ABC Thumb Index

With the help of the ABC Thumb Index at the edge of this page you can quickly find the letter you are looking for in the English-Spanish or Spanish-English section of this Dictionary.

You place your thumb on the letter you want at the edge of this page, then flip through the Dictionary till you come to the appropriate pages in the English-Spanish or Spanish-English section.

Left-handed people should use the ABC Thumb Index at the end of the book.

Abecedario Vertical

Gracias ·'
del bord
última s
damente
las dos p
Básico.

Coloque el   letra del abecedario delantero (diestros) o posterior (zurdos) que le interesa y pase rápidamente las hojas del diccionario hasta llegar a las páginas buscadas de la parte correspondiente.

A
B
C
D
E
F
G
H
I
J
K
L
M
N
Ñ
O
P
Q
R
S
T
U
V
W
Z

LANGENSCHEIDT'S POCKET SPANISH DICTIONARY

SPANISH-ENGLISH
ENGLISH-SPANISH

Edited by
THE LANGENSCHEIDT
EDITORIAL STAFF

LANGENSCHEIDT
NEW YORK · BERLIN · MUNICH

Neither the presence nor the absence of a designation that any entered word constitutes a trademark should be regarded as affecting the legal status of any trademark.

Preface

This well-known Spanish-English/English-Spanish dictionary details the latest developments in the two languages. Containing approximately 55,000 references, this comprehensive dictionary is designed for broad use and is suitable for both beginners and advanced students.

Many hundreds of up-to-date Spanish and English words have been incorporated into the present edition of this dictionary, making it ideal for everyday use in the modern world.

Special attention has been given to Latin American Spanish. Thus, the dictionary contains a wealth of expressions which, in their given meaning, are used only in Latin America and not in Spain, e.g. *baratía* (cheapness), *desrielar* (derail), *gacilla* (safety pin), *lonchería* (snack bar) and *sangriligero* (nice).

This dictionary also offers information on the conjugation of Spanish and English verbs. Each Spanish verb in the dictionary includes a reference to a corresponding verb in the grammar appendix, which is then fully conjugated. Other useful information includes lists of current Spanish and English abbreviations and proper names, a table of numerals in both Spanish and English, notes on the Spanish verb and a list of irregular verbs in English.

Based on the long-established Standard Dictionary of the English and Spanish Languages edited by C. C. Smith, G. A. Davies and H. B. Hall, it has been developed in its present form by Walter Glanze Word Books, in cooperation with Dr. Roger J. Steiner of the University of Delaware, and Dr. Gerald J. MacDonald of the Valley Forge Military Academy. To all of them our warmest appreciation.

Contents
Materias

Directions for the Use of the Dictionary
Advertencias para facilitar la consulta del diccionario

1. Arrangement. A strict alphabetical order has been maintained throughout. The following forms will therefore be found in alphabetical order:

1ˢᵗ part: the irregular forms of verbs; the various forms of the pronouns and article, etc.; and compounds.

2ⁿᵈ part: the irregular forms of verbs, nouns, comparatives and superlatives; and the inflected forms of the pronouns; and compounds.

Spanish proper names and Spanish abbreviations are collected in special lists at the end of the dictionary.

2. Vocabulary. In many cases, the rarer words formed with *-idad, -ción, -ador, -ante, -oso, in-, des-* in the 1ˢᵗ part or *-ing, -er, -ness, -ist, un-, in-,* etc. in the 2ⁿᵈ part, are excluded, to avoid extending the size of the dictionary beyond all reasonable limits. The reader having some slight acquaintance with the processes of word-formation in the two languages will be able to look up the root word and form derived words from it.

Abstract nouns are often dealt with very briefly when they are adjacent to a root-word which has been fully dealt with. Thus the entry *elegancia f* elegance *etc.* or *fineness* fineza *f etc.* means: see the adjective *elegante* resp. *fine* and form other abstract nouns accordingly.

3. Separation of different senses. The various senses of each Spanish and English word are made clear:

a) by symbols and abbreviated categories (see list on pp. 7–9);

b) by explanatory additions in italics, which may be a synonym (e.g. *emparejar [aparear]* match; *face [grimace]* mueca *f*), or a complement (e.g. *escabroso terreno* rough; *face faz f of the earth*), or the object of a transitive verb (e.g. *echar carta* post; *face danger*

arrostrar), or the subject of an intransitive verb (e.g. *empalmar [trenes]* connect; *fall [wind]* amainar), or again some other indication which while not exactly synonymous will none the less help the user in his search through the article for the required word.

Sometimes, e.g. with many abstract nouns, these explanations are omitted, but can easily be supplied from the adjacent entry for the corresponding adjective, verb or other root-word.

In the first (Spanish-English) part of the dictionary all these indications are in Spanish, and in the second (English-Spanish) part they are in English. This arrangement is in accordance with the best modern theory. The indications have been kept as simple as possible and users knowing little of the other language should not find them difficult to understand when translating from the foreign language into their own. The abbreviations, largely English but often bilingual, are of course the same in both parts.

It must be emphasized that such indications and explanations are intended only as the most elementary guide to the user, and are in no way complete definitions or exclusive rules about usage. There are many cases in which, given the limited space available, it has not been possible to provide indications of any sort.

4. The different parts of speech are indicated by numbers within each entry; the grammatical indication *adj., adv., su.,* etc., is omitted in all cases where the category is obvious.

5. The gender of every Spanish noun is indicated. Often in translating an English noun, two Spanish versions must be given, one for each gender: where the final o or e changes to *a* for the feminine, we write *passenger* pasajero (a *f*) *m*; where the *a* has to be added for the feminine, we write *teacher* profesor (-a *f*) *m*. In this second class, some endings carry an accent in the masculine which is not needed in the feminine, and this suppression is not indicated in the dictionary. The endings affected are: *-án*, *-ín*, *-ón* and *-és*, so that *loafer* haragán (-a *f*) *m* means: haragán *m*, haragana *f*.

6. Syllabification dots. The centred dots within the English word show how it should be divided in writing, e.g. **ab·do·men.** If the syllabification dot coincides with the stress mark, the former is left out. The word may therefore also be divided at the point where the stress mark stands alone, e.g. **de·nom·i'na·tion.**

See p. 13 the word division of Spanish words.

7. Phonetic transcription. In the 1st part this is given only in rare cases in which the pronunciation of a Spanish word does not correspond perfectly to its spelling. For the rest it will be sufficient for the reader to consult pp. 10–12 to know from its written form how any Spanish word is pronounced and stressed.

In the 2nd part the pronunciation of each headword and of many others is given in the alphabet of the International Phonetic Association (explanation on pp. 14–16). This is omitted only in the case of forms derived with one of the common suffixes (*-er*, *-ness*, etc.) and of compounds whose component parts are given independently elsewhere in the dictionary. In both cases, however, the stress of the word is always given.

8. Translation. In rare cases, accurate single-word translation is impossible or meaningless. Recognizing this obvious linguistic fact, we have in such cases either provided an explanation in italics in place of a translation, or have introduced the translation with the warning abbreviation *approx.* (= approximately).

9. Brackets enclosing part of a word. When certain letters stand within brackets in a Spanish word, we indicate

a) two forms that may be used indifferently, e.g. *sond(e)ar*;

b) two forms that may for convenience be run together because the translation of both is the same, e.g. *acumular(se)*, since the English word "accumulate" covers both the transitive and reflexive senses.

c) two forms which are more or less synonymous, e.g. *village* puebl(e-cit)o *m* means pueblo *m* and pueblecito *m*.

10. As appendices to the dictionary, the reader will find: a list of Spanish proper names, a list of Spanish abbreviations, a table of numerals, a table of conjugation of Spanish regular and irregular verbs (to which the numbers and letters placed after verb headwords refer, e.g. *abalanzar* [1f], *vender* [2a]), and a list of the parts of English irregular verbs.

Key to the Symbols and Abbreviations
Explicación de los signos y abreviaturas

1. Symbols

~ 2̃ ~ 2̃ is the mark of repetition or tilde (swung dash). To save space, compound catchwords are frequently given with the aid of the tilde. The thick tilde (~) stands for the catchword at the beginning of the entry. The thin tilde (~) stands for: a) the preceding catchword, which itself may have been formed with the aid of a thick tilde; b) in the phonetic transcription, the entire pronunciation of the preceding catchword, or a part of it which remains unchanged. If the preceding catchword is given without phonetic transcription, the tilde refers to the last preceding phonetic transcription or indicates only a shifting stress.

When the initial letter changes from a capital to a small letter, or vice versa, the normal tilde mark is replaced by the sign 2̃ or 2̃ respectively.

Examples:
far ... **~fetched**
fore ... **~warn:** *be ~ed*
fair¹ [fɛər] ... **fair²** [~]
favor [ˈfeivə] ... **favorable** [ˈ~vərəbl]
exchange ... *Stock* 2̃
radio...: *~captar, ~difusión*
rato ... *un buen ~, ~s pl. perdidos*
sede ... *Santa* 2̃

□ after an adjective or participle, means that from it an adverb may be formed regularly by adding -*ly*, or from adjectives ending in -*ic* by adding -*ally*, or by changing -*le* into -*ly* or -*y* into -*ily*; examples:
rich □ = *richly*
frantic □ = *frantically*
acceptable □ = *acceptably*
happy □ = *happily*

F	familiar, colloquial, *familiar, coloquial.*	🚋	railway, *ferrocarriles.*
†	archaic, *arcaico.*	✈	aviation, *aviación.*
✎	rare, little used, *raro, poco usado.*	✉	postal affairs, *correos.*
🔬	scientific, learned, *científico, culto.*	♪	music, *música.*
⚘	botany, *botánica.*	△	architecture, *arquitectura.*
⊕	technology, handicrafts, *tecnología, artes mecánicas.*	⚡	electrical engineering, *electrotecnia.*
⚒	mining, *minería.*	⚖	jurisprudence, *jurisprudencia.*
⚔	military, *milicia.*	A̶	mathematics, *matemáticas.*
⚓	nautical, *náutica.*	✶	farming, *agricultura.*
✝	commerce, *comercio.*	⚗	chemistry, *química.*
		⚕	medicine, *medicina.*

2. Abbreviations

a.	and, also, *y, también.*	*hist.*	history, *historia.*
abbr.	abbreviation, *abreviatura.*	*Hond.*	Honduras, *Honduras.*
acc.	accusative, *acusativo.*	*hunt.*	hunting, *montería.*
adj.	adjective, *adjetivo.*		
adv.	adverb, *adverbio.*	*ichth.*	ichthyology, *ictiología.*
Am.	Americanism, *americanismo.*	*indic.*	indicative, *indicativo.*
anat.	anatomy, *anatomía.*	*inf.*	infinitive, *infinitivo.*
approx.	approximately, *aproximada-*	*int.*	interjection, *interjección.*
	mente.	*Ir.*	Irish, *irlandés.*
Arg.	Argentine, *Argentina.*	*iro.*	ironical, *irónico.*
ast.	astronomy, *astronomía.*	*irr.*	irregular, *irregular.*
attr.	attributive, *atributivo.*		
		lit.	literary, *literario.*
biol.	biology, *biología.*		
Bol.	Bolivia, *Bolivia.*	*m*	masculine, *masculino.*
b.s.	bad sense, *mal sentido, peyo-*	*mar.*	maritime, *marítimo.*
	rativo.	*metall.*	metallurgy, *metalurgia.*
		meteor.	meteorology, *meteorología.*
		Mex.	Mexico, *México.*
C. Am.	Central America, *América*	*m/f*	masculine and feminine,
	central.		*masculino y femenino.*
cj., conj.	conjunction, *conjunción.*	*min.*	mineralogy, *mineralogía.*
co.	comic(al), *cómico.*	*mot.*	motoring, *automovilismo.*
Col.	Colombia, *Colombia.*	*mount.*	mountaineering, *alpinismo.*
comp.	comparative, *comparativo.*	*m/pl.*	masculine plural, *masculino*
contp.	contemptuous, *despectivo.*		*al plural.*
C.R.	Costa Rica, *Costa Rica.*	*mst*	mostly, *por la mayor parte.*
		opt.	optics, *óptica.*
dat.	dative, *dativo.*	*orn.*	ornithology, *ornitología.*
		o.s., o.s.	oneself, *uno mismo, sí mismo.*
eccl.	ecclesiastical, *eclesiástico.*	*p., p.*	person, *persona.*
Ecuad.	Ecuador, *Ecuador.*	*paint.*	painting, *pintura.*
e.g.	for example, *por ejemplo.*	*Pan.*	Panama, *Panamá.*
El Salv.	El Salvador, *El Salvador.*	*Para.*	Paraguay, *Paraguay.*
esp.	especially, *especialmente.*	*parl.*	parliamentary, *parlamenta-*
etc.	et cetera, *etcétera.*		*rio.*
euph.	euphemism, *eufemismo.*	*pharm.*	pharmacy, *farmacia.*
		phls.	philosophy, *filosofía.*
f	feminine, *femenino.*	*phonet.*	phonetics, *fonética.*
fenc.	fencing, *esgrima.*	*phot.*	photography, *fotografía.*
fig.	figurative, *figurativo, figura-*	*phys.*	physics, *física.*
	do.	*physiol.*	physiology, *fisiología.*
f/pl.	feminine plural, *femenino al*	*pl.*	plural, *plural.*
	plural.	*poet.*	poetry, poetic, *poesía, poético.*
freq.	frequently, *frecuentemente.*	*pol.*	politics, *política.*
		p.p.	past participle, *participio del*
			pasado.
gen.	generally, *generalmente.*	*P.R.*	Porto Rico, *Puerto Rico.*
geog.	geography, *geografía.*	*pred.*	predicative, *predicativo.*
geol.	geology, *geología.*	*pret.*	preterit(e), *pretérito.*
ger.	gerund, *gerundio.*	*pron.*	pronoun, *pronombre.*
gr.	grammar, *gramática.*	*prov.*	provincialism, *provincialismo.*
Guat.	Guatemala, *Guatemala.*	*prp.*	preposition, *preposición.*

rhet.	rhetoric, *retórica*.
S.Am.	Spanish Americanism, *hispanoamericanismo*.
Scot.	Scottish, *escocés*.
S.D.	Santo Domingo, *Santo Domingo*.
sew.	sewing, *costura*.
sg.	singular, *singular*.
sl.	slang, *argot, germanía*.
s.o., s.o.	someone, *alguien*.
s.t., s.t.	something, *algo*.
su.	substantive, *sustantivo*.
subj.	subjunctive, *subjuntivo*.
sup.	superlative, *superlativo*.
surv.	surveying, *topografía, agrimensura*.
tel.	telegraphy, *telegrafía*.
teleph.	telephony, *telefonía*.
th.	thing, *cosa*.

thea.	theatre, *teatro*.
typ.	typography, *tipografía*.
univ.	university, *universidad*.
Urug.	Uruguay, *Uruguay*.
v.	vide (see), *véase*.
v/aux.	auxiliary verb, *verbo auxiliar*.
Ven.	Venezuela, *Venezuela*.
vet.	veterinary, *veterinaria*.
v/i.	intransitive verb, *verbo intransitivo*.
v/r.	reflexive verb, *verbo reflexivo*.
v/t.	transitive verb, *verbo transitivo*.
W.I.	West Indies, *Antillas*.
zo.	zoology, *zoología*.

The Pronunciation of Spanish
Accentuation

1. If the word ends in a vowel, or in *n* or *s*, the penultimate syllable is stressed: *espada, biblioteca, hablan, telefonean, edificios.*

2. If the word ends in a consonant other than *n* or *s*, the last syllable is stressed: *dificultad, hablar, laurel, niñez.*

3. If the word is to be stressed in any way contrary to rules 1 and 2, an acute accent is written over the stressed vowel: *rubí, máquina, crímenes, carácter, continúa, autobús.*

4. **Diphthongs and syllable division.** Of the 5 vowels, *a e o* are considered "strong", *i* and *u* "weak":

   a) A combination of weak + strong forms a diphthong, the stress falling on the stronger element: *reina, baile, cosmonauta, tiene, bueno.*

   b) A combination of weak + weak forms a diphthong, the stress falling on the second element: *viuda, ruido.*

   c) Two strong vowels together remain as two distinct syllables, the stress falling according to rules 1 and 2: *ma/estro, atra/er.*

   d) Any word having a vowel combination not stressed according to these rules bears an accent: *traído, oído, baúl, río.*

Value of the letters

Since the pronunciation of Spanish is (in contrast with English) adequately represented by orthography, the Spanish headwords have not been provided with a transcription in the I.P.A. alphabet, except in a very few cases of recent loan-words whose spelling and pronunciation are not in accord. The sounds of Spanish are described below, each with its corresponding I.P.A. symbol.

The pronunciation described is that of educated Castilian, and does NOT refer to that of certain Spanish provinces or of Spanish America (although a few outstanding features of the latter's pronunciation are mentioned).

It should be further realized that it is impossible to explain adequately the sounds of one language in terms of another; what is said below is no more than a very approximate guide.

Vowels

Spanish vowels are clearly and sharply pronounced, and single vowels are free from the tendency to diphthongization which is noticeable in English. When they are in an unstressed position they are relaxed only very slightly, again in striking contrast to English. Stressed vowels are more open and short before *rr* (compare *parra* with *para*, *perro* with *pero*).

a [a] Not so short as in English *fat*, nor so long as in English *father*, *paz, pata.*

e [e] Like *e* in English *they* (but without the following sound of *y*): *grande, pelo.* A shorter sound when followed by a consonant in the same syllable, like *e* in English *get*: *España, renta.*

i [i] Like *i* in English *machine*, though somewhat shorter: *pila, rubí.*

o	[o]	Not so short as in English *hot*, nor so long as in English *November*: *solo*, *esposa*. A shorter sound when followed by a consonant in the same syllable, like *o* in English *hot*: *costra*, *bomba*.
u	[u]	Like *oo* in English *food*: *puro*, *luna*. Silent after *q* and in *gue*, *gui*, unless marked with a diaeresis (*antigüedad*, *argüir*).
y	[i]	when a vowel (in the conjunction *y* "and" and at the end of a word), is pronounced like *i*.

Diphthongs

ai	[aj]	like *i* in English *right*: *baile*, *vaina*.
ei	[ej]	like *ey* in English *they*: *reina*, *peine*.
oi	[oj]	like *oy* in English *boy*: *boina*, *oigo*.
au	[aw]	like *ou* in English *rout*: *causa*, *áureo*.
eu	[ew]	like the vowel sounds in English *may-you*, without the sound of the *y*: *deuda*, *reuma*.

Semiconsonants

| i, y | [j] | like *y* in English *yes*: *yelo*, *tiene*; in some cases in *S.Am.* this *y* is pronounced like the *s* [ʒ] in English *measure*: *mayo*, *yo*. |
| u | [w] | like *w* in English *water*: *huevo*, *agua*. |

Consonants

b, v		These two letters represent the same value in Spanish. There are two distinct pronunciations:
	[b]	1. At the start of the breath-group and after *m*, *n* the sound is plosive like English *b*: *batalla*, *venid*; *tromba*, *invierno*.
	[β]	2. In all other positions the sound is a bilabial fricative, unknown in English, in which the lips do not quite meet: *estaba*, *cueva*, *de Vigo*.
c	[k]	1. *c* before *a*, *o*, *u* or a consonant is like English *k*: *caló*, *cobre*.
	[θ]	2. *c* before *e*, *i* is like English *th* in *thin*: *cédula*, *cinco*. In *S.Am.* this is pronounced like English voiceless *s* in *chase* [s]. N.B. In words like *acción*, both types of *c*-sound are heard [kθ].
ch	[tʃ]	like English *ch* in *church*: *mucho*, *chocho*.
d		Three distinct pronunciations:
	[d]	1. At the start of the breath-group and after *l*, *n*, the sound is plosive like English *d*: *doy*, *aldea*, *conde*.
	[ð]	2. Between vowels and after consonants other than *l*, *n* the sound is relaxed and approaches English voiced *th* [ð] in *this*: *codo*, *guardar*; in parts of Spain it is further relaxed and even disappears, particularly in the -*ado* ending.
		3. In final position, this type 2 is further relaxed or altogether omitted: *usted*, *Madrid*.
f	[f]	like English *f*: *fuero*, *flor*.
g		Three distinct pronunciations:
	[x]	1. Before *e*, *i* is the same as the Spanish *j* (below): *coger*, *general*.

	[g]	**2.** At the start of the breath-group and after *n*, the sound is that of English *g* in get: *Granada, rango*.
	[ɣ]	**3.** In other positions the sound is as in 2 above, but with no more than a close approximation of the vocal organs: *agua, guerra*. N.B. In the group *gue, gui* the *u* is silent (*guerra, guindar*) unless marked with the diaeresis (*antigüedad, argüir*). In the group *gua* all letters are sounded.
h	[-]	always silent: *honor, buho*.
j	[x]	A strong guttural sound not found in English, but like the *ch* in Scots *loch*, Welsh *bach*, German *Achtung*: *jota, ejercer*. Silent at the end of the word: *reloj*.
k	[k]	like English *k*: *kilogramo, kerosene*.
l	[l]	like English *l*: *león, pala*.
ll	[ʎ]	approximating to English *lli* in million: *millón, calle*. In *S.Am.* like the *s* [ʒ] in English measure.
m	[m]	like English *m*: *mano, como*.
n	[n]	like English *n*: *nono, pan*; except before *v*, when the group is pronounced like *mb*: *enviar, invadir*.
ñ	[ɲ]	approximating to English *ni* in onion: *paño, ñoño*.
p	[p]	like English *p*, but without the slight aspiration which follows it: *Pepe, copa*. Silent in *septiembre, séptimo*.
q	[k]	like English *k*; always in combination with *u*, which is silent: *que, quiosco*.
r	[r]	a single trill stronger than any *r* in English, but like Scots *r*: *caro, querer*. Somewhat relaxed in final position. Pronounced like *rr* at the start of a word and after *l, n, s*: *rata*.
rr	[rr]	strongly trilled: *carro, hierro*.
s	[s]	voiceless *s*, like *s* in English chase: *rosa, soso*. But before a voiced consonant (*b, d*, hard *g, l, m, n*) is a
	[z]	voiced *s*, like English *s* in rose: *desde, mismo, asno*. Before "impure *s*" in recent loan-words, an extra *e*-sound is inserted in pronunciation: *e-sprint, e-stand*.
t	[t]	like English *t*, but without the slight aspiration which follows it: *patata, tope*.
v	[-]	see *b*.
w	[-]	found in a few recent loan-words only; usually pronounced like an English *v* or like Spanish *b, v*: *wáter*.
x	[gs]	like English *gs* in big sock: *máximo, examen*. Before a consonant like English *s* in chase: *extraño, mixto*.
z	[θ]	like English *th* in thin: *zote, zumbar*. In *S.Am.* like English voiceless *s* in chase.

The Spanish Alphabet

a [a], b [be], c [θe], (ch [tʃe]), d [de], e [e], f['efe], g [xe], h ['atʃe], i [i], j ['xota], k [ka], l ['ele], (ll ['eʎe), m ['eme], n ['ene], ñ ['eɲe], o [o], p [pe], q [ku], r ['ere], rr ['erre], s ['ese], t [te], u [u], v ['uve], x ['ekis], y [i'ɣrieɣa], z ['θeta] or ['θeda].

The letters are of the feminine gender: "Madrid se escribe con una *m* mayúscula."

Written Spanish

I. Accentuation

1. Words with more than one syllable which end in a **vowel** or in **n** or **s** are stressed on the **penultimate** syllable (**po**rque *because,* **jo**ven *young,* **Car**men, na**cio**nes *nations,* **Car**los).
2. Words with more than one syllable which end in a **consonant** other than **n** or **s**, or in a **y**, are stressed on the **last** syllable (espa**ñol** *Spanish,* ciu**dad** *town,* se**ñor** *Mr.,* es**toy** *I am*).
3. Exceptions to these two rules (including all those words stressed on the **antepenultimate** syllable) are indicated by an **accent** (´) (está *he is,* nación *nation,* francés *French,* Velázquez, fábrica *factory,* época *epoch,* Málaga, Córdoba, Lérida).
4. A number of monosyllabic words have an accent in order to distinguish them from homonyms (tú *you* – tu *your,* él *he* – el *the (masc.),* sí *yes* – si *if*).
5. Interrogatives take an accent (¿cómo? *how?,* ¿cuándo *when?,* ¿dónde? *where?,* ¿quién? *who?*).

II. Capitalization

Rules for capitalization in Spanish largely correspond to those for the English language. In contrast to English, however, adjectives derived from proper nouns are not capitalized (americano *American,* español *Spanish*).

III. Word division

Spanish words are divided according to the following rules:

1. If there is **a single consonant** between two vowels, the division is made between the first vowel and the consonant (di-ne-ro, Gra-na-da).
2. **Two consecutive consonants** may be divided (miér-co-les, dis-cur-so). If the second consonant is an l or r, however, the division comes before the two consonants (re-gla, nie-bla; po-bre, ca-bra). This also goes for ch, ll and rr (te-cho, ca-lle, pe-rro).
3. In the case of **three consecutive consonants** (usually including an l or r), the division comes after the first consonant (ejem-plo, siem-pre). If the second consonant is an s, however, the division comes after the s (cons-tan-te, ins-ti-tu-to).
4. In the case of **four consecutive consonants** (the second of these is usually an s), the division is made between the second and third consonants (ins-tru-men-to).
5. **Diphthongs** and **triphthongs** may not be divided (bien, buey). Vowels which are part of different syllables, however, may be divided (frí-o, acre-e-dor).
6. **Compounds,** including those formed with prefixes, are divided morphologically (nos-otros, des-ali-no, dis-cul-pa).

IV. Punctuation

In Spanish a comma is often placed after an adverbial phrase introducing a sentence (sin embargo, todos los esfuerzos eran inútiles *however, all efforts were in vain*). A subsidiary clause beginning a sentence is also followed by a comma (si tengo tiempo, lo haré *if I have time I'll do it,* **but**: lo haré si tengo tiempo *I'll do it if I have time*).

Questions and exclamations are introduced by an inverted question mark and exclamation mark respectively, which immediately precedes the question or exclamation (Dispense usted, ¿está en casa el señor Pérez? *Excuse me, is Mr. Pérez at home?*; ¡Que lástima! *What a shame!*)

La pronunciación del inglés

A. Vocales y Diptongos

[ɑ:] sonido parecido al de *a* en *raro*: *far* [fɑːr], *father* ['fɑːðər].

[ʌ] *a* abierta, breve y oscura, que se pronuncia en la parte anterior de la boca sin redondear los labios: *butter* ['bʌtər], *come* [kʌm], *color* ['kʌlər], *blood* [blʌd], *flourish* ['flʌriʃ], *twopence* ['tʌpəns].

[æ] sonido breve, bastante abierto y distinto, algo parecido al de *a* en *parra*: *fat* [fæt], *ran* [ræn].

[ɛə] diptongo que se encuentra únicamente delante de la *r* muda. El primer y principal elemento se parece a la *e* de *perro*, pero es más abierto y breve; el segundo es una forma débil de la 'vocal neutra' (*v.* abajo): *bare* [bɛər], *pair* [pɛər], *there* [ðɛər].

[ai] sonido parecido al de *ai* en *estáis*, *baile*: *I* [ai], *lie* [lai], *dry* [drai].

[au] sonido parecido al de *au* en *causa*, *sauce*: *house* [haus], *now* [nau].

[ei] *e* medio abierta, pero más cerrada que la *e* de *hablé*; suena como si la siguiese una [i] débil, sobretodo en sílaba acentuada: *date* [deit], *play* [plei], *obey* [ə'bei].

[e] sonido breve, medio abierto, parecido al de *e* en *perro*: *bed* [bed], *less* [les].

[ə] 'vocal neutra', siempre átona; parecida a la *e* del artículo francés *le* y a la *a* final del catalán *casa*: *about* [ə'baut], *butter* ['bʌtər], *connect* [kə'nekt].

[i:] sonido largo, parecido al de *i* en *misa*, vino: *scene* [siːn], *sea* [siː], *feet* [fiːt], *ceiling* ['siːliŋ].

[i] sonido breve, abierto, parecido al de *i* en *filfa*, *esbirro*, pero más abierto: *big* [big], *city* ['siti].

[iə] diptongo cuyo primer y princi-

pal elemento es una *i* medio abierta, medio larga, seguida de una forma débil de la 'vocal neutra' [ə]: *here* [hiər], *hear* [hiər], *inferior* [in'fiəriər].

[ou] *o* larga, más bien cerrada, sin redondear los labios ni levantar la lengua; suena como si la siguiese una [u] débil: *note* [nout], *boat* [bout], *below* [bi'lou].

[ɔ:] vocal larga, bastante cerrada, entre *a* y *o*; le es algo parecida la *o* de *por*: *fall* [fɔːl], *nought* [nɔːt], *or* [ɔːr], *before* [bi'fɔːr].

[ɔ] sonido breve y abierto, parecido al de la *o* en *porra*, *corro*, pero más cerrado: *god* [gɔd], *not* [nɔt], *wash* [wɔʃ], *hobby* ['hɔbi].

[ɔi] diptongo cuyo primer elemento es una *o* abierta, seguido de una *i* abierta pero débil; parecido al sonido de *oy* en *doy*: *voice* [vɔis], *boy* [bɔi], *annoy* [ə'nɔi].

[ə:] forma larga de la 'vocal neutra' [ə], en sílaba acentuada; algo parecida al sonido de *eu* en la palabra francesa *leur*: *word* [wəːrd], *girl* [gəːrl], *learn* [ləːrn], *murmur* ['məːrmər].

[u:] sonido largo, parecido al de *u* en *cuna*, *duda*: *fool* [fuːl], *shoe* [ʃuː], *you* [juː], *rule* [ruːl], *canoe* [kə'nuː].

[uə] diptongo cuyo primer elemento es una *u* medio larga, medio abierta, seguido de una forma débil de la 'vocal neutra' [ə]: *pure* [pjuər], *allure* [ə'ljuər].

[u] *u* pura pero muy rápida, más cerrada que la *u* de *burra*: *put* [put], *look* [luk], *careful* ['kɛərful].

B. Consonantes

[b] como la *b* de *cambiar*: *bay* [bei], *brave* [breiv].

[d] como la *d* de *andar*: *did* [did], *ladder* ['lædər].

[f] como la *f* de *filo*: *face* [feis], *baffle* ['bæfl].

[g] como la *g* de *golpe*: *go* [gou], *haggle* ['hægl].

[h] se pronuncia con aspiración fuerte, sin la aspereza gutural de la *j* en *Gijón*: *who* [hu:], *behead* [bi'hed].

[j] como la *y* de *cuyo*: *you* [ju:], *million* ['miljən].

[k] como la *c* de *casa*: *cat* [kæt], *kill* [kil].

[l] como la *l* de *loco*: *love* [lʌv], *goal* [goul].

[m] como la *m* de *madre*: *mouth* [mauθ], *come* [kʌm].

[n] como la *n* de *nada*: *not* [nɔt], *banner* ['bænər].

[p] como la *p* de *padre*: *pot* [pɔt], *top* [tɔp].

[r] es un sonido muy débil, más bien semivocal, que no tiene nada de la vibración fuerte que caracteriza la *r* española; se articula elevando la punta de la lengua hacia el paladar duro: *rose* [rouz], *pride* [praid], *there* [ðɛər].

[s] como la *s* de *casa*: *sit* [sit], *scent* [sent].

[t] como la *t* de *pata*: *take* [teik], *patter* ['pætər].

[v] inexistente en español; a diferencia de *b*, *v* en español, se pronuncia juntando el labio inferior con los dientes superiores: *vein* [vein], *velvet* ['velvit].

[w] como la *u* de *huevo*: *water* ['wɔ:tər], *will* [wil].

[z] como la *s* de *mismo*: *zeal* [zi:l], *hers* [hɔːrz].

[ʒ] inexistente en español; como la *j* de la palabra francesa *jour*: *measure* ['meʒə], *rouge* [ru:ʒ]. Aparece a menudo en el grupo [dʒ], que se pronuncia como el grupo *dj* de la palabra francesa *adjacent*: *edge* [edʒ], *gem* [dʒem].

[ʃ] inexistente en español; como *ch* en la palabra francesa *chose*: *shake* [ʃeik], *washing* ['wɔʃin]. Aparece a menudo en el grupo [tʃ], que se pronuncia como la *ch* en *mucho*: *match* [mætʃ], *natural* ['nætʃrəl].

[θ] como la *z* de *zapato*: *thin* [θin], *path* [pɑ:θ].

[ð] forma sonorizada del anterior, algo como la *d* de *todo*: *there* [ðɛər], *breathe* [bri:ð].

[ŋ] como la *n* de *banco*: *singer* ['siŋər], *tinker* ['tiŋkər].

[x] sonido que en rigor no pertenece al inglés, pero que se encuentra en palabras escocesas, alemanas, etc. que se usan en inglés: como la *j* de *jamás*: *loch* [lɔx].

Nota: Importa que el lector se dé cuenta de la casi imposibilidad de explicar de modo satisfactorio los sonidos de una lengua en términos de otra. Lo que aquí se dice es a modo de aproximación y de ayuda general, sin que pretenda tener ningún rigor científico. Importa además reconocer que los sonidos que se explican aquí pueden variar mucho en cuanto se emplean juntamente con otros sonidos o en frases enteras.

La tilde [˜], que aparece en la pronunciación figurada de ciertas palabras de origen francés, indica la nasalización de la vocal.

Los dos puntos [:] indican que la vocal anterior se pronuncia larga.

C. Acentuación

La acentuación de la palabra inglesa se indica colocando el acento ['] al principio de la sílaba acentuada, p. ej. *onion* ['ʌnjən]. Muchas palabras largas o compuestas tienen dos sílabas acentuadas (una quizá más ligeramente que la otra), lo cual se indica poniendo dos acentos: *falsification* ['fɔ:lsifi'keiʃn], *upstairs* ['ʌp'stɛərz]. Uno de los acentos que lleva la palabra compuesta puede sin embargo suprimirse cuando la palabra tiene que someterse al ritmo de una frase entera, o cuando se emplea en función distinta (p. ej. como adjetivo o adverbio): *the upstairs rooms* [ði 'ʌpstɛərz 'rumz], *on going upstairs* [ɔn 'gouiŋ ʌp'stɛərz].

Véanse también las *Advertencias*, núm. 7, y la *Explicación de los Signos*.

D. Sufijos sin pronunciación figurada

Para ahorrar espacio, las palabras derivadas mediante uno de los sufijos corrientes suelen escribirse en el diccionario sin pronunciación figurada propia. Su pronunciación puede comprobarse consultando el lector la pronunciación de la voz-guía que encabeza el párrafo, añadiendo después la pronunciación del sufijo según esta lista:

-ability [-əbiliti]	-ent [-(ə)nt]	-ize [-aiz]
-able [-əbl]	-er [-ər]	-izing [-aiziŋ]
-age [-idʒ]	-ery [-əri]	-less [-lis]
-al [-(ə)l]	-ess [-is]	-ly [-li]
-ally [-(ə)li]	-fication [-fikeiʃ(ə)n]	-ment(s) [-mənt(s)]
-an [-(ə)n]	-ial [-(ə)l]	-ness [-nis]
-ance [-(ə)ns]	-ian [-(jə)n]	-oid [-ɔid]
-ancy [-ənsi]	-ible [-əbl]	-oidic [-ɔidik]
-ant [-ənt]	-ic(s) [-ik(s)]	-or [-ər]
-ar [-ər]	-ical [-ik(ə)l]	-ous [-əs]
-ary [-(ə)ri]	-ily [-ili]	-ry [-ri]
-ation [-eiʃ(ə)n]	-iness [-inis]	-ship [-ʃip]
-cious [-ʃəs]	-ing [-iŋ]	-(s)sion [-ʃ(ə)n]
-cy [-si]	-ish [-iʃ]	-sive [-siv]
-dom [-dəm]	-ism [-iz(ə)m]	-ties [-tiz]
-ed [-d; -t; -id]*	-ist [-ist]	-tion [-ʃ(ə)n]
-edness [-dnis; -tnis;	-istic [-istik]	-tious [-ʃəs]
-idnis]	-ite [-ait]	-trous [-trəs]
-ee [-i:]	-ity [-iti]	-try [-tri]
-en [-n]	-ive [-iv]	-y [-i]
-ence [-(ə)ns]	-ization [-aizeiʃ(ə)n]	

* [-d] tras vocales y consonantes sonoras; [-t] tras consonantes sordas; [-id] tras *d* y *t* finales.

The English Alphabet – El alfabeto inglés

a [ei], b [bi:], c [si:], d [di:], e [i:], f [ɛf], g [dʒi:], h [eitʃ], i [ai], j [dʒei], k [kei], l [el], m [em], n [en], o [ou], p [pi:], q [kju:], r [ɑ:], s [es], t [ti:], u [ju:], v [vi:], w ['dʌblju:], x [eks], y [wai], z [zed].

A

a a) *lugar*: *a la mesa* at the table; *al lado de* at the side of; *a la derecha* on the right; *distancia*: *a 2 km.* (de) 2 km. away (from); *dirección*: *ir a casa* go home; b) *tiempo*: *¿a qué hora?* (at) what time?; *a las 3* at 3 o'clock; c) *manera etc.*: *a la española* in the Spanish fashion; *a escape* at full speed; *a pie* on foot; d) *modo, velocidad*: *poco a poco* little by little; *paso a paso* step by step; e) *medio, instrumento*: *bordado a mano* hand-embroidered; *girar a mano* turn by hand; *a puñetazos* with (his) fists; *a nado* (by) swimming; f) *precio*: *a 20 pesetas el kilo* at (or for) 20 pesetas a kilo; g) *propósito*: *¿a qué?* why?, for what purpose?; h) *sabor, olor*: *saber a vinagre* taste of vinegar; i) *dativo*: (*le*) *doy el libro a Juan* I give the book to John; j) *objeto personal* (*no se traduce*): *vio a su padre* he saw his father; k) *construcción con verbo*: *voy a comer* I am going to eat; l) *se lo compré a él* I bought it from him; m) *al entrar* on entering.

abacería *f* grocer's (shop), grocery store; **abacero** *m* grocer.

ábaco *m* abacus.

abadejo *m ichth.* cod(fish); (*insecto*) Spanish fly.

abadesa *f* abbess; **abadía** *f* abbey.

abajadero *m* slope, incline.

abajeño *S.Am.* 1. lowland; 2. *m, a f* lowlander.

abajo (*situación*) down, below, underneath; (*movimiento*) down, downwards; *downstairs en casa*; *¡~ X!* down with X!; *~ de* prp. below.

abalanzar [1f] weigh, balance; (*lanzar*) hurl; **~se** rush (*a* into); pounce.

abalear [1a] *S.Am.* shoot.

abalone *zo.* abalone.

abanar [1a] fan.

abanderado *m* standard-bearer, ensign; **abanderar** [1a] ♣ register; **abanderizar** [1f] organize into bands; **~se** band together.

abandonado abandoned; *lugar etc.* deserted; *aspecto etc.* forlorn; *edificio*

derelict; **abandonar** [1a] *v/t.* abandon, forsake; (*salir de*) leave; (*huir*) flee, leave; *v/i. deportes*: withdraw; **~se** (*desánimo*) give in, lose heart; **abandono** *m* abandonment; dereliction *de edificio, deber*; (*desaliño*) slovenliness.

abanicar(se) [1g] fan (o.s.); **abanico** *m* fan; fan-shaped object; **abaniqueo** *m* fanning; gesticulation *con manos.*

abaratamiento *m* cheapening; **abaratar** [1a] *v/t.* cheapen, make cheaper; **~se** get cheaper.

abarcar [1g] embrace, include, take in, extend to; contain; *S.Am.* corner, monopolize.

abarraganamiento *m* illicit cohabitation.

abarrancadero *m fig.* pitfall, difficult situation; **abarrancar** [1g] (*lluvia*) open fissures in; **~se** fall into a pit; *fig.* get into difficulties.

abarrotar [1a] ♣ stow, pack tightly; *fig.* overstock; **~se** *S.Am.* ♥ become a glut on the market; **abarrote** *m* ♣ stowing, packing; **~s** *pl. S.Am.* groceries; **abarrotero** *m S.Am.* grocer.

abastar [1a] supply; **abastecedor** *m*, **-a** *f* supplier; **abastecer** [2d] supply, provide, provision (*de* with); **abastecimiento** *m* supply, provision; (*acto*) supplying; **abasto** *m* supply; provisioning.

abatible collapsible; folding.

abatido (*ruin*) abject, despicable; *ánimo* downcast, dejected; **abatimiento** *m* ♣ *etc.* knocking down, dismantling; *fig.* dejection, low spirits; **abatir** [3a] *casa etc.* knock down, dismantle; *tienda* take down; *fig.* humble, humiliate; **~se** (*ave*) swoop, pounce; *fig.* be disheartened.

abdicación *f* abdication; **abdicar** [1g] abdicate.

abdomen *m* abdomen; **abdominal** abdominal.

abecé *m* ABC; rudiments; **abecedario** *m* alphabet; spelling-book.

abeja *f* bee; **abejar** *m* apiary; **abeja-**

rrón *m*, **abejorro** *m* bumble-bee; **abejuno** *adj.* bee(like).

aberración *f* aberration (*a. ast., opt.*); **aberrante** aberrant; **aberrar** [1k] be mistaken.

abertura *f* (*agujero*) aperture, opening, gap; (*grieta*) slit, crack; *fig.* openness, frankness.

abeto *m* fir; ~ *blanco* silver fir.

abierto 1. *p.p. of abrir*; 2. *adj.* open, opened; *p.* frank, forthcoming; *S.Am.* conceited.

abigarrado variegated, many-colored; *animal* piebald; **abigarrar** [1a] variegate; paint *etc.* in a variety of colors.

abigotado mustachioed.

abismal abysmal; **abismar** [1a] *fig.* cast down, humble; (*dañar*) spoil, ruin; ~se *S.Am.* be surprised; ~ en plunge into, sink into; **abismo** *m* abyss.

abjuración *f* abjuration; **abjurar** [1a] abjure, forswear.

ablandabrevas *m/f* good-for-nothing.

ablandar [1a] *v/t.* soften; soothe, mollify; *v/i.* (*viento*) moderate; (*frío*) become less severe; ~se soften, get soft.

ablativo *m* ablative (case).

abnegación *f* self-denial, abnegation; **abnegado** self-denying; **abnegarse** [1h *a.* 1k] deny o.s.

abobado stupid(-looking); **abobar** [1a] make stupid.

abocado *vino* smooth; **abocamiento** *m* biting; approach; meeting; **abocar** [1g] *v/t.* seize with the mouth; *vino* pour, decant; ~se approach; ~ con meet, have an interview with.

abochornado flushed, overheated; *fig.* ashamed (*de at*); **abochornar** [1a] burn up, overheat.

abofellar [1a] swell; puff out.

abofetear [1a] slap in the face.

abogacía *f* legal profession; **abogado** *m* lawyer; ~ *de secano* quack lawyer; ~ *criminalista* criminal lawyer; **abogar** [1h] advocate, plead.

abolengo *m* ancestry, lineage.

abolición *f* abolition; **abolir** [3a; *defective*] abolish; revoke.

abolladura *f* dent; (*arte*) embossing; **abollar** [1a] dent; bruise; (*arte*) emboss; ~se get dented *etc.*; **abollonar** [1a] *metal* emboss.

abolorio *m* ancestry.

abombado convex; *S.Am.* (*aturdido*)

stunned; **abombar** [1a] make convex; F stun, confuse; ~se *S.Am.* (*pudrirse*) decompose.

abominable abominable; **abominación** *f* abomination (*a. fig.*), execration; **abominar** [1a] abhor.

abonable payable; **abonado** 1. trustworthy; 2. *m*, **a** *f* subscriber season-ticket holder; **abonador** *m*, **-a** *f* ♱ guarantor.

abonanzar [1f] clear up (*a. fig.*); ♱ abate, calm down.

abonar [1a] 1. *v/t. p.* vouch for, guarantee; ♱ credit, pay; ✂ fertilize; 2. *v/i.* clear (up); 3. ~se subscribe; **abonaré** *m* promissory note; **abono** *m* ♱ *etc.* voucher, guarantee; subscription; season-ticket; manure, dressing, fertilizer; ~ *químico* (chemical) fertilizer.

abordable *p., lugar* approachable; *lugar* easy of access; **abordaje** *m* ♱ boarding; **abordar** [1a] ♱ board; (*atracar*) dock.

aborigen *adj. a. su. m* aboriginal.

aborrascarse [1g] get stormy.

aborrecer [2d] hate, detest; (*aburrir*) bore; **aborrecible** hateful, abhorrent; **aborrecido** (*aburrido*) boring; **aborrecimiento** *m* hatred, hate.

abortar [1a] abort; ✿ have a miscarriage; *fig.* miscarry, fail; **abortivo** abortive; **aborto** *m* abortion; ✿ miscarriage; ~ *de la naturaleza* monster.

abotonador *m* button-hook; **abotonar** [1a] *v/t.* button (up); *v/i.* bud.

abozalar [1a] muzzle.

abra *f* (*ensenada*) bay, cove.

abracadabra *f* hocus-pocus; **abracadabrante** amazing; breathtaking.

abrasado burnt up; *fig.* ashamed; **abrasador** burning, scorching; **abrasar** [1a] burn (up); ✿ *etc.* parch; (*frío*) nip; ~se burn; be parched.

abrasión *f* graze, abrasion; **abrasivo** *m* abrasive.

abrazadera *f* bracket, brace, clasp; paper clip.

abrazar [1f] embrace (*a. fig.*); clasp, take in one's arms, hug; ~se *a, con, de* embrace; clasp; **abrazo** *m* embrace, hug.

abrelatas *m* can opener.

abrevadero *m* drinking-trough; (*lugar*) watering-place; **abrevar** [1a] *animal* water, give a drink to; *tierra* irrigate; ~se (*animal*) quench its *etc.* thirst.

abreviación f abbreviation; reduction; **abreviadamente** in an abridged form; **abreviar** [1b] v/t. palabra etc. abbreviate; reduce; período shorten, lessen; v/i. be quick; be short; **abreviatura** f abbreviation.

abrigada f, **abrigadero** m shelter, wind-break; **abrigado** sheltered; **abrigador** adj. (vestido, etc.) warm; protective; heavy.

abrigar [1h] shelter, protect (de viento etc. from, against); (vestido etc.) keep warm, cover; (ayudar) aid, support; **se** take shelter (de aguacero etc. from); ⚓ seek shelter (de temporal from); protect o.s.; **abrigo** m shelter; esp. ⚓ haven; (sobretodo) (over)coat; (ayuda) aid.

abril m April; fig. springtime (de la vida of life); **es** pl. years (of one's youth); **abrileño** April attr.

abrillantar [1a] ⊕ cut into facets; (pulir) polish, brighten; fig. enhance.

abrir [3a; p.p. abierto] 1. v/t. open (a. fig.); ~ (con llave) unlock; ⚔ cut open; grifo etc. turn on; apetito whet; 2. v/i. ♀ etc. open, unfold; 3. **se** (puerta etc.) open; (flor etc.) open out.

abrochadura f buttoning; hooking; **abrochar** [1a] button; hook, fasten (up).

abrogación f abrogation; **abrogar** [1h] abrogate, repeal.

abrojo m thistle, thorn; **abrojos** ⚓ hidden rocks.

abroquelarse [1a] fig.: ~ con, ~ de shiled o.s. with.

abrumador overwhelming; (molesto) wearisome; **abrumar** [1a] crush, oppress; **se** get foggy.

abrupto steep, abrupt.

abrutado brutish.

absceso m abscess.

absentismo m absenteeism; absentee landlordism; **absentista** m/f absentee; absentee landlord.

absintio m absinth.

absolución f absolution; ⚖ acquittal; **absoluta** f authoritative assertion, dictum; ✕ discharge; **absolutamente** absolutely; positively; ~ nada nothing at all; **absolutismo** m absolutism; **absoluto** absolute (a. ⚛ pol.); fig. utter, absolute.

absolvederas f/pl. F tendency to absolve freely.

absolver [2h; p.p. absuelto] absolve; ⚖ acquit, clear (de of); release;

absorbente 1. absorbent; fig. absorbing; 2. m: ~ higiénico sanitary towel; **absorber** [2a] absorb (a. fig.), suck up; ✝ capital use up; **se** become absorbed (en in); **absorción** f absorption (a. fig.); **absorto** fig. absorbed, engrossed (en in); lost in thought.

abstemio abstemious, temperate.

abstención f abstention; nonparticipation; **abstencionismo** m nonparticipation; **abstencionista** m/f non-participant; **abstenerse** [2l] abstain, refrain (de inf. from ger.).

abstinencia f abstinence; (ayuno) fast; **abstinente** abstemious.

abstracción f abstraction; omission; (distracción) engrossment; **abstracto** abstract; en ~ in the abstract; **abstraer** [2p] v/t. abstract; v/i. ~ de do without, leave aside; **se** be abstracted, be absorbed; **abstraído** absentminded; withdrawn.

absurdidad f absurdity; **absurdo** 1. absurd; preposterous; farcical; 2. m absurdity; farce.

abuela f grandmother; fig. old woman; **abuelita** f F grandma, granny; **abuelito** m F grandpa, grandad; **abuelo** m grandfather; fig. (antepasado) ancestor; (viejo) old man; **es** pl. grandparents.

abulia f lack of will power; **abúlico** lacking in will power, weak-willed.

abultado bulky, massive, unwieldy; **abultar** [1a] v/t. make large, enlarge; v/i. be bulky.

abundamiento m abundance, plenty; **abundancia** f abundance, plenty; en ~ in plenty, in abundance; **abundante** abundant, plentiful; **abundar** [1a]: ~ de, ~ en abound in, be rich in.

aburguesado adj. middle-class.

aburrido wearisome, tiresome, boring; **aburrimiento** m boredom, weariness, tedium; **aburrir** [3a] bore, weary; annoy, tire; **se** be bored, get bored (con, de, por with).

abusar [1a] go too far, take an unfair advantage; ~ de autoridad, hospitalidad abuse; amigos impose upon; **abusión** f abuse; superstition; **abusionero** superstitious; **abusivo** improper, corrupt; **abuso** m abuse; misuse.

abyecto condición abject; (ruin) craven, vile.

acá here, around here, over here; ~ y a(cu)llá here and there; de ~ para allá

to and fro; *de ayer* ~ since yesterday.
acabado 1. perfect, complete; *fig.* consummate; **2.** *m* finish; **acabador** *m* ⊕ finisher; **acabamiento** *m* completion, end; (*muerte*) death.
acabar [1a] **1.** *v/t.* finish, complete; put the finishing touches to; (*matar*) kill off; **2.** *v/i.* finish, come to an end; (*morir*) die; ~ *con* make an end of; ~ *de inf.* have just *p.p.*: *acabo de hacerlo* I have just done it; ~ *mal* come to a bad (*or* sticky) end; ~**se** stop, come to an end (*a. fig.*); (*morir*) die; (*estar terminado*) be all over; *se me acabó el dinero* I ran out of money; F *el acabóse* the pay-off, the end.
acacia *f* acacia; ~ *falsa* locust tree.
academia *f* academy; **académico 1.** academic (*a. fig.*); **2.** *m* academician, member of an academy.
acaecedero possible; **acaecer** [2d] happen, occur; **acaecimiento** *m* happening, occurrence.
acajú *biol.* cashew tree.
acallar [1a] silence (*a. fig.*), hush.
acalorado heated, hot; (*fatigado*) tired (out); **acaloramiento** *m* ardour, heat; passion, anger; **acalorar** [1a] (*ejercicio*) warm, make hot; (*fatigar*) tire; ~**se** (*tomar calor*) get too hot, become overheated; (*irritarse*) get angry (*por* about).
acampar [1a] ✕ (en)camp.
acanaladura *f* groove; 🏛 fluting; **acanalar** [1a] groove; 🏛 flute; *papel etc.* corrugate.
acantilado 1. *costa* (*en escalones*) rocky; (*escarpado*) steep; **2.** *m* cliff.
acantonar [1a] quarter (en on).
acaparador *m* monopolist; profiteer; **acaparamiento** *m* monopolizing (*de* of), cornering the market (*de* in); **acaparar** [1a] monopolize; corner, corner the market in.
acaramelado *fig.* over-sweet, over-polite.
acar(e)ar [1a] *ps.* bring face to face; *peligro etc.* face (up to).
acariciar [1b] caress; *animal* pat, fondle; *esperanza* cherish, harbor.
acarrear [1a] transport, cart, haul; **acarreo** *m* haulage, cartage.
acartonarse [1a] get like cardboard; *fig.* (*p.*) become wizened.
acaso 1. *adv.* perhaps, maybe; *por si* ~ (just) in case; **2.** *m* chance, accident; *al* ~ at random.
acastañado chestnut-colored.
acatamiento *m* respect, esteem;

acatar [1a] respect, esteem; treat with deference; revere.
acatarrarse [1a] catch a cold.
acato *m* respect, esteem.
acaudalado wealthy, well-off; **acaudalar** [1a] accumulate.
acaudillar [1a] lead, command.
acceder [2a] accede, agree (*a* to).
accesible accessible; ~ *a* open to, accessible to; **accesión** *f* (*acto*) assent (*a* to); (*entrada*) access, entry; ✗ attack, **accésit** *m* second prize, consolation prize; **acceso** *m* (*acto de entrar*) admittance; (*camino*) access; **accesoria** *f* annex, outbuilding; **accesorio 1.** accessory; dependent; **2.** *m* accessory, attachment.
accidentado ✗ (*turbado*) upset; *vida* stormy, troubled; *superficie* uneven; **accidental** accidental; unintentional; **accidentarse** [1a] faint (after an accident); **accidente** *m* accident; mishap; ✗ faint(ing fit).
acción *f* action; ✝ share; ✕ action, engagement; *thea.* action, plot; ~*es pl.* ✝ stock(s), shares; ~ *de gracias* thanksgiving; ~ *liberada* stock dividend; ~ *preferente* preference share; **accionar** [1a] *v/t.* ⊕ work; *v/i.* gesticulate; **accionista** *m/f* shareholder, stockholder.
acechadura *f* ambush; **acechador** *m*, **-a** *f* spy; **acechar** [1a] spy on, lie (*or* be) in wait for; *hunt. etc.* stalk; **acecho** *m* ambush; spying; *al* ~, *en* ~ in wait.
acecinar [1a] salt, cure; ~**se** get very thin.
acedar [1a] make sour; *fig.* sour, embitter; ~**se** turn sour.
acedía *f* sourness (*a. fig.*); (*desabrimiento*) unpleasantness; ✗ heartburn; **acedo** sour (*a. fig.*), acid.
aceitar [1a] oil, lubricate; **aceite** *m* oil; (*a.* ~ *de oliva*) olive oil; ~ *combustible* fuel oil; ~ *de hígado de bacalao* cod-liver oil; ~ *de linaza* linseed oil; ~ *secante* linseed oil; **aceitera** *f* oilcan; **aceitero 1.** oil *attr.*; **2.** *m* oil merchant; **aceitoso** oily, greasy; **aceituna** *f* olive; **aceitunil** olive *attr.*; olive-colored; **aceituno 1.** *S.Am.* olive (-colored); **2.** *m* olive (tree).
aceleración *f* acceleration, speeding-up; **acelerada** *f* acceleration, speed-up; **aceleradamente** speedily, swiftly; **acelerador** *m* accelerator; **acelerar** [1a] accelerate; quicken; ~**se** hasten, hurry.

acémila f beast of burden; mule; **acemilero** m muleteer.

acendrado pure, refined (a. fig.); **acendrar** [1a] purify.

acento m accent; stress; ~ agudo acute accent; **acentuar** [1e] accent, accentuate; stress.

aceña f water-mill; **aceñero** m miller.

acepción f meaning, sense.

acepilladora f planer; **acepilladura** f (wood) shaving; **acepillar** [1a] brush; ⊕ plane.

aceptable acceptable; palatable; **aceptación** f acceptance (a. †); approval, discrimination; **aceptar** [1a] accept; trabajo accept, take on; ~ a inf. agree to inf.

acequia f irrigation ditch.

acera f pavement, sidewalk.

acerado ⊕ steel attr.; (cortante) biting, cutting (a. fig.); **acerar** [1a] ⊕ turn into steel; put a steel tip etc. on.

acerbidad f acerbity; harshness; **acerbo** sour; harsh; scathing.

acerca: ~ de about, concerning, on.

acercamiento m bringing (or drawing) near; **acercar** [1g] bring near(er); ~se approach (a acc.), come near (a to).

acería f steelworks.

acerico m small cushion; sew. pincushion.

acero m steel (a. fig.); F tener buenos ~s (ser valiente) have a lot of pluck; **acerocromo** m chrome steel.

acérrimo out-and-out, fierce.

acerrojar [1a] bolt, lock.

acertado right, correct; (prudente) wise, sound; (hábil) skilful; dicho well-aimed; apt; **acertante** m/f winner; **acertar** [1k] v/t. blanco etc. hit; solución guess right, get right; v/i. (dar en el blanco) hit the mark; (tener razón) be right.

acertijo m riddle, puzzle.

acervo m heap; store; hoard; estate.

acetato m acetate; **acético** acetic.

acetileno m acetylene.

acetona f acetone; **acetoso** acetous.

acetre m small bucket; eccl. holy water container.

achacar [1g]: ~ a attribute to, impute to; **achacoso** sickly, ailing.

achaparrado árbol dwarf, shrub-sized; p. stocky, thick-set, stumpy.

achaque m 🌿 infirmity; ailment; (asunto) matter, subject; defect, fault.

achatar [1a] flatten.

achicado child-like.

achicador m scoop, baler; **achicar** [1g] make smaller; intimidate, browbeat; ⚓ bale (out); ~se fig. eat humble pie.

achicharradero m hot-house, inferno; **achicharrar** [1a] cocina: fry crisp; (demasiado) overcook, burn; ~se get burnt.

achicoria f chicory.

achín m C.Am. peddler; door-to-door salesman.

achiquitarse S.Am. lose heart; cower.

achispado lit-up, jolly; **achisparse** [1a] get tipsy.

achocar [1g] dash (or hurl) against a wall; stone con piedra.

achocharse [1a] F get doddery, begin to dodder.

achubascarse [1g] (cielo) threatening.

achuchar [1a] F squeeze; urge on; **achuchón** m F squeeze; push.

achurar [1a] S.Am. kill; gut, disembowel.

aciago ill-fated, black, of ill omen.

acíbar m aloes; fig. bitterness, affliction; **acibarar** [1a] make bitter (with aloes); fig. embitter.

acicalado arma bright and clean; neat; **acicalar** [1a] polish, clean; fig. dress up; ~se fig. get dressed up.

acicate m spur; fig. spur, incentive.

acidez f acidity; **acidificar** [1g] acidify; **ácido 1.** fruta etc. sharp, sour, acid; **2.** m acid; **acidular** [1a] acidulate; **acídulo** acidulous.

acierto m (tiro) good shot, hit (a. fig.); fig. (acción) good choice, wise move; (habilidad) skill; (éxito) success.

aclamación f acclamation; por ~ by acclamation; **aclamar** [1a] acclaim.

aclaración f explanation; clearing; brightening (up); **aclarar** [1a] v/t. asunto clarify, explain; v/i. (tiempo) brighten (up), clear (up); **aclaratorio** explanatory; illuminating.

aclimatación f acclimatization; **aclimatar** [1a] acclimatize; ~se get acclimatized.

acné m 🌿 acne.

acobardar [1a] cow, intimidate; ~se flinch, shrink (back).

acocear [1a] kick; fig. ill-treat.

acodar [1a] vid etc. layer; ~se lean (sobre on).

acogedor ambiente, p. welcoming,

hospitable; **acoger** [2c] *visita etc.* welcome, receive; give refuge to; **se** take refuge (*a* in); avail o.s. of; **acogible** welcome; acceptable; **acogido** *f* welcome; acceptance; asylum.

acojinar [1a] ⊕ cushion.

acolchar [1a] *sew.* quilt; pad.

acólito *m* acolyte (*a. fig.*), server.

acomedido *S.Am.* obliging.

acometer [2a] attack, set upon, assail; *fig. tarea etc.* undertake; **acometida** *f* attack, assault; **acometimiento** *m* attack; **acometividad** *f* aggressiveness.

acomodable adaptable; **acomodación** *f* accommodation; **acomodadizo** accommodating, obliging; acquiescent; **acomodado** (*conveniente*) suitable; *precio* moderate; *p.* wealthy; **acomodador 1.** obliging; **2.** *m thea.* usher; **acomodadora** *f thea.* usherette.

acomodar [1a] **1.** *v/t.* (*componer*) arrange; find room for, accommodate; *acción* suit; adjust, put right; **2.** *v/i.* suit, fit; be suitable; **3.** **se** (*conformarse*) comply; adapt o.s.; **acomodo** *m* arrangement; lodgings; job; *S.Am.* neatness.

acompañado *sitio* busy, frequented; **acompañamiento** *m* accompaniment (*a. ♪*); (*p.*); escort; *thea.* extras; *sin ~* unaccompanied; **acompañanta** *f* escort; *♪* accompanist; **acompañante** *m* companion; escort; *♪* accompanist; **acompañar** [1a] accompany (*a. ♪*), go with; *mujer freq.* chaperon; enclose *en carta*; **se con ♪** accompany o.s. on.

acompasado rhythmic, regular, measured; **acompasar** [1a] *♪* mark the rhythm of; ♪ measure with a compass.

acondicionado ⊕ conditioned; (*estado*) well set-up, in good condition; **acondicionador** *m*: *~ de aire* air-conditioner; **acondicionamiento** *m*: *~ de aire* air-conditioning; **acondicionar** [1a] arrange; prepare; ⊕ condition.

aconsejable advisable, politic; **aconsejar** [1a] advise, counsel; **se** seek (*or·take*) advice.

acontecer [2d] happen, occur; **acontecimiento** *m* happening.

acopiar [1b] gather together, collect; **acopio** *m* (*acto*) gathering, collecting; abundance.

acoplado *m S.Am.* trailer; **acopla-**

dor *m radio:* coupler; **acoplamiento** *m* ⊕ coupling; joint; *⚡* hook-up; **acoplar** [1a] ⊕ (*unir*) join, couple, fit together; *S.Am.* 🚂 couple (up); **se** *zo.* mate, pair.

acorazado 1. armor-plated, ironclad; **2.** *m* battleship; **acorazamiento** *m* armor; armor plating; **acorazar** [1f] armor-plate; **se** *fig.* steel o.s. (*contra* against).

acorchado spongy, cork-like.

acordada *f* 🏛 decree; **acordadamente** by common consent; unanimously; **acordado** agreed; **acordar** [1m] **1.** *v/t.* decide, resolve; *♪* tune; *colores* blend; **2.** *v/i.* agree; correspond; **3.** **se** agree, come to an agreement (*con* with); *~* (*de*) remember; **acorde 1.** agreed; in accord; **2.** *m* harmony, chord.

acordeón *m* accordion.

acordonado corded, ribbed; **acordonar** [1a] tie up; *lugar* cordon off.

acores *m 🏥* milk crust.

acornar [1m], **acornear** [1a] butt; (*penetrando*) gore.

acorralado cornered, at bay; **acorralamiento** *m* corralling; *fig.* intimidation; **acorralar** [1a] *animales* pen, corral.

acorrer [2a] run (up), hasten (*a* to).

acortar [1a] shorten, cut down; **se** *fig.* be slow, be timid.

acosar [1a] pursue, hound (*a. fig.*); **acoso** *m* pursuit; *fig.* harrying.

acostar [1m] lay (down); *niño etc.* put to bed; **se** lie down; go to bed.

acostumbrado usual, customary; **acostumbrar** [1a] *v/t.* accustom, get *s.o.* used (*a* to); *v/i.*: *~* (*a*) *inf.* be in the habit of *ger.*; **se** accustom o.s.

acotación *f* (*mojón*) boundary mark; *surv.* elevation mark; (*apunte*) marginal note; **acotamiento** *m* boundary mark; annotation; stage direction; *S.Am.* shoulder (of road); **acotar** [1a] *terreno* survey, mark out; *página* annotate.

acotillo *m* sledge(-hammer).

acre acrid, pungent; tart, sharp.

acrecencia *f* increase, growth; **acrecentar** [1k] increase; *p.* promote; **acrecer** [2d] increase.

acreditación *f* accrediting; clearance *por policía*; **acreditado** accredited; reputable; **acreditar** [1a] *embajador etc.* accredit (*cerca de* to); *†* credit; **se** get a reputation (*de* for).

acreedor 1. deserving (*a* of); **2.** *m*, **-a** *f*

creditor; **acreencia** f S.Am. credit balance.

acribar [1a] sift, riddle; **acribillado** (balas) riddled; **acribillar** [1a] pepper, riddle (a balas etc. with); fig. pester.

acriminación f incrimination; **acriminador** incriminating; **acriminar** [1a] incriminate.

acrimonia f acridness; fig. acrimony; **acrimonioso** acrimonious.

acriollarse [1a] S.Am. go native.

acrisolar [1a] ⊕ purify, refine.

acrobacia f acrobatics (a. ✶); **acróbata** m/f acrobat; **acrobático** acrobatic.

acta f minutes; transactions; certificate de elección; ~s pl. minutes, record de reunión.

actitud f attitude (a. fig.), posture; outlook; **activar** [1a] activate, energize; speed up; **actividad** f activity; movement de muchedumbre etc.; en ~ in operation, in action; **activista** m/f activist; **activo** 1. active (a. gr.); fig. active, energetic; 2. m ✝ assets.

acto m act, action; ceremony; ♀s pl. de los Apóstoles Acts (of the Apostles); ~ de fe act of faith.

actor m actor; fig. protagonist; **actora**: parte ~ prosecution; plaintiff; **actriz** f actress.

actuación f action; performance (a. thea.); ~ en directo live performance; S.Am. role; **actual** present(-day); **actualidad** f present (time); (cuestión) question of the moment; en la ~ at the present time; ~es pl. current events; (película) news-reel; **actualmente** at present.

actuar [1e] v/t. set in motion, operate; work; v/i. act (de as); perform; ⊕ operate.

actuario m actuary.

acuarela f water color.

acuario m aquarium.

acuartelado heráldica: quartered; **acuartelar** [1a] quarter, billet.

acuático aquatic, water attr.

acuchillado knifelike; fig. experienced, wary; **acuchillar** [1a] stab (to death), knife; ~se fight with knives.

acucia f diligence; (prisa) haste; **acuciante** pressing; **acuciar** [1b] urge on, hasten, prod (on); **acucioso** diligent, keen.

acuclillarse [1a] squat (down).

acudir [3a] come up; present o.s.; (replicar) respond, answer.

acueducto m aqueduct.

acuerdo m agreement, understanding; harmony; (recuerdo) remembrance; de ~ in agreement; ¡de ~! I agree!, agreed!; estar de ~ con agree with; ponerse de ~ come to an agreement, agree.

acullá over there, yonder.

acumulación f accumulation (a. acto); pile; hoard; **acumulador** m storage battery; **acumular(se)** [1a] accumulate, gather, pile up; **acumulativo** accumulative.

acunar [1a] rock in a cradle.

acuñación f minting; **acuñar** [1a] moneda coin, mint; medalla strike.

acuoso watery; fruta juicy.

acupuntura f ✶ acupuncture.

acurrucarse [1g] squat; curl up.

acusación f accusation; esp. ⚖ charge, indictment; **acusado** 1. marked, pronounced; 2. m, a f accused, defendant; **acusador** 1. accusing, reproachful; 2. m, -a f accuser; **acusar** [1a] accuse (de of); ⚖ indict; recibo acknowledge; ~se confess (de su. to; de adj. to being); **acusativo** m accusative (case); **acusatorio** accusatory; **acuse** m acknowledgement (de recibo of receipt); **acusete** m/f S.Am. informer; **acusón** F 1. tell-tale; 2. m, -a f gossip.

acústica f acoustics; **acústico** 1. acoustic; 2. m hearing aid.

acutángulo adj. acute-angled.

adagio m adage; ♪ adagio.

adamado effeminate.

adamascado damask; **adamascar** [1g] damask.

adán m F slovenly fellow.

adaptabilidad f adaptability; **adaptable** adaptable; p. freq. versatile; **adaptación** f adaptation; **adaptador** m adapter; **adaptar** [1a] adapt; fit; ~se adapt o.s. (a to).

adarga f (oval) shield.

adecentar [1a] make decent, tidy up.

adecuado adequate, fit, suitable (a, para for); **adecuar** [1d] fit, adapt.

adefesio m F (disparate) absurdity, nonsense; outlandish dress; (p.) queer bird.

adelantado 1. precocious, advanced; ✝ por ~ in advance; 2. m ✝ governor, captain-general; **adelantamiento** m advancement; progress; **adelantar** [1a] v/t. move forward; pago advance; (pasar) overtake, outstrip;

v/i. make headway, improve; *(reloj)* be fast, gain; **~se** go forward, go ahead; **adelante** ahead; forward(s); **¡~!** *(a interlocutor)* go ahead!, go on!, *(a visita)* come in!; *más* **~** further on; later; **adelanto** *m* advance (*a.* **†**), progress.

adelfa *f* rose-bay; oleander.

adelgazamiento *m* slimming; **adelgazar** [1f] *v/t.* make thin; *fig.* purify, refine; *v/i.* grow thin; reduce; **~se** grow thin.

ademán *m* gesture; motion *de mano*; *paint. etc.* attitude; **~es** *pl.* manners; *hacer* **~es** gesture, make signs.

además 1. *adv.* besides, moreover, 2. **~** *de prp.* besides, aside from.

adentrar(se) [1a]: **~** *en* go into, get into, get inside; **adentro** 1. = *dentro*; 2. **~s** *m/pl.* innermost being.

aderezar [1f] prepare, get ready; *fig.* embellish, adorn; *comida* season; **aderezo** *m* (*acto*) preparation; dressing; *(efecto)* adornment; *cocina*: seasoning.

adeudado in debt; **adeudar** [1a] *v/t.* *dinero* owe; *impuestos* be liable for; *v/i.* become realted; **~se** run into debt; **adeudo** *m* debt.

adherencia *f* adherence; **adherente** 1.: **~** *a* adhering to, sticking to; 2. *m* follower, adherent; **adherir(se)** [3i] stick (*a* to); **~** *a fig.* espouse; **adhesión** *f* adhesion; **adhesivo** *adj. a. su. m* adhesive.

adiamantado diamondlike.

adición *f* addition; *(cuenta*) bill, check; **adicional** extra; **adicionar** [1a] *(sumar)* add (up).

adicto 1.: **~** *a* devoted to; given to; 2. *m* supporter; fan.

adiestramiento *m* training; breaking (in).

adiestrar [1a] *(enseñar)* train; *(guiar)* guide; **~se** train *en* s. *(a inf.* to *inf.*).

adinerado moneyed, well-off F.

adiós 1. *int.* good-bye!; 2. *m* goodbye; farewell.

aditivo *adj. a. su. m* additive.

adivinable guessable; **adivinación** *f* prophecy, divination; **adivinanza** *f* riddle; **adivinar** [1a] *porvenir etc.* prophesy, foretell; **adivino** *m*, **a** *f* fortune-teller.

adjetivo 1. *m* adjective; 2. adjectival; **~** *gentilicio* adjective of nationality.

adjudicación *f* award; **adjudicar** [1g] adjudge; award; **~se** *algo* appropriate.

adjuntar [1a] append; enclose *en carta*; **adjunto** 1. joined on; enclosed *en carta*; 2. *m* addition, adjunct; *(p.)* assistant.

admínículo *m* accessory; **~s** *pl.* emergency kit.

administración *f* administration; management; **administrador** *m*, **-a** *f* administrator; *(jefe)* manager; *(síndico)* steward; **administrar** [1a] administer; manage; **administrativo** administrative; managerial.

admirable admirable; **admiración** *f* admiration; wonder; **admirador** *m*, **-a** *f* admirer; **admirar** [1a] *(respetar)* admire; look up to; astonish; **~se** be surprised, wonder *(de* at); **admirativo** admiring.

admisible admissible; legitimate; **admisión** *f* admission (*a* to); *(recepción)* acceptance; **admitir** [3a] admit (*a. fig.*; *a* to, *en* into); accept, permit, allow.

admonición *f* warning; **admonitorio** warning *attr.*

adobar [1a] dress, prepare; *carne* pickle; *piel* tan, dress; **adobe** *m* adobe; **adobera** *f* *S.Am.* brick-shaped cheese; mold for brick-shaped cheese; **adobo** *m* preparation, pickle.

adocenado commonplace, ordinary.

adoctrinar [1a] indoctrinate.

adolecer [2d] fall ill (*de* with); **~** *de* suffer from (*a. fig.*).

adolescencia *f* adolescence; **adolescente** *adj. a. su. m/f* adolescent.

adonde 1. where; 2. *¿adónde?* where (to)?

adopción *f* adoption; **adoptar** [1a] adopt (*a. fig.*); *fig.* embrace; approve; **adoptivo** adoptive.

adorable adorable; **adoración** *f* worship; **adorar** [1a] adore.

adormecer [2d] send to sleep; *fig.* calm, lull; **~se** fall asleep, *(miembro)* go to sleep; **adormecido** drowsy; numb; *fig.* inactive; **adormecimiento** *m* drowsiness; numbness; **adormidera** *f* opium poppy.

adornar [1a] adorn, embellish (*de* with); *sew.* trim (*de* with); **adornista** *m/f* decorator; **adorno** *m* adornment; decoration.

adquirir [3i] acquire; obtain; **†** purchase; **adquirido** acquired; **adquisición** *f* acquisition; **†** purchase; **adquisividad** *f* acquisitiveness; **adquisitivo** acquisitive.

adrenaline f adrenalin.

adresógrafo m addressograph.

aduana f customs; custom-house; (*derechos de*) ~ customs duty; *exento de* ~ duty-free; *sujeto a* ~ dutiable; **aduanero 1.** customs *attr.*; **2.** m customs officer.

aducir [3o] adduce, bring forward; *prueba* furnish.

adulación f flattery; **adulador** m, -a f flatterer; **adular** [1a] flatter, make up to; **adulón** F **1.** fawning; **2.** m, -a f toady.

adúltera f adulteress; **adulteración** f adulteration; **adulterar** [1a] *v/t.* adulterate; *v/i.* commit adultery; **adulterino** adulterous; **adulterio** m adultery, misconduct; **adúltero** adulterous; **adultez** f *C.Am.* adulthood.

adulto *adj. a. su.* m, **a** f adult.

advenedizo 1. foreign, (from) outside; **2.** m, **a** f foreigner; *contp.* upstart; **advenimiento** m advent; accession *al trono*.

adverbial adverbial; **adverbio** m adverb.

adversario m, **a** f adversary, opponent; **adversidad** f adversity; **adverso** *suerte* adverse, untoward.

advertencia f warning; caveat; reminder; foreword *en libro*; **advertido** capable; wide-awake; **advertir** [3i] *v/t.* notice; draw attention to; advise.

Adviento m Advent.

adyacente adjacent (*a. &*).

aeración f aeration; **aéreo** aerial, air *attr.*; **aerodinámico** aerodynamic; **aerofoto** f aerial photograph; **aeromoza** f *S.Am.* air hostess, stewardess; **aeronáutica** f aeronautics; **aeronáutico** aeronautic(al); **aeronave** f airship; **aeropuerto** m airport; **aerosol** m ⚛ aerosol; **aerostática** f aerostatics; **aerostático** aerostatic(al); **aeróstato** m aerostat, balloon; **aerotaxi** m air taxi.

afabilidad f affability, geniality; **afable** affable, good-natured.

afamado famed, noted (*por* for).

afán m industry; zeal, desire, urge (*de* for); **afanarse** [1a] exert o.s., strive; *C.Am.* work for pay; **afanoso** *trabajo* laborious, heavy.

afeamiento m defacing; disfigurement; **afear** [1a] make ugly.

afección f affection (*a. &*); change, effect; ~es *pl. del alma* emotions;

afectación f affectation, pose; pretence; **afectado** affected, unnatural; **afectar** [1a] (*dejarse sentir en*) affect, have an effect on; *S.Am.* hurt, injure; **afectísimo** *mst* affectionate; *suyo* ~ yours truly; **afectivo** affective; **afecto 1.** affectionate, fond; **2.** m affection, fondness (*a* for); **afectuoso** affectionate.

afeitada f, **afeitado** m shave, shaving; **afeitar** [1a] *barba* shave; *cara* make up; ~se (have a) shave; **afeite** m make-up, cosmetic.

afeminación f effeminacy, **afeminado 1.** effeminate; **2.** m effeminate person, sissy *sl.*

aferrar [1k] *v/t.* grapple, seize; ⚓ grapple; ~se grapple (with, together).

afianzamiento m guarantee, security; ⚖ bail; **afianzar** [1f] *muro* support, prop up; (*sujetar*) fasten; *p. etc.* vouch for.

afición f fondness, liking (*a* for), taste (*a música etc.* for); hobby; **aficionado 1.** (*no profesional*) amateur; ~ *a música etc.* fond of, with a taste for; **2.** m, **a** f (*no profesional*) amateur; enthusiast; fan; **aficionar** [1a] make *s.o.* keen (*a algo* on); ~se *a*, ~ *de* get fond of, take a (fancy) to.

afiebrarse [1a] *S.Am.* get a fever.

afilada f *S.Am.* grinding, sharpening; **afiladera** f grindstone; **afilado** *filo* sharp, keen; **afilador** m (*p.*) knife-grinder; ⊕ strop; **afiladura** f sharpening, whetting; **afilalápices** m pencilsharpener; **afilar** [1a] sharpen; ~se get sharp *etc.*

afiliación f affiliation; **afiliado** affiliated (*a* to); ✝ subsidiary; **afiliarse** [1a]: ~ *a* affiliate (o.s.) to.

afilón m strop.

afín 1. bordering; related, similar; **2.** m/f relation by marriage.

afinado in tune; **afinador** m ♪ tuning-key; (*p.*) tuner; **afinar** [1a] *v/t.* perfect; polish; ♪ tune; *v/i.* sing (or play) in tune.

afinidad f affinity; kinship.

afirmación f affirmation, assertion; **afirmar** [1a] (*reforzar*) strengthen, (*declarar*) affirm, assert; ~se steady o.s.; **afirmativa** f affirmative; **afirmativo** affirmative; positive.

aflicción f sorrow, affliction; **aflictivo** distressing; **afligido 1.** distressed, heartbroken; **2.:** *los* ~s *m/pl.* the bereaved; **afligir** [3c] afflict;

Mex. beat; whip; trouble; **~se** grieve.

aflojamiento *m* slackening, loosening (*a.* 🌂); *fig.* relief; **aflojar** [1a] *v/t.* slacken; loosen; release; *fig.* relax; *v/i. fig.* (*ablandarse*) relent; get slack; **~se** slacken (off); work loose *etc.*

aflorar [1a] crop out, crop up, outcrop.

afluencia *f* (*flujo*) inflow, influx; (*gente etc.*) crowd, jam; *hora(s) de* ~ rush hour; **afluente 1.** flowing; eloquent; **2.** *m* tributary, feeder; **afluir** [3g] flow.

aforar [1a] ⊕ gauge; *fig.* appraise.

aforismo *m* aphorism; **aforístico** aphoristic.

aforrar [1a] line, face; **~se** put on plenty of underclothes.

afortunado fortunate, lucky.

afrancesado *adj. a. su. m,* **a** *f* Francophile; Frenchified; **afrancesarse** [1a] go French; become Gallicized.

afrenta *f* affront; indignity; **afrentar** [1a] affront; dishonor; **~se** be ashamed (*de* of); **afrentoso** insulting.

africano *adj. a. su. m,* **a** *f* African.

afrodisíaco *adj. a. su. m* aphrodisiac.

afrontamiento *m* confrontation; **afrontar** [1a] confront, bring face to face; *enemigo etc.* face (up to).

afuera 1. *adv.* outside; *¡~!* out of the way!; **2.** **~s** *f/pl.* outskirts; suburbs.

agachadiza *f* snipe; **agachar** [1a] *cabeza* bow; *sombrero* slouch; **~se** crouch; (*esconderse*) duck.

agalla *f* ♀ gall(-nut); *ichth.* gill; *fig. tener (muchas)* **~s** have guts.

agarrada *f* F scrap, brawl; **agarradera** *f S.Am.* hold, grip, handle; *tener* **~s** have connections; **agarradero** *m* handle, grip; ⊕ lug; **agarrado** F stingy, tight(-fisted); **agarrar** [1a] *v/t.* grip, grasp, grab *con fuerza*; *v/i.* take hold (*de* of); **~se** grasp one another, grapple; **agarro** *m* grasp, hold; **agarrón** *m S.Am.* brawl; fight.

agarrotar [1a] *fardo* tie tight; *reo* garrotte; **~se** 🌂 stiffen; ⊕ seize up.

agasajar [1a] treat kindly, make much of; (*con banquete etc.*) regale; **agasajo** *m* consideration, kindness; (*regalo*) royal welcome.

ágata *f* agate.

agavillar [1a] bind (in sheaves); **~se** F gang up, band together.

agazapar [1a] F catch, grab; **~se** F (*esconderse*) hide.

agencia *f* agency (*a. fig.*); bureau; *S.Am.* pawnshop; ~ *de turismo,* ~ *de viajes* tourist office, travel agency; **agenciar** [1b] bring about, engineer; procure, obtain; **~se** manage, get along.

agenda *f* notebook.

agente *m* agent; ~ (*de policía*) policeman; ~ *marítimo* shipping agent; *S.Am.* ~ *viajero* commercial traveller, salesman.

agible workable, feasible.

agigantado gigantic.

ágil agile, nimble, quick; **agilidad** *f* agility *etc.*; **agilitar** [1a] enable, make it easy for; **~se** limber up.

agitación *f* waving; shaking *etc.*; ♫ roughness; *fig.* ~ (*de ánimo*) agitation; **agitado** ♫ rough, *fig.* agitated, upset; **agitador** *m* agitator.

agitar [1a] *bandera etc.* wave; *brazo* shake, wave; *ala* flap; *fig.* stir up; **~se** shake, wave to and fro; *fig.* get excited.

aglomeración *f* mass, agglomeration; **aglomerado** *m* agglomerate; coal briquet; **aglomerar(se)** [1a] form a mass; (*gente*) crowd together.

aglutinación *f* agglutination; **aglutinar(se)** [1a] agglutinate.

agobiador, agobiante oppressive; overwhelming; **agobiar** [1b] weigh down; burden (*a.fig.*); exhaust, wear out; **~se con,** ~ *de* be weighed down with; **agobio** *m* burden; oppression.

agolpamiento *m* rush, crush, throng *de gente etc.*; **agolparse** [1a] crowd together, throng.

agonía *f* agony; throes (*a. fig*); **agonizante 1.** dying; **2.** *m/f* dying person; **agonizar** [1f] *v/t.* F harass, pester; *v/i.* be in the throes of death.

agorar [1n] predict, prophesy; **agorero 1.** *p.* who prophesies; **2.** *m,* **a** *f* fortune-teller.

agostar [1a] *plantas* parch, burn up; *tierra* plough (in summer); **~se** wither; **agosto** *m* August; *fig.* harvest.

agotable exhaustible; **agotado** exhausted; *libro* out of print; **agotamiento** *m* exhaustion (*a.* 🌂); depletion, draining; **agotar** [1a] exhaust (*a.* 🌂); *cisterna* drain, empty; **~se** be(come) exhausted.

agraciado graceful; nice; blessed (*de* with); **agraciar** [1b] improve the looks of, make more attractive.

agradable pleasant, nice; **agradar** [1a] please, be pleasing to.

agradecer [2d] *p.* thank; *favor* be grateful (*or* thankful) for; **agradecido** grateful (*a* to; *por* for); appreciative; **agradecimiento** *m* gratitude.

agrado *m* affability; taste, liking.

agrandar [1a] make bigger, enlarge.

agrario agrarian; land *attr.*

agravación *f*, **agravamiento** *m* aggravation, worsening; 𝒮 change for the worse; **agravante** 1. aggravating; 2. *f* additional burden; *unfortunate circumstance*; **agravar** [1a] weigh down, make heavier; **~se** worsen.

agraviar [1b] wrong, offend; **~se** take offence; **agravio** *m* offence, wrong, *a.* ⚖ grievance; **agravioso** offensive.

agraz *m* sour grape; (*zumo*) sour grape juice; *fig.* bitterness; **agrazar** [1f] *v/t.* embitter; *v/i.* taste sour.

agredir [3a; *defective*] assault.

agregado *m* (*conjunto*) aggregate; (*p.*) attaché; **agregar** [1h] (*añadir*) add (*a* to); (*juntar*) gather, collect; **~se** be joined.

agremiar [1b] form into a union.

agresión *f* aggression; **agresivo** aggressive; *fig.* assertive; **agresor** *m*, **-a** *f* aggressor, assailant.

agreste rural; *fig.* rustic.

agriar [1b *or* 1c] (make) sour; *fig.* exasperate; **~se** turn (sour).

agrícola agricultural, farming *attr.*; **agricultor** 1. farming *attr.*; 2. *m*, **-a** *f* farmer; **agricultura** *f* agriculture.

agridulce bittersweet.

agriera *f Col., P.R.* heartburn.

agrietar [1a] crack (open); **~se** get cracked; (*manos*) chap.

agrimensor *m* (land-)surveyor; **agrimensura** *f* (land-)surveying.

agringarse [1h] *S.Am.* act like a foreigner; prented to be a gringo.

agrio 1. sour, acid, tart (*a. fig.*); *fig.* disagreeable; 2. *m* (sour) juice; **~s** *pl.* citrus fruits.

agronomía *f* agronomy, agriculture; **agrónomo** 1. agricultural; 2. *m* farming expert; **agropecuario** farming and stockbreeding *attr.*

agrupación *f*, **agrupamiento** *m* association, group; (*acto*) grouping (together); **agrupar** [1a] group (together); **~se** (*ps.*) crowd (around); (*cosas*) cluster.

agrura *f* sourness (*a. fig.*).

agua *f* 1. water; (*lluvia*) rain; ⚓ (*estela*) wake; **~** *bendita* holy water; **~** *dulce* fresh water; **~** (*de*) *manantial* spring water; **~** *potable* drinking-water; **~** *abajo* downstream; **~** *arriba* upstream; *se me hace la boca* **~** my mouth waters; *¡hombre al* **~***!* man overboard!; 2. **~s** *pl.* waters; ⚓ tide; 🜄 urine; **~s** *territoriales* territorial waters; **~s** *mayores* excrement; **~s** *menores* urine; *hacer* **~s** make water, relieve o.s.

aguacate *m bot.* avocado; *pear-shaped emerald*.

aguacero *m* (heavy) shower; **aguado** watery, watered (down); *sopa* thin; *fig. fiesta etc.* spoiled, interrupted; **aguador** *m* water carrier; **aguafiestas** *m/f* wet blanket, killjoy; **aguafuerte** *f* etching; **aguaje** *m* (*marea*) (spring) tide; current; (*provisión*) water supply; *C.Am.* cloudburst; reprimand; **aguamanil** *m* ewer, water-jug; **aguamar** *m* jellyfish; **aguamarina** *f* aquamarine; **aguanieve** *f* sleet.

aguantada *f S.Am.* patience; forebearance.

aguantar [1a] *v/t. techo* hold up; *aliento* hold; *dolor etc.* endure, withstand; put up with; *v/i.* last, hold out; **~se** hold o.s. back.

aguar [1i] water (down); *fig.* mar.

aguardar [1a] *v/t.* wait for, await; *v/i.* wait; *b.s.* lie in wait.

aguardentería *f* liquor store.

aguardiente *m* brandy.

aguarrás *m* (oil of) turpentine.

aguatocha *f* pump.

aguazal *m* puddle.

agudeza *f* acuteness, sharpness (*a. fig.*); (*chiste*) witticism; **agudo** sharp, pointed; 𝒮, Å, *gr.* acute; *sentido* keen, acute; *ingenio* ready, lively.

agüero *m* (*arte*) augury; (*pronóstico*) forecast; (*señal*) omen.

aguerrido hardened; inured; **aguerrir** [3a; *defective*] inure, harden.

aguijada *f* goad; **aguijar** [1a] *v/t.* goad (*a. fig.*); *fig.* urge on; **aguijón** *m* goad; *zo.* sting; **aguijonazo** *m* prick; *zo.*, 🐝 sting.

águila *f* eagle; *fig.* superior mind.

aguileño aquiline; sharpfeatured.

aguilera *f* eyrie; **aguilón** *m* jib *de grúa*; **aguilucho** *m* eaglet.

aguinaldo *m* Christmas (*or* New Year) gift; (*propina*) gratuity.

aguja f sew. needle; (roma) bodkin; hand de reloj; ~ de zurcir darning-needle; ~ de gancho crochet hook; ~ hipodérmica hypodermic needle; ~ de (hacer) media knitting-needle; **agujazo** m jab, prick; **agujereado** full of holes; vasija leaky; **agujerear** [1a] make holes in; pierce; **agujero** m hole; (alfiletero) needle-case; **agujetas** f/pl. 🟆 stitch; **agujón** m hatpin.

agusanado maggoty.

agustin(ian)o adj. a. su. m, a f Augustinian.

aguzar [1f] sharpen (a. fig.).

ahechar [1a] sift; trigo winnow.

aherrojar [1a] fetter, put in irons.

aherrumbrarse [1a] get rusty.

ahí there, just there; de ~ que with the result that; por ~ over there, that way.

ahijado m, a f godchild; fig. protegé(e); **ahijar** [1a] p. adopt.

ahilar [1a] v/t. line up; v/i. go in single file; ~se 🟆 faint with hunger; (vino etc.) go sour, go bad.

ahincadamente earnestly, hard; **ahincado** emphatic, energetic; **ahincar** [1g] press, urge; ~se make haste; **ahinco** m earnestness, energy.

ahitar [1a] surfeit, cloy; ~se stuff o.s. (de with); **ahito 1.** surfeited, satiated; **2.** m indigestion.

ahogadero m halter, headstall de caballo; **ahogado** cuarto close, stifling; **ahogar** [1h] drown en agua; suffocate, smother por falta de aire (a. fig.); ~se drown; (suicidarse) drown o.s.; suffocate; **ahogo** m 🟆 shortness of breath, tightness of the chest.

ahondar [1a] v/t. deepen; fig. penetrate; v/i. ~ en penetrate, go (deep) into; ~se go in more deeply; **ahonde** m deepening; digging.

ahora 1. adv. now; (hace poco) (just) now; (dentro de poco) in a little while; desde ~ from now on, henceforward; **2.** cj. now; ~ bien now then.

ahorcadura f hanging.

ahorcajarse [1a] sit astride.

ahorcar [1g] hang; ~se be hanged.

ahorquillado forked; **ahorquillar** [1a] (asegurar) prop up, stay; ~se fork, become forked.

ahorrar [1a] mst save; disgusto, peligro avoid; ~se spare o.s., save o.s.; **ahorrativo** thrifty; b.s. stingy; **ahorro** m economy; ~s pl. savings.

ahuchar [1a] hoard, put by; Col., Ven.,Mex. bait; incite.

ahuecar [1g] v/t. hollow (out), make a hollow in; ~se F put on airs.

ahulado C.Am.,Mex. impermeable.

ahumado 1. tocino etc. smoked; smoky; **2.** m smoking, curing; **ahumar** [1a] v/t. tocino etc. smoke, cure; v/i. (give out) smoke; ~se (comida) taste burnt.

ahusado tapering; **ahusarse** [1a] taper.

ahuyentar [1a] drive away, scare away; ~se run away.

airado angry, furious; vida immoral, depraved; **airar** [1a] anger, irritate, ~se get angry (de, por at).

aire m air; wind, draught; ♪ tune, air; al ~ libre adj. outdoor; adv. in the fresh (or open) air; outdoors; de buen (mal) ~ in a good (bad) temper; cambiar de ~(s) have a change of air; darse ~s put on airs.

airear [1a] air, ventilate; ~se take the air; 🟆 catch a chill.

airosidad f grace(fulness), elegance; **airoso** lugar airy; tiempo blowy; fig. graceful, elegant.

aislación f insulation; ~ de sonido sound-proofing; **aislacionismo** m isolationism; **aislado** insulated; cut off; ⚡, ⊕ insulated; **aislador** ⚡ **1.** insulating; **2.** m insulator, non-conductor; **aislamiento** m insulation; ⚡ insulation; **aislar** [1a] isolate (a. fig.), separate; ⚡ insulate; ~se isolate o.s. (de from).

ajar [1a] (c)rumple, mess up; esp. vestido crush; ~se get (c)rumpled.

ajedr(ec)ista m/f chess player; **ajedrez** m chess; (fichas) chess set, chessmen; **ajedrezado** chequered.

ajenjo m wormwood; absinth.

ajeno (de otro) somebody else's, not one's own; los bienes ~s, lo ~ other people's property.

ajete m young garlic; garlic sauce.

ajetreado vida tiring, busy; **ajetrearse** [1a] bustle about; (afanarse) slave (away); **ajetreo** m (trajín) bustle.

ají m chili; red pepper; **ajiaceite** m sauce of garlic and olive oil; **ajo** m (clove of) garlic.

ajorca f bracelet, bangle.

ajornalar [1a] hire by the day.

ajuar m household furnishings.

ajuiciado sensible; **ajuiciar** [1b] bring to one's senses.

ajustable adjustable; **ajustado** right, fitting; *ropa* closefitting, tight, clinging; **ajustador** *m* waistcoat; corselet; fitter; **ajustar** [1a] **1.** *v/t.* ⊕ *(encajar etc.)* fit (a to; into); *(cerrar, ponerse etc.)* fasten; *mecanismo* adjust, regulate; **2.** *v/i.* fit; ~ bien be a good fit; **3.** ~**se** *(convenir)* fit, go; adapt o.s., get adjusted (a to); **ajustamiento** *m* ✝ settlement; **ajuste** *m* ⊕ *etc.* fitting; adjustment; *sew.* fit.

ajusticiar [1b] execute.

al = *a* + *el*; ~ *llegar* on arriving.

ala wing (a. ⚔, △, *pol. a. fig.*); ✕ wing, main plane; △ *(alero)* eaves; *caérsele a uno las* ~s lose heart; *cortar las* ~s a *fig.* clip *s.o.'s* wings.

alabador approving, eulogistic; **alabanza** *f* praise; eulogy; ~s *pl.* praises; **alabar** [1a] praise; ~se be pleased.

alabastro *m* alabaster (a. *fig.*); **alabastrino** alabaster *attr.*

alabear(se) [1a] warp; **alabeo** *m* warping; *tomar* ~ warp.

alacena *f* recess cupboard.

alacrán *m* scorpion.

alado winged; *fig.* swift.

alambicado distilled; overrefined; **alambicar** [1g] distil; *fig.* scrutinize; **alambique** *m* still.

alambre *m* wire (a. ♪); ~ *cargado* live wire; ~ *forrado* covered wire; ~ *de púas* barbed wire; **alambrar** [1a] wire; **alambrera** *f* wire mesh.

alameda *f* 🌳 poplar grove; *(paseo)* walk; **álamo** *m* poplar.

alano *m* mastiff.

alarde *m* ✕ review; *fig.* display, parade; *hacer* ~ *de* make a show of; **alardear** [1a] boast, brag; **alardeo** *m* boasting, bragging.

alargadera *f* 🔭 adapter; ⊕ extension; **alargamiento** *m* elongation, extension *etc.*; **alargar** [1h] lengthen, prolong; extend; *(estirar)* stretch; ~**se** *(días etc.)* draw out, lengthen.

alarido *m* yell, shriek, howl.

alarife *m* architect; builder; *S.Am.* sharper.

alarma *f* alarm (a. *fig.*); ~ *falsa* false alarm; **alarmante** alarming, startling; **alarmar** [1a] ✕ call to arms, alert; ~**se** be (or become) alarmed; **alarmista** *m/f* alarmist.

alba *f* dawn; *eccl.* alb.

albacea *m* executor; *f* executrix.

albacora *f* *ichth.* albacore; swordfish.

albahaca *f* basil.

albanés *adj. a. su. m*, **-a** *f* Albanian.

albañal *m* sewer, drain.

albañil *m* bricklayer; mason; **albañilería** *f* *(obra)* brickwork.

albarán *m* "to let" sign.

albarda *f* pack-saddle; **albardilla** *f* cushion, pad; *(tocino)* lard.

albaricoque *m* apricot; **albaricoquero** *m* apricot (tree).

albayalde *m* white lead.

albedrío *m* (a. *libre* ~) free will; *(capricho)* whim, fancy.

alberca *f* pond, cistern; *S.Am.* swimming-pool.

albergar [1h] *v/t.* shelter; lodge, put up; *v/i.*, ~**se** *(find)* shelter; lodge; **albergue** *m* shelter, refuge (a. *mount.*); *(alojamiento)* lodging.

albero 1. white; **2.** *m* pipeclay; *(paño)* tea towel; **albina** *f* salt lake, salt marsh; **albino** *adj. a. su. m*, **a** *f* albino.

albóndiga *f* meat ball, fish ball.

albor *m* whiteness; *(luz)* dawn (light); ~es *pl.* dawn; **alborada** *f* dawn; ✕ reveille; **alborear** [1a] dawn.

albornoz *m* bathrobe.

alborotador 1. riotous; boisterous; **2.** *m*, **-a** *f* agitator; rioter; mischiefmaker; **alborotar** [1a] *v/t.* disturb, agitate, stir up; *S.Am.* excite curiosity in; *v/i.* make a racket; ~**se** *(p.)* get excited; *(turba)* riot; **alboroto** *m* *(vocerío etc.)* disturbance, racket.

alborozar [1f] cheer (up), gladden; ~**se** be glad; **alborozo** *m* merriment, gaiety; jollification.

albricias *f/pl.* reward; ¡~! good news!

álbum *m* album.

albumen *m* 🌱 albumen; *(clara)* white of an egg; **albúmina** *f* 🔬 albumin.

albur *m* *ichth.* dace; *fig.* risk, chance.

alcabala *f* *hist.* sales tax.

alcachofa *f* artichoke.

alcahueta *f* procuress, bawd; *(mensajera)* go-between; **alcahuete** *m* procurer, pimp; **alcahuetería** *f* procuring, pandering.

alcaide *m* ✝ *castillo*: governor, castellan; warder, jailer.

alcalde *m* mayor; **alcaldesa** *f* mayoress; **alcaldía** *f* mayoralty; *(casa)* mayor's residence.

álcali *m* alkali; **alcalino** alkaline.

alcance *m* reach *de mano* (a. *fig.*); range; *fig.* scope *de programa etc.*;

capacity; *al* ~ within reach (de of; *a. fig.*); *fuera de su* ~ out of one's reach; **alcancía** *f* money-box; *S.Am. eccl.* collection box.

alcándara *f* clothes rack; *orn.* perch.

alcanfor *m* camphor.

alcantarilla *f* sewer; conduit; **alcantarillado** *m* sewer system, drains; **alcantarillar** [1a] lay sewers in.

alcanzar [1f] *v/t.* (*llegar*) reach; (*igualarse*) catch up with, overtake; *v/i.* reach (*a, hasta to* or *acc.*); ~ *a inf.* manage to *inf.*

alcaparra *f* ❦ caper.

alcaparrosa *f* ⚗ vitriol.

alcaravea *f* caraway.

alcatraz *m orn.* gannet; pelican.

alcázar *m* fortress, citadel.

alcazuz *m* liquorice.

alce *m zo.* elk; moose.

alcista † 1. bull(ish); 2. *m* bull.

alcoba *f* bedroom.

alcohol *m* alcohol; *lámpara de* ~ spirit lamp; **alcohólico** *adj. a. su. m*, **a** *f* alcoholic; **alcoholismo** *m* alcoholism.

alcornoque *m* cork oak; *fig.* blockhead.

alcorza *f cocina:* icing, frosting; **alcorzar** [1f] *cocina:* ice.

alcuza *f* olive-oil bottle; *S.Am.* cruet; water jug.

alcuzcuz *m approx.* couscous (*paste of flour and honey*).

aldaba *f* (door-)knocker; (*barra etc.*) bolt, cross-bar; **aldabada** *f* knock (on the door).

aldea *f* village; **aldeano 1.** village *attr.*; rustic; **2.** *m*, **a** *f* villager.

aleación *f* alloy; **alear**[1] [1a] *metall.* alloy.

alear[2] [1a] *orn.* flap (its wings); (*p.*) move one's arms up and down; *fig.* ✠ convalesce.

aleccionador instructive, enlightening; **aleccionar** [1a] teach, coach.

alegación *f* allegation; **alegador** *S.Am.* quarrelsome; litigious; **alegar** [1h] plead (*a. 𝔱𝔱*); allege.

alegoría *f* allegory; **alegórico** allegoric(al).

alegrar [1a] gladden, cheer (up); enliven; *fuego* stir up, brighten up; ~**se** be glad, be happy; ~ *de inf.* be happy (*or* glad) to *inf.*; **alegre** *p.*, *cara etc.* happy; *ánimo* joyful, glad; *carácter* cheerful; **alegría** *f* happiness; joy(fulness); **alegrón** *adj.* tipsy, high.

alejamiento *m* (*acto*) removal; (*lo remoto*) remoteness; distance; **alejar** [1a] move *s.t.* away (de from).

aleluya 1. *f* (*grito*) hallelujah; *paint.* Easter print; **2.** *m* Eastertime.

alemán 1. *adj. a. su. m*, **-a** *f* German; **2.** *m* (*idioma*) German.

alentador encouraging; **alentar** [1k] encourage, inspire (*a inf.* to *inf.*); ~**se** ✠ get well.

alergia *f* allergy; **alérgico** allergic.

alero *m* △ eaves; *mot.* fender; wing; **alerón** *m* aileron.

alerta 1.: ¡~! watch out!; *estar* (*ojo*) ~ be on the alert; **2.** *m* alert.

aleta *f* small wing; *ichth.* fin; flipper *de foca; mot.* wing; ⊕, 🗲 blade; ~**s** *sport* flippers; frogfeet.

aletargar [1h] benumb, drug; ~**se** become lethargic.

aletazo *m orn.* flap of the wing; *ichth.* movement of the fin; **aletear** [1a] flap its wings, flutter; **aleteo** *m* fluttering, flapping.

alevosía *f* treachery; **alevoso 1.** treacherous; **2.** *m* traitor.

alfabético alphabetic(al); **alfabetizar** [1f] teach to read and write; **alfabeto** *m* alphabet.

alfalfa *f* lucerne, alfalfa.

alfanje *m* cutlass; *ichth.* swordfish.

alfeñicarse [1g] F get awfully thin; (*remilgarse*) be finicky; **alfeñique** *m* almond paste; F (*p.*) delicate sort, mollycoddle.

alférez *m* ✗ second lieutenant; ~ *de fragata approx.* midshipman.

alfil *m ajedrez:* bishop.

alfiler *m* pin; (*broche*) brooch, clip; **alfilerar** [1a] pin (up); **alfilerazo** *m* pinprick (*a. fig.*); **alfiletero** *m* needlecase.

alfombra *f* carpet (*a. fig.*); (*esp. pequeña*) rug; ~ *de baño* bath mat; **alfombrado** *m* carpeting; **alfombrar** [1a] carpet (*a. fig.*); **alfombrilla** *f* rug; ✠ German measles; *mot.* floormat.

alforfón *m* buckwheat.

alforjas *f/pl.* saddle-bags; (*comestibles*) provisions.

alforza *f* pleat, tuck; *fig.* scar, slash.

alga *f* seaweed, alga ⚑.

algarabía *f* Arabic; *fig.* gibberish.

algarroba *f* carob (bean); **algarrobo** *m* carob tree, locust tree.

algazara *f* (Moorish) battle-cry; *fig.* unproar, din.

álgebra f algebra; **algebraico** algebraic.

algo 1. pron. something; ~ es ~ something is better than nothing; ¡por ~ será! there must be some reason behind it!; **2.** adv. rather, somewhat; es ~ grande it's rather big.

algodón m cotton; ♀ cotton plant; ✄ swab; **algodonero 1.** cotton attr.; **2.** m (p.) cotton-dealer; ♀ cotton plant.

alguacil m bailiff, constable.

alguien someone, somebody.

alguno 1. adj. (algún delante de su. m. singular) some, any; (tras su.) (not ...) any; **2.** pron. some; one; someone, somebody.

alhaja f jewel, gem; (mueble) fine piece; **alhajar** [1a] casa furnish, appoint; **alhajera** f S.Am. jewelry box.

alharaca f fuss, ballyhoo; **alharaquiento** demonstrative; strident.

alhelí m wallflower; gillyflower.

alhucema f lavender.

aliado 1. allied; **2.** m, **a** f ally; **alianza** f alliance (a. fig.); **aliar** [1c] ally; ~se become allied.

alias adv. a. su. m alias.

alicaído with drooping wings; fig. downcast, down in the mouth.

alicantino adj. a. su. m, **a** f (native) of Alicante.

alicates m/pl. pliers.

aliciente m incentive, inducement.

alienación f alienation (a. ♉); ♉ mental derangement; **alienado 1.** distracted; mentally ill; **2.** m, **a** f mad person, lunatic; **alienista** m/f psychiatrist, alienist.

aliento m (un ~) breath; (acto) breathing; fig. bravery, strength.

aligeramiento m easing; alleviation; relief; **aligerar** [1a] carga lighten (a. fig.); fig. ease, relieve, paso quicken.

alimaña f animal; esp. vermin.

alimentación f nourishment, feeding; (comida) food; ~ forzada ✄ force feeding; **alimentante** m/f ♊ person obliged to provide child support; **alimentar** [1a] feed, nourish (a. fig.); ~se feed (de, con on); **alimenticio** manjar nourishing; nutritious; **alimentista** m/f pensioner; **alimento** m food (a. fig.); fig. incentive; encouragement.

alindar [1a] v/t. surv. mark out; v/i. be adjacent, adjoin.

alineación f alignment (a. ⊕); line-up; **alineado** aligned; no ~ pol. non-

aligned; Third World; **alinear** [1a] align, line (up); ~se line up.

aliñar [1a] cocina: dress, season; S.Am. hueso set; **aliño** m dressing.

aliquebrado crestfallen.

alisador m ⊕ (p.) polisher; (instrumento) smoothing blade; **alisar** [1a] smooth (down); polish.

aliso m alder.

alistamiento m enlistment, recruitment; **alistar** [1a] (put on a) list; ~se enroll; ⚔ enlist, join up.

aliteración f alliteration; **aliterado** alliterative.

alivianar [1a] S.Am. lighten.

aliviar [1b] lighten (a. fig.); fig. relieve, soothe; speed up; ~se get (or gain) relief; **alivio** m relief (a. fig.), alleviation.

aljamía f Castilian written in Arabic characters.

aljibe m (rainwater) cistern; ♣ water tender; mot. oil tanker.

aljofaina f (wash)basin.

aljófar m pearl (a. fig.).

aljofifa f floor-cloth; **aljofifar** [1a] wash, mop (up).

allá (over) there; (tiempo) way back, long ago; más ~ de beyond, past.

allanamiento m levelling, flattening; ♊ submission (a to); **allanar** [1a] v/t. (hacer llano) level (out), flatten; even; (alisar) smooth; v/i. level out; ~se level out, level off.

allegadizo gathered at random; **allegado 1.** near, close; p. related (de to); **2.** m, **a** f (pariente) relation, relative; S.Am. foster; **allegar** [1h] gather (together), collect; ~se go up (a to).

allende beyond; ~ de besides.

allí there; ~ dentro in there; de ~ a poco shortly after(wards).

alma f soul; spirit; fig. (p.) (living) soul; heart and soul, life-blood, moving spirit; ¡~ mía! my precious!; con (toda) el ~ heart and soul; con toda mi ~ with all my heart; volver a uno el ~ al cuerpo calm down, recover one's peace of mind.

almacén m (depósito) warehouse, store (a. fig.); (tienda) shop; (tienda grande) department store; **almacenamiento** m storage; (computer) data storage; memory; **almacenaje** m storage (charge); ~ frigorífico cold-storage; **almacenar** [1a] put in store, store (up); **almacenero** m storekeeper, warehouseman; S.Am.

grocer; **almacenista** *m* warehouse (*or* shop) owner, warehouseman.

almagrar [1a] raddle, ruddle; **almagre** *m* red ochre.

almanaque *m* almanac; calendario.

almeja *f* shell-fish, clam.

almena *f* merlon; ~s *pl.* battlements; **almenado** battlemented.

almenara *f* beacon; (*araña*) chandelier.

almendra *f* ♀ almond; (*hueso*) kernel, stone; **almendrada** *f* almond shake; **almendrado** 1. almond-shaped, pear-shaped; 2. *m* macaroon; **almendral** *m* almond grove; **almendro** *m* almond (tree).

almiar *m* haycock; hayrick.

almíbar *m* syrup; fruit juice; **almibarado** syrupy (*a. fig.*); *fig.* sugary, oversweet; **almibarar** [1a] preserve (*or* serve) in syrup.

almidón *m* starch; **almidonar** [1a] starch.

alminar *m* minaret.

almirantazgo *m* admiralty; **almirante** *m* admiral.

almirez *m* (metal) mortar.

almizcle *m* musk; **almizcleño** musky; **almizclero** *m* (*ciervo*) musk-deer; (*roedor*) musk-rat.

almodrote *m* cheese and garlic sauce; F mixture; hodgepodge.

almohada *f* cushion *de silla*; pillow *de cama*; (*funda*) pillow-case; **almohadilla** *f* small cushion; ⊕ pad; **almohadillado** padded, stuffed.

almohaza *f* curry-comb; **almohazar** [1f] *caballo* curry, groom.

almoneda *f* (*subasta*) auction; (*saldo*) clearance sale.

almorranas *f/pl.* piles, hemorrhoids.

almorzada *f* double handful; heavy breakfast; **almorzar** [1f *a.* 1m] *v/t.* have for lunch, lunch on; *v/i.* (have) lunch.

almuerzo *m* lunch; luncheon.

alnado *m*, **a** *f* stepchild.

alocado mad, wild.

áloe *m* ♀ aloe; *pharm.* aloes.

alojamiento *m* lodging(s); ✕ (*acto*) billeting; (*casa*) billet, quarters (*a.* ♣); **alojar** [1a] lodge, house; alojo *m* *S.Am.* accomodations; lodging; ~se lodge; ✕ be billeted.

alondra *f* (*a.* ~ *común*) lark.

alpaca *f* zo. alpaca; alpaca wool; alpaca cloth; German silver.

alpargata *f* rope sandal; rubber and canvas sandal.

alpende *m* lean-to; tool-shed.

alpestre Alpine; *fig.* mountainous; **alpinismo** *m* mountaineering; **alpinista** *m/f* mountaineer, climber; alpinist; **alpino** Alpine.

alpiste *m* ♀ canary grass; (*semilla*) bird seed.

alquería *f* farmhouse.

alquiladizo 1. for rent; for hire; 2. *m*, **a** *f* hireling; **alquilar** [1a] (*dueño*): *casa* rent (out), let; *coche etc.* hire out; (*inquilino etc.*): *casa, garaje, televisor* rent; ~se (*casa*) be let (en *precio* at, for); **alquiler** *m* (*acto*) hiring; renting; (*precio*) rent(al); *coche de* ~ rental car.

alquimia *f* alchemy; **alquimista** *m* alchemist.

alquitara *f* still; **alquitarar** [1a] distil.

alquitrán *m* tar; ~ *mineral* coal tar; **alquitranado** *m* (*firme*) tarmac; (*lienzo*) tarpaulin; **alquitranar** [1a] tar.

alrededor 1. *adv.* around; 2. *prp.* ~ *de* around, about; *fig.* about, in the region of; 3. ~es *m/pl.* outskirts, environs *de ciudad*.

alsaciano *adj. a. su. m*, **a** *f* Alsatian.

alta *f* ♣ discharge (from hospital).

altanería *f* meteor. upper air; haughtiness; **altanero** *ave* highflying, soaring; *fig.* haughty; high-handed.

altar *m* altar; ~ *mayor* high altar.

altavoz *m* radio: loud-speaker; ⚡ amplifier.

alterabilidad *f* changeability; **alterable** alterable; **alteración** *f* alteration; (*deterioro*) change for the worse, upset, disturbance; **alterado** *fig.* agitated, upset; **alterar** [1a] alter, change; ⚡ *etc.* change for the worse, upset; ~se *fig.* be disturbed.

altercado *m* argument, altercation; **altercar** [1g] quarrel, argue.

alternación *f* alternation, rotation; (*entre sí*) interchange; **alternador** *m* ⚡ alternator; **alternar** [1a] *v/t.* alternate (con with); interchange; vary; *v/i.* alternate; **alternativa** *f* (*trabajo*) shift work; (*elección*) alternative, choice; **alternativo, alterno** alternate; alternating; *combustible* ~ alternate fuel; *energías* ~as alternate energy sources.

alteza *f* height; (*título*) highness.

altibajos *m/pl.* ups and downs, unevenness *de terreno*.

altillo *m* hillock; *S.Am.* attic.

altímetro m altimeter.

altiplanicie f high plateau.

altisonante high-flown, highsounding.

altitud f height; geog., 🛩 altitude.

altivez f haughtiness, arrogance; **altivo** haughty, arrogant.

alto[1] **1.** adj. mst high; p., edificio, árbol tall; voz loud; en (lo) ⁓ up, high (up); en lo ⁓ de up, on top of; **2.** adv. lanzar high (up); **3.** m geog. height, hill.

alto[2] m ✕ etc. halt; esp. fig. stop, standstill; ¡⁓ ahí! halt!, stop!

altoparlante m loud speaker.

altruísmo m altruism; **altruísta 1.** altruistic; **2.** m/f altruist.

altura f mst height; height, tallness; geog. latitude; ⚓ high seas; en las ⁓s on high; tiene 2 metros de ⁓ it is 2 metres high.

alucinación f hallucination, delusion; **alucinar** [1a] hallucinate; ⁓se be hallucinated, be deluded.

alud m avalanche.

aludir [3a]: ⁓ a allude to, mention (in passing).

alumbrado 1. F lit-up, tight; **2.** m lighting (system); illumination; **alumbramiento** m ⚡ lighting, illumination; **alumbrar** [1a] v/t. light (up), illuminate; v/i. ⚡ give birth; ⁓se F get tipsy.

alumbre m alum.

alúmina f alumina; **aluminio** m aluminium.

alumnado m student body; **alumno** m, **a** f univ. etc. student, pupil.

alunado lunatic, insane.

alunizaje m moon landing; **alunizar** [1f] land on the moon.

alusión f allusion, mention, reference; **alusivo** allusive.

aluvial alluvial; **aluvión** m alluvion (a. ⚖); (depósito) alluvium.

álveo m bed (of a stream).

alveolar alveolar; **alvéolo** m alveolus, cell de panal; anat. socket.

alza f ↑ rise, advance; ✕ rear sight; **alzada** f height de caballo; ⚖ appeal; **alzado 1.** elevated, raised; S.Am. insolent; brazen; rebellious; **2.** m △ front elevation; typ. gathering; **alzamiento** m (acto) lift(ing), raising; rise, **alzaprima** f (palanca) lever; (cuño) wedge; **alzar** [1f] raise, lift (up), hoist; mantel etc. put away; ⁓se rise (up); pol. revolt, rise; **alzo** m C.Am. theft.

ama f mistress de casa; (dueña) owner; (de pensión etc.) landlady; ⁓ de casa housekeeper, housewife.

amabilidad f kindness; amiability; **amable** kind; amiable, nice; **amacharse** [1a] S.Am. cohabit; get intimate.

amado, **a** f love(r), sweetheart; **amador 1.** loving; **2.** m, **a** f lover.

amadrigar [1h] welcome (with open arms); ⁓se go into its hole.

amaestrado animal trained, performing; **amaestramiento** m training etc.; **amaestrar** [1a] train; caballo break in.

amagar [1h] v/t. threaten, show signs of, portend; v/i. threaten; **amago** m threat; (indicio) sign.

amainar [1a] v/t. vela take in, shorten; v/i. abate (a. fig.); moderate; ⁓se abate; slacken.

amalgama f amalgam; fig. concoction; **amalgamación** f amalgamation; **amalgamar** [1a] amalgamate (a. fig.); fig. mix (up).

amamantar [1a] suckle.

amancebamiento m cohabitation; common-law marriage.

amanecer 1. [2d] dawn; appear (at dawn); **2.** m dawn; **amanecida** f dawn.

amanerado mannered, affected; **amanerarse** [1a] become affected.

amansado tame; **amansador** m, **-a** f tamer; S.Am. horse breaker; **amansar** [1a] animal tame; caballo break in; p. subdue; ⁓se moderate, abate.

amante 1. loving, fond; **2.** m/f lover; f mistress; ⁓s pl. lovers.

amañar [1a] do skilfully, do cleverly; fake; ⁓se be handy, be expert; **amaño** m skill, expertness; ⁓s pl. ⊕ tools.

amapola f poppy.

amar [1a] love.

amaraja m 🛩 landing (on the sea); ditching.

amaranto m amaranth.

amarar [1a] land (on the sea).

amargar [1h] make bitter; fig. embitter, spoil; ⁓se get bitter; **amargo 1.** bitter (a. fig.); fig. embittered; **2.** m bitterness; ⁓s pl. bitters; **amargor** m, **amargura** f bitterness (a. fig.).

amarillear [1a] shoe yellow; be yellowish; **amarillecer** [2d] (turn) yellow; **amarillo** adj. a. su. m yellow.

amarra f mooring line, painter; ~s pl. moorings; **amarradero** m (poste) bollard; **amarrar** [1a] v/t. barco moor.

amartelado in love; love-sick; **amartelamiento** m infatuation; **amartelar** [1a] p. woo, court; ~se fall in love.

amartillar [1a] hammer; pistola cock.

amasada f S.Am. batch of dough; batch of mortar; **amasadura** f (acto) kneading; (masa) batch; **amasamiento** m kneading; ⚘ massage; **amasar** [1a] masa knead; harina, yeso mix; patatas mash; **amasijo** m kneading.

amatista f amethyst.

amatorio love attr.; amatory.

amazona f amazon.

ambages m/pl. beating about the bush, circumlocutions; sin ~ in plain language.

ámbar m amber; ~ gris ambergris.

ambición f ambition; **ambicionar** [1a] strive after, seek; **ambicioso 1.** ambitious; b.s. pretentious; **2.** m, a f ambitious person.

ambidextro ambidextrous.

ambiente 1. ambient; **2.** m atmosphere (a. fig.); surroundings; medio~ environment.

ambigú m buffet supper; refreshment counter.

ambigüedad f ambiguity; **ambiguo** ambiguous; equivocal.

ámbito m ambit; △ confines.

ambos, ambas adj. a. pron. both.

ambrosía f ambrosia (a. fig.).

ambulancia f ambulance; ✕ field hospital; **ambulante** (que anda) walking; (que viaja) roving; **ambulatorio 1.** ambulatory; **2.** m ambulance.

amedrentar [1a] scare; intimidate.

amén 1. m amen; **2.** prp.: ~ de except (for); (además de) besides.

amenaza f threat, menace; **amenazador, amenazante** threatening, menacing; intimidating; **amenazar** [1f] v/t. threaten, menace; v/i. threaten, loom, impend.

amenguar [1i] lessen, diminish.

amenidad f pleasantness etc.; **ameno** pleasant, agreeable, nice; trato, estilo etc. pleasant.

americana f coat, jacket; **americanismo** m Americanism; **americanizar** [1f] Americanize; **americano**

adj. a. su. m, a f (norte-) American; (sud-, central-) Latin-American.

ametralladora f machine gun; ~ antiaérea antiaircraft gun.

amiba f, **amibo** m amoeba.

amiga f friend; (novia) girl friend, b.s. mistress; **amigable** friendly; fig. harmonious; **amigarse** [1h] get friendly; b.s. live in sin.

amígdala f tonsil; **amigdalitis** f tonsilitis.

amigo 1. friend; ser muy ~s be very good friends; **2.** m friend; (novio) boyfriend; sweetheart; ser ~ de fig. be fond of.

amilanar [1a] intimidate, cow; ~se be cowed, be scared.

aminorar [1a] lessen; gastos etc. cut down; paso slacken.

amistad f friendship; ~es pl. (ps.) friends, acquaintances; estrechar ~ con get friendly with; **amistar** [1a] bring together, make friends; ~se become friends; **amistoso** friendly; (de vecino) neighbourly.

amnesia f loss of memory, amnesia.

amnistía f amnesty.

amo m master de casa etc.; head of the family; (dueño) proprietor.

amodorramiento m sleepiness, drowsiness; **amodorrarse** [1a] get sleepy, get drowsy; **amodorrido** drowsy; numb; sleepy.

amohinar [1a] vex, annoy; ~se get vexed, get annoyed; (esp. niño) sulk.

amoldar [1a] mould (a. fig.); ~se fig. adapt o.s., adjust o.s.

amonestación f warning; esp. ⚖ caution; eccl. (marriage) banns; **amonestar** [1a] (advertir) warn; (recordar) remind; (reprobar) reprove, admonish.

amoníaco 1. ammoniac(al); **2.** m ammonia.

amontonamiento m accumulation, piling up; **amontonar** [1a] heap (up), pile (up), accumulate; ~se pile (up), accumulate, collect.

amor m love (a for; de of); (p.) love; ~es pl. love-affair, romance; ~ cortés courtly love; ¡~ mío! (my) darling!; por el ~ de Dios for God's sake.

amoral amoral, unmoral; **amoralidad** f amorality.

amoratado purple; blue (de frío with cold).

amordazar [1f] perro muzzle.

amorío m (a. ~s pl.) love-affair,

romance; ~ secreto intrigue; **amoroso** *p.* loving, affectionate.
amortajar [1a] shroud, lay out.
amortecer [2d] *ruido* muffle, deaden; **~se** 🪦 faint, swoon.
amortiguación *f* deadening, muffling; absorbing; cushioning;
amortiguador 1. deadening *etc.*; **2.** *m* damper; ⊕ shock-absorber;
amortiguar [1i] *mst* = amortecer.
amortización *f* 🏷️ amortization; ✝ redemption; **amortizar** [1f] 🏷️ amortize; *préstamo* pay off.
amparador 1. helping, protecting; **2.** *m*, **-a** *f* protector; **amparar** [1a] (*ayudar*) help; protect; shelter (*de* from); **~se** seek help; seek protection *etc.*; **amparo** *m* help; protection; refuge, shelter.
amperímetro *m* ammeter; **amperio** *m* ampere.
ampliación *f* enlargement (*a. phot.*); (*ensanche*) extension; **ampliadora** *f* *phot.* enlarger; **ampliar** [1c] amplify; enlarge (*a. phot.*); (*ensanchar*) extend; **amplificación** *f* amplification (*a. rhet., phys.*); ⚡ gain; **amplificador** *m radio:* amplifier; **amplificar** [1g] enlarge; amplify (*a. rhet., phys.*); **amplio** *espacio etc.* ample; *vestido* full, roomy; **amplitud** *f* ampleness; fullness *etc.*
ampolla *f* 🪦 blister; (*burbuja*) bubble; 🪦 (*vasija*) ampoule; **ampollarse** [1a] blister; **ampolleta** *f* (*vasija*) vial; (*reloj*) hour-glass.
ampulosidad *f* bombast, pomposity; **ampuloso** bombastic, pompous.
amputación *f* amputation; **amputar** [1a] amputate, cut off.
amueblado furnished; **amueblar** [1a] furnish; appoint.
amujerado effeminate.
amuleto *m* amulet, charm.
amurallar [1a] wall (in).
anacarado mother-of-pearl *attr.*
anacrónico anachronistic; **anacronismo** *m* anachronism; (*objeto*) out-of-date object.
ánade *m* duck; **anadear** [1a] waddle; **anadón** *m* duckling.
anales *m/pl.* annals.
analfabetismo *m* illiteracy; **analfabeto** *adj. a. su. m*, **a** *f* illiterate.
analgesia *f* analgesia; **analgésico** analgesic *adj. a. su. m.*
análisis *mst m* analysis; **analista** *m* 🎯 analyst; **analítico** analytic(al);

analizador *m* analyst; **analizar** [1f] analyse.
analogía *f* analogy; **análogo** analogous, similar.
ananá(s) *m* pineapple.
anaquel *m* shelf; **anaquelería** *f* shelves, shelving.
anaranjado *adj. a. su. m* orange.
anarquía *f* anarchy; **anárquico** anarchic(al); **anarquismo** *m* anarchism; **anarquista 1.** anarchic(al); *pol.* anarchic(ic); **2.** *m/f* anarchist.
anatema *mst m* anathema; **anatematizar** [1f] *eccl.* anathematize; (*maldecir*) curse; *fig.* reprimand.
anatomía *f* anatomy; ~ *macroscópica* gross anatomy; **anatómico 1.** anatomical; **2.** *m* = **anatomista** *m/f* anatomist.
anca *f* haunch; rump, croup *de caballo*; F buttock; **~s** *pl.* rump.
ancheta *f* ✝ (*géneros*) small amount; (*ganancia*) gain, profit; *Arg.* foolishness; ridiculous act.
ancho 1. wide, broad; *esp. fig.* ample, full; *ropa* loose(-fitting); *fig.* liberal, broad(-minded); **2.** *m* width, breadth; 👕 gauge.
anchoa *f* anchovy.
anchura *f* width, breadth, wideness; **anchuroso** broad; spacious.
anciana *f* old woman, old lady; **ancianidad** *f* old age; **anciano 1.** old, aged; **2.** *m* old man; *eccl.* elder.
ancla *f* anchor; *echar* (*levar*) ~s drop (weigh) anchor; **ancladero** *m* anchorage; **anclar** [1a] anchor.
andaderas *f/pl.*, **andador** *m* child's walker; **andado** worn, well-trodden; (*común*) ordinary; **andador 1.** fast-walking; (*carácter*) fond of walking; **2.** *m*, **-a** *f* walker; (*callejero*) gadabout; **3. ~es** *pl.* leading-strings; **andadura** *f* (*acto*) walking; (*paso*) gait.
andalucismo *m* Andalusianism; **andaluz** *adj. a. su. m*, **-a** *f* Andalusian; **andaluzada** *f* F tall story.
andamiada *f*, **andamiaje** *m* scaffold(ing), staging; **andamio** *m* scaffold(ing); (*tablado*) stage, stand.
andante 1. walking; *caballero* errant; **2.** *m* ♪ andante; **andanza** *f* incident; fortune, fate.
andar 1. [1q] *v/t. camino* walk; *distancia* go, cover; *v/i.* (*a pie*) walk, go; (*moverse*) move; ⊕ go, run, work; *¿cómo anda eso?* how are things going?; *¿cómo andas de dinero?* how

are you off for money?; ¡anda, anda! don't be silly!; ¡andando! that's all!; ~ a caballo etc. ride, go on; 2. m gait, pace.

andariego = andador; **andarín** m walker; **andas** f/pl. (silla) litter, sedan chair; (féretro) bier; **andén** m 🚇 platform; S.Am. (acera) sidewalk.

andinismo m S.Am. mountain climbing in the Andes; **andino** Andean.

andrajo m rag, tatter; (p.) scallywag; ~s pl. rags, tatters; **andrajoso** ragged, in tatters.

andurriales m/pl. out of the way place, wilds.

aneblar [1k] cover with mist (or cloud); ~se cloud over, get misty.

anécdota f anecdote, story; **anecdótico** anecdotal.

anegación f flooding etc.; **anegadizo** terreno subject to flooding; **anegar** [1h] (ahogar) drown (en in; a. fig.); (inundar) flood; ~se (p.) drown (a. fig.); (campos) be flooded; (barco) sink, founder.

anejo 1. attached; dependent; ~ a attached to, joined on to; 2. m △ annex, out-building.

anemómetro m anemometer.

anémona f, **anemone** f anemone.

anestesia f anaesthesia; **anestesiar** [1b] anaesthetize.

anestésico adj. a. su. m anaesthetic.

anexar [1a] annex; adjunto attach, append; **anexión** f annexation; **anexionar** [1a] annex; **anexo** 1. documento, edificio attached; 2. m annex.

anfibio 1. amphibious; amphibian (✕); 2. m amphibian.

anfiteatro m amphitheatre; thea. balcony, dress-circle.

anfitrión m lit. a. co. host; **anfitriona** f hostess.

ánfora f amphora; S.Am. ballotbox.

anfractuosidad f (desigualdad) roughness; (vuelta) bend, turning.

angarillas f/pl. hand-barrow; (cestas) panniers.

ángel m angel; ~ custodio, ~ de la guarda guardian angel; **angelical**, **angélico** angelic(al).

angina f angina, quinsy.

anglicano adj. a. su. m, a f Anglican; **anglicismo** m Anglicism; **anglófilo** adj. a. su. m, a f Anglophile; **angloparlante** English-speaking; **anglosajón** adj. a. su. m, -a f Anglo-Saxon.

angostar(se) [1a] narrow; **angosto** narrow; **angostura** f narrowness.

anguila f eel; ~ de mar conger eel.

angular angular; piedra corner attr.; **ángulo** m angle (a. ⋏); (esquina) corner, turning; phot. de ~ ancho wide-angle; en ~ at an angle; **anguloso** angular.

angurria f S.Am. raging hunger; greed.

angustia f anguish, distress; 𝒔 ~ vital anxiety state; **angustiado** distressed, anguished; (avaro etc.) mean; **angustiar** [1b] grieve, distress; ~se be distressed.

anhelante 𝒔 (a. respiración ~) panting; fig. (ansioso) eager; **anhelar** [1a] v/t. be eager for; yearn for; v/i. 𝒔 gasp, pant; ~ inf. yearn to inf.; **anhelo** m eagerness; yearning; **anheloso** 𝒔 gasping, panting; fig. eager.

anidar [1a] v/t. shelter, take in; v/i. fig. live, make one's home.

anilina f aniline.

anillo m ring (a. ast.); cigar band; ~ de boda wedding ring.

ánima f soul; soul in purgatory; eccl. las ~s sunset bell, Angelus.

animación f liveliness, life; vivacity de carácter; animation; **animado** lively, gay.

animal 1. animal; p. stupid; 2. m animal; fig. (estúpido) blockhead; F beast, brute; **animalada** f F stupidity.

animar [1a] biol. give life to, animate; fig. (alegrar) cheer up; discusión enliven, liven up; (alentar) encourage (a inf. to inf.); ~se (p.) brighten up, cheer up; **ánimo** m soul; spirit (a. fig.); (valor) courage, nerve; energy; attention, thought; ¡~! cheer up!

animosidad f (valor) courage, nerve; **animoso** spirited, brave; ready (para for).

aniñado cara etc. childlike, of a child; b.s. childish, puerile.

aniquilación f, **aniquilamiento** m annihilation, obliteration; **aniquilar** [1a] annihilate, destroy; ~se be wiped out; fig. 𝒔 waste away.

anís m ⚘ anise; (grana) aniseed; (bebida) approx. anisette; **anisete** m anisette.

aniversario m anniversary.

ano m anus.

anoche last night; **anochecer** 1. [2d] get dark; arrive at nightfall!; 2. m nightfall, dusk; **anochecida** f nightfall, dusk.

ánodo m anode.

anomalía f anomaly; **anómalo** anomalous.

anonadar [1a] annihilate, destroy; fig. overwhelm; ~**se** be humilated.

anónimo 1. anonymous; nameless; † sociedad limited; **2.** m (en general) anonymity; (p.) s.o. unknown.

anorexia f 🩺 anorexia.

anormal abnormal; **anormalidad** f abnormality.

anotación f (acto) annotation; note; S.Am. score; **anotar** [1a] annotate.

ánsar m goose; **ansarino** m gosling.

ansia f 🩺 anxiety, tension; (angustia) anguish; **ansiar** [1b] v/t. long for, yearn for, covet; **ansiedad** f anxiety (a. 🩺); solicitude; suspense; **ansioso** anxious (a. 🩺), worried.

antagónico antagonistic, opposed; **antagonismo** m antagonism; **antagonista** m/f antagonist.

antaño last year; fig. long ago.

antártico Antarctic.

ante¹ m elk; buffalo; (piel) buckskin.

ante² before, in the presence of.

anteanoche the night before last; **anteayer** the day before yesterday.

antebrazo m forearm.

antecámara f antechamber, anteroom, lobby.

antecedente 1. previous, preceding; **2.** m antecedent (a. 🅰, gr., phls.); ~s pl. record, past history; **anteceder** [2a] precede, go before; **antecesor 1.** preceding; **2.** m, -a f predecessor; (abuelo) ancestor.

antedicho aforesaid, aforementioned.

antena f zo. antenna, feeler; radio: aerial, antenna; ~ interior incorporada built-in antenna.

antenombre m title.

anteojera f spectacle case; ~s pl. blinkers; **anteojero** m spectacle maker; optician; **anteojo** m telescope, eye-glass; ~s pl. spectacles, glasses.

antepagar [1h] prepay.

antepasado 1. before last; **2.** m forbear, forefather.

antepecho m balcony, ledge de ventana; parapet, guard-rail.

antepenúltimo last but two, antepenultimate.

anteponer [2r] place s.t. in front; fig. prefer; ~**se** come in front.

anterior (orden) preceding, previous;

anterior (a. gr.); former; **anterioridad** f precedence; priority.

antes 1. adv. before; formerly; (en otro tiempo) once, previously; cuanto ~, lo ~ posible as soon as possible; **2.** prp.: ~ de before; ~ de inf. before ger.; **3.** cj.: ~ (de) que before.

antesala f antechamber.

anti... anti...; **ácido** adj. a. su. m antacid; **~adherente** nonstick; **~aéreo** anti-aircraft; cañón ~ anti-aircraft gun; **~biótico** m antibiotic; **~ciclón** m anticyclone.

anticipación f anticipation, forestalling; † advance; con ~ in advance; **anticipado** future, prospective; † advance; **anticipar** [1a] fecha etc. advance, bring forward; † advance; ~**se** take place (or happen) early; **anticipio** m foretaste; (préstamo) advance; (pago) advance payment.

anti... **~clerical** anticlerical; **~conceptivo** m contraceptive; **~congelante** m (a. solución ~) anti-freeze, de-freezer; **~corrosivo** anti-corrosive; **~constitucional** unconstitutional; **~cristo** m Antichrist.

anticuado old-fashioned, out-of-date; antiquated; obsolete; **anticuarse** [1d] become antiquated; **anticuario** m 📖 antiquarian; † antique-dealer.

anti... **~derrapante** non-skid; **~deslizante** non-slipping; mot. non-skid; **~deslumbrante** antidazzle; **~detonante** mot. antiknock.

antídoto m antidote.

anti... **~económico** uneconomic(al); wasteful; **~estético** unsightly, offensive; **~fascista** adj. a. su. m/f antifascist; **~faz** m mask; veil; **~friccional** anti-friction attr.

antigualla f antique; (cuento) old story; **antiguamente** (en lo antiguo) in ancient times, of old; (antes) formerly, once; **antiguar** [1i] attain seniority; ~**se** = **anticuarse**; **antigüedad** f antiquity; † seniority; **~es** pl. antiquities; **antiguo** old; ancient; (anterior) former, late, one-time.

antihigiénico insanitary.

antílope m antelope.

antimonio m antimony.

antioxidante anti-rust.

antipara f screen.

antiparras f/pl. F glasses, specs.

antipatía f dislike (hacia for), aversion (hacia to, from); antipathy; **an-**

tipático disagreeable, unpleasant, not nice.

antipatriótico unpatriotic.

antípoda 1. antipodal; *fig.* contrary, quite the opposite; **2.** *m* antipode; ~s *f/pl. geog.* antipodes.

antirreflejos *adj.* nonreflecting.

antirresbaladizo *mot.* nonskid.

antisemita *m/f* anti-semite; **antisemítico** anti-semitic; **antisemitismo** *m* anti-semitism.

antiséptico *adj. a. su. m* antiseptic.

antisubmarino antisubmarine.

antítesis *f* antithesis; **antitético** antithetic(al).

antitóxico antitoxic; **antitoxina** *f biol.* antitoxin.

antojadizo capricious; given to sudden fancies; **antojarse** [1a] take a fancy to.

antología *f* anthology.

antónimo *m* antonym.

antorcha *f* torch; *fig.* lamp.

antracita *f* anthracite.

ántrax *m* anthrax.

antro *m* cavern.

antropofagía *f* cannibalism; **antropófago 1.** man-eating, anthropophagous ⏚; **2.** *m, a f* cannibal; **antropoide** anthropoid; **antropología** *f* anthropology; **antropólogo** *m* anthropologist.

anual annual; **anuario** *m* yearbook.

anublar [1a] *cielo* cloud; *(oscurecer)* darken, dim *(a. fig.)*; ~se cloud over; darken; *fig.* fade away.

anudar [1a] knot, tie; join, unite *(a. fig.)*; ~se get into knots *etc.*

anulación *f* annulment *etc.*; **anular¹** [1a] annul, cancel, nullify; *ley* revoke; ~se be deprived of authority, be removed.

anular² **1.** ring(-shaped); **2.** *m* ring finger.

anunciación *f* announcement; *(día de) la* ♀ The Annunciation (25 *March*); **anunciante** *m/f* ✝ advertiser; **anunciar** [1b] announce; proclaim; ✝ advertise; **anuncio** *m* announcement; proposal; ✝ *(esp. impreso)* advertisement; *(cartel)* placard, poster.

anverso *m* obverse.

anzuelo *m* (fish)hook; *fig.* lure, bait.

añadido *m* false hair, switch; **añadidura** *f* addition; ✝ extra measure; *por* ~ besides, in addition; **añadir** [3a] add *(a* to); *(aumentar)* increase.

añagaza *f* decoy, lure *(a. fig.)*.

añal 1. *suceso* yearly; ✐ *etc.* year-old; **2.** *m* year-old lamb *etc.*

añejar [1a] age, make old; ~se age; *(vino etc.)* improve with age; **añejo** old; *vino* mellow, mature.

añicos *m/pl.* bits, pieces, shreds.

añil *m* indigo *(a. ♀)*; bluing.

año *m* year; ~s *pl. (cumpleaños)* birthday; ~ bisiesto leap-year; ~ de Cristo Anno Domini (A.D.); ~ luz lightyear.

añoranza *f* longing, nostalgia *(de* for); **añorar** [1a] long for, pine for; grieve for, mourn.

añoso aged, full of years.

aojar [1a] put the evil eye on; **aojo** *m* evil eye, hoodoo.

aovado egg-shaped, oval; **aovar** [1a] lay eggs.

apacentadero *m* pasture (land); **apacentar** [1k] pasture, graze; ~se ✐ graze; *fig.* feed *(con, de* on).

apacibilidad *f* gentleness *etc.*; **apacible** gentle, mild, meek.

apaciguamiento *m* appeasement *etc.*; **apaciguar** [1i] pacify, appease; *(aquietar)* calm down; ~se calm down, quieten down.

apadrinar [1a] *empresa etc.* sponsor; *eccl. niño* act as godfather to; *novio* be best man for.

apagado *volcán* extinct; *color* dull, lustreless, muffled; *p.* listless, spiritless; **apagafuego** *m*, **apagaincendios** *m* fire extinguisher; **apagar** [1h] *fuego* put out, extinguish; ✐ *luz* turn off; ~se go out; be extinguished; **apagón** *m* blackout; ✐ power cut.

apalabrear [1a] *S.Am.* make an appointment.

apalancar [1g] lever (up).

apaleamiento *m* beating *etc.*; **apalear** [1a] beat, thrash; *alfombra* beat; ✐ winnow.

apandillar [1a] form into a gang.

apañado *fig.* handy, skilful; **apañar** [1a] *(coger)* pick up; *(asir)* take hold of; *b.s.* steal, swipe; ~se *para inf.* contrive to *inf.*

apañuscar [1g] F rumple, crumple; *S.Am.* jam together; *(robar)* swipe.

aparador *m* sideboard, buffet; *(vitrina)* show-case; **aparar** [1a] arrange; adorn.

aparato *m* ✐, *etc.* apparatus; *(dispositivo)* device, piece of equipment; ⊕ machine; *radio etc.*: set; **aparatoso** ostentatious, showy; pretentious.

aparcamiento m parking; ~ subterráneo underground garage; **aparcar** [1g] park (a vehicle).

aparcería f partnership; **aparcero** m partner; S.Am. sharecropper.

aparear [1a] make even, level up.

aparecer [2d] appear; turn up; **aparecido** m appearance; ghost, spectre.

aparejado fit, ready (para for); **aparejador** m foreman, overseer; **aparejar** [1a] prepare, get ready; meteor. threaten; caballo harness; ♣ fit out; ~se prepare o.s., get ready (para for); **aparejo** m preparation; (caballo) harness; ~s pl. ⊕ tools, gear.

aparentar [1a] feign, affect; edad seem to be, look; ~ inf. make as if to inf.; **aparente** apparent, seeming; **aparición** f appearance; (espectro) apparition; de próxima ~ libro forthcoming; **apariencia** f appearance, look(s).

apartadero m mot. turnout; stopping place; rest area; ⛟ siding; **apartado** 1. isolated, remote, secluded; camino devious; 2. m (a. ~ de correos) post-office box; (cuarto) spare room; typ. paragraph; **apartamento** m esp. S.Am. flat; **apartamiento** m (acto) withdrawal etc.; **apartar** [1a] separate, take away (de from); isolate; ⓥ etc. sort (out); ~se (dos ps.) separate (a. casados); (alejarse) move away; withdraw, retire (de from); **aparte 1.** apart, aside (de from); 2. m thea. aside.

apasionado passionate; (fogoso) fiery, intense; **apasionamiento** m passion, enthusiasm (de, por for); **apasionante** thrilling, exciting; **apasionar** [1a] stir deeply; ~se get excited; (enamorarse) fall in love with.

apatía f apathy; ⚕ listlessness; **apático** apathetic; ⚕ listless.

apear [1a] help s.o. down (de from); (bajar) take s.t. down; ~se dismount, get down (de caballo from); ⛟ etc. get off, get out.

apechugar [1h]: ~ con F put up with, swallow.

apedazar [1f] cut (or tear) into pieces; (remendar) mend, patch.

apedrear [1a] v/t. stone, pelt with stones; v/i. hail; ~se be damaged by hail.

apegadamente devotedly; **apegado:** ~ a attached to, fond of; **ape-garse** [1h] a become attached to, grow fond of; **apego** m: ~ a attachment to, fondness for.

apelación f appeal; sin ~ without appeal, final; **apelante** m/f appellant; **apelar** [1a] ⚖ appeal (de against); **apelativo** m C.Am. family name, last name.

apellidar [1a] name; (calificar) call; ~se be called, have as a surname; **apellido** m surname; name.

apelmazar [1f] compress; ~se cake; get lumpy.

apelotonar [1a] make into a ball; ~se (gente) crowd together.

apenar [1a] trouble; ~se grieve.

apenas scarcely, hardly (a. ~ si).

apendectomía f appendectomy; **apéndice** m appendix (a. ⚕); **apendicitis** f appendicitis.

apercibimiento m preparation; provision; notice; ⚖ summons; **apercibir** [3a] prepare; provide; ánimo prepare (para for); ⚖ summon; ~se get (o.s.) ready, prepare (o.s.).

aperitivo m appetizer; aperitif.

apero m tools, equipment, gear.

apersonarse [1a] ⚖ appear; appear in person.

apertura f mst opening.

apesadumbrar [1a], **apesarar** [1a] grieve, distress; ~se be grieved etc. (con, de at).

apestar [1a] v/t. ⚕ infect (with plague); fig. corrupt; v/i. stink; **apestoso** (que huele) stinking.

apetecer [2d] crave (for), long for, hunger for; **apetecible** desirable; tempting; **apetencia** f hunger; **apetito** m appetite (a. eccl.); esp. fig. relish; abrir el ~ whet one's appetite; **apetitoso** appetizing; inviting.

apiadar [1a] move to pity; víctima = ~se de take pity on.

apicarado niño spoilt, naughty.

ápice m apex; fig. whit, iota.

apilar(se) [1a] pile up, heap up.

apiñado jammed, packed, congested; **apiñadura** f, **apiñamiento** m congestion; squeeze, squash, jam; **apiñar** [1a] squeeze (together); ~se (gente) crowd together.

apio m celery.

apiolar [1a] F (prender) nab; (matar) do away with, bump off.

apisonadora f road-roller, steamroller; **apisonar** [1a] roll; tamp.

aplacar [1g] appease, placate.

aplanacalles *S.Am. m/f* idler; lazy person.

aplanamiento *m* smoothing *etc.*; **aplanar** [1a] smooth, level, roll flat; *calles* loaf, bum around; **~se** △ collapse.

aplastante overwhelming, crushing; **aplastar** [1a] squash, flatten (out).

aplaudida *f S.Am.* applause; **aplaudir** [3a] applaud, cheer; **aplauso** *m* applause.

aplazada *f S.Am.* postponement; **aplazamiento** *m* postponement *etc.*; **aplazar** [1f] postpone, defer.

aplicable applicable; **aplicación** *f* application (*a.* 🐝); (*asiduidad*) industry; **aplicar** [1g] *mst* apply (*a* to); *manos, color etc.* lay (*sobre* on); *hombres etc.* assign (*a, para* to); **~se** *algo* claim for o.s.; **~** *a* apply to, be applicable to.

aplomar [1a] make perpendicular; **~se** collapse, fall to the ground; **aplomo** *m fig.* seriousness, aplomb.

apocado spiritless; spineless; common, mean.

apocalíptico apocalyptic.

apocar [1g] make smaller, reduce; humiliate; **~se** humble o.s.

apócrifo apocryphal.

apodar [1a] nickname, dub; label.

apoderado *m* agent, representative; **apoderamiento** *m* authorization; power of attorney; **apoderar** [1a] authorize, empower; **~se** de (*asir*) seize, take hold of.

apodo *m* nickname; label.

apogeo *m ast.* apogee; *fig.* peak.

apolilladura *f* moth-hole; **apolillado** moth-eaten; **apolillarse** [1a] get moth-eaten.

apolítico apolitical; nonpolitical.

apologética *f* apologetics; **apología** *f* defence; encomium, eulogy.

apoltronado idling, lazy; **apoltronarse** [1a] get lazy; loaf around.

apoplejía *f* stroke, apoplexy; **apoplético** apoplectic.

aporreado *vida* poor, wretched; *Cuba, Mex.* chopped beef stew; **aporrear** [1a] beat, club; beat up; **~se** slave away.

aportación *f* contribution; **~es** *pl.* de *la mujer* dowry; **aportar** [1a] *v/t.* bring; contribute; **aporte** *m S.Am.* contribution.

aposentar(se) [1a] lodge, put up; **aposento** *m* room; lodging.

aposición *f* apposition.

apostadero *m* station, stand; ⚓ naval station; **apostar**[1] [1a] ✕ post, station.

apostar[2] [1m] *v/t. dinero* lay, wager; *v/i.* bet (*a, por* on; *a que* that); *v/i.*, **~se** compete (*con* with).

apostasía *f* apostasy; **apóstata** *m/f* apostate.

apostilla *f* note, comment; **apostillar** [1a] annotate; **~se** break out in pimples.

apóstol *m* apostle; **apostólico** apostolic.

apóstrofe *m or f* apostrophe; taunt, insult; rebuke, expostulation; **apóstrofo** *m gr.* apostrophe.

apostura *f* gracefulness; neatness.

apoteosis *f* apotheosis (*a. fig.*).

apoyar [1a] *v/t. codo etc.* lean, rest (*en, sobre* on); ⚓ *etc.* support, hold up; **~se** *en base* rest on; **apoyo** *m* support (*a. fig.*); *fig.* backing, help.

apreciable appreciable, considerable; **apreciación** *f* appreciation, appraisal; ✝ valuation; **apreciador** *m* appraiser; **apreciar** [1b] value, assess (*en at*; *a. fig.*); *esp. fig.* estimate; **aprecio** *m* appreciation, appraisal; esteem.

aprehender [2a] apprehend; seize; *fig.* perceive; **aprehensión** *f* seizure; *fig.* perception.

apremiador, apremiante urgent; pressing, compelling; **apremiar** [1b] (*obligar*) compel, force; (*instar*) urge on, press; **apremio** *m* compulsion *etc.*; ⚖ writ, judgement; summons.

aprender [2a] learn (*a inf.* to *inf.*).

aprendiz *m*, **-a** *f* apprentice (*de* to); (*principiante*) learner; **aprendizaje** *m* apprenticeship.

aprensión *f* apprehension, fear, worry; **aprensivo** apprehensive.

apresamiento *m* capture *etc.*; **apresar** [1a] *p.* capture; ⚖ seize; (*asir*) seize, grasp.

aprestar ready; **aprestar** [1a] prepare, make (*or* get) ready; **~se** prepare, get ready (*para inf.* to *inf.*); **apresto** *m* (*acto*) preparation; (*equipo*) outfit; priming.

apresurado hasty, hurried; **apresuramiento** *m* haste(ning); **apresurar** [1a] hurry (up, along); accelerate; **~se** hasten, make haste (*a, en, por inf.* to *inf.*).

apretadamente hard, tight(ly); **apretadera** *f* strap, rope; **~s** *pl.* F

pressure; **apretado** *vestido etc.*
tight; *lugar (pequeño)* cramped;
dense, thick; **apretar** [1k] **1.** *v/t.*
tuerca etc. tighten; *lío etc.* squeeze;
contenido pack in, pack tight; **2.** *v/i.*
(vestido) be tight; *(zapato)* pinch;
(empeorar) get worse; insist; **3.** ⁓*se*
(estrecharse) (get) narrow; *(ps.)*
squeeze up, huddle together.

apretón *m* squeeze, pressure; *(abra-*
zo) hug; *estar en un* ⁓ be in a
quandary; **aprieto** *m* crush, jam,
squeeze; *fig. (apuro)* fix, quandary;
(aflicción) distress.

aprisa quickly, hurriedly.

aprisco *m* sheep-fold.

aprisionar *(encarcelar)* imprison;
shackle, fetter *(a. fig.)*.

aprobación *f* approval *etc.*; **apro-**
bado 1. approved; worthy, excellent; **2.** *m univ. etc.* pass (mark).

aprobar [1m] *v/t.* approve (de *as*);
endorse; consent to; *v/i. univ.* pass.

aprontamiento *m* quick service;
aprontar [1a] get ready quickly;
dinero hand over without delay.

apropiado appropriate *(a, para* to),
suitable *(a, para* for); **apropiar** [1b]
adapt, fit *(a* to); apply *(a caso, p.* to).
⁓*se algo* appropriate.

aprovechable available; useful;
aprovechado *(frugal)* thrifty; *(inge-*
nioso) resourceful; *(aplicado)* industrious; **aprovechamiento** *m* use
etc.; *(ventaja)* profit, advantage;
(adelanto) improvement, progress;
aprovechar [1a] *v/t. (explotar)* make
(good) use of, use; *oferta etc.* take
advantage of; *v/i.* be of use; progress, improve (en *in*); ⁓*se = v/t.*

aproximación *f* approach; *(efecto)*
closeness; **⅍** *etc.* approximation;
aproximado approximate; near,
rough; **aproximar** [1a] bring
near(er), draw up *(a* to); ⁓*se* approach; **aproximativo** approximate, near.

aptitud *f* suitability *(para* for);
aptitude, ability; **apto** suitable, fit
(para su. for).

apuesta *f* bet, wager.

apuesto neat, spruce.

apuntación *f* note; ♪ notation;
apuntado pointed, sharp; **apun-**
tador *m thea.* prompter.

apuntalar [1a] prop (up), shore (up),
underpin; ⊕ strut.

apuntamiento *m (apunte)* note; ⚖
aiming; ⅍ judicial report; **apuntar**

[1a] **1.** *v/t. fusil* aim *(a* at), train *(a*
on); *blanco* aim at; *(señalar)* point
out; **2.** *v/i. (bozo etc.)* begin to show;
(día) dawn; **3.** ⁓*se* turn sour; **apunte**
m note; jotting; *sacar* ⁓*s* take notes.

apuñalar [1a] stab, knife.

apuñar [1a] seize (in one's fist);
apuñ(et)ear [1a] punch, pummel.

apurado *(pobre)* needy, hard up;
(difícil) hard; **apurar** [1a] *líquido*,
vaso drain; *surtido* exhaust, finish,
use up; *(llevar a cabo)* carry out,
finish; ⊕ refine; hurry, press; ⁓*se*
fret, worry, upset; **apuro** *m (a.* ⁓*s*
pl.) hardship, need, distress.

aquejar [1a] worry, distress.

aquel, aquella *adj.* that.

aquél, aquélla *pron.* that (one); *(el*
anterior) the former; **aquél** *m (sex)*
appeal, it F.

aquello *pron.* that.

aquí here; ⁓ *dentro* in here; ⁓ *mismo*
right here; *de* ⁓ *en adelante* from now
on; *por* ⁓ *(cerca)* hereabouts, round
here.

aquietar [1a] calm; pacify.

aquilatar [1a] *metall.* assay.

aquilón *m* north wind.

ara *f* altar; *(piedra)* altar stone.

árabe 1. Arab(ic); ⚛ Moresque; **2.**
m/f Arab; **3.** *m (idioma)* Arabic; **ara-**
besco 1. Arab(ic); **2.** *m* ⊕ arabesque;
arábigo 1. Arab(ic); **2.** *m* Arabic;
arabismo *m (estudio; voz; rasgo)*
Arabism; **arabista** *m/f* Arabist.

arable arable.

arado *m* plough; *(reja)* (plough)-
share; **arador** *m* ploughman.

aragonés *adj. a. su. m,* **-a** *f* Aragonese; **aragonesismo** *m* Aragonese
expression.

arancel *m* tariff, duty; **arancelar**
[1a] *C.Am.* pay; **arancelario** customs *attr.*

arandela *f* ⊕ washer; candle-stand.

araña *f zo.* spider; *(a.* ⁓ *de luces)*
chandelier; **arañar** [1a] scratch; F
scrape together; **arañazo** *m* scratch.

arar [1a] plough; till.

arbitraje *m* arbitration; ✝ arbitrage;
arbitrar [1a] *deportes:* *(tenis)*
umpire; *(fútbol, boxeo)* referee; ⅍
etc. arbitrate; ⁓*se* get along, manage;
arbitrariedad *f* arbitrariness; **arbi-**
trario arbitrary; **arbitrio** *m (albe-*
drío) free-will; *(medio)* means, expedient; **árbitro** *m* arbiter, moderator; *deportes:* umpire, referee.

árbol *m* ♣ tree; ⊕ axle, shaft; ⚓ mast;

arbolado 1. *paisaje* wooded; **2.** *m* woodland; **arboladura** *f* ♣ masts and spars; **arbolar** [1a] *bandera* hoist; ♣ mast; ~se rear up, get up on its hind legs.

arbusto *m* shrub.

arca *f* (*caja*) chest, coffer; ✓ hutch; (*depósito*) tank, reservoir; ~s *pl.* safe.

arcadio *adj. a. su. m,* **a** *f* Arcadian.

arcaduz *m* pipe, conduit; bucket.

arcaico archaic; **arcaísmo** *m* archaism; **arcaizante** archaic; *p., estilo* given to archaisms.

arcano secret, enigmatic.

arcángel *m* archangel.

arce *m* maple (tree).

arcediano *m* archdeacon.

archidiácono *m* archdeacon.

archiduque *m* archduke; **archiduquesa** *f* archduchess.

archimillonario *m* multimillionaire.

archipiélago *m* archipelago.

archivador *m* (*p.*) filing-clerk; (*mueble*) filing-cabinet; **archivar** [1a] file (away); store away; deposit in the archives; **archivo** *m* archives; registry; ♀ *Nacional* Record Office; ~s *pl.* ♱ *etc.* files.

arcilla *f* clay.

arcipreste *m* archpriest.

arco *m* △, *anat.* arch; ♈, ✗ *arc* ✗; (long)bow; ♪ bow; hoop *de barril etc.*; ~ **iris** rainbow.

arcón *m* bin, bunker.

ardentía *f* ♣ heartburn; ♣ phosphorescence.

arder [2a] burn (*a. fig.*); (*resplandecer*) glow, blaze; ~se burn up, burn away; ♀ be parched.

ardid *m* ruse, device, scheme.

ardido spoiled; bold; *S.Am.* angry, irritated.

ardiente burning (*a. fig.*); glowing, blazing; *partidario* passionate, ardent.

ardilla *f* squirrel.

ardor *m* heat, warmth; *fig.* (*celo*) ardour, eagerness; heat *de disputa etc.*; burning, fiery.

arduo arduous, hard, tough.

área *f* area (*a.* 🅰); ~ **de descanso** rest area; ~ **de servicio** service area.

arena *f* sand; grit; (*circo*) arena; ~s *pl.* ♣ stones, gravel; ~ **movediza** quicksand; **arenal** *m* sandy ground, sands; (*cantero*) sandpit.

arenga *f* harangue (*a.* F); F scolding;

arengar [1h] harangue; F scold.

arenillas *f/pl.* ♣ gravel.

arenisca *f* sandstone; grit; **arenisco** sandy; gravelly, gritty.

arenque *m* herring.

arepa *f* *S.Am.* cornbread; corn griddlecake.

arete *m* earring.

argadijo *m* ⊕ reel, bobbin.

argado *m* prank, trick.

argamasa *f* △ mortar; plaster.

árgana *f* ⊕ crane.

argelino *adj. a. su. m,* **a** *f* Algerian.

argentar [1a] silver (*a.* ⊕, *fig.*); **argénteo** silver(y) (*a. fig.*); silver-plated; **argentería** *f* silver (*or* gold) embroidery; **argentino¹** silvery.

argentino² *adj. a. su. m,* **a** *f* Argentinian.

argolla *f* (large) ring; knocker.

argot *m* slang; cant; argot.

argucia *f* sophistry, hair-splitting.

argüir [3g] *v/t.* argue; indicate; *v/i.* argue (*contra* against, with); **argumentación** *f* argumentation; **argumentar** [1a] argue; **argumento** *m* argument; reasoning; *thea. etc.* plot.

aria *f* aria.

aridez *f* aridity, dryness (*a. fig.*); **árido 1.** arid, dry (*a. fig.*); **2.** ~s *m/pl.* dry goods (*esp.* ✓).

ariete *m* battering ram.

ario *adj. a. su. m,* **a** *f* Aryan, Indo-European.

arisco fractious, cross; surly.

arista *f* ♀ beard; edge.

aristocracia *f* aristocracy (*a. fig.*); **aristócrata** *m/f* aristocrat; **aristocrático** aristocratic.

aritmética *f* arithmetic; **aritmético 1.** arithmetical; **2.** *m* arithmetician.

aritmo arrhythmic.

arlequín *m fig.* buffoon; **arlequinada** *f* (piece of) buffoonery; **arlequinesco** *fig.* ridiculous.

arma *f* arm, weapon; ~s *pl.* arms (*a. heráldica*); ~ **arrojadiza** missile; ~ **atómica** atomic weapon; ~ **de fuego** firearm, gun.

armada *f* fleet; navy.

armadijo *m* trap, snare.

armadillo *m* armadillo.

armado ⊕ reinforced; *P.R.,Mex.* stubborn; **armadura** *f* ✗ (suit of) armour; ⊕ *etc.* frame(work); ⚡ armature; **armamentismo** *m* military preparedness; **armamentista 1.** arms *attr.*; militarist(ic); *carrera* ~ arms race; **2.** *m* arms dealer; **armamento** *m* ✗ (*acto*) arming; (*conjunto*) armament(s).

armar [1a] *p. etc.* arm (*de, con* with; *a. fig.*); *arma* load; ⊕ *etc.* mount, assemble, put together; *caballero* dub, knight; **~se** arm o.s. (*de* with; *a. fig.*); *fig.* get ready.

armario *m* cupboard; (*ropa*) wardrobe; ~ (*para libros*) bookcase.

armatoste *m contp.* hulk; *esp.* ⊕ contraption.

armazón *f* frame(work); body; ✂ chassis; △ *etc.* shell, skeleton.

armella *f* eye-bolt, screw-eye.

armenio *adj. a. su. m,* **a** *f* Armenian.

armería *f* ✗ armory; (*tienda*) gun shop; **armero** *m* gunsmith.

armiño *m zo.* stoat; ermine.

armisticio *m* armistice.

armonía *f* harmony (*a. fig.*); **en ~** in harmony (*con* with); **armónica** *f* harmonica; ~ (*de boca*) mouth organ; **armónico 1.** ♪ harmonic; *sonido* harmonious; **2.** ♫ harmonic; **armonioso** harmonious (*a. fig.*); **armonizar** [1f] harmonize.

arnés *m* ✗ armor; **~es** *pl.* harness.

aro *m* hoop, ring; ~ *de émbolo* piston ring.

aroma *m* aroma, fragrance; bouquet *de vino*; **aromático** aromatic, flavour (with herbs).

arpa *f* harp.

arpar [1a] scratch, claw (at).

arpeo *m* grapnel, grappling-iron.

arpía *f* harpy; *fig.* (*regañona*) termagant, shrew.

arpillera *f* sacking, sackcloth.

arpista *m/f* harpist.

arpón *m* gaff, harpoon; **arpon(e)ar** [1a] harpoon.

arqueología *f* archaeology; **arqueólogo** *m* archaeologist.

arquería *f* arcade; **arquero** *m* archer, bowman; ✝ cashier; *S.Am.* *sport* goalkeeper.

arquetipo *m* archetype.

arquitecto *m* architect; ~ *de jardines* landscape gardener; **arquitectónico** architectural; **arquitectura** *f* architecture.

arrabal *m* suburb; **~es** *pl.* outskirts.

arrabalero 1. suburban; F common, ill-bred; **2.** *m,* **a** *f* suburbanite; F common sort.

arraigado (firmly) rooted; *fig.* ingrained; **arraigar** [1h] *v/t.* establish, strengthen (*en f e etc.* in); *v/i.* ✿ root, take root (*a. fig.*); *v/i.,* **~se** (*p.*) become a propertyowner, settle *en lugar; fig.* establish a hold.

arrancaclavos *m* nail claw; nail puller; **arrancada** *f* sudden start; quick acceleration; **arrancadero** *m* starting-point; **arrancador** *m mot.* starter; **arrancamiento** *m* pulling out *etc.;* **arrancar** [1g] **1.** *v/t.* ✿ *etc.* pull up, root out; (*arrebatar*) snatch away (*a, de* from); **2.** *v/i.* mot. etc. start; pull away; (*salir*) start out.

arranque *m* (*sudden*) start, jerk; △, *anat.* starting-point; *fig.* impulse; (*ira*) fit, outburst.

arras *f/pl.* deposit, pledge.

arrasar [1a] raze, demolish; (*allanar*) level, flatten.

arrastradizo dangling, trailing; *fig.* maltreated; **arrastrado 1.** F poor, wretched; (*bribón*) rascally; **2.** *m* rascal; **arrastrar** [1a] drag (along), pull, haul; **~se** (*reptar*) crawl, creep; (*p.*) drag o.s. along; ~ *de espaldas* back stroke.

arrayán *m* myrtle.

¡arre! gee up!, get up!

arrear [1a] *v/t.* urge on; (*enjaezar*) harness; *v/i.* F hurry along.

arrebañar [1a] scrape together; (*comer*) eat up, clear up.

arrebatadizo excitable; hot-tempered, irascible; **arrebatado** *movimiento* sudden, violent; *rash*, reckless; **arrebatamiento** *m* snatching *etc.; fig.* fury; ecstasy; **arrebatar** [1a] snatch (away) (*a* from); wrench, wrest (*a* from); (*llevarse*) carry away (*or* off); **~se** get carried away (*en* by); *cocina:* burn; **arrebatiña** *f* = *rebatiña;* **arrebato** *m* fury; ecstasy, rapture.

arrebol *m* red, glow *de cielo;* (*afeite*) rouge; **arrebolar** [1a] redden; **~se** redden, flush; (*maquillarse*) rouge.

arreciar [1b] grow worse, get more severe; **~se** ✿ get stronger, pick up.

arrecife *m* causeway; ⚓ reef; ~ *de coral* coral reef.

arredrar [1a] drive back; *fig.* scare, daunt; **~se** draw back, move away (*de* from); *fig.* get scared.

arregazado *falda etc.* tucked up; **arregazar** [1f] tuck up.

arreglado regulated, (well-)ordered; *fig.* moderate; *vida* of moderation, orderly; **arreglar** [1a] arrange, regulate; adjust (*a* to); (*componer*) put in order, put straight; ⊕ fix, repair; *aspecto, pelo, cuarto etc.* tidy up; *disputa* settle, make up; **~se**

come to terms (*a*, *con* with; *a.* ✝); F
~as get by; manage (*para inf.* to *inf.*);
arreglo *m* arrangement *etc.*; settlement; (*regla*) rule, order; (*acuerdo*)
agreement.

arremangar [1h] turn up, roll up;
falda etc. tuck up; ~**se** roll up one's
sleeves *etc.*; *fig.* take a firm stand.

arremeter [2a] *v/t. caballo* spur on;
v/i. rush forth, attack; **arremetida**
f, **arremetimiento** *m* attack; lunge
con arma.

arremolinarse [1a] (*gente*) crowd
around; swirl; whirl.

arrendable rentable; *casa* to let;
arrendador *m*, **-a** *f* (*dueño*) lessor;
(*inquilino*) tenant.

arrendamiento *m* (*acto*) letting *etc.*;
(*precio*) rent(al); **arrendar** [1k]
(*dueño*): *casa* let, lease; *máquina etc.*
hire out.

arrendatario *m*, **a** *f* tenant, lessee.

arreo *m* adornment; ~s *pl.* harness.

arrepentido 1. regretful (*de* for); (*a.
eccl.*) repentant; **2.** *m*, **a** *f* penitent;
arrepentimiento *m* repentance;
arrepentirse [3i] repent (*de* of).

arrestado bold, daring; **arrestar**
[1a] arrest, take into custody; ~**se a**
rush boldly into; **arresto** *m* arrest.

arriba *situación*: above; on top; upstairs *en casa*; (*movimiento*) up, up-
wards; *de ~ abajo* from top to bottom;
from beginning to end; *por la calle ~*
up the street; *¡~ España!* Spain for
ever!

arribada *f* ⚓ arrival; **arribar** [1a] ⚓
put into port; arrive; (*noticia*) come
to hand; **arribista** *m/f* parvenu, upstart.

arriendo *m* = *arrendamiento.*

arriero *m* muleteer.

arriesgado risky, dangerous, hazardous; *p.* bold, daring; **arriesgar**
[1h] *vida etc.* risk, endanger; ~**se** take
a risk, expose o.s. to danger;
arriesgo *m* S.Am. risk; hazard.

arrimar [1a] (*acercar*) move up,
bring close (*a* to); *escala etc.* lean (*a*
against); ~**se** come close(r) *etc.*;
(*unirse*) join together; ~ *a* come close
to (*a. fig.*); **arrimo** *m* support.

arrinconado *fig.* forgotten, neg-
lected; **arrinconar** [1a] *fig.* lay
aside, put away; (*deshacerse de*) get
rid of; *p.* push aside; ~**se** withdraw
from the world.

arriscar [1g] risk; ~**se** take a risk;
(*engreírse*) grow conceited.

arritmia *f* ⚕ arrhythmia; **arrítmico**
arrhythmic.

arroba *f* measure of weight = 11.502
kg.; *variable liquid measure.*

arrodillado kneeling, on one's
knees; **arrodillarse** [1a] kneel
(down), go down on one's knees.

arrogancia *f* arrogance; pride; **arrogante** arrogant; brave.

arrojadizo easily thrown; for throw-
ing; **arrojado** *fig.* daring, dashing;
arrojallamas *m* flamethrower;
arrojar [1a] throw; (*con fuerza*)
fling, hurl; *deportes: pelota* bowl,
pitch; ~**se** throw o.s. (*a* into, *por* out
of); *fig.* plunge (*a*, *en* into).

arrollador *fig.* sweeping, overwhelming; devastating; **arrollar**
[1a] (*enrollar*) roll (up); *esp.* ⊕, ⚡
coil, wind.

arromar [1a] blunt, dull.

arropar [1a] wrap (up); tuck up *en
cama*; ~**se** wrap up; tuck o.s. up.

arrope *m* syrup.

arrostrar [1a] *v/t.* face (up to), brave;
v/i.: ~ *a* show a liking for; ~**se** throw
o.s. into battle.

arroyada *f* gully; (*crecida etc.*) flood;
arroyo *m* stream, brook.

arroz *m* rice; ~ *con leche* rice pudding;
arruga *f* wrinkle, line; crease, fold;
arrugado wrinkled, lined; creased,
crinkly; **arrugar** [1h] *cara* wrinkle,
line; *ropa* crease, pucker; ~**se** get
wrinkled.

arruinamiento *m* ruin(ation);
arruinar [1a] ruin (*a.* ✝, *fig.*),
destroy; ~**se** be ruined.

arrullar [1a] *niño* lull to sleep; ~**se**
bill and coo (*a. F*); **arrullo** *m* cooing;
♪ lullaby.

arsenal *m* ⚓ (naval) dockyard, shipyard; ⚔ arsenal.

arsénico 1. arsenical; **2.** *m* arsenic.

arte *m a. f* art; (*maña*) trick, cunning;
(*habilidad*) knack; *bellas ~s* fine arts;
~s *liberales* liberal arts; *malas ~s*
trickery, guile; **artefacto** *m* ⊕ appliance, contrivance.

artejo *m* knuckle, joint.

artería *f* cunning, artfulness.

arteria *f* artery (*a. fig.*); ⚡ feeder;
arterial arterial; **arteriosclerosis** *f*
arteriosclerosis.

artesanía *f* handicraft, skill; craftsmanship; **artesano** *m* artisan.

artesiano: *pozo ~* Artesian well.

ártico arctic.

articulación *f anat.*, ⊕ joint; *gr. etc.*

articulation; **articulado** anat., ⊕ articulated, joined; **articular** [1a] articulate; ⊕ join (together, up); ⚏ etc. article; **artículo** m article (a. gr., ⚏ ✝); anat. articulation, joint; entry en libro de consulta; ~s pl. de consumo consumer goods; ~s de gran consumo mass-consumption articles.

artífice m/f artist, craftsman; maker; fig. architect; **artificial** artificial; b.s. imitation attr.; **artificio** m (arte) art, skill; (hechura) workmanship, craftsmanship; ⊕ contrivance; **artificioso** artistic, fine, skilful; fig. cunning, artful.

artillado m artillery.

artillería f artillery; cannon (pl.); **artillero** m ✗ artilleryman.

artimaña f trap; fig. cunning.

artista m/f artist; thea. etc. artiste; **artístico** artistic.

artrítico arthritic; **artritis** f arthritis.

arzobispado m archbishopric; **arzobispal** archiepiscopal; **arzobispo** m archbishop.

arzón m saddle-tree.

as m ace; one en dado; fig. ace.

asa f handle; fig. handle, pretext.

asado 1. roast(ed); bien ~ well done; 2. m roast (meat); **asador** m spit, broach; **asaduras** f/pl. entrails, offal.

asalariado 1. paid; wage-earning; 2. m, a f wage-earner.

asaltar [1a] fortaleza etc. storm, rush; p. fall on, attack; assail; **asalto** m attack, assault.

asamblea f assembly.

asar [1a] roast; fig. pester, plague.

asbesto m asbestos.

ascendencia f ancestry, line; **ascendente** ascending; upward; **ascender** [2g] v/t. promote, raise (a to); v/i. (subir) go up, ascend; **ascendiente** 1. = ascendente; 2. m/f ancestor.

ascensión f ascent; eccl. ascension; fig. = ascenso; eccl. Día de la ♀ Ascension Day; **ascenso** m promotion, rise; grade; **ascensor** m elevator; ⊕ elevator.

asceta m/f ascetic; **ascético** ascetic; **ascetismo** m asceticism.

asco m loathing, disgust, revulsion.

ascua f live coal, ember; ¡~s! ouch!

aseado clean, neat, tidy, trim; **asear** [1a] adorn, embellish.

asechanza f trap, snare (a. fig.); **asechar** [1a] waylay, ambush.

asediador m besieger; **asediar** [1b] besiege; fig. pester; (amor) chase; **asedio** m siege; ✝ run (de on).

asegurable insurable; **asegurado** m, a f insured, insurant; **asegurador** m fastener; (p.) insurer, underwriter; **asegurar** [1a] (fijar) secure, fasten; cimientos etc. make firm, fig. guarantee, assure; ~se make o.s. secure (de peligro from); ~ de hechos make sure of.

asemejar [1a] v/t. make alike; fig. liken (a to); ~se be alike; ~ a be like.

asendereado camino beaten, well trodden; vida wretched.

asentada f sitting; de una ~ at one sitting; **asentaderas** f/pl. F behind, bottom; **asentado** fig. established, settled; **asentador** m △ stonemason; (suavizador) strop; **asentar** [1k] 1. v/t. p. seat, sit ~s down; cosa place; fix; tienda pitch; cimientos make firm; 2. v/i. be suitable, suit; 3. ~se seat o.s.; fig. establish o.s.; (△, líquido) settle.

asentir [3i] assent; ~ a consent to; petición grant; arreglo accept.

asentista m contractor; supplier; army contractor.

aseo m tidiness; cleanliness; cuarto de ~, ~s pl. cloakroom, toilet.

aséptico aseptic; free from infection.

asequible obtainable, available; fin attainable.

aserradero m sawmill; **aserrador** m sawyer; **aserradura** f saw-cut; ~s pl. sawdust; **aserrar** [1k] saw; **aserruchar** [1a] S.Am. saw.

aserto m assertion.

asesinar [1a] murder; pol. etc. assassinate; **asesinato** m murder; pol. assassination; **asesino** 1. murderous; 2. m murderer, killer; pol. etc. assassin; fig. thug, cutthroat.

asesor m, -a f adviser; consultant; **asesorar** [1a] advise; act as a consultant to; ~se seek (or take) advice (con, de from); consult.

asestar [1a] (apuntar) aim (a at); arma shoot, fire; fig. try to hurt.

asexual asexual.

asfaltado m asphalting; asphalt (pavement etc.); **asfaltar** [1a] asphalt; **asfalto** m asphalt.

asfixia f asphyxia ⚕; suffocation, asphyxiation; **asfixiador, asfixiante** asphyxiating, suffocating; **asfixiar** [1b] asphyxiate; suffocate; ✗ gas.

así 1. adv. a) so, in this way, thus;

thereby; ~ *pues* and so, so then; *o* ~ or so; ~ *es que* and so (is it that); ¡~ *sea!* so be it!; b) *comp. etc.*: ~ *como* (in the same way) as; **2.** *adj.*: *un hombre* ~ such a man, a man like that; ~ *es la vida* such is life; **3.** *cj.*: ~ *como*, ~ *que* as soon as.

asiático 1. Asiatic; **2.** *m*, **a** *f* Asian.

asidera *f S.Am.* ringed saddle strap; **asidero** *m* hold(er), handle.

asiduo 1. assiduous; frequent, regular; **2.** *m*, **a** *f* habitué, regular.

asiento *m* seat, place; site *de pueblo etc.*; △ settling; (*fondo*) bottom; ~ *pl.* buttocks; *tome Vd.* ~ take a seat; ~ *lanzable* ✈ ejection seat.

asignación *f* assignment *etc.*; ✝ allowance, salary; **asignar** [1a] assign, apportation; **asignatorio** *m S.Am.* heir; inheritor; **asignatura** *f univ.* course, subject.

asilo *m eccl. a. pol.* asylum; *fig.* shelter, refuge; home *de viejos*; poorhouse, workhouse *de pobres*.

asimetría *f* asymmetry; **asimétrico** asymmetric(al).

asimilación *f* assimilation; **asimilar** [1a] assimilate; = *asemejar*(se).

asimismo likewise, in like manner.

asir [3a; *present like salir*] *v/t.* seize, grasp (*con* with, *de* by); *v/i.* ♀ take root; ~*se a*, ~ *de* take hold of, seize (*a. fig.*).

asirio Assyrian.

asistencia *f* attendance (*a.* ⚙); presence (*a* at); (*ayuda*) help; *S.Am.* boarding house; *Mex.* visitors' room; ~ *social* welfare (work); **asistente** *m* assistant; ✗ orderly, ~*s pl.* people present, those present; **asistir** [3a] help, aid; *rey etc.* attend.

asma *f* asthma; **asmático** *adj. a. su. m*, **a** *f* asthmatic.

asnal asinine (*a. fig.*); F beastly; **asnería** *f* silly thing; F lousy, awful. **asno** *m* donkey, ass (*a. fig.*); F fathead.

asociación *f* association; society; ✝ partnership; **asociado 1.** associate(d); **2.** *m* associate, partner; **asociar** [1b] associate (*a, con* with); *esfuerzos etc.* pool, put together; ~*se* associate; team up.

asoleada *f*, **asoleadura** *f S.Am.* sunstroke.

asolear [1a] put (*or* keep) in the sun; ~*se* sun o.s., bask.

asomada *f* brief appearance; surprise view; **asomar** [1a] *v/t.* show,

put out, stick out; *v/i.* begin to show, appear; ~*se* show, stick out.

asombradizo easily alarmed; **asombrar** [1a] shade, cast a shadow on; *color* darken; *fig.* frighten; amaze, astonish; ~*se* be amazed (*de* at); be shocked; **asombro** *m* fear, fright; surprise; **asombroso** amazing, astonishing.

asomo *m* appearance; sign, indication.

asonancia *f* assonance; *fig. no tener* ~ *con* bear no relation to; **asonantar** [1a] assonate (*con* with); **asonante 1.** assonant; **2.** *f* assonance.

aspa *f* cross (X); △ cross-piece; sail *de molino*; **aspar** [1a] ⊕ wind, reel; F vex.

aspecto *m* aspect; look(s), appearance *de p. etc.*

aspereza *f* roughness *etc.*

áspero rough *al tacto*; *filo* jagged; *terreno* rough; *genio* sour, surly.

aspiración *f* breath; inhalation; *phonet.* aspiration; **aspirado** aspirate; **aspirador 1.** ⊕ suction *attr.*; **2.** *m*: ~ *de polvo* = **aspiradora** *f* vacuum cleaner; **aspirante 1.** ⊕ suction *attr.*; **2.** *m/f* applicant, candidate (*a* for); **aspirar** [1a] *v/t.* breathe in, inhale; *phonet.* aspirate; ⊕ suck in; *v/i.* aspire.

aspirina *f* aspirin.

asqueroso loathsome, disgusting, nasty; sickening; F lousy, awful.

asta *f* shaft *de lanza etc.*; (*lanza*) spear, lance; flag-staff *de bandera.*

aster *m* aster.

asterisco *m* asterisk.

astigmático astigmatic; **astigmatismo** *m* astigmatism.

astil *m* handle; shaft *de saeta*; beam *de balanza.*

astilla *f* splinter, chip; **astillar(se)** [1a] splinter, chip; **astillero** *m* shipyard.

astral of the stars, astral.

astringente 1. astringent, binding; **2.** *m* astringent; **astringir** [3c] *anat.* contract; ✿ bind.

astro *m* star (*a. cine*), heavenly body; F beauty; **astrología** *f* astrology; **astrológico** astrological; **astrólogo 1.** astrological; **2.** *m* astrologer; **astronauta** *m* astronaut; **astronave** *f* spaceship; ~ *tripulada* manned spaceship; **astronavegación** *f* space travel; astronavigation; **astronomía** *f* astronomy; **astronómico** astronomical (*a. fig.*); **astrónomo** *m* astronomer.

astroso dirty, untidy, shabby.

astucia f astuteness etc.; trick.

asturianismo m Asturian word or expression; **asturiano** adj. a. su. m, **a** f Asturian.

astuto astute, shrewd, smart.

asueto m (a. día de ~) day off, holiday; (tarde) afternoon off.

asumir [3a] assume, take on.

asunción f assumption.

asunto m matter, thing; (negocio) business, affair; (tema) subject; ~s pl. exteriores foreign affairs.

asustadizo easily frightened; jumpy, **asustar** [1a] frighten, scare; startle; ~se be frightened etc.

atabal m kettledrum; **atabalero** m kettledrummer.

atacar [1g] (embestir) attack (a. ♞, ♟, fig.); corner, press hard en discusión; (atar) fasten.

ataderas f/pl. F garters; **atadero** m (cuerda) rope, cord; (parte) place for tying; **atado** 1. fig. timid, shy, inhibited; 2. m bundle; (manojo) bunch; **atadura** f (acto) fastening etc.; (cuerda) string, cord; ⚓ lashing.

atajar [1a] v/t. stop, intercept; head off; deportes: tackle; v/i. take a short cut; ~se be abashed.

atalaya 1. f watch tower; fig. height, vantage point; 2. m lookout, sentinel.

atañer [2f; defective]: ~ a concern; en lo que atañe a with regard to.

ataque m attack (a, contra on; ✚ de of; a. fig.); ♞ raid; ~ al corazón, ~ cardíaco heart-attack; ✚ ~ fulminante stroke, seizure; ~ por sorpresa surprise attack.

atar [1a] tie (up), fasten; ✐ tether; fig. paralyse, root to the spot; ~se fig. get stuck (en dificultades in).

atardecer 1. [2d] get dark, get late; 2. m late afternoon, evening.

atarugar [1h] (asegurar) fasten, agujero plug, stop; ~se F swallow the wrong way, choke.

atascadero m mire, bog; fig. stumbling-block; difficulties; **atascar** [1g] agujero plug, stop; tubo obstruct (a. fig.), clog (up); ~se ⊕ etc. clog, be stopped up.

ataviar [1c] (adornar) deck, array; (vestir) dress up; **atavío** m (a. ~s pl.) dress, finery.

atavismo m atavism.

atávico atavistic; **atavismo** m atavism.

ateísmo m atheism.

atelaje m team; (arreos) harness.

atemorizar [1f] scare, frighten; ~se get scared (de, por at).

atemperar [1a] moderate, temper; adjust, accommodate (a to).

atención f attention; (cortesía) a. civility; ~es pl. attentions; duties, responsibilities; prestar ~ listen (a to); pay attention (a to); **atender** [2g] v/t. attend to, pay attention to; v/i.: take note of; see about, see to.

atenerse [2l]: ~ a verdad stand by, hold to; regla abide by, go by.

atentado 1. prudent, cautious; 2. m illegal act, offence; **atentar** [1a] v/t. acto do illegally; v/i. make an attempt on.

atento attentive (a to), observant (a of); mindful (a pormenor of); (cortés) polite, thoughtful, kind.

atenuación f attenuation; ⚖ extenuation; **atenuante**: ⚖ circunstancias ~s extenuating circumstances; **atenuar** [1e] attenuate; delito extenuate.

ateo 1. atheistic(al); 2. m, a f atheist.

aterciopelado velvety, velvet attr.; velvetized.

aterido numb; **aterirse** [3a; defective] get stiff with cold.

aterraje m ✈ landing.

aterrar¹ [1k] v/t. demolish; cover with earth; v/i. ✈ land.

aterrar² [1a] terrify, fill with terror; ~se be terrified (de at).

aterrizaje m ✈ landing; ~ forzoso forced landing; ~ a vientre pancake landing; ~ forzado, ~ forzoso forced landing; ~ violento crash landing; **aterrizar** [1f] ✈ land.

atesorar [1a] hoard (up); virtudes possess.

atestación f attestation; **atestado** m ⚖ affidavit, statement.

atestado p.p. cram-full (de of), packed (de with); **atestar¹** [1k] pack, stuff, cram (de with).

atestar² [1a] attest, testify to.

atestiguar [1i] testify to, attest.

atezado tanned, swarthy; **atezar** [1f] blacken; ~se get tanned.

ático 1. Attic; 2. m △ attic.

atierre m cave-in; S.Am. (land)fill.

atiesar [1a] stiffen; (apretar) tighten (up); ~se get stiff, stiffen.

atigrado 1. striped; gato tabby; 2. m tabby (cat).

atildado neat, spruce, stylish; **atildar** [1a] typ. put a tilde over; (asear) clean (up), put right; ~se spruce o.s. up.

atinado (*discreto*) wise; *juicio* keen; *dicho* pertinent; **atinar** [1a] v/i. find, hit on; v/i. guess (right).

atirantar [1a] make taut; brace; ~se Mex. die, pass away.

atisbar [1a] spy on, watch; peep in por *agujero* etc.; **atisbo** m watching, spying; *fig.* slight sign.

atizador m poker; ⊕ feed(er); **atizar** [1f] (*remover*) poke, stir; stoke; ¡atiza! gosh!

atlas m atlas.

atleta m/f athlete; **atlético** athletic(al); **atletismo** m athletics.

atmósfera f atmosphere; *fig.* sphere (of influence); **atmosférico** atmospheric.

atocinado F fat, well-upholstered; **atocinar** [1a] *puerco* cut up; *carne* cure; ~se F (*irritarse*) get het up.

atolladero m mire, muddy spot; **atollarse** [1a] stick in the mud.

atolón m atoll.

atolondrado thoughtless, reckless; **atolondrar** [1a] stun, bewilder.

atómico atomic; *energía* ~a atomic power; atomic energy; **atomizador** m atomizer; (scent-)spray; **átomo** m atom (a. fig.); *fig.* tiny particle.

atónito thunderstruck; aghast.

átono atonic, unstressed.

atontado dim(-witted), muddle-headed; **atontar** [1a] bewilder.

atorar [1a] obstruct, stop up.

atormentar [1a] torture (a. fig.); *fig.* torment; plague.

atornillar [1a] (*poner*) screw on; (*apretar*) screw up.

atortillar [1a] S.Am. squash; flatten.

atosigar [1h] poison; *fig.* harass, plague; put the pressure on.

atrabancado Mex. rash; thoughtless; **atrabancar** [1g] rush; ~se be in a fix; **atrabanco** m hurry.

atrabiliario *fig.* difficult, moody.

atracada f S.Am. quarrel; row; **atracador** m gangster; hold-up man; **atracar** [1g] v/t. ♣ bring alongside, tie up; ♣ waylay; v/i. come alongside, tie up.

atracción f attraction; appeal de p.; (*diversión*) amusement; ~es pl. thea. entertainment; (*cabaret*) floor show; ~ sexual sex appeal.

atraco m hold-up.

atractivo 1. attractive; *fuerza* of attraction; **2.** m = atracción; **atraer**

[2p] attract; draw; *imaginación* etc. appeal to.

atragantarse [1a] choke (con on), swallow the wrong way.

atramparse [1a] fall into a trap; (*tubo*) clog; (*pestillo*) stick, catch.

atrancar [1g] v/t. *puerta* bar; *tubo* clog, stop up; v/i. F take big steps.

atrapar [1a] F nab, catch **atrapamoscas** f Venus's-fly-trap.

atrás ir back(wards); *estar* behind; (*tiempo*) previously; **atrasado** slow (a. reloj), late, behind (time); overdue; *país* backward; **atrasar** [1a] v/t. slow up, slow down, retard; *reloj* put back; v/i. (*reloj*) lose; ~se be behind; be slow, be late; ♥ be in arrears; **atraso** m slowness de reloj; (*demora*) timelag, delay.

atravesada f S.Am. crossing; **atravesado** (*ojo*) squinting, cross-eyed; **atravesar** [1k] (*cruzar*) go over, go across, cross (over); pierce (con, de *bala* with); ~se (*espina*) get stuck.

atreverse [2a] dare (a inf. to inf.); ~ a *empresa* (dare to) undertake; **atrevido** daring, bold; **atrevimiento** m daring, boldness; (spirit of) adventure.

atribución f attribution; functions, **atribuir** [3g]; ~ a attribute to, put *s.t.* down to; ~se assume.

atribular(se) [1a] grieve.

atributivo attributive (a. gr.); **atributo** m attribute.

atril m eccl. lectern; ♪ music stand.

atrinchear [1a] entrench, fortify; ~se entrench, dig in.

atrio m inner courtyard, atrium.

atrocidad f atrocity, outrage; F (*dicho*) stupid remark.

atrofia f atrophy; **atrofiar(se)** [1b] atrophy.

atronado reckless, thoughtless; **atronador** deafening; thunderous; **atronar** [1m] deafen; *res* stun; *fig.* bewilder.

atropellado hasty en obrar; brusque; **atropellar** [1a] 1. v/t. (*pisar*) trample underfoot; (*derribar*) knock down; 2. v/i.: ~ por push one's way through; *fig.* disregard; 3. ~se act etc. hastily; **atropello** m mot. accident; *fig.* outrage, excess.

atroz atrocious, outrageous.

atufar [1a] *fig.* anger, vex; ~se (*comida*) go smelly; (*vino*) turn sour; *fig.* get vexed.

atún m tunny; F nitwit.

aturdido thoughtless, reckless; **aturdimiento** m fig. bewilderment etc.; **aturdir** [3a] stun, daze con golpe; (vino etc.) stupefy; **~se** be stunned; get bewildered etc.

atusar [1a] trim con tijeras; smooth con mano.

audacia f boldness, audacity; **audaz** bold, audacious.

audiencia f audience; hearing (a. ⚖); ⚖ (tribunal) high court; **audífono** m hearing aid; earphone; handset; **audio-visual** audiovisual; **auditor** m (a. ~ de guerra) judge-advocate; **auditorio** m (ps.) audience; (sala) auditorium.

auge m peak, summit, heyday; (aumento) increase; ✝ boom.

augurar [1a] (cosa) augur; (p.) predict; **augurio** m augury, omen; prediction; **~s** pl. fig. best wishes.

augusto august; stately.

aula f classroom; univ. lecture room; **~ magna** assembly hall.

aullar [1a] howl; **aullido** m, **aúllo** m howl.

aumentar [1a] v/t. increase, add to, augment; enlarge v/i., **~se** (be on the) increase; rise, go up; **aumento** m increase, rise; enlargement; Mex., Guat. postscript; addition.

aun even; **~** (siendo esto) así even so.

aún still, yet.

aunar [1a] join, unite; **~se** combine.

aunque although, even though.

¡aúpa! up (you get)!; **¡~** Madrid! up Madrid!

aura f (gentle) breeze; fig. popularity, popular favour.

áureo poet. golden.

auricular 1. auricular, of the ear; 2. m anat. little finger; teleph. receiver, earpiece; **~es** pl. earphones, headset.

aurora f dawn (a. fig.).

auscultar [1a] 🩺 sound; auscultate.

ausencia f absence; **ausentarse** [1a] go away, absent o.s.; stay away; **ausente** absent; missing (de from); away from home.

auspiciar [1b] S.Am. support, foster; **auspicio** m fig. protection.

austeridad f austerity etc.; **austero** austere; p. stern, severe.

austral southern.

australiano adj. a. su. m, **a** f Australian.

austríaco adj. a. su. m, **a** f Austrian.

austro m south wind.

autenticar [1a] authenticate; **auten-**

ticidad f authenticity; **auténtico** authentic, genuine, real.

auto[1] m ⚖ edict, judicial decree; thea. approx. mystery play; **~s** pl. ⚖ documents, proceedings; **~** de fe auto-da-fé; **~** del nacimiento nativity play; **~** sacramental eucharistic play.

auto[2] m mot. car.

auto[3]... self-..., auto...; **~abastecimiento** m self-sufficiency; **~adhesivo** self-adhesive; **~biografía** f autobiography; **~bote** m motorboat; **~bús** m (omni)bus; **~camión** m motor truck; **~car** m (motor-)coach; **~casa** f trailer; mobile home.

autocracia f autocracy; **autócrata** m/f autocrat; **autocrático** autocratic.

autóctono autochthonous.

autodefensa f self-defense; **auto-destrucción** f self-destruction.

autodeterminación f self-determination; **autodominio** m self-control; **auto-escuela** f driving school.

autógena f welding.

auto...: **~gestión** f self-administration; self-governance; **~gráfico** autographic; **autógrafo** adj. a. su. m autograph; **~limpiador**, **~limpiante** self-cleaning.

autómata m automaton (a. fig.), robot; **automático** automatic.

auto...: **~motor** m Diesel train; **~motriz** self-propelled; **~móvil** 1. self-propelled; 2. m car, motorcar, automobile; **~movilismo** m motoring; ⊕ car industry; **~movilista** m/f motorist.

autonomía f autonomy, home rule; **autónomo** autonomous.

autopiano m S.Am. player-piano.

autopista f motorway, motor road, turnpike.

autopropulsado self-propelled.

autopsia f postmortem, autopsy.

autor m, **-a** f author, writer; creator, originator de idea; **autoridad** f authority; fig. show, pomp; **~es** pl. authorities; **autoritario** authoritarian; dogmatic; **autorización** f authorization, licence (para inf. to inf.); **autorizado** authorized; official; **autorizar** [1f] authorize.

autorretrato m self-portrait.

autoservicio m self-service.

autostop m hitch-hiking.

auxiliar 1. auxiliary (a. gr.); 2. m/f assistant; 3. [1b] help, assist; **auxilio**

m help, assistance; relief; *primeros ~s pl.* first aid.

avalancha *f* avalanche.

avalar [1a] ✝ endorse (*a. fig.*).

avalorar [1a] = *valorar*; **avaluar** [1e] = *valorar*.

avance *m* advance (*a.* ✗); ✝ (*anticipo*) advance (payment), credit; **avanzada** *f* ✗ outpost; **avanzado** advanced (*de edad* in years); **avanzar** [1f] *v/t.* advance (*a.* ✝), move on, move forward; *v/i.*, **~se** advance (*a.* ✗); move on, push on; (*noche etc.*) advance, draw on.

avaricia *f* miserliness, avarice; greed(iness); **avaricioso, avariento** miserly, avaricious; **avaro** 1. miserly, mean; 2. *m, a f* miser.

avasallar [1a] subdue, enslave.

ave *f* bird; *~ de corral* chicken, fowl; *~s pl. a.* poultry.

avecin(d)arse [1a] take up one's residence, settle.

avellana *f* hazelnut; **avellanado** *color* hazel, nut-brown; **avellanera** *f*, **avellano** *m* hazel.

avemaría *f* Ave Maria; *al ~* at dusk; F *en un ~* in a twinkling.

avena *f* oat(s); *de ~* oaten.

avenamiento *m* drainage; **avenar** [1a] drain.

avenencia *f* agreement, bargain.

avenida *f* avenue; flood.

avenir [3s] reconcile; **~se** come to an agreement, be reconciled (*con* with); *~ a inf.* agree to *inf.*

aventador *m* ♪ winnowing fork; fan, blower *para fuego*; **aventadora** *f* winnowing machine.

aventajado outstanding, superior; *~ de estatura* very tall; **aventajar** [1a] (*exceder*) surpass, outstrip; **~se** *a* surpass; get the advantage of.

aventar [1k] ♪ winnow; fan, blow (on); **~se** fill, swell (up); F beat it; **aventón** *m S.Am. mot.* push; lift, (free) ride.

aventura *f* (*lance*) adventure; *b.s.* escapade; (*casualidad*) chance, coincidence; **aventurado** risky, hazardous; **aventurar** [1a] venture; *vida* risk, hazard; *capital* stake; **~se** venture, take a chance; **aventurero** 1. adventurous; 2. *m* adventurer; ✗ soldier of fortune.

avergonzado ashamed (*de, por* at); *expresión* shamefaced; **avergonzar** [1f *a.* 1n] (put to) shame; abash; embarrass; **~se** be ashamed.

avería[1] *f orn.* aviary.

avería[2] *f* damage; *mot. etc.* breakdown; fault; **averiado** damaged; *mot. quedar ~* have a breakdown; **averiar** [1c] damage; **~se** get damaged.

averiguar [1i] find out, ascertain; investigate, inquire into; *C.Am., Mex.* get into a fight; **~se con** F tie *s.o.* down.

aversión *f* aversion (*hacia, por algo* to; *a alguien* for); disgust, distaste.

avestruz *m* ostrich.

avezado accustomed; **avezar** [1f] accustom; **~se** get accustomed (*a* to).

aviación *f* aviation; (*cuerpo*) airforce; **aviador** *m* aviator, airman, flyer.

aviar [1c] *v/t.* get ready, prepare; equip, provide (*de* with); *S.Am.* lend; *v/i.* F hurry up.

avidez *f* greed(iness), avidity; **ávido** greedy, avid (*de* for).

avieso distorted (*a. fig.*); *p.* perverse, wicked.

avilés *adj. a. su. m*, **-a** *f* (native) of Avila.

avillanado rustic, boorish.

avinagrado sour, jaundiced; **avinagrar(se)** [1a] (turn) sour.

avío *m* preparation, provision; *S.Am.* loan; **~s** *pl.* kit, tackle, gear.

avión *m* (*aero*)plane, airplane; *orn.* martin; *~ de caza* pursuit plane; *~ de combate* fighter; *~ a chorro, ~ a reacción* jet plane; *~ de travesía* air liner; *~ supersónico* supersonic aircraft; *~ transporte* transport.

avisado prudent, wise; *mal ~* rash; **avisador** *m*, **-a** *f* informant; *b.s.* informer; **avisar** [1a] inform, notify, let *s.o.* know; (*amonestar*) warn; **aviso** *m* (*consejo*) advice; (*noticia*) piece of information, tip.

avispa *f* wasp; **avispado** F wide awake, sharp; *S.Am.* startled; scared; **avispar** [1a] *caballo* spur on; F stir up, wake up; **~se** fret, be worried; **avispón** *m* hornet.

avistar [1a] descry, sight; **~se** have an interview (*con* with).

avitaminosis *f* vitamin deficiency.

avituallar [1a] victual, provision.

avivar [1a] *fuego* stoke (up); *color, luz* make brighter; *fig.* enliven, revive; **~se** revive *etc.*

avizor 1.: *estar ojo ~* be on the alert; 2. *m* watcher; **avizorar** [1a] watch, spy on.

axioma m axiom; **axiomático** axiomatic.

ay 1. int. ¡~! dolor físico: ouch!; pena: oh!, oh dear!; rhet. alas!; admiración: oh!; ¡~ de mí! poor me!; **2.** m sigh; groan, cry de dolor.

aya f governess.

ayer yesterday.

ayo m tutor.

ayuda 1. f help, aid, assistance; ♂ enema; **2.** m page; ~ de cámara valet; **ayudador** m, -a f, **ayudante** m/f helper, assistant; esp. ⊕ mate; **ayudantía** f assistantship; **ayudar** [1a] help, aid, assist (a inf. to inf., in ger.); help out.

ayunar [1a] fast (a on); fig. go without; **ayunas: en** ~ without breakfast; **ayuno 1.** fasting; fig. without; F in the dark (de about); **2.** m fast(ing).

ayuntamiento m town (or city) council; (edificio) town (or city) hall; ~ sexual sexual intercourse.

azabache m min. jet.

azada f hoe; **azadón** m (large) hoe, mattock; **azadonar** [1a] hoe.

azafata f air hostess, stewardess.

azafrán m ♣ crocus; cocina: saffron.

azahar m orange blossom.

azalea f azalea.

azar m (el ~) chance, fate; al ~ at random; **azararse** [1a] go wrong;

rattled; **azaroso** risky, hazardous, chancy.

azogado fig. restless, fidgety; **azogue** m mercury, quicksilver.

azonzado S. Am. stupid; dumb.

azor m goshawk.

azoramiento m confusion; excitement; **azorar** [1a] disturb, upset; excite; ~se be disturbed etc.

azotacalles m loafer, lounger; gadabout; **azotar** [1a] whip, flog; niño thrash, spank; (mar, lluvia etc.) lash; **azote** m whip, lash; (golpe) spank; fig. scourge.

azotea f flat roof, terrace (roof).

azteca adj. a. su. m/f Aztec.

azúcar m a. f sugar; ~ cande rock candy; **azucarado** sugary, sweet (a. fig.); **azucarar** [1a] sugar; (bañar) coat with sugar; **azucarero 1.** sugar attr.; **2.** m sugar bowl.

azucena f (Madonna) lily.

azuela f adze.

azufre m sulphur, brimstone.

azul 1. blue; **2.** m blue; blueness; ~ celeste sky-blue; ~ de cobalto cobalt blue; **azulado** blue; bluish; **azular** [1a] dye (or colour) blue.

azulejar [1f] tile; **azulejo** m glazed tile.

azuzar [1f] perro set on; fig. irritate; (estimular) egg on.

B

baba f splittle, slobber; biol. mucus; slime de caracol; **babaza** f slime, mucus; zo. slug; **babear** [1a] slobber, drivel.

babel m or f babel, bedlam.

babero m bib.

babieca F 1. simple-minded, stupid; **2.** m/f blockhead, dolt.

babilonio adj. a. su. m, a f Babylonian.

bable m Asturian dialect.

babor m port (side), larboard.

babosa f zo. slug; **babosada** f C. Am., Mex. stupidity; foolish act; **babosear** [1a] slobber over, drool over (a. F fig.); infatuation; **baboso** slobbering etc.

babucha f slipper, mule.

bacalao m, **bacallao** m cod(fish).

bache m rut, (pot)hole.

bachiller 1. garrulous; **2.** m, -a f pupil

who has passed his school-leaving exam; † univ. bachelor; **bachillerato** m bachelor's degree; graduation examination.

bacía f (barber's) bowl; basin.

bacilo m bacillus, germ.

bacín m large chamber pot; beggar's bowl.

bacteria f bacterium, germ; **bacteriología** f bacteriology; **bacteriológico** bacteriological; **bacteriólogo** m bacteriologist.

báculo m staff; prop, support.

badajo m (bell) clapper.

badana f (dressed) sheepskin.

badén m gully, gutter.

badil m, **badila** f fire shovel.

badulaque m F nitwit, simpleton; S. Am. boor, ill-bred fellow.

bagaje m ✗ baggage; (acémila) beast of burden; fig. equipment.

bagatela f trinket, knick-knack; fig. trifle; ~s pl. trivialities.

bagre adj. S.Am. showy; gaudy; coarse.

¡bah! desprecio: bah!, pooh!

bahía f bay.

bailar [1a] v/t. dance; peonza etc. spin; v/i. dance (a. fig.); (peonza) spin (round); **bailarín** m, -a f (professional) dancer; ballet dancer; f thea. ballerina; dancing girl; **baile** m (acto) dance; dancing; (reunión) ball, dance; thea. ballet.

baja f † drop, fall; ✕ casualty; (puesto) vacancy; † etc. dar ~, ir de (or en)~ lose value.

bajada f slope; (acto) going down, descent; **bajamar** f low tide; **bajar** [1a] **1.** v/t. objecto take down, get down; lower, let down; **2.** v/i. go down, come down (a to); (†, agua) fall; ⚙ etc. get off, get out; ~ de get off, get out of; **3.** ~se bend down; fig. lower o.s.

bajeza f meanness etc; lowliness etc.

bajío m shoal, sandbank; shallows; S.Am. lowland.

bajo 1. mst low; terreno low(-lying); (inferior) lower, under(most); agua shallow; (a.~ de cuerpo) short; por lo~ secretly; **2.** m deep place, depth; ♩ = bajío; ♪ bass; △ ground-floor (flat); **3.** adv. down; hablar in a low voice; **4.** prp. under(neath).

bajón m decline (a. ♪) drop; slump en moral; ♪ bassoon.

bajorrelieve m bas-relief.

bala f ✕ bullet; † bale; ~ de cañón cannonball; ni a ~ S.Am. under no circumstances; F como una ~ like a shot; **balaceo** m S.Am. shooting, shootout.

balada f lit., ♪ ballad.

baladí trivial; material trashy.

baladrón 1. boastful; **2.** m, -a f braggart; **baladronear** [1a] boast, brag; (acto) show brave.

balance m to-and-fro motion; rocking, swinging; ♣ roll(ing); ~ de pagos balance of payments; **balancear** [1a] v/t. balance; v/i., ~se rock, swing; ♣ roll; **balanceo** m = balance; **balancín** m balance beam; ⊕ beam; see-saw de niños.

balandra f sloop; **balandro** m yacht; small sloop.

balanza f scales, weighing machine; balance (a. †, ♈); ast. ≈ Scales.

balar [1a] bleat; ~ por F pine for.

balaustrada f balustrade; banisters; **balaustre** m baluster; banister.

balazo m shot; ✸ bullet wound.

balbucear [1a], **balbucir** [3f; defective] stutter; babble; (niño) lisp; **balbuceo** m stammer etc.

balcón m balcony; (barandilla) railing; fig. vantage-point.

baldar [1a] cripple; naipes: trump.

balde[1] m esp. ♣ (canvas) pail, bucket; (zinc) bath.

balde[2]: de ~ free, for nothing; en ~ in vain, for nothing.

baldear [1a] wash (down), swill; (achicar) bale out.

baldío uncultivated; waste.

baldón m affront, insult; **baldonar** [1a] insult; stain, disgrace.

baldosa f (floor)tile; **baldosado** m tiled floor; **baldosar** [1a] tile.

balear[1] [1a] S.Am. shoot (at).

balear[2] adj. a. su. m/f, **baleárico** (native) of the Balearic Isles.

baleo m S.Am. shooting.

balido m bleat(ing).

balística f ballistics.

baliza f (lighted) buoy, marker.

ballena f whale; (lámina) whalebone; **ballenera** f whaler; **ballenero** whaling attr.

ballesta f cross bow; ⚙, mot. spring; **ballestero** m crossbowman.

ballet [bæˈle] m ballet.

balneario 1. thermal, medicinal; **2.** m health resort, spa.

balompié m football.

balón m (foot)ball; † bale; **baloncesto** m basketball.

balota f ballot; **balotar** [1a] ballot.

balsa[1] f ♥ balsa.

balsa[2] f geog. pond.

balsa[3] f ♣ raft.

bálsamo m balsam, balm (a. fig.).

balsear [1a] río cross by ferry; ps. etc. ferry across.

baluarte m bulwark (a. fig.).

balumba f (great) bulk; big pile; F confusion; row.

bambolear(se) swing, sway; (mueble) wobble; roll, reel al andar; **bamboleo** m sway(ing) etc.

bambú m bamboo.

banal banal; p. superficial, commonplace.

banana f banana (tree); prov. a. S.Am. banana; **banano** m banana (tree).

banasta f large basket, hamper.

banca f (asiento) bench; (frutería)

fruit-stall; ✝ banking; *juegos:* bank;
bancario ✝ bank *attr.*, banking *attr.*
financial; **bancarrota** *f (esp.* fraudulent) bankruptcy; *fig.* failure; *hacer*
~ go bankrupt; **banco** *m (asiento)*
bench *(a.* ⊕), form *esp. en escuela;* ✝
bank; ♣ bank; ~ de ahorros savings-
bank.

banda *f (faja)* sash, band; *(cinta)*
ribbon; zone, strip; ♪, *radio:* band;
(ps.) band, gang; *orn.* flock; **bandada** *f* flock *(a. fig.),* flight.

bandearse [1a] move to and fro; *fig.*
get along, shift for o.s.

bandeja *f* tray; salver; *S.Am.* (meat-
etc.) dish.

bandera *f* flag, banner; ⚔ colours; ~
de parlamento flag of truce, white
flag; **banderilla** *f* banderilla; **banderín** *m* little flag; pennant; ⚔
recruiting post; 🚩 signal.

bandidaje *m* banditry; **bandido** *m*
bandit; outlaw; desperado; F rascal.

bando *m* edict, proclamation; faction, party; ~s *pl.* marriage banns.

bandolerismo *m* brigandage, banditry; **bandolero** *m* brigand, bandit.

bandurria *f* bandurria.

banquero *m* banker *(a. juegos).*

banqueta *f* stool.

banquete *m* banquet; *(esp. en casa
particular)* dinner-party; **banquetear** [1a] banquet, feast.

banquillo *m* bench; footstool.

bañador 1. *m,* **-a** *f* bather; 2. *m* ⊕ tub,
trough; *(traje)* bathing-costume;
bañar [1a] bathe; bath *en bañera;*
dip *(a.* ⊕); ~**se** bath *en bañera;* bathe
en mar etc; ir a ~ go for a bathe;
bañera *f* bath(-tub); **baño** *m* bath
(a. ⊕, ♨); *(bañera)* bath(-tub); *(en
general)* bathing; **bañista** *m/f*
bather; *S.Am.* toilet; bathroom.

baque *m* thud, bump, bang; bruise.

baquelita *f* bakelite.

baqueta *f* ramrod; ~s *pl.* ♪ drum-
sticks; *a la* ~ severely, harshly.

bar *m* bar, *approx.* public house;
snackbar.

barahunda *f* uproar; racket, din.

baraja *f* pack (of cards); *fig.* confusion, mix-up; **barajar** [1a] *v/t.*
shuffle; *fig.* mix up, shuffle around;
v/i. quarrel; ~**se** get mixed up.

baranda *f* rail(ing); *billar:* cushion;
barandal *m,* **barandilla** *f* rail(ing),
hand-rail; banisters *de escalera.*

barata *f Col.,Mex.* junk shop; rum-
mage sale; **baratear** [1a] sell

cheaply; sell at a loss; **baratero** *m*
cheap; **baratía** *f S.Am.* cheapness;
baratija *f* trinket, trifle; ✝ *freq.*
novelty; ~s *pl.* cheap goods; **baratillo** *m (géneros)* second-hand goods;
(tienda) second-hand shop; **barato**
1. cheap; *de* ~ for nothing; 2. *m*
bargain sale; **baratura** *f* cheapness.

baraúnda *f* = *barahunda.*

barba 1. *f* chin; *(pelo)* beard *(a.* ♀);
whiskers; *orn.* wattle; *hacer la* ~
shave (o.s.); *hacer la* ~ a shave; 2. *m
thea.* old man's part; *(malo)* villain.

barbacoa *f S.Am.* barbecue.

barbado 1. bearded; 2. *m* ♀ seedling;
barbar [1a] grow a beard.

barbárico barbaric; **barbaridad** *f*
barbarity *(a. fig.); fig.* atrocity,
outrage; ~es *pl.* nonsense;
terrible things; *¡qué* ~! how awful!;
barbarie *f* barbarism, barbarous-
ness; *(crueldad)* barbarity; **barba-
rismo** *m gr.* barbarism; *fig.* = *barbaridad;* **bárbaro** 1. *hist.* barbarian,
barbarous; *fig.* barbarous, cruel;
(arrojado) daring.

barbechar [1a] leave fallow *(arar)*
plough for sowing; **barbechera** *f,*
barbecho *m* fallow (land).

barbería *f* barber's (shop); *(oficio)*
hairdressing; **barbero** 1. *m* barber,
hairdresser; 2. *Mex. adj.* flattering,
fawning.

barbilla *f* (tip of the) chin.

barbón *m* man with a beard; *zo.*
billy-goat; F greybeard.

barbudo bearded; with a long beard.

barbulla *f* uproar, clamour, hullabaloo; **barbullar** [1a] babble away.

barca *f* (small) boat; ~ *de pesca,* ~
pesquera fishing-boat.

barcelonés *adj. a. su. m,* **-a** *f (native)*
of Barcelona.

barco *m* boat; *(grande)* ship, vessel; ~
cisterna *m* tanker; ~ *de guerra* warship; ~ *de vela* sailing-ship.

baremo *m (escala)* scale; table of
rates.

bario *m* barium.

barítono *m* baritone.

barjuleta *f* knapsack; ⊕ tool bag.

barlovento *m* windward.

barman *m* bartender.

barniz *m* varnish; *cerámica:* glaze; ✂
dope; *(afeite)* make-up; **barnizado**
m varnishing; **barnizar** [1f] varnish;
polish; glaze.

barométrico barometric(al); **barómetro** *m* barometer.

B

barón *m* baron; **baronesa** *f* baroness; **baronía** *f* barony.

barquero *m* boatman, waterman.

barquillo *m cocina*: approx. horn, cone, rolled wafer; (*helado*) cornet.

barquinazo *m* F tumble, hard fall; *mot.* jolt; (*vuelco*) spill, overturning.

barra *f* bar; ⊕ rod; 🚉 a. dock; stick, bar *de jabón etc.*

barraca *f* hut, cabin; thatched house; *S.Am.* storage shed.

barragana *f* concubine.

barranca *f*, **barranco** *m* gully, ravine; *fig.* obstacle.

barrar [1a] daub, smear.

barrear [1a] barricade.

barredura *f* sweep(ing); ~s *pl.* sweepings; (*desperdicios*) refuse; **barreminas** *m* minesweeper.

barrena *f* auger; bit, drill *de berbiquí etc.*; **barrenar** [1a] drill (through); ⚓ scuttle.

barrendero *m*, **a** *f* sweeper.

barrer [2a] sweep (out, clean *etc.*); (*a. fig.*) sweep away.

barrera *f* barrier (*a. fig.*), rail; ✗ *etc.* barricade; ~ (*de fuego*) barrage; 🚃 level-crossing gate; *fig.* obstacle; ~ *del sonido*, ~ *sónica* sound barrier.

barrial *m S.Am.* mudhole; muddy ground.

barrica *f* large barrel.

barrido *m* = barredura.

barriga *f* belly (*a. de vasija*); △ bulge; **barrigón**, **barrigudo** potbellied.

barril *m* barrel; *de* ~ *cerveza etc.* draught *attr.*; **barrilero** *m* cooper; **barrilete** *m* keg; ⊕ dog, clamp.

barrio *m* quarter, district; suburb; ~s *pl.* bajos poor quarter; *b.s.* slums, slum area.

barrizal *m* muddy place, mire; **barro** *m* mud; *cerámica*: clay; (*búcaro*) earthenware pot; *anat.* pimple (on the face); ~s *pl.* earthenware; crockery.

barroco 1. baroque; *lit.* mannered, *b.s.* extravagant, in bad taste; 2. *m* the Baroque (style *etc.*); **barroquismo** *m* baroque style; extravagance.

barroso muddy; *cara* pimply.

barrote *m* (heavy) bar.

barruntar [1a] guess, conjecture; **barrunte** *m* sign, indication; **barrunto** *m* guess, conjecture.

bartolina *f C.Am.* cell; dungeon; jail.

bártulos *m/pl.* things, belongings, bits and pieces; goods; ⊕ tools.

barullo *m* uproar, din.

basa *f* △ base (of a column); *fig.* basis, foundation.

basáltico basaltic; **basalto** *m* basalt.

basar [1a] base; *fig.* base, found; ~se en be based on; rely on.

basca *f* 🎗 (*mst* ~s *pl.*) queasiness, nausea; F tantrum; *dar* ~s *a* make *s.o.* sick; **bascoso** 🎗 queasy; squeamish; *S.Am.* filthy.

báscula *f* scale, weighing machine.

base *f mst* base; ⊕ mount(ing); bed; *fig.* basis, foundation; ~ *aérea* air base; ~ *avanzada* forward base; ~ *naval* naval base; **básico** 🜊 basic.

basílica *f esp. hist.* basilica; *eccl.* large church, privileged church.

basilisco *m* basilisk.

basquear [1a] feel sick; *hacer* ~ *a* make *s.o.* sick, turn *s.o.'s* stomach.

basquetbol *m* basketball.

bastante 1. *adj.* enough (*para* for; *para inf.* to *inf.*); 2. *adv.* (*que basta*) enough; (*más o menos*): ~ *bueno* quite good; **bastar** [1a] be enough, be sufficient (*para inf.* to *inf.*); suffice, be (quite) enough; *¡basta!* that's enough!; stop!

bastardear [1a] *v/t.* debase; adulterate; *v/i.* ♀ *a. fig.* degenerate; **bastardilla**: (*letra*) ~ italic(s); *en* ~ in italics; **bastardo** *adj. a. su. m*, **a** *f* bastard; 🜊 *etc.* hybrid.

bastedad *f* coarseness; roughness; *C.Am.* abundance, excess.

bastidor *m* frame (*a. sew.*, ⊕); frame, case *de ventana etc.*; (*con lienzo*) stretcher; *thea.* wing.

bastilla *f* hem; **bastillar** [1a] hem.

bastimentar [1a] supply, provision; **bastimento** *m* supply, provision.

basto 1. coarse, rough; (*grosero*) rude, ill-mannered; 2. *m* packsaddle; *naipes*: ~s *pl.* clubs.

bastón *m* (walking)stick; ✗ *etc.* baton; *heráldica*: pallet, pale; *fig.* control, command; **bastonazo** *m* blow with a stick; caning; **bastonear** [1a] beat (with a stick), cane.

basura *f* rubbish, refuse; (*esp. papeles*) litter; **basural** *m S.Am.* dump; trash pile; garbage heap; **basurero** *m* (*p.*) dustman; scavenger; (*sitio*) rubbish dump; 🖉 dung-heap.

bata *f* dressing-gown; housecoat; 🜊 *etc.* laboratory coat.

bataclán *m S.Am.* burlesque show.

batahola *f* F hullabaloo, rumpus.

batalla f battle; *esp. fig.* fight, contest; *fig.* (inner) struggle; **batallar** [1a] battle, fight (con with, against; por over); 2. m battalion.

batán m fulling mill; (*máquina*) fulling hammer; **batanar** [1a] full, beat.

batata f sweet potato, yam; *S.Am.* bashfulness.

batea f (*bandeja*) tray; (*artesilla*) deep trough; ♣ flat-bottomed boat.

batel m small boat, skiff; **batelero** m boatman.

batería f mst battery; ♪ bank *de luces*; *thea.* footlights; ~ *de cocina* kitchen utensils.

baterista m/f ♪ drummer.

bati-boleo m *Cuba, Mex.* noise; confusion.

batido 1. *seda* shot, chatoyant; *camino* well-trodden, beaten; 2. m *cocina*: batter; ~ (*de leche*) milkshake; **batidor** m ⊕, *hunt.* beater; ✕ scout; (*peine*) comb; = *batidora*; **batidora** f whisk; ♪ (electric) mixer; **batintín** m gong.

batir [3a] 1. v/t. *metall., hunt.*, ✕, *adversario, alas, huevos, marca* beat; *campo, terreno* comb, reconnoitre; *casa* knock down; (*sol*) beat down on; 2. v/i. ♪ beat (violently); 3. ~se (have a) fight.

batiscafo m bathyscaphe.

batista f cambric, batiste.

batuque m *S.Am.* To-do, rumpus.

baturrillo m hotchpotch.

baturro 1. uncouth; 2. m, **a** f Aragonese peasant.

batuta f ♪ baton.

baúl m (♣ cabin) trunk; F corporation; ~ *ropero* wardrobe trunk.

bauprés m bowsprit.

bausán m dummy, straw man.

bautismo m baptism; **bautizar** [1f] baptize (*a. fig.*); *fig.* name, give a name to; **bautizo** m baptism; christening.

bauxita f bauxite.

baya f berry.

bayeta f baize; (*trapo*) floor cloth.

bayo 1. biscuit(colored); *caballo* bay; 2. m *approx.* bay (horse).

bayoneta f bayonet; **bayonetazo** m bayonet thrust, bayonet wound.

bayu(n)ca f *C.Am.* bar; tavern.

baza f *naipes*: trick; F *meter* ~ butt in.

bazar m bazaar.

bazo 1. yellowish-brown; 2. m *anat.* spleen.

bazofia f leftovers; (pig)swill, hogwash (*a. fig.*); *fig.* filth.

beata f lay sister; F devout woman; **beatificar** [1g] beatify; **beatitud** f beatitude, blessedness; *Su* ♀ His Holiness; **beato** 1. happy, blessed; pious; 2. m *approx.* lay brother; F devout man.

bebé m baby.

bebedero 1. drinkable; 2. m drinking-through; spout *de vasija*; **bebedizo** 1. drinkable; 2. m ✿ potion; (love) potion; **bebedor** 1. hard-drinking, bibulous; 2. m, **-a** f (hard) drinker, toper; **beber** 1. m drink(ing); 2. [2a] v/t. drink (up); *esp. fig.* drink in, imbibe; v/i. drink (*a. b.s.*).

bebezón m *S.Am.* drinking spree; **bebida** f drink (*a. alcohol*); beverage; ~ *alcohólica* liquor, alcoholic drink; *dado a la* ~ hard-drinking, given to drink; **bebido** tipsy, merry.

beca f scholarship, grant (for study); **becario** m, **a** f scholarship holder.

becerrillo m calf skin; **becerro** m yearling calf; ⊕ calf skin.

becuadro m ♪ natural (sign).

beduino *adj. a. su.* m, **a** f Bedouin.

befa f jeer; **befar** [1a] scoff at, jeer at.

befo 1. thick-lipped; 2. m lip.

begonia f begonia.

béisbol m baseball; **beisbolero** m, **beisbolista** m baseball player.

bejuco m liana.

beldad f beauty (*a. p.*).

belén m *eccl.* crib, nativity scene; *fig.* confusion, bedlam.

belga *adj. a. su.* m/f; **bélgico** Belgian.

belicoso warlike; militant; **beligerancia** f belligerancy; militancy, warlike spirit; **beligerante** *adj. a. su.* m/f belligerant.

bellaco 1. wicked; astute, sly, cunning; 2. m, **a** f scoundrel.

bellaquear [1a] cheat, be crooked; *S.Am.* (*caballo*) rear; **bellaquería** f (*acto*) dirty trick; (*dicho*) mean (or nasty) thing to say.

belleza f beauty, loveliness; (*p.*) beauty; **bello** beautiful, lovely.

bellota f ✿ acorn.

bemol m ♪ flat.

bencedrina f benzedrine.

bencina f *mot.* benz(ol)ine.

bendecir [*approx.* 3p] bless; consecrate; (*alabar*) praise; extol; ~ *la mesa* say grace; **bendición** f blessing, benediction; ~*es pl.* *nupciales* wedding ceremony; *echar la* ~ give one's

B

blessing (a. fig.) **bendito** saintly, blessed; *agua* holy; (*feliz*) happy; **benedictino** adj. a. su. m Benedictine.

beneficencia f (*virtud*) doing good; charity; (*obra*) benefaction; (*fundación*) charity; **beneficiar** [1b] v/t. benefit, be of benefit to; ✓ cultivate; *S.Am.* (*ganado*) slaughter; v/i. be of benefit; ~se de take advantage of; *S.Am.* shoot dead; **beneficiario** m, a f beneficiary; **beneficio** m benefit, good; (*donativo*) benefaction; *eccl.* living, benefice; ✝, ⚒, ✓ yield, profit; **benéfico** good (a, para for); *obra etc.* charitable.

benemérito worthy, meritorious.

benevolencia f benevolence, kind-(li)ness; **benévolo** benevolent.

benigno kind(ly); gracious, gentle; *clima* kindly, mild; ⚒ mild.

beodo drunk(en).

bequista m/f *C.Am.,Cuba* scholarship holder; grant winner.

berbiquí m (carpenter's) brace.

bereber adj. a. su. m/f Berber.

berenjena f aubergine, egg-plant; **berenjenal** m aubergine bed.

bergante m scoundrel, rascal.

bergantín m brig.

bermejo red(dish), russet; **bermellón** m vermilion.

berrear [1a] low, bellow; F fly off the handle; **berrido** m lowing, bellow (-ing); ♪ screech (a. fig.); **berrinche** m F rage, tantrum.

berro m water-cress.

berza f cabbage.

besar [1a] kiss; *fig.* graze, touch; ~ *la mano*, ~ *los pies fig.* pay one's respects (a to); ~**se** kiss (each other); **beso** m kiss.

besuquearse [1a] F pet, neck.

bético *lit.* Andalusian.

betún m ⚒ bitumen; (*zapatos*) shoe polish, blacking.

bezudo thick-lipped.

Biblia f Bible; F*ig. saber la* ~ know everything; **bíblico** biblical.

bibliografía f bibliography; **bibliográfico** bibliographic(al).

biblioteca f library; (*estante*) book-case; ~ *de consulta* reference library; **bibliotecario** m, a f librarian.

bicarbonato m bicarbonate of soda; cooking soda.

bicherío m *S.Am.* vermin; **bicho** m small animal, insect *etc.*, bug *S.Am.*; *toros*: fighting bull; *Mex.* cat.

bicicleta f (bi)cycle; *andar en* ~, *ir en* ~ ride a bicycle, (bi)cycle.

bicolor two-color; *mot.* two-tone.

biela f connecting rod.

bielda f *approx.* pitchfork; **bieldar** [1a] winnow.

bien 1. m good; (*beneficio*) advantage, profit; (*bienestar*) welfare, well-being; *mi* ~ (p.) my dear(est); **2.** ~*es* pl. wealth, riches; property, possessions; ~ *dotales* dowry; ~ *raíces* real estate, realty; **3.** adv. well; (*correctamente*) right; (*de buena gana*) gladly, readily; *más* ~ rather; *o* ~ or else; **4.** (*como int.*) ¡~! all right!, okay!; jolly good!; ¡*muy* ~! (*a orador etc.*) hear hear!; yes indeed; ~**aventurado** happy, fortunate; *eccl.* blessed; ~**hablado** nicely-spoken; ~**intencionado** well-meaning.

bienvenida f welcome; greeting; (*llegada*) safe arrival; **bienvenido** welcome; ¡~! welcome!

bifocal bifocal.

biftec m (beef)steak.

bifurcación f fork, junction *en camino*; branch; **bifurcarse** [1g] (*caminos etc.*) fork, branch; bifurcate; diverge.

bigamia f bigamy; second marriage *de viudo*; **bígamo 1.** bigamous; **2.** m, a f bigamist.

bigote m (a. ~*s* pl.) moustache; whiskers *de gato etc.*; **bigotudo** with a big moustache.

bigudí m hair curler.

bikini m bikini swimsuit.

bilateral bilateral (a. ✝), two-sided.

bilbaíno adj. a. su. m, a f (native) of Bilbao.

bilingüe bilingual.

bilioso bilious (a. fig.); fig. peevish, difficult; **bilis** f bile (a. fig.).

billar m billiards; (*mesa*) billiard-table.

billete m ticket; ✝ (bank-)note, bill; (*carta*) note, letter; ~ *amoroso* love letter, billet-doux; ~ *de banco* bank note, bill; ~ *de ida y vuelta* return ticket.

billón m billion; **billonésimo** billionth.

bimba f F top hat; *Mex.* drinking spree; drunkenness.

bimotor twin-engined.

binocular binocular; **binóculo** *m* binoculars; *thea.* opera-glasses.

biofísica *f* biophysics.

biografía *f* biography, life; **biográfico** biographic(al).

biología *f* biology; **biológico** biologic(al); **biólogo** *m* biologist.

biombo *m* (folding) screen.

biopsia *f* 🩺 biopsy.

bioquímica *f* biochemistry.

bípedo *adj. a. su. m*, **a** *f* biped.

biplano *m* biplane.

birlar [1a] knock down (*or* kill) with one shot; *cosa* pinch.

birlocha *f* kite.

birmano *adj. a. su. m*, **a** *f* Burmese.

birreactor *adj. a. su. m* 🛬 twin-jet.

birreta *f* biretta, cardinal's hat; **birrete** *m univ. approx.* cap, mortarboard F.

bis 1. *adv.* twice; *thea.* ¡~! encore!; **2.** *m* encore.

bisabuela *f* great-grandmother; **bisabuelo** *m* great-grandfather.

bisagra *f* hinge; F waggle *de caderas*.

bisar [1a] *thea. etc.* repeat.

bisecar [1g] bisect; **bisección** *f* bisection.

bisel *m* bevel(-edge); **biselar** [1a] bevel.

bisemanal twice-weekly.

bisiesto: *v.* año ~.

bisílabo two-syllabled.

bismuto *m* bismuth.

bisnieto *m* great-grandson.

bisojo cross-eyed, squinting.

bisonte *m* bison.

bisoño 1. green, inexperienced; raw; **2.** *m*, **a** *f* greenhorn.

bisté *m*, **bistec** *m* (beef)steak.

bisturí *m* scalpel.

bisutería *f* imitation jewellery, paste.

bitoque *m* faucet; spigot; bung; *C.Am.* sewer.

bizantino 1. Byzantine; *fig.* decadent; **2.** *m*, **a** *f* Byzantine.

bizarría *f* gallantry; generosity; (*esplendor*) show; **bizarro** gallant; generous; (*gallardo*) dashing.

bizco cross-eyed, squinting.

bizcocho *m* sponge (cake); biscuit; (*loza*) biscuit (ware); 🏴 hardtack.

bizma *f* poultice; **bizmar** [1a] poultice.

bizquear [1a] squint.

blanco 1. white; *piel* white, light; *tez* fair; *página*, *verso* blank; **2.** *m* white(ness); (*p.*) white (man); 🎯

target (*a. fig.*); ~ del ojo white of the eye; *dar en el* ~ hit the mark (*a. fig.*); **blancura** *f* whiteness.

blandear [1a] *v/t. fig.* convince, persuade; *v/i.*, **~se** soften, yield, give in.

blandir [3a; *defective*] *v/t.* brandish, wave aloft; *v/i.*, **~se** wave to and fro.

blando *mst* soft; *pasta etc.* smooth; *carne b.s.* flabby; *fig.* mild, gentle; **blanducho** F on the soft side, softish; **blandura** *f* softness *etc.*; (*halago*) flattery, flattering words.

blanqueadura *f* whitening, bleaching; whitewashing; **blanquear** [1a] *v/t. tela etc.* bleach, whiten; ⊕ blanch; *v/i.* (*volverse*) turn white, whiten; **blanqueo** *m* bleaching *etc.*

blasfemar [1a] blaspheme (*contra* against); *fig.* curse (and swear); ~ de curse, revile; **blasfemia** *f eccl.* blasphemy; insult.

blasón *m* (*en general*) heraldry; (*escudo*) coat of arms, escutcheon; **blasonar** [1a] *v/t.* (em)blazon; *v/i.* boast (*de* of being), brag.

blindaje *m* ✕, ⚓ armor(plating); **blindar** [1a] ✕ armor; ⊕ shield.

bloc *m* (writing)pad; calendar pad.

blof *m S.Am.* bluff; **blofear** [1a] bluff.

blondo blond; light.

bloque *m* △, ⊕ block; *fig.* group; *pol.* bloc; *en* ~ en bloc; **bloquear** [1a] ✕, ⚓ blockade; *mot.* brake; **bloqueo** *m* blockade; 🌡 freeze, squeeze.

blufar [1a] bluff; **bluff** *m* [bluf] bluff; *hacer un* ~ a bluff.

blusa *f* blouse; jumper; overalls.

boa *f* boa.

boato *m* show(iness), ostentation.

bobada *f* silly thing; **bobalicón** F **1.** utterly stupid, quite silly; **2.** *m*, **-a** *f* nitwit, mutt; **bobear** [1a] (*hablar*) talk (a lot of) twaddle; **bober(f)a** *f* = bobada.

bóbilis: F de ~ ~ (*gratis*) for nothing.

bobina *f* bobbin, spool (*a. phot.*), reel.

bobo 1. (*corto*) stupid, simple; (*tonto*) silly; **2.** *m*, **a** *f* fool, dolt, mutt; *thea.* clown, funny man.

boca *f* mouth; muzzle *de fusil*; *fig.* mouth, entrance; ~ *abajo* (*arriba*) face downward (upward); F ¡*cállate la* ~! shut up!, hold your tongue!

bocacalle *f* street entrance; intersection; **bocadillo** *m* snack; meat (*or* cheese *etc.*) roll, sandwich; **bocado** *m* mouthful; (*un poco de comida*) morsel, bite; (*mordedura*) bite; **bo-**

B

canada f mouthful de vino etc.; puff de humo, viento; **bocaza** f loud-mouth; gossip.

boceto m sketch, outline.

bochar [1a] Mex., Ven. turn down; reject; insult.

bochorno m sultry weather; stiftling atmosphere; (viento) hot summer breeze; **bochornoso** tiempo sultry, thundery; ambiente etc. stiftling; fig. embarrassing.

bocina f ♪ trumpet; horn (a. mot., gramófono); (portavoz) megaphone; **bocinar** [1a] mot. hoot, blow the horn, honk.

boda f wedding (a. ~s pl.), marriage; wedding reception.

bodega f wine cellar; (despensa) pantry (depósito) store room, ♣ warehouse; ♣ hold de barco; S.Am. grocery store; **bodegón** m cheap restaurant; b.s. low dive.

bodoque m pellet; lump; F nitwit.

bofe m 1. lung; ~s pl. lights de animal; 2. adj. C.Am. unpleasant; disgusting.

bofetada f slap in the face (a. fig.); **bofetón** m (hard) slap.

boga[1] f vogue (por for), popularity.

boga[2] ♣ 1. f rowing; 2. m/f rower; **bogar** [1h] row; (navegar) sail; **bogavante** m ♣ stroke; zo. lobster.

bogotano adj. a. su. m, a f (native) of Bogotá.

bohemio adj. a. su. m, a f fig., **bohemo** adj. a. su. m, a f geog. Bohemian.

boicotear [1a] boycott; **boicoteo** m boycott(ing).

boina f beret.

bola f ball; ♣ signal (with disks); naipes: slam; (betún) shoe-polish; ~s pl. ⊕ ballbearings; S.Am. hunt. bolas; **bolada** f throw; S.Am. ✝ luck break.

bolardo m bollard.

bolchev(iqu)ismo m Bolshevism; **bolchev(iqu)ista** adj. a. su. m/f Bolshevist; Bolshevik.

boleada f S.Am. hunt; **boleadoras** f/pl. S.Am. bolas; **bolear** [1a] v/t. F throw; S.Am. hunt; Mex. polish shoes; v/i. play for fun; F tell fibs; ~se (caballo) rear; fig. stumble; S.Am. make a mistake.

bolero m bolero; Mex. shoeshine (boy).

boleta f pass, ticket; ✝ authorization, permit; S.Am. ballot (paper); **bole-**

tería f S.Am. 🚄 bookingoffice; thea. box-office; **boletín** m (informe etc.) bulletin; **boleto** m S.Am. ticket.

boliche m (bola) jack; (juego) bowls; (pista) bowling green; ⊕ small furnace; S.Am. skittles.

bolígrafo m ball-point pen.

bolillo m bobbin (for making lace); S.Am. bread roll; ~s pl. toffee-bars.

bolina f ♣ bowline; F racket, row.

bolita f pellet; (canica) marble.

boliviano adj. a. su. m, a f Bolivian.

bollería f pastry shop, bakery; **bollero** m baker, muffin man; **bollo** m cocina: muffin, bun, roll; dent en metal; sew. puff; 🌩 bump, lump; F to-do, mix-up.

bolo m 1. ninepin; naipes: slam; pharm. large pill; (juego de) ~s pl. ninepins; 2. adj. C.Am., Mex. drunk.

bolsa f purse para dinero; (saquillo) bag, pouch; handbag de mujer; ✗, geol. pocket; bag en vestido, tela; S.Am. sack; anat. cavity, sac; ✝ stock exchange; ~ de agua caliente hotwater bottle; S.Am.~ negra black market; ~ de trabajo labor exchange, employment bureau; **bolsero** m S.Am. sponger; Mex. pickpocket.

bolsillo m pocket (a. fig.); (saquillo) purse, money-bag; de ~ pocket attr., pocket-size; **bolsista** m (stock-) broker; S.Am. pickpocket; **bolso** m bag, purse.

bomba f pump; glass, globe de lámpara; ✗ bomb; ✗ shell; S.Am. (burbuja) bubble; ~ de aire air-pump; ~ aspirante suction pump; ~ atómica atomic bomb; ~ de engrase grease gun; ~ estomacal stomach pump; ~ H, ~ de hidrógeno hydrogen bomb; ~ impulsora force-pump; ~ de incendios fire engine; ~ de mano grenade; ~ de relojería, ~ de retardo timebomb; ~ neutrónica neutron bomb; a prueba de ~s bombproof.

bombardear [1a] ✗, phys. bombard (a. fig.; de with); ✗ shell; ✗ bomb, raid; **bombardeo** m ✗ bombardment (a. phys.), shelling; **bombardero** 1. bombing; 2. m bomber.

bombear [1a] ✗ shell; S.Am. agua pump (out); ✗ Am. fire, dismiss; S.Am. spy on; ~se ⌂ camber; (madera etc.) bulge; **bombeo** m camber.

bombero m fireman; pumper; (cuerpo de) ~s pl. fire brigade.

bombilla f ✦ bulb; chimney de lámpara; ~ fusible flashbulb.

bombo 1. F dumbfounded; **2.** *m* ♪ bass drum; ♣ lighter; F *dar ~ a* praise to the skies; *thea.* write up, ballyhoo *S.Am.*

bombón *m* sweet, candy *S.Am.* chocolate; F (*p.*) good sort; (*mujer*) peach; (*cosa*) beauty.

bombonera *f* candy box.

bonachón good-natured, kindly; *b.s.* naïve, unsuspecting.

bonaerense *adj. a. su. m/f* (native) of Buenos Aires.

bonanza *f* ♣ fair weather; *min.* bonanza; ♥ prosperity, bonanza.

bondad *f* goodness; kind(li)ness *etc.*; *tener la ~ de inf.* be so kind (*or* good) as to *inf.*; **bondadoso** kind(ly), kind-hearted.

bonete *m eccl.* hat, biretta; *univ. approx.* cap, mortar board F; **bonetería** *f* hat shop; notions store.

bongo *m S.Am.* barge; canoa.

bonificación *f* improvement (*a.* ♪); ♥ allowance; **bonificar** [1g] improve.

bonito¹ pretty, nice (*a. fig.*).

bonito² *m* tunny, bonito.

bono *m* voucher; ♥ bond.

boom *m* (*florecimiento*) boom.

boquear [1a] *v/t.* pronounce, say; *v/i.* be at one's last gasp; *fig.* be in its last stages; **boquete** *m* gap, opening, hole; **boquiabierto** open-mouthed; *fig.* aghast; **boquilla** *f* mouthpiece; ⊕ nozzle; burner *de gas*; stem *de pipa.*

bórax *m* borax.

borboll(e)ar [1a] bubble, boil up; *fig.* splutter; **borbollón** *m* bubbling, boiling; *a ~es* impetuously.

borbotar [1a] (*fuente*) bubble up, gush forth; bubble, boil *al hervir*; **borbotón** *m =* **borbollón**.

borceguí *m* high shoe, laced boot.

borda *f* ♣ gunwale; ♣ (*vela*) mainsail; (*choza*) hut; **bordada** *f* ♣ tack; *dar ~s* ♣ tack.

bordado *m* embroidery, needlework; **bordadura** *f* embroidery; **bordar** [1a] embroider (*a. fig.*).

borde *m* edge; side *de camino etc.*; brink *de abismo*; lip *de taza*; brim, rim *de vaso*; **bordear** [1a] *v/t.* skirt, go along the edge of; *v/i.* ♣ tack.

bordo *m* ♣ side; (*bordada*) tack; *a ~* on board; *al ~* alongside.

bordón *m* pilgrim's staff; *fig.* guide, helping hand; **bordoncillo** *m* pet phrase.

Borgoña *m* (*a. vino de ~*) burgundy.

borla *f* tassel; pompon *en sombrero*; tuft *de hebras*; bob *de pelo*; powderpuff *para empolvarse.*

bornear [1a] *v/t.* twist, bend; ⚠ put in place, align; *v/i.* ♣ swing at anchor; *~se* warp, bulge.

boro *m* boron.

borra *f* (*lana*) thick wool, flock; stuffing *de almohada*; (*pelusa*) fluff; ♀ down; sediment, lees.

borrachera *f* (*estado*) drunkenness; (*a. juerga de ~*) spree, binge; **borrachería** *f Mex.* bar; tavern; **borracho 1.** drunk; (*de costumbre*) drunken; **2.** *m, a f* drunk(ard), sot.

borrador *m* rough copy, first draft; (*libro*) book for rough work; (*goma*) rubber, eraser; **borradura** *f* erasure; **borrar** [1a] erase, rub out *con borrador*; cross out *con rayas.*

borrasca *f* storm (*a. fig.*); *meteor. a.* depression, cyclone; **borrascoso** stormy (*a. fig.*); *viento* squally, gusty.

borrego *m, a f* (yearling) lamb; F simpleton.

borrico *m* donkey, ass (*a. fig.*); ⊕ saw-horse.

borrón *m* blot, smudge; (*borrador*) rough draft, sketch (*a. paint.*); **borroso** *líquido* muddy, dirty.

borujo *m* lump; pack; **borujón** *m* ♣ lump, bump; (*lío*) bundle.

boscaje *m* small wood, grove; *paint.* woodland scene; **boscoso** wooded; **bosque** *m* wood(s), woodland; (*grande*) forest.

bosquejar [1a] sketch, outline (*a. fig.*); ⊕ design; *proyecto* draft; **bosquejo** *m* sketch, outline (*a. fig.*).

bostezar [1f] yawn; **bostezo** *m* yawn.

bota *f* boot; (*odre*) leather winebottle; *~s pl. de campaña* topboots.

botafuego *m* hothead.

botánica *f* botany; **botánico 1.** botanic(al); **2.** *m, a f* botanist.

botar [1a] hurl, fling; *pelota* pitch; *barco* launch; *timón* put over; *S.Am.* throw away; fire; dismiss; *~se S.Am.* throw o.s. (*a* into); **botarate** *m* F wild fellow, madcap; *S.Am.* spendthrift.

bote¹ *m* (*golpe*) thrust, blow; buck *de caballo*; bounce *de pelota etc.*; *Mex.* prison; jail.

bote² *m* (*vasija*) can, tin; pot, jar; *naipes*: jackpot; *mot.* F jalopy.

bote³ *m* ♣ boat; *~ de paso* ferryboat; *~ de salvamento* lifeboat.

botella f bottle; ~ de Leiden Leyden jar.

botica f chemist's (shop), drug store; **boticario** m chemist, druggist.

botija f earthenware jug; S.Am. belly; F estar hecho una ~ be as fat as a sow; **botijo** m earthenware jar.

botín[1] m ✕ booty, plunder, spoils.

botín[2] m (polaina) spat; = **botina** f bootee; high shoe.

botiquín m medicine chest; (a. ~ de emergencia) first-aid kit.

boto 1. dull, blunt; fig. dull, slow (-witted); **2.** m leather wine-bottle.

botón m sew., ♪ button; ~ (de camisa) stud; ~ (de puerta) doorknob; radio: knob; **botones** m buttons, bellboy, bellhop.

bóveda f ⚖ vault; dome; cavern; ~ celeste arch of heaven.

bovino bovine.

boxeador m boxer; **boxear** [1a] box; **boxeo** m boxing.

boya f ⚓ buoy; float de red.

boyada f drove of oxen.

boyero m oxherd, drover; (perro) cattle dog.

bozal 1. (novato) raw, green; potro wild, untamed; F silly, stupid; S.Am. speaking broken Spanish; **2.** m muzzle; S.Am. halter.

bozo m (vello) down (on upper lip); (boca) mouth, lips; halter, headstall de caballo.

bracear [1a] swing one's arms; (nadar) swim, esp. crawl; **bracero** m (unskilled) laborer; **bracete**: de ~ arm in arm.

braga f ⊕ rope, sling; F diaper Am. de niño; ~s pl. breeches de hombre; **bragadura** f anat. crotch; sew. gusset; **bragazas** m henpecked husband; **braguero** m 𝕤 trus; **bragueta** f fly, flies.

bramante m twine, fine string.

bramar [1a] roar, bellow (a. fig.); **bramido** m roar, bellow etc.

brasa f (live) coal; estar en ~s fig. be on tenterhooks; **brasero** m brazier; **brasil** m brazilwood; Mex. hearth.

brasileño adj. a. su. m, ♂ f Brazilian.

bravata f threat; (piece of) bravado; **bravatear** [1a] S.Am. brag; boast; **bravear** [1a] boast, talk big; bluster.

braveza f ferocity; meteor. etc. fury; (valor) bravery, courage; **bravío 1.** fierce, ferocious; **2.** m fierceness; **bravo 1.** (valiente) brave; b.s. boastful, blustering; fine, excellent; ¡~!

¡bravo!; **2.** m thug; **bravucón** m F boaster, braggart; **bravura** f ferocity; (valor) bravery.

braza f approx. fathom (= 1,67 m.); (cabo) brace; **brazada** f (remo, natación) stroke; (brazado) armful; **brazado** m armful; **brazal** m armband; ✝ irrigation channel; **brazalete** m bracelet, wirstlet; **brazo** m arm (a. ⊕, fig.); zo. foreleg; ♀ limb, branch; (soporte) bracket; ~ de mar sound, arm of the sea; con los ~s abiertos with open arms (a. fig.); asidos de ~ arm in arm.

brea f tar, pitch; **brear** [1a] F abuse, ill-treat; (zumbar) make fun of.

brebaje m pharm. potion, mixture.

brecha f ✕ breach; ⚖ gap, opening; abrir ~ en muro breach.

brécol(es) m broccoli.

brega f (lucha) struggle; (riña) quarrel, row; **bregar** [1h] struggle, fight (con with, against; a. fig.).

breña f, **breñal** m scrub, rough ground; **breñoso** rough, scrubby.

brete m fetters, shackles; fig. tight spot, jam.

bretones m/pl. Brussels sprouts.

breve 1. idle, loafing; (esp. de duración); **2.** m ♪ breve; eccl. (papal) brief; **brevedad** f shortness; brevity; **breviario** m breviary.

bribón 1. idle, loafing; (bellaco) rascally; **2.** m, -a f loafer; rascal; scamp; **bribonada** f dirty trick; **bribonear** [1a] loaf around.

brida f bridle; ⊕ fishplate; ⊕ (anillo) collar; a toda ~ at top speed.

brigada 1. f ✕ brigade; squad, gang de obreros etc.; **2.** m approx. staff sergeant; **brigadier** m brigadier.

brillante 1. brilliant (a. fig., p.), shining, bright; joya; excesa glittering; **2.** m brilliant; **brillantez** f brilliance etc.; **brillantina** f brilliantine; metal polish; **brillar** [1a] shine (a. fig., p.); glitter, gleam, glisten; **brillo** m shine etc.; lustre, sheen esp. de superficie; sacar ~ a polish, shine.

brincar [1g] skip, jump, leap about; F go off the deep end, blow one's top (por at); **brinco** m jump, leap, skip.

brindar [1a] v/t. offer (a to; a alguien con algo s.t. to s.o.); toro etc. dedicate; invite (a inf. to inf.); v/i. invite; ~se a inf. offer to inf.; **brindis** f toast.

brío m (freq. ~s pl.) spirit, dash, nerve;

brioso spirited, dashing; resolute; jaunty.

briqueta f briquette.

brisa f breeze.

británico British; **britano 1.** esp. hist. British; **2. m, a** f Briton.

brizna f strand, thread, filament; fragment, piece.

broca f sew. reel, bobbin; ⊕ drill, bit; tack de zapato.

brocado 1. brocaded; **2. m** brocade.

brocal m curb de pozo; cigarette holder.

brocha f (large paint)brush; ~ de afeitar shaving-brush; **brochada** f, **brochazo** m brush-stroke.

broche m clasp (a. de libro), fastener; (joya etc.) brooch; ~ **de oro** punch line.

broma f (chanza) joke; prank; no estoy para ~s I'm in no mood for jokes; gastar una ~ play a joke (a on); **bromear** [1a] joke (a. ~se); rag; (burlarse) pull s.o.'s leg; **bromista 1.** fond of joking etc.; **2. m/f** (salado) joker, wag.

bromo m bromine.

bronca f F (riña) row, scrap, wrangle; armar una ~ start a row; echar una ~ a rap s.o. over the knuckles.

bronce m bronze; **bronceado 1.** bronze(-colored); piel tanned, sunburnt; **2. m** ⊕ bronze finish; tan de piel; **bronceador** m suntan lotion; **broncear(se)** [1a] ⊕ bronze; piel tan.

bronco superficie rough, unpolished; metal brittle; voz gruff, harsh; **bronquedad** f roughness etc.

bronquial bronchial.

bronquitis f bronchitis.

broquel m shield (a. fig.); **broquelarse** [1a] shield o.s.

brota f shoot, bud; **brotar** [1a] ♀ sprout, put out; bud; (agua etc.) spring up, gush forth; **brote** m ♀ shoot, bud; ✻ outbreak of enfermedad.

broza f ✓ chaff de trigo etc.; (hojas etc.) dead leaves, dead wood.

bruces: de ~ face downwards; caer de ~ fall flat on one's face.

bruja f witch; orn. owl; **brujería** f sorcery, witchcraft, magic; **brujo** m sorcerer, magician, wizard.

brújula f compass; fig. guide; ~ giroscópica gyro compass; F perder la ~ lose one's touch.

bruma f (esp. sea-)mist, fog; **brumoso** misty, foggy.

bruñido m (acto) polish(ing); (efecto) shine, gloss; **bruñir** [3h] polish, burnish; C.Am. annoy; ~se F put on make-up.

brusco ataque sudden; movimiento brusque; curva sharp; fig. brusque.

bruselas f/pl. tweezers.

brusquedad f suddenness etc.

brutal 1. brutal; (brusco) sudden, unexpected; **2. m** brute; **brutalidad** f brutality, bestiality; (acto) crime; **bruto 1.** brute, brutish; bestial; (malcriado) uncouth, coarse; en ~ (in the) rough; raw; piedra unpolished; **2. m** brute; F dolt.

bu m F bogey (man).

búa f pimple; **buba** f, **bubo** m tumor.

bucal oral, of the mouth.

bucanero m buccaneer.

bucear [1a] dive; work as a diver; fig. delve; (bocado) raw; **buceador** m diver; **buceo** m diving.

buche m orn. crop; zo. a. F maw; F belly; (bocado) mouthful.

bucle m curl, ringlet; fig. curve.

bucólica f pastoral poem, bucolic; F meal; **bucólico** pastoral, bucolic.

budín m pudding.

buenaventura f (good) luck; fortune; decir la ~ a tell s.o.'s fortune.

bueno 1. mst good; p. good, kind, nice; calentura high; constitución sound, strong; doctrina sound; sociedad polite; tiempo good, fine, fair; iro. fine, pretty; F estar de ~as be in a good mood; ¡ésa sí que es ~a! that's a good one!; **2.** (como int. etc.): ¡~! all right!, well then!; F ¡~as! hullo!; **3.** cj.: ~ que although, even though.

buey m bullock, steer; ox para labrar etc.

búfalo m buffalo.

bufanda f scarf, muffler.

bufar [1a] snort (a. fig.; de with); (gato) spit.

bufete m desk; ⚖ lawyer's office; S.Am. snack.

bufido m snort (a. fig.; de of).

bufón 1. funny, comical, clownish; **2. m, -a** f buffoon, clown; hist. jester; **bufonada** f (acto) buffoonery, clowning; (sátira) comic piece; **bufonearse** [1a] clown, play the fool; (burlarse) joke; **bufonesco** = bufón 1.

bugui-bugui m boogie-woogie.

buhard(ill)a f dormer window; (desván) garret; S.Am. skylight.

buho m (a. ~ real) (eagle) owl; fig. unsociable person, hermit.

buhonero *m* hawker; peddler.

buitre *m* vulture.

buje *m* axle box; bushing.

bujería *f* trinket, gewgaw.

bujía *f* candle; (*candelero*) candlestick; *⚡* candle power; *mot.* (sparking-)plug.

bula *f* (papal) bull.

bulbo *m ♀, ⚘* bulb; **bulboso ⚘** bulbous; bulbshaped.

bulevar *m* boulevard, avenue.

búlgaro *adj. a. su. m,* **a** *f* Bulgarian.

bulimia *f* bulimia.

bulla *f* (*ruido*) noise, uproar; (*movimiento*) bustle; **bullaje** *m* crush, crowd; **bull(ar)anga** *f* disturbance, riot, unrest; **bullebulle** *m/f* busybody, mischief-maker; (*inquieto*) fusspot; **bullicio** *m* (*ruido*) uproar; rowdiness; din, hum *de calle etc.*; **bullicioso** multitud, asamblea noisy; *calle* bustling, busy, noisy; **bullir** [3h] *v/t.* move; *v/i.* (*hervir*) boil (*a. fig.*); (*con burbujas*) bubble (up); (*moverse*) move about; *fig.* teem, swarm (*de,* en with); **se** stir, budge.

bulto *m* (*volumen*) bulk(iness), volume, mass(iveness); (*que se distingue mal*) shape, form; *⚕* swelling, lump; (*fardo*) package, bundle, bale, *S.Am.* brief case; F escurrir el **~** dodge, get out of it.

buñuelo *m approx.* doughnut, fritter; cruller; F botched job, mess.

buque *m* ship, boat, vessel; (*casco*) hull; **~-escuela** training ship; **~ de guerra** warship; man-of-war †; **~ mercante** merchantman; **~ stangue** tanker; **~ (de) vapor** steamer, steamship; **~ de vela, ~ velero** sailing-ship.

burbuja *f* bubble; *hacer* **~s** = **burbujear** [1a] bubble, form bubbles.

burdel *m* brothel.

burdo coarse.

burgalés *adj. a. su. m,* **-a** *f* (native) of Burgos.

burgués 1. middle-class, bourgeois (*a. contp.*); 2. *m,* **-a** *f* bourgeois, member of the middle class; **bur-**

guesía *f* middle class, bourgeoisie.

burla *f* (*palabra*) gibe, taunt; (*chanza*) joke; (*chasco*) trick, hoax, practical joke; (*engaño*) trick, deception; **burlador** 1. *m,* **-a** *f* wag, practical joker, leg-puller F; 2. *m* seducer.

burlar [1a] *v/t.* (*zumbar*) take in, hoax; (*engañar*) deceive; *enemigo etc.* outwit, outmanoeuvre; seduce; *v/i.,* **~se** joke, banter; scoff; **burlesco** funny, comic; (*satírico*) mock, burlesque.

burlón 1. joking, bantering; *tono* mocking; 2. *m,* **-a** *f* wag, joker, leg-puller F.

buró *m* bureau, (roll-top) desk; *Mex.* night table.

burocracia *f* public service, civil service; *fig.* red tape; **burócrata** *m/f* civil servant, administrative official; **burocrático** bureaucratic; official.

burro *m* donkey, ass, ⊕ sawhorse; *fig.* ass, dolt; **~ de carga** *fig.* glutton for work.

busca *f* search, hunt (*de* for); **buscada** *f* = *busca*; **buscapié** *m* hint; **buscapleitos** *m S.Am.* troublemaker; F shyster; ambulance chaser.

buscar [1g] 1. *v/t.* look for, search for; seek (for, after); hunt for, have a look for; *enemigo* seek out; *cita* look up; 2. *v/i.* look, search; 3. **~se**: se busca (*aviso*) wanted; **buscavidas** *m/f* snoop, busybody; *b.s.* social climber, go-getter; **buscón** *m b.s.* petty thief, smalltime crook; **buscona** *f* whore.

busilis *m* F (real) difficulty, snag; *ahí está el* **~** there's the snag.

búsqueda *f* = *busca*.

busto *m* bust.

butaca *f* armchair, easy chair; *thea.* orchestra seat.

butano *m*: *gas* **~** butane (*or* cylinder) gas.

buzo *m* diver.

buzón *m ⚘* letterbox; canal, conduit; *echar al* **~** post; mail.

C

cabal 1. *adj.* exact, right; finished, complete, consummate; **2.** *adv.* exactly; perfectly (right); **3.** *int.* quite right!

cabalgada *f* troop of riders; ✕ cavalry raid; **cabalgadura** *f* mount, horse; **cabalgar** [1h] *v/t.* *yegua* cover; *v/i.* ride (on horseback).

cabalístico cab(b)alistic(al); *fig.* occult, mysterious.

caballa *f* mackerel.

caballada *f* S.Am. dirty trick; **caballejo** *m* pony; *b.s.* nag; **caballeresco** *hist.* of chivalry, chivalric; *sentimientos* fine, noble; **caballería** *f* mount, steed; horse, mule *etc.*; ✕ cavalry; *(orden)* order of knighthood; *hist.* knighthood, chivalry; ~ *andante* knight-errantry; **caballeriza** *f* stable (*a. fig.*, *deportes*); **caballerizo** *m* groom, stable-man.

caballero 1. riding, mounted (en on); **2.** *m* gentleman; mister, sir *en trato directo*; *hist.* knight, noble, nobleman; ~ *andante* knight-errant; **caballerosidad** *f* gentlemanliness; chivalry; nobility; **caballeroso** gentlemanly; chivalrous.

caballete *m* ✍, △ ridge; *(madero)* trestle; *paint.* easel; bridge *de nariz*.

caballito *m* little horse, pony; ~ *(de niños)* hobby-horse; ~ *de mar* seahorse; ~s *pl.* merry-go-round.

caballo *m* horse; *ajedrez:* knight; *naipes:* queen; ⊕ sawhorse; ⊕ ~ *(de fuerza)* horsepower; ~ *de carrera(s)* racehorse; *a* ~ on horseback; *a* ~ *astride,* on; ✕ *de* a ~ mounted; *ir (or montar) a* ~ ride (on horseback).

cabaña *f* cabin, hut; *(rebaño)* flock; *billar:* balk; ~ *de madera* log cabin; **cabañuelas** *f/pl.* Mex. winter rain.

cabaret [kaba're] *m* cabaret; night club.

cabecear [1a] *v/t.* sew. bind; *deportes:* head; *v/i.* nod; *(negación)* shake one's head; ♣ pitch; *mot.* lurch; **cabeceo** *m* nod; shake of the head; ♣ pitching; *mot.* lurch(ing); **cabecera** *f* head *de cama, mesa, deportes;* headboard *de cama;* end *de cuarto etc.*

cabecilla 1. *m/f* F hothead, wrongheaded sort; **2.** *m* ringleader.

cabellera *f* head of hair; *(peluca)* wig; scalp *de piel roja;* ast. tail; **cabello** *m*

hair (*a.* ~s *pl.*); ~ *merino* thick curly hair; F *asirse de un* ~ use any excuse; *traído por los* ~s irrelevant, quite off the point; *símil* far-fetched; **cabelludo** hairy, shaggy; ♀ fibrous.

caber [2m] **1.** fit, go (en *caja* into); ~ *en espacio* be contained in; *cabe(n)* ✕ there is room for X; *¿cabemos todos?* is there room for us all?; **2.** *fig.* be possible; ~ *a* befall, happen to; *(suerte)* fall to (one's lot); *no cabe más* that's the limit; *cabe preguntar si* one may ask if.

cabestrillo *m* ✍ sling; **cabestro** *m* halter; *(buey)* leading ox; F pimp.

cabeza *f* mst head; top, summit *de monte;* top, head *de lista etc.; geog.* capital; *fig.* origin, beginning; *(p.)* head, chief; *a la* ~ *de* at the head of; *alzar la* ~ ♣ get on one's feet again; ✍ be up and about; *meterse de* ~ en plunge into; *metérsele a uno en la* ~ get s.t. into one's head; *perder la* ~ lose one's head; F *romperse la* ~ rack one's brains.

cabezada *f (golpe)* butt *con cabeza,* blow on the head *en cabeza; (movimiento)* nod; ♣ pitch(ing); *dar* ~s nod; **cabezal** *m* pillow; *mot.* headrest; *(imprenta)* heading; **cabezazo** *m* butt; *deportes:* header; **cabezón 1.** = *cabezudo;* **2.** *m* hole for the head; collar-band; **cabezudo** big-headed; *fig.* pigheaded.

cabida *f* space, room; capacity (*a.* ♣); extent *de terreno.*

cabildear [1a] lobby; **cabildo** *m eccl.* chapter; *pol.* town council; *(junta)* chapter *etc.* meeting.

cabina *f* ✍ etc. cabin; *(camión)* cab; ✈ *a.* cockpit; ~ *de teléfono,* ~ *telefónica* telephone box (or kiosk).

cabizbajo *fig.* crestfallen, dejected.

cable *m* cable (*a.* ♣, *medida*), rope, hawser; **cablegrafiar** [1c] cable; **cablegrama** *m* cable(gram).

cabo *m* end (*a. fig*); *geog.* cape; *(mango)* handle; ♣ cable, rope; ⊕ thread; end, bit *que queda;* tub, stump *de vela, lápiz etc.; (p.)* chief, head; ✕ corporal; ~ *suelto* loose end; *al (fin y al)* ~ in the end; *dar* ~ *a* finish off; *dar* ~ *de* put an end to; *llevar a* ~ carry s.t. out.

cabotaje *m* ♣ coasting trade.

cabra f (she-)goat, nanny-goat F;
estar como una ~ to be crazy.
cabrahigo m wild fig.
cabrero m goatherd.
cabrestante m capstan.
cabrío 1.: *macho ~* he-goat, billygoat;
2. m flock of goats.
cabriola f caper; gambol; prance; *dar
~s* = **cabriolar** [1a] cut capers;
(caballo) prance; frisk about.
cabritilla f kid(skin); **cabrito** m zo.
kid; *carne de ~* kid; **cabrón** m fig.
cuckold, complaisant husband;
(como injuria, a. co.) bastard; S.Am.
pimp; **cabronada** f F *(mala pasada)*
dirty trick; *(trabajo)* tough job.
caca f F excrement; filth.
cacahuete m peanut, monkey nut;
(planta) groundnut.
cacalote m S.Am. raven; S.Am.
popcorn; *Cuba, Mex.* blunder;
foolishness.
cacao m cocoa; S.Am. chocolate.
cacarear [1a] v/t. boast about, make
much of; v/i. *(gallina)* cackle; *(gallo)*
crow; **cacareo** m cackling; crowing
(a. fig.).
cacatúa f cockatoo.
cacería f *(partida)* shoot, hunt; *(pasatiempo)* shooting, hunting.
cacerola f (sauce)pan; casserole.
cacha f handle; S.Am. horn; F *hasta
las ~s* up to the hilt.
cacharro m earthenware pot, crock;
fig. piece of junk; C.Am.,P.R. jail; *~s
pl.* earthenware, (coarse) pottery.
cachaza f calm; *b.s.* slowness; *(bebida)* rum; **cachazudo 1.** calm,
phlegmatic; slow; **2.** m slow sort.
cachear [1a] frisk (for weapons).
cachete m punch in the face; #
swollen cheek; = **cachetero** m
dagger; **cachetina** f fist fight.
cachiporra f billy de *policía*; black-
jack de *criminal*.
cachivache m *(p.)* useless fellow; *~s
pl.* pots and pans; *contp.* junk.
cacho 1. bent, crooked; **2.** m crumb de
pan; *(pedazo)* bit, slice.
cachondo zo. in heat; *sl. mujer* hot,
sexy.
cachorr(ill)o m pocket pistol; **cachorro** m, **a** f *(perro)* pup(py); *(león
etc.)* cub.
cachupín m, **-a** f Spanish settler in
America.
cacique m S.Am. chief; *pol.* (local)
boss; **caciquismo** m *pol.* (local)
bossism.

caco m pickpocket; F coward.
cacto m cactus.
cada each; *(con número etc.)* every; *~2
semanas* every 2 weeks; *~ cual, ~ uno*
each one, everyone.
cadalso m scaffold; ⊕ platform.
cadáver m (dead) body, corpse;
carcass de *animal*; **cadavérico** *fig.*
cadaverous; ghastly, deathly pale.
cadena f chain; *~ antirresbaladiza*
skid chain; *~ de televisión* channel;
network.
cadencia f cadence, rhythm; ♪
(trozo) cadenza; **cadencioso** rhyth-
mic(al).
cadera f hip.
cadete m cadet.
caducar [1g] *(viejo)* dodder, be in
one's dotage; get out of date *por
antiguo*; ⚖, ✝ expire; **caducidad** f
feebleness; lapse, expiration; **caduco** decrepit, feeble; ♃ deciduous;
bienes perishable.
caedizo falling; weak; frail.
caer [2o] *mst* fall (down etc.; a. *~se*);
(viento, sol etc.) go down; *(cortina)*
hang; F *ya caigo* I get it; *(animal)*
pounce on; *dejar ~* drop; *tono* lower;
dejarse ~ let o.s. go (or fall).
café m coffee; *(casa)* café; *(color de)*
coffee-coloured; *~ con leche* white
coffee; *~ solo* black coffee; **cafeína** f
caffeine; **cafetal** m coffee plantation; **cafetalero** m S.Am. coffee
planter; coffee dealer; **cafetear** [1a]
drink coffee; **cafetera** f coffee pot; *~
(eléctrica, filtradora)* percolator; **cafetería** f cafeteria; milk-bar; **cafe-
tero** m, **a** f café proprietor; **cafeto** m
coffee plant.
cagar [1h] v/t. shit; *fig.* make a mess
of; v/i. (have a) shit; **cagatinta(s)** m
pen-pusher; **cagón** F *adj. a. su.* m, **-a**
f cowardly.
caída f fall (a. fig.); *(tropezando)*
tumble; *(declive)* drop; *geol.* dip; field
de *cortina*; set, hang de *vestido*; *fig.*
decline; collapse, downfall; **caído 1.**
fallen; *cabeza etc.* drooping; *cuello*
turn-down; *fig.* crestfallen, dejected; **2.** *~s m/pl.:* *los ~* the fallen; ✝
income due.
caimán m alligator, cayman.
caja f box (a. ⊕, ♪); case (a. *typ.*,
de *reloj, violín* etc.); chest; *mot.*
body; *radio:* cabinet; *(ataúd)* coffin,
casket; ✗ drum; ⊕ housing, casing; ♃ ✝ cash box; *~ (de caudales)*
safe, strong box; ✝ cash desk; cash-

ier's office; ~ *de velocidades* gear-box.
cajero *m*, **a** *f* ✝ cashier, (bank) teller;
cajeta *f* small box; **cajetilla** *f* packet,
pack; **cajón** *m* big box, case; drawer
de armario etc.; *S.A.* coffin.
cal *f* lime; ~ *apagado* slaked lime; ~
viva quicklime.
cala *f* *geog.* creek, cove, inlet; ⚓
fishing-ground; hold *de barco*.
calabaza *f* pumpkin, gourd; F dolt; F
dar ~*s a estudiante* fail; *novio* jilt;
recibir ~*s* get jilted; F *salir* ~ be a flop;
calabazada *f* butt (with the head);
blow on the head.
calabobos *m* drizzle.
calabozo *m* (*cuarto*) cell; (*cárcel*)
prison; ✕ F glasshouse; F calaboose.
calada *f* soaking *etc.*; F *dar una* ~ *a*
haul *s.o.* over the coals; **calado** *m* ⊕
fretwork.
calafatear [1a] caulk.
calamar *m* squid.
calambre *m* (*a.* ~*s pl.*) cramp.
calamidad *f* calamity; F (*p.*) dead
loss; F *es una* ~ it's a great pity.
calamitoso calamitous.
cálamo *m* *poet.* pen; ♪ reed.
calandria *f* calandria lark.
calaña *f* model, pattern; *fig.* nature,
stamp, kind.
calar [1a] **1.** *v/t.* (*líquido*) soak; pierce
con barrena; ⊕ *metal* cut openwork
in; *madera* cut fretwork in; **2.** *v/i.*
(*líquido*) sink in; (*zapato*) leak, let in
water; ⚓ draw; ~**se** get soaked (*hasta
los huesos* to the skin), get drenched.
calavera 1. *f* skull; **2.** *m* gay dog; *b.s.*
rake; *fig.* necio; **calaverada** *f* madcap escapade, foolhardy thing; **ca-
laverear** [1a] carouse; *b.s.* lead a
wild life.
calcar [1g] trace; *fig.* ~ *en* base on,
model on.
calceta *f* (knee-length) stocking;
(*grillete*) fetter, shackle; *hacer* ~ knit;
calcetería *f* hosiery; hosier's (shop);
calcetín *m* sock.
calcificar(se) [1g] calcify; **calcina** *f*
concrete; **calcinar** [1a] calcine; burn,
reduce to ashes; **calcio** *m* calcium.
calco *m* tracing; **calcomanía** *f*
transfer.
calculable calculable; **calculador 1.**
calculating; scheming; (*máquina*)
calculadora *f* computer, calculating
machine; **2.** *m* (*máquina*) calculator;
~ *de mano* hand-held calculator; ~ *de
bolsillo* pocket calculator; **calcular**
[1a] calculate; add up, work out;

cálculo *m* calculation; reckoning;
estimate; ✻ (*gall*)stone; ~ *diferencial*
differential calculus.
caldear [1a] heat (up), warm (up);
estar caldeado be very hot; ~**se** get
overheated, get very hot.
caldera *f* boiler (*a.* ⊕); kettle; *S.Am.*
coffee pot; **calderilla** *f* *eccl.* holy-
water vessel; ✝ copper(s), small
change; **calderón** *m* large boiler,
cauldron; *typ.* paragraph sign; ⚓
hold; **caldillo** *m* light broth; sauce
for fricasse; *Mex.* meat bits in broth.
caldo *m* broth; consommé, clear
soup; (*aderezo*) dressing, sauce; ~*s
pl.* liquid derived from fruit *etc.*
calefacción *f* heating; *de* ~ heating
attr.; ~ *central* central heating.
cal(e)idoscopio *m* kaleidoscope.
calendario *m* calendar; F *hacer* ~*s*
muse.
caléndula *f* marigold.
calentador *m* heater; ~ (*de inmersión*)
immersion heater; **calentar** [1k] *v/t.*
horno etc. heat (up); *comida, cuarto,
piernas, silla etc.* warm (up); *v/i.* be
hot, be warm; ~**se** heat (up), (get)
warm, get hot; warm o.s. *a la lumbre*;
fig. (*disputa*) get heated; **calentura** *f*
✻ temperature, fever; *Col.* anger;
calenturiento feverish.
calera *f* limestone quarry; (*horno*) =
calero *m* lime kiln.
caleta *f* cove, inlet.
caletre *m* F gumption.
calibrador *m* gauge; callipers; **calibrar** [1a] gauge; calibrate; **calibre** *m*
✕ calibre (*a. fig.*), bore; 🜨 gauge.
calicó *m* calico.
calidad *f* quality; ✝ *a.* grade; (social)
standing; character; ~*es pl.* (moral)
qualities; gifts; *en* ~ *de* in the capacity
of.
cálido hot; *color* warm.
calidoscopio *m* kaleidoscope.
calientacamas *m* ⚡ electric blanket;
calientapiés *m* foot warmer; **ca-
lientaplatos** *m* hotplate; **caliente**
hot; warm; *disputa* heated; *batalla*
raging; (*fogoso*) fiery; *zo.* on heat.
califa *m* caliph; **califato** *m* caliphate.
calificación *f* qualification; assessment; label; mark *en examen*; **cali-
ficado** qualified; well-known,
eminent; **calificar** [1g] qualify (*de*
as; *a. gr.*); *p.* (*acreditar*) distinguish;
examen mark; *escritos* correct; ~ *de*
call, label; characterize as, describe
as; ~**se** *S.Am.* register as a voter.

caligrafía f penmanship, calligraphy; **caligráfico** calligraphic.

calina f haze, mist.

calistenia f calisthenics.

cáliz m eccl. chalice, communion cup; poet. cup, goblet; ♀ calyx.

callado silent, quiet; reserved, secretive; **callandico** F, **callandito** F softly, stealthily; **callar** [1a] 1. v/t. secreto keep; trozo etc. pass over (in silence), not mention; cosa vergonzosa keep quiet about, hush up; 2. v/i., **~se** keep quiet, be (or remain) silent; (cesar) stop talking; ¡calla!, ¡cállate! shut up!, hold your tongue!

calle f street; road; deportes: lane; ~ de dirección única one-way street; ~ mayor high street, main street; F poner en la ~ kick out, chuck out; **calleja** f = callejuela; **callejear** [1a] stroll around; b.s. hang about, loaf; **callejero** street attr.; (p.) fond of walking about town; **callejón** m alley(way), lane, passage; ~ sin salida cul-de-sac; fig. blind alley; impasse; **callejuela** f narrow street, side street; alley(way).

callo m corn esp. en pie; callus; **~s** pl. cocina: tripe; **calloso** callous; manos horny, hard.

calma f calm; calmness; ♣ calm weather; (lentitud) slowness, laziness; **calmante** soothing, sedative (a. su. m); **calmar** [1a] v/t. calm (down), quieten (down); dolor relieve; v/i. abate, fall; **~se** calm down etc.; **calmoso** calm; F slow, lazy.

calofrío m chill.

calor m heat (a. ⊕, phys., fig. de batalla, disputa etc.); (esp. agradable) warmth (a. fig. de acogida etc.); hace (mucho) ~ it is (very) hot; tener ~ be hot, feel hot; **caloría** f calorie; **calórico** caloric; **calorífero** 1. heat-producing; 2. m heating system; furnace, stove; **calorífico** calorific; **calorífugo** heat-resistant, non-conducting; (incombustible) fireproof.

calotear [1a] S.Am. cheat; gyp.

calumnia f slander; (esp. escrito) libel (de on); **calumniar** [1b] slander; malign; libel; **calumnioso** slanderous; libellous.

caluroso warm, hot; fig. warm, enthusiastic.

calva f bald patch; ♀ clearing.

Calvario m Calvary; (estaciones del) ~ Stations of the Cross; ♀ fig. cross.

calvicie f baldness; ~ precoz premature baldness.

calvinismo m Calvinism.

calvo 1. bald; hairless; terreno barren, bare; 2. m bald man.

calza f wedge, scotch, chock; F stocking; **~s** pl. hose, breeches.

calzada f highway, roadway; causeway; (carriage-)drive a casa; **calzado** 1. p.p. ~ de shod with, wearing; 2. m footwear; **calzador** m shoehorn; **calzar** [1f] 1. v/t. p. etc. shoes on, provide with footwear; zapatos etc. put on; 2. v/i.: calza bien he wears good shoes; 3. **~se** zapatos etc. put on; wear; fig. get.

calzo m wedge; ♣ chock, skid; **calzón** m (a. **~es** pl.) breeches; shorts; S.Am. trousers; **~es** pl. blancos (under)pants, drawers; **calzoncillos** m/pl. (under)pants.

cama f bed; ✓ bedding, litter; zo. lair; floor de carro; ~ de matrimonio double-bed; **~-litera** double-decker bed; **camada** f zo. litter, brood; (capa) layer.

camafeo m cameo.

camaleón m chameleon.

cámara f room; chamber; parl. a. house; ♣ (camarote) cabin; ♣ (sala) saloon; ✕ a. breech; phot. (a. ~ fotográfica) camera; mot. (a. ~ de aire) inner tube, tire; ✗ **~s** pl. diarrhea; ♀ de Comercio Chamber of Commerce; ♀ de los Comunes (Lores) House of Commons (Lords).

camarada m comrade, companion; mate; **camaradería** f comradeship; team-spirit en deportes etc.

camarera f waitress en restaurante; (chamber)maid en hotel; ♣ stewardess; parlor-maid en casa; **camarero** m waiter; ♣ steward.

camarilla f clique, coterie; caucus de partido.

camaró(n) m shrimp; C.Am. tip.

camarote m ♣ cabin, stateroom.

camastro m rickety old bed.

cambalache m swap, exchange; **cambalach(e)ar** [1a] swap, exchange.

cambiante 1. fickle, temperamental; 2. m money changer; **~s** pl. changing colors, iridescence.

cambiar [1b] 1. v/t. change, exchange (con, por for); change, turn (en into); ✝ *a.* trade (*por* for); **2.** *v/i.*, **~se** change (*a.* ~ *de*); ~ *de sitio* shift, move; **cambio** *m* change; (*trueque*) exchange; ✝ (*tipo*) rate of exchange; (*vuelta*) (*tipo*) change; turn *de marea*, change, shift, switch *de política etc.*; ✝ *libre* ~ free trade; (*palanca de*) ~ *de marchas* gear-shift; *en* ~ instead, in return; (*por otra parte*) on the other hand; **cambista** *m* money-changer; *S.Am.* switchman.

camelia *f* camellia.

camello *m* camel (*a.* ♣).

camelo *m* F flirtation; (*chasco*) joke, hoax; (*mentira*) cock-and-bull story; (*halago*) (piece of) blarney.

camerógrafo *m* cameraman.

camilla *f* 🏥 stretcher; sofa, couch; **camillero** *m* stretcher-bearer.

caminante *m/f* traveller; walker; **caminar** [1a] *v/t. distancia* cover, travel; *v/i.* travel, journey; (*andar*) walk; (*río,fig.*) move, go; **caminata** *f* F hike, ramble; jaunt, outing.

camino *m* road; way (*de* to; *a. fig.*); *esp. fig.* course, path; ~ *de* on the way to; ~ *real* high-road (*a. fig.*); ~ *de Santiago* Milky Way; *a medio* ~ halfway; *de* ~ *attr.* travelling; (*adv.*) in passing; *2 horas de* ~ 2 hours' journey.

camión *m mot.* truck; (*carro*) heavy wagon; *S.Am.* bus; ~**-grúa** tow truck; ~ *de la basura* garbage truck; **camionero** *m* truck driver; teamster; **camioneta** *f* van.

camisa *f* shirt; ~ (*de mujer*) chemise; ⊕ jacket (*a. de libro*), sleeve; ♦ skin; ~ *de fuerza* strait jacket; *en* (*mangas de*) ~ in one's shirt-sleeves; **camiseta** *f* vest, undershirt; *deportes:* singlet; **camisón** *m* (*de noche*) nightdress, nightgown.

camomila *f* camomile.

camorra *f* F row, set-to, quarrel; **camorrista** *f* **1.** fond of scraps; **2.** *m* quarrelsome sort; hooligan.

campamento *m* camp; encampment; ~ *de trabajo* labor camp.

campana *f* bell; *eccl. fig.* parish (church); ~ *de bucear* diving-bell; ~ *de cristal* bell-glass; glass cover; **campanada** *f* stroke (of the bell); (sound of) ringing; F commotion; **campanario** *m* belfry, church tower.

campanilla *f* handbell; ⚡ electric bell; (*burbuja*) bubble; **campanillazo** *m* loud ring; **campanillear**

[1a] tinkle, ring; **campanilleo** *m* tinkling, ringing.

campanudo bell-shaped; *falda* wide; *lenguaje* high-flown, bombastic; *orador* pompous.

campaña *f geog.* (flat) countryside, plain; ✕, *pol., fig.* campaign; ♣ cruise, expedition, trip.

campar [1a] ✕ *etc.* camp; (*descollar*) stand out, excel; **campear** [1a] (*animales*) go to graze; (*trigo*) show green.

campechano hearty, good-hearted; open; generous.

campeón *m* champion; **campeonato** *m* championship.

campero (out) in the open; openair *attr.*; 🐎 sleeping in the open.

campesino **1.** country *attr.*; *zo.* field *attr.*; **2.** *m*, **a** *f* peasant (*a. contp.*); countryman (-woman); farmer; **campestre** country *attr.*; ♠ wild; **campiña** *f* farm-land; countryside.

camping *m* camping.

campo *m* 🎣 field (*a. fig., phys., heráldica*); (*despoblado*) country (-side); *deportes:* field, ground, pitch; (golf-)course; ~ *de aviación* airfield; ~ *de batalla* battlefield; ~ *de concentración* concentration camp; ~ *de deportes* playing field, recreation ground; ~ *de pruebas* testing grounds; ~ *magnético* magnetic field; *reconocer el* ~ reconnoitre; **camposanto** *m* cemetery, churchyard.

camuesa *f* pippin; **camueso** *m* pippin tree; F dolt.

camuflaje *m* camouflage; **camuflar** [1a] camouflage.

can *m zo.* dog; ✕ trigger; △ corbel.

cana *f* (*a.* ~*s pl.*) white hair, grey hair; F *echar una* ~ *al aire* let one's hair down; F *peinar* ~*s* be getting on.

canadiense *adj. a. su. m/f* Canadian.

canal *mst m geog.* ♣ channel (*a. radio*), strait(s); navigation channel *de puerto*; (*artificial*) canal, waterway; 🎣 (*a.* ~ *de riego*) irrigation channel; △ gutter, spout; drain pipe; **canalización** *f* canalization; ⊕ piping; ⚡ wiring; mains *de gas etc.*; **canalizar** [1f] *río* canalize; *aguas* harness; *aguas de riego* channel; ⊕ pipe.

canalla **1.** *f* rabble, riff-raff, mob; **2.** *m* swine, rotter.

canana *f* cartridge belt.

canapé *m* sofa, settee.

canario **1.** *adj. a. su. m*, **a** *f* (native) of

the Canary Isles; **2.** m orn. canary; **3.** int. Great Scott!

canasta f (round) basket; naipes: canasta; **canastilla** f small basket; **canastillo** m wicker tray; **canasto** m hamper; basket.

cancel m wind-proof door; (mueble) folding screen; **cancela** f lattice gate.

cancelación f cancellation; **cancelar** [1a] cancel; deuda write off, wipe out; fig. dispel, do away with.

cáncer m cancer; ast. ♋ Cancer; **cancerarse** [1a] (úlcera) become cancerous; **cancerología** f study of cancer; cancer research; **canceroso** cancerous.

cancha f field, ground; pelota: court; S.Am. caballos: racecourse, race-track; gallos: cockpit; ~ de tenis tennis-court.

canciller m chancellor; **cancillería** f chancellery.

canción f song; poet. lyric, song; ~ de cuna lullaby; cradle song; **cancionero** m ♪ song-book; poet. anthology, collection of verse.

cancro m ♠ canker; ✻ cancer.

candado m padlock; clasp de libro.

candanga f Cuba, C.Am. the Devil.

candela f candle; phys. candlepower; (candelero) candlestick; **candelero** m candlestick; (velón) oil lamp; F en ~ high up.

candente hierro white-hot, red-hot; glowing, burning; cuestión burning.

candidato m candidate (a for); **candidatura** f candidature.

candidez f candor etc.; (dicho) silly remark; **cándido** poet. snow-white.

candil m oil lamp; **candilejas** f/pl. thea. footlights.

candonga f F (lisonja) blarney; (engaño) trick; (chasco) hoax, practical joke; teasing.

candor m poet. pure whiteness; fig. innocence, guilelessness; **candoroso** innocent, guileless.

canela f cinnamon; F lovely thing; ¡~! good gracious!; **canelo 1.** cinnamon(-colored); **2.** m cinnamon (tree).

cangilón m pitcher; bucket, scoop de noria etc.

cangrejo m: ~ (de río) crayfish; ~ (de mar) crab; ♏ gaff.

canguro m kangaroo.

caníbal 1. cannibalistic, maneating; fig. savage; **2.** m cannibal; **canibalismo** m cannibalism.

canica f marble; (juego) marbles.

canícula f dog days; **canicular 1.**: calores ~s midsummer heat; **2.** ~es m/pl. dog days.

canilla f anat. shin(bone), armbone; ⊕ bobbin, spool; spout, cock de tonel; rib de tela; S.Am. tap; Mex. force; power; a ~ by force.

canino 1. canine, dog attr.; hambre ravenous; **2.** m canine (tooth).

canje m exchange, interchange; **canjear** [1a] exchange, interchange.

cano white-haired; (con algunas canas) gray(-haired); fig. aged.

canoa f canoe; boat, launch; ~ automóvil motor-launch.

canon m eccl., ♪, paint. canon; ✝ tax; ♪ rent; typ. gran ~ canon; ~es pl. ♉ canon law; **canonical** canonical; vida easy; **canónico** canonical; **canónigo** m canon; **canonización** f canonization; **canonizar** [1f] canonize; fig. applaud, show approval of.

canoro ave (sweet-)singing; voz etc. melodious.

canoso gray(-haired); barba grizzled.

cansado tired, weary (de of); ✻ exhausted; vista tired, strained; (que cansa) tedious, trying, tiresome; **cansancio** m tiredness, weariness; esp. ✻ fatigue; (tedio) boredom; **cansar** [1a] **1.** v/t. tire, weary esp. lit.; ✻ exhaust; fig. bother, bore (con with); **2.** v/i. tire; (p.) be trying, be tiresome; **3.** ~se tire, get tired (con, de of); tire o.s. out (en inf. ger.).

cansino weary; lazy; tired.

cantábrico Cantabrian.

cantador m, **-a** f folk-singer, singer of popular songs.

cantante 1. singing; v. voz; **2.** m/f (professional) singer; vocalist; **cantar** [1a] **1.** v/t. sing (fig. the praises of); chant; **2.** v/i. sing; zo. chirp; ⊕ squeak, grind; F squeal, blab; **3.** m song, poem; ~ de gesta epic; ♀ de los ♀es Song of Songs, Canticles.

cántara f large pitcher; liquid measure = 16.13 liters.

cantárida f (polvo de) ~ Spanish fly, pharm. cantharides.

cántaro m pitcher; (cabida) pitcherful; F a ~s in plenty; llover cats and dogs.

cantautor m songwriter.

cante m singing; popular song; ~ flamenco, ~ jondo Andalusian gipsy singing.

cantera f (stone) quarry, pit; fig.

talent, genius; **cantería** *f* (*arte*, *obra*) masonry, stonework.

cántico *m* *eccl.* canticle; *fig.* song.

cantidad *f* quantity; amount, number; sum *de dinero*; (*una*) **gran ~ de** a great quantity of, lots of.

cantilena *f* ballad, song.

cantimplora *f* water-bottle, canteen; decanter *para vino*; ⊕ syphon.

cantina *f* 🚂 refreshment room, buffet; ✕ *etc.* canteen; snack-bar; bar(room).

canto[1] *m* (*acto*, *arte*) singing; (*pieza*) song; *eccl.* chant(ing); *poet.* lyric, song; canto *de épica*; **~ del cisne** swan-song.

canto[2] *m* (*borde*) edge; rim; (*extremo*) end, point; (*esquina*) corner; back *de cuchillo*; crust *de pan*.

cantón *m* corner; *pol.*, *heráldica:* canton; ✕ cantonment; **cantonera** *f* corner-band *de libro*; corner table; corner cupboard; **cantonero** *m* loafer, good-for-nothing.

cantor 1. (sweet-)singing **2.** *m*, **~a** *f* singer; *orn.* singing bird, songster.

canturía *f* singing, vocal music; singing exercise; *b.s.* monotonous singing.

caña *f* 🌾 reed; (*tallo*) stem, cane; *anat.* shin(-bone); arm-bone; leg *de media*, *bota*; 🏛 gallery; (*vaso*) (long) glass; *S.Am.* rum.

cañada *f* *geog.* gully; (*grande*) glen.

cañamazo *m* canvas; burlap.

cañamiel *f* sugar cane.

cáñamo *m* hemp; (*tela*) hempen cloth; *S.Am.* string; **cañamón** *m* hemp-seed; **~es** *pl.* bird-seed.

cañaveral *m* reed field; ✔ sugar cane plantation.

cañería *f* pipe, piece of piping; pipe-line; (*desagüe*) drain; ♪ organ pipes; **cañero** *m* plumber, fitter; **cañete** *m* small pipe.

caño *m* tube, pipe (a. ♪); (*albañal*) drain, sewer; jet, spout *de fuente*; **cañón** *m* ⊕ tube, pipe (a. ♪); ✕ gun, cannon; barrel *de fusil*, *pluma*; stem *de pipa*; shaft, stack *de chimenea*; *mount.* chimney; *S.Am.* canyon; **cañonazo** *m* gunshot; **cañonear** [1a] shell; **cañoneo** *m* shelling, gunfire; **cañonero** *m* ⚓ gunboat.

cañutero *m* pincushion; **cañutillo** *m* glass tube; *sew.* gold (*or* silver) twist; **cañuto** *m* ⊕ tube, container.

caoba *f* mahogany.

caolín *m* kaolin.

caos *m* chaos; **caótico** chaotic.

capa *f* (*vestido*) cloak; *eccl.* (a. **~** *pluvial*) cope; *toros:* cape; wrapper *de cigarro etc.*; layer *de atmósfera*, *piel etc.*; *geol.* stratum, bed; **so ~ de** under the guise of.

capacha *f* frail, basket; **capacho** *m* wicker basket; ◮ hod.

capacidad *f* capacity (*a. phys.*, ✈); size *de sala etc.*; *fig.* (cap)ability, capacity; intelligence; efficiency; **~ para** aptitude for; **~** competitive competitiveness; **capacitar** [1a]: **~ para** *inf.* enable s.o. to *inf.*

capar [1a] castrate; *fig.* cut down, curtail.

caparrosa *f* vitriol.

capataz *m* foreman; *esp.* ✔ overseer, bailiff.

capaz a) *p.* (cap)able, efficient, competent (a. 🔧; *de inf.* to *inf.*); **~ de** capable of; **~ para** qualified for; b) *cabida:* large, capacious.

capear [1a] *v/t.* wave the cape at; *v/i.* ⚓ ride out the storm; lie to.

capellán *m* chaplain; (*en general*) priest; **~ castrense** army chaplain; **capellanía** *f* chaplaincy.

caperuza *f* (pointed) hood; ⊕ cowl, cowling; cowl *de chimenea*.

capicúa *f* palindrome.

capilla *f* *eccl.* chapel; ♪ choir; (*capucho*) hood, cowl; *typ.* proof-sheet; **~ ardiente** funeral chapel, oratory *en casa*; bonnet *de niño*.

capirotazo *m* flip, flick.

capirote *m* hood; hennin *de mujer*; hood *de halcón*; flip, flick *con dedos*.

capitación *f* poll-tax, capitation.

capital 1. *mst* capital; *característica* main, principal; *enemigo*, *pecado* mortal; *importancia* supreme, paramount; **2.** *f* *pol.* capital *de país*; chief town, centre *de región*; **3.** *m* ✔ capital; **~ de explotación** working capital; **~ social** share capital; **capitalismo** *m* capitalism; **capitalista 1.** capitalist(ic); **2.** *m/f* capitalist; **capitalizar** [1f] capitalize; *interés* compound.

capitán *m* captain (*a.* **~** *de navío*); **~ de fragata** commander; **~ general** *approx.* field marshal; **capitana** *f* flagship; **capitanear** [1a] captain, lead (*a. fig.*), command.

capitel *m* △ capital.

capitolio *m* capitol; *fig.* imposing edifice; F **subir al ~** get to the top.

capitoste *m* F boss; big shot.

C

capitular [1a] v/t. agree to; ⚖ charge (de with); v/i. come to terms (con with); ⚰ capitulate; **capítulo** m chapter (a. eccl.); item de presupuesto; heading.

capó m mot. hood.

capoc m kapok.

capón m (p.) eunuch; (pollo) capon; **caponera** f ⚓ chicken-coop; fig. open house; sl. clink.

capotar [1a] ✈, mot. turn over; **capote** m cloak (with sleeves); toros: bullfighter's cloak (a. ~ de brega); F frown; **capotear** [1a] fig. get out of, duck, shirk; (engañar) bamboozle.

capricho m whim, (passing) fancy, caprice (a. ♪); (deseo) keen desire, sudden urge (por for); b.s. craze, fad, pet notion; **caprichoso, caprichudo** capricious; niño etc. wayward; (inconstante) temperamental, moody; obra fanciful, whimsical.

Capricornio m Capricorn.

cápsula f cap de botella; ⚰, anat., pharm. capsule; ⚜ boll de algodón etc.; case de cartucho; **capsular** capsular.

captar [1a] confianza etc. win, get; voluntad gain control over; **captura** f capture, seizure; **capturar** [1a] capture, seize, take.

capucha f hood; eccl. cowl; **capuchina** f eccl. Capuchin sister; ⚜ nasturtium; **capuchino** m Capuchin; **capucho** m cowl, hood.

capullo m zo. cocoon; ⚜ bud; cup de bellota.

caqui m khaki.

cara f face (a. fig.); side de disco, sólido; △ façade, front; (superficie) surface, face; heads de moneda; fig. look, appearance; ~ o cruz heads or tails; a ~ descubierta openly; de ~ opposite, facing; in the face; dar ~ a face up to; tener buena ~ ⚕ look well; look nice; tener mala ~ ⚕ look ill; look bad.

carabela f ⚓ caravel.

carabina f ⚔ carbine; F chaperon; hacer etc. de ~ go as chaperon.

caracol m zo. snail; (concha) snail shell, sea-shell; (pelo) curl; ¡~es! great Scott!; de ~ escalera spiral; en ~ spiral, corkscrew attr.; **caracolear** [1a] (caballo) caracole.

carácter m character (a. biol.); typ. (una letra) character; (cursivo etc.) hand(writing); (condición) position;

caracteres pl. (de imprenta) type (-face); **característica** f characteristic; **característico** characteristic (de of); **caracterizar** [1f] characterize; distinguish, set apart; **~se** thea. make up, dress for the part.

caradura f **1.** scoundrel; **2.** adj. brazen; shameless.

carajo m F prick; ¡~! hell!

¡caramba! sorpresa: good gracious!; enfado: damn it!

carámbano m icicle.

caramelo m sweet, toffee, caramel.

caramillo m ♪ recorder, pipe; poet. reed; (montón) untidy heap; (chisme) (piece of) gossip.

carantamaula f F (cara) ugly mug; **carantoña** f F (cara) ugly mug; (mujer) mutton dressed up as lamb; ~s pl. petting, fondling.

caraqueño adj. a. su. m, a f (native) of Caracas.

carátula f mask; S.Am. title page.

caravana f caravan; fig. group; en ~ in a gang.

¡caray! F gosh!; confound it!

carbohidrato m carbohydrate.

carbólico carbolic.

carbón m min. coal (a. ~ de piedra); ⚡ carbon; ~ bituminoso soft coal; ~ de leña, ~ vegetal charcoal (a. paint.); **carbonero 1.** coal attr.; charcoal attr.; **2.** m coal merchant; charcoal-burner; **carbónico** carbonic; **carbonilla** f small coal; cinder; mot. carbon; **carbonizar** [1f] 🜍 carbonize; char; leña make charcoal of; **~se** 🜍 carbonize; be charred; be reduced to ashes; **carbono** m carbon; **carbonoso** carbonaceous.

carbunclo m min., **carbunco** m ⚕ carbuncle.

carburador m carburetor; **carburante** m fuel.

carcaj m quiver; S.Am. rifle case.

carcajada f (loud) laugh, guffaw, peal of laughter; reírse a ~s roar with laughter.

cárcel f prison, jail; ⊕ clamp; **carcelero 1.** prison attr.; **2.** m warder, jailer.

carcinógeno 1. m carcinogen; **2.** carcinogenic; cancer-causing; **carcinoma** m ⚕ carcinoma.

carcoma f woodworm; fig. anxiety; **carcomer** [2a] bore into, eat away; fig. undermine; **~se** get worm-eaten, fig. be eaten away; **carcomido** worm-eaten, wormy.

carda f (acto) carding; (instrumento) card, comb; **cardar** [1a] card, comb.

cardenal m cardinal; ♣ bruise.

cardenillo m verdigris; **cárdeno** purple, violet; lurid.

cardíaco 1. cardiac, heart attr.; 2. m, a f heart case.

cardinal cardinal.

cardo m thistle.

carear [1a] v/t. ps. bring face to face; v/i.: ~ a face towards; ~se come face to face, meet.

carecer [2d]: ~ de lack, be in need of, want (for).

carena f ♣ careening; F ragging.

carencia f lack (de of), need (de for); deficiency (a. ♣).

careo m confrontation; collation; comparison.

carero F expensive, dear; high-priced.

carestía f scarcity, shortage; famine; ✝ high price(s).

careta f mask; ✗ etc. respirator; ~ antigás gas mask, respirator.

carey m tortoise shell; zo. turtle.

carga f (acto) loading; charge de cañón, caballería, horno, ♣; (peso) load (a. ⊕, ♪); ♣ cargo; fig. load, burden, onus; obligation(s), responsibilities.

cargado loaded; esp. fig. laden (de with); ♪ charged, live; ~ de años very old; **cargador** m loader; ♣ stevedore; ✗ ramrod; filler de pluma; ~ (de acumulador) (battery) charger; **cargamento** m cargo, freight; (acto) loading.

cargar [1h] 1. v/t. load (de with; a, en on); (demasiado) overload; weigh down on; cañón load; ♪, enemigo charge; horno stoke; sl. estudiante plough; impuestos increase (a on); velas take in; S.Am. wear; fig. burden, load down (con, de with); 2. v/i. load (up), take on a load; ♣ take on (a) cargo; meteor. turn, veer (a, hacia to); (acento) fall (sobre on); (ps.) crowd together; 3. ~se peso etc. take on o.s.; meteor. become overcast; **cargareme** m (deposit) voucher.

cargazón f load; ♣ cargo; ♣ heaviness; meteor. mass of heavy cloud; ~ de espaldas stoop; **cargo** m load, weight; fig. obligation, duty; responsibility; (custodia) charge, care; (empleo) post; ✝ debit; ᵽᵗ etc. charge; alto ~ high office; high official; VIP.

carguero 1. attr. freight; of burden; 2. freighter; cargo ship; S.Am. beast of burden.

Caribe 1. Caribbean; 2. m/f Carib; savage.

cariado rotten, carious [Ⅱ]; **cariarse** [1b] decay, become decayed.

caricatura f caricature; fig. caricature (of a man); **caricaturista** m/f caricaturist; **caricaturizar** [1f] caricature.

caricia f caress; pat, stroke a perro etc.; fig. endearment.

caridad f charity, charitableness; hacer la ~ a give alms to.

caries f (dental) decay, caries.

carioca 1. of Rio de Janeiro; 2. f (dance) carioca.

cariño m affection, love; fondness, liking (a for); ~s pl. endearments, show of affection; tener ~ a be fond of; Mex.,C.Am. gift; **cariñoso** affectionate, fond.

caritativo charitable (con, para towards).

cariz m look (of the sky); F look.

carlinga f ✈ cockpit.

carlismo m Carlism; **carlista** adj. a. su. m/f Carlist.

carmesí adj. a. su. m crimson; **carmín** m carmine; ♀ dog-rose.

carnada f bait (a. fig.); **carnal** carnal, of the flesh; pariente full, blood-; **carnaval** m carnival; (época) Shrovetide.

carne f anat., ♀, eccl. flesh; meat de comer; ~ adobada salt meat; ~ congelada frozen (or chilled) meat; ~ de carnero mutton; ~ de cerdo pork; ~ de cordero lamb; ~ de gallina fig. gooseflesh; ~ picada mince(d meat); ~ de ternera veal; ~ de vaca beef; ~ de venado venison; de ~ y hueso of flesh and blood; echar ~s Mex. swear; curse.

carnear [1a] S.Am. slaughter; F take in.

carnero m zo. sheep; (macho) ram; (carne) mutton.

carnestolendas f/pl. Shrovetide.

carnet [kar'ne] m notebook; travel voucher de turista; ~ (de identidad) identity card; mot. ~ (de conducir) driving licence.

carnicería f butcher's (shop); fig. carnage, slaughter; hacer una ~ de massacre; **carnicero** m 1. zo. carnivorous; 2. m (p.) butcher (a. fig.); zo. carnivore.

carnívoro 1. carnivorous; 2. *m* carnivore.

carnoso *anat.*, ♦ fleshy; meaty; *p.* = **carnudo** beefy, fat.

caro ✝ dear, expensive; *p.* dear, beloved.

carpa *f* carp; ~ *dorada* goldfish.

carpeta *f* folder, file, portfolio; (*cartera*) briefcase; table-cover *de mesa*; *S.Am.* bookkeeping department; **carpetazo:** *dar* ~ *a* shelve, put on one side.

carpintería *f* (*arte*) carpentry, joinery; carpenter's shop; **carpintero** *m* carpenter.

carraca *f* ♣ *contp.* tub, hulk; ♪ rattle; **carraco** F 1. feeble, decrepit; 2. *m* old crock.

carraspear [1a] be hoarse, have a frog in one's throat; **carraspera** *f* hoarseness.

carrera *f* run (a. ♪, ♣, *béisbol etc.*); (*certamen*) race; (*pista*) track; (*calle*) avenue; (*raya*) parting; run, ladder *en medias*; *ast.* course; (*hilera*) row, line; △ beam; ⊕ stroke *de émbolo*; *fig.* course of human life; (*profesión*) career; *univ.* (degree)-course, studies; ~*s pl.* racing, races; ~ *armamentista* (a. *de armamentos*) arms race; *a* ~ (*abierta*) at full speed; *correr a* ~ *tendida* career, go full out; *dar* ~ *a* give s.o. his education; *dar libre* ~ *a* give free rein to.

carreta *f* cart; ~ *de mano* = **carretilla**; **carretada** *f* cart-load; *a* ~*s* in loads, galore; **carretaje** *m* cartage, haulage; **carrete** *m* reel (a. *de caña*), spool (a. *phot.*); bobbin; ≠ coil; ~ *de inducción* induction coil; **carretel** *m* reel, spool.

carretera *f* (main) road, highway; *por* ~ by road; **carretería** *f* wheelwright's; (*conjunto*) carts; **carretero** *m* carter; (*constructor*) wheelwright, cartwright; *jurar como un* ~ swear like a trooper; **carretilla** *f* truck, trolley; hand-cart, barrow; **carretón** *m* small cart.

carricoche *m* caravan, covered wagon.

carril *m* (*surco*) rut, track; ✔ furrow; (*camino*) lane; ⛫ rail.

carrillo *m* cheek, jowl; ⊕ pulley; F *comer a dos* ~*s* eat a lot.

carrizal *m* reedbed; **carrizo** *m* reed.

carro *m* cart, wagon; *S.Am.* car; ✝ (a. ~ *de guerra*) chariot; ✕ car; carriage *de máquina de escribir*; (*carga*) cart-load; ~ *alegórico* float; ~ *blindado* armored car; ~ *de combate* tank; ~*patrulla* *S.Am.* patrol car; police car.

carrocería *f* *mot.* coachwork, body; **carrocero** *attr.* body, coach; *taller* ~ *mot.* body shop.

carroña *f* carrion.

carroza *f* (state) coach, carriage; **carruaje** *m* carriage; vehicle.

carrusel *m* merry-go-round; carrousel.

carta *f* letter; document; *naipes*: (playing) card; *hist.* charter; ♣ (a. ~ *de marear*) chart; ~ *adjunta* covering letter; ~ *de amor* loveletter; ~ *blanca* carte blanche, free hand; ~ *certificada* registered letter; ~ *de crédito* letter of credit; ~ *de figura* court-card; ~ *geográfica* map; ~ *meteorológica* weather map; ~ *de naturaleza* naturalization letter; *S.Am.*: *postal* postcard; ~ *de venta* bill of sale; *a* ~ *cabal* thoroughly, in every way.

cartabón *m* set-square *de dibujante*; △ bevel; *surv.* quadrant.

cartapacio *m* (*cartera*) brief case; *escuela*: satchel.

cartearse [1a] correspond (*con* with).

cartel *m* poster, placard, bill; *escuela*: wall chart; ✝ cartel; F *tener* ~ be all the rage; **cartelera** *f* hoarding, billboard; *thea. fig.* list of plays.

cárter *m* housing, case; ~ *del cigüeñal* crankcase.

cartera *f* wallet, pocketbook; portfolio (a. *pol.*), letter file; (*bolsa*) briefcase; *sew.* (pocket) flap; *pol. sin* ~ without portfolio; **carterista** *m* pickpocket; **cartero** *m* postman.

cartílago *m* cartilage ⏱, gristle.

cartilla *f* primer; ~ (*de ahorros*) deposit book; ~ (*de identidad*) identity card; ~ (*de racionamiento*) ration book.

cartografía *f* map-making, cartography; **cartógrafo** *f* mapmaker, cartographer.

cartón *m* cardboard, pasteboard; *paint.* cartoon; board *de libro*; (*caja*) cardboard box, carton.

cartuchera *f* cartridge belt; **cartucho** *m* cartridge; roll *de monedas*; paper cone; ~ *sin bala*, ~ *en blanco* blank cartridge.

cartulina *f* fine cardboard.

casa *f* house; (*hogar*) home; (*piso*) flat, apartment; (*ps.*) household; (a. ~ *de comercio*) firm, business house;

(descendencia) house, line; square *de tablero*; ~ *de banca* banking-house; ~ *de campo* country house; ~ *de citas*, ~ *pública*, ~ *de putas* brothel; ~ *de empeños* pawnshop; ~ *de fieras* zoo, menagerie; ~ *de guarda* lodge; ~ *de huéspedes* boarding-house; ~ *de juego* casino; ~ *de locos*, ~ *de orates* asylum; ~ *de (la) moneda* mint; ~ *solariega* ancestral home, family seat; ~ *de vecindad* tenements, apartment house.

casabe *m* cassava bread; cassava flour; manioc.

casaca *f* dress coat; *cambiar de* ~, *volver* ~ be a turncoat.

casada *f* married woman; **casadero** marriageable; **casado** **1.** married; *mal* ~ unhappily married; *estar* ~ *con* be married to; **2.** *m* married man.

casal *m* country house; pair of lovers.

casamata *f* casemate.

casamentero *m*, **a** *f* matchmaker; **casamiento** *m* marriage; wedding (ceremony); *prometer en* ~ betroth.

casar [1a] *v/t. (sacerdote)* marry, join in marriage; *hija* marry (off), give in marriage *(con* to); *fig.* match; *v/i.*, **~se** marry *(con acc.),* get married *(con* to); *fig.* match.

cascabel *m* (little) bell; *de* ~ *gordo* pretentious; *poner el* ~ *al gato* bell the cat; **cascabelear** [1a] *v/t.* beguile, take *s.o.* in; *v/i.* jingle; *fig.* behave frivolously.

cascada *f* waterfall, cascade.

cascado *p.* broken down, infirm; *cosa* broken (down).

cascajo *m* (piece of) grit, (piece of) gravel; *esp.* ∆ rubble; F junk, rubbish; *(trasto)* old crock.

cascanueces *m* (*un a pair of*) nut-crackers.

cascar [1g] *v/t.* crack, split; *nueces* crack; *salud* break; F bash, slosh; *v/i.* chatter (away); **~se** crack, split; *(salud)* crack up; *(voz)* crack.

cáscara *f* shell *de huevo, nuez, edificio*; rind, peel *de fruta*; husk of grano; *S.Am.* bark; **cascarón** *m* (broken) egg shell; **cascarrabias** *m* F quick-tempered fellow.

casco *m anat.* skull; ⚒ *etc.* helmet; crown *de sombrero*; skin *de cebolla*; ⚓ hull; ⚓ *(viejo)* hulk; hoof *de caballo*; piece *de vasija*; *ligero (or alegre) de* ~s feather-brained, dim; F *romper los* ~s *a* break *s.o.'s* head; F *romperse los* ~s rack one's brains.

caseína *f* casein.

casería *f* country house; *S.Am.* ✝ clientèle; **caserío** *m* hamlet, settlement; *(casa)* country house; **casero** **1.** domestic, household *attr.*; *pan etc.* home-made; *tela* homespun; *p.* home-loving; **2.** *m*, **a** *f* *(dueño)* landlord; *(custodio)* caretaker; **caserón** *m* big tumbledown house, barracks (of a place); **caseta** *f* stall, booth *de mercado*; *deportes:* pavillion; bathing hut *de playa*.

casi nearly, almost; ~ *nada* next to nothing; ~ *nunca* hardly ever.

casilla *f* ∆ hut, cabin; ▯ cab; *thea.* box office; pigeon hole *de casillero*; compartment *de caja*; *sacar de sus* ~s shake *s.o.* up; *(irritar)* make *s.o.* go of the deep end.

casino *m* club; casino *para jugar*.

casita *f* little house; cottage *de campo*.

caso *m* case *(a. ⚕, gr.)*; *(suceso)* event, occurrence; *(ejemplo)* case, instance; *en* ~ *de* in the event of; *(en)* ~ *que, en el* ~ *de que* in case *verb.*, in the event of *ger.*; *en tal* ~ in such a case; *en todo* ~ in any case; ~ *fortuito* mischance; act of God; *hacer* ~ a mind, notice; *¡no haga Vd.* ~! never mind!; take no notice!; *hacer* ~ *omiso de* not mention, pass over; *pongamos por* ~ *que* let us suppose that; *¡vamos al* ~! let's get to the point!

casorio *m* F hasty (*or* unwise) marriage.

caspa *f* dandruff, scurf.

¡cáspita! F my goodness!; come off it!

casquete *m* ✗ helmet; skull-cap.

casquillo *m* tip, cap; ferrule *de bastón*; *S.Am.* horseshoe.

cassette *m* cassette; ~ *deck* grabador en cinta; *separable;* magnetófono separable.

casta *f* caste; *biol.* breed, race; *fig.* quality; *venir de* ~ be natural to one.

castaña *f* chestnut; ~ *(de Indias)* horse-chestnut, conker F; *(moño)* bun; **castañeta** *f* snap; ♪ ~s *pl.* castanets; **castañetear** [1a] *v/t. dedos* snap; *v/i.* ♪ play the castanets; *(dedos)* snap, click; *(dientes)* chatter, rattle; *(huesos)* crack; **castaño** **1.** chestnut (-colored); **2.** *m* chestnut (tree); ~ *(de Indias)* horse-chestnut (tree); **castañuelas** *f/pl.* castanets.

castellanizar [1f] give a Spanish form to; **castellano** *adj. a. su. m,* **a** *f* Castilian.

casticismo *m* love of purity and correctness (*in language etc.*); **casticista** *m/f* purist; **castidad** *f* chastity, chasteness.

castigar [1h] punish (*de, por* for); *deportes*: penalize; *esp. fig.* castigate, chastise; **castigo** *m* punishment, penalty (*a. deportes*).

castillete *m min.* ⊕ derrick; tower.

castillo *m* ⚓ scaffolding; go-cart *de niño*; **castillo** *m* castle.

castizo *biol.* pure-bred, pedigree; *fig.* pure, correct; authentic, genuine; **casto** chaste, pure.

castor *m* beaver; **castóreo** *m pharm.* castor.

castración *f* castration; **castrar** [1a] castrate; *animal a.* geld.

casual fortuitous, chance *attr.*; (*no esencial*) incidental; *gr.* case *attr.*; **casualidad** *f* chance, accident; *por* ~ by chance; ¡*qué* ~ *encontrarle a Vd.!* fancy meeting you!

casuc(h)a *f* hovel, slum, shack.

casulla *f* chasuble.

cataclismo *m* cataclysm.

catacumba *f* catacomb.

catador *m* taster, sampler; (*aficionado*) connoisseur; **catadura** *f* tasting, sampling; F mug; puss.

catafoto *m* (rear) reflector.

catalán 1. *adj. a. su. m,* **-a** *f* Catalan, Catalonian; **2.** *m* (*idioma*) Catalan; **catalanismo** *m* movement for Catalan autonomy.

catalejo *m* (spy)glass, telescope.

catalizador *m* catalyst.

catalogar [1h] catalogue; **catálogo** *m* catalogue.

catapulta *f* catapult.

catar [1a] (*probar*) taste, sample, try; *fig.* examine, have a look at; (*mirar*) look at.

catarata *f* waterfall; ✷ cataract.

catarro *m* cold; (*permanente*) catarrh; ~ *crónico del pecho* chest trouble.

catarsis *f* catharsis.

catástrofe *f* catastrophe; **catastrófico** catastrophic.

catecismo *m* catechism.

catecúmeno *m,* **a** *f* catechumen; *fig.* convert.

cátedra *f univ.* chair, professorship; (*asignatura*) subject; *explicar una* ~ hold a chair (*de* of); **catedral** *f* cathedral; **catedrático** *m univ.* professor, lecturer.

categoría *f* category; class, group; standing, rank *en sociedad etc.*; *de* ~ important, of importance; **categórico** categorical, positive; *mentira* downright; *orden* express.

catequizar [1f] catechize, instruct in Christian doctrine.

catódico cathode *attr.*; *tubo de rayos* ~*s* cathode-ray tube; CRT; **cátodo** *m* cathode.

catolicismo *m* (Roman) Catholicism; **católico** *adj. a. su. m,* **a** *f* (Roman) Catholic; *adj. fig.* sure, beyond doubt; F *no estar muy* ~ be none too good.

catorce fourteen; (*fecha*) fourteenth.

catre *m* cot *de niño;* ~ (*de tijera*) camp-bed, folding-bed.

Caucásico Caucasian; white.

cauce *m* river-bed; ✐ irrigation channel.

cauchero rubber *attr.*; **caucho** *m* rubber; (*impermeable*) raincoat; ~ *esponjoso* foam rubber.

caución *f* caution, wariness; ⚖ bail; (*palabra*) pledge, security; *admitir a* ~ admit to bail.

caudal *m* volume, flow *de río;* fortune, property, wealth *de p.;* **caudaloso** *río* large, carrying much water; *fig.* wealthy, rich.

caudillaje *m* leadership; **caudillo** *m* leader, chief; *pol. el* ⚥ chief of state.

causa *f* cause (*a. pol.*); reason; grounds *de queja;* ⚖ suit, case; ⚖ prosecution *de oficio;* *a* (*or por*) ~ *de* on account of, because of, owing to; **causar** [1a] cause; *gastos, trabajo* entail; *enojo, protesta* provoke.

cáustico *adj. a. su. m* caustic (*a. fig.*).

cautela *f* caution, cautiousness, wariness; (*astucia*) cunning; **cauteloso** cautious, careful, wary; (*astuto*) cunning.

cauterizar [1f] cauterize; *fig.* eradicate; *p.* reproach.

cautivar [1a] take *s.o.* prisoner; *fig.* *espíritu* enthral; *auditorio* charm, captivate, win over; **cautiverio** *m,* **cautividad** *f* captivity; *esp. fig.* bondage; **cautivo** *adj. a. su. m,* **a** *f* captive.

cauto cautious, wary, careful.

cava *f* cultivation; **cavar** [1a] *v/t.* dig; *pozo* sink; *v/i.* dig; ✷ go deep; *fig.* delve (*en* into).

caverna *f* cave, cavern; **cavernoso** cavernous; cave *attr.*; *montaña etc.* honeycombed with caves.

caviar *m* caviar(e).

cavidad *f* cavity, hollow.

cavilación f deep thought; **cavilar** [1a] ponder (deeply), brood over; be obsessed with.

cayado m ✦ crook; *eccl.* crosier.

cayo m cay; key; ♀s *de la Florida* Florida keys.

caza 1. f (*en general*) hunting; shooting *con escopeta*; (*una* ～) hunt; chase, pursuit; (*animales*) game; ～ *mayor* big game; a ～ *de* in search of; *andar a* ～ *de* go out for; *dar* ～ *a* give chase; **2.** m 🛪 fighter; ～*-bombardero* fighter-bomber; ～ *nocturno* night-fighter.

cazador m hunter, huntsman; **cazadora** f huntress, hunting jacket; **cazanoticias** m newshawk; **cazaperros** m dogcatcher; **cazar** [1f] *animales* hunt; *total de muertos* bag; (*perseguir*) chase, go after, hunt down.

cazo m ladle; ～ (*de cola*) glue pot; **cazuela** f pan, casserole (*a. plato*).

ce: ¡～! hey!; F～ *por be* down to the last detail.

cebada f barley; ～ *perlada* pearl barley; **cebadal** m barley-field; **cebadera** f nose-bag; ⊕ hopper; **cebadura** f ✦ fattening; ⊕ stoking; ✕ priming; **cebar** [1a] **1.** v/t. ✦ feed, fatten (*con* on); *arma, lámpara, máquina* prime; **2.** v/i. grip, go in, catch; **3.** ～*se en víctima* vent one's fury on, batten on.

cebellina f *zo.* sable.

cebo m ✦ feed; ✕ charge, priming; ⊕ oven load; *pesca:* bait (*a. fig.*).

cebolla f onion; bulb *de tulipán etc.*; ～ *escalonia* shallot.

cebra f zebra.

cecear [1a] lisp; *pronounce* [s] *as* [θ]; **ceceo** m lisp(ing); *pronunciation of* [s] *as* [θ]; **ceceoso** lisping, with a lisp.

cecina f dried meat.

cedazo m sieve.

ceder [2a] v/t. hand over, give up, yield; *cosa querida* part with; ✝✝ grant; v/i. give in, yield (*a* to); (*disminuir*) decline, go down.

cedro m cedar.

cédula f document, (slip of) paper, certificate; ✝ warrant; ～ *en blanco* blank check; ～ *personal,* ～ *de vecindad* identity card.

cefálico cephalic.

céfiro m zephyr (*a. tela*).

cegar [1h *a.* 1k] v/t. (make) blind; (*tapar*) block up, stop up; v/i. go blind; *fig.* = ～*se* become blinded (*de*

by); **ceguedad** f, **ceguera** f blindness (*a. fig.*).

ceja f *anat.* eyebrow; ⚠ *etc.* projection; ⊕ rim, flange; *geog.* brow, crown; *fruncir las* ～*s* knit one's brow, frown; *quemarse las* ～*s* burn the midnight oil.

cejar [1a] (move) back; *fig.* give way, back down; climb down *en discusión*; relax, weaken *en esfuerzo*.

cejijunto *fig.* scowling, frowning.

celada f ambush, trap (*a. fig.*); **celador** m guard, watchman; ⊕ maintenance man; ✗ linesman.

celaje m ⚠ skylight; *fig.* sign.

celar¹ [1a] v/t. keep a watchful eye on, keep a check on. v/i.: ～ *por* watch over, guard.

celar² [1a] (*encubrir*) conceal, hide.

celda f cell; **celdilla** f *zo.* cell; cavity, hollow; ✦ niche.

celebrar [1a] v/t. *aniversario, suceso feliz* celebrate; *misa* say; *matrimonio* perform, celebrate; *reunión* hold; *fiesta* keep; (*alabar*) praise; v/i. *eccl.* say mass; ～*se* (*tener lugar*) take place, be held; **célebre** famous, noted, celebrated (*por* for); F funny, witty; **celebridad** f celebrity; (*festejo*) celebration(s).

celeridad f speed, swiftness.

celeste celestial; *ast.* heavenly; *color* sky-blue; **celestial** heavenly (*a. fig.*), celestial; F silly.

celestina f bawd, procuress.

célibe 1. single, unmarried; **2.** m/f unmarried person; celibate.

celo m zeal, fervor; conscientiousness; *b.s.* envy, distrust; *zo.* heat; *época de* ～ mating season; ～*s pl.* jealousy.

celofán m cellophane.

celosía f lattice, blind, shutter; *fig.* jealousy; **celoso** (*con celo*) zealous (*de* for), keen (*de* about; *con*).

celta 1. Celtic; **2.** m/f Celt; **3.** m (*idioma*) Celtic; **celtibérico, celtíbero** *adj. a. su.* m, **a** f Celtiberian; **céltico** Celtic; **celtohispán(ic)o** Celto-Hispanic.

célula f cell; **celuloide** m celluloid; **celulosa** f cellulose.

cementar [1a] ⊕ case-harden.

cementerio m cemetery, graveyard.

cemento m cement (*a. anat.*); (*hormigón*) concrete.

cena f supper, evening meal; (*oficial, de homenaje etc.*) dinner.

cenagal m quagmire, morass; F sticky business; **cenagoso** muddy, boggy.

cenar [1a] *v/t.* have for supper, sup on, sup off; *v/i.* have one's supper *etc.*; dine.

cencerrada *f noisy serenade given to widower who remarries;* **cencerrear** [1a] (*cencerro*) jangle; ♪ play terribly; ⊕ *etc.* rattle, clatter; **cencerro** *m* cowbell.

cendal *m* gauze.

cenicero *m* ashtray *para cigarro;* ashpan *de hogar;* trashcan; **ceniciento** ashen, ashcolored.

cenit *m* zenith.

ceniza *f* ash(es); ~s *pl. fig.* ashes, mortal remains; **cenizoso** ashy; *fig.* ashen.

censo *m* census *de población;* (*impuesto*) tax; ground rent *de propiedad;* (*hipoteca*) mortgage; **censor** *m* censor; *fig.* critic; **censura** *f pol. etc.* censorship; (*crítica*) censure, stricture; criticism, judgement *de obra;* **censura** [1a] *pol. etc.* censor; (*criticar*) censure, condemn.

centauro *m* centaur.

centavo *adj. a. su. m* hundredth; *S.Am.* cent.

centella *f* (*chispa*) spark (*a. fig.*); (*rayo*) flash of lightning; **centelleante** sparkling (*a. fig.*); flashing; **centell(e)ar** [1a] sparkle (*a. fig.*); flash; **centelleo** *m* sparkling, flashing *etc.*

centena *f* hundred; **centenar** *m* hundred; **centenario** 1. *adj. a. su. m* centenary; 2. *m, a f* centenarian.

centeno *m* rye.

centésimo *adj. a. su. m* hundredth; **centigrado** centigrade; **centímetro** *m* centimetre; **céntimo** 1. hundredth; 2. *m* cent (*hundredth part of a peseta*).

centinela *m/f* sentry, guard, sentinel; *estar etc. de* ~ be on guard.

central 1. central, middle; *esp. fig.* pivotal; 2. *f* ✝ head office; ~ *de correos* main post-office; ~ *eléctrica* power-station; ~ *telefónica* telephone exchange; **centralista** *m/f* telephone operator; **centralita** *f teleph.* switchboard; **centralizar** [1f] centralize; **centrar** center; hit the center; ~*se en* concentrate on; **céntrico** central, middle; *lugar* central, convenient; **centrifugadora** *f* centrifuge; centrifugal machine; spindrier; **centrífugo** centrifugal; **centrípeto** centripetal; **centro** *m* center (*a. ⚛*), middle; *fig.* center, hub *de*

actividad etc.; (*objeto*) goal, purpose; ~ *de gravedad* center of gravity; **centroamericano** Central American.

ceñido *vestido* tight, close-fitting; *fig.* sparing, frugal; **ceñir** [3h a. 3l] *espada* gird on; *cinturón etc.* put on; (*llevar*) wear; *frente etc.* bind, encircle (*con,* de with); ~*se* ✝ tighten one's belt; limit o.s., be brief *en palabras.*

ceño *m* frown, scowl; *meteor.* threatening look; (*v/i.*) frown, scowl; (*v/t.*) frown at, give *s.o.* black looks; **ceñudo** frowning.

cepa *f* stump *de árbol;* stock *de vid;* (*vid*) vine; △ pier; *Mex.* pit; hole; *fig.* stock; *de buena* ~ *p.* of good stock.

cepillar [1a] brush; ⊕ plane; *S.Am.* flatter; *univ. sl.* plough; **cepillo** *m* brush; ⊕ plane; *eccl.* poor-box.

cepo *m* ⚘ branch; *hunt.* snare; trap; ✕ *etc.* mantrap; stocks *de reo.*

cequión *m Ven.* arroyo.

cera *f* (bees)wax; *Col.,Ecuad.,Mex.* candle; ~ (*de lustrar*) (wax) polish; ~s *pl.* honeycomb.

cerámica *f* (*arte*) ceramics; (*objetos*) pottery (*a.* ~s *pl.*); **cerámico** ceramic.

cerca[1] *f* fence; (*tapia*) wall; ~ (*viva*) hedge.

cerca[2] 1. *adv.* near(by), close; *de* ~ near; ✕ *etc.* at close range; 2. *prp.* ~ *de* near, close to; in the neighborhood of; ~ *de inf.* near *ger.,* on the point of *ger.*

cercado *m* enclosure; garden, orchard; = *cerca*[1].

cercanía *f* nearness; ~s *pl.* outskirts *de ciudad;* neighborhood; *de* ~s 🚉 suburban; **cercano** near, close; *pueblo etc.* nearby, next; **cercar** [1g] fence in, enclose; wall *con tapia,* hedge *con seto;* (*rodear*) surround, ring (*de* with); ✕ besiege.

cercenar [1a] cut the edge off; clip, trim; *extremo* slice off.

cerciorar [1a] inform, assure; ~*se de* find out about, make sure of, ascertain.

cerco *m* ◆ *etc.* enclosure; *S.Am.* hedge; hoop *de tonel;* rim *de rueda;* △ frame; ✕ siege; *meteor.* halo.

cerda *f* bristle; horsehair; *hunt.* noose, snare; *zo.* sow; **cerdo** *m* pig (*a. fig.*); (*carne de*) ~ pork; **cerdoso** *animal* shaggy, hairy; *barbilla etc.* bristly, stubbly.

cereal 1. cereal, grain *attr.*; **2.** *m* cereal; *~es pl.* grain, cereals.

cerebral cerebral, brain *attr.*; **cerebro** *m* brain (*a. fig.*).

ceremonia *f* ceremony; *eccl. a.* service; *sin ~ adv.* informally, with no fuss; *attr.* informal; *hacer ~* stand on ceremony; **ceremonial** *adj. a. su. m* ceremonial; **ceremonioso** ceremonious; *recepción* formal; *b.s.* stiff, overpolite.

cereza *f* cherry; (*rojo*)*~* cherry (-red); **cerezo** *m* cherry (tree).

cerilla *f* match; (*vela*) wax taper; *anat.* ear wax; **cerillo** *m S.Am.* match.

cerner [2g] *v/t.* sift (*a. fig.*); *fig.* gauge; *v/i.* 🌢 bud, blossom; *meteor.* drizzle; *~se* (*p.*) waddle; *orn.* hover, soar; *fig.* threaten.

cero *m* (*nada*) nothing; 𝔸 (*cifra*) nought; *phys. etc.* zero; *deportes:* nil; *tenis:* love; *empezar de ~* start from the beginning.

ceroso (*de cera*) waxen; (*parecido a cera*) waxy; **cerote** *m* wax.

cerquita quite near, close by.

cerrado *asunto* obscure; *p.* (*callado*) quiet, secretive; F *~* (*de mollera*) dense; all-too-typical *de carácter*.

cerradura *f* (*acto*) closing, shutting, locking *con llave*; (*aparato*) lock; *~ de combinación* combination lock.

cerrar [1k] **1.** *v/t.* close, shut; lock (up) *con llave*, bolt *con cerrojo*; *grifo etc.* turn off; **2.** *v/i.* close, shut; (*noche*) set in; *~ con* close with, close in on; *dejar sin ~* leave open; **3.** *~se* close *etc.*; 𝔸 close up, heal; 🌢 close ranks; *meteor.* cloud over; **cerrazón** *f* threatening sky.

cerrero *animal* wild; *p.* uncouth, rough; **cerro** *m* hill, height; *zo.* neck.

cerrojo *m* bolt; *táctica de ~* stone-walling; *echar el ~* bolt the door.

certamen *m* competition, contest.

certero sure, certain; *tirador* good, crack; *golpe* well-aimed; (*sabedor*) well-informed; **certeza** *f* certainty.

certidumbre *f* certainty.

certificación *f* certification; & registration; 𝔤 affidavit; **certificado 1.** & registered; **2.** *m* certificate; **certificar** [1g] certify; vouch for *s.o.*; & register.

cervato *m* fawn.

cervecería *f* brewery; (*taberna*) public house, bar; **cerveza** *f* beer.

cervical neck *attr.*, cervical 𝖦; **cerviz** *f* (nape of the) neck; *bajar (or doblar) la ~* submit, bow down.

cesación *f* cessation; suspension; stoppage; **cesante 1.** out of a job; on half-pay; **2.** *m* civil servant who has been retired; (*paga*) retirement pension; **cesantía** *f* state of being a cesante; (*paga*) retirement pension; **cesar** [1a] *v/t.* stop; *v/i.* stop, cease; (*empleado*) leave, quit; *~ de inf.* stop ger., leave off ger.; **cese** *m* stoppage; stop-payment; *~ de fuego* cease-fire.

cesión *f* 𝔤 grant(ing), cession (*a. pol.*); **cesionario** *m*, **a** *f* grantee, assign.

césped *m* grass, turf; lawn *esp. de casa*; green *para bolos*.

cesta *f* basket; *pelota:* wicker racquet; **cesto** *m* (large) basket; hamper *esp. para comida*; *~* (*de la colada*) clothes basket; *~* (*para papeles*) wastepaper basket.

cetrería *f* falconry; **cetrero** *m* falconer.

cetrino greenish-yellow; *rostro* sallow; *fig.* jaundiced.

cetro *m* sceptre; *fig.* power, dominion.

chabanería *f* (piece of) vulgarity, bad taste; (*objeto*) shoddy piece of work; **chabacano** vulgar, in bad taste; shoddy; crude.

chacal *m* jackal.

cháchara *f* F small-talk, chatter; *~s pl.*

chacota *f* fun and games, high jinks; *echar a ~*, *hacer ~ de* make fun of; **chacotear** [1a] have fun.

chacra *f S.Am.* small farm.

chacuaco *m C.Am.* **1.** cigar butt; **2.** feo; repugnante.

chafallar [1a] F botch, make a mess of.

chafar [1a] (*aplastar*) flatten; (*arrugar*) crumple; F bring *s.o.* up short.

chafarrinón *m* stain, spot; *echar un ~ a* throw dirt at (*a. fig.*).

chaflán *m* bevel, chamfer; **chaflanar** [1a] bevel, chamfer.

chal *m* shawl.

chalado F dotty, round the bend; *estar ~ por* be crazy about.

chalán *m* (*esp.* horse-)dealer.

chalanear [1a] *v/t.* beat down, haggle with; *v/i.* bargain shrewdly.

chaleco *m* waistcoat, vest; *~ salvavidas* life-jacket; *al ~ Mex.* by force; for nothing; **chalecón** *m Mex.* crook.

chalet [tʃaˈle] *m* (*rural*) villa, cottage;

(*suizo*) chalet; house *en ciudad*.
chalote *m* shallot.
chalupa 1. *f* (open) boat, launch; *S.Am.* corncake; **2.** *m sl.* madman; **3.** *adj. sl.* crazy.
chamaco *m*, **a** *f* *C.Am.,Mex.,Col.* boy; girl.
chamarasca *f* brushwood (fire).
chamarra *f* sheepskin jacket.
chambón F awkward, clumsy; (*con suerte*) lucky; **chambonada** *f* F clumsiness; (*chiripa*) fluke.
champaña *m* champagne.
champiñón *m* mushroom.
champú *m* shampoo.
champurrar [1a] *bebidas* mix.
chamuscar [1g] scorch, singe; **chamusquina** *f* F row; dispute.
chance *m S.Am.* chance.
chancear(se) [1a] crack jokes; fool around (*con* with), play about.
chancho *S.Am.* **1.** dirty; **2.** *m* pig.
chancillería *f* chancery.
chancla *f* old shoe; = **chancleta 1.** *f* slipper; **2.** *m/f* F good-for-nothing; **chanclo** *m* clog; galosh, overshoe *de goma*.
chancro *m* ⚕ chancre.
chanflón misshapen; (*basto*) coarse, crude.
changarro *m S.Am.* small shop.
chantaje *m* blackmail; **chantajista** *m* blackmailer; racketeer.
chanza *f* (*dicho*) joke; (*hecho*) piece of tomfoolery; ~s *pl.* banter; tomfoolery; de ~ in fun.
chapa *f* plate, sheet *de metal*; metal top *de botella*; check *de guardarropa etc.*; board; (*enchapado*) veneer; flush *en mejillas*; *fig.* good sense; **chapado:** ~ a la antigua old-fashioned.
chapalear [1a] splash (about); (*ola*) lap.
chapar [1a] plate, cover *con metal*; veneer *con madera*.
chaparrada *f*, **chaparrón** *m* downpour, cloudburst.
chapín *m* clog.
chapitel *m* capital; spire *de torre*.
chapotear [1a] *v/t.* sponge (down), wet; *v/i.* splash *para salpicar*; paddle *con pies*; dabble *con manos*.
chapucear [1a] botch, bungle; **chapucería** *f* botched job, shoddy piece of work; **chapucero 1.** *objeto* badly made; *trabajo* clumsy, amateurish; **2.** *m* bungling amateur.
chapurr(e)ar [1a] *bebidas* mix; *idio-*

ma speak badly.
chapuz *m* ducking; dive; (*obra mala*) botched job; (*insignificante*) odd job;
chapuzar [1f] *v/t.* dock, dip; *v/i.*, ~se duck, dive.
chaqué *m* morning coat; **chaqueta** *f* jacket.
chaquete *m* backgammon.
chaquetón *m* shootingjacket.
charca *f* pond, pool; **charco** *m* puddle; pool *de tinta etc.*
charla *f* talk (*a. radio etc.*), chat; *b.s.* chatter; (*chismes*) gossip; **charladuría** *f* small talk, gossip; **charlar** [1a] chat, talk; *b.s.* chatter; **charlatán 1.** talkative; **2.** *m*, **-a** *f* chatterbox, gossip; (*embaidor*) trickster; ⚕ quack.
charnela *f* hinge.
charol *m* varnish; (*cuero*) patent leather; **charolar** [1a] varnish.
charrada *f* (piece of) bad breeding, coarse thing.
charro 1. *p.* coarse, ill-bred; *cosa* flashy, tawdry; *vestido* loud; **2.** *m*, **a** *f* *fig.* coarse person.
chascar [1a] *v/t. lengua* click; (*ronzar*) crunch; *v/i.* crack; **chascarrillo** *m* funny story; **chasco** *m* trick, joke; (*decepción*) disappointment; llevarse un ~ be disappointed.
chasis *m* chassis.
chasquear[1] [1a] *p.* play a trick on; (*zumba*) pull *s.o.*'s leg.
chasquear[2] [1a] *v/t. látigo* crack; *lengua* click; *dedos* snap; *v/i.* (*madera*) crack; **chasquido** *m* crack; click; snap.
chatarra *f* scrap-iron, junk.
chato 1. *p.* snub-nosed; pug-nosed; *cosa* low, flat; *S.Am.* common; *S.Am.* ¡~a mía! darling!; **2.** *m* small (wine)glass.
¡chau! *S.Am.* hi there!; (*despedida*) so long!
chauvinismo *m* chauvinism; **chauvinista 1.** chauvinistic; **2.** *m/f* chauvinist.
chaval *m* F lad, boy, kid.
chaveta *f* cotter(pin).
¡che! *S.Am.* hey!
checar [1g] *Mex.* check.
checo 1. *adj. a. su. m.*, **a** *f* Czech; **2.** *m* (*idioma*) Czech; **checoslovaco** *adj. a. su. m.*, **a** *f* Czecho-Slovak.
chelín *m* shilling.
cheque *m* cheque; ~ de viajeros traveler's check; **chequear** [1a] *C.Am.,W.I.* examine; check; con-

trol; **chequeo** *m S.Am.* control; checkup.

chequera *f S.Am.* checkbook.

chica *f* girl; (*chacha*) maid.

chicha *f S.Am.* maize liquor, corn juice; F *ni ~ ni limonada* not one thing or the other.

chicharro *m* caranx, horse-mackerel; **chicharrón** *m* fried crackling; *estar hecho un ~ cocina:* be burnt to a cinder.

chichear [1a] hiss.

chichón *m* 🏷 bump, swelling.

chicle *m* chewing-gum.

chico 1. small, little; **2.** *m* boy; F (*hombre, camarada*) lad, fellow; *~ de la calle* street urchin.

chicoria *f* chicory.

chicota *f* F fine girl; **chicote** *m* F fine lad; cigar (stub); **chicotear** [1a] *S.Am.* beat up.

chifla *f* hiss(ing), whistle; **chiflado** F daft, barmy; **chifladura** *f* hissing, whistling; F daftness; (*acto*) daft thing; crazy idea; **chiflar** [1a] *thea.* hiss; *~se* go wacky.

chileno, chileño *adj. a. su. m, a f* Chilean.

chillar [1a] (*gato etc.*) howl; (*ratón*) squeak; (*ave*) squawk, screech; (*p.*) (let out a) cry, yell; **chillido** *m* howl etc.; **chillón** *niño* noisy; *sonido, voz* shrill, strident.

chimenea *f* (*exterior*) chimney; ⚓ funnel; ⚒ shaft; (*hogar*) hearth.

chimpancé *m* chimpanzee.

china[1] *f* china.

china[2] *f geol.* pebble.

china[3] *S.Am.* (*novia*) girlfriend; (*querida*) mistress; (*criada*) maid.

chinche *f* bug; F tiresome person.

chinchilla *f* chinchilla.

chinela *f* slipper; (*chanclo*) clog.

chinesco Chinese; **chino**[1] **1.** *adj. a. su. m, a f* Chinese; **2.** *m* (*idioma*) Chinese; F double Dutch.

chino[2] *m, a f S.Am.* half-breed; mulatto; Indian.

chiquero *m* pigsty; pen *de toro.*

chiquillada *f* childish prank; *contp.* childish thing (to do); **chiquillería** F (*una ~*) crowd of youngsters; *la ~* the kids; **chiquillo, a** *f* kid, youngster; **chiquito 1.** small, tiny; **2.** *m, a f* kid, youngster.

chiribita *f* spark; *~s pl.* F spots before the eyes.

chiripa *f billar:* lucky break; F fluke, stroke of luck.

chirivía *f* parsnip.

chirlo *m* gash; (*cicatriz*) long scar.

chirona *f sl.* jug; jail; klink.

chirriar [1b] (*grillo*) chirp; (*ave*) chirp, squawk; (*rueda*) creak, squeak; (*frenos*) screech; **chirrido** *m* chirp(ing) *etc.*

chirrión *m S.Am.* whip.

¡chis! sh!

chisme *m* (*murmuración*) (piece of) gossip, tale; (*trasto*) thing; ⊕ gadget; *~s pl.* gossip, tittle-tattle; (*trastos*) things, odds and ends; **chismear** [1a] gossip, tell tales; **chismería** *f* gossip, scandal; **chismoso 1.** gossipy; **2.** *m, a f* gossip, scandalmonger.

chispa 1. spark (*a.* ⚡); *fig.* sparkle; (*gota*) drop; *caen ~s* it's drizzling; F *no dar ~* be utterly dull; **2.** *adj. sl.:* *estar ~* be tight; **chispeante** *fig.* sparkling; **chispear** [1a] spark; (*relucir*) sparkle (*a. fig.*); *meteor.* spot with rain; **chisporrotear** [1a] (*leña*) crackle; (*aceite etc.*) splutter; (*tocino*) sizzle.

chiste *m* joke, funny story; (*suceso*) funny thing; *~ goma* shaggy dog story; *caer en el ~* get it; *no veo el ~* I don't see the joke.

chistera *f* F top hat.

chistoso 1. funny, witty; **2.** *m, a f* wit.

chita: *a la ~ callando* quietly.

¡chito!, ¡chitón! sh!

chivatazo *m sl.* tip-off; **chivatear** [1a] F squeal; (*contra on*), squeal; **chivato** *m zo.* kid; F stoolpigeon, informer; *S.Am.* rascal; **chivo** *m* billy goat; *Col., Ecuad., Ven.* (fit of) rage.

chocante shocking; (*sorprendente*) startling, striking; *Mex.* intolerable; **chocar** [1g] *v/t.* shock; startle; ⚡ give a shock to; *vasos* clink; *v/i.* ⚔ clash; *mot. etc.* collide; (*vasos*) clink; (*platos*) clatter.

chocarrería *f* coarse joke; **chocarrero** coarse, dirty.

chochear [1a] dodder; (*enamorado*) be soft; **chochera** *f*, **chochez** *f* dotage; (*acto*) silly thing.

chocho doddering; *enamorado* silly, soft.

chocolate *m* chocolate; drinking-chocolate; **chocolatera** *f* chocolate pot; F *mot.* crock; ⚓ hulk.

chófer *m* driver; (*empleado*) chauffeur.

cholo *adj. a. su. m, a f S.Am.* half-breed; half-civilized.

chopo *m* 🌿 black poplar; ⚔ F gun.

choque m shock (a. ⚡, 💢); impact, jar, jolt; blast de explosión; mot., 🚗 crash, smash, collision; (ruido) crash, clatter; clink de vasos; ~ eléctrico shock therapy; ~ en cadena mot. pile-up; mass collision.

chorizo m sausage, salami.

chorrear [1a] v/t. 🗡 sl. dress down; v/i. spirt, gush (forth), spout (out); (gotear) drip; **chorro** m jet (a. ⊕, 🗲), spirt, spout; fig. stream; C.Am. faucet; 🗲 a ~s fig. in plenty.

choza f hut, shack.

christmas ['krismas] m F Christmas card.

chubasco m squall, heavy shower; **chubascoso** squally, stormy.

chuchería f knick-knack; (golosina) titbit, sweet.

chufa f earth-almond, chufa.

chula f flashy sort; S.Am. girlfriend; **chulada** f vulgar thing; mean trick; (gracioso) funny thing.

chuleta f chop, cutlet; univ. sl. crib.

chulo 1. pert, saucy; C.Am.,Mex. pretty; b.s. common, flashy; 2. m lower-class madrileño; b.s. sport; (alcahuete) pimp.

chumbera f prickly pear.

chupada f suck; drag de cigarro; **chupado** F skinny; falda tight; ~ de cara lantern-jawed; **chupador** m teething ring; **chupar** [1a] suck; 🕯 absorb, take in; pipa puff at; F a. S.Am. smoke; S.Am. (beber) drink; ~se waste away; **chupón** m 🕯 sucker; drag de cigarro; (p.) swindler.

churro m fritter.

chus: no decir ~ ni mus not say a word.

chuscada f funny thing; **chusco** funny, droll.

chusma f rabble, riff-raff.

chutar [1a] deportes: shoot.

chuzo m pike; llover a ~s rain cats and dogs.

cianuro m cyanide; ~ de potasio cyanide of potassium.

ciar [1c] ♉ go astern; (bote) back water; fig. go backwards.

ciática f sciatica.

cibernética f cybernetics.

cicatería f stinginess; **cicatero** 1. stingy, mean; 2. m, a f mean sort, skinflint.

cicatriz f scar (a. fig.); **cicatrizar(se)** [1f] heal (up); heal over, form a scar.

ciclamino m cyclamen.

cíclico cyclic(al); **ciclismo** m cycling;

(carreras) cycle racing; **ciclista** m/f cyclist; **ciclo** m cycle; escuela: term; course, series de clases; **ciclón** m cyclone; **ciclotrón** m cyclotron.

cidra f citron; **cidro** m citron (tree).

ciego 1. blind (a. fig.; de with); caño etc. blocked, stopped up; a ~as blindly (a. fig.); 2. m blind man.

cielo m sky; ast. sky, heavens; eccl. heaven; climate; ~ (raso) ceiling; roof de boca; canopy de cama; ¡~s! heavens above!; a ~ abierto in the open air (a. a ~ raso).

ciempiés m centipede.

cien v. ciento; ~ por ~ fig. a hundred per cent, wholehearted.

ciénaga f marsh, bog.

ciencia f science; (saber en general) knowledge, learning; ~-ficción science fiction ~s pl. naturales natural sciences; ~s pl. ocultas occult sciences; occultism; saber a ~ cierta know for certain, know for a fact.

cieno m mud, silt, ooze.

científico 1. scientific; 2. m scientist.

ciento adj. a. su. m (a) hundred, one hundred); por ~ per cent.

cierne: en ~(s) 🌱 in blossom, in flower; fig. cosa in its infancy.

cierre m (acto) closing etc.; shutdown de fábrica; (huelga) lockout; (mecanismo) snap(lock); fastener de vestido; clasp de libro; ~ de cremallera zipper; **cierro** m = cierre; S.Am. envelope.

cierto (seguro) sure, certain, promesa definite; (verdadero) true; (determinado) a certain; ~s pl. some, certain; por ~ indeed, certainly.

cierva f hind; **ciervo** m deer; (macho) stag; ~ común red deer.

cierzo m north wind.

cifra f 🔢 number, numeral; quantity, amount; ➕ sum; (escritura) code, cipher; monogram; abbreviation; en ~ in code; fig. mysteriously; **cifrar** [1a] write in code; fig. summarize.

cigarra f cicada.

cigarrera f cigar-case; **cigarrería** f S.Am. tobacconist's (shop); **cigarrillo** m cigarette; **cigarro** m cigar (a. ~ puro); cigarette.

cigüeña f orn. stork; ⊕ crank, handle; **cigüeñal** m crankshaft.

cilampa f C.Am. drizzle.

cilíndrico cylindric(al); **cilindro** m cylinder (a. ⊕); typ. etc. roller; ~ de caminos (road)roller.

cima f top de árbol; top, summit de

monte; fig. summit, height; *dar ~ a* complete, carry *s.t.* out successfully.

cimarrón *S.Am. zo.,* ♀ wild.

címbalo *m* cymbal.

cimbor(r)io *m* (base of a) dome.

cimbr(e)ar [1a] *vara* shake, swish; bend; F thrash; **~se** sway, swing; (*doblarse*) bend; **cimbreño** pliant; *p.* willowy.

cimentar [1k] ⚔ lay the foundations of; *fig.* found.

cimera *f* crest; **cimero** top, uppermost.

cimiento *m* foundation, groundwork; *fig.* basis, source; ⚔ **~s** *pl.* foundations.

cinc *m* zinc; ✝ counter.

cincel *m* chisel; **cincelar** [1a] carve, chisel; engrave.

cincha *f* girth; **cinchar** [1a] *silla* secure; ⊕ band, hoop; **cincho** *m* (*faja*) belt, sash; ⊕ band, hoop.

cinco five (*a. su.*); (*fecha*) fifth; *las ~* five o'clock.

cincuenta fifty.

cine *m* cinema, movies *Am.*; *~ mudo* silentfilm; **cinema** *m* cinema; **cinemateca** *f* film library; **cinematografía** *f* films; film-making; **cinematográfico** cine..., film *attr.*; **cinematógrafo** *m* cinema(tograph); (*máquina*) (film) projector.

cinética *f* kinetics; **cinético** kinetic.

cínico 1. cynical; *fig.* brazen, shameless; **2.** *m,* **a** *f* cynic; *fig.* humbug; **cinismo** *m* cynicism; *fig.* shamelessness, effrontery; humbug.

cinta *f* *sew. etc.* ribbon; band, strip; tape *de papel, magnetófon,* a. *deportes; cine:* film; (*rollo*) reel; **cinto** *m* ✗ belt; girdle; *armas de ~* side-arms; **cintura** *f* *anat.* waist; waistline; (*faja*) girdle; **cinturón** *m* belt; girdle; *~ de seguridad* safetybelt; *~* retráctil retractable safety belt.

cíper *m* *Mex.* zipper.

cipo *m* memorial stone; milestone *de camino;* roadsign.

ciprés *m* cypress (tree).

circo *m* circus.

circuito *m* circuit (*a.* ⚡); *deportes:* lap; circumference; *corto ~* shortcircuit; (*circulación*) ⊕ circulation (*a.* ✝, ⚙); *mot.* (movement of) traffic; **circulante** circulating; **circular 1.** *adj. a. su. f* circular; **2.** [1a] *v/t.* circulate; *v/i.* circulate (*a.* ✝, ⚙, *fig.*); *mot.* move (freely); (*p.*) walk round, move about (*a. ~ por*); **cír-**

culo *m* circle (*a. fig.*); club; (*aro*) ring, band; (*extensión*) compass, extent; ♀ *Polar Ártico* Arctic Circle.

circun... circum...; **~ cisión** *f* circumcision; **~ dante** surrounding; **~ dar** [1a] surround; **~ ferencia** *f* circumference; **~ flejo** *m* circumflex; **~ locución** *f,* **~ loquio** *m* roundabout expression, circumlocution; **~ navegar** [1h] sail round, circumnavigate; **~ scribir** [3a; *p.p. circunscrito*] circumscribe (*a. fig.*); *fig.* limit; **~ se** *fig.* be limited, be confined (*a* to); **~ spección** *f* cautiousness, circumspection; prudence; **~ specto** circumspect, prudent, deliberate; *palabras* guarded; **~ stancia** *f* circumstance; situation; *en las ~ s* in (*or* under) the circumstances; **~ stancial** circumstantial; *arreglo* makeshift, emergency *attr.;* **~ stante 1.** surrounding; present; **2.** *m/f* onlooker, bystander; **~ vecino** adjacent, surrounding; **~ volar** ⚙ circumnavigate; fly around.

cirio *m* *eccl.* (wax) candle.

ciruela *f* plum; *~ pasa* prune; **ciruelo** *m* plum (tree); F dolt.

cirugía *f* surgery; *~ estética, ~ plástica* plastic surgery; **cirujano** *m* surgeon.

ciscar [1g] F dirty, soil; **~se** soil o.s.; **cisco** *m* slack; *Cuba,Mex.* shame; embarrass.

cisma *m* *eccl.* schism; *pol. etc.* split; *fig.* disagreement; **cismático** *eccl.* schismatic(al); *fig.* dissident.

cisne *m* swan.

cisterna *f* (water)tank, cistern; toilet tank.

cistitis *f* cystitis.

cita *f* engagement, appointment, meeting; (*lugar*) rendezvous; (*con novia etc.*) date; *lit.* quotation; reference; **citación** *f* *lit.* quotation; ⚖ summons, citation; **citar** [1a] make an appointment (*or* date) with; ⚖ summon; *lit.* quote, cite.

cítrico citric.

ciudad *f* city; town; **ciudadanía** *f* citizenship; **ciudadano 1.** civic, city *attr.;* **2.** *m,* **a** *f* city-dweller; *pol.* citizen; *~s pl. freq.* townsfolk, townspeople; **ciudadela** *f* citadel; *S.Am.* tenement; **cívico 1.** civic; *fig.* public-spirited, patriotic; domestic; **2.** *m S.Am.* policeman; **civil 1.** civil (*a. fig.*); ✗ *guerra* civil; *población* civilian; **2.** *m* policeman; **civilización** *f* civilization; **civilizar** [1f] civilize; **civismo** m good citizenship; civic-mindedness.

cizalla f (una f pair of) (metal) shears; wire cutters.

cizaña f ♃ darnel; Biblia: tares; fig. vice, harmful influence; sembrar ～ sow discord.

clamar [1a] v/t. cry out for; v/i. cry out (contra against, por for); **clamor** m (grito) cry; (protesta) outcry, clamor; (ruido) noise, clamor; **clamorear** [1a] cry out for, clamor for; **clamoreo** m clamor; (protesta) outcry; **clamoroso** noisy, loud, shrieking.

clandestino secret, clandestine.

claque m claque; hired clappers.

clara f white of an egg; bald spot en cabeza; meteor. bright interval.

claraboya f skylight; transom.

clarear [1a] v/t. brighten; color make lighter; v/i. dawn; meteor. clear up; ～se (tela) be transparent.

clarete m claret.

claridad f brightness etc.; clearness, clarity (a. fig.); ～es pl. plain speaking, blunt remarks; **claridoso** C.Am., Mex. frank; open; **clarificar** [1g] illuminate, light up; clarify (a. fig.).

clarinete m clarinet.

clarión m chalk; ～cillo crayon.

clarividencia f far-sightedness; discernment; clairvoyance; **clarividente** 1. far-sighted; discerning; 2. m/f clairvoyant(e).

claro 1. adj. día, ojos etc. bright; agua, lenguaje, prueba, voz clear; cristal clear, transparent; cuarto, cerveza, color light; ¡～! naturally!, of course!; ¡(pues) ～! I quite agree with you!; ¡～ que sí! of course it is!; 2. adv. clearly; hablar ～ fig. speak plainly; 3. m opening, gap; space; △ light, window; paint. highlight, light tone.

clase f mst class; (género) a. sort, kind; univ. a. lecture; (sala) classroom; univ. lecture-room; F fumarse la ～ cut a class.

clásico 1. classical; esp. fig. classic; traditional; typical; 2. m classic.

clasificación f classification; rating (a. ♣); **clasificador** m filing cabinet; **clasificar** [1g] classify; grade, rate; sort (out).

claudicar [1g] limp; F back down; give in; fig. act crookedly.

claustro m cloister (a. fig.); univ. approx. senate.

cláusula f clause; gr. sentence.

clausura f (acto) closing (ceremony), closure; eccl. monastic life; eccl. de ～ convento enclosed; **clausurar** [1a] close; suspend, adjourn.

clavar [1a] clavo knock in, drive in; tablas nail (together); (asegurar) fasten, pin, fix; puñal stick, thrust (en into).

clave 1. f ♪ clef; △ keystone; fig. key (de to); ～ de sol treble clef; 2. adj. key attr.

clavel m carnation; **clavellina** f pink.

clavetear [1a] puerta etc. stud; cordón etc. put a tip on.

clavícula f collar bone, clavicle.

clavija f pin, peg (a. ♪), dowel; ⚡ plug; ～ hendida cotter pin.

clavo m nail; spike; stud; ♃ clove; ⚕ (callo) corn; (dolor) sharp pain; fig. anguish; ～ de rosca screw; F dar en el ～ hit the nail on the head.

claxon m mot. horn; tocar el ～ sound one's horn, hoot.

clemencia f clemency, mercy; **clemente** merciful, forgiving; lenient.

cleptomanía f kleptomania; **cleptómano** m, a f kleptomaniac.

clerecía f priesthood; (ps.) clergy.

clerical clerical; **clérigo** m (esp. católico) priest; (esp. anglicano) clergyman; **clero** m clergy.

cliché m/f typ. stencil; lit. cliché; = ſ

cliente m/f ⚕ customer, client (a. ⚖); ⚕ patient; **clientela** f customers, clients, clientèle; ⚕ practice.

clima m climate; **climático** climatic; **climatización** f air conditioning.

clímax m rhet. climax.

clínica f clinic, hospital; (esp. privado) nursing home; ～ de reposo convalescent home; **clínico** clinical.

clip m paper clip; (joya) clip.

clisar [1a] stereotype; **clisé** m typ. cliché, plate; phot. plate.

cloaca f sewer (a.fig.).

cloquear [1a] cluck; har poon.

cloro m chlorine; **cloroformo** m chloroform; **cloruro** m chloride.

clóset m S.Am. (wall) closet.

club m club.

clueca broody (f hen).

coacción f coercion, duress; **coactivo** coercive.

coadjutor m coadjutor; **coadyuvar** [1a] assist, contribute to.

coagular(se) [1a] coagulate.

coalición f coalition.

coartada f alibi; **coartar** [1a] limit, restrict.

coba *f* F (*embuste*) neat trick; (*halago*) soft soap; F flattery.

cobalto *m* cobalt.

cobarde 1. cowardly; faint-hearted; **2.** *m/f* coward; **cobardía** *f* cowardice; faintheardness.

cobaya *f*, **cobayo** *m* guinea pig.

cobertizo *m* shed; outhouse; lean-to; (*refugio*) shelter; **cobertor** *m* bedspread; **cobertura** *f* cover(ing); bedspread *de cama*.

cobija *f* coping tile; *S. Am.* blanket; *S. Am.* ~s *pl.* bedclothes; **cobijar** [1a] cover (up), close; ~se take shelter; **cobijo** *m* fig. cover, shelter.

cobista F flattering; fawning.

cobrador *m* ✝ collector; conductor *de autobús*; (*perro*) retriever; **cobranza** *f* = *cobro*; **cobrar** [1a] **1.** *v/t.* (*recuperar*) recover; *precio* charge; *suma* collect; *cheque* cash; *sueldo* draw; get; *hunt.* retrieve; *S. Am.* press (for payment); ✝ *por* ~ outstanding; receivable; ✝ (*en empleo*) get one's pay; **3.** ~se ⚕ recover; (*volver en sí*) come to.

cobre *m* copper; ♪ brass (*a.* ~s *pl.*); *batirse el* ~ go all out (*por inf. to inf.*); (*disputa*) get really worked up; **cobrizo** coppery.

cobro *m* recovery; collection *etc.*

coca *f* F nut; (*golpe*) rap on the head; kink *en cuerda*; *Mex.* de ~ free; gratis.

cocaína *f* cocaine.

cocear [1a] kick (*a.* F).

cocer [2b *a.* 2h] *v/t.* cook; (*hervir*) boil; *pan* bake; ⊕ bake; *barros* fire; *v/i.* cook; boil; ~se ⚕ be in continual pain.

cochambre *m* F filthy thing; filth.

coche *m* (*motor-*) car, automobile; ✝ coach, carriage (*a.* 🚗); ~-cama sleeper, sleeping-car; ~-comedor dining-car; ~ (*de tipo*) *medio* medium-size car; ~ *de reparto* delivery car (*a.* van, wagon); **cochecito** *m* (de niño) pram, perambulator; **cochera** *f* garage; carport; **cochero 1.:** *puerta* ~a carriage entrance; **2.** *m* coachman.

cochinada *f* F, **cochinería** *f* F filth(iness); (*acto*) dirty trick; (*palabra*) beastly thing; **cochinilla** *f* zo. woodlouse; (*colorante*) cochineal; *de* ~ *Cuba,Mex.* unimportant; **cochinillo** *m* suckling pig; **cochino 1.** filthy, dirty (*a. fig.*); (*sin valor*) rotten, measly; **2.** *m* pig (*a. fig.*). [*tables*).}

cocido *m* stew (*of meat, bacon a vege-*}

cociente *m* quotient; ~ *intelectual* intelligence quotient (I.Q.).

cocina *f* kitchen; (*arte*, ~ *francesa etc.*) cooking, cookery, cuisine; (*aparato*) stove, cooker; ~ *económica* range, cooker; **cocinar** [1a] *v/t.* cook; *v/i.* do the cooking; **cocinero** *m*, **a** *f* cook.

coco¹ *m* ⚕ coconut; = *cocotero*.

coco² *m* bogey man; (*mueca*) face; *hacer* ~s a make faces at; (*amor*) make eyes at.

cocodrilo *m* crocodile.

cocotero *m* coconut palm.

cóctel *m* (*fiesta*) cocktail party; (*bebida*) cocktail; **coctelera** *f* cocktail shaker.

codazo *m* jab, poke (with one's elbow); (*ligero*) nudge; **codear** [1a] elbow; jostle; ~se *con* hobnob with, rub shoulders with.

códice *m* manuscript, codex.

codicia *f* greed(iness), lust (*de* for); **codiciar** [1b] covet; **codicioso** greedy, covetous; F hard-working.

codificar [1g] codify; **código** *m* ⚖ *tel.* code; ~ *de leyes* a. statute-book; ~ *penal* penal code.

codillo *m* zo. knee; ⊕ elbow (joint); ⚕ stump; (*estribo*) stirrup; **codo** *m* elbow; zo. knee; ⊕ elbow (joint); *dar de*(*l*) ~ a nudge; *fig.* despise; *Mex., Guat.* miser; tightwad.

codorniz *f* quail.

coeficiente *adj. a. su. m* coefficient.

coetáneo *adj. a. su. m*, **a** *f* contemporary.

coexistencia *f* coexistence; **coexistente** coexistent; **coexistir** [3a] coexist (*con* with).

cofrade *m* member (of a brotherhood *etc.*); **cofradía** *f* brotherhood, fraternity; (*gremio*) guild.

cofre *m* chest; **cofrecito** *m* casket.

cogedor *m* picker; gatherer; dustpan; (*pala*) shovel.

coger [2c] *flores etc.* pick, gather, collect; (*recoger*) take (up), gather (up); (*asir*) catch (hold of), take hold of, seize; ~ (*al vuelo*) snatch; *catarro, frío* catch; (*sorprender*) catch; (*encontrar*) find; (*entender*) catch, gather, take in; (*contener*) take; *extensión* cover; **cogida** *f* ✓ picking, harvesting; *toros:* goring.

cogollo *m* heart *de lechuga, col*; head *de col*.

cogotazo *m* blow on the back of the neck, rabbit punch; **cogote** *m* back of the neck, nape.

cohabitación f cohabitation; **cohabitar** [1a] live together, cohabit (a. b.s.). [bribe.\

cohechar [1a] bribe; **cohecho** m⌡

coheredero m, a f coheir(ess f).

coherencia f coherence; phys. cohesion; **coherente** coherent; **cohesión** f cohesion; **cohete** m rocket; missile. ~ de señales distress signal, flare; ~ intermedio intermediate-range missile.

cohibición f restraint; inhibition; **cohibido** restrained, restricted; (carácter) inhibited; **cohibir** [3a] restrain, check; inhibit.

cohombro m cucumber.

coima f rakeoff; bribe.

coincidencia f coincidence; **coincidir** [3a] coincide (con with).

coito m (sexual) intercourse, coitus ⨳.

cojear [1a] limp, be lame (de in); sabemos de qué pie cojea we know his weaknesses; **cojera** f lameness; (visible) limp.

cojín m cushion; **cojinete** m small cushion, pad; ⊕ ~ (a bolas) (ball-)bearing; ⊕ journal box.

cojo 1. lame, limping; crippled; mueble wobbly; fig. lame, shaky; 2. m, a f lame person; cripple.

cok m coke.

col f cabbage; ~ (rizada) kale; ~ de Bruselas Brussels sprouts.

cola¹ f zo., ✺, ast. tail (a. de frac); (extremo) (tail) end; bottom de clase; train de vestido largo; (ps. etc.) queue, line; ⊕~ de milano dovetail; a la ~ at the back, behind.

cola² f glue; ~ (de retal) size; ~ de pescado fish glue.

colaboración f collaboration; lit. contribution (a, en to); **colaborar** [1a] collaborate; ~ a lit. contribute to, write for.

colación f collation (a. eccl.); (merienda) snack; (boda) reception, wedding breakfast; S.Am. sweet; **colacionar** [1a] collate.

colada f wash(ing); (lejía) bleach; geog. defile; **coladera** m, **colador** m (tea- etc.) strainer; colander para legumbres.

colapso m collapse, breakdown.

colar [1m] v/t. líquido strain; ropa bleach; pass, squeeze (por through); F palm s.t. off, foist s.t. off (a on); v/i. (líquido) filter, percolate; = ~se slip through; (p.) slip in, sneak in.

colcha f bedspread, counterpane; **colchón** m mattress.

cole m F = colegio.

colear [1a] wag its etc. tail.

colección f collection; **coleccionar** [1a] collect; **coleccionista** m/f collector; **colecta** f collection (for charity); eccl. collect; **colectar** [1a] collect; **colectividad** f (conjunto) sum total, whole; group; pol. collective ownership; **colectivismo** m collectivism; **colectivo** collective (a. gr.); acción freq. joint, group attr.

colega m colleague.

colegial 1. school attr., college attr.; eccl. collegiate; 2. m schoolboy; Mex. greenhorn; beginner; **colegiala** f schoolgirl; **colegio** m high school; primary school; univ., eccl., ✿ etc. college.

colegir [3c a. 3l] gather, collect; conclude, gather (de from).

cólera 1. f anger; physiol. bile; 2. ✿ m cholera; **colérico** angry, irate; irascible.

colesterol m cholesterol.

coleta f pigtail; F postscript; S.Am. burlap.

coleto m leather jacket; F body; the self; decir para su ~ say to o.s.

colgadero m hook, hanger, peg; **colgadizo** 1. hanging; 2. m lean-to, penthouse; **colgadura(s)** f(pl.) hangings, drapery; **colgante** 1. hanging; drooping, floppy; puente suspension attr.; 2. m (joya) drop, pendant.

colgar [1h a. 1m] 1. v/t. hang (a. 🏛; de from, en on); ropa etc. hang up; pared decorate with hangings, drape; univ. F plough; 2. v/i. hang (de on, from); droop, dangle; teleph. hang up, ring off.

colibrí m hummingbird.

cólico m colic.

coliflor f cauliflower.

coligado allied, in league; **coligarse** [1h] join together.

colilla f stub; stump; cigarette (or cigar) butt.

colina f hill.

colindante adjoining, neighboring.

coliseo m coliseum; arena.

colisión f collision (a. fig.); fig. clash.

colitis f ✿ colitis.

collado m hill; (desfiladero) pass.

collar m (adorno) necklace; collar de perro (a. ⊕); (insignia) chain.

colmado 1. full (de of), overflowing

(de with); 2. *m* grocer's (shop); cheap restaurant; **colmar** [1a] fill (up), fill to overflowing; ~ de *fig.* shower with, overwhelm with.

colmena *f* (bee)hive; *fig.* hive; **colmenero** *m* beekeeper.

colmillo *m anat.* eyetooth, canine; *zo.* fang; tusk *de elefante*.

colmo *m fig.* height *de locura etc.*; limit; ¡es el ~! it's the limit!, it's the last straw!

colocación *f* (*acto*) placing *etc.*; position; (*puesto*) job, situation; ✝ investment; **colocar** [1g] put, place (in position); arrange; ✝ invest; *tropas etc.* position, station.

colombiano *adj. a. su. m*, **a** *f* Colombian.

colon *m anat.*, *gr.* colon.

colonia *f* colony; (*barrio*) suburb; *sew.* silk ribbon; **colonial** colonial; *productos* imported; **colonización** *f* colonization; settlement; **colonizador** *m* colonist; settler; pioneer; **colonizar** [1f] colonize; settle; **colono** *m pol.* colonist, settler; ✒ (tenant) farmer.

coloquial colloquial; **coloquio** *m* conversation, talk; *lit.* dialogue.

color *m* color; (*matiz*) hue; (*colorante*) dye; *fig.* color(ing); ~es *pl.* ✖ colors; de ~ *p. etc.* colored; so ~ de under pretext of; **coloración** *f* coloration, coloring; **colorado** colored; (*rojo*) red; *chiste* blue, rude; *argumento* plausible; *ponerse* ~ blush; **colorante** *m* coloring (matter); **colorar** [1a] color, dye (*de azul* blue); stain (*a.* ⊕); **colorear** [1a] *v/t. motivo* show in a favorable light; *acción etc.* gloss over; *v/i.* redden, show red; **colorete** *m* rouge; **colorido** *m* color(ing).

colosal colossal; **coloso** *m* colossus (*a. fig.*).

columbrar [1a] glimpse, spy, sight.

columna *f mst* column; △ *a.* pillar (*a. fig.*); *quinta* ~ fifth column; ~ vertebral spinal column; ~ de dirección *mot.* steering column; **columnista** *m* columnist.

columpiar [1b] swing; ~se swing (to and fro); seesaw; **columpio** *m* swing; (*tabla*) seesaw.

coma[1] *f gr.* comma; *sin faltar una* ~ down to the last detail.

coma[2] *f* 𝅘𝅥 coma.

comadre *f* ♀ midwife; F best friend, crony; (*chismosa*) gossip; **comadreja** *f* weasel; **comadreo** *m* F, **coma-**

drería *f* F gossip(ing); **comadrona** *f* midwife.

comandancia *f* command; (*grado*) rank of major; **comandante** *m* commandant, commander; (*grado*) major; **comandar** [1a] command; lead; **comandita** *f* silent partnership; **comando** *m* command; ✖ (*grupo*) commando.

comarca *f* region, part (of the country); **comarcano** neighboring, bordering.

comba *f* bend; *esp.* bulge, warp, sag; (*juego*) skipping; **combar** [1a] bend, curve; ~se bend, curve; (*madera*) bulge, warp, sag.

combate *m* fight, engagement, combat; *fig.* battle, struggle; **combatiente** *m* combatant; **combatir** [3a] *v/t.* ✖ attack; *costa* beat upon; *mente* assail, harass; *tendencia etc.* fight against; *v/i.*, ~se fight, struggle (*con, contra* against).

combinación *f* combination; (*arreglo*) arrangement, set-up; ~es *pl. fig.* plans, measures; **combinar** [1a] combine; *colores etc.* blend, mix; ~se combine.

combustible 1. combustible; 2. *m* fuel, combustible; **combustión** *f* combustion.

comedero 1. eatable; 2. *m* ✒ trough, manger; (*comedor*) dining room.

comedia *f* play, drama (*a. fig.*); (*festiva*) comedy; (*fingimiento*) farce, pretence; **comediante** *m*, **a** *f* (*esp. comic*) actor (actress *f*).

comedido courteous, polite; moderate.

comediógrafo *m* playwrite(r); dramatic author.

comedirse [3l] be restrained (*en* in), restrain o.s.; be moderate.

comedor 1. = *comilón* 1; 2. *m* dining room.

comején *m* termite, white ant.

comendador *m* commander (*of an order of knighthood*).

comensal *m/f* dependant; (*compañero*) companion at table.

comentador *m* commentator; **comentar** [1a] comment on; expound; **comentario** *m* comments, remarks; *esp. lit.* commentary; ~s *pl.* gossip; **comentarista** *m* commentator; **comento** *m* comment; *lit.* commentary.

comenzar [1f *a.* 1k] begin, start (*con* with; *por su.* with *su.*; *por inf.* by *ger.*).

comer [2a] **1.** v/t. eat; ⊕ etc. eat away, corrode; (consumir) use up, eat up; **2.** v/i. eat; have a meal, esp. (have) lunch; dar de ~ a feed; ser de buen ~ eat anything; **3.** ~se comida eat up (a. fig.); consonante drop; sílaba slur over; texto skip.

comercial commercial, business attr.; **comerciante** m/f trader, dealer, merchant; ~ al por mayor wholesaler; ~ al por menor retailer; **comerciar** [1b] (ps.) have dealings; ~ con mercancías, ~ en deal in, handle; **comercio** m (en general) trade, business, commerce; (negocio particular) trade, traffic; ~ exterior foreign trade; ~ sexual sexual intercourse.

comestible 1. eatable; ♀ etc. edible; **2.** m food(stuff), ~s pl. food(stuffs); (comprados) groceries.

cometa¹ m ast. comet.

cometa² f kite.

cometer [2a] crimen etc. commit; error make; negocio entrust (a to).

comezón f itch (a. fig.; de inf. to inf.; por for), itching; tingle.

cómico 1. comic(al), funny; comedy attr.; autor dramatic; **2.** m (esp. comic) actor; comedian.

comida f (alimento) food; (acto) eating; (a hora determinada) meal; esp. lunch, dinner; (manutención) keep, board; **comidilla** f F hobby, first love; ~ de la ciudad talk of the town.

comienzo m beginning, start; (a. ⚜) onset; birth, inception.

comillas f/pl. quotation marks.

comilón F **1.** fond of eating; b.s. greedy; **2.** m, -a f big eater.

comino ♀ cumin; cuminseed; no vale un ~ it's not worth tuppence.

comisaría f police station; **comisario** m commissary (a. ✕); ~ de policía police superintendent; **comisión** f commission (a. ✝); parl. etc. committee; ✝ (junta) board; (encargo) assignment, commission; **comisionado** m commissioner; parl. etc. committee member; ✝ member of the board; **comisionar** [1a] commission.

comistrajo m F awful meal; fig. hodgepodge.

comité m committee.

comitiva f retinue, suite.

como a) comp. a.: like, the same as; verb.: algo así ~ something like; ~ si as if; b) en calidad de: as; c) cj. causa: as, since; condición: if; ~ quiera as you

like; (porque) because; así ~, tan luego ~ as soon as.

cómo a) interrogative: how?; (por qué) why?; how is it that ...?; ¿~ está Vd.? how are you?; ¿~ es? what's he like?, what does he look like?; ¿~ no? why not?; ¿a ~ es el pan? how much is the bread?; b) int. ¿~? (pidiendo repetición) eh?, what did you say?; (sorpresa) what?

cómoda f chest of drawers; comode; **comodidad** f comfort, convenience; (self-)interest, advantage; ~es pl. de la vida good things of life; **comodín 1.** Col.,Mex.,P.R. adj. cozy; **2.** m naipes: wild card; joker; fig. stand-by, useful gadget; **cómodo** comfortable; cuarto etc. freq. snug, cosy; convenient, handy.

compacto compact; typ. etc. close.

compadecer [2d] (a. ~se de) pity, be sorry for; sympathize with; ~se con agree with; harmonize with.

compadre m godfather; F friend, pal; **compadrear** [1a] F be pals.

compañerismo m comradeship; deportes etc.: team spirit; **compañero** m, -a f companion; partner; mate; ~ de armas comrade in arms; ~ de clase schoolmate; ~ de cuarto roommate; **compañía** f company; society; ~ inversionista investment trust.

comparable comparable; **comparación** f comparison; **comparado** comparative; **comparar** [1a] compare (con with, to); liken (con to); **comparativo** adj. a. su. m comparative.

comparecencia f ⚖ appearance (in court); **comparecer** [2d] ⚖ appear (in court).

compartimiento m division, sharing; (departamento) a. ⚓ compartment; **compartir** [3a] divide up, share (out); ~ con share with.

compás m ♪ compasses; ♪ compass; ♪ (tiempo) time; measure; (ritmo) beat, rhythm; (división) bar; **compasado** measured, moderate.

compasión f pity, compassion; ¡por ~! for pity's sake!; **compasivo** compassionate; sympathetic.

compatibilidad f compatibility; **compatible** compatible, consistent (con with).

compatriota m/f compatriot, fellow-countryman (-woman).

compeler [2a] compel (a inf. to inf.).

compendiar [1b] abridge, sum-

marize; **compendio** *m* abridgement, summary; compendium.
compenetrarse [1a] ⚲ *etc.* interpenetrate; *fig.* share each other's feelings.
compensación *f* compensation; ⚙ redress; *esp. fig.* recompense; **compensar** [1a] *pérdida* compensate for, make up (for); *error* redeem; *p.* compensate.
competencia *f* competition (*a.* ⚙); rivalry; ⚙ competence; *hacer* ~ *con* compete against (*or* with); *ser de la* ~ *de* be within *s.o.'s* province; **competente** *trabajo*, ⚙ competent; (*apropiado*) suitable, adequate; **competidor 1.** competing; **2.** *m*, -**a** *f* competitor (*a.* ✝); rival (*a* for); **competir** [3l] compete (*a.* ✝, *deportes*; *con* with, against; *para* for); *poder* ~ ✝ be competitive.
compilación *f* compilation; **compilar** [1a] compile.
compinche *m* F pal, chum.
complacencia *f* pleasure, satisfaction; willingness *en obrar*; **complacer** [2x] please; *cliente* oblige; ~**se en** take pleasure in *su., ger.*; be pleased *to inf.*; **complacido** complacent; satisfied; **complaciente** genial, cheerful; obliging.
complejidad *f* complexity; **complejo** *adj. a. su. m* complex.
complementar [1a] complement; complete, make up; **complementario** complementary; **complemento** *m* complement (*a. gr.*, ⚛).
completar [1a] complete; make up; *fig.* perfect; **completo** complete; 🚌 *etc.* full; *por* ~ completely, utterly.
complexión *f* *physiol.* constitution; complexion.
complicado complex, complicated; *método freq.* elaborate; **complicar** [1g] complicate; ~**se** get complicated; (*embrollarse*) get tangled, get involved; **cómplice** *m/f* accomplice.
complot [kom'plo] *m* plot, intrigue; complot.
componenda *f* compromise; *b.s.* shady deal; **componente 1.** component; **2.** *m* ⚙ ⚛ component; ingredient *de bebida etc.*; **componer** [2r] compose (*a. typ.*, ♪), constitute, make up; *typ. a.* set up (in type); *lit.* write; *lo roto*, ⚙ repair, mend, overhaul; ~**se** (*mujer*) dress up; make up.
comportamentismo *m* behaviorism; **comportamiento** *m* behavior;

⊕ performance; **comportar** [1a] put up with, bear; *S.Am.* entail; cause; ~**se** behave, conduct o.s.; **comporte** *m* = *comportamiento*.
composición *f* *mst* composition; make-up; (*ajuste*) settlement; **compositor** *m* composer; **compostura** *f* composition, make-up; (*reparo*) mending, repair(ing); (*mesura*) sedateness; (*ajuste*) arrangement, settlement.
compostelano *adj.* of (or from) Santiago de Compostela.
compota *f* compote, preserve; *sauce de manzanas etc.*
compra *f* purchase; ~**s** *pl.* shopping; *ir de* ~**s** shop, go shopping; **comprador** *m*, -**a** *f* shopper, customer *en tienda*; purchaser; **comprar** [1a] buy, purchase (*a* from); *fig.* buy off, bribe.
comprender [2a] *v/t.* (*abarcar*) comprise, include; (*entender*) understand; *v/i.* understand, see; *¿comprendes?* see?; *¡ya comprendo!* I see; **comprensible** understandable, comprehensible (*para* to); **comprensión** *f* understanding; grasp; inclusion; **comprensivo** understanding; intelligent; (*que incluye*) comprehensive.
compresa *f* compress; ~ *higiénica* sanitary towel; **compresión** *f* compression; *índice de* ~ compression ratio; *de alta* ~ *attr.* high-compression; **compresor** *m* compressor; **comprimido 1.** *aire* compressed; **2.** *m* *pharm.* tablet; pill; **comprimir** [3a] compress (*a.* ⊕); squeeze, press down; *fig.* restrain, repress.
comprobación *f* checking *etc.*; (*prueba*) proof; **comprobante 1.** of proof; **2.** *m* proof; ✝ voucher, guarantee; **comprobar** [1m] check, verify; prove; ⊕ overhaul.
comprometer [2a] (*poner en peligro*) jeopardize, endanger; *reputación* compromise; put *s.o.* in a compromising situation; ~ *a* *nail s.o.* down to, hold *s.o.* to; ~**se** get involved (*en* in); ✝ commit o.s.; **comprometido** embarrassing; ✝ *etc.* estar ~ be (already) engaged; **compromiso** *m* obligation, pledge; (*cita*) engagement; compromising situation; (*aprieto*) tight corner, predicament.
compuerta *f* sluice, flood-gate; hatch *en puerta.*
compuesto *p.p. of componer; estar*

~ de be composed of, be made up of;
2. adj. 🔔, Å, gr. compound; ♀, 🔺
etc. composite; fig. composed, calm;
3. m compound (a. 🔔).

compulsión f compulsion; **compulsivo** compulsory; compulsive.

compungirse [3c] feel remorse (por
at), feel sorry (por for).

computacional computational; attr.
computing; **computador** m, **-a** f
computer; ~ de casa home computer;
~ personal personal computer; **computadora** f computer; hardware.

computar [1a] calculate, reckon;
cómputo m calculation, computation; estimate.

comulgante m/f communicant; **comulgar** [1h] v/t. administer communion to; v/i. take communion.

común 1. common (a to; a. b.s.);
opinión ~ widespread, generally
held; de ~ con in common with; en ~
in common; por lo ~ generally; Mercado ~ Common Market; **2.** m: el ~ de
las gentes most people, the common
run (of people).

comunicación f communication;
(ponencia) paper; (parte) message;
comunicado m communiqué; **comunicar** [1g] mst communicate (a
🔺; con with); noticia give, convey,
deliver (a to); (legar) bestow (a on);
periodismo: report (de from); ~se (ps.)
communicate; be in touch; 🔺 (inter)
communicate; **comunicativo** communicative; fig. sociable; rise etc. infectious; **comunidad** f community;
comunión f communion; **comunismo** m communism; **comunista 1.**
communist(ic); **2.** m/f communist.

con with; (a pesar de) in spite of,
despite; (para ~) to, towards.

conato m attempt, endeavor (de inf. to
inf.); (empeño) effort.

concatenar [1a] link together, concatenate.

concavidad f concavity; (sitio)
hollow; **cóncavo 1.** concave; hollow; **2.** m hollow, cavity.

concebible conceivable, thinkable;
concebir [3l] conceive.

conceder [2a] (otorgar) grant; concede; admit (que that).

concejal m (town) councillor; **concejo** m council; town council; town
hall.

concentrate (a. ✕), be concentrated.

concepción f conception; (facultad)
understanding; **concepto** m concept
(a. phls.), notion; opinion; lit. conceit.

concerniente: ~ a concerning, relating to.

concertar [1k] v/t. (arreglar) arrange; convenio etc. conclude; precio
fix (en at); p. reconcile (con with); v/i.
agree (a. gr.); harmonize; ~se agree.

concesión f grant, award; ♦, fig.
concession; **concesionario** m concessionaire; licensee.

concha f zo. shell; (marisco) shellfish;
thea. prompter's box; ~ de perla
mother-of-pearl.

conchabarse [1a] F gang up (contra
on); S.Am. hire out.

conciencia f (conocimiento) knowledge, awareness; phls. consciousness; (moral) conscience; moral
sense; **concienzudo** conscientious,
thorough.

concierto m order, concert; ♪ harmony; (pieza) concerto.

conciliación f conciliation; (semejanza) affinity, similarity; favor;
conciliar [1b] reconcile; respeto etc.
win; ~se algo win, gain.

concilio m eccl. council.

concisión f conciseness, terseness;
conciso concise, terse.

conciudadano m, **a** f fellowcitizen.

concluir [3g] v/t. end; conclude (de
from; a uno de s.o. to be); convince;
v/i. end (gr. etc. con, en, por in); ~ de
inf. finish ger.; **conclusión** f conclusion; en ~ lastly, in conclusion.

concordancia f concordance (a.
eccl.); gr., ♪ concord; **concordar**
[1m] v/t. reconcile; gr. make s.t.
agree; v/i. agree (a. gr.); ~ con agree
with, tally with, fit in with; **concordia** f concord, harmony; conformity, agreement.

concretar [1a] fig. make s.t. concrete;
reduce to its essentials, boil down;
~se a inf. confine o.s. to ger.; **concretera** f S.Am. concrete mixer;
concreto 1. concrete; aceite thick; en
~ to sum up; exactly, specifically;
nada en ~ nothing in particular; **2.** m
concretion; S.Am. concrete.

concubina f concubine.

concupiscencia f lust, concupiscence; **concupiscente** lewd, lustful.

concurrencia f (asistencia) attendance, turn-out; (multitud) crowd;

confidente

concurrido *lugar* crowded; *función* well attended; **concurrir** [3a] (*reunirse*) gather, meet (*a at*, *en in*); *fig.* come together, conspire (*para inf.* to *inf.*); coincide (*con* with); ✝ *etc.* compete; (*convenir*) agree; **concursante** *m/f* contestant, participant; **concurso** *m* (*reunión*) gathering; concurrence *de circunstancias*; (*ayuda*) help; competition (*a. a puesto*), contest; *deportes*: match, meeting; *tenis*: tournament.

concusión *f* ✝ extortion; **concusionario** *m* extortioner.

condado *m hist.* earldom; (*tierras, provincia*) county; **conde** *m* earl, count.

condecoración *f* ✗ *etc.* decoration; insignia; **condecorar** [1a] decorate (*con* with).

condena *f* sentence; term; ~ *a perpetuidad* life sentence; **condenación** *f* condemnation; = *condena*; *eccl.* damnation; F *¡~!* damn!; **condenado** 1. F damned, ruddy; 2. *m*, *a f* ✝ criminal, convicted person; *eccl.* one of the damned; **condenar** [1a] condemn (*a* to); *esp.* ✝ convict, find guilty (*por ladrón* of stealing); ✝ sentence (*a multa* to, *a presidio* to hard labour); *eccl.* damn; **~se** ✝ confess (one's guilt).

condensación *f* condensation; **condensador** *m* ⊕, ⚡ condenser; **condensar** [1a] condense.

condesa *f* countess.

condescendencia *f* willingness (to help); acquiescence (*a* in); **condescender** [2g] acquiesce, say yes; ~ *a* consent to, say yes to.

condición *f* condition; ~ (*social*) status, position; character, nature; ~*es pl.* ✝ conditions, terms; circumstances; *a* ~ (*de*) *que* on condition that; **condicionado, condicional** conditional (*a. gr.*).

condimentar [1a] season; flavour; (*con especias*) spice; **condimento** *m* seasoning; flavour(ing); dressing.

condiscípulo *m*, *a f* fellowstudent.

condolencia *f* condolence; **condolerse** [2h] ~ *de* be sorry for; ~ *por* sympathize with.

condominio *m* ✝ joint ownership; dual control; condominium.

condonar [1a] *acto* condone; *deuda* forgive, forget.

cóndor *m orn.* condor; *Chile, Ecuad.* gold coin.

conducción *f* leading *etc.*; transport(ation); *phys.* conduction; **conducir** [3o] 1. *v/t.* lead, guide (*a* to); conduct; *negocio* conduct, manage; *mot.* drive; 2. *v/i. mot. etc.* drive; ~ *a* lead to; 3. **~se** behave, conduct o.s.; **conducta** *f* ✝ *etc.* management, direction; conduct, behavior *de p.*; **conducto** *m* conduit (*a.* ⚡); tube; *esp. anat.* duct, canal; *fig.* agency; **conductor** 1. leading, guiding; *phys.* conductive; 2. *m phys.* conductor; ⚡ lead; 3. *m*, *-a f* leader, guide; *mot. etc.* driver.

conectar [1a] ⚡, ⊕ connect (up); (*poner*) switch on; *boxeo*: *golpe* land.

conejal *m*, **conejar** *m*, **conejera** *f* warren, burrow; F den, dive; **conejillo** *m*: ~ *de Indias* guinea pig; **conejo** *m* rabbit.

conexión *f* connexion (*a.* ⚡); relationship; **conexionar** *v/t.* connect; put in touch; *v/i.* connect; make contacts.

confección *f* (*acto*) making; (*arte*) workmanship; *pharm.* confection, concoction; **confeccionado** *ropa* readymade, ready-to-wear; **confeccionar** [1a] make (up); **confeccionista** *m/f* ready-made clothier.

confederación *f* confederacy; confederation, league; **confederarse** [1a] form a confederation.

conferencia *f* (*discurso*) lecture; *pol. etc.* meeting, conference; *teleph.* call; **conferenciante** *m/f* lecturer; **conferenciar** [1b] be in conference, confer; **conferencista** *m/f S.Am.* lecturer; **conferir** [3i] *v/t. dignidad* confer, bestow (*a* on); *premio* award (*a* to); *negocio* discuss; *v/i.* confer.

confesar [1k] *v/t.* confess (*a. eccl.*), own up to, admit; *v/i.*, **~se** confess (*con* to), make one's confession; **confesión** *f* confession; **confes(i)onario** *m* confessional; (*garita a.*) confession box; **confesor** *m* confessor.

confiado (*presumido*) vain, conceited; (*crédulo*) unsuspecting, gullible; ~ *en sí* (*mismo*) self-confident, self-reliant; **confianza** *f* confidence (*en* in); trust (*en* in); reliance (*en* on); **confiar** [1c] *v/t.*: ~ *a*, ~ *en* entrust *s.t.* to; *v/i.* (have) trust; ~ *en* trust, trust in (*or* to); rely on, count on; **confidencia** *f* confidence; *de mayor* ~ top secret; **confidencial** confidential; **confidente** *m*, *a f* confidant(e *f*); informer; detective; spy.

configuración f shape, configuration; **configurar** [1a] form, shape.

confín m limit, boundary; horizon; ~es pl. confines (a. fig.); **confinar** [1a] v/t. confine (a, en in); v/i.: ~ con border on; ~se shut o.s. up.

confirmación f confirmation (a. eccl.); **confirmar** [1a] confirm (a. eccl.; de, por as); endorse, bear out.

confiscación f confiscation; **confiscar** [1g] confiscate.

confitar [1a] preserve; frutas candy; fig. sweeten; **confite** m sweet; **confitería** f confectionery; (tienda) confectioner's, sweetshop; **confitura** f preserve; (mermelada) jam.

conflagración f conflagration; fig. flare-up.

conflictivo conflicting; anguished; troubled; **conflicto** m conflict (a. fig.); (apuro) difficulty, fix.

confluencia f confluence (a. ♫); **confluir** [3g] meet, join; fig. come together.

conformar [1a] v/t.: ~ a, ~ con adjust s.t. to, bring s.t. into line with; v/i. agree (con with); ~se conform; ~ con original conform to; regla comply with, abide by; **conforme 1.** adj. similar, in agreement, in line (con with); 3. int. ¡~! agreed!, right!, O.K.!; **conformidad** f similarity, conformity; agreement; de ~ con in accordance with; en ~ accordingly.

confort m comfort; **confortable** comfortable; comforting; **confortante** comforting; **confortar** [1a] invigorate, strengthen; afligido comfort.

confraternidad f confraternity.

confrontación f confrontation; showdown; **confrontar** [1a] v/t. ps. bring face to face, confront (con with); textos compare; v/i. border (con on); ~se con face, confront.

Confucianismo m Confucianism.

confundir [3a] (mezclar) mix, mingle (con with); b.s. mix up, jumble up; (equivocar) confuse (con with), mistake (con for), mix up; **confusión** f confusion; **confuso** mst confused; cosas a. mixed up, in disorder.

confutar [1a] confute.

conga f popular dance of Cuba; **congal** m Mex. brothel; whorehouse.

congelación f congealing; freezing;

congelado carne chilled, frozen; ✻ frost-bitten; **congelador** m freezer; **congeladora** f deep-freeze; **congelar(se)** [1a] (esp. sangre) congeal; freeze; ✻ get frost-bitten.

congenial kindred; **congeniar** [1b] get on (con with).

congénito congenital.

congestión f congestion; **congestionar** [1a] produce congestion in.

conglomeración f conglomeration; **conglomerar(se)** [1a] conglomerate.

congoja f anguish, distress.

congraciador ingratiating; **congraciarse** [1b] con get into s.o.'s good graces.

congregación f gathering, assembly; eccl. congregation; **congregar(se)** [1h] gather, congregate; **congresista** m/f delegate, member (of a congress); **congreso** m congress.

congruencia f suitability; congruence (a. ♣); **congruente** congruous.

cónico conical; ⅄ sección conic section.

conjetura f conjecture, surmise; **conjeturar** [1a] guess (at) (de, por from); ~ que surmise that, infer that.

conjugación f conjugation (a. biol.); **conjugar** [1h] conjugate.

conjunción f conjunction; **conjunto 1.** united, joint; related por afinidad; 2. m whole; grouping; (vestido, ♪) ensemble; thea. chorus; en ~ altogether, as a whole.

conjura(ción) f conspiracy, plot; **conjurado** m, a f conspirator, plotter; **conjurar** [1a] v/t. (suplicar) entreat, beseech; v/i. ~se plot, conspire (together); **conjuro** m conjuration, incantation; (súplica) entreaty.

conmemorar [1a] commemorate; **conmemorativo** commemorative; memorial attr.

conmigo with me; with myself.

conminar [1a] threaten; **conminatorio** threatening.

conmiseración f pity, sympathy; (acto) commiseration.

conmoción f geol. shock (a. fig.); fig. commotion, disturbance; **conmovedor** (enternecedor) moving, touching; poignant; (que perturba) disturbing; **conmover** [2h] shake, disturb; fig. move, touch.

conmutador m ♣ switch; commutator; S.Am. telephone exchange;

conmutar [1a] exchange (*con*, *por* for).

connatural innate, inherent.

connotación *f* connotation; (*parentesco*) distant relationship; **connotar** [1a] connote.

cono *m* cone (*a.* Ⓐ); ~ **de proa** nose cone (of rocket).

conocedor *m*, **-a** *f* connoisseur, (good) judge (*de* of); expert (*de in*).

conocer [2d] *v/t.* know; be familiar with; distinguish, tell (*en*, *por* by); *peligro etc.* recognize; (*llegar a* ~) *p.* meet; *v/i.* know; ~ **de**, ~ **en** know a lot about; ~**se** know o.s.; (*dos ps.*) (*estado*) know each other; (*acto*) meet, get to know each other; **conocido 1.** *p. etc.* well-known; familiar; noted (*por* for); **2.** *m*, **a** *f* acquaintance; **conocimiento** *m* knowledge; understanding; 🧠 consciousness; (*p.*) acquaintance; ⚓ bill of lading; ~**s** *pl.* knowledge (*de* of); information (*de* about); **poner** *s.o.* **en** ~ **a** inform, let *s.o.* know.

conque 1. (and) so, (so) then; **2.** *m* F condition (*para* of).

conquense *adj. a. su. m/f* (native) of Cuenca.

conquista *f* conquest; **conquistador** *m*, **-a** *f* conqueror; *hist.* conquistador; **conquistar** [1a] conquer (*a* from); *fig.* win over.

consabido well-known; well established; above-mentioned.

consagración *f* consecration; **consagrado** consecrated (*a* to); *expresión* time-honored; **consagrar** [1a] consecrate (*a* to); deify; ~**se a** devote o.s. to.

consanguíneo related by blood, consanguineous.

consciente conscious (*de* of).

conscrito *m S.Am.* recruit; conscript.

consecución *f* acquisition; **consecuencia** *f* consequence, outcome; consistency *de conducta*; **consecuente** *phls.* consequent; *conducta etc.* consistent; **consecutivo** consecutive (*a. gr.*); **conseguir** [3d *a.* 3l] obtain, get, secure; ~ *inf.* succeed in *ger.*

conseja *f* (fairy-)tale; **consejero** *m*, **a** *f* adviser; *pol.* councillor; **consejo** *m* (*dictamen*) advice, counsel; (*un* ~) piece of advice; hint; *pol. etc.* council; ⚖ tribunal, court; ✝ *etc.* board.

consenso *m* (unanimous) assent, consensus; **consentido** *niño* spoilt; *marido* complaisant; **consentimiento** *m* consent; **consentir** [3i] *v/t.* consent to; permit, allow (*a.* ⚖; *que alguien subj.* s.o. to *inf.*); (*tolerar*, *admitir*, *posibilidad*) admit; *niño* pamper, spoil; *v/i.* consent, say yes, agree (*en* to).

conserje *m* porter; caretaker, janitor; **conserjería** *f* porter's office.

conserva *f* (*en general*) preserved foods; (*fruta etc.*) preserve(s); (*mermelada*) jam; (*carne etc.*) pickle; ~**s** *pl.* alimenticias canned goods; **conservación** *f* preservation *etc.*; ⚠ *freq.* upkeep; **conservador 1.** preservative; *pol.* conservative; **2.** *m*, **-a** *f* *pol.* conservative; **3.** *m* 🏛 curator; **conservar** [1a] *p.*, *salud*, *frutas*, ⚠ preserve; *esp.* 🍶 conserve; can, tin *en lata*; *costumbres*, *hacienda etc.* keep up; ~**se** last (out); ~ (*bien*) keep (well); 🏥 take good care of o.s.; **conservatismo** *m* conservatism; **conservativo** preservative, conservative; **conservatorio** *m* 🎵 conservatory; *S.Am.* greenhouse.

considerable considerable, substantial, sizeable; **consideración** *f* consideration; respect, regard; **en** ~ **a** considering, in consideration of; **ser de** ~ **be** important, be of consequence; **considerado** (*amable*) considerate, thoughtful; respected; deliberate; **considerar** [1a] consider (*que* that; *como* as, to be, *or acc.*), regard (*como* as); show consideration for, respect.

consigna *f* order; slogan; ✕, *pol.* watchword; ✕ cloakroom, checkroom; **consignación** *f* consignment; deposit; **consignar** [1a] (*enviar*) consign; dispatch, remit (*a* to); deposit; *renta etc.* assign (*para* to).

consigo with him, with her, with you *etc.*

consiguiente consequent (*a* upon); *por* ~ consequently, so, therefore.

consistencia *f* consistency, consistence *etc.*; **consistente** consistent; solid, substantial; **consistir** [3a]: ~ **en** consist of (*or* in); lie in.

consocio *m* fellow-member; ✝ partner, associate.

consolación *f* consolation; **consolar** [1m] console, comfort.

consolidación *f* consolidation; **con-**

solidar [1a] consolidate (a. ✝, fig.);
fig. a. strengthen, cement.

consonancia f consonance (a. gr.),
harmony; **consonante 1.** adj. a. su. f
consonant; **2.** m rhyming word,
rhyme; **consonar** [1m] ♪ be in
harmony (a. fig.); lit. rhyme.

consorcio m ✝ consortium; association; **consorte** m/f consort.

conspicuo eminent, prominent.

conspiración f conspiracy; **conspirador** m, -a f conspirator; **conspirar** [1a] conspire, plot (contra
against); ∼ a inf. conspire to inf.

constancia f constancy; steadiness
etc.; proof, evidence; **constante 1.**
constant; steady; amigo etc. faithful,
staunch; (duradero) lasting; **2.** f Å
constant; **constar** [1a]: ∼ de be clear
from, be evident from; consist of; ∼
en be on record in; ∼ por be shown
by; hacer ∼ record; certify; reveal
(que that).

constelación f constellation; climate; **constelado** starry.

consternación f consternation, dismay; **consternar** [1a] dismay.

constipado m ✖ (head)cold; **consti-
parse** [1a] catch a cold.

constitución f constitution; **constituir** [3g] constitute; colegio etc. set
up, establish; principios etc. erect (en
into); ∼se en, ∼ por set (o.s.) up as;
constitutivo adj. a. su. m constituent; **constituyente** pol. constituent.

constreñir [3h a. 3l] force (a inf. to
inf.); ✖ constipate; **constricción** f
constriction.

construcción f building, construction (a. gr.); **constructor 1.** building, construction attr.; **2.** m builder;
construir [3g] construct (a. Å);
build; edificio freq. put up.

consuelo m consolation, solace; joy,
comfort.

consuetudinario habitual; ♄ common.

cónsul m consul; **consulado** m
consulship; consulate.

consulta f consultation; (parecer)
opinion; de ∼ libro etc. reference
attr.; **consultación** f consultation;
consultar [1a] consult; referencia
look up; asunto discuss, take up (a,
con with); (aconsejar) advise; consultant; **consultorio** m information
bureau; ✖ surgery, consulting room.

consumación f consummation; end;
consumado consummate, perfect;

accomplished (en in); **consumar**
[1a] carry out, accomplish.

consumición f consumption etc.;
food or drink taken in a café etc.;
consumidor m ✝ consumer; (cliente) customer; **consumir** [3a] mst
consume; F get on s.o.'s nerves; ∼se
burn out, be consumed en fuego; ✖
waste away (a. fig.); **consumo** m,
consunción f consumption.

contabilidad f accounting, book-
keeping; (profesión) accountancy;
contabilista m/f accountant; book-
keeper.

contacto m contact.

contado 1. adj. ∼s pl. few; rare; **2.**
adv.: al ∼ cash down. (for) cash; por
de ∼ naturally; **contador** m counter
de café; ✝ accountant, book-keeper;
⊕ meter; ∼ de Geiger Geiger counter;
∼ público titulado certified public accountant; **contaduría** f accountancy; book-keeping.

contagiar [1b] ✖ etc. infect (con with; a.
fig.); ∼se become infected; ∼ de ✖
catch; **contagio** m contagion (a.
fig.); (enfermedad) infection; **contagioso** contagious; p. infectious.

contaminación f contamination;
(baldón) stain; ∼ ambiental environ-
mental pollution; **contaminar** [1a]
contaminate (a. fig.); agua pollute;
vestido soil; texto corrupt.

contar [1m] v/t. ✖ etc. count (por
dedos on); (considerar) count (entre
among, por as); historia tell; ∼ inf.
count on ger., expect to inf.; sin ∼ not
counting, not to mention; v/i. count;
∼ con rely on, count on.

contemplación f contemplation; ∼es
pl. indulgence; **contemplar** [1a]
gaze at, look at; fig., eccl. contemplate; **contemplativo** contempla-
tive.

contemporáneo adj. a. su. m, a f
contemporary.

contender [2g] contend; compete, be
rivals (en in); ∼ con fight with, fig.
dispute with (sobre over); **contendiente** m contestant.

contenedor m container; **contener**
[2l] contain (a. ✖), hold; multitud
keep in check; rebeldes keep down;
emoción keep back; ∼se fig. hold o.s.
in check, contain o.s.; **contenido 1.**
fig. restrained; **2.** m contents.

contentamiento m contentment;
contentar [1a] satisfy, content; ✝
endorse; ∼se con, ∼ de be contented

with, be satisfied with; **contento 1.** contented; (*alegre*) pleased; glad, happy; *estar* ~ *de* be glad about; **2.** *m* joy, contentment.

conteo *m* calculation; reckoning; count.

contestación *f* answer, reply; ⚖ ~ *a la demanda* plea; **contestar** [1a] answer (*a. v/i.* ~ *a*); ⚖ corroborate; **contesto** *m* reply; answer.

contexto *m* lit. context; (*enredo*) interweaving, web; **contextura** *f* contexture; make-up *de p.*

contienda *f* struggle, contest.

contigo with you; (†, *a. Dios*) with thee.

contiguo adjacent (*a* to), adjoining.

continente 1. continent; **2.** *m geog.* continent; (*vasija*) container; *fig.* air, mien; (*porte*) bearing.

contingencia *f* contingency; **contingente 1.** contingent; **2.** *m* contingent (*a.* ✕); † *etc.* quota.

continuación *f* continuation; *a* ~ later (on); below *en texto*; **continuar** [1e] *v/t.* continue, go on with; *v/i.* continue, go on (*con* with; *ger.* ger.); ~(**se**) *con geog.*, △ adjoin, connect with; **continuidad** *f* continuity; continuance; **continuo 1.** continuous; continual; ⊕ *cinta etc.* endless; **2.** *m* continuum.

contonearse [1a] swagger, strut.

contorno *m* form, shape; *paint. etc.* outline; ~*s pl.* environs.

contorsión *f* contortion.

contra 1. *prp.* against (*a. en* ~ *de*); △ opposite, facing; **2.** *adv.* *con* ~ against; *opinar etc. en* ~ disagree; **3.** *m v. pro.*

contra...: ~**almirante** *m* rear admiral; ~**ataque** *m* counterattack; ~**bajo** *m* double bass; ~**balanza** *f* counterbalance; contrast; ~**bandista** *m/f* smuggler; ~**bando** *m* (*acto*) smuggling; (*géneros*) contraband.

contracción *f* contraction.

contra(con)ceptivo *m* contraceptive.

contracorriente *f* cross-current.

contracultura *f* counterculture.

contra...: ~**decir** [3p] contradict; ~**dicción** *f* contradiction; *fig.* incompatibility; ~**dictorio** contradictory.

contraer [2p] *mst* contract; *discurso* condense; *contrato etc.* enter into.

contra...: ~**espionaje** *m* counterespionage; ~**fuerte** *m* △ buttress; *geog.* spur; ~**hacer** [2s] copy, imitate; *moneda* counterfeit; *docu*-

~*mento* forge, fake; *p.* impersonate; ~**hecho** counterfeit, fake(d); *anat.* hunchbacked; ~**hechura** *f* counterfeit; counterfeiting *etc.*

contra...: ~**maestre** *m* ⊕ foreman; ♣ warrant-officer; ~**mandar** [1a] countermand; ~**marcha** *f* ✕ countermarch; *mot. etc.* reverse; ~**marchar** [1a] countermarch; ~**orden** *f* counter-order; ~**pelo:** *a* ~ the wrong way; *fig.* against the grain; ~**pesar** [1a] (counter)balance (*con* with); *fig.* offset, compensate for; ~**peso** *m* counterbalance, counterweight; ⊕ makeweight; ~**prestación** *f* return favor; quid pro quo; ~**producente** self-defeating.

contrariar [1c] go against, be opposed to; (*estorbar*) impede, thwart; (*molestar*) annoy; **contrariedad** *f* opposition; obstacle; (*disgusto*) bother, annoyance; **contrario 1.** contrary (*a* to); (*nocivo*) harmful (*a* to); (*enemigo*) hostile (*a* to); *lado* opposite; *suerte* adverse; *al* ~ *on* the contrary, *por lo* ~ *on* the contrary; **2.** *m*, **a** *f* (*p.*) enemy, adversary; ⚖ *etc.* opponent; **3.** *m* contrary, reverse (*de* of).

contra...: ~**rreforma** *f* Counter-reformation; ~**rrestar** [1a] counteract; offset; *pelota* return; ~**seña** *f* countersign (*a.* ✕); *thea.* ticket.

contrastar [1a] *v/t.* resist; † *metal* assay, hallmark; *medidas* check; *radio:* monitor; *v/i.* contrast (*con* with); **contraste** *m* contrast; † assay; (*marca del*) ~ hallmark; *en* ~ *con* in contrast to.

contrata *f* contract; *por* ~ by contract; **contratar** [1a] negotiate for, contract for; *p.* hire, engage; *jugador etc.* sign up.

contratiempo *m* setback, reverse.

contratista *m/f* contractor; **contrato** *m* contract.

contra...: ~**validación** *f* validation (of a document); confirmation; ~**validar** validate; confirm; ~**veneno** *m* antidote (*de* to); ~**venir** [3s]: ~ *a* contravene, infringe; ~**ventana** *f* shutter.

contribución *f* contribution; (*carga*) tax; ~*es pl.* taxes, taxation; **contribuir** [3g] contribute (*a, para* to, towards; *a inf.* to *ger.*); **contribuyente** *m* contributor; *esp.* taxpayer.

contrición *f* contrition.

contrito contrite.

control *m* control; inspection, check(ing); ✝ (*cuenta*) audit; **controlador** *m* controller; ~ **aéreo** air traffic controller; **controlar** [1a] control; check; ✝ audit.

controversia *f* controversy; **controvertir** [3i] argue (*v/t.* over).

contumacia *f* obstinacy *etc.*; ⚖ contempt (of court); **contumaz** obstinate; wayward, perverse.

contusión *f* bruising, contusion.

convalecencia *f* convalescence; **convalecer** [2d] get better, convalesce (*de* after); **convaleciente** *adj. a. su m/f* convalescent.

convección *f* convection.

convencer [2b] convince (*de* of, *de que* that); **convencimiento** *m* (act of) convincing; conviction.

convención *f* convention; **convencional** conventional.

conveniencia *f* suitability *etc.*; (*conformidad*) agreement; conformity; **conveniente** (*apropiado*) suitable; fit(ting); proper, right; **convenio** *m* agreement; **convenir** [3s] agree (*con* with; *en* about, on; *en inf.* to *inf.*; *en que* that); ~ *a* suit, be suited to; **conviene a saber** namely; **~se** come to an agreement, agree.

convento *m* monastery; ~ (*de monjas*) convent, nunnery; **conventual** conventual.

convergencia *f* convergence; *fig.* concurrence; **converger** [2a], **convergir** [3c] converge (*en* on); *fig.* concur.

conversación *f* conversation, talk; **conversar** [1a] converse.

conversión *f* conversion; **converso** *m*, *a f* convert; **convertible** convertible; **convertir** [3i] convert; *ojos, armas, pensamientos* turn; **~se** *eccl.* be(come) converted.

convexidad *f* convexity; **convexo** convex.

convicción *f* conviction; **convicto** convicted, found guilty.

convidado *m*, *a f* guest; **convidar** [1a]: ~ *a* invite *s.o.* to; *bebida esp.* treat to, stand; **~se** volunteer.

convincente convincing.

convite *m* invitation; party, banquet.

convivencia *f* living together, life together; **convivir** [3a] live together; share the same life.

convocar [1g] summon; call.

convoy *m* ⚓ convoy; 🚂 train; F procession; **convoyar** [1a] escort.

convulsión *f* convulsion (*a. fig.*); **convulsionar** [1a] convulse.

conyugal married, conjugal; **cónyug(u)e** *m/f* spouse, partner; ~s *pl.* married couple, husband and wife.

coñac *m* brandy.

¡**coño**! (*enojo*) damn it all!; (*sorpresa*) well I'm damned!; (*injuria a p.*) idiot!

cooperar [1a] cooperate (*a* in); ~ *en* take part (together) in; **cooperativa** *f* cooperative; (*mutual*) association; **cooperativo** cooperative.

cooptar [1a] coopt.

coordinación *f* coordination; **coordinar** [1a] coordinate.

copa *f mst* glass; *poet.* goblet; *deportes*: cup (*a. fig. de dolor*); crown *de sombrero*; ♣ top; *naipes*: ~s *pl.* hearts.

copete *m anat.* tuft (of hair); forelock *de caballo; orn., geog.* crest; *de nieve etc.* aristocratic; important; **tener mucho** ~ be stuck-up.

copia *f* copy; abundance; ~ *al carbón* carbon copy; **copiadora** *f* duplicator; copying machine; **copiar** [1b] copy (*a. fig.*); *dictado* take down; **copioso** copious, plentiful; **copista** *m/f* copyist.

copita *f* (small) glass.

copla *f* verse; ♪ popular song, folksong; ~s *pl.* verse(s), poetry.

copo *m* ⊕ tuft; ~ *de nieve* snowflake.

coqueta 1. flirtatious; coquettish; 2. *f* flirt, coquette; **coquetear** [1a] flirt (*con* with); **coqueteo** *m*, **coquetería** *f* flirtatiousness, coquetry.

coraje *m* (*ira*) anger; (*ánimo*) (fighting) spirit.

coral¹ ♪ 1. choral; 2. *m* chorale.

coral² *m zo.* coral.

Corán *m* Koran; **coránico** Koranic.

coraza *f hist.* cuirass; ⚓ armorplate; *zo.* shell.

corazón *m* heart (*a. fig.*); *naipes:* ~es *pl.* hearts; *duro de* ~ hardhearted; *de* ~ *adv.* willingly; *de buen* ~ kindhearted; *de todo* ~ from the heart; **corazonada** *f* rash impulse; presentiment, hunch F

corbata *f* (neck)tie; ~ *de lazo* = **corbatín** *m* bowtie.

corchete *m* snap-fastener, clasp; *sew.* hook and eye; *typ.* bracket; ⚖ † constable.

corcho *m* cork; cork mat *para mesa; perca:* float; **corchoso** corky.

corcova *f* hunchback, hump; **corcovado** 1. hunchbacked; 2. *m*, *a f* hunchback; **corcovar** [1a] bend (over); **corcovear** [1a] buck, plunge.

cordel *m* cord, line; *a ~* in a straight line.

corderillo *m*, **corderina** *f* lambskin; **cordero** *m*, **a** *f* lamb (*a. fig.*); (*piel de*) ~ lambskin.

cordial 1. cordial; heartfelt; *pharm.* tonic; 2. *m* cordial; **cordialidad** *f* warmth, cordiality; frankness.

cordillera *f* (mountain) range.

cordobán *m* cordovan (leather); **cordobés** *adj. a. su. m*, **-a** *f* Cordovan.

cordón *m* cord (*a. anat.*); (shoe-)lace *de zapato*; ✚ flex; ✚ strand *de cabo*; cordon *de policía etc.* (*a.* ✕, △).

cordoncillo *m sew.* rib; milling, milled edge *de moneda*.

cordura *f* good sense, wisdom.

cornada *f* goring; **cornadura** *f*, **cornamenta** *f* horns; antlers.

córnea *f* cornea.

cornear [1a] gore, butt.

corneja *f* crow.

corneta 1. *f* bugle; ~ (*de llaves*) cornet; ~ (*de monte*) hunting horn; 2. *m* ✕ bugler; ♪ cornet player.

cornucopia *f* cornucopia; **cornudo** 1. horned; 2. *m* cuckold.

coro *m* ♪ (*pieza*), *thea., fig.* chorus; *ps., eccl.,* △ choir; *a ~* in a chorus.

corona *f* crown; *ast.* tonsure; *meteor.* halo; *eccl.* tonsure; ~ (*de flores*) chaplet; wreath; **coronación** *f* coronation; **coronar** [1a] crown (*con, de* with; *por rey acc.*); **coronario** coronary.

coronel *m* colonel.

coronilla *f* crown, top of the head; F *estar hasta la ~* be fed up.

corotos *m/pl.* belongings; utensils; implements.

corpa(n)chón *m* F, **corpazo** *m* F carcass.

corpiño *m* bodice.

corporación *f* corporation; association; **corporal** corporal, bodily; *higiene etc.* personal; **corporativo** corporate; **corpóreo** corporeal, bodily; **corpulento** stout; *esp. p.* burly; **Corpus** *m* Corpus Christi; **corpúsculo** *m* corpuscle.

corral *m* (farm)yard; ~ *de madera* timber-yard; F ~ *de vacas* slum; **corralillo** *m* playpen.

correa *f* (leather) strap; thong; *esp.* ⊕ belt; (*calidad*) leatheriness; ~ *sin fin* endless belt.

corrección *f* correction; (*castigo*) punishment; (*formalidad*) correctness; **correcto** correct (*a. fig.*); right; *fig.* polite; *facciones etc.* regular.

corredizo sliding; *nudo* running, slip *attr.*; *grúa* travelling; **corredor**, **-a** *f* runner; ✝ agent, broker; ~ *de bolsa* (stock-)broker; ~ *de casas* house agent.

corregidor *m hist.* chief magistrate; **corregir** [3c a. 3l] correct; put right; (*castigar*) punish, reprimand.

correlación *f* correlation; **correlacionar** [1a] correlate.

correligionario *m*, **a** *f* coreligionist.

correlón *S.Am. adj.* fast; swift; *Col., Mex.* cowardly.

correo *m* ⍣ post, mail (*a. ~s pl.*); (*p.*) courier; (*p.*) postman; (*tren*) ~ mail train; (*casa de*) ~s *pl.* post office; ~ *aéreo* airmail; ~ *diplomático* courier; ~ *urgente* special delivery.

correoso leathery, tough.

correr [2a] 1. *v/t. terreno* traverse, travel over; ✕ overrun; *caballo* race; *toros* fight; (*acosar*) chase, pursue; *cortina* draw (back); *vela* (un)furl; 2. *v/i.* run (*a. líquido, plazo, fig.*); (*líquido a.*) flow; (*surtidor*) play; (*viento*) blow; (*tiempo*) pass, elapse; (*moneda*) pass; *a todo ~* at full speed; 3. *~se* (*deslizarse*) slide (*por* along); (*derretirse*) melt; (*vela*) gutter; F get embarrassed; (*excederse*) go too far; **correría** *f* ✕ raid, foray; excursion.

correspondencia *f* correspondence (*a.* ⍣); communication(s); return *de afecto*; gratitude; **corresponder** [2a] correspond (*con* to), tally (*con* with); △ communicate; **~se** correspond (*a.* ⍣; *con* with); (*en afecto etc.*) agree; have regard for one another; **correspondiente** 1. *a.* ✕ corresponding; respective; 2. *m* correspondent; **corresponsal** *m* (newspaper) correspondent.

corretaje *m* brokerage; **corretear** [1a] gad about; (*jugando*) run around; **correve(i)dile** *m* F gossip.

corrida *f* run, dash; ~ *de toros* bullfight; *de* ~ fast; **corrido** *fig.* sheepish, abashed; *S.Am.* continuous; uninterrupted; *de* ~ fluently.

corriente 1. *agua etc.* running; *estilo* flowing, fluid; *mes etc.* present; *cuenta* current; *moneda* accepted, normal; common, ordinary, everyday; *procedimiento* normal, stand-

ard; **2.** *m* current month; *el 10 del ~
the 10th inst.; estar al ~ de be
informed about; **3.** *f* current (*a. fig.*,
⚡; alterna alternating, continua
direct), stream.

corrillo *m* knot of people, huddle; *fig.*
clique, coterie.

corrimiento *m* 🐾 discharge; ~ (de
tierras) landslide; *fig.* embarrassment, sheepishness.

corro *m* ring, circle (of people).

corroboración *f* corroboration *etc.*;
corroborar [1a] strengthen; *fig.*
corroborate.

corroer [2za] corrode (*a. fig.*); *geol.*
erode.

corromper [2a] corrupt (*a. fig.*);
madera rot; comida, placeres spoil;
juez bribe; mujer seduce.

corrosión *f* corrosion; *geol.* erosion;
corrosivo *adj. a. su. m* corrosive.

corrupción *f* corruption; corrupt-
ness; ✝, 🕱 *a.* graft; rotting *etc.*;
corrupto corrupt.

corso *adj. a. su. m, a f* Corsican.

corta...: ~bolsas *m* pickpocket;
~césped *m* lawn mower; **~circuitos**
m circuit-breaker.

cortada *f* S.Am. gash; cut; **cortador
1.** cutting; **2.** *m*, **-a** *f* cutter (*a.* ⊕);
cortadura *f* cut; (*acto*) cutting (*a. de
periódico*); *geog.* pass; **cortalápices**
m pencil sharpener.

cortaplumas *m* penknife.

cortar [1a] **1.** *v/t.* cut (*a.* ♠, naipes);
(*recortar, suprimir*) cut out; (*amputar*) cut off; carne carve; árbol etc. cut
down; enemigo, provisión, región cut
off; **2.** *v/i.* cut (*a.* naipes); (*frío etc.*) be
biting; **3.** **~se** (*manos*) get chapped;
(*leche*) turn (sour); (*p.*) get embarrassed, get tongue-tied.

cortauñas *m* nail clipper.

corte[1] *m* cut; (*acto*) cutting; (*filo*)
edge; (*tela*) piece, length; *S.Am.*
harvest; 🔺, ♠ (cross) section; *⚡*
failure, cut.

corte[2] *f* court (*a. S.Am.* 🕱); (*patio*)
court(yard); (*corral*) yard; (*ciudad*)
capital (city); la ♀ freq. Madrid; ~s *pl.*
Spanish parliament.

cortedad *f* shortness *etc.*; *fig.* bashfulness; backwardness *etc.*

cortejar [1a] attend; mujer, poderoso
court; **cortejo** *m* courting; (*séquito*)
entourage.

cortés polite, courteous; amor
courtly; **cortesana** *f* courtesan; cor-
tesano 1. of the court; = cortés; **2.** *m*

courtier; **cortesía** *f* politeness; courtesy; title.

corteza *f* bark de árbol; peel, skin,
rind de fruta; crust de pan.

cortijo *m* farm(house).

cortina *f* curtain; ~ de hierro *fig.* iron
curtain.

corto short; brief; slight; (*escaso*)
scant(y), deficient; (*defectuoso*)
defective; *fig.* (*tímido*) bashful, shy;
~circuito *m* short circuit.

coruñés *adj. a. su. m,* **-a** *f* (native) of
Corunna.

corvadura *f* curve (*a.* 🔺), bend;
curvature; **corvo** curved, arched.

cosa *f* thing; (*algo*) something; (*no ...
~*) nothing; ~ de about, a matter of; es
~ de 2 horas it takes about 2 hours; *¡~s
pl. de España! contp.* what can you
expect in Spain?; otra ~ something
else; poca ~ nothing much; como si tal
~ as if nothing had happened; es poca
~, no es gran ~ it isn't up to much.

coscorrón *m* bump on the head.

cosecha *f* crop, harvest (*a. fig.*); (*acto*)
harvesting; (*época*) harvest time; de ~
propia ♀ home-grown; **cosechar** [1a]
harvest, gather (in); *esp. fig.* reap.

coseno *m* cosine.

coser [2a] sew (up, on); stitch (up; *a.*
⚡); *fig.* join closely (con to); **~se** can
become attached to; **cosido** *m*
sewing.

cosmético *adj. a. su. m* cosmetic.

cósmico cosmic; **cosmonauta** *m*
cosmonaut; **cosmonave** *f* spaceship; **cosmopolita** *adj. a. su. m/f*
cosmopolitan.

cosquillar [1a] tickle; **cosquillas**
f/pl. tickling (sensation); tener ~ be
ticklish; tener malas ~ be touchy;
cosquillear [1a] tickle; **cosquilleo**
m tickling (sensation); **cosquilloso**
ticklish; *fig.* touchy.

costa[1] *f* ✝ cost, price; ~s *pl.* 🕱 costs; a
toda ~ at any price.

costa[2] *f* ♣ coast; coastline, (sea-)
shore; **costado** *m* anat., ♣ side; ✕
flank; **costal** *m* sack, bag; F ~ de
huesos bag of bones.

costar [1m] cost (*a. fig.*); *fig.* cost
dear(ly); cuesta caro it costs a lot.

costarricense *adj. a. su. m/f,* **costa-
rriqueño** *adj. a. su. m,* **a f** Costa
Rican.

coste *m* cost, price; ~-beneficio *adj.*
cost-benefit; **costear**[1] [1a] pay for,
defray the cost of.

costear[2] [1a] ♣ (sail along the) coast.

costero coastal; coasting.
costilla f rib; ~s pl. F back.
costo m cost; ~ de la vida cost of living; **costoso** costly, expensive.
costra f crust; ✄ scab; **costroso** crusty, incrusted; ✄ scabby.
costumbre f custom, habit; ~s pl. customs, ways; (moralidad) morals; de ~ usual(ly); como de ~ as usual.
costura f sewing, needlework, dressmaking; (unión) seam; alta ~ fashiondesigning; **costur(e)ar** [1a] C.Am., Mex. sew; **costurera** f dressmaker, seamstress.
cotejar [1a] compare, collate; **cotejo** m comparison, collation.
cotidiano daily, everyday.
cotización f quotation, price en bolsa; quota; dues de asociación; **cotizar** [1f] quote (en at); cuota fix.
coto m ✔ enclosed pasture; preserve de caza; (mojón) boundary post; poner ~ a put a stop to.
cotorra f parrot; (urraca) magpie; **cotorrear** [1a] chatter (away); **cotorreo** m chatter, gabble.
coyuntura f anat. joint; fig. juncture, occasion; opportunity.
coz f kick (a. ✗); (culata) butt; F insult; dar coces, dar coces a kick.
crac m ✝ crash; ¡~! snap!, crack!
cráneo m skull, cranium Ⓜ.
crápula f drunkenness; fig. dissipation; **crapuloso** drunken; fig. dissipated.
crasitud f fatness; **craso** p. fat; líquido thick, greasy; fig. gross, crass.
cráter m crater.
creación f creation; **crear** [1a] create, make; idea etc. originate; found, establish.
crecer [2d] mst grow (a. fig.; en in); increase; (luna) wax; (precio, río) rise; ~se assume greater authority (or importance); **creces** f/pl. increase; **crecida** f spate, flood; **creciente** 1. growing, increasing; ast. cuarto ~ crescent (moon); 2. m crescent; 3. f ♁ ~ (del mar) high tide; ast. crescent moon; **crecimiento** m growth, increase; ♀ rise in value; ~ cero zero growth.
credenciales f/pl. credentials; **crédito** m mst credit; authority, standing; (creencia) belief; a ~ on credit.
credo m creed; F en menos que se canta un ~ in a jiffy; **credulidad** f credulity, gullibility; **crédulo** credulous, gullible; **creencia** f belief;

creer [2e] believe (en in; que that); think (que that); ¡ya lo creo! you bet (your life)!, rather!; ~se believe o.s. (to be); **creíble** believable, credible; **creído** credulous; S.Am. gullible.
crema f (nata) cream (a. fig.); (natillas) custard, cream; (cosmético) cold cream; ~ dental (or dentífrica) toothpaste.
cremación f cremation. [~ zipper.)
cremallera f ⊕ rack; (cierre de))
crencha f parting; part.
crepitar [1a] (leña etc.) crackle; (tocino) sizzle; crepitate (a. ✄).
crepuscular twilight; luz ~ = **crepúsculo** m twilight, dusk.
crespo curly; estilo involved; p. cross; **crespón** m crape.
cresta f crest.
creta f chalk; **cretáceo** cretaceous.
cretino m cretin (a. fig.).
cretona f cretonne.
creyente m/f believer.
creyón m crayon.
cría f keeping, breeding etc.; (pequeño) young child or animal; (conjunto) litter, young, brood; **criada** f maid, servant; **criadero** m ♀ nursery; zo. breedingground; ✗ vein; **criado** 1.: bien ~ well-bred, well brought up; mal ~ ill-bred; 2. m servant; **criador** m breeder; **crianza** f raising, rearing; **criar** [1c] ganado etc. keep, breed, raise; (educar) bring up; (cebar) fatten; ~se ♀ etc. grow; **criatura** f creature (a. fig.); (nene) infant, baby.
criba f sieve, screen; **cribar** [1a] sift, sieve, screen.
crimen m crime; **criminal** adj. a. su. m/f criminal; **criminología** f criminology.
crin f mane (a. ~s pl.); horsehair.
criollo adj. a. su. m, a f Creole.
cripta f crypt.
crisis f crisis; ~ nerviosa nervous breakdown; ~ energética energy crisis.
crisol m crucible; fig. melting pot.
crispar [1a] make s.t. twitch; ~se twitch.
cristal m glass, crystal (a. phys., poet.); (hoja) pane (of glass); (espejo) mirror; de ~ glass attr.; ~ tallado cut glass; **cristalería** f (arte) glasswork; (fábrica) glass works; (objetos) glassware; **cristalino** phys. crystalline; agua limpid; **cristalizar(se)** [1f] crystallize.

cristiandad f Christendom; **cristianismo** m Christianity; **cristianizar** [1f] Christianize; **cristiano 1.** *adj. a. su. m,* **a** f Christian; **2.** m good soul; F (p.) (living) soul; (*idioma*) Spanish; **cristo** m crucifix.

criterio m criterion; yardstick; (*juicio*) judgement.

crítica f criticism; (*reseña*) review; **criticador 1.** critical; **2.** m, **-a** f critic; **criticar** [1g] criticize; **crítico 1.** critical; **2.** m critic; **criticón 1.** faultfinding, (over)critical; **2.** m, **-a** f faultfinder, critic.

croar [1a] croak.

croata *adj. a. su. m/f* Croat(ian).

croché m crochet (work).

cromo m chromium; *paint.* transfer; F color reproduction.

crónica f chronicle; account; (*periódico*) newspaper; (*artículo*) report; **crónico** chronic; *vicio* ingrained; **cronista** m/f chronicler; (*periodista*) reporter, feature-writer; **cronología** f chronology; **cronológico** chronological; **cronómetro** m chronometer; *deportes etc.:* stop-watch.

croqueta f croquette, rissole *approx.*

croquis m sketch.

cruce m crossing; *₳ etc.* intersection; ~ *de caminos* cross-roads; **crucero** m ⚓ (*barco*) cruiser; ⚓ (*viaje*) cruise; crossing (a. ⛪); **cruceta** f crosspiece; **crucificar** [1g] crucify; *fig.* mortify; **crucifijo** m crucifix; **crucigrama** m crossword.

crudeza f rawness *etc.*; *con* ~ *hablar* harshly, roughly; **crudo** *comida, seda, tiempo etc.* raw; (*áspero*) rough; *agua, verdad* hard; *legumbres etc.* green, uncooked.

cruel cruel; **crueldad** f cruelty.

crujido m rustle *etc.*; **crujir** [3a] (*hojas, papel, seda*) rustle; (*madera*) creak; (*hueso*) crack; (*dientes*) gnash, grind.

crustáceo m crustacean.

cruz f cross (a. *fig.*); tails *de moneda*; crown *de ancla*; ⚕ Roja Red Cross; *¡~ y raya!* that's quite enough!; *hacerse cruces* cross o.s.; *fig.* show one's surprise; **cruza** f *S.Am.* intersection; crossbreeding; **cruzada** f crusade; **cruzado 1.** crossed; *chaqueta* double-breasted; *zo.* hybrid; **2.** m *hist.* crusader; **cruzar** [1f] *mst* cross; *palabras* have, exchange; **~se** pass each other.

cuaco m *S.Am.* horse.

cuaderna f ⚓ timber; ⚓ frame; **cuaderno** m notebook; (*folleto*) folder; log-book.

cuadra f 🐎 stable; *⚔* ward; (*sala*) hall; ⚔ hut; *S.Am.* ⌂ block; **cuadrado 1.** square (a. ₳); *tela* checkered; **2.** m square (*regla*) ruler; ⊕ die; *sew.* gusset; *typ.* quadrat; **cuadragésimo** fortieth; **cuadrante** m ₳, ⚓ quadrant; *radio etc.:* dial; **cuadrar** [1a] *v/t.* square (a. ₳); (*agradar*) please; (*convenir*) suit; *v/i.* ~ *con* square with, tally with; *~se* ✕ stand to attention; **cuadricular** squared; **cuadrilátero** *adj. a. su. m* quadrilateral; *boxeo:* ring.

cuadrilla f party, gang; *esp.* ✕ squad; group; *toros:* matador's team; **cuadrillero** m chief, leader.

cuadro m square (a. ₳); (*tabla*) table, chart; *⚡ etc.* panel; *paint.* picture (a. *televisión*), painting; (*marco, bastidor*) frame; *pane de vidrio*; *thea.* scene; *lit.* (vivid) picture; ~ *de mando mot.* dashboard; *2 metros en* ~ *2* metres square; **cuadrúpedo** *adj. a. su. m* quadruped; **cuádruple** quadruple.

cuajada f curd; (*requesón*) cream cheese; **cuajar** [1a] *leche* curdle; *sangre etc.* coagulate, congeal; *Mex.* tell a lie; *v/i.* ✝ (*proyecto*) take shape; (*tener éxito*) come off; *~se* curdle *etc.*; set; *fig.* sleep soundly; F ~ *de* fill with; **cuajarón** m clot.

cual 1. *adj.* (such) as, of the kind (that); **2.** *pron. el* ~ *etc.* ~ which; (*p.*) who; *lo* ~ (a fact) which; **3.** *prp.* ~ *su.* like; ~ *verb* (just) as; ~ ... *tal su.:* like ... like; *verb:* just as ... so; **4.** *cj.:* ~ *si* as if.

cuál which (one)?; ~(*es*) ... ~(*es*) some ... some.

cualidad f quality, characteristic; *phls. etc.* property.

cualquier(a), *pl.* **cualesquier(a) 1.** *adj.* any (... you like); ~ *que* whichever, whatever; **2.** *pron.* anyone; ~ *que* (*cosa*) whichever; (*p.*) whoever; *un* ~ a nobody.

cuando *cj.* when; (*aunque*) (even) if, although; (*puesto que*) since; *quiera* whenever; *de* ~ *en* ~ from time to time.

cuándo when?; ~ ... ~ sometimes ... sometimes; *¿de* ~ *acá?* how come?

cuantía f quantity; importance; **cuantioso** large, substantial; numerous; **cuantitativo** quantitative.

cuanto 1. *adj.* all that, as much as, whatever; ~s *pl.* all that; *unos* ~s a few, some; **2.** *pron.* all that (which), as much as; ~s *pl.* all those that, as many as; **3.** *adv.* a. *cj.*: en~ inasmuch as; *tiempo*: as soon as, directly; (en)~ *d* as for, with regard to.

cuánto how much?; ~s *pl.* how many?; ~ (*tiempo*) how long?; *¿a* ~s *estamos?* what is the date?

cuarenta forty; **cuarentena** *f* (about) forty; $\mathscr{F}$ quarantine.

cuaresma *f* Lent; **cuaresmal** Lenten.

cuarta *f* $\mathcal{A}$ quarter, fourth; $\mathbf{\Phi}$ point; span *de mano*; **cuartear** [1a] quarter; (*descuartizar*) cut up; *brújula* box; ~se crack, split.

cuartel *m* χ barracks; *heráldica:* quarter; $\mathbf{\Phi}$ bed; ~es *pl.* χ quarters; *general* headquarters; **cuartelazo** *m* *S.Am.* (military) takeover; putsch; **cuarteto** *m* $\mathbf{\Phi}$ quartet; *poet.* quatrain; **cuartilla** *f* (*hoja*) sheet; *anat.* pastern.

cuarto 1. fourth; **2.** *m* $\mathcal{A}$, *ast.* quarter; $\mathbf{\Phi}$ room; *joint de carne*; *las* 2 *y* ~ a quarter past 2; *las* 2 *menos* ~ a quarter to 2; F *no tener un* ~ not have a cent.

cuarzo *m* quartz.

cuatro four (*a. su.*); (*fecha*) fourth; *las* ~ four o'clock; *Mex.* deceit; swindle; **cuatrocientos** four hundred.

cuba *f* cask, barrel; (*abierta*) vat; F boozer.

cubano *adj. a. su. m*, **a** *f* Cuban.

cubertería *f* silverware; cutlery.

cubeta *f* keg; (*cubo*) pail; *phot.* tray.

cúbico cubic(al); *raíz* cube *attr.*; **cubículo** *m* cubicle.

cubierta *f* cover(ing); $\oplus$ casing; $\mathbf{\Phi}$ deck; (*sobre*) envelope; cover, jacket *de libro*; **cubierto 1.** *p.p.* of *cubrir*; **2.** *m* $\mathcal{A}$ roof; place *en mesa*; (*juego*) knife fork and spoon; *precio de* ~ cover charge; *ponerse a* ~ take cover, shelter (*de from*).

cubismo *m* cubism; **cubista** *m* cubist.

cubo *m* bucket, pail; tub; $\oplus$ drum; hub *de rueda*; $\mathcal{A}$ cube.

cubrecama *m* coverlet.

cubrir [3a; *p.p. cubierto*] *mst* cover (up, over; *con*, de with); $\mathcal{A}$ roof; *deuda* repay; *fuego* bank up; ~se (*con sombrero*) put on one's hat.

cucaracha *f* cockroach.

cuchara *f* spoon; scoop (*a.* $\mathbf{\Phi}$); $\oplus$ ladle; **cucharada** *f* spoonful; meter

su ~ butt in *en conversación*; meddle *en asunto*; **cucharilla** *f*, **cucharita** *f* small spoon, teaspoon; **cucharón** *m* ladle.

cuchichear [1a] whisper; **cuchicheo** *m* whispering.

cuchilla *f* (large) knife; chopper *de carnicero*; **cuchillada** *f* (*golpe*) slash; (*herida*) gash; ~s *pl.* sew. slash, slit; *fig.* fight; **cuchillería** *f* cutlery; $\dagger$ cutler's (shop); **cuchillero** *m* cutler; **cuchillo** *m* knife; $\mathbf{\Delta}$ upright.

cuchitril *m* den, hole; $\mathbf{\Delta}$ hovel.

cuclillas: *sentarse en* ~ squat, sit on one's heels.

cuclillo *m* cuckoo; F cuckold.

cuco 1. (*bonito*) pretty, cute; *situación* fine; (*taimado*) crafty; **2.** *m* orn. cuckoo; F gambler; *hacer* ~ *a* poke fun at.

cucurucho *m* (paper) cone, cornet; (*sombrero*) horn, hennin.

cuelga *f* $\mathbf{\Phi}$ bunch; ~**capas** *m* coat hanger; (*mueble*) hall stand.

cuello *m* neck; collar *de camisa*.

cuenca *f* wooden bowl; *anat.* (eye-) socket; *geog.* basin, catchment area *de río*; **cuenco** *m* saucer, shallow basin; *fig.* hollow.

cuenta *f* $\mathcal{A}$ calculation, count(ing), reckoning; $\dagger$ account, bill; ~ (*de banco*) bank-account; (*registro*) check, tally; (*exposición, narración*) account; bead *de rosario*; ~ *atrás* countdown; *por su propia* ~ on one's own account, for o.s.; *abonar en* ~ *a* credit to (*s.o.'s account*); *ajustar* ~s settle up (*con* with); *dar* ~ *de* (*narrar*) give an account of; (*explicar*) account for; F finish off; *dar buena* ~ *de* sí give a good account of o.s.; *darse* ~ (*de*) realize; *sin darse* ~ without noticing; *pedir* ~s *a* bring to account; *perder la* ~ lose count; *tener en* ~ bear in mind, take into account; *¡vamos a* ~s! let's get down to business!

cuentakilómetros *m approx.* milometer; speedometer.

cuentista *m/f* story-teller (*a. b.s.*); *lit.* short story writer.

cuento *m* story, tale (*a. b.s.*); *lit.* (short) story; F trouble; ~ *de hadas* fairy tale; ~ *de viejas* old wives' tale; *sin* ~ countless; *dejarse de* ~s come to the point.

cuerda *f* rope (*delgado*) string (*a.* $\mathfrak{J}$), cord (*a. anat.*); $\mathcal{A}$, *anat.*, *poet.* chord; *anat.* tendon; spring *de reloj*; ~ *floja* tight-rope; ~ *de plomada* plumbline;

cuerdo

~ *salvavidas* lifeline; *estar en su* ~ be in one's element; *dar* ~ *a reloj* wind (up).

cuerdo sensible; sane.

cuerno *m* mst horn; antler *de ciervo*; ~ *de la abundancia* horn of plenty; *poner en los* ~s place in danger; *poner los* ~s *a* cuckold.

cuero *m* leather; *zo.* skin, hide; pelt *de conejo, zorro*; *(odre)* wineskin; *en* ~s stark naked.

cuerpo *m* mst body (*a.* **A̦**, *ast.*); *(talle)* build, figure; *(grueso)* bulk; **🝐** substance; *sew.* bodice; *(libro)* volume; **△** wing, part; **✕**, *baile, diplomática*: corps; *(personal)* force, brigade; corporation; ~ *de bomberos* fire-brigade; ~ *de sanidad* medical corps; ~ *a* ~ hand to hand; *a* ~, *en* ~ without a coat.

cuervo *m* raven.

cuesta *f* slope; hill *en carretera*; ~ *abajo* downhill; ~ *arriba* uphill; *a* ~s on one's back; *echar etc. a* ~s take on one's shoulders.

cuestión *f* matter, question, issue; *b.s.* quarrel, dispute; **A̦** problem; ~ *candente, ~ palpitante* burning question; **cuestionar** [1a] question, argue about; place in doubt; **cuestionario** *m* questionnaire; question paper *en examen*.

cueva *f* cave; cellar *de casa*.

cuidado *m* *(esmero)* care; *(aprensión)* worry, concern; *(negocio)* concern, affair; *¡*~*!* look out!; mind!; *(en paquete)* with care; *¡*~ *con* ...*!* careful with ...!; beware of ...!; *¡*~ *con inf.!* be careful to *inf.*; *al* ~ *de* care of; *¡no hay* ~*!, ¡pierda Vd.* ~*!* don't worry!; *poner* ~ *en inf.* take great care in *ger.*; *tener* ~ take care; be careful (*con* of); **cuidadora** *f* *Mex.* nursemaid; **cuidadoso** careful; mindful (*de* of); solicitous (*de* for); concerned, anxious (*de, por resultado etc.* about).

cuidar [1a] *v/t.* take care of, look after (*a.* **⚘⚘**); see to; *v/i.* ~ *de* look after; *obligación* attend to; ~ *de que* see (to it) that; *~se* **⚘⚘** look after *o.s.*

cuita *f* worry, affliction; **cuitado** worried; timid.

culata *f* *zo.* haunch; butt *de fusil*; breech *de cañón*; head *de cilindro*; **culatazo** *m* kick, recoil.

culebra *f* snake; ~ *de cascabel* rattlesnake; **culebrear** [1a] wriggle (along).

culinario culinary.

culminación *f* culmination; **culmi-** **nante** highest, top(most); *fig.* outstanding; **culminar** [1a] culminate, reach its highest point.

culo *m* seat; behind; anus; bottom.

culpa *f* fault, blame; esp. **⚖⚖** guilt; *echar la* ~ *a* blame (*de* for); *tener la* ~ be to blame (*de* for); **culpabilidad** *f* guilt; **culpable 1.** *p.* to blame, at fault; esp. **⚖⚖** guilty; *acto* to be condemned, **⚖⚖** culpable; **2.** *m/f* culprit; esp. **⚖⚖** offender, guilty party; **culpado 1.** guilty; **2.** *m*, *a f* culprit; **⚖⚖** accused; **culpar** [1a] blame; condemn; ~ *de* accuse *s.o.* of being.

cultivadora *f* **⊕** cultivator; **cultivador** *m*, **-a** *f* farmer, cultivator; grower; **cultivar** [1a] cultivate (*a. fig.*); *tierras a.* work, till; **cultivo** *m* cultivation; *(plantas)* crop; *biol.* culture; **culto 1.** cultured, refined; *gr.* learned; **2.** *m* worship; cult (*a* of); *rendir* ~ *a* worship; *fig.* pay homage to; **cultura** *f* culture; education.

cumbre *f* summit, top; *fig.* summit; *conferencia en la* ~ summit meeting.

cumpa *m* *S.Am.* pal; buddy; comrade.

cumpleaños *m* birthday; **cumplido 1.** full, complete; *p.* courteous; **2.** *m* courtesy; ~s *pl.* compliments; *de* ~ *attr.* formal; *por* ~ as a compliment.

cumplimentar [1a] congratulate; *(visitar)* pay one's respects to; **⚖⚖** carry out; **cumplimiento** *m* *(acto)* fulfilment *etc.*; *(cumplido)* compliment; courtesy; *de* ~ *attr.* courtesy *attr.*

cumplir [3a] *v/t.* *amenaza, deber, promesa* carry out, fulfil; *deseo* realize; *acto* perform; *años* reach; *condena* serve; *hoy cumplo 6 años* I'm 6 (years old) today; *v/i.* *(plazo etc.)* expire; **✕** finish one's service; *~se* be fulfilled *etc.*; *(plazo)* expire.

cumulativo cumulative; **cúmulo** *m* heap; *fig.* lot; *meteor.* cumulus.

cuna *f* cradle (*a.* **⚓**, *fig.*); *(asilo)* home; *fig.* family; birth.

cundir [3a] spread (*a. fig.*); *(arroz)* swell; *fig.* multiply.

cuneiforme cuneiform.

cuña *f* wedge; chock *de rueda*.

cuñada *f* sister-in-law; **cuñado** *m* brother-in-law.

cuño *m* (die-)stamp; *fig.* stamp.

cuota *f* quota; share; tuition; fare; ~ *(de socio)* membership fee.

cupo *m* quota; share.

cupón m coupon; ~ de racimiento ration(ing) coupon.

cúpula f dome, cupola.

cura¹ m: ~ (párroco) parish priest; (en general) priest.

cura² f (acto) healing; cure; (método) cure, treatment; ~ de reposo rest-cure; first-aid; **curandero** m quack; **curar** [1a] v/t. enfermedad, p., carne cure (de of); llaga heal (a. fig.); (tratar) treat; piel tan; v/i.: ~ de look after; palabras etc. take notice of; **~se** recover (de from), get better.

curiosear [1a] v/t. (mirar) glance at, look over; (husmear) nose out; v/i. poke about, nose around; b.s. snoop; **curiosidad** f curiosity; b.s. inquisitiveness; (objeto) curio; **curioso 1.** curious; b.s. inquisitive; (aseado) neat, clean; (esmerado) careful; **2.** m, a f bystander, onlooker; b.s. busybody; S.Am. quack doctor.

curro prov. smart; b.s. showy; **currutaco** F **1.** swell, showy; **2.** m dude; sport.

cursado experienced, skilled; **cursar** [1a] lugar frequent; asignatura take; solicitud facilitate, dispatch.

cursear [1a] S.Am. have diarrhea.

cursi (de mal gusto) in bad taste, vulgar; pretentious; affected; (llamativo) loud, flashy; (deseadeo) shabby-genteel, dowdy; **cursilería** f vulgarity; pretentiousness etc.

cursivo cursive.

curso m course; univ. (ps., año) year; ~ de urgencia emergency treatment; moneda de ~ legal legal tender.

curtido 1. piel leathery; tez tanned, weather-beaten; estar ~ en be skilled in; **2.** m tanning; ~s pl. tanned hides; **curtidor** m tanner; **curtiduría** f tannery; **curtir** [3a] tan (a. fig.); (acostumbrar) inure, harden.

curva f curve; mot. etc. a. bend; ~ de nivel contour line; **curvatura** f curvature; **curvo** curved.

cúspide f geog. peak; A apex.

custodia f care, safe keeping; ✝ custody; (p.) guard; eccl. monstrance; **custodiar** [1b] keep; (vigilar) guard, watch over; **custodio** m guard(ian), keeper; caretaker.

cususa f C.Am. rum.

cutáneo cutaneous.

cúter m cutter.

cutícula f cuticle.

cutis m skin, complexion.

cuyo whose; en ~ caso in which case.

¡cuz, cuz! here boy! (dog).

D

dable possible, feasible.

¡daca! hand it over!

dactilografía f typing; **dactilógrafo** m, a f typist.

dadaísmo m Dadaism.

dádiva f gift, present; **dadivoso** generous, open-handed.

dado¹ m die; ~s pl. dice.

dado² p.p. of dar; ~ a given to; ~ que given that; granted that; **dador** m, -a f giver, donor.

daga f dagger.

dalia f dahlia.

dama f lady; (noble) lady, gentlewoman; (querida) mistress; juego de damas: king; (juego de) ~s pl. draughts; primera ~ thea. leading lady.

damajuana f demijohn.

damasco m damask; **damasquinado** ⊕ damask.

damero m checkerboard.

danés 1. adj. Danish; **2.** m, -a f Dane; **3.** m (idioma) Danish.

danza f dance; (arte) dancing; F (negocio) shady business; F (jaleo) row, rumpus; ~ de figuras square dance; **danzante** m, a f dancer; F (activo) hustler, person who is always on the go; **danzar** [1f] dance (a. fig.); **danzarín** m, -a f dancer; F = danzante F; **danzón** m danzón (Cuban dance).

dañar [1a] hurt, harm, damage; (echar a perder) spoil; **~se** get damaged; spoil; ✝ hurt o.s.; **dañino** harmful, destructive; **daño** m damage; hurt, harm, injury; ✝ loss; S.Am. witchcraft; ✝ ~s pl. y perjuicios damages; **dañoso** harmful, bad, injurious.

dar [1r] **1.** v/t. mst give; (pasar) pass, hand; permiso etc. grant, concede; fig. lend, give; batalla fight; hora strike; paseo, paso take; tema para discusión propose; ir dando cuerda pay out; ¡dale! boxeo etc.: hit him!; deportes: get on with it!; **2.:** lo mismo da it makes no odds; lo mismo me da it's all the same to me; ¿qué más da? what does it matter?; never mind!; **3.** v/i. con prp. (para muchas frases, v. el correspondiente su. o verbo): ~ a (ventana) look on to, overlook; (casa) face (towards); ~ con p. meet, run into; idea, solución etc. hit (up)on, strike; dio con la cabeza contra un árbol he hit his head against a tree; **4.** ~se (entregarse) give s.o. up; (producirse, existir) occur, be found; no se le da nada he doesn't give a damn; ~ a devote o.s. to.

dardo m dart, shaft.

dares y tomares m/pl. F arguments, bickerings; andar en ~ con argue with.

dársena f ⚓ dock.

Darvinismo m Darwinism.

data f date; ✝ item; **datar** [1a] date (de from).

dátil m ⚕ date; **datilera** f date (-palm).

dato m fact, piece of information, datum; ~s pl. data, facts, information.

de a) posesión, pertenencia: of; tras sup.: el mejor del mundo the best in the world; b) materia: una moneda de plata a silver coin, a coin of silver; tras verbo: amueblado de nogal furnished in walnut; acerca de: of, about, concerning; c) partitivo: uno de ellos one of them; ⅄ de cada 7,6 6 out of (every) 7; d) comp.: más de 20 more than 20; e) origen, procedencia: from; de A a B from A to B; f) que va a: el camino de Madrid the road to Madrid, the Madrid road; g) tiempo: a las 6 de la mañana at 6 in the morning; de día by day; edad: un niño de 8 años an 8-year old boy, a boy of 8; cuando: de niño as a child; h) causal: de miedo for fear; de puro cansado out of sheer tiredness; i) en cuanto a: mejor de salud better in health; j) aposición: la ciudad de Roma the city of Rome; el pobre de Juan poor (old) John; k) agente de pasivo: amado de todos beloved of all lit., loved by all; l) condicional: de serle a Vd. posible if you can; de no ser así if it were not so.

debajo (a. por ~) underneath, below; ~ de under(neath), below.

debate m debate, discussion; **debatir** [3a] v/t. debate, discuss.

debe m debit (side).

deber 1. [2a] v/t. owe; v/i.: ~ inf. must inf., have to inf.; debería inf., debiera inf. ought to inf., should inf.; no debe

(de) ser muy difícil it can't be very difficult; ~se a be owing to, be due to, be on account of; **2.** m duty, obligation; ✝ debt; ~es pl. escuela: homework; **debido** due, right, just; como es ~ as is only right, as is proper; ~ a owing to, due to, through.

débil mst weak; feeble; salud a. poor; esfuerzo a. half-hearted; luz dim; grito etc. a. faint; **debilidad** f weakness etc.; esp. ✿ debility; **debilitar** [1a] weaken, debilitate (esp. ✿); resistencia etc. impair, lower; ~se get weak(er).

debutante m/f debutant(e); beginner; **debutar** [1a] make one's début.

década f decade.

decadencia f decadence, decline; **decaer** [2o] decay, decline; flag; ~ de ánimo lose heart.

decaimiento m decay; weakness.

decano m univ. etc. dean; (más antiguo) doyen.

decantar praise, laud.

decapitar [1a] behead, decapitate.

decena f (about) ten.

decencia f decency etc.

decenio m decade.

decente decent, seemly, proper; (limpio) clean; modest.

decepción f disappointment; (engaño) deception; **decepcionar** [1a] disappoint.

decidido determined, decided; **decidir** [3a] decide (inf. to inf.); cuestión settle, decide; ~se decide, make up one's mind (a inf. to inf.).

décima f tenth; eccl. tithe; poet. a 10-line stanza; **decimal 1.** adj. a. su. m decimal; **2.** f: ~ periódica pura recurring decimal; **décimo 1.** tenth; **2.** m tenth; (tenth part of a) lottery ticket.

decir 1. [3p] say; tell; verdad speak, tell; misa say; (texto) say, read; (llamar) call; ~ para (or entre) sí say to o.s.; ~ que sí say yes; es ~ that is (to say); por mejor ~ or rather; por ~ lo así so to speak; querer ~ mean (con by); ¡digo, digo! just listen to this!; now wait a minute!; como quien dice, como si dijéramos so to speak, in a manner of speaking; el qué dirán what people (will) say; ¡diga(me)! teleph. hullo!; diga lo que diga whatever he says; mejor dicho rather; ~se: se dice it is said, they say; (cuento) the story goes; se me ha dicho que I have been told that; **2.** m saying.

decisión f decision; (*ánimo*) determination; *forzar una* ~ force the issue; **decisivo** decisive; *consideración* overriding; *voto* casting.

declamación f declamation; recitation; **declamar** [1a] v/t. declaim; recite; v/i. hold forth, speak out (*contra* against); *b.s.* rant.

declaración f declaration; pronouncement, statement; ⚖ evidence; *naipes:* bid; ~ *de derechos* bill of rights; ~ *de renta* tax-return; **declarar** [1a] declare; pronounce, state; profess; ⚖ (*testigo*) testify, give evidence; **~se** declare o.s.

declinación f decline, falling-off; *ast.*, ⚓ declination; *gr.* declension; **declinar** [1a] v/t. decline; refuse; ⚖ reject; *gr.* decline; inflect; v/i. decline, fall off; degenerate.

declive m slope, incline, declivity.

decoración f decoration; ~ *de interiores* interior decoration; *thea.* (*a.* ~*es pl.*) = **decorado** m *thea.* scenery, set; **decorar**¹ [1a] decorate, adorn; **decorativo** decorative, ornamental.

decoro m decorum, propriety; proprieties; **decoroso** decorous, proper, seemly.

decrecer [2d] decrease. [crepitude.]

decrépito decrepit; **decrepitud** f decrepitude.

decretar [1a] decree, ordain; *premio* award, adjudge; **decreto** m decree; *parl.* act.

dedada f thimbleful; pinch *de rapé etc.*; spot; **dedal** m thimble.

dedicación f dedication (*a* to); diligence; *fig.* devotion (*a* to); **dedicar** [1g] dedicate; *eccl. a.* consecrate; *libro* dedicate, *ejemplar* inscribe; **~se** *a* devote o.s. to; *trabajo a.* be engaged in; **dedicatoria** f inscription, dedication; **dedicatorio** dedicatory.

dedo m finger; ~ (*del pie*) toe; F spot, bit; ~ *anular* ring finger; ~ *auricular*, ~ *meñique* little finger; ~ *del corazón*, ~ *cordial* middle finger; ~ *índice* forefinger, index finger; ~ *pulgar* thumb; (*del pie*) big toe; *a dos* ~*s de* within an inch (*or* ace) of; *no mamarse el* ~ *be pretty smart.

deducción f deduction; **deducir** [3o] deduce (*de, por* from); infer.

defección f defection, desertion; **defectivo** defective (*a. gr.*); **defecto** m defect, flaw; ⊕, ⚡ fault; (*esp. moral*) shortcoming, failure; **defectuoso** defective, faulty, unsound.

defender [2g] defend (*a.* ⚖; *contra* against, de from); protect (*contra, de frío etc.* against, from); *causa* champion, uphold; **~se** defend o.s.; **defensa 1.** f defense (*a.* ⚖, *deportes*); shelter, protection; **2.** m *deportes:* back; **defensiva** f defensive; *estar a la* ~ be on the defensive; **defensivo** defensive; **defensor** m, **-a** f defender; protector; ⚖ counsel.

deferir [3i] v/t. ⚖ refer, delegate (*a* to); v/i.: ~ *a* defer to.

deficiencia f deficiency, defect; **deficiente** deficient, wanting (*en* in); defective; **déficit** m ✝ deficit.

definición f definition; **definido** definite (*a. gr.*); **definir** [3a] define; **definitiva:** *en* ~ definit(iv)ely; **definitivo** definitive.

deflación f deflation; **deflacionar** [1a] deflate.

deformación f deformation; distortion (*a. radio*); **deformar** [1a] deform; distort; ⊕ strain; **deforme** deformed, misshapen; **deformidad** f deformity, malformation; abnormality.

defraudar [1a] cheat, defraud; deceive; *esperanzas* cheat.

degeneración f degeneration; (*moral*) degeneracy; **degenerado** *adj. a. su.* m, **a** f degenerate (type); **degenerar** [1a] degenerate (*en* into).

deglución f swallowing; **deglutir** [3a] swallow.

degollación f throat-cutting; (*a.* ⚖) beheading; **degolladero** m *anat.* neck, throat; (*matadero*) slaughterhouse; **degollar** [1n] cut the throat of; behead, decapitate; *fig.* massacre.

degradación f degradation; ✗ demotion; **degradar** [1a] degrade, debase; ✗ demote.

dehesa f pasture, meadow; range.

deidad f deity; divinity; F beauty; **deificar** [1g] deify; apotheosize (*a. fig.*); **deísmo** m deism.

dejación f ⚖ abandonment; *S.Am., Col.* slovenliness; **dejadez** f neglect, slovenliness *etc.*; **dejado** slovenly; (*flojo*) lazy, slack.

dejar [1a] **1.** v/t. *mst* leave; *empresa, trabajo freq.* give up; *pasajero* drop, set down; ✝ *pérdida* show, leave; (*prestar*) lend; (*omitir*) forget, leave out; (*desamparar*) abandon, forsake; (*permitir*) let (*inf. inf.*); **2.** v/i.: ~ *de inf.* (*cesar*) stop *ger.*, leave off *ger.*;

give up *ger.*; (*omitir*) fail to *inf.*, neglect to *inf.*; **3. ~se** let o.s. go, get slovenly; ¡**déjese de eso**! stop that!, cut it out! F.

dejo *m* aftertaste, tang; *fig.* touch reminder; (*habla*) (trace of) accent.

delantal *m* apron.

delante in front (*a. por* ~); ahead; ~ **de** in front of; ahead of; **delantera** *f* front (part); *thea.* front row; (*ventaja*) lead, advantage; **delantero** **fila**, **parte** front; **pata** fore; foremost.

delatar [1a] denounce; inform against; (*traicionar*) betray (*a. fig.*); **delator** *m*, **-a** *f* accuser; informer.

delegación *f* delegation; *parl.* ~ (**de poderes**) devolution; **delegado** *m*, **a** *f* delegate; ✝ agent; **delegar** [1h] delegate (✝ to).

deleitable enjoyable, delectable; **deleitar** [1a] delight; ~**se con**, ~ **de** (take) delight in; **deleite** *m* pleasure, delight, joy; **deleitoso** delightful, pleasing.

deletrear [1a] spell out; *fig.* decipher, interpret.

deleznable fragile, brittle; (*resbaladizo*) slippery; *fig.* frail.

delfín *m* dolphin.

delgadez *f* thinness *etc.*; **delgado** thin; *p. a.* slim, slender, slight; **delgaducho** skinny; slight.

deliberación *f* deliberation; **deliberar** [1a] *v/t.* debate; ~ *inf.* decide to *inf.*; *v/i.* deliberate (**sobre** on).

delicadeza *f* delicacy *etc.*; **delicado** delicate; dainty; *color* soft, delicate; *punto* tender, sensitive; sore; *situación* delicate.

delicia *f* delight(fulness); **delicioso** delicious; delightful.

delictivo punishable; criminal.

delimitar [1a] delimit, define.

delincuencia *f* delinquency, criminality; **delincuente 1.** delinquent, criminal; **2.** *m/f* delinquent, criminal, offender.

delineación *f* delineation; **delinear** [1a] delineate, outline.

delirante delirious; light-headed; **delirar** [1a] be delirious, rave; *fig.* talk nonsense; **delirio** *m* delirium; ravings, wanderings; *fig.* frenzy.

delito *m* crime, offence; *fig.* misdeed.

delta *m* (*geog.*) *a. f* delta.

deludir [3a] delude.

demacrado emaciated; **demacrarse** [1a] waste away.

demagogia *f* demagogy; **demagogo** *m* demagogue.

demanda *f* demand (*a.* ✝), request (**de** for); inquiry; petition; *thea.* call; ⚖ action, lawsuit; **demandado** *m*, **a** *f* defendant; respondent **en divorcio**; **demandante** *m/f* plaintiff, claimant; **demandar** [1a] demand; claim; ⚖ sue.

demarcar [1g] mark out, demarcate.

demás 1. *adj.* other, rest of the; **2.** *pron.*: **lo** ~ the rest; **los** ~ the others, the rest (of them); **por lo** ~ for the rest, otherwise; **3.** *adv.*: **además** ~; **por** ~ in vain; moreover; **demasía** *f* (*superávit*) surplus; *fig.* excess, outrage; wicked thing; **demasiado 1.** *adj.* too much; overmuch; ~**s** *pl.* too many; **2.** *adv.* too; too much, excessively.

demencia *f* insanity; **dementado** *S. Am.* = demente; **demente 1.** mad, insane; **2.** *m/f* lunatic.

democracia *f* democracy; **demócrata** *m/f* democrat; **democrático** democratic.

demoler [2h] demolish (*a. fig.*), pull down; **demolición** *f* demolition.

demoníaco demoniac(al), demonic; **demonio** *m* demon; devil; ¡**qué** ~! confound it!; oh hell!; ¿**qué** ~**s**? what the hell?; **demontre** *m* F = demonio.

demora *f* delay; ⚓ bearing; **demorar** [1a] *v/t.* delay, hold up (*or* back); *v/i.* linger on, delay.

demostración *f* demonstration; show **de cariño** *etc.*; **demostrar** [1m] show, demonstrate; prove; **demostrativo** *adj. a. su. m* demonstrative.

demudar [1a] change, alter; ~**se** change color, change countenance.

dengoso affected, finicky; **dengue** *m* affectation, finickiness; prudery; **hacer** ~**s** be finicky.

denigrar [1a] denigrate, revile; insult.

denominación *f* naming, designation; denomination; **denominador** *m* denominator; **denominar** [1a] name, designate; denominate.

denotar [1a] denote; reveal, indicate, show.

densidad *f* density (*a. phys.*); thickness *etc.*; **denso** *mst* dense; *humo*, *líquido a.* thick; solid.

dentado *rueda* cogged, toothed; *filo* jagged; **dentadura** *f* denture, set of teeth; *postiza* false teeth, denture(s); **dentar** [1k] *v/t.* furnish with teeth *etc.*; ⊕ *etc.* indent; *filo* make jagged; *sello* perforate; *v/i.* teethe; **dentellada** *f* bite, nip; (*señal*) tooth-mark; **dentellar** [1a] chatter; **dentera** *f* the shivers F; F envy, jealousy; **dentición** *f* teething; dentition; *estar con la* ~ be teething; **dentífrico** 1. tooth *attr.*; 2. *m* dentifrice; **dentista** *m* dentist; **dentistería** *f* dentistry.

dentro 1. inside; *sentir etc.* inwardly; (*en casa*) indoors; (*a. hacia* ~, *para* ~) in, inwards; 2. *prp.*: ~ *de estar* in, inside, within.

dentudo toothy; large-toothed.

denudar [1a] denude; lay bare.

denuncia *f* denunciation (*a.* ⚖); ⚖ accusation; **denunciador** *m*, **-a** *f*, **denunciante** *m/f* accuser; informer; **denunciar** [1b] (*publicar*) proclaim, (*pronosticar*) announce, ⚖ denounce, accuse.

deparar [1a] provide, present (with), offer.

departamento *m* department; compartment *de caja etc.* (*a.* 🚃).

departir [3a] talk, chat.

dependencia *f* dependence (*de* on); reliance (*de* on); dependency (*a. pol.*); ⚡ branch-office; 🏠 outbuilding; **depender** [2a] depend; follow (from); **dependienta** *f* salesgirl, shop-assistant, clerk; **dependiente** 1. dependent (*de* on); 2. *m* employee; ♥ salesman, shop-assistant, clerk.

depilatorio *adj. a. su. m* depilatory.

deplorar [1a] deplore, regret.

deponente *adj.* (*gr.*) *a. su. m* (⚖) deponent.

deponer [2r] *v/t.* (*bajar*) lay down; (*apartar*) lay aside; (*quitar*) remove, take away, take down; *v/i.* ⚖ give evidence.

deportación *f* deportation; **deportar** [1a] deport.

deporte *m* sport; game; **deportista** 1. sports *attr.*; sporting; 2. *m* sportsman; 3. *f* sportswoman; **deportividad** *f* sportsmanship; **deportivo** *actitud etc.* sporting, sportsmanlike.

deposición *f* deposition (*a.* ⚖), removal; ⚖ evidence.

depositar [1a] *mst* deposit; store, put away, lodge; entrust (*en* to); ~**se** (*líquido*) settle; **depositaría** *f* depository; trust; **depositario** 1. deposit *attr.*; 2. *m*, **a** *f* depositary, trustee; repository *de secreto etc.*; **depósito** *m* (*almacén*) store (-house), warehouse;

depot; ⚒ depot, dump; reservoir, tank *de líquido*; ~ *de agua* water-tank, cistern; ~ *de gasolina* gasoline tank.

depravación *f* depravity, depravation; **depravado** depraved; **depravar** [1a] deprave.

depreciación *f* depreciation; **depreciar(se)** [1b] depreciate.

depresión *f mst* depression (*a.* 🔬, ✈, *meteor.*); drop, fall *de mercurio*; dip *de horizonte, camino*; (*hueco*) depression, hollow; **depresivo, deprimente** depressing; **deprimir** [3a] depress (*a.* 🔬, *fig.*); *nivel* lower, reduce; *fig.* humiliate; disparage.

depuración *f* purification; *pol.* purge; **depurador** cleansing; purifying; purging; *estación* ~*a* sewagedisposal plant; **depurar** [1a] purify, cleanse, purge (*a. pol.*).

derecha *f* right hand; (*lado*) right side; *pol.* right; *a* ~*s* rightly; **derechazo** *m boxeo*: right; **derechista** 1. right-wing; 2. *m/f* right-winger.

derecho 1. *adj.* *lado, mano* right; (*recto*) straight; (*vertical*) upright, erect; *C.Am.* lucky; 2. *adv.* straight, direct; (*verticalmente*) straight, upright; 3. *m* right (*a* to, *de inf.* to *inf.*); ⚖ (*ciencia*) law; (*en abstracto*) justice; right side *de papel*; ~*s pl.* ♥ due(s); (*profesionales*) fee(s); (*impuestos*) tax(es); *con* ~ rightly, justly; *con* ~ *a* with a right to; *conforme a* ~ according to law; F *¡no hay* ~*!* it's not fair!; *reservados todos los* ~*s* copyright; *tener* ~ *a* have a right to, be entitled to.

derechura *f* straightness; directness; *fig.* rightness.

derivación *f* derivation (*a. gr.*); origin, source; ⚡ shunt; **derivado** 1. derivative (*a. gr.*); 2. *m* derivative (*a. gr.*); 🧪 byproduct; **derivar** [1a] *v/t.* derive (*de* from); *v/i.*, ~**se** derive, be derived.

dermatitis *f* dermatitis; **dermatología** *f* dermatology; **dermatólogo** *m* dermatologist.

derogar [1h] repeal, abolish.

derramamiento *m* spilling *etc.*; **derramar** [1a] pour out; spill; (*esparcir*) scatter, spread; *sangre* shed; *lágrimas* weep; ~**se** spill, overflow, run over; (*sangre*) flow, be shed; **derrame** *m* spilling *etc.*; (*salida*) overflow, outflow; (*pérdida*) leakage.

derredor: *al* ~ (*de*), *en* ~ (*de*) around, about.

derrengado bent, crooked; (*cojo*) lame; **derrengar** [1h] bend, twist.

derretir [3l] melt; *nieve a.* thaw; *fortuna* squander; **~se** melt; run; thaw; **~** *por* be crazy about.

derribar [1a] *casa* knock down, pull down; *puerta* batter down; *gobierno etc.* overthrow; **~se** fall down, collapse; (*p.*) throw o.s. to the ground; **derribo** *m* knocking down *etc.*; **~s** *pl.* debris.

derrocadero *m* cliff, precipice; **derrocar** [1g] hurl down *desde lo alto*; *casa* knock down; *gobierno etc.* overthrow; oust, topple.

derrochar [1a] waste, squander; lavish; **derroche** *m* waste, squandering; extravagance.

derrota *f* defeat, rout; débâcle; **derrotar** [1a] defeat, rout.

derrotero *m* ♣ course.

derrotismo *m* defeatism; **derrotista** *m/f* defeatist.

derrumbadero *m* cliff; *fig.* pitfall, hazard; **derrumbamiento** *m* headlong fall; collapse (*a. fig.*), caving in; **derrumbar** [1a] hurl down, throw down; **~se** fall headlong (*por* down); (*edificio a. fig.*) collapse; **derrumbe** *m* C.Am. collapse; cave-in.

desabotonar [1a] *v/t.* unbotton; *v/i.* ♣ blossom; **~se** come undone.

desabrido *sabor* tasteless, insipid (*a. fig.*); (*áspero*) harsh, rough; *debate* bitter; *p.* surly.

desabrigado *fig.* unprotected, defenceless; **desabrigo** *m* bareness, exposure; *fig.* unprotectedness.

desabrimiento *m* insipidness *etc.*; (*sentimiento*) depression, uneasiness; **desabrir** [3a] *fig.* embitter.

desabrochar [1a] undo, unfasten; *fig.* penetrate; **~se** F unbosom o.s.

desacatar [1a] be disrespectful to; **desacato** *m* disrespect; *esp.* 🏛 (act of) contempt.

desacertado mistaken, wrong; (*imprudente*) unwise; **desacertar** [1k] be wrong; **desacierto** *m* mistake, miscalculation, miss.

desacomedido *S.Am.* rude; impolite.

desacomodado unemployed; badly off; **desacomodar** [1a] put out, inconvenience; *criado* discharge.

desacoplar [1a] ⚡ disconnect; ⊕ uncouple.

desacostumbrado unusual, odd; **desacostumbrar** [1a]: **~** *a uno de* break s.o. of the habit of.

desacreditar [1a] discredit, bring into disrepute; run down.

desacuerdo *m* disagreement; error; (*olvido*) forgetfulness.

desafecto *m* disaffection; ill-will, dislike.

desafiar [1c] defy; challenge; dare; **~** *a uno* challenge *s.o.* to *inf.*

desafinado out of tune, off key; **desafinar** [1a] be out of tune.

desafío *m* challenge (*a. fig.*); rivalry; defiance; ⚔ duel.

desaforado lawless, disorderly; (*grande*) huge; *grito etc.* mighty.

desafortunado unfortunate, unlucky.

desafuero *m* excess, outrage.

desagradable disagreeable, unpleasant; **desagradar** [1a] displease; dissatisfy; **desagradecido** ungrateful; **desagradecimiento** *m* ingratitude; **desagrado** *m* displeasure; dissatisfaction.

desagraviar [1b] *daño* make amends for; *p.* make amends to, indemnify; **desagravio** *m* amends, compensation.

desaguadero *m* drain (*a. fig.*; de on); **desaguar** [1i] *v/t.* drain, empty; *fig.* squander; *v/i.*: **~** *en* drain into; **desagüe** *m* drainage, draining; (*caño etc.*) outlet, drain.

desaguisado 1. illegal; 2. *m* offence, outrage.

desahogado (*descarado*) impudent, brazen; (*despejado*) free; *vida* comfortable; **desahogar** [1h] *dolor etc.* ease; *p.* console; *pasión* vent; **~se** make things more comfortable; get out of trouble (*or* debt *etc.*); (*confearse*) unbosom o.s.; **desahogo** *m* (*alivio*) relief; (*descaro*) impudence; (*libertad*) excessive freedom; comfort, comfortable circumstances.

desairado unattractive, shabby; **desairar** [1a] slight, snub; **desaire** *m* slight, snub.

desalentar [1k] make breathless; *fig.* discourage; **~se** get discouraged; **desaliento** *m* discouragement; depression; (*debilidad*) weakness.

desaliñado slovenly; (*temporalmente*) untidy, dishevelled; careless; **desaliño** *m* slovenliness *etc.*

desalmado cruel, brutal.

desalojar [1a] *v/t.* oust, eject, dislodge (*a.* ⚔); *v/i.* move out.

desalquilado vacant.

desamarrar [1a] untie; ♣ cast off.

desamor *m* coldness, indifference; dislike; **desamorado** cold-hearted.

desamparar [1a] desert, abandon, forsake; **desamparo** *m* (*acto*) desertion etc.; (*estado*) helplessness.

desamueblado unfurnished.

desangrar [1a] bleed; *lago* drain; *fig.* bleed white; ~**se** lose a lot of blood; bleed to death.

desanimado downhearted, low-spirited; lifeless; **desanimar** [1a] discourage, depress; **desánimo** *m* discouragement, despondency.

desapacible *mst* unpleasant; *ruido* sharp, jangling; *tono* harsh.

desaparecer [2d] *v/t.* hide, remove, take away; *v/i.* disappear; vanish; **desaparición** *f* disappearance.

desapasionado dispassionate.

desapego *m* coolness, indifference.

desapercibido (*desprevenido*) unprepared; (*inadvertido*) unnoticed.

desaplicación *f* slackness, laziness.

desapoderado (*precipitado*) headlong; wild; *gula etc.* excessive.

desaprensión *f* freedom from worry, nonchalance.

desapretar [1k] loosen.

desaprobación *f* disapproval; **desaprobar** [1m] disapprove of, frown on; *petición* reject.

desaprovechado unproductive, below expectations; **desaprovechar** [1a] *v/t.* waste, fail to make the best use of; *v/i.* lose ground.

desarmamiento *m* disarmament; **desarmar** [1a] *v/t.* ✕ disarm; ⊕ dismantle, take to pieces, take apart; *v/i.* disarm; **desarme** *m* disarmament; arms reduction.

desarraigar [1h] root out, uproot, dig up; *fig.* eradicate; **desarraigo** *m* fig. eradication.

desarreglado out of border; (*desaliñado*) slovenly, untidy; *conducta etc.* disorderly; **desarreglar** [1a] disarrange, disturb, upset, mess up; **desarreglo** *m* disorder; confusion.

desarrimo *m* lack of support; helplessness.

desarrollar [1a] unroll, unwind, unfold; *ecuación* expand; *tesis* expound; *fig.* develop; evolve; **desarrollo** *m* development; evolution; growth; *ayuda al* ~ developmental aid.

desarrugar [1h] smooth (out).

desarticulado disjointed; **desarticular** [1a] separate, take apart.

desaseado (*sucio*) dirty, slovenly; (*desaliñado*) untidy, unkempt, shabby; **desaseo** *m* dirtiness etc.

desasir [3a; *present like salir*] loosen, let go; ~**se** de let go of; *fig.* (*ceder*) give up; (*deshacerse de*) get rid of.

desasosegar [1h *a.* 1k] disturb, make uneasy; **desasosiego** *m* disquiet, uneasiness, anxiety.

desastrado dirty, shabby; (*infeliz*) unlucky; **desastre** *m* disaster; **desastroso** disastrous.

desatado *fig.* wild, violent; **desatar** [1a] untie, undo, unfasten; *fig.* solve; ~**se** come undone etc.; *fig.* (*hablar*) get worked up; (*obrar*) go too far; (*tempestad*) burst, break.

desatención *f* inattention; (*grosería*) discourtesy; **desatender** [2g] ignore, disregard, pay no attention to; *deber* neglect; **desatentado** thoughtless, inconsiderate; **desatento** inattentive, careless; (*grosero*) unmannerly.

desatinado foolish; nonsensical, silly; wild; **desatinar** [1a] *v/t.* perplex, bewilder; *v/i.* act foolishly; (*hablar*) talk nonsense; **desatino** *m* foolishness, folly.

desatornillar [1a] unscrew.

desautorizado unauthorized; unwarranted; discredited.

desavenencia *f* disagreement; friction, unpleasantness; **desavenido** in disagreement, incompatible; **desavenir** [3s] cause a rift between, split; ~**se** disagree (*con* with).

desaventajado unfavorable.

desavisado unadvised; ill-advised; careless.

desayunar(se) [1a] (have) breakfast (*con* on); *estar desayunado* have had breakfast; **desayuno** *m* breakfast.

desazón *f* (*soso*) tastelessness; *fig.* 🌿 trouble, discomfort; *fig.* annoyance; frustration; **desazonar** [1a] *comida* make tasteless; *fig.* upset, annoy.

desbandarse [1a] ✕ etc. (*irse*) disband; (*huir*) flee in disorder; disperse in confusion.

desbarajustar [1a] throw into confusion; **desbarajuste** *m* confusion.

desbaratar [1a] *v/t.* ruin, spoil, mess up *fig.*; *proyecto, tentativa* thwart, foil; *v/i.* talk nonsense; ~**se** F blow up, go off the deep end.

desbarrancadero *m* S.Am. precipice.

desbastar [1a] ⊕ plane (down),

smooth (out, down); **desbaste** m ⊕ planing etc.

desbocado caballo runaway; p. foulmouthed; **desbocar** [1g]: ~ en (río) run into, flow into; (calle) open into; ~se (caballo) bolt; (p.) let loose a stream of insults etc.

desbordante overflowing; uncontrolled; **desbordar(se)** [1a] overflow, run over; fig. lose one's self-control.

desbravador m horse-breaker; **desbravar** [1a] v/t. break in, tame; v/i., ~se get less wild; diminish.

descabalgar [1h] dismount.

descabellado p. dishevelled; proyecto etc. rash; mindless; crazy; **descabellar** [1a] p. etc. dishevel, rumple.

descabezado headless; fig. wild, crazy; **descabezar** [1f] behead; árbol lop, poll; planta top; ~se rack one's brains.

descalabrar [1a] hit etc. in the head; (en general) hit, hurt; **descalabro** m blow, setback, misfortune; (daño) damage; ✗ defeat.

descalcificar [1g] decalcify.

descalificación f disqualification; **descalificar** [1g] disqualify.

descalzar [1f] zapato etc. take off; p. take off s.o.'s shoes etc.; ~se take off one's shoes etc.; (caballo) lose a shoe; **descalzo** barefoot(ed), shoeless etc.; eccl. discalced.

descaminado fig. misguided, ill-advised; **descaminar** [1a] mislead, put on the wrong road.

descamisado 1. ragged, wretched; 2. m poor devil, wretch.

descansado rested, refreshed; vida free from care; (que tranquiliza) restful; **descansapié(s)** m mot. footrest; **descansar** [1a] v/t. (ayudar) help, give a hand to; (apoyar) rest, lean (sobre on); v/i. (no trabajar) rest, take a rest, have a break (de from); (dormir) rest, sleep; **descansillo** m △ landing; **descanso** m (reposo) rest; (pausa) rest, break; (alivio) relief; deportes: half-time, interval; thea. interval; △ landing; ⊕ support, rest.

descarado shameless, brazen, cheeky, saucy; blatant; **descararse** [1a] behave in an impudent way.

descarga f unloading, firing, discharge; ~ (cerrada) volley; ⚡ discharge; **descargadero** m wharf; **descargar** [1h] 1. v/t. barco, carro etc. unload; arma fire, shoot, discharge; ⚡ discharge; golpe let fly (en at), strike (en on); 2. v/i. ⚡ discharge; (tempestad) burst, break; ~ en (río) flow into; 3. ~se resign; 🏛 clear o.s. (de of); ~ de get rid of, disburden o.s. of; **descargo** m unloading de barco etc.; ✝ receipt, voucher; ✝ discharge de deuda; 🏛 (alegato) evidence; 🏛 acquittal; **descargue** m unloading.

descarnado lean; cadaverous; **descarnar** [1a] hueso remove the flesh from; fig. wear down.

descaro m shamelessness; impudence, cheek; blatancy.

descarriar [1c] misdirect, put on the wrong road; ~se stray.

descarrilar [1a] (a. ~se S.Am.) be derailed, go off the rails; fig. wander from the point.

descartar [1a] discard, reject; ~se naipes: discard; ~ de shirk.

descascar [1g] peel; shell; ~se smash to pieces; **descascarar** [1a] peel; shell; ~se peel (off).

descendencia f descent (de from), origin; (hijos) offspring; **descendente** descending, downward; tren down; **descender** [2g] v/t. get down, take down; escalera go down; v/i. descend, come down, go down; (fluir, pasar) run, flow; **descendiente** m/f descendant; **descendimiento** m descent (a. eccl.); **descenso** m descent; (disminución) fall, decline; (desnivel) slope, drop.

descentrado off center; out of plumb; **descentralizar** [1f] decentralize. [let off.∖

descerrajar [1a] break open; F tiro∫

deschavetar [1a] S.Am., get rattled; go crazy; flip one's lid.

descifrable decipherable; **desciframiento** m decoding; **descifrar** [1a] decipher, read; mensaje en cifra decode; fig. puzzle out.

desclasificación f disqualification; **desclasificar** [1g] disqualify.

descocado F cheeky; brazen, forward.

descoger [2c] spread out, unfold.

descolgar [1h a. 1m] take down, get down, unhook; ~se let o.s. down (de from; con by); come down; fig. turn up unexpectedly.

descollante outstanding; **descollar** [1m] stand out.

descolorar(se) [1a] discolor; **descolorido** faded, discolored; fig. colorless.

descomedido excessive; intemperate; (*grosero*) rude, disrespectful.
descompasado out of all proportion; **descompasarse** [1a] be rude.
descomponer [2r] *orden* disturb, upset, disarrange; *facciones* distort; *fig.* shake up, put out; (*desmontar*) take apart; *calma* ruffle, disturb; (*pudrir*) rot, decompose; **⚛** separate into its elements; **~se** (*pudrirse*) rot, decompose; (*irritarse*) lose one's temper; **descomposición** *f* disturbance *etc.*; distortion; *opt.* dispersal; (*putrefacción*) decomposition (*a.* **⚛**); **descompostura** *f* disorder, disorganization; (*deseaso*) untidiness; **descompuesto** out of order; *rostro* twisted; *fig.* (*descarado*) brazen; (*descortés*) rude.
descomunal huge, enormous.
desconcertar disconcerted, taken aback; puzzled; bewildered; **desconcertante** disconcerting, upsetting, embarrassing; **desconcertar** [1k] ⊕ put out of order, damage; *anat.* dislocate; *orden* disturb; *p.* disconcert, put out; embarrass; (*problema*) baffle.
desconcharse [1a] peel off, flake off.
desconcierto *m* disorder, confusion; ⊕ damage; *fig.* (*desavenencia*) disagreement; embarrassment; bewilderment.
desconectar [1a] ⚡, ⊕ disconnect.
desconfiado distrustful, suspicious; **desconfiar** [1c]: ~ de distrust, mistrust, suspect.
desconformar(se) [1a] disagree, dissent; **desconforme** in disagreement, dissident.
descongelación *f* thaw; **descongelador** *m* defroster; **descongelar** [1a] melt; defrost; **⚓** unfreeze.
descongestión *f* decongestion; freeing up; clearing; **descongestionar** [1a] decongest; free up.
desconocer [2d] not know; be ignorant of, be unfamiliar with; (*no reconocer*) not recognize; (*fingiendo*) pretend not to know; (*rechazar*) disown, repudiate; **desconocido 1.** unknown (*de*, *para* to); strange, unfamiliar; **2.** *m*, **a** *f* stranger; **desconocimiento** *m* ignorance; repudiation; ingratitude.
desconsiderado inconsiderate.
desconsolado disconsolate; **desconsolador** distressing; **desconsolar**

[1m] grieve, distress; **desconsuelo** *m* grief, distress.
descontaminación *f* decontamination; ~ de *radiactividad* radioactive decontamination; **descontaminar** [1a] decontaminate.
descontar [1m] take away; **⚓** discount (*a. fig.*), rebate; (*a. dar por descontado*) take for granted.
descontentadizo hard to please; restless, unsettled; **descontentar** [1a] displease; **descontento 1.** dissatisfied (*de* with); discontented; **2.** *m* dissatisfaction, displeasure.
descontinuar [1e] discontinue.
descontrolado *S.Am.* uncontrolled; unregulated; deregulated.
descorazonar [1a] *fig.* discourage.
descorchador *m* corkscrew; **descorchar** [1a] ⚘ *árbol* strip, bark; *botella* uncork, open.
descortés discourteous, rude; **descortesía** *f* discourtesy, rudeness.
descortezar [1f] *árbol* skin, bark; *pan* cut the crust off.
descoser [2a] unstitch; **~se** burst at the seams, unsew; F fart; **descosido 1.** big-mouthed; (*desastrado*) shabby, slovenly; **2.** *m sew.* tear.
descoyuntar [1a] put out of joint, dislocate; *fig.* bother, annoy.
descrédito *m* discredit; disrepute; **descreído 1.** unbelieving; godless; **2.** *m*, **a** *f* unbeliever; **descreimiento** *m* unbelief.
describir [3a; *p.p.* descrito] describe (*a.* **⚓**); **descripción** *f* description; **descriptivo** descriptive.
descuajar [1a] dissolve; ⚘ uproot.
descuartizar [1f] carve up.
descubierto *situación* open, exposed; ⚔ *freq. a.* under fire; *p.* bareheaded; *cabeza* bare; **descubridor** *m* discoverer; ⚔ scout; **descubrimiento** *m* discovery; detection; **descubrir** [3a; *p.p.* descubierto] discover; detect, spot; bring to light, unearth; uncover; **~se** take off one's hat; (*saludo*) raise one's hat.
descuento *m* discount, rebate.
descuerar [1a] *S.Am.* skin; flay; F slander; libel.
descuidado careless; slack, negligent; forgetful; (*desaseado*) slovenly, unkempt; **descuidar** [1a] *v/t.* neglect, disregard; *v/i.*, **~se** not worry, not bother (*de* about); ¡descuide Vd.! don't worry!; **descuido** *m*

carelessness, slackness *etc.*; (*un ~*) oversight, mistake.

desde *tiempo* since; *tiempo, lugar* from; *~ que* since.

desdén *m* disdain; **desdeñar** [1a] scorn, disdain, despise; *~se de inf.* not deign to *inf.*; **desdeñoso** scornful, disdainful, contemptuous.

desdicha *f* unhappiness; wretchedness; (*una ~*) misfortune; **desdichado 1.** unhappy, unlucky; wretched; **2.** *m* poor devil, wretch.

desdoblar [1a] unfold, spread out.

desdorar [1a] tarnish (*a. fig.*); **desdoro** *m* blot, stigma.

deseable desirable; **desear** [1a] want, desire, wish for.

desecación *f* desiccation; **desecar** [1g] dry up (*a. fig.*), desiccate.

desechar [1a] *desechos etc.* throw out; *lo inútil* jettison, scrap; *consejo, miedo etc.* cast aside; *proyecto, oferta* reject; **desecho** *m* residue, waste; chaff; *S.Am.* shortcut; *~ de hierro* scrap iron; *~s pl.* rubbish, debris, waste.

desembalar [1a] unpack.

desembarazar [1f] *camino, sala* clear (*de of*); *fig. ~* de rid *s.o.* of; *~se de* get rid of; **desembarazo** *m* freedom; lack of restraint.

desembarcadero *m* quay, landing-stage; **desembarcar** [1g] *v/t ps.* land, put ashore; *mercancías* unload; *v/i.* land, disembark; **desembarco** *m* landing (*a. de escarela*) *etc.*

desembargar [1h] free.

desembarque *m* unloading, landing.

desembocadura *f* mouth; outlet, outfall; opening *de calle*; **desembocar** [1g]: *~ en (río)* flow into; (*calle*) open into, meet; *fig.* end in.

desembolsar [1a] pay out; **desembolso** *m* outlay, expenditure.

desembragar [1h] disengage, disconnect; **desembrague** *m* disengagement; *mot.* declutching.

desembuchar [1a] disgorge; F spill the beans.

desemejante dissimilar; unlike (*a. ~ de*); **desemejanza** *f* dissimilarity.

desempacar [1g] unpack.

desempacho *m* ease, confidence.

desempaquetar [1a] unpack, unwrap.

desempeñar [1a] *prenda* redeem; *deudor* free from debt; *p.* get out of a jam; *papel* play; **desempeño** *m* discharge *etc. de deber*; *thea.* performance, acting.

desempleado out of work, unemployed; **desempleo** *m* unemployment; *~ en masa* mass employment.

desempolvar [1a] dust.

desenamorar [1a] alienate; *~se* get fed up (with).

desencadenar [1a] unchain; *esp. fig.* unleash; *~se fig.* break loose.

desencajado *cara* concorted; *ojos* wild; **desencajar** [1a] dislocate; ⊕ disconnect.

desencantar [1a] disenchant, disillusion; **desencanto** *m* disenchantment, disillusion(ment). [plug.⟩

desenchufar [1a] disconnect, un-⟨

desenfadar(se) [1a] calm down; **desenfado** *m* freedom, lack of inhibition.

desenfocado out of focus.

desenfrenado wild; (*vicioso*) unbridled, licentious; **desenfrenarse** [1a] lose all control; run riot; **desenfreno** *m* lack of control; (*vicio*) licentiousness.

desenganchar [1a] unhook, unfasten; ⊕ disengage.

desengañar [Na] undeceive; disabuse (*de of*); *~se* see the light; become disillusioned; **desengaño** *m* disillusion(ment).

desenlace *m* outcome; *lit.* ending, dénouement; **desenlazar** [1f] undo, unlace; *~se lit.* end, turn out.

desenmarañar [1a] unravel, disentangle.

desenmascarar [1a] unmask, expose, show up.

desenredar [1a] free, disentangle (*a. fig.*); *fig.* resolve, straighten out; **desenredo** *m* disentanglement; *fig.* dénouement.

desenrollar(se) [1a] unroll, unwind.

desentenderse [2g]: *~ de* wash one's hands of; affect ignorance of.

desenterrar [1k] unearth, dig up.

desentonar [1a] be out of tune (*con* with; *a. fig.*); *~se fig.* speak disrespectfully.

desentrañar [1a] disembowel; *fig.* puzzle out, get to the bottom of.

desenvainar [1a] *espada* unsheathe; ⚯ shell; F bring out, show.

desenvoltura *f* ease, assurance; *b.s.* boldness; **desenvolver** [2h; *p.p.* desenvuelto] *paquete* unwrap; *rollo* unwind; (*desarrollar*) develop; **desenvolvimiento** *m* development; **desenvuelto** *fig.* free and easy, self-assured; *b.s.* bold.

deseo *m* wish, desire (*de* for; *de inf.* to *inf.*); **deseoso** desirous.

desequilibrado unbalanced (*a. fig.*); (*desigual*) one-sided, lopsided; **desequilibrar** [1a] unbalance; throw off balance; **desequilibrio** *m* unbalance (*a. 𝔐*).

deserción *f* desertion; **desertar** [1a] desert (*a. ∼ de*); desertor *m* deserter.

desesperación *f* despair, desperation; **desesperado** desperate; in despair; *condición* hopeless; **desesperanzar** [1f] deprive of hope; **desesperar** [1a] drive to despair; *v/i.*, **∼se** despair (*de* of), lose hope.

desestimar [1a] have a low opinion of; belittle, disparage.

desfachatado F brazen; cheeky; **desfachatez** *f* F brazenness; cheek.

desfalcar [1g] embezzle; **desfalco** *m* embezzlement.

desfallecer [2d] *v/t.* weaken; *v/i.* get weak; faint away; **desfallecimiento** *m* weakness; faintness.

desfavorable unfavorable.

desfiguración *f* disfiguration *etc.*; **desfigurar** [1a] *rostro* disfigure; *cuadro etc.* deface; *voz* alter, disguise.

desfiladero *m* defile, pass; **desfilar** [1a] parade; (*a. ∼ ante*) file past; **desfile** *m* procession; ⚔ parade.

desflorar [1a] deflower.

desfogar [1h] vent (*a. fig.*); **∼se** let o.s. go, blow off steam.

desgajar [1a] tear off, break off; **∼se** come off, break off.

desgana *f* lack of appetite; *fig.* disinclination, reluctance.

desgarbado clumsy, ungainly; (*desaliñado*) slovenly.

desgarrador *fig.* heartbreaking, heartrending; **desgarrar** [1a] tear, rip up; *fig.* rend, shatter; **desgarro** *m* tear; *fig.* effrontery.

desgastado worn (out); used up; eroded; *llanta* treadless; *tela* threadbare.

desgastar [1a] wear away; *geol.* erode, weather; *cuerda etc.* chafe, fray; **∼se** wear away *etc.*; 𝔐 get weak, wear o.s. out; **desgaste** *m* wear; erosion *etc.*

desgobernado uncontrollable, undisciplined; **desgobernar** [1k] misgovern, misrule; *asunto* mismanage, handle badly.

desgoznar [1a] unhinge, take off the hinges; **∼se** *fig.* go off the rails.

desgracia *f* (*mala suerte*) misfortune; (*suceso*) mishap, misfortune; (*pérdida de favor*) disgrace; **desgraciado 1.** unlucky, unfortunate; wretched; (*sin gracia*) graceless; **2.** *m*, **a** *f* wretch, unfortunate.

desgranar [1a] *trigo* thresh; *racimo* pick the grapes from; *guisantes* shell; **∼se 𝔐** fall, seed.

desgreñado dishevelled; **desgreñar** [1a] tousle, ruffle.

desguarnecer [2d] ⊕ strip down; *plaza* abandon, dismantle.

deshabitado uninhabited; **deshabitar** [1a] move out of.

deshabituarse [1e] lose the habit.

deshacer [2s] *lo hecho* undo, unmake; spoil, destroy; (*dividir*) cut up; (*romper*) pull to pieces; ⊕ take apart; *maleta* unpack; *paquete* open; (*desgastar*) wear down; (*liquidar*) melt, dissolve; *agravio* right; **∼se** fall to pieces, come apart *al caer etc.*; (*liquidarse*) melt; (*afligirse*) grieve; get impatient *esperando*; 𝔐 get weak; **∼ de** get rid of; *carga* throw off; 🚢 dump, unload; **∼ por** *inf.* struggle to *inf.*

desharrapado ragged, shabby.

deshecho 1. *p.p.* of *deshacer*; undone; *salud* broken; F *estoy ∼* I'm worn out; **2.** *adj.* *lluvia* violent; *suerte* tremendous; ❄ de-ice.)

deshelar [1k] thaw, melt (*a. ∼se*).)

desherbar [1k] weed.

desheredar [1a] disinherit.

desherrarse [1k] lose its shoe.

deshidratación *f* dehydration.

deshielo *m* thaw.

deshilachar [1a] pull threads out of; **∼se** fray; **deshilar** [1a] unravel.

deshilvanar [1a] untack.

deshinchar [1a] *neumático* let down; *cólera* give vent to; **∼se 𝔐** go down.

deshojar [1a] strip the leaves (*or* petals) off; **∼se** lose its leaves *etc.*

deshonestidad *f* indecency *etc.*; **deshonesto** indecent, lewd, improper;

deshonor *m* dishonor; insult (*de* to); **deshonra** *f* dishonor, disgrace, shame; shameful act; **deshonrar** [1a] dishonor, disgrace, insult; *mujer* seduce; **deshonroso** dishonorable, ignominious.

deshora: *a ∼* at the wrong time; (*sin avisar*) unexpectedly.

deshuesador *m* pitter; boner; **∼a** *f* *frutas* pitter; pit-removing device; **deshuesar** [1a] *carne* bone; ❦ stone.

desidia f laziness, idleness; **desidioso** lazy, idle.

desierto 1. *casa etc.* deserted; *isla* desert; *paisaje* bleak, desolate; *certamen*: void; 2. *m* desert; wilderness.

designación f designation, appointment; **designar** [1a] designate, appoint; name; **designio** *m* design, plan.

desigual unequal; *superficie* uneven, rough, bumpy; *filo* ragged; *progreso etc.* erratic; *fig.* arduous, tough; **desigualdad** f inequality; unevenness *etc.*

desilusión f disappointment; disillusion(ment); **desilusionar** [1a] disappoint, let down; disillusion; **~se** get disillusioned.

desinencia f *gr.* ending.

desinfectante *m* disinfectant; **desinfectar** [1a] disinfect.

desinflación f disinflation; deflation; **desinflacionar** [1a] ✝ deflate; **desinflar** [1a] deflate.

desinsectación f (insect) extermination; **desinsectar** [1a] exterminate insects (from).

desinterés *m* disinterestedness; **desinteresado** disinterested; unselfish.

desintoxicación f sobering (up); detoxification; **desintoxicarse** [1g] sober up; be detoxified.

desistir [3a] desist; **~** de desist from; *derecho etc.* waive.

desleal disloyal; **deslealtad** f disloyalty.

desleír [3m] dissolve; dilute.

deslenguado foul-mouthed.

desliar [1c] untie, undo; **~se** come undone.

desligar [1h] untie, undo; *fig.* detach, separate; (*desenredar*) unravel; free (*de juramento*) from).

deslindar [1a] mark out; *fig.* define.

desliz *m mot.* skid; *esp. fig.* slip, lapse; **deslizadizo** slippery; **deslizamiento** *m* slide, sliding; skid; glide; **~** de *tierra* landslide; **deslizar** [1f] *v/t.* slide (*por along*), slip (*en into, por through*); *v/i.*, **~se** (*resbalar*) slip (*en up on*); slide (*por along*; *mot.* skid; (*culebra etc.*) glide, slither; (*introducirse*) squeeze in; (*huir*) slip away; (*secreto*) slip out.

deslomar [1a] break the back of.

deslucido unadorned; dull, lifeless; undistinguished; **deslucir** [3f] tarnish, dull; *fig.* spoil, fail to give life to; **~se** *fig.* be unsuccessfull.

deslumbrador dazzling (a. *fig.*), glaring; **deslumbramiento** *m* glare, dazzle; *fig.* confusion, bewilderment; **deslumbrar** [1a] dazzle (a. *fig.*), blind; *fig.* confuse.

deslustrado dull, lustreless (a. *fig.*); *vidrio* frosted, ground; **deslustrar** [1a] tarnish (a. *fig.*), dull; **deslustre** *m* dullness; *fig.* stain, stigma.

desmadejar [1a] take it out of, enervate.

desmán *m* excess; piece of bad behaviour.

desmandado uncontrollable, obstreperous; **desmandarse** [1a] behave badly, be insolent.

desmantelar [1a] dismantle; *casa* abandon, forsake; **~se** get dilapidated.

desmañado awkward, clumsy; unpractical. [(from).]

desmaquillar [1a] remove make-up]

desmayado 🌿 unconscious; *fig.* weak, faint; languid; *color* pale; **desmayar** [1a] *v/t.* dismay, distress; *v/i.* lose heart, get depressed; **~se** faint; **desmayo** *m* 🌿 faint(ing fit); 🌿 (*en general*) unconsciousness; *fig.* depression.

desmedido excessive, disproportionate; boundless; **desmedirse** [3l] forget o.s., go too far.

desmedrar [1a] *v/t.* impair; *v/i.* decline, fall off.

desmejorar [1a] spoil, impair; **~se** decline, deteriorate; 🌿 lose one's health; lose one's charms.

desmelenado dishevelled.

desmembrar [1k] dismember.

desmemoriado forgetful, absentminded.

desmentida f denial; dar una **~** a give the lie to; **desmentir** [3i] give the lie to; *acusación* deny, refute; *carácter* belie; *rumor* scotch.

desmenuzar [1f] *pan* crumble; *carne* chop (up), mince; *queso etc.* shred; *fig.* take a close look at.

desmerecer [2d] *v/t.* be unworthy of; *v/i.* deteriorate, lose value; **desmerecimiento** *m* unworthiness.

desmesura f excess; intemperance; immoderation; **desmesurado** disproportionate, inordinate; *ambición etc.* boundless.

desmigajar [1a], **desmigar** [1h] crumble.

desmilitarizado demilitarized; *zona* **~a** demilitarized zone; **desmilitarizar** [1f] demilitarize.

desmochar [1a] top; *árbol* lop, pollard; *texto etc.* cut.

desmontable detachable; **desmontar** [1a] *v/t.* ⊕ dismantle, take to pieces, strip (down); ⚔ knock down; *escopeta* uncock; *(ayudar a bajar)* help *s.o.* down; *v/i.*, **~se** dismount, alight.

desmoralizar [1f] *ejército* demoralize; *costumbres etc.* corrupt.

desmoronadizo crumbling, crumbly; **desmoronarse** [1a] *geol.* crumble; *(casa)* fall into disrepair, get dilapidated; *fig.* decline, decay.

desmovilizar [1f] demobilize.

desnatar [1a] *leche* skim; *fig.* take the cream off.

desnaturalizado unnatural; **desnaturalizar** [1f] alter fundamentally; pervert, corrupt; **~se** *(p.)* give up one's nationality.

desnivelar [1a] make uneven.

desnucar [1g] break the neck of.

desnudar [1a] strip (*a.* ♀, *fig.*; *de of*); undress; *brazo etc.* bare; *espada* draw; **~se** undress, get undressed, strip; **desnudez** *f* nakedness, nudity; bareness (*a. fig.*); **desnudismo** *m* nudism; **desnudo 1.** naked, nude; bare; *fig. (sin adorno)* bare; **2.** *m* nude.

desnutrición *f* malnutrition, undernourishment; **desnutrido** undernourished.

desobecer [2d] disobey; **desobediencia** *f* disobedience; **desobediente** disobedient.

desocupación *n f* leisure; *b.s.* idleness; *(paro)* unemployment; **desocupado** *cuarto* vacant, unoccupied; *tiempo* spare, leisure *attr.*; *p.* at leisure; *b.s.* idle; *(parado)* unemployed; **desocupar** [1a] *casa etc.* vacate; *cajón* empty.

desodorante *m* deodorant; **desodorizar** [1f] deodorize.

desoír [3q] ignore, disregard.

desolación *f* desolation; *fig.* grief; **desolar** [1m] lay waste; **~se** grieve.

desolladero *m* slaughter-house; **desollado** *f* brazen, barefaced; **desollar** [1m] skin, flay.

desorbitado: con los ojos **~s** wide-eyed, pop-eyed.

desorden *m mst* disorder; turmoil, confusion; *(objetos)* litter, mess; **desordenado** disordered; *conducta etc.* disorderly; *objetos, cuarto* untidy; *niño etc.* wild, unruly; **desordenar**

[1a] throw into confusion, mess up, disarrange.

desorganizar [1f] disorganize, disrupt.

desorientación *f* disorientation; confusion; confusedness; **desorientar** [1a] make *o.s.* lose his way; *fig.* confuse; **~se** lose one's bearings.

desovar [1a] spawn; *(insecto)* lay eggs; **desove** *m* spawning; egg-laying.

despabilado wide awake (*a. fig.*); **despabilar** [1a] *vela* snuff; *lámpara* trim; *fig. p.* wake up, liven up; **~se** wake up (*a. fig.*); *S.Am.* clear out; *¡despabílate!* get a move on!

despachar [1a] *v/t. (concluir)* dispatch, settle; *negocio* do, transact; *(enviar)* dispatch, send, post; *(dar prisa a)* expedite; *v/i.* get it settled, come to a decision; *(darse prisa)* hurry; **despacho** *m* office *para negocios*; study *en casa*; *(tienda)* shop; *(mensaje)* dispatch; **~** *(de aduana)* clearance.

despachurrar [1a] F squash, crush, squelch; *comida* mash; *p.* flatten, knock sideways.

despacio 1. slowly; gently; gradually; *¡~!* gently!, easy there!; *S.Am. (voz)* soft, low; **2.** *m S.Am.* delaying tactic; **despacioso** slow, phlegmatic.

despampanante F stunning, tremendous; **despampanar** [1a] *v/t.* ♀ prune; F knock *s.o.* sideways, bowl *s.o.* over; *v/i.* F talk freely.

desparej(ad)o uneven; odd.

desparpajo *m* ease of manner, self-confidence, charm *en el trato*; *b.s.* glibness; savoir faire *en obrar*; *b.s. (descaro)* nerve, cheek.

desparramar [1a] scatter, spread (*por over*); *fortuna* squander; **~se** F have a whale of a time.

despatarrarse [1a] F do a split; sprawl on the floor.

despavorido terrified.

despearse [1a] get footsore.

despechar [1a] spite; *(irritar)* stir up, enrage; **despecho** *m* spite; despair; *a* **~** *de* in spite of.

despectivo contemptuous, scornful; derogatory; *gr.* pejorative.

despedazar [1a] tear apart, tear to pieces; *fig. honra* ruin; *corazón* break.

despedida *f* farewell, send-off;

leave-taking; dismissal; **despedir** [31] *amigo* see off *en estación*, see out *en puerta*; *importuno* send away; *obrero* dismiss, discharge, sack; *olor* emit, give off; (*soltar*) get rid of; **~se** say good-bye, take one's leave; **~ de** say good-bye to, take leave of.

despegar [1h] *v/t.* unstick, detach; *sobre* open; *v/i.* ✈ take off; **~se** come unstuck; **despego** *m* = *desapego*; **despegue** *m* ✈ take-off; **~ vertical** vertical take-off.

despeinado dishevelled, unkempt.

despejado clear, open; *cielo* cloudless; *fig. p.* bright, smart; **despejar** [1a] clear (*a. deportes*); *fig.* clear up, clarify; ⋏ find; **~se** *meteor.* clear up; *fig.* amuse o.s., relax; **despejo** *m* self-confidence, ease of manner.

despellejar [1a] skin (*a. sl.*).

despensa *f* pantry, larder; ⚓ *etc.* storeroom; (*comida*) stock of food; daily marketing; **despensero** *m* butler, steward.

despeñadamente hastily; boldly.

despeñadero *m* cliff; *fig.* risk, danger; **despeñar** [1a] hurl (*por over, down*); **~se** hurl o.s. down; fall headlong; *fig.* **~ en** plunge into.

despepitarse [1a] bawl, shriek; **~ por** be crazy about.

desperdiciar [1b] waste, fritter away; *oportunidad* throw away; **desperdicio** *m* waste, wasting; **~s** *pl.* rubbish, refuse; waste products.

desperdigar [1h] scatter, separate.

desperezarse [1f] stretch (o.s.).

despertador *m* alarm-clock; **despertar** [1k] *v/t.* wake (up); *fig. recuerdos* revive, recall; (*excitar*) arouse, stir up; *v/i.*, **~se** wake up, awaken.

despiadado merciless, remorseless.

despicar [1g] satisfy.

despido *m* discharge; firing; termination.

despierto awake; *fig.* alert, watchful; (*listo*) wide awake.

despilfarrado(r) extravagant, wasteful; (*andrajoso*) shabby; **despilfarrar** [1a] waste, squander; **despilfarro** *m* extravagance, waste, wastefulness; (*desaseo*) shabbiness.

despintar [1a] take the paint off; *fig.* spoil, alter, distort; **~se** fade, lose its color.

despiojar [1a] delouse.

despique *m* revenge.

despistado F **1.** (all) at sea, off the

beam; absentminded; **2.** *m* absentminded sort; **despistar** [1a] *hunt. a. fig.* throw *s.o.* off the scent; *fig.* mislead; **despiste** *m* *mot.* swerve; F absence of mind; confusion.

desplacer 1. [2x] displease; **2.** *m* displeasure.

desplantador *m* trowel; **desplantar** [1a] pull up, uproot.

desplazado *m*, **a** *f* outsider; (*refugiado*) displaced person; **desplazar** [1f] displace, take the place of; **~se** move, shift; (*p.*) go, travel.

desplegar [1h *a.* 1k] open (out), unfold; *alas etc.* spread; *velas* unfurl; ⋉ deploy; **despliegue** *m* *fig.* display; ⋉ deployment.

desplomarse [1a] ⚠ lean, bulge; (*caer*) collapse, tumble (down); ✈ make a pancake landing; *fig.* (*p.*) crumple up; **desplome** *m* collapse, downfall.

desplumar [1a] pluck; *fig.* fleece.

despoblación *f* depopulation; **despoblado** *m* deserted spot, uninhabited place; **despoblar** [1m] depopulate; *fig.* lay waste.

despojar [1a]: **~ de** strip of; *esp. fig.* divest of, denude of; ⚖ dispossess of; **~se de** *ropa* strip off, take off; *hojas etc.* shed; *fig.* give up; **despojo** *m* (*acto*) spoliation, despoilment; (*lo robado*) plunder, spoils; **~s** *pl.* leavings, scraps.

despolvorear [1a] dust.

desportilladura *f* chip; **desportillar(se)** [1a] chip.

desposado recently married; **desposar** [1a] marry; **~se** get engaged; (*casarse*) get married.

desposeer [2e] dispossess (*de* of), oust (*de* from); **~se de** give up; **desposeído**: *los* **~s** *m/pl. fig.* the have-nots.

desposorios *m/pl.* engagement.

despostar [1a] *S.Am.* (*res*) cut up; carve; butcher.

déspota *m* despot; **despótico** despotic; **despotismo** *m* despotism; **~ ilustrado** enlightened despotism.

despreciable *p.* despicable; (*de baja calidad*) trashy, worthless; (*muy pequeño*) negligible; **despreciar** [1b] scorn, despise, look down on; (*desairar*) slight, spurn; **~se de** *inf.* think it beneath one to *inf.*; **desprecio** *m* scorn, contempt.

desprender [2a] unfasten, detach; separate; **~se** ⊕ *etc.* work loose, fall off, fly off; ~ de give up; *fig.* follow from; **desprendimiento** *m fig.* disinterestedness; generosity.

despreocupación *f* unconcern *etc.*; **despreocupado** unconcerned, nonchalant, carefree.

desprestigiar [1b] disparage, run down; cheapen; **~se** lose prestige; **desprestigio** *m* loss of prestige.

desprevención *f* unreadiness; lack of foresight; **desprevenido** unprepared.

desproporción *f* disproportion; **desproporcionado** disproportionate.

despropósito *m* (piece of) nonsense, silly thing.

desprovisto de devoid of.

después 1. *adv.* afterwards, later; (*en orden*) next; (*desde entonces*) since (then); (*luego*) next, then; **2.** *prp.*: ~ de after; since; ~ de *inf.* after *ger.*; **3.** *cj.*: ~ (de) que after.

despuntado blunt; **despuntar** [1a] *v/t.* blunt; *v/i.* ♀ sprout, begin to show; (*alba*) dawn, appear.

desquiciar [1b] *puerta* unhinge (a. *fig.*); *fig.* upset, turn upside down; (*turbar*) disturb.

desquitarse [1a] get satisfaction; ♰ get one's money back; (*vengarse*) get even (con with); **desquite** *m* revenge, retaliation.

desrazonable unreasonable.

desrielar [1a] *S.Am.* derail.

destacado outstanding; **destacamento** *m* ✗ detachment; **destacar** [1g] emphasize;✗ detach, detail; **~se** stand out (a. paint. *etc.*).

destajar [1a] arrange for, contract for; *baraja* cut; **destajo** *m* (*en general*) piecework, contract work; (*tarea*) job, stint; a ~ by the job; *fig.* eagerly, keenly.

destapar [1a] *botella* open, uncork; *caja* open, take the lid off; *fig.* reveal; **destaponar** [1a] uncork.

destartalado *casa* tumbledown; (*mal dispuesto*) rambling; *máquina etc.* rickety.

destazar [1f] cut up.

destejer [2a] undo, unravel.

destellar [1a] flash; sparkle; glint, gleam; **destello** *m* flash *etc.*

destemplado ♪ out of tune; *voz* harsh, unpleasant; **destemplanza** *f* *meteor.* inclemency, bleakness; ♪ indisposition; **destemplar** [1a] upset, disturb; ♪ untune; **~se** ♪ get out of tune.

desteñir [3l] fade, take the color out of.

desternillarse [1a]: *v. risa.*

desterrado *m*, **a** *f* exile; **desterrar** [1k] exile; banish (a. *fig.*). [ing.\]

destetar [1a] wean; **destete** *m* wean-\

destierro *m* exile.

destilación *f* distillation; **destilar** [1a] *v/t.* distil; *sangre etc.* ooze, exude; *v/i.* fall (drop by drop); filter through; **destilería** *f* distillery.

destinación *f* destination; goal; **destinar** [1a] destine (a, para for, to); intend, mean (a, para for); *fondos etc.* earmark (a for); *empleado* appoint, assign (a to); **destinatario** *m*, **a** *f* addressee; **destino** *m* (*suerte*) destiny, fate; (*blanco*, ✿ *etc.*) destination; (*puesto*) job, post.

destitución *f* dismissal; **destituir** [3g] dismiss, remove (de from).

destorcer [2b a. 2h] untwist; *vara etc.* straighten; **~se** ♣ get off course.

destornillador *m* screwdriver; **destornillar** [1a] unscrew.

destrabar [1a] loosen; *preso* unfetter.

destral *m* hatchet.

destreza *f* skill, handiness, dexterity.

destripar [1a] gut; disembowel; *fig.* mangle, crush; *cuento* spoil. [throw.\]

destronar [1a] dethrone; *fig.* over-\

destroncar [1g] ♀ chop off; *p.* maim; *fig.* ruin; *animal* wear out.

destrozar [1f] smash (a. ✗), shatter; mangle; tear to pieces; *esp. fig.* ravage, ruin; **destrozo** *m* destruction; massacre *ps.*

destrucción *f* destruction; **destructivo** destructive; **destructor 1.** destructive; **2.** *m* destroyer (a. ♣); **destruir** [3g] destroy; ruin, wreck; *argumento* demolish.

desunión *f* disconnection, separation; *fig.* disunity; **desunir** [3a] separate, sever; ⊕ disconnect, disengage; *fig.* cause a rift between.

desusado obsolete, out of date; **desusar** [1a] stop using; **~se** go out of use; **desuso** *m* disuse.

desvaído gaunt; *color* dull.

desvainar [1a] shell, pod.

desvalido *niño etc.* helpless; *p.* destitute; *pol.* underprivileged.

desvalijar [1a] rob, plunder.

desvalorización *f* devaluation; **desvalorizar** [1f] devalue; devaluate.

desván *m* loft, attic.

desvanecer [2d] make *s.o.* disappear;

desvanecerse 116

duda etc. dispel; ~**se** disappear, vanish; (*atenuarse*) melt away, dissolve; evaporate; **desvanecimiento** *m* disappearance *etc.*; 🎵 dizzy spell; *fig.* vanity; *radio:* fading.

desvariar [1c] rave, talk nonsense; 🎵 be delirious; **desvarío** *m* delirium; *fig.* whim, strange notion.

desvelado sleepless, wakeful; vigilant; **desvelar** [1a] keep *s.o.* awake; ~**se** stay awake, have a sleepless night; **desvelo** *m* watchfulness, vigilance; ~**s** *pl.* care, concern.

desventaja *f* disadvantage; (*estorbo*) handicap, liability; **desventajoso** disadvantageous.

desventura *f* misfortune; **desventurado** 1. unfortunate; miserable, wretched; 2. *m, a f* wretch.

desvergonzado 1. shameless, impudent; unblushing; 2. *m, a f* scoundrel; shameless person; **desvergonzarse** [1f *a.* 1n] behave in a shameless way, be impudent (*con* to); **desvergüenza** *f* shamelessness; impudence; ¡*qué* ~! what a nerve!

desvestir [3l] undress.

desviación *f* deflection, deviation (*a. de brújula*); *mot.* diversion; (*carretera*) bypass; *fig.* departure (*de* from); **desviado** astray; off the track; lost; **desviar** [1c] turn aside, deflect, divert (*a. fig., mot.; de* from); 🎵 switch; *golpe* parry, ward off; ~**se** deviate (*de curso etc.* from); turn aside, turn away; *mot. etc.* swerve; **desvío** *m* deflection, deviation; *mot. etc.* swerve; (*camino*) detour; 🎵 siding.

desvivirse [3a]: ~ *por su.* crave, be crazy about; ~ *por inf.* go out of one's way to *inf.*, be eager to *inf.*

detallado detailed; *conocimiento* intimate; **detallar** [1a] itemize, specify; *suceso etc.* tell in detail; **detalle** *m* detail; item; F token, (nice) gesture; **detallista** *m/f* retailer.

detective *m* detective.

detención *f* stoppage, hold-up; (*retraso*) delay; 🏛 detention; **detener** [2l] (*parar*) stop, hold up, check; (*guardar*) keep, hold (back), retain; 🏛 detain; ~**se** stop (*a inf.* to *inf.*); delay, linger; pause *antes de obrar*; **detenidamente** thoroughly; at (great) length; **detenido** *cuento* detailed; lengthy; *examen* thorough; **detenimiento** *m* thoroughness; care.

detergente *adj. a. su. m* detergent.

deteriorar [1a] spoil; impair; ~**se** deteriorate, spoil; **deterioro** *m* deterioration; damage.

determinación *f* determination; decision; **determinado** (*resuelto*) determined, purposeful; (*cierto*) certain, set; **determinar** [1a] *mst* determine; *fecha, precio a.* fix; *contribución, daños a.* assess; *curso a.* shape; *pleito* decide; ~**se** *a inf.* decide to *inf.*, determine to *inf.*

detestable detestable, odious; **detestar** [1a] detest, hate, loathe.

detonación *f* detonation; **detonar** [1a] detonate, explode.

detractor 1. slanderous; 2. *m, -a f* slanderer, detractor.

detrás behind; *por* ~ behind; *atacar etc.* from behind, from the rear; ~ *de* behind.

detrimento *m* damage, detriment.

deuda *f* debt; (*en general*) indebtedness; (*pecado*) sin; ~**s** *pl.* (*pasivas*) liabilities; ~ *pública* national debt; **deudo** *m* relative; **deudor** 1. *saldo* debit *attr.*; 2. *m, -a f* debtor.

devanadera *f* *sew.* reel, winding frame; **devanar** [1a] wind; *v. seso.*

devanear [1a] rave, talk nonsense; **devaneo** *m* ravings, nonsense; 🎵 delirium; (*amorío*) affair.

devastar [1a] devastate, lay waste.

devenir 1. [3s] become; 2. *m* evolution, process of development.

devoción *f* devotion (*a* to); devoutness, piety; *fig.* liking (*a* for); **devocionario** *m* prayerbook.

devolución *f* return; † repayment, refund; **devolver** [2h; *p.p.* devuelto] return, give back, send back; † repay, refund.

devorador devouring; **devorar** [1a] devour (*a. fig.*).

devoto 1. *eccl.* devout; devoted; *obra etc.* devotional; 2. *m, a f eccl.* devout person; worshipper; ~ *del volante* car enthusiast.

día *m* day; daytime; daylight; ¡*buenos* ~**s**! good morning!, good day!; *ocho* ~**s** *freq.* week; ~ *feriado,* ~ *festivo,* ~ *de fiesta* holiday; *eccl.* feast day; *al laborable* working day, week-day; *al* ~ up to date; (*proporción*) a day; *a los pocos* ~**s** within a few days; *al otro* ~ on the following day; *de* ~ by day, in the daytime; *del* ~ fashionable, up to date; *ponerse al* ~ get up to date, catch up; *vivir al* ~ live from hand to mouth.

diabetes f diabetes; **diabético** adj. a. su. m, **a** f diabetic.

diablo m devil (a. fig.); ¡(qué ~(s)! the devil!, oh hell!; ¡vete al ~! go to hell!; **diablura** f devilry; (de niño) mischief; **diabólico** diabolic(al), develish, fiendish.

diaconía f deaconry; **diaconisa** f deaconess; **diácono** m deacon.

diadema f diadem; tiara de mujer.

diáfano diaphanous, transparent; filmy; agua limpid.

diafragma m diaphragm.

diagnosis f diagnosis; **diagnosticar** [1g] diagnose.

diagrama m diagram.

dialéctica f dialectics; **dialéctico** dialectic(al); **dialecto** m dialect; **dialectología** f dialectology.

dialogar [1h] v/t. write in dialogue form; v/i. talk, converse; **diálogo** m dialogue.

diamante m diamond; **diamantino** diamond-like, adamantine; **diamantista** m diamond-cutter.

diámetro m diameter.

diana f ✕ reveille.

¡diantre! F oh hell!

diapasón m diapason; ~ (normal) tuning fork.

diapositiva f (lantern-)slide; phot. transparency.

diario 1. daily; day-to-day; everyday; **2.** m (periódico) newspaper, daily; (relación personal) diary; † daybook; (gastos) daily expenses; **diarismo** m S.Am. journalism.

diarrea f diarrhea.

diatriba f diatribe, tirade.

dibujante m ⊕ draughtsman (a. paint.), designer; cartoonist de periódico; **dibujar** [1a] draw, sketch; ⊕ design; fig. draw, depict; **~se** contra be outlined against; **dibujo** m (en general) drawing, sketching; (un ~) drawing sketch; ⊕ design; cartoon; ~s comics; comic strips; funnies.

dicción f diction; (palabra) word; **diccionario** m dictionary.

díceres m/pl. sayings; rumor(s).

dicha f happiness; (suerte) (good) luck; por ~ by chance.

dicharachero m F witty person; b.s. coarse sort; **dicharacho** m dirty thing, coarse remark.

dicho 1. p.p. of decir; ~ y hecho no sooner said than done; **2.** m (proverbio) saying; tag; (chiste) bright remark; F insult.

dichoso (feliz) happy; (con suerte) lucky; (que trae dicha) blessed (a. F).

diciembre m December.

dictado m dictation; title of honour; ~s pl. dictates; escribir al ~ take dictation, take down; **dictador** m dictator; **dictadura** f dictatorship; **dictáfono** m dictaphone; **dictamen** m opinion, dictum; judgement; **dictaminar** [1a] v/t. juicio pass; v/i. pass judgement (en on); **dictar** [1a] dictate; inspire; sentencia pass, pronounce.

didáctico didactic.

dieciséis sixteen (etc.: v. Apéndice).

diente m tooth (a. ⊕, fig.); cog de rueda; ~ de ajo clove of garlic; ♀ ~ de león dandelion; ~s pl. postizos false teeth; hablar entre ~s mumble.

Diesel: motor ~ Diesel engine; **dieseléctrico** adj. diesel-electric; **dieselización** f Dieselization; equipping with Diesel engines.

diestra f right hand; **diestro 1.** (derecho) right; (hábil) skilful (en in, at); handy, deft con manos; **2.** m toros: matador.

dieta f diet (a. pol.); ~s pl. subsistence allowance; **dietético 1.** dietary; **2.** m dietician.

diez ten (a. su.); (fecha) tenth; las ~ ten o'clock; **diezmar** [1a] decimate (a. fig.); **diezmo** m tithe.

difamación f slander, defamation; libel (de on); **difamador 1.** slanderous, libellous; defamatory; **2.** m, **-a** f defamer; scandal monger; **difamar** [1a] slander, defame; libel; **difamatorio** = difamador 1.

diferencia f difference; a ~ de unlike; in contrast to; con corta ~ more or less; **diferencial 1.** differential; impuesto discriminatory; **2.** f ⊕, mot. differential; **diferenciar** [1b] v/t. differentiate between; v/i. differ (de from), be in disagreement (en over); **~se** (discordar) differ (de from); differentiate (a. ♀ etc.); **diferente** different (de from); unlike (the acc.); ~s pl. (varios) several; **diferir** [3i] v/t. defer, put off, hold over; v/i. differ, be different (de from).

difícil difficult, hard (de inf. to inf.); **difícilmente** with difficulty; **dificultad** f difficulty; trouble; objection; **dificultar** [1a] make s.t. difficult; hinder, impede; interfere with; **dificultoso** awkward, troublesome; F ugly.

difteria f diphtheria.

difundir [3a] spread, diffuse, disseminate; *alegría etc.* radiate.

difunto dead, defunct; *día de ~s* All Souls' Day.

difusión f spread, diffusion, dissemination; (*prolijidad*) diffuseness; (*radio*) broadcasting; **difuso** widespread; *luz* diffused; (*prolijo*) discursive.

digerible digestible; **digerir** [3i] digest (*a. fig.*); (*tragar*) swallow; (*aguantar*) stomach; **digestión** f digestion; **digestivo** digestive; **digesto** m t̄z̄ digest.

digital 1. digital; 2. f ♀ foxglove; **dígito** m digit.

dignarse [1a]: ~ *inf.* condescend to *inf.*; deign to *inf.*; **dignatario** m dignitary; **dignidad** f (*gravedad*) dignity; (*cargo*) rank; (*respeto*) self-respect; **dignificar** [1g] dignify; **digno** (*honrado*) worthy; (*grave*) dignified; (*apropiado*) fitting; ~ *de* worthy of, deserving.

digresión f digression.

dije m trinket; medallion, locket; amulet; F (*p.*) treasure, gem.

dilación f delay; procrastination.

dilapidación f waste; squandering; **dilapidar** [1a] squander.

dilatado vast, extensive; numerous; (*prolijo*) long-winded; **dilatar** [1a] stretch, dilate, distend, expand (*a. phys.*); *fama etc.* spread; (*retrasar*) delay, put off; protract; ~*se* stretch *etc.*; *fig.* be long-winded.

dilema m dilemma.

diletante m/f dilettante.

diligencia f diligence; † stagecoach; (*prisa*) speed; F errand, piece of business; **diligente** diligent, assiduous; (*pronto*) quick.

dilucidación f explanation; enlightenment; **dilucidar** [1a] elucidate.

dilución f dilution; **diluir** [3g] dilute, water down (*a. fig.*).

diluviar [1b] pour (with rain); **diluvio** m deluge, flood (*a. fig.*).

dimensión f dimension; ~*es* pl. dimensions, size.

dimes y diretes: F *andar en ~ con* argue with.

diminutivo adj. a. su. m diminutive; **diminuto** tiny, minute; dwarf.

dimisión f resignation; **dimitir** [3a] resign (*de* from).

dinámica f dynamics; *fig.* dynamic; **dinámico** dynamic (*a. fig.*).

dinamita f dynamite.

dínamo f dynamo.

dinastía f dynasty; **dinástico** dynastic.

dinerada f, **dineral** m mint of money; **dinero** m money; currency; coinage *de un país; hombre de ~* man of means; ~ *contante* cash.

dintel m lintel; threshold.

diocesano adj. a. su. m diocesan; **diócesi(s)** f diocese.

Dios m God; ♀ God; ~ *mediante* God willing; *¡~ mío!* good gracious!; I ask you!; *a ~ gracias* thank heaven; *como ~ manda* as is proper; *¡plegue a ~!* please God!; *~ sabe* God knows; *¡válgame ~!* bless my soul!; *¡vaya con ~!* goodbye.

diploma m diploma; **diplomacia** f diplomacy; **diplomática** f diplomatics; (*carrera*) diplomatic corps; **diplomático** 1. diplomatic; tactful; 2. m diplomat(ist).

dipsomanía f dipsomania.

diptongo m diphthong.

diputación f deputation, delegation; **diputado** m, a f delegate; ~ (*a Cortes*) deputy, member of Parliament; **diputar** [1a] delegate, depute.

dique m (*muro*) dike, seawall; (*malecón*) jetty, mole; dam *en río;* ~ *seco* dry dock; *entrar en ~, hacer ~* dock.

dirección f (*línea de movimiento*) direction; way; (*tendencia*) trend, course; (*gobierno*) direction; ✝ *etc.* management; leading, leadership *de partido etc.;* (*despacho*) manager's office; (*señas*) address; *~ prohibida* no entry, no thoroughfare; **directivo** *junta etc.* managing, governing; *clase* managerial; administrative; **directo** 1. direct (*a. fig.*), straight; ⊕ through, nonstop; 2. m *tenis etc.:* forehand; **director** 1. leading, guiding; = *directivo;* 2. m director (*a.* ✝, *eccl.*); ✝ manager, executive; editor *de periódico;* ♪ ~ (*de orquesta*) conductor; **directorio** m (*norma*) directive; (*junta*) directorate, ✝ board of directors; (*libro*) directory.

dirigente m leader; **dirigible** 1. *buque etc.* navigable; 2. m dirigible; **dirigir** [3c] direct (*a, hacia* at, to, towards); *carta, palabra, protesta* address (*a* to); *libro* dedicate (*a* to); *mirada* turn, direct; ♄, *mot. etc.* steer; *fig. curso* shape; *esfuerzos* concentrate (*a* on), direct (*a* towards); ~*se a* go to, make one's way to; ♣ *etc.* steer for, make for; *p.* address (o.s. to).

discar [1g] *S.Am. teleph.* dial.

discernimiento *m* discernment, discrimination; **discernir** [3i] discern; distinguish (*de* from); *premio* award.

disciplina *f mst* discipline; doctrine; **disciplinar** [1a] discipline; (*enseñar*) school, train; **disciplinario** disciplinary; **discípulo** *m*, **a** *f* disciple; pupil.

disco *m* disk; ~ *vertebral* spinal disk; *deportes:* discus; 🚩 signal; *teleph.* ~ (*de marcar*) dial; ~ *microsurco* long-playing record.

díscolo uncontrollable; *niño* mischievous.

discordante discordant; **discordar** [1m] (*ps.*) disagree (*de* with), differ (*de* from); ♪ be out of tune; **discorde** discordant; *instrumento* out of tune; **discordia** *f* discord.

discoteca *f* record library; discotheque.

discreción *f* discretion, tact; discrimination; wisdom, shrewdness; **discrecional** discretionary; optional.

discrepancia *f* discrepancy, disagreement; **discrepante** divergent; dissenting; **discrepar** [1a] differ (*de* from).

discretear [1a] try to be clever, be frightfully witty; **discreto** discreet; tactful; (*sagaz*) wise, shrewd.

discriminación *f:* ~ *racial* racial discrimination; **discriminar** [1a] *S.Am.* discriminate against.

disculpa *f* excuse, plea; apology; **disculpable** pardonable, excusable; **disculpar** [1a] excuse, pardon; exonerate (*de* from); ~**se** apologize.

discurrir [3a] *v/t.* invent, think up; *v/i.* (*andar*) roam, wander; (*agua*) flow; (*tiempo*) pass; (*hablar*) discourse (*sobre* about, on); **discursista** *m/f* windbag; big talker; **discurso** *m* speech, address; (*en general, tratado*) discourse.

discusión *f* discussion; argument; **discutir** [3a] *v/t.* discuss, debate, talk over; argue about; contradict; *v/i.* argue (*sobre* about, over).

diseminar [1a] scatter; *esp. fig.* disseminate, spread.

disensión *f* dissension.

disentería *f* dysentery.

disentimiento *m* dissent; **disentir** [3i] dissent (*de* from).

diseñador *m* designer; **diseñar** [1a] draw, sketch; **diseño** *m* drawing, sketch; ⊕ *etc.* design.

disertación *f* dissertation, disquisition; **disertar** [1a] expound on.

disfavor *m* disfavor.

disforme badly-proportioned; monstrous; (*feo*) ugly.

disfraz *m* disguise; mask *de cara;* fancy dress *para baile;* **disfrazar** [1f] disguise (*de* as; *a. fig.*); *fig.* conceal, cloak; ~**se** disguise o.s. as.

disfrutar [1a] *v/t.* enjoy; *v/i.* F enjoy o.s.; **disfrute** *m* enjoyment.

disfunción *f* ⚕ dysfunction.

disgustar [1a] displease, annoy; ~**se** be annoyed, get angry (*con, de* about); (*aburrirse*) get bored (*de* with); **disgusto** *m* (*desazón*) displeasure, annoyance; (*pesadumbre*) grief, chagrin; (*molestia*) trouble, bother, difficulty; (*disputa*) quarrel.

disidencia *f* dissidence; *eccl.* dissent; **disidente 1.** dissident, dissentient; **2.** *m/f* dissident, dissenter, nonconformist.

disílabo 1. disyllabic; **2.** *m* disyllable.

disimulado furtive, covert, underhand; **disimular** [1a] *v/t.* (*ocultar, fingir no sentir*) hide; cloak, disguise; (*perdonar*) excuse; *v/i.* dissemble, pretend; **disimulo** *m* dissimulation; indulgence.

disipación *f* dissipation (*a. fig.*); **disipado** dissipated, raffish; (*manirroto*) extravagant; **disipar** [1a] dissipate; *fortuna* fritter away (*en* on); ~**se** vanish; 🔥 evaporate.

dislocación *f* dislocation; *geol.* slip; **dislocar** [1g] dislocate.

disminución *f* diminution, decrease; ~ *física* handicap; disability; **disminuir** [3g] *v/t. a. v/i.* diminish, decrease, lessen.

disociación *f* dissociation; **disociar** [1b] dissociate, separate.

disolución *f* dissolution; 🔥 solution; (*moral*) dissoluteness; **disoluto** dissolute, dissipated; **disolver(se)** [2h; *p.p. disuelto*] dissolve (*a. fig.*), melt.

disonancia *f* discord, dissonance; **disonar** [1m] ♪ be discordant, sound wrong; *fig.* lack harmony.

disparar unequal, disparate; **disparador** *m* ✕ trigger; escapement *de reloj; phot.,* ⊕ release; **disparar** [1a] ✕ shoot, fire; let off; *piedra etc.* throw; ~**se** ✕ go off; (*caballo*) bolt, run away.

disparatado absurd, nonsensical, crazy; **disparatar** [1a] talk nonsense; **disparate** _m_ silly thing, foolish remark; absurdity.

disparidad _f_ disparity.

disparo _m_ ✗ shot, report; ⊕ trip.

dispendio _m_ waste; extravagance.

dispensa _f eccl. etc._ dispensation; exemption _de examen_; **dispensación** _f_ dispensation; **dispensar** [1a] (_distribuir_) dispense; (_eximir_) exempt, excuse (_de inf._ from _ger._); _falta_ excuse, pardon; _¡dispense Vd.!_ excuse me!; **dispensario** _m_ dispensary.

dispepsia _f_ dyspepsia.

dispersar [1a] disperse, scatter; **dispersión** _f_ dispersion (_a. phys._); **disperso** scattered; straggling; (_escaso_) sparse.

displicencia _f_ bad temper, peevishness; **displicente** disagreeable, peevish, bad-tempered.

disponer [2r] _v/t._ (_arreglar_) arrange, dispose, lay out; line up _en fila_; (_preparar_) get ready (_para_ for); _v/i._: ~ _de_ (_usar_) make use of, avail o.s. of; (_tener listo_) have _s.t._ available.

disponible available; on hand, spare; **disposición** _f_ (_arreglo_) arrangement, disposition; layout (_a._ △); (_temperamento_) disposition; aptitude (_para_ for), turn (of mind); _última_ ~ last will and testament; _a la_ ~ _de_ at the disposal of; _a la_ ~ _de Vd._, _a su_ ~ at your service.

dispuesto 1. _p.p._ of disponer; _bien_ ~ well-disposed (_hacia_ towards); △ well designed; _poco_ ~ _a inf._ reluctant to _inf._, loath to _inf._; 2. _adj._ handsome; (_hábil_) clever.

disputa _f_ dispute, argument; **disputar** [1a] _v/t._ dispute, challenge; debate; _v/i._ argue (_de_, _sobre_ about; _con_ with); _se algo_ fight for.

distancia _f_ distance (_a. fig._); _a_ ~ at a distance; _a gran_ ~, _a larga_ ~ _attr._ long-distance; **distanciar** [1b] _objetos_ space out; _rival_ outdistance; _se_ (_dos ps._) be estranged; ~ _de rival_ get ahead of; **distante** _f_ distant; **distar** [1a]: _dista_ 10 km. _de aquí_ it is 10 km. (away) from here; _dista mucho_ it's a long way away.

distender [2g] distend; **distensión** _f_ distension.

distinción _f_ distinction (_a. honor_), difference; (_lo distinto_) distinctness; _fig._ elegance; _a_ ~ _de_ unlike; **distin-**

guido distinguished; _modales etc._ gentlemanly, ladylike; elegant; **distinguir** [3d] (_divisar_) distinguish, make out; (_separar_) distinguish (_de_ from, _entre_ between), tell (_de_ from); _se_ distinguish o.s.; stand out, be distinguished; **distintivo** 1. distinctive; _señal_ distinguishing; 2. _m_ badge; _fig._ distinguishing mark, characteristic; **distinto** different, distinct (_de_ from); clear, distinct.

distorsión _f radio:_ distortion.

distracción _f_ distraction; amusement; absence of mind; **distraer** [2p] distract, divert, lead _s.o._ away (_de_ from); (_entretener_) amuse; _se_ amuse o.s.; (_distraído_ absentminded; vague, dreamy; _b.s._ inattentive, lackadaisical.

distribución _f_ distribution; (_arreglo_) arrangement; **distribuidor** _m_ distributor (_a. mot._); ✝ dealer, stockist; ~ _automático_ vending machine; **distribuir** [3g] distribute; hand out; give out, send out; ✇ deliver.

distrito _m_ district, administrative area; ⚖ circuit; constituency.

disturbio _m_ disturbance.

disuadir [3a] dissuade (_de inf._ from _ger._), deter, discourage; **disuasión** _f_ disuasion _etc._

diurético diuretic _adj. a. su. m._

diurno day _attr._, diurnal ⚇.

divagación _f_ digression; _es pl._ wanderings, ramblings; **divagar** [1h] ramble _en discurso_; wander _en mente_; (_salir del tema_) digress.

diván _m_ divan. [[3c] diverge.]

divergencia _f_ divergence; **divergir**

diversidad _f_ diversity, variety; **diversificar** [1g] diversify.

diversión _f_ amusement, entertainment; pastime; ✗ diversion; **diverso** diverse; different (_de_ from); _s pl._ several, various, sundry.

divertido _libro etc._ entertaining, enjoyable; _fiesta_ merry, gay; _chiste_, _p._ funny, amusing; _S.Am._ tight; **divertir** [3i] amuse, entertain; _se_ have a good time, amuse o.s. (_en hacer_ doing).

dividendo _m_ dividend; **dividir** [3a] divide; share (out), split (up).

divinidad _f_ divinity; godhead; (_dios pagano_) god(dess _f_); _fig._ beauty; **divino** divine (_a. fig._).

divisa _f_ emblem, badge; _heráldica:_ motto, device; _s pl._ ✝ foreign exchange.

donde

divisar [1a] make out; (e)spy.

división f division (a. ✕); *pol. etc.* split; *deportes* class; category; **divisor** m: máximo común ~ highest common factor; **divisoria** f *geog.* divide;
divisorio dividing.

divorciar [1b] divorce (a. fig.); ~se get divorced, get a divorce (de from); **divorcio** m divorce.

divulgación f disclosure etc.; **divulgar** [1h] *secreto* divulge, disclose, let out; (publicar) spread, popularize; ~se (secreto) leak out.

doblado double; (cuerpo) thickset; *terreno* rough; (taimado) sly; **dobladura** f fold, crease; **doblar** [1a] v/t. double; (plegar) fold (up), crease; *página* turn down; **dobladillo** etc. turn up; *esquina* turn, round; *cine*: dub; v/i. (torcer) turn; ♪ toll; *thea.* stand in; ~se double (plegarse) fold (up); bend, buckle; (ceder) yield.

doble double (a. ♀, sentido); *fondo* false; *mando* dual; *paño extra* thick; *p.* two-faced, deceitful; 2. m (pliegue) fold, crease; ♪ knell; ♪ tolling; *tenis etc.*: juego de ~s doubles; al ~ doubly; 3. m/f *cine etc.*: double, stand-in.

doblegar [1h] (plegar) fold; (torcer) bend; *p.* persuade, sway; (rendir) force s.o. to give in; ~se (p.) give in; **doblez 1.** m fold, crease; 2. f double-dealing, duplicity.

doce twelve (a. su.); (fecha) twelfth; *las* ~ twelve o'clock; **docena** f dozen; ~ de fraile baker's dozen.

docente educational; *centro, personal* teaching attr.; **dócil** docile; obedient; gentle.

docto 1. learned; 2. m scholar; **doctor** m doctor; **doctorado** m doctorate; **doctorarse** [1a] take one's doctorate.

doctrina f doctrine; teaching; (saber) learning; **doctrinar** [1a] teach.

documentación f documentation; papers de identidad; **documental** adj. a su. m documentary; documentary film; **documento** m document; record; certificate.

dogal m halter; noose de verdugo.

dogma m dogma; **dogmático** dogmatic(al); **dogmatismo** m dogmatism.

dólar m dollar.

dolencia f ailment, complaint; **doler** [2i] ♨ hurt, pain; ache; fig. grieve, distress; ~se de be sorry for, grieve

for; (compadecer) pity, sympathize with; (a voces) moan, groan; **doliente 1.** ♨ suffering, ill; sad, sorrowful; 2. m/f sufferer; mourner en entierro.

dolor m ♨ pain, ache; pang; (pesar) grief, sorrow; regret; **dolorido** ♨ sore, tender, aching; *p.* grief-stricken; *tono* plaintive, pained; **doloroso** painful, grievous.

doloso deceitful; fraudulent.

domador m, -a f trainer, tamer; ~ de caballos horse breaker; **domar** [1a] tame, train; fig. master, control; **domeñar** [1a] = domar.

domesticado tame; (de casa) pet; **domesticar** [1g] tame, domesticate; **doméstico 1.** animal tame, pet; *vida* home attr., family attr., domestic; 2. m, a f domestic.

domiciliar [1b] domicile; house; ~se take up (one's) residence; **domicilio** m home; ⚏, 🏛 domicile, dwelling, abode; *servicio a* ~ delivery service.

dominación f domination; dominance; rule, power; **dominador** controlling; domineering; **dominante** dominant (a. ♪); *carácter* domineering, masterful; **dominar** [1a] dominate, subdue; *p. etc.* overpower; *pasión* control, master; *lengua* know well, have a command of; ~se control o.s.

domingo m Sunday; ⚭ de Resurrección Easter Sunday; **dominicano** Dominican.

dominio m dominion, power, sway (sobre over); esp. fig. grip, hold (de on); command de lengua; (superioridad) ascendancy.

dominó m (ficha, vestido) domino.

don¹ courtesy title, used before Christian names.

don² m gift (a. fig.); ~ de acierto happy knack; ~ de lenguas gift for languages; ~ de mando leadership; **donación** f donation; 🏛 gift; **donador** m, -a f donor.

donaire m charm, wit de habla; grace, elegance; (chiste) witticism.

donante m/f donor; **donar** [1a] grant, donate; **donativo** m contribution, donation.

doncella f virgin; esp. lit. maid(en); (criada) (lady's) maid.

donde where; in which; en ~ wherein; por ~ whereby; ¿dónde? where? (a. a ~); ¿por dónde? (lugar) whereabouts?; (dirección) which way?;

dondequiera 1. *adv.* anywhere; *por* ~ all over the place; **2.** *cj.* wherever.

donoso witty, funny; *iro.* fine.

doña *courtesy title, used before Christian names; mst not translated.*

dorado 1. golden; gilded; ⊕ *etc.* gilt; **2.** *m* gilding; **dorar** [1a] gild (*a. fig.*); *cocina:* brown.

dormilón 1. sleepy; **2.** *m*, **-a** *f* sleepyhead; lieabed; **dormir** [3k] *v/t.* send to sleep; *resaca etc.* sleep off; *siesta* have; *v/i.* sleep; ~**se** go to sleep (*a. miembro*), fall asleep; **dormitar** [1a] doze, snooze; **dormitorio** *m* bedroom; *dormitory de colegio etc.*

dorsal back *attr.*, dorsal ⫿⫿; **dorso** *m* back (*a. fig.*).

dos two (*a. su.*); (*fecha*) second; *las* ~ two o'clock; *los* ~ (*ambos*) both of them; **doscientos** two hundred.

dosel *m* canopy; **doselera** *f* valance.

dosis *f* dose; (*inyección*) shot; ~ *excesiva* overdose.

dotación *f* endowment; (*ps.*) staff; ⚓ complement, crew; **dotado de** ⊕ *etc.* equipped with, fitted with; (*p.*) endowed with; **dotar** [1a] *mujer* give a dowry to; *puesto* fix a salary for; ~ *de* ⚓ man with; (*taller etc.*) staff with; ⊕ equip with, fit with; **dote** *mst f* dowry, marriage portion; *fig.* gift.

dozavo *adj. a. su. m* twelfth.

draga *f* dredge; (*barco*) dredger; **dragado** *m* (*a. obras de* ~) dredging; **dragaminas** *m* minesweeper; **dragar** [1h] dredge; *minas* sweep.

dragón *m* dragon; ⚔ dragoon; **dragonear** [1a] *S.Am.* boast; flirt.

drama *m* drama (*a. fig.*); **dramática** *f* dramatic art, drama; **dramático 1.** dramatic; *p.* dramatist; **dramatizar** [1f] dramatize; **dramaturgo** *m* playwright.

drástico drastic.

drenaje *m* drainage (*a. ⚓*); **drenar** [1a] drain.

droga *f* drug (*a. b.s.*), medicine; substance; *fig.* (*trampa*) trick; (*molestia*) nuisance; **drogadicto** *m* drug addict (*a. adj.*); **droguería** *f* drugstore.

dromedario *m* dromedary.

dual *gr.* dual; **dualismo** *m* dualism.

ducado *m* duchy, dukedom; † ducat; **ducal** ducal.

ducha *f* shower(-bath); ⚕ douche;

duchar [1a] ⚕ douche; ~**se** have a shower(-bath).

dúctil soft, ductile; *fig.* easy to handle; **ductilidad** *f* softness.

duda *f* doubt; misgiving; suspense; *no cabe* ~ (*de*) *que* there can be no doubt that; **dudar** [1a] *v/t.* doubt; *v/i.* doubt (*que, si* whether); ~ *de* doubt; mistrust; ~ *en inf.* hesitate to *inf.*; **dudoso** doubtful, dubious, uncertain.

duelista *m* duellist; **duelo**[1] *m* ⚔ duel; *batirse en* ~ (fight a) duel.

duelo[2] *m* grief, sorrow; bereavement; mourning *por muerto.*

duende *m* imp, goblin; (*fantasma*) ghost.

dueña *f* owner; proprietress; mistress *de casa etc.*; (*dama*) lady; † duenna; **dueño** *m* owner; proprietor; master; ~ *de sí mismo* self-possessed; *ser* ~ *del baile* be the master of the situation.

duermevela *f* F nap, snooze.

dulce 1. *mst* sweet; *carácter, clima* mild, gentle; *agua* fresh; *metal* soft; **2.** *m* sweet, candy; **dulcera** *f* candy jar; **dulcería** *f* candy shop; **dulcificar** [1g] sweeten; *fig.* soften, make more gentle; **dulzón** sweetish; **dulzura** *f* sweetness; gentleness *etc.*

duna *f* dune.

dúo *m* duet.

duodecimal duodecimal; **duodécimo** twelfth.

duplicación *f* duplication; **duplicado** *adj. a. su. m* duplicate; *por* ~ in duplicate; **duplicar** [1g] duplicate; repeat; ⅍ double; **duplicidad** *f* deceitfulness, duplicity.

duque *m* duke; **duquesa** *f* duchess.

durabilidad *f* durability; **durable** durable, lasting; **duración** *f* duration; length of time; *de larga* ~ *disco* long-playing; **duradero** *tela* hardwearing, serviceable; durable; **durante** during; ~ *todo el año* all the year round; **durar** [1a] *cierto tiempo* last, go on for; (*recuerdo etc.*) survive, endure.

durazno *m* peach (tree).

dureza *f* hardness *etc.*

durmiente 1. sleeping; **2.** *m/f* sleeper; **3.** *m* 🚃 (cross)tie; sleeper.

duro 1. hard; *pan* stale; (*resistente*) tough; *fig. p. etc.* hard (*con* on), cruel (*con* to), callous; **2.** *m Spanish coin* = 5 *pesetas.*

E

e and.

¡ea! come on; here!, hey!

ebanista *m* cabinetmaker; **ebanistería** *f* cabinetmaking.

ébano *m* ebony.

ebrio intoxicated, drunk.

ebullición *f* boiling.

echada *f* throw, pitch, shy, cast; *S.Am.* boast; **echadizo** spying; secretly spread; waste; **echado:** estar ~ lie, be lying (down); *C.Am.,Mex., P.R.* have an easy job (or life).

echar [1a] **1.** (*arrojar*) throw; cast, pitch, fling, toss; *desperdicios etc.* throw away; *p.* eject, turn out *de un sitio*; expel *de una sociedad*; dismiss *del trabajo*; *carta* post; *cimientos* lay; *humo etc.* emit, give off; *impuesto* levy, impose; *líquido* pour (out); *suertes* cast, draw; ~ *a inf.* begin to *inf.*; ~ *abajo* demolish; *fig.* overthrow; ~ *de menos* miss; **2.** ~se (*arrojarse*) throw o.s.; (*tenderse*) lie (down), stretch out; ~ *a inf.* begin to *inf.*; ~las de pose as, fancy o.s. as.

echona *f S.Am.* sickle.

ecléctico *adj. a. su. m* eclectic.

eclesiástico 1. ecclesiastic(al); **2.** *m* clergyman, priest; ecclesiastic.

eclipsar [1a] eclipse (*a. fig.*); *fig.* outshine, overshadow; **eclipse** *m* eclipse (*a. fig.*).

eco *m* echo; *hacer* ~ *fig.* correspond.

ecología *f* ecology; **ecologista** *m/f* ecologist.

economato *m* cooperative store; company store *para empleados*.

economía *f* economy; (*un ahorro*) economy, saving; (*virtud*) thrift, thriftiness; ~ *política* economics; **económico** economic(al); (*que ahorra*) economical, thrifty; (*barato*) economical, inexpensive; **economista** *m/f* economist; **economizar** [1f] economize (*en* on); save; *b.s.* skimp, pinch.

ecuación *f* equation; **ecuador** *m* equator; **ecuánime** *carácter* equable, level-headed; *estado* calm, composed.

ecuatoriano *adj. a. su. m*, **a** *f* Ecuador(i)an.

ecuestre equestrian.

eczema *f* eczema.

edad *f* age; de ~ elderly; de corta ~ young; de mediana ~, de ~ madura middle-aged; ♀ Media Middle Ages; mayor de ~ of age, adult, grown-up; menor de ~ under age, juvenile; ~ de hierro Iron Age; ~ de oro golden age.

edecán *m* aide-de-camp.

edén *m* paradise, (garden of) Eden.

edición *f mst* edition; issue, publication.

edicto *m* edict, proclamation.

edificación *f* △ construction, building; *fig.* edification, uplift; **edificar** [1g] build; *fig.* edify, improve, uplift; **edificio** *m* building; *fig.* edifice, structure.

editar [1a] publish; edit; **editor 1.** publishing *attr.*; **2.** *m* publisher; editor; **editorial 1.** publishing *attr.*; *política etc.* editorial; **2.** *m* editorial; **3.** *f* publishing house.

edredón *m* eiderdown.

educación *f* education; training; (*crianza*) upbringing; (*modales*) manners, breeding; **educacionista** *m/f* education(al)ist; **educado** well-mannered; cultivated; *mal* ~ ill-mannered, unmannerly; **educando** *m*, **a** *f* pupil; **educar** [1g] educate; train; (*criar*) bring up.

edulcorante 1. sweetening; **2.** *m* sweetener; sweetening.

efectivamente sure enough; (*realmente*) in fact, really; (*contestación*) precisely; **efectivo 1.** effective; (*real*) actual, real; *hacer* ~ *check* cash, clear; **2.** *m* cash; specie; **efecto** *m* effect; impression, impact; ~s *pl.* (*propiedad*) effects; (*capital etc.*) assets; (*enseres*) things; *esp.* ✝ goods, articles, merchandise; *al* ~ for the purpose; *en* ~ (*como contestación*) (yes) indeed; (*en realidad*) in fact; in effect; *hacer* ~ make an impression.

efectuar [1e] effect, effectuate; *parada etc.* make; (*causar*) bring about;

proyecto, reparación carry out; **~se** take place.

efervescencia f effervescence.

eficacia f efficacy; efficiency; **eficaz** effective, efficacious, effectual; efficient; **eficiencia** f efficiency; **eficiente** efficient.

efímero adj. ephemeral, short-lived.

efluvio m effluvium.

efusión f effusion (a. fig.), outpouring; ~ de sangre bloodshed; **efusivo** effusive.

egipcio adj. a. su. m, **a** f Egyptian.

égloga f eclogue.

egocéntrico self-centered; **egoísmo** m egoism; selfishness; **egoísta** 1. egoistic(al); selfish; 2. m/f egoist; **egolatría** f self-worship, self-glorification.

egregio eminent, distinguished.

¡eh! hey!, heigh!; hi!; hoy!

eje m ⊕ axle de ruedas; (árbol, husillo) shaft, spindle; ⊕, phys., geog., pol. axis; fig. (centro) hinge, hub; (esencia) crux, core; central idea; ~ tándem dual axle, dual rear.

ejecución f execution (a. ⚡, ♪); fulfillment; enforcement de ley; ♪ performance, rendition; **ejecutar** [1a] execute (a. ⚡, ♪); perform (a. ♪); órdenes fulfil; **ejecutivo** 1. executive; (apremiante) pressing, insistent; (sin demora) prompt; 2. m executive; **ejecutor** m: ~ testamentario executor.

¡ejem! hem!

ejemplar 1. exemplary; 2. m example; copy de libro; zo. etc. specimen; (modelo) model, example; **ejemplificar** [1g] exemplify, be illustrative of; **ejemplo** m example, instance; (lección) object lesson; por ~ for example, for instance.

ejercer [2b] exercise; influencia exert, bring to bear; poder exercise, wield; profesión practise (de as); **ejercicio** m exercise (a. ✗); practice; tenure de oficio; ♱ fiscal year; **ejercitar** [1a] exercise; profesión practise; ✗ etc. train, drill; **~se** exercise; practise; train; **ejército** m army.

ejido m common.

el 1. artículo: the; 2. pron.: ~ de that of; ~ de Juan John's.

él (p.) he; (cosa) it; (tras prp.) him; it.

elaboración f elaboration etc.; **elaborar** [1a] elaborate; producto make, manufacture, prepare; metal, madera etc. work; proyecto work on.

elasticidad f elasticity; give, spring(iness); fig. resilience; **elástico** 1. elastic; superficie etc. springy; fig. resilient; 2. m elastic.

elección f choice, selection; election; **electo** elect; **elector** m, **-a** f elector; **electorado** m electorate; **electoral** electoral; voting attr.

electricidad f electricity; **electricista** m electrician; **eléctrico** electric(al); **electrificar** [1g], **electrizar** [1f] electrify (a. fig.); **electrodo** m electrode; **electrólisis** f electrolysis; **electrón** m electron; **electrónica** f electronics; **electrotecnia** f electrical engineering.

elefante m, **a** f elephant; **elefantino** elephantine.

elegancia f elegance etc.; **elegante** elegant; movimiento etc. graceful; (distintivo) stylish; (majo) smart; (de moda, sociedad) fashionable.

elegía f elegy; **elegíaco** elegiac.

elegir [3c a. 3l] choose, select; pol. etc. elect.

elemento m mst element (a. ⚡); ⚡ cell de pila; fig. ingredient; factor de situación; ~s pl. fig. means, resources; material, ingredients.

elepé 1. long-playing, LP; 2. m long-playing record.

elevación f elevation; height, altitude; fig. exaltation; rise de precios etc.; **elevador** m hoist; S.Am. elevator; ~ de granos (grain) elevator; **elevar** [1a] raise (a. ⚡, precios), lift (up), elevate; exalt a dignidad; ⚡ boost; **~se** rise; (edificio etc.) soar, tower; fig. get conceited.

eliminación f elimination, removal; **eliminar** [1a] eliminate, remove; necesidad etc. obviate.

elipse f ellipse; **elipsis** f ellipsis.

elitista elitist adj. a. su. m/f.

elixir m elixir.

ella (p.) she; (cosa) it; (tras prp.) her; it; **ellas** pl. they; (tras prp.) them.

ello etc.; ~ es que the fact is that; ~ dirá the event will show.

ellos pl. they; (tras prp.) them.

elocuencia f eloquence; **elocuente** eloquent.

elogiar [1b] praise, eulogize; **elogio** m praise, eulogy; tribute.

elucidar [1a] elucidate.

eludible avoidable; **eludir** [3a] elude, evade, escape; avoid.

emanación f emanation (a. phys.);

(*olor*) effluvium; **emanar** [1a]: ~ *de* emanate from, come from.

emancipación *f* emancipation; **emancipar** [1a] emancipate.

embaidor *m* trickster, cheat; **embaír** [3a; *defective*] impose upon.

embajada *f* embassy; **embajador** *m* ambassador.

embalador *m*, **-a** *f* packer; **embalaje** *m* packing; **embalar** [1a] pack, bale, parcel up.

embaldosado *m* tiled floor; **embaldosar** [1a] tile.

embalsamar [1a] embalm.

embalsar [1a] dam (up); **embalse** *m* dam; reservoir.

embarazada pregnant; **embarazar** [1f] obstruct, hamper, hinder; (*empreñar*) make pregnant; **embarazo** *m* (*estorbo*) obstacle, hindrance; (*preñado*) pregnancy; **embarazoso** awkward, embarrassing.

embarcación *f* craft, boat, vessel; (*embarco*) embarkation; **embarcadero** *m* pier, landing stage, jetty; **embarcar** [1g] *ps.* embark, put on board; ~**se** embark, go on board; **embarco** *m* embarkation.

embargar [1h] *propiedad* seize, impound; (*estorbar*) impede; *sentidos* blunt, paralyse; **embargo** *m* ⚓ seizure, distraint. [cargo).]

embarque *m* shipment, loading (of ƒ

embarrancarse [1g] run into a ditch, get stuck.

embarrar [1a] splash with mud; smear; *C.Am.,Mex.* involve in a dirty deal.

embate *m* ✕ sudden attack; brunt *de ataque*; breaking *de olas*.

embaucador *m*, **-a** *f* trickster, swindler; **embaucar** [1g] trick, fool, impose upon.

embaular [1a] pack (into a trunk).

embazar [1f] *v/t.* (*teñir*) dye brown; (*pasmar*) astound; *v/i.* be dumbfounded; ~**se** have had enough.

embebecer [2d] *v/t.* entertain; ~**se** be lost in wonder.

embeber [2a] *v/t.* absorb, soak up; *esp. fig.* imbibe; *v/i.* shrink; ~**se** (*absorto*) be absorbed; (*extático*) be enraptured.

embelecar [1g] deceive, cheat; **embelequería** *f W.I.,Col.,Mex.* fraud; swindle.

embelesar [1a] enrapture, enthrall, fascinate; **embeleso** *m* rapture, bliss, delight.

embellecer [2d] embellish, beautify; **embellecimiento** *m* embellishment.

embestida *f* assault, onslaught; charge *de toro etc.*; **embestir** [3l] assault, assail; rush upon.

embetunar [1a] *zapatos* blacken.

emblandecer [2d] soften; *fig.* mollify.

emblanquecer [2d] whiten, bleach.

emblema *m* emblem, device.

embobarse [1a] gape, be amazed (*con, de, en* at).

embocadura *f* mouth *de río*; tip *de cigarrillo*; ♩ mouthpiece; bit *de freno*; *thea.* proscenium arch; **embocar** [1g] put into the mouth; F *comida* cram, scoff.

embolado *m thea.* minor role; F trick; **embolar** [1a] fit with (wood) balls; polish; ~**se** *C.Am., Mex.* get drunk.

embolia *f* clot; embolism.

émbolo *m* piston; plunger.

embolsar [1a] pocket; *pago* collect.

emborrachar [1a] intoxicate, get drunk; ~**se** get drunk (*con, de, on*).

emborronar [1a] *papel* scribble over, cover with scribble.

emboscada *f* ambush; **emboscarse** [1g] lie in ambush, hide.

embotado dull, blunt (*a. fig.*); **embotar** [1a] blunt, dull (*a. fig.*); *fig.* weaken, enervate.

embotellamiento *m* traffic jam *de coches*; bottleneck *en calle estrecha* (*a. fig.*); **embotellar** [1a] bottle; *fig.* bottle up.

embozar [1f] muffle (up); *fig.* cloak, disguise; ~**se** muffle o.s. up; **embozo** *m* covering of the face, muffler, mask; (*cama*) turned-down bedclothes; *fig.* cunning.

embragar [1h] *engranaje* engage; *piezas* connect, couple; **embrague** *m* clutch; ~ *de disco* disk clutch.

embravecer [2d] *v/t.* enrage; *v/i.* ♣ flourish; ~**se** (*mar*) get rough.

embriagar [1h] make drunk, intoxicate; *fig.* enrapture; ~**se** get drunk; **embriaguez** *f* drunkenness, intoxication; *fig.* rapture.

embrión *m* embryo; *en* ~ in embryo.

embrocar [1g] *hilos* wind (on a bobbin); *zapatos* tack; (*vaciar*) empty; (*volver boca abajo*) invert.

embrollar [1a] muddle, entangle, dislocate; *esp. ps.* embroil; ~**se** get into a muddle; ~ *en* get involved in;

embrollo m (enredo) tangle, muddle; (lío) entanglement.

embromar [1a] tease, make fun of, rag; (engañar) hoodwink, kid F; **~se** S.Am. loiter; (aburrirse) get bored.

embrujar [1a] p. bewitch; casa haunt.

embrutecer [2d] brutalize, coarsen; **embrutecimiento** m coarsening; becoming brutal.

embuchar [1a] stuff (with mincemeat); F comida bolt.

embudar [1a] fit with a funnel; fig. trick; **embudo** m funnel; fig. trick.

embuste m (mentira) lie, story F; (engaño) trick, fraud; imposture, (piece of) chicanery; **~s** pl. trinkets; **embustero** 1. deceitful; 2. m, a f liar, storyteller F; cheat.

embutido m cocina: sausage; ⊕ inlay, marquetry; **embutir** [3a] stuff, cram; ⊕ inlay.

emergente resultant; **emerger** [2c] emerge; (submarino) surface.

emeritense adj. a. su. m/f (native) of Mérida.

emético adj. a. su. m emetic.

emigrante adj. a. su. m/f emigrant; **emigrar** [1a] (e)migrate.

eminencia f (colina etc., título, fig.) eminence; (lo muy alto) loftiness; fig. prominence; **eminente** (muy alto) lofty; fig. eminent; prominent, distinguished.

emisario m emissary; **emisión** f emission; issue; radio: (acto) broadcasting; (una ~) a broadcast; **emisor** m transmitter; **emisora** f radio station; **emitir** [3a] emit, give off (or forth, out); moneda, sellos issue; radio: broadcast.

emoción f emotion; (entusiasmo etc.) excitement; (estremecimiento, escalofrío) thrill; **emocionante** exciting, thrilling; moving; **emocional** emotional; **emocionar** [1a] (entusiasmar) excite, thrill; (conmover) move; **~se** get excited.

emotivo emotive; emotional.

empacar [1g] pack (up); **~se** be obstinate; (cortarse) get rattled.

empachar [1a] upset, cause indigestion to; **~se** get embarrassed; **empacho** m 🏥 indigestion; fig. embarrassment, bashfulness; **empachoso** indigestible; fig. embarrassing.

empadronar [1a] take the census of, register.

empalagar [1h] (empachar) pall (a

on; a. fig.), cloy (a. fig.); (fastidiar) bore, weary; **empalagoso** sickly, rich, gooey F; fig. wearisome.

empalar [1a] impale; **empalizada** f stockade.

empaliar decorate with bunting.

empalmar [1a] v/t. cuerda splice; fig. couple, join; v/i. (líneas) join, meet; (trenes) connect (con with); **empalme** m splice; ⊕ joint, connection; 🚂 junction de líneas.

empanada f (meat) pie, patty; fig. fraud; shady business.

empantanar [1a] flood, swamp; fig. bog down.

empañado ventana misty, steamy; **empañar** [1a] niño swaddle, wrap up; ventana mist; imagen blur; **~se** (imagen etc.) dim, blur.

empapar [1a] soak, saturate, steep (a. fig.); (lluvia etc.) drench.

empapelador m paperhanger; **empapelar** [1a] pared paper; objeto wrap in paper.

empaque m packing; fig. appearance, presence; solemnness; S.Am. brazenness; **empaquetar** [1a] pack (up), parcel up, package.

emparedado m sandwich; **emparedar** [1a] immure, confine.

emparejar [1a] v/t. (aparear) match; (allanar) level; v/i. catch up (con with); **~se** match.

emparentado related by marriage (con to); **emparentar** [1k] become related by marriage.

emparrado m (trained) vine.

empastar [1a] paste; libro bind (in stiff covers); diente fill, stop; **empaste** m filling.

empatar [1a] deportes: draw, tie; pol. etc. tie; **empate** m draw, tie; **empatía** f empathy.

empecinamiento m stubbornness; determination.

empedernido (cruel) heartless; (sin compasión) obdurate; pol. etc. diehard; **empedernir** [3a; defective] harden; **~se** harden one's heart.

empedrado 1. superficie pitted; cara pockmarked; (manchado) dappled, flecked; 2. m paving; **empedrar** [1k] pave.

empeine m groin; instep de pie.

empellón m push, shove; a **~es** roughly; dar **~es** jostle.

empelotarse [1a] F get muddled; (reñir) get involved in a row; S.Am. undress; strip.

empeñar [1a] pawn, pledge; *fig.* engage, compel; ~se insist (en on), persist (en in); *(obligarse)* bind o.s.; ~ en *inf.* insist on *ger.*, be set on *ger.*; **empeño** *m* pledge; obligation; determination, insistence; **empeñoso** diligent, eager.

empeoramiento *m* deterioration, worsening; **empeorar** [1a] make worse, worsen.

empequeñecer [2d] dwarf; *(despreciar)* belittle; *(quitar importancia a)* minimize.

emperador *m* emperor; **emperatriz** *f* empress.

empero but, yet, however.

empezar [1f *a.* 1k] begin, start *(a inf.* to *inf.; por inf.* by *ger.*).

empinado *cuesta* steep; *(alto)* high; **empinar** [1a] *v/t. vaso etc.* raise; *(enderezar)* straighten; *v. codo; v/i.* F drink; ~se *(p.)* stand on tiptoe; *(caballo)* rear; *(edificio)* tower.

empírico empiric(al); **empirismo** *m* empiricism.

emplastar [1a] plaster, poultice; *cara* make up; **emplasto** *m* plaster, poultice.

emplazamiento *m* ⚖ summons; ✕ emplacement; **emplazar** [1f] summon(s).

empleado *m*, **a** *f* employee; clerk *en oficina etc.*; **emplear** [1a] use; employ; *tiempo* occupy, spend; **empleo** *m* use; *(trabajo en general)* employment; *(puesto)* employment, job; *modo de* ~ usage; instructions for use.

emplumar [1a] *v/t.* (tar and) feather; *v/i.* = **emplumecer** [2d] fledge, grow feathers.

empobrecer [2d] *v/t.* impoverish; *v/i.*, ~se become poor.

empollar [1a] *v/t.* incubate; hatch; *v/i. (gallina)* sit, brood *(a. fig.)*.

empolvado powdery; *superficie etc.* dusty; **empolvar** [1a] *cara* powder; *superficie* cover with dust; ~se *(p.)* powder o.s., powder one's face; *(superficie)* gather dust, get dusty.

emponzoñar [1a] poison *(a. fig.); fig.* corrupt.

emporcar [1g *a.* 1m] dirty, foul.

emporio *m* emporium; mart.

emprendedor enterprising, go-ahead, pushful; **emprender** [2a] undertake, take on, tackle; *(empezar)* begin on, embark (up)on.

empreñar [1a] *p.* make pregnant, get with child; *animal etc.* impregnate; ~se become pregnant.

empresa *f* enterprise, undertaking *(a.* ✝*)*; venture; ✝ company, concern; *thea.* management; **empresario** *m thea.* manager; showman; impresario; promoter.

empréstito *m* (public) loan.

empujar [1a] push, shove; *(introducir)* push, thrust (en into); *(propulsar)* drive, propel; *botón* press; *fig. p.* sack, give the push to F; **empujatierra** *f* bulldozer; **empuje** *m* push, shove; *(presión)* pressure; *fig.* push, drive; ⊕ thrust; **empujón** *m* push, shove; dig, poke *con dedo etc.*

empulgueras *f/pl.* thumb-screw.

empuñadura *f* hilt *de espada*; grip *de herramienta*; opening *de cuento*; **empuñar** [1a] grasp, grip, clutch.

emular [1a] emulate, rival; **émulo 1.** emulous; **2.** *m* rival, competitor.

en *(dentro)* in; *(hacia dentro)* into; *(sobre)* on, upon; *(en un lugar, ciudad etc.)* in, at; *(por un precio)* for, at; *(porcentaje)* by; ~ *viéndole (pasado)* the moment I saw him; *(presente, futuro)* the moment I see him; ~ que in that; ¿~ qué lo notas? how can you tell?

enaguas *f/pl.* petticoat, slip.

enajenación *f* alienation; estrangement; *(distracción)* absentmindedness; **enajenar** [1a] *propiedad* alienate; *derechos* dispose of; *p.* drive mad; ~se *(estar absorto)* be lost in wonder.

enaltecer [2d] exalt, extol.

enamorado: *estar* ~ de be in love with; **enamorar** [1a] inspire love in, win the love of; ~se fall in love *(de* with).

enano 1. dwarf; stunted; **2.** *m* dwarf; midget; *contp.* runt.

enarbolar [1a] raise, hang out, hoist; brandish; ~se *(caballo)* rear.

enarcar [1g] *barril* hoop; *cejas* arch, raise.

enardecer [2d] *fig.* fire, inflame; ~se get excited; blaze *(de* with).

encabezamiento *m* census; tax list heading, headline; caption *de dibujo etc.*; preamble *de documento*; ~ de factura billhead; **encabezar** [1f] head, lead; *papel* put a heading to; *dibujo etc.* caption.

encadenación *f*, **encadenamiento** *m* chaining; *fig.* connexion, concatenation; **encadenar** [1a] (en)chain; (*trabar*) shackle; *fig.* connect, link.

encajadura *f* (*acto*) insertion, fitting; (*hueco*) socket; (*ranura*) groove; **encajar** [1a] 1. *v/t.* (*introducir*) insert, fit (*into* en); (*unir*) join, fit together; ⊕ encase, house (*en* in); *fig.* be appropriate; ~ con fit, match; (*cuadrar*) square with, be in line with; 3. **~se** F (*introducirse*) squeeze in; *fig.* intrude (en upon), gate-crash (*en acc.*); **encaje** *m* (*acto*) insertion, fitting; (*hueco*) socket; (*ranura*) groove; (*caja*) housing; *sew.* lace.

encajonar [1a] pack *en caja etc.*; box (up); ⊕ *etc.* box in, (en)case; squeeze in.

encalabrinar [1a] 🞽 make *s.o.* dizzy; **~se** F get an obsession.

encalar [1a] *pared* whitewash; 🞿 lime.

encalladero *m* shoal, sandbank; **encalladura** *f* stranding; **encallar** [1a] run aground, run ashore; *fig.* fail; get stuck, get tied up.

encallecido hardened.

encalmado ⚓ becalmed; 🞿 slack; **encalmarse** [1a] be becalmed.

encamarse [1a] take to one's bed; (*animal*) crouch, hide; (*trigo*) bend over.

encaminar [1a] guide, set on the right road (*a* to); *energías* direct (*a* towards); **~se** *a* set out for, take the road to), make for.

encandilar [1a] dazzle, bewilder; *lumbre* poke; *emoción* kindle.

encanecer(se) [2d] (*pelo*) grey; (*p.*) grow old; (*mohoso*) go mouldy.

encanijado puny; **encanijarse** [1a] grow weak, begin to look ill.

encantado delighted, charmed, pleased; **encantador** 1. enchanting, charming, delightful, lovely; 2. *m*, **-a** *f* magician; *fig.* charmer; **encantamiento** *m* enchantment; **encantar** [1a] bewitch; *fig.* enchant, charm, delight; **encante** *f* auction; public sale; **encanto** *m* charm, spell, enchantment, delight.

encañada *f* ravine; **encañado** *m* conduit; **encañar** [1a] *v/t. agua* pipe; *terreno* drain; *planta* stake; *v/i.* form stalks.

encapotado *cielo* overcast; *Cuba* triste; alicaído; **encapotarse** [1a] (put on a) cloak; (*p.*) frown; (*cielo*) cloud over.

encapricharse [1a] persist in one's foolishness.

encapuchado hooded.

encaramar [1a] raise, lift up; (*alabar*) extol; 🞽 elevate; **~se** perch; ~ *a* climb, get to the top of.

encarar [1a] *v/t. arma* point, aim; *problema* face; *v/i.*, **~se con** face, confront.

encarcelación *f*, **encarcelamiento** *m* imprisonment; **encarcelar** [1a] imprison, jail.

encarecer [2d] *v/t.* 🞽 put up the price of; *p.* recommend; (*alabar*) extol; exaggerate; *dificultad* stress; *v/i.*, **~se** get dearer; **encarecidamente** insistently.

encargado 1.: ~ de in charge of; 2. *m* agent, representative; person in charge; **encargamiento** *m* duty; obligation; **encargar** [1h] (*encomendar*) entrust; charge (*un deber with a* duty), commission; recommend; **~se de** (*tomar sobre si*) take charge of, take over; (*cuidar de*) look after, see about; ~ de *inf.* undertake to *inf.*, see about *ger.*; **encargo** *m* (*deber etc.*) charge, commission, assignment, job; (*pedido*) order; (*puesto*) office, post.

encariñarse [1a]: ~ con grow fond of; **encariñamiento** *m* endearment.

encarnación *f* incarnation; embodiment; **encarnado** (*color*) red, (Caucasian-) fleshcolored; *tez* florid; (*que ha encarnado*) incarnate; **encarnar** [1a] *v/t.* embody, personify; *anzuelo* bait; *v/i.* become incarnate; (*herida*) heal (up); (*arma*) enter the flesh; **encarnizar** [1f] *fig.* (*irritar*) enrage; make cruel; **~se** (*irritarse*) get angry; (*luchar*) fight fiercely.

encarrilar [1a] set on the right road, direct; *fig.* put on the right track, set right.

encasar [1a] *hueso* set.

encasillar [1a] pigeonhole; file, classify.

encastillar [1a] fortify; **~se** 🞽 take to the hills; *fig.* refuse to yield.

encauchado 1. rubberized; rubberlined; 2. *m S.Am.* rubber-lined poncho; **encauchar** [1a] rubberize.

encausar [1a] prosecute, put on trial.

encauzar [1f] channel; *fig.* channel, guide.

encenagarse [1h] get muddy; *fig.* wallow in vice.

encendedor *m* lighter; cigarette

lighter; (p.) lamplighter; **encender** [2g] light, set fire to, ignite; kindle (a. fig.); cerilla strike; luz, ⚡ switch on; fig. inflame; ~se catch (fire), ignite; (arder más) flare up; fig. (p.) get excited; **encendido 1.** adj. luz on, alambre live; (color) glowing (de with); **2.** m mot. ignition, firing; ~ transistorizado solid-state ignition.

encerado 1. waxy, wax-colored; **2.** m oilcloth; **encerar** [1a] wax; suelo polish.

encerradero m fold, pen; **encerrar** [1k] enclose, shut in, shut up; lock in, lock up con llave; fig. contain, include; **encerrona** f dilemma; tight spot; trap.

encestar [1a] put in a basket; F sink a basketball.

enchapado m plating; veneer; **enchapar** [1a] plate con metal; veneer.

encharcar [1g] swamp, cover with puddles; ~se fill with water.

enchicharse S.Am. get drunk; C.Am. get angry.

enchilada f S.Am. enchilada; corncake with chili.

enchufar [1a] connect, fit together; (como telescopio) telescope; ⚡ plug in; **enchufe** m ⊕ joint, connexion; (manguito) sleeve; (hueco) socket; ⚡ plug, point, socket; F (p. etc.) connexion, useful contact; (sinecura) cushy job; F tener ~ have pull; have connections.

encía f gum.

enciclopedia f encyclopedia; **enciclopédico** encyclopedic.

encierro m confinement, shuttingup; (lugar) enclosure; (prisión) prison; toros: corralling.

encima (en el aire) above, over, overhead; (en la cumbre) at the top; on top; (sobre) on; ~ de on, upon; on top of; por ~ over; fig. superficially.

encina f holm oak, ilex.

encinta pregnant; zo. with young; mujer ~ expectant mother.

encintado m curb(stone).

enclaustrar [1a] cloister; fig. hide away.

enclavar [1a] nail; (traspasar) pierce; F cheat; ~se interlock; **enclave** m geog. enclave.

enclenque weak(ly), sickly.

encobar [1a] brood, sit.

encoger [2c] v/i. shrink; p. intimidate, fill with fear; v/i., ~se shrink, contract; (p.) (acobardarse) cringe; ~

de hombros shrug (one's shoulders); **encogido** shrunken, contracted; p. bashful; **encogimiento** m shrinkage, contraction; fig. bashfulness.

encolar [1a] glue; size antes de pintar; (pegar) stick (down, together).

encolerizar [1f] provoke, anger, incense; ~se get angry, see red.

encomendar [1k] commend, entrust; ~se a send greetings to.

encomiar [1b] extol, praise.

encomienda f (encargo) charge, commission; recommendation.

encomio m praise, tribute.

enconar [1a] 𝔰 inflame; p. irritate, provoke; ~se fester; fig. fester, rankle; **encono** m rancour, spite.

encontrado opposed, contrary, conflicting; **encontrar** [1m] find; meet; esp. fig. encounter; ~se be, be situated (en in); (ps.) meet; (coches etc.) collide; (opiniones) clash; **encontrón** m, **encontronazo** m crash, collision.

encorchar [1a] cork; abejas hive.

encordar [1m] raqueta, violín string; (atar) lash with ropes; **encordelar** [1a] tie with string.

encornadura f horns.

encorralar [1a] corral, pen.

encorvada f stoop; slouch; **encorvadura** f bend(ing); curving, curvature; **encorvar** [1a] bend, curve; hook; inflect; ~se bend (over, down), stoop; (romperse) buckle.

encrespado curly; **encrespador** m curling-tongs; **encrespar** [1a] pelo curl; plumas ruffle; ~se curl; ripple; (mar) get rough; (p.) get angry.

encrucijada f cross roads, intersection; ambush.

encuadernación f binding; (taller) bindery; **encuadernar** [1a] bind.

encuadrar [1a] frame; (encajar) fit in, insert.

encubierta f fraud; **encubierto** hidden, under-cover; **encubridor 1.** concealing; **2.** m, -a f 𝕣𝕥𝕒 accessory (after the fact), abettor; **encubrir** [3a; p.p. encubierto] hide, conceal, cloak; 𝕣𝕥𝕒 crimen conceal, abet.

encuentro m meeting (a. deportes), encounter (a. ⚔, deportes); collision de coches etc.; clash de opiniones.

encuesta f poll; (investigación) inquiry, probe F; ~ demoscópica opinion poll.

encumbrado high, lofty, towering; **encumbrar** [1a] raise (up); p. (ele-

var) exalt; (*ensalzar*) extol; **~se** (*edificio*) tower; soar (*a. fig.*); (*p.*) be proud.

encurtido *m* pickle; **encurtir** [3a] pickle.

endeble ✚ feeble, frail; *fig.* flimsy.

endecasílabo 1. hendecasyllabic; **2.** *m* hendecasyllable.

endémico endemic; *fig.* rife.

endemoniado possessed of the devil; *fig.* devilish, fiendish; furious, wild.

endenante(s) *S.Am.* recently.

endentadura *f* serration; **endentar** [1k] ⊕ mesh, engage; **endentecer** [2d] teethe.

enderezar [1f] (*poner derecho*) straighten (out), unbend; (*poner vertical*) set up, right (*a.* ♪); *fig.* direct; dedicate; (*arreglar*) put in order; **~se** straighten (up), draw o.s. up.

endeudarse [1a] run into debt; **endeudamiento** *m* indebtedness.

endiablado devilish, fiendish; *co.* impish, mischievous.   [ness.⟩

endiosamiento *m* pride; haughti-⟩

endiosar [1a] deify; **~se** give o.s. airs; (*absorto*) be absorbed.

endocrino endocrine.

endomingado in one's Sunday best, dressed up; **endomingarse** [1h] dress up (in one's Sunday best).

endosante *m/f* endorser; **endosar** [1a] endorse; **endosatario** *m* endorsee; **endoso** *m* endorsement.

endulzar [1f] sweeten (*a. fig.*); soften, mitigate.

endurecer [2d] harden, toughen (*a. fig.*); stiffen; *fig.* inure (*a* to); **~se** harden, set; *fig.* become cruel; **endurecido** hard; *fig.* hardy, inured *a fatigas etc.*; (*cruel*) callous, hard-boiled F.

enebro *m* juniper.

enema *f* enema.

enemigo 1. enemy, hostile; *fig.* inimical; **2.** *m*, **a** *f* enemy; **enemistad** *f* enmity; **enemistar** [1a] set at odds, make enemies of; **~se** fall out (*con* with), become enemies.

energético *attr.* energy; *attr.* power; **energía** *f* energy; ⊕, ⚡ *etc.* energy; *fig.* drive, go F; **~ solar** solar energy; **enérgico** energetic; *tono etc.* emphatic; *p.* energetic, vital, active.

energúmeno *m*, **a** *f* person possessed; *fig.* madman.

enero *m* January.

enervación *f* enervation; **enervar** [1a] enervate.

enésimo n[th], umpteenth F.

enfadar [1a] annoy, anger, vex; **~se** get angry, be cross (*de* at, *con* with); **enfado** *m* annoyance, irritation; **enfadoso** annoying, irksome.

enfangar [1h] cover with mud.

énfasis *m* emphasis; stress; **enfático** emphatic; positive.

enfermar [1a] *v/t.* make ill; *v/i.* fall ill, be taken ill; **enfermedad** *f* illness, sickness, disease; *fig.* malady; **enfermería** *f* sick bay *de colegio etc.*; (*hospital*) infirmary; **enfermera** *f* nurse; **enfermero** *m* male nurse; ✚ orderly; **enfermizo** sickly, infirm; unhealthy; *mente* morbid; **enfermo 1.** ill, sick; **~ de amor** lovesick; **2.** *m*, **a** *f* patient, invalid.

enfiestarse [1a] *S.Am.* have a good time; celebrate.

enfilar [1a] ✕ enfilade; (*alinear*) line up; (*ensartar*) thread.

enflaquecer [2d] *v/t.* make thin; weaken; *v/i.*, **~se** get thin, lose weight; *fig.* weaken.

enfocar [1g] *phot. etc.* focus; *fig. problema* approach, consider, look at; size up; envisage; **enfoque** *m phot. etc.* focus(ing); *fig.* grasp.

enfrascar [1g] bottle; **~se** get entangled, get involved; bury o.s. (*en libro* in).

enfrenar [1a] *caballo* bridle; ⊕ brake; *fig.* restrain.

enfrentamiento *m* confrontation (*policía*; *masas*); **enfrentar** [1a] *v/t.* put face to face, confront; *v/i.* **~se con** face (up to).

enfrente (*en el lado opuesto*) opposite; (*delante*) in front; (*en pugna*) against, in opposition; **~ de** opposite (to).

enfriadero *m* cold storage; **enfriamiento** *m* cooling; ✚ cold; **enfriar** [1c] cool (*a. fig.*), chill; **~se** cool (down *or* off).

enfundar [1a] sheathe, (put in its) case; (*llenar*) stuff.

enfurecer [2d] enrage, madden; **~se** (*p.*) get furious; (*mar*) get rough.

enfurruñarse [1a] F get angry; (*ponerse mohíno*) sulk.

engalanar [1a] adorn, (be)deck; **~se** dress up.

enganchar [1a] hook, hitch; (*colgar*) hang up; *caballo* harness; ⊕ couple; *fig.* inveigle, rope in; **~se** get hooked up, catch; ✗ enlist; **enganche** m (*acto*) hooking (up); 🚂, ⊕ coupling; ✗ recruiting, enlisting.

engañadizo gullible; **engañador** 1. deceptive; 2. m, -a f cheat, impostor, deceiver; **engañar** [1a] deceive, fool F; (*timar*) cheat, trick; mislead *con consejos falsos*; beguile *con encantos*; delude *con promesas vanas*; ~se (*equivocarse*) be mistaken; delude o.s. *con esperanzas etc.*; **engañifa** f f trick, swindle; **engaño** m deceit; (*timo etc.*) fraud, trick; (*apariencia falsa*) sham; (*decepción*) wiles; ~s *pl.* wiles; **engañoso** p. *etc.* deceitful; *apariencia etc.* deceptive; *consejo etc.* misleading.

engarzar [1f] *cuentas* thread; *joya* mount, set; (*rizar*) curl; *fig.* link.

engastar [1a] set, mount; **engaste** m setting, mount(ing).

engat(us)ar [1a] F coax, cajole, inveigle (*para que into ger.*).

engendrar [1a] beget, breed (*a. fig.*); generate (*a. ⚡*); *fig.* engender; **engendro** m *biol.* foetus.

englobar [1a] lump together.

engolfar [1a] ⚓ lose sight of land; ~se en *fig.* plunge into; launch into.

engolosinar [1a] tempt, entice; ~se *con* grow accustomed to.

engomar [1a] gum, stick.

engordar [1a] *v/t.* fatten; *v/i.* get fat, fill out; F get rich.

engorrar [1a] *S.Am.* vex, bother; **engorroso** bothersome, vexatious, trying.

engranaje m gear(s), gearing, mesh; (*dientes*) gear-teeth; **engranar** [1a] *v/t.* gear; put into gear; ~ *con* gear into, engage (with); *v/i.* interlock; ⊕ engage (*con in*, with).

engrandecer [2d] enlarge, magnify (*a. fig.*); (*alabar*) extol; exalt; **engrandecimiento** m enlargement; *fig.* exaltation *etc.*

engrane m mesh(ing).

engrapar [1a] clamp.

engrasar [1a] grease, oil, lubricate; **engrase** m greasing, lubrication.

engreído conceited, proud, stuckup F; **engreimiento** m conceit, vanity; **engreír** [3l] make conceited; *S.Am.* spoil.

engrosar [1m] *v/t.* (*aumentar*) increase, swell; (*ensanchar*) enlarge; (*espesar*) thicken; *v/i.* get fat.

engrudar [1a] paste; **engrudo** m paste.

engullir [3a *a.* 3h] gulp (down), bolt, gobble.

enhebrar [1a] thread.

enhestar [1k] (*poner derecho*) erect; (*elevar*) hoist up; **enhiesto** (*derecho*) erect; (*p.*) bolt upright.

enhilar [1a] *aguja* thread; (*ordenar*) arrange, order.

enhorabuena f congratulations; ¡~! (*aprobación*) well and good; (*felicitación*) congratulations!, best wishes!; *dar la ~ a* congratulate; **¡enhoramala!** good riddance!

enigma m enigma; puzzle; **enigmático** enigmatic(al); puzzling.

enjabonar [1a] soap; lather; F (*dar jabón*) soap up; F (*injuriar*) abuse.

enjalbegar [1h] whitewash; *cara* paint.

enjambrar [1a] *v/t.* hive; *v/i.* swarm; **enjambre** m swarm (*a. fig.*).

enjaular [1a] cage; coop up, pen in; F jail.

enjuagar [1h] *platos, boca etc.* rinse; *cubo etc.*· swill (out); **enjuague** m rinse, rinsing; *fig.* scheme.

enjuagaparabrisas m windshield wiper; **enjuagamanos** m *S.Am.* towel; **enjugar** [1h] wipe; dry; *deuda* wipe out.

enjuiciamiento m judgement; ⚖ (*civil*) lawsuit, (*criminal*) trial; **enjuiciar** [1b] examine, judge; ⚖ (*procesar*) prosecute, try.

enjundia f *fig.* substance; (*vigor*) drive.

enjuto lean, spare; (*seco*) wizened.

enlace m link, connexion (*a.* 🚂), tieup; ✗ *etc.* liaison; ⚶ linkage.

enladrillado m brick paving; **enladrillar** [1a] pave with bricks.

enlatar [1a] can, tin; *S.Am.* put a tin roof on.

enlazar [1f] *v/t.* connect, link, tie (together), knit (together); *S.Am.* lasso; *v/i.* 🚂 connect; ~se (*unirse*) link (up), be linked.

enlodar [1a] muddy, cover with mud.

enloquecer [2d] *v/t.* madden, drive mad; *v/i.* go mad; **enloquecimiento** m madness.

enlosar [1a] pave.

enlozado 1. *S.Am.* enameled; 2. m *S.Am.* enamelware.

enlucir [3f] plaster; *metal* polish.

enlutado in mourning; **enlutar** [1a] dress in mourning; *fig.* darken.

enmarañar [1a] (en)tangle; *fig.* complicate, involve; confuse.

enmascarar [1a] mask; *fig.* mask, disguise; **~se** *fig.* masquerade.

enmendar [1k] emend, correct; *ley etc.* amend; reform *moralmente etc.*; **~se** reform, mend one's ways; **enmienda** *f* emendation; amendment.

enmohecer [2d] rust; ♀ make mouldy; **~se** rust; ♀ get mouldy.

enmudecer [2d] *v/t.* silence; *v/i.*, **~se** (*callar*) be silent; remain silent (*debiendo hablar*); (*perder el habla*) become dumb.

ennegrecer [2d] blacken, dye *etc.* black.

ennoblecer [2d] ennoble; *fig.* embellish, adorn, dignify.

enojadizo short-tempered, testy, peevish; **enojar** [1a] anger; annoy, vex; **~se** get angry, lose one's temper, get annoyed; **enojo** *m* anger; annoyance, vexation; **enojoso** irritating, annoying.

enorgullecer [2d] fill with pride; **~se** swell pride.

enorme enormous, huge; *fig.* heinous; **enormidad** *f fig.* enormity; wickedness; (*acto*) monstrous thing.

enotecnia *f* wine making; oenology.

enraizar [1f] take root.

enramada *f* arbour, bower.

enrarecer [2d] *v/t.* rarefy, thin; *v/i.*, **~se** (*gas etc.*) become rarefied, grow thin; (*escasear*) get scarce.

enredadera *f* (*en general*) creeper, climber; (*especie*) bindweed.

enredar [1a] (*coger con red*) net; (*enmarañar*) (en)tangle; (*entretejer*) intertwine; (*mezclar*) mix up, make a mess of; *fig.* (*meter en empeño*) implicate; **~se** get (en)tangled; *fig.* get involved; **enredo** *m* tangle (*a. fig.*); *fig.* (*confusión*) entanglement, mess; mix-up F, *thea. etc.* plot; **enredoso** tangled, tricky.

enrejado *m* lattice(-work) *de ventana*; trellis *de jardín*; (*cerca*) railing(s); *sew.* openwork; **enrejar** [1a] *ventana* fix a grating to; (*cercar*) fence, put railings round.

enriquecer [2d] enrich, make rich; **~se** get rich, prosper; **enriquecimiento** *m* enrichment.

enrojecer [2d] *v/t.* redden; *metal* make red-hot; *v/i.*, **~se** blush, redden.

enrolarse [1a] *S.Am.* enlist, enrol.

enrollar [1a] roll (up), wind (up), coil.

enronquecer [2d] *v/t.* make hoarse; *v/i.* grow hoarse, get hoarse.

enroscadura *f* twist; kink; coil; **enroscar(se)** [1g] twist, twine; curl (up); *alambre etc.* coil, wind.

ensacar [1g] sack, bag.

ensalada *f* salad; *fig.* (*confusión*) mix-up F; (*mezcla*) medley.

ensalmar [1a] *hueso* set; cure by quack renedies; **ensalmo** *m* ♣ quack treatment; (*fórmula*) charm, incantation.

ensalzamiento *m* exaltation; **ensalzar** [1f] exalt; (*alabar*) extol.

ensambladura *f* joint; (*arte*) joinery; **ensamblar** [1a] join; assemble.

ensanchar [1a] enlarge, widen, extend; (*estirar*) stretch; *sew.* let out; **~se** stretch, expand; **ensanche** *m* enlargement, widening; extension, expansion; stretch(ing).

ensangrentado blood-stained, gory; **ensangrentar** [1k] stain with blood; **~se** *fig.* get angry.

ensañar [1a] enrage; **~se en** vent one's anger on.

ensartar [1a] *cuentas etc.* string; *aguja* thread; *fig.* reel off, trot out.

ensayar [1a] test, try (out); *metal* assay; *thea.*, ♪ rehearse; **~se** practice; **ensaye** *m* (*metales*) assay; **ensayista** *m/f* essayist; **ensayo** *m* test, trial; assay *de metal*; (*entrenamiento*) practice; *lit. essay*; *thea.*, ♪ rehearsal; **~ de choque** *mot.* crash test.

enseguida at once, immediately.

ensenada *f* inlet, cove, creek.

enseñanza *f* teaching, instruction, education; schooling; tuition; *primera ~*, *~ primaria* elementary education; *~ superior* higher education; **enseñar** [1a] (*instruir*) teach; train; (*mostrar*) show; (*indicar*) point out; **~se** *a* accustom o.s. to.

enseres *m/pl.* goods and chattels; (*accesorios*) gear, equipment.

ensiladora *f* silo.

ensillar [1a] saddle (up).

ensimismamiento *m* reverie; **ensimismarse** [1a] be absorbed; *S.Am.* be conceited.

ensoberbecerse [2d] become proud; (*mar*) get rough.

ensombrear [1a] overshadow; **ensombrecer** [2d] darken.

ensordecer [2d] *v/t. p.* deafen; *ruido* muffle; *v/i.* go deaf.

ensortijar [1a] curl; *nariz* ring.

ensuciar [1b] soil, dirty, (be)foul; *fig.* defile, pollute; **se** soil o.s. *en vestido*, wet one's bed *en cama*.

ensueño *m* dream, reverie.

entabladura *f* boarding, planking; **entablar** [1a] ⊕ board (up); ✗ splint; ⚒ institute; *tablero* set up; *conversación etc.* enter into, strike up.

entablillar [1a] ✗ splint.

entalladura *f*, **entallamiento** *m* sculpture; carving; engraving; (*corte*) slot, groove; **entallar** [1a] *v/t.* (*esculpir*) carve; (*grabar*) engrave; (*hacer cortes en*) notch, slot; *v/i.* (*vestido*) fit.

entapizar [1f] upholster; *pared* hang with tapestry; *silla etc.* cover with fabric.

entarimado *m* (floor-)boarding; (*mosaico*) inlaid floor; **entarimar** [1a] board, plank.

ente *m* entity, being; F guy.

enteco weak(ly), sickly.

entendederas *f/pl. sl.* brains; F: tener malas ∼, ser corto de ∼ be slow on the uptake.

entender [2g] *mst* understand; (*tener intención, querer decir*) intend, mean; (*creer*) believe; *a mi* ∼ in my opinion; ∼ de know about, be good at, be experienced as (*carpintería* a carpenter); *no* ∼ *de a.* be no judge of; ∼ *en* (*versado*) be familiar with, know all about; (*que trata*) deal with; **se** have one's reasons; (*dos ps.*) understand one another, get along well together; *se entiende que* it is understood that; *eso se entiende* that is understood; ∼ *con* know how to manage *en el trato*; **entendido** (*sabio*) wise, knowing; (*enterado*) (well-)informed; **entendimiento** *m* understanding; (*inteligencia*) mind; (*juicio*) judgement.

entenebrecer [2d] darken; *asunto* fog; **se** get dark.

enterado knowledgeable, (well-)informed; *S.Am.* conceited; **enterar** [1a] inform; **se de** learn, find out, hear of, get to know (about).

entereza *f* entirety; *fig.* integrity, strength of mind; fortitude; firmness; (*severidad*) strictness.

enternecedor moving, pitiable; **enternecer** [2d] soften; *fig.* touch, move to pity *etc.*); **se** be touched, be moved.

entero 1. entire, whole; complete; *fig.* (*recto*) upright; firm; robust; ♈

integral, whole; *por* ∼ wholly, completely; **2.** *m* ♈ integer.

enterrador *m* gravedigger; **enterramiento** *m* burial, interment; **enterrar** [1k] bury (*a. fig.*), inter.

entibiar [1b] cool (*a. fig.*), take the chill off.

entidad *f* entity; ✝ firm, concern; *pol. etc.* body, organization.

entierramuertos *m* gravedigger;

entierro *m* burial, interment; (*funeral, procesión*) funeral; F treasure trove.

entintar [1a] ink (in); **entinte** *m* inking.

entoldado *m* awning; (*tienda grande*) marquee; **entoldar** [1a] put an awning over; (*adornar*) decorate (with hangings); **se** (*cielo*) cloud over; (*p.*) give o.s. airs.

entonación *f* intonation; *fig.* conceit; **entonar** [1a] *v/t. canción etc.* intone; (*afinar*) sing in tune; *phot., paint.* tone; ✗ tone up; *alabanzas* sound; *v/i.* be in tune; **se** give o.s. airs.

entonces then, at that time; (*siendo así*) and so; well then.

entornar [1a] half-close; *puerta* leave ajar; (*volcar*) upset; **entorno** *m* environment.

entorpecer [2d] dull, (be)numb, stupefy; *fig.* obstruct, slow up; **entorpecimiento** *m* numbness, torpor; *fig.* obstruction, delay.

entrada *f* (*en general*) entrance, way in; (*parte de edificio etc.*) porch, doorway, gateway, entrance-hall; (*acto*) entry (*en* into); admission (*en academia etc.* to); (*derecho*) right of entry; beginning *de año etc.*; (*ingresos*) income, receipts; ∼ *de favor*, ∼ *de regalo* complimentary ticket, pass; *dar* ∼ *a* admit; give an opening to; *prohibida la* ∼ keep out, no admittance.

entrambos *lit.* both.

entrampar [1a] trap, (en)snare; F (*enredar*) mess up; ✝ burden with debts; **se** F get into a mess.

entrañable (*querido*) dearly loved; (*afectuoso*) affectionate; **entrañar** [1a] (*introducir*) bury deep; (*contener*) contain; **se** become very intimate; **entrañas** *f/pl.* entrails, bowels; inside(s) F; *fig.* innermost parts; heart; disposition.

entrar [1a] **1.** *v/t.* (*hacer entrar*) bring in, show in; ✗ attack; (*estudio etc.*) attract; **2.** *v/i.* go in, come in, enter;

(*año etc.*) begin; ~ a *inf.* begin to *inf.*;
~ **bien** (*convenir*) be fitting; (*venir al
caso*) be to the point; ~ **en** enter, go
into; *esp. fig.* enter into; (*encajar*) fit
into.

entre between *dos*, among(st) *varios*;
(*en medio de*) in the midst of; **decir ~ sí**
say to o.s.

entre... inter...; **~abierto** halfopen;
~acto *m* interval; **~cejo** *m* space
between the eyebrows; *fig.* frown;
~cierre *m* interlock; **~coger** [2c]
catch, intercept; *fig.* press; (*hacer
callar*) silence; **~cortado** intermittent; **~cortar** [1a] partially cut; interrupt. [*biol.* interbreed.⟩

entrecruzar [1f] interlace; **~se**⟩
entre...: **~dicho** *m* prohibition, ban;
⚖ injunction.

entrega *f* (*acto*) delivery; surrender;
instalment, part *de novela etc.*; **✆**
post, delivery; ~ **contra paga** (or *reembolso*) cash on delivery; **entregar**
[1h] (*dar, poner en manos*) deliver;
hand (over), hand in; (*ceder*) surrender; give up, part with; **~se** surrender, give in; ~ **a** devote o.s. to,
indulge in.

entre...: **~lazar(se)** [1f] entwine, interlace; **~medias** (in) between; in
the meantime; **~més** *m* thea. interlude; **~es** *pl.* hors d'oeuvres; **~meter**
[2a] insert; *v.* entremeterse; **~mez-
clar** [1a] intermingle; intersperse.

entrenador *m deportes:* trainer (*a.
🏇*), coach; **entrenamiento** *m* training; **entrenar** [1a] train, coach; **~se**
train.

entre...: **~oír** [3q] half-hear; **~pier-
na(s)** *f* (*pl.*) crotch, crutch; **~ren-
glón** *m* space between lines; inter-
line; **~sacar** [1g] *pelo, árboles etc.*
thin out; (*escoger*) pick out; (*examinar*) sift; **~semana** *f S.Am.* week-
days; work days; **~suelo** *m* mez-
zanine, entresol; **~tanto 1.** *adv.*
meanwhile, meantime; **2.** *m* meantime; **~tejer** [2a] entwine, inter-
weave; (*trabar*) mat; *palabras etc.*
put in, insert.

entretener [2l] (*divertir*) entertain;
(*ocupar*) keep (occupied); keep in
suspense; engage *en conversación*;
(*demorar*) hold up, delay; **entretenido** entertaining, amusing; **entretenimiento** *m* entertainment;
amusement; recreation; (*manutención*) upkeep.

entre...: **~tiempo** *m* transition;

meantime; spring; fall; **~ver** [2v]
glimpse; *fig.* guess, suspect; **~verar**
[1a] intermingle; mix up; **~vero** *m*
jumble, mix-up.

entrevista *f* interview, conference;
entrevistar [1a] interview; **~se con**
interview, have an interview with.

entristecer [2d] sadden, grieve; **~se**
grow sad, grieve.

entrometerse [2a] meddle; intrude;
entrometido 1. meddlesome; **2.** *m*,
a *f* busybody.

entroncar [1g] be related, be con-
nected (*con* to, with), join.

entronque *m* relationship, connexion; *S.Am.* **🚂** junction.

entumecer [2d] (be)numb; **~se**
(*miembro*) get numb, go to sleep;
(*río*) swell; (*mar*) surge; **entumecido** stiff, numbed, cramped.

enturbiar [1b] *agua* muddy, disturb;
fig. obscure, fog, confuse.

entusiasmar [1a] excite, fire, fill
with enthusiasm; **~se** get excited (*por*
about, over); **entusiasmo** *m* enthusiasm (*por* for); keenness, zeal, zest;
entusiasta 1. enthusiastic; keen (*de*
on); zealous (*de* for); **2.** *m/f* enthusiast; fan **F**; **entusiástico** enthusiastic.

enumeración *f* enumeration; **enumerar** [1a] enumerate.

enunciar [1b] enunciate; declare;
enunciativo enunciative; *gr.* de-
clarative.

envainar [1a] sheathe; *sl.* **¡enváinala!**
shut your trap!

envalentonar [1a] embolden; **~se**
take courage; put on a bold front.

envanecer [2d] make vain; **~se**
grow vain; swell with pride; **en-
vanecimiento** *m* pride; vanity; conceit.

envaramiento *m* stiffness; **enva-
rarse** [1a] get stiff; get numb.

envasar [1a] *v/t.* pack(age); bottle;
can, tin; *v/i. fig.* tipple; **envase** *m*
(*acto*) packing *etc.*; (*recipiente en general*) container; (*papel*) wrapping;
bottle; ~ **de hojalata** tin can.

envejecer [2d] *v/t.* age, make old;
v/i., **~se** age, grow old, get old.

envenenamiento *m* poisoning; **envenenar** [1a] poison (*a. fig.*); *relaciones etc.* embitter.

enverdecer [2d] turn green.

envergadura *f* **⚓** breadth; (*extensión*) expanse, spread, span; *fig.*
scope, compass, reach.

envés m back, wrong side *de tela*.

enviado m envoy; **enviar** [1c] send (*por* for).

enviciar [1b] corrupt; *fig.* vitiate; **~se** *con* (*or* en) become addicted to.

envidia f envy, jealousy; *tener ~ a* envy; **envidiar** [1b] envy, begrudge; (*desear*) covet; **envidioso** envious, jealous; (*deseoso*) covetous.

envilecer [2d] debase, degrade; **~se** degrade o.s.; grovel; **envilecimiento** m degradation.

envío m (*acto*) sending, dispatch; ✝ consignment *de mercancías*, remittance *de dinero*; ♣ shipment.

envite m stake, side bet; *fig.* (*ofrecimiento*) offer; (*empujón*) push.

enviudar [1a] become a widow(er), be widowed.

envoltorio m bundle; **envoltura** f cover(ings), casing, wrapping; ♀, ✗ etc. envelope; **envolver** [2h; *p.p.* envuelto] wrap (up), tie up, do up; (*con ropa*) wrap, swathe; (*contener, ceñir*) envelop, enfold; muffle *contra frío, ruido* etc.; ✗ encircle; **~se** *fig.* become involved; **envolvimiento** m envelopment; ✗ encirclement; *fig.* involvement.

enyesado m plastering; **enyesar** [1a] plaster.

enzarzar [1f] *fig.* involve, entangle.

enzima f enzyme; **enzimología** f enzymology.

épica f epic; **épico** épic.

epidemia f epidemic; **epidémico** epidemic.

epígrafe m inscription; (*lema*) motto, device; (*título*) title.

epigrama m epigram.

epilepsia f epilepsy.

epílogo m epilogue.

episcopado m (*oficio*) bishopric; (*período*) episcopate.

episodio m episode; incident; **episódico** episodic(al).

epístola f epistle; **epistolario** m collected letters.

epitafio m epitaph.

epítome m compendium, epitome.

época f period, time, epoch; *hacer ~* be epochmaking.

epopeya f epic (*a. fig.*).

equidad f equity (*a. ⚖*); fairness.

equidistante equidistant.

equilátero equilateral.

equilibrado balanced; *p.* sensible; even-tempered; **equilibrar** [1a]

(*poner en equilibrio*) balance, poise; **equilibrio** m balance, equilibrium; *esp. fig.* poise; **equilibrista** m/f tightrope walker, acrobat.

equinoccio m equinox.

equipaje m luggage, piece of luggage; (*equipo*) equipment, kit; **equipar** [1a] equip, furnish, fit out, fit up (*con* with).

equiparar [1a] consider equal, equalize, put on a level (with).

equipo m equipment, outfit, kit; system; (*grupo, deportes* etc.) team; ~ *de alta fidelidad* stereo system; hi-fi set.

equitación f (*acto*) riding; (*arte*) horsemanship.

equitativo equitable, reasonable, *trato* fair, square.

equivalencia f equivalence; **equivalente** *adj. a. su.* m equivalent (*a* to); **equivaler** [2q]: ~ *a* be equivalent to; rank as, rank with.

equivocación f mistake, error; (*descuido*) oversight; (*malentendido*) misunderstanding; **equivocado** wrong, mistaken; *cariño* etc. misplaced; **equivocar** [1g] mistake; **~se** be wrong, make a mistake; be mistaken (*con* for); **equívoco 1.** equivocal, ambiguous; **2.** m equivocation, ambiguity; (*juego de palabras*) pun, wordplay.

era¹ etc. *v. ser*.

era² f era; age; ~ *atómica* atomic age.

era³ f ✓ threshing floor; bed, plot.

erario m treasury, exchequer.

ergotismo m argumentativeness; ergotism.

erguido erect; *cuerpo* etc. straight; **erguir** [3n] (*levantar*) raise; (*poner derecho*) straighten; **~se** straighten up; *fig.* swell with pride.

erial uncultivated.

erigir [3c] erect, build, raise; *fig.* establish; **~se** en set up as.

erizado bristly; bristling (*de* with); **erizarse** [1f] bristle; (*pelo*) stand on end; **erizo** m *zo.* hedgehog; ~ *de mar* seaurchin.

ermitaño m hermit.

erogación f distribution (of wealth); *S.Am.* payment; gift.

erosión f erosion; **erosionar(se)** [1a] erode; **erosivo** erosive.

erótico erotic; *poesía* etc. love *attr.*

errabundo wandering.

erradizo wandering; **errado** (*equivocado*) mistaken; (*inexacto*) wide of the mark; (*imprudente*) unwise; **errante** (*no fijo*) wandering, roving, itinerant; (*perdido*) stray; *fig.* errant; **errar** [11] *v/t. tiro, vocación* miss; (*no cumplir*) fail (in one's duty to); *v/i.* wander, rove, roam (about); = ~**se** err, go astray; **errata** *f* misprint, erratum.

erróneo wrong, mistaken, erroneous; **error** *m* error, mistake, fault; fallacy *en teoría etc.*

eructar [1a] belch; **eructación** *f*, **eructo** *m* belch, eructation ⓣⓣ.

erudición *f* erudition, learning, scholarship; **erudito 1.** erudite, learned; **2.** *m*, **a** *f* scholar.

erupción *f* eruption (*a.* ⚕); outbreak; ~ (*cutánea*) rash.

esbeltez *f* slenderness *etc.*; **esbelto** slim, slender, svelte.

esbozar [1f] sketch, outline; **esbozo** *m* sketch, outline.

escabechar [1a] pickle, souse; **escabeche** *m* pickle, souse; (*pescado*) soused fish; *esp.* pickled tunnyfish.

escabel *m* (foot)stool.

escabrosidad *f* roughness, ruggedness *etc.*; **escabroso** *terreno* rough, rugged; (*desigual*) uneven; *fig.* (*áspero*) harsh; *cuento* risky, scabrous.

escabullirse [3a] make o.s. scarce, slip away; ~ *por* slip through.

escafandra *f* diving suit; ~ *espacial* space helmet.

escala *f* (*escalera*) ladder; (*graduación etc.*) scale (*a.* ⚕, ♪); range *de velocidades etc.*; ⚓ port of call; (*parada*) intermediate stop; *hacer* ~ en put in at, call at; **escalada** *f* scaling, climbing; **escalafón** *m* establishment, list of officials, scale.

escalar [1a] scale, climb; *casa* burgle, break into.

escaldadura *f* scald; **escaldar** [1a] scald; *metal* make red-hot.

escalera *f* stairs, staircase *en casa*; (flight of) steps *esp. al descubierto*; (*escala*) ladder; ~ *de incendios* fire-escape; ~ *mecánica*, ~ *móvil*, ~ *rodante* escalator, moving staircase.

escalfador *m* chafing dish; **escalfar** [1a] *huevo* poach.

escalinata *f* (flight of) steps.

escalo *m* burglary; break-in; digging (to enter or escape).

escalofrío *m* chill (*a.* ⚕); (*estremecimiento*) shivering, shiver(s).

escalón *m* step, stair *de escalera*; rung *de escala*; *fig.* (*grado*) stage, grade;

escalonamiento *m* gradation; graduation; ✗ echelon; **escalonar** [1a] spread out at intervals; step; *horas*, ⊕ stagger.

escalpelo *m* scalpel.

escama *f* *zo.* scale; *fig.* (*resentimiento*) grudge; (*recelo*) suspicion; **escamar** [1a] scale; F make wary, make suspicious; ~**se** F get wary, get suspicious; **escamón** apprehensive, suspicious.

escamoso *pez* scaly; *sustancia* flaky.

escamot(e)ar [1a] whisk away, make *s.t.* vanish; *carta* palm; F steal, swipe; **escamoteo** *m* sleight of hand, conjuring.

escampar [1a] *v/t.* clear out; *v/i.* clear up, stop raining; *fig.* give up.

escanciar [1b] *vino* pour; serve.

escandalizar [1f] scandalize, shock; ~**se** be shocked; be offended; **escándalo** *m* scandal; row, uproar; bad example; *armar un* ~ make a scene; **escandaloso** scandalous, shocking; *ofensa etc.* flagrant.

escandinavo *adj. a. su.* **m**, **a** *f* Scandinavian.

escaño *m* bench, settle.

escapada *f* (*huida*) escape; (*travesura*) escapade; **escapar** [1a] escape (*a acc.*, *de* from); run away; ~ *de manos* elude; ~**se** escape; run away; get out; (*gas etc.*) leak (out); ~ *con* make off with.

escaparate *m* showcase, display cabinet, shop window *de tienda*; *Cuba,Col.,Ven.* clothes closet.

escapatoria *f* (*huida*) escape, getaway; *fig.* loophole, excuse.

escape *m* escape, flight, get-away; ⊕ exhaust (*a. tubo de* ~, *gases de* ~); leak(age) *de gas, líquido*; ⊕ escapement; *a* ~ at full speed; **escapismo** *m* escapism.

escapular scapular; **escapulario** *m* scapular(y).

escarabajo *m* beetle; ⊕ flaw; F runt, dwarf; ~**s** *pl.* F scrawl.

escaramuza *f* skirmish, brush; **escaramuzar** [1f] skirmish.

escarbadientes *m* toothpick; **escarbar** [1a] scratch; *lumbre* poke; *dientes* pick; *fig.* delve into.

escarcha *f* (hoar)frost; **escarchar** [1a] *v/t. pastel* ice; *v/i.* freeze.

escarcho *m* roach.

escarda *f* weeding-hoe; (*labor*) weeding, hoeing; **escardar** [1a] weed (out) (*a. fig.*).

escariador *m* reamer; **escariar** [1b] ream.

escarlata *f* scarlet; scarlet cloth; **escarlatina** *f* scarlet fever.

escarmenar [1a] *lana* comb; *fig.* punish; F do out of *s.t.* bit by bit.

escarmentar [1k] *v/t.* punish severely, teach a lesson (to); *v/i.* learn one's lesson; **escarmiento** *m* punishment; warning, lesson.

escarnecer [2d] scoff at, ridicule; **escarnio** *m* jibe, jeer; derision.

escarpa *f* scarp, escarpment, slope; **escarpado** steep, sheer; craggy.

escarpia *f* spike, tenterhook.

escarpín *m* (*zapato*) pump; ~es *pl.* ankle socks *de muchacha*.

escasamente barely; hardly; **escasear** [1a] *v/t.* be sparing with, skimp; *v/i.* be scarce, get scarce; **escasez** *f* scarcity, shortage; **escaso** scarce; scant(y); (*miserable*) meagre, skimpy; *cosecha, público* thin, sparse; *p.* (*tacaño*) stingy; (*económico*) sparing.

escatimar [1a] skimp, give grudgingly, stint, be sparing of; *esfuerzo* spare; **escatimoso** scrimpy, mean.

escena *f* mst scene; (*parte del teatro*) stage; ~ *muda* by-play; **escenario** *m* (*parte del teatro*) stage; scene, setting *de acción.*

escepticismo *m* scepticism; **escéptico 1.** sceptical; **2.** *m, a f* sceptic, doubter.

escindir [3a] split; **escisión** *f* scission; *fig.* split, division.

esclarecer [2d] *v/t.* (*aclarar*) explain, elucidate; *fig.* ennoble; *v/i.* dawn; **esclarecido** illustrious.

esclavitud *f* slavery, bondage; **esclavizar** [1f] enslave; **esclavo** *adj. a. su. m, a f* slave.

esclerosis *f* sclerosis.

esclusa *f* lock, sluice; floodgate.

escoba *f* broom; **escobar** [1a] sweep; **escobazo** *m* quick sweep; **escobilla** *f* whisk; brush (a. ⚡); ~ *de limpiaparabrisas* (windshield) wiper blade; **escobillón** *m* ⚔, ⊕ swab; **escobón** *m* long-handled broom; scrub brush.

escocer [2b *a.* 2h] *v/t.* annoy; *v/i.* smart, sting; ~se chafe.

escocés 1. Scots, Scotch, Scottish; **2.** *m* Scot(sman); (*idioma*) Scots.

escoger [2c] choose, select, pick out; elect *en elección*; **escogido** select, choice; *obras* selected.

---

escolar 1. scholastic; school *attr.*; **2.** *m* pupil, schoolboy; **escolástico 1.** scholastic; **2.** *m* schoolman.

escollo *m* reef, rock; *fig.* pitfall.

escolta *f* escort; **escoltar** [1a] escort, guard, protect; ⚓ convoy.

escombrar [1a] clear out, clean out; **escombro** *m ichth.* mackerel; ~s *pl.* debris, wreckage, rubble.

escondedero *m* hiding-place; **esconder** [2a] hide, conceal (*de* from); ~se hide; lurk; **escondid(ill)as:** *a* ~ by stealth, on the sly; **escondite** *m* hiding-place, cache; (*juego*) hide-and-seek; **escondrijo** *m* hiding-place, hide-out; *fig.* nook.

escopeta *f* shotgun; ~ *de dos cañones* double-barreled shotgun; ~ *de viento* air-gun; **escopetazo** *m* (*tiro*) gunshot; (*herida*) gunshot wound; *fig.* bad news, blow; *S.Am.* sarcasm; insult; **escopetear** [1a] shoot at (with a shotgun).

escoplear [1a] chisel; **escoplo** *m* chisel.

escorbuto *m* scurvy.

escoria *f metall.* slag, dross; scum; **escorial** *m* slag-heap, dump.

escorpión *m* scorpion.

escotado décolleté, low(-necked); **escotadura** *f* low neck; *thea.* large trapdoor; **escotar** [1a] *v/t. sew.* cut to fit; *v/i.* pay one's share; **escote** *m sew.*(low) neck, décolletage; share *de dinero.*

escotilla *f* hatch(way); **escotillón** *m* trapdoor.

escozor *m* smart, sting; *fig.* grief.

escriba *m* scribe; **escribanía** *f* (*escritorio*) writing-desk; writingcase; **escribano** *m* ⚖ clerk; † notary; ~ *municipal* town clerk; **escribiente** *m* amanuensis; (*empleado*) clerk; **escribir** [3a; *p.p.* escrito] write; (*ortografiar*) spell; **escrito 1.** *p.p. of* escribir; **2.** *adj.* written; **3.** *m* writing, document; manuscript; ⚖ brief; ~s *pl.* writings, works; **escritor** *m, -a f* writer; **escritorio** *m* writing desk, bureau; (*caja*) writing case; (*oficina*) office; **escritura** *f* (*acto, arte*) writing; (*símbolos*) writing, script; (*propia de p.*) (hand)writing; ⚖ deed, document; *Sagrada* ♀ Scripture.

escrófula *f* scrofula; **escrofuloso** scrofulous.

escroto *m* scrotum.

escrúpulo *m* (*inquietud*) scruple (*a. pharm.*); (*duda*) hesitation; = **es-**

crupulosidad f scrupulousness; **escrupuloso** scrupulous; precise.

escrutador 1. searching; **2.** m parl. teller; returning officer; **escrutar** [1a] scrutinize; votos count; **escrutinio** m scrutiny, count de votos; (votación) ballot.

escuadra f △ square; bracket, angle iron; ⚔ squad; ⚓ fleet, squadron; **escuadrar** [1a] square; **escuadrilla** f ⚔ squadron, flight; ⚓ flotilla; **escuadrón** m ⚔ squadron.

escuálido pale, weak; (enjuto) skinny, scraggy.

escucha 1. f (acto) listening; eccl. chaperon; estar a la ~ listen in; **2.** m ⚔ scout; radio: monitor; **escuchar** [1a] v/t. listen to; heed, pay attention to; v/i. listen.

escudar [1a] shield (a. fig.); ~se shelter, shield o.s.

escudero m hist. squire; page.

escudo m shield (a. fig.); ~ de armas coat of arms; ~ térmico heatshield (of space capsule).

escudriñar [1a] scrutinize, scan, examine; inquire into, investigate.

escuela f school; phls. school (of thought); ~ de artes y oficios trade school; ~ preparatoria prep school; ~ primaria elementary school, primary school, grade school; ~ de párvulos infant school, kindergarten; **escuelante** m/f Col.,Ven.,Mex. schoolboy (schoolgirl).

escueto plain, unadorned; bare, bald.

esculpir [3a] sculpture, carve; inscription cut; **escultor** m sculptor; **escultura** f sculpture, carving.

escupidera f spittoon; S.Am. chamber-pot; **escupidura** f spit, spittle; phlegm; **escupir** [3a] spit (a at, en on); (echar fuera) spit out; fig. llamas etc. belch, hurl forth.

escurridéro m draining board; **escurridizo** slippery; ⊕ aerodynamic; **escurridor** m wringer para ropa; plate rack para platos; **escurrir** [3a] v/t. ropa wring (out); platos, líquido drain; v/i. (líquido etc.) drip, trickle; ~se drain; slip, slide en hielo etc.; F (p. etc.) sneak off.

ese, esa adj. that; **esos, esas** pl. those. **ése, ésa** pron. that (one); (el anterior) the former; **ésos, ésas** pl. those; (los anteriores) the former.

esencia f essence; core de problema etc.; **esencial** adj. a. su. m essential.

esfera f sphere; globe; face de reloj,

dial de instrumento; fig. sphere, plane; **esférico** spherical; **esferoide** m spheroid.

esfinge f sphinx (a. fig.).

esforzado valiant; vigorous, energetic; **esforzar** [1f a. 1m] v/t. strengthen, invigorate; (animar) encourage; ~se strain, exert o.s.; ~ en inf., ~ por inf. strive to inf.; **esfuerzo** m effort, endeavor, exertion; stress; stretch, effort de imaginación; (ánimo) courage.

esfumar [1a] paint. shade, tone down; ~se fade away; (p.) make o.s. scarce.

esgrima f (deporte) fencing; (arte) swordsmanship; **esgrimir** [3a] v/t. wield (a. fig.); v/i. fence.

esguince m swerve, avoiding action.

eslabón m link de cadena; steel para sacar fuego, afilar; **eslabonar** [1a] (inter)link; fig. link, knit together.

eslálom m slalom.

eslavo 1. adj. a. su. m, **a** f Slav; **2.** m (idioma) Slavonic.

eslogan m slogan.

eslovaco 1. Slovakian; **2.** m, **a** f Slovak. [Slovene.]

esloveno 1. Slovenian; **2.** m, **a** f ∫

esmaltar [1a] enamel; uñas varnish, paint; fig. embellish; **esmalte** m enamel (a. anat.); (obra) smalt; ~ (para uñas) nail polish; fig. lustre.

esmerado painstaking, careful, neat.

esmeralda f emerald.

esmerarse [1a] take pains, take great care (en over); (lucirse) shine.

esmeril m emery; **esmerilar** [1a] polish with emery.

esmero m care(fulness), neatness; refinement, niceness.

esnob 1. p. snobbish; (de buen tono etc.) posh; **2.** m/f snob; **esnobismo** m snobbery.

eso pron. that; ~ es that's right, that's it; por ~ therefore, and so.

esófago m esophagus, gullet.

espabilado bright; intelligent; **espabilar** [1a] snuff; ~se know the ropes; be informed.

espaciador m space bar (of typewriter); **espaciar** [1b] space (out) (a. typ.); noticia spread; ~se (dilatarse) expatiate, spread o.s.; (esparcirse) relax, take one's ease; **espacio** m space (a. typ.); (lugar) space, room; ♪ interval; (tardanza) delay, slowness; ~ exterior outer space; **espacioso** spacious, roomy; capacious; slow.

espada 1. f sword; *naipes*: ~s pl. spades; **2.** m swordsman; *b.s.* bully, swashbuckler; *toros*: matador.

espadín m dress-sword, ceremonial sword; **espadón** m broadsword.

espagueti m spaghetti.

espalda f back, shoulder(s) (*mst* ~s pl.); a ~s (*vueltas*) treacherously; a ~s de uno behind one's back; ~ con ~ back to back; de ~s a with one's back to.

espaldar m back de silla; ✓ espalier, trellis; **espaldarazo** m slap on the back; accolade; **espaldilla** f shoulderblade.

espantadizo shy, timid; **espantajo** m scarecrow (a. fig.); fig. sight, fright; (*coco*) bogy; **espantapájaros** m scarecrow.

espantar [1a] scare, frighten (away, off); (*horrorizar*) appal; ~se get scared, get frightened; **espanto** m fright; terror; **espantosidad** f *S.Am.* fright; frightfulness; *S.Am.* ghost; **espantoso** frightful, dread (ful); appalling.

español 1. Spanish; **2.** m, **-a** f Spaniard; **3.** m (*idioma*) Spanish; **españolada** f Spanish mannerism (or remark); **españolería** f Spanishness; hispanophilia; **españolizar** [1f] make Spanish, hispanicize.

esparcido scattered; fig. jolly, cheerful; **esparcimiento** m scattering, spreading; fig. (*descanso*) recreation; **esparcir** [3b] scatter, spread, sow; ~se fig. relax.

espárrago m asparagus.

esparto m esparto grass.

espasmo m spasm; jerk; **espasmódico** spasmodic(al); jerky, fitful.

espátula f spatula; palette knife.

especia f spice; **especiado** spicy, spiced.

especial (e)special; en ~ especially; **especialidad** f specialty; line F; **especialista** m/f specialist; **especializarse** [1f] specialize (en in, on *Am.*).

especie f *biol.* species; (*clase*) sort, kind; (*asunto*) matter; (*noticia*) news, rumour; pretext.

especificar [1g] specify; itemize; **específico 1.** specific; **2.** m (*natural*) specific; (*fabricado*) patent medicine; **espécimen** m specimen.

espectáculo m spectacle; show, entertainment; sight; **espectador** m, **-a** f spectator; onlooker, lookeron.

especulación f speculation; **especulador** m, **-a** f speculator; **especular** [1a] v/t. contemplate, reflect on; v/i. speculate; **especulativo** speculative.

espejear [1a] shine, glint; **espejismo** m mirage (a. opt.); wishful thinking; **espejo** m mirror (a. fig.), (looking-) glass; fig. model.

espeluznante hair-raising; lurid.

espera f wait; waiting; 🕐 stay, respite; prospect; F hope; prospect; dar ~s de hold out a prospect of; **esperanzar** [1f] give hope to, buoy up (with hope); **esperar** [1a] **1.** (*tener esperanza de*) hope for; expect (de of); (*estar en espera de*) await, wait for; **2.** v/i. (*tener esperanza*) hope; (*estar en espera*) wait; (*permanecer*) stay; ~ que indic. hope that; ~ que subj. expect that; ~ (a) que subj. wait until.

esperma f sperm.

esperpento m F (p.) fright; monstrosity; freak; nonsense.

espesar [1a] thicken; tela weave tighter; ~se thicken, get thicker; coagulate, solidify; **espeso** thick, dense; **espesor** m thickness, density; **espesura** f thickness; dirtiness; ♀ thicket.

espetar [1a] carne skewer, spit; p. run through; F ~ algo a uno spring s.t. on s.o.; ~se F get on one's high horse; **espetón** m skewer, spit.

espía m/f spy; tattletale; sl. cop.

espiar [1c] spy (v/t. on).

espiga f ♀ ear de trigo, spike de flores; ⊕ spigot; (*clavo*) tenon, peg, pin; **espigado** ♀ ripe, ready to seed; p. tall, grown-up; **espigar** [1h] v/t. glean (a. fig.); ⊕ tenon; v/i. (*trigo*) form ears, come into ear; run to seed; (p.) ~se shoot up; **espigón** m zo. sting; (*púa*) spike; ♀ ear.

espina f ♀ thorn, spine, prickle; *ichth.* fish-bone; fig. suspicion, doubt; dar mala ~ a worry.

espinaca(s) f(pl.) spinach.

espinar [1a] fig. hurt s.o.'s feelings, sting; **espinazo** m spine, backbone.

espinilla f anat. shin(bone); 🦟 blackhead.

espino m hawthorn; **espinoso** ♀ thorny, prickly; pez spiny; fig. thorny, knotty.

espionaje m spying, espionage.

espiral 1. spiral, helical; corkscrew attr.; **2.** m hairspring; **3.** f spiral; wreath de humo etc.; ⊕ whorl.

E

espirar [1a] v/t. exhale, breathe out; v/i. breathe; *poet.* blow gently.

espiritismo m spiritualism; espiritista m/f spiritualist; espíritu m spirit; mind; soul; ghost; 2 Santo Holy Ghost; espiritual spiritual; unwordly; ghostly.

espita f spigot, tap, cock; F drunkard, soak; espitar [1a] tap, broach.

esplendidez f splendour; magnificence *etc.*; espléndido splendid; magnificent, grand; (*liberal*) generous, lavish; esplendor m splendour; brilliance; glory.

espolear [1a] spur; *fig.* spur on; espoleta f ✕ fuse; *anat.* wish-bone; espolón m zo., geog. spur; ♣ ram; ♣ sea-wall, dike.

espolvorear [1a] dust (off).

esponja f sponge; F sponger; esponjar [1a] make spongy; *lana etc.* make fluffy; ~se *fig.* swell with conceit; F ✿ glow with health; look prosperous; esponjoso spongy; porous.

esponsales m/pl. betrothal.

espontanearse [1a] (*falta*) own up; (*cosa íntima*) unbosom o.s.; espontaneidad f spontaneity; espontáneo spontaneous; impromptu.

esporádico sporadic.

esportillo m basket, pannier.

esposa f wife; ~s pl. handcuffs, manacles; esposar [1a] handcuff; esposo m husband; ~s pl. husband and wife.

esprínter m sprinter.

espuela f spur (*a. fig.*); espuelar [1a] *S.Am.* spur, goad (on).

espuerta f basket, pannier.

espulgar [1h] delouse, rid of fleas; *fig.* scrutinize.

espuma f foam ♣ *etc.* foam, spray, surf; froth *en cerveza etc.*; (*desechos*) scum; ~ (*de jabón*) lather; ~ de caucho, ~ de látex foam rubber; espumajoso foamy, frothy; espumar [1a] v/t. skim; v/i. foam, froth; espumarajo m froth (at the mouth); espumoso foamy, frothy; *vino* sparkling.

esputar [1a] spit; esputo m spit, spittle; ✿ sputum.

esquela f note; ~ (de defunción) announcement of death.

esqueleto m skeleton (*a. fig.*).

esquema m diagram, plan, scheme; (*dibujo*) sketch.

esquí m ski; (*deporte*) skiing; ~ acuático water-skiing; esquiador m, -a f skier; esquiar [1c] ski.

esquife m skiff.

esquila¹ f handbell; cowbell.

esquila² f shearing; esquilador m shearer; esquilar [1a] shear, clip.

esquilmar [1a] *cosecha* harvest; *suelo* exhaust, impoverish (*a. fig.*).

esquimal adj. a. su. m/f Eskimo.

esquina f corner; esquinado having corners; *fig.* unsociable, prickly; esquinazo F: dar ~ a dodge, give a p. the slip.

esquite m *C.Am.,Mex.* popcorn.

esquivar [1a] avoid, shun, elude, side-step; *inf.* avoid ger., be chary of ger.; esquivez f aloofness etc.; esquivo aloof, shy; evasive *en contestar etc.*; (*desdeñoso*) scornful.

esquizofrenia f schizophrenia; esquizofrénico schizophrenic.

estabilidad f stability; estabilizar [1f] stabilize; steady; *precios* peg; estable stable, steady; firm; ✝ regular.

establecer [2d] establish; set up, found; *gente etc.* settle; ~se establish o.s., settle *en casa, ciudad etc.*; establecimiento m mst establishment (*a. acto*); institution.

establo m cowshed; stable.

estaca f stake, paling; (tent)peg *de tienda*; (*porra*) cudgel; ✿ cutting; estacada f (*cerca*) fencing, fence; ✕ palisade, stockade; estacar [1g] *terreno* stake out (or off); *animal* tie to a stake; ~se remain rooted to the spot.

estación f ✿ *etc.* station (*a. fig.*), a. depot *Am.*; season *del año*; ~ de empalme, ~ de enlace junction; ~ meteorológica weather station; ~ muerta off season; ~ de servicio service station; ~ veraniega summer resort; estacionamiento m mot. parking; estacionar [1a] station; mot. park; ~se remain stationary; (*colocarse*) station o.s.; mot. park; estacionario stationary.

estada f stay.

estadio m *deportes*: stadium; (*fase*) stage, phase.

estadista m pol. statesman; ♀ statistician; estadística f statistics; (*official*) returns; estadístico 1. statistical; 2. m statistician.

estado m state (*a. pol.*); condition; status; class, rank; list *de empleados etc.*; ~ asistencial, ~ benefactor welfare state; en buen ~ in good condition, in good order; ~ civil marital status;

hombre de ~ statesman; ~ *llano* third estate, commoners; ~ *mayor* staff.

estadounidense United States *attr.*

estafa *f* swindle, trick; ✚ racket F; **estafador** *m* swindler, trickster; racketeer F; **estafar** [1a] swindle, cheat.

estafeta *f* post; (*oficina*) (sub) post office; (*p.*) courier.

estalactita *f* stalactite; **estalagmita** *f* stalagmite.

estallar [1a] burst, explode, go off; (*como volcán*) erupt; (*látigo*) crack; **estallido** *m* explosion, report; *fig.* outbreak.

estampa *f typ.* print, engraving; (*imprenta*) printing press; *fig.* stamp, aspect; **estampado 1.** *vestido* print(ed); **2.** *m* (cotton) print; **estampar** [1a] *typ.* print, engrave, stamp; *esp. fig.* imprint.

estampida *f S.Am.* stampede; = **estampido** *m* report; boom, crash.

estampilla *f* (rubber) stamp; *S.Am.* (postage) stamp.

estancado stagnant (*a. fig.*); *fig.* static; **estancamiento** *m* stagnancy, stagnation (*a. fig.*); *fig.* deadlock; **estancar** [1g] *aguas* stem, check; *negocio* suspend; *negociación* bring to a standstill; *b.s.* corner; ~*se* stagnate.

estancia *f* (*permanencia*) stay; (*morada*) dwelling, abode; *S.Am.* farm, ranch; **estanciero** *m S.Am.* farmer, rancher.

estanco 1. watertight; **2.** *m* state monopoly; (*tienda*) tobacconist's (shop).

estandar(d)izar [1f] standardize.

estándar *m* norm; standard.

estandarte *m* standard, banner.

estanque *m* pond, pool, small lake; reservoir *para riego etc.*

estante *m* (*mueble*) rack, stand; bookcase; (*una tabla*) shelf; **estantería** *f* shelves, shelving.

estaño *m* tin.

estaquilla *f* peg, pin.

estar [1p] be; (~ *en casa etc.*) be in; stand; (*asistir*) be present (*en at*); *estoy leyendo* I am reading; *estamos a 3 de mayo* today is the third of May; *¿a cuántos estamos?* what date is it?; *está bien* all right; ~ *de más* be superfluous; (*p.*) be in the way; ~ *mal* 🍃 be ill; ~ *para inf.* be about to *inf.*; ~ *para su.* be in the mood for; ~ *por inf.* (*dispuesto a*) be inclined to *inf.*; (*que*

queda por) be still to be *p.p.*, remain to be *p.p.*; ~*se* stay (at home *etc.*); *¡estáte quieto!* keep still!

estatal state *attr.*

estática *f* statics; **estático** static.

estatua *f* statue; **estatuaria** *f* statuary; **estatuario** statuesque.

estatura *f* stature, height; **estatutario** statutory; **estatuto** *m* statute; by-law *de municipio etc.*; (standing) order *de comité etc.*

este¹ 1. *parte* east(ern); *dirección* easterly; *viento* east(erly); **2.** *m* east.

este², esta this; **estos, estas** *pl.* these.

éste, ésta this (one); (*último*) the latter; **éstos, éstas** *pl.* these; (*últimos*) the latter.

estela *f* ⚓ wake, wash; trail *de cohete etc.*; 🜨 stela; **estelar** stellar.

estenografía *f* shorthand, stenography; **estenógrafo** *m*, **a** *f* stenographer, shorthand writer; **estenotipia** *f* stenotypy; machine stenography.

estera *f* mat, matting.

estercolar [1a] manure, dung; **estercolero** *m* dungheap, dunghill.

estero...: ~fónico stereophonic; **~scopio** *m* stereoscope; **~tipar** [1a] stereotype (*a. fig.*); **~tipo** *m* stereotype.

estéril sterile, barren; **esterilidad** *f* sterility; **esterilización** *f* 🜨 sterilization; **esterilizar** [1f] sterilize.

estero *m* matting; *geog.* estuary, inlet.

estética *f* aesthetics; **estético** aesthetic.

estetoscopia *m* stethoscope.

estevado bow legged, bandy-legged.

estibador *m* stevedore, longshoreman; **estibar** [1a] pack tight; ⚓ stow, house.

estiércol *m* dung, manure.

estigma *m* stigma; mark; brand; **estigmatizar** [1f] stigmatize.

estilar [1a] *v/t.* draw up in due form; *v/i.* ~*se* be in fashion, be worn.

estilete *m* stiletto.

estilizado stylized; **estilo** *m* style (*a.* ♀); (*pluma*) stylus; (*modo, manera*) manner.

estilográfica *f* fountain pen.

estima *f* esteem; ⚓ dead reckoning; **estimación** *f* (*acto*) estimation; (*aprecio, tasa*) estimate, estimation; (*estima*) regard, esteem; **estimar** [1a] (*juzgar, medir*) estimate, reckon, gauge; (*respetar etc.*) esteem, value, respect.

estimulante 1. stimulating; **2.** *m*

stimulant; **estimular** [1a] stimulate; encourage; excite; **estímulo** m stimulation; encouragement.

estipendio m stipend.

estipulación f stipulation; proviso, condition; **estipular** [1a] stipulate.

estirado fig. stiff, starchy; (mojigato) prim; (tacaño) tightfisted.

estirajar [1a] F = **estirar** [1a] stretch, pull out; (demasiado) strain; cuello crane; ropa run the iron over; **estirón** m pull, tug; stretch; dar un ~ fig. shoot up.

estirpe f stock, race, lineage.

estival summery, summer attr.

esto pron. this; con ~ herewith; en ~ at this point.

estocada f (sword)thrust, stab.

estofa f fig. quality, class; **estofado** m stew, hot-pot; **estofar** [1a] cocina: stew; sew. quilt.

estoicismo m stoicism; **estoico** 1. stoic(al); 2. m Stoic.

estólido stolid.

estómago m stomach; F tener buen ~ (no ofenderse) be thick-skinned; b.s. be none too scrupulous.

estoque m rapier; ♀ gladiolus; **estoquear** [1a] stab.

estorbar [1a] v/t. hinder, impede, obstruct; v/i. be in the way; **estorbo** m hindrance, obstruction.

estornudar [1a] sneeze; **estornudo** m sneeze.

estrada f road, highway.

estrado m dais, stage; ♪ bandstand; † drawing-room; ~s pl. law-courts.

estrafalario F eccentric, screwball; vestido slovenly, sloppy.

estragar [1h] corrupt, ruin; pervert; spoil; **estrago** m ruin, destruction; ~s pl. havoc, ravages.

estrangulador m ⊕ throttle; choke; **estrangular** [1a] strangle; ⚕ strangulate; ⊕ throttle; ⊕ choke.

estraperlista m black marketeer; **estraperlo** m black market.

estrapontín m jump seat; folding seat.

estratagema f stratagem; **estrategia** f strategy; generalship; **estratégico** strategic.

estrato m layer, stratum.

estratosfera f stratosphere.

estrechar [1a] narrow; vestido reduce, take in; (apretar) tighten (up); squeeze; mano grasp, shake; hug; ~se narrow; tighten (up); **estrechez** f narrowness; tightness; fig. close-

ness, intimacy de amistad; **estrecho** 1. narrow; tight; cuarto cramped; fig. amistad, relación close, intimate; strict, rigid; 2. m strait(s), narrows.

estregar [1h a. 1k] rub, scrape; (con agua etc.) scrub, scour.

estrella f star (a. fig., thea.); zo. blaze; ✕ pip, star en uniforme; **estrellado** cielo starry; vestido spangled; huevo fried; **estrellar** [1a] shatter, smash, dash; huevo fry; ~se shatter, dash (contra against); (coche etc.) smash (contra into); esp. ✕ crash (contra into).

estremecer [2d] shake (a. fig.); ~se (edificio etc.) shake; (p.) tremble, shudder; shiver (de frío with); tingle; **estremecimiento** m shaking; trembling; shudder etc.

estrenar [1a] use (or wear etc.) for the first time; thea. perform for the first time; ~se make one's début; (comedia) open; **estreno** m first appearance etc.; début esp. de p.; thea. first night; cine: première.

estreñimiento m constipation; **estreñir** [3h a. 3l] constipate, bind.

estrépito m noise, racket, row, din; **estrepitoso** noisy, loud, deafening.

estreptomicina f streptomycin.

estría f groove; ⌂ flute, fluting; **estriar** [1c] groove, striate; ⌂ flute.

estribación f geog. spur; ~es pl. foothills; **estribar** [1a]: ~ en be supported by; fig. rest (up)on.

estribillo m poet. refrain; ♪ chorus.

estribo m stirrup; ⊕ bracket, brace; geog. spur; ⌂ buttress, abutment; ⌂ pier; mot. running board, step.

estribor m starboard.

estricto strict.

estridente strident, raucous.

estrofa f verse, stanza.

estropajo m scourer para fregar; dishcloth, swab; F dirt, rubbish.

estropear [1a] p. hurt, maim; mecanismo etc. damage, tamper with; ~se get damaged; spoil, go bad.

estructura f structure; frame; **estructural** structural; **estructurar** [1a] construct, organize.

estruendo m crash, din, clatter, thunder; fig. uproar; **estruendoso** noisy; esp. p. obstreperous.

estrujadura f squeeze, press(ing); **estrujar** [1a] squeeze, press, crush; F drain; **estrujón** m squeeze, press(ing); F crush, jam.

estuario m estuary.

estuche m (caja) box, case; (vaina) sheath; ~ de afeites vanity case.

estuco m stucco, plaster.

estudiante m/f student; **estudiantil** student attr.; **estudiar** [1b] study; **estudio** m mst study; paint., cine, radio: studio; (proyecto preliminar) plan, design (de for); **estudioso** studious; bookish.

estufa f stove; heater; ✿ hothouse.

estulto stupid.

estupefaciente adj. a. su. m narcotic; **estupefacto** stupefied, thunder-struck, speechless.

estupendo stupendous; F marvellous, terrific, great; ¡~! wonderful!

estupidez f stupidity, foolishness; **estúpido** stupid, foolish.

estupor m stupor; amazement.

esturión m sturgeon.

etapa f stage, phase; deportes: lap, leg; ✕ ration.

etarra m/f supporter of ETA; Basque terrorist.

etcétera et caetera; and so on.

éter m ether; **etéreo** ethereal.

eternidad f eternity; **eternizar** [1f] etern(al)ize; perpetuate; b.s. prolong endlessly; **eterno** eternal.

ética f ethics; **ético** ethical.

etimología f etymology; ~ popular folk etymology; **etimológico** etymological.

etíope adj. a. su. m/f Ethiopian.

etiqueta f (ceremonial) etiquette; punctilio, formality; (rótulo) label, ticket; de ~ traje formal.

etnografía f ethnography; **etnología** f ethnology.

eucalipto m eucalyptus, gum tree.

Eucaristía f Eucharist.

eufemismo m euphemism.

eufonía f euphony.

euforia f euphoria, exuberance; **eufórico** euphoric, exuberant.

¡eureka! eureka!

europeizar [1f] Europeanize; **europeo** adj. a. su. m, a f European.

éuscaro adj. a. su. m Basque; **euskera** m Basque language.

evacuación f evacuation; **evacuar** [1d] evacuate; void; vientre have a movement of stove; fig. encargo fulfil; negocio transact.

evadido m fugitive; **evadir** [3a] evade; ~se escape, break out.

evaluación f evaluation; **evaluar** [1e] evaluate.

Evangelio m Gospel; **evangelizador** m evangelist; **Evangelista** m Evangelist; **evangelizar** [1f] evangelize.

evaporación f evaporation; **evaporar(se)** [1a], **evaporizar(se)** [1f] evaporate (a. fig.); vaporize.

evasión f escape; fig. evasion; **evasiva** f loophole, excuse; **evasivo** evasive, noncommittal.

evento m (unforeseen) event, eventuality, contingency; **eventual** trabajo etc. temporary, casual.

evidencia f (lo evidente) obviousness; (prueba etc.) evidence; **evidenciar** [1b] show, prove, make evident; **evidente** obvious, evident.

evitable avoidable, preventable; **evitar** [1a] peligro etc. avoid, escape; molestia save; (precaver) prevent.

evocar [1g] recuerdo etc. evoke, call up, conjure up; espíritus etc. invoke.

evolución f evolution (a. biol.); ✕ maneuvre; change de política etc.; **evolucionar** [1a] evolve (a. biol.); ✕ maneuvre; (política etc.) change; **evolucionista** adj. a. su. m/f evolutionist; evolutionary.

ex... ex-; former, late; ~ ministro ex-minister.

exacción f exaction, extortion.

exacerbar [1a] exacerbate, aggravate.

exactitud f exactness etc.; **exacto** exact, accurate, precise; right, correct; ¡~! quite right!, just so!

exagerado exaggerated; relato etc. a. highly-coloured, overdone; precio etc. excessive, steep F; (raro) peculiar, odd; **exagerar** [1a] exaggerate; overdo, overstate.

exaltación f exaltation; overexcitement; **exaltado** 1. exalted; carácter hot-headed, excitable; 2. m pol. extremist, hothead; **exaltar** [1a] exalt; (celebrar) extol; elevate a dignidad; (inflamar) excite; ~se get excited, get worked up.

examen m examination (a. univ. etc.); inspection; interrogation; **examinando** m, a f examinee; **examinar** [1a] examine; inspect, scan, go over, go through; (poner a prueba) test; ~se take an examination (de in).

exasperar [1a] exasperate, irritate; ~se lose patience.

excavadora f excavator (machine);

excavar [1a] excavate; (*ahuecar*) hollow (out).

excedente 1. excessive; (*sobrante*) excess, surplus; **2.** *m* excess, surplus; **exceder** [2a] exceed, surpass; outdo; transcend *en importancia*.

excelencia *f* excellence; **excelente** excellent.

excelso lofty, sublime.

excentricidad *f* eccentricity; **excéntrico 1.** eccentric; erratic; **2.** *m* eccentric.

excepción *f* exception; *a ~ de* with the exception of; **excepto** except (for), excepting; **exceptuar** [1e] except, exclude; ⚖ *etc.* exempt.

excesivo excessive; over...; (*indebido*) unreasonable, undue; **exceso** *m* excess (*a. fig.*); extra.

excitabilidad *f* excitability; **excitación** *f* excitation, excitement; *~ loca* hysteria; **excitador** *m* ⚡ discharger; **excitante 1.** exciting; ⚗ stimulating; **2.** *m* stimulant; **excitar** [1a] excite (*a.* ⚡); raise; *emoción* rouse, stir up; ⚡ energize.

exclamación *f* exclamation; **exclamar** [1a] exclaim; cry, shout; **exclamatorio** exclamatory.

excluir [3g] exclude; shut out; *posibilidad etc.* preclude, rule out; **exclusive** exclusively; **exclusivista** exclusive; *grupo etc.* clannish; **exclusivo** exclusive; sole.

excomulgar [1h] *eccl.* excommunicate; ban; **excomunión** *f eccl.* excommunication; ban.

excoriar [1b] skin, flay.

excreción *f* excretion; **excremento** *m* excrement; **excretar** [1a] excrete.

exculpación *f* exoneration, exculpation; ⚖ acquittal; **exculpar** [1a] exonerate, exculpate; ⚖ acquit.

excursión *f* excursion; (*mst breve*) outing, trip; *~ (a pie)* hike F; ✕ raid; **excursionismo** *m* hiking, rambling; sightseeing; **excursionista** *m/f* hiker F; sightseer.

excusa *f* excuse; apology.

excusado 1. unnecessary, superfluous; exempt (*de impuesto* from); reserved; *~ es decir* needless to say; **2.** *m* toilet; lavatory; **excusar** [1a] (*disculpar*) excuse; (*evitar*) avoid, prevent; *~se* apologize.

execrable execrable.

exención *f* exemption; immunity; **exentar** [1a] exempt (*de* from); **exento** exempt.

exhalar [1a] exhale; *vapor etc.* emit, give out; *suspiro* breathe, heave.

exhaustivo exhaustive; **exhausto** exhausted.

exhibición *f* exhibition, show; *~ venta* exhibit; **exhibir** [3a] exhibit, show.

exhortación *f* exhortation; **exhortar** [1a] exhort.

exhumación *f* exhumation.

exigencia *f* demand, requirement; exigency; **exigente** exigent, exacting; particular; demand; **exigir** [3c] *rentas etc.* exact (*a* from); (*pedir*) demand.

exilado *m*, **a** *f* exile; **exilar** [1a], **exiliar** [1b] exile; **exilio** *m* exile.

eximir [3a] exempt, free, excuse (*de* from).

existencia *f* existence; being; ✝ *en ~* in stock; *~s pl.* ✝ stock; **existente** in existence, in being, existent; **existir** [3a] exist; be.

éxito *m* result, outcome; (*buen*) *~* success; *fig., thea.,* ♪ hit; *tener (buen) ~* be successful; **exitoso** successful.

éxodo *m* exodus.

exonerar [1a]: *~ de deber etc.* relieve of, free from.

exorbitancia *f* exorbitance; **exorbitante** exorbitant.

exorcista *m/f* exorcist; **exorcizar** [1f] exorcize.

exótico exotic.

expansión *f* expansion; *fig.* (*desahogo*) expansiveness; (*solaz*) relaxation; **expansionar** [1a] expand; **expansivo** expansive (*a. fig.*); *fig.* affable, good-natured.

expatriado *m*, **a** *f* expatriate; exile; **expatriarse** [1b] go into exile.

expectación *f* expectation; **expectativa** *f* expectation; hope; prospect.

expectorar [1a] expectorate.

expedición *f* expedition (*a. fig.*); *fig.* speed; **expedicionario** expeditionary; **expediente** *m* (*medio*) expedient; ⚖ proceedings; (*papeles*) dossier.

expedir [3l] send, forward; *negocio* dispatch; *órdenes etc.* issue; **expeditar** [1a] *S.Am.* expedite; handle with speed.

expeler [2a] expel, eject.

expender [2a] (*gastar*) expend; (*vender*) sell retail; be an agent for; *moneda falsa* pass.

expensas *f/pl.* expense(s); ⚖ costs.

experiencia *f* experience; 🕮 experiment; **experimentado** experienced; **experimentar** [1a] *v/t.* experience, undergo, go through; *v/i.* experiment (*con* with, *en* on); **experimento** *m* experiment.

experto 1. expert, skilled, experienced; 2. *m* expert.

expiración *f* expiration; **expirar** [1a] expire.

explanar [1a] level; 🔧 grade; *fig.* explain, elucidate; unfold.

explayar [1a] extend, enlarge; **~se** spread, open out; *fig.* (*esparcirse*) relax; **~** *con* confide in.

explicable explicable, explainable; **explicación** *f* explanation; **explicar** [1g] (*declarar, aclarar, justificar*) explain; *doctrina etc.* expound; *curso* lecture on; *conferencia* give; **~se** explain o.s.; *no me lo explico* I can't understand it.

explícito explicit.

exploración *f* exploration; **explorador** *m* explorer; pioneer; (*niño*) **~** Boy Scout; **exploradora** *f* Girl Guide; **explorar** [1a] explore; pioneer; ✕ *etc.* scout.

explosión *f* explosion (*a. fig.*); **explosivo** *adj. a. su. m* explosive.

explotación *f* exploitation; ⚒ working etc.; **~** *abusiva geol.* overexploitation (of resources); **explotar** [1a] exploit (*a. fig.*); ⚒ work; develop.

exponente 1. *m/f* exponent; 2. *m* Å index, exponent; **exponer** [2r] expose (*a. phot.*); *vida etc.* risk; *cuadro etc.* show, exhibit; *argumento, hechos* expound; **~se** *a* expose o.s. to, lay o.s. open to.

exportación *f* (*acto*) export(ation); (*mercancías*) export(s); **exportar** [1a] export.

exposición *f* (*acto*) exposing, exposure (*a. phot.*), exposition; *paint. etc.* exhibition, show; ✝ show, fair; **~** *universal* world's fair; **exposímetro** *m* exposure meter; **expresar** [1a] express; *voice*; **~se** express o.s.; **expresión** *f* expression; **~es** *pl. fig.* greetings; **expresivo** expressive; affectionate; **expreso** 1. express, specific, clear; 2. *m* 🚂 express (train); (*p.*) special messenger.

exprimidera *f*, **exprimidor** *m* squeezer; **exprimir** [3a] squeeze out.

expropiar [1b] expropriate.

expuesto 1. *p.p.* of *exponer*; 2. *adj. lugar* exposed; (*peligroso*) dangerous; *artículo* on show, on view.

expulsar [1a] expel, eject, turn out; **expulsión** *f* expulsion, ejection.

expurgar [1h] expurgate.

exquisito exquisite; delicious; (*culto*) genteel, refined; *b.s.* affected.

extasiarse [1c] go into ecstasies, rhapsodize (*ante* over); **éxtasis** *m* ecstasy; rapture; **extático** ecstatic, rapturous.

extemporáneo unreasonable; untimely; inopportune.

extender [2g] extend; stretch, expand; (*desenvolver, desplegar*) spread (out), open (out), lay out; **~se** extend etc.; *ocupar espacio* extend, lie; (*ocupar tiempo*) extend, last (*de* from, *a* to, till); *fig.* range *entre dos puntos etc.*

extensión *f* (*acto, propagación*) extension; (*dimensión*) extent, size; duration *de tiempo*; range *entre dos puntos etc.*; ♪ range, compass; **extensivo** extensive; **extenso** extensive; broad, spacious.

extenuación *f* emaciation; **extenuado** emaciated; **extenuar** [1e] emaciate; weaken.

exterior 1. exterior, external, outer; *manifestación etc.* outward; 2. *m* exterior, outside; (*aspecto*) outward appearance; *deportes:* wing; *del* **~** *noticias, correo etc.* foreign, from abroad.

exterminar [1a] exterminate; **exterminio** *m* extermination.

externo external; outward.

extinguidor *m S.Am.* (*de incendios*) fire extinguisher; **extinguir** [3d] extinguish; exterminate; **extinto** extinct; **extintor** *m* (fire) extinguisher.

extirpación *f* extirpation, eradication; **extirpar** [1a] extirpate, eradicate, stamp out.

extra 1. extra; *horas* **~** overtime; 2. *m* extra *en cuenta*; 3. *m/f cine:* extra.

extracción *f* extraction (*a.* ✕).

extractar [1a] *libro* abridge; **extracto** *m* extract; *lit.* abstract; **extractor** *m* extractor; remover; **~** *de aire* ventilator; **~** *de humos* smoke vent.

extradición *f* extradition.

extraer [2p] extract; take out.

extra...: ~fino superfine; **~judicial** extrajudicial; **~muros** *adv.* outside the city.

extranjerismo *m* foreign word (*or* expression *etc.*); **extranjero** 1. foreign; 2. *m*, *a f* (*p.*) foreigner; 3. *m* (*un país*) foreign country; *en el* **~** abroad.

extrañamiento m estrangement; **extrañar** [1a] find strange, wonder at; *S.Am.* miss; ~se be amazed, be surprised (*de* at); **extrañeza** f strangeness, oddity; surprise, amazement; **extraño** (*raro*) strange, odd; (*extranjero*) foreign.

extraordinario extraordinary; unusual; *edición*, *número* special.

extrasensorial extrasensory.

extraterrestre extraterrestrial.

extravagancia f extravagance; eccentricity; (*capricho*) vagary; **extravagante** extravagant; eccentric.

extraviado stray, lost; **extraviar** [1c] *p.* lead astray; mislead; ~se go astray (*a. fig.*), get lost, stray, wander; **extravío** m (*pérdida*) misplacement, loss; wandering, deviation.

extremado extreme; intense; **extre-**

mar [1a] carry to extremes; ~se do one's utmost.

extremaunción f extreme unction.

extremeño adj. a. su. m, **a** f (native) of Extremadura.

extremidad f extremity; tip; edge; ~es pl. extremities del cuerpo; **extremismo** m extremism; **extremo 1.** extreme; (*sumo*) utmost; (*más remoto*) outermost; (*último*) last; **2.** m end; extreme; (*sumo grado*) highest degree; fig. great care; **extremoso** effusive, gushing.

extroversión f extroversion; **extrovertido** m, **a** f extrovert.

exuberancia f exuberance; ♀ luxuriance; **exuberante** exuberant; ♀ luxuriant.

exudar [1a] exude, ooze.

exultación f exultation; **exultar** [1a] exult.

F

fábrica f factory, works, plant, mill; △ fabric; △ masonry; (*edificio*) building, structure; ♰ (*marca*) make; **fabricación** f manufacture, making; make; ~ *en serie* mass production; **fabricante** m manufacturer, maker; **fabricar** [1g] ⊕ manufacture, make; △ build; fig. fabricate, invent; **fabril** manufacturing.

fábula f fable; rumor; (*cuento*) tale; **fabuloso** fabulous; mythical.

facción f pol. etc. faction; feature de cara; **faccioso** factious, rebellious.

faceta f facet (*a. fig.*).

facha f F look; (*p.*) sight, object.

fachada f △ façade (*a. fig.*), frontage; typ. frontispiece.

fachenda f F boasting; **fachendear** [1a] F show off; **fachendoso** F snooty, conceited.

fácil easy, simple; (*pronto*) ready; *explicación b.s.* glib; es ~ que it is likely that; **facilidad** f ease, facility; ~es pl. facilities; **facilitar** [1a] (*hacer fácil*) facilitate, help; (*proveer*) provide, supply.

facsímil(e) adj. a. su. m facsimile.

factible feasible; workable.

factor m factor (*a.* ♰, ♈); ♰ agent; ♒ clerk; **factoría** f factory; ♰ agency, trading post.

factura f invoice, bill; **facturar** [1a] ♰ invoice; ♒ register, check.

facultad f (*potencia*) faculty (*a. univ.*); (*derecho etc.*) power (de of su., to *inf.*); **facultativo 1.** optional; ♒ medical; **2.** m doctor, practitioner.

faena f task, job; (*deber*) duty; ✗ fatigue; *S.Am.* overtime; extra job; *S.Am.* gang of workers; ~s pl. chores.

faisán m pheasant.

faja f strip, band de tela etc.; (*vestido*) sash (*a.* ✗), belt; **fajar** [1a] wrap, swathe; **fajo** m sheaf de papeles; roll, wad de billetes.

falange f phalanx; ♀ *Spanish Fascist party.*

falaz p. deceitful; fallacious; *apariencia etc.* misleading.

falda f skirt; (*regazo*) lap; *geog.* slope, hillside; **faldellín** short skirt; underskirt; **faldón** m skirt; tail de traje; flap; △ gable.

falibilidad f fallibility; **falible** fallible.

fálico phallic.

falla f fault (*a. geol.*), failure.

fallar [1a] v/t. ♈ pronounce sentence on; v/i. (*tiro*) miss; (*escopeta etc.*) misfire, fail to go off; (*proyecto*) fail, miscarry; ♈ find, pass judgement.

fallecer [2d] pass away, die; **falle-**

cido late; **fallecimiento** m decease, demise.

fallido unsuccessful; ✝ (*a. su. m*) bankrupt; ⊕ (*a. su. m*) dud.

fallo m decision, ruling; ⚖ sentence; verdict; findings; ⊕ trouble; *deportes*: mistake, mix-up; ~ **humano** human error.

falo m phallus.

falsario m, a **falsear** [1a] v/t. falsify, forge, fake; juggle with; *cerradura* pick; v/i. buckle, give way; ♪ be out of tune; **falsedad** f falsity, falseness *etc.* **falsificación** f falsification; forgery; fabrication; **falsificar** [1g] falsify, forge, fake, counterfeit; *elección* rig, fiddle; *razones* misrepresent; **falso** *mst* false; counterfeit, fake; *moneda* bad; (*simulado*) bogus, sham.

falta f lack, want, need; absence; (*escasez*) shortage; (*equivocación*) fault, mistake; ⚽ default; *deportes*: foul; *tenis*: fault; *por* ~ *de* for want of, for lack of; *sin* ~ without fail; *hacer* ~ be necessary.

faltar [1a] (*estar ausente*) be missing, be lacking; be absent; (*necesitarse*) be needed; (*acabarse, fallar, dejar de ayudar a*) fail; default *en pago etc.*; *¡no faltaba más!* it's the limit!, it's the last straw!; ~ *a cita* break, not turn up for; *clase* be absent from, cut, miss.

falto short, deficient; (*apocado*) poor, wretched; ~ *de* short of.

faltriquera f fob, (watch)pocket.

fama f fame; reputation; rumour; glory; *mala* ~ *esp. de p.* notoriety.

famélico starving, famished.

familia f family; household; **familiar 1.** (*conocido*; *sin ceremonia*) familiar; (*doméstico*) homely; *palabra* colloquial; *estilo etc.* informal; **2.** m (*conocido*) close acquaintance; (*pariente*) relation, relative; **familiaridad** f familiarity *etc.*; **familiarizar** [1f] familiarize, acquaint, ~**se** become familiar.

famoso famous; F great.

fanático 1. fanatical; bigoted; **2.** m fanatic; bigot; *S. Am.* fan; devotee; **fanatismo** m fanaticism; bigotry.

fandango m fandango.

fanega f grain measure = 55.5 litres; ground area = 1.59 acres.

fanfarrón 1. blustering, boastful; **2.** m blusterer, braggart; bully; **fanfarronada** f bluster, bluff, swagger;

fanfarronear [1a] bluster, rant; swagger.

fango m mud, mire, slush; **fangoso** muddy, slushy.

fantasía f fantasy; imagination; fancy; ♪ fantasia; **fantasma 1.** m ghost, phantom; **2.** f bogey; **fantasmagoría** f phantasmagoria; **fantástico** fantastic; weird; unreal(istic); fanciful, whimsical.

farándula f ✝ troupe of strolling players; F claptrap, pack of lies.

fardel m knapsack; F ragbag; = **fardo** m bundle; bale, pack.

farfulla 1. f F splutter, jabber; **2.** m/f F gabbler, jabberer.

farináceo starchy, farinaceous.

faringe f pharynx.

fariseo m pharisee, hypocrite.

farmacéutico 1. pharmaceutical; **2.** m pharmacist, druggist; **farmacia** f (*ciencia, tienda*) pharmacy; **farmacología** f pharmacology.

farero m lighthouse keeper; **faro** m beacon; ⚓ (*torre*) lighthouse; ⚓ lantern, light; *mot.* headlamp, headlight; **farol** m lantern, lamp; street lamp; 🚂 headlight; **farola** f street lamp; **farolero** m lamp-post; (*p.*) lamplighter.

farraguista m scatterbrain; **farrear** [1a] celebrate; goof off.

farsa f farce; *fig.* humbug, masquerade; **farsante** m F humbug, fraud, fake.

fascinación f fascination; **fascinador** fascinating; **fascinar** [1a] fascinate; captivate; bewitch.

fascismo m Fascism; **fascista** adj. a. su. m/f fascist.

fase f (*a. ⚡*) phase; stage.

fastidiar [1b] annoy, bother, vex; bore; irk; **fastidio** m annoyance, bother, nuisance; boredom; *¡qué* ~*!* what a nuisance!; **fastidioso** annoying, vexing; tiresome; irksome.

fatal fatal; fateful; irrevocable; F ghastly; **fatalidad** f fate; (*desgracia*) mischance, ill-luck; fatality; **fatalismo** m fatalism; **fatalista 1.** fatalistic; **2.** m/f fatalist.

fatiga f fatigue (*a. ⊕*); weariness; (*trabajo*) toil; (*apuro*) hardship; **fatigante** tiring; **fatigar** [1h] tire, weary; (*molestar*) annoy; **fatigoso** *trabajo etc.* tiring, exhausting; F trying, tiresome.

fatuidad f inanity, fatuity; conceit; **fatuo** inane, fatuous.

fauna f fauna.

fauno m faun.

favor m favor; (servicio) favor, good turn, kindness; protection; a ~ de política in favor of; medio with the help of; p. on behalf of; por ~ please; hacer el ~ de su. oblige with su.; **favorable** favorable; auspicious; (benévolo) kind; **favorecer** [2d] favor; help; treat favorably; (fortuna etc.) smile on; (traje, retrato) flatter; **favoritismo** m favoritism; **favorito** adj. a. su. m, **a** f favorite.

faz f lit., fig. face; aspect.

fe f faith (en in); belief; fidelity; certificate; ~ de bautismo birth certificate; ~ de erratas errata.

fealdad f ugliness.

febrero m February.

febril fevered, feverish (a. fig.); fig. hectic.

fecha f date; hasta la ~ (up) to date; **fechar** [1a] date.

fechoría f misdeed.

fécula f starch; **feculento** starchy.

fecundación f fertilization; ~ artificial artificial insemination; **fecundar** [1a] fertilize; **fecundo** fertile; prolific; esp. fig. fruitful.

federación f federation; **federal** federal; **federativo** federative.

fehaciente reliable; authentic.

felicidad f happiness; good luck; success; ~es pl. congratulations; best wishes; **felicitación** f congratulation; **felicitar** [1a] congratulate.

feligrés m, **-a** f parishioner.

felino feline, catlike.

feliz mst happy; (de buena suerte) lucky; (de buen éxito) successful.

felonía f treachery; meanness.

felpar [1a] cover with plush; **felpa** f starch; **felpudo 1.** plush(y); **2.** m doormat.

femenil feminine, womanly; **femenino 1.** feminine; ♀ female; **2.** m gr. feminine.

feminidad f femininity; **feminismo** m feminism; **feminista** m/f feminist.

fenecer [2d] v/t. finish, close; v/i. (morir) die; perish; **fenecimiento** m death; end, close.

fenicio adj. a. su. m Phoenician.

fénix m phoenix; fig. marvel.

fenomenal phenomenal; F tremendous, terrific; **fenómeno** m phenomenon; (cosa anormal) freak.

feo ugly; unsightly; hideous; olor etc. nasty; juego, tiempo foul, dirty;

feote, feota F shockingly ugly.

féretro m coffin, bier.

feria f (mercado etc.) fair, market; carnival; (descanso) holiday; C.Am., Mex. tip; gratuity; **feriado:** día ~ holiday; **feriante** m/f stall-holder; **feriar** [1b] buy, sell (in a market); v/i. take time off.

fermentar [1a] ferment; **fermento** m ferment; leaven(ing).

ferocidad f fierceness etc.; **feroz** fierce, ferocious, savage, wild.

férreo iron; 🚆 rail...; **ferrería** f ironworks, foundry; **ferretería** f (material) hardware; (tienda) hardware shop; **ferrocarril** m railway, railroad; ~ elevado overhead railway; **ferroviario 1.** railway attr.; **2.** m railwayman.

ferry m ferry(boat).

fértil fertile, fruitful; rich (en in); **fertilidad** f fertility, fruitfulness; **fertilizar** [1f] fertilize; enrich.

férvido fervid, ardent; **ferviente** fervent; **fervor** m fervor, ardor; **fervoroso** fervent, ardent.

festejar [1a] entertain, fete, feast; (galantear) woo, court; S.Am. beat; **festejo** m entertainment, feast; courting; **festín** m feast, banquet; **festividad** f festivity, merrymaking; (día) holiday; **festivo** (alegre) festive, gay; (chistoso) humorous; (agudo) witty.

fetiche m fetish; mumbo jumbo F.

fétido rank, stinking, fetid.

feto m foetus.

feudal feudal; **feudalismo** m feudalism; **feudo** m fief; manor.

fiable trustworthy.

fiado: al ~ on credit, on trust; **fiador** m (p.) esp. ⚖ surety, guarantor; esp. ⚖ sponsor; ⊙ catch, trigger; (cierre etc.) fastener; ✗ safety catch.

fiambre 1. cold; noticia stale; **2.** m (carne etc.) cold meat, cold food.

fianza f surety (a. p.), security; deposit; **fiar** [1c] v/t. entrust (a to); p. guarantee, stand security for, go bail for; v/i. trust (en in).

fiasco m fiasco.

fibra f fibre; grain de madera; fig. vigor, sinews; **fibroso** fibrous.

ficción f fiction; fabrication; ciencia ~ science fiction.

ficha f juegos: counter, piece, marker; póker: chip; ~ (del dominó) domino; (como moneda) check, tally; (papeleta)

firma

etc.) (index) card; **fichero** *m* card index; (*mueble*) filing-cabinet.

ficticio fictitious, imaginary.

fidedigno trustworthy, reliable.

fidelidad *f* fidelity, loyalty; *de alta* ~ high fidelity, hi-fi.

fideos *m/pl.* vermicelli.

fiebre *f* fever (*a. fig.*); ~ *amarilla* yellow fever; ~ *del heno* hay fever.

fiel 1. faithful, loyal; (*exacto*) accurate, true; **2.** *m* pointer, needle *de balanza.*

fieltro *m* felt; (*sombrero*) felt hat.

fiera *f* wild beast; (*p.*) fiend; (*mujer*) shrew; *casa* (*or colección*) *de* ~*s* zoo, menagerie; **fiereza** *f* fierceness; cruelty; **fiero** fierce; cruel; (*horroroso*) frightful.

fierro *m S.Am.* branding iron; ~*s pl. Ecuad.,Mex.* tools.

fiesta *f* (*día*) holiday; *eccl.* feast, day *de santo etc.*; (*alegría, diversión*) festivity, celebration; party; *día de* ~ holiday; ~ *de guardar* holy day; **F** *estar de* ~ be in a good mood; **F** *no estar para* ~*s* be in no mood for jokes.

figura *f mst* figure; (*forma exterior, trazado*) shape; image; (*cara*) face; **figurado** figurative; **figurante** *m*, **a** *f thea.* super (numerary), walker-on; **figurar** [1a] *v/t.* figure, shape; represent; *v/i.* figure (*como as, entre* among); ~**se** suppose, imagine, figure; *¡figúrate!, ¡figúrese!* just imagine!

figurín *m* fashion plate, model.

fijar [1a] fix (*a. phot.*); secure, fasten; *sello etc.* stick (on), affix; *prohibido* ~ *carteles* stick no bills; ~**se** settle, lodge; *¡fíjese!* just imagine!; ~ *en* (*notar*) notice; **fijeza** *f* firmness; fixity; *mirar con* ~ stare at; **fijo** fixed; firm, steady, secure; permanent.

fila *f* row (*a. thea.*), line, file; rank (*a.* ✗); **F** dislike; *en* ~ in a row; ✗ *romper* ~*s* fall out, dismiss.

filadelfiano Philadelphian.

filamento *m* filament.

filantropía *f* philanthropy; **filántropo** *m* philanthropist.

filarmónica *f Mex.* accordeon.

filatelia *f* philately, stamp-collecting; **filatelista** *m/f* philatelist.

filete *m* △, *cocina:* fillet; ⊕ worm; thread *de tornillo*; *sew.* narrow hem.

filial 1. filial; ✝ subsidiary; **2.** *f* ✝ subsidiary.

filibustero *m* pirate, freebooter.

filigrana *f* filigree; *typ.* watermark.

filipino 1. Philippine; **2.** *m,* **a** *f* Philippine, Filipino.

filisteo *m* Philistine; *fig.* big man.

film *m* film; **filmación** *f* filming; **filmadora** *f* movie camera; **filmar** [1a] film, shot.

filo *m* edge, cutting edge, blade; dividing line.

filocomunista 1. fellow-traveling, pro-Communist; **2.** *m/f* fellow-traveler, pro-Communist.

filología *f* philology; **filológico** philological; **filólogo** *m* philologist.

filón *m* seam, vein, lode; **F** goldmine.

filosofía *f* philosophy; **filosófico** philosophic(al); **filósofo** *m* philosopher.

filtrar [1a] *v/t.* filter; strain; *v/i.,* ~**se** filter through, percolate, seep; **filtro** *m* filter; ✝ philtre.

fin *m* (*término*) end, ending; (*objeto*) purpose, aim; *a* ~ *de inf.* in order to *inf.*; *a* ~ *de que* so that; *al* ~ finally, at the end; *en* ~ (*como exclamación*) well (then), well now; *en* ~, *por* ~ (*finalmente*) finally, at last; (*en suma*) in short.

finado 1. late; **2.** *m,* **a** *f* deceased.

final 1. final, last, ultimate; eventual; **2.** *m* end; ♩ finale; **3.** *f deportes:* final; **finalidad** *f* objet, purpose; **finalizar** [1f] *v/t.* finish; *v/i.* end.

financiamiento *m S.Am.* financing; **financiar** [1b] finance; **financiero 1.** financial; **2.** *m* financier; **finanzas** *f/pl.* finance.

finca *f* property; (*country*) estate; country house; *S.Am.* ranch.

fineza *f* fineness; *naipes:* finesse; *fig.* kindness, courtesy.

fingido false, mock; sham, fake; make-believe; **fingimiento** *m* simulation; pretence; **fingir** [3c] pretend; sham, fake; invent; make believe.

finiquitar [1a] *cuenta* close, balance up; **finiquito** *m* settlement.

finlandés 1. Finnish; **2.** *m,* **-a** *f* Finn; **3.** *m* (*idioma*) Finnish.

finito finite.

fino fine; *material etc.* delicate, thin; *producto* select, quality *attr.*; *gusto* discriminating; *inteligencia etc.* acute, shrewd; *ironía etc.* subtle.

finura *f* fineness *etc.*

firma *f* signature; (*acto*) signing; ✝ firm.

firmante *adj. a. su. m/f* signatory; *el abajo*~ the undersigned; **firmar** [1a] sign.

firme 1. firm; steady, secure; *superficie etc.* hard, firm; *p.* steadfast; ✕ ¡~*s!* attention!; ✝ *en* ~ firm; 2. *m* surface; **firmeza** *f* firmness *etc.*

fiscal 1. fiscal; 2. *m* prosecutor, counsel for the prosecution, district attorney.

fisga *f fig.* banter; *hacer* ~ *a* make fun of, tease; **fisgar** [1h] *v/t.* pez harpoon; *fig.* pry into; *v/i.* pry; (*burlarse*) mock, scoff; **fisgón** nosy, prying; **fisgonear** [1a] F = *fisgar*.

física *f* physics; ~ *nuclear* nuclear physics; **físico** 1. physical; 2. *m* physicist; *anat.* physique.

fisil fissile; fissionable.

fisiografía *f* physiography.

fisiología *f* physiology.

fisión *f* fission; ~ *nuclear* nuclear fission; **fisionable** fissionable.

fisonomía *f* physiognomy, features.

fláccido flaccid, flabby.

flaco 1. thin, lean, skinny; *fig.* weak; 2. *m* weakness, weak point, foible; **flacura** *f* thinness *etc.*

flagrante flagrant; *en* ~ red-handed.

flamante brilliant; *fig.* brand-new.

flameante flamboyant (*a.* △); **flamear** [1a] flame; (*bandera*) flutter.

flamenco[1] *m orn.* flamingo.

flamenco[2] 1. Flemish; Andalusian gipsy *attr.*; F flashy, gaudy; 2. *m*, a *f* Fleming; 3. *m* (*idioma*) Flemish.

flan *m* cream caramel, caramel custard.

flanco *m* flank; **flanquear** [1a] flank; ✕ outflank.

flaquear [1a] weaken, flag; slacken; give (way); **flaqueza** *f* leanness *etc.*; weakness, frailty.

flash *m* newsflash; *phot.* flash(light); ~**back** *m* (*retrospección*) flashback.

flato *m* flatulence, wind; *S.Am.* gloominess; **flatulento** flatulent.

flauta *f* flute; **flautín** *m* piccolo.

flecha *f* arrow; *alas en* ~ swept back wings; **flechar** [1a] wound *etc.* with an arrow, wing; **flechazo** *m* arrow wound; F love at first sight.

flema *f* phlegm (*a. fig.*).

fletamento *m* charter(ing); **fletar** [1a] charter; freight; **flete** *m* freight.

flexibilidad *f* flexibility *etc.*; **flexible** 1. flexible; supple, pliable; *sombrero* soft; *p.* compliant; 2. *m* soft hat; ⚡ flex; **flexión** *f* flexion; *gr.* inflection.

flirtear [1a] flirt; **flirteo** *m* (*en general*) flirting; (*un* ~) flirtation.

flojear [1a] weaken; slacken; **flojedad** *f* looseness, slackness *etc.*; **flojo** (*no tirante*) loose, slack; *p.* lax, lazy, slack.

flor *f* flower (*a. fig.*), blossom; bloom *en fruta*; grain *de cuero*; ~ *de la vida* prime of life; ~ *y nata fig.* cream; élite, the pick; **florear** [1a] *v/t.* adorn with flowers; *v/i.* ♪ play a flourish; **florecer** [2d] ❀ flower, bloom; *fig.* flourish, thrive; **floreciente** ❀ in flower, blooming; *fig.* flourishing, thriving; **florecimiento** *m* flowering; **floreo** *m fenc.*, ♪ flourish; *fig.* witty talk; **florero** *m* vase.

florido *campo etc.* flowery; *estilo etc.* flowery, florid; **florista** *m/f* florist; **floristería** *f* florist's.

flota *f* (*en general*) shipping; (*escuadra*) fleet; **flotador** *m* float; **flotante** floating; *fig.* hanging loose; **flotar** [1a] float; ride; hang loose; stream *al viento*; **flote**: *a* ~ afloat.

fluctuación *f* fluctuation; *fig.* uncertainty; **fluctuar** [1e] fluctuate; (*p.*) waver, hesitate.

flúido 1. fluid; *fig.* fluent, smooth; 2. *m* fluid; ~ *eléctrico* electric current; **fluir** [3g] flow, run.

flujo *m* flow; flux; stream; ⚓ rising tide; ~ *de sangre* hemorrhage.

fluorescencia *f* fluorescence; **fluorescente** fluorescent.

fluorización *f* flouridation; **fluorizar** [1f] (*agua potable*) flouridate.

fobia *f* phobia.

foca *f* seal.

foco *m* focus (*a. fig.*); source *de calor, luz*; ⚡ floodlight; *fig.* center.

fofo soft, spongy; insubstantial.

fogón *m* stove, kitchen range; 🔥 firebox; **fogonazo** *m* flash; **fogonero** *m* stoker, fireman.

fogosidad *f* dash, verve; **fogoso** (high-)spirited; ardent; *caballo* fiery.

foliar [1b] foliate, number the pages of; folio *m* folio.

folklore *m* folklore; **folklórico** folk *attr.*, folklore *attr.*; **folklorista** *adj. a. su. m/f* folklorist(ic).

follaje *m* ❀ foliage, leaves.

folletín *m* newspaper serial; **folleto** *m* pamphlet; folder, brochure, leaflet.

follón 1. (*perezoso*) lazy, slack; (*arrogante*) puffed-up, blustering; 2. *m* ❀ sucker; (*p.*) good-for-nothing.

fomentar [1a] encourage, promote,

foment (a. 🐾), further, foster; **fomento** m encouragement etc.; 🐾 fomentation.

fonda f inn; restaurant; 🍴 buffet.

fondeadero m anchorage; berth.

fondero m S.Am. innkeeper.

fondillos m/pl. seat (of trousers).

fondista m/f innkeeper.

fondo m bottom (a. ⚓); (parte más lejana) back, far end; (profundidad) depth; ⚓, paint., sew. ground; paint., fig. background; ✝ ~s pl. funds; finance; a ~ thoroughly; al ~ de escena etc. at the back of; echar a ~, irse a ~ sink.

fonema m phoneme; **fonética** f phonetics; **fonético** phonetic.

fonoabsorbente sound-absorbent; sound deadening.

fonógrafo m S.Am. record player; phonograph; **fonología** f phonology.

forajido m outlaw, desperado.

forastero 1. alien, strange; 2. m, a f stranger, outsider, visitor.

forcej(e)ar [1a] struggle, wrestle; flounder (about); **forcejudo** strong, powerful.

fórceps m forceps.

forja f forge; foundry; (acto) forging; **forjado** wrought; **forjar** [1a] forge, shape; fig. concoct.

forma f form, shape; (modo) way, means; formula; typ. format; ~s pl. social forms, conventions; de esta ~ in this manner; de ~ que so that; **formación** f formation; education; training para profesión; **formal** (relativo a la forma) formal; asunto serious; official; permiso etc. formal, express; **formalidad** f formality; form; seriousness etc.; **formalismo** m conventionalism; (administrativo etc.) bureaucracy; red tape; **formalista** m/f formalist; **formalizar** [1f] formalize; formulate; put in order; ~se take offence; grow serious; **formar** [1a] form, shape; (reunir, componer) form, make up; ~se form, shape; develop; **formato** m format.

formidable formidable, redoubtable.

formón m chisel.

fórmula f formula, prescription; **formular** [1a] formulate; queja lodge; pregunta frame, pose; **formulario** 1. formulary; 2. m formulary; form.

fornicar [1g] fornicate.

fornido strapping, hefty.

foro m hist. forum; ⚖ bar; thea. backstage.

forrado m lining; padding.

forraje m fodder, forage; F hotchpotch; **forrajear** [1a] forage.

forrar [1a] mst line; ropa line, pad; libro etc. cover; ⊕ face; **forro** m lining, padding; cover; ⊕ facing, sheathing.

fortalecer [2d] strengthen; ✕ etc. fortify; moral stiffen; encourage en una opinión etc.; **fortaleza** f ✕ fortress, stronghold; (fuerza) strength; fortitude, resolution; **fortificación** f fortification; **fortificar** [1g] fortify; fig. strengthen.

fortuito fortuitous; accidental.

fortuna f mst fortune; luck; por ~ luckily.

forzar [1f a. 1m] force, compel (a inf. to inf.); puerta break open; cerradura pick; propiedad enter by force; mujer ravish, rape; **forzoso** necessary; inescapable; aterrizaje forced; **forzudo** strong, tough.

fosa f grave; anat. fosse.

fosfato m phosphate; **fosforescente** phosphorescent; **fosfórico** phosphoric; **fósforo** m match; ♆ phosphorus.

fósil adj. a. su. m fossil (a. fig.).

foso m pit; ditch, trench; ✕ fosse, moat; thea. pit.

fotinga f (a. -o m) S.Am. F jalopy.

foto f F photo; ~ aérea aerial photograph; **~copia** f photocopy, print; **~copiadora** f photocopier; **~eléctrico** photoelectric; **~génico** photogenic (a. F); **~grabado** m photogravure; **~grafía** f (arte) photography; (foto) photograph; **~grafiar** [1c] photograph; **fotógrafo** m photographer; **fotómetro** m exposure meter, photometer; **fotopila** f solar battery; **fotosíntesis** f photosynthesis; **fotostatar** [1a] photostat; **fotóstato** m photostat.

fracasar [1a] fail; fall through; **fracaso** m failure.

fracción f ♠ etc. fraction; division; (partido) faction, splinter group; **fraccionar** [1a] break up, divide; **fraccionario** fractional.

fractura f fracture, break; **fracturar** [1a] fracture, break.

fragancia f fragrance, perfume; **fragante** fragrant, sweet-smelling; crimen flagrant.

frágil fragile; brittle; fig. frail.

fragmento *m* fragment; scrap, piece, bit.

fragor *m* crash, clash; din.

fragoso rough, uneven; *terreno* difficult; *selva* dense.

fragua *f* forge; **fraguar** [1i] *v/t.* ⊕ forge; *fig. mentira* concoct.

fraile *m* friar; monk; F priest.

frambuesa *f* raspberry; **frambueso** *m* raspberry(-cane).

francés 1. French; *despedirse a la ~a* take French leave; **2.** *m* (*p.*) Frenchman; (*idioma*) French.

franciscano *adj. a. su. m* Franciscan.

francmasón *m* (free)mason; **francmasonería** *f* (free)masonry.

franco 1. frank, open, forthright; (*pleno*) full; (*liberal*) generous; ✝ free; **2.** *hist.* Frankish; *~-canadiense* French-Canadian *adj. a. su. m/f*; *~-español* Franco-Spanish; **3.** *m* franc; *hist.* Frank.

francote blunt, bluff.

francotirador *m* sniper.

franela *f* flannel; *Mex.,Ven.,Col., W.I.* undershirt. [*fig.*).\

franja *f* fringe, trimming; band (*a.*

franquear [1a] *contribuyente* exempt; *esclavo* free, liberate; *derecho* grant, allow; ✤ frank, stamp; *~se* open one's heart (*a*, con to); **franqueo** *m* franking; postage; **franqueza** *f* frankness *etc.*; **franquicia** *f* exemption; **franquista** pro-Franco; supporting Francisco Franco *adj. a. su. m/f*.

frasco *m* flask, bottle.

frase *f* sentence; (*locución*) phrase; *~ hecha* stock phrase, cliché; **fraseología** *f* phraseology.

fraternal brotherly, fraternal; **fraternidad** *f* brotherhood, fraternity; **fraternizar** [1f] fraternize; **fraterno** brotherly, fraternal.

fraude *m* fraud; false pretences; dishonesty; *~ fiscal* tax evasion; **fraudulento** fraudulent; dishonest.

frecuencia *f* frequency (*a. ∡*); *con ~* frequently; **frecuentar** [1a] frequent; haunt; **frecuente** frequent; common; *costumbre etc.* prevalent.

fregadero *m* (kitchen) sink; **fregado** *m* scrub(bing); washing-up *de platos*; **fregador** *m* (*pila*) sink; (*trapo*) dish-cloth; (*estropajo*) scrubber, scourer; **fregar** [1h *a.* 1k] scrub, scour; *suelo* scrub, mop; *platos* wash; *S.Am.* annoy; **fregona** *f* kitchen-maid.

freír [3m; *p.p.* frito] fry.

frenar [1a] brake; *fig.* check, restrain.

frenesí *m* frenzy; **frenético** frantic, frenzied; wild.

freno *m* ⊕ brake; bit *de caballo*; *fig.* check, curb; *~ de disco* disk brake; *~ de mano* hand-brake.

frente 1. *f* forehead, brow; (*cara*) face; **2.** *m todos sentidos*: front; *al ~* in front; ✝ carried forward; *de ~ mover* forward; **3.** *prp.*: *~ a* opposite (to); in front of; *fig.* as opposed to.

fresa *f* ♀ (*mst* wild) strawberry; bit, drill *de dentista*; ⊕ milling cutter.

fresca *f* fresh air, cool air; F piece of one's mind; **fresco 1.** *mst* fresh; (*algo frío*) cool; *agua* cold; *huevo* new-laid; F fresh, saucy, cheeky; **2.** *m* fresh air, cool air; ✿ *etc.* fresco; *al ~* in the open air, out of doors; **frescor** *m* freshness; coolness; **frescote** F blooming; buxom; **frescura** *f* freshness; coolness; F cheek, sauce, nerve.

fresno *m* ash (tree).

freudiano *adj. a. su. m* Freudian; **freudismo** *m* Freudianism.

frialdad *f* coldness; coolness, indifference.

fricasé *m* fricassee.

fricción *f* rubbing, rub; ⊕ friction (*a. fig.*); ⚕ massage; **friccionar** [1a] rub; ⚕ massage.

friega *f* rubbing; ⚕ massage; *S.Am.* bother, fuss; *S.Am.* thrashing; **friegaplatos** *m* dishwasher.

frigidez *f* frigidity; **frígido** frigid.

frigorífico 1. refrigerating; **2.** *m* refrigerator; *S.Am.* cold-storage plant; ⚓ refrigerator ship.

frío 1. cold; *bala* spent; **2.** *m* cold; coldness; **friolento** chilly, shivery; **friolera** *f* trifle, mere nothing.

frisar [1a] *v/t. tela* frizz, rub; *v/i.* get along; *~ en* border on.

fritada *f* fry; **frito 1.** fried; **2.** *m* fry; *~s pl. variados* mixed grill.

frivolidad *f* frivolity *etc.*; **frívolo** frivolous; trivial; *p.* shallow.

fronda *f* frond; **frondoso** leafy; luxuriant.

frontera *f* frontier, border; **fronterizo** frontier *attr.*, border *attr.*

frontis *m* façade; **frontispicio** *m* frontispiece.

frontón *m* △ pediment; *deportes*: pelota court.

frotación *f*, **frotadura** *f* rub, rubbing; ⊕ friction; **frotar** [1a] rub; *cerilla* strike; **frote** *m* rub, rubbing.

fructífero productive; *fig.* fruitful; **fructificar** [1g] produce, yield a crop; *fig.* yield (a profit).

frugal frugal; thrifty; **frugalidad** *f* frugality; thrift(iness).

fruncido *m*, **fruncimiento** *m* pleat, gather(ing), pucker; **fruncir** [3b] pucker, wrinkle, ruffle; *sew.* pleat, gather; *entrecejo* knit.

fruslería *f* trifle.

frustrar [1a] frustrate, thwart, balk; **~se** fail, miscarry.

fruta *f* fruit; *fig.* result; **~ de sartén** fritter; **frutero 1.:** *plato* **~** fruit dish; **2.** *m* fruit seller; **fruto** *m* fruit; *fig.* fruits, profit, results.

fucsia *f* fuchsia.

fuego *m* fire; light *para cigarrillo*; ⚓ beacon; ✶ rash; ✗ *¡~!* fire!; **~s** *pl.* *artificiales* fireworks; *hacer* **~** fire (*sobre* at, on).

fuelle *m* bellows (*a. phot.*); *mot.* folding hood; F gossip.

fuente *f* fountain, spring; (*plato*) large dish, bowl; *fig.* source.

fuera 1. *adv.* outside; out; away; (*equipo*) *jugar* away (from home); *¡~* (*de aquí*)! off with you!; *por* **~** on the outside; **2.** *prp.:* **~** *de* out of, outside (of); *fig.* in addition to, besides, beyond; **~** *de eso* apart from that; **~** *de servicio* out of service; inoperative; **~** *de sí* beside o.s.

fuero *m* jurisdiction; (*código*) code (of laws); charter *de ciudad*; privilege *de grupo*.

fuerte 1. strong; sturdy; vigorous; *golpe* hard; *calor etc.* intense; *comida, gasto, lluvia* heavy; *ruido* loud; **2.** *adv.* strongly; *golpear* hard; *tocar* loud, loudly; **3.** *m* ✗ fort, strongpoint; ♪, *fig.* forte.

fuerza *f* strength; force; power (*a.* ⚡); intensity; heaviness; effect *de argumento etc.*; **~s** *pl.* ✗ forces; strength *de p.*; *a* **~** *de* by dint of; *a viva* **~** *entrada* forced; *por* **~** perforce; *por* **~** *mayor* under coercion; by main force.

fuete *m* S.Am. whip; horsewhip.

fuga *f* flight, escape; leak *de gas etc.*; ♪ fugue; *poner en* **~** put to flight; **~** *de capitales* capital flight; **fugarse** [1h] flee, escape; **~** *con* run away with; **fugaz** (*pasajero*) fleeting, shortlived; (*difícil de coger*) elusive; **fugitivo** *adj. a. su. m,* **a** *f* fugitive.

fulano *m*, **a** *f* (Mr etc.) So-and-so.

fulgor *m* brilliance, glow; **fulgurante** shining, bright; **fulgurar** [1a] shine, gleam; flash; **fulguroso** shining; flashing.

fullero *m* (card)sharper; F cheat, crook; dodger.

fulminante *polvo etc.* fulminating; ✶ fulminant; F *éxito etc.* tremendous; **fulminar** [1a] *v/t.* fulminate; *amenazas etc.* thunder; **~** *con la mirada* look daggers at; *v/i.* fulminate, explode.

fumada *f* whiff (or puff) of smoke; **fumadero** *m* smoking-room; **~** *de opio* opium den; **fumador** *m*, **-a** *f* smoker; **fumar** [1a] smoke; *prohibido* **~** no smoking; **~se** F *sueldo* squander; *clase* cut.

fumigación *f* fumigation; **fumigar** [1h] fumigate.

función *f* function; duty; *thea.* show, entertainment; performance; **funcionamiento** *m* functioning; ⊕ *etc.* working, running; performance; ⊕ *en* **~** in order, in operation; **funcionar** [1a] function; work, run, go (*a.* ⊕); perform (*a.* ⊕); behave; **funcionario** *m* official, functionary; civil servant.

funda *f* case, sheath; (*bolsa*) carryall.

fundación *f* foundation; **fundador** *m*, **-a** *f* founder; **fundamentar** [1a] lay the foundations of; base (*en* on); **fundamento** *m* foundation; basis; (*trabajo preliminar*) groundwork; (*razón, motivo*) ground(s); **fundar** [1a] found, set up, establish, institute; endow *con dinero*; *argumento etc.* base (*en* on).

fundición *f* (*acto*) fusion; ⊕ (*acto*) melting, smelting; (*fábrica*) foundry, forge; **fundir** [3a] fuse; ⊕ (*derretir*) melt (down), smelt; (*formar*) found, cast; **~se** fuse (*a.* ⚡), blend; (*metal*) melt; ⚡ blow, burn out.

fúnebre funereal; (*relativo a funeral*) funeral *attr.*; *fig.* mournful; **funeral 1.** funeral *attr.*; **2.** *m*, **~es** *pl.* funeral; **funeraria** *f* undertaker's; *director de* **~** funeral director.

funesto ill-fated, unfortunate.

funicular *adj. a. su. m* funicular.

furgón *m* wagon, van; luggage van; **furgoneta** *f* van; station wagon.

furia *f* fury; rage; *a toda* **~** like fury; **furibundo, furioso** furious; violent; frantic; **furor** *m* rage; passion; frenzy; *hacer* **~** be all the rage.

furtivo furtive; stealthy; sly, shifty.

fuselaje m fuselage.
fusible 1. fusible; **2.** m fuse; *caja de* ∼s fuse box.
fusil m rifle; gun; **fusilamiento** m shooting, execution; **fusilar** [1a] shoot, execute.
fusión f fusion (a. fig.); melting de *metal*; ✝ merger; **fusionar(se)** [1a] fuse; ✝ merge.
fusta f long whip.

fuste m' wood; shaft de *arma etc.*; *(silla)* saddletree.
fustigar [1h] whip, lash (a. fig.).
fútbol m football.
fútil trifling; **futilidad** f trifling nature, unimportance.
futura f ⚖ reversion; F fiancée; **futurismo** m futurism; **futuro 1.** future; **2.** m future (a. gr.); F fiancé; ∼s pl. ✝ futures.

G

gabacho m, a f F Frenchy, froggy.
gabán m overcoat, topcoat.
gabardina f gaberdine; raincoat.
gabarro m flaw; *vet.* pip; *fig.* error; *(estorbo)* snag.
gabinete m study, library; *(despacho)* office; consulting room; *(cuarto particular)* private room.
gaceta f gazette, journal; *S.Am.* newspaper; **gacetilla** f gossip column; news in brief; F gossip; **gacetillero** m gossip columnist; *contp.* penny-a-liner.
gacha f thin paste; ∼s pl. pap; *approx.* porridge.
gacho drooping, floppy; *borde etc.* turned down; *sombrero* slouch.
gacilla f C.Am. safety pin.
gaditano adj. a. su. m, a f (native) of Cadiz.
gafa f grapple; ∼s pl. spectacles, glasses; **gafar** [1a] hook, claw; F bring bad luck to.
gaita f (a. ∼ gallega) bagpipe; *(dulzaina)* flageolet; **gaitero 1.** gaudy, flashy; *(alegre)* merry; **2.** m piper.
gaje m (mst ∼s pl.) pay, emoluments.
gajo m (torn-off) branch; small cluster de *uvas*; segment de *fruta*.
gala f full dress; elegance, gracefulness; *fig.* cream, flower, chief ornament; ∼s pl. finery, trappings; de ∼ (full-)dress, gala *attr.*; *hacer* ∼ de parade, show off.
galán m handsome fellow; ladies' man; *(amante)* gallant, beau; **galante** gallant, attentive (to women); *mujer* flirtatious; *b.s.* licentious; **galantear** [1a] court, woo; flirt with; **galanteo** m courting; flirtation; **galantería** f courtesy, compliment; gallantry.
galápago m zo. freshwater tortoise.

galardón m lit. reward, prize; **galardonar** [1a] reward.
galaxia f galaxy.
galbana f laziness; shiftlessness.
galeote m galley slave.
galera f ⚓, typ. galley; *(carro)* (covered) wagon; 🏥 hospital ward; **galerada** f galley(-proof).
galería f mst gallery; *(pasillo)* passage; ∼ de tiro shooting gallery.
galés 1. Welsh; **2.** m (p.) Welshman; *(idioma)* Welsh.
galgo m, a f greyhound.
galicismo m Gallicism.
galimatías m gibberish; double-talk.
gallardear [1a] be graceful; bear o.s. well; **gallardete** m pennant, streamer; **gallardía** f gracefulness *etc.*; **gallardo** graceful, elegant; *(bizarro)* dashing, gallant.
gallego adj. a. su. m, a f Galician.
gallera f cockpit.
galleta f biscuit; wafer; F slap.
gallina 1. f hen, fowl; ∼ ciega blind-man's-buff; ∼ de Guinea guineafowl; **2.** m/f F coward; **gallinero** m henhouse, coop; *thea.* gallery; *(voces)* babel; *(p.)* chickenfarmer; **gallo** m rooster; ♪ false note, break in the voice; *Col.,C.R.,Mex.* strong man; F boss; ∼ de pelea fighting cock.
galo 1. Gallic; **2.** m, a f Gaul.
galocha f clog, patten.
galón m braid; ✗ stripe, chevron; **galonear** [1a] (trim with) braid.
galopar [1a] gallop; **galope** m gallop; a ∼, de ∼ at a gallop.
galopín m ragamuffin, urchin; *(bribón)* rogue; ⚓ cabin boy.
galpón m S.Am. (large) shed.
galvanizar [1f] galvanize (a. fig.); electroplate; **galvanoplástico** galvanoplastic.

gama¹ f zo. doe.

gama² f (letra) gamma; ♪ scale; range, gamut de colores etc.

gamba f prawn; sl. 100 pesetas.

gamberrear [1a] F act like a hooligan; loaf; **gamberrismo** m F hooliganism; **gamberro** m F lout, hooligan.

gambito m gambit.

gamo m buck (of fallow deer).

gamuza f zo. chamois; (cuero) chamois leather.

gana f desire; appetite; inclination; de buena ~ willingly, readily; de mala ~ unwillingly, reluctantly; me da la (real) ~ de inf. I feel like ger., I want to inf.; tener ~s de inf. feel like ger., care to inf.

ganadería f livestock; (strain of) cattle; (cría) cattle raising, stock breeding; **ganadero** m stock-breeder, rancher Am.; cattle-dealer; **ganado** m livestock; (vacas) cattle; (rebaño) herd, flock.

ganador 1. winning; **2.** m, **-a** f winner; **ganancia** f gain; † profit; (aumento) increase; ~s pl. winnings, earnings; **ganancioso** (provechoso) gainful, profitable.

ganapán m (recadero) messenger, porter; (jornalero) casual laborer.

ganar [1a] v/t. gain; † earn; (vencer) win; (obtener) get; † conquer, take; (llegar a) reach; v/i. thrive, improve.

ganchillo m crochet hook; (work); **gancho** m hook; F (p.) tout; (atractivo) sex appeal, charm; S.Am. hairpin.

gandul F **1.** idle, good-for-nothing, lazy; **2.** m, **-a** f loafer, good-for-nothing; **gandulería** f F loafing, laziness.

ganga f bargain; gift F.

gangoso nasal, with a twang.

gangrena f gangrene; **gangrenarse** [1a] become gangrenous.

gángster m gunman, gangster; **-ismo** m gangsterism.

ganguear [1a] speak with a (nasal) twang; **gangueo** m (nasal) twang.

ganso 1. m gander; **2.** m, **-a** f goose; fig. dolt, dope F; (rústico) bumpkin.

ganzúa f picklock.

gañán m farmhand.

gañido m yelp, howl; **gañir** [3h] (perro) yelp, howl; (ave) croak.

garabatear [1a] hook; (escribir) scribble; F beat about the bush;

garabato m hook, meat hook; (letra) scrawl; F sex appeal.

garaje m garage.

garante m/f guarantor; surety; **garantía** f guarantee; † warranty; (prenda) security; **garantizar** [1f] guarantee, warrant, vouch for.

garañón m stud jackass.

garapiña f sugar icing; coagulated liquid; **garapiñar** [1a] ice (with sugar); (helar) freeze; fruta candy.

garbanzo m chick-pea; ~ negro fig. black sheep.

garbeo m walk; promenade.

garbera f ⚡ shock.

garbo m jauntiness; graceful bearing; elegance; glamour, attractiveness; **garboso** jaunty; sprightly, graceful; elegant; mujer glamorous, attractive.

garduña f zo. marten; **garduño** m, **a** f sneak thief.

garfa f claw; **garfada** f clawing.

garfio m hook; gaff; ⊕ grapple, grappling-iron, claw.

garganta f throat; gullet; geog. gorge, ravine; instep de pie; neck de botella; **gargantilla** f necklace.

gárgara f gargling; hacer ~s gargle; **gargarismo** m gargle; **gargarizar** [1f] gargle.

gárgola f gargoyle.

garguero m gullet; (traquea) windpipe.

garita f cabin, hut; ✕ sentry box; (portería) porter's lodge.

garito m gambling den.

garlito m fish-trap; fig. snare, trap.

garra f claw; talon; fig. hand; ~s pl. grip; strength; fig. jaws.

garrafa f carafe, decanter.

garrapatear [1a] scribble, scrawl; **garrapato** m (mst ~s pl.) scribble, scrawl.

garrido neat, graceful; (hermoso) handsome, pretty.

garrocha f goad; toros: spear; deportes: vaulting pole.

garrote m cudgel, club; ♫ tourniquet; garrote para estrangular.

garrulería f chatter; **gárrulo** garrulous, chattering; ave chirping.

garúa f S.Am., ⚓ drizzle; **garuar** [1e] drizzle.

garza f (a. ~ real) heron; ~ imperial purple heron.

gas m gas; fumes; (a. ~ del alumbrado) coal gas; ~ asfixiante poison gas; ~es pl. de escape exhaust (fumes); ~ lacrimógeno tear gas.

gasa f gauze; (*paño*) crape.

gaseosa f aerated water, mineral water; *esp*. soda (pop); soda water; ~ de limón lemonade; **gaseoso** gaseous; aerated, gassy; *bebida* fizzy; **gas oil** [ga'sojl] m diesel oil; **gasolina** f petrol, gasoline; **gasolinera** f motorboat; gas station.

gastado spent; (*usado*) worn out; *vestido* shabby, threadbare; *fig*. outworn, hackneyed; **gastador 1.** extravagant, wasteful; **2.** m, **-a** f spender, spendthrift; **gastar** [1a] *dinero* spend, expend, lay out (en on); (*perder*) waste; (*desgastar*) wear away, wear down, wear out; (*agotar*) use up; **~se** wear out; waste; (*agotarse*) run out; **gasto** m (*acto*) spending; (*lo gastado*) expenditure, expense; ✝ cost; (*desgaste*) wear; consumption; costs; ✝ ~s pl. generales overhead; ✝ ~s pl. menores petty cash.

gástrico gastric; **gastritis** f gastritis; **gastroenterología** f gastroenterology; **gastronomía** f gastronomy.

gata f (she-)cat; F Madrid woman; *Mex*. (domestic) maid; *a* ~s on all fours; **gatear** [1a] v/t. claw, scratch; F pinch, swipe; v/i. (*subir*) clamber; (*ir a gatas*) creep, crawl.

gatillo m dental forceps; ⚔ trigger, hammer; *zo*. nape; F young thief.

gato m (tom)cat; ⊕, *mot*. jack; ⊕ grab; ✝ money bag; F sneak thief; F native of Madrid; ~ montés wildcat; ~ de tornillo screw jack; dar ~ por liebre cheat, put one over on s.o.

gatuperio m (*mezcla*) hodgepodge; (*trampa*) snare, fraud.

gaucho *S.Am*. **1.** m cowboy, herdsman, gaucho; **2.** gaucho *attr*.; *fig*. (*taimado*) sly; (*grosero*) coarse.

gaveta f drawer; ✝ till.

gavia f ✔ ditch; ⚓ topsail.

gavilán m orn. sparrow-hawk.

gavilla f ✔ sheaf; (*ps*.) gang, band.

gaviota f (sea)gull.

gayola f cage; F jail.

gaza f loop; ⚓ bend, bight.

gazapera f rabbit warren; F den of thieves; (*riña*) brawl; **gazapo** m young rabbit; (*p*.) sly fellow.

gazmoñería f hypocrisy, cant; (*recato excesivo*) prudery; **gazmoñ(er)o 1.** hypocritical, canting; strait-laced; **2.** m, **a** f hypocrite; prude (*mst* f); prig.

gaznate m (*garganta*) gullet; (*traquea*) windpipe, throttle.

gazpacho m cold soup of oil, vinegar, garlic, onion, bread etc.

gelatina f gelatin(e), jelly; **gelatinoso** gelatinous.

gema f gem; ♀ bud.

gemelo 1. twin; **2.** m, **a** f twin; ~s pl. cufflinks; *opt*. binoculars; ~s pl. de teatro opera glasses.

gemido m groan; moan; wail; **gemir** [3l] groan; moan; wail; (*viento, animales*) howl; whine.

Géminis m ast., zódiaco Gemini.

gen m gene.

gendarme m gendarme.

genealogía f genealogy; pedigree; **genealógico** genealogical.

generación f generation; (*hijos*) progeny; (*descendencia*) succession; **generador 1.** generating; **2.** m generator (*a*. ⚡, ⊕).

general 1. general; universal; (*corriente*) prevailing; **2.** m general; ~ de brigada brigadier; ~ de división major general; **3.** ~es f/pl. personal particulars; **generalidad** f generality; majority; **generalizar** [1f] generalize; make widely known; **~se** become general.

generar [1a] generate (*a*. ⚡).

genérico generic; **género** m 🎭 genus; (*clase*) kind, nature; *lit*. genre; *gr*. gender; (*paño*) cloth, material; ~ chico thea. comic one-act pieces.

generosidad f generosity; nobility; valour; **generoso** generous, liberal; noble; magnanimous.

génesis 1. f genesis; **2.** m ♀ Genesis.

genética f genetics; **genético** genetic.

genial inspired, of genius; (*placentero*) pleasant, cheerful; **genialidad** f genius; temperament; eccentricity; **genio** m temper; disposition; character, nature; (*inteligencia superior*) genius; corto de ~ slow-witted.

genital genital; (*órganos*) ~es pl. genitals; **genitivo 1.** reproductive, generative; **2.** m genitive (case).

genocidio m genocide.

genovés adj. a. su. m, **-a** f Genoese.

gente f people; folk; followers; troops, nation; (*parientes*) relatives; folks; F; F ~ bien upperclass people; ~ de bien honest folk, decent people; ~ menuda (*sin importancia*) small fry; **gentecilla** f unimportant people; *contp*. riffraff; **gentil 1.** graceful, elegant; (*amable*) charming; F *iro.* remarkable, pretty; *eccl.* pagan, heathen; **2.** *m/f* gentile, heathen; **gentileza** *f* grace, charm, elegance; politeness, courtesy; **gentilicio** national; tribal; family *attr.*; **gentílico** heathen(ish), pagan; **gentío** *m* crowd, throng; mob; **gentualla** *f*, **gentuza** *f* rabble, mob; riffraff.

genuino genuine, real; pure; true.

geofísica *f* geophysics; **geografía** *f* geography; **geología** *f* geology; **geometría** *f* geometry; ~ *del espacio* solid geometry; **geopolítica** *f* geopolitics.

geranio *m* geranium.

gerencia *f* (*en general*) management; (*cargo*) managership; (*oficina*) manager's office; **gerente** *m* manager.

geriatría *f* geriatrics; **geriátrico** geriatric(al).

germanía *f* thieves' slang, cant.

germánico Germanic; **germano** German(ic).

germen *m biol.*, ❀ germ; *fig.* germ, seed, source; **germicida 1.** germicidal; **2.** *m* germicide; **germinación** *f* germination; **germinar** [1a] germinate; sprout.

gerundense *adj. a. su. m/f* (native) of Gerona.

gerundio *m* gerund, present participle.

gestación *f* gestation.

gesticulación *f* grimace; gesticulation; **gesticular** [1a] grimace; gesticulate.

gestión *f* negotiation; (*dirección*) management; conduct (of affairs); effort, measure, step; **gestionar** [1a] negotiate; manage; promote.

gesto *m* (expression of one's) face; (*mueca*) grimace; gesture *con manos*; *estar de buen* (*mal*) ~ be in a good (bad) humor.

giba *f* hump, hunch(back); F nuisance; **giboso** hunchbacked, humped.

gigante *m* giant, gigantic; **2.** *m* giant; **gigantesco** gigantic, giant, mammoth.

gilí *adj.* F foolish; stupid.

gimnasia *f* gymnastics; physical training; **gimnasio** *m* gymnasium; **gimnasta** *m/f* gymnast.

gimotear [1a] F whine; wail; (*lloriquear*) snivel, grizzle; **gimoteo** *m* F whining *etc.*

ginebra *f* gin; *fig.* confusion.

ginecología *f* gynaecology; **ginecólogo** *m* gynaecologist.

gira *f* trip, outing; picnic *con comida.*

girar [1a] *v/t.* ⊕ *etc.* turn, twist, rotate; ✝ *letra* draw, issue; *v/i.* rotate, turn (round), go round, revolve; swivel, swing; ✝ do business; ✝ ~ *a cargo de,* ~ *contra* draw on.

girasol *m* sunflower.

giratorio gyratory; *puerta etc.* revolving; *puente etc.* swivel(ling), swing *attr.*; **giro** *m* turn (*a. fig.*); revolution, rotation, gyration; *fig.* trend, course; *gr.* turn of phrase, ✝ draft; ✝ ~ *en descubierto* overdraft; ~ *postal approx.* money order, postal order; **girocompás** *m* gyrocompass; **giroscopio** *m* gyroscope.

gitanear [1a] wheedle, cajole; **gitanería** *f* (*gitanos*) band of gipsies; (*dicho*) gipsy saying; (*mimos*) wheedling, cajolery; **gitano** **1.** gipsy *attr.*; (*taimado*) sly; (*zalamero*) smooth-tongued; (*insinuante*) engaging; **2.** *m*, **a** *f* gipsy.

glacial glacial; *viento etc.* icy, freezing; *fig.* cold, stony, indifferent; **glaciar** *m* glacier.

gladio *m*, **gladíolo** *m* gladiolus.

glándula *f* gland; **glandular** glandular.

glasear [1a] *papel etc.* glaze.

glicerina *f* glycerine.

global global; total, overall; *cantidad* lump *attr.*; *investigación etc.* comprehensive, full; **globo** *m* globe, sphere; ~ (*aerostático*) balloon; ~ *del ojo* eyeball; *en* ~ all in all, as a whole; **globular** globular, spherical; **glóbulo** *m* globule; corpuscle *de sangre.*

gloria *f* glory; *estar en la* ~, *estar en sus* ~s be in one's element; **gloriarse** [1c] glory, rejoice (*en in*); boast (*de* of); **glorieta** *f* summerhouse, bower *de jardín*; **glorificar** [1g] glorify; ~**se** glory (*de, en* in); **glorioso** glorious; *santo* blessed, in glory; *la Gloriosa eccl.* the Virgin.

glosa *f* gloss; **glosar** [1a] gloss; *fig.* criticize; **glosario** *m* glossary.

glotón **1.** gluttonous; **2.** *m*, **-a** *f* glutton; **glotonear** [1a] gormandize; **glotonería** *f* gluttony.

glucosa *f* glucose, grape sugar.

gluglú *m* (*agua*) gurgle; (*pavo*) gobble; *hacer* ~ gurgle; gobble.

glutinoso glutinous.

gnomo *m* gnome.

gobernable governable; ⚓ navigable; **gobernación** f governing, government; *Ministerio de la ♀ approx.* Ministry of the Interior; **gobernador 1.** governing; **2.** m governor; **gobernalle** m rudder, helm; **gobernante 1.** ruling; **2.** m/f ruler; **gobernar** [1k] v/t. govern, rule; (*manejar*) manage, handle; guide, direct; ♣ steer, sail; v/i. govern; ♣ handle, steer; **gobierno** m government; (*puesto*) governorship; control.

goce m enjoyment; possession.

godo 1. Gothic; **2.** m, a f Goth; *S.Am. contp.* Spaniard.

gol m goal (*score*).

goleta f schooner.

golf m golf.

golfear [1a] loaf; live a street urchin's life; **golfería** f (*ps.*) street urchins; (*vida*) loafing, life in the gutter; **golfo**[1] m F loafer, tramp.

golfo[2] m *geog.* gulf, bay; open sea.

golilla f ruff.

gollería f (*golosina*) tidbit; extra, special treat.

gollete m throat; (*cuello*) neck.

golondrina f swallow; ~ *de mar* tern.

golosina f tidbit (a. fig.), delicacy, sweet; (*cosa inútil*) bauble; (*antojo*) fancy; **goloso** sweet-toothed; (*glotón*) greedy.

golpe m blow, knock (a. fig.); (*palmada*) smack; (*latido*) beat; (*choque*) shock, clash; surprise; *deportes:* stroke, hit, shot *con palo, raqueta etc.*; punch, blow *en boxeo*; kick, shot *en fútbol etc.*; ~ *de estado* coup d'état; ~ *de fortuna* stroke of luck; ~ *franco* free-kick; ~ *de gente* crowd; ~ *de gracia* coup de grâce; *de* ~ suddenly; *de un* ~ at one stroke, outright; F *dar* ~ be a sensation, be a big hit; *dar* ~s *en* thump, pound (at); **golpear** [1a] v/t. strike, knock, hit; thump, bang *con ruido*; (*repetidamente*) beat; punch *con puño*; (*zurrar*) thrash; v/i. throb; ⊕ knock; **golpecito** m tap, rap; **golpeteo** m knocking; rattling; hammering; drumming.

goma f gum; (*caucho*) rubber; (*liga*) rubber (or elastic) band; *S.Am.* F hangover; ~ *arábiga* gum arabic; **gomita** f elastic band; **gomoso 1.** gummy, sticky; **2.** m F dandy, dude.

góndola f gondola.

gong(o) m gong.

gordi(n)flón F podgy, fat, chubby.

gordo 1. fat; p. a. stout, plump; (*craso*) greasy, oily; (*grande*) big;

premio first, big; (*basto*) coarse; **2.** fat, suet; F first prize; **gordura** f corpulence, stoutness; (*grasa*) grease, fat.

gorgojo m weevil, grub; *fig.* dwarf.

gorgorito m F trill, quaver.

gorgotear [1a] gurgle; **gorgoteo** m gurgle.

gorguera f ruff; ✕ gorget.

gorila m gorilla; F tough, thug.

gorjear [1a] warble, chirp, twitter; ~se (*niño*) gurgle, crow; **gorjeo** m warble etc.

gorra 1. f (peaked) cap; bonnet; ~ *de visera* peaked cap; **2.** m (a. **gorrero** m) freeloader; sponger; F *ir etc. de* ~ scrounge, sponge; **gorrear** [1a] sponge; freeload.

gorrión m sparrow.

gorrista m/f sponger.

gorro m cap; bonnet; ~ *de baño* bathing cap; ~ *de dormir* nightcap.

gorrón[1] m pebble; ⊕ pivot, journal.

gorrón[2] m F cadger, sponger; **gorronear** [1a] F scrounge, cadge, sponge.

gota f drop; bead, blob; ⚕ gout; ~ *a* ~ drop by drop; *caer a* ~ drip; *parecerse como dos* ~s *de agua* be as like as two peas in a pod; **goteado** speckled; **gotear** [1a] drip, dribble, trickle (a. fig.); (*vela*) gutter; ~(se) leak; **goteo** m drip(ping) etc.; **gotera** f leak; drip(ping); (*cenefa*) valence; ⚕ ailment; *lleno de* ~s p. full of aches and pains.

gótico Gothic; F noble.

gozar [1f] v/t. enjoy; possess, have; v/i. enjoy o.s.; ~ *de* = v/t.; ~se rejoice; ~ *en inf.* take pleasure in ger.

gozne m hinge.

gozo m joy, gladness; pleasure, delight, enjoyment; **gozoso** glad, joyful (*con, de* about, at).

grabación f recording; ~ *en cinta* tape recording; **grabado** m engraving, print; (*esp. en libro*) illustration, picture; ~ *al agua fuerte* etching; ~ *al agua tinta* aquatint; ~ *en cobre* copperplate; ~ *en madera* woodcut; **grabador** m engraver; **grabadora** f recorder; ~ *de cinta* tape recorder; **grabador-reproductor** m cassette player; **grabar** [1a] engrave; record *en disco etc.*; *en, sobre cinta* tape-record.

gracejo m wit, humour; repartee.

gracia 1. f grace (a. eccl.); favor, pardon; gracefulness, attractiveness; (*agudeza*) wit; (*chiste*) joke; (*esencia de chiste*) point; F name; *¿cuál es su ~?* what's your name?; *¡qué ~!* what a nerve!, the very idea!; *de ~* free, for nothing; *en ~ a* on account of, for the sake of; *sin ~* graceless; *caer en ~ a* find favor with, make a hit with F; *dar en la ~ de decir* harp on; *hacer ~* strike s.o. as funny; *tener ~* be funny; **2. ~s** *pl.* thanks; *¡~!* thank you!; **grácil** slender; small; delicate; **gracioso 1.** (*elegante*) graceful; (*afable*) gracious; attractive; (*agudo*) witty; (*divertido*) funny, amusing; (*gratuito*) free; **2. m** *thea.* fool, funny man.

grada f step *de escalera*; *thea. etc.* tier, row (of seats); grandstand, bleachers; ⚓ slipway, slips; ✂ harrow; ~ *de discos* disk harrow; **gradación** f gradation; *rhet.* climax; *gr.* comparison; **gradar** [1a] harrow; **gradería** f flight of steps; *thea. etc.* rows of seats, tiers.

grado m (*peldaño*) step; *univ.*, ⚕, *phys. a. fig.* degree; (*nivel*) level; (*rango*) grade, rank; *escuela*: class; *de* (*buen*) ~ willingly; *de ~ en ~* by degrees; *de mal ~*, (*a*) *mal mi etc.* ~ unwillingly.

graduable adjustable; **graduación** f gradation; graduation; grading; ✕ rank; alcoholic strength; **graduado** m, a f graduate; **gradual** gradual; **graduar** [1e] (*clasificar*) grade; *termómetro etc.* graduate; (*medir*) gauge, measure; ⊕ calibrate; *vista* test; *univ.* confer a degree (✕ rank) on; **~se** graduate, take one's degree (*en* in).

gráfica f graph; **gráfico 1.** graphic (*a. fig.*); pictorial, illustrated; **2. m** ⚕ graph; chart; diagram.

grafito m graphite, blacklead.

gragea f colored candy; sugar-coated pill.

grajear [1a] caw; (*niño*) gurgle; **grajilla** f jackdaw; **grajo** m rook.

gramática f grammar; **gramatical** grammatical; **gramático 1.** grammatical; **2. m** grammarian.

gramo m gram(me).

gramófono m, **gramola** f Gramophone, phonograph.

gran v. *grande*.

grana[1] f ♀ seeding; (*época*) seeding time; (*semilla*) small seed.

grana[2] f *zo.* cochineal; kermes; (*color*) scarlet; (*paño*) scarlet cloth.

granada f ♀ pomegranate; ✕ grenade *de mano*, shell *de cañón*; ~ *de metralla* shrapnel; ~ *de mano* hand grenade; ~ *extintora* fire extinguisher.

granado[1] m ♀ pomegranate tree.

granado[2] notable, distinguished; select; mature; (*alto*) tall.

granate m garnet.

grande 1. big, large; (*a. fig.*) great; (*grandioso*) grand; *número, velocidad* high; (*alto*) tall; *en ~* as a whole; on a large scale, in a big way; **2. m** (*de España*) grandee; *los ~s* the great; **grandeza** f bigness; greatness; (*grandiosidad*) grandeur; (*tamaño*) size; (*nobleza*) nobility; **grandioso** magnificent, grand (*esp. b.s.*) grandiose.

graneado granulated; **granear** [1a] *semilla* sow; *cuero* grain; (*puntear*) stipple; **granel:** *a ~* (*sin orden*) at random; (*en montón*) in a heap; ✝ in bulk, loose; **granero** m granary (*a. fig.*); **granilla** f grain (in cloth).

granito m granite; ✱ pimple.

granizada f hailstorm; hail (*a. fig.*); *= granizado* ✕ iced drink; **granizar** [1f] hail; *fig.* shower; **granizo** m hail.

granja f farm; farmhouse; (*quinta*) country house; (*vaquería*) dairy; ~ *avícola* poultry farm.

granjear [1a] gain, earn; win; **~se** *algo* win (for s.o.).

granjería f farming; farm earnings; profit; **granjero** m farmer.

grano m grain (*a. pharm.*); (*semilla*) seed; (*baya*) berry; bean *de café*; (*partícula*) speck; ✱ pimple, spot; ✂ *~s pl.* grain, cereals; *ir al ~* come to the point.

granuja m ragamuffin; rogue.

granulación f granulation; **granular** granular; **granular(se)** [1a] granulate; **gránulo** m granule.

grapa f clip; paper fastener; staple *de dos puntas*; △ cramp.

grasa f fat; (*unto*) grease; (*sebo*) suet; (*aceite*) oil; (*mugre*) filth; ✕ ~s *pl.* slag; ~ *de ballena* blubber; **grasiento** greasy, oily; filthy; **graso 1.** fatty; greasy; **2. m** fattiness; greasiness.

grata f ✝ favor; **gratificación** f (*premio*) reward; (*propina*) tip, gratuity; **gratis** free (of charge), for nothing, gratis; **gratitud** f gratitude; **grato** pleasing, pleasant; welcome, gratifying; (*agradecido*) grateful; **gratuito** free; *observación etc.* gratuitous, uncalled-for; *acusación* unfounded.

grava *f* gravel; crushed stone; metal *de camino*.

gravamen *m* obligation; burden.

grave (*de peso*) heavy; *fig.* grave, serious; important, momentous; *enfermedad* grave; *herida, pérdida* grievous, severe; *p.* sedate, dignified; ♪ low, deep; *gr. palabra* paroxitone; *acento* grave.

gravedad *f* gravity.

gravitación *f* gravitation; **gravoso** onerous; oppressive, burdensome; † costly; (*molesto*) tiresome; *ser ~ a* weigh on.

greda *f geol.* clay; (*de batán*) fuller's earth; **gredoso** clayey.

gregario gregarious; herd *attr.*; (*servil*) slavish.

greña *f* (*mst pl.*) shock (or mat, mop) of hair; *fig.* entanglement, tangle; *andar a la ~* squabble; **greñudo** disheveled.

gres *m geol.* potter's clay; (*loza*) earthenware, stoneware.

gresca *f* (*jaleo*) uproar, hubbub; (*riña*) row, brawl.

grey *f eccl.* flock, congregation.

griego 1. Greek; 2. *m*, **a** *f* Greek; F cheat; 3. *m* (*idioma*) Greek; *fig.* gibberish, double Dutch.

grieta *f* fissure, crack; crevice; chink; chap *en piel*; **grietarse** [1a] = *agrietarse*.

grifo *m* tap, cock, faucet; (*servido*) *al ~* on tap, (on) draft; *Mex. estar ~* be high on pot; *Mex.* marijuana; *Mex.* pot smoker.

grillete *m* fetter, shackle.

grillo *m zo.* cricket; ♀ shoot, sprout; *~s pl.* fetters, irons.

grima *f* annoyance; horror; *me da ~ it* gets on my nerves.

gringo *m*, **a** *f contp.* foreigner.

gripe *f* influenza, flu.

gris 1. gray; *día* dull, gloomy; 2. *m* gray.

grisú *m* ⚒ firedamp.

grita *f* uproar, outcry; *dar ~ a* hoot, boo; **gritar** [1a] shout, yell, cry out; (*desaprobar*) hoot; (*bramar*) bellow; **gritería** *f*, **griterío** *m* shouting, uproar; **grito** *m* shout, yell; cry; hoot; bellow; scream.

grosella *f* (red) currant; *~ espinosa* gooseberry; **grosellero** *m* currant (bush).

grosería *f* coarseness *etc.*; (*dicho*) rude thing; **grosero** (*basto*) coarse, rough; discourteous, rude; **grosor** *m* thickness.

grotesco grotesque, bizarre, absurd.

grúa *f* ⊕ crane; derrick; *~ de auxilio* wrecking crane; *~ puente* overhead crane.

gruesa *f* gross.

grueso 1. thick; (*corpulento*) fat; *p.* stout, thick-set; (*abultado*) large, bulky; (*basto*) coarse; (*poco agudo*) dull; *artillería, mar* heavy; 2. *m* (*grosor*) thickness; (*bulto*) bulk; (*parte principal*) major portion; ✗ main body; *en ~* in bulk.

grulla *f orn.* (*a. ~ común*) crane.

grumo *m* clot *de sangre*; dollop; cluster *de uvas*; *~ de leche* curd.

gruñido *m* grunt; growl; snarl; **gruñir** [3h] (*esp. cerdo*) grunt; (*perro, oso*) growl, snarl; *fig.* grumble; (*puerta etc.*) creak; **gruñón** F grumpy.

grupa *f* crupper, horse's hindquarters; **grupera** *f* pillion.

grupo *m* group.

grupúsculo *m* splinter group.

gruta *f* cavern, grotto.

guacho *S.Am.* motherless, orphaned; *zapato etc.* odd.

guadal *m S.Am.* bog; dune.

guadaña *f* scythe; **guadañadora** *f* mowing machine; **guadañar** [1a] scythe, mow.

guagua *f* trifle; *S.Am.* bus; (*rorro*) baby; *de ~* free, for nothing.

gualdo yellow, golden.

guante *m* glove; *~s pl. fig.* tip, commission; F *echar el ~ a* lay hands on, seize; **guantelete** *m* gauntlet.

guapo 1. *mujer* pretty; *hombre* handsome; good-looking; (*aseado*) smart; (*ostentoso*) flashy; (*valiente*) dashing, bold; 2. *m* F lover, gallant; (*matón*) bully; (*fanfarrón*) braggart.

guarda 1. *m* guard; keeper, custodian; *~ de coto* gamekeeper; 2. *f* guard(ing); (*safe*) keeping, custody; observance *de ley*; flyleaf, endpaper *de libro*.

guarda...: ~barro(s) *m* mudguard; **~bosque** *m* ranger, forester; gamekeeper; **~brisa** *m mot.* windscreen.

guarda...: ~espaldas *m* henchman, bodyguard; **~fango** *m* mudguard; **~frenos** *m* brake(s)man; **~fuego** *m* fireguard; fender; **~lmacén** *m/f* storekeeper; **~lodos** *m* mudguard;

~**mano** m guard (*of sword*); ~**meta** m goalkeeper; ~**muebles** m furniture repository; ~**pelo** m locket; ~**polvo** m dust cover, dust sheet; (*vestido*) dust coat; overall(s).

guardar [1a] (*retener*) keep; (*proteger*) guard (de against, from); preserve, save (de from); (*poner aparte*) put away, lay by; (*vigilar*) watch; *ganado* tend; *fiesta, mandamiento* observe; ¡guarda! look out!; ~**se** de avoid; look out for; ~ de *inf.* keep from *ger.*, avoid *ger.*

guardarropa 1. m checkroom; (*mueble*) wardrobe; 2. m/f checkroom attendant; **guardarropía** f *thea.* wardrobe; (*accesorios*) properties, props F.

guardia 1. f (X) servicio, regimiento, esgrima) guard; police; custody; ♣ watch; *relevar la* ~ change guard; 2. m (X) guard(sman).

guardián m, **-a** f keeper, custodian, warden; (*vigilante*) watchman.

guardilla f attic, garret.

guarecer [2d] shelter, protect, take in; preserve; ~**se** take shelter.

guarida f *zo.* lair, den; (*refugio*) shelter, cover; hideout.

guarismo m figure, numeral.

guarnecer [2d] (*adornar*) garnish, embellish (de with); equip, provide; fitting (X) garrison; ⊕ packing; *sew.* trimming, binding; lining *de frenos*; setting *de joya*; guard *de espada*; fittings, fixtures.

guarra f sow; **guarro** m pig.

guatemalteco adj. a. su. m, a f Guatemalan.

guau 1. bow-wow!; 2. m bark.

guayaba f guava (jelly).

gubernativo governmental.

gubia f gouge.

guedeja f long hair, lock; mane.

guerra f war; warfare; conflict, struggle, fight; ~ *atómica* atomic warfare; ~ *bacteriológica*, ~ *bacteriana* germ warfare; ~ *fría* cold war; ~ de *guerrillas* guerrilla warfare; ~ *mundial* world war; ~ de *nervios* war of nerves; ~ *nuclear* nuclear war; ~ *relámpago* blitzkrieg; ~ *a tiros* shooting war, hot war; *de* ~ military, war *attr.*; **guerrear** [1a] wage war, fight; **guerrero** 1. fighting; war *attr.*; warlike, martial; 2. m warrior, soldier, fighting man; **guerrilla** f guerrilla band, band of partisans; **gue-**

rrillero m guerrilla, partisan, irregular.

guía 1. m/f (*p.*) guide; leader; adviser; 2. m (X) marker; 3. f (⊕, *fig.*, *libro*) guide; (*acto*) guidance; guidebook, handbook, guidepost; handlebar *de bicicleta*; (*caballo*) leader; ~**s** *pl.* reins; *cine:* ~ *sonora* sound track; ~ *telefónica*, ~ de *teléfonos* telephone directory; ~ *del viajero* guidebook; **guiar** [1c] guide; *mot.* drive; (X) pilot; ~**se** por go by, be guided by.

guija f pebble; cobblestone; **guija-rro** m pebble; boulder.

guillame m rabbet plane.

guillotina f guillotine (a. ⊕); **guillotinar** [1a] guillotine.

guinda f morello cherry.

guindaleza f hawser.

guindola f lifebuoy.

guiñada f wink; blink; ♣ yaw.

guiñapo m rag, tatter; ragamuffin.

guiñar [1a] wink; blink; ♣ yaw; **guiño** m wink.

guión m (*p. etc.*) leader; *typ.* hyphen, dash; (*escrito*) explanatory text, handout F; *cine:* script, scenario; *eccl.* processional cross (*or* banner); royal standard; **guionista** m/f script writer.

guisa f: a ~ de as, like, in the manner of; de *tal* ~ in such a way.

guisado m stew; **guisante** m pea; ~ de *olor* sweet pea; **guisar** [1a] (*cocinar*) cook; (*hervir*) stew; *fig.* prepare, arrange; **guiso** m cooked dish; seasoning; **guisote** m F hash.

guita f twine; *sl.* dough.

guitarra f guitar; **guitarrista** m/f guitarist.

gula f gluttony.

gusano m worm; maggot, grub; caterpillar *de mariposa etc.*; *fig.* meek creature; ~ de *luz* glowworm; ~ de *seda* silkworm; **gusanoso** worm-eaten.

gustación f tasting, trying; **gustar** [1a] v/t. taste, try, sample; v/i. please, be pleasing; **gustillo** m suggestion, touch, tang.

gusto m taste; (*sabor*) flavor; (*placer*) pleasure; (*afición*) liking (por for); (*capricho*) fancy, whim; ¡*tanto* ~! how do you do?; *con mucho* ~ with pleasure; *tanto* ~ glad to meet you; *tengo mucho* ~ *en conocerle* I'm very glad to meet you; *tomar* ~ *a* take a liking to; **gustoso** (*sabroso*) tasty, savory; (*agradable*) pleasant.

H

ha v. haber.

¡ha! ah!

haba f (broad) bean; lima bean.

haber 1. [2k] v/t. catch, lay hands on; † have; v/aux. have; ~ de inf. have to inf.; must inf.; be (due) to inf.; ¿qué he de hacer? what am I to do?, what must I do?; ha de ser tonto he must be a fool; ha de cantar esta noche he is to sing tonight; verbo impersonal: hay: (sg.) there is, (pl.) there are; hay sol it is sunny; ¿cuánto hay de aquí a Madrid? how far is it to Madrid?; ¡no hay de qué! you're welcome, don't mention it; ¿qué hay? what's the matter?; ¿hay plátanos? (en tienda) do you have any bananas?; años ha years ago; habrá ocho días about a week ago; ~ que inf. be necessary to inf.; hay que comer para vivir one must eat to live; ~se: tener que habérselas con have to deal with, be up against; **2.** m property, goods (mst ~es pl.); income; ✝ assets, credit (side).

habichuela f kidney bean; ~ verde string bean.

hábil clever, skilful; proficient, expert, good (en at); capable; b.s. cunning; fit (para for); ⚖ competent; **habilidad** f cleverness, skill etc.; **habilidoso** clever.

habitación f (cuarto) room; (morada) dwelling, habitation; residence; **habitante** m inhabitant; occupant de casa; **habitar** [1a] v/t. inhabit, live in, dwell in; casa occupy; v/i. live, dwell.

hábito m todos sentidos: habit; F ahorcar (or colgar) los ~s leave the priesthood.

habitual habitual, customary; mst b.s. inveterate; criminal hardened; regular; **habituar** [1e] habituate, accustom (a to); ~se a become accustomed to, get used to.

habla f (facultad) speech; (idioma) language; (regional) dialect, speech; talk, speech de clase, profesión etc.; al ~ speaking; teleph. speaking, on the line; ⚓ within hail; de ~ española Spanish-speaking; negar (or quitar)

el ~ a not be on speaking terms with; **hablador 1.** talkative; **2.** m, -a f talker, chatterbox; (y chismoso) gossip; **habladuría** f rumor; bragging.

hablar [1a] speak, talk (con to); ~ claro talk straight from the shoulder; ~ por (sólo) ~ talk for the sake of talking; ~se: se habla español Spanish (is) spoken here; se habla de inf. there is talk of ger.

hablilla f rumor; idle gossip.

hacedero practicable, feasible; **hacedor** m, -a f maker; ♀ Maker.

hacendado 1. landed, propertyowning; **2.** m, a f landowner, man etc. of property; S.Am. rancher; **hacendero** industrious, thrifty; **hacendista** m economist, financial expert; **hacendoso** diligent, hard-working; bustling, busy.

hacer [2s] **1.** v/t. a) make; create; ⊕ manufacture; 🏛 build, construct; compose, fashion, form; b) do; perform; practice; put into practice, execute; cause; compel, oblige; effect; (proveer) provide (con, de with); accustom (a to); suppose a. p. to be; c) 🏹 amount to, make; apuesta lay; ✝ balance strike; cama make; comedia perform, do; comida prepare, cook, get; corbata tie; dinero earn, make; discurso make, deliver; guerra wage; humo give off, produce; maleta pack; objeción raise; papel play, act, take; pregunta put, pose; prodigios work; sombra cast; visita pay; d) ~ adj. turn adj., render adj., send (esp. p. F) adj.; e) ~ inf. have (or make) a p. inf.; hágale entrar show him in, have him come in; me hago cortar el pelo I have (or get) my hair cut; ~ que subj. see to it that; f) ~ bien do good; ~ bien (mal) en inf. be right (wrong) to inf.; ~ bueno acusación make good; F la ha hecho buena he's made a hash of it; te hacíamos en Madrid we thought (or supposed) you were in Madrid; nos hizo con dinero he provided us with money; ¿qué (le) hemos de ~? what's to be done (about it)?; tener que ~

have s.t. to do; **2.** *v/i.* be important, matter, signify; (*convenir*) be suitable, be fitting; (*a todo* (*p.*)) be good for anything; ~ *que hacemos* pretend to be busy; *¿hace?* will it do?, is it a go? F; *no lo hace* never mind, it doesn't matter; ~ *como que*, ~ *como si* act as if; ~ *de* act as; ~ *para inf.*, ~ *por inf.* make to *inf.*; try to *inf.*; *dar que* ~ give trouble; make work; **3.** *verbo impersonal:* a) *meteor.* be; *v. calor:* b) *hace 2 horas que llegó* he arrived 2 hours ago, it is 2 hours since he arrived; *está aquí desde hace 2 horas* he has been here for 2 hours; **4.** ~*se* (*transformarse*) become, grow, get (*or* come) to be, turn (into); (*crecer*) grow; (*fingirse*) pretend to be; *cortesías* exchange; ~ *soldado* become a soldier, turn soldier; ~ *viejo* grow old, get old; ~ *a* become accustomed to; ~ *atrás* fall back: ~ *con*, ~ *de* appropriate, get hold of.

hacha 1. *f* axe, chopper; torch; **hachear** [1a] *v/t.* hew; *v/i.* wield an axe; **hachero** *m* woodcutter.

hacia toward(s); (*cerca de*) about, near; ~ *abajo* down(wards); ~ *adelante* forward(s); ~ *arriba* up(wards); ~ *atrás* back(wards); ~ *las 3* at about 3 o'clock.

hacienda *f* (landed) property; (*finca*) (country) estate; fortune; *S.Am.* ranch; (*ganado*) livestock; ~*s* pl. household chores; ~ *pública* public income.

hacina *f esp.* ♂ stack, rick; (*montón*) pile, heap; **hacinar** [1a] stack; pile (up), heap (up); accumulate.

hada *f* fairy; ~ *madrina* fairy godmother; *de* ~*s* fairy *attr.*; **hadado:** *bien* ~ lucky; *mal* ~ ill-fated; **hado** *m* fate, destiny.

haga, *v. hacer.*

halagar [1h] show affection to; (*adular*) flatter; (*agradar*) gratify; **halago** *m* caress; cajolery; blandishment(s); flattery; gratification, delight; **halagüeño** flattering; pleasing, attractive, alluring.

halar [1a] ♨ *v/t.* haul (at, on), pull.

halcón *m* falcon; *pol.* hawk.

halda *f* skirt; *poner* ~*s en cinta* F roll up one's sleeves.

hálito *m* vapor; *from the mouth* breath; *poet.* gentle breeze.

hallar [1a] *mst* find; discover; locate; come across *sin buscar*; (*averiguar*) find out; ~*se* find o.s.; be; **hallazgo** *m* (*acto*) finding; discovery; (*cosa hallada*) find; (*recompensa*) reward.

halterio *m* dumbbell; **halterofilista** *m/f* weightlifter.

hamaca *f* hammock.

hambre *f* hunger (*a. fig.; de* for); famine; starvation; *fig.* longing (*de* for); *tener* ~ be hungry; *esp. fig.* hunger (*de* after, for); **hambrear** [1a] *v/t.* starve; *v/i.* starve, go hungry; **hambriento** hungry, famished, starving.

hamburguesa *f* hamburger.

hamo *m* fishhook.

hampa *f* underworld; **hampón** *m* tough, rowdy, thug.

hámster *m* hamster.

han *v. haber.*

handicap *m* handicap.

hangar *m* hangar.

haragán 1. idle, good-for-nothing; **2.** *m*, **-a** *f* idler, loafer, good-for-nothing; **haraganear** [1a] idle; lounge, loaf (about), hang about; **haraganería** *f* idleness *etc.*

harapiento, haraposo in rags, ragged, tattered; **harapo** *m* rag, tatter; *hecho un* ~ in rags.

harén *m* harem.

harina *f* flour, meal; (*polvo*) powder; ~ *de avena* oatmeal; ~ *de huesos* bone meal; ~ *lacteada* malted milk; ~ *de maíz* corn meal; *es* ~ *de otro costal* that's (quite) another story, that's a horse of a different color; **harinero 1.** flour *attr.*; **2.** *m* (*p.*) flour merchant; flour bin; **harinoso** floury, mealy.

harnero *m* sieve.

hartar [1a] satiate; stuff, surfeit, glut (*con* with); ~*se* gorge (*con* on); **hartazgo** *m* abundance; glut; bellyful; *darse un* ~ *de* eat one's fill of; **harto 1.** *adj.* full (*de* of), glutted (*de* with); *fig.* tired (*de* of), fed up (*de* with); **2.** *adv.* quite, very; enough.

has *v. haber.*

hasta 1. *prp. espacio:* as far as, up to, down to; *tiempo:* till, until; as late as, up to; pending; *cantidad:* as much as, as many as; *v. vista:* **2.** *adv.* even; quite; **3.** *cj.* even, also; ~ *que* until.

hastiar [1c] (*cansar*) weary; (*repugnar*) disgust; (*disgustar*) annoy; (*aburrir*) bore; **hastío** *m* weariness; disgust; annoyance; boredom.

hato *m* ♂ herd; flock *de ovejas;* group *de ps.; b.s.* gang; *S.Am.* cattle ranch;

fig. lot; (*víveres*) provisions; (*ropa*) clothes; personal effects.

hay *v. haber.*

haya *f* beech (tree); **hayuco** *m* beechnut, beechmast.

haz[1] *m* ♂ sheaf *de mieses etc.*, truss *de paja*; bundle *de leña etc.*; bunch; **haces** *pl. hist.* fasces; ~ *de luz* beam of light.

haz[2] *f mst fig. or lit.* face; (*superficie*) surface; right *de tela*; ~ *de la tierra* face of the earth; *de dos haces fig.* two-faced.

haz[3] *v. hacer.*

hazaña *f* feat, exploit.

he[1] *v. haber.*

he[2]: *mst lit.* — *aquí* here is, here are; lo (and behold)!; *¡heme* (*or* héteme) *aquí* here I am; *¡helos allí!* there they are.

hebilla *f* buckle, clasp.

hebra *f* (length of) thread; strand; fibre; grain *de madera*; ♃ vein; *fig.* thread (of the conversation); ~*s pl. poet.* hair; *pegar la* ~ strike up a conversation.

hebraico Hebraic; **hebreo 1.** *adj. a. su. m,* **a** *f* Hebrew; **2.** (*idioma*) Hebrew.

hebroso fibrous; *carne* stringy.

hechicera *f* sorceress, witch; enchantress; **hechicero 1.** magic; bewitching, enchanting (*a. fig.*); *fig.* charming; **2.** *m* wizard, sorcerer; witch doctor *de salvajes*; **hechizar** [1f] bewitch (*a. fig.*), cast a spell on; *b.s.* bedevil; *fig.* charm, enchant, delight; **hechizo 1.** artificial, false; (*amovible*) detachable; ⊕ manufactured; **2.** *m* magic; charm, spell (*a. fig.*); *fig.* glamour; ~*s pl.* (woman's) charms.

hecho 1. *p.p. of hacer;* ¡~! done!, it's a deal!; **2.** *adj.* complete, mature; (*acabado*) finished; *sew.* ready-made, ready-to-wear; *frase* stock; ~ *y derecho* complete, proper, full-fledged; **3.** *m* deed, act, action; fact; (*elemento*) factor; (*asunto*) matter; (*suceso*) event; *a* ~ continuously; *all together*; indiscriminately; *de* ~ in fact, as a matter of fact.

hechura *f* make, making; creation; creature (*a. fig.*); form, shape; build *de p.*; cut *de traje*; (*artesanía*) workmanship.

hectárea *f* hectare.

heder [2g] stink, reek (*a* of).

hedor *m* stench, reek.

helada *f* frost; freeze(-up); ~ *blanca*

hoarfrost; **heladera** *f* refrigerator; **heladería** *f* ice-cream parlor; **helado 1.** frozen (*a. fig.*); freezing, icy; (*preso*) ice-bound; *fig.* chilly, disdainful; **2.** *m* ice(-cream); iced drink; **helar** [1k] freeze; water ice; chill; ~*se* freeze; be frozen; (*avión, riel etc.*) ice (up).

hélice *f* spiral; A, ♭, *anat.* helix; ♻ screw, propeller; ✈ propeller, airscrew.

helicóptero *m* helicopter.

helio *m* helium.

hembra *f* *zo.*, ♀, ⊕ female; *zo.* she-...; *orn.* hen; *sew.* eye; ⊕ nut; F woman; **hembrilla** *f* ⊕ nut.

hemiciclo *m* semicircle; semicircular theater; *parl.* floor; **hemisferio** *m* hemisphere.

hemofilia *f* hemophilia; **hemorragio** *f* hemorrhage; **hemorroides** *f/pl.* hemorrhoids.

henal *m* hayloft; **henar** *m* meadow, hayfield.

henchir [3h] fill (up), stuff, cram; ~*se* (*p.*) stuff o.s.

hendedura *f* cleft, split; (*incisión*) slit; (*grieta*) crack; *mst geol.* rift, fissure; **hender** [2g] cleave (*a. fig.*); split; crack; slit *con cuchillo.*

henil *m* hayloft; **heno** *m* hay.

heráldica *f* heraldry; **heráldico** heraldic; **heraldo** *m* herald (*a. fig.*).

herbaj(e)ar *v/t.* put to pasture, graze; *v/i.* graze, browse; **herbario 1.** herbal; **2.** *m* herbarium; (*p.*) herbalist.

heredad *f* (country) estate, farm; domain; landed property; **heredar** [1a] inherit (*de* from); *p.* name as one's heir; **heredera** *f* heiress; **heredero** *m* heir (*de* to), inheritor (*de* of); **hereditario** hereditary.

hereje *m/f* heretic; **herejía** *f* heresy.

herencia *f* inheritance; legacy; heritage; *biol.* heredity.

herético heretic(al).

herida *f* wound, injury; (*ofensa*) insult, outrage; *fig.* affliction; **herido 1.** injured; ✗ wounded; **2.** *m* injured (✗ wounded) man; ~*s pl.* the wounded; **herir** [3i] hurt, injure; *esp.* ✗ wound (*a. fig.*); (*golpear*) strike, hit; (*sol*) beat down on; (*cuerda*) pluck, strike; ♪ touch.

hermana *f* sister (*a. eccl.*); twin; ~ *de leche* foster sister; ~ *política* sister-in-law; *media* ~ half sister; **hermanar** [1a] match; (*unir*) join;

harmonize; **hermanastro** m stepbrother; **hermandad** f brotherhood (a. fig.), sisterhood; fig. close relationship; **hermano** 1. m brother (a. fig., eccl.); (cosa) twin; ~s pl. brother(s) and sister(s); ~ carnal blood brother; ~ de leche foster brother; ~ político brother-in-law; medio ~ half brother; 2. adj. similar, matching; sister attr. (fig.).

hermético hermetic, air-tight.

hermosear [1a] beautify, make beautiful; adorn; **hermoso** beautiful; esp. hombre handsome; lovely; fine, splendid; **hermosura** f beauty; loveliness; (p.) belle.

hernia f rupture, hernia.

héroe m hero; **heroicidad** f (act of) heroism; **heroico** heroic.

heroína[1] f heroine.

heroína[2] f pharm. heroin.

heroinómano m heroin addict.

heroísmo m heroism.

herpes m/pl. or f/pl. 🌿 shingles, herpes.

herradura f horseshoe; curva en ~ mot. hairpin bend; **herraje** m ironwork, metal fittings; **herramental** m tool bag, tool kit; **herramienta** f tool, implement; appliance; set of tools; ~ mecánica power tool; **herrar** [1k] caballo shoe; ganado brand; ⊕ bind (or trim) with iron; **herrería** f blacksmith's (shop), forge; (fábrica) ironworks.

herrero m (black)smith; ~ de grueso ironworker; ~ de obra steelworker.

herrete m metal tip.

herrumbre f rust; a prueba de ~ rust proof; **herrumbroso** rusty.

hervir [3i] boil, seethe (a. fig.); (mar) surge; ~ de, ~ en swarm with, teem with.

hez f: mst pl. heces sediment, less; dregs (a. fig.); excrement.

hiato m gr., 🌿 hiatus.

hibernación f hibernation.

híbrido hybrid.

hice v. hacer.

hidalga f noblewoman; **hidalgo** 1. noble, illustrious; gentlemanly; 2. m nobleman.

hidra f hydra.

hidráulica f hydraulics; **hidráulico** hydraulic, water attr.

hidro(avión) m seaplane; flying boat; **hidrocarburo** m hydrocarbon; **hidrodinámica** f hydrodynamics; **hi-**

droeléctrico hydroelectric; **hidrófilo** absorbent, F bibulous; **hidrofobia** f hydrophobia; rabies; **hidrófugo** water-repellent; **hidrógeno** m hydrogen; **hidropesía** f dropsy; **hidroplano** m seaplane; **hidrostática** f hydrostatics; **hidrostático** hydrostatic.

hiedra f ivy.

hiel f bile; fig. bitterness.

hielo m ice; frost; freezing; fig. coldness, indifference; ~ flotante drift ice; ~ seco dry ice.

hiena f hyena.

hierba f grass; esp. 🌿 herb; small plant; ~s pl. pasture; mala ~ weed; ~buena f mint.

hierro m iron; head de lanza etc.; (de marcar) brand; ~s pl. irons; ~ acanalado, ~ ondulado corrugated iron; ~ colado, ~ fundido cast iron; ~ forjado wrought iron; ~ en lingotes pig iron; ~ viejo scrap iron.

hígado m liver; ~s pl. F guts, pluck.

higiene f hygiene; **higiénico** hygienic; sanitary; healthy.

higo m 🌿 (green) fig; vet. thrush; ~ chumbo, ~ de tuna prickly pear.

higuera f fig-tree.

hija f daughter, child (a. fig.); **hijastro** m stepson; **hijito** m F sonny; **hijo** m son, child (a. fig.); ~s pl. children, son(s) and daughter(s); ~ de leche foster child; ~ político son-in-law; Juan Lanas ~ Juan Lanas Junior; **hijuela** f little girl; ⊕ accessory; 🌿 portion, inheritance; **hijuelo** m little boy; 🌿 shoot; ~s pl. zo. young.

hila f row, line; ~s pl. 🌿 lint.

hilada f row, line; △ course.

hilado m (acto) spinning; (hilo) yarn, thread; **hilar** [1a] spin; ~ delgado draw it fine.

hilarante hilarious; gas laughing; **hilaridad** f hilarity, mirth.

hilaza f yarn, (coarse) thread.

hilera f row, rank (a. ✕); line, string; sew. fine thread; ⚒ drill.

hilo m thread (a. fig.); yarn; (tejido) linen; (alambre) (thin) wire; trickle de líquido; string de perlas etc.; fig. train del pensamiento; course de la vida; a ~ uninterruptedly; ~ bramante twine; ~ dental dental floss; manejar los ~s to pull strings; perder el ~ de lose the thread of.

hilván m sew. tacking, basting; **hilvanar** [1a] sew. tack, baste.

himnario m hymnal; **himno** m hymn; ~ nacional national anthem.

H

hincapié: *hacer* ~ make a stand; *hacer* ~ *en* dwell on, insist on.

hincar [1g] thrust (in); *clavo etc.* drive (in), sink; *pie* set (firmly).

hincha F 1. *f* grudge; ill-will; (*p.*, *cosa*) pet aversion; 2. *m/f deportes:* supporter, fan, rooter; **hinchado** *lenguaje etc.* pompous, stilted; *p.* vain, puffed-up; **hinchar** [1a] swell; distend; inflate; blow up *con aire;* *fig.* exaggerate; **~se** swell (up).

hinojo[1] *m* ♥ fennel.

hinojo[2] *m* knee; *de* ~*s* on bended knee.

hipérbola *f* ⅄ hyperbola; **hipérbole** *f rhet.* hyperbole; **hiperbólico** hyperbolic(al); exaggerated.

hipnosis *f* hypnosis; **hipnótico** hypnotic; **hipnotismo** *m* hypnotism; **hipnotista** *m/f* hypnotist; **hipnotizar** [1f] hypnotize.

hipo *m* hiccup(s), hiccough(s); (*deseo*) longing; (*odio*) grudge.

hipocampo *m* sea-horse.

hipocondría *f* hypochondria; **hipocondríaco** 1. hypochondriacal; 2. *m*, **a** *f* hypochondriac.

hipocresía *f* hypocrisy; **hipócrita** 1. hypocritical; 2. *m/f* hypocrite.

hipodérmico hypodermic.

hipódromo *m* race track.

hipopótamo *m* hippopotamus.

hipoteca *f* mortgage; **hipotecar** [1g] mortgage.

hipótesis *f* hypothesis, supposition; **hipotético** hypothetical.

hirsuto hairy, hirsute, bristly; *fig. p.* brusque, rough.

hirviendo boiling; **hirviente** boiling, seething.

hispánico Hispanic; **hispanidad** *f* Spanishness; **hispanismo** *m gr.* Hispanicism; ⅃ Hispanism; **hispanista** *m/f* Hispanist; **hispano** Spanish, Hispanic; **hispanoamericano** *adj. a. su. m,* **a** *f* Spanish American, Latin American.

histérico hysteric(al); *paroxismo* ~ hysterics; **histerismo** *m* hysteria.

histología *f* histology.

historia *f* history; (*narración, cuento*) story; (*esp. inventada*) tale; ~*s pl.* (*chismes*) gossip; ~*s pl. de alcoba* bedtime stories; **historiador** *m*, **-a** *f* historian; **histórico** historical; (*notable*) historic; **historieta** *f* (short) story, tale, anecdote; ~ *gráfica* comic strip.

histrión *m* actor, player; buffoon; *b.s.*

play-actor; **histriónico** histrionic; **histrionismo** *m* histrionics; (*arte*) acting; (*ps.*) actors.

hocicar [1g] (*puerco*) root; (*con cariño*) nuzzle; (*p.*) fall on one's face; *fig.* run into trouble; **hocico** *m* snout, muzzle *de animal;* F snout.

hockey ['oki] *m* hockey; ~ *sobre patines,* ~ *sobre hielo* ice hockey.

hogaño *mst* † this year; these days.

hogar *m* hearth, fireplace; ⊕ furnace; ⛊ fire box; *fig.* home, house; family life; **hogareño** home *attr.,* family *attr.; p.* homeloving.

hoguera *f* bonfire; (*llamas*) blaze.

hoja *f* ♥ leaf (*a. de libro, puerta*); ♥ petal; sheet *de metal, papel;* blade *de espada etc.;* pane *de vidrio;* (*documento*) form; ~ *de afeitar* razorblade; ~ *de estaño* tinfoil; ~ *de guarda* flyleaf; ~ *de lata* tin(plate); ~ *plegadiza* (table)flap.

hojalata *f* tin(plate); **hojalatero** *m* tinsmith.

hojaldre *m* puff pastry.

hojarasca *f* fallen; useless words; trash, trifles.

hojear [1a] turn the pages of, skim (*or* glance) through; **hojoso** leafy; **hojuela** *f* little leaf; (*escama*) flake; *metall.* foil; *cocina:* pancake.

¡hola! *saludo:* hey!, hello!

holandés 1. Dutch; 2. *m* Dutchman; 3. *m* (*idioma*) Dutch; **holandesa** *f* Dutch woman.

holgado (*ocioso*) leisured, idle, unoccupied; *vestido etc.* loose, roomy, baggy; comfortable, cosy; (*casi rico*) well-to-do; **holganza** *f* (*ocio*) ease, leisure; (*descanso*) rest; (*placer*) enjoyment; **holgar** [1h *a.* 1m] (*descansar*) rest; (*estar ocioso*) be idle; (*cosa*) be unused; be unnecessary; (*alegrarse*) be pleased; ~*se* be glad.

holgazán 1. idle, lazy; 2. *m,* **a** *f* idler, loafer; **holgazanear** [1a] loaf; **holgazanería** *f* laziness *etc.*

holgura *f* enjoyment, merry-making; ease, comfort; looseness, roominess *de vestido;* ⊕ play.

hollar [1m] tread (on); trample underfoot (*a. fig.*); *fig.* humiliate.

hollejo *m* ♥ skin, peel.

hollín *m* soot; **holliniento** sooty.

holocausto *m* holocaust, burnt offering; *fig.* sacrifice.

hombrada *f* manly act; **hombradía** *f* manliness; courage.

hombre 1. *m* man; (*género humano*)

man, mankind; F husband; ¡~ al agua!, ¡~ a la mar! man overboard!; ~ de armas man-at-arms; ~ de bien honest man, man of honor; ~ de buenas prendas man of parts; ~ de la calle man in the street; ~ de ciencia man of science; ~ de dinero man of means; ~ de estado statesman; ~ hecho grown man; ~ de letras man of letters; ~ medio average man; ~ de mundo man of the world; ~ de negocios businessman; ~ de pro(vecho) honest man; man of worth; ~ de suposición man of straw; 2. int. man alive!, good heavens!

hombre-anuncio m sandwich man.
hombrera f shoulder-strap; ✗ epaulette.
hombre-rana m frogman.
hombría f manliness; ~ de bien honesty, uprightness.
hombro m shoulder; ~ a ~ shoulder to shoulder; ✗ sobre el ~ ¡armas! slope arms!; arrimar el ~ put one's shoulder to the wheel, lend a hand; salir en ~ to be carried off on the shoulders of the crowd.
hombruno mannish, masculine.
homenaje m homage (a. fig.); allegiance; fig. tribute, testimonial; (don) gift; en ~ a in honor of.
homicida 1. murderous, homicidal; **2.** m murderer; **3.** f murderess;
homicidio m murder, homicide.
homogéneo homogeneous; **homólogo** colleague; fig. counterpart; **homónimo** m homonym; (p.) namesake; **homosexual** adj. a. su. m/f homosexual.
honda f sling, catapult.
hondear [1a] ♣ sound; (descargar) unload.
hondo 1. deep; low; fig. profound; sentimiento deep, heartfelt; **2.** m depth(s); bottom.
honestidad f decency, decorum etc.; **honesto** decent, decorous; modest; chaste; fair, just; honest.
hongo m (en general) fungus; (comestible) mushroom; (venenoso) toadstool; (sombrero) derby.
honor m honor; virtue esp. de mujer; (reputación) good name; ~es pl. honors, honorary status; de ~ dama etc. in waiting.
honorable honorable, worthy; **honorario 1.** honorary; honorific; **2.** m honorarium; mst ~s pl. fees.
honra f self-esteem; dignity; (reputación) good name; honor; chastity; ~s

pl. (fúnebres) last honors, obsequies;
honradez f honesty, integrity; **honrado** honest, upright; **honrar** [1a] honor (a. ✝); respect, esteem, revere; do honor to; ~se be honored (con by, with; de inf. to inf.); **honroso** honourable; respectable, reputable.
hora f hour; time (of day); altas ~s pl. small hours; ~ de aglomeración rush hour; ~ de cierre closing time; ~ de comer mealtime; ~ de irse time to go; ~ de verano daylight-saving time; ~ legal, ~ oficial standard time; ~ punta peak hour; rush hour; ~s de consulta office hour; ~s de ocio leisure hours; ~s pl. extraordinarias overtime; ~-hombre man-hour; ~s pl. de oficina business hours; ~ de recreo playtime; última ~ (periódico) stop-press; a última ~ at the last moment; a buena ~ opportunely; a la ~ punctually.
horario 1. hourly; hour attr.; time attr.; **2.** m hour-hand de reloj; 🚂 etc. time-table, schedule.
horca f gallows, gibbet; ✔ (pitch-)fork; (cebollas) string; **horcadura** f fork (of a tree); **horcajadas:** a ~ astride; **horcajadura** f anat. crotch.
horda f horde; (pandilla) gang.
horero m hour hand.
horizontal horizontal; flat, level; **horizonte** m horizon.
horma f ⊕ form, mould; (a. ~ del calzado) last, boot-tree; (muro) dry stone wall.
hormiga f ant.
hormigón m concrete; ~ armado reinforced concrete; **hormigonera** f ⊕ concrete mixer.
hormiguear [1a] itch; (abundar) swarm, teem; **hormigueo** m 🐜 itch(ing), tingling, creeps F; fig. uneasiness; swarming; **hormiguero** m anthill (d. fig.).
hormón m, **hormona** f hormone.
hornada f batch (of bread), baking; fig. crop, batch; **hornero**, **a** f baker; **hornillo** m ⊕ small furnace; stove de cocina; bowl de pipa; ✗ mine; ~ eléctrico hot-plate; **horno** m ⊕ furnace; cerámica: kiln; cocina: oven; alto ~ blast furnace; ~ de cal lime kiln; ~ crematorio crematorium; ~ de fundición smelting furnace.
horóscopo m horoscope; sacar un ~ cast a horoscope.
horqueta f todos sentidos: fork; **hor-**

H

quilla f ♪ pitchfork; hairpin *para pelo*; fork *de bicicleta*; ⊕ yoke.
horrendo horrible, dire, frightful.
hórreo m *prov.* (*esp.* raised) granary.
horrible horrible, ghastly, dreadful (*a.* F); F unspeakable, nasty; **horripilante** hair-raising, horrifying; **horror** m (*sentimiento*) horror, dread; abhorrence; *tener* ~ *a* have a horror of; **horrorizar** [1f] horrify; terrify; **~se** be horrified; **horroroso** horrifying; horrible, frightful, grim.
hortaliza f vegetable; **hortelano** m, **a** f (market) gardener.
horticultura f horticulture.
hosco dark, gloomy; *p.* surly, sullen.
hospedaje m (cost of) lodging; **hospedar** [1a] put up, lodge; **~se** put up, lodge, stop, stay (*en* at); **hospedera** f hostess; innkeeper's wife; **hospedero** m host; innkeeper; **hospicio** m poor-house; hospice; (*niños*) orphanage; **hospital** m hospital, infirmary; *esp. eccl.* hospice; ~ *de primera sangre* ⚔ field hospital; **hospitalidad** f hospitality.
hostelería f restaurant and hotel business.
hostigar [1h] lash, whip; *fig.* harass, plague.
hostil hostile; **hostilidad** f hostility; hostile act; **hostilizar** [1f] ⚔ harass, attack; (*enemistar*) antagonize.
hotel m hotel; (*casa*) mansion; **hotelero** 1. hotel *attr.*; 2. *m*, **a** f hotelkeeper.
hoy today; ~ (*en*) *día* nowadays; ~ *por* ~ at the present; *de* ~ *en adelante* from now on.
hoya f pit, hole; (*tumba*) grave; *geog.* vale; *S.Am.* river basin; ♪ seedbed; **hoyo** m hole (*a. golf*), cavity; (*tumba*) grave; ⚸ pock mark; **hoyuelo** m dimple.
hoz f ♪ sickle; *geog.* defile, ravine.
hozar [1f] (*puerco*) root.
hube *v. haber.*
hucha f bin; (*arca*) chest; moneybox *para dinero*; *fig.* savings; *buena* ~ *fig.* nest-egg.
hueco 1. hollow; (*vacío*) empty; blank; (*mullido*) soft; *tierra etc.* spongy; 2. *m* hole, hollow, cavity; (*intervalo*) gap, opening.
huelga f (*laboral*) strike; (*descanso*) rest; (*ocio*) leisure, *b.s.* idleness; ⊕ play; ~ *de brazos caídos* sit-down strike; ~ *de hambre* hunger strike; ~ *patronal* lock-out; ~ *por solidaridad*

sympathetic strike; *en* ~ on strike; *declararse* (*or ponerse*) *en* ~ (go on) strike, walk out; **huelgo** m breath; space; ⊕ play; **huelguista** m/f striker.
huella f (*impresión de pie*) footprint; (*señal*) trace, imprint, ~ *dactilar*, ~ *digital* fingerprint.
huérfano 1. orphan(ed); *fig.* unprotected, uncared-for; ~ *de madre* motherless; 2. *m*, **a** f orphan.
huero *huevo* rotten; empty.
huerta f (large) market garden; ~ (*de árboles frutales*) orchard; **huerto** m (kitchen) garden, market garden; orchard *de árboles frutales.*
huesa f grave.
hueso m *anat.* bone; ♀ stone; core; *fig.* hard work; ~ *de la alegría* funny bone; ~ *de la suerte* wishbone; F *la sin* ~ the tongue; **huesoso** bony, bone *attr.*
huésped m (*invitado*) guest; boarder, lodger *que paga*; (*que invita*) host; (*amo de la casa*) landlord; **huéspeda** f guest *etc.*; hostess; landlady.
huesudo bony; *p.* raw-boned.
hueva f *ichth.* (hard) roe; ~s *pl.* spawn; **huevera** f egg-cup; **huevo** m egg; ~ *al plato*, ~ *estrellado* fried egg; ~ *en cáscara*, ~ *pasado por agua* boiled egg; ~ *duro* hard-boiled egg; ~ *escalfado* poached egg; ~s *pl. revueltos* scrambled eggs.
huida f flight, escape; shy(ing) *de caballo*; huidizo shy; elusive; (*pasajero*) fleeting; **huir** [3g] *v/t.* run away from, escape (from), flee.
hule m oilcloth, oilskin; (*caucho*) rubber; F *toros*: goring.
hulla f (soft) coal; **hullera** f colliery; **hullero** coal *attr.*
humanidad f humanity (*a. fig.*), mankind; F corpulence; ~es *pl.* humanities; **humanismo** m humanism; **humanista** m/f humanist; **humanitario** humanitarian; **humano** 1. human; (*compasivo*) humane; *ciencias* ~as humane learning; 2. *m* human (being).
humareda f cloud of smoke; **humazo** m dense (cloud of) smoke; F *dar* ~ *a* smoke out; **humeante** smoking, smoky, fuming; **humear** [1a] *v/t. S.Am.* fumigate; *v/i.* smoke; fume; steam; reek.
humedad f humidity, damp(ness), moisture, wet(ness); *a prueba de* ~ damp-proof; **humedecer** [2d]

damp, moisten, wet; **~se** get damp *etc.*; **húmedo** damp, humid, moist.
humidificador *m* air humidifier.
humildad *f* (*virtud*) humility; (*condición*) humbleness, lowliness; (*acto*) submission; **humilde** humble; *carácter* humble, meek; *condición* low(ly), low-born; *voz* small; **humillar** [1a] humiliate, humble; *cabeza* bow, bend; **~se** humble o.s.; *b.s.* grovel.
humo *m* smoke; fumes; **~s** *pl.* (*casas*) homes; *fig.* airs, conceit.
humor *m* humor (*a. anat.*); temper, mood; (*genio*) disposition; **humorada** *f* joke, witticism; **humorismo** *m* humor, humorousness; **humorista** *m/f* humorist; **humorístico** humorous, funny.
humoso smoky.

hundido sunken; *ojos* hollow; **hundimiento** *m* sinking *etc.*; **hundir** [3a] sink; submerge, engulf; plunge (en into).
huracán *m* hurricane.
huraño shy, diffident; unsociable; *animal* wild, shy.
hurgar [1h] poke; stir (up).
hurtadillas: *a* ~ stealthily, on the sly.
hurtar [1a] steal; *lit.* plagiarize; **~se** keep out of the way, make off; **hurto** *m* (*acto*) theft, robbery; (*cosa*) thing stolen; *a* ~ on the sly, by stealth.
husmear [1a] *v/t.* scent; F smell out, pry into; *v/i.* (*carne*) smell high.
huso *m* spindle (*a.* ⊕); bobbin; ~ *horario* time zone.
¡huy! ow!, ouch!; (*sorpresa*) whew!
huyo *etc. v.* huir.

I

iba *etc. v.* ir.
ibérico Iberian; **ibero, íbero** *adj. a. su. m,* **a** *f* Iberian.
iceberg *m* iceberg.
icono *m* icon; **iconoclasta** 1. iconoclastic; 2. *m/f* iconoclast.
ictericia *f* jaundice.
icurriña *f* Basque national flag.
ida *f* going; departure; *fig.* rash act; hastiness; (*rastro*) trail; (*viaje de*) ~ outward journey; ~ *y vuelta* round trip.
idea *f* idea; notion; opinion; **ideal** 1. ideal; notional, imaginary; 2. *m* ideal; **idealismo** *m* idealism; **idealista** 1. idealistic; 2. *m/f* idealist; **idealizar** [1f] idealize; **idear** [1a] think up; plan, design; invent.
ídem ditto, idem.
idéntico identical, (very) same; **identidad** *f* identity; sameness; **identificación** *f* identification; ~ *errónea* mistaken identify; **identificar** [1g] identify.
ideología *f* ideology.
idílico idyllic; **idilio** *m* idyll.
idioma *m* language; speech, idiom *de grupo*; **idiomático** idiomatic.
idiosincrasia *f* idiosyncrasy.
idiota 1. idiotic, stupid; *p.* simple; 2. *m/f* idiot; **idiotez** *f* idiocy; **idiotismo** *m* gr. idiom(atic expression).
idolatrar [1a] *ídolo* worship, adore;

fig. idolize; **idolatría** *f* idolatry; **ídolo** *m* idol (*a. fig.*).
idóneo suitable; apt, fitting.
iglesia *f* church.
iglú *m* igloo.
ígneo igneous; **ignición** *f* ignition.
ignominia *f* ignominy, shame(fulness), disgrace; **ignominioso** ignominious, shameful, disgraceful.
ignorancia *f* ignorance; **ignorante** 1. ignorant, uninformed; 2. *m/f* ignoramus; **ignorar** [1a] not know, be ignorant (or unaware) of.
igual 1. equal (*a* to); (the) same; indifferent; (*parecido*) alike, similar; uniform, constant; (*liso*) smooth, level, even; *clima* equable; *temperamento* even; ~ *que* like, the same as; en ~ *de* instead of; 2. *m/f* equal; match (de for); *al* ~, *por* ~ equally; *sin* ~ matchless; **igualdad** *f* equality; sameness; evenness, smoothness; **igualmente** equally; likewise; F the same to you.
ijada *f* flank; loin; 🞄 pain in the side, stitch; **ijar** *m* flank.
ilegal illegal, unlawful.
ilegible illegible, unreadable.
ilegítimo illegitimate; *acto* unlawful; *cosa* false, spurious.
ileso unharmed, unhurt.
iletrado uncultured, illiterate.
ilícito illicit.

ilimitado unlimited, limitless.
ilógico illogical.
ilote *m* ear of corn.
iluminación *f* illumination; lighting; *fig.* enlightenment; **iluminado 1.** illuminated; **2.** *m* visionary; **iluminar** [1a] illuminate.
ilusión *f* illusion; delusion; (*esperanza*) (unfounded) hope, (day)-dream; (*entusiasmo*) excitement, eagerness; ¡qué ∼! how thrilling!
ilusionado hopeful; excited, eager; **ilusionarse** [1a] indulge in wishful thinking; **ilusionismo** *m* wishful thinking; **iluso 1.** (easily) deluded, deceived; **2.** *m*, **a** *f* visionary, dreamer; **ilusorio** illusory.
ilustración *f* illustration; picture; *fig.* enlightenment, learning; **ilustrar** [1a] illustrate; *fig.* enlighten, instruct.
imagen *f mst* image; **imaginación** *f* imagination; (*fantasía*) fancy; **imaginar** [1a] imagine, visualize; ∼se suppose (*que* that); imagine, picture (to o.s.), fancy; ¡imagínate! just imagine; **imaginario** imaginary, fanciful; **imaginativa** *f* imagination; understanding; **imaginativo** imaginative; **imaginería** *f* statuary.
imán *m* magnet; **iman(t)ar** [1a] magnetize.
imbatible unbeatable; **imbatido** unbeaten.
imbécil 1. *p.* imbecile, feeble-minded; *cosa* silly; **2.** *m/f* imbecile, idiot.
imberbe beardless.
imborrable ineffaceable.
imbuir [3g] imbue, infuse (*de, en* with).
imitar [1a] imitate; mimic, *b.s.* ape; *cosa b.s.* counterfeit.
impaciencia *f* impatience; **impacientar** [1a] exasperate, make *s.o.* lose patience; ∼se get impatient, fret (*por* at); **impaciente** impatient (*con, de, por* at); fretful.
impacto *m* impact; ✕ hit.
impar odd (*a.* Ⓐ).
imparcial impartial.
impasible impassive, unmoved.
impávido dauntless, unflinching.
impecable impeccable, faultless.
impedido disabled, crippled; ∼ *para* unfit for; **impedir** [3l] stop, prevent (*inf. or que subj.* [from] *ger.*).
impeler [2a] propel, drive; *fig.* impel, urge (*a inf.* to *inf.*).

impenetrable impenetrable (*a. fig.*); impervious.
impensado unexpected, unforeseen; (*fortuito*) random.
imperar [1a] rule, reign; **imperativo 1.** commanding; **2.** *m* imperative (mood).
imperceptible imperceptible.
imperdible *m* safety-pin.
imperecedero undying, imperishable; eternal.
imperfección *f* imperfection, flaw; **imperfecto** imperfect (*a. gr.*).
imperial 1. imperial; **2.** *f* top, upper deck; **imperialismo** *m* imperialism; **imperialista 1.** imperialistic; **2.** *m/f* imperialist.
impericia *f* unskillfulness.
imperio *m* empire; (*autoridad*) rule, sway; *fig.* pride; **imperioso** imperious; imperative.
imperito inexpert, unskilled.
impermeabilizar [1f] waterproof; **impermeable 1.** waterproof; **2.** *m* raincoat.
impersonal impersonal.
impertérrito unafraid, unshaken.
impertinencia *f* irrelevance; impertinence *etc.*; **impertinente 1.** irrelevant; uncalled-for; (*nimio*) fussy; **2.** ∼s *m/pl.* lorgnette.
imperturbable imperturbable; **imperturbado** unperturbed.
ímpetu *m* impetus, impulse; momentum; (*movimiento*) (on)rush; (*prisa*) haste; violence; **impetuoso** *p.* impetuous; headstrong; *acto* hasty; violent; *torrente* rushing.
implacable implacable, relentless.
implantar [1a] implant, introduce.
implicar [1g] involve; *p. mst b.s.* implicate; *inferencia* imply; **implícito** implicit, implied.
implorar [1a] implore, beg.
imponente 1. imposing, impressive; **2.** *m/f* ✝ depositor; **imponer** [2r] *mst* impose (*a* on; *a. typ., eccl.*); *obediencia etc.* exact (*a* from), enforce (*a* upon); *carga etc.* lay, thrust (*a* upon); instruct (*en* in); (*impresionar*) impress; ✝ invest, deposit; ∼se get one's way, assert o.s.; prevail (*a* over); (*costumbre*) grow up; **imponible** taxable.
impopular unpopular; **impopularidad** *f* unpopularity.
importación *f* import(s); (*acto*) importation; de ∼ imported; **importador** *m*, **-a** *f* importer; **importancia** *f*

importance; **importante** important; significant; weighty; (*grande*) considerable; sizeable; *lo* (*más*) ~ the main thing; **importar**[1] *v/t.* amount to, be worth; (*llevar consigo*) involve, imply; *v/i.* matter (*a* to), be of consequence; ¡*no importa!* it doesn't matter!, never mind!; ¿*qué importa?* what of it?; **importar**[1a] **✝** import (*a*, *en* into); **importe** *m* amount, value, cost.

importuno importunate; inopportune; troublesome, annoying.

imposibilidad *f* impossibility; inability; **imposibilitado** unable (*para inf.* to inf.); **✗** disabled; (*pobre*) without means; **imposibilitar** [1a] make *s.t.* impossible; *p.* render unfit (*para* for), incapacitate; **imposible 1.** impossible; **2.** *m* the impossible.

imposición *f* imposition; tax; *typ.* make-up; **✝** deposit.

impostor *m*, **-a** *f* impostor, fraud; **impostura** *f* imposture, fraud.

impotable undrinkable.

impotencia *f* impotence (*a.* **✗**) *etc.*; **impotente** impotent (*a.* **✗**), powerless, helpless.

impracticable impracticable, unworkable; *camino* impassable.

impredictible unpredictable.

impregnar [1a] impregnate.

impremeditado unpremeditated.

imprenta *f* (*arte*) printing; (*oficina*) press, printing-house; (*letra*) print; (*lo impreso*) printed matter.

imprescindible essential.

impresión *f typ.* printing; (*letra, phot.*) print; (*tirada*) edition, impression; (*marca*) imprint; *fig.* impression; ~ *dactilar,* ~ *digital* fingerprint; **impresionable** impressionable, sensitive, susceptible; **impresionante** impressive, striking; moving; **impresionar** [1a] impress, strike; move; *disco etc.* record; **impresionista 1.** impressionist(ic); **2.** *m/f* impressionist; **impreso 1.** printed; **2.** *m* printed paper (*or* book); ~s *pl.* printed matter; **impresor** *m* printer.

imprevisible unforeseeable; **imprevisión** *f* lack of foresight; thoughtlessness; **imprevisor** thoughtless; happy-go-lucky F; **imprevisto 1.** unforeseen, unexpected; **2.** ~s *pl.* incidentals, unforeseen expenses.

imprimar [1a] *paint.* prime.

imprimir [3a; *p.p. impreso*] *typ.* print; (*estampar*) stamp; *fig.* stamp, imprint (*en* on).

improbable improbable, unlikely.

improbo dishonest; *tarea* arduous.

improperio *m* insult, taunt.

impropiedad *f* infelicity (of language); **impropio** improper (*a.* **ℝ**); (*no apto*) inappropriate, unsuitable (*de, para* to, for).

impróvido improvident.

improvisado improvised; *b.s.* makeshift; **♪** *etc.* impromptu; **improvisar** [1a] improvise; extemporize (*a.* **♪**); **improviso** unexpected, unforeseen.

imprudencia *f* imprudence *etc.*; **imprudente** unwise, imprudent; rash, reckless; *palabras* indiscreet.

impudente impudent, shameless.

impuesto 1. *p.p.* of *imponer*; **2.** *m* tax, duty, levy (*sobre* on); ~s *pl.* taxation; *sujeto a* ~ taxable; ~ *sobre el valor añadido* value-added tax; ~ *sobre la renta* income tax.

impugnar [1a] oppose, contest.

impulsar [1a] = *impeler*; **impulsión** *f* impulsion; **⊕** drive, propulsion; *fig.* impulse; ~ *por reacción* jet propulsion; **impulsivo** *fig.* impulsive; **impulso** *m* impulse (*a. fig.*), drive, thrust; impetus.

impune unpunished.

impuntual unpunctual.

impureza *f* impurity; **impurificar** [1g] adulterate; *fig.* defile; **impuro** impure.

inacabable endless, interminable; **inacabado** unfinished.

inaccesible inaccessible.

inacción *f* inaction; drift.

inacentuado unaccented.

inaceptable unacceptable.

inactividad *f* inactivity *etc.*; **inactivo** inactive.

inadecuado inadequate.

inadvertencia *f* inadvertence; (*error*) oversight, slip; **inadvertido** *p.* unobservant, inattentive; *error* inadvertent; *cosa* unnoticed.

inajenable, inalienable inalienable; not transferable.

inalámbrico wireless.

inalterable unchanging; *color* fast; **inalterado** unchanged.

inamovible irremovable, fixed.

inanición *f* inanition, starvation.

inanimado inanimate.

inapercibido unperceived.

inapetencia f lack of appetite.

inaplicable inapplicable.

inapreciable inestimable.

inapto unsuited (*para* for, to).

inarrugable crease-resisting.

inarticulado inarticulate.

inasequible unattainable, out of reach; unobtainable.

inastillable nonsplinter.

inatacable unassailable.

inaudible inaudible; **inaudito** unheard-of, unprecedented.

inauguración f inauguration *etc.*; **inaugural** inaugural, opening; *viaje* maiden; **inaugurar** [1a] inaugurate; *exposición etc.* open.

incalculable incalculable.

incalificable unspeakable.

incandescencia f incandescence; **incandescente** incandescent.

incansable tireless, unflagging.

incapacidad f incapacity; incompetence; inability (*para inf.* to *inf.*), unfitness (*para* for); **incapacitado** incapacitated; unfitted (*para* for); **incapacitar** [1a] incapacitate, render unfit; **incapaz** incapable (*de* of); unfit.

incauto unwary, incautious.

incendiar [1b] set on fire, set alight; ~se catch fire; **incendiario** 1. incendiary; 2. *m*, **a** *f* incendiary; **incendio** *m* fire.

incensar [1k] *eccl.* (in)cense; *fig.* flatter; **incensario** *m* censer.

incentivo *m* incentive.

incertidumbre f uncertainty.

incesante incessant.

incesto *m* incest; **incestuoso** incestuous.

incidencia f incidence (*a.* ♣); incident; **incidental** incidental; **incidente** 1. incidental; 2. *m* incident.

incienso *m* incense (*a. fig.*).

incierto uncertain; (*falso*) untrue; inconstant.

incineración f incineration; ~ *de cadáveres* cremation.

incipiente incipient.

incisión f incision; **incisivo** 1. cutting; *fig.* incisive; 2. *m* incisor.

inciso *m* gr. clause; comma.

incitante provoking; **incitar** [1a] incite, spur on (*a* to).

incivil uncivil, rude; **incivilidad** f incivility; **incivilizado** uncivilized.

inclemente harsh, severe.

inclinación f inclination (*a. fig.*); (*declive*) slope, incline; (*oblicuidad*) slant, tilt; stoop *de cuerpo*; nod *de cabeza*; (*reverencia*) bow; *fig.* leaning; **inclinado** sloping, slanting; *plano* inclined; **inclinar** [1a] *v/t.* incline (*a. fig.*; *a inf.* to *inf.*); slope, slant, tilt; ~se lean; slope; bend; *fig.* be inclined, tend (*a* to).

incluir [3g] include; contain, incorporate; (*insertar*) enclose; **inclusive** 1. *adv.* (*a.* **inclusivamente**) inclusive(ly); 2. *prp.* including; **inclusivo** inclusive; **incluso** 1. *adj.* enclosed; 2. *prp.* including; (*hasta*) even.

incobrable irrecoverable.

incógnita f unknown quantity; **incógnito** 1. unknown; 2. *m* incognito; *de* ~ *adv.* incognito.

incoherente incoherent.

incoloro colorless (*a. fig.*).

incólume safe, unharmed.

incombustible incombustible, fireproof.

incomible uneatable, inedible.

incomodar [1a] inconvenience, trouble, put out; ~se get annoyed; **incomodidad** f inconvenience; discomfort; annoyance; **incómodo** inconvenient; uncomfortable.

incomparable incomparable.

incompatible incompatible.

incompetencia f incompetence; **incompetente** incompetent.

incompleto incomplete, unfinished.

incomprensible incomprehensible.

incomunicación f isolation; ♣ solitary confinement; **incomunicado** incommunicado.

inconcebible inconceivable.

inconciliable irreconcilable.

inconcluso incomplete, unfinished; **inconcluyente** inconclusive.

incondicional unconditional; *fe* implicit; *apoyo* whole-hearted; *aserto* unqualified.

inconexo unconnected; *fig.* incongruous; (*incoherente*) disjointed.

inconfeso unconfessed.

inconfundible unmistakable.

incongruencia f incongruity; **incongruente, incongruo** incongruous.

inconmovible unshakable.

inconquistable unconquerable.

inconsciencia f unconsciousness; unawareness; thoughtlessness; **inconsciente** unconscious, unaware (*de* of); oblivious (*de* of, to); unwitting; (*irreflexivo*) thoughtless; *lo* ~ the unconscious.

inconsecuencia f inconsequence, inconsistency; **inconsecuente** inconsequent(ial), inconsistent.

inconsiderado thoughtless, inconsiderate; (*precipitado*) hasty.

inconsistencia f inconsistency etc.; **inconsistente** inconsistent.

inconsolable inconsolable.

inconstancia f inconstancy etc.; **inconstante** inconstant, changeable; (*poco firme*) unsteady.

inconstitucional unconstitutional.

incontable countless.

incontestable unanswerable; undeniable; **incontestado** unchallenged, unquestioned.

inconveniencia f unsuitability; inconvenience; (*dicho*) tactless remark; silly thing; **inconveniente 1.** unsuitable; inconvenient; impolite; **2.** m obstacle, difficulty; (*desventaja*) drawback; objection.

incorporación f incorporation; association; **incorporado** ⊕ built-in; **incorporar** [1a] incorporate (*a, con, en* in[to], with), embody (*a, con, en* in); mix (*con* with); make *p.* sit up; **~se** sit up; ~ *a buque etc.* join.

incorrección f incorrectness etc.; **incorrecto** wrong, incorrect; *conducta* discourteous, improper.

incredibilidad f incredibility; **incredulidad** f incredulity, unbelief; **incrédulo 1.** incredulous, sceptical; **2.** m, a f unbeliever, sceptic; **increíble** incredible, unbelievable.

incremento m increase, addition.

incrustar [1a] incrust; inlay.

incubación f incubation (*a.* ✱); **incubadora** f incubator; **incubar** [1a] incubate; hatch (*a. fig.*).

inculcar [1g] instil, inculcate.

inculpable blameless; **inculpación** f accusation; **inculpar** [1a] accuse (*de* of); blame (*de* for).

inculto uncultivated (*a. fig.*); *fig.* uncultured, uncouth; **incultura** f fig. lack of culture.

incumbencia f obligation; *no es de mi ~* it has nothing to do with me; **incumbir** [3a]: ~ *a* be incumbent upon (*inf.* to *inf.*).

incurable incurable; *fig.* irremediable.

incurrir [3a] incur; **incursión** f incursion, raid.

indagación f investigation, inquiry; **indagar** [1h] investigate, inquire into; (*descubrir*) ascertain.

indebido undue; *b.s.* improper.

indecencia f indecency etc.; **indecente** indecent, improper; obscene; F wretched, miserable.

indecible unspeakable.

indecisión f indecision, hesitation; **indeciso** undecided; hesitant; vague; *resultado* indecisive.

indefectible unfailing, infallible.

indefendible indefensible; **indefenso** defenceless.

indefinible indefinable; **indefinido** indefinite; vague.

indeleble indelible.

indemne undamaged; *p.* unhurt; **indemnización** f (*acto*) indemnification; (*pago*) indemnity; ~es pl. reparations; **indemnizar** [1f] indemnify, compensate (*de* for).

independencia f independence; self-sufficiency; **independiente 1.** independent (*de* of); *cosa a.* self-contained; *p. a.* self-sufficient; **2.** m/f independent.

indescriptible indescribable.

indesmallable runproof.

indestructible indestructible.

indeterminado indeterminate; inconclusive; *p.* irresolute.

indicación f indication, sign; ~es pl. instructions, directions; **indicado** right, suitable (*para* for); obvious; **indicador** m indicator (*a.* ⊕, ⚗); gauge *de gasolina etc.*; (*aguja*) pointer; ~ *de velocidades* speedometer; **indicar** [1g] indicate; suggest; (*señalar*) point out, point to; **índice** m mst index; (*aguja*) pointer, needle; hand *de reloj*; catalogue *de biblioteca*; **indicio** m indication, sign.

indiferencia f indifference etc.; **indiferente** indifferent (*a* to); apathetic, unconcerned (*a* about).

indígena 1. indigenous (*de* to), native; **2.** m/f native.

indignación f indignation; **indignado** indignant (*con, contra p.* with; *de, por* at, about); **indignante** outrageous, infuriating; **indignar** [1a] anger, make *s.o.* indignant; **~se** get indignant; **indignidad** f unworthiness; (*una ~*) unworthy act; (*afrenta*) indignity; **indigno** unworthy (*de* of); (*vil*) low.

indio *adj. a. su.* m, a f Indian.

indirecta f hint; insinuation; **indirecto** indirect; roundabout; oblique.

indisciplinado undisciplined; lax.

indiscreto indiscreet, tactless.
indiscutible indisputable, unquestionable.
indispensable indispensable.
indisponer [2r] *proyecto* spoil, upset; *♣* upset, make unfit; ~ **con** set *s.o.* against; **~se *♣*** fall ill; ~ **con** *p.* fall out with; **indisponible** unavailable; **indispuesto** indisposed.
indisputable indisputable.
indistinción *f* indistinctness; **indistinguible** indistinguishable; **indistintamente** indiscriminately; **indistinto** indistinct; vague; *luz etc.* faint.
individual individual; peculiar; *habitación* single; **individualidad** *f* individuality; **individualista 1.** individualistic; **2.** *m/f* individualist; **individuo** *adj. a. su. m,* **a** *f* individual (*a.* F); **indiviso** undivided.
indócil unmanageable, disobedient.
indocto unlearned, ignorant.
indocumentado without identification.
indoeuropeo *adj. a. su. m* Indo-European.
índole *f* nature; character; disposition *de p.*; class, kind *de cosa.*
indolencia *f* indolence *etc.*; **indolente** indolent, lazy; apathetic; = **indoloro** painless.
indomado untamed.
inducción *f* inducement, persuasion; *phls., ♃* induction; **inducir** [3o] induce (*a. ♂*), persuade (*a inf.* to *inf.*); **inductivo** inductive.
indudable undoubted; **indudablemente** undoubtedly, doubtless.
indulgencia *f* indulgence (*a. eccl.*); **indulgente** indulgent.
indultar [1a] *♗♘* pardon; exempt; **indulto** *m* *♗♘* pardon, exemption.
indumentaria *f,* **indumento** *m* clothing, dress.
industria *f* industry; (*destreza*) ingenuity, skill; **de** ~ on purpose; **industrial 1.** industrial; **2.** *m* industrialist, manufacturer; **industriarse** [1b] manage, find a way, get things fixed; **industrioso** industrious; (*hábil*) resourceful.
inédito unpublished.
ineducado uneducated.
inefable ineffable, indescribable.
ineficacia *f* inefficacy *etc.*; **ineficaz** ineffectual; inefficient; **ineficiente** inefficient.
inelástico inelastic.
inelegible ineligible.

ineludible inescapable.
inencogible unshrinkable.
inepcia *f* stupidity; = **ineptitud** *f* ineptitude, incompetence; **inepto** inept, incompetent; stupid.
inequívoco unequivocal.
inerme unarmed, unprotected.
inerte inert (*a. phys.*); inactive.
inesperado unexpected, unforeseen.
inestabilidad *f* instability; **inestable** unstable, unsteady.
inestimable inestimable.
inevitable inevitable, unavoidable.
inexacto inaccurate, inexact.
inexcusable inexcusable; essential.
inexhausto *parte etc.* unused; unspent; (*inagotable*) inexhaustible.
inexperiencia *f* inexperience *etc.*; **inexperto** inexperienced, raw.
inexplicable inexplicable; **inexplicado** unexplained.
inexpresable inexpressible; **inexpresivo** inexpressive; dull.
inextinguible inextinguishable, unquenchable.
infalibilidad *f* infallibility; **infalible** infallible.
infamar [1a] discredit; slander; **infamatorio** defamatory; **infame 1.** infamous; vile; **2.** *m/f* villain; **infamia** *f* infamy.
infancia *f* infancy (*a. fig.*), childhood; (*ps.*) children; **infanta** *f hist.* princess; **infante** *m hist.* prince; **infantería** *f* infantry; ~ **de marina** marines; **infantil** (*de niños*) infant, children's; (*inocente*) childlike; *b.s.* infantile, childish.
infatigable tireless.
infausto unlucky, unfortunate.
infección *f* infection (*a. fig.*); **infeccioso** infectious; **infectar** [1a] = *inficionar*; **infecto** foul.
infeliz 1. unhappy, wretched; unfortunate; **2.** *m* poor devil; good-natured simpleton.
inferior 1. lower (*a* than); *calidad, rango* inferior (*a* to); ~ **a número** under, below, less than; **2.** *m* subordinate, inferior; **inferioridad** *f* inferiority.
inferir [3i] infer, deduce (*de, por* from); *herida* inflict.
infernáculo *m* hopscotch.
infernal infernal (*a. fig.*), hellish.
infestación *f* infestation; **infestar** [1a] overrun, infest; *♣* infect.
inficionar [1a] infect, contaminate (*a. fig.*); *fig.* corrupt.

infiel 1. unfaithful, disloyal (*a, con, para* to); *relato* inaccurate; **2.** *m/f* unbeliever, unfidel.

infiernillo *m* chafing dish; **infierno** *m* hell; *fig.* inferno, hell.

infiltrar [1a] infiltrate; *fig.* inculcate; **~se** filter (*en* in, through).

ínfimo lowest.

infinidad *f* infinity; **infinitesimal** infinitesimal (*a.* Å); **infinitivo** *m* infinitive (mood); **infinito 1.** infinite; **2.** *m* infinity; **3.** *adv.* infinitely.

inflación *f* inflation (*a.* ✝); swelling; **inflacionista** inflationary.

inflamable inflammable; **inflamación** *f* ignition, combustion; *fig.*, ✿ inflammation; **inflamar** [1a] set on fire; **~se** catch fire, flame up; *fig.* become inflamed.

inflar [1a] inflate; **~se** swell.

inflexible inflexible, unyielding; **inflexión** *f* inflexion.

infligir [3c] inflict (*a* on).

influencia *f* influence (*sobre* on); **influenciar** [1b] influence; **influir** [3g] have influence (*con* with); **~ en, ~ sobre** influence, affect; **influjo** *m* influence (*sobre* on); **influyente** influential.

información *f* (*una* a piece of) information; **informador** *m*, **-a** *f* informant; **informal** incorrect, unreliable; **informalidad** *f* irregularity; unreliability; **informar** [1a] *v/t.* inform (*de* of, *sobre* about); (*dar forma a*) shape; *v/i.* report (*acerca de* on); ✝✝ plead; **~** inform (*contra* against); **~se** inquire (*de* into), find out (*de* about); **informática** *f* data processing; computer science; **informativo** informative; news *attr.*; *junta etc.* consultative.

informe[1] shapeless.

informe[2] *m* report, statement; (piece of) information; ✝✝ plea; **~s** *pl.* information; data; **~s confidenciales** inside information.

infortunado unfortunate, unlucky; **infortunio** *m* misfortune; mishap.

infracción *f* infringement; breach.

infra(e)scrito 1. undersigned; **2.** *m*, **a** *f* undersigned.

infrarrojo infrared.

infrecuente infrequent.

infringir [3c] infringe, contravene.

infructuoso fruitless.

ínfulas *f/pl. fig.* conceit; *darse* **~** put on airs.

infundado unfounded, groundless.

infundir [3a] infuse (*a, en* into); *fig.* instil (*a, en* into).

ingeniar [1b] devise, contrive; **~se** manage, contrive (*a, para inf.* to *inf.*); **ingeniería** *f* engineering; **ingeniero** *m* engineer; **ingenio** *m* ingenuity, inventiveness; talent; wit; (*p.*) clever person; ⊕ apparatus; **~ nuclear** nuclear device; *S.Am.* **~** (*de azúcar*) sugar refinery; **ingeniosidad** *f* ingenuity *etc.*; (*una* **~**) clever idea; **ingenioso** ingenious.

ingenuidad *f* ingenuousness *etc.*; **ingenuo** ingenuous, naïve; candid.

ingle *f* groin.

inglés 1. English, British; **2.** *m* (*p.*) Englishman, Briton; (*idioma*) English; F creditor; *los* **~es** the English, the British; **inglesa** *f* Englishwoman; *montar a la* **~** ride sidesaddle; **inglesismo** *m* Anglicism.

ingobernable uncontrollable.

ingratitud *f* ingratitude; **ingrato** ungrateful; *tarea* thankless.

ingravidez *f* weightlessness; **ingrávido** weightless; light.

ingrediente *m* ingredient.

ingresar [1a] *v/t. dinero* deposit, put in; *v/i.* enter; ✝ come in; **~ en** *sociedad* join, become a member of; **ingreso** *m* entry (*en* into); admission (*en sociedad*) join; **~s** *pl.* receipts, profits, revenue, income.

inhábil clumsy, unskilful; incompetent; (*inadecuado*) unfit; **inhabilidad** *f* clumsiness *etc.*; **inhabilitar** [1a] disqualify (*para* from), render *s.o.* unfit (*para* for).

inhabitable uninhabitable; **inhabitado** uninhabited.

inherente inherent (*a* in).

inhibición *f* inhibition; **inhibir** [3a] inhibit; **~se** keep out (*de* of).

inhospitalario, inhóspito inhospitable.

inhumanidad *f* inhumanity; **inhumano** inhuman; *S.Am.* filthy.

inhumar [1a] bury, inter.

iniciación *f* initiation; beginning; **iniciado** *adj. a. su.* **m**, **a** *f* initiate; **inicial** *adj. a. su. f* initial; **iniciar** [1b] initiate (*en* into); (*comenzar*) begin; originate, pioneer, set on foot; **iniciativa** *f* initiative; resource, enterprise; lead(ership); **~ privada** private enterprise.

inicuo wicked, iniquitous.

ininteligente unintelligent.

iniquidad f iniquity; injustice.

injerencia f interference, meddling; **injerir** [3i] insert, introduce; **~se** interfere, meddle (en in); **injertar** [1a] ♂, ♀ graft (en on, in); **injerto** m graft; (acto) grafting; ♂ transplant.

injuria f insult; outrage, injustice; (daño) injury; **injuriar** [1b] insult, wrong; (dañar) harm; **injurioso** insulting; harmful.

injusticia f injustice etc.; **injusto** unjust; wrong(ful).

inmaculado immaculate.

inmaduro unripe; fig. immature.

inmediaciones f/pl. neighbourhood, environs; **inmediatamente** immediately, at once; **inmediato** immediate; (contiguo) adjoining, next; ~ a next to, close to.

inmensidad f immensity etc.; **inmenso** immense, huge, vast.

inmersión f immersion.

inmigración f immigration; **inmigrado** m, **a** f, **inmigrante** adj. a. su. m/f immigrant; **inmigrar** [1a] immigrate.

inmoble immovable; fig. unmoved.

inmoderado immoderate.

inmodesto immodest.

inmoral immoral; **inmoralidad** f immorality.

inmortal adj. a. su. m/f immortal; **inmortalidad** f immortality.

inmotivado groundless, unmotivated.

inmovible, inmóvil immovable, immobile; (temporalmente) motionless, still; fig. steadfast; **inmueble** m property; ~s pl. (a. bienes ~s) real estate.

inmundicia f filth, dirt; (basura) rubbish; **inmundo** filthy, dirty.

inmune exempt (de from); ♂ immune (contra to); **inmunidad** f exemption; immunity; **inmunizar** [1f] immunize.

inmutable immutable, changeless; **inmutarse** [1a] change countenance, lose one's self-possession.

innato innate, inborn.

innecesario unnecessary.

innegable undeniable.

innoble ignoble, base.

innocuo innocuous, harmless.

innovación f innovation; novelty; **innovador** m, **-a** f innovator.

innumerable innumerable.

inobediente disobedient.

inobservado unobserved; **inobservancia** f neglect.

inocencia f innocence; **inocentada** f naïve remark etc.; (broma) practical joke; **inocente** innocent (de of); (tonto) simple.

inoculación f inoculation; **inocular** [1a] inoculate.

inodoro 1. odorless; 2. m lavatory.

inofensivo inoffensive, harmless.

inolvidable unforgettable.

inopinadamente unexpectedly; **inopinado** unexpected.

inoportuno inopportune, untimely; inconvenient; inexpedient.

inquietar [1a] disturb; (acosar) stir up; **~se** worry, fret (de, por about); **inquieto** restless; worried; **inquietud** f restlessness.

inquilino m, **a** f tenant, renter.

inquina f dislike, ill-will.

inquirir [3i] inquire into, investigate; **inquisición** f inquiry; ♀ Inquisition.

insaciable insatiable.

insalubre unhealthy, insalubrious.

insanable incurable; **insania** f insanity; **insano** insane, mad.

insatisfactorio unsatisfactory; **insatisfecho** unsatisfied.

inscribir [3a; p.p. inscrito] inscribe (a. fig., ♀, Å); register, record; **~se** enrol, register; **inscripción** f inscription; lettering; (acto) enrollment etc.

insecticida adj. a. su. m insecticide; **insecto** m insect.

inseguridad f insecurity; **inseguro** unsafe, insecure; (dudoso) uncertain.

inseminación f insemination.

insensato senseless, foolish; **insensibilidad** f insensitivity; **insensible** insensitive (a to), unfeeling.

inseparable inseparable.

inserción f insertion; **insertar** [1a] insert.

inservible useless, unusable.

insidioso insidious.

insigne illustrious, distinguished; **insignia** f badge, decoration; (bandera) flag; ~s pl. insignia.

insignificancia f insignificance; (cosa) trifle; **insignificante** insignificant; petty, trivial.

insinuación f insinuation; **insinuante** insinuating, ingratiating; **insinuar** [1e] insinuate, hint at; (observación) slip in; **~se** en creep into; ~ con ingratiate o.s. with.

insipidez f insipidness etc.; **insípido** insipid, tasteless.

insistencia f insistence; **insistente** insistent; **insistir** [3a] insist (en, sobre on; en inf. on ger.; en que that); ~ en a. stress, emphasize.

insociable unsociable.

insolación f exposure (to the sun); ✻ sunstroke; **insolar** [1a] expose to the sun; ~se ✻ get sunstroke.

insolencia f insolence; **insolentarse** [1a] be(come) insolent; **insolente** insolent.

insólito unusual, unwonted.

insolvencia f insolvency; **insolvente** insolvent, bankrupt.

insomne sleepless; **insomnio** m sleeplessness, insomnia.

insondable unfathomable.

insonorización f soundproofing; **insonorizado** soundproof; **insonorizar** [1f] v/t. soundproof; **insonoro** noiseless, soundless.

insoportable unbearable.

insospechado unsuspected.

inspección f inspection; ~ técnica de vehículos (I.T.V.) automobile inspection, car inspection; **inspeccionar** [1a] inspect; **inspector** m inspector.

inspiración f inspiration; **inspirar** [1a] breathe in; fig. inspire; ~se en be inspired by, find inspiration in.

instalación f (acto, cosas) installation; (cosas) fittings, equipment; ✻ plant; **instalar** [1a] install, set up; ~se settle, establish o.s.

instancia f request; (escrito) application; (hoja) application form; a ~ de at the request of.

instantánea f phot. snap(shot); **instantáneo** instantaneous.

instante m instant, moment; al ~ instantly; **instantemente** insistently; **instar** [1a] urge, press (a inf., a que, para que to inf.).

instigación f instigation; **instigar** [1h] instigate; p. induce (a inf. to inf.), abet.

instintivo instinctive; **instinto** m instinct; impulse, urge.

institución f institution, establishment; **instituir** [3g] institute, establish, set up; **instituto** m institute; eccl. rule; ~ (de segunda enseñanza) approx. high school; **institutriz** f governess.

instrucción f instruction; (enseñanza) education; **instructivo** instructive; **instructor** m instructor, teacher; **instructora** f instructress; **instruido** (well-)educated; **instruir** [3g] instruct (de, en, sobre in, about); ~se learn (de, en, sobre about).

instrumental 1. instrumental; 2. m instruments; **instrumentar** [1a] score; **instrumentista** m/f instrumentalist; **instrumento** m instrument (a. fig.); (herramienta, p.) tool; ~ de cuerda ♪ stringed instrument; ~ de viento ♪ wind instrument.

insubordinar [1a] rouse to rebellion; ~se rebel, be(come) insubordinate.

insuficiente insufficient, inadequate; p. incompetent.

insufrible unbearable.

insular insular.

insulina f insulin.

insulso tasteless, insipid.

insultante insulting; **insultar** [1a] insult; **insulto** m insult.

insumergible unsinkable.

insuperable insuperable; **insuperado** unsurpassed.

insurgente adj. a. su. m/f insurgent.

intachable irreproachable.

intacto untouched; (entero) intact, whole; (sin daño) undamaged.

integración f integration; **integral** adj. a. su. f ᴀ integral; **integrante** integral; **integrar** [1a] integrate; **integridad** f wholeness; fig. integrity; **íntegro** whole, complete; integral; fig. upright.

intelectiva f intellect, understanding; **intelecto** m intellect; brain(s); **intelectual** adj. a. su. m/f intellectual.

inteligencia f intelligence; **inteligente** intelligent; **inteligible** intelligible.

intemperancia f intemperance; **intemperie** f inclemency (of the weather); a la ~ in the open; **intempestivo** untimely, ill-timed.

intención f intention; **intencional** intentional.

intendente m manager.

intensar(se) [1a] intensify; **intensidad** f intensity etc.; ⊕, ⚡ etc. strength; **intensificar** [1g] intensify; **intensivo** intensive; **intenso** mst intense.

intentar [1a] attempt, try (inf. to inf.); **intento** m intention; (cosa intentada) attempt; de ~ on purpose.

inter... inter...; ~acción f interaction, interplay; ~calar [1a] intercalate, insert; ~cambiable interchangeable; **~cambiar** [1b] interchange; **~cambio** m interchange; **~ceder** [2a] intercede, plead (con with, por for); **~ceptar** [1a] intercept, cut off; (detener) hold up; **~cesión** f intercession; **~conectar** [1a] interconnect; **~confesional** interdenominational; **~continental** intercontinental; **~decir** [3p] forbid; **~dependiente** interdependent; **~dicción** f prohibition.

interés m interest; **interesado** 1. interested (en in); 2. m, **a** f person concerned, interested party; (el que firma) applicant; **interesante** interesting; **interesar** [1a] v/t. (atraer) interest (en in), be of interest to; v/i. be of interest; be important; **~se** interested, take an interest (en, por in).

inter...: **~estelar** interstellar; **~ferencia** f interference; radio: jamming; **~ferir** [3i] interfere with; radio: jam.

ínterin 1. m interim; en el ~ in the interim, in the meantime; 2. adv. meanwhile; 3. cj. while; until; **interino** 1. provisional, temporary; p. acting; 2. m, **a** f stand-in.

interior 1. interior, inner, inside; 2. m interior, inside; **~es** pl. insides.

inter...: **~jección** f interjection; **~lineal** interlinear; **~locutor** m, **-a** f speaker; mi ~ the person I was talking to; **~ludio** m interlude; **~mediario** m, **a** f intermediary; **~medio** 1. intermediate; 2. m intermission; **~mezzo** m intermezzo.

interminable unending, endless, interminable.

inter...: **~mitente** intermittent (a. ⚙); **~nacional** international; **~nacionalismo** m internationalism; **~nacionalizar** [1f] internationalize.

internamiento m internment; **internar** [1a] v/t. pol. intern; v/i., **~se** en país penetrate into; estudio go deeply into; **interno** 1. internal; inside; 2. m, **a** f boarder.

inter...: **~pelar** [1a] implore; parl. ask s.o. for explanations; (dirigirse a) address, speak to; **~planetario** interplanetary; **~polación** f interpolation; **~polar** [1a] interpolate; **~poner** [2r] interpose, insert; **~se** intervene; **~pretación** f interpretation etc.; **~pretar** [1a] mst interpret; (traducir a.) translate; **intérprete** m/f interpreter; translator.

inter...: **~rogación** f interrogation; (pregunta) question; v. punto; **~rogar** [1h] question, interrogate; **~rogativo** gr. adj. a. su. m interrogative; **~rogatorio** m questioning; (hoja) questionnaire; **~rumpir** [3a] interrupt; **~rupción** f interruption; **~ruptor** m ⚡ switch; **~secarse** [1g] intersect; **~sección** f intersection; **~sticio** m interstice; **~urbano** teleph. long-distance attr.; **~valo** m tiempo: interval; **~vención** f intervention; **~venir** [3s] intervene (en in); **~ventor** m inspector, auditor; **~viú** f interview; **~viuvar** [1a] interview.

intestinal intestinal; **intestino** 1. internal; 2. m intestine, gut; ~ ciego caecum; ~ delgado small intestine; ~ grueso large intestine.

intimación f notification etc.; **intimar** [1a] notify, announce; come intimate.

intimidación f intimidation.

intimidad f intimacy.

intimidar [1a] intimidate.

íntimo intimate.

intitular [1a] entitle, call.

intocable adj. a. su. m/f untouchable.

intolerable intolerable, unbearable.

intolerancia f intolerance etc.; **intolerante** intolerant.

intoxicar [1g] poison.

intraducible untranslatable.

intranquilizar [1f] worry; **intranquilo** restless, uneasy, worried.

intransigente intransigent; uncompromising; esp. pol. die-hard.

intransitivo intransitive.

intratable intractable; p. unsociable, difficult; cosa awkward.

intravenoso intravenous.

intrépido intrepid, undaunted.

intriga f intrigue, plot (a. lit.), scheme; **intrigante** m/f intriguer, schemer; **intrigar** [1h] v/t. intrigue.

intrincado impenetrable; intricate; **intrincar** [1g] complicate.

introducción f introduction; insertion; **introducir** [3o] introduce; objeto put in, insert; get in, slip in.

intro...: **~misión** f insertion; b.s. interference; **~spección** f introspection; **~spectivo** introspective.

intrusión f intrusion; ⚖ trespass; **intruso** 1. intrusive; 2. m, **a** f intruder, interloper; gate-crasher.

intuición f intuition; **intuir** [3g] know by intuition; **intuitivo** intuitive.

inundación f flood; **inundar** [1a] flood, inundate, swamp.

inusitado unusual.

inútil useless; **inutilidad** f uselessness; **inutilizar** [1f] make s.t. useless; disable.

invadir [3a] invade (a. fig.), overrun; fig. encroach upon.

invalidar [1a] invalidate, nullify; **invalidez** f nullity etc.; **inválido 1.** 🕂 invalid, null (and void); p. disabled; **2.** m, 🐾 a f invalid; **3.** m ✕ pensioner, disabled soldier etc.

invariable invariable.

invasión f invasion (a. 🐾, fig.); encroachment (de on); **invasor 1.** invading; **2.** m, -a f invader.

invencible invincible.

invención f invention; discovery.

invendible unsalable.

inventar [1a] invent; (fingir) make up; **inventariar** [1b] inventory, make an inventory of; **inventario** m inventory; **inventivo** inventive, ingenious, resourceful; **invento** m invention; **inventor** m, -a f inventor.

invernáculo m, **invernadero** m greenhouse; **invernal** wintry, winter attr.; **invernar** [1k] winter; zo. hibernate; **invernizo** wintry, winter attr.

inverosímil unlikely, improbable.

inversión f inversion; reversal; ✝ investment; **inversionista** m/f investor; **inverso** inverse; reverse; **inversor** m investor.

invertir [3i] invert, turn upside down; reverse (a. ⊕); ✝ invest; tiempo spend, put in.

investigación f investigation, inquiry; 🕮 research (de into); **investigador** m, -a f investigator; 🕮 research worker; **investigar** [1h] investigate, look into; 🕮 do research into.

inveterado p. inveterate.

invicto unconquered.

invidente blind.

invierno m winter; S.Am. rainy season.

inviolable inviolable; **inviolado** inviolate.

invisible invisible.

invitación f invitation; **invitado** m, a f guest; **invitar** [1a] invite (a inf. to inf.); call on (a inf. to inf.); attract, entice.

invocar [1g] invoke, call on.

involuntario involuntary.

invulnerable invulnerable.

inyección f injection; **inyectado** bloodshot; **inyectar** [1a] inject; **inyector** m injector; nozzle.

ion m ion; **ionizar** [1f] ionize.

ir [3t] **1.** go; move; (viajar) travel; (a pie) walk; (en coche) drive; (a caballo etc.) ride; 🐾 be, get along, do; be at stake en apuesta (a. fig.); de 5 a 3 van 2 3 from 5 leaves 2; con éste van 50 that makes 50; van 5 duros a que no lo dices I bet you 5 duros you don't say it; **2.** modismos: ¡voy! (I'm) coming!; a eso voy I'm coming to that; ¡vamos! let's go!, come on!; fig. well, after all; ¡vaya! sorpresa: well!, there!, I say!; aviso: now now!; ¡vaya ...! what a ...!; ¡qué va! F nonsense!, not a bit of it!; ¿quién va? who goes there?; **3.** dativo: ¿qué te va en ello? what does it matter to you!; vestido: te va muy bien it suits you; **4.** con prp.: ~ a inf. (futuro próximo) to be going to inf., be about to inf.; voy a hacerlo en seguida I am going to do it at once; fui a verle I went to see (F and saw) him; ~ de guía act (or go) as guide; ~ por go for; va por médico he's going to be a doctor; ¡vaya por X! here's to X!; ~ tras fig. chase after; **5.** v/aux. mst be; ~ ger. be ger.; van corriendo they are running; (ya) voy comprendiendo I'm beginning to understand; ~ p.p. be p.p.; iba cansado he was tired; va vendido todo el género all the goods are (already) sold; **6.** ~se go (away), leave, depart; (morir) die; (líquido) leak, ooze out; (desbordar) run over; (gastarse) wear out; (envejecer) grow old; (resbalar) slip, lose one's balance; (pared etc.) give way; ¡vete! be off with you!, go away!; ¡vámonos! let's go!

ira f anger, rage; **iracundo** irascible, irate.

iris m rainbow; opt. iris; **irisado** iridescent.

ironía f irony; **irónico** ironic(al).

irracional 1. irrational (a. 🅐); unreasoning; **2.** m brute.

irradiar [1b] (ir)radiate.

irrazonable unreasonable.

irreal unreal; **irrealidad** f unreality; **irrealizable** unrealizable.

irreconciliable irreconcilable.

irreconocible unrecognizable.

irrecuperable irrecoverable.

irrecusable unimpeachable.

irreemplazable irreplaceable.

irreflexivo thoughtless, unthinking.

irrefutable irrefutable.
irregular irregular (*a. b.s.*); **irregularidad** *f* irregularity.
irreligioso irreligious, ungodly.
irremediable irremediable.
irreparable irreparable.
irreprochable irreproachable.
irresistible irresistible.
irresoluble unsolvable; **irresoluto** irresolute, hesitant.
irrespetuoso disrespectful.
irresponsable irresponsible.
irreverente irreverent.
irrevocable irrevocable.
irrigar [1h] irrigate (*a. ⚕*).
irrisión *f* derision, ridicule; **irrisorio** derisory, ridiculous.
irritable irritable; **irritación** *f* irritation; **irritador**, **irritante 1.** irritating; **2.** *m* irritant; **irritar** [1a] irritate (*a. ⚕*), anger, exasperate; *deseos* stir up; **~se** get angry (*de* at).

irrompible unbreakable.
irrumpir [3a]: **~ en** burst into, rush into; **irrupción** *f* invasion.
isla *f* island; **△** block; **~ de peatones** island for pedestrians, safety zone (for pedestrians).
Islam *m* Islam; **islámico** Islamic.
isleño 1. island *attr.*; **2.** *m*, **a** *f* islander; **isleta** *f* islet; **islote** *m* small (rocky) island.
iso... iso...; **isótopo** *m* isotope.
israelí *adj. a. su. m/f* Israeli; **israelita** *adj. a. su. m/f* Israelite.
istmo *m* isthmus; neck.
ítem 1. *m* item; **2.** *adv.* item; also.
itinerario *m* itinerary, route.
izar [1f] ⚓ hoist; *bandera* run up.
izquierda *f* left hand; (*lado*) left side; *pol.* left; *a la* **~** *estar* on the left; *torcer etc.* (to the) left; **izquierdista 1.** left-wing; **2.** *m/f* left-winger, leftist; **izquierdo** left(-hand); (*zurdo*) left-handed.

J

J

¡ja! ha!
jabalí *m* wild boar; **jabalina** *f* ✕, *deportes:* javelin.
jabón *m* soap; (*un* **~**) piece of soap; **~ de olor**, **~ de tocador** toilet-soap; **~ en polvo** soap-powder, washing powder; *dar* **~ a** soap; F soft-soap; F *dar un* **~ a** tell *s.o.* off; **jabonado** *m* soaping; (*ropa*) wash; **jabonaduras** *f/pl.* lather, (*soap*)suds; **jabonar** [1a] soap; *ropa* wash; *barba* lather; F tell *s.o.* off; **jaboncillo** *m* toilet-soap; **~ de sastre** French chalk; **jabonoso** soapy.
jaca *f* pony.
jacinto *m* ⚘, *min.* hyacinth.
jacobino *adj. a. su. m*, **a** *f* Jacobin.
jactancia *f* boasting; (*cualidad*) boastfulness; **jactancioso** boastful; **jactarse** [1a] boast (*de* about, of).
jade *m min.* jade.
jadeante panting, gasping; **jadear** [1a] pant, puff (and blow), gasp (for breath); **jadeo** *m* pant(ing) *etc.*
jaez *m* (*piece of*) harness; *fig.* kind, sort; *jaeces pl.* trappings.
jaguar *m* jaguar.
jalar [1a] F pull, haul; ⚓ heave; **~se** *S.Am.* F get drunk; (*irse*) clear out.

jalbegar [1h] whitewash; F paint; **jalbegue** *m* whitewash(ing); F paint.
jalde, **jaldo** bright yellow.
jalea *f* jelly.
jalear [1a] *perros* urge on; *bailadores* encourage (by shouting and clapping); **jaleo** *m* F (*jarana*) spree, binge; (*ruido*) row, racket; (*lío*) row, fuss; *armar un* **~** kick up a row; *estar de* **~** make merry.
jalón *m surv.* stake, pole; jerk, jolt, yank; *fig.* stage; **jalonar** [1a] stake out, mark out.
jamás never; (not) ever.
jamón *m* ham.
japonés 1. *adj. a. su. m*, **-a** *f* Japanese; **2.** *m* (*idioma*) Japanese.
jaque *m ajedrez:* check; F bully; **~ mate** check-mate; *dar* **~ a** check; *dar* **~ mate** (*a*) (check)mate; *estar muy* **~ to** be full of pep; *tener en* **~** *fig.* hold a threat over; **jaquear** [1a] check; *fig.* harass.
jaqueca *f* headache; *dar* **~ a** bore.
jarabe *m* syrup; sweet drink; **~ de pico** mere words, lip-service.
jarana *f* F spree, binge; (*pendencia*) rumpus; *andar de* **~** = **jaranear** [1a] F roister, carouse; lark about; **jaranero** roistering, merry.

juego

jarcia f ⚓ rigging (freq. ~s pl.); (fishing-)tackle; fig. heap.

jardín m (flower) garden; ~ central baseball center field; ~ de la infancia kindergarten, nursery school; ~ derecho baseball right field; ~ izquierdo baseball left field; ~ zoológico zoo.

jardinero m, **a** f gardener; baseball fielder, outfielder.

jarra f pitcher, jar; de ~s, en ~s (with) arms akimbo.

jarrete m back of the knee; hock de animal.

jarro m jug, pitcher; F echar un ~ de agua a pour cold water on; **jarrón** m vase; ⚱ urn.

jaspe m jasper; **jaspear** [1a] marble, speckle.

jaula f cage (a. 🗡); crate de embalaje; mot. lock-up garage; cell.

jauría f pack (of hounds).

jazmín m jasmine.

jazz [dʒaz] m jazz.

jeep [dʒip] m jeep.

jefa f (woman) head; manageress; **jefatura** f leadership; (oficina) headquarters; ~ de policía police headquarters; **jefe** m chief, head, boss F; leader; (gerente) manager; 🗡 field officer; ~ de cocina chef; ~ de coro choirmaster; ~ de estación stationmaster; ~ del estado chief of state; ~ de estado mayor chief of staff; ~ de redacción editor in chief; ~ de ruta guide; ~ de taller foreman; ~ de tren conductor; ~ de tribu chieftain; en ~ in chief.

jengibre m ginger.

jeque m sheik(h).

jerarca m important person; F big shot; **jerarquía** f hierarchy.

jerez m sherry.

jerga f jargon; slang de ladrones etc.

jergón m palliasse; F ill-fitting garment; (p.) lumpish fellow.

jeringa f syringe; ~ de engrase grease gun; **jeringar** [1h] syringe; inject; squirt; F plague; ~se F get bored, get annoyed; **jeringazo** m injection; squirt; syringing.

jeroglífico 1. hieroglyphic; **2.** m hieroglyph(ic); fig. puzzle.

jersé m, **jersey** m jersey, sweater, pullover; jumper de mujer; cardigan.

jesuita adj. a. su. m Jesuit.

jeta f zo. snout; F face, mug.

jíbaro adj. a. su. m, **a** f S.Am. peasant, rustic.

jícara f small cup; S.Am. gourd.

jilguero m goldfinch, linnet.

jinete m horseman, rider; 🗡 cavalryman; **jinetear** [1a] v/t. S.Am. break in; v/i. ride around.

jira f strip de tela; excursion, outing; (merienda) picnic; (viaje) tour.

jirafa f giraffe.

jockey ['xoki] m jockey.

joder vulgar v/i. copulate; **jodienda** f dirty note.

jofaina f wash basin.

jornada f (day's) journey; (horas) working day; 🗡 expedition; thea. †act; ~ ordinaria full time; **jornal** m (day's) wage; (trabajo) day's work; a ~ by the day; ~ mínimo minimum wage; **jornalero** m (day)laborer.

joroba f hump, hunched back; fig. nuisance; **jorobado 1.** hunchbacked; **2.** m, **a** f hunchback; **jorobar** [1a] F annoy, pester, give s.o. the hump.

jota¹ f letter J; fig. jot, iota; F no entiendo ni ~ I don't understand a word of it; no saber ~ have no idea.

jota² f Spanish dance.

joven 1. young; youthful en aspecto etc.; **2.** m young man, youth; los ~es youth; young people; **3.** f young woman, girl; **jovencito** m, **a** f, **jovenzuelo** m, **a** f youngster.

jovial jolly, jovial, cheerful; **jovialidad** f joviality etc.

joya f jewel; fig. (p.) gem; ~s pl. trousseau de novia; **joyería** f jewelry; (tienda) jeweler's (shop); **joyero** m jeweler; (caja) jewelcase.

jubilación f retirement; (renta) pension; **jubilado** retired; **jubilar** [1a] v/t. p. pension off, retire; cosa discard, get rid of; v/i. rejoice; ~se retire; F play hooky; **jubileo** m jubilee; **júbilo** m jubilation, joy, rejoicing; **jubiloso** jubilant.

jubón m jerkin, close-fitting jacket.

judaísmo m Judaism; **judería** f ghetto; **judía** f Jewess; ⚘ kidney bean; ~ blanca haricot (bean).

judicial judicial.

judío 1. Jewish; **2.** m Jew (a. fig.).

judo m judo.

juego¹ etc. v. jugar.

juego² m (acto) play(ing) (diversión) game (a. fig.), sport; gambling con apuestas; (conjunto de cosas) set; suite de muebles; kit, outfit de herramientas; pack de naipes; ⊕ movement, play; play de agua, luz etc.; ~s pl. atléticos (athletic) sports;

~ de azar game of chance; ~ de bolas ball bearing; ~ de bolos ninepins; ~ de café coffee set; ~ de campanas chimes; ~ de damas checkers; ~ de la pulga tiddlywinks; ~ del corro ring-around-a-rosy; ~ del salto leapfrog; ~ limpio (sucio) fair (foul) play; ~s pl. malabares juggling; ~ de manos sleight of hand; ~ de niños cosa muy fácil child's play; ~ de mesa dinner-service; ~ de naipes card game; ♀s pl. Olímpicos Olympic Games; ~ de palabras pun, play on words; ~ de piernas footwork; ~ de prendas forfeits; ~ de salón parlor game; ~ de suerte game of chance; ~ de tejo shuffleboard; ~ de vocablos, ~ de voces play on words, pun; a ~ (con) matching; en ~ ⊕ in gear; fig. at stake; at hand; fuera de ~ (p.) offside; (pelota) out; conocer el ~ a know what s.o. is up to; hacer ~ (con) match, go (with).

juerga f F (ir de go on a) binge, spree; **juergista** m F reveller.

jueves m Thursday.

juez m judge (a. fig.); ~ árbitro arbitrator, referee; ~ de línea linesman; ~ (municipal) magistrate; ~ de paz approx. Justice of the Peace.

jugada f play; (una ~) move; (golpe) stroke, shot; (echada) throw; (mala) ~ bad turn, dirty trick; **jugador** m, **-a** f player; b.s. gambler; ~ de manos conjurer; **jugar** [1h a. 1o] v/t. mst play; (arriesgar) gamble, stake; arma handle; v/i. play (a at, con with); b.s. gamble; ~ con fig. trifle with; (hacer juego) go with, match; ~ limpio play the game; de ~ toy.

juglar m † minstrel; juggler.

jugo m juice; gravy de carne; ♀ sap (a. fig.); fig. essence; substance; **jugoso** juicy; fig. pithy, substantial.

juguete m toy, plaything; **juguetear** [1a] play, romp; **juguetería** f toyshop; **juguetón** playful.

juicio m judgement; (seso) sense; opinion; (sana razón) sanity, reason; ⁿⁿz verdict (a. fig.); ⁿⁿz (proceso) trial; perder el ~ go out of one's mind; **juicioso** judicious; wise, sensible.

julio m July.

jumento m, **a** f donkey (a. fig.).

junco[1] m ♣ rush, reed.

junco[2] m ♣ junk.

jungla f jungle.

junio m June.

junquera f rush, bulrush; **junquillo** m jonquil; (junco) reed.

junta f (reunión) meeting, assembly; session; (ps.) board (a. ✝), council, committee; (juntura) junction; ⊕ joint; ⊕ washer, gasket; ~ de comercio board of trade; ~ de sanidad board of health; ~ directiva board of management; ~ militar junta; ~ universal universal joint; celebrar ~ sit; **juntamente** together (con with); at the same time; **juntar** [1a] join, put together; (acopiar) collect, gather (together); get together; dinero raise; ~se join; (ps.) meet, gather (together); associate (con with); **junto 1.** adj. joined, together; ~s pl. together; 2. adv. together; ~ a next to, near; ~ con together with; (de) por ~ all together.

juntura f junction, join(ing); joint (a. anat.); ⊕ seam; ⊕ coupling.

jura f oath; **jurado** m jury; (p.) juryman, juror; **juramentar** [1a] swear s.o. in; ~se take an oath; **juramento** m oath; b.s. oath, swear-word; bajo ~ on oath; prestar ~ take an (or the) oath (sobre on); tomar ~ a swear s.o. in; **jurar** [1a] swear (inf. to inf.; a. b.s.); **jurisdicción** f jurisdiction; district; **jurisprudencia** f jurisprudence, law; **jurista** m/f jurist, lawyer. [test.]

justa f joust, tournament; fig. contest.

justamente justly, fairly; (exactamente) just, precisely.

justar [1a] joust, tilt.

justicia f justice; fairness; right, rightness; (ps.) police; en ~ by rights; hacer ~ a do justice to; **justiciable** actionable; **justiciero** (strictly) just; **justificable** justifiable; **justificación** f justification; **justificar** [1g] justify (a. typ.); (probar) substantiate; sospechoso clear (de of), vindicate; **justo 1.** adj. just, right, fair; (virtuoso) righteous; (legítimo) rightful; cantidad etc. exact; (ajustado) tight; **2.** adv. just; right; (ajustadamente) tightly.

juvenil young; youthful; obra early; **juventud** f youth; young people.

juzgado m court, tribunal; **juzgar** [1h] judge (a. fig.); ⁿⁿz pass sentence upon; fig. consider, deem.

K

karate *m sports* karate.
kermes(s)e [ker'mes] *f* charitable fair, bazaar.
kerosén *m*, **kerosene** *m* kerosene, coal oil.
kilo *m* kilo; **~ciclo** *m* kilocycle; **~gra-**

mo *m* kilogramme; **~metraje** *m approx.* mileage; **kilómetro** *m* kilometer; **kilovatio** *m* kilowatt; **~s-hora** *m/pl.* kilowatt-hours.
kiosco *m v.* quiosco.
knock-out [kaw] *m* knock-out.

L

la 1. *artículo:* the; **2.** *pron.* (*p.*) her; (*cosa*) it; (*Vd.*) you; **3.** *pron. relativo:* ~ de that of; ~ de Juan John's; ~ de Pérez Mrs Pérez; *v.* que.
laberinto *m* labyrinth, maze (*a. fig.*).
labia *f* F glibness, fluency; *tener mucha* ~ have the gift of the gab;
labial *adj. a. su. f* labial; **labio** *m* lip (*a. fig.*, *✿*); (*reborde*) edge, rim; *fig.* tongue; ~ *leporino* harelip; *leer en los* **~s** lip-read; **labiolectura** *f* lip reading; **labioso** *Am.* fluent, smooth.
labor *f* labor, work; (*una* ~) piece of work; job; *esp.* ✓ farm work, ploughing; *sew.* (*una a piece of*) embroidery, sewing; ~ (*de aguja*) needlework; **~es** *esp.* ✗ workings;
laborable workable; *v. día;* **laboral** labor *attr.;* **laboratorio** *m* laboratory; ~ *de idiomas* language laboratory; **laborear** [1a] work (*a.* ✗); ✓ till; **laborioso** *p.* hard-working, painstaking; *trabajo* hard, laborious;
laborterapia work therapy; **labradío** arable; **labrado 1.** worked; ⊕ wrought; *tela* patterned, emboidered; **2.** *m* cultivated field; **labrador** *m* (*dueño*) farmer; (*empleado*) farm laborer; ploughman *que ara;* (*campesino*) peasant; **labradora** *f* peasant (woman); **labrantío** arable; **labranza** *f* farming; (*hacienda*) farm; **labrar** [1a] work, fashion; ✓ farm, till; *madera etc.* carve; (*toscamente*) hew; *fig.* bring about; **labriego** *m,* **a** *f* farm hand; peasant.
laca *f* shellac (*a. goma* ~); (*barniz*) lacquer; (*color*) lake; hair spray; ~

negra japan; ~ (*para uñas*) nail polish.
lacayo *m* footman, lackey.
lacio ✙ withered; (*flojo*) limp.
lacónico laconic, terse.
lacra *f* ✿ mark; *fig.* defect, scar;
lacrar¹ [1a] ✿ strike; *fig.* damage.
lacrar² [1a] seal (with wax).
lacrimoso tearful, lachrymose.
lactar [1a] *v/t.* nurse; *v/i.* feed on milk; **lácteo** milky; **láctico** lactic.
ladear [1a] *v/t.* tilt, tip; *colina etc.* skirt; ✿ bank; *v/i.* lean, tilt; (*desviarse*) turn off; **~se** lean, incline (*a. fig.; a* to, towards); **ladera** *f* slope, hillside.
ladino shrewd, smart, wily.
lado *m* side (*a. fig.*); ✗ flank; ~ *débil* weak spot; ~ *a* ~ side by side; *al* ~ near, at hand; *al* ~ *de* by the side of, beside; (*casa*) next door to; *al otro* ~ *de* over, on the other side of; *de* ~ *adv.* sideways, edgeways; *de al* ~ *casa* next (door); *de un* ~ *a otro* to and fro; *por el* ~ *de* in the (general) direction of.
ladrar [1a] bark; **ladrido** *m* bark(ing); *fig.* scandal(-mongering).
ladrillado *m* brick floor; **ladrillo** *m* brick; (*azulejo*) tile; *de chocolate* cake; ~ *refractario* fire brick.
ladrón 1. thieving; **2.** *m,* **-a** *f* thief.
lagarta *f* lizard; F bitch.
lago *m* lake.
lágrima *f* tear; *fig.* drop; **~s** *pl. de cocodrilo* tears; **lagrimoso** tearful.
laguna *f* lagoon; gap, lacuna ⊞.
laicado *m* laity; **laical** lay; **laico 1.** lay; **2.** *m* layman.

lamentable lamentable; pitiful; **lamentación** f lamentation; **lamentar** [1a] be sorry, regret (que that); *pérdida* lament; *muerto* mourn; **~se** wail, moan (de, por over); **lamento** m lament; moan, wail.

lamer [2a] lick; *agua etc.)* lap.

lámina f sheet *de vidrio, metal etc.*; *metall., phot., typ.* plate; 🔲 lamina; **~s** *pl. de cobre etc.* sheet copper.

lámpara f lamp, light; *(bombilla)* bulb; *radio:* tube; **~** *de arco* arc lamp; **~** *de soldar* blowtorch; **~** *colgante* hanging lamp; **lamparilla** f nightlight.

lampiño hairless; *p.* clean-shaven.

lana f fleece; *(tela)* woolen cloth; **2.** *m C.Am.* man in the street; swindler; **lanar** wool *attr.*

lance m *(acto)* throw, cast *de red*; *(jugada)* stroke, move; *(cantidad pescada)* catch; *(suceso)* occurrence, incident, event; *(trance)* critical moment; *(riña)* row; **de ~** second-hand; *(barato)* cheap.

lancha f launch; *(bote)* (small) boat; lighter *para carga*; **~** *automóvil*, **~** *motora* motor launch; **~** *de desembarco* landing craft; **~** *rápida* speedboat, motor launch.

langosta f lobster; *(insecto)* locust; **langostín** m, **langostino** m prawn.

languidecer [2d] languish, pine (away); **languidez** f languor, lassitude; **lánguido** languid.

lanza f spear, lance; pole *de coche*; nozzle *de manga*; **lanzabombas** m bomb release; trench mortar; **lanzacohetes** m rocket launcher; **lanzadera** f shuttle; **lanzaespumas** m foam extinguisher; **lanzallamas** m flamethrower; **lanzamiento** m throw(ing) *etc.*; launch(ing) *de barco*; 🐿 drop (by parachute), jump; **lanzaminas** m minelayer; **lanzar** [1f] throw, fling, cast, pitch; hurl *con violencia*; drop *en paracaídas*; 🐿 vomit; *barco*, ⚓ launch; *hojas etc.* put forth; 🐎 dispossess; *grito* give; *desafío* throw down; **~se** throw o.s. *(a, en* into); rush *(sobre at, on)*, dash; 🐿 jump; *fig.* launch out *(a* into); **~** *sobre* fly at, fall upon.

laña f clamp; rivet.

lapicero m mechanical pencil; pencil holder; **~** *fuente* fountain pen.

lápida f memorial tablet, stone; **~** *mortuoria* headstone.

lápiz m· pencil, lead pencil; *min.*

black lead; **~** *labial* lipstick; **~** *estíptico* styptic pencil; *a* **~** in pencil.

lapso m lapse.

laquear [1a] lacquer; *uñas* polish.

lard(e)ar [1a] lard; **lardo** m lard.

largamente *contar* at length, fully;

largar [1h] let loose, let go; *cable* let out; *velas, bandera* unfurl; F give;

largo 1. long; *fig.* generous; abundant; F *p.* sharp; ⚓ loose, slack; **¡~** *(de aquí)!* clear off!; *tendido cuan* **~** *es etc.* full-length; *a la* **~a** in the long run; *a lo* **~** *de* along, alongside; *(tiempo)* throughout; *de* **~** in a long dress; *tirar de* **~** spend lavishly; **2.** *m* length; *tener 4 metros de* **~** be 4 metres long; **largometraje** *m* feature film; **largor** *m* length; **larguero** *m* ⚓ jamb; *deportes:* crossbar; bolster *de cama*; **largueza** f *fig.* generosity; **largucho, larguirucho** lanky; **largura** f length.

laringe f larynx; **laringitis** f laryngitis.

larva f larva 🔲, grub.

las *v. los.*

lasca f *Am.* advantage, benefit.

lascivia f lasciviousness; **lascivo** lascivious, lewd.

láser m laser.

lasitud f lassitude, weariness; **laso** weary; *(flojo)* limp, languid.

lástima f pity; *(cosa)* pitiful object; *(quejido)* complaint; *¡qué* **~***!* what a pity *(or shame)!*; **lastimar** [1a] hurt, injure; offend; *(compadecer)* pity, sympathize with; **~se** feel sorry for; **lastimero** injurious.

lastre m ballast; *fig.* steadiness, good sense.

lata f tin plate; *(envase)* tin can; *(tabla)* lath; F nuisance, bind; *en* **~** canned.

latero m *Am.* plumber; tinsmith.

latido m yelp, bark; beat(ing) *etc.*

latigazo m *(golpe)* lash *(a. fig.)*; *(chasquido)* crack (of a whip); *fig.* harsh reproof; **látigo** m whip.

latín m Latin; **latinajo** m F dog-Latin; **latino** *adj. a. su. m, a f* Latin; **latinoamericano** *adj. a. su. m,* **a** *f* Latin-American.

latir [3a] *(perro)* yelp, bark; *(corazón etc.)* beat, throb.

latitud f latitude *(a. fig.)*; *(anchura)* breadth; *(extensión)* area, extent; **lato** broad, wide.

latón m brass.

latrocinio m robbery, theft.

laúd *m* ♪ lute.
laudable laudable, praiseworthy.
laurear [1a] crown with laurel; **laurel** *m* laurel; *fig.* laurels.
lava *f* lava.
lavable washable; **lavabo** *m* washbasin; (*mesa*) washstand; (*cuarto*) lavatory; **lavadero** *m* laundry, washing place; **lavado** *m* wash(ing), laundry; ~ *cerebral*, ~ *de cerebro* brainwashing; ~ *químico* dry cleaning; ~ *de cabeza* shampoo; ~ *a seco* dry cleaning; **lavadora** *f* washing machine; ~ *de platos* dishwasher; **lavadura** *f* washing; (*agua*) dirty water; **lavamanos** *m* washbasin.
lavanda *f* lavender.
lavandera *f* laundress, washerwoman; **lavandería** *f* laundry; **lavaparabrisas** *m* ⊕ windshield washer; **lavaplatos** *m/f* ⊕ *p.* dishwasher; ⊕ dishwasher; **lavar** [1a] wash; ~se wash; ~ *las manos* wash one's hands (*a. fig.*); **lavativa** *f* enema; F annoyance, bother; **lavavajillas** *m* ⊕ dishwasher; **lavazas** *f/pl.* dishwater, slops.
laxante *adj. a. su. m* laxative; **laxar** ease; *vientre* loosen; **laxitud** *f* laxity; **laxo** lax, loose.
laya *f* spade; *fig.* kind, sort.
lazada *f* bow, knot; **lazar** [1f] lasso, rope; **lazo** *m* bow, knot, loop; lasso, lariat *para caballos etc.*; snare, trap.
le *acc.* him; (*Vd.*) you; *dat.* (to) him, (to) her, (to) it; (*a Vd.*) (to) you.
leal loyal, faithful; true; **lealtad** *f* loyalty.
lebrel *m* greyhound.
lección *f* lesson (*a. eccl., fig.*); reading *de MS etc.*
lecha *f* milt, (soft) roe; **lechada** *f* paste; (*cal*) whitewash; pulp *para papel*; **lechal** 1. sucking; 2. *m* milky juice; **leche** *f* milk; ~ *desnatada* skimmed milk; ~ *de magnesia* milk of magnesia; ~ *de manteca* buttermilk; ~ *en polvo* powdered milk; **lechecillas** *f/pl.* sweetbreads; **lechera** *f* dairymaid; (*vasija*) milk can; **lechería** *f* dairy, creamery; **lechero** 1. milk *attr.*, dairy *attr.*; 2. *m* dairyman; milkman.
lecho *m mst* bed; (*fondo*) bottom; ~ *de plumas* feather bed.
lechón *n*, **-a** *f* suckling pig; **lechoso** milky.
lechuga *f* lettuce; *sew.* frill.
lechuza *f* owl; ~ *común* barn-owl.

lectivo school *attr.*; **lector** *m*, **-a** *f* reader; foreign-language teacher; meter reader; ~ *mental* mind reader; lecturer; **lectura** *f* reading.
leer [2e] read; interpret; † lecture (*en*, *sobre* on).
legación *f* legation; **legado** *m* legate; ᵗᵗ legacy, bequest.
legal legal, lawful; *p.* trustworthy, truthful; **legalidad** *f* legality *etc.*; **legalizar** [1f] legalize.
legar [1h] ᵗᵗ bequeath (*a. fig.*), leave; **legatario** *m*, **a** *f* legatee.
legendario legendary.
legible legible, readable.
legión *f* legion (*a. fig.*).
legislación *f* legislation; **legislador** *m*, **-a** *f* legislator; **legislar** [1a] legislate; **legislativo** legislative.
legitimar [1a] legitimize; legalize; ~se prove one's identity; **legítimo** legitimate, rightful.
lego 1. lay; *fig.* ignorant, uninformed; 2. *m* layman; *los* ~s the laity.
legua *f* league; *a la* ~ far away.
legumbre *f* vegetable.
leíble legible; **leída** *f* reading; **leído** *p.* well-read.
lejanía *f* distance, remoteness; **lejano** distant, remote, far(-off).
lejía *f* lye; F dressing-down.
lejos 1. far (off, away); ~ *de* far from (*a. fig.*); *de inf.* from *ger.*); *de* ~, *desde* ~ from afar, from a distance; 2. *m* distant view; (*vislumbre*) glimpse; *paint.* background.
lelo silly, stupid.
lema *m* (*mote*) motto, device; theme; *pol. etc.* slogan.
lencería *f* draper's (shop); (*géneros*) linen, drapery; lingerie *para mujer*.
lengua *f* tongue (*a. fig.*); (*idioma*) language; ♪ clapper; *mala* ~ gossip, evil tongue; ~ *de tierra* point, neck of land; ~ *materna* mother tongue; *de* ~ *en* ~ from mouth to mouth; **lenguado** *m ichth.* sole; **lenguaje** *m* (*en general*) language, (faculty of) speech; (*modo de hablar*) idiom; diction; **lenguaraz** *b.s.* foulmouthed; **lenguaz** garrulous; **lengüeta** *f* tab; ♪, ⊕ tongue (*a. de zapato*); pointer *de balanza*; *anat.* epiglottis; barb *de saeta etc.*; **lengüetada** *f* lick.
lente *mst m* lens; ~s *pl.* glasses; ~ *de aumento* magnifying glass; ~ *de contacto* contact lens.
lenteja *f* lentil.
lentejuela *f* spangle, sequin.

lentillas *f/pl.* contact lenses.
lentitud *f* slowness; **lento** slow.
leña *f* firewood, sticks; F beating; **leñador** *m* woodcutter; **leño** *m* log; (*madera*) timber, wood; *fig.* blockhead; **leñoso** woody.
Leo *m ast.* Leo; **león** *m* lion (*a. ast. a. fig.*); *S.Am.* puma; ~ *marino* sealion; **leona** *f* lioness; **leonado** tawny; **leonera** *f* lion's cage *or* den; F gambling den.
leopardo *m* leopard.
leotardos *m/pl.* leotards.
lerdo dull, slow; clumsy *al moverse*.
les *acc.* them; (*Vds.*) you; *dat.* (to) them; (*a Vds.*) (to) you.
lesión *f* wound; injury (*a. fig.*); **lesionar** [1a] injure, hurt.
letal soporific; ⚕ deadly, lethal.
letanía *f* litany; *fig.* long list.
letargo *m* lethargy (*a. fig.*).
letra *f mst* letter; (*modo de escribir*) (hand)writing; ♪ words, lyric; ✝ *a.* bill, draft; ~s *pl.* letters, learning; ~s *pl. univ.* Arts; *bellas* ~s *pl.* literature; *primeras* ~s *pl.* elementary education, approx. three Rs; ✝~ *abierta* letter of credit; ✝~ *de cambio* bill (of exchange), draft; ~ *cursiva* script letters; ~ *gótica* black letter; ~s *pl. humanas* humanities; ~ *de imprenta typ.* type; ~ *de mano* handwriting; ~s *pl. de molde* print, printed letters; ~ *muerta* dead letter; ~s *pl. sagradas* scripture; ~ *negrilla typ.* boldface; ~ *redonda*, *redondilla typ.* roman.
letrado 1. learned; 2. *m* lawyer.
letrero *m* sign, notice; (*cartel*) placard; (*marbete*) label; (*palabras*) words; ~ *luminoso* illuminated sign.
leucemia *f* leukemia.
leva *f* ⚓ weighing anchor; ✕ levy; ⊕ cam; *mar de* ~ swell.
levadura *f* yeast, leaven.
levantamiento *m* raising *etc.*; (*sublevación*) (up)rising, revolt; ~ *del cadáver* inquest; ~ *del censo* census taking; ~ *de pesos* weight lifting; ~ *de planos* surveying; **levantar** [1a] raise, lift (up); ⚕ erect, build; (*recoger*) pick up; (*poner derecho*) straighten; *cerco*, *prohibición*, *tropa*, *voz* raise; *casa* (re)move; *caza* flush; *mesa* clear; *plano* draw (up); *sesión* adjourn; *testimonio* bear; *tienda* strike; *fig.* (*excitar*) rouse, stir up; (*animar*) hearten, uplift; ~**se** rise; get up *de cama*; (*ponerse de pie*) stand up; (*ponerse derecho*) straighten up

(*sublevarse*) rise, rebel; (*sobresalir*) stand out; ~ *con* make off with.
levante *m* east; east wind.
levantisco restless, turbulent.
levar [1a]: ~ *anclas* weigh anchor; ~**se** set sail.
leve light; *fig.* slight, trivial.
levita[1] *f* frock-coat.
levita[2] *m* Levite.
léxico 1. lexical; 2. *m* lexicon, dictionary; vocabulary; **lexicografía** *f* lexicography; **lexicógrafo** *m* lexicographer.
ley *f* law; *parl.* act, measure; (*regla*) rule; *fig.* loyalty, devotion; (*calidad*) (legal standard of) fineness; ~ *de Lynch* lynch law; ~ *marcial* martial law; ~ *del menor esfuerzo* line of least resistance; ~ *de la selva* law of the jungle; *a* ~ *de* on the word of; *de buena* ~ sterling, reliable; *de mala* ~ base, disreputable; *dar la* ~ set the tone; *tener* ~ *a* be devoted to.
leyenda *f* legend (*a. typ.*); inscription.
lezna *f* awl.
liar [1c] tie (up), wrap up; *cigarrillo* roll; F ~*las* beat it; (*morir*) kick the bucket; ~**se** *fig.* get involved (*con* with).
libar [1a] suck, sip; (*probar*) taste.
libelo *m* lampoon, libel (*contra* on).
libélula *f* dragonfly.
liberación *f* liberation, release; **liberado** ✝ paid up; **liberal** 1. liberal; generous; 2. *m/f* liberal; **liberalidad** *f* liberality.
libertad *f* liberty, freedom; ~ *de cátedra* academic freedom; ~ *de comercio* free trade; ~ *de cultos* freedom of worship; ~ *de empresa* free enterprise; ~ *de enseñanza* academic freedom; ~ *de imprenta* freedom of the press; ~ *de los mares* freedom of the seas; ~ *de palabra* freedom of speech; ~ *de reunión* freedom of assembly; ~ *vigilada* probation; *plena* ~ free hand; **libertador** *m*, **-a** *f* liberator; **libertar** [1a] set free, release, liberate (*de* from); (*eximir*) exempt; **libertinaje** *m* licentiousness; **libertino** 1. licentious; 2. *m* libertine.
libra *f* pound; ~ *esterlina* pound sterling; *ast.* ♎ Libra.
libraco *m* worthless book.
librador *m*, **-a** *f* ✝ drawer; **libramiento** *m* delivery, rescue; = **libranza** *f* ✝ draft, bill of exchange; *S.Am.* ~ *postal* money order; **librar**

[1a] save, free, deliver (de from); ⚖ exempt (de from); *confianza* place; *sentencia* pass; *batalla* join; (*expedir*) issue; ✝ draw; **~se:** ~ de get out of, escape; (*deshacerse de*) get rid of; **libre** *mst* free (de from); (*atrevido*) free, outspoken; *b.s.* loose; *aire* open.
librea *f* livery.
librería *f* (*tienda*) bookshop; ✝ bookselling, book-trade; (*biblioteca*) library; (*armario*) book case; ~ de viejo second-hand bookshop; **librero** *m* bookseller; bookshelf; **libresco** bookish; **libreta** *f* notebook; ✝ accountbook; **libreto** *m* libretto; **libro** *m* book; ~ de actas minute-book; ~ de apuntes notebook; ~ de caja cashbook; ~ de cocina cook book; ~ de cheques checkbook; ~ de chistes joke book; ~ de lance second-hand book; ~ de mayor venta best seller; ~ de oro guest book; ~ de recuerdos scrapbook; ~ de teléfonos telephone book; ~ mayor ledger; ~ de texto textbook; en rústica paperbound book; ~ talonario checkbook; hacer ~ nuevo turn over a new leaf.
licencia *f mst* licence; permission; ✕ *etc.* leave; *univ.* degree; ✕ ~ absoluta discharge; ~ de caza hunting license; de ~ on leave; **licenciado** *m*, **a** *f* licentiate, *approx.* bachelor; *S.Am.* lawyer; **licenciar** [1b] license, give a permit to; ✕ discharge; **~se** *univ.* graduate; **licenciatura** *f* degree; (*acto*) graduation; (*estudios*) degree course; **licencioso** licentious.
liceo *m* lyceum.
licitar [1a] bid for; *S.Am.* sell by auction; **lícito** lawful, legal; just; permissible.
licor *m* liquor, spirits; (*dulce*) liqueur; (*en general*) liquid; **~es** *pl.* espiritosos hard liquor.
lid *f* fight, contest.
líder *m* leader; leading; **liderar** *v/i.* lead; **liderato** *m* leadership; *deportes*: lead.
lidiar [1b] *v/t.* fight; *v/i.* fight (con, contra against).
liebre *f* hare; *fig.* coward.
lienzo *m* (un a piece of) linen; (*pañuelo*) handkerchief; *paint.* canvas.
liga *f* suspender, garter; (*faja*) band; *pol., deportes*: league; *metall.* alloy; (*mezcla*) mixture; ♀ mistletoe; *orn.* bird-lime; **ligatura** *f* tie, bond; ♪, ✿ ligature; **ligamento** *m* ligament; **ligar** [1h] tie, bind (a. *fig.*); *metall.*

alloy; (*unir*) join; ✿ ligature; **~se** band together.
ligereza *f* lightness *etc.*; (*dicho etc.*) indiscretion; **ligero** light; rapid, swift, agile; *té* weak; (*superficial*) slight; *carácter etc.* fickle; (*poco serio*) flippant; *v. casco*; a la ~a perfunctorily, quickly; without fuss.
lija *f ichth.* dogfish; ⊕ (a. papel de ~) sandpaper; **lijar** [1a] sandpaper.
lila 1. *f* ♀ lilac; **2.** *m* F boob, ninny.
lima¹ *f* ♀ lime; *jugo de ~* lime juice.
lima² *f* ⊕ file; *fig.* polish, finish; ~ para las uñas nail file; **limar** [1a] file; *fig.* polish; (*suavizar*) smooth.
limero *m* ♀ lime (tree).
limitación *f* limitation; **limitar** [1a] *v/t.* limit (a inf. to ger.); restrict; *v/i.*: ~ con border on, be bounded by; **límite** *m* limit; *geog.* boundary, border.
limo *m* slime, mud.
limón *m* lemon; **limonada** *f* lemonade; **limonero** lemon(-colored); **limonero** *m* ♀ lemon (tree).
limosna *f* alms, charity; **limosnero 1.** charitable; **2.** *m* beggar.
limpia 1. *f* cleaning *etc.*; **2.** *m* F bootblack; **~barros** *m* scraper; **~botas** *m* bootblack; **~chimeneas** *m* chimney sweep; **~dientes** *m* toothpick; **limpiadura** *f* cleaning; **~s** *pl.* scourings, dirt; **limpiaparabrisas** *m* windshield wiper; **limpiar** [1b] clean; cleanse (a. *fig.*); wipe con trapo; ♀ prune; *zapatos* polish, shine; F clean out en el juego; *sl.* swipe; ~ en seco dry-clean; **límpido** limpid; **limpieza** *f* (*acto*) cleaning *etc.*; (*calidad*) cleanness, (*a. hábito*) cleanliness; (*moral*) purity; (*destreza*) skill; fair play en juego; integrity, honesty; ~ de la casa house cleaning; ~ de sangre purity of blood; ~ en seco dry cleaning; hacer la ~ clean; **limpio** clean (a. *fig.*); pure; (*ordenado*) neat, tidy; juego fair (a. adv.).
limusina *f* limousine.
linaje *m* lineage, parentage, family; *fig.* class, sort; **~s** *pl.* (local) nobility.
linaza *f* linseed.
lince *m* lynx; *fig.* sharp-eyed (or shrewd) person.
linchar [1a] lynch.
lindante adjoining, bordering; **lindar** [1a] adjoin, border (con on); **linde** *m a. f* boundary; **lindero 1.** adjoining; **2.** *m* edge, border.
lindeza *f* prettiness *etc.*; (*dicho*) wit-

ticism; ~s *pl. iro.* insults; **lindo** pretty, fine (*a. iro.*); excellent; superb; F de lo ~ a lot, a good deal; wonderfully.

línea *f* line; figure *de p.*; (*contorno*) lines; (*linaje*) line; (*vía*) route; (*clase*) kind; ✕ ~s *pl.* lines; ✈ airline; ~ de flotación waterline; ~ de mira line of sight; ~ de montaje assembly line; ~ de puntos dotted line; ~ de tiro line of fire; ~ férrea railway; ~ internacional de cambio de fecha internacional date line; ✕ de ~ regular; en ~ in a row, in (a) line; en su ~ of its kind; en toda la ~ all along the line; leer entre ~s read between the lines; **lineal** linear; *dibujo* line *attr.*

linfa *f* lymph; **linfático** lymphatic.

lingote *m* ingot; *typ.* slug.

lingüística *f* linguistics; **lingüístico** linguistic.

lino *m* ♀ flax; (*tejido*) linen.

linóleo *m* linoleum.

linterna *f* lantern (*a.* △), lamp; ⚡ spotlight; ~ eléctrica flashlight.

lío *m* bundle, parcel, package; ⚓ truss; F mess, mix-up; F (*jaleo*) row, rumpus; F (*amorío*) affair; F armar un ~ make a fuss; F meterse en un ~ get into a jam; **liofilización** *f* freeze-drying; **liofilizar** [1f] *v/t.* freeze-dry.

liquidación *f* liquidation (*a. fig.*); settlement *de cuenta*; (*venta*) (clearance) sale; **liquidador** *m*, **-a** *f* liquidator; **liquidar** [1a] liquefy; ♗, *pol.*, *fig.* liquidate; ✝ *negocio* wind up; ✝ *cuenta* settle; **líquido** 1. liquid (*a. gr.*); ✝ net; 2. *m* liquid, fluid; ✝ net profit; ~ imponible net taxable income.

lira *f* lyre (*a. fig.*); **lírica** *f* lyrical poetry; **lírico** lyric(al); imaginary, utopian.

lirio *m* iris; lily; ~ de agua calla lily; ~ de los valles lily of the valley.

lirismo *m* lyricism; sentimentality; pipe dream.

lirón *m* dormouse; dormir como un ~ sleep like a log.

lisiado 1. injured; (*tullido*) crippled; 2. *m*, **a** *f* cripple; 3. *m*: ~ de guerra disabled veteran; **lisiar** [1b] cripple, maim.

liso smooth, even; *pelo* straight; *fig.* plain; 400 metros ~s 400 meters flat.

lisonja *f* flattery; **lisonjear** [1a] flatter; (*agradar*) please, delight; **lisonjero** 1. flattering; pleasing; 2. *m*, **a** *f* flatterer.

lista *f* list; catalogue; ✕ roll(call); (*tiro*) strip; slip *de papel*; stripe *de color*; ~ de correos general delivery; ~ (de platos) menu; ~ de precios price list; pasar ~ call the roll; **listado** striped.

listo ready (*para* for); (*avisado*) clever, smart, sharp.

listón *m* ribbon; △ lath.

lisura *f* smoothness *etc.*; *fig.* naïvety.

litera *f* litter; ⚓, 🚆 berth.

literal literal; **literario** literary; **literata** *f* literary lady; *contp.* bluestocking; **literato** *m* man of letters; **literatura** *f* literature.

litigación *f* litigation; **litigante** *adj. a. su. m/f* litigant; **litigar** [1h] go to law; *fig.* dispute, argue; **litigio** *m* lawsuit, litigation; *fig.* dispute.

litoral *adj. a. su. m* seaboard, litoral.

litro *m* liter.

liturgia *f* liturgy.

liviandad *f* fickleness *etc.*; **liviano** 1. *fig.* fickle; frivolous; (*lascivo*) wanton; 2. ~s *m/pl.* lights, lungs.

lívido livid, (black and) blue.

living ['lißin] *m* living-room.

llaga *f* ulcer, sore (*a. fig.*); (*herida*) wound; affliction; **llagar** [1h] wound, injure.

llama[1] *f* flame; *fig.* passion.

llama[2] *zo.* llama.

llamada *f* call (*a.* ✕, *teleph.*); ring (*or* knock) at the door; (*ademán*) signal, gesture; *typ.* reference (mark); **llamado** so-called; **llamamiento** *m* call; **llamar** [1a] *v/t.* call (*a. fig. a. teleph.*); (*convocar*) call, summon; (*invocar*) call upon (*a inf.* to *inf.*); (*atraer*) draw, attract; *v/i.* call; knock, ring *a puerta*; ~se be called; ¿cómo te llamas? what is your name?

llamarada *f* flare-up, blaze; flush *de cara*; *fig.* outburst, flash.

llamativo gaudy, flashy, showy.

llamear [1a] blaze, flare.

llana *f* △ trowel; = **llanada** *f* plain, level ground; **llanero** *m*, **a** *f* plaindweller; **llaneza** *f* plainness, simplicity; modesty; (*familiaridad*) informality; **llano** 1. level, smooth, even; (*sin adorno*) plain, simple; (*claro*) clear, plain; (*sin dificultad*) straightforward; *gr.* paroxytone; a la ~a simply; de ~ openly, clearly; 2. *m* plain, level ground.

llanta *f* rim (*of wheel*); (*neumático*) tyre; ~ de oruga track.

llanto *m* weeping, crying.

llanura f flatness etc.; plain.
llave f key (a. fig.); (gas- etc.) tap; ⚡ switch; ⊕ spanner; ⊕ key; ♪ stop; ✕, *lucha*: lock; ~ de caja, ~ cubo socket wrench; ~ de caño, ~ para tubos pipe wrench; ~ de cierre stopcock; mot. ~ de contacto ignition key; ~ de estufa damper; ~ de mandíbulas dentadas alligator wrench; ~ de paso stopcock; passkey; ~ inglesa (monkey) wrench; ~ maestra skeleton key, master key; bajo ~, debajo de ~ under lock and key; echar la ~ (a) lock up; **llavero** m key ring; (p.) turnkey; **llavín** m latch key.
llegada f arrival, coming; **llegar** [1h] v/t. bring up, draw up; v/i. arrive (a at), come; (alcanzar) reach; (suceder) happen; (bastar) be enough; ~ a reach; (importar) amount to; (igualar) be equal to; ~ a inf. reach the point of ger.; (lograr) manage to inf.; ~ a saber find out; ~ a ser become; hacer ~ el dinero make both ends meet; ~se approach, come near.
llenar [1a] fill, stuff (de with); espacio, tiempo occupy, take up; hoja fill in (or up, out Am.); (cumplir) fulfil; (satisfacer) satisfy; (colmar) overwhelm (de with); ~ de insultos heap insults upon; ~se fill up; F stuff o.s.; fig. get cross; ~ de polvo get covered in dust; **lleno** 1. full (de of), filled (de with); de ~ fully, entirely; 2. m fill, plenty; fig. perfection; thea. full house.
llevadero bearable; **llevar** [1a] carry (a. Ⓧ); p., cosa take (a to); p. lead (a to); casa, cuentas keep; armas, frutos, nombre bear; ropa wear; tiempo spend; precio charge; dirección follow, keep to; vida lead; premio carry off; (cercenar) take off; (aguantar) bear, stand; (dirigir) manage; ~ p.p. have (already) p.p.; llevo escritas 3 cartas I have written 3 letters; ~ mucho tiempo ger. have been ger. a long time; ¿cuánto tiempo llevas aquí? how long have you been here?; te llevo 3 años I am 3 years older than you; ~ adelante push ahead with; ~ consigo, ~ encima carry, have with one; F ~la hecha have got it all worked out; ~ las de perder be in a bad way; ~ lo mejor (peor) get the best (worst) of it; ~ puesto wear, have on; no ~ las todas consigo have the wind up; ~se algo take away, carry off; ~ bien con get on with.

llorar [1a] v/t. weep for, cry over; lament; muerte mourn; v/i. cry, weep; **lloriquear** [1a] snivel, whimper; **lloriqueo** m whimper, whimpering; **llorón** 1. snivelling, whining; 2. m, -a f cry-baby; **lloroso** tearful, sad.
llovedizo techo leaky; **llover** [2h] rain (a. fig.); como llovido unexpectedly; llueva o no rain or shine; como quien oye ~ quite unmoved; **llovizna** f drizzle; **lloviznar** [1a] drizzle; **lluvia** f rain; (cantidad) rainfall; (agua) rainwater; fig. shower; mass; hail de balas; ~ radiactiva fallout, radioactive fallout; **lluvioso** rainy.
lo 1. the, that which is etc.; ~ bueno the good, goodness; ~ ... que how; no sabe ~ grande que es he doesn't know how big it is; ~ mío what is mine; no ~ hay there isn't any; a veces no se traduce: ~ sé I know; v. que; 2. pron. (p.) him; (cosa) it.
loable praiseworthy, commendable; **loar** [1a] praise.
lobanillo m growth, tumor.
lobo m wolf; ~ de mar sea dog, old salt; ~ marino seal; ~ solitario fig. lone wolf; gritar ¡el ~! cry wolf; F pillar un ~ get drunk.
lóbrego murky, gloomy; **lobreguez** f murk, gloom(iness).
lóbulo m lobe.
local 1. local; 2. m premises, rooms; (sitio) site, scene; place; **localidad** f locality; thea. etc. seat; **localizar** [1f] locate; (limitar) localize.
loción f lotion; (acto) wash; ~ facial shaving lotion.
loco 1. mad; (disparatado) wild; ⊕ loose; ~ por mad about (or on); volver ~ drive s.o. mad; volverse ~ go mad; 2. m, -a f madman etc., lunatic.
locomoción f locomotion; **locomotora** f locomotive, engine; ~ de maniobras shifting engine.
locuacidad f loquacity etc.; **locuaz** loquacious, talkative, voluble; **locución** f expression; diction.
locuelo m, -a f madcap; **locura** f madness, lunacy; ~s pl. folly.
locutor m, -a f radio: announcer, commentator; **locutorio** m eccl. parlor; teléfono phone booth.
lodazal m muddy place, quagmire; **lodo** m mud, mire; **lodoso** muddy.
logaritmo m logarithm.

L

lógica f logic; **lógico 1.** logical; es ~ (que) it stands to reason (that); **2.** m logician.

lograr [1a] get, obtain; attain, achieve; ~ inf. succeed in ger., manage to inf.; ~ que una p. haga get s.o. to do; **logrero** m moneylender, usurer; S.Am. sponger; **logro** m achievement etc.; ✝ profit; b.s. usury; a ~ at usurious rates.

loma f hillock, low ridge.

lombriz f (earth)worm; ~ de tierra earthworm; ~ solitaria tape worm.

lomo m anat. back; (carne) loin; ✗ balk, ridge; shoulder de colina; spine de libro; ~s pl. ribs.

lona f canvas, sail cloth.

lonche m S.Am. lunch.

lonchería f S.Am. snack bar.

longaniza f pork sausage.

longevidad f longevity; **longevo** aged.

longitud f length; geog. longitude; ~ de onda wavelength; **longitudinal** longitudinal; **longitudinalmente** lengthwise.

lonja[1] f slice; rasher de tocino etc.

lonja[2] f ✝ exchange, market; (tienda) grocer's (shop).

lontananza f paint. background; en ~ in the distance (or background).

loro m parrot.

los, las 1. artículo: the; **2.** pron. them; **3.** pron. relativo: ~ de those of; ~ de Juan John's; ~ de casa those at home; v. que.

losa f stone slab, flagstone; ~ (sepulcral) tombstone; (trampa) trap.

lote m portion, share; ✝ lot; **lotería** f lottery.

loto m lotus.

loza f crockery; ~ fina china(ware).

lozanear [1a] ⚥ flourish; (p.) be full of life; **lozanía** f luxuriance; vigor, liveliness; (orgullo) pride; **lozano** ⚥ lush, luxuriant; p., animal vigorous; (orgulloso) proud.

lubri(fi)cación f lubrication; **lubri(fi)cante** adj. a. su. m lubricant; **lubri(fi)car** [1g] lubricate.

lucera f skylight.

lucerna f chandelier.

lucero m bright star, esp. Venus; ~ del alba morning star.

lucha f fight, struggle (por for); conflict; fig. dispute; deportes: ~ (libre) wrestling; ~ de clases class struggle; ~ de la cuerda tug of war; **luchador** m,

-a f fighter; wrestler; **luchar** [1a] fight, struggle (por for; por inf. to inf.); deportes: wrestle.

lúcido lucid, clear.

lucido splendid, brilliant; elegant; gallant, generous; successful.

luciente bright, shining.

luciérnaga f glowworm.

lucimiento m brilliance; show; dash; (éxito) success.

lucio[1] m ichth. pike.

lucio[2] bright, shining.

lucir [3f] v/t. show off, display, sport; v/i. shine (a. fig.); (joyas etc.) glitter, sparkle; cut a dash con vestido etc.; ~se dress up; fig. shine.

lucrativo lucrative, profitable; **lucro** m profit.

luctuoso mornful, sad.

luego immediately; (después) then, next; (dentro de poco) presently, later (on); ~ que as soon as; ¿y ~? what next?; desde ~ of course, naturally; hasta ~ see you later.

lugar m place, spot; position; (espacio) room; (pueblo) village; fig. reason (para for), cause; opportunity; retrete toilet, water closet; ~ de cita tryst; ~ común platitude, commonplace; ~ religioso place of burial; ~es pl. estrechos close quarters; en ~ de instead of; en primer ~ in the first place, firstly; for one thing; en su ~ in his place; fuera de ~ out of place; dar ~ a give rise to; dejar ~ a permit of; hacer ~ para make way (or room) for; tener ~ take place; **lugareño 1.** village attr.; **2.** m, a f village.

luge f trineo luge.

lúgubre mournful, dismal.

lujo m luxury; fig. profusion; de ~ de luxe, luxury attr.; **lujoso** luxurious; showy; **lujuria** f lust, lechery; **lujuriar** [1b] lust; **lujurioso** lustful, lewd.

lumbago m lumbago.

lumbre f fire; (luz, para cigarrillo, ⚛) light; brilliance; ⚛ skylight; ~s pl. tinderbox; **lumbrera** f luminary (a. fig.); ⚛ skylight; ⊕ vent; **luminoso** luminous, bright; idea bright.

luna f moon; (cristal) plate glass; (espejo) mirror; (lente) lens; ~ llena full moon; media ~ half moon; ~ de miel honeymoon; ~ nueva new moon; **lunar 1.** lunar; **2.** m spot, mole; (defecto) flaw, blemish; ~ postizo beauty spot; **lunático** lunatic.

lunes m Monday.

luneta *f* lens; *thea.* stall; ~ *trasera mot.* rear window.
lunfardo *m* *S.Am.* thieves' slang.
lupa *f* magnifying glass.
lupanar *m* brothel.
lúpulo *m* ♣ hop; hops.
lustrabotas *m* shoeshine boy.
lustrar [1a] shine, polish; **lustre** *m* polish, shine, gloss; *esp. fig.* lustre; ~ *para metales* metal polish; *dar* ~ *a* polish; **lustroso** glossy, bright.
luto *m* mourning; sorrow, grief.
luz *f* light (*a.* ⚡, *fig.*); *luces pl. fig.* enlightenment; intelligence; *luces*

pl. de carretera bright lights; ~ *de costado,* ~ *de situación* side light; *luces pl. de cruce* dimmers; *luces pl. de estacionamiento* parking lights; *luces pl. de tráfico* traffic lights; *a la* ~ *de* in the light of; *a todas luces* anyway; everywhere; *entre dos luces* at twilight; F mellow; *dar a* ~ give birth (*v/t.* to); *fig.* publish; ~ *de balizaje* ⚓ marker light; ~ *de magnesio* *phot.* flash bulb; ~ *de matrícula* license plate light; ~ *de parada* stop light; ~ *trasera* tail light; *mot.* *poner a media* ~ dim; *sacar a* ~ bring to light; *salir a* ~ come to light; (*libro*) appear.

M

macabro macabre.
macadán *m* macadam; **macadamizar** [1f] macadamize.
macana *f* *S.Am.* club; F (*disparate*) silly thing; F (*cuento*) fib, tale.
maceta *f* ♣ flower-pot.
machaca *m/f* (*p.*) pest, bore; **machacar** [1g] *v/t.* pound, crush, mash; F *precio* slash; *v/i.* go on, keep on; nag; **machacón 1.** tiresome; **2.** *m*, **-a** *f* pest, bore.
machado *m* hatchet.
machete *m* machete.
machihembrar [1a] ⊕ dovetail.
machismo *m* machismo; **macho 1.** *biol.,* ⊕ male; *fig.* strong, tough; **2.** *m* male; mule; *v. cabrío*; ⚥ pin; ⊕ pin, peg; (*martillo*) sledge(-hammer); *sew.* hook; F dolt; **machón** *m* buttress; **machote** *m* *sl.* he-man, tough guy.
machucar [1g] bruise.
machucho elderly; wise beyond one's years, prudent; sedate.
macilento wan, haggard.
macis *f* mace (*spice*).
macizo 1. massive; (*bien construido*) stout; *neumático, oro etc.* solid (*a. fig.*); **2.** *m* geog. mass(if); ⚘ bed.
macro... macro...
mácula *f* stain, blemish; ~ *solar* sunspot.
madeja *f* skein, hank *de lana*; mass.
madera *f* wood; (*trozo*) piece of wood; ~ (*de construcción*) timber; ~ *contrachapeada* plywood; ~ *de deriva* driftwood; *de* ~ wood(en); **maderaje** *m*, **maderamen** *m* woodwork,

timbering; **madero** *m* beam; F blockhead.
madrastra *f* stepmother; **madre** *f* mother (*a. attr., eccl., fig.*); *anat.* womb; bed *de río*; (*residuo*) sediment, dregs; *fig.* cradle *de civilización etc.*; *juegos:* la ~ home; ~ *adoptiva* foster mother; ~ *de leche* wet nurse; ~ *patria* mother country, old country; ~ *política* mother-in-law; *sin* ~ motherless; *salirse de* ~ overflow; **~selva** *f* honeysuckle.
madriguera *f* den (*a. fig.*).
madrileño *adj. a. su. m,* **a** *f* (native) of Madrid.
madrina *f* godmother; *fig.* patroness; ~ *de boda* bridesmaid.
madroño *m* strawberry tree.
madrugada *f* early morning; (*alba*) daybreak; *de* ~ early; *las 3 de la* ~ three o'clock in the morning; **madrugador 1.** that gets up early; **2.** *m*, **-a** *f* early riser, early bird; **madrugar** [1h] get up early; *fig.* get ahead.
madurar [1a] *v/t.* ripen; *fig.* mature; *p.* toughen (up), season; *proyecto etc.* think out; *v/i.* ripen; *fig.* mature; **madurez** *f* ripeness; *fig.* maturity; **maduro** ripe; *fig.* mature; *de edad ya* ~*a* middle-aged.
maestra *f* teacher (*a. fig.*); ~ (*de escuela*) schoolteacher; **maestre** *m* *hist.* (grand) master; **maestría** *f* maestry; masterliness; **maestro 1.** masterly; main, principal; *llave, obra etc.* master *attr.*; **2.** *m* master (*a. fig.*); ~ (*de escuela*) schoolteacher; ♪ maestro; ~ *de capilla* choirmaster; ~

de ceremonias master of ceremonies; ~ de equitación riding master; ~ de obras (dueño) (master) builder; foreman.

mafia f (a. fig.) Mafia.

magia f magic; **mágico** 1. magic, magical; 2. m magician.

magín m F fancy, imagination.

magisterio m (arte) teaching; teaching profession; (ps.) teachers; **magistrado** m magistrate; **magistral** magisterial; fig. masterly; authoritative.

magnético magnetic; **magnetismo** m magnetism; **magnetizar** [1f] magnetize; **magneto** f magneto; **magnetofón** m tape recorder; **magnetofónico** tape attr., recording attr.; **magnetoscopio** m video recorder.

magnificencia f magnificence, splendour; **magnificar** [1g] opt. magnify; **magnífico** splendid, wonderful, superb, magnificent; ¡~! splendid!; **magnitud** f magnitude (a. ast.); **magno** lit. great.

magra f slice; **magro** lean.

magulladura f bruise; **magullar** [1a] ✝ bruise; batter, bash, mangle.

maitines m/pl. matins.

maíz m corn; comer ~ Cuba, P.R. to accept bribes; **maizal** m cornfield.

majada f sheep fold; (estiércol) dung; **majadería** f silliness; **majadero** 1. silly; 2. m idiot.

majar [1a] pound, grind, mash.

majestad f majesty; stateliness.

mal 1. adj. = malo; 2. adv. badly; (difícilmente) hardly; (equivocadamente) wrong(ly); de ~ en peor from bad to worse; 3. m evil, wrong; (calamidad) evil; (daño) harm, hurt, damage; (desgracia) misfortune; ✝ disease; illness; ~ caduco epilepsy; ~ de la tierra homesickness; ~ de mar seasickness; ~ de ojo evil eye; ~ de rayos radiation sickness; ~ de vuelo airsickness; hacer ~ (a) harm, hurt; parar en ~ come to a bad end.

malabarista m/f juggler.

malandante unfortunate.

malaria f malaria.

malaventura f misfortune; **malaventurado** unfortunate.

malbaratar [1a] ✝ sell off cheap; fig. squander.   [**a** f malcontent.]

malcontento 1. discontented; 2. m,

malcriado ill-bred, coarse.

maldad f evil, wickedness.

maldecir [approx. 3p] v/t. curse; (difamar) = v/i.: ~ de run down, disparage; **maldiciente** 1. slanderous; 2. m slanderer; **maldición** f curse; ¡~! damn!; **maldito** damned (a. eccl.); (malo) wicked; no saber ~a la cosa de not to have the ghost of an idea of; ¡~ sea! damn it!

maleante 1. wicked; 2. m/f crook, hoodlum.

malecón m levee, dike, mole, jetty.

maledicencia f slander, scandal.

maleficio m curse, spell; **maléfico** evil, harmful.

malestar m ✝ discomfort; fig. uneasiness, malaise; pol. unrest.

maleta 1. f (suit)case; mot. trunk; hacer la(s) ~(s) pack; 2. m F bungler; thea. ham; **maletín** m valise, satchel.

malevolencia f malevolence, spite, ill-will; **malévolo** malevolent.

maleza f weeds, underbrush.

malgastar [1a] squander; tiempo waste.

malhablado foul-mouthed.

malhadado ill-starred, ill-fated.

malhecho m misdeed; **malhechor** m, -a f evil-doer, malefactor.

malhumorado cross, bad-tempered, peevish.

malicia f (maldad) wickedness; (astucia) slyness; mischief de niño etc.; (mala intención) malice, maliciousness; **malicioso** wicked; sly; mischievous; malicious.

malignidad f malignancy etc.; **maligno** malignant (a. ✝), malicious; influjo etc. evil, pernicious.

malla f mesh; network.

malo 1. mst bad; niño naughty, mischievous; (equivocado) wrong; ✝ ill; ~ de inf. hard to inf.; estar de ~as be out of luck; venir de ~as have evil intentions; 2. m thea. villain.

malogrado abortive, ill-fated; **malograr** [1a] waste; ~se fail; **malogro** m failure; (muerte) untimely end; waste de tiempo etc.

malparir [3a] have a miscarriage; **malparto** m miscarriage.

malquerencia f dislike; **malquistar** [1a] alienate; ~se become alienated; **malquisto** disliked.

malsano unhealthy; mente morbid; ✝ moral corrupt.

malsufrido impatient.

malta f malt.
maltratamiento m maltreatment;
maltratar [1a] ill-treat, maltreat;
maltrato m maltreatment etc.;
maltrecho battered.
malva f ♀ mallow; ~ *loca*, ~ *rósea*
hollyhock; (de) *color de* ~ mauve.
malvado wicked, villainous.
malvarrosa f hollyhock; **malvavisco** m ♀ marsh mallow.
malversación f embezzlement;
graft; **malversador** m embezzler;
malversar [1a] embezzle.
mamá f, **mamaíta** f F mummy,
mum, mamma.
mamar [1a] suck; fig. learn as a
child; (a. ~se) F destino wangle, land;
recursos milk; fondos pocket; susto
have; dar de ~ a feed; ~se F get tight;
~ a uno get the best of s.o.
mamífero 1. mammalian; 2. m
mammal.
mamón m ♀ sucker; zo. suckling;
Mex. baby bottle.
mampara f screen.
mampostería f △ masonry.
maná m manna.
manada f ♂ flock, herd; (de
lobos; F crowd; **manadero** m shepherd.
manantial 1. flowing, running; 2. m
spring; fig. source; **manar** [1a] v/t.
flow with; v/i. flow; fig. abound.
manceba f mistress, concubine; mistress; **mancebía** f brothel; wild
oats; **mancebo** m youth.
mancha f zo. etc. spot, mark; spot,
fleck en diseño; (suciedad) spot, stain;
smear; blot, smudge de tinta; fig.
stain en reputación; (defecto) blemish; (terreno) patch; ~ solar sunspot;
manchado spotty, smudgy etc., esp.
animal dappled, spotted; esp. ave
pied; **manchar** [1a] spot, mark;
(ensuciar) soil, stain; fig. stain,
tarnish.
mancilla f stain, spot; dishonor.
manco one-handed, one-armed; (en
general) crippled, lame.
mancomún: de ~ (con)jointly;
mancomunar [1a] recursos pool;
intereses combine; ~se merge, combine; ~ en associate in; **mancomu-
nidad** f pool; association; pol. com-
monwealth.
manda f bequest; **mandadero** m, a f
messenger; (m) errand boy; **mandado** m order; commission, errand;
ir a los ~s run errands; **manda-**

miento m order; eccl. command-
ment; ✝ writ, warrant; **mandar**
[1a] 1. v/t. order (inf. to inf.); (gobernar) rule (over); (acaudillar) lead,
command; (enviar) send; ~ a distancia remote-control; 2. v/i. be in command (or control); b.s. boss (people
about); 3. ~se △ communicate (con
with); ♂ get around (by o.s.); **mandarín** m mandarin; contp. jack-in-
office; **mandarina** f tangerine;
mandatario adj. a. su. m manda-
tory; **mandato** m order; pol. etc.
mandate; term de presidente; ✝ writ.
mandíbula f jaw, jawbone.
mando m command, rule, control;
leadership; ⊕ ~s pl. controls; ⊕ de ~
control attr.; alto ~ high command; ~
a distancia remote control; ~ a punta
de dedo finger-tip control; ~ por botón
push-button control.
mandón bossy, domineering.
manear [1a] hobble.
manecilla f ⊕ pointer, hand.
manejable manageable; herramienta
etc. handy; **manejar** [1a] manage,
handle (a. fig.); máquina a. work,
run, operate; S.Am. coche drive; ~se
♂ get around; **manejo** m management, handling etc.; b.s. intrigue;
stratagem.
manera f way, manner; ~s pl. manners de p.; a la ~ de in (or after)
the manner of; de esta ~ (in) this
way, like this; de otra ~ otherwise;
de ~ que so that; de todas ~s at any
rate.
manga f sleeve; (de riego) hose,
hose-pipe; ✈ wind-sock; ⚓ beam; ~
(de agua) cloudburst, ⚓ waterspout;
bridge: game; ~ de viento whirlwind;
F de ~ in league; de ~ ancha indulgent;
b.s. not overscrupulous; sl. pegar las
~s kick the bucket.
manganeso m manganese.
mango[1] m ♀ mango.
mango[2] m handle; **mangonear** [1a]:
F ~ meddle in; dabble in.
manguera f hose; waterspout; corral; tubo de ventilación funnel.
manguito m muff; ⊕ sleeve; ~ incandescente gas mantle.
manía f mania; fig. mania, rage,
craze (de for); (capricho) whim; (rareza) fad, peculiarity; ~ persecutoria
persecution mania; **maníaco** 1.
maniac(al); 2. m, a f maniac.
maniatar [1a] tie s.o.'s hands.
maniático 1. maniacal; fig. crazy;

(*testarudo*) stubborn; (*raro*) eccentric; 2. *m*, *a f* maniac; *fig.* eccentric; **manicomio** *m* mental hospital.

manicura *f* manicure; **manicuro** *m*, *a f* (*p.*) manicurist.

manifestación *f* manifestation; show; declaration; *pol.* demonstration; **manifestante** *m/f* demonstrator; **manifestar** [1k] show; (*por palabra*) declare, express, state; ~**se** show, be manifest; *pol.* demonstrate; ~ en be evident in; **manifiesto** 1. clear, evident; *verdad* manifest; *error etc.* glaring; *obstinacy*; *poner de* ~ make clear; 2. *m* ⚓ manifest; *pol.* manifesto.

manilla *f* bracelet; (*grillete*) handcuff, manacle; hand *de reloj*; ~**s de hierro** handcuffs; **manillar** *m* handlebar.

maniobra *f* maneuver (*a. fig.*); *fig.* move; *b.s.* stratagem; ~**s** ⚔ maneuvers; ⛟ shunting; **maniobrar** [1a] maneuver.

manipulación *f* manipulation; **manipulador** *m*, **-a** *f* manipulator; **manipular** [1a] manipulate; *fig.* handle, manage.

maniquí 1. *m* dummy, manikin; *fig.* puppet; 2. *f* mannequin.

manivela *f* crank.

manjar *m* dish; tidbit, delicacy.

mano *f* hand; *zo.* foot; coat *de pintura*; *naipes*: ser ~ lead; *yo soy* ~ it's my lead; ~ de almirez pestle; ~**s** *pl.* muertas mortmain; ~ de obra labor; man power; ~ de papel quire; *i* ~**s** quietas! hands off!; *a* ~ by hand; *escribir* in longhand; *a* (*la*) ~ at hand, on hand, handy; *a* ~**s** de dirigir care of; *i arriba las* ~**s**! hands up!; *bajo* ~ in secret, behind the scenes; *de la* ~ llevar by the hand; *de primera* ~ at first hand; *de segunda* ~ second-hand; *de* ~**s** a boca suddenly, unexpectedly; *de* ~**s** de at the hands of; *recibir* from; *entre* ~**s** in hand, on hand; *i fuera las* ~**s**! hands off!; *echar una* ~ lend a hand; *naipes etc.*: play a game (de of); *estrechar la* ~ a shake *s.o.*'s hand; *hecho a* ~ hand-made; *untar la* ~ a grease *s.o.*'s palm; *venir a las* ~**s** come to blows; *vivir de la* ~ a la boca live from hand to mouth.

manojo *m* handful, bunch.

manómetro *m* gauge.

manoseado *fig.* hackneyed; **manosear** [1a] handle, finger; (*ajar*) rumple; *b.s.* paw, fiddle with.

manotada *f*, **manotazo** *m* slap, smack; **manotear** [1a] *v/t.* slap, smack; *v/i.* gesticulate, use one's hands; **manoteo** *m* gesticulation.

mansalva: *a* ~ without risk.

mansedumbre *f* mildness *etc.*; **manso** mild, gentle; *animal* tame.

manta *f* blanket; ~ (de viaje) rug; F hiding; ~ de coche lap robe; F tirar de la ~ let the cat out of the bag; **mantear** [1a] toss in a blanket.

manteca *f* fat; *esp.* ~ (de cerdo) lard; ~ (de vaca) butter; **mantecado** *m* approx. ice cream.

mantel *m* tablecloth; **mantelería** *f* table-linen; **mantelillo** *m* table-runner.

mantener [2l] keep *en equilibrio etc.*; ⚓ *etc.* hold up, support; (*alimentar*) sustain; ⊕ maintain, service; *opinión* maintain; *costumbre, relaciones etc.* keep up; ~**se** sustain o.s., subsist (de on); *fig.* stand firm; ~ (en vigor) stand; **mantenimiento** *m* sustenance; maintenance *etc.*

mantequera *f* churn; butter-dish *de mesa*; **mantequería** *f* dairy, creamery; **mantequilla** *f* butter.

mantilla *f* mantilla; ~**s** *pl.* swaddling clothes.

manto *m* cloak (*a. fig.*); *eccl.*, ⚖ robe, gown; ~ (de chimenea) mantel; **mantón** *m* shawl.

manuable handy; **manual** 1. manual, hand *attr.*; (*manuable*) handy; 2. *m* manual, handbook; **manubrio** *m* handle, crank; winch.

manufactura *f* manufacture; (*edificio*) factory; **manufacturar** [1a] manufacture; **manufacturero** 1. manufacturing; 2. *m* manufacturer.

manuscrito 1. hand-written, manuscript; 2. *m* manuscript.

manutención *f* maintenance (*a.* ⊕).

manzana *f* apple; ⚓ block; ~ silvestre crab, crab apple; **manzano** *m* apple (tree).

maña *f* (*en general*) skill, ingenuity; *b.s.* guile, craft; (*una* ~) trick, knack; *b.s.* evil habit.

mañana 1. *f* morning; *de* ~, *por la* ~ in the morning; *muy de* ~ early in the morning; 2. *m*: el ~ the morrow, the future; 3. *adv.* tomorrow; ~ *por la* ~ tomorrow morning; *i hasta* ~! see you tomorrow!; *pasado* ~ the day after tomorrow.

mañoso skilful, clever; *b.s.* wily.

mapa *m* map.

mapache *m* rac(c)oon.

maque *m* lacquer; **maquear** [1a] lacquer.

maqueta *f* model.

maquillador *m thea.* make-up man; **maquillaje** *m* make-up; **maquillar(se)** [1a] make up.

máquina *f* machine (*a. fig.*); ⚙ engine, locomotive; ~ (*fotográfica*) camera; F bicycle; *mot.* F car; ⚓ palace, building; ⚙ scheme (of things), machinery; (*proyecto*) scheme; ~ *de afeitar* (safety) razor; ⚡ electric razor; ~ *de coser* sewing machine; ~ *de escribir* typewriter; ~ *herramienta* machine tool; ~ *de sumar* adding machine; ~ *sacaperras* slot machine; ~ *de vapor* steam engine; *a toda* ~ at full speed; *acabar* (*or coser etc.*) *a* ~ machine; *escribir a* ~ type; *hecho a* ~ machine-made; *typ.* typed; **maquinación** *f* machination, plot; **maquinador** *m*, **-a** *f* schemer; **maquinal** mechanical (*a. fig.*); **maquinar** [1a] plot; **maquinaria** *f* machinery; plant; **maquinista** *m* ⚙ operator, machinist; ⚓ *etc.* engineer; ⚙ engine driver, engineer.

mar *m a. f* sea; ~ *de fondo* (ground-) swell; F *la* ~ *adv.* a lot; F *la* ~ *de* lots of, no end of; *al* ~ *caer etc.* overboard; *a* ~*es* copiously; *en alta* ~ on the high seas; *por* ~ by sea; *hacerse a la* ~ put to sea; ~ *alta* rough sea; ~ *ancha* high seas; ~ *bonanza* calm sea; ~ *de nubes* cloud bank; ~ *llena* high tide.

maraña *f* ♠ thicket; (*enredo*) tangle; *fig.* puzzle, trick.

maravilla *f* marvel, wonder; ♠ marigold; *a* ~, *a las mil* ~*s* wonderfully, extremely well; **maravillar** [1a] surprise, amaze; ~*se* wonder, marvel (*de* at); **maravilloso** marvellous, wonderful.

marbete *m* label; tag, docket.

marca *f* mark(ing); stamp; (*fabricación*) make, brand; ♣ landmark; ♣ beat; *naipes:* bid; *deportes:* record; *hist.* march(es); ~ *de agua* watermark; ~ *de fábrica*, ~ *registrada* (registered) trademark; ~ *de reconocimiento* ♣ landmark, seamark; ~ *de taquilla* box-office record; *de* ~ outstanding; *de* ~ *mayor* most outstanding; **marcado** marked, pronounced; *acento* strong, broad; **marcador** *m* marker (*a. billar*); *deportes:* (*p.*) scorer; (*tanteador*) score-

board; **marcapasos** *m* ♥ pacemaker; **marcar** [1g] **1.** *v/t.* (*poner señal a*) mark; stamp, brand; *terreno etc.* mark out; (*señalar*) point out; (*reloj etc.*) show; (*termómetro etc.*) read, say; (*aplicar*) designate; ♪ *compás* keep, beat; *paso* mark; *deportes:* score; *teleph.* dial; **2.** *v/i. deportes:* score; *teleph.* dial.

marcha *f* ✕, ♪ *a. fig.* march; ⊕ running, functioning; ⊕ (~ *atrás etc.*) gear; *fig.* progress; (*tendencia*) trend, course; (*velocidad*) speed; ⊕ *primera* ~ low gear; ~ *atrás* reverse (gear); *dar* ~ *atrás a*, *poner en* ~ *atrás coche etc.* reverse; ~ *forzada* forced march; ~ *nupcial* wedding march; *a toda* ~ (at) full blast; *en* ~ in motion, going; ♣ *etc.* under way; *¡en* ~! ✕ forward march!; *let's go!*; *fig.* here goes!; (*a otro*) get going!; *sobre la* ~ immediately; *cerrar la* ~ bring up the rear; *poner en* ~ start; *fig.* set going; *ponerse en* ~ start.

marchar [1a] (*caminar*) go; ✕ march; ⊕ go, run, work; *fig.* go, come along; ~*se* go (away), leave.

marchitar(se) [1a] wilt, wither; **marchito** withered; faded (*o fig.*).

marcial martial; *porte* military.

marco *m paint.*, ⚓ *etc.* frame; *fig.* setting; ♣ mark; standard *de pesos etc.*; ~ *de chimenea* chimney piece; *poner* ~ *a* paint. frame.

marea *f* tide; (*viento*) sea breeze; ~ *alta* high tide, high water; ~ *baja* low tide; ~ *creciente*, ~ *entrante* flood tide; ~ *menguante* ebb tide; ~ *muerta* neap tide; ~ *viva* spring tide; **mareado** ♣ sick; ♣ seasick; *fig.* dizzy; **marear** [1a] sail, navigate; *fig.* make *s.o.* cross; ~*se* to get seasick; **marejada** *f* swell, surge; *fig.* undercurrent; **mareo** *m* seasickness; **mareta** *f* surge (*a. fig.*).

marfil *m* ivory.

margarina *f* margarine.

margarita *f* ♠ daisy; *zo.* pearl; ~ (*impresora*) ⊕ *ordenador* daisy wheel.

margen 1. *mst m* border, edge; *typ.*, ♣ *etc.* margin; ~ *de error* margin of error; ~ *de seguridad* margin of safety; *al* ~ in the margin; *dar* ~ *para* give occasion for; F *dejar al* ~ leave out in the cold; **2.** *f* bank *de río etc.*; **marginal** marginal.

marica 1. *f orn.* magpie; **2.** *m* F

milksop; sissy; **maricón** *m* F sissy, pansy.

maridaje *m fig.* marriage; **marido** *m* husband.

mariguana *f* marijuana.

marimacho *m* F mannish woman.

marina *f* (*arte*) seamanship; (*buques*) shipping; ~ (*de guerra*) navy; *paint.* sea-piece; ~ *mercante* merchant navy; **marinero 1.** seaworthy; **2.** *m* seaman, sailor; ~ *de primera* able seaman; **marino 1.** sea *attr.*; marine Ⓤ; **2.** *m* seaman, sailor.

marioneta *f* marionette; *régimen* ~ puppet régime.

mariposa *f* butterfly; ~ (*nocturna*) moth; (*luz*) nightlight; **mariposear** [1a] flutter about; *fig.* act capriciously; (*amor*) flirt.

mariscal *m* blacksmith; ~ *de campo* fieldmarshal.

marisco *m* shellfish; ~s *pl.* seafood.

marítimo maritime; marine, sea *attr.*; *ciudad etc.* seaside *attr.*

marjal *m* moor; marsh, fen.

marmita *f* pot, kettle, boiler.

mármol *m* marble; **mármoreo** marble (*a. fig.*).

marmota *f* marmot; worsted cap; sleepyhead; ~ *de Alemania* hamster; ~ *de América* ground hog.

maroma *f* rope.

marqués *m* marquis; **marquesa** *f* marchioness.

marquesina *f* marquee; canopy.

marrana *f* sow; F slut; **marrano 1.** dirty; **2.** *m* pig; F dirty pig.

marrón maroon.

marrullero smooth, glib, plausible.

marsopa *f* porpoise.

martes *m* Tuesday; ~ *de carnaval* Shrove Tuesday, Mardi Gras.

martillar [1a] hammer; **martillear** [1a] ⊕ knock; **martillo** *m* hammer; gavel *de presidente*; (*subastas*) auction room; ~ *picador* pneumatic drill.

martín *m* **pescador** kingfisher.

martinete *m* △ pile-driver; ⊕ drop hammer; ♪ hammer.

mártir *m/f* martyr; **martirio** *m* martyrdom; **martirizar** [1f] torture.

marxismo *m* Marxism.

marzo *m* March.

más 1. *comp.* more; *sup.* most; (*y*) plus, and; (*más tiempo*) longer; (*más rápidamente*) faster; ~ *quiero inf.* I would rather *inf.*; ~ *bien* rather; ~ *de*, ~ *de lo que*, ~ *que* more than; (*poco*) ~ *o menos* more or less; *a* ~ in addition (de

to), besides (*de acc.*); *a lo* ~ at (the) most; *cuando* ~ at (the) most, at the outside; *de* ~ (*adicional*) extra; (*superfluo*) too much, too many; *v. estar*; *nada* ~ nothing else; that's all; *ni* ~ *ni menos* just; *no* ~ no more; *haber llegado etc.* just; *no* ... ~ no longer, not any more; *no* ~ *que* only; just; *¿qué* ~? what else?; what next?; **2.** *m* Å plus (sign).

mas *lit.* but.

masa[1] *f* (*pasta*) dough.

masa[2] *f* mass (*a. phys., fig.*); *fig.* bulk, volume; *las* ~s *pl.* the masses; ~ *coral* choir; *en* ~ en masse.

masacrar [1a] massacre.

masaje *m* massage; *dar* ~ *a* massage; **masajista 1.** *m* masseur; **2.** *f* masseuse.

mascar [1g] chew; F mumble.

máscara *f* mask (*a. fig.*); ~ *antigás* gas mask; ~s *pl.* = **mascarada** *f* masque(rade); **mascarilla** *f* mask; (*vaciado*) death mask; **mascarón** *m*: ~ *de proa* figure head.

mascota *f* mascot.

masculinidad *f* masculinity; manliness; **masculino 1.** *biol.* male; *gr.* masculine; *fig.* masculine, manly; **2.** *m gr.* masculine.

mascullar [1a] F mumble, mutter.

masón *m* (free)mason; **masonería** *f* (free)masonry; **masónico** masonic.

masoquismo *m* masochism.

masticar [1g] masticate, chew.

mástil *m* pole, post; ♣ mast.

mastín *m* mastiff; ~ *danés* Great Dane.

mastoides *adj. a. su. f* mastoid.

mata *f* ♀ shrub; (*pie de planta*) clump, root; (*hoja*) blade, sprig; mop *de pelo*; ~s *pl.* ♀ scrub.

matadero *m* slaughterhouse; F drudgery; **matador 1.** killing; **2.** *m*, -**a** *f* killer; *toros:* matador; **matafuego** *m* fire extinguisher; **matanza** *f* slaughter; *esp.* ♂ pigkilling; *fig.* massacre; **matar** [1a] kill (*a. fig.*); *fuego* put out; *hambre* stay; *polvo* lay; *color* tone down; ~*se* kill o.s.; get killed *en accidente*; *fig.* wear o.s. out.

matarife *m* butcher; **matasanos** *m* quack doctor.

matasellar [1a] cancel, postmark; **matasello(s)** *m* postmark.

mate[1] dull, matt.

mate[2] *m* (check)mate; *dar* ~ *a* (check)mate.

mate[3] *m S.Am.* ♀ maté.

matemáticas *f/pl.* mathematics; **matemático 1.** mathematical; **2.** *m* mathematician.

materia *f* matter (*a. phys.*, ⚕); (*componentes*) material, stuff; (*asunto*) subject (matter); *escuela*: subject; ~ *prima* raw material; en ~ de as regards; ⊕ **material 1.** material; **2.** *m* material; ⊕ equipment, plant; *typ.* copy; **materialismo** *m* materialism; **materialista 1.** materialistic; **2.** *m/f* materialist; **materializar(se)** [1f] materialize.

maternal motherly; maternal; **maternidad** *f* motherhood, maternity; (*a. casa de* ~) maternity hospital; **materno** maternal; *lengua etc.* mother *attr.*; *abuelo* ~ grandfather on the mother's side.

matinal morning *attr.*

matiz *m* shade (*a. fig.*); hue, tint; **matizar** [1f] (*casar*) blend, match; (*colorar*) tinge, tint (de with); *matizado de fig.* adorned with.

matorral *m* thicket; brushwood.

matraca *f* rattle; F terrible bore, nuisance; **matraquear** [1a] rattle; *fig.* jeer at.

matrero 1. cunning; *S.Am.* suspicious; **2.** *m S.Am.* bandit.

matrícula *f* list, register (*a.* ♣); *univ. etc.* (*acto*) registration; (*permiso*) license; *mot.* registration number; **matriculación** *f* registration *etc.*; **matricular(se)** [1a] register, enroll.

matrimonial matrimonial; *vida* married; **matrimonio** *m* (*en general*) marriage, matrimony; (*acto*) marriage; (*ps.*) (married) couple; *contraer* ~ (*con*) marry.

matriz *f anat.* womb; stub *de talonario*; ⊕ mould, die; ⊕ (*tuerca*) nut; *typ.*, ♣ matrix.

matrona *f* matron.

matutino morning *attr.*

maula 1. *f* junk, trash; dirty trick; **2.** *m/f* cheat; (*pesado*) bore; **maulero** *m*, **a** *f* cheat.

maullar [1a] mew, miaow; **maullido** *m* mew, miaow.

mausoleo *m* mausoleum.

máxima *f* maxim; **máxime** especially; **máximo 1.** maximum; top; *grado etc.* highest; *esfuerzo etc.* greatest (possible); **2.** *m* = **máximum** *m* maximum.

maya *f* ♀ daisy; (*p.*) May Queen.

mayo *m* May; (*árbol*) maypole.

mayonesa *f* mayonnaise.

mayor 1. *adj. altar, calle, misa* high; *parte etc.* main, major (*a.* ♪); *p.* grown-up, of age; (*de edad avanzada*) elderly; **2.** *adj. comp.* bigger, larger, greater (*que* than); *edad:* older (*que* than), elder; senior (*que* to); *v. edad;* **3.** *adj. sup.* biggest; eldest *etc.*; **4.:** *al por* ~ wholesale; **5.** *m* chief, head; ✕ major; ~*es pl.* ancestors; *fig.* elders.

mayoral *m* ⊕ foreman, overseer; ✔ head shepherd; † coachman.

mayorazgo *m* primogeniture; (*p.*) eldest son.

mayordomo *m* steward, butler.

mayoría *f* majority; larger part; *la* ~ *de* most; *en su* ~ in the main; **mayorista** *m* wholesaler; **mayormente** chiefly, mainly.

mayúscula *f* capital letter; **mayúsculo** *letra* capital.

maza *f* mace; *deportes:* bat; ~ *de gimnasia* Indian club.

mazacote *m* ⚠ concrete; ⚕ soda; F dry doughy food; F (*p.*) bore.

mazmorra *f* dungeon.

mazo *m* mallet; (*manojo*) bunch.

mazorca *f* ♀ spike, clump; ear, cob *de maíz; sew.* spindle.

me (*acc.*) me; (*dat.*) (to) me; (*reflexivo*) (to) myself.

meandro *m* meander.

mear [1a] F *v/t.* piss on; *v/i.* piss.

mecánica *f* mechanics; (*aparato*) mechanism, works; **mecánico 1.** mechanical; machine *attr.*; *oficio* manual; **2.** *m* mechanic; engineer; machinist; ~*-dentista* dental technician; **mecanismo** *m* mechanism; works; action, movement *de pieza; esp. fig.* machinery, structure; **mecanizar** [1f] mechanize; **mecanografía** *f* typing; ~ *al tacto* touchtyping; **mecanografiado** *adj. a. su. m* typescript; **mecanografiar** [1c] type; **mecanógrafo** *m*, **a** *f* typist.

mecedora *f* rocking-chair.

mecenas *m* patron; **mecenazgo** *m* patronage.

mecer(se) [2b] *cuna etc.* rock; *rama etc.* sway; (*columpiar*) swing.

mecha *f* wick; ✕ *etc.* fuse; = *mechón;* ~ *tardía* time-fuse; **mechar** [1a] lard; **mechera** *f* F shoplifter; **mechero** *m* burner *de lámpara;* (*cada fuego*) jet; (*cigarette*) lighter; shoplifter; ~ *encendedor* pilot light; ~ *de*

M

mechón

gas gas burner, gas jet; **mechón** *m* lock (of hair).

medalla *f* medal; = **medallón** *m* medallion; locket *con pelo etc.*; *typ.* inset.

médano *m*, **medaño** *m* sand dune; sandbank.

media *f* stocking; A mean; *hacer* ~ knit; **mediación** *f* mediation; (*medio*) instrumentality; **mediado** half-full; *a* ~*s* de in the middle of; **mediador** *m*, **-a** *f* mediator; **medial** medial; **medianero** 1. *pared etc.* dividing; 2. *m* mediator; (*mensajero*) go-between; **medianía** *f* (*punto medio*) half-way (point); (*promedio*) average; (*calidad*) mediocrity; ⟊ modest means (*or* circumstances); **mediano** *punto* middle; ⚥ *etc.* median; *calidad* middling, medium, average; *b.s.* mediocre, indifferent; **medianoche** *f* midnight; **mediante** *prp.* by means of, through; **mediar** [1b] be in the middle; *fig.* mediate.

médica *f* woman doctor; **medicamento** *m* medicine, drug; **medicastro** *m* quack; **medicina** *f* medicine; **medicinal** medicinal; **medicinar** [1a] treat, prescribe.

medición *f* measuring, measurement; *surv.* survey(ing).

médico 1. medical; 2. *m* doctor; ~ *de cabecera* family doctor; ~ *dentista* dental surgeon; ~ *residente* house physician.

medida *f* A measure(ment); (*acto*) measuring; (*regla, vasija*) measure; fitting, size *de zapato etc.*; *fig.* measure, step; *fig.* moderation; *a* ~ de in proportion to, according to.

medieval medieval.

medio 1. *adj.* *punto* mid(way), middle; A mean; (*corriente*) average; (*mitad de*) half (a); ~ *pan* half a loaf; *a* ~*a tarde* in the middle of the afternoon; *las* 2 *y* ~*a* half-past 2; *ir a* ~*as* go halves (*con* with); 2. *adv.* half; ~ *dormido* half asleep; 3. *m.* (*punto*) middle; (*mitad*) half; (*ambiente*) milieu, environment; medium *de comunicación etc.*; (*método*) means, way; (*medida*) measure; *deportes:* halfback; ~ *centro* centre half; ~*s pl.* ⟊ means; ~ *ambiente* environment; ~*s de comunicación* mass media; *justo* ~ happy medium, golden mean; *de en* ~ middle; *de por* ~, *en* ~ in between; *en* ~ *de* in the middle (*or* midst) of; *por* ~ *de* by means of, through.

mediocre middling, average; *b.s.* mediocre; **mediocridad** *f* mediocrity; ⟊ modest circumstances.

mediodía *m* midday, noon; *geog.* south.

medir [3l] measure; *poet.* scan; ~*se* act with moderation.

meditabundo pensive, thoughtful; **meditación** *f* meditation *etc.*; **meditar** [1a] *v/t.* meditate, plan; *v/i.* ponder, meditate; muse.

mediterráneo Mediterranean.

medra *f* increase; improvement; ⟊ prosperity; **medrar** [1a] (*crecer*) grow; (*mejorar*) improve.

medroso timid; dreadful.

médula *f*, **medula** *f* *anat.* marrow; ⚘ pith; ~ *espinal* spinal cord.

medusa *f* jellyfish.

megáfono *m* megaphone.

megatón *m* megaton.

mejicano *adj. a. su. m*, **a** *f* Mexican.

mejilla *f* cheek.

mejor 1. *adj. comp.* better; *sup.* best; *postor* highest; *lo* ~ the best thing (*or* part *etc.*); 2. *adv. comp.* better; *sup.* best; ~ *que* rather than; **mejora** *f* improvement; **mejoramiento** *m* improvement.

mejorar [1a] *v/t.* improve; *postura* raise; *v/i.*, ~*se* improve (*a. meteor.*); ⚕ recover; ⟊ *etc.* prosper; **mejoría** *f* improvement, recovery.

melado *m* syrup.

melancolía *f* gloom(iness), melancholy; ⚕ melancholia; **melancólico** gloomy, sad, melancholy.

melaza *f* (*a.* ~*s pl.*) molasses.

melena *f* long hair; pony-tail; *zo.* mane; **melenudo** longhaired.

melifluo *fig.* mellifluous, sweet.

melindre *m* *fig.* affectation; *b.s.* affectation); squeamishness; (*moral*) prudery; **melindrear** [1a] F be affected, be finicky; **melindroso** affected; squeamish.

mella *f* notch, nick, dent; (*hueco*) gap; *hacer* ~ (*reprensión etc.*) sink in, strike home; (*dañar*) do damage (*en* to); **mellar** [1a] notch, nick, dent; *fig.* damage.

mellizo *adj. a. su. m*, **a** *f* twin.

melocotón *m* peach; **melocotonero** *m* peach (tree).

melodía *f* melody, tune; **melodioso** melodious.

melodrama *m* melodrama; **melodramático** melodramatic.

melón *m* melon; F nut; (*p.*) idiot.

meloso honeyed, sweet; *fig.* gentle.

membrana *f* membrane.

membrete *m* note, memo; *(inscripción)* letterhead, heading.

membrillo *m* ♀ quince.

membrudo burly, brawny.

memorable memorable; **memorándum** *m* memorandum; *(librito)* notebook; **memoria** *f* memory; *(relación)* report, statement; *(nota)* memorandum; *(solicitud)* petition; *(ponencia)* paper; ~s *pl.* memoirs; ~ anual annual report; de ~ aprender by heart; **memorial** *m* petition; ⚖ brief.

mención *f* mention; **mencionar** [1a] mention; sin ~ let alone.

mendicidad *f* begging; *(condición)* beggarliness; **mendigar** [1h] beg; **mendigo** *m*, **a** *f* beggar.

mendrugo *m* crust (of bread).

menear [1a] move; *cabeza etc.* shake, toss; *cola* wag; *caderas* swing, waggle; *cálamo* wield; *negocio* handle; F *peor es meneallo* leave well alone; ~se F get a move on; **meneo** *m* shaking etc.; F hiding.

menester 1.: ser ~ be necessary; 2. ~es *m/pl.* duties, jobs; F gear, tackle; **menesteroso** needy.

mengua *f* decrease, dwindling; decline; poverty; en ~ de to the discredit of; **menguado** *(cobarde)* cowardly; *(tonto)* silly; *(tacaño)* mean; **menguante** 1. dwindling etc.; 2. *f* ♄ ebb tide; waning de luna; *fig.* decline; **menguar** [1i] decrease, dwindle; *(marea etc.)* go down; *(luna)* wane.

meningitis *f* meningitis.

menor 1. *adj.* órdenes, ♪ etc. minor; 2. *adj. comp.* smaller, lesser; *edad:* younger (que than), junior (que to); v. edad; 3. *adj. sup.* smallest; least; youngest etc.; 4.: al por ~ retail; 5. *m/f* minor, young person.

menos 1. *prp.* except; & less, minus; 5 ~ 3 son 2 3 from 5 leaves 2; las 2 ~ cuarto a quarter to 2; 2. *adv. comp.* less; *sup.* least; ~ de, ~ de lo que, ~ que less than; lo de ~ the least of it; 5 de ~ 5 short; una libra de ~ a pound less; al ~, (a) lo ~, por lo ~ at least; 3. cj.: a ~ que unless; 4. *adj. signo* minus; 5. *m* minus.

menos...: ~cabar [1a] lessen, reduce; *(dañar)* damage, impair; *(deslucir)* discredit; ~cabo *m* lessening; damage, loss; en ~ de to the detriment

of; ~**preciar** [1b] *(desdeñar)* scorn, despise; *(insultar)* slight; *(subestimar)* underrate.

mensaje *m* message; **mensajero** *m*, **a** *f* messenger.

menstruación *f*, **menstruo** *m* menstruation.

mensual monthly; *100 ptas* ~es 100 ptas a month; **mensualidad** *f* monthly payment (or salary etc.); **mensualmente** monthly.

mensurable measurable; **mensuración** *f* mensuration.

menta *f* ♀ mint.

mental mental; *trabajo etc.* intellectual; **mentalidad** *f* mentality; **mentar** [1k] mention, name; **mente** *f* mind.   [idiot.]

mentecato 1. silly, stupid; 2. *m*, **a** *f*

mentir [3i] lie, tell a lie (or lies); **mentira** *f* lie; *(en general)* lying, deceitfulness; **mentirijillas:** de ~ for fun; **mentirilla** *f* fib, white lie; **mentiroso** 1. lying, false; 2. *m*, **a** *f* liar; **mentís** *m* denial; *dar un* ~ a deny, give the lie to.

mentol *m* menthol.

mentón *m* chin.

menú *m* menu.

menudear [1a] *v/t.* repeat frequently; tell in detail; *v/i.* happen frequently; go into detail *contando*; **menudeo:** ✝ al ~ retail; **menudillos** *m/pl.* giblets; **menudo** 1. small, tiny; slight, trifling; exact; a ~ often; por ~ in detail; 2. *m* small change; entrails.

meñique *m* little finger.

meollo *m anat.* marrow; *fig. (esencia)* gist; *(seso)* brains.

mercachifle *m* hawker, huckster; **mercadear** [1a] trade; **mercader** *m* merchant; **mercadería** *f* commodity; ~s *pl.* merchandise; **mercado** *m* market; ~ negro black market; **mercancía** *f* commodity; ~s *pl.* goods, merchandise; 2. ~s *m* freight train; **mercante** ⚓ 1. merchant *attr.*; 2. *m* merchant ship; **mercantil** mercantile, commercial; **mercar** [1g] buy.

merced *f*: *mst* ✝ favor; benefit; *vuestra* ~ your honor, your worship; *estar a la* ~ *de* be at the mercy of.

mercenario 1. mercenary; 2. *m* ✕ mercenary; *fig.* hack, hireling.

mercería *f* haberdashery; dry-goods store; *Chile* hardware store.

M

mercurio *m* mercury.
merecedor deserving (*de* of); **merecer** [2d] *v/t.* deserve; be worth(y of); *alabanza etc.* earn (*a. ~se*); (*necesitar*) need; *v/i.* be worthy; **merecimiento** *m* deserts; merit, worthiness.
merendar [1k] *v/t.* lunch on; *v/i.* have lunch; picnic *en el campo*.
merengue *m* meringue.
meridiana *f* couch; chaise-longue; **meridiano** *adj. a. su. m* meridian; *a la ~a* at noon; **meridional** 1. southern; 2. *m/f* southerner. [back.]
merienda *f* lunch, snack; F hunch-
mérito *m* merit; worth, value; *hacer ~ de* mention; *hacer ~s* strive to be deserving; **meritorio** meritorious, worthy.
merluza *f* hake; *sl.* estar (*con la*) ~ F be stoned, be drunk.
merma *f* decrease; wastage, loss; **mermar** [1a] *v/t.* reduce, deplete; *ración etc.* cut down on; *v/i.* decrease, dwindle; (*líquido*) go down.
mermelada *f* jam.
mero 1. *adj.* mere; pure, simple; *S.Am.* selfsame, very; 2. *adv. S.Am.* soon, in a moment.
mes *m* month.
mesa *f* table; desk *de trabajo*; counter *de oficina*; △ landing; *geog.* tableland, plateau; (*junta*) presiding committee, board; ~ *de extensión* extension table; ~ *de juego* gambling table; ~ *de noche* bedside table; ~ *de operaciones* operating table; ~ *de trucos* pool table; ~ *redonda* table d'hôte; *hist. a. pol.* round table; ~ *perezosa* drop table; *alzar* (or *levantar*) *la* ~ clear away; *poner la* ~ lay the table.
meseta *f* tableland, plateau; △ landing; **mesilla** *f* occasional table; ~ *de chimenea* mantelpiece.
mestizar [1f] cross-breed; **mestizo** *adj. a. su. m*, **a** *f* half-caste, halfbreed; *zo.* cross-bred, mongrel.
mesura *f* gravity *etc.*; **mesurado** grave; moderate, restrained; sensible; **mesurarse** [1a] restrain o.s.
meta 1. *f* goal (*a. fig.*); winningpost *en carrera*; 2. *m* goalkeeper.
metabolismo *m* metabolism.
metáfora *f* metaphor; **metafórico** metaphoric(al).
metal *m* metal; ♪ brass; timbre *de voz*; *fig.* quality; *el vil* ~ filthy lucre; **metálico** 1. metallic; metal *attr.*; 2. *m* specie, coin; *en* ~ in cash; **metalurgia** *f* metallurgy.

metamorfosear [1a] metamorphose; **metamorfosis** *f* metamorphosis.
meteórico meteoric; **meteorito** *m*, **meteoro** *m* meteor; **meteorología** *f* meteorology; **meteorológico** meteorological; **meteorologista** *m/f* meteorologist.
meter [2a] put, insert, introduce (*en* in, into); (*apretando*) squeeze in; smuggle (in) *de contrabando*; *fig.* make, cause; *~se fig.* meddle, interfere (*mucho* a lot); (*hacerse*) *monja* become; *soldado* turn; ~ *a su.* become; ~ *con* meddle with; *p.* pick a quarrel with; ~ *en* go into; get into; *fig.* interfere in; *dificultades* get into; *negocio* get involved in.
meticuloso meticulous, scrupulous.
metido 1.: *estar muy* ~ *en* be deeply involved in; 2. *m* shove, punch.
metódico methodic(al); **método** *m* method; **metodología** *f* methodology.
metraje *m*: (*cinta de*) *largo* ~ fulllength film.
metralla *f* shrapnel.
métrica *f* metrics; **métrico** metric, metrical; **metro**[1] *m* ♪, *poet.* meter; (*de cinta*) tape measure; (*plegable*) rule; (*recto*) rule.
metro[2] *m* 🚇 subway.
metrónomo *m* metronome.
metrópoli *f* metropolis; **metropolitano** *adj. a. su. m eccl.* metropolitan.
mexicano *adj. a. su. m*, **a** *f S.Am.* Mexican.
mezcla *f* mixture; *esp. fig.* blend; medley; △ mortar; *sin* ~ *bebida* neat; **mezclador** *m* mixer; **mezclar** [1a] mix (up); blend; (*unir*) merge; *cartas* shuffle; *~se* mix, mingle (*con* with); *b.s.* get mixed (*en up* in); (*entrometerse*) meddle (*en* in); **mezcolanza** *f* jumble.
mezquindad *f* meanness *etc.*; **mezquino** (*pobre*) poor, wretched; (*avaro*) mean; (*pequeño*) wretchedly small; (*insignificante*) petty, paltry.
mezquita *f* mosque.
mi, mis *pl.* my.
mí me.
miasma *m* miasma.
miau *m* mew, miaow.
mica *f min.* mica.
mico *m*, **a** *f* monkey.
micro... micro...
microbio *m* microbe.

microcosmo *m* microcosm.

microfilm *m* microfilm.

micrófono *m* microphone.

microprocesador *m* microprocessor.

microscópico microscopic; **microscopio** *m* microscope.

miedo *m* fear (*a* of); *tener* ~ be afraid (*a* of); **miedoso** scared, fearful.

miel *f* honey.

miembro *m* anat. limb; *anat.*, *gr.*, *p. etc.* member.

mientes: *parar* ~ *en* reflect on.

mientras while, as long as; ~ (*que*) whereas; ~ *más* ... *más* the more ... the more; ~ *tanto* meanwhile.

miércoles *m* Wednesday; ~ *de ceniza* Ash Wednesday.

mierda *f* F shit.

mies *f* corn, wheat, grain.

miga *f* bit; crumb *de pan*; *fig.* substance; F *hacer buenas* ~s get on well, hit it off (*con* with); **migaja** *f* bit; crumb *de pan* (*a. fig.*).

migración *f* migration.

migraña *f* migraine.

migratorio migratory.

mil a thousand; *dos* ~ two thousand; ~es *pl.* thousands.

milagro *m* miracle; *fig. a.* wonder; **milagroso** miraculous.

milenario 1. millennial; 2. *m* = **milenio** *m* millennium.

milésimo *adj. a. su. m* thousandth.

milicia *f* (*ps.*) militia; soldiery; (*profesión*) soldiering.

miligramo *m* milligram(me); **mililitro** *m* milliliter; **milímetro** *m* millimeter.

militante militant; **militar** 1. military; (*guerrero*) warlike; *arte of war*; 2. *m* soldier; serviceman; 3. [1a] serve (*in the army*), soldier; *fig.* militate (*contra* against); **militarismo** *m* militarism; **militarizar** [1f] militarize.

milla *f* mile; ~ *marina* nautical mile.

millar *m* thousand; *a* ~es in thousands, by the thousand; **millarada** *f* (about a) thousand; **millón** *m* million; **millonario** *m*, **a** *f* millionaire; **millonésimo** *adj. a. su. m* millionth.

mimar [1a] (*acariciar*) pet, fondle; *fig.* pamper, spoil.

mimbre *mst m* wicker; **mimbrear(se)** [1a] sway; **mimbrera** *f* osier willow.

mimeógrafo *m* mimeograph.

mimetismo *m* mimicry; **mímica** *f* gesticulation; sign language; (*remedo*) mimicry; (*una* ~) mime; **mímico** mimic; imitative; **mimo** 1. *m thea. etc.* mime; *hacer* ~ *de* mime; 2. *m* pampering, indulgence.

mina *f* mine (*a.* ✕, ⚓, *fig.*); lead, refill *de lápiz*; *fig.* storehouse; ~ *de carbón* coal mine; **minar** [1a] mine (*a.* ✕, ⚓); (*cavar lentamente*) undermine, wear away.

mineral 1. mineral; 2. *m* ⚙ mineral; ⚒ ore; ~ *de hierro* iron ore; **mineralogía** *f* mineralogy; **mineralogista** *m/f* mineralogist; **minería** *f* mining; **minero** 1. mining; 2. *m* miner.

miniatura *f* miniature; *en* ~ in miniature.

mínimo 1. smallest, least; minimum; minimal; tiny; 2. *m* minimum; **mínimum** *m* minimum.

minino *m*, **a** *f* F puss(y).

miniordenador *m* microcomputer.

ministerial ministerial; **ministerio** *m* ministry; **ministro** *m* minister; ~ *de asuntos exteriores* foreign minister; *primer* ~ prime minister.

minorar [1a] reduce, lessen; **minoría** *f*, **minoridad** *f* minority; **minorista** *m* retailer.

minucia *f* minuteness; ~s *pl.* details, minutiae; **minucioso** thorough, meticulous; minute.

minúscula *f* small letter; **minúsculo** small (*a. typ.*), tiny.

minuta *f* (*borrador*) first draft; (*apunte*) minute, memorandum; list; (*comida*) menu; **minutar** [1a] draft; minute; **minutero** *m* minutehand; **minuto** *m* minute.

mío, mía 1. *pron.* mine; 2. *adj.* (*tras su.*) of mine.

miope short-sighted; **miopía** *f* short-sightedness, miopia 🝙.

mira *f* ✕ (*a.* ~s *pl.*) sights; *fig.* object, aim; **mirada** *f* look; glance; gaze; expression *de cara*; **mirador** *m* △ bay window, balcony; (*lugar*) vantage point; **miramiento** *m* considerateness; caution; ~s *pl.* fuss.

mirar [1a] 1. *v/t.* look at; watch; *fig.* look on, consider (*como* as); (*reflexionar sobre*) think carefully about; (*tener cuidado con*) watch, be careful about; 2. *v/i.* look; ¡*mira*! look!; (*protesta*) look here!; (*aviso*) look out!; 3. ~*se* look at o.s.; (*recíproco*) look at each other.

mirasol *m* sunflower.

miríada *f* myriad.

mirlo *m* blackbird.

mirón 1. inquisitive; **2.** *m*, **-a** *f* onlooker, kibitzer; busybody.

mirto *m* myrtle.

misa *f* mass; ~ *del gallo* Midnight Mass; ~ *mayor* High Mass; ~ *rezada* Low Mass; **misal** *m* missal.

miscelánea *f* miscellany; **misceláneo** miscellaneous.

miserable 1. (*desdichado*) wretched; (*tacaño*) mean; *sueldo etc.* miserable, pitifully small; **2.** *m/f* wretch; (*vil*) cad; **miseria** *f* misery, wretchedness; poverty; **misericordia** *f* pity; (*perdón*) forgiveness; mercy; **misericordioso** compassionate; merciful; **mísero** wretched.

misil *m* (guided) missile.

misión *f* mission; **misionero** *adj. a. su. m*, **a** *f* missionary.

mismo *m*, **a** *f* **1.** same; own; very; *ella* ~*a* herself; **2.** *adv.* *ahora* ~ right away.

misterio *m* mystery; secrecy; *thea.* mystery play; **misterioso** mysterious; mystifying, puzzling; **mística** *f*, **misticismo** *m* mysticism; **místico 1.** mystic(al); **2.** *m*, **a** *f* mystic; **mistificación** *f* hoax.

mitad *f* half; (*medio*) middle; *mi cara* ~ my better half.

mítico mythical.

mitigación *f* mitigation *etc.*; **mitigar** [1h] *efecto* mitigate; *dolor* relieve; *cólera* appease, mollify.

mitin *m esp. pol.* meeting.

mito *m* myth; **mitología** *f* mythology; **mitológico** mythological.

mitón *m* mitten.

mitra *f* mitre.

mixto 1. mixed; **2.** *m* match; **mixtura** *f* mixture; **mixturar** [1a] mix.

mobiliario *m* suite; **moblaje** *m* (suite of) furniture.

mocedad *f* youth.

mochila *f* knapsack; ✗ pack.

mocho 1. blunt; **2.** *m* butt.

moción *f* motion (*a. parl.*).

moco *m* mucus; snot; **mocoso 1.** snotty; F ill-bred; **2.** *m* F brat.

moda *f* fashion; style; *a la* ~, *de* ~ in fashion, fashionable.

modelado *m* modelling; **modelar** [1a] model (*sobre on*); (*dar forma a*) fashion, shape; **modelo 1.** *adj.* model; **2.** *m* model (*a. fig.*); pattern; **3.** *f* model, mannequin.

moderación *f* moderation; **moderado** moderate (*a. pol.*); **moderar**

[1a] moderate; (*refrenar*) restrain; ~*se* (*p.*) control o.s.

modernizar [1f] modernize; **moderno** modern; present-day.

modestia *f* modesty; **modesto** modest.

módico reasonable, moderate.

modificación *f* modification; **modificar** [1g] modify.

modismo *m* idiom.

modista *f* dressmaker; milliner.

modo *m* way, manner, mode (*a.* ♣); method; form *de gobierno etc.*; *gr.* mood; *fig.* moderation; ~*s pl.* manners; ~ *de empleo* (*en envase*) instructions for use; *a mi* ~ *de ver* to my way of thinking; *de* ~ *que* so that; *de todos* ~*s* at any rate.

modorra *f* drowsiness; *vet.* gid.

modoso quiet, nicely behaved.

modulación *f* modulation; ~ *de frecuencia* frequency modulation; **modular** [1a] modulate.

mofa *f* mockery, derision; (*una* ~) taunt, gibe; **mofar** [1a] jeer, sneer; ~*se de* make fun of.

mogol *adj. a. su. m*, **-a** *f* Mongol, Mongolian.

mohín *m* face, grimace; **mohína** *f* (*disgusto*) annoyance; **mohíno** (*triste*) gloomy, depressed.

moho *m* rust; ♣ mold, mildew; **mohoso** rusty; ♣ moldy, musty.

mojada *f* wetting, soaking; stab; **mojado** wet; soaked; damp, moist; **mojar** [1a] *v/t.* wet; moisten; drench, soak; *pluma* dip (*en into*); (*apuñalar*) stab; ~*se* get drenched.

mojigatería *f* hypocrisy; prudery; **mojigato 1.** hypocritical; (*beato*) sanctimonious; prudish; **2.** *m*, **a** *f* hypocrite; prude.

mojón *m* landmark, boundary stone; (*de camino*) milestone.

molde *m* mold; cast *de yeso etc.*; *sew. etc.* pattern; *esp. fig.* model; *venir de* ~ be just right; **moldear** [1a] mold; (*vaciar etc.*) cast; **moldura** *f* ♙ moulding.

mole *f* mass; bulk; ♙ pile.

molécula *f* molecule; **molecular** molecular.

moledor *fig.* **1.** boring; **2.** *m* bore; **moler** [2h] grind, mill; pound; *fig.* (*fastidiar*) annoy; (*cansar*) weary; ~ *a palos* beat s.o. up.

molestar [1a] annoy, bother; ¿*le molesta a Vd. que fume?* will it bother you if I smoke?; **molestia** *f* annoy-

ance; bother, nuisance; ❊ etc. discomfort; **molesto** annoying, uncomfortable.

molicie f softness (a. fig.); fig. luxurious living; effeminacy.

molienda f grinding, milling; F weariness; (una ~) nuisance; **molinero** m miller; **molinete** m (toy) windmill, pinwheel; **molinillo** m mill, grinder para café etc.; mincer para carne; **molino** m mill; grinder; ~ de viento windmill.

mollar soft, mushy; carne lean; **molleja** f gizzard; **mollera** f anat. crown of the head.

momentáneo momentary; **momento** m moment; al ~ at once.

mona f zo. monkey; F (p.) ape; (borracho) drunk; F dormir la ~ sleep it off.

monada f (bobada) silly thing; (estupidez) silliness; (objeto) lovely thing, beauty; (p.) pretty girl.

monarca m monarch; **monarquía** f monarchy.

monasterio m monastery; **monástico** monastic.

mondadientes m toothpick; **mondaduras** f/pl. peel(ings), skin; **mondar** [1a] (limpiar) cleanse; fruta peel; árbol prune, lop; dientes pick; F p. cut s.o.'s hair; fig. fleece.

moneda f currency, coinage; (una ~) coin; ~ dura hard currency; ~ suelta change. [(mímica) mimicry.)

monería f (mueca) funny face;)

monetario monetary, financial.

monigote m rag doll; botched painting; F sap, boob.

monitorear un programa monitor.

monja f nun; **monje** m monk; **monjil** nun's, monk's, monkish.

mono[1] m zo. monkey; (p.) clown; drogas withdrawal symptom; estar de ~s be at daggers drawn.

mono[2] m overalls, coveralls.

mono[3] F pretty, nice.

monóculo m monocle.

mono...: ~**gamia** f monogamy; ~**grama** m monogram; **monólogo** m monologue.

mono...: ~**plano** m monoplane; ~**polio** m monopoly; ~**polista** m/f monopolist; ~**polizar** [1f] monopolize; ~**silábico** = ~**sílabo** 1. monosyllabic; 2. m monosyllable; ~**teísmo** m monotheism; ~**tonía** f monotony, sameness, dreariness; **monótono** monotonous.

monserga f gibberish; drivel.

monstruo m monster (a. fig.); biol. freak; **monstruosidad** f monstrosity; freak; **monstruoso** monstrous, monster attr.; biol. freakish.

monta f ✗ total; de poca ~ of small account.

montacargas m (service) lift, hoist.

montado mounted; **montadura** f mounting; (engaste) setting; **montaje** m ⊕ assembly; △ erection; **montante** m ⊕ upright, stanchion; △ transom; ✗ broadsword; ✝ total, amount.

montaña f mountain; ~ rusa switchback, scenic railway; **montañero** m, a f mountaineer; **montañés** 1. mountain attr.; 2. m, -a f highlander; native of Santander region; **montañismo** m mountaineering; **montañoso** mountainous; mountain attr.

montaplatos m dumbwaiter.

montar [1a] 1. v/t. caballo etc. (subir) mount, (ir) ride; ⊕ assemble; ✗ amount to (a. fig.); 2. v/i. mount (a, en acc.), get up (a, en on); ✗ ~ a amount to; ~ a caballo ride.

monte m mountain, hill; (bosque) woodland; (despoblado) wilds, wild country; ~ alto forest; ~ bajo scrub; ~ de piedad pawnshop; ~ pío pension fund for widows and orphans; mutual-benefit society; ~ tallar tree farm; **montecillo** m hump, hummock; **montepío** m charitable organization; mutual-fund society.

montera f cloth cap.

montería f hunting; **montero** m huntsman, hunter.

montés gato etc. wild.

montículo m hillock, mound.

montón m heap, pile; drift de nieve; F stack; a ~es in plenty, galore.

montuoso hilly.

montura f (caballo) mount; (silla) saddle; sin ~ bareback.

monumental monumental; **monumento** m monument (a. fig.); (mausoleo) memorial.

monzón m or f monsoon.

moña: sl. estar con la ~ be sozzled.

moño m bun, chignon; orn. crest.

moquero m handkerchief.

moqueta f moquette.

moquete m punch (on the nose).

moquillo m vet. distemper; orn. pip.

mora[1] f mulberry; blackberry.

mora[2]: ponerse en ~ default.

morada

morada f dwelling, home.
morado purple, dark violet.
morador m, **-a** f inhabitant.
moral¹ m ♣ mulberry (tree).
moral² 1. moral; 2. f (ciencia) ethics; (moralidad) morals; **morale** de ejército etc.; **moraleja** f moral; **moralidad** f morality, morals; **moralista** m/f, **moralizador** m, **-a** f moralist.
morar [1a] live, dwell, reside.
moratoria f moratorium.
mórbido ♠ morbid; **morboso** diseased, morbid.
mordaz fig. biting, scathing, pungent; **mordaza** f gag; ⊕ clamp, jaw; **mordedura** f bite; **morder** [2h] bite; ⊕ wear down; ✿ etc. (línea) gossip about, run down; **mordiscar** [1g] nibble; **mordisco** m nibble.
moreno (dark) brown; p. dark.
morfina f morphia, morphine.
morfinómano m drug-addict.
moribundo dying.
morir [3k; p.p. muerto] v/t.: fue muerto he was killed; v/i. die (a. fig.); (fuego etc.) die down; ✿ etc. (línea) end; (calle) come out (en in); ~ ahogado drown; ~ de frío freeze to death; ~ de hambre starve to death; ~ de risa die laughing; ~ de viejo die of old age; ~ helado freeze to death; ~ quemado burn to death; ~ vestido F die a violent death; ~se die; (miembro) go to sleep.
morisco Moorish; **moro** 1. Moorish; 2. m, Moor.
morral m haversack, knapsack.
morriña f F blues.
morsa f walrus.
mortaja f shroud; **mortal** adj. a. su. m/f mortal; herida etc. fatal; **mortalidad** f mortality; death rate; **mortandad** f mortality; death rate.
mortecino dying, failing; luz dim.
mortero m mortar (a. ✕).
mortífero deadly, lethal; **mortificar** [1g] mortify; humiliate; (despechar) spite; (doler) hurt, kill.
mosaico¹ eccl. Mosaic.
mosaico² m mosaic.
mosca f fly; F ♱ dough; F (p.) nuisance, bore; ~s pl. sparks; ~ doméstica housefly.
mosqueado spotted; brindled; **mosqueador** m fly-whisk; **mosquearse** [1a] fig. take offense.
mosquete m musket; **mosquetero** m musketeer; thea. † groundling.
mosquitero m mosquito net; **mosquito** m mosquito; gnat.

mostacho m moustache.
mostaza f mustard.
mostrador m counter; ⊕ dial; **mostrar** [1m] show.
mostrenco ownerless, unclaimed; título etc. in abeyance; F p. homeless, animal stray; obra crude.
mota f thread; speck; fig. fault.
mote m nickname; (lema) motto.
motear [1a] speckle; dapple.
motejar [1a] nickname.
motín m revolt, riot.
motivación f motivation; **motivar** [1a] cause, give rise to, motivate; justify; **motivo** 1. motive; 2. m motive, reason (de for).
moto f F motorbike; ~carro m three-wheeler; ~cicleta f motorcycle; ~ciclista m/f motor cyclist; ~ de escolta outrider.
motor 1. ⊕ motive; anat. motor; 2. m motor, engine; ~ de arranque starter; ~ de combustión interna, ~ de explosión internal combustion engine; ~ a chorro jet engine; ~ de fuera de borda outboard motor; ~ de reacción jet engine; **motora** f, **motorbote** m motorboat; **motorismo** m motor cycling; mot. motoring; **motorista** m/f motor cyclist; mot. motorist.
movedizo loose, unsteady; arenas shifting; fig. p. etc. fickle; situación etc. troubled, unsettled; **mover** [2h] move; shift; ⊕ drive; cabeza shake negando, nod asintiendo; cola wag; fig. (promover) stir up; move (a compasión to); ~se move, stir; **movible** movable; mobile; fig. changeable; **móvil** 1. = movible; 2. m motive (de for); **movilidad** f mobility; **movilización** f mobilization; **movilizar** [1f] mobilize; **movimiento** m movement; phys. etc. motion.
moza f girl; contp. wench; (criada) servant; **mozalbete** m lad.
mozárabe 1. Mozarabic; 2. m/f Mozarab; 3. m (idioma) Mozarabic.
mozo 1. young; (soltero) single; 2. m lad; (criado) servant; waiter en café; ✿ porter; buen ~ handsome fellow; ~ de caballos groom; ~ de cámara cabin boy; ~ de estación station porter; ~ de hotel bellboy; ~ de restaurante waiter; **mozuela** f girl; **mozuelo** m lad.
muchacha f girl; (criada) maid; **muchacho** m boy, lad.

mutilado

muchedumbre f crowd; mass, throng, host; *contp.* mob, herd.

mucho 1. *adj.* a lot of; much, great; ~s *pl.* many, lots of; many a; **2.** *adv.* a lot, a great deal, much; *estimar etc.* highly, greatly; *trabajar* hard.

mucilago *m* mucilage.

mucosa f mucous membrane.

muda f change of clothing; *zo.* molt; *(época)* molting season; **mudable** changeable; shifting; **mudanza** f change; ~s *pl. fig.* fickleness; *(humor)* moodiness; **mudar** [1a] *v/i.* change; *piel* slough (off), shed; *v/i.* ~se change; move; *(voz)* break; *zo.* molt.

mudez f dumbness; **mudo** dumb *(a. fig.,* de with); mute *(a. gr.);* speechless; *gr., película* silent.

mueblaje *m* = **moblaje; mueble 1.** movable; **2.** *m* piece of furniture; ~s *pl.* furniture; fittings *de tienda.*

mueca f face, grimace.

muela f millstone *de molino;* grindstone *para afilar; anat.* molar, *freq.* tooth; ~ *del juicio* wisdom tooth.

muelle¹ *m* ⚓ wharf, quay; 🚂 unloading bay. ~ *m* ⊕ spring.⟩

muelle² **1.** soft; *vida* luxurious; **2.** *f*

muérdago *m* mistletoe.

muerte f death; *(asesinato)* murder; **muerto 1.** dead; lifeless; *color* dull; **2.** *m,* **a** f dead man *etc.; (cadáver)* corpse; *los* ~s *pl.* the dead; **3.** *m naipes:* dummy.

muesca f notch, groove, slot.

muestra f † *etc.* sample; sign, signboard *de tienda etc.; (indicio)* sign, token; model; face *de reloj; dar* ~s *de* show signs of; **muestrario** *m* collection of samples.

mugido *m* moo; bellow; **mugir** [3c] *(vaca)* moo; *(toro)* bellow.

mugre f dirt; grease, grime; **mugriento** dirty; greasy, grimy.

muguete *m* lily of the valley.

mujer f woman; *(esposa)* wife; **mujeril** womanly.

mújol *m* (grey) mullet.

mula f mule.

muladar *m* dunghill; trash heap.

mulato *adj. a. su. m,* **a** f mulatto.

muleta f crutch; *fig.* prop; **muletilla** f *fig.* tag, pet phrase.

mullir [3h] pound, knead; soften.

mulo *m* mule.

multa f fine; penalty; **multar** [1a] fine; penalize.

multi...: ~**color** multicolored; ~**co-**

pista f duplicator; ~**millonario** *m,* **a** f multimillionaire; **multinacional** multinational; ~**es** f/*pl.* multinational corporations; **múltiple** manifold, multifarious; **A** multiple; *cuestión* many-sided; ~ *de admisión* intake manifold; ~ *de escape* exhaust manifold; ~ *de uso* multipurpose.

multiplicación f multiplication; **multiplicar(se)** [1g] **A** multiply; increase; ⊕ gear up; **multiplicidad** f multiplicity; **múltiplo** *adj. a. su. m* multiple; **multitud** f multitude; crowd *de gente etc.*

mundanal, mundano worldly; **mundanería** f worldliness; **mundial** world-wide; *guerra, record etc.* world *attr.;* **mundo** *m* world *(a. fig., eccl.); (ps.)* people; *(esfera)* globe; *todo el* ~ everybody.

munición f *(a.* ~**es** *pl.)* ✕ ammunition, munitions.

municipal 1. municipal; **2.** *m* policeman; **municipio** *m* municipality.

muñeca f *anat.* wrist; doll; dummy *de modista;* **muñeco** *m* dummy *de sastre; (muñeca)* doll; *fig.* puppet; F *(niño)* little angel; *(afeminado)* gay; ~ *de nieve* snowman; **muñequera** f wrist watch.

muñón *m anat.* stump.

mural mural; *mapa etc.* wall *attr.;* **muralla** f (city) wall, rampart.

murciélago *m zo.* bat.

murmullo *m* murmur; ripple *etc.;* **murmuración** f gossip, slander; **murmurar** [1a] murmur; mutter *entre dientes;* whisper *al oído; (multitud etc.)* hum.

muro *m* wall; ~ *del sonido* sound barrier.

murria f F blues; **murrio** sullen.

musa f Muse.

muscular muscular; **músculo** *m* muscle; **musculoso** muscular.

muselina f muslin.

museo *m* museum; gallery.

musgo *m* moss; **musgoso** mossy.

música f music; ~ *de fondo* background music; **musical = músico 1.** musical; **2.** *m,* **a** f musician.

musitar [1a] mumble, whisper.

muslo *m* thigh.

mustio *p.* depressed; hypocritical, sanctimonious; ♀ withered.

musulmán *adj. a. su. m,* ~**a** f Moslem.

mutilación f mutilation; **mutilado**

M

m, **a** *f* cripple, disabled person; **mutilar** [1a] mutilate (*a. fig.*); (*lisiar*) cripple, maim.

mutismo *m* dumbness; silence.

mutualidad *f* mutuality; mutual-benefit association; **mutuo** mutual (*a.* ✝), reciprocal; joint.

muy very; greatly; highly; most.

N, Ñ

nabo *m* turnip; ~ *sueco* swede.

nácar *m* mother-of-pearl; **nacarado, nacarino** mother-of-pearl *attr.*; pearly.

nacer [2d] be born (*a. fig.*); ⚹ come up, sprout; (*río*) rise; *fig.* spring, arise (*de* from); **nacido**: ~ *a*, ~ *para* born to (be); *bien* ~ of noble birth; *mal* ~ low-born; **naciente** nascent; recent; *sol* rising; **nacimiento** *m* birth (*a. fig.*); (*principio*) origin, start, beginning; source *de río*; (*manantial*) spring; (*belén*) nativity (scene); *de* ~ *ciego etc.* from birth.

nación *f* nation; *de* ~ by birth; **nacional** *adj. a. su. m/f* national; **nacionalidad** *f* nationality; **nacionalismo** *m* nationalism; **nacionalista** *adj. a. su. m/f* nationalist; **nacionalizar** [1f] nationalize; naturalize.

nada 1. *f* nothingness; *la* ~ the void; 2. *pron.* nothing; *¡~...~!* not a bit of it!; *¡~ de eso!* nothing of the kind!, far from it!; ~ *más* nothing else; (*solamente*) only; *¡de ~!* not at all!, don't mention it!; 3. *adv.*: ~ *fácil* far from easy.

nadador *m*, **-a** *f* swimmer; **nadar** [1a] swim; (*corcho etc.*) float.

nadería *f* trifle.

nadie nobody, no-one; *no ...* ~ not ... anybody; *un* (*don*) ~ a nobody.

nafta *f* naphtha; **naftaleno** *m*, **naftalina** *f* naphthalene.

naipe *m* (playing) card; ~*s pl.* cards.

nalgas *f/pl.* buttocks.

nana *f* F granny; ♪ lullaby.

naranja *f* orange; **naranjada** *f* orangeade, orange squash; **naranjado** orange; **naranjal** *m* orange grove; **naranjo** *m* orange (tree).

narciso *m* narcissus; daffodil.

narcosis *f* narcosis; **narcótico** 1. narcotic; 2. *m* narcotic; dope; **narcotismo** *m* narcotism; **narcotizar** [1f] drug, dope; **narcotraficante** *m* drug dealer.

nariz 1. *f* nose (*a. fig.*); (*cada orificio*) nostril; bouquet *de vino*; ~ *de pico de*

loro hooknose; 2. *narices pl. zo.* nostrils; F nose; *¡~!* rubbish!; *hinchársele a uno las* ~ get annoyed; *sonarse las* ~ blow one's nose; *tabicarse las* ~ hold one's nose; *tener agarrado por las* ~ lead by the nose.

narración *f* narration; narrative; **narrador** *m*, **-a** *f* narrator; **narrar** [1a] tell, narrate; **narrativa** *f* narrative; **narrativo** narrative.

nasal *adj. a. su. f* nasal; **nasalidad** *f* nasality; **nasalizar** [1f] nasalize.

nata *f* cream (*a. fig.*); skin *en natillas etc.*

natación *f* swimming; ~ *de costado* side-stroke.

natal natal; native; **natalicio** *adj. a. su. m* birthday; **natalidad** *f* birth rate; *control de* ~ birth control.

natillas *f/pl.* custard.

natividad *f* nativity; **nativo** native; natural, innate; **nato** born.

natural 1. *mst* natural (*a.* ⚹); native; 2. *m/f* native (*de* of), inhabitant; 3. *m* nature, disposition; *buen* ~ good nature; *al* ~ *descripción* true to life; (*sin arte*) rough; *bebida etc.* just as it comes; *vivir* according to nature; *del* ~ from nature, from life; **naturaleza** *f* nature; ~ *muerta* still life; *v. carta*; **naturalidad** *f* naturalness; **naturalismo** *m* naturalism; **naturalista** 1. naturalistic; 2. *m/f* naturalist; **naturalización** *f* naturalization; **naturalizar** [1f] naturalize; **naturismo** *m* nudism.

naufragar [1h] be (ship)wrecked, sink; *fig.* fail; **naufragio** *m* (ship)-wreck; *fig.* ruin; **náufrago** 1. shipwrecked; 2. *m* shipwrecked sailor.

náusea(s) *f(pl.)* nausea, sick feeling; *fig.* disgust; *dar* ~*s a* sicken; **nauseabundo** nauseating, sickening.

náutica *f* navigation, seamanship; **náutico** nautical.

navaja *f* jackknife; (*cortaplumas*) penknife; ~ (*de afeitar*) razor; **navajada** *f*, **navajazo** *m* slash.

naval naval.

níquel

nave f ship; △ nave; ~ *espacial* space ship; △ ~ *central*, ~ *principal* nave; △ ~ *lateral* aisle; **navegable** navigable; **navegación** f navigation; (*viaje*) voyage; (*buques*) shipping; **navegador** m, **navegante** m navigator; **navegar** [1h] (*ir*) sail; (*dirigir*) navigate.
Navidad f Christmas(-time); *por ~es* at Christmas(time); **¡Felices Navidades!** Merry Christmas!
naviero 1. shipping *attr.*; 2. m shipowner; **navío** m ship.
neblina f mist; **nebulosa** f nebula; **nebulosidad** f mistiness *etc.*; **nebuloso** *ast.* nebular, nebulous; *cielo* cloudy; *atmósfera* misty; (*tétrico*) gloomy; *idea etc.* nebulous.
necedad f silliness; nonsense.
necesario necessary; **neceser** m hold-all; dressing-case *de tocador;* ~ *de belleza* vanity case; ~ *de costura* workbox; **necesidad** f necessity, need (de for, of); (*hambre*) hunger; **necesitado** needy, necessitous; *los* ~s the needy; **necesitar** [1a] *v/t.* want, need; *acción etc.* necessitate; ~ *inf.* must *inf.*, need to *inf.*; *v/i.:* ~ *de* need; ~*se: necésitase* (*anuncios*) wanted.
necio silly, stupid.
nefando unspeakable.
nefasto unlucky, inauspicious.
negación f negation; denial; *gr.* negative; **negar** [1h a. 1k] *verdad etc.* deny; *permiso etc.* refuse (a *acc.*), withhold (a from); *responsabilidad* disclaim; (*vedar*) deny; ~ *que* deny that; ~*se a inf.* refuse to *inf.*; **negativa** f negative (a. *phot.*); denial, refusal; **negativo** 1. negative; A minus; 2. m *phot.* negative.
negligencia f negligence *etc.*; **negligente** negligent; neglectful.
negociable negotiable; **negociación** f negotiation; clearance *de cheque;* **negociador** m, **-a** f negotiator; **negociante** m businessman; merchant, dealer; **negociar** [1b] *v/t.* negotiate; *v/i.* negotiate; ~ *en* deal in, trade in; **negocio** m (*asunto*) affair, (piece of) business; trade, business; ~s *pl.* business.
negrita f *typ.* boldface; *en* ~ in bold type; **negro** 1. black (a. *fig.*); dark, (*sombrío*) gloomy; 2. m black; ~ *de humo* lampblack; **negrura** f blackness; **negruzco** blackish.
nenúfar m water lily.
neologismo m neologism.

nepotismo m nepotism.
nervadura f △ rib; **nervio** m nerve (a. *fig.*); ♀ rib; *fig.* sinews; vigor; stamina, toughness; **nerviosidad** f, **nerviosismo** m nervousness; (*temporal*) nerves F; **nervioso** *centro, célula* nerve *attr.*; *crisis, sistema* nervous; *p.* (*con miedo*) nervous; (*fuerte*) vigorous; *estilo* energetic; **nervudo** wiry, sinewy.
neto pure, clean; neat, clear; ♥ net.
neumático 1. pneumatic; 2. m tyre.
neuralgia f neuralgia; **neurólogo** m neurologist; **neurosis** f neurosis; **neurótico** *adj. a. su. m*, **a** f neurotic.
neutral *adj. a. su. m/f* neutral; **neutralidad** f neutrality; **neutralizar** [1f] neutralize; **neutro** neutral; *género* neuter; *verbo* intransitive.
neutrón m neutron.
nevada f (*cantidad*) snowfall; **nevado** snow-covered; *fig.* snowy; **nevar** [1k] *v/t.* whiten; *v/i.* snow; **nevasca** f snowstorm; **nevera** f refrigerator, ice box (a. *fig.*).
ni nor, neither; ~ ... ~ neither ... nor; ~ *que* even though; ~ ... *siquiera* not even.
nicho m niche, recess.
nicotina f nicotine.
nidada f (*huevos*) sitting, clutch; (*pollos*) brood; **nido** m nest (a. *fig.*).
niebla f fog; mist; *hay* ~ it is foggy.
nieta f granddaughter; **nieto** m grandson; ~s *pl.* grandchildren.
nieve f snow; *Mex.* ice cream.
nilón m nylon.
nimiedad f insignificant detail; **nimio** *detalle etc.* tiny, insignificant.
ninfa f nymph.
ningún, ninguno 1. *adj.* no; 2. *pron.* none; (*p.*) nobody, no one; ~ *de ellos* none of them.
niña f (little) girl; *anat.* pupil; *desde* ~ from childhood; ~ *expósita* foundling; ~s *pl. de los ojos de fig.* apple of *s.o.'s* eye; **niñada** f childish thing; **niñear** [1a] act childishly; **niñera** f nursemaid, nanny' F; **niñería** f childish thing; *fig.* silly thing; **niñez** f childhood; **niño** 1. young; *b.s.* childish; 2. m (little) boy; (*en general*) child; baby; infant; ~s *pl.* children; ~ *bonito*, ~ *gótico* playboy; ~ *explorador* boy scout; ~ *expósito* foundling; *desde* ~ from childhood; ~*-probeta* test-tube baby.
níquel m nickel; chromium-plating.

nitidez f spotlessness *etc.*; **nítido** bright, clean, spotless; *phot.* sharp.

nitrato m nitrate; **nítrico** nitric; **nitro** m nitre; **nitrogenado** nitrogenous; **nitrógeno** m nitrogen.

nivel m level; ~ de aire, ~ de burbuja spirit level; ~ de vida standard of living; ~ sonoro noise level; a ~ level (a. ⚙); true; **nivelado** level; ⊕ a. flush; **niveladora** f ⊕ bulldozer; **nivelar** [1a] level; ⚙ *etc.* grade; *fig.* level up, even up.

no *mst* not; (*usado solo*) no; ¿~? = ¿~ es verdad?; *compuestos*: ~ agresión nonagression; ~ sea que lest; ~ ... sino only; not ... but.

noble *adj. a. su.* m noble; **nobleza** f nobility, aristocracy.

noche f night; nighttime; (*más bien tarde*) evening; (*oscuridad*) darkness; ¡buenas ~s! good evening!; (*al despedirse o acostarse*) good night!; esta ~ tonight; de (la) ~ función *etc.* late-night *attr.*; ~ toledana sleepless night; de ~, por la ~ at night, by night; de la ~ a la mañana overnight; hacerse de ~ get dark; **nochebuena** f Christmas Eve; **noche vieja** New Year's Eve; watch night; **nochero** m sleepwalker.

noción f notion, idea; ~es pl. elements; smattering.

nocivo harmful, injurious.

nocturno night *attr.*; *zo. etc.* nocturnal.

nodriza f wet nurse.

nogal m, **noguera** f walnut (tree).

nómada 1. nomadic; 2. m/f nomad.

nombradía f fame, renown; **nombrado** *fig.* renowned; **nombramiento** m naming; designation; nomination; appointment; ⚔ commission; **nombrar** [1a] name; designate; (*proponer*) nominate; (*elegir etc.*) appoint; ⚔ commission; mention; **nombre** m name (a. *fig.*); *gr.* noun; ~ comercial firm name; ~ de lugar place name; ~ (de pila) Christian name; first name; ~ de soltera maiden name; mal ~ nickname; por mal ~ nicknamed; ~ propio proper name (*or* noun); de ~ by name; en ~ de in the name of, on behalf of; sin ~ nameless.

nomeolvides f forget-me-not.

nómina f list; ✝ payroll; **nominación** f nomination; **nominal** nominal; titular; *valor* face *attr.*

non odd; andar de ~es have nothing to do; estar de ~ be odd (man out).

nonada f trifle, mere nothing.

nordeste = *noreste*.

noreste 1. *parte* northeast(ern); *dirección* northeasterly; *viento* northeast (-erly); 2. m northeast.

noria f waterwheel, chain pump.

norma f standard, rule, norm; method; **normal** normal (a. Ⓐ); natural; regular; *ancho etc.* standard; **normalizar** [1f] normalize, standardize.

noroeste 1. *parte* northwest(ern); *dirección* northwesterly; *viento* northwest(erly); 2. m northwest.

norte 1. *parte* north(ern); *dirección* northerly; *viento* north(erly); 2. m north; *fig.* guide; lodestar; north wind; **norteamericano** *adj. a. su.* m, a f American (*of U.S.A.*); **norteño** 1. northern; 2. m, a f northerner.

nos (*acc.*) us; (*dat.*) (to) us; (*reflexivo*) (to) ourselves; (*recíproco*) (to) each other; **nosotros, nosotras** pl. we; (*tras prp.*) us.

nostalgia f nostalgia, homesickness; **nostálgico** nostalgic, homesick.

nota f note (a. ♪); *escuela:* report; mark, class *en examen*; **notable** 1. notable, noteworthy; remarkable; 2. m worthy, notable; **notación** f notation; **notar** [1a] note, notice; (*apuntar*) note down; *escrito* annotate; *fig.* criticize.

notario m notary (public).

noticia f piece of news; (news) item *en periódico*; (*noción*) knowledge, idea (de of); ~s pl. news; **noticiar** [1b] notify; **noticiario** m *radio:* news (bulletin); *cine:* newsreel; **noticioso** *fuente* well-informed; **notificación** f notification; **notificar** [1g] notify; **notorio** well-known; *b.s.* notorious; obvious.

novato 1. raw, green; 2. m beginner.

novedad f (*calidad*) newness, novelty, strangeness; (*cambio*) change, new development; (*cosa nueva*) novelty; (*noticia*) news; ~es pl. novelties; (*modas*) latest fashions; sin ~ as usual; **novel** 1. new, inexperienced; 2. m beginner; **novela** f novel; ~ por entregas serial; *policíaca* detective story, whodunit *sl.*; **novelero** p. highly imaginative, romantic; **novelesco** *género* fictional; *suceso* romantic, fantastic; **novelista** m/f novelist.

novia f girl-friend, sweetheart; (*prometida*) fiancée; (*casada*) bride; **noviazgo** m engagement.

noviciado m eccl. novitiate; apprenticeship; **novicio** m, **a** f novice (a. eccl.); beginner; apprentice.

noviembre m November.

novilla f heifer; **novillero** m toros: novice bullfighter; F truant; **novillo** m young bull; steer, bullock; fiancé; F hacer ~s play truant.

novilunio m new moon.

novio m boyfriend; (*prometido*) fiancé; (*casado*) bridegroom; los ~s (*casados*) the bridal couple.

nubarrón m storm cloud; **nube** f cloud (a. fig.); poner en (or por) las ~s praise to the skies.

núbil nubile, marriageable.

nublado 1. cloudy; 2. m storm cloud; fig. threat; (*copia*) swarm; **nubloso** cloudy; fig. gloomy.

nuca f nape.

nuclear nuclear; **núcleo** m nucleus; ⚡ core (a. fig.); ♀ kernel.

nudillo m knuckle; **nudo** m knot (a. ⚓, ♀, fig.); node; center de comunicaciones; (*enredo*) tangle; lump en garganta; fig. bond, tie; thea. plot; **nudoso** madera etc. knotty; tronco gnarled.

nuera f daughter-in-law.

nuestro 1. adj. our; (*tras su.*) of ours; 2. pron. ours.

nueva f piece of news; ~s pl. news; **nuevamente** again; recently.

nueve nine (a. su.); (*fecha*) ninth.

nuevo new; (*original*) novel; (*adicional*) further; más ~ (*p.*) junior; de ~ (all over) again.

nuez f nut; walnut; ~ de Adán Adam's apple; ~ moscada nutmeg.

nulidad f nullity; incompetence de empleado; (*p.*) nonentity; **nulo** ⚡ (null and) void; invalid.

numeral numeral; **numerar** [1a] number; **numérico** numerical; **número** m number (a. de revista etc.); thea. turn, number; item, number en programa; cargar al ~ llamado, cobrar al ~ llamado call collect, reverse the charges; mirar por el ~ uno to look out for number one; ~ atrasado back-number; ~ de serie series number; teleph. ~ equivocado wrong number; ~ extraordinario special edition; de ~ miembro full; sin ~ numberless; **numeroso** numerous.

nunca never; ever; ~ (ja)más never again; casi ~ hardly ever.

nuncio m eccl. nuncio; Papal envoy.

nupcial wedding attr.; **nupcias** f/pl. wedding.

nutria f otter.

nutrición f nutrition, nourishment; **nutrido** fig. large, considerable; **nutrimento** m nutriment, nourishment; **nutrir** [3a] feed, nourish; **nutritivo** nutritious.

nylón m nylon.

ñame m yam; dunce.

ñapa f Am. de ~ to boot.

ñaque m junk; pile of junk.

ñiquiñaque m F trash, rubbish.

ñoño 1. whining; spineless; feeble-minded; 2. m, **a** f drip.

O

o or; ~ ... ~ either ... or.

oasis m oasis.

obedecer [2d] obey; ~ a (*ceder*) yield to; **obediencia** f obedience; **obediente** obedient.

obelisco m obelisk.

obertura f overture.

obesidad f obesity; **obeso** obese.

obispo m bishop.

objeción f objection; **objetante** m/f objector; **objetar** [1a] object; **objetividad** f objectivity; **objetivo** adj. a. su. m objective; **objeto** m object (a. gr.); (*fin a.*) end, purpose.

oblea f wafer.

oblicuo oblique; mirada sidelong.

obligación f obligation; duty (a, con, para to); obligaciones pl. ♰ bonds, securities; **obligar** [1h] force, compel; ~se bind o.s. (a to); **obligatorio** obligatory, binding (a on).

oboe m oboe.

obra f work; piece of work; handi-work; ~s pl. lit. etc. works; 🏛 repairs, alterations; ~ de about, a matter of; ~s pl. de caridad good works; ~ de consulta reference book; ~ de hierro ironwork; ~ maestra masterpiece; ~s pl. públicas public works; **obraje** m

manufacture, processing; **obrar** [1a]
v/t. build, make; *madera etc.* work;
v/i. act, behave, proceed; **obrero 1.**
clase etc. working; labor *attr.*; *movimiento* working-class; **2.** *m,* **a** *f*
worker (*a. pol.*).

obscenidad *f* obscenity; **obsceno** *a.*
obscene.

obsequio *m* attention, courtesy;
(*regalo*) present, gift; **obsequioso**
attentive, obliging, helpful; *b.s.*
obsequious.

observación *f* observation; (*dicho a.*)
remark, comment; observance *de
ley;* **observador 1.** observant; **2.** *m,*
-a *f* observer; **observancia** *f* observance; **observar** [1a] (*ver*) observe;
watch; notice, spot F; **observatorio**
m observatory.

obsesión *f* obsession; **obsesionante**
haunting; **obsesionar** [1a] obsess.

obstáculo *m* obstacle; hindrance.

obstante: *no ~* **1.** *adv.* however,
nevertheless; **2.** *prp.* in spite of; **obs-
tar** [1a]: *~ a* hinder, prevent.

obstinación *f* obstinacy *etc.*; **obstinado** obstinate, stubborn; **obsti-
narse** [1a]: *~ en inf.* persist in *ger.*

obstrucción *f* obstruction (*a. parl.*);
obstructivo obstructive; **obstruir**
[3g] obstruct, block; hinder.

obtener [2l] get, obtain, secure.

obturador *m phot.* shutter; ⊕, *mot.*
choke; **obturar** [1a] plug, stop up,
seal off; *diente* fill.

obtuso blunt; A, *fig.* obtuse.

obús *m* howitzer; (*granada*) shell.

obviar [1c] *v/t.* remove; *v/i.* stand in
the way; **obvio** obvious.

oca *f* goose.

ocasión *f* occasion, time; opportunity, chance (*de inf.* to *inf.*); *de ~*
second-hand; **ocasional** accidental;
ocasionar [1a] cause, produce.

ocaso *m ast.* sunset; setting *de astro;*
geog. west; *fig.* decline.

occidental western; **occidente** *m*
west.

oceánico oceanic; **océano** *m* ocean.

ocho eight (*a. su.*); (*fecha*) eighth.

ocio *m* leisure; *ratos de ~* spare time;
ociosidad *f* idleness; **ocioso** *p. etc.*
idle, lazy; *obra* useless.

octubre *m* October.

ocular 1. ocular; *v. testigo;* **2.** *m*
eyepiece; **oculista** *m/f* oculist.

ocultar [1a] hide (*a, de from*); screen,
mask; **oculto** hidden.

ocupación *f* occupation (*a.* ✕); **ocu-**

pante *m/f* occupant; **ocupar** [1a]
mst occupy (*a.* ✕); *puesto a.* fill, hold;
espacio, tiempo a. take up; (*llenar*) fill
(up); *atmósfera* pervade.

ocurrencia *f* occurrence; (*chiste*)
witty remark; (bright) idea; **ocu-
rrente** witty; **ocurrir** [3a] happen,
occur.

oda *f* ode.

odiar [1b] hate; **odio** *m* hatred; ill-
will; *~-amor* love-hate; *~ de sangre*
feud; *tener ~ a* hate; **odioso** odious,
hateful; nasty.

odontología *f* dentistry.

odorífero sweet-smelling.

odre *m* wineskin; F old soak.

oeste 1. *parte* west(ern); *dirección*
westerly; *viento* west(erly); **2.** *m*
west.

ofender [2a] offend; wrong; *reputación etc.* injure; *vista etc.* hurt; (*injuriar*) insult; *~se* take offense (*de, por
at*); **ofensa** *f* offense; insult; **ofensiva** *f* offensive; **ofensivo** offensive
(*a.* ✕); disgusting; **ofensor** *m,* **-a** *f*
offender.

oferta *f* offer (*a.* ✝); proposal, proposition; ✝ tender, bid.

office ['ofis] *m* pantry.

oficial 1. official; **2.** *m* official, officer
(*a.* ✕); (*obrero*) skilled worker; **ofi-
ciar** [1b] officiate (*de as*); **oficina** *f*
office; ✕ orderly room; *pharm.*
laboratory; **oficinesco** office *attr.*;
clerical; white-collar; **oficinista** *m/f*
office worker, clerk; **oficio** *m* (*profesión*) occupation; ⊕ craft, trade; **ofi-
cioso** diligent; helpful; *b.s.* officious.

ofrecer [2d] *mst* offer; present; *~se*
offer o.s.; volunteer; **ofrecimiento**
m offer(ing); **ofrenda** *f eccl.* offering.

ofuscar [1g] mystify, confuse.

oída *f* hearing; **oído** *m* hearing;
anat., ♪ ear; ♪ *de ~* by ear; **oír** [3q]
hear; (*atender*) listen (to); *misa*
attend; *¡oiga! teleph.* hullo!

ojal *m* buttonhole; eyelet.

¡ojalá! 1. *int.* if only it would! *etc.*; no
such luck!; **2.** *cj. ~* (*que*) ... if only ...!;
... I hope that.

ojeada *f* glance; **ojear** [1a] eye, stare
at; *hunt.* beat; **ojeras** *f/pl.* rings
under the eyes; **ojeriza** *f* spite, ill-
will; **ojeroso** seedy; **ojete** *m sew.*
eyelet.

ojiva *f* ogive; **ojival** ogival.

ojo *m* eye (*a. fig.*); span *de puente; ~* (*de
la cerradura*) keyhole; *¡~!* look out!;

(mucho) ~ *con* be very careful about, beware of; *¡~, mancha!* wet paint!, fresh paint!; *a los ~s de* in the eyes of; *a ~s vistas* publicly; *hacer del ~* wink; **ojuelos** *m/pl.* (bright) eyes.

ola *f* wave; ~ *de calor* heat wave; ~ *de marea* tidal wave.

¡olé! bravo!

oleada *f* ✚ big wave; *(movimiento)* surge, swell; *fig.* wave *de huelgas etc.*

oleaje *m* surge, swell, surf.

óleo *m* paint., *eccl.* oil; *(cuadro)* oil-painting; *al ~ pintura* oil *attr.*, *pintar* in oils; **oleoducto** *m* pipeline.

oler [2i] smell *(a* of, like); **olfatear** [1a] sniff, smell, scent (out); *a. fig.*); *fig.* nose out; **olfativo** olfactory; **olfato** *m* (sense of) smell; scent.

oligarquía *f* oligarchy.

oliva *f* olive; **olivar** *m* olive-grove; **olivo** *m* olive (tree).

olla *f* pot, pan; pool *de río*; *mount.* chimney; ~ *podrida* stew; ~ *de presión* pressure cooker.

olmo *m* elm (tree).

olor *m* smell; odor; scent; *mal ~* stink; **oloroso** fragrant.

olvidadizo forgetful, absentminded; **olvidado** forgetful; ~ *de* forgetful of, oblivious of (*or* to); **olvidar** [1a] forget; leave behind; omit; ~**se** *(impers.)* forget o.s.; **olvido** *m (estado)* forgetfulness; oblivion; omission; slip.

ombligo *m* navel; middle, center.

omisión *f* omission; failure *(de inf.* to *inf.)*; *(dejadez)* neglect; **omitir** [3a] leave out, miss out, omit.

omóplato *m* shoulder-blade.

once eleven *(a. su.)*; *(fecha)* eleventh; *las* ~ eleven o'clock.

onda *f* wave *(a. phys., radio)*; ~ *corta* short wave; *de* ~ *corta* shortwave *attr.*; ~ *larga* long wave; ~ *luminosa* light wave; *radio:* ~ *portadora* carrier; ~ *sonora* sound wave; **ondear** [1a] *v/t.* pelo wave; *sew.* pink; *v/i. (agua)* ripple; *(movimiento)* undulate; *(bandera etc.)* flutter, wave; ~**se** wave; swing; **ondulación** *f* undulation; wave *(a. pelo)*, ripple; ~ *permanente* permanent wave; **ondulado** wavy; *camino* uneven; *hierro, papel* corrugated.

ONU: *Organización de las Naciones Unidas f* UN *(United Nations)*.

onza *f* ounce *(a. zo.)*.

opacidad *f* opacity; **opaco** opaque.

ópalo *m* opal.

opción *f* option *(a* on); *en* ~ as an option; **opcional** optional; ~ *cero* zero option.

ópera *f* opera.

operación *f* operation; **operador** *m*, **-a** *f cine etc.:* operator; ✚ surgeon; **operar** [1a] *v/t.* ✚ operate on (de for); *v/i.* operate; ~**se** ✚ have an operation (de for); **operario** *m*, **a** *f* operative; workman.

opereta *f* operetta, light opera.

opiata *f*, **opiato** *m* opiate.

opinar [1a] think; ~ *que* be of the opinion that, judge that; **opinión** *f* opinion; ~ *pública* public opinion.

opio *m* opium.

oponer [2r] *dique etc.* set up (*a* against); *objeción etc.* raise (*a* to).

oportunidad *f* opportunity *(de inf.* of *ger.*, to *inf.)*, chance; *(lo oportuno)* opportuneness, expediency; **oportunismo** *m* opportunism; **oportunista** *m/f* opportunist; **oportuno** timely, opportune.

oposición *f* opposition; *(a.* ~es *pl.)* examination, competition (*a* for); **opositor** *m*, **-a** *f* competitor.

opresión *f* oppression; oppressiveness; **opresivo** oppressive; **opresor** *m*, **-a** *f* oppressor; **oprimir** [3a] oppress; squeeze, press *con presión*; *(vestido)* be too tight for.

oprobio *m* shame, opprobrium; **oprobioso** shameful, opprobrious.

optar [1a] choose, decide (*entre* between; *por inf.* to *inf.)*.

óptica *f* optics; **óptico 1.** optic(al); **2.** *m* optician.

optimismo *m* optimism; **optimista** **1.** optimistic, hopeful; **2.** *m/f* optimist.

óptimo very good; optimum.

opuesto ⚓, *lado* opposite; *opinión etc.* contrary, opposing.

opugnar [1a] attack.

opulencia *f* opulence; affluence; **opulento** opulent; luxurious.

oquedad *f* hollow; *fig.* hollowness.

ora: ~ ... ~ now ... now (then).

oración *f* oration, speech; *eccl.* prayer; *gr.* sentence; **oráculo** *m* oracle; **orador** *m*, **-a** *f* orator; speaker; **oral** oral; **orar** [1a] speak, make a speech.

oratorio 1. oratorical; **2.** *m* ♪ oratorio; *eccl.* oratory.

orbe *m* orb; *(mundo)* world; **órbita** *f* orbit *(a. fig.)*; *entrar en* ~ go into orbit; **orbital** orbital.

O

orden[1] *m* order; ~ *del día* agenda; ~ *público* law and order; *en* ~, *por* (*su*) ~ in order; *llamar al* ~ call to order; *poner en* ~ put into order.

orden[2] *f mst* order; ⚖ *a.* writ, warrant; ~ *de allanamiento* search warrant; ~ *de colocación* word order; ✂ ~ *del día* order of the day; *de pago* money order; ✝ *a la* ~ to order; *hasta nueva* ~ till further orders; *por* ~ *de* on the orders of, by order of.

ordenación *f* order; arrangement; *eccl.* ordination; **ordenada** *f* ordinate; **ordenado** orderly, tidy; methodical; **ordenador** *m* ⊕ computer; ~ *de viaje* on-board computer; **ordenanza** 1. *f* ordinance; decree; 2. *m* ✂ orderly; **ordenar** [1a] (*arreglar*) arrange, order; marshal; (*poner en orden*) put into order; (*mandar*) order (*inf.* to *inf.*); *eccl.* ordain; **~se** take (holy) orders.

ordeñar [1a] milk; **ordeño** *m* milking.

ordinal *adj. a. su. m* ordinal.

ordinariez *f* commonness, coarseness; **ordinario** ordinary; usual; mediocre; (*vulgar*) common, coarse; *de* ~ usually.

orear [1a] air; **~se** take a breather.

orégano *m* marjoram.

oreja *f* ear; (*lengüeta*) tab; handle.

orfanato *m* orphanage; **orfandad** *f* orphanage; orphanhood.

orfebre *m* goldsmith, silversmith.

orfelinato *m Am.* orphanage.

orfeón *m* glee club, choral society.

orgánico organic; **organismo** *m* *biol. etc.* organism; *pol.* organization; **organista** *m/f* organist; **organización** *f* organization; **organizador** *m*, **-a** *f* organizer; **organizar** [1f] organize; **órgano** *m* organ; (*medio*) means, medium.

orgía *f* orgy.

orgullo *m* pride; arrogance; **orgulloso** proud.

orientación *f* orientation; **oriental** 1. oriental; eastern; 2. *m/f* oriental; **orientar** [1a] orientate; position; (*dirigir*) guide; train *para profesión*; **~se** *fig.* take one's bearings; **oriente** *m* east; ♀ Orient; *el Cercano* ♀, *el Próximo* ♀ the Near East; *el Extremo* ♀, *el Lejano* ♀ the Far East; *el* ♀ *Medio* the Middle East.

orificio *m* orifice; vent.

origen *m* origin; source; **original** 1. original; novel; (*singular*) odd, ec-

centric; 2. *m* original (*a. p.*); (*p.*) character; *typ.* copy; **originalidad** *f* originality; eccentricity; **originar(se)** [1a] originate; start, cause; **originario:** ~ *de* native to.

orilla *f* edge (*a. sew.*); bank *de río*; side *de lago*; shore *de mar*; rim *de taza*; *sew.* border, hem; ~ *del mar* seashore, ~*s f/pl. Arg., Mex.* outskirts (of the city); *a* ~*s de* on the banks of; **orillar** [1a] *sew.* edge, trim (*de* with); *lago etc.* skrit; *asunto* touch briefly on.

orín *m* rust; *tomarse de* ~ get rusty.

orina *f* urine; **orinar** [1a] urinate; **orines** *m/pl.* urine.

oriundo: ~ *de* native to; *ser* ~ *de* come from, be a native of.

orla *f* border, edging, fringe; **orlar** [1a] border, edge (*de* with).

ornamental ornamental; **ornamentar** [1a] adorn; **ornamento** *m* ornament; adornment; **ornar** [1a] adorn, decorate.

oro *m* gold; *naipes:* ~*s pl.* diamonds; ~ *en barras* bullion; ~ *batido* gold leaf; ~ *laminado* rolled gold.

oropel *m* tinsel (*a. fig.*).

orquesta *f* orchestra; **orquestar** [1a] orchestrate.

orquídea *f* orchid, orchis.

ortiga *f* (stinging) nettle.

orto...: ~**doncia** orthodontics; *aparato de* ~ orthodontic appliance, braces; ~**doxia** *f* orthodoxy; ~**doxo** orthodox; sound; ~**grafía** *f* spelling, orthography ⚇; ~**gráfico** orthographic(al).

oruga *f* *zo.* caterpillar; ⚙ rocket.

orujo *m skins and stones of grapes etc. after pressing*.

orza *f* ⚓ luff(ing); **orzar** [1f] luff.

orzuelo *m* ✱ sty (on the eye).

os (*acc.*) you; (*dat.*) (to) you; (*reflexivo*) (to) yourselves; (*recíproco*) (to) each other.

osadía *f* daring; **osado** daring, bold.

osamenta *f* bones; skeleton.

osar [1a] dare (*inf.* to *inf.*).

osario *m* ossuary, charnel-house.

oscilación *f* oscillation, swing *etc*; **oscilar** [1a] oscillate, swing, sway; (*luz*) blink; *fig.* waver.

oscurecer [2d] *v/t.* darken; *fig.* confuse, fog; *v/i.* grow dark; **oscuridad** *f* darkness; **oscuro** dark; gloomy.

oso *m* bear; ~ *blanco* polar bear; ~ *pris* grizzly bear.

ostentación f ostentation; pomp, display; **ostentar** [1a] show; *b.s.* show off, flaunt, display; **ostentativo, ostentoso** ostentatious.

ostra f oyster; *fig.* (*p.*) fixture.

ostracismo m ostracism.

ostral m oyster bed.

O.T.A.N.: *la* ~ Nato.

O.T.A.S.E.: *la* ~ Seato.

otero m hill, knoll.

otoñal autumnal, autumn *attr.*; **otoño** m autumn, fall.

otorgar [1h] grant, give (*a* to).

otramente otherwise; in a different way; **otro 1.** *adj.* other; another; *thea.* ¡~*a!* encore!; ~ que other than; **2.** *pron.* another one;

el ~ the other (one); *los* ~s the others, the rest.

ovación f ovation; **ovacionar** [1a] applaud, cheer.

oval(ado) oval; **óvalo** m oval.

ovario m *biol.* ovary.

oveja f sheep; **ovejuno** sheep *attr.*

ovillar [1a] wind; ~**se** curl up into a ball; **ovillo** m ball of wool *etc.*; *fig.* tangle; *hacerse un* ~ curl up.

ovni m: *objeto volante no identificado* UFO (*unidentified flying object*).

óvulo m ovum.

oxidado rusty; 🜛 oxidized; **oxidar** [1a] 🜛 oxidize; rust; **oxígeno** m oxygen.

ozono m ozone.

P

pabellón m (*edificio*) pavilion; (*colgadura*) canopy, (*bandera*) flag.

pábilo m, **pabilo** m wick.

paciencia f patience; forbearance; **paciente** *adj. a. su.* m/f patient; **pacienzudo** patient; longsuffering.

pacificación f peace, calm; **pacificador, -a** f peacemaker; **pacificar** [1g] pacify; ~**se** calm down; **pacífico** pacific, peaceable; **pacifismo** m pacifism; **pacifista** *adj. a. su.* m/f pacifist.

pactar [1a] agree to; **pacto** m pact, covenant, agreement.

padecer [2d] suffer (*de* from); endure; *error etc.* be a victim of; **padecimiento** m suffering.

padrastro m stepfather; *fig.* obstacle; *anat.* hangnail; **padrazo** m F indulgent father; **padre** m father (*a. eccl.*); *zo.* sire; (*tras nombre*) senior, the elder; ~s *pl.* parents, father and mother; ancestors; ~ *espiritual* confessor; ⳇ *Nuestro* Lord's Prayer; **padrino** m *eccl.* godfather; best man *en boda*.

paga f payment; (*sueldo*) pay, wages; fee; **pagadero** payable, due; **pagador** m, **-a** f payer.

paganismo m paganism; **pagano** *adj. a. su.* m, **a** f pagan, heathen.

pagar [1h] pay; repay; pay off; *compra* pay for; *favor, visita* return; *a* ~ 🜚 postage due; *a* ~, *por* ~ *cuenta* unpaid; ~**se** de be pleased with, take a liking to; **pagaré** m promissory note, IOU.

página f page; **paginación** f pagination; **paginar** [1a] paginate.

pago m payment; repayment; *fig.* return, reward; ~ *anticipado* advance payment; ~ *al contado* cash (payment); ~ *a cuenta* payment on account; ~ *a plazos* deferred payment; ~ *contra recepción* cash on delivery; *en* ~ *de* in payment for.

paila f large pan.

país m country; land, region; *del* ~ *vino etc.* local; **paisaje** m landscape; countryside; **paisanaje** m civil population; **paisano** m, **a** f fellow countryman; ✗ civilian; *S.Am.* peasant.

paja f straw; *fig.* trash; *lit.* padding; *de* ~ straw *attr.*; F *hombre de* ~ stooge; **pajar** m straw-loft; rick.

pájara f *zo.* (hen)bird; (*cometa*) paper kite; F sharp one; ~ *pinta* forfeits; **pajarear** [1a] *fig.* loaf, loiter; *S.Am.* (*caballo*) shy; **pajarera** f aviary; **pajarero 1.** F p. merry, bright; *vestido* gaudy; **2.** m bird fancier; (*cazador*) bird catcher; **pajarilla** f paper kite; **pajarita** f paper kite, paper bird; **pajarito** m fledgling; **pájaro** m bird; F chap; F (*astuto*) clever fellow; F ~ *de cuenta* bigwig; ~ *carpintero* woodpecker; ~ *mosca* hummingbird.

paje m page; ⚓ cabin-boy.

pajera f straw-loft; **pajita** f (drinking-)straw; **pajizo** straw *attr.*; straw-colored; **pajuela** f spill.

pala f shovel, spade; scoop; blade *de*

remo, hélice etc.; *deportes*: bat, racquet; upper(s) *de zapato*.

palabra *f* word; *(facultad)* (power of) speech; ~s *pl. mayores* - (strong) words; *a media* ~ at the least hint; *de* ~ by word of mouth; ~ *por* ~ word for word, verbatim; **palabrero 1.** windy, wordy; **2.** *m*, **a** *f* windbag.

palaciano, palaciego 1. palace *attr.*, court *attr.*; **2.** *m* courtier; **palacio** *m* palace; ~ *de justicia* courthouse; ~ *municipal* city hall.

paladar *m* palate (*a. fig.*), roof of the mouth; *fig.* taste; **paladear** [1a] taste (with pleasure), relish.

palanca *f* lever; crowbar; ~ *de freno* brake lever; ~ *de mando* control column.

palangana *f* washbasin; **palanganero** *m* washstand.

palco *m* box; ~ *de proscenio* stagebox; ~ *escénico* stage.

palenque *m* *(defensa)* palisade; *(público)* arena, ring.

paleta *f* small shovel, scoop; *(badil)* fire-shovel; ⚒ trowel; *paint.* palette; blade, vane; **paletilla** *f* shoulder-blade.

palidecer [2d] (turn) pale; **palidez** *f* paleness; **pálido** pale, sickly.

palillo *m* toothpick; ♪ drumstick; ~s *pl.* castanets; chopsticks; F trifles.

palio *m* cloak; canopy.

paliza *f* beating, thrashing.

palizada *f* stockade.

palma *f* ♀, *anat. a. fig.* palm; triumph; **palmada** *f* slap, pat *en el hombro etc.*; clapping, applause.

palmear [1a] clap.

palmera *f* palm(-tree).

palmeta *f* cane; *(acto)* caning.

palmípedo webfooted.

palmo *m* span; *avanzar* ~ *a* ~ go forward inch by inch.

palo *m* stick; pole; *(material)* wood; handle *de escoba etc.*; (golf- *etc.*) club; ⚓ mast; ⚓ spar; *(golpe)* blow with a stick; *naipes*: suit.

paloma *f* dove, pigeon; *fig. a. pol.* dove; ~s *pl.* ♣ whitecaps; ~ *mensajera* carrier pigeon; ~ *torcaz* wood-pigeon; **palomar** *m* dovecot(e); **palomino** *m* young pigeon; **palomitas** *f/pl.* popcorn.

palpable palpable; *(a tientas)* grope along, feel one's way; *sl.* frisk.

palpitación *f* palpitation *etc.*; **palpitante** palpitating, throbbing;

cuestión burning; **palpitar** [1a] palpitate, throb; flutter *de emoción*.

palúdico marshy; ⚘ marsh *attr.*, malarial; **paludismo** *m* malaria.

pan *m* *(en general)* bread; loaf; ♀ wheat; ⊕ gold leaf, silver leaf.

pana¹ *f* velveteen, corduroy.

pana² *f* *mot.* breakdown.

panacea *f* panacea, cure-all.

panadería *f* bakery; **panadero** *m*, **a** *f* baker.

panal *m* honeycomb.

páncreas *m* pancreas.

pandear(se) [1a] bulge, warp, sag.

pandemonio *m* pandemonium.

pandeo *m* bulge, bulging.

pandilla *f* set; *b.s.* gang, clique; ⚘ ring; **pandillero** *m* *S.Am.* gangster.

panel *m* panel; plywood.

panfleto *m* lampoon; pamphlet.

pánico *adj. a. su. m* panic.

pantalla *f* screen (*a. cine*) (lamp)-shade; *llevar a la* ~ film; *pequeña* ~ TV screen; ~ *acústica* loud-speaker.

pantalón *m*, ~es *pl.* trousers, pants *Am.*; *(de mujer, exterior)* slacks; ~es *pl. cortos* shorts.

pantano *m* marsh, bog, swamp; *(artificial)* reservoir; *fig.* obstacle; **pantanoso** marshy, swampy.

pantera *f* panther.

pantorrilla *f* calf (of the leg); **pantorrilludo** fat in the leg.

pantufla *f*, **pantuflo** *m* slipper.

panza *f* paunch, belly; **panzón** F, **panzudo** F paunchy, pot-bellied.

pañal *m* diaper *de niño*; tail *de camisa*; ~es *pl.* swaddling clothes; *fig.* early stages, infancy.

pañete *m* light cloth; ~s *pl.* shorts, trunks.

paño *m* cloth; stuff; *(medida)* breadth of cloth; duster, rag *para limpiar*; mist, cloudiness *en espejo etc.*; *sew.* panel; ~ *de cocina* dish-cloth; ~ *higiénico* sanitary napkin; ~ *de manos* towel; ~ *de mesa* tablecloth; ~s *pl. menores* F underclothes, undies; *al* ~ *thea.* off-stage.

pañolón *m* shawl; **pañuelo** *m* handkerchief; (head)scarf.

papa¹ *m* pope.

papa² *f esp. S.Am.* potato; ~s *pl.* pap, mushy food.

papá *m* F dad(dy), papa.

papagayo *m* parrot; *(p.)* chatterbox.

papal¹ papal.

papal² *m* *S.Am.* potato field.

paparrucha *f* F hoax; worthless book *etc.*

papel *m* paper; piece of paper; *thea.* part, role (*a. fig.*); ~es *pl.* (identification) papers; ~ **de calcar** tracing-paper; ~ **carbón** carbon paper; ~ **de cebolla** onionskin; ~ **cuadriculado** squared paper; ~ **de embalar,** ~ **de envolver** brown paper, wrapping paper; ~ **de empapelar** wallpaper; ~ **de estaño** tinfoil; ~ **de estraza** strong wrapping paper; ~ **de excusado** toilet paper; ~ **de filtro** filter paper; ~ **de fumar** cigarette paper; ~ **higiénico** toilet paper, toilet roll; ~ **de lija** sandpaper; ~ **moneda** paper money; ~ **ondulado** corrugated paper; ~ **de paja de arroz** rice paper; ~ **pintado** wallpaper; ~ **de plata** silver paper; ~ **secante** blotting paper, blotter; ~ **de seda** tissue paper; ~ **sellado** stamped paper; ~ **transparente** tracing paper; ~ **viejo,** ~es *pl. usados* waste paper.

papeleo *m* red tape; **papelería** *f* stationery; (*tienda*) stationer's (shop); (*lío*) sheaf of papers; **papelerío** *m* paperwork; **papelero** *m* stationer; paper manufacturer; **papeleta** *f* slip, card; *pol.* voting paper; *escuela:* report; (*empeño*) pawn ticket; **papelillo** *m* cigarette; **papelón** *m* waste paper; (*cartón*) pasteboard; F impostor; **papelote** *m,* **papelucho** *m* worthless bit of paper.

papera *f* mumps; goitre.

paquebote *m* packet (boat).

paquete *m* parcel (*a.* ✆); packet, pack(age); ⚓ packet (boat); F toff; ~s *pl. postales* parcel post.

par 1. ♈ even; equal; **2.** *m* pair, couple; (*noble*) peer; ~ **de torsión** torque; ~es o **nones** odds or evens; *a* ~es in pairs; *al* ~ equally; together; *de* ~ *en* ~ wide open; *sin* ~ unparalleled; peerless; **3.** *f* par; *a la* ~ equally; at the same time; ♈ at par; *a la* ~ *que* at the same time as; *golf:* 5 *bajo* ~ 5 under par.

para *a*) *destino, uso, fin:* for, intended for; *salir* ~ *Madrid* leave for Madrid; *b*) *tiempo:* ~ *mañana* for tomorrow; by tomorrow; *c*) *relación:* (*a.* ~ *con*) to, towards; *era amable* ~ (*con*) *todos* he was kind to everyone; *d*) *contraste:* ~ *niño, lo hace muy bien* he does it very well for a child; *e*) ~ *inf.* (*fin*) (in order) to *inf.; ahorrar* ~ *comprar algo* save (in order) to buy s.t.; *f*) ~

inf. (*resultado*): *lo encontró* ~ *volver a perderlo* he found it only to lose it again; *g*) ~ *inf.* (*con bastante, demasiado*): *tengo bastante* ~ *vivir* I have enough to live on; *h*) ~ *vivir* I am in order that, so that; *i*) *¿* ~ *qué?* why?, for what purpose?

parabién *m* congratulations; *dar el* ~ *a* congratulate.

para...: brisas *m* windscreen, windshield *Am.;* **caídas** *m* parachute; *lanzar en* ~ parachute; **caidista** *m* parachutist; ✕ paratrooper; **choques** *m mot.* bumper.

parada *f* stop; (*acto*) stopping; (*lugar*) stop, stopping place; (*taxi*) stand; shut-down, standstill.

paradero *m* whereabouts; stopping-place; *S.Am.* 🚂 halt.

parado slow, inactive; motionless; *salida* standing; *p.* unemployed; *S.Am.* standing up; *S.Am.* proud.

paradoja *f* paradox; **paradójico** paradoxical.

parador *m* † inn; (*moderno*) tourist hotel; (*p.*) heavy gambler.

parafina *f* paraffin wax.

paraguas *m* umbrella.

paragüero *m* umbrella-stand.

paraíso *m* paradise, heaven; *thea.* gallery.

paraje *m* place, spot; situation.

paralela *f* parallel line; ~s *pl.* parallel bars; **paralelo** *adj. a. su. m* parallel (*a. geog.*); ⚡ *en* ~ in parallel.

parálisis *f* paralysis; **paralítico** *adj. a. su. m,* paralytic; **paralizar** [1f] paralyse (*a. fig.*); **se** become paralysed.

parámetro *m* parameter, established boundaries.

páramo *m* bleak plateau.

parangón *m* comparison; **parangonar** [1a] compare.

paranoia *f* paranoia.

parapeto *m* parapet, breastwork.

parar [1a] **1.** *v/t.* stop; *progreso* check; *atención* fix (*en* on); *dinero* stake; **2.** *v/i.* stop; stay, put up (*en hotel* at); (*terminar*) end up; ~ *en* result in; **3.** **se** stop; *mot. etc.* stop, pull up; come to a standstill; *S.Am.* stand up; ~ *en* pay attention to.

pararrayos *m* lightening rod.

parasitario, parasítico parasitic, parasitical; **parásito 1.** parasitic (*de* on); **2.** parasite (*a. fig.*); *radio:* ~s *pl.* atmospherics, static.

parasol *m* parasol.

parcela f plot, small-holding; **parcelar** [1a] parcel out.

parcial partial, part ...; *p. etc.* partial, prejudiced, partisan; **parcialidad** f partiality, prejudice.

parcómetro m parking meter.

pardal m sparrow; F sly fellow.

¡pardiez! by Jove!

pardo 1. brown; dun; dark-skinned; *cielo* cloudy, overcast; 2. m S.Am. mulatto; **pardusco** greyish.

parear [1a] match; pair (*a. biol.*); **~se** pair off.

parecer [2d] 1. seem, look; (*presentarse*) appear, turn up; (*dejarse ver*) show; *~ inf.* seem to *inf.*; **~ bien** look well, look all right *por el aspecto*; **~se** look alike; **~ a** resemble, look like; *padre etc.* take after; 3. m opinion, view; looks *de cara*; *a mi ~* in my opinion; *al ~* apparently, evidently.

parecido 1. similar; *~ a* like; *bien ~* good-looking; personable; *mal ~* plain; 2. m resemblance, similarity.

pared f wall; *~ medianera* party wall; *~ por medio* next door; **paredaño** adjoining, next-door.

pareja f pair, couple; (dancing-) partner; *correr ~s* be on a par, keep pace, go together (*con* with); **parejero** m S.Am. race horse; **parejo** equal; *juntura etc.* even, smooth, flush; *por ~* on a par; *ir ~s* go neck and neck.

parentela f relations; **parentesco** m relationship, kinship.

paréntesis m parenthesis; (*signo*) bracket; *entre ~* fig. adj. parenthetic(al); *adv.* by the way.

paria m/f pariah.

paridad f parity; comparison.

pariente m, a f relation, relative.

parir [3a] v/t. give birth to, bear; v/i. give birth, be delivered.

parla f chatter, gossip; **parlador** talkative; *ojos etc.* expressive.

parlamentar [1a] talk, converse; (*enemigos*) parley; **parlamentario** 1. parliamentary; 2. m parliamentarian; member of parliament; **parlamento** m parl. parliament; parley *entre enemigos*.

parlanchín m, **-a** f F chatterbox; **parlante** 1. talking; 2. m loudspeaker; **parlar** [1a] chatter, talk (too much); **parlatorio** m chat, talk; **parlero** *p.* garrulous; (*chismoso*) gossiping; *pájaro* talking, song *attr.*; *ojo*

expressive; **parleta** f F small talk, idle talk; **parlotear** [1a] prattle, run on; **parloteo** m prattle.

paro[1] m orn. tit.

paro[2] m stoppage, standstill; *~ (forzoso)* unemployment.

parodia f parody, travesty (*a. fig.*), take-off F; **parodiar** [1b] parody, travesty, take off F.

parón m stop, delay.

parpadear [1a] blink, wink; (*luz*) twinkle; **parpadeo** m blink(ing); flicker *etc.*; **párpado** m eyelid.

parque m park (*a. ✕, mot.*); S.Am. ✕ ammunition; *~ de bomberos* firestation; *~ zoológico* zoo.

parquear park.

parquet [par'ke] m parquet.

parquímetro m parking meter.

parra f vine (*trained, climbing*).

párrafo m paragraph.

parral m vine arbor.

parranda F: *andar* (or *ir*) *de ~* go on a spree.

parricida m/f parricide (*p.*); **parricidio** m parricide (*act*).

parrilla f grating, gridiron; *cocina:* grill; (*restaurante*) grill-room.

párroco m parish priest; **parroquia** f parish; parish church; ✝ clientèle, custom(ers); **parroquiano** m, a f ✝ patron, client, customer.

parsimonia f parsimony; moderation; (*lentitud*) slowness; **parsimonioso** parsimonious; sparing *de palabras etc.*

parte[1] m *teleph. etc.* message; ✕ dispatch, communiqué; (*informe*) report; *~ meteorológico* weatherforecast; *dar ~ a* inform.

parte[2] f part (*a. ♪, thea.*); share *en repartimiento*; ⚖ party; side; *~s pl.* fig. parts, talents; *~s pl.* (*pudendas etc.*) private parts; *~ actora* prosecution; plaintiff.

partear [1a] *mujer* deliver.

partera f midwife.

partición f partition, division.

participación f participation; share *en repartimiento*; *deportes:* entry; fig. notification; **participante** m/f participant; *deportes:* entrant, entry; **participar** [1a] v/t. inform, notify (of); v/i. participate; *deportes:* enter (*en* for); **partícipe** m/f participant; **participio** m participle.

partícula f particle.

particular 1. particular; (e)special; private; *~ a* peculiar to; 2. m (*p.*)

pasto

private individual; (*asunto*) particular, point.

partida *f* (*salida*) departure; certificate *de bautismo etc.*; entry *en registro*; ⊕ entry, item *en lista*.

partidario 1. partisan; **2.** *m*, **a** *f* partisan; supporter (de of).

partido 1. divided, split; **2.** *m pol.* party; *deportes etc.*: game, match; (*ps.*) side; *geog.* district, administrative area; *fig.* advantage, profit.

partir [3a] *v/t.* (*rajar etc.*) split, break; *nueces etc.* crack; (*repartir*) divide up, share (out); ⊕ divide; *v/i.* set off, set out, depart, start (de from); *a ~ de* beginning from; since; *a ~ de hoy* from today.

partitura *f* score.

parto *m* (*child*)birth, delivery; labor; *fig.* product; *~ del ingenio* brain child; *estar de ~* be in labor.

párvulo 1. very small, tiny; *fig.* simple, innocent; **2.** *m*, **a** *f* child; **parvulario** *m* nursery school; kindergarten.

pasa *f* raisin; *~ de Corinto* currant.

pasable passable.

pasada *f* (*acto*) passage, passing; enough to live on; *sew.* tacking stitch; **pasadera** *f* stepping-stone; ⚓ gangway; **pasadero** passable, tolerable; **pasadizo** *m* passage, corridor; gangway; **pasado 1.** past; *semana etc.* last; (*anticuado*) out-of-date; *comida* stale, bad; *comida guisada* overdone; **2.** *m* past (*a. gr.*); *~s pl.* ancestors.

pasaje *m* (*acto, lugar, ♪, lit.*) passage; ⚓ (*travesía*) crossing, voyage; ⚓ (*precio*) fare; **pasajero 1.** *calle etc.* busy; *fig.* transient, passing, fleeting; **2.** *m* ⚓ passenger; hotel guest.

pasamano *m* rail.

pasamontañas *m* winter cap, cap with ear flaps.

pasaporte *m* passport.

pasar [1a] **1.** *v/t.* pass; *río etc.* cross, go over; (*aventajar*) surpass, excel; *apuros* suffer, endure; *armadura etc.* pierce; *contrabando* smuggle in; **2.** *v/i.* pass; go; (*tiempo*) pass, elapse, wear on; (*suceso*) happen; **3.** *~se* (*comida*) go bad; *~ al enemigo* go over to the enemy.

pasarela *f* foot-bridge; ⚓ *etc.* gangway, gangplank.

pasatiempo *m* pastime, pursuit, hobby.

Pascua *f*, **pascua** *f*: *~ de los hebreos*

Passover; *~ florida*, *~ de Resurrección* Easter; *~ de Navidad* Christmas; *~s pl.* Christmas holiday, Christmas time; ¡*Felices ~s!* Merry Christmas!

pase *m* pass.

pasear [1a] *v/t. niño etc.* walk, take for a walk; *v/i.*, *~se* stroll, walk, go for a walk; *~ a caballo* ride; *~ en coche* go for a drive; **paseo** *m* stroll, walk; outing; (*calle*) parade, avenue; (*marítimo*) promenade, esplanade.

pasillo *m* passage, corridor; ⚓ *etc.* gangway; *thea.* short piece, sketch.

pasión *f* passion; *b.s.* bias, prejudice; **pasional** *p. etc.* passionate; *crimen* passionel.

pasividad *f* passiveness, passivity; **pasivo 1.** passive; **2.** *m* ⊕ liabilities; debit side.

pasmar [1a] amaze, astound, astonish; stun, dumbfound; *~se* be amazed (*de* at) *etc.*; **pasmo** *m* amazement, astonishment; awe; *fig.* wonder, marvel; ⚕ lockjaw; **pasmoso** amazing *etc.*, breathtaking; awesome; wonderful, marvellous.

paso¹ *fruta* dried.

paso² **1.** *m* step; pace; (*sonido*) footfall, footstep; (*huella*) footprint; (*modo de andar*) walk, gait; (*velocidad*) pace, rate; step, stair *de escalera*; *geog.* pass; ⚓ *etc.* passage; ⊕, ✗ pitch; *sew.* stitch; *thea.* sketch; *fig.* (*acto*) passing; (*cambio*) passage, transition; progress, advance; incident; *~ a nivel* grade crossing; *~ de ganado* cattle crossing; *~ de ganso* goose step; **2.** *adv.* ¡*~!* not so fast!, easy there!

pasta *f* paste; dough *para pan* (*a. sl.*); pastry *para hojaldre*; pulp *de madera*; *~ dentífrica* toothpaste; *~ seca* cookie; *~s pl.* pastry, pastries; (*fideos*) noodles, spaghetti; *~ de dientes* toothpaste; *de buena ~* kindly.

pastar [1a] graze.

pastel *m* (*dulce*) cake; pie *de carne etc.*; *paint.* pastel; F plot, undercover agreement; *~es pl.* pastry, confectionery; **pastelear** [1a] F stall, spin it out to gain time; **pastelería** *f* pastry; (*conjunto*) pastries; (*tienda*) confectioner's, cake shop; **pastelero** *m*, **a** *f* pastry cook; confectioner.

pasteurizar [1f] pasteurize.

pastilla *f* tablet, pastille; cake *de jabón etc.*; bar *de chocolate*.

pasto *m* grazing; (*campo*) pasture; (*comida*) feed, grazing; *fig.* nourishment; fuel *para fuego etc.*; *a ~*

P

abundantly; *a todo* ~ freely, in great quantity; *de* ~ ordinary, everyday;
pastor *m* shepherd; herdsman; *eccl.* clergyman, pastor; **pastora** *f* shepherdess; **pastoral** *adj. a. su. f* pastoral; **pastorear** [1a] pasture; *eccl.* guide, lead; **pastorela** *f* pastoral, pastorelle; **pastoril** pastoral.

pastoso pasty; *voz* rich, mellow.

pastura *f* pasture; feed, fodder.

pata *f zo.* foot, paw, leg; leg *de mesa etc.*; *orn.* (female) duck; ~ *de cabra* crowbar; ~ *de gallo* crow's feet; ~ *de palo* peg leg, wooden leg; *a cuatro* ~s on all fours.

patada *f* stamp; (*puntapié*) kick; (*paso*) (foot)step; **patalear** [1a] stamp; kick out, kick about; **pataleo** *m* stamping; kicking.

patán *m* F rustic, yokel; *b.s.* lout.

patata *f* potato.

pateadura *f*, **pateamiento** *m* stamping; kicking; *thea.* noisy protest; **patear** [1a] F *v/t.* kick, boot; trample on; *v/i.* stamp (one's foot).

patentar [1a] patent; **patente 1.** patent (*a.* ~), obvious, (self-)evident; **2.** *f* patent (*a.* ~ *de invención*); warrant; ~ *de sanidad* bill of health; **patentizar** [1f] make evident, reveal.

paternal fatherly, paternal; **paternidad** *f* fatherhood; paternity *de niño etc.*; ~ *literaria* authorship; **paterno** paternal; *abuelo* ~ grandfather on the father's side.

patético pathetic, moving, poignant; **patetismo** *m* poignancy.

patibulario horrifying, harrowing.

patíbulo *m* gallows, gibbet.

patillas *f/pl.* whiskers, sideburns.

patín *m* skate; runner *de trineo*; ☙ skid; ☙ ~ *de cola* tail skid; ~ *de ruedas* roller skate; **patinada** *f Am. mot.* skidding; **patinadero** *m* skating rink; **patinador** *m,* ~*a f* skater; **patinaje** *m* skating; **patinar** [1a] skate; (*resbalar*) skid, slip; **patinazo** *m* skid.

patio *m* court, (court)yard, patio; *thea.* pit; ~ *de recreo* playground.

pato *m* duck; ~ (*macho*) drake.

patochada *f* F blunder.

patria *f* mother country, native land; ~ *chica* home town.

patriarca *m* patriarch; **patriarcal** patriarchal.

patrimonial hereditary; **patrimonio** *m* inheritance; *fig.* heritage.

patrio native, home *attr.*; *potestad etc.* paternal; **patriota** *m/f* patriot; **patriotería** *f* jingoism, chauvinism; **patriotero** *adj. a. su. m,* **a** *f* jingo, chauvinist; **patriótico** patriotic; **patriotismo** *m* patriotism.

patrocinador *m,* ~**a** *f* sponsor; patron; **patrocinar** [1a] sponsor; back; patronize; **patrocinio** *m* sponsorship; backing; patronage.

patrón *m* landlord *de pensión*; (*jefe*) master, boss; ♣ skipper; *eccl.* patron (saint); = *patrono*; *sew.* pattern; ♣ stock; standard *para medidas etc.*; ~ *oro* gold standard; ~ *picado* stencil.

patrona *f* landlady *de pensión*; employer, owner; *eccl.* patron (saint); (*patrocinadora*) patron, patroness; **patronato** *m* board of trustees *de obra benéfica etc.*; board *de turismo etc.*; **patrono** *m* employer, owner; *eccl.* patron (saint); (*patrocinador*) patron; sponsor.

patrulla *f* patrol; **patrullar** [1a] patrol (*por acc.*); police.

pausa *f* pause; break, respite; ♪ rest; *con* ~ slowly; **pausado** slow, deliberate; **pausar** [1a] *v/t.* slow down; interrupt; *v/i.* go slow; pause.

pauta *f* ruler *para rayar*; norm; example; outline; **pautar** [1a] *papel* rule; *fig.* give directions for.

pava *f* turkey hen; F plain woman.

pavesa *f* spark, cinder.

pavimentar [1a] pave; **pavimento** *m* pavement; paving; flooring.

pavo *m* turkey; *sl.* 5 pesetas; ~ *real* peacock; F *comer* ~ be a wallflower.

pavón *m* peacock; *metall.* bluing, bronzing; **pavonar** [1a] *metall.* blue, bronze; **pavonearse** [1a] swagger, strut, swank F.

pavor *m* terror, dread; **pavoroso** terrifying, frightful.

payasada *f* clowning, clownish stunt; ~s *pl.* tomfoolery; *thea. etc.* slapstick; **payaso** *m* clown.

paz *f* peace; peacefulness; rest; *en* ~ at peace; at rest.

pazguato simple, stupid.

peaje *m* toll; *barrera de* ~ toll gate; *puente de* ~ toll bridge.

peatón *m* pedestrian, walker; ☙ country postman.

peca *f* freckle.

pecado *m* sin; **pecador 1.** sinning,

sinful; **2.** *m*, **-a** *f* sinner; **pecaminoso** sinful; **pecar** [1g] sin.

pecera *f* fishbowl.

pechera *f* shirtfront; bosom *de vestido*; (*armadura*) chest protector.

pechero *m* commoner, plebeian.

pecho[1] *m anat.* chest; breast (*a. fig.*); (*esp. de mujer*) breast, bosom, bust; ~s *pl.* breasts, bust; *fig.* courage, spirit; *geog.* slope, gradient; *a* ~ *descubierto* unprotected; openly, frankly (*a. a* ~ *abierto*); *dar el* ~ feed, nurse; *tomar a* ~(s) take to heart.

pecho[2] *m* tax, tribute.

pechuga *f* breast *de pollo etc.*; F breast, bosom *de mujer*.

pecios *m/pl.* flotsam, wreckage.

pecoso freckled.

pecuario cattle *attr.*

peculiar peculiar; characteristic; **peculiaridad** *f* peculiarity.

pedagogía *f* pedagogy; **pedagógico** pedagogic(al); **pedagogo** *m* pedagogue (*a. b.s.*); teacher.

pedal *m* pedal; ~ *de acelerador* accelerator (pedal); ~ *de embrague* clutch (pedal); ~ *de freno* brake (pedal); **pedalear** [1a] pedal.

pedante 1. pedantic; **2.** *m* pedant; **pedantería** *f* pedantry; **pedantesco** pedantic.

pedazo *m* piece, bit; scrap; ~ *del alma etc.* darling; *hacer* ~s break to (*or* in) pieces, pull to pieces; shatter, smash.

pedernal *m* flint; flintiness.

pedestal *m* pedestal, stand, base.

pedestre *viaje* on foot; pedestrian.

pedido *m* request; ~ *de repetición* repeat order; *a* ~ on request.

pedigüeño insistent, importunate; *niño* demanding.

pedimento *m* petition; ⚖ claim, bill.

pedir [3l] **1.** *v/t.* ask for; request, require; demand, need; beg; *paz* sue for; *comida etc.*, ✝ order; **2.** *v/i.* ask; ~ (*por Dios*) beg.

pedrada *f* (*golpe*) hit with a stone; (*echada*) throw of a stone; *fig.* snide remark, dig; *matar a* ~ *s* stone to death; **pedregal** *m* stony place; **pedregoso** stony, rocky; **pedrera** *f* stone-quarry; **pedrería** *f* precious stones, jewels; **pedrisco** *m* shower of stones; heap of loose stones; *meteor.* hailstorm; **pedrusco** *m* rough stone, lump of stone.

pega *f* (*acto*) sticking *etc.*; pitch, varnish *de vasija*; F (*chasco*) trick, practical joke; F (*zurra*) beating-up; **pegadizo** sticky; 🌿 infectious; **pegajoso** sticky, adhesive; 🌿 infectious, catching; ♪ catchy; F (*suave*) soft, gentle; *vicio etc.* tempting; *p.* tiresome; (*sobón*) sloppy, oily, cloying.

pegar [1h] **1.** *v/t.* stick, glue, gum; unite, join; *botón etc.* sew on; *cartel etc.* post, stick; *p.* strike, slap, smack; *enfermedad* give; **2.** *v/i.* stick *etc.*; (*fuego*) catch; (*colores*) match, go together; ✿ take root; (*remedio etc.*) take; **3.** ~*se* stick *etc.*; 🌿 be catching; *cocina*: catch; *fig.* intrude.

pegote *m* sticking-plaster; F sticky mess; (*p.*) hanger-on, sponger; **pegotear** [1a] F sponge, cadge.

peina *f* ornamental comb, back comb; **peinada** *f* combing; *darse una* ~ comb one's hair, have a brush up; **peinado 1.** *p.* overdressed; *estilo* overdone, overnice; **2.** *m* coiffure, hair do; hair style; **peinador** *m* hairdresser; (*vestido*) dressing gown; dressing table; **peinadora** *f* hairdresser; **peinadura** *f* combing; ~s *pl.* combings; **peinar** [1a] *pelo* comb; search, comb; do; style; *pelo, pieles, caballo* dress; ~*se* comb one's hair; **peine** *m* comb.

pelado shorn, hairless; *paisaje etc.* bare, treeless, bleak; *manzana etc.* peeled; broke, penniless.

pelaje *m* coat, fur; *fig.* appearance.

pelar [1a] cut the hair off, shear; *pollo* pluck; *fruta* peel, skin; F fleece; ~*se* (*p.*) lose one's hair; (*capa*) peel off.

peldaño *m* step, stair; rung *de escala*.

pelea *f* fight, tussle; quarrel; struggle; **peleador** combative, quarrelsome; **pelear** [1a] fight; scuffle; struggle; *fig.* vie; ~*se* fight; scuffle; come to blows; (*desavenirse*) fall out.

película *f* film; movie; ~ *de terror* horror film, horror movie; ~ *en colores* color film; ~ *muda* silent film; ~ *sonora* sound movie.

peligrar [1a] be in danger; **peligro** *m* danger; risk; **peligroso** dangerous; risky.

pelillo *m* slight annoyance; F *echar* ~s *a la mar* bury the hatchet.

pelinegro black-haired; **pelirrojo** red-haired, red-headed; **pelirrubio** fair-haired.

pella *f* ball, pellet; roll, round mass; ✿ head; raw lard *de cerdo*; F sum of money; F *hacer* ~ play truant.

pelleja *f* skin, hide; **pellejería** *f* skins, hides; (*fábrica*) tannery; ~s *pl.* S.Am.

P

upsets, troubles; **pellejo** m skin, hide, pelt de animal; ♀ peel; (odre) wineskin; F drunk, toper.

pellizcar [1g] pinch, nip; comida etc. take a small bit of; **pellizco** m pinch, nip; small bit.

pelo m hair; coat, fur de animal; down de ave, fruta; nap, pile de tela, alfombra; ~ (de la barba) whisker; F a(~) ~ just right; ~ arriba, contra ~ the wrong way; en ~ bare-back; F naked; F a medios ~s tight, half-seas-over; F tomar el ~ a pull one's leg.

pelón hairless, bald; F stupid; F (sin dinero) broke; **pelona** f baldness; F death; **peloso** hairy.

pelota f ball; (juego vasco) pelota; S.Am. ferryboat; ~ base baseball; en ~ naked; **pelotari** m pelota player; **pelotear** [1a] v/t. cuenta audit; v/i. tenis etc.: knock up; fútbol: kick a ball about; F bicker, fall out; **pelotera** f F, **pelotero** m F row, quarrel, argument.

pelotón m✗ squad, party; small mat, tuft de pelo; crowd de gente; ~ de ejecución firing squad.

peluca f wig.

peludo 1. hairy, shaggy; furry; barba etc. bushy; 2. m thick mat.

peluquería f hairdresser's (shop), barber's (shop); **peluquero** m hairdresser, barber.

peluquearse Am. get a haircut.

pelusa f ♀ down; fluff de tela.

pelvis f pelvis.

pena f (aflicción) sorrow, distress, grief; ✿ pain(s); (trabajo) trouble; hardship; ⚖ punishment, penalty; ✝ forfeit, penalty; ~s pl. S.Am. ghosts; ¡qué ~! what a shame!; so under pain of; es una ~ it's a shame, it's a pity; merecer la ~ worthwhile (ir, de ir to go, going), be worth the trouble; **penable** punishable.

penacho m orn. tuft, crest; plume de casco; plume, wreath de humo; fig. pride, arrogance; panache.

penado 1. grieved; laborious, difficult; 2. m convict.

penal 1. penal; 2. m prison; **penalidad** f trouble, hardship; ⚖ penalty; **penalista** m penologist, expert in criminal law; **penalty** m penalty.

penar [1a] v/t. penalize, punish; v/i. suffer; ~ por pine for, long for; **~se** grieve, mourn.

penca f ♀ fleshy leaf; hacerse de ~s have to be coaxed into doing s.t.

pendencia f quarrel, fight, brawl; armar ~ brawl; **pendenciero** quarrelsome, cantankerous.

pender [2a] hang; dangle; droop; depend; ⚖ etc. be pending; **pendiente** 1. hanging; asunto etc. pending, unsettled; 2. m earring; 3. f geog. slope, incline; pitch de techo.

péndola f pendulum de reloj; fig. pen, quill; **pendolista** m penman, calligrapher.

pendón m banner, standard.

péndulo m pendulum.

pene m penis.

penetración f penetration (a. fig.); fig. insight, acuteness; **penetrador** penetrating, keen; **penetrante** penetrating; penetrative; **penetrar** [1a] v/t. penetrate, pierce; permeate; misterio etc. fathom, grasp; v/i. penetrate (en, entre, por acc.); sink in, soak in; **~se** become imbued with.

penicilina f penicillin.

península f peninsula; **peninsular** peninsular.

penitencia f penitence; (acto) penance; **penitencial** penitential; **penitenciar** [1b] impose a penance on; **penitenciaría** f prison, penitentiary esp. Am. (a. eccl.); **penitente** adj. a. su. m/f penitent.

penoso arduous, laborious; painful.

pensado: mal ~ evil-minded; de ~ on purpose; **pensador** m thinker; **pensamiento** m (facultad, una idea) thought; (ideas de p.) thinking; ♀ pansy; ni por ~ not on any account; **pensante** thinking; **pensar** [1k] 1. v/t. pensamiento etc. think; problema think over, give thought to; número think of (~ inf. intend to inf., plan to inf.; ~ de think of, have an opinion of; dar que ~ a give food for thought to, give pause to; ¡ni ~lo! not a bit of it!; 2. v/i. think; ~ en think of, think about, reflect on; sin ~ unexpectedly; **pensativo** thoughtful, pensive.

pensión f (renta etc.) pension; (casa) boardinghouse; fig. burden; ~ completa full board (and lodging); ~ vitalicia annuity; **pensionado** 1. m, a f (p.) pensioner; 2. m boarding-school; **pensionar** [1a] pension; **pensionista** m/f pensioner; (huésped) paying guest; (alumno) boarder.

penumbra f penumbra, half-light shadow.

peña f rock; cliff, crag; (ps.) group, circle; b.s. coterie, clique; **peñasco** m rock; crag; pinnacle of rock; **peñascoso** rocky, craggy; **peñón** m (mass of) rock, crag.

peón m (peatón) pedestrian; ✗ infantryman, foot-soldier; S.Am. farmhand, peon; (peonza) top; ajedrez: pawn; ⊕ spindle, axle.

peor adj. a. adv. comp. worse; sup. worst; cada vez ∼, ∼ que worse and worse; de mal en ∼ from bad to worse; v. tanto; **peoría** f worsening, deterioration.

pepinillos m/pl. (en vinagre) gherkins; **pepino** m cucumber.

pepita f ♀, vet. pip; metall. nugget.

pequeñez f smallness, small size; shortness de p.; infancy de niño; contp. smallmindedness; pequeñeces pl. trifles; **pequeño** little, small; estatura short; fig. modest, humble; los ∼s the children.

pera¹ adj. sl.: muy ∼ posh, classy.

pera² f pear; (barba) goatee; ♀ switch; bulb de claxon etc.; **peral** m pear (tree).

percance m mishap, mischance; hitch en proyecto etc.; † perquisite.

percatarse [1a]: ∼ de take notice of.

percepción f perception; appreciation, notion; † collection, receipt; **perceptible** perceptible, noticeable, detectable.

percha f rack, coat stand; coat hanger; **perchero** m hall-stand.

percibir [3a] sueldo etc. receive, get; impuestos collect; impresión etc. perceive, see, notice, detect.

percutir [3a] strike, tap.

perdedor m loser; buen ∼ good loser, good sport.

perder [2g] lose; tiempo waste; tren etc. miss; univ. curso fail; ⚖ etc. forfeit; (echar a ∼) ruin, spoil; ∼ por 2 a 3 lose (by) 2–3; ∼se (en camino etc.) lose o.s., get lost, stray; (material, comida) be spoiled; ∼ (de vista) pass out of sight; ∼ por be mad about.

perdición f perdition, ruin.

pérdida f loss; waste de tiempo; ⚖ etc. forfeiture; wastage de líquido; **perdidizo:** hacer ∼ hide; lose on purpose; hacerse el ∼ make o.s. scarce; **perdido 1.** bala stray; momentos idle, spare; F bebedor etc. inveterate, hardened; ∼ por mad about; dar por ∼ give up for lost; **2.** m rake.

perdigón m orn. young partridge; ✗ pellet.

perdiz f partridge.

perdón m forgiveness, pardon (a. ⚖): ¡∼! sorry!; con ∼ if I may, by your leave; hablando con ∼ if I may say so; pedir ∼ a ask s.o.'s forgiveness; **perdonable** pardonable, excusable; **perdonador** forgiving; **perdonar** [1a] pardon (a. ⚖), forgive, excuse (algo a alguien a p. a th.); vida spare.

perdulario 1. careless; sloppy; (moralmente) vicious; **2.** m rake.

perdurable (ever)lasting; abiding; **perdurar** [1a] last, endure.

perecedero perishable; vida etc. transitory; p. mortal; **perecer** [2d] perish; suffer; ∼ ahogado drown; ∼se por pine for, crave, be dying for; ∼ por mujer be mad about.

peregrinación f long tour, travels; eccl. pilgrimage; **peregrinar** [1a] travel extensively (abroad); eccl. go on a pilgrimage; **peregrino 1.** p. wandering; ave migratory; fig. strange; **2.** m, a f pilgrim.

perejil m parsley; ∼es pl. F buttons and bows, trimmings; F titles.

perendengue m trinket, cheap ornament.

perenne everlasting, undying, perennial (a. ♀); de hoja ∼ evergreen.

perentorio peremptory, authoritative; urgent.

pereza f idleness, laziness, sloth (a. eccl.); **perezoso 1.** idle, lazy, slothful; slack; movimiento sluggish, slow; **2.** m zo. sloth.

perfección f perfection; completion; a la ∼ to perfection; **perfeccionamiento** m perfection; improvement; **perfeccionar** [1a] perfect; improve; **perfectamente** perfectly; ¡∼! precisely!, just so!; **perfectibilidad** f perfectibility; **perfectible** perfectible; **perfecto** perfect.

perfidia f perfidy, treachery; **pérfido** perfidious, treacherous.

perfil m profile; phot. etc. side view; △, geol. (cross) section; outline de edificio etc.; ∼es pl. finishing touches; **perfilar** [1a] outline; avión etc. streamline; ∼se show one's profile, give a side view.

perforadora f pneumatic drill; **perforar** [1a] perforate; pierce, puncture accidentalmente; agujero drill, bore; tarjeta etc. punch.

P

perfumar [1a] scent, perfume; **perfume** m scent, perfume; **perfumería** f perfume shop; perfumery; **perfumista** m/f perfumer.

pergamino m parchment.

pergeñar [1a] (disponer) arrange, fix up; **pergeño** m rough draft.

pericia f skill, skilfulness; expertness, expertise; proficiency; **pericial** testigo expert.

perifollo m ♀ chervil; ~s pl. buttons and bows, frippery.

perilla f pear-shaped ornament; (barba) goatee; ~ (de la oreja) lobe of the ear.

perímetro m perimeter.

periódico 1. periodic(al); ⚕ recurrent; **2.** m (diario, dominical) newspaper; (revista etc.) periodical; **periodismo** m journalism; **periodista** m/f journalist; newspaperman; **periodístico** journalistic, newspaper attr.

período m period.

peripecia f lit. vicissitude; ~s pl. unforeseen changes.

periquito m parakeet.

periscopio m periscope.

peritaje m expert work; (pago) expert's fee; **perito 1.** skilled, skilful; experienced; qualified; expert, proficient (en at, in); **2.** m expert; technician.

perjudicar [1g] damage, harm, impair; posibilidades etc. prejudice; **perjudicial** harmful, injurious a salud etc.; prejudicial, detrimental (a, para intereses etc. to); **perjuicio** m (daño) damage, harm; ✝ financial loss; (injusticia) wrong; prejudice; en ~ de to the detriment of.

perjurar [1a] commit perjury; ~se perjure o.s.; **perjurio** m perjury; **perjuro 1.** perjured; **2.** m perjurer.

perla f pearl (a. fig.; de of, among); fig. gem.

permanecer [2d] stay, remain; **permanencia** f (estado) permanence; (período) stay; **permanente 1.** permanent; constant; comisión, ejército standing; **2.** f F perm.

permisible allowable, permissible; **permisivo** permissive; **permiso** m permission; ✗ etc. leave; (documento) permit, licence; ~ de conducir driving licence; ~ de convalescencia sick leave; ~ de entrada entry permit; ~ de salida exit permit; con ~ if I may; (levantándose de mesa etc.) excuse

me; con ~ de Vd. if you don't mind, by your leave; estar de ~ be on leave; **permitir** [3a] allow, permit; permit of; enable; no se permite fumar aquí you can't smoke here, no smoking here.

permuta f barter, exchange; **permutar** [1a] esp. ⚗ permute; ✝ barter, exchange.

pernear [1a] kick one's legs; **pernera** f trouser leg; **perneta**: en ~s barelegged.

pernicioso pernicious, evil.

perno m bolt.

pero 1. cj. but; yet; **2.** m objection; snag; defect; ¡no hay ~ que valga! there are no buts about it!; poner ~(s) a find fault with.

perogrullada f platitude, truism.

peroración f peroration; conclusion of a speech; **perorar** [1a] perorate, make a speech; summarize; F orate; **perorata** f long-winded speech.

perpendicular 1. perpendicular; at right angles; **2.** f perpendicular.

perpetración f perpetration; **perpetrador** m, **-a** f perpetrator; **perpetrar** [1a] perpetrate.

perpetuación f perpetuation; **perpetuar** [1e] perpetuate; **perpetuidad** f perpetuity; **perpetuo** perpetual; everlasting; ceaseless.

perplejidad f perplexity; dilemma; **perplejo** perplexed.

perra f bitch; F ~ chica 5-céntimo coin; F ~ gorda 10-céntimo coin; F ~s pl. small change; **perrada** f pack of dogs; F dirty trick; **perrera** f kennel; fig. badly-paid job; drudgery; F tantrum; **perrería** f pack of dogs; (ps.) gang of thieves; (palabra) harsh word; F dirty trick; **perrillo** m puppy; (raza pequeña) miniature dog; ✗ trigger; **perrito** m, **a** f puppy.

perro 1. m dog; ~ de aguas spaniel; ~ caliente sl. hot dog; ~ cobrador retriever; ~ danés Great Dane; ~ dogo bulldog; ~ esquimal husky; ~ faldero lap dog; ~ guardián watchdog; ~ del hortelano dog in the manger; ~ de lanas poodle; ~ lebrel whippet; ~ lobo alsatian; ~ marino dogfish; ~ de muestra pointer; setter; ~ pastor sheep dog; ~ de presa bulldog; ~ raposero foxhound; ~ rastrero tracker dog; ~ de Terranova Newfoundland dog; ~ viejo fig. old hand, wily bird; tiempo de ~s dirty weather; **2.** wretched, cruel, wicked.

perruna f dog-biscuit; **perruno** ♂ canine, dog attr.; devoción etc. dog-like.

persecución f persecution; (caza) pursuit, chase; **persecutorio:** v. manía; **perseguidor** m, -a f persecutor; pursuer; **perseguir** [3d a. 3l] persecute; (dar caza a) pursue, chase; (acosar) harass, pick on.

perseverancia f perseverance; constancy; **perseverante** persevering; **perseverar** [1a] persevere; persist (en in).

persiana f (Venetian) blind; slatted shutter; window shade.

persistencia f persistence; **persistente** persistent; **persistir** [3a] persist (en in; en inf. in ger.); persevere; continue.

persona f person; ~s pl. freq. people; buena ~ good sort, decent fellow; tercera ~ third party; en ~ in person, in the flesh; en la ~ de in the person of; por ~ per person; **personaje** m personage; thea. etc. character; F ser un ~ be somebody; **personal 1.** personal; **2.** m personnel, staff; (total) establishment; esp. ⚔ force; ⚓ complement; **personalidad** f personality; **personalismo** m selfishness, egoism; taking things in a personal way; **personalizar** [1f] personalize; embody; virtud personify; ~se become personal; **personarse** [1a] appear in person; **personificación** f personification; embodiment; **personificar** [1g] personify; embody; pick out for individual mention en discurso etc.

perspectiva f (en in) perspective; outlook, prospect para el futuro; appearance; (vista) view, scene.

perspicacia f perspicacity, discernment, perception; **perspicaz** perspicacious, discerning, perceptive; **perspicuo** clear, intelligible.

persuadir [3a] persuade; dejarse ~ be prevailed upon (a inf. to inf.); ~se be persuaded, become convinced; **persuasión** f persuasion; **persuasiva** f persuasion, persuasiveness; **persuasivo** persuasive.

pertenecer [2d] belong (a to); fig. ~ a concern, appertain to; **perteneciente:** ~ a appertaining to; **pertenencia** f ⚖ ownership; (cosa) property, possession; appurtenance.

pértiga f pole.

pertinacia f pertinacity, obstinacy; ♂ persistence; **pertinaz** pertinacious, obstinate; ♂ persistent.

pertinencia f relevance, pertinence; **pertinente** relevant, pertinent, appropriate.

pertrechar [1a] ⚔ supply with ammunition and stores etc.; equip; fig. arrange, prepare; **pertrechos** m/pl. ⚔ supplies and stores etc.; ⚔ munitions; implements.

perturbación f (mental) perturbation; pol., meteor., ♂ disturbance; **perturbar** [1a] (mentalmente) perturb; calma ruffle; orden, ♂ disturb.

perversidad f perversity, depravity; (acto) wrongdoing; **perversión** f perversion; **perverso** perverse; **pervertido** m, a f pervert; **pervertimiento** m perversion, corruption; **pervertir** [3i] pervert, corrupt; texto etc. distort; ~se become perverted.

pesa f weight; deportes: shot; dumbbell para ejercicios.

pesadez f heaviness, weight; slowness etc.

pesadilla f nightmare; (p. etc.) pet aversion.

pesado heavy, weighty; movimiento slow, sluggish; ponderous; sueño deep; libro etc. boring, tedious; **pesadumbre** f sorrow, grief.

pésame: dar el ~ express one's condolences, send one's sympathy.

pesantez f weight; gravity.

pesar [1a] **1.** v/t. weigh (a. fig.); v/i. weigh; be heavy; (tiempo) drag; (opinión etc.) count for a lot; **2.** m regret, sorrow; **pesaroso** regretful, sorrowful, sorry.

pesca f fishing; (cantidad pescada) catch; ~ submarina underwater fishing; ~ de altura deep-sea fishing; **pescadería** f fish market; **pescadilla** f whiting; fresh fish; **pescador** m fisherman; ~ de caña angler.

pescante m mot. driver's seat; ⊕ jib; ⚓ davit.

pescar [1g] v/t. (coger) catch; (tratar de coger) fish for; (sacar del fondo) dredge up (a. fig.); F puesto manage to get, land; F p. catch unawares, catch (in a lie etc.); F no saber qué se pesca not have a clue; v/i. fish.

pescuezo m neck; fig. haughtiness.

pesebre m manger, crib; stall.

pesimismo m pessimism; **pesimista 1.** pessimistic; **2.** m/f pessimist.

pésimo vile, abominable, wretched.

peso *m* weight; *(que se sostiene)* burden, load; *esp. phys.* gravity; *(balanza)* balance, scales; *S.Am.*: peso; *fig.* weight(iness); ~ *atómico* atomic weight; ~ *bruto* gross weight; ~ *específico* specific gravity; ~ *fuerte* heavyweight; ~ *gallo* bantamweight; ~ *ligero* lightweight; ~ *medio* middleweight; ~ *mosca* flyweight; ~ *de muelle* spring balance; ~ *muerto* dead weight; ~ *neto* net weight; ~ *pesado* heavyweight; ~ *pluma* featherweight; de ~ *fig.* weighty.

pesquera *f* = **pesquería** *f* fishery, fishing grounds; **pesquero** fishing *attr.*

pesquisa *f* inquiry, investigation, search; **pesquisar** [1a] inquire into, investigate.

pestaña *f* eyelash; ⊕ flange; rim *de llanta;* F no pegar ~ not get a wink of sleep; **pestañear** [1a] blink, wink; *sin* ~ without batting an eye; **pestañeo** *m* blink(ing), wink(ing).

peste *f* 🐾 plague, epidemic; *(olor)* stink, stench; *fig.* evil, menace; ~ *bubónica* bubonic plague; **pestífero** pestiferous; *olor* foul, noxious; **pestilencia** *f* pestilence, plague; **pestilencial** pestilential.

pestillo *m* bolt, latch, catch.

petaca *f* cigarette-case; tobacco pouch.

pétalo *m* petal.

petardear [1a] *v/t. fig.* cheat, swindle; *v/i. mot.* backfire; **petardista** *m/f* cheat, swindler; blackleg *en huelga;* **petardo** *m* 🅧 petard; *(fuegos artificiales)* firecracker.

petate *m* roll of bedding; F luggage; F *(p.)* trickster; *(despreciable)* poor fish; F liar el ~ pack up and go.

petición *f* request; petition *a autoridad etc.;* 🏛 suit, plea; *a* ~ by request; **peticionario** *m*, **a** *f* petitioner.

petirrojo *m* robin.

petróleo *m min.* oil, petroleum; ~ *crudo* crude oil; **petrolero** 1. oil, petroleum; 2. *m (p.)* oil man; ⚓ *(a. buque* ~*)* tanker; **petroquímico** petro-chemical.

petulancia *f* pertness, insolence; **petulante** pert, insolent.

peyorativo pejorative; depreciatory.

pez[1] *m* fish; ~ *espada* swordfish; ~ *sierra* sawfish.

pez[2] *f* pitch, tar.

pezón *m* teat, nipple; 🌿 stalk.

pezuña *f* hoof.

piada *f* cheeping; F catch-phrase.

pianista *m/f* pianist; **piano** *m* piano; ~ *de cola* grand piano; ~ *de media cola* baby grand; ~ *vertical* upright piano.

piar [1c] cheep; F ~ *por* cry for.

pica *f* pike; *poner una* ~ *en Flandes* bring off something difficult.

picada *f* sting; bite; peck; **picadillo** *m* minced meat; **picado** 1. *material* perforated; *tabaco* cut; *mar* choppy; 2. *m* 🦅 dive; **picador** *m* horse trainer; *toros:* picador; **picadura** *f* sting, bite; prick(ing); cut tobacco.

picante 1. *sabor* hot, peppery; *fig.* piquant, racy, spicy; 2. *m fig.* piquancy, spiciness; pungency.

picaporte *m* door handle; latch; *(llave)* latch-key.

picar [1g] 1. *v/t.* prick, pierce, puncture; *billete* punch, clip; *papel* perforate; *superficie* pit, pock; *caballo* prick, spur on; *toro* stick; *(insecto)* sting, bite; *(culebra, pez)* bite; *(ave)* peck; *comida* nibble, pick at; *lengua* burn; 2. *v/i.* 🦅 smart; itch; *(sol)* burn, scorch; 🦅 dive; 3. ~se *(ropa)* get moth-eaten; *(vino)* turn sour; *(fruta)* go off; *sl. drogas* get a fix, shoot up.

picaresco roguish; *lit.* picaresque; **pícaro** 1. *b.s.* crooked; sly, crafty; *mst co.* rascally; 2. *m lit.* picaro; *b.s.* rascal, rogue.

picazo *m* jab, poke; **picazón** *f* 🦅 smarting, itch(ing); sting.

picha *f* penis.

pichel *m* tankard.

pichón *m* young pigeon; *S.Am.* young bird; F kid; ~ *de barro* clay pigeon; **pichona** *f* F darling.

pico *m orn.* beak, bill; *(ave)* woodpecker; spout *de vasija etc.; geog.* peak, summit; *(punta)* sharp point, corner; *(herramienta)* pick(axe); F talkativeness; 20 y ~ 20-odd; *a las* 4 y ~ just after 4; F *callar el* ~ keep one's trap shut; *irse del* ~ talk too much; *ser un* ~ *de oro, tener mucho (or buen)* ~ have the gift of the gab.

picotada *f,* **picotazo** *m* peck; **picotear** [1a] *v/t.* peck; *v/i* F chatter; **picotero** F 1. chattering; 2. *m,* **a** *f* chatterer.

pictórico pictorial; *dotes etc.* artistic.

pie *m* foot *(a.* 🐾*, poet.)*; foot, base *de columna etc.;* stand, support; trunk *de árbol;* stem *de vaso, planta;* sediment *de líquido;* foot *de cama, página;* *thea.* cue; catchword; *fig.* foothold *al trepar;* (*estado*) footing; ~ *de atleta* athlete's foot; ~ *de imprenta* imprint; ~ *marino* sealegs; ~ *plano* flatfoot; *a* ~ on foot; *a cuatro* ~*s* on all fours; *a* ~ *enjuto* dry-shod; *fig.* without risk; *a* ~ *juntillas, a* ~ *juntillas fig. creer* firmly, absolutely; *al* ~ close, handy; ✝ *al* ~ *de fábrica* cost-price, ex works; *al* ~ *de la letra* entender, *citar* literally; *copiar* word for word, exactly; *de* ~ standing; up; *de a* ~ *soldado* foot *attr.; de* ~*s a cabeza* from head to foot.

piedad *f* piety, devoutness; (*lástima*) pity; *filial* piety; *¡por* ~*!* for pity's sake!; *tener* ~ *de* take pity on.

piedra *f* stone; rock; *meteor.* hail, hailstone; flint *de mechero;* ~ *de afilar* hone; ~ *de amolar* grindstone; ~ *angular* cornerstone (*a. fig.*); ~ *arenisca* sandstone; ~ *caliza* limestone; ~ *de escándalo* source of scandal; bone of contention; ~ *fundamental* foundation stone; ~ *de molino* millstone; ~ *pómez* pumice (stone); ~ *preciosa* precious stone; ~ *primera* ~ foundationstone; ~ *de toque* touchstone; *a tiro de* ~ within a stone's throw; *no dejar* ~ *sobre* ~ raze to the ground.

piel *f* skin; (*de animal*) skin, hide, pelt; (*con pelo*) fur; ✿ peel, rind, skin; ~ *de ante* buckskin, buff; ~ *de cerdo* pigskin; ~ *de foca* sealskin; ~ *de Rusia* Russia leather; ~ *roja m/f* redskin; ~ *de ternera* calf, calf-leather.

piélago *m lit.* ocean, deep.

pienso[1] *m* ✦ feed, fodder.

pienso[2]: *¡ni por* ~*!* the very idea!

pierna *f* leg; downstroke *con pluma;* *en* ~*s* bare-legged; *dormir a* ~ *suelta* (*or tendida*) sleep soundly.

pieza *f mst* piece; (*cuarto*) room; *hunt.* game, catch, example; *esp.* ⊕ part; *buena* ~, *linda* ~ crafty fellow; ~ *de convicción* convincing argument; ~ *fundida* cast(ing); ~ *de recambio,* ~ *de repuesto* spare part; ~ *de respeto* guest room; *de una* ~ in one piece.

pigmento *m* pigment.

pigmeo *adj. a. su. m* pigmy.

pijama *m* pyjamas.

pila *f* (*montón*) pile, heap, stack; (*abrevadero*) trough; *eccl.* font; ✿ pier of bridge *etc.;* ⚡ battery; ~ *atómica* atomic pile.

pilar *m* ✿ pillar, pier; (*mojón*) milestone; basin, bowl *de fuente.*

píldora *f* pill.

pillada *f* dirty trick; **pillaje** *m* plunder, pillage; **pillar** [1a] plunder, pillage; (*perro*) worry; F catch.

pillo F **1.** blackguardly; rotten; *niño* mischievous; (*astuto*) sly, crafty; **2.** *m* rascal, rogue; rotter, cad; (*niño*) = **pilluelo** *m* F scamp, rascal; (*golfo*) urchin.

pilón *m* (*abrevadero*) drinking trough; basin *de fuente;* (*mortero*) mortar; (*azúcar*) loaf sugar; *Mex., Ven.* tip, gratuity.

pilot(e)ar [1a] steer; *coche* drive; *avión* pilot; **pilote** *m* ✿ pile; **piloto** *m* **1.** *m* pilot; ~ *de puerto* harbor pilot; ~ *de prueba* test pilot; **2.** *luz* rear, tail *attr.*

pimentero *m* pepperbox; ✿ pepper plant; **pimentón** *m* cayenne pepper, red pepper; paprika; **pimienta** *f* black pepper; **pimiento** *m* ✿ pepper plant.

pimpollo *m* sucker, shoot *de planta;* (*árbol*) sapling; rosebud; F bonny child.

pináculo *m* pinnacle.

pinar *m* pinewood, pine-grove.

pincel *m* paint-brush; *fig.* painter; **pincelada** *f* (brush) stroke.

pinchar [1a] pierce, prick, puncture (*a. mot.*); *fig.* F prod; ~*se sl. drogas* get a fix, shoot up; **pinchazo** *m* prick, puncture.

pingajo *m* F tag; rag, shred.

pingo *m* F rag, shred; *S.Am.* horse; ~*s pl.* clothes.

pingüe rag, greasy; *fig. ganancia* rich, fat. *negocio* lucrative.

pingüino *m* penguin.

pino *m* pine (tree); ~ *albar* Scotch pine; ~ *negro* Swiss mountain pine; ~ *rodeno* cluster pine; ~ *de tea* pitchpine; **pinocha** *f* pine needle; **pinsapo** *m* Spanish fir.

pinta *f* spot, mark; (*punto*) dot, spot; F look(s); appearance.

pintado spotted, mottled; *fig.* identical; F *como el más* ~ with the best; *me sienta que ni* ~, *viene que ni* ~ it suits me a treat.

pintar [1a] *v/t.* paint (*a. fig.*); *esp. fig.* depict, picture; *v/i.* paint; ✿ begin to ripen; ~*se* put on make-up; *¡ojo, se pinta!* wet paint!

pintiparado identical (*a* to); just the

thing, just right (*para* for); **pintiparar** [1a] F compare.

pintor *m*, **-a** *f* painter; ~ *de brocha gorda* house painter; **pintoresco** picturesque; **pintura** *f* painting; (*color*) paint; *fig.* description; ~ *a la aguada* watercolor; ~ *al óleo* oil painting.

pinza *f* (*clothes*) peg; *zo.* claw; **pinzas** *f/pl.* (*unas a pair of*) ⊕ pincers; (*pequeñas*) tweezers; forceps.

pinzón *m* (*a.* ~ *vulgar*) chaffinch; ~ *real* bullfinch.

piña *f* ♀ pinecone; (*comestible*) pineapple; (*ps.*) clique, cluster; **piñón** *m* ♀ pine kernel; *orn.*, ⊕ pinion; **piñonear** [1a] click; **piñoneo** *m* click.

pío¹ *caballo* piebald.

pío² pious, devout; (*benigno*) merciful, kind.

pío³ *m orn.* cheep; F itch.

piojo *m* louse; F ~ *resucitado* jumped-up fellow; parvenu; **piojoso** verminous, lousy; *fig.* mean.

pipa *f* pipe; ♪ reed; cask *de vino*; *sl.* handgun.

pipiar [1c] chirp.

pique *m* pique, resentment; *naipes*: spades; *a* ~ *de* in danger of; on the point of; *echar a* ~ sink; *fig.* wreck.

piqueta *f* pick(axe).

piquete *m* prick, jab; small hole *en ropa*; ✂ picket.

piragua *f* canoe; shell; **piragüista** *m* canoeist; oarsman.

piramidal pyramidal; **pirámide** *f* pyramid.

pirata *m* pirate; *fig.* hard-hearted villain; ~ *aéreo* hijacker; **piratear** [1a] buccaneer; *fig.* rob; **piratería** *f* piracy; ~ *aérea* hijacking.

piro... pyro-.

piropo *m* flirtatious remark, amorous compliment; *min.* garnet, carbuncle.

pirueta *f* pirouette; **piruetear** [1a] pirouette.

pis *m* F piss; *hacer* ~ piss, pee.

pisa *f* tread(ing) *etc.*; **pisada** *f* (*ruido*) footstep, footfall, tread; (*huella*) footprint; **pisapapeles** *m* paperweight; **pisar** [1a] **1.** *v/t.* (*por descuido*) step on; (*apretando*) tread down; (*destruyendo*) trample (on, underfoot), flatten; (*estar una cosa sobre otra*) lie on, cover; ♪ *cuerda* pluck, *tecla* strike; **2.** *v/i.* tread, step.

piscina *f* swimming pool; fishpond.

Piscis *m ast.* Pisces.

piscolabis *m* F snack, bite.

piso *m* (*acto*) tread(ing); sole *de zapato*; (*suelo*) flooring; (*habitaciones*) apartment; (*segundo etc.*) floor, story; ~ *alto* top floor; ~ *bajo* ground floor; *casa de dos* ~s two-story house; **pisotear** [1a] tread down; trample (on, underfoot); stamp on; **pisotón** *m* stamp on the foot.

pista *f* track, trail (*a. fig.*); *atletismo etc.*: race track; ~ *de aterrizaje* runway; ~ *de baile* dance floor; ~ *de ceniza* dirt-track; ~ *de patinaje* skating rink; ~ *de tenis* tennis court; *estar sobre la* ~ be on the scent.

pistola *f* pistol; ~ *ametralladora* tommy gun, submachine gun; ~ *engrasadora* grease gun; **pistolera** *f* holster; **pistolero** *m* gunman, gangster.

pistón *m* ⊕ piston; ♪ key, piston.

pitar [1a] blow a whistle; *mot.* sound the horn; *S.Am.* smoke; **pitido** *m* whistle, whistling.

pitillera *f* cigarette case; **pitillo** *m* cigarette; *echar un* ~ have a smoke.

pito *m* ♪ whistle; *mot.* horn; cigarette; *S.Am.* pipe.

pizarra *f min.* slate; *escuela:* blackboard; **pizarrín** *m* slate pencil; **pizarrón** *m S.Am.* blackboard; *deportes:* scoreboard.

pizca *f cocina:* pinch; crumb *de pan etc.*; *fig.* trace, speck.

placa *f* plate (*a. phot.*); plaque *con inscripción etc.*; (*condecoración*) badge; ~ *giratoria* turntable; ~ *de matrícula* license plate.

placentero pleasant, agreeable; **placer¹ 1.** *v/t.* [2x] please; **2.** *m* pleasure, enjoyment; delight; *a* ~ at one's pleasure.

placer² *m min.* placer; ⚓ sandbank.

placero *m*, **a** *f* stall holder, market trader; *fig.* loafer, gossip.

placidez *f* placidity; **plácido** placid.

plaga *f* ✿ *etc.* plague; ✔ (*zo.*) pest, (♀) blight; *fig.* scourge, calamity; blight; hardship; abundance, glut; **plagar** [1h] infest, plague (*de* with); sow (*de minas* with); *plagado de* full of, infested with; ~*se de* become infested with.

plagiar [1b] plagiarize; *S.Am.* kidnap; **plagiario** *m*, **a** *f* plagiarist; **plagio** *m* plagiarism.

plan *m* (*disposición, intento*) plan, scheme; △, *surv.* plan; (*nivel*) level; (*altitud*) height; F set up, arrangement; F (*actitud*) attitude; ~ de estudios curriculum; ~ quinquenal five-year plan.

plana *f typ.* page; *escuela:* copywriting; ⚔, ♣ ~ *mayor* staff; *a* ~ *y renglón* line for line; *enmendar la* ~ *a* correct mistakes of.

plancha *f* plate, sheet *de metal;* slab *de madera etc.;* iron *para planchar;* (*acto*) ironing; ♣ gangway; F bloomer; ⊕~ *de garnitura* bolster; *hacer la* ~ float; **planchado** *m* ironing; **planchar** [1a] iron; *traje* press; **planchear** [1a] plate.

planeador *m* glider; **planear** [1a] *v/t.* plan; *v/i.* glide; soar; **planeo** *m* glide, gliding.

planeta *m* planet; **planetario 1.** planetary; **2.** *m* planetarium.

planificación *f* planning; **planificar** [1g] plan, organize.

plano 1. flat, level; smooth; plane (*esp.* 🅰); *de* ~ clearly, plainly; *confesar* openly; *caer de* ~ fall flat; *rechazar de* ~ turn down (flat); **2.** *m* 🅰 plane; plan *de edificio etc.;* map, street-plan *de ciudad;* flat *de espada.*

planta *f* ♀, ⊕ plant; plantation; *anat.* sole, foot; 🔺 (*piso*) floor, story; 🔺 (*ground*) plan; (*proyecto*) plan, scheme; establishment *de personal;* ~ *baja* ground floor, first floor; **plantación** *f* plantation; (*acto*) planting; **plantador** *m* (*p.*) planter.

plantar [1a] *planta, golpe* plant; *poste etc.* fix, set up; *fig.* set up; F (*a. dejar plantado*) *novio* jilt, walk out on; (*dejar en apuro*) leave high and dry; (*en cita*) stand *s.o.* up; F ~ *en la calle* pitch into the street; *obrero* sack; ~**se** plant o.s.; (*caballo*) refuse, balk; F (*llegar*) get (*en* to).

plantear [1a] establish, set up, get under way; *problema* pose.

plantel *m* ♀ nursery; (*gente*) body, group, establishment.

plantío *m* plot, bed; (*acto*) planting.

plasma *m* plasma.

plasmar [1a] mould, shape; create.

plasticidad *f* plasticity; *fig.* expressiveness, descriptiveness; **plástico 1.** plastic; *fig.* expressive, descriptive; **2.** *m* plastic.

plata *f* silver; *S.Am.* money; F *en* ~ briefly; frankly.

plataforma *f* platform (*a. fig.*); stage; 🚋 turntable.

plátano *m* plane (tree); (*fruta*) banana.

platea *f thea.* pit.

plateado 1. silver *attr.;* silvery; ⊕ silver-plated; **2.** *m* silver plating; **platear** [1a] silver; silver-plate; **platero** *m* silversmith; jeweler.

plática *f* talk, chat; *eccl.* sermon; **platicar** [1g] talk, chat, converse.

platija *f* plaice.

platillo *m* saucer; ♪ ~*s pl.* cymbals; ~ *de balanza* scale; ~ *volante* flying saucer.

platino *m* platinum; *mot.* ~*s pl.* contact points.

plato *m* plate, dish; (*primero etc.*) course; (*español, favorito etc.*) dish; (*porción*) plateful; ~ *de tocadiscos,* ~ *giratorio* turntable; ~ *fuerte* main course.

plausible acceptable, admissible; (*loable*) praiseworthy, commendable.

playa *f* (sea)shore; beach; seaside (resort) *para veranear etc.;* **playeras** *f/pl.* sandals; tennis shoes; **playero** beach *attr.*

plaza *f* square *en ciudad;* (*mercado*) market place; ⚔ (*a.* ~ *fuerte*) fortified town, stronghold; ✝ town, city, place; ✝ money market; (*sitio*) room, space; place, seat *en vehículo;* (*puesto*) post, job; (*vacante*) vacancy; ~ *de armas* parade ground; ~ *mayor* main square; ~ *de toros* bullring.

plazo *m* time, period; term, time-limit; *esp.* ✝ date; (*pago*) installment; *a* ~*s* on credit, on easy terms.

pleamar *f* high tide.

plebe *f* common people, the masses; **plebeyo 1.** plebeian; **2.** *m,* **a** *f* plebeian, commoner.

plebiscito *m* plebiscite.

plegable pliable, pliant; *silla etc.* folding, collapsible; **plegadera** *f* paper knife; **plegadizo** = *plegable;* **plegado** *m,* **plegadura** *f* fold; pleat; (*acto*) folding; pleating; **plegar** [1h *a.* 1k] fold, bend, crease; *sew.* pleat; ~**se** fold (up); bend, crease; *fig.* bow, submit.

plegaria *f* prayer.

pleito *m* lawsuit, case; *fig.* dispute, controversy; ~*s pl.* litigation.

plenipotenciario *adj. a. su. m* plenipotentiary.

plenitud *f* plenitude, fullness; abundance; **pleno 1.** *mst fig.* full, complete; *sesión* plenary, full; *en* ~

día in broad daylight; *en ~ verano* at the height of summer; *en ~a vista* in full view; 2. *m* plenum.

pliego *m* (*hoja*) sheet; folder; (*carta*) sealed letter; ~ *cerrado* sealed orders, ~ *de condiciones* details, specifications *para oferta etc.*; **pliegue** *m* fold (*a. geol.*); *sew. etc.* pleat, crease, tuck.

plomada *f* △ plumb, plummet; ⚓ sinker *de red*; ⚓ (sounding)lead *para sondar*; **plomar** [1a] seal with lead; **plomería** *f* △ lead roofing; ⊕ plumbing; **plomero** *m* plumber; **plomizo** leaden (*a. fig.*); lead-colored; **plomo** *m* ♎ lead; (*peso*) lead (weight); sinker *de red*; △ plumb-line; ✗ bullet; ⚡ fuse; *a ~* plumb, true, vertical(ly).

plugo, pluguiere *etc. v. placer*[1].

pluma *f orn.* feather; (*de escribir*) pen (*a. fig.*); (*adorno*) plume; *fig.* penmanship; ~ *esferográfica* ball-point pen; ~ *estilográfica*, ~ *fuente* fountain pen; **plumada** *f* stroke of a pen; **plumado** feathered; *pollo* fledged; **plumafuente** *f S.Am.* fountain pen; **plumaje** *m* plumage, feathers; plume, crest *de casco*; **plumazo** *m* feather mattress, feather pillow.

plúmbeo leaden; heavy as lead.

plumero *m* (feather) duster; plume; **plumón** *m* down; (*colchón*) feather-bed; **plumoso** downy.

plural *adj. a. su.* *m* plural; **pluralidad** *f* plurality; majority *de votos*.

pluriempleo *m trabajo* moonlighting.

plus *m* extra pay, bonus.

plusmarca *f* record.

pluvial rain *attr.*; **pluviómetro** *m* rain-gauge; **pluvioso** rainy.

población *f* population; (*ciudad etc.*) city, town, village; **poblado** *m* town, village; inhabited place; built-up area; **poblador** *m*, **-a** *f* settler, founder.

poblar [1m] *tierra* settle, colonize, people; stock (*de peces* with); plant (*de árboles* with); *poblado de* peopled with, populated with (*or* by); *fig.* full of; *~se* ♣ come into leaf.

pobo *m* white poplar.

pobre 1. poor (*de* in); *¡~ de mí!* poor (old) me!; 2. *m/f* poor person; pauper; beggar *que mendiga*; *los ~s pl.* the poor; *un ~* a poor man; *fig.* poor wretch; **pobrete** 1. poor, wretched; 2. *m*, **a** *f* poor thing; well-meaning but ineffective person; **pobretería** *f*

poverty; (*ps.*) poor people; **pobretón** 1. very poor; 2. *m* poor man; **pobreza** *f* poverty; want, penury.

pocilga *f* piggery, (pig)sty (*a. fig.*).

pócima *f*, **poción** *f pharm.* dose, draught; *vet.* drench; *fig.* brew.

poco 1. *adj.* little, slight; scanty; ~ *dinero* little money; *su inteligencia es ~a* his intelligence is slight; *la ganancia es ~o* the profit is small; *~s pl.* few; *~s libros* few books, not many books; 2. *m*: *un ~* a little; *un ~ de dinero* a little money, some money; *un ~* (*como adv.*): *le conozco un ~* I know him a little; *un ~ mejor* a little better; 3. *adv.* little, not much; only slightly; *sabe ~* he knows little; *cuesta ~* it doesn't cost much; *a veces se traduce por el prefijo un-*: ~ *amable* unkind, ~ *amistoso* unfriendly; *a ~* shortly (after).

poda *f* pruning (season); **podadera** *f* pruning shears; **podar** [1a] prune; lop.

podenco *m* hound, hunting-dog.

poder 1. [2t] be able, can; *puede venir* he is able to come, he can come; *no puede venir* he is unable to come, he cannot come, he can't come; (*absoluto*) *los que pueden* those who can, those that are able (to); 2. *m* power; authority; ⚖ power of attorney, proxy; ⊕ power, capacity, strength; ⊕ value; ~ *adquisitivo* purchasing power; ~ *legislativo* legislative power; (*plenos*) *~es pl.* full power, authority; *a ~ de* by dint of; *en ~ de* in the possession of, in the hands of; *por ~(es)* by proxy.

poderío *m* power; authority; jurisdiction; (*bienes*) wealth, substance.

poderoso powerful; *remedio etc.* potent, efficacious; (*rico*) rich.

podre *f* pus; **podredumbre** *f* rot, rottenness, decay, corruption; ⚕ pus; *fig.* gnawing doubt, uneasiness; **podrido** rotten, bad, putrid.

poema *m* (*esp.* long) poem; **poesía** *f* poetry; (*una ~*) (*esp.* short *or* lyrical) poem; **poeta** *m* poet; **poetastro** *m* poetaster; **poética** *f* poetics; **poético** poetic(al); **poetisa** *f* poetess.

polaina *f* gaiter, legging.

polar polar; **polaridad** *f* polarity; **polarizar** [1f] polarize.

polea *f* pulley; tackle-block.

polémica *f* polemics; controversy.

polen *m* pollen.

policía 1. *m* policeman; ~ *femenino*

policewoman; **2.** *f* police (force); *fig.*
administration, order, (good) government; (*cortesía*) politeness; ~ militar military police; ~ *secreta* secret
police.

poligamia *f* polygamy; **polígamo 1.**
polygamous; **2.** *m*, **a** *f* polygamist.

poligloto *m*, **a** *f* polyglot.

polilla *f* (clothes) moth; bookworm.

polio(mielitis) *f* polio(myelitis).

polisílabo 1. polysyllabic; **2.** *m* poly-
syllable.

política *f* politics; (*e.g.* ~ *de Carlos V*,
~ *exterior*) policy; (*cortesía*) politeness, good manners; **político 1.**
political; polite, courteous; *padre etc.*
~ father- *etc.* in-law; *familia* ~*a*
relatives by marriage, in-laws F; **po-
liticón** ceremonious, obsequious;
politiquero *m b.s.* politician.

póliza *f* certificate, voucher; (*giro*)
draft, order; (*timbre*) tax stamp; ~
dotal endowment policy; ~ *de segu-
ro(s)* insurance policy.

polizón *m* ⚓, ✈ stowaway; vagrant,
tramp; *viajar de* ~ stow away.

polizonte *m* F copper, cop *esp. Am.*

polla *f orn.* pullet; *naipes:* pool, stake;
F chick, girl; **pollada** *f* hatch, brood;
pollastro *m* F sly fellow.

pollera *f* hen coop; **pollero** *m*
chicken-farmer; (*que vende*) poult-
erer.

pollino *m*, **a** *f* donkey; F ass.

pollita *f* pullet; **pollito** *m* chick;
pollo *m* chicken; chick *de ave no
domesticada*; F young man, youth;
polluelo *m* chick.

polo *m geog.*, ⚡ pole; (*juego*) polo; ~
acuático water polo.

poltrón idle, lazy; **poltrona** *f* reclining chair, easy chair.

polvareda *f* dust cloud; F *levantar una*
~ cause a rumpus; **polvera** *f* vanity
case; **polvo** *m* dust; powder; pinch
de rapé etc.; ~*s pl.* face powder; ~(*s*)
de arroz rice powder; ~*s pl. de blanqueo* bleaching powder; ~(*s*) *de
hornear*, ~(*s*) *de levadura* baking
powder.

pólvora *f* gunpowder; *fig.* life, liveliness; (*mal genio*) bad temper; **polvorear** [1a] powder, dust, sprinkle;
polvoriento dusty, powdery; **polvorín** *m* powder-magazine; **polvo-
roso** dusty.

pompa *f* pomp; show, display,
pageantry; procession; ⚓ pump; ~
de jabón soap bubble; *director de* ~*s*

fúnebres undertaker; **pomposidad** *f*
pomposity; **pomposo** pompous.

pómulo *m* checkbone.

ponche *m* punch.

poncho *m S.Am.* poncho, blanket.

ponderación *f fig.* deliberation,
consideration; exaggeration; high
praise; **ponderar** [1a] *fig.* weigh up;
ponder (over); exaggerate; (*alabar*)
praise highly.

poner [2r] put; place; set; arrange;
cuidado take, exercise (*en* in); *dinero*
(*inversión*) put, invest; (*juego*) bet,
stake; *escaparate* dress; *huevo* lay;
impuesto impose; *luz, radio etc.*
switch on, turn on, put on; *mesa* lay,
set; *miedo* cause; *objeción* raise; *obra
dramática* perform, put on; *película*
show; *problema* set; *radio* put on;
telegrama send; *tiempo* take; *tienda*
set up; ~ *adj.* make, turn; ~ *que*
suppose that; ~*se* put o.s.; place o.s.;
(*sol*) set; ~ *adj.* turn; get, become.

ponga, pongo *etc. v. poner.*

poniente *m* west; west wind.

pontificado *m* pontificate, papacy;
pontifical pontifical, papal.

pontón *m* pontoon; bridge of planks;
pontoon bridge; ⚓ hulk.

ponzoña *f* poison; **ponzoñoso** poisonous; *fig.* noxious, harmful.

popa *f* stern, poop; *a* ~ abaft, astern;
de ~ *a proa* fore and aft.

populachero common, vulgar,
cheap; timidity *de carácter*; **populacho** *m* mob, plebs; lower orders;
popular popular; *palabra* colloquial;
popularidad *f* popularity; **popularismo** *m* colloquialism; **populari-
zar** [1f] popularize; ~*se* become
popular; **populoso** populous.

poquedad *f* scantiness, paucity; few-
ness; timidity *de carácter*; **poquísi-
mo** very little; ~*s pl.* very few; **poquito**: *un* ~ a little bit.

por 1. *prp.* **a)** *agente tu verbo pasivo*:
by; *instrumento*: *comunicar* ~ *señas*
talk by (means of) signs; ~ *ferrocarril*
by rail; *lo hizo* ~ *sí mismo* he did it by
himself; **b)** *lugar*: ~ *la ciudad* (*pasar*)
through the town; (*pasearse*) round
the town; ~ *Medina* by way of
Medina, via Medina (*a.* 🏙); ~ *el túnel*
through the tunnel; ~ *la calle* along
the street; ~ *todo el país* over the
whole country; *errar* ~ *los campos*
wander in the fields; **c)** *tiempo*: ~ *la
noche* in the night, during the night;
~ *Navidades* at (or about) Christmas

P

time; ~ **estas fechas** about this time;
d) *motivo etc.*: ~ **temor** out of fear,
from fear; *cerrado* ~ **muerte del dueño**
closed owing to (or on account of,
because of) owner's death; ~ **mí** for
me, for my sake; for myself, for my
part; ~ **la patria** for (the sake of) the
country; ~ *adj.* as being, as, because
it is *etc.*; *lo dejó* ~ *imposible* he gave it
up as impossible; e) *en nombre*: hablo
~ **todos** I speak for (or in the name of,
on behalf of) everybody; *intercedió* ~
mí he interceded for me (or on my
behalf); f) *objetivo*: **mi admiración** ~
tí my admiration for you; g) *en busca
de*: *vendrá* ~ **nosotros** he will come for
us; h) *quedar etc.*: *quedan cartas* ~
escribir there are still some letters to
be written; i) *cambio*: *lo compró* ~ *150
pesetas* he bought it for 150 pesetas;
te doy éste ~ *aquél* I'll give you one in
exchange for (or in place of) that one;
j) *manera*: ~ **docenas** in dozens, by the
dozen; ~ *escrito* in writing; ~ *persona*
per person; *120 kms.* ~ *hora* 120 kms.
an hour; *recibir* ~ *esposa* take as one's
wife; k) 🅐 *times*; 3 ~ 5 3 times 5; 2. *cj.
etc.*: ~ *inf.* (*para*) in order to *inf.*;
(*causa*) because; ~ *haber venido tarde*
through having come late, because
he came late; ~ *que subj.* in order that;
~ *difícil que sea* however hard it is; *¿~
qué?* why?; *yo sé* ~ *qué* I know why.

porcelana *f* porcelain; (*loza corriente*) china.

porcentaje *m* percentage; *esp.* ⊕ rate.

porcino porcine; *ganado* ~ pigs.

porción *f* portion; part, share; *una* ~
de cosas etc. a number of things *etc.*

pordiosear [1a] beg; **pordiosero** *m,
a f* beggar.

porfía *f* persistence, obstinacy,
stubbornness; *a* ~ in competition;
porfiado persistent, obstinate,
stubborn; **porfiar** [1c] persist (*en*
in), insist; argue obstinately; ~ *por
inf.* struggle obstinately to *inf.*

pormenor *m* detail, particular; **por-
menorizar** [1f] detail, set out in
detail.

pornografía *f* pornography; **pornográfico** pornographic.

poro *m* pore; **porosidad** *f* porosity,
porousness; **poroso** porous.

porque because; ~ *subj.* in order
that.

porqué *m* reason (*de* for), why; F
quantity, amount.

porquería *f* F (*en general*) dirt, filth;

nastiness; (*acto*) indecent act; (*mala
pasada*) dirty trick.

porra *f* stick, cudgel; truncheon *de
policía*; (*herramienta*) large hammer;
F bore, nuisance; *¡~s!* dash (it)!; (*a
otra p.*) get away!, rubbish!; F *mandar a la* ~ chuck out, send packing; F
¡vete a la ~*!* go to hell!; **porrada** *f*
thwack, thump; F stupidity; F (*montón*) pile, heap; **porrazo** *m* thwack,
thump; bump.

porreta *f* green leaf *de cebolla etc.*; F
en ~ stark naked; **porretada** *f* pile,
heap; **porrillo**: F *a* ~ in abundance,
by the ton; **porro** F dull, stupid; *sl.*
joint (or hashish cigarette); **porrón**
slow.

porta(a)viones *m* aircraft carrier.

portada *f* △ front, façade; (*puerta*)
porch, doorway; cover *de revista*;
typ. frontispiece, title-page; **por-
tado**: *bien* ~ well-dressed; well-
behaved; **portador** *m*, **-a** *f* carrier,
bearer; † bearer, payee.

porta...: **~equipajes** *m* mot. trunk;
~estandarte *m* standard bearer.

portal *m* vestibule, hall; (*puerta*)
porch, doorway; street door *que da a
calle*; gate(way) *de ciudad.*

portalámpara *m* socket, lampholder.

portalón *m* △ gate(way); ⚓ gangway.

porta...: **~monedas** *m* pocketbook;
purse; **~papeles** *m* briefcase; **~plu-
mas** *m* penholder.

portarse [1a] behave; conduct o.s.

portátil portable.

portavoz *m* megaphone; (*p.*) spokesman; *contp.* mouthpiece.

portazgo *m* toll.

portazo *m* bang, slam.

porte *m* † carriage; 🙠 postage; *fig.*
behaviour, conduct, demeanor,
bearing; disposition, character; ~
concertado mailing permit; ~ *pagado*
postage prepaid, freight prepaid;
portear[1] † carry, convey.

portear[2] [1a] slam, bang.

portento *m* marvel, prodigy; **portentoso** marvellous, extraordinary.

portero *m* porter, janitor, door-
keeper; *deportes*: goalkeeper; ~ *electrónico* automatic door opener.

pórtico *m* portico, porch; arcade *de
plaza etc.*

portilla *f* porthole; **portillo** *m* gap,
opening, breach; (*puerta*) wicket.

portón *m* large door, main door.

portorriqueño *v. puertorriqueño.*

portugués 1. adj. a. su. m, **-a** f Portuguese; **2.** m (idioma) Portuguese.

porvenir m future; en el ∼, en lo ∼ in the future.

pos: en ∼ de after, in pursuit of; ir en ∼ de chase, pursue.

posada f (mesón) inn; house, dwelling; (alojamiento) lodging.

posaderas f/pl. buttocks.

posadero m, **a** f innkeeper.

posar [1a] v/t. carga lay down; v/i. ∼**se** (ave) alight, settle, perch, rest; (modelo) sit, pose; (polvo, líquido) settle; lodge en posada.

posdata f postscript.

pose f pose; phot. time-exposure.

poseedor m, **-a** f owner, possessor; holder de marca, oficio; **poseer** [2e] have; own, possess; tema, lengua know perfectly, have a complete mastery of; ventaja (cosa) have, hold; (p.) enjoy; **poseído** possessed; fig. crazed; **posesión** f possession; tenure de oficio; **posesivo** adj. a. su. m possessive; **poseso 1.** possessed; **2.** m, **a** f person possessed.

posibilidad f possibility; chance; **posibilitar** [1a] make possible, facilitate; **posible 1.** possible, feasible; en lo ∼ as far as possible; **2.** ∼s m/pl. means, assets.

posición f position; situation; (rango) standing.

positiva f phot. positive, print; **positivo 1.** positive (a. phot.); ⊕ positive, plus; idea etc. constructive; **2.** m gr. positive; phot. print.

posponer [2r] subordinate.

posta 1. f relay de caballos; (casa) posthouse; (etapa, distancia) stage; stake en juego; hunt. slug; F a ∼ on purpose; **2.** m courier.

postal 1. postal; **2.** f post card; ∼ ilustrada picture post card.

poste m post, pole; stake de cerca etc.; (a. ∼ telegráfico) telegraph pole; ∼ indicador signpost; ∼ de llegada winning-post; ∼ de salida starting post.

postergar [1h] delay, postpone; p. pass over.

posteridad f posterity; **posterior** lugar: rear, back; posterior; tiempo: later, subsequent.

pos(t)guerra f postwar period; de (la) ∼ postwar.

postigo m wicket, postern, small door; shutter de ventana.

postizas f/pl. castanets; **postizo 1.** dentadura etc. false, artificial; cuello detachable; b.s. phony; dummy; **2.** m false hair.

postración f prostration; ∼ nerviosa nervous exhaustion; **postrado** prostrate (a. fig.); **postrar** [1a] prostrate; esp. ✚ weaken, exhaust; (derribar) overthrow; ∼**se** (acto) prostrate o.s.; (estado) be prostrate.

postre 1. m (a. ∼s pl.) dessert, sweet; **2.:** a la ∼ at last, in the end.

postremo, postrero last; rear, hindermost; **postrimerías** f/pl. dying moments; closing stages.

postulante m/f petitioner; candidate; **postular** [1a] postulate; (pedir) seek, claim, demand.

póstumo posthumous.

postura f posture, pose, stance del cuerpo; fig. position, attitude; pol. etc. agreement; bet, stake en el juego; bid en subasta; orn. (cantidad) eggs; (acto) egg-laying.

potable drinkable; v. agua.

potaje m cocina: mixed vegetables, stew; mixed drink; mixture.

pote m pot, jar; (tiesto) flower pot; (guiso) stew; a ∼ in abundance.

potencia f power (a. ✚, pol.); potency; ⊕ (horse)power, capacity; ∼ electoral voting power; ∼ mundial world power; ⊕ ∼ real effective power; **potencial 1.** potential; **2.** m potential; capacity; gr. conditional.

potente powerful; potent.

potestad f power; authority, jurisdiction; (p.) potentate.

potra f zo. filly; **potro** m zo. colt.

poyo m stone bench.

pozo m well; ✗ shaft; pool de río; S.Am. pool, puddle; ∼ artesiano Artesian well; ∼ negro cesspool; ∼ de petróleo oil well.

práctica f practice; method; **practicable** practicable; workable, feasible; **practicante** m/f practitioner; ✚ male nurse, medical assistant, orderly; **practicar** [1g] practise; exercise; (poner por obra) perform, carry out; deporte go in for; agujero cut, make; **práctico 1.** practical; handy; proyecto workable; p. practical, down-to-earth; **2.** m practitioner; ⚓ pilot.

prader(í)a f meadow(land); prairie en el Canadá etc.; **prado** m meadow, field, pasture.

pragmático pragmatic.

preámbulo *m* preamble.
precario precarious, uncertain.
precaución *f* precaution.
precaver [2a] guard against, forestall; **~se** be on one's guard (*de* against); **precavido** cautious.
precedencia *f* priority, precedence; superiority; **precedente 1.** preceding, foregoing, former; **2.** *m* precedent; *sin ~* unprecedented; **preceder** [2a] precede, go before.
precepto *m* precept; order, injunction; rule; **preceptor** *m* teacher; tutor; **preceptorado** *m* tutorship; **preceptual** tutorial.
preciar [1b] estimate, appraise; **~se** boast; **~se** *de algo* pride o.s. on, boast of; **~** *de (ser)* boast of being; **~** *de inf.* boast of *ger.*
precintar [1a] (pre)seal, prepackage; **precinto** *m* seal.
precio *m* (*que se paga*) price; cost; (*valor*) value, worth; ✝ *a.* charge, figure, rate; *fig.* worth *de p. etc.*; *control de ~s* price control; *lista de ~s* price list; *~ de compra* purchase price; *~ al contado* cash price; *~ tope* ceiling price; *~ de venta* sale price; **precioso** precious; valuable; *fig.* lovely, beautiful; charming, pretty.
precipicio *m* precipice; cliff.
precipitación *f meteor.* precipitation; rainfall; (*prisa*) haste; rashness; **precipitado 1.** *prisa* breakneck, headlong; *acción, modo* hasty; rash; **2.** *m* 🜋 precipitate.
precipitar [1a] hurl, cast down *desde lo alto*; (*acelerar*) hasten, speed up; precipitate (*a.* 🜋); **~se** rush, dash, dart; **~** *sobre* rush at.
precisamente precisely; *~ por eso* for that very reason; **precisar** [1a] *v/t.* (*necesitar*) need, require; fix, determine exactly; *detalles* state precisely; *v/i.* be necessary; **precisión** *f* precision, preciseness, accuracy; need, necessity; ⊕ *de ~* precision *attr.*; **preciso** necessary, essential; (*exacto*) precise, exact, accurate; *estilo* concise.
precitado above-mentioned.
preconcebido preconceived.
preconizar [1f] foresee.
precoz precocious, forward; *calvicie etc.* premature; ♀ *etc.* early.
precursor *m*, **-a** *f* forerunner, precursor.
predecesor *m*, **-a** *f* predecessor.
predecir [3p] foretell, predict.

predestinación *f* predestination; **predestinar** [1a] predestine.
predicación *f* preaching; sermon; **predicado** *m* predicate; **predicador** *m* preacher; **predicar** [1g] preach (*a. fig.*).
predicción *f* prediction, forecast.
predilección *f* predilection; **predilecto** favorite.
predio *m* property, estate.
predisponer [2r] predispose; prejudice (*contra* against); **predisposición** *f* predisposition, inclination.
predominante predominant; prevailing, prevalent; **predominar** [1a] predominate, prevail (*v/t.* over); **predominio** *m* predominance; prevalence; superiority (*sobre* over).
pre-estreno *m* preview, view.
prefabricado prefabricated; **prefabricar** [1g] prefabricate.
prefacio *m* preface, foreword.
preferencia *f* preference; priority; *de ~ plaza* reserved; **preferente** preferential; preferable; ✝ *acción* preference *attr.*; **preferentemente** preferably; **preferible** preferable; **preferir** [3i] prefer (*A a B A to B*).
prefijar [1a] fix beforehand, prearrange; *gr.* prefix; **prefijo** *m* prefix.
pregón *m* proclamation, announcement; ✝ street cry; **pregonar** [1a] proclaim, announce; *secreto* disclose; *méritos etc.* praise publicly.
pregunta *f* question; *hacer una ~* ask a question; **preguntar** [1a] *v/t.* ask (*algo a alguien* a p. a th., a th. of a p.); *v/i.* ask, inquire; *~ por p. etc.* ask for; *salud de p. etc.* ask after; **~se** wonder (*si* if, whether); **preguntón** inquisitive.
prejuicio *m* prejudice; bias; **prejuzgar** [1h] prejudge.
prelado *m* prelate.
preliminar 1. preliminary; preparatory; **2.** *m* preliminary.
preludiar [1b] prelude (*a. ♪*); introduce; **preludio** *m* prelude (*a. ♪*).
prematuro premature; untimely.
premeditación *f* premeditation; **premeditado** premeditated.
premeditar [1a] premeditate.
premiado 1. *adj.* prize *attr.*; **2.** *m*, **a** *f* prize winner; **premiar** [1b] reward, recompense; give an award (*or* prize) to *en certamen*; **premio** *m* reward, recompense; prize *en certamen*; ✝ premium; *~ gordo* first

prize, big prize; *a* ~ at a premium.
premioso *vestido* tight; *(molesto)* troublesome, burdensome.

premisa *f* premise.

premura *f* pressure; *(prisa)* haste, urgency.

prenda *f* *(empeño)* pledge, security; *(alhaja)* jewel; ~ *(de vestir)* garment, article of clothing; *fig.* token, sign; en ~ in pawn; ~ perdida forfeit; ~s *pl.* qualities, talents, gifts; *(juego)* forfeits; ~s interiores underwear; **prendar** [1a] pledge, pawn; *fig.* captivate, win over; ~**se** de fall in love with.

prendedero *m*, **prendedor** *m* brooch, clasp, pin.

prender [2a; *p.p. a.* preso] *v/t.* seize, grasp; *p.* capture, catch; *p.* arrest; pin, attach *con alfiler etc.*; *v/i.* ♀ take root; *(fuego)* catch; *(vacunación etc.)* take; ~**se** *(mujer)* dress up.

prendero *m* second-hand dealer; pawnbroker.

prenombrado above-mentioned, foregoing.

prensa *f* press; ⊕ gland, stuffing box; de ~ press *attr.*; dar a la ~ publish; entrar en ~ go to press; **prensado** *m* sheen, shine; **prensar** [1a] press.

preñada pregnant; **preñado** 1. *muro* bulging, sagging; ~ de full of; 2. *m* = **preñez** *f* pregnancy.

preocupación *f* worry, concern, pre-occupation; prejudice; **preocupado** worried, concerned, preoccupied; **preocupar** [1a] *(inquietar)* worry, preoccupy, exercise; *(predisponer)* prejudice; ~**se** worry, care (de, de about).

preparación *f* preparation; *(instrucción)* training; ~ militar etc. military etc. preparedness; **preparador** *m* *deportes*: trainer; **preparar** [1a] prepare; ⊕ prepare, process; *(aprestar)* get ready; *(instruir)* train; ~**se** prepare (o.s.); get ready; **preparativo** 1. preparatory; preliminary; 2. ~s *m/pl.* preparations; **preparatorio** preparatory.

preposición *f* preposition.

prepucio *m* foreskin, prepuce.

prerrogativa *f* prerogative, privilege.

presa *f* *(acto)* capture, seizure; *(cosa apresada)* prize *(esp. ♣)*, spoils, booty; *(animal que se caza)* prey, quarry; *(animal cazado)* capture, catch; weir, dam, barrage de río; ~s *pl.* fangs; hacer ~ seize.

presagiar [1b] betoken, forebode, presage; **presagio** *m* omen.

presbítero *m* priest.

prescindible dispensable, expendable; **prescindir** [3a]: ~ de do without dispense with; disregard.

prescribir [3a; *p.p.* prescrito] pre-scribe; **prescripción** *f* prescription; **prescrito** prescribed.

presencia *f* presence; ~ de ánimo presence of mind; **presenciar** [1b] be present at, witness, watch.

presentable presentable; **presentación** *f* presentation; introduction; **presentador** *m*, **-a** *f* televisión moderator; **presentar** [1a] *mst* present; *p. a otra* introduce; *p.* propose, nominate *(a puesto* for); *(mostrar)* display, show; *thea.* perform; *demanda* put in, present; *dimisión* tender; *película* show; *proyecto etc.* put forward; *pruebas* submit, present; ~**se** present o.s.; *(acudir)* turn up; report (en at).

presente 1. present; *¡*~*!* present!; los ~s those present; la ~ this letter; 2. *m* present; *gr.* present (tense).

presentimiento *m* premonition, presentiment; foreboding; **presentir** [3i] have a presentiment of; ~ que have a presentiment that.

preservación *f* preservation, protection; **preservar** [1a] preserve, protect *(contra* from, against).

presidencia *f* *pol. etc.* presidency; chairmanship; **presidencial** presidential; **presidente** *m*, **a** *f* *pol. etc.* president; chairman.

presidiario *m* convict; **presidio** *m* *(cárcel)* prison; *(condena)* hard labour; ✕ *(ps.)* garrison.

presidir [3a] preside *(acc.* at, over); take the chair *(acc.* at).

presilla *f* fastener, clip; press stud.

presión *f* pressure *(a.* ⊕, *meteor.)*; press, squeeze *con mano etc.*; ⊕ de ~ pressure *attr.*; ~ atmosférica atmospheric *(or* air) pressure; ~ sanguínea blood pressure.

preso 1. *p.p.* of prender; 2. *m*, **a** *f* prisoner, convict; ~ preventivo pretrial prisoner.

prestación *f* lending, loan; *pedir* ~, *tomar* ~ borrow; **prestador** *m*, **-a** *f* lender; **prestamista** *m* money-lender; pawnbroker; **préstamo** *m* *(acto)* lending, borrowing; *(dinero)* loan; **prestar** [1a] *v/t.* lend, loan; *atención* pay; *ayuda* give; *juramento* take, swear; *v/i.* give, stretch; **~se** (*p.*) lend o.s., (*cosa*) lend itself (*a* to); **prestatario** *m* borrower.

presteza *f* quickness, speed, agility.

prestidigitación *f* prestidigitation, sleight of hand; **prestidigitador** *m* conjurer, juggler.

prestigio *m* prestige; face; (*fascinación*) spell; (*engaño*) trick; **prestigioso** famous, captivating; illusory.

presto 1. *adj.* (*vivo*) quick, prompt; agile, nimble; (*dispuesto*) ready; **2.** *adv.* quickly; at once, right away.

presumido conceited; **presumir** [3a] *v/t.* presume; guess, surmise; *v/i.* be conceited, presume; give o.s. airs; **presunción** *f* presumption; conceit; **presunto** supposed, presumed; *heredero* presumptive; **presuntuoso** conceited, vain; presumptuous; pretentious.

presuponer [2r] presuppose; **presuposición** *f* presupposition; **presupuestar** [1a] budget for; **presupuestario** budget *attr.*, budgetary; **presupuesto** *m* † budget; estimate *para un proyecto etc.*

presura *f* speed; promptness; (*porfía*) persistence; **presuroso** quick, speedy; prompt; hasty (*a. b.s.*).

pretencioso pretentious.

pretender [2a] claim; *mujer* court; *puesto* seek, try for; *honores etc.* aspire to; *objeto* aim at, try to achieve; **~ que** *indic.* claim that, allege that; **~ que** *subj.* expect that, suggest that, intend that; **~ inf.** (*intentar*) seek to *inf.*, attempt to *inf.*, try to *inf.*; **~ decir** mean (*con* by); **pretendido** supposed, pretended; alleged; **pretendiente 1.** *m* suitor *de mujer*; **2.** *m*, **a** *f* claimant; applicant (*a puesto* for); pretender (*a trono* to).

pretensión *f* claim; aim, object; (*pretencioso*) pretension; pretense.

pretexto *m* pretext; pretence; plea, excuse; **so ~ de** under pretext of.

pretil *m* parapet *de puente*; handrail, railing.

pretina *f* girdle, belt.

prevalecer [2d] prevail (*sobre* over, against); ♀ take root.

prevalerse [2q]: **~ de** avail o.s. of.

prevención *f* (*cualidad*) forethought, foresight; (*prejuicio*) prejudice; (*estado*) preparedness; (*acto*) prevention *etc.*; safety measure, precaution; (*aviso*) warning; (*comisaría*) police station; **a ~, de ~** spare, emergency

attr.; **prevenido** prepared, ready; *fig.* cautious, forewarned; **prevenir** [3s] prepare, make ready; (*impedir*) prevent; (*prever*) foresee, anticipate; provide for; (*advertir*) (fore)warn (*contra* against); (*predisponer*) prejudice (*contra* against); **~se** make ready, get ready; **preventivo** preventive (*a.* ♣); precautionary.

prever [2v] foresee, forecast.

previo 1. *adj.* previous, preliminary; **2.** *prp.* after, following.

previsible foreseeable; **previsión** *f* foresight; far-sightedness; **previsor** farsighted; thoughtful.

prieto blackish, dark; *p.* mean; *S.Am.* dark, brunette.

prima *f* bonus, bounty; premium *de seguros*; subsidy *de exportación etc.*

primacía *f* primacy; **primada** *f* F hoax, trick; piece of stupidity; **primado** *m* primate; **primario** primary; **primato** *m* primate.

primavera *f* spring(time); ♀ primrose; **primaveral** spring.

primera *f* (*a.* **~ clase**) first class; F **de ~** first-rate, first-class; F **estar de ~** feel fine; *viajar en* **~** travel first; **primeramente** first(ly), in the first place; chiefly; **primero 1.** first; primary; foremost; *años etc.* early; (*anterior*) former; *necesidad* basic, prime; urgent; *materia* raw; *a* **~s de** at the beginning of; **2.** *adv.* first; (*preferentemente*) rather, sooner.

primicias *f/pl.* first-fruits.

primitivo primitive; original; *obra etc.* early; *color* prime.

primo 1. ♣ prime; *materia* raw; **2.** *m*, **a** *f* cousin; **~ carnal**, **~ hermano** first cousin; **3.** *m* F fool.

primor *m* beauty, elegance, exquisiteness; (*habilidad*) skill.

primoroso exquisite, fine, elegant; (*hábil*) skilful, neat.

princesa *f* princess; **principado** *m* principality.

principal 1. principal; chief, main; foremost; illustrious; **2.** *m* principal (*a.* †, ⚖); head, chief.

príncipe *m* prince; **~ consorte** prince consort; **~ heredero** crown prince.

principiante 1. learner, who is beginning; **2.** *m*, **a** *f* beginner, learner, novice; **principiar** [1b] start, begin (*a inf.* to *inf.* or *ger.*; *con* with); **principio** *m* beginning; start; origin, source; *phls.*, *ciencias etc.*:

principle; ♠ *etc.* element, constituent; *cocina*: rudiments *de tema*; *a ~s del mes* at the beginning of the month.

pringar [1h] *v/t. cocina*: dip in fat; *asado* baste; **pringoso** greasy; **pringue** *m* grease, fat, dripping; grease stain.

prioridad *f* priority; seniority.

prisa *f* hurry, haste; speed; urgency; *a ~, de ~* quickly, hurriedly; *a ~ como* as quickly as possible; *tener ~* be in a hurry.

prisión *f* (*acto*) capture, arrest; (*cárcel*) prison; (*período*) imprisonment; *~es pl.* shackles; **prisionero** *m* prisoner; *hacer ~* take prisoner.

prisma *m* prism.

pristino pristine, original.

privación *f* (*acto*) deprivation; (*falta*) privation, want; **privado 1.** private, personal; **2.** *m* favorite; *en ~* in private; **privanza** *f* favor; **privar** [1a] *v/t.* deprive (*de* of), dispossess (*de* of); starve (*de* of); (*destituir*) demote, remove (*de* from); (*vedar*) forbid; *v/i.* be in favor *en corte*; F be in vogue, be the thing; *~se de* deprive o.s. of, give up; forgo; **privativo** exclusive; particular.

privilegio *m* privilege (*de inf.* of *ger.*); *ɪ̈ɮ* sole right; *lit.* copyright; *~ de invención* patent.

pro *m a. f* profit, advantage; *hombre de ~* worthy man; *los ~s y los contras* the pros and cons; *buena ~ le haga* and much good may it do him; *en ~ de pro*, for.

proa *f* bow(s), prow; *de ~* bow *attr.*, fore.

probabilidad *f* probability, likelihood; chance, prospect; **probable** probable, likely.

probanza *f* proof, evidence; inquiry.

probar [1m] **1.** *v/t.* prove; establish; (*ensayar*) try, try out, test; *vestido* try on; *comida etc.* taste, sample, try; *no pruebo nunca el vino* I never touch wine; **2.** *v/i.*: *~ a inf.* try to *inf.*; *no me prueba bien el vino* wine doesn't agree with me; *¿probaremos?* shall we try?

probatorio probative, evidential; *documentos ~s* documents in proof of.

probeta *f* ♠ test-tube; graduated cylinder; ⊕ test specimen; *niño-~ m* test-tube baby.

probidad *f* integrity, rectitude.

problema *m* problem; puzzle; **problemático** problematic, doubtful.

procedente fitting, reasonable; *ɪ̈ɮ* proper, lawful; *~ de* coming from, originating in; **proceder 1.** [2a] proceed (*a elección* to; *a inf.* to *inf.*; *ɪ̈ɮ contra* against); (*portarse*) behave, act; (*convenir*) be proper; *~ de* proceed from, originate in; **2.** *m* course, procedure; behaviour; **procedimiento** *m* procedure; proceeding; process; *ɪ̈ɮ* proceedings.

prócer *m* important person, chief.

procesado *m*, **a** *f* accused; **procesal** procedural; *ɪ̈ɮ costas etc.* legal; **procesar** [1a] *ɪ̈ɮ* try, put on trial; prosecute; sue; *datos* process; *~ datos* data-process.

procesión *f* procession; F *la ~ va por dentro* still waters run deep.

proceso *m* process (*a. anat.*, ♠); *ɪ̈ɮ* trial; prosecution; proceedings.

proclama *f* proclamation; *~s pl.* banns; **proclamación** *f* proclamation; acclamation; **proclamar** [1a] proclaim; acclaim.

procurador *m* *ɪ̈ɮ* attorney; **procurar** [1a] get; seek; cause, produce; *~ inf.* try to *inf.*, strive to *inf.*

prodigar [1h] *b.s.* waste, squander; *alabanzas etc.* lavish.

prodigio *m* prodigy; wonder, marvel; *niño ~* child prodigy; **prodigioso** prodigious; marvellous.

pródigo 1. *b.s.* extravagant, wasteful; prodigal (*de* with), lavish (*de* with); *hijo ~* prodigal son; **2.** *m*, **a** *f* spendthrift, prodigal.

producción *f* production; yield; produce; *~ en masa*, *~ en serie* mass production; **producir** [3o] *mst* produce; cause, generate; *~ en serie* mass produce; *~se* take place, come about, arise.

productividad *f* productivity; **productivo** productive; ✝ *~ de interés* interest-bearing; **producto** *m* product (*a.* ♠, ♠, ⊕); production; ✝ yield; *~s pl.* products, produce (*esp.* ♪); *~ alimenticio* foodstuff; **productor 1.** productive; producing; **2.** *m*, **-a** *f* producer.

proeza *f* exploit, heroic deed.

profanar [1a] desecrate, profane; **profano 1.** profane; indecent, **2.** *m* layman.

profecía *f* prophecy.

proferir [3i] utter; *indirecta* throw out; *injuria* hurl, let fly (*contra* at).

profesar [1a] *v/t.* profess; show, declare; *profesión* practice; *v/i. eccl.*

P

take vows; **profesión** f profession, calling; declaration *de fe etc.*; *de ~* professional; *hacer ~ de* pride o.s. on; **profesional** *adj. a. su. m/f* professional; **profesionalismo** m professionalism; **profesor** m, **-a** f teacher *en general*; (*school*)master, (*school-*)mistress *de instituto*; *univ.* (*que tiene cátedra*) professor; (*subordinado*) lecturer; *~ adjunto, ~ auxiliar approx.* assistant lecturer; *~ agregado* visiting lecturer; **profesorado** m teaching profession; (*ps.*) teaching staff; (*puesto*) professorship.

profeta m prophet; **profético** prophetic(al); **profetizar** [1f] prophesy.

prófugo m fugitive; ✗ deserter.

profundidad f depth; *esp. fig.* profundity; ⚓ height; **profundizar** [1f] *hoyo* deepen, make deeper; (*a. v/i. ~ en*) *estudio* extend, make a careful study of; *misterio* fathom; **profundo** deep; *mst fig.* profound; *conocedor etc.* very knowledgeable.

profusión f profusion; extravagance; **profuso** profuse.

programa m program; plan; schedule; *~ de estudios* curriculum; **programación** f programing.

progresar [1a] progress, advance; **progresión** f progression (*a.* ⚓); **progresista** *adj. a. su. m/f pol.*, **progresivo** progressive; **progreso** m progress, advance; *~s pl.* progress; *hacer ~s* make progress.

prohibición f prohibition (*de* of), ban (*de* on); embargo (*de* on); **prohibir** [3a] prohibit, forbid (*algo a alguien* a p. a th.); ban; stop; *~ inf.* forbid *s.o.* to *inf.*; *se prohíbe fumar, prohibido fumar* no smoking; **prohibitivo** prohibitive.

prohijar [1a] adopt.

prójimo m neighbor, fellow man.

prole f offspring, progeny.

proletariado m proletariat(e); **proletario** *adj. a. su. m*, **a** f proletarian.

proliferación f proliferation; **proliferar** [1a] proliferate; **prolífico** prolific (*en* of).

prolijo prolix, tedious, long-winded.

prólogo [1h] preface; **prólogo** m prologue; preface, introduction *de libro etc.*

prolongación f prolongation; extension; **prolongar** [1h] prolong; extend; ⚓ *línea* produce.

promediar [1b] *v/t.* divide into two

halves; *v/i.* (*interponerse*) mediate; **promedio** m average; middle *de una distancia.*

promesa f promise; **prometedor** promising; *perspectiva* hopeful, rosy; **prometer** [2a] *v/t.* promise; pledge; *v/i.* have (*or* show) promise; *~se algo* expect, promise o.s.; (*novios*) get engaged; *estar prometido* be engaged; **prometida** f fiancée; **prometido** m promise; (*p.*) fiancé.

prominente prominent; protuberant.

promiscuo *objetos* all mixed up, in disorder; ambiguous; *vida* promiscuous.

promoción f (*ascenso*) promotion; (*fomento*) promotion, advancement, furtherance; ✗ *la ~ de 1960* the 1960 class.

promontorio m promontory, headland.

promotor m, **promovedor** m promoter; pioneer; instigator; **promover** [2h] (*ascender*) promote; (*fomentar*) promote, forward, further; *proyecto etc.* pioneer, set on foot; *rebelión* stir up, instigate.

promulgación f promulgation; **promulgar** [1h] promulgate; *fig.* proclaim, announce publicly.

pronombre m pronoun; **pronominal** pronominal.

pronosticación f prediction, prognostication; **pronosticar** [1g] forecast, predict, foretell; **pronóstico** m forecast, prediction; ⚕ prognosis; (*señal*) omen, prognostic; *~ del tiempo* weather forecast.

prontitud f promptness, speed; quickness, keenness *de ingenio*; **pronto 1.** *adj.* prompt, quick, speedy; *contestación* prompt, swift, † early; *curación* speedy; (*listo*) ready (*para inf.* to *inf.*); **2.** *adv.* quickly, promptly; soon; at once; early; **3.** m sudden movement, jerk; F strong impulse.

pronunciación f pronunciation; **pronunciado** *Am.* obvious, clear; emphasized; **pronunciamiento** m ✗ revolt, insurrection; **pronunciar** [1b] pronounce; utter; *discurso* make, deliver; ✚ *sentencia* pass, pronounce; *~se* declare (o.s.) (*en favor de* in favor of); ✗ revolt, rebel.

propagación f *biol. etc.* propagation; *fig.* spreading, dissemination; **propaganda** f propaganda; † advertising; **propagandista** m/f propagandist; **propagar** [1h] biol. etc. propagate.

propalar [1a] divulge, disclose.

propasarse [1a] go to extremes, go too far; forget o.s.

propender [2a] incline, tend (a to); **propensión** f inclination (a for), propensity (a to), tendency (a to, towards); **propenso:** ~ a inclined to; prone to, subject to; ~ a inf. apt to inf.

propiamente properly; la arquitectura ~ dicha architecture proper.

propicio propitious, auspicious; p. kind, helpful.

propiedad f (bienes, finca) property; (atributo) property (a. 🜔), attribute; (dominio) ownership; (lo propio) appositeness; paint. etc. likeness, resemblance; ~ literaria copyright, rights; en ~ properly; es ~ copyright, **propietaria** f proprietress; **propietario 1.** proprietary; **2.** m proprietor, owner; (terrateniente) landowner.

propina f tip, gratuity; F de ~ into the bargain; **propinar** [1a] bebida treat to; golpe deal; paliza give.

propincuo near.

propio (conveniente) proper, suitable, fitting (para for); (que pertenece a uno) own, one's own; characteristic (de of), peculiar (de to), special; (mismo) same; natural.

proponente m proposer; **proponer** [2r] propose; put forward; ~se inf. propose to inf., plan to inf.

proporción f proportion; ratio; rate; en ~ con in proportion to; **proporcionado** proportionate; bien ~ well-proportioned, shapely; **proporcional** proportional; **proporcionar** [1a] provide, supply, give; adjust, adapt.

proposición f proposition; proposal.

propósito m purpose, aim, intention; buenos ~s pl. good resolutions; a ~ (adj.) appropriate, fitting (para for); observación apt, apposite; a ~ (adv.) by the way, incidentally; a ~ de about; de ~ on purpose, purposely, deliberately; fuera de ~ off the point, out of place.

propuesta f proposition, proposal.

propulsión f propulsion; ~ a cohete, cohética rocket propulsion; ~ a chorro, ~ por reacción jet propulsion; **propulsor** m propellent.

prorrata f share, quota; a ~ pro rata, proportionately; **prorratear** [1a] apportion, share out; average.

prorrumpir [3a] burst forth, break forth; ~ en burst into.

prosa f prose; F idle chatter; **prosaico** prose attr.; fig. prosaic, ordinary.

prosapia f ancestry, lineage.

proscribir [3a; p.p. proscrito] (prohibir) prohibit, ban; partido etc. proscribe; (desterrar) banish; criminal outlaw; **proscripción** f ban (de on), prohibition (de of); **proscrito 1.** p.p. of proscribir; **2.** adj. banned; banished, outlawed; **3.** m exile; outlaw.

prosecución f prosecution, continuation; pursuit; **proseguir** [3d a. 3l] v/t. continue, push, proceed with, carry on; demanda push; estudio, investigación pursue; v/i. continue.

prospección f exploration; 🜔 prospecting (de for); **prospector** m prospector.

prosperar [1a] prosper, thrive, flourish; **prosperidad** f prosperity; success, good fortune; (período) good times; **próspero** prosperous, thriving, flourishing.

prosternarse [1a] prostrate o.s.

prostitución f prostitution; **prostituir** [3g] prostitute (a. fig.); **prostituta** f prostitute.

protagonista m/f protagonist; main character, (m) hero, (f) heroine.

protección f protection; **proteccionista** adj. a. su. m/f protectionist; impuesto protective; **protector 1.** protective; tono patronizing; **2.** m, -a f protector; guardian; **protectorado** m protectorate; **proteger** [2c] protect (de, contra from, against); shield, shelter.

proteína f protein.

protesta f protest; protestation de amistad etc.; **protestación** f protestation; ~ de fe profession of faith; **protestante** adj. a. su. m/f Protestant; **protestantismo** m Protestantism; **protestar** [1a] protest (a. 🜔, ⚖️; contra, de against); **protesto** m 🜔, ⚖️ protest.

protón m proton.

protoplasma m protoplasm.

prototipo m prototype.

protuberancia f protuberance.

provecho m advantage, benefit, profit (a. 🜔); negocio de ~ profitable business; persona de ~ useful person, decent sort; ¡buen ~! hoping that *those eating will enjoy their meal;* **provechoso** advantageous, beneficial, profitable (*a.* ✝).

proveedor *m,* **-a** *f* supplier, purveyor; caterer; **proveer** [2a; *p.p. provisto, a. proveído*] provide, supply (de with); *negocio* transact.

provenir [3s]: ~ de come from, arise from, stem from.

proverbio *m* proverb.

providencia *f* forethought, foresight, providence; (*Divina*) ♀ Providence; **providente, próvido** provident.

provincia *f* province; de ~(s) freq. provincial, country *attr.;* **provincial** *adj. a. su. m,* **-a** *f* (*eccl.*) provincial; **provincialismo** *m* provincialism.

provisión *f* provision; supply, store; ~es *pl.* provisions *etc.*

provocación *f* provocation; (*insulto*) affront; **provocador** provocative; **provocar** [1g] *v/t.* provoke; incite, tempt, move; (*fomentar*) promote, forward; *cambio, reacción etc.* provoke, bring about, induce; **provocativo** provocative.

próximamente approximately; (*pronto*) shortly; **proximidad** *f* proximity, nearness; **próximo** near, next; close; *el mes ~* next month; *el mes ~ pasado* last month; *en fecha ~a* at an early date.

proyección *f* projection; **proyectar** [1a] *película etc.* project, show; *sombra* cast; *casa, máquina etc.* plan, design; *viaje etc.* plan; **proyectil** *m* projectile, missile; *esp.* ✕ shell; ~ *dirigido* guided missile; **proyectista** *m/f* designer, planner; **proyecto** *m* project, scheme, plan; (*presupuesto*) detailed estimate; ~ de ley bill; **proyector** *m cine:* projector; ✈, ✕ searchlight.

prudencia *f* prudence; wisdom; sound judgement; **prudente** prudent, wise, sensible; judicious.

prueba *f* proof (*a.* ♠, typ.); (*indicio*) proof, sign, token; ⚖ proof, evidence (*a. fig.*); (*ensayo*) test, trial, try-out; *phot.* proof, print; *esp.* ♠ experiment; taste, sample; ~ de alcohol alcohol-level test (for drunken driving); ~ documental documentary evidence; ~ de fuego *fig.* acid test; ~ indiciaria circumstantial evidence; *a ~ de bala* bulletproof; *a ~ de escaladores* burglarproof; *a ~ de incendio* fireproof; *a toda ~* foolproof.

psicoanálisis *m* psychoanalysis; **psicoanalista** *m/f* psychoanalyst; **psicología** *f* psychology; **psicológico** psychological; **psicólogo** *m* psychologist; **psicosis** *f* psychosis; **psicoterapia** *f* psychotherapy; ~ de grupo group therapy; **psiquiatra** *m* psychiatrist; **psiquiatría** *f* psychiatry.

púa *f zo.,* ♣ prickle, spike, spine; quill *de erizo;* ♣ graft *para injertar.*

pubertad *f* puberty.

publicación *f* publication; **publicar** [1g] publish; (*dar publicidad a*) publicize; *secreto* disclose, divulge; **publicidad** *f* publicity; ✝ advertising; **publicista** *m/f* publicist; **público 1.** public; state *attr.; hacer ~* publish, disclose; **2.** *m* public; *thea. etc.* audience; *deportes etc.:* spectators; crowd.

pude *etc. v.* poder.

pudendo: *partes ~as* private parts.

pudibundo modest, shy; chaste.

pudiendo *v.* poder.

pudiente well-to-do; powerful.

pudor *m* modesty, shyness, virtue, chastity; (*vergüenza*) shame; **pudoroso** modest, shy; chaste.

pudrir [3a] rot; ~se rot, decay, putrefy; *fig.* rot, languish *en cárcel;* die (*de aburrimiento etc.* of).

pueblo *m* (*nación*) people, nation; (*plebe*) lower orders, common people; (*poblado*) town, village.

puedo *etc. v.* poder.

puente *m* bridge (*a.* ♪); ♠ deck; ♠ ~ (*de mando*) bridge; ~ aéreo air lift; ~ colgante suspension bridge; ~ giratorio swing bridge; ~ levadizo drawbridge; ~ de pontones pontoon bridge.

puerca *f* sow; F slut; **puerco 1.** *m* pig, hog; F pig; ~ espín porcupine; **2.** dirty, filthy.

pueril childish; **puerilidad** *f* puerility, childishness.

puerro *m* leek; *sl.* joint (*or* hashish cigarette).

puerta *f* door; doorway; gate *de jardín, ciudad etc.;* gateway (*a. fig.*); ~ accesoria side door; ~ excusada, ~ falsa private door, side door; ~ giratoria swing door, revolving door; ~ principal front door; ~ trasera back door; ~ ventana french window; ~ vidriera glass door; *a ~ cerrada* behind closed doors.

puerto *m* ♠ port, harbor; (*ciudad*) port; *esp. fig.* haven; *geog.* pass; ~ de

punto

escala port of call; ~ *franco* free port; *entrar a* ~ put in.

puertorriqueño *adj. a. su. m,* **a** *f* (native) of Puerto Rico.

pues (*ya que*) since, for, because; (*continuativo*) then; well; well then; (*afirmación*) yes, certainly; ... (*vacilando*) well ...; *ahora* ~ now, now then; ~ *bien* well then, very well; ~ *sí* well yes, yes certainly.

puesta *f* stake, bet *en el juego*; *orn.* egg-laying; ~ *a punto mot.* tune-up; ~ *del sol* sunset.

puesto 1. *p.p. of poner; ir bien* ~ be well dressed; *con el sombrero* ~ with his hat on; **2.** *m* place, position, situation; (*empleo*) post, position;✕ post; booth; (*quiosco*) stand; ~ *de socorro* first-aid post; **3.** : ~ *que* since, as.

¡puf! ugh!

púgil *m* boxer; **pugilato** *m* boxing.

pugna *f fig.* battle, struggle; *estar en* ~ *con* in conflict with; **pugnacidad** *f* pugnacity; **pugnar** [1a] struggle, fight, strive (*por inf.* to *inf.*); **pugnaz** pugnacious.

puja *f* bid; F *sacar de la* ~ *a* get ahead of; get *s.o.* out of a jam.

pujante strong, vigorous; *p.* strapping; **pujanza** *f* strength, vigor; **pujar** [1a] *v/t. precio* raise, push up; *v/i.* bid up *en subasta*; *naipes:* bid; (*pugnar*) struggle, strain; (*no lograr hablar*) be at a loss for words.

pulcro neat, tidy, smart; exquisite, delicate.

pulga *f* flea; *de malas* ~*s* peppery; *tener malas* ~*s* be bad tempered.

pulgada *f* inch.

pulgar *m* thumb; **pulgarada** *f* pinch *de rapé etc.*; flip, flick *con el pulgar*; (*medida*) inch.

pulido (*pulcro*) neat, tidy, smart; (*terso*) polished; **pulidor** *m,* **-a** *f* polisher; **pulimentar** [1a] polish; (*alisar*) smooth; **pulimento** *m* polish; **pulir** [3a] polish; *fig.* polish up, touch up; ~*se fig.* acquire polish; dress up.

pulla *f* taunt, cutting remark; dig; rude word, indecent remark.

pulmón *m* lung; **pulmonía** *f* pneumonia.

pulpa *f* pulp; soft part *de carne, fruta*; ~ *de madera* wood pulp.

pulpo *m* octopus.

pulsación *f* pulsation; throb(bing); beat(ing); ♪ touch; tap *en máquina de escribir*; **pulsador** *m* pushbutton; **pulsar** [1a] *v/t.* ♪ *instrumento* play;

tecla etc. touch, strike, play; *botón* press, push; ⚡ feel the pulse of; *fig.* sound out, explore; *v/i.* pulsate, throb, beat.

pulsera *f* wristlet, bracelet.

pulso *m anat.* pulse; (*muñeca*) wrist; *fig.* steady hand, firmness of touch; (*cuidado*) care, caution; *a* ~ by sheer strength; *a* ~ *sudando* by the sweat of one's brow; *hecho a* ~ *dibujo* freehand; *tomar el* ~ *a* feel the pulse of; *tomar a* ~ lift clean off the ground.

pulular [1a] swarm, abound.

pulverización *f* pulverization; spray(ing) *de líquido*; **pulverizador** *m* spray(er); **pulverizar** [1f] pulverize; powder; *líquido* spray.

punción ⚡ puncture.

pundonor *m* point of honor; honor; face (*fig.*); **pundonoroso** honorable; punctilious, scrupulous.

pungir [3c] prick; sting.

punible punishable; **punición** *f* punishment; **punitivo** punitive.

punta *f* point (*a. geog.*); end, tip; end, butt *de cigarro*; ⊕ nail; toe *de zapato etc.*; horn *de toro*; sourness *de vino*; (*pizca*) touch, trace, tinge; ~ *del pie* toe; ~ *de lanza* spearhead (*a. fig.*); *de* ~ on end, endways; *estar de* ~ be at odds (*con* with); *sacar* ~ *a* sharpen, point.

puntear [1a] ♪ pluck, twang; *sew.* stitch; *dibujo etc.* dot, mark with dots; stipple; fleck.

puntería *f* aim(ing); (*destreza*) marksmanship; *enmendar la* ~ correct one's aim; *hacer la* ~ *de* aim.

puntilla *f* ⊕ tack, brad; *sew.* narrow lace edging; *de* ~*s* on tiptoe.

puntillo *m* punctilio; **puntilloso** punctilious.

punto *m* point (*a. fig.; sitio, momento, detalle, rasgo, estado, etc.*); (*sitio*) spot, place; dot *señalado en papel etc.*; gr. full stop; pip *de carta*; dot, speckle, fleck *de tela; sew.* stitch; (*malla*) mesh; *fig.* point of honor; *dos* ~*s gr.* colon; ~ *y coma* semicolon; *¡*~ *en boca!* mum's the word!; ~ *por* ~ point by point; ~ *de admiración* exclamation mark; ~ *de apoyo* fulcrum; ~ *capital* crucial point, crux; ~*s pl.* cardinales cardinal points; ~ *de congelación* freezing point; ~*s pl.* de consulta terms of reference; ~ *de contacto* point of contact; ~ *de ebullición* boiling point; ~ *de fuga* vanishing point; ~ de fusión melting-point; ~ de honor point of honor; ~ de inflamación flash point; ~ de interrogación question mark; ~ de media plain knitting; ~ muerto ⊕ dead center; *mot.* neutral (*a.* ~ *neutral*); *fig.* stalemate, deadlock; ~ neutro mot. neutral; ~ de partida starting-point; ~s *pl.* suspensivos *three dots indicating hesitation etc.* (...); ~ de vista point of view; *a* ~ ready; *a* ~ *fijo* for sure; *al* ~ at once, instantly.

puntuación *f gr.* punctuation; marking de exámenes; mark, class en examen; deportes: score; **puntual** prompt; *cálculo etc.* exact; *p. etc.* reliable, conscientious; **puntualidad** *f* punctuality *etc.*; **puntualizar** [1f] fix in the mind; *suceso* give an exact account of; **puntuar** [1e] *v/t. gr.* punctuate; *examen* mark; *v/i. deportes:* score.

puntura *f* puncture, prick.

punzada *f* puncture, prick; ❃ stitch de costado; ❃ shooting pain, spasm, twinge; *fig.* pang; **punzante** *dolor* shooting, stabbing; *observación* biting, caustic; **punzar** [1f] *v/t.* puncture, pierce, prick; punch; *v/i.* (*dolor*) shoot, stab, sting.

puñada *f* punch, clout.

puñado *m* handful (*a. fig.*).

puñal *m* dagger; **puñalada** *f* stab.

puñetazo *m* punch; *dar un* ~ *a* punch; *dar de* ~s punch, pommel.

puño *m anat.* fist; (*contenido*) fistful, handful; (*mango*) handle, haft, hilt; cuff de camisa; de propio ~ in one's own handwriting; de ~ y letra de X in X's own handwriting; *como un* ~ tangible, absolutely real; por sus ~s by oneself, on one's own.

pupa *f* ❃ pimple, blister.

pupila *f anat.* pupil; (*p.*) ward; **pupilo** *m* ward; boarder.

pupitre *m* desk.

pureza *f* purity.

purga *f* purge (*a. pol.*), purgative; **purgante** *m* laxative; **purgar** [1h] purge (*a. pol.*); purify, refine; ⊕ vent, drain; ~se ❃ take a purge; *fig.* purge o.s.

purificación *f* purification; **purificar** [1g] purify; cleanse; ⊕ refine.

puro 1. pure; (*sin mezcla*) pure, unadulterated, unalloyed; *verdad* plain, simple, unvarnished; *cielo* clear; **2.** *m* cigar.

púrpura *f* purple; purple cloth.

puse *etc. v. poner.*

pústula *f* pustule, sore, pimple.

puta *f* whore, prostitute.

putativo supposed, putative.

putrefacto rotten, putrid; **putrescente** rotting; **pútrido** putrid, rotten.

Q

que 1. *pron. relativo:* (*p.*) (*sujeto*) who, (*acc.*) whom; (*cosa*) which; (*p., cosa*) that; en muchos casos se puede suprimir: el hombre ~ vi the man (whom) I saw; el ~ (*p.*) he who, whoever; who, the one who; (*cosa*) which, the one which; la ~ she who etc.; los ~, las ~ those who etc.; lo ~ what, that which; (*esp. tras coma*) which, something which, a fact which; lo ~ quiero what I want; todo lo ~ vi all (that) I saw; lo ~ es eso as for that; no tengo nada ~ hacer I have nothing to do; **2.** *cj.* a) that; en muchos casos se puede suprimir: yo sé ~ es verdad I know (that) it is true; dice ~ sí he says yes; ¡~ sí, hombre! I tell you it is!; *v. si²*) b) (*pues*) for, because; *a menudo no se traduce:* ¡cuidado!, ~ viene un coche look out! there's a car

coming; c) *con subjuntivo:* quiero ~ lo hagas I want you to do it; ¡~ lo pases bien! have a good time!; ¡~ entre! let him come in!, send him in!; d) *comparaciones:* than; más ~ yo more than I; e) el ~ *subj.* the fact that, that; f) ~ ... ~ whether ... or; yo ~ tú if I were you; F ¡*a* ~ *no!* I bet it isn't!, I bet you can't!; no, I tell you!

qué 1. *pron. interrogativo:* ¿~? what?; ¿~ hiciste entonces? what did you do then?; ¡~ perro más feo! what an ugly dog!; ¡~ bonito! how pretty!; ¡~ asco! how disgusting!; ¿de ~ tamaño es? how big is it?, what size is it?; ¿~ edad tiene? how old is he?; ¡~ de ...! how many ...!; **3.** *a* ~? why?; ¿*a* mí ~? what's that got to do with me?; ¿de ~ le conoce? how do you know him?; F ¿*y* ~? so what?; what then?;

sin ∼ *ni para* ≈ without rhyme or reason.

quebrada f gorge, ravine; gap.

quebradero m: F ∼ *de cabeza* headache, worry; **quebradizo** fragile, delicate, brittle; **quebrado 1.** *terreno* rough, broken; ☩ ruptured; ✝ bankrupt; **2.** m A fraction; **quebradura** f fissure, slit; ☛ rupture; **quebraja** f fissure, slit; **quebrantadura** f, **quebrantamiento** m breaking, breakage *etc.*; ☛ exhaustion, fatigue; **quebrantar** [1a] break (*a. fig.*); crack; *caja* break open; *cárcel* break out of; *color* tone down.

quebrar [1k] *v/t.* break, smash; *color* tone down; *v/i.* break; ✝ go bankrupt, fail; (*disminuir*) slacken, weaken; ∼ *con* break with; ∼*se* break, get broken; ☛ be ruptured.

quedar [1a] **1.** (*permanecer en un lugar etc.*) stay, remain; (*sobrar*) be left (over), remain; ∼ *adj., p.p.* be remain, stay; keep; *quedé 3 días* I stayed 3 days; *quedan 3* there are 3 left; *me quedan 3* I have 3 left; **2.** ∼*se* stay, remain; stay on, stay behind, linger (on); put up (*en hotel* at); ∼ *ciego* go blind.

quedo 1. *adj.* quiet; **2.** *adv.* softly.

quehacer m job, task, duty; ∼*es pl. domésticos* household jobs, chores; housekeeping.

queja f (*dolor*) moan, groan; whine; (*resentimiento*) complaint, grumble, grouse; ☶ *etc.* protest, complaint; *tener* ∼ *de* have a complaint to make about; **quejarse** [1a] (*dolor*) moan, groan; whine; complain (*de* about, of); **quejido** m moan, groan; **quejoso** complaining, querulous; **quejumbroso** whining.

quema f burning; **quemador** m burner; ∼ *de gas* gas-burner; **quemadura** f burn; scald *de líquido etc.*; (*insolación*) sunburn; blowout *de fusible*; **quemar** [1a] **1.** *v/t.* burn; (*pegar fuego a*) kindle, set on fire; (*líquido*) scald; *boca* burn; *plantas* (*sol*) burn, scorch; (*helada*) burn, frost; *fusible* blow, burn out; **2.** *v/i. fig.* be burning hot; **3.** ∼*se* burn; scorch; feel burning hot; F (*buscando*) be warm.

quemarropa: *a* ∼ pointblank.

quemazón f burn, burning; *fig.* intense heat; F (*comezón*) itch; F (*palabra*) cutting remark; F (*resentimiento*) pique, annoyance.

quepo *etc. v. caber.*

querella f dispute, controversy; ☶ *etc.* complaint, charge.

querencia f zo. (*guarida*) lair, haunt; zo. homing instinct; *fig.* den, haunt.

querer 1. [2u] (*amar*) love; (*tener afición a*) like; (*desear*) want, wish; *quiero hacerlo* I want to do it; *quiero que lo hagas* I want you to do it; *te quiero mucho* I love you very much; *como Vd. quiera* just as you wish; *como quiera* anyhow, anyway; *como quiera que* whereas; since, inasmuch as; *v. decir; quiere llover* it is trying to rain; *sin* ∼ inadvertently, unintentionally, by mistake; *lo hizo sin* ∼ he didn't mean to do it; **2.** m love, affection.

querida f *b.s.* mistress; *¡sí,* ∼*!* yes dear, yes darling; **querido 1.** dear, beloved, darling; **2.** m *b.s.* lover; *¡sí,* ∼*!* yes dear, yes darling.

queroseno m kerosine.

quesería f dairy *en granja*; cheese factory; **quesero** m dairyman; cheesemaker; **queso** m cheese; ∼ *crema* cream cheese; ∼ *para extender* cheese spread.

quicio m hinge; *fig. fuera de* ∼ out of joint; *sacar de* ∼ exasperate.

quiebra f (*grieta*) crack, fissure; (*pérdida*) loss, damage; ✝ bankruptcy *de p.*; failure of sociedad.

quiebro m ♪ trill; *toros:* dodge, avoiding action.

quien (*sujeto*) who, (*acc.*) whom; (*en comienzo de frase*) he *etc.* who, whoever; ∼ *...* ∼ some ... others; *hay* ∼ *dice* there are some who say.

quién (*sujeto*) who, (*acc.*) whom; *¿a* ∼ *lo diste?* to whom did you give it?; *¿de* ∼ *es este libro?* whose is this book?

quienquiera whoever.

quieto (*inmóvil*) still; (*silencioso*) quiet; *(calm, peaceful; ¡estáte* ∼*! keep still!;* **quietud** f stillness *etc.*

quijotada f quixotic act; **quijotería** f, **quijotismo** m quixotism; **quijotesco** quixotic.

quilla f ⚓, *orn.*, ⚘ keel; *colocar la* ∼ *de* lay down; *dar de* ∼ keel over.

quimera f fantastic idea, fancy, chimera; *fig.* quarrel, dispute; **quimérico** fantastic, fanciful, chimerical; **quimerista** m/f quarrelsome sort, rowdy, brawler.

química f chemistry; **químico 1.** chemical; **2.** m chemist.

quincalla f hardware, ironmongery; **quincallería** f hardware shop.
quince fifteen (a. su.); (fecha) fifteenth; ~ días freq. fortnight; **quincena** f fortnight.
quinientos five hundred.
quinina f quinine.
quinta f (casa) villa, country house; ♪ fifth; ✗ draft; ⚙ coughing fit.
quintaesencia f quintessence.
quintero m farmer; farm laborer.
quinto 1. fifth; 2. m ✗ fifth; ✗ conscript, recruit; draftee.
quiosco m stand de calle; summerhouse, pavilion de jardín; ~ (de música) bandstand; ~ (de periódicos) newsstand; ~ de necesidad public lavatory.
quiquiriquí m cock-a-doodle-doo.
quiromancia f palmistry.
quirúrgico surgical.
quise etc. v. querer.
quisquilla f trifle, triviality; (a. ~s pl.) quibbling, hair-splitting; **quisquilloso** touchy, cantankerous; fastidious, pernickety, choosy.

quiste m cyst.
quisto: bien ~ well-liked; well received; mal ~ disliked; unwelcome.
quita...: **~esmalte** m nail-polish remover; **~manchas** m (p.) dry cleaner; cleaner, stain remover; **~nieves** m: (máquina) ~ snowplough; **~pesares** m F consolation, comfort; **~piedras** m cowcatcher.
quitapón: de ~ detachable.
quitar [1a] 1. take away, remove (a from); ropa take off; pieza take out, take off, remove; golpe avert; fenc. parry; mesa clear; (robar) steal; abuso, dificultad etc. do away with, remove; ✗ subtract, take away; 2. **~se** ropa take off; (mancha) come out; (p.) withdraw (de from); ~ de algo, ~ algo de encima get rid of s.t., dispose of s.t.; ~ de en medio get out of the way; ¡quítate de ahí! come out of that!
quitasol m sunshade, parasol.
quite m hindrance; fenc. parry; (regate) dodge, dodging.
quizá(s) perhaps, maybe; I dare say.

R

rábano m radish; ~ picante horseradish.
rabia f 🐾 rabies; fig. rage, fury; **rabiar** [1b] fig. rage, rave; (dolor) be in great pain.
rabino m rabbi.
rabioso 🐾 mad, rabid; fig. furious; partidario rabid; dolor raging.
racha f meteor. squall, gust.
racial racial, race attr.
racimo m cluster, bunch.
raciocinar [1a] reason; **raciocinio** m reason; (acto) reasoning.
ración f ration; portion, helping de plato; **racional** rational (a. Å); reasonable; **racionamiento** m rationing; **racionar** [1a] ration.
racismo m racialism.
radar m radar.
radiación f radiation; radio: broadcasting; **radiactividad** f radioactivity; **radiactivo** radioactive; **radiado** radio attr., broadcast attr.; **radiador** m radiator; **radial** radial; S.Am. radio attr.; **radiante** radiant (a. fig.); **radiar** [1b] radio: broadcast; phys. radiate.

radical 1. radical; 2. m pol. radical; Å, gr. root; **radicalismo** m radicalism; **radicar** [1g] 🌱 a. fig. take root; be, be located en lugar.
radio¹ m Å, anat. radius; spoke de rueda; 🧪 radium; ♣, ✗ ~ de acción range; en un ~ de within a radius of.
radio² f radio; broadcasting; (aparato) radio (set); wireless telegram; **~aficionado** m ham (radio operator); **~captar** [1a] monitor; **~difundir** broadcast; **~difusión** f broadcasting; **~escucha** m/f listener; **~experimentador** m radio fan, ham; **~fonógrafo** m S.Am. radiogram; **~goniómetro** m direction finder; **~grafiar** [1c] ✗ X-ray; ✗ radio; **~gráfico** X-ray attr.; **~grama** m wireless message; **~gramola** f radiogram; **~logía** f radiology; **~rreceptor** m radio set (or receiver); ~ de contrastación monitor; **~teléfono** m radiophone, radio telephone; **~telescopio** m radiotelescope; **~terapia** f radiotherapy; **radioyente** m/f listener.
raedera f scraper; **raedura** f scrap-

ing; **⚙** abrasion; ~s *pl.* filings, scrapings; **raer** [2z] scrape; (*quitar*) scrape off; (*alisar*) smooth; chafe; **⚙** abrade; **~se** chafe; (*tela*) fray.

ráfaga *f* squall, gust *de viento*; burst *de balas*; flurry *de nieve*.

raído *tela* threadbare; *aspecto* shabby; *fig.* shameless.

raigón *m* **♣** large root; root, stump *de diente*.

raíz *f* root; *fig.* foundation; origin; ~ *cuadrada* square root; ~ *cúbica* cube root; *a* ~ *de* soon after; as a result of; *de* ~ root and branch; *cortar de* ~ nip in the bud.

raja *f* crack, split, slit; gash; (*astilla*) sliver, splinter; slice *de melón etc.*; **rajar** [1a] *v/t.* split, crack, slit; *melón etc.* slice; *v/i.* F shoot a line; (*hablar*) chatter; **~se** split *etc.*

ralea *f* breed, kind, sort.

rallador *m* grater; **rallar** [1a] grate.

ralo *pelo* sparse; *tela* loosely-woven; *phys.* rare.

rama *f* branch (*a. fig.*); *en* ~ *algodón* raw; *libro* unbound; *andarse por las* ~s beat about the bush; **ramaje** *m* branches; **ramal** *m* strand *de cuerda*; (*ronzal*) halter; *fig.* offshoot; **🚂** branch-line.

ramera *f* whore.

ramificación *f* ramification; **ramificarse** [1g] ramify, branch (out).

ramillete *m* bouquet, posy; corsage *en vestido*; cluster; *fig.* collection.

ramita *f* twig, sprig; spray *de flores*.

ramo *m* branch, bough; bunch, bouquet *de flores*; **⚙** touch; *fig.* branch; department *de tienda etc.*

rampa *f* ramp; ~ *de lanzamiento* launching pad.

ramplón *zapato* heavy, rough; *fig.* vulgar, coarse; **ramplonería** *f* vulgarity, coarseness.

rana *f* frog; ~ *toro* bullfrog.

ranchear [1a] *S.Am.* *v/t.* sack; *v/i.* build a camp, make a settlement; **ranchería** *f* settlement; **ranchero** *m* (*mess*) cook; *S.Am.* rancher; **rancho** *m* **✕**, **♣** mess; camp, settlement; *S.Am.* hut; (*finca*) ranch.

rancidez *f*, **ranciedad** *f* rancidness *etc.*; **rancio** rancid, rank, stale, musty; *fig. abolengo* ancient.

rango *m* rank; status; class.

ranúnculo *m* buttercup.

ranura *f* groove, slot.

rapacidad *f* rapacity, greed.

rapar [1a] shave, crop; F pinch.

rapaz[1] rapacious, greedy; thieving.

rapaz[2] *m* lad, youngster; *contp.* kid; **rapaza** *f* lass, youngster.

rapé *m* snuff.

rápido 1. rapid, speedy, quick, swift; 2. *m* express (train); ~s *pl.* rapids.

rapiña *f* robbery (with violence); *de* ~ predatory.

raposa *f* fox (*a. fig.*).

raptar [1a] abduct, kidnap; **rapto** *m* abduction, kidnapping; *fig.* sudden impulse; **raptor** *m* kidnapper.

raquero *m* beachcomber.

raqueta *f* racquet; ~ *de nieve* snowshoe.

raquítico **⚙** rickety; *fig.* stunted; (*débil*) weak, feeble; **raquitis** *f*, **raquitismo** *m* rickets.

rareza *f* rarity, rareness, scarcity; *fig.* oddity, eccentricity; **raridad** *f* rarity; **rarificar** [1g] rarefy; **raro** rare, scarce, uncommon; *fig.* strange, odd; notable.

ras *m* level(ness); ~ *con* ~ level; flush; *a* ~ *de* on a level with.

rascacielos *m* skyscraper; **rascadera** *f* scraper; **rascador** *m* rasp, scraper; hairpin *para pelo*; **rascar** [1g] scrape (*a. ♣ co.*); scratch; rasp.

rasete *m* satinet(te).

rasgado *ojos* large; *boca* wide; **rasgadura** *f* tear, rip; **rasgar** [1h] tear, rip, slash; *un papel* tear up; **rasgo** *m* stroke, flourish *de pluma*; *fig.* feature, characteristic; (*acto*) feat, deed; noble gesture; ~s *pl.* features *de cara*; ~ *de ingenio* flash of wit; stroke of genius; *a grandes* ~s in outline; **rasgón** *m* tear, rent; **rasguear** [1a] **♩** strum; **rasguñar** [1a] scratch; scrape; *paint.* outline; **rasguño** *m* scratch; *paint.* outline.

raso 1. level, flat, clear; *paisaje* bare; open; *asiento* backless; *cielo* cloudless; *soldado etc.* ordinary; *v. soldado*; 2. *m* *sew.* satin; *al* ~ in the open air; in open country.

raspador *m* scraper, rasp(er); **raspadura** *f* scrape *etc.*; erasure; ~s *pl.* filings, scrapings; **raspante** *vino* sharp; **raspar** [1a] *v/t.* scrape, rasp, file *con raspador*; *piel etc.* graze; scale; *palabra* erase; F pinch; *S.Am.* F tick off; *v/i.* (*vino*) be sharp; **raspear** [1a] (*pluma*) scratch.

rastra *f* (*señal*) track, trail; (*carro*) sledge; **♩** harrow; **♣** drag, trawl; **rastreador** *m* tracker; **♣** (*barco*) ~ trawler; **rastrear** [1a] *v/t.* (*seguir*) track, trail; (*encontrar*) track down, trace; (*llevar*) drag; ⚓ dredge, drag; *minas* sweep; *v/i.* ⚒ rake, harrow; ⚓ trawl; ⚞ *etc.* skim the ground, fly low; **rastrero** *fig.* despicable; **rastrillar** [1a] rake; *lino etc.* dress; **rastrillo** *m* rake; ⚔ portcullis; (*delantero* cowcatcher *Am.*; **rastro** *m* ⚒ rake, harrow; track, trail *de animal*, *de cosa arrastrada*; *fig.* trace, sign.

rasurador *m* (electric) razor; **rasurar** [1a] *cara* shave; ⊕ scrape.

rata 1. *f* rat; **2.** *m* F sneak-thief.

rataplán *m* drum-beat, rub-a-dub.

ratear [1a] share out; (*robar*) pilfer, lift; filch; **ratería** *f* petty larceny, pilfering; **ratero 1.** light-fingered; **2.** *m* pickpocket, small-time thief; **raticida** *m* rat poison.

ratificación *f* ratification; **ratificar** [1g] ratify.

rato *m* (short) time, while, spell; *un ~* (*como adv.*) awhile; *un buen ~* a good while; *largo ~* a long while; *~s pl. libres*, *~s perdidos* spare time, leisure.

ratón *m*, **-a** *f* mouse; *~ de biblioteca* bookworm; **ratonar** [1a] gnaw, nibble; **ratonera** *f* mousetrap.

raudal *m* torrent; *fig.* plenty, abundance; *entrar etc. a ~es* flood in *etc.*; **raudo** swift, rushing.

raya *f* stripe, streak *en tela etc.*; scratch, mark *en piedra etc.*; dash *con pluma* (*a. tel.*); line *que subraya etc.*; *deportes:* line, mark; parting *de pelo*; crease *de pantalón*; boundary, limit; *ichth.* ray, skate.

rayar [1a] *v/t.* stripe, line, streak; *piedra etc.* scratch, score; *papel* rule, draw lines across; *fusil* rifle; (*tachar*) cross out; (*subrayar*) underline; *v/i.* *~ con* border on, be next to.

rayo¹ *etc. v. raer.*

rayo² *m* (*luz*) ray, beam, shaft; (*relámpago*) flash of lightning; thunderbolt *que daña*; spoke *de rueda*; *~s pl. catódicos* cathode rays; *~s pl. cósmicos* cosmic rays; *~s pl. gama* gamma-rays; *~ de sol* sunbeam; *~s pl.* X X-rays.

rayón *m* rayon.

raza¹ *f* race (*a. biol.*); breed, stock, strain; *~ humana* human race, mankind; *de ~* *caballo* thoroughbred.

raza² *f* crack, slit; ray of light.

razón *f* reason; right, justice; ⚖ ratio; *S.Am.* message; *~ de más* all the more reason; *~ de ser* raison d'être; ✝ *~ social* trade name; *no tener ~* be

wrong; **razonable** reasonable; rational; *aviso, posibilidad etc.* fair; **razonado** reasoned; **razonamiento** *m* reasoning; argument; **razonar** [1a] *v/t.* reason; argue; *problema* reason out; *v/i.* reason.

reabrir(se) [3a; *p.p. reabierto*] reopen.

reacción *f* reaction (*ante* to); response (*a* to); *~ en cadena* chain reaction; ⚞ *a ~* jet(-propelled); **reaccionar** [1a] react (*a* to; *ante* to; *contra* against; *sobre* on); respond (*a* to); **reaccionario** *adj. a. su. m*, **a** *f* reactionary.

reacio obstinate, stubborn.

reacondicionar [1a] recondition.

reactivo *m* reagent; **reactor** *m phys.* reactor; ⚞ jet engine; *~-generador m* breeder reactor.

reajustar [1a] readjust; **reajuste** *m* readjustment.

real¹ real; genuine.

real² **1.** (*del rey*) royal; *aspecto etc.* kingly; **2.** *m* fairground; ✝ *coin of 25 cents.*

realce *m* ⊕ raised work, embossing; *paint.* highlight; *fig.* lustre, splendor; *fig.* enhancement.

realeza *f* royalty.

realidad *f* reality; truth, sincerity; *en ~* in fact, actually; **realismo** *m* realism; **realista 1.** realistic; **2.** *m/f* realist; **realizable** realizable (*a.* ✝); *objetivo etc.* attainable; **realización** *f* realization (*a.* ✝); fulfilment, achievement; **realizar** [1f] realize (*a.* ✝); *objetivo* fulfil, achieve; *promesa etc.* carry out; *~se* (*sueño etc.*) come true, materialize; **realmente** really, actually; *comer etc.* royally.

realzar [1f] ⊕ emboss, raise; *fig.* enhance, heighten, add to.

reanimar [1a] revive (*a. fig.*); *fig.* encourage; *~se* revive, rally.

reanudación *f* renewal; **reanudar** [1a] renew; *viaje etc.* resume.

reaparecer [2d] reappear; **reaparición** *f* reappearance; recurrence.

reasumir [3a] resume, reassume.

reata *f* lasso, rope; *de ~* in single file.

rebaja *f* lowering, reduction (*a.* ✝); **rebajamiento** *m* = *rebaja*; *~ de sí mismo* self-abasement; **rebajar** [1a] reduce (*a.* ✝), lower, cut down; *paint.* tone down; *fig. p.* humble.

rebanada *f* slice; **rebanar** [1a] slice.

rebaño *m* flock (*a. fig.*), herd.

rebatir [3a] *ataque* repel, ward off;

cantidad reduce; *descuento* deduct; *argumento* rebut, refute.

rebato *m* alarm; ✗ call to arms; ✗ surprise attack.

rebelarse [1a] rebel, revolt; resist; **rebelde 1.** rebellious, mutinous; **2.** *m/f* rebel; **rebeldía** *f* rebelliousness; **rebelión** *f* revolt, rebellion; **rebelón** restive.

reborde *m* ⊕ flange, rim; ledge.

rebosadero *m* overflow; **rebosante** overflowing (*a. fig.*; de with), brimful (*a. fig.*; de of); **rebosar** [1a] run over, overflow (*a. fig.*; de, en with).

rebotar [1a] *v/t. clavo etc.* clinch; *ataque* repel; F annoy, upset; *v/i.* bounce; rebound; (*bala*) ricochet; **rebote** *m* bounce; rebound; de ~ on the rebound.

rebozar [1f] muffle up; *cocina:* roll in flour (*or* batter etc.); ~**se** muffle up; **rebozo** *m* muffler; *S.Am.* shawl; *fig.* disguise; de ~ secretly.

rebullir [3h] stir; show signs of life.

rebusca *f* search; 🪶 gleaning; *fig.* leavings, remains; **rebuscado** recherché; studied, elaborate; **rebuscar** [1g] search carefully for.

rebuznar [1a] bray; **rebuzno** *m* bray(ing).

recabar [1a] manage to get.

recadero *m* messenger; errand-boy; **recado** *m* message; errand; (*regalo*) gift; (*compras*) daily shopping; (*seguridad*) safety, precaution.

recaer [2o] fall back, relapse (en into); 🩺 suffer a relapse; ~ en *heredero* pass to; ~ sobre devolve upon; **recaída** *f* 🩺 relapse (*a. fig.*).

recalar [1a] saturate.

recalcar [1g] (*apretar*) squeeze, press; cram, stuff (de with); *fig.* stress; make great play with.

recalcitrante recalcitrant; **recalcitrar** [1a] retreat, back down.

recalentar [1k] overheat.

recamado *m* embroidery; **recamar** [1a] embroider.

recapitular [1a] recapitulate, sum up.

recargado overloaded; *fig.* overelaborate; **recargar** [1h] reload; (*demasiado*) overload; recharge; (*demasiado*) overcharge; *fig.* increase; **recargo** *m* new burden; extra load; ✝ surcharge.

recatado cautious, circumspect; *mujer* shy, demure; **recatar** [1a] hide; ~**se** be cautious; refrain from taking a stand; **recato** *m* caution; shyness, demureness.

recaudación *f* collection; recovery; (*oficina*) tax office; **recaudador** *m*: ~ de contribuciones tax collector; **recaudar** [1a] *impuestos* collect; *deudas* recover; **recaudo** *m* collection; *fig.* care, protection.

recelar [1a] suspect, fear, distrust (*a.* ~ de, ~se); ~**se** *inf.* be afraid of *ger.*; **recelo** *m* suspicion, fear; **receloso** suspicious.

recepción *f* reception (*a. radio*); receipt; admission *a academia etc.*; (*cuarto*) drawing-room; reception (desk) *en hotel*; **receptáculo** *m* receptacle (*a.* ♀); holder; **receptador** *m* F fence, holder of stolen goods; **receptivo** receptive; **receptor** *m* receiver.

receta *f* *cocina:* recipe; 🩺 prescription; **recetar** [1a] 🩺 prescribe.

rechazamiento *m* rejection etc.; **rechazar** [1f] *ataque* repel, beat off; *oferta* reject, refuse, turn down; **rechazo** *m* rebound de *pelota*; recoil de *cañón*; *fig.* repulse.

rechifla *f* (*silbo*) whistle; hiss; (*silbos*) whistling etc.; **rechiflar** [1a] whistle (*v/t.* at), hiss, catcall.

rechinamiento *m* creak(ing) etc.; **rechinar** [1a] (*madera etc.*) creak; (*ludir dos cosas*) grate, grind; (*maquinaria*) clank; (*motor*) whirr, hum; **rechino** *m* creak(ing) etc.

recibidero receivable; **recibidor** *m*, **-a** *f* receiver, recipient; receptionist *en hotel*; **recibimiento** *m* (*cuarto*) hall; (*grande*) reception room; (*acto*) reception; **recibir** [3a] receive; (*acoger*) welcome, receive, greet; (*salir al encuentro de*) (go and) meet; *título* take, receive; ~**se** de qualify as; **recibo** *m* = recibimiento, recepción; ✝ receipt; (*cuenta*) bill; acusar ~ acknowledge receipt of).

reciclable recyclable; **reciclado, reciclaje** *m* recycling.

recién *adv.* newly; just; lately; ~ casado newly wed; ~ llegado **1.** newly arrived; **2.** *m,* a *f* newcomer *en lugar*; latecomer *en reunión etc.*; ~ nacido newborn; **reciente** recent; *pan etc.* new, fresh.

recinto *m* enclosure, compound; precincts; area; place.

recio 1. *adj.* (*fuerte*) strong, robust; (*grueso*) thick, bulky; (*duro*) hard;

(*áspero*) harsh, rough; *voz* loud; *tiempo* severe; **2.** *adv. hablar* loudly.

recipiente *m* (*p.*) recipient (*a. phys.*, 🜍); (*vaso*) vessel, container.

recíproca *f* 🜍 reciprocal; **reciprocar** [1g] reciprocate; **reciprocidad** *f* reciprocity; *usar* ~ reciprocate; **recíproco** reciprocal.

recitación *f* recitation; **recitado** *m* recitation; ♩ recitative; **recital** *m* recital; **recitar** [1a] recite; **recitativo** *adj. a. su. m* recitative.

reclamación *f* claim, demand; objection; protest, complaint; **reclamar** [1a] *v/t.* claim, lay claim to; *socorro etc.* beg; 🜍 reclaim; *v/i.* protest.

reclamo *m* orn. (*ave*) decoy; (*grito*) call; *typ.* catchword; *fig.* lure, inducement; (*anuncio*) advertisement; slogan; blurb *de libro*; *Am.* complaint.

reclinar(se) [1a] recline, lean back.

recluir [3g] shut away; 🜍 intern, imprison; **reclusión** *f* seclusion; ~ *perpetua* life imprisonment; **2.** *m, a* 🜍 *f* prisoner; **recluso 1.** 🜍 imprisoned; **2.** *m, a* 🜍 *f* prisoner.

recluta 1. *m* recruit; **2.** *f* = **reclutamiento** *m* recruitment; **reclutar** [1a] recruit; *ganado* round up.

recobrar [1a] recover, get back; retrieve; ~*se* 🜍 recover; (*volver en sí*) come to; **recobro** *m* recovery *etc.*

recodo *m* turn, bend, elbow.

recogedor *m* (*p.*) picker, harvester; gleaner; (*herramienta*) rake; scraper; **recoger** [2c] (*levantar*) pick up; *deportes: pelota freq.* field, stop; (*juntar*) collect, gather together; *cosecha* get in, harvest; ~*se* withdraw; (*acostarse*) go to bed, retire; **recogida** *f* withdrawal, retirement; ~ *de basuras* garbage collection; **recogimiento** *m* (*acto*) gathering; 🜍 harvesting.

recolección *f* 🜍 harvest, picking; collection *de rentas*; gathering *de información etc.*; compilation.

recomendable recommendable; (*aconsejable*) advisable; **recomendación** *f* recommendation; (*escrito*) reference, testimonial; **recomendar** [1k] recommend.

recomenzar [1f *a.* 1k] begin again.

recompensa *f* recompense; reward; compensation (*de pérdida* for); *en* ~ in return (*de* for); **recompensar** [1a] recompense (*acc.* for); compensate (*acc.* for).

reconcentrar [1a] concentrate, bring

together; *sentimiento* hide; ~*se* become absorbed in thought.

reconciliación *f* reconciliation; **reconciliar** [1b] reconcile.

reconfortar [1a] comfort; cheer.

reconocer [2d] recognize; know; *culpa, verdad etc. a.* admit, acknowledge; *hechos a.* face; inspect, examine (*a.* 🜍); *terreno* survey; ⚔ reconnoitre; spy out; **reconocible** recognizable; **reconocido** grateful; **reconocimiento** *m* recognition; admission, acknowledgement; inspection, examination.

reconstrucción *f* reconstruction *etc.*; **reconstruir** [3g] reconstruct; rebuild; *gobierno* reshuffle.

recontar [1m] recount; retell.

reconvertir [3i] reconvert.

recopilación *f* summary; compilation; 🜍 code; **recopilar** [1a] compile, collect; *leyes* codify.

récord ['rekor] *adj. a. su. m* record.

recordable memorable; **recordación** *f* remembrance; *de feliz* ~ of happy memory; **recordar** [1m] *v/t.* remember, recall, recollect; remind (*algo a alguien a p.* of a th.); ~*se* awaken; **recordativo** reminiscent; reminding; **recordatorio** *m* reminder.

recorrer [2a] *país etc.* cross, travel, tour; go through; *plaza etc.* cross; *terreno* (*buscando*) range, scour; *distancia* travel (*a.* ⊕), cover; **recorrido** *m* run, journey; (*ruta*) path, route; ✈ flight; distance travelled; run; round.

recortar [1a] *lo sobrante* cut away, trim; *figura, periódico* cut out; *pelo* trim; *paint.* outline; ~*se* stand out; **recorte** *m* cutting; trim; ~*s pl.* clippings; *álbum de* ~*s* scrapbook.

recostado reclining, recumbent; lying down; **recostar** [1m] lean; ~*se* lie back, lie down.

recoveco *m* turn, bend *de calle etc.*; ~*s pl.* ins and outs.

recreación *f* recreation; *escuela:* break, playtime; **recrear** [1a] recreate; amuse, entertain; ~*se* amuse o.s., take recreation.

recrecer [2d] *v/t.* increase; *v/i.* increase; (*ocurrir*) happen again; ~*se* recover one's good spirits.

recreo *m* recreation, relaxation; amusement; *escuela:* break.

recrudecer [2d] break out again.

recta *f* straight line; *carreras:* the

straight; ~ de *llegada* home straight; **rectangular = rectángulo 1.** rectangular, oblong; *triángulo etc.* right-angled; **2.** *m* rectangle, oblong. **rectificar** [1g] *mst* rectify (*a. fig.*); *trazado etc.* straighten; *cálculo* set right.

rectitud *f* straightness; accuracy; *fig.* rectitude, uprightness; **recto 1.** straight; *ángulo* right; *gr.* literal, proper; *fig.* upright, honest; *juicio* sound; **2.** *m* rectum.

recuento *m* recount; inventory; *hacer el* ~ *de* make a survey of.

recuerdo *m* memory, recollection; (*objeto*) souvenir, momento; ~s *pl.* (*saludo*) regards.

reculada *f* recoil; *fig.* retreat; **recular** [1a] recoil; *fig.* retreat, fall back; F back down.

recuperable recoverable, retrievable; recyclable; **recuperación** *f* recovery; **recuperar** [1a] recover, retrieve.

recurrente recurrent; **recurrir** [3a]: ~ *a algo* have recourse to, resort to, fall back on; **recurso** *m* recourse, resort.

recusar [1a] 🏛 reject; challenge.

red *f* net (*a. fig.*); (*mallas*) mesh(es) (*a. fig.*); 🕸 *etc.* network, system; *agua* 🝆 mains; *fig.* trap, snare; ~ *de alambre* wire netting.

redacción *f* (*acto*) writing, redaction; editing; wording; (*oficina*) newspaper office; (*ps.*) editorial staff; **redactar** [1a] write; draft, word; *periódico* edit; **redactor** *m*, **-a** *f* (*jefe*) editor.

redargüir [3g] turn an argument against its proposer; 🏛 impugn.

redención *f* redemption (*a.* ✝); **redentor 1.** redeeming; redemptive; **2.** *m*, **-a** *f* redeemer.

redil *m* sheep fold, pen.

redimible redeemable; **redimir** [3a] redeem; *cautivo* ransom.

rédito *m* interest, yield, return; **redituar** [1e] yield, produce.

redoblado stocky, thick-set; *paso* double-quick; **redoblante** *m* drum; **redoblar** [1a] *v/t.* redouble; (*replegar*) bend back, bend over; *clavo* clinch; *v/i.* ♪ play a roll on the drum; **redoble** *m* ♪ drumroll; roll, rumble *de trueno.*

redoma *f* flask, phial.

redonda: *a la* ~ round (about); *de la* ~ in the neighbourhood, of the area; **redondear** [1a] round off; round;

~**se** get to be well off; get clear of debts; **redondel** *m* bullring, arena; **redondo** round (*a. fig.*); *fig.* (*sin rodeos*) square, straightforward; *en* ~ around.

red(r)opelo *m* F row; *al* ~ the wrong way; against the grain.

reducción *f* reduction, cut; (*copia*) miniature version; 🎵 setting; **reducible** reducible; **reducido** reduced; limited; *número etc.* freq. small; *precio* low; *espacio* limited, confined, narrow; **reducir** [3f] reduce (*a. fig.*; *a, hasta* to); diminish, lessen, cut; *fortaleza* reduce.

reedificar [1g] rebuild.

reeditar [1a] republish, reprint.

reelegir [3c *a.* 3l] re-elect.

reembolsar [1a] *p.* reimburse, repay; ~**se** *dinero* recover; **reembolso** *m* reimbursement; repayment, refund.

reemplazar [1f] replace (*con* with, by), change (*con* for); **reemplazo** *m* (*acto, p.*) replacement.

refacción *f* refreshment; *S.Am.* repair(s); F extra, bonus.

referencia *f* reference (*a.* ✝, *recomendación sobre p.*); account, report; **referente:** ~ *a* relating to; **referir** [3i] recount, report; *cuento* tell; ~ *que* say that; ~**se** *a* refer to; apply to.

refinado refined; **refinadura** *f* refining; **refinamiento** *m* fig. refinement; nicety; neatness; **refinar** [1a] refine; polish; **refinería** *f* refinery; **refino** refined; extra fine.

reflector *m* reflector; ⚡ *etc.* searchlight; *mot.* ~ *posterior* rear reflector; **reflejar** [1a] reflect; mirror; reveal; ~**se** be reflected; **reflejo 1.** *luz* reflected; *acto* reflex; *verbo* reflexive; **2.** *m* reflection; gleam, glint; *physiol.* reflex (action); **reflexión** *f* reflection, thought; **reflexionar** [1a] *v/t.* reflect on, think about; *v/i.* reflect (*en, sobre* on), muse; think, pause *antes de obrar;* **reflexivo** thoughtful, reflective; *gr.* reflexive.

refluir [3g] flow back; **reflujo** *m* ebb (tide); *fig.* retreat.

reforma *f* reform; reformation; (*mejora*) improvement; ⚤ Reformation; ~s *pl.* △ alterations, repairs; ~ *agraria* land reform; **reformación** *f* reform(ation); **reformado** reformed; **reformador** *m*, **-a** *f* reformer; **reformar** [1a] reform; (*mejorar*) improve; revise, reorganize; *abusos* put

right; **reformatorio** *m* reformatory;
reformista *m/f* reformer.

reforzador *m* ⚡ booster; *phot.* intensifier; **reforzar** [1f *a.* 1m] reinforce (*a.* ✗), strengthen; boost (*a.* ✗); *fig.* buttress, bolster up.

refracción *f* refraction; **refractar** [1a] refract; **refractario** fireproof; *fig.* refractory, recalcitrant.

refrán *m* proverb, saying.

refrenar [1a] *caballo* rein back, rein in; *fig.* curb, restrain.

refrendar [1a] endorse, countersign; authenticate.

refrescar [1g] *v/t.* refresh; cool; *acción* renew; *memoria* refresh, jog; *v/i.*, **~se** (*tiempo*) cool down, get cooler; (*salir*) take the air; (*beber*) take a drink; **refresco** *m* soft drink; **~s** *pl.* refreshments.

refriega *f* scuffle, affray.

refrigeración *f* refrigeration; cooling *de motor*, **~** *por agua* watercooling; **refrigerador** *m* refrigerator; **refrigerante** refrigerating, cooling; 🜄, refrigerant (*a. su. m*); **refrigerar** [1a] refrigerate; cool; refresh; **refrigerio** *m* refreshment; cooling drink.

refuerzo *m* strengthening; brace; **~s** *pl.* reinforcements.

refugiado *m*, **a** *f* refugee; **refugiarse** [1b] take refuge; shelter; go into hiding; **refugio** *m* refuge, shelter (*a. fig.*); **~** *antiaéreo* air-raid shelter; **~** *antiatómico* fallout shelter.

refulgente brilliant, refulgent.

refundir [3a] ⊕ recast; *fig.* revise; *texto* remodel, adapt, rewrite.

refunfuñar [1a] grunt, growl; (*murmurar*) grumble; **refunfuño** *m* grunt, growl; grumble.

refutación *f* refutation; **refutar** [1a] refute.

regadera *f* irrigation ditch; sprinkler *para calle etc.*; **regadío 1.** irrigable; *tierra* **~a**, *tierra de* **~** = **2.** *m* irrigated land; **regadura** *f* watering, irrigation.

regala *f* gunwale.

regalar [1a] *regalo* give; (*dar gratis*) make a present of, give away; (*acariciar*) caress, fondle; (*halagar*) make a fuss of; (*convidar*) treat (*con* to), regale (*con* on, with).

regalía *f* *fig.* perquisite, privilege; bonus; **~s** *pl.* royal prerogatives.

regalo *m* gift, present; treat; pleasure; comfort, luxury; *de* **~** *entrada* complimentary.

regañadientes: *a* **~** reluctantly.

regañar [1a] *v/t.* F scold; nag (at); *v/i.* (*perro*) snarl; growl; (*dos ps.*) quarrel; **regaño** *m* snarl, growl; (*gesto*) scowl; *fig.* grouse; F scolding; **regañón** *p.* grumbling, irritable; *mujer* **~a** shrew, virago.

regar [1h *a.* 1k] *planta* water; *tierra* water, irrigate; *calle* hose; *geog.* (*río*) water; spray *con insecticida etc.*; (*esparcir*) sprinkle, scatter.

regate *m* swerve, dodge (*a.* F); **regatear¹** [1a] *v/t.* haggle over; bargain away; (*por menor*) sell retail; *v/i.* haggle, bargain.

regatear² [1a] ⛵ race.

regazo *m* lap (*a. fig.*).

regentar [1a] manage, direct; preside over; *cátedra* occupy, hold; *b.s.* domineer, boss F; **regente 1.** *príncipe* regent; *director etc.* managing; *fig.* ruling; **2.** *m/f* (*real*) regent; manager *de fábrica, finca*.

régimen *m* pol. régime; 🜨 diet; (*reglas*) rules, regulations; system, regimen; *gr.* government; **~** *alimenticio* diet; **~** *lácteo* milk diet; **regimiento** *m* administration *etc.*; ✗ regiment.

regio royal, regal; *apariencia* regal, kingly; *fig.* royal.

región *f* region; part, area; *anat.* tract, region; **regional** regional.

regir [3c *a.* 3l] *v/t.* *país etc.* rule, govern (*a. gr.*); *sociedad etc.* manage, control; (*conducir*) guide; **~se** *por* be ruled by, go by.

registrador *m* recorder, registrar; inspector; register; **registrar** [1a] *hecho* register, record; *partida etc.* enter; file *en archivo*; *voz etc.* record; **registro** *m* (*acto*) registration; (*libro, archivo*) register, record; (*archivos*) registry, record office; (*partida*) entry; recording *en disco etc.*; ♪ (*extensión, altura*) register; ♪ stop *de órgano*; ♪ pedal *de piano*; **~** *domiciliario* search of a house; **~** *parroquial* parish register.

regla *f* rule (*a.* ♣, *deportes, eccl.*); regulation; (*base*) law, principle; ruler *para trazar líneas*; order, discipline; **~s** *pl.* 🜨 period; **~** *de cálculo* slide rule; **~** *T* T-square; **~** *de tres* rule of three; *en* **~** in order.

reglamentar [1a] regulate, provide regulations for; **reglamento** *m* regulation, rule; (*código*) rules and regulations; standing order *de* asamblea; **bylaw** *de sociedad, municipio.*

reglar [1a] *línea* rule; *fig.* regulate; **~se por** conform to, be guided by.

regocijado merry; exultant; *carácter* jolly, cheerful; **regocijar** [1a] gladden, cheer (up); **~se** rejoice (*de, por* at); exult (*por* at, in); **regocijo** *m* joy, rejoicing.

regordete F chubby, dumpy.

regosto *m* craving (*de* for).

regresar [1a] go back, come back, return.

regreso *m* return.

reguera *f* irrigation ditch; ⚓ moorings; **reguero** *m* ♪ irrigation ditch; trickle *de sangre etc.*

regulable adjustable; **regulación** *f* regulation; adjustment; control; **regulador** *m* ⊕ regulator, throttle, governor; control; *radio:* (control) knob; *radio:* ~ **de volumen** volume control; **regular 1.** regular (*a.* ⚒, *eccl.*); (*mediano*) fair, middling, medium; F *salud, progreso etc.* fair, so-so; (*conveniente*) suitable; normal, usual; **por lo~** as a rule; **2.** *m eccl.* regular; **3.** [1a] regulate; *esp.* ⊕ adjust; *precios etc.* control; **regularidad** *f* regularity; **regularizar** [1f] regularize; standardize.

rehabilitación *f* rehabilitation; **rehabilitar** [1a] rehabilitate; reinstate *en oficio;* *casa* restore, renovate; ⊕ overhaul.

rehacer [2s] redo, do again; *objeto* remake; (*reparar*) mend, repair; **~se** ⚔ recover; ⚔ rally.

rehén *m* hostage.

rehuir [3g] (*apartar*) remove; (*evitar*) avoid, decline.

rehusar [1a] refuse (*inf.* to *inf.*), decline, turn down.

reina *f* queen (*a. ajedrez, abeja*); ~ **madre** queen mother; **reinado** *m* reign; **reinante** reigning; prevailing; **reinar** [1a] reign; rule.

reincidir [3a] relapse (*en* into).

reino *m* kingdom.

reinstalar [1a] reinstall; *p.* reinstate.

reintegración *f* ⚓ refund, reimbursement; restitution *etc.*; **reintegrar** [1a] ⚓ refund, pay back; restore; **~se** *a* return to; **reintegro** *m* restoration, restitution.

reinvertir [3i] reinvest; plough back.

reír(se) [3m] laugh (*de* at, over); F

(*vestido*) tear; ~ **de** laugh at, make fun of.

reja *f* grating, grid(iron); grille; bar(s) *de ventana;* ~ (**del** *arado*) ploughshare; **rejado** *m* grille, grating; **rejilla** *f* grating; lattice; screen; wickerwork *de silla etc.;* 🚂 luggage rack; *radio:* grid, grille; small stove; **rejo** *m* spike, sharp point.

rejuvenecer [2d] *v/t.* rejuvenate; *v/i.*, **~se** be rejuvenated.

relación *f* (*conexión*) relation(ship) (*con* to, with); (*narración*) account, statement, report; list, recital *de dificultades etc.;* (*informe oficial*) record, return; list; ⚖ ratio; proportion; **~es** *pl.* relation(ship); (*amorosas*) courting, courtship; **~es** *pl.* **comerciales** trade relations; **~es** *pl.* **personales** personnel management; **~es** *pl.* **públicas** public relations; **relacionado** related; ~ **con** that has to do with; bound up with; **relacionar** [1a] relate (*con* to); connect (*con* with); **~se** be related.

relajación *f* relaxation *etc.*; laxity *de moralidad;* ♪ hernia; **relajado** *vida* dissolute; **relajar** [1a] relax, slacken, loosen; *moralidad* weaken; (*distraer*) relax, amuse; **~se** relax.

relámpago 1. *m* lightning, flash (*a. fig.*); **pasar como un** ~ go by like lightning; **2.** *attr.* lightning; **relampaguear** lightning; flashing; **relampaguear** [1a] lighten; flash (*a. fig.*); **relampagueo** *m* lightning; flashing.

relanzar [1f] repel, repulse.

relatar [1a] relate, report; tell.

relatividad *f* relativity; **relativo 1.** relative; ~ *a* regarding, relating to; **2.** *m gr.* relative.

relato *m* story, tale; (*informe*) report; **relator** *m* narrator, teller.

relé *m* ⚡ relay; ~ **de televisión** television relay system.

relegar [1h] relegate; (*desterrar*) exile; banish.

relevación *f* relief (*a.* ⚒); replacement *etc.*; **relevante** outstanding; **relevar** [1a] *v/t.* ⊕ emboss, carve in relief; relieve (*de cargo etc.* of; *a.* ⚒); absolve, exonerate (*de culpa* from); *empleado* replace; *v/i.* stand up; **relevo** *m* relief (*a.* ⚒); *deportes:* **~s** *pl.* relay (race).

relicario *m* shrine; (*caja*) reliquary.

relieve *m* relief; *fig.* prominence; **~s**

pl. leftovers; *poner de* ~ set off (*contra* against); *fig.* emphasize.

religión *f* religion; religious sense, piety; *entrar en* ~ take vows; **religiosa** *f* nun; **religioso 1.** religious (*a. fig.*); **2.** *m* monk.

relinchar [1a] neigh, whinny; **relincho** *m* neigh(ing), whinny.

reliquia *f* relic; ~*s pl.* ⚕ aftereffects; *fig.* relics, remains.

rellenar [1a] refill, replenish; (*henchir*) stuff, cram; *bocado* stuff; *pollo* stuff; ~*se* F stuff o.s.; **relleno 1.** full, packed; *cocina:* stuffed; **2.** *m* filling, stuffing; padding (*a. fig.*), wadding; *cocina:* stuffing.

reloj [rei'lou] *m* (*grande*) clock; (*portátil*) watch; ⊕ clock, meter; ~ *de arena* hourglass; ~ *automático* timer; ~ *de bolsillo* pocket watch; ~ *de caja* grandfather's clock; ~ *de carillón* chime clock; ~ *de cuarzo* quartz watch; ~ *de cuclillo* cuckoo clock; ~ *despertador* alarm clock; ~ *de estacionamiento* parking meter; ~ *de pulsera* wrist watch; ~ *de sol* sundial; *como un* ~ like clockwork; *contra el* ~ against the clock; **relojería** *f* (*arte*) watchmaking; (*tienda*) watchmaker's shop; **relojero** *m* watchmaker.

reluciente shining, brilliant; glittering, gleaming, sparkling; **relucir** [3f] shine (*a. fig.*); glitter, gleam.

relumbrar [1a] shine; sparkle; glare; **relumbrón** *m* flash; glare.

remachar [1a] ⊕ *clavo* clinch; *metales* rivet; *fig.* drive home; **remache** *m* rivet; (*acto*) riveting *etc.*

remada *f* stroke; **remador** *m* oarsman.

remanente *m phys.* remanent; ♱ *etc.* surplus.

remar [1a] row; *fig.* toil.

rematado hopeless, out-and-out; *loco* raving; *tonto* utter; **rematante** *m* highest bidder; **rematar** [1a] *v/t. p., trabajo* finish off; ⚔ *etc.* top, crown; *subasta:* knock down (*a* to, *en* for); *v/i.* end (⚔ en in); *deportes:* shoot, score; ~*se* be ruined; **remate** *m* (*fin*) end; (*toque*) finishing touch; ⚔ *etc.* top, crest; (*postura*) highest bid; (*adjudicación*) sale.

remedar [1a] imitate, copy; (*para burlarse*) ape, mimic.

remediar [1b] *perjuicio etc.* remedy; *daño etc.* repair; save, help; prevent (*que* from *ger.*); **remedio** *m* remedy; help; ⚖ recourse.

remedo *m* imitation; *b.s.* poor imitation, travesty.

remendar [1k] mend, repair, patch; *fig.* correct; **remendón** *m* cobbler.

remero *m* oarsman.

remesa *f* remittance; shipment, consignment; **remesar** [1a] *dinero* remit, send; *mercancías* send, ship.

remiendo *m* (*acto*) mending *etc.*; (*tela etc.*) mend, patch; spot *en piel*; *fig.* correction; *a* ~*s* piecemeal.

remilgado (*gazmoño*) prudish, prim; (*afectado*) affected, overnice; **remilgarse** [1h] be fussy *etc.*; **remilgo** *m* prudery; affectation.

reminiscencia *f* reminiscence.

remisión *f* (*envío*) sending; forgiveness *de pecado etc.*; **remiso** slack, remiss; *movimiento* sluggish; **remitente** 1. ⚕ remittent; **2.** *m/f* sender; **remitir** [3a] *v/t.* send, remit; *pena etc.* forgive, pardon; *lector* refer (*a* to); *sesión* adjourn; *v/i.* slacken, let up; *remite* (*en sobre*) sender; ~*se a* refer to.

remo *m* oar; (*deporte*) rowing; *fig. anat.* arm, leg; *fig.* toil.

remodelación *f* remodeling.

remojar [1a] soak, steep; dip; F celebrate with a drink; **remojo** *m* soaking *etc.*; **remojón** *m* soaking *etc.*

remolacha *f* beet(root); ~ *azucarera* sugar beet.

remolcador *m* ⚓ tug; **remolcar** [1g] (take in) tow; tug.

remoler [2h] grind up small.

remolino *m* (*agua*) swirl, eddy; whirlpool; (*aire*) whirl, whirlwind; (*polvo*) whirl, cloud; (*pelo*) tuft; (*gente*) throng, crush.

remolón 1. slack, lazy; **2.** *m*, **-a** *f* shirker, slacker.

remolque *m* towing; (*cable*) towrope; (*cosa remolcada*) tow, ship *etc.* on tow; *mot.* trailer *para turismo*; *a* ~ in tow; *llevar a* ~ tow.

remonta *f* ✕ remount; cavalry horses; mending, repair; **remontar** [1a] ✕ remount; *zapatos etc.* mend, repair; *río* go up; *fig.* raise; ~*se* rise, tower; ✘ soar (*a. fig.*); *fig.* get excited; ~ *a* go (*or date*) back to.

rémora *f* fig. hindrance; loss of time.

remordimiento *m* remorse, regret; pang of conscience.

remoto remote (*a. fig.*); *control m* ~ remote control.

remover [2h] *p., cosa* remove, move; (*agitar*) stir, shake up; *tierra* turn over, dig up; *sentimientos* disturb,. upset; **removimiento** *m* removal.

rempujar [1a] F push, shove, jostle; **rempujón** *m* F push, shove.

remuneración *f* remuneration; **remunerador** remunerative; rewarding; **remunerar** [1a] remunerate; reward.

renacer [2d] be reborn; ♀ appear again; ✵ recover; *fig.* revive; ♀ revive; **renacimiento** *m* rebirth; revival; ♀ Renaissance.

rencor *m* ill-feeling, spite(fulness), rancor; *guardar ~* have a grudge, bear malice (*a* against); **rencoroso** spiteful; vicious, malicious.

rendición *f* surrender; ✝ yield, profits; **rendido** obsequious, submissive; *admirador* humble.

rendija *f* crack, crevice, chink, aperture; *fig.* rift, split.

rendimiento *m* ⊕ (*producto*) output; ⊕ efficiency, performance; ✝ yield; *fig.* obsequiousness; (*cansancio*) exhaustion; **rendir** [3l] **1.** *v/t.* (*conquistar*) *país* conquer, subdue; defeat; *fortaleza* take; (*entregar*) surrender; (*sujetar*) overcome; (*devolver*) return, give back; ✝ *producto* produce; *ganancia etc.* yield; *interés, fruto* bear; *gracias* give, render; *homenaje* pay, do; ✕ *guardia* hand over; **2.** *v/i.*: *~ bien* yield well; **3.** *~se* ✕ surrender; yield, give up.

renegado 1. renegade; F gruff, bad-tempered; **2.** *m,* **a** *f* renegade, turncoat; **renegar** [1h *a.* 1k] *v/t.* deny vigorously; detest; *v/i.* turn renegade.

renglón *m* line; *leer entre ~es* read between the lines.

reno *m* reindeer.

renombrado renowned; **renombre** *m* renown, fame.

renovable renewable; **renovación** *f* renewal; renovation; *paint.* redecoration; *etc.;* **renovar** [1m] renew; renovate; *cuarto* redecorate; *aviso etc.* repeat; *moda* reintroduce.

renquear [1a] limp.

renta *f* (*ingresos*) income; interest, return; (*acciones*) stock; *~ nacional* national income; *~s pl. públicas* revenue; *~ vitalicia* annuity; **rentar** [1a] yield, produce; **rentero** *m* tenant farmer; **rentista** *m/f* (*accionista*) stock-holder; **rentístico** financial.

renuencia *f* reluctance.

renuevo *m* ♀ shoot, sprout; (*acto*) renewal.

renuncia *f* renunciation, surrender; resignation *etc.;* **renunciar** [1b] *v/t.* (*a.* *v/i. ~ a*) *derecho etc.* renounce (*en* in favor of), surrender, relinquish; *demanda* drop, waive.

reñidero *m*: *~ (de gallos)* cockpit.

reñido *p.* on bad terms (*con* with); *batalla* bitter; **reñir** [3h *a.* 3l] *v/t.* scold; *v/i.* (*disputar*) quarrel; (*pelear*) fight, come to blows.

reo *m/f* culprit, offender, criminal; ✠ defendant, accused.

reojo: *mirar de ~* look askance (at); F look scornfully at.

reóstato *m* rheostat.

repanchigarse, repantigarse [1h] loll (about), lounge, sprawl.

reparación *f* ⊕ repair(ing), mending; *fig.* reparation; *~es pl.* repairs.

reparar [1a] *v/t.* ⊕ repair, mend; (*satisfacer*) make good, make amends for; *fortunas* retrieve; *fuerzas* restore; *error* correct; *golpe* parry; = *v/i.:* *~ en* notice; pay attention to; *~se* check o.s.

reparo *m* ⊕ *etc.* repairs; △ restoration; ✵ restorative; criticism; doubt, objection; protection.

repartimiento *m* distribution; **repartir** [3a] distribute, divide, share (out); parcel out; *tareas etc.* allot; *territorio* partition; ♣ deliver; *naipes:* deal; *thea. papeles* cast; **reparto** *m* distribution; ♣ delivery; *thea.* cast.

repasar [1a] *lugar* pass by again; *calle* go along again; *fig.* reexamine, review; *texto, lección* read (*or* go) over; *ropa* mend; *mecanismo etc.* check, overhaul; **repaso** *m* review, revision *etc.;* *sew.* mending; ⊕ check-up, overhaul; *~ general* general overhaul; *curso de ~* refresher course.

repatriado 1. repatriated; **2.** *m,* **a** *f* repatriate; **repatriar** [1b] repatriate; *~se* return home.

repelente repulsive, repellent; **repeler** [2a] repel, repulse; reject.

repente *m* start, sudden movement; *de ~* suddenly, all at once; **repentino** sudden; swift.

repercutir(se) [3a] (*cuerpo*) rebound; (*sonido*) reverberate, reecho; *fig.* *~ en* have repercussions on.

repetición *f* repetition; recurrence;

thea. encore; **repetir** [3l] *v/t.* repeat; do *etc.* again; *sonido* echo; *lo grabado* play back; *lección etc.* recite, rehearse; *v/i.* repeat; **~se** (*p.*) repeat o.s.; (*pintor etc.*) copy o.s.

repicar [1g] *campana* ring, peal; *carne* chop up small; **~se** boast.

repique *m* peal(ing), chime; F tiff, squabble; **repiquete** *m* merry (or lively) peal; ✕ clash; **repiquetear** [1a] *campana* ring merrily; **~se** F squabble, wrangle; **repiqueteo** *m* merry pealing; rapping, tapping; clatter *de máquina*.

repisa *f* ledge, shelf; bracket; **~** *de chimenea* mantelpiece; **~** *de ventana* windowsill.

replegable folding; ✈ retractable; **replegar** [1h *a.* 1k] fold over; refold; ✈ retract; **~se** ✕ fall back (*sobre on*).

repleto replete, cram-full; (*obese*).

réplica *f* answer, argument; retort, rejoinder; **replicar** [1g] retort, rejoin; *b.s.* answer back.

repliegue *m* fold, crease; convolution; ✕ retirement.

repollo *m* cabbage; **~** *morado Am.* red cabbage; **repolludo** round-headed; *fig.* tubby.

reponer [2r] replace, put back; restore; *thea.* revive; (*contestar*) reply; **~se** ✞ *etc.* recover, pick up; **~** *de* recover from, get over.

reportaje *m* report, article; **reportar** [1a] carry; *fig.* restrain; **~se** control o.s.; **reporte** *m* news item; **repórter** *m*, **reportero** *m* reporter.

reposacabezas *m* head rest.

reposado quiet, restful, solemn; **reposar** [1a] rest, repose; sleep; (*yacer*) lie; **~se** (*líquido*) settle.

reposición *f* replacement; *thea.* revival; ✞ *etc.* recovery.

repositorio *m* repository.

reposo *m* rest (*a.* ✞), repose.

reprender [2a] reprimand, take to task (*algo a alguien* s.o. for s.t.); **reprensible** reprehensible; **reprensión** *f* reprimand, rebuke.

represa *f* (*acto*) recapture; (*parada*) check, stoppage; dam.

represalia *f* reprisal; *tomar* **~s** take reprisals, retaliate.

represar [1a] (*tomar*) recapture; (*parar*) halt, check; *agua* dam.

representación *f* representation; *thea.* production; performance; acting; **representante** *m/f* representative (*a.* ✞); *thea.* performer;

representar [1a] *mst* represent; stand for; (*informar*) state, declare; (*ser la imagen de*) show, express; *edad* look; *thea.* perform, play; act; **~se** *algo* imagine, picture (to o.s.); **representativo** representative.

represión *f* repression; suppression; **represivo** repressive.

reprimenda *f* reprimand.

reprimir [3a] repress, curb; *levantamiento* suppress.

reprobar [1m] condemn, reprove; *univ. etc.* fail; **réprobo** *adj. a. su. m,* **a** *f* reprobate; *eccl.* damned.

reprochar [1a] reproach (*algo a alguien* s.o. with *or* for a th.); censure, condemn; **reproche** *m* reproach, reproof (*a* for).

reproducción *f* reproduction; **reproducir(se)** [3o] reproduce.

reptil *m* reptile.

república *f* republic; **republicanismo** *m* republicanism; **republicano** *adj. a. su. m,* **a** *f* republican.

repudiación *f* repudiation; **repudiar** [1b] repudiate; *herencia etc.* renounce; disavow, disown.

repudrirse [3a] F eat one's heart out, pine away.

repuesto *m* store, stock, supply; (*sustituto*) replacement; ⊕ refill; ⊕ (*pieza*) spare (part), extra; ⊕ *de* **~** spare, extra.

repugnancia *f* aversion (*hacia, por* from, to), loathing (*hacia, por* for); **repugnante** disgusting, revolting; **repugnar** [1a] disgust, revolt; (*estar en pugna con*) conflict with; contradict; do reluctantly.

repulir [3a] repolish; refurbish; **~se** spruce o.s. up.

repulsa *f* rejection, refusal; rebuff; **repulsar** [1a] reject, refuse; ✕ repulse, check; **repulsión** *f* = *repulsa*; (*antipatía*) repulsion (*a. phys.*); **repulsivo** repulsive.

reputación *f* reputation; name; standing; esteem; **reputar** [1a] repute, esteem.

requebrar [1k] say nice things to, try to flirt with; *fig.* flatter.

requemado *piel* tanned; parched; overdone; **requemar** [1a] ✿ *etc.* parch, scorch; *comida* overdo; burn; *lengua* burn, sting; *sangre etc.* inflame; **~se** (*piel*) get tanned; ✿ *etc.* get parched, dry up.

requerir [3i] (*necesitar*) require (*a* of),

need; (*llamar*) summon; (*enviar por*) send for; notify; investigate; ~ de *amores* a court.

requesón *m* curd; cream cheese.

requiebro *m* flirtatious remark.

requisar [1a] requisition; **requisito** *m* requisite; requirement; ~ *previo* prerequisite; *llenar los* ~s fulfil the requirements.

res *f* beast, animal; (*esp. como número*) head of cattle.

resabido would-be expert, pretentious; **resabio** *m* nasty taste; *fig.* bad habit; *tener* ~ *de* smack of.

resaca *f* ♣ undertow, undercurrent; F hangover.

resalado witty, lively, vivacious.

resaltar [1a] jut (out); *fig.* stand out; **resalte** *m*, **resalto** *m* projection.

resarcir [3b] indemnify (*de* for), repay; ~se *de* make up for, retrieve.

resbaladero *m* slippery place, slide; **resbaladizo** slippery; **resbalar** [1a] slide; skid; *fig.* slip up; **resbalón** *m* slip (*a. fig.*); slide; skid; **resbaloso** slippery.

rescatar [1a] *p.* ransom; *cosa empeñada etc.* redeem; (*salvar*) rescue; *terrenos* reclaim; retail; **rescate** *m* ransom; rescue; ~ *de terrenos* land reclamation.

rescoldo *m* embers; *fig.* scruple, lingering doubt.

resecar [1g] dry thoroughly; parch, scorch; **reseco** parched.

reseda *f* mignonette.

resentimiento *m* resentment; **resentirse** [3i]: ~ *de*, ~ *por* resent; be offended at; *defecto* suffer from; *consecuencias* feel the effects of.

reseña *f lit.*, ✕ review; *paint.* sketch; **reseñador** *m* reviewer, critic; **reseñar** [1a] review.

reserva *f* reserve (*a.* ✝, ✕); (*acto etc.*) reservation; discretion, reticence; privacy; ~ *de Indios* Indian reservation; **reservación** *f* reservation; **reservado** *p.* reserved, reticent; discreet; *lugar* private; *asiento* reserved; **reservar** [1a] reserve; set aside, keep; (*encubrir*) conceal; ~se save o.s. (*para* for); (*desconfiar*) beware.

resfriado *m* cold; chill; **resfriar** [1c] *v/t.* cool (*a. fig.*), chill; *v/i.* turn cold; ~se ✿ catch cold; *fig.* cool off.

resguardar [1a] protect, shield (*de* from); ~se shelter; safeguard o.s.; **resguardo** *m* protection; safeguard;

shelter; guard; (*documento*) certificate; (*papeleta*) slip, check.

residencia *f* residence; *univ.* hall of residence, hostel; ~ *de ancianos* home for the aged, nursing home; **residencial** residential; **residente** *adj. a. su. m/f* resident; **residir** [3a] reside; live; *fig.* lie; *fig.* ~ *en* consist in, reside in; rest with; **residual** residual, residuary; **residuo** *m* residue; ♪ remainder; ♪, ♫ residuum; ~s *pl.* refuse, remains; ~s *radiactivos* radioactive waste.

resignación *f* resignation; **resignado** resigned; **resignar** [1a] resign; renounce; *mando etc.* hand over (*en* to); ~se resign o.s. (*a* to).

resina *f* resin; **resinoso** resinous.

resistencia *f* resistance (*a.* ✕, *phys.*, ⚡); strength; endurance, stamina, staying power; opposition; (*acto*) stand; ✕ ~ *al avance* drag; ~ *pasiva* passive resistance; **resistente** resistant; tough; *tela etc.* hard-wearing; ♦ hardy; ~ *al rayado* scratch-resistant; **resistir** [3a] *v/t.* stand, bear; *tentación* resist; *v/i.* resist; (*durar*) last; *esp.* ✕ hold out; fight back; ~ *a* resist, withstand; make a stand against; ~se resist, struggle.

resollar [1m] puff (and blow); snort; wheeze.

resolución *f* resolution (*a. parl.*); (*acto*) solving; decision; *fig.* resolution, boldness; *en* ~ in short, to sum up; **resoluto** = *resuelto*; **resolver** [2h; *p.p. resuelto*] *problema* solve, do; think out, puzzle out; *cuestión* settle; *cuerpo, materia* resolve (*en* into); ~se resolve itself, work out.

resonancia *f* resonance; echo; **resonante** resonant; resounding, ringing, echoing; **resonar** [1m] resound, ring, echo (*de* with).

resoplar [1a] puff, blow, snort; **resoplido** *m* puff, snort.

resopón *m* nightcap.

resorte *m* ⊕ spring; elasticity, springiness; *fig.* expedient; ~ *espiral* coil spring; F *tocar* ~s pull wires.

respaldar [1a] endorse; *fig.* support, back; ~se lean back; sprawl; **respaldo** *m* back *de silla, hoja*; endorsement *en papel*; *fig.* support, backing.

respectar [1a] concern; **respectivo** respective; **respecto** *m* respect, relation; (*con*) ~ *de* with regard to; in relation to; *a ese* ~ on that score; *al* ~ in the matter; *bajo ese* ~ in that respect; **respetabilidad** f respectability; **respetable** respectable; worthy; **respetar** [1a] respect; **respeto** m respect, regard, consideration; ~s pl. respects.

respingado nariz snub; **respingar** [1h] shy, start; fig. kick; **respingo** m shy, start; fig. gesture of disgust.

respiración f breathing; **respiradero** m ⊕ vent, air valve; fig. respite, breathing space; **respirar** [1a] breathe; gas etc. breathe in; breathe again después de mal momento; (descansar) get one's breath; sin ~ without a break; **respiratorio** respiratory; breathing attr.; **respiro** m breathing; (descanso) breathing space; lull, respite.

resplandecer [2d] shine (a. fig.); glitter, glow, blaze; **resplandeciente** shining etc.; **resplandor** m brilliance, radiance; glitter, glow.

responder [2a] v/t. answer; injuria etc. answer with; v/i. answer, reply; esp. fig. respond; (ser respondón) answer back; ~ de, ~ por answer for, be responsible for; **respondón** F cheeky, saucy, pert.

responsabilidad f responsibility etc.; de ~ limitada limited liability attr.; bajo mi ~ on my responsibility; **responsable** responsible (de for); liable (de for).

respuesta f answer, reply; response.

resquebra(ja)dura f crack, split; **resquebrajar(se)** [1a] crack, split; **resquebrar** [1k] begin to crack.

resquicio m chink, crack; fig. chance, opening.

resta f ⩑ subtraction; (residuo) remainder.

restablecer [2d] reestablish; restore; revive; ~se recover.

restante 1. remaining; los ~s the rest; 2. m rest, remainder.

restañar [1a] stanch.

restar [1a] v/t. ⩑ subtract, take away; deduct; pelota return; autoridad, valor etc. reduce; v/i. remain.

restauración f restoration; **restaurán** [resto'ran] m, **restaurante** m restaurant; café; **restaurar** [1a] restore; repair; recover.

restitución f return, restitution; **restituir** [3g] restore, return.

resto m rest; remainder (a. ⩑); deportes: (p.) receiver; (acto) return; ~s pl. remains; cocina: leftovers.

restorán m S.Am. restaurant.

restregar [1h a. 1k] scrub, rub.

restricción f restriction; limitation; restraint; ~ mental mental reservation; **restrictivo** restrictive; **restringir** [3c] restrict.

resucitar [1a] v/t. resuscitate; fig. resurrect, revive; v/i. resuscitate; return to life; revive.

resuello m (respiración) breathing; (un ~) breath; (ruidoso, penoso) puff.

resuelto 1. p.p. of resolver; 2. resolute, determined; steadfast; prompt.

resulta: de ~s de as a result of; **resultado** m result, outcome; issue; sequel; effect; dar ~ produce results; **resultar** [1a] be, prove (to be), turn out (to be); ~ de result from, stem from; be evident from.

resumen m summary, résumé; en ~ to sum up, in short; **resumir** [3a] sum up; ~se be included.

retablo m reredos, altar-piece.

retaguardia f rearguard; a ~ in the rear.

retal m remnant, oddment.

retama f broom.

retar [1a] challenge; F tick off.

retardar [1a] slow down, slow up, retard; reloj put back; **retardo** m slowing-up; delay; time lag.

retazo m remnant; fig. bit, fragment; ~s pl. odds and ends.

retención f retention (a. ⚕); ⊢ deduction; **retener** [2l] retain, keep (back) hold (back); (deducir) withhold, deduct; ⚖ detain.

retintín m tinkle, tinkling; jingle; ring(ing); F nastily sarcastic tone; **retiñir** [3h] tinkle; jingle; ring.

retirada f ⚔ withdrawal (a. ✝), retreat (a. toque); recall de embajador; (sitio) retreat, place of refuge; batirse en ~ retreat; **retirado** oficial retired; lugar secluded, remote; **retirar** [1a] withdraw (a. ⚔, ✝; de from); take away, remove (a from); ⊕ pieza take out, take off; tapa take off; mano, cubierta draw back; embajador recall; ~se ⚔ retreat, withdraw; **retiro** m ⚔, ✝ withdrawal; (sueldo) pension, retirement pay; (jubilación) retirement.

reto m challenge; (amenaza) threat; S.Am. insult.

retocar [1g] retouch, touch up.

retoñar [1a] ♀ sprout; fig. reappear, recur; **retoño** m ♀ shoot.

retoque m retouching, touching-up; (última mano) finishing touch.

retorcer [2b a. 2h] twist; *manos* wring; *argumento* turn; *sentido* twist; **~se** twist, twine; writhe.

retórica f rhetoric; **~s** pl. quibbles.

retornar [1a] v/t. return, give back; turn back; v/i. return; *retorno* m return; (*pago*) reward, payment.

retozar [1f] frolic, frisk, gambol, romp; **retozo** m frolic etc.; **~ de la risa** giggle; **retozón** playful.

retractar [1a] retract, withdraw; **~se** recant, retract; **retráctil** retractable.

retraer [2p] bring back, bring again; *fig.* dissuade, discourage; **~se** retire, retreat; take refuge; retract; **~** de withdraw from, give up; shun; **retraído** retiring, shy; unsociable; *b.s.* backward; **retraimiento** m (*acto*) withdrawal etc.; (*lugar*) retreat, refuge.

retransmisión f *radio*: repeat (broadcast); **retransmitir** [3a] repeat; relay.

retrasar [1a] v/t. delay, defer, put off; *evolución etc.* retard, slow down; *reloj* put back; v/i. (*reloj*) be slow; **~se** (*p.*, 🜂 etc.) be late; **retrasado** (mentally) retarded; **retraso** m delay; timelag; slowness, lateness; con **~** late.

retratar [1a] portray (*a. fig.*); describe; **retrato** m portrait; *fig.* description; *fig.* (*imagen fiel*) likeness.

retreta f ✕ (*toque de*) **~** tattoo; retreat.

retrete m lavatory; toilet.

retro... retro...; **~activo** retroactive; retrospective; **~carga:** de **~** breech-loading; *arma* de **~** breech loader; **~ceder** [2a] draw back, stand back; go back, turn back *en viaje etc.*; back down, flinch (*ante peligro* from); (*agua etc.*) fall; **~ceso** m backward movement, falling back.

retruécano m play on words.

retumbante booming, resounding; **retumbar** [1a] boom, reverberate; **retumbo** m boom etc.

reuma m rheumatism; **reumatismo** m rheumatism.

reunión f meeting, gathering; reunion; *pol.* meeting, rally; (*fiesta*) party; **reunir** [3a] *cosas separadas* join (together), (re)unite; *cosas dispersas* gather (together), assemble, get together; *colección* make; *datos etc.* collect; *fondos* raise; *cualidades* combine; **~se** (*juntarse*) meet, get together; gather; (*unirse*) unite.

revancha f revenge; *deportes:* return match.

revelación f revelation; disclosure; **revelado** m *phot.* developing; **revelador 1.** revealing, telltale; **2.** m *phot.* developer; **revelar** [1a] *mst* reveal; disclose, betray, give away; *phot.* develop.

revendedor m, **-a** f retailer; *b.s.* speculator; *deportes:* ticket tout; **revender** [2a] resell, retail; *b.s.* speculate in; *entradas* tout.

reventa f resale.

reventar [1k] **1.** v/t. burst; crush, smash; *fig.* ruin; F (*cansar*) bore to tears; F (*molestar*) rile; F (*hacer trabajar*) overwork, work to death; **2.** v/i. burst; explode, pop; (*brotar*) burst forth; (*olas*) break; **3. ~se** burst etc.; **reventón** m burst; explosion; *mot.* blow-out; *fig.* steep hill, tough climb; (*apuro*) jam.

reverdecer [2d] grow green again; *fig.* acquire new vigor.

reverencia f reverence; (*saludo*) bow de hombre, curtsy de mujer; **reverencial** reverential; **reverenciar** [1b] revere, venerate; **reverendo** respected, reverend; *eccl.* reverend; **reverente** reverent.

reversible *mst* reversible; 🜂 reversionary; **reversión** f reversion; **reverso** m back, other side; reverse de moneda; el **~** de la medalla *fig.* the other side of the picture.

revés m (*cara*) back, other side, underside; (*golpe*) slap; *tenis:* backhand; *fig.* reverse, setback; al **~** *tela etc.* inside out, upside down; (*adv.*) on the contrary.

revestir [3l] *ropa* put on, wear; *superficie* clothe (de in); esp. ⊕ face, coat; line; sheathe; *fig. suelo etc.* carpet (de with); *cuento* adorn (de with); *p.* invest (con, de with); *importancia* have; **~se** be carried away; (*engreírse*) be haughty; **~** con, **~** de autoridad etc. be invested with.

revisada f *Am.* examination, revision; **revisar** [1a] revise; reexamine; review (*a.* 🜂); check; esp. ⊕ overhaul; **revisión** f revision; review (*a.* 🜂); check; esp. ⊕ overhaul.

revista f review (*a.* ♣, ✕), inspection; revision; *thea.* revue; *lit.* review, magazine; 🜂 retrial; *pasar* **~** a =

revistar [1a] ⚓, ✗ inspect, review; **revistero** m reviewer.

revivificar [1g] revitalize; **revivir** [3a] revive, be revived; live again.

revocación f revocation, repeal; reversal; **revocar** [1g] *orden etc.* revoke, repeal; *decisión* reverse; dissuade (*de* from); *casa* plaster; **revocatoria** f Am. recall; cancellation, repeal.

revolcar [1g *a.* 1m] *p. etc.* knock down, knock over, send flying; ✗ *adversario* floor; **~se** roll, flounder about; (*esp. animal*) wallow.

revoltijo m, **revoltillo** m jumble, mess, litter; *fig.* mess.

revoltoso 1. rebellious, unruly; *niño* naughty; **2.** ~ rebel; *pol.* troublemaker, agitator.

revolución f *mst* revolution (*a.* ⊕); turn; **revolucionar** [1a] revolutionize; **revolucionario** *adj. a.* su. m, **a** f revolutionary.

revólver m revolver.

revolver [2h; *p.p.* revuelto] (*agitar, sacudir*) shake; *líquido* stir (up); *tierra* turn up, turn over; *objeto* turn round, turn over (*or* upside down); *estómago* turn; **~se** turn (right) round, turn over *etc.*; toss and turn *en cama*; *ast.* revolve; (*tiempo*) change.

revuelo m disturbance; rumpus; *de ~* incidentally, in passing.

revuelta f (*motín*) revolt; disturbance; turn, bend *de camino*; change *de parecer etc.*; (*disputa*) quarrel, row; **revuelto 1.** *p.p.* of *revolver*; *agua* troubled; *v.* huevo; **2.** *adj.* in disorder; confused, complicated.

rey m king (*a. naipes, ajedrez*); los ₂es Magos the Three Wise Men.

reyerta f quarrel, fight, brawl.

rezagado m latecomer; loiterer; ✗ straggler; **rezagar** [1h] outdistance, leave behind; (*aplazar*) postpone; **~se** fall (*or* get left) behind; lag (behind); straggle.

rezar [1f] *v/t.* say; *v/i.* pray, say one's prayers; (*texto*) read, say, run; **rezo** m (*acto*) praying; (*una oración*) prayer; (*oraciones*) prayers.

rezongar [1h] grumble, mutter; growl; **rezongo** m grumble; growl; **rezongón** grumbling.

rezumar [1a] *v/t.* ooze, exude; *v/i.* ooze (out), seep, leak out (*a. fig.*).

ría[1] *etc. v.* reír.

ría[2] f estuary, mouth of a river.

riachuelo m brook, stream.

ribera f shore, beach; bank *de río*; **ribereño** riverside *attr.*

ribete m *sew. etc.* edging, border; *fig.* addition, *fig.* trimmings, embellishments *de cuento*; **~s** *pl. fig.* streak, touch; *tener sus* ~s de have some appearance of being.

rico 1. rich, wealthy; (*fértil, suntuoso*) rich (*en* in); *comida* delicious; *dulces etc.* rich; *fruto* luscious; **2.** m, **a** f wealthy man *etc.*; *nuevo* ~ nouveau riche.

ridiculizar [1f] ridicule, deride; guy; **ridículo** ridiculous, absurd, ludicrous; (*delicado*) touchy.

riego m watering; irrigation; *fig.* sprinkling; ~ *por aspersión* spray.

riel m 🚃 rail; *metall.* ingot.

rienda f rein; *a* ~ *suelta* at top speed; *fig.* without the least restraint; *dar* ~ *suelta a* give free rein to; give *s.o.* his head; *deseos* indulge; *soltar las* ~s kick over the traces.

riente laughing, merry; *paisaje* smiling, bright.

riesgo m risk; danger; *correr* ~ *de inf.* run the risk of *ger.*; **riesgoso** Am. risky.

rifa f raffle; (*riña*) quarrel; **rifar** [1a] *v/t.* raffle; *v/i.* quarrel, fight.

rifle m rifle; **riflero** m rifleman.

rigidez f rigidity *etc.*; ~ *cadavérica* rigor mortis; **rígido** rigid; stiff; *fig.* strict, stern (*con, para* towards); unbending; **rigor** m rigor, severity (*a. meteor. etc.*); harshness, strictness; *en* ~ strictly speaking; **riguroso** rigorous; *crítico, pena, tiempo etc.* severe, harsh; strict; stringent.

rima f rhyme; ~s *pl.* poems, poetry; **rimar** [1a] rhyme (*con* with).

rimbombante resounding, echoing; *fig.* bombastic; (*vistoso*) show.

rímel m mascara.

rimero m stack, heap.

rincón m (inside) corner; *fig.* corner, nook, retreat; patch *de terreno etc.*; **rinconada** f corner.

ringl(er)a f row, line; swath.

ringorrango m F flourish *de pluma*; *fig.* trimmings, frills.

riña f quarrel; (*con golpes*) fight, scuffle; ~ *de gallos* cockfight.

riñón m *anat.* kidney; *fig.* heart.

río m river; ~ *abajo* downstream; ~ *arriba* upstream; ~ *de oro fig.* goldmine; *a* ~ *revuelto* in disorder.

rió *etc. v.* reír.

ripio m residue, refuse; (*cascote*) debris, rubble; (*palabrería*) verbiage, padding.

riqueza f wealth, riches; (*fertilidad, sabor, de estilo*) richness; ~s pl. del *subsuelo* mineral resources.

risa f (*una ~*) laugh; (*en general*) laughter, laughing; *cosa de ~* joke, laughing matter; ¡*qué ~*! how funny!; *desternillarse de ~* split one's sides.

risco m cliff, bluff, crag.

risible ludicrous, laughable.

risotada f guffaw, horselaugh.

ristra f string.

risueño smiling; *disposición* cheerful, sunny; *paisaje* smiling.

rítmico rhythmic(al); **ritmo** m rhythm.

rito m rite; ceremony; **ritual** adj. a. su. m ritual.

rival 1. rival, competing; 2. m/f rival, competitor; **rivalidad** f rivalry, enmity; **rivalizar** [1f] compete, vie; ~ *con* rival.

rizado *pelo* curly; *superficie* crinkly; crisp; **rizador** m curling-iron, hair-curler; **rizar** [1f] *pelo* curl; crisp; *superficie* crinkle; *agua* ripple, ruffle; ~**se** curl etc.; **rizo** 1. curly; 2. m curl, ringlet; ripple *de agua*; ~s pl. ♣ reefs; **rizoso** curly.

roano roan.

robar [1a] *poseedor* rob (*algo a alguien* s.o. of s.t.); *posesión* steal (*a* from); (*secuestrar*) abduct, kidnap.

roblar [1a] rivet, clinch.

roble m oak (tree); **robledal** m, **robledo** m oak wood.

robo m robbery; theft, thieving.

robot m robot; **robotización** f robotization, use of robots.

robustez f robustness; **robusto** robust; strong, sturdy; tough; hardy.

roca f rock.

roce m rub(bing); *esp.* ⊕ friction; graze *en piel*; close contact; *tener ~ con* be in close contact with.

rociada f splash; shower, sprinkling; (*aspersión*) spray; shower *de piedras*, hail *de balas*; **rociador** m spray, sprinkler; **rociar** [1c] v/t. sprinkle, spray (*de* with); spatter *de lodo* etc.; *fig.* scatter, shower.

rocín m hack, nag; F lout; **rocinante** m poor old horse.

rocío m dew; (*llovizna*) drizzle; *fig.* sprinkling.

rockero m F rock singer.

rocoso rocky.

rodada f rut, (wheel) track; *S. Am.* fall.

rodado *circulación* wheeled, on wheels; *piedra* rounded; *caballo* dappled; **rodaja** f (*rueda*) small wheel, castor; disc, round; slice *de pan* etc.; **rodaje** m ⊕ (set of) wheels; *cine*: shooting, filming; *mot.* en ~ running-in; **rodante** rolling; **rodapié** m skirting board; **rodar** [1m] v/t. *vehículo* wheel; *cosa redonda* roll; *mot.* run in; *película* shoot, film; v/i. roll (*por* along, down etc.); go, run, travel *sobre ruedas*; rotate, revolve *en eje*.

rodear [1a] v/t. surround (*de* by, with); ring, encircle, shut in; *S.Am. ganado* round up; v/i. go round; (*camino*) make a detour; *fig.* beat about the bush; ~**se** turn, toss, twist; **rodeo** m detour *de camino*; round-about way, long way round; *fig.* dodge; pretext; circumlocution; ⚡ cattle-pen; ♪ roundup, rodeo; *sin* ~s outright.

rodilla f knee; *de* ~s kneeling; *caer de* ~s fall on one's knees; *estar* (*or hincarse, ponerse*) *de* ~s kneel (down); *hincar la* ~ kneel down; *fig.* bow (*ante* to).

rodillo m roller; *cocina*: rolling pin; ink roller *para entintar*.

roedor 1. gnawing (*a. fig.*); 2. m rodent; **roer** [2z] gnaw; nibble; *hueso* pick; *metal* corrode, eat into.

rogar [1h a. 1m] v/t. p. beg; plead with; *cosa* beg for, ask for, plead for; ~ *que* beg *inf.*; ask that; v/i. beg, plead (*por* for); (*orar*) pray; *hacerse* (*de*) ~ have to be coaxed.

rojez f redness; **rojillo** F pink; **rojizo** reddish; ruddy; **rojo** 1. red (*a. pol.*); ruddy; 2. m red (*a. pol.*); ~ *cereza* cherry-red; ~ *de labios* lip-stick.

rollizo p. plump; stocky, sturdy; *niño* chubby; *mujer* plump, buxom.

rollo m roll; *cocina*: rolling pin.

romadizo m head-cold.

romana f steelyard.

romance 1. *lengua* romance; 2. m romance (language); Spanish (language); **romancero** m collection of ballads; **románico** *lengua* romance; **romano** adj. a. su. m, **a** f Roman (*a. typ.*); **romanticismo** m romanticism; **romántico** adj. a. su. m romantic.

R

romería *f eccl.* pilgrimage; gathering at a shrine; *fig.* trip, excursion; **romero¹** *m*, **a** *f* pilgrim.

romero² *m* ♥ rosemary.

romo blunt; *p.* snub-nosed.

rompecabezas *m* (*problema*) puzzle, teaser; (*acertijo*) riddle; (*dibujo*) jigsaw puzzle; **rompedero** fragile, breakable; **rompedora-cargadora** *f* ☆ power loader; **rompehielos** *m* icebreaker; **rompehuelgas** *m* strike breaker; **rompeolas** *m* breakwater; **romper** [2a; *p.p.* roto] **1.** *v/t.* plato etc. break, smash, shatter; *cuerda etc.* break, snap; *presa, cerca etc.* break through, breach; *papel, tela* tear (up), rip (up); *ropa* tear; wear out; *tierra* break up; *aguas* cleave; *niebla, nubes* break through; *ayuno* break; *hostilidades* open up, start; *relaciones* break off; **2.** *v/i.* (*día, olas*) break; ♥ burst (open); (*guerra etc.*) break out; (*ps.*) fall out (*con* with); ~ *a inf.* suddenly start to *inf.*; *F de rompe y rasga* determined; **rompiente** *m* (*ola*) breaker; (*escollo*) reef; ~s *pl.* breakers, surf; **rompimiento** *m* (*acto*) breaking etc.; (*abertura*) opening, breach, crack.

ron *m* rum.

roncar [1g] snore; (*mar etc.*) roar.

roncha *f* bruise, weal; swelling *de picadura.*

ronco *p.* hoarse; throaty, husky; *sonido* harsh, raucous.

ronda *f* night patrol, (night) watch; beat *de policía*; (*ps.*) watch, patrol; (*con canto*) serenaders; round *de bebidas etc.*; ~ *negociadora* round of negotiations; **rondar** [1a] *v/t.* patrol, go the rounds of; *fig.* haunt, hang about; *v/i.* (*policía*) be on patrol, go the rounds; prowl (round), hang about.

ronquedad *f*, **ronquera** *f* hoarseness etc.; **ronquido** *m* snoring; (*un* ~) snore; *fig.* roar.

ronronear [1a] purr; **ronroneo** *m* purr(ing).

ronzal *m* halter.

ronzar [1f] crunch, munch.

roña *f vet.* scab *de oveja*, mange *de perro*; ♥ rust; (*mugre*) filth, grime; = **roñería** *f* meanness; **roñoso** scabby, mangy; dirty; stingy.

ropa *f* clothing, clothes, dress; ~ *blanca* linen; ~ *blanca* (*de mujer*) lingerie; ~ *de cama* bedclothes, bedding; ~ *dominguera* Sunday best;

~ *hecha* ready-made clothes; ~ *interior* underwear, underclothes; ~ *lavada*, ~ *por lavar*, ~ *sucia* laundry, washing; *a quema* ~ point-blank; *tentarse la* ~ think long and hard; **ropaje** *m* (*ropa*) clothing, (*vestido*) gown, robe; (*paños*) drapery; *fig.* garb; **ropavejero** *m* old-clothes dealer; **ropería** *f* clothing trade; (*tienda*) clothier's; **ropero** *m* clothier; (*mueble*) wardrobe.

rosa *f* rose; red spot, birthmark *en cuerpo*; *caminito de* ~s primrose path; ~ *de los vientos*, ~ *náutica* compass; *color* (*de*) ~ rose, pink; **rosado** pink, rosy; **rosal** *m* rose tree, rose bush; ~ *silvestre* dogrose; ~ *trepador* rambler rose; **rosaleda** *f* rose garden, rose-bed.

rosario *m* rosary, beads, chaplet; *rezar el* ~ tell one's beads.

rosbif *m* roast beef.

rosca *f* coil, spiral; ⊕ screw, thread *de tornillo*; *cocina:* ring-shaped roll etc., ♣ *en* ~ light.

róseo roseate, rosy.

roseta *f* ♥ small rose; rose *de regadera*; red patch *en mejilla*; (*adorno*) rosette; ~s *pl.* popcorn; **rosetón** *m* △ rosette; △ rose (window).

rostro *m anat.* countenance, face; ♥ beak; *hist., zo. etc.* rostrum; *hacer* ~ *a* face (up to).

rotación *f* rotation; revolution; **rotativo** rotary; revolving; **rotatorio** rotary, rotatory.

rotisería *f Am.* fast-food restaurant.

roto 1. *p.p. de romper;* **2.** broken; torn; (*andrajoso*) ragged.

rótula *f* knee-cap; ⊕ ball-and-socket joint; **rotulador** *m* felt pen.

rotular [1a] label; ticket; letter; mark, inscribe; (*titular*) head, entitle; **rotulata** *f* label, ticket, tag; **rótulo** *m* label, ticket, tag; inscription.

rotundo *negativa etc.* round, flat; *lenguaje etc.* sonorous.

rotura *f* (*acto*) breaking etc.; (*abertura*) opening, breach, break; **roturación** *f* ✔ reclamation; **roturar** [1a] ✔ break up.

rozadura *f* rub(bing); chafing; *esp.* ✖ abrasion, graze, sore spot; **rozagante** striking; *b.s.* showy; *fig.* proud; **rozamiento** *m* friction (*a.* ⊕), rubbing; **rozar** [1f] *v/t. a. v/i.* *tierra* clear; *hierba* crop, graze; nibble; (*ludir*) rub (against, on), chafe.

rutinario

scrape; *📌 piel* chafe, graze; (*tocar ligeramente*) shave, graze; *superficie* skim; **~se** *fig.* hobnob, rub shoulders (*con* with).

ruano roan.

rubéola *f* German measles.

rubí *m* ruby; jewel *de reloj*.

rubia *f* (*p.*) blonde; *mot.* shooting brake; *♀* madder; *sl.* one peseta; **~ de bote**, *♀* oxigenada peroxide blonde; **~ platino** platinum blonde; **rubicundo** reddish; ruddy; rubicund; **rubio** fair, fair-haired, blond(e).

rubor *m* bright red; blush, flush *en cara*; *fig.* bashfulness; **ruborizarse** [1f] blush (*de* at, with), flush, redden; **ruboroso** blushing, red.

rúbrica *f* rubric (*a. eccl.*), heading; (*señal*) red mark; flourish *tras firma*; **ser de ~** be in line with custom; **rubricar** [1g] sign with a flourish; (*y sellar*) sign and seal.

rucio 1. *caballo* (silver-)gray; *p.* grey-haired; **2.** *m* grey.

ruda *f* rue.

rudeza *f* coarseness *etc.*

rudo (*tosco*) coarse, rough, crude; (*áspero*) rough; *golpe* hard; (*penoso*) hard, tough; (*grosero*) rude, ill-mannered; (*bobo*) simple.

rueca *f* distaff.

rueda *f* wheel; roller, castor *de mueble etc.*; ring, circle *de ps. etc.*; (*suplicio*) rack; (*rebanada*) round; **~ de andar** treadmill; **~ de cadena** sprocket-wheel; **~ dentada** gear wheel; cog (-wheel); **~ de escape** escapement wheel; **~ de fuego** pinwheel; **~ libre** free wheel; **~ de molino** millstone; **~ motriz** drive wheel; **~ de paletas** paddle wheel; **~ de prensa** press conference; **~ de presos criminales** line-up; **~ de recambio** spare wheel; **~ de trinquete** ratchet wheel; **en ~** in a ring; **ruedecilla** *f* roller, castor; **ruedo** *m* (*giro*) turn, rotation; edge, circumference; (*estera*) mat; *toros:* bullring, arena.

ruego *m* request; entreaty.

rufián *m* pimp, pander; (*brutal*) lout, hooligan.

rugido *m* roar *etc.*; **rugir** [3c] (*león*) roar; (*toro etc.*) bellow; (*tempestad*) roar, howl; (*tripas*) rumble.

rugoso wrinkled, creased.

ruibarbo *m* rhubarb.

ruido *m* noise; sound; (*muy ruidoso*) din, row; noisiness; *fig.* repercussions; (*protestas*) outcry, stir; **ruidoso** noisy, loud; *suceso* sensational; *oposición* vocal, noisy.

ruin (*vil*) mean, despicable; (*pequeño*) small; (*mezquino*) petty; (*avaro*) mean; *trato* shabby, heartless; *animal* vicious.

ruina *f mst* ruin; downfall, collapse, wreck; **~s** *pl.* ruins.

ruindad *f* meanness *etc.*

ruinoso ruinous, tumbledown, ramshackle; *empresa* disastrous.

ruiseñor *m* nightingale.

ruleta *f* roulette; **ruletero** *m Mex.* taxi driver.

rulo *m* roll; roller; rolling pin.

rumbo *m esp.* *♣* course, direction, bearing; F show(iness), pomp; *Am.* noisy celebrating; **~ nuevo** *fig.* departure; **con ~ a** bound for, headed for; **in the direction of**; **hacer ~ a** set a course for, head for; F **de mucho ~** = **rumbón** F, **rumboso** F very fine, big, splendid.

rumiar [1b] *v/t.* chew; F chew over, brood on (*or* over); *v/i.* chew the cud; F ruminate, brood.

rumor *m* murmur, mutter, buzz *de voces*; (*voz*) rumor; **rumorear** [1a]: **se rumorea que** it is rumored that; **rumoroso** noisy, loud.

runrún *m* F purr(ing) *de gato*; (*ruido*) murmuring; (*voz*) buzz.

ruptura *f fig.* rupture; breaking *de contrato*; breaking-off *de relaciones*.

rural rural; country *attr.*

rusticidad *f* rusticity *etc.*; **rústico** rustic, country *attr.*; *b.s.* coarse, uncouth; **en ~a** paper-backed.

ruta *f* route; (*señal de carretera*) main road, through road.

rutina *f* routine; round; **por ~** as a matter of course; **rutinario** routine, everyday; humdrum.

S

sábado *m* Saturday; *(judío)* Sabbath.
sábana *f* sheet; *eccl.* altar cloth.
sabañón *m* chilblain.
saber [2n] **1.** *v/t.* know; *(estar enterado de)* know about, be aware of; *en pretérito freq.* learn, get to know, find out; ~ *inf.* know to *inf.*, can *inf.*; *hacer* ~ inform; ~ *de* know about, know of; *p. ausente* hear from; *a* ~ namely; **2.** *v/i.* ~ *d* taste of, taste like; *esp. fig.* smack of; **3.** *m* knowledge, learning.
sabidillo *m*, **a** *f* know-it-all; **sabido** well-informed, knowledgeable; *de* ~ for sure; **sabiduría** *f* wisdom; knowledge, learning; **sabiendas:** *a* ~ knowingly; *a* ~ *de que* knowing full well that; **sabihondo** *adj. a. su. m*, **a** *f* know-it-all, smart aleck; **sabio 1.** wise, learned; knowing; *animal* trained; **2.** *m*, **a** *f* learned man *etc.*, wise person; ⠏ scholar.
sablazo F: *dar un* ~ raise the wind, make a touch (*de* for).
sable *m* sabre, cutlass.
sabor *m* taste, flavor; savor(iness); *con* ~ *a miel* honey-flavored; **saborear** [1a] flavor; *(percibir el sabor de)* savor, relish, taste; ~**se** smack one's lips; **saborete** *m* F slight flavor.
sabotaje *m* sabotage; **saboteador** *m* saboteur; **sabotear** [1a] sabotage.
sabroso tasty, delicious; F salty.
sabueso *m* bloodhound (*a. fig.*).
saca¹ *f* big sack.
saca² *f (acto)* taking out; ✝ export, exporting; *estar de* ~ be on sale; F be of on age to marry.
saca...: ~**bocados** *m* ⊕ punch; ~**botas** *m* boot jack; ~**corchos** *m* corkscrew; ~**cuartos** *m* F, ~**dineros** *m* F cheap trinket; *(maña)* cheat; ~**manchas** *m/f* dry cleaner; ~**muelas** *m* F dentist; ~**puntas** *m* pencil sharpener.
sacar [1g] *(extraer)* take out, get out, pull out, draw out; extract (*a.* 🔧); withdraw; *(quitar)* remove; *(exceptuar)* exclude, remove; *(obtener)* get; *arma* draw; *billete, entrada* buy, book; *copia* make; *cuentas* make up;

dinero draw (out) *de banco*; *foto* take; *lengua, mano etc.* put out, stick out.
sacarina *f* saccharin.
sacerdocio *m* priesthood; ministry; **sacerdote** *m* priest.
saciar [1b] satiate, surfeit (*de* on, with); *hambre, deseos etc.* appease.
saco¹ *m* bag, sack; 🔧 kit bag; *S.Am.* jacket; ~ *de dormir* sleeping bag; ~ *de viaje* travelling bag.
saco² *m* 🔧 sack; *entrar a* ~ sack, loot.
sacramental sacramental; *fig.* time-honored; **sacramento** *m* sacrament; **sacrificar** [1g] sacrifice; *slaughter en matadero*; *perro etc.* put to sleep; **sacrificio** *m* sacrifice; slaughter(ing); **sacrilegio** *m* sacrilege; **sacrílego** sacrilegious; **sacristán** *m* sexton; **sacristía** *f* vestry, sacristry; **sacro** sacred, holy; **sacrosanto** most holy; sacrosanct.
sacudida *f* shake; jerk; jolt, bump *esp. de vehículo*; shock *de terremoto etc.*; blast *de explosión*; jerk, toss *de cabeza*; *pol. etc.* upheavel; **sacudidura** *f*, **sacudimiento** *m* shaking *etc.*; **sacudir** [3a] *(agitar)* shake; *brazo, pasajeros etc.* jerk, jar; jolt; *cabeza etc.* jerk, toss; *(hacer oscilar)* jerk, beat.
sádico sadistic; **sadismo** *m* sadism.
saeta *f* 🔧 arrow, dart; hand *de reloj*; magnetic needle.
saga *f* saga.
sagacidad *f* shrewdness *etc.*; **sagaz** shrewd, clever, sagacious.
Sagitario *m ast.* Sagittarius.
sagrado 1. sacred, holy; **2.** *m* sanctuary; **sagrario** *m* sanctuary.
sahumar [1a] perfume; smoke.
sal¹ *f* salt; *fig. (donaire)* charm; *(viveza)* liveliness; *(agudeza)* wit, wittiness; ~ *amoníaca* sal ammoniac; ~*es pl. (aromáticas)* smelling salts; ~ *de fruta* fruit salts; ~ *gema* rock salt; ~ *de la Higuera* Epsom salts; ~ *de la tierra* salt of the earth.
sal² *v. salir.*
sala *f (a.* ~ *de estar)* drawing room, sitting room, lounge; *(pública)* hall; *thea.* house, auditorium; ⚕ ward;

♟ court; ~ *de calderas* boiler room; ~ *del cine* movie theater; ~ *de lo civil* civil court; ~ *de conferencias* lecture room; ~ *de enfermos* infirmary; ~ *de espectáculos* concert-room, hall; ~ *de espera* waiting room; ~ *de estar* living room, sitting room; ~ *de fiestas* night club; ~ *de justicia* law court; ~ *de lectura* reading room; ~ *de máquinas* engine room; ~ *de muestras* showroom; ~ *de operaciones* operating room; ~ *de recibo* parlor; ~ *de subastas* sale room; *en* ~ *deporte* indoor.

saladar *m* salt marsh; **salado** salt(y); *fig.* (*encantador*) charming, cute; (*vivo*) lively; *lenguaje etc.* racy; (*agudo*) witty.

salar [1a] salt, cure.

salario *m* wage(s).

salaz salacious, prurient.

salchicha *f* (pork) sausage; **salchichería** *f* pork butcher's; **salchichón** *m* (salami) sausage.

saldar [1a] *cuenta* settle; *cuentas* balance; *existencias* sell off; *libros* remainder; **saldo** *m* (*acto*) settlement; (*cantidad*) balance; (*venta*) (clearance) sale; (*géneros*) remnant(s); ~ *acreedor* credit balance; ~ *deudor* debit balance.

salero *m* salt-cellar; (*almacén*) salt store; F wit; charm; (*gancho*) sex appeal; **saleroso** F = *salado*.

salida *f* (*puerta etc.*) way out, exit; ⊕ *etc.* outlet, vent; *geog.* outlet (*al mar* to the sea); (*acto*) going out *etc.*; emergence; 🚂, ✈ departure; rising *de sol; deportes:* start; leak *de gas, líquido;* ✗ sally, sortie; ⊕ output; † (*inversión*) outlay; (*venta*) sale; (*mercado*) outlet, opening; (*resultado*) issue, outcome, result; ⚓ projection; (*escapatoria*) loophole, way out; F crack, joke; ~ *de baño* bathrobe; ~ *de emergencia* emergency exit; ~ *fácil* ready market; ~ *lanzada* flying start, running start; ~ *del sol* sunrise; ~ *de teatro* evening wrap; ~ *de teatros* after-theater party; ~ *de tono* remark out of place; *dar* ~ *a cólera etc.* vent; † place, find an outlet for; † *tener* ~ sell well.

salido projecting, bulging; *hembra* on heat; **salidizo** *m* projection; **saliente 1.** ⚓ *etc.* projecting; *sol* rising; **2.** *m* projection.

salir [3r] (*pasar fuera*) come out, go out; appear; emerge (*de* from); issue; arise; (*sol*) rise; *thea.* (*a.* ~ *a escena*) come on, go on; (*partir*) leave, depart (*a.* 🚂, ✈; *para* for); ⚓ sail; ♀ come up (*a. puesto*); (*escapar*) get out (*de* of), escape (*de* from); (*mancha*) come off; (*sobresalir*) project, jut out, stick out *etc.; deportes:* start; *ajedrez:* have first move; *naipes:* lead; (*lotería*) win a prize (*a.* ~ *premiado*); (*resultar*) prove, turn out (*to be*); *le salió un diente* he cut a tooth; ~ *corriendo etc.* run *etc.* out; ~ *ganando deportes:* win; *fig.* be the gainer; † be in pocket; ~ *perdiendo deportes:* lose; *fig.* be the loser; † be out of pocket; ~ *elegido* be elected; ~ *bien* (*p.*) succeed, make good; pass *en examen;* (*suceso*) go off well.

saliva *f* spit, spittle, saliva; (*no*) *gastar* ~ (not) waste one's breath (*en* on).

salivar [1a] salivate.

salmo *m* psalm; **salmodia** *f* psalmody; F singsong, drone.

salmón *m* salmon.

salmuera *f* pickle, brine.

salón *m* lounge; (*público*) hall; *paint.* salon; (*a.* ~ *de baile*) ballroom, dance hall; ~ *de belleza* beauty parlor; ~ *de demostraciones* showroom; ~ *de pintura* art exhibition; ~ *de sesiones* assembly hall; *juego de* ~ parlor game.

salpicadero *m mot.* dashboard.

salpicadura *f* splash(ing) *etc.;* **salpicar** [1g] splash, spatter (*de* with); sprinkle (*de* with).

salpimentar [1a] season.

salsa *f* sauce; gravy *para carne asada;* dressing *para ensalada; fig.* appetizer; ~ *de tomate* tomato sauce; **salsera** *f* gravy boat.

saltamontes *m* grasshopper.

saltar [1a] **1.** *v/t.* leap (over), jump (over); vault; skip *en lectura.* **2.** *v/i.* leap, jump, spring (*a* on, *por* over); vault; dive, plunge (*a agua* into); hop, skip *a la comba etc.;* (*rebotar*) bounce, fly up; (*tapón*) pop out; (*botón*) come off; ⊕ (*pieza*) fly off; (*líquido*) spurt up, shoot up; (*vaso*) break, crack; burst; explode; *biol.* ~ *atrás* revert; ~ *sobre* pounce on.

salteador *m*: ~ *de caminos* highwayman, robber; **salteamiento** *m* hold up; **saltear** [1a] hold up.

salto *m* leap, jump, spring, bound; vault; hop, skip; dive, plunge; pounce *sobre presa;* (*sima*) chasm; passage skipped, part missed *en lec-*

tura; ~ *de agua* waterfall; ⊕ chute; ~ *de altura* high jump; ~ *de ángel* swan dive; ~ *de cabeza* header; ~ *de cama* négligée, dressing gown; ~ *de carpa* jackknife (dive); ~ *a ciegas* leap in the dark; ~ *con garrocha,* ~ *con pértiga* pole vault; ~ *de esquí* ski jump; ~ *de longitud* long jump; ~ *mortal* somersault; ~ *ornamental* fancy dive; ~ *de palanca* highdive; *triple* ~ hop step and jump; ~ *de trampolín* (springboard) dive; ~ *de viento* ⚓ sudden shift in the wind; *a* ~*s* by leaps and bounds; *(a empujones)* by fits and starts; *de un* ~ in one bound; *bajar etc. de un* ~ jump down *etc.;* *en un* ~ *fig.* in a jiffy; **saltón** [1] *ojos* bulging; *dientes* protruding; 2. *m* grasshopper.

salubre healthy, salubrious; **salubridad** *f* healthiness; *S.Am.* (public) health; **salud** *f* ⚕ health; *fig.* welfare, wellbeing; *eccl.* salvation; *¡(a su) ~!* good health!; *beber a la* ~ *de* drink (to) the health of; *estar bien (mal) de* ~ be in good (bad) health; **saludable** healthy; *fig.* salutary; **saludar** [1a] greet; say hullo to F; hail; *esp.* ✕ salute; **saludo** *m* greeting; *esp.* ✕ salute; ~*s (en carta)* best wishes; *un* ~ *afectuoso* kind regards; **salutación** *f* greeting.

salva *f* ✕ salute, salvo; *(bienvenida)* greeting; volley, salvo *de aplausos.* **salvación** *f eccl. etc.* salvation; rescue; delivery (de from).

salvador *m,* **-a** *f* rescuer, deliverer.
salvaguardar [1a] safeguard; **salvaguardia** *f* safe conduct.
salvajada *f* barbarity, savage deed *etc.;* **salvaje 1.** *mst* wild; *(feroz)* savage; 2. *m/f* savage; **salvajería** *f* savagery; *(acto)* barbarity; **salvajino** *≈* wild; savage; *carne* gamy.
salvamento *m* rescue; salvage; *fig.* salvation; *(lugar)* place of safety; *de* ~ life-saving; *v. bote etc.;* **salvar** [1a] save *(a. eccl.),* rescue *(de* from); *barco etc.* salvage; *arroyo etc.* jump over, clear; *rápidos* shoot; *distancia* cover; *obstáculo* negotiate, clear; *dificultad* get round; resolve; *~se* save o.s., escape *(de* from); **salvavidas** *m:* *(cinturón)* ~ lifebelt.
salvo 1. *adj.* safe; saved; 2. *adv., prp.* except (for), save, barring; *a* ~ safely; out of danger; *a* ~ *de* safe from; *en* ~ out of danger; ~ *que* except that; unless; **salvoconducto** *m* safe conduct.

san saint *(mst escrito* St.); F *¡voto a* ~*es!* in heaven's name!
sanable curable; **sanalotodo** *m fig.* panacea, cure-all; **sanar** [1a] *v/t.* cure (de of), heal; *v/i. (p.)* recover; *(herida)* heal; **sanativo** healing; **sanatorio** *m* sanatorium.
sanción *f* sanction; penalty; **sancionar** [1a] sanction.
sandalia *f* sandal.
sandez *f* foolishness.
sandía *f* watermelon.
saneamiento *m* ⚖ surety; indemnification; drainage; sanitation *de casa;* **sanear** [1a] ⚖ guarantee; indemnify; *terreno* drain.
sangradera *f* ✚ lancet; **sangradura** *f* ✚ bleeding, blood-letting; outlet, draining; **sangrar** [1a] *v/t.* ✚ bleed; *fig. ✐ etc.* drain; *árbol, horno* tap; *typ.* indent; *v/i.* bleed; **sangre** *f* blood; ~ *azul* blue blood; ~ *fría* sangfroid, coolness; *a* ~ *fría* in cold blood; *a* ~ *y fuego* by fire and sword; *without mercy; mala* ~ bad blood; *pura* ~ *m/f* thoroughbred; *de pura* ~ thoroughbred; ~ *vital* life-blood; *echar* ~ bleed; *se me heló la* ~ my blood ran cold; **sangría** *f* bleeding; tapping *etc.; (bebida)* sangría; **sangriento** bloody; gory; *arma etc.* bloodstained; *p.* bloodthirsty; *injuria* deadly; **sangrigordo** *Am.* unpleasant; **sangriligero** *Am.* nice; **sangripesado** *Am.* unpleasant; **sanguijuela** *f* leech *(a. fig.);* **sanguinario** bloodthirsty; bloody; **sanguíneo** *vaso etc.* blood attr.

sanidad *f* sanitation; *(lo sano)* health (-iness); ~ *pública* public health; *inspector de* ~ sanitary inspector; **sanitario** sanitary; *instalación* ~ sanitation; **sano** *p.* healthy, fit; *comida etc.* wholesome; *fruta, doctrina etc.* sound; ~ *y salvo* safe and sound.
santa *f* saint.
santidad *f* holiness, sanctity; saintliness; *su* ♀ His Holiness; **santificar** [1g] sanctify; hallow.
santiguar [1i] make the sign of the cross over; F slap; ~*se* cross o.s.
santo 1. holy; *esp. p.* saintly; *mártir* blessed *(a.* F); 2. *m* saint; saint's day; ~ *y seña* password; *fig.* watchword; F *¿a ~ de qué?* what on earth for?; *desnudar a un* ~ *para vestir a otro* rob Peter to pay Paul; **santuario** *m* sanctuary.

saña f anger, fury (a. fig.); cruelty; **sañoso, sañudo** furious.

sapo m toad; F echar ~s y culebras swear black and blue.

saque m tenis etc.: service, serve; base line; (p.) server; ~ inicial kickoff; ~ de esquina corner kick; ~ de portería goal kick.

saqueador m looter; **saquear** [1a] loot, sack, plunder; fig. rifle ransack; **saqueo** m looting etc.

sarampión m measles.

sarcasmo m sarcasm; **sarcástico** sarcastic.

sardina f sardine.

sardo adj. a. su. m, a f Sardinian.

sargento m sergeant.

sarmiento m vine shoot.

sarna f itch, scabies; vet. mange.

sarro m incrustation; fur de vasija, lengua; tartar de dientes; **sarroso** furry; covered with tartar.

sarta f, **sartal** m string (a. fig.); line, series.

sartén f frying-pan.

sastre m tailor; ~ de teatro costumier; hecho por ~ tailor-made; **sastrería** f tailoring.

satélite 1. satellite; ~ de comunicaciones communications satellite; 2. m satellite (a. pol.); (p.) minion, henchman.

satén m sateen; **satinado** glossy.

sátira f satire; **satírico** satiric(al); **satirizar** [1f] satirize.

sátiro m satyr (a. fig.).

satisfacción f satisfaction; ~ de sí mismo self-satisfaction, smugness; a ~ to one's satisfaction; **satisfacer** [2s] mst satisfy; deuda pay; necesidad, petición meet; (dar placer a) gratify, please; ~se satisfy o.s., be satisfied; (vengarse) take revenge; **satisfactorio** satisfactory; **satisfecho** satisfied; pleased.

saturar [1a] saturate; permeate.

sauce m willow; ~ llorón weeping willow.

sazón f ripeness, maturity; (ocasión) season, time; a la ~ then, at that time; en ~ 🍏 ripe; **sazonado** 🍏 etc. mellow; plato tasty; frase witty; **sazonar** [1a] v/t. season, flavor; v/i. ripen.

se 1. pron. reflexivo: a) sg. himself, herself, itself; (con Vd.) yourself; pl. themselves (con Vds.) yourselves; b) recíproco: each other, one another; c) con inf.: oneself, e.g. hay que protegerse one must protect oneself; d)

impersonal: freq. se traduce por la voz pasiva, por one, por people: se dice que it is said that, people say that; no se sabe por qué it is not known why; se habla español Spanish (is) spoken here; 2. pron. personal que corresponde a le, les: se lo di I gave it to him; se lo buscaré I'll look for it for you.

sé v. saber, ser.

sebo m grease, fat; tallow para velas; suet para cocina; **seboso** greasy, fatty; tallowy; suety.

seca f drought; (época) dry season; (arena) sandbank; **secador** m: ~ para el pelo hair-dryer; **secadora** f wringer; **secano** m (a. tierras de ~) dry land, unirrigated land; region having little rain; ⚓ sandbank; fig. very dry thing; **secante** 1. drying; S.Am. annoying; papel ~ = 2. m blotting paper; **secar** [1g] dry (up); superficie wipe dry; frente wipe, mop; blot; mop up; ~se (río etc.) dry up, run dry; (p.) dry o.s.

sección f section; ⚓ (corte) cross-section; fig. section (a. ✂).

seco mst dry; legumbres etc. dried; planta dried-up; (flaco) lean; (áspero) sharp, harsh; golpe etc. sharp; (riguroso) strict; respuesta curt; estilo plain, bare.

secretaría f secretariat(e); (oficio) secretaryship; (oficina) secretary's office; **secretario** m, a f secretary; **secretear** [1a] F talk confidentially; **secreto** 1. secret; (no visible) hidden; 2. m secret; (lo ~) secrecy; (escondrijo) secret drawer.

secta f sect; denomination; **sectario** 1. sectarian; denominational; 2. m, a f follower, devotee.

secuaz m follower; partisan.

secuestrador m, -a f kidnapper; **secuestrar** [1a] kidnap; bienes seize; **secuestro** m kidnapping.

secular secular; (viejo) age-old, ancient; **secularización** f secularization; **secularizar** [1f] secularize.

secundar [1a] second, help; **secundario** mst secondary; minor.

sed f thirst (de for; a. fig.); apagar la ~ quench one's thirst; tener ~ be thirsty; fig. tener ~ de thirst for.

seda f silk; (cerda) bristle; (adv.) smoothly; **sedal** m fishing line.

sedante sedative; fig. soothing.

sede f eccl. see; seat de gobierno; headquarters de sociedad etc.; ~ social head office; Santa ⚲ Holy See.

S

sedeño silken; silky; **sedería** f silks, silk goods; (*comercio*) silk trade; **sedero** silk *attr.*

sedición f sedition; **sedicioso 1.** seditious; **2.** m, **a** f rebel.

sedimentar [1a] deposit (sediment); **~se** settle; **sedimentario** sedimentary; **sedimento** m sediment.

seducción f (*acto*) seduction *etc.*; (*aliciente*) lure, charm; **seducir** [3o] seduce; entice, lure, lead astray; (*cautivar*) charm; (*sobornar*) bribe; **seductivo** seductive; *fig.* captivating; **seductor 1.** = *seductivo*; **2.** m seducer.

segador m harvester, reaper; **segadora** f reaper; mower, mowing machine; **~-atadora** f binder; **~-trilladora** f combine (harvester); **~** de césped lawn mower; **segar** [1h a. 1k] *trigo etc.* reap, cut; *heno, hierba* mow; *fig.* cut off.

seglar 1. secular, lay; **2.** m layman.

segmento m segment.

segregación f segregation; **segregacionista** segregationist; **segregar** [1h] segregate.

seguida: de **~** uninterruptedly, straight off; en **~** at once, right away; **seguido** continued, successive; *camino etc.* straight; **~s** pl. in a row, in succession; *3 días* **~s** 3 days running; *todo* **~** adv. straight ahead; **seguimiento** m chase, pursuit; continuation; **seguir** [3d a. 3l] **1.** v/t. follow; (*cazar*) chase, pursue; (*acosar*) hound; *pasos* dog; *consejo* follow, take; *curso* pursue; continue; **2.** v/i. follow; come after, come next; go on, continue; (*caminar etc.*) proceed; *como sigue* as follows; **3.** **~se** follow, ensue; follow one another; *síguese que* it follows that.

según 1. prp. according to; in accordance with; **~** lo que dice from what he says; **~** este modelo on this model; **2.** adv. depending on circumstances; **~** (y como), **~** (y conforme) it (all) depends; **3.** cj. as; **~** esté el tiempo depending on the weather.

segunda f (**🎵**) second; **~** (*intención*) second (or veiled) meaning; hidden purpose; **segundante** m boxeo: second; **segundero** m second-hand; **segundo 1.** second; **2.** m second; **♟** mate; sin **~** unrivaled.

seguridad f safety, safeness; security; reliability; (*certeza*) certainty; **⚖** security, surety; **~** colectiva collective security; **~** contra incendios fire precautions; de **~** cinturón etc. safety *attr.*; **seguro 1.** (*sin peligro*) safe, sure; secure; (*confiable*) reliable, dependable; (*cierto*) certain, sure; (*firme*) stable, steady; ¿está Vd. **~**? are you sure?; estar **~** de que be sure that; **2.** m safety; certainty; confidence; **†** insurance; (*lugar*) safe place; tumbler of cerradura; **⚔** safetycatch; **⊕** pawl, catch; **~** de desempleo, **~** de desocupación unemployment insurance; **~** de enfermedad health insurance; **~** de incendios fire insurance; **~** social social insurance (or security); **~** de vida life insurance; (*póliza de*) **~** sobre la vida life insurance (policy); a buen **~**, de **~** surely, truly; sobre **~** without risk.

seis six (a. su.); (*fecha*) sixth; las **~** six o'clock; **seiscientos** six hundred.

seísmo m earthquake.

selección f selection (a. biol.); **♪ ~es** pl. selections; **seleccionador** m selector; **seleccionar** [1a] pick, choose; **selectivo** selective (a. radio); **selecto** calidad select, choice; obras etc. selected.

selladura f seal(ing); **sellar** [1a] seal; stamp con timbre etc.; **sello** m seal; signet; **☘** stamp; **†** brand, seal; *fig.* (*huella*) impression, mark; hallmark de calidad; **💊** capsule, pill; **~** fiscal revenue stamp.

selva f forest, wood(s); (*esp. tropical*) jungle; **selvático 🌿** wild; escena etc. sylvan; *fig.* rustic.

semáforo m semaphore; **🚦** signal; *mot.* traffic light.

semana f week; **semanal, semanario** adj. a. su. m weekly.

semántica f semantics.

semblante m lit. visage; *fig.* appearance, look; **semblanza** f biographical sketch.

sembradera f, **sembradora** f drill; **sembrado** m sown field; **sembrador** m, **-a** f sower; **sembradura** f sowing; **sembrar** [1k] sow; *fig.* sprinkle, scatter.

semejante 1. similar (a. ♣); **~s** pl. alike, similar; **~** a like; **2.** m fellow man, fellow creature; no tiene **~** it has no equal; **semejanza** f similarity, resemblance; **semejar(se)** [1a] be alike, be similar, resemble each other.

semen m semen; **semental 1.** caballo stud, breeding; **2.** m sire.

señor

semestral half-yearly; **semestre** *m* period of six months.

semi... semi...; half...; **~breve** *f* semibreve; **~círculo** *m* semicircle; **~conductor** *m* ⚡ semiconductor; **~corchea** *f* semiquaver; **~final** *f* semi-final.

semilla *f* seed; **semillero** *m* seedbed; nursery; *fig.* hotbed.

seminario *m* seminary; *univ.* seminar; ♀ seedbed; nursery.

semita 1. Semitic; **2.** *m/f* Semite; **semítico** Semitic.

sempiterna *f* evergreen; **sempiterno** everlasting.

senado *m* senate; **senador** *m* senator.

sencillez *f* simplicity *etc.*; **sencillo 1.** simple, easy; *billete,* ♀ single; *p. etc.* unsophisticated, natural; *b.s.* simple; *vestido, estilo etc.* simple, plain; **2.** *m S.Am.* loose change.

senda *f*, **sendero** *m* (foot)path, track, lane (*a. mot.*).

senil senile; **senilidad** *f* senility.

seno¹ *m* (*pecho*) breast; (*pechos*) bosom, bust; (*útero*) womb; (*frontal*) sinus; *fig.* bosom; lap; (*hueco*) hollow; *geog.* small bay.

seno² *m* ♈ sine.

sensación *f* sensation (*a. fig.*); sense, feeling; feel; thrill; **sensacional** sensational.

sensatez *f* good sense, sensibleness; **sensato** sensible.

sensibilidad *f* sensitivity (*a* to); **sensibilizado** *phot.* sensitive; sensitized; **sensible** (*que siente*) sensitive; *aparato etc.* sensitive; (*que se conmueve*) sensitive, responsive (*a* to); (*apreciable*) perceptible, noticeable; (*lamentable*) regrettable; *pérdida* considerable; ♣ tender, sore; *phot.* sensitive; **sensibilería** *f* sentimentality; **sensiblero** sentimental; **sensitiva** *f* mimosa; **sensitivo** *órgano etc.* sense *attr.*; sensitive; *ser* sentient; **sensual** sensual, sensuous; **sensualidad** *f* sensuality; **sensualismo** *m* sensualism; **sensualista** *m/f* sensualist.

sentada *f* sitting; *de una ~* at one sitting; **sentadero** *m* seat; **sentado** sitting, seated; (*establecido*) settled; permanent; *carácter* sedate; sensible; *dar por ~* take for granted, assume; *dejar ~* leave a clear impression of; **sentar** [1k] **1.** *v/t. p.* seat, sit; (*asentar*) set up, establish; **2.** *v/t. a. v/i.* (*vestido*) fit *por tamaño,*

suit *por estilo;* ~ *bien fig.* go down well; **3.** **~se** (*down*); settle (o.s.).

sentencia *f* ⚖ sentence; (*máxima*) dictum, saying; **sentenciar** [1b] *v/t.* ⚖ sentence (*a* to); *v/i.* pronounce, give one's opinion.

sentidamente regretfully; **sentido 1.** (*hondo*) heartfelt, keen; (*que se ofende*) sensitive; (*convincente*) moving, feeling; **2.** *m* (*facultad*) sense; (*significado*) sense, meaning; (*juicio*) sense, good sense; (*aprecio*) feeling (*de música* for); way, direction; ~ *común* common sense; *doble* ~ double meaning; *en cierto* ~ in a sense; *sin* ~ meaningless.

sentimental sentimental; *mirada* soulful; *aventura, vida etc.* love *attr.*; **sentimentalismo** *m* sentimentality; **sentimiento** *m* feeling; sentiment; (*pesar*) regret, regret.

sentir 1. [3i] *v/t.* feel; sense, perceive; (*oír*) hear; (*tener pesar*) regret, be sorry for; *lo siento* (*mucho*) I am (very or so) sorry; **~se** feel, *e.g.* ~ *enfermo* feel ill, ~ *obligado a* feel obliged to; **2.** *m* feeling; opinion; *a mi* ~ in my opinion.

seña *f* sign, token; mark *en cara etc.*; ✕ password; **~s** *pl.* address; **~s** *pl. personales* personal description; *por más* ~s to clinch the matter.

señal *f* sign, mark; (*indicio*) sign, token, indication; mark(ing) *de identidad;* brand *de animal;* sign, signal *con mano; radio, mot.*, 🚗 *etc.* signal; (*mojón*) landmark; bookmark *en libro;* 🌟 scar, mark; (*huella*) trace; ✝ deposit; (*prenda*) pledge(m token); ~ *de carretera* road sign; ~ *digital* fingerprint; ~ *horaria* time signal; **~s** *pl. luminosas,* **~es** *pl. de tráfico* traffic signales; ~ *para marcar* dial tone; ~ *de ocupado* busy signal; ~ *de peligro* danger signal; ✝ *en* ~ as a deposit; *en* ~ *de* as a token of; **señaladamente** especially; **señalado** notable, distinguished; **señalar** [1a] point out, point to, indicate *con dedo;* (*mostrar*) show; (*comunicar*) signal; mark, stamp; *animal* brand; denote; *fecha etc.* fix, set; *p. etc.* appoint, name; 🌟 leave a scar (on); **~se** *fig.* make one's mark.

señor *m* gentleman, man; (*dueño*) master, owner; (*noble, feudal, dueño fig.*) lord; *delante de apellido:* Mister (*escrito* Mr); *en trato directo:* sir; (*a noble*) my lord; *¡sí* ~*!* yes indeed!;

S

pues sí ~ well that's how it is; *El* ♀ The Lord; *muy* ~ *mío* Dear Sir; *hacer el* ~*es* pl. gentlemen; ✝ Messrs; *los* ~*es* Smith the Smiths.

señora *f* lady; (*dueña*) mistress, owner; (*noble*) lady; (*esposa*) wife; *delante de apellido:* Mrs ['misiz] *en trato directo:* madam; (*a noble*) my lady; *la* ~ *de* Smith Mrs Smith; *Nuestra* ♀ Our Lady *para católicos,* the Virgin (Mary) *para protestantes.*

señoría *f* rule, sway; lordship.

señorita *f* young lady; *delante de apellido:* Miss; *en trato directo* Miss. *no se traduce;* **señorito** *m* young gentleman; (*young*) master; (*de mucho mundo*) man about town; *contp.* playboy.

señuelo *m* decoy; *fig.* bait, lure.

separable separable; ⊕ detachable; **separación** *f* separation (*a.* ⚖); dismissal (*de puesto* from); ⊕ removal; *eccl.* disestablishment; ~ *del matrimonio* legal separation; **separado** separate; *esp.* ⊕ detached; *por* ~ separately; ✂ under separate cover; **separador** *m* separator; **separar** [1a] separate (*de* from); sever; divide; (*clasificar*) sort; *mueble etc.* move away (*de* from); ⊕ *pieza* remove, detach; (*despedir*) dismiss; ~*se* separate (*de* from); part company (*de* with); (*piezas*) come apart; retire, withdraw; (*estado etc.*) secede; **separata** *f* offprint.

septentrional north(ern).

se(p)tiembre *m* September.

sepulcral sepulchral (*a. fig.*); *fig.* gloomy, dismal; **sepulcro** *m* tomb, grave; (*Biblia*) sepulchre; **sepultar** [1a] bury; *fig.* entomb; *fig.* hide away; **sepultura** *f* (*acto*) burial; (*tumba*) grave; **sepulturero** *m* gravedigger, sexton.

sequedad *f* dryness *etc.*; **sequía** *f* drought; (*temporada*) dry season.

séquito *m* retinue, entourage; party.

ser 1. [2w] be; a) *identidad:* soy yo it's me, it is I *lit.;* *teleph.* ¡soy Pérez! Pérez speaking, this is Pérez; b) *origen:* yo soy de Madrid I am from Madrid; c) *materia:* la moneda es de oro it is a gold coin; d) *hora:* es la una it is one o'clock; son las 2 it is 2 o'clock; serán las 9 it will be about 9; serían las 9 it would be (*or* have been) about 9; e) *posesión:* el coche es de mi padre the car belongs to my father; f) *destino:* ¿qué ha sido de él? what has

become of him?; F ¿qué es de tu vida? what's the news?; g) *pasivo:* ha sido asesinado he has been murdered; h) *frases:* ~ *para poco* be of next to no use; *de no* ~ *así* were it not so; *a no* ~ *por* but for; were it not for; *a no* ~ *que* unless; *¡cómo ha de* ~*!* what else do you expect?; *es de esperar que* it is to be hoped that; *es de creer que* it may be assumed that; *es que* the fact is that; *soy con Vd.* I'll be with you in a moment; *siendo así que* so that; *o sea* that is to say, or rather; *sea ... sea* whether ... or whether; *sea lo que sea* (*or fuere*) be that as it may; *no sea que* lest; *érase que se era* once upon a time (there was); *era de ver* you ought to have seen it, it was worth seeing; *presidente que fue* expresident; former(ly) president; **2.** *m* being; (*vida*) life; essence; ~ *humano* human being.

serenar [1a] calm, quieten, pacify; *líquido* clarify; ~*se* grow calm; *meteor.* clear up; (*p.*) calm down.

serenidad *f* serenity *etc.*; **sereno**[1] serene, calm; *tiempo* settled, fine; *cielo* cloudless; *temperamento* even.

sereno[2] *m* (night) watchman; (*rocío*) dew; *al* ~ in the open (air).

serial *m* serial; **serie** *f* series (*a.* A, ⚡, *biol.*); sequence; set; soap opera, serial (on radio or TV); ⚡ *arrollado en* ~ series-wound.

seriedad *f* seriousness *etc.*; **serio** *mst* serious; grave; solemn; sober, staid; (*confiable*) reliable, trustworthy; (*justo*) fair, fair-minded; (*genuino*) true, real; *en* ~ seriously.

sermón *m* sermon (*a. iro.*); **sermonear** [1a] F *v/t.* lecture.

serpentear [1a] *zo.* wriggle, snake; (*camino*) wind; (*río*) wind, meander; **serpentín** *m* coil; **serpentino** snaky, sinous; winding; **serpiente** *f* snake; (*mitológica, fig.*) serpent; ~ *de cascabel* rattlesnake; ~ *de mar* sea serpent.

serraduras *f/pl.* sawdust.

serranía *f* hill country; **serrano 1.** highland; **2.** *m* highlander.

serrar [1k] saw; **serrín** *m* sawdust; **serruchar** [1a] *S.Am.* saw; **serrucho** *m* handsaw.

servible serviceable; **servicial** helpful, obliging; dutiful; **servicio** *m* service (*a.* ⚔, *eccl., hotel, tenis*); service, set *de vajilla;* *hotel:* service (charge); *S.Am.* lavatory; ~*s* pl. sanitation *de casa;* ~ *activo* active service;

~ de café coffee-set; ~ doméstico (domestic) service; domestic help; (ps.) servants; ~ militar military service; ~ postventa customer service; ~ social social service, welfare work; al ~ de in the service of; ✕ etc. de ~ on duty; ✕ en condiciones de ~ operational.

servidor m, **-a** f servant; un ~ my humble self; ~ de Vd. at your service; su seguro ~ yours faithfully; **servidumbre** f servitude; fig. self-control; compulsion; ~ de paso right of way; **servil** servile.

servilleta f serviette, napkin.

servir [3l] 1. v/t. mst serve; ps. a la mesa wait on; cargo carry out, fulfil; cañon man; máquina tend; (hacer un servicio a) do a favor to, oblige; ser servido de inf. be pleased to inf.; 2. v/i. serve (a. ✕, tenis; de as, for); (ser servible) be useful, be of use; 3. ~se help o.s. a la mesa; ~ de make use of; put to use.

sesear [1a] pronounce c (before e, i) and z [θ] as [s].

seseo m pronunciation of c (before e, i) and z [θ] as [s].

sesgado slanting, oblique; gorra etc. awry; **sesgar** [1h] slant, slope; (cortar) cut on the slant; sew. cut (on the) bias; ⊕ bevel; (torcer) twist to one side; **sesgo** m slant, slope; esp. sew. bias; (torcimiento) warp, twist; fig. (mental) twist, turn; fig. compromise; al ~ slanting; awry; cortar ~ on the bias.

sesión f session, sitting; ~ continua continuous showing; ~ de espiritismo séance; levantar la ~ adjourn.

seso m brain; fig. sense, brains; ~s pl. brains (a. cocina); devanarse los ~s rack one's brains.

sestear [1a] take a siesta (or nap).

sesudo sensible, wise.

seta f mushroom.

setiembre m September.

seto m fence; ~ (vivo) hedge.

seudo... pseudo...; **seudónimo** 1. pseudonymous; 2. m pseudonym.

severidad f severity etc.; **severo** mst severe; stringent, exacting.

sexo m sex; el bello ~ the fair sex; el ~ débil the gentle sex.

sextante m sextant.

sexto adj. a. su. m sixth.

sexual sexual; sex attr.; **sexualidad** f sexuality.

sí[1] 1. adv. yes; indeed; enfático etc.: él ~ fue he did go, he certainly went; por

~ o por no in any case; ¡eso ~ que no! not on any account!; un día ~ y otro no every other day; 2. m yes; consent; dar el ~ say yes.

sí[2] pron. sg. himself, herself, itself; (con Vd.) yourself; pl. themselves; (con Vds.) yourselves; recíproco: each other; ~ mismo himself etc.; (con inf.) oneself; de ~ in itself; spontaneous; de por ~ separately, individually; per se; in itself etc.; fuera de ~ beside o.s.

si cj. if; whether; ~ no if not; otherwise; ¿~...? what if...?, suppose...?; ¡~ fuera verdad! if only it were true!

siamés adj. a. su. m, **-a** f Siamese.

siderurgia f iron and steel industry; **siderúrgico** iron and steel attr.

sidra f cider.

siega f reaping, mowing; (época) harvest.

siembra f (acto) sowing; (campo) sown field; (época) sowing time; patata de ~ seed potato.

siempre always; all the time; ever; como ~ as usual; lo de ~ the same old thing; (de una vez) para ~ once and for all; para ~ for ever; ~ que indic. whenever, as often as; subj. provided that.

sien f anat. temple.

sierpe f snake, serpent.

sierra f ⊕ saw; geog. mountain range; ~ de arco (para metales), ~ de armero hacksaw; ~ cabrilla whip saw; ~ de calados fretsaw; ~ circular circular saw; buzz saw; ~ continua, ~ sin fin band saw; ~ de espigar tenon saw; ~ de vaivén jig saw.

siervo m, **a** f slave; serf; servant.

siesta f siesta, (afternoon) nap; (calor) hottest part of the day; dormir (or echar) la ~ take a nap.

siete seven (a. su.); (fecha) seventh; las ~ seven o'clock; F hablar más que ~ talk nineteen to the dozen.

sífilis f syphilis; **sifilítico** syphilitic.

sifón m siphon; ⊕ trap.

sigilo m secrecy, discretion; **sigiloso** discreet, secret; reserved.

sigla f symbol, abbreviation.

siglo m century; (mucho tiempo) age; (época) age, time(s); eccl. world; ♀ de Oro Golden Age.

signarse [1a] cross o.s.; **signatura** f typ., ♪ signature; (catalogue)number de biblioteca.

significación f significance; **significado** 1. S.Am. well-known; important; 2. m meaning de palabra;

intention; (*importancia*) significance; **significante** significant; **significar** [1g] v/t. (*hacer saber*) make known, signify; (*querer decir*) mean (*para to*), signify; v/i. be important; **significativo** significant; *mirada etc.* meaning, expressive.

signo m mst sign; ♀ a. symbol; mark *en lugar de firma*; ~ de admiración exclamation mark; ~ de interrogación question mark.

sigo etc. v. seguir.

siguiente next, following.

sílaba f syllable; **silábico** syllabic.

silba f hiss(ing), catcall; **silbar** [1a] v/t. melodía whistle; *silbato* blow; v/i. ♪ etc. whistle; (*bala etc.*) whine; **silbato** m whistle; **silbido** m, **silbo** m whistle; whistling; hiss.

silenciador m silencer; **silenciar** [1b] *hecho* keep silent about; p. silence; **silencio** m silence; quiet; hush; ♪ rest; ¡~! quiet!; **silencioso** 1. silent, quiet; soundless; *esp.* ⊕ noiseless; 2. m ⊕ muffler, silencer.

silla f (*en general*) seat; (*mueble*) chair; ~ (*de montar*) saddle; ~ eléctrica electric chair; ~ de manos sedan chair; ~ plegadiza, ~ de tijera camp stool, folding chair; ~ de ruedas wheel chair.

sillón m armchair, easy chair; ~ (*de montar*) side saddle; ~ de orejas wing chair.

silueta f silhouette; skyline *de ciudad*; (*talle de p.*) figure.

silvestre *esp.* ♀ wild; uncultivated; *fig.* rustic; **silvicultura** f forestry.

sima f abyss, pit; chasm.

simbolismo m symbolism; **simbolizar** [1f] symbolize; **símbolo** m symbol; *eccl.* creed.

simetría f symmetry; *fig.* harmony; **simétrico** symmetrical.

símil 1. similar; 2. m simile; comparison; **similar** similar; **similitud** f similarity, resemblance.

simpatía f (*afecto*) liking (*hacia, por* for), friendliness (*hacia, por* towards); congeniality *de ambiente*; (*correspondencia*) sympathy; fellowfeeling; (*lo atractivo*) charm; (*no*) tener ~ a (dis)like; **simpático** p. nice, likeable; pleasant; *ambiente* congenial, agreeable; ⚕, *phys. etc.* sympathetic; **simpatizante** m/f sympathizer (de with); **simpatizar** [1f] get on well together; ~ con p. get on

well with; *carácter etc.* harmonize with, be congenial to.

simple 1. mst simple; (*no doble*) single; (*incauto*) gullible, simple; (*corriente*) ordinary; por ~ descuido through sheer carelessness; 2. m simpleton; ♀ ~s pl. simples; **simpleza** f silliness; (*acto etc.*) silly thing; (*pequeñez*) mere trifle; decir ~s talk nonsense; **simplificar** [1g] simplify; **simplón** F 1. gullible, simple; 2. m, -a f simple soul.

simulación f simulation; **simulacro** m image, idol; (*fantasma*) vision; **simular** [1a] simulate; feign, sham.

simultáneo simultaneous.

sin without; with no; ...less; un...; apart from, not counting; ~ gasolina out of petrol; ~ sombrero without a hat, hatless; ~ inf. without ger.; ~ hablar without speaking; ~ almidonar unstarched; ~ lavar unwashed; *cuenta* ~ pagar bill to be paid, unpaid bill; ~ que subj. without ... ger.

sinagoga f synagogue.

sinceridad f sincerity; **sincero** sincere; genuine, heartfelt.

síncopa f ♪ syncopation; *gr.* syncope; **síncope** [1a] syncopate.

sincronizar [1f] synchronize.

sindicar [1g] syndicate; *propiedad* put in trust; **sindicato** m syndicate; (*laboral*) labor union; **síndico** m trustee; (*quiebra*) receiver.

sinfonía f symphony; **sinfónico** symphonic.

singular 1. mst singular (a. gr.); (*destacado*) outstanding; *combate* single; (*raro*) peculiar, odd; 2. m gr. singular; **singularidad** f singularity, peculiarity etc.; **singularizar** [1f] single out; ~se stand out, distinguish o.s.; be conspicuous.

siniestrado disaster; damaged; hurt by an accident.

siniestro 1. left; *fig.* sinister; (*funesto*) disastrous; 2. m accident, catastrophe, disaster.

sinnúmero: un ~ de a great many, a great amount of.

sino[1] m fate, destiny.

sino[2] ... (*chino*) sino...

sino[3] but; except; ~ que but.

sinónimo 1. synonymous; 2. m synonym.

sinrazón f wrong, injustice.

sinsabor m trouble, unpleasantness; (*pesar*) sorrow.

sintaxis f syntax.

síntesis *f* synthesis; **sintético** synthetic(al); **sintetizar** [1f] synthesize.

síntoma *m* symptom; sign; **sintomático** symptomatic.

sintonía *f radio:* tuning; ♪ signature tune; **sintonización** *f* tuning; **sintonizar** [1f] *radio:* tune; *programa* tune in to; ⚡ syntonize.

sinuoso winding, sinuous; wavy.

siquiera 1. *adv.* at least; *dame un beso* ~ give me a kiss at least; *ni* ~ not even, not so much as; *ni me besó* ~ he didn't even kiss me; *tan* ~ even; **2.** *cj.* even if, even though.

sirena *f (p.)* mermaid; *(clásica)* siren; ♪ siren; ~ *de la playa* bathing beauty; ~ *de niebla* foghorn.

sirvienta *f* servant, maid; **sirviente** *m* servant; waiter.

sisa *f* petty theft; *sew.* dart; **sisar** [1a] pilfer; *sew.* put darts in, take in.

sisear [1a] hiss; **siseo** *m* hiss.

sísmico seismic; **sismógrafo** *m* seismograph.

sistema *m mst* system; method; framework; **sistemático** systematic; **sistematizar** [1f] systematize.

sitiar [1b] besiege; *S.Am.* surround, hem in; **sitio** *m (lugar determinado)* place, spot; site, location; *(espacio)* room; ✗ siege; *situación f* situation; position; location, locality; *(social)* position, standing; *S.Am. precios de* ~ bargain prices; **situado** situated, placed; **situar** [1e] place, put, set; *esp. edificio* locate; ✗ *etc.* post, station; ~se take place.

slogan [ez'logan] *m* slogan.

so¹ *prp.* under.

¡so!² whoa!

sobaco *m* armpit; armhole *de vestido.*

sobar [1a] *masa etc.* knead; squeeze; F *(zurrar)* tan; F *(manosear)* paw, finger, feel; *Am. huesos* set; *(novios, a.* ~) pet, cuddle.

soberanía *f* sovereignty; **soberano** *adj. a. su. m, a f* sovereign.

soberbia *f* pride *etc.*; **soberbio** *(orgulloso)* proud; arrogant; magnificent, grand; *(colérico)* angry.

sobra *f* excess, surplus; ~s *pl.* leftovers; scraps; *de* ~ *(adj.)* surplus, extra; *(adv.)* more than enough; **sobradamente** too; (only) too well; **sobradillo** *m* penthouse; **sobrado 1.** excessive, more than enough; *p.* wealthy; **2.** *m* attic, garret.

sobrante 1. spare, extra; surplus; **2.** *m*

surplus *(a.* ✝); ✝ balance in hand; margin; **sobrar** [1a] *v/t.* exceed, surpass; *v/i.* be left over; remain; be more than enough.

sobre¹ *m* envelope; letter cover; *(señas)* address.

sobre² on, upon; on top of; *(encima de)* over, above; *(acerca de)* about; *1* ~ *4* 1 in 4; ~ *las 5* about 5 o'clock.

sobre³... super...; over...; ~**abundante** superabundant; ~**abundar** [1a] superabound *(en in,* with); ~**alimentado** ⊕ supercharged; ~**alimentador** *m* ⊕ supercharger; ~**alimentar** [1a] ⊕ supercharge; *p.* overfeed; ~**calentar** [1k] overheat; ~**cama** *f* bedspread; ~**carga** *f* extra load; *(soga)* rope; ✝ surcharge; ~**cargar** [1h] *carro* overload; ✝ *etc.* overcharge; ✝, ⚓ surcharge; ~**cargo** *m* ⚓ supercargo; ~**cejo** *m*, ~**ceño** *m* frown.

sobrecoger [2c] startle, (take by) surprise; ~**se** be startled, start *(a* at, *de* with); *(achicarse)* be overawed.

sobre...: ~**cubierta** *f* outer cover; jacket *de libro*; ~**dicho** above (-mentioned); ~**dorar** [1a] gild; *fig.* gloss over; ~**dosis** *f* overdose; ~**estimar** overestimate.

sobre(e)ntender [2g] understand; deduce, infer; ~**se** be implied *etc.*

sobre...: ~**(e)xcitado** overexcited; ~**(e)xcitar** [1a] overexcite; ~**(e)xponer** [2r] *phot.* overexpose; ~**faz** *f* surface, outside; ~**giro** *m* overdraft; ~**haz** *f* = ~*faz*; *(cubierta)* cover; ~**humano** superhuman; ~**llevar** [1a] (help to) carry; *fig. carga de otro* ease; *molestias* bear, endure; *faltas de otro* be tolerant towards; ~**manera** exceedingly; ~**marcha** *f mot.* overdrive; ~**mesa** *f (tapete)* table cover; *(postre)* dessert; *(tiempo)* sitting on after a meal; *de* ~ *charla etc.* after-dinner; *reloj etc.* table *attr.*; ~**nadar** [1a] float; ~**natural** supernatural; unearthly, weird; *ciencia* occult; ~**nombre** *m* nickname.

sobre...: ~**paga** *f* rise, bonus; ~**parto** *m* ⚕ confinement; *morir de* ~ die in childbirth; ~**pasar** [1a] surpass; *límite* exceed; *marca* beat; ✗ *pista* overshoot; ~**pelliz** *f* surplice; ~**peso** *m* overweight; ~**población** *f* overcrowding.

sobreponer [2r] put on top, put *one thing* on *another*, superimpose; ~**se** *fig.* pull o.s. together; make the best

S

of a bad job; ~ a dificultad overcome; rival etc. triumph over.

sobre...: ~precio m surcharge; **~producción** f overproduction; **~puesto** 1. superimposed; 2. m addition; **~pujar** [1a] outdo; outbid.

sobrero extra, spare.

sobre...: ~saliente 1. outstanding, brilliant; 2. m/f substitute; thea. understudy; 3. m distinction; **~salir** [3r] ⚠ etc. project, jut out; stick out (or up~), potrude; fig. stand out, excel (en at).

sobresaltar [1a] fall upon, rush at; (asustar etc.) startle; shock; **~se** start, be startled (con, de at); **sobresalto** m shock; de ~ suddenly.

sobre...: ~sanar [1a] 🦵 heal superficially; defecto hide, gloss over; **~scrito** m superscription; address en carta; **~stante** m overseer; foreman; **~stimar** [1a] overestimate; **~sueldo** m extra pay, bonus; **~tasa** f surcharge; **~todo** m overcoat; **~venir** [3s] supervene, ensue; happen (unexpectedly); **~viviente** 1. surviving; 2. m/f survivor; **~vivir** [3a] survive; ~ a survive; outlive; outlast; **~volar** [1m] fly over.

sobriedad f sobriety etc.

sobrina f niece; **sobrino** m nephew.

sobrio sober, moderate; temperate.

socarrón sly, crafty, artful; (guasón) mocking, with sly humor; malicious; **socarronería** f slyness.

socavón m 🔨 mine gallery, tunnel; hole en calle; ⚠ sudden collapse.

social social; ✝ company attr.; **~cialismo** m socialism; **socialista** adj. a. su. m/f socialist; **socializar** [1f] socialize, nationalize.

sociedad f society; association; ✝ company, firm; ✝ etc. partnership de dos ps.; alta ~, buena ~ (high) society; ~ anónima stock company, corporation; Pérez y García ⚲ Anónima Pérez y García Limited (Incorporated); ~ de control holding company; ⚲ de las Naciones League of Nations; ~ secreta secret society; ~ de socorro mutuo friendly (or provident) society.

socio m, a f member de club etc.; fellow de sociedad científica etc.; ✝ partner; ✝ associate; ~ de honor, ~ honorario honorary member; ~ de número full member; **sociología** f sociology; **sociológico** sociological; **sociólogo** m sociologist.

socorrer [2a] help; necesidades, ciudad relieve; **socorrido** p. etc. helpful, cooperative; cosa útil handy; (bien provisto) well-stocked; (trillado) hackneyed; **socorrismo** m first aid; **socorro** m help, aid; relief (a. ✖); ¡~! help!

soda f 🥃 soda; (bebida) soda(-water).

soez dirty, obscene; crude.

sofá m sofa; **~cama** m day bed.

sofistería f (piece of) sophistry; **sofisticación** ⊕ sophistication; **sofisticado** p. etc. sophisticated; ⊕ sophisticated; **sofístico** sophistic, sophistical; false, fallacious.

sofocación f suffocation; fig. vexation; annoying rebuff; **sofocante** stifling, suffocating; **sofocar** [1g] choke, stifle, suffocate; incendio smother, put out; fig. make s.o. blush; (irritar) make s.o. angry; F bother; **~se** choke etc.; (corriendo etc.) get out breath; fig. flush, get embarrassed; (encolerizarse) get hot under the collar; **sofoco** m embarrassment.

sofrenar [1a] rein back suddenly; fig. restrain; F bawl out.

soga f rope; halter; F dar ~ a make fun of.

soja f soya; semilla de ~ soya bean.

sojuzgar [1h] subjugate, subdue.

sol m sun; sunshine, sunlight; de ~ a ~ sunny; de ~ a ~ from sunrise to sunset; hacer ~ be sunny.

solamente only; solely.

solana f sunny spot; (cuarto) sun lounge; **solanera** f 🦵 sunburn.

solapa f lapel; flap de sobre; fig. excuse; **solapado** sly, sneaky; **solapar** [1a] fig. v/t. overlap; (ocultar) cover up, keep dark; v/i. overlap; **~se** get hidden underneath; **solapo** m sew. lapel; overlap; F a ~ by underhand methods.

solar[1] m ⚠ lot, site, piece of ground; (casa) ancestral home, family seat; Am. backyard.

solar[2] solar, sun attr.

solar[3] [1m] calzado sole; suelo floor.

solariego casa ancestral; familia ancient and noble; hist. manorial.

solario m sun porch.

solaz m relaxation, recreation; (consuelo) solace; **solazar** [1f] give relaxation to, amuse; (consolar) solace, comfort; **~se** enjoy o.s., amuse o.s.

soldado m soldier; ~ de a pie foot soldier; ~ de infantería infantryman; ~ de juguete toy soldier; ~ de marina

son

marine; ~ de *plomo* tin soldier; ~ de *primera* private first class; ~ *raso* buck private.

soldador *m* soldering-iron; (*p.*) welder; **soldadura** *f* (*metal*) solder; (*acto*) soldering, welding; (*juntura*) soldered joint, welded seam; ~ *autógena* welding; **soldar** [1a] ⊕ solder, weld; *fig.* join; *disputa* patch up; correct; **~se** (*huesos*) knit.

soleado sunny; sunned.

soledad *f* solitude; loneliness; (*lugar*) lonely place.

solemne solemn; dignified; grave, weighty; F *error* terrible; **solemnidad** *f* solemnity *etc.*; (*acto*) solemn ceremony; formalities; **solemnizar** [1f] solemnize; celebrate.

soler [2h; *defective*]: ~ *inf.* be in the habit of *ger.*; *suele venir a las 5 he* generally (or usually) comes at 5; *solía hacerlo* I used to do it; *como se suele* as is customary.

solicitador *m*, **-a** *f*, **solicitante** *m/f* applicant; petitioner; **solicitar** [1a] request, solicit (*algo a* th.; *algo a alguien* a th. of a p.); *puesto etc.* apply for, put in for; **solícito** diligent, careful; solicitous (*por* about, for); **solicitud** *f* care, concern; (*acto, petición*) request; application (*de puesto* for); *a* ~ on request, on demand.

solidaridad *f* solidarity; **solidario** jointly liable; jointly binding; ~ *de* integral with; **solidez** *f* solidity *etc.*; **solidificar(se)** [1g] solidify; harden; **sólido** 1. solid (*a.* ♣, *fig.*); stable, firm; (*robusto*) strong, stout; hard; *aspecto* solid, massive; (*duradero*) solid, lasting; *argumento* sound; *color* fast; 2. *m* solid.

soliloquiar [1b] soliloquize, talk to o.s.; **soliloquio** *m* soliloquy, monologue.

solista *m/f* soloist.

solitaria *f* tapeworm; **solitario** 1. solitary; desolate, lonely, bleak; *en* ~ solo; 2. *m*, **a** *f* (*p.*) recluse, hermit; 3. *m* solitaire.

sollozar [1f] sob; **sollozo** *m* sob.

solo 1. (*único*) only, sole; (*sin compañía*) alone, by o.s.; single; (*solitario*) lonely; ♪ solo; *a solas* by o.s., alone; 2. *m* ♪, *naipes*: solo.

sólo only, solely; just; *tan* ~ only.

soltar [1m] (*desatar*) untie, unfasten; (*aflojar*) loose(n), slacken; (*desenmarañar*) free; (*dejar caer*) drop, let

go of; *mano etc.* release; (*poner en libertad*) release, let go, (set) free; *animal etc.* let out, let (or set, turn) loose; *amarras* cast off; *carcajada* let out; *dificultad* solve; ⊕ *embrague* disengage, *freno* release; *exclamación* let out; *golpe* let fly; *injurias* utter, let fly (a string of); *presa* let go of; **~se** (*pieza*) (*aflojarse*) work loose; (*desprenderse*) come off, come undone.

soltera *f* spinster, unmarried woman; **soltero** 1. single, unmarried; 2. *m* bachelor, unmarried man; **solterón** *m* old (or confirmed) bachelor; **solterona** *f* spinster, maiden lady; *contp.* old maid.

soltura *f* (*acto*) release *etc.*; ⊕ looseness *de pieza*; agility, freedom of movement; ease, fluency; ♣ ~ *de vientre* looseness of the bowels.

soluble soluble; **solución** *f mst* solution; answer (*de problema* to); **solucionar** [1a] (re)solve.

solventar [1a] † settle, pay; *dificultad* resolve; **solvente** *adj.* (♥) *a. su. m* (♠) solvent; (*juicioso*) discerning; credible, believable.

sombra *f* (*que proyecta un objeto*) shadow; (*para resguardarse del sol*; *luz y* ~) shade; (*oscuridad*) darkness, shadow(s); (*fantasma*) ghost, shade; *fig.* shadow *de duda etc.*; **sombraje** *m*, **sombrajo** *m* shelter from the sun; **sombreado** *m* shading; **sombrear** [1a] shade; *fig.* overshadow.

sombrerera *f* milliner; (*caja*) hatbox; **sombrerería** *f* millinery, hats; (*tienda*) hat shop; **sombrerero** *m* hatter; **sombrero** *m* hat; headgear; ~ *de candil*, ~ *de tres picos* three-cornered hat, cocked hat; ~ *de copa* top hat; ~ *flexible* soft hat, trilby; ~ *gacho* slouch hat; ~ *hongo* derby; ~ *de paja* straw hat; ~ *de pelo Am.* high hat.

sombrilla *f* parasol, sunshade.

sombrío shady; *fig.* sombre, dismal; *p.* gloomy, morose.

somero superficial, shallow.

someter [2a] *informe etc.* submit, present; conquer; ~ *a prueba etc.* subject to; **~se** yield, submit.

somnámbulo *m*, **a** *f* sleepwalker; **somnífero** sleep inducing; **somnolencia** *f* sleepiness.

son *m* (pleasant) sound; *fig.* news, rumor; *¿a qué* ~?, *¿a* ~ *de qué* why?; *a* ~ *de* to the sound of; *en* ~ *de* like, as, in the manner of; **sonado** famous; sensational.

sonaja f little bell; **sonajear** [1a] jingle; **sonajero** m rattle.

sonámbulo 1. adj. moonstruck; 2. m sleepwalker.

sonar [1m] 1. v/t. sound; campana ring; ♪ play; sirena, narices blow; 2. v/i. sound; (campana) ring; ♪ play; (reloj) strike; gr. be pronounced; F fig. sound familiar, ring a bell; ~ a sound like; ~ a hueco sound hollow; 3. ~se (a. ~ las narices) blow one's nose; se suena que it is rumored that.

sonda f (acto, medida) sounding; (instrumento) ♣ lead; ⊕ bore; ♂ probe; **sondaje** m ♣ sounding; ⊕ boring; fig. de ~ exploratory; organismo de ~ public opinion poll; **sond(e)ar** [1a] ♣ sound, take soundings of; probe, sound; ⊕ drill, bore into; fig. terreno explore; p., intenciones sound out; **sondeo** m sounding etc.; fig. (encuesta) poll, inquiry; pol. etc. feeler, overture.

sonido m sound (a. gr., phys.); noise; ~ silencioso ultrasound.

sonorizar(se) [1f] gr. voice; **sonoro** sonorous; loud, resounding.

sonreír(se) [3m] smile (de at); **sonriente** smiling; **sonrisa** f smile.

sonrojarse [1a] blush, flush (de at); **sonrojo** m blush(ing).

sonrosado rosy, pink.

sonsacar [1g] remove s.t. surreptitiously (or craftily); p. entice away; fig. p. pump, draw out.

sonsonete m (golpecitos) tapping; din, jangling, rumbling; fig. singsong, chant; (frase con rima) jingle.

soñar [1m] dream (con about, of; con inf. of ger.); **soñera** f drowsiness; **soñoliento** sleepy, drowsy.

sopa f soup; sop en leche; F hecho una ~ soaked to the skin.

sopapo m F punch; slap; tap.

sopetón m punch; de ~ unexpectedly; entrar de ~ rush in, drop in.

soplar [1a] 1. v/t. (apartar) blow away; blow up, inflate; fig. inspire; (apuntar) prompt, help s.o. along with; (robar) pinch; F (zampar) hog, guzzle; sl. split on; 2. v/i. blow (a viento); puff; sl. split (contra on), blab; **soplete** m blowlamp, torch; ~ oxiacetilénico oxyacetylene burner; **soplido** m = **soplo** m blow(ing), puff de boca; puff, gust de viento; esp. ⊕ blast; fig. instant; F (aviso) tip; F

(delación) tales; = **soplón** m, -a f F (niño) tell-tale; informer de policía.

soportal m porch; ~es pl. arcade con tiendas; colonnade.

soportar [1a] (apoyar) carry, hold up; (aguantar) endure, bear, stand; **soporte** m support; mount(ing).

sorber [2a] sip; (chupar) suck (in); ~ (por las narices) sniff; medicamento inhale; absorb, soak up; (tragar) swallow (up); **sorbete** m sherbet; (bebida) iced fruit drink; **sorbo** m sip; gulp, swallow; sniff.

sordera f, **sordez** f deafness.

sórdido nasty, dirty; fig. mean.

sordina f ♪ mute, muffler.

sordo 1. p. deaf (a. fig.); (silencioso) quiet, noiseless; sonido muffled, dull; gr. voiceless; a la ~a, a ~as noiselessly; 2. m, a f deaf person; **sordomudo** 1. deaf and dumb; 2. m, a f deaf-mute.

sorprendente surprising; amazing; startling; **sorprender** [2a] (maravillar) surprise; amaze; (sobresaltar) startle; (coger desprevenido) (take by) surprise, catch; conversación overhear; secreto discover; ~se be surprised (de at); **sorpresa** f surprise; ¡qué ~!, ¡vaya ~! what a surprise!; coger de ~ take by surprise; ✕ coger por ~ surprise; **sorpresivo** surprising.

sortear [1a] v/t. rifar) raffle; deportes etc.: toss up for; (evitar) dodge; v/i. toss up; draw lots.

sortija f ring; curl, ringlet de pelo; ~ de sello signet ring.

sortilegio m spell, charm; (brujería) sorcery; fortunetelling.

sosa f soda.

sosegado quiet, calm, peaceful; gentle; restful; **sosegar** [1h a. 1k] v/t. calm (down); reassure; dudas allay; v/i. rest; ~se calm down.

sosiego m quiet(ness), calm, peace, peacefulness.

soslayar [1a] put s.t. sideways, place s.t. obliquely; dificultad get round; pregunta dodge; **soslayo**: al ~, de ~ obliquely; at a slant, sideways; mirada sidelong.

soso tasteless, insipid; (sin azúcar) unsweetened; fig. dull, flat.

sospecha f suspicion; **sospechar** [1a] v/t. suspect; v/i.: ~ suspect, have one's suspicions about; **sospechoso** 1. suspicious; (no confiable) suspect; 2. m, a f suspect.

s

sostén *m* △ *etc.* support, prop; stay; stand; *bra(ssière) de mujer*; *fig.* support, prop; **sostener** [2l] △, ⊕ support, hold up; *lo inestable* prop up; *peso* bear; *carga* carry; *fig.* sustain (*a.* ♪); (*entretener*) maintain; (*tolerar*) bear; *p. etc.* sustain *con comida*; maintain *con dinero*; *opinión* uphold; *proposición* maintain; *presión* keep up, sustain; *resistencia* bolster up; ~ *que* hold that; **~se** support o.s. *etc.*; (*perdurar*) last (out); ~ (*en pie*) stand up; **sostenimiento** *m* support; maintenance *etc.*

sota *f* jack, knave.

sotana *f* cassock; F hiding.

sótano *m* basement; (*almacén*) cellar.

soterrar [1k] bury; *fig.* hide away.

soto *m* thicket; copse; grove.

soya *f Am.* soy bean.

su, sus (*un poseedor*) his, hers, its, one's; (*de Vd.*) your; (*varios poseedores*) their; (*de Vds.*) your.

suave (*blando*) soft; (*liso*) smooth; (*dulce, agradable*) sweet; *aire* soft, mild; *carácter* gentle, docile; **suavidad** *f* softness *etc.*; **suavizar** [1f] soften; (*alisar*) smooth (out), smooth; *fig. dureza* ease, soften; temper; relax; *color* tone down.

sub... *mst* sub...; under...

subalimentado undernourished.

subalterno 1. subordinate; auxiliary; **2.** *m* subordinate.

subasta *f* auction sale, (sale by) auction; **subastador** *m* auctioneer; **subastar** [1a] auction (off).

subcomisión *f* subcommittee.

subconsciencia *f* subconsciousness.

subconsciente subconscious.

subdesarrollado underdeveloped.

súbdito *adj. a. su. m*, **a** *f* subject.

subestimar [1a] *capacidad, contrario* underestimate, underrate; *propiedad* undervalue.

subida *f* (*acto*) climb(ing) *etc.*; (*cuesta*) slope, hill; (*aumento*) rise, increase; promotion; **subido** *color* bright; *olor* strong; *precio* high, stiff; *calidad* superior; ~ *de color cara* florid, rosy; flushed.

subir [3a] **1.** *v/t.* (*levantar*) raise, lift up; (*llevar*) take up; get up; *escalera* climb, go up; *montaña* climb; *p.* promote; *precio, sueldo* raise, put up; ✝ *artículo* put up the price of; ♪ raise the pitch of; **2.** *v/i.* go up, come up; move up; climb; (*aumentarse*) rise, increase; (*precio, río, temperatura*)

rise; (*fiebre*) get worse; (*ser ascendido*) rise, move up; ~ *a* (*precio*) come to; **3. ~se** rise, go up; ~ *a*, ~ *en* get into *etc.*

súbito sudden; *de* ~ suddenly.

sublevación *f* (up)rising; **sublevar** [1a] stir up a revolt among; **~se** rise, revolt.

sublime sublime; high, lofty; noble; grand; *lo* ~ the sublime; **subliminal** subliminal.

submarinismo *m* scuba diving; **submarinista** *m/f* scuba diver; **submarino 1.** underwater; **2.** *m* submarine.

subnormal (mentally) retarded.

subordinado *adj. a. su. m*, **a** *f* subordinate; **subordinar** [1a] subordinate.

subproducto *m* by-product.

subrayar [1a] underline (*a. fig.*); *lo subrayado es mío* my italics.

subrepticio surreptitious.

subsanar [1a] *falta* overlook; *error* put right; *pérdida* make up.

subscr... *v. suscr...*

subsidiarias *f/pl.* feeder industries.

subsidiario subsidiary.

subsidio *m* subsidy, grant; aid; (*de seguro social*) benefit; ~ *familiar* family allowance; ~ *de paro* unemployment insurance; ~ *de vejez* old-age pension.

subsiguiente subsequent.

subsistir [3a] (*vivir*) subsist, live; (*existir aún*) endure, last (out); (*ley etc.*) be still in force; (*edificio*) still stand.

subst... *v. sust...*

subsuelo *m* subsoil.

subterfugio *m* subterfuge; way out.

subterráneo 1. underground, subterranean; **2.** *m* cavern; cellar.

subtítulo *m* subtitle, subhead(ing); caption.

suburbano suburban; **suburbio** *m* suburb; *b.s.* outlying slum.

subvención *f* subsidy, grant; **subvencionar** [1a] subsidize, aid.

subversión *f* subversion; (*acto*) overthrow; **subversivo** subversive; **subvertir** [3i] subvert; *orden* disturb; undermine.

subyacente underlying.

subyugar [1h] subdue, subjugate; overpower; dominate.

succión *f* suction; **succionar** [1a] suck; apply suction to.

suceder [2a] (*ocurrir*) happen; (*se-*

guir) succeed, follow; (_heredar_) inherit; ~ _a p._ succeed; _puesto, trono_ succeed to; _bienes_ inherit; **~se** follow one another; **sucesión** _f_ sucession (_a to_), sequence; (_hijos_) issue, offspring; **sucesivamante** successively; _y así_ ~ and so on; **sucesivo** successive; consecutive; _en lo_~ in the future; (_desde entonces_) thereafter; **suceso** _m_ event, happening; incident; (_resultado_) outcome; **sucesor** _m_, **-a** _f_ successor.

suciedad _f_ dirt(iness) etc.; (_palabra_) dirty word, obscene remark.

sucinto succinct, concise.

sucio dirty, filthy; grimy, grubby, soiled; _fig._ dirty, obscene.

sucumbir [3a] succumb (_a to_).

sucursal _f_ branch (office); subsidiary.

sud _m_ south; **sudamericano** _adj. a. su. m_, **a** _f_ South American.

sudar [1a] sweat (_a._ F).

sudor _m_ sweat (_a. fig._); **sudoriento, sudo(ro)so** sweaty, sweating.

suegra _f_ mother-in-law; **suegro** _m_ father-in-law.

suela _f_ sole; sole leather.

sueldo _m_ salary, pay; _a_ ~ on a salary; _gangster_ hired, on a contract (to kill).

suelo _m_ (_tierra_) ground, soil, land; (_superficie de la tierra_) ground; (_piso_) floor; (_material de piso_) flooring; _bottom de vasija_; hoof _de caballo_; ~ _natal_ native land.

suelto 1. (_no atado_) loose, free; (_libre_) free, at large; (_sin trabas_) unhampered; (_separado_) detached, unattached; (_no en serie_) odd, separate; _ejemplar, número_ single; _fig._ (_ligero_) light, quick; (_hábil_) expert; (_libre, atrevido_) free, daring; _estilo_ easy, fluent; _verso_ blank; 2. _m_ small change; news item.

sueño _m_ sleep; (_fantasía_) dream (_a. fig._); _en(tre)_ ~s in a dream; ~ _hecho realidad_ dream come true; ~s _dorados_ daydreams.

suero _m_ ✚ serum; whey _de leche_.

suerte _f_ (_good_) luck; fortune, chance; (_hado_) fate, destiny, lot; condition, state; (_género_) kind; _toros_: stage; (_capa_) play with the cape; ~s _pl._ juggling; _buena_ ~ (good) luck; _mala_ ~ bad luck, hard luck; _de mala_ ~ unlucky; _de_ ~ _que_ so that; (_en principio de frase_) (and) so; _por_ ~ luckily; by chance.

suéter _m_ jumper, sweater.

suficiencia _f_ adequacy, fitness; (_aire de_) ~ self-importance; smugness, self-satisfaction; **suficiente** enough, sufficient; (_apto_) adequate, fit; _b.s._ smug, self-satisfied, superior.

sufijo _m_ suffix.

sufragar [1h] _v/t._ aid, support; ✚ defray (the costs of); _v/i. S.Am._ vote; **sufragio** _m_ (_derecho de votar_) suffrage, franchise; (_voto_) vote; ballot; (_ayuda_) aid; ~ _universal_ universal suffrage.

sufrido 1. patient, long-suffering; _color, tela etc._ hard-wearing; _marido_ complaisant; 2. _m_ F complaisant husband; **sufrimiento** _m_ patience; tolerance; (_padecimiento_) suffering, misery; **sufrir** [3a] _v/t._ (_padecer_) suffer; _pérdida_ suffer, sustain; (_experimentar_) undergo, experience; (_soportar_) bear, put up with; _v/i._ suffer.

sugerencia _f_ suggestion; **sugerir** [3i] suggest; hint; _pensamiento etc._ prompt; **sugestión** _f_ suggestion; hint; **sugestionar** [1a] hypnotize; **sugestivo** attractive; thought-provoking.

suicida 1. suicidal; 2. _m/f_ suicide (_p._); **suicidarse** [1a] commit suicide; **suicidio** _m_ suicide (_act_).

sujeción _f_ subjection (_acto de fijar_) fastening etc.; **sujetador** _m_ fastener; bra; clip _de pluma_; ~ _de libros_ bookend; **sujetapapeles** _m_ paperclip; **sujetar** [1a] (_fijar etc._) fasten, hold in place; (_agarrar_) lay hold of, seize; (_dominar_) subdue; keep down, keep under; **~se** _a subject o.s. to, submit to; **sujeto** 1.: ~ _a subject to, liable to; 2. _m gr._ subject; F fellow, character.

sulfurar [1a] 🜍 sulphurate; _fig._ annoy, rile; **~se** blow up, see red; **sulfúreo** sulphur(e)ous; **sulfúrico** sulphuric; **sulfuro** _m_ sulphide.

sultán _m_ sultan; **sultana** _f_ sultana.

suma _f_ (_agregado_) sum, total; (_dinero_) sum; (_acto_) adding-up; (_resumen_) summary; **sumadora** _f_ adding machine; **sumamente** extremely, highly; **sumar** [1a] add up, total; (_compendiar_) summarize; sum up; **~se** _a join, become attached to; **sumario** _adj. a. su. m_ summary.

sumergir [3c] submerge; sink; dip, plunge, immerse; _fig._ plunge (_en into_); **~se** submerge; sink _etc._

sumidero _m_ drain, sewer; sink.

suministrar [1a] supply.

sumir [3a] sink; plunge, immerse; *fig.* plunge (en into); **~se** sink.

sumisión *f* submission; *(cualidad)* submissiveness; **sumiso** submissive, obedient; unresisting.

sumo great, extreme; *sacerdote* high; *pontífice* supreme.

suntuoso *mst* sumptuous; lavish, rich.

super... super...; over...

superar [1a] surpass *en cantidad*; excel *en calidad*; *dificultad* overcome, surmount; *expectativa* exceed; *límites* transcend.

superávit *m* surplus.

supercarburante *m* high-test fuel.

superficial *medida* surface attr.; *fig. mst* superficial (*a.* 🎣); facile; perfunctory; *p. etc.* shallow; **superficie** *f* surface; area; outside; face; ~ **inferior** underside.

superfluo superfluous.

super...: ~hombre *m* superman; **~intendencia** *f* supervision; **~intendente** *m* superintendent, supervisor; overseer.

superior 1. upper, higher; *fig.* superior, better; high, higher; first-rate; *clase social etc.* upper; *p.* chief, head ...; *master* ...; ~ **a cifra** more than, larger than; *calidad* better than; *nivel etc.* above, higher than; 2. *m* superior; *mis* **~es** my superiors *en categoría*; *fig.* my betters.

superlativo adj. a. su. *m* superlative.

super...: ~mercado *m* supermarket; **~numerario** adj. a. su. *m, a f* supernumerary; **~poblado** *barrio etc.* overcrowded, congested; *región* overpopulated; **~poner** [2r] superimpose; **~producción** *f* overproduction; **~sónico** supersonic.

superstición *f* superstition; **supersticioso** superstitious.

supervisar [1a] supervise.

supervivencia *f* survival; **superviviente** *m/f* survivor.

suplantar [1a] supplant.

suplemental supplemental; **suplementario** *mst* supplementary; *precio etc.* extra; **suplemento** *m* supplement; 🚋 excess fare; ~ **dominical** *diario* Sunday supplement.

suplente 1. substitute, deputy, reserve; *maestro* supply attr.; 2. *m/f* substitute, deputy; *thea. etc.* understudy; *deportes:* reserve.

súplica *f* supplication; ⚖️ petition; **~s** *pl.* pleading(s); **suplicante** 1. *tono etc.* imploring; 2. *m/f* ⚖️ *etc.* petitioner; applicant; **suplicar** [1g] *p.* plead with, implore; beg.

suplicio *m* (*castigo*) punishment; (*tormento*) torture; (*dolor*) torment.

suplir [3a] *necesidad, omisión* supply; *falta* make good, make up for; supplement; *p. etc.* (*mst* ~ *a*) replace.

suponer [2r] *v/t.* suppose, assume; entail, imply *como consecuencia*; *v/i.* be important; **suposición** *f* supposition; surmise.

supremacía *f* supremacy; **supremo** supreme.

supresión *f* suppression etc.; **supresor** *m radio:* suppressor; **suprimir** [3a] *rebelión, crítica etc.* suppress; *costumbre, derecho* abolish; *dificultad, desechos* remove, eliminate; *restricciones* lift.

supuesto 1. *p.p.* of **suponer**; 2. *adj.* supposed, ostensible; (*sedicente*) self-styled; *nombre* assumed; ~ **que** since, granted that; 3. *m* assumption, hypothesis; *por* ~ of course.

supurar [1a] discharge, run, suppurate 🩹.

sur 1. *parte* south(ern); *dirección* southerly; *viento* south(erly); 2. *m* south.

surcar [1g] *tierra etc.* furrow, plough (through *etc.*); (*hacer rayas*) score, groove; *agua* cleave; **surco** *m* ✒️ *etc.* furrow; (*raya*) groove, line; groove *de disco;* (*arruga*) wrinkle; track *en agua.*

surgir [3c] arise, emerge, appear; (*líquido*) spout, spurt (up); spring up; loom up; (*dificultad etc.*) arise, crop up; (*p.*) appear unexpectedly.

suroeste 1. *parte* south-west(ern); *dirección* south-westerly; *viento* south-west(erly); 2. *m* south-west.

surrealismo *m* surrealism; **surrealista** *m/f* surrealist.

surtido 1. mixed, assorted; 2. *m* (*gama*) range, selection, assortment; (*provisión*) stock, supply; *de* ~ stock; **surtidor** *m* fountain; (*chorro*) jet; ~ **de gasolina** gas(oline) pump; **surtir** [3a] *v/t.* supply, stock; *esp. fig.* provide; *efecto* have, produce; *bien surtido* well stocked (de with); *v/i.* spout, spurt; **~se de** provide o.s. with.

susceptible susceptible; sensitive, touchy; impressionable; ~ **de mejora** etc. capable of, open to.

suscitar [1a] *rebelión etc.* stir up; provoke; *cuestión, duda etc.* raise.

S

suscribir [3a; *p.p. suscrito*] subscribe (*a* to); *opinión* subscribe to; (*firmar*) sign; **~se** subscribe (*a* to, for); **suscripción** *f* subscription; **suscriptor** *m*, **-a** *f* subscriber.

susodicho above(-mentioned).

suspender [2a] hang (up), suspend; *fig. mst* suspend; *candidato* fail; (*admirar*) astonish; **suspensión** *f* hanging (up), suspension (*a. mot.*); ⚡ stay; **suspenso** suspended, hanging; *candidato* failed; *fig.* amazed; bewildered.

suspicaz suspicious, distrustful.

suspirar [1a] sigh (*por* for); **suspiro** *m* sigh.

sustancia *f* substance; essence; *en ~* in substance; **sustancial** substantial; important, vital; **sustancioso** substantial; *comida* nourishing; **sustantivo 1.** substantive; **2.** *m* noun, substantive.

sustentar [1a] sustain; maintain; support; (*alimentar*) feed, nourish; *tesis* defend; **~se** sustain o.s.; subsist (*con* on); **sustento** *m* sustenance, food; maintenance.

sustitución *f* substitution; replacement; **sustituir** [3g] *v/t.* substitute (*A por B* B for A), replace (*A por B* A by B, A with B); *v/i.* substitute; deputize; **~** a replace; deputize for; **sustituto** *m*, **a** *f* substitute; deputy; replacement.

susto *m* fright, scare; *¡ay qué ~!* what a fright you gave me!; *darse un ~* have a fright.

sustracción *f* ➗ substraction; deduction; **sustraer** [2p] ➗ subtract; deduct; (*robar*) steal; **~se a** withdraw from, contract out of.

sustrato *m* substratum.

susurrar [1a] whisper; *fig.* (*arroyo*) murmur; (*hojas*) rustle; (*viento*) whisper; **~se** *fig.* be whispered about; **susurro** *m fig.* whisper; murmur; rustle.

sutil *tela etc.* thin, fine; tenuous; (*perspicaz*) keen, sharp; *distinción etc.* subtle; **sutileza** *f* thinness *etc.*; subtlety; finesse; **sutilizar** [1f] *v/t.* thin down, fine down; *fig.* polish, perfect; refine.

suyo, suya 1. *pron. a. adj.* (*tras verbo ser*) (*un poseedor*) his, hers, its, one's; (*de Vd.*) your; (*varios poseedores*) theirs; (*de Vds.*) yours; **2.** *adj.* (*tras su.*) of his *etc.*; *de ~* naturally; intrinsically; per se.

svástica *f* swastika.

T

taba *f* anklebone; (*juego*) knucklebones; F *tomar la ~* show who is the boss.

tabacal *m* tobacco field; **tabacalero 1.** tobacco *attr.*; **2.** *m* tobacconist; **tabaco** *m* tobacco; (*puro*) cigar; (*cigarrillos*) cigarettes; *~ en polvo* snuff; *~ rubio* Virginian tobacco; **tabacoso** *dedos* tobacco-stained.

tabalear [1a] *v/t.* shake, rock; *v/i.* drum (with one's fingers).

tábano *m* horsefly.

tabaquería *f* tobacconist's (shop); **tabaquero** *m* tobacconist.

taberna *f* pub(lic house), bar.

tabernario *fig.* rude, dirty; **tabernero** *m* landlord; barman.

tabicar [1g] wall up, partition off; **tabique** *m* partition, wall.

tabla *f* (*madera*) plank, board; (*piedra*) slab; *paint.* panel; *anat.* flat (or wide) part; 𝄞 bed, patch; *sew.* broad pleat; ✝ meat stall; ➗ *etc.* table; (*lista*) table, list; chart; index *de libro*; *~s pl. thea.* boards, stage; *fig.* theater; *~s pl. ajedrez etc.*: draw; *~ de dibujo* drawing board; *~ de materias* table of contents; *~ de multiplicar* multiplication table; *~ de planchar* ironing board; *~ de salvación* last resort; lifesaver; **tablado** *m* plank floor, platform, stand; *thea. etc.* stage; (*cadalso*) scaffold; **tablaje** *m*, **tablazón** *f* planks, planking, boards; **tablero** *m* boards, planks; *ajedrez etc.*: board; (*encerado*) blackboard; counter *de tienda*; ⚡ switchboard; *~* (*de instrumentos*) instrument panel, *mot.* dashboard; *~ de ajedrez* chessboard; *~ de dibujo* drawing board; **tableta** *f* small board; (*taco*) tablet; bar *de chocolate*.

tabú *m* taboo.

tabular [1a] tabulate.

taburete *m* stool, footstool.

tacañería *f* meanness; **tacaño** mean, stingy, close-fisted.

tacha[1] *f* ⊕ large tack, stud.

tacha² f flaw, blemish, defect; *sin ~* flawless; *poner ~ a* find fault with; **tachar** [1a] cross out; *fig.* fault, criticize, attack.

tachón¹ m ⊕ stud; *sew.* trimming; **tachonar** [1a] ⊕ stud.

tachón² m stroke, crossing-out.

tachoso defective, faulty.

tachuela f tack.

tácito tacit; *observación etc.* unspoken; *ley* unwritten; **taciturno** taciturn; (*triste*) moody, sulky.

taco m plug, bung, stopper; (*empaquetadura*) wad(ding); *billar:* cue.

tacón m heel; **taconear** [1a] click one's heels *al saludar etc.*

táctica f tactics; gambit; **táctico 1.** tactical; **2.** m tactician.

táctil tactile; **tacto** m (*sentido*) (sense of) touch; touch *de mecanógrafa etc.*; (*acto*) touch(ing), feel.

tafetán m taffeta; *~es pl. fig.* flags; *~ adhesivo*, *~ inglés* court plaster.

tahúr m gambler; *b.s.* cardsharper.

taifa f F gang of thieves; *hist.* band.

taimado sly, crafty.

taja f cut; division; **tajada** f slice, cut *de carne etc.*; *S.Am.* cut, slash; F (*ronquera*) hoarseness; F (*borrachera*) drunk; F ✝ rake-off; **tajar** [1a] *carne etc.* slice, cut; chop; hew; **tajo** m (*corte*) cut; slash *con espada*; (*filo*) cutting edge; *geog.* sheer cliff; (*tajadero*) chopping-block; block *de verdugo*; (*tarea*) job.

tal 1. *adj.* such (a); (*con su. abstracto*) such; *~es pl.* such; *el ~ Pérez* this Pérez, that fellow Pérez; *un ~ Pérez a* man called Pérez, one Pérez; **2.** *pron.* (*p.*) such a one, someone; (*cosa*) such a thing, something; F *en la calle de ~* in such-and-such a street; *el ~* this man *etc.* (we're talking about); such a person; *~ como* such as; *como ~* as such; *~ cual libro* an odd book, one or two books; *~ o cual* such-and-such; *~ para cual* two of a kind; *sí ~*, yes indeed; *y ~* and such; *~ hay que* there are those who; *no hay ~* nothing of the sort; *no hay ~ como inf.* there's nothing like *ger.*; **3.** *adv.* so, in such a way; *~ como* just as; *~ cual* (*adv.*) just as it is; *era ~ cual deseaba* it was just what he wanted; (*como adj.*) middling, so-so; *¿qué ~?* how goes it?, how's things?; *¿qué ~ el libro?* what do you think of the book?; *¿qué ~ te gustó?* how did you like it?; **4.** *cj.:* *con ~ que* provided (that).

taladradora f drill; *~ de fuerza* power-drill; **taladrar** [1a] bore, drill, punch, pierce; **taladro** m drill; gimlet; auger.

talante m (*semblante*) look; (*ánimo*) frame of mind; will, pleasure; (*modo de hacer*) method, way.

talar [1a] *árbol* fell, cut down; ⚠ *etc.* pull down; *fig.* devastate.

talco m talcum powder; *min.* talc.

talega f bag, sack; nappy *de niño*; **talego** m long sack, poke.

talento m talent (*a. hist.*); gift; (*inteligencia*) brains, ability; *~s pl.* talents; accomplishments; **talentoso** talented, gifted.

talla f (*escultura*) carving, (*grabado*) engraving; height, stature *de p.*; size *de traje etc.*; rod, scale *para medir*; ⚖ reward; *diamante* cut, polish; **tallado 1.** carved *etc.*; *diamante* cut, polished; *bien ~* shapely, well-formed; **2.** m carving *etc.*; **tallar** [1a] *v/t.* carve; shape, work; (*grabar*) engrave; *diamante* cut; *p.* measure; *fig.* value.

tallarín m noodle.

talle m (*cintura*) waist; (*cuerpo*) figure *esp. de mujer*; build, physique *esp. de hombre*; *fig.* outline; look.

taller m ⊕ workshop, shop; (*grande*) mill, factory; workroom *de sastre*; studio *de pintor*; *~es pl.* gráficos printing works; *~ de máquinas* machine shop; *~ de montaje* assembly shop; *~ de reparaciones* repair shop.

tallo m ♀ stem, stalk; blade *de hierba*; (*renuevo*) shoot.

talón m *anat.* heel; stub, counterfoil *de cheque etc.*; 🚆 receipt for luggage; **talonar** [1a] heel; **talonario** m (*a. libro ~*) book of tickets; **talonear** [1a] hurry along.

tamaño 1. (*grande*) big, such a big; huge; (*pequeño*) so small *etc.*; *~ como* as big as; **2.** m size; capacity, volume; *de ~ extra(ordinario)* outsize; *de ~ natural* full-size, life-size.

tambalear(se) [1a] (*p.*) stagger, reel; (*vehículo*) lurch, sway.

también also, as well, too; beside(s); *¡~!* that as well?, not that too!; *yo ~* so am I, me too.

tambor m ♪, ⊕ drum; *sew.*, ▲ tambour; *anat.* eardrum; (*p.*) drummer; *a ~ batiente* with flying colors; **tambora** f bass drum; **tamborileo** m drumming; patter; **tamborilero** m drummer.

T

tamiz *m* sieve; **tamizar** [1f] sift, sieve.

tampoco neither, not ... either; nor; *ni éste ni aquél* ~ neither this one nor that one; *yo ~ lo sé* I don't know either; *ni yo ~* nor I.

tan so; ~ *bueno* so good; *coche* ~ *grande* such a big car; ~ ... *como* ~ as ... as; ~ *es así que* so much so that; *un* ~ such a.

tanda *f* shift, gang, relay *de ps.*; shift, turn, spell *en el trabajo*; turn *de riego etc.*; (*tarea*) job; (*capa*) layer, coat; (*partida*) game.

tangible tangible.

tanteador *m* scoreboard; (*p.*) scorer; **tantear** [1a] *v/t.* (*examinar*) weigh up; (*ensayar*) feel, test; (*comparar*) measure, weigh; *deportes:* keep the score of; *v/i. deportes:* score, keep (the) score; (*ir a tientas*) grope; **tanteo** *m* weighing-up; calculation; trial, test(ing); trial and error; *deportes:* score; *al* ~ by guesswork.

tanto 1. *adj.* so much; ~*s pl.* so many; ~ *como* as much as; ~*s como* as many as; *20 y* ~*s* 20-odd; *a* ~*s de mayo* on such-and-such a day in May; *a las* ~*as* in the small hours; **2.** *adv.* so much; as much; *trabajar etc.* so hard; *permanecer etc.* so long; *él come* ~ *como yo* he eats as much as I do; ~ *A como B* both A and B; ~ *más* the more, all the more ... as; ~ *más cuanto que* all the more (...) because; ~ *mejor* all the better; ~ *peor* so much the worse; *en(tre)* ~ meanwhile; *por (lo)* ~ so, therefore; **3.** *cj.:* *con* ~ *que* provided (that); **4.** *m* ✝ *etc.* so much, a certain amount; (*ficha*) counter, chip; *deportes:* point, goal; ~ *por ciento* percentage, rate; ✝ *al* ~ at the same price; *algún* ~, *un* ~ rather.

tañer [2f] ♪ play; *campana* ring; **tañido** *m* sound *de instrumento;* ring-ing; twang; tinkle.

tapa *f* lid; (*tapón*) top, cap; cover.

tapacubos *m* hubcap.

tapadera *f* lid, cover, cap.

tapar [1a] *vasija* put the lid on; *botella* put the cap on, stopper; *cara* cover up; *muffle up;* (*cegar etc.*) stop (up), block (up); *visión* obstruct, hide; *fig.* conceal; *defecto* cover up; *fugitivo* hide; *delincuente* cover up for; ~*se* wrap (o.s.) up.

taparrabo *m* loincloth *de indio etc.*; (*bathing*) trunks.

tapete *m* rug; (table-)runner; ~ *verde* card table.

tapia *f* (garden) wall; mud wall; **tapiar** [1b] wall in; *fig.* stop up.

tapicería *f* (*colgada*) tapestry, tapestries, hangings; upholstery.

tapiz *m* tapestry; carpet; **tapizar** [1f] *pared* hang with tapestries; *mueble* upholster; *suelo* carpet.

tapón *m* stopper, cap *de botella;* (*corcho*) cork; ⊕ plug, bung; wad; 🚿 tampon; ~ *de algodón* 🚿 swap; ~ *de cubo mot.* hubcap; ~ *de desagüe* drain plug; ~ *de tráfico* traffic jam; **taponar** [1a] stopper, cork; *conducto* plug, stop up.

taquigrafía *f* shorthand, stenography; **taquígrafo** *m*, **a** *f* shorthand writer, stenographer.

taquilla *f* 🎫 booking office; *thea.* box-office; (*carpeta*) file; **taquillero 1.** *éxito etc.* box-office *attr.*; **2.** *m*, **a** *f* clerk.

taquimeca(nógrafa) *f* shorthand typist.

taquímetro *m* speedometer; *surv.* tachymeter.

tarabilla 1. *f* F chatter; *soltar la* ~ F talk a blue streak; **2.** *m*/*f* F (*hablador*) chatterbox.

tararear [1a] hum.

tarascada *f* bite; F tart reply; **tarascar** [1g] bite, snap at.

tardanza *f* slowness; (*retraso*) delay; **tardar** [1a] take a long time, be long; delay; (*sin partir de*) linger (on); (*llegar tarde*) come late, be late; *a más* ~ at the latest.

tarde 1. *adv.* late; (*demasiado*) too late; *de* ~ *en* ~ from time to time; ~ *o temprano* sooner or later; *más* ~ later (on); *se hace* ~ it is getting late; **2.** *f* (*de 12 a 5 o 6*) afternoon; (*de 5 o 6 al anochecer*) evening; *¡buenas* ~*s!* good afternoon, good evening; *de la* ~ *a la mañana* overnight; *fig.* in no time at all; **tardecita** *f* dusk.

tardío *tardío* (*lento*) slow; (*que llega o madura tarde*) late; (*atrasado*) belated, overdue; **tardo** slow, sluggish; **tardón** F slow; (*lerdo*) dim.

tarea *f* job, task; duty, duties; (*cuidado*) worry; ~ *de ocasión* chore; ~ *suelta* odd job.

tarifa *f* tariff; rate, charge; price list *en café etc.*; (*pasaje*) fare; ~ *turística* tourist class.

tarima *f* platform; (*soporte*) stand; (*asiento*) stool, bench; (*cama*) bunk.

tarja *f* tally; F swipe, slash; **tarjar** [1a] keep a tally of.

T

tarjeta f card; ~ de crédito credit card; ~ de felicitación, ~ de buen deseo greeting card; ~ de identidad identity card; ~ navideña Christmas card; ~ postal postcard; ~ de visita visiting card.

tarro m pot, jar.

tarta f tart, cake.

tartamudear [1a] stutter, stammer; **tartamudeo** m stutter(ing); **tartamudez** f stutter, speech defect; **tartamudo 1.** stuttering; **2.** m, a f stutterer.

tarugo m wooden peg; (tapón) plug, stopper.

tasa f (fixed, official) price; rate; fig. estimate; (acto) valuation etc.; (medida, norma) measure, standard; sin ~ boundless, unstinted; **tasable** ratable; **tasación** f valuation; fixing de precios; fig. appraisal; **tasadamente** in moderation, sparingly; **tasador** m valuer; **tasar** [1a] artículo fix a price for, price (en at); trabajo etc. assess, rate (en at).

tatarabuelo m great-great-grandfather.

¡tate! 1. admiración: goodness!, well well!; (ya caigo) oh I see; cuidado: look out!; **2.** m sl. drug addict, smoker of hashish.

tatuaje m tattoo; (acto) tattooing; **tatuar** [1d] tattoo.

taurino bullfighting attr.; zo. bull attr.

Tauro m ast. Taurus; **tauromaquia** f bullfighting; **tauromáquico** bullfighting.

taxi m taxi (cab).

taxidermista m/f taxidermist.

taxista m taxi driver.

taza f cup; basin de fuente.

tazón m large cup, bowl; prov. wash basin.

te (acc.) you; (dat.) to you; (reflexivo) (to) yourself; (†, a Dios) thee, (to) thee, (to) thyself.

té m tea.

tea f torch.

teatral of the theater, theatrical; fig. dramatic; esp. b.s. histrionic, stagey; **teatro** m theater (a. ✕); scene de acontecimiento; (profesión) the theater, the stage; (obras) dramatic works.

techado m roof; bajo ~ indoors, under cover; **techar** [1a] roof (in, over); **techo** m roof; **techumbre** f roof; ceiling de habitación (a. ✒).

tecla f key; F dar en la ~ get the hang of a thing; **teclado** m keyboard; manual de órgano; **tecleo** m fingering etc.; touch, fingerwork.

técnica f technique; **tecnicidad** f technicality; **tecnicismo** m technicality, technical term; **técnico 1.** technical; **2.** m technician; expert, specialist; **tecnología** f technology; **tecnológico** technological.

tedio m boredom; tedium.

teja f tile; a toca ~ on the nail, in hard cash; **tejadillo** m top, cover; **tejado** m (tiled) roof; fig. housetop; **tejar** [1a] tile.

tejedor m, -a f weaver; **tejedura** f weaving, weave, texture; **tejeduría** f weaving; (fábrica) textile mill; **tejer** [2a] weave (a. fig.); S.Am. knit; fig. scheme; **tejido** m fabric, material; tissue (a. anat.); web; (textura) weave, texture.

tela f cloth, fabric, material; web de araña etc.; (nata) skin, film; skin de fruta; sl. dough; fig. subject, matter; ~ de araña spider web; ~s pl. del corazón heartstrings; ~ cruzada twill; ~ metálica wire fencing, chicken wire; ~ de punto stockinet; hay ~ que cortar (or para rato) it's an awkward business, it's a long job; poner en ~ de juicio (call in) question, test, look closely at.

telar m loom; thea. gridiron.

telaraña f spider's web, cobweb.

tele...: ~comando m remote control; **~control** m remote control; **~diario** m daytime television news; **~fonear** [1a] telephone; **~fonema** m telephone message; **~fónico** telephonic; telephone attr.; **~fonista** m/f (telephone) operator, telephonist; **teléfono** m telephone; llamar al (or por) ~ telephone, ring (up).

tele...: ~fotografía f telephoto; **~grafía** f telegraphy; **~grafiar** [1c] telegraph; **~gráfico** telegraphic; telegraph attr.; **~grafista** m/f telegraphist; **telégrafo** m telegraph; **~s** m F telegram boy; **telegrama** m telegram; **teleimpresor** m teleprinter; **~loca** f F television; **telémetro** m range finder.

tele...: ~patía f telepathy; **~pático** telepathic; **~scopar(se)** [1a] telescope; **~scópico** telescopic; **~scopio** m telescope; **~spectador** m, -a f (tele)viewer; **~squí** m ski lift; **~tipo** m teletype; **~visar** [1a] televise; **~vi-**

T

sión f television; ~ por cable cable television; aparato de ~ = **~visor** m television set.

telón m curtain; pol. ~ de acero iron curtain; ~ de boca front curtain; drop (curtain); ~ de fondo, ~ de foro backcloth, backdrop; ~ de seguridad safety curtain.

tema¹ m theme (a. ♪); subject (a. paint.), topic; motif; gr. stem.

tema² m fixed idea, mania; tener ~ be stubborn; tener ~ a have a grudge against.

temblar [1k] tremble (ante a, de at, with); shake, quiver, shiver; (tambalearse) totter, sway; ~ de frío shiver with cold; ~ por su vida fear for one's life; **temblequear** [1a] F be all of a quiver; **temblón 1.** trembling; álamo ~ = **2.** m aspen; **temblor** m tremble, trembling etc.; tremor, shiver(ing) esp. de frío; ~ de tierra earthquake; **tembloroso** trembling.

temer [2a] v/t. be afraid of, fear; dread; v/i. be afraid; ~ por fear for; ~ inf. fear to inf.; ~ que fear that; no temas don't be afraid.

temerario p., acto rash, reckless; **temeridad** f rashness.

temeroso timid; = **temible** dreadful, frightful; adversario etc. redoubtable; **temor** m fear, dread; (recelo) misgiving; sin ~ a fearless of.

témpano m: ~ (de hielo) ice floe; (grande) iceberg.

temperamento m temperament, nature; fig. compromise; **temperancia** f temperance; **temperante** S.Am. **1.** teetotal; **2.** m/f teetotaller; **temperar** [1a] v/t. temper, moderate; pasión etc. calm; v/i. S.Am. go on holiday; **temperatura** f temperature.

tempestad f storm (a. fig.); **tempestuoso** stormy (a. fig.), rough.

templado moderate, restrained; agua tepid; clima mild, temperate; ♪ in tune; **templanza** f temperance, mildness; **templar** [1a] temper, moderate; (suavizar) soften; temperatura cool; solución dilute; metal temper; colores blend; ♪ tune (up); **~se** (p.) control o.s.; (tiempo) moderate; **temple** m temper(ing) of metal; ♪ tuning; meteor. (state of the) weather; temperature.

templo m temple; (cristiano) church, chapel.

temporada f time, period; spell (a.

meteor.); (social, deportiva etc.) season; ~ alta midseason; en plena ~ at the height of the season; **temporal 1.** eccl. etc. temporal; (provisional) temporary; **2.** m storm; **temporáneo** temporary; **temporero** temporary; **tempranal** ♀ etc., **tempranero**, **temprano** early.

tenacidad f toughness etc.

tenacillas f/pl. tongs para azúcar etc.; curling-tongs para pelo; ✄ etc. tweezers, forceps.

tenaz tough, resistant; (pegajoso) that sticks fast; creencia, resistencia stubborn; p. tenacious.

tenazas f/pl. ⊕ (unas a pair of) pliers, pincers; tongs para carbón.

tendencia f tendency, trend; inclination; tenor de observación etc.

tender [2g] **1.** v/t. stretch; spread (out), lay out; paint., ⚒ put on; arco draw; cable, vía lay; ferrocarril, puente build; mano stretch out; ropa hang out; trampa set (a for); **2.** v/i.: ~ a su. tend to, tend towards, incline to; ~ a inf. tend to inf.; **3.** **~se** lie down, stretch (o.s.) out; (caballo) run at a full gallop; naipes: lay down.

tendero m, a f shopkeeper.

tendido 1. lying (down), flat; **2.** m laying de cable etc.; (ropa) washing; (yeso) coat of plaster.

tendón m tendon, sinew.

tendré etc. v. tener.

tenebroso dark, gloomy, dismal; asunto sinister, dark; negocio shady.

tenedor m fork; (p.) holder, bearer; ~ de acciones stockholder; ~ de libros bookkeeper; ~ de obligaciones boldholder; **teneduría** f: ~ de libros bookkeeping.

tener [2l] have; have got; (tener en la mano, asir etc.) hold; (retener) keep; (contener) hold, contain; ¿qué tienes? what's the matter with you?; ~ 9 años be 9 (years old)?; ¿cuántos años tienes? how old are you?; **~se** hold (fast); stand firm; catch o.s. al caer; (detenerse) stop.

tengo etc. v. tener.

teniente m lieutenant.

tenis m tennis; ~ de mesa table tennis; **tenista** m/f tennis player.

tenor¹ m ♪ tenor.

tenor² m state; (sentido) tenor, purport; a este ~ like this.

tensar [1a] tauten; tense; **tensión** f tension; stress, strain; rigidity; alta ~

high tension; ~ *arterial,* ~ *sanguínea* blood pressure; ~ *superficial* surface tension; **tenso** tense, taut.

tentación f temptation.

tentáculo m tentacle, feeler.

tentador 1. tempting; **2.** m tempter; **tentadora** f temptress; **tentar** [1k] (*palpar*) touch, feel; ⚕ probe; *camino* feel; (*intentar*) try, attempt; (*emprender*) undertake; (*seducir*) tempt; **tentativa** f try, attempt; effort; **tentativo** tentative.

tenue (*delgado*) thin, slender; *hilo* fine; *esp. fig.* tenuous, slight.

teñir [3h *a.* 3l] mst dye (*de negro* black); color; stain, tinge.

teología f theology.

teorema m theorem; **teoría** f theory; ~ *atómica* atomic theory; ~ *cuántica,* ~ *de los cuanta* quantum theory; **teórico** theoretic(al); **teorizar** [1f] theorize.

tequila f *Mex.* brandy.

terapeuta m/f therap(eut)ist; **terapéutica** f therapeutics; = **terapia** f therapy; ~ *laboral* occupational therapy.

tercera f ♪ third; **tercería** f mediation; *b.s.* procuring; **tercermundista** Third World; **tercermundo** m Third World; **tercero 1.** *adj. a. su.* m ♂ third; **2.** m, a f go-between; (*árbitro*) mediator; ⚖ third person (or party); *b.s.* procurer, pimp; **terciado** *azúcar* brown; **terciar** [1b] v/t. slope, slant; ⚖ divide into three; v/i. fill in, stand in; **tercio** m third.

terciopelo m velvet.

terco obstinate, stubborn.

tergiversar [1a] v/t. distort, misrepresent; v/i. prevaricate; be undecided, blow hot and cold.

terminal *adj. a. su.* m (♫), f (*puerto*) terminal; **terminante** final, definitive; (*claro*) conclusive; *negativa* flat; *prohibición* strict; **terminar** [1a] end, finish; ~se draw to a close, stop; **término** m end, finish; (*mojón*) boundary, limit; ⚙ etc. terminus; (*plazo*) period, time; outlying part *de ciudad*; (*palabra, phls.,* ♂) term; (*árbitro*) compromise solution; *primer* ~ foreground; *segundo* ~ middle distance; *último* ~ background; *en último* ~ *fig.* in the last analysis; *en medio* compromise, middle way; (*promedio*) average.

termómetro m thermometer; **termonuclear** thermonuclear; **ter-**

mos m vacuum (*or* thermos) flask; **termóstato** m thermostat.

ternera f (heifer) calf; (*carne*) veal; **ternero** m (bull) calf.

terno m set of three, trio; (*traje*) three-piece suit; F swear word.

ternura f tenderness.

terquedad f obstinacy.

terraplén m ⚙ etc. embankment; ✈ terrace; mound; ⚔ rampart.

terraza f terrace; (*tejado*) flat roof; balcony *de piso*; ✈ flowerbed.

terremoto m earthquake.

terrenal = **terreno 1.** earthly, worldly; **2.** m geol. etc. (*superficie*) terrain; (*naturaleza del suelo*) soil, land; (*extensión*) piece of ground, grounds; ✈ plot, patch, field; *deportes:* pitch, ground; *fig.* field.

terrible terrible, dreadful; **terrífico** terrifying.

terrón m clod; lump (*a. azúcar*).

terror m terror, dread; **terrorífico** terrifying; **terrorismo** m terrorism; **terrorista** m terrorist.

terroso earthy; (*sucio*) dirty.

terso (*liso*) smooth; (*y brillante*) glossy; (*brillante*) shining, bright.

tertulia f (*reunión*) social gathering, get-together F; (*grupo*) party, group, circle; set *de café etc.*; **tertuliano** m, a f member of a social gathering *etc.*

tesis f thesis.

teso tense, taut.

tesón m insistence; tenacity, firmness *en resistir.*

tesorería f treasury; (*oficio*) treasurership; **tesorero** m, a f treasurer; **tesoro** m treasure; hoard; (*edificio, ministerio*) treasury; (*diccionario*) thesaurus.

testa f head; (*frente, cara*) front; F brains; ~ *coronada* crowned head.

testamento m will, testament; *Antiguo* (*Nuevo*) ♀ Old (New) Testament; **testar** [1a] make a will.

testarudez f stubbornness; **testarudo** stubborn.

testera f front, face; forehead *de animal.*

testículo m testicle.

testificar [1g] give evidence, testify; *fig.* attest; **testigo** m/f witness; ~ *de cargo* witness for the prosecution; ~ *de descargo* witness for the defense; ~ *ocular,* ~ *presencial,* ~ *de vista* eye witness; **testimoniar** [1b] testify to, bear witness to; **testimonio** m testimony, evidence.

teta f breast; (*pezón*) teat.

tétano m tetanus.

tetera f teapot; teakettle.

tétrico gloomy; sullen, sad.

textil 1. textile; **2.** ~es m/pl. textiles.

texto m text; **textual** textual.

textura f texture (a. fig.).

tez f complexion, skin.

ti you; (†, *a Dios*) thee.

tía f aunt; (*grosera*) coarse woman; (*vieja*) old bag; (*puta*) whore; ~ **abuela** great-aunt.

tibia f tibia.

tiburón m shark.

tic m tic.

tiempo m time; *meteor.* weather; *gr.* tense; ♪ (*parte*) movement; ♪ (*compás*) time, tempo; *deportes:* half; *los buenos* ~s the good old days; *en mis buenos* ~s in my prime; ~ *libre* spare time, leisure; *deportes:* primer ~ first half; *a* ~ in (good) time, early; *a un* ~, *al mismo* ~ at the same time; *a su debido* ~ in due course; *al poco* ~ very soon; *con* ~ in (good) time, early; *con el* ~ eventually, in time; *de 4* ~s *motor* 4-stroke; *el* ♀ Father Time; *en* ~ *de Maricastaña*, *en* ~ *del rey que rabió* long ago, in the year dot; *fuera de* ~ at the wrong time; *más* ~ *quedar etc.* longer; *¿cuánto* ~ *más?* how much longer?; *mucho* ~ a long time.

tienda f shop, store; ~ (*de campaña*) tent; (*toldo*) awning.

tienta f ✿ probe; *fig.* cleverness; *a* ~s gropingly; *andar a* ~s grope, feel one's way (a. fig.); **tiento** m (*tacto*) touch, feel(ing); stick *de ciego*; *zo.* feeler; *fig.* (*seguridad*) steady hand; (*cuidado*) wariness.

tierno mst tender; (*blando*) soft.

tierra f *ast.* earth; *geog.* world, earth; (*no mar*) land; (*finca, terreno*) land; (*materia del suelo*) ground, earth, soil; (*patria*) native land, one's (own) country; region; ⚡ earth; ~ *de batán* fuller's earth; ~ *firme* mainland; dry land; ~ *de nadie* no man's land; ~ *de pan llevar* corn land; ~ *prometida*, ~ *de promisión* promised land; ~ *quemada* scorched earth; ♀ *Santa* Holy Land; ~ *adentro* inland; *por* ~ by land, overland.

tieso 1. adj. stiff, rigid (a. fig.); (*tirante*) taut; *fig.* brave; grave; **2.** adv. strongly, hard.

tiesto m flower pot; (*fragmento*) piece of pottery, sherd.

tifón m typhoon; water spout.

tifus m typhus; *thea. sl.* free seats.

tigre m tiger; **tigresa** f tigress.

tijera f (p.) gossip; *tener una* ~ have a sharp tongue; **tijeras** f/pl. scissors; (*grandes, de jardín*) shears, clippers; *de* ~(s) folding; **tijereta** f ♀ vine tendril; *zo.* earwig; **tijeretada** f, **tijeretazo** m snip, cut; **tijeretear** [1a] snip, cut, snick.

tildar [1a] *letra* put a tilde over; (*tachar*) cross out; *fig.* brand, stigmatize (*de as*); **tilde** mst f typ. tilde (~); *fig.* jot.

timbal m ♪ (kettle)drum; *cocina:* meat pie.

timbrar [1a] stamp; ✉ postmark; **timbre** m ✉ stamp; tax stamp; (*campanilla*) bell; timbre *de voz etc.*

timidez f timidity *etc.*; **tímido** timid, shy, nervous; bashful, coy.

timón m ♣, ✈ rudder; *esp. fig.* helm; ~ *de dirección* rudder.

tímpano m eardrum; kettledrum.

tina f vat, tub; (*baño*) bath-tub; large jar; ~ *de lavar* washtub; **tinaja** f vat; (large earthen) jar.

tinieblas f/pl. darkness (a. fig.), dark, shadows.

tino m (*habilidad*) skill, knack; feel, (*sure*) touch; (*juicio*) good judgment; *a buen* ~ by guesswork.

tinta f ink; dye *para teñir*; (*matiz*) tint, shade, hue; ~ *china* India ink; ~ *de imprenta* printer's ink; ~ *de marcar* marking ink; ~ *simpática* invisible ink; *de buena* ~ on good authority; **tinte** m (*acto*) dyeing; (*materia*) dye(-stuff); (*color*) tint, hue, tinge; ⊕ stain; (*tintorería*) dry-cleaner's; *fig.* disguise; **tintero** m inkstand; inkwell.

tintín m clink, chink, jingle, tinkle; **tintinear** [1a] clink *etc.*

tinto dyed; *vino* red; **tintorería** f dry cleaner's *que limpia*; dyer's *que tiñe*; (*arte*) dyeing; (*fábrica*) dyeworks; **tintura** f dye; rouge *de cara*; ⊕ stain; *pharm.* tincture.

tiña f ✿ ringworm; F meanness; **tiñoso** scabby, mangy; F mean.

tío m uncle; F (*viejo*) old fellow; F (*sujeto*) fellow, chap; ~s pl. uncle and aunt; ~ *abuelo* great-uncle; **tiovivo** m merry-go-round.

típico typical; *fig.* picturesque.

tipo m mst type; (*clase a.*) sort, kind; (*físico*) shape, figure, build; F fellow, chap; ~s pl. typ. type; ~ *de cambio* rate of exchange; ~ de ensayo, ~ de prueba eye-test chart; ~ de impuesto tax rate; ~ de interés rate of interest; ~ de letra typeface; ~ menudo small print; ~ (de) oro gold standard; **tipografía** f printing; typography; **tipográfico** printing attr.; typographical.

tira f (long or narrow) strip; slip of papel; ~ cómica comic strip; ~ proyectable film strip.

tirada f (acto) throw; distance, stretch; typ. printing, edition; ~ aparte offprint; de una ~ at one stroke, at a stretch; **tirado** ✝ dirt cheap; ⚓ rakish; letra cursive; **tirador** m handle, knob de puerta etc.; bell-rope; ✂ cord; ✕ (p.) shot, marksman; ~ apostado, ~ certero, ~ emboscado sniper.

tiranía f tyranny; **tiránico** tyrannical; amor possessive; encanto irresistible; **tiranizar** [1f] v/t. tyrannize; v/i. be a tyrant, domineer; **tirano** 1. tyrannical; domineering; 2. m, a f tyrant.

tirante 1. taut, tight; relaciones etc. tense, strained; ✝ tight; 2. m ⚠ tie, brace; ⊕ strut; trace de guarnición; shoulder strap de vestido; ~s pl. braces, suspenders Am.; **tirantez** f tautness etc.; fig. tension.

tirar [1a] 1. v/t. throw; cast, toss, sling; desperdicios throw away; (disipar) waste; alambre draw out; (arrastrar) haul; línea draw; ✕ shoot, fire; typ. print, run off; beso blow; 2. v/i. (chimenea) draw; ✕ fire (a at, on), shoot (a at); (atraer) appeal; (have a) pull; (durar) last; ~ a su. tend towards; ~ a color approach, have a touch of; ~ a inf. aim to inf.; ~ a la derecha turn to the right, keep right; ~ a viejo be elderly; ~ de (arrastrar) pull, haul; cuerda etc. pull on, tug; (imán) attract; espada draw; 3. ~se throw o.s., jump; (abalanzarse) rush.

tiritar [1a] shiver (de with); **tiritón** m shiver.

tiro m throw; ✕ shot (a. deportes, p.); (alcance) range; ✕ (sitio) riflerange; shooting gallery de feria; team de caballos; trace de guarnición; (cuerda) rope; sew. length; flight de escalera; (broma) practical joke; ~ con arco archery; ~ al blanco target practice; a ~ within range; a ~ de fusil within gunshot.

tiroideo thyroid; **tiroides** m (a. glándula ~) thyroid (gland).

tirón m pull, tug; jerk; hitch; (estirón) stretch; mover etc. a ~es tug, jerk.

tirotear [1a] blaze away at; ~se exchange shots repeatedly; **tiroteo** m firing, shooting.

tirria f dislike; tener ~ a have a grudge against.

tísico adj. a. su. m, a f tubercular; **tisis** f tuberculosis.

titán m titan; **titánico** titanic.

títere m marionette, puppet; (teatro de) ~s pl. puppets, puppet show.

titubear [1a] (tambalear) reel, stagger, totter; (vacilar) hesitate, stammer; **titubeo** m hesitation etc.

titular 1. titular, official; 2. m typ. headline; 3. m/f holder; 4. [1a] (en)title, call; **titulillo** m running title, page heading; **título** m mst title; headline; (certificado) diploma, qualification; univ. degree; ✝ bond; ~ (de nobleza) title; ~ de propiedad deed; a ~ de by way of; in the capacity of; ¿a ~ de qué? by what right?; ~s credentials.

tiza f chalk.

tizna f black, grime; paint. crayon; **tiznar** [1a] blacken; smudge; (manchar) spot, stain; fig. stain, tarnish; brand; **tizne** mst m (hollín) soot; (suciedad) smut, grime.

toalla f towel; ~ de rodillo roller towel; **toallero** m towel rack.

tobillo m ankle.

tocadiscos m record player; ~ automático record changer.

tocado head-dress; (pelo) coiffure.

tocador[1] m, -a f ♪ player.

tocador[2] m (mueble) dressing table; (cuarto) boudoir, dressing room; (estuche) toilet case; de ~ freq. toilet attr.

tocante: ~ a with regard to.

tocar[1] [1g] 1. v/t. (palpar, estar en contacto con) touch; (palpar) feel; (manosear) touch, handle; (chocar) collide with, hit; ⚓ go aground on; ♪ play; trompeta blow; tambor beat; disco play; timbre ring; tema touch on; 2. v/i.: ~ a puerta knock at; (caber en suerte) fall to one's lot (or share); le tocó el premio he got the prize; (importar a) concern, affect; 3. v/i.: ~ en ⚓ touch at, call at; (estar junto) next to.

tocar[2] [1g] pelo do; arrange, set; ~se cover one's head.

tocayo m, a f namesake.

tocino m bacon; salt pork.

T

tocón *m* ♀, *anat.* stump.

todavía still, yet; ~ *no* not yet; ~ *en 1900* as late as 1900.

todo 1. all; whole, entire; every; *velocidad etc.* full; ~ *el dinero* all the money, the whole of the money; *por* ~*a Europa* all over Europe, throughout Europe; ~*s los días* every day; ~ *el que* everyone who; *lo comió* ~ he ate it all; *lo sabe* ~ he knows everything; (*nada menos que*) ~ *un hombre* every inch (*or* bit) a man; ~ *cuanto* all that which; ~*s cuantos* all those who; 2. *adv.*: *ante* ~ first of all; primarily; *a pesar de* ~, *así y* ~ even so, in spite of everything; all the same; *con* ~ still; however; *del* ~ wholly, completely; *no del* ~ not quite; *después de* ~ after all; *sobre* ~ above all, especially, most of all; 3. *m* all, everything; (*el* ~) whole; ~*s pl.* everybody; every one of them.

todopoderoso almighty.

toga *f hist.* toga; *univ. etc.* gown.

toldo *m* sunshade, awning; (*pabellón*) marquee; cloth, tarpaulin *de carro*.

tole *m* hubbub, uproar; outcry.

tolerable tolerable; **tolerancia** *f* tolerance (*a.* ⊕), toleration; **tolerante** tolerant; broad-minded; **tolerar** [1a] tolerate; endure.

toma *f* taking; ✗ capture; ⚡ dose; (*entrada*) inlet, intake; (*salida*) tap, outlet; ⚡ (*a.* ~ *de corriente*) (*enlace*) lead; (*enchufe*) plug, point; ~ *de declaración* taking of evidence; ~ *de hábito* taking of vows; ~ *de posesión* taking-over; (*presidente etc.*) inauguration; ~ *de tierra* ⚡ groundwire; ✈ landing.

tomar [1a] 1. *v/t. mst* take; *ánimo, fuerzas* get, gain; *aspecto* take on; *bebida, comida, lecciones* have; *costumbre* get into, acquire; *frío* get, catch; ~ *por* take *s.o.* for; ~*la con* pick a quarrel with; 2. *v/i.*: ~ *por la derecha* turn to the right; *toma y daca* give and take; 3. ~*se*: ~ (*de orin*) go rusty.

tomate *m* tomato.

tomavistas *m phot.* motion-picture camera; cameraman.

tomillo *m* thyme; ~ *salsero* savory.

tomo *m* volume; (*lo grueso*) bulk; *fig.* importance; *de* ~ *y lomo* bulky.

ton: *sin* ~ *ni son* without rhyme or reason.

tonada *f* tune, song; **tonadilla** *f* little tune; merry tune; *thea.* interlude;

tonalidad *f* shade *de color*; *radio:* control *de* ~ tone control.

tonel *m* barrel, cask; **tonelada** *f* ton; **tonelaje** *m* tonnage; **tonelero** *m* cooper; **tonelete** *m* cask, keg; (*falda*) short skirt; kilt *de hombre*.

tónica *f* ♪ tonic; (*nota*) ~ keynote; **tónico** 1. ✗, ♪, *acento* tonic; *sílaba* accented; 2. *m* ✗ tonic (*a. fig.*); **tonificar** [1g] tone up, fortify; **tonillo** *m* singsong, monotonous note; **tono** *m mst* tone; ♪ (*calidad etc.*) tone; ♪ (*altura*) pitch; ♪ (*de fa etc.*) key; ♪ (*pieza*) slide; (*matiz*) shade; *teleph.* ~ *de marcar* dialling tone; ~ *mayor* (*menor*) major (minor) key; ♪ *a* ~ *in key; a* ~ *con* in tune with; *de buen* ~ fashionable; elegant; genteel; *de mal* ~ vulgar; *bajar el* ~ lower one's voice.

tontería *f* (*lo tonto*) silliness; (*acto*) silly thing; (*palabra; a.* ~*s pl.*) nonsense, rubbish; **tonto** 1. silly, foolish; 2. *m*, *a f* fool, idiot; (*payaso*) funny man, clown.

topar [1a] *v/t.* (*chocar*) bump (against, into), knock (against, into); (*encontrar, a. v/i.* ~ *con*) run into, bump into; *v/i. zo.* butt (each other); (*juego*) take a bet; (*tropezar*) stumble; (*dificultad*) lie; (*salir bien*) succeed, manage it; **tope** *m* (*cabo*) butt, end; ♠ masthead; ⛵ buffer; *mot.* bumper; ⊕ stop, check; (*choque*) collision; bump, knock; *fig.* snag; (*riña*) quarrel; *hasta el* ~ to the brim; *estar hasta los* ~*s* ♠ be loaded to the gunwales; *fig.* be fed up.

topetada *f*, **topetazo** *m* butt, bump; **topetar** [1a] butt, bump; *fig.* bump into; **topetón** *m* bump.

tópico 1. local; 2. *m* commonplace, cliché, catch-phrase; *S.Am.* topic.

topo *m* mole; ℱ great lump.

topografía *f* ▥ topography; surveying; **topográfico** topographic.

toque *m* (*acto*) touch (*a. paint.*); (*ensayo*) test, trial; peal(ing) *de campana*; ring *de timbre*; beat *de tambor*; hoot *de sirena*.

toquilla *f* headscarf; shawl.

torbellino *m* (*viento*) whirlwind; (*agua*) whirlpool; *fig.* whirl.

torcedura *f* twist(ing); ✗ sprain, strain; (*vino*) weak wine; **torcer** [2b a. 1l] 1. *v/t.* twist; (*encorvar*) bend, curve; (*alabear*) warp; *manos, cuello* wring; *cara* screw up; *músculo* strain; *tobillo* sprain, twist; *esquina* turn; *fig.*

sentido twist; *justicia* pervert; **2.** *v/i.* turn (*a* to); (*pelota*) swerve, spin; **3.** **~se** twist; bend; (*alabearse*) warp; (*cambiar de lugar*) slew (round); (*extraviarse*) go astray; (*vino etc.*) turn sour; **torcida** *f* wick; **torcido 1.** twisted; *bent*; *camino etc.* full of turns, twisty; *fig.* crooked; *S.Am.* unlucky; **2.** *m* curl *de pelo*; twist *de seda etc.*; **torcimiento** *m* twisting.

tordo 1. dappled; **2.** *m* thrush.

torear [1a] *v/t. toro* fight, play; *fig.* deceive; (*burlarse*) tease, draw on; *v/i.* fight (bulls); (*como profesión*) be a bullfighter; **toreo** *m* (art of) bullfighting; **torería** *f* (class of) bullfighters; F prank; **torero** *m* bullfighter; **torete** *m* young bull; F bouncing child; **toril** *m* bull pen.

tormenta *f* storm; *fig.* misfortune; (*confusión*) turmoil, upheaval; **tormento** *m* torment; anguish, agony.

tornar [1a] *v/t.* give back; (*volver*) turn, make; *v/i.* go back, return; **~ a escribir** write again; **~se** turn, become; **tornasol** *m* ♀ sunflower; ↗ litmus; sheen *de tela*; **tornasolado** iridescent, sheeny; *seda* shot; **tornavía** *f* turntable; **tornavoz** *f* sounding board; *eccl.* canopy.

tornear [1a] turn (on a lathe).

torneo *m* tournament; competition; *hist.* tourney, joust.

tornillo *m* (*rosca*) screw; (*torno*) small lathe; ⚒ F desertation; **~ de banco** vice, clamp; **~ sin fin** worm (gear); *apretar los* **~s** *a p* put the screws on; *le falta un* **~**, *tiene flojos los* **~s** he has a screw loose; **~ de mariposa**, **~ de orejas** thumbscrew; **~ de presión** setscrew; **~ para metales** machine screw.

torno *m* ⊕ lathe; ⊕, ⚓ winch, drum; (*freno*) brake; bend *de río*; (*vuelta*) turn; **~ de alfarero** potter's wheel; **~ de asador** spit; **~ de banco** vice, clamp; **~ de hilar** spinning wheel; **~ revolvedor** turret lathe; **~ de tornero** turning lathe; **en ~** around, round about; **en ~ suyo** about him; **en ~ a** around, about.

toro *m* bull; **~s** *pl.* bullfight; (*arte*) bullfighting; **~ de lidia** fighting bull; *echar* (*or soltar*) *el* **~** *a* pull no punches with; *irse a la cabeza del* **~** take the bull by the horns; *ver los* **~s** *desde la barrera* sit on the fence.

toronja *f* grapefruit.

torpe *movimiento* ungainly, heavy; *mente* slow; (*desmañado*) clumsy, awkward; (*tosco*) crude; indecent.

torpedear [1a] torpedo (*a. fig.*); **torpedo** *m* torpedo (*a. ichth.*).

torpeza *f* slowness *etc.*

torre *f* △ tower; ⚒, ⚓, ↗ turret; *radio:* mast; *ajedrez:* rook; **~ de conducción eléctrica** pylon; **~ del homenaje**, **~ maestra** donjon, keep; **~ de lanzamiento** launching tower; **~ de marfil** *fig.* ivory tower; ⊕ **~ de mando** conning tower; **~ de perforación** oil derrick; **~ de refrigeración** cooling tower; **~ reloj** clock tower; ⚓ **~ de vigía** crow's nest.

torrente *m* mountain stream, torrent; *fig.* torrent, rush, flood *de palabras etc.*

tórrido torrid.

torsión *f* ⊕ torsion; twist; *esp.* ↗ warping; **torsional** torsional.

torso *m* torso; *paint.* head and shoulders; *escultura:* bust.

torta *f cocina:* cake, tart; *fig.* cake.

tortícolis *m* stiff neck.

tortilla *f* omelet(te).

tortita *f* pancake.

tórtola *f* turtledove; **tórtolo** *m* turtledove; F lovebird.

tortuga *f* tortoise; **~** (*marina*) turtle.

tortuoso winding, tortuous.

tortura *f* torture (*a. fig.*); **torturar** [1a] torture.

tos *f* cough(ing); **~ ferina** whooping cough.

tosco coarse, rough, crude.

toser [2a] cough.

tosquedad *f* coarseness.

tostada *f* (piece of) toast; **tostado 1.** *pan* toasted; *color* dark brown; **~** (*por el sol*) sunburnt, tanned; **2.** *m* tan; **tostador** *m* toaster; roaster; **tostadora** *f* ⚡ toaster; toaster; **tostar** [1m] *pan* toast; *café* roast; *fig.* (*calentar*) toast; *p.* tan; **~se** (*al sol*) tan, get brown.

total 1. *adj.* total; whole; *esp.* ↑ gross; *ruina etc.* utter; **2.** *adv.* all in all; and so; **3.** *m* total; whole; sum; **en ~** in all; **totalidad** *f* whole; totality; **totalitario** totalitarian; **totalitarismo** *m* totalitarianism; **totalizar** [1f] add up.

tóxico 1. toxic, poisonous; **2.** *m* poison; **toxicómano 1.** addicted to drugs; **2.** *m*, **a** *f* drug addict; **toxina** *f* toxin.

traba *f* link, bond *que une*; lock *que cierra*, sujeta; ↙ hobble; *fig.* hindrance, obstacle; **trabado** strong.

trabajado worn out; *estilo etc.* strained; **trabajador 1.** hardworking, industrious; **2.** *m* worker;

laborer; **trabajar** [1a] v/t. *madera etc.* work; work on; *p.* work, drive; *p.* (*con maña*) get to work on; *caballo* train; *mente* trouble; v/i. work (*de as*; *en at*); (*torcerse*) warp; ~ *mucho* work hard; ~ *con fig.* (get to) work on; ~ *por inf.* strive to *inf.*; *hacer* ~ *dinero* make work; *agua, recursos* harness; **trabajo** m (*en general, a. phys.*) work; (*un* ~) piece of work; (*tarea, colocación*) job; (*fermentación*) working(s); (*los obreros*) labor, the workers; *fig.* trouble, difficulty; ~**s** *pl. fig.* hardships; ~ *en el propio campo* fieldwork; ~ *a destajo* piece work; ~**s** *pl.* forzados hard labor; **trabajoso** hard, laborious, deficient; ⚕ sickly.

trabalenguas m tongue twister; **trabar** [1a] join, link; (*aherrojar*) shackle, fetter (*a. fig.*); (*sujetar*) lock, fasten; (*asir*) seize; *caballo* hobble; *sierra* set; *amistad* strike up; *batalla* join; *conversación* start; ~**se** (*cuerdas*) get tangled; ⊕ lock.

tracción f traction; haulage; ~ *a las 4 ruedas* 4-wheel drive.

tractor m tractor; ~ *de oruga* caterpillar tractor.

tradición f tradition; **tradicional** traditional; *costumbre freq.* time-honored; *ley* unwritten.

traducción f translation; rendering; *thea. etc.* translate; **traducir** [3f] translate; express; **traductor** m, **-a** f translator.

traer [2p] bring, get, fetch; (*atraer*) attract, draw; *ropa* wear; (*llevar consigo*) have, carry; (*causar*) bring (about); (*acarrear*) involve; *autoridades* adduce; ~**se:** ~ *bien* (*mal*) be well (badly) dressed; (*comportarse*) behave properly (badly).

tráfago m 🕇 traffic, trade; (*faena*) drudgery, routine job; **traficante** m trader; **traficar** [1g] trade, deal (*en* in); buy and sell; F come and go; **tráfico** m *mot. etc.* traffic; 🕇 trade, business, traffic.

tragaderas f/pl. throat; **tragadero** m throat, gullet; **tragaluz** m skylight; **tragar** [1h] 1. *mst* swallow; (*y terminar*) drink up, swallow down; (*engullir*) gulp (down); (*con dificultad*) get down; 2. *fig.* (*a.* ~**se**) *barco etc.* swallow up, engulf; *material* use up, take; *cosa desagradable, increíble* swallow; *p.* stick, stand; 3. v/i. *sl.* sleep around.

tragedia f tragedy; **trágico** 1. tragic(al); 2. m tragedian.

trago m drink, swallow, gulp; *a* ~**s** little by little.

traición f treachery; treason (*a.* 🏛); (*una* ~) betrayal; *alta* ~ high treason; **traicionar** [1a] betray; **traicionero** treacherous.

traída f: ~ *de aguas* water supply; **traído** worn, threadbare; ~ *y llevado* knocked about; *fig.* wellworn.

traidor 1. *p.* treacherous; *acto* treasonable; 2. m traitor; betrayer; *thea.* villain; **traidora** f traitress.

traje[1] *etc. v.* traer.

traje[2] m (*en general*) dress; costume (*a. de mujer*); suit *de hombre*; *fig.* garb, guise; ~ *de baño* bathing-costume; ~ *de calle* lounge suit; *en* ~ *de calle policía* in plain clothes; ~ *de campaña* battledress; ~ *de ceremonia*, ~ *de etiqueta* full-dress; dress suit, evening dress; ~ *de cuartel* undress; ~ *hecho* readymade suit; ~ *de luces* bullfighter's costume; ~ *de malla* tights; ~ *de montar* riding-habit; ~ *de novia* wedding dress; ~ *de paisano* civilian clothes; **trajear** [1a] clothe, dress; *co.* get up, rig out; ~**se** dress up *etc.*

trajín m haulage, transport; F coming and going; (*bullicio*) bustle.

trama f weft, woof; *fig.* plot, scheme; *thea. etc.* plot; **tramar** [1a] weave; *fig.* plot, contrive.

tramitación f transaction; steps, procedure; **tramitar** [1a] transact, negotiate; **trámite** m (*paso*) movement, transit; (*en negocio*) step, move; ~**s** *pl.* procedure; ~**s** *pl.* oficiales official channels.

tramo m flight *de escalera*; length, section *de camino etc.*; stretch; span *de puente*; (*terreno*) plot.

trampa f *hunt.* trap, snare; trapdoor *en suelo*; 🛱 fender; *fig.* snare, catch, pitfall; (*ardid*) trick, ruse; (*criminal*) fraud; fiddle F, wangle F; 🕇 bad debt; ~ *explosiva* booby trap; *armar* ~ *a* set a trap for; *caer en la* ~ fall for it; *hacer* ~**s** cheat; (*con manos*) juggle; *hay* ~ there's a catch somewhere; **trampear** [1a] v/t. cheat, swindle; v/i. get money by false pretenses; **trampolín** m springboard (*a. fig.*). **tramposo** 1. crooked; 2. m crook.

tranca f beam, pole; (*cross-*)bar *de puerta*; *S.Am.* binge; *a* ~**s** *y barrancas* through fire and water; **trancada** f stride; **trancar** [1g] v/t. *puerta* bar; v/i. F stride along.

trance *m* moment, juncture; (*mal paso, apuro*) critical juncture; ~ *mortal* dying moments.

tranco *m* big step, stride; *a* ~s pellmell; *en dos* ~s in a couple of ticks.

tranquilidad *f* stillness *etc.*; *con toda* ~ with one's mind at ease; **tranquilizador** *noticia* reassuring; *música etc.* soothing; **tranquilizante** *m* ₰ tranquillizer; **tranquilizar** [1f] still, calm; *ánimo* reassure, relieve; *¡tranquilícese!* calm yourself!; don't worry!; **tranquilo** still, calm, tranquil; quiet, calm, untroubled.

trans... trans...; *v. a.* tras...; **~acción** *f* compromise, settlement; ✝ transaction; (*volumen de*) ~es *pl.* turnover; **~atlántico 1.** transatlantic; **2.** *m* liner; **~bordador** *m* ferry; (*puente*) transporter bridge; **~bordar** [1a] *v/t. etc.* transfer; ⚓ tranship; ferry *en río*; *v/i.* ⚓ change; **~bordo** *m* transfer; change; ⚓ transhipment; ☊ *hacer* ~ change (*en* at); **~cribir** [3a; *p.p. transcrito*] transcribe; **~cripción** *f* transcription; **~currir** [3a] go by, elapse; **~curso** *m*: *en el* ~ *de* in the course of; **~eúnte 1.** transitory, transient; **2.** *m/f* passer-by; (*que vive fuera*) nonresident; **~ferencia** *f* transfer (*a.* ✞); **~ferencie; **~ferible** transferable; **~ferir** [3i] transfer; **~figurar** [1a] transfigure; **~formable** *mot.* convertible; **~formación** *f* transformation, change; **~formador** *m* ⚡ transformer; **~formar** [1a] transform; change.

trans...: **~fusión** *f* transfusion; ~ *de sangre* blood transfusion; **~gredir** [3a] transgress; **~gresor** *m*, **-a** *f* transgressor.

transición *f* transition; **transicional** transitional.

transido: ~ *de dolor* racked with pain; ~ *de hambre* overcome with hunger.

transigente accommodating, compromising; **transigir** [3c] compromise (*con* with); be tolerant (*con* towards).

transistor *m* ⚡ transistor.

transitable passable; **transitar** [1a] travel, go from place to place; **transitivo** transitive; **tránsito** *m* (*acto*) transit, passage; (*parada*) stop(pingplace); traffic; *transfer a puesto*; *horas de máximo* ~ rush hours; *de* ~, *en* ~ in transit; **transitorio** transitory.

trans...: **~lúcido** translucent; **~ma-**

~rino overseas; **~migrar** [1a] (trans)-migrate; **~misión** *f* transmission (*a.* ⊕, ✍); *radio a.* broadcast; ~ *en circuito* hook-up; ✕ (*cuerpo de*) ~es *pl.* signals; **~misor 1.:** *estación* ~ transmitting station; **2.** *m* transmitter; **~mitir** [3a] *mst* transmit (*a. radio*); *posesión* pass on, hand down; **~mutación** *f* transmutation; **~mutar** [1a] transmute; **~parencia** *f* transparency; **~parentarse** [1a] (*vidrio etc.*) be transparent; (*objeto visto*) show through; (*intención*) be clear; **~parente 1.** transparent (*a. fig.*); limpid; filmy; *aire etc.* clear; **2.** *m* curtain, blind; **~piración** *f* *anat.* perspiration; ♀ transpiration; **~pirar** [1a] *anat.* perspire; ♀ transpire.

transponer [2r] move, change the places of, transpose; *esquina* disappear round; **~se** hide behind s.t.

transportable transportable; **transportación** *f* transportation; **transportador** *m* ⚗ protractor; **transportar** [1a] transport; haul, carry; ⚓ *a.* ship; *diseño etc.* transfer; ♩ transpose; **~se** *fig.* get carried away; **transporte** *m* transport (*a. buque*); (*a.* ~s *pl.*) transportation; *fig.* transport, ecstasy; ~ *colectivo* public transportation.

transposición *f* transposition (*a.* ♩); move, change of places.

transversal, transverso transverse, oblique; *calle etc.* cross.

tranvía *m* streetcar.

trapo *m* rag; duster; ⚓ canvas, sails; F ~s *pl.* clothes, dresses; *a todo* ~ full sail; *soltar el* ~ burst out laughing; (*llorar*) burst into tears.

traque *m* crack, bang.

tráquea *f* windpipe, trachea ⚕ (*a. zo.*).

traque(te)ar [1a] *v/t.* (*agitar*) shake; rattle *con ruido*; F muck about with; *v/i.* crackle, bang *como cohete*; (*máquina, vehículo etc.*) rattle; jolt, joggle.

tras 1. *prp. lugar*: behind, after; *tiempo*: after; **2.** *cj.*: ~ *de inf.* besides *ger.*, in addition to *ger.*; **3.** *int.* ¡~, ~! bang, bang!

tras... trans...; *v. a.* tras...; **~alcoba** *f* dressing room; **~cendencia** *f* importance; result; implications; *esp. phls.* transcendence; *de* ~ important, significant; **~cendental** far-reaching, momentous, of great significance; *esp. phls.* transcendent(al); **~colar**

[1m] strain; *fig.* get *s.t.* across; **~conejarse** [1a] get lost; **~corral** *m* back yard; F bottom.

trasegar [1h *a.* 1k] *v/t.* decant; pour into another bottle; *botellas* rack; *fig.* upset, turn upside down; *puestos* reshuffle; *v/i.* F booze.

trasera *f* back, rear; **trasero 1.** back, rear, hind; **2.** *m* hind quarters, rump *de animal*; bottom *de p.*

trasfondo *m* background; (*honduras*) uttermost depths; undertone.

trasgo *m* goblin; imp.

trasladar [1a] transfer, move (*a* to); *función* postpone; *documento* copy; (*traducir*) translate; **~se** move; **~** *a puesto etc.* transfer to, move to; *otro sitio* move to, go on to, proceed to; **traslado** *m* transfer, move; copy.

tras...: ~lapar(se) [1a] overlap; **~lapo** *m* overlap; **~latício** *sentido* figurative; **~lucirse** [3f] (*cuerpo*) be translucent; (*hecho*) be plain to see; (*noticia*) leak out; **~luz** *m* diffused light; reflected light; *al ~* against the light; **~nochada** *f* last night; (*vela*) sleepless night; (*vigilia*) watch; **~** night attack; **~nochado** *comida*, *cuento* stale; *p.* hollow-eyed, run down; **~nochador** *m* (*p.*) night owl; **~nochar** [1a] *v/i.* *problema* sleep on; *v/i.* (*sin dormir*) have a sleepless night; (*pernoctar*) spend the night; (*estar fuera*) stay out all night, have a night on the tiles F; **~oír** [3q] mishear; **~ojado** haggard, hollow-eyed; **~país** *m* hinterland, interior; **~palar** [1a] shovel; **~papelar** [1a] mislay.

traspasar [1a] (*trasladar*) move; (*cruzar*) cross (over); *negocio* make over, transfer; *jugador* transfer; *esp.* ⚖ convey; *cuerpo* pierce, run through, transfix; *ley* violate; (*dolor*) rack, torture; **~se** go too far; **traspaso** *m* move; transfer; *esp.* ⚖ conveyance; (*dolor*) anguish, pain.

traspié *m* stumble, slip; (*zancadilla*) trip; *dar un* **~** stumble.

trasplantar [1a] transplant.

tras...: ~puesta *f* transposition, changing over; removal; *geog.* fold, rise; (*escondite*) hiding place; (*patio*) back yard; (*huida*) escape; **~quilar** [1a] *oveja* shear.

trastazo *m* whack, thump; **traste** *m* ♪ fret.

trasto *m* (*mueble*) piece of furniture; (*utensilio*) crock; (*cosa inútil*) piece of junk; *thea.* furniture and properties;

F (*p. inútil*) dead loss; (*p. molesta*) nuisance; (*p. rara*) queer type; **~s** *pl.* tools, tackle; **~s** *pl. de matar* weapons; **~s** *pl. de pescar* fishing-tackle; **~s** *pl. viejos* junk; F *coger los* **~s** pack up and go.

trastornar [1a] (*volcar*) turn upside down; overturn; *orden de objetos* mix up; *fig.* (*inquietar*) trouble; *sentidos* daze, make dizzy; *nervios* shatter; *orden político etc.* disturb; **trastorno** *m* (*acto*) overturning *etc.*; *fig. pol. etc.* upheaval; ⚕ upset, disorder; **~** *mental* mental disorder, breakdown.

trastrocar [1g *a.* 1m] reverse, invert, change round.

trasunto *m* copy; *fig.* (*a.* **~** *fiel*) faithful copy, exact image.

trasvolar [1m] fly over.

trata *f* slave trade; **~** *de blancas* white slave trade.

tratable tractable, manageable; *p.* sociable, easy to get on with.

tratado *m* *lit.* treatise, tract; *pol.* treaty; ✝ *etc.* agreement.

tratamiento *m* treatment (*a.* ⚕, ⊕); ⊕ processing; treatment.

tratante *m* dealer, trader (*en* in).

tratar [1a] **1.** *v/t.* mst treat (*a.* ⊕; **~** *con*, *por* with; *de loco etc.* as); ⊕ *a.* process; (*manejar*) handle, deal with; **~** *de p.* (*con título*, *de tú*) address as; **2.** *v/i.:* **~** *con* have dealings with; **~** (*acerca*) *de*, **~** *sobre* deal with, treat of; **3.** **~se** bien live well, do o.s. well; *se trata de su.* it is about su.

trato *m* treatment; (*entre ps.*) intercourse, dealings; relationship; manner; title, style (of address); ✝ deal, bargain; **~** *colectivo* collective bargaining; **~** *comercial* business deal; **~** *doble* double-dealing; **~** *sexual* sexual intercourse; *de fácil* **~** easy to get on with; *cerrar un* **~** strike a bargain, do a deal; *hacer un buen* **~** drive a good bargain.

través *m* bend, turn; (*torcimiento*) bias; △ cross-beam; △ traverse; *fig.* upset; *a(l)* **~** *de* through; across; over; *de* **~** sideways; crooked; **travesaño** *m* △, ⊕ transome, crossbar (*a. deportes*); bolster *de cama*; **travesía** *f* (*calle*) crossstreet; main road *dentro de pueblo*; **travesura** *f* prank, lark, (*piece of*) mischief; clever trick.

trayecto *m* (*espacio*) distance, way; (*viaje*) journey *de p.*, run *de vehículo*; flight *de bala etc.*; **trayectoria** *f* trajectory, path.

traza f △ etc. plan, design; (medio) device, scheme; (aspecto) looks; por las ⁓s by all the signs; **trazado 1.:** bien ⁓ goodlooking; mal ⁓ unattractive; 2. m (dibujo) outline, sketch; (plano) plan, layout; (línea) route; **trazador 1.** phys., ✕ tracer attr.; 2. m (p.) planner, designer; phys. etc. tracer; **trazar** [1f] sketch, outline, design, plan, lay out; límites mark out; línea draw, trace; curso etc. plot; medios contrive, devise; **trazo** m sketch, outline; line, stroke.

trébol m clover, trefoil (a. △); naipes: ⁓es pl. clubs.

trece thirteen; (fecha) thirteenth.

trecho m stretch, way; (tiempo) while; un buen ⁓ a good way; **de ⁓ en ⁓** at intervals.

tregua f ✕ truce; fig. respite, lull, let-up; no dar ⁓ give no respite.

treinta thirty; (fecha) thirtieth.

tremendo (horrendo) dreadful, frightful; (digno de respeto) imposing.

trementina f turpentine.

tremolar [1a] v/t. (agitar) wave; fig. make a show of; v/i. flutter, wave; **trémulo** quivering, tremulous; luz flickering; voz timid, small.

tren m 🚂 train; ✕ convoy; ⊕ set of engranajes etc.; outfit, equipment de viaje; (ps.) retinue; (boato) pomp; ⁓ ascendente up train; ⁓ de aterrizaje landing gear; ⁓ botijo, ⁓ de recreo excursion train; ⁓ correo mail train; slow train; ⁓ descendente down train; ⁓ expreso express train; ⁓ de laminación rolling mill; ⁓ de mercancías freight train; ⁓ ómnibus accommodation train, local train; ⁓ de viajeros passenger train; **en ⁓** by train.

trena f sl. clink.

trenza f plait, pigtail, pony tail; braid; twist de hebras; **trenzar** [1f] pelo plait, braid; hebras etc. twist, intertwine, weave.

trepar [1a] v/t. climb; ⊕ drill, bore; sew. trim; v/i. (a. ⁓ a) climb (up); clamber up; scale; ❦ climb (por up).

trepidar [1a] shake, vibrate.

tres three (a. su.); (fecha) third; las ⁓ three o'clock.

treta f fenc. feint; fig. trick, stratagem; wheeze F; gimmick publicitaria etc.; S.Am. bad habit.

triangular triangular, three-cornered; **triángulo** m triangle (a. ♪).

tribal tribal; **tribu** f tribe (a. zo.).

tribuna f rostrum de orador; hist. tribune; platform en mitin; gallery (a. eccl.); deportes: (grand)stand; ⁓ del acusado dock; ⁓ del jurado jury box; ⁓ de la prensa press box; **tribunal** m ⚖ court; (ps.) court, bench; tribunal de investigación etc.

tributar [1a] todos sentidos: pay; **tributario** adj. a. su. m tributary; **tributo** m tribute (a. fig.).

trigo m wheat; sl. dough; ⁓ sarraceno buck wheat; **de ⁓ entero** wholemeal.

triguero 1. wheat attr.; 2. m cornsieve.

trilla f threshing; **trillado** camino beaten, well-trodden; fig. trite, hack(neyed); **trillador** m thresher; **trilladora** f threshing machine; **trilladura** f threshing.

trimestral revista etc. quarterly; univ. terminal, termly; **trimestre** m quarter, period of three months; univ. term; † quarterly payment.

trinado m ♪ trill; orn. warble; **trinar** [1a] trill; orn. sing, warble.

trinchar [1a] carve, slice; F do in; **trinchera** f ✕ etc. trench; entrenchment; 🧥 cutting.

trineo m sled(ge), sleigh; ⁓ balancín bobsleigh.

tripa f intestine, gut; (panza) belly; ⁓s pl. anat. insides, guts; cocina: tripe; hacer de ⁓s corazón pluck up courage; put on a bold front.

triple 1. triple; threefold; 2. m triple; es el ⁓ de lo que era it is three times (or treble) what is was.

tripulación f crew; **tripulante** m crew member, man.

trique m crack, swish; a cada ⁓ at every turn.

tris m (ruido) crack, tinkle; F trice; en un ⁓ within an inch.

trisca f crushing noise; (retozo) romp; (jaleo) rumpus, row; **triscar** [1g] v/t. (mezclar) mix, mingle; (enredar) mix up; sierra set; v/i. stamp one's feet; (retozar) romp.

trismo m lockjaw.

triste mst sad; aspecto sad-looking, gloomy; carácter melancholy; (afligido) sorrowful; (sombrío) gloomy, dismal; paisaje etc. desolate, dreary; (despreciable) wretched, miserable

triunfador 1. triumphant; 2. m victor, winner; **triunfal** triumphal; **triunfante** triumphant; (jubiloso) jubilant, exultant; **triunfar** [1a] triumph (de over); exult (de, sobre

T

triunfo

over); *naipes*: trump; **triunfo** *m* triumph (*a. fig.*); *fig.* success; *naipes*: trump; *sin* ~ no trumps.

trivial trivial; (*trillado*) trite; (*grosero*) vulgar; **trivialidad** *f* triviality; triteness.

triza *f* shred, bit; ~s *pl. fig.* ribbons; *hacer* ~s shred, tear up.

trocar [1g *a.* 1m] ✝ *etc.* exchange, barter; change (*con, por* for); *palabras* exchange; (*equivocar*) mix up, twist; ~**se** change.

trocha *f* by-path, narrow path.

trofeo *m* trophy; *fig.* victory.

troglodita *m* caveman, troglodyte; *fig.* brute; (*comilón*) glutton.

troj(e) *f* barn, granary.

trole *m* trolley.

tromba *f* whirlwind; column *de polvo etc.*; ~; (*marina*) waterspout.

trombón *m* trombone.

trompa *f* horn; (*trompo*) humming-top; trunk *de elefante*; proboscis *de insecto etc.*; *sl.* hooter, conk; *anat.* tube, duct; *sl. cogerse una* ~ get boozed.

trompeta **1.** *f* trumpet; **2.** *m* = trompetero; **trompetazo** *m* trumpet blast; blast, blare; **trompetear** [1a] (play the) trumpet; **trompetero** *m* ♪ trumpet player.

tronada *f* thunderstorm; **tronado** F broke; **tronar** [1m] thunder; (*cañón etc.*) thunder, rumble; F fail, be ruined; ~ *contra* denounce, fulminate against; storm at.

tronchar [1a] chop off, lop off.

tronco *m* ♀ (*de árbol*), *anat.* trunk; stem, stalk *de flor*; (*leño*) log.

tronera *f* ✕ loophole, embrasure; △ narrow window; *billar*: pocket.

tronido *m* thunderclap; ~s *pl.* thunder.

trono *m* throne.

tropa *f* (*gente*) troop, flock, body; ✕ (*soldados*) troop; (*no oficiales*) men, rank and file; *S.Am.* herd; ~s *pl.* troops; **tropel** *m* (*movimiento*) rush, bustle; (*prisa*) rush, hurry; (*confusión*) jumble, mess; (*muchedumbre*) throng; *de* ~, *en* ~ in utter chaos; in a mad rush.

tropezar [1f *a.* 1k] trip, stumble (*con, en* on, over); (*reñir*) fall out (*con* with); *fig.* ~ *con*, ~ *en dificultad* run into, run up against; (*encontrar*) stumble upon; *p.* run into; **tropezón** *m* stumble, trip; *a* ~*es* by fits and starts; *hablar etc.* falteringly.

tropical tropic(al); **trópico** *m* tropic; ~s *pl.* tropics.

tropiezo *m* stumble, trip; *fig.* snag, obstacle; (*falta*) slip.

trotar [1a] trot; F be on the go, hustle; **trote** *m* trot; ~ *cochinero*, ~ *de perro* jog trot; *al* ~ at a trot; quickly.

trozo *m* bit, piece; ♪, *lit. etc.* passage; *a* ~s piecemeal, in bits.

trucha *f* trout; ⊕ derrick, crane.

truco *m* F trick, wheeze, dodge; ~ *de naipes* card trick; ~ *de propaganda* gimmick.

trueno *m* thunder; (*un* ~) clap of thunder; bang, report.

trueque *m* exchange; barter; *a* ~ *de* in exchange for.

trufa *f* truffle; F fib, story; **trufar** [1a] *v/i.* F fib.

truhán *m* rogue, crook; (*gracioso*) clown, funny man; **truhanesco** crooked; funny.

tú you; (✝, *a Dios*) thou; *tratar etc. de* ~ = *tutear.*

tu, tus *pl.* your; (✝, *a Dios*) thy.

tubérculo *m* ♀ tuber; *anat., zo.*, 🍎 tubercle; **tuberculosis** *f* tuberculosis; **tuberculoso** tubercular.

tubería *f* tubing; piping, pipes; **tubo** *m* tube (*a. anat., televisión*); pipe; ~ *acústico* speaking tube; ~ *de aspiración* breathing tube; ~ *capilar* capillary; ~ *de chimenea* chimney pot; ~ *de desagüe* waste pipe; drain pipe; ~ *digestivo* alimentary canal; ~ *de ensayo* test tube; ~ *de escape* exhaust (pipe); ~ *de humo* flue; ~ *de imagen televisión* picture tube; ~ *de lámpara* lampglass; ~ *de paso* bypass; ~ *de rayos catódicos* cathode ray tube; ~ *sonoro* chime; ~ *de vacío* vacuum tube; **tubular** tubular.

tuerca *f* nut; ~ *mariposa* wing nut.

tuerto 1. (*torcido*) twisted, crooked; (*de ojo*) one-eyed; **2.** *m*, *a* f one-eyed person; **3.** *m* wrong.

tuétano *m anat.* marrow; ♀ pith; *hasta los* ~s through and through.

tufo *m* gas; (*olor*) stink.

tul *m* tulle, net.

tulipán *m* tulip.

tullido 1. crippled; paralytic; **2.** *m*, *a* f cripple; **tullir** [3h] cripple, maim; paralyse; *fig.* abuse.

tumba¹ *f* grave, tomb.

tumba² *f* (*voltereta*) somersault; **tumbar** [1a] *v/t.* knock down, knock over; F (*vino*) lay *s.o.* out; *v/i.* fall down; ♣ capsize; ~**se** lie down;

stretch out, sprawl; **tumbo** m fall, tumble; (*vaivén*) shake, lurch; *fig.* critical moment; *dar un ~* tumble; (*a. dar ~s*) lurch.

tumor m tumour, growth.

tumulto m tumult; *pol. etc.* riot; **tumultuario, tumultuoso** tumultuous; riotous.

tunante 1. crooked; **2.** m rogue, crook; *esp. co.* scamp, villain.

tunda f shearing; F hiding; **tundir** [3a] *paño* shear; *hierba* mow, cut.

túnel m tunnel; ~ *aerodinámico,* ~ *del viento* wind tunnel; ~ *de lavado* automatic car wash.

túnica f *hist., anat. etc.* tunic; (*vestido largo*) robe, gown.

tupido thick, dense (*a.* F); *paño* closewoven; *paño* [3a] pack tight.

turba[1] f *geol.* peat, turf.

turba[2] f crowd; swarm; mob.

turbación f confusion; disturbance; (*de p.*) embarrassment; distress; trepidation; **turbador** disturbing.

turbamulta f mob, rabble.

turbante m turban.

turbar [1a] *orden etc.* disturb, upset; *agua* stir up; *fig.* darken; *p., ánimo* disturb, upset, worry; (*desconcertar*) embarrass; **~se** get embarrassed, feel awkward; get all mixed up; (*inquietarse*) get upset.

turbio *agua* muddy, turbid; *líquido* thick, cloudy; *aguas fig.* dark,

troubled; *época, vida* unsettled; *negocio* shady; *medio* dubious.

turbión m heavy shower, squall; *fig.* shower; swarm; hail *de balas.*

turbocompresor m turbocompressor; **turbohélice** adj. a. su. m turboprop; **turborreactor** adj. a. su. m turbo-jet.

turbulento turbulent; *niño* noisy, unruly; *espíritu etc.* restless; *época* troubled; *ejército etc.* mutinous, disorderly.

turismo m tourism; tourist trade; touring; sightseeing; (*coche de*) ~ tourer; **turista** m/f tourist; sightseer; **turístico** tourist *attr.*

turnar [1a] take turns; **turno** m (*vez*) turn; (*tanda*) spell, shift; turn, go *en juegos*; *por ~* in rotation, in turn; *por ~s* by turns; *esperar su ~* take one's turn.

turrón m nougat; F plum, easy job.

tusar [1a] *S.Am.* cut, shear.

tutear [1a] address *as tú*; be on familiar terms with.

tutela f 🏛 guardianship; *fig.* protection, tutelage; *bajo ~* in ward.

tuteo m addressing a *p. as tú.*

tutor m guardian, tutor; **tutora** f guardian; **tutoría** f guardianship.

tuve *etc. v.* tener.

tuyo, tuya 1. *pron.* yours, (†, *a Dios*) thine; **2.** *adj.* (*tras su.*) of yours.

U

u or (*before words beginning with o or ho*).

ubicación f location, position, situation; **ubicar** [1g] *v/t. S.Am.* place, put; *v/i.,* **~se** be located.

ubre f udder; (*cada pezón*) teat.

ufanarse [1a] boast; ~ *de* pride o.s. on, boast of; **ufanía** f pride; *b.s.* vanity, conceit; **ufano** proud; exultant; (*alegre*) cheerful.

ujier m usher, attendant.

úlcera f ulcer; (*esp. externo*) sore; **ulceración** f ulceration; **ulcerar** [1a] ulcerate, **~se** ulcerate, fester; **ulceroso** ulcerous; full of sores.

ulterior *lugar*: farther, further; *tiempo*: later, subsequent.

ultimación f conclusion; **últimamente** lastly, finally; (*recientemente*) lately, of late; **ultimar** [1a] end,

finish; *trato etc.* conclude; **ultimátum** m *pol.* ultimatum; **último** (*en ~ lugar*) last; latter *de dos*; (*más reciente*) latest; (*más remoto*) furthest; (*extremo*) utmost; *piso* top; *calidad* finest, superior; *este ~* the latter; *a ~s de mes* in the latter part of.

ultra... ultra...

ultrajador, ultrajante outrageous; insulting, offensive; **ultrajar** [1a] outrage; insult; **ultraje** m outrage; insult; **ultrajoso** outrageous.

ultramar *de ~,* *en ~* overseas; **ultramarino 1.** overseas; **2.** *~s m/pl.* groceries, delicatessen.

ultramoderno ultramodern.

ultravioleta ultraviolet.

ulular [1a] howl, shriek; (*búho*) hoot; **ululato** m howl, shriek; hoot.

umbilical umbilical.

U

umbral m threshold (a. ~es pl. fig.).

umbrío, umbroso shady; shadowy.

un, una 1. artículo: a, (delante de vocal y h muda) an; **2.** adj. numeral: one; ¡a la una, a las dos, a las tres! (subasta) going, going, gone!; (carreras) ready, steady, go!

unánime unanimous; **unanimidad** f unanimity; por ~ unanimously.

unción f eccl. a. fig. unction.

uncir [3b] yoke.

ungir [3c] anoint (a. eccl.), apply ointment to; **ungüento** m ointment, salve.

uni... uni...; one-...

únicamente only; solely.

único only; sole, single, solitary; (singular, extraordinario) unique; distribuidor etc. sole, exclusive; hijo ~ only child; este ejemplar es-~ this specimen is unique.

unidad f unity; oneness; ✕, ⚕, ⊕ etc. unit; **unido** united; (liso) smooth; **unificación** f unification; **unificar** [1g] unite, unify.

unifamiliar casa one-family.

uniformar [1a] make uniform; p. put into uniform; **uniforme 1.** mst uniform; velocidad etc. a. steady, unvarying, regular; superficie a. level, even, true; **2.** m uniform; **uniformidad** f uniformity etc.

unilateral one-sided, unilateral.

unión f union (a. ✝); (unidad) unity; (casamiento) union, marriage; ⊕ union, joint; (punto de) ~ junction.

unir [3a] cosas join; mst fig. unite; sociedades, intereses merge; ~se join (together) unite; esp. ✝ merge.

universal universal; world-wide; **universalidad** f universality; generality; **universidad** f university; **universitario 1.** university; **2.** m/f university student; **3.** m university professor; **universo** m universe.

uno 1. adj. one; identical, one and the same; Dios es ~ God is one; la verdad es una truth is one and indivisible; ~s pl. some, a few; unos 20 km some 20 km, about 20 km; **2.** pron. one; ~ que vino a verme someone who came to see me; ~ no sabe one does not know; ~ necesita amigos a man needs friends; ~ a ~ one by one; ~(s) a otro(s) one another, each other; ~ que otro an occasional, the odd; ~ y otro both; cada ~ each one, everyone; en~ at one; una de dos either one (thing) or the

other; a una all together; la una one o'clock; **3.** m one.

untar [1a] smear, dab (de with); (engrasar) grease, oil; pan, mantequilla spread; fig. bribe, grease the palm of; **unto** m grease; fat de animal; **untuoso** greasy, sticky; mst fig. unctuous.

uña f anat. nail; (garra) claw; hoof de caballo; sting de alacrán; ⚓ fluke, bill; ⊕ pallet; ♘ claw; ⚓ ~ de caballo coltsfoot; a ~ de caballo at full gallop; largo de ~s light-fingered; comerse las ~s bite one's nails; **uña(ra)da** f nailmark; **uñero** m ingrowing nail; 🌿 whitlow.

uranio m uranium.

urbanidad f refinement, urbanity; **urbanismo** m town planning; **urbanización** f urbanization; development; **urbanizado** built-up; **urbanizar** [1f] terreno urbanize, develop, build on; p. civilize; **urbano** urban, city attr.; fig. polite, refined, urbane; **urbe** f large city, metropolis; La ♀ esp. Madrid.

urdimbre f warp; **urdir** [3a] warp; fig. contrive, plot, scheme.

urgencia f urgency; pressure; haste; emergency; pressing need; de ~ emergency; salida emergency attr.; botiquín etc. first-aid attr.; en caso de ~ in case of necessity; pedir con ~ press for; **urgente** (que corre prisa) urgent; (apremiante) pressing; demanda etc. imperative, insistent; pedido rush attr.; carta express; **urgir** [3c] be urgent, press; urge inf. it is absolutely necessary to inf.

urna f urn; glass case; ~ electoral ballot box; ~s pl. electorales fig. voting place; acudir a las ~s vote, go to the polls.

urraca f magpie.

usado used; (gastado) worn; p. skilled, experienced.

usanza f custom; a ~ de according to the custom of.

usar [1a] v/t., a. v/i. ~ de use, make use of; sin~ unused; sello etc. mint; ~ inf. be accustomed to inf.; ~se be used, be in use; (estilarse) be in fashion; (gastarse) wear out.

uso m (empleo) use; (usufructo) use, enjoyment; (deterioro) wear (and tear); (costumbre) custom, usage; (moda) fashion, style; al ~ in keeping with custom; al ~ de hacer etc. for the use of; vestir etc. in the style of; en ~ in use.

usted, ustedes pl. you.

usual usual, customary; **usuario** *m*, **a** *f* user; **usufructo** *m* usufruct, use; ~ (*vitalicio*) life interest (*de* in).
usura *f* usury; (*ganancia excesiva*) profiteering; **usurario** usurious; **usurear** [1a] profiteer; **usurero** *m* usurer, loan shark.
usurpación *f* usurpation; *fig* encroachment (*de* upon), inroad (*de* into); **usurpador** *m* usurper; **usurpar** [1a] usurp (*a. fig.*); *fig.* encroach upon, make inroads into.
utensilio *m* tool, implement; utensil.
útero *m* womb, uterus.
útil 1. useful; helpful, handy; usable, serviceable; **2.** *m* usefulness; ~**es** *pl.* (set of) tools, implements, equipment; **utilidad** *f* use(fulness), utility; (*provecho*) profit, benefit, good; **utilitario** utilitarian; *ropa etc.* utility *attr.*; **utilizable** usable; fit for use, ready to use; ⊕ *desechos* reclaimable; **utilización** *f* use, utilization; ⊕ reclamation; **utilizar** [1f] use, make use of, utilize.
utopía *f* Utopia; **utópico, utopista** *m/f* Utopian.
uva *f* grape; ~ *espina* gooseberry; ~ *pasa* raisin; ~ *de Corinto* currant; *estar hecho una* ~ be stoned, be high.
úvula *f* uvula; **uvular** uvular.

V

va *etc. v. ir.*
vaca *f* cow; (*carne*) beef; (*cuero*) cowhide; ~ *lechera* milker; ~ *marina* sea cow; ~ *de San Antón* ladybird.
vacación *f* holiday(s), vacation (*mst* ~**es** *pl.*); (*puesto*) vacancy; **vacacionista** *m/f* vacationist.
vacada *f* herd of cows.
vacante 1. vacant, unoccupied; **2.** *f* vacancy; **vacar** [1g] be vacant.
vaciar [1c] *v/t. vasija, bolsillo etc.* empty; *vaso etc.* drain; *contenido* empty out; *líquido* pour away, run off; (*ahuecar*) hollow out; (*afilar*) grind, sharpen; *v/i.* (*río*) flow, empty (*en* into); ~**se** F spill the beans.
vacilante *luz* flickering; *movimiento* unsteady; *habla* halting; *fig.* hesitant, vacillating; **vacilar** [1a] (*luz*) flicker; (*mueble etc.*) be unsteady, shake; (*habla*) falter; *fig.* hesitate, waver, vacillate.
vacío 1. empty; *puesto etc.* vacant, unoccupied; *papel* blank; *charla* idle; (*inútil*) vain, useless; (*presuntuoso*) vain, proud; **2.** *m phys.* vacuum; (*el espacio, la nada*) void; (*ijada*) side, ribs; (*puesto*) vacancy.
vacuidad *f* emptiness; vacancy.
vacuna *f* vaccine; **vacunación** *f* vaccination; **vacunar** [1a] vaccinate; **vacuno** bovine.
vadear [1a] *v/t. río* ford; *aqua* wade through; *fig. dificultad* get around, overcome.
vado *m* ford; *fig.* way out, expedient; *no hallar* ~ see no way out.
vagabundo 1. vagabond; wandering, vagrant; **2.** *m*, **a** *f* wanderer, rover; *b.s.* tramp, bum *Am.*; vagabond, vagrant; **vagancia** *f* vagrancy; idleness; **vagante** vagrant; **vagar 1.** [1h] wander, rove, roam; prowl; **2.** *m* leisure.
vagido *m* wail, cry.
vago 1. vague, indeterminate; *perfil etc.* ill-defined, indistinct; *ideas* vague, woolly; *control etc.* loose, lax; (*holgazán*) lazy; (*errante*) roving; **2.** *m* (*holgazán*) lazy sort; (*no confiable*) unreliable sort.
vagón *m* car, railroad car; ~ *cama* sleeping car; ~ *carbonero* coal car; ~ *de carga* freight car; ~ *cerrado* boxcar; ~ *cisterna* tank car; ~ *de cola* caboose; ~ *frigorífico* refrigerator car; ~ *de mercancías* freight car; ~ *de plataforma* flatcar; ~ *salón* parlor car; ~ *tolva* hopper-bottom car; ~ *volquete* dump car.
vagoneta *f* ⚒ *etc.* tip car; *S.Am.* delivery van.
vaharada *f* puff; whiff, reek; **vah(e)ar** [1a] steam, send out vapor; **vahido** *m* queer turn, dizzy spell; **yaho** *m* vapor, steam, fumes.
vaina *f* sheath, scabbard; ⚘ pod, husk, shell; **vainilla** *f* vanilla.
vaivén *m* oscillation, rocking; swing, sway; movement to and fro.
vajilla *f* (*en general*) crockery; (*una* ~) set of dishes, service; ~ *de oro* gold plate; ~ *de plata* silver plate; ~ *de*

porcelana chinaware; *lavar la* ~ wash the dishes.

valdré etc. v. **valer**.

vale m promissory note, IOU; (*cédula*) voucher, warrant; **valedero** valid, binding.

valentía f courage, bravery; b.s. boastfulness; **valentón 1.** boastful; arrogant; **2.** m braggart.

valer [2q] **1.** v/t. (*tener el valor de*) be worth, be valued at; cost; (*sumar*) amount to; be equal to, be equivalent to; *castigo* etc. earn; (*ayudar, servir*) avail, be of help to, protect; ¿*cuánto vale?* how much is it?; **2.** v/i. (*ser valioso*) be valuable; (*ser valedero*) be valid; (*p.* etc.) have one's merits; count *en juegos* etc.; **3.** ~**se:** *no poder* ~ be helpless; ~ *de* make use of; *derecho* exercise; ~ *por sí mismo* help o.s.; **4.** m value, worth.

valeroso brave; effective, powerful.

valía f value, worth; influence.

validar [1a] ratify; validate; **validez** f validity; **válido** valid; (*sano*) strong, fit; **valido** m pol. favorite.

valiente brave, gallant; (*excelente*) fine, first-rate; iro. fine.

valija f case; 𝄞 (*saco*) mail bag; (*correo*) mail, post; ~ *diplomática* diplomatic bag.

valioso valuable; useful, worthwhile; (*rico*) wealthy.

valla f fence; (*defensa*) barricade, stockade; roadside advertising sign; ~ (*de construcción*) hoarding; fig. obstacle; *deportes:* hurdle.

valle m valley; ~ *de lágrimas* vale of tears.

valor m value (a. ♪, ♫), worth; price; value, denomination *de moneda* etc.; importance; (*sentido*) meaning; (*ánimo*) courage; (*atrevimiento*) nerve, audacity; ✝ ~es pl. securities, bonds, stock; ~es pl. *en cartera* investments; ~es pl. *habidos* holdings; ~ *nominal* face value.

valoración f ✝ valuation; fig. assessment; 🜪 titration; **valorar** [1a] value; price; esp. fig. assess, rate.

vals m waltz; **valsar** [1a] waltz.

válvula f valve; ~ *de admisión* intake valve; ~ *de escape* exhaust valve; ~ *de purga* vent; ~ *de seguridad* safety valve.

vamos v. **ir**.

vampiresa f vamp; **vampiro** m vampire; fig. vampire, bloodsucker.

vanidad f vanity; uselessness etc.;

vanidoso vain, conceited, smug;
vano useless, vain, idle; (*ilusorio*) vain; (*frívolo*) inane, idle, frivolous.

vapor m steam (a. ⊕), vapor; (*natural*) vapor, mist; (*con olor*) fumes; 🜪 faintness, giddiness; ~ *de ruedas* paddle steamer; ~ *volandero* tramp (steamer); *al* ~ by steam; *de* ~ steam attr.; **vaporizador** m vaporizer; spray *de perfume* etc.; **vaporizar** [1f] vaporize; *perfume* etc. spray; **vaporoso** steamy, misty, vaporous; fig. light, airy.

vaquería f dairy; (*vacada*) herd of cows; **vaquer(iz)o** m herdsman, cowman, cowboy; **vaqueta** f cowhide; **vaquill(on)a** f heifer.

vara f stick, rod (a. ⊕), bar; wand *de mando*; shaft *de coche*; (*medida*) approx. yard (2.8 feet); ~ *alta* authority, power; ~ *de adivinar* divining rod; ~ *de oro* goldenrod; ~ *de pescar* fishing rod; **varada** f launching; (*encalladura*) stranding; **varadero** m shipyard; **varal** m long pole, long stick; **varapalo** m long pole.

varar [1a] v/t. (*botar*) launch; beach *en playa* etc.; v/i. ~**se** run aground, be stranded; fig. get bogged down.

varazo m blow with a stick; **varear** [1a] p. beat, strike; beat.

variable variable (a. 🜪), changeable, up-and-down; **2.** f 🜪 variable; **variación** f variation (a. ♪); **variado** varied; mixed; *superficie* etc. variegated, chequered; **variante** adj. a. su. f variant; **variar** [1c] v/t. vary, change; alter, modify; v/i. vary; change; range (*de* from; *a* to).

várices f/pl. varicose veins.

varicela f chicken pox.

variedad f variety (a. biol.).

vario various, varied; *colorido* variegated, motley; *actividades* multifarious; (*inconstante*) changeable; ~ pl. several, some, a number of.

varón m (*hombre*) man; (*macho*) male; (*de edad viril*) adult male; (*respetable*) worthy man, great man; *hijo* ~ male child, boy; **varonil** manly, virile; biol. male, masculine.

vase = **se va**; v. **ir**.

vaselina f Vaseline; petroleum jelly.

vasija f vessel; container.

vaso m glass, tumbler; (*en general*) vessel; hist. vase; (*cantidad*) glassful; anat., 🜪 vessel; duct; hoof *de caballo*; ~ *capilar* capillary; ~ *de engrase* ⊕ grease cup; ~ *graduado* measuring

V

vengar

glass, measuring cup; ~ de noche chamber pot; ~ sanguíneo blood vessel.

vástago m ⊕ rod, stem; ⚘ shoot, bud; fig. scion, offspring.

vasto vast, immense.

vaya v. ir.

vecinal camino local; **vecindad** f neighborhood, vicinity; (ps.) neighborhood, neighbors; **vecindario** m neighborhood; community; (cifra etc.) population, inhabitants; **vecino 1.** neighboring, adjoining; casa etc. next; (cercano) near, close; fig. close, similar (a to); **2.** m, **a** f (de al lado) neighbor; (habitante) resident, inhabitant.

veda f (acto) prohibition; (tiempo) close season; **vedar** [1a] forbid, prohibit; (impedir) stop.

vedette [beˈðet] f star.

vegetación f vegetation; (desarrollo) growth; **vegetal 1.** plant attr., vegetable; **2.** m plant, vegetable; **vegetar** [1a] grow; esp. fig. vegetate; **vegetariano** adj. a. su. m, **a** f vegetarian; **vegetativo** vegetative.

vehemencia vehemence etc.; **vehemente** vehement, passionate.

vehículo m vehicle (a. fig.).

veinte twenty; (fecha) twentieth; **veintena** f a score, (about) twenty.

vejación f vexation; **vejamen** m vexation; (represión) sharp rebuke.

vejar [1a] vex, annoy.

vejez f old age; fig. old story.

vejiga f anat. bladder (a. de pelota); (ampolla) blister.

vela[1] f ⚓ sail; (toldo) awning; ~ de cruz square sail; ~ mayor mainsail; ~ romana Roman candle; F entre dos ~s half-seas-over; darse (or hacerse) a la ~ (set) sail, get under way.

vela[2] f wakefulness, being awake; (trabajo) night work; (romería) pilgrimage; (velación) vigil; candle; pasar la noche en ~ have a sleepless night; **velada** f evening party, soirée; party, social para divertirse; = vela; ~ musical musical evening; **velador** m candlestick; (p.) watchman, caretaker.

velar[1] [1a] veil (a. fig.); phot. fog veil; fig. shroud; ~se phot. fog.

velar[2] [1a] v/t. keep watch over, watch; enfermo sit up with; v/i. (no dormir) stay awake; stay up.

veleidad f fickleness; (capricho) whim; **veleidoso** fickle, inconstant.

velero 1. swift; **2.** m ⚓ sailingship.

veleta f weather vane, weathercock.

vello m down, hair; ⚘ bloom; **vellocino** m fleece; ~ de oro Golden Fleece; **vellón** m (lana) fleece; (piel) sheepskin; metall. copper alloy; **vellosidad** f hairiness etc.; **velloso** hairy; **velludo** shaggy.

velo m veil; fig. veil, shroud, film; pretext; phot. fog, veil(ing); ~ del paladar soft palate.

velocidad f speed, pace, rate; velocity; (ligereza) swiftness; ⊕, mot. speed; (engranaje) gear; de alta ~ high-speed; ~ de crucero cruising speed; ~ económica cruising speed; límite de ~, ~ máxima permitida speed limit; primera ~ low gear, bottom gear; segunda ~ second gear; a toda ~ at full speed; **velocímetro** m speedometer.

veloz fast, speedy; (ligero) swift.

vena f anat. vein; (filón) vein, seam; grain de piedra, madera; streak.

venablo m dart, javelin.

venado m deer, stag; venison.

vencedor 1. equipo etc. winning; general, país conquering, victorious; **2.** m, **-a** f winner; victor, conqueror.

vencer [2b] v/t. enemigo defeat, beat, conquer; deportes: beat; rival surpass, outdo; v/i. win; ✝ (plazo) expire; (obligaciones) mature, fall due; ~se control o.s.; **vencido** equipo etc. losing; ✝ mature; due, payable; **vencimiento** m ✝ expiration; maturity.

venda f bandage; **vendaje** m dressing, bandaging; ~ provisional first-aid bandage; **vendar** [1a] herida bandage, dress; ojos etc. cover.

vendedor m seller, vendor; salesman de tienda etc.; ~ ambulante pedlar, hawker; **vendedora** f seller; salesgirl, saleswoman en tienda etc.; **vender** [2a] sell; market; fig. sell, betray, give away; ~se sell (bien etc.); be sold; ~ a, ~ por sell at, sell for; **vendible** saleable, marketable.

vendré etc. v. venir.

veneno m poison, venom; **venenoso** poisonous, venomous.

venera f zo. scallop; (cáscara) scallop shell.

venerable venerable; **veneración** f veneration; **venerar** [1a] venerate.

venéreo venereal.

venero m spring; min. lode.

vengador 1. avenging; **2.** m, **-a** f avenger; **venganza** f vengeance, revenge; retaliation; **vengar** [1h] avenge; **~se** take revenge (de for, en on); retaliate (en on, against); **vengativo** vindictive.

vengo etc. v. venir.

venia f pardon, forgiveness; (permiso) leave, consent; (saludo) nod.

venida f (llegada) arrival, coming; (regreso) return; fig. impetuosity, rashness; **venidero** coming, forthcoming, future.

venir [3s] come (a to; de from); el mes que viene next month; vengo cansado I'm tired; ¿a qué viene ...? what's the point of ...?; ¡venga! come along!; ¡venga un beso! let's have a kiss!; ¡venga el libro ese! let's have a look at that book!; venga lo que viniere come what may; (estar a) ~ sit on the fence, wait and see; ~ a su. agree to, consent to; ~ a inf. come to inf.; (terminar) end by ger., end up ger.; (suceder) happen to inf.; (acertar) manage to inf.; ~ a ser (sumar) amount to, work out at; (resultar) turn out to be; ~ a menos come down in the world; ~ bien ⚘ etc. do well, grow well; (objeto) come in handy; ~ bien a (vestido) fit, suit; **~se** ferment; ~ abajo, ~ a tierra collapse, tumble down.

venta f selling, marketing; (mesón) inn; ~ al contado cash sale; ~ de liquidación clearance sale; ~ a plazos installment plan; ~ por balance clearance sale; ~ pública (public) auction; precio de ~ selling price; de ~ on sale, on the market; en ~ for sale; poner a la ~ put on sale.

ventaja f advantage; asset; start en carrera; tenis: vantage; odds en juego; (sobresueldo) bonus; (ganancia) gain, profit; **ventajoso** advantageous; ✝ profitable.

ventana f window; ~ de guillotina sash window; ~ de la nariz nostril; ~ salediza bay window; **ventanaje** m windows; **ventanal** m large window; **ventanilla** f small window; ticket window; window de coche etc.; anat. nostril; **ventanillo** m small window; peephole en puerta.

ventarrón m gust (of wind).

ventear [1a] v/t. (perro etc.) sniff, scent; ropa air, put out to dry; fig. smell out; v/i. snoop, come sniffing around; **~se** (henderse) split; (arruinarse) spoil.

ventilación f ventilation (a. fig.); fig. airing, discussion; **ventilado** drafty, breezy; **ventilador** m ventilator,

(electric) fan; **ventilar** [1a] ventilate; fig. air, discuss.

ventisca f blizzard, snowstorm.

ventosear [1a] break wind; **ventosidad** f wind, flatulence; **ventoso** windy.

ventrílocuo m, **a** f ventriloquist; **ventriloquia** f ventriloquism.

ventura f luck, (good) fortune; (dicha) happiness; a la (buena) ~ at random; hit or miss; por ~ by chance; (quizá) perhaps; **venturoso** lucky, fortunate, happy.

ver [2v] **1.** mst see; (mirar) look at; (examinar) look into; ⚖ hear, try; le vi llegar I saw him arrive; **véase** see, vide; ¡a ~! let's see, let's have a look; a mi modo de ~ in my opinion; ~ y creer seeing is believing; dejarse ~ (p.) show one's face, show up; (efecto) become apparent; dejarse ~ en tell on; no dejarse ~ keep away; echar de ~ notice; estar por ~ remain to be seen; hacer ~ que make s.o. see that; make the point that en dispute; no poder ~ not be able to stand; ser de ~ be worth seeing; **2.** **~se** become (p.); (reflexivo) see o.s.; (recíproco) see each other; (encontrarse) (una p.) find o.s., be; (dos ps.) meet; ya se ve naturally; ya se ve que it is obvious that; **3.** m sight, vision; (aspecto) looks, appearance, opinion; a mi ~ in my opinion.

vera f edge, verge; a la ~ de near.

veracidad f truthfulness, veracity.

veranear [1a] spend the summer (vacation), vacation; **veraneo** m summer vacation; lugar de ~, punto de ~ summer resort; **veraniego** summer attr.; **veranillo** m: ~ de San Martín Indian summer; **verano** m summer.

veras f/pl. truth, reality; (seriedad) earnestness; serious matters, hard facts; de ~ really; (en serio) in earnest; ¿de ~? really?, indeed?

veraz truthful, veracious.

verbena f fair; (velada) evening party; eccl. night festival.

verbo m gr. verb; el ♀ the Word; **verboso** wordy, verbose.

verdad f truth; la ~ lisa y llana the plain truth; la pura ~ es the fact of the matter is; a la ~ really, in truth; de ~ real, proper; en ~ really, truly; es ~ it is true (que that); ¿no es ~?, ¿~? isn't it?, don't you? etc.; isn't that so?; **verdaderamente** really, truly, indeed; **verdadero** historia etc. true, truthful; *p.* truthful; (*real, cierto*) true, real, veritable.

verde 1. green; *fruta* green, unripe; *madera* unseasoned; (*fresco*) fresh; (*lozano*) young, vigorous, lusty; *cuento etc.* dirty, smutty; ¡están ~s! sour grapes!; **2.** *m* green; 💚 greenery, foliage; **verdear** [1a], **verdecer** [2d] (*estar*) look green; (*hacerse*) turn green, grow green; **verdor** *m* greenness; **verdoso** greenish.

verdugo *m* executioner, hangman.

verdura *f* greenness; *esp.* 💚 greenery, verdure; ~s *pl.* vegetables.

vereda *f* path, lane.

verga *f* ⚓ yard (arm), spar; *anat.* penis; **vergajo** *m* whip.

vergonzante shame-faced; **vergonzoso** (*tímido*) bashful, shy; (*pudoroso*) modest; (*que causa vergüenza*) shameful, disgraceful; *anat. partes* private; **vergüenza** *f* shame; bashfulness, shyness, modesty; (*oprobio*) shame; ¡qué ~! shame (on you)!, what a disgrace!; ~s genitals, privates, private parts.

verídico true, truthful; **verificable** verifiable; **verificación** *f* checking, check-up, verification; proving; **verificar** [1g] (*comprobar*) check (up on), verify; *hechos* substantiate; *testamento* prove; *contador etc.* inspect; (*efectuar*) carry out; ~se (*tener lugar*) take place; (*ser verdad*) prove true, come true.

verismo *m* realism, truthfulness.

verja *f* (*reja*) grating, grill.

vernal spring *attr.*, vernal.

verosímil likely, probable; *relato* credible; **verosimilitud** *f* likeliness, probability.

verraco *m* boar; **verraquear** [1a] F grunt; (*niño*) howl with rage.

verruga *f* wart (*a.* 💚); *fig.* defect; (*p.*) bore, nuisance.

versal *adj. a. su. f typ.* capital; **versalitas** *f/pl. typ.* small capitals.

versar [1a] turn, go round; ~ *sobre fig. materia* deal with, discuss.

versátil *miembro etc.* mobile, easily turned; (*inconstante*) changeable, fickle; (*talentoso*) versatile; (*arma*) multipurpose; **versatilidad** *f* changeableness *etc.*

versículo *m* verse; **versificar** [1g] *v/t.* versify; *v/i.* write verses.

versión *f* version; draft; translation.

verso *m* (*en general*) verse; (*un* ~) line; ~ suelto blank verse.

vértebra *f* vertebra; **vertebrado** *adj. a. su. m* vertebrate.

vertedero *m* (*canal*) overflow, drain; spillway *de río*; **verter** [2g] *v/t. líquido, sal etc.* pour (out); (*por accidente*) spill; *luz, lágrimas* shed; *desechos* dump, tip; *vasija* empty, tip up; (*traducir*) translate (*a* into); *v/i.* flow, run.

vertical vertical (*a.* 📐), upright.

vertiginoso giddy, dizzy, vertiginous; **vértigo** *m* giddiness.

vesícula *f* vesicle; (*ampolla*) blister; ~ biliar gall bladder.

vestíbulo *m* vestibule; hall, lobby.

vestido *m* (*en general*) dress, clothing; dress, frock *de mujer*; (*conjunto*) costume, suit; ~ *de ceremonia* dress suit; ~ *de etiqueta*, ~ *de serio* evening clothes; ~ *de noche*, ~ *de etiqueta* evening gown; ~ *de gala* 🎖 full dress; ~ *de tarde-noche* cocktail dress; **vestidor** *m* dressing room; **vestidura** *f* clothing; ~s *pl. eccl.* vestments.

vestigio *m* vestige, trace, sign; relic; ~s *pl.* (*restos*) remains.

vestir [3l] **1.** *v/t. p. etc.* dress, clothe (*de* in); (*cubrir*) dress, cover, drape (*de* in, with); (*adornar*) dress up; embellish, trim; *vestido* (*ponerse*) put on, (*llevar*) wear; (*sastre*) make clothes for; *vestido de* dressed in, clad in; (*como disfraz etc.*) dressed as; **2.** *v/i.* dress (*bien* well); ~ *de* dress in, wear; **3.** ~se (*p.*) dress, get dressed.

vestuario *m* (*vestidos*) clothes, wardrobe; *thea.* (*trajes*) wardrobe; (*cuarto*) dressing room.

veta *f* seam, vein; grain *en madera etc.*; *fig.* talents, inclinations.

vetar [1a] veto.

veterano *adj. a. su. m* veteran.

veterinario *m* vet(erinary surgeon).

veto *m* veto; *poner* ~ *a* veto.

vetusto *adj.* very old, ancient; hoary.

vez *f* **1.** time, occasion; (*caso*) instance; (*turno*) turn; *a la* ~ at a time, at the same time; *a su* ~ in his turn; *alguna* ~ sometimes; (*alg*)*una* (*que otra*) ~ occasionally; *cada* ~ every time; *de una* ~ in one go, at once, outright; *de una* ~ (*para siempre*) once and for all, for good; *de* ~ *en cuando* from time to time; *en* ~ *de* instead of; *otra* ~ again; *tal* ~ perhaps; **2.** *veces* *pl.* times *etc.*; *dos veces* twice; *dos veces tanto* twice as much; *a veces* at times; *algunas veces* sometimes; *¿cuántas veces?* how many times?, how often?; *muchas veces* often; *pocas veces* seldom.

vía *f* road; route, way; **🚂** *(rieles)* track, line; *(ancho) gauge; (número de andén)* platform; *anat.* passage, tract; *fig.* way, means; *(oficial etc.)* channel; **✈** *aérea* airmail; *~ de agua* leak; *~ ancha* broad gauge; *~ doble* double track; *de ~ estrecha* narrow-gauge; *~ férrea* railway; *~ fluvial* waterway; *~ Láctea* Milky Way; *~ muerta* siding; *~ normal* standard gauge; *~ pública* thoroughfare; *en ~ de* in process of; *por ~ de* via, by way of; *por ~ bucal* orally.

viajante 1. traveling; **2.** *m/f* traveler; **3.** *m* **🚂** commercial traveler, salesman; **viajar** [1a] travel (*a.* **✈**); go; *~ en coche etc.* ride; *~ por* travel (through); tour *de vacaciones;* **viaje** *m* journey; **⚓** voyage; *(breve, de excursión)* trip; *(jira, de vacaciones)* tour; *(en general)* travel (*mst ~s pl.*); *~ en coche etc. a.* ride; *~ de ensayo* trial run, trial trip; *~ de ida y vuelta* return journey; *~ de novios* honeymoon; *~ de recreo* pleasure trip; *¡buen ~!* have a good trip!, bon voyage!; *estar de ~* be away (on one's travels); be on tour; **viajero** *m*, **a** *f* traveler; **🚂** *etc.* passenger.

viático *m* travel allowance.

víbora *f* viper (*a. fig.*).

vibración *f* vibration; throb(bing); *phonet.* roll, trill; **vibrante** vibrating; *phonet.* rolled, trilled; **vibrar** [1a] *v/t.* vibrate; *phonet.* roll, trill; *v/i.* vibrate.

vice... vice...; **~cónsul** *m* vice-consul; **~gerente** *m* assistant manager; **~presidente** *m* *pol. etc.* vice-president; vice-chairman *de comité.*

viceversa vice versa.

viciado aire foul, thick, stale; *texto* corrupt; **viciar** [1b] aire make foul; *comida etc.* taint, spoil; *texto* corrupt, falsify; *costumbres* corrupt, pervert; *contrato*, **⚖** nullify; **vicio** *m* mst vice; defect; *gr. etc.* mistake; *de ~, por ~ (de mimo)* from being spoiled; **vicioso 1.** mst vicious (*a. phls.*); *gusto etc.* depraved; **⊕** defective, faulty; *niño* spoiled; **♣** rank, luxuriant; **2.** *m*, **a** *f* addict, fiend.

víctima *f* victim; *(p. o animal sacrificado)* sacrifice; prey *de ave.*

victoria *f* victory; **victorioso** victorious.

vid *f* vine.

vida *f* mst life; *(duración)* life(time); *(modo de vivir)* way of life, living; *(modo de sustentarse)* livelihood; *~ airada* loose-living; *~ de perros* dog's life; *¡~ mía!* my darling!; *¡por ~ mía!* upon my soul!; *de por ~* for life; *de toda la ~* lifelong; *en la ~, en mi ~* never in my life; *en ~* in his *etc.* lifetime; *ganarse la ~* earn a living; *hacer ~ b.s.* live together.

vidente *m/f* seer; clairvoyant.

videocassette *m* videocassette; **videodisco** *m* video disk; **video-juego** *m* video game; **videotocadiscos** *m* video-disk player.

vidriado 1. glazed; **2.** *m* glaze, glazing; *(loza)* glazed earthenware; **vidriar** [1b] glaze, glass; **vidriera** *f* *eccl.* stained-glass window; *S.Am.* show window; *(puerta)* glass door; **vidriería** *f* glass-works; *(vasos)* glassware; **vidriero** *m* glazier; **vidrio** *m* glass; *~ cilindrado* plate glass; *~ de color* stained glass; *~ deslustrado* frosted glass, ground glass; *~ tallado* cut glass; **vidrioso** glassy; *mirada* glazed, glassy; *(resbaladizo)* like glass; *(quebradizo)* brittle; delicate.

vieja *f* old woman; **viejo 1.** old; *(anticuado)* old(-fashioned); **2.** *m* old man.

viento *m* wind (*a. ♪, fig.,* F); air; *hunt.* scent; *(cuerda)* guy (rope); *fig.* vanity; *~s pl. alisios* trade winds; **✈** *~ ascendente* up-current; *☁ ~ de cola* tail wind; *~ contrario* headwind; *~ de la hélice* slipstream; *~ en popa* tail wind; *ir ~ en popa fig.* get along splendidly; F *beber etc. los ~s por* be crazy about; *hacer ~* be windy.

vientre *m* belly (*a. fig.*); *(útero)* womb; *(intestino)* bowels; **♐** *~ flojo* looseness of the bowels.

viernes *m* Friday; **♀** *Santo* Good Friday.

viga *f* **🔨** beam, rafter; girder *de metal;* *(madero)* balk, timber.

vigencia *f* operation, validity; *en ~ =* **vigente** in force, valid.

vigésimo twentieth.

vigía 1. *f* watchtower; **⚓** reef; **2.** *m* lookout, watch.

vigilante 1. vigilant, watchful; **2.** *m* watchman, caretaker; warder *de cárcel;* shopwalker *en tienda; ~ de noche* night-watchman; **vigilar** [1a] watch (over), keep an eye on (*a.* ~ *por*); *trabajo etc.* supervise, superintend; *máquina* tend; *frontera* guard, police.

vigor *m mst* vigor; validity; (*resistencia*) stamina, hardiness; (*ímpetu*) drive; **en** ~ in force, operative; **entrar en** ~ come into force; **poner en** ~ put into effect, enforce; **vigoroso** *mst* vigorous; strong, forceful.

viguería *f* beams, rafters; (*metal*) steel frame; **vigueta** *f* joist.

vil villainous, blackguardly; low, base; *hecho* vile, foul; *tratamiento* shabby; **vileza** *f* vileness *etc.*

vilipendiar [1b] vilify; despise, scorn; **vilipendioso** contemptible.

villa *f* (*romana, quinta, de veraneo*) villa; (*población*) small town; *La* ♀ *esp.* Madrid; **villanaje** *m* peasantry, villagers.

villanesco peasant *attr.*; *fig.* rustic.

villano 1. rustic; *fig.* coarse; **2.** *m, a f hist.* villein; low-born person; peasant (*a. fig.*).

vinagre *m* vinegar; **vinagrera** *f* vinegar bottle; ~**s** *pl.* cruet-stand; **vinagroso** bad-tempered.

vinatero 1. wine *attr.*; **2.** *m* wine merchant; vintner.

vínculo *m* link, bond, tie; ⚖ entail.

vindicación *f* vindication; **vindicar** [1g] vindicate.

vine *etc. v.* venir.

vínico wine *attr.*; **vinícola** wine (-growing) *attr.*; **vinicultor** *m* wine grower; **vinicultura** *f* wine-growing, production of wine; **vino** *m* wine; ~ **añejo** mellow wine; ~ **blanco** white wine; ~ **espumoso** sparkling wine; ~ **generoso** strong wine, full-bodied wine; ~ **de Jerez** sherry; ~ **de mesa**, ~ **de pasto** table wine; ~ **de Oporto** port (wine); ~ **de postre** dessert wine; ~ **seco** dry wine; ~ **tinto** red wine.

viña *f* vineyard; **viñador** *m* vine-grower; wine-grower.

violación *f mst* violation; ~ (**de la ley**) offence, infringement; rape; **violador** *m,* **-a** *f* violator *etc.*; **violar** [1a] *mst* violate; *ley* a. break, offend against; (*ultrajar*) outrage; *mujer* rape.

violencia *f* violence (*a. fig.*); *fig.* fury; embarrassment; embarrassing situation; ⚖ assault, violence; *hacer* ~ *a* = **violentar** [1a] *casa* break into; ⚖ assault; *fig.* do violence to, outrage; ~**se** force o.s.; **violento** *mst* violent;

fig. a. wild; *postura* awkward, unnatural.

violeta *f* violet.

violín *m* violin; (*p.*) = **violinista** *m/f* violinist; **violón** *m* double-bass; **violoncelo** *m* cello.

vira *f* dart; welt *de zapato.*

virada *f* tack(ing); **viraje** *m* ⚓ tack, turn; bend *de camino;* swerve, turn *de coche; pol.* swing *de votos,* volte-face *de política;* ~ **en horquilla** hairpin bend; **virar** [1a] *v/t.* put about; *v/i.,* ~**se** ⚓ go about, tack; veer (round) (*a. fig.*); *mot.,* ⚒ turn, swerve; *pol.* (*votos*) swing.

viral virus.

virgen *adj. a. su. f* virgin; **virginal** virginal; **virginidad** *f* virginity; **virgo** *m* virginity; *ast.* ♀ Virgo.

viril virile; *esp. carácter* manly; **virilidad** *f* virility.

virtual virtual; *fuerza* potential; *imagen etc.* apparent.

virtud *f* virtue; efficacy; **en** ~ **de** in virtue of, by reason of; **virtuoso 1.** virtuous; **2.** *m* virtuoso.

viruela *f* smallpox, variola.

virus *m* virus.

visado *m* visa; ~ **de permanencia** residence permit.

visaje *m* face, grimace.

visar *m* pasaporte visa.

viscosidad *f* 🔵 viscosity; stickiness *etc.;* **viscoso** 🔵 viscous; sticky.

visibilidad *f* visibility; **visible** visible; (*manifiesto*) evident, in evidence; *¿está* ~ *el duque?* is the duke available?

visión *f* sight, vision (*a. eccl.*); (*imaginación vana*) fantasy; *fig.* (*p.*) sight, scarecrow; **visionario** *adj. a. su. m,* **a** *f* visionary.

visita *f* visit; call; (*p.*) visitor, caller; *hacer* (*pagar*) *una* ~ pay (return) a visit; **visitador** *m,* **-a** *f* frequent visitor; (*oficial*) inspector; **visitante 1.** visiting; **2.** *m/f* visitor; **visitar** [1a] visit; call on, (go and) see; (*en viaje oficial*) inspect; **visiteo** *m* frequent visiting; **visitero 1.** forever visiting; **2.** *m,* **a** *f* constant visitor.

vislumbrar [1a] glimpse, catch a glimpse of; *fig.* get some idea of, conjecture; **vislumbre** *f* glimpse; (*reflejo*) gleam, glimmer.

viso *m* sheen, gloss *de tela;* gleam, glint *de metal;* ~**s** *pl. fig.* appearance; **a dos** ~**s** having a double purpose.

visón *m* (*a. piel de* ~) mink.

víspera f eve, day before; ~s pl. vespers, evensong; la ~ de, en ~s de on the eve of.

vista f (facultad, sentido) sight, vision, eyesight; (que se dirige a un punto) eyes, glance, gaze; (cosa vista) sight; (panorama) view, scene, vista; (apariencia) appearance, looks; (perspectiva) outlook, prospect; intention; † sight; ⚖ trial de p., hearing de pleito; ~s pl. view, outlook; corto de ~ shortsighted; doble ~ second sight; cine: ~ fija still; ~ de pájaro bird's-eye view; † a la ~ at sight, on sight; a la ~ de (with)in sight of; a ~ de in sight of; (ante) in the presence of; a primera ~ at first sight, on the face of it; a simple ~ with the naked eye; con ~s al mar overlooking the sea; con ~s al norte with northerly aspect; de ~ (conocer etc.) by sight; en plena ~ in full view; ¡hasta la ~! so long!; aguzar la ~ look more closely; clavar la ~ en stare at; clap eyes on; hacer la ~ gorda a turn a blind eye to, wink at; medir con la ~ size up; perder de ~ lose sight of; torcer la ~ a squint.

vistazo m look, glance, glimpse; de un ~ at a glance.

visto 1. p.p. of ver; ~ bueno passed, approved, O.K.; bien ~ approved of, thought right; mal ~ thought wrong; ~ que seeing that; por lo ~ evidently, by the look of things; ~ todo esto in view of all this; 2.: ~ bueno m approval, authorization.

vistoso showy, attractive.

visual 1. visual; 2. f line of sight.

vital vital; espacio living; **vitalidad** f vitality; **vitamina** f vitamin.

viticultor m vine grower; **viticultura** f vine growing, viticulture.

vítreo glassy, vitreous ⬚; **vitrificar(se)** [1g] vitrify; **vitrina** f glass case, show case; display cabinet.

vituperar [1a] condemn, inveigh against, vituperate; **vituperio** m condemnation, vituperation; insult.

viuda f widow; **viudedad** f widow's pension; **viudez** f widowhood; **viudo** 1. widowed; 2. m widower.

¡viva! v. vivir.

vivacidad f vivacity, liveliness.

vivar m (conejos) warren; (peces) fish pond.

vivaz (de larga vida) long-lived; ♀ perennial; (lleno de vida) lively; (agudo) quick-witted.

víveres m/pl. provisions, supplies.

vivero m fish-pond; ♀ nursery.

viveza f liveliness etc. (v. vivo).

vivienda f housing, accommodation; (morada) dwelling; escasez de ~s housing shortage.

viviente living; los ~s the living.

vivificar [1g] revitalize, enliven, bring to life.

vivir 1. [1a] live (de by, off, on; en at, in); ¡viva! hurrah!; ¡viva X! long live X!, hurrah for X!; ¿quién vive? who goes there?; ~ para ver live and learn; 2. m life; living; way of life.

vivo 1. (no muerto) alive, living; live; lengua modern, living; (lleno de vida) lively, bright; dolor sharp, acute; emoción keen, deep, intense; inteligencia sharp; imaginación lively; ingenio ready; paso quick, smart; escena, recuerdo, colorido etc. vivid; color rich, bright; carne raw; los ~s the living; al ~ to the life; 2. m sew. edging, border.

vocablo m word; jugar del ~ (make a) pun; **vocabulario** m vocabulary.

vocación f calling, vocation; **vocacional** vocational.

vocal 1. vocal; 2. m voting member; 3. f vowel; **vocálico** vocalic, vowel attr.; **vocalizar** [1f] v/t. vocalize; voice; v/i. ♪ hum; ~se vocalize; **vocativo** m vocative (case).

voceador 1. vociferous, loudmouthed; 2. m town crier; **vocear** [1a] v/t. (publicar) shout, announce loudly; acclaim loudly; (llamar) shout to; v/i. shout, bawl; **vocería** f, **vocerío** m shouting, uproar, hullabaloo F; **vocero** m spokesman; **vociferar** [1a] vociferate, scream.

voladero flying, that can fly; **voladizo** △ projecting; **volador** 1. flying; fig. swift; 2. m rocket; ichth. flying fish; **voladura** f blowing-up, demolition.

volandero fledged, ready to fly; p. restless; **volante** 1. flying; fig. unsettled; 2. m mot. steering wheel; ⊕ flywheel; balance de reloj; (juego) badminton; shuttlecock con que se juega; sew. ruffle, frill, flounce; (papel) note; un buen ~ a good driver; **volantón** m fledgeling.

volar [1m] v/t. explode; edificio etc. blow up, demolish; mina explode, spring; blast en cantera; v/i. fly (a. fig.); flutter; hurtle; (irse volando) fly away, disappear; (ir rápidamente) fly, run fast, go fast; (*noticia*) spread quickly; (*tiempo*) fly.

volatería *f* (*aves*) birds, fowls; (*caza*) falconry; fowling *con señuelo*.

volátil ⚗ volatile; changeable.

volatín *m*, **volatinero** *m*, **a** *f* tightrope walker, acrobat.

volcán *m* volcano; **volcánico** volcanic.

volcar [1g *a*. 1m] *v/t*. overturn, tip over; upset, knock over *por accidente*; *coche etc*. overturn, turn over; ⚓ capsize; *contenido* empty out, dump; *fig*. (*turbar*) make *s.o.* dizzy; tease, irritate; *v/i*., **se** overturn.

volear [1a] volley; **voleo** *m* volley.

voltaico voltaic; **voltaje** *m* voltage.

volteador *m*, **-a** *f* acrobat; **voltear** [1a] *v/t*. (*girar*) swing, whirl; (*poner al revés*) turn round; (*volcar*) upset, overturn; transform; *S.Am*. turn; *v/i*. roll over, somersault; **voltereta** *f* somersault, roll; tumble; ~ *sobre las manos* hand spring.

voltio *m* volt.

volubilidad *f fig*. fickleness; instability; **voluble** (*que gira*) revolving, ⚘ winding; *fig*. fickle.

volumen *m mst* volume; (*bulto*) bulk (-iness); *radio*: ~ *sonoro* volume (of sound); **voluminoso** voluminous, bulky, big.

voluntad *f mst* will; (*energía*) willpower; (*cariño*) affection, fondness; *buena* ~ goodwill; *mala* ~ illwill, malice; *su santa* ~ his own sweet will; *última* ~ last wish; ⚰ last will and testament; *a* ~ *obrar etc*. at will; (*cantidad*) ad-lib ⌐; **voluntario 1.** voluntary; ~ volunteer *attr*.; **2.** *m* volunteer.

voluptuoso 1. voluptuous; *b.s.* sensual; **2.** *m*, **a** *f* voluptuary.

volver [2h; *p.p.* vuelto] **1.** *v/t*. turn; turn round; *página etc*. turn (over); (*invertir*) turn upside down; *ojos etc*. turn, cast; *arma etc*. turn (*a* on), direct, aim (*a* at); *puerta* close, pull to; (*devolver*) send back; *favor, visita* return, repay; (*reponer*) put back, replace (*a* in); (*restablecer*) restore (*a* to); ~ *adj*. turn, make, render; *v. loco*. **2.** *v/i*. return, come back, go back, get back; (*torcer*) turn, bend; ~ *a hábito, tema etc*. revert to, return to; ~ *a hacer* do again; ~ *atrás* turn back; ~ *en sí* come to, regain consciousness; ~ *por* stand up for; ~ *sobre sí* recover one's calm; **3.** **se** turn (round);

(*regresar*) = *v/i*.; (*vino*) turn (sour); (*opinión*) change one's mind; ~ *adj*. turn, become, go, get; ~ *atrás fig*. look back; (*cejar*) back out.

vomitado ⸋ sickly, seedy; **vomitar** [1a] vomit, bring up, throw up; *fig*. *llamas etc*. belch forth, spew; *ganancias* disgorge; *injurias* hurl; **vomitivo** *m* emetic; **vómito** *m* vomit; (*acto*) being sick, vomiting.

voraz voracious, greedy, ravenous.

vórtice *m* whirlpool, vortex.

vos † *you*; *S.Am*. you; **vosear** [1a] *S.Am*. address as *vos* (*i.e.*, treat familiarly).

vosotros, vosotras *pl*. you.

votación *f* vote, voting; *esp. parl*. division; ~ *por manos levantadas* show of hands; **votante 1.** voting; **2.** *m/f* voter; **votar** [1a] *v/t*. *ley* pass; *candidato* vote for; *v/i*. vote (*por* for); **votivo** votive; **voto** *m* vote; (*p*.) voter; vow *a Dios etc*.; (*reniego*) curse, swear-word; ~**s** *pl. fig*. (good) wishes; ~ *de calidad* casting vote; ~ *de confianza* vote of confidence; ~ *informativo* straw vote; *echar* ~**s** curse, swear.

voy *etc*. *v*. **ir**.

voz *f* voice (*a*. *gr*.); (*vocablo*) word; (*voto*) vote, support; (*grito*) shout; noise *de trueno etc*.; rumor, report; *voces pl*. (*gritos*) shouting; ~ *común* hearsay, rumor; *a una* ~ with one voice; *a media* ~ in a low voice; *de viva* ~ *viva voce*; by word of mouth; *en* ~ in (good) voice; *en* ~ *alta* aloud, out loud; *en* ~ *baja* in an undertone; *aclarar la* ~ clear one's throat; *dar voces* shout, call out; *dar la* ~ *de alarma* sound the alarm; *dar cuatro voces* make a great fuss.

vudú *m* voodoo; **vudismo** *m* voodoo cult.

vuelco *m* upset, spill, overturning; *dar un* ~ overturn; (*corazón*) jump.

vuelo *m* ⸙ flight; fullness *de vestido*; (*adorno*) lace, frill; △ projecting part; *de mucho* ~ *falda* full; ~ *a ciegas* blind flying; ~ *de enlace* connecting flight; ~ *de ensayo* test flight; ~ *sin motor*, ~ *a vela* gliding; ~ *en picado* dive; *al* ~ on the wing, in flight; *fig*. at once; *alzar el* ~ take flight; ⸙ dash off; *tocar a* ~ peal; *tomar* ~ grow, develop.

vuelta *f* turn, revolution; *deportes*: lap, circuit *en carrera*; round *de torneo*; (*jira*) tour; (*paseo*) stroll; (*recodo*) bend, curve; (*regreso*) return; (*devolución*) return, giving back; (*dinero*) change; (*revés*) back, other side; (*repetición*) repeat; sew. cuff; F hiding; ♣ ~ de cabo hitch; ~ de campana somersault; ~ del mundo journey around the world; *a la* ~ (*de regreso*) on one's return; (*página*) on the next page, overleaf; *a la* ~ *de esquina* round; *años etc.* after, at the end of; *dar* ~ *a llave* turn; *coche etc.* reverse, turn round; *dar la* ~ *a* go round; *dar una* ~ take a stroll; *dar una* ~ *de campana* turn completely over; *dar media* ~ face about; ✗ about turn; *dar* ~s turn, go round, revolve; (*camino*) twist and turn; (*cabeza*) (be in a) whirl; *dar* ~s *a manivela etc.* wind, turn; *botón* turn; twirl *en dedos*.

vuelto 1. *p.p.* of *volver*; **2.** *m S.Am.* change.
vuestro 1. *adj.* your; (*tras su.*) of yours; **2.** *pron.* yours.
vulgar *lengua* vulgar; *opinión etc.* common, general; *término* ordinary, accepted; (*corriente*) ordinary, everyday; banal; trivial, trite; **vulgaridad** *f* commonness *etc.*; (*cosa vulgar*) triviality; ~es *pl. freq.* small-talk; platitudes; **vulgarismo** *m* popular form; *b.s.* slang (word); vulgarism; **vulgarizar** [1f] popularize, vulgarize; *texto etc.* translate into the vernacular; **Vulgata** *f* Vulgate; **vulgo** *m* common people, lower orders, common herd.

W

wáter [ˈbater] *m* lavatory, toilet, water closet.

wélter [ˈbelter] *m boxeo:* welterweight.
whisk(e)y [ˈwiski] *m* whisk(e)y.

X

xilófono [s-] *m* xylophone.
xilografía [s-] *f* xylography, wood engraving.

xilógrafo [s-] *m* xylographer, wood engraver.

Y

y and; *las 2 y media* halfpast two.
ya (*en momento pasado*) already, before now; (*ahora*) now; (*más adelante*) in due course, sometime; (*en seguida*) at once; ¡~! now I remember, of course!; ~, ~ yes, yes; ~ ..., ~ ... (*ora*) now ..., now ...; (*si*) whether ..., or ...; ~ *en 1984* as long ago as 1984, as early as 1984; ~ *no* no longer, not any more.
yacaré *m* crocodile.
yacente *estatua* recumbent; **yacer** [2y] †, *lit.* lie; *aquí yace* here lies; **yacija** *f* bed; (*tumba*) grave, tomb; *ser de mala* ~ sleep badly; (*inquieto*) be restless; (*carácter*) be a bad lot; **yacimiento** *m* bed, deposit; ~ *de petróleo* oil field.
yanqui *adj. a. su. m/f* Yankee.
yate *m* yacht.
yedra *f* ivy.
yegua *f* mare; **yeguada** *f* stud.
yelmo *m* helmet.
yema *f* yolk *de huevo*; ♀ (leaf-)bud, eye; (*lo mejor*) best part; ~ *del dedo* fingertip; ~ *mejida* eggnog.
yendo *v. ir.*
yerba *f v.* hierba.
yermar [1a] lay waste; **yermo 1.** uninhabited; **2.** *m* wilderness.
yerno *m* son-in-law.
yerro *m* error, mistake.
yerto stiff, rigid.
yesca *f* tinder (*a. fig.*); fuel *de pasión etc.*; ~s *pl.* tinder box.
yesero *m* plasterer; **yeso** *m* gypsum; △ plaster; (*vaciado*) plaster cast; ~ *mate* plaster of Paris.
yip *m S.Am.* jeep.
yo I; *el* ~ the self, the ego.
yódico iodic; **yodo** *m* iodine.
yonqui *m sl. drogas* junkie (drug addict).
yugo *m* yoke (*a. fig.*).
yungla *f* jungle.
yunque *m* anvil; *fig.* tireless worker.
yunta *f* yoke, team *de bueyes*; (*pareja*) couple, pair.
yute *m* jute.

Z

zafado *S.Am.* (*vivo*) wide awake; (*descarado*) brazen.

zafar [1a] loosen, untie; ~se keep out of the way, hide o.s. away; ~ de *p. etc.* shake off, dodge, ditch F.

zafio coarse, loutish.

zafiro *m* sapphire.

zafo: salirse ~ come out (*de* of) unharmed.

zaga *f* rear; *a la* ~, *en* ~ behind, in the rear; *no ir en* ~ *a nadie* be second to none.

zagal *m* lad, youth; ♂ shepherd boy; **zagala** *f* lass, girl; ♀ shepherdess.

zaguán *m* vestibule, hall(way).

zaherir [3i] attack, criticize (sarcastically); reproach, upbraid.

zaino *animal* chestnut; *p.* false.

zalamería *f* flattery, cajolery *etc.*; **zalamero 1.** flattering, cajoling; unctuous, suave, oily; **2.** *m,* **a** *f* flatterer; servile person.

zalea *f* sheepskin.

zalema *f* salaam, bowing and scraping.

zambo 1. knock-kneed; **2.** *m,* **a** *f* Indian-black half-breed.

zambullida *f* dive, plunge; duck, ducking; **zambullir** [3h] duck, plunge; ~se dive, plunge; duck; *fig.* hide, cover o.s. up.

zampabollos *m/f* F (*comilón*) greedy pig, glutton; **zampar** [1a] F (*comer*) wolf, put away; ~se whip, vanish (*en* into); **zampón** F greedy.

zanahoria *f* carrot.

zanca *f* shank; ~s *pl.* F long shanks; **zancada** *f* stride; F *en dos* ~s in a couple of ticks; **zancadilla** *f* trip *con pie*; (*aparato*) booby trap; (*engaño*) trick; *echar la* ~ *a* trip (up); **zancajear** [1a] rush around; **zancarrón** *m* F leg bone; big bone; (*p.*) old bag of bones; **zanco** *m* stilt; *en* ~s *fig.* well up, in a good position; **zancudo** long-legged; *orn.* wading; *ave* ~a wader.

zangolotear [1a] F *v/t.* fidget with; *v/i.* fidget; ~se (*ventana*) rattle.

zanguanga: F *hacer la* ~ swing the lead; **zanguango** F lazy; silly.

zanja *f* ditch, trench; *Am.* irrigation ditch; **zanjar** [1a] trench, ditch; *dificultad* get round.

zapallo *m S.Am.* gourd, pumpkin.

zapapico *m* pick(axe); **zapar** [1a] sap, undermine.

zapata *f* shoe *de freno etc.*; **zapatazo** *m* bump, bang; **zapateado** *m* tap dance; **zapatear** [1a] *v/t.* kick, prod with one's foot; tap with one's foot; F give *s.o.* a rough time; *v/i.* tap-dance; **zapatería** *f* shoe-shop; (*arte*) shoemaking; **zapatero** *m* shoemaker; ~ remendón, ~ de viejo cobbler; **zapatilla** *f* slipper *para casa*; pump *para bailar*; ⊕ washer; **zapato** *m* shoe.

zar *m* tsar, czar.

zaranda *f* sieve; **zarandajas** *f/pl.* F trifles, odds and ends; **zarandear** [1a] sift, sieve; shake up; ~se be on the go, never be still; **zarandillo** *m* F active person, lively sort; F *traer como un* ~ keep *s.o.* on the go.

zarcillo *m* ♀ tendril; (*joya*) earring.

zarigüeya *f* opossum.

zarpa *f* claw, paw; F *echar la* ~ grab hold (*a* of); **zarpada** *f* clawing, blow with the paw; **zarpar** [1a] weigh anchor, set sail; **zarpazo** *m* = zarpada; *fig.* thud, bump.

zarrapastrón F, **zarrapastroso** ragged, slovenly, shabby.

zarza *f*, **zarzamora** *f* blackberry.

zarzuela *f* operetta, light opera.

zepelín *m* Zeppelin.

zigzag *m* zigzag; *en* ~ *relámpago* forked; **zigzaguear** [1a] zigzag.

zinc *m* zinc.

zócalo *m* socle, base of a pedestal; *Mex.* public square, center square.

zoclo *m* clog, wooden shoe; galosh, overshoe *de goma*.

zodiacal zodiacal; **zodíaco** *m* zodiac.

zona *f* zone; belt, area; ~ edificada built-up area; ~ de pruebas testing ground; ~ siniestrada disaster area; ~ tórrida torrid zone; **zonal** zonal.

zoo... zoo...; **zoología** *f* zoology; **zoológico** zoological; **zoólogo** *m* zoologist.

zopenco F **1.** stupid, silly; **2.** m nitwit, dunce, blockhead.

zoquete m (madera) block, piece; (pan) bit of bread; F (tonto) chump, duffer; (grosero) oaf, lout.

zorra f (en general) fox; (hembra) vixen; F whore; **zorrera** f foxhole; F worry, anxiety; **zorrería** f foxiness, craftiness; **zorrero** foxy, crafty; **zorro 1.** m (dog) fox; F old fox, crafty sort; F hacerse el ~ act dumb; **2.** foxy, crafty, slippery.

zorzal m thrush; F sly fellow.

zozobra f ♣ sinking, capsizing; fig. worry, anxiety; unrest; **zozobrar** [1a] ♣ sink, capsize, overturn; fig. (peligrar) be in danger.

zulú m Zulu.

zumba f fig. banter, teasing; hacer ~ a tease; **zumbador** m ⚡ buzzer; **zumbar** [1a] v/t. F rag, chaff; univ. sl. plough; golpe let s.o. have; S.Am. throw, chuck; v/i. (abeja) buzz, hum, drone; (oídos) sing, ring; (máquina) whirr, drone, hum; (zumbador) buzz; ~se de rag, chaff; **zumbido** m buzz(ing) etc.; F punch, biff; **zum-**

bón 1. p. funny; tono etc. bantering; **2.** m, **-a** f funny man etc.; banterer, tease.

zumo m juice; (como bebida) juice, squash; fig. solid profit, real benefit; ~ de limón lemon squash; ~ de uva grape juice; **zumoso** juicy.

zuncho m band, hoop, ring.

zupia f muddy wine; fig. trash.

zurcido m darn, mend; **zurcidura** f (acto) darning, mending; = zurcido; **zurcir** [3b] darn, mend, sew up; fig. put together; mentira concoct, think up.

zurdo left-handed.

zurra f dressing, tanning; F (paliza) tanning, spanking; (trabajo) grind, drudgery; (riña) set-to; **zurrador** m tanner.

zurrar [1a] dress, tan; F tan, wallop, spank; ~se dirty o.s.

zurriaga f whip; **zurriagar** [1h] whip; **zurriagazo** m lash; fig. stroke of bad luck; **zurriago** m whip.

zurrón m pouch, bag.

zutano m, **a** f (Mr etc.) So-and-so.

A

a [ei; ə] *article*: un, una; *10 miles an hour* 10 millas por hora; *2 shillings a pound* 2 chelines la libra.

A 1 ['ei 'wʌn] F de primera calidad; F *feel* ~ estar como un reloj.

a·back [ə'bæk] F atrás, hacia atrás; ♦ en facha; F *taken* ~ desconcertado.

a·ban·don [ə'bændən] abandonar, desamparar; renunciar a, dejar; ~ *o.s. to* abandonarse a, entregarse a.

a·base [ə'beis] humillar, degradar; envilecer.

a·bash [ə'bæʃ] confundir, avergonzar.

a·bate [ə'beit] *v/t*. disminuir, reducir; ⚖ suprimir, abolir; *v/i*. menguar, disminuir; moderarse; (*price*) bajar; (*wind*) amainar.

ab·bey ['æbi] abadía *f*, convento *m*; **ab·bot** ['æbət] abad *m*.

ab·bre·vi·ate [ə'bri:vieit] abreviar; & simplificar; **ab·bre·vi·a·tion** abreviatura *f*.

ABC [ei 'bi: 'si:] abecé *m*, abecedario *m*; rudimentos *m/pl*.

ab·di·cate ['æbdikeit] *v/t*. abdicar, renunciar; *v/i*. abdicar (*in favor of* en favor de).

ab·do·men ['æbdəmen; ♂ æb'dou-men] abdomen *m*, vientre *m*.

ab·duct [æb'dʌkt] raptar.

ab·er·ra·tion [æbə'reiʃn] aberración *f* (*a. ast. a. opt.*).

a·bet [ə'bet] incitar, instigar; ⚖ (*mst aid and* ~) encubrir, ser cómplice.

a·bey·ance [ə'beiəns] suspensión *f*; ⚖ *in* ~ en suspenso, en desuso.

ab·hor [əb'hɔ:] aborrecer, abominar; **ab'hor·rent** □ repugnante, detestable (*to* a).

a·bide [ə'baid] [*irr*.] *v/i. lit*. morar; ~ *by* atenerse a; conformarse con, cumplir con; ~ *t/u.* aguardar; conformarse con; *I cannot* ~ *him* no le puedo ver; **a'bid·ing** □ permanente, perdurable.

a·bil·i·ty [ə'biliti] habilidad *f*, capacidad *f*, talento *m*; aptitud *f*; *to the best of one's* ~ lo mejor que pueda (*or* sepa) uno; **a'bil·i·ties** *pl*. dotes *f/pl*. intelectuales.

ab·ject ['æbdʒekt] □ abyecto, vil, ruin; ~ *poverty* la mayor miseria.

ab·la·tive ['æblətiv] ablativo *m*.

a·blaze [ə'bleiz] ardiendo; *fig*. ardiente, ansioso.

a·ble ['eibl] □ hábil, capaz; *be* ~ poder; (*know how to*) saber; ~ *to pay* solvente; ~**bod·ied** ['·'bɔdid] sano, robusto; ♦ ~ *seaman* marinero *m* de primera.

ab·nor·mal [æb'nɔ:ml] □ anormal; deforme; **ab·nor'mal·i·ty** anormalidad *f*; deformidad *f*.

a·board [ə'bɔ:d] ♦ a bordo; *all* ~ ¡señores viajeros, al tren! (*etc.*).

a·bode [ə'boud] 1. *pret. a. p.p. of abide*; 2. morada *f*, domicilio *m*.

a·bol·ish [ə'bɔliʃ] abolir, anular, suprimir; **ab·o·li·tion** [æbo'liʃn] abolición *f*; **ab·o'li·tion·ist** abolicionista *m/f*.

A-bomb ['eibɔm] = *atomic bomb* bomba *f* atómica.

a·bom·i·na·ble [ə'bɔminəbl] □ abominable, detestable; *taste etc*. pésimo; **a·bom·i·na·tion** abominación *f*; asco *m*.

ab·o·rig·i·ne [æbə'ridʒini:] aborigen *m*.

a·bort [ə'bɔ:t] abortar (*a. fig.*); **a'bor·tion** aborto *m*; engendro *m*; *fig*. malogro *m*, fracaso *m*.

a·bound [ə'baund] abundar (*with*, *in* en).

a·bout [ə'baut] 1. *prp*. (*nearly*) casi; *place* junto a; (*relating to*) acerca de; ~ *6 o'clock* a eso de las 6; ~ *6 days* unos 6 días; ~ *the end* casi al final; *speak* ~ *the matter* hablar del asunto; *ask questions* ~ *s.t.* hacer preguntas acerca de algo; *what is it* ~? ¿de qué se trata?; *v. how, what*; 2. *adv*.: *be* ~ estar levantado; estar por aquí; *be* ~ *to do* estar para (*or* a punto de) hacer.

a·bove [ə'bʌv] 1. *prp*. encima de, superior a; ~ *300* más de 300; ~ *all* sobre todo; *not to be* ~ *doing s.t.* ser capaz de hacer algo; *fig. get* ~ *o.s.* engreírse; *fig. it is* ~ *me* no lo entiendo; 2. *adv*. (por) encima; arriba; 3. *adj*. susodicho; **a'bove-'board** sin rebozo; legítimo; **a·bove-'men·tioned** sobredicho, antedicho, susodicho.

ab·ra·sion [ə'breiʒn] raedura f, rozadura f, raspadura f; abrasión f; **ab·ra·sive** ⊕ abrasivo m.

a·breast [ə'brest] de frente, de fondo; fig. ~ of or with al corriente de; al día de.

a·bridge [ə'bridʒ] abreviar; compendiar; privar; **a'bridg·ment** abreviación f; compendio m; privación f of rights.

a·broad [ə'brɔːd] fuera; en el extranjero; go ~ ir al extranjero; there is a rumor ~ that corre el rumor de que; it has got ~ se ha divulgado.

ab·ro·gate ['æbrougeit] revocar, abrogar.

ab·rupt [ə'brʌpt] □ brusco, rudo; event precipitado; terrain escarpado; style cortado.

ab·scess ['æbsis] absceso m.

ab·scond [əb'skɔnd] huir de la justicia; F zafarse.

ab·sence ['æbsns] ausencia f; falta f; ~ of mind distracción f, despiste m (F).

ab·sent 1. ['æbsnt] □ ausente; be ~ faltar; fig. = '·'·mind·ed □ distraído; **2.** [æb'sent] ~ o.s. ausentarse (from de); **ab·sen·tee** [æbsn'tiː] absentista m/f; **ab·sen'tee·ism** absentismo m.

ab·sinth ['æbsinθ] ajenjo m.

ab·so·lute ['æbsəluːt] □ absoluto (a. gr.); total; denial categórico, rotundo; liar redomado; nonsense puro; ~ly absolutamente etc.; ~ly! ¡perfectamente!

ab·solve [əb'zɔlv] absolver (from de).

ab·sorb [əb'sɔːb] absorber (a. fig.); shock etc. amortiguar; ~ed in absorto en; **ab'sorb·ent** absorbente, hidrófilo.

ab·sorp·tion [əb'sɔːpʃn] absorción f (a. fig.).

ab·stain [əb'stein] abstenerse (from de); freq. abstenerse de las bebidas alcohólicas.

ab·sti·nence ['æbstinəns] abstinencia f (from de); **'ab·sti·nent** □ abstinente, abstemio.

ab·stract 1. ['æbstrækt] □ abstracto (a. gr.); recóndito; in the ~ en abstracto; **2.** [~] resumen m, extracto m; **3.** [æb'strækt] abstraer (mentally); euph. hurtar; ⚚ extraer; book compendiar.

ab·struse [æb'struːs] □ abstruso.

ab·surd [əb'seːd] □ absurdo, irrazonable; ridículo; necio; **ab'surd·i·ty** disparate m, absurdo m; tontería f, locura f.

a·bun·dance [ə'bʌndəns] abundancia f, copia f, caudal m; plenitud f of heart etc.; riqueza f; **a'bun·dant** □ abundante, copioso; water caudaloso; ~ in abundante en, rebosante de; **a'bun·dant·ly** copiosamente; ~ clear plenamente claro.

a·buse 1. [ə'bjuːs] abuso m; (insults) denuestos m/pl., improperios m/pl.; injurias f/pl.; **2.** [~z] abusar de; denostar; maltratar; **a'bu·sive** □ abusivo; insultante; be ~ soltar injurias.

a·bys·mal [ə'bizməl] □ abismal; fig. profundo; **a·byss** [ə'bis] abismo m, sima f.

ac·a·dem·ic [ækə'demik] □ académico; universitario; ~ costume toga f, traje m de catedrático; ~ freedom libertad f de catedrático.

a·cad·e·mi·cian [əkædə'miʃn] académico m; **a·cad·e·my** [ə'kædəmi] academia f.

ac·cede [æk'siːd] ~ to consentir en, acceder a; the throne subir a.

ac·cel·er·ate [æk'seləreit] acelerar; apresurar; **ac·cel·er·a·tion** aceleración f; **ac'cel·er·a·tor** mot. acelerador m.

ac·cent 1. ['æksnt] acento m; **2.** [æk'sent] acentuar; recalcar (a. fig.).

ac·cept [ək'sept] aceptar (a. ~ of, a. ♱); p. admitir; **ac·cept·a·ble** [ək'septəbl] □ aceptable; grato; **ac'cept·ance** aceptación f (a. ♱); acogida f; (ideas) acogida f, asenso m; **ac·cep·ta·tion** [æksep'teiʃn] acepción f (de una palabra); **ac'cept·ed** □ acepto.

ac·cess ['ækses] acceso m, entrada f (to a); ⚕ acceso m, ataque m; easy of ~ abordable, tratable; accesible; **ac'ces·si·ble** [~əbl] □ accesible (to a); asequible; **ac'ces·sion** acceso m, entrada f; subida f to the throne.

ac·ces·so·ry [æk'sesəri] **1.** □ accesorio; **2.** accesorio m; ⚖ cómplice m/f; **ac'ces·so·ries** [~riz] pl. accesorios m/pl.

ac·ci·dent ['æksidənt] accidente m; ~ insurance seguro m contra accidentes; by ~ por casualidad; **ac·ci·den·tal** [æksi'dentl] **1.** □ accidental, fortuito; ~ death muerte f accidental; **2.** ♪ accidente m.

ac·claim [ə'kleim] 1. aclamar, ovacionar; 2. aclamación *f*.

ac·cli·mate [ə'klaimit] aclimatar.

ac·com·mo·date [ə'kɔmədeit] (*adapt*) acomodar, adaptar (*to* a); ajustar; *differences* reconciliar, acomodar; proveer (*with de*); (*house*) alojar; **ac'com·mo·dat·ing** ☐ acomodadizo; **ac·com·mo·da·tion** acomodación *f*; **ac·com·mo·da·tions** *pl.* facilidades *f/pl.*, comodidades *f/pl.*; *in a train* localidad *f*; *in a hotel* alojamiento *m*.

ac·com·pa·ni·ment [ə'kʌmpənimənt] acompañamiento *m* (*a.* ♪); accesorio *m*; **ac'com·pa·nist** acompañante (*a* f) *m*; **ac'com·pa·ny** acompañar (*by*, *with* de).

ac·com·plice [ə'kɔmplis] cómplice *m/f*, fautor *m*.

ac·com·plish [ə'kɔmpliʃ] acabar, completar; efectuar; *prophesy etc.* cumplir; **ac'com·plished** consumado, logrado; *fact* realizado; *p.* hábil; **ac'com·plish·ment** (*end*) conclusión *f*; logro *m*; éxito *m*; *mst pl.* talentos *m/pl.*, habilidades *f/pl.*

ac·cord [ə'kɔːd] 1. acuerdo *m*, convenio *m*; armonía *f*; *of one's own* ~ espontáneamente, de su propio acuerdo; *with one* ~ de común acuerdo; 2. *v/i.* conceder (*with con*); *v/t.* conceder; **ac'cord·ance** conformidad *f*; *in* ~ *with* conforme a, de acuerdo con; **ac'cord·ant** ~ *to*, ~ *with* conforme a; **ac'cord·ing**: ~ *to* según; conforme a; ~ *as* según; **ac'cord·ing·ly** en conformidad; *and* ~ así pues, y por lo tanto.

ac·cor·di·on [ə'kɔːdiən] acordeón *m*.

ac·cost [ə'kɔst] abordar.

ac·count [ə'kaunt] 1. narración *f*, relato *m*; cuenta *f* (*a.* ✝), cálculo *m*; estimación *f*, importancia *f*; *payment on* ~ pago *m* a cuenta; *by all* ~s por lo que dicen; *of no* ~ de poca importancia; *on his* ~ por él; *on his own* ~ por su propia cuenta; *on no* ~ de ninguna manera; *on* ~ *of* a causa de, por; *bring to* ~ pedir cuentas a; *give* (*or render*) *an* ~ *of* dar cuenta de; *give a good* ~ *of o.s.* dar buena cuenta de sí; *settle an* ~ liquidar una cuenta; *take into* ~, *take* ~ *of* tener en cuenta; *turn to* ~ aprovechar, sacar provecho de; 2. *v/i.*: ~ *for* dar cuenta de, explicar; justificar; *I cannot* ~ *for it* no me lo explico; *v/t.* considerar, tener por; **ac·count·a'bil·i·ty** responsabilidad *f*; **ac·**

'count·a·ble ☐ responsable; **ac'count·ant** contador *m*; contable *m*; **ac'count·ing** contabilidad *f*.

ac·cred·it [ə'kredit] acreditar.

ac·crue [ə'kruː] aumentarse.

ac·cu·mu·late [ə'kjuːmjuleit] acumular(se), amontonar(se); **ac·cu·mu·la·tion** acumulación *f*, aumento *m*; montón *m*; **ac·cu·mu·la·tive** [ə'kjuːmjulətiv] ☐ acumulativo; **ac·'cu·mu·la·tor** ⚡ acumulador *m*.

ac·cu·ra·cy ['ækjurəsi] exactitud *f*, precisión *f*; **ac·cu·rate** ['~rit] ☐ exacto, preciso; correcto.

ac·curs·ed [ə'kəːsid], **ac·curst** [ə'kəːst] maldito.

ac·cu·sa·tion [ækjuː'zeiʃn] acusación *f*; ⚖ denuncia *f*, delación *f*; **ac·cu·sa·tive** [ə'kjuːzətiv] acusativo *m* (*a.* ~ *case*); **ac·cuse** [ə'kjuːz] acusar (*of* de); denunciar, delatar; *the* ~*d* ⚖ el acusado; **ac'cus·er** acusador *m*.

ac·cus·tom [ə'kʌstəm] acostumbrar, avezar (*to* a); **ac'cus·tomed** acostumbrado; usual.

ace [eis] as *m*.

ac·e·tate ['æsitit] acetato *m*; **a·ce·tic** [ə'siːtik] acético; **a·cet·y·lene** [ə'setiliːn] acetileno *m*.

ache [eik] 1. doler; 2. dolor *m*; *full of* ~*s and pains* lleno de goteras.

a·chieve [ə'tʃiːv] lograr, conseguir; acabar; **a'chieve·ment** realización *f*, logro *m*; *fact* hazaña *f*, proeza *f*.

ac·id ['æsid] 1. ☐ ácido, agrio; *v. test*; 2. ácido *m*; **a·cid·i·fy** [ə'sidifai] acidificar; **a'cid·i·ty** acidez *f*; acedía *f* of *stomach*.

ac·knowl·edge [ək'nɔlidʒ] reconocer; *crime etc.* confesar; *favor etc.* agradecer; ✝ ~ *receipt* acusar recibo; **ac'knowl·edg·ment** reconocimiento *m*; confesión *f*; agradecimiento *m*; ✝ acuse *m* de recibo.

ac·me ['ækmi] cima *f*, apogeo *m*.

ac·ne ['ækni] acné *m*.

a·corn ['eikɔːn] bellota *f*.

a·cous·tic, **a·cous·ti·cal** [ə'kuːstik(l)] ☐ acústico; **a'cous·tics** *mst pl.* acústica *f*.

ac·quaint [ə'kweint] enterar, avisar (*with*, *of* de); *be* ~*ed* conocerse; *be* ~*ed with* conocer; saber, estar al corriente de; *become* ~*ed with* (llegar a) conocer; ponerse al tanto de; **ac'quaint·ance** conocimiento *m* (*with* de); (*p.*) conocimiento *m*, conocido *m*.

ac·qui·esce [ækwi'es] asentir (*in* a), conformarse (*in* con).

ac·quire [əˈkwaiə] adquirir, obtener; *language* aprender; **ac·quire·ment** adquisición *f*; ~s *pl.* conocimientos *m/pl.*

ac·qui·si·tion [ækwiˈziʃn] adquisición *f*; ganancia *f*.

ac·quit [əˈkwit] absolver (*a.* 🏛); exculpar (*of* de); ~ *o.s. of duty etc.* desempeñar, cumplir; ~ *o.s. well* (*ill*) hacerlo bien (mal); **ac·quit·tal** 🏛 absolución *f*; descargo *m of debt*; desempeño *m*; **ac·quit·tance** 🏛 quita *f*; descargo *m of debt*.

a·cre [ˈeikə] acre *m* (= 40.47 áreas).

ac·ri·mo·ni·ous [ækriˈmounjəs] áspero, desabrido.

ac·ro·bat [ˈækrəbæt] acróbata *m/f*; **ac·ro·bat·ic** □ acrobático; **ac·ro·bat·ics** acrobacia *f*; ✈ vuelo *m* acrobático.

a·cross [əˈkrɔs] 1. *adv.* a través, de través; de una parte a otra, de un lado a otro; del otro lado; en cruz, transversalmente; 2. *prp.* a(l) través de; del otro lado de.

act [ækt] 1. *v/i.* actuar, obrar; funcionar, marchar; comportarse, conducirse; *thea.* trabajar; ~ *as* actuar de, hacer de; ~ (*up*)*on* obrar con arreglo a; influir en; 🔫 atacar; ~ *for* representar; F ~ *up* travesear; *v/t. thea.* representar; desempeñar (un papel); 2. acto *m*, acción *f*, obra *f*; *parl.* decreto *m*, ley *f*; *thea.* acto *m*, jornada *f*; F *in the* ~ con las manos en la masa; **ʹact·ing** 1. *thea.* representación *f*; desempeño *m*; 2. interino, suplente.

ac·tion [ˈækʃn] acción *f* (*a.* ⚔, *thea.*), acto *m*, hecho *m*; ⊕ mecanismo *m*; funcionamiento *m*, marcha *f*; (*horse*) marcha *f*; gesto *m*; 🏛 acción *f*, demanda *f*; *put into* ~ poner en marcha; *put out of* ~ inutilizar; parar; *take* ~ tomar medidas.

ac·tive [ˈæktiv] □ activo (*a. gr. a.* ↑); enérgico; vigoroso; *be on the* ~ *list* estar en activo; **ac·tiv·i·ty** actividad *f*; energía *f*; vigor *m*.

ac·tor [ˈæktə] actor *m*, cómico *m*; **ac·tress** [ˈæktris] actriz *f*.

ac·tu·al [ˈæktjuəl] □ verdadero, real, efectivo; actual; **ac·tu·al·i·ty** [æktjuˈæliti] realidad *f*; actualidad *f*; **ac·tu·al·ly** [ˈæktjuəli] en realidad.

ac·tu·ar·y [ˈæktjuəri] actuario *m* de seguros.

ac·u·punc·ture [ˈækjupʌŋkʃə] acupuntura *f*.

a·cute [əˈkjuːt] □ *all senses:* agudo; **aʹcute·ness** agudeza *f*.

ad [æd] F = *advertisement* anuncio *m*; *classified* ~s *pl.* anuncios *m/pl.* por palabras.

a·dapt [əˈdæpt] adaptar, acomodar, ajustar; *text* refundir; **aʹdapt·a·ble** adaptable; **ad·ap·ta·tion** adaptación *f* (*to* a); refundición *f*; **aʹdapt·er** *radio:* adaptador *m*.

add [æd] *v/t.* añadir, agregar (*to* a); 🅰 sumar; *v/i.* ~ *to* aumentar; realzar; ~ *up to* subir a.

ad·dict 1. [əˈdikt] ~ *o.s.* entregarse (*to* a), enviciarse (*to* en, con); 2. [ˈædikt] adicto (*a f*) *m*; (*drugs*) toxicómano (*a f*) *m*; **ad·dict·ed:** ~ *to* aficionado a, adicto a; entregado a; **ad·dic·tion** (*drugs*) toxicomanía *f*.

ad·di·tion [əˈdiʃn] añadidura *f*; adición *f*; 🅰 suma *f*; *in* ~ además, a más; *in* ~ *to* además de; **ad·di·tion·al** □ adicional.

ad·di·tive [ˈæditiv] aditivo.

ad·dress [əˈdres] 1. *p.* dirigir la palabra a; *letter, protest etc.* dirigir (*to* a); ✝ consignar; ~ *o.s. to p.* dirigirse a; *th.* aplicarse a; 2. (*house*) dirección *f*, señas *f/pl.*; sobrescrito *m*; ✝ consignación *f*; (*speech*) discurso *m*; (*skill*) destreza *f*; (*behavior*) maneras *f/pl.*, modales *m/pl.*; *give an* ~ pronunciar un discurso; **ad·dress·ee** [ædreˈsiː] destinatario *m*.

ad·e·noids [ˈædənɔidz] *pl.* vegetaciones *f/pl.* adenoides.

ad·ept [ˈædept] 1. diestro, experto (*at*, *in* en); 2. perito *m*; *be an* ~ *at* ser maestro en (*or* de).

ad·e·quate [ˈædikwit] □ suficiente; apropiado, adecuado.

ad·here [ədˈhiə] ~ *to* adherir a, pegarse a; *fig.* adherirse a, allegarse a; **ad·her·ence:** ~ *to* adherencia *f* a, adhesión *f* a; (*rule*) observancia *f* de; **ad·her·ent** 1. adhesivo; 2. partidario (*a f*) *m*.

ad·he·sion [ədˈhiːʒn] *mst* = *adherence*; ☇ adherencia *f*.

ad·he·sive [ədˈhiːsiv] □ adhesivo; ~ *plaster* esparadrapo *m*; ~ *tape* cinta *f* adhesiva.

ad·ja·cent [əˈdʒeisənt] □ adyacente, contiguo, inmediato (*to* a).

ad·jec·tive [ˈædʒiktiv] adjetivo *m*.

ad·join·ing [əˈdʒɔiniŋ] colindante, lindero.

ad·journ [əˈdʒəːn] v/t. prorrogar, diferir; *session* clausurar, suspender; v/i.: ~ *to* trasladarse a; **ad'journ·ment** aplazamiento *m*; clausura *f*.

ad·junct [ˈædʒʌŋkt] auxiliar *m*, adjunto *m*; accesorio *m*.

ad·just [əˈdʒʌst] ajustar; arreglar; *quarrel* conciliar; *apparatus etc.* ajustar, regular; ~ *o.s.* adaptarse a; **ad'just·a·ble** □ ajustable, graduable, regulable; **ad'just·ment** ajuste *m*, regulación *f*; acuerdo *m*, convenio *m*; arreglo *m*.

ad·ju·tant [ˈædʒətənt] ayudante *m*.

ad-lib [ædˈlib] F **1.** a voluntad; a discreción; **2.** improvisar.

ad·min·is·ter [ədˈministə] *mst* administrar; *shock etc.* proporcionar; ~ *an oath* tomar juramento; **ad'min·is'tra·tion** administración *f*; gobierno *m*; dirección *f*; **ad'min·is·tra·tive** [~trətiv] administrativo; **ad'min·is·tra·tor** [~treitə] administrador *m*.

ad·mi·ra·ble [ˈædmərəbl] □ admirable; excelente.

ad·mi·ral [ˈædmərəl] almirante *m*.

ad·mi·ra·tion [ædmiˈreiʃn] admiración *f*.

ad·mire [ədˈmaiə] admirar; **ad'mir·er** admirador (-a *f*) *m*.

ad·mis·si·ble [ədˈmisibl] □ admisible; **ad'mis·sion** admisión *f*, entrada *f* (*to* a); confesión *f* (*of* de); ~ *free* entrada *f* libre (*or* gratis).

ad·mit [ədˈmit] v/t. admitir; aceptar; confesar, reconocer; *be ~ted to academy etc.* ingresar en; v/i.: ~ *of* admitir, dar lugar a; ~ *to* confesarse culpable de; **ad'mit·tance** entrada *f*, admisión *f*; £ admitancia *f*; *no ~* prohibida la entrada; **ad'mit·ted·ly** indudablemente; de acuerdo que..., es verdad que...

ad·mon·ish [ədˈmɔniʃ] amonestar; reprender; aconsejar (*to inf.*); **ad·mo·ni·tion** [ædməˈniʃn] amonestación *f*; reprensión *f*; consejo *m*; advertencia *f*.

a·do [əˈduː] ruido *m*; aspaviento *m*.

ad·o·les·cence [ædouˈlesns] adolescencia *f*; **ad·o'les·cent** adolescente *adj. a. su. m/f*.

a·dopt [əˈdɔpt] adoptar; *~ed son* hijo *m* adoptivo; **a'dop·tion** adopción *f*; *country of ~* patria *f* adoptiva; **a'dop·tive** adoptivo.

a·dor·a·ble [əˈdɔːrəbl] □ adorable;

ad·o·ra·tion [ædɔːˈreiʃn] adoración *f*; **a·dore** [əˈdɔː] adorar.

ad·re·nal [ədˈriːnl] suprarrenal; ~ **'gland** glándula *f* suprarrenal.

ad·ren·al·in [ədˈrenəlin] adrenalina *f*.

a·drift [əˈdrift] ♣ al garete, a la deriva (*a. fig.*).

a·droit [əˈdrɔit] □ diestro, hábil; mañoso.

ad·u·la·tion [ædjuˈleiʃn] adulación *f*.

a·dult [ˈædʌlt] adulto.

a·dul·ter·ate [əˈdʌltəreit] adulterar, falsificar; **2.** [~rit] adulterado, falsificado; **a'dul·te·ry** adulterio *m*.

ad·vance [ədˈvɑːns] **1.** v/i. avanzar, adelantar(se); ascender *in rank*; (*price*) subir; v/t. avanzar, adelantar; *fig. cause etc.* fomentar, promover; *idea etc.* proponer; **2.** ⚔ *etc.* avance *m*; *fig.* progreso *m*, adelanto *m*; (*money*) anticipo *m*; *~s pl.* requerimiento *m* amoroso; *in ~* por adelantado, de antemano; *be in ~ of* adelantarse a; *thank in ~* anticipar las gracias; **3.** *adj.* adelantado, anticipado; *~ guard* avanzada *f*; **ad'vanced** *adj. gen. a. pol.* avanzado; adelantado; *study* superior, alto; *~ in years* entrado en años; **ad'vance·ment** progreso *m*; adelantamiento *m*; fomento *m*; ascenso *m*.

ad·van·tage [ədˈvɑːntidʒ] ventaja *f* (*a. tennis*); beneficio *m*, provecho *m*; *take ~ of* aprovechar(se de), sacar ventaja de; *b.s.* embaucar, valerse de, abusar de; *have the ~ of s.o.* llevar ventaja a alguien; *show to ~* lucir; **ad·van·ta·geous** [ædvənˈteidʒəs] □ ventajoso, provechoso.

ad·ven·ture [ədˈventʃə] **1.** aventura *f*; lance *m*; **2.** aventurar(se); arriesgarse; **ad'ven·tur·ous** □ aventurero, arrojado, emprendedor.

ad·verb [ˈædvəːb] adverbio *m*; **ad·ver·bi·al** [ədˈvəːbiəl] □ adverbial.

ad·ver·sar·y [ˈædvəsəri] adversario (a *f*) *m*, contrario (a *f*) *m*; **ad·verse** [ˈ~vəːs] □ adverso, contrario; hostil; desfavorable; **ad·ver·si·ty** [ədˈvəːsiti] adversidad *f*; infortunio *m*.

ad·ver·tise [ˈædvətaiz] v/t. anunciar; publicar; v/i. poner un anuncio; **ad·ver·tise·ment** [ədˈvəːtismənt] anuncio *m*; **ad·ver·tis·er** [ˈædvətaizə] anunciante *m/f*; **'ad·ver·tis·ing** publicidad *f*, propaganda *f*, anuncios *m/pl*.

ad·vice [ədˈvais] consejo *m*; aviso *m*, informe *m*, noticia *f*.

ad·vis·a·ble [əd'vaizəbl] □ aconsejable, prudente, conveniente; **ad·vise** v/t. aconsejar (to inf.); v/i.: ∼ on ser asesor en; **ad·vis·er** consejero m, asesor m; **ad·vi·so·ry** [∼əri] consultivo.

ad·vo·cate 1. ['ædvəkit] ⅀⅜ abogado m; defensor m; **2.** ['∼keit] abogar por; propugnar, defender; proponer.

aer·ate ['ɛəreit] v/t. airear.

a·e·ri·al ['ɛəriəl] □ aéreo; ∼ camera aparato m de fotografía aérea; ∼ photograph aerofoto f.

aer·i·al·ist ['ɛəriːəlist] volatinero m.

a·er·o·dy·nam·ic [ɛəroudai'næmik] aerodinámico; **aer·o·plane** avion m, aeroplano m; **aer·o·sol** aerosol m; **aer·o·space** aeroespacial.

aes·thet·ic, aes·thet·i·cal [es'θetik(l)] v. esthetic, esthetical.

a·far [ə'faː] (mst ∼ off) lejos, en (la) lontananza; from ∼ (des)de lejos.

af·fa·ble ['æfəbl] □ afable.

af·fair [ə'fɛə] asunto m, negocio m; F cosa f; amorío m.

af·fect [ə'fekt] afectar; conmover, enternecer, impresionar; tener que ver con; influir en; **af·fec·ta·tion** [æfek'teiʃn] afectación f; amaneramiento m; cursilería f; melindre m; dengue m; **af·fect·ed** [ə'fektid] □ afectado; conmovido; amanerado; cursi; melindroso; **af·fec·tion** afecto m, cariño m, amor m; esp. ⅀⅜ afección f; **af·fec·tion·ate** [∼kʃnit] □ cariñoso, afectuoso.

af·fi·da·vit [æfi'deivit] declaración f jurada.

af·fil·i·ate [ə'filieit] v/t. (a)filiar; v/i. afiliarse (with, to a); **af·fil·i·a·tion** afiliación f.

af·fin·i·ty [ə'finiti] afinidad f.

af·firm [ə'fəːm] afirmar, aseverar, declarar; **af·fir·ma·tion** [æfə'meiʃn] afirmación f, aseveración f, declaración f; **af·firm·a·tive** [ə'fəːmətiv] **1.** □ afirmativo; **2.** answer in the ∼ dar una respuesta afirmativa.

af·fix [ə'fiks] fijar; pegar, unir; añadir.

af·flict [ə'flikt] afligir, acongojar; be ∼ed with sufrir de; **af·flic·tion** aflicción f, congoja f; miseria f.

af·flu·ent ['æfluənt] **1.** □ opulento, acaudalado; **2.** afluente m.

af·flux ['æflʌks] aflujo m.

af·ford [ə'fɔːd] dar, proporcionar, proveer; (pay for) costear.

af·front [ə'frʌnt] **1.** afrentar, injuriar,

ultrajar; (verbally) denostar; arrostrar; **2.** afrenta f, injuria f.

a·float [ə'flout] a flote; en el mar; a nado; inundado.

a·foot [ə'fut] a pie; en pie; en marcha.

a·fore [ə'fɔː] ⅌ v. before; **'∼·mentioned, '∼·named, '∼·said** antedicho, susodicho, precitado; **'∼·thought** premeditado; malice ∼ premeditación f.

a·fraid [ə'freid] temeroso, miedoso; be ∼ tener miedo (of de, a), temer.

a·fresh [ə'freʃ] de nuevo, otra vez.

Af·ri·can ['æfrikən] africano adj. a. su. m (a f); **Af·ri·kaans** [∼'kɑːns] africaans m; **Af·ri·kan·der** ['∼kændə] africander m.

aft [ɑːft] a popa; en popa.

aft·er ['ɑːftə] **1.** adj. (time) después; (place) detrás; **2.** prp. (time) después de; (place) detrás de; ∼ all después de todo, con todo; day ∼ day día tras día; ∼ hours fuera de horas; **3.** cj. después (de) que; **4.** adj. posterior, ⅌ de popa; **'∼·din·ner 'speak·er** orador m de sobremesa; **'∼·din·ner 'speech** discurso m de sobremesa; **'∼·glow** celajes m/pl.; **'∼·math** consecuencias f/pl.; repercusiones f/pl.; **'∼·noon** tarde f; good ∼! ¡buenas tardes!; **'∼·shave 'lo·tion** loción f para después del afeitado; **'∼·taste** dejo m, resabio m; **'∼·thought** ocurrencia f tardía; **'∼·wards** ['∼wədz] después, más tarde.

a·gain [ə'gen] otra vez, de nuevo, nuevamente; ∼ and ∼, time and ∼ repetidas veces; as much (many) ∼ otro (os, as) tanto (os, as); now and ∼ de vez en cuando, una que otra vez; never ∼ nunca más; do it ∼ volver a hacerlo.

a·gainst [ə'genst] contra; cerca de, al lado de; (as) ∼ en contraste con; ∼ his coming para su venida; over ∼ enfrente de; be ∼ oponerse a; he was ∼ it estaba en contra.

a·gape [ə'geip] boquiabierto.

ag·ate ['ægət] ágata f.

a·ga·ve [ə'geivi] agave f, pita f.

age [eidʒ] **1.** edad f; época f, siglo m; (old) ∼ vejez f, senectud f; come of ∼ llegar a mayor edad; over ∼ demasiado viejo; under ∼ menor de edad; what is your ∼? ¿qué edad tiene Vd.?, ¿cuántos años tiene Vd.?; F wait for ∼s esperar una eternidad; **2.** envejecer(se); **'∼ 'brack·et, '∼ 'group** grupo m de personas de la misma edad;

ag·ed ['ᴧid] viejo; anciano; [eidȝd]: ~ 20 de 20 años; **'age·less** que no tiene edad, inmemorial; eternamente joven; **'age lim·it** edad f mínima or máxima; edad f de jubilación.

a·gen·cy ['eidȝənsi] agencia f; acción f; medio m, mediación f.

a·gen·da [ə'dȝendə] orden m del día.

a·gent ['eidȝənt] agente m; apoderado m; representante m; jefe m de estación.

age-old ['eidȝould] secular.

age-worn ['eidȝwɔːn] caduco.

ag·gran·dize ['ægrəndaiz] engrandecer, agrandar; **ag·gran·dize·ment** [ə'grændizmənt] engrandecimiento m, agrandamiento m.

ag·gra·vate ['ægrəveit] agravar, exacerbar; F irritar, exasperar; **ag·gra·'va·tion** agravación f, exacerbación f.

ag·gre·gate ['ægrigit] □ agregado, unido, global.

ag·gres·sion [ə'greʃn] agresión f; **ag·'gres·sive** [ə'gresiv] □ agresivo; fig. emprendedor; ~ war guerra f agresiva; **ag'gres·sor** agresor (-a f) m.

ag·grieved [ə'griːvd] ofendido, desairado; agraviado.

a·ghast [ə'gæst] espantado, horrorizado; pasmado (at de).

ag·ile ['ædȝəl] □ ágil.

a·gil·i·ty [ə'dȝiliti] agilidad f.

a·ging ['eidȝin] envejecimiento m.

ag·i·tate ['ædȝiteit] v/t. agitar; perturbar, alborotar; **ag·i·'ta·tion** agitación f; perturbación f; **'ag·i·ta·tor** agitador (-a f) m, instigador (-a f) m.

a·glow [ə'glou] encendido.

a·go [ə'gou]: (it is) a year ~ hace un año; long ~ hace mucho tiempo, tiempo ha.

ag·o·nize [ə'gonaiz] v/t. atormentar; v/i. retorcerse de dolor.

ag·o·ny ['ægəni] angustia f, congoja f.

a·gree [ə'griː] v/i. concordar (esp. gr.), estar de acuerdo (with con, that en que); ponerse de acuerdo; ~ on, ~ to convenir en, quedar en, acordar; it does not ~ with me no me sienta (bien); v/t. be ~d estar de acuerdo (on en, that en que); ~d convenido, aprobado; ~d! ¡Conforme!; **a·'gree·a·ble** □ agradable, ameno; p. simpático; conforme (to con), dispuesto (to a); **a·'gree·a·ble·ness** agrado m; amenidad f; **a·'gree·ment** acuerdo m; convenio m; concordancia f; conformidad f.

ag·ri·cul·tur·al [ægri'kᴧltʃurəl] agrícola; ~ adviser agrónomo m; **ag·ri·cul·ture** ['·tʃə] agricultura f.

a·ground [ə'graund] varado, encallado; run ~ varar, encallar.

a·gue ['eigjuː] fiebre f intermitente; escalofrío m.

a·head [ə'hed] delante, al frente; ⚓ por la proa; adelante; straight ~ todo seguido.

aid [eid] **1.** ayudar, auxiliar, socorrer; **2.** ayuda f, auxilio m, socorro m.

ail [eil] v/i. estar enfermo; sufrir; v/t. afligir; inquietar; what ~s him? ¿qué tiene?

ail·e·ron ['eilərɔn] alerón m.

ail·ment ['eilmənt] achaque m, dolencia f, enfermedad f.

aim [eim] **1.** v/i. apuntar (at a); fig. ~ at aspirar a, ambicionar; ~ to aspirar a, intentar; fig. ~ high picar muy alto; v/t. gun, remark etc. apuntar (at a); blow etc. asestar (at a); **2.** puntería f; fig. mira f, meta f, blanco m, designio m; take ~ apuntar; **'aim·less** □ sin objeto; desatinado; ~ly a la buena ventura, a la deriva.

ain't [eint] F = is not, are not etc.; has not, have not.

air¹ [ɛə] **1.** aire m; by ~ por avión; in the ~ fig. en el aire, indefinido; en proyecto; in the open ~ al aire libre, al raso; **2.** airear, orear, ventilar (a. fig.).

air² [~] aire m, aspecto m; ademán m; porte m.

air³ [~] ♪ aire m, tonada f.

air...: '~ **base** base f aérea; '~**borne** ✈ en el aire, despegado; ✈ aerotransportado; germs etc. transmitido por el aire; '~ **brake** freno m neumático; '~**con·di·tioned** con aire acondicionado, refrigerado; '~ **con·di·tion·er** acondicionador m de aire; '~**craft** avión m; ~ carrier porta(a)viones m; '~ **drop** **1.** lanzamiento m; **2.** v/t. lanzar; '~**field** campo m de aviación; '~ **force** aviación f, fuerzas f/pl. aéreas.

air·i·ness ['ɛərinis] buena ventilación f; airosidad f; fig. ligereza f.

air...: '~**lift** puente m aéreo; '~**line** línea f aérea; línea f recta; '~**lin·er** avión m de pasajeros, transaéreo m; '~ **mail** correo m aéreo; '~**plane** avión m; ~ carrier porta(a)viones m; ~ pilot piloto m; '~ **pock·et** bache m aéreo; '~**port** aeropuerto m; '~ **pres·sure** presión f atmosférica; '~ **raid**

ataque *m* aéreo; ∼ *shelter* refugio *m* antiaéreo; ∼ *warning* alarma *f* aérea; '∼**sick** mareado (en el aire); '∼**speed** velocidad *f* relativa al aire; ∼ *indicator* velocímetro *m* aéreo; '∼**strip** pista *f* de aterrizaje; '∼**tight** hermético; '∼**worthy** en condiciones de vuelo.

air·y ['ɛəri] □ airoso; *esp. room* bien ventilado, ancho; *fig.* etéreo, ligero; (*rude*) impertinente.

aisle [ail] nave *f* lateral; *thea. etc.* pasillo *m*.

a·jar [ə'dʒɑ:] entreabierto, entornado; *fig.* en desacuerdo.

a·larm [ə'lɑːm] **1.** alarma *f*; sobresalto *m*; **2.** alarmar, inquietar, asustar; **a'larm clock** (reloj *m*) despertador *m*.

a·las [ə'læs] ¡ay!

al·be·it [ɔːl'biːit] aunque, bien que.

al·bum ['ælbəm] álbum *m*.

al·co·hol ['ælkəhɔl] alcohol *m*; **al·co-'hol·ic** alcohólico *adj. a. su. m* (a *f*), alcoholizado *adj. a. su. m* (a *f*); '**al·co-hol·ism** alcoholismo *m*.

al·cove ['ælkouv] nicho *m*, hueco *m*; gabinete *m of library*; cenador *m in garden*.

al·der·man ['ɔːldəmən] regidor *m*, concejal *m* (de cierta antigüedad).

ale [eil] cerveza *f* (inglesa).

ale·house ['eilhaus] taberna *f*.

a·lert [ə'ləːt] **1.** □ vigilante; vivo, listo; **2.** alarma *m*; be on the ∼ estar alerta, estar sobre aviso.

a·li·as ['eiliæs] alias *adv. a. su. m*.

al·i·bi ['ælibai] coartada *f*; F excusa *f*, pretexto *m*.

al·ien ['eiliən] **1.** ajeno, extraño (*to* a); extranjero; **2.** extranjero (a *f*) *m*; **al·ien·ate** ['∼eit] enajenar, alienar; *be* ∼*d from* enajenarse de.

a·light¹ [ə'lait] ardiendo, encendido, iluminado.

a·light² [∼] bajar, apearse; ✈ aterrizar; ∼ *on* posarse sobre; ∼ *on one's feet* caer de pie.

a·lign [ə'lain] alinear; ∼ *o.s. with* alinearse con; ponerse al lado de.

a·like [ə'laik] **1.** *adj.* semejante, parecido; *look* ∼ parecerse (*a f*); **2.** *adv.* igualmente, del mismo modo.

a·li·mo·ny ['æliməni] alimentos *m/pl*.

a·live [ə'laiv] vivo, viviente, con vida; *fig.* vivaz, activo; sensible (*to* a); *keep* ∼ mantener(se) en vigor.

al·ka·li ['ælkəlai] álcali *m*; **al·ka·line** ['∼lain] alcalino.

all [ɔːl] **1.** *adj.* todo; ∼ *day* (*long*) (durante) todo el día; ∼ *kind(s) of books* toda clase de libros, libros de toda clase; *for* ∼ *that* con todo, no obstante, así y todo; ∼*purpose* para todo uso, universal; ∼*weather* para todo tiempo; **2.** todo *m*; todos *m/pl.*, todas *f/pl.*; *my* ∼ todo lo que tengo; ∼ *of them* (ellos) todos; *at* ∼ de cualquier manera; en lo más mínimo; siquiera un poco; *not at* ∼ de ninguna manera; no hay de qué; *for* ∼ *(that)* I *care* igual me da; *for* ∼ I *know* que yo sepa; quizá; **3.** *adv.* enteramente, del todo; ∼ *the better* tanto mejor; ∼ *but* casi, por poco; menos.

al·lay [ə'lei] apaciguar, aquietar; *pain* aliviar, mitigar.

al·le·ga·tion [æle'geiʃn] aseveración *f*, alegación *f*, alegato *m*; **al·lege** [ə'ledʒ] declarar, sostener; (*as proof, excuse, etc.*) alegar.

al·le·giance [ə'liːdʒəns] fidelidad *f*, lealtad *f*, (a ∼) homenaje *m*.

al·le·gor·ic, al·le·gor·i·cal [æle'gɔrik(l)] □ alegórico; '**al·le·go·ry** alegoría *f*.

al·le·lu·ia [æli'luːjə] aleluya *f*.

al·ler·gy ['ælədʒi] alergia *f*.

al·le·vi·ate [ə'liːvieit] aliviar.

al·ley ['æli] callejuela *f*, callejón *m*.

al·li·ance [ə'laiəns] alianza *f*; *form an* ∼ formar una alianza.

al·li·ga·tor ['æligeitə] caimán *m*.

al·lo·cate ['æləkeit] asignar; repartir.

al·lot [ə'lɔt] asignar, adjudicar; repartir; **al·lot·ment** asignación *f*; reparto *m*; lote *m*, porción *f*.

all-out ['ɔːl'aut] **1.** *adj. supporter etc.* acérrimo; *effort etc.* total, máximo; **2.** *adv.* con todas las fuerzas; a máxima velocidad.

al·low [ə'lau] (*permit*) permitir, dejar (*to inf.*); (*grant*) conceder, dar; (*admit*) confesar; *discount* descontar; **al·low·a·ble** □ permisible, admisible; **al·low·ance** (*grant*) concesión *f*; ración *f*, pensión *f*; (*discount*) descuento *m*, rebaja *f*; ⊕ tolerancia *f*; *make* ∼ *for p.* disculpar; *th.* tener en cuenta.

al·loy [ə'lɔi] **1.** aleación *f*, liga *f*; *fig.* mezcla *f*; **2.** alear, ligar; *fig.* mezclar, adulterar.

al·lude [ə'luːd]: ∼ *to* aludir a.

al·lure [ə'ljuə] atraer, fascinar; **al-'lure·ment** atractivo *m*, aliciente *m*; fascinación *f*; **al'lur·ing** □ atractivo, tentador.

al·lu·sion [əˈluːʒn] alusión *f*, referencia *f* (*to* a).

al·ly 1. [əˈlai] aliarse, unirse; *fig.* emparentarse (*to*, *with* con); *allied fig.* conexo, parecido; *allied to* fig. relacionado con; **2.** [ˈælai] aliado *m*.

al·ma·nac [ˈɔːlmənæk] almanaque *m*.

al·might·y [ɔːlˈmaiti] □ todopoderoso; F imponente, grandísimo.

al·mond [ˈɑːmənd] almendra *f*; (*a.* ~ *tree*) almendro *m*.

al·most [ˈɔːlmoust] casi.

alms [ɑːmz] *sg. a. pl.* limosna *f*.

a·loft [əˈlɔft] hacia arriba, en alto.

a·lone [əˈloun] **1.** *adj.* solo; **2.** *adv.* solamente, sólo.

a·long [əˈlɔŋ] **1.** *adv.* a lo largo; adelante; *all* ~ desde el principio; ~ *with* junto con; **2.** *prp.* a lo largo de; por; al lado de; **a·long·side 1.** *adv.* ⚓ al costado, costado con costado; *bring* ~ costar; **2.** *prp.* fig. junto a, al lado de.

a·loof [əˈluːf] reservado, huraño; *keep* ~ apartarse, alejarse (*from* de); *stand* ~ mantenerse apartado, mantenerse a distancia; **a·loof·ness** reserva *f*.

a·loud [əˈlaud] en voz alta.

al·pha·bet [ˈælfəbit] alfabeto *m*; **al·pha·bet·ic**, **al·pha·bet·i·cal** [~ˈbetik(l)] □ alfabético.

al·read·y [ɔːlˈredi] ya; previamente, antes.

al·so [ˈɔːlsou] también, además; *racing*: ~ *ran* (caballo *m*) que no logró colocarse; F fracasado *m*.

al·tar [ˈɔːltə] ara *f* (*lit.*); *high*~ altar *m* mayor; **'~·piece** retablo *m*.

al·ter [ˈɔːltə] cambiar(se), alterar, modificar; F *animal* castrar; **'al·ter·a·ble** mudable; **al·ter·a·tion** alteración *f*, cambio *m* (*of*, *to* de); △ ~*s pl.* reformas *f/pl.*

al·ter·nate 1. [ˈɔːltəːneit] alternar; *alternating current* corriente *f* alterna; **2.** [ɔːlˈtəːnit] □ alterno, alternativo; *on* ~ *days* cada dos días, un día sí y otro no; **3.** suplente *m*, sustituto *m*; **al·ter·na·tion** [~ˈneiʃn] alternación *f*; **al·ter·na·tive** [~ˈnətiv] **1.** □ alternativo; **2.** alternativa *f*.

al·though [ɔːlˈðou] aunque; si bien.

al·ti·tude [ˈæltitjuːd] altitud *f*; altura *f*, elevación *f*.

al·to [ˈæltou] contralto *f*.

al·to·geth·er [ɔːltəˈgeðə] enteramente, del todo; en conjunto.

al·u·mi·num [əˈluːminəm] aluminio *m*.

a·lum·nus [əˈlʌmnəs] *m*, *pl.* **a·lum·ni** [~nai]; **a·lum·na** [~nə] *f*, *pl.* **a·lum·nae** [~niː] graduado (a *f*) *m*.

al·ways [ˈɔːlwəz] siempre; *as* ~ como (de) siempre.

am [æm; *in phrases freq.* əm] soy; estoy (*v. be*).

a·mal·gam·ate [əˈmælɡəmeit] amalgamar(se).

a·mass [əˈmæs] acumular, amontonar.

am·a·teur [ˈæmətə:] aficionado (a *f*) *m*; *b.s.* chapucero *m*, principiante *m/f*; **am·a·teur·ish** superficial, inexperto, chapucero.

a·maze [əˈmeiz] asombrar, pasmar; **a'mazed** □ asombrado, pasmado (*at* de); *be* ~ at asombrarse de; **a'maze·ment** asombro *m*, aturdimiento *m*; pasmo *m*; **a'maz·ing** □ asombroso, pasmoso.

am·bas·sa·dor [æmˈbæsədə] embajador *m*.

am·ber [ˈæmbə] **1.** ámbar *m*; **2.** ambarino, de ámbar.

am·bi·gu·i·ty [æmbiˈɡjuiti] ambigüedad *f*, doble sentido *m*; **am·big·u·ous** [~ˈbigjuəs] □ ambiguo; equívoco.

am·bi·tion [æmˈbiʃn] ambición *f* (*to*, *for* por), anhelo *m* (*to*, *for* de); **am·bi·tious** □ ambicioso.

am·bu·lance [ˈæmbjuləns] (*coche m*) ambulancia *f*.

am·bu·la·to·ry [ˈæmbjulətəri] ambulatorio, móvil.

am·bus·cade [æmbəsˈkeid], **am·bush** [ˈæmbuʃ] **1.** emboscada *f*; *lie in* ~ estar en acecho (*or* en celada); **2.** acechar; tomar (*or* coger) por sorpresa.

a·mel·io·rate [əˈmiːliəreit] mejorar (-se); **a·mel·io·ra·tion** mejora *f*, mejoramiento *m*.

a·men [ˈɑːˈmen] amén.

a·me·na·ble [əˈmiːnəbl] sumiso, dócil; 🏛 responsable.

a·mend [əˈmend] enmendar (*a.* 🏛 *a. parl.*); rectificar, reformar; **a'mend·ment** enmienda *f*; **a'mends** [~dz] reparación *f*, recompensa *f*; *make* ~ *for* compensar, igualar; expiar.

A·mer·i·can [əˈmerikən] **1.** americano; **2.** americano (a *f*) *m*; **a'mer·i·can·ism** americanismo *m*; **a'mer·i·can·ize** americanizar(se).

Am·er·in·di·an, **Am·er·ind** [æməˈrindjən, ˈæmərind] amerindio *m*.

am·e·thyst [ˈæmiθist] amatista *f*.

a·mi·a·ble [ˈeimiəbl] □ afable, amable; bonachón; simpático.

am·i·ca·ble ['æmikəbl] □ amigable, amistoso.

a·mid(st) [ə'mid(st)] entre, en medio de.

a·miss [ə'mis] mal, fuera de propósito; impropio; *take* ~ llevar a mal.

am·i·ty ['æmiti] amistad *f*.

am·mo·ni·a [ə'mounjə] amoníaco *m*; *liquid* ~ amoníaco *m* líquido.

am·mu·ni·tion [æmju'niʃn] **1.** municiones *f*/*pl*.; *fig.* pertrechos *m*/*pl*.; **2.** *attr.* de municiones.

am·nes·ty ['æmnesti] **1.** amnistía *f*, indulto *m*; **2.** indultar.

a·moe·ba [ə'mi:bə] amiba *f*.

a·mong(st) [ə'mʌŋ(st)] entre, en medio de; *from* ~ de entre.

a·mor·phous [ə'mɔ:fəs] *min.* amorfo.

a·mount [ə'maunt] **1.:** ~ *to* valer, hacer, ascender a; *fig.* equivaler a, significar; **2.** cantidad *f*, suma *f*.

am·pere ['æmpɛə] amperio *m*.

am·phib·i·an [æm'fibiən] **1.** anfibio *m*; **2.** = **am'phib·i·ous** □ anfibio.

am·phi·the·a·ter ['æmfiθiətə] anfiteatro *m*.

am·ple ['æmpl] amplio; abundante; liberal; bastante.

am·pli·fi·ca·tion [æmplifi'keiʃn] amplificación *f* (*a. rhet. a. phys.*); **am·pli·fi·er** ['~faiə] *radio*: amplificador *m*; **'am·pli·fy** amplificar, ampliar; dilatar, extender; *radio*: ~*ing valve* lámpara *f* amplificadora *f*; **am·pli·tude** ['~tju:d] amplitud *f*.

am·pu·tate ['æmpjuteit] amputar; **am·pu'ta·tion** amputación *f*.

a·muck [ə'mʌk]: *run* ~ enloquecer, desbocarse (*a. fig.*), desmandarse.

am·u·let ['æmjulit] amuleto *m*.

a·muse [ə'mju:z] divertir, entretener; distraer, solazar; **a'muse·ment** diversión *f*, entretenimiento *m*; pasatiempo *m*, recreo *m*; *for* ~ para divertirse; **a·mus·ing** □ divertido, entretenido; gracioso.

an [æn, ən] *article*; *v*. una, una.

a·nach·ro·nism [ə'nækrənizm] anacronismo *m*.

a·nae·mi·a [ə'ni:miə] *v*. anemia.

an·aes·the·si·a [ænis's'θi:zjə] *v*. anesthesia.

an·al·ge·si·a [ænəl'dʒi:ziə] analgesia *f*.

an·a·log·ic, an·a·log·i·cal [ænə'lodʒik(l)] □, **a·nal·o·gous** [ə'næləgəs] análogo; afín; **a'nal·o·gy** analogía *f*; afinidad *f*; *on the* ~ *of* por analogía con.

an·a·lyse ['ænəlaiz] analizar; **a·nal·y·sis** [ə'næləsis], *pl.* **a·nal·y·ses** ['~i:z] análisis *mst m*; **an·a·lyst** ['ænəlist] analizador *m*; *public* ~ jefe *m* del laboratorio municipal; **an·a·lyt·ic, an·a·lyt·i·cal** [ænə'litik(l)] □ analítico.

an·ar·chic, an·ar·chi·cal [æ'nɑ:kik(l)] □ anárquico; **an·arch·ist** anarquista *m*/*f*; **'an·arch·y** anarquía *f*; desorden *m*.

a·nath·e·ma [ə'næθimə] anatema *m*.

an·a·tom·i·cal [ænə'tɔmikl] □ anatómico; **a'nat·o·my** anatomía *f* (*a. fig.*).

an·ces·tor ['ænsistə] antepasado *m*, progenitor *m*; **an·ces·tral** [~'sestrəl] ancestral, hereditario; **'an·ces·try** ascendencia *f*, linaje *m*, abolengo *m*.

an·chor ['æŋkə] **1.** ⚓ *a. fig.* ancla *f*; *at* ~ al ancla, anclado; *cast* (*or drop*) ~ echar anclas; *weigh* ~ zarpar; **2.** *v*/*t*. anclar; sujetar; *v*/*i*. anclar, fondear; **'an·chor·age** ancladero *m*, fondeadero *m*.

an·cho·vy ['æntʃəvi] anchoa *f*.

an·cient ['einʃənt] **1.** □ antiguo; vetusto; **2.** *the* ~*s pl.* los antiguos *m*/*pl*.

an·cil·lar·y [æn'siləri] auxiliar; subordinado (*to* a).

and [ænd, ənd F ən] y; (*before* i-, hi-) e; *thousands* ~ *thousands* miles y miles, millares; *try* ~ *inf.* tratar de *inf.*; *try* ~ *take it* cógelo si puedes; *after verbs of motion*: a (*e.g.*, *go* ~ *see him* ir a verle).

and·i·ron ['ændaiən] morillo *m*.

an·ec·dote ['ænikdout] anécdota *f*.

a·ne·mi·a [ə'ni:miə] anemia *f*; **a'ne·mic** anémico.

an·es·the·si·a [ænis'θi:ziə] anestesia *f*; **an·es·thet·ic** [ænis'θetik] anestésico *adj. a. su. m.*; **an·es·thet·ize** [ə'ni:sθətaiz] anestesiar.

a·new [ə'nju:] de nuevo, otra vez.

an·gel ['eindʒl] ángel *m*; **an·gel·ic, an·gel·i·cal** [æn'dʒelik(l)] □ angélico.

an·ger ['æŋgə] **1.** cólera *f*, ira *f*, saña *f*; **2.** enojar, encolerizar, provocar.

an·gi·na [æn'dʒainə] angina *f*; ~ *pectoris* angina *f* de pecho.

an·gle ['æŋgl] **1.** ángulo *m*; *fig.* punto *m* de vista; **2.** pescar con caña (*for acc.*); ~ *for* F ir a la caza de; **'an·gler** pescador (-a *f*) *m* con caña.

An·glo-Sax·on ['æŋglou'sæksn] anglosajón *adj. a. su. m.* (-a *f*).

an·gry ['æŋgri] □ colérico; enojado,

enfadado; ⚓ inflamado; get~ encolerizarse, montar en cólera (*with p.* con); *it makes me* ~ me enoja mucho.

an·guish ['æŋgwiʃ] angustia *f.*

an·gu·lar ['æŋgjulə] □ angular.

an·i·mal ['æniməl] **1.** animal *m;* bestia *f;* **2.** animal; ~ *spirits pl.* vitalidad *f.*

an·i·mate 1. ['ænimeit] animar, alentar; **2.** ['~mit] vivo; **'an·i·mat·ed** □ *fig.* vivo, vivaz, animado; '~d **car·toon** película *f* de dibujos, dibujo *m* animado; **an·i·ma·tion** [æni'meiʃn] vivacidad *f*, animación *f.*

an·ise ['ænis] anís *m;* **an·i·seed** ['~siːd] **1.** anís *m;* **2.** *attr.* de anís.

an·kle ['æŋkl] tobillo *m.*

an·klet ['æŋklit] ajorca *f* para el pie.

an·nals ['ænlz] *pl.* anales *m/pl.; fig. a. lit.* fastos *m/pl.*

an·nex 1. [ə'neks] añadir, adjuntar (to a); *esp. territory* anexar, apoderarse de; **2.** ['æneks] apéndice *m*, aditamento *m;* **an'nex·a·tion** anexión *f.*

an·ni·hi·late [ə'naiəleit] aniquilar; **an·ni·hi·la·tion** aniquilamiento *m.*

an·ni·ver·sa·ry [æni'vəːsəri] aniversario *m.*

an·no·tate ['ænouteit] anotar; comentar, glosar; **an·no'ta·tion** anotación *f;* comentario *m* (on, to sobre).

an·nounce [ə'nauns] anunciar, proclamar; **an'nounce·ment** anuncio *m*, aviso *m*, proclama *f;* **an'nounc·er** *radio:* locutor (-a *f*) *m.*

an·noy [ə'nɔi] molestar, fastidiar, jorobar (F); **an'noy·ance** molestia *f*, fastidio *m;* enojo *m;* **an'noyed** enfadado, irritado, enojado; **an'noy·ing** □ molesto, fastidioso.

an·nu·al ['ænjuəl] **1.** □ anual; ♀ ~ **ring** cerco *m;* anuario *m;* ♀ planta *f* anual, anual *m.*

an·nu·i·ty [ə'njuiti] renta *f* vitalicia.

an·nul [ə'nʌl] anular, cancelar.

an·nul·ment [ə'nʌlmənt] anulación *f*, cancelación *f;* abrogación *f.*

a·noint [ə'nɔint] *mst eccl.* untar, ungir; consagrar.

a·nom·a·lous [ə'nɔmələs] □ anómalo; **a'nom·a·ly** anomalía *f.*

a·non [ə'nɔn] **1.** † luego, dentro de poco; *poet.* ever and ~ de vez en cuando; **2.** *abbr.* = **anonymous.**

an·o·nym·i·ty [ænə'nimiti] anónimo *m;* **a·non·y·mous** [ə'nɔniməs] □ anónimo.

an·oth·er [ə'nʌðə] otro; *just such* ~ otro tal.

an·swer ['ɑːnsə] **1.** *v/t. p., question* contestar a, responder a, replicar a; *v/i.* responder, contestar, replicar; (*suffice*) servir, convenir; **2.** respuesta *f*, contestación *f* (to a); ⚓ solución *f;* ⚙ réplica *f.*

ant [ænt] hormiga *f.*

an·tag·o·nism [æn'tægənizm] antagonismo *m*, rivalidad *f* (between entre); **an'tag·o·nist** antagonista *m/f*, adversario *m.*

an·tag·o·nize [æn'tægənaiz] enemistarse con, contrariar.

ant·arc·tic [ænt'ɑːktik] antártico; ♀ **Circle** Círculo *m* Polar Antártico.

an·te ['ænti] *poker:* **1.** tanto *m*, apuesta *f;* **2.** F (*mst* ~ up) *v/t. a. v/i.* poner un tanto, apostar.

an·te·ced·ent [ænti'siːdənt] **1.** □ precedente, antecedente (to a); **2.** antecedente *m* (*a. gr.*); *his* ~s *pl.* sus antecedentes *m/pl.*

an·te·lope ['æntiloup] antílope *m.*

an·ten·na [æn'tenə], *pl.* **an·ten·nas** [~əs], **an·ten·nae** [~niː] *all senses:* antena *f.*

an·te·ri·or [æn'tiəriə] anterior (to a).

an·them ['ænθəm] motete *m; national* ~ himno *m* nacional.

an·thol·o·gy [æn'θɔlədʒi] antología *f.*

an·thra·cite ['ænθrəsait] antracita *f.*

an·thro·pol·o·gist [ænθrə'pɔlədʒist] antropólogo *m;* **an·thro·pol·o·gy** antropología *f.*

an·ti... ['ænti] *in compounds* anti...

an·ti·air·craft ['ænti'eəkrɑːft]: ~ *de·fense* defensa *f* antiaérea; ~ *gun* cañón *m* antiaéreo.

an·ti·bi·ot·ic ['æntibai'ɔtik] antibiótico *m.*

an·tics ['æntiks] *pl.* bufonadas *f/pl.*, payasadas *f/pl.;* travesuras *f/pl.*

an·tic·i·pate [æn'tisipeit] (*forestall*) anticipar, prevenir; (*foresee*) prever; (*expect*) esperar; (*look forward to*) prometerse; **an·tic·i·pa·tion** anticipación *f*, prevención *f;* previsión *f;* expectación *f;* esperanza *f;* in ~ de antemano; in ~ o esperando.

an·ti·dote ['æntidout] antídoto *m* (against, for contra).

an·ti·freeze ['ænti'friːz] *mot.* (solución *f*) anticongelante.

an·ti·knock ['ænti'nɔk] *mot.* antidetonante.

an·tip·a·thy [æn'tipəθi] antipatía *f.*

an·ti·quar·i·an [ænti'kwεəriən] anticuario *adj. a. su. m;* **an·ti·quat·ed** ['~kweitid] anticuado.

an·tique [ænˈtiːk] 1. antiguo, viejo; 2. antigüedad f, antigualla f; **an·tiq·ui·ty** [ˌtikwiti] antigüedad f; vetustez f.

an·ti·sem·i·tism [ˈæntiˈsemitizm] antisemitismo m.

an·ti·sep·tic [æntiˈseptik] antiséptico adj. a. su. m.

an·tith·e·sis [ænˈtiθisis], pl. **an·tith·e·ses** [ˌsiːz] antítesis f; **an·ti·thet·ic, an·ti·thet·i·cal** [ˌˈθetik(l)] □ antitético.

ant·ler [ˈæntlə] cuerna f, ~s pl. cornamenta f, cuernas f/pl.

an·to·nym [ˈæntənim] antónimo m.

a·nus [ˈeinəs] ano m.

an·vil [ˈænvil] yunque m (a. fig.).

anx·i·e·ty [æŋˈzaiəti] cuidado m; inquietud f, ansiedad f (about sobre); (yearning) ansia f, anhelo m (for, to de); ⚕ ansiedad f.

anx·ious [ˈæŋkʃəs] □ inquieto, preocupado, ansioso; (desirous) deseoso (for, to de).

an·y [ˈeni] 1. pron. alguno; cualquiera; (negative sense) ninguno; 2. adj. algún; cualquier; (negative sense) ningún; are there ~ nails? ¿hay clavos?; ~ book you like cualquier libro; 3. adv. mst not translated: ~ more más; '~·bod·y, '~·one alguien, alguno; not ~ nadie; '~·how en todo caso, de todos modos; con todo; de cualquier modo; '~·thing algo, cualquier cosa; ~ but (that) todo menos (eso); not ~ nada; '~·way = anyhow; '~·where en todas partes, en cualquier parte, dondequiera.

a·part [əˈpɑːt] aparte, separadamente; aislado, separado; **a·part·ment** habitación f, aposento m; piso m; ~ house casa f de pisos; ~s pl. alojamiento m, casa f.

ap·a·thy [ˈæpəθi] apatía f; indiferencia f (to a).

ape [eip] 1. mono m (esp. los antropomorfos), fig. mono (a f) m de imitación; remedador (-a f) m; 2. imitar, remedar.

ap·er·ture [ˈæpətjuə] abertura f.

a·pex [ˈeipeks], pl. freq. **ap·i·ces** [ˈeipisiːz] ápice m; fig. cumbre f.

aph·ro·dis·i·ac [æfrouˈdiziæk] afrodisíaco adj. a. su. m.

a·piece [əˈpiːs] cada uno; por persona.

ap·o·gee [ˈæpoudʒiː] apogeo m.

a·pol·o·get·ic [əpɔləˈdʒetik] □ lleno de disculpas; **a·pol·o·gize** [ˌdʒais]

disculparse (for de; to con); pedir perdón; **a·pol·o·gy** disculpa f, excusa f; lit. apología f, defensa f.

ap·o·plec·tic, ap·o·plec·ti·cal [æpəˈplektik(l)] □ apopléctico.

a·pos·tle [əˈpɔsl] apóstol m.

a·pos·tro·phe [əˈpɔstrəfi] gr. apóstrofo m; rhet. apóstrofe m or f.

ap·pal [əˈpɔːl] espantar; infundir pasmo (or horror); **ap·pall·ing** □ espantoso; taste etc. pésimo.

ap·pa·ra·tus [æpəˈreitəs] aparato m.

ap·par·el [əˈpærəl] lit. 1. ataviar, vestir (esp. p.p.); 2. atavío m, vestido m; (a. wearing ~) ropa f.

ap·par·ent [əˈpærənt] □ aparente; claro, manifiesto; v. heir; ~ly según parece, por lo visto; aparentemente; **ap·pa·ri·tion** [æpəˈriʃn] aparición f; fantasma m.

ap·peal [əˈpiːl] ⚖ apelar (to a; against de); suplicar (to a p. for a th. a una p. por algo); ~ to llamar la atención de s.o.; atraer, interesar acc.; recurrir a.

ap·pear [əˈpiə] parecer; aparecer (mst suddenly); esp. ⚖ comparecer; **ap·pear·ance** apariencia f, aspecto m; (act) aparición f; ⚖ comparecencia f; ~s pl. apariencias f/pl.; keep up (or save) ~s salvar las apariencias; thea. make an ~ salir.

ap·pease [əˈpiːz] apaciguar; p. desenojar; hunger etc. satisfacer, saciar; passion mitigar, aquietar; **ap·pease·ment** pacificación f.

ap·pend [əˈpend] añadir; adjuntar; colgar; **ap·pen·di·ci·tis** [ˌsaitis] apendicitis f; **ap·pen·dix** [ˌdiks], pl. a. **ap·pen·di·ces** [ˌdisiːz] apéndice m (a. ⚕).

ap·per·tain [æpəˈtein] ~ to pertenecer a; atañer a; relacionarse con.

ap·pe·tite [ˈæpitait] apetito m, apetencia f (a. fig.); fig. deseo m.

ap·pe·tiz·er [ˈæpitaizə] aperitivo m; **ap·pe·tiz·ing** □ apetitoso.

ap·plaud [əˈplɔːd] v/t. aplaudir (a. fig.); fig. celebrar; v/i. aplaudir.

ap·plause [əˈplɔːz] aplauso m (a. fig.); fig. aprobación f, elogio m.

ap·ple [ˈæpl] manzana f; (a. ~ tree) manzano m; Adam's ~ nuez f de la garganta; ~ of one's eye niñas f/pl. de los ojos; '~·cart: F upset a p.'s ~ dar al traste con los planes de una p.; '~·jack aguardiente m de manzana; '~ pie pastel m (or empanada f) de manzanas; F in ~ order en perfecto orden; '~·sauce compota *f* de manzanas; *sl.* coba *f*, jabón *m.*

ap·pli·ance [ə'plaiəns] instrumento *m*, herramienta *f*; dispositivo *m.*

ap·pli·ca·ble ['æplikəbl] aplicable (*to* a); **'ap·pli·cant** suplicante *m/f*; aspirante *m/f*, pretendiente (*a f*) *m* (*for a post* a un puesto); **ap·pli·ca·tion** aplicación *f* (*to* a; *a.* = *industry*); solicitud *f* (*for* por), petición *f* (*for de, por*); *make an ∼* solicitar; dirigirse (*to* a).

ap·ply [ə'plai] *v/t.* aplicar (*to* a); *∼ o.s. to* aplicarse a; *v/i.* ser aplicable; *for* solicitar, pedir *acc.*

ap·point [ə'pɔint] *date etc.* señalar, designar; *p.* nombrar; *house* amueblar; proveer; **ap'point·ment** señalamiento *m*, designación *f*; nombramiento *m to post;* (*post*) oficio *m*; cita *f with p.*

ap·por·tion [ə'pɔ:ʃn] prorratear; **ap'por·tion·ment** prorrateo *m.*

ap·prais·al [ə'preizl] tasación *f*, valoración *f*; *fig.* aprecio *m*; **ap'praise** [∼eiz] tasar, valorar; *fig.* apreciar.

ap·pre·ci·a·ble [ə'pri:ʃəbl] □ apreciable, estimable; sensible, perceptible; **ap'pre·ci·ate** [∼ʃieit] *v/t.* apreciar, estimar; percibir; *v/i.* aumentarse en valor; **ap·pre·ci·a'tion** aprecio *m*, estimación *f*; percepción *f*; (*value*) aumento *m* en valor.

ap·pre·hend [æpri'hend] aprehender, prender; *fig.* percibir, entender; temer, sospechar; **ap·pre'hen·sion** aprehensión *f*, prendimiento *m*; percepción *f*, comprensión *f*; temor *m*, recelo *m*, aprensión *f*; **ap·pre'hen·sive** □ aprensivo, miedoso (*of*; *that* de que); tímido; perspicaz, comprensivo.

ap·pren·tice [ə'prentis] **1.** aprendiz (*-a f*) *m*; *fig.* novicio (*a f*) *m*; **2.** poner de aprendiz.

ap·prise [ə'praiz] informar, avisar.

ap·proach [ə'prout] **1.** *v/i.* acercarse, aproximarse (*a. fig.*; *freq.* *to* a); *v/t.* acercarse a, aproximarse a (*a. fig.*); *p.* abordar; *firm etc.* dirigirse a; **2.** acercamiento *m*; aproximación *f* (*to* a); acceso *m* (*a. fig.*); método *m*, camino *m*; camino *m* de entrada.

ap·pro·ba·tion [æprə'beiʃn] aprobación *f*; consentimiento *m.*

ap·pro·pri·ate **1.** [ə'prouprieit] apropiar(se); *funds etc.* destinar (*for* a); **2.** [∼priit] apropiado (*to* a), a propósito; apto, pertinente; **ap·pro·pri'a·tion** apropiación *f*; consignación *f.*

ap·prov·al [ə'pru:vəl] aprobación *f*; consentimiento *m*; visto *m* bueno; *on ∼* a prueba; **ap'prove** aprobar, sancionar, confirmar; *∼ of* aprobar, dar por bueno; **ap'proved** probado, acreditado.

ap·prox·i·mate **1.** [ə'prɔksimeit] aproximar(se) (*to* a); **2.** [∼mit] □ aproximado, aproximativo; cercano, inmediato (*to* a); **ap·prox·i·ma·tion** [∼'meiʃn] aproximación *f*; **∼·ly** aproximadamente, poco más o menos.

a·pri·cot ['eiprikɔt] albaricoque *m.*

A·pril ['eiprəl] abril *m.*

a·pron ['eiprən] delantal *m.*

ap·ro·pos [æprə'pou] **1.** *adj.* oportuno; **2.** *adv.* a propósito; **3.** *prp. ∼ of* a propósito de; acerca de.

apse [æps] ábside *m.*

apt [æpt] □ apto; *remark etc.* a propósito; propenso (*to* a); listo (*at* en); **ap·ti·tude** ['∼titju:d] aptitud *f.*

aq·ua·lung ['ɑkwəlʌŋ] aparato *m* de aire comprimido (que suministra aire al buzo).

a·quar·i·um [ə'kweəriəm] acuario *m.*

a·quat·ic [ə'kwætik] acuático.

aq·ue·duct ['ækwidʌkt] acueducto *m.*

Ar·ab ['ærəb] árabe *adj. a. su. m/f*; **Ar·a·bic** ['ærəbik] árabe.

ar·bi·ter ['ɑ:bitə] árbitro (*a f*) *m*; arbitrador (*-a f*) *m*; **'ar·bi·trar·y** □ arbitrario; **ar·bi·trate** [∼treit] arbitrar; **ar·bi'tra·tion** arbitraje *m*; ⚖ arbitramento *m*; tercería *f.*

arc [ɑ:k] *all senses:* arco *m*; **ar·cade** [ɑ:'keid] arcada *f*; (*with shops*) pasaje *m*, soportales *m/pl.*

arch[1] [ɑ:tʃ] △ *a. anat.* arco *m*; bóveda *f.*

arch[2] [∼] □ zumbón; chancero; travieso; astuto; *woman* coqueta.

arch[3] [∼] principal; consumado.

ar·chae·ol·o·gist [ɑ:ki'ɔlədʒist] arqueólogo *m*; **ar·chae·ol·o·gy** arqueología *f.*

ar·cha·ic [ɑ:'keiik] □ arcaico; **'ar·cha·ism** arcaísmo *m.*

arch·an·gel ['ɑ:keindʒl] arcángel *m.*

arch·bish·op ['ɑ:tʃ'biʃəp] arzobispo *m.*

arch·er ['ɑ:tʃə] arquero *m.*

ar·che·type ['ɑ:kitaip] arquetipo *m.*

ar·chi·pel·a·go [ɑ:ki'peligou] archipiélago *m.*

ar·chi·tect ['ɑ:kitekt] arquitecto *m*; *fig.* artífice *m/f*; **ar·chi·tec·ture** ['∼tʃə] arquitectura *f.*

ar·chives ['ɑ:kaivz] *pl.* archivo *m*; **'ar·chiv·ist** archivero (*a f*) *m.*

arch·way [ˈɑːtʃwei] arcada *f.*

arc·tic [ˈɑːktik] **1.** ártico; frígido; ♀ *Circle* Círculo *m* Polar Ártico; ♀ *Ocean* Océano *m* Boreal; **2.** zona *f* ártica; chanclo *m.*

ar·dent [ˈɑːdənt] □ *mst fig.* ardiente, caluroso; fogoso; fervoroso, entusiasmado.

ar·dor [ˈɑːdə] ardor *m; fig.* fervor *m,* celo *m;* ahinco *m.*

ar·du·ous [ˈɑːdjuəs] □ arduo, penoso; riguroso.

are [ɑː] somos; estamos *etc.* (*v.* be).

a·re·a [ˈɛəriə] área *f,* extensión *f; geog.* región *f,* comarca *f.*

a·re·na [əˈriːnə] arena *f,* redondel *m; esp. bullfighting:* ruedo *m; fig.* lid *f.*

aren't [ɑːnt] = are not.

ar·gue [ˈɑːgjuː] *v/t.* argüir; sostener; ~ *into* persuadir a; ~ *out of* disuadir de; *v/i.* disputar, argumentar.

ar·gu·ment [ˈɑːgjumənt] argumento *m;* discusión *f;* disputa *f.*

a·ri·a [ˈɑːriə] aria *f.*

ar·id [ˈærid] árido, seco (*a. fig.*).

a·right [əˈrait] correctamente; acertadamente; a derechas.

a·rise [əˈraiz] [*irr.*] *lit.* levantarse, alzarse; *fig.* surgir, aparecer; ~ *from* provenir de (*a. fig.*); been *p.p. of* arise.

ar·is·toc·ra·cy [ærisˈtɔkrəsi] aristocracia *f* (*a. fig.*); **a·ris·to·crat** [ˈæristəkræt] aristócrata *m/f;* **a·ris·to·crat·ic** □ aristocrático.

a·rith·me·tic [əˈriθmətik] aritmética *f.*

ark [ɑːk] arca *f;* ♀ *of the Covenant* arca *f* de la alianza; *Noah's* ♀ arca *f* de Noé.

arm¹ [ɑːm] brazo *m* (*a. of sea, chair*); ♣ rama *f,* gajo *m;* ~ *in* ~ de bracete; *fig. with open* ~s con los brazos abiertos; *within* ~'s *reach* al alcance del brazo; *keep a p. at* ~'s *length* mantener a una p. a distancia.

arm² [~] **1.** ✕ arma *f* (*mst in pl.*); *heraldry:* ~s *pl.* escudo *m,* blasón *m; take up* ~s tomar las armas; **2.** ✕ armar(se); ⊕ armar.

ar·ma·da [ɑːˈmɑːdə] armada *f.*

ar·ma·ment [ˈɑːməmənt] armamento *m;* **ar·ma·ture** [ˈɑːˌtjuə] armadura *f.*

arm·chair [ˈɑːmtʃɛə] silla *f* de brazos; butaca *f,* sillón *m.*

arm·ful [ˈɑːmful] brazado *m.*

ar·mi·stice [ˈɑːmistis] armisticio *m.*

ar·mor [ˈɑːmə] **1.** ✕ armadura *f* (*a. suit of* ~; *a. zo. a. fig.*); blindaje *m;* escafandro *m;* **2.** blindar; ~ed car carro *m* blindado; '**~-clad**, '**~-plat-**

-ed blindado, acorazado; '**armor·er** armero *m;* '**ar·mor·y** armería *f;* arsenal *m.*

arm·pit [ˈɑːmpit] sobaco *m;* '**arm-rest** apoyo *m* para el brazo.

ar·my [ˈɑːmi] ejército *m* (*a. fig.*); ~ *command,* ~ *staff* estado *m* mayor; '**~·corps** cuerpo *m* de ejército.

a·ro·ma [əˈroumə] aroma *m,* fragancia *f;* **ar·o·mat·ic** [ærouˈmætik] □ aromático, fragante.

a·rose [əˈrouz] *pret. of* arise.

a·round [əˈraund] **1.** *adv.* alrededor; a la redonda; por todos lados; F *be* ~ andar por allí; **2.** *prp.* alrededor de, en torno de; *number* cerca de.

a·rouse [əˈrauz] despertar (*a. fig.*); *fig.* mover, excitar.

ar·raign [əˈrein] ᵗᵗₛ procesar; denunciar; reprender; **ar·raign·ment** ᵗᵗₛ auto *m* de procesamiento; denuncia *f;* represión *f.*

ar·range [əˈreindʒ] *v/t.* arreglar, componer, ordenar; *time* fijar, citar; *dispute, agreement etc.* ajustar, componer; ♪ adaptar, refundir; *v/i.* hacer un arreglo (*with* con); convenir (*to* en); ~ *for* prevenir, disponer; **ar-range·ment** arreglo *m,* ordenación *f;* concierto *m,* convenio *m;* ajuste *m;* orden *m,* disposición *f;* ♪ adaptación *f,* refundición *f; come to an* ~ llegar a un acomodo, entenderse (*with* con).

ar·ray [əˈrei] ✕ orden *m* de batalla; *fig.* aparato *m,* pompa *f; poet.* gala *f,* atavío *m.*

ar·rear [əˈriə] *mst* ~s *pl.* atrasos *m/pl.; in* ~s atrasado en pagos.

ar·rest [əˈrest] **1.** arresto *m,* detención *f;* secuestro *m of goods;* parada *f;* prórroga *f of judgment;* **2.** arrestar, detener; parar; prorrogar; *attention* llamar; **ar·rest·ing** impresionante.

ar·riv·al [əˈraivl] llegada *f;* persona *f or* cosa *f* que ha llegado; **ar·rive** [əˈraiv] llegar, arribar (*at* a).

ar·ro·gance [ˈærəgəns] arrogancia *f,* soberbia *f;* '**ar·ro·gant** □ arrogante, soberbio.

ar·row [ˈærou] flecha *f,* saeta *f;* '**~-head** punta *f* de flecha.

ar·se·nal [ˈɑːsinl] arsenal *m.*

ar·se·nic [ˈɑːsnik] arsénico *m.*

ar·son [ˈɑːsn] delito *m* de incendiar.

art [ɑːt] arte *mst in sg., f in pl.,* destreza *f; black* ~s *pl.* magia *f* negra; *fine* ~s *pl.* bellas artes *f/pl.*

ar·te·ri·al [ɑːˈtiəriəl] arterial; **ar-ter·y** [ˈɑːtəri] arteria *f* (*a. fig.*).

art·ful ['ɑːtful] □ artero, mañoso.

ar·thrit·ic [ɑː'θritik] artrítico.

ar·ti·choke ['ɑːtitʃouk] alcachofa f.

ar·ti·cle ['ɑːtikl] artículo m.

ar·tic·u·late 1. [ɑː'tikjuleit] speech articular; joints enlazar; **2.** [∼lit] □ (a. **ar'tic·u·lat·ed** [∼leitid]) articulado; distinto; capaz de hablar; **ar·tic·u·'la·tion** articulación f.

ar·ti·fice ['ɑːtifis] artificio m; destreza f, maña f; **ar·ti·fi·cial** [∼'fiʃəl] □ artificial; postizo; afectado; ⚥ person persona f jurídica.

ar·til·ler·y [ɑː'tiləri] artillería f; **ar·'til·ler·y·man** artillero m.

ar·ti·san [ɑːti'zæn] artesano (a f) m.

art·ist ['ɑːtist] artista m/f; **ar·tis·tic, ar·tis·ti·cal** [ɑː'tistik(l)] □ artístico; artificioso.

art·less ['ɑːtlis] □ natural, sencillo; ingenuo; b.s. desmañado.

as [æs, əz] adv. a. cj. como; porque, ya que; a medida que; tal como; (temporal) cuando; (result) que, de manera que; ∼ ... ∼ tan ... como; it is ∼ good ∼ lost puede darse por perdido; v. far; ∼ for, ∼ to en cuanto a; ∼ from date a partir de; ∼ if, ∼ though como si subj.; ∼ if to inf. como para inf.; ∼ it were to decirlo así; ∼ per según; ∼ well también; ∼ well así como; tan bien como; ∼ yet hasta ahora.

as·bes·tos [æz'bestɔs] asbesto m.

as·cend [ə'send] v/i. subir (a. ♪); elevarse, encaramarse; (time) remontarse; v/t. river subir; mountain, throne subir a.

as·cen·sion [ə'senʃn] ascensión f.

as·cent [ə'sent] ascenso m; subida f of mountain etc.; (slope) cuesta f, pendiente f; tramo m of stairs.

as·cer·tain [æsə'tein] averiguar.

as·cet·ic [ə'setik] **1.** □ ascético; **2.** asceta m/f.

as·cribe [əs'kraib] atribuir; imputar; achacar.

a·sep·tic [ei'septik] aséptico.

a·sex·u·al [ei'seksjuəl] asexual.

ash[1] [æʃ] ♀ fresno m.

ash[2] [∼] (freq. pl. **ash·es** ['æʃiz] ceniza f; ∼es pl. cenizas f/pl. of dead.

a·shamed [ə'ʃeimd] □ avergonzado; be (or feel) ∼ avergonzarse, sonrojarse (at, of de; for por); be ∼ of o.s. tener vergüenza de sí.

ash·can ['æʃkæn] cubo m de la basura.

ash·en[1] ['æʃn] ♀ de fresno.

ash·en[2] [∼] ceniciento; face pálido.

a·shore [ə'ʃɔː] a tierra; en tierra; come ∼, go ∼ desembarcar.

ash...: ∼ pan guardacenizas m; **∼·tray** cenicero m.

A·sian ['eiʃn], **A·si·at·ic** [eiʃi'ætik] asiático adj. a. su. m (a f).

a·side [ə'said] **1.** aparte, a un lado; ∼ from además de; ∼ thea. aparte m.

ask [ɑːsk] v/t. preguntar (a th. algo; a p. a th. algo a una p.); pedir, rogar (of, from a); ∼ a p. for a th. pedir algo a una p.; ∼ that pedir que; invitar (to a); ∼ (a p.) a question hacer una pregunta (a una p.); v/i. ∼ about, ∼ after, ∼ for preguntar por; ∼ for pedir, reclamar.

a·skance [ə'skæns], **a·skant** [ə'skænt] al soslayo, al sesgo; look con recelo.

a·skew [ə'skjuː] al soslayo, ladeado.

a·sleep [ə'sliːp] dormido, durmiendo; fall ∼ dormirse.

as·par·a·gus [əs'pærəgəs] espárrago m.

as·pect ['æspekt] aspecto m; apariencia f.

as·per·sion [əs'pɜːʃən] difamación f.

as·phalt ['æsfælt] **1.** asfalto m; **2.** asfaltar.

as·phyx·i·a [æs'fiksiə] asfixia f; **as·'phyx·i·ate** asfixiar.

as·pi·rate 1. ['æspərit] aspirado; **2.** [∼] aspirada f; **3.** [∼reit] aspirar: **as·pi·'ra·tion** ⚥ aspiración f; fig. anhelo m (after, for por); **as'pire** [əs'paiə] aspirar (after, to a), anhelar (after, to acc.); **as'pir·in** ['æspərin] aspirina f; **as'pir·ing** [əs'paiəriŋ] □ ambicioso.

ass [æs] asno m, burro m; fig. burro m, mentecato m; make an ∼ of o.s. ponerse en ridículo; F culo m.

as·sail [ə'seil] acometer, arremeter contra; fig. asaltar; fig. inundar (with de); task acometer, emprender; **as·'sail·ant, as·'sail·ler** asaltador (-a f) m, agresor (-a f) m.

as·sas·sin [ə'sæsin] asesino (a f) m; **as'sas·si·nate** [∼neit] asesinar (esp. por motivos políticos); **as·sas·si·'na·tion** asesinato m.

as·sault [ə'sɔːlt] **1.** asalto m (a. fig.); [up]on sobre); ⚔ carga f, ataque m; ⚥ violencia f; atraco m; **2.** asaltar; ⚔ cargar, atacar; ⚥ violentar.

as·say [ə'sei] **1.** ensaye m; **2.** metals ensayar; intentar, tratar (de).

as·sem·blage [ə'semblidʒ] asamblea f, reunión f; ⊕ montaje m; **as·'sem·ble** convocar; juntar(se), reunir(se);

troops formar; ⊕ montar; **as'sem·bly** reunión *f*; asamblea *f* (a. ✕), junta *f*; senado *m*; ⊕ montaje *m*, armadura *f*; ~ **line** cadena *f* de montaje.

as·sent [ə'sent] **1.** asenso *m*, consentimiento *m*; aprobación *f*; **2.** consentir (*to* en), asentir (*to* a).

as·sert [ə'sə:t] afirmar, declarar; hacer valer; **asser·tion** afirmación *f*, declaración *f*.

as·sess [ə'ses] gravar (con impuestos); *damage, tax etc.* fijar, determinar; valorar; apreciar; **as'sess·ment** gravamen *m*; valoración *f*; aprecio *m*.

as·set ['æset] posesión *f*; F ventaja *f*; *fig.* valor *m*; **as·sets** *pl.* ✝ activo *m*.

as·sid·u·ous [æ'sidjuəs] ☐ asiduo, diligente, concienzudo.

as·sign [ə'sain] **1.** asignar, señalar; *goods* consignar, traspasar; achacar (*to a cause etc.*); **2.** ⚖ cesionario *m*, consignatorio *m*; **as'sign·ment** [ə'sainmənt] asignación *f*; consignación *f*; (*task*) comisión *f*, encargo *m*.

as·sim·i·late [ə'simileit] asimilar(se) (*a. physiol. a. gr.*), asemejar(se); **as·sim·i·la·tion** asimilación *f*.

as·sist [ə'sist] ayudar, auxiliar; ~ *at* asistir a; ~ *in* tomar parte en; ~ *in ger.* ayudar a *inf.*; **as'sist·ance** ayuda *f*, socorro *m*, auxilio *m*; **as'sist·ant 1.** auxiliar, ayudante; sub-; **2.** ayudante *m*, adjutor *m*.

as·so·ci·ate 1. [ə'souʃieit] asociar(se), juntar(se) (*with* a, con); ~ *in* mancomunarse en; **2.** [~ʃiit] asociado, coligado; con-; **3.** [~ʃiit] asociado *m*, socio *m* (*a.* ✝), consocio *m*; miembro *m* correspondiente (de una academia); compañero *m*, camarada *m/f*; **as·so·ci·a·tion** [~si'eiʃn] asociación *f*; agrupación *f*, sociedad *f*.

as·sort [ə'sɔ:t] *v/t.* clasificar, compaginar; **as'sort·ment** clasificación *f*; ✝ surtido *m*.

as·suage [ə'sweidʒ] apaciguar.

as·sume [ə'sju:m] *aspect* tomar; *authority etc.* apropiarse, agregarse; *burden* asumir; dar por sentado, suponer (*that* que); *assuming that* dado que; **as'sum·ing** ☐ presuntuoso, presumido; **as·sump·tion** [ə'sʌmpʃn] suposición *f*; presunción *f*; *eccl.* 2 Asunción *f*.

as·sur·ance [ə'ʃuərəns] aseguramiento *m*; declaración *f*; garantía *f*; ✝ seguro *m*; confianza *f* en sí mismo; *b.s.* descoco *m*; **as'sure** asegurar;

afirmar; **as'sur·ed·ly** [~ridli] seguramente, sin duda.

as·ter·isk ['æestərisk] asterisco *m*.

asth·ma ['æsmə] asma *f*.

a·stig·ma·tism [æ'stigmətizm] astigmatismo *m*.

a·stir [ə'stə:] en movimiento.

as·ton·ish [əs'tɔniʃ] asombrar, sorprender; pasmar; *be ~ed* asombrarse, maravillarse (*at* de, con); **as'ton·ish·ing** ☐ asombroso, sorprendente; **as'ton·ish·ment** asombro *m*, sorpresa *f*; pasmo *m*.

as·tound [əs'taund] pasmar; aturdir.

a·stray [ə'strei] extraviado, descarriado, despistado; *go ~* extraviarse, descarriarse (*a. fig.*); *lead ~* llevar por mal camino.

a·stride [ə'straid] **1.** *adv.* (*ride* montar) a horcajadas; **2.** *prp.* a caballo sobre, a horcajadas sobre.

as·trol·o·ger [əs'trɔlədʒə] astrólogo *m*; **as·tro·log·i·cal** [æstrə'lɔdʒikl] ☐ astrológico, astrológo; **as·trol·o·gy** [əs'trɔlədʒi] astrología *f*; **as·tron·o·mer** [əs'trɔnəmə] astrónomo *m*; **as·tro·nom·i·cal** [æstrə'nɔmikl] ☐ astronómico; *fig.* tremendo; **as·tron·o·my** [əs'trɔnəmi] astronomía *f*.

as·tro·naut ['æstrənɔt] astronauta *m/f*; **as·tro'phys·ics** *sg.* astrofísica *f*.

as·tute [əs'tju:t] ☐ sagaz, perspicaz, astuto.

a·sun·der [ə'sʌndə] separadamente; en dos; *lit.* tear ~ hacer pedazos.

a·sy·lum [ə'sailəm] asilo *m*.

at [æt, *unstressed* ət] en; a; hacia; por; ~ *Mérida* en Mérida; ~ *school* en la escuela; ~ *midday* a mediodía; ~ *Christmas* en (*or* por) Navidades; ~ *a low price* a un precio bajo; ~ *Mary's* en casa de María; ~ *that time* en aquella época; ~ *the door* a la puerta; ~ *table* a la mesa; ~ *peace* en paz; ~ *one blow* de un golpe.

ate [et; eit] *pret. of eat.*

a·the·ism ['eiθiizm] ateísmo *m*; **'a·the·ist** ateo (a *f*) *m*.

ath·lete ['æθli:t] atleta *m/f*; ♂ ~'s *foot* pie *m* de atleta; **ath·let·ic** [æθ'letik], **ath'let·i·cal** ☐ atlético; ~ *sports* *pl.* ejercicios *m/pl.* atléticos; **ath'let·ics** *pl.*, **ath'let·i·cism** [~tisizəm] atletismo *m*.

at·las ['ætləs] atlas *m*.

at·mos·phere ['ætməsfiə] atmósfera *f*; *fig.* ambiente *m*; **at·mos·pher·ic**, **at·mos·pher·i·cal** [~'ferik(l)] ☐ atmosférico.

auspice

at·oll [ˈætɔl] atolón m.

at·om [ˈætəm] átomo m (a. fig.); **a·tom·ic** [əˈtɔmik] atómico; ∼ age era f atómica; ∼ bomb bomba f atómica; ∼ energy energía f atómica; ∼ fission fisión f nuclear; ∼ nucleus núcleo m atómico; ∼ pile pila f atómica; ∼ research investigaciones f/pl. atómicas; **a'tom·ic·'pow·ered** impulsado por energía atómica; **'at·om·ize** reducir a átomos; liquid pulverizar; **'at·om·izer** pulverizador m.

a·tone [əˈtoun] v/t. † conciliar; v/i.: ∼ for expiar acc.; **a'tone·ment** expiación f.

a·tro·cious [əˈtrouʃəs] □ atroz; F malísimo, infame; **a·troc·i·ty** [əˈtrɔsiti] atrocidad f (a. F).

at·tach [əˈtætʃ] 1. atar, pegar, prender (to a); † adjuntar; importance, value etc. dar, conceder (to a); ⚖ p. arrestar; th. incautarse; ∼ o.s. to agregarse a; pegarse a; ∼ value to conceder valor a, estimar; fig. be ∼ed to p. etc. tener cariño a; v/i. ∼ to corresponder a; **at'tach·ment** atadura f; ⊕ accesorio m; (affection) cariño m (to por, a), apego m (to a); (loyalty) adhesión f, lealtad f; ⚖ arresto m; incautación f.

at·tack [əˈtæk] 1. acometer, embestir (a. fig.); atacar (a. ✗ a. 🔎); 2. ataque m (on contra, a, sobre; a. fig.); ✗ ataque m, acceso m; **at'tack·er** agresor (-a f) m.

at·tain [əˈtein] v/t. alcanzar, lograr, conseguir; v/i.: ∼ to llegar a; **at'tain·ment** logro m, obtención f; ∼s pl. talentos m/pl., conocimientos m/pl.

at·tempt [əˈtempt] 1. ensayar, intentar (to inf.), tentar (to de); 2. tentativa f, conato m (to de); atentado m (on life a, contra).

at·tend [əˈtend] v/t. acompañar; cortejar, servir; † aguardar; course etc. asistir a; ✗ atender a, asistir; well attended (muy) concurrido; v/i. prestar atención (to a); asistir (at a); ∼ on servir; sick atender a, asistir; ∼ to work etc. atender a; **at'tend·ance** (presence) presencia f (at en), asistencia f (at a); (gathering) concurrencia f; ✗ asistencia f; obsequio m (on de); be in ∼ asistir; **at'tend·ant** 1. concomitante (upon a); asistente (at a); 2. criado (a f) m, sirviente (a f) m; mozo (a f) m; ordenanza m.

at·ten·tion [əˈtenʃn] atención f (a. fig.); ∼! ¡atención!; ✗ ∼! ¡firmes!;

call ∼ to llamar la atención sobre; give (or pay) ∼ prestar atención (to a); **at'ten·tive** □ atento (to a).

at·ten·u·ate [əˈtenjueit] atenuar.

at·test [əˈtest] atestiguar; dar fe (to de); juramentar.

at·tire [əˈtaiə] lit. 1. ataviar; adornar, componer; 2. atavío m; adorno m.

at·ti·tude [ˈætitjuːd] actitud f (a. fig.; to a); además m; ⚔ posición f.

at·tor·ney [əˈtɔːni] abogado m; † apoderado (a f) m; † 🔎 procurador m.

at·tract [əˈtrækt] atraer; attention llamar; **at'trac·tion** [∼kʃən] atracción f; aliciente m; atractivo m of p. esp.; thea. programa m; **at'trac·tive** [∼tiv] □ mst fig. atractivo, atrayente; agradable.

at·trib·ute 1. [əˈtribjuːt] atribuir, achacar; 2. [ˈætribjuːt] atributo m.

at·tri·tion [əˈtriʃn] roce m, desgaste m; eccl. atrición f.

au·burn [ˈɔːbən] castaño rojizo.

auc·tion [ˈɔːkʃn] 1. almoneda f, subasta f; sell by (at) ∼, put up for ∼ subastar, poner en pública subasta; sale by ∼ subasta f; 2. subastar (freq. ∼ off); **auc·tion·eer** [∼ˈniə] subastador m.

au·da·cious [ɔːˈdeiʃəs] □ audaz, osado; b.s. descarado, fresco; **au·dac·i·ty** [ɔːˈdæsiti] audacia f, osadía f; b.s. descaro m.

au·di·ble [ˈɔːdəbl] □ audible.

au·di·ence [ˈɔːdjəns] auditorio m, público m; audiencia f (with, of con).

au·di·o·fre·quen·cy [ˈɔːdiouˈfriːkwənsi] radio: audiofrecuencia f.

au·dit [ˈɔːdit] 1. intervención f; 2. intervenir; **au'di·tion** audición f; **'au·di·tor** interventor m; censor m de cuentas; **au·di·to·ri·um** [∼ˈtɔːriəm] sala f, anfiteatro m; **au·di·to·ry** [∼ˈtɔri] auditivo.

au·ger [ˈɔːgə] barrena f.

aught [ɔːt] algo; (with negation) nada; for ∼ I care igual me da; for ∼ I know que yo sepa.

aug·ment [ɔːɡˈment] aumentar(se).

au·gur [ˈɔːgə] 1. augur m; 2. agorar, pronosticar; prometer (well bien, ill mal).

Au·gust [ˈɔːɡəst] 1. agosto m; 2. ♀ [ɔːˈɡʌst] augusto.

aunt [ɑːnt] tía f; **aunt·ie, aunt·y** [∼ti] F tía f.

au·ra [ˈɔːrə] ambiente m; emanación f.

aus·pice [ˈɔːspis] auspicio m; protección *f*; *under the* ~s *of* bajo los auspicios de; **aus·pi·cious** [ɔː'piʃəs] □ propicio, favorable.

aus·tere [ɔː'tiə] □ austero, severo; *style etc.* austo; *taste* acerbo; **aus·ter·i·ty** [ʌˈteriti] austeridad *f*, severidad *f*; adustez *f*.

au·then·tic [ɔːˈθentik] □ auténtico.

au·thor ['ɔːθə] autor (-a *f*) *m*; **au·thor·i·tar·i·an** [ɔːθɔriˈteəriən] autoritario; **au·thor·i·ta·tive** [ʌˈteitiv] □ autorizado; perentorio; autoritario; **au·thor·i·ty** autoridad *f*; *the authorities* las autoridades; *on good* ~ de buena tinta; *under the* ~ *of* bajo la autoridad de; *in* ~ *over* al mando de; **au·thor·i·za·tion** [ɔːθərai'zeiʃn] autorización *f*; '**au·thor·ize** autorizar.

au·tis·tic [ɔːˈtistik] autístico.

au·to [ɔːˈtou] automóvil *m*, coche *m*.

au·to·bi·og·ra·phy [ɔːtoubaiˈɔgrəfi] autobiografía *f*.

au·to·cade ['ɔːtoukeid] caravana *f* de automóviles.

au·to·graph ['ɔːtəgrɑːf] 1. autógrafo *adj. a. su. m*; 2. firmar; dedicar.

au·to·mat·ic [ɔːtəˈmætik] 1. □ automático; 2. pistola *f* automática.

au·tom'a·tion automatización *f*; **au·tom·a·ton** [ɔːˈtɔmətən] *pl. mst* **au'tom·a·ta** [ʌtə] autómata *m* (*a. fig.*).

au·to·mo·bile ['ɔːtəmoubiːl] *esp.* automóvil *m*, coche *m*.

au·ton·o·mous [ɔːˈtɔnəməs] □ autónomo; **au'ton·o·my** autonomía *f*.

au·top·sy ['ɔːtɔpsi] autopsia *f*.

au·tumn ['ɔːtəm] otoño *m*.

aux·il·ia·ry [ɔːgˈziliəri] 1. auxiliar (*a. gr.*); subalterno; 2. **aux'il·ia·ries** [ʌiz] *pl.* tropas *f*/*pl.* auxiliares.

a·vail [əˈveil] 1. beneficiar, valer; ~ *o.s. of* valerse de, aprovechar; **2.**: *of no* ~ inútil; *of what* ~ *is it?* ¿de qué sirve? (*to* *inf.*); **a·vail·a·bil·i·ty** disponibilidad *f*; calidad *f* de asequible (*or* accesible); **a'vail·a·ble** □ disponible, asequible; *p.* accesible, tratable.

av·a·lanche ['ævəlɑːntʃ] alud *m*; *fig.* torrente *m*.

av·a·rice ['ævəris] avaricia *f*, mezquindad *f*; **av·a·ri·cious** □ avaro, avariento.

a·venge [əˈvendʒ] vengar, vindicar.

av·e·nue ['ævinjuː] avenida *f*; autopista *f*; *fig.* camino *m*, acceso *m*.

a·ver [əˈvəː] afirmar, declarar.

av·er·age ['ævəridʒ] 1. promedio *m*,

término *m* medio; ♣ avería *f* (*general* gruesa, *particular* particular); *on* (*an or the*) ~ por regla general; 2. medio, de término medio; *a.b.s.* mediano, ordinario; 3. *v/t.* calcular el término medio de; prorratear; *v/i.* (*work etc.*) resultar por término medio.

a·ver·sion [əˈvəːʃən] aversión *f* (*for, from, to* hacia), repugnancia *f*.

a·vert [əˈvəːt] apartar; *blow etc.* impedir, quitar.

a·vi·a·tion [eiviˈeiʃn] aviación *f*; '**a·vi·a·tor** aviador (-a *f*) *m*.

av·id ['ævid] □ ávido, ansioso.

av·o·ca·do [ɑːvɔkɑːˈdou] aguacate *m*.

av·o·ca·tion [ævouˈkeiʃn] ocupación *f* accesoria; † distracción *f*.

a·void [əˈvɔid] evitar (*doing* hacer); salvarse de; *duty etc.* eludir; ⚖ anular.

a·vouch [əˈvautʃ] afirmar.

a·vow [əˈvau] reconocer, confesar, admitir.

a·wait [əˈweit] *lit. a. fig.* aguardar, esperar.

a·wake [əˈweik] 1. despierto; *fig.* despabilado, listo; *keep* ~ (*coffee etc.*) desvelar; *wide* ~ completamente despierto (*a. fig.*); *fig.* astuto; 2. [*irr.*] *v/t.* (*mst* **a'wak·en**) despertar; ~ *a p. to a th.* ponerle a uno al corriente de algo; *v/i.* despertar(se) (*a. fig.*); ~ *to* darse cuenta de.

a·ward [əˈwɔːd] 1. adjudicación *f*; ⚖ sentencia *f*, fallo *m*; ✕ *etc.* condecoración *f*; (*prize*) premio *m* (*chief* gordo); 2. adjudicar; decretar; *prize etc.* conferir, conceder.

a·ware [əˈwɛə] consciente (*of* de); *be* ~ *of* estar enterado de; *become* ~ *of* enterarse de; darse cuenta de.

a·way [əˈwei] ausente; lejos; en otro lugar; (*with verbs, e.g. work* ~) con ahinco, sin cesar; *be* ~ estar fuera; ~ *with you!* ¡quita allá!; ¡lárgate!; F ~ *back* hace mucho tiempo.

awe [ɔː] temor *m* reverencial.

aw·ful ['ɔːful] □ tremendo, pasmoso, impresionante; F malísimo, muy feo; ~**ly** *adv.* F excesivamente; terriblemente.

a·while [əˈwail] un rato; algún tiempo.

awk·ward ['ɔːkwəd] □ *p. etc.* desmañado, torpe, lerdo; *situation* embarazoso; violento; *problem* peliagudo, difícil, delicado; '**awk·ward·ness** desmaña *f*, torpeza *f*.

awl [ɔːl] lezna *f*, subilla *f*.

awn·ing ['ɔːniŋ] toldo *m*; (*cart*) entalamadura *f*; (*window*) marquesina *f*; ♣ toldilla *f*.

a·woke [ə'wouk] *pret. a. p.p. of awake 2.*

axe [æks] **1.** hacha *f*; *fig.* (*costs etc.*) reducción *f*, cercenamiento *m*; *have an ~ to grind* actuar de una manera

interesada; **2.** *fig.* reducir, cercenar.

ax·i·om ['æksiəm] axioma *m*.

ax·is ['æksis], *pl.* **ax·es** ['ˌsiːz] eje *m* (*a.* ♈ *a.* ♀); *physiol.* axis *m*.

ax·le ['æksl] eje *m*, árbol *m*.

ay(e) [ai] *parl. a.* ♣ sí.

az·i·muth ['æzimɔθ] acimut *m*.

az·ure ['æʒə] azul *adj. a. su. m.*

B

baa [bɑː] **1.** balar; **2.** balido *m*.

bab·ble ['bæbl] **1.** barbullar, barbotear; *fig.* charlar, parlar; hablar indiscretamente; (*stream*) murmurar; **2.** barboteo *m*; parloteo *m*; murmullo *m*; **'bab·bler** charlatán (-a *f*) *m*; **'bab·bling** *adj. talk* descosido.

babe ['beibi] niño *m*; *sl.* chica *f*.

ba·boon [bə'buːn] mandril *m*.

ba·by ['beibi] niño (a *f*) *m*; nene (a *f*) *m*, rorro (a *f*) *m*; F (*woman*) rica *f*; *b.s.* aniñado (a *f*) *m*; ~ **car·riage** cochecillo *m* para niños; ~ **grand** piano *m* de media cola; **'~·hood** [ˌhud] infancia *f*; niñez *f*; **'~·ish** infantil; **'~·sit·ter** niñero (a *f*) *m*, cuidaniños *m/f S.Am.*; **'~·talk** habla *f* infantil.

bach·e·lor ['bætʃələ] soltero *m*; *old* ~ solterón *m*; *univ.* bachiller *m* (†), licenciado (a *f*) *m*; ~ *girl* soltera *f* (que tiene sus propios recursos); **'~·hood** [ˌhud] soltería *f*.

ba·cil·lus [bə'siləs], *pl.* **ba·cil·li** [ˌlai] bacilo *m*.

back [bæk] **1.** espalda *f*, dorso *m*; (*mountain*) lomo *m*; respaldo *m* of *chair*; dorso *m* of *check*, *hand etc.*; final *m* of *book*; *sport*: defensa *m*; (*at the*) ~ of tras, detrás de; *stage etc.* al fondo de; *behind one's* ~ a espaldas de uno (*a. fig.*); *on one's* ~ postrado, en cama; (*carrying s.t.*) a cuestas; *with one's* ~ *to the wall* entre la espada y la pared; *turn one's* ~ *on* volver la espalda a; **2.** *adj.* trasero, posterior, de atrás; ~ *issue* número *m* atrasado; ~ *pay* sueldo *m* retrasado; **3.** *adv.* (hacia) atrás; otra vez; de vuelta; ~ *and forth* de una parte a otra; *some months* ~ hace unos meses; **4.** *v/t.* apoyar (*a.* ~ *up*); *pol.* respaldar; *car* dar marcha atrás a; *horse* montar; (*bet*) apostar a; ♈ endosar; ~ *up* mover hacia atrás; ♣ ~ *water* ciar; *v/i.* retroceder, moverse hacia atrás; (*esp. horse*) cejar; F ~

down ceder; rajarse; F ~ *out* echarse atrás, desdecirse; **'~·ache** dolor *m* de espalda; ~ *al·ley* callejón *m* de atrás; **'~·bite** [*irr. bite*] cortar de vestir, murmurar; **'~·bone** espinazo *m*; *fig.* firmeza *f*; **'~·break·ing** deslomador; **~ 'door** puerta *f* trasera; **'back·er** sostenedor (-a *f*) *m*; ♈ suscriptor (-a *f*) *m*.

back...: **'~·fire 1.** *mot.* petardeo *m*, falsa explosión *f*; **2.** *mot.* petardear; *fig.* salir el tiro por la culata; **'~·gam·mon** chaquete *m*; **'~·ground** fondo *m*, último término *m*; *fig.* antecedentes *m/pl.*; educación *f*; ~ *music* música *f* de fondo; **'~·hand 1.** *tennis etc.*: revés *m*; **2.** = **'~·hand·ed** dado con la vuelta de la mano; *fig.* falto de sinceridad, irónico; **'back·ing** apoyo *m*; *esp.* ♈ reserva *f*.

back...: **'~·lash** ⊕ contragolpe *m*; *fig.* reacción *f* violenta; **'~·log** atrasos *m/pl.* (de pedidos pendientes); **'~·num·ber** número *m* atrasado; *fig.* cero *m* a la izquierda; ~ *pay* sueldo *m* retrasado; **'~·ped·al** dar marcha atrás con los pedales, contrapedalear; **'~·seat** asiento *m* de atrás; F *take a* ~ ceder su puesto, perder influencia; **'~·side** trasero *m*; nalgas *f/pl.*; **'~·slap·per** tipo *m* guasón, campechano *m*; **'~·slap·ping** espaldarazos *m/pl.*; *mutual* ~ bombo *m* mutuo; **'~·stairs 1.** escalera *f* de servicio; **2.** F por enchufe; por intriga; clandestino; **'~·stitch 1.** perpunte *m*; **2.** pespuntar; **'~·stage** detrás del telón; entre bastidores; **'~·stop** reja *f* (*or* red *f*) para detener la pelota; **'~·stroke** arrastre *m* de espaldas; ~ *talk* F contestación *f* insolente; ~ *to back* dándose las espaldas; F sucesivamente; **'~·track** F volver pies atrás, retirarse.

back·ward ['bækwəd] **1.** *adj.* vuelto

hacia atrás; *country*, *pupil* atrasado; *p.* (*shy*) retraído, corto; **2.** *adv.* (*a.* **'back·wards**) (hacia) atrás; al revés; ~s *and forwards* de acá para allá; **'back·ward·ness** atraso *m*; cortedad *f*.

back...: **'·~wa·ter** brazo *m* de río estancado; remanso *m*; *fig.* lugar *m* (*or* condición *f*) atrasado(a); **'·~woods** *pl.* región *f* apartada; **'·~yard** patio *m* trasero, corral *m* trasero.

ba·con ['beikən] tocino *m*; *sl.* bring home the ~ sacarse el gordo.

bac·te·ri·um [bæk'tiəriəm], *pl.* **bac·'te·ri·a** [~iə] bacteria *f*.

bad [bæd] □ malo; infeliz, desgraciado; (*rotten etc.*) dañado, podrido; (*harmful*) nocivo, dañoso; ⚕ indispuesto, enfermo; *coin* falso; *debt* incobrable; F *not* ~ bastante bueno; F *too* ~ así así; ~ *blood* mala sangre *f*; ~ *breath* mal aliento *m*; F *be in* ~ *with* tener enojada a una persona (*over a causa de*); *go* ~ (*food*) pasarse; *look* ~ tener mala cara; ~*ly adv.* mal; con urgencia; gravemente; ~*ly off* malparado; muy enfermo; *want* ~*ly* desear mucho; perderse por.

bade [beid] *pret. of* bid.

badge [bædʒ] insignia *f*, divisa *f*.

badg·er ['bædʒə] **1.** tejón *m*; **2.** molestar; fastidiar, acosar.

bad·min·ton ['bædmintən] volante *m*.

bad-tem·pered ['bæːd'tempəd] de mal genio.

baf·fle ['bæfl] **1.** ⊕ (*a.* ~*-plate*) deflector *m*; *radio:* pantalla *f* acústica; **2.** frustrar, impedir; chasquear; desconcertar; **baf·fling** ['bæfliŋ] perplejo; desconcertador.

bag [bæg] **1.** maleta *f*, bolsa *f* (*a. zo.*, ⚓); (*hand-*) bolso *m*; (*big*) saco *m*; (*shoulder*) zurrón *m*, mochila *f*; *hunt.* cacería *f* (de animales muertos de una vez); F ~*s pl.* pantalón *m*; F *it's in the* ~ es cosa segura; *pack* ~ *and baggage* tomar el tole; **2.** [bæg] *v/t.* ensacar; ⚓ coger, asegurarse; *hunt.* cazar; *v/i.* (*garment etc.*) hacer bolsa.

bag·gage ['bægidʒ] equipaje *m*; ⚔ bagaje *m*; *contp.* mujercilla *f*; *fulana f*; ~ *car* ⚒ vagón *m* de equipajes; **'·~ check** talón *m* de equipajes; **'·~ rack** red *f* de equipajes; **'·~ room** sala *f* de equipajes.

bag·gy ['bægi] holgado.

bag...: **'·~pipe** gaita *f*; **'·~ snatch·er** ladrón *m* de bolsos, ratero (a *f*) *m*.

bail [beil] ⚖ **1.** caución *f*, fianza *f*; *be* (*or go, stand*) ~ *for* salir fiador por; **2.** caucionar; ~ *out* poner en libertad bajo fianza.

bail·iff ['beilif] ⚖ alguacil *m*, corchete *m*; mayordomo *m* *on estate*.

bait [beit] **1.** cebo *m*, carnada *f*; *fig.* aliciente *m*; (*deceitful*) señuelo *m*, añagaza *f*; *swallow the* ~ tragar el anzuelo; **2.** *trap. etc.* poner cebo en; *fig.* acosar, atormentar.

baize [beiz] bayeta *f*.

bake [beik] cocer al horno.

ba·ke·lite ['beikəlait] baquelita *f*.

bak·er ['beikə] panadero *m*; **bak·er·y** panadería *f*; **'bak·ing** hornada *f*; cocción *f*; **'bak·ing pow·der** polvos *m/pl.* de levadura, polvo *m* de hornear; **'bak·ing so·da** bicarbonato *m* de sosa.

bal·ance ['bæləns] **1.** (*scales*) balanza *f*; equilibrio *m* (*a. fig.*); ✝ balance *m*; ✝ saldo *m* *of account etc.*; (*watch*) volante *m*; F resto *m*; ~ *of power* equilibrio *m* político; ~ *of trade* balance *m* de comercio; *fig. in the* ~ en la balanza; *v. strike*; **2.** *v/t.* equilibrar; contrapesar (*with con*); ✝ saldar, finiquitar; *v/i.* equilibrarse, balancearse; menearse; ✝ ~ *up* finiquitar; **'·~ sheet** ✝ balance *m*, avanzo *m*.

bal·co·ny ['bælkəni] balcón *m*.

bald [bɔːld] □ calvo; *fig.* franco; **'·~-head·ed** calvo; **'·~ness** calvicie *f*.

bale [beil] ✝ **1.** fardo *m*, bala *f*; **2.** embalar.

bale² [~] ⚓ achicar; ✈ ~ *out* lanzarse en paracaídas.

bale·ful ['beilful] □ funesto.

balk [bɔːk] **1.** ✓ lomo *m* (entre surcos); *fig.* obstáculo *m*, estorbo *m*; (*timber*) viga *f*; (*billiards*) cabaña *f*; **2.** *v/t.* frustrar; evitar, perder.

ball¹ [bɔːl] **1.** bola *f*; globo *m*, esfera *f*; (*tennis etc.*) pelota *f*; (*football*) balón *m*; (*cannon*) bala *f*; (*wool*) ovillo *m*; *baseball:* tiro *m* falso; F *keep the* ~ *rolling* mantener en marcha (*esp.* la conversación); F *play* ~ cooperar (*with con*); **2.** convertir en bolas; *sl.* ~ *up* echarlo todo a rodar.

ball² [~] baile *m*; *dress* ~ baile *m* de etiqueta.

bal·lad ['bæləd] romance *m*; ♪ balada *f*.

bal·last ['bæləst] **1.** ⚓ lastre *m* (*a. fig.*); ⚒ balasto *m*; **2.** ⚓ lastrar; balastar.

ball...: **'·~ bear·ing** cojinete *m* a bolas;

'~ game juego *m* de pelota; F béisbol *m*.

bal·let ['bælei] ballet *m*, baile *m*.

bal·lis·tics [bə'listiks] *mst sg.* balística *f*.

bal·loon [bə'luːn] **1.** 🔎 *a.* 🎈 globo *m*; *mot.* ~ tyre llanta *f* balón; **2.** subir en un globo; ~ (*out*) hincharse como un globo.

bal·lot ['bælət] **1.** balota *f*, papeleta *f* (para votar); sufragio *m*; votación *f*; **2.** balotar, votar; **'~ box** urna *f* electoral.

ball-point pen ['bɔːlpɔint'pen] bolígrafo *m*, polígrafo *m*, pluma *f* esferográfica; *Arg.* birome *f*; *Bol.* punto *m* bola; *Col.* esfero *m*.

ball·room ['bɔːlrum] salón *m* de baile.

bal·ly·hoo [bæli'huː] **1.** F alharaca *f*; bombo *m*; propaganda *f* sensacional; **2.** F dar bombo a.

balm [bɑːm] bálsamo *m* (*a. fig.*).

balm·y ['bɑːmi] □ balsámico, fragante; *sl.* chiflado.

ba·lo·ney [bə'louni] *sl.* sandez *f*, tontería *f*.

bal·sam ['bɔːlsəm] bálsamo *m*; **bal·sam·ic** [~'sæmik] □ balsámico.

bam·boo [bæm'buː] bambú *m*.

bam·boo·zle [bæm'buːzl] F embaucar, capotear.

ban [bæn] **1.** bando *m*, edicto *m*; prohibición *f* (*on* de); **2.** prohibir.

ba·nan·a [bə'nɑːnə] plátano *m*; banana *f*.

band [bænd] **1.** banda *f* (*a. radio*), faja *f*; (*edge of garment*) cenefa *f*; (*hat-*)cintillo *m*; (*group*) cuadrilla *f*, banda *f*; ♪ banda *f*, música *f*; **2.** orlar; rayar *with stripes*; (*group*) apandillar(se), acuadrillarse; ~ *together* asociarse.

band·age ['bændidʒ] **1.** vendaje *m*, venda *f*; *first aid* ~ vendaje *m* provisional; **2.** vendar.

ban·dan·na [bæn'dænə] pañuelo *m* de hierbas.

ban·dit ['bændit] bandido *m*.

bane·ful ['beinful] □ funesto; nocivo.

bang [bæŋ] **1.** ¡pum!; **2.** F precisamente (~ *across etc.*); **3.** detonación *f*; estallido *m*; golpe *m* *on head etc.*; contusión *f*; (*hair*) flequillo *m*; **4.** golpear, cerrar *etc.* con estrépito.

ban·ish ['bæniʃ] desterrar (*a. fig.*).

ban·is·ter ['bænistə] balaustre *m*; **ban·is·ters** [~z] *pl.* barandilla *f*.

ban·jo ['bændʒou] banjo *m*.

bank [bæŋk] **1.** ribera *f*, orilla *f*, margen *f*; banda *f*, montón *m* *of clouds*; banco *m* *of sand*; (*hill*) loma *f*; batería *f* *of lamps*; hilera *f* *of oars*; ✈ banco *m*; (*in games*) banca *f*; (piggy-) ~ hucha *f*, alcancía *f*; ~ *of deposit* banco *m* de depósito; ~ *of issue* banco *m* de emisión; **2.** *v/t.* fire cubrir (*a.* ~ *up*); *water* represar, estancar; *pile* amontonar (*a.* ~ *up*); ✈ depositar; ✈ ladear; *v/i.* dedicarse a negocios de banca; depositar dinero (*with* en); ✈ ladearse; F ~ *on* contar con; **'bank ac·count** cuenta *f* de banco; **'bank·er** banquero *m* (*a. in games*); **bank·rupt** ['~rʌpt] **1.** quebrado *m*, fallido *m*; ~'s estate activo *m* de la quiebra; **2.** quebrado, insolvente; *fig.* ~ *in* (*or* ~ *of*) falto de; *go* ~ hacer bancarrota, quebrar; **3.** hacer quebrar, arruinar.

ban·ner ['bænə] bandera *f*, estandarte *m*.

ban·quet ['bæŋkwit] **1.** banquete *m*; **2.** banquetear (*v/i. a. v/t.*); ~*ing hall* comedor *m* de gala.

ban·tam ['bæntəm] gallinilla *f* (de) Bantam; *fig.* persona *f* de pequeña talla y amiga de pelear; **'~·weight** peso *m* gallo.

ban·ter ['bæntə] **1.** zumba *f*, chanza *f*; **2.** chancear(se con); burlar(se de).

bap·tism ['bæptizm] bautismo *m* (*a. fig.*); (*act*) bautizo *m*.

bap·tize [bæp'taiz] bautizar (*a. fig.*).

bar [bɑː] **1.** barra *f* (*a.* ⚜ *a. heraldry*); vara *f*, varilla *f*; (*securing*) tranca *f*; (*window*) reja *f*; (*tavern*) bar *m*; (*counter*) mostrador *m*; (*river*) barra *f*; ♪ compás *m*; *fig.* impedimento *m* (*to* para); *fig.* tribunal *m of public opinion etc.*; *parallel* ~*s pl.* (barras) paralelas *f/pl.*; **2.** *door* atrancar; barrear; impedir, obstruir; prohibir; (*a.* ~ *out*) excluir.

barb [bɑːb] lengüeta *f of arrow etc.*; *zo.* púa *f*; ~*ed wire* alambre *m* de puas, alambre *m* de espino.

bar·bar·i·an [bɑː'bɛəriən] bárbaro *adj. a. su. m* (*a f*) (*a. fig.*); **bar·bar·ic** [~'bærik] □ barbárico; de ruda magnificencia; **'bar·ba·rous** □ bárbaro.

bar·be·cue ['bɑːbikjuː] barbacoa *f*.

bar·ber ['bɑːbə] barbero *m*, peluquero *m*; ~ *shop* peluquería *f*, barbería *f*.

bard [bɑːd] bardo *m*.

bare [bɛə] **1.** □ desnudo; *head* descubierto; *landscape* pelado, raso; *clothes etc.* raído; *style* escueto; *room* con pocos muebles; desprovisto (of de); mero; v. lay; 2. desnudar, descubrir; '**⁓back** montado en pelo; adv. en pelo, sin montura; '**bare·foot·ed** descalzo; '**bare·head·ed** descubierto; '**bare·ly** apenas, solamente.

bar·gain ['bɑːgin] 1. pacto m, convenio m; (cheap th.) ganga f; negocio m ventajoso (para el comprador); ⁓ **counter** baratillo m; ⁓ **price** precio m irrisorio; F it's a ⁓! ¡hecho!; into the ⁓ de añadidura; por más señas; make (or strike) a ⁓ cerrar un trato; make the best of a bad ⁓ poner a mal tiempo buena cara; 2. negociar.

barge [bɑːdʒ] 1. gabarra f, barcaza f; (esp. ceremonial) falúa f; 2. F ⁓ in entrar sin pedir permiso; irrumpir; ⁓ into entrometerse en, inmiscuirse en.

bar·i·tone ['bæritoun] barítono m.

bar·i·um ['bɛəriəm] bario m.

bark[1] 1. corteza f; ⊕ casca f for tanning; 2. descortezar; skin raer.

bark[2] [⁓] 1. ladrar (a. fig.: at a); ⁓ up the wrong tree tomar el rábano por las hojas; 2. ladrido m; sl. tos f.

bar·ley ['bɑːli] cebada f.

barn [bɑːn] granero m, troje f; establo m, cuadra f.

bar·na·cle ['bɑːnəkl] cirrópodo m.

ba·rom·e·ter [bə'rɔmitə] barómetro m; **bar·o·met·ric, bar·o·met·ri·cal** [bærə'metrik(l)] □ barométrico.

bar·on ['bærən] barón m.

ba·roque [bə'rɔk] barroco adj. a. su. m.

bar·rack ['bærək] (mst ⁓s pl.) cuartel m; F approx. caserón m.

bar·rage ['bærɑːʒ] (water) presa f; ✕ barrera f de fuego.

bar·rel ['bærl] 1. tonel m, cuba f; (gun, pen) cañón m; (capstan, watch) cilindro m; ⊕ tambor m; 2. embarrilar, entonelar; '**bar·rel or·gan** ♪ organillo m.

bar·ren ['bærən] □ estéril, árido; fig. infructuoso; '**bar·ren·ness** esterilidad f; aridez f.

bar·ri·cade [bæri'keid] 1. barricada f; 2. barrear, cerrar con barricadas.

bar·ri·er ['bæriə] barrera f (a. fig.); ✝ fielato m.

bar·ring ['bɑːriŋ] F excepto, salvo.

bar·tend·er ['bɑːtendə] tabernero m, barman m.

bar·ter ['bɑːtə] 1. permutación f,

trueque m (de bienes); 2. trocar, permutar (for por, con).

base[1] [beis] □ bajo, humilde; vil, ruin; infame; metals bajo de ley.

base[2] [⁓] 1. base f; ⌂ basa f; 2. basar, fundar ([up]on en; a. fig.); ✕ aterrizar; ⁓ o.s. on apoyarse en; be ⁓d[up]on estribar en, basarse en.

base...: '**⁓·ball** béisbol m; '**⁓·less** infundado; '**base·ment** sótano m.

base·ness ['beisnis] bajeza f, vileza f.

bash·ful ['bæʃful] □ tímido, encogido; vergonzoso.

bas·ic ['beisik] básico.

ba·sil·i·ca [bə'zilikə] basílica f.

ba·sin ['beisn] (small) escudilla f, cuenca f; (wash) jofaina f; (river) cuenca f; (port) dársena f; (fountain) taza f.

ba·sis ['beisis], pl. **ba·ses** ['⁓iːz] base f, fundamento m; on the ⁓ of a base de.

bask [bɑːsk] asolearse, tomar el sol.

bas·ket ['bɑːskit] cesta f; (big) cesto m; (with two handles) canasta f; '**⁓·ball** baloncesto m.

Basque [bæsk] 1. vasco adj. a. su. m (a f); 2. (language) vascuence m.

bass·re·lief [beisri'liːf] bajorrelieve m.

bass[1] [beis] ♪ bajo m.

bass[2] [bæs] corteza f de tilo; ⁓ **wood** tilo m americano.

bas·soon [bə'suːn] bajón m.

bas·tard ['bɑːstəd] □ bastardo adj. a. su. m (a f).

baste[1] [beist] sew. hilvanar.

baste[2] [⁓] joint pringar; F dar de palos.

bas·tion ['bæstiən] baluarte m.

bat[1] [bæt] zo. murciélago m; blind as a ⁓ más ciego que un topo.

bat[2] [⁓] 1. sport: maza f; of one's own ⁓ sin ayuda; de suyo; F right off the ⁓ de repente, sin deliberación; 2. golpear (con un palo etc.); F come (or go) to ⁓ for ayudar.

bat[3] [⁓] guiñar; without ⁓ting an eyelid sin emoción, sin pestañear.

batch [bætʃ] cooking: hornada f; colección f, grupo m; (set) tanda f.

bath [bɑːθ] 1. (pl. **baths** [bɑːðz]) baño m; piscina f for swimming; fig. blood ⁓ carnicería f; take a ⁓ tomar un baño; 2. v/t. bañar; v/i. bañar; 2. bañar.

bathe [beið] 1. bañar(se); 2. baño m (en el mar etc.).

bath·ing ['beiðiŋ] 1. baño m; 2. attr. de baño; '**⁓ 'beau·ty** sirena f de playa; '**⁓ cap** gorro m de baño; '**⁓ re'sort** estación f balnearia; '**⁓ suit** traje m de baño, bañador m.

bath...: '**~-robe** albornoz m; '**~-room** cuarto m de baño; **~** fixtures pl. aparatos m/pl. sanitarios; '**~ salts** sales f/pl. de baño; '**~ tow·el** toalla f de baño; '**~-tub** bañadera f, bañera f.

ba·ton ['bætən] ✗ bastón m; ♪ batuta f.

bat·tal·ion [bə'tæljən] batallón m.

bat·ter ['bætə] **1.** pasta f, batido m; sport: bateador m; **2.** apalear, magullar; ✗ cañonear; '**bat·ter·y** ✗, ⚡, baseball: batería f; ⚡ pila f, acumulador m; ⚙ violencia f (esp. assault and ~).

bat·tle ['bætl] **1.** batalla f; combate m; **2.** batallar (against contra; with con); luchar (for por).

bat·tle...: '**~-field** campo m de batalla; '**~-front** frente m de combate; '**~-ground** campo m de batalla; '**~-ship** acorazado m.

bau·ble ['bɔːbl] chuchería f.

bawd·y ['bɔːdi] □ obsceno, impúdico.

bawl [bɔːl] v/i. vocear, desgañitarse (freq. ~ out); ~ at s.o. reñir a una p. en voz alta; v/t. sl. ~ out reñir, regañar.

bay[1] [bei] horse (caballo m) bayo approx.

bay[2] [~] ♣ bahía f, abra f; (large) golfo m; ~ salt sal f morena.

bay[3] [~] △ crujía f; ⛵ nave f.

bay[4] [~] ♣ laurel m.

bay[5] [~] **1.** ladrar, aullar; **2.** ladrido m, aullido m; at ~ acosado, acorralado; keep at ~ mantener a raya.

bay·o·net ['beiənit] **1.** bayoneta f; **2.** herir (or matar) con la bayoneta.

bay win·dow ['bei'windou] ventana f salediza, mirador m; sl. barriga f.

ba·zaar [bə'zaː] bazar m.

ba·zoo·ka [bə'zuːkə] bazuca f.

be [biː; bi] [irr.]: a) ser; estar; encontrarse; haber; existir; he is a doctor es médico; (location) he is in Madrid está en Madrid; (temporary state) he is ill está (or se encuentra) enfermo; there is, there are hay; so be it (or be it so) así sea; be that as it may sea como fuere; b) auxiliary verb with present participle: I am working trabajo, estoy trabajando; he is coming tomorrow viene mañana; c) auxiliary verb with inf.: I am to go to Spain he de ir a España; d) auxiliary verb with p.p.: ser, estar, quedar; passive (action): he was followed by the police fue seguido por la policía; passive (state): the door

is closed la puerta está (or queda) cerrada; e) idioms: mother to ~ futura madre f; my wife to ~ mi futura (esposa); f) for phrases with prp., v. the prp.

beach [biːtʃ] **1.** playa f; **2.** v/t. ♣ varar; '**~-comb·er** raquero m; '**~-head** ✗ cabeza f de playa.

bea·con ['biːkn] **1.** almenara f, alcandora f; faro m; (hill) hacho m; fig. amonestación f, guía f; **2.** iluminar, guiar.

bead [biːd] **1.** cuenta f, abalorio m; gota f; (gun) mira f globular; ~s pl. sarta f de cuentas; rosario m; tell one's ~s rezar el rosario; **2.** v/t. adornar con abalorios.

beak [biːk] pico m; nariz f (corva esp.); ♣ rostro m; sl. magistrado m.

beam [biːm] **1.** △ viga f; ♣ bao m; ♣ (width) manga f; (plough) timón m; ⚡ etc. a. elgc. rayo m; (balance) astil m; ⊕ balancín m; F on the ~ siguiendo el buen camino; **2.** brillar, fig. sonreír alegremente.

bean [biːn] ♣ haba f; judía f; sl. cabeza f; F full of ~s rebosando de vitalidad.

bear[1] [bɛə] **1.** oso m; fig. hombre m ceñudo; ♥ bajista m/f; ♦ ~ market mercado m bajista; **2.** ♥ jugar a la baja; ~ hacer bajar el valor.

bear[2] [~] [irr.] v/t. llevar; (endure) soportar, aguantar; arms, date, inscription, name llevar; interest devengar; child parir; inspection etc. tolerar, sufrir; fruit etc. rendir, producir; costs etc. pagar, costear; ~ away llevarse; ganarse; ~ down postrar; ~ out confirmar, apoyar; v/i. dirigirse (a); ♣ ~ down upon correr sobre; caer sobre; F ~ up cobrar ánimo; bring to ~ pressure etc. ejercer ([up]on sobre); '**~-a·ble** □ llevadero.

beard [biəd] **1.** barba f; ♣ arista f; **2.** hacer cara a; retar; '**beard·ed** barbudo; ♣ aristado; '**beard·less** imberbe, lampiño.

bear·er ['bɛərə] portador (-a f) m (a. ♣).

bear·ing ['bɛəriŋ] aguante m; sustentamiento m; p.'s porte m, modales m/pl.; heraldry: blasón m; aspecto m of th.; relación f (on con); ♣ marcación f; ⊕ cojinete m, apoyo m; take one's ~s ♣ marcarse; fig. orientarse; lose one's ~s desorientarse.

beast [biːst] bestia f; fig. hombre m brutal; fig. persona f molesta; F th.

cosa *f* mala (*or* molesta); ~ of burden bestia *f* de carga.

beat [biːt] **1.** [*irr.*] *v/t.* batir, golpear, pegar; (*defeat*) vencer; *record* batir, superar; F sobrepasar, aventajar; F ~ confundir; *path* abrir; *hunt.* ojear; *drum* tocar; *carpet* apalear; ♪ *time* llevar; *v.* retreat; *sl.* ~ it! ¡lárgate!; F *to* ~ *the band* hasta más no poder; F ~ *one's way* hacer un viaje sin pagar; ~ *down* abatir; ✝ *price* rebajar; ~ *off* rechazar; ~ *up egg* batir; *sl.* ~ apo- rrear; *v/i.* batir; (*heart*) latir; F ~ *about the bush* andarse por las ramas, ir por rodeos; **2.** golpe *m*; (*heart-*) latido *m*; (*rhythm*) marca *f*; ♪ compás *m*; (*police*) ronda *f*; **3.** F deslumbrado, perplejo; engañado; *dead* ~ *sl.* ren- dido; '**beat·en** *p.p. of beat* 1; *track* trillado.

beau·ti·cian [bjuːˈtiʃən] embellece- dora *f*, esteta *m/f*, esteticista *m/f*.

beau·ti·ful [ˈbjuːtəful] □ hermoso, bello; ~*ly* F maravillosamente, muy bien.

beau·ti·fy [ˈbjuːtifai] embellecer.

beau·ty [ˈbjuːti] belleza *f*, hermosura *f*; (*woman*) beldad *f*; F *it's a* ~ es bárbaro; *sleeping* ♀ *la* Bella Dur- miente (*del bosque*); ~ *contest* con- curso *m* de belleza; ~ *parlor* salón *m* de belleza; ~ *queen* reina *f* de la be- lleza; ~ *spot* (*face*) lunar *m* postizo; (*place*) sitio *m* pintoresco.

bea·ver [ˈbiːvə] *zo.* castor *m*.

be·came [biˈkeim] *pret. of become.*

be·cause [biˈkɔz] porque; ~ *of* a causa de.

beck [bek] seña *f*; *at the* ~ *and call of* a disposición de.

beck·on [ˈbekn] hacer seña (*to* a); llamar con señas; *fig.* atraer.

be·come [biˈkʌm] [*irr.* (*come*)] *v/i.* ser, hacerse (*of* de); *what will* ~ *of me?* ¿qué será de mí?; *v/t. mst with su.* hacerse; *mst with adj.* ponerse; llegar a ser; convertirse en; (*action*) con- venir a; (*clothes esp.*) sentar a, favo- recer; **be'com·ing** □ decoroso; *clothes* que sienta bien.

bed [bed] cama *f*; (*a. animals*) lecho *m*; (*river-*) cauce *m*; ✝ macizo *m*, arriate *m*; ⊕ base *f*, apoyo *m*; *geol.* capa *f*, yacimiento *m*; ~ *and board* comida *f* y casa; *go to* ~ acostarse; *make the* ~ hacer la cama; *stay in* ~ guardar cama.

bed·clothes [ˈbedklouðz] *pl.* ropa *f* de cama.

bed·ding [ˈbedin] ropa *f* de cama; colchón *m*; (*animals*) lecho *m*.

bed·fel·low [ˈbedfelou] compañero *m* de cama.

bed·lam [ˈbedləm] manicomio *m*; *fig.* belén *m*.

bed·lin·en [ˈbedlinin] ropa *f* de cama; las sábanas.

bed·pan [ˈbedpæn] silleta *f*.

be·drag·gle [biˈdrægl] ensuciar; *clothes etc.* manchar.

bed...: '~**rid**(**·den**) postrado en cama; '~ '**rock** *geol.* lecho *m* de roca; *fig.* fundamento *m*; '~**room** dormitorio *m*, alcoba *f*; '~**side**: *at the* ~ *of* a la cabecera de; *good* ~ *manner* mano *f* izquierda, diplomacia *f*; ~ *table* mesa *f* de noche; '~**sore** úlcera *f* de decú- bito; '~**spread** colcha *f*, sobrecama *m*; '~**stead** cuja *f*; '~**time** hora *f* de acostarse; '~ **warm·er** calientaca- mas *m*.

bee [biː] abeja *f*.

beech [biːtʃ] haya *f*; '~**nut** hayuco *m*.

beef [biːf] **1.** carne *f* de vaca; F fuerza *f* muscular; **2.** F quejarse; ~**steak** [ˈbiːfsteik] biftec *m*, bistec *m*.

bee...: '~**hive** colmena *f*; '~ **keep·ing** apicultura *f*; '~ **line** línea *f* recta.

been [biːn, bin] *p.p. of be.*

beer [biə] cerveza *f*; *small* ~ cerveza floja; *dark* ~ cerveza *f* parda, cerveza *f* negra; *light* ~ cerveza *f* clara.

beet [biːt] remolacha *f*.

bee·tle¹ [biːtl] ⊕ **1.** pisón *m*; **2.** api- sonar.

beet·le² [~] *zo.* **1.** escarabajo *m*; **2.** *sl.* ~ *off* largarse, volver la cara.

bee·tle³ [~] **1.** (sobre)saliente; ceñu- do; **2.** sobresalir.

be·fit [biˈfit] cuadrar a, convenir a; **be·fit·ting** □ propio, conveniente.

be·fore [biˈfɔː] **1.** *adv.* (*place*) (a)de- lante; *go* ~ ir adelante; ~ *and behind* por delante y por detrás; (*time*) an- tes; anteriormente; **2.** *cj.* antes (de que); **3.** *prp.* (*place*) delante de; (*judge etc.*) ante; (*time*) antes de; *be* (*or go*)~ *a p.* ir delante de una p., ir primero; **be'fore·hand** de antemano; *be* ~ *with* anticipar.

be·friend [biˈfrend] ofrecer amistad a; patrocinar.

beg [beg] *v/t.* suplicar, rogar (*of* a); (*as beggar*) mendigar; *v. pardon, question*; *v/i.* mendigar, pordiosear.

be·gan [biˈgæn] *pret. of begin.*

be·get [biˈget] [*irr.* (*get*)] engendrar, ...

beg·gar [ˈbegə] mendigo (*a f*) *m*, ...

pordiosero (a f) m; F contp. tío m.

be·gin [bi'gin] [irr.] comenzar, empezar (to a); iniciar; ~ by comenzar por; ~ on s.t. emprender algo; ~ with comenzar con, principiar con; to ~ with para empezar; en primer lugar; ~ning from date a partir de; **be·gin·ner** principiante m/f; **be·gin·ning** comienzo m, principio m; from ~ to end del principio al fin, de cabo a rabo (F).

be·grudge [bi'grʌdʒ] dar de mala gana; (envy) envidiar.

be·guile [bi'gail] engañar, seducir; fig. entretener.

be·gun [bi'gʌn] p.p. of begin.

be·half [bi'hɑ:f]: on ~ of a favor de, en nombre de; por.

be·have [bi'heiv] (com)portarse; ⊕ etc. funcionar, actuar; ~ o.s. portarse bien; **be·hav·ior** [~jə] conducta f, comportamiento m.

be·head [bi'hed] descabezar; decapitar.

be·held [bi'held] pret. a. p.p. of behold.

be·hest [bi'hest] orden f.

be·hind [bi'haind] 1. adv. (por) detrás; (hacia) atrás; be ~ (late) retrasarse; 2. prp. detrás de.

be·hold [bi'hould] [irr. (hold)] lit. 1. contemplar; advertir, columbrar; 2. ¡he aquí!; ¡mira(d)!

be·ing ['bi:iŋ] ser m; existencia f, in ~ existente; come into ~ producirse; nacer.

be·la·ted [bi'leitid] ☐ demorado, tardío.

belch [beltʃ] 1. eructar, regoldar; fig. echar, arrojar; 2. regüeldo m.

be·lea·guer [bi'li:gə] sitiar.

bel·fry ['belfri] campanario m.

be·lie [bi'lai] desmentir.

be·lief [bi'li:f] creencia f, crédito m; fe f (in en; that de que).

be·liev·a·ble [bi'li:vəbl] creíble.

be·lieve [bi'li:v] creer (in en); ~ in story etc. dar crédito a; F (not) ~ in e.g. drink (no) aprobar; don't you ~ it! ¡no lo crea(s)!; **be·liev·er** creyente m/f.

be·lit·tle [bi'litl] fig. deprimir, despreciar.

bell [bel] campana f; (hand-) campanilla f (a. ♀); (electric) timbre m; (animal's) cencerro m; cascabel m; ♪ pabellón m of trumpet etc.; fig. that rings a ~ eso me suena.

bell·boy ['belboi] botones m.

belle [bel] beldad f, guapetona f.

bell...: '~**flow·er** campanilla f; '~**hop** botones m.

bel·li·cose ['belikous] belicoso.

bel·lig·er·ent [bi'lidʒərənt] ☐ beligerante adj. a. su. m/f.

bel·low ['belou] 1. bramar; (p.) gritar, dar voces; 2. bramido m.

bel·lows ['belouz] pl. (a pair of un) fuelle m (a. phot.).

bell...: '~**rope** cuerda f de campana; '~**shaped** acampanado.

bel·ly ['beli] 1. vientre f; barriga f (a. of vessel); 2. combarse; (sail) hacer bolso; '~ **but·ton** F ombligo m; '~**dance** danza f del vientre; **'bel·ly·ful** [~ful] sl. panzada f.

be·long [bi'lɔŋ] pertenecer (to a); corresponder (to a); **be·long·ings** [~iŋz] pl. efectos m/pl.; F cosas f/pl.

be·lov·ed [bi'lʌvid] querido adj. a. su. m (a f).

be·low [bi'lou] 1. adv. abajo, debajo; here ~ en este mundo; 2. prp. debajo de; fig. inferior a.

belt [belt] 1. cinturón m (a. ✕), cinto m; (corset) faja f; ⊕ correa f, cinta f; fig. zona f; fig. below the ~ sucio, suciamente; fig. tighten one's ~ ceñirse; 2. sl. golpear con correa.

be·moan [bi'moun] lamentar.

be·muse [bi'mju:z] aturdir.

bench [bentʃ] banco m (a. ⊕); ⴵⴳ tribunal m; ⴵⴳ judicatura f; be on the ~ ser juez (or magistrado); v. treasury.

bend [bend] 1. curva f; recodo m, curva f in road; 2. [irr.] combar(se), encorvar(se); body etc. inclinar(se); efforts etc. dirigir (to a).

beneath [bi'ni:θ] = below; fig. ~ me indigno de mí.

ben·e·dic·tion [beni'dikʃn] bendición f.

ben·e·fac·tion [beni'fækʃn] beneficencia f; (gift) beneficio m; '**ben·e·fac·tor** bienhechor m.

ben·e·fi·cial [beni'fiʃl] ☐ beneficioso; ⴵⴳ que goza el usufructo de una propiedad.

ben·e·fit ['benifit] 1. beneficio m (a. thea.); (insurance) lucro m; for the ~ of a beneficio de; 2. beneficiar, aprovechar; sacar provecho.

be·nev·o·lence [bi'nevələns] benevolencia f; **be·nev·o·lent** ☐ benévolo; society caritativo.

be·nign [bi'nain] ☐ benigno (a. ✳).

bent [bent] 1. pret. a. p.p. of bend 2; ~ on resuelto a, empeñado en; 2. inclinación f, propensión f (for a).

B

ben·zene [ˈbenziːn] benceno *m*.

ben·zine [ˈbenziːn] bencina *f*.

be·queath [biˈkwiːð] legar (*a. fig.*), manda *f*.

be·quest [biˈkwest] legado *m* (*a. th.*), manda *f*.

be·reave [biˈriːv] [*irr.*] despojar; *esp. the* ∼*d* los afligidos; **be·reave·ment** *mst* aflicción *f*, duelo *m*.

be·ret [ˈberei] boina *f*.

ber·ry [ˈberi] baya *f*.

berth [bəːθ] 1. ⚓ fondeadero *m*, amarradero *m for ship*; ♣ F (*cabin*) camarote *m*; ⚓, 🚂 (*bunk*) litera *f*; F *fig.* puesto *m*; *give a wide* ∼ *to* esquivar, evitar; 2. anclar, atracar.

be·seech [biˈsiːtʃ] suplicar (*for acc.*); **be·seech·ing** □ suplicante.

be·set [biˈset] [*irr.* (*set*)] acosar (*a. fig.*), perseguir.

be·side [biˈsaid] 1. *adv. v.* ∼*s*; 2. *prp.* cerca de, junto a; en comparación con; ∼ *o.s.* fuera de sí (*with con*); **be·sides** [∼dz] 1. *adv.* además, también; 2. *prp.* además de; excepto.

be·siege [biˈsiːdʒ] asediar (*a. fig.*), sitiar.

best [best] 1. *adj. sup.* mejor; óptimo; ∼ *girl* novia *f*; ∼ *man* padrino *m de* boda; 2. *adv. sup.* mejor; *at* ∼ *a lo* más; *I had* ∼ *go* más vale que yo vaya; 3. *su.* lo mejor; *do one's* ∼ hacer como mejor pueda uno; *for the* ∼ con la mejor intención; *be for the* ∼ conducir al bien; F *get the* ∼ *of it* vencer; *make the* ∼ *of* salir lo mejor posible de.

bes·tial [ˈbestjəl] □ bestial, brutal.

be·stow [biˈstou] conferir, otorgar ([*up*]*on a*).

bet [bet] 1. apuesta *f*; (*sum*) postura *f*; 2. apostar (*on a*).

be·tray [biˈtrei] traicionar; delatar (*a. fig.*); *fig.* revelar, dejar ver; **be·tray·al** traición *f*; *fig.* revelación *f*; ∼ *of trust* abuso *m* de confianza; **be·tray·er** traicionero (*a f*) *m*, traidor (-*a f*) *m*.

be·troth [biˈtrouð] prometer en matrimonio; *be* (*or become*) ∼*ed* desposarse; **be·troth·al** desposorio *m*.

bet·ter¹ [ˈbetə] 1. *adj. comp.* mejor; *he is* ∼ está mejor; *get* ∼ mejorarse; *v/i. half*; 2. *adv. comp.* mejor; ∼ *off* más acomodado; *so much the* ∼ tanto mejor; *I had* ∼ *go* más vale que yo vaya; *think* ∼ *of it* mudar de parecer; 3. *su.* superior *m*; *my* ∼*s pl.* mis superiores; *get the* ∼ *of* llevar la ventaja a; 4. *v/t.* mejorar; ∼ *o.s.* mejorar su posición; *v/i.* progresar, mejorar(se).

bet·ter² [∼] *adj.* apostador (-*a f*) *m*.

bet·ter·ment mejoramiento *m*.

bet·ting [ˈbetiŋ] apostar *m*; juego *m*.

be·tween [biˈtwiːn] (*poet. or prov. a.* ∼) en medio, entremedias; *betwixt and* ∼ entre lo uno y lo otro, ni fu ni fa (F); 2. *prp.* entre; ∼ *ourselves* entre nosotros.

be·twixt [biˈtwikst] 1. *adv.* (*freq. in* ∼) en medio, entremedias; *betwixt and* ∼ entre lo uno y lo otro, ni fu ni fa (F); 2. *prp.* entre.

bev·el [ˈbevl] 1. biselado; 2. *v/t.* ⊕ biselar; *v/i.* inclinarse.

bev·er·age [ˈbevəridʒ] bebida *f*.

bev·y [ˈbevi] (*birds*) bandada *f*; (*ladies*) grupo *m*.

be·wail [biˈweil] lamentar.

be·ware [biˈwɛə] precaverse (*of de*); ∼! ¡atención!

be·wil·der [biˈwildə] aturdir, aturrullar; desconcertar; **be·wil·der·ment** aturdimiento *m*; perplejidad *f*.

be·witch [biˈwitʃ] hechizar (*a. fig.*), embrujar.

be·yond [biˈjɔnd] 1. *adv.* más allá (*a. fig.*), más lejos; 2. *prp.* más allá de; además de; fuera de; superior a; *it is* ∼ *me* está fuera de mi alcance; 3. más allá *m*.

bi·an·nu·al [baiˈænjəl] semestral.

bi·as [ˈbaiəs] 1. sesgo *m*, diagonal *f*; *fig.* pasión *f*, predisposición *f*, prejuicio *m*; *cut on the* ∼ cortar al sesgo; 2. sesgar; *fig.* influir en, torcer; *be* ∼*sed* tener prejuicio, ser partidista.

bib [bib] babador *m*, babero *m*.

Bi·ble [ˈbaibl] Biblia *f*.

bib·li·cal [ˈbiblikəl] □ bíblico.

bib·li·og·ra·pher [bibliˈɔgrəfə] bibliógrafo *m*; **bib·li·o·graph·ic**, **bib·li·o·graph·i·cal** [∼ouˈgræfik(l)] □ bibliográfico; **bib·li·og·ra·phy** [∼ˈɔgrəfi] bibliografía *f*.

bi·car·bon·ate of so·da [baiˈkɑːbənitəvˈsoudə] bicarbonato *m* sódico.

bi·ceps [ˈbaiseps] bíceps *m*.

bick·er [ˈbikə] (*quarrel*) altercar, pararse en quisquillas.

bi·cy·cle [ˈbaisikl] 1. bicicleta *f*; 2. andar en bicicleta; **bi·cy·clist** ciclista *m/f*.

bid [bid] 1. [*irr.*] *lit.* mandar; ordenar; *cards*: pujar, marcar; licitar *at auction*; *adieu etc.* decir, dar; ∼ *fair to inf.* prometer *inf.*, dar indicios de *inf.*; ∼ *up* pujar; 2. (*auction etc.*) oferta *f*, postura *f*; (*cards*) marca *f*; tentativa *f* (*to de*, *para*); *cards*: *no* ∼ paso; **bid·den** *p.p. of bid*; **bid·der** licitador *m*, postor *m*; *highest* ∼ mejor postor *m*; **bid·ding** orden *f*; (*auction*) licitación *f*, postura *f*.

bide [baid] † aguardar; ~ one's time esperar la hora propicia.

bi·en·ni·al [bai'enjəl] ♀ (planta f) bienal, bianual m.

bier [biə] féretro m, andas f/pl.

bi·fo·cal [bai'foukl] 1. bifocal 2. ~s pl. anteojos m/pl. bifocales.

big [big] grande (a. fig.); abultado, voluminoso; (mst ~ with child) encinta; F engreído; fig. importante; ~ shot sl. pájaro m de cuenta, señorón m; sl. talk ~ echar bravatas.

big·a·mist ['bigəmist] bígamo (a f) m; '**big·a·my** bigamia f.

big·ot ['bigət] fanático (a f) m, intolerante m/f; '**big·ot·ed** fanático, intolerante; '**big·ot·ry** fanatismo m, intolerancia f.

big toe [big'tou] dedo m gordo o grande del pie.

big·wig ['bigwig] F pájaro m de cuenta, espadón m.

bike [baik] F bici f.

bile [bail] bilis f; fig. displicencia f.

bi·lin·gual [bai'lingwəl] bilingüe.

bill¹ [bil] 1. zo. pico m; una f of anchor; ✍ podadera f (a. ~hook); geog. promontorio m; 2. esp. fig. ~ and coo acariciarse, besuquearse.

bill² [~] 1. † cuenta f, factura f; parl. proyecto m de ley; † billete m; † letra f de cambio (a. ~ of exchange); (notice) cartel m; anuncio m; thea. programa m; ‡‡ alegato m; pedimento m; ~ of fare minuta f; ♣ ~ of health patente m de sanidad; ~ of lading conocimiento m de embarque; ~ of rights declaración f de derechos; ley f fundamental; ‡‡ ~ of sale escritura f de venta; 2. thea. etc. anunciar.

bill·board ['bil'bɔːd] cartelera f, tablón m de anuncios.

bill·fold ['bilfould] billetera f.

bil·liard ['biljəd] de billar; '~ **cue** taco m; '**bil·liards** pl. billar m.

bil·lion ['biljən] American mil millones m/pl.; British billón m.

bil·low ['bilou] 1. oleada f; poet. ~s pl. piélago m; 2. ondular, ondear.

bil·ly goat ['biligout] macho m cabrio.

bin [bin] hucha f, arcón m; (bread) nasa f.

bi·na·ry ['bainəri] binario.

bind [baind] [irr.] 1. v/t. liar, atar (to a); ceñir (with, con, de); wound vendar; book encuadernar; cloth ribetear; corn agavillar; ✍ estreñir; fig. obligar; v/i. atiesarse, aglutinarse,

adherirse; 2. sl. lata f; '**bind·ing** 1. obligatorio; food que estriñe; 2. ligadura f; (book-) encuadernación f; sew. ribete m.

bin·oc·u·lars [bi'nɔkjuləz] pl. gemelos m/pl.

bi·o·chem·i·cal ['baiou'kemikl] bioquímico.

bi·og·ra·pher [bai'ɔgrəfə] biógrafo (a f) m; **bi·o·graph·ic, bi·o·graph·i·cal** [~ou'græfik(l)] □ biográfico; **bi·og·ra·phy** [~'ɔgrəfi] biografía f.

bi·o·log·ic, bi·o·log·i·cal [baiə'lɔd-ʒik(l)] □ biológico; **bi·ol·o·gist** [~-'ɔlədʒist] biólogo m; **bi·ol·o·gy** biología f.

bi·par·ti·san [bai'pɑːtizn] de dos partidos políticos.

birch [bəːtʃ] 1. ♀ abedul m; vara f de abedul, férula f; 2. varear.

bird [bəːd] ave f, pájaro m; sl. sujeto m, tío m; ~ in the hand pájaro m en mano; ~s of a feather gente f de una calaña; kill two ~s with one stone matar dos pájaros de una pedrada; '~ **cage** jaula f; '~ **call** reclamo m; '~ **lime** liga f; '~ **of pas'sage** ave f de paso; '~ **of 'prey** ave f de rapiña; '~ **seed** alpiste m; '**bird's-eye view** vista f de pájaro; '~ **shot** perdigones m/pl.; '**bird's nest** 1. nido m de pájaro; 2. buscar nidos.

birth [bəːθ] nacimiento m (a. fig.); ♀ parto m; linaje m; fig. origen m, comienzo m; by ~ de nacimiento; give ~ to parir, dar a luz; ~ control control m de natalidad; '~ **day** cumpleaños m; ~ **cake** pastel m de cumpleaños; ~ **present** regalo m de cumpleaños; '~ **mark** antojo m, nevo m materno; '~ **place** lugar m de nacimiento; '~ **rate** natalidad f; '~ **right** derechos m/pl. de nacimiento; primogenitura f.

bis·cuit ['biskit] 1. galleta f; bizcocho m (a. pottery); 2. bayo, pardusco.

bi·sect [bai'sekt] bisecar; **bi·sec·tion** bisección f.

bish·op ['biʃəp] obispo m; (chess) alfil m; '**bish·op·ric** obispado m.

bi·son ['baisn] bisonte m.

bit [bit] 1. trozo m, porción f; (horse's) freno m; ⊕ barrena f; ~ by ~ poco a poco; a good ~ bastante; F (p.) a ~ of a hasta cierto punto; not a (or one) ~ ni pizca; 2. pret. of bite.

bitch [bitʃ] 1. perra f; zorra f, loba f; (woman) zorra f, mujer f de mal genio; 2. sl. chapucear.

bite [bait] **1.** mordedura *f*, dentellada *f*; bocado *m* to eat; (*snack*) refrigerio *m*; picadura *f* of insect etc.; fig. mordacidad *f*; take a ~ F comer algo; **2.** morder; (*fish, insect*) picar; ⊕ asir; (*acid*) corroer.

bit·ten [bitn] *p.p.* of bite.

bit·ter [bitǝ] □ amargo (*a. fig.*); *fight etc.* encarnizado; *cold* cortante.

bit·ter·ness ['bitǝnis] amargura *f*, amargor *m*; encarnizamiento *m*.

bit·ter·sweet ['bitǝ:swiːt] agridulce.

bi·zarre [bi'zɑː] raro, grotesco.

black [blæk] **1.** □ negro (*a. fig.*); *fig.* aciago; *look* ceñudo; *look* ~ at mirar con ceño; ~ and blue amoratado, acardenalado; in ~ and white en blanco y negro; por escrito; *v. eye, market;* **2.** negro *m* (*a. race*); color negro *m*.

black...: '~·ber·ry zarzamora *f*; '~·bird mirlo *m*; '~·board pizarra *f*; '~·board e'ras·er cepillo *m*; '~·'black·en v/t. in airplanes registrador *m* de vuelo; '~·en v/t. ennegrecer; fig. denigrar; '~·guard ['blægɑːd] **1.** pícaro *m*, bribón *m*, canalla *m*; **2.** (*mst* '~·guard·ly) pillo, vil; **3.** injuriar, vilipendiar; '~·head ['blækhed] 🐞 comedón *m*; '**black·ish** negruzco; '~·list **1.** lista *f* negra; **2.** v/t. poner en lista negra; '~·mail **1.** chantaje *m*; **2.** amenazar con chantaje; '~·mail·er chantajista *m/f*; '**black·ness** negrura *f*; '~·out **1.** apagón *m*; 🐞 amnesia *f* (or ceguera *f*) temporal; **2.** v/t. apagar; v/i. padecer un ataque de amnesia (or ceguera) temporal; '~·smith herrero *m*.

blad·der ['blædǝ] vejiga *f*.

blade [bleid] hoja *f* of knife etc.; (*cutting edge*) filo *m*; paleta *f* of propeller; hoja *f* of grass; pala *f* of oar, axe, hoe; (*p.*) buen mozo *m*.

blame [bleim] **1.** culpa *f*; put (or lay) the ~ on echar la culpa a (for de); **2.** culpar; be to ~ for tener la culpa de.

blame·ful ['bleimful] censurable; '**blame·less** □ inculpable, intachable.

blanch [blɑːntʃ] cooking: blanquear; blanquecer; (*p.*) palidecer.

bland [blænd] □ suave, blando.

blank [blæŋk] **1.** □ paper etc. en blanco, vacío; fig. desconcertado; *look* sin expresión; *verse* blanco, suelto; ~ cartridge cartucho *m* sin bala; ~ check firma *f* en blanco; fig. carta *f* blanca; *fire* ~ usar municiones

de fogueo; **2.** (*space etc.*) blanco *m*; (*coin*) cospel *m*; fig. falta *f* de sensaciones etc.; billete *m* de lotería no premiado; fig. draw (a) ~ no encontrar nada.

blan·ket ['blæŋkit] **1.** manta *f*, cobija *f* S.Am.; fig. manto *m*; fig. wet ~ aguafiestas *m/f*; **2.** cubrir con manta; ♣ quitar el viento a; fig. suprimir; (*p.*) mantear; **3.** comprensivo, general.

blare [blɛǝ] **1.** (*trumpet*) sonar; sonar muy fuerte; ~ (out) vociferar; **2.** trompetazo *m*; estrépito *m*.

blas·pheme [blæs'fiːm] blasfemar; '**blas·phe·my** blasfemia *f*.

blast [blɑːst] **1.** ráfaga *f*; soplo *m* of bellows; trompetazo *m* from trumpet; carga *f* de pólvora; (*explosion*) sacudida *f*; presión *f*; ♀ tizón *m*, añublo *m*; v. full·-; **2.** volar, barrenar; ♀ añublar, marchitar; fig. arruinar; ~ (it)! ¡maldito sea!

blaze [bleiz] **1.** llamarada *f*, hoguera *f*; F incendio *m*; fig. ardor *m*; fig. resplandor *m*; **2.** v/i. arder, encenderse en llamas; fig. enardecerse; F ~ away ⚔ seguir tirando; trabajar con ahínco; v/t. trail abrir; publicar, proclamar (*mst* ~ abroad); '**blaz·er** chaqueta *f* ligera.

bla·zon ['bleizn] **1.** blasón *m* (*a. fig.*); **2.** blasonar; proclamar.

bleach [bliːtʃ] **1.** blanquear(se); **2.** 🐞 lejía *f*; ~s pl. gradas *f/pl.* al aire libre.

bleak [bliːk] □ desierto, solitario; (*bare*) pelado; *weather* frío, crudo; fig. prospect nada prometedor; *welcome* inhospitalario.

bleat [bliːt] **1.** balido *m*; **2.** balar.

bled [bled] pret. a. p.p.of bleed.

bleed [bliːd] [*irr.*] **1.** v/i. sangrar; ~ to death morir de desangramiento; **2.** v/t. sangrar, desangrar; ~ (white) desangrar; '**bleed·ing 1.** 🐞 sangría *f*; **2.** sl. maldito.

blem·ish ['blemiʃ] **1.** mancha *f*, tacha *f* (*a. fig.*); **2.** manchar, tachar (*a. fig.*).

blend [blend] **1.** mezclar(se), combinar(se); (*colors*) casar; **2.** mezcla *f*, combinación *f*.

bless [bles] bendecir; **blessed** [blest] *p.p.* of bless; agraciado (with con); **bles·sed** ['blesid] □ bendito; bienaventurado; '**bless·ing** bendición *f* (*a. fig.*); beneficio *m*.

blest [blest] poet. v. blessed.

blew [bluː] pret. of blow².

blight [blait] 1. ♀ añublo *m*; ♀ tizón *m*, roya *f*; *fig.* plaga *f*, infortunio *m*; 2. ♀ atizonar; arruinar.

blind [blaind] 1. ☐ ciego (*a.* △ *a. fig.*; *with* de, *to* a); oculto; ~ *in one eye* tuerto; *fig.* ~ *alley* callejón *m* sin salida; ~ *date* cita *f* a ciegas; ~*ly fig.* a ciegas; 2. venda *f*; (*window*) celosía *f*, persiana *f*; *fig.* pretexto *m*; *sl.* pantalla *f*; 3. cegar; deslumbrar.

blind...: '~**fold** 1. con los ojos vendados; *fig.* sin reflexión; 2. vendar los ojos a; '~ **land·ing** aterrizaje *m* a ciegas; '**~·man's-buff** gallina *f* ciega; '**blind·ness** ceguedad *f*; '**blind·worm** lución *m*.

blink [bliŋk] 1. parpadeo *m*; (*gleam*) destello *m*; *sl. on the* ~ incapacitado, desconcertado; 2. *v/t.* guiñar, cerrar momentáneamente; *v/i.* parpadear; (*light*) oscilar.

blip [blip] bache *m*.

bliss [blis] bienaventuranza *f*; arrobamiento *m*.

blis·ter ['blistə] 1. ampolla *f*, vejiga *f*; 2. ampollar(se).

blitz [blits] 1. guerra *f* relámpago; *esp.* bombardeo *m* aéreo (alemán); 2. ✠ bombardear.

bliz·zard ['blizəd] ventisca *f*.

bloat [blout] hinchar(se), abotagarse; ~*ed* abotagado.

blob [blɔb] gota *f*; burbuja *f*.

block [blɔk] 1. *stone, a. pol. a. mot.* bloque *m*; zoquete *m of wood*; (*butcher's, executioner's*) tajo *m*; (*pulley*) polea *f*, aparejo *m*; △ manzana *f*, cuadra *f* S.Am.; ▆ bloqueo *m*; *fig.* obstáculo *m*; *fig.* grupo *m*; ~ *and tackle* aparejo *m* de poleas; 2. obstruir, cerrar; ♱ bloquear; ~ *in*, ~ *out* esbozar; ~ *up* tapar, cegar; '~ **bust·er** F bomba *f* rompedora.

block·ade [blɔ'keid] 1. bloqueo *m*; *v. run*; 2. bloquear.

blond [blɔnd] 1. rubio; blondo; 2. F rubia *f*; (*a.* ~ *lace*) blonda *f*.

blood [blʌd] sangre *f*; linaje *m*, parentesco *m*; *b. s.* ira *f*, cólera *f*; (*p.*) currutaco *m*, galán *m*; *in cold* ~ a sangre fría; ~ *royal* estirpe *f* regia; *his* ~ *ran cold* se le heló la sangre; '~ **bank** banco *m* de sangre; '~ **curd·ling** horripilante; '~ **hound** sabueso *m* (*a. fig.*); '**blood·less** ☐ exangüe; *fig.* pacífico.

blood...: '~ **let·ting** sangría *f*; '~ **poi·son·ing** envenenamiento *m* de la sangre; '~ **pres·sure** tensión *f* arterial; (*high*) hipertensión *f*; '~ **re·la·tion** pariente *m/f* consanguíneo; '~ **shed** efusión *f* de sangre; matanza *f*; '~ **shot** *eye* inyectado (de sangre); '~ **stream** corriente *f* sanguínea; '~ **test** análisis *m* de sangre; '~ **thirst·y** ☐ sanguinario; '~ **trans·fu·sion** transfusión *f* de sangre; '~ **ves·sel** vaso *m* sanguíneo; '**blood·y** ☐ sangriento; *sl.* puñetero; *sl. as adv.* muy.

bloom [blu:m] 1. flor *f*; florecimiento *m*, floración *f*; vello *m on fruit*; *fig.* lozanía *f*; 2. florecer.

blos·som ['blɔsəm] 1. flor *f*; flores *f/pl.*; *in* ~ en flor; 2. florecer; *fig.* ~ *into* convertirse en.

blot [blɔt] 1. borrón *m* (*a. fig.*); 2. manchar; borrar; (*mst* ~ *out*) *light, view* oscurecer; *writing* borrar, tachar; *fig.* destruir; secar *with blotting-paper*.

blotch [blɔtʃ] mancha *f*; erupción *f on skin*.

blot·ter ['blɔtə] papel *m* secante; borrador *m*.

blouse [blauz] blusa *f*.

blow¹ [blou] golpe *m*; bofetada *f with hand*; choque *m*; *at one* ~ de un golpe; *come to* ~*s* venir a las manos.

blow² [~] [*irr.*] 1. *v/i.* soplar (*a. whale*); (*puff*) jadear, resoplar; (*hooter etc.*) sonar; *sl.* irse; *sl.* ~ *in* entrar de sopetón; ~ *on s.t.* enfriar soplando; ¿come abrirse (por el viento); ~ *over* pasar; ser olvidado; ~ *up* estallar; *sl.* reventar (de ira); *v/t.* soplar; ♪ sonar, tocar; *fuse* quemar; *nose* sonar; (*fly*) depositar larvas en; *sl. money* despilfarrar; ~ *out* apagar; ~ *up* volar, hacer saltar; *balloon etc.* inflar; 2. soplo *m*; '~**out** *tire* reventón *m*; *fuse* quemazón *f*; *sl.* tertulia *f* concurrida, festín *m*; '~**torch** antorcha *f* a soplete, lámpara *f* de soldar.

blub·ber ['blʌbə] 1. grasa *f* de ballena; (*weeping*) llanto *m*; 2. lloriquear.

bludg·eon ['blʌdʒn] 1. cachiporra *f*; 2. aporrear; *fig.* obligar a porrazos (*into ger. a inf.*).

blue [blu:] 1. azul; *bruise etc.* lívido, amoratado; F abatido, melancólico; *talk a* ~ *streak* F soltar la tarabilla; 2. azul *m*; ♙ añil *m*; *pol.* conservador (-a *f*) *m*; 3. azular; *washing* dar azulete a, añilar.

B

blue...: '~ **'chip** valor *m* de primera fila; '~**ber·ry** mirtilo *m*; '~**jay** cianocita *f*; '~ **'moon** cosa *f* muy rara; *once in a ~ moon* cada muerte de obispo; de Pascuas a Ramos; '~**pen·cil** marcar o corregir con lapiz azul; **'blue·print** cianotipo *m*, ferroprusiato *m*; *fig.* programa *m*, bosquejo *m*, anteproyecto *m*; **blues** *pl.* morriña *f*, murrias *f|pl.*; ♪ *música de jazz melancólica.*

bluff [blʌf] **1.** □ escarpado; *p.* brusco, francote; **2.** risco *m*, promontorio *m* escarpado; amenaza *f* que no se puede realizar, bluf *m*; fanfarronada *f*; *call s.o.'s ~* cogerle la palabra a uno; **3.** engañar, embaucar.

blu·ish ['bluːiʃ] azulado, azulino.

blun·der ['blʌndə] **1.** patochada *f*, coladura *f*, patinazo *m*; **2.** hacer una patochada *etc.*

blunt [blʌnt] **1.** □ embotado (*a. fig.*), despuntado; *fig.* obtuso, torpe; *manner* francote; **2.** embotar, despuntar; **'blunt·ness** embotamiento *m*; *fig.* brusquedad *f*, franqueza *f*.

blur [bləː] **1.** borrón *m*; contorno *m* borroso; **2.** manchar; borrar.

blurb [bləːb] *sl.* anuncio *m* efusivo.

blurt [bləːt] (~ *out*) descolgarse con.

blush [blʌʃ] **1.** rubor *m*, sonrojo *m*; color *m* de rosa; *at first ~* a primera vista; **2.** sonrojarse, ruborizarse (*at* de); ponerse colorado.

blus·ter ['blʌstə] **1.** borrasca *f* ruidosa; *fig.* jactancia *f*, fanfarronada *f*; **2.** *v|i.* (*wind etc.*) bramar; fanfarronear.

boar [bɔː] verraco *m*; *wild ~* jabalí *m.*

board [bɔːd] **1.** tabla *f*, tablero *m*; (*notice-*) tablón *m*; cartón *m for binding*; ♣ bordo *m*; ✝ *etc.* junta *f*, consejo *m* de administración; ~ *of health* junta *f* de sanidad; ~ *of trade* junta *f* de comercio; ~ *of trustees* consejo *m* de administración; ~*walk* paseo *m* entablado a la orilla del mar; **2.** *v|t.* entablar (*a. ~ up*); ♣ abordar; ₲ *etc.* subir a; *p.* dar pensión completa a.

boast [boust] **1.** jactancia *f*; baladronada *f*; **2.** jactarse (*about*, *of* de); ~ *about*, ~ *of* hacer alarde de; *fig. th.* enorgullecerse de, cacarear; **'boast·ful** □ jactancioso.

boat [bout] **1.** barca *f*, bote *m*; (*large*) barco *m*; *be in the same ~* correr los

mismos peligros; **2.** ir en bote; '~ **hook** bichero *m*; '~**house** casilla *f* para botes; **'boat·ing** canotaje *m.*

bob [bɔb] **1.** (*jerk*) sacudida *f*, meneo *m*; (*hair*) borla *f*; pelo *m* cortado corto; *sl.* chelín *m*; (*plumb-line*) plomo *m*; **2.** *v|t.* menear, sacudir; hair cortar corto; *v|i.* menearse; (*a. ~ up and down*) fluctuar.

bob·bin ['bɔbin] carrete *m* (*a.* ⚡); bobina *f* (*a.* ⚡); *sew.* canilla *f.*

bob·sled ['bɔbsled], **bob·sleigh** ['bɔbslei] trineo *m* de balancín, bobsleigh *m.*

bode [boud]: ~ *well* (*ill*) ser buena (mala) señal.

bod·ice ['bɔdis] corpiño *m*, almilla *f*; (*dress*) cuerpo *m.*

bod·i·ly ['bɔdili] **1.** *adj.* corpóreo, corporal; **2.** *adv.* corporalmente; en conjunto; *lift etc.* en peso.

bod·y ['bɔdi] cuerpo *m*; persona *f*; (*dead*) cadáver *m*; ⊕ armazón *f*; *mot.* carrocería *f*, caja *f*; *in a ~* en bloque, todos juntos; ✂ *main ~* grueso *m*; '~**guard** guardia *m* de corps; guardaespaldas *m.*

bog [bɔg] **1.** pantano *m*, ciénaga *f*; **2.**: *get ~ged down* enfangarse (*fig.* empantanarse, atrancarse.

bo·gus ['bougəs] falso, superchero.

Bo·he·mi·an [bou'hiːmjən] bohemio *adj. a. su. m* (*a f*); *fig.* bohemio *adj. a. su. m* (*a f*).

boil¹ [bɔil] ✦ divieso *m*, furúnculo *m.*

boil² [~] hervir [*a. fig.*]; *cooking*: cocer, salcochar; ~ *down* reducir por cocción; ~ *over* (*liquid*) irse; **'boil·ing** hervor *m*; cocción *f*; ~ *point* punto *m* de ebullición.

bois·ter·ous ['bɔistərəs] □ *wind etc.* borrascoso, proceloso; *p.* alborotador, bullicioso; *voices* vocinglero.

bold [bould] □ atrevido, osado; *b.s.* desenvuelto, descocado; *fig.* claro, vigoroso; **bold·face** *typ* negrilla *f*; negrita *f*; **'bold·ness** osadía *f*; *b.s.* desenvoltura *f*, descoco *m.*

bol·ster ['boulstə] **1.** (*pillow*) travesero *m*; ⊕ plancha *f* de garnitura, cojín *m*; **2.** (*mst ~ up*) sostener, reforzar; *fig.* alentar.

bolt [boult] **1.** (*door*) cerrojo *m*, pestillo *m*; ✂ saeta *f*; (*thunder-*) rayo *m*; ⊕ perno *m*; salida *f* (*or* fuga *f*) repentina (*for* para alcanzar); ~ *upright* erguido; *fig.* ~ *from the blue* acontecimiento *m* inesperado, *b.s.*

bore

rayo *m*; 2. *v/t.* door acerrojar; ⊕ sujetar con perno, empernar; F *food* engullir; *v/i.* fugarse, escaparse (*esp. horse*).

bomb [bɔm] 1. bomba *f*; (*hand*) granada *f*; *v.* atomic, incendiary *etc.*; *fig.* fall like a ~(*shell*) caer como una bomba; 2. bombardear.

bom·bard [bɔm'bɑːd] bombardear; *fig.* llenar (*with* de); **bom'bard·ment** bombardeo *m*.

bom·bast ['bɔmbæst] ampulosidad *f*, rimbombancia *f*.

bomb·er ['bɔmə] bombardero *m*.

bomb·proof ['bɔmpruːf] a prueba de bombas.

bo·na fi·de ['bɔnə'faidə] de buena fe.

bo·nan·za [bou'nænzə] F 1. *fig.* filón *m*; 2. lucrativo.

bond [bɔnd] 1. lazo *m*, vínculo *m* (*a. fig.*); ✝ obligación *f*; ✝ bono *m*; ✝ fianza *f* (de aduana); ⚓ aparejo *m*; *in* ~ en depósito; 2. ✝ obligar por fianza.

bone [boun] 1. hueso *m*; (*fish*-) espina *f*; ~s *pl. a.* esqueleto *m*; huesos *m/pl. of the dead*; ~ *of contention* manzana *f* de la discordia; *feel in one's* ~s saber a buen seguro, estar totalmente seguro de; F *have a* ~ *to pick with* tener que habérselas con; F *make no* ~s *about* no andarse con rodeos en; 2. *meat, fish* deshuesar; F (*a.* ~ *up*) quemarse las cejas, empollar.

bon·fire ['bɔnfaiə] hoguera *f*.

bon·net ['bɔnit] (*woman's*) gorra *f*, papalina *f*; (*child's*) capillo *m*.

bo·nus ['bounəs] adehala *f*; ✝ prima *f*.

bon·y ['bouni] huesudo; ✍ *etc.* huesoso.

boo [buː] 1. *speaker etc.* silbar; 2.: *not to say* ~ no decir chus ni mus.

boo·by ['buːbi] bobo *m*, mentecato *m*; *orn.* bubía *f*; ~ *prize* premio *m* de consolación; ~ *trap* trampa *f* explosiva; zancadilla *f*.

boo·hoo [buː'huː] lloriquear.

book [buk] 1. libro *m*; libreta *f for notes etc.*; libro *m* talonario *of cheques, tickets*; *bring s.o. to* ~ pedirle cuentas a una p.; ✝ *close the* ~s cerrar el borrador; 2. ✝ asentar, anotar; *artist* escriturar; *room* reservar; *ticket* sacar; F (*police*) reseñar; ~ *through to* sacar un billete hasta; ~ *case* armario *m* para libros, estante *m*; ~ *end* sujetador *m* de libros; **'book·ie** F = *bookmaker*; **'book·keep·er** tene-

dor *m* de libros; **'book·keep·ing** teneduría *f* de libros; **'book·let** folleto *m*, opúsculo *m*.

book...: **'~·mak·er** corredor *m* profesional de apuestas; **'~·mark** señal *f* de libros; **'~·plate** ex libris *m*; **'~·sell·er** librero *m*; **'~·worm** polilla *f*; *fig.* ratón *m* de biblioteca.

boom¹ [buːm] ⚓ (*jib*) botalón *m*; botavara *f*.

boom² [~] ✝ 1. auge *m*, prosperidad *f* repentina; 2. ascender (los negocios), estar en bonanza.

boom³ [~] 1. estampido *m*; 2. hacer estampido; estallar; (*voice*) resonar, retumbar.

boom·er·ang ['buːməræŋ] bumerang *m*; *fig.* lo contraproducente.

boon¹ [buːn] merced *f*, gracia *f*; (*gift*) dádiva *f*; favor *m*.

boon² [~] generoso, liberal.

boor [buə] patán *m* (*a. fig.*); tosco *m*.

boost ['buːst] 1. empujar; ✍ elevar; *fig.* promover, fomentar; ayudar; 2.: *give a* ~ *to* dar bombo a; **'boost·er** reforzador *m*; (*enthusiastic backer*) bombista *m/f*; *elec.* elevador *m* de tensión; *radio* repetidor *m*; ~ *rocket* cohete *m* lanzador; ~ *shot* inyección *f* secundaria; ~ *station* repetidor *m*.

boot¹ [buːt] ✝ 1.: *to* ~ también; 2. aprovechar.

boot² [~] 1. bota *f*; *mot.* maleta *f*; 2. patear; *sl.* ~ *out* poner en la calle; **'~·black** limpiabotas *m*.

booth [buːð] caseta *f*; (*market*) puesto *m*; *teleph.* cabina *f*.

boot...: **'~·lace** cordón *m*; **'~·leg·ger** contrabandista *m* en licores.

boo·ty ['buːti] botín *m*, presa *f*.

booze [buːz] F 1. emborracharse; borrachear; 2. bebida *f* (alcohólica); borrachera *f*.

bo·rax ['bɔːræks] bórax *m*.

bor·der ['bɔːdə] 1. borde *m*, margen *m*, orilla *f*; (*frontier*) frontera *f*; ✍ arriate *m*; *sew.* orla *f*, orilla *f*; (*embroidered etc.*) cenefa *f*; 2.: ~ *on* rayar en, frisar en; ~ *upon* lindar con, confinar con; 3. fronterizo; **'~·line** dudoso, incierto.

bore¹ [bɔː] 1. ⊕ taladro *m*, barreno *m*; ✗ calibre *m*, alma *f*; *geol.* sonda *f*; *fig.* (*p.*) pelmazo *m*, pesado (a *f*) *m*, machaca *m/f*; (*th.*) molestia *f*, lata *f*; 2. ⊕ taladrar, perforar; *fig.* aburrir; fastidiar, dar la lata a; *be*

~d **to death** aburrirse como una almeja.

bore² [~] *pret. of* bear².

bore·dom ['bɔːdəm] aburrimiento *m*, fastidio *m*.

bo·ric ac·id ['bɔːrik'æsid] ácido *m* bórico.

bor·ing ['bɔːriŋ] □ aburrido, pesado.

born [bɔːn] 1. *p.p. of* bear²; **be** ~ nacer; *I was* ~ nací; 2. *adj.* actor nato; liar innato.

borne [bɔːn] *p.p. of* bear² llevar *etc.*

bor·ough ['bʌrə] villa *f*.

bor·row ['bɔrou] pedir prestado (*of, from* a); *idea etc.* apropiarse; '**bor·row·er** prestario (a *f*) *m*, comodatorio *m*; el (la) que pide (*or* toma) prestado.

bos·om ['buzəm] seno *m* (*a. fig.*), pecho *m*; (*garment*) pechera *f*; ~ **friend** amigo (a *f*) *m* íntimo (a).

boss¹ [bɔs] ⊕ clavo *m*, tachón *m*, protuberancia *f*; △ crucería *f*.

boss² [~] F 1. jefe (a *f*) *m*, patrón (-a *f*) *m*; *esp. pol.* cacique *m*; 2. dirigir, mandar, dominar.

boss·y ['bɔsi] □ F mandón; tiránico.

bo·tan·ic, bo·tan·i·cal [bə'tænik(l)] □ botánico; '**bot·a·ny** botánica *f*.

botch [bɔtʃ] 1. chapucería *f*, chafallo *m*; 2. chapucear, chafallar.

both [bouθ] ambos, los dos, ... *and* tanto ... como *~ of them* ambos, los dos.

both·er ['bɔðə] F 1. molestia *f*, lata *f*; pejiguera *f*; 2. molestar; ~ **to** tomarse la molestia de.

bot·tle ['bɔtl] 1. botella *f*; frasco *m*; (*water-*) cantimplora *f*; (*baby's*) biberón *m*; (*scent-*) pomo *m*; F **hit the** ~ emborracharse; 2. embotellar (*a.* ~ *up*; *esp. fig.*); ~ *up emotion* contener; '~·**neck** cuello *m* (de una botella); *fig.* embotellamiento *m*; '~ **'o·pen·er** abrebotellas *m*.

bot·tom 1. fondo *m* (*a. fig.*); lecho *m*, cauce *m* of *river*; asiento *m* of *chair, bottle*; ⊕ (*ship's*) quilla *f*, casco *m*; F trasero *m*; *fig.* base *f*, fundamento *m*; **at the** ~ en el fondo; **in the other extreme**; *fig.* **at** ~ en el fondo; *fig.* **be at the** ~ **of** ser causa (*or* motivo) de; 2. ínfimo, más bajo; último; ~ *dollar* último dólar *m*.

bough [bau] rama *f*.

bought [bɔːt] *pret. a. p.p. of* buy.

boul·der ['bouldə] canto *m* rodado.

bounce [bauns] 1. (re)bote *m*; F fanfarronería *f*; 2. (re)botar; F fanfarronear; ~ *in* (*out*) entrar (salir) sin ceremonia.

bound¹ [baund] 1. *pret. a. p.p. of* bind; 2. *adj.* atado; *fig.* obligado; *fig.* ~ **to** seguro de *inf.*; ~ *up with* estrechamente relacionado con.

bound² [~]: ~ *for* con rumbo a, con destino a.

bound³ [~] 1. límite *m*, linde *m a. f.*; *in* ~**s** a raya; *out of* ~**s** fuera de los límites; *fig.* fix (*the*) ~**s** fijar los jalones; 2. limitar, deslindar.

bound⁴ [~] 1. salto *m*, brinco *m*; 2. saltar, brincar.

bound·ary ['baundəri] límite *m*, linde *m a. f.*; lindero *m*.

bound·less ['baundlis] □ ilimitado.

boun·te·ous ['bauntiəs] □, **boun·ti·ful** ['~tiful] □ liberal, generoso.

boun·ty ['baunti] munificencia *f*; ⚔ *etc.* gratificación *f*, enganche *m*; (*esp. royal*) merced *f*, gracia *f*.

bou·quet [bu'kei] 💐 ramillete *m*, ramo *m*; (*wine*) aroma *m*, nariz *f*.

bour·geois ['buəʒwɑː] burgués *adj. a. su. m* (-a *f*).

bout [baut] turno *m*, vez *f*; *fenc.* asalto *m*.

bow¹ [bau] 1. reverencia *f*, inclinación *f*; *make one's* ~ presentarse, debutar; 2. *v/i.* hacer una reverencia *f* (*to* a); *v/t.* inclinar; *fig.* agobiar.

bow² [~] ⚓ proa *f*.

bow³ [bou] 1. arco *m* (*a.* ♪); (*tie, knot*) lazo *m*; 2. ♪ hacer pasos *m* del arco.

bow·el ['bauəl] intestino *m*; ~**s** *pl.* entrañas *f/pl.* (*a. fig.*).

bowl¹ [boul] (*large*) (al)jofaina *f*, palangana *f*; (*small*) escudilla *f*, tazón *m*; *fig.* copa *f* of *wine*; hornillo *m* of *pipe*; pala *f* of *spoon*.

bowl² [~] 1. bola *f*, bocha *f*; ~**s** *sg. a. pl.* juego *m* de las bochas; 2. *v/t.* rodar; *sport:* arrojar; *v/i.* rodar; *sport:* jugar a las bochas; arrojar la pelota.

bow·leg·ged ['bou'legid] estevado.

bow-wow ['bau'wau] ¡guau!

box¹ [bɔks] 1. ♀ boj *m*; caja *f* (*a.* ⚙); (*large*) cajón *m*; cofre *m*, arca *f*; (*jewel-*) estuche *m*; ⊕ caja *f*, cojinete *m*; (*coach*) pescante *m*; *thea.* palco *m*; 2. encajonar (*a. fig.*; *esp.* ~ *up*); *compass* cuartear.

box² [~] boxear; '**box·er** boxeador *m*; *zo.* boxer *m*.

box·ing ['bɔksiŋ] boxeo *m*; '~ **gloves** *pl.* guantes *m/pl.* de boxeo; '~ **match** partido *m* de boxeo; '~ **ring** cuadrilátero *m* de boxeo.

box...: '~ **num·ber** apartado *m*; '~ **of·fice** 1. taquilla *f*; 2. *adj.* seguro de éxito popular; '~ **pleat** pliegue *m* de taquilla; '~ **pleat** pliegue *m* de tabla; '~ **seat** asiento *m* de palco; '~ **wood** boj *m*.

boy [bɔi] 1. niño *m*; muchacho *m*, chico *m*; (son) hijo *m*; (servant) criado *m*, botones *m*; 2. *adj.* joven; *v.* scout.

boy·cott ['bɔikət] 1. boicotear; 2. boicoteo *m*.

boy·hood ['bɔihud] muchachez *f*, puericia *f*; juventud *f*.

boy·ish ['bɔiiʃ] □ amuchachado; juvenil.

brace [breis] 1. ⊕ abrazadera *f*; refuerzo *m*, laña *f*; △ tirante *m*, riostra *f*; (carriage) sopanda *f*; typ. corchete *m*; ♣ braza *f*; (pair) par *m*; ~s *pl.* tirantes *m/pl.*; ~ *and bit* berbiquí *m* y barrena; 2. asegurar, reforzar; ♣ bracear; *fig.*, *esp.* ~ *o.s.* vigorizar(se); prepararse.

brace·let ['breislit] pulsera *f*, brazalete *m*.

brack·et ['brækit] 1. △ ménsula *f*, repisa *f*; (gas) mechero *m*; (light) brazo *m*; typ. corchete *m*; 2. poner entre corchetes; *fig.* asociar, agrupar.

brag [bræg] 1. fanfarronada *f*; 2. fanfarronear; ~ *of*, ~ *about* jactarse de.

brag·gart ['brægət] fanfarrón *m*.

braid [breid] 1. (hair) trenza *f*; trencilla *f*; ✕ galón *m*; 2. trenzar; galonear.

braille [breil] alfabeto *m* de los ciegos.

brain [brein] 1. cerebro *m*, sesos *m/pl.*; *fig.* (mst ~s *pl.*) intelecto *m*, cabeza *f*; *rack one's ~s* devanarse los sesos; 2. *sl.* romper la crisma a.

brain...: '~ **child** parto *m* del ingenio; '~ **drain** éxodo de técnicos; '~ **fe·ver** meningitis *f* cerebroespinal; '~ **less** □ tonto, insensato; '~ **storm** frenesí *m*; '**brain-trust** consultorio *m* intelectual; '~ **wash·ing** lavado *m* cerebral; '~ **wave** onda *f* encefálica.

braise [breiz] guisar; estofar.

brake[1] [breik] ♣ helecho *m*; soto *m*.

brake[2] [~] 1. ⊕ freno *m* (a. *fig.*); (flax) agramadera *f*; mot. rubia *f*; ~ *lining*

forro *m* del freno, guarnición *f* del freno; ~ *pedal* pedal *m* de freno; ~ *shoe* zapata *f*; 2. ⊕ frenar; flax agramar.

bram·ble ['bræmbl] zarza *f*.

bran [bræn] salvado *m*.

branch [brɑ:ntʃ] 1. ♣ rama *f*; *fig.* ramo *m*, dependencia *f*, sección *f*; brazo *m* of river; ✝ sucursal *f*; 2. (a. ~ *out*) ramificarse; ♣ echar ramas; extenderse; (a. ~ *off*) bifurcarse; separarse (from de); '**branch 'of·fice** sucursal *f*.

brand [brænd] 1. tizón *m*; ✒ etc. hierro *m* de marcar; *esp. poet.* tea *f*; poet. espada *f*; ✝ marca *f*, sello *m*; 2. marcar (con hierro candente); *fig.* tiznar (acc. de).

bran·dish ['brændiʃ] blandir.

brand-new ['brænd'nju:] enteramente nuevo, flamante.

bran·dy ['brændi] coñac *m*.

brash [bræʃ] insolente, respondón; descarado; inculto; tosco.

brass [brɑ:s] latón *m*; F pasta *f*; plancha *f* conmemorativa (de latón); *fig.* descaro *m*; ♪ *the* ~ el cobre; ~ *band* charanga *f*, banda *f*; ✕ F ~ *hat* espadón *m*; F ~ *knuckles* boxeador *m*; *sl.* ~ *tacks pl.* lo esencial; *get down to* ~ *tacks* ir al grano.

brassière ['bræsiɛə] sostén *m*.

brat [bræt] F mocoso *m*.

bra·va·do [brə'vɑ:dou] bravata *f*, baladronada *f*.

brave [breiv] 1. □ valiente, animoso; *lit.* magnífico, vistoso; 2. desafiar, arrostrar; '**brav·er·y** valor *m*, valentía *f*.

brawl [brɔ:l] 1. pendencia *f*; alboroto *m*; *poet.* murmullo *m*; 2. alborotar, armar pendencia.

brawn [brɔ:n] músculo *m*; *fig.* fuerza *f* muscular.

bray [brei] 1. rebuzno *m*; 2. rebuznar.

bra·zen ['breizn] □ de latón; *fig.* descarado.

bra·zier ['breiziə] brasero *m*.

Bra·zil-nut [brə'zil'nʌt] castaña *f* de Pará.

breach [bri:tʃ] 1. rompimiento *m* (a. *fig.*), rotura *f*; violación *f*, infracción *f* of rule; ✕ brecha *f*; ~ *of contract* infracción *f* de contrato; ~ *of faith* abuso *m* de confianza, infidencia *f*; 2. romper; ✕ abrir brecha en.

bread [bred] pan *m* (a. *fig.*); *know*

B

which side one's ~ is buttered saber a qué carta quedarse; '~ **bas·ket** panera f, cesto m para el pan; *fig.* granero m; '~**board** tablero m para cortar el pan; '~**box** caja f para pan; '~**fruit** fruto m del pan; '~ **knife** cuchillo m para cortar el pan; '~ **line** cola f del pan.

breadth [bredθ] anchura f; ♣ (*beam*) manga f; *fig.* amplitud f; tolerancia f.

bread-win·ner ['bredwinə] el (la) que se gana la vida.

break [breik] 1. ruptura f; abertura f, grieta f; pausa f, intervalo m; interrupción f; (*rest*) descanso m; (*holiday*) asueto m; (*voice*) gallo m; (*carriage*) break m; partida f *at billiards*; ✝ (*price*) baja f; ~ of day alba f; amanecer m; *without a* ~ sin parar; F *give a p. a* ~ abrirle a uno la puerta; 2. [*irr.*] v/t. romper, quebrantar (a. *fig.*); ⚡ interrumpir; *bank* quebrar; *horse* domar, amansar; *impact* amortiguar, suavizar; *news* comunicar; v/i. arruinar; *record* batir, superar; ✎ abrir (*freq. fig.*: ~ *new ground* emprender algo nuevo); ~ *down* derribar; *destruir;* ~ *in* forzar, romper; ~ *in pieces* hacer pedazos; ~ *up* desmenuzar; v/i. romperse, quebrantarse; (*bank*) hacer bancarrota; (*day*) reventar; (*day*) apuntar; (*health*) desfallecerse; (*voice*) mudar; ~ *away* desprenderse; separarse; ~ *down* perder la salud, decaer; prorrumpir en lágrimas; *mot.*, ⊕ tener averías; ~ *out* (*war*) estallar; ✎ declararse; ~ *up* hacerse pedazos; disolverse; v. a. *broken;* '**break·a·ble** quebradizo, frágil; '**break·down** ✎ colapso m; ✎ (*nervous*) crisis f nerviosa; interrupción f, cesión f.

break...: ~**fast** ['brekfəst] 1. desayuno m; 2. desayunar(se); ~**neck** ['breiknek] precipitado; arriesgado; *at* ~ *speed* a mata caballo; '~**through** ✕ ruptura f; *fig.* descubrimiento m sensacional; '~**up** desmoronamiento m; desintegración f; disolución f.

breast [brest] pecho m (a. *fig.*); seno m; *fig.* corazón m; pechuga f *of bird;* *make a clean* ~ *of* confesar con franqueza.

breast...: '~**bone** esternón m; '~**plate** peto m; '~**stroke** brazada f de pecho.

breath [breθ] aliento m, respiración f; (*animals*) hálito m (a. *poet.* = *breeze*); (*pause*) respiro m, pausa f; *out of* ~ sin aliento; *short of* ~ corto de resuello; *under one's* ~ en voz baja; *waste one's* ~ *on* gastar saliva en.

breathe [bri:ð] v/i. respirar (a. *fig.*); (*heavily*) resollar; aspirar (~ *in*); v/t. inspirar, respirar; exhalar; sugerir; v. *last, word;* '**breath·er** respiro m.

breath·ing ['bri:ðiŋ] respiración f.

breath·less ['breθlis] □ falto de aliento.

breath-tak·ing ['breθteikiŋ] □ *speed* vertiginoso; pasmoso.

bred [bred] *pret. a. p.p. of breed.*

breech [bri:tʃ] ⊕ recámara f; **breeches** ['~iz] *pl.* calzones *m/pl.*

breed [bri:d] 1. casta f, progenie f; raza f. 2. [*irr.*] v/t. criar, engendrar; *fig.* ocasionar, producir; educar; v/i. reproducirse; '**breed·er** criador (-a f) m; ~ *reactor* reactor-generador m; '**breed·ing** cría f; crianza f (a. *fig.*).

breeze [bri:z] brisa f; F bronca f.

breez·y ['bri:zi] □ ventilado; (*windy*) ventoso; *p.* animado, jovial.

breth·ren ['breðrin] hermanos *m/pl.*

brev·i·ty ['breviti] brevedad f.

brew [bru:] 1. v/t. hacer, preparar; *fig.* urdir; v/i. prepararse; (*storm*) amenazar; 2. poción f, brebaje m; mezcla f; '**brew·er** cervecero m; '**brew·er·y** fábrica f de cerveza.

bribe [braib] 1. soborno m, cohecho m; 2. sobornar, cohechar; '**brib·er·y** soborno m, cohecho m.

brick [brik] 1. ladrillo m; F *a regular* ~ un buen sujeto; 2. (*mst* ~ *up*) cerrar (con ladrillos); '~**bat** trozo m de ladrillo.

brid·al ['braidl] 1. □ nupcial; 2. *mst poet.* boda f.

bride [braid] novia f, desposada f; '~**groom** novio m, desposado m; '**brides·maid** madrina f de boda, pronuba f.

bridge¹ [bridʒ] 1. puente m (a. ♪); (*nose*) caballete m; (*billiards*) violín m; 2. tender un puente sobre.

bridge² [~] *cards:* bridge m.

bridge·head ['bridʒhed] cabeza f de puente.

bri·dle ['braidl] 1. brida f, freno m; 2. v/t. enfrenar; *fig.* refrenar, reprimir; v/i. levantar la cabeza; *fig.* picarse (*at* por); *fig.* erguirse; '~**path** camino m de herradura.

brief [bri:f] **1.** □ breve, conciso; *(fleeting)* fugaz, pasajero; **2.** epítome *m*, resumen *m*; *(papal)* breve *m*; ⚖ escrito *m*, memorial *m*; *hold a ~ for* abogar por *(a. fig.)*; '**~ case** cartera *f*; '**~ing** órdenes *f/pl.*; *(of the press)* informe *m*; reunión *f* en que se dan las órdenes.

bri·gade [bri'geid] brigada *f*.

bright [brait] **1.** □ luminoso, brillante; *surface* lustroso, pulido; *color* subido; *fig. (cheerful)* vivo, alegre; *(clever)* listo, talentoso; '**bright·en** *v/t.* pulir, abrillantar; *fig.* mejorar, avivar, animar; *v/i. (freq. ~ up)* avivarse, animarse; mejorar; '**brightness** claridad *f*, brillantez *f*; resplandor *m*; lustre *m*; lo subido *of color*; *fig.* viveza *f*; talento *m*, viveza *f* de ingenio.

brill [bril] rodaballo *m*.

bril·liance [ˈbriljəns] *or* **bril·lian·cy** [ˈbriljənsi] brillantez *f*, brillo *m*; '**bril·liant 1.** □ brillante, refulgente; *fig.* excelente, sobresaliente; *(showy)* vistoso; **2.** brillante *m*.

brim [brim] **1.** borde *m*, orilla *f*; ala *f of hat*; **2.** *(a. ~ over)* rebosar *(with de; a. fig.)*; '**~·ful, '~·full** lleno hasta el borde; rebosante *(with de)*; '**~·less** *hat* sin ala.

brim·stone [ˈbrimstən] azufre *m*.

brine [brain] salmuera *f*.

bring [briŋ] llevar; traer; conducir; ⚖ *charge* exponer; ⚖ *suit* entablar, armar; *~ about* ocasionar, originar; *~ along* llevar consigo; *~ away* llevarse; *~ back* devolver; *p., th.* volver con; *~ down price* rebajar; *~ derribar; thea. ~ down the house* hacer que se venga abajo el teatro; *~ forth* dar a luz, parir; *fig.* producir; *~ forward* presentar; *date* adelantar; † llevar a otra cuenta; *~ s.t. home to s.o.* hacer que alguien se dé cuenta de algo; *~ in* presentar; *fashion etc.* introducir; *income etc.* producir, rendir; *p.* hacer entrar; *verdict* dar; *~ off* ⚖ exculpar; *success* conseguir; *~ on* causar, inducir; *~ out th.* sacar, hacer salir; *book* sacar a luz, publicar; *p.* hacer más afable, ayudar a adquirir confianza; *~ round (win over)* ganar, convertir; ✗ hacer volver en sí; *~ a p. to do s.t.* inducir a alguien a hacer algo; *~ o.s. to inf.* resignarse a *inf.*, cobrar suficiente ánimo para *inf.*; ⚓ *~ to* ponerse en facha; *~ together* reunir; *enemies* re-

conciliar; *~ under* sojuzgar, someter; *~ up p.* criar, educar; *subject* sacar a colación; *(stop)* parar; ✗ vomitar, arrojar.

brink [briŋk] borde *m*, orilla *f*; *fig. on the ~* of a punto de.

brin·y [ˈbraini] salado, salobre.

brisk [brisk] **1.** □ enérgico, vigoroso; despejado; animado, activo; *gait etc.* gallardo, airoso; **2.** *(mst ~ up)* avivar, animar.

bris·tle [ˈbristl] **1.** cerda *f*; **2.** erizarse; *fig. (freq. ~ up)* montar en cólera; *fig.* estar erizado *(with de)*.

Brit·ish [ˈbritiʃ] británico; inglés; *the ~ pl.* los ingleses.

brit·tle [ˈbritl] quebradizo, frágil.

broach [broutʃ] **1.** asador *m*; *(spire)* aguja *f*; ⊕ broca *f*; **2.** *cask* espitar; *fig.* mencionar por primera vez.

broad [brɔːd] □ ancho, amplio; extenso, vasto; *outline etc.* claro, explícito; *(coarse)* grosero; *story* verde; *mind, view* liberal, tolerante; *accent* marcado, cerrado; *~ly* en general; '**~·cast 1.** ✗ sembrado al vuelo; *fig.* diseminado, divulgado; **2.** *[irr. (cast)]* *v/t.* ✗ sembrar al vuelo; *fig.* diseminar, divulgar; *radio:* emitir, radiar; *v/i.* hablar *etc.* por la radio; *~ing* radiodifusión *f*; *~ing station* emisora *f*; **3.** *radio:* emisión *f*, programa *m*; '**~·cloth** paño *m* fino; '**broad·en** ensanchar(se); '**broad-'mind·ed** liberal, tolerante; de miras amplias; '**broadness** anchura *f*; *esp. fig.* amplitud *f*; liberalismo *m*, tolerancia *f*.

broad...: '**~·side** ⚓ andanada *f*.

bro·cade [brəˈkeid] brocado *m*.

broc·co·li [ˈbrɔkəli] brécol *m*.

bro·chure [ˈbrɔʃjuə] folleto *m*.

broil [brɔil] asar sobre ascuas *(or a la parrilla)*; tostar *(al sol)*; '**broil·er** pollo *m* para asar.

broke [brouk] *pret. of break; sl.* sin blanca.

bro·ken [ˈbroukən] *p.p. of break; adj.* quebrado accidentada, desigual; *health* estropeado, deshecho; *language* chapurreado; *voice* cascado; *(despairing)* desesperado; '**~·hearted** traspasado de dolor; '**bro·ken·ly** con la voz cascada; acongojado.

bro·ker [ˈbroukə] † corredor *m*; † agente *m* de negocios; prendero *m*; '**bro·ker·age**, '**bro·king** corretaje *m*.

bron·chi·al [ˈbrɔŋkiəl] bronquial;

bron·chi·tis [brɔŋˈkaitis] bronquitis *f*.

bronze [brɔnz] **1.** bronce *m* (*a. fig.*); **2.** *attr.* de bronce; **3.** *v/t.* broncear; F (*beat*) zurrar.

brooch [brout∫] broche *m*.

brood [bru:d] **1.** camada *f*, cría *f*; *fig.* progenie *f*; **2.** empollar; *fig.* ~ on, ~ over rumiar *acc.*; meditar *acc.* melancólicamente.

brook[1] [bruk] arroyo *m*.

brook[2] [~] *lit.* (*mst negative*) sufrir, aguantar.

broom [bru:m] escoba *f*; ♥ hiniesta *f*, retama *f*; **~·stick** [ˈbrumstik] palo *m* de escoba.

broth [brɔθ] caldo *m*.

broth·el [ˈbrɔθl] burdel *m*, lupanar *m*.

broth·er [ˈbrʌðə] hermano *m* (*a. fig.*). **~·hood** [ˈ~hud] fraternidad *f*; (*a. guild*) hermandad *f*; **'~-in-law** cuñado *m*; **'broth·er·ly** fraternal.

brought [brɔːt] *pret. a. p.p. of* **bring**.

brow [brau] ceja *f*; (*forehead*) frente *f*; cumbre *f* of hill; knit one's ~ fruncir las cejas; **'~·beat** [*irr.* (*beat*)] intimidar (con palabras); (*dominate*) imponerse a.

brown [braun] **1.** pardo, castaño, moreno; *bread* moreno; *paper* de embalar, de estraza; *shoes* de color; ~ *sugar* azúcar *f* terciada; **2.** color *m* pardo *etc.*; **3.** (*skin etc.*) broncear(se); poner(se) moreno; *cooking:* dorar (-se); *sl.* be ~ed off estar harto (with de).

browse [brauz] **1.** pimpollos *m/pl.*; **2.** herbajar; ramonear, rozar (on *acc.*); *fig.* leer por gusto.

bruise [bru:z] **1.** contusión *f*, cardenal *m*, magulladura *f*; **2.** magullar; (*batter*) majar, machacar.

bru·nette [bru:ˈnet] morena, trigueña *adj. a. su. f*.

brunt [brʌnt]✕ embate *m*, acometida *f*; *fig.* bear the ~ of aguantar lo más recio de.

brush [brʌ∫] **1.** cepillo *m*; (*large*) escoba *f*; *paint.* pincel *m*, brocha *f*; (*fox*) rabo *m*; ⚡ escobilla *f*; ✕ escaramuza *f*; = **~·wood**; (*stroke*) pincelada *f*; *give a p. a* ~ cepillar a una *p.*; *have a* ~ *with a p.* desavenirse con una *p.*; **2.** *v/t.* (a)cepillar; rozar *in passing*; ~ *aside* echar a un lado; ~ *away*, ~ *off* quitar con cepillo (*or* con la mano); ~ *down* (a)cepillar, limpiar, almohazar; ~ *up* acicalar; *fig.* repasar, refrescar; *v/i.*:

~ *against* rozar; ~ *by*, ~ *past* pasar rozando (*or* muy cerca); **'~·wood** matorral *m*, breñal *m*.

brusque [brusk] ☐ brusco, rudo.

bru·tal [ˈbru:tl] ☐ brutal; feroz; **bru·tal·i·ty** [bruˈtæliti] brutalidad *f*; ferocidad *f*; **brute 1.** brutal; bruto; **2.** bruto *m*, bestia *f*; monstruo *m*.

bub·ble [ˈbʌbl] **1.** burbuja *f*, ampolla *f*; *fig.* bagatela *f*; **2.** burbujear, borbotar; ~ *over fig.* rebosar (with de).

buck [bʌk] *zo.* gamo *m*; (*goat*) macho *m* cabrío; (*rabbit*) conejo *m* macho; (*p.*) petimetre *m*; *sl.* dólar *m*; F *pass the* ~ echar la carga a otro; **2.** *v/i.* corcovear; F ~ *up* animarse, cobrar ánimo; F ~ *up!* ¡apúrate!; *v/t.* F hacer frente a; F embestir, arrojarse sobre; F ~ *up* animar.

buck·et [ˈbʌkit] cubo *m*, balde *m*; ⊕ paleta *f*; F *a drop in the* ~ una nonada; *sl.* kick the ~ estirar la pata.

buck·le [ˈbʌkl] **1.** hebilla *f*; **2.** *v/t.* hebillar; ~ *to* doblarse, encorvarse; ~ *down to* (*prp.*) dedicarse con empeño a.

buck...: **'~·shot** balines *m/pl.*; perdigón *m* zorrero; **'~·skin** cuero *m* de ante; **'~·wheat** alforfón *m*.

bud [bʌd] **1.** pimpollo *m*, brote *m*; chica *f* que se presenta en la sociedad; *in* ~ en brote; *fig.* nip in the ~ cortar de raíz; **2.** *v/t.* ✿ injertar de escudete; *v/i.* brotar, echar pimpollos.

bud·dy [ˈbʌdi] F camarada *m*, compinche *m*.

budge [bʌdʒ] mover(se); he did not dare to ~ no osaba bullirse.

budg·et [ˈbʌdʒit] **1.** presupuesto *m*; *attr.* presupuestario; **2.** *v/i.*: ~ *for* presupuestar; **'budg·et·ar·y** presupuestario.

buff [bʌf] **1.** piel *f* de ante; in (one's) ~ en cueros; **2.** color de ante.

buf·fa·lo [ˈbʌfələu], *pl.* **buf·fa·loes** [ˈ~z] búfalo *m*.

buff·er [ˈbʌfə] 🚃 tope *m*; amortiguador *m*; F mastuerzo *m*; ~ *state* estado *m* tapón.

buf·fet[1] [ˈbʌfit] **1.** bofetada *f*; golpe *m*; **2.** abofetear; golpear.

buf·fet[2] [ˈbufei] 🍴 fonda *f*, cantina *f*; (*sideboard*) aparador *m*; (*meal*) ambigú *m*.

buf·foon [bʌˈfu:n] bufón *m*; **buf·'foon·er·y** bufonada *f*.

bug [bʌg] chinche *f*; *esp.* bicho *m*,

insecto *m*; *sl.* microbio *m*; *sl.* estorbo *m*, traba *f*; **'bug·gy 1.** lleno de chinches; **2.** calesa *f*.

bu·gle[1] ['bju:gl] ♪ corneta *f*.

bu·gle[2] [∼] abalorio *m*.

bu·gler ['bju:glə] corneta *m*.

build [bild] **1.** [*irr.*] construir, fabricar; *fig.* edificar (on sobre); fundar, establecer, componer; ⊕ ∼ in emportar; ∼ up componer *from parts*; armar; ✠ fortalecer; *fig.* crear; **2.** estructura *f*; *anat.* talle *m*; **'build·er** arquitecto *m*; constructor *m*; maestro *m* de obras; **'build·ing** edificio *m*; construcción *f*; *attr.* de construcción; relativo a edificios; ∼ lot solar *m*; ∼ site terreno *m* para construir; ∼ trades *pl.* oficios *m*/*pl.* de edificación; **'build-up** composición *f*, acumulación *f*; *fig.* propaganda *f* previa.

built [bilt] *pret. a. p.p. of* build 1; **'built-'in** ⚙ empotrado; ⊕ incorporado, montado; ⚡ interior; **'built-'up** urbanizado.

bulb [bʌlb] ♣ bulbo *m*; ⚡ bombilla *f*; ampolleta *f of thermometer*.

bulge [bʌldʒ] **1.** bombeo *m*, comba *f*, pandeo *m*; **2.** bombearse, combarse.

bulk [bʌlk] bulto *m*, volumen *m*; grueso *m*; *fig.* la mayor parte; ⚓ carga *f*; in ∼ a granel.

bull[1] [bul] **1.** *zo.* toro *m*; ✝ *sl.* alcista *m*; *Am. sl.* detective *m*, policía *m*; take the ∼ by the horns irse a la cabeza del toro; *attr.* macho; **2.** ✝ *sl.* jugar al alza; *sl.* chapucear.

bull[2] [∼] *eccl.* bula *f*.

bull[3] [∼] disparate *m*.

bull·dog ['buldɔg] dogo *m*.

bull·doze ['buldouz] ⱻ intimidar; *opposition* arrollar; **'bull·doz·er** empujadora *f* niveladora, motoniveladora *f*.

bul·let ['bulit] bala *f* (de fusil); **'∼-proof** a prueba de balas, blindado.

bul·le·tin ['bulitin] boletín *m*; anuncio *m*; ∼ board tablón *m* de anuncios; tablilla *f*.

bull...: **'∼-fight** corrida *f* de toros; **'∼-finch** camachuelo *m*; **'∼-frog** rana *f* toro; **'∼-head·ed** obstinado, terco.

bul·lion ['buljən] oro *m* (or plata *f*) en barras (or lingotes); (*fringe*) entorchado *m*.

bull's-eye ['bulzai] centro *m* del blanco; ⚓ cristal *m* de patente, portilla *f*.

bul·ly ['buli] **1.** matón *m*, valentón *m*; **2.** intimidar, tiranizar.

bul·rush ['bulrʌʃ] junco *m*; espadaña *f*.

bul·wark ['bulwək] baluarte *m* (*a. fig.*); ⚓ macarrón *m*.

bum [bʌm] F **1.** (*p.*) holgazán *m*, vagabundo *m*; **2.** holgazanear, vagabundear; **3.** *sl.* inferior, chapucero; feel ∼ sentirse muy malo.

bum·ble-bee ['bʌmblbi:] abejorro *m*.

bump [bʌmp] **1.** topetón *m*; batacazo *m in falling*; sacudida *f*; (*lump etc.*) chichón *m*, hinchazón *f*; protuberancia *f*; comba *f on surface*; **2.** chocar contra, topetar (*a.* ∼ against); F ∼ into *p.* topar; *sl.* ∼ off asesinar, despenar; **bump·er** ['bʌmpə] tope *m*; 🚗 *a.* mot. parachoques *m*; copa *f* llena; *attr.* muy grande, abundante.

bump·kin ['bʌmpkin] patán *m*.

bump·y ['bʌmpi] abollado; *land* desigual; *air* agitado; *road* lleno de baches.

bun [bʌn] bollo *m*; (*hair*) moño *m*.

bunch [bʌntʃ] **1.** manojo *m*, atado *m*; ramo *m of flowers*; racimo *m of grapes*; F grupo *m*; F montón *m*; **2.** agrupar, juntar.

bun·dle ['bʌndl] **1.** lío *m*, bulto *m*; legajo *m of papers*; haz *f of sticks*; **2.** *v/t.* arropar, envolver (*mst* ∼ up); *v/i.* escaparse, irse.

bun·ga·low ['bʌŋgəlou] bungalow *m*, casa *f* de campo.

bun·gle ['bʌŋgl] **1.** chapucería *f*; **2.** chapucear.

bun·ion ['bʌnjən] hinchazón *f* en el pie, juanete *m*.

bunk[1] [bʌŋk] *sl.* palabrería *f*, música *f* celestial.

bunk[2] [∼] camastro *m*, tarima *f* para dormir; F cama *f*.

bunk·er ['bʌŋkə] (*coal*) carbonera *f*; ⚓ pañol *m* del carbón.

bun·ny ['bʌni] conejito *m*.

bun·ting[1] ['bʌntiŋ] *orn.* escribano *m*; corn ∼ triguero).

bun·ting[2] [∼] ⊕ estameña *f*; ⚓ etc. banderas *f*/*pl.*, empavesado *m*.

buoy [bɔi] **1.** boya *f*; **2.** abøyar; ∼ up mantener a flote; *fig.* alentar.

buoy·an·cy ['bɔiənsi] fluctuación *f*, facultad *f* de flotar; ⚡ fuerza *f* ascensional; **'buoy·ant** □ boyante; *fig.* alegre, animado; ✝ al alza.

bur [bə:] ♣ erizo *m*; *fig.* persona *f* muy pegadiza.

bur·den ['bə:dn] **1.** carga *f* (*a. fig.*),

B

gravamen m; ⚓ arqueo m; ⚓ peso m de la carga; 2. cargar (a. fig.; with de); '**bur·den·some** oneroso, gravoso.

bu·reau [bjuəˈrou], pl. a. **bu·reaux** [ˈ‑z] escritorio m; oficina f, agencia f; ramo m, departamento m; **bu·reauc·ra·cy** [‑ˈrɔkrəsi] burocracia f; **bu·reau·crat** [ˈbjuəroukræt] burócrata m/f; **bu·reau·crat·ic** □ burocrático.

bur·glar [ˈbəːglə] escalador m; '**∼ alarm** alarma f de ladrones; '**∼‑proof** a prueba de escaladores; **bur·gla·ry** [ˈ‑əri] allanamiento m de morada.

bur·i·al [ˈberiəl] entierro m; '**∼‑ground** cementerio m.

bur·lap [ˈbəːlæp] harpillera f.

bur·lesque [ˈbəːˈlesk] 1. burlesco, festivo; 2. parodia f; 3. parodiar.

bur·ly [ˈbəːli] membrudo, fornido.

burn [bəːn] 1. quemadura f; Scot. arroyo m; 2. [irr.] v/t. quemar; (sun) abrasar; ⊕ fuel funcionar con; house etc. (a. ∼ down) incendiar; ⚡ ∼ out fundir, quemar; ∼ up consumir (a. fig.); with con, en); v/i. quemar(se); arder; incendiarse (a. ∼ down); ∼ out apagarse; ⚡ fundirse; quemarse; ∼ up consumirse; arder mejor; fig. ∼ with arder en (or de); the light is ∼ing la luz está encendida; '**burn·er** mechero m; (gas etc.) quemador m, fuego m; '**burn·ing** □ ardiente (a. fig.).

bur·nish [ˈbəːniʃ] bruñir.

burnt [bəːnt] pret. a. p.p. of burn 2; ∼ almond almendra f dulce tostada; ∼ offering holocausto m.

bur·row [ˈbʌrou] 1. madriguera f; (rabbit's) conejera f; 2. socavar; (a. ∼ through) horadar.

burst [bəːst] 1. reventón m; estallido m; (leak) fuga f; ✕ ráfaga f of fire; fig. arranque m, ímpetu m; 2. [irr.] v/i. reventar(se); estallar (a. fig.); ∼ into room irrumpir en; tears prorrumpir en, deshacerse en; threats etc. desatarse en; ∼ out laughing echarse a reír; ∼ with laughing reventar de risa; v/t. reventar; romper.

bur·y [ˈberi] enterrar, sepultar; fig. ocultar.

bus [bʌs] F autobús m; sl. miss the ∼ perder la ocasión; '**∼‑boy** ayudante m de camarero; '**∼ driv·er** conductor m de autobús; '**∼ stop** parada f de autobús.

bush [buʃ] arbusto m; matorral m; ⊕ forro m de metal; **bush·el** [ˈbuʃl] medida de áridos (American = 35.24 litros; British = 36.36 litros); **bush·y** [ˈbuʃi] p. peludo; ground matoso.

busi·ness [ˈbiznis] negocio m, comercio m; (firm) empresa f; negocios m/pl.; (calling) empleo m, ocupación f; (matter) asunto m, cuestión f; big ∼ comercio m en gran escala; on ∼ de negocios; ∼ connections pl. relaciones f/pl. comerciales; ∼ deal trato m comercial; ∼ district barrio m comercial; ∼ hours pl. horas f/pl. de oficina; ∼ trip viaje m de negocios; do ∼ with comerciar con; have no ∼ to inf. no tener derecho a inf.; F mean ∼ actuar (or hablar) en serio; mind one's own ∼ no meterse donde no le llaman; '**∼‑like** metódico, eficaz; negocioso; '**∼‑man** hombre m de negocios; '**∼ suit** traje m de calle.

bust[1] [bʌst] busto m; pecho m de mujer.

bust[2] [∼] F 1. reventón m; ✝ fracaso m; go ∼ quebrar; 2. romper(se), entropear(se).

bus·tle [ˈbʌsl] 1. bullicio m, animación f; (esp. crowd) bulla f; (dress) polisón m; 2. v/i. menearse, apresurarse; (a. ∼ about) bullir; v/t. impeler (a trabajar etc.).

bus·y [ˈbizi] 1. □ ocupado (at, with en); activo; b.s. entrometido; bullicioso; place muy concurrido, de mucha actividad; keep ∼ (v/t.) ocupar, (v/i.) estar ocupado; 2. (mst ∼ o.s.) ocupar(se) (about, at, in with en, de, con); '**∼‑body** buscavidas m/f, entrometido (a f) m.

but [bʌt] 1. cj. pero, mas (lit.); (after negative) sino; sino que; que no subj. (e.g., not so busy ∼ he can come no tan ocupado que no pueda venir); he never walks ∼ he falls nunca anda sin caer; 2. prp. excepto; solamente; I cannot ∼ inf. no puedo menos de inf.; v. last; ∼ for a no ser por; 3. adv. solamente; v. all; nothing ∼ nada más que; ∼ little muy poco; 4. su. pero m, objeción f.

butch·er [ˈbutʃə] 1. carnicero m (a. fig.); asesino m; 2. cattle matar; dar muerte a; '**∼ knife** cuchilla f de carnicero; '**∼ shop** carnicería f.

but·ler [ˈbʌtlə] despensero m; mayordomo m.

butt[1] [bʌt] 1. cabo m, extremo m;

mocho *m*; culata *f* of gun; colilla *f* of *cigarette*; ⊕ cabeza *f* de biela; (*target*) blanco *m*; *fig.* hazmerreír *m*; cabezada *f with head*; 2. dar cabezadas (*v/t.* contra); F ~ in interrumpir; *b.s.* entrometerse.

butt² [~] tonel *m*.

but·ter ['bʌtə] 1. mantequilla *f*; 2. untar con mantequilla; F (*a.* ~ up) lisonjear; '~**cup** ranúnculo *m*; '~**fin·gered** desmañado en coger (la pelota *etc.*); '~**fly** mariposa *f* (*a. fig.*); '~**milk** leche *f* de manteca; '**but·ter·y** despensa *f*.

but·tock ['bʌtək] nalga *f* (*mst pl.*).

but·ton ['bʌtn] 1. botón *m* (*a.* ♀); 2. abotonar (*a.* ~ up); '~**hole** 1. ojal *m*; 2. *sew.* abrir ojales en; *fig.* obligar a escuchar.

but·tress ['bʌtris] 1. contrafuerte *m* (*a. geog.*); *fig.* sostén *m*, apoyo *m*; flying ~ arbotante *m*; 2. apoyar, reforzar (*a. fig.*).

bux·om ['bʌksəm] rolliza; frescachona.

buy [bai] [*irr.*] *v/t.* comprar (*from* a); *fig.* (*a.* ~ off) comprar, sobornar; ~ *out partner* comprar la parte de; ~ *up* ⊕ acaparar; *v/i. mst* ~ *and sell* traficar, comerciar; '**buy·er** comprador (-a *f*) *m*; '**buy·ing** compra *f*.

buzz [bʌz] 1. zumbido *m*; 2. *v/i.* zumbar; ~ *about* cazcalear; '~ **bomb** bomba *f* volante; '~ **saw** sierra *f* circular.

buz·zard ['bʌzəd] ratonero *m* común, águila *f* ratonera.

buzz·er ['bʌzə] ⚡ zumbador *m*.

by [bai] 1. *prp.* por; *norm* según, de acuerdo con; (*in respect of*) de; (*time*) ~ *day* de día; ~ *3 o'clock* para las 3; ~ *now* ya, ahora; ~ *then* para entonces; antes de eso; *day* ~ *day* día por día; (*place*) ~ *me* cerca de mí, a mi lado; *north* ~ *east* norte por este; *side* ~ *side* lado a lado; (*manner*) ~ *easy stages* en cortas etapas; ~ *leaps and bounds* a pasos agigantados; ~ *lamplight* a la luz de una lámpara; ~ *land* por tierra; *the dozen fig.* a docenas; ~ *twos* en pares; ♈ (*multiplication*) por; ~ *far*, ~ *half* con mucho; ~ *o.s.* solo; ~ *the* ~ a propósito; ~ *the way* de paso; a propósito; 2. *adv.* cerca; a un lado; aparte; ~ *and* ~ luego, pronto; ~ *and large* de un modo general; *close* ~ cerca; 3. *adj.* secundario, incidente.

bye·bye ['bai'bai] F ¡adiosito!; (*lulling children*) ¡ro ro!

by...: '~**gone** 1. pasado; 2. ~*s pl.*: *let* ~ *be* ~ olvidemos lo pasado; '~**law** estatuto *m*, reglamento *m*; '~**pass** 1. desviación *f*; ⊕ tubo *m* de paso; 2. desviar; evitar (*a. fig.*); '~**prod·uct** subproducto *m*; 🜂 derivado *m*; '~**stand·er** espectador (-a *f*) *m*, circunstante *m/f*; '~**word** objeto *m* de burla (*or* aprobio); refrán *m*; *be a* ~ *for* ser notorio por.

C

cab [kæb] taxi *m*.
cab·a·ret ['kæbərei] cabaret *m*.
cab·bage ['kæbidʒ] col *f*; repollo *m*.
cab·by ['kæbi] F taxista *m*.
cab·in ['kæbin] cabaña *f*; ⚓ camarote *m*; *lorry*, ✈ cabina *f*; '~ **boy** mozo *m* de cámara; grumete *m*.
cab·i·net ['kæbinit] vitrina *f*; armario *m*; (*radio*) caja *f*; *pol.* gabinete *m*, consejo *m* de ministros; *medicine* ~ botiquín *m*; '~ **mak·er** ebanista *m*.
ca·ble ['keibl] 1. ⚓, *tel.* cable *m* (*a.* F); 2. cablegrafiar; '~**gram** cablegrama *m*.
cab·stand ['kæbstænd] parada *f* de taxis.

cache [kæʃ] escondite *m*; ~ *of arms* alijo *m* de armas.
ca·chet ['kæʃei] sello *m*; *fig.* marca *f* de distinción.
cack·le ['kækl] 1. cacareo *m*; risa *f* aguda; *sl.* cháchara *f*; 2. cacarear; *sl.* chacharear.
cac·tus ['kæktəs] cacto *m*.
cad [kæd] F sinvergüenza *m*, pillo *m*.
cad·dy ['kædi] cajita *f* para té.
ca·dence ['keidəns] cadencia *f*; compás *m*.
ca·det [kə'det] cadete *m*; hijo *m* menor.
cadge [kædʒ] *v/t.* obtener mendigando; *v/i.* gorronear.
ca·fé ['kæfei] café *m*; restaurante *m*.

caf·e·te·ri·a [kæfi'tiəriə] cafetería f.

caf·fe·ine ['kæfiːn] cafeína f.

cage [keidʒ] **1.** jaula f (a. ⚔); **2.** enjaular.

cage·y ['keidʒi] ☐ F astuto, taimado; cauteloso, reservado.

cais·son ['keisn] ⚒ cajón m; ⊕ cajón m hidráulico; ⚓ cajón m de suspensión.

ca·jole [kə'dʒoul] halagar, camelar; ~ s.o. into s.t. conseguir por medio de halagos que una p. haga algo.

cake [keik] **1.** pastelillo m, bollo m; bizcocho m; (soap) pastilla f; sl. take the ~ ganar el premio; ser el colmo; **2.** apelmazarse; endurecerse.

ca·lam·i·tous [kə'læmitəs] ☐ calamitoso; **ca·lam·i·ty** calamidad f.

cal·ci·fy ['kælsifai] calcificar(se); **cal·ci·um** ['~siəm] calcio m.

cal·cu·late ['kælkjuleit] v/t. calcular; ~d to inf. aprestado para inf.; v/i. calcular, conjeturar; ~ on contar con; calculating machine máquina f de calcular; sumadora f; **cal·cu·la·tion** cálculo m, calculación f.

cal·en·dar ['kælində] calendario m; lista f; ~ month mes m del año.

cal·en·der [~] ⊕ **1.** calandria f; **2.** calandrar.

calf [kɑːf], pl. **calves** [kɑːvz] ternero m; fig. F bobo m; (or '~·leath·er) piel f de becerro; anat. pantorrilla f.

cal·i·brate ['kælibreit] calibrar.

cal·i·co [kælikou] calicó m.

calk [kɔːk] **1.** poner ramplones; **2.** ramplón m (a. **calk·in** ['kælkin]).

call [kɔːl] **1.** llamada f; grito m; visita f (pay back); ⚖⚖ citación f; ⚔ toque m, llamada f; (bird's, birdcatcher's) reclamo m; hunt. chilla f; ✝ demanda f; fig. (~ to) obligación f (a, de), necesidad f (de); thea. llamamiento m; demanda f (for por); ~ girl prostituta f, mujer f de lujo; ✝ ~ money dinero m a la vista; radio: ~ sign indicativo m; port of ~ puerto m de escala; on ~ disponible; ✝ a solicitud; within ~ al alcance de la voz; v/t. llamar; meeting convocar; invitar; calificar de; considerar, juzgar; roll pasar; llamar por teléfono; cards: (bid) marcar; poker: exigir la exposición de una mano; attention llamar (to sobre, a); be ~ed llamarse; ~ back hacer volver; teleph. volver a llamar; ~ down pedir al cielo; F regañar; ~ forth sacar; protest originar, motivar; ~ in

p. hacer entrar; police llamar; pedir la ayuda de; thing issued retirar; ~ off cancelar, abandonar; ~ together convocar; ~ up memory evocar; teleph. llamar; ⚔ llamar (al servicio militar); v/i. llamar (a. teleph.), dar voces; venir; hacer una visita; ~ at house etc. pasar por; ⚓ port hacer escala en; ~ for ir (or venir) por; exigir; pedir; ~ on acudir a (for en busca de).

call·ing ['kɔːliŋ] vocación f, profesión f; acción f de llamar etc.; ~ card tarjeta f de visita.

cal·lis·then·ics [kælis'θeniks] mst sg. calistenia f.

cal·lous ['kæləs] ☐ calloso; fig. duro, insensible.

cal·low ['kælou] inexperto, sin plumas.

call-up [kɔːl'ʌp] movilización f; servicio m militar; llamamiento m.

calm [kɑːm] **1.** ☐ weather calmoso, bonancible; p. etc. tranquilo, sosegado; **2.** calma f; tranquilidad f, sosiego m; v. dead; **3.** (a. ~ down) calmar(se); tranquilizar(se), sosegar(se); ~ down! ¡tente quieto!

came [keim] pret. of come.

cam·el ['kæml] zo. a. ⚓ camello m.

ca·mel·li·a [kə'miːlje] camelia f.

cam·e·o ['kæmiou] camafeo m.

cam·er·a ['kæmərə] máquina f (fotográfica); cámara f (de televisión); in ~ en secreto; '~·man camarógrafo m, tomavistas m.

cam·ou·flage ['kæmuflɑːʒ] **1.** camuflaje m; **2.** camuflar.

camp [kæmp] **1.** campamento m; ~-bed catre m de tijera; ~-chair, ~ stool silla f plegadiza; **2.** acampar; F alojarse temporalmente.

cam·paign [kæm'pein] **1.** campaña f; election ~ campaña f electoral; **2.** hacer campaña (for a favor de).

cam·phor ['kæmfə] alcanfor m.

cam·pus ['kæmpəs] recinto m (de la Universidad).

cam·shaft ['kæmʃɑːft] árbol m de levas.

can¹ [kæn] [irr.] puedo; sé; etc.

can² [~] **1.** lata f, bote m; vaso m (de lata); **2.** enlatar, conservar; sl. poner en la calle; sl. carry the ~ pagar el pato; ~·ning industry industria f conserva.

ca·nal [kə'næl] canal m (a. ⚛).

ca·nar·y [kə'nɛəri] canario m.

can·cel ['kænsl] v/t. cancelar (a. fig.); stamp matar; v/i. ℛ ~ out destruirse;

capture

can·cel·la·tion [kænseˈleiʃn] cancelación f, supresión f.

can·cer [ˈkænsə] *ℳ* cáncer m; ♀ ast. Cáncer m; **ˈcan·cer·ous** canceroso.

can·did [ˈkændid] ☐ franco; ~ly francamente.

can·di·date [ˈkændidit] candidato m (for para); opositor (-a f) m; **can·di·da·ture** [~ʃə] candidatura f.

can·died [ˈkændid] azucarado.

can·dle [ˈkændl] candela f, bujía f; vela f; eccl. cirio m; ~ power bujía f; **ˈcan·dle·stick** candelero m; (low) palmatoria f.

can·dor [ˈkændə] candor m; franqueza f.

can·dy [ˈkændi] **1.** azúcar m cande; bombón m, dulce m; ~ floss caramelo m americano; **2.** v/t. azucarar; v/i. cristalizarse.

cane [kein] ♀ caña f; ♀ caña f de azúcar; (stick) bastón m; school: palmeta f; ~ chair silla f de mimbre.

ca·nine [ˈkeinain] **1.** canino; **2.** canino m, colmillo m (a. ~ tooth).

can·is·ter [ˈkænistə] bote m, lata f.

canned [kænd] envasado; en lata; sl. ~ music música f en discos.

can·ner·y [ˈkænəri] fábrica f de conservas alimenticias.

can·ni·bal [ˈkænibl] **1.** caníbal m; **2.** antropófago.

can·non [ˈkænən] ✕ cañón m; artillería f; billiards: carambola f.

can·not [ˈkænɔt] no puedo; no sé; etc.

can·ny [ˈkæni] ☐ Scot. astuto, frugal, económico.

ca·noe [kəˈnuː] **1.** canoa f; **2.** pasear en canoa.

can·on [ˈkænən] canon m; (p.) canónigo m; typ. gran canon m; ~ law derecho m canónico.

can·o·py [ˈkænəpi] dosel m; ♙ baldaquin m; cielo m of bed.

cant [kænt] lenguaje m insincero, gazmoñería f; (jargon) jerga f, germanía f.

can't [~] = cannot.

can·ta·loup [ˈkæntəluːp] cantalupo m, melón m.

can·tan·ker·ous [kənˈtæŋkərəs] ☐ F arisco, intratable; quejumbroso.

can·teen [kænˈtiːn] cantina f; (bottle) cantimplora f.

can·ter [ˈkæntə] **1.** medio galope m; **2.** andar a medio galope.

can·vas [ˈkænvəs] cañamazo m, lona f; paint. lienzo m; under ~ en tiendas.

can·vass [~] **1.** solicitación f (esp. de votos); sondeo m; escrutinio m, pesquisa f; **2.** v/t. escudriñar; votes solicitar; opinion sondear; v/i. solicitar.

cap [kæp] gorra f; (with peak) gorra f de visera; (cover) tapa f, tapón m; caballete m of chimney; ⊕ casquete m; ♣ tamborete m; cápsula f of gun, bottle; ~ and bells gorro m con campanillas; ~ and gown toga f y bonete; ~ in hand con el sombrero en la mano; the ~ fits viene de perilla; polar ~ casquete m polar; put on one's thinking ~ meditarlo bien.

ca·pa·bil·i·ty [keipəˈbiliti] capacidad f, habilidad f; **ˈca·pa·ble** ☐ capaz (of de), hábil.

ca·pac·i·ty 1. capacidad f; mot. cilindrada f; in my ~ as en mi calidad de; **2.** attr. máximo; thea. lleno.

cape[1] [keip] geog. cabo m, promontorio m.

cape[2] [~] capa f, esclavina f.

cap·il·lar·y [kəˈpiləri] **1.** capilar; **2.** tubo m (or vaso m) capilar.

cap·i·tal [ˈkæpitl] **1.** ☐ capital; ✝ de capital; F excelente, magnífico; **2.** ✝ capital m; (town) capital f; ♙ capitel m; typ. (or ~ letter) mayúscula f; fig. make ~ out of aprovechar; **ˈcap·i·tal·ism** capitalismo m; **ˈcap·i·tal·ist** capitalista m/f; **cap·i·tal·is·tic** capitalista; **cap·i·tal·ize** capitalizar; typ. escribir (or imprimir) con mayúscula; ~ on aprovecharse de.

ca·pit·u·late [kəˈpitjuleit] capitular.

ca·price [kəˈpriːs] capricho m; **ca·pri·cious** [kəˈpriʃəs] ☐ caprichoso, caprichudo.

Cap·ri·corn [ˈkæprikɔːn] Capricornio m.

cap·size [kæpˈsaiz] v/i. volcar, zozobrar; v/t. tumbar, volcar.

cap·sule [ˈkæpsjuːl] ♀ a. *ℳ* cápsula f.

cap·tain [ˈkæptin] capitán m.

cap·tion [ˈkæpʃn] **1.** encabezamiento m; pie m; film: subtítulo m; **2.** intitular.

cap·tious [ˈkæpʃəs] ☐ criticón, reparador; quisquilloso; falso.

cap·ti·vate [ˈkæptiveit] fig. cautivar, fascinar; **ˈcap·tive** cautivo adj. a. su. m (a f); **cap·tiv·i·ty** [~ˈtiviti] cautiverio m.

cap·tor [ˈkæptə] apresador (-a f) m; **cap·ture** [~ˈtʃə] **1.** apresamiento m; captura f; toma f of city etc.; (p.) prisionero (a f) m; presa f; **2.** apresar, capturar; *city etc.* tomar; *fig.* captar.

car [kɑː] coche *m*, carro *m S.Am.*; *(tram-)* tranvía *m*; 🚃 vagón *m*, coche *m*.

ca·rafe [kəˈrɑːf] garrafa *f*.

car·a·mel [ˈkærəmel] caramelo *m*.

car·at [ˈkærət] quilate *m*.

car·a·van [kærəˈvæn] caravana *f*; carricoche *m*; *mot.* remolque *m*.

car·a·way [ˈkærəwei] alcaravea *f*.

car·bide [ˈkɑːbaid] carburo *m*.

car·bine [ˈkɑːbain] carabina *f*.

car·bo·hy·drate [ˈkɑːbouˈhaidreit] 🌾 hidrato *m* de carbono *m*; 🧪 carbohidrato *m*, fécula *f*.

car·bol·ic ac·id [kɑːˈbɔlikˈæsid] ácido *m* carbólico.

car·bon [ˈkɑːbən] carbono *m*; 💧 carbón *m*; *(a. ~ paper)* papel *m* carbón; *~ copy* copia *f* al carbón.

car·bun·cle [ˈkɑːbʌŋkl] *min.* carbunclo *m*; 🧪 carbunco *m*; F grano *m*.

car·bu·re·tor [ˈkɑːbjuretə] carburador *m*.

car·cass [ˈkɑːkəs] cadáver *m* (de un animal); res *f* muerta; *(frame)* armazón *f*.

card¹ [kɑːd] ⊕ **1.** carda *f*; **2.** *wool* cardar.

card² [~] *(playing-)* carta *f*; 🃏 *etc.* tarjeta *f*, postal *f*; *(index)* ficha *f*; F *(tipo m)* salado *m*; ~ *catalogue* catálogo *m* de fichas, fichero *m*; ~ *game* juego *m* de naipes; *game of* ~*s* partida *f* de cartas; *like a house of* ~*s* como un castillo de naipes; F *on the* ~*s* probable; *have a* ~ *up one's sleeve* tener ayuda en reserva; *put one's* ~*s on the table* poner las cartas boca arriba.

card·board [ˈkɑːdbɔːd] cartón *m*; ~ *box* caja *f* de cartón.

car·di·ac [ˈkɑːdiæk] cardíaco *m*.

car·di·nal [ˈkɑːdinl] **1.** ☐ cardinal; **2.** cardenal *m (a. orn.)*.

card...: '~ **in·dex** fichero *m*; '~**sharp·er** fullero *m*.

care [kɛə] **1.** cuidado *m*, solicitud *f*; esmero *m*, atención *f*; cargo *m*, custodia *f*; ~ *of (abbr* c/o*)* ... a manos de; *in care of* cuidado; *take* ~ tener cuidado; *take* ~ *of* cuidar de; F atender a; *with* ~ ¡atención!; ¡cuidado!; **2.** tener cuidado; ~ *about* preocuparse de (*or* por); ~ *for* cuidar de; *(love)* querer, amar; desear; ¿ *I don't* ~ *for that* no me gusta eso; ~ *to* tener ganas de; *would you* ~ *to say?* ¿quiere Vd. decirme?; F *I don't* ~ *(twopence etc.)* ¡no se me da

un bledo! *(for* de*)*; *well* ~*d for* bien cuidado.

ca·reen [kəˈriːn] ⚓ carenar; volcar, inclinar.

ca·reer [kəˈriə] **1.** carrera *f*; ~ *diplomat* diplomático *m* de carrera; **2.** correr a carrera tendida.

care·free [ˈkɛəfriː] despreocupado.

care·ful [ˈkɛəful] ☐ cuidadoso; esmerado; cauteloso; *appearance* acicalado; *be* ~ *to inf.* poner diligencia en *inf.*

care·less [ˈkɛəlis] ☐ descuidado, desatento, desaplicado; alegre, sin cuidado.

ca·ress [kəˈres] **1.** caricia *f*; **2.** acariciar *(a. fig.)*.

care·tak·er [ˈkɛəteikə] custodio *m*, conserje *m*; guardesa *f*.

care·worn [ˈkɛəwɔːn] agobiado de inquietudes.

car·fare [ˈkɑːfɛə] pasaje *m*.

car·go [ˈkɑːgou] carga *f*, cargamento *m*; *mixed (or general)* ~ carga *f* mixta.

car·i·ca·ture [ˈkærikətjuə] **1.** caricatura *f*; *(newspaper)* dibujo *m*; **2.** caricaturizar.

car·nage [ˈkɑːnidʒ] carnicería *f*, mortandad *f*; ¹**car·nal** ☐ carnal; **car·na·tion** [~ˈneiʃn] **1.** clavel *m*; **2.** encarnado.

car·ni·val [ˈkɑːnivl] carnaval *m*; fiesta *f*, feria *f*.

car·ol [ˈkærl] **1.** villancico *m*; **2.** cantar villancicos.

carp¹ [kɑːp] *ichth.* carpa *f*.

carp² [~] criticar, censurar; ~ *at* quejarse de.

car·pen·ter [ˈkɑːpintə] **1.** carpintero *m*; **2.** carpintear.

car·pet [ˈkɑːpit] **1.** alfombra *f*, tapete *m*; F *be on the* ~ estar sobre el tapete; F ser reprobado; **2.** alfombrar; *fig.* cubrir, revestir; F reprobar; '**car·pet·ing** alfombrado *m*.

car·riage [ˈkæridʒ] carruaje *m*; 🚃 vagón *m*; ⚔ cureña *f*; † porte *m*; ⊕ carro *m*; *(bearing)* andares *m/pl.*, modo *m* de andar.

car·ri·er [ˈkæriə] porteador *m*, trajinante *m*; empresa *f* de transportes; ⚓ porta(a)viones *m*; 🧪 portador (-a *f*) *m*; *radio:* onda *f* portadora; '~**pi·geon** paloma *f* mensajera.

car·rot [ˈkærət] zanahoria *f*.

car·ry [ˈkæri] **1.** *v/t.* llevar, traer; transportar; llevar encima *on p.*; *goods* acarrear; *burden* sostener; *prize, election* ganar, lograr; ⚔ *for-*

tress conquistar, tomar; *proposition* hacer aceptar; ✝ *stock* tener en existencia; (*extend*) extender, llevar más lejos; ⚓ llevar; *fig.* comprender, implicar; *v. day, effect, weight; ~ o.s.* andar (con garbo *etc.*); ~ *along* llevar consigo; ~ *away* llevarse; *fig.* encantar, arrebatar; ~ *everything before one* arrollarlo todo; ✝ ~ *forward* pasar; ~ *off* llevarse; (*kill*) matar; ~ *s.t. off well* salir airoso; ~ *on* continuar; *esp.* ✝ dirigir; promover; ~ *out (or through) plan* realizar, llevar a cabo; *repairs* hacer; ~ *over* guardar para más tarde; ✝ pasar; ~ *through p.* sostener hasta el fin; *v/i.* (*reach*) alcanzar; ~ *on* continuar; F (*complain*) quejarse sin motivo; (*misbehave*) travesar; insistir; machacar (*about on*); ~ *on* ¡adelante!; ¡siga!; F ~ *on with* tener un amorío con; ~*ing capacity* capacidad *f* de carga; ⚔ alcance *m*.

cart [kɑ:t] **1.** carro *m*, carreta *f*; ~ *horse* caballo *m* de tiro; *hand* ~ carretilla *f*, carretón *m*; *fig.* *put the* ~ *before the horse* trastrocar las cosas; **2.** carretear.

car·tel [ˈkɑːtel] ✝ *a.* ⚔ cartel *m*.

car·ti·lage [ˈkɑːtilidʒ] cartílago *m*.

car·ton [ˈkɑːtən] caja *f* de cartón, envase *m*.

car·toon [kɑːˈtuːn] **1.** *paint.* cartón *m*; caricatura *f*, dibujo *m*; *film*: dibujo *m* animado; **2.** caricaturizar.

carve [kɑːv] *meat* trinchar; *stone etc.* esculpir, tallar (*in en*); *fig.* ~ *one's way through* hacerse un camino por.

carv·ing [ˈkɑːviŋ] acción *f* de trinchar; ⚓ *etc.* escultura *f*; obra *f* de talla.

cas·cade [kæsˈkeid] cascada *f*.

case[1] [keis] **1.** caja *f* (*a. typ.*); estuche *m*; funda *f*; (*window etc.*) marco *m*, bastidor *m*; (*cartridge- etc.*) cápsula *f*; (*glass*) vitrina *f*; *typ. lower* ~ caja *f* baja; *upper* ~ caja *f* alta; **2.** encajonar; enfundar.

case[2] [~] caso *m* (*a.* ♟ *a. gr.*); 🏛 causa *f*, pleito *m*; F persona *f* divertida; *argumento m convincente; a* ~ *for* una razón por; *have a strong* ~ tener un argumento fuerte; *as the* ~ *may be* según el caso; *in* ~ en caso (que); *por si acaso; in* ~ *of* en caso de; *in any* ~ en todo caso; *in such a* ~ en tal caso.

cash [kæʃ] **1.** dinero *m* contante; pago *m* al contado; ~ *down, for* ~ al contado; *in* ~ en metálico; *be out of* ~ estar sin blanca; ~ *payment* pago *m* al

contado; ~ *on delivery* pagar contra recepción; ~ *register* caja *f* registradora; **2.** *check* cobrar, hacer efectivo; F ~ *in on* sacar provecho de; **cash·ier** [kæˈʃiə] **1.** cajero (*a f*) *m*; **2.** destituir; degradar.

cash·mere [kæʃˈmiə] casimir *m*.

ca·si·no [kəˈsiːnou] casino *m*.

cask [kɑːsk] tonel *m*, barril *m*.

cas·ket [ˈkɑːskit] cajita *f*, cofrecito *m*; ataúd *m*.

cas·se·role [ˈkæsəroul] cacerola *f*.

cast [kɑːst] **1.** echada *f*; lance *m* of net; molde *m*, forma *f*; *fig.* apariencia *f*, estampa *f*; *thea.* reparto *m*, personal *m*; ⊕ pieza *f* fundida; ✝ balance *m*; (*eye*) mirada *f* or bizca; (*color*) tinte *m*; **2.** [*irr.*] *v/t.* echar, lanzar; desechar; *eyes* volver; *shadow* proyectar; ⊕ fundir; *thea. parts* repartir; *lots* echar; *sum* (*a.* ~ *up*) calcular, sumar; ~ *iron* hierro *m* colado; ~ *steel* acero *m* colado; ~ (*a th.*) *in a p.'s teeth* echar a uno en la cara; ~ *away* desechar, abandonar; ♻ *be* ~ *away* ser un náufrago; ~ *down* derribar; *fig.* desanimar; *eyes* bajar; ~ *forth* despedir; ~ *loose* soltar; ~ *off* abandonar; ~ *on* (*knitting*) empezar con; ~ *out* arrojar; despedir; *v/i.* (*fishing*) lanzar, arrojar; ⊕ fundir; ~ *about for* buscar; ♻ ~ *off* desamarrar.

cas·ta·net [kæstəˈnet] castañuela *f*.

caste [kɑːst] casta *f*; *lose* ~ desprestigiarse.

cas·ti·gate [ˈkæstigeit] castigar.

cast·i·ron [ˈkɑːstˈaiən] hecho de hierro fundido; *fig.* fuerte, duro.

cas·tle [ˈkɑːstl] **1.** castillo *m*; *chess*: torre *f*, roque *m*; ~ *in Spain* castillo *m* en el aire; **2.** *chess*: enrocar.

cas·tor[1] [ˈkɑːstə] *pharm.* castóreo *m*; *sl.* sombrero *m*; ~ *oil* aceite *m* de ricino.

cas·tor[2] [~] ruedecilla *f* de mueble; vinagrera *f*; ~ *pl.* angarillas *f/pl.*

cas·trate [kæsˈtreit] castrar; **cas'tra·tion** castración *f*.

cas·u·al [ˈkæʒjuəl] ☐ casual; descuidado, indiferente; **'cas·u·al·ty** accidente *m*; ⚔ baja *f*; víctima *f*.

cat [kæt] gato *m*; azote *m* con nueve ramales; F *let the* ~ *out of the bag* revelar el secreto, cantar.

cat·a·clysm [ˈkætəklizm] cataclismo *m*.

cat·a·comb [ˈkætəkoum] catacumba *f*.

cat·a·log, *a.* **cat·a·logue** [ˈkætələg] **1.** catálogo *m*; fichero *m*; **2.** catalogar.

cat·a·lyst ['kætəlist] catalizador *m*.
cat·a·pult ['kætəpʌlt] catapulta *f*; honda *f*.
cat·a·ract ['kætərækt] catarata *f* (*a. ♣*).
ca·tas·tro·phe [kə'tæstrəfi] catástrofe *f*; **cat·a·stroph·ic** [kætə'strɔfik] □ catastrófico.
cat·call ['kætkɔːl] **1.** rechifla *f*, silba *f*; **2.** rechiflar, silbar.
catch [kætʃ] **1.** cogida *f*; presa *f*, botín *m*; pesca *f* (*of fish*); (*lock*) pestillo *m*, aldabilla *f*; *♪* canon *m* de carácter cómico; (*deceit*) trampa *f*; **2.** *irr.*] *v/t.* coger, atrapar; agarrar, asir; *fig.* comprender; llegar a oír; *fig.* sorprender; *breath* suspender; *~* it merecerse un regaño; *~ in the act* coger con las manos en la masa; *~* cold, fire, hold etc.; F *~ out p.* cazar, sorprender; coger en una falta; *~ up p.* alcanzar; *th.* asir; **3.** *v/i.* enredarse, engancharse; ⊕ engranar; (*fire*) encenderse; *♣ be ~ing* ser contagioso; *~ at* tratar de asir (*or* coger); *~ on* prender en; F coger el tino; caer en la cuenta; *~ up fig.* ponerse al día; *~ up with* alcanzar, emparejar con; **'catch·er** *sport*: receptor *m*, parador *m*; **'catch·ing** *♣* contagioso, atrayente; *♪* pegajoso.
cat·e·chism ['kætikizm] catecismo *m*; (*method*) catequismo *m*.
cat·e·go·ry ['kætigəri] categoría *f*.
ca·ter ['keitə]: *~ for* abastecer, proveer; *fig.* proveer a; **'ca·ter·er** abastecedor *m*; proveedor *m*; **'ca·ter·ing** abastecimiento *m*.
ca·ter·pil·lar ['kætəpilə] oruga *f*.
cat·gut ['kætgʌt] cuerda *f* de tripa.
ca·the·dral [kə'θiːdrl] catedral *f*.
cath·ode ['kæθoud] cátodo *m*; *~ ray tube* tubo *m* de rayos catódicos.
cath·o·lic ['kæθəlik] **1.** □ *eccl.* católico; liberal, de amplias miras; **2.** católico (*a f*) *m*; **ca·thol·i·cism** catolicismo *m*.
cat·sup ['ketsəp; kætsəp] salsa *f* de tomate condimentada.
cat·tle ['kætl] ganado *m* (vacuno).
cau·cus ['kɔːkəs] camarilla *f* política.
caught [kɔːt] *pret. a. p.p. of catch 2 a.* 3.
caul·dron ['kɔːldrən] calderón *m*.
cau·li·flow·er ['kɔliflauə] coliflor *f*.
caulk [kɔːk] calafatear; **'caulk·er** calafate *m*.
cause [kɔːz] **1.** causa *f* (*a. ⚖*); *make*

common ~ with hacer causa común con; **2.** causar.
cau·tion ['kɔːʃn] **1.** cautela *f*; (*warning*) amonestación *f*; F persona *f* extraordinaria; *~ money* caución *f*; **2.** advertir, amonestar.
cau·tious ['kɔːʃəs] □ cauteloso, precavido.
cav·al·cade [kævl'keid] cabalgata *f*.
cav·a·lier [kævə'liə] **1.** caballero *m*; galán *m*; **2.** altivo, desdeñoso.
cav·al·ry ['kævlri] caballería *f*.
cave [keiv] **1.** cueva *f*; **2.** *~ in: v/i.* hundirse, derrumbarse; *v/t.* F quebrar.
cave·man ['keivmæn] troglodita *m*; hombre *m* de las cavernas.
cav·ern ['kævən] caverna *f*, antro *m*.
cav·il ['kævil] **1.** crítica *f*, reparo *m*; **2.** sutilizar, criticquizar; *~ at, about* poner peros a.
cav·i·ty ['kæviti] cavidad *f*.
ca·vort [kə'vɔːt] cabriolar.
caw [kɔː] **1.** graznar; **2.** graznido *m*.
cease [siːs] *v/i.* cesar (*from* de); *~ from* dejar de; *v/t.* suspender, cesar; **'~ fire** cese *m* de hostilidades; **'cease·less** □ incesante.
ce·dar ['siːdə] cedro *m*.
cede [siːd] ceder.
ceil·ing ['siːliŋ] techo *m*, cielo *m* raso; *≼* techo *m*; *fig.* punto *m* más alto; *~ price* precio *m* tope.
cel·e·brate ['selibreit] celebrar (*a. eccl.*); **'cel·e·brat·ed** célebre, famoso (*for* por); **cel·e·bra·tion** celebración *f*; (*party*) reunión *f*.
ce·leb·ri·ty [si'lebriti] celebridad *f* (*a. p.*).
cel·er·y ['seləri] apio *m*.
ce·les·tial [si'lestjəl] celestial (*a. fig.*).
cel·i·ba·cy ['selibəsi] celibato *m*.
cell [sel] (*prison*) celda *f*; *biol.* célula *f*; *pol.* célula *f* (de comunistas); *⚡* elemento *m*; (*bees*) celdilla *f*.
cel·lar ['selə] **1.** sótano *m*; (*wine*) bodega *f*; **2.** embodegar.
cel·lo·phane ['seləfein] (papel *m*) celofán *m*.
ce·ment [si'ment] **1.** cemento *m*; **2.** cementar; *fig.* consolidar.
cem·e·ter·y ['semitri] cementerio *m*.
cen·sor ['sensə] **1.** censor *m*; **2.** censurar; **cen·sor·ship** ['~ʃip] censura *f*.
cen·sure ['senʃə] **1.** censura *f*; **2.** censurar.
cen·sus ['sensəs] censo *m*.
cent [sent] centavo *m* (= $^1/_{100}$ dólar); *per ~* por ciento.

cen·ten·ni·al [sen'tenjəl] centenario *adj. a. su. m.*

cen·ti... ['senti] '~**grade** centígrado; '~**gramme** centigramo *m;* '~**me·ter** centímetro *m;* '~**pede** ['~pi:d] ciempiés *m.*

cen·tral ['sentrəl] □ central; ~ *heat·ing* calefacción *f* central; '**cen·tral·ize** centralizar.

cen·ter ['sentə] 1. centro *m;* ~ *forward* delantero *m* centro; ~ *half* medio centro *m;* 2. central; 3. concentrarse (*on, about* en); ⊕ ~ *punch* punzón *m* de marcar.

cen·trif·u·gal [sen'trifjugl] □ centrífugo.

cen·tu·ry ['sentʃuri] siglo *m.*

ce·ram·ic [si'ræmik] cerámico; **ce·ram·ics** *pl.* cerámica *f.*

ce·re·al ['siəriəl] cereal *adj. a. su. m.*

cer·e·bral ['seribrəl] cerebral.

cer·e·mo·ni·al [seri'mounjəl] □ ceremonial *adj. a. su. m;* **cer·e·mo·ny** ['serimənı] ceremonia *f; Master of Ceremonies* maestro *m* de ceremonias.

cer·tain ['sə:tn] □ cierto; *know for* ~ saber a buen seguro; *make* ~ asegurarse (de), cerciorarse (de); ~*ly* ciertamente; sin falta; '**cer·tain·ty** certeza *f.*

cer·tif·i·cate 1. [sə'tifikit] certificado *m,* título *m;* ~ *of baptism* (*death, marriage*) partida *f* de bautismo (defunción, casamiento); 2. [sə'tifikeit] certificar; **cer·ti·fy** ['~fai] certificar; garantizar.

ces·sa·tion [se'seiʃn] cesación *f;* ~ *of hostilities* suspensión *f* de hostilidades.

cess·pool ['sespu:l] pozo *m* negro.

chafe [tʃeif] 1. *v/t.* rozar, raer; calentar (frotando); *fig.* irritar, enfadar; 2. *v/i.* desgastarse (*against* contra); *fig.* irritarse, enfadarse; *chafing dish* escalfador *m.*

chaff [tʃæf] 1. barcia *f,* aechaduras *f/pl.; b.s.* broza *f,* desecho *m;* (*banter*) zumba *f,* chanza *f;* 2. *p.* zumbarse de, dar chasco a.

cha·grin ['ʃægrin] 1. desazón *f,* disgusto *m;* 2. desazonar, apesadumbrar.

chain [tʃein] 1. cadena *f; phys.* ~ *reaction* reacción *f* en cadena; ~ *store* tienda *f* de una cadena; 2. encadenar; '~**gang** cadena *f* de presidiarios, collera *f,* cuerda *f* de presos; '~ **re·ac·tion** reacción *f* en cadena; '~

smoke fumar un pitillo tras otro; '~ **store** empresa *f* con una cadena de tiendas; tienda *f* de una cadena de tiendas.

chair [tʃeə] 1. silla *f;* cátedra *f* (*a. professorial* ~); presidencia *f of meet·ing; take the* ~ presidir; 2. *p. in authority* asentar; llevar en una silla; *meeting* presidir; '~**man,** '~**wom·an** presidente *m;* '~**man·ship** presidencia *f.*

chalk [tʃɔ:k] *geol.* creta *f;* tiza *f for drawing; French* ~ jaboncillo *m* de sastre; esteatita *f.*

chal·lenge ['tʃælindʒ] 1. desafío *m* (*a. fig.*), reto *m;* ✗ quién vive *m;* ⚖ recusación *f;* 2. desafiar (*a. fig.*), retar; ✗ dar el quién vive *m;* ⚖ recusar; disputar; dudar; '**chal·leng·er** desafiador (-a *f*) *m;* retador (-a *f*) *m.*

cham·ber ['tʃeimbə] cámara *f;* recámara *f of gun; lit.* aposento *m;* ~ *music* música *f* de cámara; ~*s pl.* despacho *m* de un abogado (*or* juez).

champ¹ [tʃæmp] morder; mordiscar.

champ² [~] campeón *m.*

cham·pagne [ʃæm'pein] champaña *m.*

cham·pi·on ['tʃæmpjən] 1. campeón *m* (*a. fig.*); paladín *m* (*of a cause etc.*); 2. defender; abogar por; '**cham·pi·on·ship** campeonato *m.*

chance [tʃɑ:ns] 1. ocasión *f,* oportunidad *f;* posibilidad *f,* probabilidad *f;* suerte *f;* riesgo *m; by* ~ por casualidad; *stand a* ~ tener una probabilidad (*of* de); *take a* (*or one's*) ~ aventurarse; *take no* ~*s* obrar con cautela; 2. casual; fortuito; 3. *v/i.* acontecer, suceder; ~ *upon* tropezar con; *v/t.* F arriesgar.

chan·de·lier [ʃændi'liə] araña *f* (de luces).

change [tʃeindʒ] 1. cambio *m;* transformación *f;* muda *f of clothing;* (*a. small* ~) moneda *f* suelta; (*money returned*) vuelta *f;* 2. *v/t.* cambiar; transformar; (*replace*) reemplazar; *clothes, opinion* cambiar de; *color* demudarse; ~ *places* trocarse (*with* con); ~ *the subject* volver la hoja; *v/i.* cambiar, mudar; 🚂 transbordar, hacer transbordo.

chan·nel ['tʃænl] 1. canal *m* (*a. radio*); brazo *m of river;* (*irrigation-*) cacera *f; fig.* vía *f;* 2. acanalar; *fig.* encauzar.

chant [tʃɑ:nt] 1. canto *m* llano;

(*talking*) sonsonete *m*; 2. cantar (el canto llano).

cha·os ['keiɔs] caos *m*; **cha'ot·ic** □ caótico.

chap¹ [tʃæp] 1. grieta *f*, hendedura *f*; 2. agrietar(se).

chap² [~] mandíbula *f*, quijada *f*.

chap³ [~] F tipo *m*, pájaro *m*.

chap·el ['tʃæpl] capilla *f*; templo *m*.

chap·er·on ['ʃæpəroun] 1. acompañanta *f* de señorita, carabina *f*; 2. acompañar (a una señorita), ir de carabina.

chap·lain ['tʃæplin] capellán *m*.

chap·ter ['tʃæptə] capítulo *m*; *eccl. mst* cabildo *m*.

char·ac·ter ['kæriktə] carácter *m*; *thea.* personaje *m*; F tipo *m*, sujeto *m*; *in* ~ conforme al tipo; **char·ac·ter'is·tic** 1. □ característico; propio (of de); 2. característica *f*; distintivo *m*.

cha·rade [ʃəˈrɑːd] charada *f*.

char·coal ['tʃɑːkoul] carbón *m* vegetal; carboncillo *m* for drawing.

charge [tʃɑːdʒ] 1. carga *f* of gun (*a.* ⚡); *fig.* cargo *m*; ✕ carga *f*; *eccl.,* ⚖ exhortación *f*, exhorto *m*; ⚖ acusación *f*; (*price*) precio *m*; *heraldry*: blasón *m*; ~*s pl.* coste *m*; honorarios *m/pl.*; *in* ~ of *p.* a cargo de; *th.* encargado de; *free of* ~ gratis; *give a p. in* ~ entregar a la policía; *take* ~ *of* hacerse cargo de; ~ *account* cuenta *f* corriente; 2. *v/t.* cargar (*a.* ✕, ⚡); *price* cobrar; *ordenar,* mandar (*to inf.*); *p.* cargar (*with* con, de); *v/i.* cobrar (*freq.* mucho).

char·i·ot ['tʃæriət] carro *m* romano, carro *m* de guerra.

char·i·ta·ble ['tʃæritəbl] □ caritativo; benéfico.

char·i·ty ['tʃæriti] caridad *f*; *out of* ~ por caridad.

char·la·tan ['ʃɑːlətən] charlatán *m*, curandero *m*.

charm [tʃɑːm] 1. hechizo *m*, encanto *m*; amuleto *m*; *fig.* encanto *m*; ~*s pl.* hechizos *m/pl. of woman*; 2. hechizar, encantar (*a. fig.*); ~ *away* hacer desaparecer como por magia; llevarse misteriosamente; **'charm·ing** □ encantador.

chart [tʃɑːt] 1. ⚓ carta *f* de marear; tabla *f*, cuadro *m*; 2. poner en una carta de marear; ~ *a course* trazar un derrotero.

char·ter ['tʃɑːtə] 1. carta *f*; carta *f* de privilegio, encartación *f*; 2. estatuir; *ship* fletar; *bus etc.* alquilar.

chase¹ [tʃeis] 1. caza *f*; persecución *f*; *give* ~ dar caza; 2. perseguir; ~ *after* ir en pos de; *fig.* ir tras; ~ *away* ahuyentar.

chase² [~] grabar; *jewel* engastar.

chase³ [~] *typ.* rama *f*.

chasm ['kæzm] grieta *f*; sima *f*; *fig.* abismo *m*.

chas·sis ['ʃæsi] chasis *m*, armazón *f*.

chaste [tʃeist] □ casto; *fig.* castizo, sin adorno.

chas·ten ['tʃeisn] castigar; *style* acendrar, apurar (*mst p.p.*); templar; ~*ed p.* escarmentado.

chas·tise [tʃæsˈtaiz] *lit.* castigar.

chas·ti·ty ['tʃæstiti] castidad *f*.

chat [tʃæt] 1. charla *f*, palique *m*; 2. charlar.

chat·ter ['tʃætə] 1. (*p.*) chacharrear; (*birds*) chirriar; (*teeth*) castañetear; 2. cháchara *f*; chirrido *m*; castañeteo *m*.

chauf·feur ['ʃoufə] chófer *m*.

cheap [tʃiːp] □ barato; (*selling cheap*) baratero; *fig.* de mal gusto, chabacano; F *feel* ~ sentirse avergonzado; *hold* ~ despreciar; **'cheap·en** abaratar; *fig.* desprestigiar; ~ *o.s.* aplebeyarse; **'cheap·skate** *sl.* tacaño (a *f*) *m*.

cheat ['tʃiːt] 1. trampa *f*, fraude *m*; (*p.*) tramposo (a *f*) *m*, petardista *m/f*; 2. trampear, petardear; defraudar; estafar ([*out*] *of acc.*); **'cheat·ing** trampa *f*, engaño *m*.

check [tʃek] 1. parada *f* (súbita); rechazo *m*, repulsa *f* (*a.* ✕); impedimento *m* (*on* para), estorbo *m* (*on* a); control *m*, inspección *f* (*on* de); (*luggage*) talón *m*; billete *m* de reclamo, ficha *f* in games; ⊕ tope *m*; (*square*) cuadro *m*; (*cloth*) paño *m* a cuadros; *chess*: jaque *m*; jaque *m*; cuenta *f*; *hold in* ~ contener, refrenar; 2. parar, rechazar, repulsar; impedir, estorbar; controlar, inspeccionar; *document* compulsar; *facts* comprobar; *baggage* facturar; *chess*: dar jaque a; ~ *in* inscribir el nombre (en el registro de un hotel); ~ *up* comprobar, verificar (*on acc.*); **'~·book** talonario *m* de cheques; **'check·ers** *pl.* juego *m* de damas; **'check girl** moza *f* de guardarropa; **'check·ing** control *m*, verificación *f*; **'check(·ing) ac·count** cuenta *f* corriente; **'check(·ing)-room** guardarropa *f*; **'check·mate** 1. mate *m*; 2. dar mate a; **'check·out** *from a hotel* salida *f*; *time* hora *f* de salida; *in a self-service retail store* revisión *f* de pago; **'check·out**

chocolate

'**coun·ter** mostrador *m* de revisión; '**check·point** punto *m* de inspección; '**check·up** verificación *f*; ⚕ reconocimiento *m* general.

cheek [tʃi:k] mejilla *f*, carrillo *m*; F descaro *m*, frescura *f*; ⊕ quijada *f*; '**cheek·y** F descarado.

cheep [tʃi:p] piar.

cheer [tʃiə] *v/t.* alegrar, consolar (*a.* ~ up); aplaudir; animar con aplausos (*a.* ~ on); *v/i.* alegrarse, animarse (*a.* ~ up); ~ up! ¡ánimo!; '**cheer·ful** □ alegre; '**cheer·ful·ness** alegría *f*, complacencia *f*.

cheese [tʃi:z] queso *m*; *cream* ~ requesón *m*; '~**cloth** estopilla *f*.

chef [ʃef] jefe *m* de cocina.

chem·i·cal ['kemikl] 1. □ químico; 2. sustancia *f* química.

chem·ist ['kemist] 🕭 químico (a *f*) *m*; '**chem·is·try** química *f*.

cher·ish ['tʃeriʃ] estimar, apreciar; *hopes etc.* acariciar, abrigar.

cher·ry ['tʃeri] 1. cereza *f*; (*a.* ~ *tree*) cerezo *m*; 2. *attr.* rojo cereza.

chess [tʃes] ajedrez *m*; '~**board** tablero *m* (de ajedrez); '~**man** trebejo *m*, pieza *f*.

chest [tʃest] arca *f*, cofre *m*; *anat.* pecho *m*; (*money-*) caja *f*; ~ *of drawers* cómoda *f*; *get a th. off one's* ~ desahogarse.

chest·nut ['tʃesnʌt] 1. castaña *f*; (*a.* ~ *tree*) castaño *m*; F chiste *m* ya conocido; 2. castaño, marrón.

chev·a·lier [ʃevə'liə] caballero *m*.

chev·ron ['ʃevrən] ✕ galón *m*; *heraldry*: cheurón *m*.

chew [tʃu:] 1. mascar, masticar; ~ *the cud* rumiar (*a.* fig.; *a.* ~ *s.t. over*); *sl.* ~ *the rag* dar la lengua; 2. mascadura *f*; '**chew·ing-gum** chicle *m*.

chick [tʃik] pollito *m*; F crío (a *f*) *m*; **chick·en** ['tʃikin] pollo *m*, gallina *f*; '~ **farm·er** avicultor *m*; '~ **feed** *sl.* pan *m* comido; *sl.* breva *f*; '~ **pox** varicela *f*; '**chick·pea** garbanzo *m*.

chic·o·ry ['tʃikəri] chicoria *f*.

chide [tʃaid] [*irr.*] *lit.* reprobar.

chief [tʃi:f] 1. □ principal; primero; 2. jefe *m*; ...*in*-~ ... en jefe; ~ *of staff* jefe *m* de estado mayor; **chief·tain** ['~tən] jefe *m*, cacique *m*.

chil·blain ['tʃilblein] sabañón *m*.

child [tʃaild] niño (a *f*) *m*; hijo (a *f*) *m*; *attr.* muy joven; '~**birth** parto *m*; '**child·hood** niñez *f*, infancia *f*; '**child·ish** □ pueril; *b.s.* aniñado; '~ **la·bor** trabajo *m* de menores;

'**child·like** *fig.* propio de un niño; **children** ['tʃildrən] *pl.* of *child*; '~'s **play** juego *m* de niños.

chill [tʃil] 1. *lit.* frío; *manner* desapacible; 2. frío *m*; escalofrío *m* (*a.* 🎇); 3. *v/t.* enfriar (*a. metal*); *fig.* desalentar; *v/i.* enfriarse; *esp.* 🎇 calofriarse; **chill·y** frío (*a. fig.*); *p.* friolero; *feeling* escalofriado.

chime [tʃaim] 1. campaneo *m*; (*peal*) repique *m*; carillón *m*; *fig.* conformidad *f*, acuerdo *m*; 2. repicar, sonar; *fig.* estar en armonía.

chim·ney ['tʃimni] chimenea *f* (*exterior*); tubo *m* de lámpara; *mount.* olla *f*, cañón *m*.

chim·pan·zee [tʃimpən'zi:] chimpancé *m*.

chin [tʃin] barba *f*, barbilla *f*; *double* ~ papada *f*; F *keep one's* ~ *up* no desanimarse; F *take it on the* ~ mantenerse firme.

chin² [~] *sl.* parlotear.

chi·na ['tʃainə] porcelana *f*.

Chi·nese ['tʃai'ni:z] 1. chino *adj. a. su. m* (a *f*); 2. (*language*) chino *m*.

chink¹ [tʃiŋk] grieta *f*, hendedura *f*; resquicio *m* (*a. fig.*).

chink² [~] 1. sonido *m* metálico; tintineo *m*; 2. sonar, tintinear.

chip [tʃip] 1. astilla *f*, brizna *f*; lasca *f* *of stone*: (*defect*) saltadura *f*; ~ *off the old block* de tal palo tal astilla; F *have a* ~ *on one's shoulder* ser un resentido; 2. desportillar(se), astillar(se); F ~ *in* interrumpir (una conversación) (*with* diciendo); **chip·munk** ['tʃipmʌŋk] ardilla *f* listada.

chirp [tʃə:p] 1. gorjear, pipiar; (*cricket*) chirriar; F hablar alegremente; 2. gorjeo *m*; chirrido *m*.

chis·el ['tʃizl] 1. formón *m*, escoplo *m* *for wood*; cincel *m* *for stone*; 2. escoplear; cincelar; *sl.* timar; '**chis·el·er** F gorrón *m*.

chiv·al·rous ['ʃivlrəs] □ caballeroso; '**chiv·al·ry** caballería *f*; (*spirit*) caballerosidad *f*.

chive [tʃaiv] cebollino *m*.

chlo·ral ['klɔ:rl] cloral *m*; **chlo·ride** ['~aid] cloruro *m*; ~ *of lime* cloruro *m* de cal; **chlo·rine** ['~i:n] cloro *m*; **chlo·ro·form** ['~əfɔ:m] 1. cloroformo *m*; 2. cloroformizar.

chock [tʃɔk] 1. cuña *f*, combo *m* *of barrel*; ⚓ calzo *m*; 2. acuñar; afianzar con combos (*or* calzos).

choc·o·late ['tʃɔkəlit] chocolate *m*.

C

choice [t∫ɔis] 1. elección f; preferencia f; 2. selecto, escogido.

choir [ˈkwaiə] coro m.

choke [t∫ouk] 1. v/t. estrangular; sofocar (a. fig.); tapar, atascar (a. ~ up); fig. ~ back retener; F ~ off p. parar; reprobar; v/i. sofocarse, ahogarse (a. fig.); atascarse, obstruirse; 2. ⊕ cierre m, obturador m; mot. estrangulador m; mot. aire m.

chol·er·a [ˈkɔlərə] cólera m.

choose [t∫uːz] [irr.] escoger; elegir; seleccionar; ~ between optar entre; ~ to inf. optar por inf.; **ˈchoos·y** F melindroso, quisquilloso.

chop [t∫ɔp] golpe m cortante; tajada f; (meat) chuleta f.

chop·per [ˈt∫ɔpə] person tajador m; tool hacha f; of butcher cortante m; sl. helicóptero m.

ˈchop·stick palillo m para comer (de los chinos).

cho·ral [ˈkɔːrl] □ coral; **cho·ral(e)** [kɔˈrɑːl] coral m.

chord [kɔːd] acorde m.

chore [t∫ɔː] tarea f de ocasión; (household) ~s pl. quehaceres m/pl. domésticos.

cho·rus [ˈkɔːrəs] 1. coro m; ~ girl corista f, conjuntista f; 2. hablar (or cantar) en coro.

chose [t∫ouz] pret., **ˈcho·sen** p.p. of choose.

chough [t∫ʌf] chova f.

chow [t∫au] chao m; sl. comida f.

chris·ten [ˈkrisn] bautizar; **ˈchris·ten·ing** bautismo m, bautizo m.

Chris·tian [ˈkristjən] □ cristiano adj. a. su. m (a. ~ religion); ~ name nombre m de pila; **Chris·ti·an·i·ty** [~ˈti·æniti] cristianismo m.

Christ·mas [ˈkrisməs] Navidad(es) f(pl.); ~ Day Día m de Navidad; ~ Eve Noche f Buena.

chrome [kroum] [a. ~ yellow] amarillo m de cromo; **ˈchro·mi·um** [ˈ~jəm] cromo m.

chron·ic [ˈkrɔnik] □ crónico; F terrible, muy serio; **ˈchron·i·cle** 1. crónica f; 2. anotar; narrar.

chron·o·log·i·cal [krɔnəˈlɔdʒikl] □ cronológico; ~ly en orden cronológico; **chron·ol·o·gy** [krəˈnɔlədʒi] cronología f.

chrys·an·the·mum [kriˈsænθəməm] crisántemo m.

chub [t∫ʌb] cacho m; **ˈchub·by** rechoncho; face mofletudo.

chuck·le [ˈt∫ʌkl] 1. reír entre dientes,

soltar una risa sofocada; 2. risa f sofocada.

chum [t∫ʌm] F compinche m.

chump [t∫ʌmp] F zoquete m.

chunk [t∫ʌŋk] F pedazo m grueso.

church [t∫əːt∫] iglesia f.

churn [t∫əːn] 1. mantequera f; 2. batir en una mantequera; hacer (mantequilla); revolver, agitar.

chute [∫uːt] salto m de agua; canalón m in house; tolva f in mill.

ci·der [ˈsaidə] sidra f.

ci·gar [siˈgɑː] (cigarro) puro m.

cig·a·rette [sigəˈret] cigarrillo m; pitillo m; **ˈ~ case** petaca f, pitillera f; **ˈ~ hold·er** boquilla f; **ˈ~ light·er** mechero m; **ˈ~ pa·per** papel m de fumar.

cinch [sint∫] sl. breva f.

cin·der [ˈsində] carbonilla f; ~s pl. cenizas f/pl.

cin·e·ma [ˈsinimə] cine m.

cin·na·mon [ˈsinəmən] canela f.

ci·pher [ˈsaifə] 1. cifra f; cero m; (p.) cero m a la izquierda; in ~ en cifra; 2. cifrar; calcular.

cir·cle [ˈsəːkl] 1. círculo m (a. fig.); thea. anfiteatro m; 2. circundar, cercar; (go round) dar vueltas (a); girar.

cir·cuit [ˈsəːkit] circuito m (a. ⚡); approx. distrito m; sport: pista f; v. short ~; ⚡ ~-breaker cortacircuitos m; **cir·cu·i·tous** [səˈkjuitəs] □ tortuoso.

cir·cu·lar [ˈsəːkjulə] 1. □ circular; 2. circular f (a. ~ letter).

cir·cu·late [ˈsəːkjuleit] circular; **cir·cu·la·tion** circulación f (a. ⚕).

cir·cum [ˈsəːkəm] circum, circun...;

cir·cum·cise [ˈ~saiz] circuncidar; **cir·cum·ci·sion** [ˈ~siʒn] circuncisión f; **cir·cum·fer·ence** [səˈkʌmfərəns] circunferencia f; **cir·cum·flex** [ˈsəːkəmfleks] circunflejo m; **cir·cum·spect** [ˈ~spekt] □ circunspecto; **cir·cum·stance** [ˈ~stəns] circunstancia f; in (or under) the ~s en las circunstancias; under no ~s de ninguna manera; **cir·cum·stan·tial** [ˈ~ˈstæn∫l] □ circunstancial; ⚖ ~ evidence prueba f indiciaria; **cir·cum·vent** [ˈ~ˈvent] embaucar; burlar.

cir·cus [ˈsəːkəs] circo m; (in town) plaza f redonda.

cis·tern [ˈsistən] arca f, depósito m; (rainwater) aljibe m.

cit·a·del [ˈsitədl] ciudadela f.

ci·ta·tion [saiˈtei∫n] citación f (a. ⚖); ✕ mención f; **cite** [sait] citar; ✕ mencionar.

cit·i·zen [ˈsitizn] ciudadano (a f) m;

clear–cut

Am. ✕ paisano *m;* **cit·i·zen·ship** ['∼ʃip] ciudadanía *f.*

cit·ric ac·id ['sitrik'æsid] ácido *m* cítrico; **cit·rus** ['∼rəs] **1.** auranciáceo; **2.** cidro *m (el género Citrus).*

cit·y ['siti] **1.** ciudad *f;* **2.** ciudadano; ∼ *hall* palacio *m* municipal.

civ·ic ['sivik] cívico; ∼ *centre* casa *f* consistorial; conjunto *m* de edificios municipales; ∼s *sg.* ciencia *f* de los derechos *etc.* del ciudadano.

civ·il ['sivl] □ civil; ∼ *servant* funcionario *(a f) m* del Estado; ♀ *service* burocracia *f* oficial; **ci·vil·ian** [si'viljən] paisano *(a f) m;* ∼ *clothes pl.* traje *m* de paisano; **civ·i·li·za·tion** [∼lai'zeiʃn] civilización *f;* **civ·i·lize** ['∼laiz] civilizar.

clack [klæk] **1.** chasquido *m;* (*p.*) tarabilla *f;* **2.** hacer chasquido; sonar; *(chatter)* charlar.

clad [klæd] *lit. pret. a. p.p. of clothe.*

claim [kleim] **1.** demanda *f (a.* ⚖*);* petición *f;* pretensión *f (to a);* ✕ pertinencia *f; lay* ∼ *to* reclamar; **2.** demandar; reclamar; pretender *(to inf.);* afirmar; *attention* merecer.

clair·voy·ance [klɛə'vɔiəns] clarividencia *f.*

clam [klæm] almeja *f.*

clam·ber ['klæmbə] gatear, trepar, subir gateando *(up a).*

clam·my ['klæmi] □ frío y húmedo.

clam·or·ous ['klæmərəs] □ clamoroso; **'clam·or,** clamor *m,* clamoreo *m;* **2.** clamorear, clamar *(for por).*

clamp [klæmp] **1.** abrazadera *f, (screw)* tornillo *m* de banco; **2.** afianzar con abrazadera; *fig.* ∼ *down on* apretar los tornillos a; suprimir.

clan [klæn] clan *m (a. fig.).*

clan·des·tine [klæn'destin] □ clandestino.

clang [klæŋ] **1.** sonido *m* metálico fuerte, clamoreo *m;* ∼! ¡tolón!; **2.** (re)sonar.

clank [klæŋk] **1.** sonido *m* metálico seco, rechino *m;* **2.** rechinar.

clan·nish ['klæniʃ] exclusivista.

clap [klæp] **1.** palmoteo *m,* aplauso *m; (thunder)* trueno *m;* golpe *m* seco; *sl.* gonorrea *f;* **2.** dar palmadas, aplaudir; **'clap·trap 1.** faramalla *f;* farfolla *f;* **2.** faramalloso.

clar·i·fi·ca·tion [klærifi'keiʃn] aclaración *f;* **clar·i·fy** ['∼fai] clarificar, aclarar.

clar·i·net [klæri'net] clarinete *m.*

clar·i·ty ['klæriti] claridad *f.*

clash [klæʃ] **1.** choque *m;* fragor *m;* **2.** chocar *(a. fig.; with* con*); (colors)* desentonar *(with* con*).*

clasp [klɑːsp] **1.** broche *m,* corchete *m; (book)* broche *m,* manecilla *f; (shoe)* hebilla *f;* agarro *m* of *hand etc.; (handshake)* apretón *m;* **2.** abrochar; abrazar; agarrar; *hand* apretar; **'∼ 'knife** navaja *f.*

class [klɑːs] **1.** clase *f;* **2.** clasificar; ∼ *with* comparar con.

clas·sic ['klæsik] clásico *adj. a. su. m;* *the* ∼s *pl.* las obras clásicas *(esp.* griegas y latinas); las humanidades; **'clas·si·cal** □ clásico.

clas·si·fi·ca·tion [klæsifi'keiʃn] clasificación *f;* **clas·si·fy** ['∼fai] clasificar.

class...: **'∼·room** aula *f,* clase *f.*

clat·ter ['klætə] **1.** martilleo *m;* repiqueteo *m;* estruendo *m;* trápala *f* of *hooves;* choque *m* of *plates;* rumor *m* of *conversation;* **2.** martillear; *(esp. metal)* guachapear; chocar; mover con estruendo confuso.

clause [klɔːz] cláusula *f (a. gr.).*

clav·i·cle ['klævikl] clavícula *f.*

claw [klɔː] **1.** garra *f;* garfa *f esp. of bird of prey; (lobster's etc.)* pinza *f;* ⊕ garfio *m,* gancho *m;* **2.** arañar; agarrar; *(tear)* desgarrar.

clay [klei] arcilla *f;* ∼ *pigeon* pichón *m* de barro.

clean [kliːn] **1.** *adj.* □ limpio *(a. fig.);* neto, distinto; *surface etc.* despejado, desembarazado; *limb etc.* bien formado; *fig.* diestro; *sl. come* ∼ cantar; **2.** *adv.* enteramente; **3.** limpiar; ∼ *out* limpiar vaciando; *sl.* be ∼ed *out* quedar limpio; ∼ *up* arreglar; *sl.* sacar de ganancia; **4.** *su.* limpia *f;* **'clean·ing** limpia *f,* limpiadura *f; attr.* de limpiar; ∼ *woman* asistenta *f;* **'clean·li·ness** ['klenlinis] limpieza *f;* esmero *m;* **clean·ly** *adj.* ['klenli] esmerado; limpio; **cleanse** [klenz] *lit.* limpiar, purificar *(of* de*);* **clean·up** ['kliːnʌp] limpiadura *f; sl.* ganancia *f.*

clear [kliə] **1.** □ claro; *sky* despejado; libre *(of* de*);* completo, total; *v/t.* aclarar, clarificar *(a.* ∼ *up); table* despejar; *(a.* ∼ *away)* levantar; *site* desmontar; quitar *(a.* ∼ *away,* off); limpiar *(of* de*); (jump)* saltar por encima de; ⚖ absolver; probar la inocencia de; *ball* despejar; ✝ *check* hacer efectivo; ✝ *debt* liquidar *(a.* ∼ *off); v/i.* abonanzar *(a.* ∼ *up); (sky)* despejarse; F ∼ *off* irse, escabullirse *(a.* ∼ *out);* **'clear-'cut** claro, bien definido.

clem·en·cy ['klemənsi] clemencia *f.*

clench [klentʃ] apretar, cerrar.

cler·gy ['klɜːdʒi] clero *m*, clerecía *f*; **'~·man** clérigo *m*, sacerdote *m*.

cler·i·cal ['klerikəl] □ clerical; oficinista, *b.s.* oficinesco; ~ **error** error *m* de pluma.

clerk [klɑːk] oficinista *m/f*; dependiente (*a f*) *m*.

clev·er ['klevə] □ inteligente; hábil; listo; *b.s.* habilidoso.

cli·ché ['kliːʃei] cliché *m*.

click [klik] 1. golpecito *m* seco; piñoneo *m of gun*; chasquido *m of tongue*; taconeo *m of heels*; 2. piñonear; chasquear.

cli·ent ['klaiənt] cliente *m/f*; **cli·en·tele** [kliːɑːnˈtel] clientela *f*.

cliff [klif] risco *m*; (*sea*) acantilado *m*.

cli·mate ['klaimit] clima *m*; *fig.* ambiente *m*.

cli·max ['klaimæks] *rhet.* clímax *m*; colmo *m*; cima *f* de intensidad.

climb [klaim] [*irr.*] 1. trepar, escalar; subir (*a*); F *fig.* ~ **down** cejar; desdecirse; 2. subida *f*.

clinch [klintʃ] 1. agarro *m*; ⊕ remache *m*; *boxing*: clincha *f*; 2. agarrar; remachar; luchar cuerpo a cuerpo; *fig. argument* remachar; *v.* clench.

cling [kliŋ] [*irr.*] adherirse (*to* a), pegarse (*to* a) (*a. fig.*); ~ *to p.* abrazarse a, quedar abrazado a.

clin·ic ['klinik] 1. clínica *f*; 2. = **'clin·i·cal** □ clínico.

clink [kliŋk] 1. tintín *m*; choque *m of glasses*; *sl.* trena *f*; 2. tintinear; chocar.

clip¹ [klip] 1. esquileo *m of wool*; F golpe *m*; 2. trasquilar, esquilar.

clip² [~] grapa *f*; (*paper*) sujetapapeles *m*; sujetador *m of pen*; (*brooch*) alfiler *m* de pecho, clip *m*.

clip·per ['klipə] (*a pair of* ~s una) cizalla *f*; 🔪 tijeras *f/pl.* podadoras; ⚓, 🛩 clíper *m*; **'clip·pings** *pl.* recortes *m/pl.*; trasquilones *m/pl. of wool*; retales *m/pl. of cloth*.

clique [kliːk] pandilla *f*; peña *f*.

cloak [klouk] 1. capa *f* (*a. fig.*), capote *m*; ~ **and dagger** de capa y espada; 2. encapotar; *fig.* encubrir, disimular.

clock [klɔk] 1. reloj *m*; *sport*: cronómetro *m*; *against the* ~ contra el reloj; 2.: ~ **in** fichar; **'~·wise** en la dirección de las agujas del reloj; **'~·work** aparato *m* de relojería; *like* ~ como un reloj.

'clog [klɔg] 1. zueco *m*; *fig.* traba *f*;

estorbo *m*; 2. atascar(se) (*a. fig.*); (*hamper*) estorbar.

clois·ter ['klɔistə] 1. claustro *m*; 2. enclaustrar (*a. fig.*).

close 1. a) [klouz] fin *m*; conclusión *f*; *at the* ~ *of* day a la caída de la tarde; b) [klous] recinto *m*, cercado *m*; 2. [klouz] *v/t.* cerrar (*a. ⚡*); ~**d shop** *fig.* coto *m* cerrado; ~ **down** cerrar definitivamente; *closing date* fecha *f* tope; *v/i.* cerrar(se); terminar; ~ **in** acercarse rodeando; ~ **in** *on* todear; ~ **up** ponerse más cerca; (*wound*) cicatrizarse; 3. [klous] □ cercano, próximo; *friendship etc.* estrecho, intimo; *weave etc.* compacto, tupido; *argument* minucioso; *atmosphere* sofocante, mal ventilado; *imitation* arrimado; *score* igual, casi empatado; *translation* fiel; F (*mean*) avaro, mezquino; ~ *by,* ~ *to* cerca de; **'~ call** F escape *m* por un pelo; **'~-fist·ed** tacaño; **'~-fit·ting** ajustado; **'~ shave** afeitado *m* a ras; F *escape m* por un pelo.

clos·et ['klɔzit] retrete *m*, gabinete *m*; (*cupboard*) armario *m*.

close-up ['klousʌp] vista *f* de cerca.

clot [klɔt] 1. grumo *m*; cuajarón *m of blood etc.*; *sl.* papanatas *m*; 2. cuajarse, coagularse.

cloth [klɔθ], *pl.* **cloths** [klɔθs, klɔːðz] tela *f*, paño *m*; (*table*) mantel *m*; *fig.* clero *m*.

clothe [klouð] [*irr.*] vestir; *p.* trajear; *fig.* revestir; investir (*with* de).

clothes [klouðz] ropa *f*, vestidos *m/pl.*; **'~-bas·ket** cesto *m* de la colada; **'~ hang·er** colgador *m*, perchero *m*; **'~-line** cuerda *m* para tender la ropa; **'~-pin** pinza *f*.

cloth·ing ['klouðiŋ] ropa *f*, vestidos *m/pl.*; ropaje *m*; *attr.* textil.

cloud [klaud] 1. nube *f* (*a. fig.*); *storm* ~ nubarrón *m*; 2. anublar (*a. fig.*); ~ (*over*) anublarse; **'~-burst** chaparrón *m*; **'cloud·less** sin nubes, despejado; **'cloud·y** □ anublado, nuboso; *liquid* turbio.

clout [klaut] 1. F dar de bofetadas; 2. F bofetada *f*; † trapo *m*.

clo·ver ['klouvə] trébol *m*; F *be in* ~ vivir holgadamente; **'~ leaf** hoja *f* de trébol; *intersection* cruce *m* de trébol.

clown [klaun] 1. payaso *m in circus*; palurdo *m*; 2. bufonearse.

cloy [klɔi] empalagar(se), hartar(se).

club [klʌb] 1. porra *f*, cachiporra *f*; (*golf-*) palo *m*; (*society*) club *m*; casino *m*; *cards*: ~s *pl.* tréboles *m/pl.*, (*Spanish*) bastos *m/pl.*; 2. *v/t.* aporrear; '~**house** *golf*: chalet *m.*

cluck [klʌk] cloquear.

clue [kluː] indicio *m*; pista *f.*

clump [klʌmp] 1. grupo *m* de árboles, arboleda *f*; masa *f* informe; 2. andar pesadamente (*a.* ~ *along*).

clum·si·ness ['klʌmzinis] desmaña *f*, torpeza *f*; '**clum·sy** □ desmañado, torpe; (*badly done*) chapucero.

clung [klʌŋ] *pret. a. p.p. of* **cling**.

clus·ter ['klʌstə] 1. grupo *m*; ♀ racimo *m*; 2. agruparse; ♀ arracimarse; (*people*) apiñarse.

clutch [klʌtʃ] 1. agarro *m*; *mot.* (*pedal m de*) embrague *m*; 2. agarrarse (*at* a); empuñar.

clut·ter ['klʌtə] 1. desorden *m*, confusión *f*; (*with noise*) barahunda *f*; 2. poner en confusión; *be* ~*ed up with* estar atestado de.

coach [koutʃ] 1. coche *m*; diligencia *f*; *sport:* entrenador *m*; 2. *team etc.* entrenar; *student* enseñar, preparar.

co·ag·u·late [kouˈægjuleit] coagular.

coal [koul] acu(a) hulla *f*; (*freq.* ~s *pl.*) ascua *f*, brasa *f*; ~ *industry* industria *f* hullera; '~**bin** carbonera *f*; '~ **car** vagón *m* carbonero; '~ **deal·er** carbonero *m.*

co·a·lesce [kouəˈles] unirse; combinarse; *pol. etc.* incorporarse.

coal·field ['koulfiːld] yacimiento *m* de carbón; cuenca *f* minera.

co·a·li·tion [kouəˈliʃn] *pol.* coalición *f*; unión *f*, combinación *f.*

coarse [kɔːs] □ basto, tosco; *fig.* grosero, rudo.

coast [koust] 1. costa *f*; litoral *m*; 2. costear; *mot.* ir en punto muerto; ~ *along* avanzar sin esfuerzo; '**coast guard** guardacostas *m.*

coat [kout] 1. chaqueta *f*, americana *f*; (*overcoat*) abrigo *m*; (*layer*) capa *f*; mano *f* (*of paint*); (*animal's*) pelo *m*; ~ *of arms* escudo *m* de armas; ~ *of mail* cota *f* de malla; 2. cubrir, revestir (*with con, de*); dar una mano de pintura a; '~ **hang·er** colgador *m.*

coax [kouks] engatusar; persuadir por medio de halagos (*into ger.* que *subj.*); '**coax·ing** □ lenguaje *m* almibarado; coba *f*; halagos *m/pl.*

co·balt [kəˈbɔːlt] cobalto *m.*

cob·web ['kɔbweb] telaraña *f.*

co·caine [kəˈkein] cocaína *f.*

cock [kɔk] 1. gallo *m*; macho *m* de ave; ⊕ grifo *m*, espita *f*; martillo *m* of

gun; 2. **gun** amartillar; enderezar; volver hacia arriba; ~*ed hat* sombrero *m* de tres picos (*or* de candil).

cock-and-bull sto·ry ['kɔkəndˈbul-stɔːri] cuento *m*, camelo *m.*

cock...: '~**eyed** ['kɔkaid] bizco; *sl.* ladeado; *sl. fig.* incomprensible, estúpido; '~**fight(·ing)** pelea *f* de gallos.

cock·pit ['kɔkpit] cancha *f*, reñidero *m* de gallos; ✈ cabina *f*, carlinga *f*; *fig.* sitio *m* de muchos combates.

cock·roach ['kɔkroutʃ] cucaracha *f.*

cocks·comb ['kɔkskoum] cresta *f* de gallo; '**cock·sure** *F* demasiado seguro; presuntuoso; '**cock·tail** combinación *f*; ~ *party* cóctel *m*; '**cock·y** □ *F* engreído, hinchado.

co·co ['koukou] cocotero *m.*

co·coa ['koukou] cacao *m*; (*drink*) chocolate *m.*

co·co·nut ['koukənʌt] coco *m.*

co·coon [kɔˈkuːn] capullo *m.*

cod [kɔd] bacalao *m.*

cod·dle ['kɔdl] mimar.

code [koud] 1. código *m* (🕱 *a. fig.*); cifra *f*; *tel.* alfabeto *m* Morse; *in* ~ en cifra; 2. cifrar.

cod·fish ['kɔdfiʃ] bacalao *m.*

codg·er ['kɔdʒə] *F* (*freq. old* ~) tipo *m*, sujeto *m.*

cod·i·cil ['kɔdisil] codicilo *m*; **cod·i·fy** ['kɔdifai] codificar.

cod·liv·er oil ['kɔdlivərˈɔil] aceite *m* de hígado de bacalao.

co·ed ['kouˈed] *F* 1. coeducacional; 2. alumna *f* de un colegio coeducacional.

co·ed·u·ca·tion [kouedjuˈkeiʃn] coeducación *f.*

co·erce [kouˈəːs] obligar, apremiar (*into ger.* a *inf.*); coercer.

co·ex·ist ['kouigˈzist] coexistir (*with* con); '**co·ex·ist·ence** coexistencia *f*, convivencia *f.*

cof·fee ['kɔfi] café *m*; '~**bean** grano *m* de café; '~**grounds** heces *f/pl.* del café; '~**pot** cafetera *f.*

cof·fer ['kɔfə] cofre *m*, arca *f*; ⌂ artesón *m*; ~s *pl. fig.* fondos *m/pl.*

cof·fin ['kɔfin] ataúd *m.*

cog [kɔg] diente *m*; rueda *f* dentada.

co·gen·cy ['koudʒənsi] fuerza *f.*

cog·i·tate ['kɔdʒiteit] *v/i.* meditar, reflexionar; *v/t.* recapacitar.

co·gnac ['kounjæk] coñac *m.*

cog·nate ['kɔgneit] cognado *adj. a. su. m* (*a f*); afín.

cog·wheel ['kɔgwiːl] rueda *f* dentada.

co·hab·it [kou'hæbit] cohabitar.

co·here [kou'hiə] adherirse, pegarse; (ideas etc.) enlazarse; **co'her·en·cy** coherencia f; **co'her·ent** □ coherente.

co·he·sion [kou'hi:ʒn] cohesión f (a. fig.); **co'he·sive** □ cohesivo.

coif·feur [kwɑː'fəː] peluquero m; **coif·fure** [~'fjuə] peinado m.

coil [kɔil] 1. rollo m; ⚓ aduja f of rope; ✗ carrete m; ⚕ serpentín m; † desorden m, barahunda f; ~ spring resorte m espiral; 2. arrollar(se), enrollar(se); serpentear; ⚓ rope adujar.

coin [kɔin] 1. moneda f; ⚒ acuñar; fig. forjar; word etc. inventar, idear; **'coin·age** acuñación f; amonedación f; sistema m monetario; fig. invención f.

co·in·cide [kouin'said] coincidir (with con); **co·in·ci·dence** [kou'insidəns] coincidenca f; **co·in·ci'dent·al** □ coincidente; fortuito.

coke [kouk] 1. coque m; F Coca-Cola f; 2. convertir en coque.

cold [kould] 1. □ frío (a. fig.); ~ meat carne f fiambre; be ~ (p.) tener frío; (weather) hacer frío; (th.) estar frío; have ~ feet encogérsele a uno el ombligo; 2. frío m; ⚕ resfriado m; catch ~ resfriarse; F leave out in the ~ dejar al margen; **'~·blood·ed** zo. de sangre fría; fig. insensible; (cruel) desalmado; **'cold·ness** frialdad f; indiferencia f; **'~·'shoul·der** tratar con frialdad; **'~·'stor·age** almacenaje m frigorífico.

cole·slaw ['koul'slɔː] ensalada de coles.

col·ic ['kɔlik] cólico m.

col·lab·o·rate [kə'læbəreit] colaborar; **col·lab·o·ra·tion** colaboración f; **col'lab·o·ra·tor** colaborador (-a f) m; ✗ colaboracionista m.

col·lapse [kə'læps] 1. ⚕ sufrir colapso; F desmayarse; ⚕ etc. hundirse; fig. fracasar; 2. ⚕ colapso m; hundimiento m; fracaso m; **col'laps·i·ble** plegable.

col·lar ['kɔlə] 1. cuello m; (animals a. ⊕) collar m; F slip the ~ escaparse; 2. prender por el cuello; sl. coger, prender; **'~·bone** clavícula f.

col·late [kɔ'leit] colacionar (a. eccl.); text cotejar.

col·lat·er·al [kɔ'lætərəl] □ colateral; ~ security garantía f subsidiaria.

col·league ['kɔliːg] colega m.

col·lect 1. ['kɔlekt] eccl. colecta f; 2.

[kə'lekt] v/t. acumular; reunir; antiques etc. coleccionar; taxes colectar, recaudar; ~ o.s. recobrarse; ~ one's wits reconcentrarse; v/i. acumularse; reunirse; coleccionar; **col'lect 'call** llamada f por cobrar; **col'lec·tion** colección f; montón m; recaudación f of taxes etc.; **col'lec·tive** □ colectivo (a. gr.); ~ bargaining trato m colectivo; **col'lec·tor** coleccionador m; (tax-) recaudador m; ✗ colector m.

col·lege ['kɔlidʒ] colegio m; colegio m de universidad; **col·le·gi·an** [kə'liːdʒiən] colegial m.

col·lide [kə'laid] chocar (with con; a. fig.); fig. entrar en conflicto.

col·lier ['kɔliə] minero m de carbón; ⚓ barco m minero.

col·li·sion [kə'liʒn] colisión f, choque m (a. fig.).

col·lo·qui·al [kə'loukwiəl] □ popular, familiar; **col'lo·qui·al·ism** popularismo m.

co·lon ['koulən] typ. dos puntos; anat. colon m.

colo·nel ['kəːnl] coronel m.

co·lo·ni·al [kə'lounjəl] 1. colonial; colono m; **col·o·nist** ['kɔlənist] colonizador m; colono m; **col·o·ni·za·tion** [kɔlənai'zeiʃn] colonización f; **'col·o·nize** colonizar.

col·o·ny ['kɔləni] colonia f.

col·or ['kʌlə] 1. color m (a. fig.); ✗ ~s pl. bandera f; F be off ~ estar indispuesto; change ~ mudar de color, demudarse; ~ film película f en colores; call to the ~s llamar al servicio militar; show one's ~s dejar ver uno su verdadero carácter; fig. with flying ~s con lucimiento; 2. v/t. colorear (a. fig.), colorar; v/i. sonrojarse (a. ~ up); **'~ bar** barrera f racial; **'~·blind** daltoniano; **'~ blind·ness** daltonismo m; **col·or·ful** ['~ful] □ lleno de color; vivo, animado; **'~ 'tel·e·vi·sion** televisión f en colores.

co·los·sal [kə'lɔsl] □ colosal.

colt [koult] potro m; fig. mozuelo m.

col·umn ['kɔləm] columna f; **col·um·nist** ['kɔləmnist] periodista m, columnista m.

co·ma ['koumə] ⚕ coma m.

comb [koum] 1. peine m; almohaza f for horse; (cock's) cresta f; ⊕ carda f; v. honey·~; 2. peinar; wool cardar; fig. registrar (or explorar) con minuciosidad.

com·bat ['kɔmbət] 1. combate m (a. fig.); ~ duty servicio m de frente; 2.

combatir(se); **'com·bat·ant** combatiente *m*.

com·bi·na·tion [kɔmbi'neiʃn] combinación *f* (*a. garment, mst* ~s *pl*.); ~ *lock* cerradura *f* de combinación; **com·bine 1.** [kəm'bain] combinar (-se); **2.** ['kɔmbain] ✛ monopolio *m*; ✛ (*a.* ~ *harvester*) cosechadora *f*.

com·bus·tion [kəm'bʌstʃən] combustión *f*.

come [kʌm] [*irr.*] venir; ir; ~! ¡ven!, ¡venga!; *oh,* ~! ¡pero mire!; *how* ~ *?* ¿cómo eso?; *coming!* ¡voy!; ~ *about* pasar; suceder (*that que*); realizarse; ~ *across p.* topar a; *th.* encontrar, dar con; ~ *along* venir, ir; ~ *back* volver; ~ *before* anteponerse a; llegar antes; ~ *by* conseguir; ~ *down* bajar; *fig.* desplomarse; ~ *down on* osar sobre; F regañar; ~ *down with* ✛ enfermar de; ~ *for* venir por; ~ *forward* presentarse, acudir; ~ *in* entrar; *fig.* presentarse en uso, ponerse de moda; empezar; llegar *in race*; ~ *in!* ¡adelante!; ~ *in useful* servir, ser útil; ~ *off* (*part*) soltarse; desprenderse; *fig.* (*event*) verificarse, celebrarse; (*succeed*) tener éxito, verse logrado; ~ *off well* salir airoso; ~ *on!* ¡vamos!, ¡despabílate!; (*encouragement*) ¡ánimo!; ~ (*up*)*on* encontrarse con; descubrir; ~ *out* salir; salir a luz; ~ *out with* decir, revelar; ~ *over: what's* ~ *over you?* ¿qué te pasa?; ~ *round* ✛ volver en sí; (*visit*) ir a ver; (*agree*) convenir, asentir; dejarse persuadir; ~ *to a*) *adv.* ✛ volver en sí, ✛ parar, fachear; b) *prp.* heredar; *sum* subir a; ~ *to mind* ocurrirse; ~ *up* subir; aparecer; acercarse (*to a*); mencionarse *in conversation*; *univ.* matricularse; ~ *up to* estar a la altura de; ~ *up with* th. proponer; **'~·back** F rehabilitación *f*; respuesta *f* aguda.

co·me·di·an [kə'miːdiən] cómico *m*; autor *m* de comedias; **co·me·di·enne** [~i'en] cómica *f*.

come·down ['kʌmdaun] F desazón *f*, humillación *f*; desgracia *f*.

com·e·dy ['kɔmidi] comedia *f*; (*musical*) zarzuela *f*.

come·on ['kʌmɔn] *sl.* añagaza *f*; desafío *m*; (*p.*) bobo *m*.

com·et ['kɔmit] cometa *m*.

com·fort ['kʌmfət] **1.** consuelo *m*, alivio *m*; (*physical*) confort *m*, comodidad *f*; bienestar *m*; ~ *loving* comodón; **2.** consolar, aliviar; ✛ ayudar; **'com·fort·a·ble** ☐ cómodo, confortable; *living* desahogado, holgado; **'com·fort·er** consolador (-a *f*) *m*; (*scarf*) bufanda *f* de lana; (*baby's*) chupete *m*; colcha *f*, cobertor *m*.

com·ic ['kɔmik] **1.** ☐ (*mst* **'com·i·cal** ☐) cómico; divertido, entretenido; **2.** (*p.*) cómico *m*; revista *f* cómica (*infantil*), tebeo *m*; **'com·ic book** tebeo *m*; **'com·ic strip** tira *f* cómica.

com·ma ['kɔmə] coma *f*.

com·mand [kə'mɑːnd] **1.** orden *f*, mandato *m*; mando *m*, mando *m*; ✕ comando *m*; ✛ comandancia *f*; dominio *m* *of language*; *be at the* ~ *of* estar a la disposición de; *be in* ~ estar al mando; **2.** mandar, ordenar (*to a*); *respect* merecer, imponer; ✕, ✛ comandar; **com·man·dant** [kɔmən'dænt] comandante *m*; **com·man·deer** [~'diə] ✕ *men* reclutar por fuerza; *stores etc.* expropiar; F apoderarse de; **com·mand·er** [kə'mɑːndə] ✕ comandante *m*; ✛ capitán de fragate; comendador *m* *of Order*; **com·'mand·er·in·'chief** generalísimo *m*; **com·'mand·ment** mandamiento *m*.

com·mem·o·rate [kə'meməreit] conmemorar; **com·mem·o·'ra·tion** conmemoración *f* (*in* ~ *of* en ... de); **com·'mem·o·ra·tive** ☐ conmemorativo.

com·mence [kə'mens] comenzar, empezar (*ger. or to inf.* a *inf.*); **com·'mence·ment** comienzo *m*, principio *m*.

com·mend [kə'mend] encomendar (*to a*); recomendar, alabar.

com·ment ['kɔment] **1.** comento *m*; comentario *m* (*on* sobre); observación *f* (*on* sobre); (*conversational*) dicho *m*; **2.** comentar (*on acc.*); observar (*that* que); **'com·men·tar·y** comentario *m*; **'com·men·ta·tor** comentador *m*, comentarista *m*; *radio:* locutor *m*.

com·merce ['kɔmə:s] comercio *m*; *Chamber of* ♀ Cámara *f* de Comercio; **com·mer·cial** [kə'mə:ʃl] **1.** ☐ comercial; ~ *traveller* viajante *m*, agente *m* viajero *S.Am.*; **2.** *radio:* anuncio *m*, programa *m* publicitario; **com·'mer·cial·ism** mercantilismo *m*; **com·'mer·cial·ize** comercializar.

com·mis·er·ate [kə'mizəreit] compadecer; ~ *with* condolerse de.

com·mis·sion [kə'miʃn] **1.** comisión *f* (*a.* ✛); ✕ nombramiento *m*; ⚖ perpetración *f* *of crime*; ✛ ~ *merchant* comisionista *m*; **2.** comisionar; ✕

nombrar; *ship* poner en servicio activo.

com·mit [kə'mit] cometer; *business* confiar; *parl. bill* someter (a una comisión); (*o.s.*) comprometer(se); ⚖ *p.* encarcelar, internar; **com'mit·ment** obligación *f*; compromiso *m*; ⚖ auto *m* de prisión; *parl.* traslado *m* a una comisión; **com'mit·tal** ⚖ auto *m* de prisión; entierro *m* of *body*; **com'mit·tee** comité *m*, comisión *f*.

com·mode [kə'moud] cómoda *f*; (*a. night~*) sillico *m*; **com'mo·di·ous** [~] cómodo, espacioso, holgado; **com·mod·i·ty** [kə'mɔditi] mercancía *f*; cosa *f* útil.

com·mon ['kɔmən] 1. común; F ordinario; ~ *law* derecho *m* de consuetudinario; *in ~* en común; *in ~ with* de común cún; 2. campo *m* común, ejido *m*; '~ **law** derecho *m* consuetudinario; '~**law mar·riage** matrimonio *m* consensual; '**com·mon·place** 1. perogrullada *f*; lugar *m* común; 2. común, trivial; '~ '**sense** sentido *m* común; '~**sense** cuerdo, razonable; '~ '**stock** acción *f* ordinaria; acciones *f/pl.* ordinarias.

com·mo·tion [kə'mouʃn] conmoción *f*, tumulto *m*.

com·mu·ni·cate [kə'mju:nikeit] comunicar (*with* con); *eccl.* comulgar; (*buildings*) mandarse (*with* con); **com·mu·ni·ca·tion** comunicación *f*; *be in ~ with* estar en contacto con.

com·mun·ion [kə'mju:njən] comunión *f*.

com·mu·ni·qué [kə'mju:nikei] comunicado *m*, parte *m*.

com·mu·nism ['kɔmjunizm] comunismo *m*; '**com·mu·nist** 1. = **com·mu·nis·tic** □ comunista *m/f*; 2. = **com·mu·nis·tic** □ comunista.

com·mu·ni·ty [kə'mju:niti] comunidad *f*; sociedad *f*; (*local*) vecindario *m*.

com·mute [kə'mju:t] *v/t.* conmutar (*for, to* por, *into* en); *v/i.* ser abonado al ferrocarril; viajar con billete de abono (*esp.* al trabajo); **com'mut·er** abonado *m* al ferrocarril.

com·pact 1. ['kɔmpækt] pacto *m*, convenio *m*; (*make-up*) estuche *m* de afeites; 2. [kəm'pækt] compacto; conciso, breve; 3. [~] condensar, hacer compacto.

com·pan·ion [kəm'pænjən] compañero (a *f*) *m*; campañía *f*; ⚓ lumbrera *f*.

com·pa·ny ['kʌmpəni] compañía *f* (*a. ✕ a. thea.*); ✝ sociedad *f*, empresa *f*; F (*p.*) visita *f*; *bad~* amistades *f/pl.* sospechosas; F *good ~* compañero *m* simpático (or entretenido); *keep s.o. ~* acompañar a, estar con; *ir juntos*; *part ~* separarse, tomar rumbos distintos.

com·pa·ra·ble ['kɔmpərəbl] □ comparable; **com'par·a·tive** [kəm-'pærətiv] 1. *gr.* comparativo *m*; 2. □ comparado; *gr.* comparativo.

com·pare [kəm'pɛə] 1. *beyond ~, without ~, past ~* sin comparación; 2. *v/t.* comparar (*with, to* con); *as ~d with* comparado con; *v/i.* compararse (*with* con); **com·par·i·son** [~'pærisn] comparación *f*; *in ~ with* en comparación con.

com·part·ment [kəm'pɑ:tmənt] compartimiento *m*; 🚃 departamento *m*.

com·pass ['kʌmpəs] 1. ⚓ brújula *f*; ♪ extensión *f*, límites *m/pl.* (de la voz *etc.*); confín *m*, circuito *m*; *fig.* alcance *m*; 2. rodear, ceñir; (*contrive*) conseguir; *fig.* alcanzar.

com·pas·sion [kəm'pæʃn] compasión *f*, piedad *f*; *have ~ on* tener piedad de; **com'pas·sion·ate** [~ʃə-nit] □ compasivo.

com·pat·i·bil·i·ty [kəmpætə'biliti] compatibilidad *f*; **com'pat·i·ble** □ compatible.

com·pel [kəm'pel] *p.* compeler (*to* a); *respect* imponer.

com·pen·sate ['kɔmpenseit] *v/t.* compensar (*with* con); indemnizar (*for* de); *v/i.* ~ *for* compensar; **com·pen·sa·tion** compensación *f*; indemnización *f*; ⊕ retribución *f*, recompensa.

com·pete [kəm'pi:t] competir, hacer competencia (*for* para; *with* con).

com·pe·tence, com·pe·ten·cy ['kɔmpitəns(i)] competencia *f* (*a.* ⚖); capacidad *f*; aptitud *f*; '**com·pe·tent** □ competente (*a.* ⚖); capaz, hábil.

com·pe·ti·tion [kɔmpi'tiʃn] competencia *f*; concurso *m*; (*Civil Service etc.*) oposiciones *f/pl.*; *in ~ with* en competencia con; **com·pet·i·tive** [kəm'petitiv] □ competidor; *price* competitivo; *post* de (or por) concurso (or oposición); **com·pet·i·tor** competidor (-a *f*) *m*; opositor (-a *f*) *m* *for post*.

com·pi·la·tion [kɔmpi'leiʃn] compilación f; **com·pile** [kəm'pail] compilar.

com·pla·cence, **com·pla·cen·cy** [kəm'pleisns(i)] complacencia f; b.s. satisfacción f de sí mismo; **com·pla·cent** ☐ satisfecho (con poca razón) (about de).

com·plain [kəm'plein] quejarse (about, of de; that de que); ✠ demandar; **com·plaint** queja f; ✠ querella f, demanda f; ✠ enfermedad f, mal m.

com·ple·ment ['kɔmplimənt] 1. complemento m (a. gr., ♣); ♣ personal m; 2. complementar.

com·plete [kəm'pli:t] 1. ☐ completo, entero; consumado; llevar a cabo; form llenar; **com·ple·tion** cumplimiento m, terminación f.

com·plex ['kɔmpleks] 1. ☐ complejo; complicado; 2. ✠ complejo m; F idea f fija, prejuicio m irracional; **com·plex·ion** [kəm'plekʃn] tez f, color m de la cara; aspecto m, carácter m; **com·plex·i·ty** complejidad f.

com·pli·ance [kəm'plaiəns] sumisión f (with a), condescendencia f (with a); in ~ with accediendo a.

com·pli·cate ['kɔmplikeit] complicar; embrollar; **com·pli·ca·tion** complicación f.

com·plic·i·ty [kəm'plisiti] complicidad f.

com·pli·ment 1. ['kɔmplimənt] cumplimiento m, cumplido m; piropo m to woman; send ~s enviar saludos; 2. ['~ment] cumplimentar; felicitar (on sobre); **com·pli·men·ta·ry** lisonjero; ticket etc. de regalo, de cortesía.

com·ply [kəm'plai] conformarse (with con); obedecer (with a); ~ with obrar de acuerdo con.

com·po·nent [kəm'pounənt] componente adj. a. su. m (a. ~ part).

com·pose [kəm'pouz] componer (a. ♪ a. typ.); **com'posed**, adv. spirit sosegado; compuesto (of de); be ~ of componerse de, estar compuesto de; **com'pos·er** ♪ compositor m; autor m; **com·pos·ite** ['kɔmpəzit] 1. compuesto; 2. compuestas f/pl.; **com·pos·i·tion** [kɔmpə'ziʃn] composición f; ✝ arreglo m, ajuste m; **com·po·sure** [kəm'pouʒə] compostura f, serenidad f.

com·pound¹ 1. ['kɔmpaund] compuesto; ~ fracture fractura f complicada; ~ interest interés m compuesto; 2. [~] compuesto m (a. ♠); gr. (~ word) vocablo m compuesto; 3. [kəm'paund] v/t. componer; v/i.: ~ with capitular con.

com·pound² ['kɔmpaund] comprender; encerrar, incluir.

com·pre·hen·si·ble [kɔmpri'hensəbl] ☐ comprensible; **com·pre·hen·sion** [~'henʃn] comprensión f; **com·pre·hen·sive** ☐ comprensivo (se).

com·press 1. [kəm'pres] comprimir; 2. ['kɔmpres] compresa f; **com·pres·sion** [~'preʃn] compresión f; **com·pres·sor** compresor m.

com·prise [kəm'praiz] comprender; constar de; range abarcar.

com·pro·mise ['kɔmprəmaiz] 1. compromiso m, componenda f; 2. v/t. affair arreglar; p. comprometer; v/i. comprometer(se).

com·pul·sion [kəm'pʌlʃn] compulsión f; **com·pul·so·ry** [~səri] ☐ obligatorio; compulsivo.

com·pu·ta·tion [kɔmpju:'teiʃn] cómputo m, cálculo m; **com·pute** [kəm'pju:t] computar, calcular; **com·put·er** calculadora f, computador m.

com·rade ['kɔmreid] camarada m; ~ in arms compañero m de armas.

con·cave ['kɔn'keiv] ☐ cóncavo.

con·ceal [kən'si:l] ocultar (from a, de); ✠ encubrir.

con·cede [kən'si:d] conceder.

con·ceit [kən'si:t] presunción f, engreimiento m, ínfulas f/pl.; lit. concepto m; **con'ceit·ed** ☐ engreído, afectado; style conceptuoso.

con·ceiv·a·ble [kən'si:vəbl] ☐ concebible; **con'ceive** v/i. concebir; v/t. imaginar, formar concepto de; child concebir; plan idear.

con·cen·trate 1. ['kɔnsentreit] concentrar(se); 2. ['~trit] esp. 🦅 sustancia f concentrada; **con·cen·tra·tion** concentración f (a. ♠); ~ camp campo m de concentración; **con·cen·tric** ☐ concéntrico.

con·cep·tion [kən'sepʃn] concepción f; idea f, concepto m.

con·cern [kən'sə:n] 1. asunto m, negocio m; interés m; preocupación f (for, with por); inquietud f (for por); ✝ empresa f; 2. concernir, atañer; preocupar, inquietar; ~ o.s. with ocuparse de, interesarse por; be ~ed in estar interesado en; estar metido en;

C

be ~ed estar preocupado (*with* por; *that* porque); be ~ed to *inf.* (me *etc.*) interesa *inf.*; *as far as he is* ~ed en cuanto le toca a él; *as* ~s respecto de; **con'cerned** □ interesado (*in* en); ocupado; inquietado (*at, about, for* por); *those* ~ los interesados; **con'cern·ing** *prp.* concerniente a; respecto de.

con·cert 1. ['kɔnsət] concierto *m* (*a.* ♪); *in* ~ de concierto; **2.** [kən'sɔːt] concertar; **con·cer·ti·na** [kɔnsə'tiːnə] concertina *f.*

con·ces·sion [kən'seʃn] concesión *f*; privilegio *m*; **con·ces·sion·aire** [kənseʃə'nɛə] concesionario *m.*

con·cil·i·ate [kən'silieit] conciliar; (*win over*) ganar, granjear; **con·cil·i·a·tion** conciliación *f.*

con·cise [kən'sais] □ conciso.

con·clude [kən'kluːd] concluir, terminar; sacar una consecuencia; *agreement* llegar a; *business* finalizar; **con'clud·ing** final.

con·clu·sion [kən'kluːʒn] conclusión *f*; *in* ~ en conclusión; **con'clu·sive** (*decisive*) decisivo.

con·coct [kən'kɔkt] mezclar, confeccionar; *fig.* tramar, urdir.

con·cord ['kɔnkɔːd] concordia *f*; *gr.*, ♪ concordancia *f*; **2.** [kən'kɔːd] concordar (*with* con); **con'cord·ance** concordancia *f* (*a. eccl.*).

con·course ['kɔŋkɔːs] confluencia *f* of *rivers*; concurso *m*, reunión *f* of *people*; 🚇 gran salón *m.*

con·crete 1. ['kɔnkriːt] □ concreto; ⊕ de hormigón; **2.** [~] ⊕ hormigón *m*; ~ *mixer* hormigonera *f*; **3.** [kən'kriːt] cuajarse; solidificarse.

con·cur [kən'kɔː] concurrir; convenir (*with* con; *in* en); **con·cur·rence** [~'kʌrəns] concurrencia *f*; unión *f*; (*agreement*) acuerdo *m*; (*assent*) asenso *m.*

con·cus·sion [kən'kʌʃn] sacudimiento *m*; 🩺 commoción *f* cerebral.

con·demn [kən'dem] condenar (*to* a); censurar; **con·dem·na·tion** [kɔndem'neiʃn] condenación *f*; 🔧 condena *f*; censura *f.*

con·den·sa·tion [kɔnden'seiʃn] condensación *f*; (*a.* 🔲) compendio *m* of *material*; **con·dense** [kən'dens] condensar; *material* abreviar.

con·de·scend [kɔndi'send] condescender (*to* en); dignarse (*to inf.*); **con·de'scend·ing** □ condescen-

diente; **con·de'scen·sion** dignación *f*, condescendencia *f.*

con·di·tion [kən'diʃn] **1.** condición *f*; ~s *pl.*; condiciones *f/pl.*, circunstancias *f/pl.*; **2.** condicionar, acondicionar; determinar; **con·di·tion·al** □ condicional (*a. gr.*).

con·do·min·i·um [kɔndə'miniəm] condominio *m.*

con·done [kən'dəun] condonar.

con·duct 1. ['kɔndʌkt] conducta *f*; **2.** [kən'dʌkt] conducir; llevar; *orchestra* dirigir; ♪ (*v/i.*) llevar la batuta; ~ *o.s.* comportarse; **con·duc·tor** [kən'dʌktə] conductor *m* (*a. phys.*); ♪ director *m*; (*bus*) cobrador *m*; 🚍 revisor *m*; (*lightning*) pararrayos *m.*

con·duit ['kɔndjuit] conducto *m*, canal *m.*

cone [kəun] cono *m* (*a.* ♣); (*ice-cream* ~) barquillo *m.*

con·fec·tion [kən'fekʃn] confección *f*, hechura *f*; (*sweetmeat*) confite *m.*

con·fed·er·a·cy [kən'fedərəsi] confederación *f*; 🔧 complot *m*; **con'fed·er·ate 1.** [~rit] confederado; **2.** [~] confederado *m*; cómplice *m*; **3.** [~reit] confederarse.

con·fer [kən'fɔː] *v/t.* conferir (*on* a); *v/i.* conferir (*with* con; *about, upon* acerca de, sobre); **con·fer·ence** ['kɔnfərəns] conferencia *f*; (*assembly*) congreso *m.*

con·fess [kən'fes] confesar (*to p.* a); ~ *to* th. reconocer, admitir; **con·fes·sion** [~'feʃn] confesión *f* (*a. eccl.*); *eccl.* (*a.* ~ *of faith*) credo *m*; ~ *box* confesonario *m.*

con·fi·dant [kɔnfi'dænt] confidente *m*; **con·fi·dante** [~] confidenta *f.*

con·fide [kən'faid] *v/i.*: ~ *in* confiar en, fiarse de; ~ *to* hacer confidencias a; *v/t. th.* confiar (*to* a, en); **con·fi·dence** ['kɔnfidəns] confianza *f* (*in* en); confidencia *f*, secreto *m*; *in* ~ en confianza; *gain* ~ adquirir confianza; ~ *man* timador *m*; **'con·fi·dent** □ seguro (*of* de; *that* de que); lleno de confianza; *b.s.* confiado; **con·fi·den·tial** □ confidencial; ~*ly* en confianza.

con·fine 1. ['kɔnfain] *mst* ~s *pl.* confines *m/pl.* (*a. fig.*); **2.** [kən'fain] confinar (*s.o. to* en); encerrar; limitar.

con·firm [kən'fɔːm] confirmar (*a. eccl.*); ratificar, revalidar; **con·fir·ma·tion** [kɔnfə'meiʃn] confirmación *f* (*a. eccl.*); **con'firmed** confirmado (*a. eccl.*); (*by habit*) inveterado.

consent

con·fis·cate ['kɔnfiskeit] confiscar; con·fis·ca·tion [confiscación f.

con·fla·gra·tion [kɔnfləˈgreiʃn] conflagración f.

con·flict 1. ['kɔnflikt] conflicto m (a. fig.); 2. [kɔnˈflikt] ~ with estar en pugna con.

con·form [kɔnˈfɔːm] v/t. conformar (to con); v/i. ~ to conformarse con, allanarse a; con·for·ma·tion [kɔn-fɔːˈmeiʃn] conformación f.

con·found [kɔnˈfaund] confundir; vencer; F ~ it! ¡demonio!; con·found·ed □ F condenado.

con·front [kɔnˈfrʌnt] afrontar, carear; s.o. confrontar (with con); hacer cara a; manuscripts cotejar; be ~ed with encararse con; salírsele a uno; con·fron·ta·tion [kɔnfrʌnˈteiʃn] confrontación f; cotejo m.

con·fuse [kɔnˈfjuːz] confundir (s.t. with con); ~ the issue oscurecer las cosas; con·fused □ confuso; perturbado, aturrullado; con·fu·sion confusión f; (mental) aturdimiento m; desorden m.

con·geal [kɔnˈdʒiːl] congelar(se); (blood) coagular(se).

con·ge·la·tion [kɔndʒiˈleiʃn] congelación f.

con·gen·ial [kɔnˈdʒiːniəl] □ congenial; atmosphere etc. agradable; con·gen·i·tal [kɔnˈdʒenitl] □ congénito.

con·gest [kɔnˈdʒest] congestionar(se) (a. 🐾); (people) apiñarse; con·ges·tion congestión f.

con·grat·u·late [kɔnˈgrætjuleit] felicitar ([up]on por); con·grat·u·la·tion felicitación f, parabién m; ~s! ¡enhorabuena!

con·gre·gate ['kɔngrigeit] congregar (-se); con·gre·ga·tion eccl. congregación f.

con·gress ['kɔngres] congreso m; 2 Congreso m (de Estados Unidos); ~man congresista m; con·gres·sion·al [~ˈgreʃnl] congresional; '~·man congresista m.

con·ic, con·i·cal ['kɔnik(l)] □ cónico; Å ~ section sección f cónica.

con·jec·ture [kɔnˈdʒektʃə] 1. conjetura f; 2. conjeturar (from de, por).

con·ju·gal ['kɔndʒugl] □ conjugal; con·ju·gate ['~geit] 1. v/t. conjugar; v/i. biol. reproducirse; 2 conjugado; con·ju·ga·tion ['~geiʃn] conjugación f (a. biol.).

con·junc·tion [kɔnˈdʒʌŋkʃən] conjunción f; con·junc·tive [kɔn-ˈdʒʌŋktiv] conjuntivo; ~ mood modo m conjuntivo; con·junc·ti·vi·tis [~-ˈvaitis] conjuntivitis f.

con·ju·ra·tion [kɔndʒuəˈreiʃn] conjuro m; con·jure 1. [kɔnˈdʒuə] v/t. conjurar, pedir con instancia; 2. ['kʌndʒə] v/t. conjurar, exorcizar (~ away); ~ up hacer aparecer; fig. evocar; v/i. escamotear; practicar las artes mágicas.

con·nect [kɔˈnekt] conectar(se), conexionar(se), asociar(se), enlazar (-se); 🐾 empalmar (with con); teleph. poner en comunicación (with con); con·nect·ed □ conexo; asociado; enlazado (with con); be ~ with estar asociado con; con·nec·tion [kɔ-ˈnekʃn] conexión f (a. ⚡); fig. relación f; (family ~) parentesco m; unión f, enlace m; ⚓ correspondencia f (with con), empalme m; ⊕ acoplamiento m; in ~ with a propósito de; in this ~ con respecto a esto.

con·niv·ance [kɔˈnaivəns] connivencia f; confabulación f (at, in para).

con·nois·seur [kɔniˈsɔː] conocedor (-a f) m; catador m of wine.

con·no·ta·tion [kɔnəˈteiʃn] connotación f; con·note connotar.

con·quer ['kɔŋkə] conquistar (a. fig.), vencer; con·quer·or conquistador (-a f) m; vencedor (-a f) m.

con·quest ['kɔŋkwest] conquista f.

con·science ['kɔnʃns] conciencia f; F in all ~ en realidad de verdad.

con·sci·en·tious [kɔnʃiˈenʃəs] □ concienzudo; ~ objector pacifista m que se niega a tomar las armas.

con·scious ['kɔnʃəs] □ consciente; intencional; be ~ hacerse cargo, tener conocimiento (of de; that de que); 🐾 tener conocimiento; 'con·scious·ness conciencia f; 🐾 conocimiento m; phls. conciencia f; lose (regain) ~ perder (recobrar) el conocimiento.

con·script [kɔnˈskript] reclutar; con·script ['kɔnskript] recluta m, quinto m; con·scrip·tion reclutamiento m.

con·se·crate ['kɔnsikreit] consagrar (a. fig.); con·se·cra·tion consagración f.

con·sec·u·tive [kɔnˈsekjutiv] consecutivo (a. gr.), sucesivo; con·sec·u·tive·ly sucesivamente.

con·sen·sus [kɔnˈsensəs] consenso m.

con·sent [kɔnˈsent] 1. consentimiento m (to en); by common ~ según la opinión unánime; 2. consentir (to en).

con·se·quence [ˈkɔnsikwəns] consecuencia *f*; **ˈcon·se·quent 1.** consiguiente; *phls.* consecuente; *be ~ on*
ser consecuencia de; **2.** *gr.* consiguiente *m*; *phls.*, Ⱥ consecuente *m*;
ˈcon·se·quent·ly [ˈ∼kwentli] por consiguiente.

con·ser·va·tion [kɔnsəˈveiʃn] conservación *f*; **con·serv·a·tism** [kən-
ˈsə:vətizm] conservatismo *m*; **con-
ˈserv·a·tive** □ conservativo *a.* ; *pol.*
conservador (*a. su. m*); moderado,
cauteloso; **conˈserve 1.** conserva *f*,
compota *f*; **2.** conservar.

con·sid·er [kənˈsidə] considerar;
conˈsid·er·a·ble □ considerable;
conˈsid·er·ate [∼rit] □ considerado;
con·sid·er·a·tion [∼ˈreiʃn] consideración *f*; ✝ remuneración *f*; *in ~ of* en
consideración a; *take into ~* tomar en
cuenta; *without due ~* sin reflexión;
conˈsid·er·ing 1. *prp.* en consideración a; **2.** F *adv.* teniendo en cuenta
las circunstancias.

con·sign [kənˈsain] consignar (*a.* ✝);
confiar, entregar; **conˈsign·ment**
[kənˈsainmənt] consignación *f* (*a.*
✝); ✝ envío *m*, remesa *f*.

con·sist [kənˈsist] consistir (*in*, of en);
constar (*of* de); **conˈsist·en·cy** consistencia *f*; consecuencia *f of actions*;
conˈsist·ent □ consistente; consonante (*with* con); *conduct* consecuente; *~ly* sin excepción, continuamen-
te.

con·so·la·tion [kɔnsəˈleiʃn] consolación *f*, consuelo *m*.

con·sole 1. [kənˈsoul] consolar; **2.**
[ˈkɔnsoul] Ⱥ consola *f*.

con·sol·i·date [kənˈsɔlideit] consolidar (*a.* ✝); **con·sol·i·da·tion** consolidación *f*.

con·so·nant [ˈkɔnsənənt] consonante.

con·sort [ˈkɔnsɔːt] consorte *m/f*; ⚓
buque *m* que acompaña a otro.

con·spic·u·ous □ [kənˈspikjuəs] □ visible, evidente; que llama la atención.

con·spir·a·cy [kənˈspirəsi] conspiración *f*, complot *m*; **conˈspir·a·tor**
[∼tə] conspirador (*-a f*) *m*; **conˈspire**
[∼ˈspaiə] *v/t.* urdir, maquinar; *v/i.*
conspirar (*to* a).

con·stant [ˈkɔnstənt] **1.** □ constante;
incesante; (*persistent*) porfiado; **2.** Ⱥ
constante *f*.

con·stel·la·tion [kɔnstəˈleiʃn] constelación *f* (*a. fig.*).

con·ster·na·tion [kɔnstəˈneiʃn] consternación *f*.

con·sti·pate [ˈkɔnstipeit] estreñir;
con·sti·pa·tion estreñimiento *m*.

con·sti·tute [ˈkɔnstitjuːt] constituir (*a
p. judge* a una p. juez); **con·sti·tu-
tion** constitución *f*.

con·strain [kənˈstrein] constreñir,
obligar (*to* a); imponer; **conˈstraint**
coacción *f*, constreñimiento *m*; encierro *m*; *fig.* desconcierto *m*.

con·strict [kənˈstrikt] apretar.

con·struct [kənˈstrʌkt] construir (*a.
gr.*); **conˈstruc·tion** construcción *f*;
interpretación *f*, explicación *f*; *under
~* en construcción.

con·sul [ˈkɔnsl] cónsul *m*; **con·su·lar**
[ˈkɔnsjulə] consular; **con·su·late**
[ˈ∼lit] consulado *m*.

con·sult [kənˈsʌlt] consultar (*with*
con), *~ing attr.* consultor; ⚕ *~ing
room* consultorio *m*; **conˈsult·ant**
consultor *m*; ⚕ especialista *m*; **con-
sul·ta·tion** [kɔnsəlˈteiʃn] consulta *f*
(*a.* ⚕), consultación *f*.

con·sume [kənˈsjuːm] consumir (*a.
fig.*); **conˈsum·er** consumidor *m*; *~
goods pl.* artículos *m/pl.* de consumo.

con·sump·tion [kənˈsʌmpʃn] consunción *f*; ⚕ *of goods*.

con·tact [ˈkɔntækt] **1.** contacto *m* (*a.
fig.*, *ⳋ*); *~ lenses* microlentillas *f/pl.*
get in ~ with = **2.** [kɔnˈtækt] F ponerse
en contacto con; **ˈ~ break·er** ⚡ rup-
tor *m*.

con·ta·gion [kənˈteidʒn] contagio *m*
(*a. fig.*); **conˈta·gious** □ contagioso
(*a. fig.*).

con·tain [kənˈtein] contener (*a.* ✕);
space abarcar; **conˈtain·er** continente *m*; ✝ *etc.* envase *m*, caja *f*.

con·tam·i·nate [kənˈtæmineit] contaminar (*a. fig.*); **con·tam·i·na·tion**
contaminación *f*; refundición *f*, fusión *f of text*.

con·tem·plate [ˈkɔntempleit] contemplar; proponerse (*doing* hacer);
con·tem·pla·tion contemplación *f*;
mira *f*, intención *f*.

con·tem·po·ra·ne·ous [kəntempə-
ˈreinjəs] □ contemporáneo; **con-
ˈtem·po·rar·y** contemporáneo *adj.
a. su. m* (*a f*); coetáneo *adj. a. su. m*
(*a f*).

con·tempt [kənˈtempt] desprecio *m*,
desdén *m*; ⚖ *~ of court* contumacia *f*,
rebeldía *f*; *hold in ~* despreciar; **con-
ˈtempt·i·ble** □ despreciable; **con-
ˈtemp·tu·ous** [∼juəs] □ desprecia-

tivo, despectivo; desdeñoso (*of* para, hacia).

con·tend [kən'tend] *v/i.* contender (*with* ... *over* con ... sobre); luchar (*for* por); (*argument*) sostener; *v/t.* afirmar, sostener.

con·tent [kən'tent] **1.** contento (*with* de, con); **2.** contentar; **3.** contento *m*; *to one's heart's* ~ a gusto, hasta más no poder; **4.** ['kɔntent] contenido *m* (*freq.* ~*s pl.*); (*capacity*) cabida *f*; (*esp.* 🔊) componente *m*.

con·ten·tion [kən'tenʃn] contienda *f*, disputa *f*; argumento *m*, aseveración *f* (*that* de que).

con·tent·ment [kən'tentmənt] contento *m*, satisfacción *f*.

con·test 1. ['kɔntest] debate *m*, disputa *f*; (*fight*) contienda *f*, lid *f* (*a. fig.*); (*competition*) concurso *m*; **2.** [kən'test] disputar, impugnar; tomar parte en un concurso; *election* ser candidato en; **con·test·ant** contendiente *m/f*; contrincante *m*; rival *m/f*.

con·text ['kɔntekst] contexte *m*.

con·ti·nent ['kɔntinənt] **1.** □ continente; **2.** continente *m*; *the* ♀ la Europa continental; **con·ti·nen·tal** [~'nentl] □ continental.

con·tin·gent [kən'tindʒənt] **1.** □ contingente, eventual; dependiente (*on* de); **2.** contingente *m*.

con·tin·u·al [kən'tinjuəl] □ continuo, incesante; **con·tin·u·a·tion** continuación *f*; 🌱 prórroga *f*; **con·tin·ue** *v/t.* continuar; mantener; 🏛 aplazar; *to be* ~*d* continuará; *v/i.* continuar(se); **con·ti·nu·i·ty** [kɔnti'nju:iti] continuidad *f*; **con·tin·u·ous** [kən'tinjuəs] □ continuo (*a.* 🎬).

con·tour ['kɔntuə] contorno *m*; ~ *line* curva *f* de nivel.

con·tra·band ['kɔntrəbænd] (*attr.* de) contrabando *m*.

con·tract 1. [kən'trækt] *v/t.* contraer; *v/i.* contraerse; comprometerse por contrato (*to* a); **2.** ['kɔntrækt] contrato *m*; ♯ contrata *f*; **con·tract·ed** [kən'træktid] contraído; encogido; **con·trac·tion** contracción *f*; **con·trac·tor** contratista *m/f*; contratante *m*.

con·tra·dict [kɔntrə'dikt] contradecir; **con·tra·dic·tion** contradicción *f*; **con·tra·dic·to·ry** □ contradictorio; *p.* contradictor.

con·trap·tion [kən'træpʃn] dispositivo *m*, artificio *m*; *contp.* armatoste *m*.

con·tra·ry ['kɔntrəri] **1.** contrario; F [kən'treəri] obstinado, terco; *que lleva la contra*; *adv.* en contrario; ~ *to* contrario a; **2.** contrario *m*; *on the* ~ al contrario; *to the* ~ en contrario.

con·trast 1. ['kɔntræst] contraste *m*; *in* ~ *por* contraste; *in* ~ *to* en contraposición a; **2.** [kən'træst] *v/t.* poner en contraste; *v/i.* contrastar (*with* con).

con·trib·ute [kən'tribju:t] contribuir (*towards* a, para; *to ger. a inf.*); ~ *to paper* colaborar en; **con·tri·bu·tion** [kɔntri'bju:ʃn] contribución *f*; artículo *m*, escrito *m* *to paper*; **con·trib·u·tor** [kən'tribju:tə] contribuidor (-a *f*) *m*, contribuyente *m*; colaborador (-a *f*) *m to paper*.

con·trite ['kɔntrait] □ contrito; **con·tri·tion** [kən'triʃn] contrición *f*.

con·trol [kən'troul] **1.** mando *m*, gobierno *m*; inspección *f*, intervención *f* (*esp.* 🌱); control *m*; ⊕ regulador *m*; 🎛 norma *f* de comprobación; dirección *f*; *attr.* de mando, de control; ~*s pl. esp.* ✈ aparatos *m/pl.* de mando; *remote* ~ comando *m* a distancia, telecontrol *m*; *be in* ~ tener el mando, mandar; *get out of* ~ perder control; *get under* ~ conseguir dominar; **2.** mandar, gobernar; controlar, comprobar; ⊕ regular; *price* controlar; ~ *o.s.* dominarse.

con·tro·ver·sial [kɔntrə'vɔ:ʃl] □ controvertible; contencioso; **con·tro·ver·sy** controversia *f*.

co·nun·drum [kə'nʌndrəm] acertijo *m*, adivinanza *f*.

con·va·lesce [kɔnvə'les] convalecer; **con·va·les·cence** convalecencia *f*; **con·va·les·cent** convaleciente *adj. a. su. m/f*; ~ *home* clínica *f* de reposo.

con·vene [kən'vi:n] *v/i.* juntarse, reunirse; *v/t. meeting* convocar.

con·ven·ience [kən'vi:njəns] conveniencia *f*; comodidad *f*; (*time*) oportunidad *f*; *at your earliest* ~ cuando le sea conveniente; **con·ven·ient** □ conveniente; cómodo; *time* oportuno; apto.

con·vent ['kɔnvənt] convento *m* (de religiosas); **con·ven·tion** convención *f*; (*meeting*) asamblea *f*.

con·verge [kən'və:dʒ] convergir.

con·ver·sant [kən'və:sənt] versado (*with* en); *become* ~ *with* familiarizarse con; **con·ver·sa·tion** [~'seiʃn] conversación *f*, plática *f*; **con·ver·sa·tion·al** □ de conversación; *p.*

hablador, expansivo; **con·verse 1.** ['kɔnvəːs] □ contrario, inverso; **2.** [~] plática *f*; *A* inversa *f*; **3.** [kən'vəːs] conversar (*with* con); **con'ver·sion** conversión *f* (*to a*) into en); **†** cambio *m*, conversión *f*; **†**, ⊕ reorganización *f*; **g̶r̶** apropiación *f* ilícita.

con·vert 1. ['kɔnvəːt] converso (*a f*) *m*, convertido (*a f*) *m*; **2.** [kən'vəːt] convertir (*to a*) into en); **g̶r̶** apropiarse ilícitamente (*to one's own use* para uso propio); **con'vert·er** ⊕, ⊕ convertidor *m*; **con·vert·i·bil·i·ty** [~ə'biliti] convertibilidad *f*.

con·vex ['kɔn'veks] □ convexo.

con·vey [kən'vei] transportar, llevar; *current* transmitir; *news* comunicar; dar a entender (*to a*) into en); **g̶r̶** traspasar; **con'vey·ance** transporte *m*; vehículo *m*; (*a. ⚡*) transmisión *f*; comunicación *f*; **g̶r̶** (escritura *f* de) traspaso *m*.

con·vict 1. ['kɔnvikt] presidiario *m*; **2.** [kən'vikt] condenar; declarar culpable (*of* de); **con·vic·tion** [kən'vikʃn] convencimiento *m*; **g̶r̶** condena *f*; ~*s pl.* convicciones *f/pl.*

con·vince [kən'vins] convencer (*of* de); **con·vinc·ing** □ convincente.

con·viv·i·al [kən'viviəl] □ festivo, jovial.

con·vo·ca·tion [kɔnvə'keiʃn] convocación *f*; (*meeting*) asamblea *f*.

con·voy ['kɔnvɔi] **1.** convoy *m*; **2.** convoyar.

con·vulse [kən'vʌls] agitar(se); *nerves* convulsionar; *be* ~*d with laughter* desternillarse de risa; **con'vul·sion** convulsión *f* (*a. fig.*); ~*s pl.* (*of laughter*) paroxismo *m* de risa.

coo [kuː] arrullar.

cook [kuk] **1.** cocinero (*a f*) *m*; **2.** cocinar; cocer, guisar; *meal* preparar; *sl.* ~ *up* maquinar; tramar; ~ *book* libro *m* de cocina; **'cook·ie** pastelito *m* dulce; **'cook·ing** cocina *f*; *attr.* de cocina(*r*).

cool [kuːl] **1.** □ fresco; tibio (*a. fig.*); *fig.* indiferente, frío; sereno, tranquilo; *b.s.* descarado, audaz; F sin exageración; *a* ~ *thousand* mil libras contantes y sonantes; **2.** fresco *m*; **3.** refrescar(se); (*a.* ~ *down*) moderarse; ~ *off* fig. enfriarse; *sl.* trena *f*; **'cool-'head·ed** sereno, sosegado.

cool·ing ['kuːlin] refrigeración *f*; *attr.* refrigerante; *drink* refrescante; ~ *tower* torre *f* de refrigeración; **'cool·ness** frescura *f*; tibieza *f* (*a. fig.*), etc.

coop [kuːp] **1.** gallinero *m*, caponera *f*; **2.** ~ *up* encerrar, enjaular.

co-op [kou'ɔp] F = cooperative.

co·op·er·ate [kou'ɔpəreit] cooperar; **co·op·er·a·tion** cooperación *f*; **co·op·er·a·tive** [~pərətiv] cooperativo; *p.* socorrido.

co·or·di·nate 1. [kou'ɔːdinit] □ coordenado; (*equal*) igual; *gr.* coordinante; **2.** [~] *Å* coordenada *f*; **3.** [~neit] coordinar; **co·or·di·na·tion** coordinación *f*.

co·part·ner ['kou'pɑːtnə] consocio *m*; copartícipe *m/f*.

cope¹ [koup] **1.** *eccl.* capa *f* pluvial; *Δ* albardilla *f*; **2.** *Δ* poner albardilla *a*; abovedar.

cope² [~]: ~ *with* poder con, vencer.

co·pi·lot ['kou'pailət] copiloto *m*.

co·pi·ous ['koupjəs] □ copioso.

cop·per¹ ['kɔpə] **1.** cobre *m*; (*utensil*) caldero *m*; (*money*) calderilla *f*; **2.** cubrir con cobre; **3.** de cobre, cobreño; (*color*) cobrizo.

cop·per² [~] *sl.* polizonte *m*, esbirro *m*.

cop·u·late ['kɔpjuleit] tener ayuntamiento; **cop·u·la·tion** ayuntamiento *m* carnal; coito *m*.

cop·y ['kɔpi] **1.** copia *f*; ejemplar *m* of *book*; número *m* of *journal*; *typ.* material *m*, original *m*; *v. fair, rough*; **2.** copiar; imitar; (*counterfeit*) contrahacer; **'~·book** cuaderno *m*; **'~·cat** F imitador (-a *f*) *m*; **'cop·y·ist** copista *m/f*; **'cop·y·right** derecho *m* de propiedad literaria, copyright *m*; **'cop·y·writ·er** escritor *m* de anuncios.

cor·al ['kɔrəl] coral *m*; *attr.* coralino.

cord [kɔːd] **1.** cuerda *f*; *anat.* cordón *m*; (*cloth*) pana *f*; **2.** acordonar.

cor·di·al ['kɔːdiəl] □ cordial *adj. a. su. m*; **cor·di·al·i·ty** [~di'æliti] cordialidad *f*.

cor·du·roy ['kɔːdərɔi] pana *f*; ~ *road* camino *m* de troncos.

core [kɔː] corazón *m*, centro *m*; *fig.* quid *m*, esencia *f*; **☞** foco *m*; alma *f* of *cable*; núcleo *m* of *electromagnet*.

cork [kɔːk] **1.** corcho *m*; tapón *m* (de corcho); **2.** tapar con corcho (*a.* ~ *up*); **'~·screw** **1.** sacacorchos *m*; **2.** en caracol, en espiral; **3.** zigzaguear, moverse en espiral; **'~·tipped** *cigarette* emboquillado.

corn¹ [kɔːn] **1.** maíz *m*; *sl.* broma *f* gastada; ~ *bread* pan *m* de maíz; **2.** acecinar; ~*ed beef* carne *f* de vaca conservada en lata.

corn² [~] *☞* callo *m*.

corn...: '~**cob** mazorca *f* de maíz.

cor·ner ['kɔ:nə] 1. ángulo *m*; esquina *f* (*esp.* street-~); (*inside*) rincón *m* (*a. fig.*); *fig.* apuro *m*, aprieto *m*; *sport*: córner *m*; **♠** acaparamiento *m*; *cut* ~**s** atajar; 2. arrinconar (*a. fig.*); **†** acaparar; '~**cup·board** rinconera *f*; '~**stone** piedra *f* angular (*a. fig.*).

corn...: '~**ex·change** bolsa *f* de granos; '~**field** maizal *m*; *in England* trigal *m*; '~**flour** harina *f* de maíz; '~**flow·er** cabezuela *f*; '~**husk** perfolla *f*; '~ **meal** harina *f* de maíz; '~ **on the 'cob** maíz *m* en la mazorca; '~**stalk** tallo *m* de maíz; '~**starch** almidón *m* de maíz.

cor·nu·co·pi·a [kɔ:nju'koupjə] cornucopia *f*.

corn·y ['kɔ:ni] de maíz; **♪** calloso; *sl.* **♪** muy sentimental; *sl. joke etc.* pesado, gastado, trivial.

co·ro·na [kə'rounə], *pl.* **co·ro·nae** [~ni:] corona *f*; **△** cornisa *f*, coronamiento *m*; '**co·ro·na·ry ♂** coronario; ~ *thrombosis* trombosis *f* coronaria; **cor·o·na·tion** [kɔrə'neiʃn] coronación *f*; **cor·o·ner** ['kɔrənə] juez *m* de primera instancia e instrucción.

cor·po·ral ['kɔ:pərəl] 1. □ corporal; 2. ✕ cabo *m*; *eccl.* corporal *m*; **cor·po·rate** ['~rit] □ corporativo; incorporado; **cor·po·ra·tion** [~'reiʃn] corporación *f*; **F** panza *f*, tripa *f*; **th** sociedad *f* anónima.

corps [kɔ:], *pl.* **corps** [kɔ:z] cuerpo *m*; ~ *de ballet* cuerpo *m* de baile.

corpse [kɔ:ps] cadáver *m*.

cor·pu·lence, cor·pu·len·cy ['kɔ:pjuləns(i)] corpulencia *f*; '**cor·pu·lent** corpulento.

cor·pus ['kɔ:pəs], *pl.* **cor·po·ra** ['~pərə] cuerpo *m* (de leyes, escritos *etc.*); ~ *delicti* cuerpo *m* de delito; **cor·pus·cle** ['~pʌsl] (*blood*) glóbulo *m*.

cor·ral [kə'rɑ:l] 1. corral *m*; 2. acorralar, encerrar.

cor·rect [kə'rekt] 1. □ exacto, justo; *behaviour* correcto, cumplido; *be* ~ *freq.* tener razón, acertar; 2. corregir; *exam* puntuar, calificar; **cor·rec·tion** corrección *f*; calificación *f* of *exam paper*.

cor·re·late ['kɔrileit] 1. correlacionar; 2. correlativo *m*; **cor·re·la·tion** correlación *f*.

cor·re·spond [kɔris'pɔnd] corresponder (*to* a); corresponderse, catearse (*with p.* con); **cor·re·spond·ence** correspondencia *f*; (*collected letters*) epistolario *m*; **cor·re·spond·ent** 1. □ correspondiente; 2. correspondiente *m*; (*newspaper*) corresponsal *m*; el (la) que escribe cartas.

cor·ri·dor ['kɔridɔ:] pasillo *m*, corredor *m*.

cor·rob·o·rate [~'reit] corroborar; **cor·rob·o·ra·tion** corroboración *f*.

cor·rode [kə'roud] corroer (*a. fig.*); **cor·ro·sion** corrosión *f*.

cor·ru·gate ['kɔrugeit] arrugar(se); **⊕** acanalar; ~*d iron* hierro *m* ondulado; ~*d paper* papel *m* ondulado.

cor·rupt [kə'rʌpt] 1. □ corrompido; *manners* estragado; *text* viciado, depravado; 2. *v/t.* corromper; estragar; *v/i.* corromperse; (*rot*) podrirse; **cor·rup·tion** corrupción *f* (*a. fig.*).

cor·sage [kɔ:'sɑ:ʒ] corpiño *m*, jubón *m*; **♀** ramillete *m* para la cintura.

co·sine ['kousain] coseno *m*.

cos·met·ic [kɔz'metik] 1. cosmético; 2. cosmético *m*, afeite *m*.

cos·mic ['kɔzmik] □ cósmico; ~ *rays* rayos *m/pl.* cósmicos.

cos·mo·pol·i·tan [kɔzmə'pɔlitən] cosmopolita *adj. a. su. m/f.*

cost [kɔst] 1. precio *m*; coste *m*, costa *f*; **†** *at* ~ a costa; ~ *of living* costo *m* de la vida; ~*s pl.* **th** costas *f/pl.*; *at all* ~*s* a todo trance; 2. [*irr.*] costar.

cos·tume ['kɔstju:m] 1. traje *m*; (*fancy dress*) disfraz *m*; 2. trajear.

co·sy ['kouzi] = cozy.

cot [kɔt] catre *m*; camita *f* de niño, cuna *f*; **♧** coy *m*.

co·te·rie ['koutəri] grupo *m*, camarilla *f*.

cot·tage ['kɔtidʒ] casita *f*, chalet *m*; (*labourer's etc.*) barraca *f*, choza *f*, cabaña *f*; ~ *cheese* requesón *m*, naterón *m*.

cot·ton ['kɔtn] algodón *m*; (*plant*) algodonero *m*.

couch [kautʃ] 1. sofá *m*, canapé *m*, meridiana *f*; *poet.* lecho *m*; 2. acostar(se) (*now only p.p.*); *thoughts* expresar, formular; (*crouch*) agacharse; (*lie in wait*) emboscarse.

cough [kɔf] 1. tos *f*; 2. toser; ~ *up* expectorar; *sl.* descolgarse con; *sl.* sacar, producir; (*money*) desdinerarse.

could [kud] *pret. of* can.

couldn't ['kudnt] = could not.

coun·cil ['kaunsl] junta *f*, consejo *m*; *eccl.* concilio *m*; (*town*) concejo *m*, ayuntamiento *m*; **coun·ci·(l)·lor** ['~ilə] concejal *m*.

coun·sel [ˈkaunsəl] 1. consejo m; deliberación f, consulta f; ⚖ abogado m; *take ~ with* consultar; 2. aconsejar;
coun·se(l)·lor [ˈ~lə] consejero (a f) m; *Ir.* abogado m (a. '**~·at-'law**).

count[1] [kaunt] 1. cuenta f, cálculo m; suma f, total m; ⚖ cargo m; *boxing:* cuenta f; *lose ~* perder la cuenta; 2. v/t. contar; *~ out* no incluir, no tener en cuenta; *boxing:* declarar vencido; v/i. contar; valer (a. *~ for*); *that doesn't ~* eso no vale; *~ on* contar con.

count[2] [~] conde m.

coun·te·nance [ˈkauntinəns] 1. semblante m, figura f; 2. dar aprobación a; (*encourage*) apoyar.

count·er[1] [ˈkauntə] (*shop etc.*) mostrador m, contador m; (*check*) ficha f, chapa f; (*horse's*) pecho m; ⚓ bovedilla f, *fenc.* contra f; *Geiger ~* contador m Geiger; *sl. under the ~* por la trastienda.

count·er[2] [~] 1. en contra; *~ to* lo contrario a, opuesto a; *run ~ to* oponerse a, ser contrario a; 2. oponerse a, contradecir; contrarrestar; *blow* parar; *~ with* contestar con.

coun·ter·act [kauntəˈrækt] contrarrestar; neutralizar.

coun·ter·at·tack [ˈkauntərətæk] 1. contraataque m; 2. contraatacar.

coun·ter·clock·wise [ˈkauntəˈklɒkwaiz] en sentido contrario al de las agujas del reloj.

coun·ter·cur·rent [ˈkauntəˈkʌrənt] contracorriente f.

coun·ter·es·pi·o·nage [ˈkauntərˈespiənaːʒ] contraespionaje m.

coun·ter·feit [ˈkauntəfiːt] 1. falsificado, falseado, contrahecho; 2. falsificación f, contrahechura f; 3. falsificar, falsear, contrahacer; '**coun·ter·feit·er** falsificador (-a f) m, falseador (-a f) m; '**coun·ter·feit 'mon·ey** moneda f falsa.

coun·ter·part [ˈkauntəpaːt] copia f, imagen f; (*complement*) contraparte f, complemento m.

coun·ter·point [ˈkauntəpɔint] contrapunto m.

coun·ter·sign [ˈkauntəsain] 1. contraseña f (a. ⚔); ✝ *etc.* contramarca f; 2. refrendar.

count·ess [ˈkauntis] condesa f.

count·less [ˈkauntlis] sin cuento.

coun·try [ˈkʌntri] 1. país m; patria f; (*not town*) campo m; 2. attr. de campo, rural; *~ club* club m campestre; *~ estate* finca f; *~ folk* gente f del campo; *~ house* quinta f, casa f de campo; *~ life* vida f del campo; '**~·man** campesino m; *fellow ~* compatriota m; '**~·side** campo m; (*open ~*) campiña f.

coun·ty [ˈkaunti] condado m; *~ seat* cabeza f de partido.

coup [kuː] golpe m; *~ d'état* golpe m de estado; *~ de grâce* golpe m de gracia.

cou·ple [ˈkʌpl] 1. par m; (*people*) pareja f; F dos más o menos; *married ~* matrimonio m; 2. juntar, unir; *animals* aparear; ⊕ acoplar, enganchar; F casar; '**cou·pler** *radio:* acoplador m; '**cou·plet** pareado m; par m de versos.

cou·pling [ˈkʌpliŋ] ⊕ acoplamiento m; 🚃 enganche m.

cou·pon [ˈkuːpɔn] cupón m; (*football*) boleto m.

cour·age [ˈkʌridʒ] valor m, valentía f; *~!* ¡ánimo!; *pluck up ~* hacer de tripas corazón; **cou·ra·geous** [kəˈreidʒəs] □ valiente.

cou·ri·er [ˈkuriə] estafeta f, correo m diplomático; agente m de turismo.

course [kɔːs] 1. curso m; ✕ trayectoria f; *fig.* proceder m, camino m; ⚓ rumbo m; plato m *of meal;* transcurso m, paso m *of time;* hilada f *of bricks;* corriente f *of water;* (*golf*) campo m; (*race*) pista f; *in due ~* a su tiempo; andando el tiempo; *in the ~ of* durante; *of ~* por supuesto, desde luego; *give ~ to* dar curso a; 2. v/t. dar caza a, perseguir; v/i. correr (*freq. ~ along*).

court [kɔːt] 1. corte f; ⚖ tribunal m; *sport:* pista f; ⚘ patio m; (*house*) palacete m, mansión f suntuosa; 2. cortejar, galantear; **cour·te·ous** [ˈkəːtiəs] □ cortés; **cour·te·san** [kɔːtiˈzæn] cortesana f, hetera f; **cour·te·sy** [ˈkəːtisi] cortesía f, gentileza f; **court·house** [ˈkɔːthaus] palacio m de justicia; **court·i·er** [ˈkɔːtiə] cortesano m; '**court·ly** urbano, elegante; *b.s.* obsequioso, halagüeño; *~ love* amor m cortés.

court...: '**~·'mar·tial** 1. consejo m de guerra; 2. someter a consejo de guerra; '**~·ship** cortejo m; noviazgo m; '**~·yard** patio m, atrio m.

cous·in [ˈkʌzn] primo (a f) m; *first ~*, *~ german* primo (a f) m carnal.

cove[1] [kouv] 1. ⚓ cala f, ensenada f; escondrijo m; ⚘ bovedilla f; 2. abovedar.

cove[2] [~] *sl.* tío m, tipo m.

cov·e·nant ['kʌvinənt] **1.** pacto m, convenio m; **2.** pactar, convenir.

cov·er ['kʌvə] **1.** (lid) tapa f, cubierta f; (cutlery) cubierto m; colcha f on bed; forro m, cubierta f of book; portada f of magazine; (insurance) cobertura f; mot. (a. outer ~) cubierta f; fig. b.s. disimulación f, pretexto m; ~ charge precio m del cubierto; take ~ abrigarse (from de); esconderse; under ~ clandestinamente; under ~ of so pretexto de; under separate ~ por separado; **2.** cubrir (a. fig.); revestir; tapar with lid etc.; (hide) ocultar; fig. disimular; fig. incluir; distance recorrer; ⚔ apuntar a, dominar; retreat cubrir; (stallion) cubrir; ~ in llenar; ~ over revestir (with de, con); ~ up tapar, correr el velo sobre; fig. ocultar; disimular; '**cov·ered** ['kʌvəd] '**wag·on** carromato m; '**cov·er·ing** cubierta f, envoltura f; ~ letter carta f adjunta; **cov·er·let** ['ʌlit] cubrecama m, colcha f.

cov·ert ['kʌvət] **1.** ☐ cubierto, secreto, disimulado; **2.** zo. guarida f; abrigo m; ♀ soto m.

cov·et ['kʌvit] codiciar; '**cov·et·ous** ☐ codicioso (of de); avaro.

cov·ey ['kʌvi] nidada f de perdices; fig. grupo m, peña f.

cow[1] [kau] vaca f; hembra f del elefante etc.

cow[2] [~] intimidar, acobardar.

cow·ard ['kauəd] ☐ cobarde adj. a. su. m; '**cow·ard·ice**, '**cow·ard·li·ness** cobardía f; '**cow·ard·ly** cobarde.

cow·boy ['kaubɔi] vaquero m; gaucho m S.Am.

cow·er ['kauə] agacharse (esp. por causa de miedo).

cow·hide ['kauhaid] cuero m; (whip) zurriago m.

cox·comb ['kɔkskoum] farolero m, mequetrefe m.

cox·swain ['kɔkswein, 'kɔksn] timonel m.

coy [kɔi] ☐ reservado, tímido, recatado.

co·zy ['kouzi] **1.** ☐ cómodo; room acogedor; **2.** cubretetera f.

crab[1] [kræb] cangrejo m, centolla f.

crab[2] [~] ♀ (freq. ~ **ap·ple**) manzana f silvestre; (tree) manzano m silvestre; F persona f desabrida; **crab·bed** ['kræbid] ☐ avinagrado, amargado; (disagreeable) desabrido; '~ **grass** garranchuelo m.

crack [kræk] **1.** grieta f, hendedura f; (sound) crujido m; chasquido m (a. of whip), estallido m; F instante m; sl. chiste m, cuchufleta f; attr. F de primera; F andar certero; at (the) ~ of dawn al romper el alba; **2.** v/t. agrietar, hender; hacer chasquear; safe, bottle abrir; joke decir, contar; nut cascar; sl. ~ up elogiar; v/i. agrietarse, henderse; chasquear; (window) rajarse; (voice) cascarse; F ~ down on castigar severamente; F ~ up fracasar; (⚔ etc.) desbaratarse; ⚑ perder la salud; '~**brained** chiflado, loco; '**cracked** agrietado; window rajado; F chiflado; '**crack·er** triquitraque m, petardo m; (biscuit) cracker m; blanco m de baja clase; '**crack·er·jack** F la monda, el non plus ultra; '**crack·le 1.** crujir, crepitar; **2.** crujido m, crepitación f; '**crack·up** F fracaso m, ⚑ colapso m; ✈ aterrizaje m violento.

cra·dle ['kreidl] **1.** cuna f (a. ⚓ a. fig.); ⚒ artesa f oscilante; ⚖ plataforma f colgante; ~ song canción f de cuna; **2.** poner en la cuna; fig. criar.

craft [krɑːft] oficio m, empleo m; (skill) destreza f; b.s. maña f, astucia f; ⚓ embarcación f, barco m; '**crafts·man** artesano m, artífice m; '**crafts·man·ship** artesanía f, artificio m; '**craft·y** ☐ astuto, socarrón.

crag [kræg] peñasco m, risco m, despeñadero m.

cram [kræm] embutir, rellenar; hen cebar; F empollar; F ~ o.s. (with food) hartarse; '~**full** atestado, repleto (of de).

cramp [kræmp] **1.** ⊕ grapa f; ⊕ abrazadera f; ⚑ calambre m; **2.** engrapar, lañar; ~ (one's style) cortarle ias alas a uno; '**cramped** estrecho, apretado; ⚑ entumecido.

cran·ber·ry ['krænbəri] arándano m agrio.

crane [krein] **1.** orn. grulla f (común); ⊕ grúa f; **2.** levantar (or mover) con grúa; neck estirar.

cra·ni·um ['kreiniəm] cráneo m.

crank [kræŋk] **1.** ⊕ manivela f, manubrio m; F persona f rara, maniático m; extravagante m; concepto m raro m; **2.** mot. hacer arrancar con la manivela (a. ~ up); '~ **case** cárter m del cigüeñal; '**crank·shaft** eje m del cigüeñal; '**crank·y** chiflado, extravagante.

crash [kræʃ] **1.** (noise) estrépito m,

estallido *m*; *mot.*, 🚗 *etc.* accidente *m*, choque *m*, encontronazo *m*; *fig.* fracaso *m*; ♦ quiebra *f*; ~ **dive of submarine** sumersión *f* instantánea; ~ **helmet** casco *m* protector; ~ **landing** aterrizaje *m* violento; ~ **program** programa *m* intensivo; **2.** romperse con estrépito; *mot.*, 🚗 tener un accidente; 🚗 estrellarse; ♦ quebrar; ~ **a party** *sl.* colarse, entrar de gorra; ~ **into** chocar con, estrellarse contra.

crass [kræs] tupido, espeso; *fig.* craso.

crate [kreit] caja *f*, cajón *m* (de embalaje); jaula *f* (de listones).

cra·ter ['kreitə] cráter *m*.

crave [kreiv] implorar, solicitar; ansiar, anhelar (*for*, *after acc.*).

cra·ven ['kreivn] cobarde.

crav·ing ['kreiviŋ] ansia *f*; regosto *m*, deseo *m* vehemente (*for* de).

crawl [krɔːl] **1.** arrastramiento *m*; (*on all fours*) gateamiento *m*; *swimming*: crol *m*, crawl *m*; **2.** arrastrarse; gatear, ir a gatas; F (*a.* ~ **along**) ir a paso de tortuga.

cray·fish ['kreifiʃ] ástaco *m*.

cray·on ['kreiən] creyón *m*, tizna *f*; **2.** dibujar con creyón.

craze [kreiz] **1.** manía *f* (*for* por), locura *f*; (*fashion*) moda *f*; **2.** estriar; **'crazed** enloquecido, alocado; **'cra·zy** ☐ loco (*for*, *about* por); chiflado; *idea* disparatado; ~ **quilt** centón *m*.

creak [kriːk] **1.** crujido *m*, chirrido *m*; rechinamiento *m*; **2.** crujir, chirriar; rechinar.

cream [kriːm] **1.** crema *f*; nata *f*; *fig.* flor *f* y nata (*of* de); *cold* ~ crema *f*; ~ **of tartar** crémor *m* (tártaro); **2.** formar nata; *milk* desnatar; *butter* batir; **'cream·y** ☐ cremoso.

crease [kriːs] **1.** pliegue *m*, arruga *f*; (*fold*) doblez *m*; (*trouser*) raya *f*; ~ **resisting** inarrugable; **2.** arrugar(se), plegar(se).

cre·ate [kriˈeit] crear; originar, ocasionar; *sl.* hacer alharacas; **cre'a·tion** creación *f*; **cre'a·tive** creador; fecundo; **cre'a·tor** creador *m*; **crea·ture** ['kriːtʃə] criatura *f*.

cre·den·tials [kriˈdenʃlz] *pl.* credenciales *f/pl.*

cred·i·ble ['kredəbl] ☐ creíble.

cred·it ['kredit] **1.** crédito *m* (*a.* ♦); *on* ~ a crédito; *give* ~ *to* creer; **2.** *attr.* ♦ crediticio; **3.** creer; ♦ acreditar; **'cred·it·a·ble** ☐ estimable, honorable; **'cred·i·tor** acreedor (-a *f*) *m*.

creed [kriːd] credo *m*.

creek [kriːk] cala *f*, ensenada *f*; río *m*, riachuelo *m*.

creep [kriːp] **1.** [*irr.*] arrastrarse; gatear; moverse despacio y con cautela; (*flesh*) sentir hormigueo; **2.** arrastramiento *m*; *sl.* **be a** ~ reptar; ~**s** *pl.* hormigueo *m*; *give the* ~**s** horripilar.

cre·mate [kriˈmeit] incinerar; **cre'ma·tion** incineración *f* (de cadáveres).

Cre·ole ['kriːoul] criollo *adj. a. su. m* (*a f*).

crept [krept] *pret. a. p.p.* de *creep* 1.

cres·cent ['kresnt] **1.** creciente; **2.** cuarto *m* creciente (*or* menguante); *heraldry*: creciente *m*.

crest [krest] cresta *f*; **'crest·fall·en** alicaído, abatido.

cre·tin ['kretin] cretino *m*.

crev·ice ['krevis] grieta *f*.

crew¹ [kruː] 🚢 tripulación *f*; equipo *m*; (*gang*) banda *f*, pandilla *f*.

crew² [~] *pret.* de *crow* 2.

crib [krib] **1.** pesebre *m*; cama *f* pequeña para niños; F plagio *m*; hucha *f* para maíz; **2.** F plagiar; F usar una chuleta.

crick [krik] tortícolis *m* (*esp.* ~ **in the neck**); calambre *m*.

crick·et¹ ['krikit] *zo.* grillo *m*.

crick·et² [~] **1.** cricquet *m*; F juego *m* limpio; **2.** jugar al cricquet.

crime [kraim] crimen *m*.

crim·i·nal ['kriminl] criminal *adj. a. su. m/f.*

crim·son ['krimzn] **1.** carmesí *adj. a. su. m*; **2.** enrojecer(se).

cringe [krindʒ] **1.** agacharse, encogerse; *fig.* reptar; **2.** servilismo *m.*

crin·kle ['kriŋkl] **1.** arruga *f*; *sl.* parné *m*; **2.** arrugar(se).

crip·ple ['kripl] **1.** lisiado (*a f*) *m*, mutilado *m* (*a f*), tullido (*a f*) *m*; **2.** lisiar, mutilar.

cri·sis ['kraisis] *pl.* **cri·ses** ['~siːz] crisis *f.*

crisp [krisp] **1.** ☐ crespo, rizado; frágil pero duro; tostado; *style* cortado; **2.** encrespar, rizar; tostar *in oven.*

criss·cross ['kriskrɔs] **1.** cruz *f*; líneas *f/pl.* cruzadas; **2.** *adv.* en cruz; **3.** trazar líneas cruzadas (*sobre*); entrecruzarse.

cri·te·ri·on [kraiˈtiəriən] *pl.* **cri·te·ri·a** [~ə] criterio *m.*

crit·ic ['kritik] crítico *m*; *b.s.* criticón

(-a f) m; '**crit·i·cal** □ crítico; (*hyper-*) criticón; be ~ of criticar; **crit·i·cism** ['~sizm], **cri·ti·que** [kri'ti:k] crítica f; **crit·i·cize** ['~saiz] criticar.

croak [krouk] 1. (*crow*) graznar; (*frog*) croar; (*p.*) gruñir; *sl.* estirar la pata; 2. graznido m.

crock [krɔk] vasija f de barro; F (*p.*) carcamal m; (*car*) cacharro m; '**crock·er·y** loza f; vajilla f, los platos.

croc·o·dile ['krɔkədail] cocodrilo m; ~ tears lágrimas f/pl. de cocodrilo.

crone [kroun] vieja f arrugada.

cro·ny ['krouni] F compinche m.

crook [kruk] 1. (*shepherd's*) cayado m; ⊕ gancho m; (*bend*) curva f; F criminal m, fullero m; 2. encorvar(se); **crook·ed** ['~kid] □ encorvado, curvo; *fig.* torcido.

croon [kru:n] canturrear; '**croon·er** vocalista m/f (*sentimental*).

crop [krɔp] 1. cosecha f (a. *fig.*); *orn.* buche m; (*hair*) cabellera f, corte m de pelo; (*whip*) látigo m mocho; 2. *v/t.* cortar; desorejar; *top* desmochar; trasquilar (a. *fig.*); *grass* pacer; *v/i.* ~ up *geol.* aflorar; F manifestarse inesperadamente; salir.

cro·quet ['kroukei] juego m de croquet.

cross [krɔs] 1. cruz f; *biol.* cruzamiento m; (*burden*) cruz f; on the ~ diagonalmente; *make the sign of the* ~ hacer la señal de la cruz; 2. □ transversal, opuesto (*to* a); F malhumorado, F arisco, de mal genio; *get* ~ enfadarse, ponerse furioso; 3. *v/t.* atravesar, cruzar; *p.* contrariar; *breed* cruzar; ~ o.s. santiguarse; ~ out tachar; ~ one's mind ocurrírsele a uno; *v/i.* cruzar (a. *letters*); ~ over atravesar de un lado a otro; '**~·beam** viga f transversal; '**~·bow** ballesta f; '**~·breed** 1. híbrido; 2. cruzar; '**~·coun·try** a campo traviesa; ~ *race* cross m; '**~·cur·rent** contracorriente f; '**~·cut saw** sierra f de trazar; '**~·ex·am·i'na·tion** ♣ repregunta f; interrogatorio m severo; **~·ex·am·ine** ['krɔsig'zæmin] ♣ repreguntar; interrogar; '**~·eyed** bizco; '**cross·ing** ♣ travesía f; (*roads*) cruce m; (*ford*) vado m. **cross...:** '**~·patch** F malhumorado (a. f) m; '**~·ref·er·ence** contrarreferencia f, remisión f; '**~·road** camino m que cruza; '**~·s** pl.) cruce m, encrucijada f; '**~·sec·tion** sección f transversal; *fig.* sección f representa-

tativa; '**~·wise** al través; en cruz; '**~·word** (a. ~ *puzzle*) crucigrama m.

crotch [krɔtʃ] bifurcación f; *anat.* horcajadura f; **crotch·et** ['~it] ♪ negra f; capricho m.

crouch [krautʃ] agacharse, encogerse.

croup[1] [kru:p] (*horse's*) grupa f.

croup[2] [~] ♣ crup m.

crou·pi·er ['kru:piə] coime m.

crow [krou] 1. corneja f; *as the* ~ *flies* en derechura; F *eat* ~ cantar la palinodia; 2. [*irr.*] cantar (el gallo); *fig.* alardear, exultar; '**~·bar** palanca f.

crowd [kraud] 1. multitud f, muchedumbre f; gentío m; *contp.* vulgo m; *sport:* espectadores m/pl.; *follow the* ~ irse tras el hilo de la gente; *fig. pass in* a ~ no descollar; 2. *v/t.* amontonar, atestar; *people* apiñar (a. ~ *together*); ~ed atestado (with de); concurrido; *be* ~ed *out* (*place*) estar de bote en bote; (*p.*) ser excluido; *v/i.* agolparse, arremolinarse (a. ~ *together*, ~ *around*).

crow·foot ['kroufut] ranúnculo m.

crown [kraun] 1. corona f; cruz f *of anchor*; copa f *of hat*; cima f *of hill*; ♣ coronamiento m; 2. coronar; completar, terminar; (*reward*) premiar; *sl.* golpear en la cabeza.

crow's-nest ['krouznest] ♣ torre f de vigía.

cru·cial ['kru:ʃiəl] □ decisivo, crítico; *shape* cruciforme; **cru·ci·ble** ['kru:sibl] crisol m (a. *fig.*); **cru·ci·fix** ['~fiks] crucifijo m, cruz f; **cru·ci·fix·ion** [~'fikʃn] crucifixión f; **cru·ci·fy** ['~fai] crucificar; *fig.* mortificar.

crude [kru:d] □ (*raw*) crudo; *fig.* tosco, grosero.

cru·el ['kruəl] □ cruel (a. *fig.*); '**cru·el·ty** crueldad f.

cruise [kru:z] 1. viaje m por mar, crucero m; 2. cruzar; *cruising speed* velocidad f de crucero; '**cruis·er** ♣ crucero m.

crul·ler ['krʌlə] Am. buñuelo m.

crumb [krʌm] 1. migaja f (a. *fig.*); miga f *of loaf*; 2. desmigar; cubrir con migajas; **crum·ble** ['~bl] *v/t.* desmigar; *v/i.* desmoronarse (a. *fig.*; a. ~ *away*); '**crum·bling** desmenuzable, desmoronadizo.

crum·my ['krʌmi] *sl.* sucio; *joke* gastado; *bar etc.* de baja categoría.

crum·ple ['krʌmpl] arrugar(se), plegar(se); (*dress*) ajar(se); *fig.* (a. ~ *up*) ceder, desplomarse.

crunch [krʌntʃ] ronzar; *(ground)* crujir.

cru·sade [kruˈseid] **1.** cruzada *f (a. fig.)*; **2.** participar en una cruzada; ~ *for* hacer campaña en pro de (*or* por); **cru·sad·er** cruzado *m.*

crush [krʌʃ] **1.** aplastar; *grapes etc.* prensar, estrujar; *stones etc.* moler; *dress* ajar; *fig.* abrumar, anonadar; ~*ing fig.* aplastante; **2.** presión *f* violenta, aplastamiento *m*; *(crowd)* agolpamiento *m*, bullaje *m*; *sl.* have a ~ on perder la chaveta por.

crust [krʌst] **1.** corteza *f*; *(& a. wine)* costra *f*; *& escara f; (old bread)* mendrugo *m*; **2.** encostrarse; **'crust·y** □ costroso; *fig.* áspero, desabrido.

crutch [krʌtʃ] muleta *f (a. fig.)*.

crux [krʌks] enigma *m*; lo esencial.

cry [krai] **1.** grito *m*; lloro *m*, lamento *m*; *be a far* ~ estar lejos, ser mucho camino; **2.** gritar; llorar; *wares* pregonar; ~ *for* clamar por; ~ *for joy* llorar de alegría; *s.t.* renunciar (a), romper; ~ *out* gritar, publicar en voz alta; ~ *out (against)* protestar (contra); **'~·ba·by** llorón (-a *f*) *m*; **'cry·ing** *fig.* atroz, enorme.

crypt [kript] cripta *f*; **'cryp·tic** □ oculto, misterioso.

crys·tal [ˈkristl] **1.** cristal *m*; *as clear as* ~ tan claro como el agua; ~ *ball* bola *f* de cristal; **2.** = **crys·tal·line** [ˈ~təlain] cristalino.

cub [kʌb] cachorro *m*; *fig.* rapaz *m.*

cub·by·hole [ˈkʌbihoul] chiribitil *m.*

cube [kjuːb] **1.** cubo *m*; ~ *root* raíz *f* cúbica; **2.** cubicar; **'cu·bic, 'cu·bi·cal** □ cúbico.

cu·bi·cle [ˈkjubikl] cubículo *m.*

cuck·old [ˈkʌkəld] **1.** cornudo *m*; **2.** encornudar, poner los cuernos a.

cuck·oo [ˈkukuː] **1.** cuc(lill)o *m*; **2.** *sl.* chiflado.

cu·cum·ber [ˈkjuːkʌmbə] cohombro *m*, pepino *m*; *cool as a* ~ fresco como una lechuga; *fig.* sosegado.

cud [kʌd] bolo *m* alimenticio; *v.* chew.

cud·dle [ˈkʌdl] **1.** abrazo *m*, caricia *f*; **2.** acariciar, abrazar; ~ *up* arrimarse *(to a)*.

cudg·el [ˈkʌdʒl] **1.** porra *f*; *take up the* ~*s for* ir a la defensa de; **2.** aporrear, apalear.

cue [kjuː] *billiards*: taco *m*; *thea.* pie *m*, apunte *m*; *(hair)* coleta *f*; *take one's* ~ *from* seguir el ejemplo de.

cuff¹ [kʌf] **1.** bofetada *f*; **2.** abofetear, dar de bofetadas.

cuff² [~] *(shirt-, etc.)* puño *m*; *(hand-)* ~*s pl.* esposas *f/pl.*; **'~ links** *pl.* gemelos *m/pl.*

cui·rass [kwiˈræs] coraza *f.*

cui·sine [kwiˈziːn] cocina *f.*

cu·li·nar·y [ˈkʌlinəri] culinario.

cull [kʌl] *lit.* entresacar, espigar.

cul·mi·nate [ˈkʌlmineit] culminar *(a. ast.)*; ~ *in* terminar en.

cul·prit [ˈkʌlprit] culpado (a *f*) *m*; reo *m*; *F* bribón *m.*

cult [kʌlt] culto *m.*

cul·ti·vate [ˈkʌltiveit] cultivar *(a. fig.)*; *fig.* ~*d* culto, refinado; **cul·ti·va·tion** cultivo *m.*

cul·tur·al [ˈkʌltʃərəl] □ cultural.

cul·ture [ˈkʌltʃə] cultura *f*; cultivo *m (a. ☊)*; **'cul·tured** culto.

cul·vert [ˈkʌlvət] alcantarilla *f.*

cun·ning [ˈkʌniŋ] **1.** □ astuto, taimado; *Am.* precioso, mono; **2.** astucia *f*; sagacidad *f.*

cup [kʌp] **1.** taza *f*; *eccl. a. ♥* cáliz *m; (fig. a. prize)* copa *f*; **2.** ahuecar; poner en forma de taza (*or* bocina); **'~·board** [ˈkʌbəd] armario *m*; aparador *m*; ~ *love* amor *m* interesado.

cu·pid·i·ty [kjuˈpiditi] codicia *f.*

cu·po·la [ˈkjuːpələ] cúpula *f.*

cur [kəː] perro de mala raza; *(p.)* canalla *m.*

curb [kəːb] **1.** barbada *f* (de la brida); *(pavement)* encintado *m*; *(well)* brocal *m*; *fig.* impedimento *m*, estorbo *m* (*on* para); **2.** proveer de barbada (*or* encintado); *fig.* refrenar.

curd [kəːd] cuajada *f*; **cur·dle** [ˈ~dl] cuajar(se); ~ *the blood* horripilar.

cure [kjuə] **1.** cura *f*; *fig.* curato *m*; **2.** curar; **'~·all** panacea *f.*

cur·few [ˈkəːfjuː] queda *f.*

cu·ri·o [ˈkjuəriou] curiosidad *f*; **cu·ri·os·i·ty** [~ˈɔsiti] curiosidad *f*; **'cu·ri·ous** □ curioso.

curl [kəːl] **1.** rizo *m*, bucle *m* of *hair*; espiral *f* of *smoke*; ondulación *f*; **2.** rizar(se), encrespar(se); ondular(se); *lips* fruncir; *(waves)* encresparse; ~ *up* arrollarse; *(p.)* acurrucarse; *F* abatirse.

curl·ing [ˈkəːliŋ] *sport:* curling *m (juego sobre un campo de hielo)*; **'~ i·ron,** **'~ tongs** *pl.* encrespador *m*; **'curl·y** crespo, encrespado, rizado.

cur·mudg·eon [kəːˈmʌdʒn] erizo *m*, mezquino *m*, cicatero *m.*

cur·rant [ˈkʌrənt] *(dried)* pasa *f* de

Corinto; *(fresh)* grosella *f*; ~ *(bush)* grosellero *m*.

cur·ren·cy ['kʌrənsi] moneda *f* (en circulación); *fig.* uso *m* corriente; *fig.* extensión *f*, propagación *f*; **'cur·rent 1.** □ corriente; *be* ~ correr, ser de actualidad; ~ *events* actualidades *f/pl.*; ~*ly* actualmente; **2.** corriente *f (a. ⚡)*.

cur·ric·u·lum [kəˈrikjuləm], *pl.* **cur·'ric·u·la** [~lə] programa *m* de estudios.

cur·ri·er ['kʌriə] curtidor *m*.

cur·ry[1] ['kʌri] **1.** cari *m*, curry *m*; **2.** preparar con cari.

cur·ry[2] [~] *leather* curtir; *horse* almohazar; ~ *favor* buscar favores.

curse [kə:s] **1.** maldición *f*; blasfemia *f*; *(oath)* palabrota *f*; **2.** *v/t.* maldecir; echar pestes de; *be* ~*d with* padecer de; tener que aguantar; *v/i.* blasfemar; *(a.* ~ *and swear)* soltar palabrotas.

cur·so·ry ['kə:səri] □ precipitado, apresurado; *glance* rápido.

curt [kə:t] □ brusco, áspero; conciso; **'curt·ness** brusquedad *f*.

cur·tail [kə:'teil] cercenar *(a. fig.)*, reducir; privar *(of* de).

cur·tain ['kə:tn] **1.** cortina *f (a. ⚔)*; *(heavy)* cortinón *m*; *thea.* telón *m*; *pol. iron* ~ telón *m* de acero; **2.** proveer de cortina; separar con cortina *(a.* ~ *off)*; **'~ rais·er** pieza *f* preliminar; **'~ ring** anilla *f*; **'~ rod** barra *f* de cortina.

curt·sy ['kə:tsi] **1.** reverencia *f*; *drop a* ~ = **3.** hacer una reverencia *(to* a.).

cur·va·ture ['kə:vətʃə] curvatura *f*.

curve [kə:v] **1.** curva *f*; **2.** encorvar (-se); voltear en curva *through air*.

cush·ion ['kuʃn] **1.** cojín *m*, almohadón *m*; *billiards:* baranda *f*; *fig.* ⊕ colchón *m*; **2.** amortiguar; proteger con cojines; ⊕ acojinar.

cuss [kʌs] F **1.** blasfemia *f*, ajo *m*; *sl.* tipo *m*, tío *m*; **2.** blasfemar, soltar un ajo; **'cuss·ed** ['kʌsid] maldito.

cus·tard ['kʌstəd] natillas *f/pl.*; flan *m*.

cus·to·di·an [kʌs'toudiən] custodio *m*; **cus·to·dy** ['kʌstədi] custodia *f*; *in* ~ en prisión; *take into* ~ arrestar.

cus·tom ['kʌstəm] costumbre *f*; ✝ clientela *f*, parroquia *f*; ~ *pl.* aduana *f*; derechos *m/pl.* de aduana; ~*s house* aduana *f*; **cus·tom·ar·y** ['~əri] □ acostumbrado, de costumbre; **'cus·tom·er** cliente *m*; F tío *m*; **'cus·tom·made** hecho a la medida.

cut [kʌt] **1.** corte *m*; *(blow)* golpe *m*

cortante, tajo *m*; tajada *f of meat*; *(deletion)* corte *m*; ✝ reducción *f*; ♂ herida *f*, incisión *f*; corte *m*, hechura *f of dress*; *(proportion)* parte *f*; *(insult)* desaire *m*, zaherimiento *m*; ⚡ apagón *m*; *sl.* tajada *f*; *short* ~ atajo *m*; **2.** *[irr.] v/t.* cortar; *esp. hole* practicar, hacer; *stone etc.* tallar; *(divide)* partir, dividir; ✝ *losses* abandonar; *class* fumarse; *p.* desairar, zaherir; fingir no ver; *tooth* salirle a uno (un diente); ~ *across* cortar al través; atravesar; *fig.* ir en contra de; ~ *down* cortar, derribar; *costs* aminorar; *price* rebajar; ~ *off* cortar *(a. ⚡)*; *leg* amputar; ~ *open* abrir (cortando); ~ *out* (re)cortar; *hole etc.* practicar, hacer; *stone* tallar, labrar; *fig.* suprimir; *be* ~ *out for* tener talento especial para; *have one's work* ~ *out* tener trabajo de sobra *(to inf.* para poder *inf.)*; F ~ *it out!* ¡déjese de eso!; ~ *up* desmenuzar; *meat* picar; F *fig.* criticar severamente; F *be* ~ *up* acongojarse, afligirse *(about por)*; *v/i.* cortar; ~ *in* interrumpir, interponerse; **3.** cortado; ⊕ labrado; ~ *glass* cristal *m* tallado; ~ *and dried* preparado *(or* convenido) de antemano; ~ *off* aislado, incomunicado.

cute [kju:t] □ F mono; astuto.

cut·lass ['kʌtləs] chafarote *m*.

cut·let ['kʌtlit] chuleta *f*.

cut...: '~**off** atajo *m*; '~**out** diseño *m* para recortar; ✝ portafusible *m*; ⊕ válvula *f* de escape; '~**rate** de precio reducido; '**cut·throat 1.** asesino *m*; **2.** sanguinario, cruel; *competition* intenso, implacable; **'cut·ting 1.** □ cortante; *fig.* mordaz; ~ *edge* filo *m*; **2.** corte *m*, cortadura *f*; *(paper)* recorte *m*; ✂ etc. trinchera *f*, desmonte *m*; 🚂 zanja *f* ferroviaria.

cy·a·nide ['saiənaid] cianuro *m*.

cy·cle ['saikl] **1.** ciclo *m (a. ♩ etc.)*; F bicicleta *f*; **2.** montar *(or* ir) en bicicleta; **cy·clic, cy·cli·cal** ['saiklik(l)] □ cíclico; **'cy·cling** ciclismo *m*; **'cy·clist** ciclista *m/f*.

cy·clone ['saikloun] ciclón *m*; borrasca *f*.

cyl·in·der ['silində] cilindro *m*; **cy'lin·dric, cy'lin·dri·cal** □ cilíndrico.

cyn·ic ['sinik] **1.** *(a.* **'cyn·i·cal** □*)* cínico; **2.** cínico *m*; **cyn·i·cism** ['~sizm] cinismo *m*.

cy·press ['saipris] ciprés *m*.

cyst [sist] quiste *m*.

Czar [zɑ:] zar *m*; **Czar·i·na** [zɑ:'ri:nə] zarina *f*.

D

'd F = *had*; *would*.

dab [dæb] **1.** golpe *m* ligero; soba *f*; untadura *f of liquid*; brochazo *m of paint*; pizca *f*, porción *f* pequeña; *ichth.* lenguado *m*; **2.** golpear (*or* tocar) ligeramente; sobar; untar.

dab·ble ['dæbl] salpicar; mojar; *feet etc.* chapotear; ~ *in* interesarse en, ser aficionado a.

dad [dæd], **dad·dy** ['~i] F papá *m*, papaíto *m*.

dad·dy-long·legs ['dædi'lɔŋlegz] F típula *f*.

daf·fo·dil ['dæfədil] dafodelo *m*; narciso *m*.

dag·ger ['dægə] daga *f*, puñal *m*; *look* ~*s at* apuñalar con la mirada.

dahl·ia ['deiljə] dalia *f*.

dai·ly ['deili] diario *adj. a. su. m.*

dain·ty ['deinti] **1.** □ delicado, regalado; de buen gusto, precioso; *b.s.* quisquilloso, esmerado; **2.** golosina *f*.

dair·y ['dɛəri] † lechería *f*; (*farm*) quesería *f*, vaquería *f*.

da·is ['deiis] estrado *m*.

dai·sy ['deizi] margarita *f*, maya *f*; *sl.* primor *m*.

dale [deil] valle *m*.

dal·ly ['dæli] coquetear (*with* con); (*sport*) juguetear; (*delay*) tardar; (*idle*) holgar.

dam¹ [dæm] madre *f* (de un animal).

dam² [~] **1.** presa *f*; embalse *m*; **2.** represar (*a. fig.*); ~ *up* cerrar, tapar.

dam·age ['dæmidʒ] **1.** daño *m*, perjuicio *m*; ⊕ *etc.* avería *f*; ⚖ ~*s pl.* daños *m/pl.* y perjuicios; **2.** dañar, perjudicar; averiar; *mot. etc.* causar daño a; *mot. etc. be* ~*d* sufrir daño.

dame [deim] dama *f*; *sl.* tía *f*.

damn [dæm] **1.** condenar (*a. eccl.*), censurar; maldecir; ~ *it!* ¡maldito sea!; **2.** terno *m*, palabrota *f*; **damned** *eccl.* condenado; F maldito, condenado; *adv.* extremadamente; **damn·ing** ['dæmiŋ] damnificador.

damp [dæmp] **1.** húmedo; mojado; **2.** humedad *f*; *fig.* abatimiento *m*, desaliento *m*; **3.** (*a.* '**damp·en**) humedecer, mojar; (*dull*) amortiguar, amortecer; *fig.* desalentar; (*a.* ~ *down*) cubrir; '**damp·er** registro *m*; ♪ sordina *f*; tiro *m* (de chimenea).

dam·sel ['dæmzl] †, *lit.* damisela *f*.

dance [dɑːns] **1.** baile *m*, danza *f*; *formal* ~ baile de etiqueta; **2.** bailar, danzar (*a. fig.*); '~ **floor** pista *f* de baile; '**danc·er** bailador (-a *f*) *m*; danzante (a *f*) *m*; (*professional*) bailarín (-a *f*) *m*.

danc·ing ['dɑːnsiŋ] baile *m*.

dan·de·li·on [dændi'laiən] diente *m* de león.

dan·driff ['dændrif], **dan·druff** ['dændrəf] caspa *f*.

dan·dy ['dændi] **1.** currutaco *m*; *sl.* cosa *f* excelente; **2.** *sl.* de primera.

dan·ger ['deindʒə] peligro *m*; '**dan·ger·ous** □ peligroso; '**dan·ger sig·nal** señal *f* de peligro.

dan·gle ['dæŋgl] colgar(se) en el aire.

dank [dæŋk] húmedo, liento.

dap·per ['dæpə] □ apuesto, gallardo.

dare [dɛə] *v/i.* osar (*to inf.*), atreverse (*to* a); *I* ~ *say* quizá; concedo (*that* que); *v/t. s.o.* desafiar; *gaze* resistir; '~**dev·il** temerario (a *f/m*; '**dar·ing** □ **1.** atrevido, osado; **2.** atrevimiento *m*, osadía *f*.

dark [dɑːk] **1.** □ oscuro; *complexion* moreno, trigueño; enigmático, secreto; ignorante; (*evil*) malvado, alevoso; ⚥ *Ages* edades *f/pl.* bárbaras; ~ *horse fig.* ganador *m* inesperado; candidato *m* poco conocido; ~ *room* cuarto *m* oscuro; *get* ~ hacerse de noche; **2.** oscuridad *f*, tinieblas *f/pl.*; *in the* ~ a oscuras (*a. fig.*); *keep s.o. in the* ~ no revelar a una p. cierta noticia; '**dark·en** oscurecer(se); *fig.* entristecer; *fig.* confundir, turbar; '**dark·ness** oscuridad *f*.

dar·ling ['dɑːliŋ] **1.** querido (a *f*) *m*; *my* ~! ¡amor mío!; **2.** querido.

darn¹ [dɑːn] F = *damn*.

darn² [~] **1.** zurcido *m*, zurcidura *f*; **2.** zurcir.

darn·ing ['dɑːniŋ] acción *f* de zurcir; zurcidura *f*; cosas *f/pl.* por zurcir; '~ **nee·dle** aguja *f* de zurcir.

dart [dɑːt] **1.** ⚔ dardo *m*, venablo *m*; (*game*) rehilete *m*; movimiento *m* rápido; ~*board* blanco *m*; **2.** lanzarse, precipitarse; moverse rápidamente.

dash [dæʃ] **1.** choque *m*; rociada *f of water etc.*; pequeña cantidad *f*; raya *f with pen*; *typ.* guión *m*; *fig.* arrojo *m*, brío *m*; carrera *f* corta (*for* hasta *etc.*); **2.** *v/t.* romper, estrellar (*against* contra); rociar, salpicar; despedazar (*mst* ~ *to pieces*); *hope* frustrar; ~ *off letter* escribir de prisa; *v/i.* estre-

deathless

llarse; (*waves*) romperse; correr; F ~ *away*, ~ *off* marcharse; '**~board** tablero *m* de instrumentos, panel *m*; '**dash·ing** □ brioso, arrojado; apuesto, guapo.

da·to ['deitə] *pl.* datos *m/pl.*

date[1] [deit] ♀ dátil *m*; (*tree*) datilera *f* (*a.* ~ *palm*).

date[2] [~] 1. fecha *f*; F cita *f*; F plazo *m*; F novio (a *f*) *m*; *what is the* ~? ¿a cuántos estamos?; F *make a* ~ citar (*with a*); *out of* ~ anticuado; (*up*) *to* ~ hasta la fecha; *up to* ~ al día; moderno; 2. fechar; F citar; ~ *back to* remontarse a; ~ *from* datar de; ~d fechado; *fig.* anticuado.

daub [dɔ:b] 1. embadurnar; *paint.* pintorrear; 2. embadurnamiento *m*; *paint.* pintarrajo *m*.

daugh·ter ['dɔ:tə] hija *f*; **~·in·law** ['dɔ:tərinlɔ] nuera *f*.

daunt [dɔ:nt] acobardar, desalentar; '**~·less** □ intrépido, impávido.

daw·dle ['dɔ:dl] F *v/i.* holgazanear; andar muy despacio; *v/t.* ~ *away* malgastar.

dawn [dɔ:n] 1. amanecer *m*, alba *f*; *from* ~ *to dusk* de sol a sol; 2. amanecer, apuntar el día; *fig.* ~ *on s.o.* caer uno en la cuenta.

day [dei] día *m*; *eccl.* fiesta *f*; *fig.* palma *f*, victoria *f*; *fig.* ~ *after* ~, *in*, ~ *out* día tras día; *the* ~ *after* el día siguiente; *the* ~ *before* el día anterior; la víspera de *event etc.*; *by* ~ de día; *by the* ~ a journal; *good* ~! ¡buenos días!; *to this* ~ hasta el día de hoy; *call it a* ~ dejar de trabajar *etc.*; *carry the* ~ ganar la victoria; *v. off etc.*; '**~·break** amanecer *m*; '**~·dream** ensueño *m*; '**~·light** luz *f* del día; *in broad* ~, *en pleno* día; *fig. see* ~ comprender; ver el final de un trabajo; '**~·nurse·ry** guardería *f* para niños; '**~·time** *m*; '**~·to-'day** diario, cotidiano.

daze [deiz] 1. aturdir, ofuscar; deslumbrar; 2. aturdimiento *m*; *in a* ~ aturdido.

daz·zle ['dæzl] 1. deslumbrar (*a. fig.*), ofuscar; 2. deslumbramiento *m*.

dead [ded] 1. muerto; difunto; insensible (*to* a); *leaf* marchito, seco; *hands etc.* entumecido; *color* apagado; *sound* sordo; ⚡ sin corriente; (*obsolete*) anticuado, obsoleto; ~ *bolt* cerrojo *m* dormido; ~ *calm* calma *f* chicha; ~ *center* punto *m* muerto; *letter fig.* letra *f* muerta; ~ *load* carga *f* fija; ~ *march* marcha *f* fúnebre; ~ *stop*

parada *f* en seco; ~ *water* agua *f* tranquila; ~ *weight* peso *m* muerto; *fig.* carga *f* onerosa; ~ *wood leña f* seca; *fig.* material *m* inútil; 2. *adv.* completamente, absolutamente; ~ *drunk* borracho como un tronco; ~ *set* empeñado (*on* en); ~ *tired* hecho polvo, muerto de cansancio; 3.: *the* ~ *pl.* los muertos; *fig.* lo más profundo; *in the* ~ *of night* en las altas horas; *in the* ~ *of winter* en lo más recio del invierno; '**~·beat** 1. hecho polvo, agotado; 2. *sl.* gorrón (-a *f*) *m*; holgazán (-a *f*) *m*; '**dead·en** amortiguar, amortecer; '**dead·end** callejón *m* sin salida (*a. fig.*); ~ *kids* chicos *m/pl.* de las calles; '**dead·line** fecha *f* tope, línea *f* tope; '**dead·lock** *fig.* punto *m* muerto; '**dead·ly** 1. mortal; fatal (*a. fig.*); *fig.* abrumador; 2. *adv.* sumamente; '**~·pan** *sl.* (*semblante m*) sin expresión.

deaf [def] sordo (*to* a); '**deaf·en** ensordecer; (*noise*) asordar; '**deaf-'mute** sordomudo (a *f*) *m*.

deal[1] [di:l] tabla *f* de pino (*or* de abeto).

deal[2] [~] 1. negocio *m*, negociación *f*; F ♀ trato *m*, transacción *f*; convenio *m*, acuerdo *m*; *cards*: reparto *m*, mano *f*; (*turn*) turno *m*; porción *f*; *a good* ~ bastante; *a great* ~ mucho; *it's a* ~! ¡trato hecho!; *make a great* ~ *of* p. estimar mucho a; *th.* dar importancia a; 2. (*irr.*) *v/t. blow* asestar, dar; (*esp.* ~ *out*) repartir; *cards* dar; *v/i.* negociar, comerciar (*in* en); *cards*: ser mano; ~ *with p.* tratar a (*or* con); *subject* tratar de; '**deal·er** comerciante *m* (*in* en); *cards*: mano *f*; '**deal·ing** (*mst* ~*s pl.*) comercio *m*, trato *m*; relaciones *f/pl.*

dealt [delt] *pret. a. p.p. of deal*[2].

dean [di:n] *univ. etc.* decano *m*.

dear [diə] 1. □ *p. etc.* querido; *fig. pay* ~*ly for* pagar caro *acc.*; 2. querido (a *f*) *m*; persona *f* simpática; *my* ~! ¡querido (a) mío (a)!; ¡hombre!; 3. F *oh* ~!, ~ *me!* ¡Dios mío!; ¡caramba!; **dearth** [dɔ:θ] carestía *f*, escasez *f*.

death [deθ] muerte *f*; fallecimiento *m*, defunción *f*; *be at* ~*'s door* estar a la muerte; *do* (*put*) *to* ~ dar la muerte a; ~ *penalty* pena *f* de muerte; *tired to* ~ rendido, fatigado; *fig.* harto (*of* de); *to the* ~ a muerte; '**~·bed** lecho *m* de muerte; '**~·blow** golpe *m* mortal; '**~·less** inmortal.

de·base [di'beis] degradar, envilecer; *coinage* adulterar.

de·bat·a·ble [di'beitəbl] ☐ discutible, contestable; dudoso; **de'bate 1.** debate *m*, discusión *f*; **2.** discutir, debatir (*with* con); disputar (*on* de, sobre; *with* con); (*think*) deliberar.

de·bauch [di'bɔːtʃ] **1.** libertinaje *m*; **2.** corromper; viciar.

de·bil·i·tate [di'biliteit] debilitar.

deb·it ['debit] **1.** debe *m* (*a. ~ side*); (*entry*) cargo *m*; **2.** cargar.

de·bris ['debriː] escombros *m/pl.*, desechos *m/pl.*

debt [det] deuda *f*; *deeply in ~* lleno de deudas; *be in ~* tener deudas; *run into ~* contraer deudas, endeudarse; **'debt·or** deudor (-a *f*) *m*.

de·bunk [diː'bʌŋk] F p. desenmascarar; desacreditar.

dé·but ['deibuː] estreno *m*, debut *m*; *make one's ~ thea.* estrenarse, debutar; (*in society*) ponerse de largo, presentarse en la sociedad.

dec·ade ['dekeid] década *f*; decenio *m*, década *of years.*

de·ca·dence ['dekədəns] decadencia *f*; **'de·ca·dent** decadente.

de·cap·i·tate [di'kæpiteit] degollar.

de·cay [di'kei] **1.** decadencia *f*, decaimiento *m*; caries *f of teeth*; podredumbre *f*; **2.** decaer; *esp.* △ *a. fig.* desmoronarse; cariarse; pudrirse.

de·cease [di'siːs] *esp.* ✝ **1.** fallecimiento *m*; **2.** fallecer; *the ~d* el (la) difunto (a).

de·ceit [di'siːt] engaño *m*; fraude *m*; **de'ceit·ful** ☐ engañoso; (*lying*) mentiroso.

de·ceive [di'siːv] engañar; defraudar; *be ~d freq.* equivocarse; **de'ceiv·er** engañador (-a *f*) *m*.

De·cem·ber [di'sembə] diciembre *m*.

de·cen·cy [diːsnsi] decencia *f*; **'de·cent** decente.

de·cen·tral·i·za·tion [diːsentrəlai-'zeiʃn] descentralización *f*; **de'cen·tral·ize** descentralizar.

de·cep·tion [di'sepʃn] engaño *m*, fraude *m*, decepción *f*; **de'cep·tive** ☐ engañoso; ilusorio.

de·cide [di'said] decidir (*to inf. or -se a inf.*; *in favor of* a favor de; [*up*]*on* por); *attitude* determinar; **de'cid·ed** ☐ decidido, resuelto; indudable; **~ly** indudablemente.

dec·i·mal ['desiml] decimal *adj. a. su. m*; *~ point* punto *m* decimal, coma *f*.

de·ci·pher [di'saifə] descifrar.

de·ci·sion [di'siʒn] decisión *f*; ✝✝ resolución *f*, fallo *m*; (*resoluteness*) firmeza *f*; *make* (*or take*) *a ~* tomar una decisión; **de·ci·sive** [di'saisiv] ☐ decisivo; (*conclusive*) terminante.

deck [dek] **1.** ♣ cubierta *f*; (*omnibus*) planta *f*; *cards:* baraja *f*; **2.** *lit.* ataviar, engalanar; **'~·chair** hamaca *f*, tumbona *f*.

de·claim [di'kleim] declamar; *~ against* protestar contra.

dec·la·ma·tion [deklə'meiʃn] declamación *f*.

dec·la·ra·tion [deklə'reiʃn] declaración *f* (*a.* ✝✝); **de·clare** [di'kleə] declarar; afirmar; *nothing to ~* nada de pago; **de'clared** ☐ manifiesto.

de·clen·sion [di'klenʃn] declinación *f* (*a. gr.*).

dec·li·na·tion [dekli'neiʃn] declinación *f* (*ast. a.* ♣); denegación *f*; **de·cline** [di'klain] **1.** *v/t.* rehusar, no aceptar; *gr.* declinar; *v/i.* declinar (*a. fig.*); negarse (*to* a); **2.** declinación *f* (*a. fig.*); ♂ *etc.* bajón *m*; ocaso *m of sun*; baja *f of prices*; F tisis.

de·code [diː'koud] descifrar.

de·con·tam·i·nate [diːkən'tæmineit] descontaminar.

dec·o·rate ['dekəreit] decorar, adornar; *room* empapelar, pintar; ✗ condecorar; **dec·o'ra·tion** adorno *m*, ornato *m*; ✗ condecoración *f*; **dec·o·ra·tive** [di'dekərətiv] ☐ decorativo; bonito; **dec·o·ra·tor** ['~reitə] adornista *m/f*; (*pintor m*) decorador *m*.

de·co·rum [di'kɔːrəm] decoro *m*.

de·coy [di'kɔi] **1.** señuelo *m* (*a. fig.*); (*a.* **de'coy duck**) reclamo *m*; trampa *f*; **2.** atraer con señuelo.

de·crease 1. [diː'kriːs] disminución *f*; **2.** [di'kriːs] disminuir(se).

de·cree [di'kriː] **1.** decreto *m*; **2.** decretar.

de·crep·it [di'krepit] decrépito.

de·cry [di'krai] desacreditar; rebajar.

ded·i·cate ['dedikeit] dedicar; **ded·i'ca·tion** dedicación *f*; dedicatoria *f in book*; **'ded·i·ca·to·ry** dedicatorio.

de·duce [di'djuːs] deducir.

de·duct [di'dʌkt] restar; **de'duc·tion** deducción *f*; ✝ descuento *m*.

deed [diːd] **1.** hecho *m*, acto *m*, hazaña *f*; ✝✝ escritura *f*, documento *m*; **2.** traspasar por escritura.

deem [diːm] juzgar, considerar; (*believe*) creer.

deep [diːp] **1.** ☐ hondo, profundo; ♪ grave, bajo; *color* oscuro; subido; *p.*

delightful

insondable, astuto; ~ *in debt* lleno de deudas; F *go off the* ~ *end* montar en cólera; 2. *poet.* piélago *m*; '**deep·en** profundizar(se); *voice* ahuecar; *color* hacer(se) más oscuro (*or* subido).

deer [diə] ciervo *m*.

de·face [di'feis] desfigurar, deformar.

def·a·ma·tion [defə'meiʃn] difamación *f*; **de·fame** [di'feim] difamar; mancillar.

de·fault [di'fɔ:lt] 1. omisión *f*, descuido *m*; falta *f*, incumplimiento *m*; ⚖ rebeldía *f*; *in* ~ *of* por falta de; 2. faltar; ⚖ caer en rebeldía; ponerse en mora; † demorar los pagos.

de·feat [di'fi:t] 1. derrota *f*; 2. vencer (*a. fig.*); derrotar; *fig. e.g. hopes* frustrar.

de·fect [di'fekt] defecto *m*; **de·fec·tive** □ defectuoso; defectivo (*a. gr.*); *child etc.* anormal.

de·fend [di'fend] defender (*from* de); **de·fen·dant** (*civil*) demandado (a *f*) *m*; (*criminal*) acusado (a *f*) *m*, reo *m*; **de'fend·er** defensor *m*.

de·fense [di'fens] defensa *f* (*a. sport*).

de·fen·si·ble [di'fensəbl] defendible; **de'fen·sive** 1. □ defensivo; 2. defensiva *f*.

de·fer[1] [di'fə:] diferir, aplazar.

de·fer[2] [~] deferir (*to* a); **def·er·ence** ['defərəns] deferencia *f*; *in* ~ *to, out of* ~ *to* obedeciendo a, teniendo respeto a.

de·fer·ment [di'fə:ment] aplazamiento *m*; prórroga *f* (*a.* ⚔).

de·fi·ance [di'faiəns] desafío *m*; oposición *f* terca; **de'fi·ant** □ desafiador; provocativo.

de·fi·cien·cy [di'fiʃənsi] deficiencia *f*, carencia *f*; **de'fi·cient** insuficiente; incompleto; deficiente; *be* ~ *in* carecer de.

def·i·cit ['defisit] déficit *m*.

de·fin·a·ble [di'fainəbl] definible; **de'fine** definir; delimitar; determinar; **def·i·nite** ['definit] □ definido (*a. gr.*); *statement etc.* categórico; distinto, preciso; *quite* ~ indudable; **def·i'ni·tion** definición *f*; claridad *f*; *by* ~ por definición; **de'fin·i·tive** □ definitivo; categórico.

de·flate [di'fleit] desinflar; † deflacionar.

de·flect [di'flekt] desviar.

de·fraud [di'frɔ:d] defraudar (*of* de).

de·fray [di'frei] *costs* sufragar, costear.

deft [deft] □ diestro (*at* en); *touch* ligero.

de·funct [di'fʌŋkt] difunto.

de·fy [di'fai] desafiar (*a. fig.*); oponerse a.

de·gen·er·a·cy [di'dʒenərəsi] depravación *f*; **de'gen·er·ate** [~rit] □ degenerado *adj. a. su. m* (a *f*); 2. [~reit] degenerar (*into* en).

deg·ra·da·tion [degrə'deiʃn] degradación *f*, envilecimiento *m*; **de·grade** [di'greid] degradar, envilecer; ~ *o.s. freq.* aplebeyarse.

de·gree [di'gri:] grado *m* (*a. fig.*); *univ.* título *m*, licenciatura *f*; † grada *f*; rango *m*, condición *f* social; *by* ~*s* poco a poco.

de·hy·drat·ed [di:'haidreitid] deshidratado; **de·hy'dra·tion** deshidratación *f*.

de·ice ['di:'ais] ✈ deshelar.

de·i·fy ['di:ifai] deificar.

deign [dein]: ~ *to* dignarse *inf*.

de·i·ty ['di:iti] deidad *f*; *the* ♀ Dios.

de·ject [di'dʒekt] abatir, desanimar; **de'ject·ed** □ abatido.

de·lay [di'lei] 1. tardanza *f*, retraso *m*; dilación *f*; 2. *v/i.* tardar (*in* en); *v/t.* diferir, dilatar.

del·e·gate 1. ['deligeit] delegar (*to* a); *p.* diputar; 2. ['deligit] delegado (a *f*) *m*; diputado (a *f*) *m*; **del·e·ga·tion** [~'geiʃn] delegación *f* (*a. body*); diputación *f*.

de·lete [di:'li:t] tachar, suprimir, borrar; **de·le·tion** [di:'li:ʃn] supresión *f*.

de·lib·er·ate 1. [di'libəreit] *v/t. s.t.* meditar; *v/i.* deliberar (*on* sobre); 2. [~rit] □ premeditado, reflexionado; (*cautious*) cauto, circunspecto; *movement etc.* lento, espacioso; ~*ly freq.* de propósito, con premeditación; **de·lib·er·a·tion** [~'reiʃn] deliberación *f*; premeditación *f*.

del·i·ca·cy ['delikəsi] delicadeza *f*; (*tidbit*) golosina *f*; **del·i·cate** ['~kit] □ delicado; *food* exquisito; *action* considerado; **del·i·ca·tes·sen** [delikə'tesn] tienda *f* que se especializa en manjares exquisitos.

de·li·cious [di'liʃəs] □ delicioso, exquisito.

de·light [di'lait] 1. deleite *m*, delicia *f*; 2. deleitarse (*in* en, con); *be* ~*ed to* tener mucho gusto en; **de'light·ful** [~ful] □ delicioso, precioso.

de·lin·e·ate [di'linieit] delinear; bosquejar (a. fig.).

de·lin·quen·cy [di'liŋkwənsi] 🏛 delincuencia f; (guilt) culpa f; (omission) descuido m; **de·lin·quent** delincuente adj. a. su. m/f; culpable adj. a. su. m/f.

de·lir·i·ous [di'liriəs] 🗆 delirante.

de·liv·er [di'livə] librar (from de); (a. ~ up, ~ over) entregar; ⚙ distribuir, repartir; speech pronunciar; blow asestar; 🥼 woman partear; message comunicar; ball lanzar; be ~ed of parir acc.; **de'liv·er·ance** liberación f, rescate m; **de'liv·er·y** liberación f, salvación f; ⚙ repartido m; 🥼 parto m, alumbramiento m; entrega f of goods, writ; modo m de expresarse; attr. de entrega; de reparto; ~ man mozo m de reparto; ~ room sala f de alumbramiento; ~ truck sedán m de reparto.

dell [del] vallecito m.

de·louse [di:'laus] despiojar, espulgar.

del·ta ['deltə] delta f; geog. delta m.

de·lude [di'lu:d] engañar, deludir (into para que); easily ~d iluso.

del·uge ['delju:dʒ] 1. diluvio m; 2. inundar (with de).

de·lu·sion [di'lu:ʒn] engaño m, ilusión f, alucinación f.

de luxe [di'lʌks] de lujo.

delve [delv] cavar (into en; a. fig.).

dem·a·gog·ic, **dem·a·gog·i·cal** [demə'gɔgik(l)] 🗆 demagógico; **dem·a·gogue** ['demagɔg] demagogo m.

de·mand [di'mɑ:nd] 1. demanda f (a. ✝, 🏛); exigencia f; on ~ a solicitud; 2. demandar; exigir (of a), solicitar perentoriamente (of de); **de'mand·ing** exigente.

de'mean·or [~ə] porte m, conducta f.

de·ment·ed [di'mentid] 🗆 demente.

de·mer·it [di:'merit] demérito m.

de·mil·i·ta·ri·za·tion [di:militərai'zeiʃn] desmilitarización f; **de'mil·i·ta·rize** desmilitarizar.

de·mise [di'maiz] 1. 🏛 transferencia f; traspaso m of title or estate; fallecimiento m of p. 2. transferir, traspasar.

de·mo·bi·li·za·tion ['di:moubilai'zeiʃn] desmovilización f; **de'mo·bi·lize** desmovilizar.

de·moc·ra·cy [di'mɔkrəsi] democracia f; **dem·o·crat** ['deməkræt] demócrata m/f; **dem·o'crat·ic,** **dem·o'crat·i·cal** 🗆 democrático.

de·mol·ish [di'mɔliʃ] demoler, derribar; argument etc. destruir; F zamparse; **dem·o·li·tion** [demə'liʃn] demolición f, derribo m.

de·mon ['di:mən] demonio m; **de·mon·ic** [di:'mɔnik] demoníaco.

de·mon·stra·ble ['demənstrəbl] 🗆 demostrable; **dem·on·strate** ['~streit] demostrar; pol. hacer una manifestación; **dem·on'stra·tion** demostración f; pol. manifestación f; **de·mon·stra·tive** [di'mɔnstrətiv] 1. 🗆 demostrativo (a. gr.); p. exagerado, exaltado; 2. demostrativo m; **dem·on·stra·tor** ['demənstreitə] demostrador (-a f) m; pol. manifestante m.

de·mor·al·i·za·tion [dimɔrəlai'zeiʃn] desmoralización f; **de'mor·al·ize** desmoralizar.

de·mur [di'mə:] 1. reparo m, pega f; 2. poner pegas, objetar.

de·mure [di'mjuə] 🗆 grave, solemne; (modest) recatado; b.s. gazmoño.

den [den] (animal's, robber's) madriguera f; F (room) cuchitril m; F cuarto m de estudio.

de·ni·a·ble [di'naiəbl] negable; **de·ni·al** negación f; (refusal) denegación f; (a. self-~) abnegación f.

den·i·grate ['di:nigreit] denigrar.

den·im ['denim] (freq. ~s pl.) dril m de algodón.

den·i·zen ['denizn] habitante m/f; extranjero (a f) m naturalizado (a).

de·nom·i·nate [di'nɔmineit] denominar; **de·nom·i·na·tion** denominación f; categoría f; eccl. secta f, confesión f; valor m of coin etc.; **de'nom·i·na·tor** [~neitə] denominador m; common ~ denominador m común.

de·note [di'nout] denotar; señalar, designar; significar.

de·nounce [di'nauns] denunciar; censurar, reprender.

dense [dens] 🗆 denso, compacto; undergrowth etc. tupido; **'den·si·ty** densidad f (a. phys.).

dent [dent] 1. abolladura f; mella f in edge; 2. abollar(se); mellar.

den·tal ['dentl] 1. dental; odontológico; 2. 📖 dental f; **dent·ti·frice** ['~tifris] dentífrico m; **'den·tist** dentista m, odontólogo m; **'den·tist·ry** odontología f; **den·ture** ['~tʃə] dentadura f; (esp. ~s pl.) dentadura f postiza.

de·nun·ci·a·tion [dinʌnsi'eiʃn] denuncia *f* (a. ⚖), denunciación *f*. **de·ny** [di'nai] negar; *request etc.* denegar; *report* desmentir; ~ *o.s.* abnegarse; ~ *o.s. th.* negarse, no permitirse.

de·o·dor·ize [di:'oudəraiz] desodorizar; **de·o·dor·ant** desodorante *m*.

de·part [di'pɑːt] *v/i.* partir, marcharse; *(train etc.)* salir, tener su salida; **de·part·ment** departamento *m*; sección *f*, ramo *m*; ministerio *m*; ~ **store** grandes almacenes *m/pl.*; **de·part·men·tal** ☐ departamental; **de·par·ture** [~t∫ə] partida *f*, salida *f*; *fig.* desviación *f*.

de·pend [di'pend] ⚕ pender, colgar; ~ *(up)on* depender de; *p. etc.* contar con, confiar en; F it ~s eso depende; **de·pend·a·ble** ☐ *p.* formal, confiable; seguro; **de·pend·ence** dependencia *f* (*on* de); confianza *f* (*on* en); apoyo *m* (*on* sobre); **de·pend·ent** ☐ dependiente (*on* de); pendiente (*on* de); *gr.* subordinado.

de·pict [di'pikt] representar, describir; *paint.* pintar, dibujar.

de·plete [di'pliːt] agotar; *stock etc.* mermar; ♣ depauperar.

de·plor·a·ble [di'plɔːrəbl] ☐ deplorable; **de·plore** [di'plɔː] deplorar.

de·ploy [di'plɔi] ✗ desplegar; *fig.* organizar.

de·port [di'pɔːt] deportar; ~ *o.s.* comportarse; **de·por·ta·tion** deportación *f*; **de·port·ment** porte *m*, continente *m*; conducta *f*.

de·pose [di'pouz] deponer (a. ⚖).

de·pos·it [di'pozit] 1. depósito *m* (a. ♦); *geol.* yacimiento *m*; ✝ señal *f*; *(house etc.)* desembolso *m* inicial; ⚱ poso *m*; 2. depositar (*with* en); ✝ dar para señal; ⚱ sedimentar; **de·pos·i·tor** [di'pozitə] depositador (-a *f*) *m*; ✝ cuentacorrentista *m/f*, imponente *m*.

de·pot ['depou] depósito *m*, almacén *m*; 🚂 estación *f*.

de·prave [di'preiv] depravar; **de·praved** depravado; **de·prav·i·ty** [di'præviti] depravación *f*, estragamiento *m*.

de·pre·ci·ate [di'priː∫ieit] depreciar (-se); desestimar, despreciar; **de·pre·ci·a·tion** depreciación *f*.

dep·re·da·tion [depri'dei∫n] depredación *f*; ~*s pl.* estragos *m/pl.*

de·press [di'pres] deprimir (a. *fig.*); *(dispirit)* desalentar, desanimar; *price* hacer bajar; ~ed alicaído, aba-

tido; **de·press·ing** ☐ deprimente; triste; **de·pres·sion** [di'pre∫n] depresión *f* (a. ⚓, ♣); ✝ flojedad *f*; *crisis f* económica.

dep·ri·va·tion [depri'vei∫n] privación *f*; **de·prive** [di'praiv] privar (*of* de).

depth [depθ] profundidad *f* (a. *fig.*); fondo *m of building*; ~ **charge** carga *f* de profundidad; *in the* ~ *of* en lo más recio de, en pleno ....

dep·u·ta·tion [depju'tei∫n] diputación *f*; **dep·u·tize** ['depjutaiz] diputar; ~ *for s.o.* sustituir a; **dep·u·ty** diputado *m* (a. *pol.*); sustituto *m*.

de·range [di'reind3] desarreglar, descomponer; *p.* volver loco; **de·range·ment** desarreglo *m*, descompostura *f*; ♣ trastorno *m* mental.

der·e·lict ['derilikt] 1. abandonado; negligente; 2. *esp.* ♣ derrelicto *m*; pelafustán (-a *f*) *m*; **der·e·lic·tion** [deri'lik∫n] abandono *m*; desamparo *m*.

de·ride [di'raid] ridiculizar, mofarse de.

de·ri·sion [di'riʒn] mofa *f*, befa *f*; **de·ri·sive** [di'raisiv] ☐ mofador; **de·ri·so·ry** [~səri] mofador; *quantity etc.* irrisorio, ridículo.

der·i·va·tion [deri'vei∫n] derivación *f*; **de·riv·a·tive** [di'rivətiv] 1. ☐ derivativo, derivado (a. *gr.*); 2. derivativo *m* (a. *gr.*, ♣); **de·rive** [di'raiv] derivar(se) (*from* de); *profit* sacar (*from* de); *be* ~d *from* provenir de.

der·ma·tol·o·gist [dəːmə'tɔlədʒist] dermatólogo *m*; **der·ma·tol·o·gy** dermatología *f*.

de·rog·a·to·ry [di'rɔgətəri] ☐ despreciativo, despectivo.

der·rick ['derik] grúa *f*; *(oil)* torre *f* de perforación, derrick *m*.

de·scend [di'send] descender, bajar *(from* de); ~ *(up)on* caer sobre; *fig.* ~ *to* rebajarse a; ~ *(or be* ~*ed) from* descender de; **de·scend·ant** descendiente *m/f*.

de·scent [di'sent] descendimiento *m* (a. *eccl.*); *(fall)* descenso *m* (a. *fig.*); *(origin)* descendencia *f* (*from* de); ⚖ herencia *f*; *geog.* declive *m*; *esp.* ♣ invasión *f*.

de·scribe [dis'kraib] describir (a. 📐); ~ *as* calificar de.

de·scrip·tion [dis'krip∫n] descripción *f*; clase *f*, género *m*; **de·scrip·tive** ☐ descriptivo; *style* pintoresco.

des·e·crate [desikreit] profanar; **des·e'cra·tion** profanación f.

des·ert 1. ['dezət] a) desierto; inhabitado; b) desierto m, yermo m; 2. [di'zə:t] v/t. ⚔, desertar; abandonar, desamparar; v/i. ⚔, desertar (from de; to a).

de·sert·er [di'zə:tə] desertor m; **de'ser·tion** deserción f, abandono m.

de·serve [di'zə:v] merecer (of de, para con); he got what he ~d llevó su merecido; **de'serv·ed·ly** [~vidli] merecidamente; **de'serv·ing** □ merecedor (of de); digno (of de).

de·sign [di'zain] 1. ⊕ etc. diseño m, traza f; (pattern) dibujo m; (sketch) bosquejo m; (purpose) designio m, intención f; by ~ intencionalmente; F have ~s on tener sus proyectos sobre; 2. diseñar, trazar; dibujar; (purpose) idear, proyectar.

des·ig·nate 1. ['dezigneit] designar; nombrar; (point to) señalar; 2. ['~nit] designado, nombrado; **des'ig·na·tion** nombramiento m; (title etc.) denominación f.

de·sign·er [di'zainə] dibujante m; diseñador m.

de·sir·a·ble [di'zaiərəbl] □ deseable, apetecible; **de·sire** [di'zaiə] 1. deseo m (for, to de); 2. desear (to inf.; a p. to que una p. subj.).

de·sist [di'zist] desistir (from de).

desk [desk] pupitre m; (a. writing ~) escritorio m; mesa f.

des·o·late 1. ['desəleit] asolar; p. entristecer; 2. ['~lit] □ desierto, solitario; despoblado; (in ruins) arruinado; (forlorn) lúgubre, triste; **des·o'la·tion** soledad f; desolación f; (act) arrasamiento m.

de·spair [dis'pεə] 1. desesperación f; 2. desesperar (of de).

des·per·a·do [despə'ra:dou] bandido m; forajido m.

des·per·ate ['despərit] □ desesperado; situation etc. grave; fight encarnizado; (bold) temerario; **des·per·a·tion** [despə'reiʃn] desesperación f; in ~ desesperado.

des·pi·ca·ble [di'spikəbl] □ despreciable; vil, ruin.

de·spise [dis'paiz] despreciar; desdeñar.

de·spite [dis'pait] prp. a despecho de.

de·spond·ent [dis'pondənt] □ abatido, alicaído; be ~ andar de capa caída.

des·pot ['despɔt] déspota m; **des-**

'pot·ic □ despótico; **des·pot·ism** ['~pətizm] despotismo m.

des·sert [di'zə:t] postre m.

des·ti·na·tion [desti'neiʃn] destino m (a. 🌑), paradero m; **des·tine** ['~tin] destinar (to, for a, para); be ~d to estar destinado a; **'des·ti·ny** destino m, hado m.

des·ti·tute ['destitju:t] indigente; desprovisto (of de); **des·ti'tu·tion** indigencia f.

de·stroy [dis'trɔi] destruir (a. fig.); matar; (annihilate) aniquilar; **de'stroy·er** destructor m (a. ⚓).

de·struc·ti·ble [di'strʌktəbl] destructible; **de·struc·tion** destrucción f (a. fig.); ⚔ etc. estragos m/pl.; **de'struc·tive** □ destructivo (a. fig.); child revoltoso; nocivo (of a).

de·tach [di'tætʃ] separar, desprender; ⚔ destacar; **de'tach·a·ble** separable, desmontable; suelto; **de'tached** separado, desprendido; fig. imparcial, objetivo; ~ house hotel m; become ~ desprenderse, separarse; **de'tach·ment** separación f, desprendimiento m; fig. objetividad f (of mind de ánimo).

de·tail ['di:teil] detalle m, pormenor m; ⚔ destacamento m; in ~ en detalle; go into ~ menudear; 2. [di'teil] detallar; ⚔ destacar; **de'tailed** account etc. detallado, detenido.

de·tain [di'tein] detener (a. 🌑); (delay) retener.

de·tect [di'tekt] descubrir, percibir; **de'tect·a·ble** perceptible; **de'tec·tion** descubrimiento m; **de'tec·tive** detective m; attr. policíaco, de detective; **de'tec·tor** descubridor m; radio a. ⚓ detector m.

dé·tente [dei'tã:nt] pol. détente f.

de·ten·tion [di'tenʃn] detención f, arresto m.

de·ter [di'tə:] disuadir (from de); impedir (from que subj.).

de·ter·gent [di'tə:dʒənt] detergente adj. a. su. m.

de·te·ri·o·rate [di'tiəriəreit] v/t. deteriorar; v/i. empeorarse; **de·te·ri·o·'ra·tion** deterioro m, empeoramiento m.

de·ter·ment [di'tə:mənt] disuasión f.

de·ter·mi·na·tion [ditə:mi'neiʃn] determinación f; (resolve) empeño m; **de'ter·mine** [~min] determinar (to inf.); determinarse (to a); ocasionar, dar motivo a; ~ on optar por;

did

resolverse a; **de'ter·mined** □ resuelto; (*stubborn*) porfiado.

de·ter·rent [di'terənt] **1.** disuasivo; **2.** lo que disuade; impedimento *m*; (*threat*) amenaza *f*.

de·test [di'test] detestar; **de'test·a·ble** □ detestable.

det·o·nate ['detouneit] (hacer) detonar; **'det·o·nat·ing-cap** cápsula *f* fulminante; **det·o'na·tion** detonación *f*.

de·tour [di'tuə], **dé·tour** ['deituə] desvío *m*, rodeo *m*.

de·tract [di'trækt]: ~ *from* quitar atractivo a; rebajar, quitar mérito a; **det·ri·ment** ['detrimənt] perjuicio *m*, detrimento *m*; *to the* ~ *of* en perjuicio de; **det·ri·men·tal** [detri'mentl] □ perjudicial (*to*, a, para).

deuce [dju:s] **1.** dice: dos *m*; *tennis*: a dos; **2.** *F* diantre *m*, demonio *m*; *what the* ~ ...? ¿qué demonios ...?

de·val·u·a·tion [di:vælju'eiʃn] desvalorización *f*; **de'val·ue** desvalorizar.

dev·as·tate ['devəsteit] devastar; **'dev·as·tat·ing** □ *fig.* arrollador; **dev·as'ta·tion** devastación *f*.

de·vel·op [di'veləp] *v/t.* desarrollar (*a.* Ⓐ), desenvolver; *phot.* revelar; *land* urbanizar; ⚒ *etc.* explotar; *v/i.* desarrollarse (*esp. be* ~ing) ir, progresar; **de'vel·op·ment** desarrollo *m*, desenvolvimiento *m*; *phot.* revelado *m*; (*a. urban* ~) urbanización *f*; ⚒ explotación *f*.

de·vi·ate [di:'vieit] desviar(se) (*from* de); **de·vi'a·tion** desviación *f* (*a. compass*).

de·vice [di'vais] ⊕ dispositivo *m*, aparato *m*; *fig.* recurso *m*, ardid *m*; emblema *m*; (*motto*) lema *m*; *nuclear* ~ ingenio *m* nuclear.

dev·il ['devl] diablo *m* (*a. fig.*); *F* arrojo *m*, ardor *m*; ⚖ abogado *m* principiante; *typ.* mozo *m* recadero; plato *m* picante; *the* ~! ¡diablos!; *F there'll be the* ~ *to pay* nos sentarán las costuras; *F raise the* ~ armarla; **'dev·il·ish** □ diabólico; *adv.* F extremadamente; **'dev·il-may-'care** F despreocupado; temerario.

de·vi·ous ['di:viəs] □ apartado, aislado; *path.* tortuoso.

de·vise [di'vaiz] **1.** ⚖ legado *m*; **2.** idear, proyectar; hacer proyectos; ⚖ legar.

de·void [di'vɔid] desprovisto (*of* de).

de·vote [di'vout] dedicar; ~ *o.s.* to dedicarse a; **de'vot·ed** □ devoto;

dedicado (*to* a); (*letter*) *your* ~ *servant* suyo afmo.; **de·vo·tion** [di'vouʃn] devoción *f* (*to* a); **de'vo·tion·al** □ piadoso, devoto.

de·vour [di'vauə] devorar (*a. fig.*); *F food* zamparse.

de·vout [di'vaut] □ devoto, piadoso; (*earnest*) cordial.

dew [dju:] **1.** rocío *m*; **2.** rociar; '~·**drop** gota *f* de rocío; '~·**lap** papada *f*.

dex·ter·i·ty [deks'teriti] destreza *f*.

di·a·be·tes [daiə'bi:ti:z] diabetes *f*; **di·a'be·tic** diabético *adj. a. su. m* (*a f*).

di·a·bol·ic, **di·a·bol·i·cal** [daiə'bɔlik(l)] □ diabólico.

di·a·dem ['daiədem] diadema *f*.

di·ag·nose ['daiəgnouz] diagnosticar; **di·ag'no·sis** [~·sis], *pl.* **di·ag'no·ses** [~·si:z] diagnosis *f*.

di·ag·o·nal [dai'ægənl] □ diagonal *adj. a. su. f* (Ⓧ *a. cloth*).

di·a·gram ['daiəgræm] diagrama *m*, esquema *m*.

di·al ['daiəl] **1.** esfera *f*, cuadrante *m*; *teleph.* disco *m*; *radio:* dial *m*; **2.** *teleph.* marcar; ~ing *tone* tono *m* (de marcar).

di·a·lect ['daiəlekt] dialecto *m*.

di·a·logue, *a.* **di·a·log** ['daiəlɔg] diálogo *m*.

di·am·e·ter [dai'æmitə] diámetro *m*.

di·a·mond ['daiəmənd] diamante *m*; (*shape*) *losange m*; *cards:* ~ *pl.* diamantes *m/pl.*, (*Spanish*) oros *m/pl.*

di·a·per ['daiəpə] pañal *m*.

di·a·phragm ['daiəfræm] diafragma *m* (*a. teleph.*).

di·ar·rhe·a [daiə'riə] diarrea *f*.

di·a·ry ['daiəri] diario *m*.

di·a·tribe ['daiətraib] diatriba *f*.

dice [dais] [*pl. of die*²] **1.** dados *m/pl.*; (*shape*) cubitos *m/pl.*, cuadritos *m/pl.*; *load the* ~ cargar los dados; **2.** jugar a los dados; *vegetables* cortar en cuadritos.

dick·er ['dikə] regatear.

dic·ta·phone ['diktəfoun] dictáfono *m*.

dic·tate 1. ['dikteit] mandato *m*; **2.** [dik'teit] dictar; mandar, disponer (*a. fig.*); **dic'ta·tion** dictado *m*; = *dictate*; *take* ~ escribir al dictado; **dic'ta·tor** dictador *m*; **dic'ta·tor·ship** [dik'teiteʃip] dictadura *f*.

dic·tion ['dikʃn] dicción *f*, lenguaje *m*; **dic·tion·ar·y** ['dikʃənri] diccionario *m*.

did [did] *pret. of.* do.

didactic

di·dac·tic [di'dæktik] □ didáctico.

didn't ['didnt] = did not.

die[1] [dai] [*ger. dying*] morir (*of, from* de); ~ *away* acabarse gradualmente; desaparecer.

die[2] [~] [*pl.* dice] dado *m*; (*pl.* dies [daiz]) ⊕ troquel *m*; matriz *f*, molde *m*.

die...: '~-hard intransigente (*a. su. m*); acérrimo, empedernido.

di·et ['daiət] 1. régimen *m*, dieta *f*; *pol. etc.* dieta *f*; 2. *v/t.* poner a dieta; *v/i.* estar a dieta (*a. be on a ~*).

dif·fer ['difə] diferenciar, discordar (*with, from* de); diferenciarse (*from* de); **dif·fer·ence** ['difrəns] diferencia *f* (*a.* Ⓐ); *it makes no* ~ lo mismo da; *split the* ~ partir la diferencia; **'dif·fer·ent** □ diferente, distinto (*from* de); **dif·fer·en·tial** [~'ʃl] 1. □ diferencial; ~ *calculus* cálculo *m* diferencial; 2. diferencial *f* (Ⓐ *a. mot.*); **dif·fer·en·ti·ate** [~'ʃieit] *v/t.* distinguir (*between* entre); *v/i.* diferenciarse (*a.* Ⓐ *etc.*).

dif·fi·cult ['difikəlt] □ difícil; **'dif·fi·cul·ty** dificultad *f*; aprieto *m*; *difficulties pl.* ✝ *etc.* aprietos *m/pl.*, apuros *m/pl.*

dif·fuse 1. [di'fju:z] difundir(se) (*a. fig.*); 2. [~s] □ difuso (*a. fig.*); **dif·fused** [~zd] *light etc.* difuso.

dig [dig] 1. [*irr.*] cavar, excavar; ✕ empellar, empujar; ✕ ~ *in* atrincherarse; ~ *up* desenterrar; 2. empujón *m*; F *fig.* indirecta *f*, zumba *f*.

di·gest 1. [di'dʒest] digerir (*a. fig.*); compendiar, resumir; 2. ['daidʒest] resumen *m*; ⚕ digesto *m*; **di·gest·i·ble** digerible; **di·ges·tion** digestión *f*; **di·ges·tive** digestivo.

dig·it ['didʒit] Ⓐ dígito *m*; **'dig·it·al** digital.

dig·ni·fied ['dignifaid] grave, solemne; **dig·ni·fy** ['~fai] significar.

dig·ni·tar·y ['dignitəri] dignatario *m*; **'dig·ni·ty** dignidad *f*; *beneath one's* ~ impropio.

di·gress [dai'gres] hacer una digresión, apartarse del tema.

dike [daik] 1. dique *m* (*a. fig. a. geol.*); 2. contener con un dique.

di·lap·i·date [di'læpideit] *furniture etc.* desmantelar(se); *house* desmoronar(se); **di·lap·i·dat·ed** desmoronado.

di·late [dai'leit] dilatar(se) (*upon* sobre); **dil·a·to·ry** ['dilətəri] □ dilativo; tardón (F).

di·lem·ma [di'lemə] dilema *m* (*a. phls.*), perplejidad *f*, apuro *m*.

dil·i·gence ['dilidʒens] diligencia *f*; **'dil·i·gent** □ diligente, trabajador.

di·lute [dai'lju:t] 1. diluir (*a. fig.*); 2. diluido; **di'lu·tion** dilución *f*.

dim [dim] 1. □ *light* débil, mortecino; *fig.* confuso, indistinto; 2. amortiguar; *mot.* poner a media luz; *fig.* ofuscar.

dime [daim] *moneda de diez centavos (de un dólar)*.

di·men·sion [di'menʃn] dimensión *f*.

di·min·ish [di'miniʃ] disminuir(se); **dim·i·nu·tion** [dimi'nju:ʃn] disminución *f*; **di·min·u·tive** [~jutiv] 1. □ *gr.* diminutivo; (*small*) diminuto, menudo; 2. *gr.* diminutivo *m*.

dim·ple ['dimpl] 1. hoyuelo *m*; 2. formar(se) hoyuelos; (*water*) rizar(se).

din [din] 1. estruendo *m* continuo; 2. atolondrar con reiteraciones.

dine [dain] *v/i.* cenar; ~ *out* cenar fuera; *v/t.* dar de cenar a; **'din·er** convidado *m*; comensal *m*; ⚒ cochecomedor *m*.

din·gy ['dindʒi] □ deslustrado, desmejorado; sórdido.

din·ing... ['dainiŋ...]: '~ *car* coche comedor *m*; '~ *hall* comedor *m*; '~ *room* comedor *m*; '~ *suite* comedor *m*; ~ *ta·ble* mesa *f* de comer.

dink·y ['dinki] F mono; pequeñito.

din·ner ['dinə] cena *f*; comida *f* (*at midday*); banquete *m*; '~ *jack·et* smoking *m*; '~ *par·ty* banquete *m*.

dint [dint] 1. † golpe *m*; *by* ~ *of* a fuerza de; 2. abollar.

dip [dip] 1. *v/t.* bañar, sumergir (*a.* ⊕); *flag* bajar, saludar con; *pen* mojar; *cloth* teñir; meter, mojar (*into* en); *mot.* poner a media luz; *v/i.* sumergirse; inclinarse hacia abajo, ladearse; (*disappear*) desaparecer, bajar; *geol.* buzar; F ~ *into* meterse en; *book* hojear; 2. baño *m* (*a. liquid*), inmersión *f*; inclinación *f*, ladeo *m*; depresión *f in road, horizon*; baño *m* de mar; (*candle*) vela *f* de sebo; *geol.* buzamiento *m*.

diph·the·ri·a [dif'θiəriə] difteria *f*.

diph·thong ['difθɔŋ] diptongo *m*.

di·plo·ma [di'plouma] diploma *m*; **di·plo·ma·cy** diplomacia *f*; **dip·lo·mat** ['dipləmæt] diplomático *m*; **dip·lo'mat·ic** □ diplomático.

dip·per ['dipə] cazo *m*; *orn.* mirlo *m* acuático; **'dip·py** *sl.* loco.

dire ['daiə] horrendo, calamitoso; extremado.

di·rect [di'rekt] **1.** ☐ directo (*a. gr.*); sincero, abierto; ~ *current* corriente *f* continua; **2.** *adv.* derecho, en derechura; = ~*ly*; **3.** dirigir (*to, towards, at a,* hacia); mandar, ordenar (*to inf.*); **di·rec·tion** dirección *f*; (*order*) orden *f*, instrucción *f*; ~*s* for use modo *m* de empleo; *in the* ~ *of* en la dirección de; **di·rec·tion·al** *radio:* direccional; ~ *aerial* antena *f* orientable; **di·rec·tive** [~tiv] **1.** directivo; **2.** directorio *m*; **di·rect·ly 1.** *adv.* en el acto, en seguida; precisamente; **2.** *cj.* en cuanto; **di·rect·ness** derechura *f*; franqueza *f*.

di·rec·tor [di'rektə] director *m* (*a. film*); ✝ *board of* ~*s* consejo *m* de administración; **di·rec·to·ry** directorio *m*; *teleph.* guía *f* telefónica.

dirge [də:dʒ] endecha *f*.

dir·i·gi·ble ['diridʒəbl] dirigible *adj. a. su. m.*

dirk [də:k] puñal *m*.

dirt [də:t] mugre *f*, suciedad *f*; (*mud*) lodo *m*; (*filth, a. fig.*) porquería *f*; obscenidad *f*; '~-'cheap F tirado; ~ **road** camino *m* de tierra; '**dirt·y 1.** ☐ sucio (*a. fig.*); (*stained*) manchado; indecente, obsceno; **2.** ensuciar; manchar.

dis·a·bil·i·ty [disə'biliti] inhabilidad *f*, impedimento *m*.

dis·a·ble [dis'eibl] inhabilitar, incapacitar (*for, from* para); **dis·a·bled** incapacitado; impedido; mutilado.

dis·ad·van·tage [disəd'vɑːntidʒ] desventaja *f*; **dis·ad·van·ta·geous** [disædvɑːn'teidʒəs] ☐ desventajoso.

dis·a·gree [disə'griː] desavenirse (*with* con); discrepar (*with* de); no estar de acuerdo (*on* sobre); (*quarrel*) altercar; ~ *with* (*food*) sentar mal a; **dis·a·gree·a·ble** ☐ desagradable; *p.* displicente, de mal genio; desabrido (*to* con); **dis·a·gree·ment** desacuerdo *m*; discrepancia *f*; disconformidad *f* (*with* con); (*quarrel*) altercado *m*.

dis·ap·pear [disə'piə] desaparecer; **dis·ap·pear·ance** [~'piərəns] desaparición *f*.

dis·ap·point [disə'point] decepcionar; desilusionar; *hopes* frustrar; **dis·ap·point·ing** ☐ decepcionante; **dis·ap·point·ment** decepción *f*, desilusión *f*, chasco *m*.

dis·ap·prov·al [disə'pruːvl] desapro-

bación *f*; **dis·ap·prove** desaprobar (*of the acc.*); ~ *of p.* tener poca simpatía a.

dis·arm [dis'ɑːm] desarmar; **dis·ar·ma·ment** desarme *m*.

dis·ar·range ['disə'reindʒ] desarreglar, descomponer.

dis·ar·ray [disə'rei] desorden *m*, descompostura *f*.

dis·as·ter [di'zɑːstə] desastre *m*; **dis·as·trous** ☐ desastroso, catastrófico.

disband [dis'bænd] *v/t.* troops licenciar; *organization* disolver; *v/i.* desbandarse.

dis·bar [dis'bɑː] 🏛 excluir del foro.

dis·be·lief ['disbi'liːf] incredulidad *f* (*a. eccl.*).

dis·burse [dis'bəːs] desembolsar; **dis·burse·ment** desembolso *m*.

disc [disk] = disk.

dis·card 1. [dis'kɑːd] (*a. cards*) descartar, echar a un lado; **2.** ['diskɑːd] descarte *m*.

dis·cern [di'sə:n] discernir, percibir; **dis·cern·ment** discernimiento *m*, perspicacia *f*.

dis·charge [dis'tʃɑːdʒ] **1.** *v/t.* descargar; *duty* desempeñar; *worker* despedir; *patient* dar de alta; *v/i.* (*river, ⚡*) descargar; 🏥 supurar; **2.** descarga *f*; descargo *m of debt*; desempeño *m*; despedida *f*, desacomodo *m*; 🏥 supuración *f*.

dis·ci·ple [di'saipl] discípulo (*a f*) *m*; **dis·ci·ple·ship** discipulado *m*.

dis·ci·pline ['disiplin] **1.** disciplina *f*; (*punishment*) castigo *m*; **2.** disciplinar; castigar.

dis·claim [dis'kleim] desconocer, negar; 🏛 renunciar; **dis·claim·er** negación *f*; renuncia *f*.

dis·close [dis'klouz] revelar; divulgar, propalar; **dis·clo·sure** [~ʒə] revelación *f*; divulgación *f*.

dis·col·or·a·tion [diskʌlə'reiʃn] descoloramiento *m*; **dis·col·or** descolorar(se).

dis·con·cert [diskən'səːt] desconcertar.

dis·con·nect ['diskə'nekt] ⚡, ⊕ desconectar; desacoplar; **dis·con·nect·ed** ☐ desconectado; *speech* inconexo.

dis·con·so·late [dis'kɔnsəlit] ☐ desconsolado (*a. fig.*).

dis·con·tent ['diskən'tent] **1.** descontento *m*; **2.** descontentar; **dis·con·tent·ed** ☐ descontento; **dis·con·tent·ment** descontento *m*.

dis·con·tin·u·ance ['diskən'tinjuəns]

(*a.* **dis·con·tin·u'a·tion**) descontinuación *f*; **'dis·con'tin·ue** [∿nju:] descontinuar; cesar de; *paper* anular el abono de.

dis·cord ['diskɔ:d], **dis'cord·ance** discordia *f*; ♪ disonancia *f*; *fig.* sow ∿ sembrar cizaña; **dis'cord·ant** □ discorde (*a. fig.*); *fig.* disonante.

dis·count 1. ['diskaunt] descuento *m*, rebaja *f*; *at a ∿* al descuento; *fig. be at a ∿* no valorarse en su justo precio; **2.** [dis'kaunt] descontar (*a. fig.*); desestimar; *report* considerar exagerado.

dis·cour·age [dis'kʌridʒ] desalentar, desanimar; disuadir (*from* de); desaprobar; **dis'cour·age·ment** desaliento *m*; disuasión *f*; desaprobación *f*.

dis·course 1. ['diskɔ:s] discurso *m*; *hold ∿ with* platicar con; **2.** [dis'kɔ:s] discurrir (*about, upon* sobre).

dis·cour·te·ous [dis'kɔ:tiəs] □ descortés; **dis'cour·te·sy** [∿tisi] descortesía *f*.

dis·cov·er [dis'kʌvə] descubrir; revelar; manifestar; **dis'cov·er·er** descubridor *m*; **dis'cov·er·y** descubrimiento *m*; revelación *f*; manifestación *f*.

dis·cred·it [dis'kredit] **1.** descrédito *m*; (*doubt*) duda *f*, desconfianza *f*; **2.** desacreditar; (*disbelieve*) descreer.

dis·creet [dis'kri:t] □ discreto.

dis·crep·an·cy [dis'krepənsi] discrepancia *f*.

dis·crete [dis'kri:t] ▯ discreto; discontinuo.

dis·cre·tion [dis'kreʃn] discreción *f*; *at one's ∿* a discreción.

dis·crim·i·nate [dis'krimineit] distinguir (*between* entre); *∿ against* hacer distinción en perjuicio de; **dis'crim·i·nat·ing** □ discernidor, perspicaz; de buen gusto, fino; † *duty* diferencial; parcial; **dis·crim·i·na·tion** discernimiento *m*, discreción *f*; *b.s.* tratamiento *m* parcial (*against* de); *racial ∿* discriminación *f* racial; **dis'crim·i·na·tive** [∿neitiv] ▯, **dis·crim·i·na·to·ry** □ discernidor; *b.s.* parcial.

dis·cuss [dis'kʌs] hablar de, tratar de; *theme etc.* versar sobre; (*argue*) discutir; **dis'cus·sion** discusión *f*; tratamiento *m*, exposición *f* of *theme*.

dis·dain [dis'dein] **1.** desdén *m*; **2.** desdeñar; **dis'dain·ful** [∿ful] □ desdeñoso.

dis·ease [di'zi:z] enfermedad *f*; **dis-**'**eased** enfermo; morboso; *fig.* depravado.

dis·em·bark ['disim'ba:k] desembarcar.

dis·en·chant ['disin'tʃɑ:nt] desencantar (*a. fig.*).

dis·en·gage ['disin'geidʒ] ⊕ soltar, desenganchar; *p.*, † *etc.* desempeñar(se); ✗ retirar(se); **'dis·en'gage·ment** *mot.* desembrague *m*; ⊕ desunión *f*; † *etc.* desempeño *m*; ✗ retirada *f*; *pol.* neutralización *f*.

dis·en·tan·gle ['disin'tæŋgl] librar (*from* de); desenredar; *fig. ∿ o.s. from* desenredarse de.

dis·fa·vor ['dis'feivə] **1.** disfavor *m*; desaprobación *f*; *fall into ∿* caer en la desgracia; **2.** desfavorecer; *action* desaprobar.

dis·fig·ure [dis'figə] desfigurar; **dis-**'**fig·ure·ment** desfiguración *f*.

dis·grace [dis'greis] **1.** desgracia *f*, disfavor *m*; ignominia *f*; escándalo *m*; **2.** deshonrar, desacreditar; **dis-**'**grace·ful** [∿ful] □ ignominioso, vergonzoso; *∿!* ¡qué vergüenza!

dis·grun·tled [dis'grʌntld] descontento (*at* de); (*moody*) veleidoso.

dis·guise [dis'gaiz] **1.** disfrazar (*as* de; *a. fig.*); *voice* cambiar, disfrazar; **2.** disfraz *m*.

dis·gust [dis'gʌst] **1.** repugnancia *f*, aversión *f* (*at* hacia); **2.** repugnar, dar asco a; **dis'gust·ing** □ repugnante, asqueroso; ofensivo.

dish [diʃ] **1.** plato *m*, fuente *f*; *cooking*; plato *m*, manjar *m*; **2.** servir en un plato; *sl.* vencer, burlar.

dish·cloth ['diʃklɔθ] paño *m* de cocina; *approx.* estropajo *m*.

dis·heart·en [dis'hɑ:tn] desalentar, abatir.

di·shev·el(l)ed [di'ʃevld] *hair* despeinado, desgreñado; desaliñado.

dis·hon·est [dis'ɔnist] □ fraudulento; no honrado; **dis·hon·est·y** [∿'ɔnisti] fraude *m*; falta *f* de honradez.

dis·hon·or [dis'ɔnə] **1.** deshonra *f*, deshonor *m*; **2.** deshonrar, afrentar; *check, etc.* negarse a aceptar (*or* pagar); **dis'hon·or·a·ble** □ deshonroso.

dish...: '*∿·pan* jofaina *f* para fregar los platos; '*∿·wash·er* friegaplatos *m*; ⊕ lavadora *f* de platos; '*∿·wa·ter* lavazas *f/pl.*

dis·il·lu·sion [disi'lu:ʒn] **1.** desilusión *f*; **2.** desilusionar; **dis·il·lu·sion·ment** desilusión *f*.

dis·in·fect ['disin'fekt] desinfectar; **'dis·in'fect·ant** desinfectante *m*.

dis·in·her·it ['disin'herit] desheredar.

dis·in·te·grate ['dis'intigreit] desagregar(se), disgregar(se).

dis·in·ter ['disin'tə:] desenterrar.

dis·in·ter·est·ed [dis'intristid] □ desinteresado.

disk [disk] disco *m*.

dis·like [dis'laik] **1.** *p.*: I ∼ him le tengo aversión, me es antipático; *th.*: I ∼ *that* eso no me gusta; I ∼ *walking* no me gusta ir a pie; **2.** aversión *f*, antipatía *f* (*for*, of hacia, a); *take a ∼ to* coger antipatía a; ∼*d* malquisto; poco grato.

dis·lo·cate ['dislokeit] dislocar.

dis·lodge [dis'lɔdʒ] desalojar (*a.* ✕); quitar de su sitio, hacer caer.

dis·loy·al [dis'lɔiəl] □ desleal.

dis·mal ['dizməl] □ *fig.* sombrío, tenebroso, tétrico; (*sad*) triste, lúgubre; F pésimo.

dis·man·tle [dis'mæntl] desmontar, desarmar; *house* desmantelar; ⚓ desaparejar; ✕ desguarnecer.

dis·may [dis'mei] **1.** consternación *f*, conturbación *f*; (*discouragement*) desánimo *m*; **2.** consternar, turbar (*a. fill with* ∼); desanimar.

dis·mem·ber [dis'membə] desmembrar.

dis·miss [dis'mis] *v/t.* despedir, destituir; dar permiso a *p.* para irse; *possibility etc.* descartar, echar a un lado; ∼ (*from one's mind*) poner en olvido; **dis'miss·al** despedida *f*, destitución *f*.

dis·mount [dis'maunt] desmontar (-se).

dis·o·be·di·ence [disə'bi:djəns] desobediencia *f*; **dis·o'be·di·ent** □ desobediente; **'dis·o'bey** desobedecer.

dis·or·der [dis'ɔ:də] **1.** desorden *m*; ⚕ trastorno *m*; (*indisposition*) destemplanza *f*; tumulto *m*, motín *m*; *mental* ∼ trastorno *m* mental; **2.** desordenar, desarreglar.

dis·or·gan·ize [dis'ɔ:gənaiz] desorganizar.

dis·own [dis'oun] repudiar, desconocer; renegar de.

dis·par·age [dis'pæridʒ] desacreditar; (*with words*) menospreciar, hablar mal de; **dis'par·ag·ing** □ despreciativo.

dis·pa·rate ['dispərit] □ dispar, distinto; **dis·par·i·ty** [dis'pæriti] disparidad *f*.

dis·patch [dis'pætʃ] **1.** despachar; *goods* consignar, enviar; (*deathblow*) rematar; *meal* despabilar; **2.** despacho *m*; consignación *f*; (*speed*) prontitud *f*.

dis·pel [dis'pel] disipar, dispersar; *esp. fig.* desvanecer.

dis·pen·sa·ble [dis'pensəbl] dispensable; prescindible; **dis'pen·sa·ry** dispensario *m*; **dis·pen·sa·tion** [dispen'seiʃn] dispensación *f*; *eccl. etc.* dispensa *f*; designio *m* divino.

dis·pense [dis'pens] *v/t.* dispensar; *v/i.:* ∼ *with* deshacerse de; prescindir de; *oath etc.* eximir de; **dis'pens·er** dispensador *m*.

dis·perse [dis'pə:s] dispersar(se); **dis'per·sal, dis'per·sion** dispersión *f* (*a.* of Jews).

dis·pir·it [dis'pirit] desalentar; **dis'pir·it·ed** □ desalentado; abatido.

dis·place [dis'pleis] sacar de su sitio; destituir; (*replace*) suplir, reemplazar; *phys.* desplazar; ∼*d person* (*abbr.* D. P.) desplazado (a *f*) *m*.

dis·play [dis'plei] **1.** despliegue *m* of *quality*; exhibición *f*; pompa *f*, aparato *m*; ostentación *f* (*esp. b.s.*); ∼ *window* escaparate *m*; **2.** desplegar; exhibir; ostentar; *quality* revelar.

dis·please [dis'pli:z] desagradar, desplacer; (*annoy*) enojar, enfadar; **dis'pleased** □ disgustado (*at*, *with* de, con); enfadado, indignado; **dis'pleas·ing** □ desagradable, ingrato; **dis·pleas·ure** [∼'pleʒə] desagrado *m*; disgusto *m* (*at por*, a causa de); enojo *m*, indignación *f*; *incur s.o.'s* ∼ incurrir en el enojo de una p.

dis·pos·a·ble [dis'pouzəbl] disponible; **dis'pos·al** disposición *f*; arreglo *m*, ajuste *m* of *a matter*; ✝ *etc.* consignación *f*, donación *f*; (*sale*) venta *f*; *at one's* ∼ a su disposición; **dis'pose** *v/t.* disponer, arreglar; inducir, mover (*to* a); determinar, decidir; *v/i.* ∼ *of* disponer de; (*rid*) deshacerse de, quitarse de; *rights* enajenar; *problem etc.* solucionar; *food* comer; *property* vender; **dis·po·si·tion** [∼pə'siʃn] disposición *f*, orden *m*; (*character*) índole *f*, natural *m*; decreto *m*; ⚖ (*will*) legado *m*; propensión *f* (*to* a); plan *m*; ✕ *make* ∼*s* hacer preparativos.

dis·pos·sess [dispə'zes] desposeer, privar (*of* de); *tenant* desahuciar.

dis·prove ['dis'pru:v] confutar, refutar.

dis·pute [dis'pju:t] **1.** disputa f, contienda f; *beyond* (*or without*) ~ sin disputa; *in* ~ disputado; **2.** v/t. disputar; v/i. disputar, discutir (*about, over* sobre).

dis·qual·i·fy ['dis'kwɔlifai] inhabilitar, incapacitar (*for* para); *sport:* descalificar.

dis·qui·et·ing [dis'kwaiətiŋ] inquietante.

dis·qui·si·tion [diskwi'ziʃn] disertación f, disquisición f.

dis·re·gard ['disri'gɑːd] **1.** indiferencia f (*for* a); (*neglect*) descuido m; **2.** desatender, descuidar; (*ignore*) no hacer caso de.

dis·re·pair ['disri'pɛə] mal estado m; *fall into* ~ desmoronarse.

dis·rep·u·ta·ble [dis'repjutəbl] □ de mala fama, mal reputado; *house* de mal vivir; **dis·re·pute** ['ˌri'pju:t] mala fama f, descrédito m; *bring into* ~ desacreditar.

dis·re·spect ['disris'pekt] desacato m, falta f de respeto; **dis·re·spect·ful** ['ˌ'pektful] □ irrespetuoso, desacatador.

dis·robe ['dis'roub] desnudar(se) (*of* de; *a. fig.*).

dis·rupt [dis'rʌpt] romper; *fig.* desbaratar, desorganizar; **dis·rup·tion** rompimiento m; desordenamiento m, confusión f; desbaratamiento m, desorganización f.

dis·sat·is·fac·tion ['dissætis'fækʃn] descontento m; desagrado m.

dis·sect [di'sekt] disecar; *fig.* hacer la disección de; **dis·sec·tion** [di'sekʃn] disección f; análisis m minucioso.

dis·sem·ble [di'sembl] v/t. disimular, encubrir; v/i. disimular, ser hipócrita.

dis·sem·i·nate [di'semineit] diseminar, difundir; **dis·sem·i·na·tion** difusión f.

dis·sen·sion [di'senʃn] disensión f, discordia f; *eccl.* disidencia f.

dis·sent [di'sent] **1.** disentir (*from* de); *eccl.* disidir; **2.** disentimiento m; *eccl.* disidencia f.

dis·ser·ta·tion [disə'teiʃn] disertación f (*on* sobre).

dis·serv·ice ['dis'sə:vis] deservicio m (*to* a); *render a* ~ perjudicar.

dis·si·pate ['disipeit] v/t. disipar; *money* despilfarrar; v/i. disiparse;

(*p.*) entregarse a los vicios; **'dis·si·pat·ed** disoluto.

dis·so·ci·ate [di'souʃieit] disociar; ~ *o.s. from* hacerse insolidario de.

dis·so·lute ['disəlu:t] □ disoluto.

dis·solve [di'zɔlv] v/t. disolver (*a. fig.*); v/i. disolverse; *fig.* desvanecerse.

dis·suade [di'sweid] disuadir (*from* de).

dis·taff ['distæf] rueca f; *fig. on the* ~ *side* por parte de madre.

dis·tance ['distəns] **1.** distancia f (*a. fig.*); lejanía f, lontananza f; *fig.* reserva f, recato m; *paint.* término m; *at a* ~ a distancia; *in the* ~ a lo lejos, en lontananza; *from a* ~ de lejos; *fig. keep at a* ~ no tratar con familiaridad; *keep one's* ~ mantenerse a distancia; *striking* ~ alcance m; **2.** distanciar; *sport:* dejar atrás (*a. fig.*); **'dis·tant** □ distante; lejano; (*slight*) leve, ligero; *fig.* indiferente, frío; *relation* lejano; *be* ~ *with s.o.* tratar con frialdad.

dis·taste ['dis'teist] aversión f, repugnancia f (*for, towards* hacia, por); **dis·taste·ful** [ˌful] □ desagradable, poco grato (*to* a); (*annoying*) enfadoso.

dis·tend [dis'tend] dilatar(se), distender(se), hinchar(se).

dis·til(l) [dis'til] destilar (*a. 🝆*); **dis·till·er** destilador m; **dis·till·er·y** destilería f.

dis·tinct [dis'tiŋkt] □ distinto; claro, inequívoco; positivo; *as* ~ *from* a diferencia de; **dis·tinc·tion** distinción f; individualidad f *of style*; *have the* ~ *of ger.* haberse distinguido por *inf.*; **dis·tinc·tive** □ distintivo, característico.

dis·tin·guish [dis'tiŋgwiʃ] distinguir (*between* entre); ~ *o.s.* distinguirse; *be* ~*ed from* distinguirse de; **dis·tin·guished** distinguido; conocible (*by* por).

dis·tort [dis'tɔːt] torcer (*a. fig.*), deformar; **dis·tor·tion** torcimiento m, deformación f; *radio etc.:* distorsión f.

dis·tract [dis'trækt] distraer; (*confuse*) aturdir, confundir; (*madden*) volver loco; **dis·trac·tion** distracción f; diversión f; aturdimiento m, perplejidad f; locura f.

dis·tress [dis'tres] **1.** pena f, angustia f; (*straits*) apuro m, miseria f; (*danger*) peligro m; 🝆 agotamiento m; ~ *signal* señal f de peligro; **2.** apenar, afligir; agotar; **dis'tressed** *freq.* preocupado (*for* por); **dis'tress·ing** □ penoso, que da pena.

dis·trib·ute [dis'tribju:t] distribuir, repartir (*among* entre); **dis·tri'bu·tion** distribución *f*, repartimiento *m*; **dis'trib·u·tor** distribuidor (-a *f*) *m*.

dis·trict [distrikt] comarca *f*, región *f*; *pol.* distrito *m*; ⚖ jurisdicción *f*; **'~ at·tor·ney** fiscal *m*.

dis·trust [dis'trʌst] **1.** desconfianza *f*, recelo *m*; **2.** desconfiar de, recelar; **dis'trust·ful** [~ful] □ desconfiado; (*suspicious*) receloso.

dis·turb [dis'tə:b] *p.* molestar, estorbar; inquietar, perturbar; *order* alborotar; *balance of mind* trastornar; **dis'turb·ance** alboroto *m*, disturbio *m*; (*disquiet*) desasosiego *m*; trastorno *m of mind*.

ditch [ditʃ] **1.** zanja *f*; (*road*) cuneta *f*; ⚔ foso *m*; *to the last* ~ hasta quemar el último cartucho; **2.** *v/i.* abrir zanjas; *v/t. sl.* zafarse de; ✈ *sl.* ~ *a plane* amarar, tomar agua.

dith·er ['diðə] F estremecimiento *m*; nerviosismo *m*.

dit·o ['ditou] idem, ídem.

dit·ty ['diti] cancioneta *f*.

di·van [di'væn] diván *m*; ~ *bed* cama *f* turca.

dive [daiv] **1.** sumergirse; *swimming:* zambullirse *into water*, bucear *under water*; ✈ picar; **2.** *swimming:* salto *m* de trampolín, zambullida *f*; ✈ picado *m*; F (*esp. low*) ~ tasca *f*; **'div·er** buzo *m*; *orn.* colimbo *m*.

di·verge [dai'və:dʒ] divergir; (*road*) bifurcarse; **di'ver·gent** □ divergente; discrepante.

di·verse [dai'və:s] □ diverso; variado; **di'ver·sion** [~ʃn] diversión *f* (*a.* ⚔); (*traffic*) desviación *f*; **di'ver·si·ty** diversidad *f*.

di·vert [dai'və:t] divertir; *traffic* desviar.

di·vest [dai'vest] desnudar; *fig.* despojar (*of* de); ~ *o.s. of fig.* renunciar a.

di·vide [di'vaid] **1.** *v/t.* partir, dividir (*freq.* ~ *up*; *into* en); ⚖ dividir (*by* por); *fig.* dividir, sembrar la discordia entre; ~ *out* repartir; *v/i.* dividirse (*into* en); **2.** *geog.* divisoria *f*; **div·i·dend** ['dividend] ✝, ⚖ dividendo *m*; **di·vid·ing** [di'vaidiŋ] divisorio; ~ *line* línea *f* divisoria.

di·vine [di'vain] **1.** □ divino (*a. fig.*); *v. service;* **2.** sacerdote *m*; teólogo *m*; **3.** adivinar (*a. fig.*).

div·ing ['daiviŋ] salto *m* de trampolín, el bucear *etc.*; '~ **bell** campana *f* de bucear; '~ **suit** escafandra *f*.

di·vin·i·ty [di'viniti] divinidad *f*; teología *f*.

di·vi·sion [di'viʒn] división *f* (*a.* ⚔, ⚒); sección *f*; *fig.* discordia *f*; división *f*; *parl.* votación *f*.

di·vorce [di'vɔːs] **1.** disolución *f* del matrimonio; divorcio *m*; *fig.* separación *f*, divergencia *f*; *get a* ~ divorciarse; **2.** divorciar; *fig.* separar; **di·vor'cee** [~sei] divorciado (a *f*) *m*.

di·vulge [dai'vʌldʒ] divulgar.

diz·zi·ness ['dizinis] vértigo *m*; '**diz·zy** □ vertiginoso; aturdido, confuso.

do [du:] [*irr.*] (*v. a. done*) **1.** *v/t.* hacer; obrar; ejecutar; terminar; *thea.* desempeñar, representar; *cooking:* asar, cocer; *distance* recorrer; *duty* cumplir con; *hair* peinar; *homage* rendir, tributar; *problem* resolver; *room* limpiar; *sl.* visitar de turista; *sl.* estafar, timar (*a.* ~ *down*); F ~ *o.s. well* regalarse; ~ (*over*) *again* repetir; *sl.* ~ *in* apalear; asesinar; F ~ *out* decorar; F ~ *out of* hacer perder; ~ *up laces etc.* liar, atar; *parcel* empaquetar; *room* renovar el papel *etc.* de; **2.** *v/i.* actuar, proceder; convenir, ser suficiente; estar, encontrarse; *that will* ~ basta ya; eso sirve; *that won't* ~ no sirve; no vale; *how do you* ~? encantado, mucho gusto; ¿*cómo está Vd.?;* ~ *away with* quitar, suprimir; *have nothing to* ~ *with* no tener nada que ver con; ~ *without* pasarse sin, prescindir de; **3.** *v/aux.* a) *question:* ~ *you know him?* ¿le conoce Vd.?; b) *negation with not:* I ~ *not know him* no le conozco; c) *emphasis:* I ~ *feel better* ciertamente me encuentro mejor; ~ *come and see me* le ruego que venga a verme; I ~ *tell truth* yo sí que digo la verdad; d) *to avoid repetition of a verb:* ~ *you like London?–I* ~ ¿le gusta Londres?–Sí; *you write better than I* ~ Vd. escribe mejor que yo; *I take a bath every day–so* ~ me baño todos los días–yo también; e) *inversion after adv.:* *seldom does she come here* (ella) rara vez viene por aquí; **4.** *su.* F (*swindle*) estafa *f*; (*party*) reunión *f*, guateque *m*; *make* ~ *with* conformarse con; hacer lo posible con.

doc [dɔk] F = *doctor*.

doc·ile ['dousail] dócil.

dock¹ [dɔk] recortar; *tree* desmochar; *pay* reducir, rebajar.

dock² [~] ♣ acedera f, romaza f.
dock³ [~] 1. ♣ (with gates) dique m; dársena f; esp. muelle m; 🚂 barra f; ~s pl. puerto m; dry ~ dique m seco; floating ~ dique m flotante; 2. (hacer) entrar en dique; atracar al muelle; '~hand portuario m; '~yard arsenal m, astillero m.

doc·tor ['dɔktə] 1. doctor m (a ⚕); médico m; 2. ℱ medicinar; reparar; ℱ castrar; adulterar, falsificar; **doc·tor·ate** ['~rit] doctorado m.

doc·trine ['dɔktrin] doctrina f.

doc·u·ment 1. ['dɔkjumənt] documento m; 2. [~ment] documentar; **doc·u·men·ta·tion** documentación f.

dodge [dɔdʒ] 1. regate m (a. fig.); (trick) truco m; ⊕ ingenio m, artificio m; 2. v/t. evadir (moviéndose bruscamente); (elude) dar esquinazo a; v/i. ℱ fig. escurrir el bulto; ~ around andar a saltos.

do·er ['du:ə] hacedor m.

does [dʌz] hace etc. (v. do).

dog [dɔg] 1. perro m; hunt. sabueso m; (male of fox) zorro m; (wolf) lobo m; ℱ tío m; ℱ b.s. tunante m; ⊕ grapa f; (a fire ~) morillo m; ℱ go to the ~s arruinarse; entregarse al vicio; ℱ put on the ~ darse ínfulas; 2. seguir de cerca, perseguir.

dog·ged ['dɔgid] ☐ tenaz, terco.

dog·ma ['dɔgmə] dogma m; **dog·mat·ic, dog·mat·i·cal** ['mætik(l)] ☐ dogmático (a. fig.); arrogante, autoritario.

dog...: '~('s)-eared book sobado, muy usado; '~ show exposición f canina; '~'s life vida f miserable; '~tired rendido, cansadísimo; '~wood cornejo m.

doi·ly ['dɔili] pañito m (de adorno).

do·ing ['du:iŋ] present participle of do; nothing ~! de ninguna manera!; 2.: esp. ~s pl. actos m/pl., hechos m/pl.; conducta f.

dol·drums ['dɔldrəmz] pl. ♣ zona f de las calmas; fig. be in the ~ tener murria; (th.) languidecer.

dole [doul] 1. limosna f; subsidio m de paro; 2. repartir, distribuir (mst ~ out).

dole·ful ['doulful] ☐ triste, lúgubre.

doll [dɔl] 1. muñeca f; sl. mozuela f; 2. ℱ engalanarse, emperejilarse (a. ~ up).

dol·lar ['dɔlə] dólar m.

doll·y ['dɔli] ℱ muñequita f.

dol·phin ['dɔlfin] delfín m.

do·main [də'mein] dominio m; fig. campo m.

dome [doum] cimborrio m; cúpula f.

do·mes·tic [də'mestik] 1. ☐ doméstico; casero; 2. doméstico m, **do·mes·ti·cate** [~keit] domesticar; ~d p. hogareño.

dom·i·cile ['dɔmisail] 1. esp. 🚂 domicilio m; 2. domiciliar(se).

dom·i·nance ['dɔminəns] dominación f; **'dom·i·nant** dominante adj. a. su. (♪); **dom·i·nate** ['~neit] dominar; **dom·i·na·tion** dominación f; **dom·i·neer** [dɔmi'niə] dominar, tiranizar (over acc.); **dom·i·neer·ing** ☐ dominante, dominador.

do·min·ion [də'minjən] dominio m.

dom·i·no ['dɔminou] (carnival) dominó m; ficha f del dominó; **dom·i·noes** ['~z] pl. (juego de) dominó m.

do·nate [dou'neit] donar; **do·na·tion** donación f.

done [dʌn] 1. p.p. of do; freq. ser hecho, estar hecho (th. cooking); have ~ haber terminado; have ~ with th. haber terminado con; p. freq. no tener nada que ver con; ger. haber terminado de inf., haber dejado de inf.; well ~! ¡bien!; 2. adj. terminado; ℱ (a. ~ in, ~ up) rendido, hecho cisco; ℱ ~ for fuera de combate; ⚕ desahuciado; ✝ ¡terminado!; ✝ ¡trato hecho!

don·key ['dɔŋki] burro m.

do·nor ['dounə] donador m; donante m/f; blood ~ donante m/f de sangre.

don't [dount] 1. = do not; 2. ℱ prohibición f.

doom [du:m] 1. mst b.s. destino m, hado m; perdición f, muerte f; juicio m final; 2. predestinar (a la muerte, a la perdición); condenar (a muerte); **dooms·day** ['du:mzdei] día m del juicio final.

door [dɔ:] puerta f (a. fig.); (street) portal m; portezuela f of vehicle; front ~, main ~ puerta f principal; side ~ puerta f accesoria; behind closed ~s a puertas cerradas; next ~ en la casa de al lado; next ~ to al lado de; fig. que raya en; out of ~s al aire libre, afuera; lay the blame at s.o.'s ~ echarle a uno la culpa (for de); '~bell campanilla f de puerta, timbre m de puerta; '~knob botón m de puerta, pomo m de puerta; '~man portero m; '~way portal m, puerta f.

dope [doup] 1. grasa f lubricante;

draft

barniz *m* (*a.* 🖌); *sl.* narcótico *m*; *sl.* informe *m*; *sl.* (*p.*) bobo *m*; **2.** *sl.* dar (*or* poner) un narcótico a; *sl.* pronosticar; '~ **fiend** *sl.* toxicómano; '~ **sheet** *sl.* hoja *f* confidencial sobre los caballos de carreras.

dor·mant ['dɔːmənt] *mst* *fig.* durmiente, inactivo; latente.

dor·mer (**win·dow**) ['dɔːmə('windou)] buhardilla *f*.

dor·mi·to·ry ['dɔːmitəri] dormitorio *m*; ⚔ compañía *f*.

dose [dous] **1.** dosis *f*; **2.** administrar una dosis a (*a.* ~ *a* *p. with*).

dos·si·er ['dɔsiei] expediente *m*; (*police etc.*) ficha *f*.

dot [dɔt] **1.** punto *m*; F *on the* ~ *in* punto; **2.** poner punto a; puntear, salpicar de puntos; *fig.* esparcir, desparramar (*a.* ~ *about*); *sl.* ~ *s.o.* one dar de bofetadas a; ~ted *with* salpicado de.

dot·age ['doutidʒ] chochez *f*; *be in one's* ~ chochear; **dote** [dout] chochear; ~ (*up*)*on* estar loco por (*or* con); '**dot·ing** ☐ chocho (*a.* *fig.*); (*doltish*) lelo.

dou·ble ['dʌbl] **1.** doble (*a.* ♧); dos veces; doblado; *fig.* doble, falso; ~ *meaning* doble sentido *m*; **2.** doble *m* (*a.* *p.*); ~s *pl.* tennis: juego *m* de dobles; *at the* ~ a paso ligero; **3.** *v/t.* doblar (*a.* bridge); *p.* ser el doble de; ~*d up* doblado; agachado; *v/i.* doblarse; (*a.* ~ *up*) agacharse; F ~ compartir dos la misma habitación (*a.* ~ *back*) virar; '~**bar·reled** de dos cañones; *fig.* ambiguo; '~ **bass** contrabajo *m*; '~ **bed** cama *f* de matrimonio; '~**breast·ed** *jacket* cruzado, de dos filas; '~**cross** *sl.* hacer una mala faena a; '~**edged** de dos filos; '~ **en·try** ✝ partida *f* doble; '~**head·er** tren *m* con dos locomotoras; *baseball* dos partidos *m/pl.* jugados sucesivamente; '~**joint·ed** de articulaciones dobles; '~**park** aparcar en doble fila; '~**talk** F galimatías *m*; F habla *f* ambigua para engañar.

doubt [daut] **1.** *v/i.* dudar (*whether* que *subj.*); tener dudas; *v/t.* dudar; *I* ~ *it* lo dudo; **2.** duda *f*; *beyond* ~ sin duda; *in* ~ dudoso; *no* ~ sin duda; *without* ~ indudablemente; *call in* ~ poner en duda; **doubt·ful** ['~ful] ☐ dudoso (*a.* character); '**doubt·less** *adv.* sin duda, indudablemente.

dough [dou] masa *f*, pasta *f*; *sl.* pasta

f, guita *f*; '~**boy** F soldado *m* de infantería; '~**nut** buñuelo *m*.

dour ['duə] severo, austero; (*obstinate*) terco.

douse [daus] mojar, calar *with water*; *v.* dowse.

dove [dʌv] paloma *f*; '~**cot(e)** palomar *m*; '~**tail** ⊕ **1.** cola *f* de milano; **2.** ensamblar a cola de milano; *fig.* corresponder, ajustarse.

dow·dy ['daudi] ☐ *p.*, *dress* poco elegante, poco atractivo.

down¹ [daun] vello *m*; plumón *m*.

down² [~] **1.** *adv.* abajo; hacia abajo, para abajo; (*to ground*) en tierra; (*south*) hacia el sur; ~ *below* allá abajo; ~ *from* desde; ~ *to* hasta; *be* ~ (*price*) haber bajado; F estar abatido; (*battery etc.*) estar agotado; *sport*: quedarse atrás, perder; F *be* ~ *on p.* tener una inquina a; tratar severamente; *be* ~ *and out* estar arruinado; **2.** *prp.* abajo de; ~ *the street* calle abajo; **3.** *int.* ¡abajo!; ~ *with* …! ¡muera …!; **4.** *adj.* estar en las últimas; descendente; **5.** F echar a tierra; *food* tragar; '~**cast** alicaído, abatido; '~**fall** caída *f*, ruina *f*; '~**grade** F *be on the* ~ ir cuesta abajo (*fig.*); '~**heart·ed** abatido, desanimado; '~**hill** **1.** *adj.* en declive; **2.** *adv.* cuesta abajo (*a.* *fig.*); '~**pour** chaparrón *m*; aguacero *m*; '~**right** **1.** *lie etc.* categórico, absoluto; *p.* patente, evidente; *p.* franco, abierto; **2.** *adv.* absolutamente, completamente; '~**stairs** **1.** abajo; en el piso de abajo; **2.** piso *m* inferior; '~**stream** aguas abajo, río abajo; '~**stroke** (*pen*) palote *m*, pierna *f*; ⊕ carrera *f* descendente; '~**town** en el centro de la ciudad; '~**trod·den** pisoteado (*a.* fig.); oprimido; '~**ward 1.** descendente; **2.** (*a.* '~**wards**) hacia abajo.

down·y ['dauni] velloso; plumoso; *sl.* despabilado, taimado.

dow·ry ['dauəri] dote *f*.

dowse [dauz] *light* apagar; '**dows·er** zahorí *m*; '**dows·ing rod** varilla *f* de zahorí.

doze [douz] **1.** dormitar (*a.* ~ *away*); ~ *off* quedarse medio dormido; **2.** sueño *m* ligero.

doz·en ['dʌzn] docena *f*; *baker's* ~ docena *f* de fraile.

drab [dræb] **1.** gris amarillento; *fig.* monótono; **2.** ramera *f*.

draft [dræft] **1.** tiro *m* (*a.* chimney); corriente *f* de aire; (*drink*) trago *m*;

♣ calado *m of ship*; ♣ (*net*) rastreo *m*; ✝ giro *m*, letra *f* de cambio; ✕ quinta *f*; (*sketch*) bosquejo *m*; borrador *m*, versión *f of article etc.*; *attr.* horse etc. de tiro; *beer* de barril, al grifo; *v.* draught; **2.** *article* redactar; *plan* bosquejar; ✕ quintar; ✕ destacar; '**~ age** edad *f* de quintas; '**~ beer** cerveza *f* a presión; '**~ board** ✕ junta *f* de reclutamiento; '**~ dodg·er** ✕ emboscado *m*; **draft·ee** [dræf'tiː] **1.** quinto *m*; '**drafts·man** dibujante *m*; (*professional*) delineante *m*; '**drafts·man·ship** arte *m* del dibujante (*or* delineante); '**draft·y** airoso; *house* ventilado, aireado, lleno de corrientes de aire.

drag [dræg] **1.** rastra *f* (*a.* ♣); ✎ grada *f*; narria *f for wood etc.*; ♣ (*a.* ~ *net*) red *f* barredera; ✖ resistencia *f* al avance; *fig.* estorbo *m*, demora *f*; F cuesta *f* dura; *sl.* influencia *f*; **2.** *v/t.* arrastrar; ♣ rastrear; ~ *along* arrastrar consigo (*or* tras sí); ~ *out* hacer demasiado largo (*or* lento); *v/i.* arrastrarse (*along the ground* por el suelo); ♣ rastrear (*for* en busca del suelo); ✝ decaer; (*time*) pesar.

drag·on ['drægən] dragón *m*; F *fig.* fiera *f*; F (*duenna*) carabina *f*; '**~·fly** libélula *f*, caballito *m* del diablo.

drain [dreɪn] **1.** (*outlet*) desaguadero *m*; alcantarilla *f*, boca *f* de alcantarilla *in street*; *fig.* desaguadero *m* (*on* de); ~ *pipe* tubo *m* de desagüe (*a. fig.*); **2.** *v/t.* desaguar; ✎ avenar; ✖ *wound* drenar; *glass* apurar; *lake* desangrar (*a.* ~ *off*); *vessel* escurrir *v/i* desaguar (*into* en); '**drain·age** desagüe *m*, avenamiento *m*; (*system*) alcantarillado *m*; ~ *basin* cuenca *f* de un río; ✎ ~ *channel* zanja *f*.

drake [dreɪk] pato *m* macho.

dram [dræm] dracma *f*; cantidad *f* pequeña *of brandy etc.*

dra·ma ['drɑːmə] drama *m* (*a. fig.*); **dra·mat·ic** [drə'mætɪk] ☐ dramático (*a. fig.*); **dram·a·tist** ['dræmətɪst] dramaturgo *m*; '**dram·a·tize** dramatizar.

drank [dræŋk] *pret. of* drink.

drape [dreɪp] colgar, adornar con colgaduras; vestir (con telas de muchos pliegues; *in* de).

dras·tic ['dræstɪk] ☐ drástico.

draught [drɑːft] tiro *m* (*a. chimney*); corriente *f* de aire; (*drink*) trago *m*; ♣ calado *m of ship*; ♣ (*net*) rastreo *m*; *attr.* horse de tiro; *beer* de barril, al

grifo; ~*s pl.* juego *m* de damas; *v.* draft; *at a* ~ de un trago; '**~·board** tablero *m* (del juego de damas); '**~·horse** caballo *m* de tiro.

draw [drɔː] **1.** [*irr.*] *v/t.* arrastrar, tirar de (*a.* ~ *along*); (*take out*) sacar; (*lengthen*) alargar; atraer; *bow* tender; *breath* aspirar; *cheque* girar, librar; *curtain* correr; *drawing* dibujar; *fowl* destripar; *line* trazar, tirar; *lots* echar; *money, prize* sacar; *salary* cobrar; *sword, water* sacar; ♣ *water* calar; ~ *aside p.* apartar; ~ *back* retirar; *curtain* descorrer; ~ *forth* hacer salir, producir; ~ *off* sacar, extraer; *liquid* trasegar; ~ *on p.* engatusar; *glove* ponerse; ~ *out* sacar; *p.* hacer hablar; *b.s.* sonsacar; ~ *up* redactar; *chair* acercar; ✕ ordenar para el combate; ~ *o.s. up* enderezarse, ponerse en su lugar; ~ (*up*)*on* ✝ girar a cargo de; *fig.* inspirarse en; *v/i.* (*chimney*) tirar; *sport:* empatar; atraer; (*artist*) dibujar; moverse (*aside* a un lado *etc.*); ~ *back* retroceder, cejar (*a. fig.*); ~ *near* acercarse (*to* a); ~ *up* pararse (*sharp* en seco); ~ *to a close* estar para terminar; **2.** *sport:* empate *m*; *chess:* tablas *f/pl.*; *lottery:* sorteo *m*; F función *f* taquillera (*or* de mucho éxito); '**~·back** inconveniente *m* (*to* en); ✝ (*excise*) reembolso *m*; '**~·bridge** puente *m* levadizo; '**draw·er 1.** ['drɔːə] dibujante *m*; ✝ girador *m*, librador *m*; **2.** ['drɔː] cajón *m*; ~*s pl.* calzoncillos *m/pl.*; *bragas f/pl.* de mujer.

draw·ing ['drɔːɪŋ] dibujo *m*; ~ *instruments pl.* instrumentos *m/pl.* de dibujar; '**~·board** tablero *m* de dibujo; '**~·card** polo *m* de atracción popular; '**~·room** salón *m*; recepción *f*.

drawl [drɔːl] **1.** *v/t. words* arrastrar; *v/i.* hablar lentamente arrastrando las palabras; **2.** habla *f* lenta y pesada.

drawn [drɔːn] **1.** *p.p. of* draw 1; **2.** *adj. game* empatado; *face* ojeroso, cansado; *sew.* ~ *work* calado *m*; '**~·butter** mantequilla *f* derretida.

dread [dred] **1.** pavor *m*, temor *m*; **2.** temer; **3.** espantoso; '**dread·ful** ['~ful] ☐ terrible, espantoso; F desagradable; F malísimo.

dream [driːm] **1.** sueño *m* (*a. fig.*); (*a. day-*) ensueño *m*; **2.** [*irr.*] soñar (*of* con); ~ *away* (*e.g. the day*) pasar (el día) soñando; '**dream·er** soñador (*-a f*) *m*; *fig.* fantaseador (*-a f*) *m*; '**dream·like** de ensueño; **dreamt**

pret. a. p.p. of dream 2; **'dream·y** □ *p.* distraído, muy en las nubes; entre sueños, nebuloso.

drear·i·ness ['driərinis] tristeza *f*; monotonía *f*; **'drear·y** □ triste, melancólico, monótono.

dredge [dredʒ] ⚓ **1.** draga *f*, rastra *f*; **2.** dragar; rastrear; ~ *up* pescar (*a. fig.*).

dregs [dregz] *pl.* heces *f/pl.* (*a. fig.*).

drench [drentʃ] **1.** *vet.* poción *f*; (*shower*) chaparrón *m*; **2.** mojar, empapar; F *be ~ed* calarse, estar calado.

dress [dres] **1.** vestido *m*, ropa *f*; (*a. fig.*) atavío *m*; (*woman's*) vestido *m*; ~ *ball* baile *m* de etiqueta; *thea.* ~ *rehearsal* ensayo *m* general; *full* ~ traje *m* de etiqueta; *v. fancy*; **2.** *v/t.* vestir (*a. fig.*; *in black* de negro); (*a.* ~ *up*) ataviar, adornar (*in* con, de); *hair* peinar; *horse*, *skins* peinar, almohazar; *stone* labrar; *window* poner; *wound* curar, vendar; ✗ abonar; ✗ alinear; F ~ *down* dar un rapapolvo a; *v/i.* (*a. get* ~*ed*) vestirse; ~ (*well*) vestir(se) (bien); ~ *up* acicalarse; vestirse de etiqueta; ~ **'cir·cle** *thea.* anfiteatro *m*; '~ **'coat** frac *m*; **de'sign·er** modisto *m*; '**dress·er** aparador *m* con estantes; cómoda *f* con espejo.

dress·ing ['dresiŋ] (*act*) el vestir(se); ✗ vendaje *m*; (*food*) salsa *f*, condimento *m*; ✗ abono *m*; '~**'down** F repasata *f*, regaño *m*; '~ **gown** bata *f*; '~ **room** vestidor *m*; *thea.* camarín *m*, camerino *m*; '~ **ta·ble** tocador *m*.

dress...: '~**mak·er** costurera *f*, modista *f*; '~**mak·ing** costura *f*; '~ **pa·rade** ✗ parada *f*; '~ **re'hears·al** ensayo *m* general; '~ **'shirt** camisa *f* de pechera dura; '~ **'suit** traje *m* de etiqueta; '**dress·y** F acicalado; elegante.

drew [dru:] *pret. of* draw 1.

drib·ble ['dribl] gotear, caer gota a gota; (*mouth*) babear; *football*: driblar.

drib·let ['driblit] adarme *m*; *in* ~*s* por adarmes.

dried [draid] secado; *fruit* paso; *vegetables* seco.

drift [drift] **1.** (impulso *m* de una) corriente *f*; ⚓ deriva *f*; *fig.* sentido *m*, tendencia *f*; *fig.* giro *m*; *b.s.* (*esp. pol.*) inacción *f*; (*snow etc.*) montón *m*; *geol.* terrenos *m/pl.* de acarreo; ✗ galería *f* horizontal que sigue el filón; **2.** *v/t.* impeler, llevar; amontonar;

v/i. ir a la deriva (*a.* ~ *along*); *fig.* vivir sin rumbo; '~ **ice** hielo *m* a la deriva; '~ **wood** madera *f* de deriva.

drill [dril] **1.** ⊕ taladro *m*; (*pneumatic*) ~ perforadora *f*, martillo *m* picador; ✗ hilera *f*; ✗ (*machine*) sembradora *f*; ✗ instrucción *f*; *fig.* disciplina *f*; *sl.* rutina *f*; **2.** *v/t.* ⊕ taladrar; ✗ sembrar con sembradora; ✗ enseñar instrucción a; *v/i.* perforar (*for oil en* busca de); ✗ hacer instrucción; '**drill·ing** perforación *f for oil etc.*

drink [driŋk] **1.** bebida *f*; beber *m* (en exceso); (*swing*) trinquis *m*, trago *m*; *have a* ~ tomar unas copas, tomar algo; *take a* ~ echar un trago; **2.** beber (*a. fig.*); ~ *to a p.'s health* brindar por alguien.

drink·ing...: '~ **bout** juerga *f* de borrachera; '~ **foun·tain** fuente *f*; '~ **song** canción *f* de taberna; '~ **wa·ter** agua *f* potable.

drip [drip] **1.** goteo *m*; △ alero *m*; *sl.* bobalicón (-a *f*) *m*; tontaina *m/f*; **2.** gotear, caer gota a gota.

drive [draiv] **1.** *mot.* paseo *m* (en coche); calzada *f up to* house; *sport*: golpe *m* fuerte (*tennis*: a ras de la red); *fig.* vigor *m*, energía *f*; campaña *f* vigorosa (*to* para); ⊕ mecanismo *m* de transmisión; ✝ venta *f* de liquidación; *hunt.* ✗ batida *f*; ~ *way* calzada *f*; camino *m* de entrada para coches; **2.** [*irr.*] *v/t.* impeler, empujar; mover, actuar (*a. fig.*); ⊕ impulsar; *mot. etc.* conducir, guiar; *p.* llevar en coche; *fig. p.* forzar (*to* a); *sport*: golpear con gran fuerza; *p. crazy etc.* volver; ~ *away* (*or off*) ahuyentar; ~ *back* obligar a retroceder; ~ *in* (*or home*) hincar, remachar; ~ *a good bargain* hacer un buen trato; *v/i.* conducir; ~ *at th. fig.* insinuar, querer decir; ~ *away* trabajar mucho; *mot.* ~ *on* seguir adelante.

drive-in ['draiv'in] motocine *m*; auto-teatro *m*; *restaurant* restaurante *m* donde los clientes no necesitan dejar sus coches.

driv·el ['drivl] **1.** babear; **2.** música *f* celestial, monserga *f*.

driv·en ['drivn] *p.p. of* drive 2.

driv·er ['draivə] conductor *m*; 🚂 maquinista *m*; ⊕ rueda *f* motriz; persona *f* despótica; '~**'s li·cense** carnet *m* de chófer, permiso *m* de conducir.

driv·ing ['draiviŋ] **1.** conducción *f*; **2.** *adj. freq.* motriz; *rain* torrencial, recio; '~ **school** auto-escuela *f*.

driz·zle ['drɪzl] **1.** llovizna *f*; **2.** lloviznar.

droll [droul] (*adv.* drolly) gracioso, festivo; (*odd*) raro; **'droll·er·y** chuscada *f*.

drone [droun] **1.** *zo.* zángano *m* (*a. fig.*); (*noise*) zumbido *m*; **2.** zumbar; hablar monótonamente.

drool [druːl] **1.** babear; **2.** F bobería *f*.

droop [druːp] *v/t.* inclinar, dejar caer; *v/i.* inclinarse; pender, colgar; *fig.* decaer; *fig.* (*lose heart*) desalentarse; **'droop·ing** □ caído, inclinado, lánguido.

drop [drɔp] **1.** gota *f* (*a.* ⚕); (*fall*) baja *f*, caída *f* repentina; (*slope*) cuesta *f*, declive *m*, pendiente *f*; *mount.* precipicio *m*; lanzamiento *m by parachute*; *thea.* (*a.* ~ curtain) telón *m* de boca; ~ by ~ gota a gota; ~ light lámpara *f* colgante; F get (have) the ~ on coger (llevar) la delantera a; **2.** *v/t.* dejar caer; inclinar; *hunt.* derribar; abandonar; omitir, suprimir; *claim* renunciar a; *consonant* comerse; *curtsy* hacer; *money* perder; *passenger, voice* bajar; ~ that! ¡deja eso!; ~ a hint soltar una indirecta; *v/i.* caer; bajar (*a.* ~ down); (*crouch*) agacharse; *fig.* cesar, terminar; (*drip*) gotear; ~ behind quedarse atrás; ~ dead caer muerto; ~ in (*or* by, over) visitar de paso; ~ off esp. quedarse dormido; ~ out darse de baja, retirarse; ~ out of sight desaparecer; **'drop·let** gotita *f*; **'drop·ping** goteo *m*; ~s *pl.* excremento *m* (de los animales).

dross [drɔs] escoria *f* (*a. fig.*).

drought [draut] sequía *f*; **'drought·y** árido, seco.

drove [drouv] **1.** manada *f*, piara *f*; *fig.* muchedumbre *f*; **2.** *pret.* of drive 2.

drown [draun] *v/t.* anegar (*a. fig.*, en); *sound* apagar; *v/i.* (*or be* ~ed) ahogarse; perecer ahogado, anegarse.

drowse [drauz] adormecer(se); **'drow·sy** □ soñoliento; *be* ~ tener sueño.

drudge [drʌdʒ] **1.** esclavo *m* del trabajo (*or* de la cocina), azacán (-a *f*) *m*; **2.** azacanarse, afanarse; **'drudg·er·y** perrera *f*, trabajo *m* penoso.

drug [drʌg] **1.** droga *f* (*a. b.s.*), medicamento *m*; (*esp. to sleep*) narcótico *m*; ~ store farmacia *f*, droguería *f*; **2.** administrar narcóticos a, narcotizar;

aletargar; **drug·gist** ['drʌgɪst] farmacéutico *m*.

dru·id ['druːɪd] druida *m*.

drum [drʌm] **1.** tambor *m* (*a.* ⊕); (*big*) timbal *m*; (*ear-*) tímpano *m*; (*oil- etc.*) bidón *m*; **2.** *v/i.* ♪ tocar el tambor; tamborilear *with fingers*; *v/t.* ~ into s.o. meterle a uno en la cabeza; ⚔ ~ out expulsar; **'~head** piel *f* (*or* parche *m*) de tambor; **'drum·mer** tambor *m*; **'drum·stick** palillo *m*, maza *f*.

drunk [drʌŋk] **1.** *p.p.* of drink 2; **2.** borracho (*a. fig.*); *get* ~ emborracharse; **drunk·ard** ['~əd] borracho (a *f*) *m*; **'drunk·en** borracho, dado a la bebida; **'drunk·en·ness** embriaguez *f*.

dry [draɪ] **1.** □ seco; *climate etc.* árido; *fig.* aburrido, sin interés; F ~ goods *pl.* lencería *f*; **2.** secar(se) (*a.* ~ up); *sl.* ~ up callarse, dejar de hablar.

dry-clean ['draɪ'kliːn] limpiar en seco; **'dry-'clean·ing** limpieza *f* en seco.

dry·ness ['draɪnɪs] sequedad *f*; (*climate*) aridez *f*.

du·al ['djuːəl] *gr.* dual; doble; ~ control doble mando *m*.

dub [dʌb] *film* doblar; *knight* armar caballero; apodar *with name*; **'dub·bing** *film:* doblaje *m*.

du·bi·ous ['djuːbiəs] □ dudoso; *be* ~ dudar, tener dudas (*of, about, over* sobre, de).

duch·ess ['dʌtʃɪs] duquesa *f*.

duck[1] [dʌk] *orn.* pato *m*; ánade *m*; F ~! ¡querida!

duck[2] [~] **1.** zambullida *f in water*; agacharse *f to escape*; **2.** chapuzar(se) *in water*; agachar(se) *to escape*; F ~ out esfumarse.

duck[3] [~] (*cloth*) dril *m*, brin *m*; ~s *pl.* pantalón *m* de dril.

duck·ling ['dʌklɪŋ] patito *m*, anadón *m*.

duck·y ['dʌki] F **1.** ¡querida!; **2.** mono, majo.

duct [dʌkt] conducto *m* (*a.* ⚕).

dud [dʌd] **1.** ⚔ granada *f etc.* fallida; *fig.* fallo *m*; (*fake*) filfa *f*; **2.** fallido, huero; falso.

dude [djuːd] petimetre *m*, cursi *m*; ~ ranch rancho *m* para turistas.

due [djuː] **1.** *adj.* debido; † pagadero, conveniente, oportuno; ⚓ *etc.* (*que*) debe llegar; ~ to por causa de; debido a; (*time*) estar para *inf.*; *fall* ~ vencer; **2.** *adv.* ♣ derecho, en derechura;

precisamente; **3.** su. (*right*) derecho *m*; (*desert*) merecimiento *m*; (*debt*) deuda *f*; ~s *pl.* ✝ derechos *m/pl.*

du·el ['dju:əl] **1.** duelo *m*; **2.** batirse en duelo.

duff·el ['dʌfl] paño *m* de lana basta.

duff·er ['dʌfə] tonto *m*, zoquete *m*.

dug [dʌg] *pret. a. p.p.* of dig.

duke [dju:k] duque *m*.

dull [dʌl] **1.** (*adv.* dully) lerdo, estúpido; insensible; (*tedious etc.*) insulso, aburrido; *color* apagado; *day* gris; *edge* embotado; *pain, sound* sordo; *surface* deslustrado, mate; ✝ inactivo, flojo; **2.** embotar (*a. fig.*); deslustrar; *enthusiasm* enfriar; *p.* entorpecer.

du·ly ['dju:li] *v.* due; debidamente; a su (debido) tiempo.

dumb [dʌm] □ mudo; F estúpido, lerdo; *deaf and* ~ sordomudo; *v. show; strike* ~ dejar sin habla, pasmar; '~·**bell** pesa *f*; *sl.* estúpido *m*; ~'**found** dejar sin habla, pasmar; '**dumb·ness** mudez *f*; F estupidez *f*; '**dumb·wait·er** estante *m* giratorio; montaplatos *m*.

dum·my ['dʌmi] **1.** (*tailor's*) maniquí *m*; ✝ envase *m* vacío; (*baby's*) chupete *m*; *bridge*: (be hacer de) muerto *m*; ✝ (*p.*) testaferro *m*; **2.** falso, postizo.

dump [dʌmp] **1.** descargar de golpe; (*rid*) deshacerse de; *rubbish* vaciar; ✝ *goods* inundar el mercado con; F ~ *down meter*; **2.** basurero *m*, escorial *m*; ✗ depósito *m*; *sl. contp.* pueblucho *m*, poblachón *m*; F (be [down] in the tener) ~s *pl.* murria *f*; '**dump·ing** ✝ dumping *m*; '**dump·ing-ground** basurero *m*.

dun[1] [dʌn] pardo, castaño oscuro.

dun[2] [~] **1.** acreedor *m* importuno; **2.** molestar, dar la lata a.

dunce [dʌns] zopenco (a *f*) *m*; '~·**cap** capirote *m* que se le pone al alumno torpe.

dune [dju:n] duna *f*.

dung [dʌŋ] **1.** estiércol *m*; **2.** estercolar.

dun·geon ['dʌndʒən] mazmorra *f*, calabozo *m*.

dung·hill ['dʌŋhil] estercolero *m*.

duo ['dju:ou] dúo *m*.

dupe [dju:p] **1.** primo *m*, inocentón *m*; **2.** embaucar; (*swindle*) timar.

du·plex ['dju:pleks] dúplice, doble; ~ *house* casa *f* para dos familias.

du·pli·cate **1.** ['dju:plikit] a) (*in* por)

duplicado; b) duplicado *m*; **2.** ['~keit] duplicar; **du·pli·ca·tion** [~'keiʃn] duplicación *f*; '**du·pli·ca·tor** duplicador *m*, multicopista *m*.

du·ra·ble ['djuərəbl] □ durable, duradero; ~ *goods pl.* artículos *m/pl.* duraderos; **du·ra·tion** [~'reiʃn] duración *f*.

du·ress [djuə'res] (*under* por) coacción *f*.

du·ring ['djuəriŋ] durante.

dusk [dʌsk] crepúsculo *m*, anochecer *m*; *poet.* oscuridad *f*; '**dusk·y** □ oscuro, sombrío; *complexion* moreno.

dust [dʌst] **1.** polvo *m*; (*refuse*) basura *f*; *fig.* cenizas *f/pl.*; *sl.* pasta *f*; **2.** quitar el polvo, despolvorear; *cooking*: espolvorear; '~ **bowl** estepa *f*, terreno *m* estéril a causa de la erosión; '~ **cov·er** guardapolvo *m*; sobrecubierta *f* of *book*; '**dust·er** plumero *m*; (*rag*) gamuza *f*, trapo *m*; guardapolvo *m*; '**dust jack·et** sobrecubierta *f* of *book*; '**dust·pan** cogedor *m*; '**dust·y** polvoriento, empolvado.

Dutch [dʌtʃ] holandés *m*; *in* ~ en desgracia; '~ **treat** F convite *m* a escote.

du·ti·ful ['dju:tiful] □ obediente, respetuoso; (*obliging*) servicial.

du·ty ['dju:ti] deber *m*, obligación *f* (*to* a, para con); (*esp.* duties *pl.*) tarea *f*, faena *f*; ✝ derechos *m/pl.* de aduana; *off* ~ libre; ✗ franco de servicio; *on* ~ de servicio; de guardia; *in* ~ *bound* obligado (*to* a); *do* ~ *for* servir en lugar de; '~·**free** ✝ libre de derechos de aduana.

dwarf [dwɔ:f] **1.** enano *m*; **2.** enano; diminuto; **3.** achicar; *fig.* empequeñecer.

dwell [dwel] [*irr.*] morar, habitar; ~ (*up*)*on* explayarse en; hacer hincapié en; '**dwell·ing** morada *f*, vivienda *f*; **dwelt** [dwelt] *pret. a. p.p.* of dwell.

dwin·dle ['dwindl] disminuirse, menguar (*a.* ~ *away*); quedar reducido (*into* a).

dye [dai] **1.** tinte *m*; matiz *m*, color *m*; *fig.* of *deepest* ~ de lo más vil; **2.** teñir (*s.t. black* de negro); *v. wool*; '**dy·er** tintorero *m*.

dy·ing ['daiiŋ] **1.** moribundo; agonizante; *moments* final; **2.** *ger.* of die[1].

dy·nam·ic [dai'næmik] **1.** □ dinámico (*a. fig.*); **2.** *fig.* dinámica *f*; **dy'nam·ics** *sg.* dinámica *f*; **dy·na-**

mite ['dainəmait] 1. dinamita f; 2. volar con dinamita; **dy·na·mo** ['dainəmou] dínamo f.

dy·nas·ty ['dinəsti] dinastía f.

dys·en·ter·y ['disntri] disentería f.

dys·pep·sia [dis'pepsiə] dispepsia f.

E

each [i:tʃ] 1. adj. cada; todo; 2. pron. cada uno; ~ other uno(s) a otro(s), el uno al otro; mutuamente; 3. adv. por persona.

ea·ger ['i:gə] □ ansioso; anhelante; impaciente; vehemente; be ~ for anhelar; be ~ to tener vivo deseo de; **'ea·ger·ness** ansia f; anhelo m etc.

ea·gle ['i:gl] águila f; eye (de) lince.

ear[1] [iə] ♥ espiga f.

ear[2] [~] oreja f; (sense) oído m; ♪ by ~ de oído; be all ~s ser todo oídos; **~ache** ['iəreik] dolor m de oídos; **'~drum** tímpano m.

ear·ly ['ə:li] 1. adj. temprano (a. ♥); primero, primitivo; precoz; reply pronto; at an ~ date en fecha próxima; ~ bird madrugador (-a f) m; ~ life juventud f; 2. adv. temprano; con tiempo; arrive 5 minutes ~ llegar con 5 minutos de anticipación; ~ last century a principios del siglo pasado; ~ in the morning muy de mañana.

ear·mark ['iəmɑːk] fig. reservar, poner aparte (for para); destinar (for a).

earn [ə:n] ganar(se); adquirir, obtener; praise etc. merecer(se), granjearse; † (bonds) interest devengar.

ear·nest[1] ['ə:nist] prenda f, señal f; (a. '~ mon·ey) arras f/pl.

ear·nest[2] [~] □ serio; formal; desire ardiente; in (good) ~ (muy) de veras, en serio; **'ear·nest·ness** seriedad f; formalidad f.

earn·ings ['ə:niŋz] pl. sueldo m; ingresos m/pl.; ganancias f/pl.

ear·...'~·phones pl. auriculares m/pl.; **'~·ring** (long) pendiente m; (round) arete m; **'~·shot**: within ~ al alcance del oído; **'~·split·ting** shout desaforado; noise que rompe el tímpano.

earth [ə:θ] 1. tierra f (a. ♀); zo. madriguera f; down-to-~ práctico; ♪ conectar a tierra; ♪ ~ up acollar; **'earth·en** de tierra; pot de barro; **'earth·en·ware** loza f de barro; cacharros m/pl.; **'earth·ly** terrenal, mundano; be of no ~ use no servir para nada en absoluto; **'earth-**

quake terremoto m; **'earth·worm** lombriz f.

ease [i:z] 1. facilidad f; soltura f; comodidad f of living etc.; alivio m from pain; naturalidad f of manner; at ~ cómodo; a sus anchas; ill at ~ incómodo; ✕ at ~! en su lugar ¡descanso!; life of ~ vida f desahogada; take one's ~ descansar; with ~ fácilmente, con facilidad; 2. v/t. aliviar, mitigar; (soften) suavizar; weight aligerar; pressure aflojar; mind tranquilizar; v/i. (wind) amainar; (rain) moderarse; ~ up suavizarse, aligerarse.

ea·sel ['i:zl] caballete m.

ease·ment ['i:zmənt] ⚖ servidumbre f.

eas·i·ness ['i:zinis] facilidad f; soltura f.

east [i:st] 1. este m, oriente m; 2. adj. del este, oriental; 3. adv. al este, hacia el este.

East·er ['i:stə] pascua f florida (or de Resurrección); (period) semana f santa; attr. ... de pascua; ~ Day, ~ Sunday Domingo m de Resurrección.

east·er·ly ['i:stəli] direction hacia el este; wind del este; **east·ern** ['~tən] oriental; **'east·ern·er** habitante m/f del este; **east·ward(s)** ['i:stwəd(z)] hacia el este.

eas·y ['i:zi] 1. □ fácil; conditions cómodo, holgado; manner natural, afable; pace lento, pausado; virtue laxo; p. de moralidad laxa; † money abundante; F p. fácil de engañar; ~ to get on with muy afable; ~ to run de fácil manejo; 2. adv. F fácilmente; take it ~ descansar; b.s. haraganear; i.e. despacio; take it ~! ¡cálmese! ¡'~·chair butaca f, sillón m.

eat [i:t] [irr.] comer; meal tomar; consumir with envy etc.; sl. what's ~ing you? ¿qué mosca te ha picado?; ~ away, ~ into corroer; fig. carcomer; fig. mermar; ~ up comerse; devorar; **'eat·a·ble** comestible; **'eat·en** p.p. of eat; **'eat·er**: be a big ~ tener siempre buen apetito; ser comilón.

eaves [i:vz] *pl.* alero *m*; **'eaves·drop** escuchar a las puertas; fisgonear.

ebb [eb] **1.** menguante *m*, reflujo *m*; ~ *tide* marea *f* menguante; *at a low* ~ decaído; **2.** bajar; *fig.* decaer, disminuir.

e·bul·li·ent [i'bʌljənt] *fig.* exaltado, entusiasta.

ec·cen·tric [ik'sentrik] **1.** □ excéntrico; **2.** ⊕ excéntrica *f* (*a. fig.*); **(p.)** excéntrico *m*.

ec·cle·si·as·tic [ikli:zi'æstik], *adj.* mst **ec·cle·si·as·ti·cal** □ eclesiástico *adj. a. su. m.*

ech·e·lon ['eʃəlɔn] **1.** escalón *m*; **2.** escalonar.

ech·o ['ekou] **1.** eco *m*; **2.** *v/t.* repetir; *opinion* hacerse eco de; *v/i.* resonar.

ec·lec·tic [ek'lektik] □ ecléctico *adj. a. su. m.*

e·clipse [i'klips] **1.** eclipse *m* (*a. fig.*); **2.** eclipsar (*a. fig.*).

e·co·nom·ic [i:kə'nɔmik], **e·co'nom·i·cal** □ económico; frugal; *rent* justo; **e·co'nom·ics** *pl.* economía *f* política; **e·con·o·mist** [i'kɔnəmist] economista *m/f*; **e'con·o·mize** [~maiz] economizar (*on* en); **e'con·o·my** economía *f*, frugalidad *f*.

ec·sta·sy ['ekstəsi] éxtasis *m*; *go into ecstasies* extasiarse (*over* ante); **ec·stat·ic** [eks'tætik] □ extático.

ec·ze·ma ['eksimə] eczema *m*.

ed·dy ['edi] **1.** remolino *m*; **2.** arremolinarse.

edge [edʒ] **1.** *(cutting)* filo *m*, corte *m*; *(border)* margen *m*, borde *m*, orilla *f*; canto *m* of table etc.; *(end)* extremidad *f*; *on* ~ de canto; *fig.* nervioso; *put an* ~ *on* afilar; **2.** *v/t.* afilar; orlar; *sew.* ribetear; *v/i.* ~ *along* avanzar de lado.

edg·ing ['edʒiŋ] orla *f*, ribete *m*.

edg·y ['edʒi] F nervioso.

ed·i·ble ['edibl] comestible.

e·dict ['i:dikt] edicto *m*.

ed·i·fi·ca·tion [edifi'keiʃn] edificación *f*; **ed·i·fice** ['~fis] edificio *m* (imponente).

ed·it ['edit] *script* preparar (*or* corregir) para la imprenta; *paper* dirigir, redactar; *book* editar; ~*ed by* (en) edición de; **e·di·tion** [i'diʃn] edición *f*; *typ.* tirada *f*; **ed·i·tor** ['editə] director *m*, redactor *m* of paper; editor *m* of book; **ed·i·to·ri·al** [~'tɔ:riəl] artículo *m* de fondo; ~ *staff* redacción *f*; **ed·i·tor·ship** ['~təʃip] dirección *f*.

ed·u·cate ['edjukeit] educar; instruir; ~*d* culto; **ed·u·ca·tion** [~'keiʃn] educación *f*; instrucción *f*; cultura *f*; *elementary* ~ primera enseñanza *f*; *secondary* ~ segunda enseñanza *f*; **ed·u'ca·tion·al** □ educacional; docente; *film etc.* instructivo; **'ed·u·ca·tor** educador (-a *f*) *m*.

eel [i:l] anguila *f*.

e'en [i:n] = *even*.

e'er [ɛə] = *ever*.

ee·rie, ee·ry ['iəri] □ misterioso; horripilante; inquietante.

ef·face [i'feis] borrar.

ef·fect [i'fekt] **1.** efecto *m*; resultado *m*; impresión *f*; fuerza *f*; ~*s pl.* efectos *m/pl.*; *in* ~ en efecto, en realidad; *law* vigente; *of no* ~ inútil; *to this* ~ con este propósito; *carry into* ~ poner en ejecución; *feel the* ~ *of* estar resentido de; *put into* ~ poner en vigor; *take* ~ *(law)* ponerse en vigor; *(remedy)* surtir efecto; **2.** efectuar, llevar a cabo; **ef'fec·tive 1.** □ eficaz; potente, impresionante; efectivo; ✗, ⚓ útil para todos servicios; ⚖ *become* ~ entrar en vigor; **2.** ✗ ~*s pl.* efectivos *m/pl.*

ef·fem·i·nate [i'feminit] □ afeminado.

ef·fete [e'fi:t] gastado; decadente.

ef·fi·ca·cious [efi'keiʃəs] □ eficaz.

ef·fi·cien·cy [i'fiʃnsi] eficiencia *f*; eficacia *f*; capacidad *f*; ⊕ rendimiento *m*; **ef'fi·cient** [~ʃnt] □ eficiente; eficaz; capaz; ⊕ de buen rendimiento.

ef·fi·gy ['efidʒi] efigie *f*.

ef·fort ['efət] esfuerzo *m* (*to* por); F tentativa *f*; resultado *m*; *spare no* ~ to no regatear medio para; **'ef·fort·less** □ fácil, nada penoso.

ef·fron·ter·y [e'frʌntəri] descaro *m*, impudencia *f*.

ef·fu·sion [i'fju:ʒn] efusión *f*; **ef·fu·sive** [~siv] □ efusivo.

egg¹ [eg]: ~ *on* incitar (*to* a), impulsar (*to* a).

egg² [~] huevo *m*; *sl.* tío *m*; *sl. bad* ~ calavera *f*, sinvergüenza *m*; *as sure as* ~*s* sin duda alguna; '~ **beat·er** batidor *m* de huevos; '~**cup** huevera *f*; '~**head** intelectual *m* erudito; '~**nog** caldo *m* de la reina; yema *f* mejida; '~**plant** berenjena *f*; '~**shell** cáscara *f* de huevo.

e·go ['egou] (el) yo; **'e·go·ism** egoísmo *m*; **'e·go·ist** egoísta *m/f*; **e·go·is·tic, e·go·is·ti·cal** □ egoísta; **e·go·tism** ['egoutizm] egoísmo *m*; **'e·go·tist** egotista *m/f*; **e·go·tis·tic, e·go·tis·ti·cal** □ egotista.

E

e·gre·gious [i'gri:dʒes] □ enorme, chocante.

eh [ei] ¿cómo?; ¿qué?; ¿no?

eight [eit] ocho (a. su. m); **eight·een** ['ei'ti:n] dieciocho; **'eight·eenth** [~θ] decimoctavo; **eighth** [~θ] octavo (a. su. m); **eight·i·eth** ['~iiθ] octogésimo; **'eight·y** ochenta.

either ['aiðə, 'i:ðə] 1. adj. cualquier ... de los dos; 2. pron. uno u otro, cualquiera de los dos; 3. cj. ~ ... or o ... o; 4. adv. tampoco.

e·jac·u·late [i'dʒækjuleit] exclamar, proferir (de repente).

e·ject [i'dʒekt] expulsar, echar, arrojar; tenant desahuciar; **e·jec·tion** expulsión f; desahucio m from house.

eke [i:k]: ~ out hacer llegar; suplir las deficiencias de (with con); livelihood ganar a duras penas.

e·lab·o·rate 1. [i'læbərit] □ complicado; primoroso; detallado; rebuscado; 2. [~reit] v/t. elaborar; v/i. explicarse (~ on explicar) con muchos detalles; ~ on ampliar; **e·lab·o·ra·tion** [~'reiʃn] elaboración f; complicación f etc.

e·lapse [i'læps] pasar, transcurrir.

e·las·tic [i'læstik] □ elástico (a. su. m; ~ band gomita f); **e·las·tic·i·ty** [~'tisiti] elasticidad f.

e·late [i'leit] regocijar, exaltar; be ~d alegrarse (at, with de); **e'la·tion** regocijo m, viva alegría f, júbilo m.

el·bow ['elbou] 1. codo m (a. ⊕); (bend) recodo m; at one's ~ a la mano, muy cerca; 2. empujar con el codo; ~ one's way (through) abrirse paso codeando; **'~ grease** F codo m; esfuerzo m, aplicación f; **'~·room** espacio m suficiente; libertad f de acción.

eld·er¹ ['eldə] 1. mayor; 2. mayor m/f; eccl. anciano m; ~s pl. jefes m/pl. (de tribu); my ~s pl. mis mayores.

eld·er² [~] ♀ saúco m.

eld·er·ly ['eldəli] mayor, de edad.

eld·est ['eldist] (el) mayor.

e·lect [i'lekt] 1. elegir, escoger; ~ to optar por inf.; decidir inf.; 2. elegido; eccl. electo; the ~ los elegidos; president ~ presidente m electo; **e'lec·tion** elección f; **e'lec·tive** 1. □ electivo; 2. asignatura f electiva.

e·lec·tric [i'lektrik] □ eléctrico; fig. cargado de emoción; muy tenso, candente; ~ blanket caliente-camas m; ~ chair silla f eléctrica; ~ fan ventilador m eléctrico; ~ percolator cafetera f eléctrica; ~ shaver eléctro-afeitadora f; ~ tape cinta f aislante; **e'lec·tri·cal** □ eléctrico; ~ engineer ingeniero m electricista; ~ engineering electrotecnia f; **e·lec·tri·cian** [~'triʃn] electricista m; **e·lec·tric·i·ty** [~siti] electricidad f; **e·lec·tri·fy** [~fai] electrificar; electrizar (a. fig.).

e·lec·tro [i'lektrou] electro...; **e'lec·tro·cute** [~trəkjut] electrocutar; **e·lec·tro'cu·tion** electrocución f; **e'lec·trode** [~troud] electrodo m.

e·lec·tron [i'lektron] electrón m; attr. = **e·lec'tron·ic** □ electrónico; ~ brain cerebro m electrónico; **e·lec·'tron·ics** sg. electrónica f.

el·e·gance ['eligəns] elegancia f; **'el·e·gant** □ elegante.

el·e·gi·ac [eli'dʒaiæk] elegíaco.

el·e·gy ['elidʒi] elegía f.

el·e·ment ['elimənt] all senses: elemento m; ~s pl. elementos m/pl., nociones f/pl.; **el·e'men·tal** □ elemental; **el·e'men·ta·ry** □ elemental; ~ school escuela f primaria.

el·e·phant ['elifənt] elefante m; white ~ maula f.

el·e·vate ['eliveit] elevar; p. exaltar; ascender in rank; **'el·e·vat·ed** elevado (a. fig.); F (a. ~ railroad) ferrocarril m elevado; **el·e'va·tion** all senses: elevación f; **'el·e·va·tor** ascensor m; (goods) montacargas m; ♪ elevador m de granos; ✈ timón m de profundidad.

e·lev·en [i'levn] once (a. su. m); **e'lev·enth** [~θ] undécimo, onceno.

elf [elf] duende m; (dwarf) enano m.

e·lic·it [i'lisit] (son)sacar, lograr obtener.

e·lide [i'laid] elidir.

el·i·gi·bil·i·ty [elidʒə'biliti] elegibilidad f; **'el·i·gi·ble** □ elegible; aceptable, adecuado.

e·lim·i·nate [i'limineit] eliminar; solution etc. descartar; suprimir; **e·lim·i'na·tion** eliminación f etc.

e·li·sion [i'liʒn] elisión f.

e·lite [ei'li:t] élite f; lo selecto, flor f y nata.

e·lix·ir [i'liksə] elixir m.

elk [elk] alce m.

el'lip·tic, el'lip·ti·cal [i'liptik(l)] □ elíptico.

elm [elm] olmo m.

e·lon·gate ['i:lɔŋgeit] alargar, extender.

e·lope [i'loup] fugarse (con un amante); **e'lope·ment** fuga f.

el·o·quence ['eləkwəns] elocuencia f; **'el·o·quent** □ elocuente.

else [els] **1.** adj. otro; all ~ todo lo demás; anyone ~ (cualquier) otro; nobody ~ ningún otro; nothing ~ nada más; how ~? ¿de qué otra manera?; what ~? ¿qué más?; **2.** adv. (ade)más; F de otro modo; or ~ o bien, si no; **'else'where** en (or a) otra parte.

e·lu·ci·date [i'lu:sideit] aclarar, dilucidar, elucidar.

e·lude [i'lu:d] blow etc. eludir, esquivar, evitar; grasp escapar de; **e·lu·sive** [i'lu:siv] □ fugaz; evasivo; p. difícil de encontrar.

elves [elvz] pl. of elf.

e·ma·ci·at·ed [i'meiʃieitid] demacrado, extenuado.

em·a·nate ['eməneit] emanar.

e·man·ci·pate [i'mænsipeit] emancipar; **e·man·ci·pa·tion** emancipación f.

em·balm [im'ba:m] embalsamar.

em·bank·ment [im'bæŋkmənt] terraplén m; dique m.

em·bar·go [em'ba:gou] **1.** embargo m; prohibición f (on de), suspensión f; **2.** embargar.

em·bark [im'ba:k] v/t. embarcar; v/i. embarcarse (for con rumbo a); ~ (up)on emprender.

em·bar·rass [im'bærəs] desconcertar, turbar, azorar; molestar; poner en un aprieto; **em·bar·rass·ing** □ embarazoso, desconcertador; vergonzoso; molesto; moment, situation violento; **em·bar·rass·ment** desconcierto m, (per)turbación f, azoramiento m; apuro m; estorbo m.

em·bas·sy ['embəsi] embajada f.

em·bat·tled [im'bætld] en orden de batalla; city sitiado; △ almenado.

em·bel·lish [im'beliʃ] embellecer; adornar, guarnecer.

em·bez·zle [im'bezl] malversar, defalcar.

em·bit·ter [im'bitə] amargar; relations envenenar.

em·blem ['embləm] emblema m.

em·bod·i·ment [im'bɔdimənt] encarnación f, personificación f; **em·'bod·y** encarnar, personificar; (include) incorporar.

em·bo·lism ['embəlizm] embolia f.

em·brace [im'breis] **1.** abrazar(se); (include) abarcar; offer aceptar; **2.** abrazo m.

em·broi·der [im'brɔidə] bordar, recamar; fig. adornar con detalles ficticios; **em'broi·der·y** bordado m.

em·broil [im'brɔil] embrollar, enredar; ~ with indisponer con.

em·bry·o [i'embriou] **1.** embrión m; in ~ en embrión; **2.** = **em·bry·on·ic** [~'ɔnik] □ embrionario.

e·mend [i'mend] enmendar; **e·men'da·tion** enmienda f.

em·er·ald ['emərəld] **1.** esmeralda f; **2.** esmeraldino.

e·merge [i'mə:dʒ] salir, surgir, emerger; aparecer; **e·mer·gen·cy** necesidad f urgente, aprieto m, situación f imprevista; ~ brake freno m de auxilio; ~ exit salida f de urgencia; ~ landing aterrizaje m forzoso.

em·er·y ['eməri] esmeril m; **'~ cloth** tela f de esmeril; **'~ wheel** esmeriladora f, rueda f de esmeril, muela f de esmeril.

e·met·ic [i'metik] emético adj. a. su. m.

em·i·grant ['emigrənt] emigrante adj. a. su. m/f; **em·i·grate** ['~greit] emigrar; **em·i'gra·tion** emigración f.

em·i·nence ['eminəns] eminencia f (a. little); **'em·i·nent** □ eminente.

em·is·sar·y ['emisəri] emisario m; **e·mis·sion** [i'miʃn] emisión f.

e·mit [i'mit] emitir; smoke etc. arrojar, despedir; cry dar; sound producir.

e·mo·tion [i'mouʃn] emoción f; **e·'mo·tion·al** □ emocional; moment de mucha emoción; p. exaltado; demasiado sensible.

em·per·or ['empərə] emperador m.

em·pha·sis ['emfəsis] pl. **em·pha·ses** ['~si:z] énfasis m; **em·pha·size** ['~saiz] acentuar (a. fig.); fig. subrayar, recalcar; **em·phat·ic** [im'fætik] □ enfático; enérgico; be ~ that insistir en que.

em·pire ['empaiə] imperio m.

em·ploy [im'plɔi] **1.** emplear; servirse de; **2.** empleo m; servicio m; ocupación f; **em·ploy·ee** [emplɔi'i:] empleado (a f) m, dependiente (a f) m; **em·ploy·er** [im'plɔiə] patrón m; **em'ploy·ment** empleo m; ocupación f; servicio m; full~ pleno empleo m; ~ agency agencia f de colocaciones.

em·pow·er [im'pauə] autorizar (to a); habilitar (to para que).

em·press ['empris] emperatriz f.

emp·ti·ness ['emptinis] vacío m; vaciedad f, vacuidad f; **emp·ty** ['empti] **1.** vacío; (fruitless) vano, inútil;

house, place desocupado; post vacante; vehicle sin carga; F hambriento; 2. v/t. vaciar; contents descargar, verter; place desocupar, dejar vacío; v/i. vaciar; (drain away) desaguar; (place) ir quedando vacío (or desocupado); ~ into (river) desembocar en; 3. botella f etc. vacía; empties pl. envases m/pl.; **'emp·ty-han·ded** con las manos vacías, manivacío.

em·u·late ['emjuleit] emular.

en·a·ble [i'neibl] permitir (to inf.); habilitar (to para que); poner en condiciones (to para).

en·act [i'nækt] decretar; law promulgar; thea. representar, realizar; **en'act·ment** ley f, estatuto m; promulgación f of law.

en·am·el [i'næml] 1. esmalte m; 2. esmaltar, pintar al esmalte.

en·am·or [i'næmə] enamorar.

en·chant [in't ʃ ɑːnt] encantar (a. fig.); **en'chant·er** hechicero m; **en'chant·ing** □ encantador.

en·cir·cle [in'səːkl] cercar; rodear; circunvalar; waist ceñir; ✕, pol. envolver; **en'cir·cle·ment** ✕, pol. envolvimiento m.

en·close [in'klouz] cercar, encerrar; (include) incluir; remitir adjunto, adjuntar with letter; **en'clo·sure** [~ʒə] (place) cercado m, recinto m; (act) encerramiento m; cosa f etc. inclusa in letter.

en·com·pass [in'kʌmpəs] abarcar; (surround) rodear; (bring about) lograr.

en·core [ɔŋ'kɔː] 1. ¡bis!; 2. pedir la repetición de a th., a a p.; 3. repetición f, bis m.

en·coun·ter [in'kauntə] 1. all senses: encuentro m; 2. encontrar(se con), tropezar con.

en·cour·age [in'kʌridʒ] animar, alentar (to a); industry fomentar, reforzar; growth estimular; fortalecer in a belief; **en'cour·age·ment** estímulo m, incentivo m; aliento m; fomento m; **en'cour·ag·ing** □ alentador, esperanzador; favorable.

en·croach [in'krout ʃ] pasar los límites (on de); invadir (on acc.); fig. usurpar (on acc.).

en·crust [in'krʌst] incrustar(se).

en·cum·ber [in'kʌmbə] estorbar; gravar, cargar with debts etc.; place llenar.

en·cy·clo·pe·di·a [ensaiklou'piːdiə] enciclopedia f; **en·cy·clo·pe·dic** enciclopédico.

end [end] 1. fin m, final m; extremo m, cabo m; remate m; límite m; sport: lado m; desenlace m of play; (object) fin m, objeto m; at the ~ al cabo de; century etc. a fines de; in the ~ al fin y al cabo; on ~ de punta, de canto; 3 days on ~ 3 días seguidos; for days on ~ durante una infinidad de días; no ~ of un sinfín de, la mar de; to the ~ that a fin de que; to this ~ con este propósito; be at an ~ estar terminado; come to an ~ terminarse; make an ~ of acabar con; make both ~s meet hacer llegar el dinero; put an ~ to poner fin a; stand on ~ poner(se) de punta; 2. final; 3. v/t. acabar, terminar; v/i. terminar (in en; with con; by present participle); acabar; (route) morir; ~ up acabar; ir a parar (at en).

en·dan·ger [in'deindʒə] poner en peligro, comprometer.

en·dear [in'diə] hacer querer; ~ o.s. to hacerse querer de; **en'dear·ing** □ atractivo, simpaticonísima.

en·deav·or [in'devə] 1. esfuerzo m, empeño m; tentativa f; 2. esforzarse (to por), procurar (to inf.).

end·ing ['endiŋ] fin m, conclusión f; desenlace m of book etc.; gr. desinencia f.

en·dive ['endiv] escarola f, endibia f.

end·less ['endlis] □ inacabable, interminable; ⊕ sin fin.

en·dorse [in'dɔːs] endosar; fig. aprobar, confirmar; licence poner nota de inhabilitación en; **en·dorse·ment** [in'dɔːsmənt] endoso m; fig. aprobación f, confirmación f.

en·dow [in'dau] dotar (a. fig.) (with con, fig. de); fundar; **en'dow·ment** dotación f; fundación f; fig. dote f, prenda f.

en·dur·ance [in'djuərəns] resistencia f, paciencia f; aguante m; past ~ inaguantable; **en·dure** [in'djuə] v/t. aguantar, soportar, tolerar; resistir; v/i. (per)durar; sufrir sin rendirse.

en·e·ma ['enimə] enema f.

en·e·my ['enimi] enemigo adj. a. su. m (a f) (of de).

en·er·get·ic [enə'dʒetik] □ enérgico; **'en·er·gize** activar; excitar (a. ⚡); **'en·er·gy** energía f.

en·er·vate ['enəːveit] enervar.

en·fold [in'fould] envolver, abrazar; estrechar (entre los brazos).

en·force [in'fɔːs] law hacer cumplir, poner en vigor; demand insistir en; imponer (upon a); **en'force·ment**

ejecución *f of law*; imposición *f*.

en·fran·chise in'fræntʃaiz] conceder el derecho de votar a; (*free*) emancipar.

en·gage [in'geidʒ] *v/t.* (*contract*) apalabrar; *taxi etc.* alquilar; *servant* ajustar, tomar a su servicio; *attention* atraer, ocupar; *p.* entretener in *conversation*; ⊕ (*a. ~ with*) engranar con; ⊕ *coupling* acoplar; ⚔ *enemy* trabar batalla con; *be ~d* estar prometido (*to* para casarse con); *teleph.* estar comunicando; *be ~d in* estar ocupado en, dedicarse a; *get ~d* prometerse; *v/i.* (*promise*) comprometerse (*to* a); ⊕ engranar (*in, with* con); *~ in* ocuparse en, dedicarse a; **en'gage·ment** (*contract*) contrato *m*, ajuste *m*; (*appointment*) compromiso *m*, cita *f*; (*to marry*) palabra *f* de casamiento; (*period of ~*) noviazgo *m*; ⚔ combate *m*, acción *f*.

en·gag·ing [in'geidʒiŋ] □ simpático, atractivo, agraciado.

en·gine [in'dʒin] motor *m*; 🚂 máquina *f*, locomotora *f*.

en·gi·neer [endʒi'niə] **1.** ingeniero *m* (*a.* ⚔, ⚓); mecánico *m*; 🚂 maquinista *m*; **2.** F lograr, agenciar, gestionar; **en·gi'neer·ing** ingeniería *f*.

Eng·lish ['iŋgliʃ] inglés *adj. a. su. m*; *the ~* los ingleses; '~ **Chan·nel** Canal *m* de la Mancha; '~**Eng·lish·man** inglés *m*; '~ **speak·ing** de habla inglesa; '**Eng·lish·wom·an** inglesa *f*.

en·grave [in'greiv] grabar (*a. fig.*); burilar; **en'grav·ing** grabado *m*.

en·gross [in'grous] absorber; ♰♱ redactar en forma legal; poner en limpio.

en·gulf [in'gʌlf] sumergir, hundir, tragar(se).

en·hance [in'hæns] realzar; *price* aumentar.

e·nig·ma [i'nigmə] enigma *m*; **e·nig·mat·ic**, **e·nig·mat·i·cal** [enig'mætik(l)] □ enigmático.

en·join [in'dʒɔin] mandar, ordenar (*to inf.*); imponer (*on* a); ♰♱ prohibir (*from inf.*).

en·joy [in'dʒɔi] *health, possessions* gozar de, disfrutar de; *advantages* poseer; *meal* comer con gusto; *I ~ swimming* me gusta nadar; *b.s. ~ ger.* gozarse in *inf.*; *~ o.s.* divertirse mucho, pasarlo bien; *did you ~ the play?* ¿le gustó la comedia?; **en'joy·a·ble** □ deleitable, agradable; divertido; **en'joy·ment** placer *m*; goce *m*; gusto *m*; disfrute *m of inheritance etc.*

en·lace [in'leis] en(tre)lazar; ceñir.

en·large [in'lɑːdʒ] *v/t.* agrandar, ensanchar; aumentar; ampliar (*a. phot.*); *v/i.: ~ upon* tratar con más extensión; exagerar; **en'large·ment** ensanche *m*; extensión *f*; aumento *m*; ampliación *f* (*a. phot.*).

en·light·en [in'laitn] ilustrar, iluminar; instruir (*in* en); *can you ~ me?* ¿puede Vd. ayudarme? (*about* en el asunto de).

en·list [in'list] ⚔ alistar(se); *support* conseguir.

en·liv·en [in'laivn] vivificar, avivar, animar.

en·mesh [in'meʃ] coger en la red; ⊕ engranar.

en·mi·ty ['enmiti] enemistad *f*.

en·no·ble [i'noubl] ennoblecer.

e·nor·mi·ty [i'nɔːmiti] *fig.* enormidad *f*; **e·nor·mous** □ enorme.

e·nough [i'nʌf] bastante; suficiente; *be kind ~ to* tener la amabilidad de; *that's ~!* ¡basta!

en·rage [in'reidʒ] enfurecer, hacer rabiar.

en·rap·ture [in'ræptʃə] embelesar.

en·rich [in'ritʃ] enriquecer; *soil* fertilizar; **en'rich·ment** enriquecimiento *m*; fertilización *f*.

en·rol(l) [in'roul] alistar(se) (*a.* ⚔), inscribir(se), matricular(se); **en'rol(l)·ment** alistamiento *m*; inscripción *f*.

en·sign ['ensain] bandera *f*; alférez *m*.

en·slave [in'sleiv] esclavizar; **en'slave·ment** esclavitud *f*; (*act*) avasallamiento *m*.

en·tail [in'teil] **1.** vínculo *m*, vinculación *f*; **2.** ocasionar, causar; suponer; ♰♱ vincular.

en·tan·gle [in'tæŋgl] enmarañar, enredar.

en·ter ['entə] *v/t.* entrar en; penetrar en; *society* ingresar en, matricularse en; *member* matricular; asentar, registrar in *records*; *protest* formular; ♰ *order* asentar, anotar; *child* inscribir como futuro alumno (*for* de); *~ a p.'s head* ocurrírsele a uno; *~ up* ♰ *ledger* hacer, llevar; *diary* poner al día; *v/i.* entrar; *thea.* entrar en escena; *sport:* participar (*for* en); presentarse (*for* a); *~ into* participar en; *agreement* firmar; *conversation* entablar; *plans* formar parte de; *relations* establecer; *~ into the spirit of* dejarse emborrachar por; empaparse en; *~ (up)on career* emprender; *office* tomar posesión de; *term* empezar.

en·ter·prise [ˈentəpraiz] empresa *f*; (*spirit*) iniciativa *f*; *private* ~ iniciativa *f* privada; **en·ter·pris·ing** □ emprendedor.

en·ter·tain [entəˈtein] (*amuse*) entretener, divertir; *guest* recibir; festejar, agasajar; *idea, hope* abrigar; considerar; **en·ter·tain·er** actor *m*, músico *m* (*etc.*); **en·ter·tain·ing** □ entretenido, divertido; **en·ter·tain·ment** entretenimiento *m*, diversión *f*; espectáculo *m*; función *f*.

en·thral(l) [inˈθrɔːl] *fig.* encantar, embelesar; cautivar.

en·thu·si·asm [inˈθjuːziæzm] entusiasmo *m* (*for* por); **en·thu·si·as·tic** entusiasta; entusiástico; lleno de entusiasmo (*about, over* por).

en·tice [inˈtais] tentar, atraer (con maña); seducir.

en·tire [inˈtaiə] entero; completo; **en·tire·ly** enteramente, completamente; **en·tire·ty**: *in its* ~ enteramente, completamente; en su totalidad.

en·ti·tle [inˈtaitl] *book* intitular; ~ *to* dar derecho a (*acc., inf.*); *be* ~*d to* tener derecho a.

en·ti·ty [ˈentiti] entidad *f*, ente *m*.

en·tour·age [ɒntuˈrɑːʒ] séquito *m*.

en·trails [ˈentreilz] *pl.* entrañas *f/pl.*

en·trance¹ [ˈentrəns] entrada *f*; ingreso *m*; *thea.* entrada *f* en escena.

en·trance² [inˈtræns] encantar, embelesar, hechizar; extasiar.

en·trant [ˈentrənt] principiante *m/f*; *sport:* participante *m/f*.

en·treat [inˈtriːt] rogar, suplicar (insistentemente) (*to inf.*).

en·tree [ɒnˈtriː] entrada *f*, ingreso *m*; *of meal* entrada *f*, principio *m*.

en·trench(se) [inˈtrentʃ] ⚔ atrincherar(se); *fig.* ~ o.s. establecerse firmemente.

en·trust [inˈtrʌst] confiar (*to* a; *a p. with a th.* algo a uno).

en·try [ˈentri] entrada *f*; ingreso *m*, (*street*) bocacalle *f*; ⚖ toma *f* de posesión (*on* de); *sport:* (*total*) participación *f*; (*p.*) participante *m/f*; artículo *m in dictionary*; apunte *m in diary*; † partida *f*.

en·twine [inˈtwain] entretejer; entrelazar.

e·nu·mer·ate [iˈnjuːməreit] enumerar; **e·nu·mer·a·tion** enumeración *f*.

e·nun·ci·ate [iˈnʌnsieit] enunciar; pronunciar; **e·nun·ci·a·tion** enunciación *f*; pronunciación *f*.

en·vel·op [inˈveləp] envolver (*in* en); **en·ve·lope** [ˈenviloup] sobre *m*.

en·vi·ron·ment [inˈvaiərənmənt] medio *m* ambiente.

en·vis·age [inˈvizidʒ] prever; concebir, representarse; contemplar.

en·voy [ˈenvɔi] enviado *m*.

en·vy [ˈenvi] **1.** envidia *f*; **2.** envidiar (*a p. a th.* algo a alguien); *p.* tener envidia a.

en·zyme [ˈenzaim] enzima *f*.

e·phem·er·al [iˈfiːmərəl] efímero.

ep·ic [ˈepik] **1.** □ épico; **2.** épica *f*, epopeya *f*.

ep·i·dem·ic [epiˈdemik] **1.** □ epidémico; **2.** epidemia *f*.

ep·i·lep·sy [ˈepilepsi] epilepsia *f*; **ep·i·lep·tic** epiléptico *adj. a. su. m* (*a f*).

ep·i·log, ep·i·logue [ˈepilɒg] epílogo *m*.

ep·i·sode [ˈepisoud] episodio *m*.

ep·i·taph [ˈepitɑːf] epitafio *m*.

ep·i·thet [ˈepiθet] epíteto *m*.

e·pit·o·me [iˈpitəmi] epítome *f*, compendio *m*.

ep·och [ˈiːpɒk] época *f*.

e·qual [ˈiːkwl] **1.** □ igual (*to* a); *fig.* ~ *to ask* con fuerzas para; *occasion* al nivel de; **2.** igual *m/f*; **3.** ser igual a; **e·qual·i·ty** [iˈkwɒliti] igualdad *f*; **e·qual·ize** *v/t.* igualar; *v/i. sport:* lograr el empate.

e·quate [iˈkweit] igualar, considerar equivalente (*to, with* a); **e·qua·tion** ecuación *f*; **e·qua·tor** ecuador *m*.

e·qui·lib·ri·um [iːkwiˈlibriəm] equilibrio *m*.

e·qui·nox [ˈiːkwinɒks] equinoccio *m*.

e·quip [iˈkwip] equipar; ⊕ ~*ped with* dotado de; **e·quip·ment** [iˈkwipmənt] equipo *m*; material *m*; avíos *m/pl.*; equipaje *m*; pertrechos *m/pl.*

eq·ui·ta·ble [ˈekwitəbl] □ equitativo; **eq·ui·ty** equidad *f* (*a.* ⚖).

e·quiv·a·lence [iˈkwivələns] equivalencia *f*; **e·quiv·a·lent** equivalente *adj. a. su. m* (*to* a).

e·quiv·o·cal [iˈkwivəkl] □ equívoco, ambiguo.

e·ra [ˈiərə] era *f*, época *f*.

e·rad·i·cate [iˈrædikeit] desarraigar, extirpar.

e·rase [iˈreiz] borrar (*a. fig.*); **e·ras·er** goma *f* de borrar; **e·ra·sure** [~ʒə] borradura *f*.

e·rect [iˈrekt] **1.** □ erguido, derecho; *hair etc.* erizado; **2.** erigir, construir, levantar; ⊕ montar; *principles* formular; constituir (*into* en); **e·rec·tion** construcción *f*, estructura *f*; (*act*) erección *f*; ⊕ montaje *m*.

er·mine ['ə:min] armiño *m*.

e·rode [i'roud] *soil* erosionar(se), causar erosión en.

e·ro·sion [i'rouʒn] erosión *f*; desgaste *m*.

e·rot·ic [i'rɔtik] □ erótico; erotómano; (*obscene*) sicalíptico.

err [ə:] errar, equivocarse; (*sin*) pecar.

er·rand ['erənd] recado *m*, mandado *m*; *run* ~ ir a los mandados; '~ **boy** mandadero *m*, recadero *m*.

er·rant ['erənt] errante; *knight* andante; (*erring*) equivocado.

er·rat·ic [i'rætik] □ irregular, inconstante; *performance, record etc.* desigual; *behavior* excéntrico; *geol.*, 🌿 errático; **er·ra·tum** [i'rɑ:təm], *pl.* **er·ra·ta** [~ə] errata *f*.

er·ro·ne·ous [i'rounjəs] □ erróneo.

er·ror ['erə] error *m*, yerro *m*; equivocación *f*; *in* ~ por equivocación.

er·u·dite ['erudait] □ erudito.

e·rupt [i'rʌpt] (*volcano*) entrar en erupción; 🩺 hacer erupción; *fig.* irrumpir (*into* en); (*anger*) estallar; **e'rup·tion** erupción *f* (*a.* 🩺); explosión *f* of anger *etc.*

es·ca·la·tor ['eskəleitə] escalera *f* móvil (*or* rodante).

es·ca·pade [eskə'peid] travesura *f*, aventura *f*; **es·cape** [is'keip] **1.** *v/t.* evitar, eludir; *death* escapar a; *vigilance* burlar; (*forget*) olvidársele (a uno); (*meaning*) p. escaparse a; *v/i.* escapar(se); evadirse; (*gas etc.*) fugarse; ~ *from* p. escaparse a; *prison* escaparse de; **2.** escape *m*, fuga *f*; fuga *f* of gas *etc.*; *fig.* escapatoria *f* (*from duties etc.*); *have a narrow* ~ escaparse por un pelo.

es·cort 1. ['eskɔ:t] ✕ escolta *f*; acompañante *m/f*; **2.** [is'kɔ:t] escoltar; acompañar.

Es·ki·mo ['eskimou] esquimal *m/f*.

e·so·ter·ic [esou'terik] □ esotérico.

es·pe·cial [is'peʃl] □ especial; particular; **es'pe·cial·ly** especialmente; sobre todo; máxime.

es·pi·o·nage [espiə'nɑ:ʒ] espionaje *m*.

es·pous·al [is'pauzl] *fig.* adhesión *f* (*of* a); **es'pouse** [~z] casarse con; *fig.* adherirse a; abrazar.

es·say 1. [e'sei] intentar (*to inf.*); (*test*) ensayar; **2.** ['esei] ensayo *m*; '**es·say·ist** ensayista *m/f*.

es·sence ['esns] esencia *f*; **es·sen·tial** [i'senʃl] **1.** □ esencial; indispensable, imprescindible; ~ *oil* aceite *m* esencial; **2.** esencial *m*.

es·tab·lish [is'tæbliʃ] establecer; fundar; *facts* verificar; ~ *that* comprobar que; ℒ*ed Church* iglesia *f* del Estado; **es'tab·lish·ment** establecimiento *m*; fundación *f*.

es·tate [is'teit] (*land etc.*) finca *f*, hacienda *f*, heredad *f*; 🏛 (*property*) bienes *m/pl.* (relictos); herencia *f*; *pol.* estado *m*; *real* ~ bienes *m/pl.* raíces.

es·teem [is'ti:m] **1.** estima *f*; consideración *f*, aprecio *m*; **2.** estimar, apreciar.

es·ti·ma·ble ['estiməbl] estimable.

es·ti·mate 1. ['estimeit] estimar; apreciar; calcular (*that* que); computar, tasar (*at* en); hacer un presupuesto (*for* de); **2.** [~mit] estimación *f*; tasa *f*; cálculo *m*; presupuesto *m* *for work*; **es·ti·ma·tion** estimación *f*; *in my* ~ según mis cálculos; en mi opinión.

es·trange [is'treindʒ] enajenar, apartar; *become* ~*d* malquistarse.

et·cet·er·a [it'setrə] etcétera; ~*s* *pl.* adiciones *f/pl.*, adornos *m/pl.*

etch [etʃ] grabar al agua fuerte; '**etch·ing** aguafuerte *f*.

e·ter·nal [i'tə:nl] □ eterno; (*a. b.s.*) sempiterno; **e'ter·ni·ty** eternidad *f*.

e·ther ['i:θə] éter *m*; **e·the·re·al** [i'θiəriəl] etéreo (*a. fig.*).

eth·i·cal ['eθikl] □ ético; honrado; '**eth·ics** *mst sg.* ética *f*; moralidad *f*.

et·i·quette [eti'ket] etiqueta *f*; honor *m* profesional.

eu·lo·gy ['ju:lədʒi] elogio *m*, encomio *m*.

eu·nuch ['ju:nək] eunuco *m*.

eu·phe·mism ['ju:fimizm] eufemismo *m*.

Eu·ro·pe·an [juərə'pi:ən] europeo *adj. a. su. m* (a *f*).

eu·tha·na·si·a [ju:θə'neiziə] eutanasia *f*.

e·vac·u·ate [i'vækjueit] evacuar; desocupar; **e·vac·u·a·tion** evacuación *f*; **e·vac·u·ee** evacuado (a *f*) *m*.

e·vade [i'veid] evadir, eludir; *v. issue*.

e·val·u·ate [i'væljueit] evaluar; **e·val·u·a·tion** evaluación *f*.

e·van·gel·ic [i:væn'dʒelik(l)] evangélico; **e·van·ge·list** [i'vændʒilist] evangelizador *m*.

e·vap·o·rate [i'væpəreit] evaporar(se) (*a. fig.*); ~*d milk* leche *f* evaporada; **e·vap·o·ra·tion** evaporación *f*.

e·va·sion [i'veiʒn] evasiva *f*, evasión *f*; **e'va·sive** [~siv] □ evasivo.

eve [i:v] víspera *f*.

e·ven¹ ['iːvn] **1.** *adj.* □ llano, liso; igual; *temperature etc.* constante, invariable; *treatment* imparcial; *temper* sereno, apacible; ⚭ par; *be ~* estar en paz (*with* con); *get ~* desquitarse (*with* con); *that makes us ~* (*game*) eso iguala el tanteo; **2.** *adv.* aun, hasta; incluso; *~ as* precisamente cuando, en el mismo momento en que; *~ if, ~ though* aunque, aun cuando; *~ so* aun así; *not ~* ni (...) siquiera; F *break ~* salir sin ganar ni perder; **3.** *v/t.* igualar, allanar; *~ out ps.* hacer iguales; *th.* repartir con justicia; *~ up score etc.* igualar, nivelar; *v/i.:* ~ *up* pagar, ajustar cuentas (*with* con).

e·ven² [~] *poet.* anochecer *m.*

e·ven...: '~**hand·ed** imparcial; '~**tem·pered** apacible, ecuánime.

eve·ning ['iːvnin] tarde *f;* anochecer *m;* noche *f; good ~!* ¡buenas tardes! ; *~ gown* vestido m de noche *de mujer; ~ star* estrella *f* vespertina, lucero *m* de la tarde.

e·ven·ness ['iːvnnis] igualdad *f;* lisura *f;* uniformidad *f;* imparcialidad *f;* serenidad *f.*

e·vent [i'vent] suceso *m,* acontecimiento *m;* caso *m;* consecuencia *f; sport:* prueba *f,* carrera *f etc.; ~s pl.* (*program*) programa *m; at all ~s, in any ~* en todo caso; *in the ~ of* en caso de; **e·vent·ful** [~ful] □ *life* azaroso, accidentado; memorable; *match etc.* lleno de emoción, lleno de incidentes.

e·ven·tu·al [i'ventjuəl] □ final; consiguiente; eventual; *~ly* finalmente, con el tiempo; al fin y al cabo; **e·ven·tu·al·i·ty** [~'æliti] eventualidad *f.*

ev·er ['evə] siempre; alguna vez; (*negative sense*) jamás, nunca; *~ after, ~ since* desde entonces; (*cj.*) después (de) que; F *~ so* (~ *adj.*) muy; F *~ so* (*much*) (*adv.*) muchísimo; F *~ so many things* la mar de cosas; *as ~* como siempre; (*in letter*) tu amigo, un abrazo; *as soon as ~ I can* lo más pronto que pueda; *for ~* para siempre; *for ~ and ~* por siempre jamás; *hardly ~* casi nunca; *better than ~* mejor que nunca; F *the best ~* el mejor que se ha visto nunca; F *did you ~?* ¿se vió jamás tal cosa?; *did you ~ meet him?* ¿llegó Vd. a conocerle?; *~green* (planta *f*) de hoja perenne; *~last·ing* □ sempiterno, perpetuo,

perdurable; *b.s.* aburrido; '~**more** eternamente; *for ~* por siempre jamás.

ev·er·y ['evri] cada, todo; todos (los *etc.*); *~ now and then* de vez en cuando; *~ one* cada uno; *~ one of them* todos ellos; *~ other day* un día sí y otro no, cada dos días; *~ ten years* cada diez años; '~**bod·y** todos, todo el mundo; '~**day** diario; rutinario; acostumbrado, corriente; '~**thing** todo; *he paid for ~* lo pagó todo; '~**where** en (por, a) todas partes.

e·vict [i'vikt] desahuciar; **e'vic·tion** [~kʃn] desahucio *m.*

ev·i·dence ['evidəns] **1.** ⚖ prueba *f,* declaración *f,* testimonio *m,* deposición *f;* (*sign*) prueba *f,* indicio *m;* evidencia *f; in ~* manifiesto, visible; *give ~* deponer, prestar declaración, dar testimonio; **2.** evidenciar; *be ~d by* estar probado por; **'ev·i·dent** □ evidente, claro; manifiesto; *be ~ in* manifestarse en.

e·vil ['iːvl] **1.** □ *p.* malo, malvado, perverso; *th.* pernicioso; **2.** mal *m,* maldad *f.*

e·vince [i'vins] dar señales de, mostrar; indicar.

e·voke [i'vouk] evocar.

ev·o·lu·tion [iːvə'luːʃn] evolución *f.*

e·volve [i'vɔlv] *v/t.* evolucionar, desarrollar; *heat etc.* desprender; *v/i.* evolucionar, desarrollarse.

ewe [juː] oveja *f.*

ex [eks] **1.** *prp. dividend* sin participación en; *works etc. ~ officio* de oficio; **2.** antiguo;... que fue, ex...; *~minister* ex ministro *m.*

ex·act [ig'zækt] **1.** □ exacto; puntual; **2.** exigir (*from* a); *obedience etc.* imponer (*from* a); **ex'act·ing** exigente; *conditions* severo; **ex'act·ly** exactamente; (*time*) en punto; (*as answer*) exacto.

ex·ag·ger·ate [ig'zædʒəreit] exagerar; **ex·ag·ger·a·tion** [ig'zædʒə'reiʃn] exageración *f.*

ex·alt [ig'zɔːlt] exaltar; elevar; ensalzar.

ex·am [ig'zæm] F examen *m.*

ex·am·i·na·tion [igzæmi'neiʃn] examen *m;* ⚕ reconocimiento *m;* ⚖ interrogación *f;* investigación *f* (*into* de); registro *m of baggage;* **ex'am·ine** [~min] examinar; ⚖ interrogar; (*closely*) escudriñar; *baggage* registrar.

ex·am·ple [ig'zɑːmpl] ejemplo *m;* ejemplar *m;* ⚭ problema *m; for ~* por ejemplo; *make an* ~ *of* castigar de modo ejemplar; *set an* ~ dar ejemplo.

ex·as·per·ate [ig'sɑ:spəreit] exasperar, irritar, sacar de quicio; **ex·as·per·a·tion** exasperación *f*.

ex·ca·vate ['ekskəveit] excavar; **ex·ca·va·tion** excavación *f*.

ex·ceed [ik'si:d] exceder (de); *limit* rebasar; *speed limit* sobrepasar; *expectations* superar.

ex·cel [ik'sel] *v/t*. aventajar, superar; *v/i*. sobresalir (*in en*); **ex·cel·lence** ['eksələns] excelencia *f*; **'ex·cel·lent** □ excelente.

ex·cept [ik'sept] **1.** exceptuar, excluir; **2.** *cj*. † ~ (*that*) a menos que; **3.** *prp*. excepto, salvo, fuera de; ~ *for* excepto; dejando aparte, sin contar; **ex·cept·ing** *prp*. excepto, a excepción de; **ex·cep·tion** excepción *f*; *with the* ~ *of* a excepción de; *take* ~ ofenderse (*to* por); **ex·cep·tion·al** □ excepcional.

ex·cerpt ['eksə:pt] citar; sacar; **2.** ['eksə:pt] cita *f*, extracto *m*; separata *f from journal*.

ex·cess [ik'ses] exceso *m* (*a. fig*.); *fig*. desmán *m*, desafuero *m*; † excedente *m*; *attr*. excedente, sobrante; *in* ~ *of* superior a; **ex·ces·sive** □ excesivo; sobrado.

ex·change [iks't∫eindʒ] **1.** cambiar (*for* por); *prisoners, stamps etc.* canjear; *shots* cambiar; *courtesies* hacerse; **2.** cambio *m*; canje *m*; (*cultural etc.*) intercambio *m*; *teleph.* central *f* telefónica; † (*Stock ⊘*) Bolsa *f*; (*corn etc.*) lonja *f*; *in* ~ a cambio (de por); *bill of* ~ letra *f* de cambio; (*rate of*) ~ (tipo *m* de) cambio *m*.

ex·cite [ik'sait] emocionar; entusiasmar; (*stimulate*) excitar, estimular; (*rouse*) provocar; *get* ~*d* emocionarse; alborotarse; entusiasmarse (*about, over* por); **ex·cite·ment** emoción *f*; entusiasmo *m*; excitación *f*; **ex·cit·ing** □ emocionante; conmovedor; apasionante; excitante.

ex·claim [iks'kleim] *v/t*. decir con vehemencia; *v/i*. exclamar.

ex·cla·ma·tion [ekslə'mei∫n] exclamación *f*; ~ *mark* punto *m* de admiración.

ex·clude [iks'klu:d] excluir; exceptuar.

ex·clu·sion [iks'klu:ʒn] exclusión *f*; *to the* ~ *of* con exclusión de; **ex·clu·sive** □ [~siv] exclusivo; privativo; *policy*

etc. exclusivista; (*sole*) único; *club etc.* selecto.

ex·com·mu·ni·cate [ekskə'mju:nikeit] excomulgar.

ex·cre·ment ['ekskrimənt] excremento *m*.

ex·crete [eks'kri:t] excretar.

ex·cru·ci·at·ing [iks'kru:∫ieitiŋ] □ agudísimo, atroz.

ex·cur·sion [iks'kə:∫n] excursión *f*.

ex·cus·a·ble [iks'kju:zəbl] □ perdonable, disculpable; **ex·cuse 1.** [iks'kju:z] disculpar, perdonar (*a p. a th.* algo a alguien); excusar; dispensar (*from* de); ~ *me!* ¡dispense Vd.!; ~ *I dispense* Vd.!; **2.** [iks'kju:s] excusa *f*; disculpa *f*; pretexto *m*.

ex·e·cute ['eksikju:t] ejecutar (*a. ♪*); llevar a cabo, cumplir; ‡‡ *man* ejecutar, ajusticiar; *document* otorgar; legalizar; **ex·e·cu·tion** ejecución *f* (*a. ♪ t a. ‡‡*); ‡‡ otorgamiento *m*; legalización *f*; **ex·e·cu·tion·er** verdugo *m*; **ex·ec·u·tive** [ig'zekjutiv] **1.** □ ejecutivo; **2.** † gerente *m*, director *m*; *pol.* poder *m* ejecutivo; autoridad *f* suprema; ejecutivo *m*; **ex·ec·u·tor** [~tə] albacea *m*, ejecutor *m* testamentario.

ex·em·pli·fy [ig'zemplifai] ejemplificar; ‡‡ hacer copia notarial de.

ex·empt [ig'zempt] **1.** exento (*from* de); **2.** exentar, eximir (*from* de); dispensar, exceptuar; **ex·emp·tion** exención *f*.

ex·er·cise ['eksəsaiz] **1.** *all senses*: ejercicio *m*; **2.** *v/t*. *power, profession* ejercer; *care* poner (*in* en); *right* valerse de; *mind, p.* preocupar; *dog* llevar de paseo; *horse* entrenar; *v/i*. ejercitarse; hacer ejercicios.

ex·ert [ig'zə:t] ejercer; ~ *o.s.* esforzarse; afanarse; trabajar *etc.* demasiado; **ex·er·tion** esfuerzo *m*; afán *m*; trabajo *m etc.* excesivo.

ex·hale [eks'heil] *air* espirar; exhalar.

ex·haust [ig'zɔ:st] **1.** agotar (*a. fig*.); *fig*. apurar; debilitar; (*tire*) cansar; *be* ~*ed* (*tired*) estar rendido; **2.** ⊕ (tubo *m* de) escape *m*; *gases m/pl.* de escape; *attr.* de escape; ~ *pipe* tubo *m* de escape; ~ *valve* válvula *f* de escape; **ex·haust·ing** □ duro, que agota; **ex·haus·tion** agotamiento *m* (*a. fig*.); *fig*. postración *f*; **ex·haus·tive** □ exhaustivo, comprensivo.

ex·hib·it [ig'zibit] **1.** *signs etc.* mostrar, manifestar, exhibir; *exhibit* exponer; *film etc.* presentar; **2.** objeto *m* expuesto; pieza *f* de museo; 🕮 documento *m*; on ~ expuesto; **ex·hi·bi·tion** [eksiˈbiʃn] *paint. etc.* exposición *f*; exhibición *f*; demostración *f*; on ~ expuesto; **ex·hi·bi·tion·er** becario *m*; **ex·hi·bi·tion·ist** exhibicionista *m/f*; **ex·hib·i·tor** [igˈzibitə] expositor *m*.

ex·hil·a·rate [igˈziləreit] alegrar, regocijar; exaltar; levantar el ánimo de; **ex·hil·a·rat·ing** □ que regocija *etc*; tónico, vigorizante; **ex·hil·a·'ra·tion** alegría *f*, regocijo *m*; excitación *f*.

ex·hort [igˈzɔːt] exhortar (*to* a).

ex·i·gence, ex·i·gen·cy [ˈeksidʒəns(i)] exigencia *f*, necesidad *f* (*urgente*); caso *m* de urgencia.

ex·ile [ˈeksail] **1.** destierro *m*, exilio *m*; (*p.*) desterrado (a *f*) *m*, exilado (a *f*) *m*; **2.** desterrar, exil(i)ar.

ex·ist [igˈzist] existir; **ex·ist·ence** existencia *f*; vida *f*; *be in* ~ existir; *in* ~ = **ex·istent** existente; actual.

ex·it [ˈeksit] **1.** salida *f*; *thea.* mutis *m*; ~ *permit* permiso *m* de salida; **2.** *thea.* hacer mutis; ~ *Macbeth* váse Macbeth.

ex·o·dus [ˈeksədəs] éxodo *m*.

ex·on·er·ate [igˈzɔnəreit] exculpar, disculpar (*from blame* de); exonerar (*from duty* de).

ex·or·bi·tant [igˈzɔːbitənt] □ exorbitante, excesivo.

ex·ot·ic [egˈzɔtik] **1.** □ exótico; **2.** 🌿 planta *f* exótica.

ex·pand [iksˈpænd] *v/t.* extender; ensanchar; dilatar; *market etc.* expansionar; 🅰 *equation* desarrollar; *v/i.* extenderse; dilatarse; (*p.*) hacerse más expansivo; **ex·panse** [~ˈpæns] extensión *f*; envergadura *f of wings*; **ex·pan·sion** expansión *f*; dilatación *f*; ensanche *m of town etc.*; ✝ desarrollo *m*.

ex·pa·tri·ate [eksˈpætrieit] **1.** desterrar; ~ *o.s.* expatriarse; **2.** expatriado (a *f*) *m*.

ex·pect [iksˈpekt] esperar (*of* de; *that* que *subj.*); contar con; prometerse; *baby* esperar; (*foresee*) prever; F suponer; F *be* ~*ing* estar encinta; **ex·pect·ant** □ expectante; ~ *mother* mujer *f* encinta; **ex·pec·ta·tion** expectación *f*; expectativa *f*; ~*s pl.* esperanza *f* de heredar *in will*; *beyond* ~ mejor de lo que se esperaba; *in* ~ *of* esperando.

ex·pec·to·rate [eksˈpektəreit] expectorar.

ex·pe·di·ence, ex·pe·di·en·cy [iksˈpiːdiəns(i)] conveniencia *f*; oportunidad *f*; **ex·pe·di·ent 1.** □ conveniente; oportuno; ventajoso; **2.** expediente *m*, recurso *m*; **ex·pe·dite** [ˈekspidait] *progress* facilitar; *business* despachar; (*speed up*) acelerar; **ex·pe·di·tion** [~ˈdiʃn] expedición *f*; **ex·pe·di·tion·ar·y** expedicionario.

ex·pel [iksˈpel] expeler, despedir; arrojar; *p.* expulsar.

ex·pend [iksˈpend] expender, gastar (*on en; in doing* haciendo); *time* pasar; *resources* consumir, agotar; **ex·pend·a·ble** prescindible; **ex·pend·i·ture** [~ˈitʃə] gasto(s) *m* (*pl.*); desembolso *m*; **ex·pense** [~ˈpens] gasto *m*; costa *f*; expensas *f/pl.*; *at my* ~ corriendo y con los gastos; *at the* ~ *of fig.* a expensas de; *at great* ~ gastándose muchísimo dinero; ~ *account* cuenta *f* de gastos; *go to* ~ meterse en gastos; **ex·pen·sive** □ caro, costoso; *shop etc.* carero.

ex·pe·ri·ence [iksˈpiəriəns] **1.** experiencia *f*; **2.** experimentar; *loss, fate* sufrir; *difficulty* tener; **ex·pe·ri·enced** experimentado; perito; versado (*in* en).

ex·per·i·ment 1. [iksˈperimənt] experimento *m*; prueba *f*; **2.** [~mənt] hacer experimentos, experimentar (*on* en, *with* con); **ex·per·i·men·tal** [eksperiˈmentl] □ experimental.

ex·pert [ˈekspəːt] **1.** experto, perito (*at, in* en); hábil; 🕮 *witness* pericial; **2.** experto *m*, perito *m* (*in* en); **ex·per·tise** [ekspəːˈtiːz], **'ex·pert·ness** pericia *f*; habilidad *f*.

ex·pi·ate [ˈekspieit] expiar.

ex·pi·ra·tion [ekspiˈreiʃn] vencimiento *m*, expiración *f of term*; espiración *f of air*; **ex·pire** [eksˈpaiə] *v/i.* (*die*) expirar; (*term*) vencer, expirar, cumplirse; (*ticket*) caducar; *v/t. air* expeler, espirar.

ex·plain [iksˈplein] explicar; *mystery* aclarar; *plan* exponer; *conduct* explicar, justificar; ~ *o.s.* explicarse; hablar más claro; justificar su conducta; ~ *away* justificar hábilmente, dar razones convincentes de; *difficulty* salvar hábilmente.

ex·pla·na·tion [ekspləˈneiʃn] explicación *f*; aclaración *f, etc.*; **ex·plan·a·to·ry** [iksˈplænətəri] explicativo.

ex·ple·tive [eksˈpliːtiv] voz *f* expletiva, reniego *m*; (*oath*) palabrota *f*.

ex·pli·ca·ble [ˈeksplikəbl] explicable.

ex·plic·it [iks'plisit] □ explícito.

ex·plode [iks'ploud] *v/t.* volar, hacer saltar; *theory* refutar, desmentir; *v/i.* estallar, hacer explosión; reventar *with anger etc.*

ex·ploit 1. [iks'ploit] explotar; 2. ['eksploit] hazaña *f*, proeza *f*; **ex·ploi·ta·tion** explotación *f*.

ex·plo·ra·tion [eksplɔː'reiʃn] exploración *f*; **ex·plor·a·to·ry** [~rətəri] preparatorio, de sondaje; **ex·plore** [iks'plɔː] explorar; *fig.* examinar, sondar; **ex·plor·er** explorador *m*.

ex·plo·sion [iks'plouʒn] explosión *f* (a. fig.); **ex·plo·sive** [~siv] 1. explosivo *a. su. m.* (a. fig.).

ex·po·nent [eks'pounənt] exponente *m/f*; partidario (a *f*) *m*; intérprete *m/f*; ℞ exponente *m*.

ex·port 1. [eks'pɔːt] exportar; 2. ['ekspɔːt] exportación *f* (a. ~s *pl.*); **ex·port·er** exportador *m*.

ex·pose [iks'pouz] exponer (*a. phot.*); *plot etc.* desenmascarar; **ex·posed** *adj. position* expuesto, desabrigado, al descubierto; *flank* desguarnecido; **ex·po·si·tion** [ekspə'ziʃn] exposición *f*.

ex·po·sure [iks'pouʒə] exposición *f* (*a. phot.*); desenmascaramiento *m* of *plot etc.*; ~ meter fotómetro *m*.

ex·pound [iks'paund] exponer, explicar; comentar.

ex·press [iks'pres] 1. □ expreso; explícito, categórico; *letter* urgente; ~ train rápido *m*; 2. rápido *m* (a. ~ train); 3. *adv.* por carta (*etc.*) urgente; 4. expresar; ~ o.s. expresarse; **ex·pres·sion** *all senses:* expresión *f*, **ex·pres·sive** □ expresivo.

ex·pro·pri·ate [eks'prouprieit] expropiar; **ex·pro·pri·a·tion** expropiación *f*.

ex·pul·sion [iks'pʌlʃn] expulsión *f*.

ex·qui·site ['ekskwizit] 1. □ exquisito, primoroso; *pain* agudísimo; 2. petimetre *m*.

ex·tant [eks'tænt] existente.

ex·tem·po·rar·y [iks'tempərəri], **ex·tem·po·re** [eks'tempəri] 1. *adj.* improvisado; 2. *adv.* de improviso, sin preparación.

ex·tend [iks'tend] extender(se); *building etc.* ensanchar, ampliar; *hand* tender; *term etc.* prolongar(se); *thanks, welcome* dar, ofrecer; *athlete* exigir el máximo esfuerzo a.

ex·ten·si·ble [iks'tensibl] extensible; **ex·ten·sion** extensión *f*; ♧ *etc.* en-

sanche *m*, ampliación *f*; prolongación *f* of *term etc.*; ✝ prórroga *f*; *teleph.* línea *f* derivada; ∠ ~ cord cordón *m* de extensión; **ex·ten·sive** □ extenso; vasto, dilatado; *use etc.* abundante, general.

ex·tent [iks'tent] extensión *f*; alcance *m*; amplitud *f*; *to the* ~ *of* hasta el punto de; *to the full* ~ en toda su extensión; *to a certain* ~, *to some* ~ hasta cierto punto; *to a great* ~ en gran parte.

ex·ten·u·ate [eks'tenjueit] atenuar, disminuir, mitigar; *extenuating circumstances pl.* circunstancias *f/pl.* atenuantes.

ex·te·ri·or [eks'tiəriə] exterior *adj. a. su. m.*

ex·ter·mi·nate [eks'təːmineit] exterminar; **ex·ter·mi·na·tion** exterminio *m*.

ex·ter·nal [eks'təːnl] 1. □ externo; exterior; ~ *trade* comercio *m* exterior; 2. ~s *pl.* exterioridad *f*, aspecto *m* exterior.

ex·tinct [iks'tiŋkt] *volcano etc.* extinto, apagado; *animal* extinto, extinguido; **ex·tinc·tion** extinción *f*.

ex·tin·guish [iks'tiŋgwiʃ] extinguir; apagar; *right etc.* suprimir.

ex·tir·pate ['ekstəːpeit] extirpar.

ex·tol [iks'tɔl] ensalzar, celebrar.

ex·tort [iks'tɔːt] obtener (*or* sacar) por fuerza; **ex·tor·tion** *all senses:* exacción *f*.

ex·tra ['ekstrə] 1. *adj.* extra (...); de más, de sobra; *charge etc.* extraordinario, suplementario; *part* de repuesto; adicional; 2. *adv.* especialmente, extraordinariamente; *with verbs:* más; de sobra; 3. *su.* extra *m on bill*; exceso *m*; *cosa f* adicional; (*pieza f* de) repuesto *m*; *thea.* comparsa *m/f*; ~s *pl.* comparsería *f*.

ex·tract 1. ['ekstrækt] cita *f*, trozo *m*; *pharm.* extracto *m*; 2. [iks'trækt] extraer (*a. ℞*); sacar; **ex·trac·tion** extracción *f*.

ex·traor·di·nar·y [iks'trɔːdnri] □ extraordinario.

ex·trav·a·gance [iks'trævigəns] prodigalidad *f*, despilfarro *m*, gasto *m* (*or* lujo *m*) excesivo; extravagancia *f*; **ex·trav·a·gant** □ *p.* pródigo, despilfarrado(r); *price* exorbitante; *praise* excesivo; *living* muy lujoso.

ex·treme [iks'triːm] 1. □ extremo; *case freq.* excepcional; ~*ly* extremadamente, sumamente; 2. extremo *m*;

extremidad f; **ex·trem·ist** extremista m/f; **ex·trem·i·ty** [ˌtremiti] extremidad f; medida f extrema; rigor m; **ex·trem·i·ties** [ˌz] pl. extremidades f/pl. of body); medidas f/pl. extremas; be driven to ∼ estar muy apurado.

ex·tri·cate [ˈekstrikeit] librar, extraer, sacar (from de).

ex·tro·vert [ˈekstrouvəːt] extrovertido m.

ex·u·ber·ance [igˈzju:bərəns] exuberancia f; euforia f.

ex·ult [igˈzʌlt] exultar; regocijarse (at, in por; to find al encontrar); triunfar (over sobre).

eye [ai] 1. mst ojo m; sew. corcheta f; ✿ yema f; ✿ black ∼ ojo m amoratado; in the ∼s of a los ojos de; with an ∼ to ger. con la intención de inf.; pensando en acc.; be all ∼s ser todo ojos; catch the ∼ llamar la atención; catch s.o.'s ∼ atraer la atención de uno; cry one's ∼s out llorar a mares; have an ∼ for tener gusto por; saber apreciar acc.; have

an ∼ to vigilar; tener en cuenta; F have one's ∼ on tener los ojos en; vigilar; (desire) echar el ojo a; keep an ∼ on vigilar; echar una mirada a; make ∼s at hacer guiños a; open s.o.'s ∼s to hacer que uno se dé cuenta de; (not to) see ∼ to ∼ (with) (no) estar completamente de acuerdo (con); shut one's ∼s to hacer la vista gorda a; 2. ojear; mirar (detenidamente etc.); '∼**ball** globo m del ojo; '∼**brow** ceja f; '∼**cup** ojera f, lavaojos m; '∼**ful** buena ojeada f; '∼**glass** anteojo m; lente m; monóculo m; '∼**lash** pestaña f; '**eye·let** ojete m.

eye...: '∼**lid** párpado m; '∼**o·pen·er** revelación f, sorpresa f grande; acontecimiento m asombroso; '∼**shade** visera f; '∼ **shad·ow** crema f para los párpados; '∼**shot** alcance m de la vista; '∼**sight** (alcance m de la) vista f; '∼**sore** monstruosidad f, cosa f que ofende la vista; '∼**strain** vista f fatigada; '∼**tooth** colmillo m; '∼**wit·ness** testigo m presencial.

F

fa·ble [ˈfeibl] fábula f.

fab·ric [ˈfæbrik] tejido m, tela f; △ fábrica f; **fab·ri·cate** [ˈkeit] fabricar (a. fig.); fig. inventar, falsificar.

fab·u·lous [ˈfæbjuləs] □ fabuloso.

fa·çade [fəˈsɑːd] fachada f; fig. apariencia f, barniz m.

face [feis] 1. cara f; semblante m, rostro m; superficie f; faz f of the earth; (grimace) mueca f; (effrontery) desfachatez f; (prestige) prestigio m, apariencias f/pl.; esfera f of watch; ✕ cara f de trabajo; ∼ downwards boca abajo; ∼ to ∼ cara a cara; in (the) ∼ of ante; luchando contra; a pesar de; on the ∼ of it a primera vista; lose ∼ desprestigiarse; F make (or pull) ∼s hacer carantoñas (at a), hacer muecas (at a); save (one's) ∼ salvar las apariencias; say s.t. to one's ∼ decir algo por (or en) la cara de uno; F show one's ∼ dejarse ver; ∼ value ✝ valor m nominal; fig. valor m aparente, significado m literal; 2. v/t. danger arrostrar, hacer cara a; p., enemy encararse con; problem afrontar; facts reconocer, aceptar; (building) mirar hacia, estar enfrente de; ⊕ revestir; (a)fo-

rrar; ⊕ (a. ∼ off) alisar; be ∼d with presentársele a uno; v/i.: ∼ about dar media vuelta; ∼ on to dar a, dar sobre; ∼ up to dar cara a; '∼ **card** figura f, naipe m de figura; '∼**lift** cirugía f estética; '∼ **pow·der** polvos m/pl.

fa·cial [ˈfeiʃl] 1. □ facial; 2. masaje m facial.

fac·ile [ˈfæsail] fácil, vivo; b.s. ligero, superficial; **fa·cil·i·tate** [fəˈsiliteit] facilitar; **fa·cil·i·ty** facilidad f.

fac·ing [ˈfeisiŋ] ⊕ revestimiento m; sew.: ∼s pl. vueltas f/pl.

fac·sim·i·le [fækˈsimili] facsímil adj. a. su. m.

fact [fækt] hecho m; realidad f; ∼s pl. ◻ datos m/pl.; the ∼ is that ello es que; '∼**find·ing** ... de investigación, de indagación.

fac·tion [ˈfækʃn] facción f; disensión f.

fac·tor [ˈfæktə] factor m (ᴀ a. fig.); fig. elemento m, hecho m; ✝ agente m; '**fac·to·ry** fábrica f, factoría f.

fac·tu·al [ˈfæktjuəl] □ objetivo; que consta de hechos (or datos).

fac·ul·ty [ˈfækəlti] all senses: facultad f.

fad [fæd] F manía *f*, capricho *m*.

fade [feid] desteñir(se), descolorar (-se); *(flower)* marchitar(se); ∼ *away*, ∼ *out* desdibujarse; desvanecerse (*a. radio*); apagarse; ∼ *in*, ∼ *up* (hacer) aparecer gradualmente; *film*: ∼ *to* fundir a.

fail [feil] **1.** *v/i.* fracasar, frustrarse, malograrse; no surtir efecto; *(supply)* acabarse; *(voice)* desfallecer; ser suspendido *in exam*; † quebrar, hacer bancarrota; ∼ *to* dejar de; no lograr; *v/t.* faltar a; *p.* faltar a sus obligaciones a; *pupil* suspender; *exam* salir mal en, no aprobar; *(strength etc.)* abandonar; **2.** *without* ∼ sin falta; **'fail·ing 1.** falta *f*, defecto *m*, flaqueza *f*; **2.** *prp.* a falta de; **fail·ure** ['feiljər] fracaso *m*; malogro *m*; falta *f*, omisión *f*; *(p.)* fracasado (a *f*) *m*; ∉ corte *m*; suspenso *m in exam*.

faint [feint] **1.** □ débil; *sound etc.* indistinto, casi imperceptible; *resemblance* ligero; *line etc.* tenue; ∉ *feel* ∼ tener vahídos; **2.** desmayarse, desfallecer (*with* de); **3.** desmayo *m*, desfallecimiento *m*.

fair[1] [fɛə] **1.** □ *(beautiful)* hermoso, bello; *hair* rubio; *skin* blanco; *(just)* justo, equitativo; *hearing* imparcial; *name* honrado; *prospects* favorable; *sky* sereno, despejado; *weather* bueno; *chance, warning* razonable; *(middling)* regular, mediano; *the* ∼ *(sex)* el bello sexo; *it's not* ∼ ! ¡no hay derecho!; ∼ *copy* copia *f* en limpio; *by* ∼ *means* por medios rectos; ∉ ∼ *play* juego *m* limpio; ∼ *sex* bello sexo *m*; **2.** *adv.* directamente, exactamente; justamente; *play* ∼ jugar limpio; *speak a p.* ∼ hablar a una p. cortésmente.

fair[2] [∼] feria *f*; *(fun-)* parque *m* de atracciones; verbena *f*; **'∼-ground** real *m*.

fair·ly ['fɛəli] *v. fair*[1]; bastante; medianamente; completamente; **'fair·ness** justicia *f*, imparcialidad *f*; blancura *f of skin*; *in all* ∼ para ser justo.

fair·y ['fɛəri] **1.** hada *f*; **2.** feérico, mágico; de hada(s); **'∼ god·moth·er** hada *f* madrina; **'fair·y tale** cuento *m* de hadas; fantástico, de ensueño.

faith [feiθ] fe *f*; confianza *f* (*in* en); *in good* ∼ de buena fe; *break* ∼ faltar a la palabra (*with* dada a); *keep* ∼ cumplir su palabra (*with* dada a); **faith·ful** ['∼ful] □ fiel, leal; puntual; *the* ∼ *pl.*

los fieles; *yours* ∼*ly* atentamente le saluda; **'faith·ful·ness** fidelidad *f*, lealtad *f*; **'faith·less** □ infiel, desleal; falso.

fake [feik] F **1.** falsificación *f*, impostura *f*; filfa *f*; *(p.)* impostor *m*, farsante *m* (*a.* **'fak·er**); **2.** falso, fingido; **3.** contrahacer, falsificar, fingir.

fal·con ['fɔːlkən] halcón *m*; **'fal·con·ry** halconería *f*, cetrería *f*.

fall [fɔːl] **1.** caída *f*; † baja *f*; otoño *m*; declive *m*, desnivel *m in ground*; *(water)* salto *m* de agua, cascada *f*, catarata *f* (*a.* ∼*s pl.*); *the* ♀ la Caída; *ride for a* ∼ ir a acabar mal; **2.** *[irr.]* caer(se); disminuir; *(level, price)* bajar; ⚔ caer, rendirse; *(enemy)* amainar; sucumbir (*to* ante); *his face fell* se inmutó; ∼ *asleep* dormirse; ∼ *away* enflaquecer; apostatar; ∼ *back* retroceder; ⚔ replegarse (*on* sobre); ∼ *back (up)on* recurrir a; ∼ *behind* quedarse atrás; *v. stool*; ∼ *down* caerse; ∼ *due* vencer; ∼ *flat* caer de bruces, caer de boca; *(suggestion)* caer en el vacío; ∼ *for p.* enamorarse de; *trick* dejarse engañar por; ∼ *in (roof)* desplomarse; ⚔ alinearse; ∼ *in love* enamorarse (*with* de); ∼ *in with p.* encontrarse con; *idea* convenir en; ∼ *into error etc.* incurrir en; *category* estar incluido en; *conversation* entablar; *habit* adquirir; *three parts etc.* dividirse en; ∼ *off* desprenderse; caerse; *(quantity)* disminuir; *(quality)* empeorar; ∼ *on* ⚔ *etc.* caer sobre, echarse sobre; ∼ *out* reñir (*with* con), pelearse (*with* con), indisponerse (*with* con); resultar (*that* que); ⚔ romper filas; *v. short*; ∼ *through* fracasar, quedar en nada; ∼ *to* empezar a comer; *(duty)* competer a, corresponder a; ∼ *to ger.* empezar a *inf.*

fal·la·cious [fə'leiʃəs] □ erróneo, ilusorio, ilusorio; *b.s.* sofístico.

fal·la·cy ['fæləsi] error *m*; sofisma *m*.

fall·en ['fɔːlən] *p.p. of fall* 2.

fall guy ['fɔːlgai] *sl.* pato *m*, cabeza *f* de turco.

fal·li·bil·i·ty [fæli'biliti] falibilidad *f*; **fal·li·ble** ['fæləbl] □ falible.

false [fɔːls] □ falso; *p.* desleal, pérfido; *teeth etc.* postizo; *be* ∼ *to play* ∼ traicionar; ∼ *bottom* doble fondo *m*; **false·hood** ['∼hud] mentira *f*, falsedad *f*.

fal·set·to [fɔːl'setou] falsete *m*.

fal·ter ['fɔːltə] *v/i.* vacilar, titubear;

(*voice*) desfallecer, empañarse; v/t. decir titubeando.

fame [feim] fama f; **famed** famoso (*for* por), afamado.

fa·mil·iar [fəˈmiljə] 1. □ familiar (*to* a) (*a.b.s.*); conocido; íntimo; 2. familiar m (*a. eccl.*; *a.* ~ *spirit*); **fa·mil·i·ar·i·ty** [ˌʌliˈæriti] familiaridad f (*a. b.s.*); conocimiento m; intimidad f.

fam·i·ly [ˈfæmili] 1. familia f; 2. familiar; casero; *business* de familia; *butcher etc.* doméstico; *in the* ~ *way* en estado de buena esperanza, encinta; ~ *tree* árbol m genealógico.

fam·ine [ˈfæmin] hambre f; carestía f *of goods*.

fa·mous [ˈfeiməs] □ famoso, célebre (*for* por); F ~*ly* a las mil maravillas.

fan¹ [fæn] 1. abanico m; ventilador m; ♪ aventador m; (*machine*) aventadora f; 2. abanicar; ventilar; ♪ aventar; *fire* avivar, soplar; *fig.* excitar, atizar.

fan² [~] F aficionado (a f) m, entusiasta m/f; admirador (-a f) m.

fa·nat·ic, fa·nat·i·cal [fəˈnætik(l)] □ fanático *adj. a. su. m* (a f).

fan·cy [ˈfænsi] 1. fantasía f; imaginación f; capricho m, antojo m; afición f, gusto m; quimera f, suposición f arbitraria; *take a* ~ *to* aficionarse a; *p.* prendarse de; 2. de fantasía; de lujo, de adorno; *ideas etc.* extravagante; *price* exorbitante; ~ *dress* disfraz m; ~ *dress ball* baile m de trajes; 3. imaginar(se), figurarse; antojarse; aficionarse a, encapricharse por.

fan·fare [ˈfænfɛə] *approx.* toque m de trompeta, fanfarria f.

fang [fæŋ] colmillo m; ⊕ diente m.

fan·tas·tic [fænˈtæstik] □ fantástico; **fan·ta·sy** [ˈʌtəsi] fantasía f.

far [fɑː] 1. *adj.* lejano, distante; más lejano; 2. *adv.* lejos, a lo lejos (*a.* ~ *away, off*); how ~ *is it* (*to*)? ¿cuánto hay de aquí (a)?; ~ *and near*, ~ *and wide* por todas partes; ~ *better* mucho mejor; ~ *the best* con mucho el mejor; ~ *from ger.* lejos de *inf.*; ~ *from it!* ¡nada de eso!; *as* ~ *as* hasta; *as* ~ *as I know* que yo sepa; *in so* ~ *as* en tanto que; *so* ~ hasta aquí; (*time*) hasta ahora.

farce [fɑːs] farsa f; *fig.* tontería f, absurdo m.

fare [fɛə] 1. precio m (del billete); billete m; ♣ pasaje m; (*p.*) pasajero (a f) m; (*food*) comida f; 2. pasarlo, irle a uno (*bien etc.*); suceder; ~*well* 1. ¡adiós!; 2. adiós m, despedida f; *bid* ~ despedirse (*to* de); 3. ... de despedida.

far-... [fɑː]: ~*fetched* inverosímil, poco probable; forzado, traído por los cabellos; ~*flung* extenso.

farm [fɑːm] 1. granja f; cortijo m; estancia f *S.Am.*; (*oyster- etc.*) criadero m; = ~*house*; 2. v/t. cultivar, labrar; ~ *out* arrendar, dar en arriendo; v/i. cultivar la tierra; ser agricultor; **farm·er** granjero m, agricultor m; labrador m; estanciero m *S.Am.*; **farm hand** labriego m; peón m *S.Am.*; **farm·house** alquería f, cortijo m; **farm·ing** 1. agricultura f; labranza f, cultivo m; 2. agrícola; *land* labrantío, de labor.

far-off [ˈfɑːˈrɔf] lejano, remoto.

far-reach·ing [ˈfɑːˈriːtʃiŋ] trascendental; de mucho alcance.

far·ther [ˈfɑːðə], **far·thest** [ˈʌðist] *comp. a. sup. of* far.

fas·ci·nate [ˈfæsineit] fascinar, encantar; **fas·ci·nat·ing** □ fascinador, encantador; **fas·ci·na·tion** fascinación f, encanto m.

fash·ion [ˈfæʃn] 1. moda f; estilo m; uso m, manera f; buen tono m; *in* ~ de moda; *out of* ~ pasado de moda; 2. formar; labrar; forjar; adaptar; modelar; **fash·ion·a·ble** □ de moda; de buen tono, elegante; **fash·ion pa·rade**, ~ **show** desfile m de modelos; **fash·ion plate** figurín m de moda.

fast¹ [fɑːst] 1. *adj.* rápido, veloz; ligero; (*firm*) fijo, firme; *color* sólido, inalterable; *friend* leal; *living* disoluto; F *woman* muy coqueta; fresca; *make* ~ sujetar, amarrar; F *pull a* ~ *one* jugar una mala pasada (*on* a); 2. *adv.* rápidamente; de prisa; ~ *asleep* profundamente dormido; *be* ~ (*clock*) adelantar; *hold* ~ mantenerse firme.

fast² [~] 1. ayuno m; 2. ayunar; ~*day* día m de ayuno.

fas·ten [ˈfɑːsn] v/t. asegurar, fijar; atar; sujetar; pegar.

fas·tid·i·ous [fæsˈtidiəs] □ quisquilloso, delicado; exigente.

fat [fæt] 1. gordo, grueso; *land* fértil; *living, profits* pingüe; *meat* poco magro; 2. grasa f.

fa·tal [ˈfeitl] □ fatal, funesto (*to* para); **fa·tal·ism** [ˈʌlizm] fatalismo m; **fa·tal·i·ty** [fəˈtæliti] fatalidad f; (*p.*) muerto m, muerte f.

fellow

fate [feit] hado *m*; suerte *f*, destino *m*; the ℥s *pl.* las Parcas.

fat·head ['fæthed] F tronco *m*, estúpido *m*.

fa·ther ['fɑːðə] 1. padre *m*; 2. engendrar; prohijar; servir de padre a; **'fa·ther-in-law** suegro *m*; **'fa·ther-land** patria *f*; **'Fa·ther 'Time** el Tiempo *m*.

fath·om ['fæðəm] 1. braza *f*; 2. ⚓ sond(e)ar (*a. fig.*); *fig.* penetrar; profundizar; entender.

fa·tigue [fə'tiːg] 1. fatiga *f* (*a.* ⊕), cansancio *m*; ✕ faena *f*; 2. fatigar, cansar.

fat·ness ['fætnis] gordura *f*; fertilidad *f*; **'fat·ten** engordar (*a. v/i.*).

fau·cet ['fɔːsit] grifo *m*.

fault [fɔːlt] 1. falta *f* (*a. sport*); culpa *f*; imperfección *f in manufacture etc.*; ⊕, ⚡ avería *f*, desperfecto *m*, defecto *m*; *geol.* falla *f*; at ℥ culpable; to a ℥ excesivamente, sumamente; find ℥ criticar, censurar (*with acc.*); 2. tachar, encontrar defectos en; **'℥·find-er** criticón (-a *f*) *m*; **'fault·less** □ impecable, intachable; **'fault·y** □ defectuoso, imperfecto.

fa·vor ['feivə] 1. favor *m*; (*approval*) aprobación *f*; (*support*) amparo *m*; privanza *f at court*; (*token*) prenda *f*; ✝ grata *f*, atenta *f*; do a ℥ hacer un favor; 2. favorecer; apoyar; **fa·vor-a·ble** ['℥rəbl] □ favorable; **fa·vor·ite** ['℥vərit] favorito, predilecto; 2. favorito (a *f*) *m* (*a. sport*); **'fa·vor·it·ism** favoritismo *m*.

fawn¹ [fɔːn] *zo.* cervato *m*; color *m* de cervato.

fawn² [℥] adular, lisonjear (*on acc.*); (*animal*) acariciar (*on acc.*).

faze [feiz] F inquietar, molestar.

fear [fiə] 1. miedo *m* (*of a, de*), temor *m*; aprensión *f*; *for* ℥ of temiendo, por miedo de; 2. *v/t.* temer; *v/i.* tener miedo (*to inf.* de *inf.*); **fear·ful** ['℥ful] □ *p.* temeroso (*of* de), tímido, aprensivo; *th.* pavoroso, horrendo; **'fear·less** □ intrépido, audaz.

fea·si·ble ['fiːzəbl] factible, posible; *make* ℥ posibilitar.

feast [fiːst] 1. banquete *m*, festín *m*; (*day*) fiesta *f*; 2. *v/t.* festejar; agasajar; banquetear; *v/i.* banquetear; ℥ on regalarse con.

feat [fiːt] hazaña *f*, proeza *f*.

feath·er ['feðə] 1. pluma *f*; ⊕ lengüeta *f*; ⊕ cuña *f*; *in fine etc.* ℥ de buen humor; 2. emplumar; ℥ one's nest

ponerse las botas, hacer su agosto; **'℥ bed** plumón *m*; 2.; **'℥-brained** cascabelero; **'feath·ered** plumado; alado.

fea·ture ['fiːtʃə] 1. rasgo *m*; característica *f*; facción *f of face*; (*film*) atracción *f* principal; artículo *m in paper*; ℥s *pl.* facciones *f/pl.*; 2. delinear; representar; *film* ofrecer; destacar; *actor* presentar.

Feb·ru·ar·y ['februəri] febrero *m*.

fed [fed] *pret. a. p.p. of feed* 2; be ℥ up estar harto (*with* de).

fed·er·al ['fedərəl] □ federal.

fee [fiː] derechos *m/pl.*; honorarios *m/pl.*; (*entrance*) cuota *f*; (*tip*) gratificación *f*.

fee·ble ['fiːbl] □ débil; flojo; irresoluto; **'℥-'mind·ed** imbécil.

feed [fiːd] 1. comida *f*; 🐎 pienso *m*, pasto *m*; F cuchipanda *f*, comilona *f*; ⊕ (*tubo m*, dispositivo *m* de) alimentación *f*; 2. [*irr.*] *v/t.* dar de comer a; nutrir; alimentar (*a.* ⊕); *fire* cebar; *v/i.* comer; alimentarse (*on* de); 🐎 pacer; **'℥-back** *radio*: realimentación *f*.

feel [fiːl] 1. [*irr.*] *v/t.* sentir; experimentar, percibir; (*touch*) palpar, tocar; *pulse* tomar; reconocer; ℥ that creer que, parecerle a uno que; *v/i.* sentirse; ℥ bad, ℥ ill sentirse mal; ℥ cold (*p.*) tener frío; (*th.*) estar frío; ℥ for condolerse de; ℥ like doing tener ganas de hacer; ℥ rough etc. estar áspero etc. al tacto; ℥ up to creerse capaz de; 2. tacto *m*; sensación *f*; **'feel·er** *zo.* antena *f*; *zo.* tentáculo *m*; *pol. etc.* sondeo *m*; tentativa *f*; **'feel·ing 1.** □ sensible; compasivo; ℥ly con honda emoción; 2. tacto *m*; sensación *f*; sentimiento *m*; sensibilidad *f*; (*opinion*) parecer *m*; (*foreboding*) presentimiento *m*; *with* ℥ con emoción; (*angrily*) con pasión; *hurt one's* ℥s herir los sentimientos de uno.

feet [fiːt] *pl. of foot* pies *m/pl.*

feign [fein] fingir.

feint [feint] 1. artificio *m*, engaño *m*; (*fencing*) finta *f*; 2. hacer una finta.

fe·line ['fiːlain] felino.

fell [fel] 1. *pret. of fall* 2; 2. *tree* talar; derribar; *cattle* acogotar.

fel·low ['felou] compañero *m*; prójimo *m*; (*equal*) igual *m/f*; (*other half*) pareja *f*; *univ. approx.* miembro *m* de la junta de gobierno de un colegio; *univ.* becario *m*; socio *m*, miembro *m of society*; F tipo *m*, sujeto *m*, individuo *m*; *nice* ℥ buen chico *m*; *poor* ℥ (!)

pobrecito *m*; young ~ chico *m*; '~ **be·ing** prójimo *m*; '~ **cit·i·zen** conciudadano *m*; '~ **coun·try·man** compatriota *m*; '~ **crea·ture** prójimo *m*; '~ **feel·ing** simpatía *f*, afinidad *f*; '~ **mem·ber** consocio *m*; **~ship** ['~ʃip] compañerismo *m*; compañía *f*; hermandad *f*; univ. (of-fice) dignidad *f* del fellow; univ. (grant) beca *f*; '~ **trav·el·er** compañero *m* de viaje (a. *fig.*); pol. filocomunista *m/f*.

fel·on ['felən] criminal *m*, delincuente *m/f* de mayor cuantía; **fel·o·ny** ['feləni] crimen *m*, delito *m* de mayor cuantía.

felt[1] [felt] pret. a. p.p. of feel 1.

felt[2] [~] 1. fieltro *m* (a. ~ hat); 2. cubrir con fieltro.

fe·male ['fi:meil] hembra adj. a. su. *f* (a. ⊕); femenino.

fem·i·nine ['feminin] femenino; *contr.* afeminado; **fem·i·nin·i·ty** femineidad *f*; **fem·i·nism** feminismo *m*; **fem·i·nist** feminista *m/f*.

fence [fens] 1. cerca *f*, valla *f*, cercado *m*; *sl.* receptor *m* de cosas robadas; *sit on the* ~ ver los toros desde la barrera; (estar a) ver venir; 2. *v/t.* cercar, proteger, defender (*from* de); ~ **in** encerrar con cerca; ~ **off** separar con cerca; *v/i.* *fig.* defenderse con evasivas; *sport*: esgrimir; **fenc·ing** ['fensiŋ] esgrima *f*; *attr.* de esgrima; ~ **post** poste *m* de cerca.

fend [fend]: ~ **for o.s.** defenderse (a sí mismo), apañárselas por su cuenta; ~ **off** parar; desviar; **fend·er** guardafuego *m*; *mot.* parachoques *m*; guardafango *m*; '~ **trompa** *f*; ♣ defensa *f*.

fer·ment 1. ['fə:mənt] fermento *m*; fermentación *f*; *fig.* agitación *f*; 2. [fə'ment] (hacer) fermentar; **fer·men·ta·tion** [fə:men'teiʃn] fermentación *f*.

fern [fə:n] helecho *m*.

fe·ro·cious [fə'rouʃəs] □ feroz; **fe·roc·i·ty** [fə'rɔsiti] ferocidad *f*.

fer·ret ['ferit] 1. hurón *m* (a. *fig.*); 2. cazar con hurones; ~ **about** buscar revolviéndolo todo; ~ **out** husmear; *secret* lograr saber.

Fer·ris wheel ['feriswi:l] rueda *f* de feria, noria *f*.

fer·ry ['feri] 1. pasaje *m*; balsadero *m*; (*boat*) balsa *f*, barca *f* (de pasaje); 2. pasar ... a través del río *etc.*; '~ **boat** balsa *f*, barca *f*.

fer·tile ['fə:tail] fértil (*of*, in en; a.

fig.), fecundo; **fer·til·i·ty** [fə:'tiliti] fertilidad *f*, fecundidad *f*; **fer·ti·lize** fertilizar, fecundar; ✓ abonar; **fer·ti·liz·er** fertilizante *m*, abono *m*.

fer·vent ['fə:vənt] □, **fer·vid** ['fə:vid] □ fervoroso, ardiente.

fer·vor ['fə:və] fervor *m*, ardor *m*.

fes·ter ['festə] ulcerarse, enconarse (a. *fig.*).

fes·ti·val ['festəvl] 1. fiesta *f*; ♪ festival *m*; 2. festivo; **fes·tive** ['~iv] □ festivo; regocijado; **fes·tiv·i·ty** fiesta *f*; festividad *f*; regocijo *m*.

fetch [fetʃ] *v/t.* traer; ir por, ir a buscar; hacer venir.

fet·id ['fetid] □ fétido.

fet·ish ['fetiʃ] fetiche *m*.

fet·ter ['fetə] 1. grillete *m*; ~s *pl.* grillos *m/pl.* (a. *fig.*); 2. encadenar; trabar (a. *fig.*); *fig.* estorbar.

feud [fju:d] enemistad *f* heredada (entre dos familias *etc.*); vendetta *f*, odio *m* de sangre; **feu·dal** ['~dl] □ feudal; **feu·dal·ism** ['~dəlizm] feudalismo *m*.

fe·ver ['fi:və] fiebre *f*; calentura *f*; **fe·ver·ish** □ febril (a. *fig.*) calenturiento.

few [fju:] pocos; (alg)unos; *a* ~ unos cuantos; *not a* ~ no pocos; ~ *and far between* muy raros; *the* ~ la minoría.

fi·an·cé(e) [fi'ānsei] approx. novio (a *f*) *m*, prometido (a *f*) *m*.

fi·as·co [fi'æskou] fiasco *m*.

fi·at ['faiæt] fiat *m*, autorización *f*.

fib [fib] F 1. mentirilla *f*, bola *f*; 2. decir mentirillas; **fib·ber** F mentirosillo (a *f*) *m*.

fi·bre ['faibə] fibra *f*; *fig.* carácter *m*; **fi·brous** □ fibroso.

fick·le ['fikl] inconstante, mudable, veleidoso.

fic·tion ['fikʃn] ficción *f*; novelas *f/pl.*, género *m* novelístico; **fic·tion·al** □ novelesco.

fic·ti·tious [fik'tiʃəs] □ ficticio.

fid·dle ['fidl] 1. ♪ violín *m*; F trampa *f*; *be fit as a* ~ andar como un reloj; *play second* ~ desempeñar un papel secundario; 2. ♪ tocar el violín; *sl.* agenciarse; ~ *away* desperdiciar; ~ *with* jugar con, manosear.

fi·del·i·ty [fi'deliti] fidelidad *f*.

fidg·et ['fidʒit] F 1. (*p.*) persona *f* inquieta; ~s *pl.* agitación *f* nerviosa; 2. agitarse nerviosamente; ~ *with* manosear, jugar con.

fief [fi:f] feudo *m*.

field [fi:ld] 1. campo *m* (a. ✕, ⚡,

find

sport); prado *m*, pradera *f*; esfera *f of activities*; competidores *m/pl. in race*; **take the ~** salir a la palestra; **2. ball** parar, recoger; *team* presentar; '**~ day** día *m* de maniobras; *fig.* día *m* de gran éxito.

field...: '~ glass·es *pl.* gemelos *m/pl.* (de campo); '**~ 'mar·shal** *approx.* mariscal *m* de campo; capitán *m* general del ejército; '**~ work** trabajo *m* en el propio campo.

fiend [fiːnd] demonio *m*, diablo *m*; desalmado *m*; fanático *m* (*for* de); **'fiend·ish** □ diabólico.

fierce [fiəs] □ feroz, fiero; furioso; *heat* intenso; *supporter etc.* acérrimo.

fi·er·y ['faiəri] □ ardiente; caliente; *fig.* vehemente; *horse* fogoso; *speech* apasionado.

fife [faif] pífano *m*.

fif·teen ['fifˈtiːn] quince (*a. su. m*); **'fif·teenth** [~θ] decimoquinto; **fifth** [fifθ] **1.** □ quinto; **2.** quinto *m*; quinta parte *f*; ♪ quinta *f*; **'fifth 'col·umn** quinta columna *f*; **'fifth 'col·um·nist** quintacolumnista *m/f*; **fif·ti·eth** ['-tiiθ] quincuagésimo; **'fif·ty** cincuenta; **'fif·ty-'fif·ty: go ~** ir a medias, pagar a escote.

fig [fig] (*green*) higo *m*; (*early*) breva *f*; **~-leaf** *fig.* hoja *f* de parra.

fight [fait] **1.** pelea *f*, combate *m*; lucha *f* (*for* por); combatividad *f*, brío *m*; riña *f*; *put up a good ~* dar buena cuenta de sí; *show ~* enseñar los dientes; **2.** [*irr.*] *v/t.* combatir; batirse con; luchar con(tra); *battle* dar; *bull* lidiar; *~ it out* decidirlo luchando; *~ off* rechazar; *v/i.* batirse, pelear; luchar (*against* con, contra; *for* por); *~ back* resistir; *~ing chance* posibilidad *f* de éxito; *~ing fit* en excelente salud; **'fight·er** combatiente *m/f*; luchador (-a *f*) *m*; ⚔ caza *m*; **'fight·ing** combate *m*; lucha *f*; pendencia *f*; *attr.* guerrero; *cock of pelea*.

fig·ment ['figmənt] ficción *f*, invención *f*.

fig·ur·a·tive ['figərətiv] □ *sense* figurado; figurativo.

fig·ure ['figə] **1.** figura *f*; tipo *m of body*; (*sketch etc.*) dibujo *m*, figura *f*; ♣ figura *f*; (*number*) cifra *f*; número *m*; ✝ precio *m*; (~ *of speech*) figura *f*, tropo *m*; *fig.* exageración *f*; **2.** *v/t.* figurar; representar; imaginar; calcular (*a.* ~ *up*); *~ out* calcular; resolver; descifrar; *v/i.* figurar (*as* como,

among entre); figurarse; '**~·head** ⚓ mascarón *m* (de proa); *fig.* figurante (*a f*) *m*; '**~ skat·ing** patinaje *m* de figura.

fig·u·rine ['figjuriːn] figurina *f*.

fil·a·ment ['filəmənt] *all senses:* filamento *m*.

fil·bert ['filbəːt] avellana *f*.

filch [filtʃ] sisar, ratear.

file¹ [fail] **1.** carpeta *f*; fichero *m*; archivo *m*; legajo *m*; (*row*) fila *f*, hilera *f*, *the ~s pl.* los archivos; **2.** *v/t.* archivar (*a.* ~ *away*); clasificar; registrar; *v/i.* ~ *past* desfilar; ~ *out* salir en fila; ~ *case* fichero *m*; ~ *clerk* fichador *m*; **filing cabinet** archivador *m*; **filing clerk** archivero *m*.

file² [~] ⊕ **1.** lima *f*; **2.** limar.

fill [fil] **1.** llenar(se) (*with* de); rellenar(se); *post* ocupar; *vacancy* cubrir; *sails* hinchar(se); *space* llenar (*or* ocupar) completamente; *tooth* empastar; *tyre* inflar; *details* añadir; *outline etc.* completar; ~ *out form* llenar; (*p.*) engordar; *fig.* completar; ~ *up* llenar; colmar; **2.** hartazgo *m*; *eat one's* ~ hartarse.

fill·ing ['filin] relleno *m*; ⊕ empaquetadura *f*; empaste *m of tooth*; *mot.* ~ **station** estación *f* de servicio.

film [film] **1.** película *f*; capa *f of dust*; *fig.* velo *m*; *phot. a. thea.* película *f*, film *m*; **2.** filmar; hacer una película de; rodar; '**~ star** estrella *f* (*or astro m*) de cine.

fil·ter ['filtə] **1.** filtro *m*; **2.** filtrar(se); ~ *in*, ~ *through* infiltrarse; *fig.* introducirse; '**~ pa·per** papel *m* de filtro; '**~ tip** embocadura *f* de filtro.

filth [filθ] inmundicia *f*, suciedad *f*, mugre *f*; **'filth·y** □ inmundo (*a. fig.*); sucio, mugriento.

fin [fin] *all senses:* aleta *f*.

fi·nal ['fainl] **1.** □ final, último; decisivo, definitivo, terminante; *~ly* finalmente, por último; **2.** *sport:* final *f*; *univ. ~s pl.* examen *m* final; **fi·na·le** [fiˈnɑːli] ♪ final *m*; **fi·nal·ist** ['fainəlist] finalista *m/f*.

fi·nance [fiˈnæns] **1.** finanzas *f/pl.*; fondos *m/pl.*; asuntos *m/pl.* financieros; **2.** financiar; **fi·nan·cial** [~ʃl] □ financiero; bancario; monetario; **fi·nan·cier** [~siə] financiero *m*.

find [faind] **1.** [*irr.*] encontrar, hallar; dar con; descubrir; ⚖ declarar, fallar; (*supply*) proveer; lograr obtener, lograr reunir; ~ *o.s. fig.* descubrir su verdadera vocación; *all found* todo incluido; ~ **out** averiguar; (llegar a) saber; F conocer el juego de, calar; ~ **out** *about* informarse sobre; 2. hallazgo *m*.

fine[1] [fain] 1. □ fino; bello, hermoso; escogido, primoroso; refinado; *p.* admirable; magnífico; *iro.* bueno, lindo; *be* ~ *(weather)* hacer buen tiempo; *that's* ~! ¡estupendo!; *have a* ~ *time* divertirse mucho; ~ *arts* f/pl.; ~ *print* letra *f* menuda, tipo *m* menudo; 2. *adv.* F muy bien; *feel* ~ estar de primera; 3. *meteor.* buen tiempo *m*.

fine[2] [~] 🏛 1. multa *f*; *in* ~ en resumen; 2. multar.

fine-drawn ['fain'drɔːn] fino, sutil.

fine·ness ['fainnis] fineza *f* etc. (v. fine[1]); ley *f* of metals.

fi·nesse [fi'nes] discriminación *f* sutil; artificio *m*, sutileza *f*; tino *m*; *cards*: impase *m*.

fine-toothed comb ['faintuːθd'koum] lendrera *f*, peine *m* de púas finas; *go over with a* ~ escudriñar minuciosamente.

fin·ger ['fiŋɡə] 1. dedo *m*; *little* ~ dedo *m* meñique; *middle* ~ dedo *m* del corazón; *ring* ~ dedo *m* anular; *have a* ~ *in the pie* meter su cucharada; *put one's* ~ *on* señalar acertadamente; *slip through one's* ~s escaparse de entre los dedos de uno; *twist s.o. round one's little* ~ hacer con uno lo que le da la gana; 2. manosear; ♪ pulsar; ♪ teclear *(v/i.)*; ~ **board** teclado *m*; ~ **bowl** lavadedos *m*, lavafrutas *m*; **'fin·gered** con ... dedos; **'fin·ger·ing** ♪ digitación *f*.

fin·ger...: '~**nail** uña *f*; '~**nail 'pol·ish** esmalte *m* para las uñas; '~**print** 1. huella *f* dactilar; 2. tomar las huellas dactilares de; '~**tip** punta *f* del dedo; *have at one's* ~s saber al dedillo.

fin·ish ['finiʃ] 1. *v/t.* acabar *(a.* ⊕, *a.* ~ *up)*; terminar; concluir; consumar; ~ *off* completar; rematar; acabar con; F *p.* despachar; ~*ing touch* última mano *f*, aderezo *m* final; 2. *v/i.* acabar (*by* por); *ger. de inf.)*; 2. fin *m*, final *m*; conclusión *f*; remate *m*; *sport:* poste *m* de llegada; ⊕ acabado *m*.

fi·nite ['fainait] □ finito *(a. gr.)*.

fir [fəː] abeto *m*; *Scotch* ~ pino *m*; '~**cone** piña *f* (de abeto).

fire ['faiə] 1. fuego *m*; *(damaging)* incendio *m*; *(warming)* fuego *m*, lumbre *f*; *fig.* ardor *m*; viveza *f*; *be on* ~ estar ardiendo; *catch* ~ encenderse;

open ~ abrir fuego; *play with* ~ *fig.* jugar con fuego; *set on* ~, *set* ~ *to* pegar fuego a; 2. *v/t.* encender, incendiar, quemar; *pottery etc.* cocer; *gun, shot* disparar; F *p.* despedir; *fig.* excitar, enardecer; ~ *off* descargar; *v/i.* encenderse; ✕ hacer fuego; *mot.* dar explosiones; ~ *at*, ~ *(up)on* hacer fuego sobre, tirar a; ~ *away!* ¡adelante!; 3. ¡fuego!; '~**a·larm** alarma *f* de incendios; '~**arm** arma *f* de fuego; '~**brand** *fig.* partidario *m* violento; '~**com·pa·ny** cuerpo *m* de bomberos; compañía *f* de seguros; '~**crack·er** triquitraque *m*; '~**damp** ⚒ grisú *m*; '~ **de·part·ment** servicio *m* de bomberos; '~**dog** morillo *m*; '~ **drill** ejercicio *m* para caso de incendio; '~ **en·gine** bomba *f* de incendios; '~ **es·cape** escalera *f* de incendios; '~ **ex·tin·guish·er** extintor *m*; '~**fly** luciérnaga *f*; '~**house** cuartel *m* de bomberos, estación *f* de incendios; '~ **hy·drant** boca *f* de incendio; '~ **in·sur·ance** seguro *m* de incendios; '~ **i·rons** *pl.* útiles *m/pl.* de chimenea; '~**less** '~**cook·er** cocinilla *f* sin fuego; '~**man** bombero *m*; 🚂 fogonero *m*; '~**place** chimenea *f*; hogar *m*; '~**plug** boca *f* de agua; '~**proof** incombustible, a prueba de fuego; '~**sale** venta *f* de mercancías averiadas en un incendio; '~ **screen** pantalla *f* de chimenea; '~ **ship** brulote *m*; '~**side** 1. hogar *m*; 2. familiar, hogareño, doméstico; '~ **sta·tion** parque *m* de bomberos; '~**trap** edificio *m* sin medios adecuados de escape en caso de incendio; '~ **wall** cortafuego *m*; '~ **war·den** vigía *m* de incendios; '~ **wa·ter** aguardiente *m*; '~**wood** leña *f*; '~**works** fuegos *m/pl.* artificiales; *fig.* explosión *f* de cólera *etc.*

fir·ing ['faiəriŋ] *(fuel)* combustible *m*; *(act)* incendio *m*; cocción *f* of *pottery etc.*; *mot.* encendido *m*; ✕ disparo *m*; tiroteo *m*; ~ *squad* pelotón *m* de ejecución.

firm[1] [fəːm] 1. □ firme; 2. firma *f*, casa *f* de comercio, empresa *f*.

fir·ma·ment ['fəːməmənt] firmamento *m*.

firm·ness ['fəːmnis] firmeza *f*.

first [fəːst] 1. *adj.* primero; original, primitivo; 2. *adv.* primero; en primer lugar; ~ *of all*, ~ *and foremost* ante todo; *at* ~ al principio; 3. primero (*a f) m*; ✝ ~s *pl.* artículos *m/pl.* de primera calidad; '~ **aid** primera curación f, primeros auxilios m/pl.; ~ **kit** botiquín m; ~ **post or station** puesto m de socorro; '~**born** primogénito (a f, a) m; '~**class** de primera (clase); '~ **e'di·tion** edición f príncipe; '~ **fruits** pl. primicias f/pl.; '~**hand** de primera mano; **'first·ly** en primer lugar; **first mate** piloto m; **first name** nombre m de pila; **first night** estreno m; **'first-rate** excelente, de primera.

fis·cal ['fiskl] fiscal; monetario.

fish [fiʃ] 1. pez m; (as food) pescado m; F tipo m, tío m; **have other ~ to** fry tener cosas más importantes que hacer; 2. v/t. pescar; river pescar; F ~ **out** sacar; v/i. pescar; ~ **for** tratar de pescar; F compliment etc. andar a la pesca de; '~**bone** raspa f, espina f (de pez); '~**bowl** pecera f.

fish·er·man ['fiʃəmən] pescador m.

fish·hook ['fiʃhuk] anzuelo m.

fish·ing ['fiʃiŋ] pesca f; '~ **boat** barca f pesquera; '~ **grounds** pl. pesquera f; '~ **reel** carrete m; '~ **rod** caña f (de pescar); '~ **tack·le** aparejo m de pescar.

fish...: '~ **line** sedal m; '~ **mar·ket** pescadería f; '~**plate** 🚂 elisa f; '~**pond** piscina f; '~ **sto·ry** F andaluzada f, patraña f; **tell ~ stories** mentir por la barba; '~**tail** 1. 🚗 coleadura f; 2. 🚗 v/i. colear; '~**wife** pescadera f; **foul-mouthed woman** verdulera f; '~**worm** lombriz f de tierra (cebo para pescar); **'fish·y** eye vidrioso; F dudoso, inverosímil; it's ~ me huele a camelo.

fis·sion ['fiʃn] phys. fisión f; biol. escisión f; **'fis·sion·a·ble** fisionable; **fis·sure** ['fiʃə] 1. grieta f, hendedura f; 2. agrietar(se), hender(se).

fist [fist] puño m; F escritura f; ~**ful** puñado m; '~ **fight** pelea f con los puños; **fist·i·cuffs** ['~ikʌfs] pl. pelea f a puñetazos.

fit[1] [fit] 1. □ apto, a propósito; adecuado, conveniente, apropiado; listo (for para); hábil (for a post para); digno (for a king de); 🚑 sano, bien de salud; ~ **to eat** bueno de comer; see ~ juzgar conveniente (to inf.); survival of the ~**test** supervivencia f de los mejor dotados; 2. v/t. ajustar, acomodar (to a); encajar (a. ⊕); adaptar (for para); clothes probar (a.); p. (clothes) sentar a, venir bien a; description cuadrar con; facts estar de acuerdo con; ⊕ ~ in(to) encajar en; ~ out, ~ up equipar (with con); ⚓ armar; v/i. ajustar(se); (clothes) entallar, encajar in place; (facts) estar de acuerdo; ~ in caber; ⊕ encajarse en; F fig. acomodarse; ~ in with cuadrar con, concordar con; (p.) llevarse bien con; 3. ajuste m, corte m; ⊕ encaje m; it's a good ~ le sienta bien.

fit[2] [~] acceso m, ataque m; arranque m of anger; by ~s and starts a saltos, a rachas.

fit·ful ['fitful] □ espasmódico, caprichoso; **'fit·ness** aptitud f; conveniencia f; 🚑 (buena) salud f; **'fit·ting** 1. □ conveniente, apropiado; it is not ~ that no está bien que subj.; 2. prueba f of dress; ajuste m; (size) medida f.

five [faiv] cinco (a. su. m).

fix [fiks] 1. fijar (a. phot.), asegurar; attention fijar (on en); bayonet calar; blame colgar (on a); date fijar, señalar (a. ~ on); eyes clavar (on en); price determinar, decidir; (establish) precisar; sl. pagar en la misma moneda; F = ~ up arreglar; componer; decidir, organizar; F ~ (up)on escoger, elegir; F ~ up with arreglarlo con; p. proveer de; F 2. aprieto m, apuro m; sl. (adv. **fix·ed·ly** ['~idli]) all senses: fijo; **fix·ture** ['~tʃə] cosa f fija; instalación f fija; sport: (fecha f de un) partido m; fig. (p.) ostra f; lighting ~s pl. guarniciones f/pl. de alumbrado.

fizz [fiz] 1. sisear; 2. siseo m; F gaseosa f; **'fiz·zle** 1. sisear débilmente; F ~ **out** (candle) apagarse; fig. no dar resultado, fracasar; 2. siseo m débil; F fracaso m.

flab·ber·gast ['flæbəgɑːst] pasmar.

flab·by ['flæbi] □ flojo; blanducho.

flag[1] [flæg] 1. bandera f, pabellón m; (small) banderín m; 2. hacer señales con bandera (a).

flag[2] [~] △ 1. losa f; 2. enlosar.

flag[3] [~] ♀ lirio m.

flag[4] [~] flaquear, decaer; (conversation etc.) languidecer; (enthusiasm etc.) aflojar, enfriarse.

flag...: '~**pole** asta f de bandera.

fla·grant ['fleigrənt] □ notorio, escandaloso.

flag...: '~**ship** capitana f; '~**staff** asta f de bandera; '~**stone** losa f.

flail [fleil] 1. 🌾 mayal m; 2. v/t. fig. golpear, azotar; v/i.: ~ **about** debatirse.

flair [fleə] instinto m, aptitud f especial (for para).

flake [fleik] **1.** escama *f*; hojuela *f*; copo *m* of snow; **2.** *v/t.* separar en escamas; desprenderse en escamas; **'flak·y** escamoso; desmenuzable.

flam·boy·ant [flæm'bɔiənt] □ extravagante (*a.* ⚘).

flame [fleim] **1.** llama *f*; fuego *m*; co. novio (a *f*) *m*; **2.** llamear; brillar; *fig.* estallar, encenderse (*a.* ~ up); ~ up inflamarse; '~·throw·er lanzallamas *m*.

flank [flæŋk] **1.** costado *m*; ijada *f* of animal; ✕ flanco *m*; **2.** flanquear.

flan·nel ['flænl] franela *f*; (face- ~ up) paño *m*; ~s *pl.* pantalones *m/pl.* de franela; ropa *f* interior de lana.

flap [flæp] **1.** fald(ill)a *f* on dress; cartera *f* of pocket; hoja *f* plegadiza of table; solapa *f* of envelope; aletazo *m* of wing; *sl.* lío *m*; estado *m* nervioso; **2.** *v/t.* sacudir; agitar; *v/i.* aletear; *sl.* ponerse nervioso.

flare [flɛə] **1.** *v/i.* resplandecer, llamear, destellar; ~ up encenderse; *fig.* (*p.*) encolerizarse; estallar; *v/t.* skirt nesgar; **2.** llamarada *f*, destello *m*; (signal) cohete *m* de señales; (skirt) nesga *f*; '~·up llamarada *f*; *fig.* arranque *m* of anger; manifestación *f* súbita, estallido *m* of trouble.

flash [flæʃ] **1.** relámpago *m* of lightning (*a. fig.*); destello *m*, ráfaga *f* of light; fogonazo *m* of gun; rayo *m* of hope etc.; (moment) instante *m*; phot. = ~·light; flash *m*, noticia *f* de última hora, mensaje *m* urgente; in a ~, en un instante; ~ of wit rasgo *m* de ingenio; **2.** *v/i.* relampaguear; destellar; ~ past pasar como un rayo; *v/t.* light despedir; look dirigir rápidamente; message transmitir rápidamente; F hacer ostentación de (*a.* ~ about); '~·back film: escena *f* retrospectiva; '~·bulb bombilla *f* fusible (or de flash); '~·light phot. flash *m*, relámpago *m*; held in hand linterna *f* eléctrica, lámpara *f* eléctrica de bolsillo; of lighthouse luz *f* intermitente, fanal *m* de destellos; '**flash·light 'bat·ter·y** pila *f* de linterna; '**flash·light** bombilla *f* de linterna; '**flash·y** chillón, llamativo.

flask [flɑːsk] frasco *m*; redoma *f*; ⚗ matraz *m*.

flat [flæt] **1.** □ llano (smooth) liso; (even) igual; horizontal; (stretched out) tendido; denial terminante; drink muerto; feeling of abatimien-

to; *p.* alicaído; taste insípido; tone monótono; tyre desinflado; voice desafinado; ♪ bemol; ↑ flojo; **2.** adv.: sing ~ desafinar; turn down ~ rechazar de plano; **3.** piso *m*; palma *f* of hand; ♪ bemol *m*; ⚓ banco *m*; pantano *m*; mot. *sl.* pinchazo *m*; '~·foot *sl.* polizonte *m*; '~·i·ron plancha *f*; '**flat·ness** llanura *f*; *fig.* insipidez *f*; '**flat·ten** allanar; aplanar (-se); ✕ ~ out enderezarse.

flat·ter ['flætə] adular, lisonjear, (clothes, picture) favorecer; '**flat·ter·y** adulación *f*, lisonja *f*.

flaunt [flɔːnt] *v/t.* ostentar, lucir; *v/i.* pavonearse.

fla·vor ['fleivə] **1.** sabor *m*; gusto *m*, condimento *m* (*a.* ~·ing); **2.** sazonar, condimentar; *fig.* dar un sabor característico a.

flaw [flɔː] tacha *f*; imperfección *f*; desperfecto *m*; defecto *m* (*a.* ⚙ *a.* ⊕); (crack) grieta *f*; '**flaw·less** □ intachable, perfecto.

flax [flæks] lino *m*; '**fla·xen** de lino; hair muy rubio.

flay [flei] desollar; *fig.* azotar.

flea [fliː] pulga *f*.

fled [fled] pret. a. p.p. of flee.

fledge [fledʒ] emplumar; ~d plumado; full-~d *fig.* hecho y derecho.

flee [fliː] [irr.] huir (from de).

fleece [fliːs] **1.** vellón *m*; lana *f*; **2.** esquilar; F pelar, mondar.

fleet [fliːt] **1.** □ poet. veloz, ligero; **2.** flota *f*; armada *f*; escuadra *f* of cars; '**fleet·ing** □ fugaz, efímero, pasajero.

flesh [fleʃ] carne *f* (*a. fig.*); in the ~ en persona; of ~ and blood de carne y hueso; '**flesh·ly** carnal, sensual; '**fleshwound** herida *f* superficial.

flew [fluː] pret. of fly 2.

flex [fleks] **1.** doblar(se); ⚡ hilo *m*, cordón *m* (de la luz); **flex·i·bil·i·ty** [~'biliti] flexibilidad *f* (*a. fig.*); '**flex·i·ble** □ flexible (*a. fig.*).

flick [flik] **1.** dar un capirotazo a; rozar levemente; whip chasquear; ~ away quitar etc. rápidamente; **2.** capirotazo *m* of finger; chasquido *m* of whip; golpe *m* rápido y ligero.

flick·er ['flikə] **1.** (light) parpadear; brillar con luz mortecina; (flame) vacilar; (movement) oscilar, vibrar; *fig.* fluctuar; **2.** parpadeo *m*; luz *f* mortecina.

flight [flait] ✕ vuelo *m*; (distance) recorrido *m*; (unit) escuadrilla *f*; ✕

trayectoria f of bullet etc.; (flock of birds) bandada f; (escape) huida f, fuga f; escalera f, tramo m of steps; ~ of fancy sueño ~, ilusión f; put to ~ ahuyentar; take ~ alzar el vuelo; take to ~ ponerse en fuga; '~ deck ⚓ cubierta f de vuelo.

flim·flam ['flimflæm] 1. F engaño m, trampa f; tontería f; 2. F engañar, trampear.

flim·sy ['flimzi] 1. □ débil, endeble; fig. baladí, frívolo; cloth muy delgado; 2. papel m muy delgado.

flinch [flintʃ] acobardarse, retroceder (from ante); desistir de miedo (from de); without ~ing sin vacilar.

fling [fliŋ] 1. baile m escocés; have a ~ at intentar; 2. [irr.] v/i. arrojarse; ~ out salir muy enfadado; v/t. arrojar, tirar (a. ~ away); echar (a. ~ out); ~ o.s. arrojarse; ~ down echar al suelo; ~ open abrir de golpe.

flint [flint] pedernal m; piedra f of lighter; '**flint·y** fig. empedernido.

flip [flip] 1. capirotazo m; ✗ sl. vuelo m; 2. coin etc. echar de un capirotazo; mover de un tirón.

flip·pant ['flipənt] □ ligero, frívolo.

flip·per ['flipə] aleta f (a. sl.).

flirt [flə:t] 1. coqueta f; mariposón m; 2. coquetear (with con), flirtear, mariposear.

flit [flit] revolotear; volar con vuelo cortado; pasar rápidamente.

float [flout] 1. boya f, corcho m; balsa f; carroza f in procession; 2. v/t. poner a flote; ⊕ emitir; company lanzar; v/i. flotar; (bather) hacer la plancha.

flock¹ [flɔk] 1. rebaño m; bandada f of birds; eccl. grey f; gentío m of people; 2. congregarse, reunirse; come ~ing venir en masa.

flock² [~] (wool) borra f.

floe [flou] témpano m de hielo.

flog [flɔg] azotar.

flood [flʌd] 1. inundación f; diluvio m; avenida f in river; fig. torrente m, plétora f; (a. ~ tide) pleamar f; 2. v/t. inundar (with de; a. fig.), anegar; v/i. desbordar; ~ in etc. entrar a raudales; '~-gate compuerta f, esclusa f; '~-light 1. foco m; 2. iluminar con foco(s).

floor [flɔ:] 1. suelo m; (storey) piso m; fondo m of sea; parl. hemiciclo m; first ~ primer piso m, piso m principal; ground ~ piso m bajo, planta f baja; have the ~ tener la palabra; ~ show atracciones f/pl. (en la pista de

baile); 2. solar, entarimar; p. derribar; fig. dejar sin réplica posible, confundir; '**floor·ing** entarimado m, piso m, suelo m; '~ **lamp** lámpara f de pie; '~ **mop** fregasuelos m, estropajo m; '~ **plan** planta f; '**floor-walk·er** superintendente m/f de división; '~ **wax** cera f de pisos.

flop [flɔp] 1. dejarse caer pesadamente; sl. fracasar; thea. venirse al foso; 2. thea. caída f; sl. fracaso m; sl. ~-house posada f de baja categoría; '**flop·py** flojo, colgante.

flo·ra ['flɔ:rə] flora f.

flo·ral ['flɔ:rəl] floral; de flores.

flo·res·cence [flɔ:'resns] florescencia f.

flor·id ['flɔrid] □ florido; face encarnado, subido de color.

flo·rist ['flɔrist] florista m/f; ~'s floristería f.

flo·til·la [flə'tilə] flotilla f.

floun·der¹ ['flaundə] ichth. platija f.

floun·der² [~] revolcarse, forcejear (a. ~ about).

flour ['flauə] harina f; ~ mill molino m de harina.

flour·ish ['flʌriʃ] 1. rúbrica f, rasgo m in writing; ♪ floreo m; ♪ toque m de trompeta; ademán m of hand; with a ~ triunfalmente; 2. v/i. florecer; prosperar; crecer rápidamente; v/t. weapon blandir; stick menear; fig. hacer alarde de, mostrar orgullosamente; '**flour·ish·ing** □ floreciente; (healthy) como un reloj.

flout [flaut] mofarse de, burlarse de.

flow [flou] 1. corriente f; flujo m; (amount) caudal m; curso m; torrente m of words etc.; 2. fluir; correr; (tide) subir.

flow·er ['flauə] 1. flor f; fig. flor f (y nata); in ~ en flor; 2. florecer; '~ **bed** cuadro m, macizo m; '~ **girl** florera f; at a wedding damita f de honor; '~ **pot** tiesto m, maceta f; '~ **shop** floristería f; '~ **show** exposición f de flores; '**flow·er·y** florido, cubierto de flores; fig. florido.

flown [floun] p.p. of fly 2.

flu [flu:] F = influenza gripe f.

fluc·tu·ate ['flʌktjueit] fluctuar.

flue [flu:] humero m, (cañón m de) chimenea f.

flu·en·cy ['flu:ənsi] fluidez f, facilidad f; dominio m (in language de); '**flu·ent** □ flúido, fácil; corriente.

fluff·y ['flʌfi] velloso; que tiene mucha pelusa.

fluid

flu·id ['fluːid] flúido *adj. a. su. m* (*a. ⚡*); líquido *m*.

fluke [fluːk] *zo.* trematodo *m*; *ichth.* platija *f*; ⚓ uña *f*, F chiripa *f*.

flung [flʌŋ] *pret. a. p.p. of* fling 2.

flunk [flʌŋk] F *v/t. p.* reprobar, dar calabazas a; *exam* perder; *v/i.* salir mal.

flu·o·res·cence [fluə'resns] fluorescencia *f*; **flu·o'res·cent** fluorescente.

flur·ry ['flʌri] **1.** agitación *f*; conmoción *f*; nevisca *f*, ráfaga *f of snow*; **2.** agitar, hacer nervioso.

flush [flʌʃ] **1.** ⊕ nivelado; igual, parejo; F adinerado; **2.** rubor *m*, sonrojo *m*; abundancia *f*; *fig.* vigor *m*, plenitud *f*; *cards:* flux *m*; **3.** *v/t.* limpiar con chorro de agua (*a. ~ out*); *game* levantar; *v/i.* ruborizarse, sonrojarse; '**~ tank** depósito *m* de limpia; '**~ toi·let** inodoro *m* con chorro de agua.

flus·ter ['flʌstə] **1.** confusión *f*, aturdimiento *m*; **2.** confundir, aturdir.

flute [fluːt] **1.** ♪ flauta *f*; △ estría *f*; **2.** estriar, acanalar.

flut·ter ['flʌtə] **1.** revoloteo *m of wings*; palpitación *f of heart*; *fig.* agitación *f*; emoción *f*; *sl.* apuesta *f*; **2.** *v/t.* agitar, menear; *v/i.* (*bird etc.*) revolotear; (*heart*) palpitar; (*flag*) ondear; agitarse.

flux [flʌks] *fig.* flujo *m*; ⚗ fundente *m*; (*state*) continua mudanza *f*.

fly [flai] **1.** mosca *f*; (*trouser-*) bragueta *f*; *thea.* flies *pl.* bambalinas *f/pl.*; die like flies morir como chinches; **2.** [*irr.*] *v/i.* volar; (*rush*) precipitarse; (*escape*) evadirse, huir; *I must ~* tengo que darme prisa; *~ at* lanzarse sobre; *~ away* irse volando; *~ off* (*part*) desprenderse; (*bird*) alejarse volando; *~ open* abrirse de repente; *v/t.* hacer volar; ✈ dirigir; transportar en avión; *ocean etc.* atravesar (en avión); *distance* recorrer (en avión); *flag* llevar, tener izado; *danger* huir (de); *country* abandonar; *let ~* descargar, proferir (*at* contra); **3.** F despabilado, avispado.

fly·er ['flaiə] aviador *m*; tren *m etc.* rápido; *sl.* empresa *f* arriesgada.

fly·ing ['flaiiŋ] **1.** vuelo *m*; aviación *f*; **2.** *attr.* de vuelo; de aviación; *adj.* volante, volador; rápido, veloz; *visit* muy breve; *~ colors pl.* gran éxito *m*; *~ fish* pez *m* volador; *~ saucer* platillo *m* volante; *~ start* salida *f* lanzada.

fly...: '**~·leaf** hoja *f* de guarda; '**~·paper** papel *m* matamoscas; '**~·speck** macha *f* de mosca; '**~·swat·ter** matamoscas *m*; '**~·trap** atrapamoscas *m*; '**~·wheel** volante *m* (*de motor*).

foam [foum] **1.** espuma *f*; **~ rubber** espuma *f* de látex (*or* de caucho); **2.** espumar; echar espuma; *~ at the mouth* espumajear; '**foam·y** espum(aj)oso.

fo·cal ['foukl] focal; *phot.* **~ distance** distancia *f* focal; *phot.* **~ plane** plano *m* focal; **~ point** punto *m* focal.

fo·cus ['foukəs] **1.** foco *m* (*a. fig.*); *in ~* enfocado; *out of ~* desenfocado; **2.** enfocar; *attention* fijar, concentrar (*on* en).

fod·der ['fɔdə] forraje *m*.

foe [fou] *lit.* enemigo *m*.

foe·tus ['fiːtəs] feto *m*.

fog [fɔg] **1.** niebla *f* (*a. fig.*); *fig.* confusión *f*; *phot.* velo *m*; **2.** *fig.* oscurecer; *issue* entenebrecer; *phot.* velar(se).

fog·gy ['fɔgi] brumoso, nebuloso (*a. fig.*); *phot.* velado; *it is ~* hay niebla. '**fog·horn** sirena *f* (*de niebla*).

foi·ble ['fɔibl] flaco *m*.

foil¹ [fɔil] hojuela *f* (*de metal*); *fig.* contraste *m*.

foil² [~] **1.** frustrar; *attempt* desbaratar; **2.** *fenc.* florete *m*.

foist [fɔist]: *~ on* encajar a, lograr con engaño que ... acepte; imputar a.

fold¹ [fould] ♪ **1.** redil *m*, aprisco *m*; *eccl.* rebaño *m*; **2.** apriscar.

fold² [~] **1.** doblez *m*, pliegue *m* (*a. geol.*); arruga *f*; **2.** plegar(se), doblar(se); envolver (*in* en); *wings* recoger; *~ one's arms* cruzar los brazos; *~ up* doblar(se); F ✝ quebrar; entrar en liquidación.

fold·ing ['fouldiŋ] plegadizo; plegable; '**~ bed** *or* **cot** catre *m* de tijera; '**~ chair** silla *f* de tijera; '**~ door** puerta *f* plegadiza; '**~ rule** metro *m* plegadizo.

fo·li·age ['fouliidʒ] follaje *m*.

fo·li·o ['fouliou] folio *m*; libro *m* en folio.

folk [fouk] *pl.* gente *f*; nación *f*; raza *f*; tribu *f*; (*~s pl.*) familia *f*.

folk·lore ['fouklɔ:] folklore *m*; '**folk song** canción *f* popular.

fol·low ['fɔlou] *v/t.* seguir; seguir la pista a; *news* interesarse en; *profession* ejercer; *p.* comprender; *argu-*

ment seguir el hilo de; ~ *through*, ~ *up* llevar hasta el fin; proseguir; *v. suit*; *v/i.* seguirse; resultar; *as* ~*s* como sigue; *it* ~*s that* síguese que; **'fol·low·er** partidario (a *f*) *m*; secuaz *m*; imitador (-a *f*) *m*; discípulo *m*; **'fol·low·ing 1.** partidarios *m/pl.*; secuaces *m/pl.*; séquito *m*; **2.** siguiente; *the* ~ lo siguiente; ~ *wind* viento *m* en popa.

fol·ly ['fɔli] locura *f*, desatino *m*.

fo·ment [fou'ment] fomentar (*a.* ⚓); provocar; nutrir.

fond [fɔnd] □ cariñoso, afectuoso; *be* ~ *of* ser aficionado a, ser amigo de.

fon·dle ['fɔndl] acariciar.

fond·ness ['fɔndnis] cariño *m*; afición *f* (*for a*).

font [fɔnt] pila *f*.

food [fuːd] comida *f*; alimento *m*, alimentación *f*; provisiones *f/pl.*; (*dish*) manjar *m*; (*material*) comestible *m*; *fig.* alimento *m*, pábulo *m*; *give* ~ *for thought* dar materia en que pensar; **'~·poi·son·ing** botulismo *m*; **'~·stuffs** *pl.* comestibles *m/pl.*, artículos *m/pl.* alimenticios.

fool [fuːl] **1.** tonto (a *f*) *m*, necio (a *f*) *m*; (*jester*) bufón *m*; *make a* ~ *of* poner en ridículo; ~*'s errand* empresa *f* descabellada; misión *f* inútil; **2.** F tonto; **3.** *v/t.* engañar, embaucar; confundir; F ~ *away* malgastar; *v/i.* chancear; tontear; (*a.* ~ *about*) juguetear (*with* con), divertirse (*with* con); F no ~*ing* en serio; F ~ *around* malgastar el tiempo neciamente.

fool·hard·y ['fuːlhɑːdi] □ temerario; **'fool·ish** □ tonto, necio; *remark etc.* disparatado; indiscreto; ridículo; **'fool·proof** ⊕ a prueba de mal trato; F infalible.

foot [fut] **1.** (*pl.* feet) pie *m*; pata *f* of *animal etc.*; ⚔ infantería *f*; *on* ~ a pie; *fig.* en marcha; *put one's* ~ *down* adoptar una actitud firme; F *mot.* acelerar; F *put one's* ~ *in it* meter la pata; *set on* ~ promover, iniciar; **2.:** ~ *the bill* pagar la cuenta; *fig.* pagar el pato; ~ *it* ir andando; **'~-and-mouth (dis·ease)** fiebre *f* aftosa; **'~·ball** fútbol *m*; (*ball*) balón *m*; ~ *player* futbolista *m*; ~ *pool* quiniela *f/pl.*; **'~ brake** pedal *m* del freno; freno *m* de pie; **'~·bridge** puente *m* para peatones; **'foot·ed** de ... pies; **'foot·fall** pisada *f*, paso *m*; **'foot·hills** *pl.* colinas *f/pl.* al pie de una sierra; estribaciones *f/pl.*; **'foot·hold**

(asidero *m* para el) pie *m*, pie *m* firme; **foot·ing** ['futiŋ] pie *m*; posición *f* estable(cida); condición *f*.

foot...: **'~·lights** *pl.* candilejas *f/pl.*; **'~·loose** libre; andariego; **'~·man** lacayo *m*; **'~·note** nota *f*; apostilla *f*; **'~·print** huella *f*; **'~·rest** apoyapié *m*; **'~·sore** con los pies cansados; **'~·step** paso *m*; **'~·stool** escabel *m*; **'~·wear** calzado *m*.

for [fɔː, fə, fo, f] **1.** *prp.* para; por; a causa de; en honor de; en lugar de; ~ *all that* con todo; ~ 3 *days (past)* (durante) 3 días; *(present a. future)* por 3 días; *as* ~ en cuanto a; *as* ~ *me* por mi parte; *but* ~ a no ser por; *time* ~ *dinner* hora *f* de comer; *were it not* ~ *that* si no fuera por esto; **2.** *cj.* pues, ya que.

for·age ['fɔridʒ] **1.** forraje *m*; **2.** forrajear; dar forraje a; *fig.* buscar (*for acc.*).

for·ay ['fɔrei] correría *f*, incursión *f*.

for·bade [fə'beid] *pret. of* forbid.

for·bear [fɔː'bɛə] [*irr.*] abstenerse (*from* de); contenerse.

for·bid [fə'bid] [*irr.*] prohibir (*to inf.*; *a p. a th.* algo a alguien); *God* ~! ¡no lo permita Dios!; **for·bid·den** *p.p. of* forbid; **for·bid·ding** □ formidable; repugnante.

for·bore, for·borne [fɔː'bɔː(n)] *pret. a. p.p. of* forbear.

force [fɔːs] **1.** fuerza *f*; personal *m*; ⚔ cuerpo *m*; ⚔ ~*s pl.* fuerzas *f/pl.* (armadas); *by* ~ *of* a fuerza de; *in* ~ en gran número; *in* ~ (*law*) vigente, en vigor; **2.** *mst* forzar (*to a inf.*; *upon a p.* a uno a aceptar); obligar; violentar; 🌶 hacer madurar temprano; ✈ obligar a aterrizar; ~ *in* introducir por fuerza; ~ *open* forzar; **'forced** (*adv. a.* p.p.p. *of* forced); **'forc·ed·ly** ['~idli] *mst* forzado; *smile* que no le sale a uno; **'forced 'land·ing** aterrizaje *m* forzado *or* forzoso; **'forced 'march** marcha *f* forzada; **'force·ful** ['~ful] □ vigoroso, poderoso.

for·ceps ['fɔːseps] fórceps *m*; tenacillas *f/pl.*

ford [fɔːd] **1.** vado *m*; **2.** vadear.

fore [fɔː] **1.** *adv.:* *to the* ~ en la delantera; destacado; *come to the* ~ empezar a destacar; ♣ ~ *and aft* de (*etc.*) popa a proa; **2.** *adj.* anterior, delantero; ♣ de proa; **'~·arm** antebrazo *m*; **'~·bod·ing** presagio *m*, presentimiento *m*; **'~·cast 1.** pronóstico *m*; **2.** [*irr.* (*cast*)] pronosticar, prever;

foreclose

416

~'close excluir; ⚖ extinguir el derecho de redimir; **'~fa·thers** pl. antepasados m/pl.; **'~fin·ger** dedo m índice; **'~foot** pata f delantera; **'~front** vanguardia f; sitio m de actividad más intensa; **~'go** [irr. (go)] renunciar, privarse de; **~'go·ing** anterior, precedente; **'~ground** primer plano m; **~head** ['fɒrid] frente f.

for·eign ['fɒrin] extranjero; trade etc. exterior; extraño, ajeno (to a); **~ exchange** divisas f/pl. (currency); cambio m extranjero; **~ trade** comercio m exterior; **'for·eign·er** extranjero (a f) m.

fore...: **'~leg** pata f delantera; **'~man** capataz m; maestro m de obras; ⚖ presidente m del jurado; **'~mast** trinquete m; **'~most** delantero; primero; principal; **'~noon** mañana f.

fo·ren·sic ['fɒrensik] forense.

fore...: **'~run·ner** precursor (-a f) m; **~sail** ['~seil, ⚓ '~sl] trinquete m; **~'see** [irr. (see)] prever; **~'see·a·ble** ☐ previsible; **~'shad·ow** prefigurar; prever, anunciar; **~'shorten** escorzar; **'~sight** previsión f; **'~skin** prepucio m.

for·est ['fɒrist] bosque m; attr. forestal, del bosque.

fore·stall [fɔː'stɔːl] th. prevenir; p. anticipar (e impedir).

for·est·er ['fɒristə] silvicultor m; ingeniero m forestal (or de montes); (keeper) guardabosques m; **'for·est·ry** silvicultura f.

fore...: **'~taste** anticipo m; **'~tell** [irr. (tell)] predecir, pronosticar; presagiar; **'~thought** providencia f, prevención f; b.s. premeditación f; **~'warn** prevenir; **be ~ed** precaverse; **'~word** prefacio m.

for·feit ['fɔːfit] **1.** perdido; **2.** (fine) multa f; ✝ pena f; prenda f in game; **~s** pl. juego m de prendas; **3.** perder (el derecho a); **for·fei·ture** ['~tʃə] pérdida f.

for·gath·er [fɔː'gæðə] reunirse.

for·gave [fə'geiv] pret. of forgive.

forge¹ [fɔːdʒ] **1.** (fire) fragua f; (blacksmith's) herrería f; (factory) fundición f; **2.** metal forjar, fraguar; money etc. falsificar, contrahacer; **'forg·er** falsificador m; **'for·ger·y** falsificación f.

forge² [~]: **~ ahead** avanzar constantemente; adelantarse muchísimo a todos.

for·get [fə'get] [irr.] v/t. olvidar(se de) (to inf.); **~ o.s.** propasarse; F **~ it!** ¡no se preocupe!; v/i. olvidarse; **for·get·ful** [~ful] ☐ olvidadizo; descuidado; **for·get·ful·ness** olvido m; descuido m; **for·get-me-not** no-meolvides f.

for·give [fə'giv] [irr.] perdonar (acc.; a p. [for] a th. algo a uno); **for·give·n** p.p. of forgive; **for·give·ness** perdón m; misericordia f; **for·giv·ing** ☐ perdonador; magnánimo.

for·go [fɔː'gou] [irr. (go)] renunciar, privarse de.

for·got [fə'gɒt], **for·got·ten** [~n] pret. a. p.p. of forget.

fork [fɔːk] **1.** tenedor m; ⚒ horca f; horquilla f (a. ⊕); bifurcación f in road; horcajo m in river; horcadura f in tree; anat. horcajadura f, entrepierna f; **2.** v/i. (road) bifurcarse; v/t. cultivar (cavar, hacinar etc.) con horquilla; F **~ out** desembolsar de mala gana; F **~ over** entregar; **'forked** ahorquillado; road bifurcado; lightning en zigzag.

for·lorn [fə'lɔːn] abandonado, desamparado; appearance triste, de abandono.

form [fɔːm] **1.** forma f; figura f; (condition) estado m; (formality) formalidad f; (seat) banco m; school: clase f; (document) hoja f, formulario m; **be in (good) ~** sport: estar en forma, (witty) estar de vena; **be bad ~** ser de mal gusto; **for ~'s sake** por pura fórmula; **2.** formar(se); habit adquirir; ✕ alinearse.

for·mal ['fɔːml] ☐ formal; manner etc. ceremonioso; visit de cumplido; dress etc. de etiqueta; **for·mal·i·ty** [fɔː'mæliti] formalidad f; etiqueta f.

for·mat ['fɔːmæt] formato m.

for·ma·tion [fɔː'meiʃn] all senses: formación f.

for·mer ['fɔːmə] antiguo; anterior, primero, precedente; ex...; **the ~** ése etc., aquél etc.; **'for·mer·ly** antes, antiguamente.

form·less ['fɔːmlis] ☐ informe.

for·mu·la ['fɔːmjulə], pl. mst **for·mu·lae** ['~liː] fórmula f; **for·mu·late** ['~leit] formular.

for·sake [fə'seik] [irr.] abandonar, dejar; desamparar; opinion renegar de; **for·sak·en** p.p. of forsake.

for·sook [fə'suk] pret. of forsake.

for·swear [fɔː'swɛə] [irr. (swear)] abjurar; **~ o.s.** perjurarse.

fort [fɔːt] fuerte *m*, fortín *m*.

forte [\] *fig.* fuerte *m*.

forth [\ːθ] (a)delante, (a)fuera; *v. so; from this day* ~ de hoy en adelante; **~'com·ing** venidero, próximo; *book etc.* de próxima aparición; *p.* abierto, afable; **'~'right** directo; franco; terminante; **'~'with** en el acto, sin dilación.

for·ti·eth ['fɔːtiiθ] cuadragésimo.

for·ti·fi·ca·tion [fɔːtifi'keiʃn] fortificación *f*; **for·ti·fy** ['\fai] ⚔ fortificar; *wine* encabezar; *opinion* corroborar; *p.* animar; *p.* confirmar (*in belief en*); **for·ti·tude** ['\tjuːd] fortaleza *f*, valor *m*, resistencia *f*.

fort·night ['fɔːtnait] quince días *m/pl.*, quincena *f*; *this day* ~ de hoy en quince (días).

for·tress ['fɔːtris] fortaleza *f*, plaza *f* fuerte.

for·tu·nate ['fɔːtʃnit] ☐ afortunado; feliz; **~ly** afortunadamente.

for·tune ['fɔːtʃn] fortuna *f*; suerte *f*; *cost a* ~ valer un dineral; *tell one's* ~ decirle a uno la buenaventura; **'~'tel·ler** adivina *f*.

for·ty ['fɔːti] cuarenta.

fo·rum ['fɔːrəm] foro *m*; *fig.* tribunal *m*.

for·ward ['fɔːwəd] **1.** *adj.* delantero; adelantado; precoz; ⚓ de proa; F descarado, impertinente; **2.** *adv.* (hacia) adelante; ⚓ hacia la proa; *march!* de frente ¡mar!; **3.** *sport:* delantero *m*; **4.** *project* fomentar, promover, favorecer; & hacer seguir; expedir; enviar.

for·went [fɔː'went] *pret. of* forgo.

fos·sil ['fɒsl] fósil *adj. a. su. m* (*a. fig.*); **'fos·sil·ized** fosilizado.

fos·ter ['fɒstə] **1.** fomentar, favorecer; criar; **2.:** ~ *brother* hermano *m* de leche; ~ *home* hogar *m* de adopción; ~ *mother* madre *f* adoptiva; (*nurse*) ama *f* de leche.

fought [fɔːt] *pret. a. p.p. of* fight 2.

foul [faul] **1.** ☐ sucio, puerco; asqueroso; *air* viciado; *blow*, *play* sucio, feo; *breath* fétido; *deed* vil; *weather* feo, muy malo; **2.** falta *f*, juego *m* sucio; **3.** ensuciar; chocar contra; enredarse en; obstruir; *sport:* cometer una falta contra; **'~'mouthed** [\mauðd] deslenguado.

found¹ [faund] *pret. a. p.p. of* find 1.

found² [\] ⚓ fundar, establecer; basar.

found³ [\] ⊕ fundir.

foun·da·tion [faun'deiʃn] fundación *f*; *fig.* fundamento *m*, base *f*; ~s *pl.* △ cimientos *m/pl.*

found·er ['faundə] **1.** fundador (-a *f*) *m*; **2.** ⊕ fundidor *m*; **3.** ⚓ irse a pique, hundirse (*a. fig.*).

found·ling ['faundliŋ] niño *m* expósito.

found·ry ['faundri] fundición *f*.

fount *poet.* [faunt] fuente *f*.

foun·tain ['fauntin] fuente *f* (*a. fig.*); surtidor *m*; **'~'head** *fig.* fuente *f*, origen *m*; **~'pen** (pluma *f*) estilográfica *f*; plumafuente *f S.Am.*

four [fɔː] cuatro (*a. su. m*); *on all* ~s a gatas; *fig.* en completa armonía (*with con*); **'~'flush·er** *sl.* impostor *m*, embustero *m*; **'~'fold 1.** *adj.* cuádruple; **2.** *adv.* cuatro veces; **'~'foot·ed** cuadrúpedo; **'four'square** *fig.* firme, fuerte, sincero; **four'teen** ['\ˈtiːn] catorce; **four'teenth** ['\ˈtiːnθ] decimocuarto; **fourth** [fɔːθ] **1.** cuarto *f*; **2.** cuarto *m*; cuarta parte *f*; ♪ cuarta *f*; **'fourth·ly** en cuarto lugar.

fowl [faul] ave *f* (de corral); gallina *f*; pollo *m*; ~ *pest* peste *f* aviar.

fox [fɒks] **1.** zorra *f*; (*dog*-) zorro *m* (*a. fig.*); **2.** F desconcertar, confundir.

fox···: '~'glove dedalera *f*; **'~'hole** zorrera *f*; ✕ pozo *m* de lobo, hoyo *m* de protección; **'~'hound** perro *m* raposero; **'~'hunt** cacería *f* de zorras; **~'trot** fox *m*; **'fox·y** *fig.* taimado, astuto.

foy·er ['fɔiei] vestíbulo *m*, hall *m*.

fra·cas ['fræka:] gresca *f*, riña *f*.

frac·tion ['frækʃn] ℵ fracción *f*, quebrado *m*.

frac·ture ['fræktʃə] **1.** fractura *f*; **2.** fracturar(se), quebrar(se).

frag·ile ['frædʒail] frágil; quebradizo; delicado.

frag·ment ['frægmənt] fragmento *m*.

fra·grance ['freigrəns] fragancia *f*; **'fra·grant** ☐ fragante.

frail [freil] ☐ frágil; *fig.* débil, endeble.

frame [freim] **1.** estructura *f*; esqueleto *m*; marco *m of picture*; *sew.*, ⊕ bastidor *m*; armadura *f of spectacles*; ⊕ armazón *f*; *p.'s* forma *f*, figura *f*; ⚓ cuaderna *f*; ~ *house* casa *f* de madera; ~ *of mind* estado *m* de ánimo; **2.** formar, inventar, construir; *picture* poner un marco a; *fig.* servir de marco a; *question* formular, expresar; *esp. Am. sl.* incriminar por medio de una estratagema; arreglar bajo cuerda; **'frame-up** *esp. Am.* F estratagema *f* para incriminar a alguien; complot *m*; **'frame-work** ⊕ armazón *f*, esqueleto *m*, armadura *f*; *fig.* sistema *m*, organización *f*.

fran-chise ['fræntʃaiz] derecho *m* de votar, sufragio *m*.

frank-furt-er ['fræŋkfə:tə] salchicha *f* de carne de vaca y de cerdo.

frank-ness ['fræŋknis] franqueza *f*.

fran-tic ['fræntik] □ frenético, furioso; F desquiciado *with worry*.

fra-ter-nal [frə'tə:nl] □ fraternal, fraterno; **fra-ter-ni-ty** fraternidad *f*, hermandad *f*; *univ.* club *m* de estudiantes.

fraud [frɔ:d] fraude *m*; (*p.*) impostor *m*, farsante *m*; **'fraud-u-lent** □ fraudulento.

fray[1] [frei] *v/i.* deshilacharse; *~ed* raído; *v/t.* desgastar.

fray[2] [~] combate *m*; refriega *f*, riña *f*.

freak [fri:k] **1.** capricho *m of imagination*; (*p.*) fenómeno *m*; (*a. ~ of nature*) monstruo *m*, monstruosidad *f*; curiosidad *f*; **2.** = **'freak-ish** □ caprichoso; imprevisto.

freck-le ['frekl] peca *f*; **'freck-led** pecoso.

free [fri:] **1.** □ *mst* libre (*from*, of de); franco, exento (*from* de); inmune (*from* contra); *p.* liberal; (*not fixed*) suelto; (*untied*) desatado; (*for nothing*) gratuito; *be* ~ *on inf.* poder libremente *inf.*; *set* ~ libertar; ~ *and easy* despreocupado, poco ceremonioso; ~ *of charge* gratis; ✝ ~ *on board* franco a bordo; ~ *fight*, F ~ *for all* sarracina *f*, riña *f* general; **2.** liberar (*from* de), libertar; eximir, exentar (*from*, of de); *place etc.* desembarazar, despejar; *knot etc.* soltar, desenredar; **'free-dom** libertad *f*; exención *f*, inmunidad *f*; ~ *of speech* libertad *f* de la palabra; ~ *of the press* libertad *f* de imprenta; ~ *of the seas* libertad *f* de los mares; ~ *of worship* libertad *f* de cultos.

free…: '~ **'en-ter-prise** libertad *f* de empresa; **'~-lance** (periodista *m etc.*) independiente; **'~-man** hombre *m* libre; ciudadano *m* de honor *f city*; **'𝔉-ma-son** francmasón *m*; **'𝔉-ma-son-ry** francmasonería *f*; *fig.* compañerismo *m*; **'~-think-er** librepensador (-a *f*) *m*; **'~-'will** libre albedrío *m*; *of one's own* ~ por voluntad propia.

freeze [fri:z] **1.** [*irr.*] helar(se); con-

gelar(se) (*a. fig.,* ✝ *etc.*); ~ *to death* morir de frío; **2.** helada *f*; congelación *f of wages etc.*; **'freez-er** heladora *f*, sorbetera *f*; **'freez-ing** □ glacial (*a. fig.*), helado; ~ *point* punto *m* de congelación.

freight [freit] **1.** flete *m*, carga *f*; *attr.* de mercancías; **2.** fletar, cargar; **'freight car** vagón *m* de mercancías; **'freight-er** buque *m* de carga; **'freight 'sta-tion** estación *f* de carga; **'freight train** mercancías *m/pl.*, tren *m* de mercancías; **'freight yard** patio *m* de carga.

French [frentʃ] francés *adj. a. su. m*; ~ *bean* judía *f*; *take* ~ *leave* despedirse a la francesa; ~ *window* puerta *f* ventana; **'~-man** francés *m*; **'~-wom-an** francesa *f*.

fren-zied ['frenzid] □ frenético; **'fren-zy** frenesí *m*, delirio *m*.

fre-quen-cy ['fri:kwənsi] frecuencia *f* (*a. ⚡*); **fre-quent 1.** ['~kwənt] □ frecuente; **2.** [~'kwent] frecuentar.

fresh [freʃ] □ fresco; nuevo, reciente; *air* puro; *face* de buen color; *water* dulce; *wind* recio; *p.* nuevo, novicio; F fresco, descarado; *in the* ~ *air* al aire libre; **'fresh-en** refrescar (-se).

fret[1] [fret] ⊕ **1.** calado *m*; **2.** adornar con calados.

fret[2] [~] **1.** *v/t.* raer, rozar, corroer; *p.* irritar, molestar; *v/i.* inquietarse, apurarse, impacientarse (*at* por); **2.** estado *m* inquieto.

fret[3] [~] ♪ traste *m*.

fret-work ['fretwə:k] calado *m*.

fri-ar ['fraiə] fraile *m*; fray *in titles*.

fric-tion ['frikʃn] rozamiento *m* (*a. fig.*), fricción *f*; *fig.* desavenencia *f*; ~ *tape* cinta *f* aislante.

Fri-day ['fraidi] viernes *m*.

friend [frend] amigo (*a f*) *m*; ♀ cuáquero (*a f*) *m*; ~*!* ¡gente de paz!; *be* ~*s with* ser amigo de; *make* ~*s with* trabar amistad con; **'friend-less** sin amigos; **'friend-li-ness** cordialidad *f*, amigabilidad *f*; **'friend-ly** amistoso; cordial, amigable; *place etc.* acogedor; **'friend-ship** amistad *f*.

frieze [fri:z] friso *m*.

frig-ate ['frigit] fragata *f*.

fright [frait] susto *m*, sobresalto *m*; terror *m*; (*p.*) espantajo *m*; **'fright-en** asustar, espantar, sobresaltar; ~ *away*, ~ *off* ahuyentar, espantar; *be* ~*ed of* tener miedo a; **fright-ful**

full-time

['~ful] □ espantoso, horrible, horroroso (*a. fig.*); F tremendo.

frig·id ['fridʒid] □ frío; frígido; **fri·gid·i·ty** frialdad *f*; frigidez *f*.

frill [fril] lechuga *f*, volante *m*; ~s *pl. fig.* afectación *f*, adornos *m/pl.*

fringe [frindʒ] **1.** franja *f*; borde *m*; orla *f*; flequillo *m of hair*; **2.** orlar (*with the*) (*a. fig.*).

frisk [frisk] *v/i.* retozar, cabriolar, juguetear; *v/t. sl.* palpar, registrar, cachear; **'frisk·y** □ retozón, juguetón; *horse* fogoso.

frit·ter ['fritə] **1.** fruta *f* de sartén, buñuelo *m*; **2.:** ~ *away* desperdiciar, disipar.

friv·o·lous ['frivələs] □ frívolo; trivial.

fro [frou]: *to and* ~ de un lado a otro, de aquí para allá.

frog [frɔg] rana *f*; ~ *in the throat* carraspera *f*; **'~·man** hombre-rana *m*.

frol·ic ['frɔlik] **1.** juego *m* alegre; travesura *f*; **2.** retozar, juguetear.

from [frɔm, frəm] de; desde; *message de parte de; date a partir de; price* desde ... en adelante; ~ *above* desde encima; ~ *among* de entre; ~ *afar* desde lejos; ~ *memory* de memoria; ~ *what he says* según lo que dice; *judging* ~ juzgando por; *take s.t.* ~ *s.o.* quitar algo a alguien.

front [frʌnt] **1.** frente *m* (*a. ✕, meteor., pol.*); parte *f* delantera (*or* anterior); fachada *f of house*; principio *m of book*; pechera *f of shirt; fig.* apariencia *f* falsa; *in* ~ delante (*of de*); **2.** delantero; anterior; primero; ~ *door* puerta *f* principal; ✕ ~ *line* primera línea *f*; ~ *wheel drive* tracción *f* a las ruedas delanteras; **3.:** ~ *on* (*to*) dar a; **fron·tier** ['~jə] **1.** frontera *f*; **2.** fronterizo; **'~ page** primera plana *f*.

frost [frɔst] **1.** helada *f*; escarcha *f* (*a. hoar* ~, *white* ~); *sl.* fracaso *m*; **2.** cubrir de escarcha; *plant* quemar; *~ed glass* vidrio *m* deslustrado; **'~·bite** congelación *f*; **'frost·bit·ten** congelado, helado; **'frost·y** □ helado; escarchado; *fig.* glacial.

froth [frɔθ] **1.** espuma *f*; *fig.* bachillerías *f/pl.*; **2.** espumar; ~ *at the mouth* espumajear.

frown [fraun] **1.** ceño *m*; entrecejo *m*; **2.** fruncir el entrecejo; ~ *at* mirar con ceño; ~ *on* desaprobar.

froze [frouz] *pret. of freeze 1*; **'froz·en** □

p.p. of freeze 1 a. adj.; ~ *foods* alimentos *m/pl.* congelados.

fru·gal ['fru:gəl] □ frugal.

fruit [fru:t] **1.** fruto *m* (*a. fig.*); fruta *f*; ~ *tree* árbol *m* frutal; **2.** dar fruto, frutar; **'~ cake** torta *f* de frutas; **'~ cup** compota *f* de frutas picadas; **'~ fly** mosca *f* del vinagre; mosca *f* de las frutas; **fruit·ful** ['~ful] □ fructífero; *fig.* fructuoso, provechoso; **fru·i·tion** [fru'iʃn] cumplimiento *m*; fruición *f*; *come to* ~ verse logrado; **'~ juice** jugo *m* de frutas; **'fruit·less** □ infructuoso.

frus·trate [frʌs'treit] frustrar; *plot* desbaratar; **frus'tra·tion** frustración *f*; desazón *f*.

fry [frai] **1.** fritada *f*; **2.** *ichth.* pececillos *m/pl.*; F *small* ~ gente *f* menuda; **3.** freír(se); *fried fish* pescado *m* frito; **'fry·ing pan** sartén *f*.

fu·el ['fjuəl] **1.** combustible *m*; carburante *m*; *fig.* pábulo *m*; **2.** aprovisionar(se) de combustible.

fu·gi·tive ['fju:dʒitiv] **1.** fugitivo; fugaz; *de interés* pasajero; **2.** fugitivo (*a f*) *m*, evadido *m*.

fugue [fju:g] fuga *f*.

ful·crum ['fʌlkrəm] fulcro *m*.

ful·fil [ful'fil] cumplir; realizar; *condition etc.* llenar; *orders* ejecutar; **ful'fil·ment** cumplimiento *m*; realización *f*; ejecución *f*.

full¹ [ful] **1.** (*adv. fully*) muy lleno; *fig.* pleno; (*complete*) cabal, íntegro; *account* extenso; *bus* completo; *dress* (*formal*) de etiqueta; *meal* abundante; *member* de número; *session* plen(ari)o; *skirt* amplio; ~ *moon* luna *f* llena, plenilunio *m*; *at* ~ *speed* a máxima velocidad, a toda máquina; ~ *stop* punto *m*; *fig.* parada *f* completa; *in* ~ *view* totalmente visible; **2.** *adv.* de lleno; *well* muy bien, sobradamente; **3.:** *in* ~ sin abreviar, por extenso; *pay in* ~ pagar la deuda entera; *to the* ~ completamente, al máximum.

full² [~] ⊕ abatanar.

full...: '~ **blast** a máxima velocidad (*or* capacidad); en plena actividad; '~**bod·ied** fuerte; *wine* generoso.

full...: ~**fledged** *fig.* hecho y derecho; '~**grown** crecido; '~ **length** de cuerpo entero.

full-time ['fultaim] (*adj.* que trabaja) jornada *f* completa, jornada *f* de costumbre; *adj.* en plena dedicación.

fulsome

ful·some ['fulsəm] ☐ exagerado; repugnante; servil.

fum·ble ['fʌmbl] v/t. manosear, revolver etc. torpemente; ball dejar caer; v/i. ~ for buscar con las manos; ~ with tocar (or manejar etc.) torpemente.

fume [fju:m] 1.: ~s pl. humo m, gas m, vapor m; 2. humear; (p.) enfadarse; echar pestes (at th. contra, p. de).

fu·mi·gate ['fju:migeit] fumigar; **fu·mi'ga·tion** fumigación f.

fun [fʌn] diversión f; alegría f; be (good, great) ~ ser (muy) divertido; for ~, in ~ en broma; have ~ divertirse; make ~ of burlarse de, hacer chacota de.

func·tion ['fʌŋkʃn] 1. función f; acto m, ceremonia f; cargo m; 2. funcionar; **'func·tion·al** ☐ funcional.

fund [fʌnd] 1. fondo m (a. fig.); ~s pl. fondos m/pl.; be in ~s estar en fondos; 2. debt consolidar.

fun·da·men·tal [fʌndə'mentl] ☐ fundamental; **fun·da'men·tals** [~z] pl. fundamentos m/pl.

fu·ner·al ['fju:nərəl] 1. entierro m, funerales m/pl.; ~ director director m de funeraria; 2. funeral, fúnebre.

funk [fʌŋk] F 1. canguelo m, jindama f; (p.) gallina m/f, mandria m/f; in a ~ aterrado; 2. retraerse por miedo de.

fun·nel ['fʌnl] embudo m; ⚓, 🚂 chimenea f.

fun·ny ['fʌni] ☐ cómico, gracioso, divertido; chistoso; (strange) raro, curioso; '~ bone F hueso m de la alegría.

fur [fə:] 1. piel f; pelo m; saburra f on tongue; sarro m in kettle etc.; 2. de piel(es); ~ coat abrigo m de pieles; 3. guarnecer etc. con pieles; depositar sarro en.

fur·bish ['fə:biʃ] pulir; ~ up renovar, restaurar.

fu·ri·ous ['fjuəriəs] ☐ furioso; frenético; violento.

furl [fə:l] ⚓ aferrar; arrollar.

fur·lough ['fə:lou] 1. licencia f; 2. dar licencia a.

fur·nace ['fə:nis] horno m; lugar m de mucho calor.

fur·nish ['fə:niʃ] suministrar, proporcionar (with acc.); equipar (with con); proof aducir; room amueblar (with de); **'fur·nish·ings** pl., **fur·ni·ture** ['fə:nitʃə] muebles m/pl., mueblaje m, mobiliario m; piece of ~ mueble m; **'fur·ni·ture 'store** mueblería f.

fur·ri·er ['fʌriə] peletero m.

fur·row ['fʌrou] 1. surco m; 2. surcar.

fur·ry ['fə:ri] peludo.

fur·ther ['fə:ðə] 1. adj. más lejano; nuevo, adicional; till ~ orders hasta nueva orden; 2. adv. más lejos, más allá (a. ~ on); además; 3. promover, fomentar; adelantar; **'fur·ther 'more** además.

fur·thest ['fə:ðist] 1. adj. más lejano; extremo; 2. adv. (lo) más lejos.

fur·tive ['fə:tiv] ☐ furtivo.

fu·ry ['fjuəri] furor m, furia f; frenesí m; like ~ a toda furia.

fuse [fju:z] 1. fundir(se) (a. ⚡); fusionar(se); 2. ⚡ plomo m, fusible m, tapón m; ✕ espoleta f, mecha f; ~ box caja f de fusibles.

fu·se·lage ['fju:zila:ʒ] fuselaje m.

fu·sion ['fju:ʒn] fusión f (a. fig.), fundición f.

fuss [fʌs] 1. (noisy) bulla f, alharaca f; (excessive display) aspaviento m, hazañería f; (trouble) lío m; (formalities) ceremonia f; there's no need to make such a ~ no es para tanto; 2. agitarse, inquietarse (por pequeñeces); **'fuss·y** ☐ F exigente; remilgado.

fu·tile ['fju:tail] ☐ inútil, vano, infructuoso; frívolo; **fu·til·i·ty** [fju:'tiliti] inutilidad f, lo inútil; frivolidad f.

fu·ture ['fju:tʃə] 1. futuro; 2. porvenir m, futuro m; ✝ ~s pl. futuros m/pl.; in (the) ~ en el futuro, en lo sucesivo; in the near ~ en fecha próxima.

fuzz [fʌz] tamo m, pelusa f; **'fuzz·y** ☐ borroso; hair muy ensortijado.

G

gab [gæb] F locuacidad f; cháchara f; *have the gift of* ~ tener mucha labia, ser un pico de oro.

ga·ble ['geibl] aguilón m.

gad [gæd] (*mst* ~ *about*) andar de aquí para allá; corretear; viajar mucho.

gadg·et ['gædʒit] F artilugio m, chisme m.

gag [gæg] 1. mordaza f (*a. fig.*); *thea.* morcilla f; *parl.* clausura f; F chiste m; *sl.* timo m; 2. amordazar (*a. fig.*); *thea.* meter morcillas.

gai·e·ty ['geiəti] alegría f, regocijo m; diversión f alegre.

gai·ly ['geili] alegremente.

gain [gein] 1. ganancia f; aumento m; provecho m; ⚡ amplificación f; 2. v/t. ganar; conseguir; (*clock*) adelantarse; v/i. crecer, medrar; ganar terreno; ~ *on* ir alcanzando; **gain·ful** ['~ful] □ ganancioso; ~ *employment* trabajo m remunerado.

gain·say [gein'sei] *lit.* contradecir, negar.

gait [geit] paso m, andar m.

gai·ter ['geitə] polaina f.

gal [gæl] *sl.* chica f.

ga·la ['ga:lə] fiesta f.

gal·ax·y ['gæləksi] *ast.* galaxia f; *fig.* constelación f, pléyade f.

gale [geil] ventarrón m; (*esp. southerly*) vendaval m; *poet.* brisa f.

gall¹ [ɡɔːl] bilis f, hiel f (*a. fig.*); vejiga f de la bilis; *fig.* rencor m; *sl.* descaro m; ~ *bladder* vejiga f de la bilis, vesícula f biliar.

gall² [~] ⚘ agalla f.

gall³ [~] 1. *vet.* matadura f; 2. lastimar rozando; *fig.* irritar, mortificar.

gal·lant ['gælənt] 1. □ (*brave*) gallardo, valiente; lucido; 2. [*mst* ɡə'lænt] □ galante; 3. [~] galán m.

gal·ler·y ['gæləri] galería f (*a.* 🎭, *thea.*); *art* ~ museo m de arte.

gal·ley ['gæli] ⚓ *a. typ.* galera f; ⚓ cocina f, fogón m; '~ **proof** galerada f; '~ **slave** galeote m.

gal·lon ['gælən] galón m (= *American* 3,785 *litros, British* 4,546 *litros*).

gal·lop ['gæləp] 1. galope m; galopada f; *at full* ~ a galope tendido, a uña de caballo; 2. galopar.

gal·lows ['gæləuz] *sg.* horca f; '~ **bird** carne f de horca.

gam·bit ['gæmbit] gambito m; *fig.* táctica f.

gam·ble ['gæmbl] 1. jugar; 2. jugada f; empresa f arriesgada; '**gam·bler** jugador (-a f) m, tahur m.

gam·bling ['gæmbliŋ] juego m.

gam·bol ['gæmbl] 1. brinco m; retozo m; 2. brincar, retozar, juguetear.

game [geim] 1. juego m (*a.* F); partida f; (*match*) partido m; deporte m; *bridge:* manga f; *hunt.* caza f; *big* ~ caza f mayor; ~ *of chance* juego m de azar; 2. F animoso, valiente; *leg* cojo; *be* ~ *for anything* atreverse a todo; 3. jugar (por dinero).

gam·ma ['gæmə] gama f; '~ **rays** *pl.* rayos m/*pl.* gama.

gam·ut ['gæmət] gama f.

gam·y ['geimi] manido, salvajino.

gan·der ['gændə] ganso m (macho).

gang [gæŋ] 1. cuadrilla f; pandilla f; brigada f (*of workers*); juego m (*of tools*). 2. ~ *up* conspirar, obrar de concierto (*against, on* contra); 3. ⊕ múltiple; '**gang·plank** ⚓ plancha f.

gan·grene ['gæŋgriːn] gangrena f.

gang·ster ['gæŋstə] pistolero m, atracador m, gángster m.

gang·way ['gæŋwei] paso m, pasadizo m, pasillo m; ⚓ plancha f, pasadera f; ⚓ (*opening*) portalón m; ⚓ pasamano m; ~! ¡abran paso!

gap [gæp] portillo m, abertura f; brecha f, boquete m; quebrada f *in mountains*; vacío m, hueco m.

gape [geip] 1. bostezo m; abertura f, hendedura f; 2. bostezar; embobarse, estar boquiabierto; ~ *at* mirar boquiabierto.

ga·rage ['gæra:ʒ; 'gærid3] 1. garaje m; 2. dejar en garaje.

garb [ga:b] 1. traje m, vestido m; ropaje m (*a. fig.*); 2. vestir.

gar·bage ['ga:bidʒ] basura f, bazofia f, desperdicios m/*pl.*; ~ *can* cubo m de basuras.

gar·ble ['ga:bl] mutilar; falsear (*por selección*).

gar·den ['ga:dn] 1. jardín m; (*fruit a. vegetables*) huerto m; 2. cultivar un huerto (*or* jardín); trabajar en el huerto (*or* jardín); '**gar·den·er** jardinero (a f) m; hortelano (a f) m; '**gar·den·ing** jardinería f; horticultura f.

gar·gle ['ga:gl] 1. gargarizar, hacer gárgaras; 2. gargarismo m.

gar·goyle ['ga:gɔil] gárgola f.

gar·land ['gɑːlənd] 1. guirnalda *f*; 2. enguirnaldar.

gar·lic ['gɑːlik] ajo *m*.

gar·ment ['gɑːmənt] prenda *f* (de vestir).

gar·nish ['gɑːniʃ] adornar, guarnecer; aderezar (*a. cooking*).

gar·ri·son ['gærisn] 1. guarnición *f*; 2. guarnecer, guarnicionar.

gar·ru·lous ['gæruləs] □ gárrulo.

gar·ter ['gɑːtə] liga *f*; ~**belt** portaligas *m*.

gas [gæs] 1. *pl.* **gas·es** ['~iz] gas *m*; F parloteo *m*; = *gasoline*; *mot.* step on the ~ acelerar la marcha; 2. asfixiar con gas; F parlotear; '~**bag** ⚡ cámara *f* de gas; F charlatán (-a *f*) *m*; '~ **heat** calefacción *f* por gas; '~ **jet** mechero *m* de gas; llama *f* de gas.

gash [gæʃ] 1. cuchillada *f*, chirlo *m*; raja *f*, hendedura *f*; 2. acuchillar, herir.

gas·ket ['gæskit] ⚓ tomador *m*; ⊕ empaquetadura *f*.

gas...: '~**light** luz *f* de gas, alumbrado *m* de gas; '~**main(s)** cañería *f* (maestra) de gas; '~ **man·tle** manguito *m* incandescente; '~**mask** careta *f* antigás; **gas·o·line** ['gæsəliːn] *mot.* gasolina *f*; **gas·o·line pump** poste *m* distribuidor de gasolina, surtidor *m* de gasolina; '**gas ov·en** cocina *f* de (*or* a) gas.

gasp [gæsp] 1. (*esp. last* ~) boqueada *f*; grito *m* entrecortado; 2. boquear; ~ **for breath** jadear.

gas-proof ['gæs'pruːf] a prueba de gas; '**gas range** cocina *f* de (*or* a) gas; '**gas 'sta·tion** estación *f* de gasolina; '**gas stove** cocina *f* de (*or* a) gas.

gat [gæt] *sl.* arma *f* de fuego, revólver *m*.

gate [geit] puerta *f*; verja *f* of iron; portal *m* of town; (*wicket*) portillo *m*; (*level crossing*) barrera *f*; *sport*: entrada *f*; '~**crash·er** *sl.* intruso (a *f*) *m*; '~**leg(·ged) ta·ble** mesa *f* de alas abatibles; '~**way** portal *m*; entrada *f*.

gath·er ['gæðə] 1. *v/t.* recoger, reunir; acumular; *wood, flowers* coger; *crops* cosechar; *sew.* fruncir; *fig.* colegir, inferir, sacar la consecuencia (*that que*); ~ *strength* cobrar fuerzas; ~ *in* recoger; *money* recaudar; ~ *together* reunir, juntar; ~ *up* recoger; *v/i.* reunirse, juntarse, congregarse (*a.* ~ *together*); acumularse; condensarse; (*clouds*) amontonarse; 🌢 formar plus; 2. (*mst*

~*s pl.*) frunce *m*; '**gath·er·ing** reunión *f*, asamblea *f*.

gaud·y ['gɔːdi] □ chillón, llamativo.

gauge [geidʒ] 1. (*norma f de*) medida *f*; calibre *m*; indicador *m*; manómetro *m*; ⊕ calibrador *m*; *carpentry*: gramil *m*; ❀ entrevía *f*, ancho *m*; 2. medir; calibrar; aforar; *fig.* estimar.

gaunt [gɔːnt] □ flaco, desvaído, macilento; sombrío.

gaunt·let ['gɔːntlit] guantelete *m*; guante *m*; *fig.* ~ correr baquetas; *take up the* ~ recoger el guante; *throw down the* ~ arrojar el guante.

gauze [gɔːz] gasa *f*; '**gauz·y** diáfano.

gave [geiv] *pret.* of give.

gav·el ['gævl] martillo *m* de los presidentes y subastadores.

gawk [gɔːk] F 1. zote *m*, bobo *m*; 2. papar moscas.

gay [gei] 1. *adj. a. su.* homosexual *m/f*; 2. † alegre, festivo; (*brilliant*) vistoso; (*pleasure-loving*) amigo *m* de los placeres.

gaze [geiz] 1. mirada *f* fija; contemplación *f*; 2. *a.* ~ *at*, ~ *on* mirar con fijeza, contemplar.

gear [giə] 1. aparejo *m*, pertrechos *m/pl.*, herramientas *f/pl.*; F cosas *f/pl.*, chismes *m/pl.*; (*attire*) atavío *m*; (*harness*) arreos *m/pl.*, arneses *m/pl.*; ⊕ aparato *m*, mecanismo *m*; ⊕ engranaje *m*, rueda *f* dentada; *mot.* marcha *f* (*low, bottom* primera, *second* segunda, *top* tercera *or* cuarta), velocidad *f*; *in* ~ en juego; *put into* ~ engranar; *throw out of* ~ desengranar; *fig.* desconcertar; 2. aparejar; ⊕ engranar; '~**box**, '~**case** caja *f* de velocidades (*or* de engranajes); '**gear-le·ver**, '**gear-shift** (palanca *f* de) cambio *m* de marchas.

gee [dʒiː] *esp.* ~ *up!* ¡arre!; ¡caramba!

geese [giːs] *pl. of* goose.

gel·a·tin(e) ['dʒelətin] gelatina *f*.

gem [dʒem] gema *f*, piedra *f* preciosa; *fig.* joya *f*, preciosidad *f*.

gen [dʒen] *sl.* información *f*.

gen·der ['dʒendə] género *m*.

gene [dʒiːn] *biol.* gen *m*.

gen·e·al·o·gy [dʒiːni'ælədʒi] genealogía *f*.

gen·er·al ['dʒenərəl] 1. □ general; *become* ~ generalizarse; *in* ~, *as a* ~ *rule* en general, por lo general, por regla general; 2. 🞱 general *m*; '**gen·er·al·ly** generalmente, en general, por lo común; '**gen·er·al·ship** generalato *m*; dirección *f*.

gen·er·ate ['dʒenereit] engendrar (*a.* Ⓐ), generar (*a.* ⚡); **gen·er·a'tion** generación *f*; **'gen·er·a·tor** generador *m* (*a.* ⚡, ⊕).

ge·ner·ic [dʒi'nerik] genérico.

gen·er·os·i·ty [dʒenə'rɔsiti] generosidad *f*; **'gen·er·ous** □ generoso; dadivoso; amplio, abundante.

ge·net·ic [dʒi'netik] □ genético, genésico; **ge'net·ics** genética *f*.

gen·ial ['dʒi:njəl] □ afable, complaciente, cordial; suave.

gen·i·tals ['dʒenitlz] *pl.* órganos *m*/*pl.* genitales.

gen·i·tive ['dʒenitiv] genitivo *m* (*a.* ~ *case*).

gen·ius ['dʒi:njəs] *pl.* **gen·i·i** ['~niai] (*deidad, espíritu tutelar*), *pl.* **gen·iuses** ['~nəsiz] (*facultad, persona*) genio *m*.

gen·o·cide ['dʒenəsaid] genocidio *m*.

gen·teel [dʒen'ti:l] *mst iro.* fino, cortés, elegante, de buen tono.

gen·tile ['dʒentail] no judío *adj. a. su. m* (*a f*); (*pagan*) gentil *adj. a. su. m*/*f*.

gen·til·i·ty [dʒen'tiliti] *mst iro.* fineza *f*, buen tono *m*; cursilería *f*.

gen·tle ['dʒentl] □ suave, dulce; benigno; sosegado; *esp. animals* manso, dócil; moderado; ligero, lento, pausado; bien nacido; † caballeroso; **'~·man** caballero *m*, señor *m*; (*at court*) gentilhombre *m*; *he is no* ~ es un mal caballero; ~'s *agreement* acuerdo *m* verbal; **'~·man·ly** caballeroso; **'gen·tle·ness** suavidad *f*, dulzura *f*; mansedumbre *f*; **'gen·tly** suavemente; poco a poco, despacio; ~! ¡paso!

gen·u·ine ['dʒenjuin] □ auténtico, legítimo, genuino; sincero.

ge·nus ['dʒi:nəs] *pl.* **gen·er·a** [dʒenərə] género *m*.

ge·og·ra·pher [dʒi'ɔgrəfə] geógrafo *m*; **ge·o·graph·i·cal** [~ə'græfikl] □ geográfico; **ge·og·ra·phy** [~'ɔgrəfi] geografía *f*.

ge·o·log·ic, ge·o·log·i·cal [dʒiə'lɔdʒik(l)] □ geológico; **ge·ol·o·gist** [dʒi'ɔlədʒist] geólogo *m*.

ge·o·met·ric, ge·o·met·ri·cal [dʒiə'metrik(l)] □ geométrico; **ge·om·e·try** [~'ɔmitri] geometría *f*.

ge·o·phys·ics [dʒiou'fiziks] geofísica *f*.

ge·o·pol·i·tics [dʒiou'pɔlitiks] geopolítica *f*.

ge·ra·ni·um [dʒi'reinjəm] geranio *m*.

ger·i·a·trics [dʒeri'ætriks] geriatría *f*.

germ [dʒə:m] *biol.*, *fig. a.* 🌡 germen *m*; 🌡 microbio *m*.

Ger·man¹ ['dʒə:mən] **1.** alemán *adj. a. su. m* (-a *f*); 🌡 ~ *measles* rubéola *f*; ⊕ ~ *silver* plata *f* alemana; ~ *text* typ. letra *f* gótica; **2.** (*language*) alemán *m*.

ger·man² [~]: *brother etc.* ~ hermano *m etc.* carnal; **ger·mane** [dʒə:'mein] relacionado (*to* con); pertinente (*to* a); oportuno.

Ger·man·ic [dʒə:'mænik] germánico.

ger·mi·nate ['dʒə:mineit] (hacer) germinar; **ger·mi'na·tion** germinación *f*.

ges·tic·u·late [dʒes'tikjuleit] accionar, gesticular, manotear.

ges·ture ['dʒestʃə] **1.** gesto *m*, ademán *m*; demostración *f*; (*small token*) muestra *f*, detalle *m*; *empty* ~ pura formalidad *f*; **2.** hacer ademanes.

get [get] [*irr.*] **1.** *v/t.* adquirir, lograr, conseguir; coger; (*grasp*) asir, agarrar *S.Am.*; recibir; *wage etc.* cobrar; ganar; tomar, prender; (*hit*) dar en; captar; comprender; alcanzar; cazar; hallar; (*fetch*) buscar; traer; sacar; (dis)poner; procrear; *have got* tener; *have got to inf.* tener que *inf.*; ~ *it sl.* ser castigado; *F* (*do you*) ~ *it?* ¿comprendes?; *I'll* ~ *him one day! sl.* ¡algún día me lo cargaré!; ~ *a p. to do s.t.* lograr que una p. haga algo; *F* ~ *religion* darse a la religión; ~ *s.t. done* hacer (*or* mandar) hacer una cosa; *that's what* ~*s me! sl.* ¡eso es lo que me irrita!; *F* ~ *across* hacer entender; ~ *away* quitar (de en medio); separar; conseguir que (una p.) se escape; ~ *back* recobrar; ~ *down* bajar; descolgar; tragar; apuntar; *F* (*state of mind*) abatir; ~ *in* hacer entrar; *harvest* recoger; *word* decir; *blow* dar; ~ *off clothes etc.* quitar(se); *stain* sacar; despachar; (*punishment*) librar; aprender; ~ *on clothes etc.* ponerse; ~ *out* sacar; publicar; *problem* resolver; ~ *over* hacer pasar por encima de; *F* hacer entender; terminar; *let's* ~ *it over with!* ¡vamos a concluir de una vez!; ~ *through* conseguir pasar (por); ~ *up* levantar; (hacer) subir; organizar; presentar; (*dress*) ataviar; (*disguise*) disfrazar *P*. **2.** *v/i.* hacerse, llegar a ser, ponerse, volverse, quedar(se); ir; *sl.* largarse; venir; llegar; ~ *going* ponerse en marcha; empezar; ~ *going!* ¡menearse!; ~ *dark* oscurecer; ~ *old* envejecer(se); ~ *angry* enfadarse; ~ *married* casarse; ~ *about* ir a muchos sitios; *(after sickness etc.)* estar levantado y moverse; *(report)* divulgarse; ~ *across* lograr cruzar; F *thea.* surtir efecto, tener éxito; F indisponerse con; ~ *ahead (of)* adelantar(se a); ~ *along* seguir andando; *(depart)* marcharse; *(manage)* ir tirando; *how are you ~ting along?* ¿cómo te va?; ~ *along with* avenirse con; ~ *along with you!* ¡no digas bobadas! ~ *along without* pasarse sin; ~ *around* viajar mucho; *(report)* divulgarse; ~ *around to s.t.* llegar a una cosa (con el tiempo); ~ *at* alcanzar, llegar a; atacar; descubrir, averiguar; querer decir; F apuntar a; F sobornar; *(spoil)* estropear; ~ *away* escapar(se); conseguir marcharse; alejarse; ~ *away with* fig. hacer algo impunemente; ~ *back* volver; retroceder; ~ *behind* penetrar; quedarse atrás; ~ *by* lograr pasar; eludir; F arreglárselas; ~ *down* bajar; ~ *down to work* ponerse a trabajar; ~ *in* (lograr) entrar (en); llegar, volver a casa; *pol.* ser elegido; ~ *into* (lograr) entrar (en); *vehicle* subir a; *difficulties etc.* meterse en; *clothes* ponerse; ~ *off* apearse (de); bajar (de); marcharse; *punishment* librarse de; escaparse; ✂ despegar; ~ *off!* ¡suelta!; ¡fuera!; ~ *off with* sl. enamorar; ~ *on* subir a; ponerse encima de; *(make progress)* adelantar; *(continue)* seguir; *(prosper)* medrar, tener éxito; ~ *on with a p.* congeniar con; llevarse (bien) con; ~ *out* salir; escaparse; *(news)* hacerse público; ~ *out of vehicle* bajar de; *responsibility etc.* librarse de; evadir; ~ *over* atravesar; *obstacle* vencer, superar; *illness etc.* reponerse de, salir de; *fright* sobreponerse a; ~ *round* dar la vuelta a; *difficulty* soslayar; *p.* persuadir; ~ *through* (conseguir) pasar por; *money* gastar; llegar al final de; terminar; penetrar; *exam* aprobar; ~ *through to* comunicar con; ~ *to* llegar a; empezar a; aprender a; ~ *together* reunirse; ~ *up* levantarse; ponerse de pie; subir; *(wind)* empezar a soplar fuerte; *(fire)* avivarse; **get-away** ['getəweɪ] *sport:* salida *f*; escapatoria *f*; *make one's* ~ escaparse; **'get-up** *(dress)* atavío *m*; presentación *f*.

gey-ser ['gaɪzə] géiser *m*; ['gi:zə] calentador *m*.

ghast-ly ['gɑ:stlɪ] horrible; pálido; cadavérico; F malo, desagradable.

gher-kin ['gə:kɪn] pepinillo *m*.

ghet-to ['getoʊ] judería *f*.

ghost [goʊst] fantasma *m*, aparecido *m*, espectro *m*; alma *f*, espíritu *m*; sombra *f*; *Holy* ⚜ Espíritu *m* Santo; ~ *(writer)* escritor *m* fantasma; *not the ~ of a chance* ni la más remota posibilidad; **'ghost-write** componer escritos por otra persona.

gi-ant ['dʒaɪənt] 1. gigante *m*; 2. gigantesco; **'gi-ant-ess** giganta *f*.

gid-dy ['gɪdɪ] □ vertiginoso; mareado; atolondrado; ligero de cascos.

gift [gɪft] 1. regalo *m*, dádiva *f*; *(esp. spiritual)* don *m*; *(personal quality)* dote *f*, talento *m*, prenda *f*; *eccl.* ofrenda *f*; ⚖ donación *f*; *sl.* ganga *f*; 2. dotar; **'gift-ed** talentoso; **'~ horse:** *never look a ~ in the mouth* a caballo regalado no se le mira el diente; **'~-of 'gab** F facundia *f*, labia *f*.

gi-gan-tic [dʒaɪ'gæntɪk] □ gigantesco.

gig-gle ['gɪgl] (reír con una) risilla *f* sofocada *(or* tonta).

gild [gɪld] 1. = guild; 2. *[irr.]* (sobre-) dorar.

gilt [gɪlt] 1. *pret. a p.p. of* gild; 2. dorado *m*; *fig.* atractivo *m*; **'~-edged** con los cantos dorados; *fig.* de toda confianza, de primer orden.

gim-let ['gɪmlɪt] barrena *f* de mano.

gim-mick ['gɪmɪk] *sl.* treta *f*, artilugio *m*; *thea.* truco *m* característico; ✝ truco *m* publicitario.

gin¹ [dʒɪn] *(drink)* ginebra *f*.

gin² [~] 1. trampa *f*; ⊕ desmotadera *f* de algodón; 2. coger con trampa; ✝ desmotar.

gin-ger ['dʒɪndʒə] 1. jengibre *m*; F brío *m*, viveza *f*; 2. rojo; 3. F *(mst ~ up)* animar, estimular; **'~ 'ale** gaseosa *f*; **'~-bread** pan *m* de jengibre; **'gin-ger-ly** 1. *adj.* cuidadoso, delicado; 2. *adv.* con tiento, con pies de plomo; **'gin-ger-snap** galleta *f* de jengibre.

gip-sy ['dʒɪpsɪ] gitano *adj. a. su. m* (a *f*).

gi-raffe [dʒɪ'rɑ:f] jirafa *f*.

gird [gə:d] *[irr.]* ceñir; rodear.

gird-er ['gə:də] viga *f*.

gird-le ['gə:dl] 1. cinto *m*; *(belt a. fig.)* cinturón *m*; *(corset)* faja *f*; 2. ceñir; cercar.

girl [gə:l] *(mst young)* niña *f*; muchacha *f*, chica *f*; *(young woman)* joven *f*; *(servant)* criada *f*; **'~ 'friend** amiguita *f*; novia *f*; **girl·hood** ['ˌhud] niñez *f*; mocedad *f*; **'girl·ish** □ de niña; juvenil; afeminado.

girt [gɔːt] *pret. a. p.p.* of gird.

girth [gɔːθ] **1.** (*horse's*) cincha *f*; cintura *f*; corpulencia *f*; circunferencia *f*; **2.** (*a. ~ up*) cinchar.

gist [dʒist] esencia *f*, quid *m*, meollo *m*.

give [giv] **1.** [*irr.*] *v/t.* dar; proporcionar; ofrecer; (*as present*) regalar; (*pass on*) transmitir; *disease* contagiar con; *punishment* imponer, condenar a, castigar con; *aid* prestar; (*produce*) dar por resultado, arrojar, producir; (*cause*) ocasionar; (*hand over*) entregar; (*grant*) otorgar, conceder; *time, energy* dedicar, consagrar; sacrificar; (*impart*) comunicar; *lecture* explicar; *thea.* representar; *speech* pronunciar; *~ it to a p.* regañar a una p.; pegar a una p.; *~ us a song!* ¡cántanos algo!; *~ away* regalar; (*get rid of*) deshacerse de; (*sell cheaply*) malvender; (*disclose*) revelar; (*betray*) traicionar; *~ back* devolver; *~ forth* publicar, divulgar; emitir, despedir; *~ in* entregar; *~ off* emitir, despedir, echar; *~ out* distribuir, repartir; anunciar; divulgar; afirmar; emitir; despedir; *~ over* entregar; transferir; F cesar (de); dejar (de); *~ up* entregar; ceder; cesar (de), dejar (de); renunciar (a); 🏴 desahuciar; (*for lost*) dar por perdido; *~ o.s. up to* entregarse a; dedicarse a; **2.** [*irr.*] *v/i.* dar; ceder; (*weaken*) flaquear; (*break*) romperse; (*cloth etc.*) dar de sí; *~ in* ceder; consentir; darse por vencido; *~ out* agotarse; fallar; F *~ over* cesar; *~ up* rendirse, darse por vencido; perder la esperanza; **3.** elasticidad *f*; **give-and-take** ['givənˈteik] toma y daca *m*; concesiones *f/pl.* mutuas; **give-a·way** ['givəˈwei] revelación *f* indiscreta; *~ price* precio en obsequio; **'giv·en** *p.p.* of give; *~ that* dado que, *~ to* dado a, adicto a; **'giv·er** dador (-a *f*) *m*, donador (-a *f*) *m*.

glad [glæd] □ contento, satisfecho, alegre, gozoso; *be ~* alegrarse (*of*, to de); tener mucho gusto (to en); *~ly* con mucho gusto; alegremente; **glad·den** ['ˌdn] alegrar, regocijar.

glad·i·a·tor ['glædieitə] gladiador *m*.

glad·i·o·lus ['glædiˈouləs], *pl.* **glad·i·o·li** [ˌˈoulai] estoque *m*, gladiolo *m*.

glad·ness ['glædnis] alegría *f*, gozo *m*; contento *m*.

glam·or·ous ['glæmərəs] □ encantador, hechicero; **glam·our** ['ˌmə] encanto *m*, hechizo *m*; *~ girl* glamour *f*, chica *f* picante.

glance [glɑːns] **1.** (*look*) ojeada *f*, vistazo *m*; (*light*) destello *m*; golpe oblicuo; resbalón *m*, rebote *m* of *projectile*; *at a ~* de un vistazo; *at first ~* a primera vista; **2.** destellar; (*a. ~ off*) rebotar de soslayo; *~ at* ojear, echar un vistazo a; *book* (*a. ~ over, ~ through*) hojear; examinar de paso.

gland [glænd] *anat.*, 🌿 glándula *f*; ⊕ prensaestopas *m*.

glare [glɛə] **1.** luz *f* deslumbradora; deslumbramiento *m*; mirada *f* feroz; **2.** relumbrar, deslumbrar; mirar ferozmente, echar fuego por los ojos; **glar·ing** ['ˌriŋ] □ deslumbrador; *color* chillón; de mirada feroz; *fig.* manifiesto, craso.

glass [glɑːs] **1.** vidrio *m*, cristal *m*; (*drinking*) vaso *m*; (*wine*) copa *f*; (*beer*) caña *f*; (*spyglass*) catalejo *m*; barómetro *m*; (*mirror*) espejo *m*; *~es pl.* gafas *f/pl.*, anteojos *m/pl.*, lentes *m/pl.*; (*binoculars*) gemelos *m/pl.*; **2.** de vidrio, de cristal; **'~ware** cristalería *f*; **'glass·y** □ vítreo; *water* espejado; *eyes* vidriosos.

glaze [gleiz] **1.** vidriado *m*, barniz *m*; **2.** vidriar; poner vidrio a.

gleam [gliːm] **1.** rayo *m*, destello *m*; *a. fig.* vislumbre *f*; brillo *m*; **2.** brillar, destellar.

glean [gliːn] espigar (*a. fig.*).

glee [gliː] regocijo *m*, júbilo *m*; ♪ canción *f* para voces solas; *~ club* orfeón *m*.

glen [glen] cañada *f*.

glib [glib] □ de mucha labia; *explanation* fácil; **'glib·ness** labia *f*.

glide [glaid] **1.** deslizamiento *m*; ✈ planeo *m*; **2.** deslizarse; ✈ planear; *~ away*, *off* escurrirse; **'glid·er** planeador *m*; (*light*) velero *m*; **'glid·ing** vuelo *m* a vela.

glim·mer ['glimə] **1.** luz *f* trémula; *a. fig.* vislumbre *f*; **2.** brillar con luz tenue y vacilante.

glimpse [glimps] **1.** vistazo *m*, vislumbre *f*; *catch a ~ of* vislumbrar; **2.** vislumbrar, entrever; ver por un momento.

glint [glint] **1.** destello *m*, reflejo *m*, centelleo *m*; **2.** destellar, centellear.

glis·ten ['glisn] relucir, brillar, centellear.

glit·ter ['glitə] **1.** resplandecer, rutilar; 2. resplandor *m*; brillo *m*; **'glit·ter·ing** resplandeciente, brillante, reluciente.

gloat [glout] (*mst ~ over*) deleitarse (en); relamerse.

glob·al ['gloubl] mundial, global; **globe** [gloub] globo *m*; esfera *f*; *geog.* bola *f* del mundo; **'globe·trot·ter** trotamundos *m*.

gloom [glu:m], **'gloom·i·ness** tenebrosidad *f*, lobreguez *f*, oscuridad *f*; melancolía *f*, abatimiento *m*; **'gloom·y** □ tenebroso, lóbrego; abatido, melancólico.

glo·ri·ous ['glɔ:riəs] □ glorioso; *F* magnífico, estupendo.

glo·ry ['glɔ:ri] 1. gloria *f*; 2. (*rejoice*) gloriarse (*in* en); (*boast*) gloriarse (*in* de).

gloss[1] [glɔs] 1. glosa *f*; 2. glosar.

gloss[2] [~] 1. lustre *m*, brillo *m*; *put a ~ on* sacar brillo a; 2. pulir, lustrar; *~ over* paliar, colorear.

glos·sa·ry ['glɔsəri] glosario *m*.

gloss·y ['glɔsi] □ lustroso, pulido; *paper*, *cloth* satinado.

glove [glʌv] guante *m*.

glow [glou] 1. incandescencia *f*; brillo *m*; calor *m*; luz *f* (difusa); arrebol *m* of *sky*; color *m* vivo; sensación *f* de bienestar; 2. estar candente; brillar; estar encendido.

glow·er ['glauə] *~ at* mirar con ceño.

glow·ing ['glouiŋ] candente; encendido; ardiente; *fig.* entusiasta.

glow·worm ['glouwə:m] luciérnaga *f*.

glue [glu:] 1. cola *f*; 2. encolar, pegar.

glum [glʌm] □ taciturno, sombrío.

glut [glʌt] 1. hartazgo *m*; superabundancia *f*; 2. hartar; *market* inundar.

glut·ton ['glʌtn] glotón (-a *f*) *m*; glotón *m*; *be a ~ for* ser insaciable de.

glyc·er·in(e) ['glisərin] glicerina *f*.

gnarled [na:ld] nudoso, rugoso; (*weather-beaten*) curtido.

gnash [næʃ] rechinar (los dientes).

gnat [næt] mosquito *m*; jején *m* S.Am.

gnaw [nɔ:] roer; **'gnaw·ing** 1. roedura *f*; 2. roedor.

gnome [noum] gnomo *m*; **gnom·ic** ['noumik] gnómico.

gnu [nu:] ñu *m*.

go [gou] 1. [*irr.*] (*v. a. going, gone*) ir; viajar, caminar; (*no direction indicated*) andar; (*depart*) irse, marcharse; desaparecer; eliminarse; (*give*

way) ceder, romperse; hundirse; ⊕ funcionar, trabajar, marchar; seguir; hacer (gestos *or* movimientos); (*be current*) correr; (*be habitually*) andar; (*turn out*) resultar, salir; (*become*) hacerse, ponerse, volverse; (*food*) pasarse; (*milk*) cortarse; (*be sold*) venderse; (*time*) pasar; (*reach*) alcanzar, llegar; (*fit*) ajustarse, caber; (*belong*) (deber) colocarse; *as far as it ~es* dentro de sus límites; *as they etc. ~* considerando lo que corre; *F here ~es!* ¡vamos a ver!; *F how ~es it?* ¿qué tal?; *the story ~es* se dice; *who ~es there?* ¿quién vive?; *~ and* (*or to*) *see* ir a ver; *v. bad*; *~ blind* quedarse ciego; *~ hungry* pasar hambre; *~ hunting* ir de caza; *sl. ~ it alone* obrar sin ayuda; *~ one better* quedar por encima (*than* de); *~ about* andar (de un sitio para otro); circular; ocuparse en; emprender; hacer las gestiones para; ♣ virar; *~ abroad* ir al extranjero; salir; *~ against* ir en contra de; oponerse a; *~ ahead* ir adelante, continuar, avanzar; *~ ahead!* ¡adelante!; *~ along* ir por; marcharse; seguir andando; *~ at* lanzarse sobre; acometer; *~ away* irse, marcharse; desaparecer; *~ back* volver, regresar; retroceder; *F ~ back on* desdecirse de; faltar a; *~ before* ir a la cabeza de; anteceder; comparecer ante; *~ between* interponerse; mediar (entre); *~ beyond* ir más allá (de); exceder; *~ by* pasar (por); atenerse a; juzgar por; regirse por; *~ by the name of* conocerse por el nombre de; *~ down* bajar; (*sun*) ponerse; (*ship*) hundirse; sucumbir (*before* ante); *F aceptarse, tragarse; pasar a la historia; *~ for* ir por; *F atacar*; *~ in* entrar (en); (*fit*) caber (en); *~ in for* dedicarse a; tomar parte en; *exam* tomar, presentarse para; comprar; *~ into* entrar en; caber en; investigarse; *~ in with* asociarse con; *~ off* irse, marcharse; (*gun*) dispararse; (*explosion*) estallar; deteriorarse; *~ on* seguir (adelante); durar; pasar; *F machacar*; *F echar pestes*; *thea.* salir a escena; *F ~ on!* ¡anda!; *~ on to inf.* pasar luego a *inf.*; *~ on to say* decir a continuación; *~ on with* continuar, proseguir; *~ out* salir; (*light*) apagarse; *F pasar de moda*; *~ over* recorrer, atravesar; examinar, repasar; (*to another party, etc.*) pasarse a; *~ round* dar la vuelta a; circular; (*re-*

volve) girar; *(suffice)* alcanzar para todos; ~ *round* to hacer una visita a; ~ *through* pasar por; atravesar; penetrar; sufrir; experimentar; *(spend)* (mal)gastar; examinar; ~ *through with* llevar a cabo; ~ *to (bequest)* pasar a; servir para, ayudar a; destinarse a; ~ *under (ship)* hundirse; arruinarse; fracasar; *name* pasar por; ~ *up* subir (a); *(explode)* estallar; ~ *with* acompañar; *(agree)* estar de acuerdo con; hacer juego con; ~ *without* pasarse sin; 2. F *(occurrence)* suceso *m*; *(fix)* lío *m*; energía *f*; turno *m*; F be on the ~ trajinar; F have a ~ probar suerte; tentar; *in on* ~ de una vez, de un tirón; F *is it a* ~? ¿hace?; F *it's a* ~! ¡trato hecho!; *no* ~ es inútil; no puede ser; F *it's your* ~ te toca a ti; *make a* ~ *of* tener éxito en.

goad [goud] 1. aguijada *f*; *(a. fig.)* aguijón *m*; 2. aguijonear; *fig.* irritar, incitar; ~ *into* provocar a.

go-a·head ['gouəhed] 1. emprendedor; 2. permiso *m* (or señal *f*) para seguir adelante.

goal [goul] meta *f*; *sport:* portería *f*, meta *f*; *(score)* gol *m*, tanto *m*; '~keep·er portero *m*, guardameta *m*; '~post poste *m* de la portería, larguero *m*.

goat [gout] cabra *f*, macho *m* cabrío; *sl. get a p.'s* ~ irritar a una p.; **goat·ee** perilla *f*.

gob [gob] salivazo *m*; *sl.* boca *f*; F marino *m*.

gob·ble ['gobl] 1. engullir; *(turkey)* gluglutear; 2. gluglú *m* of *turkey*; **gob·ble·dy·gook** ['gobldiguk] *sl.* jerga *f* burocrática.

go-be·tween ['goubitwi:n] medianero (a *f*) *m*, tercero (a *f*) *m*; *b.s.* alcahuete (a *f*) *m*.

gob·let ['goblit] copa *f*.

gob·lin ['goblin] duende *m*.

god [god] dios *m*; 2 Dios *m*; *thea.* F paraíso *m*, gallinero *m*; *please* 2 plegue a Dios; 2 *willing* Dios mediante; '**god·child** ahijado (a *f*) *m*; '**god·daugh·ter** ahijada *f*; '**god·dess** diosa *f*; '**god·fa·ther** padrino *m*; '**god·fear·ing** timorato; '**god·less** descreído; '**god·like** (de aspecto) divino; '**god·li·ness** piedad *f*, santidad *f*; '**god·ly** piadoso; '**god·moth·er** madrina *f*; *fairy* ~ hada madrina *f*; '**god·par·ents** *pl.* padrinos *m/pl.*

go·er ['gouə] corredor (-a *f*) *m*.

go-get·ter ['gou'getə] *sl.* persona *f* emprendedora, buscavidas *m/f*.

go·ing ['gouiŋ] 1. yendo, que va; en marcha, funcionando; F en venta; F disponible; F existente; be ~ of inf. ir a *inf.*; keep ~ seguir; no cejar; set ~ poner en marcha; ~ *concern* empresa *f* en pleno funcionamiento (or que marcha bien); ~, ~, gone! ¡a la una, a las dos, a las tres!; 2. ida *f*; partida *f*, salida *f*; marcha *f*, velocidad *f*; estado *m* del camino *(sport:* de la pista); *good* ~! ¡bien hecho!; '**go·ings-on** *pl.* F actividades *f/pl.* (dudosas); jarana *f*.

goi·tre ['goitə] bocio *m*.

gold [gould] 1. oro *m*; 2. de oro, áureo; *sl.* ~ *brick* estafa *f*; '~ *leaf* oro *m* batido; '~ *plate* vajilla *f* de oro; '~ *standard* patrón *m* oro; '~ **dig·ger** *sl.* aventurera *f*; '**gold·en** áureo, de oro; dorado; *fig.* excelente, próspero, feliz; ~ *jubilee* quincuagésimo aniversario *m*; ~ *mean* justo medio *m*; ~ *wedding* bodas *f/pl.* de oro; '**gold·finch** jilguero *m*; '**gold·fish** pez *m* de colores; ~ *bowl* pecera *f*; '**gold mine** mina *f* de oro; *fig.* rio *m* de oro, potosí *m*; '**gold·smith** orfebre *m*.

golf [golf] golf *m*; ~ *club (stick)* palo *m* de golf; club *m* de golf; '**golf·er** jugador (-a *f*) *m* de golf; '**golf links** terreno *m* de golf.

gon·do·la ['gondələ] & góndola *f*; barquilla *f*.

gone [gon] *(p.p. of go)* ido; pasado; desaparecido; arruinado; *(lost)* perdido; *(used up)* agotado; muerto; F chiflado; be ~!, get you ~! ¡vete!; F *far* ~ muy adelantado; cerca de la muerte; muy borracho; *sl.* ~ *on* loco por; enamorado de; ~ *(with child)* encinta; '**gon·er** *sl.* persona *f* (dada por) muerta.

gong [gon] gong(o) *m*, batintín *m*.

good [gud] 1. bueno; F ~ *and adj. or adv.* bien, muy; ~ *at* hábil en; be ~ *for* ser bueno para; servir para; F tener fuerzas para; F ser capaz de (hacer or pagar or dar); *that's a* ~ *one!* ¡ésa sí que es buena!; 2. bien *m*; provecho *m*, utilidad *f*; ~*s pl.* bienes *m/pl.*; † géneros *m/pl.*, mercancías *f/pl.*; *do* ~ hacer bien; sentar bien; *for* ~ *(and all)* (de una vez) para siempre; *for the* ~ *of* en bien de, para el bien de; *it is no* ~ es inútil, no sirve (para nada); *he is up to no* ~ está urdiendo algo malo; *the* ~ bueno; los buenos; *to the* ~ en el haber, de sobra; '~ **af·ter·noon!**

¡buenas tardes!; **~bye 1.** [gud'bai] adiós *m*; **2.** ['gud'bai] ¡adiós!; **'~'eve·ning!** ¡buenas noches!; **'~·for-'noth·ing 1.** inútil; **2.** haragán (-a *f*) *m*; **'~'hu·mored de buen** humor; afable; **'good·li·ness** hermosura *f*; excelencia *f*; **'good-look·ing** bien parecido; **'good·ly** hermoso; considerable; **'~ morn·ing!** ¡buenos días!; **'good-'na·tured** bondadoso; bonachón; **'good·ness** bondad *f*; (*food*) sustancia *f*, lo mejor; **~!** ¡válgame Dios!; **for ~' sake!** ¡por Dios!; **'~ night!** ¡buenas noches!; **'~-sized** [-saizd] bastante grande, de buen tamaño; **'~ time** rato *m* agradable; **have a ~ time** divertirse; **'~ turn** favor *m*, servicio *m*; **'good'will** buena voluntad *f* (*towards* hacia); buena gana *f*; **✝** clientela *f*, buen nombre *m*.

goo·ey ['guːi] *sl.* pegajoso, empalagoso.

goof [guːf] *sl.* bobo (a *f*) *m*; **'goof·y** *sl.* bobo.

goon [guːn] *sl.* zoquete *m*; gángster *m*, gorila *m*.

goose [guːs], *pl.* **geese** [giːs] ganso (a *f*) *m*, oca *f*, ánsar *m*; plancha *f* de sastre; **cook a p.'s ~** pararle los pies a una p.; **'~ flesh**, **'~ pim·ples** carne *f* de gallina; **'~ step** paso *m* de ganso.

gore¹ [gɔː] sangre *f* (derramada).

gore² [~] **1.** *sew* nesga *f*; **2.** cornear, acornar; *sew.* nesgar.

gorge [gɔːdʒ] **1.** garganta *f*, barranco *m*; (*meal*) atracón *m*; **2.** *v/t.* engullir; *v/i.* atracarse.

gor·geous ['gɔːdʒəs] □ magnífico, brillante, vistoso; **F** maravilloso, hermoso.

gor·y ['gɔːri] □ ensangrentado; sangriento.

gosh [gɔʃ] *sl.* ¡caray!

gos·pel ['gɔspəl] evangelio *m*.

gos·sip ['gɔsip] **1.** hablador (-a *f*) *m*; *b.s.* chismoso (a *f*) *m*, murmurador (-a *f*) *m*; ✝ comadre *f*; (*conversation*) charla *f*; comadreo *m*, murmuración *f*, chismes *m/pl.*, habladurías *f/pl.*; *piece of ~* chisme *m*, habililla *f*; *~ column* gacetilla *f*; **2.** charlar; *b.s.* chismear.

got [gɔt], **⚓** *or* **got·ten** ['~tn] *pret.* y *p.p.* of **get**.

gouge [gaudʒ] **1.** ⊕ gubia *f*; **2.** (*mst ~ out*) excavar con gubia, acanalar; *sl.* estafar.

gourd ['guəd] calabaza *f*.

gour·mand ['guəmənd] glotón *m*.

gour·met ['guəmei] gastrónomo *m*.

gout [gaut] **⚕** gota *f*.

gov·ern ['gʌvən] *v/t.* gobernar, regir (*a. fig., gr.*); dominar; *v/i.* gobernar; **'gov·ern·ess** institutriz *f*; **'gov·ern·ment** gobierno *m*; (*a. gr.*) régimen *m*; *attr.* = **gov·ern·men·tal** [~'mentl] gubernativo, gubernamental, del gobierno; **'gov·er·nor** gobernador *m*; director *m*; alcaide *m* of *prison*; **F** jefe *m*; **F** (*father*) progenitor *m*, viejo *m* *S.Am.*

gown [gaun] **1.** (*dress*) vestido *m*; **⚖** *univ.* toga *f*; traje *m* talar; **2.** vestir (con toga).

grab [græb] **1.** arrebatar, agarrar, coger; *fig.* apropiarse; **~ at** tratar de agarrar; **2.** arrebatiña *f*; agarro *m*; **F** robo *m*; ⊕ gancho *m* arrancador; ⊕ cubeta *f* draga, cuchara *f* de dos mandíbulas.

grace [greis] **1.** (*favor, attractiveness, a. eccl.*) gracia *f*; elegancia *f*; armonía *f*, decoro *m*; (*at table*) bendición *f* de la mesa; (*deferment*) respiro *m*, demora *f*; **~ note** nota *f* de adorno; **with** (*a*) **good** (**bad**) **~** de buen (mal) talante; **good ~s** favor *m*; **get into a p.'s good ~s** congraciarse con una p.; **period of ~** plazo *m*; **2.** adornar, embellecer; favorecer; honrar; **grace·ful** ['~ful] □ agraciado, gracioso.

gra·cious ['greiʃəs] □ clemente, benigno, graciable; gracioso; **good(ness) ~!** ¡Dios mío!

gra·da·tion [grə'deiʃn] graduación *f*; gradación *f*; paso *m* (gradual).

grade [greid] **1.** grado *m*; (*quality*) clase *f*, calidad *f*; (*mark*) nota *f*; (*slope*) pendiente *f*; **make the ~** vencer los obstáculos, tener éxito; **'~ cross·ing** paso *m* a nivel; **~ school** escuela *f* primaria; **2.** graduar, clasificar; *cattle* cruzar; **⚒** *etc.* nivelar, explanar.

grad·u·al ['grædjuəl] □ gradual; **grad·u·ate 1.** ['~eit] graduar(se); **2.** ['~it] graduado *adj. a. su. m* (a *f*); **grad·u·a·tion** [~'eiʃn] graduación *f*.

graft¹ [grɑːft] **1.** ✿, **ᵱ** injerto *m*; **2.** ✿, **ᵱ** injertar (*in, upon* en).

graft² [~] **1.** corrupción *f*, soborno *m*, chanchullos *m/pl.*; *sl.* **hard ~** trabajo *m* muy duro; **'graft·er** **F** chanchullero *m*.

grain [grein] **1.** grano *m*; cereales *m/pl.*; fibra *f*, hebra *f* of *wood*; vena *f*, veta *f* of *stone*; flor *f* of *leather*; granilla *f* of *cloth*; (*particle*) pizca *f*;

against the ~ fig. a contrapelo; *with a ~ of salt* con un grano de sal; 2. vetear.
gram·mar ['græmə] gramática *f*; *~ school* instituto *m* (de segunda enseñanza); *(private)* colegio *m*; escuela *f* intermedia; **gram·mar·i·an** [grə'meəriən] gramático *m*; **gram·mat·i·cal** [grə'mætikl] □ gramático, gramatical.
gram(me) [græm] gramo *m*.
gran·a·ry ['grænəri] granero *m*.
grand [grænd] 1. □ magnífico, imponente, grandioso; esplédido; *p.* distinguido, soberbio; *style* elevado, sublime; noble; magno; gran(de); estupendo; *2 Duke* gran duque *m*; *~ opera* ópera *f* seria; 2. *♪ (a. ~ piano)* piano *m* de cola; *sl.* mil dólares *m/pl.*
gran·dad ['grændæd] F abuelito *m*; **'grand·child** nieto (a *f*) *m*; **'grand·daugh·ter** nieta *f*; **'grand·fa·ther** abuelo *m*; *~('s) clock* reloj *m* de caja (*or* de pie).
gran·di·ose ['grændious] □ grandioso; *b.s.* exagerado, hinchado.
grand·ma ['grændma] F abuelita *f*.
grand·moth·er ['grændmʌðə] abuela *f*.
grand·pa ['grændpa] F abuelito *m*.
grand...: '**~par·ents** *pl.* abuelos *m/pl.*; '**~son** nieto *m*; '**~stand** tribuna *f*.
gran·u·lar ['grænjulə] granular.
grape [greip] uva *f*; *sour ~s!* ¡están verdes!; '**~fruit** toronja *f*, pomelo *m*; '**~ juice** zumo *m* de uva, jugo *m* de uvas; '**~shot** metralla *f*; '**~vine** vid *f*, parra *f*; *sl.* sistema *m* de comunicación clandestina, rumores *m/pl.*
graph [græf] gráfico *m*; *~ paper* papel *m* cuadriculado; '**graph·ic** □ gráfico; *~ arts* artes *f/pl.* gráficas.
grap·ple ['græpl] 1. *♣* arpeo *m*, rezón *m*; asimiento *m*; *wrestling:* presa *f*;

⊕ garfio *m*; 2. *v/t.* *♣* aferrar con; luchar (a brazo partido) con; *fig.* esforzarse por resolver.
grasp [grɑːsp] 1. agarro *m*, asimiento *m*; *(handclaps)* apretón *m*; *(power)* poder *m*; *(range)* alcance *m*; comprensión *f*; *have a good ~ of* saber a fondo; *within the ~ of* al alcance de; 2. *v/t.* agarrar, asir, empuñar; *hand* estrechar; apoderarse de; *fig.* comprender; *v/i.:* ~ *at* hacer por asir; '**grasp·ing** □ codicioso, tacaño.
grass [grɑːs] 1. hierba *f*; *(sward)* césped *m*; *(grazing)* pasto *m*; *go to ~* ir al pasto; *fig.* descansar; *put out to ~* echar al pasto; 2. cubrir de hierba, apacentar; '**~hop·per** saltamontes *m*; '**~land** pradera *f*; '**~plot** césped *m*; '**~roots** básico; rústico, provinciano; popular; '**~ wid·ow·(er)** F mujer *f* cuyo marido (hombre *m* cuya mujer) está ausente; '**grass·y** herboso; herbáceo.
grate¹ [greit] parrilla *f*; reja *f*; *(fireplace)* hogar *m*.
grate² [~] *v/t. food* rallar; *teeth* hacer rechinar; *v/i.* rechinar; ~ *(up)on fig.* irritar; ~ *on the ear* herir el oído.
grate·ful ['greitful] □ agradecido, reconocido; *th.* grato, agradable; *be ~ for* agradecer.
grat·i·fy ['grætifai] satisfacer; complacer; '**grat·i·fy·ing** satisfactorio, grato.
grat·ing ['greitin] 1. □ rechinador, áspero; irritante; 2. reja *f*, verja *f*; rechinamiento *m*.
gra·tis ['greitis] 1. *adv.* gratis; 2. *adj.* gratuito.
grat·i·tude ['grætitjuːd] agradecimiento *m*, reconocimiento *m*, gratitud *f*.
gra·tu·i·tous [grə'tjuːitəs] □ gratuito; **gra·tu·i·ty** gratificación *f*.
grave¹ [greiv] grave *(a. gr.)*; solemne; serio.
grave² [~] 1. fosa *f*, sepultura *f*; *(esp. monument)* tumba *f*, sepulcr *m*; 2. *[irr.]* grabar, esculpir; '**~dig· r** sepulturero *m*, enterrador *m*.
grav·el ['grævl] 1. grava *f*, recebo *m*; *𝔰* litiasis *f*, arenillas *f/pl.*; 2. engravar, recebar; desconcertar.
grav·en ['greivən] *p.p. of grave*; ~ *image* ídolo *m*.
grave...: '**~stone** lápida *f* sepulcral; '**~yard** cementerio *m*, campo *m* santo.
grav·i·tate ['græviteit] gravitar; *fig.*

dejarse atraer [to(wards) por]; **grav·i·ta·tion** gravitación f.

grav·i·ty ['græviti] gravedad f; seriedad f, solemnidad f.

gra·vy ['greivi] salsa f; jugo m (de la carne); sl. ganga f.

gray [grei] **1.** □ gris (a. fig.); horse rucio; weather pardo; gray-haired cano, canoso; gray hairs canas f/pl.; matter anat. materia f gris, seso m; **2.** (color) gris m; (horse) rucio m; **3.** volver(se) gris; (hair) encanecer; '~**beard** anciano m, viejo m; '~**haired**, '~**head·ed** canoso; '~**hound** galgo m; '**gray·ish** grisáceo; hair entrecano.

graze [greiz] **1.** v/t. grass pacer; cattle etc. apacentar, pastar; v/i. pacer; **2.** a) v/t. rozar; raspar; b) su. roce m, abrasión f, desolladura f.

grease 1. [gri:z] engrasar; v. palm²; **2.** [gri:s] grasa f; (dirt) mugre f; '~**box**, '~**cup** vaso m de engrase, caja f de sebo; '~**gun** mot. engrasador m de compresión; '~**paint** maquillaje m.

greas·y ['gri:zi] □ grasiento, pringoso; surface resbaladizo; F adulón.

great [greit] **1.** gran(de), enorme, vasto; importante; lit. magno; principal; mucho; time largo; F excelente, estupendo; F ~ at fuerte en; F ~ on aficionado a; **2.** the ~ los grandes; '~**aunt** tía abuela f; '~**coat** sobretodo m; '~'**grand·child** bisnieto (a f) m; '~'**grand·fa·ther** bisabuelo m; '~'**grand·moth·er** bisabuela f; '~'**grand·fa·ther** tarabuelo m; '~'**grand·son** tataranieto m; '**great·ly** grandemente, mucho, muy; '**great·ness** grandeza f.

Gre·cian ['gri:ʃn] griego.

greed [gri:d], '**greed·i·ness** codicia f, avaricia f; voracidad f, gula f; '**greed·y** □ codicioso, avaro; (for food) goloso, voraz.

Greek [gri:k] **1.** griego adj. a. su. m (a f); **2.** (language) griego m; that is ~ to me no lo entiendo palabra.

green [gri:n] **1.** verde; fresco; complexion pálido; (raw) crudo; F (inexperienced) novato; F (credulous) crédulo, bobo; grow~, look~ verdear; **2.** verde m; prado m; césped m; ~s pl. verduras f/pl.; bright~ verdegay adj. a. su. m; dark~ verdinegro; '~**horn** bisoño m; bobo m; '~**house** invernáculo m; '**green·ish** verdoso.

greet [gri:t] saludar; recibir; senses presentarse a; (welcome) dar la bienvenida a; '**greet·ing** saludo m, salutación f; (welcome) bienvenida f; ~s (in letters) recuerdos m/pl.

gre·gar·i·ous [gre'gɛəriəs] □ gregario; sociable.

grew [gru:] pret. of grow.

grey [grei] = gray.

grid [grid] reja f; parrilla f; ∮ red f; radio: rejilla f; mot. sl. armatoste m, rácano m; '**grid·i·ron** parrilla f; reja f; campo m de fútbol; ⛗ emparrillado m.

grief [gri:f] dolor m, pesar m, aflicción f; come to ~ malograrse; sobrevenirle a una p. una desgracia.

griev·ance ['gri:vəns] agravio m, motivo m de queja; **grieve** [gri:v] afligir(se), acongojar(se) (at, over de, por); ~ for llorar; '**griev·ous** □ doloroso, penoso; opresivo; lamentable, grave.

grill [gril] **1.** parrilla f; (meat) asado m a la parrilla; **2.** asar a la parrilla; sl. atormentar, interrogar.

grim [grim] □ severo; ceñudo; feroz; inflexible; horroroso; F muy aburrido, desagradable.

gri·mace [gri'meis] **1.** mueca f, gesto m, visaje m; **2.** hacer muecas.

grime [graim] **1.** mugre f; tizne mst m; **2.** enmugrecer.

grin [grin] **1.** sonrisa f (abierta or burlona or feroz); (grimace) mueca f; **2.** sonreír (mostrando los dientes or irónicamente or ferozmente).

grind [graind] **1.** [irr.] v/t. moler; pulverizar; (sharpen) amolar, afilar; teeth etc. hacer rechinar; dentistry: desgastar; (oppress) oprimir; ~ down desgastar; pulverizar; F oprimir, agobiar; ~ out (re)producir mecánicamente (or laboriosamente); v/i. moler(se); trabajar (or estudiar) laboriosamente; F quemarse las cejas; **2.** molienda f; F rutina f; '**grind·ing** fig. agobiante.

grip [grip] **1.** asir, agarrar; (squeeze) apretar; wheel agarrarse (a); fig. absorber la atención (a); **2.** asimiento m, agarro m; (handle) agarradero m, empuñadura f; (clutches) garras f/pl.; (handshake) apretón m; fig. dominio m, comprensión f; (bag) maletín m (con cremallera); come to ~s with luchar (a brazo partido) con; F lose one's ~ estar desbordado.

gripe [graip] **1.** esp. ~s pl. retortijón m de tripas; **2.** F quejarse.

gris·ly ['grizli] horripilante, espantoso; F desagradable.

grit [grit] **1.** arena f, cascajo m; geol. arenisca f; F valor m, firmeza f; ~s cereales m/pl. a medio moler; **2.** (hacer) rechinar.

griz·zly ['grizli] **1.** gris, grisáceo; canoso; **2.** oso m gris.

groan [groun] **1.** gemido m, quejido m; **2.** gemir, quejarse; (with weight) crujir.

gro·cer ['grousə] tendero (a f) m (de ultramarinos), abacero (a f) m; abarrotero (a f) m S.Am.; **gro·cer·ies** ['~riz] pl. comestibles m/pl., ultramarinos m/pl.; abarrotes m/pl. S.Am.; **'gro·cer·y store** tienda f de ultramarinos (or de comestibles), abacería f, colmado m; tienda f de abarrotes S.Am.

groin [grɔin] anat. ingle f; △ arista f de encuentro.

groove [gru:v] **1.** ranura f, estría f, acanaladura f; record: surco m; fig. rutina f; **2.** estriar, acanalar.

grope [group] andar a tientas; ~ one's way tentar el camino.

gross [grous] □ size: grueso, espeso; enorme; total; † bruto; character grosero; error etc. craso; **2.** gruesa f; by the ~ en gruesas; in (the) ~ en grueso; al por mayor.

gro·tesque [grou'tesk] □ grotesco.

grot·to ['grɔtou] gruta f.

grouch [grautʃ] Am. F **1.** mal humor m; **2.** estar de mal humor, refunfuñar.

ground[1] [graund] pret. a. p.p. of grind; ~ glass vidrio m deslustrado.

ground[2] [~] **1.** suelo m; (earth a. ⚡) tierra f; terreno m (a. fig.); sport: campo m; ⚓ fondo m; (reason) causa f, motivo m; (basis) fundamento m; paint. primera capa f, fondo m; ~s pl. terreno m, jardines m/pl.; fig. fundamento m, motivo m; (sediment) poso m; F down to the ~ completamente, como un guante; on the ~ sobre el terreno; on the ~(s) of con motivo de, en virtud de; on the ~(s) that porque, pretextando que; give ~ ceder terreno; **2.** ⚡ (hacer) varar; poner en tierra; ⚡ conectar con tierra; establecer; basar; enseñar los rudimentos (in de); ✈ ~ed no poder despegar; well ~ed bien fundado; versado (in en); '~ **floor** piso m bajo, planta f baja; '~·less infundado; '~·nut cacahuete m.

group [gru:p] **1.** grupo m, agrupación f; **2.** agrupar(se); **3.** colectivo.

grouse[1] [graus] orn. black ~ gallo m lira; red ~ lagópodo m escocés.

grouse[2] [~] F **1.** (motivo m de) queja f; **2.** quejarse, refunfuñar.

grove [grouv] soto m, arboleda f, boscaje m.

grov·el ['grɔvl] arrastrarse.

grow [grou] [irr.] v/i. crecer; cultivarse; (become) hacerse, ponerse, volverse; ~ a. adj. is often translated by v/i. or v/r. corresponding to adj.: ~ angry enfadarse; ~ cold enfriarse; ~ dark oscurecer(se); ~ fat engordar; ~ old envejecer(se); ~ into hacerse, llegar a ser; F ~ on a p. gustar cada vez más a una p.; (habit) arraigar en una p.; ~ out of resultar de; clothes hacérsele pequeña a una p. la ropa; habit perder (con el tiempo); ~ to inf. llegar a inf.; ~ up hacerse hombre (or mujer); (custom) imponerse; **'grow·er** cultivador (-a f) m.

growl [graul] **1.** gruñido m; rezongo m; **2.** gruñir, regañar; rezongar; decir rezongando.

grown [groun] **1.** p.p. of grow; **2.** adj. crecido, adulto, maduro; ~ over with cubierto de; '~·**up 1.** adj. mayor de edad; adulto; **2.** su. persona f mayor; **growth** [grouθ] crecimiento m; desarrollo m; aumento m; cobertura f, vegetación f; ❀ tumor m.

grub [grʌb] **1.** larva f, gusano m; contp. puerco (a f) m; sl. alimento m, comida f; **2.** v/t. desmalezar; (a. ~ out, ~ up) arrancar, desenterrar; v/i. cavar; afanarse (a. ~ away); emplearse en oficios bajos.

grudge [grʌdʒ] **1.** (motivo m de) rencor m, inquina f, resentimiento m; bear (or have) a ~ against guardar rencor a; **2.** escatimar, dar de mala gana; envidiar.

gru·el ['gruəl] approx. gachas f/pl.; **'gru·el·(l)ing 1.** castigo m; **2.** riguroso, penoso.

grue·some ['gru:səm] □ pavoroso, horripilante.

gruff [grʌf] □ voice (b)ronco; manner brusco, malhumorado.

grum·ble ['grʌmbl] **1.** queja f, regaño m; ruido m sordo; **2.** quejarse (at de); murmurar; refunfuñar; (thunder) retumbar (a lo lejos).

grunt [grʌnt] **1.** gruñido m; **2.** gruñir.

guar·an·tee [gærən'ti:] **1.** garantía f; persona f de quien se sale fiador;

garante *m/f*, fiador (-a *f*) *m*; **2.** garantizar; F asegurar.

guard [gɑːd] **1.** (*in general, p., act, a. of sword*) guarda *f*; (*fencing, ✕ duty, regiment*) guardia *f*; (*soldier*) guardia *m*; (*sentry*) centinela *m*; (*safeguard*) resguardo *m*; 🚄 jefe *m* de tren; *~'s van* furgón *m*; *off* (*one's*) *~* desprevenido; *on ~* en guardia; ✕ de guardia; *alerta*; *change ~* relevar la guardia; *mount ~* montar la guardia; **2.** *v/t.* guardar, proteger, defender (*against, from* de); vigilar, escoltar; *v/i.* *~ against* guardarse de; **'guard·ed** □ guardado; cauteloso, reservado, circunspecto; **'guard·i·an** guardián (-a *f*) *m*; ♃ tutor (-a *f*) *m*; *~ angel* ángel *m* custodio (*or* de la guarda).

gua·va ['gwɑːvə] guayaba *f*.

gue(r)·ril·la [gə'rilə] guerrilla *f*; guerrillero (a *f*) *m*.

guess [ges] **1.** adivinación *f*, conjetura *f*, suposición *f*; **2.** adivinar, conjeturar, suponer; creer; *~ at* conjeturar, estimar aproximadamente; **'guess·work** conjetura(s) *f(pl.)*.

guest [gest] huésped (-a *f*) *m*; (*at meal*) convidado (a *f*) *m*; *~ book* libro *m* de oro; **'~·room** cuarto *m* de reserva.

guf·faw [gʌ'fɔː] **1.** risotada *f*; **2.** reírse a carcajadas.

guid·ance ['gaidəns] gobierno *m*, conducta *f*, dirección *f*; consejo *m*.

guide [gaid] **1.** (*p.*) guía *m/f*; (*book, ⊕, fig. etc.*) guía *f*; *attr.* de guía; **2.** guiar, orientar; *⊕* gobernar; *~d missile* proyectil *m* (tele)dirigido; **'~·book** guía *f* (del viajero); **'~ dog** perro-lazarillo *m*; **'~·line** cuerda *f* de guía; norma *f*, pauta *f*, directorio *m*; **'~·post** poste *m* indicador.

guild [gild] gremio *m*; cofradía *f*.

guile [gail] astucia *f*, maña *f*, malicia *f*, engaño *m*.

guil·lo·tine [gilə'tiːn] **1.** guillotina *f* (*a. ⊕*); **2.** guillotinar.

guilt [gilt] culpa(bilidad) *f* (*a.* **'guilt·i·ness**); **'guilt·less** □ libre de culpa, inocente (*of* de); **'guilt·y** □ culpable; *plead ~* confesarse culpable.

guin·ea ['gini] guinea *f* (= 21 *chelines*); **'~ fowl** gallina *f* de Guinea; **'~ pig** cobayo *m*.

guise [gaiz] apariencia *f*; traje *m*; manera *f*; pretexto *m*; *in the ~ of* disfrazado de.

gui·tar [gi'tɑː] guitarra *f*; **guit·ar·ist** guitarrista *m/f*.

gulch [gʌltʃ] barranco *m*.

gulf [gʌlf] golfo *m*; abismo *m* (*a. fig.*); vorágine *f*.

gull¹ [gʌl] *orn.* gaviota *f*.

gull² [~] **1.** primo *m*, bobo *m*; **2.** engañar; inducir con engaños (*into* a).

gul·let ['gʌlit] esófago *m*; garganta *f*.

gul·li·ble ['gʌlibl] crédulo, simplón.

gul·ly ['gʌli] barranco *m*, hondonada *f*; canal *m*.

gulp [gʌlp] **1.** trago *m*, sorbo *m*; **2.** *v/t.* (*a. ~ down*) tragar, engullir; *emotion* ahogar; *v/i.* ahogarse momentáneamente.

gum¹ [gʌm] *anat.* encía *f*.

gum² [~] **1.** goma *f*; (*chewing-*) chicle *m*; (*adhesive*) cola *f*; *~s pl.* chanclos *m/pl.* de goma; **2.** engomar, pegar con goma; F (*esp. ~ up*) atascar.

gump·tion ['gʌmpʃn] F sentido *m* común; energía *f*.

gun [gʌn] **1.** arma *f* de fuego; cañón *m*; (*sporting*) escopeta *f*; (*rifle*) fusil *m*; F revólver *m*, pistola *f*; (*shot*) cañonazo *m*; F *big* (*or great*) *~* pájaro *m* gordo; *stick to one's ~s* seguir en sus trece; *a 21-~ salute* una salva de 21 cañonazos; **2.** F nadar a caza (*for* de); **'~·boat** cañonero *m*; **'~·fire** cañoneo *m*; **'gun·ner** cañonero *m*, ♣, ✕ artillero *m*; **'~·pow·der** pólvora *f*; **'~·run·ning** contrabando *m* de armas; **'~·shot** cañonazo *m*, escopetazo *m*, tiro *m* de fusil.

gur·gle ['gəːgl] **1.** (*liquid*) gluglú *m*, gorgoteo *m*; (*baby*) gorjeo *m*; **2.** gorgotear, hacer gluglú.

gush [gʌʃ] **1.** chorro *m*, borbotón *m*; *fig.* efusión *f.*; **2.** chorrear, borbotar; manar a borbotones (*from* de); *fig.* hacer extremos; **'gush·er** pozo *m* de petróleo; *fig.* persona *f* efusiva; **'gush·ing** □ *fig.* efusivo.

gust [gʌst] ráfaga *f*, racha *f*; *fig.* acceso *m*, arrebato *m*; *~ explosión f.*

gus·to ['gʌstou] usto *m*; entusiasmo *m*.

gus·ty ['gʌsti] borrascoso.

gut [gʌt] **1.** intestino *m*, tripa *f*; cuerda *f* de tripa; ♣ estrecho *m*; *sl.* descaro *m*; *~s sl.* agallas *f/pl.*; F sustancia *f*; **2.** destripar; saquear (*or* destruir) lo interior de.

gut·ter ['gʌtə] **1.** *street:* arroyo *m*; *roadside:* cuneta *f*; *roof:* canal *m*, gotera *f*; *fig.* barrios *m/pl.* bajos; **2.** *v/t.* acanalar; *v/i.* gotear; (*candle*) correrse; **'~·snipe** golfillo *m*.

gut·tur·al ['gʌtərəl] □ gutural.

guy[1] [gai] muñeco *m*, mamarracho *m*; espantajo *m*; F tío *m*, tipo *m*.

guy[2] [~] (*a.* ~ *rope*) viento *m*; retenida *f*; ~ **wire** cable *m* de retén.

guz·zle ['gʌzl] tragar, engullir; beber con exceso.

gym [dʒim] = *gymnasium*.

gym·na·si·um [dʒim'neizjəm] gimnasio *m*; **gym·nast** ['dʒimnæst] gimnasta *m/f*; **gym'nas·tic** 1. □

gym·nástico; 2. ~**s** *pl.* gimnasia *f*.

gyp [dʒip] *sl.* 1. estafa *f*; estafador *m*; 2. estafar.

gyp·sum ['dʒipsəm] yeso *m*.

gy·rate [dʒai'reit] girar; **gy'ra·tion** giro *m*, vuelta *f*.

gy·ro·com·pass ['dʒaiərə'kʌmpəs] brújula *f* giroscópica, girocompás *m*; **gy·ro·scope** ['gaiərəskoup] giroscopio *m*.

H

h [eitʃ]: *drop one's h's* hablar con poca corrección.

ha [hɑ:] ¡ah!

hab·it ['hæbit] costumbre *f*; hábito *m* (*a. dress*); *be in the* ~ *of gr.* acostumbrar *inf.*, soler *inf.*; **hab·i·tat** ['~tæt] habitat *m*, habitación *f*.

ha·bit·u·al [hə'bitjuəl] □ habitual, acostumbrado; **ha'bit·u·ate** [~eit] habituar, acostumbrar (*to* a).

hack[1] [hæk] 1. ⊕ piqueta *f*; corte *m*, hachazo *m*; mella *f*; puntapié *m* (en la espinilla); 2. cortar, acuchillar; picar; mellar; dar un puntapié (en la espinilla).

hack[2] [~] 1. caballo *m* de alquiler; rocín *m*; (*a.* ~*-writer*) escritorzuelo (*a f*) *m*, plumífero (*a f*) *m*; 2. de alquiler; mercenario; *fig.* trillado, gastado, sin originalidad.

hack·le ['hækl] ⊕ rastrillo *m*; *orn.* plumas *f/pl* del pescuezo.

hack·neyed ['hæknid] trillado, gastado.

hack·saw ['hæksɔ:] sierra *f* de armero, sierra *f* de cortar metales.

had [hæd, həd] *pret. a. p.p. of have*.

had·dock ['hædək] eglefino *m*.

hag [hæg] (*mst fig.*) bruja *f*; F callo *m*.

hag·gard ['hægəd] □ macilento; trasojado, trasnochado.

hag·gle ['hægl] (*a.* ~ *over*) regatear.

hail[1] [heil] 1. granizo *m*, pedrisco *m*; *fig.* granizada *f*; 2. granizar (*a. fig.*).

hail[2] [~] 1. *v/t.* llamar; saludar; aclamar; *v/i.*: ~ *from* proceder de, ser natural de; 2. llamada *f*, grito *m*; saludo *m*; ~! ¡salud!, ¡salve!; *within* ~ al habla.

hail·stone ['heilstoun] piedra *f* de granizo; **'hail·storm** granizada *f*.

hair [hɛə] pelo *m*; cabello *m*; (*head of*) ~ cabellera *f*; (*down*) vello *m*; F *let*

one's ~ *down* echar una cana al aire; *tear one's* ~ mesarse los cabellos; *escape by a* ~*'s breadth* escapar por un pelo; **'~·brush** cepillo *m* para el cabello; **'~·cut** corte *m* de pelo; *get a* ~ hacerse cortar el pelo; **'~·do** F peinado *m*; **'~·dress·er** peluquero (*a f*) *m*; ~*'s (shop)* peluquería *f*; **'~ dry·er** secador *m* para el pelo; **'~ dye** tinte *m* para el pelo.

hair...: **'~·less** sin pelo; pelón, calvo; **'~ net** redecilla *f*; **'~·pin** horquilla *f*; ~ *bend* viraje *m* en horquilla; **'~ rais·ing** horripilante, espeluznante; **'~ rib·bon** cinta *f* para el cabello; **'~·split·ting** quisquilla *f*, argucia *f*; 2. quisquilloso; **'~·spring** espiral *f*; **'~ style** peinado *m*; **'~ ton·ic** vigorizador *m* del cabello; **'hair·y** peludo, velloso.

hake [heik] merluza *f*.

hal·cy·on ['hælsiən] 1. alción *m*; 2. apacible, feliz; **'~ days** días *m/pl.* tranquilos, época *f* de paz.

hale [heil] sano, robusto; ~ *and hearty* sano y fuerte.

half [hɑ:f] 1. *su.* mitad *f*; *school*: trimestre *m*; parte *f*; ~ *and* ~ mitad y mitad; F *better* ~ cara mitad *f*; *by* ~ con mucho; ~ *halves* a medias; *go halves with* ir a medias con; *in* ~ en dos mitades; 2. *adj.* medio, semi...; *two and a* ~ *hours*, *two hours and a* ~ dos horas *f/pl.* y media; 3. *adv.* medio, a medias, mitad, semi...; casi; ~ *asleep* medio dormido, semidormido, dormido a medias; ~ *dressed* a medio vestir; *not* ~ *bad* bastante bueno; ~ **baked** ['~'beikt] *fig.* poco maduro, incompleto; ~ **breed** mestizo (*a f*) *m*; **'~ 'broth·er** medio hermano *m*; **'~·caste** mestizo *adj. a. su.* (*a f*); **'~ fare** medio billete *m*; **'~ 'full** a medio llenar, mediado; '**~·length** de medio cuerpo; '**~·'mast:** (at) ~ a media asta; '**~·'moon** media luna f; '~ **note ♪** nota f blanca; '~ **'pay** media paga f; '~ **'price** a mitad de precio; **~·seas o·ver** ['hɑːfsiːz'ouvə] F calamocano; '~ **'time** sport: descanso m; '**~·tone** fotograbado m a media tinta; '**~·'truth** verdad f a medias; '**~·way** 1. adv. a medio camino; 2. adj. intermedio; ~ between equidistante de; '**~·'wit·ted** imbécil.

hal·i·but ['hælibət] halibut m.

hall [hɔːl] vestíbulo m; sala f; recibimiento m; casa f señorial; ~ **guild~,** music~, town ~; univ.: residencia f; comedor m; paraninfo m.

hal·le·lu·jah [hæli'luːjə] aleluya f.

hall·mark ['hɔːlmɑːk] 1. marca f del contraste; fig. sello m; 2. contrastar; fig. sellar.

hal·low ['hælou] santificar; **Hal·low·e'en** ['...iːn] víspera f de Todos los Santos.

hal·lu·ci·na·tion [həluːsi'neiʃn] alucinación f.

ha·lo ['heilou] halo m; fig. aureola f.

halt [hɔːlt] 1. alto m, parada f; call a ~ to atajar; come to a ~ pararse; interrumpirse; 2. hacer alto, parar(se); (hesitate) vacilar; 3. cojo m; 4. ~! ¡alto!

hal·ter ['hɔːltə] cabestro m, ronzal m; (noose) dogal m.

halt·ing ['hɔːltiŋ] □ vacilante, titubeante.

halve [hɑːv] 1. partir por mitad; 2. **halves** [~z] pl. of half.

ham [hæm] jamón m, pernil m; sl. ~ (actor) comicastro m, maleta m; sl. radio: radioaficionado m.

ham·burg·er ['hæmbəːgə] hamburguesa f.

ham·let ['hæmlit] aldehuela f, caserío m.

ham·mer ['hæmə] 1. martillo m; ♪ macillo m; percusor m of firearm; 2. martillar; batir; (a. ~ in) clavar (con martillo).

ham·mock ['hæmək] hamaca f; ♣ coy m.

ham·per ['hæmpə] 1. cesto m, canasta f, excusabaraja f; 2. estorbar, embarazar, impedir.

ham·ster ['hæmstə] hámster m.

ham·string ['hæmstriŋ] 1. tendón m de la corva; 2. desjarretar; fig. incapacitar.

hand [hænd] 1. mano f; (worker) operario (a f) m, obrero (a f) m, peón m; (measure) palmo m; manecilla f of clock; aguja f of instrument; (writing) escritura f; (signature) firma f; aplausos m/pl.; fig. habilidad f; fig. influencia f; at ~ a mano; at first ~ de primera mano, directamente; ~ in glove uña y carne; by ~ a mano; change ~s cambiar de dueño; live from ~ to mouth vivir de la mano a la boca; get one's ~ in hacerse a la mano; have a ~ in tomar parte en, tener mano en; have a free ~ tener carta blanca; in ~ entre manos; money contante; dominado; take in ~ hacerse cargo de; disciplinar; entrenar; lend a ~ arrimar el hombro; ~s off! ¡fuera las manos!; on ~ a la mano; entre manos; disponible; on one's ~s a su cargo; on the one ~ por una parte; on the other ~ por otra parte; out of ~ en seguida; desmandado; ~ over fist rápidamente; take a ~ tomar parte, intervenir (at, in en); to (one's) ~ a mano; ~ to ~ cuerpo a cuerpo; put one's ~ to emprender; firmar; ~s up! ¡arriba las manos!; 2. dar; entregar; alargar; ~ down bajar; p. ayudar a bajar; transmitir; ⚖ dictaminar; ~ in entregar; p. ayudar a entrar; ~ out distribuir; p. ayudar a salir; ~ over entregar; ~ round repartir; (hacer) pasar de uno a otro; '**~·bag** bolso m, bolsa f; '**~·ball** balonmano m; '**~·bill** hoja f volante; '**~·book** manual m; (guide) guía f; '~ **brake** freno m de mano; '**~·cuff** 1. ~s pl. esposas f/pl.; 2. poner las esposas a; **hand·ful** ['~ful] puñado m, manojo m.

hand·i·cap ['hændikæp] 1. desventaja f, obstáculo m; handicap m (a. sport); 2. perjudicar, dificultar; handicapar.

hand·i·craft ['hændikrɑːft] artesanía f; destreza f manual.

hand·ker·chief ['hæŋkətʃif] pañuelo m.

han·dle ['hændl] 1. mango m, puño m; asidero m; (lever) palanca f; asa f of basket, jug etc.; tirador m of door, drawer etc.; (winding) manubrio m; fig. F título m; fig. pretexto m; sl. fly off the ~ salirse de sus casillas; 2. tocar, manosear; manejar, manipular; gobernar; (deal in) comerciar en; '**~·bar** manillar m.

han·dling ['hændliŋ] manejo m; gobierno m; tratamiento m; manoseo m.

hand...: '~**'made** hecho a mano; '~**out** F limosna f; F distribución f; F nota f de prensa; '~**'picked** escogido a mano; '~**rail** pasamano m, barandal m; '~**saw** serrucho m, sierra f de mano; '~**shake** apretón m de manos.

hand·some ['hænsəm] □ hermoso, guapo; buen mozo; *treatment etc.* generoso; *fortune etc.* considerable.

hand...: '~**'spring** voltereta f sobre las manos; '~**writ·ing** escritura f, letra f; '**hand·y** □ a mano; conveniente, práctico, manuable; útil; *p.* diestro, hábil; ~ *man* factótum m; *come in* ~ venir bien.

hang [hæŋ] **1.** [*irr.*] v/t. colgar; suspender; *wallpaper* pegar; *head* inclinar; (*execute*) ahorcar; (*drape*) poner colgaduras en; ~ *out* tender; ~ *up* colgar; interrumpir; suspender; v/i. colgar, pender; estar suspendido; (*be executed*) ser ahorcado; (*garments*) caer; ~ *in the balance* estar pendiente de un hilo; ~ *about* frecuentar, rondar; (*idle*) haraganear; ~ *back* resistirse a pasar adelante; vacilar; ~ *on* colgar de; agarrarse (*to* a); persisitir; depender; estar pendiente de; **2.** caída f *of garment*; F modo m de manejar; F sentido m; *get the* ~ *of* (lograr) entender.

hang·ar ['hæŋə] hangar m.

hang·er ['hæŋə] percha f, colgadero m; ~**on** ['~r'ɔn] *contp. fig.* parásito m, pegote m.

hang·man ['hæŋmən] verdugo m.

hang·out ['hæŋ'aut] *sl.* guarida f, nidal m.

hang·o·ver ['hæŋouvə] F resto m; *sl.* resaca f *after drinking.*

han·ker ['hæŋkə]: ~ *after* ambicionar, añorar; ~ *for* anhelar.

hap·haz·ard ['hæp'hæzəd] **1.** casualidad f; **2.** fortuito, casual.

hap·pen ['hæpən] pasar, suceder, ocurrir, acontecer, acaecer; *as it* ~s, *it* ~s *that* da la casualidad que; ~ *in(to)* entrar por casualidad; ~ *(up)on* tropezar con; acertar con; '**hap·pen·ing** suceso m, acontecimiento m.

hap·pi·ly ['hæpili] felizmente, afortunadamente.

hap·pi·ness ['hæpinis] felicidad f, dicha f.

hap·py ['hæpi] □ feliz, dichoso; *sl.* entre dos luces; *be* ~ alegrarse de, tener gusto en; *be* ~ *about* estar contento con; *v. medium*; '~**go-**

-luck·y despreocupado, imprevisor.

ha·rangue [hə'ræŋ] **1.** arenga f; **2.** arengar.

har·ass ['hærəs] acosar, hostigar; preocupar; agobiar; ✕ picar.

har·bor ['hɑːbə] **1.** puerto m; **2.** abrigar (*a. fig.*); encubrir.

hard [hɑːd] **1.** *adj.* duro, endurecido; sólido, firme; difícil, arduo, penoso; fuerte; recio; severo, inflexible; *water* crudo; *climate* áspero; *blow* rudo; *it is* ~ *to know* es difícil saber; *he is* ~ *to beat* es malo de vencer, es difícil de vencer; ~ *to deal with* intratable; *be* ~ (*up*)*on p.* estar muy duro con; *clothing etc.* gastar, echar a perder; ~ *and fast* inflexible; ~ *cash* dinero m contante; ~ *currency* moneda f dura; ~ *drinker* bebedor (-a f) m empedernido (a); ~ *liquor* licor m espiritoso; ~ *of hearing* duro de oído; **2.** *adv.* duro, duramente; de firme; difícilmente; con ahinco; *look* fijamente; ~ *by* muy cerca; F ~ *up* apurado; *be* ~ *put to it* encontrar difícil; estar en un aprieto; **3.** F = *hard labor*; '~**'bit·ten** terco; '~**'boiled** *egg* duro; F endurecido; '~**coal** antracita f; '**hard·en** endurecer(se) (*a.* ↑); solidificar(se).

hard...: '~**'heart·ed** □ duro de corazón, sin entrañas; '~**la·bor** trabajos m/pl. forzados; '~**luck** mala suerte f; ~**luck story** cuento m de penas; '**hard·ly** duramente; difícilmente; mal; (*scarcely*) apenas, casi no; ~ *ever* casi nunca; '**hard·ness** dureza f, dificultad f; fuerza f; rigor m; '**hard·ship** penas f/pl., penalidad f; infortunio m; apuro m, privación f; '**hard·ware** ferretería f, quincalla f; ~ *shop* quincallería f, ferretería f; '**hard·'work·ing** trabajador, hacendoso; '**har·dy** □ robusto; audaz; ♀ resistente.

hare [hɛə] liebre f; '~**brained** ligero de cascos; '~**lip** *anat.* labio m leporino.

ha·rem ['hɛərem] harén m.

har·lot ['hɑːlət] ramera f.

harm [hɑːm] **1.** daño m; mal m; perjuicio m; *out of* ~'s *way* a (*or* en) salvo; **2.** hacer mal (a), hacer daño (a); dañar; perjudicar; **harm·ful** ['~ful] □ dañino, dañoso, perjudicial, nocivo; **harm·less** □ inocuo, inofensivo.

har·mon·ic [hɑː'mɔnik] **1.** □ armónico; **2.** armónica f; **har'mon·i·ca** [~ikə] armónica f; **har·mo·ni·ous**

H

[hɑːˈmouniəs] armonioso; **'har·mo·ny** armonía f.

har·ness ['hɑːnis] **1.** guarniciones f/pl., arreos m/pl.; + ✕ arnés m; **2.** enjaezar, poner guarniciones a; *fig.* hacer trabajar constantemente.

harp [hɑːp] **1.** arpa f; **2.** tañer el arpa; ∼ *on* repetir constantemente.

har·poon [hɑːˈpuːn] **1.** arpón m; **2.** arpon(e)ar.

har·ry ['hæri] acosar; asolar; atormentar, inquietar.

harsh [hɑːʃ] □ áspero; *color* chillón, duro, severo, cruel.

hart [hɑːt] ciervo m.

har·vest ['hɑːvist] **1.** cosecha f, recolección f; (*reaping*) siega f; vendimia f *of grape*; ∼ *festival*, ∼ *thanksgiving* fiesta f de la cosecha; **2.** cosechar (a. *fig.*); recoger; **'har·vest·er** segador (-a f) m; (*machine*) cosechadora f.

has [hæz, həz] ha; tiene (v. *have*); **'∼-been** F persona f (*or cosa f*) que ya no sirve; vieja gloria f.

hash [hæʃ] picadillo m; F embrollo m, lío m.

haste [heist] prisa f, apresuramiento m, precipitación f.

has·ten ['heisn] v/t. apresurar, abreviar, acelerar; v/i. apresurarse (*to* a), darse prisa (*to* para, en).

hat [hæt] sombrero m; *talk through one's* ∼ decir disparates; **'∼-box** sombrerera f.

hatch¹ [hætʃ] **1.** *orn.* nidada f, pollada f; (*door*) media puerta f, postigo m; (*trap*) trampa f; compuerta f; ⚓ escotilla f; **2.** v/t. empollar, sacar del cascarón; *fig.* tramar, idear; v/i. salir del huevo; empollarse; *fig.* madurarse.

hatch² [∼] plumear.

hatch·et ['hætʃit] destral m, machado m, hacha f; *bury the* ∼ echar pelillos a la mar.

hatch·way ['hætʃwei] ⚓ escotilla f.

hate [heit] **1.** odio m (*for* a), aborrecimiento m (*for* de); **2.** odiar, aborrecer; **ha·tred** ['heitrid] = *hate* 1.

haugh·ty ['hɔːti] □ altanero, altivo.

haul [hɔːl] **1.** tirón m; (*journey*) recorrido m, trayecto m; redada f *of fish* (a. *fig.*); *fig.* botín m, ganancia f; **2.** tirar (de); arrastrar; acarrear.

haunt [hɔːnt] **1.** nidal m, querencia f, lugar m frecuentado (*of* por); (*animal's*) guarida f; **2.** frecuentar, rondar; *fig.* preseguir; (*ghost*) aparecer

en, andar por; ∼*ed house* casa f de fantasmas.

have [hæv, həv] **1.** [*irr.*] v/t. tener; poseer; gozar de; contener; obtener; *food, drink, lessons* tomar; (*cause*) hacer; sentir; pasar; decir; coger; vencer; dejar perplejo; engañar; tolerar, permitir; *child* tener, dar a luz; ∼ *just p.p.* acabar de *inf.*; ∼ *to do* tener que hacer; ∼ *to do with* tener que ver con; *I* ∼ *my hair cut* me hago cortar el pelo; *he had a suit made* mandó hacer un traje; *he had his leg broken* se (le) rompió una pierna; *I would* ∼ *you know* sepa Vd.; *as Plato has it* según Platón; *he will* ∼ *it that* sostiene que; *I had (just) as well…* lo mismo da que yo …; *I had better* go más vale que yo vaya; *it is not to be had* no se puede conseguir; *no se vende*; F *I* ∼ *been had* me han engañado; *sl.* he has had it se acabó para él; ya perdió la oportunidad; *we can't* ∼ *that* no se puede consentir (eso); *let a p.* ∼ *it* facilitárselo a una p.; F dar una paliza a una p.; F decircle cuatro verdades a una p.; F ∼ *it in for* tener tirria a; ∼ *on* F p. tomar el pelo a; *th.* llevar puesto; ∼ *it out* resolverlo discutiendo (*or* peleando); **2.** v/aux. haber; **3.** *mst the* ∼s los ricos m/pl.

ha·ven ['heivn] puerto m; abrigo m, refugio m.

have-not ['hævnɔt]: *mst the* ∼s pl. los desposeídos m/pl.

haven't ['hævnt] = *have not*.

hav·oc ['hævək] estrago m, destrucción f, ruina f; *make* ∼ *of, play* ∼ *with* (*or among*) hacer estragos en (*or* entre).

haw¹ [hɔː] ⚘ baya f del espino.

haw² [∼] **1.** *mst hem and* ∼ vacilar (al hablar); **2.** tosecilla f (falsa).

hawk¹ [hɔːk] **1.** *orn.* halcón m; **2.** cazar con halcones.

hawk² [∼] carraspear.

hawk³ [∼] vender por las calles; pregonar (a. *fig.*).

haw·thorn ['hɔːθɔːn] espino m.

hay [hei] **1.** heno m; ∼ *fever* fiebre f del heno; *sl. hit the* ∼ acostarse; *make* ∼ *of* confundir, desbaratar; **2.** segar el heno; **'∼-field** henar m; **'∼-loft** henil m; **'∼-mow** henil m; acopio m de heno; **'∼-rick, '∼-stack** almiar m; **'∼-ride** paseo m de placer en carro de heno; **'∼-seed** simiente f de heno; *sl.* patán m; **'∼-wire** *sl.* en desorden; loco.

haz·ard ['hæzəd] **1.** azar m; riesgo m,

peligro *m*; *run a* ~ correr riesgo; **2.** arriesgar; *remark etc.* aventurar; **'haz·ard·ous** □ peligroso, arriesgado.

haze[1] [heiz] calina *f*; *fig.* confusión *f*, vaguedad *f*.

haze[2] [~] vejar; dar novatada a.

ha·zel ['heizl] **1.** avellano *m*; **2.** avellanado; **'~·nut** avellana *f*.

ha·zy ['heizi] calinoso; *fig.* confuso, vago.

H-bomb ['eitʃbɔm] = *hydrogen bomb* bomba *f* de hidrógeno.

he [hi:] **1.** él; ~ *who* el que, quien; **2.** macho *m*, varón *m*.

head [hed] **1.** cabeza *f*; *lit. or iro.* testa *f*; cabecera *f* of *bed*; espuma *f* of *beer*; punta *f* of *arrow*; altura *f* de caída of *water*; culata *f* of *cylinder*; ♣ proa *f*; *geog.* punta *f*; ♀ cabezuela *f* (*p.*) jefe *m*, director (-a *f*) *m*; (*title*) encabezamiento *m*; sección *f*; *fig.* crisis *f*; ~s *or tails* cara o cruz; *I can't make* ~ *or tail of it* no le veo ni pies ni cabeza; *from* ~ *to foot* de pies a cabeza; ~ *over heels* patas arriba; *fig.* completamente, perdidamente; *off one's* ~ delirante, fuera de sí, loco; (*up*)*on one's (own)* ~ a su responsabilidad; *over one's* ~ fuera de su alcance; *por encima de uno*; *bring to a* ~ ☞ ultimar; *provocar*; *come to a* ~ madurar, llegar a la crisis; ☞ supurar; *it goes to his* ~ se le sube a la cabeza; *keep one's* ~ ser dueño de sí mismo; *lose one's* ~ perder los estribos; *talk one's* ~ *off* hablar por los codos; *he took it into his* ~ *to* se le ocurrió *inf.*; **2.** principal, primero; delantero, de frente; ♣ de proa; superior; **3.** *v/t.* encabezar, estar a la cabeza de; acaudillar; dirigir; poner cabeza a; *football* cabecear; *~ed for* con rumbo a; ~ *off* interceptar; desviar; distraer; atajar; *v/i.* dirigirse (*for, towards* hacia); (*stream*) nacer; *~ing for* ♣ con rumbo a; **'head·ache** dolor *m* de cabeza; *fig.* quebradero *m* de cabeza; **'head·dress** toca *f*, tocado *m*; **'~·first** de cabeza; precipitadamente; **'head·gear** tocado *m*; sombrero *m*, gorro *m*; cabezada *f* of *horse*; **'~·hunt·er** cazador *m* de cabezas; **'head·ing** encabezamiento *m*, título *m*; **'head·land** promontorio *m*.

head···: **'~·light** 🚗 farol *m*; *mot.* faro *m*; **'~·line** titular *m*, cabecera *f*; **'~·long 1.** *adj.* de cabeza, precipitado;

2. *adv.* de cabeza, precipitadamente; **'~ 'of·fice** oficina *f* central; **'~·'on** de frente; **'~·phones** *pl.* auriculares *m*/*pl.*; **'~·'quar·ters** *pl.* ✕ cuartel *m* general; sede *f*; jefatura *f*; oficina *f* central; **'~·stone** lápida *f* mortuoria; **'~·strong** voluntarioso, impetuoso, cabezudo; **'~·wait·er** jefe *m* de camareros, encargado de comedor; **'~·wat·ers** *pl.* cabecera *f* (de un río); **'~·way**: *make* ~ adelantar, hacer progresos; **'~·wind** viento *m* contrario; **'head·y** □ impetuoso, fogoso; terco; *wine* cabezudo, embriagador.

heal [hi:l] curar, sanar (*of* de); *cut etc.* cicatrizar(se); *fig.* remediar; ~ *up* cicatrizarse.

health [helθ] salud *f*; (*public*) sanidad *f*; *be in good* (*bad*) ~ estar bien (mal) de salud; *drink* (*to*) *the* ~ *of* beber a la salud de; **health·ful** ['~·ful] □ sano; saludable, higiénico; **'health·y** □ sano, saludable; *place etc.* salubre.

heap [hi:p] **1.** montón *m* (*a. fig.*); pila *f*, hacina *f*; **2.** amontonar, hacinar, apilar (*a.* ~ *up*); **3.** *adv.* F ~s mucho.

hear [hiə] [*irr.*] oír, sentir; escuchar; ~ *about*, ~ *of* oír hablar de, enterarse de; *I won't* ~ *of it* no lo permito; ¡ni hablar!; ~ *that* oír decir que; **heard** [hə:d] *pret. a. p.p. of* hear; **hear·er** ['hiərə] oyente *m*/*f*; **'hear·ing** (*sense*) oído *m*; audiencia *f*; ☞ vista *f*; *within* ~ al alcance de oído; ~ *aid* aparato *m* del oído; **heark·en** ['hɑːkən] *mst* ~ *to* escuchar; hacer caso de; **hear·say** ['hiəsei] rumor *m*, voz *f* común; *by* ~ de oídas.

hearse [hə:s] coche *m* (or carro *m*) fúnebre.

heart [hɑːt] corazón *m* (*a. fig.*); cogollo *m* of *lettuce*; (*soul*) alma *f*; prenda *f* (*a. dear* ~); *cards:* ~s *pl.* corazones *m*/*pl.*, copas *f*/*pl.* (*Spanish*); ~ *and soul* con toda el alma; *at* ~ en el fondo; *by* ~ de memoria; *from the* ~ de todo corazón; *lose* ~ descorazonarse; *set one's* ~ *on* tener la esperanza puesta en; poner el corazón en; *take* ~ cobrar ánimo; *take to* ~ tomar a pecho(s); *wear one's* ~ *on one's sleeve* llevar el corazón en la mano; *with all my* ~ con toda mi alma; **'~·ache** angustia *f*, pesar *m*; **'~·at-'tack** ataque *m* cardíaco; **'~·beat** latido *m* del corazón; **'~·break** congoja *f*, angustia *f*; **'~·break·ing** □ angustioso, desgarrador; **'~·bro·ken** con el corazón partido, acongojado, afli-

gido; '**~·burn** ⚕ acedía f; '**heart·en**
alentar, animar; '**~ fail·ure** debilidad f coronaria; (death) desfallecimiento m, desmayo m; '**heart·felt** cordial,
sincero, hondo.

hearth [hɑːθ] hogar m (a. fig.), chimenea f.

heart·i·ness ['hɑːtinis] cordialidad f,
sinceridad f; vigor m; campechanía
f; '**heart·less** ☐ despiadado, empedernido; '**heart-rend·ing** angustioso, desgarrador.

heart...: '**~·sick** afligido, desconsolado; '**~·strings** pl. fig. fibras f/pl. del
corazón; '**~ trou·ble** debilidad f coronaria; I have ~ soy enfermo del
corazón; '**heart·y** ☐ cordial, sincero; vigoroso, robusto; campechano.

heat [hiːt] 1. calor m (a. fig.); ardor m;
calefacción f; zo. celo m; sport: elimi-
natoria f; dead ~ empate m; in ~ en
celo; 2. calentar(se) (a. ~ up); acalo-
rar(se) (a. fig.); '**heat·ed** ☐ acalorado; '**heat·er** calentador m.

heath [hiːθ] brezal m; ♀ brezo m;
native ~ patria f chica.

hea·then [hiːðən] gentil adj. a. su.
m/f, pagano adj. a. su. m (a f); F
bárbaro adj. a. su. m (a f).

heath·er ['heðə] brezo m.

heat·ing ['hiːtiŋ] 1. calefacción f, cal-
deo m; 2. de calefacción.

heave [hiːv] 1. esfuerzo m (para levantar); echada f; henchidura f; náusea
f; jadeo m; 2. v/t. levantar; cargar;
lanzar; tirar; ⚓ jalar; sigh exhalar;
v/i. levantarse con esfuerzo; subir y
bajar; palpitar; ⚓ basquear; ⚓ (at
capstan) virar; ⚓ ~ in(to) sight aparecer.

heav·en ['hevn] (a. ~s pl.) cielo m;
(good) ⚹s! ¡Dios mío!; '**heav·en·ly**
celestial (a. fig.); ast. celeste.

heav·y ['hevi] ☐ pesado; atmosphere
opresivo; burden fig. oneroso; cloth,
line, sea grueso; ⚡ current, ⚹ fire
intenso; emphasis, expense, meal, rain
fuerte; feeling aletargado; heart triste;
liquid espeso; loss considerable; movement lento, torpe; population, traffic
denso; responsibility grave; sky encapotado; soil arcilloso; surface difícil;
task duro, penoso; yield abundante;
'**~·weight** boxing: peso m pesado.

He·brew ['hiːbruː] hebreo adj. a. su.
m (a f).

heck·le ['hekl] interrumpir (a un orador).

hec·tic ['hektik] ☐ F agitado, febril;
⚕ hé(c)tico.

hedge [hedʒ] 1. seto m (vivo); cerca f;
2. v/t. cercar con seto; ~ about, ~ in
rodear, encerrar; poner obstáculos
a; v/i. eludir la respuesta, contestar
con evasivas; vacilar; '**~·hog** erizo m;
puerco m espín; '**~·hop** ✈ sl. volar a
ras de tierra.

heed [hiːd] 1. atención f, cuidado m;
give ~ to poner atención en; 2. atender (a), hacer caso (de); '**heed·less** ☐
desatento, descuidado; distraído.

heel[1] [hiːl] 1. anat. calcañar m; anat. a.
fig. talón m; heel of shoe; parte f
inferior; parte f trasera; restos m/pl.;
sl. sinvergüenza m; cool one's ~s hacer
antesala; take to one's ~s poner pies
en polvorosa; 2. shoe poner tacón a;
football talonar.

heel[2] [~] ⚓ escorar; ~ over zozobrar.

heft·y ['hefti] F pesado; fuerte, fornido.

heif·er ['hefə] novilla f, vaquilla f.

heigh-ho ['hei'hou] ¡ay!

height [hait] altura f; elevación f;
altitud f; (top) cima f; p.'s estatura f;
(hill) cerro m; crisis f; '**height·en**
elevar; hacer más alto; aumentar;
(enhance) realzar; intensificar, avivar.

hei·nous ['heinəs] ☐ atroz, nefando.

heir [ɛə] heredero m; be ~ to heredar;
~ apparent, ~ at law heredero m
forzoso; '**hair·ess** heredera f; F soltera f adinerada; '**heir·loom** ['~·luːm]
reliquia f de familia.

held [held] pret. a. p.p. of hold 2.

hel·i·cop·ter ['helikɔptə] helicóptero
m.

he·li·um ['hiːliəm] helio m.

hell [hel] infierno m; (a. gambling-~)
garito m; sl. like~! ¡ni hablar!; F oh~!
¡demonio!; go to~! ¡vete al diablo!; F
what the ~...? ¿qué demonios...?; F
raise ~ armar la de Dios o Cristo.

hel·lo ['hʌ'lou; he'lou] teleph. ¡oiga!;
(answering teleph.) ¡diga!

helm [helm] (caña f or rueda f del)
timón m.

hel·met ['helmit] casco m; † yelmo m.

helms·man ['helmzmən] timonel m.

help [help] 1. ayuda f, auxilio m;
socorro m; remedio m; (p.) criada f;
(servants) servidumbre f; ~! ¡socorro!; call for ~ pedir socorro; 2. v/t.
ayudar (to a); auxiliar; socorrer; pain
aliviar; remediar; facilitar; (at table)
servir; ~ a p. to a th. servirle algo a

una p.; ~ o.s. servirse; valerse por sí mismo; *(not) if I can* ~ si puedo evitarlo; *it can't be* ~ed no hay (más) remedio; ~ *out* ayudar (a salir *or* a bajar); *v/i.* ayudar (a. ~ *out*); **'help·er** ayudador (-a *f*) *m*; ayudante *m*; asostente (a. ~ *out*) *f*; colaborador (-a *f*) *m*; **'help·ful** ['~ful] □ útil, provechoso; *p.* servicial, comprensivo; **'help·ing** ración *f*, porción *f*; plato *m*; **'help·less** □ impotente; incapaz; desamparado; **'help·mate** buen(a) compañero (a *f*) *m*; esposo (a *f*) *m*.

hel·ter-skel·ter ['heltə'skeltə] atropelladamente.

hem[1] [hem] **1.** dobladillo *m*, bastilla *f*; *(edge)* orilla *f*; **2.** dobladillar, bastillar; ~ *in* encerrar, cercar.

hem[2] [\~] **1.** destoserse; **2.** ¡ejem!

hem·i·sphere ['hemisfiə] hemisferio *m*.

hem·lock ['hemlɔk] cicuta *f*.

hem·or·rhage ['hemɔridʒ] hemorragia *f*; **hem·or·rhoids** ['~rɔidz] *f/pl.* hemorroides *f/pl.*

hemp [hemp] cáñamo *m*.

hen [hen] gallina *f*; *(female bird)* hembra *f*.

hence [hens] *(a. from ~)* *(place)* de aquí, desde aquí; fuera de aquí; *(time)* desde ahora; *(therefore)* por lo tanto, por eso; ~! ¡fuera (de aquí)!; **'~·forth**, **'~·for·ward** de aquí en adelante.

hen·house ['henhaus] gallinero *m*.

hen·pecked ['henpekt] dominado por su mujer.

her [hə:, hə] **1.** *possessive* su(s); **2.** *pron. acc.* la; *dat.* le; *(after prp.)* ella.

her·ald ['herəld] **1.** heraldo *m*; *fig.* anunciador *m*, precursor *m*; **2.** anunciar, proclamar; ser precursor de; **her·al·dry** ['herəldri] heráldica *f*.

herb [hə:b] hierba *f*.

herd [hə:d] **1.** manada *f*, hato *m*, rebaño *m*; piara *f* of swine; *fig.* muchedumbre *f*; **2.** *v/t.* guardar; reunir (*or* llevar) en manada; *v/i.* (a. ~ *together*) reunirse en manada; ir juntos.

here [hiə] aquí; acá; ~! ¡presente!; ~ *and there* aquí y allá; ~ *below* aquí abajo; ~'s *to...!* ¡vaya por...!; ¡a la salud de...!; ~ *it is* aquí lo tiene Vd.; *come* ~! ¡ven acá!; *that's neither* ~ *nor there* eso no viene al caso.

here·a·bout(s) ['hiərəbaut(s)] por aquí (cerca); **here·af·ter** [hiər'ɑːftə] **1.** de aquí en adelante; en lo futuro; en la vida futura; **2.** lo futuro; vida *f*

futura; **'here·by** por este medio; por la presente.

he·red·i·tar·y [hi'reditəri] hereditario; **he·red·i·ty** herencia *f*.

here·in [hiər'in] aquí dentro; en esto.

her·e·sy ['herəsi] herejía *f*.

he·ret·ic ['heretik] **1.** *(mst* **he·ret·i·cal** □ [hi'retikl]) herético; **2.** hereje *m/f*.

here·to·fore ['hiətu'fɔ:] hasta ahora; antes; **here·up·on** ['hiərə'pɔn] en esto; en seguida; **'here·with** con esto; adjunto.

her·it·age ['heritidʒ] herencia *f*.

her·mit ['hə:mit] ermitaño *m*.

her·ni·a ['hə:njə] hernia *f*.

he·ro ['hiərou], *pl.* **he·roes** ['~z] héroe *m*; **he·ro·ic** [hi'rouik] □ heroico; **her·o·ine** ['herouin] heroína *f*; **'her·o·ism** heroísmo *m*.

her·o·in ['herouin] *pharm.* heroína *f*.

her·on ['herən] garza *f* real.

her·ring ['heriŋ] arenque *m*; **'her·ring-bone** ⊕ espinapez *m*.

hers [hə:z] (el) suyo, (la) suya *etc.*

her·self [hə:'self] *(subject)* ella misma; *acc., dat.* se; *(after prp.)* sí (misma).

hes·i·tance, **hes·i·tan·cy** ['hezitəns(i)] vacilación *f*; **hes·i·tant** ['~tənt] □ vacilante, irresoluto; **hes·i·tate** ['~teit] vacilar *(about, over, to* en*)*; **hes·i·ta·tion** vacilación *f*, irresolución *f*; titubeo *m*.

hew [hju:] *[irr.]* cortar, tajar; hachear; labrar; picar; **hewn** [hju:n] *p.p. of* hew.

hey [hei] ¡eh!, ¡oye!

hey·day ['heidei] auge *m*, apogeo *m*; buenos tiempos *m/pl.*

hi [hai] ¡oye!, ¡eh!, ¡hala!

hi·a·tus [hai'eitəs] laguna *f*; interrupción *f*; *gr.,* ✠ hiato *m*.

hi·ber·nate ['haibəneit] *biol.* hibernar; invernar.

hic·cup, **a. hic·cough** ['hikʌ] **1.** hipo *m*; **2.** *v/t.* decir con hipos; *v/i.* hipar.

hick [hik] *sl.* palurdo *m*; *attr.* de aldea.

hick·o·ry ['hikəri] nogal *m* americano.

hid [hid] *pret. a.* **hid·den** ['hidn] *p.p. of* hide[2].

hide[1] [haid] piel *f*, pellejo *m*; *(esp. tanned)* cuero *m*.

hide[2] [\~] *[irr.]* **1.** *v/t.* esconder *(from* de*)*, ocultar *(from* de*)*; (en)cubrir; disimular; *v/i.* esconderse, ocultarse *(from* de*)*; **2.** *hunt.* trepa *f*; **'hide-and-'seek** escondite *m*.

hid·e·ous ['hidiəs] □ horrible; feo; monstruoso.

hide-out ['haidaut] F escondrijo *m*, guarida *f*.

hid·ing[1] ['haidiŋ] F paliza *f*, tunda *f*.

hid·ing[2] [~] ocultación *f*; *in* ~ escondido; *go into* ~ ocultarse, refugiarse; '~ **place** escondrijo *m*.

hi·er·arch·y ['haiəraːki] jerarquía *f*.

hi-fi ['hai'fai] = *high fidelity* (de) alta fidelidad *f*.

high [hai] **1.** *adj.* □ (*v. a.* ~ly) alto; *altar, mass, street* mayor; *color, price* subido; *game* manido; *manner* altanero; *meat* pasado; *number, speed* grande; *polish* brillante; *priest* sumo; *quality* superior; F *intoxicated* embriagado; *3 feet* ~ 3 pies de alto; ~ *and dry* en seco; F ~ *and mighty* encopetado; ~*est bid* mejor postura *f*; *with a* ~ *hand* arbitrariamente, despóticamente; ~ *antiquity* antigüedad *f* remota; ♀ *Church* Alta Iglesia *f*; ✕ ~ *command* alto mando *m*; ♀ *Court* tribunal *m* supremo; ~ *diving* saltos *m/pl.* de palanca; ≴ ~ *frequency* alta frecuencia *f*; ~ *life* alta sociedad *f*; ~ *living* vida *f* regalada; *v. spirit, tension etc.*; ~ *treason* alta traición *f*; ~ *wind* ventarrón *m*; ~ *words* palabras *f/pl.* airadas; **2.** *meteor.* (zona *f* de) alta presión *f*; ♀ = *High Street*; ♀ = *High School*; *on* ~ en las alturas, en el cielo; **3.** *adv.* altamente; (en) alto; fuertemente; a gran precio; lujosamente; ~ *and low* por todas partes; *aim* ~ *fig.* picar muy alto; *fly* ~ ✈ volar por alto; *fig.* picar muy alto; '~**-backed** de respaldo alto; '~**-ball** highball *m*; '~**-born** linajudo; '~**-boy** cómoda *f* alta con patas altas; '~**-brow** F intelectual *adj. a. su. m/f*; '~**-chair** silla *f* alta; '~**-class** de marca, de clase superior; '~**-grade** de calidad superior; '~**-hand·ed** arbitrario, despótico; '~**hat** *sl.* **1.** esnob *m/f*; **2.** encopetado; **3.** tratar con desdén; '~**-heeled** *shoes* de tacones altos; '~**jump** salto *m* de altura; '~**lands** tierras *f/pl.* altas, montañas *f/pl.*; '~**light** toque *m* de luz; *fig.* momento *m* culminante; '**high·ly** altamente; mucho, muy; sumamente; muy favorablemente; '**high·ness** altura *f*; ♀ Alteza *f*; '~ **noon** pleno mediodía *m*; '~**-pitched** agudo; tenso, impresionable.

high...: '~**-pow·ered** de gran potencia; '~**-pres·sure** de alta presión; *fig.* enérgico, urgente; '~**-priced** de precio elevado; '~ **rise** edificio *m* de muchos pisos; '~ **so'ci·e·ty** alta sociedad *f*, gran mundo *m*; '~**-sound·ing** altisonante; '~**-speed** de alta velocidad; '~**-spir·it·ed** animoso; *horse* fogoso; '~**-test fuel** supercarburante *m*; '~ **tide** pleamar *f*, marea *f* alta; *fig.* punto *m* culminante; '~ **time** hora *f*; *it is* ~ *for you to go* ya es hora de que Vd. se marche; *sl.* jarana *f*, parranda *f*; '~ **trea·son** alta traición *f*; '~**way** carretera *f*.

hi(gh)·jack ['haidʒæk] F *an airplane* robar; '~**er** F atracador *m*.

hike [haik] F **1.** caminata *f*, excursión *f* a pie; **2.** dar una caminata, ir de excursión; '**hik·er** F excursionista *m/f*.

hi·lar·i·ous [hi'lɛəriəs] □ hilarante.

hill [hil] colina *f*, cerro *m*, otero *m*, collado *m*; (*slope*) cuesta *f*; '~**bil·ly** ['~bili] F rústico *m* montañés; '**hill·side** ladera *f*; '**hill·y** accidentado, montuoso; *road* de fuertes pendientes.

hilt [hilt] puño *m*, empuñadura *f*; *ip to the* ~ hasta las cachas.

him [him] *acc.* lo, le; *dat.* le; (*after prp.*) él.

him·self [him'self] (*subject*) él mismo; *acc., dat.* se; (*after prp.*) sí (mismo); *by* ~ solo, por sí (solo).

hind[1] [haind] cierva *f*.

hind[2] [~] trasero, posterior; ~ *leg* pata *f* trasera; '**hin·der** ['hində] *v/t.* estorbar, dificultar.

hin·drance ['hindrəns] obstáculo *m*, estorbo *m*, impedimento *m* (*to* para).

hinge [hindʒ] **1.** gozne *m*, pernio *m*, bisagra *f*; *a. zo.* charnela *f*; *fig.* eje *m*; **2.** *v/t.* engoznar, embisagrar; *v/i.*: ~ (*up*)*on* girar sobre.

hint [hint] **1.** indirecta *f*; indicación *f*; consejo *m*; **2.** echar indirectas; (*a.* ~ *at*) insinuar.

hin·ter·land ['hintəlænd] traspaís *m*.

hip[1] [hip] *anat.* cadera *f*; ~ *and thigh* sin piedad.

hip[2] [~] ♀ escaramujo *m*.

hip[3] [~]: *int.* ~! ... ~! hurra(h)! ¡hurra! ¡viva!

hip·bone ['hipboun] cía *f*.

hire ['haiə] **1.** alquiler *m*, arriendo *m*; salario *m*, jornal *m* *of p.*; *for* (*or on*) ~ de alquiler; **2.** alquilar, arrendar (*a.* ~ *out*); tomar en arriendo; *p.* contratar.

his [hiz] **1.** su(s); **2.** *pron.* (el) suyo, (la) suya *etc.*

hiss [his] **1.** siseo *m*, silbido *m*; **2.** silbar, sisear (*a.* ~ *off*).

his·to·ri·an [his'tɔːriən] historiador (-a *f*) *m*; **his·tor·ic, his·tor·i·cal** [~'tɔrik(l)] □ histórico; **his·to·ry** ['~təri] historia *f*.

his·tri·on·ic [histri'ɔnik] □ histriónico, teatral.

hit [hit] **1.** golpe *m* (bien dado); tiro *m* certero; acierto *m*; *fig.*, *thea.*, ♪ éxito *m*, sensación *f*; ✗ impacto *m*; sátira *f*; **make a ~ with** caer en gracia a; **2.** golpear, pegar; (*collide with*) chocar con(tra), dar con; *target* dar en, acertar; (*wound*) herir; (*damage*) hacer daño a; afectar; **F** llegar a; **~ at** dirigir (un) golpe(s) a; *fig.* satirizar, apuntar a; **~ it off with** hacer buenas migas con; **~ or miss** a la buena ventura; **~ (up)on** dar con; tropezar con; **~ and run** atacar y retirarse; **~ the nail on the head** dar en el clavo; **'~-and-'run driv·er** *mot.* conductor *m* que atropella y huye.

hitch [hitʃ] **1.** tirón *m*; ♪ cote *m*, vuelta *f* de cabo; obstáculo *m*, dificultad *f*; **without a ~** a pedir de boca; **2.** mover de un tirón; amarrar; enganchar; atar; **~ up** *trousers* alzar; **'~-hike** hacer autostop.

hith·er ['hiðə] *mst lit.* acá, hacia acá; **~ and thither** acá y acullá; **hith·er·to** ['~'tuː] hasta ahora.

hive [haiv] **1.** *a. fig.* colmena *f*; **~s** ✗ urticaria *f*; **2.** enjambrar; acopiar (miel); *fig.* vivir aglomerados.

ho [hou] ¡eh!; ¡alto!; ¡hola!

hoard [hɔːd] **1.** tesoro *m* (escondido); provisión *f*; acumulación *f*; **2.** (*a. ~ up*) atesorar; acumular.

hoar-frost ['hɔː'frɔst] escarcha *f*.

hoarse [hɔːs] □ ronco, enronquecido; **'hoarse·ness** ronquedad *f*; ✗ ronquera *f*.

hoar·y ['hɔːri] cano; vetusto.

hoax [houks] **1.** mistificación *f*, burla *f*; engaño *m*; **2.** mistificar; burlar.

hob·ble ['hɔbl] **1.** cojera *f*; maniota *f*; **2.** *v/i.* cojear; *v/t.* manear.

hob·by ['hɔbi] pasatiempo *m*, afición *f*; tema *f*, manía *f*; *orn.* alcotán *m*; **'~-horse** caballito *m* (de niños); caballo *m* mecedor; *fig.* tema *f*.

hob·nob ['hɔbnɔb] **F** codearse.

ho·bo ['houbou] vagabundo *m*.

hock¹ [hɔk] **1.** *zo.* corvejón *m*; **2.** desjarretar.

hock² [~] *sl.* **1.** empeño *m*; **2.** empeñar; **'~-shop** casa *f* de empeños.

hock·ey ['hɔki] hockey *m*.

ho·cus-po·cus ['houkəs'poukəs] abracadabra *m*, mistificación *f*.

hoe [hou] **1.** azada *f*, azadón *m*; sacho *m*; **2.** azadonar; sachar.

hog [hɔg] **1.** cerdo *m*, puerco *m* (*a. fig.*); **2.** *sl.* acaparar; tragarse lo mejor de; *credit etc.* atribuirse todo; **'hog·wash** bazofia *f*.

hoist [hɔist] **1.** montacargas *m*; elevador *m S.Am.*; cabria *f*; poleame *m*; **2.** alzar; *flag* enarbolar; ♪ izar.

hold [hould] **1.** agarro *m*; asimiento *m*; *wrestling*: presa *f*; *fig.* dominio *m*, influencia *f*; *fig.* arraigo *m*; (*place to grip*) asidero *m*, asa *f*; ♪ bodega *f*; ♪ calderón *m*; **catch** (or **get, lay, take**) **~ of** agarrar, coger; apoderarse de; **have a ~ on** (or **over**) dominar; **keep ~ of** seguir agarrado a; **2.** *v/t.* tener; retener, guardar; detener; (*in place*) sujetar; agarrar, coger; contener, tener cabida para; mantener; sostener (*a.* ♪); juzgar; *post* ocupar; *meeting* celebrar; **this box won't ~ them all** en esta caja no caben todos; **~ back** retener; detener; refrenar; **~ down** sujetar; oprimir; **~ forth** perorar; **~ down a** *suport* apoyar, sostener; (*raise*) levantar; (*stop*) detener; parar; suspender; interrumpir; (*rob*) saltear; (*gangsters*) atracar; **3.** (*irr.*) *v/i.* mantenerse firme, resistir, aguantar; (de)tenerse; ser valedero; (*weather*) continuar; (*stick*) pegarse; **~ back** refrenarse; vacilar; **~ forth** perorar (*about*, on sobre); **~ good** (or **true**) ser valedero; **~ off** mantenerse a distancia; esperar; **~ on** agarrarse bien; aguantar; persistir; **~ on!** ¡espera!; **~ out** resistir; durar; **~ out for** s.t. no cejar hasta que se conceda algo; insistir en algo; **~ to** atenerse a; afirmarse en; **~ up** mantenerse en pie; (*weather*) seguir bueno; **'hold·er** (*p.*) tenedor (-a *f*) *m*; (*tenant*) arrendatario (a *f*) *m*; (*office, title*) titular *m*/*f*; (*handle*) asidero *m*; receptáculo *m*; ⊕ soporte *m*; (*pad*) agarrador *m*; (*in compounds*) porta...; **'hold·ing** posesión *f*; tenencia *f*; propiedad *f*; ✝ **~s** valores *m*/*pl.* en cartera; ✝ **~ company** sociedad *f* de control; compañía *f* tenedora; **'hold·o·ver** resto *m*, sobras *f*/*pl.*; consecuencias *f*/*pl.*; **'hold·up** **F** detención *f*; interrupción *f*; (*gangsters*) atraco *m*.

hole [houl] 1. agujero *m*; cavidad *f*; (*a. golf*) hoyo *m*; bache *m* in *road*; rotura *f* in *clothes*; boquete *m* in *wall*; guarida *f* of *animals*; *fig.* cuchitril *m*; F in a ~ en un aprieto; 2. agujerear; *ball* meter en el hoyo.

hol·i·day ['hɔlədi] día *m* de fiesta, día *m* festivo; asueto *m*.

hol·low ['hɔlou] 1. □ hueco, ahuecado; *eyes* hundido; *fig.* vacío, falso; *voice* sepulcral, cavernoso; 2. F *adv. beat* (*all*) ~ cascar, vencer completamente; 3. hueco *m*; (con)cavidad *f*; depresión *f*; hondón *m* in *terrain*; 4. (*a.* ~ *out*) ahuecar, excavar, vaciar.

hol·ly ['hɔli] acebo *m*.

hol·o·caust ['hɔləkɔːst] holocausto *m*.

hol·ster ['houlstə] pistolera *f*.

ho·ly ['houli] santo; sagrado; ~ *water* agua *f* bendita.

hom·age ['hɔmidʒ] homenaje *m*; *do, pay, or render* ~ rendir homenaje (*to a.*).

home [houm] 1. hogar *m*; domicilio *m*, casa *f*; patria (*chica*); (*institution*) asilo *m*; (*habitat*) habitación *f*; *sport:* meta *f*; *children's games:* la madre; *at* ~ en casa; *fig.* a gusto; 2. *adj.* casero, doméstico; de casa; nativo; nacional; ~ *life* vida *f* de familia; ~ *team* equipo *m* de casa; 3. *adv.* a casa; en casa; a fondo; *be* ~ estar de vuelta; *come* ~ volver a casa; *hit* ~ herir en lo vivo; dar en el blanco; ⊕ meter a fondo; 4. volver a casa; buscar la querencia; '~**baked** hecho en casa; '~**com·ing** regreso *m* al hogar; ~ **de·liv·er·y** distribución *f* a domicilio; '~ **front** frente *m* doméstico; '~**grown** de cosecha propia; del país; '**home·less** sin casa ni hogar; '**home·ly** sencillo, llano; casero; feo. **home···**: '~**made** casero, de fabricación casera; '~**mak·er** ama *f* de casa; '~**plate** in *baseball* puesto *m* metal; ~ **run** in *baseball* jonrón *m*, cuadrangular *m*; '~**sick** nostálgico; *be* ~ tener morriña; '~**stead** hacienda *f*, granja *f*; heredad *f*; casa *f*, caserío *m*; '~ **stretch** esfuerzo *m* final, último trecho *m*; '~ **town** ciudad *f* natal; '~**ward** 1. de regreso; 2. *adv.* hacia casa; hacia su país; '~**work** deberes *m/pl.*

hom·i·cide ['hɔmisaid] homicidio *m*; (*p.*) homicida *m/f*.

hom·i·ly ['hɔmili] homilía *f*.

hom·ing ['houmiŋ] vuelta *f* (al palomar); ~ *pigeon* paloma *f* mensajera; ~ *rocket* cohete *m* autodirigido buscador del blanco.

ho·mo·sex·u·al ['houmou'seksjuəl] homosexual.

hone [houn] 1. piedra *f* de afilar; 2. afilar.

hon·est ['ɔnist] □ honrado, recto, probo; (*chaste, decent, reasonable*) honesto; sincero, genuio; '**hon·es·ty** honradez *f*, rectitud *f* etc.

hon·ey ['hʌni] miel *f*; (*my*) ~*!* ¡vida mía!; '~**bee** abeja *f* (obrera); '**hon·ey·comb** panal *m*; '**hon·ey·combed** apanalado; acribillado; '**hon·eyed** ['hʌnid] meloso, melifluo; '**hon·ey·moon** 1. luna *f* de miel, viaje *m* de novios; 2. pasar la luna de miel; '**hon·ey·suck·le** ['~sʌkl] madreselva *f*.

honk [hɔŋk] 1. graznido *m* of *goose*; bocinazo *m* of *horn*; 2. graznar; bocinar.

hon·or ['ɔnə] 1. honor *m*; (*esp. good name*) honra *f*; condecoración *f*; ~*s pl.* honores *m/pl.*; *in* ~ *of* en honor de; (*up*)*on my* ~ a fe mía; 2. honrar (*a.* ✝); *signature etc.* hacer honor a.

hon·or·a·ble ['ɔnərəbl] □ honorable; honrado; (*conferring honour*) honroso.

hon·o·rar·i·um [ɔnə'rɛəriəm] honorario *m* (*mst pl.*); **hon·or·ar·y** ['ɔnərəri] honorario; no remunerado.

hood [hud] capucha *f*, capilla *f*; (*univ., penitent's, hawk's*) capirote *m*; *mot.* capota *f*; *mot.* capó *m*; *sl.* criminal *m*; '**hood·ed** encapuchado; encapirotado.

hood·lum ['huːdləm] F matón *m*, gorila *m*.

hood·wink ['hudwiŋk] vendar los ojos a; engañar.

hoof [huːf] casco *m*, pezuña *f*.

hook [huk] 1. gancho *m* (*a. boxing*); garfio *m*; (*fishing*) anzuelo *m*; (*door etc.*) aldabilla *f*; (*hanger*) colgadero *m*; ~*s and eyes* corchetes *m/pl.*; *by* ~ *or by crook* por fas o por nefas; ~, *line and sinker* totalmente; 2. *v/t.* enganchar (*a. fishing*); pescar (*a. fig.*); encorvar; *sl.* hurtar; *sl.* ~ *it* largarse; ~ *up* enganchar; abrochar; *v/i.* engancharse; encorvarse; '**hooked** [~t] ganchudo; '**hook·up** combinación *f*; conexión *f*; ⚡ acoplamiento *m*; *radio:* estaciones *f/pl.* conjugadas; '**hook·y** *play* ~ hacer novillos.

hoop [hu:p] **1.** aro *m*; ~ *skirt* miriñaque *m*; **2.** encarcar.

hoot [hu:t] **1.** ululato *m* of owl; bocinazo *m* of horn; ♫, ⊕ toque *m* de sirena; (*laugh*) risotada *f*; grito *m*; **2.** *v/i.* ulular; gritar; *mot.* tocar la bocina; ♫, ⊕ tocar la sirena; *v/t.* manifestar a gritos; dar grita a.

hop¹ [hɔp] ♀ lúpulo *m* (*a.* ~s *pl.*).

hop² [~] **1.** salt(it)o *m*, brinco *m*; ~ vuelo *m*, etapa *f*; F baile *m*; ~, *skip and jump* triple salto *m*; **2.** *v/i.* brincar, saltar; danzar; F ~ *off* marcharse; bajar de; *v/t.* atravesar (de un salto).

hope [houp] **1.** esperanza *f*; **2.** esperar (*for acc.*, *to inf.*); ~ *in* confiar en; ~ *against* ~ esperar desesperando; **hope·ful** ['~ful] □ esperanzado; optimista; esperanzador; **'hope·less** □ desesperanzado; desesperado; imposible; ☞ desahuciado.

hop·scotch ['hɔpskɔtʃ] infernáculo *m*.

horde [hɔ:d] horda *f*.

ho·ri·zon [hə'raizn] horizonte *m*; **hor·i·zon·tal** [hɔri'zɔntl] □ horizontal.

hor·mone ['hɔ:moun] hormona *f*.

horn [hɔ:n] **1.** cuerno *m*; asta *f* of stag, bull; ♫ trompa *f*; *mot.* bocina *f*, claxon *m*; ~ *of plenty* cuerno *m* de la abundancia; **2.** *sl.* ~ *in* entrometerse.

hor·net ['hɔ:nit] avispón *m*.

hor·o·scope ['hɔrəskoup] horóscopo *m*; *cast a* ~ sacar un horóscopo.

hor·ri·ble ['hɔrəbl] □ horrible, horroroso; **hor·rid** ['hɔrid] □ horroroso, horrible; F muy antipático; **hor·ry·fy** ['~fai] horrorizar; **hor·ror** ['hɔrə] horror *m* (*of a*).

hors d'œuvres [ɔ:'dɔ:vr] entremeses *m/pl.*

horse [hɔ:s] **1.** *zo.*, *gymnastics*: caballo *m*; ✕ caballería *f*; ⊕ caballete *m*; ~ *of a different color* harina *f* de otro costal; *eat like a* ~ comer como una vaca; *get on one's high* ~ darse aires de suficiencia; F *hold your* ~s! ¡para!; ¡despacito!; *take* ~ montar a caballo; ~ *artillery* artillería *f* montada; **2.** montar; proveer de caballos; **'~·back**: *on* ~ a caballo; **'~ chest·nut** castaña *f* de Indias; (*a.* ~ *tree*) castaño *m* de Indias; **'~·col·lar** collera *f*; **'~·hair** crin *f*; **'~·laugh** F risotada *f*; **'~·man** jinete *m*, caballista *m*; **'~ play** payasadas *f/pl.*, travesuras *f/pl.*, pela *f* amistosa; **'~·pow·er** caballo *m* (de fuerza); **~ race** carrera *f* de caballos; **'~·rad·ish** rábano *m* picante; **'~ sense** sentido *m* común; **'~·shoe** herradura *f*; **'~ show** concurso *m* hípico; **'~·whip** látigo *m*; **'~·wom·an** amazona *f*.

hose [houz] **1.** † calzas *f/pl.*; ✝ medias *f/pl.*, calcetines *m/pl.*; **2.** regar (*or* limpiar) con manga.

ho·sier·y ['houʒəri] calcetería *f*; géneros *m/pl.* de punto.

hos·pice ['hɔspis] hospicio *m*.

hos·pi·ta·ble ['hɔspitəbl] □ hospitalario.

hos·pi·tal ['hɔspitl] hospital *m*; **hos·pi·tal·i·ty** [~'tæliti] hospitalidad *f*; **hos·pi·tal·ize** ['~təlaiz] hospitalizar.

host¹ [houst] huésped *m* (*a.* *zo.*, ♀); anfitrión *m* *at meal*; hospedero *m* of *inn*.

host² [~] ✕ hueste *f*, ejército *m*; muchedumbre *f*; sinnúmero *m*.

host³ [~] *eccl.* hostia *f*.

hos·tage ['hɔstidʒ] rehén *m*.

hos·tel ['hɔstəl] albergue *m*; residencia *f* (de estudiantes).

hos·tess ['houstis] huéspeda *f* (*v.* host¹); ✈ azafata *f*.

hos·tile ['hɔstail] hostil; **hos·til·i·ty** [hɔs'tiliti] hostilidad *f*.

hot [hɔt] caliente; *climate* cálido; *day* caluroso, de calor; *sun* ardiente, abrasador; *taste* picante; ⊕ en caliente; *fig.* dispute acalorado; *supporter* vehemente, acérrimo; *p.* enérgico; apasionado; lujurioso; F *situation* difícil, de mucho peligro; *sl.* robado; *sl.* radiactivo; *be* ~ (*p.*) tener calor; (*weather*) hacer calor; (*th.*) estar caliente; F ~ *air* palabrería *f*; F ~ *dog* perro *m* caliente; *go like* ~ *cakes* venderse como pan bendito; *sl.* ~ *stuff* caliente; de rechupete; experto; **'hot·bed** almajara *f*; *fig.* semillero *m*, foco *m*.

ho·tel [hou'tel] hotel *m*.

hot...: **'~·head** persona *f* exaltada (*or* impetuosa); **'~·house** invernáculo *m*; ~ *rod* *sl.* bólido *m*; **'~·wa·ter**: ~ *bottle* bolsa *f* de agua caliente!

hound [haund] **1.** perro *m* (de caza); podenco *m*; sabueso *m* de Artois; *fig.* canalla *m*; **2.** acosar, perseguir.

hour ['auə] hora *f*; *fig.* momento *m*; *after* ~s fuera de horas; *by the* ~ por horas; *the small* ~s las altas horas; **'~·glass** reloj *m* de arena; **~ hand** horario *m*; **'hour·ly** (de) cada hora; por hora.

house 1. [haus], *pl.* **hous·es** ['hauziz] casa *f* (*a.* ✝); *thea.* sala *f*, público *m*, entrada f; edificio m; parl. cámara f; univ. colegio m; ~ and home hogar m; F it's on the ~ está pagado (por el dueño); keep ~ llevar la casa; ~ of cards castillo m de naipes; tener casa propia; attr. de (la) casa, domiciliario, doméstico; 2. [hauz] v/t. alojar; domiciliar; almacenar; meter (en) ⊕ encajar; ⚓ estibar; v/i. vivir, alojarse; '~ar·rest arresto m domiciliario; '~boat habitación f flotante; '~break·er ladrón m con escala; demoledor m de casas; '~bro·ken ['~brokǝn] dog or cat enseñado a hábitos de limpieza; '~coat bata f; '~fly mosca f doméstica; '~hold casa f; familia f; menaje m; attr. casero, doméstico; '~keep·er ama f de casa (or de llaves); '~phy'si·cian médico m residente; '~to-'house de casa en casa; a domicilio; '~top tejado m; shout from the ~s proclamar a los cuatro vientos; '~trained bien enseñado, limpio; '~warm·ing (a. ~ party) fiesta f de estreno de una casa; ~wife ['~waif] ama f de casa; madre f de familia; mujer f casada.

hous·ing ['hauziŋ] alojamiento m; (provisión f de) vivienda f; casas f/pl.; (storage) almacenaje m; ⊕ encaje m; ⊕ cárter m, caja f.

hove [houv] pret. a. p.p. of heave 2.

hov·el ['hovl] casucha f, cuchitril m.

hov·er ['hovǝ] cernerse; revolotear; planear; estar suspendido; flotar (en el aire); rondar; vacilar.

how [hau] cómo; price: a cómo; before adj. or adv. qué, cuán; ~ large it is! ¡qué grande es!, ¡cuán grande es!; ~ large is it? ¿cómo es de grande?, ¿de qué tamaño es?; ~ are you? ¿cómo está Vd.?; ¿qué tal? (F); ~ about ...? ¿qué tal si ...?; ¿qué te parece ...?; ¿qué tal anda ...?; v. else, far; ~ long cuánto tiempo; ~ many cuántos; ~ much cuánto; ~ often cuántas veces; ~ old is he? ¿cuántos años tiene?, ¿qué edad tiene?; '~ev·er 1. adv. comoquiera que; por más que; (with adj. or adv.) por (muy) ... que; ~ much por mucho que; 2. conj. sin embargo, no obstante, con todo.

how·itz·er ['hauitsǝ] obús m.

howl [haul] 1. aullido m; alarido m; chillido m; ⚡ silbido m; 2. aullar; dar alaridos; F reír a carcajadas.

hub [hʌb] cubo m; fig. eje m, centro m; '~cap tapacubos m.

hub·bub ['hʌbʌb] baraúnda f, batahola f, alboroto m.

hub(·by) ['hʌb(i)] F marido m.

huck·ster ['hʌkstǝ] 1. buhonero m; mercachifle m; 2. (re)vender; regatear.

hud·dle ['hʌdl] 1. pelotón m, montón m; grupo m apretado; sl. go into a ~ ir aparte para conferenciar; 2. v/t. amontonar; confundir; hacer precipitadamente; v/i. amontonarse, apretarse (a. ~ together, up) acurrucarse (a. ~ up).

hue[1] [hju:] color m, tinte m; matiz m; tono m.

hue[2] [~]: ~ and cry alarma f; protesta f clamorosa.

huff [hʌf] mal humor m, pique m; rabieta f; in a ~ ofendido.

hug [hʌg] 1. abrazo m; 2. abrazar; apretujar; coast etc. no apartarse de; fig. afirmarse en; fig. acariciar; ~ o.s. congratularse (on de, por).

huge [hju:dʒ] □ enorme, inmenso, descomunal.

hulk [hʌlk] ⚓ casco m (arrumbado); pontón m, carraca f; fig. armatoste m; 'hulk·ing grande y pesado.

hull [hʌl] 1. ⚓ casco m; ♃ vaina f, cáscara f; 2. mondar; desvainar; ⚓ dar en el casco de.

hul·la·ba·loo [hʌlǝbǝ'lu:] baraúnda f, batahola f, vocería f.

hum [hʌm] 1. zumbido m; tarareo m; murmullo m; 2. zumbar; tune tararear; v. haw; F make things ~ avivarlo, desplegar gran actividad.

hu·man ['hju:mǝn] □ humano adj. a. su. m; hu·mane [hju:'mein] □ humano; compasivo; hu·man·ism ['hju:mǝnizm] humanismo m; 'hu·man·ist humanista m/f; hu·man·i·tar·i·an [hjumæni'tɛǝriǝn] humanitario adj. a. su. m (a f); hu·man·i·ty [hju:'mæniti] humanidad f; humanities pl. humanidades f/pl.

hum·ble ['hʌmbl] 1. □ humilde; 2. humillar.

hum·bug ['hʌmbʌg] 1. bola f, farsa f; embaucamiento m; 2. embaucar.

hum·drum ['hʌmdrʌm] monótono; rutinario; aburrido.

hu·mid ['hju:mid] húmedo; hu·mid·i·ty [hju:'miditi] humedad f.

hu·mil·i·ate [hju:'milieit] humillar; hu·mil·i·a·tion [hju:mili'eiʃn] humillación f; hu·mil·i·ty [hju:'militi] humildad f.

hum·ming-bird ['hʌmiŋbǝːd] colibrí m.

hu·mor·ist ['hju:mərist] humorista *m/f*; persona *f* chistosa.

hu·mor·ous ['hju:mərəs] □ festivo, chistoso, humorístico.

hu·mor ['hju:mə] 1. humor *m*; humorismo *m*; capricho *m*; (*situation*) comicidad *f*; *in a good* (*bad*) ~ de buen (mal) humor; 2. seguir el humor a; complacer; mimar.

hump [hʌmp] joroba *f*, corcova *f*, giba *f*; montecillo *m*; 2. corcovar(se); *fig.* jorobar.

humph [mm] ¡bah!, ¡qué va!

hunch [hʌntʃ] 1. tajada *f*, pedazo *m* grande; F idea *f* corazonado *f*, sospecha *f*; 2. encorvar (*a.* ~ *up*); **'hunch·back** corcova *f*, joroba *f*; (*p.*) corcovado (a *f*) *m*, jorobado (a *f*) *m*; **'hunch·backed** corcovado, jorobado.

hun·dred ['hʌndrəd] 1. cien(to); 2. ciento *m*; centenar *m*; centena *f*; *in* (*by*) ~s a centenares; **'hun·dred·fold** 1. *adj.* céntuplo; 2. *adv.* cien veces; **hun·dredth** ['~θ] centésimo (*a. su. m*).

hung [hʌŋ] *pret. a. p.p. of hang* 1.

hun·ger ['hʌŋgə] 1. hambre *f* (*a. fig.*) (*for* de); ~ *strike* huelga *f* de hambre; 2. hambrear; tener hambre (*after, for* de).

hun·gry ['hʌŋgri] □ hambriento; *land* pobre, estéril; *be* ~ tener hambre, tener ganas (*for* de).

hunk [hʌŋk] F buen pedazo *m*, rebanada *f* gruesa.

hunt [hʌnt] 1. (partida *f* de) caza *f*, cacería *f*; montería *f*; 2. *v/t.* cazar; perseguir; buscar; *hounds etc.* emplear en la caza; *country* recorrer de caza; ~ *out*, ~ *up* rebuscar; *v/i.* cazar, buscar (*a.* ~ *for*); *go* ~*ing* ir de caza; **'hunt·er** cazador *m*; caballo *m* de caza; (*watch*) saboneta *f*; **'hunt·ing** 1. caza *f*; montería *f*; 2. cazador; de caza; **'hunt·ing ground** cazadero *m*.

hur·dle ['hə:dl] valla *f* (*a. sport*).

hurl [hə:l] 1. lanzamiento *m*; 2. lanzar, arrojar.

hur·ra(h) [hu'rɑ:] ¡hurra!; ~ *for* ...! ¡viva ...!

hur·ri·cane ['hʌrikən] huracán *m*.

hur·ried ['hʌrid] □ apresurado; hecho de (or a) prisa.

hur·ry ['hʌri] 1. prisa *f*; *in a* ~ de prisa; *be in a* ~ (o) tener prisa (*for* de); 2. *v/t.* apresurar, dar prisa a, acelerar (*a.* ~ *on*, ~ *up*); ~ *away*, ~ *off* hacer marchar de prisa; *v/i.* apresurarse (*to* a), darse

prisa (*a.* ~ *up*) (*to* para, en); ~ *away*, ~ *off* marcharse de prisa; ~ *over* pasar rápidamente por; concluir a prisa; hacer con precipitación.

hurt [hə:t] 1. daño *m*, mal *m*; dolor *m*; herida *f*; 2. [*irr.*] *v/t.* lastimar, dañar; herir; perjudicar; hacer mal a; doler; ofender; *get* ~ lastimarse; *v/i.* doler; hacer mal; F sufrir daño; **hurt·ful** ['~ful] □ dañoso, perjudicial.

hur·tle ['hə:tl] arrojarse con violencia; volar; caer con violencia.

hus·band ['hʌsbənd] 1. marido *m*, esposo *m*; 2. economizar; manejar con economía.

hush [hʌʃ] 1. silencio *m*; quietud *f*; 2. *v/t.* acallar; apaciguar; ~ *up* echar tierra a; *v/i.* callar(se); 3. ¡chito!, ¡chitón!

husk [hʌsk] 1. cascabillo *m*; cáscara *f* (*a. fig.*); 2. descascarar; desvainar.

hus·ky¹ ['hʌski] □ ronco, ♀ cascarudo; F fornido.

hus·ky² ['hʌski] esquimal *adj. a. su. m/f*; perro *m* esquimal, husky *m*.

hus·sar [hu'zɑ:] húsar *m*.

hus·tle ['hʌsl] 1. prisa *f*; actividad *f* (febril); empuje *m*; 2. *v/t.* empujar; atropellar; apresurar; dar prisa a; *v/i.* apresurarse; F menearse.

hut [hʌt] cabaña *f*; barraca *f* (*a.* ✕); casucha *f*; casilla *f*; cobertizo *m*.

hy·a·cinth ['haiəsinθ] jacinto *m*.

hy·brid ['haibrid] híbrido *adj. a. su. m* (*a f*).

hy·dra ['haidrə] hidra *f*.

hy·dran·gea [hai'dreindʒə] hortensia *f*.

hy·drant ['haidrənt] boca *f* de riego.

hy·drau·lic [hai'drɔ:lik] 1. □ hidráulico; 2. ~s hidráulica *f*.

hy·dro... ['haidrou...] hidr(o)...; '~**car·bon** hidrocarburo *m*; '~**chlo·ric ac·id** ácido *m* clorhídrico; '~**e'lec·tric** hidroeléctrico; **hy·drogen** ['haidridʒən] hidrógeno *m*; ~ *bomb* bomba *f* de hidrógeno; '~**pho·bi·a** hidrofobia *f*; '~**plane** hidroplano *m*.

hy·drox·ide [hai'drɔksaid] hidróxido *m*.

hy·e·na [hai'i:nə] hiena *f*.

hy·giene ['haidʒi:n] higiene *f*; **hy·'gi·en·ic** □ higiénico.

hymn [him] 1. himno *m*; 2. *v/t.* ensalzar con himnos; *v/i.* cantar himnos; **hym·nal** ['~nəl], **'hymn book** himnario *m*.

hy·per·bo·le [hai'pə:bəli] *rhet.* hipérbole *f*; **hy·per·crit·i·cal** ['⌣'kri-tikl] □ hipercrítico.

hy·phen ['haifən] guión *m*; **hy·phen·ate** ['⌣eit] unir (*or* separar *or* escribir) con guión.

hyp·no·sis [hip'nousis] hipnosis *f*.

hyp·not·ic [hip'nɒtik] □ hipnótico *adj. a. su. m* (a *f*); **hyp·no·tism** ['⌣nətizm] hipnotismo *m*; **hyp·no·tist** hipnotista *m/f*; **hyp·no·tize** ['⌣taiz] hipnotizar.

hy·po·chon·dri·a [haipou'kɒndriə]

hipocondría *f*; **hy·poc·ri·sy** [hi'pɒkrəsi] hipocresía *f*; **hyp·o·crite** ['hipəkrit] hipócrita *m/f*; **hyp·o'crit·i·cal** [haipə'dɔːmik] hipodérmico; **hy·po·der·mic** [haipə'dɔːmik] hipodérmico; **hy·poth·e·sis** [⌣θisis], *pl.* **hy'poth·e·ses** [⌣θisiːz] hipótesis *f*; **hy·po·thet·i·cal** [⌣pə'θetik(l)] □ hipotético.

hys·te·ri·a [his'tiəriə] ♂ histerismo *m*; excitación *f* loca; **hys·ter·i·cal** [his'terik(l)] □ histérico; **hys·ter·ics** paroxismo *m* histérico; *go into* ~ ponerse histérico.

I

I [ai] yo.

ice [ais] **1.** hielo *m*; (*to eat*) helado *m*; *break the* ~ romper el hielo; F *cut no* ~ pinchar ni cortar; **2.** *v/t.* helar; (*with sugar*) alcorzar, garapiñar; *v/i.* helarse (*a.* ~ *up*); **ice·berg** ['⌣bəːg] témpano *m*, iceberg *m*; '~·**bound** helado; preso entre los hielos; '~·**box** nevera *f*; '~·**break·er** ♣ rompehielos *m*; '~ **cap** bolsa *f* para hielo; manto *m* de hielo; '~ **cream** helado *m*, mantecado *m*; '~·**cream cone** cucurucho *m* de helado, barquillo *m* de helado; '~ **cube** cubito *m* de hielo; '~ **floe** témpano *m*; '~ '**hock·ey** hockey *m* sobre hielo.

i·ci·cle ['aisikl] carámbano *m*.

i·ci·ness ['aisinis] frialdad *f* (de hielo).

ic·ing ['aisiŋ] formación *f* de hielo; alcorza *f*, capa *f* de azúcar *on cake*.

i·con ['aikɒn] icono *m*; **i·con·o·clast** [ai'kɒnəklæst] iconoclasta *m/f*.

i·cy ['aisi] □ helado; glacial (*a. fig.*); gélido (*mst lit.*).

i·de·a [ai'diə] idea *f*, concepto *m*; *bright* ~ ocurrencia *f*, idea *f* luminosa; F *the very* ~! ¡ni hablar! **i·de·al** [ai'diəl] **1.** □ ideal; perfecto; **2.** ideal *m*; **i·de·al·ism** idealismo *m*; **i·de·al·ist** idealista *m/f*; **i·de·al'is·tic** □ idealista.

i·den·ti·cal [ai'dentikl] □ idéntico; **i·den·ti·fi·ca·tion** identificación *f*; ~ *mark* señal *f* (*or* marca *f*) de identificación; ~ *card* carta *f* de identificación; ~ *disc* disco *m* de identificación; **i'den·ti·fy** [⌣fai] identificar; **i'den·ti·ty** identidad *f*.

id·e·o·log·i·cal [aidiə'lɒdʒikl] □

ideológico; **id·e·ol·o·gy** [⌣'ɒlədʒi] ideología *f*.

id·i·o·cy ['idiəsi] idiotez *f*, imbecilidad *f*.

id·i·om ['idiəm] modismo *m*, idiotismo *m*; lenguaje *m*; idioma *m*; estilo *m*; **id·i·o·mat·ic** [idiə'mætik] □ idiomático.

id·i·o·syn·cra·sy [idiə'siŋkrəsi] idiosincrasia *f*.

id·i·ot ['idiət] idiota *m/f*, tonto (a *f*) *m*, imbécil *m/f*; **id·i·ot·ic** [idi'ɒtik] □ idiota, necio, imbécil.

i·dle ['aidl] **1.** □ ocioso; desocupado; ⊕ parado; inactivo; *p. contp.* holgazán, perezoso; vano, inútil; *talk* vacío, frívolo; ~ *question* pregunta *f* ociosa; ⊕ *run* ~ marchar en vacío; **2.** *v/t.* (*mst* ~ *away*) gastar ociosamente; perder; *v/i.* haraganear; vagar; ⊕ marchar en vacío.

i·dol ['aidl] ídolo *m*; **i'dol·a·try** idolatría *f*; **i'dol·ize** [aidəlaiz] idolatrar.

i·dyll ['aidil] idilio *m*; **i'dyl·lic** □ idílico.

if [if] **1.** si; ~ *only...!* ¡ojalá (que)...!; ~ *so* si es así; **2.** hipótesis *f*; duda *f*; ~*s and buts* peros *m/pl.*, dudas *f/pl.*; **'if·fy** F dudoso.

ig·loo ['iglu] iglú *m*.

ig·nite [ig'nait] encender(se); **ig·ni·tion** [⌣'niʃn] ignición *f*; *mot.* encendido *m*; ~ *key* llave *f* de contacto.

ig·no·ble [ig'noubl] □ innoble.

ig·no·min·i·ous [ignə'miniəs] □ ignominioso.

ig·no·ra·mus [ignə'reiməs] ignorante *m/f*; **ig·no·rance** ['ignərəns] ignorancia *f*; **'ig·no·rant** ignorante; F inculto; *be* ~ *of* ignorar, desconocer;

ig·nore [ig'nɔ:] desatender, no hacer caso de (*a p.*).

ilk [ilk] (mismo) nombre *m*; F especie *f*, jaez *m*.

ill [il] **1.** *su.* mal *m*; desgracia *f*; daño *m*; **2.** *adj.* malo; enfermo; *fall (or take)* ~ caer (*o* ponerse) enfermo; **3.** *adv.* mal; *v. ease*; *take it* ~ tomarlo a mal; '**~·ad·vised** ['iləd'vaizd] mal aconsejado; '**~·bred** malcriado; '**~·dis·posed** malintencionado; mal dispuesto (*to[wards]* a, hacia).

il·le·gal [i'li:gəl] □ ilegal.

il·leg·i·ble [i'ledʒəbl] □ ilegible.

il·le·git·i·mate [ili'dʒitimit] □ ilegítimo.

ill...: '**~·fat·ed** aciago; malhadado; malogrado; '**~·fa·vored** feo, mal parecido; '**~·feel·ing** hostilidad *f*, rencor *m*; '**~·got·ten** mal adquirido.

il·lic·it [i'lisit] □ ilícito.

il·lit·er·a·cy [i'litərəsi] analfabetismo *m*; **il·lit·er·ate** ['~·rit] □ analfabeto *adj. a. su. m* (*a f*); iletrado.

ill...: '**~·man·nered** grosero, mal educado; '**~·na·tured** malicioso; malhumorado.

ill·ness ['ilnis] enfermedad *f*, mal *m*.

il·log·i·cal [i'lodʒikl] □ ilógico.

ill...: '**~·starred** malhadado; '**~·tem·pered** de mal genio; malhumorado; '**~·timed** intempestivo.

il·lu·mi·na·tion [ilju:mi'neiʃn] iluminación *f*; alumbrado *m*.

ill-use ['il'ju:z] maltratar.

il·lu·sion [i'lu:ʒn] ilusión *f*; **il·lu·sive** [~siv] □, **il·lu·so·ry** [~səri] □ ilusorio.

il·lus·trate ['iləstreit] ilustrar; **il·lus·tra·tion** ilustración *f*; '**il·lus·tra·tive** □ ilustrativo; *de* ejemplificar; '**il·lus·tra·tor** ilustrador (-a *f*) *m*.

il·lus·tri·ous [i'lʌstriəs] □ ilustre.

ill-will ['il'wil] mala voluntad *f*; rencor *m*, odio *m*.

I'm [aim] = *I am*.

im·age ['imidʒ] **1.** imagen *f*; *be the very* (F *spitting*) ~ *of* ser el vivo retrato de; **2.** representar; retratar; imaginar; reflejar; '**im·age·ry** imaginería *f*.

im·ag·i·na·ble [i'mædʒinəbl] imaginable; **im'ag·i·nar·y** imaginario; **im·ag·i·na·tion** [~'neiʃən] imaginación *f*; **im'ag·ine** [~dʒin] imaginar (-se), figurarse; *just* ~! ¡imagínese!

im·be·cile ['imbisi:l] □ imbécil *adj. a. su. m/f*.

im·bibe [im'baib] (em)beber; *fig.* embeberse de (*or* en).

im·i·tate ['imiteit] imitar; *b.s.* remedar; **im·i·ta·tion** imitación *f*; *b.s.* remedo *m*; *attr.* imitado, artificial; '**im·i·ta·tor** imitador (-a *f*) *m*.

im·mac·u·late [i'mækjulit] □ sin mancha, limpísimo; inmaculado; correcto.

im·ma·ture [imə'tjuə] immaturo; verde.

im·me·di·ate [i'mi:djət] inmediato; **im'me·di·ate·ly 1.** *adv.* inmediatamente, luego, en seguida; **2.** *cj.* así que, luego que.

im·mense [i'mens] □ inmenso, enorme, vasto; *sl.* estupendo.

im·merse [i'mə:s] sum(erg)ir; ~ *o.s. in fig.* sumergirse en; ~*ed in fig.* absorto en.

im·mi·grant ['imigrənt] inmigrante *adj. a. su. m/f*; **im·mi·gra·tion** inmigración *f*.

im·mi·nent ['iminənt] inminente.

im·mo·bile [i'moubail] inmóvil, inmoble.

im·mod·er·ate [i'modərit] □ inmoderado.

im·mod·est [i'modist] □ inmodesto, impúdico.

im·mor·al [i'morəl] □ inmoral.

im·mor·tal [i'mɔ:tl] □ inmortal *adj. a. su. m/f*; **im·mor·tal·i·ty** [~'tæliti] inmortalidad *f*.

im·mov·a·ble [i'mu:vəbl] □ inmoble, inmóvil; inalterable.

im·mune [i'mju:n] inmune (*from, to* contra); exento (*from* de); **im'mu·ni·ty** inmunidad *f*; exención *f*; '**im·mu·nize** [~aiz] inmunizar.

imp [imp] trasgo *m*, duende *m*, diablillo *m* (*a. fig.*).

im·pact ['impækt] impacto *m* (*a. fig.*), choque *m*; *fig.* efecto *m*.

im·pair [im'pɛə] perjudicar, menoscabar, deteriorar, debilitar.

im·pale [im'peil] empalar, espetar.

im·pan·el [im'pænl] inscribir en la lista de los jurados; *a juror* elegir.

im·part [im'pa:t] comunicar, hacer saber; impartir.

im·par·tial [im'pa:ʃl] □ imparcial.

im·pass·a·ble [im'pa:səbl] □ intransitable, impracticable.

im·passe [æm'pa:s] callejón *m* sin salida (*a. fig.*).

im·pa·tience [im'peiʃns] impaciencia *f*; **im'pa·tient** □ impaciente (*at, with* con, de, por); intolerante (*of* con, para); be(come) (or get, grow) ~ impacientarse (at, with ante, con; to por); make ~ impacientar.

im·peach [im'piːtʃ] acusar (de alta traición); prosesar; censurar; tachar; **im'peach·ment** procesamiento m (por alta traición); acusación f.

im·pec·ca·ble [im'pekəbl] □ impecable, intachable.

im·pede [im'piːd] dificultar, estorbar; impedir.

im·ped·i·ment [im'pedimənt] impedimento m (a. ⚖); estorbo m (to para); speech: defecto m del habla.

im·pel [im'pel] impeler, impulsar (to a).

im·pend·ing [im'pendiŋ] inminente; pendiente.

im·per·a·tive [im'perətiv] 1. □ imperativo; imperioso; indispensable; gr. ~ mood = 2. gr. (modo) imperativo m.

im·per·cep·ti·ble [impə'septəbl] □ imperceptible.

im·per·fect [im'pəːfikt] □ imperfecto (a. gr.); deficiente, defectuoso; **im·per·fec·tion** [ˌ~pə'fekʃn] imperfección f; desperfecto m.

im·pe·ri·al [im'piəriəl] 1. □ imperial; imperatorio; 2. (beard) perilla f.

im·per·il [im'peril] poner en peligro, arriesgar.

im·per·son·al [im'pəːsnl] □ impersonal.

im·per·son·ate [im'pəːsəneit] hacerse pasar por; hacer el papel de; thea. imitar; **im·per·son·a·tion** representación f; thea. imitación f.

im·per·ti·nent [im'pəːtinənt] □ impertinente; insolente.

im·per·vi·ous [im'pəːviəs] □ impermeable, impenetrable (to a); fig. insensible (to a).

im·pet·u·ous [im'petjuəs] □ impetuoso; irreflexivo; **im·pe·tus** [ˌ~pitəs] ímpetu m; impulso m (a. fig.).

im·pinge [im'pindʒ] incidir ([up]on en); chocar ([up]on con).

im·pi·ous ['impiəs] □ impío.

imp·ish ['impiʃ] □ endiablado; travieso; juguetón.

im·pla·ca·ble [im'plækəbl] □ implacable.

im·plant [im'plɑːnt] implantar; inculcar.

im·plau·si·ble [im'plɔːzəbl] inverosímil.

im·ple·ment 1. ['implimənt] utensi-

lio m, herramienta f, instrumento m; ~s pl. ✍ apero m; 2. ['~ment] poner por obra; llevar a cabo; cumplir.

im·pli·cate ['implikeit] implicar; comprometer; enredar; **im·pli·ca·tion** inferencia f; insinuación f; complicidad f; ~s pl. trascendencia f, consecuencias f/pl.

im·plic·it [im'plisit] □ implícito; faith etc. absoluto, incondicional, ciego.

im·plied [im'plaid] implícito; be ~ sobre(e)ntenderse.

im·plore [im'plɔː] implorar.

im·ply [im'plai] implicar; (pre)suponer; dar a entender; insinuar.

im·po·lite [impə'lait] □ descortés, mal educado.

im·port 1. ['impɔːt] ✛ importación f; mercancía f importada; importancia f; significado m; ~ duty derechos m/pl. de entrada; 2. [im'pɔːt] importar (a. ✛); significar; **im·por·tance** importancia f; **im·por·tant** □ importante; de categoría; **im·port·er** importador (-a f) m.

im·pose [im'pouz] imponer; cargar; hacer aceptar; ~ upon embaucar; abusar de; molestar; **im·pos·ing** □ imponente, impresionante, majestuoso.

im·pos·si·bil·i·ty [imposə'biliti] imposibilidad f; **im·pos·si·ble** □ imposible.

im·pos·tor [im'postə] impostor (-a f) m, embaucador (-a f) m.

im·po·tence ['impətəns] impotencia f; 'im·po·tent impotente.

im·pov·er·ish [im'povəriʃ] empobrecer.

im·prac·ti·ca·ble [im'præktikəbl] □ impracticable; intratable.

im·preg·na·ble [im'pregnəbl] □ inexpugnable; **im·preg·nate** [ˌ~neit] impregnar; empreñar; biol. fecundar; imbuir.

im·pre·sa·ri·o ['imprəsɑːriəu] empresario m, empresario m de teatro.

im·press 1. ['impres] impresión f; huella f; fig. sello m; 2. [im'pres] imprimir; estampar; (of emotions) impresionar, imponer; **im·pres·sion** [ˌ~ʃn] impresión f (a. fig.); huella f; fig. efecto m; make an ~ hacer efecto; make an ~ on impresionar; be under the ~ that tener la impresión de que; **im·pres·sive** □ impresionante, imponente.

im·print 1. [im'print] imprimir; estampar; *fig.* grabar; **2.** ['imprint] impresión *f*; huella *f*; *typ.* pie *m* de imprenta.

im·pris·on [im'prizn] encarcelar, aprisionar; **im'pris·on·ment** encarcelamiento *m*; prisión *f*.

im·prob·a·ble [im'prɔbəbl] □ improbable, inverosímil.

im·promp·tu [im'prɔmtju:] **1.** *su.* improvisación *f*; **2.** *adj.* improvisado; espontáneo; **3.** *adv.* de improviso.

im·prop·er [im'prɔpə] □ impropio, incorrecto; indecoroso; ∼ *fraction* fracción *f* impropia; **im·pro·pri·e·ty** [imprə'praiəti] inconveniencia *f*, indecencia *f*; indecoro *m*; impropiedad *f* *of language*.

im·prove [im'pru:v] *v/t.* mejorar, perfeccionar; ✗ abonar; enmendar, reformar; *opportunity* aprovechar; *yield etc.* aumentar; *v/i.* mejorar(se), medrar; perfeccionarse; aumentar (-se); hacer progresos *in studies etc.*; ∼ *upon* mejorar, perfeccionar; aventajar; **im'prove·ment** mejora *f*, mejoría *f*; perfeccionamiento *m*; ✗ abono *m*; enmienda *f*, reforma *f*; aprovechamiento *m*; aumento *m*; progreso *m*.

im·pro·vise ['imprəvaiz] improvisar.

im·pru·dent [im'pru:dənt] □ imprudente, malaconsejado.

im·pu·dent ['impjudənt] ⊡ impudente, descarado, insolente, desvergonzado.

im·pugn [im'pju:n] impugnar; poner en tela de juicio.

im·pulse ['impʌls] impulso *m*, impulsión *f*; ímpetu *m*; arranque *m*, arrebato *m*; **im'pul·sive** □ impulsivo; irreflexivo.

im·pu·ni·ty [im'pju:niti] impunidad *f*; *with* ∼ impunemente.

im·pure [im'pjuə] □ impuro; adulterado; deshonesto; **im'pu·ri·ty** [∼riti] impureza *f*.

in [in] **1.** *prp.* en; dentro de; ∼ *Spain* en España; ∼ *1984* en (el año) 1984; ∼ *the box* en (*or* dentro de) la caja; ∼ *a week* dentro de una semana, de aquí a 8 días; *the biggest* ∼ *Spain* el más grande de España; ∼ *this way* de esta manera; *dressed* ∼ *white* vestido de blanco; ∼ *the morning* por la mañana; *at 7* ∼ *the morning* a las 7 de la mañana; ∼ *the daytime* de día, durante el día; ∼ *writing* por escrito; ∼ *my opinion* a mi parecer; ∼ (*good*) *time* (*early*) a tiempo, con tiempo; (*eventually*) andan-

do el tiempo, con el tiempo; ∼ *the rear* a retaguardia; ∼ *the reign of* bajo el reinado de; *one* ∼ *four* uno sobre cuatro; *day* ∼, *day out* día tras día; F *there's nothing* ∼ *it* van muy iguales; no da ningún resultado; no tiene importancia; *it is not* ∼ *him to* no es capaz de; *he has it* ∼ *him to* tiene capacidad (*or* predisposición) para; ∼ *that* en que, por cuanto; ∼ *saying this* al decir esto; **2.** *adv.* (a)dentro; *be* ∼ estar en casa (*or* en su oficina *etc.*); haber llegado; *parl.* estar en el poder; F estar en sazón; F estar de moda; *is John* ∼? ¿está Juan?; F *be* ∼ *for* estar expuesto a; *exam* presentarse a; *post* ser candidato a, solicitar; *competition* concurrir a; F *you're* ∼ *for it now* la vas a pagar; F *you don't know what you're* ∼ *for* no sabes lo que te pescas; F *be* ∼ *on* (*it*) estar en el secreto, estar al tanto de; ∼ *here* aquí dentro; ∼ *there* allí dentro; **3.** *su.* ∼*s and outs pl.* recovecos *m*/*pl.*; pormenores *m*/*pl.*

in·a·bil·i·ty [inə'biliti] incapacidad *f*; impotencia *f*; imposibilidad *f*.

in·ac·ces·si·ble [inæk'sesəbl] □ inaccesible; inasequible.

in·ac·cu·ra·cy [in'ækjurəsi] inexactitud *f*; incorrección *f*; **in'ac·cu·rate** [∼rit] □ inexacto; incorrecto.

in·ac·tive [in'æktiv] □ inactivo.

in·ad·e·quate [in'ædikwit] □ insuficiente, inadecuado.

in·ad·vert·ent [inəd'və:tənt] □ inadvertido; accidental; ∼*ly a.* sin querer.

in·ad·vis·a·ble [inəd'vaizəbl] □ imprudente, no aconsejable.

in·ane [i'nein] □ necio, fatuo, inane.

in·ap·pro·pri·ate [inə'proupriit] □ impropio, inoportuno, inadecuado.

in·ar·tic·u·late [ina:'tikjulit] □ *p.* incapaz de expresarse; inarticulado.

in·as·much [inəz'mʌtʃ]: ∼ *as* ya que; en cuanto.

in·at·ten·tion [inə'tenʃn] desatención *f*; **in·at'ten·tive** □ desatento; distraído; descuidado.

in·au·di·ble [in'ɔ:dəbl] □ inaudible, imperceptible.

in·au·gu·ral [i'nɔ:gjurəl] inaugural; **in'au·gu·rate** [∼reit] inaugurar; **in·au·gu·ra·tion** inauguración *f*.

in·born ['in'bɔ:n] innato.

in·cal·cul·a·ble [in'kælkjuləbl] □ incalculable.

in·ca·pa·ble [in'keipəbl] □ incapaz; inhábil; imposibilitado; **in·ca·pac-**

i·tate [inkə'pæsiteit] incapacitar (*for, from* para); imposibilitar.

in·cen·di·ar·y [in'sendjəri] incendiario *adj. a. su. m* (*a f*); ~ *bomb* bomba *f* incendiaria.

in·cense[1] ['insens] **1.** incienso *m* (*a. fig.*); **2.** incensar.

in·cense[2] [in'sens] encolerizar, indignar.

in·cen·tive [in'sentiv] incentivo *adj. a. su. m.*

in·cep·tion [in'sepʃn] principio *m*, comienzo *m*; inauguración *f*.

in·ces·sant [in'sesnt] □ incesante.

in·cest ['insest] incesto *m*; **in·ces·tu·ous** [in'sestjuəs] □ incestuoso.

inch [intʃ] **1.** pulgada *f* (= 2,54 *cm.*); *fig.* pizca *f*; ~*es pl. a.* estatura *f*; ~ *by* ~, *by* ~*es* palmo a palmo; *every* ~ *a man* nada menos que todo un hombre; *within an* ~ *of* a dos dedos de; **2.:** ~ *forward etc.* avanzar *etc.* palmo a palmo.

in·ci·dence ['insidəns] incidencia *f*; frecuencia *f*; extensión *f*; *angle of* ~ ángulo *m* de incidencia; **'in·ci·dent 1.** incidente *m*; episodio *m*; ocurrencia *f*; suceso *m*; **2.** incidente; propio (*to* de); **in·ci·den·tal** [~'dentl] **1.** cosa *f* accesoria (*or* sin importancia); **2.** ~ incidental, incidente; accesorio, casual; ~*ly a.* a propósito.

in·cin·er·ate [in'sinəreit] incinerar; **in·cin·er·a·tion** incineración *f*; **in·cin·er·a·tor** incinerador *m*.

in·cip·i·ent [in'sipiənt] incipiente.

in·ci·sion [in'siʒn] incisión *f*; **in·ci·sive** [~'saisiv] □ incisivo; *fig.* tajante; **in'ci·sor** [~zə] incisivo *m*.

in·cite [in'sait] incitar, mover (*to* a).

in·cli·na·tion [inkli'neiʃn] inclinación *f*; declive *m*; tendencia *f*; afición *f* (*for* a); gana(s) *f(pl.)* (*to, for* de); **in·cline** [~'klain] **1.** *v/t.* inclinar (*a. fig.*), ladear; ~*ed plane* plano *m* inclinado; *fig.* be ~*ed to* inclinarse a; *v/i.* inclinarse (*to* a); ladearse; estar inclinado, estar ladeado; **2.** *su.* [*mst* '~*klain*] declive *m*, pendiente *f*.

in·clude [in'klu:d] incluir; adjuntar, comprender; *be* ~*d in* figurar en; *everything* ~*d* todo comprendido; *including* incluso, inclusive; *not including* no comprendiendo.

in·clu·sion [in'klu:ʒn] inclusión *f*; **in·clu·sive 1.** □ *adj.* inclusivo; completo; *be* ~ *of* incluir; ~ *terms* todo incluido; **2.** *adv.* inclusive.

in·co·her·ent [inkou'hiərənt] □ incoherente; sin pies ni cabeza.

in·come ['inkəm] ingreso(s) *m(pl.)*; renta *f*; entrada *f*; *annual* ~ ingresos *m/pl.* anuales; *family* ~ entradas *f/pl.* familiares; **in·come tax** ['inkəmtæks] impuesto *m* sobre la renta.

in·com·mu·ni·ca·do [inkəmjuni-'ka:dou] incomunicado.

in·com·pa·ra·ble [in'kɔmpərəbl] □ incomparable.

in·com·pat·i·ble [inkəm'pætəbl] □ incompatible.

in·com·plete [inkəm'pli:t] □ incompleto; defectuoso; inconcluso.

in·com·pre·hen·si·ble [inkəmpri-'hensəbl] □ incomprensible.

in·con·ceiv·a·ble [inkən'si:vəbl] □ inconcebible.

in·con·clu·sive [inkən'klu:siv] □ inconcluyente; poco convincente; indeterminado.

in·con·sid·er·ate [inkən'sidərit] □ desconsiderado.

in·con·sist·en·cy [inkən'sistənsi] inconsistencia *f*, inconsecuencia *f*; **in·con'sist·ent** □ inconsistente, inconsecuente.

in·con·spic·u·ous [inkən'spikjuəs] □ que no llama la atención; ~*ly* poco aparente; modesto.

in·con·test·a·ble [inkən'testəbl] □ incontestable.

in·con·ven·ience [inkən'vi:njəns] **1.** incomodidad *f*, inconveniencia *f*, molestia *f*; inoportunidad *f*; **2.** incomodar, molestar; **in·con'ven·ient** □ incómodo, inconveniente, molesto; inoportuno.

in·cor·po·rate 1. [in'kɔ:pəreit] incorporar (*in[to], with* a, con, en); incluir; comprender; *r𝔱s* constituir(se) en corporación (*or* sociedad anónima); **2.** [in'kɔ:pərit] incorpóreo; asociado, incorporado; **in'cor·po·rat·ed** [~reitid] *✝* sociedad *f* anónima (*abbr.* S.A.); **in·cor·po·ra·tion** incorporación *f*; constitución *f* en sociedad anónima.

in·cor·rect [inkə'rekt] □ incorrecto; inexacto; erróneo.

in·cor·ri·gi·ble [in'kɔridʒəbl] □ incorregible, empecatado.

in·crease 1. [in'kri:s] *v/t.* aumentar; acrecentar; multiplicar; *v/i.* aumentarse; crecer; multiplicarse; *increasing* creciente; *increasingly* cada vez más; **2.** [ˈinkriːs] aumento *m*, incremento *m*; crecimiento *m*.

in·cred·i·ble [inˈkredibl] □ increíble.

in·cre·du·li·ty [inkriˈdjuːliti] incredulidad *f*; **in·cred·u·lous** [inˈkredjuləs] □ incrédulo.

in·cre·ment [ˈinkrimənt] incremento *m*; añadidura *f*; (*a.* ~ *value*) plusvalía *f*.

in·crim·i·nate [inˈkrimineit] acriminar, incriminar.

in·crust [inˈkrʌst] incrustar(se).

in·cu·bate [ˈinkjubeit] empollar, incubar; **in·cu·ba·tion** incubación *f*; **ˈin·cu·ba·tor** incubadora *f*; **in·cu·bus** [ˈ~bəs] íncubo *m*.

in·cul·cate [ˈinkʌlkeit] inculcar (*in* en); **in·cul·ca·tion** inculcación *f*.

in·cul·pate [ˈinkʌlpeit] inculpar.

in·cum·bent [inˈkʌmbənt] **1.** *eccl.* beneficiado *m*; **2.** incumbente, obligatorio; *be* ~ *upon* incumbir a.

in·cur [inˈkəː] incurrir en; *debt* contraer.

in·cur·a·ble [inˈkjuərəbl] □ incurable.

in·cur·sion [inˈkəːʃn] incursión *f*, invasión *f*; *fig.* penetración *f*.

in·debt·ed [inˈdetid] adeudado; reconocido; obligado; *be* ~ *to* estar en deuda con; **in·debt·ed·ness** deuda *f*, obligación *f*.

in·de·cent [inˈdiːsənt] □ indecente.

in·de·ci·sive [indiˈsaisiv] □ indeciso, inconcluyente; dudoso.

in·deed [inˈdiːd] verdaderamente, de veras; por cierto; en efecto (*a. yes*, ~); ~? ¿de veras?; *yes*, ~! ¡sí, por cierto!

in·de·fat·i·ga·ble [indiˈfætigəbl] □ infatigable, incansable.

in·de·fen·si·ble [indiˈfensəbl] □ indefendible.

in·de·fin·a·ble [indiˈfainəbl] indefinible.

in·def·i·nite [inˈdefinit] □ indefinido; incierto; vago.

in·del·i·ble [inˈdelibl] □ indeleble; ~ *pencil* lápiz tinta *m*.

in·del·i·cate [inˈdelikit] □ poco delicado, indecoroso, grosero.

in·dem·ni·ty [inˈdemniti] (*compensation*) indemnización *f*; indemnidad *f*.

in·dent [inˈdent] mellar; (en)dentar; *typ.* sangrar.

in·de·pend·ence [indiˈpendəns] independencia *f*; **in·de·pend·ent** □ independiente *adj. a. su. m/f*.

in·de·scrib·a·ble [indisˈkraibəbl] □ indescriptible; *b.s.* incalificable.

in·de·struct·i·ble [indisˈtrʌktəbl] □ indestructible.

in·de·ter·mi·nate [indiˈtəːminit] □ indeterminado; vago.

in·dex [ˈindeks] **1.** (*pl. a.* **in·di·ces** [ˈindisiːz]) (*finger, of book*) índice *m*; ~ *card* ficha *f* catalográfica; *A* exponente *m*; ♁ *eccl.* índice *m* expurgatorio; **2.** *book* poner índice a; *entry* poner en un índice.

In·di·a [ˈindjə]: ~ *ink* tinta *f* china; ~ *paper* papel *m* de China, papel *m* biblia; ~ *rubber* goma *f* de borrar; caucho *m*.

In·di·an [ˈindjən] **1.** indio (*a f*) *m*; (*Red*) ~ piel roja *m/f*; **2.** indio; ~ *club* maza *f* (de gimnasia); ~ *corn* maíz *m*; ~ *file* fila *f* india; *F* ~ *giver* dador *m* interesado (*or* de toma y daca); ~ *ink* tinta *f* china; ~ *summer* veranillo *m* de San Martín.

in·di·cate [ˈindikeit] indicar, señalar; **in·di·ca·tion** indicio *m*, señal *f*; indicación *f*; **in·dic·a·tive** [inˈdikətiv] indicativo *adj. a. su. m*; *be* ~ *of* indicar; **in·di·ca·tor** [ˈ~keitə] indicador *m* (*a.* ⊕).

in·di·ces [ˈindisiːz] *pl. of* index.

in·dict [inˈdait] acusar (ante el juez) (*for, on a charge of* de); encausar; **in·dict·ment** acusación *f*; ⚖ sumaria *f*.

in·dif·fer·ence [inˈdifrəns] indiferencia *f*; desapego *m*; falta *f* de importancia; **in·dif·fer·ent** □ indiferente; desinteresado; imparcial; *quality* mediano, ordinario.

in·dig·e·nous [inˈdidʒinəs] indígena (*to* de).

in·di·gent [ˈindidʒənt] indigente.

in·di·gest·i·ble [indiˈdʒestəbl] □ indigestible, indigesto; **in·di·ges·tion** indigestión *f*, empacho *m*.

in·dig·nant [inˈdignənt] indignado (*at a p.* con[tra]; *at a th.* de, por); **in·dig·na·tion** indignación *f*; ~ *meeting* mitin *m* de protesta; **in·dig·ni·ty** [~niti] indignidad *f*, afrenta *f*.

in·di·rect [indiˈrekt] □ indirecto; ~ *discourse* estilo *m* indirecto.

in·dis·creet [indisˈkriːt] □ indiscreto.

in·dis·crim·i·nate [indisˈkriminit] □ promiscuo, sin distinción; falto de discernimiento.

in·dis·pen·sa·ble [indisˈpensəbl] □ indispensable, imprescindible.

in·dis·pose [indis'pouz] indisponer (*for* para); **in·dis'posed** ✗ indispuesto; mal dispuesto.

in·dis·pu·ta·ble ['indis'pju:təbl] □ indisputable, incontestable.

in·dis·tinct [indis'tiŋkt] □ indistinto.

in·dis·tin·guish·a·ble [indis'tiŋgwiʃəbl] indistinguible.

in·di·vid·u·al [indi'vidjuəl] **1.** individuo *m; mst contp.* sujeto *m;* **2.** □ individual; personal; particular.

in·di·vis·i·ble [indi'vizbl] □ indivisible.

in·doc·tri·nate [in'dɔktrineit] adoctrinar (*with* en).

in·dom·i·ta·ble [in'dɔmitəbl] □ indómito, indomable.

in·door ['indɔ:] interior; de casa; de puertas adentro; *sport:* en sala; **in·doors** ['in'dɔ:z] en casa; (a)dentro; bajo techado.

in·duce [in'dju:s] inducir (*a.* ✍) (*to* a); producir; ocasionar; *sleep* provocar; **in'duce·ment** incentivo *m;* aliciente *m;* estímulo *m.*

in·dulge [in'dʌldʒ] *v/t.* desires gratificar, dar rienda suelta a; *p.* consentir, mimar; dar gusto a; *v/i.:* ~ in darse a, entregarse a; darse el lujo de, permitirse; **in'dul·gence** indulgencia *f (a. eccl.);* mimo *m;* gratificación *f;* abandono *m (in* a); desenfreno *m;* **in'dul·gent** □ indulgente.

in·dus·tri·al [in'dʌstriəl] industrial; **in'dus·tri·al·ist** industrial(ista) *m;* **in'dus·tri·ous** □ industrioso, aplicado.

in·dus·try ['indəstri] industria *f;* laboriosidad *f,* diligencia *f.*

in·e·bri·ate 1. [i'ni:brieit] embriagar, emborrachar; **2.** [i'ni:briit] borracho *adj. a. su. m* (a *f*).

in·ed·i·ble [in'edibl] incomible.

in·ef·fa·ble [in'efəbl] □ inefable.

in·ef·fec·tive [ini'fektiv], **in·ef·fec·tu·al** [~tjuəl] □ ineficaz; vano; *p.* incapaz.

in·ef·fi·ca·cy [in'efikəsi] ineficacia *f.*

in·ef·fi·cien·cy [ini'fiʃənsi] ineficiencia *f;* **in·ef'fi·cient** □ ineficiente, ineficaz.

in·el·e·gance [in'eligəns] inelegancia *f;* **in'el·e·gant** □ inelegante.

in·el·i·gi·ble [in'elidʒəbl] □ inelegible.

in·ept [i'nept] □ inepto.

in·e·qual·i·ty [ini'kwɔliti] desigualdad *f.*

in·eq·ui·ta·ble [in'ekwitəbl] injusto.

in·ert [i'nə:t] □ inerte; **in·er·tia** [i'nə:ʃiə], **in'ert·ness** inercia *f.*

in·es·cap·a·ble [inis'keipəbl] ineludible.

in·es·ti·ma·ble [in'estiməbl] inestimable.

in·ev·i·ta·ble [in'evitəbl] □ inevitable, ineludible.

in·ex·act [inig'zækt] inexacto.

in·ex·cus·a·ble [iniks'kju:zəbl] □ inexcusable, imperdonable.

in·ex·haust·i·ble [inig'zɔ:stəbl] □ inagotable, inexhausto.

in·ex·pen·sive [iniks'pensiv] □ barato, económico.

in·ex·pe·ri·ence [iniks'piəriəns] inexperiencia *f,* falta *f* de experiencia; **in·ex'pe·ri·enced** inexperto, novel.

in·ex·pli·ca·ble [in'eksplikəbl] □ inexplicable.

in·ex·press·i·ble [iniks'presəbl] □ inexpresable, indecible.

in·fal·li·bil·i·ty [infælə'biliti] infalibilidad *f;* **in'fal·li·ble** □ infalible.

in·fa·mous ['infəməs] □ infame; ♊ infamante; **in·fa·my** [~.mi] infamia *f.*

in·fan·cy ['infənsi] infancia *f (a. fig.);* ♊ menor edad *f; from* ~ desde niño; **in·fant** ['~fənt] **1.** criatura *f,* infante *m;* niño (a *f*) *m;* ♊ menor *m/f;* ~ *school* escuela *f* de párvulos; **2.** infantil.

in·fan·ti·cide [in'fæntisaid] infanticidio *m; (p.)* infanticida *m/f;* **in·fan·tile** ['infəntail] infantil; pueril; aniñado; ~ *paralysis* parálisis *f* infantil.

in·fan·try ['infəntri] infantería *f.*

in·fat·u·ate [in'fætjueit] apasionar, amartelar; *be* ~*d with* apasionarse de (*or* por); *F* estar chiflado por.

in·fect [in'fekt] infectar; inficionar (*a. fig.);* contagiar (*a. fig.);* *fig.* influenciar; **in'fec·tion** infección *f;* contagio *m (a. fig.);* **in'fec·tious** □ infeccioso; contagioso (*a. fig.*).

in·fer [in'fə:] inferir; deducir, colegir; *F* conjeturar; **in'fer·ence** ['infərəns] inferencia *f.*

in·fe·ri·or [in'fiəriə] inferior *adj. a. su. m/f;* **in·fe·ri·or·i·ty** [~ri'ɔriti] inferioridad *f;* ~ *complex* complejo *m* de inferioridad.

in·fest [in'fest] infestar; *be* ~*ed with* estar plagado de.

in·fi·del ['infidəl] infiel *adj. a. su. m/f;* pagano *adj. a. su. m* (a *f*).

in·fil·trate ['infiltreit] infiltrar(se en); **in·fil'tra·tion** infiltración *f.*

in·fi·nite ['infinit] □ infinito; **in-fin·i·tes·i·mal** [~'tesiml] infinitesimal (a. Å); **in·fin·i·tive** infinitivo m (a. ~ mood); **in·fin·i·ty** infinidad f; sinfín m; Å infinito m.

in·firm [in'fə:m] enfermizo, achacoso; débil; inestable; ~ of purpose irresoluto; **in·fir·ma·ry** enfermería f; hospital m; **in·fir·mi·ty** achaque m; enfermedad f; debilidad f; (moral) flaqueza f.

in·flame [in'fleim] inflamar (a. fig. a.).

in·flam·ma·ble [in'flæmbl] □ inflamable; **in·flam·ma·tion** [inflə'meiʃn] inflamación f (a.); **in-flam·ma·to·ry** [in'flæmətəri] inflamatorio; inflamador; speech incendiario.

in·flate [in'fleit] hinchar (a. fig.); inflar; **in·fla·tion** inflación f (a. ✝); **in·fla·tion·ar·y** inflacionista.

in·flect [in'flekt] torcer, encorvar; voice modular; gr. declinar, conjugar; ~ed gr. flexional; **in·flec·tion** inflexión f.

in·flict [in'flikt] inferir, infligir (on a); damage causar.

in·flu·ence ['influəns] 1. influencia f, influjo m ([up]on sobre); valimiento m (with cerca de); ascendiente m (over sobre); 2. influir en, influenciar; **in·flu·en·tial** [~'enʃl] □ influ(y)ente; p. prestigioso.

in·flu·en·za [influ'enzə] gripe f, trancazo m.

in·form [in'fɔ:m] v/t. informar (of de, about sobre); avisar, comunicar; enterar; v/i.: ~ against delatar; **in·for·mal** □ de confianza, sin ceremonia, familiar; sencillo; (unofficial) extraoficial; (irregular) informal; **in·for·mal·i·ty** [~'mæliti] falta f de ceremonia; familiaridad f; sencillez f; informalidad f; **in·form·ant** [~ənt] informante m/f; informador (-a f) m; = informer; **in·for·ma·tion** [infə'meiʃən] información f (a. piece of ~); informe(s) m(pl.); noticia(s) f(pl.); dato(s) m(pl.); conocimientos m/pl.; **in·form·a·tive** [in'fɔ:mətiv] informativo; **in·form·er** denunciante m/f, delator (-a f) m; F soplón m.

in·frac·tion [in'frækʃn] infracción f.

in·fre·quent [in'frikwənt] □ poco frecuente, infrecuente.

in·fringe [in'frindʒ] infringir, violar (a. ~ upon); **in·fringe·ment** infracción f, transgresión f.

in·fu·ri·ate [in'fjuərieit] enfurecer, poner furioso.

in·fuse [in'fju:z] all senses: infundir (into a, en).

in·gen·ious [in'dʒi:njəs] □ ingenioso, inventivo, hábil; listo; **in·ge·nu·i·ty** [indʒi'njuiti] ingenio m, ingeniosidad f; inventiva f; maña f.

in·got ['iŋgət] lingote m.

in·grain [in'grein] teñido en rama; fig. (a. **in·grained** [~d]) arraigado, inveterado; innato.

in·gra·ti·at·ing [in'greiʃieitiŋ] □ insinuante; congraciador; **in·grat·i·tude** [~'grætitju:d] ingratitud f, desagradecimiento m.

in·gre·di·ent [in'gri:diənt] ingrediente m, componente m.

in·hab·it [in'hæbit] habitar; **in·hab·it·a·ble** habitable; **in·hab·it·ant** habitante m/f.

in·hale [in'heil] inspirar; ✈ inhalar.

in·her·ent [in'hiərənt] □ inherente (in a).

in·her·it [in'herit] heredar; **in·her·it·ance** herencia f; patrimonio m.

in·hib·it [in'hibit] inhibir; impedir (from inf.); eccl. prohibir; **in·hi·bi·tion** [~'biʃn] inhibición f.

in·hos·pi·ta·ble [in'hɔspitəbl] □ inhospitalario, inhóspito.

in·hu·man [in'hju:mən] □ inhumano.

in·hume [in'hju:m] inhumar.

in·im·i·cal [i'nimikəl] enemigo (to de); contrario (to a).

in·im·i·ta·ble [i'nimitəbl] □ inimitable.

in·iq·ui·tous [i'nikwitəs] □ inicuo.

in·i·tial [i'niʃl] 1. □ inicial adj. a. su. f; 2. marcar (or firmar) con iniciales; **in·i·ti·ate** 1. [i'niʃieit] iniciado adj. a. su. m (a f); 2. [i'niʃieit] iniciar (into en); **in·i·ti·a·tion** iniciación f; **in·i·ti·a·tive** [~iətiv] 1. iniciativa f; on one's own ~ por su propia iniciativa; take the ~ tomar la iniciativa; 2. iniciativo.

in·ject [in'dʒekt] inyectar (into en); fig. introducir; injertar; **in·jec·tion** inyección f.

in·junc·tion [in'dʒʌŋkʃn] mandato m, precepto m; 🏛 entredicho m.

in·jure ['indʒə] body lastimar, herir; ✈ lesionar; (esp. permanently) lisiar; (damage) dañar, perjudicar, averiar; feelings, reputation injuriar, ofender; **in·ju·ri·ous** [in'dʒuəriəs] □ dañoso, perjudicial; nocivo; injurioso; **in-**

jury ['indʒəri] herida *f*, lesión *f*; perjuicio *m*, daño *m*; injuria *f*.

in·jus·tice [in'dʒʌstis] injusticia *f*.

ink [iŋk] 1. tinta *f*; 2. entintar.

ink·ling ['iŋkliŋ] atisbo *m*; sospecha *f*; indicio *m*; idea *f*.

in·laid ['inleid] *pret. a. p.p. of inlay.*

in·lay ['in'lei] 1. [*irr.* (*lay*)] taracear, embutir, incrustar; 2. taracea *f*, embutido *m*.

in·mate ['inmeit] residente *m/f*; inquilino (a *f*) *m*; preso (a *f*) *m*.

in·most ['inmoust] (más) interior; más íntimo, más recóndito.

inn [in] posada *f*, mesón *m*; (*poor*, *wayside*) venta *f*; (*bigger*) fonda *f*.

in·nate ['i'neit] innato.

in·ner ['inə] interior, interno; secreto, oculto; *mot. etc.* ~ *tube* cámara *f*; **'in·ner·most** = *inmost.*

inn·keep·er ['inki:pə] posadero (a *f*) *m*, mesonero (a *f*) *m*; ventero (a *f*) *m*; fondista *m/f*.

in·no·cence ['inəsns] inocencia *f*; **inno·cent** ['~snt] inocente *adj. a. su. m/f* (of de).

in·noc·u·ous [i'nɔkjuəs] □ inocuo.

in·no·vate ['inouveit] innovar; **in·no'va·tion** innovación *f*.

in·nu·en·do [inju'endou] indirecta *f*, insinuación *f*, pulla *f*.

in·nu·mer·a·ble [i'nju:mərəbl] □ innumerable.

in·oc·u·late [i'nɔkjuleit] inocular; **in·oc·u'la·tion** inoculación *f*.

in·of·fen·sive [inə'fensiv] □ inofensivo.

in·op·er·a·tive [in'ɔpərətiv] inoperante.

in·op·por·tune [in'ɔpɔtju:n] □ inoportuno; ~ly a deshora.

in·or·di·nate [i'nɔːdinit] □ desmesurado, excesivo; inordenado.

in·put ['input] ⊕, ⚡ (potencia *f* de) entrada *f*.

in·quire [in'kwaiə] preguntar (*about*, *after*, for por; of a); pedir informes (*about* sobre); ~ *into* inquirir, averiguar, indagar; **in'quir·y** pregunta *f*; encuesta *f*; (*esp.* ⚖) pesquisa *f*.

in·qui·si·tion [inkwi'ziʃn] inquisición *f*; **in'quis·i·tive** □ *b.s.* curioso, preguntón; especulativo.

in·road ['inroud] incursión *f*; *fig.* invasión *f*, usurpación *f* (*into*, on de).

in·sane [in'sein] □ insano, loco, demente; (*senseless*) insensato; **in'san·i·ty** insania *f*, locura *f*, demencia *f*.

in·sa·ti·a·ble [in'seiʃiəbl] insaciable.

in·scribe [in'skraib] inscribir (*a. fig.*, ☩, A); *book* dedicar.

in·scrip·tion [in'skripʃn] inscripción *f*; dedicatoria *f in book.*

in·sect ['insekt] insecto *m*; **in'sec·ti·cide** [~isaid] insecticida *adj. a. su. m.*

in·se·cure [insi'kjuə] □ inseguro; **in·se'cu·ri·ty** [~riti] inseguridad *f*.

in·sen·si·tive [in'sensətiv] insensible (to a).

in·sep·a·ra·ble [in'sepərəbl] □ inseparable.

in·sert 1. [in'sət] insertar, inserir; introducir; 2. ['insət] inserción *f*; hoja *f* insertada; **in'ser·tion** inserción *f*; *sew.* entredós *m*.

in·set ['inset] inserción *f*; intercalación *f*, encaje *m*; *typ.* medallón *m*, mapa *m* (*or* grabado *m*) en la esquina de la página.

in·side ['in'said] 1. interior *m*; parte *f* de dentro; F entrañas *f/pl.*; *on the* ~ por dentro; F ~ *out* al revés; *turn* ~ *out* volver(se) al revés; 2. *adj.* interior; interno; F secreto, confidencial; 3. *adv.* (a)dentro, hacia dentro; por dentro; 4. *prp.* dentro de.

in·sid·i·ous [in'sidiəs] □ insidioso.

in·sight ['insait] penetración *f* (psicológica); perspicacia *f*; intuición *f*.

in·sig·ni·a [in'signiə] *pl.* insignias *f/pl.*

in·sig·nif·i·cance [insig'nifikəns] insignificancia *f*; **in·sig'nif·i·cant** □ insignificante.

in·sin·cere [insin'siə] □ poco sincero, falso; **in·sin'cer·i·ty** [~'seriti] falta *f* de sinceridad, falsedad *f*.

in·sin·u·ate [in'sinjueit] insinuar; **in'sin·u·at·ing** □ insinuador; **in·sin·u'a·tion** insinuación *f*; indirecta *f*, pulla *f*.

in·sip·id [in'sipid] □ insípido, soso.

in·sist [in'sist] insistir ([up]on en, sobre; *on ger.* en *inf.*; *that* en que); empeñarse (en); porfiar; **in'sist·ence** insistencia *f*, empeño *m*, porfía *f*; **in'sist·ent** □ insistente, porfiado; urgente.

in·so·la·tion [insou'leiʃn] 🌣 insolación *f*.

in·so·lence ['insələns] insolencia *f*, descaro *m*; **'in·so·lent** □ insolente, descarado.

in·sol·u·ble [in'sɔljəbl] □ insoluble; *problem* indescifrable.

in·som·ni·a [in'sɔmniə] insomnio *m*.

in·spect [in'spekt] inspeccionar; examinar; registrar; ⚔ pasar revista a;

in·spec·tion [insˈpɛkʃən] inspección f; examen m; registro m; ✕ revista f; ✕ pit foso m de reconocimiento; **in·spec·tor** inspector m; interventor m; 🚢 revisor m.

in·spi·ra·tion [inspəˈreiʃn] inspiración f; **in·spire** [ˈspaiə] inspirar; mover (a to).

in·stall instalar; **in·stal·la·tion** [instəˈleiʃn] instalación f.

in·stal(l)·ment [inˈstɔːlmənt] entrega f; 🕇 plazo m; payment by (or in) ~s pago m a plazos; ~ plan pago m a plazos, compra f a plazos; on the ~ plan con facilidades de pago.

in·stance [ˈinstəns] 1. ejemplo m, caso m; vez f, ocasión f; petición f; for ~ por ejemplo; 2. poner por caso, citar (como ejemplo).

in·stant [ˈinstənt] 1. instante m, momento m; in an ~, on the ~, this ~ al instante, en seguida; 2. cj.: the ~ luego que, en cuanto; 3. ☐ inmediato, urgente; corriente; the 10th ~ (mst inst.) el 10 del (mes) corriente; **in·stan·ta·ne·ous** [ˈteinjəs] ☐ instantáneo; **in·stant·ly** [ˈinstəntli] inmediatamente, al instante.

in·stead [insˈted] en cambio; en lugar de ello (or él, ella, etc.); ~ of en lugar de, en vez de.

in·sti·gate [ˈinstigeit] instigar.

in·stil(l) [inˈstil] instilar; infundir, inculcar (into en).

in·stinct 1. [ˈinstiŋkt] instinto m; 2. [inˈstiŋkt] ~ with animado de, lleno de; **in·stinc·tive** ☐ instintivo.

in·sti·tute [ˈinstitjuːt] 1. instituto m; 2. instituir; **in·sti·tu·tion** institución f; fundación f; establecimiento m; iniciación f; instituto m; asilo m; costumbre f.

in·struct [insˈtrʌkt] instruir (about, in de, en, sobre); mandar (to a); **in·struc·tion** instrucción f; ~s pl. instrucciones f/pl.; indicaciones f/pl.; orden f; ~s for use modo m de empleo; **in·struc·tive** ☐ instructivo; **in·struc·tor** instructor m; univ. profesor m (auxiliar).

in·stru·ment [ˈinstrumənt] all senses: instrumento m; **in·stru·men·tal** [ˈmentl] instrumental; be ~ in contribuir (materialmente) a, intervenir en, ayudar a.

in·suf·fi·cient [insəˈfiʃnt] ☐ insuficiente.

in·su·lar [ˈinsjulə] insular, isleño; fig. de miras estrechas; **in·su·lar·i·ty** [ˈlæriti] insularidad f; fig. estrechez f de miras; **in·su·late** [ˈleit] aislar; **in·su·la·tion** aislamiento m.

in·su·lin [ˈinsjulin] insulina f.

in·sult 1. [ˈinsʌlt] insulto m, ultraje m, injuria f; 2. [inˈsʌlt] insultar, ultrajar, injuriar; **in·sult·ing** ☐ insultante, injurioso.

in·sur·ance [inˈʃuərəns] aseguramiento m; 🕇 seguro m; ~ company compañía f de seguros; ~ policy póliza f; ~ premium prima f, premio m; **in·sure** [inˈʃuə] asegurar; **in·sured** asegurado (a f) m.

in·sur·gent [inˈsɔːdʒənt] insurgente adj. a. su. m/f, insurrecto adj. a. su. m (a f).

in·sur·mount·a·ble [insəˈmauntəbl] insuperable.

in·sur·rec·tion [insəˈrekʃn] insurrección f, levantamiento m.

in·tact [inˈtækt] intacto, íntegro, ileso.

in·take [ˈinteik] ⊕ admisión f, toma f, entrada f; cantidad f admitida; número m admitido; ~ manifold multiple m de admisión, colector m de admisión; ~ valve válvula f de admisión.

in·tan·gi·ble [inˈtændʒəbl] ☐ intangible.

in·te·ger [ˈintidʒə] (número m) entero m; **in·te·gral** [ˈgrəl] 1. ☐ (whole) íntegro; (component) integrante; 𝔄 integral; 2. 𝔄 integral f; **in·te·grate** [ˈgreit] integrar (a. 𝔄); combinar en un todo (with con); **in·te·gra·tion** integración f; **in·teg·ri·ty** [ˈtegriti] integridad f, probidad f.

in·tel·lect [ˈintilekt] intelecto m, entendimiento m; **in·tel·lec·tu·al** [ˈtjuəl] ☐ intelectual adj. a. su. m/f.

in·tel·li·gence [inˈtelidʒəns] inteligencia f; información f; noticias f/pl.; ~ quotient cociente m intelectual; ~ service ✕ servicio m de información; ~ test prueba f (or test m) de inteligencia.

in·tel·li·gent [inˈtelidʒənt] ☐ inteligente; **in·tel·li·gent·si·a** [ˈdʒentsiə] intelectualidad f; **in·tel·li·gi·ble** ☐ inteligible.

in·tem·per·ance [inˈtempərəns] intemperancia f; inmoderación f; exceso m en la bebida; **in·tem·per·ate** [ˈrit] ☐ intemperante; inmoderado; descomedido.

in·tend [inˈtend] pensar, proponerse; (mean) querer decir (by con); destinar (*for* a, para); ~ *to do* pensar hacer; **in'tend·ed** pensado; deseado; *be* ~ *to* tener por fin.

in·tense [in'tens] ☐ intenso; fuerte; extremado; *p.* apasionado.

in·tent [in'tent] **1.** absorto (*on* en); resuelto (*on* a); **2.** intento *m*, propósito *m*; **in'ten·tion** intención *f*; intento *m*, propósito *m*; significado *m*; **in'ten·tion·al** [~ʃnl] ☐ intencional; ~*ly* adrede, de propósito.

in·ter [in'tɜː] enterrar, sepultar.

in·ter... ['intə] inter...; entre.

in·ter·cede [intə'siːd] interceder, mediar (*with* con, *for* por).

in·ter·cept [intə'sept] interceptar; detener; ⅄ cortar.

in·ter·ces·sion [intə'seʃn] intercesión *f*.

in·ter·change 1. [intə'tʃeindʒ] (inter)cambiar(se), trocar(se); alternar (-se); **2.** ['ʌ'tʃeindʒ] intercambio *m*; canje *m* *of prisoners, publications*; alternación *f*; **in·ter'change·a·ble** intercambiable.

in·ter·com [intə'kɔm] F sistema *m* de intercomunicación.

in·ter·course ['intəkɔːs] (*social*) trato *m*; comercio *m*; intercambio *m*; (*sexual*) coito *m*, trato *m* sexual.

in·ter·de·nom·i·na·tion·al [intədi-nɔmi'neiʃnl] interconfesional.

in·ter·est ['intrist] **1.** interés *m* (*a.* ♥); ♥ rédito *m*; participación *f*; influencia *f* (*with* sobre); ~*s pl.* intereses *m/pl.*; personas *f/pl.* interesadas; *bear* ~ devengar intereses; *be of* ~ *to* interesar; *take an* ~ interesarse (*in* th. en, *p.* por); **2.** interesar; *be* ~*ed in*, ~ *o.s. in* interesarse por (*or* en); **'in·ter·est·ed** ☐ interesado; **'in·ter·est·ing** ☐ interesante.

in·ter·fere [intə'fiə] (entro)meterse, mezclarse, intervenir (*in* en); ~ *with* estorbar; dificultar; meterse con; F tocar, manosear; *phys.* interferir; **in·ter'fer·ence** entrometimiento *m*; intervención *f*; estorbo *m*; *phys.*, ⅄ interferencia *f*.

in·ter·im ['intərim] **1.** intervalo *m*, intermedio *m*, interín *m*; *in the* ~ entretanto, en el ínterin, interinamente; **2.** interino; provisional.

in·te·ri·or [in'təriə] **1.** interior *m*; **2.** interior, interno; ~ *decoration* decoración *f* de interiores.

in·ter·ject [intə'dʒekt] interponer; interrumpir (con); **in·ter'jec·tion** *gr.* interjección *f*; exclamación *f*.

in·ter·lude ['intəluːd] ♪ interludio *m*; *thea.* intermedio *m*; intervalo *m*; descanso *m*.

in·ter·mar·riage [intə'mæridʒ] matrimonio *m* entre parientes; matrimonio *m* entre personas de distintas razas o religiones.

in·ter·me·di·a·ry [intə'miːdiəri] intermediario *adj.* *a.* *su.* *m* (*a* *f*); **in·ter·me·di·ate** [~'miːdiət] ☐ (inter-) medio; intermediario.

in·ter·ment [in'tɜːmənt] entierro *m*.

in·ter·mi·na·ble [in'tɜːminəbl] ☐ interminable, inacabable.

in·ter·mis·sion [intə'miʃn] interrupción *f*; intervalo *m*, pausa *f*; *thea.* entreacto *m*; ☐ intermisión *f*.

in·ter·mit·tent [intə'mitənt] ☐ intermitente (*a.* ♣); ~*ly* a intervalos.

in·tern [in'tɜːn] recluir, internar.

in·tern(e) ['intɜːn] ♣ practicante *m* de hospital.

in·ter·nal [in'tɜːnl] ☐ interno, interior; ~**com'bus·tion en·gine** motor *m* de explosión, motor *m* de combustión interna.

in·ter·na·tion·al [intə'næʃnl] ☐ internacional; ~ *law* derecho *m* internacional (*or* de gentes).

in·ter·plan·e·tar·y [intə'plænitəri] interplanetario.

in·ter·play ['intə'plei] interacción *f*.

in·ter·po·late [in'tɜːpouleit] interpolar.

in·ter·pret [in'tɜːprit] interpretar; **in·ter'pre·ta·tion** interpretación *f*; **in'ter·pret·er** intérprete *m/f*.

in·ter·ro·gate [in'terəgeit] interrogar, examinar; **in·ter·ro'ga·tion** interrogación *f*, examen *m*.

in·ter·rupt [intə'rʌpt] interrumpir; (entre)cortar; **in·ter'rup·tion** interrupción *f*.

in·ter·sect [intə'sekt] *v/t.* cortar; *v/i.* intersecarse; **in·ter'sec·tion** intersección *f*; cruce *m*.

in·ter·sperse [intə'spəːs] esparcir, entremezclar; salpicar (*with* de).

in·ter·val ['intəvəl] intervalo *m* (*a.* ♪); *thea.* entreacto *m*; descanso *m* (*a.* *sport*); pausa *f*; *at* ~*s* de vez en cuando, a intervalos.

in·ter·vene [intə'viːn] intervenir, interponerse, mediar; **in·ter·ven·tion** [~'venʃn] intervención *f*.

in·ter·view ['intəvjuː] **1.** entrevista *f*; (*press etc.*) interviú *f*; *have an* ~ *with* = **2.** entrevistarse con, interviuvar; **'inter·view·er** interviuvador (-a f) m; interrogador (-a f) m.

in·tes·tine [in'testin] intestino adj. a. su. ~ large ~ intestino m grueso; small ~ intestino m delgado.

in·ti·ma·cy ['intiməsi] intimidad f; F trato m sexual; **in·ti·mate 1.** ['~meit] intimar; dar a entender; 2. ['~mit] a) □ íntimo; estrecho; knowledge profundo, detallado; become ~ intimarse (with con); b) amigo (a f) m de confianza; **in·ti·ma·tion** [~'meiʃn] intimación f; insinuación f, indirecta f; indicio m.

in·tim·i·date [in'timideit] intimidar, amedrentar, acobardar.

in·to ['intu, before consonant 'intə] en; a; dentro de; hacia el interior de.

in·tol·er·a·ble [in'tɔlərəbl] □ intolerable, inaguantable; **in·tol·er·ance** intolerancia f; **in·tol·er·ant** □ intolerante (of con, para).

in·to·na·tion [intou'neiʃn] entonación f.

in·tox·i·cant [in'tɔksikənt] 1. embriagador; 2. bebida f alcohólica; **in·tox·i·cate** [~keit] embriagar (a. fig.); ⚕ intoxicar; **in·tox·i·ca·tion** embriaguez f (a. fig.); ⚕ intoxicación f.

in·tra·mu·ral [intrə'mjuərəl] interior, situado intramuros.

in·tran·si·gent [in'trænsidʒənt] intransigente.

in·tran·si·tive [in'trɑːnsitiv] □ intransitivo adj. a. su.

in·tra·ve·nous ['intrə'viːnəs] intravenoso.

in·trench [in'trentʃ] v. entrench.

in·trep·id [in'trepid] □ intrépido.

in·tri·cate ['intrikit] □ intrincado.

in·trigue [in'triːg] 1. intriga f; amorío m secreto, lío m; thea. enredo m; 2. intrigar; tener la intriga.

in·tro·duce [intrə'djuːs] introducir; meter, insertar; **in·tro·duc·tion** [~'dʌkʃn] introducción f; inserción f; presentación f (de p.); prólogo m to book; letter of ~ carta f de recomendación; **in·tro·duc·to·ry** [~tɔri] introductor; preliminar; ~ offer ofrecimiento m de presentación, oferta f preliminar.

in·tro·spec·tion [introu'spekʃn] introspección f.

in·trude [in'truːd] v/t. introducir (sin derecho), meter, encajar (in en); imponer (upon a); v/i. (entro)meterse, encajarse (upon en); pegarse, estorbar; **in·trud·er** intruso (a f) m.

in·tru·sion [in'truːʒn] intrusión f.

in·trust [in'trʌst] v. entrust.

in·tu·i·tion [intju'iʃn] intuición f.

in·vade [in'veid] invadir (a. fig.); **in·vad·er** invasor (-a f) m.

in·val·id 1. [in'vælid] inválido, nulo; 2. ['invæli(ː)d] ✕, ⚓ inválido adj. a. su. m (a f); enfermo adj. a. su. m (a f); 3. [invə'liːd] incapacitar; ✕, ⚓ (~ out) licenciar por invalidez; **in·val·i·date** [in'vælideit] invalidar.

in·val·u·a·ble [in'væljuəbl] □ inestimable, inapreciable.

in·var·i·a·ble [in'vɛəriəbl] □ invariable.

in·va·sion [in'veiʒn] invasión f (a. fig., ✕).

in·vent [in'vent] inventar; idear; fingir; **in·ven·tion** invención f, invento m; (faculty) inventiva f; ficción f; **in·ven·tor** inventor (-a f) m; **in·ven·to·ry** ['inventri] 1. inventario m; existencias f/pl.; 2. inventariar.

in·ver·sion [in'veːʃn] inversión f.

in·vert [in'veːt] invertir; trastrocar; volver al revés; ~ed commas gr. pl. comillas f/pl.; ~ed exclamation point principio m de admiración; ~ed question mark principio m de interrogación; 2. ['inveːt] invertido (a f) m.

in·vest [in'vest] v/t. ✝ invertir, colocar; v/i.: ~ in poner (or invertir) dinero en; F comprar.

in·ves·ti·gate [in'vestigeit] investigar; averiguar; examinar; **in·ves·ti·ga·tion** investigación f; averiguación f; pesquisa f; **in·ves·ti·ga·tor** [~geitə] investigador (-a f) m.

in·vest·ment ✝ inversión f, colocación f (de fondos); ~ s ✝ valores m/pl. en cartera, fondos m/pl. invertidos; **in·ves·tor** inversionista m/f; accionista m/f, inversor (-a f) m.

in·vig·or·ate [in'vigəreit] vigorizar, tonificar; **in·vig·or·a·ting** vigorizador; tonificante; **in·vig·or·a·tion** tonificación f.

in·vin·ci·ble [in'vinsəbl] □ invencible.

in·vis·i·ble [in'vizbl] □ invisible; ~ ink tinta f simpática.

in·vi·ta·tion [invi'teiʃn] invitación f, convite m; **in·vite** [in'vait] invitar (to a); (esp. to food, drink) convidar (to a); **in·vit·ing** □ atrayente; incitante; provocativo; food apetitoso.

in·vo·ca·tion [invou'keiʃn] invocación f; evocación f of spirits.

in·voice ['invɔis] 1. factura f; 2. facturar.

in·voke [in'vouk] invocar; *spirits* evocar.

in·vol·un·tar·y [in'vɔləntəri] □ involuntario.

in·volve [in'vɔlv] envolver; (*entangle*) enredar, enmarañar; complicar; (*entail*) traer consigo, acarrear; implicar; comprometer; get ~d in meterse en, embrollarse en; **in'volve·ment** envolvimiento m; enredo m; complicación f; compromiso m; apuro m, dificultad f.

in·ward ['inwəd] 1. adj. interior, interno; 2. adv. hacia dentro, para dentro, interiormente; **'in·ward·ly** interiormente; (hacia) dentro; para sí.

i·o·dide ['aiədaid] yoduro m; **i·o·dine** ['~diːn] yodo m.

i·on ['aiən] ion m; ~ trap ⚡ trampa f, de iones.

I·o·ni·an [ai'ounjən] jonio adj. a. su. m (a f), jónico adj. a. su. m (a f).

I·on·ic [ai'ɔnik] jónico.

i·on·ize ['aiənaiz] ionizar.

i·o·ta [ai'outə] (*letter*) iota f; *fig.* jota f, ápice m, pizca f.

I·ra·ni·an [i'reinjən] iranio adj. a. su. m (a f), iranés adj. a. su. m (a -a f).

I·ra·qi [i'rɑːki] iraki adj. a. su. m/f.

i·ras·ci·ble [i'ræsibl] □ irascible, iracundo.

i·rate [ai'reit] airado, colérico.

ire [ai'ə] poet. ira f, cólera f.

ir·i·des·cent [iri'desnt] iridescente, irisado; tornasolado.

i·ris ['aiəris] opt. iris m; ⚘ lirio m.

I·rish ['aiəriʃ] irlandés adj. a. su. m; the ~ pl. los irlandeses; **'I·rish·ism** idiotismo m irlandés; **'I·rish·man** irlandés m.

irk [əːk] fastidiar, molestar.

irk·some ['əːksəm] □ fastidioso, molesto, pesado; **'irk·some·ness** fastidio m, molestia f, tedio m.

i·ron ['aiən] 1. hierro m (a. fig., tool, weapon, golf); (a. flat~) plancha f; ~ pl. hierros m/pl., grillos m/pl.; 2. de hierro; férreo (a. fig.); ~ curtain telón m de acero; ~ lung pulmón m de hierro; ~ ore mineral m de hierro; 3. clothes planchar; aherrojar; ⁱ²ᵗ 'Age Edad f de Hierro; '~·bound zunchado con hierro; fig. férreo, inflexible; '~·clad acorazado adj. a. su. m.

i·ron·ic, **i·ron·i·cal** [ai'rɔnik(l)] □ irónico.

i·ron·ing ['aiəniŋ] planchado m.

i·ron...: '~·stone mineral m de hierro;

'~·willed de voluntad f férrea; '~·work herraje m; obra f de hierro; '~·works herrería f; fábrica f de hierro.

i·ro·ny ['aiərəni] ironía f.

ir·ra·di·ant [i'reidiənt] luminoso, radiante.

ir·ra·di·ate [i'reidieit] v/t. phys., ⚡ irradiar; iluminar(se de); fig. derramar; v/i. irradiar; **ir·ra·di·a·tion** irradiación f.

ir·ra·tion·al [i'ræʃnl] □ irracional (a. Ⓐ); **ir·ra·tion·al·i·ty** [~ʃə'næliti] irracionalidad f.

ir·re·claim·a·ble [iri'kleiməbl] □ irrecuperable; irredimible.

ir·re·con·cil·a·ble [i'rekənsailəbl] □ irreconciliable, intransigente.

ir·re·cov·er·a·ble [iri'kʌvərəbl] irrecuperable; incobrable.

ir·re·duc·i·ble [iri'djuːsəbl] irreducible.

ir·ref·u·ta·ble [i'refjutəbl] □ irrefutable.

ir·reg·u·lar [i'regjulə] 1. □ irregular; 2. ✕ guerrillero m; **ir·reg·u·lar·i·ty** [~'læriti] irregularidad f.

ir·rel·e·vance, **ir·rel·e·van·cy** [i'relivəns(i)] impertinencia f; inaplicabilidad f; **ir'rel·e·vant** □ fuera de propósito; impertinente; inaplicable.

ir·re·li·gious [iri'lidʒəs] □ irreligioso.

ir·re·me·di·a·ble [iri'miːdiəbl] □ irremediable.

ir·rep·a·ra·ble [i'repərəbl] □ irreparable.

ir·re·place·a·ble [iri'pleisəbl] insustituible, irreemplazable.

ir·re·press·i·ble [iri'presəbl] indomable; incorregible, incontrolable.

ir·re·proach·a·ble [iri'proutʃəbl] □ irreprochable.

ir·re·sist·i·ble [iri'sistəbl] □ irresistible.

ir·res·o·lute [i'rezəluːt] □ irresoluto, irresuelto, indeciso; **ir'res·o·lute·ness** indecisión f.

ir·re·spec·tive [iris'pektiv] □: ~ of aparte de, prescindiendo de.

ir·re·spon·si·ble [iris'pɔnsəbl] □ irresponsable.

ir·re·triev·a·ble [iri'triːvəbl] irrecuperable, irreparable.

ir·rev·er·ence [i'revərəns] irreverencia f; **ir'rev·er·ent** □ irreverente.

ir·re·vers·i·ble [iri'vəːsəbl] irreversible; irrevocable.

ir·rev·o·ca·ble [i'revəkəbl] □ irrevocable.
ir·ri·gate ['irigeit] regar; irrigar (*a.*
♚); **ir·ri·ga·tion** riego *m*; irrigación *f*.
ir·ri·ta·bil·i·ty [iritə'biliti] irritabili-
dad *f*; **ir·ri·tate** ['ʌteit] irritar; exasperar; molestar; '**ir·ri·tat·ing** □
irritador, irritante; enojoso; molesto.
ir·rup·tion ['irʌpʃn] irrupción *f*.
is [iz] es; está (*v. be*).
Is·lam ['izlɑ:m] islam *m*; **Is·lam·ic**
[iz'læmik] islámico.
is·land ['ailənd] **1.** isla *f*; refugio *m in
road*; **2.** isleño.
isle [ail] *mst poet.* isla *f*; **is·let** ['ailit]
isleta *f*; islote *m*.
ism [izm] F *mst contp.* ismo *m*; teoría
f; sistema *m*.
isn't ['iznt] = *is not.*
i·so·late ['aisəleit] aislar; apartar;
'**i·so·lat·ed** aislado; insulado; alejado; **i·so·la·tion** aislamiento *m*; apartamiento *m*; **i·so·la·tion·ism** aislacionismo *m*.
i·so·met·ric [aisə'metrik] isométrico;
ʌs isométrica.
i·so·sce·les [ai'sɔsəli:z] isósceles.
i·so·tope ['aisoutoup] isótopo *m*.
Is·ra·el·i [iz'reili] israelí, israelita *adj.
a. su. m/f.*
is·sue ['isjuː, 'iʃuː] **1.** salida *f*; distribución *f*; ♾ emisión *f of coins, shares,
stamps; publishing:* edición *f*, impresión *f*; (*copy*) número *m*, entrega *f*;
(*question*) cuestión *f*, problema *m*,
punto *m* en disputa; **evade the ～**
esquivar la pregunta; **face the ～**
afrontar la situación; **2.** *v/t.* distribuir; expedir; ♾ emitir; poner en
circulación; publicar; *decree* promulgar; *v/i.* salir; brotar; provenir;
emanar; fluir.

isth·mus ['isməs] istmo *m*.
it [it] **1.** (*subject, but gen. omitted*) él,
ella, ello; *acc.* lo, la; *dat.* le; *after prp.*
él, ella, ello; *～ is I (or F ～'s me)* soy yo;
～ is raining llueve; *～ is said that* se dice
que; *～ is 2 o'clock* son las 2; **2.** F aquél
m; atracción *f* sexual; lo necesario; **3.**
F *pred.:* **you're ～** *children's games:* tú
te quedas.
I·tal·ian [i'tæljən] **1.** italiano *adj.
a. su. m* (*a f*); **2.** (*language*) italiano
m.
i·tal·ic [i'tælik] **1.** (*a. 2*) itálico; **2.** *typ.
mst ～s* (letra *f*) bastardilla *f*; *in ～s* en
bastardilla; en cursiva; **i·tal·i·cize**
[i'tælisaiz] poner en (letra) bastardilla; subrayar.
itch [itʃ] **1.** ♚ sarna *f*; picazón *f*;
comezón *f*, prurito *m* (*a. fig.* for pon,
to de); **2.** picar; sentir comezón; **my
arm ～es** me pica el brazo; '**itch·ing**
prurito *m*, comezón *f* (*a. fig.*).
i·tem ['aitem] **1.** ítem *m*, artículo *m*;
(*newspaper*) noticia *f*, detalle *m*; **2.**
adv. ítem; **i·tem·ize** ['aitəmaiz] ole-
tallar; especificar.
i·tin·er·ant [i'tinərənt] ambulante,
errante; **i·tin·er·ar·y** [ai'tinərəri] **1.**
itinerario *m*; ruta *f*; guía *f*; **2.** itinerario.
its [its] su(s); **2.** *pron.* (el) suyo, (la)
suya *etc.*
it's [its] = *it is, it has.*
it·self [it'self] (*subject*) él mismo, ella
misma; ello mismo; *acc., dat.* se;
(*after prp.*) sí (mismo [a]).
i·vied ['aivid] cubierto de hiedra.
i·vo·ry ['aivəri] **1.** marfil *m*; *～ tower*
torre *f* de marfil; *fig.* inocencia *f*; *sl.
ivories pl.* teclas *f/pl.* de piano; can de
marfil; *poet.* ebúrneo.
i·vy ['aivi] hiedra *f*.

J

jab [dʒæb] **1.** (*poke*) hurgonazo *m*;
(*prick*) pinchazo *m*; (*with elbow*) codazo *m*; *boxing:* golpe *m* rápido; **2.**
hurgonear; pinchar; dar un codazo
a; golpear.
jab·ber ['dʒæbə] **1.** (*a. ～ing*) jerigonza *f*; farfulla *f*; **2.** farfullar.
jack [dʒæk] **1.** ⊕, *mot.* gato *m*; ⚡
enchufe *m* hembra; *cards:* sota *f*;
zo. macho *m*; ♣ bandera *f* de proa;

2.: *～ up* alzar con el gato; *price* subir,
aumentar.
jack·al ['dʒækɔːl] *zo.* chacal *m*.
jack·ass ['dʒækæs] burro *m* (*a. fig.*).
jack·et ['dʒækit] chaqueta *f*, americana *f*; saco *m S.Am.*; cubierta *f*;
envoltura *f*; ⊕ camisa *f*.
jack...: *～-in-the-box* caja *f* sorpresa;
'*～-knife* navaja *f*; '*～-of-'all-trades*
factótum *m*; hombre *m* de muchos
oficios; '*～-o'-lan·tern* fuego *m* fa-

tuo; '**~·pot** *cards*: bote *m*; premio *m* gordo; '**~ rab·bit** liebre *m* grande.

Jac·o·bite ['dʒækəbait] jacobita *adj. a. su. m/f.*

jade¹ [dʒeid] **1.** *contp.* mujerzuela *f*, picarona *f*; **2.** saciar.

jade² [~] *min.* jade *m*.

jag·ged ['dʒægid] dentado, desigual, mellado; áspero; rasgado (en sietes).

ja·gu·ar ['dʒægwɑːr] jaguar *m*.

jail [dʒeil] **1.** cárcel *f*; **2.** encarcelar; '**~·bird** presidiario *m*; encarcelado *m*; '**~·break** escaparoria *f* de encarcelado.

jail·er ['dʒeilə] carcelero *m*.

ja·lop·y [dʒə'lɔpi] *F mot.*, 🚂 cacharro *m*, armatoste *m*.

jam¹ [dʒæm] *approx.* mermelada *f*, confitura *f*, compota *f*.

jam² [~] **1.** apiñadura *f*; *(stoppage)* atasc(amient)o *m*; agolpamiento *m of people*; *sl.* aprieto *m*, lío *m*; traffic ~ aglomeración *f* de tráfico; *F* ~ *session* concierto *m* improvisado de jazz; **2.** apiñar(se); apretar(se); atascar(se); *radio*: interferir; ~ *on brakes* echar (or poner) con violencia; '**~·packed** apiñado, apretujado.

Ja·mai·can [dʒə'meikən] jamaicano *adj. a. su. m* (a *f*).

jam·bo·ree [dʒæmbə'riː] *F* francachela *f*, juerga *f*; congreso *m* de (niños) exploradores.

jan·gle ['dʒæŋgl] **1.** sonido *m* discordante, cencerreo *m*; **2.** cencerrear, (hacer) sonar de manera discordante; '**jan·gling** discordante, estridente, desapacible.

jan·i·tor ['dʒænitə] portero *m*, conserje *m*.

Jan·u·ar·y ['dʒænjuəri] enero *m*.

ja·pan [dʒə'pæn] **1.** laca *f* negra; **2.** barnizar con laca japonesa.

Jap·a·nese [dʒæpə'niːz] **1.** japonés *adj. a. su. m* (-a *f*); the ~ *pl.* los japoneses; **2.** *(language)* japonés *m*.

jar¹ [dʒɑː] tarro *m*; pote *m*; jarra *f*; *(narrow-necked)* botija *f*; *(large)* tinaja *f*.

jar² [~] **1.** choque *m*, sacudida *f*; sorpresa *f* desagradable; **2.** chocar; sacudir; (hacer) vibrar.

jar·gon ['dʒɑːgən] jerigonza *f*; *(specialist)* jerga *f*.

jas·min(e) ['dʒæsmin] jazmín *m*.

jas·per ['dʒæspə] jaspe *m*.

jaun·dice ['dʒɔːndis] 🩺 icteticia *f*; '**jaun·diced** 🩺 ictérico; cetrino.

jaunt [dʒɔːnt] **1.** caminata *f*, excur-

sión *f*, paseo *m*; **2.** hacer una caminata, ir de excursión; '**jaun·ti·ness** viveza *f*, garbo *m*, soltura *f*; '**jaun·ty** □ garboso, airoso, ligero.

Jav·a·nese [dʒɑːvə'niːz] javanés *adj. a. su. m* (-a *f*).

jave·lin ['dʒævlin] jabalina *f*.

jaw [dʒɔː] **1.** quijada *f*, mandíbula *f*, maxilar *m*; *sl.* cháchara *f*, ~s *pl.* fauces *f/pl.*; **2.** *F v/i.* chismear, charlar; *v/t.* regañar; '**~·bone** maxilar *m*, quijada *f*.

jay [dʒei] *orn.* arrendajo *m*; *F* necio (-a *f*) *m*; '**~·walk** cruzar la calle sin cuidar; '**~·walk·er** peatón *m* imprudente.

jazz [dʒæz] **1.** jazz *m*; **2.** de jazz; **3.** *v/t.* sincopar; *v/i.* tocar (or bailar) el jazz; '**~ band** orquesta *f* de jazz, jazz-band *m*; '**jazz·y** *F* sincopado; de colores chillones.

jeal·ous ['dʒeləs] □ celoso, envidioso; cuidadoso, vigilante; *be* ~ *of a p.* tener celos de una p.; '**jeal·ous·y** celos *m/pl.*; envidia *f*.

jeans [dʒiːnz] *pl. F* pantalones *m/pl.* de dril.

jeep [dʒiːp] jeep *m*.

jeer [dʒiə] **1.** escarnio *m*; *(shout)* grito *m* de sarcasmo (or protesta *etc.*); **2.** mofarse (*at* de); befar; '**jeer·ing** □ mofador.

jell [dʒel] cuajarse; ponerse gelatinoso.

jel·ly ['dʒeli] **1.** jalea *f*, gelatina *f*; **2.** convertir(se) en jalea; '**~·bean** frutila *f*; '**~·fish** medusa *f*.

jeop·ard·ize ['dʒepədaiz] arriesgar, comprometer; '**jeop·ard·y** riesgo *m*, peligro *m*.

jerk [dʒəːk] **1.** tirón *m*, sacudida *f*, arranque *m*; espasmo *m* muscular; *by (or in)* ~s a sacudidas; **2.** *v/t.* sacudir; mover a tirones; arrojar; *v/i.* sacudirse; avanzar a tirones.

jer·kin ['dʒəːkin] justillo *m*.

jerk·wa·ter ['dʒəːkwɔːtə] *F* de poca monta.

jerk·y ['dʒəːki] □ espasmódico, desigual; que se mueve a tirones.

jer·ry-built ['dʒeriːbilt] mal construido, de pacotilla.

jer·sey ['dʒəːzi] jersey *m*.

jest [dʒest] **1.** chanza *f*, broma *f*; *(esp. verbal)* chiste *m*; **2.** bromear, chancear(se); '**jest·er** bufón *m*.

Jes·u·it ['dʒezjuit] jesuita *adj. a. su. m*; **Jes·u·it·ic, Jes·u·it·i·cal** □ jesuítico.

jet¹ [dʒet] *min.* azabache *m*.

jet² [~] **1.** chorro *m*, surtidor *m*; (*burner*) mechero *m*; ⊕, ⚙ *attr.* a reacción, a chorro; ~ *engine* reactor *m*, motor *m* a chorro; ~ *fighter* cazarreactor *m*; ~ *plane* avión *m* a reacción; **2.** *v/t.* echar en chorro; *v/i.* chorrear.

jet-black ['dʒet'blæk] azabachado.

jet... '~-'pow·ered, '~-'pro·pelled a reacción.

jet·sam ['dʒetsəm] ⚓ echazón *f*.

jet·ti·son ['dʒetisn] ⚓ echazón *f*; **2.** ⚓ echar al mar; *fig.* desechar.

jet·ty ['dʒeti] malecón *m*; muelle *m*; embarcadero *m*.

Jew [dʒu:] judío (a *f*) *m*; ~'s *harp* birimbao *m*.

jew·el ['dʒu:əl] **1.** joya *f*; alhaja *f* (*a. fig.*); piedra *f* preciosa; **2.** enjoyar; '~·**case** joyero *m*; '**jew·el·er** joyero *m*; ~'s (*shop*) joyería *f*; '**jew·el·ry** joyas *f/pl.*; † joyería *f*.

Jew·ish ['dʒu:iʃ] judío; **Jew·ry** ['dʒuəri] judería *f*, los judíos *m/pl.*

jib [dʒib] ⚓ foque *m*; ⊕ aguilón *m*; *fig. the cut of his* ~ su pergeño *m*.

jibe [dʒaib] F concordar.

jif·fy ['dʒifi] F instante *m*; *in a* ~ en un santiamén.

jig [dʒig] **1.** jiga *f*; ⊕ plantilla *f* (de guía); **2.** bailar (la jiga); mover(se) a saltitos.

jig·gle [dʒigl] F zangolotear; vibrar.

jig·saw ['dʒigsɔ:] sierra *f* de vaivén; ~ *puzzle* rompecabezas *m*.

jilt [dʒilt] dar calabazas a, dejar plantado.

jim·my ['dʒimi] palanqueta *f*.

jin·gle ['dʒiŋgl] **1.** (re)tintín *m*, cascabeleo *m*; rima *f* infantil; **2.** *v/t.* hacer sonar; *v/i.* cascabelear, tintinear.

jin·go ['dʒiŋgou] patriotero (a *f*) *m*, jingoísta *m/f*; F *by* ~! ¡caramba!; '**jin·go·ism** jingoísmo *m*, patriotería *f*.

jinx [~] *sl.* cenizo *m*, pájaro *m* de mal agüero, duendecillo *m*.

jit·ter ['dʒitə] *sl.* **1.** temblar, estremecerse; bailar; **2.** ~*s pl.* inquietud *f*, nerviosidad *f*; '~·**bug** ['~bʌg] *sl.* (aficionado [a *f*] *m*) bailar el jazz; '**jit·ter·y** *sl.* nervioso, inquieto.

jiu-jit·su [dʒu:'dʒitsu:] jiu-jitsu *m*.

jive [dʒaiv] *sl.* (modo *m* de) bailar el jazz.

job [dʒɔb] tarea *f*, quehacer *m*; labor *m*; trabajo *m*; (*post*) empleo *m*, puesto *m*; F cosa *f* difícil, faena *f*; *sl.*

crimen *m*, robo *m*; *be on the* ~ estar trabajando; *sl.* estar al pie; *be out of a* ~ estar sin trabajo; *a bad* ~ mala situación *f*, caso *m* desahuciado; ~ *security* garantía *f* de empleo continuo; *odd* ~ tarea *f* suelta.

job·ber ['dʒɔbə] destajista *m/f*; † agiotista *m*; † corredor *m*; † intermediario *m*; *b.s.* chanchullero *m*; '**job·less** desempleado; desocupado; '**job mar·ket** oportunidades *f* de empleo.

jock·ey ['dʒɔki] **1.** jockey *m*; **2.** *v/t.* embaucar (*into* para que); *v/i.* maniobrar (*for* para obtener).

jock·strap ['dʒɔk'stræp] suspensorio *m* de atleta.

jo·cose [dʒə'kous] □, **joc·u·lar** ['dʒɔkjulə] □ jocoso.

joc·und ['dʒɔkənd] □ jocundo.

jodh·purs ['dʒɔdpʌrz] pantalones *m* de equitación.

jog [dʒɔg] **1.** empujoncito *m*, cidazo *m*, sacudimiento *m* (ligero); trote *m* corto, paso *m* lento; *fig.* estímulo *m*; **2.** *v/t.* empujar (*or* sacudir) levemente; *fig.* estimular; *memory* refrescar; *v/i.* (*mst* ~ *along*, ~ *on*) andar a trote corto; '~·**ging** recreo; *calisténica*: trote *m* (corto).

jog·gle [dʒɔgl] **1.** traqueo *m*, sacudimiento *m*; ⊕ ensambladura *f* dentada; **2.** traquear, sacudir.

john [dʒɔn] F retrete *m*; inodoro *m*.

john·ny ['dʒɔni] F tipo *m*, chico *m*; currutaco *m*; ~ *cake* pan *m* de maíz.

join [dʒɔin] **1.** juntura *f*, costura *f*; **2.** *v/t.* unir, juntar; ⊕ ensamblar, acoplar; ✂ alistarse en; ~ *hands* darse las manos; ~ *one's regiment* (*ship*) incorporarse a su regimiento (barco); ~ *a p. in* acompañar a una *p.* en; *v/i.* juntarse, unirse; (*lines*) empalmar; ~ *in* tomar parte (en), participar (en).

join·er ['dʒɔinə] carpintero *m* (de blanco); ensamblador *m*.

joint [dʒɔint] **1.** junt(ur)a *f*; *anat.* articulación *f*, coyuntura *f*; ♥ nudo *m*; ⚡ empalme *m*; ⊕ ensambladura *f*; *sl.* garito *m*; *sl.* fonducho *m*; *out of* ~ descoyuntado; *fig.* fuera de quicio; **2.** □ (en) común; mutuo; colectivo; conjunto; combinado; (*in compounds*) co...; **3.** juntar, unir; ⊕ ensamblar; articular; '**joint·ed** articulado; ♥ nudoso; '**joint-stock com·pa·ny** sociedad *f* anónima; '**joint·ure** ⚖ bienes *m* parafernales.

joist [dʒɔist] vig(uet)a *f*.

joke [dʒouk] **1.** broma *f*, chanza *f*; (*esp. verbal*) chiste *m*; (*laughing matter*) cosa *f* de reír; (*p.*) hazmerreír *m*; **2.** bromear, chancear(se); decir chistes; hablar en broma; F chunguear; *cards*: comodín *m*; **'jok·er** bromista *m/f*; guasón (-a *f*) *m*; *cards*: comodín *m*; **jol·li·ty** ['dʒɔliti] alegría *f*, regocijo *m*; diversión *f*.

jol·ly ['dʒɔli] **1.** □ alegre, regocijado, jovial; divertido; F agradable, estupendo; **2.** *adv.* F muy.

jolt [dʒoult] **1.** sacudida *f*, choque *m*; (*a.* ~*ing*) traque(te)o *m*; **2.** sacudir; traque(te)ar.

josh [dʒɔʃ] *sl.* **1.** broma *f*; **2.** burlarse de, tomar el pelo a.

jos·tle ['dʒɔsl] **1.** empujón *m*, empellón *m*; **2.** empujar; codear.

jot [dʒɔt] **1.** jota *f*, pizca *f*; **2.**: ~ *down* apuntar; **'jot·ting** apunte *m*.

jour·nal ['dʒə:nl] (✝ *libro m*) diario *m* (✪ *de navegación*); (*newspaper*) periódico *m*; (*review*) revista *f*; **'jour·nal·ese** [‿nə'li:z] lenguaje *m* periodístico; **'jour·nal·ism** periodismo *m*; **'jour·nal·ist** periodista *m/f*.

jour·ney ['dʒə:ni] **1.** viaje *m*; **2.** viajar; **'‿·man** oficial *m*.

joust [dʒaust] **1.** justa *f*, torneo *m*; **2.** justar.

jo·vi·al ['dʒouviəl] □ jovial.

jowl [dʒaul] quijada *f*; carrillo *m*.

joy [dʒɔi] alegría *f*, júbilo *m*, regocijo *m*; deleite *m*; **joy·ful** [‿ful] □ alegre, regocijado; **'joy·ous** □ alegre; **'joy·ride** F excursión *f* (desautorizada) en coche *etc.*; **'joy·stick** ✈ *sl.* palanca *f* de gobierno.

ju·bi·lant ['dʒu:bilənt] □ jubiloso, triunfante; **ju·bi·la·tion** júbilo *m*; **ju·bi·lee** [‿li:] *hist., eccl.* jubileo *m*; (*rejoicing*) júbilo *m*.

Ju·da·ism ['dʒu:deiizm] judaísmo *m*; **'Ju·da·ize** *v/i.* convertir al judaísmo; *v/t.* judaizar.

judge [dʒʌdʒ] **1.** juez *m*; *fig.* conocedor (-a *f*) *m*; *sport:* árbitro *m*; **2.** juzgar; considerar; opinar; *judging by* a juzgar por; **'‿·'ad·vo·cate** ⚔ auditor *m* de guerra.

judge·ship ['dʒʌdʒʃip] judicatura *f*; **judg·ment** [‿mənt] juicio *m*; ⚖ sentencia *f*, fallo *m*; entendimiento *m*, discernimiento *m*; opinión *f*; *in my* ~ a mi parecer; *pronounce* ~ pronunciar sentencia (*on en, sobre*); ♀ *Day* día *m* del juicio (final).

ju·di·ca·ture ['dʒu:dikətʃə] judicatura *f*.

ju·di·cial [dʒu'diʃl] □ judicial; juicioso; ~ *murder* asesinato *m* legal.

ju·di·cious [dʒu'diʃəs] □ juicioso, sensato.

jug [dʒʌg] **1.** jarro *m*; pote *m*; *sl.* chirona *f*; **2.** *sl.* encarcelar.

jug·ger·naut ['dʒʌgənɔ:t] *fig.* monstruo *m* destructor de los hombres.

jug·gle ['dʒʌgl] **1.** juego *m* de manos; *b.s.* engaño *m*; **2.** *v/t.* escamotear; *b.s.* falsear; *v/i.* hacer juegos malabares (*or* de manos); *b.s.* hacer trampas; **'jug·gler** malabarista *m/f*, jugador (-a *f*) *m* de manos; *b.s.* tramposo (a *f*) *m*; **'jug·gler·y** juegos *m/pl.* malabares (*or* de manos); *b.s.* trampas *f/pl.*; fraude *m*.

Ju·go·slav ['ju:gou'sla:v] yugo(e)slavo *adj. a. su. m* (a *f*).

jug·u·lar ['dʒʌgjulə] yugular.

juice [dʒu:s] (*esp. fruit*) zumo *m*; jugo *m*; ⚡ *sl.* corriente *f*; **juic·i·ness** [‿inis] jugosidad *f*; **'juic·y** □ zumoso, jugoso; F picante, sabroso.

ju·jube ['dʒu:dʒu:b] ♀ azufaifa *f*; pastilla *f*.

juke-box ['dʒu:kbɔks] tocadiscos *m* (tragamonedas).

ju·lep ['dʒu:lep] julepe *m*.

Ju·ly [dʒu'lai] julio *m*.

jum·ble ['dʒʌmbl] **1.** revoltijo *m*; confusión *f*; mezcolanza *f*; **2.** mezclar, emburujar; confundir; **jum·bly** ['dʒʌmbli] revuelto, emburujado.

jum·bo ['dʒʌmbou] F elefante *m*; *attr.* enorme.

jump [dʒʌmp] **1.** salto *m*, brinco *m*; F *get* (*have*) *the* ~ *on* llevar la ventaja a; **2.** *v/t.* saltar; *horse* hacer saltar; F ~ *the gun* madrugar; ~ *the rails* descarrilar; ~ *ship* desertar del buque; *v/i.* saltar; brincar; dar saltos; bailar; ~ *lanzarse*; ~ *to conclusions* juzgar al (buen) tuntún; **'jump·er** saltador (-a *f*) *m*; (*dress*) suéter *m*, jersey *m*; blusa *f*; ⚡ hilo *m* de cierre; **'jump seat** *mot.* asiento *m* desmontable; traspuntín *m*; **'jump suit** vestido *m* unitario (como de paracaidista); **'jump·y** saltón *m*; *fig.* asustadizo, nervioso.

junc·tion ['dʒʌŋkʃn] juntura *f*, unión *f*; conexión *f*; confluencia *f* of *rivers*; ⛟ (estación *f* de) empalme *m*; ⚡ ~ *box* caja *f* de empalmes; **junc·ture** ['‿tʃə] coyuntura *f*; (*critical*) trance *m*; ⚒ juntura *f*.

June [dʒu:n] junio *m*.

keep

jun·gle ['dʒʌŋgl] jungla f; selva f; fig. maraña f.

jun·ior ['dʒuːnjə] 1. menor, más joven; más nuevo; subalterno; juvenil; *Paul Jones,* ~ *Paul Jones,* hijo; 2. menor m/f; joven m/f; hijo m.

ju·ni·per ['dʒuːnipə] enebro m.

junk¹ [dʒʌŋk] ⚓ junco m.

junk² [~] F trastos m/pl. viejos; (*iron*) chatarra f; (*cheap goods*) baratijas f/pl.; sl. heroína (*pharm.*); ~ **yard** parque m de chatarra.

junk·et ['dʒʌŋkit] 1. dulce m de leche cuajada; (*a.* ~*ing*) francachela f, festividades f/pl.; jira f; 2. festejar; banquetear; ir de jira.

junk·ie (*a.* **junk·y**) ['dʒʌŋki] sl. toxicómano m; narcotómano m.

jun·ta ['dʒʌntə] junta f; camarilla f.

ju·rid·i·cal [dʒuə'ridikl] □ jurídico.

ju·ris·dic·tion [dʒuəris'dikʃn] jurisdicción f; **ju·ris·pru·dence** ['~pruː-dəns] jurisprudencia f.

ju·rist ['dʒuərist] jurista m.

ju·ror ['dʒuərə] (miembro m de un) jurado m.

ju·ry ['dʒuəri] jurado m; **'ju·ry box** tribuna f del jurado; **'ju·ry·man** (miembro m de un) jurado m.

ju·ry rig ['dʒuəirig] ⚓ aparejar temporariamente.

just [dʒʌst] 1. *adj.* □ justo; recto;

exacto; 2. *adv.* justamente, exactamente, ni más ni menos; precisamente; F absolutamente, completamente; *it's* ~ *perfect!* ¡es absolutamente perfecto!; ~ *as* en el momento en que; (tal) como; ~ *as you wish* como Vd. quiera.

jus·tice ['dʒʌstis] justicia f; juez m; ♀ *of the Peace* juez m de paz; *court of* ~ tribunal m de justicia.

jus·ti·fi·a·ble ['dʒʌstifaiəbl] justificable; **'jus·ti·fi·a·bly** con razón, con justicia; **'jus·ti·fi·er** *tip.*: justificador m; **'jus·ti·fy** justificar (*a. typ.*); dar motivo para; ~ *o.s.* sincerarse; acreditarse.

just·ly ['dʒʌstli] justamente, con justicia; con derecho; debidamente.

just·ness ['dʒʌstnis] justicia f; rectitud f; exactitud f.

jut [dʒʌt] 1. saliente m, saledizo m; 2. (*a.* ~ *out*) sobresalir, resaltar.

jute [dʒuːt] yute m.

ju·ve·nile ['dʒuːvənail] 1. joven m/f; niño (a f) m; 2. juvenil; de (or para) niños (or menores); ♀ *Court* tribunal m juvenil; ~ *delinquency* delincuencia f de menores; ~ *lead thea.*: galancete m.

jux·ta·pose [dʒʌkstə'pouz] yuxtaponer; **jux·ta·po·si·tion** [~pə'ziʃn] yuxtaposición f.

K

kale [keil] col f (rizada); sl. guita f.

ka·lei·do·scope [kə'laidəskoup] cal(e)idoscopio m; fig. escena f animada y variadísima.

kan·ga·roo [kæŋgə'ruː] canguro m.

ka·pok ['keipɔk] capoc m; lana f de ceiba.

ka·put [kə'put] sl. inutil; gastado; roto.

kay·ak ['kaiæk] ⚓ kayak m.

keel [kiːl] 1. ⚓, *orn.*, ♀ quilla f; *on an even* ~ ⚓ en iguales calados; en equilibrio (*a. fig.*); fig. derecho, estable; 2.: ~ *over* ⚓ dar de quilla; volcar(se); F caerse patas arriba.

keen [kiːn] □ agudo; *edge* afilado; *wind* penetrante; sutil; perspicaz; *emotion* vivo, ardiente, sentido; *appetite* bueno; p. entusiasta, celoso; ansioso; F *be* ~ *on th.* ser muy aficionado a; p. estar prendado de; **'keen-**

ness agudeza f; perspicacia f; viveza f; entusiasmo m.

keep [kiːp] 1. mantenimiento m; subsistencia f; comida f; *hist.* torreón m, torre f del homenaje; F *for* ~s para siempre, para guardar; 2. [*irr.*] *v/t.* guardar; tener guardado; (re)tener; reservar; (*not give back*) quedarse con; preservar, conservar, mantener; defender; cuidar; custodiar; (*delay a p.*) detener, entretener; *promise* cumplir; ~ *a p. waiting* hacer esperar a una p.; ~ *away* mantener a distancia; no dejar acercarse; ~ *a p. from ger.* no dejar *inf.* a una p.; ~ *s.t. from a p.* ocultar algo a una p.; ~ *in* p. no dejar salir, tener encerrado; *feelings* contener; ~ *up* mantener, conservar; sostener; p. hacer trasnochar; ~ *it up* no cejar; 3. [*irr.*] *v/i.* quedar(se); permanecer; seguir, continuar; mantenerse; conservarse; estar(se); ~ *doing* seguir haciendo, continuar haciendo; ~ *still!* ¡estáte quieto!; F ~ *at it* machacar; ~ *away* mantenerse alejado (*from place* de); no dejarse ver; ~ *off* mantenerse a distancia; *grass* no pisar; no tocar; ~ *out!* ¡prohibida la entrada!; ~ *up* continuar; no rezagarse; ~ *up with* ir al paso de; emular; proseguir.

keep·er ['kiːpə] guarda *m*; custodio *m*; (*park etc.*) guardián (-a *f*) *m*; (*owner*) dueño (a *f*) *m*; (*a. game* ~) guardabosques *m*; archivero *m*; cerradero *m*; culata *f*; **'keep·ing** custodia *f*; guarda *f*; protección *f*; mantenimiento *m*; **'keep·sake** ['~seik] recuerdo *m*.

keg [keg] cuñete *m*, barrilete *m*.

ken·nel ['kenl] 1. perrera *f*; jauría *f* of *hounds*; *fig.* cuchitril *m*; 2. tener (*or* encerrar *or* estar) en perrera.

kept [kept] *pret. a. p.p.* of *keep* 2.

ker·chief ['kəːtʃif] pañuelo *m*, pañoleta *f*.

ker·nel ['kəːnl] almendra *f*, núcleo *m*; grano *m*; *fig.* meollo *m*.

ker·o·sene ['kerəsiːn] keroseno *m*.

ketch·up ['ketʃəp] salsa *f* de tomate *etc.*; *v.* catsup.

ket·tle ['ketl] *approx.* olla *f* en forma de cafetera, tetera *f*; pava *f* *S.Am.*; **'~·drum** timbal *m*.

key [kiː] 1. llave *f* (*a. fig.*); tecla *f* of *piano, typewriter*; *tel.* manipulador *m*; ⊕ chaveta *f*, cuña *f*; *fig.*, △ clave *f*; ♪ tonalidad *f*, tono *m*; ~ *man* hombre *m* indispensable; 2. ⊕ enchavetar, acuñar; ♪ afinar; **'~·board** teclado *m*; **'~·hole** ojo *m* (de la cerradura); **'~ saw** sierra *f* de punta; **'~ money** pago *m* ilícito al casero; **'~·note** (nota *f*) tónica *f*; *fig.* idea *f* fundamental; **'~·ring** llavero *m*; **'~·stone** △ clave *f*; *fig.* piedra *f* angular.

khak·i ['kaːki] (de) caqui *m*.

kib·itz·er ['kibitsə] F entrometido (a *f*) *m*; mirón (-a *f*) *m*.

kick [kik] 1. puntapié *m*, patada *f*; coz *f* of *animal*; culatazo *m* of *firearm*; *fig.* (fuerza *f* de) reacción *f*; *sl.* fuerza *f* of *drink*; F queja *f*, protesta *f*; 2. *v/t.* dar un puntapié a; dar de coces a; *goal* marcar; ~ *out* echar (a puntapiés); F ~ *the bucket* morir; ~ *up the dust* levantar una polvareda; ~ *up a row* meter bulla; armar camorra; *v/i.* dar coces; cocear (*a. fig.*); patalear; *fig.* respingar, quejarse; **'~·back** 1. ⊕ contra-

golpe *m*; 2. ✝ comisión *f* ilícita; propina *f* ilícita; **'kick·er** caballo *m* coceador; F reparón (-a *f*) *m*, persona *f* quejumbrosa; **'kick·'off** *football*: saque *m* inicial.

kid [kid] 1. (*meat* carne *f* de) cabrito *m*, chivo *m*; (*leather*) cabritilla *f*; F crío *m*, niño (a *f*) *m*, chico (a *f*) *m*; F *the* ~*s* la chiquillería *f*; ~ *gloves* guantes *m/pl.* de cabritilla; 2. *sl.* embromar, tomar el pelo a; *I was only* ~*ding* lo decía en broma; **'kid·dy** F niño (a *f*) *m*.

kid·nap ['kidnæp] secuestrar; **'kid·nap·(p)er** secuestrador (-a *f*) *m*, ladrón *m* de niños.

kid·ney ['kidni] riñón *m*; ~ *bean* judía *f*, habichuela *f*.

kill [kil] 1. matar (*a. fig.*); destruir; eliminar; *feeling* apagar; *parl. bill* ahogar; F hacer morir de risa; 2. matanza *f*; golpe *m* (*or* ataque *m*) final; **'kill·er** matador (-a *f*) *m*; asesino *m*; **'kill·ing** 1. matanza *f*; F éxito *m* financiero; 2. □ matador; destructivo; abrumador; **'kill·joy** aguafiestas *m/f*.

kiln [kiln, ⊕ kil] horno *m*; **'~·dry** secar al horno.

kil·o·cy·cle ['kilousaikl] kilociclo *m*; **kil·o·gram** ['~græm] kilo (gramo) *m*; **kil·o·me·ter** ['kiləmiːtə] kilómetro *m*; **kil·o·watt** ['kiləwɔt] kilovatio *m*; **'kil·o·watt-'hours** kilovatioshora *m/pl.*

kilt [kilt] tonelete *m* (de los montañeses de Escocia).

kin [kin] familia *f*, parientes *m/pl.*, parentela *f*; *next of* ~ pariente(s) *m(pl.)* más próximo(s).

kind [kaind] 1. clase *f*, género *m*, especie *f*, suerte *f*; *a* ~ *of* uno a modo de; F ~ *of* casi, vagamente; 2. □ bondadoso, bueno; benigno; amable.

kin·der·gar·ten ['kindəgɑːtn] jardín *m* de (la) infancia.

kind-heart·ed ['kaind'hɑːtid] de buen corazón, bondadoso.

kin·dle ['kindl] encender(se).

kind·li·ness ['kaindlinis] bondad *f*, benignidad *f*, benevolencia *f*.

kin·dling ['kindliŋ] (*act*) encendimiento *m*; (*wood*) leña *f* menuda.

kind·ly ['kaindli] 1. *adj.* bondadoso, benévolo; *climate* benigno; 2. *adv.* bondadosamente; benignamente.

kind·ness ['kaindnis] bondad *f*; benevolencia *f*; amabilidad *f*.

kin·dred ['kindrid] 1. (*kinship*) parentesco *m*; parientes *m/pl.*; 2. allegado; afín.

kin·e·scope ['kinəskoup] cinescopio *m*.

ki·net·ic [kai'netik] cinético; **ki'net·ics** cinética *f*.

king [kiŋ] rey *m* (*a. fig., chess, cards*); *draughts*: dama *f*; ♀'s *English* inglés *m* correcto; **'king·dom** reino *m*; **'king·fish·er** martín *m* pescador; **'king·ly** real, regio; digno de un rey; **'king·pin** perno *m* real, perno *m* pinzote; pivote *m*; *fig.* persona *f* principal, elemento *m* fundamental; **'king-size** F de tamaño extra.

kink [kiŋk] 1. coca *f*, enroscadura *f*; *fig.* chifladura *f*, peculiaridad *f*; 2. formar cocas; **'kink·y** enroscado, ensortijado; *sl.* inortodoxo; raro.

kin...: **'~·ship** parentesco *m*, afinidad *f*; **'~s·man** pariente *m*.

ki·osk ['kiːɔsk] quiosco *m*; *teleph.* cabina *f*.

kip·per ['kipə] arenque *m* ahumado.

kiss [kis] 1. beso *m*; ósculo *m* (*lit.*); *fig.* roce *m*; 2. besar(se).

kit [kit] avíos *m/pl.*; ✗ equipo *m*; (*travel*) equipaje *m*; (*tools*) herramental *m*; (*first aid*) botiquín *m*.

kitch·en ['kitʃin] cocina *f*; ~ *utensils* batería *f* de cocina; **kitch·en·ette** [~'net] cocina *f* pequeña.

kitch·en...: **'~ maid** fregona *f*; **'~ range** cocina *f* económica; ~ **sink** fregadero *m*; F including the ~ sin faltar nada; completísimo.

kite [kait] *orn.* milano *m* real; cometa *f*; ✝ giro *m* ficticio.

kit·ten ['kitn] gatito (a *f*) *m*; **'kit·ten·ish** juguetón; coquetón.

kit·ty ['kiti] F minino *m*; *cards etc.*: puesta *f*, bote *m*.

klax·on ['klæksn] claxon *m*.

klep·to·ma·ni·a [kleptou'meiniə] cleptomanía *f*; **klep·to'ma·ni·ac** [~niæk] cleptómano (a *f*) *m*.

knack [næk] tino *m*; maña *f*, destreza *f*; hábito *m*; truco *m*.

knap·sack ['næpsæk] mochila *f*, barjuleta *f*.

knave [neiv] bellaco *m*, bribón *m*; **knav·er·y** ['~əri] bellaquería *f*.

knav·ish ['neiviʃ] ☐ bellaco, bribón, ruin.

knead [niːd] amasar, sobar.

knee [niː] 1. rodilla *f*; ⊕ ángulo *m*, cod(ill)o *m*; on bended ~, on one's ~s de rodillas; 2. dar un rodillazo a; **'~**

'deep metido hasta las rodillas; **'~ joint** articulación *f* de la rodilla; **kneel** [niːl] [*irr.*] (*a. ~ down*) arrodillarse, hincar la rodilla (*to* ante); estar de rodillas.

knell [nel] doble *m*, toque *m*.

knelt [nelt] *pret. a. p.p. of* kneel.

knew [njuː] *pret. of* know.

knick·ers ['nikəz] *pl.* F bragas *f/pl.*

knick-knack ['niknæk] chuchería *f*.

knife [naif] 1. [*pl.* knives] cuchillo *m*; navaja *f*; ⊕ cuchilla *f*; 2. acuchillar, apuñalar; **'~ edge** filo *m* (de cuchillo); **'~ grind·er** amolador *m*; **'~ switch** ⚡ interruptor *m* de cuchilla.

knight [nait] 1. caballero *m*; *chess*: caballo *m*; 2. armar caballero; **knight-er·rant** ['nait'erənt] caballero *m* andante; **'knight-'er·rant·ry** caballería *f* andante; **knight·hood** ['~hud] caballería *f*; título *m* de caballero; **'knight·li·ness** caballerosidad *f*; **'knight·ly** caballeroso, caballeresco.

knit [nit] [*irr.*] *v/t.* hacer (a punto de aguja); *brows* fruncir; (*a. ~ together*) enlazar, unir; *v/i.* hacer calceta (*or* media *or* punto); (*bone*) soldarse; **'knit·ting** labor *f* de punto; **'knit·ting nee·dle** aguja *f* de hacer calceta; **'knit·wear** géneros *m/pl.* de punto.

knives [naivz] *pl. of* knife.

knob [nɔb] protuberancia *f*, bulto *m*; botón *m*, perilla *f*; tirador *m* of door, drawer; puño *m* of stick; (*fragment*) terrón *m*; **'knobbed**, **'knob·by** nudoso.

knock [nɔk] 1. golpe *m*; porrazo *m*; aldabonazo *m*, llamada *f* on door; ⊕ golpeo *m*; 2. *v/t.* golpear; chocar contra; *sl.* criticar, calumniar; ~ *off* quitar (de un golpe); hacer caer; F *work* terminar, suspender; ✝ rebajar; F ejecutar prontamente; *sl.* apropiarse, robar; ~ *out mst boxing:* poner fuera de combate, noquear; eliminar; suprimir; ~ *over* volcar; *v/i.* llamar a la puerta; ⊕ golpear, martillear; F ~ *about* vagabundear, ver mucho mundo; **'knock·er** aldaba *f*; **'knock-kneed** patizambo; *fig.* débil, irresoluto; **'knock·out** *boxing:* (*a. ~ blow*) knockout *m*, noqueada *f*; *sl.* moza *f* (*or* cosa *f*) estupenda.

knoll [noul] otero *m*, montículo *m*.

knot [nɔt] 1. nudo *m* (*a. fig.*, ♣, ♠); (*bow*) lazo *m*; corrillo *m* of people; tied up in ~s confuso, enmarañado; perplejo; 2. *v/t.* anudar, atar; *v/i.* hacer nudos; enmarañarse; **'knot-hole** agujero *m in wood*; **'knot·ty** nudoso; *fig.* difícil, complicado, espinoso.

know [nou] 1. [*irr.*] saber; (*be acquainted with*) conocer; (*recognize*) reconocer; ~ *best* saber lo que más conviene; ~ *how to inf.* saber inf.; ~ *of* saber de; tener conocimiento de; 2. F *be in the* ~ estar enterado (*about* de); **know·a·ble** ['nouǝbl] conocible; **'know-how** F habilidad *f*, destreza *f*; experiencia *f*; **'know·ing** □ inteligente; sabio; entendido; *b.s.* astuto; ~*ly* a sabiendas; **'know-it-all** sabe-

lotodo *m/f*; **knowl·edge** ['nɔlidʒ] conocimiento(s) *m(pl.)*; saber *m*; **'knowl·edge·a·ble** □ enterado, conocedor.

knuck·le ['nʌkl] 1. nudillo *m*; jarrete *m of meat*; 2.: ~ *down to inf.* ponerse a *inf.* con ahinco; ~ *under* someterse.

kook [ku:k] tipo *m* raro; (*p.*) excéntrico *m*.

Ko·ran [kɔ'rɑːn] Alcorán *m*, Corán *m*.

ko·sher ['kouʃǝ] de ortodoxia judía; *sl.* genuino.

kow·tow ['kau'tau] saludar humildemente; humillarse (*to* ante).

ku·dos ['kjuːdɔs] F renombre *m*, prestigio *m*.

L

lab [læb] F = *laboratory*.

la·bel ['leibl] 1. rótulo *m*, marbete *m*, etiqueta *f*; *fig.* calificación *f*, apodo *m*; 2. rotular, poner etiqueta a.

la·bi·al ['leibiǝl] labial *adj a. su. f.*

la·bor ['leibǝ] 1. trabajo *m*; labor *f*; faena *f*; esfuerzo *m*; pena *f*; (*a. ~ force*) mano *f* de obra; clase *f* obrera; (dolores *m/pl.* del) parto *m*; *be in* ~ estar de parto; 2. *attr.* de trabajo; laboral; obrero; *pol.* ♀ laborista; ~ *union* sindicato *m* (de trabajadores de la misma rama) industrial; 3. *v/t.* insistir en; *v/i.* trabajar (*at* en); afanarse (*to* por); moverse penosamente.

lab·o·ra·to·ry ['læbrǝtɔri] laboratorio *m*; ~ *assistant* ayudante (a *f*) *m* (or mozo *m*) de laboratorio.

la·bor...: ~*ed* penoso, dificultoso; fatigoso; *style* premioso; **'~·er** trabajador *m*; obrero *m*; (*day*) jornalero *m*; (*unskilled*) peón *m*; bracero *m*; (*farm*) labriego *m*; **~·i·ous** [lǝ'bɔːriǝs] □ laborioso; que ahorra trabajo.

lab·y·rinth ['læbǝrinθ] laberinto *m*.

lace [leis] 1. cordón *m of shoes etc.*; encaje *m*; (*trimming*) puntilla *f*; 2. atar; enlazar(se).

lac·er·ate ['læsǝreit] lacerar; *feelings* herir; **lac·er·a'tion** laceración *f*.

lach·ry·mose ['lækrimous] lacrimoso.

lack [læk] 1. carencia *f*; falta *f*; necesidad *f*; ausencia *f*; *for* (or *through*) ~ *of* por falta de; 2. *v/t.* carecer de;

necesitar; *he* ~*s money* le (hace) falta dinero.

lack·a·dai·si·cal [lækǝ'deizikl] □ lánguido; indiferente; distraído.

lack·ey ['læki] lacayo *m*; *fig.* secuaz *m* servil.

lack·ing ['lækiŋ] sin, carente de; *be* ~ faltar.

lack·lus·ter ['læklʌstǝ] deslustrado, inexpresivo, apagado.

la·con·ic [lǝ'kɔnik] □ lacónico.

lac·quer ['lækǝ] 1. (*a.* ~ *work*) laca *f*, maque *m*; 2. laquear, maquear.

lac·tic ['læktik] láctico.

lac·tose ['læktouz] lactosa *f*.

la·cu·na [lǝ'kjuːnǝ] laguna *f*.

lad [læd] muchacho *m*, mozalbete *m*, zagal *m*, rapaz *m*, chico *m*.

lad·der ['lædǝ] escala *f* (*a.* ♣); escalera *f* de mano; *fig.* escalón *m*.

lad·en ['leidn] cargado; **lad·ing** ['leidiŋ] cargamento *m*, flete *m*.

la·dle ['leidl] 1. cucharón *m*, cazo *m*; 2. sacar (or servir) con cucharón.

la·dy ['leidi] señora *f*; (*noble*) dama *f*; *young* ~ señorita *f*; *ladies and gentlemen!* ¡(señoras y) señores!; **'~·bird** mariquita *f*, vaca *f* de San Antón; **'~-in-'wait·ing** dama *f* (de honor); **'~-kill·er** F tenorio *m*; **'~-like** delicado; elegante; *contp.* afeminado; **'~-love** amada *f*, querida *f*.

lag [læg] 1. retraso *m*, retardo *m*; 2. (*a.* ~ *behind*) rezagarse; retrasarse; **lag·gard** ['lægǝd] rezagado (a *f*) *m*; holgazán (-a *f*) *m*; persona *f* irresoluta.

la·goon [lǝ'guːn] laguna *f*

laid [leid] *pret. a. p.p.* of *lay*⁴ 2; be ~ up tener que guardar cama (*with* a causa de).

lain [lein] *p.p.* of *lie*² 2.

lair [lɛə] cubil *m*, guarida *f*.

la·i·ty [ˈleiiti] legos *m/pl.*, laicado *m*.

lake [leik] lago *m*.

lam [læm] *sl.* pegar, tundir (*a* ~ *into*).

lamb [læm] 1. cordero (*a f*) (*a. fig.*); (*older*) borrego (*a f*) *m*; (*meat*) carne *f* de cordero; 2. parir (*la oveja*).

lam·baste [læmˈbeist] F dar una paliza; poner como un trapo.

lamb...: '~**chop** chuleta *f* de cordero; '~**like** (manso) como un cordero; '~**skin** corderina *f*, piel *f* de cordero; '~**s·wool** añinos *m/pl.*

lame [leim] 1. □ cojo; lisiado; ~ *duck* persona *f* incapacitada (*or* ✝ insolvente); político *m* derrotado; ~ *excuse* disculpa *f* de poco crédito; 2. lisiar, encojar; '**lame·ness** cojera *f*; incapacidad *f*.

la·ment [ləˈment] 1. lamento *m*, queja *f*; *poet. etc.* elegía *f*; 2. lamentar (se *de*); **lam·en·ta·ble** [ˈlæməntəbl] □ lamentable, deplorable; **lam·en·ta·tion** lamentación *f*.

lamp [læmp] lámpara *f*; linterna *f*; (*street*) farol *m*, farola *f*; *mot.* faro *m*; (*bulb*) bombilla *f*; *fig.* antorcha *f*; '~**black** negro *m* de humo; '~**chim·ney**, '~ **glass** tubo *m* (de lámpara); '~**hold·er** portalámparas *m*; '~**light** luz *f* de (la) lámpara; '~**light·er** farolero *m*.

lam·poon [læmˈpuːn] 1. pasquín *m*; 2. pasquinar.

lamp·shade [ˈlæmpʃeid] pantalla *f*.

lance [lɑːns] 1. lanza *f*; 2. (a)lancear; *✗* abrir con lanceta; '~**cor·po·ral** soldado *m* (de) primera; **lanc·er** [ˈlɑːnsə] lancero *m*.

lan·cet [ˈlɑːnsit] lanceta *f*.

land [lænd] 1. *all senses:* tierra *f*; (*soil*) suelo *m*; (*nation*) pais *m*; (*a. tract of* ~) terreno *m*; *native* ~ patria *f*; *promised* ~ tierra *f* de promisión; ~ *forces* fuerzas *f/pl.* terrestres; ~ *reform* reforma *f* agraria; 2. *v/t. passengers* desembarcar; *goods* descargar; ✗ poner en tierra; F conseguir; *v/i.* desembarcar; ✈ aterrizar; ✗ (*on sea*) amerizar; '**land·ed** hacendado; que consiste en tierras; '~**fall** aterraje *f*; '~**hold·er** terrateniente *m/f*.

land·ing [ˈlændiŋ] aterraje *m*; desembarco *m of passengers*; desembarque

m of cargo; ✈ aterrizaje *m*; (*stairs*) descanso *m*; '~ **field** pista *f* de aterrizaje; '~ **gear** tren *m* de aterrizaje; '~ **stage** (des)embarcadero *m*.

land...: '~**la·dy** dueña *f*; patrona *f*, huéspeda *f of boardinghouse*; '~**locked** cercado de tierra; '~**lord** propietario *m*, dueño *m of property*; '~**lub·ber** ♣ *contp.* marinero *m* de agua dulce; '~**mark** ♣ marca *f* (de reconocimiento); mojón *m*; punto *m* destacado; *fig.* monumento *m*; '~**owner** terrateniente *m/f*, propietario (*a f*) *m*; '~**scape** [ˈlænskeip] paisaje *m*; '~**slide** corrimiento *m* de tierras (*a.* '~**slip**); *pol.* victoria *f* electoral arrolladora; ~ **tax** contribución *f* territorial.

lane [lein] (*country*) camino *m* (vecinal), vereda *f*; (*town*) callejón *m*; ♣ ruta *f* de navegación.

lan·guage [ˈlæŋgwidʒ] lenguaje *m* (*faculty of speech, particular mode of speech, style*); lengua *f*, idioma *m of nation*; '~ **lab·o·ra·to·ry** laboratorio *m* de idiomas.

lan·guid [ˈlæŋgwid] □ lánguido; '**lan·guid·ness** languidez *f*.

lan·guish [ˈlæŋgwiʃ] languidecer; afectar languidez; '**lan·guish·ing** □ lánguido; sentimental.

lank·y [ˈlæŋki] □ zancudo.

lan·tern [ˈlæntən] linterna *f* (*a.* △); fanal *m of lighthouse*; ♣ farol(a) *m*; '~ **jawed** chupado de cara; '~ **slide** diapositiva *f*.

lap¹ [læp] 1. regazo *m*; falda *f*; *fig.* seno *m*; *sport:* vuelta *f*; 2. envolver (*in* en); traslapar(se) (*a.* ~ *over*).

lap² [læp] 1. lametada *f*; chapaleteo *m*; 2. lamer; (*waves*) chapalear.

lap dog [ˈlæpdɔg] perro *m* faldero.

la·pel [ləˈpel] solapa *f*.

lap·i·dar·y [ˈlæpidəri] lapidario *adj. a. su. m*.

Lap·land·er [ˈlæplændə], **Lapp** [læp] lapón (*a f*) *m*.

lapse [læps] 1. (*moral, of time*) lapso *m*; desliz *m*; recaída *f* (*into* en); 2. (*time*) transcurrir; pasar; recaer (*into* en); ⚖ caducar.

lar·board [ˈlɑːbəd] (de) babor.

lar·ce·ny [ˈlɑːsni] latrocinio *m*; petty ~ robo *m* de menor cuantía.

larch [lɑːtʃ] alerce *m*.

lard [lɑːd] 1. manteca *f* (de cerdo), lardo *m*; 2. lard(e)ar, mechar; *fig.* adornar (*with* con); '**lard·er** despensa *f*.

large [lɑːdʒ] grande; *as ~ as* life de tamaño natural; en persona; **'largely** en gran parte; **'large·ness** grandeza *f*; gran tamaño *m*; **'large-'scale** en gran(de) escala; **'large-'sized** de gran tamaño.

lar·iat [ˈlæriət] lazo *m*.

lark [lɑːk] *orn.* alondra *f* común.

lark² [~] juerga *f*; travesura *f*; broma *f*.

lar·va [ˈlɑːvə], *pl.* **lar·vae** [ˈ~viː] larva *f*; **lar·val** [ˈ~vl] larval.

lar·yng·i·tis [lærinˈdʒaitis] laringitis *f*.

lar·ynx [ˈlærinks] laringe *f*.

las·civ·i·ous [ləˈsiviəs] *f* lascivo.

la·ser [ˈleizə] *f* láser *m*.

lash [læʃ] 1. tralla *f*; azote *m*; *(whip)* látigo *m*; *(stroke)* latigazo *m (a. fig.)*. *anat.* pestaña *f*; 2. azotar, fustigar *(a. fig.)*; provocar *(into hasta)*; *tail* agitar; chocar con; *(bind)* atar, ♣ trincar; *~ out* dar golpes furiosos; estallar; **'lash·ing** azotamiento *m*; atadura *f*; ♣ trinca *f*.

lass [læs] chica *f*, muchacha *f*; zagala *f*; moza *f*; **las·sie** [ˈ~i] muchachita *f*.

las·si·tude [ˈlæsitjuːd] lasitud *f*.

las·so [ˈlæsəu] 1. lazo *m*; 2. lazar.

last¹ [læst] 1. *adj.* último; postrero, final; extremo; *week etc.* pasado; the *~ to* el último en; *at the ~ moment* a última hora; 2. último (*a f*) *m*; última cosa *f*; fin *m*; *my ~* mi última carta; *at ~* por fin; *at long ~* al fin y al cabo; *to the ~* hasta el fin; *breathe one's ~* exhalar el último suspiro; 3. *adv.* por último; por última vez; finalmente; *~ but not least* el último pero no el peor.

last² [~] (per)durar; continuar; permanecer; resistir; subsistir.

last³ [~] horma *f* (del calzado).

last·ing [ˈlæstiŋ] □ duradero, perdurable; constante; *color* sólido.

last·ly [ˈlæstli] por último, finalmente.

latch [lætʃ] picaporte *m*; pestillo *m* de golpe; aldabilla *f*.

late [leit] 1. *adj.* tardío; *hour* avanzado; reciente, de ha poco; *(dead)* fallecido, difunto; *(former)* antiguo, *ex…*; *he is ~* llega tarde; *I was ~ in ger.* tardé en *inf.*; *be 2 minutes ~ ⚡ etc.* llegar con 2 minutos de retraso; *get (or grow) ~* hacerse tarde; 2. *adv.* tarde; *~ in life* a una edad avanzada; *~ in the year* hacia fines del año; *at the ~st* a más tardar; *~r on* más tarde; *of ~* últimamente, recientemente; **'~-**

com·er recién llegado (a *f*) *m*; rezagado (a *f*) *m*; **'late·ly** últimamente, recientemente.

late·ness [ˈleitnis] retraso *m*; lo avanzado *of the hour*; lo tarde; lo reciente.

la·tent [ˈleitənt] □ latente.

lat·er·al [ˈlætərəl] □ lateral.

la·tex [ˈleiteks] ♀ látex *m*.

lath [lɑːθ] listón *m*.

lathe [leið] torno *m*.

lath·er [ˈlɑːðə] 1. jabonadura(s) *f(pl.)*, espuma *f* (de jabón); 2. *v/t.* (en)jabonar; *v/i.* hacer espuma.

Lat·in [ˈlætin] 1. latino *adj. a. su. m* (a *f*); 2. *(language)* latín *m*; **'~ A'mer·i·can** latinoamericano *adj. a. su. m* (a *f*); **'Lat·in·ism** latinismo *m*.

lat·i·tude [ˈlætitjuːd] latitud *f*; *fig.* libertad *f*.

la·trine [ləˈtriːn] letrina *f*.

lat·ter [ˈlætə] más reciente; posterior; último; segundo *of 2*; *the ~* éste *etc.*; **'~-day** moderno, reciente.

lat·tice [ˈlætis] 1. enrejado *m* (a. **'~-work**); celosía *f*; 2. enrejar.

Lat·vi·an [ˈlætviən] letón *adj. a. su. m* (a *f*).

laud [lɔːd] *mst lit.* 1. alabanza *f*; *~s eccl.* laudes *f/pl.*; 2. alabar, loar, elogiar; **'laud·a·ble** □ laudable, loable; **laud·a·to·ry** [ˈ~ətəri] □ laudatorio.

laugh [lɑːf] 1. risa *f*; *(loud)* carcajada *f*, risotada *f*; 2. reír(se); *~ at* reírse de, burlarse de; *~ off* tomar a risa; *~ out (loud)* reírse a carcajadas; **'laugh·ing** 1. risa *f*; 2. risueño, reidor; *~ matter* cosa *f* de risa; **'laugh·ing-stock** hazmerreír *m*; **'laugh·ter** risa(s) *f* (*pl.*).

launch [lɔːntʃ] 1. botadura *f*; *(boat)* lancha *f*; 2. *v/t. ship* botar, echar al agua, *(throw, publicize, set up)* lanzar; dar principio a; poner en operación; ♣ emitir; *v/i.*: *~ forth*, *~ out* lanzarse, salir; *~ (out) into* lanzarse a; emprender; **'launch·ing** botadura *f*; lanzamiento *m*; iniciación *f*; ♣ emisión *f*; **'launch·(ing) 'pad** paraje *m* de lanzamiento.

laun·der [ˈlɔːndə] *v/t.* lavar (y planchar); *v/i.* resistir el lavado.

laun·dress [ˈlɔːndris] lavandera *f*; **'laun·dry** lavadero *m*; lavandería *f* *S.Am.*; *(clothes)* ropa *f* lavada (*or* por lavar).

lau·rel [ˈlɔrl] laurel *m*; *win ~s* cargarse de laureles, laurearse.

la·va [ˈlɑːvə] lava *f*.

lav·a·to·ry [ˈlævətəri] wáter *m*, excusado *m*, inodoro *m*, retrete *m*; *(wash-*

place) lavabo *m*; *public* ~ evacuatorio *m* (público).

lav·en·der ['lævində] espliego *m*, lavanda *f*.

lav·ish ['læviʃ] **1.** □ pródigo (*of* de, *in* en); profuso; **2.** prodigar; ~ *s.t. upon* a *p.* colmar a una p. de algo; '**lav·ish·ness** prodigalidad *f*; profusión *f*.

law [lɔ:] ley *f*; (*study*, *body of*) derecho *m*; jurisprudencia *f*; *sport*: regla *f*; ~ *and order* orden *m* público; *by* ~ según la ley; *in* ~ según derecho; *...-in-* ~ político; *lay down the* ~ hablar autoritariamente; *practice* ~ ejercer (la profesión) de abogado; *take the* ~ *into one's own hands* tomarse la justicia por su mano; '~-a·bid·ing observante de la ley; morigerado; '~-break·er infractor (-a *f*) *m* de la ley; '~ court tribunal *m* de justicia; '**law·ful** □ lícito, legítimo, legal; '**law·mak·er** legislador (-a *f*) *m*.

lawn[1] [lɔ:n] linón *m*.

lawn[2] [~] césped *m*; '~ **mow·er** cortacésped *m*; '~ **ten·nis** tenis *m*.

law·suit ['lɔ:su:t] pleito *m*, litigio *m*, proceso *m*; **law·yer** ['lɔ:jə] abogado *m*; jurisconsulto *m*.

lax [læks] (*morally*) laxo; indisciplinado; negligente; **lax·a·tive** [~ətiv] laxante *adj. a. su. m*; '**lax·i·ty**, '**lax·ness** negligencia *f*.

lay[1] [lei] *pret. of* lie[2] 2.

lay[2] [~] *lit.* trova *f*, romance *m*.

lay[3] [~] laico, lego, seglar; profano.

lay[4] [~] **1.** disposición *f*, situación *f*; **2.** [*irr.*] *v/t.* poner, colocar, dejar; (*ex-*)tender; acostar; derribar; acabar con; *blame*, *foundations* echar; *eggs*, *table* poner; ~ *aside*, ~ *away* echar a un lado, arrinconar; ahorrar; ~ *bare* poner al descubierto; ~ *before* presentar a; exponer ante; ~ *by* poner a un lado; guárdar; ahorrar; ~ *in* (*stocks of*) proveerse de; almacenar; ~ *low* derribar; poner fuera de combate; ~ *off* poner a un lado; *workers* despedir (temporalmente); F ~ *it on* (*thick*) (*beat*) zurrar; (*exaggerate*) recargar las tintas; (*flatter*) adular; ~ *up* almacenar, guardar, ahorrar; <sup>s<sup> obligar a guardar cama; *v/i.* (*hens*) poner; apostar (*a.* ~ *a wager*) (*that* a que); *sl.* ~ *into* atacar, dar una paliza a; ~ *off sl.* dejar en paz, quitarse de encima; *sl.* dejar; '~-a·bout holgazán (-a *f*) *m*.

lay·er 1. ['leiə] capa *f*; lecho *m*; *geol.* estrato *m*; (*gallina f*) ponedora *f*; ✓ acodo *m*; **2.** ['lɛə] acodar.

lay·ette [lei'et] canastilla *f*, ajuar *m* (de niño).

lay·ing ['leiiŋ] colocación *f*; tendido *m of cable*; postura *f of eggs*.

lay·man ['leimən] seglar *m*, lego *m*.

lay...: '~-**off** paro *m* involuntario; '~-**out** trazado *m*; disposición *f*; equipo *m*.

laze [leiz] holgazanear; '**laz·i·ness** pereza *f*, indolencia *f*, holgazanería *f*; '**la·zy** □ perezoso, indolente, holgazán; '**la·zy·bones** gandul (-a *f*) *m*.

lead[1] [led] **1.** plomo *m*; ♫ sonda *f*, escandallo *m*; *typ.* regleta *f*; mina *f in pencil*; **2.** emplomar; *typ.* regletear; ~*ed gasoline* gasolina *f* con plomo.

lead[2] [li:d] **1.** delantera *f*, cabeza *f* (*a. sport*); iniciativa *f*; dirección *f*, mando *m*; ejemplo *m*; guía *f*; **2.** *v/t.* conducir; guiar; encabezar; dirigir; mandar; *life* llevar; mover (*to inf.* a *inf.*); *v/i.* llevar la delantera; tener el mando; conducir (*to* a).

lead·en ['ledn] plúmbeo, de plomo; *color* plomizo; *fig.* pesado.

lead·er ['li:də] jefe (*a f*) *m*, líder *m*, caudillo *m*; guía *m/f*; conductor (-a *f*) *m*; director *m of band*; primer violín *m of orchestra*; artículo *m* de fondo *in newspaper*; '**lead·er·ship** jefatura *f*, liderado *m*; mando *m*, dirección *f*; iniciativa *f*.

lead·ing ['li:diŋ] **1.** dirección *f*; **2.** principal, capital; primero; ~ *article* artículo *m* de fondo; ~ *lady* dama *f*, primera actriz *f*; ~ *man* primer galán *m*; ~ *question* 🏛 pregunta *f* capciosa.

leaf [li:f] **1.** (*pl. leaves*) hoja *f*; *turn over a new* ~ reformarse; **2.** ~ *through* hojear; '**leaf·age** follaje *m*; '**leaf·less** deshojado, sin hojas; **leaf·let** ['~lit] hoja *f* volante, folleto *m*; '**leaf·y** frondoso.

league [li:g] **1.** (*measure*) legua *f*; *pol.*, *sport*: liga *f*; ♀ *of Nations* Sociedad *f* de las Naciones; *in* ~ *with* de acicate con; **2.** (co)ligar(se).

leak [li:k] **1.** ♫ vía *f* de agua; gotera *f in roof*; (*aperture*) agujero *m*, rendija *f*; salida *f*; **2.** ♫ hacer agua; salirse; gotear(se); ~ *out* rezumarse (*a. fig.*); *fig.* filtrarse; '**leak·age** escape *m*; derrame *m*; filtración *f*; '**leak·y** ♫ que hace agua; *roof* llovedizo; agujereado.

lean[1] [li:n] flaco; *meat* magro.

lean[2] [~] **1.** [*irr.*] ladear(se), inclinar(se); ~ *against* arrimar(se) a; ~ (*up*)*on* apoyarse en; **2.** (*a. fig.*

lean·ing) inclinación f; tendencia f.
lean·ness ['li:nnis] flaqueza f; magrez f; fig. carestía f.
lean-to ['li:n'tu:] colgadizo m.
leap [li:p] 1. salto m, brinco m; 2. saltar (a. ~ over); dar un salto (a. fig.); '**~frog** 1. fil derecho m, pídola f; 2. jugar a la pídola; saltar; **leapt** [lept] pret. a. p.p. of leap 2; '**leap year** año m bisiesto.
learn [lə:n] [irr.] aprender (to a); instruirse (about en); enterarse de a fact; **learn·ed** ['~id] □ docto, sabio; erudito; profession liberal; '**learn·er** principiante m/f, aprendiz (-a f) m; '**learn·ing** el aprender; estudio m; erudición f, saber m.
lease [li:s] 1. (contrato m de) arrendamiento m; 2. arrendar; dar (or tomar) en arriendo; '**~hold·er** arrendatario (a f) m.
leash [li:ʃ] traílla f.
least [li:st] 1. adj. menor; más pequeño; mínimo; 2. adv. menos; 3. su. lo menos; menor m/f; at~ a lo menos, al menos, por lo menos; at the (very) ~ lo menos; not in the ~ de ninguna manera; nada; to say the ~ para no decir más.
leath·er ['leðə] 1. cuero m; piel f; F pellejo m; 2. de cuero; 3. F zurrar; **leath·er·ette** [~'ret] cuero m artificial; '**leath·er·neck** sl. soldado m de la infantería de marina norteamericana; '**leath·er·y** correoso; skin curtido.
leave [li:v] 1. permiso m; ✕ (a. ~ of absence) licencia f; (a. ~-taking) despedida f; by your ~ con permiso de Vd.; take (one's) ~ despedirse (of de); 2. [irr.] v/t. dejar; abandonar; salir de; marcharse de; legar in will; ~ it to me yo me encargaré de eso; it ~s much to be desired deja mucho que desear; ~ alone p. dejar en paz; no meterse con; th. no tocar, no manosear; ~ it alone ¡déjalo!; ~ behind dejar atrás; olvidar; ~ out omitir; v/i. irse, marcharse; salir (for para); ~ off ger. cesar de inf., dejar de inf.
leav·en ['levn] 1. levadura f; fig. influencia f, estímulo m, mezcla f; 2. (a)leudar; fig. entremezclar.
leaves [li:vz] pl. of leaf.
leav·ings ['li:viŋz] pl. sobras f/pl.
Leb·a·nese ['lebəni:z] libanés adj. a. su. m (-a f).
lech·er·ous ['letʃərəs] □ lascivo; '**lech·er·y** lascivia f.

lec·tern ['lektən] atril m.
lec·ture ['lektʃə] 1. conferencia f; univ. mst lección f, clase f; fig. sermoneo m; 2. dar una conferencia, dar conferencias (or lecciones) (on sobre); fig. sermonear; '**lec·tur·er** conferenciante m/f; conferencista m/f S.Am.; univ. approx. profesor m adjunto; '**lec·ture room** sala f de conferencias; univ. aula f, sala f de clase.
ledge [ledʒ] repisa f, (re)borde m; (shelf) anaquel m; retallo m.
ledg·er ['ledʒə] ✝ libro m mayor.
lee [li:] ♣ (attr. de) sotavento m; (shelter) socaire m.
leech [li:tʃ] sanguijuela f (a. fig.).
leek [li:k] puerro m.
leer [liə] 1. mirada f (de reojo) con una sonrisa impúdica (or maligna); 2. mirar (de reojo) con una sonrisa impúdica (or maligna) (at acc.).
leer·y ['liəri] sl. suspicaz; cauteloso.
lees [li:z] pl. heces f/pl., poso m.
lee·ward ['li:wəd] (attr. de, adv. a) sotavento m.
lee·way ['li:wei] ♣ deriva f; fig. atraso m, pérdida f de tiempo; F sobra f de tiempo, libertad f.
left¹ [left] pret. a. p.p. of leave 2; be ~ quedar(se); be ~ over sobrar; ~overs sobra f/pl.
left² [~] 1. su. izquierda f; pol. izquierda(s) f(pl.); on (or to) the ~ a la izquierda; 2. adj. izquierdo; pol. izquierdista; siniestro (lit.); 3. adv. a (or hacia) la izquierda; '**~-hand**: ~ drive mot. conducción f a la izquierda; '**~-hand·ed** □ zurdo; fig. p. torpe, desmañado; compliment ambiguo, insincero; '**left·ist** izquierdista adj. a. su. m/f; '**~-wing** pol. izquierdista.
leg [leg] pierna f; pata f of animals, furniture; (support) pie m; pernil m of pork, trousers; caña f of stocking; (stage) etapa f, recorrido m; ~ bail sl. fuga f; evasión f; ~ room espacio m para las piernas of a car etc.
leg·a·cy ['legəsi] legado m, herencia f.
le·gal ['li:gəl] □ legal; lícito; **le·gal·i·za·tion** [li:gəlai'zeiʃn] legalización f; '**le·gal·ize** legalizar.
le·ga·tion [li'geiʃn] legación f.
leg·end ['ledʒənd] leyenda f; '**leg·end·ar·y** legendario.
leg·er·de·main ['ledʒədə'mein] juego m de manos; trapacería f.

leg·gings ['legiŋz] *pl.* polainas *f/pl.*; 'leg·gy zanquilargo.
leg·i·bil·i·ty [ledʒi'biliti] legibilidad *f*; **leg·i·ble** ['ledʒəbl] □ legible.
le·gion ['li:dʒən] legión *f* (*a. fig.*).
leg·is·late ['ledʒisleit] legislar; **leg·is·la·ture** [~tʃə] legislatura *f*.
le·git·i·ma·cy [li'dʒitiməsi] legitimidad *f*; **le·git·i·mate** [~mit] □ legítimo; admisible; **le·git·i·ma·tion** legitimación *f*.
leg·ume ['legju:m] legumbre *f*.
lei·sure ['leʒə] 1. ocio *m*, tiempo *m* libre, desocupación *f*; 2. de ocio, desocupado, de pasatiempo; ~ *activities* recreo(s) *m*; pasatiempos *m*; ~ *time* horas *f/pl.* de ocio; ~ *wear* ropa *f* de recreo; traje *m* informal; 'lei·sure·ly 1. *adj.* pausado, lento; 2. pausadamente, despacio, con calma.
lem·on ['lemən] 1. limón *m*; (*a.~ tree*) limonero *m*; 2. *attr.* de limón; (*color*) limonado; *sl.* cosa *f* de fábrica defectuosa; **lem·on·ade** [~'neid] limonada *f*, gaseosa *f* de limón; **lem·on-'squeez·er** exprimelimones *m*.
lend [lend] [*irr.*] prestar; *fig.* dar, añadir; ~ *o.s. to* prestarse a; ~*ing library* biblioteca *f* circulante; '**lend·er** prestador (-a *f*) *m*; '**Lend-'Lease Act** ley *f* de préstamos y arriendos.
length [leŋθ] largo(r) *m*, longitud *f*; ♣ eslora *f*; *racing*: cuerpo *m*; duración *f* *of time*; corte *m* *of cloth*; '**length·en** alargar(se), prolongar(se); '**length·wise** longitudinal(mente); a lo largo; '**length·y** largo; prolongado.
le·ni·ent ['li:niənt] □ indulgente, clemente, poco severo; **le·ni·ence, le·ni·en·cy** ['~niəns(i)] lenidad *f*.
lens [lenz] lente *f*; *anat.* cristalino *m*.
Lent [lent] cuaresma *f*.
Lent·en ['lentən] cuaresmal.
len·til ['lentil] lenteja *f*.
leop·ard ['lepəd] leopardo *m*.
le·o·tard ['li:ətɑ:d] *baile, gimnástica*: traje *m* ajustado de ejercicio.
lep·er ['lepə] leproso (a *f*) *m*.
lep·ro·sy ['leprəsi] lepra *f*.
Les·bi·an ['lezbiən] lesbia *f*; lesbiana *f*; mujer *f* homosexual; '**~ism** lesbianismo.
less [les] 1. *adj.* (*size, degree*) menor, inferior; (*quantity*) menos; 2. *adv.*, *prp.* menos; ~ *and* ~ cada vez menos; *grow* ~ menguar, disminuir(se); **...less** [lis] sin...
less·en ['lesn] *v/t.* disminuir, reducir; *v/i.* disminuir(se).

less·er ['lesə] menor, más pequeño; inferior.
les·son ['lesn] lección *f*; *fig.* escarmiento *m*; ~*s pl.* clases *f/pl.*
lest [lest] para que no, no sea que.
let [let] [*irr.*] *v/t.* dejar, permitir; *property* alquilar, arrendar; ~ *inf.* = *imperative*: ~ *him come!* ¡que venga!; ~*'s go!* ¡vamos!; ~ *alone* no tocar; dejar en paz; F ~ *be* dejar en paz; ~ *by* dejar pasar; ~ *down* (dejar) bajar; ~ *o.s. down by* descolgarse con; ~ *fly* disparar (*at* contra); soltar (palabras duras) (*at* contra); ~ *go* soltar; *property* vender; (*miss, pass*) dejar pasar; F ~ *o.s. go* desfogarse; dejar de cuidarse *in appearance*; ~ *a p. know* hacer saber a una p., avisar a una p.; ~ *out* dejar salir; poner en libertad; ~ *through* dejar pasar (por); *v/i.* alquilarse (*at, for* en); F ~ *up* moderarse (*on* en); trabajar menos, cesar; **let-down** ['letdaun] desilusión *f*; chasco *m*.
le·thal ['li:θl] □ mortífero; letal.
le·thar·gic, le·thar·gi·cal [le'θɑ:dʒik(l)] □ letárgico.
let·ter ['letə] 1. carta *f*; letra *f* *of alphabet, typ. a. fig.*; ~*s pl.* (*learning etc.*) letras *f/pl.*; ~ *of credit* carta *f* de crédito; *small* ~ minúscula *f*; *to the* ~ a(l pie de) la letra; 2. rotular; estampar con letras; '**~box** buzón *m*; '**~·car·rier** cartero *m*; '**let·tered** *p.* letrado; rotulado, marcado con letras; '**let·ter-file** carpeta *f*, archivo *m*; '**~·head** membrete *m*; pliego *m* con membrete; '**let·ter·ing** inscripción *f*, letras *f/pl.*; '**~·press** texto *m* impreso; '**~ press** prensa *f* de copiar cartas.
let·tuce ['letis] lechuga *f*.
let up ['letʌp] cesación *f*; F calma *f*, tregua *f*, descanso *m*.
leu·ke·mia [lju:ki:miə] leucemia *f*.
lev·ee ['levi] ribero *m*, dique *m*.
lev·el ['levl] 1. (*flat place*) llano *m*; llanura *f*; (*instrument, altitude, degree*) nivel *m*; *fig.* uniformidad *f*, monotonía *f*; *sl.* *on the* ~ honrado; sin engaño, en serio; 2. *v/t.* nivelar (*a. surv.*); igualar; allanar; derribar; *site* desmontar; *v/i.*: ~ *at*, ~ *against* apuntar a; ~ *off* nivelarse; ⚡ enderezarse; (*prices*) estabilizarse; 3. raso, llano, plano; a nivel; nivelado; igual; 4. *adv.* a nivel; ras con ras; '**~'head·ed** sensato, juicioso.
le·ver ['li:və] 1. palanca *f* (*a. fig.*); 2. apalancar; '**le·ver·age** apalanca-

miento *m*; *fig.* influencia *f*, ventaja *f*.
le·vi·a·than [liˈvaiəθən] leviatán *m*.
lev·i·ty [ˈleviti] frivolidad *f*, levedad *f*.
lev·y [ˈlevi] **1.** exacción *f* (de tributos); impuesto *m*; ✕ leva *f*; **2.** *tax* exigir, recaudar; ✕ reclutar.
lewd [luːd] ☐ lascivo, impúdico; **ˈlewd·ness** lascivia *f*, impudicia *f*.
lex·i·cog·ra·pher [leksiˈkɔgrəfə] lexicógrafo *m*; **lex·i·cog·ra·phy** [~ˈkɔgrəfi] lexicografía *f*; **lex·i·con** [ˈleksikən] léxico *m*.
li·a·bil·i·ty [laiəˈbiliti] obligación *f*, compromiso *m*; responsabilidad *f*; riesgo *m*.
li·a·ble [ˈlaiəbl] responsable (*for de*); obligado; expuesto, sujeto.
li·ai·son [liˈeizɔ(ː)n] enlace *m* (*a.* ✕); (*affair*) lío *m*.
li·ar [ˈlaiə] mentiroso (*a f*) *m*.
li·bel [ˈlaibl] **1.** (*written*) libelo *m* (on contra); difamación *f*, calumnia *f* (on de); **2.** difamar, calumniar; **ˈli·bel·(l)ous** ☐ difamatorio.
lib·er·al [ˈlibərəl] **1.** ☐ liberal (*a. pol.*); generoso; tolerante; abundante; **2.** liberal *m/f*; **ˈlib·er·al·ism** liberalismo *m*; **lib·er·al·i·ty** [~ˈræliti] liberalidad *f*.
lib·er·ate [ˈlibəreit] libertar, librar (*from de*); **lib·er·a·tion** liberación *f*; **ˈlib·er·a·tor** libertador (*-a f*) *m*.
lib·er·tar·i·an [libəˈtæriən] libertarianista *adj. a. su. m/f*.
lib·er·tine [ˈlibətain] libertino; **ˈlib·er·tin·ism** libertinaje *m*; **lib·er·ty** [ˈlibəti] libertad *f*; ⚓ *take liberties* permitirse (*or tomar*) libertades; *be at* ~ estar en libertad; *set at* ~ poner en libertad.
li·bid·i·nous [liˈbidinəs] ☐ libidinoso.
li·bi·do [liˈbiːdou] libido *f*; libidine *f*.
li·brar·i·an [laiˈbrɛəriən] bibliotecario (*a f*) *m*; **li·brar·y** [ˈlaibrəri] biblioteca *f*; (*esp. private*) librería *f*; ~ *science* bibliotecnia *f*; biblioteconomía *f*.
li·bret·to [liˈbretou] libreto *m*.
Lib·y·an [ˈlibiən] **1.** libio (*a f*) *m*; **2.** *p.* libio; líbico.
lice [lais] *pl. of* **louse**.
li·cense [ˈlaisəns] **1.** licencia *f*; permiso *m*; autorización *f*; título *m*; **2.** licenciar; autorizar; ~ *plate* placa *f* de matrícula; **li·cen·see** [~ˈsiː] concesionario (*a f*) *m*.
li·cen·tious [laiˈsenʃəs] ☐ licencioso.
lick [lik] **1.** lamedura *f*; lamida *f*

S.Am.; lengüetada *f*; **2.** lamer; F vencer; F zurrar; habilitar; ~ *one's lips* relamerse; **ˈlick·ing** lamedura *f*; F zurra *f*.
lic·o·rice [ˈlikəris] regaliz *m*.
lid [lid] tapa(dera) *f*; cobertera *f* of pan *etc.*; *anat.* párpado *m*.
lie¹ [lai] **1.** mentira *f*; *give the* ~ *to* desmentir; *tell a* ~ **2.** mentir.
lie² [~] **1.** disposición *f*; **2.** [*irr.*] echarse, acostarse; estar echado; yacer, estar enterrado *in grave*; ~ *back*, ~ *down* echarse, acostarse; tenderse; ~ *in wait for* acechar; F ~ *low* agacharse, no chistar.
liege [liːdʒ] *hist.* **1.** feudatario; **2.** (*a.* **ˈ~man** [ˈ~mæn] vasallo *m*.
li·en [ˈliːən] derecho *m* de retención.
lieu [ljuː]: *in* ~ *of* en lugar de.
lieu·ten·ant [luˈtenənt] lugarteniente *m*; ✕ teniente *m*; ⚓ teniente *m* de navío; ✕ *second* ~ alférez *m*; ⚓ *sub*-~ alférez *m* de navío; **ˈ~ colo·nel** teniente coronel *m*; **ˈ~ com·mand·er** capitán *m* de corbeta; **ˈ~ gen·er·al** teniente general *m*; ~ *gov·er·nor* vicegobernador *m*; **lieu·ten·an·cy** lugartenencia *f*; tenencia *f*.
life [laif] (*pl.* **lives**) vida *f*; (*modo m de*) vivir *m*; ser *m*, existencia *f*; vivacidad *f*, animación *f*; (*period of validity*) vigencia *f*; **ˈ~ an·nu·i·ty** vitalicio *m*; **ˈ~ belt** (cinturón *m*) salvavidas *m*; **ˈ~ blood** sangre *f* vital; *fig.* alma *f*, nervio *m*, sustento *m*; **ˈ~ boat** lancha *f* de socorro; (*ship's*) bote *m* salvavidas, bote *m* de salvamento; **ˈ~ buoy** guíndola *f*; ~ *ex·pect·an·cy* expectación *f* de vida; **ˈ~ guard** ✕ guardia *m* de corps; **ˈ~ jack·et** chaleco *m* salvavidas; **ˈ~ less** ☐ sin vida, muerto; exánime; *fig.* desanimado; flojo; deslucido; **ˈ~ like** natural; **ˈ~ line** cuerda *f* salvavidas; **ˈ~ long** de toda la vida; **ˈ~ pre·serv·er** cachiporra *f*; **ˈ~ raft** balsa *f* salvavidas; **ˈ~ sav·ing** (de) salvamento *m*; **ˈ~ size** de tamaño natural; **ˈ~ span** período *m* de la vida; **ˈ~ time** (transcurso *m* de la) vida *f*; **lif·er** *sl.* presidiario de por vida.
lift [lift] **1.** alzamiento *m*; esfuerzo *m* para levantar, empuje *m* para arriba; ayuda *f* (para levantar); (*cargo*) montacargas *m*; F viaje *m* en coche ajeno; ✈ sustentación *f*; **2.** *v/t.* levantar, alzar, elevar (*a.* ~ *up*); transportar (en avión); *v/i.* levantarse; (*clouds etc.*) disiparse; **ˈ~ off** despegue *m* (vertical); alzamiento *m*.

light¹ [lait] **1.** luz *f* (*a. fig. a.* window); lumbre *f*; fuego *m* for cigarette etc.; ~*s pl.* luces *f/pl.*, conocimientos *m/pl.*; bring (come) to ~ sacar (salir) a luz, descubrir(se); ~ bulb bombilla *f*; ~ meter exposímetro *m*; ~ wave onda *f* luminosa; **2.** claro; hair rubio; skin blanco; **3.** [*irr.*] *v/t.* (ignite) encender; alumbrar, iluminar (*a.* ~ up); *v/i.* (mst ~ up) encenderse; alumbrarse.

light² [~] **1.** adj. □ *a.* adv. ligero; (slight) leve; (bearable) llevadero; (unencumbered) desembarazado; (fickle, wanton) liviano; ~ opera opereta *f*, zarzuela *f*; **2.** tropezar con; (bird) posarse en.

light·en¹ [laitn] iluminar(se).

light·en² [~] load etc. aligerar(se).

light·er [laitə] encendedor *m*; (petrol-) mechero *m*.

light...: '~·fin·gered largo de uñas; '~·head·ed mareado; '~·heart·ed □ alegre de corazón; poco serio; '~·house faro *m*.

light·ing [laitiŋ] alumbrado *m*; iluminación *f*; ~ engineering luminotecnia *f*.

light·ly [laitli] adv. ligeramente; levemente; frívolamente; sin pensarlo bien; **light-mind·ed** tonto; atolondrado; **light·ness** ligereza *f*; agilidad *f*; claridad *f*.

light·ning [laitniŋ] relámpago *m*, rayo *m* (*a.* ~ flash); relampagueo *m*; ~ bug luciérnaga *f*; '~ rod pararrayos *m*.

light·ship [laitʃip] buque *m* faro.

light·weight [laitweit] persona *f* de poco peso (*a. fig.*); boxing: peso *m* ligero.

light-year [laitjɔ:] año *m* luz.

lik·a·ble [laikəbl] simpático.

like [laik] **1.** adj. parecido (a), semejante (a); igual; propio de, característico de; como; feel ~ ger. tener ganas de inf.; something ~ algo así como; what is he ~? ¿cómo es?; **2.** adv. or prp. como; del mismo modo (que); igual (que); **3.** conj. F como, del mismo modo que; **4.** su. semejante *m/f*, semejanza *f*; ~*s pl.* simpatías *f/pl.*, gustos *m/pl.*; **5.** vb. gustar; querer; estar aficionado a; I ~ bananas me gustan los plátanos; I don't ~ bullfighting no estoy aficionado a los toros; how do you ~ Madrid? ¿qué te parece Madrid?; as you ~ como quieras, como gustes.

like·able v. likable.

like·li·hood [laiklihud] probabilidad *f*; **like·ly 1.** adj. probable; verosímil; prometedor; **2.** adv. probablemente.

lik·en [laikn] comparar (to con), asemejar (to a); **like·ness** parecido *m*, semejanza *f*; imagen *f*; (portrait) retrato *m*; **like·wise** asimismo, igualmente.

lik·ing [laikiŋ] gusto *m* (for por); afición *f* (for a); simpatía *f* (for p. hacia), cariño *m* (for p. a).

li·lac [lailək] (de color de) lila *f*.

lil·y [lili] lirio *m*; azucena *f*.

limb [lim] miembro *m* of body; rama *f* of tree.

lim·ber [limbə] **1.** ágil, flexible; **2.** hacer flexible; ~ up agilitarse.

lim·bo [limbou] limbo *m*.

lime¹ [laim] **1.** cal *f*; (*a.* bird-~) liga *f*; **2.** encalar; untar con liga.

lime² [~] ♀ (*a.* ~ tree) tilo *m*.

lime³ [~] ♀ lima *f*; (tree) limero *m*; '~ juice jugo *m* de lima.

lime...: '~·light luz *f* de calcio; be in the ~ estar a la vista del público; '~·stone (piedra *f*) caliza *f*.

lim·er·ick [limərik] especie de quintilla *f* jocosa.

lim·it [limit] **1.** límite *m*, confín *m*; to the ~ hasta no más; **2.** limitar (to a), restringir; **lim·i·ta·tion** limitación *f*, restricción *f*; ⚖ prescripción *f*; **lim·it·ed** limitado, restringido; **lim·it·less** □ ilimitado.

lim·ou·sine [limuzi:n] limousine *f*, limusina *f*.

limp¹ [limp] **1.** cojera *f*; **2.** cojear.

limp² [~] □ flojo, lacio; flexible.

lim·pid [limpid] □ límpido, cristalino, transparente.

linch·pin [lintʃpin] pezonera *f*.

line¹ [lain] **1.** línea *f*; cuerda *f*; ♣ cordel *m*; fishing: sedal *m*; ✝ ramo *m*, género *m*; 🖂 vía *f*; typ. renglón *m*; poet. verso *m*; draw the ~ no pasar más allá (at de); drop a ~ poner unas letras (to a); teleph. hold the ~! ¡un momento ito!; ¡no cuelgue Vd.!; in ~ with conforme a, de acuerdo con; **2.** v/t. rayar; linear; face etc. arrugar; alinear (*a.* ~ up); v/i.: ~ up alinearse; ponerse en fila.

line² [~] clothes forrar; ⊕ revestir; brakes guarnecer.

lin·e·age [liniidʒ] linaje *m*; **lin·e·al** [liniəl] □ lineal; en línea recta.

lin·e·ar [~·iə] lineal; de longitud.

lin·en [linin] **1.** lino *m*, hilo *m*; (*a.*

piece of un) lienzo m; (sheets, underclothes etc.) ropa f blanca; dirty ~ ropa f sucia; 2. de lino; '~ **clos·et** armario m para ropa blanca.

lin·er ['lainə] ♃ vapor m de línea, transatlántico m; **lines·man** ['lainzmən] (a. **line·man**) sport: juez m de línea; '**line-up** alineación f, formación f.

lin·ger ['liŋgə] (a. ~ on) tardar en marcharse [or morirse]; quedarse; persistir; '**lin·ger·ing** □ prolongado, dilatado, lento.

lin·ge·rie ['lɛ̃nʒəri:] ropa f blanca (or interior) de mujer, lencería f.

lin·go ['liŋgou] F lengua f, jerga f, galimatías m.

lin·gua fran·ca ['liŋgwa 'fræŋkə] lengua f franca.

lin·guist ['liŋgwist] poligloto (a f) m; lingüista m/f; **lin·guis·tics** lingüística f.

lin·i·ment ['linimənt] linimento m.

lin·ing ['lainiŋ] forro m of clothes; ⊕ revestimiento m.

link [liŋk] 1. eslabón m; fig. enlace m; ⊕ varilla f, corredera f; 2. eslabonar(se), enlazar(se) (a. ~ up).

link·age ['liŋkidʒ] enlace m, eslabonamiento m; ⊕ varillaje m.

links [liŋks] pl. campo m de golf.

link-up ['liːŋkʌp] conexión f; acoplamiento m in space.

li·no·le·um [li'nouljəm] linóleo m.

li·no·type ['lainoutaip] linotipia f.

lin·seed ['linsi:d] linaza f; ~ oil aceite m de linaza.

lint [lint] hilas f/pl.

li·on ['laiən] león m (a. astr. a. fig.); fig. celebridad f; ~'s share parte f del león; '**li·on·ize** tratar como una celebridad.

lip [lip] labio m (a. fig., ♣); pico m of jug; borde m of cup; sl. insolencia f; keep a stiff upper ~ no inmutarse; '~-**read** leer en los labios; '~-**serv·ice** jarabe m de pico; '~-**stick** rojo m de labios.

liq·ue·fy ['likwifai] liquidar(se).

liq·uid ['likwid] 1. líquido m; gr. líquida f; 2. □ líquido; fig. límpido; ♦ realizable.

liq·ui·date ['likwideit] all senses: liquidar(se).

liq·uor ['likə] licor m; bebida f alcohólica.

lisp [lisp] 1. ceceo m; balbuceo m as of child; 2. cecear; balbucear.

list¹ [list] 1. lista f, relación f; (regis-

tration) matrícula f; 2. poner en una lista; hacer una lista de; inscribir.

list² [~] ♦ 1. escora f; 2. escorar.

lis·ten ['lisn] escuchar, oír (to acc.); prestar atención, dar oídos, atender (to a); (eavesdrop) escuchar a hurtadillas; '**lis·ten·er** oyente m/f.

lis·ten·ing ['lisniŋ] escucha f; attr. de escucha; '~ **post** puesto m de escucha.

list·less ['listlis] □ lánguido, apático, indiferente; ~**ness** apatía f; indiferencia f.

lit·a·ny ['litəni] letanía f.

li·ter ['li:tə] litro m.

lit·er·a·cy ['litərəsi] capacidad f de leer y escribir.

lit·er·al·ism ['litərəlizm] literalismo m.

lit·er·ar·y ['litərəri] □ literario; **lit·er·ate** ['litərit] que sabe leer y escribir; **lit·er·a·ture** ['litəritʃə] literatura f.

lith·o·graph ['liθəgræf] 1. litografía f; 2. litografiar; **li·thog·ra·phy** [li-'θɔgrəfi] litografía f.

Lith·u·a·ni·an [liθju'einjən] lituano adj. a. su. m (a f).

lit·i·gate ['litigeit] litigar; **lit·i'ga·tion** litigio m, litigación f; **li·ti·gious** [li'tidʒəs] □ litigioso.

lit·mus (pa·per) ['litməs (peipə)] (papel m de) tornasol m.

lit·ter ['litə] 1. litera f; ♣ camilla f; lecho m, cama f de paja for animals; (rubbish) desperdicios m/pl., basura f; 2. poner en desorden; esparcir (cosas por); ~ **bas·ket** basurero m; cubo m para desechos; ~**bug** caminante m desperdiciador.

lit·tle ['litl] 1. adj. pequeño; chico; menudo; poco; escaso; (mean) mezquino; ~ ones los pequeños, los chiquillos, la gente menuda; ~ people hadas f/pl.; 2. adv. poco; a ~ better un poco mejor, algo mejor; 3. su. poco; he knows ~ sabe poco; a ~ un poco; ~ by ~ poco a poco.

lit·ur·gy ['litədʒi] liturgia f.

liv·a·ble ['livəbl] life llevadero; F habitable.

live 1. [liv] v/i. vivir; long ~! ¡viva(n)!; ~ high (or well) darse buena vida; ~ up to promise cumplir; standard vivir (or ser) en conformidad con; ~ up to one's income gastarse toda la renta; ~ within one's means vivir con arreglo a los ingresos; v/t. life llevar; experience vivir; ~ down lograr borrar; 2. [laiv]

vivo; ardiente, encendido; *issue etc.* de actualidad; ≶ con corriente; ⚔ cargado; **live·li·hood** ['laivlihud] vida *f*, sustento *m*; **live·li·ness** ['ˌlinis] viveza *f*; **live·ly** ['laivli] vivo, vivaz; animado, bullicioso; alegre.

liv·en ['laivən] avivar; animar.

liv·er ['livə] hígado *m*.

liv·er·y ['livəri] librea *f*.

lives [laivz] *pl. of life*; **'live·stock** ganado *m*, ganadería *f*.

liv·id ['livid] lívido; F furioso.

liv·ing ['livin] 1. vivo, viviente; vital; 2. vida *f*; sustento *m*; modo *m* de vivir; '~ room sala *f* de estar, living *m*; '~ space espacio *m* vital of a nation.

liz·ard ['lizəd] lagarto *m*.

load [loud] 1. carga *f* (*a. fig.*, ⊕, ≶); peso *m*; 2. *v/t.* cargar; (*oppress*) agobiar; (*favor*) colmar (*with* de); ~ed *question* intencionado; *v/i.* (*a. ~ up*) cargar(se); tomar carga; **'load·ing 1.** cargamento *m*, carga *f*; 2. de carga; cargador; '~ **zone** zona *f* de carga; **'load·stone** piedra *f* imán.

loaf¹ [louf] (*pl. loaves*) pan *m*; (*large*) hogaza *f*; ~ *sugar* azúcar *m* de pilón.

loaf² [~] F haraganear, gandulear.

loaf·er ['loufə] haragán (-a *f*) *m*.

loam [loum] marga *f*.

loan [loun] 1. préstamo *m*; (*public*) empréstito *m*; *ask for the ~ of* pedir prestado *acc.*; 2. prestar.

loath [louθ] poco dispuesto (*to* a); *be ~ for a p.* to no querer que una p. *subj.*; **loathe** [louð] abominar, detestar, aborrecer; *I ~ cheese* me da asco el queso; **loath·ing** ['~ðin] asco *m*, detestación *f*, repugnancia *f*; **'loath·some** ['~ðsəm] asqueroso, repugnante; '~**ness** repugnancia *f*.

loaves [louvz] *pl. of loaf¹*.

lob·by ['lɔbi] 1. vestíbulo *m*; antecámara *f*; *parl.* camarilla *f* de cabilderos; 2. *parl.* cabildear; **'lob·by·ist** *parl.* cabildero *m*.

lob·ster ['lɔbstə] langosta *f*.

lo·cal ['loukəl] 1. local; vecinal; 2. ⛟ (*a. ~ train*) tren *m* ómnibus (*or* suburbano); **lo·cale** [lou'kɑːl] lugar *m*; escenario *m* (*de acontecimientos*); **lo·cal·i·ty** ['~kæliti] localidad *f*; situación *f*; **lo·cal·ize** ['~kəlaiz] localizar.

lo·cate ['lou'keit] situar; colocar; localizar, hallar; **lo'ca·tion** localidad *f*; situación *f*; colocación *f*.

lock¹ [lɔk] 1. cerradura *f*; traba *f*;

retén *m*; (*wrestling a.* ⚔) llave *f*; esclusa *f on canal etc.*; 2. *v/t.* cerrar con llave; encerrar; ⊕ trabar, enclavar; *v/i.* cerrarse con llave; ⊕ trabarse.

lock² [~] mechón *m*; guedeja *f*.

lock·er ['lɔkə] armario *m* (particular); cajón *m* cerrado con llave; **lock·et** ['~it] guardapelo *m*.

lock...: '~**jaw** trismo *m*; '~ **keep·er** esclusero *m*; '~ **nut** contratuerca *f*; '~**out** cierre *m*, paro *m* voluntario de patronos; '~**smith** cerrajero *m*; '~ **up** cierre *m*; cárcel *f*.

lo·co·mo·tion [loukə'mouʃn] locomoción *f*; **lo·co·mo·tive** ['~tiv] 1. locomotora *f*; 2. locomotor.

lo·cust ['loukəst] langosta *f* (*a. fig.*).

lode [loud] filón *m*; '~**star** estrella *f* polar; *fig.* norte *m*; '~**stone** piedra *f* imán.

lodge [lɔdʒ] 1. casita *f*; casa *f* de campo; 2. *v/t.* alojar, hospedar; colocar, depositar; *v/i.* alojarse; hospedarse; **'lodg·er** huésped (-a *f*) *m*; **'lodg·ing** alojamiento *m*, hospedaje *m*; (*a. ~s pl.*) habitación *f*.

loft [lɔft] desván *m*; pajar *m*; **loft·i·ness** ['~inis] altura *f*; eminencia *f*; **'loft·y** ☐ alto, elevado; eminente; noble; sublime.

log [lɔg] 1. leño *m*, tronco *m*, troza *f*; ♣ corredera *f*; 2. cortar (y transportar) leños; apuntar, registrar.

log·a·rithm ['lɔgəriθm] logaritmo *m*.

log...: '~**book** ♣ cuaderno *m* de bitácora, diario *m* de navegación; ≼ libro *m* de vuelo(s); ⊕ cuaderno *m* de trabajo; '~ **cab·in** cabaña *f* de madera.

log·ic ['lɔdʒik] lógica *f*; **lo·gis·tic** [lɔ'dʒistik] logístico; ~**s** logística *f*.

log·roll·ing ['lɔgroulin] trueque *m* de favores políticos.

loin [lɔin] ijada *f*; lomo *m*; '~**cloth** taparrabo *m*.

loi·ter ['lɔitə] holgazanear, perder el tiempo; **'loi·ter·er** holgazán (-a *f*) *m*; vago (a *f*) *m*.

loll [lɔl] repantigarse (*a. ~ about*); apoyarse con indolencia.

lol·li·pop ['lɔlipɔp] F gilda *f*.

Lon·don·er ['lʌndənə] londinense *m/f*.

lone [loun] solo, solitario; soltero; aislado; **'lone·li·ness** soledad *f*; **'lone·ly**, **lone·some** ['~səm] solitario, solo; aislado, remoto; ~ **wolf** lobo *m* solitario.

long¹ [lɔŋ] **1.** adj. largo; extenso; prolongado; F alto; *it is 4 feet* ∼ tiene 4 pies de largo; *in the* ∼ *run* a la larga; ∼ *wave radio:* (de) onda f larga; **2.** su. largo (or mucho) tiempo m; **3.** adv. largo (or mucho) tiempo; largo rato; largamente; ∼ *before* mucho antes; *as* ∼ *as* mientras; con tal que *subj.*; F *so* ∼! ¡hasta luego!; *so* ∼ *as* con tal que.

long² [∼] anhelar (*for acc.*, *to inf.*).

long...: '∼'dis·tance a (larga or gran) distancia; *sport:* de fondo; *teleph.* ∼ *call* conferencia f interurbana; ∼ *flight* vuelo m a distancia; **lon·gev·i·ty** [lɔn'dʒeviti] longevidad f; **'long·hair** *sl.* aficionado a la música clásica adj. a. su.; **'long·hand** escritura f normal (or sin abreviaturas).

long·ing ['lɔŋiŋ] **1.** anhelo m, añoranza f; **2.** □ anhelante.

lon·gi·tude ['lɔndʒitjuːd] longitud f.

long...: '∼ *johns* F ropa f interior que cubre brazos y piernas; **'∼'jump** salto m de longitud; **'∼'leg·ged** zancudo; '∼'**lived** ['∼'laivd] de larga vida, duradero; '∼'**play·ing** de larga duración; ✈ de gran alcance; ✕ de gran autonomía; '∼'**shore·man** estibador m, obrero m portuario; '∼'**stand·ing** existente desde hace mucho tiempo; '∼'**suf·fer·ing** sufrido; '∼'**term** a largo plazo; '∼'**wind·ed** □ prolijo.

look [luk] **1.** mirada f, vistazo m; (a. ∼ pl.) aspecto m, apariencia f; aire m; *good* ∼s pl. buen parecer m; **2.** v/i. mirar; parecer; tener aire (de); buscar; considerar; ∼ *before you leap* antes que te cases, mira a los que vas; ∼ *here!* ¡oye!; ∼ *like* parecerse a; *it* ∼s *well on you* te sienta bien; ∼ *about* mirar alrededor; ∼ *about for* andar buscando; ∼ *down on* dominar; *fig.* mirar por encima del hombro, despreciar; ∼ *for* buscar; esperar; ∼ *forward to* anticipar con placer, esperar con ilusión; F ∼ *in* hacer una visita breve (on a), pasar por la casa *etc.* (on de); ∼ *out!* ¡cuidado!, ¡ojo!; ∼ *out for* buscar; estar a la expectativa de; tener cuidado con; ∼ *out on* dar a, caer a; ∼ (*up*)*on fig.* considerar, estimar; ∼ *up to* respetar, admirar; **3.** v/t. *emotion* expresar con la mirada; ∼ *a p. in the face* mirar a una p. cara a cara (*a. fig.*); ∼ *over* examinar; recorrer; ∼ *up* buscar, averiguar, consultar; F visitar; ∼ *a p. up and down* mirar

a una p. de arriba abajo; '∼'**a·like** doble; parecido adj. a. su. m (a f).

look·out ['luk'aut] (*p.*) vigía m, atalaya m; (*tower*) atalaya f; observación f, vigilancia f; perspectiva f; *be on the* ∼ (*for*) estar a la mira (de); '∼'**o·ver** *sl.* vistazo m; ojeada f.

loom¹ [luːm] telar m.

loom² [∼] surgir, asomar(se), aparecer (*a.* ∼ *up*); vislumbrarse; *fig.* amenazar.

loon·y ['luːni] *sl.* loco adj. a. su. m (a f); '∼ *bin sl.* manicomio m.

loop [luːp] **1.** gaza f, lazo m; (*fastening*) presilla f; (*bend*) curva f, vuelta f, recodo m; **2.** v/t. hacer gaza con; asegurar con gaza (or presilla); enlazar; ✈ *the* ∼ hacer (or rizar) el rizo; v/i. formar lazo(s); serpentear; '∼'**hole** ✕ aspillera f, tronera f; *fig.* escapatoria f, evasiva f.

loose [luːs] **1.** □ (*free; separate*) suelto, desatado; (*not tight*) flojo, movedizo; (*unpacked*) sin envase; *dress* holgado; *wheel, pulley etc.* loco; *connexion* desconectado; poco exacto; aproximado; negligente; *morals* relajado; *woman* fácil; ∼ *change* suelto m; ∼ *end* cabo m suelto; **2.** soltar; desatar; aflojar; (*a.* ∼ *off*) disparar; ∼ *one's hold on* soltar; *be on the* ∼ estar en libertad; estar de juerga; '∼ *leaf:* ∼ *book* cuaderno m de hojas sueltas (or *movibles*); **loos·en** ['luːsn] desatar(se), aflojar(se), soltar(se); ∼ *up muscles* desentumecer; **'loose·ness** soltura f; flojedad f; holgura f.

loot [luːt] **1.** botín m; F ganancias f/pl.; **2.** saquear, pillar; **'loot·er** saqueador (-a f) m.

lop [lɔp] *tree* (des)mochar; cercenar.

lop...: '∼ *sid·ed* desproporcionado; ladeado; desequilibrado (*a. fig.*).

lo·qua·cious [louˈkweiʃəs] □ locuaz.

lo·ran ['lɔːræn] ⚓ lorán m.

lord [lɔːd] **1.** señor m; (*title*) lord m; *the* ⸰ el Señor; *my* ∼ señor; Su Señoría; ⸰'s *Prayer* padrenuestro m; ⸰'s *Supper* (última) Cena f; *parl. the* (*House of*) ⸰s (la Cámara de) los Lores; **2.** ∼ *it* hacer el señor; mandar despóticamente; **'lord·ly** señoril; altivo; imperioso; espléndido; **'lord·ship** (*title*) señoría f; (*rule*) señorío m.

lore [lɔː] saber m (popular), ciencia f.

lose [luːz] v/t. perder; hacer perder; *that lost us the war* eso nos hizo perder la guerra; ∼ *o.s.* perderse;

v/i. perder; ser vencido; (*clock*) atrasar; **'los·er** perdidoso (a *f*) *m*, perdedor (-a *f*) *m*; *sl.* persona *f* sin atractivo.

loss [lɔs] pérdida *f*; *be a total* ~ considerarse totalmente perdido; *at a* ~ ✝ con pérdida; *be at a* ~ estar perplejo, no saber qué hacer; ~ **lead·er** artículo *m* vendido a gran descuento.

lost [lɔst] *pret. a p.p. of lose*; ~ *in* abismado en, absorto en; ~ *to* insensible a; inaccesible a.

lot [lɔt] ✝ lote *m*; porción *f*; (*fate*) suerte *f*; solar *m for building*; F gran cantidad *f*.

lo·tion ['louʃn] loción *f*.

lo·ter·y ['lɔtəri] lotería *f*.

loud [laud] □ alto; fuerte, recio; ruidoso, estrepitoso; *color* chillón; **'loud-mouth** bocón *m* (a *f*); **'loud-ness** (gran) ruido *m*; sonoridad *f*; **loud'speak·er** altavoz *m*, altoparlante *m*.

lounge [laundʒ] **1.** salón *m*; sala *f* (de estar); sofá *m*; **2.** arrellanarse, repantigarse; pasearse perezosamente; haraganear.

louse [laus] (*pl.* lice) piojo *m*; **lous·y** ['lauzi] piojoso; *sl.* asqueroso, vil.

lout [laut] patán *m*; gamberro *m*; **'lout·ish** grosero, zafio.

lov·a·ble ['lʌvəbl] □ amable.

love [lʌv] **1.** amor *m* (*of, for, towards* de, a); querer *m*; cariño *m*; *tennis:* cero *m*; *attr.* de amor, amoroso; *in* ~ *with* enamorado de; *fall in* ~ enamorarse (*with* de); *make* ~ *to* hacer el amor a; cortejar; **2.** amar, querer; tener cariño a; ser muy aficionado a; **'~ af·fair** amores *m/pl.*; amorío(s) *m(pl.)* (F); **'~ bird** periquito *m*; *fig.* palomito *m*; **'~ child** hijo (a *f*) *m* del amor; **'~ feast** ágape *m*; **love·li·ness** belleza *f*, hermosura *f*; encanto *m*; exquisitez *f*; **love·lorn** ['lʌvlɔːn] suspirando de amor, abandonado de su amante; **'love·ly** bello, hermoso; encantador; exquisito; precioso; simpático; **'love·mak·ing** galanteo *m*; trato *m* sexual; **'lov·er** amante *m/f*; aficionado (a *f*) *m* (*of* a), amigo (a *f*) *m* (*of* de); **~** *pl.* amantes *m/pl.*, novios *m/pl.*; **'love·sick** enfermo de amor, amartelado.

low¹ [lou] **1.** bajo; *bow* profundo; *blow* sucio; *dress* escotado; *price* módico; ~ *comedy* farsa *f*; **2.** *meteor.* área *f* de baja presión; F punto *m* bajo; *mot.* primera marcha *f*; **3.**

adv. bajo; bajamente; en voz baja.

low² [~] **1.** mugir; **2.** mugido *m*.

low…: '~**born** de humilde cuna; '~**brow** F (persona *f*) nada intelectual; '~**'cost** económico; '~**'down 1.** bajo, vil; **2.** [~] *sl.* verdad *f*, informes *m/pl.* confidenciales; pormenores *m/pl.*

low·er¹ ['louə] **1.** más bajo *etc.*; inferior; bajo; ~ *classes* clase *f* baja; **2.** bajar; disminuir; *price* rebajar; ♣ arriar; ♣ debilitar.

low·er² ['lauə] fruncir el entrecejo, mirar con ceño.

low-key ['louki:] modesto; retirado; **'low·land** ['loulənd] tierra *f* baja; **'low·li·ness** humildad *f*; **'low·ly** humilde; **'low-necked** escotado; **'low·ness** bajeza *f etc.*

loy·al ['lɔiəl] □ leal, fiel; **'loy·al·ist** legitimista *adj. a. su. m/f*; **'loy·al·ty** lealtad *f*, fidelidad *f*.

loz·enge ['lɔzindʒ] pastilla *f*.

lub·ber ['lʌbə] ♣ marinero *m* de agua dulce; bobalicón *m*.

lu·bri·cant ['lu:brikənt] lubri(fi)cante *adj. a. su. m*; **lu·bri·cate** ['~keit] lubri(fi)car, engrasar.

lu·cid ['lusid] □ lúcido; **lu·cid·i·ty** lucidez *f*.

luck [lʌk] suerte *f*, ventura *f*; fortuna *f*; azar *m*; **'luck·i·ly** afortunadamente, por fortuna; **'luck·less** desafortunado, desdichado; **'luck·y** □ afortunado; de buen agüero; *be* ~ tener (buena) suerte; tener buena sombra.

lu·cra·tive ['lu:krətiv] □ lucrativo, provechoso.

lu·di·crous ['lu:dikrəs] □ absurdo, ridículo.

lug [lʌg] **1.** oreja *f*; ⊕ orejeta *f*; agarradera *f*; (*movement*) (es)tirón *m*; **2.** arrastrar; tirar de.

lug·gage ['lʌgidʒ] equipaje *m*; **'~ car·ri·er** portaequipajes *m*; **'~ rack** rejilla *f*.

lu·gu·bri·ous [lu:'gju:briəs] □ lúgubre.

luke·warm ['lu:kwɔːm] tibio (*a. fig.*), templado; *fig.* indiferente; '~**ness** tibieza *f*.

lull [lʌl] recalmón *m*, intervalo *m* de calma; *fig.* tregua *f*, respiro *m*.

lull·a·by ['lʌləbai] nana *f*, canción *f* de cuna.

lum·ba·go [lʌm'beigou] lumbago *m*.

lum·ber ['lʌmbə] **1.** maderos *m/pl.*, maderas *f/pl.* (de sierra); **2.** moverse pesadamente (*or* con ruido sordo);

'lum·ber·ing pesado; **'lum·ber·jack,** **'lum·ber·man** hachero *m*, maderero *m*; leñador *m*; **'lum·ber·yard** corral *m* de madera.
'lu·mi·nous ['lu:minəs] □ luminoso.
lump [lʌmp] **1.** terrón *m* (*a. of sugar*); masa *f*; borujo *m*; (*swelling*) bulto *m*, hinchazón *f*; protuberancia *f*; ~ *sugar* azúcar *m* en terrón; ~ *sum* suma *f* global; **2.** *v/t.* amontonar; aborujar; ~ *together* agrupar, mezclar; *v/i.* aborujarse; **'lump·y** □ aterronado; borujoso.
lu·na·cy ['lu:nəsi] locura *f*.
lu·nar ['lu:nə] lunar; **'~ mod·ule** (*semiindependent spaceship*) módulo *m* lunar.
lu·na·tic ['lu:nətik] loco *adj. a. su. m* (*a f*), demente *adj. a. su. m/f*; ~ *asylum* manicomio *m*; F ~ *fringe* elementos *m/pl.* fanáticos.
lunch [lʌntʃ] **1.** almuerzo *m*, comida *f* (*a. more formally* **'lunch·eon** ['~ən]); lonche *m S.Am.*; (*snack*) merienda *f*; **2.** almorzar, merendar; **'~ hour** hora *f* del almuerzo.
lung [lʌŋ] pulmón *m*.
lunge [lʌndʒ] **1.** *fenc.* estocada *f*; arremetida *f*; **2.** dar una estocada; arremeter (*at* contra).
lurch [ləːtʃ] **1.** sacudida *f*, tumbo *m*,

tambaleo *m* repentino; **2.** dar sacudidas, dar un tumbo, tambalearse.
lure [ljuə] **1.** cebo *m*; señuelo *m* (*a. fig.*); aliciente *m*, seducción *f*; **2.** atraer (con señuelo); tentar; seducir.
lu·rid ['ljuərid] □ lívido, cárdeno; sensacional; espeluznante.
lurk [ləːk] ocultarse; estar en acecho.
lus·cious ['lʌʃəs] □ delicioso, rico, exquisito, suculento.
lust [lʌst] **1.** lujuria, lascivia *f*; (*greed*) codicia *f*; **2.** lujuriar; **'lust·ful** □ lujurioso, lascivo.
lus·ter ['lʌstə] lustre *m*, brillo *m*.
lus·trous ['lʌstrəs] □ lustroso.
lust·y ['lʌsti] □ vigoroso, lozano.
Lu·ther·an ['lu:θərən] luterano *adj a. su. m* (*a f*).
lux·u·ri·ance [lʌgˈzjuəriəns] lozanía *f*, exuberancia *f*; **lux·u·ri·ant** □ lozano, exuberante; **lux·u·ri·ous** [~riəs] □ lujoso; lascivo; **lux·u·ry** ['lʌkʃeri] lujo *m*; *attr.* de lujo.
lye [lai] lejía *f*.
ly·ing ['laiiŋ] **1.** *ger. of lie*[1] *a. lie*[2]; **2.** *adj.* mentiroso; **'~·in** parto *m*.
lynch [lintʃ] linchar; **'~·law** ley *f* de Lynch; ley *f* de la soga.
lynx [liŋks] lince *m*.
lyr·ic ['lirik] **1.** lírico; **2.** poesía *f* lírica; letra *f* (de una canción); **'lyr·i·cal** □ lírico; F elocuente.

M

ma'am [mæm, F məm, m] = *madam*.
ma·ca·bre [məˈkɑːbr] macabro.
mac·ad·am [məˈkædəm] macadán *m*; **mac·ad·am·ize** macadamizar.
mac·a·ro·ni [mækəˈrouni] macarrones *m/pl.*
mac·a·roon [mækəˈruːn] macarrón *m* (de almendras), mostachón *m*.
mach·i·na·tion [mækiˈneiʃn] maquinación *f*; **ma·chine** [məˈʃiːn] **1.** máquina *f* (*a. fig.*); aparato *m*; *mot.* coche *m*; *pol.* organización *f*, camarilla *f*; **2.** elaborar (*or* acabar, coser) a máquina; **ma'chine gun 1.** ametralladora *f*; **2.** ametrallar; **ma'chine-made** hecho a máquina; **ma'chine·ry** maquinaria *f*; mecanismo *m* (*a. fig.*); **ma'chine shop** taller *m* de máquinas; **ma'chine trans·la·tion** traducción *f* automática; **ma'chine·wash·able** lavable en lavadora au-

tomática; **ma'chin·ist** maquinista *m/f*.
mack·in·tosh ['mækintɔʃ] impermeable *m*.
mad [mæd] □ loco, demente; F furioso; *dog* rabioso; *idea* insensato; *drive* ~ enloquecer.
mad·am ['mædəm] señora *f*.
mad·cap ['mædkæp] locuelo; **mad·den** ['mædn] enloquecer; enfurecer.
made-to-order ['meidtuːɔːdə] hecho a la medida.
made-up ['meidˈʌp] hecho; compuesto; *story* ficticio; *face* pintado.
mad·house ['mædhaus] manicomio *m*; **'mad·man** loco *m*; **'mad·ness** locura *f*, demencia *f*.
mag·a·zine [mægəˈziːn] revista *f*; ✕ almacén *m*; ✕ polvorín *m* *for powder*.
mag·got ['mægət] cresa *f*, gusano *m*.

mag·ic ['mædʒik] 1. magia *f; as if by ~* (como) por ensalmo; 2. mágico; **ma·gi·cian** [mə'dʒiʃn] mágico *m; (conjuror)* prestidigitador *m.*

mag·is·tra·cy ['mædʒistrəsi] magistratura *f;* **mag·is·trate** ['~trit] magistrado *m;* juez *m* (municipal).

mag·na·nim·i·ty [mægnə'nimiti] magnanimidad *f;* **mag·nan·i·mous** [~'nænimes] magnánimo.

mag·ne·sia [mæg'ni:ʃə] magnesia *f;* **mag·ne·sium** [~ziəm] magnesio *m.*

mag·net ['mægnit] imán *m;* **mag·net·ism** ['~nitizm] magnetismo *m;* **'mag·net·ize** magnetizar, iman(t)ar.

mag·nif·i·cent [mæg'nifisnt] magnífico; **mag·ni·fy** ['~fai] *opt.* aumentar, magnificar; agrandar; *fig.* exagerar; **~ing** *glass* lupa *f,* lente *f* de aumento.

mag·no·li·a [mæg'nouljə] magnolia *f.*

mag·pie ['mægpai] urraca *f,* marica *f.*

ma·hog·a·ny [mə'hɔgəni] caoba *f.*

maid [meid] criada *f,* camarera *f; mst lit.* doncella *f,* virgen *f.*

maid·en ['meidn] 1. *mst lit.* doncella *f,* virgen *f;* muchacha *f;* soltera *f* 2. virginal, intacto; (de) soltera; *speech* primero; *voyage* inaugural.

mail [~] 1. ✆ correo *m;* correspondencia *f;* 2. echar al correo; **'~bag** valija *f,* mala *f;* **'~box** buzón *m;* **'~man** cartero *m;* **'~-or·der house** casa *f* de ventas por correo; **'~ train** (tren *m*) correo *m;* **'mail·ing** lista *f* de direcciones.

maim [meim] tullir; mutilar.

main [mein] 1. principal; maestro; mayor; 2. cañería *f* (maestra); *poet.* océano *m;* **'~land** tierra *f* firme, continente *m;* **~mast** ['~mɑ:st, ♃ '~məst] palo *m* mayor; **~sail** ['~seil, ♃ '~sl] vela *f* mayor; **~spring** muelle *m* real; *fig.* causa *f* (*or* motivo *m*) principal; **~stream** vía *f* principal.

main·tain [mein'tein] mantener, sostener; ⊕ entretener.

main·te·nance ['meintinəns] mantenimiento *m;* sustento *m.*

maize [meiz] maíz *m.*

ma·jes·tic [mə'dʒestik] □ majestuoso; **maj·es·ty** ['mædʒisti] majestad *f.*

ma·jor ['meidʒə] 1. mayor (*a.* ♩); principal; importante; 2. ✕ comandante *m; phls.* mayor *f; univ.* especia-

lidad *f;* 3. *univ.* especializarse (*in* en); **~ 'gen·er·al** general *m* de división; **ma·jor·i·ty** [mə'dʒɔriti] mayoría *f,* mayor número *m;* mayor edad *f.*

make [meik] 1. [*irr*] *v/t.* hacer; crear; formar; construir; practicar, ejecutar, efectuar; constituir; causar, ocasionar; componer; producir; (*compel*) forzar, obligar, compeler (*inf. a inf.);* (*equal*) ser (igual a); (*induce*) inclinar, inducir (*inf. a inf.);* (*manufacture*) fabricar, confeccionar, elaborar; (*prepare*) aderezar, preparar, disponer, arreglar; *mistake* cometer; *speech* pronunciar; **~** *believe* fingir (-se); **~** *good damage* reparar; *loss* compensar, indemnizar; **~** *up* hacer; preparar; fabricar; inventar; componer, formar; *collection* reunir; *clothes* confeccionar; *face* pintar, maquillar; 2. [*irr*] *v/i.:* **~** *as if to,* **~** *as though to inf.* hacer como si quisiese *inf.,* fingir que va a *inf.,* aparentar *inf.;* **~** *after* (per)seguir; **~** *away with* llevarse, hurtar; **~** *off* largarse, escaparse; **~** *off with* alzarse con, llevarse; escaparse con; *mst* F **~** *out* arreglárselas, salir bien; *how did you ~ out?* ¿cómo te fue?; **~** *up* pintarse, maquillarse; *thea.* caracterizarse; **~** *up for* compensar; suplir; *lost time* recobrar; **~** *up to* (procurar) congraciarse con; halagar; adular; galantear; 3. hechura *f;* confección *f;* corte *m* of *clothes;* (*brand*) marca *f;* modelo *m; sl.* be on the **~** echar el agua a su molino; *our own ~* de fabricación propia; **'~be·lieve** 1. ficción *f,* simulación *f;* 2. simulado, falso, fingido; **'mak·er** hacedor (-a *f*) *m,* creador (-a *f*) *m;* fabricante *m;* artífice *m/f;* **'~shift** improvisado, provisional; **'~up** composición *f;* carácter *m,* modo *m* de ser; hechura *f,* confección *f* of *clothes;* maquillaje *m,* cosmético(s) *m(pl.)* for *face; thea.* caracterización *f;* **mak·ing** creación *f;* formación *f;* fabricación *f,* confección *f.*

mal·ad·just·ment ['mælə'dʒʌstmənt] mal ajuste *m;* inadaptación *f.*

mal·a·dy ['mælədi] mal *m,* enfermedad *f.*

mal·aise [mæ'leiz] malestar *m.*

mal·a·prop·ism ['mæləprɔpizm] despropósito *m.*

ma·lar·i·a [mə'lɛəriə] paludismo *m,* malaria *f;* **ma·lar·i·al** palúdico.

M

ma·lar·key [məˈlɑːki] *sl.* habla *f* necia; tontería(s) *f(pl.)*; mentira(s) *f(pl.)*.

Ma·lay [məˈlei] 1. malayo (a *f*) *m*; (*language*) malayo *m*; 2. malayo (*a.* **Ma·lay·an**).

mal·con·tent [ˈmælkəntent] malcontento *adj. a. su. m* (a *f*).

male [meil] 1. macho; masculino; ~ *child* hijo *m* varón; ~ *nurse* enfermero *m*; 2. macho; varón *m*.

ma·lev·o·lence [məˈlevələns] malevolencia *f*; **ma·lev·o·lent** □ malévolo.

mal·func·tion [mælˈfʌŋkʃn] 1. malfuncionamiento *m*; 2. ir de través; estropearse.

mal·ice [ˈmælis] malicia *f*, mala voluntad *f*; ⚖ intención *f* delictuosa.

ma·li·cious [məˈliʃəs] □ malicioso.

ma·lign [məˈlain] 1. □ maligno; 2. calumniar, difamar; **ma·lig·nan·cy** [məˈlignənsi] malignidad *f*; **ma·lig·nant** maligno.

mal·le·a·ble [ˈmæliəbl] maleable (*a. fig.*).

mal·let [ˈmælit] mazo *m*, mallo *m*.

mal·nu·tri·tion [ˈmælnjuːˈtriʃn] desnutrición *f*.

mal·prac·tice [mælˈpræktis] procedimientos *m/pl.* ilegales; abuso *m* de autoridad.

malt [mɔːlt] 1. malta *f*; 2. preparar la malta.

Mal·tese [mɔːlˈtiːz] maltés *adj. a. su. m* (-a *f*); ~ *cross* cruz *f* de Malta.

mal·treat [mælˈtriːt] maltratar.

ma·ma, mam·ma [məˈmɑː] mamá *f*.

mam·mal [ˈmæməl] mamífero *m*.

mam·moth [ˈmæməθ] 1. mamut *m*; 2. gigantesco.

man [mæn, *in compounds* ... mən] 1. (*pl.* men) hombre *m*; varón *m*; el género humano; (*servant*) criado *m*; (*workman*) obrero *m*; ✕ soldado *m*; pieza *f in chess, etc.*; ~ *in the street* hombre *m* medio, hombre *m* de la calle; ~ *of the world* hombre *m* de mundo; *no* ~ nadie; 2. ⚓ tripular; ✕ guarnecer; proveer de gente (armada); *guns* servir.

man·a·cle [ˈmænəkl] manilla *f*; ~s *pl.* esposas *f/pl.*

man·age [ˈmænidʒ] *v/t.* manejar; manipular; llevar; conseguir (hacer); guiar; regir; administrar; *business* dirigir; *house* gobernar; *v/i.* arreglárselas, componérselas; ir tirando; ~ *to inf.* lograr *inf.*; **man·age·ment**

dirección *f*, gerencia *f*; administración *f*; **man·ag·er** director *m*, gerente *m*; administrador (-a *f*) *m*; jefe *m*; **man·a·ge·ri·al** [ˌ~dʒiəriəl] □ directivo; administrativo.

man·da·rin [ˈmændərin] mandarín *m*; ♣ mandarina *f*.

man·date [ˈmændeit] 1. mandato *m*; 2. asignar por mandato; ~*d territory* país *m* bajo mandato; **man·da·to·ry** [ˈ~dətəri] obligatorio; conferido por mandato.

man·do·lin [ˈmændəlin] mandolina *f*.

man·drake [ˈmændreik] mandrágora *f*.

mane [mein] crin(es) *f(pl.)*; melena *f of lion*.

man·eat·ing [ˈmæniːtiŋ] antropófago; caníbal.

ma·neu·ver [məˈnuːvə] 1. maniobra *f*; 2. *v/t.* hacer maniobrar, manipular; lograr con maniobras; *v/i.* maniobrar.

man·ful [ˈmænful] □ valiente, resuelto; **~·ness** virilidad *f*.

man·ga·nese [ˈmæŋgəˈniːz] manganeso *m*; ~ *steel* acero *m* al manganeso.

mange [meindʒ] *vet.* roña *f*, sarna *f*.

man·ger [ˈmeindʒə] pesebre *m*.

man·gle [ˈmæŋgl] 1. exprimidor *m* de la ropa; rodillo *m*; 2. pasar por el exprimidor.

man·gle² [~] lacerar, destrozar; mutilar (*a. fig.*); magullar.

man·go [ˈmæŋgou] mango *m*.

man·gy [ˈmeindʒi] sarnoso, roñoso.

man...: **~·han·dle** ⊕ mover a brazo; (*roughly*) maltratar; **~·hole** registro *m*, pozo *m* de visita; **~·hood** virilidad *f*; naturaleza *f* humana; hombres *m/pl.*; **~·hunt** persecución *f* de un criminal.

ma·ni·a [ˈmeiniə] manía *f*; **ma·ni·ac** [ˈ~iæk] maníaco (a *f*) *m*; **man·ic-de·press·ive** maníacodepresivo.

man·i·cure [ˈmænikjuə] 1. manicura *f*; 2. hacer manicura a.

man·i·fest [ˈmænifest] 1. □ manifiesto; *make~* poner de manifiesto; 2. ⚓ manifiesto *m*; 3. manifestar; hacer patente, revelar; **man·i·fes·to** [ˌ~ˈfestou] manifiesto *m*.

man·i·fold [ˈmænifould] □ múltiple; multiforme; numeroso; *exhaust* ~ múltiple *m* de escape.

ma·nip·u·late [məˈnipjuleit] manipular, manejar.

man·kind [mænˈkaind] humanidad

f, raza f humana; [~] sexo m masculino; '**man·li·ness** virilidad f, masculinidad f; hombr(ad)ía f; '**man·ly** varonil; masculino; valiente; '**man-made** hecho por el hombre; manufacturado.

man·ne·quin ['mænikin] maniquí m/f, modelo f; ~ **parade** desfile m de modelos.

man·ner ['mænə] manera f, modo m; además m, aire m of p.; clase f; ~s pl. modales m/pl., crianza f, educación f; costumbres f/pl.; he has no ~s tiene malos modales, no tiene crianza, es un mal criado; *after* (or *in*) *the ~ of* a la manera de; *all ~ of* toda clase de; '**man·nered** *style* amanerado; de modales...; '**man·ner·ism** amaneramiento m *of style*; hábito m; idiosincrasia f; '**man·ner·ly** cortés, bien criado.

man·nish ['mæni] hombruno.

man·or ['mænə] solar m, finca f solariega, señorío m; (a. ~ **house**) casa f señorial, casa f solariega.

man·pow·er ['mænpauə] mano f de obra; potencial m humano.

man·sion ['mænʃn] palacio m, hotel m, casa f grande; casa f solariega.

man·slaugh·ter ['mænslɔːtə] homicidio m (sin premeditación).

man·tel ['mæntl] manto m (de chimenea); '~**piece** repisa f de chimenea.

man·til·la [mæn'tilə] mantilla f.

man·tle ['mæntl] 1. manto m (a. fig., zo.); (incandescent ~) manguito m incandescente; 2. cubrir, ocultar.

man·u·al ['mænjuəl] 1. □ manual; 2. manual m; ♪ teclado m de órgano.

man·u·fac·ture [mænju'fæktʃə] 1. fabricación f; (product) manufactura f; 2. fabricar (a. fig.); manufacturar, elaborar.

ma·nure [mə'njuə] estiércol m.

man·u·script ['mænjuskript] manuscrito adj. a. su. m.

man·y ['meni] 1. muchos (a. ~ a, ~ one); ~ a time muchas veces; ~ people mucha gente; *as ~ as* tantos como; *how ~* cuántos; *so ~* tantos; *too ~* demasiados; 2. gran número m; muchos (as f/pl.) m/pl.; a good ~ un buen número (de).

map [mæp] 1. mapa m, carta f geográfica; 2. trazar el mapa (or plano) de; fig. planear.

ma·ple ['meipl] arce m.

map-mak·ing ['mæp'meikiŋ],

11 Pocket Sp.-E.

map·ping ['mæpiŋ] cartografía f.

mar [mɑː] estropear; desfigurar.

mar·a·schi·no [mɑːrəs'kiːnou] (liqueur) marrasquino.

Mar·a·thon ['mærəθən] (or ~ **race**) carrera f de Maratón.

ma·raud [mə'rɔːd] merodear.

mar·ble ['mɑːbl] 1. mármol m; canica f in game; 2. marmóreo (a. fig.); de mármol; 3. crispir; jaspear.

March¹ [mɑːtʃ] marzo m.

march² [~] 1. marcha f (a. ♪, fig.); 2. v/i. marchar; caminar con resolución; ~ *past* desfilar (ante); v/t. p. etc. hacer marchar; llevar.

mare [mɛə] yegua f.

mar·ga·rine [mɑːdʒə'riːn] margarina f.

mar·gin ['mɑːdʒin] margen mst m (a. typ., ♥ of profit); reserva f; sobrante m; ~ *of error* margen m de error; ~ *of safety* margen m de seguridad; *in the ~* al margen.

mar·i·gold ['mærigould] caléndula f, maravilla f.

mar·i·jua·na [mæri'wɑːnə] mariguana f.

ma·ri·na [mə'riːnə] dársena f; **mar·i·nade** ['mærəneid] 1. escabeche; 2. escabechar; marinar.

ma·rine [mə'riːn] 1. marino, marítimo; 2. marina f; soldado m de marina; ~s pl. infantería f de marina.

mar·i·o·nette [mæriə'net] marioneta f, títere m.

mar·i·tal ['mæritl] □ marital; matrimonial; ~ *status* estado m civil.

mar·i·time ['mæritaim] marítimo.

mark¹ [mɑːk] (coin) marco m.

mark² [~] 1. señal f; (distinguishing, trade-) marca f; impresión f; (trace) huella f; (stain) mancha f; (sign) indicio m; (target) blanco m; (label) marbete m; exam: calificación f, nota f; distinción f, categoría f; 2. v/t. señalar; marcar; (stain) manchar; notar; apuntar; distinguir; exam: dar nota a, calificar; (label) rotular; indicar (el precio de); ~ *down* ♥ rebajar (el precio de); apuntar; fig. señalar, escoger; ~ *off* señalar; separar; definir; jalonar; ~ *out* trazar; marcar; definir; jalonar; '**mark·ed·ly** ['mɑːkidli] marcadamente; notablemente; '**mark·er** marcador m (a. billiards); ficha f; registro m in book.

mar·ket ['mɑːkit] 1. mercado m (a. place) plaza f (del mercado); ♥ bolsa f; fig. tráfico m; venta f; be in the ~

for estar dispuesto a comprar; black~ estraperlo *m*, mercado *m* negro; bolsa *f* negra *S.Am.*; ~ research análisis *m* de mercados; on the ~ de venta; en la bolsa; play the ~ jugar a la bolsa; ready ~ fácil salida *f*; ~ 2. vender, poner a la venta; llevar al mercado; '**mar·ket·a·ble** □ vendible, comerciable; **mar·ket·eer** [~'tiə]: black~ estraperlista *m/f*; **mar·ket·ing** venta *f*, comercialización *f*; '**mar·ket price** precio *m* corriente; '**mar·ket re·search** investigación *f* mercológica.

mark·ing ['mɑːkin] señal *f*, marca *f*; pinta *f* on animals; coloración *f*.

marks·man ['mɑːksmən] tirador (-a *f*) *m*; **marks·man·ship** buena puntería *f*.

mar·ma·lade ['mɑːməleid] mermelada *f* (de naranjas amargas).

ma·roon¹ [mə'ruːn] 1. (color) marrón *m*; 2. marrón.

ma·roon² [~] abandonar (en una isla desierta).

mar·quee [mɑː'kiː] entoldado *m*; marquesina *f*.

mar·riage ['mæridʒ] matrimonio *m*; (wedding) boda(s) *f* (pl.), casamiento *m*; *fig.* unión *f*; by ~ político; civil ~ matrimonio *m* civil; ~ licence licencia *f* para casarse; ~ settlement capitulaciones *f/pl.*

mar·ried ['mærid] *p.* casado; state etc. conyugal; get ~ casarse (to con).

mar·row ['mærou] médula *f* (or medula *f*), tuétano *m*; meollo *m* (a. *fig.*); to the ~ hasta los tuétanos.

mar·ry ['mæri] *v/t.* (give or join in marriage) casar (to con); (take in marriage) casar(se) con; *fig.* unir; *v/i.* casarse; ~ into family emparentar con.

marsh [mɑːʃ] pantano *m*, marjal *m*; marisma *f*; ciénaga *f*; ~ fever paludismo *m*.

mar·shal ['mɑːʃəl] 1. mariscal *m*; maestro *m* de ceremonias; 2. ordenar; conducir con ceremonia; dirigir; '**marsh·mal·low** 🌢 malvavisco *m*; bombón *m* de merengue blando; '**marsh·y** pantanoso.

mar·su·pi·al [mɑː'sjuːpiəl] marsupial *adj. a. su. m.*

mart [mɑːt] emporio *m*; (auction-room) martillo *m*.

mar·tial ['mɑːʃəl] □ marcial; castrense; ~ law ley *f* marcial.

Mar·tian ['mɑːʃn] marciano *adj. a. su. m* (a *f*).

mar·tin ['mɑːtin] *orn.* avión *m*.

mar·ti·net [mɑːti'net] ordenancista *m/f*.

mar·ti·ni [mɑː'tiːni] cóctel *m* compuesto de ginebra con vermut.

mar·tyr ['mɑːtə] 1. mártir *m/f*; 2. martirizar; '**mar·tyr·dom** martirio *m*; '**mar·tyr·ize** martirizar.

mar·vel ['mɑːvəl] 1. maravilla *f*; prodigio *m*; 2. maravillarse.

mar·vel·(l)ous ['mɑːviləs] □ maravilloso.

Marx·ian ['mɑːksjən] marxista; **Marx·ism** ['mɑːksizm] marxismo *m*; **Marx·ist** marxista *adj. a. su. m/f*.

mar·zi·pan [mɑːzi'pæn] mazapán *m*.

mas·ca·ra [mæs'kɑːrə] tinte *m* para las pestañas.

mas·cot ['mæskət] mascota *f*.

mas·cu·line ['mæskjulin] masculino; varonil.

mash [mæʃ] 1. mezcla *f*; amasijo *m*; baturrillo *m*; brewing: malta *f* remojada; 2. majar, machacar; mezclar; amasar.

mask [mɑːsk] 1. máscara *f* (a. *fig.*); careta *f*, antifaz *m*; (p.) máscara *m/f*; 2. enmascarar; ocultar.

mas·och·ism ['mæzəkizm] masoquismo *m*.

ma·son ['meisn] 🔺 cantero *m*, albañil *m*; (free-) (franc)masón *m*; '**ma·son·ry** albañilería *f*; (franc)masonería *f*.

mas·quer·ade [mæskə'reid] 1. mascarada *f*; (baile *m* de) máscaras *f/pl.*; *fig.* farsa *f*; 2. enmascararse, ir disfrazado (as de).

mass¹ [mæs] *eccl.* misa *f*.

mass² [~] 1. masa *f* (a. *phys.*); bulto *m* (informe); masa *m* of mountains; montón *m*, gran cantidad *f*; muchedumbre *f*; the ~es *pl.* las masas; ~ meeting mitin *m* popular; ~ production producción *f* en serie; 2. juntar(se) en masa, reunir(se); concentrar(se).

mas·sa·cre ['mæsəkə] 1. matanza *f*; carnicería *f*; 2. hacer una carnicería de, masacrar.

mas·sage ['mæsɑːʒ] 1. masaje *m*; 2. dar masaje a.

mas·seur [mæ'səː] masajista *m*; **mas'seuse** [~z] masajista *f*.

mas·sive ['mæsiv] macizo, sólido.

mass me·di·a ['mæs 'miːdjə] (press, radio, television etc.) medios *m* de comunicación de gran escala.

mast [mɑːst] ⚓ mástil *m*, palo *m*, árbol *m*; radio: torre *f*.

may

mas·ter ['mɑ:stə] 1. señor m; amo m of house etc.; (owner) dueño m; (graduate, expert, teacher a. fig.) maestro m; profesor m in secondary school; director m of college; ♣ capitán m; 2. maestro m; fig. magistral, superior, principal; 3. dominar (a. fig.); llegar a ser maestro m; vencer; **'mas·ter·'build·er** arquitecto m; maestro m de obras; constructor m; **mas·ter·ful** ['~ful] □ imperioso, dominante; **'mas·ter·ly** magistral; maestro; perfecto; **'mas·ter·mind** mente f directora; **'~·piece** obra f maestra; **~·stroke** golpe m maestro; **'mas·ter·y** maestría f; dominio m; autoridad f.

mas·ti·cate ['mæstikeit] mas(ti)car.

mas·tiff ['mæstif] mastín m; perro m alano.

mast·oid ['mæstɔid] mastoides.

mat [mæt] 1. estera f; esterilla f; (round) ruedo m; felpudo m at door; salvamanteles m for table; (lace etc.) tapetito m; greña f of hair; 2. esterar; enmarañar(se), entretejerse.

match¹ [mætʃ] cerilla f, fósforo m, cerillo m S.Am.

match² [~] 1. igual m/f; compañero (a f) m; pareja f; matrimonio m; sport: partido m; concurso m; good ~ buena pareja f; buen partido m in marriage; 2. v/t. (pair) emparejar; parear; igualar; competir con; v/i. hacer juego, casar.

match·box ['mætʃbɔks] cajita f de cerillas, fosforera f.

match·less ['mætʃlis] sin par, incomparable; **'match·mak·er** casamentero (a f) m.

mate¹ [meit] chess: 1. mate m; 2. dar jaque mate (a).

mate² [~] 1. compañero m, camarada m; (married) cónyuge m/f, consorte m/f; ♣ primer oficial m, segundo m, piloto m; 2. casar(se); zo. parear(se), acoplar(se).

ma·te·ri·al [mə'tiəriəl] 1. □ material; importante, esencial; 2. material m; (substance) materia f; fig. datos m/pl.; (cloth) tejido m, tela f; ~s pl. material(es) m(pl.); raw ~s materias f/pl. primas; **ma·te·ri·al·ism** materialismo m; **ma·te·ri·al·ize** materializar (-se); realizarse.

ma·ter·nal [mə'tə:nl] □ materno; affection etc. maternal; **ma·ter·ni·ty** [~niti] maternidad f; ~ benefit subsidio m de natalidad.

math [mæθ] sl. matemática f.

math·e·mat·i·cal [mæθi'mætikl] □ matemático; **math·e·ma·ti·cian** [~mə'tiʃn] matemático m; **math·e·mat·ics** [~'mætiks] mst sg. matemática(s) f(pl.).

mat·i·née ['mætinei] función f de tarde.

ma·tri·arch ['meitriɑ:k] matriarca f.

ma·tric·u·late [mə'trikjuleit] matricular(se).

mat·ri·mo·ny ['mætriməni] matrimonio m; vida f conyugal.

ma·trix ['meitriks] matriz f.

ma·tron ['meitrən] matrona f; ~ of honor dama f de honor; **'ma·tron·ly** matronal; respetable; maduro y algo corpulento.

mat·ter ['mætə] 1. materia f (a. ♠); material m; tema m; asunto m, cuestión f; motivo m; cosa f; printed ~ impresos m/pl.; a ~ of cosa de; obra de; as a ~ of course por rutina; to make ~s worse para colmo de desgracias; for that ~ en cuanto a eso; what ~? ¿qué importa? what's the ~? ¿qué hay?; what's the ~ with you? ¿qué te pasa?; 2. importar; it does not ~ no importa; what does it ~? ¿qué importa?; **'~-of-'fact** prosaico; práctico, positivista; flemático.

mat·ting ['mætiŋ] estera f.

mat·tres ['mætris] colchón m.

ma·ture [mə'tjuə] 1. □ maduro (a. fig.); ✝ vencido; 2. madurar; ✝ vencer; **ma'tu·ri·ty** madurez f.

maud·lin ['mɔ:dlin] sensiblero; llorón.

maul [mɔ:l] magullar; maltratar.

mau·so·le·um [mɔ:sə'li:əm] mausoleo m.

mauve [mouv] (de) color m de malva.

mav·er·ick ['mævərik] res f sin marcar; pol. disidente m.

mawk·ish ['mɔ:kiʃ] □ insulso; empalagoso, dulzarrón; sensiblero; **'mawk·ish·ness** sensiblería f etc.

max·im ['mæksim] máxima f; **'max·i·mal** máximo; **max·i·mum** ['~əm] 1. máximo; 2. máximo m, máximum m.

May [mei] mayo m; ~ Queen maya f; ♀ flor f del espino blanco.

may [~] (irr.) poder; ser posible; tener permiso para; I ~ come puede (ser) que yo venga; if I ~ si me lo permites; ~ I come in? ¿se puede (pasar)?; it ~ be that puede ser que, tal vez.

M

may·be ['meibi:] quizá(s), tal vez, acaso.

May Day ['meidei] (fiesta f del) primero m de mayo; **May·day** ¡socorro! (naves, aviones).

may·on·naise [meiə'neiz] mayonesa f.

may·or [mɛə] alcalde m; **may·or·al** de alcalde; **may·or·al·ty** alcaldía f.

may·pole ['meipoul] mayo m.

maze [meiz] laberinto m; fig. enredo m, perplejidad f.

me [mi:, mi] (after prp.) mí; with ~ conmigo.

mead·ow ['medou] prado m; (big) pradera f; henar m for hay.

mea·ger ['mi:gə] □ escaso, exiguo, pobre; magro, flaco; **mea·ger·ness** escasez f etc.

meal[1] [mi:l] comida f.

meal[2] [~] harina f (a medio moler).

meal·time ['mi:ltaim] hora f de comer.

meal·y ['mi:li] harinoso; pálido; '~-mouthed mojigato.

mean[1] [mi:n] □ humilde, pobre; bajo; sórdido; mezquino, tacaño; F malo, desconsiderado.

mean[2] [~] 1. medio; 2. medio m; promedio m, término m medio; & media f; ~s sg. or pl. medio(s) m(pl.); manera f; ~s pl. recursos m/pl., medios m/pl., dinero m; by fair ~s or foul por las buenas o por las malas; by ~s of por medio de, mediante; by this ~s por este medio, de este modo; ~s to an end medio m para conseguir un fin.

mean[3] [~] [irr.] querer decir (by con); significar (to para); destinar (for para); decir en serio; ~ to inf. pensar inf., proponerse inf.

me·an·der [mi'ændə] serpentear.

mean·ing ['mi:niŋ] 1. □ significativo; 2. significado m, sentido m; what's the ~ of ...? ¿qué significa ...?; '**mean·ing·less** sin sentido; insignificante; insensato.

mean·ness ['mi:nnis] humildad f; mezquindad f.

mean·time ['mi:ntaim], **mean·while** ['mi:nwail] entretanto, mientras tanto.

mea·sles ['mi:zlz] sarampión m; '**mea·sly** F pobre, despreciable.

meas·ure ['meʒə] 1. medida f (a. fig.); (rule) regla f; ♪ compás m; parl. (proyecto m de) ley f; made to ~ hecho a medida; take a p.'s ~ fig. tomarle las medidas a una p.; 2. medir (a. ~ off, ~

out); p. for height tallar; p. for clothes tomar las medidas a; '**meas·ure·ment** medida f; medición f.

meat [mi:t] carne f; † comida f; fig. meollo m, sustancia f; cold ~ fiambre m; ~ ball albóndiga f; ~ head sl. tonto m; '**meat·y** carnoso; fig. sustancioso.

me·chan·ic [mi'kænik] mecánico m; **me·chan·i·cal** □ mecánico; maquinal (a. fig.); ~ engineering ingeniería f mecánica; **me·chan·ics** [mi'kæniks] mst sg. mecánica f; mecanismo m, técnica f.

mech·a·nism ['mekənizm] mecanismo m; phls. mecanicismo m; **mech·a·nize** ['~naiz] mecanizar.

med·al ['medl] medalla f; **me·dal·lion** [mi'dæljən] medallón m.

med·dle ['medl] entrometerse (in en); meterse (with con); '**med·dler** entrometido (a f) m; **med·dle·some** ['~səm] □ entrometido.

me·di·a = mass media.

me·di·al ['mi:djəl] □ medial; '**me·di·an** mediano; ~ strip faja f divisora of highway.

me·di·ate 1. □ ['mi:diit] mediato; 2. ['mi:dieit] mediar (between entre, for por, in en).

med·i·cal ['medikəl] médico; de medicina; medicinal; ~ board tribunal m médico; ~ certificate certificado m médico; ~ corps cuerpo m de sanidad; ~ student estudiante m/f de medicina; **me'dic·a·ment** medicamento m; '**med·i·care** seguros m/pl. de enfermedad para los viejos en Estados Unidos.

med·i·cate ['medikeit] medicar; impregnar.

med·i·cine ['medsin] medicina f; medicamento m; ~ chest botiquín m; ~ man curandero m; hechizador m.

me·di·e·val [medi'i:vəl] □ medieval; **me·di·e·val·ist** medievalista m/f.

me·di·o·cre ['mi:di'oukə] mediano, mediocre; **me·di·oc·ri·ty** [~'ɔkriti] mediocridad f, medianía f (a. p.).

med·i·tate ['mediteit] meditar (on acc.); reflexionar (on en, sobre).

me·di·um ['mi:diəm] 1. pl. a. **me·dia** ['~diə] medio m; (p.) médium m; happy ~ justo medio m; through the ~ of por medio de; 2. mediano, intermedio, regular; '~-sized de tamaño medi(an)o.

med·ley ['medli] mezcla f, mezcolanza f; miscelánea f; ♪ popurrí m.

meek [miːk] ☐ manso, dócil, humilde; '**meek·ness** mansedumbre f.

meet [miːt] 1. [irr.] v/t. encontrar(se con); (come across) tropezar con; (on arrival) ir a recibir, esperar; (become acquainted with) conocer; (fight) batirse con; sport: enfrentarse con; expense hacer frente a; go to ~ ir al encuentro de; ~ p. half-way fig. partir la diferencia, hacer concesiones a una p.; v/i. encontrarse; reunirse; 2. concurso m de cazadores (or deportistas).

meet·ing ['miːtiŋ] reunión f; sesión f; (public) mitin m; encuentro m; (by appointment) cita f; ~ house iglesia f de disidentes; iglesia f de los cuáqueros.

meg·a·cy·cle ['megəsaikl] megaciclo m; **meg·a·lo·ma·ni·a** ['ˌlou'meinjə] megalomanía f; **meg·a·phone** ['ˌfoun] megáfono m; **meg·a·ton** ['ˌtʌn] megatón m.

mel·an·chol·y ['melənkəli] 1. melancolía f; 2. melancólico.

mê·lée ['melei] pelea f confusa, refriega f.

mel·low ['melou] 1. ☐ maduro, sazonado; fig. blando, suave; 2. madurar(se); suavizar(se); '**mel·low·ness** madurez f etc.

me·lo·di·ous [mi'loudjəs] ☐ melodioso; '**mel·o·dra·ma** melodrama m; **mel·o·dra'mat·ic** melodramático; '**mel·o·dy** melodía f.

mel·on ['melən] melón m.

melt [melt] (snow) derretir(se); (metal) fundir(se); disolver(se); fig. ablandar(se); ~ away disolverse.

melt·ing ['meltiŋ] 1. fusión f; derretimiento m; 2. ☐ fundente; '~ point punto m de fusión; '~ pot crisol m (a. fig.).

mem·ber ['membə] miembro m (a. parl.); socio (a f) m, individuo m of society; parl. diputado m (Spanish: a Cortes); '**mem·ber·ship** calidad f de miembro (or socio); asociación f.

mem·brane ['membrein] membrana f.

me·men·to [me'mentou] recuerdo m.

mem·oir ['memwaː] memoria f.

mem·o·ran·dum [memə'rændəm] apunte m, memoria f.

me·mo·ri·al [mi'mɔːriəl] 1. conmemorativo; 2. monumento m (conmemorativo); (document) memorial m; **me'mo·ri·al·ize** conmemorar; dirigir un memorial a.

mem·o·rize ['meməraiz] aprender de memoria.

mem·o·ry ['meməri] memoria f.

men·ace ['menəs] 1. amenaza f; F sujeto m peligroso (or fastidioso); 2. amenazar.

me·nag·er·ie [mi'nædʒəri] casa f (or colección f) de fieras.

mend [mend] v/t. remendar; componer, reparar; mejorar.

men·di·cant ['mendikənt] mendicante adj. a. su. m/f; **men'dic·i·ty** [ˌsiti] mendicidad f.

mend·ing ['mendiŋ] compostura f; reparación f; (darning) zurcidura f.

me·ni·al ['miːniəl] mst contp. bajo; servil; doméstico.

men·in·gi·tis [menin'dʒaitis] meningitis f.

men·stru·al ['menstruəl] menstrual; **men·stru'a·tion** menstruación f.

men·tal ['mentl] ☐ mental; ~ arithmetic cálculo m mental; ~ derangement trastorno m mental; ~ home, ~ hospital manicomio m; ~ hygiene higiene f mental; **men·tal·i·ty** [ˌ'tæliti] mentalidad f.

men·tion ['menʃən] 1. mención f; alusión f; 2. mencionar, mentar.

men·u ['menjuː] lista f (de platos), minuta f, menú m.

me·ouw [mi'au] 1. miau m; 2. maullar.

mer·can·tile ['məːkəntail] mercantil, comercial.

mer·ce·nar·y ['məːsinəri] ☐ mercenario (✕, a. su. m); interesado.

mer·chan·dise ['məːtʃəndaiz] mercancía(s) f(pl.); géneros m/pl.

mer·chant ['məːtʃənt] 1. comerciante m/f, negociante m; 2. mercantil; ♣ mercante; '**mer·chant bank** banco m mercantil; '**mer·chant·man** buque m mercante; '**mer·chant mar·ine** marina f mercante.

mer·ci·ful ['məːsiful] ☐ misericordioso, piadoso; clemente.

mer·ci·less ['məːsilis] ☐ despiadado, inhumano; '**~·ness** inhumanidad f; crueldad f.

mer·cu·ri·al [məːˈkjuəriəl] mercurial; (changeable) veleidoso.

mer·cu·ry ['məːkjuri] mercurio m.

mer·cy ['məːsi] ☐ misericordia f, compasión f; clemencia f; merced f; ~ killing eutanasia f.

mere [miə] ☐ mero; simple; solo.

merge [məːdʒ] v/t. unir; mezclar; ✝ fusionar; v/i. fundirse, ✝ fusionarse; '**merg·er** fusión f.

M

me·rid·i·an [mə'rɪdɪən] 1. *geog.*, *ast.* meridiano *m*; mediodía *m*; 2. meridiano.

me·ringue [mə'ræŋ] merengue *m*.

mer·it ['merɪt] 1. mérito *m*, merecimiento *m*; ~s 🏦 méritos *m/pl.*; circunstancias *f/pl.* (de cada caso); 2. merecer.

mer·maid ['mɜːmeɪd] sirena *f*.

mer·ri·ment ['merɪmənt] alegría *f*.

mer·ry ['merɪ] ☐ alegre, regocijado, alborozado; ~ *Christmas!* ¡felices pascuas!; '~-go-round tiovivo *m*, caballitos *m/pl.*; '~-mak·ing festividades *f/pl.*; alborozo *m*.

me·sa ['meɪsə] meseta *f*.

mesh [meʃ] 1. malla *f*; ⊕ engran(aj)e *m*; *fig.* (*freq.* ~es) red *f*; 2. *v/i.* engranar (*with* con).

mes·mer·ize ['mezməraɪz] hipnotizar.

mess¹ [mes] 1. revoltijo *m*, lío *m*, confusión *f*; suciedad *f*; 2. (*a.* ~ *up*) echar a perder; desordenar; ensuciar.

mess² [~] comida *f*; ✕, ⚓ rancho *m*; '~·kit utensilios *m/pl.* de rancho.

mes·sage ['mesɪdʒ] recado *m*, mensaje *m*.

mes·sen·ger ['mesɪndʒə] mensajero (a *f*) *m*; mandadero (a *f*) *m*, recadero (a *f*) *m*.

mes·sy ['mesɪ] desarreglado; sucio.

met·a·bol·ic [metə'bɔlɪk] metabólico; **me·tab·o·lism** metabolismo *m*.

met·al ['metl] metal *m*; *fig.* temple *m*; *fig.* ánimo *m*; ~ *polish* lustre *m* para metales; 2. metálico; **me·tal·lic** [mɪ'tælɪk] ☐ metálico; **met·al·lur·gic, met·al·lur·gi·cal** [~'lɜːdʒɪk(l)] metalúrgico; '**met·al·lur·gy** metalurgia *f*.

met·a·mor·pho·sis [metə'mɔːfəsɪs], *pl.* **met·a·mor·pho·ses** [~fəsiːz] metamorfosis *f*.

met·a·phor ['metəfə] metáfora *f*.

met·a·phys·i·cal [metə'fɪzɪkl] ☐ metafísico; **met·a·phys·ics** *mst sg.* metafísica *f*.

mete [miːt] repartir, distribuir.

me·te·or ['miːtjə] meteorito *m*; *fig.* meteoro *m*; **me·te·or·ite** ['miːtjəraɪt] bólido *m*; **me·te·or·o·log·i·cal** [miːtjərə'lɔdʒɪkl] ☐ meteorológico; **me·te·or·ol·o·gy** meteorología *f*.

me·ter ['miːtə] 1. contador *m*; medidor *m S.Am.*; metro *m*; 2. medir (con contador).

meth·ane ['meθeɪn] metano *m*.

meth·od ['meθəd] método *m*, procedimiento *m*, sistema *m*; orden *m*; **Meth·od·ism** ['meθədɪzm] metodismo *m*; '**Meth·od·ist** metodista *m/f*; **meth·od·ol·o·gy** [~'dɔlədʒi] metodología *f*.

meth·yl ['meθɪl] metilo *m*; **meth·yl·at·ed spir·it** ['meθɪleɪtɪd 'spɪrɪt] alcohol *m* metilado.

me·tic·u·lous [mɪ'tɪkjuləs] ☐ meticuloso; minucioso.

met·ric ['metrɪk] métrico; ~ *system* sistema *m* métrico; '**met·rics** *pl. a. sg.* métrica *f*.

me·trop·o·lis [mɪ'trɔpəlɪs] metrópoli *f*; **me·tro·pol·i·tan** [metrə'pɔlɪtən] metropolitano.

met·tle ['metl] ánimo *m*, brío *m*; temple *m*.

mew [mjuː] 1. maullido *m* of cat; 2. maullar.

Mex·i·can ['meksɪkən] mejicano (*in Mexico* mexicano) *adj. a. su. m* (a *f*).

mez·za·nine ['mezəniːn] entresuelo *m*.

mi·cro... ['maɪkrou] micro...

mi·cro·bi·ol·o·gy [maɪkroubaɪ'ɔlədʒi] microbiología *f*.

mi·cro·bus ['maɪkroubʌs] microbus *m*; **mi·cro·card** (*a.* ~·fiche) microficha *f*; **mi·cro·cosm** ['~kɔzm] microcosmo *m*; '**mi·cro·film** microfilm *m*; '**mi·cro·groove** microsurco; **mi·crom·e·ter** [maɪ'krɔmɪtə] micrómetro *m*; **mi·cro·phone** ['maɪkrəfoun] micrófono *m*; '**mi·cro·scope** ['~skoup] microscopio *m*; '**mi·cro·wave** microonda *f*.

mid [mɪd] medio; ~·air: *in* ~ en medio del aire; '~·day 1. mediodía *m*; 2. de(l) mediodía.

mid·dle ['mɪdl] 1. centro *m*, medio *m*, mitad *f*; (*waist*) cintura *f*; *in the* ~ *of* en medio de, en pleno; 2. medio, intermedio; de en medio; central; ♀ *Ages Edad f Media*; ~ *class*(es *pl.*) clase *f* media; '~·aged de mediana edad, de edad madura; '~·class de la clase media; '~·man intermediario *m*; corredor *m*; '~·sized de tamaño mediano; *p.* de estatura mediana.

mid·dling ['mɪdlɪŋ] 1. *adj.* mediano, mediocre; 2. *adv.* medianamente.

midg·et ['mɪdʒɪt] 1. enano (a *f*) *m*; 2. (en) miniatura.

mid·land ['mɪdlənd] del interior, del centro (de un país); '**mid·night** (*the* ~ *oil*) medianoche *f*; *burn the* ~ *oil* quemarse las cejas; **mid·riff** ['∼rif] diafragma *m*; **'mid·ship·man** guardia marina *m*; **midst** [midst]: *in the* ∼ *of* entre, en medio de; *in our* ∼ entre nosotros; **'mid·stream**: *in* ∼ en medio de la corriente; **'mid·way 1.** (situado) a mitad del camino; **2.** mitad *f* del camino; avenida *f* central; **'mid·wife** comadrona *f*, partera *f*; **mid·wife·ry** ['midwifri] partería *f*.

might [mait] **1.** fuerza *f*, poder(ío) *m*; *with* ∼ *and main* con todas sus *etc.* fuerzas; **2.** *pret. of may*; podría *etc.*; ser posible; *they* ∼ *arrive today* es posible que lleguen hoy; **might·i·ness** ['∼inis] fuerza *f*, poder(ío) *m*; grandeza *f*; **mighty 1.** □ fuerte, potente; F enorme; **2.** *adv.* F muy.

mi·graine ['miːgrein] jaqueca *f*, migraña *f*.

mi·grant ['maigrənt] migratorio *m*.

mi·grate [mai'greit] emigrar; **mi·gra·to·ry** ['∼grətəri] migratorio *m*.

mike [maik] *sl.* micrófono *m*.

mild [maild] □ suave; manso; blando; apacible; dulce.

mil·dew ['mildjuː] **1.** moho *m*; añublo *m on wheat*; **2.** enmohecer(se).

mild·ness ['maildnis] suavidad *f etc.*

mile [mail] milla *f*.

mil(e)·age ['mailidʒ] número *m* de millas; distancia *f* en millas; *approx.* kilometraje *m*.

mile·stone ['mailstoun] piedra *f* miliar(ia); mojón *m*.

mil·i·tant ['militənt] □ militante; belicoso; agresivo; **mil·i·ta·rism** ['∼rizəm] militarismo *m*; **'mil·i·tar·y 1.** □ militar; de guerra; **2.** *the* ∼ los militares; **mi·li·tia** [mi'liʃə] milicia *f*.

milk [milk] **1.** leche *f*, ∼ *diet* régimen *m* lácteo; ∼ *of magnesia* leche *f* de magnesia; **2.** *v/t.* ordeñar; *fig.* chupar; *v/i.* dar leche; **'milk·ing** ordeño *m*; **'milk·ing ma'chine** ordeñadora *f* (mecánica).

milk...: '∼**maid** lechera *f*; '∼**man** lechero *m*; '∼ **'shake** batido *m* de leche; **'milk·y** lechoso; ♀ *Way* Vía *f* Láctea.

mill[1] [mil] **1.** molino *m*; molinillo *m for coffee etc.*; (*factory*) fábrica *f*; '∼**end** retazo *m* de hilandería; **2.** moler; ⊕ fresar.

mill[2] [∼] milésimo *m* de dólar.

mil·len·ni·al [mi'leniəl] milenario *m*; **mil'len·ni·um** [∼iəm] milenario *m*, milenio *m*.

mil·le·pede ['milipiːd] miriápodo *m*.

mill·er ['milə] molinero *m*.

mil·les·i·mal [mi'lesiməl] milésimo *m*.

mil·li·gram ['miligræm] miligramo *m*.

mil·li·me·ter ['milimiːtə] milímetro *m*.

mil·li·ner ['milinə] sombrerera *f*, modista *f* (de sombreros).

mill·ing ['miliŋ] molienda *f*; cordoncillo *m of coin*.

mil·lion ['miljən] millón *m*; *three* ∼ *men* tres millones de hombres; **mil·lion·aire** [∼'nɛə] millonario (a *f*) *m*; **mil·lionth** ['miljənθ] millonésimo *adj. a. su. m.*

mill...: '∼ **'pond** represa *f* de molino, cubo *m*; '∼**stone** piedra *f* de molino, muela *f*.

mil·om·e·ter [mai'lɔmitə] *approx.* cuentakilómetros *m*.

mime [maim] **1.** mimo *m*; pantomima *f*, mímica *f*; **2.** *v/t.* remedar, hacer en pantomima; *v/i.* hacer de mimo.

mim·e·o·graph ['mimiəgrɑːf] **1.** mimeógrafo *m*; **2.** mimeografiar.

mim·ic ['mimik] **1.** mímico; fingido; **2.** remedador (-a *f*) *m*; **3.** imitar; **'mim·ic·ry** mímica *f*, remedo *m*.

mince [mins] **1.** *v/t.* picar; desmenuzar; *not to* ∼ *matters, not to* ∼ *one's words* no tener pelos en la lengua; *v/i.* andar con pasos menudites; **2.** carne *f* picada; **'∼·meat** (*carne picada con frutas*) cuajado *m*; '∼ **'pie** pastel *m* de mincemeat.

mind [maind] **1.** mente *f*; (*intellect*) inteligencia *f*, entendimiento *m*; (*not matter*) espíritu *m*; ánimo *m*; juicio *m*; (*opinion*) parecer *m*; *change one's* ∼ cambiar de opinión, mudar de parecer; *bear (or keep) in* ∼ tener presente, tener en cuenta; *be in one's right* ∼ estar en sus cabales; *make up one's* ∼ resolverse, decidirse (*to a*); determinar (*to inf.*); *it slipped my* ∼ se me escapó de la memoria; *speak one's* ∼ decir su parecer, hablar con franqueza; **2.** *v/t.* (*heed*) fijarse en, hacer caso de; (*bear in* ∼) tener en cuenta; cuidar; *do you* ∼ *the noise?* ¿le molesta el ruido?; *v/i.* tener cuidado; sentir molestia; tener inconveniente; ∼! ¡cuidado!; *never* ∼! ¡no haga Vd. caso!; ¡no importa!; ¡no se preocupe!; **'mind·bend·ing** *sl.* alucinante; **'mind-blow·ing** *sl.* alucinante en exceso; *sl.* deslumbrante *in general sense*; **'mind-bog·gling** des-

M

lumbrante; abrumador; **'mind·ful** □ atento (*of* a), cuidadoso (*of* de); **'mind·less** □ estúpido; negligente (*of* de).

mine¹ [main] (el) mío, (la) mía *etc*.

mine² [\] 1. mina *f* (a. ♣, ⚔, *fig*.); 2. *v/t.* extraer; minar (*mst* ⚔); ⚔, ♣ sembrar minas en; *v/i.* extraer minerales; ⚔ minar; **'~·field** campo *m* de minas; **'~·lay·er** buque *m* minador; **'min·er** minero *m*.

min·er·al ['minərəl] mineral *adj. a. su. m*; ~ *water* agua *f* mineral; gaseosa *f*; **min·er'al·o·gy** mineralogía *f*.

mine·sweep·er ['mainswi:pə] barreminas *m*, dragaminas *m*.

min·gle ['miŋgl] mezclar(se) (*in*, *with* con).

min·i·a·ture ['minjətʃə] 1. miniatura *f*; 2. diminuto.

mi·ni·com·put·er [mini:kəm'pju:tər] minicomputadora *f*.

min·i·mal ['miniməl] mínimo; **'min·i·mize** minimizar, reducir al mínimo; **min·i·mum** ['~iməm] 1. mínimo *m*, mínimum *m*; 2. mínimo.

min·ing ['mainiŋ] minería *f*; extracción *f*.

min·i·skirt ['mini:skə:t] minifalda *f*.

min·i·ster ['ministə] 1. ministro *m*; 2. ministrar; atender (*to* a); **min·is·te·ri·al** [~'tiəriəl] □ *pol.* ministerial; de ministro.

min·is·tra·tion [minis'treiʃn] ayuda *f*; servicio *m*; **'min·is·try** ministerio *m*; *eccl.* sacerdocio *m*.

mink [miŋk] (piel *f* de) visón *m*.

min·now ['minou] pececillo *m* de agua dulce.

mi·nor ['mainə] 1. menor (*a.* ♪); menor de edad; secundario; 2. menor *m/f* de edad; *phls.* menor; *univ.* asignatura *f* secundaria; **mi·nor·i·ty** [mai'nɔriti] minoría *f*; (*age*) minoridad *f*.

min·strel ['minstrəl] juglar *m*, trovador *m*; cantor *m*.

mint¹ [mint] ♀ hierbabuena *f*.

mint² [\] 1. casa *f* de moneda; *a* ~ *of money* un dineral; 2. sin usar; 3. acuñar; *fig.* inventar.

mi·nus ['mainəs] 1. *prp.* menos; F sin; 2. *adj.* negativo.

mi·nute [mai'nju:t] diminuto, menudo; **'~·ly** minuciosamente.

min·ute ['minit] minuto *m*; *fig.* instante *m*, momento *m*; ~ *s* acta(s) *f(pl.)*; **'min·ute hand** minutero *m*.

minx [miŋks] picaruela *f*.

mir·a·cle ['mirəkl] milagro *m*; **mi·rac·u·lous** [mi'rækjuləs] □ milagroso.

mi·rage ['mira:ʒ] espejismo *m*.

mire ['maiə] fango *m*, lodo *m*.

mir·ror ['mirə] 1. espejo *m* (*a. fig.*); *mot.* retrovisor *m*; 2. reflejar.

mirth [mə:θ] regocijo *m*, alegría *f*; hilaridad *f*, risa *f*; **mirth·ful** ['~ful] □ alegre; reidor.

mis·ad·ven·ture ['misəd'ventʃə] desgracia *f*, accidente *m*.

mis·an·thrope ['mizənθroup] misántropo *m*; **mis·an·throp·ic, mis·an·throp·i·cal** [~'θrɔpik(l)] □ misantrópico; **mis·an·thro·py** misantropía *f*.

mis·ap·ply [misə'plai] aplicar mal; abusar de.

mis·ap·pre·hend ['misæpri'hend] entender mal; **'mis·ap·pre·hen·sion** equivocación *f*; concepto *m* erróneo.

mis·ap·pro·pri·ate ['misə'prouprieit] malversar.

mis·be·got·(ten) ['misbi'gɔt(n)] bastardo, ilegítimo.

mis·be·have ['misbi'heiv] portarse mal; (*child*) ser malo; **'mis·be·hav·ior** [~jə] mala conducta *f*, mal comportamiento *m*.

mis·be·lief ['misbi'li:f] error *m*; creencia *f* heterodoxa.

mis·cal·cu·late ['mis'kælkjuleit] calcular mal.

mis·car·riage ['mis'kæridʒ] malparto *m*, aborto *m*; malogro *m*; ⚑ extravío *m*; **mis'car·ry** malparir, abortar; malograrse.

mis·cel·la·ne·ous [misi'leinjəs] misceláneo.

mis·cel·la·ny [mi'seləni] miscelánea *f*.

mis·chance [mis'tʃɑ:ns] mala suerte *f*; infortunio *m*; accidente *m*.

mis·chief ['mistʃif] daño *m*; mal *m*; malicia *f*; travesura *f*, diablura *f* '~·mak·er** enredador (-a *f*) *m*, chismoso (a *f*) *m*.

mis·chie·vous ['mistʃivəs] dañoso, perjudicial; malo; *child* travieso.

mis·con·ceive ['miskən'si:v] entender mal, formar un concepto erróneo de.

mis·con·duct ['mis'kɔndəkt] mala conducta *f*; adulterio *m*.

mis·con·strue [miskən'stru:] interpretar mal.

mis·count ['mis'kaunt] 1. contar mal; 2. cuenta *f* errónea.

M

mis·date [mis'deit] fechar erróneamente.

mis·deed ['mis'di:d] malhecho *m*, delito *m*.

mis·de·mean·or ['misdi'mi:nə] mala conducta *f*; 🏛 delito *m* de menor cuantía.

mis·di·rect ['misdi'rekt] dirigir mal; extraviar.

mi·ser ['maizə] avaro (*a f*) *m*.

mis·er·a·ble ['mizərəbl] □ triste; miserable; lastimoso; despreciable.

mi·ser·ly ['maizəli] avariento, tacaño.

mis·er·y ['mizəri] sufrimiento *m*; aflicción *f*; infelicidad *f*; miseria *f*.

mis·fire ['mis'faiə] 1. falla *f* de tiro (*mot.* de encendido); 2. fallar.

mis·fit ['misfit] cosa *f* mal ajustada; (*p.*) inadaptado (*a f*) *m*.

mis·for·tune [mis'fɔ:tʃn] desgracia *f*, infortunio *m*, desventura *f*.

mis·giv·ing [mis'givin] recelo *m*.

mis·guide [mis'gaid] dirigir mal; aconsejar mal.

mis·han·dle ['mis'hændl] manejar mal; maltratar.

mis·hap ['mishæp] contratiempo *m*.

mish·mash ['miʃmæʃ] baturrillo *m*, mezcolanza *f*.

mis·in·form ['misin'fɔ:m] informar mal, dar informes erróneos a.

mis·in·ter·pret ['misin'tə:prit] interpretar mal.

mis·judge ['mis'dʒʌdʒ] juzgar mal.

mis·lay [mis'lei] [*irr.* (*lay*)] extraviar, perder.

mis·lead [mis'li:d] [*irr.* (*lead*)] extraviar; despistar; engañar; **mis'lead·ing** engañoso.

mis·man·age ['mis'mænidʒ] administrar mal, manejar mal; **'mis'man·age·ment** mala administración *f*, desgobierno *m*.

mis·no·mer ['mis'noumə] nombre *m* equivocado (*or* inapropiado).

mis·place [mis'pleis] colocar mal; poner fuera de su lugar; extraviar.

mis·print ['mis'print] 1. error *m* de imprenta; 2. imprimir mal.

mis·pro·nounce ['misprə'nauns] pronunciar mal.

mis·quote [mis'kwout] citar mal.

mis·read ['mis'ri:d] leer mal.

mis·rep·re·sent ['misrepri'zent] falsificar; describir engañosamente; **'mis·rep·re·sen'ta·tion** falsificación *f*; descripción *f* falsa.

mis·rule ['mis'ru:l] 1. desgobierno *m*; desorden *m*; 2. desgobernar.

miss¹ [mis] señorita *f*; muchacha *f*.

miss² [~] 1. tiro *m* errado; (*mistake*) desacierto *m*; (*failure*) malogro *m*, fracaso *m*; 2. *v/t.* aim, target, vocation errar; chance, train etc. perder; solution no acertar; (*regret absence of*) echar de menos; (*overlook*) pasar por alto; *v/i.* errar el blanco; fallar, salir mal; *mot.* ratear.

mis·sal ['misəl] misal *m*.

mis·shap·en ['mis'ʃeipən] deforme.

mis·sile ['misl] proyectil *m*; arma *f*; arrojadiza.

miss·ing ['misin] ausente; perdido; ⚔ desaparecido; *be* ~ faltar.

mis·sion ['miʃn] misión *f*; **'mis·sion·ar·y** misionero *adj. a. su. m* (*a f*).

mis·spell ['mis'spel] [*irr.* (*spell*)] deletrear (*or* escribir) mal; **'mis'spell·ing** error *m* de ortografía.

mis·spend ['mis'spend] malgastar, desperdiciar, perder.

mis·state ['mis'steit] relatar mal.

mist [mist] niebla *f*; (*low*) neblina *f*; bruma *f at sea*; (*slight*) calina *f*.

mis·tak·a·ble [mis'teikəbl] confundible, equívoco; **mis·take** [~'teik] 1. *v/t.* entender mal; confundir, equivocar(se en); *be* ~n engañarse; equivocarse (*for* con); *v/i.* ⚗ equivocarse; 2. equivocación *f*; error *m*; falta *f in exercise*; *by* ~ por equivocación; sin querer; **mis'tak·en** □ equivocado; erróneo, incorrecto.

mis·ter ['mistə] señor *m* (*abbr.* **Mr**).

mis·tle·toe ['misltou] muérdago *m*.

mis·trans·late ['mistræns'leit] traducir mal.

mis·tress ['mistris] ama *f* de casa; dueña *f*; maestra *f* (de escuela); amante *f*, querida *f*.

mis·tri·al [mis'traiəl] 🏛 pleito *m* o juicio *m* viciado de nulidad.

mis·trust [mis'trʌst] 1. desconfiar de; 2. desconfianza *f*, recelo *m*; **'mis'trust·ful** [~ful] □ receloso.

mist·y ['misti] □ nebuloso, brumoso; *fig.* vaporoso; **'~·ness** nebulosidad *f*.

mis·un·der·stand ['misʌndə'stænd] entender mal, comprender mal; **'mis·un·der'stand·ing** equivocación *f*; malentendido *m*.

mis·use 1. ['mis'ju:z] emplear mal; maltratar; 2. ['~'ju:s] abuso *m*; maltratamiento *m*.

mite [meit] (*coin*) ardite *m*; pizca *f*.

mi·ter ['maitə] 1. mitra *f*; ⊕ inglete *m*; ~ **box** caja *f* de ingletes; ~ **joint** ensambladura *f* de inglete; 2. ⊕ ingletear.

mit·i·gate ['mitigeit] mitigar.

mitt [mit] guante *m* forreado; *sl.* mano *f*; **'mit·ten** mitón *m*, guante *m* con solo el pulgar separado.

mix [miks] mezclar, mixturar; *flour, plaster etc.* amasar; *drinks* preparar; *salad* aderezar; combinar; confundir; ~*ed* mixto; mezclado; *v/i.* mezclarse; (*p.*) asociarse; (*get on well*) llevarse bien; **mix·ture** ['ʌtʃə] mezcla *f*, mixtura *f*; F lío *m*, enredo *m*; **'mix-'up** confusión *f*.

moan [moun] 1. gemido *m*, quejido *m*; 2. gemir; F quejarse.

mob [mɔb] 1. gentío *m*, muchedumbre *f*; *b.s.* chusma *f*; 2. atropellar.

mo·bile ['moubil] móvil, movible; **mo·bil·i·ty** [mou'biliti] movilidad *f*; **'mo·bi·lize** movilizar.

mob·ster ['mɔbstə] *sl.* gángster *m*; panderillero *m*.

moc·ca·sin ['mɔkəsin] mocasín *m*.

mock [mɔk] 1. fingido, simulado; burlesco; 2. *v/t.* burlarse de, mofarse de; (*mimic*) remedar; *v/i.* mofarse (at de); **'mock·er** mofador (-a *f*) *m*; **'mock·er·y** mofa *f*, burla *f*; hazmerreír *m*; parodia *f*; **'mock-'he'ro·ic** heroicocómico; **'mock-up** maqueta *f*, modelo *m* en escala natural.

mod·al ['moudl] □ modal.

mode [moud] modo *m* (*a. phls.*, ♪); manera *f*; (*fashion*) moda *f*.

mod·el ['mɔdl] 1. modelo *m* (*a. fig.*); ▲ maqueta *f*; (*fashion*) ~ modelo *m*/*f*; *attr.* modelo; 2. *v/t.* modelar (*on* sobre); planear (*after* según); *v/i.* servir de modelo.

mod·er·ate 1. ['mɔdərit] □ moderado (*pol. a. su. m*); mediocre; *price* módico; 2. ['ʌreit] moderar(se), templar(se).

mod·ern ['mɔdən] 1. moderno; 2.: *the* ~*s pl.* los modernos; **'mod·ern·ism** modernismo *m*; **'mod·ern·ize** modernizar(se).

mod·est ['mɔdist] □ modesto; moderado; **'mod·es·ty** modestia *f*.

mod·i·fi·a·ble ['mɔdifaiəbl] modificable; **mod·i·fy** ['ʌfai] modificar (-se).

mod·ish ['moudiʃ] de moda, elegante.

mod·u·late ['mɔdjuleit] modular; **mod·u·la·tion** modulación *f*; *radio:*

frequency ~ modulación *f* de frecuencia.

mo·hair ['mouhɛə] moer *m*.

Mo·ham·med·an [mou'hæmidən] mahometano *adj. a. su. m* (*a f*).

moist [mɔist] húmedo; mojado; **mois·ten** ['mɔisn] humedecer(se); mojar(se); **'moist·ness, mois·ture** ['ʌtʃə] humedad *f*.

mo·lar ['moulə] molar *m*, muela *f*.

mo·las·ses [mə'læsiz] melaza(s) *f*(*pl.*).

mold [mould] *v.* mo(u)ld.

mole [moul] *zo.* topo *m*; (*spot*) lunar *m*; **♣** mola *f*.

mol·e·cule ['mɔlikjuːl] molécula *f*.

mole·hill ['moulhil] topera *f*; *make a mountain out of a* ~ hacer de una pulga un elefante.

mo·lest [mou'lest] importunar; molestar; **mo·les·ta·tion** [moules'teiʃn] importunidad *f*, molestia *f*.

moll [mɔl] *sl.* amiga *f*, ramera *f*.

mol·li·fy ['mɔlifai] apaciguar, mitigar.

mol·ly·cod·dle ['mɔlikɔdl] 1. niño *m* mimado; marica *m*; 2. mimar.

mo·ment ['moumənt] momento *m*; instante *m*; importancia *f*; *at any* ~ de un momento a otro; **'mo·men·tar·y** □ momentáneo; **mo·men·tous** [~'mentəs] □ grave, trascendental, de suma importancia; **mo'men·tum** [ʌtəm] *phys.* momento *m*; ímpetu *m*.

mon·arch ['mɔnək] monarca *m*; **mon·arch·ism** ['mɔnəkizm] monarquismo *m*; **mon·arch·y** ['ʌki] monarquía *f*.

mon·as·ter·y ['mɔnəstri] monasterio *m*; **mon·as·ti·cism** monacato *m*; monaquismo *m*.

Mon·day ['mʌndi] lunes *m*.

mon·e·tar·y ['mʌnitəri] monetario.

mon·ey ['mʌni] dinero *m*; plata *f esp. S.Am.*; (*coin*) moneda *f*; *make* ~ ganar dinero; (*business*) dar dinero; **'~·chang·er** cambista *m*/*f*; **mon·eyed** ['mʌnid] adinerado.

mon·ey-...: ~ **grub·ber** avaro (*a f*) *m*; **'~·lend·er** prestamista *m*/*f*; **~·mar·ket** mercado *m* monetario; **~ 'or·der** *approx.* giro *m* postal.

mon·ger ['mʌŋgə] traficante *m*/*f*.

Mon·gol ['mɔŋgɔl], **Mon·go·lian** [~'gouljən] 1. mogol *adj. a. su. m* (*a f*); 2. (*language*) mogol *m*.

mon·grel ['mʌŋgrəl] 1. perro *m* callejero; mestizo (*a f*) *m*; 2. mestizo.

mon·i·tor ['mɔnitə] 1. *school:* monitor *m*; *radio*: (*p.*) escucha *m/f*; **2.** vigilar; regular.

monk [mʌŋk] monje *m*.

mon·key ['mʌŋki] **1.** mono (a *f*) *m*, mico (a *f*) *m*; *fig.* diablillo *m*; F ~ *business* trampería *f*, malas mañas *f/pl.*; **2.** F hacer payasadas; ~ (*about*) *with* manosear; meterse con; '~ **shine** *sl.* monada *f*; '~ **wrench** ⊕ llave *f* inglesa.

monk·ish ['mʌŋkiʃ] *mst contp.* frailuno, de monje.

mo·no... ['mɔnou] mono...; **mon·o·chrome** ['mɔnəkroum] monocromo *adj. a. su. m*; **mon·o·cle** ['mɔnɔkl] monóculo *m*; **mo·nog·a·my** [~gəmi] monogamia *f*; **mon·o·gram** ['mɔnəgræm] monograma *m*; **mon·o·graph** ['~grɑ:f] monografía *f*; **mon·o·lith** ['mɔnəliθ] monolito *m*; **mon·o·logue** ['mɔnəlɔg] monólogo *m*; **mon·o·ma·ni·a** ['mɔnou'meiniə] monomanía *f*; **mon·o·plane** ['mɔnəplein] monoplano *m*; **mo·nop·o·list** [mə'nɔpəlist] monopolista *m/f*; acaparador (-a *f*) *m*; **mo·nop·o·lize** [~laiz] monopolizar; acaparar (*a. fig.*); **mo·nop·o·ly** monopolio *m*; **mon·o·syl·lab·ic** ['mɔnousi'læbik] *word* monosílabo; monosilábico; **mon·o·syl·la·ble** ['~ləbl] monosílabo *m*; **mon·o·the·ism** ['mɔnouθi:izm] monoteísmo *m*; **mon·o·tone** ['mɔnətoun] monotonía *f*; **mo·not·o·nous** [mə'nɔtənəs] ☐ monótono; **mo·not·o·ny** [~təni] monotonía *f*.

mon·soon [mɔn'su:n] monzón *m* or *f*.

mon·ster ['mɔnstə] monstruo *m*.

mon·stros·i·ty [mɔns'trɔsiti] monstruosidad *f*; '**mon·strous** ☐ monstruoso.

month [mʌnθ] mes *m*; *100 pesetas a* ~ 100 pesetas mensuales, '**month·ly 1.** mensual(mente); **2.** revista *f* mensual.

mon·u·ment ['mɔnjumənt] monumento *m*.

moo [mu:] **1.** mugido *m*; **2.** mugir.

mooch [mu:tʃ] pedir de gorra; F ~ *about* vagar, haraganear.

mood¹ [mu:d] *gr.* modo *m*.

mood² [~] humor *m*; capricho *m*; *be in a good* (*bad*) ~ estar de buen (mal) humor.

mood·y ['mu:di] ☐ de mal humor; melancólico; caprichoso.

moon [mu:n] luna *f*; *poet.* mes *m*; '~**beam** rayo *m* de luna; '**moon·light 1.** luz *f* de la luna; **2.** tener

empleo segundo; '~**shine** F pamplinas *f/pl.*, música *f* celestial; F licor *m* destilado ilegalmente; '~**shin·er** F fabricante *m* de licor ilegal.

Moor¹ [muə] moro (a *f*) *m*.

moor² [~] páramo *m*, brezal *m*.

moor³ [~] ♣ *v/t.* amarrar; *v/i.* echar las amarras.

moor·ings ['muəriŋz] *pl.* ♣ amarras *f/pl.*; (*place*) amarradero *m*.

Moor·ish ['muəriʃ] moro; ▲ *etc.* árabe.

moose [mu:s] alce *m* de América.

moot [mu:t]: ~ *point*, ~ *question* punto *m* discutible.

mop [mɔp] **1.** fregasuelos *m*; mata *f*, greña *f of hair*; **2.** fregar; limpiar.

mope [moup] estar abatido (or aburrido); andar alicaído.

mo·ped ['mouped] moto *f*.

mo·raine [mə'rein] *geol.* morena *f*.

mor·al ['mɔrəl] **1.** ☐ moral, ético; virtuoso; **2.** moraleja *f*; ~*s pl.* moral *f*; moralidad *f*; costumbres *f/pl.*; **mo·rale** [mə'rɑ:l] estado *m* de ánimo; **mo·ral·ist** ['mɔrəlist] moralista *m/f*; moralizador (-a *f*) *m*; **mo·ral·i·ty** [mə'ræliti] moralidad *f etc.*; **mor·al·ize** ['mɔrəlaiz] moralizar.

mor·a·to·ri·um [mɔrə'tɔ:riəm] moratoria *f*.

mor·bid ['mɔ:bid] ☐ mórbido, morboso; *mind* malsano, enfermizo; **mor·bid·i·ty** morbosidad *f*.

mor·dant ['mɔ:dənt] mordaz.

more [mɔ:] *adj., adv., su.* más; ~ *and* ~ cada vez más; ~ *or less* (poco) más o menos; *no* (*or not any*) ~ ya no, no más; *the* ~ ... *the* ~ ... cuanto más ... (tanto) más ...

more·o·ver [mɔ:'rouvə] además (de eso), por otra parte.

morgue [mɔ:g] depósito *m* de cadáveres.

mor·i·bund ['mɔribʌnd] moribundo.

Mor·mon ['mɔ:mən] **1.** mormón (-a *f*) *m*; **2.** mormónico.

morn·ing ['mɔ:niŋ] **1.** mañana *f*; *good* ~! ¡buenos días!; *in the* ~ por la mañana; *at 6 o'clock in the* ~ a las 6 de la mañana; *to-morrow* ~ mañana por la mañana; **2.** matutino, matinal, de (la) mañana.

Mo·roc·can [mə'rɔkən] marroquí *adj. a. su. m/f*, marrueco *adj. a. su. m* (a *f*).

mo·ron ['mɔ:rɔn] imbécil *m/f*.

mo·rose [mə'rous] ☐ malhumorado, sobrio.

M

morphine

mor·phine ['mɔːfiːn] morfina f.

mor·phol·o·gy [mɔːˈfɔlədʒi] morfología f.

mor·sel ['mɔːsəl] pedazo m; bocado m.

mor·tal ['mɔːtl] □ mortal adj. a. su. m/f; **mor·tal·i·ty** [mɔːˈtæliti] mortalidad f; mortandad f.

mor·tar ['mɔːtə] mortero m (a. ⚔).

mort·gage ['mɔːgidʒ] 1. hipoteca f; 2. hipotecar; **mort·ga·gee** [ˌmɔːgəˈdʒiː] acreedor (-a f) m hipotecario (a); **mort·ga·gor** [ˌmɔːgəˈdʒɔː] deudor (-a f) m hipotecario (a).

mor·ti·cian [mɔːˈtiʃn] director m de pompas fúnebres.

mor·ti·fi·ca·tion [mɔːtifiˈkeiʃn] mortificación f; humillación f.

mor·ti·fy ['mɔːtifai] v/t. mortificar; humillar; v/i. 🌺 gangrenarse.

mor·tu·ar·y ['mɔːtjuəri] 1. depósito m de cadáveres; 2. mortuorio.

mo·sa·ic¹ [məˈzeiik] mosaico m.

Mo·sa·ic² [~] mosaico.

Mos·lem ['mɔzlem] musulmán adj. a. su. m (-a f); islámico.

mosque [mɔsk] mezquita f.

mos·qui·to [məsˈkiːtou], pl. **mos·qui·tos** [~z] mosquito m.

moss [mɔs] musgo m; geog. pantano m; **moss·y** musgoso.

most [moust] 1. adj. □ más; la mayor parte de; los más, la mayoría de; 2. adv. más; muy, sumamente; de lo más; ~ of all sobre todo; a ~ interesting book un libro interesantísimo; 3. su. la mayor parte; el mayor número, los más.

most·ly ['moustli] por la mayor parte; principalmente; en general.

mo·tel [mouˈtel] motel m.

moth [mɔθ] mariposa f (nocturna); polilla f in clothes etc.; '~·ball bola f de naftalina; '~·eat·en apolillado.

moth·er ['mʌðə] 1. madre f; attr. madre, maternal, materno; ♀ Church la santa madre iglesia; iglesia f metropolitana; 2. servir de madre a; mimar; animal ahijar; **moth·er·hood** ['~hud] maternidad f; madres f/pl.; '**moth·er-in-law** suegra f; '**moth·er·land** (madre) patria f; '**moth·er·less** huérfano de madre, sin madre; '**moth·er·ly** maternal; '~-of-'**pearl** nácar m; 2. nacarado; '~ **tongue** lengua f materna; lengua f madre.

mo·tif [mouˈtiːf] ♩, art: motivo m; tema m; sew. adorno m.

mo·tion ['mouʃn] 1. movimiento m; ⊕ marcha f, operación f; ⊕ mecanismo m; parl. moción f; además m; señal f; (set) in ~ (poner) en marcha; 2. v/t. indicar a una p. con la mano etc. (to inf. que subj.); v/i. hacer señas; '**mo·tion·less** inmóvil; '**mo·tion pic·ture** 1. película f; 2. cinematográfico.

mo·ti·vate ['moutiveit] motivar.

mo·tive ['moutiv] 1. motivo m; 2. motor, motivo; motriz.

mot·ley ['mɔtli] 1. abigarrado; vario; 2. botarga f; mezcla f.

mo·tor ['moutə] 1. motor m; 2. motor; ~ ship, ~ vessel motonave f; 3. ir (or viajar) en automóvil; '~·bike F moto f; '~·boat gasolinera f, motora f, motorbote m; '~ 'bus autobús m; '~·cade f caravana f de automóviles; '~ coach autocar m; '~·cy·cle moto(cicleta) f; **mo·tor·ing** ['moutəriŋ] automovilismo m; '**mo·tor·ist** automovilista m/f; **mo·tor·i·za·tion** [ˌraiˈzeiʃn] motorización f; '**mo·tor·ize** motorizar; '**mo·tor launch** lancha f (or canoa f) automóvil; '~·man 🔧 conductor m (de locomotora eléctrica); '~ 'scoot·er vespa f; motoneta f.

mot·tled ['mɔtld] jaspeado, abigarrado.

mot·to ['mɔtou], pl. **mot·toes** ['~z] lema m; heraldry: divisa f.

mo(u)ld¹ [mould] mantillo m; (fungus) moho m; (iron ~) mancha f de orín.

mo(u)ld² [~] 1. molde m; cosa f moldeada; fig. carácter m; 2. moldear; vaciar; amoldar (a. fig.).

mo(u)ld·er ['mouldə] (a. ~ away) desmoronarse; convertirse en polvo.

mo(u)ld·ing ['mouldiŋ] amoldamiento m; vaciado m; △ moldura f.

mo(u)ld·y ['mouldi] mohoso, enmohecido; fig. rancio, anticuado.

moult [moult] mudar (la pluma).

mound [maund] montón m; montículo m; terraplén m.

mount [maunt] 1. poet. a. geog. monte m; engaste m of jewel; base f; 2. v/t. montar (a. ⊕); (climb) subir; (get on to) subir a (or en); poner a caballo; jewel engastar; v/i. subir a caballo; montar(se); aumentar.

moun·tain ['mauntin] 1. montaña f; (pile) montón m; ~ chain cordillera f; ~ range sierra f; 2. montañés, de montaña; **moun·tain·eer** [ˌ~iˈniə] montañés (-a *f*) *m*; montañero (a *f*) *m*, alpinista *m*/*f*; **moun·tain'eer·ing 1.** montañismo *m*; alpinismo *m*; **2.** montañero; **'moun·tain·ous** montañoso; *fig.* enorme.

mount·ing ['mauntiŋ] montadura *f*; ⊕ montaje *m*; base *f*.

mourn [mɔːn] *v*/*t*. llorar (la muerte de); lamentar; *v*/*i*. lamentarse; estar de luto; **mourn·ful** ['ful] □ triste, lastimero; **'mourn·ful·ness** tristeza *f*, melancolía *f*.

mourn·ing ['mɔːniŋ] **1.** luto *m*, duelo *m*; lamentación *f*; *be in* ~ estar de luto; **2.** de luto.

mouse 1. [maus] (*pl. mice* mice). **2.** [mauz] cazar ratones; **'mouse·trap** ratonera *f*.

mous·tache [məs'taːʃ] bigote(s) *m*(*pl.*), mostacho *m*.

mous·y ['mausi] tímido.

mouth [mauθ] **1.** boca *f* (*a. fig.*); (des)embocadura *f* of river; boquilla *f* of wind-instrument; **2.** [mauð] *v*/*t*. pronunciar (con rimbombancia), proferir; *v*/*i*. hablar exagerando los movimientos de la boca; **mouth·ful** ['ful] bocado *m*; '~·or·gan armónica *f* (de boca); '~·piece boquilla *f*; *teleph.* micrófono *m*; *fig.* portavoz *m*; '~·wash enjuague *m*; '~·wa·ter·ing apetitoso.

mov(e)·a·ble ['muːvəbl] **1.** movible; **2.** ~s *pl.* bienes *m*/*pl.* muebles.

move [muːv] **1.** *v*/*t*. mover; poner en marcha; trasladar *from one place to another*; *house* mudar de; *emotion*: conmover, enternecer; *parl.* proponer; *v*/*i*. moverse; trasladarse; caminar; ponerse en marcha; menearse; mudar de casa; ~ *forward* avanzar; ~ *in* instalarse (en); ~ *out* salir; abandonar la casa; ~ *up* ascender, subir; **2.** movimiento *m*; paso *m*; acción *f*; maniobra *f*; *game*: jugada *f*; mudanza *f* of *house*; F *get a* ~ *on* menearse, darse prisa; F *get a* ~ *on!* ¡anda, espabílate!; **'move·ment** movimiento *m* (*a. fig.*); ⊕ mecanismo *m*; juego *m*; ♪ tiempo *m*; ♂ defecación *f*; ❦ actividad *f*; **'mov·er** movedor (-a *f*) *m*; móvil *m*; (*proposer*) autor (-a *f*) *m*; *prime* ~ ⊕ máquina *f* motriz.

mov·ie ['muːvi] F película *f*; ~*s pl.* cine *m*; '~·go·er aficionado *m* al cine.

mov·ing ['muːviŋ] □ motor; movedor; movedizo; *fig.* conmovedor.

mow [mou] [*irr.*] segar (*a.* ~ *down*);

'**mow·er** segador (-a *f*) *m*; '**mow·ing 1.** siega *f*; **2.** segador; '**mow·ing ma·chine** segadora *f* mecánica; cortacésped *m for lawn*; **mown** *p*.*p*. of mow.

much [mʌtʃ] *adj.* mucho; *adv.* mucho; (*before p.p.*) muy; (*almost*) casi, más o menos; *as* ~, *so* ~ tanto; *as* ~ *again*, *as* ~ *more* otro tanto más; *as* ~ *as* tanto como; *how* ~ cuánto; *think* ~ *of* estimar en mucho; *not to think* ~ *of* tener en poco; *I thought as* ~ ya me lo figuraba; *too* ~ demasiado.

mu·ci·lage ['mjuːsilidʒ] mucílago *m*.

muck [mʌk] ⚷ estiércol *m*; suciedad *f*; F porquería *f* (*a. fig.*); '**muck·rak·er** escarbador (-a *f*) *m* de vidas ajenas.

mu·cus ['mjuːkəs] moco *m*, mucosidad *f*.

mud [mʌd] lodo *m*, barro *m*; fango *m* (*a. fig.*); *sling* ~ *at* F vilipendiar; ~*slinger* F menospreciador *m*; *stick in the* ~ aguafiestas *m*/*f*.

mud·dle ['mʌdl] **1.** embrollo *m*, confusión *f*; F lío *m*; *get into a* ~ embrollarse; **2.** *v*/*t*. embrollar, confundir; *v*/*i*. obrar confusamente (*or* sin ton ni son); ~ *through* salir del paso sin saber cómo; '~·head·ed atontado, estúpido; confuso.

mud·dy ['mʌdi] **1.** □ lodoso, fangoso; **2.** enlodar; enturbiar.

mud...: '~·guard guardabarros *m*; '~·lark F galopín *m*.

muff[1] [mʌf] *sport:* dejar escapar (la pelota); perder (la ocasión).

muff[2] [~] manguito *m*.

muf·fin ['mʌfin] *approx.* mollete *m*.

muf·fle ['mʌfl] embozar(se), tapar (-se) (*a.* ~ *up*) muff; amortiguar (el ruido de); '**muf·fler** bufanda *f*; ♪ sordina *f*; ⊕ silenciador *m*.

muf·ti ['mʌfti] traje *m* de paisano; *in* ~ vestido de paisano.

mug [mʌg] **1.** taza *f* (alta sin platillo); barro *m*, jarra *f* of *beer*; *sl.* (*face*) hocico *m*, jeta *f*; *sl.* bruto *m*; **2.** asaltar para robar; **mug·ger** ['mʌgə] ladrón *m* asaltador.

mug·gy ['mʌgi] húmedo y sofocante.

mu·lat·to [mjuˈlætou] mulato *adj.* a. su. *m* (a *f*).

mul·ber·ry ['mʌlbəri] mora *f*.

mulch [mʌlʃ] ⚷ (cubrir con) estiércol *m*, paja *f* y hojas *f*/*pl*.

mule [mjuːl] mulo (a *f*) *m*; (*slipper*) babucha *f*; *fig.* sujeto *m* terco.

mul·ish ['mjuːliʃ] □ terco, obstinado.

M

mul·let ['mʌlit] (red) salmonete m.

mul·lion ['mʌljən] 1. ⌂ parteluz m; 2. dividir con parteluz.

mul·ti·col·ored ['mʌltikʌləd] multicolor; **mul·ti·far·i·ous** [ˌ·'fɛəriəs] □ múltiple, vario; **mul·ti·form** ['ˌ·fɔːm] multiforme; **mul·ti·lat·er·al** [ˌ·'lætərəl] □ multilátero; **mul·ti·mil·lion·aire** [ˌ·miljə'nɛə] multimillonario (a f) m; **mul·ti·ple** ['mʌltipl] 1. múltiple; múltiplo; 2. múltiplo m; lowest common ~ mínimo común múltiplo m; **mul·ti·plex** múltiple; **mul·ti·pli·ca·tion** multiplicación f; ~ table tabla f de multiplicar; **mul·ti·plic·i·ty** [ˌ·'plisiti] multiplicidad f; **mul·ti·pli·er** ['ˌ·plaiə] multiplicador m; **mul·ti·ply** ['ˌ·plai] multiplicar (-se); **mul·ti·tude** ['ˌ·tjuːd] multitud f, muchedumbre f.

mum·ble ['mʌmbl] mascullar, musitar; hablar entre dientes.

mum·bo jum·bo ['mʌmbou 'dʒʌmbou] F fetiche m; conjuro m; mistificación f; galimatías m.

mum·mer ['mʌmə] máscara m/f; contp. comicastro m; **'mum·mer·y** momería f, mojiganga f.

mum·mi·fi·ca·tion [mʌmifi'keiʃn] momificación f; **mum·mi·fy** ['ˌ·fai] momificar(se).

mum·my ['mʌmi] momia f.

mumps [mʌmps] sg. papera f, parótidas f/pl.

munch [mʌntʃ] ronzar.

mu·nic·i·pal [mju:'nisipl] □ municipal; **mu·nic·i·pal·i·ty** [ˌ·'pæliti] municipio m; **mu·nic·i·pal·ize** [ˌ·əlaiz] municipalizar.

mu·ni·tions ['mju:'niʃnz] pl. municiones f/pl.

mu·ral ['mjuərəl] 1. mural; 2. pintura f mural.

mur·der ['mɜːdə] 1. asesinato m; homicidio m; 2. asesinar; fig. arruinar, **'mur·der·er** asesino m; **'mur·der·ous** □ asesino, homicida; sanguinario; intolerable.

murk·y ['mɜːki] □ oscuro, lóbrego; tenebroso (a. fig.).

mur·mur ['mɜːmə] 1. murmullo m, murmurio m (a. fig.); 2. murmurar.

mus·cle ['mʌsl] 1. músculo m; fig. fuerza f muscular; 2.: sl. ~ in entrar (or establecerse) por fuerza (en un negocio ilegal); **'ˌ·bound** de musculatura desarrollada en exceso.

Muse¹ [mju:z] musa f.

muse² [ˌ·] meditar, reflexionar.

mu·se·um [mju:'ziəm] museo m.

mush [mʌʃ] gacha(s) f(pl.); fig. disparates m/pl.; fig. sensiblería f.

mush·room ['mʌʃrum] 1. seta f, hongo m; champiñón m; 2. crecer rápidamente.

mush·y ['mʌʃi] pulposo, mollar; fig. sensiblero.

mu·sic ['mju:zik] música f; F face the ~ pagar el pato; **'mu·si·cal** □ músico, musical; ~ comedy zarzuela f; ~ instrument instrumento m músico.

mu·sic hall ['mju:zikhɔ:l] teatro m de variedades; salón m de conciertos.

mu·si·cian [mju:'ziʃn] músico (a f) m; **'ˌ·ship** musicalidad f.

musk [mʌsk] (olor m de) almizcle m; ♀ almizcleña f; **'ˌ·deer** almizclero m.

mus·ket ['mʌskit] mosquete m; **mus·ket·eer** [ˌ·'tiə] mosquetero m; **'mus·ket·ry** mosquetes m/pl.; (troops) mosquetería f.

musk·y ['mʌski] almizcleño, almizclado.

Mus·lim ['mʌzlim] v. Moslem.

mus·lin ['mʌzlin] muselina f.

muss [mʌs] F 1. desaliño m, confusión f; 2. desarreglar.

must¹ [mʌst, məst] deber; tener que; haber de; probability: deber (de); I ~ do it now tengo que hacerlo ahora; I ~ keep my word debo cumplir lo prometido; he ~ be there by now ya debe (de) estar allí.

must² [ˌ·] moho m.

mus·tache [məs'tæʃ] v. moustache.

mus·tard ['mʌstəd] mostaza f; **'ˌ·gas** gas m mostaza; **'mus·tard pot** mostacera f.

mus·ter ['mʌstə] 1. asamblea f; ✗ revista f; lista f, matrícula f; 2. v/t. llamar a asamblea; v/i. juntarse.

mus·ti·ness ['mʌstinis] moho m; rancidez f; **'mus·ty** mohoso; rancio.

mu·ta·bil·i·ty [mju:tə'biliti] mutabilidad f; **'mu·ta·ble** □ mudable.

mute [mju:t] 1. □ mudo; silencioso; 2. mudo (a f) m; ♪ sordina f; 3. poner sordina a; apagar.

mu·ti·late ['mju:tileit] mutilar.

mu·ti·neer [mju:ti'niə] amotinado(r) m; **'mu·ti·nous** □ amotinado, turbulento, rebelde; **'mu·ti·ny** 1. motín m; 2. amotinarse.

mut·ter ['mʌtə] 1. murmullo m; 2. v/t. murmurar; v/i. murmurar.

mut·ton ['mʌtn] carne f de carnero; **'ˌ·chop** chuleta f de carnero.

mu·tu·al ['mju:tjuəl] □ mutuo; F

común; ~ *consent* común acuerdo *m*; ~ *fund* sociedad *f* inversionista mutualista.

muz·zle ['mʌzl] 1. hocico *m*; bozal *m* *for dog*; 2. abozalar; (*gag*) amordazar.

my [mai, *a*. mi] mi(s).

my·op·ic [mai'ɔpik] □ miope *adj. a. su. m/f*; **my·o·pi·a** [~'oupiə], **my·o·py** [~'oupi] miopía *f*.

myr·tle ['mɔːtl] arrayán *m*, mirto *m*.

my·self [mai'self] (*subject*) yo mismo, yo misma; *acc., dat.* me; (*after prp.*) mí (mismo, misma).

mys·te·ri·ous [mis'tiəriəs] □ misterioso.

mys·ter·y ['mistəri] misterio *m*; arcano *m*; *thea.* auto *m*, misterio *m*; (*a.* ~ *novel*) novela *f* policíaca; '~ **play** auto *m*; misterio *m*.

mys·tic ['mistik] 1. (*a.* '**mys·ti·cal**) □ místico; 2. místico (*a f*) *m*; **mys·ti·cism** ['~sizm] misticismo *m*, mística *f*; **mys·ti·fi·ca·tion** [~fi'keiʃn] mistificación *f*; **mys·ti·fy** ['~fai] dejar perplejo; ofuscar.

myth [miθ] mito *m*; **myth·ic, myth·i·cal** ['~ik(l)] □ mítico; fabuloso.

myth·o·log·ic, myth·o·log·i·cal [miθə'lɔdʒik(l)] □ mitológico; **my·thol·o·gy** [~'θɔlədʒi] mitología *f*.

N

nab [næb] coger, atrapar, prender.

na·dir ['neidiə] *ast.* nadir *m*; *fig.* punto *m* más bajo.

nag[1] [næg] jaca *f*; *contp.* rocín *m*.

nag[2] [~] regañar; *fig.* hostigar.

nail [neil] 1. *anat.* uña *f*; ⊕ clavo *m*; *bite one's ~s* comerse las uñas; 2. clavar (*a. fig.*), enclavar; clavetear; F coger; '~ **clip·pers** cortauñas *m*; '~ **file** lima *f* para las uñas; '~ **pol·ish** laca *f* de uñas.

na·ïve [nai'iːv] □ ingenuo, cándido, sencillo; **na·ïve·té** [nai'iːvtei] ingenuidad *f* etc.

na·ked ['neikid] desnudo (*a. fig.*), en cueros; obvio; *fig.* desvergonzado; '**na·ked·ness** desnudez *f*.

nam·by-pam·by ['næmbi'pæmbi] 1. soso, ñoño; melindroso; 2. insulseces *f/pl*.

name [neim] 1. nombre *m* (*a. fig.*); (*surname*) apellido *m*; reputación *f*; *b.s.* apodo *m*; título *m* *of book etc.*; *my* ~ *is* me llamo; *what is your* ~? ¿cómo se llama?; 2. nombrar; designar; (*mention*) mentar; *date, price etc.* fijar, señalar; bautizar *with Christian name*; '**name·less** □ anónimo, sin nombre; *vice* nefando; '**name·ly** a saber (*abbr. viz.*); '**name·plate** placa *f* rotulada, letrero *m* con nombre; '**name·sake** tocayo (*a f*) *m*, homónimo (*a f*) *m*.

nan·ny ['næni] F niñera *f*; '~ **goat** F cabra *f*.

nap[1] [næp] *cloth*: lanilla *f*, flojel *m*.

nap[2] [~] 1. sueño *m* ligero, dormirela *m*; (*afternoon*) siesta *f*; 2. dormitar.

na·palm ['neipɑːm] jalea *f* de gasolina.

nape [neip] cogote *m*, nuca *f*.

naph·tha ['næfθə] nafta *f*; **naph·tha·lene** ['~liːn] naftaleno *m*, naftalina *f*.

nap·kin ['næpkin] servilleta *f* (*a. table-*~); pañal *m* (*a. baby's* ~); '~ **ring** servilletero *m*.

nar·cis·sus [nɑːˈsisəs] narciso *m*.

nar·co·sis [nɑːˈkousis] narcosis *f*, narcotismo *m*; **nar·cot·ic** [~ˈkotik] narcótico *adj. a. su. m*; **nar·co·tize** ['nɑːkətaiz] narcotizar.

nar·rate [næˈreit] narrar, referir, relatar; **nar·ra·tive** ['~rətiv] 1. □ narrativo; 2. narrativa *f*, narración *f*.

nar·row ['nærou] 1. □ estrecho (*a. fig.*); *passage etc.* angosto; *p.* de miras estrechas; 2. ~s *pl.* ⚓ estrecho *m*; desfiladero *m*; 3. estrechar(se), (en-)angostar(se); '~-**gauge** 🚂 de vía estrecha; '~-**mind·ed** □ intolerante; de miras estrechas; '**nar·row·ness** angostura *f*; intolerancia *f*.

na·sal ['neizl] □ nasal *adj. a. su. f*; **na·sal·i·ty** [~ˈzæliti] nasalidad *f*; **na·sal·ize** ['~zəlaiz] nasalizar.

nas·ty ['nɑːsti] □ sucio, asqueroso; feo; horrible; áspero; F peligroso; F difícil.

na·tal ['neitl] natal.

na·tion ['neiʃn] nación *f*.

na·tion·al ['næʃ(ə)nl] □ nacional *adj. a. su. m/f*; ~ *debt* deuda *f* pública; ♀ *Socialism* nacionalsocialismo *m*; **na·tion·al·i·ty** [næʃə'næliti] nacionalidad *f*; **na·tion·al·ize** ['næʃnəlaiz] nacionalizar.

na·tion-wide ['neiʃnwaid] por (or de) toda la nación.

na·tive ['neitiv] **1.** ☐ nativo (a. ⚒); natural; indígena, originario (to de); **2.** natural m/f; indígena m/f; nacional m/f.

na·tiv·i·ty [nə'tiviti] natividad f; (Christmas) Navidad f; ~ play auto m del nacimiento.

nat·ty ['næti] ☐ F elegante; majo.

na·tu·ral ['nætʃrəl] **1.** ☐ natural (a. ♪); nativo; innato; p. sencillo, llano; normal; **2.** ♪ nota f natural; ♪ becuadro m; F cosa f de éxito certero; **'nat·u·ral·ism** naturalismo m; **'nat·u·ral·ist** naturalista m/f; **nat·u·ral·i·za·tion** [~lai'zeiʃn] naturalización f; ~ papers carta f de naturaleza; **'nat·u·ral·ize** naturalizar.

na·ture ['neitʃə] naturaleza f; p.'s temperamento m; (kind) género m, clase f.

naught [nɔːt] nada; cero m; **naugh·ti·ness** ['~tinis] travesura f etc.; **'naugh·ty** travieso, pícaro; desobediente.

nau·se·a ['nɔːsiə] náusea f, asco m; **'nau·se·ate** ['~sieit] dar asco (a); **'nau·se·at·ing, 'nau·seous** ☐ nauseabundo; asqueroso.

nau·ti·cal ['nɔːtikl] ☐ náutico, marítimo; ~ mile milla f marina.

na·val ['neivəl] naval, de marina.

na·vel ['neivəl] ombligo m; **'~ or·ange** navel m; naranja f umbilicada.

nav·i·ga·ble ['nævigəbl] river etc. navegable; ship etc. gobernable; **'nav·i·gate** ['~geit] navegar; ship marear; **nav·i·ga·tion** navegación f, náutica f; mareaje m; **'nav·i·ga·tor** navegante m.

na·vy ['neivi] marina f de guerra; armada f; ~ blue azul m marino.

Naz·a·rene [næzə'riːn] nazareno adj. a. su. m (a f).

Na·zi ['nɑːtsi] nazi adj. su. m/f; **Na·zism** nazismo m.

Ne·a·pol·i·tan [niə'pɔlitən] napolitano adj. a. su. m (a f).

near [niə] **1.** adj. cercano, próximo; inmediato, vecino; relationship estrecho, íntimo; **2.** adv. cerca; ~ at hand a la mano, cerca; **3.** prp. (a. ~ to) cerca de; próximo a, cerca; **4.** acercarse a; **near·by** ['~bai] **1.** adj. próximo, cercano; **2.** adv. cerca; **'near·ly** casi; de cerca; aproximadamente; **'near·ness** proximidad f, cercanía f; **'near-**

'sight·ed miope, corto de vista.

neat [niːt] ☐ pulcro, esmerado, aseado; primoroso; (shapely) bien proporcionado; **'neat·ness** pulcritud f; aseo m.

neb·u·la ['nebjulə] nebulosa f; **'neb·u·lous** ☐ nebuloso.

nec·es·sar·y ['nesisəri] **1.** ☐ necesario, preciso, indispensable; **2.** cosa f necesaria, requisito m indispensable; **ne·ces·si·tate** [ni'sesiteit] necesitar, exigir; **ne'ces·si·ty** necesidad f; requisito m indispensable.

neck [nek] **1.** cuello m; pescuezo m of animal; gollete m of bottle; **2.** sl. acariciarse, besuquearse; **neck·lace** ['~lis] collar m; **'neck·tie** corbata f.

ne·crol·o·gy [ne'krɔlədʒi] necrología f; **nec·ro·man·cy** ['nekroumænsi] necromancía f.

nec·tar ['nektə] néctar m.

née [nei] nacida; Rosa Bell, ~ Martin Rosa Martin de Bell.

need [niːd] **1.** necesidad f (for, of de); requisito m; urgencia f; carencia f; if ~ be si fuera necesario; in ~ necesitado; **2.** v/t. necesitar; requerir; exigir; carecer de; deber inf.; tener que inf.; v/i. estar necesitado; **need·ful** ['~ful] ☐ necesario; **'need·i·ness** necesidad f, estrechez f.

nee·dle ['niːdl] **1.** aguja f; **2.** F aguijar; fastidiar; **'~ case** alfiletero m.

need·less ['niːdlis] innecesario, superfluo, inútil; ~ to say excusado es decir, huelga decir; **'~·ly** inútilmente.

needs [niːdz] necesariamente; **'need·y** ☐ necesitado, indigente.

ne'er-do-well ['nɛədu:wel] holgazán m, perdulario m.

ne·gate [ni'geit] negar; anular, invalidar; **neg·a·tive** ['negətiv] **1.** ☐ negativo; **2.** negativa f; phot. negativo m; gr. negación f; ≠ electricidad f negativa; **3.** negar; desaprobar; anular.

neg·lect [ni'glekt] **1.** negligencia f, descuido m; abandono m; **2.** descuidar, desatender; abandonar; duty etc. faltar a; ~ to inf. dejar de inf., olvidarse de inf.; **neg'lect·ful** [~ful] ☐ negligente, descuidado.

neg·li·gence ['neglidʒəns] negligencia f, descuido m; **'neg·li·gent** ☐ negligente, descuidado.

neg·li·gi·ble ['neglidʒəbl] insignificante; despreciable.

ne·go·ti·ate [ni'gouʃieit] v/t. negociar; gestionar; agenciar; pasar por; **ne·go·ti·a·tion** negociación f; gestión f; *enter into ~ with* entrar en tratos con.

Ne·gri·tude ['negrɪtuːd] negrura f; calidad f de ser identificada con la raza negra; **Ne·gro** ['niːgrou] *mst contp.* negro *adj. a. su. m*; **Ne·groid** ['niːgroid] negroide.

neigh [nei] 1. relincho *m*; 2. relinchar.

neigh·bor ['neibə] 1. vecino (a f) *m*; prójimo (a f) *m*; 2. (*a. ~ upon*) colindar con, estar contiguo a; **'neigh·bor·hood** vecindad f, vecindario *m*; barrio *m*; **'neigh·bor·ing** vecino, colindante.

nei·ther ['naiðə, 'niːðə] 1. ninguno (de los dos), ni (el) uno ni (el) otro; 2. *adv.* ni; ~ ... *nor* ni ... ni; tampoco ni ... tampoco. 3. *conj.* ni; tampoco.

ne·o·lo·gism [niːˈɔlədʒizm] neologismo *m*.

ne·on ['niːɔn] neón *m*, neo *m*; **'~ light** lámpara f neón.

ne·o·phyte ['niːoufait] neófito (a f) *m*.

neph·ew ['nevju] sobrino *m*.

nerve [nəːv] relincho *m* (*a. fig.*); (*courage*) valor *m*, ánimo *m*; *sl.* descaro *m*; **'~ cell** neurona f, célula f nerviosa; **'nerve·rack·ing** irritante; exasperante.

nerv·ous ['nəːvəs] □ nerv(i)oso; tímido; ~ *breakdown* crisis f nerviosa; **'nerv·ous·ness** nerviosidad f, nerviosismo *m*; timidez f.

nerv·y ['nəːvi] F nervioso; *sl.* descarado.

nest [nest] 1. nido *m* (*a. fig.*); nidada f *of eggs or young birds*; nidal *m of hen*; 2. anidar; buscar nidos; **'nest egg** nidal *m*; *fig.* ahorros *m/pl.*; **nes·tle** ['nesl] abrigar(se); anidar(se); arrimar(se) (*up to a*).

net[1] [net] 1. red f (*a. fig.*); (*fabric*) tul *m*; redecilla f *for hair etc.*; 2. coger (con red); enredar.

net[2] [~] ✝ neto, líquido; ~ *income* renta f neta; ~ *price* precio *m* neto; ~ *weight* peso *m* neto.

net·tle ['netl] 1. ortiga f; 2. irritar, provocar.

net·work ['netwəːk] red f (*a. fig.*); malla f.

neu·ral·gia [njuəˈrældʒə] neuralgia f; **neu·ras·the·ni·a** [njuərəsˈθiːniə] neurastenia f; **neu·ri·tis** [njuəˈraitis] neuritis f; **neu·rol·o·gist** [~ˈrɔlədʒist] neurólogo *m*; **neu·rol·o·gy** [~ˈrɔlədʒi] neurología f; **neu·ron** ['niː-

rɔn] neurona f; **neu·ro·sis** [~ˈrousis] neurosis f; **neu·rot·ic** [~ˈrɔtik] □ neurótico *adj. a. su. m* (a f).

neu·ter ['njuːtə] neutro.

neu·tral ['njuːtrəl] 1. □ neutral; ⚥, ✝, 🜋 zo. neutro; 2. neutral *m/f*; *mot. in* ~ en punto muerto; **neu·tral·i·ty** [njuːˈtræliti] neutralidad f; **'neu·tral·ize** neutralizar.

neu·tron ['njuːtron] neutrón *m*.

nev·er ['nevə] nunca, jamás; de ningún modo; **'nev·er·more** nunca más; **nev·er·the·less** [ˌ~ðə'les] sin embargo, no obstante, con todo.

new [njuː] 1. *adj.* nuevo; (*fresh*) fresco; *bread* tierno; *p.* inexperto; F *what's ~?* ¿qué hay de nuevo?; 2 *Testament* Nuevo Testamento; 2 *Yorker* neoyorquino (a f) *m*; 2 *Zealander* neozelandés (-a f) *m*; 2. *adv.* recién; **'new·born** recién nacido; **'new·com·er** recién llegado (a f) *m*; **new·fan·gled** ['~fæŋgld] *contp.* recién inventado, moderno; **'newish** bastante nuevo; **'new·ly** nuevamente, recién; ~ *wed* recién casado; **'new·ness** novedad f; inexperiencia f.

news *mst sg.* noticia(s) f(*pl.*); nueva(s) f (*pl.*), novedad f; *radio:* noticiario *m*; **'~ a·gen·cy** agencia f de información; **'~ bul·le·tin** (boletín *m* de) noticias f/*pl.*, noticiario *m*; **'~cast** noticiario *m*; **'~cast·er** reportero *m* radiofónico; **'~ con·fer·ence** conferencia f de prensa; **'~let·ter** circular f noticiera; **'~pa·per** periódico *m*, diario *m*; *attr.* periodístico; **'~pa·per·man** periodista *m*; **'~print** papel *m* prensa; **'~reel** noticiario *m*, actualidades f/*pl.*; **'~stand** quiosco *m* de periódicos; **news·y** ['njuːzi] noticioso.

next [nekst] 1. *adj.* próximo, siguiente; *year etc.* que viene; inmediato; *house etc.* de al lado, vecino; ~ *time* la próxima vez; ~ *week* la semana que viene; 2. *adv.* luego, inmediatamente, después; ~ *to* junto a, al lado de.

nib·ble ['nibl] (*a. ~ at*) mordiscar; (*fish*) picar; roer, rozar.

nice [nais] □ ameno, agradable; bonito (*a. iro.*); bueno; *p.* simpático, amable; **'~-look·ing** F mono, guapo; **'nice·ness** amenidad f; lo simpático, simpatía f *etc.*; **nice·ty** ['~iti] exactitud f; sutileza f; refinamiento *m*.

niche [nitʃ] nicho *m*.

nick [nik] 1. mella *f*; muesca *f*; 2. mellar, hacer muescas en.

nick·el ['nikl] 1. níquel *m* (*a. moneda de 5 centavos*); 2. niquelar (*a.* '**~-plate**).

nick·name ['nikneim] 1. apodo *m*, sobrenombre *m*, mote *m*; 2. apodar.

nic·o·tine ['nikəti:n] nicotina *f*.

niece [ni:s] sobrina *f*.

nif·ty ['nifti] □ *sl.* elegante, pera.

nig·gard ['nigəd] tacaño; '**~·ly** tacaño, avariento.

night [nait] 1. noche *f*; *attr.* nocturno; at ~, by ~, in the ~ de noche, por la noche; good ~! ¡buenas noches!; last ~ anoche; '**~·cap** gorro *m*; F resopón *m*; '**~·club** cabaret *m*; '**~·fall** anochecer *m*; at ~ al anochecer; '**~·gown** camisa *f* de dormir, camisón *m*; **night·in·gale** ['naitiŋgeil] ruiseñor *m*; '**night·ly** de noche; (de) todas las noches; '**~·mare** pesadilla *f* (*a. fig.*); '**~ school** escuela *f* nocturna; '**~ shift** turno *m* de noche; '**~·spot** cabaret; '**~·time** noche *f*; '**~ watch(·man)** sereno *m*; guardia *m* de noche.

ni·hil·ism ['naiilizm] nihilismo *m*.

nim·ble ['nimbl] □ ágil, activo.

nine [nain] nueve (*a. su. m*); **nine·teen** ['~'ti:n] diecinueve; '**nine·teenth** [~θ] decimonoveno, decimonono; **nine·tieth** ['~tiiθ] nonagésimo; '**nine·ty** noventa.

ninth [nainθ] noveno, nono.

nip[1] [nip] 1. pellizco *m*, mordisco *m*; viento *m* frío; 2. pellizcar, mordiscar; helar; (*wind*) picar.

nip[2] [~] trago *m*, sorb(it)o *m*.

nip[3] [~] F correr; ~ off pirarse; ~ in the bud salvar en el principio.

nip·ple ['nipl] pezón *m*; tetilla *f* of male *or* bottle; ⊕ boquilla *f* roscada, manguito *m* de unión.

nip·py ['nipi] ágil, listo; helado.

nir·va·na [niə'va:nə] nirvana *m*.

nit [nit] liendre *f*.

ni·trate ['naitreit] nitrato *m*.

ni·tric ac·id ['naitrik'æsid] ácido *m* nítrico.

ni·tro·gen ['naitridʒən] nitrógeno *m*; **ni·tro·glyc·er·in** [naitrou'glisərin] nitroglicerina *f*.

nit·wit ['nitwit] *sl.* bobalicón *m*.

no [nou] 1. *adv.* no; 2. *adj.* ninguno; ~ one nadie, ninguno; with ~ sin; 3. *su.* no *m*; voto *m* negativo.

no·bil·i·ty [nou'biliti] nobleza *f*.

no·ble ['noubl] 1. □ noble; hidalgo, caballeroso; sublime; 2. (*a.* '**~·man**)

noble *m*; hidalgo *m*; '**no·ble·ness** nobleza *f*; hidalguía *f*.

no·bod·y ['noubədi] nadie, ninguno; *a* ~ un (don) nadie, un cualquiera.

noc·tur·nal [nɔk'tə:nl] nocturno.

nod [nɔd] 1. menear la cabeza de arriba abajo; cabecear; indicar con la cabeza; 2. cabezada *f*; inclinación *f* de la cabeza.

node [noud] protuberancia *f*; nudo *m*; ♂, *ast.*, *phys.* nodo *m*.

nod·ule ['nɔdju:l] nódulo *m*.

nog·gin ['nɔgin] vaso *m* pequeño; medida *f* de licor (= 1,42 decilitros); *sl.* cabeza *f*.

noise [nɔiz] 1. ruido *m*; clamor *m*; 2.: ~ about divulgar, publicar.

noise·less ['~lis] □ silencioso, sin ruido.

nois·i·ness ['nɔizinis] ruido *m*, estrépito *m*; lo ruidoso.

nois·y ['nɔizi] □ ruidoso, estrépitoso, clamoroso.

no·mad ['nɔməd] nómada *adj. a. su. m/f*; **no·mad·ic** [nou'mædik] □ nómada.

nom·i·nal ['nɔminl] □ nominal; **nom·i·nate** ['~neit] nombrar, proponer como candidato (*for* a); **nom·i·na·tive** ['~nətiv] nominativo *adj. a. su. m*; **nom·i·nee** [~'ni:] candidato *m* nombrado.

non [nɔn] *in compounds*: no, des..., in..., falta *f* de.

non·ac·cept·ance [nɔnæk'septəns] rechazo *m*; falta *f* de aceptación.

non·a·ge·nar·i·an [nounədʒi'neəriən] nonagenario (a *f*) *m*.

non·ag·gres·sion [nɔnə'greʃn]: no agresión *f*; ~ pact pacto *m* de no agresión.

non·al·co·hol·ic [nɔnælkə'hɔlik] no alcohólico.

non·a·ligned [nɔnə'laind] *country* no comprometido *to a major power.*

non·cha·lant [nɔnʃə'lɑ:nt] □ indiferente; descuidado.

non·com·bat·ant [nɔn'kɔmbətənt] no combatiente *adj. a. su. m/f*.

non·com·mis·sioned ['nɔnkə'miʃənd]: ~ officer ✗ sargento *m or* cabo *m*; suboficial *m* de marina.

non·com·mit·al ['nɔnkə'mitl] que no compromete; ambiguo, evasivo.

non·com·pli·ance ['nɔnkəm'plaiəns] falta *f* de cumplimiento, desobediencia *f* (*with* de).

non·con·form·ist ['nɔnkən'fɔ:mist]

disidente *adj. a. su. m/f*; **'non-con-form·i·ty** disidencia *f*.

non·de·script ['nɔndiskript] indefinido, inclasificable; *b.s.* mediocre.

none [nʌn] 1. *pron.* (*p.*) nadie; (*p.*, *th.*) ninguno; (*th.*) nada; 2. *adv.* no; de ninguna manera.

non·en·ti·ty [nɔ'nentiti] nulidad *f*.

non·ex·ist·ence [nɔnek'zistəns] inexistencia *f*.

non·fic·tion ['nɔn'fikʃn] literatura *f* no novelesca.

non·in·ter·ven·tion ['nɔnintə'venʃn] no intervención *f*.

non·par·ti·san ['nɔn'pɑ:tizn] imparcial.

non·plus ['nɔn'plʌs] dejar perplejo, confundir.

non·prof·it(-making) ['nɔn'prɔfit (meikiŋ)] sin fin *m* lucrativo.

non·res·i·dent ['nɔn'rezidənt] transeúnte *adj. a. su. m/f*.

non·sense ['nɔnsəns] disparate *m*, desatino *m*, tontería *f*; ~! ¡tonterías!; **non'sen·si·cal** desatinado.

non·shrink ['nɔn'ʃriŋk] inencogible.

non·skid ['nɔn'skid] antideslizante.

non·smok·er ['nɔn'smoukə] no fumador *m*.

non·stop ['nɔn'stɔp] 1. *adj.* 🚃 directo; ✈ sin escalas; continuo; 2. *adv.* sin parar.

non·un·ion [nɔn'ju:njən] no sindicalizado.

noo·dle ['nu:dl] F cabeza *f*; *cooking*: tallarín *m*; fideo *m*; ~ **soup** sopa *f* de pastas.

nook [nuk] rincón *m*, escondrijo *m*.

noon [nu:n] 1. mediodía *m*; 2. de mediodía, meridional.

noose [nu:s] lazo *m* (corredizo); (*hangman's*) dogal *m*.

nope [noup] F no.

nor [nɔ:] ni, no, tampoco; *neither ...* ~ *... ni ... ni ...*; ~ *I* ni yo tampoco.

Nor·dic ['nɔ:dik] nórdico.

norm [nɔ:m] norma *f*; modelo *m*; **'nor·mal** □ normal (*a.* Ⓐ); regular, corriente.

north [nɔ:θ] 1. norte *m*; 2. *adj.* del norte, septentrional; 3. *adv.* hacia el norte; **'~east** noreste *adj. a. su. m*; **north·er·ly** ['~ðəli] *direction* hacia el norte; *wind* del norte; **north·ern** ['~ðən] (del) norte, norteño, septentrional; **'north·ern·er** habitante *m/f* del norte; **'north·ward(s)** hacia el norte; **'~west** noroeste *adj.*

Nor·we·gian [nɔ:'wi:dʒən] noruego *adj. a. su. m* (*a.f*).

nose [nouz] 1. nariz *f*; narices *f/pl.* (F); hocico *m* *of animals*; (*sense of smell*) olfato *m*; *under the* (*very*) ~ *of* en las barbas de; 2. husmear, olfatear (*a.* ~ *out*); restregar la nariz contra; '~ **cone** cono *m* de proa *of a rocket*; '~ **dive** ✈ picado *m* vertical; (*involuntary*) caída *f* de bruces.

no·show ['nou'ʃou] F persona *f* que no se presenta cuando debe.

nos·y ['nouzi] F curioso.

nos·tal·gi·a [nɔs'tældʒiə] nostalgia *f*, añoranza *f*.

nos·tril ['nɔstril] (ventana *f* de la) nariz *f*.

not [nɔt] no; ~ *I* yo no; ~ *to say* por no decir; *why* ~? ¿cómo no?

no·ta·ble ['noutəbl] 1. □ notable, señalado; 2. notabilidad *f*; ~**s** *pl.* notables *m/pl.*

no·ta·ry ['noutəri] notario *m*.

no·ta·tion [nou'teiʃn] notación *f*.

notch [nɔtʃ] 1. muesca *f*, mella *f*; 2. mellar, cortar muescas en.

note [nout] 1. nota *f* (*a.* ♪); apunte *m*; marca *f*, señal *f*; (*letter*) esquela *f*, recado *m*; (*bank*) billete *m*; ✝ vale *m*; *of* ~ notable; 2. notar, observar, anotar, apuntar (*a.* ~ *down*); '~**book** cuaderno *m*, libro *m* de apuntes, libreta *f*; **'not·ed** conocido, célebre (*for* por); **'note·wor·thy** notable, digno de notarse.

noth·ing ['nʌθiŋ] 1. nada; Ⓐ cero *m*; friolera *f*, nadería *f*; *sweet* ~**s** *pl.* ternezas *f/pl.*; ~ *else* nada más; *think* ~ *of* tener en poco; tener por fácil; no hacer caso de; 2. *adv.* de ninguna manera, en nada; **'noth·ing·ness** nada *f*, inexistencia *f*.

no·tice ['noutis] 1. aviso *m*; (*poster etc.*) letrero *m*, anuncio *m*, cartel *m*; (*review*) reseña *f*, observación *f*, atención *f*; *take* ~ *of* observar, hacer caso de; *until further* ~ hasta nuevo aviso; 2. notar, observar; hacer caso de; advertir, fijarse en.

no·ti·fy ['noutifai] notificar, comunicar, intimar, avisar.

no·tion ['nouʃn] noción *f*, idea *f*; capricho *m*; ~**s** *pl.* mercería *f*.

no·to·ri·e·ty [noutə'raiəti] mala fama *f*; notoriedad *f*; **no·to·ri·ous** [nou-'tɔ:riəs] □ de mala fama; notorio; célebre (*for* por).

not·with·stand·ing [nɔtwiθ'stændiŋ] 1. *prp.* a pesar de; 2. *adv.* no obstante; **3.** *cj.* a pesar de que.

nought [nɔːt] Ⓐ cero *m*; nada.

noun [naun] nombre *m*, sustantivo *m*.

nour·ish ['nʌriʃ] nutrir, alimentar, sustentar; **'nour·ish·ing** nutritivo, alimenticio; **'nour·ish·ment** nutrimento *m*, alimento *m*.

nov·el ['nɔvl] **1.** nuevo, original, insólito; **2.** novela *f*; **'nov·el·ist** novelista *m/f*; **nov·el·ty** ['nɔvlti] novedad *f*; ✝ baratija *f*.

No·vem·ber [nou'vembə] noviembre *m*.

nov·ice ['nɔvis] principiante *m/f*.

now [nau] **1.** ahora; ya; *before* ∼ antes, ya; *from* ∼ *on(ward)* de aquí en adelante; *just* ∼ ahora mismo; hace poco; **2.** *cj.* ahora bien, pues; ∼ (*that*) ya que.

now·a·days ['nauədeiz] hoy en día.

no·way(s) ['nouwei(z)] Ⓕ de ninguna manera.

no·where ['nouwɛə] en (*or* a) ninguna parte.

nox·ious ['nɔkʃəs] ☐ nocivo, dañoso; pestífero.

nu·cle·ar ['njuːkliə] nuclear; ∼ *fission* fisión *f* nuclear, escisión *f* nuclear; ∼ *physics* física *f* nuclear; ∼*-powered* accionado por la energía nuclear; **nu·cle·us** ['∼kliəs] núcleo *m*.

nude [njuːd] desnudo *adj. a. su. m*.

nudge [nʌdʒ] **1.** codazo *m* (ligero); **2.** dar una codazo a.

nud·ism ['njuːdizm] desnudismo *m*; **'nud·ist** desnudez *f*.

nug·get ['nʌgit] pepita *f* (de oro).

nui·sance ['njuːsns] molestia *f*, fastidio *m*; plaga *f*; lata *f* (Ⓕ).

nuke [nuːk] *sl.* **1.** arma *f* atómica; **2.** atacar con arma atómica.

null [nʌl] nulo, inválido (*a.* ∼ *and void*); **'nul·li·fy** ['∼ifai] anular, invalidar; **'nul·li·ty** nulidad *f* (*a. p.*).

numb [nʌm] **1.** ☐ entumecido; insensible; **2.** entumecer; entorpecer.

num·ber ['nʌmbə] **1.** número *m*; (*figure*) cifra *f*; *a* ∼ *of* una porción

de, varios; **2.** numerar; contar; poner número a; (*total*) ascender a; **'num·ber·less** innumerable, sin número.

nu·mer·al ['njuːmərəl] **1.** numeral; **2.** número *m*, cifra *f*, guarismo *m*; **'nu·mer·a·tor** numerador *m*.

nu·mer·i·cal [njuːˈmerikl] ☐ numérico.

nu·mer·ous ['njuːmərəs] ☐ numeroso; muchos.

nu·mis·mat·ic [njuːmizˈmætik] ☐ numismático; **nu·mis·mat·ics** *mst sg.* numismática *f*.

num·skull ['nʌmskʌl] Ⓕ zote *m*.

nun [nʌn] monja *f*, religiosa *f*.

nup·tial ['nʌpʃəl] **1.** nupcial; **2.** ∼*s* ['∼lz] *pl.* nupcias *f/pl.*

nurs·er·y ['nɔːsri] cuarto *m* de los niños; ✹ criadero *m*, semillero *m*; ∼ *school* jardín *m* de la infancia; **'∼ rhyme** canción *f* infantil.

nurs·ing ['nɔːsin] crianza *f*; profesión *f* de enfermera; ∼ *home* casa *f* de inválidos.

nur·ture ['nɔːtʃə] **1.** nutrición *f*; crianza *f*; **2.** nutrir; alimentar.

nut [nʌt] nuez *f*; ⊕ tuerca *f*; *sl.* cabeza *f*; *sl.* excéntrico *m*; loco *m*; *sl. be* ∼*s on* estar loco por.

nut·crack·er ['nʌtkrækə] cascanueces *m*; **nut·meg** ['∼meg] nuez *f* moscada.

nu·tri·ent ['njuːtriənt] **1.** nutritivo; **2.** nutrimento *m*.

nu·tri·tion [njuːˈtriʃn] nutrición *f*; alimentación *f*; **nu·tri·tious, nu·tri·tive** ['∼tiv] ☐ nutritivo.

nut·shell ['nʌtʃel] cáscara *f* de nuez; **nut·ty** *sl.* loco.

nuz·zle ['nʌzl] hocicar; acariciar con el hocico.

ny·lon ['nailɔn] nylón *m*.

nymph [nimf] ninfa *f*.

O

o [ou] ¡oh!, ¡ay!; ∼ *that ...!* ¡ojalá (que) ...!

oaf [ouf] zoquete *m*, bobalicón *m*, patán *m*.

oak [ouk] **1.** roble *m*; **2.** de roble.

oa·kum ['oukəm] estopa *f*.

oar [ɔː] remo *m*; (*p.*) remero (a *f*) *m*; **oars·man** ['ɔːzmən] remero *m*.

o·a·sis [ou'eisis], *pl.* **o'a·ses** [∼siːz] oasis *m*.

occupation

oat [out] avena *f* (*mst* ~s *pl.*); rolled ~s copos *m/pl.* de avena.

oath [ouθ], **oaths** [ouðz] juramento *m*, jura *f*; *b.s.* blasfemia *f*, reniego *m*.

oat·meal ['outmi:l] harina *f* de avena.

ob·du·rate ['ɔbdərit] ☐ obstinado, terco; empedernido.

o·be·di·ence [ə'bi:djəns] obediencia *f*; **o·be·di·ent** ☐ obediente.

o·bei·sance [ou'beisns] reverencia *f*, acato *m*; homenaje *m*.

ob·e·lisk ['ɔbilisk] obelisco *m*.

o·bese [ou'bi:s] obeso.

o·bey [ə'bei] obedecer; *instructions* cumplir, observar.

o·bit·u·ar·y [ə'bitjuəri] necrología *f*; *eccl.* obituario *m*.

ob·ject 1. ['ɔbdʒikt] objeto *m*; (*thing*) cosa *f*, artículo *m*; *gr.* complemento *m*; **2.** [əb'dʒekt] *v/t.* objetar; *v/i.* poner reparos, hacer objeciones, oponerse (*to* a).

ob·jec·tion [əb'dʒekʃn] objeción *f*, reparo *m*; dificultad *f*, inconveniente *m*; **ob'jec·tion·a·ble** ☐ molesto, desagradable; ofensivo.

ob·jec·tive [əb'dʒektiv] ☐ objetivo *adj.* a. *su. m*; **ob·jec'tiv·i·ty** objetividad *f*.

ob·ject...: '~ **lens** objetivo *m*; '~ **les·son** lección *f* práctica, ejemplo *m*.

ob·li·ga·tion [ɔbli'geiʃn] obligación *f*; deber *m*; compromiso *m*; **ob·lig·a·to·ry** ['~gətəri] obligatorio.

o·blige [ə'blaidʒ] obligar, forzar (*to* a); complacer, hacer un favor a; *much* ~d muy agradecido (*for* por); **o'blig·ing** ☐ atento, servicial, complaciente.

ob·lique [ə'bli:k] ☐ oblicuo; indirecto, evasivo.

ob·lit·er·ate [ə'blitəreit] borrar; destruir, aniquilar; *✍* obliterar; **ob·lit·er'a·tion** borradura *f*; destrucción *f*; aniquilación *f*.

ob·liv·i·on [ə'bliviən] olvido *m*; **ob·liv·i·ous** ☐ olvidado, inconsciente (*of*, *to* de).

ob·long ['ɔblɔŋ] **1.** oblongo, rectangular, cuadrilongo; **2.** rectángulo *m*.

ob·nox·ious [əb'nɔkʃəs] ☐ detestable, ofensivo, odioso.

o·boe ['oubou] oboe *m*.

ob·scene [ɔb'si:n] ☐ obsceno, indecente; **ob'scen·i·ty** [~iti] obscenidad *f*.

ob·scure [əb'skjuə] **1.** ☐ oscuro (*a. fig.*); **2.** oscurecer; eclipsar; esconder; **ob'scu·ri·ty** oscuridad *f* (*a. fig.*).

ob·se·qui·ous [əb'si:kwiəs] ☐ servil; obsequioso; **ob'se·qui·ous·ness** servilismo *m*; obsequiosidad *f*.

ob·serv·a·ble [əb'zɔ:vəbl] ☐ observable; **ob'serv·ance** observancia *f*; práctica *f*, costumbre *f*; **ob'serv·ant** ☐ observador; atento; perspicaz; vigilante; **ob·ser·va·tion** [ɔbzɔ:'veiʃn] observación *f*, experiencia *f*; **ob·serv·a·to·ry** [əb'zɔ:vətəri] observatorio *m*; **ob'serve** observar; decir; *festival, silence* guardar; *p.* vigilar.

ob·sess [əb'ses] obsesionar; **ob·ses·sion** [əb'seʃn] obsesión *f*.

ob·so·lete ['ɔbsəlit] anticuado, desusado; *biol.* rudimentario.

ob·sta·cle ['ɔbstəkl] obstáculo *m*; impedimento *m*; inconveniente *m*.

ob·ste·tri·cian [ɔbste'triʃn] obstétrico *m*; **ob'stet·rics** [~riks] obstetricia *f*.

ob·sti·na·cy ['ɔbstinəsi] obstinación *f* *etc.*; **ob·sti·nate** ['~nit] ☐ obstinado, terco, porfiado; pertinaz.

ob·struct [əb'strʌkt] *v/t.* obstruir; *action* estorbar; *pipe etc.* atorar; *v/i.* estorbar; **ob'struc·tion** obstrucción *f* (*a. parl.*); estorbo *m*; **ob'struc·tion·ist** obstruccionista *m/f*.

ob·tain [əb'tein] *v/t.* obtener; adquirir; lograr, conseguir; *v/i.* existir, prevalecer.

ob·trude [əb'tru:d] *opinions* imponer (*on* a), introducir a la fuerza; **ob'tru·sive** [~siv] ☐ entrometido, intruso.

ob·tuse [əb'tju:s] ☐ obtuso (*a. ⅋, fig.*); *p.* estúpido, duro de mollera); **ob'tuse·ness** embotadura *f*; *fig.* estupidez *f*.

ob·vi·ate ['ɔbvieit] obviar, evitar, eliminar.

ob·vi·ous ['ɔbviəs] ☐ evidente, obvio, patente; transparente.

oc·ca·sion [ə'keiʒn] **1.** ocasión *f*; vez *f*; coyuntura *f*, sazón *f*; motivo *m*; *on* ~ de vez en cuando; **2.** ocasionar; **oc'ca·sion·al** ☐ poco frecuente; uno que otro.

oc·ci·dent ['ɔksidənt] *lit.* occidente *m*; **oc·ci·den·tal** [~'dentl] ☐ occidental.

oc·cult [ɔ'kʌlt] ☐ oculto, secreto; misterioso; sobrenatural; **oc·cul·ta·tion** [~'eiʃn] *ast.* ocultación *f*; **oc·cult·ism** ['ɔkəltizm] ocultismo *m*.

oc·cu·pan·cy ['ɔkjupənsi] ocupancia *f*, tenencia *f*; **'oc·cu·pant** ocupante *m/f*; (*tenant*) inquilino (a *f*) *m*; **oc·cu·pa·tion** ocupación *f* (*a. ✗*); tenencia f, inquilinato m; **oc·cu'pa-tion·al** de oficio, profesional; ~ *haz-ard* riesgo m ocupacional; ~ *therapy* terapia f vocacional; **oc·cu·py** ['~pai] ocupar; *house* habitar; *time* emplear, pasar.

oc·cur [ə'kə:] (*happen*) ocurrir, suceder, acontecer; (*be found*) encontrarse; **oc'cur·rence** [ə'kʌrəns] acontecimiento m, ocurrencia f; *caso* m, aparición f.

o·cean ['oun] océano m; *fig.* ~s of la mar de; **'~-go·ing** transoceánico.

o'clock [ə'klɔk] = *of the clock*; *it is 1* ~ es la una; *it is 5* ~ son las cinco; *at 2* ~ a las dos.

oc·ta·gon ['ɔktəgən] octágono m.

oc·tane ['ɔktein] octano m.

oc·tave ['ɔktiv] octava f; **oc·ta·vo** [~'teivou] (libro m) en octavo.

Oc·to·ber [ɔk'toubə] octubre m.

oc·to·ge·nar·i·an ['ɔktoudʒi'nɛəriən] octogenario adj. a. su. m (a f).

oc·to·pus ['ɔktəpəs] pulpo m.

oc·u·list ['ɔkjulist] oculista m/f.

odd [ɔd] *number* impar; desigual; (*isolated*) suelto, desparejado; (*extra*) sobrante; (*queer*) raro, extraño, estrambótico; (*occasional*) tal cual; **'odd·ball** excéntrico; disidente adj. a. su. m/f; **'odd·i·ty** rareza f, excentricidad f; ente m singular; cosa f rara; **'odd 'job(s)** empleo m al azar; pequeña(s) tarea(s) f (pl.); **odds** [ɔdz] *mst pl.* (*advantage*) ventaje f, superioridad f; (*chances*) probabilidades f/pl.; *betting*: puntos m/pl. de ventaja; ~ *and ends* retazos m/pl.

ode [oud] oda f.

o·di·ous ['oudjəs] □ odioso, detestable, infame; **o·di·um** ['oudiəm] oprobio m; odio m.

o·dor·if·er·ous [oudə'rifərəs] □ odorífero; **'o·dor·ous** oloroso.

o·dor ['oudə] olor m; fragancia f; *fig.* sospecha f; *fig.* estimación f; **'o·dor·less** inodoro.

o'er [ouə] = *over*.

of [ɔv, *unstressed* əv, v] de; *I was robbed* ~ *my money* me robaron el dinero; *how kind* ~ *you to* inf. qué amable ha sido Vd. en *inf.*; *a friend* ~ *mine* un amigo mío; *I dream* ~ *you* sueño contigo; *I think* ~ *you* pienso en ti.

off [ɔf] **1.** *adv.* lejos, a distancia; fuera; *mst in combination with vb.*: *be* ~ *go* ~ marcharse *etc.*; *3 miles* ~ a 3 millas (de distancia); *the exam is 3 days* ~ faltan 3 días para el examen; *far* ~, (*a long*) *way* ~ muy lejos; *hands* ~! ¡fuera las manos!; *be well* ~ estar acomodado; *there is nothing* ~ ~ ✝ no hay descuento; **2.** *prp.* lejos de; fuera de; separado de; de, desde; **3.** *adj.* separado; terminado; quitado; ✝ desconectado; ⊕ parado; *water etc.* cortado; *brake* desapretado; *light* apagado; *tap* cerrado; *day* ~ día m libre; ~ *season* estación f muerta.

off·beat ['ɔf'bi:t] *sl.* insólito; original.

off-col·or ['ɔf'kʌlə] detenido; F arriesgado; de mal gusto.

off-du·ty hours ['ɔf'dju:ti'auəz] horas f/pl. libres (de servicio).

of·fend [ə'fend] ofender; *be* ~ed *tomarlo a mal;* **of'fend·er** delincuente m/f; culpable m/f; ofensor (-a f) m.

of·fense [ə'fens] ofensa f; ✝ ✝ violación f de la ley; delito m; ✗ ofensiva f; **of·fen·sive** [ə'fensiv] **1.** □ ofensivo, injurioso; repugnante; agresivo; ✗ ofensiva f; **of·fen·sive·ness** repugnancia f; insolencia f.

of·fer ['ɔfə] **1.** oferta f (a. ✝), ofrecimiento m; **2.** ofrecer (a. ~ *up*); *prospect etc.* deparar, brindar; **'of·fer·ing** ofrecimiento m.

of·fer·to·ry ['ɔfətəri] ofertorio m.

off-hand ['ɔf'hænd] **1.** *adj.* informal, brusco; despreocupado; **2.** *adv.* de improviso, sin pensarlo.

of·fice ['ɔfis] oficina f; (*room*) despacho m, escritorio m; (*lawyer's*) bufete m; (*function*) oficio m (a. *eccl.*); ~ *boy* mandadero m; ~ *force* gente f de la oficina; ~ *hours* horas de oficina or de negocio; ~ *seeker* aspirante m; ~ *worker* oficinista m/f.

of·fi·cer ['ɔfisə] **1.** oficial m (a. ✗); funcionario m; dignatario m; (*agente* m *de*) policía m; **2.** mandar.

of·fi·cial [ə'fiʃl] **1.** □ oficial; formal; autorizado; ☞ oficial; **2.** oficial m (público), funcionario m.

of·fi·cious [ə'fiʃəs] entrometido.

off...: '~**-'peak** (*horas, estación, etc.*) de valle; de menor tránsito; '~**-'print** separata f, tirada f aparte; '~**-'set 1.** compensación f; △ retallo m; *typ.* offset m; **2.** compensar; '~**-'shoot** vástago m; *fig.* ramal m; '~**-'shore** costanero; costeño; '~**-'side** *sport:* fuera de juego, offside; '~**-'spring** vástago m; prole f; '~**-'stage** (de) entre bastidores; '~**-the-'record** confidencial.

of·ten ['ɔfn, 'ɔftən] a menudo, muchas veces, con frecuencia; *as* ~ *as* siempre que, tantas veces como.

o·gre ['ougə] ogro *m*.

oh [ou] ¡oh!, ¡ay!

ohm [oum] ohmio *m*.

oil [ɔil] **1.** *mst* aceite *m*; *geol. etc.* petróleo *m*; *paint.*, *eccl.* óleo *m*; **2.** lubri(fi)car, engrasar; aceitar; '**~·can** aceitera *f*; '**~ cloth** hule *m*; F linóleo *m*; '**~ field** campo *m* petrolífero; '**~·glut** exceso *m* de petróleo; '**~ paint·ing** pintura *f* al óleo; '**~ tank·er** ⚓ (buque) petrolero *m*; tanquero *m* S.Am.; '**~ well** pozo *m* de petróleo; '**oil·y** □ aceitoso.

oint·ment ['ɔintmənt] ungüento *m*.

O.K., o·kay ['ou'kei] **1.** ¡está bien!; **2.** aprobar; **3.** aprobado; satisfactorio; **4.** visto *m* bueno.

old [ould] viejo; anciano (*p. only*); (*long-standing, former*) antiguo; wine añejo; grow ~ envejecer(se); how ~ is he? ¿cuántos años tiene?, ¿qué edad tiene?; he is 6 years ~ tiene 6 años (de edad); ♀ Glory bandera de los EE.UU.; ♀ Testament Antiguo Testamento *m*; '**old·en** † *or poet.* antiguo; '**old·'fash·ioned** anticuado, pasado de moda.

ol·fac·to·ry [ɔl'fæktəri] olfativo, olfatorio.

ol·i·garch·y ['ɔligɑːki] oligarquía *f*.

ol·ive ['ɔliv] **1.** aceituna *f*, oliva *f*; ~ oil aceite *m* (de oliva); **2.** aceitunado; '**~ grove** olivar *m*.

O·lym·pi·an [ou'limpiən] olímpico; **O'lym·pic Games** *pl.* Juegos *m/pl.* Olímpicos.

om·e·let, om·e·lette ['ɔmlit] tortilla *f*.

o·men ['oumen] agüero *m*, presagio *m*.

om·i·nous ['ɔminəs] □ ominoso.

o·mis·sion [ou'miʃn] omisión *f*.

o·mit [ou'mit] omitir; olvidar.

om·nip·o·tent [ɔm'nipətənt] □ omnipotente.

om·ni·pres·ence ['ɔmni'prezns] omnipresencia *f*.

om·ni·science [ɔm'nisiəns] omnisciencia *f*; **om'nis·cient** □ omnisciente, omniscio.

on [ɔn] **1.** *prp.* en, sobre, encima de; (*concerning*) sobre, (acerca de); ~ arriving al llegar; ~ Sunday el domingo; ~ Sundays los domingos; ~ his arrival a su llegada; ~ holiday de vacaciones; get a train subir a un tren; F have you any change ~ you? ¿tienes cambio encima?; F this is ~ me esto corre por mi cuenta; **2.** *adv.*

(hacia) adelante; encima; *vb.* ~ seguir ger.; ~ read ~ seguir leyendo; farther ~ más allá, más adelante; **3.** *adj. clothes* puesto; *light* encendido; ⚡ conectado; ⊕ (puesto) en marcha; *brake* apretado; *tap* abierto.

once [wʌns] **1.** *adv.* una vez; (*formerly*) antes, antiguamente; at ~ en seguida, inmediatamente; (*in one go*) de una vez; all at ~ (*suddenly*) de repente; ~ in a while de tarde en tarde, de vez en cuando; ~ more otra vez; ~ upon a time there was érase que se era, había una vez; **2.** *su.* (una) vez *f*; this ~ esta vez; **3.** *cj.* una vez que.

once·o·ver ['wʌnsouvə] *sl.* vistazo *m*, examen *m* (rápido).

on·col·o·gy [ɔn'kɔlədʒi] oncología *f*.

on·com·ing ['ɔnkʌmiŋ] inminente; pendiente.

one [wʌn] **1.** un(o); solo, único; un tal; igual; **2.** uno (a *f*) *m*; alguno (a *f*) *m*; (*hour*) la una; (*indefinite*) se, uno; the little ~s los pequeños, los chiquillos, la gente menuda; ~ and all todos; ~ another se, uno(s) a otro(s); this ~ éste (a *f*) *m*; '**~·eyed** tuerto; '**~·hand·ed** manco; '**~·piece** enterizo, de una pieza.

on·er·ous ['ɔnərəs] □ oneroso.

one...: ~·'self (*subject*) uno mismo, una misma; (*acc., dat.*) se; (*after prp.*) sí (mismo), sí (misma); '**~·'sid·ed** □ unilateral; desequilibrado; parcial; '**~·way:** ~ street calle *f* de dirección única; ~ traffic dirección *f* obligatoria.

on·ion ['ʌnjən] cebolla *f*.

on·look·er ['ɔnlukə] mirón (-a *f*) *m*, espectador (-a *f*) *m*.

on·ly ['ounli] **1.** *adj.* solo, único; **2.** *adv.* (tan) sólo, solamente; únicamente; if ~...! ¡ojalá...!; **3.** *cj.* ~ (*that*) sólo que, pero.

on·rush ['ɔnrʌʃ] arremetida *f*.

on·set ['ɔnset] ataque *m*; acceso *m*, comienzo *m* (*a.* ⚔).

on·slaught ['ɔnslɔːt] embestida *f* furiosa.

on·ward ['ɔnwəd] **1.** *adj.* progresivo; hacia adelante; **2.** *adv.* (hacia) adelante (*a.* **on·wards** ['~z]).

oo·dles ['uːdlz] F: ~ of la mar de.

oomph [uːmf] *sl.* vigor *m*; atracción *f* sexual.

ooze [uːz] **1.** lama *f*, cieno *m*; **2.** rezumarse (*a.* ~ out), exudar.

o·pal ['oupəl] ópalo *m*.

o·paque [ou'peik] □ opaco.

o·pen ['oupən] **1.** ☐ abierto; (*uncovered*) descubierto, destapado; (*unfolded*) desplegado, extendido; *event etc.* público; libre; *p.* franco; *mind* receptivo, sin prejuicios; ~ *question* cuestión *f* pendiente (*or* sin resolver); ~ *secret* secreto *m* a voces; **2.:** *in the* ~ al aire libre; en el campo; al descubierto; *bring into the* ~ hacer público; **3.** *v/t.* abrir; (*uncover*) descubrir, destapar; *v/i.* abrir(se) (*a.* ~ *out*); comenzar; extenderse; (*play*) estrenarse; ~ *on* (*to*) dar a, mirar a; '~·**end·ed** sin límite *m*; sin término *m* fijo; '~·**hand·ed** ☐ liberal, dadivoso; '**o·pen·ing 1.** abertura *f*; brecha *f in wall*; claro *m in woods*; **2.** de apertura; inaugural; '**o·pen·'mind·ed** ☐ receptivo; imparcial; '**o·pen·'mouthed** boquiabierto; **o·pen·ness** ['oupnis] espaciosidad *f*; *fig.* franqueza *f*.

op·er·a ['ɔpərə] ópera *f*; '~ **glass(·es** *pl.*) gemelos *m/pl.* de teatro; '~ **house** teatro *m* de la ópera; '~ **sing·er** cantante *m/f* de la ópera.

op·er·ate ['ɔpəreit] *v/t.* hacer funcionar; actuar; impulsar; manejar, dirigir; *v/i.* funcionar; ✝, ⚔, ✕ operar; **op·er·at·ing** ['ɔpəreitiŋ] operante; ~ *expenses pl.* gastos *m/pl.* de explotación; **op·er·a·tion** operación *f* (*a.* ✿, ✝, ✕); funcionamiento *m*; explotación *f*, manejo *m*; procedimiento *m*; **op·er·a·tor** ['~reitə] ⊕ maquinista *m/f*; ✿, *film:* operador (-a *f*) *m*; ✝ agente *m*, corredor *m* de bolsa; *teleph.* telefonista *m/f*.

op·er·et·ta [ɔpə'retə] opereta *f*; *Spain:* zarzuela *f*.

oph·thal·mol·o·gist [ɔfθæl'mɔlə-dʒist] oftalmólogo *m*.

o·pi·ate ['oupiit] **1.** opiata *f*, narcótico *m*; **2.** opiato.

o·pine [ou'pain] opinar; **o·pin·ion** [ə'pinjən] opinión *f*, parecer *m*, juicio *m*, concepto *m*; *public* ~ opinión *f* pública; *be of (the)* ~ opinar; **o'pin·ion·at·ed** [~eitid] porfiado, pertinaz; dogmático.

o·pi·um ['oupjəm] opio *m*; ~ *den* fumadero *m* de opio; ~ *poppy* ♀ adormidera *f*.

op·po·nent [ə'pounənt] adversario (a *f*) *m*, contrincante *m*.

op·por·tune ['ɔpətjuːn] ☐ oportuno, tempestivo; '**op·por·tun·ism** oportunismo *m*; '**op·por'tu·ni·ty** oportunidad *f*, ocasión *f*.

op·pose [ə'pouz] oponerse a; resistir, combatir; (*set against*) oponer; **op'posed** opuesto; *be* ~ *to* oponerse a; **op'pos·ing** opuesto, contrario; **op·po·site** ['ɔpəzit] **1.** ☐ opuesto, contrario; de enfrente; **2.** *prp.* (*a.* ~ *to*) enfrente de, frente a; **3.** *adv.* enfrente; **op·po'si·tion** oposición *f*; resistencia *f*; ✝ competencia *f*.

op·press [ə'pres] oprimir; agobiar.

opt [ɔpt] optar (*for* por).

op·tic ['ɔptik], **op·ti·cal** ☐ óptico; **op·ti·cian** [ɔp'tiʃn] óptico *m*; '**op·tics** *sg.* óptica *f*.

op·ti·mism ['ɔptimizm] optimismo *m*; '**op·ti·mist** optimista *m/f*; **op·ti'mis·tic** ☐ optimista; '**op·ti·mize** mejorar todo lo posible.

op·tion ['ɔpʃn] opción *f* (*on* a); '**op·tion·al** ☐ opcional, discrecional.

op·u·lence ['ɔpjuləns] opulencia *f*; '**op·u·lent** ☐ opulento.

o·pus ['oupəs] ♪ obra *f*; opus *m*.

or [ɔː] o; (*before* o-, ho-) u; *after negative* ni; *either* ... ~ ... o ... o ...

or·a·cle ['ɔrəkl] oráculo *m*.

o·ral ['ɔːrəl] oral; *anat.* bucal.

or·ange ['ɔrindʒ] **1.** naranja *f*; **2.** (a)naranjado; **or·ange·ade** ['~'eid] naranjada *f*.

o·rate [ɔː'reit] *co.* perorar; **o'ra·tion** oración *f*, discurso *m*; **or·a·to·ri·o** [~'tɔːriou] ♪ oratorio *m*; **or·a·to·ry** ['ɔrətəri] oratoria *f*; *eccl.* oratorio *m*.

orb [ɔːb] orbe *m*, globo *m*; **or·bit 1.** órbita *f* (*a. fig.*); *go into* ~ entrar en órbita; **2.** girar (alrededor de).

or·chard ['ɔːtʃəd] huerto *m*, huerta *f* (de árboles frutales).

or·ches·tra ['ɔːkistrə] orquesta *f*.

or·chid ['ɔːkid] orquídea *f*.

or·dain [ɔː'dein] ordenar (*a. eccl.*); decretar; disponer.

or·deal [ɔː'diːl] prueba *f* rigurosa, experiencia *f* penosa.

or·der ['ɔːdə] **1.** orden *m*; (*command, society*) orden *f*; ✝ pedido *m for goods*; ✝ libranza *f for money*; ~ ✝ hoja *f* de pedidos; *in* ~ *that* para que; *in* ~ *to* para; *of the* ~ *of* del orden de; *on the* ~*s of* por orden de; *out of* ~ desarreglado, descompuesto; ⊕ que no funciona; *keep* ~ mantener el orden; *put in* ~ poner en orden, arreglar; *take* (*holy*) ~*s* ordenarse; **2.** ordenar; mandar; (*arrange*) disponer; *goods* encargar, pedir; '**or·der·ly 1.** ordenado, metódico; regular;

tranquilo; obediente; **2.** ⚔ ordenanza *m*; ⚔ enfermero *m*.

or·di·nance ['ɔːdinəns] ordenanza *f*, decreto *m*.

or·di·nar·y ['ɔːdnri] □ común, corriente, normal; ordinario (*a. b.s.*).

or·di·na·tion ['ɔːdi'neiʃn] ordenación *f*.

ord·nance ['ɔːdnəns] artillería *f*; pertrechos *m/pl.* de guerra (*a. ~ stores*).

ore [ɔː] mineral *m*, mena *f*.

or·gan ['ɔːgən] *all senses:* órgano *m*; '**~grind·er** organillero (*a f*) *m*; **or·gan·ism** ['ɔːgənizm] organismo *m*; '**or·gan·ist** organista *m/f*; **or·gan·i·za·tion** [ˌ~nai'zeiʃn] organización *f*, organismo *m*; '**or·gan·ize** organizar(se); *sl.* agenciar.

or·gasm ['ɔːgæzm] orgasmo *m*.

or·gy ['ɔːdʒi] orgía *f*.

o·ri·ent ['ɔːriənt] **1.** ♀ Oriente *m*; oriente *m* (*of pearl*); **2.** ['~ent] orientar; **o·ri·en·ta·tion** orientación *f*.

or·i·gin ['ɔridʒin] origen *m*.

o·rig·i·nal [ə'ridʒənl] **1.** □ original, primitivo, primordial; *b.s.* *sin pecado m* original; **2.** original *m* (*a. p.*); prototipo *m*; **o·rig·i·nal·i·ty** [ˌ~'næliti] originalidad *f*.

o·rig·i·nate [ə'ridʒineit] originar(se); ~ *from*, ~ *in* a *th.* traer su origen de; **o·rig·i·na·tive** creador; inventivo; **o·rig·i·na·tor** creador (-a *f*) *m*, inventor (-a *f*) *m*.

o·ri·ole ['ɔːrioul] oropéndola *f*.

or·na·ment 1. ['ɔːnəmənt] adorno *m*, ornato *m*; ornamento *m* (*a. fig.*); **2.** ['~ment] adornar, ornamentar; **or·na·men·tal** □ ornamental.

or·nate [ɔː'neit] □ muy ornado; *language* florido.

or·ni·tho·log·i·cal [ɔːniθə'lɔdʒikl] □ ornitológico; **or·ni·thol·o·gist** [ˌ~'θɔlədʒist] ornitólogo *m*; **or·ni·thol·o·gy** ornitología *f*.

or·phan ['ɔːfən] huérfano *adj. a. su. m* (a *f*) (*adj. a. ~ed*); **or·phan·age** ['~idʒ] orfanato *m*.

or·tho·dox ['ɔːθədɔks] ortodoxo.

or·thog·ra·phy [ɔː'θɔgrəfi] ortografía *f*.

or·tho·pe·dic [ɔːθou'piːdik] ortopédico; **or·tho·pe·dics** *sg.* ortopedia *f*; **or·tho·pe·dist** ortopedista *m/f*.

os·cil·late ['ɔsileit] *mst co.* oscilar; **os·cil·la·to·ry** [ˌ~təri] oscilatorio; **os·cil·lo·graph** ['ˌ~græf] ⚡ oscilógrafo *m*.

os·cu·late ['ɔskjuleit] *mst co.* besar (-se).

os·si·fy ['ɔsifai] osificar(se); **os·su·ar·y** ['ɔsjuəri] osario *m*.

os·ten·si·ble [ɔs'tensəbl] □ supuesto, pretendido, aparente.

os·ten·ta·tion [ɔsten'teiʃn] ostentación *f*; aparato *m*, boato *m*; **os·ten·ta·tious** □ ostentoso, aparatoso.

os·te·o·path ['ɔstiəpæθ] osteópata *m/f*; **os·te·op·a·thy** [ɔsti'ɔpəθi] osteopatía *f*.

os·tra·cism ['ɔstrəsizm] ostracismo *m*; **os·tra·cize** ['ˌ~saiz] condenar al ostracismo, excluir de la sociedad.

os·trich ['ɔstritʃ] avestruz *m*.

oth·er ['ʌðə] **1.** otro (*than que*); *the ~ day* el otro día; *some ~ day* otro día; *the ~ (one)* el otro; **2.** *adv.:* ~ *than* de otra manera que; otra cosa que; '**~wise** de otra manera; si no; (*in other respects*) por lo demás.

ot·ter ['ɔtə] nutria *f*.

ought [ɔːt] **1.** = *aught* algo; **2.** *v/aux. mst* deber; *I ~ to do it* debo (debiera *or* debería) hacerlo; *I ~ to have done it* debiera haberlo hecho; *one ~ to drink water* conviene beber agua.

ounce [auns] onza *f* (= 28,35 *gr.*).

our ['auə] nuestro(s), nuestra(s); **ours** ['auəz] (el) nuestro, (la) nuestra *etc.*; **our'selves** (*subject*) nosotros mismos, nosotras mismas; (*acc., dat.*) nos; (*after prp.*) nosotros (mismos), nosotras (mismas).

oust [aust] desposeer; expulsar.

out [aut] **1.** *adv.* afuera, fuera, hacia fuera; *a. in combination with vb.: come ~, go ~* salir; *run ~* salir corriendo; *be ~* haber salido; estar fuera (de casa); (*fire*) estar apagado; *Mr Jones is ~* no está el señor Jones; *be ~ for* buscar; ambicionar; *be ~ to inf.* esforzarse por *inf.*; proponerse *inf.*; **2.** *prp.* ~ *of* fuera de; de; entre; de entre; por; sin; **3.** *int.* ~ *with him!* ¡fuera con él!; F ~ *with it!* ¡habla sin rodeos!

out...: [ˌ~] '**~and-...** perfecto, rematado; *b.s.* redomado; '**~board** (*motor* motor *m*) fuera de borda; '**~break** erupción *f*; estallido *m*; rompimiento *m of war*; brote *m of disease*; '**~burst** explosión *f*, arranque *m*, acceso *m*; '**~cast** paria *m/f*, proscrito (a *f*) *m*; '**~class** ser muy superior a, aventajar con mucho; '**~come** resultado *m*, consecuencia *f*; '**~cry** grito *m*, clamoreo *m*; protesta *f* (ruidosa); **~'dat·ed** fuera de moda, anticuado; '**~do** [*irr.*(*do*)] exceder, sobrepujar; *he was not to be outdone* no se quedó en menos; '**.door** adj. al aire libre; externo; '**.doors 1.** adv. fuera de casa, al aire libre; **2.** su. aire m libre; campo m raso.

out·er ['autə] exterior, externo; ~ space espacio m exterior.

out...: '**.fit** equipo m; (suit) traje m; (tools) juego m de herramientas; F×, cuerpo m; F organización f; '**.flow** efusión f, derrame m, desagüe m; '**.go** gasto m; '**.go·ing** saliente; p. sociable; **.grow** [irr. (grow)] crecer más que; '**.growth** excrecencia f, fig. consecuencia f.

out·ing ['autiŋ] excursión f, paseo m.

out...: **.land·ish** estrafalario; ~ '**last** durar más que; sobrevivir a; '**.law 1.** proscrito m, forajido m; **2.** proscribir; declarar fuera de la ley; '**.lay** desembolso m; '**.let** salida f (a. fig., ✝); ⚡ toma f de corriente; '**.line 1.** contorno m, perfil m; trazado m; bosquejo m; **2.** perfilar, trazar; bosquejar (a. fig.); policy prefigurar; '**.live** sobrevivir a; durar más que; '**.look** perspectiva(s) f(pl.) (a. fig.); punto m de vista; actitud f; '**.ly·ing** remoto; exterior, de las afueras; ~ '**mod·ed** anticuado, fuera de moda; '**.num·ber** exceder en número; '**.of-the-way** apartado; poco concurrido; '**.pa·tient** paciente m/f externo (a) (del hospital); '**.post** avanzada f, puesto m avanzado; '**.pour·ing** chorro m; efusión f (a. fig.); '**.put** producción f; ⊕ rendimiento m.

out·rage ['autreidʒ] **1.** atrocidad f; ultraje m, atropello m; **2.** ultrajar; violentar; **out·ra·geous** □ ultrajoso.

out...: '**.right 1.** ['autrait] adj. completo, cabal, franco; **2.** [aut'rait] adv. de una vez, de un golpe; enteramente; '**.run** [irr. (run)] correr más que; fig. exceder; '**.set** principio m, comienzo m; '**.shine** [irr. (shine)] brillar más que; fig. eclipsar; '**.side 1.** exterior m; superficie f; apariencia f; **2.** adj. exterior, externo; superficial; ajeno; **3.** adv. (a)fuera; **4.** prp. fuera de; más allá de; '**.sid·er** forastero (a f) m; intruso (a f) m; desplazado (a f) m; '**.skirts** pl. afueras f/pl., alrededores m/pl.; '**.spok·en** □ franco, abierto; '**.stand·ing** destacado, descollante; sobresaliente; ✝ pendiente, sin pagar; '**.stretched** extendido, '**.strip** dejar atrás, aventajar.

out·ward ['autwəd] **1.** □ exterior,

externo; aparente; **2.** adv. (mst **out·wards** ['ˌz]) hacia fuera.

out...: '**.weigh** pesar más que; valer más que; ~ '**wit** ser más listo que; burlar.

o·val ['ouvl] **1.** oval(ado); **2.** óvalo m.

o·va·ry ['ouvəri] ovario m.

ov·en ['ʌvn] horno m, cocina f.

o·ver ['ouvə] **1.** adv. (por) encima; al otro lado; de un lado a otro; al revés; patas arriba; otra vez; de añadidura; all ~ por todas partes; **2.** prp. sobre, (por) encima de; al otro lado de; por, a través de; más allá de; number más de; (concerning) acerca de; por causa de; **3.** adicional, excesivo; acabado, concluido; it's ~ se acabó.

o·ver...: '**.bear·ing** □ despótico, dominante; '**.board** ♫ al mar, al agua; man ~! ¡hombre al agua!; '**.charge** sobrecargar; ✝ cobrar un precio excesivo (a); '**.coat** abrigo m, sobretodo m, gabán m; '**.come** [irr. (come)] vencer; superar; (sleep etc.) rendir; '**.crowd·ing** sobrepoblación f, congestionamiento m; ~ '**do** [irr. (do)] exagerar; llevar a exceso, excederse en; food recocer, requemar; ~ it F trabajar demasiado, fatigarse; '**.done** [ouvə'dʌn] exagerado; ['ouvə'dʌn] food muy hecho, requemado, pasado; '**.dose** dosis f excesiva; '**.drive** mot. superdirecta f; '**.due** atrasado; ✝ vencido y no pagado; '**.eat** [irr. (eat)] comer con exceso, atracarse; '**.ex'pose** phot. sobreexponer; '**.ex'po·sure** phot. sobreexposición f; '**.flow 1.** [ouvə'flou] [irr. (flow)] desbordar(se); rebosar (a. fig.); **2.** ['ouvəflou] desbordamiento m; derrame m; (pipe) vertedor m, cañería f de desagüe; '**.grown** revestido, cubierto (with de); '**.haul 1.** revisar; rehabilitar, componer; (catch up) alcanzar, **2.** repaso m, revisión f; '**.head 1.** [ouvə'hed] adv. por lo alto, por encima de la cabeza; **2.** ['ouvəhed] adj. de arriba; aéreo; ✝ general; **3.** ✝ ~s pl. gastos m/pl. generales; '**.hear** [irr. (hear)] oír (por casualidad); acertar a oír; conversation sorprender; '**.heat** recalentar; '**.in'dulge** mimar demasiado; ~ in tomar con exceso; '**.kill 1.** exceso m de potencia (or eficacia); **2.** fig. exceder lo necesario; '**.lap 1.** traslapar(se); fig. coincidir en parte; **2.** solapo m, traslapo m; fig. coincidencia f (parcial);

~·lay 1. ['ouvə'lei] [irr. (lay)] cubrir (with con); **2.** ['ouvəlei] capa f; cubierta f; **~·load 1.** ['ouvə'loud] sobrecargar; **2.** ['ouvəloud] sobrecarga f; **~·look** (p.) dominar con la vista; vigilar; (leave out) pasar por alto, no hacer caso de; (tolerate) disimular; (forgive) perdonar; **'~·night** de la noche a la mañana; **~·pow·er** vencer; subyugar; dominar; senses embargar; **~·ride** [irr. (ride)] no hacer caso de; anular; poner a un lado; **~·rid·ing** predominante, decisivo; **~·rule** anular; **~** denegar; **~·run** [irr. (run)] invadir; **'~·sea(s) 1.** adj. de ultramar; **2.** adv. allende el mar, en ultramar; **~·see** [irr. (see)] superentender, fiscalizar; **'~·shoe** chanclo m; **'~·shoot** [irr. (shoot)] tirar más allá de; ♐ sobrepasar; **'~·sight** descuido m, inadvertencia f; equivocación f; (supervision) vigilancia f; **'~·sleep** [irr. (sleep)] dormir demasiado; **'~·step** exceder; **~** the mark sobrepasarse; **'~·sup·ply** proveer en exceso.

o·vert ['ouvə:t] □ abierto, manifiesto.

over...: **~·take** [irr. (take)] alcanzar, pasar, adelantar(se) a; fig. sorprender; **'~·tax** oprimir con tributos; fig. agobiar; **~·throw 1.** [ouvə'θrou] [irr. (throw)] echar abajo; volcar; **2.** ['ouvəθrou] derrocamiento m, derribo m; **'~·time** horas f/pl. extraordinarias; **'~·tone** ♩ armónico m; fig. sugestión f.

over·ture ['ouvətjuə] ♩ obertura f; fig. proposición f; sondeo m.

o·ver...: **~·turn** [ouvə'tə:n] v/t. volcar, trastornar; v/i. volcar; ♐ zozobrar; **'~·weight 1.** sobrepeso m, peso m de añadidura; **2.** excesivamente pesado; be ~ pesar demasiado; **'~·whelm** abrumar; anonadar; inundar; **'~·work 1.** trabajo m excesivo; **2.** [irr. (work)] (hacer) trabajar demasiado.

owe [ou] v/t. deber; estar agradecido por; v/i. tener deudas.

ow·ing ['ouiŋ] sin pagar; debido; ~ to debido a, por causa de.

owl [aul] (barn-) lechuza f común; (little) mochuelo m común.

own [oun] **1.** propio; particular; my ~ self yo (after prp. mí) mismo; yo por mi parte; **2.** my ~ (lo) mío; come into one's ~ entrar en posesión de lo suyo; on one's ~ por su propia cuenta; a solas; a house of one's ~ una casa propia; **3.** poseer; ser dueño de.

own·er ['ounə] amo (a f) m, dueño (a f) m, poseedor (-a f) m; **'own·er·less** sin dueño; abandonado; **'own·er·ship** posesión f, propiedad f.

ox [ɔks], pl. **ox·en** ['~ən] buey m.

ox·ide ['ɔksaid] óxido m; **ox·i·diza·tion** [ɔksidi'zeiʃən] oxidación f; **ox·i·dize** ['ɔksidaiz] oxidar(se).

ox·y·gen ['ɔksidʒən] oxígeno m; **ox·y·gen·ate** [ɔk'sidʒineit] oxigenar.

oys·ter ['ɔistə] ostra f; **'~ bed** ostral m; **~ 'catch·er** orn. ostrero m.

o·zone ['ouzoun] ozono m.

P [piː]: mind one's Ps and Qs andar con cuidado con lo que dice uno.

pa [pɑː] F papá m.

pace [peis] **1.** paso m; marcha f; velocidad f; keep ~ with llevar el mismo paso con; fig. correr parejas con; **2.** v/t. distance medir a pasos (a ~ out); room pasearse por; v/i.: ~ up and down pasearse de un lado a otro; **'pace-mak·er** el que marca el paso; ⚕ marcapasos.

pa·cif·ic [pə'sifik] □ pacífico; **'pac·i·fism** pacifismo m; **'pac·i·fist** pacifista m/f; **pac·i·fy** ['pæsifai] pacificar; apaciguar, calmar.

pack [pæk] **1.** (bundle) lío m, fardo m; (animal's) carga f; (rucksack) mochi-

la f (a. ✕); paquete m; cajetilla f of cigarettes; ~ animal bestia f de carga; **2.** v/t. case etc. hacer; embaular in trunk, encajonar in box; (a. ~ up) empacar, empaquetar; (wrap) envasar; ~ off despachar; v/i. hacer las maletas; ~ up hacer el equipaje; F terminar; **'pack·age 1.** paquete m; bulto m; **2.** empaquetar, envasar; **'pack·er** embalador (-a f) m; **pack·et** ['~it] paquete m; cajetilla f of cigarettes etc.

pact [pækt] **1.** pacto m; **2.** pactar.

pad¹ [pæd] (about etc.) andar, pisar (sin hacer ruido).

pad² [~] **1.** almohadilla f, cojinete m; (ink-) tampón m; bloc m of paper; sl.

vivienda *f*; **2.** rellenar, forrear; **'pad·ding** relleno *m*; paja *f in book etc.*

pad·dle ['pædl] **1.** canalete *m*, zagual *m*; **2.** *v/i.* remar con canalete; chapotear *in sea*; *v/t.* impulsar con canalete; **'∼ steam·er** vapor *m* de ruedas; **'∼ wheel** rueda *f* de paletas.

pad·dy wag·on ['pædiwægən] *sl.* camión *m* de policía.

pad·lock ['pædlɔk] **1.** candado *m*; **2.** cerrar con candado.

pa·gan ['peigən] pagano *adj. a. su. m* (a *f*); **'pa·gan·ism** paganismo *m*.

page¹ [peidʒ] **1.** (*boy*) paje *m*; **2.** (*in hotel*) buscar llamando.

page² [∼] **1.** página *f*; *typ.* plana *f of newspaper etc.*; **2.** paginar.

pag·eant ['pædʒənt] espectáculo *m* brillante; desfile *m*; **'pag·eant·ry** pompa *f*, boato *m*.

pa·go·da [pə'goudə] pagoda *f*.

pail [peil] cubo *m*, balde *m*.

pain [pein] **1.** dolor *m*; *⚕ ∼s pl.* (*labor*) dolores *m/pl.* del parto; *∼s fig.* trabajo *m*; **2.** doler; dar lástima; **pain·ful** ['∼ful] □ doloroso; *decision* muy difícil; **'pain·kil·ler** calmante *m* de dolor; analgésico *m*; **'pain·less** □ indoloro; sin dolor; **'pains·tak·ing** □ *p.*, *th.* esmerado; cuidadoso; laborioso.

paint [peint] **1.** pintura *f*; colorete *m for face*; **2.** pintar; *face* pintarse; **'∼·brush** (*small*) pincel *m*; (*large*) brocha *f*.

paint·er ['peintə] pintor (-a *f*) *m*.

paint·ing ['peintiŋ] pintura *f*; cuadro *m*; **'paint roll·er** rodillo *m* pintor.

pair [pɛə] **1.** par *m*; pareja *f*; **2.** aparear(se) (*a. zo.*, *a. ∼ off*).

pa·ja·mas [pə'dʒɑːməz] *pl.* pijama *m*.

pal [pæl] **F 1.** compañero (a *f*) *m*; amigo (a *f*) *m*; **2.:** ∼ *up with* hacerse amigo de.

pal·ace ['pælis] palacio *m*.

pal·at·a·ble ['pælətəbl] □ sabroso, apetitoso; F comible; *fig.* aceptable.

pal·ate ['pælit] paladar *m* (*a. fig.*).

pa·la·tial [pə'leiʃəl] □ suntuoso.

pa·la·ver [pə'lɑːvə] (*discussion*) conferencia *f*, parlamento *f*; (*words*) palabrería *f*.

pale [peil] **1.** □ pálido; *color* claro; *grow* ∼ **= 2.** palidecer; descolorarse; **'pale·face** F rostropálido *m*.

pale·ness ['peilnis] palidez *f*.

pa·le·og·ra·phy [peili'ɔgrəfi] paleografía *f*.

Pal·es·tin·i·an [pæles'tiniən] palestino *adj. a. su. m* (a *f*).

pal·ette ['pælit] paleta *f*.

pal·i·sade [pæli'seid] estacada *f*.

pall¹ [pɔːl] paño *m* mortuorio; *eccl.* palio *m*; capa *f of smoke*; **'∼·bear·er** portaféretro *m*.

pall² [∼] perder su sabor (*on para*), dejar de gustar (*on a*).

pal·lid ['pælid] □ pálido; **'pal·lid·ness**, **pal·lor** ['pælə] palidez *f*.

palm¹ [pɑːm] ♀ palma *f* (*a. fig.*), palmera *f*; ♀ *Sunday* Domingo *m* de Ramos.

palm² [∼] **1.** palma *f of hand*; *grease s.o.'s* ∼ untar la mano a alguien; **2.** *card etc.* escamotear; ∼ *off* encajar (*on a*); **palm·is·try** ['∼istri] quiromancia *f*; **'palm tree** palmera *f*.

pal·pa·ble ['pælpəbl] □ palpable (*a. fig.*).

pal·pi·tate ['pælpiteit] palpitar.

pal·try ['pɔːltri] □ insignificante, mezquino, baladí; **'pal·tri·ness** mezquindad *f*; insignificancia *f*.

pam·pas ['pæmpəs] pampas *f/pl.*

pam·per ['pæmpə] mimar.

pam·phlet ['pæmflit] octavilla *f*; folleto *m*, panfleto *m*; **pam·phlet·eer** [∼'tiə] folletista *m/f*.

pan¹ [pæn] **1.** cazuela *f*; cacerola *f*; **2.** *v/t. gold* separar en la gamella; F *play* criticar severamente; *v/i.:* ∼ *out* tener éxito; resultar.

pan²... [∼] pan...

pan·a·ce·a [pænə'siə] panacea *f*.

pan·cake ['pænkeik] hojuela *f*, tortita *f*; ∼ *landing* aterrizaje *m* a vientre.

pan·da ['pændə] *zo.* panda *m/f.*

pan·der ['pændə] **1.** alcahuetear; **2.** alcahuete *m*.

pane [pein] cristal *m*, (hoja *f* de) vidrio *m*.

pan·el ['pænl] panel *m*; (*door*) entrepaño *m*; (*ceiling*) artesón *m*; (*wall*) panel *m*; ∼ *discussion* coloquio *m* ante un auditorio; tribunal *m of experts etc.*; **'pan·eled** artesonado; con paneles; de tableros; **'pan·el·ing** entrepaños *m/pl. of door*; artesonado *m*; paneles *m/pl.*

pang [pæŋ] punzada *f*, dolor *m*.

pan·han·dle ['pænhændl] F pedir limosna; **'pan·han·dler** F mendigo *m*.

pan·ic ['pænik] **1.** pánico *m*; **2.** (*terror m*) pánico *m*; **3.** llenarse (sin motivo) de terror; aterrarse; **'∼-strick·en** lleno de terror.

pan·o·ra·ma [pænə'rɑːmə] panorama *m*.

pan·sy ['pænzi] ♀ pensamiento *m*; F maricón *m*.

pant [pænt] jadear; resollar.

pan·the·ism ['pænθiizm] panteísmo *m*; **pan·the·is·tic** □ panteísta; **pan·the·on** ['pænθiən] panteón *m*.

pan·ther ['pænθə] pantera *f*.

pant·ies ['pæntiz] *pl.* F (*a pair of* unas) bragas *f/pl.*; pantaloncillos *f/pl.*

pan·to·mime ['pæntəmaim] pantomima *f*.

pan·try ['pæntri] despensa *f*.

pants [pænts] *pl.* F calzoncillos *m/pl.*; pantalones *m/pl.*

pa·pa [pə'pɑː] papá *m*.

pa·pa·cy ['peipəsi] papado *m*, pontificado *m*.

pa·per ['peipə] **1.** papel *m*; (*news-*) periódico *m*; (*learned*) comunicación *f*, ponencia *f*; (*written*) artículo *m*; ~s *pl.* (*identity etc.*) documentación *f*; *brown* ~ papel *m* de embalar, papel *m* de estraza; *on* ~ sobre el papel; **2.** *attr.* ... de papel; ~ *money* papel *m* moneda; **3.** *wall* empapelar; '~·back libro *m* en rústica; '~ bag saco *m* de papel; '~ clip sujetapapeles *m*; clip *m*; '~·hang·er empapelador *m*; '~ knife cortapapeles *m*; '~ mill fábrica *f* de papel; '~ work preparación *f* de escritos; papeleo *m*.

pa·pier mâché ['pæpjeimɑː'ʃei] (*attr. de*) cartón *m* piedra.

pa·py·rus [pə'paiərəs] papiro *m*.

par [pɑː] **1.** par *f*; *above* ~ a premio; *below* ~ ♣ a descuento; **2.** *value* nominal; *standard* normal.

pa·rab·o·la [pə'ræbələ] parábola *f*.

par·a·chute ['pærəʃuːt] **1.** paracaídas *m*; **2.** lanzar(se) en paracaídas; '**par·a·chut·ist** paracaidista *m*.

pa·rade [pə'reid] **1.** ✕ desfile *m*, parada *f*; (*road*) paseo *m*; **2.** *v/t.* ✕ formar; *streets* desfilar por; *th.* pasear (*through the streets* por las calles); *v/i.* desfilar.

par·a·dise ['pærədais] paraíso *m*.

par·a·dox ['pærədɔks] paradoja *f*; *fig.* persona *f etc.* enigmática.

par·a·gon ['pærəgən] dechado *m*.

par·a·graph ['pærəɡrɑːf] párrafo *m*.

Pa·ra·guay·an [pærə'gwaijən] paraguayo *adj. a. su. m* (*a f*).

par·a·keet ['pærəkiːt] perico *m*, periquito *m*.

par·al·lel ['pærəlel] **1.** paralelo; ≠ en paralelo; ~ *bars* paralelas *f/pl.*; **2.** (*linea f*) paralela *f*; *geog.*, *fig.* paralelo *m*; ≠ in ~ en paralelo; '**par·al·lel·ism** paralelismo *m*; **par·al·lel·o·gram** [~ə-græm] paralelogramo *m*.

par·a·lyse ['pærəlaiz] paralizar (*a. fig.*); **pa·ral·y·sis** [pə'rælisis] parálisis *f*.

par·a·mil·i·tar·y ['pærə'militəri] seudomilitar; semimilitar.

par·a·mount ['pærəmaunt] supremo; *importance* capital.

par·a·noi·a [pærə'nɔijə] paranoia *f*; **par·a·noid** ['~nɔid] paranoico *adj. a. su.* (*a f*).

par·a·pet ['pærəpit] parapeto *m*.

par·a·pher·na·li·a [pærəfə'neiljə] F avíos *m/pl.*, chismes *m/pl.*

par·a·phrase ['pærəfreiz] **1.** paráfrasis *f*; **2.** parafrasear.

par·a·ple·gia [pærə'pliːdʒə] paraplejía *f*.

par·a·site ['pærəsait] parásito *m* (*a. fig.*); **par·a·sit·ic**, **par·a·sit·i·cal** [~'sitik(l)] □ parasítico.

par·a·sol [pærə'sɔl] sombrilla *f*, quitasol *m*.

par·a·troop·er ['pærətruːpə] paracaidista *m*.

par·cel ['pɑːsl] **1.** paquete *m*; lío *m*; parcela *f* of *land*; **2.** parcelar; repartir; embalar; '**par·cel post** (servicio *m* de) paquetes *m/pl.* postales.

parch [pɑːtʃ] (re)secar, (re)quemar.

par·don ['pɑːdn] **1.** perdón *m*; ✠ indulto *m*; *I beg your* ~ le pido perdón, perdone; **2.** perdonar, dispensar; ✠ indultar.

pare [pɛə] adelgazar; *fruit etc.* mondar; *fig.* reducir.

par·ent ['pɛərənt] **1.** padre *m*, madre *f*; ~s *pl.* padres *m/pl.*; **2.** madre.

pa·ren·the·sis [pə'renθisis] paréntesis *m*; **par·en·thet·i·cal** [pærən-'θetikl] □ entre paréntesis; explicativo.

par·ent·hood ['pɛərənthud] paternidad *f* or maternidad *f*.

par·ish ['pæriʃ] **1.** parroquia *f* (*a.* ~ *church*); **2.** *attr.* parroquial; ~ *priest* párroco *m*.

Pa·ri·sian [pə'rizjən] parisiense *adj. a. su. m/f*, parisino *adj. a. su. m* (*a f*).

par·i·ty ['pæriti] paridad *f*, igualdad *f*.

park [pɑːk] **1.** parque *m*; jardines *m/pl.*; **2.** *v/t.* estacionar; aparcar; F parquear, dejar; *v/i.* estacionarse; aparcar; '**park·ing** estacionamiento *m*; aparcamiento *m*; *no* ~ prohibido estacionarse; ~ *fee* costa *f* de estacionamiento; ~ **lot** parque *m* de estacionamiento; ~ **meter** reloj *m* de estacionamiento.

par·lia·ment ['pɑ:ləmənt] parlamento *m*; (*Spanish*) Cortes *f/pl.*; *Houses of* ♀ Cámara *f* de los Lores y la de los Comunes; *member of* ~ diputado *m*, miembro *m* del parlamento; **par·lia·men·ta·ry** [~'mentəri] parlamentario.

par·lor ['pɑ:lə] salón *m*, saloncito *m*; *eccl.* locutorio *m*.

pa·ro·chi·al [pə'roukjəl] □ parroquial; *fig.* de miras estrechas.

par·o·dy ['pærədi] 1. parodia *f*; 2. parodiar.

pa·role [pə'roul] 1. palabra *f* (de honor); libertad *f* bajo palabra; 2. dejar libre bajo palabra.

par·rot ['pærət] 1. loro *m*, papagayo *m*; 2. remedar; imitar.

par·ry ['pæri] *fenc.* parar, quitar; *fig.* esquivar, desviar (hábilmente).

par·si·mo·ni·ous [pɑ:si'mounjəs] □ parsimonioso.

pars·ley ['pɑ:sli] perejil *m*.

pars·nip ['pɑ:snip] chirivía *f*.

par·son ['pɑ:sn] clérigo *m*, cura *m*.

part [pɑ:t] 1. parte *f*; porción *f*; ⊕ pieza *f*; *thea. a. fig.* papel *m*; ♪ parte *f*; (*place*) lugar *m*, comarca *f*; (*duty*) deber *m*; ~ *of speech* parte *f* de la oración; *for my* (*own*) ~ por mi parte; *for the most* ~ por la mayor parte; *in* ~ en parte; *take* ~ *in* tomar parte en; 2. *adv.* (en) parte; 3. *adj.* parcial; co~..., con~; ~ *author* coautor (-a *f*) *m*; 4. *v/t.* separar; dividir; partir; *v/i.* separarse; (*come apart*) desprenderse; romperse; ~ *from* despedirse de.

par·take [pɑ:'teik] [*irr.* (*take*)]: ~ *of food etc.* comer *etc.*, aceptar.

par·tial ['pɑ:ʃl] □ parcial; ~ *to* aficionado a; **par·ti·al·i·ty** [pɑ:ʃi'æliti] (*bias*) parcialidad *f*.

par·tic·i·pant [pɑ:'tisipənt] *mst* partícipe *m/f*; combatiente *m/f in fight*; **par·tic·i·pate** [~peit] participar, tomar parte (*in* en); **par·ti·ci·ple** ['pɑ:tisipl] participio *m*; *past* ~ participio *m* de pasado; *present* ~ participio *m* de presente.

par·ti·cle ['pɑ:tikl] partícula *f*; pizca *f*; ~ *physics* física *f* de partículas.

par·tic·u·lar [pə'tikjulə] 1. □ particular; detallado, minucioso; (*scrupulous*) escrupuloso; (*fastidious*) exigente, quisquilloso; 2. particularidad *f*; detalle *m*; **par·tic·u·lar·i·ty**

[~'læriti] particularidad *f*; **par·tic·u·lar·ize** *v/t.* particularizar; *v/i.* dar todos los detalles.

part·ing ['pɑ:tiŋ] 1. separación *f*; despedida *f*; 2. ... de despedida.

par·ti·san [pɑ:ti'zæn] 1. partidario (a *f*) *m*; ✕ partisano *m*, guerrillero *m*; 2. partidista; '~·ship parcialidad *f*; partidismo *m*.

par·ti·tion [pɑ:'tiʃn] 1. partición *f*, división *f*; 2. (*share*) repartir; *country, room* dividir.

part·ly ['pɑ:tli] en parte; en cierto modo.

part·ner ['pɑ:tnə] 1. ♥ socio (a *f*) *m*; compañero (a *f*) *m* (*a. cards*); pareja *f in dance, tennis etc.*; 2. acompañar; '**part·ner·ship** ♥ sociedad *f*, asociación *f*.

part...: '~·own·er condueño (a *f*) *m*; '~·**pay·ment** pago *m* en parte.

part-time ['pɑ:t'taim] 1. *adj.* parcial, que trabaja por horas; 2. *adv.*: *work* ~ trabajar por horas.

par·ty ['pɑ:ti] 1. *pol.* partido *m*; grupo *m*; *hunt. etc.* partida *f*; (*gathering*) reunión *f*; (*informal*) tertulia *f*; (*merry*) fiesta *f*; ⚖ parte *f*; interesado (a *f*) *m*; 2. *attr. pol.* de partido; *dress* de gala; ~ *leader* jefe *m* de partido; ~ *politics b.s.* politiqueo *m*, partidismo *m*; ~ *ticket* candidatura *f* apoyada por un partido.

pass [pɑ:s] 1. *geog.* puerto *m*, paso *m*, desfiladero *m*; ✕ *etc.* pase *m* (*a. fenc., sport*); salvoconducto *m*; *thea.* entrada *f* de favor; *univ. etc.* nota *f* de aprobado; 2. *v/i.* pasar; *univ. etc.* aprobar, ser aprobado; *come to* ~ suceder, acontecer; *let* ~ dejar pasar, no hacer caso de; ~ *away* fallecer; ~ *out* F desmayarse; caer redondo; *v/t.* pasar; pasar por delante de; (*overtake*) pasar, dejar atrás; *p.* cruzarse con *on street etc.*; *bill, candidate, exam, proposal* aprobar; *opinion* expresar; ~ *over* pasar por alto; F ~ *up* renunciar a, rechazar; '**pass·a·ble** □ (*tolerable*) soportable, pasable.

pas·sage ['pæsidʒ] paso *m*; ♣, ♪ pasaje *m*; △ pasillo *m*, galería *f*; (*alley*) callejón *m*; (*underground*) pasadizo *m*; trozo *m of book.*

pass·book ['pɑ:sbuk] libreta *f* de banco.

passé ['pæsei] pasado (de moda).

pas·sen·ger ['pæsindʒə] pasajero (a *f*) *m*, viajero (a *f*) *m*; ~ *train* tren *m* de pasajeros.

pass·er-by, *pl.* **pass·ers-by** [ˈpɑːs-ə(z)ˈbai] transeúnte *m/f*.

pas·sing [ˈpɑːsiŋ] **1.** paso *m*; (*death*) fallecimiento *m*; **2.** pasajero.

pas·sion [ˈpæʃən] pasión *f*; (*arranque m de*) cólera *f*; *have a* ~ *for* tener pasión por; **pas·sion·ate** [ˈ~ʃənit] □ apasionado; (*angry*) colérico; *believer*, *desire* vehemente, ardiente; **'pas·sion·less** sin pasión; frío; **'pas·sion play** drama *m* de la Pasión.

pas·sive [ˈpæsiv] **1.** □ pasivo; **2.** voz *f* pasiva.

pass·key [ˈpɑːskiː] llave *f* maestra.

Pass·o·ver [ˈpɑːsouvə] Pascua *f* de los hebreos.

pass·port [ˈpɑːspɔːt] pasaporte *m*.

pass·word [ˈpɑːswəːd] santo *m* y seña.

past [pɑːst] **1.** *adj.* pasado (*a. gr.*); *all that is now* ~ todo eso se acabó ya; **2.** *adv.* por delante; *rush* ~ pasar precipitadamente; **3.** *prp. place (beyond)* más allá de; *time etc.* después de; *half* ~ 2 las 2 y media; *F I wouldn't put it* ~ *him* le creo capaz de eso; **4.** *su.* pasado *m* (*a. gr.*); antecedentes *m/pl*.

paste [peist] **1.** pasta *f*; engrudo *m for sticking*; **2.** engrudar; pegar (con engrudo); *sl.* pegar.

pas·tel [ˈpæstəl] pastel *m*; pintura *f* al pastel; ~ *shade* tono *m* pastel.

paste-up [ˈpeistʌp] montaje *m*; arreglo *m* compósito.

pas·teur·ize [ˈpæstəraiz] pasteurizar.

pas·time [ˈpɑːstaim] pasatiempo *m*.

pas·tor [ˈpɑːstə] pastor *m*.

pas·try [ˈpeistri] pasta *f*; pastas *f/pl.*, pasteles *m/pl.*; (*art*) pastelería *f*; *flaky (or puff-)* ~ hojaldre *m*; **'~ cook** pastelero (*a f*) *m*; repostero (*a f*) *m*.

pas·ture [ˈpɑːstʃə] **1.** pasto *m*, pastura *f*; (*land*) dehesa *f*; **2.** *v/t. animals* apacentar, pastorear; *herbage* comer; *v/i.* pastar, pacer.

pat [pæt] **1.** palmadita *f*; caricia *f*; palmada *f*; pastelillo *m of butter*; **2.** dar una palmadita a; *dog etc.* acariciar (con la mano).

patch [pætʃ] **1.** remiendo *m in dress*; parche *m on tire, wound*; lunar *m postizo on face*; (*stain etc.*) mancha *f*; (*small area*) pequeña extensión *f*; **2.** remendar; ~ *up quarrel* componer; **'~·work** [ˈpætʃwəːk] labor *f* de retazos; ~ *quilt* centón *m*; **'patch·y** desigual, poco uniforme.

pat·ent [ˈpætnt] **1.** □ patente, pal-

mario; ✝ *de patente*, patente, patentado; **2.** patente *f*, privilegio *m* de invención; ~ *office* oficina *f* de patentes; **3.** patentar.

pa·ter·nal [pəˈtəːnl] □ paternal, *relation* paterno; **pa·ter·ni·ty** paternidad *f*.

path [pɑːθ] senda *f*, sendero *m*; *fig.* camino *m*, trayectoria *f*; curso *m*; **'~·less** sin camino *m*; desconocido.

pa·thet·ic [pəˈθetik] □ patético, conmovedor.

path·o·log·i·cal [pæθəˈlɔdʒikl] □ patológico; **pa·thol·o·gy** patología *f*.

pa·thos [ˈpeiθɔs] patetismo *m*.

pa·tience [ˈpeiʃns] paciencia *f*; *cards:* solitario *m*; **'pa·tient 1.** □ paciente, sufrido; **2.** paciente *m/f*, enfermo (*a f*) *m*.

pa·ti·o [ˈpɑːtiou] patio *m*.

pa·tri·arch [ˈpeitriɑːk] patriarca *m*.

pat·ri·mo·ny [ˈpætriməni] patrimonio *m*.

pa·tri·ot [ˈpætriət] patriota *m/f*; **pa·tri·ot·ism** [ˈ~ɔtizm] patriotismo *m*.

pa·trol [pəˈtroul] **1.** ✕ *etc.* patrulla *f*; ronda *f*; **2.** patrullar (*v/t.* por); *fig.* rondar, pasearse (por); **~·man** [pəˈtroulmæn] guardia *m* municipal.

pa·tron [ˈpeitrən] *lit.* mecenas *m*; *eccl.* patrono (*a f*) *m* (*a.* ~ *saint*); patrocinador (*-a f*) *m of enterprise*; **pa·tron·age** [ˈpætrənidʒ] *lit.* mecenazgo *m*; *eccl.* patronato *m*; patrocinio *m of enterprise*; **pa·tron·ize** [ˈpætrənaiz] *shop* ser parroquiano de; *enterprise* patrocinar; *b.s.* tratar con aire protector.

pat·ter [ˈpætə] **1.** andar con pasos ligeros; (*rain*) tamborilear; **2.** pasos *m/pl.* ligeros *of feet*; tamborileo *m of rain etc.*; (*rapid speech*) parloteo *m*.

pat·tern [ˈpætən] **1.** (*design*) diseño *m*, dibujo *m*; modelo *m*; patrón *m for dress etc.*; **2.** modelar (*on sobre*).

pau·ci·ty [ˈpɔːsiti] escasez *f*.

paunch [pɔːntʃ] panza *f*; **'paunch·y** panzudo.

pau·per [ˈpɔːpə] pobre *m/f*, indigente *m/f*.

pause [pɔːz] **1.** pausa *f*; **2.** hacer una pausa, detenerse (brevemente).

pave [peiv] pavimentar, enlosar; **'pave·ment** acera *f*; pavimento *m*.

pa·vil·ion [pəˈviljən] pabellón *m*.

paw [pɔː] **1.** pata *f*; (*cat's etc.*) garra *f*; (*lion's*) zarpa *f*; **2.** (*lion etc.*) dar zarpazos a; *F* manosear.

P

pawn¹ [pɔːn] *chess:* peón *m*; *fig.* instrumento *m*.

pawn² [~] empeñar, dejar en prenda; '**~·bro·ker** prestamista *m*, prendero *m*; '**~·bro·ker's**, '**~·shop** casa *f* de empeños, prendería *f*; monte *m* de piedad.

pay [pei] **1.** paga *f*; sueldo *m*; *on half* ~ a medio sueldo; **2.** [*irr.*] *v/t.* pagar; *account* liquidar; (*be profitable*) ser provechoso a, rendir (bien, etc.); *attention* prestar; *respects* ofrecer; ~ *out* desembolsar; *rope* ir dando; *v/i.* pagar (*for acc.*); (*be profitable*) rendir, ser provechoso; *it doesn't* ~ *to* vale más no *inf.*; '**pay·a·ble** pagadero *m*; '**pay·load** carga *f* útil; '**pay·mas·ter** oficial *m* pagador; '**pay·ment** paga *f* (*a. fig.*); *in* ~ *for* en pago de; *on* ~ *of* pagando; *monthly* ~ mensualidad *f*; '**~·off** F colmo *m*; resultado *m*, momento *m* decisivo.

pea [piː] guisante *m*; *as like as 2* ~*s* parecerse como dos gotas de agua.

peace [piːs] paz *f*; *at* ~ en paz; '**peace·a·ble** ☐ pacífico; sosegado; **Peace Corps** Cuerpo *m* de Paz; '**peace·ful** [~ful] ☐ tranquilo.

peach [piːtʃ] ☘ melocotón *m*; (*a.* ~ *tree*) melocotonero *m*; *sl.* monada *f*; *sl.* (*girl*) botón *m*, real moza *f*.

pea·cock ['piːkɔk] pavo *m* real, pavón *m*.

peak [piːk] pico *m*; cima *f*; cumbre *f* (*a. fig.*); visera *f* *of cap*; ~ *hours* pl. horas *f/pl.* punta; ~ *season* época *f* más popular del año; ~ *traffic* movimiento *m* máximo; '**peaked** [piːkt] *cap* con visera.

peal [piːl] **1.** repique(teo) *m*; (*set*) juego *m* de campanas; ~ *of laughter* carcajada *f*; ~ *of thunder* trueno *m*; **2.** *v/i. a. v/t.* repicar, tocar a vuelo.

pea·nut ['piːnʌt] cacahuete *m*; ~ *butter* manteca *f* de cacahuete.

pear [pɛə] pera *f*; (*a.* ~ *tree*) peral *m*.

pearl [pɜːl] perla *f* (*a. fig.*); '**pearl·y** de perla (s); color de perla; nacarado.

peas·ant ['pezənt] campesino (a *f*) *m*, labrador (-a *f*) *m*.

pea soup ['piːsuːp] puré *m* de guisantes.

peat [piːt] turba *f*; '~ *bog* turbera *f*.

peb·ble ['pebl] guija *f*, guijarro *m*.

pe·can [pi'kæn] ♣ pacana *f*.

peck¹ [pek] *medida de áridos* (= 9,087 *litros*).

peck² [~] **1.** picotazo *m*; F beso *m* poco cariñoso; **2.** picotear.

pec·to·ral ['pektərəl] pectoral *m*.

pe·cul·iar [pi'kjuːljə] ☐ peculiar; singular; ~ *to* propio de, privativo de; **pe·cu·li·ar·i·ty** [~liː'æriti] peculiaridad *f*; rasgo *m* característico.

ped·a·gog·ic, ped·a·gog·i·cal [pedə'gɔdʒik(l)] ☐ pedagógico; '**ped·a·gogue** [~gɔg] pedagogo *m* (*a. b.s.*); **ped·a·go·gy** ['~gi] pedagogía *f*.

ped·al ['pedl] **1.** pedal *m*; **2.** impulsar pedaleando.

ped·ant ['pedənt] pedante *m*.

ped·dle ['pedl] andar vendiendo (de puerta en puerta); '**ped·dler** vendedor *m* ambulante.

ped·er·as·ty ['pedəræsti] pederastia *f*.

ped·es·tal ['pedistl] pedestal *m*.

pe·des·tri·an [pi'destriən] **1.** de (*or* para) peatones; pedestre (*a. fig.*); **2.** peatón *m*; paseante *m/f*.

ped·i·gree ['pedigriː] **1.** genealogía *f*, linaje *m*; **2.** de raza.

pe·dom·e·ter [pi'dɔmitə] podómetro *m*.

peek [piːk] **1.** mirada *f* furtiva; *take a* ~ (*at*) = **2.** mirar furtivamente.

peel [piːl] **1.** piel *f*; (*removed*) pieles *f/pl.*, monda *f*, peladura(s) *f(pl.)*; **2.** pelar, mondar.

peep [piːp] **1.** mirada *f* (rápida, furtiva, por una rendija *etc.*); **2.** (*a.* ~ *at*) mirar (rápidamente, furtivamente, por una rendija *etc.*); atisbar; '**peep·hole** mirilla *f* *in door*, atisbadero *m*; **Peep·ing Tom** mirón *m*; '**peep show** mundonuevo *m*.

peer¹ [piə] (*a.* ~ *at*) mirar de cerca.

peer² [~] (*noble*) par *m*; (*equal*) igual *m*; '**peer·less** incomparable.

peeved [piːvd] irritado; **pee·vish** ['piːviʃ] ☐ malhumorado, displicente; '**pee·vish·ness** mal humor *m*, displicencia *f*.

peg [peg] **1.** clavija *f*, claveta *f*; (*tent-etc.*) estaca *f*; (*clothes-*) pinza *f*; colgadero *m* *for coats*; **2.** enclavijar; (*a.* ~ *down*) estaquillar.

pe·jo·ra·tive ['piːdʒərətiv] ☐ peyorativo.

pel·i·can ['pelikən] pelícano *m*.

pel·let ['pelit] bolita *f*; bodoque *m*.

pelt¹ ['pelt] (*skin*) pellejo *m*.

pelt² [~] tirar, arrojar; apedrear *with stones*; *they* ~*ed him with tomatoes* le tiraron tomates.

pel·vis ['pelvis] pelvis *f*.

pen¹ [pen] **1.** pluma *f*; (*fountain-*) estilográfica *f*; **2.** escribir; redactar; ~ *pal* F amigo *m* por correspondencia.

perfume

pen² [~] 🖋 corral *m*, redil *m*.

pe·nal ['pi:nl] penal; ~ *code* código *m* penal; **pe·nal·ize** ['ˌɔlaiz] penar; (*accidentally, unfairly*) perjudicar; *sport*: castigar; **pen·al·ty** ['penlti] pena *f*; multa *f*; castigo *m*.

pen·ance ['penəns] penitencia *f*.

pen·chant ['pɑːnʃɑːn] predilección *f* (*for* por), afición *f* (*for* a).

pen·cil ['pensl] 1. lápiz *m*; rayo *m* of *light*; 2. escribir con lápiz; **'pen·cil sharp·en·er** sacapuntas *m*.

pend·ant, pend·ent ['pendənt] 1. pendiente; 2. pendiente *m*, medallón *m*.

pend·ing ['pendiŋ] pendiente.

pen·e·trate ['penitreit] penetrar; **'pen·e·trat·ing** □ penetrante (*a. fig.*); **pen·e'tra·tion** penetración *f*.

pen·guin ['peŋgwin] pingüino *m*.

pen·i·cil·lin [peni'silin] penicilina *f*.

pen·in·su·la [pi'ninsjulə] península *f*; **pen·in·su·lar** peninsular.

pe·nis ['pi:nis] pene *m*.

pen·i·tence ['penitəns] penitencia *f*, arrepentimiento *m*; **'pen·i·tent** □ penitente *adj. a. su. m/f*; **pen·i·ten·tia·ry** [~'tenʃəri] cárcel *f*, presidio *m*.

pen·knife ['pennaif] navaja *f*, cortaplumas *m*.

pen·man·ship ['penmənʃip] caligrafía *f*.

pen name ['pen neim] seudónimo *m*.

pen·nant ['penənt] ⚓ gallardete *m*; banderola *f*.

pen·ny ['peni] penique *m*; centavo *m*; **'~·weight** *peso* (= 1,555 gr.).

pen·sion ['penʃn] 1. pensión *f*; jubilación *f*; 2. pensionar; jubilar (*a. ~ off*); **'pen·sion·er** pensionado (a *f*) *m*, pensionista *m/f*.

pen·sive ['pensiv] □ pensativo; melancólico; preocupado.

pent-up ['pent'ʌp] contenido; reprimido.

pen·ta·gon ['pentəgən] pentágono *m*.

Pen·te·cost ['pentikɔst] Pentecostés *f*; **pen·te'cos·tal** de Pentecostés.

pent·house ['penthaus] colgadizo *m*; casa *f* de azotea.

pe·o·ny ['piəni] peonía *f*.

peo·ple ['pi:pl] 1. (*nation*) pueblo *m*, nación *f*; (*lower orders*) pueblo *m*, plebe *f*; (*in general*) gente *f*; personas *f/pl.*; the English ~ el pueblo inglés; old ~ los viejos; some ~ algunos; ~ *say that* se dice que; *I like the* ~ *here* aquí la gente es muy simpática; 2. poblar.

pep [pep] *sl.* ánimo *m*, vigor *m*; ~ *talk* palabras *f* alentadoras.

pep·per ['pepə] 1. pimienta *f*; (*plant*) pimiento *m*; 2. sazonar con pimienta; *fig.* salpicar; acribillar *with shot*; **'~·corn** grano *m* de pimienta; **'~·mint** (pastilla *f etc.* de) menta *f*; **'pep·per·y** picante; *fig.* enojadizo, de malas pulgas.

pep·tic ['peptik] péptico.

per [pə:] por; ~ *annum* al año; ~ *cent* por ciento.

per·am·bu·late [pə'ræmbjuleit] pasearse, deambular; **per·am·bu·la·tor** ['præmbjuleitə] cochecito *m* de niño.

per·ceive [pə'si:v] percibir; ver; notar; comprender.

per·cent·age [pə'sentidʒ] porcentaje *m*; proporción *f*; *sl.* tajada *f*.

per·cep·ti·ble [pə'septəbl] □ perceptible; **per'cep·tion** percepción *f*; comprensión *f*; perspicacia *f*.

perch¹ [pə:tʃ] *ichth.* perca *f*.

perch² [~] 1. (*bird's*) percha *f*; posición *f* elevada; 2. *v/i.* posar(se); encaramarse; *v/t.* colocar (en una posición elevada).

per·co·late ['pə:kəleit] filtrar(se), infiltrar(se); **'per·co·la·tor** *approx.* cafetera *f* filtradora.

per·cus·sion [pə:'kʌʃn] (♪ *attr.* de) percusión *f*.

per·di·tion [pə:'diʃn] perdición *f*; infierno *m*.

per·en·ni·al [pə'renjəl] □ perenne *adj. a. su. m* (*a.* ♧).

per·fect 1. ['pə:fikt] □ perfecto (*a. gr.*); 2. [~] (*a.* ~ *tense*) perfecto *m*; 3. [pə'fekt] perfeccionar; **per'fec·tion** perfección *f*; *to* ~ a la perfección; **per'fec·tion·ist** persona *f* que lo quiere todo perfecto; detallista *m/f*.

per·fid·i·ous [pə'fidiəs] □ pérfido; **per·fi·dy** ['pə:fidi] perfidia *f*.

per·fo·rate ['pə:fəreit] perforar, horadar; ~ *stamp* dentado; **per·fo'ra·tion** perforación *f*; trepado *m* of *stamp*; **'per·fo·ra·tor** perforador (-a *f*) *m*.

per·form [pə'fɔ:m] *v/t.* task *etc.* realizar, cumplir, hacer; *functions* desempeñar; ♪ *etc.* ejecutar; *v/i.* ♪ tocar; *thea.* representar, actuar; **per'form·ance** ejecución *f* (*a.* ♪); desempeño *m*; *thea.* representación *f*; función *f*; actuación *f* (brillante *etc.*); ⊕ funcionamiento *m*.

per·fume 1. ['pə:fju:m] perfume *m*; 2. [pə'fju:m] perfumar.

per·haps [pə'hæps, præps] tal vez, quizá(s); puede que.

per·il ['peril] peligro *m*, riesgo *m*; **'per·il·ous** ☐ peligroso, arriesgado.

pe·ri·od ['piəriəd] período *m* (*a. gr.*); época *f*; término *m*; *typ.* punto *m*; *school:* clase *f*, hora *f*; *♂* ~s *pl.* reglas *f/pl.*; **pe·ri·od·i·cal 1.** ☐ periódico; **2.** periódico *m*, publicación *f* periódica.

per·i·pa·tet·ic [peripə'tetik] ☐ ambulante; *phls.* peripatético.

pe·riph·ra·sis [pə'rifrəsis] perífrasis *f*; **per·i·phras·tic** [peri'fræstik] ☐ perifrástico.

per·i·scope ['periskoup] periscopio *m*.

per·ish ['periʃ] *v/i.* parecer; (*material*) deteriorarse; *v/t.* deteriorar, echar a perder; **'per·ish·a·ble 1.** perecedero; *food etc.* corruptible, que no se conserva bien; **2.** ~s *pl.* mercancías *f/pl.* corruptibles.

per·i·win·kle ['periwiŋkl] ♀ (vinca)pervinca *f*; *zo.* litorina *f*.

per·jure ['pə:dʒə] ~ *o.s.* perjurar(se); **'per·ju·ry** perjurio *m*.

perk [pə:k] F: ~ *up* reanimarse, sentirse mejor; **'~·i·ness** viveza *f*; gallardía *f*.

perk·y ['pə:ki] F de excelente humor; despabilado.

perm [pə:m] F permanente *f*.

per·ma·nence ['pə:mənəns], **'per·ma·nen·cy** permanencia *f*; **'per·ma·nent** ☐ permanente; fijo; duradero; ~ *press* planchado *m* permanente.

per·me·a·bil·i·ty [pə:miə'biliti] permeabilidad *f*; **per·me·ate** ['~mieit] penetrar; saturar; impregnar.

per·mis·si·ble [pə'misəbl] ☐ permisible; **per·mis·sive** [~'misiv] permisivo.

per·mit 1. [pə'mit] permitir (*to inf.*, que *subj.*); **2.** ['pə:mit] permiso *m*; licencia *f*; *✝* permiso *m* de importación *etc.*

per·mu·ta·tion [pə:mju:'teiʃn] permutación *f*.

per·ni·cious [pə'niʃəs] ☐ pernicioso, funesto.

per·ox·ide [pə'rɔksaid] peróxido *m*; F ~ *blonde* rubia *f* de bote.

per·pen·dic·u·lar [pə:pən'dikjulə] ☐ perpendicular *adj. a. su. f*.

per·pe·trate ['pə:pitreit] perpetrar.

per·pet·u·al [pə'petjuəl] ☐ perpetuo; **per'pet·u·ate** [~eit] perpetuar;

per·pe·tu·i·ty [pə:pi'tjuiti] perpetuidad *f*; *in* ~ para siempre.

per·plex [pə'pleks] confundir, dejar perplejo; **per'plexed** ☐ perplejo; **per'plex·ing** ☐ confuso, que causa perplejidad; **per'plex·i·ty** perplejidad *f*.

per·qui·site ['pə:kwizit] gaje *m*; ~s *pl.* gajes *m/pl.*; *salary and* ~s un sueldo y lo que cae.

per·se·cute ['pə:sikju:t] perseguir, acosar; **per·se'cu·tion** persecución *f*; ~ *mania* manía *f* persecutoria.

per·se·vere [pə:si'viə] perseverar, persistir (*in* en); **per·se'ver·ing** ☐ perseverante.

Per·sian ['pə:ʃn] persa *adj. a. su. m/f*.

per·sist [pə'sist] persistir; porfiar, empeñarse (*in* en); **per'sist·ent** ☐ porfiado; *disease etc.* pertinaz.

per·son ['pə:sn] persona *f*; *in* ~ en persona; **'per·son·a·ble** bien parecido; **'per·son·age** personaje *m*; **'per·son·al** ☐ personal; (*private*) privado; de uso personal; *cleanliness etc.* corporal; *interview etc.* en persona; **per·son·al·i·ty** [~sə'næliti] personalidad *f*; **per·son·i·fi·ca·tion** [~sɔnifi'keiʃn] personificación *f*; **per·son·i·fy** [~'sɔnifai] personificar; **per·son·nel** [~sə'nel] personal *m*; ~ *manager* jefe *m* del personal.

per·spec·tive [pə'spektiv] (*in* en) perspectiva *f*.

per·spi·ca·cious [pə:spi'keiʃəs] ☐ perspicaz.

per·spi·ra·tion [pə:spə'reiʃn] transpiración *f*, sudor *m*; **per·spire** [pəs'paiə] transpirar, sudar.

per·suade [pə'sweid] persuadir, inducir (*to* a); convencer.

per·sua·sion [pə'sweiʒən] persuasiva *f*; (*act*) persuasión *f*.

pert [pə:t] ☐ impertinente, respondón; fresco.

per·tain [pə:'tein] referirse a, tener que ver con; pertenecer con.

per·ti·nence, **per·ti·nen·cy** ['pə:tinəns(i)] pertinencia *f*; **'per·ti·nent** ☐ pertinente, oportuno.

pert·ness ['pə:tnis] frescura *f*.

per·turb [pə'tə:b] perturbar, inquietar.

pe·ruse [pə'ru:z] leer (con atención), examinar.

Pe·ru·vi·an [pə'ru:viən] peruano *adj. a. su. m* (*a f*); ~ *bark* quina *f*.

per·vade [pə:'veid] extenderse por,

difundirse por; impregnar, ocupar; **per'va·sive** [ˌ·siv] penetrante.

per·verse [pəˈvɜːs] ☐ perverso; avieso; contumaz; **per'ver·si·ty** perversidad f; contumacia f.

per·vert 1. [pəˈvɜːt] pervertir; *taste etc.* estragar; *talent* emplear mal; 2. [ˈpɔːvɜːt] 🛩 pervertido (a f) m; (*apostate*) apóstata f.

pes·ky [ˈpeski] molesto.

pes·si·mism [ˈpesimizm] pesimismo m; **'pes·si·mist** pesimista m/f; **pes·si'mis·tic** ☐ pesimista.

pest [pest] zo. plaga f; insecto m etc. nocivo; *fig.* (*p.*) machaca f; ~ *control* control m de los insectos; **'pes·ter** molestar, acosar (con preguntas *etc.*), importunar; **'pes·ti·cide** [ˈ~said] insecticida m; **'pes·ti·lence** pestilencia f; **'pes·ti·lent** pestilente; *fig.* engorroso.

pet [pet] 1. animal m doméstico (or de casa); (*p.*) favorito (a f) m, persona f muy mimada; 2. *animal* doméstico, de casa, domesticado; (*favourite*) favorito; 3. *v/t.* acariciar; (*spoil*) mimar; *v/i.* F besuquearse, sobarse.

pet·al [ˈpetl] pétalo m.

pe·ter [ˈpiːtə] ~ *out* (*supply*) agotarse; ir disminuyendo.

pe·ti·tion [pəˈtiʃn] 1. petición f, memoria f, instancia f; 2. suplicar, rogar (*for acc.*; *to inf.* que *subj.*); **pe'ti·tion·er** suplicante m/f.

pet·rel [ˈpetrəl] petrel m, paíño m.

pet·ri·fac·tion [petriˈfækʃn] petrificación f.

pet·ri·fy [ˈpetrifai] petrificar(se) (a. *fig.*).

pet·rol [ˈpetrəl] gasolina f; bencina f for lighter.

pe·tro·le·um [piˈtrouliəm] petróleo m; ~ *jelly* vaselina f, jalea f de petróleo.

pet·ti·coat [ˈpetikout] enagua(s) f(pl.); (*slip*) combinación f; (*stiff*) falda f.

pet·ti·fog·ger [ˈpetifɔɡə] picapleitos m; trapacister m.

pet·ti·ness [ˈpetinis] insignificancia f etc.

pet·ty [ˈpeti] ☐ insignificante, pequeño; despreciable; *p.* intolerante; rencoroso; reparón; ~ *cash* gastos m/pl. menores.

pet·u·lance [ˈpetjuləns] mal humor m; **pet·u·lant** [ˈ~lənt] ☐ malhumorado, enojadizo.

pew [pjuː] banco m de iglesia.

pew·ter [ˈpjuːtə] (*attr.* de) peltre m; **'~·er** peltrero m.

pha·lanx [ˈfælæŋks] falange f.

phan·tom [ˈfæntəm] 1. fantasma m; 2. fantasmal.

phar·i·sa·ic, phar·i·sa·i·cal [færiˈseiik(l)] ☐ farisaico.

Phar·i·see [ˈfærisiː] fariseo m.

phar·ma·ceu·tics [fɑːməˈsuːtiks] farmacéutica f; farmacia f; **pharma·cist** [ˈfɑːməsist] farmacéutico m; **phar·ma·col·o·gy** [ˈkɔlədʒi] farmacología f; **'phar·ma·cy** farmacia f.

phar·inx [ˈfæriŋks] faringe f.

phase [feiz] fase f, etapa f.

pheas·ant [ˈfeznt] faisán m.

phe·nom·e·nal [fiˈnɔminl] ☐ fenomenal; **phe'nom·e·non** [ˌ·nən], *pl.* **phe'nom·e·na** [ˌ·nə] fenómeno m.

phi·lan·der [fiˈlændə] flirtear, mariposear; **phi'lan·der·er** tenorio m.

phil·an·throp·ic [filənˈθrɔpik] ☐ filantrópico; **phi·lan·thro·pist** [fiˈlænθrəpist] filántropo (a f) m; **phi·lan·thro·py** filantropía f.

phi·lat·e·list [fiˈlætəlist] filatelista m/f; **phi'lat·e·ly** filatelia f.

Phi·lip·pine [ˈfilipain] filipino adj. a. su. m (a f).

phi·lol·o·gist [fiˈlɔlədʒist] filólogo m; **phi'lol·o·gy** filología f.

phi·los·o·pher [fiˈlɔsəfə] filósofo m; **phil·o·soph·ic, phil·o·soph·i·cal** [filəˈsɔfik(l)] ☐ filosófico; **phi·los·o·phize** [fiˈlɔsəfaiz] filosofar; **phi'los·o·phy** filosofía f.

phlegm [flem] flema f (a. *fig.*); **phleg·mat·ic** [fleɡˈmætik] ☐ flemático.

phone [foun] F = *telephone*; ~ *call* llamada f telefónica.

pho·net·ic [fouˈnetik] ☐ fonético; **pho·net·ics** [fouˈnetiks] fonética f.

pho·no·graph [ˈfounəɡrɑːf] fonógrafo m.

pho·nol·o·gy [founˈɔlədʒi] fonología f.

pho·ny [ˈfouni] sl. 1. farsante m/f; persona f insincera; 2. falso, postizo; sospechoso; insincero.

phos·pho·resce [fɔsfəˈres] fosforecer; **phos·pho·res·cent** fosforescente; **phos·pho·rus** [ˈ~fərəs] fósforo m.

pho·to [ˈfoutou] F foto f; **'~·cop·ier** fotocopiador m; fotóstato m; **'~·co·py** 1. fotocopia f; 2. fotocopiar; **'~·e·lec·tric 'cell** célula f fotoeléctrica; **~·en·grav·ing** [ˌ·inˈɡreivin] fotograbado *m*; '~ **'fin·ish** (resultado *m* comprobado por) fotocontrol *m*; *fig.* final *m* muy reñido; **pho·to·gen·ic** [ˌ~'dʒenik] fotogénico (*a.* F).

pho·to·graph ['foutəgrɑːf] 1. fotografía *f* (*foto*); 2. fotografiar; **pho·tog·ra·pher** [fə'tɔgrəfə] fotógrafo (a *f*) *m*; **pho·tog·ra·phy** [fə'tɔgrəfi] fotografía *f* (*arte*).

pho·to·gra·vure [foutəgrə'vjuə] fotograbado *m*, huecograbado *m*; **'pho·to·play** fotodrama *m*; **pho·to·stat** ['foutoustæt] 1. fotóstato *m*; 2. fotostatar; **pho·to·syn·the·sis** fotosíntesis *f*; **pho·to·type** ['~taip] fototipo *m*.

phrase [freiz] 1. frase *f* (*a.* ♪); expresión *f*, locución *f*; 2. expresar; **phrase·ol·o·gy** [ˌ~i'ɔlədʒi] fraseología *f*.

phys·ic ['fizik] purgante *m*; ~**s** *sg.* física *f*; **'phys·i·cal** □ físico; **physi·cian** [fi'ziʃn] médico *m*; **phys·i·cist** ['~sist] físico *m*.

phys·i·og·no·my [fizi'ɔnəmi] fisonomía *f*; **phys·i·og·ra·phy** [ˌ~'ɔgrəfi] fisiografía *f*; **phys·i·ol·o·gy** [ˌ~'ɔlədʒi] fisiología *f*.

phy·sique [fi'ziːk] físico *m*.

pi·an·ist ['pjænist, 'piənist] pianista *m/f*.

pi·an·o [pi'ænou, 'pjaːnou, pi'ænou] piano(forte) *m*.

pi·az·za [pi'ædʒə] pórtico *m*, galería *f*.

pic·a·resque [pikə'resk] picaresco.

pick [pik] 1. (~axe) (zapa)pico *m*, piqueta *f*; (*choice*) derecho *m* de elección; 2. *v/t.* escoger (con cuidado); *bone* roer; *flower* coger; *fruit* recoger; ~ out escoger; ~ up recoger *from floor etc.*; (*recover*) recobrar; (*casually*) saber o encontrar *etc.*) por casualidad; (*learn*) lograr aprender; *radio:* captar; *v/i.* escoger; F~ on perseguir, criticar; ~ up *F* reponerse; '~axe *v. pick* 1; **picked** [pikt] escogido; **'pick·er** recogedor *m*.

pick·et ['pikit] 1. estaca *f*; ✕ piquete *m*; (*guardia f* de) vigilante(s) *m(pl.)* huelguista(s); 2. *factory* cercar con un cordón de huelguistas.

pick·ing ['pikiŋ] recolección *f of fruit etc.*; ~**s** *pl.* sobras *f/pl.*

pick·le ['pikl] 1. (*as condiment*) encurtido *m* (*a.* ~**s** *pl.*); (*fish, olives*) escabeche *m*; F apuro *m*; lío *m*; 2. escabechar; adobar.

pick...: '~-me-up F reconstituyente *m*; ✚ tónico *m*; '~-pock·et ratero *m*,

carterista *m*; '~-up pick-up *m*; ~ arm palanca *f*.

pic·nic ['piknik] 1. jira *f*, excursión *f* campestre, picnic *m*; *sl.* cosa *f* fácil; 2. merendar *etc.* en el campo.

pic·to·ri·al [pik'tɔːriəl] □ pictórico.

pic·ture ['piktʃə] 1. cuadro *m*, pintura *f*; (*portrait*) retrato *m*; (*photo*) fotografía *f*; lámina *f in book; television:* cuadro *m*; 2. pintar; describir; ~ (*to o.s.*) imaginarse, representarse; '~ **frame** marco *m*; '~ **gal·ler·y** museo *m* de pintura; '~ **post·card** postal *f* ilustrada.

pic·tur·esque [piktʃə'resk] □ pintoresco.

pie [pai] (*sweet*) pastel *m*; (*meat etc.*) empanada *f*.

piece [piːs] 1. (*fragment*) pedazo *m*, fragmento *m*; trozo *m*; ♪, *thea.*, ✕, ⊕, *coin, chess* etc.: pieza *f*; *in* ~**s** hecho pedazos, roto; desmontado; ~ *of advice* consejo *m*; ~ *of furniture* mueble *m*; ~ *of ground* terreno *m*; solar *m*; ~ *of news* noticia *f*; 2. (*a.* ~ *together*) juntar (las piezas de); *fig.* atar cabos; '~**meal** *adv.* a trozos; sin sistema fijo; '~**work** trabajo *m* a destajo.

pier [piə] △ estribo *m*, pila *f of bridge*; pilar *m*, columna *f*; ⚓ muelle *m*.

pierce [piəs] penetrar, taladrar; horadar; perforar; **pierc·ing** ['piəsiŋ] □ penetrante, agudo.

pi·e·ty ['paiəti] piedad *f*, devoción *f*.

pig [pig] cerdo *m*, puerco *m*, cochino *m*; F (*p.*) marrano *m*; F *make a* ~ *of o.s.* comer demasiado.

pi·geon ['pidʒin] paloma *f*; '~**hole** 1. casilla *f*; 2. encasillar; clasificar.

pig-head·ed ['pig'hedid] □ terco, cabezudo.

pig i·ron ['pigaiən] hierro *m* en lingotes.

pig·ment ['pigmənt] pigmento *m*.

pig·my ['pigmi] pigmeo *adj. a. su. m.*

pig...: '~**skin** piel *f* de cerdo; *sl.* balón *m* de fútbol; '~**sty** ['~stai] pocilga *f*, cochiquera *f* (*a. fig.*); '~**tail** trenza *f*, coleta *f*.

pike [paik] ✕ pica *f*; *ichth.* lucio *m*; '**pik·er** *sl.* cicatero *m*; cobarde *m*.

pile[1] [pail] 1. montón *m*, pila *f*; *mole f of buildings; phys.* (*atomic* ~) pila *f*; 2. (*a.* ~ *up*) amontonar(se), apilar(se).

pile[2] [~] pelo *m of carpet*; pelillo *m of cloth*.

pile driv·er ['paildraivə] martinete *m*.

piles [pailz] *pl.* ✚ almorranas *f/pl.*

pil·fer ['pilfə] ratear; **'pil·fer·ing** ratería f.

pil·grim ['pilgrim] peregrino (a f) m; romero (a f) m; **'pil·grim·age** peregrinación f, romería f.

pill [pil] píldora f; sl. pelota f; sl. persona f molesta.

pil·lar ['pilə] pilar m, columna f; fig. sostén m.

pill·box ['pilbɔks] fortín m; estuche m para píldoras.

pil·low ['pilou] 1. almohada f; 2. apoyar sobre una almohada; **'~·case**, **'~·slip** funda f de almohada.

pi·lot ['pailət] 1. ✈ piloto m; ⚓ práctico m; mechero m encendedor on stove; 2. pilotar; fig. guiar; conducir.

pi·men·to [pi'mentou] pimienta f.

pimp [pimp] 1. alcahuete m; 2. alcahuetear.

pim·ple ['pimpl] grano m; **'pim·ply** granujoso.

pin [pin] 1. alfiler m; ⊕ perno m; (wooden) clavija f; **~** pl. sl. piernas f/pl.; **~ball** billar m romano; 2. prender con alfiler(es); sujetar (con perno etc.); **~** down fig. inmovilizar; p. obligar a que concrete.

pinch [pintʃ] 1. pellizco m with fingers; cooking: pizca f; pulgarada f of snuff; 2. v/t. pellizcar with fingers; finger cogerse in door etc.; (shoe) apretar; sl. (steal) birlar, guindar; (arrest) prender; v/i. (shoe) apretar.

pinch-hit ['pintʃhit] 1. batear de emergente; 2. sl. servir de sustituto (for para).

pin cush·ion ['pinkuʃin] acerico m.

pine¹ [pain] ♀ pino m.

pine² [~] languidecer, consumirse.

pine...: **'~·ap·ple** ananás m, piña f; **'~·cone** piña f; **'~·need·le** aguja f de pino.

ping [piŋ] 1. sonido m metálico; 2. hacer un sonido metálico (como una bala).

ping-pong ['piŋpɔŋ] ping-pong m.

pin·ion ['pinjən] 1. ⊕ piñón m; 2. p. atar los brazos de.

pink [piŋk] 1. ♀ clavel m, clavellina f; 2. rosado; color de rosa (a. su. m); pol. rojillo, procomunista m/f.

pin mon·ey ['pinmʌni] alfileres m/pl.

pin·na·cle ['pinəkl] △ pináculo m, chapitel m; cumbre f (a. fig.).

pin...: **'~·point** fig. indicar con toda precisión; **'~·prick** alfilerazo m; fig. molestia f pequeña.

pint [paint] pinta f (= 0,473 litros).

pin-up ['pinʌp] F foto f de muchacha guapa, pin-up f; fig. mujer f ideal.

pi·o·neer [paiə'niə] 1. explorador m; (early settler) colonizador m; 2. v/i. explorar; v/t. settlement etc. preparar el terreno para; scheme, study iniciar, promover.

pi·ous ['paiəs] ☐ piadoso, devoto.

pipe [paip] 1. tubo m, caño m, cañería f; conducto m; cañón m of organ; ♪ caramillo m; pipa f for tobacco; 2. v/t. conducir en cañerías etc.; v/i. tocar el caramillo; sl. **~** down callarse; **'~ line** (oil) oleoducto m; cañería f.

pip·ing ['paipiŋ] cañería(s) f(pl.).

pip·squeak ['pipskwi:k] persona f sin importancia.

pi·quant ['pi:kənt] ☐ picante.

pique [pi:k] 1. pique m, resentimiento m; 2. picar, herir.

pi·ra·cy ['paiərəsi] piratería f; **pi·rate** ['~rit] 1. pirata m; 2. pillar, robar; publicar fraudulentamente.

pi·rou·ette [piru'et] 1. pirueta f; 2. piruetear.

piss [pis] 1. orina f; 2. mear.

pis·tol ['pistl] pistola f; revólver m; sl. persona f descarada.

pis·ton ['pistən] émbolo m, pistón m; **'~ ring** aro m (or segmento m) de pistón; **'~ dis·place·ment** cilindrada f.

pit [pit] 1. hoyo m, hoya f, foso m; ⚒ mina f (de carbón); (quarry) cantera f; thea. parte f posterior del patio; hueso m of a fruit; 2. marcar (con hoyas); (match) oponer (against a).

pitch¹ [pitʃ] pez f, brea f; **~** dark negro como boca de lobo.

pitch² [~] 1. (throw) lanzamiento m, echada f; ⚓ cabezada f; ♪ tono m; 2. v/t. arrojar, echar; lanzar; tent armar; ♪ graduar el tono de; note entonar, dar; v/i. caerse (into en); ⚓ cabecear.

pitch·er¹ ['pitʃə] cántaro m, jarro m.

pitch·er² [~] lanzador m of baseball team.

pitch·fork ['pitʃfɔ:k] horca f, tornadera f, bielda f.

pit·e·ous ['pitiəs] ☐ lastimero, lastimoso.

pit·fall ['pitfɔ:l] fig. escollo m, trampa f.

pith [piθ] ♀ médula f (a. fig.).

pith·y ['piθi] ☐ fig. sucinto, expresivo, lacónico.

pit·i·a·ble ['pitiəbl] □ enternecedor, digno de compasión.

pit·i·ful ['pitiful] □ lastimero, lastimoso; (*contemptible*) despreciable, lamentable.

pit·i·less ['pitilis] □ despiadado, implacable.

pi·tu·i·tar·y [pi'tjuːitəri] 1. pituitario; 2. (a. ~ gland) glándula f pituitaria.

pit·y ['piti] 1. piedad f, compasión f; lástima f; for ~'s sake! ¡por piedad!; it is a ~ (that) es lástima (que *subj.*); what a ~! ¡qué lástima!; 2. tener piedad de, compadecer(se de).

piv·ot ['pivət] 1. pivote m, gorrón m; fig. punto m central; 2. v/t. montar sobre un pivote; v/i. girar (on sobre).

pix·ie ['piksi] duende m.

pla·card ['plækɑːd] cartel m.

pla·cate [plə'keit] aplacar.

place [pleis] 1. sitio m, lugar m; (*enclosed*) local m; (*post*) puesto m, empleo m; (*rank*) lugar m, puesto m; (*seat*) plaza f; cubierto m at table; ~ mat estera f de cubierto; in ~ of en lugar de; in the first ~ en primer lugar; out of ~ fuera de (su) lugar; fuera de serie; fuera de propósito; take ~ tener lugar; verificarse; 2. colocar, poner; fijar; colocar in post etc.; '~-name topónimo m.

plac·id ['plæsid] □ plácido; **pla·cid·i·ty** placidez f.

pla·gia·rism ['pleidʒiərizm] plagio m; **'pla·gia·rist** plagiario (a f) m; **'pla·gia·rize** plagiar.

plague [pleig] 1. peste f, plaga f; 2. plagar, infestar; fig. atormentar.

plaid [plæd] plaid m, manta f escocesa; (*cloth*) tartán m.

plain [plein] 1. □ sencillo, llano; sin adornos; (*unmixed*) natural, puro; face sin atractivo, ordinario; it is ~ that es evidente que; ~ truth verdad f lisa y llana; 2. adv. claro, claramente; 3. llano m, llanura f; '~·clothes man agente m de policía que lleva traje de calle; 'plain·ness llaneza f; falta f de atractivo of face etc.

plains·man ['pleinzmən] llanero m.

plain·tiff ['pleintif] demandante m/f; **'plain·tive** □ dolorido, plañidero.

plait [plæt] 1. trenza f; 2. trenzar.

plan [plæn] 1. proyecto m, plan m; △ plano m; 2. v/t. planear, planificar; proyectar; idear; v/i. hacer proyectos (for para); ~ to proponerse inf.

plane [plein] 1. plano m; 2. ⅌ plano m;

avión m; ala f; ⊕ cepillo m (de carpintero); 3. ⊕ acepillar.

plan·et ['plænit] planeta m.

plan·e·tar·i·um [plæni'teəriəm] planetario m; **plan·e·tar·y** ['~təri] planetario.

plank [plæŋk] 1. tablón m, tabla f (gruesa); ~s pl. tablaje m; 2. entablar, entarimar.

plan·ning ['plænin] planificación f.

plant [plɑːnt] 1. ♀ planta f (a. ⊕); ⊕ instalación f, maquinaria f; ∉ grupo m electrógeno; (*factory*) fábrica f; 2. plantar; (*sow*) sembrar; sentar, colocar.

plan·tain ['plæntin] llantén m.

plan·ta·tion [plæn'teiʃn] plantación f; vega f S.Am. of tobacco; arboleda f of trees; **plant·er** ['plɑːntə] plantador m; colono m.

plaque [plɑːk] placa f.

plas·ma ['plæzmə] plasma m.

plas·ter ['plɑːstə] 1. yeso m; △ argamasa f; (*layer*) enlucido m; ⚕ emplasto m; 2. enyesar, enlucir; ⚕ emplastar; fig. cubrir, llenar (with de).

plas·tic ['plæstik] 1. plástico; ~ surgery cirugía f estética (or plástica); 2. plástico m.

plate [pleit] 1. plato m; (*plaque*) placa f; ⊕ lámina f, chapa f, plancha f; (*silver*) vajilla f de plata; 2. planchear, chapear; niquelar etc.; ~ glass vidrio m cilindrado.

pla·teau ['plætou] meseta f.

plate·ful ['pleitful] plato m.

plat·form ['plætfɔːm] plataforma f; tablado m; tribuna f at meeting; ⅏ andén m; pol. programa m electoral.

plat·ing ['pleitin] enchapado m.

plat·i·num ['plætinəm] platino m; ~ blonde rubia f platino.

plat·i·tude ['plætitjuːd] lugar m común, perogrullada f, platitud f.

pla·toon ['plə'tuːn] pelotón m.

plat·ter ['plætə] fuente f; sl. ♪ disco m.

plau·si·ble ['plɔːzəbl] □ especioso, aparente.

play [plei] 1. juego m (a. ⊕), recreo m; thea. obra f dramática, pieza f; fair (foul) ~ juego m limpio (sucio); ~ on words juego m de palabras; sport: in ~ en juego; 2. v/i. jugar (at a); divertirse; ♪ tocar; thea. representar; v/t. card jugar, game, cards etc. jugar a; opponent jugar con(tra); ♪ tocar; thea. play representar, poner; '~

back ✍ lectura f; '**~·bill** cartel m; '**~·boy** señorito m amante de los placeres; '**play·er** jugador (-a f) m; thea. actor m, actriz f; ♪ músico (a f) m; '**~** '*piano* autopiano m; **play·ful** ['~ful] □ juguetón; '**~·go·er** aficionado (a f) m al teatro; '**~·ground** patio m de recreo; '**~·house** teatro m; casita f de muñecas.

play·ing...: '**~** **card** carta f; '**~** **field** campo m de deportes.

play...: '**~·mate** compañero (a f) m de juego; '**~·off** (partido m de) desempate m; '**~·pen** parque m (de niño), corral m; '**~·thing** juguete m (a. fig.).

plea [pli:] pretexto m, disculpa f; ⚖ (alegato m de) defensa f; contestación f a la demanda.

plead [pli:d] v/i. suplicar (with acc.), rogar (with s.o. for a uno que conceda); ⚖ abogar; **~** *guilty* confesarse culpable; '**plead·ing** (a. ~s pl.) súplicas f/pl.; ⚖ alegatos m/pl.

pleas·ant ['pleznt] □ agradable; surprise etc. grato; manner, style ameno.

please [pli:z] v/i. gustar; dar satisfacción; ~ *tell me* haga Vd. el favor de decirme, dígame por favor; as you ~ como Vd. quiera; v/t. gustar, dar gusto a, caer en gracia; be ~d to complacerse en; we are ~d to inform you nos es grato informarle; I am ~d to meet you tengo mucho gusto en conocerle; **pleas·ing** ['pli:ziŋ] □ agradable, grato.

pleas·ur·a·ble ['pleʒərəbl] □ agradable, deleitoso.

pleas·ure ['pleʒə] placer m; gusto m; deleite m; (will) voluntad f; it is a ~ es un placer.

pleat [pli:t] 1. pliegue m, plisar.

ple·be·ian [pli'bi:ən] plebeyo adj. a. su. m (a f).

pledge [pledʒ] 1. (security) prenda f (a. fig.); (promise) promesa f; (toast) brindis m; 2. (pawn) empeñar; (promise) prometer; (toast) brindar por.

ple·na·ry ['pli:nəri] plenario.

plen·te·ous ['plentiəs] □, **plen·ti·ful** ['plentiful] □ copioso, abundante.

plen·ty ['plenti] 1. abundancia f; in ~ en abundancia; 2. F: know ~ saber (lo) bastante; ~ of people do hay muchos que lo hacen.

pleu·ri·sy ['pluərisi] pleuresía f.

plex·i·glass ['pleksiglæs] plexiglás m.

pli·a·ble ['plaiəbl] □, **pli·ant** ['plai-

ənt] □ flexible, plegable; fig. dócil, manejable.

pli·ers ['plaiəz] pl. (a pair of ~ unos) alicates m/pl.

plight [plait] apuro m, aprieto m; condición f (inquietante), situación f (difícil).

plod [plɔd] avanzar (or caminar) laboriosamente; trabajar laboriosamente (away at en); '**plod·der** estudiante m/f etc. más aplicado que brillante; '**plod·ding** □ perseverante, laborioso.

plot[1] [plɔt] parcela f, terreno m; (building-) solar m; cuadro m.

plot[2] [~] 1. complot m, conspiración f; thea. etc. argumento m, trama f; 2. v/t. course etc. trazar; maquinar; v/i. conspirar, intrigar (to para); '**plot·ter** conspirador (-a f) m.

plough [plau] = **plow**.

plow [~] 1. arado m; 2. v/t. arar; v/i. arar; fig. ~ *through* snow etc. abrirse con dificultad paso por; book leer con dificultad; '**~·ing** arada f; '**~·share** reja f del arado.

ploy [plɔi] maniobra f; artimaña f.

pluck [plʌk] 1. valor m, ánimo m; 2. coger; arrancar; bird desplumar; **pluck·y** ['plʌki] □ valiente, animoso.

plug [plʌg] 1. tapón m, taco m; tampón m (a. ⚕); mot. bujía f; ⚡ enchufe m; ⚡ (wall) toma f; (fire-) boca f de agua; 2. v/t. tapar, obturar; ⚡ ~ *in* enchufar; v/i. sl. (a. ~ away) trabajar con ahinco (at en), seguir trabajando a pesar de todo; '**~·in** enchufable.

plum [plʌm] ciruela f; ciruelo m.

plumb [plʌm] 1. plomada f; 2. adj. vertical, a plomo; 3. adv. verticalmente, a plomo; 4. fig. sond(e)ar; **plumb·er** ['~mə] fontanero m; **plumb·ing** ['~miŋ] (craft) fontanería f; (piping) instalación f de cañerías; '**plumb line** cuerda f de plomada.

plume [plu:m] pluma f; penacho m.

plump[1] [plʌmp] rechoncho, rollizo; fowl etc. gordo.

plump[2] [plʌmp] □ dejar(se) caer pesadamente; ~ *for* optar por.

plump·ness ['plʌmpnis] gordura f.

plum pud·ding [plʌm 'pudiŋ] pudín m inglés (de Navidad).

plun·der ['plʌndə] 1. botín m, pillaje m; 2. saquear, pillar.

plunge [plʌndʒ] 1. zambullida f; salto m; 2. zambullir(se); sumergir(se);

fig. arrojar(se); precipitar(se); hundir.

plu·per·fect ['pluː'pɜːfikt] pluscuamperfecto *m*.

plu·ral ['pluərəl] plural *adj. a. su. m*; **plu·ral·i·ty** [ˌ'ræliti] pluralidad *f*.

plus [plʌs] 1. *prp.* más, y; 2. *adj.* positivo; adicional; F y algo más, y pico.

plush [plʌʃ] 1. felpa *f*; 2. F lujoso, de buen tono.

plu·to·ni·um [pluː'touniəm] plutonio *m*.

ply [plai] 1.: *three* ~ de tres capas; *wool* de tres cordones; 2. *v/t.* tool manejar, menear (vigorosamente); *trade* ejercer; *v/i.*: ~ *between* hacer el servicio entre; '~·**wood** madera *f* contrachapeada, panel *m*.

pneu·mat·ic [njuˈmætik] □ neumático; ~ *drill* perforadora *f*, martillo *m* picador; ~ *tire* neumático *m*.

pneu·mo·ni·a [njuˈmounjə] pulmonía *f*.

poach¹ [poutʃ] *v/t. a. v/i.* cazar (or pescar) en vedado.

poach² [~] *v/t.* escalfar.

poach·er ['poutʃə] cazador *m* furtivo; **'poach·ing** caza *f* furtiva.

pock·et ['pɔkit] 1. bolsillo *m*; *fig.* bolsa *f* (*a.* ⚡, *geol.*), cavidad *f*; *pick s.o.'s* ~ robar la cartera etc. a alguien; 2. embolsar; *b.s.* apropiarse; 3. *attr.* ... de bolsillo; '~·**book** (*purse*) bolsa *f*; portamonedas *m*; '~ **cal·cu·la·tor** calculadora *f* de bolsillo; '~·**knife** cortaplumas *m*; '~ **mon·ey** dinero *m* para pequeños gastos personales; '~·**size** de bolsillo.

pock·marked ['pɔkmɑːkt] picado de viruelas; *fig.* marcado de hoyos.

pod [pɔd] vaina *f*.

po·di·um ['poudiəm] △ podio *m*.

po·em ['pouim] poesía *f*, poema *m*.

po·et ['pouit] poeta *m*; **'po·et·ry** poesía *f*; *attr.* de poesía.

poign·an·cy ['pɔinənsi] patetismo *m*; **'poign·ant** □ conmovedor.

point [pɔint] 1. punto *m* (*a. sport, typ.*, ⚡); (*sharp*) punta *f*; puntilla *f* of *pen*; *geog.* punta *f*, cabo *m*; cuarta *f* of *compass*; (*objective*) propósito *m*, finalidad *f*; *the* ~ *is that* lo importante es que; *there is no* ~ *in* no vale la pena *inf.*; ~ *of order* cuestión *f* de procedimiento; *up to a* ~ hasta cierto punto; *be beside the* ~ no venir al caso; *see the* ~ caer en la cuenta; *I do not see the* ~ *of ger.* no creo que sea

necesario *inf.*; *speak to the* ~ hablar al caso; 2. *v/t.* (*sharpen*) afilar, aguzar; *pencil* sacar punta a; *gun etc.* apuntar (*at* a); ~ *a finger at* señalar con el dedo; ~ *out* indicar, señalar; *v/i.*: *it* ~*s west* está orientado hacia el oeste; '~·**blank** (*adj.* hecho *etc.*) a quemarropa (*a. fig.*); '**point·ed** □ puntiagudo; *remark* inequívoco; lleno de intención; '**point·er** indicador *m on gauge*; (*dog*) perro *m* de muestra.

poise [pɔiz] 1. equilibrio *m*; aplomo *m*; confianza *f* en sí mismo; 2. *v/t.* equilibrar; balancear.

poi·son ['pɔizn] 1. veneno *m* (*a. fig.*); 2. *attr.* venenoso; ~ *gas* gas *m* asfixiante; '~·**pen** letter carta *f* calumniosa; 3. envenenar (*a. fig.*); '**poi·son·ous** □ venenoso; F pésimo.

poke [pouk] 1. empuje *m*, empujón *m*; codazo *m*; hurgonazo *m* of *fire*; 2. empujar; *hole* hacer a empujones; *fire* hurgar, atizar.

pok·er¹ ['poukə] *approx.* atizador *m*, badila *f*.

po·ker² [~] *cards*: póker *m*, póquer *m*; ~ *face* cara *f* impasible.

po·lar ['poulə] polar; ~ *bear* oso *m* blanco; **po·lar·i·ty** [~'læriti] polaridad *f*; '**po·lar·ize** polarizar.

Pole¹ [poul] polaco (*a f*) *m*.

pole² [~] *geog.*, ⚡ *etc.* polo *m*.

pole³ [~] palo *m*, vara *f* larga; (*flag*) asta *f*; (*tent*) mástil *m*; (*telegraph*) poste *m*; (*vaulting etc.*) pértiga *f*; '~·**cat** turón *m*; mofeta *f*.

pole·star ['poulstɑː] estrella *f* polar; *fig.* norte *m*.

pole vault ['poulvɔːlt] salto *m* con pértiga.

po·lice [pəˈliːs] 1. policía *f*; ~ *court* tribunal *m* de policía; ~ *force* (cuerpo *m* de) policía *f*; ~ *state* estadopolicía *m*; 2. *frontier* vigilar, patrullar; *area* mantener servicio de policía en; '~·**man** guardia *m*, policía *m*; agente *m* de policía; '~ **re·cord** ficha *f*; '~·**sta·tion** comisaría *f*; '~·**wom·an** policía *m* femenino.

pol·i·cy ['pɔlisi] política *f*; programa *m* político; normas *f/pl.* de conducta *of newspaper etc.*; (*insurance*) póliza *f*.

Pol·ish ['pouliʃ] polaco *adj. a. su. m*.

pol·ish ['pɔliʃ] 1. (*shine*) lustre *m*, brillo *m*, bruñido *m*; (*shoe*) betún *m*; (*floor*) cera *f* de lustrar; 2. *floor etc.* encerar, sacar brillo a; *pans etc.* abrillantar; *shoes* limpiar; *silver etc.* pulir; '**pol·ished** *fig.* fino, elegante,

pol·ish·ing 1. el pulir *etc.*; **2.** *attr.* de lustrar *etc.*; ~ *machine* enceradora *f*.

po·lite [pəˈlait] □ cortés, atento, fino; **po·lite·ness** cortesía *f etc.*

pol·i·tic [ˈpɔlitik] □ prudente, aconsejable; *body* ~ el estado; **pol·i·tician** [pɔliˈtiʃn] político *m*; *b.s.* politiquero *m*; **pol·i·tics** [ˈpɔlitiks] política *f*.

pol·ka [ˈpɔlkə] polca *f*; diseño *m* de puntos.

poll [poul] (*election*) votación *f*, elección *f*; (*total votes*) votos *m/pl.*; (*public opinion* ~) organismo *m* de sondaje; (*inquiry*) encuesta *f*, sondeo *m*.

pol·len [ˈpɔlin] polen *m*; **pol·lin·ate** [ˈpɔlineit] fecundar (con polen).

poll·ing [ˈpoulin] votación *f*; **'~ booth** caseta *f* de votar; **'~ day** día *m* de elecciones; **'~ place** urnas *f/pl.* electorales; **'~ sta·tion** urnas *f/pl.* electorales; **'poll tax** capitación *f*.

pol·lu·tant [pəˈluːtənt] contaminante *m*; **pol·lute** [pəˈluːt] *water etc.* contaminar, ensuciar.

po·lo [ˈpoulou] polo *m*.

po·lyg·a·mist [pəˈligəmist] polígamo (*a f*) *m*; **po·lyg·a·my** [pəˈligəmi] poligamia *f*; **pol·y·glot** [ˈpɔliglɔt] poligloto *adj. a. su. m* (*a f*); **pol·y·phon·ic** [~ˈfɔnik] □ polifónico; **pol·y·syl·la·ble** [ˈ~siləbl] polisílabo *m*; **pol·y·tech·nic** [~ˈteknik] escuela *f* de formación profesional; **pol·y·the·ism** [ˈ~θiizm] politeísmo *m*.

pome·gran·ate [ˈpɔmigrænit] granada *f*.

pom·mel [ˈpʌml] **1.** pomo *m*; **2.** apuñear, dar de puñetazos.

pomp [pɔmp] pompa *f*; **pom·pos·i·ty** [pɔmˈpɔsiti] pomposidad *f etc.*; **'pomp·ous** □ pomposo.

pond [pɔnd] charca *f*; estanque *m*.

pon·der [ˈpɔndə] *v/t. a. v/i.* ponderar, considerar con especial cuidado; **'pon·der·ous** □ pesado; laborioso.

pon·tiff [ˈpɔntif] pontífice *m*; **pon·tif·i·cal** □ pontificio, pontifical.

pon·toon [pɔnˈtuːn] pontón *m*.

po·ny [ˈpouni] jaca *f*, caballito *m*, poney *m*; F chuleta *f*.

pooch [puːtʃ] *sl.* perro *m*.

poo·dle [ˈpuːdl] perro *m* de lanas.

pooh-pooh [puːˈpuː] rechazar con desdén; negar importancia a.

pool [puːl] **1.** charca *f*, (*artificial*) estanque *m*; (*swimming-*) piscina *f*; *billiards:* trucos *m/pl.*; fusión *f* de intereses; ✝ fondo *m* común; **2.** *resources* juntar, mancomunar; **'~ room** sala *f* de trucos; **'~ table** mesa *f* de trucos.

poor [pue] □ pobre; *quality* malo, bajo; *spirit* mezquino; **'~ box** cepo *m* para los pobres; **'~ house** asilo *m* de los pobres; **'poor·ly 1.** *adj.* enfermo; **2.** *adv.* pobremente; mal.

pop¹ [pɔp] **1.** ligera detonación *f*; taponazo *m of cork*; F gaseosa *f*; **2.** *v/t.* ~ *corn* hacer palomitas de maíz; F ~ *the question* declararse; *v/i.* estallar (con ligera detonación); reventar; **3.** ¡pum!

pop² [~] F (*abbr. of popular*): ~ *concert* concierto *m* popular.

pop³ [~] F papá *m*.

pop·corn [ˈpɔpkɔːn] rosetas *f/pl.*, palomitas *f/pl.*

pope [poup] papa *m*.

pop·eyed [ˈpɔpaid] de ojos saltones.

pop·gun [ˈpɔpgʌn] taco *m*, fusil *m* de juguete.

pop·lar [ˈpɔplə] (*white*) álamo *m*; (*black*) chopo *m*.

pop·lin [ˈpɔplin] popelín *m*, popelina *f*.

pop·py [ˈpɔpi] amapola *f*, adormidera *f*; **'~ cock** F ¡tonterías! (*a. su. f/pl.*).

pop·u·lace [ˈpɔpjuləs] pueblo *m*; *contr.* populacho *m*.

pop·u·lar [ˈpɔpjulə] □ popular; **pop·u·lar·ize** [~ˈləraiz] vulgarizar.

pop·u·late [ˈpɔpjuleit] poblar; **pop·u·la·tion** población *f*.

por·ce·lain [ˈpɔːslin] porcelana *f*.

porch [pɔːtʃ] pórtico *m*; entrada *f*.

por·cu·pine [ˈpɔːkjupain] puerco *m* espín.

pork [pɔːk] carne *f* de cerdo (*or* puerco); ~ *chop* chuleta *f* de puerco; **'pork·er** cerdo *m*.

por·no·graph·ic [pɔːnəˈgræfik] pornográfico; **por·nog·ra·phy** [pɔːˈnɔgrəfi] pornografía *f*; F **'por·no queen** actriz *f* de películas pornográficas.

po·rous [ˈpɔːrəs] □ poroso.

por·poise [ˈpɔːpəs] marsopa *f*.

port¹ [pɔːt] ♣ (*harbor*) puerto *m*.

port² [~] ♣ (~*hole*) portilla *f*; ⊕ lumbrera *f*.

port³ [~] ♣ (*a.* ~ *side*) babor *m*.

port⁴ [~] vino *m* de Oporto.

port·a·ble [ˈpɔːtəbl] portátil.

por·tend [pɔːˈtend] pronosticar.

por·tent [ˈpɔːtent] presagio *m*, augurio *m*; **por·ten·tous** □ portentoso.

por·ter ['pɔːtə] portero *m*, conserje *m*; 🚂 mozo *m* (de estación); '**por·ter·house**: ~ steak bistec *m* de filete.

port·fo·li·o [pɔːt'fouljou] cartera *f*; carpeta *f*; *without* ~ sin cartera.

port·hole ['pɔːthoul] portilla *f*.

por·tion ['pɔːʃn] 1. porción *f*, parte *f*; (*dowry*) dote *f*; (*helping*) ración *f*; 2. (*a.* ~ *out*) repartir, dividir.

port·li·ness ['pɔːtlinis] corpulencia *f*; '**port·ly** corpulento; grave.

por·trait ['pɔːtrit] retrato *m*; **por·tray** ['pɔː'treɪ] retratar; *fig.* describir.

Por·tu·guese [pɔːtju'giːz] 1. portugués *adj. a. su. m* (-a *f*); 2. (*language*) portugués *m*.

pose [pouz] 1. postura *f of body*; *fig.* afectación *f*, pose *f*; 2. *v/t. problem* plantear; *v/i.* (*model*) posar.

posh [pɔʃ] F elegante, de lujo, lujoso.

po·si·tion [pə'zɪʃn] 1. posición *f*, situación *f*; categoría *f*; (*post*) puesto *m*, colocación *f*; 2. colocar, disponer.

pos·i·tive ['pɔzətiv] 1. □ positivo (*a.* Å, ⚡, phot.); (*affirmative*) afirmativo; (*emphatic*) enfático, categórico; ~*ly* realmente, absolutamente; 2. *phot.* positiva *f*; '**pos·i·tiv·ism** positivismo *m*.

pos·sess [pə'zes] poseer; apoderarse de; *be* ~*ed by idea* estar dominado por; **pos·sessed** [pə'zest] poseído, poseso; **pos·ses·sion** [pə'zeʃn] posesión *f*; ~*s pl.* bienes *m/pl.*; *in the* ~ *of* en poder de; **pos·ses·sor** poseedor (-a *f*) *m*.

pos·si·bil·i·ty [pɔsə'biliti] posibilidad *f*; '**pos·si·ble** □ posible; *as soon as* ~ cuanto antes; *do as much as* ~ *to* hacer lo posible para; '**pos·si·bly** posiblemente; tal vez; *if I* ~ *can* a serme posible.

post[1] [poust] poste *m*.

post[2] [~] 1. (*job*) puesto *m*; destino *m*; cargo *m*; ✕ *etc.* puesto *m*; ✆ correo *m*; (*casa f de*) correos; 2. *poster etc.* fijar, pegar; ✆ echar al correo; mandar por correo, despachar.

post·age ['poustidʒ] franqueo *m*; ~ *stamp* sello *m* (de correo), estampilla *f S.Am.*

post...: '~ **card** (tarjeta *f*) postal *f*; '~'**date** poner fecha adelantada *f*.

post·er ['poustə] cartel *m*.

pos·te·ri·or [pɔs'tiəriə] 1. posterior; 2. F *co.* asentaderas *f/pl.*

pos·ter·i·ty [pɔs'teriti] posteridad *f*.

post-free ['poust'friː] porte pagado.

post·grad·u·ate ['poust'grædjuit] postgraduado *adj. a. su. m* (a *f*).

post·hu·mous ['pɔstjuməs] □ póstumo.

post...: '~**man** cartero *m*; '~**mark** 1. matasellos *m*; 2. matar (el sello de); '~**mas·ter** administrador *m* de correos.

post·me·rid·i·an ['poustmə'ridiən] postmeridiano; **post-mor·tem** ['~'mɔːtəm] autopsia *f*.

post...: '~**of·fice** (casa *f* de) correos; ~ *box* apartado *m* (de correos); '~**paid** porte pagado.

post·pone [poust'poun] aplazar.

post·script ['pousskript] posdata *f*.

pos·tu·late 1. ['pɔstjulit] postulado *m*; 2. ['~leit] postular; '**pos·tu·lant** *eccl.* postulante (a *f*) *m*.

pos·ture ['pɔstʃə] 1. postura *f*, actitud *f*; 2. adoptar una actitud (afectada).

post-war ['poust'wɔː] de (la) post(e)-guerra.

po·sy ['pouzi] ramillete *m*; flor *f*.

pot [pɔt] 1. (*cooking*) olla *f*, puchero *m*, marmita *f*; (*preserving*) tarro *m*, pote *m*; (*flower-*) tiesto *m*; F *go to* ~ echarse a perder, arruinarse; 2. *plant* poner en tiesto.

po·tas·si·um [pə'tæsiəm] potasio *m*.

po·ta·to [pə'teitou], *pl.* **po·ta·toes** [~z] patata *f*, papa *f S.Am.*; '~ '**om·e·let** tortilla *f* a la española.

pot...: '~'**bel·lied** barrigón; '~'**boil·er** obra *f* mediocre compuesta para ganar dinero; '~ '**cheese** requesón *m*.

po·ten·cy ['poutənsi] potencia *f*; '**po·tent** □ potente; poderoso, eficaz; **po·ten·tial** [pə'tenʃl] potencial *adj. a. su. m*.

pot·hole ['pɔthoul] bache *m in road*; *geol.* marmita *f* de gigante.

pot·luck ['pɔt'lʌk]: *take* ~ comer (*fig.* tomar) lo que haya.

pot shot ['pɔtʃɔt] tiro *m* a corta distancia; tiro *m* al azar.

pot·ter ['pɔtə] alfarero *m*; ~'*s clay* arcilla *f* de alfarería; '**pot·ter·y** (*works, art*) alfarería *f*; (*pots*) cacharros *m/pl.*; (*archaeological etc.*) cerámicas *f/pl.*

pouch [pautʃ] bolsa *f*; *hunt. etc.* morral *m*, zurrón *m*; (*tobacco-*) petaca *f*.

poul·tice ['poultis] 1. cataplasma *f*, emplasto *m*; 2. emplastar.

poul·try ['poultri] aves *f/pl.* de corral; ~ *farm* granja *f* avícola.

pounce [pauns] 1. salto *m*; ataque *m* súbito; 2. atacar súbitamente.

pound[1] [paund] libra *f* (= 453,6 gr.); ~ (*sterling*) libra *f* (esterlina).

pound² [~] corral m de concejo.

pound³ [~] v/t. machacar, martillar, aporrear; (grind) moler; ✕ bombardear; v/i. dar golpes (at en).

pour [pɔː] v/t. echar, verter, derramar (a. fig.); v/i. correr, fluir (abundantemente); (rain) diluviar; llover a torrentes.

pout [paut] **1.** puchero m, mala cara f; **2.** hacer pucheros.

pov·er·ty ['pɔvəti] pobreza f, miseria f; escasez f.

pow·der ['paudə] **1.** polvo m; (face) polvos m/pl.; (gun) pólvora f; **2.** pulverizar(se); (dust with ~) polvorear; face, o.s. empolvarse; ponerse polvos; '~ **com·pact** polvera f; '~ **puff** borla f para empolvarse; '~ **room** cuarto m tocador; '**pow·der·y** substance en polvo; pulverizado.

pow·er ['pauə] poder m (a. ✍); poderío m; autoridad f; pol., ⚔ potencia f; ⊕ potencia f, energía f; ⚡ fuerza f; '~ **brake** mot. servofreno m; '~ **drill** taladradora f de fuerza; '~ **fail·ure** interrupción f de fuerza; '**pow·er·ful** [~ful] □ poderoso; ⊕ potente; build fuerte; '**pow·er·house** central f eléctrica; '**pow·er·less** □ impotente; sin fuerzas (to para); '~ **line** ⚡ línea f de fuerza; '~ **plant** grupo m electrógeno; '~ **saw** motosierra f; '~ **sta·tion** central f eléctrica; '~ **steer·ing** mot. servodirección f; '~ **strug·gle** lucha f por control; '~ **tool** herramienta f mecánica.

prac·ti·ca·ble ['præktikəbl] □ practicable, hacedero; '**prac·ti·cal** □ práctico; ~ joke trastada f, broma f pesada.

prac·tice ['præktis] **1.** práctica f; costumbre f; ejercicio m; ✒ clientela f; **2.** v/t. practicar; profession etc. ejercitar, ejercer; piano etc. hacer prácticas de; sport: hacer ejercicios de, entrenarse en; v/i. ensayarse, hacer ensayos (on en); (professionally) ejercer (as de); ✒ practicar la medicina.

prag·mat·ic [præg'mætik] □ pragmático.

prai·rie ['prεəri] pradera f, pampa f.

praise [preiz] **1.** alabanza f; elogio(s) m(pl.); **2.** alabar, elogiar; '~**·wor·thy** □ loable, digno de alabanza.

prance [prɑːns] encabritarse.

prank [præŋk] travesura f; broma f.

prat·tle ['prætl] **1.** parloteo m; (child's) balbuceo m; **2.** parlotear; (child) balbucear.

prawn [prɔːn] gamba f.

pray [prei] v/i. rezar; orar (for por, to a); v/t. rogar, pedir, suplicar (for acc.).

pray·er ['prεə] oración f, rezo m; (entreaty) súplica f, ruego m.

preach [priːtʃ] predicar (a. F, b.s.); advantages etc. celebrar; '~**·y** moralizador.

pre·am·ble [priː'æmbl] preámbulo m.

pre·ar·range [priːə'reindʒ] arreglar (or fijar) de antemano.

pre·car·i·ous [pri'kεəriəs] □ precario.

pre·cau·tion [pri'kɔːʃn] precaución f; **pre'cau·tion·ar·y** de precaución, preventivo.

pre·cede [pri'siːd] preceder; **prec·e·dence** ['presidəns] precedencia f; take ~ over primar sobre; **prec·e·dent** ['presidənt] precedente m; **pre'ced·ing** precedente.

pre·cept ['priːsept] precepto m.

pre·cinct ['priːsiŋkt] recinto m; distrito m electoral; barrio m; ~s pl. contornos m/pl.

pre·cious ['preʃəs] □ **1.** precioso; p. amado, querido; style afectado.

prec·i·pice ['presipis] precipicio m, despeñadero m; **pre'cip·i·tate 1.** [~teit] precipitar (a. 🜊); **2.** [~] 🜊 precipitado m; **3.** [~tit] precipitado; **pre'cip·i·tous** □ escarpado, cortado a pico.

pre·cise [pri'sais] □ preciso, exacto; (too ~) afectado; p. escrupuloso; **pre'cise·ness, pre·ci·sion** [pri'siʒn] (attr. de) precisión f, exactitud f.

pre·clude [pri'kluːd] excluir.

pre·co·cious [pri'kouʃəs] □ precoz.

pre·con·ceived ['priːkən'siːvd] preconcebido.

pre·cur·sor [pri'kɔːsə] precursor (-a f) m.

pred·e·ces·sor ['priːdisesə] predecesor (-a f) m, antecesor (-a f) m.

pre·des·ti·na·tion [pridesti'neiʃn] predestinación f.

pre·de·ter·mine ['priːdi'təːmin] predeterminar.

pre·dic·a·ment [pri'dikəmənt] apuro m, situación f difícil.

pred·i·cate ['predikit] gr. predicado m.

pre·dict [pri'dikt] pronosticar, predecir; **pre·dic·tion** [~'dikʃn] pronóstico m, predicción f.

pre·di·lec·tion [priːdiˈlekʃn] predilección f.

pre·dis·pose [ˈpriːdisˈpouz] predisponer; **pre·dis·po·si·tion** [ˈ~dispəˈziʃn] predisposición f.

pre·dom·i·nance [priˈdɔminəns] predominio m; **pre·dom·i·nate** [~neit] predominar.

pre·em·i·nence [priːˈeminəns] preeminencia f; **pre·em·i·nent** □ preeminente.

pre·ex·ist [ˈpriːigˈzist] preexistir; **ˈpre·ex·ist·ent** preexistente.

pre·fab [ˈpriːfæb] F casa f prefabricada; **ˈpre·fab·ri·cate** [~rikeit] prefabricar; **~d** prefabricado.

pref·ace [ˈprefis] **1.** prólogo m, prefacio m; **2.** book etc. prologar; fig. decir etc. a modo de prólogo a.

pref·a·to·ry [ˈprefətəri] preliminar, a modo de prólogo.

pre·fer [priˈfəː] preferir (to inf.; A to B A a B); p. ascender, promover to post; charge etc. hacer, presentar; **pref·er·a·ble** [ˈprefərəbl] □ preferible; **ˈpref·er·ence** preferencia f; **~ shares** p. acciones f/pl. preferentes.

pre·fix 1. [ˈpriːfiks] prefijo m; **2.** [priːˈfiks] prefijar.

preg·nan·cy [ˈpregnənsi] embarazo m; **ˈpreg·nant** □ embarazada, encinta, en estado; fig. preñado.

pre·his·tor·ic [ˈpriːhisˈtɔrik] prehistórico.

pre·ig·ni·tion [ˈpriːigˈniʃn] preignición f.

pre·judge [ˈpriːˈdʒʌdʒ] prejuzgar.

prej·u·dice [ˈpredʒudis] **1.** prejuicio m; parcialidad f; **2.** chances etc. perjudicar; prevenir, predisponer (against contra); **~d** parcial.

prej·u·di·cial [predʒuˈdiʃl] □ perjudicial.

pre·lim·i·nar·y [priˈliminəri] preliminar adj. a. su. m; **pre·lim·i·na·ries** [~z] pl. preliminares m/pl.; **pre·lim** [ˈpriːlim] F examen m preliminar.

prel·ude [ˈpreljuːd] preludio m.

pre·ma·ture [preməˈtjuə] prematuro; **~ baldness** calvicie f precoz.

pre·med·i·tate [priˈmediteit] premeditar.

pre·mier [ˈpremjə] **1.** primero, principal; **2.** primer ministro m; **pre·mi·ère** [ˈpremiɛə] estreno m.

prem·ise [ˈpremis] premisa f; **~s** pl. local m, casa f, tienda f etc.

pre·mi·um [ˈpriːmjəm] ✝ premio m; (insurance) prima f; be at a ~ fig. estar en gran demanda.

pre·mo·ni·tion [priːməˈniʃn] presentimiento m, premonición f.

pre·na·tal [ˈpriːˈneitl] prenatal.

pre·oc·cu·pied [priːˈɔkjupaid] preocupado; **pre·oc·cu·py** [~pai] preocupar.

prep [prep] F = **1.** preparation, preparatory; **2.** prepare, ready.

pre·pack·aged [priˈpækidʒd] precintado.

pre·paid [ˈpriːˈpeid] pagado por adelantado.

prep·a·ra·tion [prepəˈreiʃn] preparación f; **~s** pl. preparativos m/pl.; **pre·par·a·to·ry** [~təri] **1.** preparatorio, preliminar; **2.** adv.: **~ to** con miras a, antes de.

pre·pare [priˈpɛə] preparar(se), disponer(se), prevenir(se); **pre·par·ed·ness** preparación f (militar etc.).

pre·pay [ˈpriːˈpei] pagar por adelantado; **ˈpre·pay·ment** pago m adelantado.

pre·pon·der·ance [priˈpɔndərəns] preponderancia f.

prep·o·si·tion [prepəˈziʃn] preposición f.

pre·pos·ter·ous [priˈpɔstərəs] □ absurdo, ridículo.

pre·re·cord [priːriˈkɔːd] grabar de antemano.

pre·req·ui·site [ˈpriːˈrekwizit] requisito m previo.

pre·rog·a·tive [priˈrɔgətiv] prerrogativa f.

pres·age [ˈpresidʒ] presagio m.

Pres·by·te·ri·an [prezbiˈtiəriən] presbiteriano adj. a. su. m (a f).

pre·sci·ence [ˈpreʃiəns] presciencia f; **ˈpre·sci·ent** presciente.

pre·scribe [prisˈkraib] prescribir, ordenar; ✚ recetar.

pre·scrip·tion [prisˈkripʃn] prescripción f; ✚ receta f.

pres·ence [ˈprezns] presencia f; asistencia f (at a).

pres·ent[1] [ˈpreznt] **1.** □ presente, actual; **~!** ¡presente!; be ~ asistir (at a); **2.** presente m; actualidad f; gr. tiempo m presente.

pre·sent[2] [priˈzent] presentar, ofrecer, dar; case exponer; **~ o.s.** presentarse.

pres·ent[3] [ˈpreznt] regalo m, presente m; **make a ~ of** regalar.

pres·en·ta·tion [prezenˈteiʃn] presentación f; (present) obsequio m.

pres·ent·day ['prezntdei] actual.

pre·sen·ti·ment [pri'zentimənt] presentimiento *m*, corazonada *f*.

pres·ent·ly ['prezntli] luego, dentro de poco.

pres·er·va·tion [prezə'veiʃn] conservación *f*; preservación *f*; **pre·serv·a·tive** [pri'zə:vətiv] preservativo *adj. a. su. m.*

pre·serve [pri'zə:v] 1. conservar; preservar (*from* contra); guardar (*from* de); 2. conserva *f*; confitura *f*, compota *f*.

pre·side [pri'zaid] presidir (*at, over acc.*).

pres·i·den·cy ['prezidənsi] presidencia *f*; **'pres·i·dent** presidente *m*; † director *m*; ~-**elect** presidente *m* electo (*todavía no gobierno*).

press [pres] 1. ⊕ *etc.* prensa *f*; imprenta *f*; (*pressure*) presión *f*; urgencia *f* of affairs; apiñamiento *m* of people; **be in** ~ estar en prensa; 2. *v/t.* ⊕ *etc.* prensar; apretar; *button etc.* pulsar, presionar, empujar; *clothes* planchar; *fig.* abrumar, acosar; ~ **the point** insistir (*that* en que); ~ **into service** utilizar; *v/i.* urgir, apremiar; ~ **forward**, ~ **on** seguir adelante (a pesar de todo); '~ **agent** agente *m* de publicidad; '~ **box** tribuna *f* de la prensa; '~ **con·fer·ence** conferencia *f* de prensa; **'press·ing** □ urgente, apremiante, aciciante; **'press·mark** signatura *f*; **'press re·lease** comunicado *m* de prensa.

pres·sure ['preʃə] presión *f* (*a.* ⊕, *meteor.*); *fig.* urgencia *f*, apremio *m*; 🇦 tensión *f* (nerviosa); '~ **gauge** manómetro *m*; '~ **group** grupo *m* de presión; **'pres·sur·ize** ⚚ sobrecargar; **'pres·sur·ized cab·in** cabina *f* a presión (*or* altimática).

pres·ti·dig·i·ta·tion ['prestidid3i-'teiʃn] prestidigitación *f*.

pres·tige [pres'ti:3] prestigio *m*.

pre·sum·a·bly [pri'zju:məbli] *adv.* según cabe presumir; **pre'sume** presumir, suponer; ~ **to** atreverse a.

pre·sump·tion [pri'zʌmpʃn] presunción *f*; pretensión *f*; **pre'sump·tive** *heir* presunto; **pre'sump·tu·ous** [ˌtjuəs] □ presuntuoso, presumido.

pre·sup·pose [pri:sə'pouz] presuponer.

pre·tend [pri'tend] (*feign*) fingir,

aparentar; (*claim*) pretender (*to acc.*); **pre'tend·ed** □ pretendido; **pre'tend·er** pretendiente *m/f*; **pre'tense** [pri'tens] (*claim*) pretensión *f*; (*display*) ostentación *f*; (*pretext*) pretexto *m*; **pre'ten·sion** [pri'tenʃn] pretensión *f*; **pre·ten·tious** [pri'tenʃəs] □ pretencioso, presuntuoso; ambicioso.

pret·er·it(e) ['pretərit] pretérito *m*.

pre·text ['pri:tekst] pretexto *m*; *under* ~ *of* so pretexto de.

pret·ti·fy ['pritifai] embellecer; **pret·ti·ness** ['pritinis] lindeza *f*.

pret·ty ['priti] 1. □ bonito, guapo, lindo; precioso, mono; 2. *adv.* bastante, algo; ~ **difficult** bastante difícil; *be sitting* ~ estar en posición muy ventajosa.

pre·vail [pri'veil] prevalecer, imponerse; (*conditions*) reinar; **pre'vail·ing** reinante, imperante; predominante; general.

prev·a·lence ['prevələns] uso *m* corriente, costumbre *f*; frecuencia *f*; **'prev·a·lent** □ corriente; extendido; frecuente.

pre·vent [pri'vent] impedir ([*from*] *ger. inf.*), evitar, estorbar; **pre'vent·a·ble** evitable; **pre'ven·tion** prevención *f*; el impedir; **pre'ven·tive** □ preventivo, impeditivo; ~ *medicine* medicina *f* preventiva.

pre·view ['pri:vju:] pre-estreno *m*.

pre·vi·ous ['pri:viəs] □ previo, anterior; ~ *to* antes de.

pre·war ['pri:'wɔ:] de (la) preguerra.

prey [prei] 1. presa *f*, víctima *f*; *bird of* ~ ave *f* de rapiña; 2.: ~ (*up*)*on* atacar, alimentarse de, pillar.

price [prais] 1. precio *m*; *at any* ~ a toda costa; ~ *control* control *m* de precios; 2. tasar, fijar el precio de; **'price·less** inapreciable; **'price war** guerra *f* de precios; **'price·y** F caro.

prick [prik] 1. pinchazo *m*, punzada *f*; alfilerazo *m with pin*; 2. *v/t.* pinchar, punzar; agujerear; *v/i.*: ~ *up* prestar atención; **prick·le** ['▪] espina *f*, pincho *m*, púa *f*; **'prick·ly** espinoso, lleno de púas.

pride [praid] 1. orgullo *m*; *b.s.* soberbia *f*, arrogancia *f*; 2.: ~ *o.s. on* enorgullecerse de, preciarse de.

priest [pri:st] sacerdote *m*; cura *m*; **'priest·ess** sacerdotisa *f*; **'priest·hood** ['▪hud] (*function*) sacerdocio *m*; (*priests collectively*) clero *m*; **'priest·ly** sacerdotal.

prig [prig] presumido (a f) m; '**prig-gish** □ presumido; pedante.

prim [prim] □ remilgado; estirado.

pri·ma·cy ['praiməsi] primacía f; **pri·ma·ri·ly** ['⁓rili] ante todo; '**pri·ma·ry** 1. primario; 2. elección f preliminar; **pri·mate** ['⁓mit] zo. primate m.

prime [praim] 1. primero; principal; fundamental; *quality* selecto; 2. flor f, lo mejor; ⁓ *of life* la flor de la vida; 3. *gun, pump* cebar; *surface etc.* preparar.

prim·er ['praimə] cartilla f; libro m de texto elemental.

pri·me·val [prai'mi:vəl] primitivo, prístino.

prim·ing ['praimiŋ] preparación f; primera capa f of paint.

prim·i·tive ['primitiv] □ primitivo, rudimentario, sencillo; F sucio.

prince [prins] príncipe m; '**prince·ly** principesco, magnífico; **prin·cess** ['prinsis] princesa f.

prin·ci·pal ['prinsəpəl] 1. □ principal; *gr.* ⁓ *parts pl.* partes f/pl. principales; 2. principal m (*a.* ♰, ⚖); director (-a f) m of school, etc.

prin·ci·ple ['prinsəpl] principio m; in ⁓ en principio; on ⁓ por principio.

print [print] 1. (*mark*) marca f, impresión f; *typ.* tipo m; (*picture*) estampa f, grabado m; *phot.* impresión f, positiva f; (*cloth, dress*) estampado m; 2. *dress* estampado; 3. (hacer) imprimir (*a. phot.*); (*write*) escribir en caracteres de imprenta; '**print·ed** impreso; *dress etc.* estampado; in ⁓ *matter;* '**print·er** impresor m.

print·ing ['printiŋ] impresión f; tipografía f; (*quantity*) tirada f; '⁓ **press** prensa f de imprenta; '**print-out** (*computer*) impreso m derivado.

pri·or ['praiə] 1. anterior; previo; 2. *adv.:* ⁓ *to* antes de; hasta; 3. *eccl.* prior m; **pri·or·i·ty** [⁓'ɔriti] prioridad f.

prism ['prizm] prisma m; **pris·mat·ic** [priz'mætik] □ prismático.

pris·on ['prizn] cárcel f, prisión f; *put in* ⁓ encarcelar; '**pris·on·er** ⚖ preso (a f) m; ⚔ prisionero m; *take* ⁓ hacer prisionero.

pris·sy ['prisi] F remilgado, melindroso.

pri·va·cy ['praivəsi] secreto m, reserva f, retiro m; aislamiento m.

pri·vate ['praivit] 1. □ privado; particular; secreto, reservado; *report*

etc. confidencial; *conversation etc.* íntimo; ⁓*!* prohibida la entrada; ⁓ *enterprise* iniciativa f privada; 2. ⚔ (or ⁓ *soldier*) soldado m raso; ⁓*s pl.*, ⁓ *parts pl.* partes f/pl. pudendas; *in* ⁓ en privado.

pri·va·tion [prai'veiʃn] estrechez f, miseria f; privación f.

pri·va·tive ['privətiv] privativo.

priv·i·lege ['privilidʒ] 1. privilegio m, prerrogativa f; 2. privilegiar; *be* ⁓*d to* tener el privilegio de.

priv·y ['privi] 1. □: *be* ⁓ *to* estar enterado secretamente de; 2. retrete m.

prize [praiz] 1. premio m; ♱ *etc.* presa f; 2. premiado; digno de premio; 3. apreciar, estimar.

prize...: '⁓ **fight·er** boxeador m profesional; '⁓ **mon·ey** bolsa f; '⁓ **win·ner** premiado (a f) m.

pro¹ [prou] en pro de.

pro² [⁓] F profesional m/f.

prob·a·bil·i·ty [prɔbə'biliti] probabilidad f; *in all* ⁓ según toda probabilidad; '**prob·a·bly** probablemente; *he* ⁓ *forgot* lo habrá olvidado.

pro·ba·tion [prə'beiʃn] probación f; ⚖ *approx.* libertad f condicional; *on* ⁓ a prueba; ⚖ bajo libertad condicional; **pro'ba·tion·ar·y** de prueba.

probe [proub] 1. ⚕ sonda f; (*rocket*) cohete m, proyectil m; *fig.* F investigación f (*into* de), encuesta f; 2. ⚕ sondar, tentar; *fig.* indagar.

prob·lem ['prɔbləm] problema m; *attr.* difícil; **prob·lem·at·ic, prob·lem·at·i·cal** [⁓bli'mætik(l)] problemático, dudoso.

proce·dure [prou'si:dʒə] procedimiento m; trámites m/pl.

pro·ceed [prə'si:d] proceder; (*continue*) seguir, continuar; obrar; ⁓ *against* proceder contra, procesar; **pro'ceed·ing** procedimiento m; ⁓*s pl.* actos m/pl.; transacciones f/pl.; (*published*) actas f/pl.; ⁓ *proceso m,* procedimiento m; **pro·ceeds** ['prou-si:dz] pl. ganancia f, producto m; ingresos m/pl.

process ['prouses] 1. procedimiento m, proceso m; *in* ⁓ *of construction* bajo construcción; 2. ⊕ preparar, tratar (*into* para hacer); '**proc·ess·ing** tratamiento m; **pro·ces·sion** [prə'seʃn] desfile m; *eccl.* procesión f.

pro·claim [prə'kleim] proclamar.

pro·cliv·i·ty [prə'kliviti] propensión f, inclinación f.

pro·cras·ti·nate [prə'kræstineit] hablar *etc.* para aplazar una decisión, no decidirse; **pro·cras·ti·na·tion** falta *f* de decisión, dilación *f*.

pro·cre·ate ['proukrieit] procrear.

pro·cur·a·ble [prə'kjuərəbl] asequible.

pro·cure [prə'kjuə] *v/t.* obtener; conseguir; lograr; gestionar; *girl* obtener para la prostitución; *v/i.* alcahuetear; **pro'cure·ment** obtención *f*; **pro'cur·er** alcahuete *m*; **pro'cur·ess** alcahueta *f*.

prod [prɔd] **1.** empuje *m*; codazo *m*; estímulo *m*; **2.** empujar; codear; *fig.* pinchar; estimular.

prod·i·gal ['prɔdigəl] □ pródigo (*of* de); *the* ~ *son* el hijo pródigo.

pro·di·gious [prə'didʒəs] □ prodigioso; enorme, ingente; **prod·i·gy** ['prɔdidʒi] prodigio *m*.

pro·duce 1. ['prɔdjuːs] producto(s) *m(pl.)*; (*esp.* agrícolas); **2.** [prə'djuːs] producir; (*show*) presentar, mostrar; sacar; (*cause*) causar, ocasionar, motivar; **pro'duc·er** productor (-a *f*) *m*; *thea.* director *m* de escena.

prod·uct ['prɔdʌkt] producto *m*; **pro·duc·tion** [prə'dʌkʃn] producción *f*; *thea.* (re)presentación *f*; **pro'duc·tive** □ productivo; **pro·duc·tiv·i·ty** [prɔdʌk'tiviti] productividad *f*.

prof [prɔf] F profesor *m*.

pro·fane [prə'fein] **1.** profano; impío; *language etc.* fuerte; **2.** profanar; **pro·fan·i·ty** [prə'fæniti] blasfemia *f*, impiedad *f*, F lenguaje *m* indecente.

pro·fess [prə'fes] profesar; declarar, confesar; *regret etc.* manifestar; **pro·'fessed** □ declarado; *b.s.* supuesto; *eccl.* profeso.

pro·fes·sion·al [prou'feʃnəl] □ profesional (*a. su. m/f*), de profesión; **pro'fes·sion·al·ism** [~əlizm] *sport:* profesionalismo *m*.

pro·fes·sor [prə'fesə] profesor (-a *f*) *m* (universitario [a]), catedrático (a *f*) *m*; **pro'fes·sor·ship** cátedra *f*.

pro·fi·cien·cy [prə'fiʃənsi] pericia *f*, habilidad *f*; **pro'fi·cient** □ perito, hábil (*at, in* en).

pro·file ['proufail] **1.** perfil *m*; **2.** perfilar.

prof·it ['prɔfit] **1.** ganancia *f* (↑, *a.* ~s *pl.*); *fig.* provecho *m*, beneficio *m*; utilidad *f*; ~ *margin* excedente *m* de ganancia; **2.** *v/t.* servir a, aprovechar

a; **'prof·it·a·ble** □ provechoso; **prof·it·eer** [~'tiə] **1.** acaparador *m*; **2.** hacer ganancias excesivas; **prof·it·'eer·ing** (negocios *m/pl.* que dan) ganancias *f/pl.* excesivas; **'prof·it·less** □ inútil; **prof·it shar·ing** ['~ʃɛəriŋ] participación *f* en los beneficios.

prof·li·gate ['prɔfligit] □ libertino *adj. a. su. m*.

pro·found [prə'faund] □ profundo; **pro·fun·di·ty** [~'fʌnditi] profundidad *f*.

pro·fuse [prə'fjuːs] □ profuso, abundante; prodigio.

prog·no·sis [prɔg'nousis] *pl.* **prog·'no·ses** [~siːz] pronóstico *m*.

prog·nos·tic [prəg'nɔstik] **1.** pronóstico *m*; **2.** pronosticador, pronóstico; **prog'nos·ti·cate** [~keit] pronosticar.

pro·gram ['prougræm] **1.** programa *m*; **2.** *computer, etc.* programar; **pro·gram·(m)er** ['prougræmə] programador *m*.

pro·gram·(m)ing ['prougræmiŋ] programación *f*; *computer* ~ programación *f* de computadoras.

prog·ress 1. ['prougres] progreso(s) *m(pl.)*; marcha *f*; **2.** **pro·gress** [prə'gres] progresar, hacer progresos; **pro'gres·sive** □ progresivo; *pol.* progresista (*a. su. m/f*).

pro·hib·it [prə'hibit] prohibir; **pro·hi·bi·tion·ist** prohibicionista *m/f*; **pro·hib·i·tive** [prə'hibitiv] □ prohibitivo; *price* exorbitante.

proj·ect ['prɔdʒekt] proyecto *m*.

pro·ject [prə'dʒekt] *v/t.* proyectar; *v/i.* (sobre)salir; resaltar; **pro·jec·tile** [prə'dʒektil] proyectil *m*; **pro·'ject·ing** saliente.

pro·le·tar·i·an [proule'tɛəriən] proletario *adj. a. su. m* (a *f*).

pro·lif·ic [prə'lifik] □ prolífico (*of* en).

pro·logue, *a.* **pro·log** ['proulɔg] prólogo *m* (*a. fig.*).

pro·long [prə'lɔŋ] prolongar, alargar.

prom·e·nade [prɔmi'nɑːd] **1.** paseo *m*; **2.** pasear(se).

prom·i·nence ['prɔminəns] prominencia *f*; *fig.* eminencia *f*; **'prom·i·nent** □ saliente, prominente.

pro·mis·cu·ous [prə'miskjuəs] □ promiscuo.

prom·ise ['prɔmis] **1.** promesa *f*; **2.** prometer (*to inf.*); asegurar; **'prom·is·ing** □ prometedor, que promete; **'prom·is·so·ry note** pagaré *m*.

P

prom·on·to·ry ['prɔmǝntri] promontorio m.

pro·mote [prǝ'mout] promover, fomentar; ascender in rank; discussion etc. estimular, facilitar; **pro'mot·er** promotor m; ⚔ fundador m; boxing: empresario m, promotor m; **pro'mo·tion** promoción f, fomento m; ascenso m in rank.

prompt [prɔmpt] 1. ☐ pronto, puntual; 2. adv. puntualmente; 3. v. mover, incitar, estimular (to a); thea. apuntar; **'prompt·er** apuntador m; **'prompt·ness** prontitud f, puntualidad f.

pro·mul·gate ['prɔmǝlgeit] promulgar.

prone [proun] postrado (boca abajo); fig. ~ to propenso a.

prong [prɔŋ] punta f, púa f.

pro·noun ['prounaun] pronombre m.

pro·nounce [prǝ'nauns] v/t. pronunciar (a. 🔤); (with adj.) declarar, juzgar; v/i.: ~ on expresar una opinión sobre, juzgar acc; **pro'nounced** marcado, fuerte; decidido.

proof [pruːf] 1. prueba f (a. typ.); graduación f normal of alcohol; in ~ of en prueba de, en comprobación de; 2. drink of graduación normal; bullet~ a prueba de balas; 3. impermeabilizar; **'proof·read** ['pruːfriːd] corregir; **'~·read·er** corrector m (de pruebas); **'~ sheets** pruebas f/pl.

prop [prɔp] 1. ♠ puntal m, sostén m (a. fig.); 🔨 entibo m; 2. (a. ~ up) apuntalar; apoyar.

prop·a·gan·da [prɔpǝ'gændǝ] propaganda f; **prop·a'gan·dist** propagandista m/f; **prop·a·gate** ['prɔpǝgeit] propagar.

pro·pel [prǝ'pel] ⊕ impeler, impulsar; empujar; **pro'pel·lent** propulsor m; **pro'pel·ler** hélice f.

prop·er ['prɔpǝ] ☐ propio (to de); conveniente, apropiado, (decent) decente, decoroso; (prim and ~) relamido, etiquetero; in the ~ sense of the word en el sentido estricto de la palabra; ~ name nombre m propio; **'prop·er·ly:** do s.t. ~ hacer algo bien (or como hace falta); (correctly) correctamente, debidamente; **'prop·er·ty** (estate, quality) propiedad f; hacienda f; bienes m/pl.; ~ owner propietario m de bienes raíces; **'prop·er·ty tax** impuesto m sobre la propiedad.

proph·e·cy ['prɔfisi] profecía f;

proph·e·sy ['~sai] profetizar; fig. augurar, prever.

proph·et ['prɔfit] profeta m; **proph·et·ic, proph·et·i·cal** [prǝ'fetik(l)] ☐ profético.

pro·phy·lac·tic [prɔfi'læktik] ☐ profiláctico adj. a. su. m.

pro·pi·tious [prǝ'piʃǝs] ☐ propicio.

prop·jet ['prɔp'dʒet] turbohélice m.

pro·po·nent [prǝ'pounǝnt] defensor m; patrocinador m.

pro·por·tion [prǝ'pɔːʃn] 1. proporción f; in ~ as a medida que (to de) etc. ~ed bien etc. proporcionado; **pro'por·tion·ate** [~it] ☐ proporcionado.

pro·pos·al [prǝ'pouzǝl] propuesta f, proposición f; oferta f; **pro'pose** v/t. proponer; ofrecer; v/i. proponer; (marriage) pedir la mano; ~ to inf. proponerse inf.; **pro·po·si·tion** [prɔpǝ'ziʃn] proposición f; oferta f; F empresa f, problema m.

pro·pri·e·tar·y [prǝ'praiǝtǝri] propietario; article patentado; **pro'pri·e·tor** propietario m; dueño m; **pro'pri·e·ty** corrección f; conveniencia f; decoro m.

pro·pul·sion [prǝ'pʌlʃn] propulsión f.

pro·rate [prou'reit] 1. prorrata f; 2. prorratear.

pro·sa·ic [prou'zeiik] ☐ prosaico.

prose [prouz] 1. prosa f; 2. attr. de (or en) prosa.

pros·e·cute ['prɔsikjuːt] 🔤 procesar, enjuiciar; **pros·e'cu·tion** [~ʃn] (case) proceso m, causa f; 🔤 (side) parte f actora; prosecución f; **'pros·e·cu·tor** acusador m.

pros·e·lyte ['prɔsilait] prosélito (a f) m.

pros·o·dy ['prɔsǝdi] métrica f, prosodia f.

pros·pect 1. ['prɔspekt] perspectiva f; (view) vista f; (expectation) expectativa f, esperanza f; 2. [prǝs'pekt] v/t. explorar; v/i.: ~ for buscar; **pro'spec·tive** ☐ anticipado, esperado; futuro; **pros'pec·tor** ⚒ prospector m.

pros·per ['prɔspǝ] prosperar, medrar; **pros·per·i·ty** [prɔs'periti] prosperidad f; **pros·per·ous** ['~pǝrǝs] ☐ próspero.

pros·tate ['prɔsteit] 🔬 1. próstata f; 2. prostático; ~ gland glándula f prostática.

pros·ti·tute ['prɔstitjuːt] 1. prostituta f; 2. prostituir.

pros·trate 1. ['prɔstreit] postrado (*a. fig.*); *fig.* abatido (with por); **2.** postrar (*a. fig.*); *fig.* abatir.

pro·tag·o·nist [prou'tægənist] protagonista *m/f.*

pro·tect [prə'tekt] proteger (*from* de, contra); **pro·tec·tion·ist** proteccionista *adj. a. su. m/f;* **pro·tec·tive** □ protector; **pro·tec·tor·ate** [~tərit] protectorado *m.*

pro·té·gé(e) ['prɔteiʒei] protegido (*a f*) *m,* ahijado (*a f*) *m.*

pro·te·in ['prouti:n] proteína *f.*

pro·test 1. ['proutest] protesta *f;* queja *f;* **2.** [prə'test] protestar (*against* de, *that* de que); quejarse.

Prot·es·tant ['prɔtistənt] protestante *adj. a. su. m/f;* '**Prot·es·tant·ism** protestantismo *m.*

prot·es·ta·tion [proutes'teiʃn] protesta *f.*

pro·to·col ['proutəkɔl] protocolo *m.*

pro·ton ['proutɔn] protón *m.*

pro·to·type ['proutətaip] prototipo *m.* ♦

pro·tract [prə'trækt] prolongar.

pro·trude [prə'tru:d] *v/t.* sacar fuera; *v/i.* (sobre)salir, salir fuera.

pro·tu·ber·ance [prə'tju:bərəns] protuberancia *f,* saliente *m;* **pro·tu·ber·ant** □ protuberante, saliente.

proud [praud] □ orgulloso; *b.s.* soberbio, engreído; (*imposing*) espléndido, imponente.

prove [pru:v] *v/t.* (com)probar; demostrar; *will verdical; v/i.* resultar (*that* que; *true* verdadero).

prov·erb ['prɔvəb] refrán *m,* proverbio *m.*

pro·vide [prə'vaid] *v/t.* suministrar, surtir; proporcionar; abastecer (*with* de); *v/i.: ~ against* precaverse de; *~ for* prevenir; *~ that* disponer que, estipular que; **pro·vid·ed (that)** con tal que.

prov·i·dence ['prɔvidəns] providencia *f;* previsión *f;* ♀ (Divina) Providencia; '**prov·i·dent** □ providente, previsor.

pro·vid·er [prə'vaidə] proveedor (*-a f*) *m.*

prov·ince ['prɔvins] provincia *f; fig.* competencia *f,* jurisdicción *f.*

pro·vin·cial [prə'vinʃl] **1.** provincial; *contp.* provinciano; **2.** provinciano (*a f*) *m;* **pro'vin·cial·ism** provincialismo *m.*

prov·ing ground ['pru:viŋgraund] campo *m* de ensayos.

pro·vi·sion [prə'viʒn] **1.** provisión *f;* estipulación *f; ~s pl.* provisiones *f/pl.,* víveres *m/pl.;* **2.** aprovisionar, abastecer.

pro·vi·so [prə'vaizou] estipulación *f;* salvedad *f.*

pro·voke [prə'vouk] provocar (*to* a), incitar (*to* a); causar, motivar; (*anger*) irritar; **pro'vok·ing** □ enojoso.

prov·ost ['prɔvəst] preboste *m.*

prow [prau] proa *f.*

prow·ess ['prauis] valor *m;* habilidad *f,* destreza *f.*

prowl [praul] rondar (en busca de presa *etc.*); vagar (*v/t.* por); '~ **car** coche *m* de policía; '~·**er** rondador *m* sospechoso.

prox·im·i·ty [prɔk'simiti] proximidad *f;* inmediaciones *f/pl.*

prox·y ['prɔksi] poder *m;* (*p.*) apoderado (*a f*) *m;* *by ~* por poder(es).

pru·dence ['pru:dəns] prudencia *f;* '**pru·dent** □ prudente.

prud·er·y ['pru:dəri] remilgo *m,* gazmoñería *f;* '**prud·ish** □ gazmoño.

prune¹ [pru:n] ciruela *f* pasa.

prune² [~] podar; escamondar (*a. fig.*); '**prun·ing** poda *f.*

pru·ri·ence, pru·ri·en·cy ['pruəriəns(i)] salacidad *f,* lascivia *f.*

Prus·sian ['prʌʃn] prusiano *adj. a. su. m* (*a f*); *~* blue azul *m* de Prusia.

pry [prai] fisgar, fisgonear; curiosear; entrometerse (*into* en); *~ up, apart, etc.* apalancar; '**pry·ing** □ fisgón, entrometido; curioso.

psalm [sɑ:m] salmo *m.*

pseu·do... ['psju:dou] seudo...; falso, fingido; **pseu·do·nym** ['~dənim] seudónimo *m;* **pseu·don·y·mous** [~'dɔniməs] □ seudónimo.

psy·che ['saiki] psique *f.*

psy·chi·a·trist [sai'kaiətrist] psiquiatra *m/f;* **psy'chi·a·try** psiquiatría *f.*

psy·chic ['saikik] □ psíquico.

psy·cho·a·nal·y·sis [saikouə'næləsis] psicoanálisis *m;* **psy·cho·an·a·lyst** [~'ænəlist] psicoanalista *m/f.*

psy·chol·o·gist [sai'kɔlədʒist] psicólogo *m;* **psy·chol·o·gy** psicología *f.*

psy·cho·sis [sai'kousis] psicosis *f.*

pto·maine ['toumein] ptomaína *f.*

pub [pʌb] □ taberna *f,* tasca *f;* '~·**crawl** *sl.* **1.** chateo *m* (de tasca en tasca); **2.** ir de chateo, copear.

pu·ber·ty ['pju:bəti] pubertad *f.*

pub·lic ['pʌblik] **1.** □ público; *~ address system* sistema *m* amplificador (de discursos públicos); *~ house* taberna f; posada f; ~ library biblioteca f pública; ~ relations relaciones f/pl. públicas; 2. público m; in ~ en público; **pub·li·cist** ['~sist] publicista m; **pub·lic·i·ty** [~siti] publicidad f; **pub·li·cize** ['~saiz] publicar, dar publicidad a, anunciar; '**pub·lic·'spir·it·ed** □ action de buen ciudadano; p. lleno de civismo.

pub·lish ['pʌbliʃ] publicar; **pub·lish·er** editor m; **pub·lish·ing** publicación f de libros.

puck·er ['pʌkə] 1. sew. frunce m, fruncido m; 2. (a. ~ up) v/t. sew., brow fruncir; v/i. arrugarse.

pud·ding ['pudin] pudín m.

pud·dle ['pʌdl] 1. charco m; 2. ⊕ pudelar.

pudg·y ['pʌdʒi] F gordinflón; rechoncho.

pu·er·ile ['pjuərail] pueril.

puff [pʌf] 1. resoplido m, resuello m; soplo m of air, racha f of wind; bocanada f, humareda f of smoke; 2. v/t. soplar; ~ out smoke etc. echar, arrojar; ~ up hinchar, inflar; v/i. soplar; jadear, acezar, resollar.

puff·pas·try ['pʌfˌpeistri] hojaldre m; '**puf·fy** hinchado.

pu·gil·ism ['pju:dʒilizm] pugilato m; '**pu·gil·ist** púgil m; pugilista m.

pug-nosed ['pʌgnouzd] chato, braco.

puke [pju:k] vomitar.

pull [pul] 1. tirón m; estirón m; chupada f at pipe; cuerda f of bell; F (influence) buenas aldabas f/pl.; 2. v/t. tirar de; (drag) arrastrar; muscle torcerse, dislocarse; ~ along arrastrar; ~ back tirar hacia atrás; ~ out sacar; arrancar; ~ (stretch) estirar; o.s. together sobreponerse, recobrar la calma; v/i. tirar, dar un tirón; ~ at pipe chupar; rope etc. tirar de; ~ through ✗ recobrar la salud; salir de un apuro; ~ up pararse, detenerse; mejorar su posición.

pul·let ['pulit] poll(it)a f.

pul·ley ['puli] polea f.

pull·o·ver ['pulouvə] jersey m; pulóver m.

pul·mo·nar·y ['pʌlmənəri] pulmonar.

pulp [pʌlp] pulpa f; pasta f.

pul·pit ['pulpit] púlpito m.

pulp·y ['pʌlpi] pulposo.

pul·sate [pʌl'seit] pulsar, latir.

pulse [pʌls] 1. pulso m; feel one's ~ tomar el pulso a; 2. pulsar, latir.

pul·ver·ize ['pʌlvəraiz] pulverizar (-se); F cascar.

pum·ice ['pʌmis] (a. '~-stone) piedra f pómez.

pump¹ [pʌmp] 1. bomba f; 2. sacar (or elevar etc.) con bomba; F p. sonsacar; ~ dry secar con bomba(s); ~ up tire inflar.

pump² [~] (shoe) zapatilla f.

pump·kin ['pʌmpkin] calabaza f.

pun [pʌn] 1. juego m de palabras (on sobre); 2. jugar del vocablo.

punch¹ [pʌntʃ] 1. ⊕ punzón m; 2. punzar, taladrar; ticket picar.

punch² [~] 1. (blow) puñetazo m; F empuje m, vigor m; pull one's ~es no emplear toda su fuerza; 2. dar un puñetazo a; golpear; cattle guiar; cuidar.

punch³ [~] (drink) ponche m.

punch-drunk ['pʌntʃ'drʌnk] boxer atontado.

punc·tu·al ['pʌnktjuəl] □ puntual; **punc·tu·al·i·ty** [~'æliti] puntualidad f.

punc·tu·ate ['pʌnktjueit] puntuar.

punc·ture ['pʌnktʃə] 1. mot. etc. pinchazo m; puntura f, punzada f; 2. pinchar; perforar, punzar.

pun·ish ['pʌniʃ] castigar; F maltratar; (tax) exigir esfuerzos sobrehumanos a; '**pun·ish·ment** castigo m; F tratamiento m severo.

punk [pʌnk] 1. basura f, fruslerías f/pl.; sl. pillo m; 2. sl. malo, baladí; **punk rock** ['pʌnkrɔk] música f rock de efectos deliberadamente chocantes.

punt [pʌnt] ⚓ 1. batea f; 2. v/i. ir en batea; v/t. impeler con botador.

pu·ny ['pju:ni] encanijado; insignificante; effort etc. débil.

pup [pʌp] cachorro (a f) m.

pu·pil ['pju:pl] alumno (a f) m; anat. pupila f.

pup·pet ['pʌpit] títere m; (p.) marioneta f; '~ show (función f de) títeres m/pl.

pup·py ['pʌpi] cachorro (a f) m; perrito (a f) m.

pur·chase ['pəːtʃəs] 1. compra f; fig. agarre m firme; ⊕ apalancamiento m; 2. comprar, adquirir; purchasing power poder m adquisitivo.

pure [pjuə] □ puro; '~-bred de pura sangre; '**pure·ness** pureza f.

pur·ga·tive ['pəːgətiv] purgativo; purgante (a. su. m); '**pur·ga·to·ry** purgatorio m.

puzzle

purge [pə:dʒ] **1.** ⚕ purga *f*, purgante *m*; *pol.* purga *f*; **2.** purgar; purificar, depurar; *pol. party* purgar.

pu·ri·fi·er ['pjuərifaiə] (*water-*) depurador *m*; **pu·ri·fy** ['ˊfai] purificar, depurar; **'pu·rist** purista *m/f*, casticista *m/f*.

pu·ri·tan ['pjuəritən] puritano *adj. a. su. m* (a *f*); **pu·ri·tan·ism** ['ˊtənizm] puritanismo *m*.

pu·ri·ty ['pjuəriti] pureza *f*.

pur·ple ['pə:pl] **1.** purpúreo, morado; **2.** púrpura *f*.

pur·port 1. ['pə:pət] significado *m*, tenor *m*; intención *f*; **2.** [pə'pɔ:t] significar, dar a entender (*that* que).

pur·pose ['pə:pəs] propósito *m*, intención *f*; resolución *f*; *novel with a* ~ novela *f* de tesis; *for the* ~ *of ger.* con el fin de *inf.*; *on* ~ adrede, de propósito; **'pur·pose·ful** ['ˊful] □ determinado, resuelto; **'pur·pose·less** □ sin propósito fijo, sin fin determinado; **'pur·pose·ly** *adv.* adrede, de propósito.

purr [pə:] **1.** (*cat, motor*) ronronear; **2.** ronroneo *m*.

purse [pə:s] **1.** bolsa *f*; bolso *m*; (*prize*) premio *m*; **2.** *lips* fruncir; **'purs·er** contador *m* de navío; **'purse-strings:** *hold the* ~ tener las llaves de la caja.

pur·sue [pə'sju:] (*hunt*) seguir (la pista de), cazar; (*a. fig.*) perseguir; acosar; *pleasures etc.* dedicarse a; **pur·suit** [ˊsju:t] caza *f*, busca *f*; (*occupation*) ocupación *f*; (*pastime*) pasatiempo *m*; *in* ~ *of* en pos de; ~ *plane* avión *m* de caza.

pur·vey [pə:'vei] suministrar, abastecer, proveer; **pur'vey·or** abastecedor (-a *f*) *m*, proveedor (-a *f*) *m*.

pur·view ['pə:vju:] alcance *m*, esfera *f*.

pus [pʌs] pus *m*.

push [puʃ] **1.** empuje *m*, empujón *m*; ✗ ofensiva *f*, avance *m*; F agresividad *f*; **2.** *v/t.* empujar; *enterprise* promover, fomentar; *claim* proseguir; F *product* hacer una campaña publicitaria a favor de; ~ *away* apartar con la mano; empujar; ~ *back* echar atrás; *v/i.* empujar, dar un empujón; hacer esfuerzos; ~ *on* seguir adelante, continuar (a pesar de todo); avanzar; **'ˊbut·ton** botón *m* de llamada *etc.*; ~ *control* mando *m* por botón; **'ˊcart** carretilla *f* de mano; **'push·o·ver** F cosa *f* muy fácil; persona *f* muy fácil

de (con)vencer *etc.*; breva *f*; **push·y** F agresivo; presumido.

pu·sil·lan·i·mous [pju:si'læniməs] □ pusilánime.

puss(·y) ['pus(i)] minino *m*, micho *m*; **'puss·y·foot** F moverse a paso de gato, andar a tientas; no declararse.

put [put] [*irr.*] **1.** *v/t.* poner; colocar; (*insert*) meter; *question* hacer; *motion* proponer, someter a votación; (*expound*) exponer, presentar; expresar, redactar *in words*; ~ *across meaning* comunicar, hacer entender; *idea, product* hacer aceptar; ~ *aside* (*reject*) rechazar; (*save*) poner aparte, ahorrar; ~ *away* (*keep*) guardar; (*save*) ahorrar; volver a poner en su lugar; (*imprison*) encarcelar; *lunatic* meter en un manicomio; ~ *back th.* devolver a su lugar; *clock, process* retardar, atrasar; *function etc.* aplazar; ~ *forth book etc.* publicar; *bud etc.* producir, echar; *effort* emplear; ~ *forward* presentar, proponer; *function, date* adelantar; *time* dedicar; ~ *off* (*postpone*) aplazar, dejar para después; *p.* quitar las ganas de, hacer perder el sabor de; ~ *on clothes* ponerse; *shoes* calzarse; F ~ *it on* exagerar; emocionarse demasiado; *fire, light* apagar; (*expel*) poner en la calle; (*inconvenience*) molestar, incomodar; (*disconcert*) desconcertar; ~ *over idea, product* hacer aceptar; *meaning* comunicar; *teleph.* poner (*to* con); ~ *it to p.* decirlo a; sugerirlo a; proponerlo a; *be hard* ~ *to* tener mucha dificultad en *inf.*; ~ *together* añadir; juntar; ⊕ montar; ~ *up building* construir; *umbrella* abrir; *price* aumentar; *money* poner, contribuir; *candidate* nombrar; apoyar; *guest* hospedar; **2.** *v/i.:* ~ *about* ⚓ cambiar de rumbo; ~ *in* ⚓ entrar a puerto; ~ *in at* ⚓ hacer escala en; ~ *up with* aguantar, resignarse a.

pu·tre·fy ['pju:trifai] pudrirse.

pu·tres·cence [pju:'tresns] pudrición *f*; **pu'tres·cent** putrescente.

pu·trid ['pju:trid] □ podrido, putrefacto; F malísimo, pésimo.

putt [pʌt] **1.** golpe *m* corto; **2.** golpear con poca fuerza.

put·ty ['pʌti] **1.** masilla *f*; **2.** enmasillar.

put-up job ['putʌp'dʒɔb] *sl.* cosa *f* proyectada y preparada de antemano; asunto *m* fraudulento.

puz·zle ['pʌzl] **1.** problema *m*, enigma *m*; (*game*) rompecabezas *m*, acertijo

P

m; 2. *v/t.* intrigar, confundir, dejar perplejo; *v/i.*: ~ **over** tratar de resolver, devanarse los sesos para descifrar; **'puz·zled** intrigado; perplejo; **'puz·zling** enigmático, misterioso.

pyg·my ['pɪgmɪ] pigmeo *adj. a. su. m.*

py·lon ['paɪlən] pilón *m*; ⚡ torre

f de conducción eléctrica.

pyr·a·mid ['pɪrəmɪd] pirámide *f*; **pyram·i·dal** [pɪ'ræmɪdl] piramidal.

py·ri·tes [paɪ'raɪtiːz] pirita *f*.

py·ro... ['paɪərəu] piro...; **py·ro·'tech·nics** *pl.* pirotecnia *f*.

py·thon ['paɪθən] pitón *m*.

Q

quack[1] [kwæk] *approx.* 1. graznido *m*; 2. graznar.

quack[2] [~] 1. charlatán *m*, curandero *m*; 2. falso; *remedy* de curandero.

quad·ra·gen·ar·ian [kwɔdrədʒə'neəriən] cuadragenario *adj. a. su. m* (*a f*).

quad·ran·gle ['kwɔdræŋgl] cuadrángulo *m*; △ patio *m*.

quad·rant ['kwɔdrənt] cuadrante *m*.

quad·ra·phon·ic [kwɔdrə'fɔnɪk] cuadrafónico; **quad·rat·ic** [kwɔ'drætɪk] de segundo grado.

quad·ri·lat·er·al [kwɔdrɪ'lætərəl] cuadrilátero *adj. a. su. m.*

quad·ru·ped ['kwɔdruped] 1. cuadrúpedo *m*; 2. cuadrúpedo; **quadru·ple** 1. ['kwɔdrupl] cuádruple *m*; [~] cuádruplo *m*; 3. [~'rupl] cuadruplicar(se); **quad·ru·plets** [kwɔd'ruːplɪts] *pl.* cuatrillizos (as *f/pl.*) *m/pl.*; **quad·ru·pli·cate** 1. [kwɔ'druːplɪkɪt] (*in pair*) cuadruplicado; 2. [~keit] cuadruplicar.

quail [kweil] *orn.* codorniz *f*.

quaint [kweint] □ curioso, original; pintoresco; típico.

quake [kweik] 1. temblor *m*; terremoto *m*; 2. temblar, trepidar, estremecerse (**with**, for de).

Quak·er ['kweikə] cuáquero *m*; **'Quak·er·ism** cuaquerismo *m*.

qual·i·fi·ca·tion [kwɔlɪfɪ'keɪʃn] calificación *f*; requisito *m*; **qual·i·fied** ['~faɪd] *p.* c(u)alificado, habilitado, capacitado; competente; **qual·i·fy** ['~faɪ] *v/t.* calificar (*a. gr.*); habilitar, modificar, limitar; *v/i.* habilitarse, capacitarse; llenar los requisitos; **'qual·i·ty** (*type, character*) calidad *f*, categoría *f*, clase *f*; (*characteristic*) cualidad *f*, virtud *f*.

qualm [kwɔːm, kwɑːm] 🌊 bascas *f/pl.*, náusea *f*; duda *f*.

quan·ti·ta·tive ['kwɔntɪteɪtɪv] □ cuantitativo; **'quan·ti·ty** cantidad *f*.

quan·tum ['kwɔntəm] cantidad *f*.

quar·an·tine ['kwɔrəntiːn] 1. cuarentena *f*; 2. poner en cuarentena.

quar·rel ['kwɔrəl] 1. riña *f*, disputa *f*; 2. (*violent*) reyerta *f*, pendencia *f*; 2. reñir, disputar; pelear; **quar·rel·some** ['~səm] □ pendenciero.

quar·ry ['kwɔri] *hunt.* presa *f*.

quart [kwɔːt] *cuarto de galón* (= *1,136 litros*).

quar·ter ['kwɔːtə] 1. cuarto *m*, cuarta parte *f*; (*3 months*) trimestre *m*; cuarto *m* of moon; barrio *m* of town; moneda de 25 centavos; ~s *pl.* vivienda *f*; ✗ cuartel *m*, alojamiento *f*; 2. cuartear; *meat* descuartizar; *heraldry*: cuartelar; ✗ acuartelar; **be ~ed** (*up*) on estar alojado en casa de; **'~·deck** alcázar *m*; **'quar·ter·ly** 1. trimestral; 2. publicación *f* trimestral; 3. cada tres meses, por trimestres; **'quar·ter·mas·ter** *approx.* furriel *m*, comisario *m*.

quartz [kwɔːts] cuarzo *m*.

quash [kwɔʃ] anular, invalidar.

qua·ver ['kweivə] 1. temblor *m*; ♪ trémolo *m*; (*note*) corchea *f*; 2. temblar, vibrar; ♪ gorjear.

quay [kiː] muelle *m*, desembarcadero *m*.

quea·si·ness ['kwiːzɪnɪs] bascas *f/pl.*; propensión *f* a la náusea; **'quea·sy** □ bascoso; delicado.

queen [kwiːn] 1. reina *f* (*a.* chess); *cards*: dama *f*, (*Spanish*) caballo *m*; ~ **bee** abeja *f* reina; ~ **mother** reina *f* madre; 2. *pawn* coronar; ~ **it** pavonearse.

queer [kwiə] □ raro, extraño; misterioso; excéntrico, extravagante; F ♂ enfermo; F maricón (*a. su. m*).

quell [kwel] reprimir, domar.

quench [kwentʃ] *thirst etc.* apagar; extinguir, ahogar; ⊕ templar; **'quench·er** F trago *m*.

quotient

quer·u·lous [ˈkwerʊləs] □ quejumbroso, quejicoso.

que·ry [ˈkwɪəri] 1. pregunta f; duda f; punto m de interrogación [?]; 2. preguntar; dudar de.

quest [kwest] 1. busca f; búsqueda f; pesquisa f; 2. buscar.

ques·tion [ˈkwestʃn] 1. pregunta f; (affair) asunto m, cuestión f; problema m; ~ mark punto m de interrogación; it is a ~ of se trata de; the ~ is el caso es; that is the ~ ahí está el problema; that is out of the ~ es totalmente imposible; there is no ~ of no se trata de; 2. interrogar, hacer preguntas a; examinar; (doubt) poner en duda; desconfiar de; **ques·tion·naire** [kestiəˈneə, kwestʃəˈneə] cuestionario m.

queue [kjuː] 1. cola f; 2. hacer cola.

quib·ble [ˈkwibl] 1. evasión f, sofistería f; retruécano m; 2. sutilizar; jugar del vocablo; buscar evasivas; **ˈquib·bler** sofista m/f.

quick [kwik] 1. rápido, veloz; pronto; vivo; ágil; ear fino; eye, wit agudo; 2. carne f viva; the ~ los vivos; cut to the ~ herir en lo vivo; **ˈquick·en** acelerar(se), apresurar; vivificar; **ˈquick·froz·en** de congelación rápida; **ˈquick·ie** [~i] F pregunta f (or acción) relámpago f; **ˈquick·lime** cal f viva; **ˈquick·ly** pronto; de prisa, rápidamente; **ˈquick·ness** presteza f, celeridad f; prontitud f.

quick···: **~sand** arena f movediza; **~-sil·ver** azogue m, mercurio m; **~-tem·pered** de genio vivo; **~-wit·ted** agudo, perspicaz.

qui·es·cence [kwaiˈesns] quietud f, tranquilidad f; **qui·es·cent** □ quieto, inactivo; latente.

qui·et [ˈkwaiət] 1. □ (silent) silencioso, callado; (motionless, not excited) quieto, tranquilo; reposado; color no llamativo; celebration etc. sin ceremonias, más bien privado; all ~ sin novedad; be ~, keep ~ (p.) callarse; 2. silencio m; tranquilidad f, reposo m; F on the ~ a la sordina; 3. calmar(se); 4. ~! ¡silencio! **ˈqui·et·ness, qui·e·tude** [ˈ~tjuːd] tranquilidad f, quietud f; silencio m.

quill [kwil] 1. pluma f; cañón m (de pluma); (spine) púa f; (bobbin) canilla f; 2. plegar; **ˈquill pen** pluma f de ave (para escribir).

quilt [kwilt] 1. colcha f; 2. acolchar; estofar; pespunt(e)ar; **ˈquilt·ing** colchadura f; (art) piqué m.

qui·nine [ˈkwainain] quinina f.

quin·qua·gen·ar·ian [kwinkwədʒəˈneəriən] quincuagenario adj. a. su. (a f) m.

quin·quen·ni·um [kwinˈkweniəm] quinquenio m.

quint·es·sence [kwinˈtesns] quinta esencia f.

quin·tet(te) [kwinˈtet] quinteto m.

quin·tu·ple [ˈkwintjupl] 1. quíntuplo; 2. quintuplicar(se); **quin·tu·plets** [~plits] pl. quintillizos (as f/pl.) m/pl.

quip [kwip] 1. agudeza f, pulla f, chiste m; 2. echar pullas.

quire [ˈkwaiə] mano f de papel.

quirk [kwɜːk] (oddity) capricho m, peculiaridad f; (quip) agudeza f.

quit [kwit] v/t. dejar, abandonar; salir de; desocupar; ~ ger. dejar de inf., desistir de inf.; v/i. retirarse, despedirse; rajarse; cejar.

quite [kwait] totalmente, completamente; (rather) bastante ~ a hero todo un héroe; ~ (so)! efectivamente, perfectamente.

quits [kwits] en paz (with con); en conclusión; cry ~ hacer las paces; call it ~ no seguir; descontinuar.

quit·ter [ˈkwitə] F approx. faltón m, remolón m; catacaldos m.

quiv·er [ˈkwivə] 1. temblar, estremecerse; 2. temblor m.

quix·ot·ic [kwikˈsɔtik] □ quijotesco.

quiz [kwiz] 1. encuesta f, acertijo m; prueba f; ~ show torneo m radiofónico; torneo m televisado; 2. interrogar; mirar con curiosidad; **ˈquiz·zi·cal** □ burlón.

quo·rum [ˈkwɔːrəm] quórum m.

quo·ta [ˈkwoutə] cuota f; contingente m, cupo m.

quo·ta·tion [kwouˈteiʃn] cita f, citación f; † cotización f; **quo·ta·tion marks** pl. comillas f/pl.

quote [kwout] citar; † cotizar (at en).

quo·tient [ˈkwouʃənt] cociente m.

R

rab·bi [ˈræbai] rabino *m*; (*before name*) rabí *m*.
rab·bit [ˈræbit] conejo *m*.
rab·ble [ˈræbl] canalla *f*, chusma *f*; **ˈ~-rous·er** agitador *m*.
rab·id [ˈræbid] ☐ rabioso (*a. fig.*); *fig.* fanático.
ra·bies [ˈreibiːz] rabia *f*.
race[1] [reis] raza *f* (*a. biol.*); estirpe *f*, casta *f*; *human* ~ género *m* humano.
race[2] [~] **1.** carrera *f*; regata *f on water*; (*current*) corriente *f* fuerte; **2.** *v/i.* competir; ir a máxima velocidad; *v/t.* hacer correr; competir con; **ˈ~-course** hipódromo *m*, cancha *f* *S.Am.*
race ha·tred [ˈreisˈheitrid] odio *m* racial.
race horse [ˈreishɔːs] caballo *m* de carrera.
rac·er [ˈreisə] caballo *m* (*or* coche *m* *etc.*) de carrera.
race ri·ot [ˈreisˈraiə] disturbio *m* racista.
race track [ˈreistræk] pista *f*, cancha *f* *S.Am.*; *mot.* autódromo *m*.
ra·cial [ˈreiʃl] ☐ racial.
rac·i·ness [ˈreisinis] sal *f*, vivacidad *f*, picante *m*.
rac·ing [ˈreisiŋ] carreras *f/pl.*; *attr.* de carrera(s).
rac·ism [ˈreisizm] actitud *f* discriminatoria hacia razas específicas; racismo *m*.
rac·ist [ˈreisist] practicante *m/f* o creyente *m/f* del racismo; racista *adj. a. su. m/f*.
rack [ræk] **1.** estante *m*, anaquel *m*; (*hat- etc.*) percha *f*, cuelgacapas *m*; **2.** atormentar.
rack·et[1] [ˈrækit], **racqu·et** [~] raqueta *f*.
rack·et[2] [~] **1.** alboroto *m*, baraúnda *f*, jaleo *m*, estrépito *m*; F estafa *f*; **rack·et·eer** [~ˈtiə] F estafador *m*, chantajista *m*, trapacista *m*; **rack·etˈeer·ing** F chantaje *m* sistematizado.
rac·y [ˈreisi] ☐ espiritoso; picante; castizo; *style* salado, vivaz.
ra·dar [ˈreidɑː] radar *m*; ~*scope* radarscopio *m*; ~ *scanner* explorador *m* de radar.
ra·di·al [ˈreidiəl] ☐ radial.
ra·di·ance, ra·di·an·cy [ˈreidiəns(i)] brillantez *f*, resplandor *m*; **ˈra·di·ant** ☐ radiante (*a. fig.*); brillante.
ra·di·ate [ˈreidieit] (ir)radiar; *happiness etc.* difundir; **ra·di·a·tor** [ˈ~eitə] radiador *m*.
rad·i·cal [ˈrædikəl] ☐ *all senses*: radical *adj. a. su. m*; **ˈrad·i·cal·ism** radicalismo *m*.
ra·di·o [ˈreidiou] **1.** radio *f* (*a.* ~ set); radio(tele)fonía *f*; *on* (*or over*) *the* ~ por radio; ~ *station* emisora *f*; ~ *studio* estudio *m* (de emisión); **2.** radiar, transmitir por radio; **ˈ~ˈac·tive** radiactivo; **ˈ~acˈtiv·i·ty** radiactividad *f*; **ra·di·o·gra·phy** [reidiˈɔgrəfi] radiografía *f*; **ra·di·ol·o·gy** [reidiˈɔlədʒi] radiología *f*; **ra·di·os·co·py** [~ˈɔskəpi] radioscopia *f*; **ra·di·oˈtel·e·scope** radiotelescopio *m*; **ˈra·di·oˈther·a·py** radioterapia *f*.
rad·ish [ˈrædiʃ] rábano *m*.
ra·di·us [ˈreidiəs], *pl.* **ra·di·i** [ˈ~ai] *all senses*: radio *m*.
raf·fle [ˈræfl] **1.** rifar, sortear; **2.** rifa *f*.
raft [rɑːft] **1.** balsa *f*, almadía *f*; **2.** transportar en balsa; **ˈraft·er** ⚠ cab(r)io *m*; traviesa *f*.
rag[1] [ræg] trapo *m*; andrajo *m*, harapo *m*; F (*newspaper*) periodicucho *m*; *sl.* *chew the* ~ platicar.
rag[2] [~] *sl.* *v/t.* embromar, dar guerra a; *v/i.* guasearse, bromear.
rag·a·muf·fin [ˈrægəmʌfin] granuja *m*, galopín *m*.
rage [reidʒ] **1.** rabia *f*, furor *m*; manía *f*, afán *m* (*for* de); **2.** rabiar.
rag·ged [ˈrægid] ☐ harapiento, andrajoso; *edge* desigual, mellado.
rag·ing [ˈreidʒiŋ] rabioso, furibundo.
rag...: **ˈ~·tag** F chusma *f* (*freq.* ~ *and bobtail*); **ˈ~·time** ♪ tiempo *m* sincopado.
raid [reid] **1.** correría *f*, incursión *f*; ✈ ataque *m*, bombardeo *m*; **2.** invadir; atacar; ✈ bombardear.
rail[1] [reil] **1.** baranda *f*, barandilla *f*, pasamanos *m*; 🚂 riel *m*, carril *m*; ~ *car* automotriz *m*; *by* ~ por ferrocarril; **2.** (*a.* ~ *in*, ~ *off*) poner cerca (*or* barandilla) a.
rail[2] [~]: ~ *at*, ~ *against* protestar amargamente contra.
rail·ing [ˈreiliŋ] (*a.* ~*s pl.*) verja *f*, barandilla *f*.
rail·road **1.** [ˈreilroud] ferrorcarril *m*; **2.** *attr.* ... ferroviario; **3.** (*through*) llevar a cabo muy precipitadamente; *sl.* encarcelar falsamente.

rashness

rain [rein] **1.** lluvia f (a. fig.); **2.** llover (a. fig.); ~ cats and dogs llover a cántaros; '~**bow** arco iris m; '~**coat** impermeable m; '~**drop** gota f de agua; '~**fall** precipitación f; (cantidad f de) lluvia f; ~ **gauge** ['~geidʒ] pluviómetro m; '**rain·y** □ lluvioso; ~ day día m de lluvia.

raise [reiz] levantar, alzar, elevar, subir, erguir; ⚤ elevar (a una potencia); building erigir; crop cultivar; livestock criar; money reunir.

rai·sin ['reizin] pasa f, uva f seca.

rake¹ [reik] **1.** (garden) rastrillo m; (farm) rastro m; (fire) hurgón m; **2.** v/t. rastrillar; fire hurgar; ~ together (off) reunir (quitar) con el rastrillo; v/i. rastrear.

rake² [~] libertino m, calavera m. '**rake-off** sl. tajada f.

rak·ish ['reikiʃ] **1.** ⚓ de palos inclinados; veloz, ligero; gallardo (a. fig.); at a ~ angle hat echado al lado, a lo chulo; **2.** □ p. libertino.

ral·ly ['ræli] **1.** mst pol. reunión f, manifestación f; ⚔, ♛ recuperación f; **2.** v/i. reunirse; ⚔, ♛ recuperarse; ⚔ replegarse, rehacerse; v/t. reanimar.

ram [ræm] **1.** zo. carnero m; ast. Aries m; ⚔ ariete m; ⚓ espolón m; ⊕ pisón m; **2.** dar contra.

ram·ble ['ræmbl] **1.** paseo m por el campo, excursión f a pie; **2.** salir de (or hacer una) excursión a pie; '**ram·bler** excursionista m/f; vagabundo m; rosal m trepador; '**rambling** □ errante; ♠ trepador; speech divagador.

ram·i·fi·ca·tion [ræmifi'keiʃn] ramificación f; **ram·i·fy** ['~fai] ramificarse.

ram·jet (en·gine) ['ræmdʒet ('endʒən)] ≍ motor m autorreactor; estatorreactor m.

ramp [ræmp] rampa f; descendedero m; '**ram·page** co. **1.** v/i. = **2.**: be on the ~ desbocarse, desenfrenarse; '**ramp·ant** □ prevaleciente; exuberante; desenfrenado.

ram·part ['ræmpaːt] muralla f, terraplén m.

ram·shack·le ['ræmʃækl] desvencijado, destartalado, ruinoso.

ranch [rænʃ] hacienda f, rancho m S.Am.; '**ranch·er** ganadero m.

ran·cid ['rænsid] □ rancio; **ran'cid·i·ty**, '**ran·cid·ness** rancidez f, ranciedad f.

ran·cor ['rænkə] rencor m; **ran·cor·ous** ['rænkərəs] □ rencoroso.

ran·dom ['rændəm] **1.**: at ~ al azar; **2.** fortuito, casual, impensado; aleatorio.

rang [ræŋ] pret. of ring² 2.

range [reindʒ] **1.** alcance m; extensión f; serie f; ⚤ gama f (de frecuencias); ♥ surtido m; (cattle-) dehesa f; (mountain-) sierra f, cordillera f; (stove) fogón m; ≍ campo m de tiro; within ~ al alcance (a. fig.); **2.** v/t. ordenar; clasificar; v/i. variar; alinearse; '~ **find·er** telémetro m; '**rang·er** guardabosques m.

rank¹ [ræŋk] **1.** (row) fila f (a. ≍), hilera f; (status) grado m, graduación f, rango m; **2.** v/t. clasificar, ordenar; v/i. clasificarse; figurar; ~ above ser superior a; ~ with equipararse con.

rank² [~] □ growth lozano, exuberante; smell etc. maloliente, rancio.

rank·ness ['ræŋknis] exuberancia f of growth; fetidez f of smell.

ran·sack ['rænsæk] saquear; registrar (de arriba abajo).

ran·som ['rænsəm] **1.** rescate m; **2.** rescatar; redimir.

rant [rænt] **1.** lenguaje m campanudo (or declamatorio); **2.** despotricar, delirar, hablar con violencia.

rap [ræp] **1.** golpecito m; not to care a ~ no importarle un bledo a uno; sl. take the ~ pagar la multa; **2.** golpear.

ra·pa·cious [rə'peiʃəs] □ rapaz; **ra·pac·i·ty** [rə'pæsiti] rapacidad f.

rape [reip] **1.** violación f, estupro m; **2.** violar, forzar, estuprar; '**rap·ist** violador m; estuprador m.

rap·id ['ræpid] **1.** □ rápido, veloz; **2.** ~s pl. rápidos m/pl., recial m, rabión m; **ra·pid·i·ty** [rə'piditi] rapidez f.

rapt [ræpt] arrebatado, transportado; ~ attention atención f fija.

rap·ture ['ræptʃə] rapto m, éxtasis m, arrobamiento m; in ~ extasiado; '**rap·tur·ous** □ extático.

rare [rɛə] □ raro, poco común; peregrino; phys. ralo; esp. meat poco hecho; poco asado; ~ly rara vez.

rar·e·fy ['rɛərifai] enrarecer; '**rare·ness**, '**rar·i·ty** rareza f.

ras·cal ['raːskəl] pillo m, pícaro m; **ras·cal·i·ty** ['~'kæliti] picardía f.

rash¹ [ræʃ] □ temerario; precipitado.

rash² [~] ⚕ erupción f (cutánea); salpullido m.

rash·ness ['ræʃnis] temeridad f; precipitación f.

rasp [rɑːsp] **1.** escofina f; **2.** escofinar, raspar; decir en voz áspera.

rasp·ber·ry [ˈrɑːzbəri] frambuesa f.

rasp·ing [ˈrɑːspiŋ] **1.** □ *voice* áspero.

rat [ræt] **1.** rata f; *sl.* canalla m; *pol.* desertor m; *rat race sl.* lucha f diaria por ganarse el pan; **2.** cazar ratas; *pol. a. sl.* ~ *on* chivatear contra.

ratch·et [ˈrætʃit] trinquete m; '~ **wheel** rueda f de trinquete.

rate [reit] **1.** proporción f; relación f; tanto m (por ciento); (*speed*) velocidad f, paso m; (*price*) tasa f, precio m; *at any* ~ de todas formas; *at that* ~ de ese modo; ~ *of exchange* cambio m; ~ *of interest* tipo m de interés; **2.** tasar (*at* en), valorar; clasificar; imponer contribución (municipal) a.

rate pay·er [ˈreitpeiə] contribuyente m/f.

rath·er [ˈrɑːðə] (*more*) mejor, primero, más bien; (*somewhat*) algo, bastante; F ~! [ˈrɑːˈðə] ¡ya lo creo!; ~ *mejor dicho.

rat·i·fi·ca·tion [rætifiˈkeiʃn] ratificación f; **rat·i·fy** [ˈ~fai] ratificar.

rat·ing [ˈreitiŋ] clasificación f; contribución f; ⚓ (*ship*) clase f.

ra·tio [ˈreiʃiou] relación f, razón f, proporción f.

ra·tion [ˈræʃn] **1.** ración f; ✕ ~s *pl.* suministro m; **2.** racionar.

ra·tion·al [ˈræʃnl] □ racional, razonable; **ra·tion·al·ism** [ˈ~nəlizm] racionalismo m; **ra·tion·al·i·ty** [~ˈnæliti] racionalidad f; 'ra·tion·al·ize hacer racional, organizar racionalmente; buscar pretexto racional a.

ra·tion·ing [ˈræʃniŋ] racionamiento m.

rat·tle [ˈrætl] **1.** golpeteo m; traqueteo m; crujido m; sonsonete m; (*instrument*) matraca f, carraca f; (*child's*) sonajero m; **2.** *v/i.* sonar, crujir, castañetear; F ~ *on* parlotear; *v/t.* agitar, sacudir; ~ *off* enumerar rápidamente; **'rat·tler** F = **'rat·tle·snake** serpiente f de cascabel; **'rat·tle·trap 1.** desvencijado; **2.** armatoste m.

rat·tling [ˈrætliŋ] ruidoso; desconcertante.

rat·ty [ˈræti] *sl.* amostazado; *clothing* ruin, vil.

rau·cous [ˈrɔːkəs] □ estridente, ronco.

rav·age [ˈrævidʒ] **1.** estrago m, destrozo m; **2.** destrozar, asolar; pillar.

rave [reiv] delirar, desvariar.

rav·en [ˈreivn] cuervo m.

rav·en·ous [ˈrævnəs] □ famélico, voraz, hambriento; *be* ~*ly hungry* tener una hambre canina.

rav·ings [ˈreiviŋz] *pl.* delirio m, desvarío m.

rav·ish [ˈræviʃ] encantar, embelesar; *lit.* robar, violar; **'rav·ish·ing** □ encantador, embelesador.

raw [rɔː] **1.** □ *food, weather* crudo; *spirit* puro; *substance* en bruto, sin refinar, crudo; (*inexperienced*) novato; **2.** carne f viva; **'~-boned** huesudo; **'~ deal** *sl.* mala pasada f; **'~-hide** cuero m en verde; **'raw·ness** crudeza f; inexperiencia f.

ray¹ [rei] **1.** rayo m; ⚘ bráctea f; **2.** emitir rayos.

ray² [~] *ichth.* raya f.

ray·on [ˈreiɔn] rayón m.

raze [reiz] arrasar, asolar.

ra·zor [ˈreizə] (*open*) navaja f; (*safety*-) maquinilla f de afeitar; ⚡ maquina f de afeitar, rasurador m; '~ **blade** hoja f (*or* cuchilla f) de afeitar.

razz [ræz] *sl.* echar un rapapolvo a; ridiculizar.

raz·zle(-daz·zle) [ˈræzl(ˈdæzl)] *sl.* ostentación f; confusión f.

re [riː] respecto a, con referencia a.

reach [riːtʃ] **1.** alcance m; extensión f, distancia f; capacidad f; *within* (*easy*) ~ al alcance; **2.** *v/i.* extenderse; *with hand* (*freq.* ~ *out*) alargar (*or* tender) la mano (*for* para tomar); *v/t.* alcanzar; llegar a; lograr.

re·act [riˈækt] reaccionar (*against* contra; *to* a, ante; *upon* sobre).

re·ac·tion [riˈækʃn] reacción f; **re·'ac·tion·ar·y** *esp. pol.* reaccionario *adj. a. su. m* (a f).

re·ac·tive [riˈæktiv] reactivo; **re·'ac·tor** *phys.* reactor m.

read [riːd] [*irr.*] *v/t.* leer; interpretar; descifrar; *typ.* corregir; *v/i.* leer; (*notice etc.*) rezar, decir; (*thermometer etc.*) indicar, marcar; ~ *aloud* leer en alta voz; ~ *between the lines fig.* leer entre líneas.

read·a·ble [ˈriːdəbl] □ legible; digno de leerse, entretenido.

read·er [ˈriːdə] (-*a* f) m; *typ.* corrector m; (*book*) libro m de lectura; **'read·er·ship** número m total de lectores (de un periódico).

read·i·ly [ˈredili] *adv.* de buena gana; fácilmente; **'read·i·ness** prontitud f; alacridad f; buena disposición f.

read·ing [ˈriːdiŋ] lectura f (*a. parl.*);

interpretación *f*; ~ **room** sala *f* de lectura.

re·ad·just ['ri:ə'dʒʌst] reajustar; *pol. etc.* reorientar; '**re·ad·just·ment** reajuste *m*; reorientación *f*.

read·y ['redi] 1. □ listo, preparado (*for* para; *to* para *inf.*); pronto; (*inclined*) dispuesto (*to* a); ✝ contante, efectivo; *answer* fácil; *wit* agudo, vivo; *get* (*or* make) ~ preparar(se), disponer(se); 2.: *at the* ~ ✕ listo para tirar; apercibido; *en* ristre; '**~-made**, '**~-to-**'**wear** ya hecho, confeccionado.

re·af·firm ['ri:ə'fə:m] reafirmar, reiterar.

re·a·gent ['ri:'eidʒənt] reactivo *m*.

re·al [riəl] 1. □ real; verdadero; auténtico; genuino; legítimo; 2. *F adv.* verdaderamente; muy; '**re·al·ism** realismo *m*; '**re·al·is·tic** □ realista; **re·al·i·ty** [ri:'æliti] realidad *f*; **re·al·iz·a·ble** ['riəlaizəbl] □ realizable; '**re·al·ize** darse cuenta de; reconocer; ✝ realizar; *plan etc.* realizar, llevar a cabo; '**re·al·ly** en realidad; verdaderamente, realmente; ~? ¿de veras?

realm [relm] reino *m*; *fig.* campo *m*.

re·al·tor ['riəltə] corredor *m* de bienes raíces (*or* de fincas); '**re·al·ty** ᵻᵻ bienes *m*/*pl.* raíces.

ream[1] [ri:m] (*paper*) resma *f*; F montón *m*.

ream[2] [~] ⊕ escariar; '**ream·er** escariador *m*.

reap [ri:p] segar; cosechar (*a. fig.*); '**reap·er** segador (-a *f*) *m*; (*machine*) segadora *f*; '**reap·ing** siega *f*.

re·ap·pear ['ri:ə'piə] reaparecer.

re·ap·point ['ri:ə'pɔint] volver a nombrar.

rear[1] [riə] *v/t.* criar; alzar; *v/i.* encabritarse, ponerse de manos.

rear[2] [~] 1. parte *f* posterior (*or* trasera); cola *f*; ✕ última fila; ✕ retaguardia *f*; *bring up the* ~ cerrar la marcha; 2. trasero, posterior; de cola; ~ **wheel drive** mando *m* de las ruedas traseras; '**~ ad·mi·ral** contraalmirante *m*; '**~ guard** retaguardia *f*.

re·arm ['ri:'ɑ:m] rearmar(se); '**re·ar·ma·ment** [~məmənt] rearme *m*.

re·ar·range ['ri:ə'reindʒ] ordenar de nuevo; ✝ volver a adaptar.

rear-view ['riə'vju:] *adj.* retrovisor, de retrovisión.

rear·ward ['riəwəd] 1. *adj.* trasero,

de atrás; 2. *adv.* (*a.* '**rear·wards** [~z]) hacia atrás.

rea·son ['ri:zn] 1. razón *f*; motivo *m*; causa *f*; sensatez *f*; moderación *f*; *by* ~ *of* a causa de; en virtud de; 2. *v/i.* razonar, discurrir; *v/t.* razonar; resolver pensando (*a.* ~ **out**); '**rea·son·a·ble** □ razonable; justo, equitativo; *p.* sensato; '**rea·son·ing** razonamiento *m*; argumento *m*.

re·as·sur·ance ['ri:ə'ʃuərəns] noticia *f* (*or* promesa *f etc.*) tranquilizadora; **re·as·sure** ['~'ʃuə] tranquilizar; alentar; **re·as·sur·ing** □ tranquilizador.

re·bate ['ri:beit] 1. rebaja *f*, descuento *m*; 2. rebajar, descontar.

reb·el 1. ['rebl] rebelde *m*/*f*; 2. [~] rebelde (*mst* **re·bel·lious** [ri'beljəs]); 3. [ri'bel] rebelarse, sublevarse; **re·bel·lion** [~jən] rebelión *f*.

re·birth ['ri:'bə:θ] renacimiento *m*.

re·bound [ri'baund] 1. rebotar; resaltar; 2. rebote *m*.

re·buff [ri'bʌf] 1. repulsa *f*, desaire *m*; 2. rechazar, desairar.

re·build ['ri:'bild] [*irr.* (*build*)] reedificar, reconstruir.

re·buke [ri'bju:k] 1. reprensión *f*, reprimenda *f*; 2. reprender, censurar.

re·but [ri'bʌt] rebatir, refutar.

re·cal·ci·trant [ri'kælsitrənt] recalcitrante, refractorio.

re·call [ri'kɔ:l] 1. revocación *f*; retirada *f* (*of ambassador, capital*); llamada *f* (*para que vuelva una p.*); 2. revocar; *ambassador, capital* retirar; llamar; hacer volver; recordar.

re·can·ta·tion [ri:kæn'teiʃn] retractación *f*.

re·cap [ri'kæp] *tires* recauchutar.

re·ca·pit·u·late [ri:kə'pitjuleit] recapitular; '**re·ca·pit·u·la·tion** recapitulación *f*.

re·cap·ture ['ri:'kæptʃə] 1. represa *f*, recobro *m*; 2. represar, recobrar.

re·cede [ri'si:d] retroceder, retirarse.

re·ceipt [ri'si:t] 1. recibo *m*; ✝ ~s *pl.* ingresos *m*/*pl.*; 2. dar recibo (por).

re·ceiv·a·ble [ri'si:vəbl] admisible; recibidero; ✝ por cobrar; **re·ceive** recibir, admitir; *guest etc.* acoger; *money* cobrar; **re·ceiv·er** recibidor (-a *f*) *m*; destinatario (a *f*) *m*; *radio:* receptor *m*; *teleph.* auricular *m*; *phys.*, 🜨 recipiente *m*; ᵻᵻ (*official* ~) *approx.* síndico *m*; **re·ceiv·er·ship** ᵻᵻ sindicatura *f*.

re·cent ['riːsnt] □ reciente, nuevo.

re·cep·ta·cle [ri'septəkl] receptáculo m (a. ♀).

re·cep·tion [ri'sepʃn] recepción f (a. radio); recibimiento m; **re'cep·tion·ist** recibidor (-a f) m; **re'cep·tion room** sala f de recibo.

re·cep·tive [ri'septiv] □ receptivo.

re·cess [ri'ses] vacaciones f/pl., intermisión f; esp. parl. suspensión f; intermedio m; ⊕ rebajo m; △ hueco m.

re·ces·sion [ri'seʃn] retirada f, retroceso m (a. ✝); ✝ recesión f.

re·ci·pe ['resipi] receta f.

re·cip·i·ent [ri'sipiənt] recibidor (-a f) m, recipiente m/f.

re·cip·ro·cal [ri'siprəkəl] 1. □ recíproco, mutuo; 2. ♠ recíproca f, inverso m; **re'cip·ro·cate** [~keit] v/i. ⊕ oscilar, alternar; v/t. intercambiar; corresponder a; **rec·i·proc·i·ty** [resi'prɒsiti] reciprocidad f.

re·cit·al [ri'saitl] relación f, narración f; ♪ recital m; **rec·i·ta·tive** [~tə'tiːv] ♪ recitativo adj. a. su. m; recitado m; **re·cite** [ri'sait] recitar; declamar; narrar, referir.

reck·less ['reklis] □ temerario; imprudente; inconsiderado; **'reck·less·ness** temeridad f.

reck·on ['rekn] v/t. contar, calcular; estimar; considerar (as como); v/i. calcular; F estimar, creer; **'reck·on·ing** cuenta f; cálculo m.

re·claim [ri'kleim] reclamar; amansar, reformar; land recuperar.

rec·la·ma·tion [reklə'meiʃn] reclamación f; recuperación f; land ~ rescate m de terrenos.

re·cline [ri'klain] reclinar(se), recostar(se); **re'clin·ing chair** sillón m reclinable, poltrona f.

re·cluse [ri'kluːs] recluso, solitario adj. a. su. m (a f).

rec·og·ni·tion [rekəg'niʃn] reconocimiento m; **rec·og·ni·zance** [ri'kɒgnizəns] ꝛ́ꝛ reconocimiento m; obligación f contraída; **rec·og·nize** ['rekəgnaiz] reconocer; confesar.

re·coil [ri'kɔil] 1. recular, retroceder (de espanto); ✗ retroceder; 2. reculada f, retroceso m (a. ✗).

rec·ol·lect [rekə'lekt] recordar, acordarse de; **rec·ol·lec·tion** [rekə'lekʃn] recuerdo m.

rec·om·mend [rekə'mend] recomendar, encarecer; **rec·om·men·da·tion** recomendación f.

re·com·mit [riːkə'mit] volver a confiar; volver a internar.

rec·om·pense ['rekəmpens] 1. recompensa f, compensación f; 2. recompensar (for acc.).

rec·on·cil·a·ble ['rekənsailəbl] reconciliable; **'rec·on·cile** (re)conciliar; ~ o.s. to resignarse a, acomodarse con.

re·con·di·tion [riːkən'diʃn] reacondicionar.

re·con·nais·sance [ri'kɒnisəns] reconocimiento m.

rec·on·noi·ter [rekə'nɔitə] reconocer.

re·con·quer [riː'kɒnkə] reconquistar; **'re'con·quest** [~kwest] reconquista f.

re·con·sid·er ['riːkən'sidə] repensar, reconsiderar.

re·con·sti·tute ['riː'kɒnstitjuːt] reconstituir.

re·con·struct ['riːkəns'trʌkt] reconstruir; reedificar.

re·con·ver·sion ['riːkən'vɔːʃn] reconversión f, reorganización f.

re·cord 1. ['rekɔːd] registro m; partida f; documento m; relación f; (p.'s history) historial m, curriculum vitae m, carrera f; ~ archivos m/pl.; esp. off the ~ no oficial, confidencial (-mente); ~ card ficha f; ~ library discoteca f; 2. [~] attr. sin precedentes, máximo; ~ time tiempo m record; 3. [~'kɔːd] registrar; hacer constar, consignar; inscribir; **re·cord break·er** ['rekɔːd'breikə] plusmarquista m/f; **re'cord·er** registrador m, archivero m; ꝛ́ꝛ approx. juez m municipal; ♪ caramillo m; **re'cord·ing** grabación f; **'re'cord 'play·er** tocadiscos m.

re·count [ri'kaunt] (re)contar, referir.

re·course [ri'kɔːs] recurso m; have ~ to recurrir a.

re·cov·er¹ [ri'kʌvə] v/t. recobrar, recuperar; money reembolsarse, recaudar; v/i. ♣ restablecerse (a. ✝), reponerse.

re·cov·er² ['riː'kʌvə] recubrir.

re·cov·er·a·ble [ri'kʌvərəbl] recuperable; **re'cov·er·y** recobro m, recuperación f; ♣ restablecimiento m, mejoría f.

rec·re·ate ['rekrieit] recrear(se), divertir(se); **rec·re·a·tion** recreación f; school: recreo m; ~ ground campo m de deportes; ~al vehicle vehículo m de recreo.

re·crim·i·nate [ri'krimineit] recriminar; **re·crim·i'na·tion** recriminación f.

re·cruit [ri'kru:t] **1.** recluta m; fig. novicio m; **2.** reclutar, alistar; **re'cruit·ment** reclutamiento m.

rec·tan·gle [⹂rektæŋgl] rectángulo m; **rec'tan·gu·lar** [⹂gjulə] rectangular.

rec·ti·fi·a·ble [rektifaiəbl] rectificable; **rec·ti·fi·er** [⹂faiə] mst rectificador m; ⊕ (crankshafts etc.) rectificadora f; **rec·ti·fy** [⹂fai] all senses: rectificar; **rec·ti·lin·e·al** [rekti'linjəl], **rec·ti·lin·e·ar** [⹂njə] □ rectilíneo; **rec·ti·tude** [⹂tju:d] rectitud f, probidad f.

rec·to·ry ['rektəri] rectoría f; casa f del cura.

rec·tum ['rektəm] recto m.

re·cu·per·ate [ri'kju:pəreit] v/t. recuperar; v/i. ✚ restablecerse; **re'cu·per·a·tive** [⹂rətiv] recuperativo.

re·cur [ri'kə:] repetirse, producirse de nuevo, volver a ocurrir; **re·cur·rence** [ri'kʌrəns] repetición f, reaparición f; **re'cur·rent** □ repetido; recurrente (a. anat., 𝄢); Ⱥ periódico.

red [red] **1.** rojo (a. pol.); colorado; encarnado; wine tinto; face encendido with anger, ruboroso with shame; sl. paint the town ~ echar una cana al aire; ~ herring fig. pista f falsa, ardid m para apartar la atención del asunto principal; ~ tape papeleo m, formalidades f/pl.; burocracia f; **2.** (color m) rojo m; (pol.) rojo m; comunista m/f; be in the ~ estar adeudado.

red·breast ['redbrest] (freq. robin ~) petirrojo m; **'red·cap** mozo m de estación; **red·den** ['redn] v/t. enrojecer, teñir de rojo; v/i. enrojecer(se) with anger; ponerse colorado; **'red·dish** rojizo.

re·deem [ri'di:m] redimir; promise cumplir; pledge etc. rescatar, desempeñar; **Re'deem·er** Redentor m.

re·demp·tion [ri'dempʃn] redención f; rescate m; desempeño m; ✚ amortización f.

red...: '~·faced vergonzado; '~·hand·ed con las manos en la masa, en flagrante; '~·head·ed pelirrojo; '~·hot candente; fig. vehemente, acérrimo.

re·dis·cov·er ['ri:dis'kʌvə] volver a descubrir.

red-let·ter day ['redletə'dei] día m festivo; fig. día m señalado.

red-light dis·trict ['redlait'distrikt] barrio m de los lupanares, barrio m chino.

red·ness ['rednis] rojez f; inflamación f.

red·o·lence ['redələns] fragancia f, perfume m; **'red·o·lent** perfumado (of como); fig. be ~ of recordar.

re·dound [ri'daund] redundar.

re·dress [ri'dres] **1.** reparación f, compensación f, resarcimiento m; **2.** reparar, resarcir; enmendar.

red...: '~·skin piel roja m/f indio m norteamericano; '~ 'tape papeleo m.

re·duce [ri'dju:s] v/t. reducir (to a, hasta; a. Ⱥ, ♞); disminuir; abreviar; price rebajar; degradar in rank; v/i. ❧ adelgazar; **re·duc·tion** [ri'dʌkʃn] reducción f; di(s)minución f; abreviación f; rebaja f of price.

re·dun·dance, re·dun·dan·cy [ri'dʌndəns(i)] redundancia f; **re'dun·dant** □ redundante.

red·wood ['redwud] secoya f.

re·ech·o [ri'ekou] repercutirse.

reed [ri:d] ♣ carrizo m, junco m, caña f; ♪ lengüeta f (pipe) caramillo m.

reed·y ['ri:di] place cañoso; voice alto y delgado.

reef [ri:f] escollo m, arrecife m.

reef·er [⹂] sl. pitillo m de mariguana.

reek [ri:k] **1.** vaho m; hedor m; **2.** vahear, humear; heder, oler (of a).

reel [ri:l] **1.** carrete m, tambor m; (fishing) carrete(l) m; sew. broca f, devanadera f; phot., film: rollo m, cinta f, película f; **2.** v/t. devanar; ~ off enumerar rápidamente, ensartar; v/i. tambalear(se).

re·e·lect ['ri:i'lekt] reelegir.

re·en·act ['ri:i'nækt] 𝄐𝄐 volver a promulgar; thea. volver a representar.

re·en·list ['ri:in'list] reenganchar(se).

re·en·ter ['ri:'entə] reingresar en, reentrar en; **re'en·try** [⹂tri] reingreso m; into earth's atmosphere reentrada f.

re·es·tab·lish ['ri:is'tæbliʃ] restablecer; **'re·es'tab·lish·ment** restablecimiento m.

re·fer [ri'fə:] v/t. remitir (a th. to a p. algo a una p., a p. to a th. una p. a algo); v/i.: ~ to referirse a, hacer referencia (or alusión) a; **ref·er·ee** [refə'ri:] **1.** all senses: árbitro m; **2.** arbitrar; **ref·er·ence** ['refrəns] referencia f; alusión f; recomendación *f*; *(a. ~ mark)* llamada *f*; *with (or in)* ~ *to* en cuanto a, respecto a *(or de)*; ~ *book library* room *m* de consulta; ~ *library* biblioteca *f* de consulta.

ref·er·en·dum [refə'rendəm] referéndum *m*.

re·fill ['riː'fil] **1.** repuesto *m*, recambio *m*; mina *f (for pencil)*; **2.** rellenar.

re·fine [ri'fain] *v/t.* refinar *(a. ⊕)*; purificar; ⊕ acrisolar; *v/i.*: ~ *(up)on* sutilizar *acc.*; mejorar *acc.*; **re'fined** fino, refinado; *b.s.* redicho; **re'fine·ment** refinamiento *m*; esmero *m*, urbanidad *f*; **re'fin·er·y** refinería *f*.

re·flect [ri'flekt] *v/t.* reflejar; *v/i. (think)* reflexionar; **re'flec·tion** reflejo *m*, reflexión *f*; *(thinking)* reflexión *f*, consideración *f*, meditación *f*; **re'flec·tive** □ reflexivo; **re'flec·tor** reflector *m*.

re·flex ['riː'fleks] reflejo *adj. a. su. m*; ~ *action physiol.* (acto *m*) reflejo *m*; **re·flex·ive** [ri'fleksiv] □ reflexivo.

re·for·est·a·tion ['riː'fɔris'teiʃn] repoblación *f* forestal.

re·form [ri'fɔːm] **1.** reforma(ción) *f*; **2.** reformar(se), enmendar(se); re-constituir; **ref·or·ma·tion** [refə-'meiʃn] reformación *f*; *eccl.* 2 Reforma *f*; **re·form·a·to·ry** [ri'fɔːmətəri] reformatorio *adj. a. su. m (mst* de jóvenes).

re·fract [ri'frækt] refractar; ~*ing tele-scope* telescopio *m* de refracción; **re'frac·tion** refracción *f*; **re·frac·to·ri·ness** lo refractario *(a. ⚛)*, obstinación *f*; **re'frac·to·ry** refractario *(a. ⚛)*, obstinado.

re·frain[1] [ri'frein] abstenerse *(from de)*.

re·frain[2] [~] estribillo *m*.

re·fresh [ri'freʃ] refrescar; **re'fresh·ing** □ refrescante; **re'fresh·ment** refresco *m*; ~*s pl.* refrescos *m/pl.*

re·frig·er·ant [ri'fridʒərənt] refrigerante *adj. a. su. m*; **re'frig·er·ate** [~reit] refrigerar; **re'frig·er·a·tor** nevera *f*, refrigerador *m*; ⚛ refrigerante *m*.

re·fu·el [riː'fjuəl] reabastecer(se) de combustible, rellenar (de combustible).

ref·uge ['refjuːdʒ] refugio *m*, asilo *m*; *fig.* recurso *m*, amparo *m*; *mount.* albergue *m*; **ref·u·gee** [~'dʒiː] refugiado *(a f) m*.

re·fund **1.** [riː'fʌnd] devolver, re-integrar; **2.** ['riː'fʌnd] devolución *f*.

re·fus·al [ri'fjuːzl] negativa *f*; dene-gación *f*; rechazamiento *m*.

re·fuse **1.** [ri'fjuːz] *v/t.* rehusar, (de-)negar, rechazar; no querer aceptar; *v/i.* ~ *to inf.* negarse a *inf.*, rehusar *inf.*; **2. ref·use** ['refjuːs] desechado; **3.** [~] basura *f*; desperdicios *m/pl.*; sobras *f/pl.*

re·fute [ri'fjuːt] refutar, rebatir.

re·gain [ri'gein] (re)cobrar.

re·gal ['riːgəl] □ regio; real.

re·gale [ri'geil] regalar(se) *(on con)*; agasajar, festejar.

re·gard [ri'gɑːd] **1.** consideración *f*, respeto *m*; estimación *f*; *(gaze)* mira-da *f*; ~*s pl.* recuerdos *m/pl.*; *in (or with)* ~ *to* con respeto a, en cuanto a; **2.** considerar *(as como)*; observar; respetar; mirar; **re'gard·ing** en cuanto a; relativo a; **re'gard·less 1.:** ~ *of* indiferente a; sin hacer caso de; sin miramientos de; **2.** *adv.* F pese a quien pese, a pesar de todo.

re·gen·cy ['riːdʒənsi] regencia *f*.

re·gen·er·ate 1. [ri'dʒenəreit] regene-rar; **2.** [~rit] regenerado; **re'gen·er·a·tive** [~rətiv] regenerador.

re·gent ['riːdʒənt] regente *adj. a. su. m/f*; '~·ship regencia *f*.

ré·gime [rei'ʒiːm], **reg·i·men** ['re-dʒimen] régimen *m*.

reg·i·ment 1. ['redʒimənt] regimien-to *m*; **2.** ['~ment] *fig.* organizar muy estrictamente, reglamentar; **reg·i·men·ta·tion** organización *f* estricta.

re·gion ['riːdʒən] región *f*, comarca *f*; zona *f*; *in the* ~ *of* alrededor de.

reg·is·ter ['redʒistə] **1.** registro *m (a. ♪)*; lista *f*, padrón *m of members*; *univ.*, ♣ matrícula *f*; ⊕ indicador *m*, registrador *m*; **2.** *v/t.* registrar; ins-cribir, matricular; ⊕ indicar; *v/i.* inscribirse, matricular; '**reg·is·tered** *letter* certificado.

reg·is·trar [redʒis'trɑː] registrador *m*, archivero *m*; **reg·is·tra·tion** [~-'treiʃn] registro *m*, inscripción *f*; matrícula *f*; '**reg·is·try** registro *m*, archivo *m*; ~ *office* approx. juzgado *m*.

re·gress 1. ['riːgres] retroceso *m*; **2.** [~'gres] perder terreno; retroce-der; **re·gres·sion** [ri'greʃn] regre-sión *f*.

re·gret [ri'gret] **1.** sentimiento *m*, pesar *m*; remordimiento *m*; **2.** sentir, lamentar; arrepentirse de; **re'gret·ful** [~ful] □ pesaroso; arrepentido; **re'gret·ta·ble** □ lamentable, deplo-rable.

re·group [riːˈgruːp] reagrupar(se).

reg·u·lar [ˈreɡjulə] **1.** ☐ regular; normal; uniforme; ordenado; *attender etc.* asiduo; F cabal, verdadero; **2.** obrero *m* permanente; ✕ soldado *m* de línea; F parroquiano *m*, asiduo *m*.

reg·u·late [ˈreɡjuleit] regular (*a.* ⊕), arreglar, ajustar; **ˈreg·u·lat·ing** ⊕ regulador; **reg·u·lat·ion 1.** regulación *f*; regla *f*, reglamento *m*; **2.** reglamentario; **ˈreg·u·la·tor** regulador *m* (*a.* ⊕).

re·gur·gi·tate [riːˈɡəːdʒiteit] *v/t.* vomitar; *v/i.* regurgitar.

re·ha·bil·i·tate [riːəˈbiliteit] rehabilitar.

re·hash [ˈriːˈhæʃ] *fig.* **1.** refundir, rehacer; **2.** refundición *f*; repetición *f* sin novedad.

re·hears·al [riˈhəːsl] repetición *f*, *thea.*, ♪ ensayo *m*; **re·hearse** [riˈhəːs] repetir; *thea.*, ♪ ensayar.

re·heat [riːˈhiːt] recalentar.

reign [rein] **1.** reinado *m*; *fig.* (pre-)dominio *m*; **2.** reinar; *fig.* imperar.

re·im·burse [riːimˈbəːs] reembolsar; **ˈre·im·burse·ment** reembolso *m*.

rein [rein] **1.** rienda *f*; *give ~ to* dar rienda suelta a; **2.** *v/t.*: *~ in* refrenar.

rein·deer [ˈreindiə] reno *m*.

re·in·force [riːinˈfɔːs] reforzar (*a. fig.*); **ˈre·in·force·ments** *pl.* refuerzos *m/pl.*

re·in·state [riːinˈsteit] reinstalar; rehabilitar.

re·in·sur·ance [ˈriːinˈʃuərəns] reaseguro *m*; **re·in·sure** [ˈ◡ˈʃuə] reasegurar.

re·it·er·ate [riːˈitəreit] reiterar.

re·ject [riˈdʒekt] *offer etc.* rechazar; *application* denegar; *plan etc.* desechar; **re·jec·tion** rechazamiento *m*; denegación *f*, desestimación *f*.

re·joice [riˈdʒɔis] alegrar(se), regocijar(se) (*at, by* de); **re·joic·ing** regocijo *m*, júbilo *m*, alegría *f*.

re·join 1. [ˈriːˈdʒɔin] reunirse con, volver a juntarse con; **2.** [riˈdʒɔin] replicar; **re·join·der** réplica *f*.

re·ju·ve·nate [riˈdʒuːvineit] rejuvenecer; **re·ju·ve·na·tion** rejuvenecimiento *m*.

re·lapse [riˈlæps] **1.** ☞ recaída *f*, recidiva *f*; reincidencia *f*; **2.** ☞ recaer; reincidir.

re·late [riˈleit] *v/t.* relatar, contar; *v/i.*: *~ to* relacionarse con; **re·lat·ed** *subject* afin, conexo.

re·la·tion [riˈleiʃn] (*narration*) relato *m*, relación *f*; (*~ship*) conexión *f*, relación *f* (*to, with* con); **re·la·tion·ship** conexión *f*, afinidad *f* (*to, with* con); (*kinship*) parentesco *m*.

rel·a·tive [ˈrelətiv] **1.** ☐ relativo (*to* a); **2.** *gr.* relativo *m*; (*kin*) pariente *m/f*; **rel·a·tiv·i·ty** relatividad *f*.

re·lax [riˈlæks] *v/t.* relajar, aflojar; suavizar; *v/i.* esparcirse, expansionarse, descansar; F *~!* ¡cálmate!; **re·lax·a·tion** esparcimiento *m*, recreo *m*, descanso *m*.

re·lay [riˈlei] **1.** parada *f*, posta *f* of *horses etc.*; tanda *f* of *workmen*; relevo *m*; ⚡ relé *m*; **2.** *radio:* retransmitir.

re·lease [riˈliːs] **1.** liberación *f*; excarcelación *f from prison*; descargo *m from obligation*; **2.** soltar, libertar; descargar, absolver; *brake* soltar.

rel·e·gate [ˈreliɡeit] relegar.

re·lent [riˈlent] ablandarse, ceder; **re·lent·less** ☐ implacable.

rel·e·vance, **rel·e·van·cy** [ˈrelivəns(i)] pertinencia *f*; **ˈrel·e·vant** ☐ pertinente.

re·li·a·bil·i·ty [rilaiəˈbiliti] confiabilidad *f*; seguridad *f*; integridad *f*; **re·li·a·ble** ☐ confiable; seguro; de fiar, de confianza; *p.* formal.

re·li·ance [riˈlaiəns] confianza *f* (*on* en); dependencia *f* (*on* de).

re·li·ant [riˈlaiənt] confiado.

rel·ic [ˈrelik] reliquia *f* (*a. eccl.*), vestigio *m*; **rel·ict** [ˈrelikt] viuda *f*.

re·lief [riˈliːf] alivio *m*; desahogo *m*; consuelo *m*; (*a. poor ~*) socorro *m*, auxilio *m*; ✕ (*troops*) relevo *m*; △ relieve *m*; *~ map* mapa *m* en relieve.

re·lieve [riˈliːv] aliviar; (*reassure*) tranquilizar; *burden* aligerar; *poor* socorrer; *headache etc.* quitar, suprimir; ✕ *men* relevar; *~ one's feeling* desahogarse.

re·li·gion [riˈlidʒən] religión *f*.

re·li·gious [riˈlidʒəs] ☐ religioso; *~ly fig.* puntualmente.

re·lin·quish [riˈliŋkwiʃ] abandonar, renunciar (a); **re·lin·quish·ment** abandono *m*, renuncia *f*.

rel·ish [ˈreliʃ] **1.** sabor *m*, gusto *m*, apetito *m*; (*sauce*) salsa *f*; **2.** saborear; gustar de.

re·lo·cate [riːˈloukeit] mudar(se); cambiar de lugar.

re·luc·tance [riˈlʌktəns] desgana *f*, renuencia *f*, aversión *f*; *with ~* a desgana; **re·luc·tant** ☐ maldispuesto.

re·ly [ri'lai]: ~ (up)on confiar en, fiarse de; contar con.

re·main [ri'mein] 1. quedar(se), permanecer; (be left over) sobrar; 2.~s pl. restos m/pl.; sobras f/pl.; **re'main·der** resto m; & residuo m, resta f; (books) restos m/pl. de edición.

re·mark [ri'ma:k] 1. observación f; 2. v/t. observar, notar; v/i. hacer una observación ([up]on sobre); **re'mark·a·ble** □ notable; raro.

re·me·di·a·ble [ri'mi:diəbl] □ remediable; **re·me·di·al** [ri'mi:diəl] □ remediador.

rem·e·dy ['remidi] 1. remedio m; 2. remediar.

re·mem·ber [ri'membə] acordarse de, recordar; **re'mem·brance** [-brəns] recuerdo m, memoria f; recordación f.

re·mind [ri'maind] recordar (a p. of a th. algo a una p.); **re'mind·er** recordatorio m, advertencia f.

rem·i·nisce [remi'nis] contar los recuerdos; **rem·i·nis·cence** [remi'nisns] reminiscencia f; **rem·i·nis·cent** □ evocador; recordativo.

re·miss [ri'mis] □ negligente, descuidado; **re'mis·si·ble** [-əbl] remisible; **re·mis·sion** [-'miʃn] remisión f; perdón m.

re·mit [ri'mit] all senses: remitir; **re'mit·ance** remesa f; **re·mit·tee** consignatorio (a f) m.

rem·nant ['remnənt] resto m, residuo m; ✝ retazo m of cloth.

re·mon·strate [ri'mɔnstreit] reconvenir (with a); protestar (against contra).

re·morse [ri'mɔ:s] remordimiento m; **re'morse·ful** [-ful] □ arrepentido; **re'morse·less** □ implacable.

re·mote [ri'mout] □ remoto.

re·mov·a·ble [ri'mu:vəbl] separable; amovible; **re'mov·al** [-əl] removimiento m, remoción f; mudanza f of furniture; deposición f from office; ⊕ separación f **re·move** [ri'mu:v] quitar, remover; trasladar (to a); furniture mudar; ✽ part separar, retirar; obstacle, waste eliminar; ✽ extirpar; **re'mov·er** agente m de mudanzas; spot ~ quitamanchas m.

re·mu·ner·ate [ri'mju:nəreit] remunerar.

Ren·ais·sance [ri'neisəns] Renacimiento m.

re·nal ['ri:nl] renal.

re·nas·cence [ri'næsns] renacimiento m; **re'nas·cent** renaciente.

rend [rend] [irr.] lit. rasgar, hender.

ren·der ['rendə] hacer, volver; service, honour, thanks dar; ♪ interpretar, ejecutar.

ren·dez·vous ['rɔndivu:] (lugar m de una) cita f.

ren·di·tion [ren'diʃn] ♪ ejecución f.

ren·e·gade ['renigeid] renegado adj. a. su. m (a f).

re·new [ri'nju:] renovar; reanudar; **re'new·al** [-əl] renovación f.

re·nounce [ri'nauns] renunciar.

ren·o·vate ['renouveit] renovar.

re·nown [ri'naun] lit. renombre m, nombradía f; **re'nowned** renombrado, ínclito.

rent[1] [rent] rasgón m; fig. cisma m.

rent[2] [~] 1. alquiler m; arriendo m; 2. alquilar; arrendar; **'rent·al** alquiler m, arriendo m; **'rent-'free** exento de alquiler.

re·o·pen ['ri:'oupn] reabrir(se); **'re-'o·pen·ing** reapertura f.

re·or·gan·ize [ri:'ɔ:gənaiz] reorganizar.

re·paint ['ri:'peint] repintar.

re·pair [ri'pεə] 1. reparación f; compostura f; (esp. shoes) remiendo m; 2. reparar; componer; shoes etc. remendar; '~·man reparador m; mecánico m; '~ shop taller m de reparaciones.

rep·a·ra·tion [repə'reiʃn] reparación f; satisfacción f; ~s pol. indemnizaciones f/pl.; make ~s dar satisfacción f.

re·pa·tri·ate 1. [ri:'pætrieit] repatriar; 2. [ri:'pætriit] repatriado m.

re·pay [ri:'pei] [irr. (pay)] pagar, devolver; reembolsar; p. resarcir; **re·'pay·ment** reembolso m; devolución f.

re·peal [ri'pi:l] 1. revocación f, abrogación f; 2. revocar, abrogar.

re·peat [ri'pi:t] 1. v/t. repetir; thanks etc. reiterar; (aloud) recitar; v/i. repetirse; (rifle, clock, taste) repetir; 2. ♪ repetición f; **re'peat·er** reloj m (rifle m etc.) de repetición.

re·pel [ri'pel] rechazar, repeler; fig. repugnar; **re'pel·lent** repugnante.

re·pent [ri'pent] arrepentirse (of de). **re·pent·ance** [ri'pentəns] arrepentimiento m; **re'pent·ant** □ arrepentido.

re·per·cus·sion [ri:pə'kʌʃn] repercusión f (a. fig.); fig. resonancia f.

rep·er·toire ['repətwa:], **rep·er·to·ry** ['repətəri] repertorio m (a. fig.).

rep·e·ti·tion [repi'tiʃn] repetición f; **re'pet·i·tive** □ reiterativo.

re·place [ri'pleis] reemplazar, sustituir (*with*, by por); **re'place·ment** (*th.*) repuesto *m*; (*p.*) sustituto *m*.

re·plen·ish [ri'pleniʃ] rellenar, reaprovisionar; **re'plen·ish·ment** rellenado *m*, reaprovisionamiento *m*.

re·plete [ri'pli:t] repleto (*with* de); **re'ple·tion** hartazgo *m*.

rep·li·ca ['replikə] *paint. etc.* copia *f*, reproducción *f* (exacta).

re·ply [ri'plai] 1. responder, contestar; 2. respuesta *f*, contestación *f*.

re·port [ri'pɔːt] 1. (*official*) informe *m*; parte *m*; relato *m*; (*newspaper*) información *f*, reportaje *m*; ~ **card** certificado *m* escolar; 2. *v/t.* relatar; *event etc.* dar cuenta acerca de; *v/i.* hacer un informe (*on* acerca de); presentarse (*at* en); **re'port·er** reportero *m*; repórter *m*.

re·pose [ri'pouz] 1. reposo *m*; 2. descansar, reposar; **re·pos·i·to·ry** [ri'pozitəri] repositorio *m*; depósito *m*.

rep·re·hend [repri'hend] reprender; **rep·re'hen·si·ble** ☐ reprensible.

rep·re·sent [repri'zent] representar; ♊ ser apoderado de; ✝ ser agente (*or* representante) de; **rep·re'sent·a·tive** [~ətiv] 1. ☐ representativo; 2. representante *m/f*; ♊ apoderado *m*; *House of* ♊s Cámara *f* de Representantes.

re·press [ri'pres] reprimir; **re·pres·sion** [ri'preʃn] represión *f*.

re·prieve [ri'priːv] 1. respiro *m*; ♊ indulto *m*; 2. indultar.

rep·ri·mand ['reprimɑːnd] 1. reprimenda *f*; 2. reprender.

re·print ['riː'print] 1. reimprimir; 2. reimpresión *f*.

re·pris·al [ri'praizl] represalia *f*.

re·proach [ri'proutʃ] 1. reproche *m*; oprobio *m*; baldón *m*; 2. reprochar (*s.o. for, with* th. algo a uno); **re'proach·ful** [~ful] ☐ acusador.

re·pro·cess [riː'prɔses] elaborar de nuevo; confeccionar de nuevo; reproducir.

re·pro·duce [riːprə'djuːs] reproducir(se); **re·pro'duc·tive** ☐ reproductor; *organ etc.* de la generación.

re·proof [ri'pruːf] reproche *m*, reprensión *f*.

re·prov·al [ri'pruːvl] reprobación *f*.

re·prove [~'pruːv] reprobar, reprender (*s.o. for s.t.* algo a uno).

rep·tile ['reptail] reptil *adj. a. su. m.*

re·pub·lic [ri'pʌblik] república *f*; **re'pub·li·can·ism** *m*.

re·pu·di·ate [ri'pjuːdieit] *charge etc.* desechar, negar, rechazar; *obligation etc.* desconocer.

re·pug·nance [ri'pʌgnəns] repugnancia *f*; **re'pug·nant** ☐ repugnante.

re·pulse [ri'pʌls] 1. repulsión *f*, rechazo *m*; 2. rechazar, repulsar; **re'pul·sive** ☐ repulsivo, repelente.

rep·u·ta·ble ['repjutəbl] ☐ *firm* acreditado; *p.* honroso, estimable; **rep·u'ta·tion** [~'teiʃn] reputación *f*, fama *f*; **re·pute** [ri'pjuːt] 1. reputación *f*; **re'put·ed** supuesto.

re·quest [ri'kwest] 1. petición *f*, instancia *f*, solicitud *f*; ✝ demanda *f*; 2. pedir; solicitar; suplicar.

re·quire [ri'kwaiə] necesitar; exigir; **re'quired** requisito; obligatorio; **re'quire·ment** requerimiento *m*; requisito *m*; necesidad *f*.

req·ui·site ['rekwizit] 1. preciso, indispensable; 2. requisito *m*; **req·ui'si·tion** 1. requisición *f* (*a.* ✕). 1. requerimiento *m*; 2. ✕ requisar; exigir.

re·quite [ri'kwait] (re)compensar; desquitarse; corresponder a.

re·run ['riːrʌn] exhibición *f* repetida *of film*, programa *m* grabado repetido.

re·scind [ri'sind] rescindir.

res·cue ['reskjuː] 1. salvamento *m*; liberación *f*; rescate *m*; 2. salvar; librar, libertar; rescatar.

re·search [ri'səːtʃ] 1. investigación *f* (*in*, *into* de); 2. investigar; indagar.

re·sem·blance [ri'zembləns] semejanza *f*, parecido *m* (*to* a); **re'sem·ble** [~bl] asemejarse a, parecerse a.

re·sent [ri'zent] resentirse de (*or* por); tomar a mal; **re'sent·ful** [~ful] ☐ resentido, ofendido (*at*, *of* por).

res·er·va·tion [rezə'veiʃn] (*act*) reserva *f*; reservación *f*; (*mental*) reserva *f*.

re·serve [ri'zəːv] 1. reserva *f* (*a.* ✕, ✝); *sport:* suplente *m/f*; *in* ~ de reserva; 2. reservar; **re'served** ☐ reservado, callado; sigiloso.

res·er·voir ['rezəvwɑː] embalse *m*, pantano *m of water*; depósito *m*.

re·set·tle ['riː'setl] *p.* restablecer; *land* colonizar; **'re'set·tle·ment** restablecimiento *m*; colonización *f*.

re·side [ri'zaid] residir (*fig. in* en); **res·i·dence** ['rezidəns] residencia *f*; ~ *permit* visado *m* de permanencia; **'res·i·dent** 1. residente; 2. residente *m/f*, vecino (*a f*) *m*.

re·sid·u·al [ri'zidjuəl] residual; **re-'sid·u·ar·y** restante; residual; **res-i·due** ['rezidju:] residuo m; resto m.

re·sign [ri'zain] v/t. dimitir, renunciar, resignar; ~ o.s. resignarse (to a); v/i. dimitir (*from* de); **res·ig·na-tion** [rezig'neiʃn] dimisión f (*from* de), renuncia f; resignación f.

re·sil·i·ence [ri'ziliəns] resistencia f; elasticidad f; *fig.* resistencia f; **re-'sil·i·ent** elástico; resistente (a. *fig.*).

res·in ['rezin] 1. resina f; 2. tratar con resina; **'res·in·ous** resinoso.

re·sist [ri'zist] resistir (a); oponerse a; **re'sist·ance** resistencia f (a. *phys.*, ⚡); **re'sist·or** ⚡ resistor m.

res·o·lute ['rezəlu:t] □ resuelto; **'res·o·lute·ness** resolución f.

res·o·lu·tion [rezə'lu:ʃn] resolución f; *parl. etc.* acuerdo m.

re·solve [ri'zɔlv] 1. v/t. *all senses:* resolver (*into* en); v/i. resolverse (*into* en; *to* a); *parl. etc.* acordar (*to do* hacer); 2. resolución f; **re'solved** resuelto.

res·o·nance ['rezənəns] resonancia f.

re·sort [ri'zɔ:t] 1. recurso m; punto m de reunión; *health* ~ balneario m; *as a last* ~ en último caso; 2. ~ *to* recurrir a, acudir a; *place* frecuentar.

re·sound [ri'zaund] resonar, retumbar; **re'sound·ing** □ sonoro.

re·source [ri'sɔ:s] recurso m, expediente m; inventiva f; ~ *s pl.* recursos m/pl.; **re'source·ful·ness** inventiva f, iniciativa f.

re·spect [ris'pekt] 1. (*esteem*) respeto m, consideración f (*for* por); (*aspect, relation*) respecto m; *with* ~ *to* con respecto a; *pay one's* ~ *s to* cumplimentar a; 2. respetar; estimar; *law etc.* atenerse a; **re·spect·a·bil·i·ty** respetabilidad f; **re'spect·ful** [~ful] □ respetuoso; *Yours* ~ly le saluda atentamente; **re'spect·ing** con respecto a, en cuanto a; **re'spec·tive** □ respectivo.

res·pi·ra·tion [respə'reiʃn] respiración f.

re·spir·a·to·ry [ris'paiərətəri] respiratorio.

re·spire [ris'paiə] respirar.

res·pite ['respait] 1. respiro m, respiradero m; ♟♟ prórroga f; 2. aplazar, prorrogar.

re·splend·ent [ris'plendənt] □ resplandeciente.

re·spond [ris'pɔnd] responder; ~ *to*

treatment etc. reaccionar a, ser sensible a.

re·sponse [ris'pɔns] respuesta f; *fig.* reacción f (*to* a); *eccl.* responsorio m.

re·spon·si·bil·i·ty [rispɔnsi'biliti] responsabilidad f (*for* de); **re'spon-si·ble** responsable (*for* de).

rest[1] [rest] 1. descanso m, reposo m; *fig.* paz f; (*support*) apoyo m; ♪ silencio m, pausa f; 2. v/i. descansar; holgar; posar(se) (*on* en); apoyarse (*on* en); (*matter*) quedar; v/t. descansar; apoyar (*on* en).

rest[2] [~] resto m; ✝ reserva f; *the* ~ lo demás, los demás *etc.*

res·tau·rant ['restərɔ:ŋ] restaurante m, restorán m; ~ *car* coche m restaurante, coche-comedor m.

rest·ful ['restful] □ descansado, sosegado; tranquilizador.

rest home ['resthoum] casa f de reposo.

res·ti·tu·tion [resti'tju:ʃn] restitución f; *make* ~ indemnizar.

res·tive ['restiv] □ intranquilo, inquieto; *horse etc.* rebelón; **'res·tive-ness** intranquilidad f.

rest·less ['restlis] □ inquieto; desasosegado; **'rest·less·ness** inquietud f; desasosiego m; insomnio m.

res·to·ra·tion [restə'reiʃn] restauración f; **re·stor·a·tive** [ris'tɔrətiv] reconstituyente *adj. a. su. m.*

re·store [ris'tɔ:] restaurar; devolver; ~ *a p. to liberty* (*health*) devolver la libertad (la salud) a una p.

re·strain [ris'train] contener, refrenar, reprimir; ~ *s.o. from ger.* impedir que alguien *subj.*; **re'straint** moderación f, comedimiento m; restricción f.

re·strict [ris'trikt] restringir, limitar.

rest room ['rest'ru:m] sala f de descanso; excusado m.; retrete m.

re·sult [ri'zʌlt] 1. resultado m; *as a* ~ por consiguiente; 2. resultar (*from* de); ~ *in* terminar en, parar en.

ré·su·mé ['rezju:mei] resumen m.

re·sume [ri'zju:m] reasumir; *journey etc.* reanudar; **re·sump·tion** [ri-'zʌmpʃn] reasunción f; reanudación f.

re·sur·gence [ri'sɔ:dʒəns] resurgimiento m.

res·ur·rect [rezə'rekt] resucitar.

re·sus·ci·tate [ri'sʌsiteit] resucitar (v/t. a. v/i.).

re·tail 1. ['ri:teil] venta f al por menor; ~ *price* precio m al por menor (*or* al detall); ~ *bookseller* librero *m* al por menor; **2.** [~] *adj.*, *adv.* al (por) menor; **3.** [ri:'teil] *v/t.* vender al (por) menor (*or* al detall); *v/i.* venderse al (por) menor (*at a*); **re'tail·er** detallista *m/f*.

re·tain [ri'tein] retener; conservar; quedarse con; **re'tain·er** *hist.* adherente *m*; *ztz* (*a. retaining fee*) ajuste *m*, anticipo *m*.

re·tal·i·ate [ri'tælieit] desquitarse; vengarse (*on* en); **re·tal·i'a·tion** represalias *f/pl.*; venganza *f*; **re'tal·i·a·to·ry** [~ori] vengativo.

re·tard [ri'tɑ:d] retardar, retrasar; **re·tard·a·tion** retardación *f*.

retch [ri:tʃ] (esforzarse por) vomitar.

re·ten·tion [ri'tenʃn] retención *f* (*a.* *), conservación *f*; **re'ten·tive** □ retentivo.

ret·i·cence ['retisəns] reserva *f*; **'ret·i·cent** □ reservado.

ret·i·na ['retinə] retina *f*.

re·tire [ri'taiə] *v/i.* retirarse (*a.*); recogerse *to bed* etc.; jubilarse *from post*; *v/t.* jubilar; **re'tired** jubilado, retirado; **re'tire·ment** retiro *m*; retirada *f*; jubilación *f from post*; **re'tir·ing** □ retraído, reservado.

re·touch ['ri:'tʌtʃ] retocar (*a.* *phot.*).

re·trace [ri'treis] volver a trazar; repasar.

re·tract [ri'trækt] retractar(se); traer(se); ⊕ replegar; **re'tract·a·ble** retractable; *⚓* replegable.

re·tread 1. [ri:'tred] llanta *f* recauchutada; **2.** [ri:'tred] recauchutar.

re·treat [ri'tri:t] retiro *m* (*a. eccl.*); retraimiento *m*; *⚔* retirada *f*; **2.** *⚔* retirarse.

re·trench [ri'trentʃ] cercenar; **re·trench·ment** cercenadura *f*.

ret·ri·bu·tion [retri'bju:ʃn] justo castigo *m*; desquite *m*.

re·trieve [ri'tri:v] (re)cobrar; *fortunes* reparar; *v/t.* (re)cobrar; **re'triev·al** recobro *m*; cobra *f*; **re'triev·er** perro *m* cobrador.

ret·ro... ['retrou] retro...; **re·tro'ac·tive** □ retroactivo; **ret·ro'cede** retroceder; **'ret·ro·grade 1.** retrógrado; **2.** *ast.* retrogradar; **'ret·ro'rock·et** retrocohete *m*; **ret·ro·spect** ['~spekt] retrospección *f*; *in* ~ retrospectivamente; **ret·ro'spec·tion** retrospección *f*, consideración *f* de lo pasado.

re·turn [ri'tə:n] **1.** vuelta *f*, regreso *m*; devolución *f of book* etc.; *⚕* etc. reaparición *f*; *pol.* elección *f*; resultado *m* (del escrutinio); *✝* (*freq.* ~s *pl.*) ganancia *f*, rédito *m on capital* etc.; ingresos *m/pl.*; ~s *pl.* (*official*) estadística *f* (*tax* ~) declaración *f* (de renta); *in* ~ en cambio, en recompensa (*for* de); **2.** *v/i.* volver, regresar; (*reply*) responder; (*reappear*) reaparecer; *ztz* revertir; *v/t.* devolver; *✝* producir, rendir; *parl.* elegir; **re'turn·a·ble** restituible; *ztz* devolutivo.

re·un·ion [ri:'ju:njən] reunión *f*; **re·u·nite** ['ri:ju:'nait] reunir(se); reconciliar(se).

re·val·u·a·tion [ri:vælju'eiʃn] revalor(iz)ación *f*; **re·val·ue** [~'vælju:] revalorizar.

re·vamp ['ri:'væmp] renovar; remendar (*se*).

re·veal [ri'vi:l] revelar; **re'veal·ing** □ revelador.

re·veille [ri'væli] diana *f*.

rev·el ['revl] **1.** (*freq.* ~s *pl.*) jarana *f*, juerga *f*, fiesta *f* bulliciosa; **2.** juerguear; ir de paranda.

rev·e·l(l)er ['revlə] jaranero *m*, juerguista *m/f*; **'rev·el·ry** jolgorio *m*.

re·venge [ri'vendʒ] **1.** venganza *f*; **2.** vengar(se); ~ *o.s.* (*or* be ~ed) on vengarse en; **re'venge·ful** [~ful] □ vengativo.

rev·e·nue ['revinju:] rentas *f/pl.* públicas; (*a.* ~s *pl.*) ingresos *m/pl.*

re·ver·ber·ate [ri'və:bəreit] retumbar; (*light*) reverberar.

re·vere [ri'viə] reverenciar, venerar; **rev·er·ence** ['revərəns] **1.** reverencia *f*; **2.** reverenciar; **'rev·er·end 1.** reverendo; **2.** pastor *m*.

rev·er·ent ['revərənt] □ reverente.

re·ver·sal [ri'və:səl] inversión *f*; cambio *m* completo *of policy* etc.; *ztz* revocación *f*; **re·verse 1.** (*the* ~) lo contrario; *fig.* revés *m*, contratiempo *m*; reverso *m of coin*; revés *m of cloth*; ⊕ marcha *f* atrás; **2.** inverso, invertido; contrario; *mot.* ~ *gear* cambio *m* de marcha atrás; **3.** *v/t.* invertir; *opinion* cambiar completamente de; trastrocar; *v/i.* dar la marcha atrás.

re·ver·sion [ri'və:ʃn] reversión *f*.

re·vert [ri'və:t] volver(se) (*to* a); revertir (*a.* *ztz*); *biol.* saltar atrás.

re·view [ri'vju:] **1.** revista *f* (⚓, *⚔*, *magazine*); repaso *m*; *ztz* revisión *f*; reseña *f of book*; **2.** rever (*a. ztz*); repasar; *book* reseñar; **re'view·er** crítico *m*.

re·vile [ri'vail] ultrajar, injuriar.

re·vise [ri'vaiz] revisar; *lesson* repasar; *book* corregir, refundir.

re·vi·sion [ri'viʒn] revisión *f*; repaso *m*; corrección *f*, refundición *f*; '**~·ism** revisionismo *m*; '**~·ist** revisionista *adj. a. su. m/f*.

re·vi·tal·ize ['ri:'vaitəlaiz] revivificar.

re·viv·al [ri'vaivl] reanimación *f*, renacimiento *m*; *thea.* reposición *f*; '**~·ist** predicador *m* del renacimiento del sentimiento religioso.

re·vive [~'vaiv] *v/t.* reanimar; restablecer; *v/i.* reanimarse; volver en sí; renacer.

re·voke [ri'vouk] *v/t.* revocar; *v/i. cards:* renunciar.

re·volt [ri'voult] **1.** rebelión *f*, sublevación *f*; **2.** *v/i.* rebelarse, sublevarse; *v/t. fig.* dar (or causar) asco a; **re'volt·ing** □ repugnante.

rev·o·lu·tion [revə'lu:ʃn] revolución *f* (*a.* ⊕, *pol.*); vuelta *f*, rotación *f*.

re·volve [ri'vɔlv] *v/i.* girar, dar vueltas; *ast.* revolverse; *fig.* depender (*round* de); *v/t.* (hacer) girar; **re'volv·er** revólver *m*; **re'volv·ing** giratorio; rotativo.

re·vul·sion [ri'vʌlʃn] 𝐬 revulsión *f*; asco *m*; reacción *f*.

re·ward [ri'wɔ:d] **1.** recompensa *f*, premio *m*, galardón *m*; **2.** recompensar, premiar.

re·write ['ri:'rait] (*irr. write*) refundir; escribir de nuevo.

rhap·so·dize ['ræpsədaiz] *fig.:* ~ *over* entusiasmarse por, extasiarse ante; '**rhap·so·dy** rapsodia *f*; *fig.* transporte *m* (de admiración *etc.*).

rhet·o·ric ['retərik] retórica *f*; **rhe·tor·i·cal** [ri'tɔrikl] □ retórico.

rheu·mat·ic [ru:'mætik] □ reumático; **rheu·ma·tism** ['ru:mətizm] reumatismo *m*.

rhi·no ['rainou] = **rhi·noc·er·os** [rai'nɔsərəs] rinoceronte *m*.

rhu·barb ['ru:bɑ:b] ruibarbo *m*.

rhyme [raim] **1.** rima *f*; poesía *f*; *without* ~ *or reason* sin ton ni son; **2.** rimar.

rhythm ['riðm] ritmo *m*; '**rhyth·mic**, '**rhyth·mi·cal** □ rítmico.

rib [rib] **1.** costilla *f*; ♀ nervio *m*; **2.** F tomar el pelo a.

rib·ald ['ribəld] obsceno; irreverente y regocijado; '**rib·ald·ry** obscenidad *f*; irreverencia *f*.

rib·bon ['ribən] cinta *f* (*a.* typewriter ~); ✂ galón *m*.

ri·bo·fla·vin [raibou'fleivin] riboflavina *f*.

rice [rais] arroz *m*; ~ *field* arrozal *m*.

rich [ritʃ] □ rico; (*lavish*) suntuoso; exquisito; *color* vivo; *food* rico, sabroso; **rich·es** ['~iz] *pl.* riqueza *f*; '**rich·ness** riqueza *f*; fertilidad *f* of soil *etc.*

rick·ets ['rikits] 𝐬 raquitismo *m*, raquitis *f*; '**rick·et·y** 𝐬 raquítico.

rick·shaw ['rikʃɔ:] rikscha *f*.

ri·co·chet ['rikəʃei] rebotar.

rid [rid] (*irr.*) librar, desembarazar (of de); *be* ~ *of* estar libre de; '**rid·dance** libramiento *m*; *good* ~! ¡enhoramala!

rid·dle[1] ['ridl] acertijo *m*, adivinanza *f*; (*p. etc.*) enigma *m*.

rid·dle[2] [~] **1.** criba *f* (gruesa); (*potato* ~) escogedor *m*; **2.** cribar; acribillar *with shot*.

ride [raid] **1.** cabalgata *f*; paseo *m*, viaje *m* (a caballo, en coche *etc.*); **2.** *v/i.* montar, cabalgar; ir, viajar, pasear(se) (en coche *etc.*); ~ *a horse etc.* montar; *bicycle* ir en; *a distance* recorrer (a caballo *etc.*); '**rid·er** jinete (*a f*) *m*, caballero *m*; (*cyclist*) ciclista *m/f*.

ridge [ridʒ] cadena *f*, sierra *f* of hills; cresta *f* of hill; ⌂ caballete *m*.

rid·i·cule ['ridikju:l] **1.** irrisión *f*, burlas *f/pl.*; **2.** ridiculizar, poner en ridículo; **ri'dic·u·lous** [~juləs] □ ridículo.

rid·ing ['raidiŋ] **1.** equitación *f*; **2.** ... de montar; '**~ hab·it** traje *m* de montar.

rife [raif] corriente, frecuente; general; endémico.

riff·raff ['rifræf] chusma *f*, bahorrina *f*; canalla *f*.

ri·fle[1] ['raifl] robar; saquear.

ri·fle[2] [~] **1.** rifle *m*, fusil *m*; **2.** ⊕ rayar; '~ *range* tiro *m* de rifle.

rift [rift] hendedura *f*, rendija *f*; *fig.* desavenencia *f*.

rig[1] [rig] *sl.* falsificar; subvertir.

rig[2] [~] **1.** ♣ aparejo *m*; **2.** ♣ aparejar, enjarciar; F ~ *out* ataviar; F ~ *up* improvisar; '**rig·ger** ♣ aparejador *m*; '**rig·ging** jarcia *f*, aparejo *m*; cordaje *m*.

right [rait] **1.** □ *side* derecho; (*correct*) correcto, exacto; (*true*) verdadero; (*just*) justo, equitativo; (*proper*) indicado, debido; *conditions* favorable; *be* ~ (*p.*) tener razón; *that's* ~ eso es; **2.** *adv.* derechamente; directamente; bien; completamente; a la derecha; ~ away en seguida; ~ here aquí mismo; **3.** derecho m (to a su., inf.); justicia f; título m; privilegio m (of ger. de inf.); (side) derecha f (a. pol.); **4.** enderezar (a. ⚓); corregir, rectificar; '~ **'an·gle** Ⓐ ángulo m recto; '~·**'an·gled** ['~ʃəs] □ justo; **'right·eous** ['~ʃəs] □ justo, honrado, probo; **'right·eous·ness** honradez f, probidad f; **'right·ful** ['~ful] □ justo; legítimo; **'right-'hand:** ~ drive mot. conducción f a la derecha; ~ man mano f derecha; ~ side derecha f; **'right-'hand·ed** que usa (or ⊕ para) la mano derecha; **'right·ist** derechista adj. a. su. m/f; **'right-wing** pol. derechista.

rig·id ['ridʒid] □ rígido; **ri'gid·i·ty** rigidez f.

rig·ma·role ['rigməroul] galimatías m, relación f disparatada.

rig·or·ous ['rigərəs] □ riguroso.

rig·or ['rigə] rigor m, severidad f.

rim [rim] borde m, canto m; llanta f of wheel.

rind [raind] corteza f; cáscara f; piel f.

ring¹ [riŋ] **1.** (finger) anillo m; círculo m; (iron) argolla f; (boxing) cuadrilátero m; (bull) redondel m, plaza f; pandilla f; **2.** cercar, rodear (by, with de).

ring² [~] **1.** campanilleo m; toque m (de timbre); teleph. telefonazo m; v/i. sonar; resonar (with con); (bell) repicar; campanillear; v/t. small bell tocar; large bell tañer; (hacer) sonar; ~ **'bind·er** cuaderno m de hojas sueltas; **'ring·lead·er** cabecilla m; **'ring·let** ['~lit] rizo m; **'ring·worm** tiña f.

rink [riŋk] pista f.

rinse [rins] **1.** aclarar; enjuagar (a. ~ out); **2.** enjuague m.

ri·ot ['raiət] **1.** tumulto m, alboroto m, motín m; orgía f (a. fig.); run ~ desenfrenarse; **2.** amotinarse, alborotarse; **'ri·ot·er** manifestante m/f; amotinado(r) m; **'ri·ot·ous** □ alborotado; life desenfrenado; party bullicioso; **'ri·ot 'squad** pelotón m de asalto.

rip [rip] **1.** rasgón m, rasgadura f; **2.** rasgar(se); ~ off arrebatar; ~ up desgarrar, romper.

ripe [raip] □ maduro; **'rip·en** madurar; **'ripe·ness** madurez f.

rip-off ['ripɔf] sl. estafa f; timo m.

rip·ple ['ripl] **1.** rizo m; ondulación f; (sound) murmullo m; **2.** rizar(se), encrespar(se); (sound) murmurar.

rise [raiz] **1.** subida f, alza f, elevación f

f of prices etc.; ascenso m in rank; crecida f of river; **2.** [irr.] subir; alzarse; levantarse; ponerse en pie; ascender in rank; (sun) salir; **'ris·er:** early ~ madrugador (-a f) m.

ris·ing ['raiziŋ] **1.** (revolt) sublevación f; levantamiento m; salida f of sun; **2.** naciente, ascendiente; sun saliente.

risk [risk] **1.** riesgo m; peligro m; run a (or the) ~ of ger. correr riesgo de inf.; **2.** arriesgar, exponer(se a); **'risk·y** □ arriesgado, aventurado.

rite [rait] rito m; last (or funeral) ~s pl. exequias f/pl.; **rit·u·al** ['ritjuəl] □ ritual adj. a. su. m.

ri·val ['raivl] **1.** rival m/f, competidor (-a f) m; **2.** rival, competidor (a. ♥); **3.** rivalizar con, competir con; **'ri·val·ry** rivalidad f.

riv·er ['rivə] río m; down ~ río abajo; up ~ río arriba; attr. fluvial; '~·**ba·sin** cuenca f de río; '~·**horse** caballo m marino; hipopótamo m.

riv·et ['rivit] **1.** roblón m, remache m; **2.** ⊕ remachar; fig. clavar.

roach [routʃ] ichth. escarcho m; zo. cucaracha f.

road [roud] camino m (to a. fig.); carretera f; (in town) calle f; '~ **hog** conductor m poco considerado, asesino m de carretera; '~·**house** taberna f; posada f; '~·**race** carrera f sobre carretera; '~·**side** borde m del camino; **road·ster** ['~stə] coche m (or bicicleta f etc.) de turismo; **'road·way** calzada f.

roam [roum] v/i. vagar; callejear in town; v/t. vagar por, recorrer.

roar [rɔ:] **1.** rugir; bramar; (with laughter) reírse a carcajadas; **2.** rugido m; bramido m; **roar·ing** ['~riŋ] □ rugiente; bramante.

roast [roust] **1.** asar; coffee tostar; **2.** asado; coffee tostado; ~ beef rosbif m; **3.** carne f asada, asado m.

rob [rɔb] robar (s.o. of s.t. algo a alguien); saltear on highway; **'rob·ber** ladrón m; salteador m (de caminos); **'rob·ber·y** robo m.

robe [roub] túnica f, manto m; ⚖ toga f; vestido m talar.

rob·in ['rɔbin] petirrojo m.

ro·bot ['roubɔt] autómata m, robot m; **ro·bot·ics** ['rou'bɔtiks] ciencia o uso del robot; robótica f.

ro·bust [rou'bʌst] □ robusto; recio, vigoroso; **ro'bust·ness** robustez f.

rock¹ [rɔk] roca f; peña f; ⚓ escollo m; sl. diamante m; the ⚳ el Peñón (de

Gibraltar); get down to ~ bottom llegar a lo más bajo; ~ crystal cristal m de roca; ~ salt sal f gema.

rock² [~] mecer(se), balancear(se); (violently) sacudir(se).

rock-bot·tom ['rɔk'bɔtəm] F price más bajo, mínimo.

rock·er ['rɔkə] (eje m de) balancín m; chair mecedora f.

rock·et ['rɔkit] 1. cohete m; sl. peluca f; ~ propulsion propulsión f a cohete; 2. subir como cohete; **rock·et·ry** cohetería f.

rock·ing... ['rɔkiŋ]: '~ chair mecedora f; '~ horse caballo m de balancín.

rock-'n'-roll (rock²) ['rɔkən'roul] música popular de compás intenso, poca melodía y mucha percusión; rock m.

rock·y ['rɔki] rocoso, peñascoso; sl. inestable; dificultoso.

rod [rɔd] medida de longitud (= 5,029 m); var(ill)a f; barra f; vástago m; (fishing) caña f; sl. pistola f.

ro·dent ['roudnt] roedor m.

ro·de·o ['roudiou, rou'deiou] rodeo m.

roe¹ [rou] hueva f; soft ~ lecha f.

roe² [~] zo. corzo (a f) m; '~·buck corzo m.

rogue [roug] pícaro m, pillo m; canalla m; ~s' gallery fichero m de delincuentes; **'ro·guer·y** picardía f; **'ro·guish** □ pícaro, picaruelo; travieso.

role [roul] thea. papel m (a. fig.); play (or take) a ~ hacer un papel.

roll [roul] 1. rollo m; ⊕ rodillo m; (bread-) panecillo m; bollo m; (list) lista f; retumbo m of thunder; ⚓ balance(o) m; 2. v/t. hacer rodar; soil allanar; cigarette liar; eyes poner en blanco; v/i. rodar; revolcarse on ground; (land) ondular; (thunder) retumbar; '~ call (acto m de pasar) lista f; '**roll·er** ✓, ⊕ rodillo m; ⚓ ola f larga; ~ coaster montaña f rusa; ~ skates patines m/pl. de ruedas; '**roll film** película f en rollo.

roll·ing ['roulin] 1. rodante; rodadero; ground ondulado; 2. rodadura f; ⚓ balanceo m; ~ pin rodillo m; '~ stock material m rodante.

ro·ly-po·ly ['rouli'pouli] regordete.

Ro·man ['roumən] mármon adj. a. su. m (a f); typ. (mst 2) tipo m romano.

ro·mance [rə'mæns] 1. novela f; ficción f; sentimentalismo m; F amoríos m/pl., amores m/pl.; 2. soñar; exage-

rar; 3. románico, romance; 2 **languages** lenguas f/pl. romances or románicas.

ro·man·tic [rə'mæntik] 1. □ romántico; affair novelesco; p. sentimental; place pintoresco, encantado; 2. romántico m; **ro'man·ti·cism** romanticismo m.

romp [rɔmp] 1. retozo m, trisca f; 2. retozar, juguetear, triscar; '**romp·ers** traje m infantil de juego.

roof [ru:f] 1. tejado m, techo m; (flat) azotea f; 2. (freq. ~ in, over) techar.

rook¹ [ruk] 1. orn. graja f; 2. trampear, estafar.

rook² [~] chess: torre f, roque m.

room [ru:m] cuarto m, habitación f; pieza f; (large) aposento m; (space) sitio m, espacio m; cabida f; ~s pl. alojamiento m; ~ and board pensión f completa; '**room·er** subinquilino (a f) m; huésped m/f; '**room·ing house** casa f donde se alquilan cuartos; **room·mate** compañero (a f) m de cuarto; '**room·y** □ espacioso, holgado.

roost [ru:st] 1. percha f; gallinero m; rule the ~ mandar; 2. (bird) descansar (en una percha); '**roost·er** gallo m.

root [ru:t] 1. all senses: raíz f; take (or strike) ~ echar raíces, arraigar; 2. v/t.: ~ out, ~ up arrancar, desarraigar, extirpar; v/i. ⚓ arraigar(se); (pig) hozar, hocicar; sl. ~ for gritar por el éxito de.

rope [roup] 1. cuerda f; soga f; (esp. ⚓) maroma f, cable m; know the ~s saber cuántas son cinco; 2. atar, amarrar con cuerda(s) etc.; ~ off cercar con cuerdas; '~·lad·der escala f de cuerda.

ro·sa·ry ['rouzəri] eccl. rosario m.

rose¹ [rouz] ♀ rosa f; (color) color m de rosa; ⚓ rosetón m (a. ~ window).

rose·bud ['rouzbʌd] capullo m de rosa; '**rose bush** rosal m; '**rose hip** ♀ cinarrodón m; eterio m.

rose·mar·y ['rouzməri] romero m.

ro·sette [rou'zet] escarapela f; ⚓ rosetón m.

ros·ter ['rɔstə] lista f.

ros·y ['rouzi] □ (son)rosado.

rot [rɔt] 1. putrefacción f, podredumbre f; sl. tonterías f/pl.; 2. pudrir(se), corromper(se).

ro·ta·ry ['routəri] rotativo, rotatorio; ~ press prensa f rotativa; **ro·tate** [rou'teit] (hacer) girar; alternar(se).

ro·tor ['routə] rotor m.

rot·ten ['rɔtn] ☐ podrido, corrompido; *food* putrefacto; *wood* carcomido; *sl.* vil, ruin; **'rot·ten·ness** podredumbre *f*, putrefacción *f*.

rot·ter ['rɔtə] *sl.* canalla *m*, sinvergüenza *m*.

ro·tund [rou'tʌnd] ☐ rotundo; *figure* corpulento.

rouge [ru:ʒ] **1.** colorete *m*, arrebol *m*; **2.** ponerse colorete, arrebolarse.

rough [rʌf] **1.** ☐ áspero; tosco; *estimate* aproximado; *ground* quebrado; *manners* grosero; *material* crudo, bruto; *play* duro; *sea* bravo; *treatment* brutal; *weather* tempestuoso; ∼ *copy*, ∼ *draft* borrador *m*; **2.** terreno *m* áspero; superficie *f* áspera; **3.** F ∼ it pasar apuros, vivir sin comodidades; **'rough·age** alimento *m* poco digerible; **'rough·en** poner(se) áspero (*or* tosco).

rough...: '-hewn ['∼'hju:n] desbastado; **'∼-house** *sl.* trapatiesta *f*, trifulca *f*; **'∼-neck** *sl.* canalla *m*, matón *m*; **'rough·ness** aspereza *f*, tosquedad *f etc.*; **'rough-shod**: *ride* ∼ *over* tratar sin miramientos, imponerse.

rou·lette [ru:'let] ruleta *f*.

round [raund] **1.** ☐ redondo (*a. number, sum*); *denial etc.* rotundo, categórico; ∼ *trip* viaje *m* de ida y vuelta; **2.** *adv.* alrededor; (*freq.* ∼ *about*) a la redonda; 2 *feet* ∼ 2 pies en redondo; **3.** *prp.* alrededor de; cerca de, cosa de; ∼ *the corner* a la vuelta de esquina; ∼ *the town* por la ciudad; **4.** esfera *f*; círculo *m*; (*daily*) rutina *f*; (*tradesman's etc.*) recorrido *m*; (*drinks*) ronda *f*; **5.** redondear (*a. ∼ off, ∼ out*); *corner etc.* doblar; ∼ *up* acorralar, rodear *S.Am.*

round·a·bout ['raundəbaut] indirecto; ambaguoso; **round·house** ['raundhaus] depósito *m* de locomotoras; **'round·ness** redondez *f*; **'round-'shoul·dered** cargado de espaldas; repartidor *m*; **'round-table con·fer·ence** reunión *f* de mesa redonda; **'round-up** rodeo *m*.

rouse [rauz] despertar(se); excitar; *provocar to fury etc.*; **'rous·ing** conmovedor.

rout [raut] **1.** derrota *f* completa, fuga *f* desordenada; *put to* ∼ = **2.** derrotar (completamente).

route [ru:t, ⚔ raut] ruta *f*, itinerario *m*, camino *m*.

rou·tine [ru:'ti:n] **1.** rutina *f*; **2.** rutinario.

rove [rouv] vagar, errar; **'rov·er** vagabundo (a *f*) *m*; **'rov·ing** errante; ambulante.

row[1] [rou] fila *f* (*a. thea. etc.*), hilera *f*; *in a* ∼ seguidos.

row[2] [∼] ⚓ **1.** *v/i.* remar; *v/t.* conducir remando; **2.** paseo *m* en bote.

row[3] [rau] F (*noise*) ruido *m*, jaleo *m*, tremolina *f*, estrépito *m*; (*quarrel*) bronca *f*, pelea *f*, camorra *f*; lío *m*.

row·boat ['roubout] bote *m* (de remos).

row·dy ['raudi] quimerista *adj. a. su. m*; gamberro *m*.

row·er ['rouə] remero (a *f*) *m*.

roy·al ['rɔiəl] ☐ real; regio; **'roy·al·ist** monárquico (a *f*) *m*; **'roy·al·ty** realeza *f*; personaje *m/pl.* reales; derechos *m/pl.* (de autor).

rub [rʌb] **1.** frotamiento *m*; roce *m*, rozadura *f*; **2.** *v/t.* frotar; (*hard*) (r)estregar; limpiar frotando; ∼ *down horse* almohazar; ∼ *out* borrar; *sl.* asesinar; *v/i.*: ∼ *against*, ∼ *on* rozar *acc.*

rub·ber ['rʌbə] caucho *m*, goma *f*; (*eraser*) goma *f* de borrar; ⊕ paño *m etc.* de pulir; *bridge*: juego *m* (primero *etc.*); ∼*s pl.* chanclos *m/pl.*; *sl.* ∼ *check* cheque *m* no cobradero; **'∼-neck** *sl.* **1.** mirón (-a *f*) *m*; **2.** curiosear; **'∼-stamp 1.** estampilla *f* (*or* sello *m*) de goma; **2.** F aprobar maquinalmente.

rub·bish ['rʌbiʃ] basura *f*; desperdicios *m/pl.*; desecho(s) *m(pl.)*; *fig.* disparates *m/pl.*, tonterías *f/pl.*

rub·ble ['rʌbl] cascote *m*, escombros *m/pl.*; (*filling*) cascajo *m*.

ru·bric ['ru:brik] rúbrica *f* (*a. eccl.*).

ru·by ['ru:bi] **1.** rubí *m*; **2.** de color de rubí.

ruck·sack ['ruksæk] mochila *f*.

rud·der ['rʌdə] timón *m* (*a.* ✈), gobernalle *m*.

rud·dy ['rʌdi] rubicundo; rojizo.

rude [ru:d] ☐ grosero, descortés; ofensivo; (*rough*) inculto, rudo; **'rude·ness** grosería *f*; rudeza *f*.

ru·di·ment ['ru:dimənt] *biol.* rudimento *m*; ∼*s pl. fig.* rudimentos *m/pl.*; **ru·di·men·ta·ry** [∼'mentəri] *biol.* rudimental; *fig.* rudimentario.

rue [ru:] *v/t.* arrepentirse de, lamentar.

rue·ful ['ru:ful] ☐ triste; arrepentido; lamentable; **'rue·ful·ness** tristeza *f*.

ruff [rʌf] gorguera *f*.

ruf·fi·an ['rʌfjən] rufián *m*; canalla *m*; pillo *m*; bribón *m*.

ruf·fle ['rʌfl] 1. *sew.* volante *m*; 2. descomponer; perturbar.

rug [rʌg] alfombr(ill)a *f*; tapete *m*; manta *f* (de viaje).

rug·by ['rʌgbi] rugby *m*.

rug·ged ['rʌgid] □ *country* áspero, escabroso; *character* robusto; **'rug·ged·ness** escabrosidad *f etc.*

ru·in ['ru:in] 1. ruina *f*; arruinamiento *m*; perdición *f*; ∼ *pl.* ruinas *f/pl.*; 2. arruinar; perder; estropear; estragar.

rule [ru:l] 1. regla *f* (*a. eccl.*); reglamento *m*; norma *f*; mando *m*; dominio *m*; ⊕ metro *m* (plegable *etc.*); *as a* ∼ por regla general; 2. *v/t.* mandar, gobernar (*a.* ∼ *over*); regir; *line* trazar, tirar; *paper* rayar, reglar; *v/i.* gobernar; reinar; prevalecer; † *(price)* regir; **'rul·er** gobernante *m/f*; *(for lines)* regla *f*; **'rul·ing** 1. *esp.* ₷ fallo *m*; 2. † *price* que rige; imperante.

rum [rʌm] ron *m*; aguardiente *m*.

Ru·ma·nian [ru:'meinjən] 1. rumano *adj. a. su. m* (*a f*); 2. *(language)* rumano *m*.

rum·ble ['rʌmbl] 1. retumbo *m*; ruido *m* sordo; ∼ *seat* asiente *m* trasero *(descubierto)*; 2. retumbar; F *(stomach)* sonar.

ru·mi·nant ['ru:minənt] rumiante *adj. a. su. m*; **ru·mi·nate** ['∼neit] rumiar (*a. fig.*).

rum·mage ['rʌmidʒ] buscar (*in* en) revolviéndolo todo; registrar.

rum·my ['rʌmi] *cards:* rummy *m*.

ru·mor ['ru:mə] 1. rumor *m*; 2. rumorear.

rump [rʌmp] *anat.* trasero *m*, ancas *f/pl.*; *cooking:* cuarto *m* trasero.

rump·steak ['rʌmp'steik] biftec *m* del cuarto trasero.

rum·pus ['rʌmpəs] F tumulto *m*, batahola *f*, revuelo *m*; ∼ *room* ['∼ru:m] cuarto *m* para juegos y fiestas.

run [rʌn] 1. *[irr.] v/i.* correr; apresurarse; *(continue)* seguir; *(reach)* extenderse; *(liquid)* correr, fluir; ⊕ funcionar, marchar, andar; ⚓ supurar; *parl.* ser candidato; ∼ *away* huir; escaparse; ∼ *in the family* venir de familia; ∼ *into* extenderse a; *(meet)* topar a; *(crash)* chocar con; ∼ *up against* tropezar con, chocar con; 2. *[irr.] v/t.* correr; *blockade* forzar, burlar; *business* dirigir, organizar; *city* gobernar; *contraband* pasar; *distance, race* correr; *machine* manejar;

∼ *down (car)* atropellar; *(police)* acorralar, cazar; *reputation* desacreditar, desprestigiar, denigrar; *be* ∼ *down* estar debilitado; ∼ *over text* repasar; *(search)* registrar a la ligera; *p.* atropellar; ∼ *one's eye over* examinar *acc.*; ∼ *one's hand over* pasar la mano por, recorrer con la mano; 3. carrera *f* (*a. sport*); corrida *f*; *mot.* paseo *m* en coche; trayecto *m*, recorrido *m* of *vehicle*; ♪ glisado *m*, fermata *f*; ♣ (*a. day's* ∼) singladura *f*; *thea.* serie *f* de representaciones; *(progress)* marcha *f*, progreso *m*; *the common* ∼ el común (de las gentes); *in the long* ∼ a la larga; *on the* ∼ en fuga desordenada; *(prisoner)* fugado; *have the* ∼ *of* tener libre uso de.

run·a·bout ['rʌnəbaut] *mot.* coche *m* pequeño.

run·a·way ['rʌnəwei] 1. fugitivo *m*; caballo *m* desbocado; 2. *victory* fácil; *marriage* clandestino.

run-down ['rʌn'daun] desmantelado; inculto.

rung [rʌŋ] escalón *m* (*a. fig.*).

run·ner ['rʌnə] corredor (*-a f*) *m*; caballo *m*; ✗ ordenanza *m*, mensajero *m*; *part of sledge*; **∼·up** ['∼r'ʌp] subcampeón *m*.

run·ning ['rʌniŋ] 1. corriente; *writing* cursivo; *commentary* continuo; ⚓ supurante; ∼ *start* salida *f* lanzada; 2. carrera *f*; ⊕ marcha *f*, funcionamiento *m* of *machine*; administración *f*, dirección *f* of *business*; *be in the* ∼ tener posibilidades de ganar; **'∼-board** *mot.* estribo *m*; **'∼·in** *mot.* (*adv.* en) rodaje *m*; **'∼·mate** compañero *m* de candidatura.

run-of-the-mill ['rʌnəvðəmil] F ordinario; mediocre.

runt [rʌnt] redrojo *m*, enano *m* (*a. fig.*); animal *m* achaparrado.

run·way ['rʌnwei] ✗ pista *f* de aterrizaje; *hunt.* trocha *f*.

rup·ture ['rʌptʃə] 1. ♣ hernia *f*, quebradura *f*; *fig.* ruptura *f*; 2. ♣ quebrarse (*a.* ∼ *o.s.*).

ru·ral ['ruərəl] □ rural.

rush [rʌʃ] 1. ímpetu *m*; ataque *m* (*a.* ✗), acometida *f*; torrente *m* of *words etc.*; *(haste)* prisa *f*, precipitación *f*; aglomeración *m* of *people*; 2. *v/i.* precipitarse; lanzarse; venir *etc.* de prisa; *v/t. work* despachar (*or* ejecutar) de prisa; ✗ asaltar.

Rus·sian ['rʌʃən] 1. ruso *adj. a. su. m* (*a f*); 2. *(language)* ruso *m*.

rust [rʌst] **1.** orín *m*, herrumbre *f*; **2.** aherrumbrar(se), oxidar(se).

rus·tic [ˈrʌstik] **1.** □ rústico, palurdo; **2.** rústico *m*, palurdo *m*.

rus·tle [ˈrʌsl] **1.** (hacer) susurrar; (hacer) crujir; F hurtar; **2.** (*a.* **'rustling**) crujido *m* of *paper*; susurro *m* of *wind*.

rust...: '**~·less** inoxidable; **~ 'proof**, '**~·re·sist·ant** a prueba de herrum-

bre; **'rust·y** mohoso, enmohecido, oxidado; *fig.* torpe; empolvado.

rut [rʌt] rodera *f*, rodada *f*, carril *m*; bache *m*; *fig.* rutina *f*.

ruth·less [ˈruːθlis] □ despiadado; implacable; '**ruth·less·ness** implacabilidad *f*.

rut·ted [ˈrʌtid] *road* lleno de baches.

rye [rai] centeno *m*; whisky *m* de centeno.

S

sab·bath [ˈsæbəθ] (*Christian*) domingo *m*; (*Jewish*) sábado *m*.

sab·o·tage [ˈsæbətɑːʒ] **1.** sabotaje *m*; **2.** sabotear; **sab·o·teur** [sæbəˈtəː] saboteador *m*.

sa·bre [ˈseibə] sable *m*.

sac·cha·rin [ˈsækərin] sacarina *f*; **sac·cha·rine** [ˈ~rain] sacarino; *fig.* azucarado.

sack[1] [sæk] **1.** saco *m*, costal *m*; (*a. ~ coat*) saco *m*, americana *f*; **2.** ensacar; F despedir.

sack[2] [~] **1.** saqueo *m*; **2.** saquear.

sack·cloth [ˈsækkləθ], '**sack·ing** (h)arpillera *f*.

sac·ra·ment [ˈsækrəmənt] sacramento *m*.

sa·cred [ˈseikrid] □ sagrado; '**sa·cred·ness** santidad *f*.

sac·ri·fice [ˈsækrifais] **1.** sacrificio *m*; víctima *f*; **2.** sacrificar.

sac·ri·lege [ˈsækrilidʒ] sacrilegio *m*; **sac·ri·le·gious** [~ˈlidʒəs] sacrílego.

sac·ris·tan [ˈsækristən] sacristán *m*.

sad [sæːd] □ triste; lamentable.

sad·den [ˈsædn] entristecer.

sad·dle [ˈsædl] **1.** silla *f*, (*cycle-*) sillín *m*; (*hill*) collado *m*; **2.** ensillar (*a. ~ up*); '**~·bag** alforja *f*; '**~·cloth** sudadero *m*; '**sad·dler** talabartero *m*, guarnicionero *m*.

sad·ism [ˈsædizm] sadismo *m*; **sa·dis·tic** □ sádico.

sad·ness [ˈsædnis] tristeza *f*.

sa·fa·ri [səˈfɑːri] safari *f*.

safe [seif] **1.** □ seguro; intacto, ileso; *p.* digno de confianza; ~ *from* a salvo de, al abrigo de; ~ *and sound* sano y salvo; **2.** caja *f* de caudales; ~ *deposit* cámara *f* acorazada; ~ *keeping* custodia *f*; ~·**'con·duct** salvoconducto *m*; '**~·crack·er** ladrón *m* de cajas de caudales; '**~·de·pos·it box** caja *f* de

seguridad; '**~·guard 1.** salvaguardia *f*; protección *f*; **2.** salvaguardar; '**safe·ly** con toda seguridad; '**safe·ness** seguridad *f*.

safe·ty [ˈseifti] **1.** seguridad *f*; **2.** *attr.* de seguridad; ~ **belt** ⚒ cinturón *m* de seguridad; ~ **match** fósforo *m* de seguridad; ~ **pin** imperdible *m*; ~ **ra·zor** maquinilla *f* de afeitar; ~ **valve** válvula *f* de seguridad.

sag [sæg] **1.** combarse, hundirse; ✝ bajar; *fig.* aflojarse; **2.** comba *f*.

sa·ga [ˈsɑːgə] saga *f*.

sail [seil] **1.** vela *f*; paseo *m* en barco (de vela); aspa *f* of *mill*; **2.** *v/i.* navegar; darse a la vela; flotar; *v/t. boat* gobernar; *sea* navegar; '**~·boat** barco *m* de vela; '**~·cloth** lona *f*; '**sail·ing:** *be plain* ~ ser cosa de coser y cantar; '**sail·ing ship** velero *m*; '**sail·or** marinero *m*, marino *m*; '**sail·plane** velero *m*, planeador *m*.

saint [seint] santo (*a f*) *m*; (*before most m names*) San ...; '**saint·li·ness** santidad *f*; '**saint·ly** santo.

sake [seik]: *for the* ~ *of* por, por motivo de, en atención a; *for God's* ~ por el amor de Dios.

sa·la·cious [səˈleiʃəs] □ salaz.

sal·ad [ˈsæləd] ensalada *f*; ~ *bowl* ensaladera *f*; ~ *dressing* mayonesa *f*.

sal·a·ried [ˈsælərid] *post* retribuido; *p.* asalariado; '**sal·a·ry** sueldo *m*; '**sal·a·ry earn·er** persona *f* que gana un sueldo.

sale [seil] venta *f*; (*clearance* ~) saldo *m*, liquidación *f*; *for* ~, *on* ~ de venta, en venta; *se vende*; '**sale·a·ble** vendible.

sales... [seilz]: '**~·man** dependiente *m*, vendedor *m*; viajante *m*; '**~·man·ship** arte *m* de vender; '**~·room** salón *m* de ventas; '**~·wom·an** dependienta *f*, vendedora *f*.

sa·li·ent ['seiliənt] □ (fig. sobre)saliente adj. a. su. m.

sa·li·va [sə'laivə] saliva f; **sal·i·var·y** ['sælivəri] salival.

sal·low [sælou] cetrino, amarillento.

sal·ly ['sæli] 1. ⚔ salida f (a. fig.); 2. hacer una salida.

salm·on ['sæmən] (color m) salmón m.

sa·loon [sə'lu:n] salón m; ⚓ cámara f; bar m, taberna f; **sa'loon car** 🚂 coche-salón m.

salt [sɔ:lt] 1. sal f; ~s pl. sales f/pl. medicinales; 2. salado; salobre; 3. salar.

salt...: '~·cel·lar salero m; 'salt·ness salinidad f; 'salt·pe·ter salitre m; 'salt shak·er salero m; 'salt·works salinas f/pl.; 'salt·y salado.

sa·lu·bri·ous [sə'lu:briəs] □ salubre.

sal·u·tar·y ['sæljutəri] □ saludable.

sa·lute [sə'lu:t] 1. saludo m; co. beso m; salva f of guns; 2. saludar.

sal·vage ['sælvidʒ] 1. salvamento m; objetos m/pl. salvados; 2. salvar.

sal·va·tion [sæl'veiʃn] salvación f; ♀ Army Ejército m de Salvación.

salve [sɑ:v] 1. mst fig. ungüento m; 2. curar (con ungüento); fig. tranquilizar.

sal·vo ['sælvou] ⚔ salva f.

Sa·mar·i·tan [sə'mæritn] samaritano adj. a. su. m (a f).

same [seim] mismo; igual, idéntico; the ~ ... as el mismo ...; the ~ to you igualmente; 'same·ness igualdad f; identidad f; monotonía f.

sam·ple ['sɑ:mpl] 1. esp. ♣ muestra f; 2. probar; wine etc. catar; ⚕ muestrear.

san·a·to·ri·um [sænə'tɔ:riəm] sanatorio m.

sanc·ti·fi·ca·tion [sæŋktifi'keiʃn] santificación f; **sanc·ti·fy** ['~fai] santificar; **sanc·ti·mo·ni·ous** [~'mounjəs] □ mojigato, santurrón; **sanc·tion** ['sæŋkʃn] 1. sanción f; 2. sancionar, autorizar; **sanc·ti·ty** ['~titi] santidad f; inviolabilidad f; **sanc·tu·ar·y** ['~tjuəri] santuario m; (high altar) sagrario m; fig. refugio m.

sand [sænd] 1. arena f; ~s pl. arenal m, playa f (arenosa); 2. enarenar; lijar.

san·dal ['sændl] sandalia f.

sand...: '~·bag saco m terrero; '~·bank banco m de arena; '~·blast ⊕ chorro m de arena; '~·pa·per 1. papel m de lija; 2. lijar; '~·pit arenal m; '~·stone piedra f arenisca.

sand·wich ['sændwidʒ, '~witʃ] 1. sándwich m; bocadillo m; 2. poner (entre dos cosas o capas).

sand·y ['sændi] arenoso; hair rojo.

sane [sein] □ cuerdo, sensato.

san·gui·nary ['sæŋgwinəri] □ sanguinario; sangriento; **san·guine** ['~gwin] optimista.

san·i·tar·y ['sæniteri] □ sanitario; ~ napkin compresa f higiénica, paño m higiénico.

san·i·ta·tion [sæni'teiʃn] sanidad f; instalación f sanitaria, servicios m/pl.; saneamiento m in house; 'san·i·ty cordura f, sensatez f.

San·skrit ['sænskrit] sánscrito adj. a. su. m.

sap[1] [sæp] ♀ savia f; jugo m; fig. vitalidad f; sl. simplón m.

sap[2] [~] 1. ⚔ zapa f; 2. ⚔ zapar, socavar; strength minar.

sap·ling ['sæpliŋ] pimpollo m, árbol m nuevo; fig. jovenzuelo m.

sap·phire ['sæfaiə] zafiro m.

sap·py ['sæpi] jugoso; fig. enérgico; sl. tonto.

sar·casm ['sɑ:kæzm] sarcasmo m; **sar·cas·tic**, sarcástico.

sar·dine [sɑ:'di:n] ictio. sardina f.

Sar·din·i·an [sɑ:'dinjən] sardo adj. a. su. m (a f).

sar·don·ic [sɑ:'dɔnik] □ burlón, irónico; sardónico S.Am.

sash[1] [sæʃ] marco m (corredizo) de ventana.

sash[2] [~] faja f; ⚔ fajín m.

satch·el ['sætʃl] cabás m; cartapacio m.

sat·el·lite ['sætəlait] satélite adj. a. su. m; ~ country país m satélite.

sa·ti·ate ['seiʃieit] saciar, hartar.

sat·in ['sætin] raso m.

sat·ire ['sætaiə] sátira f; **sat·i·rist** ['sætərist] escritor m satírico; 'sat·i·rize satirizar.

sat·is·fac·tion [sætis'fækʃn] satisfacción f; **sat·is·fac·to·ry** [~'təri] □ satisfactorio.

sat·is·fied ['sætisfaid] satisfecho; **sat·is·fy** ['~fai] satisfacer.

sat·u·rate ['sætʃəreit] saturar; empapar; **sat·u·ra·tion** saturación f.

Sat·ur·day ['sætədi] sábado m.

sauce [sɔ:s] salsa f; (sweet) crema f; '~·pan cacerola f, cazo m; 'sauc·er platillo m.

sau·ci·ness ['sɔ:sinis] F impertinencia f, desfachatez f; **sau·cy** ['sɔ:si] impertinente, descarado.

saun·ter ['sɔːntə] **1.** paseo *m* lento y tranquilo; **2.** pasearse despacio y tranquilamente; deambular.

sau·sage ['sɔsidʒ] embutido *m*, salchicha *f*, chorizo *m*.

sav·age ['sævidʒ] **1.** □ salvaje; *attack* feroz; **2.** salvaje *m/f*; **'sav·age·ness, 'sav·age·ry** salvajismo *m*; salvajería *f*; ferocidad *f*.

save [seiv] **1.** *v/t.* salvar (*from* de); *time, money* ahorrar; *trouble* evitar; (*keep*) guardar; *v/i.* ahorrar, economizar; **2.** *lit. prp. a. cj.* salvo, excepto.

sav·ing ['seiviŋ] **1.:** ~ *grace* único mérito *m*; **2.** economía *f*; ~s *pl.* ahorros *m/pl.*; **'~s ac·count** cuenta *f* de ahorros; **'~s bank** caja *f* de ahorros.

sav·ior ['seivjə] salvador (-a *f*) *m*; ♀ Salvador *m*.

sa·voir faire ['sævwɑ:'fɛə] desparpajo *m*, destreza.

sa·vor ['seivə] **1.** sabor *m*, gust(ill)o *m*; **2.** *v/i.* saber (*of* a), oler (*of* a) (*a. fig.*); *v/t.* saborear; **'sa·vor·y 1.** sabroso; salado; **2.** entremés *m* salado.

sav·vy ['sævi] *sl.* **1.** comprender; **2.** comprensión *f*.

saw [sɔː] ⊕ **1.** sierra *f*; **2.** (a)serrar; **'~·buck** cabrilla *f*; *sl.* billete *m* de diez dólares; **'~·dust** serrín *m*; **'~·fish** pez *m* sierra; **'~·horse** burro *m*; **'~·mill** aserradero *m*.

Sax·on ['sæksn] sajón *adj. a su. m* (-a *f*).

sax·o·phone ['sæksəfoun] saxofón *m*.

say [sei] **1.** [*irr.*] decir; afirmar; (*text*) rezar; ~ *grace* bendecir la mesa; ~ *mass* decir misa; *that is to* ~ es decir; *I should* ~ *so!* ¡ya lo creo!; ~ *to o.s.* decir para sí; *it is said to* ~, *uso m* de la palabra *f*; **'say·ing** dicho *m*, refrán *m*.

scab [skæb] costra *f*; *vet.* roña *f*; F esquirol *m*.

sca·brous ['skeibrəs] escabroso.

scaf·fold ['skæfəld] cadalso *m*; andamiaje *m*, andamio *m*.

scald [skɔːld] **1.** escaldadura *f*; **2.** escaldar; *milk* calentar.

scale¹ [skeil] **1.** (*fish*) escama *f*; **2.** *v/t.* escamar; descostrar; ⊕ raspar; *v/i.* descamarse.

scale² [~] platillo *m* de balanza; (*a pair of* una) ~s *pl.* balanza *f*.

scale³ [~] **1.** escala *f* (*a. ♪*); *to* ~ según escala; *on a large* ~ en gran(de) escala; **2.** *mountain* escalar, trepar a; ~ *down* reducir según escala; graduar.

scal·lop ['skɔləp] **1.** *zo.* venera *f*; *sew.* festón *m*; **2.** *sew.* festonear.

scalp [skælp] **1.** cuero *m* cabelludo; cabellera *f*; **2.** escalpar; *sl. billetes* revender a precio subido.

scal·y ['skeili] escamoso.

scamp [skæmp] tunante *m/f*, bribón (-a *f*) *m*; (*child*) diablillo *m*; golfo *m*; **'scamp·er** (*a.* ~ *away,* ~ *off*) escabullirse, escaparse precipitadamente.

scan [skæn] escudriñar, examinar; explorar (*a. television*); *verse* escandir.

scan·dal ['skændl] escándalo *m*; ⚖ difamación *f*; **'scan·dal·ize** escandalizar; **'scan·dal·mon·ger** chismoso (a *f*) *m*; difamador (-a *f*) *m*; **'scan·dal·ous** □ escandaloso.

Scan·di·na·vi·an [skændi'neivjən] escandinavo *adj. a. su. m* (a *f*).

scan·ner ['skænə] (*radar*) antena *f* direccional giratoria; (*television*) dispositivo *m* explorador.

scant [skænt] escaso; poco.

scant·i·ness ['skæntinis] escasez *f*, insuficiencia *f*.

scant·y ['skænti] □ escaso, corto; insuficiente.

scape·goat ['skeipgout] cabeza *f* de turco.

scar [skɑː] **1.** ⚕ cicatriz *f*, señal *f* (*a. fig.*); **2.** *v/t.* señalar; *v/i.* cicatrizarse.

scar·ab ['skærəb] escarabajo *m*.

scarce [skɛəs] escaso; raro; F *make o.s.* ~ escabullirse, esfumarse; **'scarce·ly** apenas; con dificultad; **'scar·ci·ty** escasez *f*; carestía *f*.

scare [skɛə] **1.** espantar, asustar; ~ *away* ahuyentar; **2.** susto *m*, sobresalto *m*; **'~·crow** espantapájaros *m*; *fig.* espantajo *m*; **'~·mon·ger** alarmista *m/f*.

scarf [skɑːf] bufanda *f*; (*head*) pañuelo *m*; tapete *m*.

scar·i·fy ['skɛərifai] ⚕, ✔ escarificar; *fig.* criticar severamente.

scar·la·ti·na [skɑːlə'tiːnə] escarlatina *f*.

scar·let ['skɑːlit] **1.** escarlata *f*, grana *f*; **2.** de color escarlata, de grana); ~ *fever* escarlatina *f*.

scarred [skɑːd] señalado de cicatrices; abusado.

scar·y ['skɛəri] F asustadizo.

scath·ing ['skeiðiŋ] □ acerbo, mordaz.

scat·ter ['skætə] **1.** esparcir, desparramar(se); ✕ dispersar(se); ~ed disperso; 2. ⚙ dispersión f; '**~·brain** F cabeza m/f de chorlito.

scav·enge ['skævindʒ] limpiar (las calles), recoger la basura.

sce·nar·i·o [si'næriou] guión m; escenario m.

scene [si:n] escena f (a. thea.); vista f, perspectiva f; paisaje m; teatro m of events; escenario m of crime; **scen·er·y** ['~əri] paisaje m; thea. decoración(es) f(pl.); decorado m.

sce·nic ['si:nik] □ pintoresco; escénico; ~ railway montaña f rusa.

scent [sent] 1. perfume m, olor m; (sense) olfato m; hunt. rastro m, pista f; 2. perfumar; danger etc. percibir; olfatear, husmear; '**scent·ed** perfumado.

scep·tic ['skeptik] escéptico (a f) m; **scep·ti·cism** ['~sizm] escepticismo m.

sched·ule ['skedju:l] 1. lista f; esp. 🄰 inventario m, apéndice m; programa m; horario m; 2. catalogar; fijar la hora de; proyectar.

scheme [ski:m] 1. esquema m; plan m, proyecto m; (plot) ardid m, intriga f; 2. v/t. proyectar; b.s. tramar; v/i. b.s. intrigar; '**schem·er** intrigante m/f.

schism ['sizm] cisma m; **schis·mat·ic** [siz'mætik] 1. cismático; 2. cismático m.

schiz·o·phre·nia [skitsə'fri:njə] esquizofrenia f; **schiz·o·phren·ic** [~'frenik] □ esquizofrénico.

schol·ar ['skɔlə] (pupil) colegial (-a f) m, escolar m/f; (learned p.) erudito (a f) m; '**schol·ar·ship** erudición f; univ. beca f.

scho·las·tic [skə'læstik] □ escolástico adj. a. su. m.

school [sku:l] 1. escuela f (a. ~ of thought); colegio m; high ~ instituto m; primary ~ escuela f primaria; secondary ~ escuela f secundaria; 2. instruir, enseñar; disciplinar; '**~·boy** colegial m, escolar m; '**~·girl** colegiala f, escolar f; '**school·ing** instrucción f, enseñanza f; '**~·mate** compañero (a f) m de clase.

school···: '**~·room** (sala f de) clase f; '**~·teach·er** maestro (a f) m.

schoon·er ['sku:nə] ⚓ goleta f.

sci·ence ['saiəns] ciencia f; '**~·fic·tion** literatura f fictiva; novela f científica.

sci·en·tif·ic [saiən'tifik] □ científico.

sci-fi ['saifai] sl. literatura f fictiva.

scin·til·late ['sintileit] centellear, chispear; fig. brillar.

scis·sors ['sizəz] pl. (a pair of unas) tijeras f/pl.

scle·ro·sis [skliə'rousis] esclerosis f.

scoff [skɔf] 1. mofa f, befa f; 2. mofarse, burlarse (at de); sl. engullir.

scold [skould] regañar, reprender; '**scold·ing** reprensión f, regaño m.

scoop [sku:p] 1. pal(et)a f; (water) achicador m; cuchara f (de draga); sl. primera publicación f de una noticia; 2. sacar con pal(et)a; water achicar; hole excavar.

scoot·er ['sku:tə] (child's) patinete m; (adult's) vespa f; monopatín m.

scope [skoup] alcance m; extensión f; envergadura f; oportunidad f; esfera f de acción.

scorch [skɔ:tʃ] chamuscar; (sun, wind) abrasar; '**scorch·er** F día m de mucho calor.

score [skɔ:] 1. (cut) muesca f, entalladura f; (line) raya f; ♪ partitura f; (20) veintena f; sport: tanteo m; 2. v/t. rayar; hacer cortes en; ♪ instrumentar; sport: goal marcar; points ganar; total apuntar (a. ~ up); F criticar severamente; v/i. marcar (un tanto), ganar (puntos); '**score·board** tanteador m; '**score card** anotador m; '**scor·er** (player) marcador m; (recorder) tanteador m.

scorn [skɔ:n] 1. desprecio m, desdén m; 2. despreciar, desdeñar; **scorn·ful** ['~ful] □ desdeñoso.

scor·pi·on ['skɔ:pjən] alacrán m.

Scot [skɔt] escocés (-a f) m.

Scotch [skɔtʃ] 1. escocés; the ~ los ecoceses; 2. F whisk(e)y m escocés.

scot-free ['skɔt'fri:] impune.

Scots [skɔts] escocés; '**Scots·man** escocés m.

Scot·tish ['skɔtiʃ] escocés.

scoun·drel ['skaundrl] canalla m.

scour ['skauə] dish fregar, estregar; channel limpiar; ⚕ purgar.

scourge [skə:dʒ] lit. 1. azote m (a. fig.); 2. azotar, hostigar.

scout [skaut] 1. explorador m, escucha m; F busca f, reconocimiento m; Boy ♀ (niño m) explorador m; 2. explorar; reconocer.

scow [skau] gabarra f.

scowl [skaul] 1. ceño m, sobrecejo m; 2. fruncir el ceño; mirar con ceño.

scram [skræm] sl. 1. largarse, dar un zarpazo; 2. int. ¡lárgate!

scram·ble ['skræmbl] 1.: ~ up trepar

a, subir gateando a; **∼d eggs** huevos *m/pl.* revueltos; **2.** subida *f* (*up* a); arrebatiña *f*, pelea *f* (*for* por).

scrap [skræp] **1.** pedazo *m*, fragmento *m*; *sl.* riña *f*, bronca *f*; **∼s** desperdicios *m/pl.*; **2.** *v/t.* desechar; ⚓ reducir a chatarra; *v/i. sl.* reñir; **'∼book** álbum *m* de recortes.

scrape [skreip] **1.** raspadura *f*, F aprieto *m*, lío *m*; **2.** *v/t.* raspar, raer; ♪ *co.* rascar; (*a. ∼ against*) rozar; *v/i.*: **∼ along** ir tirando; F **∼ through exam** aprobar justo; **'scrap·er** (*tool*) raspador *m*, rascador *m*; limpiabarros *m for shoes.*

scrap...: '∼ heap montón *m* de desechos; **'∼ i·ron** chatarra *f*, hierro *m* viejo; **'scrap·py** ☐ fragmentario; *sl.* combativo.

scratch [skrætʃ] **1.** rasguño *m*, arañazo *m*; raya *f on stone etc.*; *sport:* línea *f* de partida; **start from ∼** empezar sin nada, empezar desde el principio; **2.** *competitor* sin ventaja; *team etc.* reunido de prisa; **3.** *v/t.* rasguñar; rascar; *stone* rayar; *earth* escarbar; *v/i.* rasguñar; rascarse; (*pen*) raspear; **'scratch·y** *pen* que raspea; *tone* áspero.

scrawl [skrɔːl] **1.** garrapatear; **2.** garrapatos *m/pl.*

scraw·ny ['skrɔːni] F descarnado.

scream [skriːm] **1.** chillido *m*, grito *m*; **2.** chillar, gritar (*a. ∼ out*); *abuse etc.* vociferar.

screech [skriːtʃ] *v.* scream; **'∼ owl** lechuza *f* común.

screen [skriːn] **1.** (*cinema etc.*) pantalla *f*; (*folding*) biombo *m*; (*sieve*) tamiz *m*; ✕ cortina *f*; **2.** (*sift*) tamizar; *film* proyectar; *suspects* investigar; **∼play** cinedrama *m*.

screw [skruː] **1.** tornillo *m*; (*thread*) rosca *f*; ⚓, ✈ hélice *f*; F **he has a ∼ loose** le falta un tornillo; **2.** atornillar; **∼ down** fijar con tornillos; **'∼ball** *sl.* estrafalario, excéntrico *adj. a. su. m*; **'∼·driv·er** destornillador *m*; **'∼ jack** gato *m* de tornillo; **'∼ pro·pel·ler** hélice *f*; **'screw·y** *sl.* chiflado.

scrib·ble ['skribl] **1.** garrapatos *m/pl.*; **2.** garrapatear; **∼ over** emborronar; **'scrib·bler** autorzuelo *m*.

scrim·mage ['skrimidʒ] arrebatiña *f*, pelea *f*.

scrimp [skrimp] escatimar.

script [skript] escritura *f*, letra *f* (cursiva); manuscrito *m*; *film:* guión *m*; **∼ writer** guionista *m/f*.

Scrip·tur·al ['skriptʃərəl] escriturario; bíblico; **Scrip·ture** ['∼tʃə] Sagrada Escritura *f*.

scroll [skroul] rollo *m* de pergamino *etc.*; ⚠ voluta *f*.

scro·tum ['skroutəm] escroto *m*.

scrounge [skraundʒ] *sl. v/i.* ir de gorra, gorronear, sablear; *v/t.* sacar por medio de gorronería.

scrub [skrʌb] **1.** fregar, (r)estregar; **2.** fregado *m* (*a.* **'scrub·bing**); jugador *m* no adiestrado; **scrub brush** ['skrʌbrʌʃ] bruza *f*, estregadera *f*.

scrub·by ['skrʌbi] achaparrado, enano.

'scrub wom·an fregona *f*.

scruff of the neck ['skrʌfəvðə'nek] pescuezo *m*; **'scruf·fy** F sucio; desaliñado, piojoso.

scrump·tious ['skrʌmpʃəs] *sl.* de rechupete.

scru·ple ['skruːpl] **1.** escrúpulo *m*; **2.** escrupulizar, vacilar (*to* en); **scru·pu·lous** ['∼juləs] ☐ escrupuloso (*about* en cuanto a); **'scru·pu·lous·ness** escrupulosidad *f*.

scru·ti·nize ['skruːtinaiz] escudriñar; examinar; *votes* escrutar; **'scru·ti·ny** escrutinio *m*; examen *m*.

scuff [skʌf] **1.** rascadura *f*; **2.** rascar; desgastar.

scuf·fle ['skʌfl] **1.** refriega *f*, riña *f*; **2.** pelear(se).

scul·ler·y ['skʌləri] trascocina *f*, fregadero *m*; **'∼ maid** fregona *f*.

sculp·tor ['skʌlptə] escultor *m*.

sculp·tur·al ['skʌlptʃərəl] ☐ escultural; **sculp·ture** ['skʌlptʃə] **1.** escultura *f*; **2.** esculpir; **'sculp·tur·ing** escultura *f*.

scum [skʌm] espuma *f*; *metall.* escoria *f*; *fig.* heces *f/pl.*; canalla *f*.

scur·ril·i·ty [skʌ'riliti] grosería *f*; **'scur·ril·ous** ☐ grosero, procaz.

scur·ry ['skʌri] **1.** escabullirse; **2.** carrera *f* precipitada.

scur·vy ['skʌːvi] ☞ escorbuto *m*.

scut·tle ['skʌtl] (*coal-*) cubo *m*.

scythe [saið] **1.** guadaña *f*; **2.** guadañar.

sea [siː] mar *m or f*; océano *m*; (*waves*) marejada *f*; *fig.* (*all*) **at ∼** despistado, perplejo; **put to ∼** hacerse a la mar; **'∼·board** litoral *m*; **'∼·dog** lobo *m* de mar; **'∼·far·ing** marinero; **∼ food** (*a. ∼s pl.*) mariscos *m/pl.*; **'∼·go·ing** de alta mar; **'∼ green** verdemar; **'∼·gull** gaviota *f*; **'∼ horse** caballito *m* de mar.

seal¹ [si:l] zo. foca f.

seal² [∿] 1. sello m; great∿ sello m real; 2. sellar; cerrar; lacrar with wax; ∿ off obturar; ∿ up cerrar.

sea legs ['si:legz] pie m marino.

sea lev·el ['si:levl] nivel m del mar.

seal·ing ['si:liŋ] caza f de la foca.

sea·ling wax ['si:liŋwæks] lacre m.

sea li·on ['si:laiən] león m marino.

seal·skin ['si:lskin] piel f de foca.

seam [si:m] sew. costura f; ⊕ juntura f; geol. filón m, veta f.

sea·man ['si:mən] marinero m; **'sea·man·ship** marina f, náutica f.

seam·stress ['semstris] costurera f.

seam·y ['si:mi] vil; burdo; soez.

sé·ance ['seiɑːns] sesión f de espiritismo.

sea...: **'∿·plane** hidroavión m; **'∿·port** puerto m de mar; **'∿·po·wer** potencia f naval.

sear [siə] chamuscar; (wind) abrasar; fig. marchitar; ✶ cauterizar.

search [sɔːtʃ] 1. busca f, buscada f, búsqueda f (for de); registro m; 🕵 pesquisa f; 2. buscar (a. ∿ for); place explorar, registrar; conscience examinar; ✶ tentar; ¡qué sé yo!; **'search·er** buscador (-a f) m; **'search·light** reflector m; **'search war·rant** mandamiento m judicial.

sea...: **'∿·scape** ['si:skeip] marina f; **'∿·ser·pent** serpiente f de mar; **'∿·shore** playa f; orilla f del mar; **'∿·sick** mareado; be ∿ marearse; **'∿·sick·ness** mareo m; **'∿·side** playa f (a. ∿ place, ∿ resort); orilla f del mar.

sea·son ['si:zn] 1. estación f of year; (indefinite) época f; social, sport: temporada f; (opportune time) sazón f; at this ∿ en esta época (del año); 2. sazonar, condimentar; wood curar; fig. templar; **'sea·son·a·ble** propio de la estación; oportuno; **'sea·son·al** ['si:znl] □ estacional; según la estación; **'sea·son·ing** condimento m; aderezo m; **'sea·son 'tick·et** abono m (de temporada); ∿ holder abonado m.

seat [si:t] 1. asiento m, silla f; thea. localidad f; parl. escaño m; 🏇 etc. plaza f; residencia f; sede f; ∿ belt cinturón m de asiento; 2. (a)sentar; establecer, fijar; chair poner asiento a; **'seat·er** mot., 🏇 de ... plaza(s); **'seat·ing ca·pac·i·ty** número m de asientos.

SEATO ['si:to] (la) O.T.A.S.E.

sea ur·chin ['si:'ɔːtʃin] erizo m de mar; **'sea 'wall** dique m (marítimo); **sea·ward** ['si:wəd] 1. adj. del lado del mar; 2. adv. (a. **sea·wards** ['∿z]) hacia el mar.

sea...: **'∿·weed** alga f (marina); **'∿·wor·thy** marinero, en condiciones de hacerse a la mar.

se·cede [si'si:d] separarse; **se'ced·er** separatista m.

se·ces·sion [si'seʃn] secesión f.

se·clud·ed [si'klu:did] retirado, apartado; **se'clu·sion** [∿ʒn] recogimiento m, retiro m.

sec·ond ['sekənd] 1. □ segundo; 2. segundo m; duel: padrino m; boxing: segundante m; ♪ segunda f; ♣ ∿s pl. artículos m/pl. de segunda calidad; 3. apoyar, secundar; p. [si'kɔnd] trasladar temporalmente; **'sec·ond·a·ry** □ secundario (a. school); **'sec·ond-'best** 1. expediente m, sustituto m; 2. (el) mejor después del primero; **'sec·ond-'hand** 1. de segunda mano, de lance; ∿ bookseller librero m de viejo; 2. segundero m of watch; **'sec·ond·ly** en segundo lugar; **'sec·ond-'rate** de segunda categoría; de calidad inferior.

se·cre·cy ['si:krisi] secreto m; discreción f; **se·cret** ['∿krit] 1. □ secreto; oculto; clandestino; 2. secreto m.

sec·re·tar·y ['sekrətri] secretaria (a f) m; ♀ of State Ministro m de Asuntos Exteriores; **'sec·re·tar·y·ship** secretaría f.

se·crete [si'kri:t] esconder; physiol. secretar; **se'cre·tive** □ callado, reservado; sigiloso.

sect [sekt] secta f; **sec·tar·i·an** [∿'teəriən] secretario adj. a. su. m (a f).

sec·tion ['sekʃn] mst sección f; región f of country; barrio m of city; tramo m of road etc.; sector m of opinion; **'sec·tion·al** párrafo m.

sec·tor ['sektə] sector m.

sec·u·lar ['sekjulə] □ secular; seglar; **'sec·u·lar·ize** secularizar.

se·cure [si'kjuə] 1. □ seguro; firme, fijo; 2. asegurar; (obtain) conseguir.

se·cu·ri·ty [si'kjuəriti] seguridad f; protección f; † fianza f on loan, prenda f; **se'cu·ri·ties** pl. valores m/pl., obligaciones f/pl.; acciones f/pl.

se·date [si'deit] 1. □ sosegado, sentado, grave; 2. dar sedante a; **se'date·ness** compostura f, gravedad f.

sed·a·tive ['sedətiv] sedante adj. a. su. m; calmante adj. a. su. m.

sed·en·tar·y ['sedntəri] □ sedentario.

sed·i·ment ['sedimənt] sedimento m (a. geol.); poso m; **sed·i·men·ta·ry** [~'mentəri] sedimentario (a. geol.).

se·di·tious [si'diʃəs] □ sedicioso.

se·duce [si'djuːs] seducir; **se'duc·er** seductor m; **se'duc·tion** □ seductor.

see¹ [siː] [irr.] v/i. a. v/t. ver; observar; percibir; fig. comprender; (visit) visitar; (receive) recibir; let's ~ a ver; let me ~ vamos a ver; ~ about a th. atender a; encargarse de; ~ off despedir(se de); ~ to atender a; ~ (to it) that hacer que, cuidar de que; ~ home acompañar a casa.

see² [~] sede f; Holy ♎ Santa Sede f.

seed [siːd] 1. semilla f, simiente f; fig. germen m; 2. v/t. land sembrar; sport: seleccionar; v/t. dejar caer semillas; '**~bed** (or '**~plot**) semillero m; **seed·i·ness** [~inis] aspecto m raído; '**seed·ling** planta f de semillero; '**seed·y** andrajoso; raído; place asqueroso.

see·ing ['siːiŋ] vista f, visión f; worth ~ que vale la pena de verse.

seek [siːk] [irr.] (a. ~ after, ~ for) buscar; post pretender, solicitar; honor ambicionar; '**seek·er** buscador (-a f) m.

seem [siːm] parecer; '**seem·ing 1.** □ aparente; 2. apariencia f; '**seem·li·ness** decoro m; '**seem·ly** decoroso, decente, correcto.

seen [siːn] p.p. of see¹.

seep [siːp] rezumarse, filtrar(se); '**seep·age** filtración f.

see·saw ['siːˈsɔː] 1. columpio m; balancín m; fig. vaivén m; 2. columpiarse; vacilar.

seg·ment ['segmənt] segmento m.

seg·re·gate ['segrigeit] segregar; **seg·re'ga·tion** segregación f; **seg·re·ga·tion·ist** segregacionista adj. a. su. m/f.

seis·mo·graph ['saizməgrɑːf] sismógrafo m.

seize [siːz] agarrar, asir, coger; apoderarse de; ⚖ p. prender; property embargar; '**sei·zure** [~ʒə] asimiento m; captura f; ⚖ prendimiento m; embargo m; ⚕ ataque m.

sel·dom ['seldəm] rara vez, raramente.

se·lect [si'lekt] 1. escoger, elegir; 2. selecto, escogido; **se'lec·tion** selec-

ción f (a. ⚘, zo.); elección f; ♪ selecciones f/pl.; ✝ surtido m; **se'lect·man** concejal m; **se'lec·tor** radio: selector m; sport: seleccionador m.

self [self] 1. pron. se etc.; (after prps.) sí mismo etc.; ✝ or F = myself etc.; 2. su. (pl. selves [selvz]) uno mismo; the ~ el yo; (all) by one's ~ (unaided) sin ayuda de nadie; (alone) completamente a solas; '**~'act·ing** automático; '**~as'sur·ance** confianza f en sí mismo; '**~'cen·tered** egocéntrico; '**~con'ceit** presunción f, arrogancia f; '**~con'fi·dence** confianza f en sí mismo; '**~'con·scious** □ cohibido, tímido; '**~con'tained** ['~kən'teind] independiente; reservado; '**~con'trol** autodominio m, dominio m sobre sí mismo; '**~de'fence** (in en) defensa f propia; '**~de'ni·al** abnegación f; '**~deter·mi'na·tion** autodeterminación f; '**~'ed·u·cat·ed** autodidacto; '**~'evi·dent** patente, palmario; '**~'in·ter·est** egoísmo m; '**self·ish** □ egoísta; '**self·ish·ness** egoísmo m.

self...: '**~'made man** hijo m de sus propias obras; '**~'por·trait** autorretrato m; '**~pos'sessed** sereno, dueño de sí mismo; '**~preser'va·tion** propia conservación f; '**~pro'pelled** autopropulsado; automotriz (f only); '**~re'li·ant** confiado en sí mismo; '**~re'spect** amor m propio, dignidad f; '**~'right·eous** □ santurrón; '**~'sat·is·fied** pagado de sí mismo; '**~'seek·ing** egoísta; '**~'serv·ice res·tau·rant** autoservicio m; '**~'start·er** mot. arranque m automático; '**~'styled** supuesto, sediciente; '**~suf'fi·cien·cy** independencia f; confianza f en sí mismo; '**~'willed** terco, obstinado; '**~wind·ing** de cuerda automática.

sell [sel] [irr.] v/t. vender (a. fig.); F idea hacer aceptar; ✝ ~ off liquidar; ~ out saldar; be sold out estar agotado; v/i. venderse, estar de venta; 2. F decepción f, estafa f; '**sell·er** vendedor (-a f) m; best-~ éxito m de librería; '**sell·ing price** precio m de venta.

se·man·tics [si'mæntiks] semántica f.

sem·a·phore ['seməfɔː] 1. semáforo m; 2. comunicar por semáforo.

sem·blance ['sembləns] apariencia f; simulacro m.

sem·i... ['semi] semi...; medio...; '**~cir·cle** semicírculo m; '**~co·lon**

punto *m* y coma; '~·de'tached semiseparado; '~·'fi·nal semifinal *f*.

sem·i·of·fi·cial ['semio'fiʃl] □ semioficial.

Sem·ite [si'mait] semita *m/f*; **Sem·it·ic** [si'mitik] semítico.

se·mi·week·ly ['semi'wi:kli] bisemanal.

sen·ate ['senit] senado *m*; *univ.* approx. claustro *m*.

sen·a·tor ['senətə] senador *m*; **sen·a·to·ri·al** [ˌ'tɔ:riəl] □ senatorial.

send [send] [*irr.*] enviar, mandar, despachar; remitir; expedir; *telegram* poner; ~ *off p.* despedir; expedir; *signal* emitir; *invitations* mandar; distribuir; '**send·er** remitente *m/f*; ⚡ transmisor *m*; '**send·'off** despedida *f*; principio *m*.

se·nile ['si:nail] senil, caduco; **se·nil·i·ty** [si'niliti] vejez *f*; ⚡ debilidad *f* senil.

sen·ior ['si:njə] 1. mayor (de edad); más antiguo *in post* (to que); 2. mayor *m/f*; *univ.* alumno *m* del último año; **sen·ior·i·ty** [si:ni'ɔriti] antigüedad *f*; prioridad *f*.

sen·sa·tion [sen'seiʃn] sensación *f*; **sen·sa·tion·al** □ sensacional; **sen·sa·tion·al·ism** sensacionalismo *m*.

sense [sens] 1. sentido *m*; sensación *f*; juicio *m*; opinión *f* of *meeting*; ~ of *humor* sentido *m* de humor; *common (or good)* ~ sentido *m* común; *make* ~ tener sentido; *talk* ~ hablar con juicio; *in a* ~ en cierto sentido; 2. sentir, percibir; intuir.

sense·less ['senslis] □ sin sentido; (*mad*) insensato; '**sense·less·ness** insensatez *f*.

sen·si·bil·i·ty [sensi'biliti] sensibilidad *f* (to a).

sen·si·ble ['sensəbl] □ (*reasonable*) sensato, cuerdo; (*feeling*) sensible.

sen·si·tive ['sensitiv] □ sensitivo; sensible (to a); impresionable; '**sen·si·tive·ness**, **sen·si·tiv·i·ty** [ˌ'tiviti] sensibilidad *f* (to a); susceptibilidad *f*.

sen·si·tize ['sensitaiz] sensibilizar.

sen·su·al·ism ['sensjuəlizm] sensualismo *m*; '**sen·su·al·ist** sensualista *m/f*; **sen·su·al·i·ty** [ˌ'æliti] sensualidad *f*.

sen·su·ous ['sensjuəs] □ sensual.

sent [sent] *pret. a. p.p. of send.*

sen·tence ['sentəns] 1. ⚖ sentencia *f*, condena *f*; fallo *m*; 2. sentenciar, condenar (to a).

sen·ti·ment ['sentimənt] sentimiento *m*; **sen·ti·men·tal·i·ty** [ˌ'tæliti] sentimentalismo *m*; sensibilería *f*.

sen·ti·nel ['sentinl], **sen·try** ['sentri] centinela *m*.

sen·try box ['sentriboks] garita *f* de centinela.

sep·a·rate 1. ['seprit] □ separado; distinto; suelto; 2. ['~əreit] separar(se) (from de); desprender(se); apartar(se); **sep·a·ra·tist** ['~ərətist] separatista *m/f*.

se·phar·dic [sə'fa:dik] sefardí *adj. a. su. m/f*; sefardita *adj. a. su. m/f*.

Sep·tem·ber [sep'tembə] se(p)tiembre *m*.

sep·tic ['septik] séptico.

sep·tu·a·ge·nar·i·an ['septjuedʒi'nɛəriən] septuagenario *adj. a. su. m* (a *f*).

se·pul·chral [si'pʌlkrəl] sepulcral (*a. fig.*); **se·pul·chre** ['sepəlkə] *lit.* 1. sepulcro *m*; 2. sepultar en sepulcro.

se·quel ['si:kwəl] continuación *f* of *story*; resultado *m* (to *act* de).

se·quence ['si:kwəns] (orden *m* de) sucesión *f*; serie *f*; *film:* secuencia *f*.

se·ques·ter [si'kwestə] secuestrar.

se·ques·trate [si'kwestreit] ⚖ secuestrar; **se·ques·tra·tion** [si:kwes'treiʃn] secuestro *m*.

se·quoi·a [si'kwɔiə] secoya *f*.

ser·aph ['serəf], *pl. a.* **ser·a·phim** ['~fim] serafín *m*; **se·raph·ic** [se'ræfik] □ seráfico.

Serb, Ser·bi·an [sə:b, '~jən] servio *adj. a. su. m* (a *f*).

ser·e·nade [seri'neid] 1. serenata *f*; 2. dar serenata a.

serf [sə:f] siervo (a *f*) *m* (de la gleba); '**serf·dom** servidumbre *f* (de la gleba).

ser·geant ['sa:dʒnt] sargento *m*; '**~·ma·jor** approx. sargento *m* mayor, brigada *m*.

se·ri·al ['siəriəl] 1. □ consecutivo; en serie; *number* de serie; *story* por entregas; 2. serial *m*, novela *f* por entregas.

se·ries ['siəri:z] *sg. a. pl. all senses:* serie *f*; ⚡ *connect or join in* ~ conectar en serie.

se·ri·ous ['siəriəs] □ serio; *news, condition* grave; '**se·ri·ous·ness** seriedad *f*; gravedad *f*.

ser·mon ['sə:mən] sermón *m*.

ser·pent ['sə:pənt] serpiente *f*, sierpe *f*; **ser·pen·tine** ['~ain] 1. serpentino; 2. *min.* serpentina *f*.

sex

se·rum ['siərəm] suero m.

serv·ant ['sɜːvənt] criado (a f) m; sirviente (a f) m; servidor (-a f) m; ~s pl. servidumbre f.

serve 1. [sɜːv] p. servir (a); estar al servicio de; food service (a. ~ out, ~ up); abastecer; ser útil a; sacar; **2.** tennis: saque m; '**serv·er** tennis: saque m; pala f for fish etc.; eccl. acólito m.

serv·ice ['sɜːvis] **1.** servicio m; vajilla f, juego m, servicio m of crockery; tennis: saque m; ⚓ forro m de cable; ⚡ entrega f; (a. divine ~) oficio m divino; misa f; **2.** ⊕ atender, mantener, reparar; '**serv·ice·a·ble** □ servible; útil; duradero.

serv·ice...: '~ line tennis: línea f de saque; '~·man militar m; mecánico m; ~ sta·tion estación f de servicio; taller m de reparaciones.

ser·vi·ette [sɜːvi'et] servilleta f.

ser·vi·tude ['sɜːvitjuːd] servidumbre f.

ses·sion ['seʃn] sesión f; univ. curso m; to be in ~ celebrarse.

set [set] **1.** [irr.] v/t. poner, colocar; situar; establecer; arreglar, preparar; alarm-clock regular; 🦴 bone reducir; dog azuzar (at, on a que embista a); example dar; hair fijar, marcar; jewel engastar, montar; ~ apart separar, segregar; ~ aside poner aparte; reservar; petition desatender; ⚖ anular; ~ at ease, at rest tranquilizar; ~ back detener; entorpecer; poner obstáculos a; ~ down poner por escrito; depositar; passenger dejar (apearse); ~ forth exponer; ~ off (explode) hacer estallar; (contrast) hacer resaltar, poner de relieve (against contra); ~ up fundar; house, shop poner; establecer, instalar; p. erigir (as en); ⊕ armar, montar; v/i. (sun) ponerse; (jelly, mortar) cuajarse; (gum etc.) endurecerse; ~ about ger. ponerse a inf.; ~ about th. emprender; ~ forth salir, partir; ponerse en camino; ~ off partir; ~ on atacar; ~ out partir, ponerse en camino; ~ out to inf. ponerse a inf.; tener la intención de inf.; **3.** adj. purpose resuelto, determinado; inflexible in belief, (rigid) rígido; (usual) reglamentario; price etc. fijo, firme; **4.** su. juego m; serie f; servicio m (de mesa); tendencia f of mind; pandilla f, clase f of people; caída f of dress; thea. decorado m, decoración f; (radio-) (aparato m de)

radio f; jet ~, smart ~ mundo m elegante.

set·back ['setbæk] contratiempo m, revés m; ⚓ retranqueo m.

set·ter ['setə] el que pone etc.; hunt. perro m de muestra.

set·ting ['setiŋ] puesta f of sun; engaste m, montadura f of jewels; ⊕ ajuste m; alrededores m/pl. of place; '~·up establecimiento m; ⊕ ajuste m; composición f of type.

set·tle ['setl] **1.** banco m (largo); **2.** v/t. colocar; fijar; establecer; arreglar; calmar, sosegar; account ajustar, liquidar (a. ~ up); fig. saldar cuentas con (a. ~ with); date fijar; quarrel componer; question decidir, resolver; v/i. (freq. ~ down) asentarse (liquid, building); (a. ~ o.s.) sentarse, reposarse; (bird etc.) posar(se); (p.) instalarse, establecerse in house, in town.

set·tle·ment ['setlmənt] establecimiento m; ⚡ ajuste m, pago m, liquidación f of account; ⚖ asignación f (on a); (agreement) convenio m; colonización f of land.

set·tler ['setlə] colono (a f) m; colonizador m.

set...: '~·to F disputa f; pelea f; '~·up F tinglado m, sistema m, organización f.

sev·en ['sevn] siete (a. su. m); **sev·en·teen** ['~'tiːn] diecisiete; **sev·en·teenth** [~θ] decimoséptimo; **sev·enth** ['~θ] □ séptimo (a. su. m); **sev·en·ti·eth** ['~tiiθ] septuagésimo; **sev·en·ty** setenta.

sev·er ['sevə] separar, cortar.

sev·er·al ['sevrəl] □ diversos, varios, respectivos; distintos; '**sev·er·al·ly** respectivamente; separadamente.

se·vere [si'viə] □ severo; riguroso; storm violento; loss, wound grave; pain intenso; **se·ver·i·ty** [~'veriti] severidad f; rigor m etc.

Se·vil·lian [se'viljən] sevillano adj. a. su. m (a f).

sew [sou] [irr.] coser; ~ up zurcir.

sew·age ['sjuːidʒ] aguas f/pl. residuales.

sew·er ['sjuə] albañal m, alcantarilla f; '**sew·er·age** alcantarillado m.

sew·ing ['souiŋ] **1.** (labor m de) costura f; **2.** ... de coser; '~ ma·chine máquina f de coser.

sewn [soun] p.p. of sew.

sex [seks] sexo m; attr. sexual; ~ appeal atracción f sexual, gancho m.

sex·a·ge·nar·i·an [seksədʒiˈnɛəriən] sexagenario *adj. a. su. m* (a *f*); **sex·en·ni·al** □[sekˈsenjəl] sexenal; **sex·tant** [ˈsekstənt] sextante *m*.

sex·tu·ple [ˈsekstjupl] séxtuplo.

sex·u·al [ˈseksjuəl] □ sexual; ~ *desire* instinto *m* sexual; **sex·u·al·i·ty** [ˌ~ˈæliti] sexualidad *f*; **sex·y** erótico; lozano; F provocativo.

sh [ʃ]: ~! ¡chitón!, ¡chis!

shab·by [ˈʃæbi] □ *p.* pobremente vestido; *dress* raído, gastado; *treatment* ruin, vil.

shack [ʃæk] chabola *f*, choza *f*; casucha *f*.

shack·le [ˈʃækl] 1. grillete *m*, grillos *m/pl.* (a. *fig.*); *fig.* (*mst* ~s *pl.*) trabas *f/pl.*; ⊕, ♣ eslabón *m*; 2. encadenar; trabar; *fig.* poner trabas a.

shade [ʃeid] 1. sombra *f*; matiz *f* of *color, meaning, opinion*; tonalidad *f* of *color*; (*fraction*) poquito *m*; (*lamp-*)pantalla *f*; (*eye-*) visera *f*; 2. dar sombra a; (*protect*) resguardar; *paint.* sombrear; **shades** F gafas *f/pl.* de sol.

shad·ow [ˈʃædou] 1. *all senses*: sombra *f*; *the* ~s las tinieblas; ~ *boxing* boxeo *m* (*fig.* disputa *f*) con un adversario imaginario; 2. sombrear; (*follow*) seguir y vigilar; **shad·ow·y** umbroso, sombroso; *fig.* vago, indefinido.

shad·y [ˈʃeidi] sombreado, umbroso; F turbio, sospechoso.

shaft [ʃɑːft] (*arrow*) flecha *f*, dardo *m*; (*handle*) mango *m*; rayo *m of light*; ⊕ eje *m*; árbol *m*; ✗ pozo *m*.

shag·gy [ˈʃægi] velludo, peludo; *sl.* ~ *dog story* chiste *m* goma.

shake [ʃeik] 1. [*irr.*] *v/t.* sacudir (*a.* ~ *off*); agitar; *head* mover, menear; *building* hacer retemblar; (*perturb*) perturbar; F sorprender; *hand* estrechar; ~ *hands* estrecharse la mano; ~ *up* agitar; *fig.* descomponer; F reorganizar; *v/i.* agitarse; (*earth*) (re)temblar (*at, with* de); bambolear; ♪ trinar; 2. sacudida *f*, sacudimiento *m*; meneo *m*, movimiento *m of head*; **~·down** *sl.* exacción *f* de dinero; ~ *cruise* ♣ viaje *m* de pruebas; **shak·er** (*cocktail*) coctelera *f*.

shake-up [ˈʃeikˌʌp] F conmoción *f*; reorganización *f*.

shak·i·ness [ˈʃeikinis] falta *f* de solidez; **shak·y** □ tembloroso; *fig.* poco sólido; *fig.* débil, debilitado.

shall [ʃæl] [*irr.*] *v/aux.* que forma el futuro etc.

shal·low [ˈʃælou] 1. poco profundo; *fig.* somero, superficial; *p.* frívolo; 2. ~s *pl.* bajío *m*; **shal·low·ness** poca profundidad *f*; *fig.* superficialidad *f*.

sham [ʃæm] 1. falso, fingido, postizo; 2. impostura *f*, engaño *m*; (*p.*) impostor *m*, farsante *m*; 3. *v/i. a. v/t.* fingir(se), simular.

sham·bles [ˈʃæmblz] *pl. or sg.* (lugar *m* de gran) matanza *f*; ruina *f*, escombrera *f*; lío *m*; desorden *m*.

shame [ʃeim] 1. vergüenza *f*; oprobio *m*, deshonra *f*; (*for*) ~! ~ *on you!* ¡qué vergüenza!; *what a* ~! ¡qué lástima!; 2. avergonzar.

shame-faced [ˈʃeimfeist] □ vergonzoso, avergonzado.

shame·ful [ˈʃeimful] □ vergonzoso; ignominioso; **shame·ful·ness** ignominia *f*.

shame·less [ˈʃeimlis] □ descarado, desvergonzado; **shame·less·ness** descaro *m*, desvergüenza *f*.

sham·poo [ʃæmˈpuː] 1. lavar la cabeza (*v/t. a.*); 2. champú *m*.

sham·rock [ˈʃæmrɔk] trébol *m*.

shang·hai [ʃæŋˈhai] ♣ *sl.* embarcar emborrachando.

shank [ʃæŋk] zanca *f of bird*; caña *f of leg*; ♣ tallo *m*; ⊕ mango *m*.

shan·ty [ˈʃænti] choza *f*, cabaña *f*; ♪ saloma *f*.

shape [ʃeip] 1. forma *f*; figura *f*; contorno *m*; configuración *f*; 2. formar(se); modelar; tallar; *fig. course etc.* determinar; dirigir; **shape·less** □ informe; **shape·li·ness** buen talle *m*; elegancia *f*; **shape·ly** (bien) proporcionado, elegante; de buen talle.

share [ʃɛə] 1. parte *f*, porción *f*; participación *f*; interés *m*; cuota *f*, contribución *f*; ✝ acción *f*; *have a* ~ *in* participar en; 2. *v/t.* (com)partir, dividir; *fig.* poseer en común; *v/i.*: ~ *in* tener parte en, participar en (*te de*); **~·crop·per** aparcero *m*; **~·hold·er** accionista *m/f*.

shark [ʃɑːk] *ichth.* tiburón *m*; F estafador *m*; *sl.* perito *m*; estafador *m*.

sharp [ʃɑːp] 1. □ agudo; *fig.* puntiagudo; *appearance* elegante; *bend* fuerte; *edge* afilado; *feature* bien marcado; *mind* listo, vivo; *outline* definido;

*p*ain agudo; F astuto, mañoso; avispado; 2. *adv.* ♪ desafinadamente; F 4 o'clock ~ las 4 en punto; '**sharp·en** afilar, aguzar (*a. fig.*); *pencil* sacar punta a; *feeling* agudizar; '**sharp-en·er** afilador *m*, máquina *f* de afilar; '**sharp·ness** agudeza *f etc.*

sharp...: '~**shoot·er** tirador *m* certero; '~**sight·ed** de vista penetrante; '~**wit·ted** perspicaz.

shat·ter [ˈʃætə] romper(se), hacer(se) pedazos, estrellar(se); *health* quebrantar; *nerves* destrozar; '~**proof** inastillable.

shave [ʃeiv] 1. [*irr.*] afeitar(se); ⊕ (a)cepillar; 2. afeitada *f*, afeitado *m*; *have a close* ~ escaparse por un pelo.

shawl [ʃɔːl] chal *m*.

she [ʃiː] 1. ella; 2. hembra *f*.

sheaf [ʃiːf] (*pl.* sheaves) ⚼ gavilla *f*; *haz m*; *fajo m of papers*.

shear [ʃiə] 1. [*irr.*] esquilar, trasquilar; 2. (*a pair of unas*) ~s *pl.* tijeras *f/pl.* (de jardín).

sheath [ʃiːθ] vaina *f* (*a.* ♀); estuche *m*, funda *f*; cubierta *f*; '**sheathe** [ʃiːð] envainar; ⊕ revestir; '**sheath·ing** ⊕ revestimiento *m*, forro *m*.

sheaves [ʃiːvz] *pl. of* sheaf.

shed[1] [ʃed] [*irr.*] *tears, light* verter; *blood* derramar; *skin etc.* mudar; *clothes, leaves* despojarse de.

shed[2] [~] cobertizo *m*; (*industrial*) nave *f*.

sheen [ʃiːn] lustre *m*, brillo *m*.

sheep [ʃiːp] oveja *f*; carnero *m*; *pl.* ganado *m* lanar; '~**dog** perro *m* pastor; '~**fold** redil *m*, aprisco *m*; '**sheep·ish** □ corrido; tímido; '**sheep·ish·ness** timidez *f*.

sheep...: '~**man** dueño *m* de ganado lanar; '~**skin** zamarra *f*, badana *f*; *sl.* diploma *m*.

sheer[1] [ʃiə] 1. *adj.* completo, cabal; puro; *cloth* diáfano; fino; 2. *adv.* directamente, completamente.

sheer[2] [~] 1. ♏ desviarse; ~ *off fig.* largarse; 2. ♏ desviación *f*.

sheet [ʃiːt] sábana *f*; hoja *f of paper, tin*; lámina *f of metal, glass*; (*news*-) periódico *m*; extensión *f of water etc.*; '**sheet·ing** tela *f* para sábanas; '**sheet light·ning** relámpago *m* difuso.

sheik(h) [ʃeik] jeque *m*.

shelf [ʃelf] (*pl.* shelves) estante *m*, anaquel *m*; ♏ banco *m* de arena, bajío *m*.

shell [ʃel] 1. cáscara *f of egg, nut, building*; concha *f*, caparazón *m*, ca-

rapacho *m of mollusc, tortoise etc.*; ⚔ granada *f*, proyectil *m*, bomba *f*; 2. des(en)vainar, descascarar; ⚔ bombardear.

shel·lac [ʃeˈlæk] (goma *f*) laca *f*.

shell...: '~**fire** cañoneo *m*; '~**fish** mariscos *m/pl.*; ☿ crustáceo *m*; '~**proof** a prueba de granadas; '~**shock** neurosis *f* de guerra.

shel·ter [ˈʃeltə] 1. abrigo *m*, asilo *m*, refugio *m*; (*mountain*-) albergue *m*; 2. *v/i.* abrigarse, refugiarse; *v/t.* abrigar; guarecer.

shelve [ʃelv] *fig.* arrinconar; aplazar indefinidamente.

she·nan·i·gans [ʃiˈnænigənz] *pl.* F embustes *m/pl.*; travesuras *f/pl.*

shep·herd [ˈʃepəd] 1. pastor *m*; 2. guiar; dirigir.

sher·bet [ˈʃɔːbət] sorbete *m*.

sher·iff [ˈʃerif] sheriff *m*; alguacil *m* mayor.

sher·ry [ˈʃeri] jerez *m*.

shield [ʃiːld] 1. escudo *m* (*a. fig.*); ⊕ blindaje *m*; 2. escudar (*a. fig.*), proteger; '~**bear·er** escudero *m*.

shift [ʃift] 1. cambio *m*; movimiento *m*, cambio *m* de sitio; tanda *f*, turno *m at work*; astucia *f*; recurso *m*, expediente *m*; 2. *v/t.* cambiar (de sitio); mover; *v/i.* cambiar (de sitio, de puesto, de marcha); moverse; (*move house*) mudar; (*wind*) cambiar; '**shift·less** □ agalbanado, indolente, inútil; '**shift·y** □ taimado, furtivo.

shil·ling [ˈʃiliŋ] chelín *m*.

shim·mer [ˈʃimə] 1. reflejo *m* (*or* resplandor *m*) trémulo; 2. rielar.

shim·my [ˈʃimi] *sl.* shimmy *m* (*baile*); *mot.* vibración *f*.

shin [ʃin] 1. (*or* ~**bone**) espinilla *f*; 2.: ~ *up* trepar a.

shine [ʃain] 1. lustre *m*, brillo *m*; 2. [*irr.*] *v/i.* brillar (*a. fig.*), lucir (*a. fig.*); *v/t. shoes* limpiar; sacar brillo a.

shin·gle [ˈʃiŋgl] 1. ripia *f*; 2. cubrir con ripias.

shin·gles [ˈʃiŋglz] ⚕ *pl.* herpes *m/pl. or f/pl.*; zona *f*.

shin·y [ˈʃaini] □ brillante, lustroso.

ship [ʃip] 1. buque *m*, navío *m*, barco *m*; ~s *company* tripulación *f*; *merchant* ~ mercante *m*; 2. *v/t.* embarcar; ♏ transportar; enviar, expedir; *v/i.* embarcar(se); '~**board**: *on* ~ a bordo; '~**build·er** constructor *m* de buques, ingeniero *m* naval; '~ **chandler** abastecedor *m* de buques; '**ship·ment** embarque *m*; envío *m*, remesa *f*; '**ship·own·er** naviero *m*; '**ship·per** exportador *m*; remitente *m*; '**ship·ping** buques *m/pl.*, flota *f*, marina *f*.

ship...: '**~shape** en buen orden; '**~wreck** 1. naufragio *m*; 2. naufragar (*a. be ~ed*); '**~wrecked** náufrago; '**~yard** astillero *m*.

shirk [ʃəːk] *v/t.* eludir, esquivar, desentenderse de; *v/i.* faltar al deber, gandulear; '**shirk·er** gandul *m*.

shirt [ʃəːt] camisa *f*; *sl.* keep one's ~ on quedarse sereno; '**shirt-sleeve:** *in* ~ *s* en mangas de camisa.

shit [ʃit] *sl.* 1. mierda *f*; excremento *m*; 2. evacuar el vientre; cagar.

shiv·er [ˈʃivə] 1. (*fear*) temblor *m*; (*cold*) tiritón *m*; F *the* ~*s pl.* dentera *f*, grima *f*; *it gives me the* ~*s* me da miedo; 2. estremecerse; temblar *with fear*; tiritar *with cold*; '**shiv·er·y** estremecido.

shoal [ʃoul] 1. bajío *m*, banco *m* de arena; 2. disminuir en profundidad.

shock¹ [ʃɔk] ♪ tresnal *m*.

shock² [~] 1. choque *m* (*a. ⚡*); sacudida *f*; temblor *m* de tierra; sobresalto *m*; *toxic* ~ *syndrome* síndrome *m* de choque tóxico; ⚔ ~ *troops pl.* tropas *f/pl.* de asalto; 2. *fig.* chocar; sobresaltar; escandalizar.

shock³ [~] greña *f* of hair.

shock ab·sorb·er [ˈʃɔkəbsɔːbə] *mot.* amortiguador *m*.

shock·er [ˈʃɔkə] *sl.* película *f* horripilante.

shock·ing [ˈʃɔkiŋ] □ chocante; escandaloso; *taste* pésimo.

shod·dy [ˈʃɔdi] de pacotilla, de pésima calidad.

shoe [ʃuː] 1. zapato *m*; (*horse-*) herradura *f*; 2. [*irr.*] calzar; *horse* herrar; '**~horn** calzador *m*; '**~lace** cordón *m*; '**~mak·er** zapatero *m*; '**~pol·ish** betún *m*; bola *f*; '**~shine** brillo *m*; lustre *m*; '**~shop** zapatería *f*.

shoo [ʃuː] 1. *birds* oxear; ahuyentar; 2. ¡zape!, ¡ox!

shook [ʃuk] *pret. of* **shake** 1.

shoot [ʃuːt] 1. ⚘ renuevo *m*, vástago *m*; cacería *f*; tiro *m* (*al blanco*); 2. [*irr.*] *v/t.* disparar; tirar; herir (*or* matar) con arma de fuego; (*execute*) fusilar; *film* rodar; ~ *down* derribar; ~ *up sl.* destrozar a tiros; *v/i.* tirar (*at* a).

shoot·ing [ˈʃuːtiŋ] 1. tiros *m/pl.*; tiroteo *m*, cañoneo *m*; caza *f* con escopeta; rodaje *m* of film; 2. *pain* punzante; '**~gal·ler·y** galería *f* de tiro (al blanco); '**~match** certamen *m* de tiro al blanco; *sl.* conjunto *m*; asunto *m*; '**~star** estrella *f* fugaz.

shoot-out [ˈʃuːtaut] pelea *f* a tiros.

shop [ʃɔp] 1. tienda *f*; (*large*) almacén *m*; ⊕ taller *m*; 2. ir de compras (*mst go* ~*ping*); '**~as·sist·ant** dependiente (*a f*) *m*; '**~keep·er** tendero (*a f*) *m*; '**~lift·er** mechera *f*; '**shop·per** comprador (*-a f*) *m*; '**shop·ping** compras *f/pl.*; ~ *center* zona *f* de tiendas.

shop...: '**~soiled** deteriorado; '**~stew·ard** representante *m* de los obreros en la sección de una fábrica; '**~walk·er** vigilante (*a f*) *m*; '**~win·dow** escaparate *m*, vidriera *f S.Am.*

shore¹ [ʃɔː] playa *f*, orilla *f*, ribera *f*.

shore² [~] 1. puntal *m*; 2. apuntalar; *fig.* apoyar.

short [ʃɔːt] 1. corto, breve; *p.* bajo; (*brusque*) brusco, seco; *memory* flaco; ~ *wave radio*: onda *f* corta; ~ *of* falto de, escaso de; *nothing* ~ *of* nada menos que; *run* ~ acabarse; *run* ~ *of* acabársele a uno; *stop* ~ parar de repente; *stop* ~ *of* detenerse antes de llegar a; 2. *film*: corto metraje *m*; ⚡ cortocircuito *m*; F ~*s pl.* pantalones *m/pl.* cortos; 3. *v. circuit*; '**short·age** escasez *f*, falta *f*, carestía *f*; ⚕ déficit *m*.

short...: '**~bread**, '**~cake** torta *f* seca y quebradiza; '**~cir·cuit** 1. cortocircuito *m*; 2. poner(se) en cortocircuito; '**~com·ing** defecto *m*; '**~cut** atajo *m*; '**~en** acortar(se), reducir(se); '**short·en·ing** acortamiento *m*; (*lard*) manteca *f*, grasa *f*.

short...: '**~fall** déficit *m*; '**~hand** taquigrafía *f*; ~ *writer* taquígrafo (*a f*) *m*; '**~hand·ed** falto de mano de obra; '**~lived** [~laivd] efímero; '**short·ly** *adv.* en breve, dentro de poco.

short...: '**~sight·ed** miope, corto de vista; *fig.* falto de previsión; '**~sto·ry** cuento *m*; '**~tem·pered** enojadizo; '**~term** a plazo corto; '**~wave** *radio*: ... de onda corta; '**~wind·ed** corto de resuello.

shot [ʃɔt] tiro *m*, disparo *m*; balazo *m*; (*a. small* ~) perdigones *m/pl.*; (*p.*) tirador (*-a f*) *m*; *sport*: tiro *m at goal*; *phot.* fotografía *f*; *film*: fotograma *m*; ⚕ inyección *f*; dosis *f*; *sl.* trago *m* of rum *etc.*; F *big* ~ pez *m* gordo; '**~gun** escopeta *f*; F ~ *marriage* casamiento *m* a la fuerza.

should [ʃud] *v/aux.* que forma el

condicional etc.: I ~ do it if I could lo haría si pudiese; **2.** deber: *he* ~ *be here soon* debe llegar dentro de poco; *he* ~ *know that* debiera saberlo.

shoul·der ['ʃouldə] **1.** hombro *m*; espaldas *f/pl.*; lomo *m of hill etc.*; **2.** llevar al hombro; *fig.* cargar con; empujar con el hombro; '~ **blade** omóplato *m*.

shout [ʃaut] **1.** grito *m*; voz *f*; **2.** gritar; dar voces.

shove [ʃʌv] **1.** empujón *m*; **2.** *v/i.* dar empujones; ~ *off* ⚓ alejarse; *sl.* marcharse; *v/t.* empujar.

shov·el ['ʃʌvl] **1.** pala *f*; cogedor *m*; **2.** traspalar.

show [ʃou] **1.** [*irr.*] *v/t.* mostrar, enseñar; (*prove*) probar, demostrar; señalar; manifestar; *film* poner, proyectar; *goods, pictures* exhibir; ~ *off* hacer gala de; ~ *out* acompañar a la puerta; *v/i.* mostrarse, (a)parecer; (*film*) representarse; ~ *off* lucirse; fachendear; F ~ *up* acudir, presentarse; **2.** (*display*) exhibición *f*; exposición *f*; (*outward*) apariencia *f*; (*pomp*) boato *m*; manifestación *f*, demostración *f of feeling*; *thea.* función *f*, espectáculo *m*; *sl. run the* ~ ser el todo; mandar; '~ **bus·i·ness** comercio *m* de los espectáculos; '~**case** vitrina *f* (de exposición); '~**down** momento *m* decisivo, revelación *f* decisiva.

show·er ['ʃauə] **1.** chaparrón *m*, chubasco *m*; aguacero *m*; *fig.* rociada *f*; **2.** llover; derramar; *fig.* ~ *with* colmar de; ~ **bath** ['~bɑːθ] ducha *f*; '**show·er·y** lluvioso.

show·i·ness ['ʃouinis] boato *m*; aparatosidad *f*; '**show·man** empresario *m*; *fig.* hombre *m* ostentoso; '**show·man·ship** teatralidad *f*; '**show·room** salón *m* de demostraciones; '**show win·dow** escaparate *m*; '**show·y** □ vistoso, llamativo; *p.* ostentoso.

shrap·nel ['ʃræpnl] metralla *f*.

shred [ʃred] **1.** triza *f*, jirón *m*; fragmento *m*; *fig.* pizca *f*; **2.** [*irr.*] hacer trizas; desmenuzar.

shrew [ʃruː] *zo.* musaraña *f*; *fig.* mujer *f* regañona, fierecilla *f*.

shrewd [ʃruːd] □ astuto, sagaz; '**shrewd·ness** astucia *f*, sagacidad *f*.

shriek [ʃriːk] **1.** alarido *m*, chillido *m*; **2.** chillar (*a. fig.*).

shrill [ʃril] □ chillón (*a. fig.*), agudo y penetrante.

shrimp [ʃrimp] *zo.* camarón *m*; *fig.* enano *m*.

shrine [ʃrain] relicario *m*; capilla *f*, sepulcro *m* (de santo).

shrink [ʃriŋk] [*irr.*] *v/i.* encogerse, contraer(se); mermar; (*a.* ~ *back*) acobardarse; *v/t.* encoger; contraer; '**shrink·age** encogimiento *m*, contracción *f*.

shriv·el ['ʃrivl] (*a.* ~ *up*) marchitar(se), arrugar(se); avellanarse.

shroud [ʃraud] **1.** sudario *m*, mortaja *f*; **2.** amortajar; *fig.* velar.

shrub [ʃrʌb] arbusto *m*; **shrub·ber·y** ['~əri] plantío *m* de arbustos.

shrug [ʃrʌg] **1.** encogerse de hombros; **2.** encogimiento *m* (de hombros).

shud·der ['ʃʌdə] **1.** estremecerse; **2.** estremecimiento *m*.

shuf·fle ['ʃʌfl] **1.** *v/t.* mezclar, revolver; *cards* barajar; **2.** *v/i.* arrastrar los pies; andar (bailar *etc.*) arrastrando los pies; **3.** *cards:* (*act*) barajadura *f*.

shun [ʃʌn] esquivar, evitar.

shunt [ʃʌnt] **1.** ⚡ derivación *f*, shunt *m*; cambio *m* de vía; **2.** ⚡ poner en derivación; 🚂 maniobrar; apartar.

shut [ʃʌt] [*irr.*] cerrar; ~ *down factory* cerrar; *machine* parar; ~ *in* encerrar; cercar, rodear; ~ *off water etc.* cortar; aislar (*from* de); F ~ *up* callarse; F ~ *up!* ¡cállate!; '~**down** cierre *m*; ~**out** *sport:* victoria *f* en que el contrario no gana un tanto; '**shut·ter** contraventana *f*; *phot.* obturador *m*.

shut·tle ['ʃʌtl] **1.** lanzadera *f*; ~ *service* tren *m etc.* que hace viajes cortos entre dos puntos; *space* ~ astronave *f* dirigible; **2.** hacer viajes cortos entre dos puntos.

shy [ʃai] □ tímido; recatado; huraño; vergonzoso.

shy·ness ['ʃainis] timidez *f*; recato *m*; vergüenza *f*.

shy·ster ['ʃaistə] *sl.*, abogado *m* trampista.

Si·a·mese [saiə'miːz] siamés *adj. a. su. m* (*-a f*).

Si·be·ri·an [sai'biəriən] siberiano *adj. a. su. m* (*-a f*).

sib·ling ['sibliŋ] hermano *m*; hermana *f*.

sib·yl ['sibil] sibila *f*.

Si·cil·i·an [si'siljən] siciliano *adj. a. su. m* (*-a f*).

sick [sik] enfermo; mareado; *be* ~ estar enfermo; sentirse mareado; *be* ~ *of* estar harto de; *sl.* perverso;

mórbido; '**~bay** enfermería f; '**~bed** lecho m de enfermo; '**sick·en** v/i. enfermar; ~ **at** sentir náuseas ante; v/t. dar asco a; '**sick·en·ing** □ asqueroso, nauseabundo.

sick leave ['sikli:v] permiso m de convalecencia; '**sick·li·ness** achaque m; palidez f; '**sick·ly** p. enfermizo, achacoso; pálido; *smell* nauseabundo; '**sick·ness** enfermedad f, mal m; náusea f; '**sick pay** subsidio m de enfermedad.

side [said] **1.** lado m; costado m of body, ship; cara f of solid, record; falda f, ladera f of hill; ~ **by** ~ lado a lado; by the ~ al lado de; on all ~s por todas partes; **2.** lateral; secundario; indirecto; **3.**: ~ **with** declararse por; '**~arms** armas f/pl. de cinto; '**~board** aparador m; '**~car** sidecar m.

side...: '**~kick** compañero m; '**~light** detalle m (or información f) incidental; '**~line** 🚂 apartadero m; *sport:* línea f lateral; *fig.* empleo m (or negocio m) suplementario.

side...: '**~sad·dle 1.** silla f de mujer; **2.** *adv.* a mujeriegas, a la inglesa; '~ **show** caseta f (de feria); '**~step 1.** esquivada f lateral; **2.** *fig.* evitar, esquivar; '**~stroke** natación f de costado; '**~track 1.** 🚂 apartadero m, vía f muerta; **2.** *fig.* desviar, apartar; '**~walk** acera f; S.Am. vereda; ('**side·ways**, '**side·wise**) de lado, hacia un lado.

siege [si:dʒ] cerco m, sitio m; *lay* ~ *to* asediar (a. fig.).

sieve [siv] cedazo m, tamiz m; (*kitchen*) coladera f.

sift [sift] tamizar, cerner.

sigh [sai] **1.** suspiro m; **2.** suspirar.

sight [sait] **1.** vista f (a. ✝); visión f; escena f; espectáculo m; cosa f digna de verse; ✕ puntería f; F espantajo m; *catch* ~ *of* alcanzar a ver; *lose* ~ *of* perder de vista (a. fig.); **2.** avistar, divisar; *gun* apuntar; '**~less** ciego; '**~see·ing** excursionismo m, turismo m; '**~se·er** excursionista m/f, turista m/f.

sign [sain] **1.** señal f; indicio m; ♪, ♏, etc. signo m; (*trace*) huella f, vestigio m; (*notice*) letrero m; (*shop-*) rótulo m; ~s pl. señas f/pl.; **2.** v/t. firmar; usar el alfabeto de los sordomudos; ~ **off** terminar.

sig·nal ['signl] **1.** señal f; *teleph.* busy~ señal f de ocupado; ~s pl. ✕ (cuerpo m de) transmisiones f/pl.; **2.** □ seña-

lado, notable; **3.** hacer señales (*to* a); comunicar por señales (*that* que); **sig·nal·ize** ['~nəlaiz] distinguir, marcar; '**sig·nal·man** 🚂 guardavía m; ✕ soldado m de transmisiones.

sig·na·to·ry ['signətəri] firmante *adj. a. su. m* (a f), signatorio *adj. a. su. m* (a f); **sig·na·ture** ['signitʃə] firma f; *typ.*, ♪ signatura f.

sig·net ['signit] sello m; '~ **ring** sortija f de sello.

sig·nif·i·cance, sig·nif·i·can·cy [sig-'nifikəns(i)] significación f, significado m; **sig·nif·i·cant** □ significante, significativo.

sig·ni·fy ['signifai] significar; querer decir.

sign...: '~ **paint·er** rotulista m; '~ **post** poste m indicador.

si·lence ['sailəns] **1.** silencio m; ~! ¡silencio!; **2.** acallar (a. fig.), imponer silencio a.

si·lent ['sailənt] □ silencioso, callado; *be* ~, *remain* ~ callarse; ~ *film* película f muda.

sil·hou·ette [silu'et] silueta f.

silk [silk] **1.** seda f; **2.** *attr.* de seda; ~ *hat* sombrero m de copa; '**silk·en** de seda; sedoso; '**silk·'stock·ing 1.** aristócrata m/f; **2.** aristocrático; '**silk·worm** gusano m de seda; '**silk·y** □ sedoso.

sill [sil] (*window-*) alféizar m; antepecho m; (*door-*) umbral m.

sil·li·ness ['silinis] necedad f, tontería f; **sil·ly** ['sili] □ tonto, necio.

si·lo ['sailou] silo m, ensiladora f.

silt [silt] **1.** sedimento m, aluvión m; **2.** obstruirse con sedimentos.

sil·ver ['silvə] **1.** plata f; **2.** platear (a. ⊕ '~ **plate**); *mirror* azogar; **3.** de plata; plateado; '**~ware** vajilla f de plata; '**silver·y** plateado; *voice* argentino.

sim·i·lar ['similə] □ parecido, semejante; **sim·i·lar·i·ty** ['~læriti] semejanza f.

si·mil·i·tude [si'militju:d] similitud f.

sim·mer ['simə] v/i. hervir (v/t. cocer) a fuego lento.

si·mon·y ['saiməni] simonía f.

sim·ple ['simpl] □ sencillo; simple; *style* llano; F bobo; '~'**mind·ed** □ estúpido, idiota; candoroso; **sim·ple·ton** ['~tən] inocentón m.

sim·plic·i·ty [sim'plisiti] sencillez f; llaneza f *of style*; F simpleza f; **sim·pli·fy** ['~fai] simplificar.

sim·u·late ['simjuleit] simular.

si·mul·ta·ne·i·ty [siməltə'niəti] simultaneidad *f*; **si·mul·ta·ne·ous** [~'lʹteinjəs] ☐ simultáneo.

sin [sin] 1. pecado *m*; 2. pecar.

since [sins] 1. *prp*. desde, a partir de, después de; 2. *adv*. desde entonces, después; 3. *cj*. desde que; puesto que, ya que.

sin·cere [sin'siə] ☐ sincero; *Yours* ~*ly* le saluda afectuosamente; **sin·cer·i·ty** [~'seriti] sinceridad *f*.

sin·ful ['sinful] ☐ pecaminoso; *p*. pecador; **'sin·ful·ness** maldad *f*.

sing [sin] [*irr*.] cantar; (*birds*) trinar; (*ears*) zumbar; ~ *to sleep* arrullar, adormecer cantando; *sl*. confesar.

singe [sindʒ] chamuscar; *hair* quemar las puntas de.

sing·er ['siŋə] cantor (-a *f*) *m*; (*profesional*) cantante *m/f*.

sin·gle ['siŋgl] 1. ☐ único, solo; simple; *room* individual; *ticket* sencillo; (*unmarried*) soltero; 2. (*mst* ~ *out*) distinguir, singularizar; escoger; señalar; 3. *tennis*: ~*s pl*. juego *m* de individuales; F ~*s* (los) no casados *a. adj*.; '~**breast·ed** sin cruzar; '~**cham·ber** *pol*. unicameral; '~**en·gined** ☐ monomotor; '~**hand·ed** sin ayuda (de nadie); '~**mind·ed** ☐ resuelto, firme; sincero; **'sin·gle·ness** resolución *f*, firmeza *f* *of purpose*; **'sin·gle·seat·er** monoplaza *m*; **sin·gle·ton** ['~tən] semi-fallo *m*, carta *f* única de un palo; **'sin·gle·track** de vía única.

sin·gly ['siŋgli] *adv*. individualmente.

sing·song ['siŋsɔŋ] 1. (*tone*) salmodia *f*, sonsonete *m*; 2. *tone* monótono, cantarín.

sin·gu·lar ['siŋgjulə] ☐ singular *adj*. *a. su. m*; **sin·gu·lar·i·ty** [~'læriti] singularidad *f*.

sin·is·ter ['sinistə] ☐ siniestro.

sink [siŋk] 1. [*irr*.] *v/i*. menguar, declinar; (*ship*) hundirse; (*sun*) ponerse; ☼ debilitarse; dejarse caer *into chair*; *v/t*. sumergir; *ship* hundir; ☼ *shaft* abrir, cavar; 2. fregadero *m*, pila *f*; ☼ sumidero *m*; *fig*. sentina *f*; **'sink·er** (*fishing*) plomo *m*; **'sink·ing** hundimiento *m*.

sin·ner ['sinə] pecador (-a *f*) *m*.

si·nol·o·gy [sai'nɔlədʒi] sinología *f*; **si·nol·o·gist** sinólogo *m*.

si·nus ['sainəs] *anat*. seno *m*; **si·nus·i·tis** [~'saitis] sinusitis *f*.

sip [sip] 1. sorbo *m*; 2. sorber.

si·phon ['saifən] 1. sifón *m*; 2. sacar con sifón (*a.* ~ *off*).

sir [sə:] señor *m* (*in direct address*); sir *m* (*as title*); *Dear* ♀ Muy señor mío.

si·ren ['saiərin] *all senses*: sirena *f*.

sir·loin ['sə:lɔin] solomillo *m*.

sis·sy ['sisi] marica *m*, mariquita *m*.

sis·ter ['sistə] hermana *f* (*a. eccl*.); *eccl*. (*as title*) Sor *f*; **sis·ter·hood** ['~hud] hermandad *f*; cofradía *f* de mujeres; **'sis·ter·in·law** cuñada *f*.

sit [sit] *v/i*. sentarse (*a.* ~ *down*); estar sentado; (*assembly*) reunirse, celebrar junta; (*clothes*) sentar; ~ *up* incorporarse; velar *at night*; **sit·com** ['sitkɔm] telecomedia *f* serial; **'~down strike** huelga *f* de brazos caídos.

site [sait] sitio *m*; solar *m*, local *m*.

sit·in ['sitin] manifestación *f* pacífica a modo de bloqueo.

sit·ting ['sitiŋ] sesión *f*; nidada *f* of eggs; '~ **room** sala *f* de estar.

sit·u·at·ed ['sitjueitid] situado; sito; **sit·u·a·tion** situación *f*; (*post*) puesto *m*, colocación *f*.

six [siks] seis (*a. su. m*); *at* ~*es* and *sevens* en confusión; **six·teen** ['~'ti:n] dieciséis; **'six·teenth** [~θ] decimosexto; **sixth** [~θ] sexto (*a. su. m*); **six·ti·eth** ['~tiəθ] sexagésimo; **'six·ty** sesenta.

size [saiz] 1. tamaño *m*; talla *f*; dimensiones *f/pl*.; número *m* of *shoes etc.*; 2. clasificar según el tamaño.

siz·zle ['sizl] chisporrotear, churruscar, crepitar (al freírse).

skate [skeit] 1. patín *m*; *ichth*. raya *f*; 2. patinar; **'skat·ing rink** pista *f* de patinaje.

ske·dad·dle [ski'dædl] F poner pies en polvorosa, largarse.

skein [skein] madeja *f*.

skel·e·ton ['skelitn] esqueleto *m*; *fig*. esquema *m*; ⊕ armazón *f*; ~ *key* llave *f* maestra.

skep·tic ['skeptik] *v*. sceptic.

sketch [sketʃ] 1. bosquejo *m*, boceto *m*; *thea*. pieza *f* corta; 2. dibujar; **'sketch·y** ☐ incompleto.

skew·er ['skuə] 1. broqueta *f*, espetón *m*; 2. espetar.

ski [ski:] 1. esquí *m*; 2. esquiar.

skid [skid] 1. derrape *m*, patinazo *m*; 2. derrapar, patinar, deslizarse.

skid row ['skid'rou] barrio *m* de mala vida.

ski·er ['ski:ə] esquiador (-a *f*) *m*.

ski·ing ['ski:iŋ] esquí *m*; **'ski jump**

S

salto *m* de esquí; **'ski lift** telesquí *m*, telesilla *f*.

skil(l)·ful ['skilful] □ diestro, hábil; experto; **'skil(l)·ful·ness, skill** [skil] destreza *f*, habilidad *f*; pericia *f*; **skilled** [skild] hábil, experto; *work, man* especializado.

skil·let ['skilit] sartén *f*.

skim [skim] *v/t. milk* desnatar; espumar; (*graze*) rozar, rasar; *v/i.*: ∼ *over* pasar rasando.

skimp [skimp] *v/t.* escatimar; *work* chapucear, frangollar; *v/i.* economizar; **'skimp·y** □ escaso; tacaño.

skin [skin] **1.** piel *f*; cutis *m*; (*animal's*) pellejo *m*; ♣ corteza *f*; **2.** despellejar (*a. sl.*); desollar; *fruit* pelar; **'∼·deep** superficial; **'∼·flint** cicatero *m*, tacaño *m*; **'skin·ny** flaco, magro.

skip [skip] **1.** brinco *m*, salto *m*; **2.** *v/i.* brincar, saltar; *f* escabullirse (*a.* ∼ *over*) omitir, saltar.

skir·mish ['skə:miʃ] **1.** escaramuza *f*; **2.** escaramuzar.

skirt [skə:t] **1.** falda *f*; faldón *m of coat*; (*edge*) orilla *f*, borde *m*; **2.** orillar, ladear.

skit [skit] sátira *f*, pasquín *m* (on contra); *thea.* número *m* corto burlesco; **'skit·tish** □ asustadizo (*esp. horse*).

skul·dug·ger·y [skʌl'dʌgəri] F trampa *f*, embuste *m*.

skulk [skʌlk] acechar; remolonear.

skull [skʌl] cráneo *m*; calavera *f*.

skunk [skʌŋk] *zo.* mofeta *f*; F canalla *m*.

sky [skai] cielo *m*; **'∼·blue** azul celeste; **∼·div·ing** ['skaidaiviŋ] paracaidismo *m* con una plomada suelta inicial; **'∼·high** por las nubes; **'∼·light** tragaluz *m*; claraboya *f*; **'∼·line** (línea *f* del) horizonte *m*, silueta *f of building etc.*; **'∼·rock·et 1.** cohete *m*; **2.** F subir (como un cohete); **'∼·scrap·er** rascacielos *m*; **sky·ward(s)** ['∼wəd(z)] hacia el cielo; **'sky·writ·ing** escritura *f* aérea.

slab [slæb] tabla *f* (*a.* ⊕), plancha *f*; losa *f of stone*.

slack [slæk] **1.** flojo (*a.* ♣); (*lax*) descuidado, negligente; (*lazy*) perezoso; *student* desaplicado; **2.** lo flojo; ♣ estación *f* (*or* temporada *f*) de inactividad; ✗ cisco *m*; ∼s *pl.* pantalones *m/pl.* (flojos; *mst* de mujer); **'slack·en** *v/t.* aflojar (*a.* ∼ *off*); disminuir; *v/i.* aflojarse; (*wind*) amainar.

sla·lom ['slɔːləm] eslálom *m*.

slam [slæm] **1.** golpe *m*; (*door*) portazo *m*; *cards*: bola *f*; **2.** (*door*) cerrar (-se) de golpe; golpear.

slan·der ['slɑːndə] **1.** calumnia *f*, difamación *f*; **2.** calumniar, difamar; **'slan·der·ous** □ calumnioso.

slang [slæŋ] argot *m*, jerga *f*; (*thieves'*) germanía *f*; vulgarismo *m*.

slant [slɑːnt] **1.** inclinación *f*, sesgo *m*; F punto *m* de vista, parecer *m*; **2.** inclinar(se), sesgar(se); **'slant·ing** □ inclinado, sesgado; **'slant·wise** oblicuamente.

slap [slæp] **1.** palmada *f*, manotada *f*; **2.** dar una palmada (*or* bofetada) a; pegar; **3.** *adv.* (*full*) de lleno, directamente; **'∼·dash** descuidado, de brocha gorda; **'∼·stick** payasadas *f/pl.*

slash [slæʃ] **1.** cuchillada *f*, latigazo *m*; **2.** *v/t.* acuchillar, rasgar; azotar *with whip*; F *price* machacar; cortar; reducir; *v/i.* tirar tajos (*at* a); **'slash·ing** □ *criticism* severo.

slate [sleit] **1.** pizarra *f*; lista *f* de candidatos; **2.** cubrir de pizarra(s).

slaugh·ter ['slɔːtə] **1.** sacrificio *m*, matanza *f*; **2.** sacrificar, matar; carnear *S.Am.*; **'slaugh·ter·er** jifero *m*; **'slaugh·ter·house** matadero *m*; **'slaugh·ter·ous** mortífero.

Slav [slɑːv] eslavo *adj. a. su. m* (a *f*).

slave [sleiv] **1.** esclavo (a *f*) *m*; **2.** trabajar como un negro, sudar tinta.

slav·er·y ['sleivəri] esclavitud *f*.

Slav·ic ['slævik] eslavo *adj. a. su. m* (a. Slav·on·ic).

slav·ish ['sleiviʃ] □ servil; **'slav·ish·ness** servilismo *m*.

slaw [slɔː] ensalada *f* de col.

slay [slei] [*irr.*] matar; **'slay·er** asesino *m*; matador *m*.

sled [sled], *mst* **sledge**[1] [sledʒ] **1.** trineo *m*; **2.** ir en trineo.

sledge[2] [∼] acotillo *m*, macho *m* (*a.* '∼·ham·mer).

sleek [sliːk] **1.** □ liso y brillante; pulido; **2.** alisar, pulir.

sleep [sliːp] **1.** [*irr.*] *v/i.* dormir; *v/t.* pasar durmiendo (*a.* ∼ *away*); **2.** sueño *m*; go to ∼ dormirse (*a. of limb*); **'sleep·er** durmiente *m/f*; 🚃 traviesa *f*; (*coach*) coche-cama *m*; cama *f*; **'sleep·i·ness** somnolencia *f*; modorra *f*.

sleep·ing ['sliːpiŋ]: 🚃 ∼ *partner* socio *m* comanditario; '∼ **bag** saco *m* de dormir; '∼ **car** 🚃 coche-cama *m*; '∼

pill, '~ **'tab·let** comprimido *m* para dormir, somnífero *m*; '~ **'sick·ness** enfermedad *f* del sueño.

sleep·less ['sli:plis] □ *p.* insomne; **'sleep·less·ness** insomnio *m*.

sleep·walk·er ['sli:pwɔ:kə] somnámbulo (a *f*) *m*.

sleep·y ['sli:pi] *p.* soñoliento; '~**head** F dormilón (-a *f*) *m*.

sleet [sli:t] **1.** aguanieve *f*, nevisca *f*; **2.** caer aguanieve, neviscar.

sleeve [sli:v] manga *f*; ⊕ manguito *m*, enchufe *m*; **'sleeve·less** sin mangas.

sleigh [slei] *v.* sled.

slen·der ['slendə] □ delgado; escaso, limitado; **'slen·der·ness** delgadez *f*.

sleuth [slu:θ] (*a.* '~**hound**) sabueso *m*; *fig.* detective *m*.

slew [slu:] *pret. of* slay.

slice [slais] **1.** tajada *f*, lonja *f* *of meat etc.*; raja *f* *of sausage*; trozo *m* *of bread*; **2.** cortar, tajar; *bread* rebanar; **'slic·er** rebanador *m*.

slick [slik] F *p.* astuto, mañoso.

slick·er ['slikə] (*coat*) impermeable *m*.

slid [slid] *pret. a. p.p. of* slide 1.

slide [slaid] **1.** [*irr.*] *v/i.* resbalar; deslizarse (*along* por); *v/t.* correr, deslizar; **2.** resbaladero *m* *on ice*; ⊕ cursor *m*; corredera *f* (*lantern-*) diapositiva *f*; **'slide rule** regla *f* de cálculo.

slid·ing ['slaidiŋ] **1.** deslizamiento *m*; **2.** corredizo.

slight [slait] **1.** □ leve, ligero; insignificante; escaso, tenue; *stature* delgado; **2.** desaire *m*, desatención *f*; **3.** desatender; menospreciar.

slim [slim] **1.** □ delgado, esbelto; escaso; **2.** adelgazar.

slime [slaim] limo *m*, légamo *m*; cieno *m*; baba *f* *of snail*; **slim·i·ness** ['slaiminis] lo limoso; viscosidad *f*.

slim·y ['slaimi] □ limoso, legamoso; baboso; viscoso; *p.* rastrero; adulón.

sling [sliŋ] **1.** ⋊ honda *f*; ⚑ cabestrillo *m*; **2.** [*irr.*] lanzar, tirar; (*a.* ~ *away*) colgar, suspender.

slink [sliŋk] [*irr.*] *v/i.* andar furtivamente; ~ *away* irse cabizbajo.

slip [slip] **1.** *v/i.* deslizarse; (*freq.* ~ *up*) resbalar; F declinar; ~ *away*, ~ *off* escabullirse; ~ *by* pasar inadvertido; ~ *through* colarse; ~ *up* *fig.* equivocarse; *v/t.* deslizar; *bone* dislocarse; *guard* eludir; ~ *in remark* deslizar, insinuar; *it* ~*ped my mind* se me olvidó; **2.** resbalón *m*; desliz *m* (*a. fig.*); *fig.* lapso *m*, equivocación *f*;

✐ esqueje *m*; (*dress*) combinación *f*; *geol.*~ *of paper* tira *f*, papeleta *f*; F~ *of a girl* jovenzuela *f*; '~**knot** lazo *m* corredizo; **'slip·per** zapatilla *f*, babucha *f*; **'slip·per·y** □ resbaladizo; *skin* viscoso; F *p.* astuto, zorro; **slip·shod** ['.ʃɔd] descuidado; desaseado; **'slip-up** F error *m*, desliz *m*.

slit [slit] **1.** hendedura *f*, raja *f*; **2.** [*irr.*] hender, rajar, cortar.

sliv·er ['slivə] raja *f*.

slob [slɔb] sujeto *m* desaseado.

slob·ber ['slɔbə] **1.** baba *f*; **2.** babear.

slog [slɔg] F *v/i.* afanarse, sudar tinta; *v/t.* golpear (sin arte).

slo·gan ['slougən] slogan *m*, lema *m*.

sloop [slu:p] balandra *f*, corbeta *f*.

slop [slɔp] **1.**: ~*s pl.* agua *f* sucia, lavazas *f/pl.*; **2.** (*a.* ~ *over*) derramar (-se), desbordarse.

slope [sloup] **1.** cuesta *f*, declive *m*; inclinación *f*; vertiente *f*; ladera *f* *of hill*; **2.** *v/t.* inclinar; sesgar; formar en declive; *v/i.* inclinarse; declinar; **'slop·ing** □ inclinado; en declive.

slop·py ['slɔpi] □ lleno de charcos; mojado; *fig. work* descuidado; *dress* desgalichado; F sentimental.

slosh [slɔʃ] *v.* slush.

slot [slɔt] ⋊ muesca *f*, ranura *f*.

sloth [slouθ] pereza *f*; *zo.* perezoso *m*; **sloth·ful** ['.ful] □ perezoso.

slot ma·chine ['slɔtməʃi:n] tragamonedas *m*; máquina *f* tragaperras.

slouch [slautʃ] **1.** *v/i.* estar sentado (*or* andar *etc.*) con un aire gacho; agacharse; *v/t. hat* agachar; **2.** postura *f* desgarbada.

slough [slʌf] *v/i.* desprenderse; *v/t.* mudar, echar de sí (*a.* ~ *off*).

Slo·vak ['slouvæk] **1.** eslovaco (a *f*) *m*; **2.** = **Slo'va·ki·an** eslovaco.

slov·en·li·ness ['slʌvnlinis] desaseo *m*, dejadez *f*; **'slov·en·ly** desaseado, desaliñado, dejado.

slow [slou] **1.** □ lento; pausado; *clock* atrasado; (*dull*) torpe, lerdo; **2.** *adv.* (*a.* ~*ly*) despacio, lentamente; **3.** *v/t.* retardar; ⊕ reducir la velocidad de, moderar la marcha de; *v/i.* ir más despacio; moderarse la marcha; '~**lane** vía *f* de velocidad reducida; '~**'mo·tion** *film* a cámara lenta; **'slow·ness** lentitud *f*; torpeza *f*.

sludge [slʌdʒ] lodo *m*, fango *m*.

slug¹ [slʌg] *zo.* babosa *f*; *sl.* **1.** porrazo *m*; puñetazo *m*; **2.** apuñear.

slug² [~] ⋊ posta *f*; *typ.* lingote *m*.

slug·gard ['slʌgəd] haragán (-a *f*) *m*; **'slug·gish** □ perezoso; tardo.

S

sluice [sluːs] **1.** esclusa *f*; (*a. ~·way*) canal *m*; (*a. ~ gate*) compuerta *f*; **2.** regar, lavar (abriendo la compuerta).

slum [slʌm] barrio *m* bajo; (*house*) casucha *f*, tugurio *m*; **'~ lord** dueño *m* desinteresado de casas del barrio bajo.

slum·ber [ˈslʌmbə] **1.** (*a. ~s pl.*) *lit.* sueño *m* (*mst* tranquilo); *fig.* inactividad *f*; **2.** dormir, dormitar.

slump [slʌmp] **1.** bajar repentinamente; dejarse caer pesadamente (*into chair*); **2.** ✝ baja *f* repentina *in price*; (*general*) declive *m* económico.

slur [sləː] **1.** reparo *m*; borrón *m* (en la reputación); ♪ ligado *m*; **2.** ocultar (*a. ~ over*); *syllable* comerse.

slush [slʌʃ] nieve *f* a medio derretir; fango *m*; F sentimentalismo *m*; **'slush·y** fangoso; F sentimental.

slut [slʌt] marrana *f*, mujer *f* desaseada; **'slut·tish** sucio; inmoral.

sly [slai] socarrón, taimado; astuto; furtivo; **'sly·ness** socarronería *f*.

smack¹ [smæk] **1.** sabor(cillo) *m*; **2.** saber (*of a*).

smack² [~] **1.** (*slap*) manotada *f*; golpe *m*; **2.** dar una manotada a, pegar; golpear; *lips* relamerse.

small [smɔːl] **1.** pequeño; chico; menudo; corto, exiguo; insignificante; *print* minúsculo; **2.:** *~ of the back* parte *f* más estrecha (de la espalda); **'~ arms** *pl.* armas *f/pl.* cortas; **'small·ness** pequeñez *f*; **'small·pox** ✠ viruela *f*; **'small talk** cháchara *f*; vulgaridades *f/pl.*

smart [smɑːt] **1.** ☐ listo, vivo; inteligente; *b.s.* ladino, astuto; *dress etc.* elegante; *appearance* pulcro; **2.** escozor *m*; **3.** escocer; picar; **'~ al·eck** fatuo; sabihondo *adj. a. su.* (a *f*) *m*; **'smart·ness** elegancia *f*; vivacidad *f etc.*; **'smart 'mon·ey** *fig.* inversionistas *m/pl.* astutos.

smash [smæʃ] **1.** hacer(se) pedazos; destrozar(se), aplastar (*freq. ~ up*); ✝ quebrar; **2.** ✠ *etc.* choque *m* (violento), accidente *m*; ✝ quiebra *f*; *tennis:* golpe *m* violento; *~ hit sl.* exitazo *m*; **'smash·ing** *sl.* imponente, bárbaro; **'smash-up** colisión *f* violenta.

smat·ter·ing [ˈsmætərin] nociones *f/pl.*; tintura *f*.

smear [smiə] **1.** manchar(se) (*a. fig.*), embarrar(se), untar(se); **2.** mancha *f* (*a. fig.*), embarradura *f*.

smell [smel] **1.** olor *m* (*of a*); (*bad*)

hedor *m*; (*sense of*) olfato *m*; **2.** [*irr.*] oler (*of a*); (*dog*) olfatear.

smelt [smelt] fundir; **'smelt·er** fundidor *m*; **'smelt·ing 'fur·nace** horno *m* de fundición.

smile [smail] **1.** sonrisa *f*; **2.** sonreír (-se) (*at de*); **'smil·ing** ☐ risueño.

smirk [sməːk] **1.** sonreírse satisfecho; sonreírse afectadamente; **2.** sonrisa *f* satisfecha.

smite [smait] [*irr.*] † golpear (con fuerza); herir; castigar; afligir.

smith [smiθ] herrero *m*.

smit·ten [ˈsmitn] *fig. ~ with* afligido por; F *idea* entusiasmado por; *p.* chalado por.

smock [smɔk] blusa *f*; bata *f*.

smog [smɔg] niebla *f* espesa con humo.

smoke [smouk] **1.** humo *m*; F pitillo *m*, tabaco *m*; **2.** *v/i.* fumar; (*chimney*) echar humo, humear; *v/t.* fumar; *bacon etc.* ahumar; *~ out* ahuyentar con humo; **'smoke·less** ☐ sin humo; **'smok·er** fumador (-a *f*) *m*; ✠ coche *m* fumador; **'smoke screen** cortina *f* de humo; **'smoke-stack** chimenea *f*.

smok·ing [ˈsmoukin] **1.** el fumar; *no ~* prohibido fumar; **2.** ... de fumador(es); **'~ com·part·ment** departamento *m* de fumadores; **'~ room** salón *m* de fumar.

smok·y [ˈsmouki] ☐humeante; lleno de humo; ahumado.

smooth [smuːð] **1.** ☐ liso, terso; suave; llano, igual; *manner* afable; *style* fluido; *p.*, *b.s.* zalamero, meloso, astuto; **2.** (*a. ~ out*, *~ down*) alisar; suavizar; allanar; ⊕ desbastar; *p.* ablandar; **'smooth·ness** lisura *f*; suavidad *f etc.*

smote [smout] *pret. of* smite.

smoth·er [ˈsmʌðə] (*a. ~ up*) sofocar, ahogar; *fire* apagar; *yawn* contener; *doubts etc.* suprimir.

smoul·der [ˈsmouldə] arder sin llama; *fig.* estar latente.

smudge [smʌdʒ] **1.** manchar(se), tiznar(se); **2.** mancha *f*; **'smudg·y** ☐ manchado; borroso.

smug [smʌg] ☐ pagado de sí mismo; presumido, vanidoso; farisaico.

smug·gle [ˈsmʌgl] pasar de contrabando; **'smug·gler** contrabandista *m/f*; **'smug·gling** contrabando *m*.

smut [smʌt] tizne *m*; tiznón *m*; ♀ tizón *m*; *fig.* obscenidad *f*.

smut·ty ['smʌti] □ tiznado; ♥ atizonado; fig. obsceno, verde.

snack [snæk] bocadillo m, tentempié m; '**~bar** bar m; cafetería f, cantina f.

snag [snæg] nudo m in wood; tocón m of tree; raigón m of tooth; fig. tropiezo m; obstáculo m.

snail [sneil] caracol m.

snake [sneik] culebra f, serpiente f.

snap [snæp] 1. castañetazo m of fingers; chasquido m of whip; (fastener) corchete m; F vigor m; cold ~ ola f de frío; 2. repentino, imprevisto; 3. v/i. (break) romperse; saltar; (sound) chasquear; ~ at querer morder; fig. contestar groseramente; F ~ out of it! ¡menéate!, ¡ánimo!; v/t. romper; hacer saltar; whip etc. chasquear; fingers castañetear; phot. sacar una foto (or instantánea) de; ~ up asir; 4. ¡crac!; '~·drag·on cabeza f de dragón; '~ fas·ten·er corchete m (de presión); '**snap·py** F enérgico; F make it ~! ¡pronto!; '**snap·shot** disparo m rápido sin apuntar; phot. instantánea f.

snare [snɛə] 1. trampa f, lazo m; fig. engaño m; 2. coger con trampas.

snarl [snɑːl] 1. gruñir; regañar; 2. gruñido m; regaño m; enredo m.

snatch [snætʃ] 1. arrebatamiento m; 2. (~ at tratar de) arrebatar (from a); coger (al vuelo); ~ up asir.

sneak [sniːk] 1. v/i. ir (~ in entrar) a hurtadillas; v/t. F hacer a hurtadillas; 2. soplón (-a f) m; '**sneak·ers** pl. F zapatos m/pl. ligeros de goma; '**sneak thief** ratero m.

sneer [sniə] 1. visaje m de burla y desprecio; 2. hacer un visaje de burla y desprecio; ~ at mofarse de, mirar a desgaire; '**sneer·ing** □ burlador y despreciativo.

sneeze [sniːz] 1. estornudar; 2. estornudo m.

sniff [snif] 1. v/i. oler, ventear; ~ at husmear; v/t. husmear, olfatear; 2. husmeo m; venteo m.

snip [snip] 1. tijeretada f; recorte m; 2. tijeretear; recortar (a. ~ off).

snipe [snaip] 1. orn. agachadiza f; 2. ✕ tirar desde un escondite; ~ at paquear; '**snip·er** tirador m escondido.

snip·pets ['snipits] pl. recortes m/pl.; fig. retazos m/pl.

snitch [snitʃ] soplar, hurtar; sl. escamotear.

sniv·el ['snivl] lloriquear; gimotear; '**sniv·el·(l)ing** llorón.

snob [snɔb] (e)snob m/f; '**snob·ber·y** (e)snobismo m; '**snob·bish** □ (e)snob, (e)snobista.

snoop [snuːp] sl. 1. curiosear, fisgonear, ventear; 2. fisgón (-a f) m.

snoot·y ['snuːti] F fachendón.

snooze [snuːz] F 1. siestecita f, sueñecillo m; 2. dormitar.

snore [snɔː] 1. ronquido m (a. '**snor·ing**); 2. roncar.

snort [snɔːt] 1. bufido m; 2. bufar.

snot [snɔt] F mocarro m; '**snot·ty** F mocoso; sl. insolente.

snout [snaut] hocico m, morro m.

snow [snou] 1. nieve f; sl. cocaína f; 2. nevar; sl. engañar; '**~·ball** 1. bola f de nieve; 2. fig. aumentar progresivamente; '**~·bound** aprisionado por la nieve; '**~·drift** ventisquero m; '**~·drop** campanilla f blanca; '**~·fall** nevada f; '**~·flake** copo m de nieve; sl.: '**~·job** decepción f; engaño m; '**~·man** figura f de nieve; '**~·plow** (máquina f) quitanieves m; '**~·shoe** raqueta f de nieve; '**~·storm** nevasca f; '**~ tire** llanta f de invierno; '**snow·'white** níveo; '**snow·y** □ nevoso; fig. níveo.

snub [snʌb] 1. desairar; 2. desaire m; '**snub-nosed** chato.

snuff [snʌf] 1. rapé m, tabaco m en polvo; 2. aspirar, sorber por la nariz (a. take ~); candle despabilar; fig. extinguir.

snug [snʌg] □ cómodo; abrigo; dress ajustado; '**snug·gle** ['~l] arrimarse (up to a); apretarse (para calentarse).

so [sou] así; por tanto, por consiguiente; (and ~) conque; ~ much tanto; ~ many tantos; I think ~ creo que sí; ~ as to, ~ that (purpose) para inf., para que subj.; (result) de modo que.

soak [souk] 1. remojar(se), empapar (-se); sl. desplumar, clavar un precio exorbitante a; 2. F borrachín m; '**soak·ing** remojón m.

so-and-so ['souənsou] (p.) fulano (a f) m; F tío m; Mr ♀ Don Fulano (de Tal).

soap [soup] 1. jabón m; soft ~ sl. coba f; 2. (en)jabonar; '**~·box** fig. caja f vacía empleada como tribuna (en la calle); '**~ dish** jabonera f; '**~ op·er·a** sl. serial m radiofónico (chabacano); telenovela f; serial m lacrimógeno; '**~ suds** pl. jabonaduras f/pl.; '**soap·y** □ jabonoso.

soar [sɔː] encumbrarse (*a. fig.*); cernerse; volar a gran altura.

sob [sɔb] 1. sollozo *m*; 2. sollozar.

so·ber ['soubə] 1. □ sobrio; serio; (*sensible*) cuerdo; moderado; (*not drunk*) no embriagado; 2. calmar(se) (*a. ~ down*); F ~ *up* desintoxicar(se).

so-called ['sou'kɔːld] llamado.

soc·cer ['sɔkə] F fútbol *m*.

so·cia·ble ['souʃəbl] □ sociable.

so·cial ['souʃl] 1. □ social; ~ *democrat* socialdemócrata *m/f*; 2. reunión *f* (social), velada *f*; **'so·cial·ism** socialismo *m*; **'so·cial·ist** socialista *adj. a. su. m*; **'so·cial·ize** socializar; **'So·cial Se'cu·ri·ty** Seguro *m* Social.

so·ci·e·ty [sə'saiəti] sociedad *f*; asociación *f*; (*high ~*) buena sociedad *f*.

so·ci·o·log·i·cal [sousiə'lɔdʒikl] □ sociológico; **so·ci·ol·o·gy** sociología *f*.

sock[1] [sɔk] calcetín *m*.

sock[2] [~] *sl.* 1. tortazo *m*; golpe *m* fuerte; 2. pegar; golpear con fuerza.

sock·et ['sɔkit] cuenca *f of eye*; alvéolo *m of tooth*; ⚡, ⊕ enchufe *m*.

sod [sɔd] césped *m*, terrón *m*.

so·da ['soudə] sosa *f*, soda *f* (*a. drink*); '~ **foun·tain** fuente *f* de sodas; '~ **wa·ter** agua *f* de seltz.

sod·den ['sɔdn] empapado, saturado.

so·di·um ['soudjəm] sodio *m*.

so·fa ['soufə] sofá *m*.

soft [sɔft] 1. □ blando; muelle; suave; *water* blando; *metal* dúctil; F *heart* tierno; F *job* fácil; 2. (*a. ~ly*) suavemente, blandamente *etc.*; **soft·en** ['sɔfn] ablandar(se); reblandecer; **'soft·ness** ['sɔftnis] blandura *f*; suavidad *f*; molicie *f*; **'soft·ware** programas *m/pl.* (u operaciones *f/pl.*) de computadoras.

sog·gy ['sɔgi] empapado; esponjoso.

soil[1] [sɔil] tierra *f* (*a. fig.*), suelo *m*.

soil[2] [~] ensuciar(se); manchar(se).

so·journ ['sɔdʒəːn] 1. permanencia *f*, estancia *f*; 2. pasar una temporada.

sol·ace ['sɔləs] 1. consuelo *m*; 2. consolar.

so·lar ['soulə] solar; ~ *battery* fotopila *f*.

sold [sould] *pret. a. p.p. of sell*.

sol·der ['sɔldə] 1. soldadura *f*; 2. soldar; **sol·der·ing-i·ron** ['~riŋaiən] soldador *m*.

sol·dier ['souldʒə] soldado *m*; **'sol·dier·like**, **'sol·dier·ly** militar.

sole[1] [soul] □ único, solo; exclusivo.

sole[2] [~] suela *f*; planta *f*.

sole[3] [~] *ichth.* lenguado *m*.

sol·emn ['sɔləm] □ solemne; **so·lem·ni·ty** [sə'lemniti] solemnidad *f*; **'sol·em·nize** solemnizar.

so·lic·it [sə'lisit] solicitar; importunar; intentar seducir; **so·lic·i·tor** ⚖ *approx.* abogado *m*; procurador *m*; (*oaths, wills etc.*) notario *m*; **so·lic·it·ous** □ solícito (*about, for* por); ansioso; **so·lic·i·tude** [~tjuːd] solicitud *f*, ansiedad *f*.

sol·id ['sɔlid] 1. □ sólido (*a. fig.*, Ⓐ); *gold, tire etc.* macizo; *crowd* denso; *vote* unánime; Ⓐ ~ *geometry* geometría *f* del espacio; 2. sólido *m*; **sol·i·dar·i·ty** [~'dæriti] solidaridad *f*; **so·lid·i·fy** [~fai] solidificar(se); **'sol·id-state** transistorizado.

so·lil·o·quy [sə'liləkwi] soliloquio *m*.

sol·i·taire [sɔli'tɛə] solitario *m* (*game, gem*); **sol·i·tar·y** ['~təri] □ solitario; retirado; único; **sol·i·tude** [~tjuːd] soledad *f*.

so·lo ['soulou] ♪, *cards*: solo *m*; **'so·lo·ist** solista *m*.

sol·u·ble ['sɔljubl] soluble.

so·lu·tion [sə'luːʃn] *all senses*: solución *f*.

solv·a·ble ['sɔlvəbl] soluble; **solve** [sɔlv] resolver; solucionar; *riddle* adivinar; **'sol·vent** solvente.

som·ber, **som·bre** ['sɔmbə] □ sombrío.

some [sʌm, *unstressed* səm] 1. *pron. a. adj.* un poco (de); alguno(s); unos; ciertos; *for* ~ *reason (or other)* por alguna que otra razón, por no sé qué razón; 2. *adv.* algo; F muy, mucho; '~**bod·y**, '~**one** alguien; F *be* ~ ser un personaje; '~**how** de algún modo; ~ *or other* de un modo u otro.

some...: ~**thing** ['sʌmθiŋ] algo; alguna cosa; ~ *else* otra cosa; ~**times** [~z] algunas veces; a veces; '~**what** algo, algún tanto; '~**where** en (*motion a*) alguna parte; ~ *else* en (*motion a*) otra parte.

som·nam·bu·lism [sɔm'næmbjulizm] somnambulismo *m*; **som·nam·bu·list** somnámbulo (a *f*) *m*.

son [sʌn] hijo *m*.

so·na·ta [sə'nɑːtə] sonata *f*.

song [sɔŋ] canción *f*; canto *m*; cantar *m*; F ~ *and dance* alharaca *f*; '~**bird** pájaro *m* cantor; '~ **book** cancionero *m*; '~ **hit** canción *f* de moda.

son·ic bar·ri·er ['sɔnik 'bæriə] barrera f del sonido; '~ **boom** estampido m sónico.

son-in-law ['sʌninlɔ:] yerno m, hijo m político.

son·net ['sɔnit] soneto m.

son·ny ['sʌni] F hijito m.

so·no·rous [sə'nɔ:rəs] □ sonoro, resonante.

soon [su:n] pronto, temprano; ~ *after* poco después; *as* (*or* so) ~ *as* tan pronto como (*a. cj.*), luego que; *as* ~ *as possible* cuanto antes; '**soon·er** más temprano; ~ *or later* tarde o temprano.

soot [sut] hollín m.

soothe [su:ð] calmar; aliviar; '**sooth·ing** □ calmante; tranquilizador.

soot·y ['suti] □ holliniento.

sop [sɔp] 1. sopa f; 2. empapar; ~ *up* absorber.

soph·ist ['sɔfist] sofista m; **so·phis·tic, so·phis·ti·cal** [sə'fistik(l)] □ sofístico; **so'phis·ti·cat·ed** □ sofisticado.

soph·o·more ['sɔfəmɔ:] estudiante m/f de segundo año.

sop·ping ['sɔpiŋ]: ~ *wet* hecho una sopa.

so·pran·o [sə'prɑ:nou] soprano f, tiple f.

sor·cer·er ['sɔ:sərə] hechicero m, brujo m; '**sor·cer·y** brujería f.

sor·did ['sɔ:did] □ asqueroso; vil.

sore [sɔ:] 1. □ dolorido; doloroso; sensible; inflamado; 2. llaga f (*a. fig.*), úlcera f; '**sore·head** F persona f resentida; '**sore·ness** dolor m; inflamación f.

so·ror·i·ty [sə'rɔriti] *univ.* hermandad f (de estudiantas).

sor·row ['sɔrou] 1. pesar m, dolor m, pena f; 2. apenarse, afligirse; '**sor·row·ful** ['~ful] □ afligido.

sor·ry ['sɔri] □ pesaroso, apesadumbrado; apenado; arrepentido (*for th.* de); *condition, plight* desastrado, lastimoso; *be* ~ sentirlo; *be* ~ *for p.* compadecer; *be* ~ *that* sentir que *subj.*; *be* ~ *to inf.* sentir *inf.*; (*I am*) (*so*) ~! lo siento (mucho).

sort [sɔ:t] 1. clase f, especie f; *a* ~ *of* una a modo de; *in some* ~, F ~ *of* algo; en cierta medida; *of all* ~ *s* de toda clase; *something of the* ~, *that* ~ *of thing* algo por el estilo; *of* ~ *s* de poco valor; 2. clasificar (*a. ~ out*); escoger; separar.

so-so ['sousou] F regular.

sought [sɔ:t] *pret. a. p.p. of* seek; '~**'aft·er** solicitado.

soul [soul] alma f (*a. fig.*); *upon my* ~! ¡por vida mía!; '**soul·ful** □ sentimental; conmovedor.

sound¹ [saund] □ sano; firme, sólido; *opinion* razonable, bien fundado, ortodoxo.

sound² [~] 1. sonido m; son m; ruido m; *I don't like the* ~ *of it* no me gusta la idea; *me inquieta la noticia*; ~ *barrier* barrera f del sonido; ~ *track film:* banda f sonora; ~ *wave* onda f sonora; 2. *v/i.* (re)sonar; (*seem*) parecer; *v/t.* sonar; tocar; *alarm* dar la voz de.

sound³ [~] 1. ♪ sonda f; 2. ⚓, ♪ sondar; *chest* auscultar.

sound·less ['saundlis] □ silencioso; ⊕ insonorizado.

sound·ness ['saundnis] firmeza f, solidez f *etc.*

sound·proof ['saundpru:f] insonorizado.

soup [su:p] (*thin*) caldo m, consomé m; (*thick*) puré m, sopa f.

sour ['sauə] 1. □ agrio; acre (*a. fig.*); *milk* cortado; 2. agriar(se).

source [sɔ:s] fuente f, nacimiento m *of river*; *fig.* fuente f; procedencia f.

sour·ish ['sauəriʃ] agrete; '**sour·ness** agrura f (*a. fig.*); acidez f; '**sour·puss** *sl.* cascarrabias m/f.

souse [saus] 1. escabechar; *sl.* ~ *d* ajumado; 2. escabeche m.

south [sauθ] 1. sur m, mediodía m; 2. *adj.* del sur, meridional; 3. *adv.* al sur, hacia el sur.

South A·mer·i·can ['sauθ ə'merikən] sudamericano.

south...: '~'**east** sudeste *adj.* (*a.* '~·**east·er·ly**, '~·**east·ern**) *a. su. m.*

south·er·ly ['sʌðəli] *direction* hacia el sur; *wind* del sur; '**south·ern** [~ən] meridional.

south·paw ['sauθpɔ:] jugador m zurdo; lanzador m zurdo.

south...: '~'**west** suroeste; '~·**west·er** (*wind*) suroeste m.

sou·ve·nir ['su:vəniə] recuerdo m.

sov·er·eign ['sɔvrin] soberano *adj. a. su. m* (*a f.*).

so·vi·et ['souviet] 1. soviet m; 2. soviético.

sow¹ [sau] *zo.* cerda f.

sow² [sou] [*irr.*] sembrar (*a. fig.*); esparcir; plagar *with mines*; '**sow·er** sembrador (-a f) m; '**sow·ing** siembra f.

soy bean ['sɔi 'bi:n] soja f; semilla f de soja.

space [speis] **1.** espacio *m* (*a. typ.*); ~ *helmet* casco *m* sideral; **2.** (*a. ~ out*) espaciar (*a. typ.*); '~**ship** nave *f* espacial, astronave *f*; '~**shut·tle** astronave *f* dirigible; '~**sta·tion** apostadero *m* espacial; '~**suit** escafandra *f* espacial.

spa·cious ['speiʃəs] □ espacioso; *room* amplio; *living* holgado.

spade [speid] laya *f*, pala *f*; *cards:* ~s *pl.* picos *m/pl.*, pique *m*, (*Spanish*) espadas *f/pl.*

spag·het·ti [spəɡ'eti] *approx.* fideos *m/pl.*; espagueti *m*.

span [spæn] **1.** palmo *m* of hand; ojo *m* of bridge; ≶ envergadura *f*; *fig.* extensión *f*, duración *f*; **2.** (*bridge*) extenderse sobre; tender (un puente) sobre.

span·gle ['spæŋɡl] **1.** lentejuela *f*; **2.** adornar con lentejuelas.

Span·iard ['spænjəd] español (-a *f*) *m*.

span·iel ['spænjəl] perro *m* de aguas.

Span·ish ['spæniʃ] español *adj. a. su. m.*

spank [spæŋk] F **1.** zurrar; manotear; **2.** manotada *f*; '**spank·ing** F zurra *f*.

spar [spɑ:] *boxing:* hacer fintas; amagar (*at* a) (*a. fig.*).

spare [spɛə] **1.** □ (*lean*) enjuto; (*left over*) sobrante; *room* disponible; *para convidados*; *time* libre, desocupado; *part* de repuesto; **2.** ⊕ (pieza *f* de) repuesto *m* (or recambio *f*); **3.** ahorrar, economizar; pasarse sin; dispensar de, excusar.

spar·ing ['spɛəriŋ] □ escaso; parco (*in*, of en); económico.

spark [spɑ:k] **1.** chispa *f*; *fig.* chispazo *m* of wit; átomo *m* of life; **2.** chispear.

spar·kle ['spɑ:kl] **1.** centelleo *m*, destello *m*; *fig.* viveza *f*; **2.** centellear, chispear; relucir; '**spar·kling** centelleante; chispeante.

spark plug ['spɑ:k plʌɡ] bujía *f*.

spar·row ['spærou] gorrión *m*.

sparse [spɑ:s] □ disperso; escaso; *hair* ralo.

spasm ['spæzm] ⚕ espasmo *m*; *fig.* arranque *m*; **spas·mod·ic** espasmódico.

spat [spæt] disputa *f*; riña *f*.

spa·tial ['speiʃl] □ espacial.

spat·ter ['spætə] salpicar, rociar.

spawn [spɔːn] **1.** freza *f*, huevas *f/pl.*; *fig.* prole *f*; **2.** *v/i.* desovar, frezar; *v/t. contp.* engendrar.

speak [spiːk] [*irr.*] hablar (*to* con, a);

truth decir; *parl. etc.* hacer uso de la palabra; ~ *out* hablar claro; *osar hablar*; ~ *up* hablar alto; ~ *up!* ¡más fuerte!; '~**eas·y** *sl.* taberna *f* clandestina; '**speak·er** orador (-a *f*) *m*; hablante *m/f* of language; *parl.* presidente *m*; *radio:* (*loud-*) altavoz *m*.

speak·ing ['spiːkiŋ] hablante; '~**tube** tubo *m* acústico.

spear [spiə] **1.** lanza *f*; (*fishing-*) arpón *m*; **2.** alancear, herir con lanza; '~**head 1.** punta *f* de lanza (*a. fig.*); **2.** encabezar; dar impulso a.

spe·cial ['speʃl] **1.** □ especial, particular; **2.** *approx.* guardia *m* auxiliar, F oferta *f* extraordinaria; plato *m* del día; **spe·cial·ize** ['speʃəlaiz] especializarse; **spe·cial·ty** ['~ʃlti] ⚖ contrato *m* sellado; especialidad *f*.

spe·cies ['spiːʃiːz] *sg. a. pl.* especie *f*.

spe·cif·ic [spi'sifik] □ específico *adj.* (*all senses*) *a. su. m.*; expreso.

spec·i·fi·ca·tion [spesifi'keiʃn] especificación *f*; plan *m* detallado; **spec·i·fy** ['~fai] especificar; designar (en un plan).

spec·i·men ['spesimin] espécimen *m*, ejemplar *m*.

speck [spek] manchita *f*, mota *f*; grano *m* of dust; partícula *f*; **speck·le** ['~kl] **1.** punto *m*, mota *f*; **2.** motear, salpicar de manchitas.

specs [speks] F gafas *f/pl.*

spec·ta·cle ['spektəkl] espectáculo *m*; (*a pairs of unas*) ~s *pl.* gafas *f/pl.*, anteojos *m/pl.*

spec·tac·u·lar [spek'tækjulə] □ espectacular; aparatoso.

spec·ta·tor [spek'teitə] espectador.

spec·trum ['spektrəm] *opt.* espectro *m*.

spec·u·late ['spekjuleit] especular (*on* en); † *in* sobre).

spec·u·lum ['spekjuləm] ⚕ espéculo *m*; *opt.* espejo *m* (metálico).

sped [sped] *pret. a. p.p.* of speed 2.

speech [spiːtʃ] (*faculty*) habla *f*; idioma *m*; (*style, manner*) lenguaje *m*; (*oration*) discurso *m*, *thea.*, ⚖ parlamento *m*; '**speech·less** □ mudo; estupefacto.

speed [spiːd] **1.** velocidad *f* (*a.* ⊕, *mot.*); prisa *f*, presteza *f*; *at full* ~ a máxima velocidad, a todo máquina; **2.** *v/i.* apresurarse, darse prisa; *mot.* exceder la velocidad permitida; *v/t.* ~ *up* ⊕ acelerar; *p.* dar prisa a; *process* activar; '~**boat** lancha *f* rápida; **speed lim·it** velocidad *f* máxima permitida; límite *m* de velocidad; **speed·om·e·ter** [spi'dɔmitə] velocímetro *m*, cuentakilómetros *m*; **'speed·way** carretera *f* para carreras; **'speed·y** □ veloz, rápido; *answer* pronto.

spell[1] [spel] 1. tanda *f*, turno *m* of *work*; rato *m*, temporada *f*; 2. reemplazar; relevar.

spell[2] [~] 1. encanto *m*, hechizo *m*; 2. *(irr.) word* escribir; ~ out deletrear; **'~bind·er** F orador *m* fascinante; **'~bound** *fig.* embelesado, hechizado; **'spell·er**: be a bad ~ no saber escribir correctamente las palabras; F abecedario *m*.

spell·ing ['spelin] ortografía *f*; **'~ bee** certamen *m* de ortografía; **'~ book** abecedario *m*.

spelt [spelt] *pret. a. p.p.* of spell[2] 2.

spend [spend] *[irr.] v/t. money, effort* gastar; *time* pasar; *anger (v/r.)* consumir(se); *v/i.* gastar dinero; **'~ing mon·ey** dinero *m* para gastos menudos.

spend·thrift ['spendθrift] derrochador (-a *f*) *m*, pródigo *m*.

spent [spent] 1. *pret. a. p.p.* of spend; 2. *adj.* agotado; gastado.

sperm [spɔːm] esperma *f*; **sper·ma·to·zo·on** [~ətou'zouɔn], *pl.* **sper·ma·to·zo·a** [~'zouə] espermatozoo *m*.

sperm whale ['spɔːm'weil] cachalote *m*.

sphere [sfiə] esfera *f* (*a. fig.*); **spher·i·cal** ['sferikl] □ esférico.

sphinx [sfiŋks] esfinge *f*.

spice [spais] 1. especia *f*; *fig.* picante *m*; aliciente *m*; 2. condimentar.

spick-and-span ['spikən'spæn] impecablemente limpio; pulcro.

spic·y ['spaisi] □ especiado; picante.

spi·der ['spaidə] araña *f*; **~'s web** telaraña *f*.

spig·ot ['spigət] espita *f* of cask.

spike [spaik] 1. pincho *m*, púa *f*; escarpia *f*, espigón *m*; 2. sujetar con pincho *etc.*; *gun* clavar.

spill [spil] 1. *[irr.]* derramar(se); verter(se); 2. caída *f* from horse; vuelco *m*.

spill·way ['spilwei] derramadero *m*; bocacaz *m*.

spin [spin] 1. *[irr.] thread* hilar; (*a. ~ round*) girar, hacer girar; *top* (hacer) bailar; ~ out alargar; 2. vuelta *f*; ✈ barrena *f*; F paseo *m* en coche *etc.*

spin·ach ['spinidʒ] espinaca *f*.

spi·nal ['spainl] espinal; ~ column columna *f* vertebral.

spin·dle ['spindl] (*spinning-*) huso *m*; ⊕ eje *m*.

spin-dri·er ['spin'draiə] secador *m* centrífugo.

spine [spain] *anat.* espinazo *m*; *zo.* púa *f*; ♀ espina *f*; **'spine·less** □ *fig.* flojo, falto de voluntad.

spin·ner ['spinə] hilandero (a *f*) *m*.

spin·ning...: **~ mill** hilandería *f*; **~ top** peonza *f*; **~ wheel** torno *m* de hilar.

spin...: **'~off** ⊕, ✝ byproduct, derivative rendir; **'~-off** ⊕, ✝ derivado *m*; subproducto *m*.

spin·ster ['spinstə] soltera *f*; *contp.* solterona *f*.

spin·y ['spaini] espinoso (*a. fig.*).

spi·ral ['spaiərəl] 1. □ (en) espiral; helicoidal; 2. espiral *f*, hélice *f*; 3. dar vueltas en espiral.

spire ['spaiə] aguja *f*; chapitel *m*.

spir·it ['spirit] 1. espíritu *m*; ánimo *m*; brío *m*; temple *m*, humor *m*; espectro *m*; 🜊 alcohol *m*; in (high) ~s animado; in low ~s abatido; 2. ~ away, ~ off hacer desaparecer, llevarse misteriosamente.

spir·it·ed ['spiritid] □ animoso, brioso; *horse* fogoso.

spir·it·less ['spiritlis] □ apocado, sin ánimo.

spir·it·u·al ['spiritjuəl] 1. □ espiritual; 2. tonada *f* espiritual; **'spir·it·u·al·ism** espiritualismo.

spit[1] [spit] espetón *m*, asador *m*.

spit[2] [~] 1. saliva *f*; 2. *[irr.] v/i.* escupir (*at a, on en*); *(cat)* bufar; *v/t.* (*mst ~ out*) escupir.

spite [spait] 1. rencor *m*, ojeriza *f*, despecho *m*; in ~ of a pesar de, a despecho de; 2. causar pena a.

spite·ful ['spaitful] □ rencoroso, malévolo; **'spite·ful·ness** rencor *m*, malevolencia *f*.

spit·fire ['spitfaiə] fierabrás *m*.

spit·toon [spi'tuːn] escupidera *f*.

splash [splæʃ] 1. salpicadura *f*, rociada *f*; mancha *f* of color; F make a ~ impresionar; 2. *v/t.* salpicar; *v/i.* chapotear (*a. ~ about*); F ~ out derrochar dinero; **'~down** (*astronave*) aterrizaje *m* en la mar; **'splash·y** □ fangoso; llamativo.

spleen [spliːn] *anat.* bazo *m*; *fig.* esplín *m*, spleen *m*; rencor *m*.

splen·did ['splendid] □ espléndido.

splen·dor ['~də] esplendor *m*, brillantez *f*.

splice [splais] 1. empalme *m*; ⊕

splint

(*wood*) junta *f*; 2. empalmar; ⊕ juntar; *sl.* casar.

splint [splint] 1. tablilla *f*; 2. entablillar.

splin·ter ['splintə] 1. astilla *f*; ~ group grupo *m* disidente, facción *f*; 2. astillar(se), hacer(se) astillas.

split [split] 1. hendedura *f*, raja *f*, *fig.* división *f*; cisma *m*; 2. partido; hendido; *fig.* dividido; 3. partir(se); hender(se), rajarse; dividir(se); *sl.* irse; huir; **'split·ting** *headache* enloquecedor.

splotch [splɔtʃ] borrón *m*, mancha *f*.

splurge [splə:dʒ] F 1. fachenda *f*; 2. fachendear.

splut·ter ['splʌtə] 1. farfulla *f* *of speech*; ⊕ chisporroteo *m*; 2. (*p.*) farfullar; ⊕ chisporrotear.

spoil [spɔil] 1. (*mst* ~*s pl.*) despojo *m*, botín *m*; *pol.* ~*s system* enchufismo *m*; 2. [*irr.*] echar(se) a perder; estropear(se); dañar(se); *child* mimar; **'spoil·sport** aguafiestas *m/f.*

spoke [spouk] rayo *m*, radio *m*.

spo·ken ['spoukən] *p.p. of* speak.

spokes·man ['spouksmən] portavoz *m*; vocero *m*.

sponge [spʌndʒ] 1. esponja *f*; (*a.* ~ *cake*) bizcocho *m*; *boxing* etc. *fig.*: *throw in the* ~ darse por vencido; 2. lavar con esponja; *F* vivir de gorra; ~ *up* absorber; **'spong·er** F gorrón *m*, sablista *m/f.*

spon·gy ['spʌndʒi] esponjoso.

spon·sor ['spɔnsə] 1. patrocinador *m*; ✝ fiador *m*; 2. patrocinar; **sponsor·ship** ['~ʃip] patrocinio *m.*

spon·ta·ne·i·ty [spɔntə'niːiti] espontaneidad *f*; **spon·ta·ne·ous** [~'teiniəs] □ *all senses:* espontáneo.

spoof [spuːf] *sl.* 1. *v/t.* engañar; *v/i.* bromear; 2. engaño *m*; broma *f.*

spook [spuːk] F espectro *m*; **'~·y** horripilante.

spool [spuːl] carrete *m*; canilla *f.*

spoon [spuːn] 1. cuchara *f*; 2. cucharear (*a.* ~ *out*); *sl.* besuquearse; **'spoon-fed** *fig.* muy mimado; **'spoon·ful** [~'ful] cucharad(it)a *f.*

spo·rad·ic [spə'rædik] □ esporádico.

sport [spɔːt] 1. deporte *m*; juego *m*, diversión *f*; juguete *m*; ~*s pl.* juegos *m/pl.* (atléticos); 2. *v/i.* divertirse; juguetear; *v/t. clothes* lucir; **'sport·ing** □ deportivo; *gun* de caza; *offer* arriesgado; **'spor·tive** □ juguetón; **sports·man** ['~smən] deportista *m*;

persona *f* honrada; **'sports·wear** trajes *m/pl.* de deporte.

spot [spɔt] 1. (*place*) sitio *m*, lugar *m*; (*mark*) punto *m*; (*stain*) mancha *f*; lunar *m*; F ten ~ billete *m* de 10 dólares; *F a* ~ *of* un poco de; *on the* ~ en el acto; al punto; *sl.* (*put*) *on the* ~ (poner) en un aprieto; 2. ✝ contante; 3. manchar(se); salpicar; F notar, observar; descubrir; **'spot·less** □ nítido; sin manchas; inmaculado; **'spot·less·ness** nitidez *f*; **'spot·light** arco *m*, proyector *m*; *mot.* faro *m* auxiliar; **'spot·ted** manchado; moteado; **'spot·ter** observador *m*; **'spot·ty** manchado (*face* de granos).

spouse [spauz] cónyuge *m/f.*

spout [spaut] 1. pico *m*; pitón *m*; caño *m*; chorro *m* *of water*; 2. *v/t.* arrojar (en chorro); F declarar; *v/i.* chorrear.

sprain [sprein] 1. torcedura *f*; 2. torcer(se).

sprang [spræŋ] *pret. of* spring 2.

sprawl [sprɔːl] arrellanarse; tumbarse; (♧, *town*) extenderse.

spray [sprei] 1. rociada *f*, ⚓ espuma *f*; 2. rociar; regar; pulverizar.

spread [spred] 1. [*irr.*] extender(se); esparcir(se), desparramar(se); propagar(se), difundir(se); *butter* untar; 2. extensión *f*; propagación *f*, difusión *f*; ✝ diferencia *f*; envergadura *f* *of wings*; **'~·ea·gled** con los miembros extendidos.

spree [spriː] F juerga *f*, parranda *f*; *go on the* ~ ir de juerga.

sprig [sprig] ramita *f*; ⊕ puntilla *f.*

spright·li·ness ['spraitlinis] viveza *f*; **'spright·ly** vivo, animado.

spring [spriŋ] 1. (*season*) primavera *f*; (*water*) fuente *f*, manantial *m*; (*jump*) salto *m*, brinco *m*; ⊕ muelle *m*; 2. *v/t.* *trap* hacer saltar; *mine* volar; ⚓ ~ *a leak* abrirse una (vía de) agua; ~ *a th.* (*up*)*on a p.* espetarle algo a alguien; *v/i.* saltar (*over acc.*); brincar; moverse rápidamente; brotar; ~ *up* levantarse de un salto; ♧, *fig.* brotar; (*breeze*) levantarse de pronto; 3. primaveral; ⊕ de muelle; **'~·board** trampolín *m*; **'~·clean·ing** limpieza *f* en primavera.

spring·i·ness ['spriŋinis] elasticidad *f*; **spring mat·tress** somier *m*; **'spring·time** primavera *f*; **'spring·y** □ elástico; *turf* muelle.

sprin·kle ['spriŋkl] *v/t.* salpicar, rociar (*with* de); asperjar *with holy* water; v/i. (*rain*) lloviznar; **'sprin-kler** regadera f; **'sprin·kling** rociada f; aspersión f; salpicadura f.

sprint [sprint] **1.** sprint m; **2.** sprintar; **'sprint·er** esprínter m.

sprite [sprait] duende m, hada f.

sprock·et ['sprɔkit] rueda f de cadena.

sprout [spraut] v/i. brotar, germinar; crecer rápidamente; v/t. echar, hacerse; **2.** vástago m.

spruce [spruːs] ♀ pícea f (a ~ *fir*).

sprung [sprʌŋ] *pret.* (†) a. *p.p. of* spring 1.

spry [sprai] ágil, activo.

spun [spʌn] *pret. a. p.p. of* spin 1.

spunk [spʌŋk] coraje m, ánimo m; **'spunk·y** animoso.

spur [spɔː] **1.** espuela f (a. *fig.*); zo. espolón m; *geog.* estribo m; *fig.* estímulo m, aguijón m; **2.** espolear; ~ *on* estimular.

spurge [spɔːdʒ] euforbio m.

spu·ri·ous ['spjuəriəs] □ espurio, falso; **'spu·ri·ous·ness** falsedad f.

spurn [spɔːn] desdeñar, rechazar.

spurt [spɔːt] **1.** chorreada f; *sport etc.* esfuerzo m supremo; **2.** salir a chorros; hacer un esfuerzo supremo.

sput·nik ['sputnik] sputnik m; satélite m artificial.

spy [spai] **1.** espía m/f; **2.** espiar (*on acc.*); columbrar, divisar; ~ *out land* reconocer; **'~·glass** catalejo m.

squab·ble ['skwɔbl] **1.** riña f, disputa f; **2.** reñir, disputar.

squad [skwɔd] escuadra f, pelotón m; **squad·ron** ['~rən] ⚔ escuadrón m; ✈ escuadrilla f; ⚓ escuadra f.

squal·id ['skwɔlid] □ miserable, sucio; mezquino.

squall [skwɔːl] ⚓ ráfaga f, racha f, chubasco m; **'squall·y** chubascoso.

squal·or ['skwɔlə] suciedad f.

squan·der ['skwɔndə] malgastar.

square [skweə] **1.** cuadrado (*measure, mile,* ⚗ *root, etc.*); en ángulo recto (*to, with* con); *p.* honrado; *meal* abundante; F ~ *shooter* persona f honrada; *2 feet* ~ 2 pies en cuadro; **2.** cuadrado m (a. ⚗); cuadro m (a. ⚗); △, ⊕ escuadra f; plaza f (*in town*); **3.** cuadrar (a. ⚗); △, ⊕ escuadrar; ajustar (*with* con; a. ↑); **'~·ly** *adv.* honradamente; directamente.

squash [skwɔʃ] **1.** aplastamiento m; ♀ calabaza f; frontón m con raqueta; **2.** aplastar; apretar, apiñar.

squat [skwɔt] **1.** *p.* rechoncho; *build-*

ing desproporcionadamente bajo; **2.** agacharse, sentarse en cuclillas; *sl.* establecerse (sin derecho) *on property*; **'squat·ter** colono m usurpador.

squaw [skwɔː] india f norteamericana.

squawk [skwɔːk] **1.** graznar, chillar; **2.** graznido m, chillido m.

squeak [skwiːk] **1.** chirriar, rechinar; **2.** chirrido m; **'squeak·y** □ chirriador.

squeal [skwiːl] **1.** chillido m; **2.** chillar; *sl.* cantar; delatar (*on* a).

squeam·ish ['skwiːmiʃ] □ remilgado, escrupuloso, delicado.

squee·gee ['skwiːdʒiː] enjugador m de goma (a. *phot.*).

squeeze [skwiːz] **1.** apretar, estrujar; oprimir; ~ *out* exprimir; **2.** estrujón m, estrujadura f; presión f; apretón m of hand; ✝ restricción f of credit; **'squeez·er** exprimidor m.

squelch [skwseltʃ] F despachurrar.

squid [skwid] calamar m.

squint [skwint] **1.** bizquear; cerrar casi los ojos; **2.** estrabismo m; mirada f bizca.

squirm [skwɔːm] retorcerse.

squir·rel ['skwirəl] ardilla f.

squirt [skwɔːt] **1.** chorro m; jeringazo m; **2.** v/t. jeringar; arrojar a chorros; v/i. salir a chorros.

stab [stæb] **1.** puñalada f; F tentativa f; **2.** apuñalar.

sta·bil·i·ty [stə'biliti] estabilidad f.

sta·bi·lize ['steibilaiz] estabilizar; **'sta·bi·liz·er** estabilizador m.

sta·ble ['steibl] □ estable.

sta·ble [~] **1.** establo m; (*racing*) caballeriza f; **2.** poner (*or* guardar) en una cuadra.

stack [stæk] **1.** hacina f; montón m, pila f; cañón m of chimney; **2.** ⚡ hacinar; amontonar.

sta·di·um ['steidiəm] estadio m.

staff [stɑːf] **1.** bastón m; palo m; ♪ pentagrama m; ⚔ estado m mayor; personal m of office; **2.** proveer de personal.

stag [stæg] zo. ciervo m, venado m; F soltero m.

stage [steidʒ] **1.** plataforma f, estrado m, tablado m; *thea.* escena f; (*stop*) parada f; posta f; fase f, etapa f of progress; **2.** play representar; **'~·box** palco m de proscenio; **'~·coach** diligencia f; ~ **fright** miedo m al público; **'~·hand** tramoyista m; ~ **man-**

ag·er director m de escena; '∼**struck** loco por el teatro.

stag·ger ['stægə] 1. v/i. tambalear, titubear; v/t. asombrar, sorprender; 2. tambaleo m; '**stag·ger·ing** □ titubeante; fig. asombroso.

stag·nant ['stægnənt] □ estancado (a. fig.); paralizado; ✝ inactivo; **stag·nate** ['∼neit] estancarse; paralizarse.

stag par·ty ['stægpɑːti] F tertulia f de solteros.

staid [steid] □ serio, formal; '**staid·ness** seriedad f.

stain [stein] 1. mancha f (a. fig.); tinte m, tintura f (a. ⊕); 2. manchar(se) (a. fig.); teñir; ⊕ inoxidable.

stair [steə] peldaño m, escalón m; (flight of tramo de m) ∼s pl. escalera f; '**∼·case**, a. '**∼·way** escalera f; moving ∼ escalera f móvil.

stake [steik] 1. estaca f, poste m; (bet) (a)puesta f; fig. interés m; 2. (bet) apostar (on a); ✝ aventurar.

stale [steil] food rancio, añejo, pasado; bread duro.

stale·mate ['steilmeit] 1. chess: tablas f/pl. por ahogo; fig. paralización f; 2. dar tablas por ahogo a; paralizar.

stalk[1] [stɔːk] ♀ tallo m; (cabbage-) troncho m.

stalk[2] [∼] v/i. andar con paso majestuoso; v/t. hunt. etc. cazar al acecho.

stall [stɔːl] 1. ♂ pesebre m; establo m; (market-) puesto m; 2. v/t. ⊕ parar, atascar; ♂ encerrar en establo; v/i. ⊕ pararse, atascarse.

stal·lion ['stæljən] caballo m padre.

stal·wart ['stɔːlwət] □ (sturdy) fornido; supporter etc. leal.

stam·i·na ['stæminə] vigor m, resistencia f.

stam·mer ['stæmə] 1. tartamudear, balbucir; 2. tartamudeo m, balbuceo m.

stamp [stæmp] 1. (postage-) sello m, estampilla f S.Am.; (fiscal) timbre m; marca f, impresión f; ⊕ cuño m; 2. v/i. patear; patalear disapprovingly; '∼ al·bum álbum m (para sellos); '∼ col·lect·ing filatelia f; '∼ pad tampón m.

stam·pede [stæm'piːd] 1. fuga f precipitada, estampida f S.Am.; 2. (hacer) huir en desorden.

stance [stɑːns] postura f.

stan·chion ['stɑːnʃn] puntal m, montante m.

stand [stænd] 1. [irr.] v/i. estar de pie; levantarse; (be situated) estar (situado); (remain) quedarse; (remain in force) mantenerse (en vigor); ∼ firm resistir, mantenerse firme; ∼ by estar alerta; estar cerca; estar a la expectativa; (abide by) atenerse a; ∼ for representar; significar; apoyar, apadrinar, F aguantar; ∼ out destacarse (against sky etc. contra); esp. fig. descollar, sobresalir; ∼ up levantarse, ponerse de pie; ∼ up for defender; ∼ up to resistir resueltamente a; test salir muy bien de; 2. [irr.] v/t. poner derecho; colocar; (bear) aguantar, soportar; examination resistir a; I can't ∼ him no lo puedo ver; 3. posición f, postura f; resistencia f; (stall) puesto m; quiosco m; sport: tribuna f; ⊕ sostén m, pedestal m; estante m; (taxi-) parada f, punto m; make a ∼ resistir (against a).

stand·ard ['stændəd] 1. patrón m, norma f, pauta f; nivel m; modelo m; (flag) estandarte m, bandera f; ∼ of living nivel m de vida; 2. normal; corriente; standard, estándar; ∼ measure medida f y tipo; '∼·bear·er abanderado m; fig. jefe m; caudillo m; ∼ gauge [∼geidʒ] vía f normal; '**stand·ard·ize** normalizar, regularizar, estandar(d)izar.

stand-by ['stændbai] 1. recurso m seguro, persona f confiable; 2. de sustituto; disponible; alternativo.

stand·ee [stæn'diː] espectador m que asiste de pie.

stand-in ['stændin] doble m/f.

stand·ing ['stændiŋ] 1. derecho, en (or de) pie; army, committee permanente; order vigente; 2. posición f; reputación f; importancia f; (of) long ∼ de mucho tiempo; '∼-room sitio m para estar de pie.

stand...: '∼-off reserva f; empate m; '∼-off·ish □ reservado; endiosado; poco amable; '∼-pipe columna f de alimentación; '∼-point punto m de vista; '∼ still parada f, paro m; alto m.

stank [stæŋk] pret. of stink 2.

stan·za ['stænzə] estancia f, estrofa f.

sta·ple[1] ['steipl] 1. producto m principal; materia f prima; fibra f (textil); 2. sujetar con grapas; 3. principal; corriente.

sta·ple[2] [∼] grapa f.

sta·pler ['steiplə] grapadora f; cosepapeles m.

star [stɑː] 1. estrella f (a. fig.); thea.

steam

estrella *f*, astro *m*; *typ.* asterisco *m*; *north* ~ estrella *f* polar; 2. *v/t.* adornar con estrellas; *v/i.* ser la estrella.

star·board ['stɑːbəd] 1. estribor *m*; 2. a estribor.

starch [stɑːtʃ] 1. almidón *m*; *biol.* fécula *f*; 2. almidonar; **'starch·y** □ feculento; *fig.* estirado, entonado.

star·dom ['stɑːdəm] fama *f* of an actor or comedian.

stare [steə] 1. mirada *f* fija; 2. mirar fijamente (*at* acc.).

star·fish ['stɑːfiʃ] *zo.* estrella *f* de mar.

stark [stɑːk] (*stiff*) rígido; (*sheer*) completo, puro; ~ *naked* en cueros.

star·ling ['stɑːliŋ] estornino *m* pinto.

star·ry ['stɑːri] estrellado; **'~·eyed** *fig.* inocentón, ingenuo.

star-span·gled ['stɑːspæŋgld]: ♀ *Banner* bandera *f* estrellada.

start [stɑːt] 1. comienzo *m*, principio *m*; (*departure*) salida *f* (*a.* of race); (*surprise*) sobresalto *m*; ~ *of horse*; 2. *v/i.* empezar, comenzar, principiar (*to* inf. or ger. *a* inf.); sobresaltarse, sobrecogerse *with surprise* (*at* a); (*motor*) arrancar; *v/t.* empezar, principiar, iniciar; *motor* arrancar.

start·er ['stɑːtə] *sport:* stárter *m*, juez *m* de salida; *mot.* arranque *m*.

start·ing ['stɑːtiŋ]: **'~ point** punto *m* de partida; **'~ post** poste *m* de salida; **'~ switch** botón *m* de arranque.

star·tle ['stɑːtl] asustar, sobrecoger; **'star·tling** □ alarmante; sorprendente.

star·va·tion [stɑːˈveiʃn] inanición *f*, hambre *f*; ~ *diet* régimen *m* de hambre; **starve** [stɑːv] *v/i.* morir de hambre; padecer hambre; F tener mucha hambre; *v/t.* morir de hambre.

state [steit] 1. estado *m* (*a.* pol.), condición *f*; pompa *f*, fausto *m*; 2. estatal; del estado; público; *occasion* de gala; ♀ *Department* Ministerio *m* de Asuntos Exteriores; 3. declarar, manifestar, afirmar; exponer; **'state·less** desnacionalizado; **'state·li·ness** majestad *f*, majestuosidad *f* etc.; **'state·ly** majestuoso, imponente; augusto; *carriage* etc. majestuoso, garboso; ~ *home* casa *f* solariega; **'state·ment** declaración *f*; informe *m*; exposición *f*; relación *f*; **'state·room** camarote *m*; **'state·side** F *adv.* en (*or* a) los Estados Unidos.

states·man ['steitsmən] estadista *m*,

hombre *m* de estado; **'states·man·like** digno de estadista; **'states·man·ship** habilidad *f* de estadista; arte *m* de gobernar.

stat·ic ['stætik] □ *phys.* estático; *fig.* estancado, inactivo; **'stat·ics** *pl.* or *sg. phys.* estática *f*.

sta·tion ['steiʃn] 1. ⊞ *etc.* estación *f*; ⚓ apostadero *m* naval; puesto *m*; situación *f*; 2. colocar, situar; ⚔ apostar, estacionar; **'sta·tion·ar·y** □ estacionario; **'sta·tion·er·y** papelería *f*, papel *m* de escribir; **'sta·tion-mas·ter** jefe *m* de estación; **sta·tion wag·on** ['steiʃn] F furgoneta *f*.

stat·is·ti·cian [stætisˈtiʃn] estadístico *m*; **sta·tis·tics** [stəˈtistiks] *pl.* (*as science*), *sg.*) estadística *f*.

stat·u·ar·y ['stætjuəri] 1. estatuario; 2. (*p.*) estatuario *m*; (*art*) estatuaria *f*; **stat·ue** ['stætjuː] estatua *f*; **stat·u·esque** [~tjuˈesk] □ estatuario; **stat·u·ette** [~tjuˈet] figurina *f*.

stat·ure ['stætʃə] estatura *f*, talla *f*.

sta·tus ['steitəs] condición *f*, rango *m*; **'~ seek·er** ambicioso *m/f*; **'~ symbol** símbolo *m* de categoría social.

stat·ute ['stætjuːt] estatuto *m*; ~ *law* derecho *m* escrito.

staunch [stɔːntʃ] 1. □ leal, firme, constante; 2. estancar; restañar.

stay [stei] 1. estancia *f*, permanencia *f*; visita *f*; ⚖ suspensión *f*, prórroga *f*; 2. *v/t.* detener; poner freno a; ⚖ suspender; ⊕ sostener; *v/i.* quedar (-se), permanecer; hospedarse (*at* en); esperar (*for* hasta); *fig.* ~ *put* mantenerse en su lugar.

stead [sted]: *in his* ~ en su lugar.

stead·fast ['stedfəst] □ constante, firme, resuelto.

stead·i·ness ['stedinis] constancia *f*.

stead·y ['stedi] 1. □ firme, fijo; estable; regular; constante; 2. estabilizar; afirmar; *nerves* calmar; 3. F novio (*a f*) *m* formal.

steak [steik] *meat:* bistec *m*; tajada *f*.

steal [stiːl] 1. [*irr.*] *v/t.* hurtar, robar; cautivar; *v/i.*: ~ *away* escabullirse; marcharse sigilosamente; F *ganga f* extraordinaria.

stealth [stelθ] cautela *f*, sigilo *m*; **'~·i·ness** clandestinidad *f*; **'stealth·y** □ furtivo; clandestino.

steam [stiːm] 1. vapor *m*; vaho *m*; *let off* ~ ⊕ descargar vapor; *fig.* desahogarse; 2. ... *de vapor*; 3. *v/i.* echar vapor; marchar (*or* funcionar) a vapor; *v/t.* cocer al vapor; *window* empañar; **'steam en·gine** máquina f de vapor; **'steam·er ⚓** (buque m de) vapor m; **'steam-roll·er 1.** apisonadora f; **2.** fig. aplastar, arrollar; **'steam·ship** = steamer; **'steam·y** ☐ lleno de vapor; window empañado.

steel [sti:l] **1.** acero m; (sharpener) chaira f, eslabón m; **2.** de acero; acerado; **3.** ⊕ acerar; fig. ~ o.s. acorazarse; **'~-clad** revestido de acero; **'steel·y** mst fig. inflexible.

steep [sti:p] ☐ empinado, escarpado, abrupto; F exorbitante.

stee·ple ['sti:pl] campanario m; **'~-chase** (horses) carrera f de vallas; **'~-jack** eacalatorres m.

steer¹ [stiə] ✍ buey m; novillo m.

steer² [~] dirigir; car conducir; ship gobernar; ~ clear of evitar.

steer·ing ['stiəriŋ] dirección f; ⊕ gobierno m; **'~ col·umn** columna f de dirección; **'~ com·mit·tee** comité m (a. planeador); **'~ wheel** volante m.

steers·man ['stiəzmən] timonero m.

stel·lar ['stelə] estelar.

stem [stem] **1.** ♀ tallo m; ⊕ vástago m; gr. tema m; pie m of glass; cañón m of pipe; **2.** ~ from resultar de.

stench [stentʃ] hedor m.

sten·cil ['stensl] **1.** ⊕ patrón m picado; estarcido m; **2.** estarcir.

ste·nog·ra·pher [ste'nɔgrəfə] taquígrafo (a f) m; **ste·nog·ra·phy** [ste'nɔgrəfi] taquigrafía f.

step [step] **1.** paso m (a. fig.); (stair) peldaño m, escalón m, grada f; estribo m of car; fig. medida f, gestión f; (a. flight of) ~s pl. escalera f, escalinata f; watch one's ~ ir con tiento; **2.** v/i. dar un paso; andar, ir; pisar; ~ on pisar; F ~ on it! ¡date prisa!; v/t. escalonar; distance medir a pasos (a. ~ out); ~ up aumentar, elevar.

step² [~]: **'~-fa·ther** padrastro m; **'~-son** hijastro m; etc.

steppe [step] estepa f.

ster·e·o... ['steriə]: **'~-phon·ic** ☐ estereofónico; **'~-scope** estereoscopio m; **'~-type** clisé m, estereotipo m; F concepción f tradicional.

ster·ile ['sterail] estéril; **ster·i·lize** ['~rilaiz] esterilizar.

ster·ling ['stə:liŋ] **1.** genuino, de ley; **2.** libras f/pl. esterlinas.

stern¹ [stə:n] ☐ severo, rígido; austero.

stern² [~] ⚓ popa f.

stern·ness ['stə:nnis] severidad f, rigidez f.

steth·o·scope ['steθəskoup] estetoscopio m.

ste·ve·dore ['sti:vidɔ:] estibador m.

stew [stju:] **1.** v/t. estofar; guisar; v/i. F contener el enojo; **2.** estofado m, guisado m; F apuro m.

stew·ard ['stjuəd] mayordomo m; administrador m; ⚓, ✈ camarero m; **'stew·ard·ess ⚓** camarera f; ✈ azafata f, aeromoza f.

stick¹ [stik] palo m, vara f; porra f; (walking-) bastón m; barra f of soap etc.; ~s pl. leña f.

stick² [~] (irr.) **1.** v/i. pegarse, adherirse (to a); atascarse in mud etc.; estar prendido; pararse, quedar parado; (stay) permanecer; F ~ around esperar por ahí; ~ at persistir en; F ~ to principle aferrarse a; p. permanecer fiel a; (follow) p. pegarse a, seguir de cerca; ~ together quedarse unidos; **2.** v/t. (gum etc.) pegar, encolar (a. ~ down, ~ together); (thrust) clavar, hincar; (pierce) picar; F poner, meter; **'stick·er** etiqueta f engomada; **'stick·i·ness** pegajosidad f; viscosidad f; **'stick-in-the-mud** tardón m; sl. aguafiestas m/f.

stick·ler ['stiklə] rigorista m/f.

stick-up ['stikʌp] sl. atraco m.

stick·y ['stiki] ☐ pegajoso; viscoso; difícil; obstinado; sl. end triste.

stiff [stif] **1.** ☐ tieso, rígido; collar duro, almidonado; aterido with cold; paste espeso; F scared ~ muerto de miedo; **2.** sl. cadáver m; **'stiff·en** atiesar; endurecer(se); **'stiff·ness** entumecimiento m of limb; tiesura f etc.

sti·fle ['staifl] sofocar(se), ahogar(se); fig. suprimir; **'sti·fling** sofocante.

stig·ma ['stigmə] all senses: estigma m; **'stig·ma·tize** estigmatizar.

sti·let·to [sti'letou] estilete m.

still¹ [stil] **1.** adj. inmóvil; quieto; tranquilo; **2.** silencio m; film: vista f fija; **3.** adv. todavía, aún; **4.** cj. sin embargo, con todo; **5.** calmar, tranquilizar.

still² [~] alambique m.

still...: **'~-born** nacido muerto; ~ life bodegón m, naturaleza f muerta.

stilt [stilt] zanco m; **'stilt·ed** hinchado, afectado.

stim·u·lant ['stimjulənt] estimulante adj. a. su. m; **stim·u·late** ['~leit] estimular (to a); **stim·u·lus** ['~ləs] estímulo m.

sting [stiŋ] **1.** ♀, zo. aguijón m; picadura f; fig. punzada f; 2. [irr.] picar; punzar; **stin·gi·ness** ['stindʒinis] tacañería f; **stin·gy** ['stindʒi] □ tacaño, cicatero.

stink [stiŋk] 1. hedor m, mal olor m; 2. heder, oler mal (of a); '**~·er** sl. p sinvergüenza m/f.

stint [stint] 1. límite m, restricción f; tarea f; 2. limitar, restringir.

sti·pend ['staipend] estipendio m.

stip·u·late ['stipjuleit] estipular (for acc.); **stip·u'la·tion** estipulación f.

stir¹ [stəː] 1. agitación f; alboroto m; conmoción f; 2. v/t. (re)mover; agitar; fire hurgar; liquid revolver; v/i. moverse; menearse.

stir² [~] sl. chirona f; cárcel f.

stir·ring ['stəːriŋ] □ emocionante, conmovedor.

stir·rup ['stirəp] estribo m.

stitch [stitʃ] 1. punto m, puntada f; ✚ punzada f; 2. coser (a. ✿), hilvanar.

stock [stɔk] 1. (family) estirpe f, raza f; ♀ tronco m de tree, cepa f de vine; (handle) mango m; ✕ caja f; ♣ surtido m, existencias f/pl.; ✔ (a. live ~) ganado m; ♣ ~s pl. acciones f/pl., valores m/pl.; 2. consagrado; acostumbrado; phrase hecho; ♣ proveer, abastecer; ♣ tener existencias de.

stock·ade [stɔ'keid] estacada f.

stock...: '~·breed·er ganadero m; '~·brok·er bolsista m, agente m de bolsa; '~·ex·change bolsa f; '~·hold·er accionista m/f.

stock·ing ['stɔkiŋ] media f; (knee-length) calceta f.

stock...: '~·pile acumular; '~·still completamente inmóvil; '~·tak·ing inventario m, balance m; **stock·y** rechoncho, achaparrado.

stodg·y ['stɔdʒi] □ pesado.

sto·ic ['stouik] estoico adj. a. su. m; '**sto·i·cism** estoicismo m.

stoke [stouk] cargar, echar carbón a; atizar; '**stok·er** fogonero m.

stole¹ [stoul] estola f.

stole² [~] pret., **sto·len** p.p. of steal.

stol·id ['stɔlid] □ impasible, imperturbable.

stom·ach ['stʌmək] 1. estómago m; fig. apetito m, deseo m (for de); 2. fig. tragar, aguantar; '~·ache dolor m de estómago; ~·pump bomba f estomacal.

stomp [stɔmp] pisar muy fuerte.

stone [stoun] 1. piedra f; hueso m of fruit; ✚ cálculo m; (weight) catorce libras f/pl.; 2. ... de piedra; 3. lapi-

dar, apedrear; fruit deshuesar; '~·broke arrancado; sin blanca; '~·dead más muerto que una piedra; '~·deaf sordo como una tapia; '~·ma·son albañil m; cantero m; '~·pit, '~·quar·ry cantera f; '~·wall·ing fig. táctica f de cerrojo); '~·ware gres m.

stoned [stound] sl. borracho.

ston·y ['stouni] ground pedregoso; pétreo; heart empedernido.

stood [stud] pret. a. p.p. of stand.

stool [stuːl] taburete m, escabel m; ♀ planta f madre; ✚ evacuación f; (folding) silla f de tijera; '~·pi·geon soplón m, espía m.

stoop [stuːp] 1. v/i. encorvarse, inclinarse; (permanently) cargarse de espaldas; fig. rebajarse (to a); 2. inclinación f; escalinata f de entrada.

stop [stɔp] 1. v/t. detener, parar; abuse, process etc. poner fin a; payment suspender; supply cortar, interrumpir; (a. ~ up) tapar, cegar; obstruir; v/i. parar(se), detenerse; hacer alto; terminar(se), acabarse; 2. parada f; alto m; ⊕ tope m, retén m; '~·gap recurso m provisional; (p.) tapa(a)gujeros m; '~ light luz f de parada; '~·off, '~·o·ver parada f intermedia; '**stop·page** cesación f; detención f; paro m; ⊕ obstrucción f; '**stop·per** tapón m; ⊕ taco m; '**stop·watch** cronómetro m.

stor·age ['stɔːridʒ] almacenaje m, depósito m; ~ battery acumulador m.

store [stɔː] 1. provisión f; (reserve) repuesto m; (~house) almacén m, depósito m; tienda f; ~s pl. provisiones f/pl., víveres m/pl.; 2. almacenar; abastecer; ~ away tener en reserva, guardar, archivar; ~ up amontonar, acumular; '~·house almacén m, depósito m; fig. mina f; '~·keep·er almacenero m; tendero m; '~·room despensa f; cuarto m de almacenar.

sto·rey ['stɔːri] = story².

stork [stɔːk] cigüeña f.

storm [stɔːm] 1. tormenta f, tempestad f (a. fig.), borrasca f; take by ~ tomar por asalto; ~ troops pl. tropas f/pl. de asalto; 2. v/t. ✕ asaltar, tomar por asalto; v/i. enfurecerse, tronar (at contra); '**storm·y** □ tempestuoso, borrascoso (a. fig.).

sto·ry¹ ['stɔːri] cuento m, histori(et)a f; (joke) chiste m; anécdota f; argumento m, trama f of novel etc.; F mentira f; embuste m; short ~ cuento m.

sto·ry², a. **sto·rey** [~] piso m.

13*

S

sto·ry·tell·er ['stɔːritelə] cuentista m/f; F embustero (a f) m.
stout [staut] **1.** □ robusto, sólido, macizo; p. corpulento; fig. valiente; **2.** stout m (cerveza fuerte); '**~·heart·ed** □ valiente.
stove [stouv] estufa f; hornillo m; cocina f de gas etc.; '**~·pipe** tubo m de estufa; F (top hat) chistera f.
stow [stou] v/t. meter; esconder; ♣ arrumar; v/i.: **~ away** viajar de polizón; '**stow·age** ♣ arrumaje m; (place) bodega f; '**stow·a·way** polizón m.
strad·dle ['strædl] esparrancarse encima de; horse montar a horcajadas.
strafe [strɑːf] bombardear.
strag·gle ['strægl] rezagarse; extraviarse; '**strag·gler** rezagado m; '**strag·gling** □ disperso.
straight [streit] **1.** adj. derecho, recto; back erguido; hair lacio; (honest) honrado; answer franco, directo; drink sin mezcla; **2.** adv. derecho, directamente; con franqueza; **~ ahead**, **~ on** todo seguido; F **go ~** enmendarse; '**straight·en** v/t. enderezar (a. **~ out**); fig. arreglar; v/i.: **~ up** enderezarse; **straight·for·ward** ['~'fɔːwəd] □ honrado, franco; (easy) sencillo; '**straight·'out** cabal; completo.
strain¹ [strein] **1.** tensión f, tirantez f; esfuerzo m grande; ⊕ deformación f; ⚕ torcedura f of muscle; ⚕ agotamiento m nervioso; **2.** v/t. estirar, tender con fuerza; poner tirante; ⊕ (filter) colar, filtrar; v/i. esforzarse.
strain² [~] (race) linaje m, raza f; vena f of madness.
strain·er ['streinə] colador m.
strait [streit] **1.** geog. estrecho m (a. **~s** pl.); fig. **~s** pl. estrecheces f/pl., apuro m; **2.**: **~ jacket** camisa f de fuerza; '**strait·en** estrechar; **strait-laced** ['~leist] gazmoño.
strand¹ [strænd] **1.** poet. playa f, ribera f; **2.** ♣ varar(se), encallar.
strand² [~] hebra f; hebra f.
strange [streindʒ] □ extraño, raro, peregrino; desconocido; nuevo; '**strange·ness** extrañeza f, rareza f, novedad f; '**stran·ger** desconocido (a f) m; forastero (a f) m.
stran·gle ['strængl] estrangular; fig. ahogar; '**~·hold** sport: collar m de fuerza; fig. dominio m completo.
strap [stræp] **1.** correa f; tira f, banda f; **2.** (tie) atar con correa; '**~·hang·er**

pasajero m sin asiento; '**strap·ping** robusto, fornido.
strat·a·gem ['strætidʒəm] estratagema f.
stra·te·gic [strə'tiːdʒik] □ estratégico; '**strat·e·gy** estrategia f.
strat·i·fy ['strætifai] estratificar(se).
stra·to·cruis·er ['streitoukruːzə] avión m estratosférico.
strat·o·sphere ['streitousfiə] estratosfera f.
straw [strɔː] **1.** paja f; (drinking-) pajita f; **2.** ... de paja; (color) pajizo; '**~·ber·ry** fresón m; (wild) fresa f; '**~ man** figura f de paja.
stray [strei] **1.** extraviarse; perderse; **2.** extraviado; errante; aislado; bullet perdido; **3.** animal m extraviado.
streak [striːk] **1.** raya f, lista f; **~ of lightning** rayo m (a. fig.); **2.** v/t. rayar, listar; v/i. pasar etc. como un rayo; '**streak·y** □ rayado.
stream [striːm] **1.** arroyo m; corriente f; flujo m, chorro m; on **~** instalado; puesto en operación; **2.** v/i. correr, fluir; ondear, flotar in wind; **~ forth**, **~ out** brotar, chorrear; v/t. arrojar, derramar; '**stream·er** flámula f.
stream·line ['striːmlain] aerodinamizar; fig. coordinar, perfeccionar; **~d** aerodinámico.
street [striːt] calle f; attr. callejero; '**~·car** tranvía m; **~ floor** planta f baja; '**~·walk·er** prostituta f de calle.
strength [streŋθ] fuerza f; intensidad f; resistencia f; '**strength·en** fortalecer(se), reforzar(se).
stren·u·ous ['strenjuəs] □ vigoroso, enérgico; arduo.
strep·to·my·cin [streptou'maisin] estreptomicina f.
stress [stres] **1.** esfuerzo m; presión f; compulsión f; ⚕ fatiga f (nerviosa) ⊕ tensión f; **2.** ⊕ cargar; gr. acentuar.
stretch [stretʃ] **1.** extender(se); estirar(se); alargar(se); dilatar(se), ensanchar(se); desperezarse after sleep; limb desentorpecerse; **2.** extensión f; (act of stretching) estirón m; ensanche m; esfuerzo m of imagination; '**stretch·er** ⊕ ensanchador m; ⚕ camilla f.
strick·en ['strikən] afligido (with por).
strict [strikt] □ estricto; riguroso; '**strict·ness** rigor m; severidad f.
stride [straid] **1.** [irr.] caminar a paso largo (a. **~ along**), andar a trancos; **2.** zancada f, tranco m.

stumble

stri·dent ['straidnt] □ estridente.

strife [straif] *lit.* disensión *f*, contienda *f*.

strike [straik] 1. huelga *f*; F descubrimiento *m* repentino *of oil etc.*; *baseball:* golpe *m*; be on ~ estar en huelga; go on ~ ponerse en huelga; 2. [*irr.*] *v/t.* golpear; pegar; herir; *fig.* impresionar; *(clock)* hour dar; *match* frotar, encender; *oil* descubrir; ♀ *root* echar; ~ out borrar, tachar; ~ up iniciar, empezar a tocar; *v/i.* golpear; chocar; ponerse (*or* estar) en huelga; *(clock)* dar (la una *etc.*); '~**break·er** esquirol *m*; '~ **pay** sueldo *m* de huelguista; '**strik·er** huelguista *m/f*; ⊕ percutor *m*.

strik·ing ['straikiŋ] □ impresionante; sorprendente; *color etc.* llamativo.

string [striŋ] 1. cuerda *f* (*a.* ♪, *a. bow-*); sarta *f of pearls, lies;* (*row*) hilera *f*, fila *f*; ristra *f of onions etc.;* ~s *pl.* ♪ instrumentos *m/pl.* de cuerda; F *pull* ~s tocar resortes, mover palancas; 2. *violin* encordar; *pearls etc.* ensartar; F ~ *along* traer el retortero; '~ **band** orquesta *f* de cuerdas; '~ **bean** habichuela *f* verde; **stringed** ♪ ... de cuerda(s).

strin·gen·cy ['strindʒənsi] rigor *m*, severidad *f*; '**strin·gent** □ riguroso, estricto, severo; ♥ tirante.

string·y ['striŋi] fibroso.

strip [strip] 1. *v/t.* despojar (*of* de); desnudar; *clothes* quitar, despojarse de (*a.* ~ *off*); *gears* estropear; *v/i.* desnudarse; 2. tira *f*; faja *f*; *comic* ~ tira *f* cómica.

stripe [straip] 1. raya *f*, lista *f*; banda *f*; ✕ galón *m*; 2. rayar, listar.

strip-tease ['striptiːz] espectáculo *m* de desnudamiento sensual.

strive [straiv] [*irr.*] esforzarse (*to* por); luchar (*against* contra).

strode [stroud] *pret.* of stride 1.

stroke [strouk] 1. golpe *m* (*a. sport*); jugada *f*; estilo *m of swimming;* brazada *f of swimmer;* remada *f of oar;* 𝒮 ataque *m* fulminante, apoplejía *f;* ~ *of luck* racha *f* de suerte; *at a* ~ de un golpe; 2. acariciar; *chin* pasar la mano sobre.

stroll [stroul] 1. pasearse, callejear; 2. paseo *m*; *take a* ~ dar un paseo; '**stroll·er** paseante *m/f*; cochecito *m*; '**stroll·ing** ambulante.

strong [strɔŋ] □ fuerte; recio, robusto; *accent* marcado; *conviction* profundo; *drink* alcohólico; *emotion* intenso; *language* indecente; '~ **box** caja *f* de caudales; '~ **hold** fortaleza *f*, plaza *f* fuerte; *fig.* baluarte *m*; '~ **point** fuerte *m*; '~-**willed** obstinado.

strove [strouv] *pret.* of strive.

struck [strʌk] *pret. a. p.p.* of strike 2.

struc·ture ['strʌktʃə] estructura *f*; construcción *f*.

strug·gle ['strʌgl] 1. luchar (*to, for* por); esforzarse (*to* por); 2. lucha *f* (*for* por); contienda *f*; esfuerzo *m*.

strum [strʌm] *guitar* rasguear.

strum·pet ['strʌmpit] ramera *f*.

strung [strʌŋ] *pret. a. p.p.* of string 2.

strut [strʌt] 1. *v/i.* pavonearse, contonearse; *v/t.* ⊕ apuntalar; 2. (*walk*) contoneo *m*; ⊕ puntal *m*, riostra *f*.

stub [stʌb] 1. ♪ tocón *m*; colilla *f of cigarette;* cabo *m of pencil;* 2. ~ *one's toe* dar un tropezón.

stub·ble ['stʌbl] rastrojo *m*.

stub·born ['stʌbən] □ tenaz, inflexible; *b.s.* terco, porfiado; '**stub·born·ness** tenacidad *f*.

stuc·co ['stʌkou] 1. estuco *m*; 2. estucar.

stuck [stʌk] *pret. a. p.p.* of stick 2; F ~ *on* chalado por; '~-**up** empingorotado, engreído.

stud¹ [stʌd] 1. tachón *m*; (*boot-*) taco *m*; botón *m* (de camisa); 2. tachonar; *fig.* sembrar (*with* de).

stud² [~] caballeriza *f*; yeguada *f*; '~-**horse** caballo *m* padre.

stu·dent ['stjuːdənt] estudiante *m/f*; alumno (a *f*) *m*; ~ *body* estudiantado *m*.

stud·ied ['stʌdid] □ *insult* premeditado; *pose* afectado.

stu·di·o ['stjuːdiou] estudio *m* (*a. radio*); taller *m*.

stu·di·ous ['stjuːdjəs] □ estudioso.

stud·y ['stʌdi] 1. estudio *m*; despacho *m*, gabinete *m*; 2. estudiar.

stuff [stʌf] 1. materia *f*, material *m*; (*cloth*) tela *f*, paño *m*; *fig.* cosa *f*; 2. *v/t.* llenar, hinchar, atestar, atiborrar (*with* de); meter sin orden (*into* en); *fowl* rellenar; *sl.* ~ed shirt tragaviriotes *m*; *v/i.* F atracarse, hartarse; '**stuff·ing** borra *f*; *cooking:* relleno *m*; '**stuff·y** □ *room* mal ventilado, sofocante; F relamido.

stul·ti·fy ['stʌltifai] anular; hacer parecer ridículo.

stum·ble ['stʌmbl] 1. tropezón *m*, traspié *m*; 2. tropezar (*a. fig.*);

'stum·bling block *fig.* tropiezo *m*.

stump [stʌmp] 1. tocón *m* of tree; muñón *m* of leg etc.; cabo *m*; ~ *speaker* orador *m* callejero; 2. *v/t.* F confundir, dejar confuso; **'stump·y** □ achaparrado.

stun [stʌn] aturdir, atolondrar (*a. fig.*).

stung [stʌŋ] *pret. a. p.p. of* sting 2.

stunk [stʌŋk] *p.p. of* stink 2.

stun·ning ['stʌniŋ] □ F estupendo, bárbaro, imponente.

stunt[1] [stʌnt] F 1. ✈ vuelo *m* acrobático; treta *f* publicitaria; maniobra *f* sensacional; 2. ✈ lucirse haciendo maniobras acrobáticas.

stunt[2] [~] atrofiar, impedir el crecimiento de; **'stunt·ed** enano.

stu·pe·fy ['stju:pifai] atolondrar; pasmar; dejar estupefacto.

stu·pen·dous [stju:'pendəs] □ estupendo.

stu·pid ['stju:pid] □ estúpido; **stu·pid·i·ty** [stju:'piditi] estupidez *f*.

stu·por ['stju:pə] estupor *m* (*a. fig.*).

stur·dy ['stə:di] □ robusto, fuerte, vigoroso; tenaz.

stut·ter ['stʌtə] 1. *v/t.* tartamudear; *v/t.* balbucear; 2. tartamudeo *m*; **'~·er** tartamudo *adj. a. su.* (*a f*) *m*.

sty [stai] ✗ pocilga *f*, zahúrda *f*.

style [stail] 1. estilo *m* (*a.* ☙); moda *f*; elegancia *f*; título *m*; *live in* ~ darse buena vida; 2. nombrar; *dress* cortar a la moda.

styl·ish ['stailiʃ] □ elegante; a la moda; **'styl·ish·ness** elegancia *f*.

styl·ist ['stailist] estilista *m/f*; **styl·ized** ['stailaizd] estilizado.

sty·lo·graph ['stailəgræf] estilógrafo *m*.

suave [swɑ:v] □ afable, fino; *b.s.* zalamero.

sub·com·mit·tee ['sʌbkəmiti] subcomisión *f*.

sub·con·scious ['sʌb'kɔnʃəs] 1. □ subconsciente; 2. subcon(s)ciencia *f*.

sub·di·vide ['sʌbdi'vaid] subdividir (-se), **sub·di·vi·sion** ['~'viʒn] subdivisión *f*.

sub·due [səb'dju:] sojuzgar, avasallar, amansar; **sub'dued** *color* amortiguado; *emotion* templado; *light* tenue; *p.* deprimido, manso.

sub·head·(ing) ['sʌbhed(iŋ)] subtítulo *m*.

sub·ject ['sʌbdʒikt] 1. sujeto; *people* subyugado, esclavizado; ~ *to* (*liable*) propenso a; ~ *to* (*exposed*) expuesto a;

~ *to a fee* sujeto a derechos; 2. *gr.* sujeto *m*; *pol.* súbdito (*a f*) *m*; (*-matter*) tema *m*, materia *f*; materia *f*, asignatura *f in school*; 3. [səb'dʒekt] someter to test etc.; (*conquer*) dominar, sojuzgar; ~ *o.s. to* sujetarse a; **sub'jec·tion** sujeción *f*; avasallamiento *m*.

sub·ju·gate ['sʌbdʒugeit] subyugar.

sub·junc·tive [səb'dʒʌŋktiv] (*or* ~ *mood*) subjuntivo *m*.

sub·lease ['sʌb'li:s], **sub·let** ['~'let] realquilar, subarrendar.

sub·lime [sə'blaim] 1. □ (*the lo*) sublime; 2. sublimar; **sub·lim·i·ty** [sə'blimiti] sublimidad *f*.

sub·ma·chine gun ['sʌbmə'ʃi:n'gʌn] subfusil *m* ametrallador.

sub·ma·rine [sʌbmə'ri:n] submarino *adj. a. su. m*; **'~·'chas·er** cazasubmarinos *m*.

sub·merge [səb'mə:dʒ] sumergir.

sub·mis·sion [səb'miʃn] sumisión *f*; **sub·mis·sive** [~'misiv] □ sumiso.

sub·mit [səb'mit] *v/t.* someter; *evidence* presentar; *esp. parl.* proponer; *v/i.* (*a.* ~ *o.s.*) someterse; *fig.* resignarse (*to* a).

sub·or·di·nate 1. [sə'bɔ:dnit] □ subordinado (*a. gr.*), inferior; 2. [~] subordinado (*a f*) *m*; 3. [~'bɔ:dineit] subordinar.

sub·poe·na [sə'pi:nə] 1. comparendo *m*; 2. mandar comparecer.

sub·scribe [səb'skraib] su(b)scribir (-se), abonarse (*to a paper* a un periódico); ✝ su(b)scribir (*for*, *to* acc.); **sub'scrib·er** su(b)scriptor (-a *f*) *m*; abonado (*a f*) *m*.

sub·se·quent ['sʌbsikwənt] □ subsecuente, posterior (*to* a); **~·ly** con posterioridad, después.

sub·ser·vi·ent [səb'sə:viənt] □ subordinado; servil.

sub·side [səb'said] (*water*) bajar; (*house*) hundirse; (*excitement*) calmarse; **sub·sid·i·ar·y** [~'sidjəri] 1. □ subsidiario; auxiliar; ✝ filial; 2. sucursal *f*; **sub·si·dize** ['sʌbsidaiz] subvencionar; **'sub·si·dy** subvención *f*.

sub·sist [səb'sist] subsistir; sustentarse (*on* con); **sub·sist·ence** subsistencia *f*; ~ *allowance* dietas *f/pl*.

sub·son·ic [sʌb'sɔnik] subsónico.

sub·stance ['sʌbstəns] sustancia *f*.

sub·stand·ard [sʌb'stændəd] inferior al nivel normal, deficiente.

sub·stan·tial [səb'stænʃl] □ sustancial, sustancioso; considerable.

sub·stan·ti·ate [səb'stænʃieit] establecer, verificar, justificar.

sub·stan·tive ['sʌbstəntiv] □ sustantivo *adj. a. su. m (a. gr.)*.

sub·sta·tion ['sʌbˌsteiʃn] ⚡ subestación *f*; subcentral *m*.

sub·sti·tute ['sʌbstitjuːt] **1.** *v/t.* substituir (*A for B* B por *A*); *v/i.* F suplir (*for* a); **2.** sustituto (a *f*) *m*; suplente *m/f*; reemplazo *m*; **3.** sucedáneo; de reemplazo.

sub·ten·ant ['sʌb'tenənt] subarrendatario (a *f*) *m*.

sub·ter·ra·ne·an [sʌbtə'reinjən] subterráneo.

sub·ti·tle ['sʌbtaitl] subtítulo *m*.

sub·tle ['sʌtl] □ sutil; astuto; **'sub·tle·ty** sutileza *f*; astucia *f*.

sub·tract [səb'trækt] ♫ sustraer, restar.

sub·urb ['sʌbəːb] suburbio *m*, arrabal *m*, barrio *m*; **sub·ur·ban** [sʌ'bəːbən] suburbano; **sub'ur·bi·a** los arrabales; vida *f* arrabalera.

sub·ver·sion [sʌb'vəːʃn] subversión *f*; **sub'ver·sive** □ subversivo.

sub·vert [sʌb'vəːt] subvertir.

sub·way ['sʌbwei] paso *m* subterráneo; metro *m*.

suc·ceed [sək'siːd] tener (buen) éxito, salir bien; ~ *in ger.* lograr *inf.*; **suc'ceed·ing** subsiguiente.

suc·cess [sək'ses] (buen) éxito *m*; triunfo *m*; prosperidad *f*; it was a (*great*) ~ salió (muy) bien; **suc'cess·ful** [~ful] □ próspero, afortunado, feliz; *be* ~ tener (buen) éxito *esp.* † prosperar, medrar; **suc·ces·sion** [~'seʃn] sucesión *f* (*to* a); descendencia *f*.

suc·cinct [sək'siŋkt] □ sucinto.

suc·cor ['sʌkə] **1.** socorro *m*; **2.** socorrer.

suc·cu·lent ['sʌkjulənt] □ suculento.

suc·cumb [sə'kʌm] sucumbir (*to* a).

such [sʌtʃ] **1.** *adj.* tal, semejante; ~ a *man* tal hombre; no ~ *thing* no hay tal cosa; **2.** *adv.*: ~ a *big dog* un perro tan grande; **3.** *pron.*: ~ as los que.

suck [sʌk] **1.** chupar; mamar; ~ *in* sorber; *air* aspirar; ~ *up* absorber; **2.** chupada *f*; **'suck·er** ⊕ émbolo *m*; ♀ serpollo *m*, mamón *m*; *sl.* inocente *m/f*; bobo.

suc·tion ['sʌkʃn] **1.** succión *f*; **2.** ... de succión; aspirante.

sud·den ['sʌdn] □ repentino, súbito; imprevisto; (*all*) *of a* ~ de repente; *~ly* de repente, de pronto.

suds [sʌds] *pl.* jabonaduras *f/pl.*; *sl.* cerveza.

sue [sjuː] *v/t.* procesar; demandar; *v/i.* poner pleito.

suede [sweid] suecia *f*.

suf·fer ['sʌfə] sufrir; padecer (⚔ *from* de); aguantar; (*allow*) permitir; ~ *from* fig. adolecer de; **suf·fer·er** víctima *f*; paciente *m/f*; **'suf·fer·ing** dolor *m*.

suf·fice [sə'fais] *v/i.* bastar; *v/t.* satisfacer.

suf·fi·cient [sə'fiʃənt] □ suficiente.

suf·fix 1. [sʌ'fiks] añadir (como sufijo); **2.** ['sʌfiks] sufijo *m*.

suf·fo·cate ['sʌfəkeit] sofocar(se), asfixiar(se); **'suf·fo·cat·ing** sofocante.

suf·frage ['sʌfridʒ] sufragio *m*; aprobación *f*.

suf·fuse [sə'fjuːz] bañar (*with* de); difundirse por.

sug·ar ['ʃugə] **1.** azúcar *m a. f*; **2.** azucarar; **'~ bowl** azucarero *m*; **'~ cane** caña *f* de azúcar; **'~ coat** azucarar; **'~ plum** confite *m*; **'sug·ar·y** azucarado; *fig.* almibarado.

sug·gest [sə(g)'dʒest] sugerir; indicar.

sug·ges·tive [sə'dʒestiv] □ sugerente; sugestivo; *b.s.* sicalíptico.

su·i·cid·al [sjui'saidl] □ suicida; **su·i·cide** ['~said] suicidio *m*; (*p.*) suicida *m/f*.

suit [sjuːt] **1.** traje *m* (*a.* ~ *of clothes*); (*courtship*) galanteo *m*, cortejo *m*; ⚖ pleito *m*, petición *f*; *cards:* palo *m*; **2.** *v/t.* adaptar, ajustar, acomodar (*to* a); convenir, satisfacer; *v/i.* convenir; **suit·a·bil·i·ty** conveniencia *f*; idoneidad *f*; **'suit·a·ble** □ conveniente, apropiado; idóneo; **'suit·case** maleta *f*; **suite** [swiːt] séquito *m*, comitiva *f*; mobiliario *m*; **'suit·or** pretendiente *m*, galán *m*; ⚖ demandante *m/f*.

sulk [sʌlk] amohinarse; **sulk·i·ness** ['~nis] mohina *f*, murria *f*; **'sulk·y** □ mohíno; resentido.

sul·len ['sʌlən] □ hosco, malhumorado; **'sul·len·ness** hosquedad *f* etc.

sul·phate ['sʌlfeit] sulfato *m*; **sul·phide** ['~faid] sulfuro *m*.

sul·phur ['sʌlfə] **1.** azufre *m*; **2.** azufrar.

sul·tan ['sʌltən] sultán *m*.

sul·try ['sʌltri] □ bochornoso; sofocante; *fig.* seductor.

sum [sʌm] **1.** suma *f*; total *m*; F problema *m* de aritmética; **2.** (*mst* ~ *up*) sumar; *fig.* resumir; *to* ~ *up* en resumen.

S

sum·ma·rize ['sʌmaraiz] resumir; '**sum·ma·ry 1.** ☐ sumario (a. ᵼᵗ₂); **2.** resumen m, sumario m.

sum·mer ['sʌmə] **1.** verano m, estío m; **2.** ... de verano; veraniego; estival; **3.** veranear.

sum·mer·like ['sʌməlaik], **summer·y** [‿ri] veraniego, estival; '**sum·mer re·sort** lugar m de veraneo.

sum·ming-up ['sʌmiŋʌp] recapitulación f.

sum·mit ['sʌmit] cima f, cumbre f (a. fig.); '‿ **con·fer·ence** conferencia f en la cumbre.

sum·mon ['sʌmən] convocar; llamar; **sum·mons** [‿z] **1.** ᵼᵗ₂ citación f; llamamiento m; **2.** citar.

sump·tu·ous ['sʌmptjuəs] ☐ suntuoso; '**sump·tu·ous·ness** suntuosidad f.

sun [sʌn] **1.** sol m; **2.** ... solar; **3.** asolear; ‿ o.s. asolearse, tomar el sol (a. '‿**bathe**); '‿**baked** asoleado; muy expuesto al sol; '‿**beam** ['sʌnbi:m] rayo m de sol.

sun·burn ['sʌnbə:n] solanera f; quemadura f del sol y; '**sun·burnt** tostado (por el sol), bronceado.

sun·dae ['sʌnd(e)i] helado con frutas, jarabes o nueces.

Sun·day ['sʌndi] domingo m; attr. dominical.

sun·di·al ['sʌndaiəl] reloj m de sol.

sun·down ['sʌndaun] puesta f del sol; at ‿ al anochecer.

sun·dry ['sʌndri] **1.** varios, diversos; **2. sun·dries** ['‿driz] pl. esp. ♣ géneros m/pl. diversos.

sun·flow·er ['sʌnflauə] girasol m.

sung [sʌŋ] p.p. of sing.

sun·glass·es pl. gafas f/pl. de sol.

sunk [sʌŋk] p.p. of sink 1; **sunk·en** ['sʌŋkən] **1.** p.p.c. of sink 1; **2.** adj. sumido, hundido (a. fig.).

sun lamp ['sʌnlæmp] lámpara f de rayos ultravioletas.

sun·light ['sʌnlait] luz f solar.

sun·lit ['sʌnlit] iluminado por el sol; '**sun·ny** ☐ place (a)soleado.

sun...: '‿**rise** salida f del sol; '‿**set** puesta f del sol; ocaso m; '‿**shade** quitasol m; toldo m; '‿**shine** sol m; mot. ‿ roof techo m corredizo; '‿**spot** mancha f solar; '‿**stroke** 𝒔 insolación f; '‿**up** salida f del sol.

su·per¹ ['sju:pə] (abbr.) **1.** superintendente m; **2.** ♣ F superfino; sl. bárbaro, de rechupete.

su·per...:² [‿] super...; sobre...; ‿**a'bun·dant** ☐ sobreabundante; ‿**an'nu·ate** [‿njueit] jubilar; ‿d jubilado; fig. anticuado.

su·perb [sju'pə:b] ☐ soberbio; magnífico.

su·per...: '‿**charged** sobrealimentado; **su·per·cil·i·ous** [‿'silios] ☐ desdeñoso, altanero, arrogante; **su·per·fi·cial** [‿'fiʃl] ☐ superficial; **su·per·fi·ci·al·i·ty** [‿fiʃi'æliti] superficialidad f; '**su·per'fine** extrafino, superfino; **su·per·flu·i·ty** [‿'fluiti] superfluidad f; **su·per·flu·ous** [sju'pə:fluəs] ☐ superfluo; **su·per'heat** sobrecalentar.

su·per...: '‿**hu·man** ☐ sobrehumano; ‿**im'pose** sobreponer; ‿**in'tend** dirigir; vigilar; supervisar; ‿**in'tend·ent** superintendente m; inspector m; supervisor m.

su·pe·ri·or [sju'piəriə] **1.** ☐ superior; b.s. orgulloso; **2.** superior m; (eccl. a.) superior m; **su·pe·ri·or·i·ty** [‿'ɔriti] superioridad f.

su·per·la·tive [sju'pə:lətiv] ☐ superlativo adj. a. su. m; '**su·per·man** superhombre m; '**su·per·mar·ket** supermercado m; **su·per'nat·u·ral** ☐ (the lo) sobrenatural; **su·per·nu·mer·ar·y** [‿'nju:mərəri] supernumerario adj. a. su. m (a f); **su·per·sede** [‿'si:d] reemplazar; sustituir; **su·per·son·ic** [‿'sɔnik] supersónico; **su·per·sti·tion** [‿'stiʃn] superstición f; **su·per'sti·tious** [‿'ʃəs] ☐ supersticioso; **su·per·struc·ture** ['‿strʌktʃə] superestructura f; **su·per·tank·er** ['‿tæŋkə] superpetrolero m; S.Am. supertanquero m; **su·per·vise** [‿'vaiz] dirigir; vigilar; supervisar; **su·per·vi·sion** [‿'viʒn] superintendencia f, vigilancia f; **su·per·vi·sor** ['‿vaizə] superintendente m; inspector m.

su·pine [su:'pain] **1.** gr. supino m; **2.** ☐ supino; fig. letárgico.

sup·per ['sʌpə] cena f.

sup·plant [sə'plɑ:nt] suplantar.

sup·ple ['sʌpl] ☐ flexible; b.s. dócil.

sup·ple·ment 1. ['sʌplimənt] suplemento m; **2.** ['‿ment] suplir, complementar.

sup·pli·cate ['sʌplikeit] suplicar.

sup·pli·er [sə'plaiə] suministrador (-a f) m; ♣ proveedor (-a f) m.

sup·ply [sə'plai] **1.** suministrar, facilitar; surtir; **2.** provisión f; suministro m; ♣ surtido m; mst supplies

swallow

pl. provisiones *f/pl.*, víveres *m/pl.*; ♥ ~ *and demand* oferta y demanda.

sup·port [sə'pɔːt] 1. sostén *m*, apoyo *m* (⊕ *a. fig.*); ♠ soporte *m*, pilar *m*; 2. apoyar (⊕ *a. fig.*); sostener, mantener; *campaign* respaldar; ~ *o.s.* mantenerse; **sup'port·er** partidario (a *f*) *m*; *sport:* seguidor (-a *f*) *m*; ⊕ soporte *m*, sostén *m*.

sup·pose [sə'pouz] suponer; presumir; figurarse, imaginarse; F *he is* ~*d to go* debe ir; *let us* ~ pongamos por caso.

sup·posed [sə'pouzd] □ supuesto; pretendido.

sup·pos·i·to·ry [sʌ'pɔzitɔːri] supositorio *m*.

sup·press [sə'pres] suprimir; **sup'pres·sor** *radio:* supresor *m*.

su·preme [sə'priːm] □ supremo.

sur·charge 1. [sɔː'tʃɑːdʒ] sobrecargar; 2. ['sɔː'tʃɑːdʒ] sobrecarga *f*.

sure [ʃuə] 1. □ seguro; cierto; *aim etc.* certero; *manner, touch* firme; *I am* ~ estoy seguro (*that* de que); *make* ~ asegurar(se) (*that* de que); *make* ~ *of facts* verificar, cerciorarse de; ~ *thing* cosa *f* cierta; certeza *f*; 2. *adv.:* *he* ~ *was mean* ése sí que era tacaño; '~- **foot·ed** de pie firme; '**sure·ty** seguridad *f*, fianza *f*; (*p.*) fiador (-a *f*) *m*.

surf [sɔːf] oleaje *m*; espuma *f*, rompientes *m/pl.*

sur·face ['sɔːfis] 1. superficie *f*; firme *m* *of road*; *v/t.* ⊕ alisar; recubrir; *v/i.* (*submarine*) emerger.

surf·board ['sɔːfbɔːd] patín *m* de mar.

sur·feit ['sɔːfit] 1. hartura *f*; exceso *m*; 2. hartar(se), saciar(se).

surf·rid·ing ['sɔːfraidiŋ] patinaje *m* sobre las olas.

surge [sɔːdʒ] 1. oleada *f*, oleaje *m*; 2. agitarse, hervir.

sur·geon ['sɔːdʒən] cirujano *m*; **sur·ger·y** ['sɔːdʒəri] cirugía *f*; **sur·gi·cal** ['sɔːdʒikl] □ quirúrgico.

sur·li·ness ['sɔːlinis] malhumor *m*; '**sur·ly** □ áspero, hosco.

sur·mise 1. ['sɔːmaiz] conjetura *f*; 2. [~'maiz] conjeturar; suponer.

sur·mount [sɔː'maunt] superar, vencer; ~*ed by* coronado de.

sur·name ['sɔːneim] 1. apellido *m*; 2. apellidar.

sur·pass [sɔː'pɑːs] *fig.* aventajar, exceder, sobrepujar.

sur·plus ['sɔːpləs] 1. sobrante *m*; ♥ superávit *m*; 2. ... sobrante.

sur·prise [sə'praiz] 1. sorpresa *f*;

asombro *m*; ✗ (*a.* ~ *attack*) rebato *m*; 2. sorprender; ✗ coger por sorpresa; **sur'pris·ing** □ sorprendente.

sur·re·al·ism [sə'riəlizm] surrealismo *m*; **sur're·al·ist** surrealista *m*.

sur·ren·der [sə'rendə] 1. rendición *f*; abandono *m*; entrega *f* *of documents*; 2. rendir(se).

sur·rep·ti·tious [sʌrəp'tiʃəs] □ subrepticio.

sur·round [sə'raund] cercar, circundar, rodear (*by* de); ✗ sitiar; **sur'round·ing** circundante.

sur·tax ['sɔːtæks] impuesto *m* adicional (*sobre ingresos excesivos*).

sur·veil·lance [sɔː'veiləns] vigilancia *f*.

sur·vey 1. [sɔː'vei] reconocer, registrar; *surv.* medir; 2. ['sɔːvei] reconocimiento *m*; inspección *f*, examen *m*; *surv.* medición *f*; **sur'vey·ing** planimetría *f*; agrimensura *f*; **sur'vey·or** agrimensor *m*.

sur·vive [sɔː'vaiv] sobrevivir (*acc. a acc.*); perdurar.

sus·cep·ti·bil·i·ty [səseptə'biliti] susceptibilidad *f*; delicadeza *f*; **sus'cep·ti·ble** □ susceptible.

sus·pect 1. [səs'pekt] sospechar, recelar; 2. ['sʌspekt] sospechoso (a *f*) *m*; 3. [~] sospechado, sospechoso.

sus·pend [səs'pend] *all senses:* suspender; **sus'pend·ers** *pl.* ligas *f/pl.*; tirantes *m/pl.*

sus·pense [səs'pens] incertidumbre *f*, duda *f*; ansiedad *f*.

sus·pen·sion [səs'penʃn] *all senses:* suspensión *f*; ~ *bridge* puente *m* colgante.

sus·pi·cion [səs'piʃn] sospecha *f*; recelo *m*; suspicacia *f*; *fig.* sombra *f*, **sus·pi·cious** [~'piʃəs] □ (*causing suspicion*) sospechoso; (*feeling suspicion*) receloso; suspicaz.

sus·tain [səs'tein] sostener (*a.* ♩), apoyar; sustentar; *loss, injury* sufrir.

sus·te·nance ['sʌstinəns] sustento *m*, subsistencia *f*.

su·ture ['sjuːtʃə] 1. *all senses:* sutura *f*; 2. ✄ suturar, coser.

swab [swɔb] 1. estropajo *m*; ⚓ lampazo *m*; ✄ algodón *m*; 2. lampacear.

swad·dle ['swɔdl] 1. empañar; 2. pañal *m*.

swag [swæg] *sl.* botín *m*, robo *m*.

swag·ger ['swægə] 1. fanfarronear; pavonearse; 2. fanfarronada *f*.

swal·low[1] ['swɔlou] *orn.* golondrina *f*.

swal·low[2] [~] 1. trago *m*; 2. tragar.

S

swamp [swɔmp] **1.** pantano *m*; marisma *f*; **2.** sumergir; inundar; ⚓ hundir; **'swamp·y** pantanoso.

swan [swɔn] cisne *m*; **'~ dive** salto *m* de ángel.

swank [swæŋk] *sl.* **1.** ostencación *f*; fachenda *f*; (*p.*) currutaco *m*; **2.** (*a.* **'swank·y**) ostentoso, fachendoso.

swan song ['swɔnsɔŋ] canto *m* del cisne.

swap [swɔp] F **1.** intercambio *m*, cambalache *m*, canje *m*; **2.** intercambiar, cambalachear, canjear.

swarm [swɔːm] **1.** enjambre *m*; *fig.* muchedumbre *f*, hormigueo *m*; **2.** enjambrar; (*people etc.*) hormiguear, pulular.

swarth·y ['swɔːði] □ atezado, moreno.

swash·buck·ler ['swɔʃbʌklə] espadachín *m*, matón *m*.

swas·ti·ka ['swɔstikə] svástica *f*.

swat [swɔt] *fly etc.* aplastar.

sway [swei] **1.** vaivén *m*, balanceo *m*; coletazo *m of train etc.* (*a.* **'sway·ing**); *fig.* imperio *m*, dominio *m*; **2.** *v/t.* hacer oscilar; *fig.* influir en; *v/i.* oscilar, ladearse.

swear [swɛə] [*irr.*] *v/i.* jurar (*by* por); decir palabrotas; ~ *at* maldecir *acc.*; *v/t.* jurar; juramentar; **'~word** palabrota *f*; voto *m*; F taco *m*.

sweat [swet] **1.** sudor *m* (*a. fig.* F); ~ *shirt* pulóver *m* de mangas largas; **2.** *v/i.* sudar; *v/t.* sudar; *workmen* explotar; **'sweat·er** suéter *m*; **'sweat·shop** taller *m* de trabajo afanoso y poco sueldo.

Swede [swiːd] sueco (*a f*) *m*; ♀♈ nabo *m* sueco.

Swed·ish ['swiːdiʃ] sueco *adj. a. su. m.*

sweep [swiːp] **1.** [*irr.*] *v/t.* barrer; *chimney* deshollinar; ⚓ *mines* rastrear; *fig.* ~ *away* arrebatar, arrastrar; *v/i.* barrer; (*mst with adv.*, ~ *by* etc.) pasar rápidamente, pasar majestuosamente; **2.** barredura *f*, escobada *f*; (*p.*) deshollinador *m*; redada *f by police*; **'sweep·er** barrendero (*a f*) *m*; (*machine*) barredera *f*; **sweep·stake** ['~steik] lotería *f* de premio único.

sweet [swiːt] **1.** □ dulce; azucarado; suave; *smell* fragante; (*pleasing*) grato; *have a* ~ *tooth* ser goloso; **2.** dulce *m*; caramelo *m*; (*course*) postre *m*; ~*s pl.* dulces *m/pl.*, bombones *m/pl.*, golosinas *f/pl.*; **'~breads** *pl.* lechecillas *f/pl.*; **'sweet·en** azucarar; en-

dulzar (*a. fig.*); **'sweet·heart** novio (*a f*) *m*; **'sweet·meats** *pl.* confites *m/pl.*; dulces *m/pl.*; **'sweet·ness** dulzura *f*, suavidad *f etc.*; **'sweet po'ta·to** batata *f*; camote *m*; **'sweet shop** confitería *f*.

swell [swel] **1.** [*irr.*] hinchar(se), inflar(se); crecer (*v/i.*); **2.** F muy elegante; **3.** ♪ crescendo *m*; ⚓ marejada *f*; **'swell·ing** hinchazón *f*; ✿ chichón *m*.

swel·ter ['sweltə] sofocarse de calor, abrasarse; chorrear de sudor; **'swel·ter·ing** *heat* sofocante, abrasador.

swept [swept] *pret. a. p.p. of* sweep 1.

swerve [swəːv] **1.** *v/t.* desviarse (bruscamente); torcer; *v/t.* desviar; **2.** desvío *m* (brusco).

swift [swift] □ rápido, veloz; repentino; **'swift·ness** rapidez *f etc.*

swill [swil] **1.** bazofia *f*; *contp.* aguachirle *f*; **2.** *v/t.* (*mst* ~ *out*) enjuagar; beber a grandes tragos; F emborracharse.

swim [swim] **1.** [*irr.*] *v/i.* nadar; (*head*) dar vueltas; *v/t.* (*a.* ~ *across*) pasar a nado; **2.** *go for a* ~ ir a nadar. **swim·mer** ['swimə] nadador (*-a f*) *m*.

swim·ming ['swimiŋ] natación *f*; **'swim·ming pool** piscina *f*; **'swim·suit** traje *m* de baño.

swin·dle ['swindl] **1.** estafar, timar; **2.** estafa *f*, timo *m*.

swine [swain] *zo. pl.* puercos *m/pl.*, cerdos *m/pl.*; F *sg.* canalla *m*.

swing [swiŋ] **1.** [*irr.*] columpiar(se); balancear(se); (*hacer*) oscilar; *arm* menear; *door* girar; F *he'll* ~ *for it* le ahorcarán; **2.** columpio *m*; (*movement*) vaivén *m*; ♪ swing *m*; ♪ ritmo *m* agradable; *boxing:* golpe *m* lateral; *in full* ~ en plena actividad; **'~ bridge** puente *m* giratorio; **'~ing door** puerta *f* giratoria.

swipe [swaip] **1.** golpear fuertemente; *sl.* hurtar; **2.** golpe *m*.

swirl [swəːl] **1.** arremolinarse; **2.** remolino *m*; torbellino *m*.

swish [swiʃ] **1.** *v/t.* (*flog*) zurrar; *cane* agitar; *v/i.* silbar; (*dress*) crujir; **2.** silbido *m*; crujido *m of dress*.

Swiss [swis] suizo *adj. a. su. m* (*a f*).

switch [switʃ] **1.** (*stick*) varilla *f*; cambio *m of policy*; ⚓ agujas *f/pl.*, desviación *f*; ⚡ interruptor *m*; llave *f*; **2.** *v/t.* ⚓ desviar; *policy, positions* cambiar; ~ *on* ⚡ encender, conectar; ~ *off* ⚡ apagar, cortar; *v/i.:* ~ *from A to B* (*or* ~ *over*) *to B*) dejar A para tomar *etc.*

B; **'⁓·board** cuadro *m* de distribución; *teleph.* cuadro *m* de conexión manual.

swiv·el ['swivl] **1.** eslabón *m* giratorio; **2.** (hacer) girar.

swol·len ['swouln] *p.p.* of swell 1.

swoop [swu:p] **1.** (*a.* ⁓ down) precipitarse (*on* sobre); (*bird*) calar; **2.** descenso *m* súbito.

sword [sɔ:d] espada *f*; **'⁓·fish** pez *m* espada; **'⁓ rat·tling** fanfarronería.

swords·man ['sɔ:dzmən] esgrimidor *m*; espadachín *m*; **'swords·man·ship** esgrima *f*.

swore [swɔ:] *pret.* of swear.

sworn [swɔ:n] *p.p.* of swear; *enemy* implacable.

swum [swʌm] *p.p.* of swim 1.

swung [swʌŋ] *pret. a. p.p.* of swing 1.

syc·a·more ['sikəmɔ:] sicomoro *m*.

syc·o·phant ['sikəfænt] adulador *m*; **syc·o·phan·tic** [sikə'fæntik] □ adulatorio.

syl·la·ble ['siləbl] sílaba *f*.

syl·la·bus ['siləbəs] programa *m*.

syl·lo·gism ['silədʒizm] silogismo *m*.

sym·bol ['simbəl] símbolo *m*; **sym·bol·ic, sym·bol·i·cal** [⁓'bɔlik(l)] □ simbólico; **sym·bol·ism** ['⁓bəlizm] simbolismo *m*; **'sym·bol·ize** simbolizar.

sym·me·try ['simitri] simetría *f*.

sym·pa·thet·ic [simpə'θetik] □ compasivo; simpático; **sym·pa·thize** ['⁓θaiz] compadecerse; ⁓ *with* compadecer(se de); **sym·pa·thiz·er** ['⁓θaizə] simpatizante *m/f* (*with* de); partidario (a *f*) *m*; **sym·pa·thy**

['⁓θi] compasión *f*, conmiseración *f*.

sym·phon·ic [sim'fɔnik] sinfónico; **sym·pho·ny** ['simfəni] sinfonía *f*.

symp·tom ['simptəm] síntoma *m*; **symp·to·mat·ic** [⁓'mætik] □ sintomático.

syn·a·gogue ['sinəgɔg] sinagoga *f*.

syn·chro·mesh gear ['siŋkroumeʃ·'giə] engranaje *m* sincronizado.

syn·chro·nize ['siŋkranaiz] *v/i.* ser sincrónico; *v/t.* sincronizar.

syn·co·pate ['siŋkəpeit] sincopar; **syn·co·pa·tion, syn·co·pe** ['⁓pi] síncopa *f*.

syn·di·cate 1. ['sindikit] sindicato *m*; **2.** ['⁓keit] sindicar.

syn·drome ['sindroum] síndrome *m*; *toxic shock* ⁓ síndrome *m* del choque tóxico.

syn·er·gism ['sinədʒizm] sinergia *f*.

syn·od ['sinəd] sínodo *m*.

syn·o·nym ['sinənim] sinónimo *m*; **syn·on·y·mous** [si'nɔniməs] □ sinónimo.

syn·op·sis [si'nɔpsis] sinopsis *f*.

syn·tax ['sintæks] sintaxis *f*.

syn·the·sis ['sinθisis] síntesis *f*; **syn·the·size** ['⁓saiz] sintetizar.

syn·thet·ic, syn·thet·i·cal [sin'θetik(l)] □ sintético.

syph·i·lis ['sifilis] sífilis *f*.

syph·i·lit·ic [sifi'litik] sifilítico.

Syr·i·an ['siriən] sirio *adj. a. su. m* (a *f*).

syr·up ['sirəp] jarabe *m*.

sys·tem ['sistim] sistema *m* (*a.* ⚙); ⚙ constitución *f*; ⊕ mecanismo *m*; ⚡ circuito *m*, instalación *f*.

T

T [ti:]: F *to a* ⁓ exactamente.

tab·by ['tæbi] **1.** (*male*) gato *m* atigrado; (*female*) gata *f*; F solterona *f*; **2.** atigrado.

tab·er·nac·le ['tæbənækl] tabernáculo *m*.

ta·ble ['teibl] **1.** mesa *f*; ⚹ *etc.* tabla *f*; (*statistical*) cuadro *m*; △ tablero *m*; **2.** *motion etc.* poner sobre la mesa, presentar; (*index*) catalogar.

ta·ble...: **'⁓·cloth** mantel *m*; **'⁓·land** meseta *f*; **'⁓ lin·en** mantelería *f*; **'⁓ mat** apartador *m*, salvamanteles *m*; **'⁓ nap·kin** servilleta *f*; **'⁓·spoon** cuchara *f* grande.

tab·let ['tæblit] pastilla *f* of soap *etc.*; tableta *f*; bloc *m* (de papel); ⚹ comprimido *m*.

ta·ble...: **'⁓ talk** conversación *f* de sobremesa; **'⁓ ten·nis** tenis *m* de mesa.

tab·loid ['tæblɔid] periódico *m* de formato reducido.

ta·boo [tə'bu:] **1.** tabú, prohibido; **2.** tabú *m*; **3.** prohibir.

tab·u·late ['tæbjuleit] exponer en forma de tabla, tabular.

tac·it ['tæsit] □ tácito; **tac·i·turn** ['⁓tə:n] □ taciturno.

tack [tæk] **1.** (*nail*) tachuela *f*; *sew.*

hilván m; ♣ virada f, bordada f; *fig.* rumbo m; 2. *v/t.* clavar con tachuelas; *sew.* hilvanar; *fig.* añadir *v/i.* ♣ virar.

tack·le ['tækl] 1. ♣, ⊕ aparejo m; ♣ jarcia f; avíos m/pl.; *sport:* atajo m; 2. agarrar; *sport:* atajar.

tack·y ['tæki] pegajoso; F desaseado, cursi.

tact [tækt] tacto m, discreción f; **tact·ful** ['⁓ful] □ discreto.

tac·tics ['tæktiks] pl. táctica f.

tact·less ['tæktlis] □ indiscreto.

taf·fe·ta ['tæfitə] tafetán m.

tag [tæg] 1. (*label*) etiqueta f, marbete m; herrete m; (*rag*) pingajo m; 2. *v/t.* pegar una etiqueta a.

tail [teil] 1. (*label*) cola f (*a. fig.*), rabo m; trenza f of hair; cabellera f of comet; faldón m, faldillas f/pl. of coat; 2. *v/t.* (*follow*) seguir de cerca, vigilar; *v/i.*: ⁓ *away*, ⁓ *off* ir disminuyendo; **tailed** con rabo; *long-*⁓ rabilargo; **tail end** cola f; extremo m; *fig.* parte f que queda; porción f restante; **tail·less** sin rabo; **tail·light** luz f piloto (*or* trasera).

tai·lor ['teilə] 1. sastre m; 2. *suit* confeccionar; **tai·lor·ing** sastrería f; corte m; **tai·lor-made** hecho por sastre.

tail...: '⁓*piece* typ. florón m; *fig.* apéndice m; '⁓*pipe* mot. tubo m de escape; '⁓ *skid* ⊁ patín m de cola; '⁓*un·it* conjunto m de cola; '⁓'*wind* viento m de cola.

taint [teint] 1. infección f; mancha f; 2. manchar(se); corromper(se).

take [teik] 1. [*irr.*] *v/t.* tomar; coger; *p.* llevar; (*by force*) asir; arrebatar; (*steal*) robar; (*accept*) aceptar; (*tolerate*) aguantar; (*catch*) coger; *advice* seguir; *oath* prestar; *opportunity* aprovechar; *photo, ticket* sacar; *step, walk etc.* dar; *trip* hacer; it ⁓s 2 men to lift it se necesita 2 hombres para levantarlo; F *we can* ⁓ *it* lo aguantamos todo; *the devil* ⁓ *it!* ¡maldición!; ⁓ *apart* desmontar, descomponer; ⁓ *away* quitar; llevarse; ⅍ restar; ⁓ *back* recibir devuelto; ⁓ *down* bajar; descolgar; ⊕ desmontar; *note* apuntar, poner por escrito; ⁓ *from* quitar a; privar de; ⅍ restar de; ⁓ *in* (*understand*) comprender; (*include*) abarcar; *clothes* achicar; *p.* acoger, recibir; ⁓ *off clothes* quitarse; *discount* descontar; F contrahacer, parodiar; ⁓ *on* (*assume*) tomar; *duties* tomar

sobre sí; ⁓ *out* (*extract*) extraer, sacar; *children* llevar de paseo; *girl* escoltar, invitar; cortejar; ⁓ *it out on a p.* desahogarse riñendo a una p.; vengarse en una p.; ⁓ *over* tomar posesión de; encargarse de; ⁓ *upon o.s.* tomar sobre sí; encargarse de; ⁓ *it upon o.s.* to atreverse a; 2. [*irr.*] *v/i.* pegar; ser eficaz; resultar; ♀ arraigar (*a. fig.*); (*set*) cuajar; (*vaccination*) prender; ⁓ *after* parecerse a; salir a; ⁓ *off* salir; ⊁ despegar; F ⁓ *up with* relacionarse con, estrechar amistad con; 3. toma f; *phot.* exposición f; '⁓ **home pay** salario m neto.

tak·en ['teikn] *p.p.* of take; be ⁓ *with* estar cautivado por; be ⁓ *ill* enfermar; be ⁓ *up with* estar ocupado en; estar absorto en; F be ⁓ *in* tragar el anzuelo; '**take·off** ⁓ despegue m; ⊕ toma f de fuerza; F caricatura f, parodia f (of, on de).

tak·ing ['teikin] 1. □ F atractivo, encantador; 2. toma f; '**tak·ings** pl. ingresos m/pl.

talc [tælk], **tal·cum pow·der** ['tælkəm 'paudə] talco m.

tale [teil] cuento m (*a. b.s.*); fábula f; relación f; historia f; tell ⁓s (*out of school*) soplar; chismear; '⁓'**bear·er** ['⁓bɛərə] soplón (-a f) m.

tal·ent ['tælənt] talento m.

talk [tɔːk] 1. conversación f, charla f; F palabras f/pl.; there is ⁓ of ger. se habla de inf.; ⁓ of the town comidilla f de la ciudad; 2. hablar (to con); charlar; *sense etc.* decir; ⁓ *into* persuadir a; convencer; ⁓ *out of* disuadir de; ⁓ *over* discutir; hablar de; **talk·a·tive** ['⁓ətiv] □ locuaz, hablador; **talk·ie** ['⁓i] F película f sonora; '**talk·ing** parlante; *bird* parlero; **talk·ing-to** ['⁓tuː] F rapapolvo m.

tall [tɔːl] alto; grande; be 6 feet ⁓ tener 6 pies de alto; *sl.* ⁓ *order* cosa f muy difícil; *sl.* ⁓ *story*, ⁓ *tale* cuento m exagerado; '**tall·ness** altura f.

tal·ly ['tæli] 1. (*stick*) tarja f; (*account*) cuenta f; número m; 2. cuadrar, concordar (with con).

Tal·mud ['tælmuːd] Talmud m; ⁓*ic* [tæl'muːdik] talmúdico.

tal·on ['tælən] garra f.

tam·a·ble ['teiməbl] domable.

ta·ma·le [tə'mæli a. tə'mɑːli] tamal m.

tam·bou·rine [tæmbə'riːn] pandereta f.

tame [teim] 1. □ domesticado; manso; doméstico; *fig.* inocuo; F abu-

rrido; 2. domar, amansar; **'tame-
ness** mansedumbre *f.*

tamp [tæmp] apisonar; ⚔ atacar.

tam·per ['tæmpə]: ~ *with* descomponer, estropear; *document* falsificar; *witness* sobornar.

tam·pon ['tæmpən] tapón *m.*

tan [tæn] 1. bronceado *m*; (*bark*) casca *f*; 2. *leather* curtir, adobar; (*sun*) tostar(se), broncear(se).

tan·dem ['tændəm] 1. tándem *m*; 2. *adj. a. adv.* ⚡ en tándem.

tang [tæŋ] *fig.* gustillo *m*, dejo *m*; sabor *m* fuerte y picante.

tan·gent ['tændʒənt] tangente *adj. a. su. f*; go (*or* fly) off at a ~ cambiar súbitamente de rumbo.

tan·ger·ine [tændʒə'ri:n] mandarina *f.*

tan·gi·ble ['tændʒəbl] □ tangible; *fig. a.* concreto.

tan·gle ['tæŋgl] 1. enredo *m* (*a. fig.*), nudo *m*, maraña *f*; 2. enredar(se); F pelear (*with* con).

tank [tæŋk] tanque *m* depósito *m*; ⚔ tanque *m*, carro *m* de combate.

tank·er ['tæŋkə] petrolero *m*; tanquero *m S.Am.*

tan·ner ['tænə] curtidor *m.*

tan·ner·y ['tænəri] curtiduría *f.*

tan·ta·lize ['tæntəlaiz] atormentar, tentar, dar dentera; **'tan·ta·liz·ing** □ atormentador.

tan·trum ['tæntrəm] F rabieta *f.*

tap¹ [tæp] 1. palmadita *f*, golpecito *m*; 2. golpear ligeramente.

tap² [~] 1. (*water*) grifo *m*; (*gas*) llave *f*, espita *f* *of barrel*; ⊕ macho *m* de terraja; on ~ servido al grifo; 2. *barrel* espitar; *tree* sangrar; *resources* explotar; *teleph. wire* escuchar clandestinamente.

tap dance ['tæpdɑːns] 1. zapateado *m*; 2. zapatear.

tape [teip] 1. cinta *f* (*a. sport*); cinta *f* adhesiva; cinta *f* magnetofónica *for recording*; 2. F grabar sobre cinta; '~ **meas·ure** cinta *f* métrica.

ta·per [teipə] 1. cerilla *f*; 2. ahusado; 3. ~ ahusarse; *v/t.* afilar, ahusar.

tape...: '~ **re·cord** grabar sobre cinta; '~ **re·cord·er** magnetofón *m*; grabador *m* en cinta; '~ **re·cord·ing** grabación *f* en cinta.

tap·es·try ['tæpistri] tapiz *m*; tapicería *f.*

tape·worm ['teipwəːm] tenia *f*, solitaria *f.*

ta·pi·o·ca [tæpi'oukə] tapioca *f.*

tap·pet ['tæpit] ⊕ alza-válvulas *m.*

tap·room ['tæprum] bodegón *m.*

taps [tæps] toque *m* de silencio; *sl.* conclusión *f*; muerte *f.*

tar [tɑː] 1. alquitrán *m*; brea *f*; F ⚓ marinero *m*; 2. alquitranar.

ta·ran·tu·la [tə'ræntjulə] tarántula *f.*

tar·dy ['tɑːdi] □ tardío; lento.

tar·get ['tɑːgit] blanco *m* (*a. fig.*); ~ *practice* tiro *m* al blanco.

tar·iff ['tærif] tarifa *f*; arancel *m.*

tar·mac ['tɑːmæk] alquitranado *m.*

tar·nish ['tɑːniʃ] 1. deslustrar(se) (*a. fig.*); 2. deslustre *m.*

tar·pau·lin [tɑː'pɔːlin] alquitranado *m*; lienzo *m* alquitranado.

tar·ry¹ ['tæri] *lit.* tardar; detenerse.

tar·ry² ['tɑːri] alquitranado; embreado.

tart [tɑːt] 1. □ ácido, agrio; *fig.* áspero; 2. tarta *f*, torta *f*; *sl.* puta *f.*

tar·tan ['tɑːtən] tartán *m.*

Tar·tar¹ ['tɑːtə] tártaro *m*; *fig.* arpía *f*, mujer *f* regañona.

tar·tar² [~] 🜄 tártaro *m*, sarro *m.*

task [tɑːsk] tarea *f*; faena *f*; *take to* ~ reprender (*for acc.*); **task force** agrupación *f* de fuerzas (para operación especial); **'task·mas·ter** capataz *m*; superintendente *m*; amo *m.*

taste [teist] 1. gusto *m*; sabor *m* (of *a*); (*sip*) sorbo *m*; (*sample*) muestra *f*; (*good*) ~ (buen) gusto *m*; 2. *v/t.* gustar; notar (un gusto de); (*try*) probar; *v/i.*: ~ *of* saber a; ~ *good* estar muy rico, estar sabroso; **taste·ful** ['~ful] □ de buen gusto.

taste·less ['teistlis] □ insípido, soso; (*in bad taste*) de mal gusto.

tast·y ['teisti] □ F sabroso.

ta·ta ['tæ'tɑː] F adiós.

tat·tered ['tætəd] andrajoso; en jirones; **tat·ters** ['tætəz] *pl.* andrajos *m/pl.*; jirones *m/pl.*

tat·tle ['tætl] 1. parlotear, *b.s.* chismear; 2. charla *f*, *b.s.* chismes *m/pl.*

tat·too¹ [tə'tuː] ⚔ (toque *m* de) retreta *f*; espectáculo *m* militar.

tat·too² [~] 1. tatuar; 2. tatuaje *m.*

taunt [tɔːnt] 1. mofa *f*; pulla *f*; dicterio *m*; 2. mofar.

taut [tɔːt] tieso, tenso, tirante.

tav·ern ['tævən] taberna *f*; mesón *m.*

taw·dry ['tɔːdri] □ charro; barato; deslucido; cursi; de oropel.

tax [tæks] 1. impuesto *m* (on sobre), contribución *f*; *fig.* carga *f* (on sobre); ~ *evasion* evasión *f* fiscal; 2. *p.* imponer contribuciones a; *th.* imponer contribución sobre; ⚖ *costs* tasar; **'tax·a·ble** imponible; sujeto a impuesto; **tax'a·tion** impuestos *m/pl.*; contribuciones *f/pl.*; sistema *m* tributario; **'tax-col·lec·tor** recaudador *m* de contribuciones; **'tax de·duc·tion** exclusión *f* de contribución; **'tax e·va·sion** evasión *f* fiscal; **tax-'free** exento de contribuciones; **'tax·ha·ven** asilo *m* de los impuestos.

tax·i ['tæksi] **1.** = '~·cab taxi *m*; **2.** ir en taxi; ⚔ carretear, taxear.

'tax···: '~ **loss** pérdida *f* reclamable; **tax·pay·er** ['tækspeiə] contribuyente *m/f*; **'tax re·lief** aligeramiento *m* de impuestos; **'tax re·turn** declaración *f* de renta.

tea [ti:] té *m*; (*meal*) merienda *f*; high~ merienda-cena *f*; '~ **bag** muñeca *f*.

teach [ti:tʃ] [*irr.*] enseñar (*to* a); instruir; **'teach·er** profesor (-a *f*) *m*; maestro (a *f*) *m*; **'teach·er 'train·ing** formación *f* pedagógica; **'teach·ing** enseñanza *f*; doctrina *f*.

tea·cup ['ti:kʌp] taza *f* para té.

team [ti:m] **1.** equipo *m*; tiro *m* of *horses*; yunta *f* of *oxen*; **2.:** formar un equipo; '~ **spir·it** compañerismo *m*; camaradería *f*; **team·ster** ['stə] tronquista *m*; conductor *m* de camión; **'team·work** cooperación *f*, colaboración *f*; solidaridad *f*.

tea·pot ['ti:pɔt] tetera *f*.

tear[1] [teə] **1.** [*irr.*] *v/t.* rasgar, desgarrar; romper; *flesh* lacerar; ~ *apart* despedazar; ~ *down building* derribar; *v/i.* rasgarse; F ir con toda prisa; **2.** rasgón *m*, desgarrón *m*.

tear[2] [tiə] lágrima *f*.

'tear·ful ['tiəful] □ lloroso, llorón.

'tear-gas ['tiə'gæs] gas *m* lacrimógeno.

tease [ti:z] **1.** *wool* cardar; *fig.* embromar, tomar el pelo a; **2.** embromador (-a *f*) *m*, guasón (-a *f*) *m*.

tea···: '~ **set** servicio *m* de té; '~·**spoon** cucharita *f*; '~·**strain·er** colador *m* de té.

teat [ti:t] pezón *m*; teta *f*.

tech·ni·cal ['teknikl] □ técnico; **tech·ni·cian** [tek'niʃn] técnico *m*.

tech·ni·col·or ['teknikʌlə] (*attr.* en) tecnicolor *m*.

tech·nique [tek'ni:k] técnica *f*.

tech·nol·o·gy [tek'nɔlədʒi] tecnología *f*.

ted·dy bear ['tedibeə] osito *m* de felpa, oso *m* de juguete.

te·di·ous ['ti:diəs] □ aburrido, fastidioso; cansado.

teem [ti:m] hormiguear; hervir (*with* de); llover a cántaros.

teen·ag·er ['ti:neidʒə] joven *m/f* de 13 a 19 años.

teens [ti:nz] *pl.* edad *f* de 13 a 19 años; F juventud *f* de 13 a 19 años.

tee·ter ['ti:tə] F balancear, oscilar.

teethe [ti:ð] echar los (primeros) dientes; **'teeth·ing** dentición *f*.

tee·to·tal·er ['ti:toutələ] abstemio (a *f*) *m*.

tel·e·gram ['teligræm] telegrama *m*.

tel·e·graph ['teligraːf] **1.** telégrafo *m*; **2.** telegrafiar; **te'leg·ra·phy** telegrafía *f*.

tel·e·pa·thy [ti'lepəθi] telepatía *f*.

tel·e·phone ['telifoun] **1.** teléfono *m*; ~ *booth* locutorio *m*, cabina *f* de teléfono; ~ *call* llamada *f*; ~ *directory* guía *f* telefónica; ~ *exchange* central *f* telefónica; ~ *operator* telefonista *m/f*; **2.** llamar por teléfono, telefonear.

tel·e·pho·to lens ['teli'foutou 'lenz] lente *f* telefotográfica.

tel·e·print·er ['teliprintə] teleimpresor *m*.

tel·e·scope ['teliskoup] **1.** telescopio *m*; catalejo *m*; **2.** telescopar(se); enchufar(se); **tel·e·scop·ic** ['~'kɔpik] □ telescópico; de enchufe.

tel·e·type ['telitaip] **1.** teletipo *m*; **2.** transmitir por teletipo.

tel·e·vise ['telivaiz] televisar; **tel·e·vi·sion** ['~viʒn] (*attr.* de) televisión *f*; ~ *set* aparato *m* de televisión, televisor *m*; *cable* ~ televisión *f* emitida por cable.

tel·ex ['teleks] servicio *m* comercial de teletipo.

tell [tel] [*irr.*] *v/t.* decir; *story* contar; distinguir (*from* de); determinar; ~ *a p. to inf.* decirle a uno que sabe; ~ *off* mandar (*to inf.*); F reñir, regañar; *v/i.* hablar (*about, of* de); hacer mella, surtir efecto (*on* en); **'tell·er** narrador (-a *f*) *m*; (*bank*) cajero *m*; **tell·tale** ['~teil] **1.** revelador; indicador; **2.** soplón (-a *f*) *m*.

tem·per ['tempə] **1.** *all senses:* templar; *fig. a.* mitigar, moderar; *humor m*; disposición *f*; natural *m*; (*anger*) mal genio *m*; **tem·per·a·men·tal** ['~mentl] □ complexional; caprichoso, excitable; *be* ~ tener genio; **'tem·per·ance** templanza *f*; abstinencia *f* (del alcohol); **tem·per·ate** ['~rit] □ templado; sobrio,

abstemio; **tem·per·a·ture** ['temprit∫ə] temperatura *f*; ⚕ calentura *f*.
tem·pest ['tempist] tempestad *f*.
tem·ple¹ ['templ] templo *m*.
tem·ple² [~] *anat.* sien *f*.
tem·po·ral ['tempərəl] □ temporal;
'**tem·po·rar·y** □ temporáneo, provisional.
tempt [tempt] tentar, provocar, inducir (*to* a); '**tempt·ing** □ tentador; *food* apetitoso.
ten [ten] diez (*a. su. m*); decena *f*.
te·na·cious [ti'neiʃəs] □ tenaz; **te·nac·i·ty** [ti'næsiti] tenacidad *f*.
ten·an·cy ['tenənsi] inquilinato *m*, arriendo *m*.
ten·ant ['tenənt] **1.** arrendatario (a *f*) *m*, inquilino (a *f*) *m*; *fig.* habitante *m/f*; **2.** alquilar; *fig.* ocupar.
tend¹ [tend] tender (*to, towards* a).
tend² [~] *sick etc.* cuidar; vigilar; *machine* manejar; *cattle* guardar.
tend·en·cy ['tendənsi] tendencia *f*.
ten·der¹ ['tendə] tierno; *spot* delicado, sensible; ⚕ dolorido.
ten·der² [~] **1.** † oferta *f*, proposición *f*; *legal* ~ moneda *f* de curso legal; **2.** *v/i.* † ofertar; *v/t.* ofrecer.
ten·der·foot ['tendəfut] recién llegado *m*; novato *m*; **ten·der·loin** ['~lɔin] filete *m*; '**ten·der·ness** ternura *f*; sensibilidad *f*.
ten·don ['tendən] tendón *m*.
ten·e·ment ['tenimənt] vivienda *f*; habitación *f*; ~*s pl.* = ~ *house* casa *f* de vecindad.
ten·et ['ti:net] dogma *m*, credo *m*.
ten·fold ['tenfould] **1.** *adj.* décuplo; **2.** *adv.* diez veces.
ten·nis ['tenis] tenis *m*; '~ **court** pista *f* de tenis, cancha *f* de tenis *S.Am.*; '~ **play·er** tenista *m/f*.
ten·or ['tenə] tenor *m* (*a.* ♪); curso *m*; tendencia *f*.
tense¹ [tens] *gr.* tiempo *m*.
tense² [~] **1.** tieso, tenso; *situation* crítico, lleno de emoción; **2.** te(n)sar; estirar; '**tense·ness** tirantez *f*; **ten·sile** ['tensail] tensor; tenso; **ten·sion** ['~ʃn] tensión *f*; tirantez *f* (*a. fig.*); ⚡ *high* ~ alta tensión *f*.
tent [tent] tienda *f* (de campaña).
ten·ta·cle ['tentəkl] tentáculo *m*.
ten·ter·hook ['tentəhuk] escarpia *f*; *fig.* be on ~*s* estar en ascuas.
tenth [tenθ] décimo (*a. su. m*).
ten·u·ous ['tenjuəs] □ tenue; sutil.
ten·ure ['tenjuə] posesión *f*; tenencia *f*, ejercicio *m* of office.

tep·id ['tepid] □ tibio.
term [tə:m] **1.** término *m* (*end, word, &c, phls.*); (*period*) plazo *m*, período *m*; (*of imprisonment*) mandato *m* of president; ⚖, *univ., school*: trimestre *m*; semestre *m*; *fig.* come to ~*s* with conformarse con; **2.** nombrar, llamar; calificar (de).
ter·mi·nal ['tə:minəl] **1.** □ terminal (*a.* ⚘); **2.** ⚡ borne *m*; ⚡ polo *m*; (*port*) terminal *f*; 🚂 estación *f* de cabeza; **ter·mi·nate** ['~neit] *v/t. a. v/i.* terminar.
ter·mi·nol·o·gy [tə:mi'nɔlədʒi] terminología *f*.
ter·mite ['tə:mait] termita *m*, comején *m*; termite *m*.
ter·race ['terəs] **1.** terraza *f*, terraplén *m*; hilera *f* of houses; (*roof*) azotea *f*; **2.** terraplenar.
ter·rain ['terein] terreno *m*.
ter·res·tri·al [ti'restriəl] □ terrestre.
ter·ri·ble ['terəbl] □ terrible; F malísimo, pésimo.
ter·rif·ic [tə'rifik] □ tremendo; F estupendo; imponente; **ter·ri·fy** ['terifai] aterrar, aterrorizar.
ter·ri·to·ri·al [teri'tɔ:riəl] **1.** □ territorial; ~ *waters pl.* aguas *f/pl.* territoriales (*or* jurisdiccionales); **2.** reservista *m*; **ter·ri·to·ry** ['~təri] territorio *m*.
ter·ror ['terə] terror *m*, espanto *m*; '**ter·ror·ism** terrorismo *m*; '**ter·ror·ist** terrorista *m*; **ter·ror·ize** aterrorizar.
ter·ry cloth ['teri'klɔθ] albornoz *m*.
terse [tə:s] □ breve, conciso, lacónico; '**terse·ness** laconismo *m*.
test [test] **1.** prueba *f*, ensayo *m*; examen *m*; *psychological etc.*: test *m*; *acid* ~ *fig.* prueba *f* de fuego; ~ *flight* vuelo *m* de ensayo; **2.** probar, ensayar; examinar.
tes·ta·ment ['testəmənt] testamento *m*.
test ban ['test'bæn] prohibición *f* contra pruebas de armas nucleares.
test case ['test keis] pleito *m* de ensayo.
test·er ['testə] (*p.*) ensayador *m*.
tes·ti·cle ['testikl] testículo *m*.
tes·ti·fy ['testifai] testificar (*that* que); atestiguar (*to* acc.); atestar.
tes·ti·mo·ny ['testimouni] testimonio *m*.
test·ing ground ['testiŋ 'graund] zona *f* de pruebas.
test...: '~ **pa·per** *school*: papel *m* de

test pilot

examen; **☊** papel *m* reactivo; '~ **pi·lot** piloto *m* de pruebas; '~ **print** *phot.* copia *f* de prueba; '~ **tube** tubo *m* de ensayo; probeta *f*; ~ **baby** niñoprobeta *m*.

tes·ty ['testi] ☐ enojadizo, picajoso.

te·ta·nus ['tetənəs] tétano *m*.

teth·er ['teðə] 1. atadura *f*, traba *f*; 2. apersogar, atar.

text [tekst] texto *m*; tema *m*; '~**book** libro *m* de texto.

tex·tile ['tekstail] 1. textil; 2. *mst* ~s *pl.* tejidos *m/pl.*

tex·ture ['tekstʃə] textura *f* (*a. fig.*).

than [ðæn, *unstressed* ðən] que; *more* ~ *I* más que yo; *more* ~ *ten* más de diez; *no more* ~ *ten* no más que diez.

thank [θæŋk] 1. dar las gracias a; agradecer (*for acc.*); (*no*) ~ *you* (no) gracias; 2. ~s *pl.* gracias *f/pl.*; agradecimiento *m*; ~s to gracias a; **thank·ful** ['~ful] ☐ agradecido; **thank·less** ~ *p.* ingrato; *task* ímprobo, sin recompensa; **thanks·giv·ing** ['~sgivin] acción *f* de gracias.

that [ðæt, *unstressed* ðət] 1. *pron.* (*pl. those*) *m:* ése, aquél (*more remote*); *f:* ésa, aquélla; *neuter:* eso, aquello; (*relative*) que, el cual *etc.*; ~ *is* es decir; 2. *adj.* (*pl. those*) *m:* ese, aquel (*more remote*); *f:* esa, aquella; 3. *adv.* tan; 4. *cj.* que; para que; *in* ~, *so* ~ (*purpose*) para *inf.*, para que *subj.*; (*result*) de modo que.

thaw [θɔ:] 1. deshielo *m*; 2. deshelar (-se), derretir(se); *fig.* ablandar(se).

the [ði:; *before vowel* ði, *before consonant* ðə] 1. *article:* el, la; *pl.* los, las; 2. *adv.* ~ ... ~ cuanto más ... (tanto) más.

the·a·ter ['θiətə] teatro *m* (*a. fig.*); *operating* ~ quirófano *m*, sala *f* de operaciones.

theft [θeft] hurto *m*, robo *m*.

their [ðɛə] su(s); **theirs** [~z] (el) suyo, (la) suya *etc.*

them [ðem, ðəm] *acc.* los, las; *dat.* les; (*after prp.*) ellos, ellas.

theme [θi:m] tema *m*; ~ **song** motivo *m* principal, tema *m* central.

them·selves [ðəm'selvz] (*subject*) ellos mismos, ellas mismas; *acc., dat.* se; (*after prp.*) sí (mismos, mismas).

then [ðen] 1. *adv.* entonces; luego; después; *by* ~ para entonces; 2. *cj.* pues; conque; 3. *adj.* (de) entonces.

thence·forth ['ðens'fɔ:θ] *lit.* de allí en adelante; desde entonces.

the·o·lo·gi·an [θiə'loudʒiən] teólogo *m*; **the·ol·o·gy** [θi'ɔlədʒi] teología *f*.

the·o·rize ['θiəraiz] teorizar; **the·o·ry** teoría *f*; *in* ~ teóricamente.

ther·a·peu·tic [θerə'pju:tik] 1. ☐ terapéutico; 2. ~s *pl.* terapéutica *f*; **ther·a·py** terapia *f*; terapéutica *f*.

there [ðɛə] *adv.* allí, allá, ahí; F all ~ despierto, vivo; ~ *is*, ~ *are* [ðə'riz, ðə'rɑ:] hay.

there...: '~·a·bout(s) por ahí; '~·aft·er después de eso; '~·by por eso, de ese modo; '~·fore por (lo) tanto, por consiguiente; '~·up·on por consiguiente; al momento, en seguida.

ther·mal ['θə:məl] ☐ termal; **ther·mic** ['~mik] ☐ térmico.

ther·mo·dy·nam·ics ['θə:moudai'næmiks] *sg.* termodinámica *f*.

ther·mom·e·ter [θə'mɔmitə] termómetro *m*; **ther·mo·nu·cle·ar** ['~'nju:kliə] termonuclear; **ther·mo·pile** ['~moupail] termopila *f*; **Ther·mos** ['~mɔs] (*a.* ~ *flask*, ~ *bottle*) termos *m*; **ther·mo·stat** ['~moustæt] termóstato *m*.

these [ði:z] (*pl. of this*) 1. *pron. m:* éstos; *f:* éstas; 2. *adj. m:* estos; *f:* estas.

the·sis ['θi:sis] tesis *f*.

they [ðei] ellos, ellas; ~ *who* los que.

thick [θik] 1. ☐ espeso; denso; *air* (*misty*) brumoso; (*foul*) viciado; *liquid* (*cloudy*) turbio; (*stiff*) viscoso; 2 *inches* ~ 2 pulgadas de espesor; F *be* ~ (*as thieves*) intimar mucho, ser uña y carne; 2.: *in the* ~ *of* en medio de; (*battle*) en lo más reñido de; **thick·en** espesar(se); (*plot*) complicarse; **thick·et** ['~it] matorral *m*, espesura *f*; **thick-head·ed** estúpido, torpe; **thick·ness** espesura *f*; espesor *m*; grueso *m*; densidad *f*; **thick-skinned** *fig.* insensible.

thief [θi:f] ladrón (-a *f*) *m*; **thieve** [θi:v] hurtar, robar; **thiev·er·y** ['~vəri], **thiev·ing** robo *m*, latrocinio *m*.

thigh [θai] muslo *m*; '~·bone fémur *m*.

thim·ble ['θimbl] dedal *m*.

thin [θin] 1. ☐ delgado; *p.* flaco; *covering* ligero; transparente; *air, scent, sound* tenue; *crop, crowd* escaso; 2. (*slim*) adelgazar(se); aclarar; (*crowd etc.*) reducir(se).

thing [θiŋ] cosa *f*; asunto *m*; ~s *pl.* (*possessions*) efectos *m/pl.*; cosas *f/pl.*; F *the* ~ *is* es el caso es que; *the best* ~ lo mejor; F *know a* ~ *or two* saber cuántas son cinco; *not to know the first* ~ *about* no saber nada en absoluto de.

think [θiŋk] [*irr.*] *v/i.* pensar; (*believe*) creer; reflexionar; meditar; *I ~ so* creo que sí; *I should ~ so!* ¡ya lo creo!; *v/t.* pensar; acordarse de; *~ little of* tener en poco; *~ up* idear; imaginar; **'think·a·ble** concebible; **'think·ing 1.** intelectual, mental; **2.** pensamiento *m*.

thin·ness ['θinnis] delgadez *f*; tenuidad *f etc.*

third [θəːd] **1.** tercero; F *~ degree* interrogatorio *m* brutal; ☪ *World* Tercero Mundo *m*; **2.** tercio *m*; tercera parte *f*; ♪ tercera *f*; **'~·rate** de tercer orden.

thirst [θəːst] **1.** sed *f*; **2.** tener sed (*after, for* de); **'thirst·y** ☐ sediento; *be ~* tener sed.

thir·teen ['θəː'tiːn] trece (*a. su. m*); **'thir'teenth** [~θ] decimotercio, decimotercero; **'thir·ti·eth** ['~tiiθ] trigésimo; **'thir·ty** treinta.

this [ðis] (*pl.* **these**) **1.** *pron. m*: éste; *f*: ésta; *neuter*: esto; **2.** *adj. m*: este; *f*: esta.

thong [θɒŋ] correa *f*.

tho·rax ['θɔːræks] tórax *m*.

thorn [θɔːn] espina *f*; **'thorn·y** espinoso (*a. fig.*).

thor·ough ['θʌrə] ☐ completo; cabal; concienzudo, minucioso; **'~·bred** (de) pura sangre *m/f*; **'~·fare** vía *f* pública; carretera *f*; **'~·go·ing** cabal, totalista, de cuerpo entero; **'thor·ough·ness** minuciosidad *f*; lo concienzudo *etc.*

those [ðouz] (*pl.* of **that** 1, 2) **1.** *pron. m*: ésos, aquéllos (*more remote*); *f*: ésas, aquéllas (*more remote*); ~ *who* los que, aquellos que *etc.*; **2.** *adj. m*: esos, aquellos; *f*: esas, aquellas.

though [ðou] **1.** *cj.* aunque; si bien; *as ~ como si subj.*; **2.** *adv.* sin embargo.

thought [θɔːt] pensamiento *m*; reflexión *f*; solicitud *f*; **thought·ful** ['θɔːtful] ☐ (*thinking*) pensativo; (*kind*) atento; considerado; **'thought·ful·ness** atención *f*; solicitud *f*; previsión *f*.

thought·less ['θɔːtlis] ☐ irreflexivo; descuidado; inconsiderado.

thou·sand ['θauzənd] **1.** mil *m*; **2.** mil *m* millar *m*; **thou·sandth** ['~zenθ] milésimo (*a. su. m*).

thrash [θræʃ] *v/t.* golpear, azotar, zurrar; *v/i.*: ~ *about etc.* sacudirse, dar vueltas; **'thrash·ing** paliza *f*.

thread [θred] **1.** hilo *m* (*a. fig.*); hebra *f of silkworm*; filete *m*, rosca *f of*

screw; **2.** *needle* enhebrar; *beads* ensartar; **'~·bare** raído, gastado.

threat [θret] amenaza *f*; **'threat·en** amenazar (*to* con); **'threat·en·ing** ☐ amenazante, amenazador.

three [θriː] tres (*a. su. m*); **'~·col·or** de tres colores; **'~·cor·nered** triangular; ~ *hat* tricornio *m*; **'~·di·men·sion·al** tridimensional; **'~·fold 1.** *adj.* triple; **2.** *adv.* tres veces; **~ pence** ['θrepəns] tres peniques *m/pl.*; **'~·phase** ['θrifeiz] ⚡ trifásico; **'~·ply** *wood* de 3 capas; *wool* triple; **'~·way switch** conmutador *m* de tres terminales.

thresh [θreʃ] ♪ trillar; **thresh·ing** ['θreʃiŋ] ♪ trilla *f*; **'~·floor** era *f*; **'~·ma·chine** trilladora *f*.

threw [θruː] *pret.* of **throw** 1.

thrice [θrais] † tres veces.

thrift, thrift·i·ness ['θrift(inis)] economía *f*, frugalidad *f*; **'thrift·y** ☐ económico, frugal.

thrill [θril] **1.** emocionar(se), conmover(se); **2.** emoción *f*; estremecimiento *m*; **'thrill·er** F novela *f* (*or* película *f or* pieza *f*) escalofriante; novela *f* policíaca; **'thrill·ing** ☐ emocionante, apasionante.

thrive [θraiv] [*irr.*] medrar, florecer; **thriv·ing** ['θraiviŋ] ☐ próspero.

throat [θrout] garganta *f*; cuello *m*; **'throat·y** ☐ gutural, ronco.

throb [θrɒb] **1.** latir, palpitar; (*engine*) vibrar; **2.** latido *m*, pulsación *f*.

throes [θrouz] *pl.* agonía *f*, dolores *m/pl.*

throne [θroun] trono *m*.

throng [θrɒŋ] **1.** tropel *m*, muchedumbre *f*; **2.** atestar; apiñarse.

throt·tle ['θrɒtl] **1.** ahogar, estrangular (*a.* ⊕); **2.** gaznate *m*; **'~ valve** regulador *m*; *mot.* acelerador *m*.

through [θruː] **1.** *prp.* por; a través de; por medio de, debido a; **2.** *adv.* de parte a parte; (*desde el principio*) hasta el fin; **3.** *adj. train* directo; F *be ~* haber terminado; haber acabado (*with* con); **'~·out 1.** *prp.* durante todo, por todo; **2.** *adv.* todo el tiempo, desde el principio hasta el fin; **'~·way** (*a.* **thru·way**) carretera *f* troncal.

throve [θrouv] *pret.* of **thrive**.

throw [θrou] **1.** [*irr.*] echar, lanzar, arrojar, tirar; F *fight* perder con premeditación; ~ *away* echar; malgastar; *chance* desperdiciar; ~ *out* echar; *p.* poner en la calle; *hint* proferir;

parl. bill rechazar; ~ *up* F devolver, vomitar; **2.** tirada *f*, tiro *m*, echada *f*; '**~back** *biol.* reversión *f*; **thrown** [θroun] *p.p.* of *throw*.

thrum [θrʌm] ♪ *v/t.* *guitar* rasguear.

thrush [θrʌʃ] *orn.* zorzal *m*.

thrust [θrʌst] **1.** estocada *f* *of sword*; ✕ avance *m*; ataque *m*; ⊕ *a. fig.* empuje *m*; **2.** *v/t.* empujar (*forward etc.* hacia adelante *etc.*); ~ *aside* rechazar bruscamente; *v/i.*: ~ *at* asestar un golpe a; ~ *forward* seguir adelante; ✕ avanzar.

thud [θʌd] **1.** golpear con ruido sordo; **2.** ruido *m* sordo.

thug [θʌg] asesino *m*; ladrón *m* brutal; hombre *m* brutal, desalmado *m*.

thumb [θʌm] **1.** pulgar *m*; ✍ manosear; F ~ *a ride* hacer autostop; '**~in·dex** escalerilla *f*; índice *m* con pestañas; '**~screw** *hist.* empulgueras *f/pl.*; ⊕ tornillo *m* de orejas; '**~tack** chinche *m*.

thump [θʌmp] **1.** golpazo *m*; porrazo *m*; **2.** *v/t.* golpear; aporrear; *v/i.* caer *etc.* con golpe pesado.

thun·der ['θʌndə] **1.** trueno *m*; *fig.* estruendo *m*; **2.** tronar; *threats etc.* fulminar; '**~bolt** rayo *m* (*a. fig.*); '**~clap** trueno *m*; '**~cloud** nubarrón *m*; '**thun·der·ous** □ atronador; '**thun·der·storm** tronada *f*, tempestad *f* de truenos; '**thun·der·struck** *fig.* pasmado, estupefacto.

Thurs·day ['θəːzdei] jueves *m*.

thus [ðʌs] así; ~ *far* hasta aquí.

thwart [θwɔːt] frustrar, impedir, desbaratar.

thyme [taim] tomillo *m*.

thy·roid ['θairɔid] **1.** tiroideo; **2.** tiroides *m* (*a. ~ gland*).

tib·i·a ['tibiə] tibia *f*.

tic [tik] ✍ tic *m*.

tick¹ [~] *zo.* garrapata *f*.

tick² [~] **1.** tictac *m of clock*; (*mark*) señal *f*, marca *f*; **2.** hacer tictac.

tick·er ['tikə] teleimpresor *m*; *sl.* corazón *m*.

tick·er tape ['tikəteip] cinta *f* de cotizaciones.

tick·et ['tikit] **1.** billete *m*; *S.Am.* boleto *m*; *thea. etc.* entrada *f*, localidad *f*; (*counterfoil*) talón *m*; (*label*) etiqueta *f*, rótulo *m*; F multa *f* (*de conductor*); **2.** rotular, poner etiqueta a; '**~ col·lec·tor** revisor *m*; '**~ scal·per** revendedor *m* de billetes con mucha ganancia; '**~ win·dow** ventanilla *f*; taquilla *f*; 🚂 despacho *m* de billetes.

tick·le ['tikl] cosquillear, hacer cosquillas a; (*amuse*) divertir; '**tick·lish** □ cosquilloso; *fig.* peliagudo; F difícil; delicado.

tid·bit ['tidbit] golosina *f*; bocadito *m*.

tide [taid] **1.** marea *f*; *fig.* corriente *f*; marcha *f*; *low* ~ bajamar *f*; *fig.* punto *m* más bajo; *high* ~ pleamar *f*; *fig.* apogeo *m*; **2.**: *fig.* ~ *over* sacar temporalmente de apuro; '**~wa·ter 1.** agua *f* de marea; **2.** *adj.* costanero.

ti·di·ness ['taidinis] aseo *m*, buen orden *m*.

ti·dy ['taidi] **1.** aseado; ordenado; pulcro; **2.** (*a. ~ up*) asear; arreglar.

tie [tai] **1.** corbata *f*; lazo *m*; ♪ ligado *m*; 🏛 tirante *m*; (*bond*) vínculo *m*; *sport, voting:* empate *m*; **2.** *v/t.* atar; liar; enlazar; ♪ *a. fig.* ligar; confinar; (*hinder*) estorbar; ~ *up* atar; envolver; *v/i. sport etc.:* empatar; '**~pin** alfiler *m* de corbata.

tier [tiə] fila *f*, grada *f*, grado *m*.

tie·up ['taiʌp] enlace *m*; paralización *f* *by strike:* bloqueo *m*.

ti·ger ['taigə] tigre *m*.

tight [tait] □ apretado; estrecho; *clothes* ajustado; (*taut*) tirante; *situation* difícil; ✝ *money* escaso; F (*mean*) agarrado; F (*drunk*) borracho; '**tight·en** apretar(se); atiesar(se); estrechar(se); '**tight·fist·ed** agarrado; '**tight·fit·ting** muy ajustado; '**tight·lipped** callado; que sabe guardar secretos; '**tight·rope walk·er** funámbulo *m*, equilibrista *m/f*; **tights** [~s] *pl.* traje *m* de malla; '**tight·squeeze** aprieto *m*; '**tight·wad** *sl.* cicatero *m*.

ti·gress ['taigris] tigresa *f*.

tile [tail] **1.** (*roof*) teja *f*; (*floor*) baldosa *f*; (*colored*) azulejo *m*; **2.** *roof* tejar; *floor* embaldosar.

till¹ [til] caja *f* registradora, cajón *m*.

till² [~] *prp.* hasta; *cj.* hasta que.

till³ [~] ✍ cultivar, labrar.

tilt [tilt] **1.** inclinación *f*; ✕ torneo *m*; (*at*) *full* ~ a toda velocidad; **2.** inclinar(se), ladear(se).

tim·ber ['timbə] **1.** madera *f* (*de construcción*); (*beam*) viga *f*; árboles *m/pl.* de monte; **2.** enmaderar; '**~line** límite *m* forestal.

time [taim] **1.** tiempo *m*; hora *f* *of day*; (*occasion*) vez *f*; época *f*; plazo *m*; horas *f/pl.* de trabajo; ♪ compás *m*; ~! ¡la hora!; ℞ ~s por; *what is the* ~? ¿qué hora es?; *it is high* ~ *that* ya es hora de que; *at no* ~ nunca; *at* ~s a veces; *behind* ~ atrasado; *behind the* ~s anticuado; *from* ~ *to* ~ de vez en cuando, con el tiempo; *in (good)* ~ *(early)* a tiempo, con tiempo; *on* ~ puntual(mente); *beat (or keep)* ~ llevar el compás; F *do* ~ cumplir una condena; *have a bad* ~ pasarlo mal; *have a good* ~ divertirse (mucho); darse buena vida; *take one's* ~ no darse prisa; **2.** *race* cronometrar; medir el tiempo de; '~ **bomb** bomba f de relojería, bomba-reloj f; '~ **ex·po·sure** *phot.* pose f; '~**hon·ored** tradicional, consagrado; '~**keep·er** reloj m; cronómetro m; (p.) cronometrador m; '~**lag** intervalo m, retraso m, retardo m; '**time·ly** oportuno; '**time 'pay·ment** pago m a plazos; '**time·piece** reloj m; '**tim·er** ⊕ reloj m automático; ⊕ distribuidor m de encendido *in engine*.

time...: '~ **'sig·nal** *radio:* señal f horaria; '~**ta·ble** horario m; programa m; '~ **zone** huso m horario.

tim·id ['timid] □ tímido; **ti·mid·i·ty** [ti'miditi] timidez f.

tim·ing ['taimiŋ] medida f del tiempo; ⊕ cronometraje m.

tin [tin] **1.** estaño m; *(can)* lata f; ⊕ hoja f de lata, hojalata f; **2.** de estaño, de hojalata; **3.** ⊕ estañar.

tinc·ture ['tiŋktʃə] **1.** tintura f; *pharm.* tintura f; **2.** turar, teñir.

tin·foil ['tin'fɔil] papel m de estaño.

tinge [tindʒ] **1.** tinte m; matiz m (a. *fig.*); **2.** teñir (*with* de).

tin·gle ['tiŋgl] **1.** sentir comezón; *fig.* estremecerse (*with* de); **2.** comezón f; estremecimiento m.

tin hat ['tin'hæt] casco m de acero.

tink·er ['tiŋkə] **1.** calderero m remendón; **2.** v/t. remendar chapuceramente (a. ~ *up*); v/i. jugar con; (*spoil*) estropear.

tin·kle ['tiŋkl] **1.** (hacer) retiñir; **2.** retintín m; campanilleo m.

tin·ny ['tini] ♪ cascado, que suena a lata; F desvencijado; '**tin·plate** hojalata f.

tin·sel ['tinsl] oropel m (a. *fig.*).

tin·smith ['tin'smiθ] hojalatero m.

tint [tint] **1.** tinte m, matiz m; media tinta f; **2.** teñir, matizar.

ti·ny ['taini] menudo, diminuto, chiquitín.

tip [tip] **1.** punta f, extremidad f; casquillo m *of stick etc.*; embocadura f *of cigarette*; F *(gratuity)* propina f; F aviso m; soplo m; **2.** inclinar(se),

ladear(se); F dar propina (*v/t.* a); F ~ *off* advertir clandestinamente; '~**off** F advertencia f clandestina.

tip·ple ['tipl] envasar, empinar el codo; '**tip·pler** bebedor m.

tip·sy ['tipsi] □ achispado.

tip·toe ['tip'tou]: *on* ~ de puntillas.

tip·top ['tip'tɔp] F de primera, excelente.

ti·rade [tai'reid] diatriba f, invectiva f.

tire[1] [taiə] neumático m; llanta f; calce m *of metal*; ~ *chain* cadena f antirresbaladiza.

tire[2] [~] cansar(se); aburrir(se).

tired ['taiəd] □ cansado (*fig.* de de).

tire·less ['taiəlis] □ infatigable, incansable.

tire·some ['taiəsəm] □ molesto, fastidioso; aburrido.

tis·sue ['tisju:] tejido m (a. *anat.*); † *(cloth)* tisú m; '~ **'pa·per** papel m de seda.

tit·il·late ['titileit] estimular, excitar, titilar; **tit·il'la·tion** estimulación f.

ti·tle ['taitl] **1.** título m; ⚖ título m de propiedad; *sport:* campeonato m; **2.** *(in)*titular; '~d titulado; '~**deed** título m de propiedad; '~**hold·er** *sport:* campeón m, titular m; '~ **page** portada f; '~ **role** papel m titular of a *play*.

tit·ter ['titə] **1.** reírse a disimulo; **2.** risa f disimulada.

tit·u·lar ['titjulə] titular; nominal.

to [tu:] **1.** *not translated before infinitive:* *to do* hacer; *I have letters* ~ *write* tengo cartas que escribir; *the book is still* ~ *be written* el libro está todavía por escribir; **2.** *prp.* a; hacia; para; *I am going* ~ *Madrid (Spain)* voy a Madrid (España); *from door* ~ *door* de puerta en puerta.

toad [toud] sapo m; '~**stool** hongo m *(freq. venenoso).*

toad·y ['toudi] **1.** pelotillero m, adulador m servil; **2.** adular servilmente (a to).

toast [toust] **1.** pan m tostado; tostada f; brindis m (to por); **2.** tostar; '**toast·er** *(electric)* tostadora f.

to·bac·co [tə'bækou] tabaco m; ~ *pouch* petaca f.

to·bog·gan [tə'bɔgən] **1.** tobogán m; **2.** deslizarse en tobogán.

to·day ['tu'dei] hoy; hoy día; *a week from* ~ de hoy en ocho días.

tod·dle ['tɔdl] hacer pinos, andar a tatas; '**tod·dler** pequeño (a f) m (que aprende a andar).

to-do [tə'du:] F lío *m*, alharaca *f*, alboroto *m*.

toe [tou] 1. *anat.* dedo *m* del pie; punta *f* del pie; 2. tocar con la punta del pie; ~ *the (party) line* conformarse; someterse.

tof·fee ['tɔfi] caramelo *m*.

to·geth·er [tə'geðə] 1. *adj.* juntos; *all* ~ todos juntos; 2. *adv.* juntamente, junto; a la vez.

tog·gle ['tɔgl] 1. cazonete *m* de aparejo; 2. asegurar con cazonete; '~**switch** interruptor *m* a palanca.

togs [tɔgz] *pl.* F ropa *f*.

toil [tɔil] 1. fatiga *f*; afán *m*; 2. fatigarse; afanarse.

toi·let ['tɔilit] atavío *m*, tocado *m*; inodoro *m*; retrete *m*; '~ **bowl** inodoro *m*; '~ **pa·per** papel *m* higiénico; '~ **set** juego *m* de tocador; '~ **wa·ter** agua *f* de tocador.

to·ken ['toukən] señal *f*; muestra *f*; prenda *f*; prueba *f*; *attr.* simbólico.

told [tould] *pret. a. p.p.* of *tell*; *all* ~ en total.

tol·er·a·ble ['tɔlərəbl] □ tolerable; (*fair*) mediano, regular; **tol·er·ate** ['~reit] tolerar; aguantar.

toll[1] [toul] peaje *m*; pontazgo *m*; *fig.* mortalidad *f*, número *m* de víctimas; *teleph.* ~ *call* conferencia *f* interurbana; '~**bridge** puente *m* de peaje; '~**gate** barrera *f* de peaje.

toll[2] [~] doblar (a muerto).

to·ma·to [tə'meitou] tomate *m*.

tomb [tu:m] tumba *f*, sepulcro *m*.

tom·boy ['tɔmbɔi] muchacha *f* traviesa, moza *f* retozona.

tomb·stone ['tu:mstoun] lápida *f* sepulcral.

tome [toum] tomo *m*; *co.* librote *m*.

tom·my ['tɔmi] F soldado *m* inglés; ~ *gun* pistola *f* ametralladora.

to·mor·row [tə'mɔrou] mañana *f*.

ton [tʌn] tonelada *f*.

tone [toun] 1. *all senses:* tono *m*; *radio:* ~ *control* control *m* de tonalidad; 2. ♪, *paint.* entonar; *phot.* virar; ~ *down* suavizar (el tono de).

tongs [tɔŋz] *pl.* (*sugar*) tenacillas *f/pl.*; (*coal*) tenazas *f/pl.*

tongue [tʌŋ] *mst* lengua *f*; ⊕ lengüeta *f* (*a. of scales*); '**tongue-tied** de lengua trabada; *fig.* premioso, tímido; '**tongue twist·er** trabalenguas *m*.

ton·ic ['tɔnik] 1. □ tónico; 2. ♪ tónica *f*; ✆ tónico *m* (*a. fig.*).

to·night [tə'nait] esta noche.

ton·nage ['tʌnidʒ] tonelaje *m*.

ton·sil ['tɔnsl] amígdala *f*; **ton·sil·li·tis** [~'laitis] amigdalitis *f*.

ton·y ['touni] *sl.* aristocrático, elegante.

too [tu:] demasiado; (*also*) también; ~ *much* demasiado.

took [tu:k] *pret.* of *take*.

tool [tu:l] 1. herramienta *f*; utensilio *m*; *fig.* instrumento *m*; 2. filetear *leather*; '~ **bag**, '~ **kit** herramental *m*, bolsa *f* de herramientas; '~**box** caja *f* de herramientas.

toot [tu:t] 1. sonar (*v/i.* la bocina *etc.*); 2. sonido *m* breve.

tooth [tu:θ] (*pl. teeth*) diente *m*; (*molar*) muela *f*; púa *f* of *comb*; *false teeth* dentadura *f* postiza; '~**ache** dolor *m* (*or* mal *m*) de muelas; '~**brush** cepillo *m* de dientes; **toothed** [~θt] dentado; '**tooth·paste** pasta *f* dentífrica (*or* de dientes); '**tooth·pick** palillo *m*; mondadientes *m*.

top[1] [tɔp] 1. cima *f*, cumbre *f*, ápice *m*; cabeza *f* of *page, list*; copa *f* of *tree*; remate *m* of *roof etc.*; (*lid*) tapa *f*; capuchón *m* of *pen*; *mot.* capota *f*; ~ *banana sl.* jefe *m*; persona *f* principal; *from* ~ *to bottom* de arriba abajo; *de cabo a rabo; on* ~ *of* encima de; *fig. además de; fig. on* ~ *of that* por añadidura; 2. (*lid*) tapa *f*; más alto; *cimero; floor* último; 3. coronar, rematar; *fig.* superar, aventajar; F ~ *off* rematar.

top[2] [~] peonza *f*; peón *m*.

to·paz ['toupæz] topacio *m*.

top·coat ['tɔpkout] sobretodo *m*.

top...: '~**flight** F sobresaliente; ~ *hat* chistera *f*; '~**heav·y** demasiado pesado por arriba.

top·ic ['tɔpik] asunto *m*, tema *m*; '**top·i·cal** □ corriente; ✆ tópico. **top...:** '~**most** (el) más alto; '**notch** F sobresaliente.

to·pog·ra·pher [tə'pɔgrəfə] topógrafo *m*; **to·pog·ra·phy** [tə'pɔgrəfi] topografía *f*.

top·per ['tɔpə] *sl.* chistera *f*; '**top·ping:** *cake* ~ garapiña *f*.

top·ple ['tɔpl] *v/t.* derribar, volcar; *v/i.* volcar(se), tambalear.

top-se·cret ['tɔp'si:krit] ✕ de máxima confidencia.

top·sy-tur·vy ['tɔpsi'tə:vi] trastornado; en desorden.

torch [tɔ:tʃ] antorcha *f*; '~**bear·er** portaachón *m*; '~**light** luz *f* de antorcha; ~ *procession* desfile *m* de portaachones; '~ *song* canción *f* de murria; fado *m*.

tore [tɔː] *pret. of* tear[1] 1.

tor·ment 1. ['tɔːmənt] tormento *m*; **2.** [tɔː'ment] atormentar.

torn [tɔːn] *p.p. of* tear[1] 1.

tor·na·do [tɔː'neidou], *pl.* **tor·na·does** [~z] huracán *m*, tornado *m*.

tor·pe·do [tɔː'piːdou], *pl.* **tor·pe·does** [~z] *all senses:* torpedo *m*; **2.** torpedear (*a. fig.*); '~ **boat** torpedero *m*; '~ **tube** (tubo *m*) lanzatorpedos *m*.

tor·pid ['tɔːpid] □ aletargado, inactivo; *fig.* torpe, entorpecido.

torque [tɔːk] par *m* de torsión.

tor·rent ['tɔrənt] torrente *m* (*a. fig.*); **tor·ren·tial** [tɔ'renʃl] □ torrencial.

tor·rid ['tɔrid] tórrido; ~ **zone** zona *f* tórrida.

tor·sion [tɔːʃn] torsión *f*.

tor·so ['tɔːsou] torso *m*.

tort [tɔːt] agravio *m*.

tor·toise ['tɔːtəs] tortuga *f*; '~-**shell** carey *m*.

tor·ture ['tɔːtʃə] **1.** tortura *f*; **2.** torturar; *fig.* torcer, violentar; '**tor·tur·er** verdugo *m*.

toss [tɔs] **1.** meneo *m*, sacudida *f of head*; cogida *f by bull*; echada *f of coin*; *it's a* ~ *up* puede ser lo uno tanto como lo otro; *win the* ~ ganar el sorteo; **2.** *v/t.* echar, tirar; lanzar al aire; agitar, menear; sacudir; *v/i.* agitarse; (~ *and turn*) revolverse *in bed*.

tot [tɔt] nene (a *f*) *m*; peque *m/f*.

to·tal ['toutl] **1.** □ total; **2.** total *m*; **3.** *v/t.* sumar; *v/i.* ascender a; **to·tal·i·tar·i·an** [toutæli'tɛəriən] totalitario; **to·tal·i·ty** totalidad *f*; **to·tal·ize** ['~təlaiz] totalizar.

tote [tout] F llevar, acarrear.

tot·ter ['tɔtə] tambalear(se); estar para desplomarse.

touch [tʌtʃ] **1.** *v/t.* tocar; palpar; (*reach*) alcanzar; *food* tomar, probar; *emotions* conmover, enternecer; *sl.* dar un sablazo a (*for* para sacar); ~ *off* hacer estallar (*a. fig.*); ~ *up* retocar (*a. phot.*); *v/i.* estar contiguo; tocarse; pasar rozando; aludir brevemente a; **2.** tacto *m*; toque *m*; contacto *m*; ♪ pulsación *f*; *paint.* pincelada *f*; (*master's*) mano *f*; *be in* ~ *with p.* estar en comunicación con; *keep in* ~ *with p.* mantener relaciones con; *th.* mantenerse al corriente de; '~-**and**-**go** difícil; dudoso; **touched** conmovido; F chiflado; '**touch·ing** □ conmovedor; '**touch**-**stone** piedra *f* de toque (*a. fig.*); '**touch typ·ing** me-

canografía *f* al tacto; '**touch·y** □ quisquilloso, susceptible.

tough [tʌf] **1.** duro; resistente; tenaz; *task* difícil; F *luck* malo; F *p.* duro; malvado; criminal; **2.** F machote *m*, gorila *m*; '**tough·en** endurecer; '**tough·ness** dureza *f*.

tour [tuə] **1.** viaje *m* (largo); excursión *f*; vuelta *f*; **2.** *v/t.* viajar por, recorrer; *v/i.* viajar (de turista); '**tour·ing** **1.** turismo *m*; **2.** turístico; ~ *car* coche *m* de turismo; '**tour·ist** turista *m/f*.

tour·na·ment ['tuənəmənt] torneo *m*; concurso *m*.

tout [taut] **1.** (*agent*) gancho *m*; (*ticket-*) revendedor *m*; *racing:* pronosticador *m*; **2.** solicitar.

tow [tou] **1.** (*on a*) remolque *m*; **2.** remolcar, llevar al remolque.

to·ward(s) [tə'wɔːd(z)] hacia; (*attitude*) para con; (*time*) cerca de.

tow·boat ['toubout] remolcador *m*.

tow·el ['tauəl] **1.** toalla *f*; **2.** secar con toalla; '~ **rack** toallero *m*.

tow·er ['tauə] **1.** torre *f*; (*church-*) campanario *m*; **2.** elevarse, encumbrarse; '**tow·er·ing** □ encumbrado.

town [taun] ciudad *f*; población *f*; pueblo *m*; ~ *hall* ayuntamiento *m*; '**towns·folk**, '**towns·peo·ple** ciudadanos *m/pl.*; '**town·ship** municipio *m*; '**towns·man** ['taunzmən] ciudadano *m*, vecino *m*.

tow·rope ['touroup] sirga *f*; cable *m* de remolque.

tox·ic ['tɔksik] □ tóxico; ~ **shock syndrome** síndrome *m* del choque tóxico; **tox·in** ['tɔksin] toxina *f*.

toy [tɔi] **1.** juguete *m*; chuchería *f*; **2.** *attr.* de jugar; **2.**: ~ *with* jugar con; '~ **shop** juguetería *f*.

trace [treis] **1.** huella *f*, rastro *m*; (*small amount*) pizca *f*; **2.** rastrear; (*find*) encontrar; **tra·cer** ['treisə] *phys. etc.* trazador; ~ *bullet* bala *f* trazadora.

track [træk] **1.** huella *f*; pista *f*; (*path*) senda *f*, camino *m*; 🚋 vía *f*; 🏃 *etc.* trayectoria *f*; *keep* ~ *of fig.* estar al tanto de; **2.** (*a.* ~ *down*) rastrear; averiguar el origen de; '**track·er** rastreador *m*; ~ *dog* perro *m* rastrero; '**track·ing** seguimiento *m* of space vehicles; ~ *station* estación *f* de seguimiento; '**track·less** sin caminos; '**track meet** concurso *m* de carreras y saltos.

tract[1] [trækt] región *f*; extensión *f*; *digestive* ~ canal *m* digestivo.

tract² [~] tratado m; folleto m.

trac·tion ['trækʃn] tracción f; **'trac·tor** tractor m; **'trac·tor·'trail·er** tractocamión m.

trade [treid] **1.** comercio m; industria f; negocio m; (calling) oficio m; by ~ de oficio; **2.** v/i. comerciar (in en, with con); v/t. trocar, cambiar (for por); ~ in dar como parte del pago; '~ **fair** feria f de muestras; '~**in** trueque m; ~**mark** marca f registrada; '~ **name** razón f social; nombre m de fábrica; ~ **price** precio m al por mayor; **'trad·er** comerciante m, traficante m; **'trade school** escuela f de artes y oficios; **'trades·man** tendero m; artesano m; **trade un·ion** sindicato m; gremio m; attr. sindical, gremial; **trade 'un·ion·ism** sindicalismo m; **trade 'un·ion·ist** sindicalista m/f.

trade winds ['treid windz] pl. vientos m/pl. alisios.

tra·di·tion [trə'diʃn] tradición f.

traf·fic ['træfik] **1.** tráfico m; (mot. etc.) circulación f; (trade) comercio m; **2.** traficar (in en); b.s. tratar (in en); **'traf·fick·er** traficante m.

trag·e·dy ['trædʒidi] tragedia f.

trag·ic ['trædʒik] ☐ trágico.

trail [treil] **1.** rastro m, pista f; (path) sendero m; **2.** v/t. rastrear; seguir la pista de; v/i. arrastrar(se) (a. ♥); (be last) rezagarse; **'trail·er** mot. etc. remolque m.

train [trein] **1.** ⚙ tren m; (following) séquito m; recua f (of mules); **2.** adiestrar(se) (a. ⚔); preparar; child etc. enseñar; sport: entrenar(se); **train'ee** approx. aprendiz m; **'train·er** sport: entrenador m (a. ⚞); (circus) domador m.

train·ing ['treiniŋ] educación f; preparación f; instrucción f; sport: entrenamiento m; '~ **ship** buque-escuela m.

trait [trei(t)] rasgo m.

trai·tor ['treitə] traidor m; be a ~ to traicionar acc.

tra·jec·to·ry ['trædʒiktəri] trayectoria f.

tram·mel ['træml] **1.** ~s pl. fig. trabas f/pl.; **2.** poner trabas a.

tramp [træmp] **1.** marcha f pesada of feet; paseo m largo, excursión f a pie; (p.) vagabundo m; **2.** v/i. marchar pesadamente; viajar a pie; v/t. pisar con fuerza; recorrer a pie; **tram·ple** ['~l] v/i. patullar; v/t. hollar, pisotear.

trance [trɑːns] éxtasis m; estado m hipnótico, trance m.

tran·quil ['træŋkwil] ☐ tranquilo; **'tran·quil·ize** tranquilizar; **'tran·quil·iz·er** calmante m; **tran'quil·li·ty** tranquilidad f.

trans·act [træn'zækt] tramitar; despachar; **trans'ac·tion** negocio m, transacción f; tramitación f.

trans·at·lan·tic ['trænzət'læntik] transatlántico.

tran·scend [træn'send] exceder, superar; **tran'scend·ence, tran'scend·en·cy** [~dəns(i)] superioridad f; phls. tra(n)scendencia f.

tran·scribe [træns'kraib] transcribir.

trans·fer 1. [træns'fəː] v/t. transferir (a. ⚖); trasladar; transbordar; v/i. trasladarse; **2.** ['trænsfə] transferencia f (a. ⚖), traspaso m (a. ♣, sport); transbordo m; traslado m to post; **trans·fer'ee** [~fə'riː] ⚖ cesionario (a f) m; **trans'fer·ence** [~fərəns] transferencia f.

trans·fix [træns'fiks] traspasar, espetar; ~ed fig. atónito, pasmado.

trans·form [træns'fɔːm] transformar; **trans'form·er** ⚡ transformador m.

trans·fuse [træns'fjuːz] transfundir; blood hacer una transfusión de.

trans·gress [træns'gres] v/t. violar, traspasar; v/i. pecar.

tran·ship [træn'ʃip] transbordar.

tran·sient ['trænziənt] **1.** pasajero, transitorio; **2.** transeúnte m.

tran·sis·tor [træn'sistə] ⚡ transistor m; **tran'sis·tor·ize** transistorizar.

tran·sit ['trænsit] tránsito m.

tran·si·tion [træn'siʒn] transición f, paso m.

tran·si·tive ['trænsitiv] ☐ transitivo.

trans·late [træns'leit] traducir (into a); trasladar to post; **trans'la·tion** traducción f; **trans'la·tor** traductor (-a f) m.

trans·lu·cent [trænz'luːsnt] ☐ translúcido.

trans·mi·grate ['trænzmaigreit] transmigrar.

trans·mis·si·ble [trænz'misəbl] transmisible; **trans'mis·sion** transmisión f; microwave ~ emisión f en microonda.

trans·mit [trænz'mit] all senses: transmitir; **trans'mit·ter** transmisor m; radio: emisora f.

trans·mu·ta·tion [trænzmju'teiʃn] transmutación f; biol. transformismo *m*; **trans·mute** [‿'mjuːt] transmutar.

tran·som ['trænsəm] travesaño *m*.

trans·par·en·cy [træns'pɛərənsi] transparencia *f*; **trans·par·ent** □ transparente (*a. fig.*).

tran·spire [træns'paiə] transpirar; *fig.* revelarse, divulgarse.

trans·plant [træns'plɑːnt] 1. trasplantar; 2. ['trænsplɑːnt] trasplante *m*.

trans·port 1. [træns'pɔːt] transportar (*a. fig.*); 2. ['trænspɔːt] *all senses*: transporte *m*; **trans·por'ta·tion** transportación *f*; transporte(s) *m(pl.)*.

trans·pose [træns'pouz] transponer; ♪ transportar.

trans·ship [træns'ʃip] transbordar.

tran·sub·stan·ti·ate [trænsəb'stænʃieit] transubstanciar.

trans·ver·sal [trænz'vɔːsl] □ (& línea *f*) transversal; **trans·verse** ['‿vɔːs] □ transverso, transversal.

trans·ves·tite [trænz'vestait] transvestido *adj. a. su. m/f*; **trans·vestism** transvestismo *m*.

trap [træp] 1. trampa *f*; ⊕ bombillo *m*, sifón *m*; *sl.* boca *f*; 2. entrampar; atrapar; coger (en una trampa); **'trap·door** trampa *f*; *thea.* escotillón *m*.

tra·peze [trə'piːz] trapecio *m*; **trap·ezoid** ['træpizoid] trapezoide *m*.

trap·per ['træpə] cazador *m*.

trap·pings ['træpiŋz] *pl.* arreos *m/pl.*; *fig.* adornos *m/pl.*

trash [træʃ] pacotilla *f*, hojarasca *f*, cachivaches *m/pl.*; **'trash·y** □ baladí, despreciable; cursi.

trav·el ['trævl] 1. *v/i.* viajar (*a.* ✦); ir *at a speed*; *v/t.* recorrer; viajar por; 2. viaje(s) *m(pl)*; el viajar; ⊕ recorrido *m*; **'trav·el·er** viajero (*a f*) *m*; ✦ viajante *m*; ~'s check cheque *m* de viajeros.

trav·e·log(ue) ['trævəlɔg] película *f* de viajes.

trav·erse ['trævəːs] 1. ⊕ travesaño *m*; ✕ través *m*; 2. atravesar, cruzar.

trav·es·ty ['trævisti] 1. parodia *f* (*a. fig.*); 2. parodiar.

trawl [trɔːl] 1. red *f* barredera; 2. rastrear, pescar a la rastra; **'trawl·er** barco *m* rastreador.

tray [trei] bandeja *f*; cubeta *f*.

treach·er·ous ['tretʃərəs] □ traidor, traicionero; *fig.* engañoso, incierto; **'treach·er·y** traición *f*.

tread [tred] 1. [*irr.*] *v/i.* andar;

poner el pie; ~ (*up*)*on* pisar; *v/t.* pisar, pisotear; 2. pisada *f*; paso *m*; huella *f of stair*; **trea·dle** ['‿l] pedal *m*.

trea·son ['triːzn] traición *f*.

treas·ure ['treʒə] 1. tesoro *m*; ~ trove tesoro *m* hallado; 2. atesorar (*a.* ~ *up*); apreciar mucho.

treas·ur·y ['treʒəri] tesoro *m*, tesorería *f*; 2 *Department* Ministerio *m* de Hacienda.

treat [triːt] 1. *v/t.* tratar; (*invite*) convidar (*to* a); *v/i.*: ~ *of* tratar de; 2. placer *m*, alegría *f*; recompensa *f* (*especial*); **trea·tise** ['‿iz] tratado *m*; **'trea·ty** tratado *m*.

tree [triː] 1. árbol *m*; 2. ahuyentar por un árbol.

trek [trek] 1. emigrar; viajar; 2. migración *f*; F viaje *m* largo y aburrido.

trem·ble ['trembl] 1. temblar, estremecerse (*at* ante, *with* de); 2. temblor *m*, estremecimiento *m*.

tre·men·dous [tri'mendəs] □ tremendo, formidable, imponente.

trem·or ['tremə] temblor *m*.

trem·u·lous ['tremjuləs] □ trémulo; tímido.

trench [trentʃ] 1. zanja *f*, foso *m*; ✕ trinchera *f*; 2. zanjar; hacer zanjas *etc.* en; **'trench·ant** □ mordaz.

trend [trend] 1. tendencia *f*; dirección *f*; marcha *f*; 2. tender; **trend·y** F de (última) moda.

tres·pass ['trespəs] 1. intrusión *f*, entrada *f* sin derecho; violación *f*; 2. entrar sin derecho (*on* en); no ~*ing* prohibida la entrada; **'tres·pass·er** intruso (*a f*) *m*.

tress [tres] trenza *f*.

tres·tle ['tresl] caballete *m*.

tri·al ['traiəl] prueba *f*, ensayo *m*; *fig.* aflicción *f*; ♃ proceso *m*, juicio *m*; ~*s sport*, ⊕ *etc.*: pruebas *f/pl.*; ~ run viaje *m* de ensayo.

tri·an·gle ['traiæŋgl] triángulo *m* (*a.* ♪); **tri'an·gu·late** [‿leit] triangular.

trib·al ['traibl] □ tribal; **tribe** [traib] tribu *f* (*a. zo.*); *contp.* tropel *m*; ralea *f*.

tri·bu·nal [trai'bjuːnl] tribunal *m* (*a. fig.*); **trib·une** ['tribjuːn] tribuna *f*; (*p.*) tribuno *m*.

trib·ute ['tribjuːt] tributo *m*; *fig.* homenaje *m*; elogio *m*.

trick [trik] engaño *m*; truco *m*; burla *f*; trampa *f*; maña *f*; (*harmless*) travesura *f*; (*illusion*) ilusión *f*; (*conjuring*) juego *m* de manos; 2. engañar,

T

trampear, burlar; '**trick·er·y** astucia *f*; fraude *m*; malas artes *f/pl*.

trick·le ['trikl] **1.** gotear, escurrir; **2.** hilo *m*, chorro *m* delgado.

trick·ster ['trikstə] estafador *m*.

trick·y ['triki] □ *p.* tramposo; astuto; *situation etc.* delicado, difícil.

tri·cy·cle ['traisikl] triciclo *m*.

tri·dent ['traidənt] tridente *m*.

tri·en·ni·al ['trai'enjəl] □ trienal.

tri·fle ['traifl] **1.** friolera *f*, bagatela *f*, fruslería *f*; fig. pizca *f*; **2.** chancear; jugar (*with* con); '**tri·fler** persona *f* frívola.

tri·fling ['traiflin] □ insignificante, fútil.

tri·fo·cal [trai'foukl] **1.** trifocal *m*; *fig.* lente *f* trifocal.

trig·ger ['trigə] **1.** gatillo *m*; ⊕ disparador *m*; **2.** hacer estallar (*a. fig.*); *fig.* provocar.

trig·o·no·met·ric [trigənə'metrik] □ trigonométrico; **trig·o·nom·e·try** ['∼'nɒmitri] trigonometría *f*.

tri·lin·gual ['trai'lingwəl] □ trilingüe.

trill [tril] **1.** trino *m* (*a. ♪*), gorjeo *m*; quiebro *m*; vibración *f* of R; **2.** trinar, gorjear; *R* pronunciar con vibración.

tril·lion ['triljən] trillón *m*; un millón de billones.

trim [trim] **1.** □ elegante; aseado; □ disposición *f*; (buena) condición *f*; recorte *m* of hair etc.; **3.** arreglar; ajustar; componer; (re)cortar; ✄ podar; '**trim·ming** guarnición *f*, adorno *m*; orla *f*; '**trim·ness** buen orden *m*; elegancia *f*.

Trin·i·ty ['triniti] Trinidad *f*.

trin·ket ['trinkit] dije *m*; *contp.* ∼s *pl.* baratijas *f/pl.*, chucherías *f/pl.*

tri·o ['tri:ou] trío *m*.

trip [trip] **1.** excursión *f*; viaje *m*; tropiezo *m*, zancadilla *f with foot*; ⊕ trinquete *m*; **2.** *v/i.* tropezar (*on, over* en); *v/t.* (*mst* ∼ *up*) echar la zancadilla a.

tri·par·tite ['trai'pɑ:tait] tripartito.

tripe [traip] tripa *f* (*mst* ∼s *pl.*); *sl.* tonterías *f/pl.*

trip·li·cate 1. ['triplikit] (*in por*) triplicado; **2.** ['∼keit] triplicar.

tri·pod ['traipɒd] trípode *m*.

tris·yl·lab·ic ['traisi'læbik] □ trisílabo; **tri·syl·la·ble** ['∼'siləbl] trisílabo *m*.

trite [trait] □ trillado, trivial, vulgar; '**trite·ness** trivialidad *f*.

tri·umph ['traiəmf] **1.** triunfo *m*; **2.**

triunfar (*over* de); **tri·um·phant** □ triunfante.

triv·i·al ['triviəl] □ trivial; frívolo.

triv·i·al·i·ty [∼'æliti] trivialidad *f*.

Tro·jan ['troudʒn] troyano *adj. a. su. m* (*a f*).

trol·ley ['trɔli] carretilla *f*; (*a.* '∼-car) tranvía *m*; ⊕ corredera *f* elevada; '∼-bus trolebús *m*.

trol·lop ['trɔləp] marrana *f*, ramera *f*.

trom·bone [trɔm'boun] trombón *m*.

troop [tru:p] **1.** tropa *f*; escuadrón *m* of cavalry; *thea.* compañía *f*; ∼s *pl.* tropas *f/pl.*; **2.** reunirse; ∼ off marcharse en tropel; '∼ **car·ri·er** ⊕ transporte *m*; ✗ camión *m* blindado; '**troop·er** soldado *m* de caballería; policía *m* de a caballo; '**troop·ship** transporte *m*.

tro·phy ['troufi] trofeo *m*.

trop·ic ['trɔpik] trópico *m*; ∼s *pl.* trópicos *m/pl.*

trot [trɔt] **1.** trote *m*; *school sl.* chuleta *f*; **2.** trotar; F ∼ out sacar (para mostrar).

trot·ter ['trɔtə] (caballo *m*) trotón *m*.

trou·ble ['trʌbl] **1.** aflicción *f*, congoja *f*; (*misfortune*) desgracia *f*, apuro *m*; dificultad *f*, disgusto *m*; (*unpleasantness*) sinsabor *m*; (*inconvenience*) molestia *f*; *be in* ∼ verse en un apuro; *be worth the* ∼ valer la pena; **2.** *v/t.* turbar; trastornar; afligir; molestar; fastidiar; incomodar; *v/i.* molestarse; '**trou·bled** *p.* inquieto; apenado; *times* turbulento; **trouble·some** ['∼səm] □ molesto; dificultoso.

trough [trɔf] (*drinking-*) abrevadero *m*; (*feeding-*) comedero *m*.

trounce [trauns] zurrar, pegar.

troupe [tru:p] compañía *f*.

trou·sers [trauzəz] (*a pair of* un) pantalón *m*; pantalones *m/pl.*

trous·seau ['tru:sou] ajuar *m*.

trout [traut] trucha *f*.

trow·el ['trauəl] ✄ desplantador *m*; △ paleta *f*, llana *f*.

tru·an·cy ['tru:ənsi] ausencia *f* de clase sin permiso; '**tru·ant 1.** haragán; **2.** novillero *m*.

truce [tru:s] tregua *f*.

truck¹ [trʌk] **1.** camión *m*; (*hand*) carretilla *f*; ➡ vagón *m* (de mercancías); vagoneta *f*; **2.** transportar en camión.

truck² [∼] cambio *m*, trueque *m*; *contp.* baratijas *f/pl.*; *have no* ∼ *with* no tratar con.

truc·u·lent ['trʌkjulənt] □ áspero, hosco, arisco; agresivo.

turbosupercharger

trudge [trʌdʒ] caminar trabajosamente.

true [tru:] (adv. truly) verdadero; account verídico; p. leal; copy fiel, exacto; genuino; auténtico; come ~ realizarse; '~'**blue** sumamente leal; '~'**bred** de casta legítima; '~'**love** fiel amante m/f, novio (a f) m.

truf·fle ['trʌfl] trufa f.

tru·ly ['tru:li] verdaderamente; fielmente; Yours ~ su seguro servidor.

trump [trʌmp] 1. triunfo m; 2. fallar; ~ up forjar, falsificar.

trum·pet ['trʌmpit] 1. trompeta f; ~ blast trompetazo m; 2. trompetear; (elephant) barritar; '**trum·pet·er** trompetero m, trompeta f.

trun·cate ['trʌŋkeit] truncar.

trun·cheon ['trʌntʃn] (cachi)porra f.

trun·dle ['trʌndl] 1. ruedecilla f; 2. (hacer) rodar (a. ~ along).

trunk [trʌŋk] ♀, anat. tronco m; (case) baúl m; (elephant's) trompa f; maleta f; '~ **line** 🚂 línea f troncal; teleph. línea f principal; **trunks** pl. taparrabo m.

truss [trʌs] 1. 🌾 haz m, lío m; 🏥 braguero m; 🏛 entramado m; 2. atar, liar.

trust [trʌst] 1. confianza f; crédito m; obligación f, cargo m; 🏦 fideicomiso m; ✝ trust m; ~ **company** banco m fideicomisario; 2. v/t. confiar en, fiarse de; v/i. confiar (in, to en).

trus·tee [trʌs'ti:] síndico m; depositario m; 🏦 fideicomisario m.

trust·ful ['trʌstful] □, '**trust·ing** □ confiado.

trust·wor·thi·ness ['trʌstwə:ðinis] confiabilidad f; '**trust·wor·thy** p. confiable; news etc. fidedigno.

truth [tru:θ, pl. ~ðz] verdad f. **truth·ful** ['tru:θful] □ verídico; veraz; '**truth·ful·ness** veracidad f.

try [trai] 1. v/t. intentar; (test) probar, ensayar (a. ~ out); 🏛 p. procesar (for por); (sorely) afligir; ~ on clothes probarse; v/i. probar; esforzarse; 2. F tentativa f, ensayo m (a. rugby), prueba f; '**try·ing** □ molesto; cansado; penoso; '**try'out** experimento m; prueba f (a. sport).

tryst [traist, trist] (lugar m de una) cita f.

Tsar [zɑ:] zar m.

T-square ['ti:skweə] regla f T.

tub [tʌb] tina f; cubo m; cuba f; '**tub·by** rechoncho.

tu·ba ['tu:bə] tuba f.

tube [tu:b] tubo m (a. television); radio: lámpara f; (a. inner ~) cámara f; '~·**less** mot. sin cámara; 🚲 sin tubo.

tu·ber ['tu:bə] tubérculo m; **tu·ber·cle** ['tu:bə:kl] all senses: tubérculo m; **tu·ber·cu·lo·sis** [tubə:kju'lousis] tuberculosis f.

tub·ing ['tu:bin] tubería f.

tuck [tʌk] 1. alforza f; pliegue m; 2. alforzar; plegar; ~ away encubrir, ocultar.

tuck·er [tʌkə] F agotar, cansar.

Tues·day ['tu:zdi] martes m.

tuft [tʌft] copete m; penacho m; manojo m of grass etc.

tug [tʌg] 1. tirón m; estirón m; ⚓ remolcador m; ~ of war lucha f de la cuerda; 2. tirar de; arrastrar; '~·**boat** remolcador m.

tu·i·tion [tu'iʃn] cuota f de enseñanza.

tu·lip ['tu:lip] tulipán m.

tum·ble ['tʌmbl] 1. v/i. caer; tropezar (over en); desplomarse, hundirse; v/t. derribar; derrocar; desarreglar; 2. caída f; voltereta f; take a ~ caerse; '~·**down** destartalado, ruinoso; '**tum·bler** (glass) vaso m; (p.) volteador (-a f) m.

tum·my ['tʌmi] F estómago m.

tu·mor ['tu:mə] tumor m.

tu·mult ['tu:mʌlt] tumulto m.

tu·na ['tu:nə] atún m.

tune [tu:n] 1. aire m, tonada f; armonía f; tono m; in ~ templado, afinado; adv. afinadamente; fig. be in ~ with concordar con; out of ~ destemplado, desafinado; 2. ♪ afinar, acordar, templar (a. ~ up); radio: ~ (in) sintonizar (to acc.); mot. ~ up poner a punto; '**tune·less** □ disonante; '**tun·er** afinador m; radio: sintonizador m.

tung·sten ['tʌŋstən] tungsteno m.

tu·nic ['tu:nik] túnica f.

tun·ing ['tu:nin] ♪ afinación f; radio: sintonización f; '~·**coil** bobina f sintonizadora; '~·**fork** diapasón m.

tun·nel ['tʌnl] 1. túnel m; ⛏ galería f; 2. v/t. construir un túnel bajo; v/i. construir un túnel.

tur·ban ['tə:bən] turbante m.

tur·bid ['tə:bid] turbio.

tur·bine ['tə:bin] turbina f.

tur·bo·fan ['tə:boufæn] turboventilador m; **tur·bo·jet** turborreactor (a. su. m); '**tur·bo'prop** turbohélice (a. su. m); **tur·bo'ram'jet** turborreactor m a postcombustión; **tur·bo'su·per·charg·er** turbosupercargador m.

tur·bu·lence ['tɔːbjuləns] turbulencia *f*.

turf [tɔːf] césped *m*; (*sod*) tepe *m*; (*peat*) turba *f*; *sport*: turf *m*.

tur·gid ['tɔːdʒid] □ turgente.

Turk [tɔːk] turco (*a f*) *m*; *fig*. pícaro *m*.

tur·key ['tɔːki] pavo (*a f*) *m*.

Turk·ish ['tɔːkiʃ] turco *adj*. *a*. *su*. *m*; ~ *bath* baño *m* turco.

tur·moil ['tɔːmɔil] desorden *m*; alboroto *m*, tumulto *m*; disturbio *m*.

turn [tɔːn] **1.** *v/t*. volver; ⊕ tornear; *ankle* torcer; *corner* doblar; *handle* girar, dar vueltas a; *key* dar vuelta a; ~ *aside* desviar; ~ *away* apartar; despedir; ~ *into* convertir en, cambiar en; (*translate*) verter a; ~ *off light* apagar; *tap* cerrar; *gas* cortar; ~ *on light* encender; *radio* poner; *tap* abrir; ~ *out light* apagar; *p.* echar, expulsar; **2.** *v/i*. volver(se); girar, dar vueltas; *mot.*, 🚞 virar; torcer; (*become*) hacerse *su*., ponerse, volverse *adj*.; (*milk*) agriarse, cortarse; ~ *back* volver (atrás), retroceder; ~ *from* apartarse de; ~ *out to be* resultar; ~ *out well* salir bien; ~ *over* revolver (-se) *mot.*, 🚞 capotar; volcar; ~ *round* volverse; girar; ~ *to* (*for help*) recurrir a, acudir a; **3.** vuelta *f*; giro *m*; revolución *f*; curva *f*, recodo *m* in *road etc.*, 🚢 *etc.* viraje *m*; *mot. etc.* giro *m*; (*change*) cambio *m*; repunte *m*, cambio *m of tide*; (*spell*) turno *m*; oportunidad *f*; *it is my* ~ me toca a mí; *take a* ~ dar una vuelta; *take a* ~ contribuir con su trabajo a; *take a* ~ *at the wheel* conducir por su turno; *take one's* ~ esperar su turno; *take* ~*s* turnar, alternar; **'~-coat** renegado (*a f*) *m*; **'~-down** doblado hacia abajo; negativa *f*.

turn·ing ['tɔːniŋ] vuelta *f*; ángulo *m*; *the first* ~ la primera bocacalle; **'~ lathe** torno *m* (de tornero); **'~ point** *fig*. punto *m* decisivo, coyuntura *f* crítica.

tur·nip ['tɔːnip] nabo *m*.

turn·key ['tɔːnkiː] llavero *m* (de cárcel); **'turn·off** salida *f*, desviación *f of road*; *sl*. rechazamiento *m*; negativa *f*; **'turn·out** concurrencia *f*; entrada *f*; ✝ producción *f*; F atuendo *m*; **'turn·o·ver** *f* (volumen *m* de) transacciones *f/pl.*; movimiento *m* de mercancías *f/pl.*; *cooking*: pastel *m* con repulgo; **'turn·pike** barrera *f* de portazgo; autopista *f* de peaje; **'turn sig·nal** *mot*. señal

f de dirección; **'turn·stile** torniquete *m*; **'turn·ta·ble** 📻, *Gramophone*: placa *f* giratoria; **'turn·up** vuelta *f of trousers*.

tur·pen·tine ['tɔːpəntain] trementina *f*.

tur·quoise ['tɔːkwɑːz] turquesa *f*.

tur·ret ['tʌrit] △ torreón *m*; ✕ torre *f*; ⚓ torreta *f* (acorazada).

tur·tle ['tɔːtl] tortuga *f* marina.

tusk [tʌsk] colmillo *m*.

tus·sle ['tʌsl] **1.** lucha *f*; agarrada *f*, pelea *f*; **2.** luchar; reñir.

tu·te·lage ['tjuːtilidʒ] tutela *f*.

tu·tor ['tjuːtə] **1.** preceptor *m*; ayo *m*; maestro *m* particular; 🎓 instruir; **tu·to·ri·al** [tjuːˈtɔːriəl] **1.** preceptoral; 🎓 tutelar; **2.** *univ*. clase *f* particular.

tux·e·do [tʌkˈsiːdou] smoking *m*.

twad·dle ['twɔdl] disparates *m/pl.*

twang [twæŋ] tañido *m*, punteado *m of guitar*; (*mst nasal* ~) gangueo *m*, timbre *m* nasal.

tweak [twiːk] pellizcar retorciendo.

tweez·ers ['twiːzəz] *pl*. (*a pair of* ~ *unas*) bruselas *f/pl.*, pinzas *f/pl.*

twelfth [twelfθ] duodécimo.

twelve [twelv] doce (*a*. *su*. *m*).

twen·ti·eth ['twentiiθ] vigésimo.

twen·ty ['twenti] veinte; **~-fold** ['~fould] *adv*. veinte veces (*adj*. *mayor*).

twerp [twɔːp] *sl*. tonto *m*; papanatas *m*.

twice [twais] dos veces; ~ *the sum* el doble; ~ *as much* dos veces tanto.

twid·dle ['twidl] **1.** girar; jugar con, revolver ociosamente; **2.** vuelta *f* (ligera).

twig [twig] ramita *f*; ~*s pl*. leña *f* menuda.

twi·light ['twailait] **1.** crepúsculo *m* (*a*. *fig*.); **2.** crepuscular.

twill [twil] **1.** tela *f* cruzada; **2.** cruzar.

twin [twin] gemelo *adj*. *a*. *su*. *m* (*a f*); **'~-en·gined** ['~endʒind] bimotor; **'~-jet** birreactor *adj*. *a*. *su*. *m*.

twine [twain] **1.** guita *f*, bramante *m*; **2.** enroscar(se); retorcer(se).

twinge [twindʒ] punzada *f*.

twin·ing ['twainiŋ] 🌿 sarmentoso.

twin·kle ['twiŋkl] **1.** centellear, titilar, parpadear; *fig*. moverse rápidamente; **2.** centelleo *m*, parpadeo *m*; *in a* ~ en un instante.

twirl [twɔːl] **1.** vuelta *f* (rápida), giro *m*; **2.** girar rápidamente.

twist [twist] **1.** torcedura *f* (*a*. 🎣);

torsión f; enroscadura f; torzal m; rollo m of tobacco; F baile m de rock-'n'-roll; 2. torcer(se) (a. fig.); retorcer(se); enroscar(se); **'twist·er** torcedor m; meteor. tromba f; tornado m.

twit [twit] **1.**: ~ a p. with a th. reprender (para divertirse) algo a alguien; **2.** F papanatas m.

twitch [twitʃ] **1.** v/i. crisparse; temblar; v/t. tirar ligeramente de; **2.** sacudida f repentina; ✄ tic m.

twit·ter ['twitə] **1.** (bird) gorjear; fig. agitarse; **2.** gorjeo m; fig. agitación f.

two [tu:] dos (a. su. m); in ~ en dos; **'~·bit** sl. inferior; cursi; **'~·edged** de doble filo (a. fig.); **'~·faced** fig. doble, falso; **'~·fist·ed** fig. fuerte; viril; **'~·fold 1.** adj. doble; **2.** adv. dos veces; **'~·hand·ed** de (or para) dos manos; **'~·phase** ✄ bifásico; **'~·ply** de dos capas; **'~·seat·er** mot. de dos plazas; **'~·step** paso m doble; **'~·sto·ry** de dos pisos; **'~·stroke** de dos tiempos; **'~·time** sl. engañar en amor; **'~·tone** mot. bicolor; **'~·way 'switch** ✄ conmutador m de dos direcciones.

ty·coon [tai'ku:n] F magnate m.

tyke [taik] F chiquillo m.

type [taip] **1.** tipo m; typ. tipo m, carácter m; tipos m/pl.; **2.** escribir a máquina, mecanografiar; **'~·script** (original m) mecanografiado; **'~·set·ter** (p.) cajista m; (machine) máquina f de componer; **'~·write** [irr. (write)] = type 2; **'~·writ·er** máquina f de escribir; **'~·writ·ten** escrito a máquina.

ty·phoid ['taifɔid] fiebre f tifoidea.

ty·phoon [tai'fu:n] tifón m.

ty·phus ['taifəs] tifus m.

typ·i·cal ['tipikl] □ típico; **typ·i·fy** ['tipifai] simbolizar; representar; ser ejemplo de; **typ·ing** ['taipiŋ] mecanografía f, dactilografía f; **typ·ist** ['taipist] mecanógrafo (a f) m, dactilógrafo (a f) m.

ty·pog·ra·phy [tai'pɔgrəfi] tipografía f.

tyr·an·ni·cide [ti'rænəsaid] tiranicidio m; **tyr·an·nize** ['tirənaiz] tiranizar (over acc.); **'tyr·an·ny** tiranía f.

tyr·ant ['taiərənt] tirano (a f) m.

Tzar [zɑ:] zar m.

U

u·biq·ui·tous [ju'bikwitəs] □ ubicuo; **u'biq·ui·ty** ubicuidad f.

ud·der ['ʌdə] ubre f.

UFO ['ju:'ef'ou; 'ju:fou] ovni m.

ugh [ʌx, ux, ə:h] ¡puf!

ug·li·ness ['ʌglinis] fealdad f.

ug·ly ['ʌgli] □ feo; wound, situation peligroso; vice etc. feo, asqueroso, repugnante; sky etc. amenazado; rumor etc. inquietante; be in an ~ mood (p.) estar de muy mal humor; (mob) amenazar violencia; turn ~ (situation) ponerse peligroso; F (p.) mostrarse violento, ponerse negro.

ul·cer ['ʌlsə] úlcera f; fig. llaga f.

ul·te·ri·or [ʌl'tiəriə] ulterior; motive oculto.

ul·ti·mate ['ʌltimit] □ último, final; fundamental; sumo; **ul·ti·mate·ly** últimamente; a la larga.

ul·ti·ma·tum [ʌlti'meitəm] ultimátum m.

ul·tra ['ʌltrə] ultra...; **'~·high** ✄ ultraelevado; **~·ma·rine 1.** ultrama-

rino; **2.** ⌗, paint. azul m de ultramar; **'~·mod·ern** ultramoderno; **~·vi·o·let** ultravioleta.

um·bil·i·cal [ʌm'bilikl] umbilical; ~ cord cordón m umbilical.

um·brel·la [ʌm'brelə] paraguas m; ⊠ cortina f de fuego (antiaéreo).

um·pire ['ʌmpaiə] **1.** árbitro m; **2.** arbitrar.

un... [ʌn...] in...; des...; no; poco.

UN ['ju:'en] ONU f.

un·a·bashed ['ʌnə'bæʃt] descarado, desvergonzado.

un·a·ble [ʌn'eibl] imposibilitado, incapaz (to inf. de inf.); be ~ to inf. no poder inf.

un·a·bridged ['ʌnə'bridʒd] íntegro.

un·ac·cent·ed ['ʌnæk'sentid] inacentuado, átono.

un·ac·cept·a·ble ['ʌnək'septəbl] inaceptable.

un·ac·count·a·ble ['ʌnə'kauntəbl] □ inexplicable.

un·ac·cus·tomed ['ʌnə'kʌstəmd] insólito; no acostumbrado (*to* a).

un·ac·quaint·ed ['ʌnə'kweintid]: be ~ *with* desconocer, ignorar.

un·a·dul·ter·at·ed ['ʌnə'dʌltəreitid] sin mezcla; puro.

un·af·fect·ed ['ʌnə'fektid] □ no afectado (*by* por); *fig.* sin afectación, natural.

un·a·fraid ['ʌnə'freid] impertérrito.

un·aid·ed ['ʌn'eidid] sin ayuda.

un·al·ter·a·ble [ʌn'ɔːltərəbl] □ inalterable.

un·am·big·u·ous ['ʌnæm'bigjuəs] □ inequívoco.

un·A·mer·i·can ['ʌnə'merikən] antiamericano.

u·na·nim·i·ty [juːnə'nimiti] unanimidad *f*; **u·nan·i·mous** [juː'næniməs] □ unánime.

un·an·swer·a·ble [ʌn'ɑːnsərəbl] □ incontestable; irrebatible.

un·ap·pe·tiz·ing ['ʌn'æpitaiziŋ] poco apetitoso.

un·ap·proach·a·ble ['ʌnə'prəutʃəbl] □ inaccesible; *p.* intratable.

un·armed ['ʌn'ɑːmd] inerme, desarmado.

un·a·shamed ['ʌnə'ʃeimd]; *adv.* ~midli] □ desvergonzado; sin remordimiento.

un·as·sum·ing ['ʌnə'sjuːmiŋ] □ modesto, sin pretensiones.

un·at·tached ['ʌnə'tætʃt] suelto; *p.* no prometido; *fig.* no embargado.

un·at·tain·a·ble ['ʌnə'teinəbl] □ inasequible.

un·at·trac·tive ['ʌnə'træktiv] □ poco atractivo.

un·au·thor·ized ['ʌn'ɔːθəraizd] desautorizado.

un·a·void·a·ble ['ʌnə'vɔidəbl] □ inevitable, ineludible.

un·a·ware ['ʌnə'wɛə]: be ~ ignorar (*of* *acc.*, *that* que); **un·a·wares** de improviso; inopinadamente; *catch a p.* ~ coger a una p. desprevenida.

un·bal·ance ['ʌn'bæləns] desequilibrio *m*; **un·bal·anced** desequilibrado.

un·bear·a·ble [ʌn'bɛərəbl] □ inaguantable, insufrible.

un·beat·a·ble ['ʌn'biːtəbl] imbatible; *price* inmejorable.

un·beat·en ['ʌn'biːtn] *track* no trillado; *team* imbatido; *price* no mejorado.

un·be·com·ing ['ʌnbi'kʌmiŋ] □ indecoroso; impropio (*for*, *to* de); *dress* que sienta mal.

un·be·known ['ʌnbi'nəun]: ~ *to me* sin saberlo yo.

un·be·lief ['ʌnbi'liːf] descreimiento *m*; **un·be·liev·a·ble** □ increíble; **un·be·liev·er** no creyente *m/f*, descreído (*a f*) *m*; **un·be·liev·ing** □ incrédulo.

un·bend·ing ['ʌn'bendiŋ] □ inflexible (*a. fig.*); *fig.* inconquistable, poco afable.

un·bi·ased ['ʌn'baiəst] imparcial.

un·blem·ished [ʌn'blemiʃt] sin tacha.

un·bos·om [ʌn'buzm] ~ *o.s.* desahogarse, abrir su pecho (*to* a).

un·bound ['ʌn'baund] *book* sin encuadernar.

un·bound·ed [ʌn'baundid] ilimitado.

un·break·a·ble ['ʌn'breikəbl] irrompible.

un·bri·dled ['ʌn'braidld] desenfrenado (*a. fig.*).

un·bro·ken ['ʌn'brəukn] *seal* intacto; *time* no interrumpido; *horse* no domado.

un·busi·ness·like ['ʌn'biznislaik] poco práctico; informal.

un·but·ton ['ʌn'bʌtn] desabotonar.

un·called-for ['ʌn'kɔːldfɔː] gratuito, inmerecido; impropio.

un·can·ny [ʌn'kæni] □ misterioso; extraordinario.

un·ceas·ing [ʌn'siːsiŋ] □ incesante.

un·cer·tain [ʌn'səːtn] □ incierto, dudoso; *be* ~ *of* no estar seguro de; **un·cer·tain·ty** incertidumbre *f*.

un·chain ['ʌn'tʃein] desencadenar.

un·change·a·ble [ʌn'tʃeindʒəbl], **un·chang·ing** □ incambiable, inalterable.

un·char·i·ta·ble [ʌn'tʃæritəbl] □ poco caritativo; despiadado.

un·civ·il ['ʌn'sivl] □ incivil; **un·civ·i·lized** [~vilaizd] incivilizado, inculto.

un·claimed ['ʌn'kleimd] sin reclamar.

un·clas·si·fied ['ʌn'klæsifaid] sin clasificar.

un·cle ['ʌŋkl] tío *m*.

un·clean ['ʌn'kliːn] □ sucio.

un·clothed ['ʌn'kləuðd] desnudo.

un·coil ['ʌn'kɔil] desenrollar(se).

un·com·fort·a·ble [ʌn'kʌmfətəbl] □ incómodo.

un·com·mon [ʌn'kɔmən] 1. □ poco común, raro; 2. *adv.* F extraordinariamente.

un·com·mu·ni·ca·tive [ˈʌnkəˈmjuː-nikətiv] poco comunicativo.

un·com·plain·ing [ˈʌnkəmˈpleiniŋ] □ resignado, sumiso.

un·com·pli·men·ta·ry [ʌnˈkɔmpli-ˈmentəri] poco lisonjero; ofensivo.

un·com·pro·mis·ing [ˈʌnˈkɔmprə-maiziŋ] □ intransigente.

un·con·cern [ˈʌnkənˈsəːn] despreocupación f; indiferencia f; **un·con·cerned** [adv. ~idli] □ despreocupado; indiferente (about a).

un·con·di·tion·al [ˈʌnkənˈdiʃnl] □ incondicional.

un·con·firmed [ˈʌnkənˈfəːmd] no confirmado.

un·con·gen·ial [ˈʌnkənˈdʒiːnjəl] antipático; incompatible.

un·con·nect·ed [ˈʌnkəˈnektid] □ inconexo; no relacionado (with con).

un·con·quer·a·ble [ʌnˈkɔŋkərəbl] □ inconquistable, invencible.

un·con·scion·a·ble [ʌnˈkɔnʃənəbl] □ desmedido, desrazonable.

un·con·scious [ʌnˈkɔnʃəs] **1.** □ inconsciente (of de); no intencional; sin sentido, desmayado; **2.** the ~ lo inconsciente; **un·con·scious·ness** inconsciencia f; ⚕ insensibilidad f.

un·con·sti·tu·tion·al [ˈʌnkɔnsti-ˈtjuːʃnl] □ inconstitucional.

un·con·test·ed [ˈʌnkənˈtestid] incontestado.

un·con·trol·la·ble [ʌnkənˈtroulabl] □ ingobernable.

un·con·ven·tion·al [ˈʌnkənˈvenʃnl] □ poco formalista, desenfadado, poco convencional; original.

un·con·vinced [ˈʌnkənˈvinst] no convencido; **un·con·vinc·ing** □ poco convincente.

un·cooked [ˈʌnˈkukd] sin cocer.

un·cork [ˈʌnˈkɔːk] descorchar.

un·cou·ple [ˈʌnˈkʌpl] desacoplar.

un·couth [ʌnˈkuːθ] □ grosero; rústico; tosco.

un·cov·er [ʌnˈkʌvə] descubrir.

un·crit·i·cal [ˈʌnˈkritikl] □ falto de sentido crítico; poco juicioso.

unc·tion [ˈʌŋkʃn] unción f (a. fig.); fig. fervor m afectado; zalamería f; eccl. extreme ~ extremaunción f; **unc·tu·ous** [ˈʌŋktuəs] □ untuoso (a. fig.); fig. afectadamente fervoroso; zalamero.

un·cul·ti·vat·ed [ˈʌnˈkʌltiveitid] inculto (a. fig.).

un·cut [ˈʌnˈkʌt] sin cortar; diamond en bruto, sin tallar; book intonso.

un·dam·aged [ˈʌnˈdæmidʒd] ileso, indemne.

un·dat·ed [ˈʌnˈdeitid] sin fecha.

un·daunt·ed [ʌnˈdɔːntid] □ impávido; intrépido.

un·de·feat·ed [ˈʌndiˈfiːtid] invicto.

un·de·fined [ˈʌndiˈfaind] indefinido.

un·de·ni·a·ble [ˈʌndiˈnaiəbl] □ innegable.

un·de·pend·a·ble [ˈʌndiˈpendəbl] poco confiable.

un·der [ˈʌndə] **1.** adv. debajo; abajo; **2.** prp. (less precise; a. fig.) bajo, (more precise) debajo de; number inferior a; aged ~ 21 que tiene menos de 21 años; **3.** in compounds: ... inferior; ... interior; ... inferior(mente); ... (clothes) ... interior; **~bid** [irr. (bid)] ofrecer precio más bajo que; **~clothes**, **~cloth·ing** ropa f interior; **~coat** paint. primera capa f; **~cur·rent** corriente f submarina, contracorriente f; fig. nota f callada; **~cut** competitor competir con (rebajando los precios); **~de·vel·oped** subdesarrollado; **~dog** desvalido m; **~done** poco hecho; medio asado; **~es·ti·mate** subestimar; p. tener en menos de lo que merece; **~foot** debajo de los pies; **~go** [irr. (go)] sufrir, experimentar; **~grad·u·ate** estudiante m/f (no graduado [a]); **~ground 1.** adj. subterráneo; fig. clandestino; **2.** adv. bajo tierra; **3.** (= ~ railway) metro m; ✕ resistencia f; **~growth** maleza f; **~hand** turbio, poco limpio; clandestino; **~lay** [irr. (lay)] reforzar; typ. calzar; **~lie** [irr. (lie)] estar debajo de; servir de base a (a. fig.); **~line** subrayar (a. fig.).

un·der·mine [ʌndəˈmain] socavar; minar (a. fig.); **un·der·most** (el) más bajo; **un·der·neath** [ʌˈniːθ] **1.** prp. debajo de, bajo; **2.** adv. debajo; **3.** su. superficie f inferior; **un·der·nour·ished** desnutrido.

un·der...: **~pants** pl. calzoncillos m/pl.; **~pass** paso m inferior; **~pin·ning** apuntalamiento m; **~priv·i·leged** desvalido; **~rate** menospreciar; subestimar; **~score** subrayar; **~sell** [irr. (sell)] p. vender a menor precio que; th. malvender; **~shirt** camiseta f; **~side** superficie f inferior; revés m; **~signed** infra(e)-scrito (a f) m; abajo firmante m/f; **~sized** de dimensión insuficiente; p. sietemesino; **~skirt** enaguas f/pl.;

~**'staffed** sin el debido personal; ~**'stand** [*irr.* (*stand*)] comprender, entender; sobre(e)ntender; *it is understood that* se entiende que; ~**'stand·a·ble** ☐ comprensible; ~**'stand·ing 1.** entendimiento *m*; comprensión *f*; interpretación *f*; (*agreement*) acuerdo *m*; *on the ~ that* con tal que, bien entendido que; **2.** ☐ inteligente; razonable, compasivo; comprensivo; ~**'state·ment** exposición *f* incompleta; subestimación *f*.

un·der...: ~**'stud·y** *thea.* **1.** suplente *m/f*; **2.** aprender un papel para poder suplir a; ~**'take** [*irr.* (*take*)] *task etc.* emprender; *duty etc.* encargarse de, ~**'tak·er** director *m* de pompas fúnebres; ~**'s** funeraria *f*; ~**'tak·ing** empresa *f*; (*pledge*) compromiso *m*, garantía *f*; promesa *f*; ~**'tone** voz *f* baja; trasfondo *m* (*of criticism etc.*); *in an ~* en voz baja; ~**'tow** resaca *f*; ~**'wa·ter** submarino *m*; ~**'wa·ter 'fish·ing** pesca *f* submarina; ~**'wear** ropa *f* interior; ~**'weight** (*adj.* de) peso *m* insuficiente; ~**'world** infierno *m*; (*criminal*) hampa *f*; ~**'write** [*irr.* (*write*)] † (re)asegurar.

un·de·sir·a·ble [ˈʌndiˈzaiərəbl] ☐ indeseable.

un·de·vel·oped [ˈʌndiˈveləpt] sin desarrollar; *land* sin explotar.

un·dig·ni·fied [ʌnˈdignifaid] indecoroso; poco digno.

un·dis·ci·plined [ʌnˈdisiplind] indisciplinado.

un·dis·mayed [ˈʌndisˈmeid] impávido; sin desanimarse.

un·dis·put·ed [ˈʌndisˈpjuːtid] ☐ incontestable.

un·dis·turbed [ˈʌndisˈtəːbd] sin tocar; *p.* imperturbable.

un·di·vid·ed [ˈʌndiˈvaidid] ☐ indiviso; entero.

un·do [ˈʌnˈduː] [*irr.* (*do*)] *work* deshacer; *knot* desatar; *clasp* desabrochar; **'un·do·ing** perdición *f*, ruina *f*; **un·done** [ˈʌnˈdʌn]: *leave ~* dejar sin hacer; *come ~* desatarse.

un·doubt·ed [ʌnˈdautid] ☐ indudable.

un·dress [ˈʌnˈdres] desnudar(se).

un·drink·a·ble [ʌnˈdriŋkəbl] impotable.

un·due [ˈʌnˈdjuː] (*adv. unduly*) indebido; excesivo.

un·du·late [ˈʌndjuleit] ondular, ondear; **'un·du·lat·ing** ondeante.

un·dy·ing [ʌnˈdaiiŋ] imperecedero, inmarcesible.

un·earned [ʌnˈəːnd] no ganado.

un·earth [ʌnˈəːθ] desenterrar.

un·eas·i·ness [ʌnˈiːzinis] inquietud *f*, desasosiego *m*; **un·eas·y** ☐ inquieto (*about* por), desasosegado.

un·ed·u·cat·ed [ʌnˈedjukeitid] ineducado.

un·e·mo·tion·al [ˈʌniˈmouʃnl] ☐ impasible; objetivo.

un·em·ployed [ˈʌnimˈplɔid] parado, sin empleo, desocupado; **'un·em·ploy·ment** paro *m* (forzoso), desempleo *m*, desocupación *f*.

un·end·ing [ʌnˈendiŋ] ☐ interminable, inacabable.

un·e·qual [ˈʌnˈiːkwəl] ☐ desigual, ~ *to* sin fuerzas para; **un·e·qualed** inigualado.

un·e·quiv·o·cal [ˈʌniˈkwivəkl] ☐ inequívoco.

un·err·ing [ˈʌnˈəːriŋ] ☐ infalible.

un·es·sen·tial [ˈʌniˈsenʃl] ☐ no esencial.

un·e·ven [ˈʌnˈiːvn] ☐ desigual; ~ *number* impar; *road* ondulado.

un·e·vent·ful [ˈʌniˈventful] ☐ sin incidentes notables.

un·ex·pect·ed [ˈʌniksˈpektid] ☐ inesperado; inopinado.

un·ex·posed [ˈʌniksˈpouzd] *phot.* inexpuesto.

un·ex·pur·gat·ed [ʌnˈekspəːgeitid] sin expurgar, íntegro.

un·fad·ing [ʌnˈfeidiŋ] ☐ *mst fig.* inmarcesible.

un·fail·ing [ʌnˈfeiliŋ] ☐ *zeal* infalible; *supply* inagotable.

un·fair [ˈʌnˈfɛə] ☐ *comment* injusto; *practice* sin equidad; *play* sucio.

un·faith·ful [ʌnˈfeiθful] ☐ infiel.

un·fal·ter·ing [ʌnˈfɔːltəriŋ] ☐ resuelto; sin desconocer.

un·fa·mil·iar [ˈʌnfəˈmiljə] desconocido (*to a*); poco familiar.

un·fash·ion·a·ble [ˈʌnˈfæʃnəbl] ☐ fuera de moda.

un·fas·ten [ˈʌnˈfɑːsn] desatar, soltar.

un·fa·vor·a·ble [ˈʌnˈfeivərəbl] ☐ desfavorable.

un·feel·ing [ʌnˈfiːliŋ] ☐ insensible.

un·fin·ished [ˈʌnˈfiniʃt] inacabado, sin acabar; incompleto.

un·fit 1. [ˈʌnˈfit] incapaz (*for* de, *to* de); no apto (*for* para); *player* lesionado; **2.** [ʌnˈfit] inhabilitar; **un·fit·ted** incapacitado (*for* para).

607 **unity**

un·flag·ging [ʌn'flægiŋ] □ incansable.

un·flat·ter·ing ['ʌn'flætəriŋ] □ poco lisonjero.

un·flinch·ing [ʌn'flintʃiŋ] □ impávido.

un·fold ['ʌn'fould] desplegar(se); desdoblar(se); desarrollar(se) (a. fig.); revelar; idea exponer.

un·fore·seen ['ʌnfɔː'siːn] imprevisto.

un·for·get·ta·ble ['ʌnfə'getəbl] □ inolvidable.

un·for·giv·a·ble ['ʌnfə'givəbl] □ imperdonable; **un'for'giv·ing** implacable.

un·for·tu·nate [ʌn'fɔːtʃənit] 1. □ p. desgraciado, desafortunado; malogrado; event funesto. 2. desgraciado (a f) m; **un·for·tu·nate·ly** por desgracia, desafortunadamente.

un·found·ed ['ʌn'faundid] infundado.

un·fre·quent·ed ['ʌnfri'kwentid] poco frecuentado.

un'friend·ly ['ʌn'frendli] poco amistoso, hostil.

un·fruit·ful ['ʌn'fruːtful] infructuoso.

un·furl ['ʌn'fɔːl] desplegar.

un·fur·nished ['ʌn'fɔːniʃt] desamueblado, sin muebles.

un·gain·ly ['ʌn'geinli] torpe, desgarbado.

un·gen·tle·man·ly [ʌn'dʒentlmənli] poco caballeroso.

un·glazed ['ʌn'gleizd] no vidriado.

un·god·ly [ʌn'gɔdli] impío, irreligioso; F atroz.

un·gov·ern·a·ble [ʌn'gʌvənəbl] □ ingobernable.

un·grate·ful [ʌn'greitful] □ desagradecido, ingrato.

un·grudg·ing ['ʌn'grʌdʒiŋ] □ generoso.

un·guard·ed ['ʌn'gɑːdid] □✕ indefenso; words imprudente; moment de descuido.

un·guent ['ʌngwənt] ungüento m.

un·ham·pered ['ʌn'hæmpəd] no estorbado; libre, sin estorbos.

un·hand [ʌn'hænd] soltar.

un·hap·py [ʌn'hæpi] □ p. infeliz, desdichado; desgraciado; event infausto.

un·harmed ['ʌn'hɑːmd] ileso, incólume.

un·health·y [ʌn'helθi] □ p. enfermizo; place malsano.

un·heard-of [ʌn'hɔːdɔv] inaudito.

un·heed·ed [ʌn'hiːdid] desatendido.

un·hes·i·tat·ing [ʌn'heziteitiŋ] □ resuelto; pronto, inmediato; ~ly sin vacilar.

un·ho·ly [ʌn'houli] impío; F atroz.

un·hook ['ʌn'huk] desenganchar; descolgar.

un·horse ['ʌn'hɔːs] desarzonar.

un·hurt ['ʌn'hɔːt] ileso, incólume.

un·i·den·ti·fied ['ʌnai'dentifaid] sin identificar.

u·ni·form ['juːnifɔːm] 1. uniforme adj. a. su. m; 2. uniformar; **u·ni·form·i·ty** uniformidad f.

u·ni·fy ['juːnifai] unificar.

u·ni·lat·er·al ['juːni'lætərəl] □ unilateral.

un·i·mag·i·na·ble ['ʌni'mædʒinəbl] □ inimaginable; **un·i·mag·i·na·tive** [~nətiv] □ poco imaginativo.

un·im·paired ['ʌnim'pɛəd] no disminuido, no deteriorado; intacto.

un·im·peach·a·ble [ʌnim'piːtʃəbl] □ irrecusable.

un·im·por·tant ['ʌnim'pɔːtənt] □ insignificante; sin importancia.

un·in·jured ['ʌn'indʒəd] ileso.

un·in·sured ['ʌnin'ʃuəd] no asegurado.

un·in·tel·li·gent ['ʌnin'telidʒənt] ininteligente; **un·in·tel·li·gi·ble** □ ininteligible.

un·in·ten·tion·al ['ʌnin'tenʃnl] □ involuntario, no intencional; ~ly sin querer.

un·in·ter·est·ing ['ʌn'intristiŋ] □ falto de interés.

un·in·ter·rupt·ed ['ʌnintə'rʌptid] □ ininterrumpido.

un·in·vit·ed ['ʌnin'vaitid] guest no convidado, (adv.) sin ser convidado; comment gratuito; **un·in·vit·ing** □ poco atractivo.

un·ion ['juːnjən] unión f (a. ⊕); (marriage) enlace m; pol. etc. sindicato m, gremio m (obrero); attr. gremial; ~ suit traje m interior de una sola pieza; **un·ion·ize** agremiar(se); **un·ion shop** taller m de obreros agremiados.

u·nique [juː'niːk] □ único.

u·ni·son ['juːnizn] ♪ unisonancia f; armonía f (a. fig.); in ~ al unísono.

u·nit ['juːnit] unidad f (a. ✕, ✗); ⚡ (measurement) unidad f; ⊕, ⚡ grupo m; ~ite unir(se), unir(se), juntar(se); (marry) casar, enlazar; 2d Nations Naciones f/pl. Unidas; **u·ni·ty** ['~niti] unidad f; unión f.

u·ni·ver·sal [ju:ni'vɔ:sl] □ universal; ~ **heir** heredero *m* único; ⊕ ~ **joint** junta *f* cardán, junta *f* universal; ♀ *Postal Union* Unión *f* Postal Universal; ~ *suffrage* sufragio *m* universal; **u·ni·verse** ['ʌvɔ:s] universo *m*; **u·ni·ver·si·ty** universidad *f*; *attr.* universitario.

un·just ['ʌn'dʒʌst] □ injusto; **un·jus·ti·fi·a·ble** [ʌn'dʒʌstifaiəbl] □ injustificable.

un·kempt ['ʌn'kempt] despeinado; *fig.* desaseado, descuidado.

un·kind [ʌn'kaind] □ poco amable, poco compasivo; cruel, despiadado; *remark etc.* malintencionado.

un·known ['ʌn'noun] 1. desconocido; incógnito; *adv.* ~ to me sin saberlo yo; 2. desconocido *m*; Å *a. fig.* (*a.* ~ *quantity*) incógnita *f*; '~ **'sol·dier** soldado *m* desconocido.

un·law·ful ['ʌn'lɔ:ful] □ ilegítimo, ilegal.

un·leash ['ʌn'li:ʃ] destraillar; *fig.* desencadenar.

un·less [ən'les, ʌn'les] a menos que, a no ser que.

un·let·tered ['ʌn'letəd] indocto.

un·li·censed ['ʌn'laisənst] sin permiso, sin licencia.

un·like ['ʌn'laik] 1. desemejante; diferente (*a p.* de una p.); ∮ de signo contrario; 2. *prp.* a diferencia de; **un'like·ly** improbable; inverosímil.

un·lim·it·ed [ʌn'limitid] ilimitado.

un·load ['ʌn'loud] descargar; ✝ deshacerse de.

un·lock ['ʌn'lɔk] abrir (con llave); *fig.* resolver.

un·loose, un·loos·en ['ʌn'lu:s(n)] aflojar, desatar, soltar.

un·luck·y [ʌn'lʌki] □ desgraciado; desdichado; (*ill-starred*) nefasto, de mala suerte.

un·man·age·a·ble [ʌn'mænidʒəbl] □ inmanejable; *esp. p.* incontrolable.

un·man·ly ['ʌn'mænli] cobarde; afeminado.

un·marked ['ʌn'ma:kt] sin marca(r); intacto; (*unnoticed*) inadvertido; *sport:* desmarcado.

un·mar·ried ['ʌn'mærid] soltero.

un·mask ['ʌn'ma:sk] desenmascarar.

un·matched ['ʌn'mætʃt] incomparable.

un·mer·ci·ful [ʌn'mɔ:siful] □ despiadado.

un·mind·ful [ʌn'maindful] □ descuidado; *be* ~ *of* no pensar en.

un·mis·tak·a·ble ['ʌnmis'teikəbl] □ inconfundible; inequívoco.

un·mit·i·gat·ed [ʌn'mitigeitid] no mitigado; *rogue* redomado.

un·moved ['ʌn'mu:vd] *mst fig.* impasible, inmóble.

un·named ['ʌn'neimd] sin nombre.

un·nat·u·ral [ʌn'nætʃrl] □ innatural; desnaturalizado; afectado.

un·nec·es·sar·y [ʌn'nesisəri] □ innecesario, superfluo.

un·neigh·bor·ly [ʌn'neibəli] poco amistoso.

un·nerve ['ʌn'nɔ:v] acobardar.

un·no·ticed [ʌn'noutist] inadvertido.

un·ob·serv·ant ['ʌnəb'zɔ:vənt] □ inadvertido; distraído, que no se fija; '**un·ob·served** inadvertido.

un·ob·tain·a·ble ['ʌnəb'teinəbl] inasequible.

un·ob·tru·sive ['ʌnəb'tru:siv] □ discreto; modesto.

un·oc·cu·pied ['ʌn'ɔkjupaid] *house* deshabitado; *territory* sin colonizar; *seat* libre; *post* vacante; *p.* desocupado.

un·of·fi·cial ['ʌnə'fiʃl] □ extraoficial, no oficial.

un·o·pened ['ʌn'oupənd] sin abrir.

un·op·posed ['ʌnə'pouzd] sin oposición.

un·or·gan·ized ['ʌn'ɔ:gənaizd] no organizado.

un·or·tho·dox ['ʌn'ɔ:θədɔks] poco ortodoxo; *eccl.* heterodoxo.

un·pack ['ʌn'pæk] desembalar, desempaquetar; *case* deshacer.

un·paid ['ʌn'peid] *bill* a pagar, por pagar; *work* no retribuido.

un·pal·at·a·ble [ʌn'pælətəbl] desabrido (*a. fig.*), intragable (*a. fig.*).

un·par·al·leled [ʌn'pærəleld] incomparable, sin par.

un·par·don·a·ble [ʌn'pa:dnəbl] □ imperdonable.

un·pa·tri·ot·ic ['ʌnpætri'ɔtik] □ antipatriótico.

un·paved ['ʌn'peivd] sin pavimentar.

un·pleas·ant [ʌn'pleznt] □ desagradable; *p.* antipático; **un'pleas·ant·ness** lo desagradable; (*quarrel etc.*) desavenencia *f*, disgusto *m*.

un·po·lished ['ʌn'poliʃt] sin pulir; *stone* en bruto; *fig.* grosero, tosco.

un·pol·lut·ed ['ʌnpə'lu:tid] impoluto.

un·pop·u·lar [ˈʌnˈpɔpjulə] impopular; **un·pop·u·lar·i·ty** [ˈ‿ˈlæriti] impopularidad f.

un·prec·e·dent·ed [ʌnˈpresidantid] ☐ inaudito, sin precedente.

un·pre·dict·a·ble [ˈʌnpriˈdiktəbl] ☐ impredicible, incierto; p. de (re)acciones imprevisibles.

un·prej·u·diced [ʌnˈpredʒudist] imparcial.

un·pre·med·i·tat·ed [ˈʌnpriˈmediteitid] ☐ impremeditado.

un·pre·pared [ˈʌnpriˈpɛəd, adv. ~ridli] ☐ no preparado; p. desprevenido.

un·pre·ten·tious [ˈʌnpriˈtenʃəs] ☐ modesto, sin pretensiones.

un·prin·ci·pled [ʌnˈprinsəpld] nada escrupuloso, sin conciencia.

un·print·a·ble [ʌnˈprintəbl] intranscribible.

un·pro·duc·tive [ˈʌnprəˈdʌktiv] ☐ improductivo.

un·pro·fes·sion·al [ˈʌnprəˈfeʃnl] ☐ conduct indigno de su profesión; (unskilled) inexperto.

un·prof·it·a·ble [ʌnˈprɔfitəbl] ☐ poco provechoso, nada lucrativo.

un·prom·is·ing [ʌnˈprɔmisin] ☐ poco prometedor.

un·pro·tect·ed [ʌnprəˈtektid] indefenso.

un·proved [ʌnˈpruːvd] no probado. **un·pro·voked** [ʌnprəˈvoukt] sin provocación.

un·pub·lished [ʌnˈpʌbliʃt] inédito. **un·pun·ished** [ʌnˈpʌniʃt] impune; go ~ escapar sin castigo.

un·qual·i·fied [ʌnˈkwɔlifaid] p. incompetente; teacher sin título; success, assertion incondicional; F liar redomado.

un·quench·a·ble [ʌnˈkwentʃəbl] ☐ inextinguible, insaciable (a. fig.).

un·ques·tion·a·ble [ʌnˈkwestʃənəbl] ☐ incuestionable; **un·ques·tioned** incontestable; **un·ques·tion·ing** incondicional.

un·rav·el [ʌnˈrævl] desenmarañar (a. fig.).

un·re·al [ʌnˈriəl] irreal, ilusorio; **un·re·al·is·tic** [ˈʌnriəˈlistik] ☐ impracticable; fantástico; p. poco realista; **un·re·al·i·ty** [ˈ‿ˈæliti] irrealidad f; **un·re·al·iz·a·ble** [~laizəbl] irrealizable.

un·rea·son·a·ble [ʌnˈriːznəbl] ☐ irrazonable; demand excesivo; **un·rea·son·ing** irracional.

un·rec·og·niz·a·ble [ʌnˈrekəgnaizəbl] ☐ irreconocible; **un·rec·og·nized** no reconocido.

un·re·cord·ed [ˈʌnriˈkɔːdid] no registrado.

un·re·deemed [ˈʌnriˈdiːmd] promise sin cumplir; pledge no desempeñado.

un·reg·is·tered [ʌnˈredʒistəd] no registrado; letter no certificado.

un·re·lat·ed [ˈʌnriˈleitid] inconexo.

un·re·lent·ing [ˈʌnriˈlentiŋ] ☐ inexorable, implacable.

un·re·li·a·ble [ˈʌnriˈlaiəbl] p. poco confiable; informal; news nada fidedigno.

un·re·lieved [ˈʌnriˈliːvd] ☐ no aliviado.

un·re·peat·a·ble [ˈʌnriˈpiːtəbl] que no puede repetirse.

un·re·pent·ant [ˈʌnriˈpentənt] ☐ impenitente.

un·re·quit·ed [ˈʌnriˈkwaitid] ☐ no correspondido.

un·re·spon·sive [ˈʌnrisˈpɔnsiv] insensible.

un·rest [ʌnˈrest] malestar m, zozobra f; pol. desorden m.

un·re·strained [ˈʌnrisˈtreind] ☐ desenfrenado.

un·re·strict·ed [ˈʌnrisˈtriktid] ☐ sin restricción.

un·re·ward·ed [ˈʌnriˈwɔːdid] sin recompensa; **un·re·ward·ing** sin provecho, infructuoso.

un·right·eous [ʌnˈraitʃəs] ☐ injusto; malvado.

un·ripe [ʌnˈraip] inmaduro, verde.

un·ri·val(l)ed [ʌnˈraivəld] sin rival, incomparable.

un·roll [ʌnˈroul] desenrollar.

un·ruf·fled [ʌnˈrʌfld] imperturbable.

un·ruled [ʌnˈruːld] paper sin rayar.

un·rul·y [ʌnˈruːli] revoltoso, ingobernable.

un·safe [ʌnˈseif] ☐ inseguro.

un·said [ʌnˈsed] sin decir.

un·sal·a·ble [ʌnˈseiləbl] invendible.

un·sat·is·fac·to·ry [ˈʌnsætisˈfæktəri] ☐ insatisfactorio; **un·sat·is·fied** insatisfecho; **un·sat·is·fy·ing** ☐ insuficiente.

un·sa·vor·y [ʌnˈseivəri] desabrido; repugnante; p. indeseable.

un·scathed [ʌnˈskeiðd] ileso.

un·sci·en·tif·ic [ˈʌnsaiənˈtifik] ☐ poco científico.

un·screw [ʌnˈskruː] destornillar.

un·scru·pu·lous [ʌn'skru:pjuləs] □ desaprensivo, poco escrupuloso.

un·sea·soned [ʌn'si:znd] sin sazonar; sin madurar; *wood* verde.

un·seat [ʌn'si:t] *rider* desarzonar; destituir *from post*; *parl.* expulsar.

un·seem·ly [ʌn'si:mli] *adj.* indecoroso.

un·seen [ʌn'si:n] **1.** invisible; inadvertido; **2.** (*a. ~ translation*) traducción *f* hecha a primera vista.

un·self·ish [ʌn'selfiʃ] □ desinteresado, altruista.

un·serv·ice·a·ble [ʌn'sə:visəbl] □ inservible.

un·set·tle [ʌn'setl] desarreglar; *p.* inquietar; **un·set·tled** *p.* inquieto; *weather* variable; *question* pendiente; *land* inhabitado, no colonizado; † *market* in(e)stable; † *account* por pagar.

un·shack·le [ʌn'ʃækl] desencadenar.

un·shak·en [ʌn'ʃækən] impertérrito.

un·shav·en [ʌn'ʃeivn] sin afeitar.

un·sight·ly [ʌn'saitli] feo.

un·signed [ʌn'saind] sin firmar.

un·skil(l)·ful [ʌn'skilful] □, **un·skilled** inexperto, desmañado; *worker* no cualificado.

un·so·cia·ble [ʌn'souʃəbl] □ insociable.

un·sold [ʌn'sould] sin vender.

un·so·phis·ti·cat·ed [ʌnsə'fisti-keitid] sencillo, cándido.

un·sound [ʌn'saund] □ defectuoso; *opinion* falso, erróneo; *fruit* podrido; *of ~ mind* insano, demente.

un·spar·ing [ʌn'spɛəriŋ] □ generoso, pródigo; *effort* incansable; (*cruel*) despiadado; *be ~ of* no escatimar *acc.*

un·speak·a·ble [ʌn'spi:kəbl] □ indecible; F horrible.

un·spec·i·fied [ʌn'spesifaid] no especificado.

un·spoiled [ʌn'spoild] sin menoscabo, intacto.

un·spo·ken [ʌn'spoukn] tácito.

un·sports·man·like [ʌn'spɔ:tsmən-laik] antideportivo; nada caballeroso.

un·sta·ble [ʌn'steibl] inestable.

un·stead·y [ʌn'stedi] □ inestable, inseguro; inconstante; *p.* irresoluto.

un·stint·ed [ʌn'stintid] ilimitado, liberal.

un·stressed [ʌn'strest] inacentuado, átono.

un·suc·cess·ful [ʌnsək'sesful] □ *p.* fracasado; *effort etc.* infructuoso, ineficaz; *be ~* malograrse; *be ~ in ger.* no lograr *inf.*

un·suit·a·ble [ʌn'sju:təbl] □ inconveniente, inadecuado; impropio (*for a p.* de una p.); *p.* incompetente; **un·suit·ed** inapto (*for, to* para); inadecuado.

un·sure [ʌn'ʃuə] poco seguro.

un·sur·passed [ʌnsə'pɑ:sd] insuperado.

un·sus·pect·ed [ʌnsəs'pektid] insospechado; **un·sus·pect·ing** □ confiado, nada suspicaz.

un·swerv·ing [ʌn'swə:viŋ] □ *resolve* inquebrantable; *course* sin vacilar.

un·sym·pa·thet·ic [ʌnsimpə'θetik] □ incompasivo, indiferente.

un·taint·ed [ʌn'teintid] □ incorrupto; inmaculado.

un·tamed [ʌn'teimd] indomado.

un·tan·gle [ʌn'tæŋgl] desenmarañar.

un·tar·nished [ʌn'tɑ:niʃt] inmaculado.

un·teach·a·ble [ʌn'ti:tʃəbl] indócil.

un·ten·a·ble [ʌn'tenəbl] insostenible.

un·think·a·ble [ʌn'θiŋkəbl] inconcebible; **un·think·ing** □ irreflexivo.

un·ti·dy [ʌn'taidi] □desaliñado, desaseado; *room* en desorden.

un·tie [ʌn'tai] desatar; soltar.

un·til [ən'til, ʌn'til] **1.** *prp.* hasta; **2.** *cj.* hasta que.

un·tilled [ʌn'tild] inculto.

un·time·ly [ʌn'taimli] intempestivo, prematuro.

un·tir·ing [ʌn'taiəriŋ] □ incansable.

un·to ['ʌntu] † = *to a etc.*

un·told [ʌn'tould] *story* nunca contado; *wealth* incalculable.

un·touch·a·ble [ʌn'tʌtʃəbl] (*India*) intocable *adj. a. su. m/f*; **un·touched** intacto; incólume; *food* sin probar; *phot.* sin retocar; *fig.* insensible.

un·trained [ʌn'treind] no adiestrado, no entrenado.

un·trans·lat·a·ble [ʌn'trænsleitəbl] intraducible.

un·tried [ʌn'traid] no probado; *tʃʒ p.* no procesado, *case* no visto.

un·trou·bled [ʌn'trʌbld] tranquilo.

un·true [ʌn'tru:] □ falso; inexacto; *p.* infiel.

un·trust·wor·thy [ʌn'trʌstwə:ði] □ indigno de confianza.

un·truth [ʌn'tru:θ] mentira *f*; **un·truth·ful** □ mentiroso.

un·tu·tored [ˈʌnˈtjuːtəd] no instruido, indocto.

un·used [ˈʌnˈjuːzd] inusitado; *stamp etc.* sin usar; no acostumbrado (*to a*).

un·u·su·al [ʌnˈjuːʒʊəl] □ insólito, extraordinario; nada usual, poco común.

un·veil [ˈʌnˈveil] quitar el velo a; *statue etc.* descubrir.

un·versed [ˈʌnˈvəːst] poco ducho (*in* en).

un·voiced [ˈʌnˈvɔist] *opinion* no expresado; *gr.* sordo.

un·want·ed [ˈʌnˈwɔntid] superfluo; *child* no deseado.

un·war·like [ˈʌnˈwɔːlaik] pacífico.

un·war·rant·ed [ʌnˈwɔrəntəd] injustificado; desautorizado.

un·war·y [ˈʌnˈwɛəri] □ imprudente, incauto.

un·wa·ver·ing [ʌnˈweivəriŋ] □ inquebrantable, resuelto.

un·wea·ry·ing [ʌnˈwiəriiŋ] □ incansable.

un·wel·come [ʌnˈwelkəm] importuno, molesto.

un·well [ˈʌnˈwel] indispuesto.

un·whole·some [ˈʌnˈhoulsəm] insalubre; *p. etc.* indeseable.

un·wield·y [ʌnˈwiːldi] pesado; abultado.

un·will·ing [ˈʌnˈwiliŋ] □ desinclinado; *be* ~ *to* estar poco dispuesto a; ~*ly* de mala gana.

un·wind [ˈʌnˈwaind] [*irr.* (*wind*)] desenvolver.

un·wise [ˈʌnˈwaiz] □ imprudente, malaconsejado.

un·wit·ting [ʌnˈwitiŋ] □inconsciente; ~*ly* sin saber.

un·wont·ed [ʌnˈwountid] □insólito, inusitado.

un·work·a·ble [ˈʌnˈwəːkəbl] impracticable.

un·world·ly [ˈʌnˈwəːldli] no mundano, espiritual.

un·wor·thy [ʌnˈwəːði] □ indigno.

un·wrap [ˈʌnˈræp] desenvolver; *parcel* deshacer.

un·writ·ten [ˈʌnˈritn] no escrito; *law* tradicional, tácito.

un·yield·ing [ʌnˈjiːldiŋ] □ inflexible.

up [ʌp] 1. *adv.* arriba; hacia arriba; en el aire, en (lo) alto; (*out of bed*) levantado; (*sun*) salido; (*standing*) de pie, en pie; (*time*) expirado; F *hard* ~ apurado; F ~ *against it* en apuros; *be* ~ *against p.* tener que habérselas con; F

what's ~? ¿qué pasa?; ~ *to* hasta; *v. date*; *be* ~ *to* ser capaz de; *it is* ~ *to me* me toca a mí; *what are you* ~ *to?* ¿qué haces allí?; 2. *int.* ¡arriba!; 3. *prp.* en lo alto de; encima de; ~ *a tree* en un árbol; ~ *the street* calle arriba; 4. *adj.*: ~ *train* tren *m* ascendente; 5. *su.*: F *on the* ~ *and* ~ cada vez mejor; *the* ~*s and downs* vicisitudes *f/pl.*, altibajos *m/pl.*; 6. *vb.*: F *to* ~ *and inf.* ponerse de repente a *inf.*

up-and-com·ing [ˈʌpənˈkʌmiŋ] F joven y prometedor.

up-and-down [ˈʌpənˈdaun] variable; accidentado.

up-and-up [ˈʌpənˈʌp]: *on the* ~ F (*without fraud*) abiertamente, sin dolo; F (*improving*) mejorándose.

up·braid [ʌpˈbreid] reprochar, censurar (*a. p. with a th.* algo a alguien).

up·bring·ing [ˈʌpbriŋiŋ] educación *f*, crianza *f*.

up·date [ʌpˈdeit] poner al día.

up·end [ˈʌpˈend] volver de arriba abajo.

up·grade [ʌpˈgreid] mejorar.

up·heav·al [ʌpˈhiːvl] *geol.* solevantamiento *m*; *fig.* cataclismo *m*, sacudida *f*.

up·hill [ˈʌpˈhil] 1. *adv.* cuesta arriba; 2. *adj.* task arduo.

up·hold [ʌpˈhould] [*irr.* (*hold*)] sostener, defender.

up·hol·ster [ʌpˈhoulstə] (en)tapizar; **up·hol·ster·er** tapicero *m*; **up·hol·ster·y** tapicería *f*; tapizado *m*.

up·keep [ˈʌpkiːp] (gastos *m/pl.* de) conservación *f*, entretenimiento *m*.

up·land [ˈʌplənd] 1. (*mst pl.*) tierras *f/pl.* altas; meseta *f*; 2. de la meseta.

up·lift 1. [ʌpˈlift] *fig.* inspirar, edificar; 2. [ˈʌplift] *fig.* inspiración *f*.

up·on [əˈpɔn] = *on* en, sobre *etc.*

up·per [ˈʌpə] 1. superior; ~ *berth* litera *f* alta, cama *f* alta; ~ *case typ.* caja *f* alta; ~ *class* clase *f* alta; ~ *deck* (*bus*) piso *m* de arriba; ~ *hand* ventaja *f*, dominio *m*; *have the* ~ *hand* tener vara alta; 2. (*mst* ~*s pl.*) pala *f*; ~-**class** de la clase alta; '~-**cut** *boxing*: golpe *m* de abajo arriba; '~-**most** (el) más alto; predominante *in mind*.

up·raise [ʌpˈreiz] levantar.

up·right 1. [ˈʌpˈrait] □ vertical; derecho (*a. adv.*); *fig.* honrado, probo; 2. [ˈʌprait] montante *m*.

up·ris·ing [ʌpˈraiziŋ] alzamiento *m*, sublevación *f*.

up·roar [ˈʌprɔː] *fig.* alboroto *m*, tu-

U V

multo *m*; grita *f*; **up·roar·i·ous** □ tumultuoso; clamoroso.

up·root [ʌpˈruːt] desarraigar (*a. fig.*), arrancar.

up·set [ʌpˈset] **1.** *irr.* (set) (*overturn*) volcar, trastornar; (*spill*) derramar; *fig. p. etc.* desconcentrar, perturbar, trastornar; *plans* dar al traste con; *stomach* hacer daño a; *F ~ o.s.* congojarse, apurarse; **2.** vuelco *m*; trastorno *m* (*a. &*); contratiempo *m*; **3.** perturbado, preocupado; *&* indispuesto; **up·set·ting** inquietante; desconcertante.

up·shot [ˈʌpʃɔt] resultado *m*; *in the ~* al fin y al cabo.

up·side [ˈʌpsaid]: *~ down* al revés; lo de arriba abajo; *fig.* en confusión; *turn ~ down* trastornar(se).

up·stage [ˈʌpˈsteidʒ] **1.** *adv.* (*be*) en el fondo de la escena; (*go*) hacia el fondo de la escena; **2.** *adj.* F altanero; **3.** *v/t.* mirar por encima del hombro, desairar.

up·stairs [ˈʌpˈstɛəz] **1.** *adv.* arriba; **2.** *adj.* de arriba; **3.** piso *m* de arriba.

up·start [ˈʌpstɑːt] arribista *adj. a. su. m*; advenedizo *adj. a. su. m*.

up·stream [ˈʌpˈstriːm] río arriba.

up·take [ˈʌpteik]: F *be quick* (*slow*) *on the ~* ser muy listo (torpe).

up-to-date [ˈʌptəˈdeit] corriente; reciente, moderno; de última hora, de última moda.

up-to-the-min·ute [ˈʌptəθəˈminit] al día, de actualidad.

up·turn [ˈʌpˈtɜːn] volver(se) hacia arriba; volcar.

up·ward [ˈʌpwəd] **1.** *adj.* ascendente, ascensional; **2.** *adv.* = **up·wards** [ˈ∼z] hacia arriba; *~ of* más de.

u·ra·ni·um [juəˈreiniəm] uranio *m*.

ur·ban [ˈɜːbən] urbano; *ur·bane* [ɜːˈbein] □ urbano; **ur·ban·i·ty** [ɜːˈbæniti] urbanidad *f*.

ur·chin [ˈɜːtʃin] galopín *m*, golf(ill)o *m*.

urge [ɜːdʒ] **1.** impeler, instar (*to a inf.*, *a que subj.*); incitar (*a p. to a th.*, *a th. on a p.* a una p. a algo); *~ on* animar; **2.** impulso *m*; instinto *m*; **ur·gen·cy** [ˈ∼ənsi] urgencia *f*; **ur·gent** [ˈ∼ənt] □ urgente.

u·ri·nal [ˈjuərinl] urinario *m*; (*vessel*) orinal *m*; **u·ri·nate** [ˈ∼neit] orinar; **u·rine** [ˈ∼rin] orina *f*, orines *m/pl*.

urn [ɜːn] urna *f*; (*mst tea-~*) tetera *f*.

us [ʌs, əs] nos; (*after prp.*) nosotros, nosotras.

us·a·ble [ˈjuːzəbl] utilizable.

us·age [ˈjuːzidʒ] uso *m*; tratamiento *m*.

use 1. [juːs] uso *m*; utilidad *f*; manejo *m*, empleo *m*; *in ~* en uso; *be of ~* ayudar; *be of no ~* no servir; *it is (of) no ~ ger.* (*or to inf.*) es inútil *inf.*; *have no ~ for* no necesitar; F tener en poco; *make ~ of* servirse de; *make good ~ of* aprovecharse de; *put to ~* servirse de, sacar partido de; **2.** [juːz] usar; emplear, utilizar; utilizar; *~ up* consumir, agotar; *~d* usado; **used** [ˈjuːst]: *be ~ to* estar acostumbrado a; *get ~ to* acostumbrarse a; *I ~ to do* solía hacer, hacía; **use·ful** [ˈjuːsful] □ útil; ⊕ *~ capacity*, *~ efficiency* capacidad *f* útil; *~ load* carga *f* útil; **use·ful·ness** utilidad *f*; **use·less** □ inútil; inservible; *p.* inepto; **use·less·ness** inutilidad *f*; **us·er** [ˈjuːzə] usuario (*a f*) *m*.

ush·er [ˈʌʃə] **1.** ujier *m*; portero *m*; *thea.* acomodador *m*; **2.** (*mst ~ in*) anunciar; introducir; hacer pasar; *thea.* acomodar.

ush·er·ette [ʌʃərˈet] acomodadora *f*.

u·su·al [ˈjuːʒuəl] □ usual, acostumbrado; corriente; *as ~* como de costumbre.

u·su·rer [ˈjuːʒərə] usurero *m*.

u·surp [juːˈzɜːp] usurpar.

u·su·ry [ˈjuːʒuri] usura *f*.

u·ten·sil [juːˈtensl] utensilio *m*.

u·ter·us [ˈjuːtərəs] útero *m*.

u·til·i·tar·i·an [juːtiliˈtɛəriən] **1.** utilitarista *m/f*; **2.** utilitario; **u·til·i·ty** utilidad *f*; *public ~* empresa *f* de servicio público.

u·ti·lize [ˈjuːtilaiz] utilizar.

ut·most [ˈʌtmoust] extremo; último; supremo; *do one's ~* hacer todo lo posible; *to the ~* hasta no más poder.

U·to·pi·an [juːˈtoupjən] **1.** utópico; **2.** utopista *m/f*.

ut·ter [ˈʌtə] **1.** □ completo, absoluto, total; *fool etc.* de remate; **2.** pronunciar, proferir; *cry* dar; *money* poner en circulación; **ut·ter·ance** declaración *f*; palabras *f/pl.*; *give to ~* expresar; **ut·ter·ly** totalmente, del todo; **ut·ter·most** [ˈ∼moust] más remoto; *v. utmost*.

u·vu·la [ˈjuːvjulə] úvula *f*; **u·vu·lar** [ˈ∼] uvular.

V

va·can·cy ['veikənsi] vacuidad f; vacío m; vaciedad f of mind; cuarto m vacante in boarding-house etc.; (office) vacante f; fill a ~ proveer una vacante; **va·cant** ['~kənt] □ vacante; vacío; seat libre; desocupado; p. estólido; look vago.

va·cate [və'keit, 'veikeit] house desocupar; post dejar (vacante); **va·ca·tion 1.** vacación f, vacaciones f/pl.; **2.** tomar vacaciones.

vac·ci·nate ['væksineit] vacunar; **vac·ci·na·tion** vacunación f; **vac·cine** ['~si:n] vacuna f.

vac·il·late ['væsileit] vacilar.

vac·u·um ['vækjuəm] vacío m; ~ brake freno m de vacío; ~ cleaner aspirador m; ~ bottle termos m; ~ tube tubo m al vacío.

vag·a·bond ['vægəbənd] vagabundo adj. a. su. m ♂.

va·gran·cy ['veigrənsi] vagancia f; **'va·grant 1.** vagabundo; vagante; fig. errante; **2.** vagabundo (a f) m.

vague [veig] □ vago; p. indeciso, distraído; **'vague·ness** vaguedad f.

vain [vein] □ vano; p. vanidoso; in ~ en vano; **~'glo·ry** vanagloria f.

vale [veil] poet. or in names: valle m.

val·en·tine ['væləntain] tarjeta f del día de San Valentín (14 febrero); novio (a f) m (escogido en tal día).

val·et ['vælit] ayuda m de cámara.

val·iant ['væljənt] □ lit. esforzado, valiente.

val·id ['vælid] □ válido; valedero; ♂♂ vigente; be ~ valer; **val·i·date** ['~deit] validar; **va·lid·i·ty** [və'liditi] validez f; ♂♂ vigencia f.

val·ley ['væli] valle m.

val·or·ous ['vælərəs] □ lit. valeroso.

val·or ['vælə] lit. valor m.

val·u·a·ble ['væljuəbl] **1.** □ valioso; precioso; estimable; **2.** ~s pl. objetos m/pl. de valor.

val·u·a·tion [vælju'eiʃn] valuación f; tasación f.

val·ue ['vælju:] **1.** valor m; **2.** valorar, tasar (at en); estimar, apreciar; tener en mucho; **'val·ue·less** sin valor; **'val·u·er** tasador m.

valve [vælv] anat., ⊕ válvula f; ♫, zo. valva f; of a trumpet llave f; ~ cap capuchón m; ~ stem vástago m de válvula; **'~-in-'head 'en·gine** motor m con válvulas en cabeza.

vam·pire ['væmpaiə] vampiro m; fig. vampiresa f.

van[1] [væn] camioneta f; furgoneta f; ⛟ furgón m.

van[2] [~] ⚔ a. fig. vanguardia f.

van·dal·ism ['vændəlizm] vandalismo m.

vane [vein] (weather) veleta f; paleta f of propeller; aspa f of mill.

van·guard ['vænɡɑːd] vanguardia f.

va·nil·la [və'nilə] vainilla f.

van·ish ['væniʃ] desvanecerse, desaparecer.

van·i·ty ['væniti] vanidad f; engreimiento m; ~ case neceser m de belleza, polvera f de bolsillo.

van·quish ['væŋkwiʃ] lit. vencer.

van·tage ['vɑːntidʒ] tennis: ventaja f; '~ ground posición f ventajosa; '~ point lugar m estratégico.

vap·id ['væpid] □ insípido.

va·por ['veipə] **1.** vapor m; vaho m; exhalación f; ~ trail ♒ estela f de vapor, rastro m de condensación; **2.** fig. fanfarronear.

va·por·ize ['veipəraiz] vaporizar(se); **'va·por·iz·er** vaporizador m.

var·i·a·ble ['vɛəriəbl] □ variable adj. a. su. f (Ⓐ); **'var·i·ance** desacuerdo m; desavenencia f; variación f; ♂♂ discrepancia f; at ~ en desacuerdo (with con); **'var·i·ant** variante adj. a. su. f; **var·i·a·tion** variación f (a. ♪).

var·i·cose ['værikous] varicoso; ~ veins varices f/pl.

var·ied ['vɛərid] □ variado.

va·ri·e·ty [və'raiəti] variedad f (a. biol.); diversidad f.

var·i·ous ['vɛəriəs] □ vario, diverso.

var·nish ['vɑːniʃ] **1.** barniz m (a. fig.); fig. capa f, apariencia f; nail ~ laca f, esmalte m (para uñas); **2.** barnizar; nails laquear, esmaltar; fig. paliar, dar apariencia respetable a.

var·si·ty ['vɑːsiti] **1.** sports universitario; **2.** sports equipo m principal de la universidad.

var·y ['vɛəri] variar (v/i. a. v/t.); decisión modificar.

vase [vɑːz] jarrón m; florero m.

Vas·e·line ['væsəliːn] vaselina f.

vas·sal ['væsl] vasallo m.

vast [vɑːst] □ vasto, inmenso; ~ly sumamente, en sumo grado.

vat [væt] tina f, tinaja f.

vau·de·ville ['voudəvil] vaudeville m.

vault[1] [vɔːlt] 1. ∆ bóveda f; (wine-) bodega f; (tomb) tumba f; 2. above-dar.

vault[2] [~] 1. saltar (v/i. a. v/t.); 2. salto m.

vaunt [vɔːnt] lit. v/i. jactarse; v/t. jactarse de, hacer alarde de; **'vaunted** cacareado, alardeado.

veal [viːl] carne f de ternera.

veer [viə] virar (a. fig., a. ~ round); (wind) cambiar.

veg·e·ta·ble [ˈvedʒitəbl] 1. vegetal; 2. legumbre f, hortaliza f; (in general) vegetal m; ~ garden huerto m de hortalizas, huerto m de verduras; ~ soup menestra f, sopa f de hortalizas; ~s pl. freq. verduras f/pl.; **veg·e·tar·i·an** [~ˈteəriən] vegetariano adj. a. su. m (a f); **veg·e·tate** [~teit] vegetar (a. fig.); **veg·e·ta·tion** vegetación f.

ve·he·mence [ˈviːiməns] vehemencia f; **'ve·he·ment** □ vehemente.

ve·hi·cle [ˈviːikl] vehículo m.

veil [veil] 1. velo m (a. fig. a. phot.); 2. velar (a. fig.).

vein [vein] all senses: vena f; be in the ~ estar en vena (para).

ve·loc·i·ty [viˈlɔsiti] velocidad f.

vel·vet [ˈvelvit] terciopelo m; hunt. piel f velluda; sl. ganancia f limpia; 2. aterciopelado; de terciopelo; **'vel·vet·y** aterciopelado.

ve·nal [ˈviːnl] sobornable, venal.

vend [vend] mst ⚖ vender; vender como buhonero; **'vend·er**, **'vend·or** vendedor (-a f) m; buhonero m; **'vend·ing ma·chine** distribuidor m automático.

ve·neer [vəˈniə] 1. chapa f, enchapado m; fig. apariencia f, barniz m; 2. (en)chapar; fig. disfrazar.

ven·er·a·ble [ˈvenərəbl] □ venerable; **ven·er·ate** [~reit] venerar.

ve·ne·re·al [viˈniəriəl] □: ~ disease enfermedad f venérea.

Ve·ne·tian [viˈniːʃn] veneciano adj. a. su. m (a f); ~ blind persiana f.

venge·ance [ˈvendʒəns] venganza f; F with a ~ con creces, con extremo.

ven·i·son [ˈvenzn] carne f de venado.

ven·om [ˈvenəm] veneno m; fig. virulencia f, malignidad f.

vent [vent] 1. respiradero m; salida f; ⊕ válvula f de purga, orificio m, lumbrera f; orn. cloaca f; give ~ to desahogar, dar salida a f; 2. ⊕ purgar; fig. desahogar, descargar.

ven·ti·late [ˈventileit] ventilar (a. fig.); **ven·ti·la·tion** ventilación f

(a. fig.); **'ven·ti·la·tor** ventilador m.

ven·tril·o·quism [venˈtriləkwizm] ventriloquia f; **ven·tril·o·quist** ventrílocuo (a f) m.

ven·ture [ˈventʃə] 1. empresa f (arriesgada); riesgo m; especulación f; 2. v/t. aventurar; v/i. aventurarse (to a).

ve·ra·cious [vəˈreiʃəs] □ veraz; **ve·rac·i·ty** [~ˈræsiti] veracidad f.

ve·ran·da [vəˈrændə] veranda f.

verb [vəːb] verbo m; **'ver·bal** □ verbal; **ver·ba·tim** [~ˈbeitim] palabra por palabra; **ver·bose** [~ˈbous] □ verboso.

ver·dict [ˈvəːdikt] ⚖ veredicto m; fallo m, juicio m; fig. opinión f, juicio m (on sobre); bring in (or return) a ~ dictar un veredicto.

ver·dure [ˈvəːdʒə] verdura f.

verge[1] [vəːdʒ] vara f of office.

verge[2] [~] 1. borde m, margen m; fig. on the ~ of of disaster a dos dedos de, en el mismo borde de; madness al borde de; discovery, triumph en la antesala de; fig. be on the ~ of ger. estar a punto de inf.; 2.: ~ on acercarse a, rayar en.

ver·i·fi·ca·tion [verifiˈkeiʃn] verificación f; **ver·i·fy** [~fai] verificar; **ver·i·si·mil·i·tude** [~siˈmilitjuːd] verosimilitud f; **'ver·i·ta·ble** □ verdadero.

ver·mil·ion [vəˈmiljən] 1. bermellón m; 2. de color rojo vivo.

ver·min [ˈvəːmin] bichos m/pl.; sabandijas f/pl.; parásitos m/pl. (a. fig.); (fox etc.) alimañas f/pl.

ver·mo(u)th [ˈvəːmuːt] vermut m.

ver·nac·u·lar [vəˈnækjulə] 1. vernáculo; 2. lengua f vernácula; F idioma m corriente.

ver·sa·tile [ˈvəːsətail] □ versátil, flexible, adaptable, hábil para muchas cosas; **ver·sa·til·i·ty** [~ˈtiliti] versatilidad f, flexibilidad f.

verse [vəːs] (stanza) estrofa f; (poetry) poesías f/pl.; (line, genre) verso m; versículo m of Bible; **versed** versado (in en).

ver·sion [ˈvəːʃn] versión f.

ver·sus [ˈvəːsəs] contra.

ver·te·bra [ˈvəːtibrə], pl. **ver·te·brae** [~briː] vértebra f; **ver·te·brate** [~brit] vertebrado adj. a. su. m.

ver·ti·cal [ˈvəːtikəl] □ vertical.

verve [vɛəv] energía f, entusiasmo m, brío m.

ver·y [ˈveri] 1. adv. muy; (alone, in

reply to question) mucho; ~ *much* mucho, muchísimo; *the* ~ *best* el mejor (de todos); ~ *good* mst muy bueno, *but sometimes translated by absolute superlative of adj.*, *e.g.* buenísimo, bonísimo, *and by prefix* re(quete)..., *e.g.* re(quete)bueno; **2.** *adj.* mismo; mismísimo; † verdadero; *it is* ~ *cold* hace mucho frío; *the* ~ *same* el idéntico; *to the* ~ *bone* hasta el mismo hueso; *the* ~ *idea!* ¡ni hablar!

ves·pers ['vespəz] vísperas *f/pl.*

ves·sel ['vesl] vasija *f*, recipiente *m*; *anat.*, ♣ vaso *m*; ♣ buque *m*.

vest [vest] **1.** camiseta *f*; chaleco *m*; **2.** investir (*with* de); conferir (*in* a), conceder (*in* a); ~*ed rights pl.* derechos *m/pl.* inalienables; ~*ed interests pl.* intereses *m/pl.* creados.

ves·ti·bule ['vestibju:l] vestíbulo *m*; zaguán *m*.

ves·tige ['vestidʒ] vestigio *m*.

vest·ment ['vestmənt] vestidura *f*.

vest-pock·et ['vest'pɒkit] *attr.* en miniatura, de bolsillo; diminuto.

ves·try ['vestri] sacristía *f*; '~·**man** miembro *m* de la junta parroquial.

vet [vet] **F 1.** veterinario *m*; **2.** repasar, corregir; examinar, investigar.

vet·er·an ['vetərən] veterano *adj. a. su. m.*

vet·er·i·nar·y ['vetnəri] veterinario *adj. a. su. m* (*mst* ~ *surgeon*).

ve·to ['vi:tou] **1.** *pl.* **ve·toes** ['~z] veto *m*; *put a (or one's)* ~ *on* = **2.** vedar, vetar.

vex [veks] vejar, fastidiar, enojar.

vex·ing ['veksiŋ] ☐ fastidioso, molesto.

vi·a ['vaiə] por (vía de).

vi·a·ble ['vaiəbl] viable.

vi·a·duct ['vaiədʌkt] viaducto *m*.

vi·al ['vaiəl] frasco *m* (pequeño).

vi·ands ['vaiəndz] *pl. lit.* manjares *m/pl.* (exquisitos).

vi·brant ['vaibrənt] vibrante (*with* de).

vi·brate [vai'breit] vibrar; **vi'bra·tion** vibración *f*.

vic·ar ['vikə] vicario *m*; **vi·car·i·ous** [vai'kɛəriəs] vicario.

vice[1] [vais] vicio *m*.

vice[2] [~] ⊕ torno *m* (*or* tornillo *m*) de banco.

vice[3] **1.** ['vaisi] *prp.* en lugar de; que sustituye a; **2.** [vais] vice...; '~·**'chair·man** vicepresidente *m*; '~·**'con·sul** vicecónsul *m*; '~·**'pres·i-**

dent vicepresidente *m*; '~·**roy** ['~rɔi] virrey *m*.

vi·ce ver·sa ['vaisi'vɔ:sə] viceversa; *a* la inversa.

vi·cin·i·ty [vi'siniti] vecindad *f*; proximidad *f* (*to* a); *in the* ~ cerca.

vi·cious ['viʃəs] ☐ vicioso; *criticism* virulento, rencoroso; *dog* bravo; *phls.* ~ *circle* círculo *m* vicioso.

vi·cis·si·tude [vi'sisitju:d]: *mst* ~*s pl.* vicisitud *f*.

vic·tim ['viktim] víctima *f*; **'vic·tim·ize** hacer víctima; escoger y castigar, tomar represalias contra.

vic·tor ['viktə] vencedor *m*; **Vic·to·ri·an** [vik'tɔ:riən] victoriano; **vic·'to·ri·ous** ☐ victorioso; **vic·to·ry** ['~təri] victoria *f*.

vid·e·o ['vidiou] *radio*: ... de vídeo; ~ *signal* señal *f* de vídeo; ~ *tape* cinta *f* grabada de televisión; '~ **tape re·'cord·ing** videograbación *f*.

vie [vai] rivalizar (con), competir (con); ~ *with s.o. for s.t.* disputar algo a alguien, disputarse algo.

view [vju:] **1.** vista *f*; prespectiva *f*; aspecto *m*; *paint.*, *phot.* panorama *m*; paisaje *m*; (*opinion*) opinión *f*, parecer *m*; *in* ~ visible, *in full* ~ totalmente visible; *in* ~ *of* en vista de; *have (or keep) in* ~ no perder de vista; *be on* ~ estar expuesto; *with a* ~ *to* a *ger.* con miras a *inf.*, con el propósito de *inf.*; **2.** mirar; examinar; contemplar; considerar; **'view·er** espectador (-a *f*) *m*; telespectador (-a *f*) *m*; **'view·find·er** *phot.* visor *m*; **'view·point** mirador *m*, punto *m* panorámico; *fig.* punto *m* de vista.

vig·il ['vidʒil] vigilia *f*, vela *f*; **'vig·i·lance** vigilancia *f*; ~ *committee* comité *m* de vigilancia; **'vig·i·lant** ☐ vigilante; **vig·i·lan·te** [~'lænti] vigilante *m*.

vig·or·ous ['vigərəs] ☐ vigoroso; **'vig·or** vigor *m*.

vile [vail] ☐ vil; (*very bad*) horrible, pésimo; asqueroso.

vil·la ['vilə] villa *f*, quinta *f*.

vil·lage ['vilidʒ] aldea *f*, puebl(ecit)o *m*; lugar *m*; *attr.* aldeano; **'vil·lag·er** aldeano (a *f*) *m*.

vil·lain ['vilən] malvado *m*; *thea. etc.* malo *m*, traidor *m*; *hist.* villano *m*; *co.* tunante *m*; **'vil·lain·ous** ☐ vil, malvado; *F* pésimo, malísimo.

vim [vim] *F* fuerza *f*, energía *f*.

vin·di·cate ['vindikeit] vindicar; justificar; ~ *o.s.* justificarse; **vin·di·'ca·tion** vindicación *f*.

vin·dic·tive [vin'diktiv] □ vengativo, vindicativo.

vine [vain] vid f; (climbing) parra f; **vin·e·gar** ['viniɡə] 1. vinagre m; 2. avinagrar (a. fig.); **vine·yard** ['vinjəd] viña f, viñedo m.

vin·tage ['vintidʒ] 1. (season) vendimia f; the 1949 ~ la cosecha de 1949; 2.: ~ wine vino m añejo; vino m de marca, vino m de buena cosecha; ~ year año m de buen vino; F car etc. de época, clásico; **vint·ner** ['vintnə] vinatero m.

vi·o·late ['vaiəleit] all senses: violar; **vi·o·la·tion** violación f.

vi·o·lence ['vaiələns] violencia f; do ~ to violentar; **vi·o·lent** □ violento.

vi·o·let ['vaiəlit] 1. ♣ violeta f; (color) violado m; 2. violado.

vi·o·lin [vaiə'lin] violín m; **vi·o·lin·ist** violinista m/f.

vi·per ['vaipə] víbora f.

vir·gin ['vɔːdʒin] virgen af; s.f.; ~ birth parto m virginal de María Santísima; zo. partenogénesis f; **vir·gin·al** □ virginal; **vir·gin·i·ty** [vəː'dʒiniti] virginidad f.

vir·ile ['virail] □ viril; **vi·ril·i·ty** [vi-'riliti] virilidad f.

vir·tual ['vɔːtʃʊəl] □ virtual; **vir·tue** ['.tjuː] virtud f; **vir·tu·os·i·ty** [.tjuː'ɔsiti] virtuosismo m; **vir·tu·o·so** [.'ouzou] esp. ♪ virtuoso m; **vir·tu·ous** □ virtuoso.

vi·rus ['vaiərəs] virus m.

vi·sa ['viːzə] 1. visado m; 2. visar.

vis·age ['vizidʒ] lit. semblante m.

vis-à-vis ['viːzɑː'viː] respecto de.

vis·cous ['viskəs] □ viscoso.

vis·i·bil·i·ty [vizi'biliti] visibilidad f; **vis·i·ble** ['vizəbl] □ visible.

vi·sion ['viʒn] visión f; **vi·sion·ar·y** ['viʒnəri] visionario adj. a. su. m (a f).

vis·it ['vizit] 1. v/t. visitar; ~ s.t. upon a p. castigar una p. con algo; mandar algo a una p.; v/i. hacer visitas; F visitarse; 2. visita f; pay (return) a ~ hacer (pagar) una visita; **vis·it·ing** ... visitante; ... de visita; ~ card tarjeta f de visita; ~ hours horas f/pl. de visita; ~ nurse enfermera f ambulante; **vis·i·tor** visitante m/f; visita f to house; turista m/f; forastero (a f) m.

vi·sor ['vaizə] visera f.

vis·ta ['vistə] perspectiva f, vista f.

vis·u·al ['vizjuəl] □ visual; **vis·u·al·ize** representar (en la mente); imaginarse; situation prever.

vi·tal ['vaitl] □ vital; esencial; p.

enérgico; ~s pl., ~ parts pl. partes f/pl. vitales; ~ statistics pl. estadística f vital; co. medidas f/pl. vitales; **vi·tal·i·ty** [.'tæliti] vitalidad f.

vi·ta·min ['vaitəmin], **vi·ta·mine** ['.miːn] vitamina f; attr. vitamínico.

vi·tu·per·a·tion [vitjuːpəˈreiʃn] vituperio m, injurias f/pl.

vi·va·cious [vi'veiʃəs] □ vivaz, animado; alegre; vivaracho.

viv·id ['vivid] □ vivo; color, light intenso; description gráfico.

viv·i·fy ['vivifai] vivificar; **viv·i·sec·tion** [.'sekʃn] vivisección f.

vo·cab·u·lar·y [vəˈkæbjuləri] vocabulario m.

vo·cal ['voukl] □ vocal (a. ♪); gr. vocálico; fig. ruidoso, expresivo; ~ cords pl. cuerdas f/pl. vocales; **vo·cal·ist** cantante m/f; (in cabaret etc.) vocalista m/f; **vo·cal·ize** ♪ vocalizar; gr. vocalizar(se).

vo·ca·tion [vouˈkeiʃn] vocación f; **vo·ca·tion·al** □ vocacional; ~ guidance guía f vocacional.

vogue [voug] boga f, moda f; in ~ en boga.

voice [vɔis] 1. voz f (a. gr.); in (good) ~ en voz; with one ~ a una voz, al unísono; give ~ to expresar; have no ~ in a matter no tener voz en capítulo; 2. expresar; hacerse eco de; gr. sonorizar(se); **voiced** gr. sonoro; **voice·less** □ gr. sordo.

void [vɔid] 1. vacío; nulo, inválido; ~ of falto de, desprovisto de; 2. vacío m; hueco m; bridge: fallo m; the ~ la nada; 3. evacuar, vaciar.

vol·a·tile ['vɔlətail] volátil (a. fig.).

vol·can·ic [vɔl'kænik] □ volcánico; **vol·ca·no** [.'keinou], pl. **vol·ca·noes** [.z] volcán m.

vo·li·tion [vouˈliʃn] volición f; of one's own ~ por voluntad propia.

vol·ley ['vɔli] 1. ✕ descarga f; lluvia f of stones etc.; salva f of applause; retahíla f of abuse; tennis: voleo m; 2. tennis: volear; ✕ lanzar una descarga; **vol·ley·ball** balón m volea.

volt [voult] voltio m; **volt·age** voltaje m.

vol·u·ble ['vɔljubl] □ locuaz.

vol·ume ['vɔljəm] volumen m; tomo m of book; fig. masa f; radio: ~ control control m del volumen sonoro; speak ~s for evidenciar de modo inconfundible; **vo·lu·mi·nous** [vəˈljuː-minəs] □ voluminoso.

vol·un·tar·y ['vɔləntəri] 1. □ voluntario; ~ **manslaughter** homicidio *m* intencional sin premeditación; **2.** solo *m* de órgano; **vol·un·teer** [~'tiə] **1.** voluntario *m*; **2.** voluntario, de voluntarios; **3.** *v/i.* ofrecerse; ✗ alistarse como voluntario; *v/t.* ofrecer; *remark* permitirse hacer.

vo·lup·tu·ous [və'lʌptjuəs] □ voluptuoso.

vom·it ['vɔmit] **1.** vomitar; **2.** vómito *m*.

vo·ra·cious [və'reiʃəs] □ voraz.

vor·tex ['vɔːteks], *pl. mst* **vor·ti·ces** ['~tisiz] vórtice *m*.

vote [vout] voto *m*; sufragio *m*; (*a. voting*) votación *f*; *cast a* ~ dar un voto; *put to the* ~, *take a* ~ on someter a votación; **2.** *v/t.* votar; ~ *in* elegir; *v/i.* votar (*for, por*); F proponer, sugerir (*that* que); ~ *that* resolver (*por* voto) que; **'vot·er** votante *m/f*; **'vot·ing** votación *f*; ~ **machine** máquina *f* registradora de votos.

vouch [vautʃ] atestiguar; garantizar; confirmar; ~ *for th.* responder de; *p.* responder por; **'vouch·er** documento *m* justificativo; † comprobante *m*; vale *m*; **vouch'safe** conceder, otorgar; dignarse hacer.

vow [vau] **1.** voto *m*; promesa *f* solemne; **2.** hacer voto (*to* de); jurar.

vow·el ['vauəl] vocal *f*.

voy·age ['vɔiidʒ] **1.** viaje *m* (*por mar*); travesía *f*; **2.** viajar (*por mar*); navegar; **voy·ag·er** ['vɔidʒə] viajero (*a f*) *m*.

vul·gar ['vʌlgə] **1.** □ vulgar; *b.s.* grosero; (*in bad taste, showy*) cursi; *joke etc.* verde, indecente; ~ *tongue* lengua *f* vulgar; **2.:** *the* ~ el vulgo; **vul·gar·i·ty** [~'gæriti] vulgaridad *f*; grosería *f*; indecencia *f*.

vul·ner·a·ble ['vʌlnərəbl] □ vulnerable.

vul·ture ['vʌltʃə] buitre *m*.

vy·ing ['vaiiŋ] *ger. of* vie.

W

wack·y ['wæki] *sl.* chiflado.

wad [wɔd] **1.** taco *m*, tapón *m*; lío *m* of *papers*; F fajo *m* of *notes*; **2.** rellenar; acolchar; tapar; **'wad·ding** algodón *m* (en rama); taco *m*.

wad·dle ['wɔdl] anadear.

wade [weid] *v/i.* caminar por el agua *etc.*; ~ *ashore* llegar a tierra vadeando; ~ *into* meterse en; *v/t.* vadear; **'wad·er** *orn.* ave *f* zancuda; ~s *pl.* botas *f/pl.* altas.

wa·fer ['weifə] galleta *f*; barquillo *m*; oblea *f* *for sealing*.

waft [wɑːft] **1.** traer, llevar (*por el aire*); **2.** soplo *m*.

wag[1] [wæg] **1.** menear(se) o agitar (se); **2.** meneo *m*.

wag[2] [~] bromista *m*, zumbón *m*.

wage [weidʒ] **1.** *war* hacer; proseguir; **2.** (*a.* **wag·es** ['~iz] *pl.*) salario *m*; (*mst day-*) jornal *m*; **wage earn·er** ['~ɔːnə] asalariado (*a f*) *m*; **'wage in·crease** aumento *m* de sueldo.

wa·ger ['weidʒə] *lit.* **1.** apuesta *f*; **2.** apostar (*on a, that a* que).

wag·on ['wægən] carro *m*; 🚃 vagón *m*, furgón *m*.

waif [weif] niño (*a f*) *m* abandonado (a).

wail [weil] **1.** lamento *m*, gemido *m*; **2.** lamentarse, gemir; gimotear.

waist [weist] cintura *f*; talle *m*; ⚓ combés *m*; **'~band** pretina *f*; **'~coat** chaleco *m*; **'~deep** hasta la cintura; **'~line** talle *m*.

wait [weit] **1.** *v/i.* esperar, aguardar (*for acc.*); (*a.* ~ *at table*) servir (*on acc.*); *keep s.o.* ~*ing* hacer que uno espere; ~ *and see!* espera y verás; *v/t.* esperar; **2.** espera *f*; *have a long* ~ tener que esperar mucho tiempo; *be* (*or lie*) *in* ~ acechar (*for acc.*); **'wait·er** camarero *m*; mozo *m*.

wait·ing ['weitiŋ] espera *f*; servicio *m*; **'~list** lista *f* de espera; **'~room** sala *f* de espera.

wait·ress ['weitris] camarera *f*.

waive [weiv] *right* renunciar; *claim* desistir de; **'waiv·er** renuncia *f*.

wake[1] [weik] ⚓ estela *f*; *fig. in the* ~ *of* siguiendo, como consecuencia de.

wake[2] [~] **1.** [*irr.*] *v/i.* despertar(se) (*a.* ~ *up*); *v/t.* despertar; *corpse* velar; **2.** vela *f over corpse*; **wake·ful** ['~ful] □ despierto; desvelado; **'wak·en** *v/i.* despertar(se); *v/t.* despertar.

walk [wɔːk] **1.** *v/i.* andar; caminar; (*stroll*) pasear(se); (*not ride*) ir a pie; ~ *about* pasearse; ~ *away with* llevarse; ~ *off with* llevarse; robar; ~ *out* (*strike*) declararse en huelga; *v/t. child etc.*

pasear; *horse* llevar al paso; *distance* recorrer (a pie); 2. (*stroll*) paseo *m*; (*gait*) andar *m*, paso *m*; (*place*) paseo *m*, alameda *f*; '**walk·er** paseante *m/f*, peatón *m*; '**walk·er·on** F figurante (a *f*) *m*.

walk·ie-talk·ie ['wɔːki'tɔːki] transmisor-receptor *m* portátil.

walk·ing ['wɔːkiŋ] 1. excursionismo *m* a pie; el pasearse; 2. ambulante; F ~ *papers pl.* despedida *f*; ~ *race* carrera *f* pedestre; '~·**stick** bastón *m*.

walk...: '~·**out** huelga *f*; salida *f*; '~·**up** *house* sin ascensor.

wall [wɔːl] 1. (*mst interior*) pared *f*; muro *m*; (*garden*) tapia *f*; (*city*) muralla *f*; 2. murar; *city* amurallar; ~ *up* emparedar; cerrar con muro.

wal·let ['wɔlit] cartera *f*.

wall...: '~·**eyed** de ojos incoloros; '~·**flow·er** alhelí *m*; *fig.* be a ~ comer pavo; '~ **map** mapa *m* mural.

wal·lop ['wɔləp] F 1. golpear fuertemente; zurrar; 2. golpazo *m*; zurra *f*; *sl.* fuerza *f* of a drink; '**wal·lop·ing** F grandote.

wall...: '~·**pa·per** papel *m* pintado, papel *m* de empapelar; '~ **sock·et** enchufe *m* de pared.

wal·nut ['wɔːlnʌt] nuez *f*; (*tree, wood*) nogal *m*.

wal·rus ['wɔːlrəs] morsa *f*.

waltz [wɔːls] 1. vals *m*; 2. valsar.

wan [wɔn] □ pálido, macilento.

wan·der ['wɔndə] errar, vagar; extraviarse; deambular (*a.* ~ *about*); '**wan·der·er** vagabundo (a *f*) *m*; nómada *m/f*; '**wan·der·ing** □ errante; errabundo; *fig.* distraído; '**wan·der·lust** ['~lʌst] ansia *f* de viajar.

wane [wein] 1. (*moon*) menguar; *fig.* disminuir; 2. (*a.* '**wan·ing**) menguante *f*; mengua *f*.

wan·ness ['wɔnnis] palidez *f*.

want [wɔnt] 1. (*lack*) falta *f*, carencia *f*; (*need*) necesidad *f*; (*poverty*) indigencia *f*; for ~ of por falta de; F ~ *ad* anuncio *m* clasificado; 2. *v/i.*: be ~ing faltar; be ~ing in estar falto de; *v/t.* querer, desear; (*need*) necesitar; (*lack*) carecer de; ~ed (*in adverts*) necesítase; (*police*) se busca; '**want·ing** defectuoso; deficiente (*in en*), falto (*in de*).

wan·ton ['wɔntən] 1. □ (*playful*) juguetón; (*rank*) lozano; caprichoso; *b.s.* lascivo; 2. libertino (a *f*) *m*; 3. retozar; '**wan·ton·ness** lascivia *f* etc.

war [wɔː] 1. guerra *f*; *attr.* ... de guerra, bélico; *at* ~ en guerra; *cold* ~ guerra *f* fría; *hot* ~ guerra *f* a tiros; ~ *of nerves* guerra *f* de nervios; ~ *criminal* criminal *m* de guerra; ~ *dance* danza *f* guerrera; 2. *lit.* guerrear.

war·ble ['wɔːbl] 1. trinar, gorjear; 2. trino *m*, gorjeo *m*; '**war·bler** mosquitero *m*, curruca *f* etc.

ward [wɔːd] 1. (*p.*) pupilo (a *f*) *m*; (*wardship*) tutela *f*, custodia *f*; (*hospital*) sala *f*, crujía *f*; distrito *m* (*electoral*) of *city*; F ~ *heeler* muñidor *m*; 2.: ~ *off* desviar, parar; '**ward·en** carcelero *m*; guardián *m*; '**ward·robe** guardarropa *m*; vestidos *m/pl.*; *thea.* vestuario *m*; '**ward·room** ♣ cuarto *m* de los oficiales.

ware [wɛə] loza *f*; ~s *pl.* mercancías *f/pl.*; *small* ~s *pl.* mercería *f*.

ware·house 1. ['wɛəhaus] almacén *m*, depósito *m*; 2. ['~hauz] almacenar; '~·**man** ['~hausmən] almacenista *m*.

war...: '~·**fare** guerra *f*; '~·**head** punta *f* de combate of *torpedo*; cabeza *f* de guerra of *rocket*.

war·i·ly ['wɛərili] cautelosamente; '**war·i·ness** ['~inis] cautela *f*, precaución *f*.

war·like ['wɔːlaik] guerrero, belicoso; castrense.

warm [wɔːm] 1. □ caliente (*a.* F = *near*); *day, greeting* caluroso; *climate* cálido; *heart* afectuoso; *argument* acalorado; be ~ (*p.*) tener calor; (*weather*) hacer calor; 2. *v/t.* calentar; *heart* alegrar, regocijar; *v/i.* (*a.* ~ *up*) calentarse; (*argument*) acalorarse; *sport:* hacer ejercicios (para entrar en calor); '~·**heart·ed** cariñoso; simpático.

war·mon·ger ['wɔːmʌŋgə] incendiario *m* de la guerra.

warmth [wɔːmθ] calor *m*; *fig.* cordialidad *f*; entusiasmo *m*; ardor *m*.

warn [wɔːn] avisar; advertir (*of acc.*); prevenir (*against contra*); amonestar (*to inf.*); '**warn·ing** aviso *m*; advertencia *f*; *attr.* de aviso; de alarma; admonitorio.

warp [wɔːp] 1. (*weaving*) urdimbre *f*; alabeo *m* of *wood*; ♣ espía *f*; *fig.* sesgo *m*; 2. (*wood*) alabearse, tocerse.

war·plane ['wɔːplein] avión *m* militar.

war·rant ['wɔrənt] 1. garantía *f*; autorización *f*, justificación *f*; ✝ mandato *m*; 2. *esp.* ✝ garantizar; autorizar, justificar; '**war·rant·ed** ✝ garantizado; '**war·rant-of·fi·cer**

♆ contramaestre *m*; ⚔ suboficial *m*;
'war·ran·tor [⌐ɔː] garante *m/f*;
'war·ran·ty ✝ garantía *f*; *v.* warrant.
war·ri·or ['wɔriə] guerrero *m*.
war·ship ['wɔːʃip] buque *m* de
guerra.
wart [wɔːt] verruga *f* (*a.* ⚘).
war·y ['wɛəri] □ cauto, cauteloso,
prudente.
was [wɔz, wəz] *pret. of* be.
wash [wɔʃ] 1. *v/t.* lavar (*a. ~ up, ~ out*);
dishes a. fregar; bañar; *~ away* quitar
lavando; *v/i.* lavarse; lavar la ropa;
(*water*) moverse; 2. lavado *m*; ropa *f*
(para lavar); (*hung to dry*) tendido *m*;
✈ disturbio *m* aerodinámico;
'wash·a·ble lavable; **'wash-and-**
wear *adj.* de lava y pon; **'wash-**
ba·sin palangana *f*, lavabo *m*.
washed-up ['wɔʃdʌp] *sl.* fracasado.
wash·er ['wɔʃə] ⊕ arandela *f*; (*tap-*)
zapatilla *f*; **'~·wom·an** lavandera *f*.
wash·ing ['wɔʃiŋ] 1. ropa *f* (para
lavar); lavado *m*; *~s pl.* lavadura *f*; 2.
~ machine lavadora *f*; **'~·up** fregado
m, lavado *m* (de platos).
wash...: '~·out *sl.* fracaso *m*; **'~·rag**
paño *m* de cocina; **'~·stand** lavabo *m*,
lavamanos *m*; **'~·tub** tina *f* (de lavar).
wasp [wɔsp] avispa *f*; **'wasp·ish** □
irascible; punzante.
waste [weist] 1. (*rejected*) desechado;
(*useless*) inútil; (*left over*) sobrante;
land baldío, yermo; *lay ~* asolar,
devastar; *~ paper* papel *m* viejo; 2.
despilfarro *m*, derroche *m*; pérdida *f*
of time; desgaste *m*; desperdicio(s)
m(pl.); desecho *m*, basura *f*; 3. *v/t.*
malgastar; desperdiciar; derrochar;
time perder; *v/i.* (des)gastarse; perderse; *~ away* consumirse, mermar;
'waste·ful ['~ful] □ pródigo; des-
pilfarrado; antieconómico; **'waste-**
ful·ness despilfarro *m* etc.; **'waste-**
pa·per bas·ket cesto *m* (para papeles); **'waste-pipe** tubo *m* de desagüe; **'waste prod·uct** producto *m*
de desecho.
watch [wɔtʃ] 1. reloj *m*; vigilia *f*;
vigilancia *f*; ⚔, ♆ guardia *f*, ♆
vigía(s) *m(pl.)*; *keep ~ over p.* sth.;
vigilar por; 2. *v/i.* velar; *~ for* esperar;
acechar; *~ out* tener cuidado (*for*
con); *v/t.* mirar; observar; vigilar;
guardar; *~* **chain** cadena *f* de reloj;
'~·dog perro *m* guardián; **'watch·er**
observador *m*; **watch·ful** ['~ful] □
vigilante; **'watch·ful·ness** vigilancia
f, desvelo *m*.

watch...: '~·mak·er relojero *m*;
'~·man guardián *m*, (*night-*) sereno
m; **'~·tow·er** atalaya *f*; **'~·word** ⚔
santo *m* y seña.
wa·ter ['wɔːtə] 1. agua *f*; *high ~* pleamar *f*; *low ~* bajamar *f*; *by ~* por agua;
por mar; F *get into hot ~* cargárseса
(*for, over* en el asunto de); *hold ~*
retener el agua; *fig.* ser lógico; 2.
acuático; de agua, para agua; *~ supply*
abastecimiento *m* de agua; 3. *v/t.*
land, plant regar; *cattle* abrevar; *wine*
aguar (*a. ~ down*); *v/i.* (*mouth*) hacerse agua; (*eyes*) llorar; **'~·borne**
llevado por barco *etc.*; **'~ bot·tle**
cantimplora *f*; **'~ can·non** cañón *m*
de agua; **'~·col·or** acuarela *f*;
'~·cooled refrigerado por agua;
'~·cool·ing refrigeración *f* por agua;
'~·fall cascada *f*, salto *m* de agua;
'~·fowl *z.* aves *f/pl.* acuáticas;
'~·front terreno *m* ribereño;
wa·ter·ing ['wɔːtəriŋ] riego *m*; **'~·can**
regadera *f*; **'~·place** (*spa*) balneario
m; 🐎 abrevadero *m*.
water...: '~·jack·et camisa *f* de agua;
'~·lev·el nivel *m* del agua; ♆ línea *f* de
agua; **'~ lil·y** nenúfar *m*; **'~·logged**
anegado, empapado; **'~ main** cañería *f* maestra; **'~·mark** filigrana *f*;
'~·mel·on sandía *f*; **'~ mill** molino *m*
de agua; **'~ pipe** caño *m* de agua; **'~**
po·lo polo *m* acuático; **'~ pow·er**
fuerza *f* hidráulica; **'~·proof** 1. impermeable *adj. a. su. m*; 2. impermeabilizar; **'~·ski·ing** esquí *m* acuático; **'~·spout** tromba *f* marina; **'~**
tank cisterna *f*; **'~ ta·ble** retallo *m* de
derrame; **'~·tight** estanco, hermé-
tico; *fig.* irrecusable; completamente lógico; *~ compartment* compartimiento *m* estanco; **'~·way** canal
m, vía *f* fluvial; **'~ wings** *pl.* nada-
deras *f/pl.*; **'~·works** *pl., a. sg.* central
f depuradora; **'wa·ter·y** acuoso.
watt [wɔt] vatio *m*.
wave [weiv] 1. ola *f*; onda *f*; (*hair*)
ondulación *f*; ademán *m of hand*; *cold*
~ ola *f* de frío; 2. *v/t.* agitar; *weapon*
etc. blandir; *hair* ondular; *v/i.* ondear; agitar el brazo; *~ to a p.* hacer
señales (con la mano) a una p.;
'~·length longitud *f* de onda.
wa·ver ['weivə] vacilar, titubear.
wave...: '~ the·o·ry teoría *f* ondula-
toria; *radio:* trampa *f* de ondas.
wav·y ['weivi] ondulado; ondeado.
wax¹ [wæks] 1. cera *f*; 2. encerar.
wax² [~] [*irr.*] (*moon*) crecer.

way [wei] camino m (to de); vía f; dirección f, sentido m; distancia f, trayecto m; viaje m; by ~ of por vía de; fig. a título de; in a ~ en cierto modo; in no ~ de ningún modo; in a bad ~ en mal estado; F in a big ~ en grande, en gran escala; on the ~ en el camino; on the ~ to camino de; out of the ~ arrinconado, aislado; insólito; under ~ en marcha; go one's own ~ ir a la suya; go out of one's ~ desviarse del camino; fig. darse la molestia (to inf. de inf.); have a ~ with manejar bien; have a ~ with people tener don de gentes; lead the ~ ir primero; lose one's ~ extraviarse, errar el camino; ~ station estación f de paso; ~ lay [irr. (lay)] asechar; detener; '~ side 1. (by the al) borde m del camino; 2. junto al camino.

way·ward ['weiwəd] voluntarioso; caprichoso; '**way·ward·ness** voluntariedad f; lo caprichoso.

we [wi:, wi] nosotros, nosotras.

weak [wi:k] □ débil; flojo; sound tenue; '**weak·en** debilitar(se); atenuar(se); enflaquecer(se); '**weak·ling** ♂ canijo m; cobarde m; '**weak·ly** enclenque, achacoso; '**weak·mind·ed** □ imbécil; vacilante; '**weak·ness** debilidad f.

wealth [welθ] riqueza f; caudal m; fig. abundancia f; '**wealth·y** □ rico, acaudalado.

wean [wi:n] destetar; fig. ~ from, ~ of apartar gradualmente.

weap·on ['wepən] arma f; '**~·less** desarmado; inerme; '**~·ry** armamento m.

wear [wɛə] 1. [irr.] v/t. llevar; shoes calzar; ~ away, ~ down, ~ out (des)gastar; consumir; patience cansar, agotar; ~ o.s. out matarse; v/i. (well) durar; ~ well conservarse bien; ~ away desgastarse; 2. desgaste m, deterioro m, uso m; (clothes) ropa f; moda f.

wea·ri·ness ['wiərinis] cansancio m; aburrimiento m.

wea·ri·some ['wiərisəm] □ fastidioso; aburrido.

wea·ry ['wiəri] 1. □ (tired) cansado (of de), fatigado; (tiring) fastidioso; 2. v/t. cansar; aburrir.

wea·sel ['wi:zl] comadreja f.

weath·er ['weðə] 1. tiempo m; (harsh) intemperie f; 2. attr. ♣ de barlovento; meteorológico; 3. v/t. aguan-

tar (a. fig.); ~ beat·en ['~bi:tn] curtido por la intemperie; '~ bu·reau servicio m meteorológico; '~ chart mapa m meteorológico; '~ cock veleta f; '~ fore·cast parte m (or boletín m) meteorológico; '~ proof a prueba de la intemperie; '~ sta·tion estación f meteorológica; '~ strip burlete m; '~ vane veleta f.

weave [wi:v] 1. [irr.] tejer; trenzar; fig. urdir, tramar; 2. tejido m.

web [web] tela f; tejido m; (spider's) telaraña f; orn. membrana f; ⊕ alma f; '**web·foot·ed** palmípedo.

wed [wed] v/t. casarse con; fig. casar; v/i. casarse; '**wed·ded** conyugal; fig. ~ to aferrado a; '**wed·ding 1.** boda f, bodas f/pl.; casamiento m; 2. attr. nupcial; de boda.

wedge [wedʒ] 1. cuña f; calce m; 2. calzar, acuñar.

wed·lock ['wedlɔk] matrimonio m.

Wednes·day ['wenzdi] miércoles m.

weed [wi:d] 1. mala hierba f; F tabaco m; 2. escardar; desherbar; '**~ kill·er** herbicida m.

weed·y ['wi:di] lleno de malas hierbas; F flaco; desmirriado.

week [wi:k] semana f; a ~ today de hoy en ocho días; '**~ day** día m laborable; '**~ end** fin m de semana, weekend m; '**week·ly 1.** semanal; 2. semanalmente.

weep [wi:p] (irr.) llorar, lamentar; '**weep·ing** lloroso.

weigh [wei] 1. v/t. pesar (a. fig., ~ up, words etc.); ~ against considerar en relación con; ~ anchor zarpar; v/i. pesar; he ~s 80 kilos pesa 80 kilos; 2.: ♣ under ~ en marcha; '**weigh·ing ma·chine** báscula f.

weight [weit] 1. peso m (a. fig.); pesa f; ~s and measures pl. pesos m/pl. y medidas; carry great ~ influir poderosamente (with en); ~ lifting halterofilia f; 2. (sobre)cargar; sujetar con un peso; ponderar statistically; '**weight·i·ness** pesar m; fig. importancia f; '**weight·less** ingrávido; '**weight·less·ness** ingravidez f; gravedad f nula; '**weight·y** □ pesado; fig. importante, de peso.

weird [wiəd] □ fantástico, sobrenatural; horripilante; F extraño.

wel·come ['welkəm] 1. □ bienvenido; grato; F you're ~! no hay de qué; iro. ¡buen provecho le haga!; 2. bienvenida f; (buena) acogida f; 3. acoger; recibir.

wherewithal

weld [weld] 1. ⊕ soldar; *fig.* unir, unificar (*into* para formar); 2. soldadura *f*; '**weld·er** soldador *m*; '**weld·ing** ⊕ soldadura *f*; *attr.* ... soldador.

wel·fare ['welfɛə] bienestar *m*; prosperidad *f*; asistencia *f* social; ~ **state** estado *m* benefactor.

well¹ [wel] 1. pozo *m*; *fig.* fuente *f*, manantial *m*; ⊕ pozo *m* (de petróleo); 2. brotar, manar.

well² [~] 1. *adv.* bien; ~ *done!* ¡bien!; ~ *and good* enhorabuena; 2. *pred. adj.* bien (de salud); *it is just as* ~ *that* menos mal que; 3. *int. etc.* ¡vaya!; bien; pues; ~ *then* pues bien; '~·**ad·vised** bien aconsejado; '~·**be·haved** bien educado; '~·**be·ing** bienestar *m*; '~·**bred** bien criado; cortés; '~·**dis·posed** bien dispuesto; benévolo (*to, towards* con); '~·**in·formed** (*in general*) instruido; bien enterado (*about matter* de).

well...: '~·**in·ten·tioned** bienintencionado; '~·**known** familiar, conocido; '~·**man·nered** cortés, urbano; '~·**mean·ing** bienintencionado; '~·**nigh** casi; '~·**off** F acomodado; '~·**read** muy leído; '~·**spoken** bienhablado; '~·**timed** oportuno; '~·**to·do** acomodado, pudiente.

Welsh [welʃ] 1. galés, de Gales; 2. (*language*) galés *m*; '~·**man** galés *m*.

wel·ter ['weltə] confusión *f*; mar *m* of *blood etc.*; '~·**weight** wélter *m*.

wench [wentʃ] moza *f*, mozuela *f*.

went [went] *pret.* of *go* 1.

were [wəː, wə] *pret.* of *be*.

west [west] 1. oeste *m*, occidente *m*; 2. *adj.* del oeste, occidental; 3. *adv.* al oeste, hacia el oeste.

west·er·ly ['westəli] *direction* hacia el oeste; *wind* del oeste.

west·ern ['westən] 1. occidental; 2. ♀ película *f* que se desarrolla en el Oeste de EE. UU.; '**west·ern·er** habitante *m/f* del oeste.

west·ward(s) ['westwəd(z)] hacia el oeste.

wet [wet] 1. mojado; *place* húmedo; *weather* lluvioso; *day* de lluvia; *paint* fresco; ~ *paint* ¡ojo, se pinta!; 2. humedad *f*; (*rain*) lluvia *f*; 3. mojar; ~ *one's whistle* remojar el gaznate.

wet·back ['wetbæk] *sl.* inmigrante *m/f* ilegal (desde Méjico).

wet cell ['wet'sel] ⚡ pila *f* húmeda.

wet·ness ['wetnis] humedad *f*; (*raininess*) lo lluvioso.

whack [wæk] F 1. golpear (ruidosamente); pegar; 2. golpe *m* (ruidoso); *sl.* tentativa *f*; '**whack·ing** F 1. zurra *f*; 2. grandote, imponente.

whale [weil] ballena *f*; F *a* ~ *of* ... un enorme ...; F *have a* ~ *of a time* pasarlo en grande; '~·**bone** ballena *f*; '**whal·er** (*p.*) ballenero *m*; (*boat*) ballenera *f*; '**whale oil** aceite *m* de ballena.

whal·ing ['weiliŋ] pesca *f* de ballenas; ~ *station* estación *f* ballenera.

wharf [wɔːf] muelle *m*.

what [wɔt] 1. *relative* lo que; *know* ~'s ~ saber cuántas son cinco; ... *and* ~ *not* y saber de qué no más; 2. *interrogative* qué; cuál; ~? (*surprise etc., asking for repetition*) ¿cómo?; ~ *about* ...? ¿qué te parece ...?; ~ *for*? ¿para qué?; ¿por qué?; ~ *of it*?, *so* ~? y eso ¿qué importa?; 3.: ~ *luck!* ¡qué suerte!; ~ *a* ...! ¡qué ...!; '**what(·so)·ev·er** 1. cual(es)quiera que; todo lo que; 2.: *he says* diga lo que diga; *nothing* ~ nada en absoluto.

wheat [wiːt] trigo *m*; *attr.* triguero; '**wheat·en** de trigo.

whee·dle ['wiːdl] engatusar (*into* ger. para *subj.*); sonsacar.

wheel [wiːl] 1. rueda *f*; (*steering-*) volante *m*; ♣ timón *m*; ✗ conversión *f*; 2. *v/t.* hacer girar, hacer rodar; *bicycle* empujar; *child* pasear; *v/i.* girar, rodar; '~·**bar·row** carretilla *f*; '~·**base** *mot.* distancia *f* entre ejes; '~·**chair** silla *f* de ruedas; '**wheel·er·'deal·er** *contp.* explotador *m* tramoyista; empresario *m* pretendido.

wheeze [wiːz] 1. resollar (*con ruido*); 2. resuello *m* (ruidoso); '**wheez·y** □ que resuella (con ruido).

when [wen] 1. ¿cuándo?; 2. cuando.

whence [wens] *lit.* 1. ¿de dónde?; 2. por consiguiente.

when(·so)·ev·er [wen(sou)'evə] siempre que, cuandoquiera que.

where [wɛə] 1. ¿(a)dónde?; 2. donde; ~·**a·bouts** 1. ['wɛərə'bauts] ¿dónde?; 2. ['~] paradero *m*; ~ *as* mientras (que); por cuanto; ⚖ considerando que; ~·**at** con lo cual; ~·**by** por lo cual, por donde; '~·**fore** por eso; por tanto; ~·**in** en donde; ~·**of** de que; ~·**on** en que; ~·**up·on** acto seguido, después de lo cual; **wher·'ev·er** 1. dondequiera que; 2. F ¿dónde?; **where·with·al** [wɛəwi'ðɔ:l] F medios *m/pl.*, conquibus *m.*

whet [wet] *tool* afilar, amolar.

wheth·er ['weðə] si; ~ ... or sea ... sea; ~ or no en todo caso.

whew [hwu:] ¡vaya!

which [witʃ] **1.** ¿cuál(es)?; ¿qué?; ~ *book do you want?* ¿cuál de los libros quieres?; **2.** que; el (la, los, las) que; el (la) cual, los (las) cuales; lo cual; ~**ev·er** [.'evə] **1.** *pron.* cualquiera; el (la) que; **2.** *adj.* cualquier.

whiff [wif] soplo *m* (fugaz); vaharada *f*; fumada *f* of *smoke.*

while [wail] **1.** rato *m*; for *a* ~ durante un rato; F *worth* ~ que vale la pena; **2.** ~ *away* entretener, pasar; **3.** mientras (que).

whim [wim] capricho *m*, antojo *m.*

whim·per ['wimpə] **1.** *v/i.* lloriquear, gimotear; gimoteo *m.*

whim·si·cal ['wimzikl] □ caprichoso, fantástico; **whim·si·cal·i·ty** [.'kæliti] capricho *m*, fantasía *f.*

whine [wain] **1.** *v/i.* gimotear, quejarse; *v/t.* decir gimoteando; **2.** gimoteo *m etc.*

whin·ny ['wini] **1.** relinchar; **2.** relincho *m.*

whip [wip] **1.** *v/t.* azotar; fustigar (*a. fig.*); *fig.* F derrotar; *cream* batir; ~ *out* sacar de repente; ~ *up* avivar; *v/i.* agitarse; **2.** látigo *m*; azote *m*; *parl.* llamada *f*; (*p.*) oficial *m* disciplinario de partido; '~**ped 'cream** crema *f* (*or* nata *f*) batida.

whip·per... ['wipə]: '~**snap·per** mequetrefe *m*; rapaz *m.*

whip·ping ['wipiŋ] flagelación *f*; vapuleo *m*; '~ *boy* cabeza *f* de turco'; '~ **post** poste *m* de flagelación.

whip-saw ['wipsɔ:] sierra *f* cabrilla.

whirl [wə:l] **1.** *v/i.* arremolinarse; (*head*) dar vueltas; *v/t.* hacer girar; agitar; **2.** giro *m*, vuelta *f*; remolino *m*; serie *f* vertiginosa *of pleasures*; **whirl·i·gig** [.'igig] tiovivo *m*; '**whirl·pool**, '**whirl·wind** torbellino *m*, remolino *m*; '**whir·ly·bird** F helicóptero *m.*

whir(r) [wə:] **1.** zumbar, rechinar; **2.** zumbido *m*, rechino *m.*

whisk [wisk] **1.** (*brush*) escobilla *f*; (*fly*) mosqueador *m*; **2.** *dust* quitar; *cooking*: batir; ~ *away* escamotear, arrebatar; '**whisk·er** pelo *m* (de la barba); bigotes *m/pl.* (*a. zo.*).

whis·k(e)y ['wiski] whisky *m.*

whis·per ['wispə] **1.** *v/i.* cuchichear;

susurrar (*a. fig., leaves*); *v/t.* decir al oído (*to* a); **2.** cuchicheo *m.*

whis·tle ['wisl] **1.** silbar (*at acc.*); ~ *up* llamar con un silbido; **2.** ♪ silbato *m*, pito *m*; (*sound*) silbido *m*, silbo *m*; ~ **stop** población *f* pequeña.

white [wait] **1.** blanco; *face* pálido; *turn* ~ (*p.*) palidecer; ~ *coffee* café *m* con leche; ~ *heat* candencia *f*; **2.** blanco *m* (*a. of eye*); clara *f* del huevo; (*p.*) blanco (*a f*) *m*; '~**col·lar** profesional; de oficina; ~ *crime* crímenes de oficinistas (contra la empresa); '~**hot** candente; *fig.* violento, ardiente; **whit·en** blanquear (*v/i. a. v/t.*); (*p.*) palidecer; '**white·ness** blancura *f.*

white...: '~ *tie* (*attr.* de) traje *m* de etiqueta; '~**wash 1.** jalbegue *m*; F encubrimiento *m* de faltas; **2.** enjalbegar, blanquear.

whit·ish ['waitiʃ] blanquecino.

whit·tle ['witl] *stick* cortar pedazos a; *fig.* ~ *away*, ~ *down* mermar.

whiz [wiz] **1.** silbar; (*arrow*) rehilar; **2.** silbido *m*, zumbido *m.*

who [hu:] **1.** que; quien(es); **2.** ¿quién(es)?; ~ *goes there?* ¿quién vive?

who·dun·it [hu:'dʌnit] *sl.* novela *f* policíaca.

who·ev·er [hu:'evə] **1.** quienquiera que, cualquiera que; **2.** F ¿quién?

whole [houl] **1.** □ todo; entero; total; ❧ sano; intacto; *the* ~ *world* el mundo entero; ~ *milk* leche *f* sin desnatar; **2.** todo *m*; conjunto *m*; total *m*; totalidad *f*; *on the* ~ en general; '~**heart·ed** □ incondicional; cien por cien; '~**sale 1.** (*a.* ~ *trade*) venta *f* al (por) mayor; **2.** al (por) mayor; *fig.* en masa; general; '**whole·sal·er** mayorista *m*; '**whole·some** □ [.'səm] □ saludable, sano; apetitoso; '**whole wheat** trigo *m* entero.

whol·ly ['houli] enteramente.

whom [hu:m] *acc. of* who.

whoop [hu:p] **1.** alarido *m*, grito *m*; **2.** gritar (fuertemente); **whoop·ee** ['wu:pi:] F: *make* ~ divertirse una barbaridad; **whoop·ing-cough** ['hu:piŋkɔf] tos *f* ferina.

whop·per ['wɔpə] *sl.* enormidad *f*; (*lie*) mentirón *m*; '**whop·ping** *sl.* enorme, grandísimo.

whore [hɔ:] puta *f.*

whorl [wə:l] ⊕ espiral *f*; *zo.* espira *f.*

whose [hu:z] *genitive of* who: **1.** cuyo; de quien; **2.** ¿de quién?; **who·so-**

ev·er [hu:sou'evə] quien(es)quiera que.

why [wai] **1.** ¿por qué?; ¿para qué?; **2.** vamos; pero; **3.** *su.* porqué *m.*

wick·ed ['wikid] □ malo, malvado; inicuo; *co.* F horroroso; **'wick·ed·ness** maldad *f etc.*

wick·et ['wikit] postigo *m*, portillo *m.*

wide [waid] **1.** □ ancho; extenso; amplio; *difference* considerable; **2.** *adv.* lejos; ~ **open** abierto de par en par; **'~an·gle** phot. de ángulo ancho; **wid·en** ['waidn] ensanchar(se); **'wide·ness** anchura *f*; **'wide·spread** extenso, muy difundido.

wid·ow ['widou] viuda *f*; **'wid·ow·er** viudo *m*; **wid·ow·hood** ['~hud] viudez *f.*

width [widθ] anchura *f*; extensión *f.*

wield [wi:ld] *lit.* manejar, empuñar; *power* ejercer.

wife [waif] (*pl. wives*) mujer *f*, esposa *f*; **'wife·ly** de esposa.

wig [wig] peluca *f*; *big* ~ F pájaro *m* de cuenta.

wig·gle ['wigl] menear(se) rápidamente.

wild [waild] **1.** □ salvaje; ♀ silvestre; feroz; violento; *child etc.* desmandado, desgobernado; (*rash, foolish*) insensato, temerario; ~ *beast* fiera *f*; F *be* ~ *about* andar loco por; **2.** ~*s pl. v. wilderness;* **'wild·cat 1.** *zo.* gato *m* montés; empresa *f* arriesgada; pozo *m* de petróleo de exploración; **2.** *fig.* quimérico; arriesgado; indisciplinado; ~ *strike* huelga *f* espontánea; **wil·der·ness** ['wildnis] desierto *m*, yermo *m*; **'wild-goose chase** empresa *f* desatinada; **'wild·ness** ferocidad *f*; violencia *f etc.*

wiles [wailz] engaños *m/pl.*, mañas *f/pl.*

wil·ful ['wilful] □ *p.* voluntarioso; *act* premeditado, intencionado.

will [wil] **1.** voluntad *f*; placer *m*; ⚖ testamento *m*; **2.** [*irr.*] *v/aux. que forma el futuro etc.:* he ~ **come** vendrá; I ~ **do** it sí que lo haré; **3.** querer; ⚖ legar.

will·ing ['wiliŋ] □ complaciente; gustoso; **'will·ing·ness** buena voluntad *f.*

wil·low ['wilou] sauce *m*; **'wil·low·y** *fig.* esbelto, cimbreño.

will pow·er ['wilpauə] fuerza *f* de voluntad.

wil·ly-nil·ly ['wili'nili] a la fuerza, quiera o no quiera.

wilt [wilt] marchitar(se); *fig.* acobardarse; languidecer.

wil·y ['waili] □ astuto, mañoso.

win [win] **1.** [*irr.*] *v/t.* ganar; lograr; *v/i.* ganar; triunfar; **2.** victoria *f.*

wind¹ [wind, *poet. a.* waind] **1.** viento *m*; *fig.* (*breath*) aliento *m*; ♪ flatulencia *f*; ♪ instrumento *m* de viento; *throw to the* ~s desechar; **2.** *hunt.* husmear; ♪ dejar sin aliento.

wind² [waind] [*irr.*] *v/t.* enrollar, envolver (*a.* ~ *up*); *handle* dar vueltas a; *watch* dar cuerda a; ~ *up* concluir; † liquidar; *v/i.* serpentear; dar vueltas.

wind... [wind]: **'~bag** charlatán *m*; **'~ed** sin aliento; **'~fall** fruta *f* caída; *fig.* golpe *m* de suerte inesperado.

wind·ing ['waindiŋ] **1.** (*handle*) vuelta *f*; (*watch*) cuerda *f*; **2.** serpentino; sinuoso; tortuoso; ~ *staircase* escalera *f* de caracol; **'~·up** conclusión *f*; † liquidación *f.*

wind in·stru·ment ['windinstrumənt] instrumento *m* de viento.

wind·lass ['windlas] torno *m.*

wind·mill ['windmil] molino *m* (de viento); (*toy*) molinete *m.*

win·dow ['windou] ventana *f*; (*shop*) escaparate *m*; ventanilla *f* of *vehicle*; **'~ dress·ing** decoración *f* de escaparates; *fig.* camuflaje *m*; **'~ frame** marco *m* (de ventana); **'~pane** cristal *m*; **'~shade** visillo *m*, transparente *m*; **'~shop** curiosear en las tiendas.

wind...: **'~pipe** tráquea *f*; **'~shield** parabrisas *m*; ~ *wiper* limpiaparabrisas *m*; **'~ tun·nel** ✈ túnel *m* aerodinámico.

wind·y ['windi] □ ventoso; *day* de mucho viento; *place* expuesto al viento; *fig. speech* palabrero.

wine [wain] vino *m*; **'~ cel·lar** bodega *f*; **'~er·y** lagar *m*; **'~glass** vaso *m* para vino; **'~grow·er** viñador *m.*

wing [wiŋ] **1.** ala *f*; ♪ brazo *m*; *sport:* exterior *m*; *thea.* ~s *pl.* bastidores *m/pl.*; *be on the* ~ estar volando; *take* ~ irse volando; **2.** *v/t. p.* herir en el brazo; *v/i.* volar; **'~ chair** sillón *m* de orejas; **winged** [~ŋd] alado; **'wing nut** tuerca *f* mariposa.

wink [wiŋk] **1.** guiño *m*; pestañeo *m*; F *have* (*or take*) 40 ~s descabezar el sueño; **2.** *v/t. eye* guiñar; *v/i.* guiñar el ojo; parpadear.

win·ner ['winə] ganador (-a *f*) *m*, vencedor (-a *f*) *m.*

win·ning ['winiŋ] □ vencedor, victorioso.

win·ter ['wintə] 1. invierno m; attr. invernal, de invierno; 2. invernar.

win·try ['wintri] invernal; fig. frío.

wipe [waip] 1. enjugar; limpiar; ~ off quitar frotando; ~ out destruir, extirpar; 2. limpión m; limpiadura f.

wire ['waiə] 1. alambre m; F telegrama m; 2. v/t. house instalar el alambrado de; fence alambrar; F telegrafiar; v/i. F poner un telegrama; '~ cut·ters pl. cizalla f; '~ gauge calibre m para alambres; '~-haired de pelo áspero; 'wire·less 1. radio f, radiorreceptor m (a. ~ set); radiotelegrafía f; 2. attr. radiofónico; ~ operator (radio)telegrafista m; 'wire 'net·ting red f de alambre; 'wire serv·ice servicio m telegráfico y telefónico; 'wire·tap·ping intercepción f secreta de comunicaciones telefónicas.

wir·ing ['waiəriŋ] instalación f de alambres; alambrado m; 'wir·y □ delgado pero fuerte; nervudo.

wis·dom ['wizdəm] sabiduría f; prudencia f.

wise [waiz] □ (learned) sabio; (sensible etc.) prudente; juicioso; acertado; sl. ~ guy sabelotodo m; F be ~ to conocer el juego de.

wise·a·cre ['waizeikə] sabihondo m; 'wise·crack 1. cuchufleta f; 2. cuchufletear.

wish [wiʃ] 1. desear (for acc.; anhelar (for acc.); 2. deseo m (for de; to inf. de inf.); anhelo m; best ~es enhorabuena f; 'wish·ful □ deseoso (to inf. de inf.); ~ thinking espejismo m, ilusionismo m.

wish·y-wash·y ['wiʃi'wɔʃi] F soso, insípido.

wist·ful ['wistful] □ pensativo.

wit [wit] 1. ingenio m (a. p.); agudeza f; sal f; (p.) chistoso m; 2.: to ~ a saber.

witch [witʃ] bruja f, hechicera f; ~ doctor hechicero m; '~·craft brujería f; '~ hunt persecución f (política).

with [wið] con; en compañía de; (towards) para con; de (e.g., tremble with fear temblar de miedo); covered with cubierto de.

with·draw [wið'drɔː] [irr. (draw)] v/t. retirar; sacar; retractar; v/i. retirarse (from de); recogerse; **with'draw·al** retirada f; abandono m.

with·er ['wiðə] v/i. marchitarse; v/t. marchitar; fig. aplastar, confundir.

with·hold [wið'hould] [irr. (hold)] retener; negar (from a); payment suspender; ~ing tax descuento m anticipado de los impuestos; **with'in** 1. adv. lit. dentro; 2. prp. dentro de; al alcance de (a. ~ reach of); **with'out** 1. adv. lit. (a)fuera; from ~ desde fuera; 2. prp. sin; 3. cj. sin que; **with'stand** resistir a, aguantar.

wit·less ['witlis] □ tonto, insensato.

wit·ness ['witnis] 1. (p.) testigo m/f; testimonio m; 2. presenciar; atestiguar (to acc.); will etc. firmar como testigo; '~ stand barra f (or puesto m) de los testigos.

wit·ti·cism ['witisizm] agudeza f, chiste m; 'wit·ti·ness agudeza f, gracia f; 'wit·ting·ly a sabiendas; 'wit·ty □ ingenioso, chistoso, gracioso.

wives [waivz] pl. of wife.

wiz·ard ['wizəd] hechicero m, brujo m; F as m; '~·ry magia f.

wob·ble ['wɔbl] bambolear, tambalearse; ⊕ oscilar; fig. vacilar.

woe [wou] lit. or co. aflicción f, dolor m; ~ is me! ¡ay de mí!; '~·be·gone abatido, desconsolado; **woe·ful** □ triste, afligido.

woke [wouk] pret. a. p.p. of wake².

wolf [wulf] 1. lobo (a f) m; sl. mujeriego m; 2. F zampar, engullir; 'wolf·ish □ lobuno.

wolves [wulvz] pl. of wolf 1.

wom·an ['wumən] 1. mujer f; F criada f; 2. femenino; de mujer; ~ doctor médica f; 'wom·an-hat·er misógino m; **wom·an·hood** ['~hud] (quality) feminidad f; (age) edad f adulta; 'wom·an·ish □ afeminado; mujeril; 'wom·an·like mujeril; 'wom·an·ly femenino, mujeril.

womb [wuːm] matriz f, útero m; fig. seno m.

wom·en ['wimin] pl. of woman; ~'s liberation movimiento m feminista; ~'s rights pl. derechos m/pl. de la mujer; ~'s team equipo m femenino.

won [wʌn] pret. a. p.p. of win 1.

won·der ['wʌndə] 1. maravilla f, prodigio m; (feeling) admiración f; work ~s hacer milagros; 2. admirarse, maravillarse (at de); preguntarse; **won·der·ful** ['~ful] □ maravilloso; 'won·der·ment asombro m, admiración f.

won't [wount] = will not.

wont [wount] acostumbrado.

woo [wu:] *lit.* cortejar, galantear; *fig.* tratar de conquistar.

wood [wud] (*trees*) bosque *m*; (*material*) madera *f*; (*fire-*) leña *f*; ♪ instrumento *m* de viento de madera; '~·**carv·ing** escultura *f* en madera; '~·**cut** grabado *m* en madera; '~·**cut·ter** leñador *m*; '**wood·ed** arbolado, enselvado; '**wood·en** □ de madera; *fig.* inexpresivo; rígido; ~ *shoe* zueco *m*; '**wood en·grav·ing** grabado *m* en madera.

wood...: '~·**land** 1. bosque *m*, arbolado *m*; monte *m*; 2. selvático; '~·**man** leñador *m*; '~·**peck·er** *orn.* carpintero *m*; '~·**pile** montón *m* de leña; '~·**pulp** pulpa *f* de madera; '~·**shav·ings** *pl.* virutas *f/pl.*; '~·**shed** leñera *f*; '~·**wind** (*or instruments*) *pl.* instrumentos *m/pl.* de viento de madera; '~·**work** carpintería *f*, ebanistería *f*; △ maderaje *m*; '~·**worm** carcoma *f*; '**wood·y** *tissue* leñoso; *country* arbolado.

wool [wul] lana *f*; *attr.* de lana, lanar; *dyed in the* ~ *fig.* acérrimo, intransigente; '**wool·en** 1. de lana; lanero; 2. ~s *pl.* géneros *m/pl.* de lana; '**wool·ly** lanudo, lanoso.

word [wə:d] 1. palabra *f*; vocablo *m*; (*news*) noticia *f*; ✗ santo *m* y seña; *the* ♀ el Verbo; '♪ letra *f*; *by* ~ *of mouth* de palabra; ~ *for* ~ palabra por palabra; *give one's* ~ dar (*or* empeñar) su palabra; 2. redactar; expresar; '~·**book** vocabulario *m*; '**word·i·ness** verbosidad *f*; '**word·ing** fraseología *f*, términos *m/pl.*; '**word proc·ess·ing** redacción *f* por medios electrónicos.

word·y ['wə:di] □ verboso.

wore [wɔ:] *pret. of* **wear** 1.

work [wə:k] 1. trabajo *m*; labor *f*; (*lit. etc.*) obra *f*; ~s *pl.* ⊕ fábrica *f*; (*mechanism*) mecanismo *m*; (*lit. etc.*) obras *f/pl.*; *public* ~s *pl.* obras *f/pl.* públicas; *be out of* ~ estar desempleado; *make short of* ~ concluir con toda rapidez; 2. *v/i.* trabajar (*at* en; *hard* mucho); ⊕ funcionar, marchar; obrar; (*remedy*) surtir efecto, ser eficaz; *land* cultivar; *mine* explotar.

work·a·ble ['wə:kəbl] □ practicable; factible; práctico; **work·a·hol·ic** ⊦ individuo *m* con compulsión al trabajo; '**work·bench** banco *m* de taller; '**work·day** día *m* laborable; '**work·er** trabajador (-a *f*) *m*; obrero (a *f*) *m*; operario (a *f*) *m*; *zo.* abeja *f*

obrera; '**work force** personal *m* obrero; '**work·ing** 1. funcionamiento *m*; explotación *f*; ⚒ ~s *pl.* labores *f/pl.*; 2. obrero; de trabajo; *in* ~ *order* funcionado; ~ *capital* capital *m* de explotación; ~ *class* clase *f* obrera; ~ *hypothesis* hipótesis *f* de guía.

work·man ['wə:kmən] obrero *m*; trabajador *m*; operario *m*; '~·**like** bien ejecutado; competente; '**work·man·ship** hechura *f*; confección *f*; arte *m*, artificio *m*.

work...: ~·**out** ['wə:kaut] entrenamiento *m*, ejercicio *m*; '~·**shop** taller *m*.

world [wə:ld] mundo *m*; *attr.* mundial; *fig. a* ~ *of* la mar de; ~ *champion* campeón *m* mundial; ~ *power* potencia *f* mundial; ♀ *Series* Serie *f* Mundial; '**world·li·ness** mundanería *f*.

world·ly ['wə:ldli] mundano; '~·**wis·dom** mundología *f* (F), astucia *f*; '~·**wise** que tiene mucho mundo; astuto.

world-wide ['wə:ld'waid] mundial, universal.

worm [wə:m] 1. gusano *m*; (*earth-*) lombriz *f*; *fig.* (-p.) persona *f* vil; ⊕ filete *m*; 2. *fig.* insinuarse (*into* en); '~·**drive** transmisión *f* por tornillo sin fin; '~·**eat·en** *wood* carcomido; *cloth* apolillado; '~ **gear** engranaje *m* de tornillo sin fin; '**worm·y** gusanoso; carcomido.

worn [wɔ:n] *p.p. of* **wear** 1; '~·**out** gastado; inservible; anticuado.

wor·ry ['wari] 1. inquietar(se), preocupar(se) (*about, over* por); molestar(se); 2. inquietud *f*, preocupación *f*; cuidado *m*.

worse [wə:s] 1. peor (*a.* 🐾); ~ *and* cada vez peor; ~ *than ever* peor que nunca; 2. peor *m*; *from bad to* ~ de mal en peor; '**wors·en** empeorar.

wor·ship ['wə:ʃip] 1. culto *m*; adoración *f*; oficio *m*; 2. adorar; venerar; **wor·ship·ful** ['~·ful] *in titles:* excelente; '**wor·ship·(p)er** adorador (-a *f*) *m*; devoto (a *f*) *m*.

worst [wə:st] 1. *adj.* & *adv.* peor; 2. lo peor; *at* (*the*) ~ en el peor de los casos; *the* ~ *of it is* (*that*) lo malo es que; 3. vencer.

worth [wə:θ] 1. (*worthy of*) digno de; (*equal to*) equivalente a; *be* ~ valer; merecer; 2. valor *m*; valía *f*; mérito *m*; **wor·thi·ness** ['~·ðinis] mérito *m*, merecimiento *m*; **worth·less** ['~·θlis]

□ sin valor; indigno; inútil; despreciable; '**worth·while** valioso; **wor·thy** ['wəːði] □ digno (*of* de); meritorio; benemérito.

would [wud] [*pret. of will*] *v/aux.* que forma el condicional etc.; ~ *that* ...! ¡ojalá (que)...!

would-be ['wudbiː] supuesto; llamado; que presume de; aspirante a.

wouldn't ['wudnt] = *would not*.

wound[1] [wuːnd] **1.** herida *f*; **2.** herir; '**wound·ing** □ *tone* hiriente.

wound[2] [waund] *pret. a. p.p. of wind*[2].

wove *pret.*, **wo·ven** ['wouv(n)] *p.p. of weave* [1].

wow [wau] F **1.** (*exclamation*) ¡cielos!; **2.** impresionar mucho a.

wran·gle ['ræŋgl] **1.** reñir indecorosamente; **2.** riña *f* indecorosa; '**wran·gler** disputador *m*; F vaquero *m*.

wrap [ræp] **1.** *v/t.* envolver (*a.* ~ *up*); *fig.* be ~*ped up in* estar absorto en; *v/i.*: ~ *up* arroparse, arrebujarse; **2.** bata *f*, abrigo *m*; '**wrap·per** envase *m*; (*postal*) faja *f*; '**wrap·ping** envase *m*, envoltura *f*; ~ *paper* papel *m* de envolver (*or* embalar); '**wrap-up** F conclusión *f*; resumen *m*.

wrath [rɔːθ] *lit. or co.* cólera *f*, ira *f*.

wreak [riːk] *lit. vengeance* tomar (*on* en); *wrath* descargar (*on* en).

wreath [riːθ] (*funeral*) corona *f*; guirnalda *f*; **wreathe** [riːð] [*irr.*] *v/t.* enguirnaldar; ceñir; *v/i.* enroscarse, formar espirales.

wreck [rek] **1.** ♫ (*act*) naufragio *m*; (*ship*) buque *m* naufragado; *fig.* ruina *f*; F *mot.* choque *m*; automóvil *m* destruido; *p.* quebrado (*a f*) *m*; **2.** ♫ hacer naufragar; ♫ hacer descarrilar; *fig.* arruinar, acabar con; '**wreck·age** restos *m/pl.*; escombros *m/pl. of house etc.*; (*act*) naufragio *m* (*a. fig.*), ruina *f*; '**wreck·er** ♫ raquero *m*; demoledor *m*; *sl.* camión *m* de grúa.

wrench [rentʃ] **1.** arrancar; arrebatar (*from a p.* a una p.); torcer (*a. ♫*); **2.** arranque *m*; ♫ torcedura *f*; ⊕ llave *f* inglesa; *fig.* sacudida *f*, choque *m*.

wrest [rest] arrancar, arrebatar.

wres·tle ['resl] **1.** *v/i.* luchar (*a. fig.*); *v/t.* luchar contra; **2.** = '**wres·tling** lucha *f* (*libre*).

wretch [retʃ] desgraciado (*a f*) *m*.

wretch·ed ['retʃid] □ miserable, desgraciado; *th.* pobre, mezquino;

taste etc. pésimo; '**wretch·ed·ness** miseria *f*; vileza *f etc.*

wrig·gle ['rigl] menearse; culebrear.

wring [riŋ] [*irr.*] *clothes* escurrir, exprimir el agua de; *hands* retorcer; *neck* torcer; '**wring·er** secadora *f*, escurridor *m*.

wrin·kle ['riŋkl] **1.** arruga *f*; **2.** arrugar(se); *brow* fruncir.

wrist [rist] muñeca *f*; ~ *watch* reloj *m* de pulsera; '**~·band** puño *m*; bocamanga *f*.

writ [rit] *mst ♫* orden *f*, mandato *m*, auto *m*; *Holy* ♀ Sagrada Escritura *f*.

write [rait] [*irr.*] *v/t.* escribir; redactar; ~ *down* poner por escrito; ♀ bajar el precio de; *v/i.* escribir; ~ *back* contestar; '**~-off** ♀ carga *f* por depreciación; F pérdida *f* total.

writ·er ['raitə] escritor (-*a f*) *m*, autor (-*a f*) *m*; ~'*s cramp* calambre *m* de los escribientes.

write-up ['raitˌʌp] F (*report*) crónica *f*; *b.s.* bombo *m*, valoración *f* excesiva.

writhe [raið] retorcerse, contorcerse, debatirse.

writ·ing ['raitiŋ] el escribir; (*hand etc.*) escritura *f*, letra *f*; (*thing written*, *work*) escrito *m*; profesión *f* de autor; *in* ~ por escrito; *attr.* ... de escribir; '~ *desk* ♫ tapa *f* de papel, bloc *m*; '~ *pa·per* papel *m* de escribir.

writ·ten ['ritn] *p.p. of write*; *adj.* escrito.

wrong [rɔŋ] **1.** □ erróneo, incorrecto, equivocado; (*unfair*) injusto; (*wicked*) malo; inoportuno, impropio; *be* ~ (*p.*) no tener razón; equivocarse; F *what's* ~ *with* ...? ¿qué le pasa a ...?; **2.** *adv.* mal; al revés; injustamente; *go* ~ funcionar mal; *fig.* extraviarse; **3.** mal *m*; injusticia *f*, entuerto *m*, agravio *m*; perjuicio *m*; *be in the* ~ no tener razón, equivocarse; **4.** agraviar, ofender; ser injusto con; '~·*do·er* malhechor (-*a f*) *m*; '~·*do·ing* maldad *f*, perversidad *f*; **wrong·ful** ['~ful] □ injusto; ilegal; '**wrong-'head·ed** □ obstinado, perversamente equivocado; '**wrong·ness** injusticia *f*; error *m*; '**wrong 'num·ber** *teleph.* número *m* equivocado.

wrote [rout] *pret. of write*.

wrought [rɔːt] **1.** † *pret. a. p.p. of work* **2**; *lit.* he ~ *great changes* llevó a cabo

(*or* efectuó) grandes reformas; **2.** *adj.*
⊕ forjado, labrado; ~ **iron** hierro *m*
forjado (*or* batido).

wrung [rʌŋ] *pret. a. p.p. of* wring.
wry [rai] ☐ torcido, tuerto; *fig.* pervertido; ~ **face** mueca *f.*

X

X [eks] ⋏ *a. fig.* X.
xer·o·graph·y [ziːˈrɔgræfi] xerogra-
fía *f.*; proceso *m* de producir fotoco-
pias instantáneas en seco.
X-mas [ˈeksməs, ˈkrisməs] F Navidad *f.*
X-rat·ed [ˈeksˈreitid] F *film* no reco-
mendado; condenado; pornográfico.

X-ray [ˈeksˈrei] **1.** F radiografía *f.*; ~**s**
pl. rayos *m/pl.* X; **2.** radiográfico; **3.**
radiografiar.
xy·log·ra·pher [zaiˈlɔgrəfə] xilógrafo
m; **xy·lo·graph·ic, xy·lo·graph·i-**
cal [ˌ-ləˈgræfik(l)] xilográfico; **xy-**
log·ra·phy [ˌ-ˈlɔgrəfi] xilografía *f.*
xy·lo·phone [ˈzailəfoun] xilófono *m.*

Y

yacht [jɔt] **1.** yate *m*, (*small*) balandro
m; **2.** pasear en yate; **'yacht club**
club *m* náutico; **'yacht·ing** paseo *m*
en yate; regatas *f/pl.* de balandros;
attr. de balandros; de balandristas;
'yachts·man deportista *m* náutico;
balandrista *m.*
yam [jæm] batata *f,* ñame *m.*
yank [jæŋk] F **1.** *mst* ~ **out** sacar de un
tirón; **2.** tirón *m.*
Yan·kee [ˈjæŋki] F yanqui *adj. a. su.*
m.
yap [jæp] **1.** dar ladridos agudos; F
charlar neciamente; **2.** ladrido *m*
agudo.
yard[1] [jɑːrd] yarda *f* (= 91,44 cm.);
approx. vara *f;* ♠ verga *f.*
yard[2] [ˌ] corral *m;* patio *m.*
yard... [ˈ~·arm] verga *f;* penol *m;* '~·
stick yarda *f; fig.* criterio *m,* norma *f.*
yarn [jɑːn] hilo *m,* hilaza *f;* F cuento *m*
(inverosímil).
yaw [jɔː] **1.** ♠ guiñada *f;* ✈ derrape
m; **2.** ♠ hacer una guiñada; ✈ derrapar.
yawn [jɔːn] **1.** bostezar; *fig.* ~**ing** muy
abierto; **2.** bostezo *m.*
yea [jei] † sí (*a. su. m*); sin duda.
year [jiːr, jiə] año *m;* ~ *of grace* año *m*
de gracia; '~·**book** anuario *m;* **'year-**
ling primal *adj. a. su. m* (-a *f*);
'year·ly anual(mente *adv.*).
yearn [jəːn] anhelar, añorar, ansiar
·(*after, for acc.*); suspirar (*for* por);
'yearn·ing anhelo *m,* añoranza *f.*

yeast [jiːst] levadura *f;* **'yeast·y** ☐
espumoso; *fig.* frívolo.
yegg [jeg] *sl.* ladrón *m* (de cajas fuertes).
yell [jel] **1.** gritar; chillar; decir a
gritos; **2.** grito *m,* alarido *m.*
yel·low [ˈjelou] **1.** amarillo; F (*cow-*
ardly) blanco; ~ *fever* fiebre *f* amarilla; ~ *press* periódicos *m/pl.* sen-
sacionales; **2.** amarillo *m;* **3.** *v/i.*
amarillecer, amarillear; *v/t.* volver
amarillo; '~·**jack·et** avispa *f;* avispón
m; **'yel·low·ish** amarillento.
yelp [jelp] **1.** gañido *m;* **2.** gañir.
yen [jen] *sl.* deseo *m* vivo.
yep [jep] F sí.
yes [jes] sí (*a. su. m*); ~ **man** *sl.*
pelotillero *m.*
yes·ter·day [ˈjestədi] ayer (*a. su. m*); ~
afternoon ayer por la tarde.
yet [jet] **1.** *adv.* todavía, aún; *as* ~
hasta ahora; *not* ~ todavía no; **2.** *cj.*
sin embargo; con todo.
Yid·dish [ˈjidiʃ] lengua *f* de los judíos
askenazis.
yield [jiːld] **1.** *v/t.* producir, dar (de
sí); *profit* rendir; (*give up*) entregar;
v/i. ✿ *etc.* producir, rendir; (*sur-*
render) rendirse, someterse; ceder;
consentir (*to* en); **2.** ✿ cosecha *f;*
producción *f;* ✝ rendimiento *m;*
'yield·ing ☐ flexible (*a. fig.*); *fig.*
complaciente, dócil.
yo·del, yo·dle [ˈjoudl] **1.** canto *m* a la
tirolesa; **2.** cantar a la tirolesa.
yo·ga [ˈjougə] yoga *f;* **'yo·gi** yogui *m.*

yo·gurt [ˈjougət] yogurt *m*.
yoke [jouk] **1.** ✶ yunta *f*; *fig*. yugo *m*; ⊕ horquilla *f*; **2.** ✶ uncir; acoplar; *fig*. unir.
yo·kel [ˈjoukl] F palurdo *m*, patán *m*.
yolk [jouk] yema *f* (de huevo).
you [juː] **1.** (*nominative*) *sg*. tú, *pl*. vosotros, vosotras; (*acc. dat.*) *sg*. te, *pl*. os; (*after prp.*) *sg*. ti, *pl*. vosotros, vosotras; with ∼ (*sg. reflexive*) contigo; **2.** *formal, with third p. verb*: (*nominative*) *sg*. usted, *pl*. ustedes; (*acc. dat.*) *sg*. le, la, *pl*. les; (*after prp.*) *sg*. usted, *pl*. ustedes; with ∼ (*sg. a. pl. reflexive*) consigo.
young [jʌŋ] **1.** joven; *brother etc*. menor; ∼ **man** joven *m*; **2.** *zo*. cría *f*, hijuelos *m/pl.*; *the* ∼ *pl*. los jóvenes;

ˈyoung·ish bastante joven; **ˈyoung-ster** joven *m/f*, jovencito (a *f*) *m*.
your [jɔː, juə, jə] tu(s); vuestro(s), vuestra(s); su(s); **yours** [jɔːz, juəz] (el) tuyo, (la) tuya *etc*.; (el) vuestro, (la) vuestra *etc*.; (el) suyo, (la) suya *etc*.; **yourˈself**, *pl*. **yourˈselves** [∼ˈselvz] (*subject*) tú mismo, vosotros mismos; usted(es) mismo(s); *acc.*, *dat*. te, os, se; (*after prp.*) ti, vosotros, sí (mismo[s]); *f forms have* a(s).
youth [juːθ] juventud *f*; (*p*.) joven *m*, mozo *m*; **youth·ful** [∼ˈful] □ juvenil; joven; **ˈyouth·ful·ness** juventud *f*; vigor *m*, espíritu *m* juvenil.
Yu·go·slav [ˈjuːɡousla:v] yugo(e)slavo *adj. a. su. m* (a *f*).
Yule [juːl], **Yule·tide** [ˈjuːltaid] *lit*. Navidad *f*; ∼ *log* leño *m* de Navidad.

Z

za·ny [ˈzeini] F tonto; loco.
zeal [ziːl] celo *m*, entusiasmo *m*; **ˈzeal·ot** [ˈzelət] fanático *m*; **ˈzeal-o·try** fanatismo *m*; **ˈzeal·ous** □ entusiasta (*for* de); apasionado (*for* por).
ze·bra [ˈziːbrə] cebra *f*.
ze·nith [ˈzeniθ] cenit *m*; *fig*. apogeo *m*.
zeph·yr [ˈzefə] céfiro *m* (a. ✦ *cloth*).
ze·ro [ˈziərou] **1.** cero *m*; **2.** nulo; ∼ *growth adj*. sin aumento; estable; ∼ **hour** ✕ hora *f* de ataque.
zest [zest] gusto *m*, entusiasmo *m*.
zig·zag [ˈzigzæg] **1.** zigzag *m*; **2.** (en) zigzag; **3.** zigzaguear, hacer eses.
zinc [ziŋk] **1.** cinc *m*; **2.** cubrir con cinc.
Zi·on·ism [ˈzaiənizm] sionismo *m*;

ˈZi·on·ist sionista *adj. a. su. m*.
zip [zip] **1.** pasar volando; **2.** silbido *m*, zumbido *m*; F energía *f*; **zip code** ✉ número de zona postal; **ˈzip·per** (cierre *m* de) cremallera *f*, cierre *m* relámpago; **ˈzip·py** F enérgico; rápido.
zo·di·ac [ˈzoudiæk] zodíaco *m*; **zo-di·a·cal** [zouˈdaiəkl] zodiacal.
zone [zoun] zona *f*.
zoo [zuː] F jardín *m* (*or* parque *m*) zoológico; casa *f* de fieras.
zo·o·log·i·cal [zouəˈlɔdʒikl] □ zoológico; **zo·ol·o·gist** [zouˈblədʒist] zoólogo *m*; **zoˈol·o·gy** zoología *f*.
zoom [zuːm] F **1.** zumbar; ✈ empinarse; **2.** zumbido *m*; ✈ empinadura *f*.
Zu·lu [ˈzuːluː] zulú *m*.

Spanish Abbreviations
Abreviaturas españolas

Cada artículo contiene la forma desarrollada de la abreviatura, y, en cuanto ha sido posible, la abreviatura inglesa correspondiente, desarrollándose también ésta entre paréntesis.

A

a *área.*
A: bomba A *bomba atómica* A-bomb (atomic bomb).
(a) *alias* alias.
ab.¹ *april* Apl. (April).
a.c. *año corriente* current year, present year.
A. (de) C. *año de Cristo* A.D. (Anno Domini).
a/c *al cuidado* c/o (care of).
acr. *acreedor* creditor.
adj. *adjunto* Enc. (enclosure, enclosed).
adm(ón). *administración* admin. (administration).
a/f. *a favor* in favor.
afmo. *afectísimo: suyo ~* yours truly.
ag. *agosto* Aug. (August).
a. (de) J.C. *antes de Jesucristo* B.C. (before Christ).
AI *Amnistía Internacional* Amnesty International.
Al.º *Alonso personal name.*
amp. *amperios* amp. (ampères).
Ant.º *Antonio personal name.*
ap. *thea.* aparte aside.
apdo. *apartado (de correos)* P.O.B. (Post Office Box).
art., art.º *artículo* art. (article).
arz. *arzobispo* abp. (archbishop).
A.T. *Antiguo Testamento* O.T. (Old Testament).
atmo. *atentísimo: suyo ~* yours truly.
atta. *atenta.*
atte. *atentamente.*
a/v. *a vista* at sight.
Av., Av.ᵈᵃ *Avenida* Av., Ave. (Avenue).

B

B. *eccl.* beato blessed.
B.A. *Buenos Aires capital of Argentina.*
Bº *banco* bk. (bank).
Bón. *batallón* Battn, Bn. (battalion).

C

c. *capítulo* ch. (chapter).
C. *compañía* Co. (company).
c³ *centímetro cúbico* c.c. (cubic centimeter).
c.ª *compañía* Co. (company).
c.a. *corriente alterna* A.C. (alternating current).
C.A.E. *cóbrese al entregar* C.O.D. (cash on delivery).
cap. *capítulo* ch. (chapter).
Cap.ⁿ *Capitán* Capt. (Captain).
cap.º *capítulo* ch. (chapter).
c.c. *centímetro cúbico* c.c. (cubic centimeter).
c.c. *corriente continua* D.C. (direct current).
c/c *cuenta corriente* C/A (current account).
C.D. *Club Deportivo* S.C. (Sports Club).
c/d *con descuento* with discount.
C. de J. *Compañía de Jesús* S.J. (Society of Jesus).
CECA *Comunidad Europea del Carbón y del Acero* ECSC (European Coal and Steel Community).
CEE *Comunidad Económica Europea* E(E)C (European [Economic] Community).
C.F. *Club de Fútbol* F.C. (Football Club).
cg. *centigramo* centigramme.

Cía *compañía* Co. (company).
c.i.f. *costo, seguro y flete* c.i.f. (cost, insurance, freight).
cl. *centilitro* centiliter.
cm. *centímetro* cm. (centimeter).
cm² *centímetro cuadrado* sq. cm. (square centimeter).
cm³ *centímetro cúbico* c.c. (cubic centimeter).
Cnel *Coronel* Col. (Colonel).
COI *Comité Olímpico Internacional* IOC International Olympic Committee.
col., col.ª *columna* col. (column).
comp. *compárese* cf. (confer).
comp.ª *compañía* Co. (company).
corrte. *corriente, de los corrientes* inst. (instant).
C.P. *contestación pagada* R.P. (reply paid).
cs. *céntimos; centavos* cents.
c.s.f. *costo, seguro, flete* c.i.f. (cost, insurance, freight).
cta, c.ta *cuenta* A/C (account).
cte *corriente, de los corrientes* inst. (instant).
cts. *céntimos; centavos* cents.
c/u *cada uno* ea. (each).
c.v. *caballo(s) de vapor* HP (horse-power).

Ch

ch. *cheque* chq. (cheque).

D

D. *debe* debit side.
D. *Don* Esq. (Esquire) (*Sr D., en el sobre delante del nombre de pila*; Esq., *en el sobre después del apellido*).
Da. *Doña title of courtesy to ladies: no equivalent.*
dcho., dcha. *derecho, derecha* right.
d. (de) J.C. *después de Jesucristo* A.D. (Anno Domini).
D.F. *Méjico: Distrito Federal* Federal District.
dg. *decigramo* decigramme.
Dg. *decagramo* decagramme.
D.G.T. *Dirección General del Turismo state tourist organization.*
dho. *dicho* aforesaid.
dic.e *diciembre* Dec. (December).
dl. *decilitro* deciliter.
Dl. *decalitro* decaliter.
dm. *decímetro* decimeter.

D.n *Don* (v. D.).
d.na *docena* doz. (dozen).
do. *descuento* dis., dist (discount).
doc. *docena* doz. (dozen).
dom.o *domingo* Sun. (Sunday).
d/p. *días plazo* days' time.
Dr. *Doctor* Dr (doctor).
dro., dra. *derecho, derecha* right.
d.to *descuento* dis., dist (discount).
dup.do *duplicado* duplicate.
d/v. *días vista* d.s., d/s. (days after sight).

E

E *este* E. (East[ern]).
ed. *edición* ed. (edition).
EE.UU. *Estados Unidos* U.S., U.S.A. (United States [of America]).
E.M. *Estado Mayor* staff.
Encia. *Eminencia* Eminence.
en.o *enero* Jan. (January).
E.P.D. *en paz descanse* R.I.P. (requiescat in pace).
Es *Ejército de Salvación* S.A. (Salvation Army).
esq. *esquina* corner.
etc. *etcétera* etc. (et caetera, etcetera).
EU *Estados Unidos* US (United States).
Exc. *Excelencia* Excellency.
Exmo. *Excelentísimo courtesy title.*

F

f. *femenino* f., fem. (feminine).
fa *factura* bill, account.
f.a.b. *franco a bordo* f.o.b. (free on board).
f.c. *ferrocarril* Rly. (railway).
feb.o *febrero* Feb. (February).
Fern.do *Fernando personal name.*
fha. *fecha* d. (date).
FMI *Fondo Monetario Internacional* I.M.F. (International Monetary Fund).
f.o, fol. *folio* fo., fol. (folio).
Fr. *Fray* Fr. (Friar).
Fran.co *Francisco personal name.*

G

g. *gramo(s)* gr(s). (gramme[s]).
G *giro* draft, money-order.
gde. *guarde: que Dios guarde* whom God protect.

Genl *General* Gen. (General).
G.º *Gonzalo personal name.*
gob.ⁿᵒ *gobierno* Govt. (Government).
Gral, gral. *General* Gen. (General).
grs. *gramos* grs. (grammes).

H

h. *habitantes* pop. (population).
h. *hacia* c. (circa).
H. *haber* Cr. (credit).
H: bomba H *bomba de hidrógeno* H-bomb (hydrogen bomb).
hect. *hectárea* hectare.
Hg. *hectogramo* hectogramme.
Hl. *hectolitro* hectoliter.
Hnos. *Hermanos* Bros. (Brothers).
H.P. *(inglés* = *horse-power) caballos, caballaje* H.P. (horse-power).

I

ib., ibíd. *ibídem* ibid. (ibidem).
igl.ᵃ *iglesia* church.
Il. *ilustre courtesy title.*
Ilmo. *ilustrísimo courtesy title.*
Imp. *Imprenta* printers, printing works.
I.N.I. *Instituto Nacional de Industria state industrial council.*
IVA *Impuesto sobre el valor agregado (o añadido)* VAT (valued-added tax).
izdo., izda. *izquierdo, izquierda* left.

J

J.C. *Jesucristo* Jesus Christ.
JJ.OO. *Juegos Olímpicos* Olympic Games.
juev. *jueves* Thurs. (Thursday).

K

k/c *kilociclos* k/c. kilocycles.
Kg. *kilogramo* kg. (kilogramme).
Kl. *kilolitro* kiloliter.
Km. *kilómetro* km. (kilometer).
Km./h. *kilómetros por hora* kilometers per hour.
kv. *kilovatio* kw. (kilowatt).

L

l. *ı̤̈̇* *ley* law.

l. *libro* bk. (book).
l. *litro* l. (litre).
lbs. *libras* lbs. (pounds).
lib. *libra* lb. (pound).
lib., lib.º *libro* bk. (book).
Lic. en Fil. y Let. *Licenciado en Filosofía y Letras* B.A. (Bachelor of Arts).
lun. *lunes* Mon. (Monday).

M

m. *minuto* m. (minute).
m. *metro* m. (meter).
m. *masculino* m., masc. (masculine).
m. *muerto, murió* d. (died).
m² *metro cuadrado* sq. m. (square meter).
m³ *metro cúbico* cu. m. (cubic meter).
M. *Madrid capital of Spain.*
Ma. *María personal name.*
mart. *martes* Tues. (Tuesday).
M.C. *Mercado Común* C.M. (Common Market).
Md. *Madrid capital of Spain.*
M.F. *modulación de frecuencia* F.M. (frequency modulation).
mg *miligramo* mg. (milligramme).
miérc. *miércoles* Weds. (Wednesday).
mm *milímetro* mm. (millimeter).
Mons. *Monseñor* Mgr. (Monsignor).
MS *manuscrito* MS (manuscript).
MSS *manuscritos* MSS (manuscripts).

N

n. *nacido, nació* b. (born).
N *norte* N. (North[ern]).
nal. *nacional* national.
Na. Sra. *Nuestra Señora* Our Lady, The Virgin.
N.B. *nótese bien* N.B. (nota bene).
NE *noreste* N.E. (North East[ern]).
NNE *nornordeste* NNE (north-north-east).
NNO *nornordoeste* NNW (north-northwest).
NN.UU. *Naciones Unidas* U.N. (United Nations).
n.º *número* No. (number).
NO *noroeste* N.W. (North West [-ern]).
nov.ᵉ *noviembre* Nov. (November).
nro., nra. *nuestro, nuestra* our.
N.S. *Nuestro Señor* Our Lord.
N.T. *Nuevo Testamento* N.T. (New Testament).

ntro., ntra. *nuestro, nuestra* our.
N.U. *Naciones Unidas* U.N. (United Nations).
Núm. *número* No. (number).

O

O *oeste* W. (West[ern]).
O.A.A. *Organización de Agricultura y Alimentación* F.A.O. (Food and Agriculture Organization).
O.A.C.I. *Organización de Aviación Civil Internacional* I.C.A.O. (International Civil Aviation Organization).
ob., obpo. *obispo* Bp. (bishop).
obr. cit. *obra citada* op. cit. (opere citato).
OCDE *Organización de Cooperación y Desarrollo Económico* O.E.C.D. (Organization for Economic Cooperation and Development).
oct.^e *octubre* Oct. (October).
OEA *Organización de los Estados Americanos* O.A.S. (Organization of American States).
OIT *Organización Internacional de Trabajo* ILO (International Labor Organization).
OLP *Organización para la Liberación de Palestina* P.L.O. (Palestine Liberation Organization).
OMS *Organización Mundial de la Salud* W.H.O. (World Health Organization).
ONU *Organización de las Naciones Unidas* UNO (United Nations Organization).
O.P. *Orden de Predicadores* O.S.D. (Order of St. Dominic).
O.P. *Obras Públicas* P.W.D. (Public Works Department).
OPEP *Organización de Países Exportadores de Petróleo* OPEC (Organization of Petroleum-Exporting Countries).
O.S.B. *Orden de San Benito* O.S.B. (Order of St. Benedict).
OTAN *Organización del Tratado del Atlántico del Norte* NATO (North Atlantic Treaty Organization).
OTASE *Organización del Tratado del Sudeste Asiático* (*or del Asia Sudeste*) SEATO (South East Asia Treaty Organization).
OVNI *u* **ovni** *objeto volante* (*o volador no identificado*) UFO (unidentified flying object).

P

p. *punto, puntada* st. (stitch).
P. *papa* pope.
P. *padre* Fr. (Father).
P% *por cien(to)* %, p. c. (per cent).
pág. *página* p. (page).
págs. *páginas* pp. (pages).
p.c. *por cien(to)* %, p.c. (per cent).
PC *Partido Comunista* C.P. (Communist Party).
P.D. *posdata* P.S. (postscript).
PDC *Partido Demócrata Cristiano* Christian Democratic Union.
pdo. *pasado* ult. (ultimo).
Pe. *Padre* Fr. (Father).
PED *Procesamiento Electrónico de Datos* E.D.P. (electronic data processing).
p. ej. *por ejemplo* e.g. (exempli gratia, for example).
pmo. *próximo* prox. (proximo).
PNB *producto nacional bruto* G.N.P. (gross national product).
P.º *Pedro personal name.*
P.º *Paseo* Avenue.
p.º n.º *peso neto* nt. wt. (net weight).
p.o. *por orden* per pro(c)., p.p. (per procurationem, by proxy).
p.p. *por poder* per pro(c)., p.p. (per procurationem, by proxy).
P.P. *porte pagado* C.P. (carriage paid).
p.pdo. (*el mes*) *próximo pasado* ult. (ultimo).
pral. *principal* first.
pr. fr. *próximo futuro* prox. (proximo).
Prof. *Profesor* Prof. (Professor).
prov. *provincia* province.
PS *Partido Socialista* Socialist Party.
ps. *pesos* pesos.
P.S. *postscriptum* (*posdata*) P.S. (postscript).
ptas. *pesetas* pesetas.
P.V.P. *precio de venta al público* retail price.
pzs *piezas* pcs. (pieces).

Q

q.D.g. *que Dios guarde* whom God protect (*used after mention of king*).
q.e.p.d. *que en paz descanse* R.I.P. (requiescat in pace).
q.e.s.m. *que estrecha su mano courtesy formula.*
quil. *quilates* carats.
qts. *quilates* carats.

R

R. *Real* Royal.
R. *Reverendo* Rev. (Reverend).
R.A.C.E. *Real Automóvil Club de España* equivalent to British A.A. and R.A.C.
Rdo *Reverendo* Rev. (Reverend).
RENFE *Red Nacional de Ferrocarriles Españoles* Spanish railway company.
RFA *República Federal de Alemania* FRG Federal Republic of Germany.
R.M. *Reverenda Madre* Reverend Mother.
R.O. *real orden* royal decree.
R.P. *Reverendo Padre* Reverend Father.
rúst. *en rústica* paper-backed.

S

s/ *su* yr. (your).
S. *San(to), Santa* St. (Saint).
S *sur* S. (South[ern]).
s.a. *sin año* s.a. (sine anno).
S.A. *Su Alteza* H.H. (His [or Her] Highness).
S.A. ✝ *Sociedad Anónima* Ltd. (Limited); Inc. *Am.* (Incorporated).
sáb. *sábado* Sat. (Saturday).
SE *sudeste* S.E. (South East[ern]).
sept.ᵉ *septiembre* Sept. (September).
s.e.u.o. *salvo error u omisión* E. & O.E. (errors and omissions excepted).
s.f. *sin fecha* n.d. (no date).
sgte. *siguiente* f. (following).
sigs. *(y) siguientes* et seq. (et sequentia), ff. (following).
S.I.M. *Servicia de Información Militar* M.I. (Military Intelligence).
s.l. ni f. *sin lugar ni fecha* n.p. or d. (no place or date).
s/n. *sin número* not numbered.
S.M. *Su Majestad* H.M. (His [or Her] Majesty).
SO *suroeste* S.W. (South West[ern]).
Sr. *Señor* Mr (Mister).
Sra. *Señora* Mrs (Mistress).
S.R.C. *se ruega contestación* R.S.V.P. (répondez s'il vous plaît).
Sres. *Señores* Messrs (Messieurs).
Srio. *Secretario* Sec. (Secretary).
S.R.M. *Su Real Majestad* H.M. (His [or Her] Majesty).
Srta. *Señorita* Miss.
SS *Seguridad Social Br.* N.I. (National Insurance); *Am.* (Social Security).
S.S. *Su Santidad* His Holiness.

SS *Santos* SS (Saints).
SSE *sudsudeste* SSE (south-south-east).
SSO *sudsudoeste* SSW (south-south-west).
s.s.s. *su seguro servidor* yours truly.

T

t. *tomo(s)* vol(s). (volume[s]).
Tel. *teléfono* Tel. (Telephone).
Tente. *Teniente* Lieut. (Lieutenant).
Tlf. *teléfono* Tel. (Telephone).
T.R.B. *toneladas registradas brutas* G.R.T. (gross register tonnage).
Tte *Teniente* Lieut. (Lieutenant).
TV *televisión* T.V. (television).

U

Ud. *Usted* you.
Uds. *ustedes* you.
U.E.P. *Unión Europea de Pagos* E.P.U. (European Payments Union).
U.P.U. *Unión Postal Universal* U.P.U. (Universal Postal Union).
URSS *hist. Unión de las Repúblicas Socialistas Soviéticas* U.S.S.R. (Union of Soviet Socialist Republics).

V

v. *voltio* v. (volt).
v. *véase* see.
V. *Usted* you.
Vd. *Usted* you.
Vda de *viuda de* widow of.
Vds. *Ustedes* you.
verso *versículo* v. (verse).
v.g., v. gr. *verbigracia* viz. (videlicet).
vid. *vide* see.
vier. *viernes* Fri. (Friday).
V.M. *Vuestra Majestad* Your Majesty.
V.º B.º *visto bueno* O.K. (all correct?).
v(t)ro., v(t)ra. *vuestro, vuestra* yr. (your).

W

w. *watio* w. (watt).

X

Xpo. *Cristo* Christ.

American and British Abbreviations

Abreviaturas americanas y británicas

Cada artículo contiene el texto completo de la abreviatura inglesa y, a ser posible, la abreviatura española con su texto completo entre paréntesis.

A

AA Automobile Association *equivalente de* Real Automóvil Club *m* de España.

abbr. abbreviated abreviado; abbreviation abreviatura *f*.

ABC American Broadcasting Company *Compañía americana de radiotelevisión*.

A/C account (current) c.ta (c.te) (cuenta *f* [corriente]).

AC alternating current c.a. (corriente *f* alterna).

acc(t). account c.ta, cta (cuenta *f*).

AEC Atomic Energy Commission Comisión *f* de la Energía Atómica.

AFL–CIO American Federation of Labor and Congress of Industrial Organizations Confederación general de los sindicatos de EE.UU.

AFN American Forces Network Red de radiodifusión de las Fuerzas Armadas de EE.UU.

AIDS acquired immune-deficiency syndrome SIDA (síndrome *m* de inmunidad deficiente adquirida).

Ala Alabama Estado de EE.UU.

Alas Alaska Estado de EE.UU.

a.m. ante meridiem (*Latin* = before noon) de la mañana, antes del mediodía.

AP Am. Associated Press Agencia de información.

ARC American Red Cross Cruz *f* Roja Americana.

Ariz Arizona Estado de EE.UU.

Ark Arkansas Estado de EE.UU.

arr. arrival Ll. (llegada *f*).

B

BA 1. Bachelor of Arts Lic. en Fil. y Let. (Licenciado [a *f*] *m* en Filosofía y Letras); 3. British Airways Compañía británica de aviación.

BBC British Broadcasting Corporation BBC *f* (Radiotelevisión nacional de Gran Bretaña).

BE bill of exchange letra *f* de cambio.

BFN British Forces Network Red de radiodifusión de las Fuerzas Armadas de Gran Bretaña.

BL 1. bill of lading conocimiento *m*; 2. Bachelor of Law Licenciado (a *f*) *m* en Derecho.

BM 1. British Museum Museo *m* Británico; 2. Bachelor of Medicine Licenciado (a *f*) *m* en Medicina.

BOT Board of Trade Ministerio *m* de Comercio (británico).

BR British Rail Ferrocarriles británicos.

Br(it). 1. Britain Gran Bretaña *f*; 2. British británico.

Bros. brothers Hnos. (hermanos *m/pl.*).

BS British Standard norma (industrial) británica.

BS Am., **B.Sc.** Bachelor of Science Licenciado (a *f*) *m* en Ciencias.

Bucks. Buckinghamshire Condado inglés.

C

c. l. cent(s) céntimo(s) *m(pl.)* (moneda americana); 2. circa h. (hacia); aproximadamente; 3. cubic cúbico.

C. Celsius, centigrade termómetro centígrado.

C/A current account c/c (cuenta *f* corriente).

Cal(if) California Estado de EE.UU.

Cambs. Cambridgeshire Condado inglés.

Can. 1. Canada (el) Canadá; 2. Canadian canadiense.

CC *continuous current* c.c. (corriente *f* continua).

cf. *confer* comp. (compárese).

Ches. *Cheshire* Condado inglés.

CIA *Central Intelligence Agency* CIA (Servicio *m* Secreto de Información de EE.UU.).

CID *Criminal Investigation Department* Departamento de Investigación Criminal (británico), equivalente de Brigada *f* Criminal.

c.i.f. *cost, insurance, freight* c.i.f., c.s.f. (costo, seguro, flete).

Co. 1. *Company* C., Cía. (compañía *f*); **2.** *county* condado *m* (*en EE.UU. e Irlanda*).

c/o. *care of* c/d (en casa de); a/c (al cuidado de).

COD *cash* (*Am. collect*) *on delivery* cóbrese a la entrega, contra re(e)mbolso.

Col *Colorado* Estado de EE.UU.

Conn *Connecticut* Estado de EE.UU.

cp. *compare* comp. (compárese).

c.w.o. *cash with order* pago *m* al contado.

cwt. *hundredweight* (= *50,8 kg.*) *approx.* quintal *m*.

D

DA 1. *deposit account approx.* cuenta *f* de ahorro; **2.** *Am. District Attorney* fiscal *m* de distrito.

DC 1. *direct current* c.c. (corriente *f* continua); **2.** *District of Columbia Washington, capital de EE.UU., y sus alrededores.*

Del *Delaware* Estado de EE.UU.

dep. *departure* S. (salida *f*).

Dept. *Department* dep. (departamento *m*).

Derby. *Derbyshire* Condado inglés.

disc(t). *discount* d.^{to} (descuento *m*).

doz. *dozen* d.^{na} (docena *f*).

Dur(h.) *Durham* Condado inglés.

dz. *dozen* d.^{na} (docena *f*).

E

E. 1. *east(ern)* E (este [*m*]); **2.** *English* inglés.

EC *East Central* Parte este del centro de Londres (distrito postal).

ECE *Economic Commission for Europe* Comisión *f* Económica para Europa (de las Naciones Unidas).

ECOSOC *Economic and Social Council* Consejo *m* Económico y Social (de las Naciones Unidas).

Ed., ed. 1. *edition* ed. (edición *f*); **2.** *editor* director *m*, editor *m*, redactor *m*; **3.** *edited* editado.

EEC *European Economic Community* CEE (Comunidad *f* Económica Europea).

e.g. *exempli gratia* (*Latin = for example*) p.ej. (por ejemplo).

enc(l). *enclosure(s)* adjunto; anexo(s) *m(pl.)*.

Esq. *Esquire* D. (Don); (*Esq., en el sobre después del apellido*).

F

f. 1. *fathom* (= *1,8288 m.*) braza *f*; **2.** *female, feminine* f. (femenino); **3.** *following sgte.* (siguiente).

F(ahr). *Fahrenheit* termómetro *Fahrenheit.*

FBI *Federal Bureau of Investigation* Departamento de Investigación Criminal, equivalente de Brigada *f* Criminal.

FC *Football Club* CF (Club *m* de Fútbol).

Fla *Florida* Estado de EE.UU.

fo(l). *folio* f.°, fol. (folio *m*).

f.o.b. *free on board* f.a.b. (franco a bordo).

for. *foreign* extranjero.

f.o.r. *free on rail* libre en la estación ferroviaria.

fr. *franc(s)* franco(s) *m(pl.)*.

ft. *foot, pl. feet* (= *30,48 cm.*) pie(s) *m(pl.)*.

G

g. *gram(me[s])* gr(s). (gramo[s] *m[pl.]*).

Ga *Georgia* Estado de EE.UU.

gal. *gallon* (= *4,546 litros, Am. 3,785 litros*) galón *m*.

GB *Great Britain* Gran Bretaña *f*.

GI *Am. government issue* propiedad *f* del Estado; *por extensión, el soldado raso americano.*

Glos. *Gloucestershire* Condado inglés.

GMT *Greenwich Mean Time* T.M.G. (Tiempo *m* Medio de Greenwich).

GOP *Am. Grand Old Party* Partido *m* Republicano.

Govt. *Government* gob.^{no} (gobierno *m*).

GPO *General Post Office* Oficina *f* Central de Correos.

gr. *gross* bruto.

H

h. *hour(s)* hora(s) *f[pl.].*

Hants. *Hampshire* Condado *inglés.*

HBM *His (Her) Britannic Majesty* Su Majestad Británica.

HC *House of Commons* Cámara *f* de los Comunes.

Herts. *Hertfordshire* Condado *inglés.*

hf. *half* medio.

HI *Hawaii(an Islands)* (Islas *f[pl.]*) Hawai.

HL *House of Lords* Cámara *f* de los Lores.

HM *His (Her) Majesty* S.M. (Su Majestad).

HMS 1. *His (Her) Majesty's Ship (Steamer)* buque *m* ([buque *m* de] vapor *m*) de Su Majestad; **2.** *His (Her) Majesty's Service* servicio *m* (de Su Majestad); & oficial.

HO *Home Office* Ministerio *m* del Interior (*británico*).

Hon. *Honourable* Título de la nobleza británica.

h.p. *horse-power* approx. c.v. (caballo[s] *m[pl.]* de vapor).

HQ *Headquarters* Cuartel *m* General.

HR *Am. House of Representatives* Cámara *f* de Representantes (= *Diputados*).

HRH *His (Her) Royal Highness* S.A.R. (Su Alteza Real).

hrs. *hours* horas *f[pl.*

I

Ia *Iowa* Estado de EE.UU.

ID *Intelligence Department* Servicio *m* Secreto.

Id *Idaho* Estado de EE.UU.

i.e. *id est* (*Latin = that is*) es decir.

Ill *Illinois* Estado de EE.UU.

ILO *International Labour Organization* OIT (Organización *f* Internacional del Trabajo).

in. *inch(es)* (= *2,54 cm.*) pulgada(s) *f[pl.].*

Inc. *Am. Incorporated* S.A. (Sociedad *f* Anónima).

Ind *Indiana* Estado de EE.UU.

inst. *instant* cte (corriente, de los corrientes).

IOC *International Olympic Committee* COI (Comité *m* Olímpico Internacional).

IQ *Intelligence Quotient* cociente *m* intelectual.

Ir. 1. *Ireland* Irlanda *f*; **2.** *Irish* irlandés.

IRA *Irish Republican Army* Ejército *m* Republicano Irlandés.

IRC *International Red Cross* Cruz *f* Roja Internacional.

J

JP *Justice of the Peace* juez *m* de paz.

Jr., Jun(r). *junior* hijo.

K

Kans *Kansas* Estado de EE.UU.

KO 1. *knock-out* k.o. (fuera *m* de combate); **2.** *knocked out* k.o. (fuera de combate).

Ky *Kentucky* Estado de EE.UU.

L

l. 1. *left* izquierdo; a la izquierda; **2.** *liter* l. (litro *m*).

La *Louisiana* Estado de EE.UU.

LA *Los Angeles* Los Ángeles.

Lancs. *Lancashire* Condado *inglés.*

lb. *pound* (= *453,6 gr.*) libra *f.*

LC *letter of credit* carta *f* de crédito.

Leics. *Leicestershire* Condado *inglés.*

Lincs. *Lincolnshire* Condado *inglés.*

LP 1. *long-playing* (de) larga duración *f*; **2.** *long-playing record* LP, elepé *m* (disco *m* de larga duración).

Ltd. *Limited* S. A. (Sociedad *f* Anónima).

M

m. 1. *male, masculine* m. (masculino); **2.** *meter* m. (metro *m*); **3.** *mile* (= *1609,34 m.*) milla *f*; **4.** *minute* m. (minuto *m*).

MA *Master of Arts* Maestro *m* en Artes.

Mass *Massachusetts* Estado de EE.UU.

MD *medicine doctor* (*Latin = Doctor of Medicine*) Doctor *m* en Medicina.

Md *Maryland* Estado de EE.UU.

Me *Maine* Estado de EE.UU.

mi. *mile* (= *1609,34 m.*) milla *f.*
Mich *Michigan Estado de EE.UU.*
Middx. *Middlesex Condado inglés.*
Minn *Minnesota Estado de EE.UU.*
Miss *Mississippi Estado de EE.UU.*
Mo *Missouri Estado de EE.UU.*
MO *money order* giro *m* postal.
Mont *Montana Estado de EE.UU.*
MP 1. *Member of Parliament* miembro *m* del Parlamento; **2.** *Military Police* policía *f* militar.
m.p.h. *miles per hour* millas por hora.
Mr *Mister* Sr. (Señor *m*).
Mrs ['misiz] Sra. (Señora *f*).
MS 1. *manuscript* MS (manuscrito *m*); **2.** *motorship* motonave *f.*
Mt. *Mount* montaña *f*, monte *m.*

N

n. 1. *neuter* neutro; **2.** *noun* sustantivo *m*; **3.** *noon* mediodía *m.*
N. *North(ern)* N (norte [*m*]).
NASA *National Aeronautics and Space Administration* NASA (Administración *f* Nacional de Aeronáutica y del Espacio).
NATO *North Atlantic Treaty Organization* OTAN (Organización *f* del Tratado del Atlántico Norte).
NBC *National Broadcasting Company* Compañía americana de radiotelevisión.
NC *North Carolina Estado de EE.UU.*
ND(ak) *North Dakota Estado de EE.UU.*
NE *northeast(ern)* NE (noreste [*m*]).
Neb(r) *Nebraska Estado de EE.UU.*
Nev *Nevada Estado de EE.UU.*
NF *Newfoundland* Terranova *f.*
NH *New Hampshire Estado de EE.UU.*
NHS *National Health Service* Servicio *m* Nacional de Sanidad.
NJ *New Jersey Estado de EE.UU.*
NMex *New Mexico Estado de EE.UU.*
Norf. *Norfolk Condado inglés.*
Northants. *Northamptonshire Condado inglés.*
Northumb. *Northumberland Condado inglés.*
Notts. *Nottinghamshire Condado inglés.*
nt. *net* n.º (neto).
NW *northwest(ern)* NO (noroeste [*m*]).
NY *New York Estado de EE.UU.*
NYC *New York City* Ciudad *f* de Nueva York.

O

O *Ohio Estado de EE.UU.*
o/a *on account* (*of*) a/c. (de) (a cuenta [de]).
OAS *Organization of American States* OEA (Organización *f* de los Estados Americanos).
OECD *Organization for Economic Cooperation and Development* OCDE (Organización *f* para la Cooperación y el Desarrollo Económico).
OHMS *On His (Her) Majesty's Service* en el servicio de Su Majestad.
Okla *Oklahoma Estado de EE.UU.*
OPEC *Organization of Petroleum Exporting Countries* OPEP (Organización *f* de los Países Exportadores de Petróleo).
Ore(g) *Oregon Estado de EE.UU.*
Oxon. *Oxfordshire Condado inglés.*

P

Pa *Pennsylvania Estado de EE.UU.*
p.a. *per annum* (*Latin* = *yearly*) por año.
PanAm *PanAmerican Airways* Compañía (Pan)americana de aviación.
PAU *Panamerican Union* Unión *f* Panamericana.
PC *police constable* guardia *m.*
p.c. 1. *per cent* P%, %, p. c. (por cien[to]); **2.** *postcard* tarjeta *f* postal.
pd. *paid* pagado.
PEN Club *Poets, Playwrights, Editors, Essayists and Novelists* PEN (Asociación internacional de escritores, etc.).
Penn(a) *Pennsylvania Estado de EE.UU.*
per pro(c). *per procurationem* (*Latin* = *by proxy*) p.o. (por orden), p.p. (por poder).
Ph.D. *philosophiae doctor* (*Latin* = *Doctor of Philosophy*) Doctor *m* en Filosofía.
PLO *Palestine Liberation Organization* OLP (Organización *f* para la Liberación de Palestina).
p.m. *post meridiem* (*Latin* = *after noon*) de la tarde.
PO 1. *Post Office* (Oficina *f* de) Correos *m/pl.*; **2.** *postal order* giro *m* postal.
POB *Post Office Box* apartado *m.*
p.o.d. *pay on delivery* (contra) re(e)mbolso.

638

p.p. 1. *v.* per pro(c); **2.** *past participle* participio *m* del pasado.
PS *postscript* PD (posdata *f*).
PTO *please turn over* véase al dorso.

Q

quot. *quotation* cotización *f*.

R

r. *right* derecho, a la derecha.
RAC *Royal Automobile Club* equivalente de Real Automóvil Club *m* de España.
RAF *Royal Air Force* Fuerzas *f/pl.* Aéreas Británicas.
Rd. *road* carretera *f*; c. (calle *f*).
ref. (*in*) *reference* (*to*) (con) referencia (a).
regd. *registered* certificado.
reg.tn. *register ton* tonelada *f* de arqueo.
resp. *respective(ly)* respectivamente.
ret. *retired* retirado.
Rev. *Reverend* R., Rdo (Reverendo).
RI *Rhode Island* Estado de EE.UU.
RN *Royal Navy* Marina *f* Real.
RP *reply paid* CP (contestación *f* pagada).
r.p.m. *revolutions per minute* r.p.m. (revoluciones *f/pl.* por minuto).
RR *Am. railroad* f.c. (ferrocarril *m*).
Ry. *railway* f.c. (ferrocarril *m*).

S

s. 1. *second(s)* segundo(s) *m(pl.)*; **2.** *shilling(s)* chelín(es) *m(pl.)*.
S. *south(ern)* S (sur [*m*]).
SA 1. *South Africa* Africa *f* del Sur; **2.** *South America* América *f* del Sur; **3.** *Salvation Army* Ejército *m* de Salvación.
SALT *Strategic Arms Limitation Talks* SALT (Conversaciones *f/pl.* para la limitación de las armas estratégicas).
SC 1. *South Carolina* Estado de EE.UU.; **2.** *Security Council* Consejo *m* de Seguridad (*de las Naciones Unidas*).
SD(ak) *South Dakota* Estado de EE.UU.
SE 1. *southeast(ern)* SE (sudeste [*m*]); **2.** *Stock Exchange* Bolsa *f*.
SEATO *South East Asia Treaty Organization* OTASE (Organización *f* del Tratado de Asia de Sudeste).

SHAPE *Supreme Headquarters Allied Powers Europe* Cuartel *m* General Supremo de los Aliados en Europa.
SJ *Society of Jesus* C. de J. (Compañía *f* de Jesús).
Soc. *Society* sociedad *f*.
Som. *Somerset* Condado *inglés*.
Sq. *square* plaza *f*.
sq. *square* cuadrado.
Sr. *senior* padre.
SS *steamship* vapor *m*.
St. 1. *Saint* S. (San[ta]); **2.** *Street* calle *f*; **3.** *station* estación *f*.
Staffs. *Staffordshire* Condado *inglés*.
St. Ex. *Stock Exchange* Bolsa *f*.
stg. *sterling* moneda *f* esterlina.
Suff. *Suffolk* Condado *inglés*.
suppl. *supplement* suplemento *m*.
SW *southwest(ern)* SO (suroeste [*m*]).

T

t. *ton(s)* tonelada(s) *f(pl.)*.
Tenn *Tennessee* Estado de EE.UU.
Tex *Texas* Estado de EE.UU.
TO *Telegraph* (*Telephone*) *Office* Oficina *f* de Telégrafos (Teléfonos).
TU *Trade Union* sindicato *m*.
TUC *Trades Union Congress* Confederación *f* de Sindicatos.
TWA *Trans World Airlines* Compañía americana de aviación.

U

UFO *unidentified flying object* OVNI (objeto *m* volante no identificado).
UK *United Kingdom* RU (Reino *m* Unido: Inglaterra, Escocia, Gales e Irlanda del Norte).
UMW *Am. United Mine Workers* Sindicato *m* de Mineros.
UN *United Nations* NU, NN.UU. (Naciones *f/pl.* Unidas).
UNESCO *United Nations Educational, Scientific and Cultural Organization* UNESCO (Organización *f* de las Naciones Unidas para la Educación, la Ciencia y la Cultura).
UNICEF *United Nations (International) Children's (Emergency) Fund* UNICEF (Fondo *m* Internacional de Emergencia de las Naciones Unidas para la Infancia).
UNO *United Nations Organization* ONU (Organización *f* de las Naciones Unidas).

UPI *United Press International Agencia de información americana.*

US(A) *United States (of America)* EE.UU. (Estados *m/pl.* Unidos [de América]).

USAF(E) *United States Air Force (Europe)* Fuerzas *f/pl.* Aéreas de Estados Unidos (en Europa).

USN *United States Navy* Marina *f* Estadounidense.

USSR *hist. Union of Soviet Socialist Republics* URSS (Unión *f* de las Repúblicas Socialistas Soviéticas).

UT *Utah Estado de EE.UU.*

V

v. 1. *verse* verso *m;* estrofa *f; (biblical)* vers.° (versículo *m);* **2.** *versus (Latin = against)* contra; **3.** *vide (Latin = see)* v. (véase), vid. (vide); **4.** *volt* v. (voltio *m).*

Va *Virginia Estado de EE.UU.*

VAT *value-added tax* IVA (impuesto *m* sobre el valor añadido).

VHF *very high frequency* MF (modulación *f* de frecuencia).

VIP *very important person* personaje *m* importante.

viz. *videlicet (Latin = namely)* v.gr. (verbigracia).

Vt *Vermont Estado de EE.UU.*

v.v. *vice versa (Latin = conversely)* viceversa.

W

W. *west(ern)* O (oeste [*m*]).

War. *Warwickshire Condado inglés.*

Wash *Washington Estado de EE.UU.*

WC 1. *West Central Parte* oeste del centro de Londres *(distrito postal);* **2.** *water closet* WC (wáter *m*, inodoro *m*).

WHO *World Health Organization* OMS (Organización *f* Mundial de la Salud).

WI *West Indies* Antillas *f/pl.*

Wilts. *Wiltshire Condado inglés.*

Wis *Wisconsin Estado de EE.UU.*

wt. *weight* peso *m.*

WVa *West Virginia Estado de EE.UU.*

Wyo *Wyoming Estado de EE.UU.*

X

Xmas *Christmas* Navidad *f.*

Y

yd. *yard(s)* (= *91,44 cm.)* yarda(s) *f(pl.).*

YMCA *Young Men's Christian Association* Asociación *f* Cristiana para los Jóvenes.

Yorks. *Yorkshire Condado inglés.*

yr(s). *year(s)* año(s) *m(pl.).*

YWCA *Young Women's Christian Association* Asociación *f* Cristiana para las Jóvenes.

Spanish Proper Names

Nombres propios españoles

A

Abisinia *f* Abyssinia.
Abrahán Abraham.
Adán Adam.
Adén Aden.
Adolfo Adolf, Adolphus.
Adriano Hadrian.
Adriático *m* Adriatic.
Afganistán *m* Afghanistan.
Africa *f* Africa; ~ *del Norte* North Africa.
Agustín Augustine.
Aladino Aladdin.
Albania *f* Albania.
Alberto Albert.
Albión *f* Albion.
Alejandría Alexandria.
Alejandro Alexander; ~ *Magno* Alexander the Great.
Alemania *f* Germany.
Alfredo Alfred.
Alicia Alice.
Alpes *m/pl.* Alps.
Alsacia *f* Alsace.
Alto Volta *m* Upper Volta.
Amalia Amelia.
Amazonas *m* Amazon.
Amberes Antwerp.
América *f* America; ~ *Central* Central America; ~ *del Norte* North America; ~ *del Sur* South America; ~ *Latina* Latin America.
Ana Ann(e).
Anacreonte Anacreon.
Andalucía *f* Andalusia.
Andes *m/pl.* Andes.
Andrés Andrew.
Angola *f* Angola.
Aníbal Hannibal.
Antártida *f* Antarctic.
Antillas *f/pl.* West Indies, Antilles; *Grandes* ~ Greater Antilles; *Pequeñas* ~ Lesser Antilles.
Antioquía Antioch.
Antonio Anthony.

Apeninos *m/pl.* Apennines.
Aquiles Achilles.
Arabia *f* Arabia; ~ *Saudita o Saudí* Saudi Arabia.
Aragón *m* Aragon.
Arcadia *f* Arcady.
Ardenas *m/pl.* Ardennes.
Argel Algiers.
Argelia *f* Algeria.
Argentina *f* the Argentine.
Aristófanes Aristophanes.
Aristóteles Aristotle.
Arlequín Harlequin.
Armenia *f* Armenia.
Arquimedes Archimedes.
Arturo Arthur.
Artús: *el Rey* ~ King Arthur.
Asia *f* Asia; ~ *Menor* Asia Minor.
Asiria *f* Assyria.
Asunción *Capital of Paraguay.*
Atenas Athens.
Atila Attila.
Atlántico *m* Atlantic.
Augusto Augustus.
Australia *f* Australia.
Austria *f* Austria.
Auvernia *f* Auvergne.
Aviñón Avignon.
Azores *m/pl.* Azores.

B

Babia: *estar en* ~ go woolgathering, have one's mind somewhere else.
Babilonia *f* Babylon.
Baco Bacchus.
Bahamas *f/pl.* Bahamas.
Balcanes *m/pl.* Balkans.
Baleares *f/pl.* Balearic Isles.
Báltico *m* Baltic.
Bangla Desh *m* Bangladesh.
Barba Azul Bluebeard.
Bartolomé Bartholomew.
Basilea Bâle, Basle.
Baviera *f* Bavaria.
Beatriz Beatrice.

Belcebú Beelzebub.
Belén Bethlehem; *estar en* ~ daydream, go woolgathering.
Bélgica *f* Belgium.
Belgrado Belgrade.
Belice *m* Belize.
Benedicto Benedict.
Bengala *f* Bengal.
Benito Benedict.
Benjamín Benjamin.
Berlín Berlin.
Berna Berne.
Bernardo Bernard.
Birmania *f* Burma.
Bizancio Byzantium.
Blancanieves Snow-white.
Bocacio Boccaccio.
Bogotá *Capital of Colombia.*
Bolivia *f* Bolivia.
Borbón Bourbon.
Borgoña *f* Burgundy.
Bósforo *m* Bosphorus.
Brasil *m* Brazil.
Bretaña *f* Brittany.
Brígida Bridget.
Briján: *saber más que* ~ be very bright.
Brujas Bruges.
Bruselas Brussels.
Bruto Brutus.
Buda Buddha.
Buenos Aires *Capital of Argentina.*
Bulgaria *f* Bulgaria.
Burdeos Bordeaux.
Burundi *m* Burundi.

C

Cabo *m* **de Buena Esperanza** Cape of Good Hope.
Cabo *m* **de Hornos** Cape Horn.
Cabo *m* **Cañaveral** Cape Canaveral.
Cabo: (Ciudad *f* **de) El** ~ Cape Town.
Cachemira *f* Kashmir.
Cádiz Cadiz.
Caín Cain; F *pasar las de* ~ have a terrible time.
Cairo: El ~ Cairo.
Camboya *f* Cambodia.
Camerún *m* Cameroons.
Canadá *m* Canada.
Canal *m* **de la Mancha** English Channel.
Canal *m* **de Panamá** Panama Canal.
Canal *m* **de Suez** Suez Canal.
Canarias *f/pl.* Canaries.
Cantórbery Canterbury.
Caperucita Roja Red Riding-Hood.

Caracas *Capital of Venezuela.*
Caribe *m* Caribbean (Sea).
Carlitos Charlie.
Carlomagno Charlemagne.
Carlos Charles.
Carlota Charlotte.
Cárpatos *m/pl.* Carpathians.
Cartago Carthage.
Casa Blanca, *la* the White House.
Casandra Cassandra.
Castilla *f* Castile.
Catalina Catherine, Catharine; Katherine; Kathleen.
Cataluña *f* Catalonia.
Catón Cato.
Catulo Catullus.
Cáucaso *m* Caucasus.
Cecilia Cecily.
Ceilán *m* Ceylon.
Cenicienta: (La) ~ Cinderella.
Cerdeña *f* Sardinia.
César Caesar.
Cicerón Cicero.
Cíclope *m* Cyclops.
Clemente Clement.
Colombia *f* Colombia.
Colón Columbus.
Colonia Cologne.
Concha, Conchita *pet names for Concepción.*
Congo *m* the Congo.
Constantinopla Constantinople.
Constanza Constance.
Copenhague Copenhagen.
Córcega *f* Corsica.
Córdoba Cordova.
Corea *f* Korea; ~ *del Norte* North Korea; ~ *del Sur* South Korea.
Corinto Corinth.
Cornualles *m* Cornwall.
Coruña: La ~ Corunna.
Costa *f* **de Marfil** Ivory Coast.
Costa Rica *f* Costa Rica.
Creta *f* Crete.
Creso Croesus.
Cristo Christ.
Cristóbal Christopher.
Cuba *f* Cuba.
Cupido Cupid.

Ch

Chad *m* Chad.
Champaña *f* Champagne.
Checoslovaquia *f hist.* Czechoslovakia.
Chile *m* Chile, Chili.
China *f* China; ~ *Nacionalista* Taiwan.
Chipre *f* Cyprus.

D

Dafne Daphne.
Dahomey o **Dahomé** m Dahomey.
Dalmacia f Dalmatia.
Damasco Damascus.
Dámocles Damocles.
Danubio m Danube.
Dardanelos m/pl. Dardanelles.
Darío Darius.
David David.
Delfos Delphi.
Demóstenes Demosthenes.
Diego James.
Dinamarca f Denmark.
Domiciano Domitian.
Don Quijote Don Quixote.
Dorotea Dorothy.
Dublín Dublin.
Dunquerque Dunkirk.
Durero Dürer.
Durmiente: *la* **Bella** ~ Sleeping
Beauty.

E

Ecuador m Ecuador.
Edén m Eden.
Edimburgo Edinburgh.
Edipo Oedipus.
Eduardo Edward.
Egeo (Mar) m Aegean Sea.
Egipto m Egypt.
Elena Helen.
Elíseo m Elysium.
Emilia Emily.
Emilio Emil(e).
Eneas Aeneas.
Enrique Henry, Harry.
Erasmo Erasmus.
Ernesto Ernest.
Escandinavia f Scandinavia.
Escipión Scipio.
Escocia f Scotland.
Esmirna Smyrna.
Esopo Aesop.
España f Spain.
Esparta Sparta.
Esquilo Aeschylus.
Estados m/pl. **Unidos (de América)** United States (of America).
Esteban Stephen.
Estocolmo Stockholm.
Estonia f Estonia.
Estrasburgo Strasbourg.
Estuardo Stuart.
Etiopía f Ethiopia.
Euclides Euclid.
Eugenio Eugene.

Eurípedes Euripedes.
Europa f Europe.
Eva Eve.

F

Federico Frederick.
Felipe Philip.
Fernando Ferdinand.
Filadelfia Philadelphia.
Filipinas f/pl. Philippines.
Finlandia f Finland.
Flandes m Flanders.
Florencia Florence.
Francfort-del-Meno Frankfurt on
Main.
Francia f France.
Francisca Frances.
Francisco Francis.

G

Gabón m Gaboon.
Galeno Galen.
Gales m Wales.
Galilea f Galilee.
Gante Ghent.
Garona m Garonne.
Gascuña f Gascony.
Génova Genoa.
Geofredo Geoffrey.
Gertrudis Gertrude.
Getsemaní Gethsemane.
Ghana f Ghana.
Gibraltar m Gibraltar; *Estrecho de* ~
Straits of Gibraltar; *Peñón de* ~ Rock
of Gibraltar.
Gil Giles.
Ginebra Geneva; (p.) Guinevere.
Godofredo Godfrey.
Golfo m **Pérsico** Persian Gulf.
Golfo m **de Vizcaya** Bay of Biscay.
Goliat Goliath.
Gran Bretaña f Great Britain.
Granada Granada; Grenada.
Gran Cañón m Grand Canyon.
Grecia f Greece.
Gregorio Gregory.
Groenlandia f Greenland.
Guadalupe f Guadeloupe.
Gualterio Walter.
Guatemala f Guatemala.
Guayana f **(Francesa)** (French)
Guiana.
Guido Guy.
Guillermo William; ~ *el Conquistador*
William the Conqueror.
Guinea f Guinea; ~ *Ecuatorial* Equatorial Guinea.
Gustavo Gustave.
Guyana f Guyana.

H

Habana: La ~ Havana.
Habsburgo Hapsburg.
Haití m Haiti.
Hamburgo Hamburg.
Hawai m Hawaii.
Haya: La ~ The Hague.
Hébridas f/pl. Hebrides.
Helena Helen.
Hércules Hercules.
Herodes Herod.
Himalaya m the Himalayas.
Hipócrates Hippocrates.
Hispanoamérica f Spanish America.
Holanda f Holland.
Homero Homer.
Honduras m Honduras.
Horacio Horace.
Hugo Hugh, Hugo.
Hungría f Hungary.

I

Iberia f Iberia.
Ignacio Ignatius.
India: La ~ India.
Indias f/pl. Indies; ~ *Occidentales* West Indies.
Indonesia f Indonesia.
Indostán m Hindustan.
Inés Agnes.
Inglaterra f England.
Irak m Irak, Iraq.
Irán m Iran.
Irlanda f Ireland; ~ *del Norte* Northern Ireland.
Isabel Isabel, Elizabeth.
Isabelita Bess(ie), Bessy, Betty.
Iseo Isolde.
Islandia f Iceland.
Islas f/pl.: ~ *Bahamas* Bahamas; ~ *Baleares* Balearic Islands; ~ *Bermudas* Bermuda; ~ *Británicas* British Isles; ~ *de Cabo Verde* Cape Verde Islands; ~ *Canarias* Canary Islands; ~ *Hawai* Hawaii; ~ *Normandas* Channel Islands; ~ *de Sotavento* Leeward Islands.
Isolda Isolde.
Israel m Israel.
Italia f Italy.

J

Jacob Jacob.
Jacobo (*reyes de Escocia e Inglaterra*) James.
Jaime James.
Jamaica f Jamaica.
Japón m Japan.
Jehová Jehovah.
Jenofonte Xenophon.

Jeremías Jeremy.
Jericó Jericho.
Jerónimo Jerome.
Jerusalén Jerusalem.
Jesús Jesus; ¡~! good heavens!; (*estornudo*) bless you!; *en un decir ~* in a trice; *Jesucristo* Jesus Christ.
Joaquín m Joachim.
Job Job.
Jordán m Jordan (*river*).
Jordania f Jordan (*country*).
Jorge George.
José Joseph.
Josefina Josephine.
Josué Joshua.
Juan John; *un buen ~, ~ Lanas* simple soul.
Juana Jane; Joan; ~ *de Arco* Joan of Arc.
Juanito Jack; Johnny.
Judá f Judah.
Judas Judas.
Judea f Judaea.
Julieta Juliet.
Julio Julius.
Júpiter Jupiter; Jove.

K

Kenia f Kenya.
Kuwait m Kuwait.

L

Lacio m Latium.
Lanzarote Lancelot.
Laos m Laos.
La Paz *Capital of Bolivia.*
Laponia f Lapland.
Lausana Lausanne.
Lázaro Lazarus.
Leandro Leander.
Leida, Leide(n) Leyden.
Leningrado Leningrad.
Leonor Eleanor.
Lepe: *saber más que* ~ be pretty smart.
Letonia f Latvia.
Levante m Levant; *South-east part (or coasts) of Spain.*
Líbano m Lebanon.
Liberia f Liberia.
Libia f Libya.
Lieja Liège.
Lima *Capital of Peru.*
Liorna Leghorn.
Lisboa Lisbon.
Lituania f Lithuania.
Livio Livy.
Loira m Loire.
Lola, Lolita *pet names for Dolores.*
Lombardía f Lombardy.

Londres London.
Lorena f Lorraine.
Lorenzo Laurence.
Lovaina Louvain.
Lucano Lucan.
Lucas Luke.
Lucerna Lucerne.
Lucrecia Lucretia.
Lucrecio Lucretius.
Luis Louis.
Lutero Luther.
Luxemburgo m Luxembourg.
Lyón Lyons.

M

Madera f Madeira.
Magallanes m Magellan; *Estrecho de* ~ Magellan Straits.
Magdalena f Magdalen.
Maguncia Mainz.
Mahoma Mahomet.
Málaga Malaga.
Malawi m Malawi.
Malaysia f Malaysia.
Malí m Mali.
Mallorca f Majorca.
Malvinas f/pl. Falkland Isles.
Managua *Capital of Nicaragua*.
Manolo *pet name for Manuel*.
Manuel Emmanuel.
Mar m: ~ *Adriático* Adriatic Sea; ~ *Báltico* Baltic Sea; ~ *Caribe* Caribbean (Sea); ~ *Caspio* Caspian Sea; ~ *de las Indias* Indian Ocean; ~ *Mediterráneo* Mediterranean Sea; ~ *Muerto* Dead Sea; ~ *Negro* Black Sea; ~ *del Norte* North Sea; ~ *Rojo* Red Sea.
Marcial Martial.
Marcos Mark.
Margarita Margaret.
María Mary; ~ *Antonieta* Marie Antoinette.
Maricastaña: en tiempo de ~ long ago, in the year dot.
Marruecos m Morocco.
Marsella Marseilles.
Marsellesa f Marseillaise.
Marte Mars.
Martín Martin.
Martinica f Martinique.
Mateo Matthew.
Matilde Mat(h)ilda.
Mauricio Mauritius; (p.) Maurice.
Mauritania f Mauretania.
Meca: La ~ Mecca.
Mediterráneo m Mediterranean.
Méjico m Mexico.
Menorca f Minorca.
Mercurio Mercury.

Mesías Messiah.
México m *Am.* Mexico.
Midas Midas.
Miguel Michael; ~ *Angel* Michelangelo.
Milán Milan.
Misisipí m Mississippi.
Misuri m Missouri.
Moisés Moses.
Montevideo *Capital of Uruguay*.
Moscú Moscow.
Mosela m Moselle.
Montañas f/pl. **Rocosas** Rocky Mountains.
Montes m/pl. **Apalaches** Appalachian Mountains.
Mozambique f Mozambique.

N

Napoleón Napoleon.
Nápoles Naples.
Narbona Narbonne.
Navarra f Navarre.
Nazaret Nazareth.
Nepal m Nepal.
Neptuno Neptune.
Nerón Nero.
Niágara Niagara.
Níger m Niger.
Nigeria f Nigeria.
Nilo m Nile.
Niza Nice.
Noé Noah.
Normandía f Normandy.
Noruega f Norway.
Nueva Escocia f Nova Scotia.
Nueva Gales f **del Sur** New South Wales.
Nueva Guinea f New Guinea.
Nueva York New York.
Nueva Zelanda f New Zealand.

O

Océano m: ~ *Atlántico* Atlantic Ocean; ~ *glacial Antártico* Southern Ocean; ~ *glacial Ártico* Arctic Ocean; ~ *Índico* Indian Ocean; ~ *Pacífico* Pacific Ocean.
Octavio Octavian.
Oliverio Oliver.
Orcadas f/pl. Orkney Islands.
Orfeo Orpheus.
Oriente m East; *Extremo* ~ Far East; ~ *Medio* Middle East; *Próximo* ~ Near East.
Ostende Ostend.
Ovidio Ovid.

P

Pablo Paul.
Pacífico *m* Pacific.
Paca *pet name for Francisca* Frances.
Paco *pet name for Francisco* Frank.
País *m* **Vasco** Basque Country.
Países *m/pl.* **Bajos** Netherlands.
Pakistán *m* Pakistan.
Palestina *f* Palestine.
Panamá *m* Panama.
Paquita *pet name for Francisca* Frances.
Paquito *pet name for Francisco* Frank.
Paraguay *m* Paraguay.
París Paris.
Parnaso Parnassus.
Patillas F the devil, Old Nick; *ser un~* be a poor fish, be a nobody.
Patricio Patrick.
Pedro Peter.
Pegaso Pegasus.
Pekín Pekin(g).
Península *f* **Ibérica** Iberian Peninsula.
Pensilvania *f* Pennsylvania.
Pepa *pet name for Josefa.*
Pepe *pet name for José* Joe.
Pepita *pet name for Josefa.*
Perico *pet name for Pedro* Pete; *~ el de los Palotes* somebody, so-and-so, any Tom, Dick and Harry.
Pero Grullo: *frase de ~ =* perogrullada.
Perpiñán Perpignan.
Perú *m* Peru.
Petrarca Petrarch.
Piamonte *m* Piedmont.
Picardía *f* Picardy.
Pilatos Pilate.
Píndaro Pindar.
Pío Pius.
Pirineos *m/pl.* Pyrenees.
Pitágoras Pythagoras.
Platón Plato.
Plinio Pliny.
Plutarco Plutarch.
Plutón Pluto.
Polichinela Punch.
Polinesia *f* Polynesia.
Polonia *f* Poland.
Pompeya Pompeii.
Poncio Pilato(s) Pontius Pilate.
Portugal *m* Portugal.
Praga Prague.
Provenza *f* Provence.
Prusia *f* Prussia.
Psique Psyche.
Puerto Rico *m* Porto Rico.
Pulgarcito Tom Thumb.

Q

Quito *Capital of Ecuador.*

R

Rafael Raphael.
Raimundo, Ramón Raymond.
Raquel Rachel.
Rebeca Rebecca.
Reginaldo, Reinaldos Reginald.
Reino *m* **Unido** United Kingdom.
Renania *f* Rhineland.
República *f* **Centroafricana** Central African Republic.
República *f* **Dominicana** *f* Dominican Republic.
República *f* **Malgache** Republic of Madagascar.
República *f* **Popular de China** People's Republic of China.
Ricardo Richard.
Rin *m* Rhine.
Roberto Robert.
Ródano *m* Rhône.
Rodas *f* Rhodes.
Rodesia *f hist.* Rhodesia.
Rodrigo Roderick.
Roldán, Rolando Roland.
Roma Rome.
Rosa Rose.
Rosellón *m* Roussillon.
Ruán Rouen.
Ruanda *f* Ruanda.
Rumania *f* Rumania.
Rusia *f* Russia.

S

Saboya *f* Savoy.
Sahara *m* Sahara.
Sajonia *f* Saxony.
Salomón Salomon.
Salvador: El ~ El Salvador.
Samuel Samuel.
San José *Capital of Costa Rica.*
San Salvador *Capital of El Salvador.*
Sansón Samson.
Santiago Saint James; *Capital of Chile.*
Santo Domingo *Capital of the Dominican Republic.*
Sarre *m* Saar.
Satanás Satan.
Saturno Saturn.
Saúl Saul.
Sena *m* Seine.
Senegal *m* Senegal.

Servia f Serbia.
Sevilla Seville.
Siberia f Siberia.
Sibila Sibyl.
Sicilia f Sicily.
Sierra Leona f Sierra Leone.
Simbad Sin(d)bad.
Singapur Singapore.
Sión m Zion.
Siracusa Syracuse.
Siria f Syria.
Sócrates Socrates.
Sofía Sofia.
Sófocles Sophocles.
Somalia f Somaliland.
Sri Lanka m Sri Lanka.
Sudán m S(o)udan.
Suecia f Sweden.
Suiza f Switzerland.
Surinam m Surinam.

T

Tácito Tacitus.
Tailandia f Thailand.
Tajo m Tagus.
Támesis m Thames.
Tanganica f Tanganyika.
Tánger Tangier.
Tanzania f Tanzania.
Tegucigalpa *Capital of Honduras.*
Tejas m Texas.
Terencio Terence.
Teresa Theresa.
Terranova f Newfoundland.
Tesalia f Thessaly.
Tíber m Tiber.
Tibet m Tibet.
Ticiano Titian.
Tierra f **Santa** Holy Land.
Timoteo Timothy.
Togo m Togo.
Toledo Toledo.
Tolomeo Ptolemy.
Tolón Toulon.
Tolosa (de Francia) Toulouse.
Tomás Thomas.
Trento Trent.
Trinidad f **y Tobago** m Trinidad and Tobago.
Trípoli Tripoli.
Tristán Tristram.
Troya Troy; ¡*arda* ~! press on regardless!; ¡*aquí fue* ~! now there's nothing but ruins; that's where the

trouble began; that was a battle royal.
Túnez Tunis; Tunisia.
Tunicia f Tunisia.
Turquía f Turkey.

U

Ucrania f Ukraine.
Uganda m Uganda.
Unión f **de Emiratos Arabes** United Arab Emirates.
Unión f **de India** Union of India.
Unión f **de Repúblicas Socialistas Soviéticas (U.R.S.S.)** *hist.* Union of Soviet Socialist Republics (U.S.S.R.).
Unión f **Soviética** Soviet Union.
Unión f **Sudafricana** Union of South Africa.
Uruguay m Uruguay.
Utopia f Utopia.

V

Varsovia Warsaw.
Vascongadas f/pl. Basque Provinces.
Vaticano m Vatican.
Velázquez Velasquez.
Venecia Venice.
Venezuela f Venezuela.
Venus Venus.
Versalles Versailles.
Vesubio m Vesuvius.
Vicente Vincent.
Viena Vienna.
Vietnam o **Viet Nam** m Vietnam.
Villadiego: F *tomar las de* ~ beat it.
Virgilio Virgil.
Vizcaya f Biscay.
Vosgos m/pl. Vosges.
Vulcano Vulcan.

Y

Yemen m Yemen.
Yugo(e)slavia f Jugoslavia.

Z

Zaire m Zaïre.
Zambia f Zambia.
Zaragoza Saragossa.
Zimbabwe m Zimbabwe.

English Proper Names
Nombres propios ingleses

A

Ab·er·deen [æbər'di:n] *Ciudad de Escocia.*

Ad·am ['ædəm] Adán.

Ad·e·laide ['ædəleid] 1. *Ciudad de Australia;* 2. Adelaida.

A·den ['eidn] Adén.

Ad·olf ['ædɔlf], **A·dol·phus** [ə'dɔlfəs] Adolfo.

Af·ghan·i·stan [æf'gænistæn] Afganistán *m.*

Af·ri·ca ['æfrikə] Africa *f.*

Agnes ['ægnis] Inés.

Al·a·bam·a [ælə'bæmə] *Estado de EE.UU.*

A·las·ka [ə'læskə] *Estado de EE.UU.*

Al·ba·ni·a [æl'beinjə] Albania *f.*

Al·bert ['ælbərt] Alberto.

Al·ber·ta [æl'bərtə] *Provincia de Canadá.*

Al·der·ney ['ɔ:ldərni] *Isla británica de las Islas Normandas.*

Al·ex·an·der [ælig'zændər] Alejandro.

Al·fred ['ælfrid] Alfredo.

Al·ge·ri·a [æl'dʒiriə] Argelia *f.*

Al·giers [æl'dʒiərz] Argel.

Al·ice ['ælis] Alicia.

Alps [ælps] *pl.* Alpes *m/pl.*

Am·a·zon ['æməzn] Amazonas *m.*

A·mer·i·ca [ə'merikə] América *f.*

An·des ['ændi:z] *pl.* Andes *m/pl.*

An·drew ['ændru:] Andrés.

Ann(e) [æn] Ana.

An·nap·o·lis [ə'næpəlis] *Capital del Estado de Maryland. Sede de la Academia de Marina.*

An·tho·ny ['æntəni] Antonio.

An·til·les [æn'tili:z] *pl.* Antillas *f/pl.*

Ap·pa·lach·i·ans [æpə'lei(t)ʃənz] *pl.* Apalaches *m/pl.*

A·ra·bia [ə'reibjə] Arabia *f.*

Ar·gen·ti·na [ɑ:rdʒən'ti:nə], **the Ar·gen·tine** ['ɑ:rdʒəntin] (1a) Argentina.

Ar·i·zo·na [ærə'zounə] *Estado de EE.UU.*

Ar·kan·sas ['ɑ:rkənsɔ:] *Estado, y* [ɑ:r'kænzəs] *Río de EE.UU.*

As·cot ['æskət] *Pueblo de Inglaterra con hipódromo de fama.*

A·sia ['eiʃə] Asia *f;* ~ Minor Asia *f* Menor.

Ath·ens ['æθɔnz] Atenas.

At·lan·tic (O·cean) [ət'læntik ('ouʃn)] (Océano *m*) Atlántico *m.*

Auck·land ['ɔ:kländ] *Puerto de Nueva Zelanda.*

Aus·tra·lia [ɔ:s'treiljə] Australia *f.*

Aus·tri·a ['ɔ:striə] Austria *f.*

A·von ['eivən, 'ævən] *Río de Inglaterra.*

A·zores [ə'zɔ:rz] Azores *f/pl.*

B

Ba·ha·mas [bə'hɑ:məz] *pl.* Islas *f/pl.* Bahama, las Bahamas.

Ba·le·ar·ic Is·lands [bæli'ærik 'ailəndz] *pl.* Islas *f/pl.* Baleares.

Bal·kans ['bɔ:lkənz] Balcanes *m/pl.*

Bal·ti·more ['bɔ:ltəmɔ:r] *Puerto en la costa oriental de EE.UU.*

Be·a·trice ['biətris] Beatriz.

Bed·ford·shire ['bedfərdʃər] *Condado inglés.*

Bel·fast ['belfæst] *Capital de Irlanda del Norte.*

Bel·gium ['beldʒəm] Bélgica *f.*

Bel·grade [bel'greid] Belgrado.

Ben·ja·min ['bendʒəmin] Benjamín.

Ben Ne·vis [ben'nevis] *Pico más alto de Gran Bretaña (1343 m).*

Berk·shire ['bɑ:rkʃər] *Condado inglés.*

Ber·lin [bər'lin] Berlín.

Ber·mu·das [bər'mju:dəz] Islas *f/pl.* Bermudas.

Bess(·y) ['bes(i)] Isabelita.

Beth·le·hem ['beθlihem] Belén.

Bet·ty ['beti] Isabelita.

Bill, Bil·ly ['bil(i)] *nombre cariñoso de* William.

Bir·ming·ham ['bɑ:rmiŋhæm] *Ciudad industrial de Inglaterra; Ciudad industrial de Alabama.*

Bis·cay ['bisk(e)i]: Bay of ~ Golfo *m* de Vizcaya.

Bob(·by) ['bɔb(i)] *nombre cariñoso de* Robert.

Bo·liv·i·a [bə'livjə] Bolivia *f.*

Bos·ton ['bɔstən] *Ciudad de EE.UU. con la Universitaria de Harvard en el barrio de Cambridge.*

Bra·zil [brə'zil] (el) Brasil.

Bridg·et ['bridʒit] Brígida.

Brigh·ton ['braitn] *Ciudad en el sur de Inglaterra.*

Bris·tol ['bristl] *Puerto y ciudad industrial en el suroeste de Inglaterra.*

Bri·tain ['britn] Gran Bretaña *f.*

Brook·lyn ['bruklin] *Barrio de Nueva York.*

Brus·sels ['brʌslz] Bruselas.

Buck·ing·ham(·shire) ['bʌkiŋəm (-ʃər)] *Condado inglés.*

Bul·gar·i·a [bʌl'geriə] Bulgaria *f.*

Bur·ma ['bəːrmə] Birmania *f.*

C

Cal·i·for·nia [kæli'fɔːrnjə] California *f (Estado de EE.UU.).*

Cam·bridge ['keimbridʒ] *Ciudad universitaria inglesa; v. Boston; ~ shire* [~ʃər] *Condado inglés.*

Can·a·da ['kænədə] (el) Canadá.

Can·ar·y Is·lands [kə'neri 'ailəndz] Islas *f/pl.* Canarias.

Can·ter·bur·y ['kæntərbəri] Cantórbery.

Cape Horn [keip'hɔːrn] Cabo *m* de Hornos.

Car·diff ['kɑːrdif] *Capital de Gales.*

Ca·rib·be·an (Sea) [kæri'biːən 'siː) (Mar *m*) Caribe *m.*

Car·o·li·na [kærə'lainə]: *North ~* Carolina *f* del Norte; *South ~* Carolina *f* del Sur *(Estados de EE.UU.).*

Cath·e·rine, Cath·a·rine ['kæθərin] Catalina.

Cec·i·ly ['sesəli] Cecilia.

Cey·lon [si'lɔn] Ceilán *m.*

Chan·nel Is·lands ['tʃænl 'ailəndz] *pl.* Islas *f/pl.* Normandas.

Charles [tʃɑːrlz] Carlos.

Char·lotte ['ʃɑːrlət] Carlota.

Chesh·ire ['tʃeʃər] *Condado inglés.*

Chi·ca·go [ʃi'kɑːgou] *Ciudad industrial de EE.UU.*

Chil·e, Chil·i ['tʃili] Chile *m.*

Chi·na ['tʃainə] China *f.*

Christ [kraist] Cristo.

Chris·to·pher ['kristəfər] Cristóbal.

Cin·cin·na·ti [sinsi'næti] *Ciudad de EE.UU.*

Cleve·land ['kliːvlənd] *Ciudad indus-*

trial y de comercio de EE.UU.

Co·lom·bi·a [kə'lʌmbiə] Colombia *f.*

Col·or·a·do [kɔlə'rædou] Colorado *m (Nombre de dos ríos y de un Estado de EE.UU.).*

Co·lum·bi·a [kə'lʌmbiə] *Capital del Estado de Carolina del Sur.*

Co·lum·bus [kə'lʌmbəs] Colón.

Con·nect·i·cut [kə'netikət] *Río y Estado de EE.UU.*

Co·pen·ha·gen [koupn'heign] Copenhague.

Cor·do·va ['kɔːrdəvə] Córdoba.

Corn·wall ['kɔːrnwəl] Cornualles *m.*

Co·sta Ri·ca ['kɔstə 'riːkə] Costa Rica *f.*

Cov·en·try ['kʌvəntri] *Ciudad industrial de Inglaterra.*

Crete ['kriːt] Creta *f.*

Cu·ba ['kjuːbə] Cuba *f.*

Cy·prus ['saiprəs] Chipre *f.*

Czech·o·slo·va·ki·a ['tʃekouslou-'vækiə] *hist.* Checoslovaquia *f.*

D

Da·ko·ta [də'koutə]: *North ~* Dakota *f* del Norte; *South ~* Dakota *f* del Sur *(Estados de EE.UU.).*

Da·niel ['dænjəl] Daniel.

Da·nube ['dænjuːb] Danubio *m.*

Da·vid ['deivid] David.

Del·a·ware ['deləwər] *Río y Estado de EE.UU.*

Den·mark ['denmɑːrk] Dinamarca *f.*

Der·by(·shire) ['dəːrbi(ʃər)] *Condado inglés.*

De·troit [di'trɔit] *Ciudad industrial de EE.UU.*

Dev·on(·shire) ['devn(ʃər)] *Condado inglés.*

Di·a·na [dai'ænə] Diana.

Dick [dik] *nombre cariñoso de Richard.*

Do·mi·ni·can Re·pub·lic [də'minikən ri'pʌblik] República *f* Dominicana.

Dor·set(·shire) ['dɔːrsit(ʃər)] *Condado inglés.*

Do·ver ['douvər] *Puerto en el sur de Inglaterra.*

Down·ing Street ['dauniŋ 'striːt] *Calle de Londres con la sede del Primer Ministro.*

Dub·lin ['dʌblin] Dublín *(Capital de Irlanda).*

Dun·kirk [dʌn'kəːrk] Dunquerque.

Dur·ham ['dʌrəm] *Condado inglés.*

649

E

Ed·in·burgh ['ed(i)nbərə] Edimburgo (*Capital de Escocia*).

E·gypt ['i:dʒipt] Egipto *m.*

Ei·re ['eərə] *Nombre irlandés de Irlanda.*

E·li·za·beth [i'lizəbəθ] Isabel.

El Sal·va·dor [el 'sælvədɔːr] El Salvador.

Em·m(an)·u·el ['mænjuəl] Manuel.

Eng·land ['ingland] Inglaterra *f.*

Ep·som ['epsəm] *Pueblo inglés donde se verifican célebres carreras de caballos.*

Es·sex ['esiks] *Condado inglés.*

E·thi·o·pi·a [i:θi'oupiə] Etiopía *f.*

E·ton ['i:tn] *Pueblo inglés con colegio del mismo nombre.*

Eu·gene ['juːdʒiːn] Eugenio.

Eu·rope ['jurəp] Europa *f.*

Eve [iːv] Eva.

F

Falk·land Is·lands ['fɔːklənd 'ailəndz] (*Islas f/pl.*) Malvinas *f/pl.*

Fer·di·nand ['fɔːdinənd] Fernando.

Fin·land ['finlənd] Finlandia *f.*

Flor·i·da ['floridə] *Península y Estado de EE.UU.*

France [frɑːns] Francia *f.*

Fran·ces ['frænsis] Francisca.

Fran·cis ['frænsis] Francisco.

Frank [fræŋk] Paco.

Fred·e·rick ['fredrik] Federico.

G

Ge·ne·va [dʒi'niːvə] Ginebra.

Gen·o·a ['dʒenouə] Génova.

George [dʒɔːdʒ] Jorge.

Geor·gia ['dʒɔːrdʒə] *Estado de EE.UU.*

Ger·ma·ny ['dʒɔːrməni] Alemania *f.*

Get·tys·burg ['getizbərg] *Pueblo del Estado de Pensilvania (EE.UU.).*

Gib·ral·tar [dʒib'rɔːltər] Gibraltar; *Rock of* ~ Peñón *m* de Gibraltar; *Straits of* ~ *pl.* Estrecho *m* de Gibraltar.

Giles [dʒailz] Gil.

Glas·gow ['glæsgou] *Puerto de Escocia.*

Glouces·ter ['glɔːstər] *Ciudad de Inglaterra;* ~**shire** ['~ʃər] *Condado inglés.*

Grand Can·yon [grænd 'kæniən]

Gran Cañón *m del rio Colorado (EE.UU.).*

Great Brit·ain ['greit 'britn] Gran Bretaña *f.*

Greece [griːs] Grecia *f.*

Green·land ['griːnlənd] Groenlandia *f.*

Green·wich ['grinidʒ] *Barrio de Londres;* ~ *Village* ['~'vilidʒ] *Barrio de los artistas de Nueva York.*

Gua·te·ma·la [gwɑːtə'mɑːlə] Guatemala *f.*

Guern·sey ['gɔːrnzi] Guernesey *m.*

Gui·a·na [gai'ænə] Guayana *f.*

Guin·ea ['gini] Guinea *f.*

Guy [gai] Guido.

H

Hague [heig] *The* ~ La Haya.

Hai·ti ['heiti] Haití *m.*

Hamp·shire ['hæmpʃər] *Condado inglés.*

Har·ry ['hæri] Enrique.

Har·vard U·ni·ver·si·ty ['hɑːrvərd juːni'vɔːrsiti] *Universidad de fama de los EE.UU.*

Has·tings ['heistiŋz] *Ciudad en el sur de Inglaterra.*

Ha·van·a [hə'vænə] La Habana.

Ha·wai·i [hɑː'waiiː] (*Islas f/pl.*) Hawai.

Heb·ri·des ['hebridiːz] *pl.* Hébridas *f/pl.*

Hel·en ['helin] Elena.

Hen·ry ['henri] Enrique.

Her·e·ford(·shire) ['herifərd(ʃər)] *Condado inglés.*

Hert·ford(·shire) ['hɑːrfərd(ʃər)] *Condado inglés.*

Hol·ly·wood ['hɔliwud] *Ciudad de California y centro de la industria del cine de EE.UU.*

Hon·du·ras [hɔn'durəs] Honduras *f.*

Hud·son ['hʌdsn] *Río en el este de EE.UU.*

Hugh [hjuː] Hugo.

Hun·ga·ry ['hʌŋgəri] Hungría *f.*

Hu·ron ['hjurən] *Lake* ~ el lago Huron.

Hyde Park ['haid 'pɑːrk] *Parque público de Londres.*

I

Ice·land ['aislənd] Islandia *f.*

I·da·ho ['aidəhou] *Estado de EE.UU.*

Il·li·nois [ili'nɔi] *Río y Estado de EE.UU.*

In·dia ['indjə] (la) India.

In·di·an·a [indi'ænə] *Estado de EE.UU.*

In·dian O·cean ['indjən 'ouʃn] Océano *m* Indico.

In·dies ['indiz] Indias *f/pl.*

In·do·ne·sia [indou'ni:ʒə] Indonesia *f.*

I·o·wa ['aiouə, 'aiəwə] *Estado de EE.UU.*

I·raq [i'rɑ:k, i'ræk] (el) Irak.

I·ran [i'rɑ:n, i'ræn] (el) Irán.

Ire·land ['aiərlənd] Irlanda *f.*

Is·rael ['izriəl] Israel *m.*

It·a·ly ['it(ə)li] Italia *f.*

I·vo·ry Coast ['aivəri 'koust] Costa *f* de Marfil.

J

Jack [dʒæk] Juan(ito).

Ja·mai·ca [dʒə'meikə] Jamaica *f.*

James [dʒeimz] Diego; Jaime.

Jane [dʒein] Juana.

Ja·pan [dʒə'pæn] (el) Japón.

Jer·e·my ['dʒerəmi] Jeremías.

Jer·ome [dʒə'roum] Jerónimo.

Jer·sey ['dʒɔ:rzi] *Isla británica de las Islas Normandas;* ~ *City Ciudad a orillas del Hudson (EE.UU.).*

Je·ru·sa·lem [dʒə'ru:sələm] Jerusalén.

Je·sus ['dʒi:zəs] Jesús; *Jesus Christ* ['dʒi:zəs 'kraist] Jesucristo.

Jim(·my) ['dʒim(i)] *nombre cariñoso de James.*

Joan [dʒoun] Juana.

Joe [dʒou] Pepe.

John [dʒɔn] Juan.

Jor·dan ['dʒɔ:rdn] *(river)* Jordán *m;* *(country)* Jordania *f.*

Jo·seph ['dʒouzif] José.

Jo·se·phine ['dʒouzifi:n] Josefina.

Ju·go·sla·vi·a [ju:gou'slɑ:vjə] Jugo(e)slavia *f.*

Ju·lian ['dʒu:ljən] Juliano.

K

Kan·sas ['kænzəs] *Río y Estado de EE.UU.*

Kate [keit] *nombre cariñoso de Catherine.*

Kent [kent] *Condado inglés.*

Ken·tuck·y [ken'tʌki] *Río y Estado de EE.UU.*

Kit(·ty) ['kit(i)] *nombre cariñoso de Catherine.*

Ko·re·a [kə'riə] Corea *f.*

L

Lab·ra·dor ['læbrədɔ:r] Labrador *m (Canadá).*

Lan·ca·shire ['læŋkəʃər] *Condado inglés.*

Lap·land ['læplənd] Laponia *f.*

Lat·in A·mer·i·ca ['lætn ə'merikə] América *f* Latina.

Leb·a·non ['lebənən] Líbano *m.*

Leeds [li:dz] *Ciudad industrial de Inglaterra.*

Leices·ter ['lestər] *Capital de Leicestershire;* ~**shire** ['~ʃər] *Condado inglés.*

Lew·is ['lu:is] Luis.

Lib·y·a ['libiə] Libia *f.*

Lin·coln·shire ['liŋkənʃər] *Condado inglés.*

Lis·bon ['lizbən] Lisboa.

Liv·er·pool ['livərpu:l] *Puerto y ciudad industrial de Inglaterra.*

Lon·don ['lʌndən] Londres.

Los An·ge·les [lɔs 'ændʒələs] Los Angeles *(Ciudad de EE.UU.).*

Lou·i·si·an·a [lu:zi'ænə] Luisiana *f (Estado de EE.UU.).*

Luke [lu:k] Lucas.

Lux·em·bourg ['lʌksəmbərg] Luxemburgo *m.*

M

Ma·dei·ra [mə'dirə] Madera *f.*

Mad·i·son ['mædisn] *Capital del Estado de Wisconsin (EE.UU.).*

Ma·gel·lan [mə'gelən] Magellanes; ~ *Straits pl.* Estrecho *m* de Magellanes.

Ma·hom·et [mə'hɔmət] Mahoma *(Fundador del Islam).*

Maine [mein] *Estado de EE.UU.*

Ma·jor·ca [mə'dʒɔ:rkə] Mallorca *f.*

Man·ches·ter ['mæntʃestər] *Ciudad industrial de Inglaterra.*

Man·hat·tan [mæn'hætn] *Isla y centro de la ciudad de Nueva York.*

Man·i·to·ba [mæni'toubə] *Provincia de Canadá.*

Mar·ga·ret ['mɑ:rgərit] Margarita.

Mark [mɑ:rk] Marcos.

Mar·tin·ique [mɑːrtnˈiːk] Martinica f.

Mar·y ['meri] María.

Mar·y·land ['merilənd] *Estado de EE.UU.*

Mas·sa·chu·setts [mæsə'tʃuːsəts] *Estado de EE.UU.*

Mat·thew ['mæθjuː] Mateo.

Mau·rice ['mɔːrəs] Mauricio.

Mau·ri·tius [mɔːˈriʃəs] Mauricio m (isla).

Med·i·ter·ra·ne·an (Sea) [meditə-'reinjən (siː)] (Mar m) Mediterráneo m.

Mel·bourne ['melbərn] Melbourne (Australia).

Mex·i·co ['meksikou] Méjico m, México m.

Mi·am·i [mai'æmi] *Ciudad en el Estado de Florida (EE.UU.).*

Mich·ael ['maikl] Miguel.

Mich·i·gan ['miʃigən] *Estado de EE.UU.; Lake ~ el lago Michigan (el tercero de los cinco Grandes Lagos de Norteamérica).*

Mid·dle·sex ['midlseks] *Condado inglés.*

Min·ne·ap·o·lis [mini'æpəlis] *Ciudad en el Estado de Minnesota (EE.UU.).*

Min·ne·so·ta [mini'soutə] *Estado de EE.UU.*

Mi·nor·ca [mi'nɔːrkə] Menorca f.

Mis·sis·sip·pi [misi'sipi] Misisipí m (Estado y río de EE.UU.).

Mis·sou·ri [mi'zuri] Misuri m (Río y Estado de EE.UU.).

Mo·ham·med [mou'hæmed] Mahoma.

Mon·tan·a [mɔn'tænə] *Estado de EE.UU.*

Mont·re·al [mɔntri'ɔːl] *Ciudad de Canadá.*

Mo·roc·co [mə'rɔkou] Marruecos m.

Mos·cow ['mɔskou] Moscú.

Mo·ses ['mouziz] Moisés.

New·cas·tle ['n(j)uːkæsl] *Puerto en Gran Bretaña.*

New Eng·land [n(j)uː 'iŋglənd] Nueva Inglaterra f.

New·found·land ['n(j)uːfəndlənd] Terranova f.

New Guin·ea [n(j)uː 'gini] Nueva Guinea f.

New Hamp·shire [n(j)uː 'hæmpʃər] *Estado de EE.UU.*

New Jer·sey [n(j)uː 'dʒərzi] *Estado de EE.UU.*

New Mex·i·co [n(j)uː 'meksikou] *Estado de EE.UU.*

New Or·le·ans [n(j)uː 'ɔːrliːnz] Nueva Orleans f.

New South Wales [n(j)uː'sauθ-'weilz] Nueva Gales f del Sur (Australia).

New York [n(j)uː 'jɔːrk] Nueva York (Ciudad y Estado de EE.UU.).

New Zea·land [n(j)uː'ziːlənd] Nueva Zelanda f.

Ni·ag·a·ra [nai'ægərə] Niágara m.

Nic·a·ra·gua [nikə'rɑːgwə] Nicaragua f.

Nice [niːs] Niza.

Nich·o·las ['nikələs] Nicolás.

Ni·ge·ri·a [nai'dʒiːriə] Nigeria f.

Nile [nail] Nilo m.

No·ah ['nɔːə] Noé.

Nor·folk ['nɔːrfək] 1. *Condado inglés;* 2. *Puerto en Virginia (EE.UU.).*

North·amp·ton·shire [nɔːr'θæmp-tənʃər] *Condado inglés.*

North·ern Ire·land ['nɔːrθərn 'aiər-lənd] Irlanda f del Norte.

North Sea ['nɔːrθ'siː] Mar m del Norte.

North·um·ber·land [nɔːr'θʌmbər-lənd] *Condado inglés.*

Nor·way ['nɔːrwei] Noruega f.

Not·ting·ham·shire ['nɔtiŋəmʃər] *Condado inglés.*

No·va Sco·tia ['nouvə'skouʃə] Nueva Escocia f (Provincia de Canadá).

N

Ne·bras·ka [ni'bræskə] *Estado de EE.UU.*

Neth·er·lands ['neðərləndz] *pl.* (los) Países *m/pl.* Bajos.

Ne·vad·a [nə'vædə] *Estado de EE.UU.*

New Bruns·wick [n(j)uː 'brʌnzwik] *Provincia de Canadá.*

O

O·hi·o [ou'haiou] Ohío m (Río y Estado de EE.UU.).

O·kla·ho·ma [ouklə'houmə] *Estado de EE.UU.*

On·tar·i·o [ɔn'teriou] *Provincia de Canadá; Lake ~ el lago Ontario.*

Or·e·gon ['ɔrigən] *Estado de EE.UU.*

Ork·ney Is·lands ['ɔːrkni 'ailəndz]

pl. (las) Orcadas *f/pl.* (*Archipiélago situado al norte de Escocia*).

Ot·ta·wa ['ɔtəwə] *Capital de Canadá.*

Ox·ford ['ɔksfərd] *Ciudad universitaria inglesa.*

Ox·ford·shire ['-ʃər] *Condado inglés.*

P

Pa·cif·ic (O·cean) [pə'sifik ('ouʃn) (Océano *m*) Pacífico *m*.

Pa·ki·stan [pæki'stæn] Pakistán *m*.

Pal·es·tine ['pælistain] Palestina *f*.

Pall Mall ['pel'mel] *Nombre de una calle de Londres.*

Pan·a·ma [pænə'mɑ:] Panamá *m*.

Par·a·guay ['pærəgwai] (el) Paraguay.

Par·is ['pæris] París.

Pat·rick ['pætrik] Patricio.

Paul [pɔ:l] Pablo.

Pearl Har·bor ['pərl 'hɑːrbər] *Puerto cerca de Honolulú, Hawai.*

Pe·kin(g) [piː'kiŋ] Pekín.

Penn·syl·va·nia [pensil'veinjə] Pensilvania *f* (*Estado de EE.UU.*).

Pe·ru [pə'ruː] (el) Perú.

Pe·ter ['piːtər] Pedro.

Phil·a·del·phi·a [filə'delfjə] Filadelfia (*Gran ciudad de EE.UU.*).

Phil·ip ['filip] Felipe.

Phil·ip·pines ['filipiːnz] *pl.* Filipinas *f/pl.*

Phoe·nix ['fiːniks] *Capital de Arizona* (*EE.UU.*).

Pic·ca·dil·ly [pikə'dili] *Avenida principal en la parte occidental de Londres.*

Pitts·burgh ['pitsbərg] *Ciudad de EE.UU.*

Pi·us ['paiəs] Pío.

Plym·outh ['pliməθ] **1.** *Puerto de Inglaterra;* **2.** *Ciudad de EE.UU.*

Po·land ['poulənd] Polonia *f*.

Ports·mouth ['pɔːrtsməθ] *Puerto de Inglaterra.*

Por·tu·gal ['pɔːrtʃigəl] Portugal *m*.

Po·to·mac [pə'toumək] *Río de EE.UU.*

Prague [prɑːg] Praga.

Puer·to Ri·co ['pwertə 'riːkou] Puerto Rico *m*.

Pyr·e·nees [pirə'niːz] Pirineos *m/pl.*

Q

Que·bec [kwi'bek] *Provincia y ciudad de Canadá.*

R

Ra·phael ['ræfiəl] Rafael.

Rhine [rain] Rin *m*.

Rhode Is·land [roud'ailənd] *Estado de EE.UU.*

Rhone [roun] Ródano *m*.

Rich·ard ['ritʃərd] Ricardo.

Rich·mond ['ritʃmənd] **1.** *Capital de Virginia* (*EE.UU.*); **2.** *Barrio de Nueva York; barrio de Londres.*

Rob·ert ['rɔbərt], **Rob·in** ['rɔbən] Roberto.

Rock·y Moun·tains ['rɔki'mauntnz] *pl.* Montañas *f/pl.* Rocosas (*Sierra principal en el oeste de EE.UU.*).

Rome [roum] Roma.

Rose [rouz] Rosa.

Ru·ma·ni·a [ruː'meinjə] Rumania *f*.

Rus·sia ['rʌʃə] Rusia *f*.

S

Sa·har·a [sə'hɑːrə] Sáhara *m*.

Sam [sæm] *nombre cariñoso de Samuel.*

Sam·u·el ['sæmjəl] Samuel.

San Fran·cis·co [sænfrən'siskou] San Francisco (*EE.UU.*).

Sar·a·gos·sa [særə'gɔsə] Zaragoza.

Sar·di·nia [sɑːr'dinjə] Cerdeña *f*.

Sas·katch·e·wan [səs'kætʃiwən] *Río y provincia de Canadá.*

Sau·di A·ra·bia ['sɔːdi ə'reibjə] Arabia *f* Saudita.

Scan·di·na·via [skændi'neivjə] Escandinavia *f*.

Scot·land ['skɔtlənd] Escocia *f*; New ~ Yard *Oficina central de la policía de Londres.*

Se·at·tle [si'ætl] *Puerto en el noroeste de EE.UU.*

Seine [sein] Sena *m*.

Se·ville ['səvil] Sevilla.

Shef·field ['ʃefiːld] *Ciudad industrial de Inglaterra.*

Si·be·ri·a [sai'biriə] Siberia *f*.

Sic·i·ly ['sisili] Sicilia *f*.

Si·er·ra Le·one [si'erə li'oun] Sierra *f* Leona.

Si·er·ra Ne·va·da [si'erə ni'vɑːdə] Sierra Nevada *en España y California.*

Si·mon ['saimən] Simón.

Sin·ga·pore [siŋgə'pɔːr] Singapur.

Snow·don ['snoudn] *Pico en Gales.*

Som·er·set·shire ['sʌmərsitʃər] *Condado inglés.*

Sou·dan [suː'dæn] Sudán *m*.

South Af·ri·ca: Re·pub·lic of ~ [ri'pʌblik əvsauθ'æfrikə] República *f* Sudafricana.

South A·mer·i·ca ['sauθ ə'merikə] América *f* del Sur.

South·amp·ton [sauθ'æmptən] *Puerto en Inglaterra.*

So·vi·et Un·ion ['souvjət 'ju:njən] Unión *f* Soviética.

Spain [spein] España *f.*

Sri Lan·ka [sri: 'lɑːŋkə] Sri Lanka *m.*

Staf·ford·shire ['stæfərdʃər] *Condado inglés.*

Ste·phen ['sti:vn] Esteban.

St. Lou·is [seint 'lu:əs] *Ciudad industrial de EE.UU.*

Stock·holm ['stɔkholm] Estocolmo.

Stras·bourg ['stræzbɔrg] Estrasburgo.

Strat·ford ['strætfɔrd] *Nombre de varias poblaciones de Inglaterra y de EE.UU.;* **~on-Avon** *Lugar de nacimiento de Shakespeare.*

Stu·art ['st(j)u:ərt] Estuardo.

Su·dan [su:'dæn] Sudán *m.*

Su·ez Ca·nal ['su:ez kə'næl] Canal *m* de Suez.

Suf·folk ['sʌfək] *Condado inglés.*

Sur·rey ['sʌri] *Condado inglés.*

Su·san ['su:zn] Susana.

Sus·sex ['sʌsiks] *Condado inglés.*

Swe·den ['swi:dn] Suecia.

Swit·zer·land ['switsərlənd] Suiza *f.*

Syd·ney ['sidni] *Puerto y ciudad industrial de Australia.*

Sy·ri·a ['siriə] Siria *f.*

T

Ta·gus ['teigəs] Tajo *m.*

Tan·gier [tæn'dʒiər] Tánger.

Ten·nes·see [tenə'si:] *Río y Estado de EE.UU.*

Tex·as ['teksəs] Tejas *m (Estado de EE.UU.).*

Thames [temz] Támesis *m.*

Thom·as ['tɔməs] Tomás.

To·kyo ['toukjou] Tokio.

Tom(·my) ['tɔm(i)] *nombre cariñoso de Thomas.*

Ton·y ['touni] *nombre cariñoso de Anthony.*

To·ron·to [tə'rɔntou] *Ciudad de Canadá.*

Tra·fal·gar [trə'fælgər] *Promontorio cerca de Gibraltar.*

Tu·nis ['tu:nəs] Túnez.

Turk·ey ['tɔːrki] Turquía *f.*

U

U·kraine [ju:'krein] Ucrania *f.*

Ul·ster ['ʌlstər] *Provincia de Irlanda.*

U·nit·ed King·dom [ju:'naitid 'kiŋdəm] (el) Reino Unido *(Gran Bretaña e Irlanda del Norte).*

U·nit·ed States (of A·mer·i·ca) [ju:'naitid 'steits (əvə'merikə)] *pl.* (los) Estados *m/pl.* Unidos (de América).

U·ru·guay ['urugwai] (el) Uruguay.

U·tah ['ju:tɑː] *Estado de EE.UU.*

V

Van·cou·ver [væn'ku:vər] *Isla y ciudad en la costa occidental de Canadá.*

Vat·i·can ['vætikən] Vaticano *m.*

Ven·e·zue·la [venə'zweilə] Venezuela *f.*

Ven·ice ['venis] Venecia.

Ver·mont [vər'mɔnt] *Estado de EE.UU.*

Ver·sailles [ver'sai] Versalles.

Vi·en·na [vi'enə] Viena.

Vietnam ['vjet'næm] Vietnam *m.*

Vir·gin·ia [vər'dʒinjə] *Estado de EE.UU.*

W

Wales [weilz] Gales *f.*

Wall Street ['wɔːlstri:t] *Calle de Nueva York y centro financiero de EE.UU.*

War·saw ['wɔːrsɔ:] Varsovia.

War·wick(·shire) ['wɔrik(ʃər)] *Condado inglés.*

Wash·ing·ton ['wɔʃiŋtən] **1.** *Estado de EE.UU.;* **2.** *Capital federal y sede del gobierno de EE.UU.*

Wa·ter·loo [wɔ:tər'lu:] *Pueblo cerca de Bruselas (Bélgica).*

Wel·ling·ton ['weliŋtən] *Capital y puerto principal de Nueva Zelanda.*

West In·dies ['west 'indiz] *pl.* Antillas *f/pl.*

West·min·ster ['westminstər] *Barrio de Londres.*

West·mor·land ['westmərlənd] *Antiguo condado inglés.*

White·hall ['wait'hɔ:l] *Calle de Londres con edificios del gobierno inglés.*

White House ['wait 'haus]: **the ~ la** Casa Blanca *(sede oficial y residencia*

654

del presidente de EE.UU).

Wight: Isle of ~ [wait] *Isla en la costa meridional de Inglaterra.*

Will [wil], **Will·iam** ['wiljəm] *Guillermo.*

Wim·ble·don ['wimbldən] *Barrio de Londres (campeonatos de tenis).*

Wis·con·sin [wis'kɔnsn] *Estado de EE.UU.*

Worces·ter·shire ['wustərʃər] *Antiguo condado inglés.*

Wy·o·ming [wai'oumiŋ] *Estado de EE.UU.*

Yale U·ni·ver·si·ty ['jeil juːni'vɔːrsiti] *Universidad de Yale (en el Estado norteamericano de Connecticut).*

Yel·low·stone ['jeloustoun] *Río y parque nacional de EE.UU.*

York [jɔːrk] *Ciudad y sede arzobispal en Inglaterra.*

York·shire ['jɔːrkʃər] *Condado inglés.*

Yo·sem·i·te [jou'semiti] *Valle y parque nacional de EE.UU.*

Yu·go·sla·vi·a [juːgou'slɑːvjə] *Yugo(e)slavia f.*

Numerals — Numerales

Cardinal Numbers — Números cardinales

0	cero *nought*	40	cuarenta *forty*
1	uno, una *one*	50	cincuenta *fifty*
2	dos *two*	60	sesenta *sixty*
3	tres *three*	70	setenta *seventy*
4	cuatro *four*	80	ochenta *eighty*
5	cinco *five*	90	noventa *ninety*
6	seis *six*	100	cien(to) *a (one) hundred*
7	siete *seven*	101	ciento uno *a hundred and one*
8	ocho *eight*	110	ciento diez *a hundred and ten*
9	nueve *nine*	200	doscientos, -as *two hundred*
10	diez *ten*	300	trescientos, -as *three hundred*
11	once *eleven*	400	cuatrocientos, -as *four hundred*
12	doce *twelve*	500	quinientos, -as *five hundred*
13	trece *thirteen*	600	seiscientos, -as *six hundred*
14	catorce *fourteen*	700	setecientos, -as *seven hundred*
15	quince *fifteen*	800	ochocientos, -as *eight hundred*
16	dieciséis *sixteen*	900	novecientos, -as *nine hundred*
17	diecisiete *seventeen*	1000	mil *a thousand*
18	dieciocho *eighteen*	1959	mil novecientos cincuenta y nueve *nineteen hundred and fifty-nine*
19	diecinueve *nineteen*		
20	veinte *twenty*	2000	dos mil *two thousand*
21	veintiuno *twenty-one*	1 000 000	un millón (de) *a (one) million*
22	veintidós *twenty-two*	2 000 000	dos millones (de) *two million*
30	treinta *thirty*		
31	treinta y uno *thirty-one*		

Ordinal Numbers — Números ordinales

(The ordinal numbers in Spanish agree with the noun in number and gender, *primero -a -os -as etc.*)

1	primero *first*	13	decimotercero, decimotercio *thirteenth*
2	segundo *second*	14	decimocuarto *fourteenth*
3	tercero *third*	15	decimoquinto *fifteenth*
4	cuarto *fourth*	16	decimosexto *sixteenth*
5	quinto *fifth*	17	decimoséptimo *seventeenth*
6	sexto *sixth*	18	decimoctavo *eighteenth*
7	séptimo *seventh*	19	decimonoveno, decimonono *nineteenth*
8	octavo *eighth*	20	vigésimo *twentieth*
9	noveno, nono *ninth*	21	vigésimo prim(er)o *twenty-first*
10	décimo *tenth*	22	vigésimo segundo *twenty-second*
11	undécimo *eleventh*		
12	duodécimo *twelfth*		

30 trigésimo *thirtieth*	**200** ducentésimo *two hundredth*
31 trigésimo prim(er)o *thirty-first*	**300** trecentésimo *three hundredth*
40 cuadragésimo *fortieth*	**400** cuadringentésimo *four hundredth*
50 quincuagésimo *fiftieth*	**500** quingentésimo *five hundredth*
60 sexagésimo *sixtieth*	**600** sexcentésimo *six hundredth*
70 septuagésimo *seventieth*	**700** septingentésimo *seven hundredth*
80 octogésimo *eightieth*	**800** octingentésimo *eight hundredth*
90 nonagésimo *ninetieth*	**900** noningentésimo *nine hundredth*
100 centésimo *hundredth*	**1000** milésimo *thousandth*
101 centésimo primero *hundred and first*	**2000** dos milésimo *two thousandth*
110 centésimo décimo *hundred and tenth*	**1000000** millonésimo *millionth*
	2000000 dos millonésimo *two millionth*

En inglés, los números ordinales suelen abreviarse 1st., 2nd., 3rd., 4th., 5th. *etc.*; in Spanish, the ordinal numbers may be written 1°, 2° *etc.*

Fractions and other Numerals — Números quebrados y otros

$1/2$ medio, media *one (a) half*;
$1^1/_2$ uno y medio *one and a half*;
$2^1/_2$ dos y medio *two and a half*; $1/2$ hora *half an hour*;
$1^1/_2$ kilómetros *a kilometer and a half*

$1/3$ un tercio, la tercera parte *one (a) third*; $2/3$ dos tercios, las dos terceras partes *two thirds*

$1/4$ un cuarto, la cuarta parte *one (a) quarter*; $3/4$ tres cuartos, las tres cuartas partes *three-quarters*; $1/4$ hora *a quarter of an hour*; $1^1/_4$ horas *an hour and a quarter*

$1/5$ un quinto *one (a) fifth*; $3^4/_5$ tres y cuatro quintos *three and four fifths*

$1/11$ un onzavo *one (an) eleventh*; $5/_{12}$ cinco dozavos *five twelfths*; $75/_{100}$ setenta y cinco centésimos *seventy-five hundredths*

$1/_{1000}$ un milésimo *one (a) thousandth*

simple *single*
doble, duplo *double*
triple *treble, triple, threefold*
cuádruplo *fourfold*
quíntuplo *fivefold etc.*
una vez *once*
dos veces *twice*
tres veces *three times etc.*
siete veces más grande *seven times as big*; doce veces más *twelve times more*
en primer lugar *firstly*
en segundo lugar *secondly etc.*

$7 + 8 = 15$ siete y (or más) ocho son quince *seven and eight are fifteen*

$10 - 3 = 7$ diez menos tres resta siete, de tres a diez van siete *three from ten leaves seven*

$2 \times 3 = 6$ dos por tres son seis *two times three are six*

$20 \div 4 = 5$ veinte dividido por cuatro es cinco *twenty divided by four is five.*

Note on the Spanish Verb

The simple tenses and parts of the three conjugations and of irregular verbs are set out in the following pages, but certain general points may be summarized here:

1. **Compound tenses** etc. are formed with the auxiliary *haber* and the past participle:

   perfect: he mandado (*subj.*: haya mandado)

   pluperfect: había mandado (*subj.*: hubiera mandado, hubiese mandado)

   future perfect: habré mandado

   perfect infinitive: haber mandado

   perfect gerund: habiendo mandado

2. The **imperfect** is regular for all verbs except *ser* (*era* etc.) and *ir* (*iba* etc.).

3. The **conditional** is formed like the future on the infinitive: *mandaría*. If the future is irregular, so will be the conditional: *salir — saldré, saldría; decir — diré, diría*.

4. The **imperfect subjunctives** I and II are formed from the 3rd person plural of the preterite, using as a stem what remains after removing the final *-ron* syllable, and adding *-ra* or *-se*:

   mandar: manda/ron — mandara, mandase

   querer: quisie/ron — quisiera, quisiese

   traer: traje/ron — trajera, trajese

   conducir: conduje/ron — condujera, condujese

5. **Imperative.** The "true" imperative is limited to the familiar forms or true second persons (*tú, vosotros*) used affirmatively: *habla, mándamelo, hacedlo*. The imperative affirmative with *Vd., Vds*. is formed with the subjunctive: *mándemelo Vd., háganlo Vds*. The imperative negative for all persons is formed with the subjunctive: *no lo hagas (tú), no vayan Vds*.

6. **Continuous tenses** are formed with *estar* and the gerund: *estoy trabajando, estábamos discutiendo*. Other auxiliary verbs may be used according to sense: *vamos avanzando, según voy viendo, vengo diciendo eso*.

7. The **passive** is formed with tenses of *ser* and the past participle: *es recibido, será vencido, fue construido*. In passive uses the past participle agrees in number and gender with the subject: *las casas fueron derribadas*.

First Conjugation

[1a] **mandar**

Infinitive: mandar **Gerund:** mandando **Past Participle:** mandado

Indicative

Present	*Imperfect*	*Preterite*
mando	mandaba	mandé
mandas	mandabas	mandaste
manda	mandaba	mandó
mandamos	mandábamos	mandamos
mandáis	mandabais	mandasteis
mandan	mandaban	mandaron

Future	*Conditional*
mandaré	mandaría
mandarás	mandarías
mandará	mandaría
mandaremos	mandaríamos
mandaréis	mandaríais
mandarán	mandarían

Subjunctive

Present	*Imperfect I*	*Imperfect II*
mande	mandara	mandase
mandes	mandaras	mandases
mande	mandara	mandase
mandemos	mandáramos	mandásemos
mandéis	mandarais	mandaseis
manden	mandaran	mandasen

Imperative

Affirmative	*Negative*
manda (tú)	no mandes (tú)
mande Vd.	no mande Vd.
mandad (vosotros)	no mandéis (vosotros)
manden Vds.	no manden Vds.

Infinitive	Present Indicative	Present Subjunctive	Preterite
[1b] **cambiar.** The *i* of the stem is not stressed and the verb is regular	cambio cambias cambia cambiamos cambiáis cambian	cambie cambies cambie cambiemos cambiéis cambien	cambié cambiaste cambió cambiamos cambiasteis cambiaron
[1c] **variar.** In forms stressed on the stem, the *i* is accented	varío varías varía variamos variáis varían	varíe varíes varíe variemos variéis varíen	varié variaste varió variamos variasteis variaron

Infinitive	Present Indicative	Present Subjunctive	Preterite
[1d] evacuar. The *u* of the stem is not stressed and the verb is regular	evacuo evacuas evacua evacuamos evacuáis evacuan	evacue evacues evacue evacuemos evacuéis evacuen	evacué evacuaste evacuó evacuamos evacuasteis evacuaron
[1e] acentuar. In forms stressed on the stem, the *u* is accented	acentúo acentúas acentúa acentuamos acentuáis acentúan	acentúe acentúes acentúe acentuemos acentuéis acentúen	acentué acentuaste acentuó acentuamos acentuasteis acentuaron
[1f] cruzar. The stem consonant *z* is written *c* before *e*	cruzo cruzas cruza cruzamos cruzáis cruzan	cruce cruces cruce crucemos crucéis crucen	crucé cruzaste cruzó cruzamos cruzasteis cruzaron
[1g] tocar. The stem consonant *c* is written *qu* before *e*	toco tocas toca tocamos tocáis tocan	toque toques toque toquemos toquéis toquen	toqué tocaste tocó tocamos tocasteis tocaron
[1h] pagar. The stem consonant *g* is written *gu* (*u* silent) before *e*	pago pagas paga pagamos pagáis pagan	pague pagues pague paguemos paguéis paguen	pagué pagaste pagó pagamos pagasteis pagaron
[1i] fraguar. The *u* of the stem is written *ü* (so that it should be pronounced) before *e*	fraguo fraguas fragua fraguamos fraguáis fraguan	fragüe fragües fragüe fragüemos fragüéis fragüen	fragüé fraguaste fraguó fraguamos fraguasteis fraguaron
[1k] pensar. The stem vowel *e* becomes *ie* when stressed	**pie**nso **pie**nsas **pie**nsa pensamos pensáis **pie**nsan	**pie**nse **pie**nses **pie**nse pensemos penséis **pie**nsen	pensé pensaste pensó pensamos pensasteis pensaron
[1l] errar. As [1k], but the diphthong is written *ye* at the start of the word	**ye**rro **ye**rras **ye**rra erramos erráis **ye**rran	**ye**rre **ye**rres **ye**rre erremos erréis **ye**rren	erré erraste erró erramos errasteis erraron

Infinitive	Present Indicative	Present Subjunctive	Preterite
[1m] contar. The stem vowel *o* becomes *ue* when stressed	cuento cuentas cuenta contamos contáis cuentan	cuente cuentes cuente contemos contéis cuenten	conté contaste contó contamos contasteis contaron
[1n] agorar. The stem vowel *o* becomes *üe* when stressed	agüero agüeras agüera agoramos agoráis agüeran	agüere agüeres agüere agoremos agoréis agüeren	agoré agoraste agoró agoramos agorasteis agoraron
[1o] jugar. The stem vowel *u* becomes *ue* when stressed; the stem consonant *g* is written *gu* (*u* silent) before *e*; *conjugar, enjugar* are regular	juego juegas juega jugamos jugáis juegan	juegue juegues juegue juguemos juguéis jueguen	jugué jugaste jugó jugamos jugasteis jugaron
[1p] estar. Irregular. Imperative: *está* (*tú*)	estoy estás está estamos estáis están	esté estés esté estemos estéis estén	estuve estuviste estuvo estuvimos estuvisteis estuvieron
[1q] andar. Irregular.	ando andas anda andamos andáis andan	ande andes ande andemos andéis anden	anduve anduviste anduvo anduvimos anduvisteis anduvieron
[1r] dar. Irregular.	doy das da damos dais dan	dé des dé demos deis den	di diste dio dimos disteis dieron

Second Conjugation

[2a] vender
Infinitive: vender **Gerund:** vendiendo **Past Participle:** vendido

Indicative

Present	*Imperfect*	*Preterite*
vendo	vendía	vendí
vendes	vendías	vendiste
vende	vendía	vendió
vendemos	vendíamos	vendimos
vendéis	vendíais	vendisteis
venden	vendían	vendieron

Future	*Conditional*
venderé	vendería
venderás	venderías
venderá	vendería
venderemos	venderíamos
venderéis	venderíais
venderán	venderían

Subjunctive

Present	*Imperfect I*	*Imperfect II*
venda	vendiera	vendiese
vendas	vendieras	vendieses
venda	vendiera	vendiese
vendamos	vendiéramos	vendiésemos
vendáis	vendierais	vendieseis
vendan	vendieran	vendiesen

Imperative

Affirmative	*Negative*
vende (tú)	no vendas (tú)
venda Vd.	no venda Vd.
vended (vosotros)	no vendáis (vosotros)
vendan Vds.	no vendan Vds.

Infinitive	Present Indicative	Present Subjunctive	Preterite
[2b] vencer. The stem consonant *c* is written *z* before *a* and *o*	venzo vences vence vencemos vencéis vencen	venza venzas venza venzamos venzáis venzan	vencí venciste venció vencimos vencisteis vencieron
[2c] coger. The stem consonant *g* is written *j* before *a* and *o*	cojo coges coge cogemos cogéis cogen	coja cojas coja cojamos cojáis cojan	cogí cogiste cogió cogimos cogisteis cogieron

	Infinitive	Present Indicative	Present Subjunctive	Preterite
[2d]	**merecer.** The stem consonant *c* becomes *zc* before *a* and *o*	mere**zc**o mereces merece merecemos merecéis merecen	mere**zc**a mere**zc**as mere**zc**a mere**zc**amos mere**zc**áis mere**zc**an	merecí mereciste mereció merecimos merecisteis merecieron
[2e]	**creer.** Unstressed *i* between vowels is written *y*. Past participle: *creído* Gerund: *creyendo*	creo crees cree creemos creéis creen	crea creas crea creamos creáis crean	creí creíste cre**y**ó creímos creísteis cre**y**eron
[2f]	**tañer.** Unstressed *i* after *ñ* and *ll* is omitted. Gerund: *tañendo*	taño tañes tañe tañemos tañéis tañen	taña tañas taña tañamos tañáis tañan	tañí tañiste ta**ñ**ió tañimos tañisteis ta**ñ**eron
[2g]	**perder.** The stem vowel *e* becomes *ie* when stressed	p**ie**rdo p**ie**rdes p**ie**rde perdemos perdéis p**ie**rden	p**ie**rda p**ie**rdas p**ie**rda perdamos perdáis p**ie**rdan	perdí perdiste perdió perdimos perdisteis perdieron
[2h]	**mover.** The stem vowel *o* becomes *ue* when stressed. Verbs in *-olver* form their past participle in *-uelto*	m**ue**vo m**ue**ves m**ue**ve movemos movéis m**ue**ven	m**ue**va m**ue**vas m**ue**va movamos mováis m**ue**van	moví moviste movió movimos movisteis movieron
[2i]	**oler.** As [2h], but the diphthong is written *hue* at the start of the word	**hue**lo **hue**les **hue**le olemos oléis **hue**len	**hue**la **hue**las **hue**la olamos oláis **hue**lan	olí oliste olió olimos olisteis olieron
[2k]	**haber.** Irregular throughout. Future: *habré*	he has ha hemos habéis han	haya hayas haya hayamos hayáis hayan	hube hubiste hubo hubimos hubisteis hubieron
[2l]	**tener.** Irregular throughout. Future: *tendré* Imperative: *ten* (*tú*)	tengo tienes tiene tenemos tenéis tienen	tenga tengas tenga tengamos tengáis tengan	tuve tuviste tuvo tuvimos tuvisteis tuvieron

Infinitive	Present Indicative	Present Subjunctive	Preterite
[2m] **caber.** Irregular throughout. Future: *cabré*	quepo cabes cabe cabemos cabéis caben	quepa quepas quepa quepamos quepáis quepan	cupe cupiste cupo cupimos cupisteis cupieron
[2n] **saber.** Irregular throughout. Future: *sabré*	sé sabes sabe sabemos sabéis saben	sepa sepas sepa sepamos sepáis sepan	supe supiste supo supimos supisteis supieron
[2o] **caer.** Irregular. Unstressed *i* between vowels is written *y*, as [2e]. Past participle: *caído* Gerund: *cayendo*	caigo caes cae caemos caéis caen	caiga caigas caiga caigamos caigáis caigan	caí caiste cayó caimos caisteis cayeron
[2p] **traer.** Irregular throughout. Past participle: *traído* Gerund: *trayendo*	traigo traes trae traemos traéis traen	traiga traigas traiga traigamos traigáis traigan	traje trajiste trajo trajimos trajisteis trajeron
[2q] **valer.** Irregular. Future: *valdré*	valgo vales vale valemos valéis valen	valga valgas valga valgamos valgáis valgan	valí valiste valió valimos valisteis valieron
[2r] **poner.** Irregular throughout. Future: *pondré* Past participle: *puesto* Imperative: *pon (tú)*	pongo pones pone ponemos ponéis ponen	ponga pongas ponga pongamos pongáis pongan	puse pusiste puso pusimos pusisteis pusieron
[2s] **hacer.** Irregular throughout. Future: *haré* Past participle: *hecho* Imperative: *haz (tú)*	hago haces hace hacemos hacéis hacen	haga hagas haga hagamos hagáis hagan	hice hiciste hizo hicimos hicisteis hicieron
[2t] **poder.** Irregular throughout. In present tenses like [2h]. Future: *podré* Gerund: *pudiendo*	puedo puedes puede podemos podéis pueden	pueda puedas pueda podamos podáis puedan	pude pudiste pudo pudimos pudisteis pudieron

Infinitive	Present Indicative	Present Subjunctive	Preterite
[2u] querer. Irregular. In present tenses like [2g]. Future: *querré*	quiero quieres quiere queremos queréis quieren	quiera quieras quiera queramos queráis quieran	quise quisiste quiso quisimos quisisteis quisieron
[2v] ver. Irregular. Past participle: *visto* Gerund: *viendo* Imperfect: *veía etc.* Imperative: *ve (tú)* *ved (vosotros)*	veo ves ve vemos veis ven	vea veas vea veamos veáis vean	vi viste vio vimos visteis vieron
[2w] ser. Irregular throughout. Past participle: *sido* Gerund: *siendo* Future: *seré* Imperfect: *era, eras etc.* Imperative: *sé (tú), sed (vosotros)*	soy eres es somos sois son	sea seas sea seamos seáis sean	fui fuiste fue fuimos fuisteis fueron

[2x] placer. Used only in 3rd person sg. Irregular forms: Present subj. *plega, plegue* or *plazca*; Preterite *plugo* or *plació*; Imperfect subj. I *pluguiera* or *placiera*, Imperfect subj. II *pluguiese* or *placiese*.

[2y] yacer. (Mostly †). Irregular forms: Present indic. *yazco, yazgo* or *yago*; Present subj. *yazca, yazga, yaga* etc. Imperative *yace (tú)* or *yaz (tú)*.

[2z] raer. Alternative forms in present tenses: Present indic. *raigo* or *rayo* etc.; Present subj. *raiga* or *raya* etc.

[2za] roer. Alternative forms in present tenses: Present indic. *roigo* or *royo*; Present subj. *roiga* or *roya*.

Third Conjugation

[3a] recibir

Infinitive: recibir **Gerund:** recibiendo **Past Participle:** recibido

Indicative

Present	Imperfect	Preterite
recibo	recibía	recibí
recibes	recibías	recibiste
recibe	recibía	recibió
recibimos	recibíamos	recibimos
recibís	recibíais	recibisteis
reciben	recibían	recibieron

Future	Conditional
recibiré	recibiría
recibirás	recibirías
recibirá	recibiría
recibiremos	recibiríamos
recibiréis	recibiríais
recibirán	recibirían

Subjunctive

Present	Imperfect I	Imperfect II
reciba	recibiera	recibiese
recibas	recibieras	recibieses
reciba	recibiera	recibiese
recibamos	recibiéramos	recibiésemos
recibáis	recibierais	recibieseis
reciban	recibieran	recibiesen

Imperative

Affirmative	Negative
recibe (tú)	no recibas (tú)
reciba Vd.	no reciba Vd.
recibid (vosotros)	no recibáis (vosotros)
reciban Vds.	no reciban Vds.

Infinitive	Present Indicative	Present Subjunctive	Preterite
[3b] esparcir. The stem consonant *c* is written *z* before *a* and *o*	esparzo	esparza	esparcí
	esparces	esparzas	esparciste
	esparce	esparza	esparció
	esparcimos	esparzamos	esparcimos
	esparcís	esparzáis	esparcisteis
	esparcen	esparzan	esparcieron
[3c] dirigir. The stem consonant *g* is written *j* before *a* and *o*	dirijo	dirija	dirigí
	diriges	dirijas	dirigiste
	dirige	dirija	dirigió
	dirigimos	dirijamos	dirigimos
	dirigís	dirijáis	dirigisteis
	dirigen	dirijan	dirigieron

	Infinitive	Present Indicative	Present Subjunctive	Preterite
[3d]	**distinguir.** The *u* after the stem consonant *g* is omitted before *a* and *o*	distingo distingues distingue distinguimos distinguís distinguen	distinga distingas distinga distingamos distingáis distingan	distinguí distinguiste distinguió distinguimos distinguisteis distinguieron
[3e]	**delinquir.** The stem consonant *qu* is written *c* before *a* and *o*	delinco delinques delinque delinquimos delinquís delinquen	delinca delincas delinca delincamos delincáis delincan	delinquí delinquiste delinquió delinquimos delinquisteis delinquieron
[3f]	**lucir.** The stem consonant *c* becomes *zc* before *a* and *o*	luzco luces luce lucimos lucís lucen	luzca luzcas luzca luzcamos luzcáis luzcan	lucí luciste lució lucimos lucisteis lucieron
[3g]	**concluir.** The *i* of *-ió* and *-ie-* changes to *y*; a *y* is inserted before endings not beginning with *i*. Gerund: *concluyendo*	concluyo concluyes concluye concluimos concluís concluyen	concluya concluyas concluya concluyamos concluyáis concluyan	concluí concluiste concluyó concluimos concluisteis concluyeron
[3h]	**gruñir.** Unstressed *i* after *ñ*, *ll* and *ch* is omitted. Gerund: *gruñendo*	gruño gruñes gruñe gruñimos gruñís gruñen	gruña gruñas gruña gruñamos gruñáis gruñan	gruñí gruñiste gruñó gruñimos gruñisteis gruñeron
[3i]	**sentir.** The stem vowel *e* becomes *ie* when stressed; unstressed *e* becomes *i* in 3rd persons of Preterite, 1st and 2nd persons pl. of Present Subjunctive. In *adquirir etc.* the stem vowel *i* becomes *ie* when stressed Gerund: *sintiendo*	siento sientes siente sentimos sentís sienten	sienta sientas sienta sintamos sintáis sientan	sentí sentiste sintió sentimos sentisteis sintieron
[3k]	**dormir.** The stem vowel *o* becomes *ue* when stressed; unstressed *o* becomes *u* in 3rd persons of Preterite, 1st and 2nd persons pl. of Present Subjunctive. Gerund: *durmiendo*	duermo duermes duerme dormimos dormís duermen	duerma duermas duerma durmamos durmáis duerman	dormí dormiste durmió dormimos dormisteis durmieron

Infinitive	Present Indicative	Present Subjunctive	Preterite
[3l] medir. The stem vowel *e* becomes *i* when stressed, and also when unstressed in 3rd persons of Preterite, 1st and 2nd persons pl. of Present Subjunctive. Gerund: *midiendo*	mido mides mide medimos medís miden	mida midas mida midamos midáis midan	medí mediste midió medimos medisteis midieron
[3m] reír. Irregular. Past participle: *reído* Gerund: *riendo*	río ríes ríe reímos reís ríen	ría rías ría riamos riáis rían	reí reíste rió reímos reísteis rieron
[3n] erguir. Irregular. Gerund: *irguiendo* Imperative: *irgue (tú)* or *yergue (tú)*	irgo irgues irgue erguimos erguís irguen *or* yergo yergues yergue erguimos erguís yerguen	irga irgas irga irgamos irgáis irgan *or* yerga yergas yerga yergamos yergáis yergan	erguí erguiste irguió erguimos erguisteis irguieron
[3o] conducir. The stem consonant *c* becomes *zc* before *a* and *o*, as [3f]. Irregular preterite in *-uje*	conduzco conduces conduce conducimos conducís conducen	conduzca conduzcas conduzca conduzcamos conduzcáis conduzcan	conduje condujiste condujo condujimos condujisteis condujeron
[3p] decir. Irregular throughout. Future: *diré* Past participle: *dicho* Gerund: *diciendo* Imperative: *di (tú)*	digo dices dice decimos decís dicen	diga digas diga digamos digáis digan	dije dijiste dijo dijimos dijisteis dijeron
[3q] oír. Irregular. Unstressed *i* between vowels becomes *y*. Past participle: *oído* Gerund: *oyendo*	oigo oyes oye oímos oís oyen	oiga oigas oiga oigamos oigáis oigan	oí oiste oyó oímos oísteis oyeron

	Infinitive	Present Indicative	Present Subjunctive	Preterite
[3r]	**salir.** Irregular.	salgo	salga	salí
	Future: *saldré*	sales	salgas	saliste
	Imperative: *sal (tú)*	sale	salga	salió
		salimos	salgamos	salimos
		salís	salgáis	salisteis
		salen	salgan	salieron
[3s]	**venir.** Irregular	vengo	venga	vine
	throughout.	vienes	vengas	viniste
	Future: *vendré*	viene	venga	vino
	Gerund: *viniendo*	venimos	vengamos	vinimos
	Imperative: *ven (tú)*	venís	vengáis	vinisteis
		vienen	vengan	vinieron
[3t]	**ir.** Irregular	voy	vaya	fui
	throughout.	vas	vayas	fuiste
	Imperfect: *iba, ibas*	va	vaya	fue
	etc.	vamos	vayamos	fuimos
	Gerund: *yendo*	vais	vayáis	fuisteis
	Imperative: *ve (tú),*	van	vayan	fueron
	id (vosotros)			

Notas sobre el verbo inglés

a) Conjugación

Modo indicativo.

1. **El tiempo presente** tiene la misma forma que el infinitivo en todas las personas menos la 3a del singular; en ésta, se añade una -s al infinitivo, p.ej. *he brings*, o se añade -es si el infinitivo termina en sibilante (ch, sh, ss, zz), p. ej. *he passes*. Esta s tiene dos pronunciaciones distintas: tras consonante sorda se pronuncia sorda, p.ej. *he paints* [peints]; tras consonante sonora se pronuncia sonora, p.ej. *he sends* [sendz]; -es se pronuncia también sonora, sea la e parte de la desinencia o letra final del infinitivo, p.ej. *he washes* ['wɔʃiz], *he urges* ['ɔːrdʒiz]. Los verbos que terminan en -y la cambian en -ies en la tercera persona, p.ej. *he worries, he tries*, pero son regulares los verbos que en el infinitivo tienen una vocal delante de la -y, p.ej. *he plays*. El verbo *be* es irregular en todas las personas: *I am, you are, he is, we are, you are, they are.* Tres verbos más tienen forma especial para la tercera persona del singular: *do—he does, go—he goes, have—he has.*

   En los demás tiempos, todas las personas son iguales. **El pretérito** y el **participio del pasado** se forman añadiendo -ed al infinitivo, p.ej. *I passed, passed*, o añadiendo -d a los infinitivos que terminan en -e, p.ej. *I faced, faced.* (Hay muchos verbos irregulares: *v.* abajo). Esta -(e)d se pronuncia generalmente como [t]: *passed* [pæst], *faced* [feist]; pero cuando se añade a un infinitivo que termina en consonante sonora o en sonido consonántico sonoro o en r, se pronuncia como [d]: *warmed* [wɔːrmd], *moved* [muːvd], *feared* [fird]. Si el infinitivo termina en -d o -t, la desinencia -ed se pronuncia [id]. Si el infinitivo termina en -y, ésta se cambia en -ie antes de añadirse la -d: *try—tried* [traid], *pity—pitied* ['pitid]. **Los tiempos compuestos del pasado** se forman con el verbo auxiliar *have* y el participio del pasado, como en español: **perfecto** *I have faced*, **pluscuamperfecto** *I had faced.* Con el verbo auxiliar *will* (*shall*) y el infinitivo se forma **el futuro**, p.ej. *I shall face*, y con el verbo auxiliar *would* (*should*) y el infinitivo se forma **el condicional**, p.ej. *I should face.*

   En cada tiempo existe además una forma continua que se forma con el verbo *be* (= estar) y el participio del presente (*v.* abajo): *I am going, I was writing, I had been staying, I shall be waiting*, etc.

2. **El subjuntivo** ha dejado casi de existir en inglés, salvo en algún caso especial (*if I were you, so be it, it is proposed that a vote be taken*, etc.). En el presente, tiene en todas las personas la misma forma que el infinitivo, *that I go, that he go*, etc.

3. **El participio del presente** y **el gerundio** tienen la misma forma en inglés, añadiéndose al infinitivo la desinencia -ing: *painting, sending.* Pero **1)** Los verbos cuyo infinitivo termina en -e muda la pierden al añadir -ing, p.ej. *love—loving, write—writing* (excepciones que conservan la -e: *dye—dyeing, singe—singeing, shoe—shoeing*); **2)** El participio del presente de los verbos *die, lie, vie*, etc. se escribe *dying, lying, vying*, etc.

4. Existe una clase de verbos ligeramente irregulares, que terminan en consonante simple precedida de vocal simple acentuada; en éstos, antes de añadir la desinencia *-ing* o *-ed*, se dobla la consonante:

to lob	lob*bed*	lob*bing*
to wed	wed*ded*	wed*ding*
to beg	beg*ged*	beg*ging*
to step	step*ped*	step*ping*
to quit	quit*ted*	quit*ting*
to compel	compel*led*	compel*ling*
to control	control*led*	control*ling*
to bar	bar*red*	bar*ring*
to stir	stir*red*	stir*ring*

Los verbos que terminan en *-l*, *-p*, aunque precedida de vocal átona, tienen doblada la consonante en los dos participios en el inglés escrito en Gran Bretaña, aunque no en el de Estados Unidos:

to travel	travel*led*	travel*ling*
	Am. traveled	*Am.* traveling
to worship	worship*ped*	worship*ping*
	Am. worshiped	*Am.* worshiping

Los verbos que terminan en *-c* la cambian en *-ck* al añadirse las desinencias *-ed*, *-ing*:

to traffic	traffic*ked*	traffic*king*

5. **La voz pasiva** se forma exactamente como en español, con el verbo *be* y el participio del pasado: *I am obliged, he was fined, they will be moved*, etc.

6. Cuando se dirige uno directamente a otra(s) persona(s) en inglés se emplea únicamente el pronombre *you*, con las formas correspondientes del verbo (2a persona del plural). *You* traduce por tanto el *tú, vosotros, usted y ustedes* del español. La segunda persona del singular en inglés (*thou*) no se emplea más que dialectalmente o en el rezo.

b) Los verbos irregulares ingleses

Se citan las tres partes principales de cada verbo: infinitivo, pretérito, participio del pasado.

abide - abode - abode
arise - arose - arisen
awake - awoke - awoke, awaked
be (am, is, are) - was (were) - been
bear - bore - borne (*llevado*), born (*nacido*)
beat - beat - beaten, beat
become - became - become
beget - begot, † begat - begotten
begin - began - begun
belay - belayed, belaid - belayed, belaid
bend - bent - bent
bereave - bereaved, bereft - bereaved, bereft
beseech - besought - besought
bestrew - bestrewed - bestrewed, bestrewn
bestride - bestrode - bestridden

bet - bet, betted - bet, betted
bid - bade, bid - bidden, bid
bind - bound - bound
bite - bit - bitten
bleed - bled - bled
blow - blew - blown
break - broke - broken
breed - bred - bred
bring - brought - brought
build - built - built
burn - burnt, burned - burnt, burned
burst - burst - burst
buy - bought - bought
can - could
cast - cast - cast
catch - caught - caught
chide - chid - chid, chidden
choose - chose - chosen

cleave - clove, cleft - cloven, cleft
cling - clung - clung
clothe - clothed, *lit.* clad - clothed, *lit.* clad
come - came - come
cost - cost - cost
creep - crept - crept
cut - cut - cut
dare - dared, † durst - dared
deal - dealt - dealt
dig - dug - dug
do - did - done
draw - drew - drawn
dream - dreamt, dreamed - dreamt, dreamed
drink - drank - drunk
drive - drove - driven
dwell - dwelt - dwelt
eat - ate - eaten
fall - fell - fallen
feed - fed - fed
feel - felt - felt
fight - fought - fought
find - found - found
flee - fled - fled
fling - flung - flung
fly - flew - flown
forbear - forbore - forborne
forbid - forbad(e) - forbidden
forget - forgot - forgotten
forgive - forgave - forgiven
forsake - forsook - forsaken
freeze - froze - frozen
geld - gelded, gelt - gelded, gelt
get - got - got, *Am.* gotten
gild - gilded, gilt - gilded, gilt
gird - girded, girt - girded, girt
give - gave - given
go - went - gone
grave - graved - graved, graven
grind - ground - ground
grow - grew - grown
hang - hung, 𝕣𝕥 hanged - hung, 𝕣𝕥 hanged
have - had - had
hear - heard - heard
heave - heaved, ⚓ hove - heaved, ⚓ hove
hew - hewed - hewed, hewn
hide - hid - hidden, hid
hit - hit - hit
hold - held - held
hurt - hurt - hurt
keep - kept - kept
kneel - knelt, kneeled - knelt, kneeled
knit - knitted, knit - knitted, knit
know - knew - known

lade - laded - laded, laden
lay - laid - laid
lead - led - led
lean - leaned, leant - leaned, leant
leap - leaped, leapt - leaped, leapt
learn - learned, learnt - learned, learnt
leave - left - left
lend - lent - lent
let - let - let
lie - lay - lain
light - lighted, lit - lighted, lit
lose - lost - lost
make - made - made
may - might
mean - meant - meant
meet - met - met
mow - mowed - mowed, mown
must - must
falta el presente - **ought**
pay - paid - paid
pen - penned, pent - penned, pent
put - put - put
read [ri:d] - read [red] - read [red]
rend - rent - rent
rid - rid - rid
ride - rode - ridden
ring - rang - rung
rise - rose - risen
rive - rived - riven
run - ran - run
saw - sawed - sawn, sawed
say - said - said
see - saw - seen
seek - sought - sought
sell - sold - sold
send - sent - sent
set - set - set
sew - sewed - sewed, sewn
shake - shook - shaken
shall - should
shave - shaved - shaved, (*mst adj.*) shaven
shear - sheared - shorn
shed - shed - shed
shine - shone - shone
shoe - shod - shod
shoot - shot - shot
show - showed - shown
shred - shredded - shredded, shred
shrink - shrank - shrunk
shut - shut - shut
sing - sang - sung
sink - sank - sunk
sit - sat - sat
slay - slew - slain
sleep - slept - slept

slide - slid - slid
sling - slung - slung
slink - slunk - slunk
slit - slit - slit
smell - smelt, smelled - smelt, smelled
smite - smote - smitten
sow - sowed - sown, sowed
speak - spoke - spoken
speed - sped, ⊕ speeded - sped, ⊕ speeded
spell - spelt, spelled - spelt, spelled
spend - spent - spent
spill - spilt, spilled - spilt, spilled
spin - spun, span - spun
spit - spat - spat
split - split - split
spoil - spoiled, spoilt - spoiled, spoilt
spread - spread - spread
spring - sprang - sprung
stand - stood - stood
stave - staved, stove - staved, stove
steal - stole - stolen
stick - stuck - stuck
sting - stung - stung
stink - stunk, stank - stunk
strew - strewed - (have) strewed, (be) strewn
stride - strode - stridden

strike - struck - struck
string - strung - strung
strive - strove - striven
swear - swore - sworn
sweep - swept - swept
swell - swelled - swollen
swim - swam - swum
swing - swung - swung
take - took - taken
teach - taught - taught
tear - tore - torn
tell - told - told
think - thought - thought
thrive - throve - thriven
throw - threw - thrown
thrust - thrust - thrust
tread - trod - trodden
wake - woke, waked - waked, woke(n)
wear - wore - worn
weave - wove - woven
weep - wept - wept
wet - wetted, wet - wetted, wet
will - would
win - won - won
wind - wound - wound
work - worked, ⊕ wrought - worked, ⊕ wrought
wring - wrung - wrung
write - wrote - written